Making Literature Matter

An Anthology for Readers and Writers

Making Literature Matter

AN ANTHOLOGY FOR READERS AND WRITERS

John Schilb
Indiana University

John Clifford
University of North Carolina at Wilmington

BEDFORD/ST. MARTIN'S   Boston   •   New York

FOR BEDFORD/ST. MARTIN'S

Developmental Editor: Stephen A. Scipione
Production Editor: Lori Chong Roncka
Production Supervisor: Catherine Hetmansky
Marketing Director: Karen Melton
Editorial Assistant: Nicole Simonsen
Production Assistant: Helaine Denenberg
Copyeditor: Lisa A. Wehrle
Text Design: Geri Davis, The Davis Group, Inc.
Cover Design: Trudi Gershenov Design
Cover Art: Bill Jacklin, *The Park,* 1996 (tapestry detail)
Composition: Stratford Publishing Services
Printing and Binding: Quebecor Printing Kingsport

President: Charles H. Christensen
Editorial Director: Joan E. Feinberg
Director of Editing, Design, and Production: Marcia Cohen
Managing Editor: Elizabeth M. Schaaf

Library of Congress Catalog Card Number: 99–62002

Manufactured in the United States of America.

4   3   2   1   0   9
f   e   d   c   b   a

For information, write: Bedford/St. Martin's, 75 Arlington Street, Boston, MA 02116
(617-426-7440)

ISBN: 0–312–09726–3

For Wendy and Janet

Preface for Instructors

Why a new introductory literature textbook when so many already exist? Because the introduction to literature course is changing. Increasingly, it is taught as part of a first-year composition sequence. Students learn to read literature in the context of the critical thinking and writing goals of a composition course. While traditional introductory literature anthologies continue to add writing instruction to their new editions, we believe that such retrofitting is not the best way to serve the needs of today's students, many of whom are taking the course as a writing requirement, and some of whom have to be convinced that literature matters. It seemed to us, then, that the time was ripe for a genuine rethinking of how such textbooks work.

What would this literature anthology, prepared from its inception to be used in a composition class, have to do? We realized that it would need to include a writing text, thereby integrating composition pedagogy with the traditional *and* contemporary concerns of literary studies. We decided, too, that the anthology itself would need to be re-envisioned so that every literary work in it presented an occasion — or, better still, *multiple* occasions — for critical thinking and writing. *Making Literature Matter* provides such a text, wrapped around such an anthology. Through the many years we have taught composition and literature, we have constantly sought to fuse these subjects. Our belief is that students make literature matter to themselves, and to others, when they write about it. *Making Literature Matter*, therefore, combines a great deal of advice on writing about literature with a great deal of literature — fifty-one stories, ninety poems, twelve plays, and twenty essays — chosen, arranged, and supported by apparatus that stimulates students' own critical prose.

A Text for Writing

Students learn to write by writing. Accordingly, *Making Literature Matter* prompts them to write almost immediately and keeps them writing as they work through the activities and assignments in the text and the anthology. We depict writing as a perpetually useful and rewarding means of exploring various dimensions of a literary work.

Although writing projects, from informal exercises to formal paper assignments, are integrated throughout the book, we discuss writing most in Part One, "Ways of Making Literature Matter," using each of its six chapters to take students step by step through the process of writing about literature. In part, our discussions draw on classical rhetoric; for instance, we build on Aristotle's definition of rhetoric as "the discovery of the available means of persuasion." We also incorporate insights from contemporary rhetoricians like Stephen Toulmin, who has influenced our treatment of claims and warrants.

As these rhetorical influences suggest, our text is distinguished by its emphasis on how to write *arguments* about literature. Literature textbooks tend to be hazy about argumentation, when they refer to it at all. Students, encouraged by the media, tend to believe that an argument is necessarily aggressive and hostile. In such a climate of opinion, instructors may fear that emphasizing argument can only lead to classroom donnybrooks about the meaning of a poem or a story. But *Making Literature Matter* elaborates a much different view of argument. We encourage students to see argument as civil inquiry, a process requiring writers to clarify, support, and often revise their ideas. This concept of argument is, we believe, vital to classes in literature and composition. Quite simply, students need to see argument as careful, well-grounded thought. To help them see this, our first two chapters refer continually to several poems about work, as a way of showing students how to write arguments about particular texts. Chapters 3 through 6 move through all four genres in this book — stories, poems, plays, and essays — using works in each genre to explain the process of arguing about that genre. Throughout Part One, the brief writing tasks help students to formulate issues and claims. We also include five sample arguments by students, showing how these writers developed informal jottings into full-fledged drafts.

Another distinctive feature of Part One is our emphasis on specific *issues* currently pursued in literary studies. Typically, literature textbooks refer to the discipline's present state by identifying schools of critical thought, such as feminism, New Historicism, psychoanalysis, or cultural studies. But the average critic is more eclectic than these categories suggest, and the time spent explaining these categories is better spent cultivating students' own reading and writing. Therefore, instead of taking a "schools" approach, Chapter 1 introduces students to the kinds of questions that literature specialists now address: questions of fact, definition, genre, pattern, symbolism, evaluation, history, cause and effect, and policy. Similarly, we point out particular subjects that currently engage the discipline — what classical rhetoricians would call its special topics. These include gender, race, memory, subversion, and the body as well as relations between "high" culture and mass culture. Again, we do more than just list these issues and topics. Rather, we demonstrate their usefulness by applying them to particular literary works and provide opportunities for students actually to implement the principles and strategies we discuss.

The final writing project in a literature-based composition course is often a research paper, and the final section of this book is an appendix on how to develop a well-researched argument about literature. The appendix follows the research process of a student, offering detailed advice on finding a topic, locating and working with library and electronic sources, and drafting and documenting. It concludes with the student's research paper, annotated to call out important features of her argument.

An Anthology for Readers and Writers

Students learn to read literature by reading literature. The heart of *Making Literature Matter* is Part Two, where most of the stories, poems, plays, and essays are gathered in an anthology titled "Literature and Its Issues." The authors presented here range from canonical figures like Sophocles, William Shakespeare, John Donne, John Milton, Jonathan Swift, Walt Whitman, and Emily Dickinson to well-known and emerging contemporary voices like Marge Piercy, Amy Tan, Julia Alvarez, Leslie Marmon Silko, Margaret Atwood, Haruki Murakami, and Don DeLillo. As we hope you can tell from these examples, we have tried to make sure that our selections represent many eras and social backgrounds.

The overall structure of Part Two is thematic, with the stories, poems, plays, and essays broadly grouped in six chapters focusing on subjects relevant to students today: living in families, teaching and learning, loving, considering outsiders, making judgments, and confronting mortality. A thematic organization, which emphasizes what literature is *about* rather than its formal features, is more inviting than a strictly generic organization. Students are more comfortable reading literature and responding to it in writing if they are not immediately set to hunting formal elements. Moreover, such an organization puts students on the path to making comparisons of how different literary works treat the same subjects. When students start to think about how one work resembles and differs from another, they are more likely to sense issues raised by the work, to understand its author's options, and to advance thoughtful claims about it. In other words, comparing works helps students devise better arguments, even if the paper they eventually write deals with just one text.

Because we believe so strongly that comparison leads to critical thinking and writing, we have made it central to our book in a way that no other introductory literature text does. Throughout *Making Literature Matter*, but especially in the anthology, we cluster small groupings of literary works around provocative issues. Overall, our book contains sixty-five such clusters, with sixty appearing in the anthology alone. Each thematic chapter in Part Two is divided into clusters that deal with issues emerging from the chapter's theme. For instance, we juxtapose two stories of fraternal conflict, James Baldwin's "Sonny's Blues" and Tobias Wolff's "The Rich Brother." We gather poems about schoolchildren by Louise Glück, Toi Derricotte, and Philip Levine. We pair essays by Maxine Hong Kingston and Naomi Wolf on women who defy sexual taboos. We couple William Shakespeare's *The Tempest* with Aimé Césaire's postcolonial version of the play. We link stories of revenge by Edgar Allan Poe, Louise Erdrich, and Andre Dubus. As you can tell from these examples, our clusters usually consist of works in the same genre, as an aid to teachers who prefer a genre-based approach.

Of the nine to twelve clusters within each thematic chapter, three are dedicated to special pedagogical purposes. The first kind, called "Collections of Writings," presents multiple works by the same author. Spotlighted in this way are the Brothers Grimm, Jamaica Kincaid, Kate Chopin, Franz Kafka, Alice Walker, and Emily Dickinson. The second kind features a single work and selected professional commentaries on it. Works highlighted by "Critical Commentaries" include Sylvia Plath's "Daddy," Richard Rodriguez's "Aria," Henrik Ibsen's play *A Doll House*, Herman Melville's story "Bartleby, the Scrivener," Sophocles' play *Antigone*, and Marsha Norman's play *'night, Mother*. The third kind focuses on a single work and documents that illuminate its "Cultural Contexts." For example, we accompany David Mamet's *Oleanna*, a play about a college teacher accused of sexual harassment, with a real university's pamphlet about sexual harassment; an essay about a college student's use of mediation to resolve a harassment complaint she had made; and an article proposing ways to protect college faculty's right to free speech. Similarly contextualized are Lorraine Hansberry's play *A Raisin in the Sun*, David Henry Hwang's *M. Butterfly*, Ralph Ellison's story "Battle Royal," Charlotte Perkins Gilman's story "The Yellow Wallpaper," and Bharati Mukherjee's story "The Management of Grief."

The apparatus for Part Two, as extensive as you would find in a composition textbook, is designed to help students continually associate reading with writing and critical thinking. Each chapter begins with a discussion of its overall theme and a preview of the specific works it includes. Each cluster within a chapter begins the same way. Also at the start of each cluster is a set of prereading questions, which can spark class discussion and informal writing. For instance, the cluster on "Punishment" in the "Making Judgments" chapter begins by asking students to recall and reflect on a punishment they consider unjust. We also provide informative biographical headnotes on each writer. Naturally, we seek to stimulate inquiry *after* students read a selection. Each literary work in Part Two is followed by five questions about it, as well as three questions comparing it to any other texts preceding it in its cluster. Each cluster concludes by suggesting four writing assignments related to its contents. These assignments call for various types of essays: interpretations of single texts; comparative analyses; connections between literature and the reader's personal history; and projects based primarily on archival or ethnographic research.

Resources for Teaching Making Literature Matter

Instructors will find additional prompts for writing and discussion in the accompanying instructor's manual, *Resources for Teaching MAKING LITERATURE MATTER*. There, we have more to say about each of the selections in this book. Just as important, the manual elaborates our ideas about how to mesh literary studies with composition. Our effort to link them has been influenced not only by our classroom experiences but also by several other books and articles, so the manual includes an annotated bibliography of these. Classes using our book will also find guidance at our publisher's Web site, **www.bedfordstmartins.com.** Among other things, this Web site provides additional information on the authors we feature, as well as links to other Web sites about them.

As we noted at the outset, *Making Literature Matter* reflects careerlong interests of ours. During our more than two decades as English faculty, we have enjoyed reading literature, teaching about it, and writing about it. We have also dedicated ourselves to writing instruction, both in our classroom practice and our research. We know that literary studies and composition studies can be difficult to synthesize, especially given their different institutional circumstances. Yet we seek in this book to connect reading, writing, and critical thinking, and we encourage readers to do the same. We hope the book itself makes literature matter; we hope it makes students' writing matter, too.

Acknowledgments

Any book like this takes years of work, but the labor is made considerably more pleasant when the publisher is Bedford/St. Martin's. *Making Literature Matter* grew out of conversations John Schilb had with Chuck Christensen and Joan Feinberg at various CCCC and MLA meetings; after all this time, we are still grateful for their enthusiasm, encouragement, and sheer companionship. We value the persistent sympathy, wisdom, and good humor of our editor, Steve Scipione. Lori Chong Roncka and her production team provided indispensable help. We are grateful to the many other people at Bedford/St. Martin's who worked behind the scenes to produce this book, including Maura Shea, Nicole Simonsen, Elizabeth Schaaf, John Amburg, Lisa Wehrle, and Meg Hyre.

John Schilb thanks his former colleagues at the University of Maryland. He is especially indebted to Jeanne Fahnstock, whose knowledge of rhetoric and argumentation continues to awe and inspire him. John appreciates, too, the support of his new colleagues at Indiana University, especially Christine Farris. John Clifford thanks his colleague at the University of North Carolina at Wilmington, Joyce Hollingsworth. Joyce did professional research and editing on the development of this textbook, including valuable class-testing, and we are profoundly grateful for her insightful and pedagogically savvy work on the instructor's manual. Our thanks go also to Janet E. Gardner of the University of Massachusetts at Dartmouth for her fine work on the research appendix.

We thank those who reviewed our manuscript at various stages. Their observations and suggestions were extremely useful. They include Jonathan Alexander, University of Southern Colorado; Virginia Anderson, University of Texas at Austin; Carolyn Baker, San Antonio College; Rance G. Baker, San Antonio College; Barbara Barnard, Hunter College; Linda Bensel-Meyers, University of Tennessee, Knoxville; Kevin J. H. Dettmar, Southern Illinois University at Carbondale; Thomas Dukes, University of Akron; Irene R. Fairley, Northeastern

University; Iris Rose Hart, Santa Fe Community College; Carol Peterson Havi-
land, California State University, San Bernardino; John Heyda, Miami University–
Middletown; Margaret Lindgren, University of Cincinnati; Phillip Mayfield,
Fullerton College; Julie Segedy, Chabot College; Sharon Winn, Northeastern
State University; Bertha Wise, Oklahoma City Community College.

    What matters most to John Schilb is Wendy Elliot; what matters most to
John Clifford is Janet Ellerby. We dedicate this book to our wives, in acknowledgment of their unflagging love and support.

J.S.

J.C.

Brief Contents

Contents

PART TWO
Literature and Its Issues

9. Loving   714

10. Considering Outsiders   935

Making Literature Matter

AN ANTHOLOGY FOR
READERS AND WRITERS

INTRODUCTION

What Is Literature? How and Why Does It Matter?

> Art lives upon discussion, upon experiment, upon curiosity, upon variety of
> attempt, upon the exchange of views and the comparison of standpoints. . . .
> — Henry James, "The Art of Fiction"

The title of this book, *Making Literature Matter,* may seem curious to you.
Presumably your school assumes that literature already matters, for otherwise it
would hardly offer courses in the subject. Quite possibly you are taking this
course because you think literature is important or hope it will become so for
you. But with our title, we want to emphasize that literature does not exist in a
social vacuum. Rather, literature is part of human relationships; people *make* literature matter to other people. We will be especially concerned with how you
can make literature matter to others as well as to yourself. Above all, we will point
out ways you can argue about literature, both in class discussions and in your own
writing.

First, though, we need to address three questions:

+ How have people defined literature?
+ What about literature has mattered to people?
+ What can you do to make literature matter?

How Have People Defined Literature?

Asked to define *literature,* probably most people would say that the term
encompasses fiction (novels and short stories), poetry, and drama. Although this
definition is common, it is somewhat misleading. It fails to acknowledge that fiction, poetry, and drama are rooted in everyday life. Often these genres make use
of ordinary forms of talk, although they may play around with such forms and
even satirize them. Our book includes several works that, in one way or another,
incorporate familiar types of speech. For example, Daniel Orozco's short story
"Orientation" is a bizarre version of a ritualistic conversation: the guided tour
that office workers receive when they join a firm.

The genres regarded as "literary" are tied in other ways to daily behavior.
Most likely you are often poetic, in the sense that you use metaphors in your

1

conversations and you quote or sing lyrics of songs. Probably you are often theatrical, too, carrying out various kinds of scripts and performing any number of roles. Furthermore, you probably engage in storytelling even when you are not actually writing works of fiction. Imagine this familiar situation: You are late for a meeting with friends because you got stuck in traffic, and now you must explain to them your delay. Your explanation may very well become a tale of suspense, with you the hero racing against time to escape the bumper-to-bumper horde. As the writer Joan Didion has observed, "We tell ourselves stories in order to live." Almost all of us spin narratives day after day, because doing so helps us meaningfully frame our lives.

Many people would admit that literature is grounded in real life and yet still insist on applying the term only to written texts of fiction, poetry, and drama. But this attitude is distinctly modern, for the term *literature* has not always been applied so restrictively. *Literature* was at first a characteristic of *readers*. From the term's emergence in the fourteenth century to the middle of the eighteenth, *literature* was more or less a synonym for *literacy*. People of literature were assumed to be well read.

In the late eighteenth century, however, the term's meaning changed. Increasingly it referred to books and other printed texts rather than to people who read them. At the beginning of this shift, the scope of literature was broad, encompassing practically all public writing. But as the nineteenth century proceeded, the term's range shrank. More and more people considered literature to be imaginative or creative writing, and they distinguished it from nonfiction. This trend did take years to build; in the early 1900s, literature anthologies still featured essays as well as excerpts from histories and biographies. By the mid-1900s, though, the narrower definition of literature prevailed.

As we have noted, many people still associate literature with just fiction, poetry, and drama. Nevertheless, this limited definition has become newly vulnerable. From the early 1970s on, a significant number of literature faculty have called for widening it. In 1979, for instance, a National Endowment for the Humanities–Modern Language Association summer institute entitled "Women's Nontraditional Literature" applied the term *literature* to genres that had not been thought of as such. Participants studied essays, letters, diaries, autobiographies, and oral testimonies. To each of these genres, women have contributed much; in fact, the institute's participants concluded that a literature curriculum slights many works by women if it focuses on fiction, poetry, and drama alone.

Of course, even within these three categories, the term *literature* has been selectively applied. Take the case of novelist and short-story writer Stephen King, whose books have sold millions of copies. Despite his commercial success, a lot of readers — including some of his fans — refuse to call King's writing literature. They assume that to call something literature is to say it has artistic merit, and for them King's tales of horror fall short.

Yet people who use the term *literature* as a compliment may still disagree about whether a certain text deserves it. Plenty of readers praise King's writing as literature, while others deem it schlock. In short, artistic standards differ. To be sure, some works have been constantly admired through the years; regarded as classics, they are frequently taught in literature classes. *Hamlet, Othello, The Tempest,* and other plays by William Shakespeare are perhaps the most obvious examples. But in the last twenty years, much controversy has arisen over the literary canon, those works taught again and again. Are there good reasons why the canon has consisted mostly of texts by white men? Or have the principles of selection been skewed by sexism and racism? Should the canon be changed to accommodate a greater range of authors? Or should literary studies resist having any canon at all? These questions have provoked various answers, the result being continued debate. Nowadays even Shakespeare's works are not universally beloved. In our "Considering Outsiders" chapter, we follow his original *Tempest* with a version of it by Aimé Césaire, a writer from Martinique who associates Shakespeare with the dominant colonialism of the Elizabethan age. Shakespeare still has legions of defenders, as do many writers long acclaimed as great, but disputes about what constitutes greatness are likely to persist.

Also in question are attempts to separate literature from nonfiction. Our notion of the literariness of everyday life acknowledges that much "nonfiction" shows imagination and relies on devices found in novels, short stories, poems, and plays. The last few years have seen the emergence of the term *creative nonfiction* as a synonym for essays, autobiographies, and histories that use evocative language and strong narratives. Conversely, works of fiction, poetry, and drama may center on real-life events. One example included in our book is Seamus Heaney's poem "Punishment." It juxtaposes two actual incidents: the discovery of an ancient woman's body and the violence suffered by women of Northern Ireland for consorting with British soldiers.

Works like Heaney's confirm that poetry can embrace actual history. Some people, however, argue that poems about real events are still "literary" because they inspire contemplation rather than action. This view of literature has traditionally been summed up as "art for art's sake." Yet this notion brushes aside all the poems, novels, short stories, and plays that do encourage audiences to undertake certain acts. Right after "Punishment," for example, we present Sherman Alexie's "Capital Punishment," a poem obviously designed to spark resistance to the death penalty.

In this book, we resist endorsing a single definition of *literature.* Rather, we encourage you to review and perhaps rethink what the term means to you. At the same time, we do want to expand the realm of literature, so we include several essays in addition to short stories, poems, and plays. We also present numerous critical commentaries as well as various historical documents. Throughout the book, we invite you to make connections among these different kinds of texts: You need not treat them as altogether separate species.

What about *Literature Has Mattered to People?*

People have studied literature for all sorts of reasons. You may be surprised to learn that in the late 1800s, English departments in American universities taught Shakespeare's plays mostly by having students trace the origins of particular words he used. Shakespeare's plots, characters, and themes received little attention. Today, by contrast, most classes in Shakespeare consider these things important; they are not content to use his plays as a springboard for dictionary research. In fact, literary history can be seen as a history of changing responses to literature. Nevertheless, if you were to ask people today why they read literature, probably you would get several common answers. The following are some we have heard. As we list them, compare them with what you might say.

One common reason for reading literature has to do with proving sophistication. Ever since the eighteenth century, people have sought to join the cultural elite by proving their familiarity with literature. Read Shakespeare's plays, their thinking goes, and you can then impress high society with quotations from him. The desire to raise one's status is understandable. Still, this motive is rarely enough to sustain a person's interest in literature. Frankly, we hope you will find other reasons for reading it. At the same time, we encourage you to analyze how knowledge of literature has served as *cultural capital*: that is, as a sign of a person's worth. In coining the term *cultural capital*, sociologist Pierre Bourdieu suggested there is something wrong when a society makes literature a means of achieving status. Do you agree?

Another common reason for reading literature has to do with institutional requirements. Millions of students read literature simply because they have to take courses in it. Probably Roland Barthes, the French critic, had this situation in mind when he wryly defined *literature* as "what gets taught in schools." Barthes was being provocatively reductive; if pressed, perhaps he would have conceded that people read literature outside school, too. Across the United States, college graduates and others meet regularly in book discussion groups, studying literature together. Even if you are taking this course only because you must, the obligation may turn out enjoyable. When required to read literature, students have found value in it. While inevitably they end up preferring some works to others, they learn that literature provides them with more pleasures and insights than they had expected. Stay open to the possibility that you will find the same rewards.

Still another popular reason for reading literature is the enjoyment it provides. Quite simply, lots of people find the experience entertaining. Specifically, they may revel in literature's ability to render human existence concretely. They may delight in its often eloquent and evocative language. They may like finding all the various patterns in a literary text. They may prize the moments when literature makes them think, laugh, or cry.

People have also turned to literature because, as scholar and critic Kenneth Burke has noted, it serves as "equipment for living." Perhaps you have found that a certain story, poem, play, or essay helped you understand your life and conduct it better. Of course, even readers who look to literature for guidance may have different tastes. While some readers prefer literature that reflects their own lives, others like it most when it explores situations that they have not experienced or have not pondered much. "When it's the real thing," critic Frank Lentricchia notes, "literature enlarges us, strips the film of familiarity from the world; creates bonds of sympathy with all kinds, even with evil characters, who we learn are all in the family."

Some people *dislike* literature because they find it too indirect. They resent that it often forces them to figure out symbols and implications, when they would rather have the truth presented straight. But in life, truth can be complicated and elusive. In many ways, literature is most realistic when it suggests the same. Besides, many readers appreciate literature most when it resists simple decoding, forcing them to adopt new assumptions and learn new methods of analysis. Indeed, throughout this book we will suggest that the most interesting and profitable conversations about literature are those in which the issues are not easily resolved. One of the best things your course will provide you is the chance to exchange insights with other students about texts whose issues prove challenging.

We hope that any literature you read in this book strikes you as "equipment for living." If a particular selection leaves you cold, use the occasion to identify and review the standards you are judging it by. Even if you like a piece, think about the values you are applying. Probably your values will grow clearer to you in class debates, especially if you have to support your own view of a work.

What Can You Do to Make Literature Matter to Others?

Look again at our opening quotation, which comes from an 1895 essay called "The Art of Fiction" by the American novelist, short-story writer, and critic Henry James. When James declared that "art lives upon discussion, upon experiment, upon curiosity, upon variety of attempt, upon the exchange of views and the comparison of standpoints," certainly he was suggesting that the creators of literature play a big role in making it matter. But James was suggesting, too, that plenty of other people contribute to literature's impact. Today, these people include publishers, printers, agents, advertisers, librarians, professional reviewers, bookstore staff, and even show business figures such as Oprah Winfrey, who got millions of viewers to participate in her "book club." Teachers of literature also make it matter — or at least they try to! Perhaps your parents or other family members have contributed to your appreciation of certain literary texts; many adults introduce their children and grandchildren to books they loved when young. Moreover, friends often recommend works of literature to one another.

We concede that some people think of literature negatively, believing that it matters in a way they don't like. The ancient Greek philosopher Plato wanted to ban poets from his ideal republic because he thought they merely imitated truth. Today, reviewers sometimes want to stop a book from being widely read, believing it will do more harm than good. One recent example is Kathryn Harrison's *The Kiss*, a memoir about the author's incestuous relationship with her father. Many reviewers hated the book, regarding it as a superficial and tasteless treatment of its subject. At the same time, some of these reviewers feared that *The Kiss* would attract a large audience, so they made their criticisms of it sound like public health warnings.

Throughout history, various forces have worked actively to censor or abolish a great deal of literature. In communities across the contemporary United States, pressure groups have succeeded in getting particular novels removed from library shelves. These novels include such classics as *The Catcher in the Rye* and *Adventures of Huckleberry Finn*. History has also seen many writers of literature killed, jailed, or harassed for their work. In recent years, the most conspicuous example of such persecution has been the Ayatollah Khomeini's indictment of author Salman Rushdie. The ayatollah was so enraged by the portrayal of Islam in Rushdie's novel *The Satanic Verses* that he commanded his followers to hunt Rushdie down and slay him. Even after the ayatollah died, Rushdie was still in danger, for the *fatwa* against him remained in effect. Not until eight years after the original edict did the Iranian government back away from it, thereby granting Rushdie at least a measure of safety. But the Rushdie affair stands as a reminder that some writers of literature risk their lives. Ironically, the ayatollah's execution order was a sort of homage to literature, a fearsome way of crediting it with the power to shape minds.

Our book aims to help you join the conversations that Henry James saw as nourishing literature. More specifically, our book focuses on helping you argue about literature, whether your audience is your classmates, your teacher, or other people. While arguments involve real or potential disagreement, they need not be waged like wars. When we use the term *argument* in this book, we have in mind civilized efforts through which people try to make their views persuasive. When you argue about literature, you are carefully reasoning with others, helping them see how a certain text should matter to them.

In particular, we will say much about you as a writer. The main goal of your course is to help you compose more effective texts of your own. By writing arguments about literature, you make it matter to others. Moreover, you learn about yourself as you analyze a literary text and negotiate other readers' views of it. We will emphasize that, at its best, arguing is indeed a process of inquiry for all involved. This process entails a great deal of re-vision: Both you and your audience may wind up changing your minds.

The Rest of This Book

In Part One, Chapters 1 and 2 introduce you to activities that are at the heart of making literature matter: reading, thinking, and writing. Chapters 3 through 6 focus on writing about the four literary genres we include in this book. Each of these four chapters identifies traditional features of each genre — fiction, poetry, drama, and essays — and lays out strategies for developing, drafting, and revising the sorts of papers you will write in this course. As examples, we include writing by other students of literature.

Part Two features six chapters filled with literary works for you to read, think, and write about. Each chapter's selections treat the same general subject and its various issues. In Chapter 7, it is "Living in Families"; in Chapter 8, "Teaching and Learning"; in Chapter 9, "Loving"; in Chapter 10, "Considering Outsiders"; in Chapter 11, "Making Judgments"; and in Chapter 12, "Confronting Mortality." Within each chapter, the selections are arranged in clusters that address aspects of the chapter's subject.

After each selection, we raise questions designed to help you think about what you have just read. Often these questions raise issues you can build on in constructing arguments about the work. Moreover, often the questions invite you to compare the work with others in its cluster. Then, at the end of every cluster, we suggest ways of writing about the various texts it includes.

Finally, an appendix explains how to write a literary research paper: how to discover and focus on a topic; how to find and use sources; and how to draft, revise, and document the paper.

WRITING ASSIGNMENTS

1. Write a brief essay in which you explain what you value in literature by focusing on a literary work you have liked and why you liked it. Don't worry about whether you are defining *literature* correctly. The aim of this exercise is for you to begin reviewing the values you hold as you read a work that you regard as literary.

2. Sometimes a literary work matters to you in one way, and then, when you read it again, it matters to you in another way. Write a brief essay in which you discuss a work that did, in fact, matter to you differently when you reread it. In what way did it matter to you the first time? What significance did it have for you later? What about your life had changed in the meantime? If you cannot think of a literary work, choose a film you have seen.

3. Write a brief essay in which you identify the values that a previous literature teacher of yours seemed to hold. Be sure to identify, too, ways in which the teacher expressed these values. You may want to bring up one or more specific events that took place in the teacher's classroom.

4. Many bookstores sell computer instruction manuals. Examine one of these. Do you consider the manual literature? Write a brief essay answering this question. Be sure to explain how you are defining *literature* and refer to the manual's specific features.

5. Visit your school's bookstore or another bookstore. Spend at least a half hour looking at books in various sections, noting how the publishers of these works try to make them matter. Look at such things as the books' physical formats, the language on their covers, and any introductory material they include. Then, write a brief essay in which you identify and evaluate the strategies for "mattering" used by at least three books you came across.

6. Visit a Web site that includes readers' comments about particular works of fiction. A good example is www.amazon.com, a commercial online "bookstore." Choose a novel or short story collection on the site that readers have commented about a lot. Then, write a brief essay in which you identify the values that seem reflected in the comments. In what respects, apparently, does literature matter to these readers? What do they evidently hope to find in it?

7. Write a brief essay in which you recall an occasion when someone made something matter to you. Presumably this exercise will get you thinking about what it means to "make something matter." At some point in your essay, try to define this phrase, using your specific experience as an example.

8. Write a brief essay in which you summarize your history as a writer. What are the main kinds of writing you have done? What successes and problems have you experienced as a writer? How might this course help your writing most?

PART ONE

Ways of Making
Literature Matter

1

Reading and Thinking

Reading Comparatively: Three Poems about Work

This book presents many poems, short stories, plays, and essays. At the same time, it invites you to **compare** texts. Let's assume that you are analyzing a poem. How might you develop ideas about it? One good way is to see how the poem resembles, and differs from, others on the same topic. To get a better sense of this method, read the following three poems, each of which concerns work.

JOHN MILTON
When I consider how my light is spent

When I consider how my light is spent,
    Ere half my days in this dark world and wide,
    And that one talent which is death to hide
Lodged with me useless, though my soul more bent
To serve therewith my Maker, and present   5
    My true account, lest He returning chide;
    "Doth God exact day-labor, light denied?"
I fondly ask. But Patience, to prevent
That murmur, soon replies, "God doth not need
    Either man's work or His own gifts. Who best   10
    Bear His mild yoke, they serve Him best. His state
Is kingly: thousands at His bidding speed,
    And post o'er land and ocean without rest;
    They also serve who only stand and wait."   [c. 1652]

FRANCES E. W. HARPER
Free Labor

I wear an easy garment,
    O'er it no toiling slave
Wept tears of hopeless anguish,
    In his passage to the grave.

And from its ample folds   5
    Shall rise no cry to God,
Upon its warp and woof shall be
    No stain of tears and blood.

Oh, lightly shall it press my form,
    Unladen with a sigh,   10
I shall not 'mid its rustling hear,
    Some sad despairing cry.

This fabric is too light to bear
    The weight of bondsmen's tears,
I shall not in its texture trace   15
    The agony of years.

Too light to bear a smother'd sigh,
    From some lorn woman's heart,
Whose only wreath of household love
    Is rudely torn apart.   20

Then lightly shall it press my form,
    Unburden'd by a sigh;
And from its seams and folds shall rise,
    No voice to pierce the sky,

And witness at the throne of God,   25
    In language deep and strong
That I have nerv'd Oppression's hand,
    For deeds of guilt and wrong.   [1874]

MARGE PIERCY
To be of use

The people I love the best
jump into work head first
without dallying in the shallows
and swim off with sure strokes almost out of sight.
They seem to become natives of that element,   5

the black sleek heads of seals
bouncing like half-submerged balls.

I love people who harness themselves, an ox to a heavy cart,
who pull like water buffalo, with massive patience,
who strain in the mud and the muck to move things forward,   10
who do what has to be done, again and again.

I want to be with people who submerge
in the task, who go into the fields to harvest
and work in a row and pass the bags along,
who are not parlor generals and field deserters   15
but move in a common rhythm
when the food must come in or the fire be put out.

The work of the world is common as mud.
Botched, it smears the hands, crumbles to dust.
But the thing worth doing well done   20
has a shape that satisfies, clean and evident.
Greek amphoras for wine or oil,
Hopi vases that held corn, are put in museums
but you know they were made to be used.
The pitcher cries for water to carry   25
and a person for work that is real.   [1974]

These poems differ in their styles and cultural references, in part because they come from different historical periods. Whereas John Milton wrote his poem around 1652 and published it in 1673, the other two poems were published much later: Frances Harper's in 1874, Marge Piercy's in 1974. But if you look at the poems together, you can better see the specific approach each takes to the subject of work.

A WRITING EXERCISE

Once you have read the three poems as a group, write brief responses to each. You might jot down things you especially notice about them, feelings they evoke in you, and questions you have about them. You might also note work experiences of your own that they lead you to recall. With each poem, write for ten minutes without stopping — off the top of your head, so to speak. Don't feel that you have to pour forth terrific insights right away. This exercise, often called **freewriting**, simply helps you begin responding to a text.

If the poems puzzle you at first, take heart. Few people make brilliant observations about a work of literature when they first read it. Examining literature is best seen as a process, during which you gradually construct, test, revise, and refine your sense of a text. Practically everyone would need to reflect on these three poems a while before developing substantial ideas about them. We think literature is most worth reading when it challenges your current understanding of the world, pressing you to expand your knowledge and review your beliefs.

You need not read in isolation, relying solely on yourself to figure out a text. If you have trouble understanding a literary work, try consulting other readers. In the course you are taking, you will have plenty of chances to exchange insights with your classmates and teacher. All these people are resources for your thinking. Encourage them to see you as a resource, too.

Still another good way to ponder a literary work is to write about it. Again, do not feel obliged to churn out a polished, profound analysis of the text right away. If reading literature is best seen as a process, so too is writing about it. To begin your study of a work, you might freewrite in a notebook or journal. Then, you might try extended drafts, in which you experiment with sustained analysis. Only later might you attempt a whole formal paper on the text, aiming to show others that you have arrived at a solid, credible view of it. In each of these activities, your thinking might be helped by class discussions. Perhaps classmates will even be able to give you direct feedback on your writing, including the freewriting you have just done on the three poems about work.

In your course, you will read many of the literary selections we present. Naturally, we hope that you will find them emotionally engaging as well as thought-provoking. Moreover, we hope the course helps you become a more learned and thoughtful reader of whatever literature you read later. But we have yet another goal. With the texts we present, the background information we provide, the questions we raise, and the assignments we suggest, we seek to help you become a more thoughtful and effective writer. That is why we began by asking you to freewrite about the three poems.

Probably you have already taken courses that required you to write a great deal. On your own, perhaps you have enjoyed writing poems, short stories, plays, essays, or other kinds of texts. Actually, almost everyone does some kind of writing outside of school, whether it's merely a letter or a full-fledged essay. Nevertheless, you may hesitate to call yourself a writer out of a belief that your writing is often flawed. Yet everyone brings strengths to the act of writing, and we hope this course helps you recognize yours. While obviously the course is a chance for you to improve as a writer, believing that you deserve to be called a writer is an important step in your growth.

A WRITING EXERCISE

Introduce yourself to the rest of the class through a letter that describes your career as a writer. You might recall particular works you have written and memorable writing teachers you have had. Also, you might identify whatever kinds of writing you like to do, your current strengths as a writer, and aspects of your writing that you hope to strengthen in this course.

LITERATURE AS SOCIAL ACTION

We began this chapter with poems by Milton, Harper, and Piercy because each of these poets views writing as we would like you to view it: as a form of social action. Perhaps you see writing as a form of communication, a way to express your ideas. This is a logical and important concept of writing to hold. But these three poets also see writing as a way to have impact on other people. They write not just to express themselves but also to shape the world around them. As writers, they contributed especially to the political debates of their day.

John Milton (1608–1674) played a leading role in England's Puritan revolution, which sought to make dominant its own version of Christianity. Ultimately, the Puritans executed King Charles I and installed their leader Oliver Cromwell as head of state. Milton supported the Puritan movement through his poetry and prose. He wrote "When I consider how my light is spent" while working as an official in Cromwell's government. Obviously autobiographical, the poem refers to Milton's growing blindness, which threatened to prevent him from serving both his political leader and his religious one, God. Milton was further discouraged a few years later when the monarchy was restored with the crowning of Charles II. Even then, however, Milton remained active as a social critic. In 1667, with the publication of his epic poem *Paradise Lost*, he aimed "to justify the ways of God to man."

Like Milton, African American writer Frances Ella Watkins Harper (1825–1911) saw social injustice as a sin to be eradicated. Through her poems, essays, fiction, and speeches, she specifically challenged the oppression of African Americans and women. Born free, Harper spent the pre–Civil War period campaigning against slavery. After emancipation, she worked on behalf of the former slaves, striving to help them prosper and to secure their legal rights. During this post–Civil War period, she wrote "Free Labor." At the same time, Harper participated in the campaign to obtain voting rights for women, although she had to fight racial prejudice even within the suffrage movement.

Marge Piercy (b. 1936) is a veteran of the contemporary civil rights and women's movements. During the 1960s and 1970s, she also protested America's involvement in Vietnam. Subsequently she has used her writing to promote various social causes, especially feminism. Piercy is the author of several novels, including the 1976 science-fiction classic *Woman on the Edge of Time*. But she has published several books of poetry as well. The title "To be of use" suggests how Piercy conceives a poet's responsibilities. In her introduction to *Circles on the Water*, a 1982 collection of her poems, Piercy hopes that her readers "will find poems that speak to and for them, will take those poems into their lives and say them to each other and put them up on the bathroom wall and remember bits and pieces of them in stressful or quiet moments" (xii).

In presenting these three poems by Milton, Harper, and Piercy, we are not asking you to adopt the writers' political beliefs. Were these writers to meet, probably they would disagree among themselves about various issues. Nor is all their writing explicitly political: Each has written poems focused more on private life than on public affairs. And yet, each of these writers has often explored how the private and public realms are related. For instance, even as Milton wrote about the loss of his sight, he raised the question of how to define public service and prodded his readers to share his abiding faith in God. Furthermore, each of these poets wrote to affect readers' hearts and minds. Each of them is a good model for thinking about the social context and possible effects of your writing as you produce your own texts.

Thinking Critically: The Value of Argument

Our writing assignments are designed to help you reflect on the literature you read. Although these assignments are varied, mostly we encourage you to argue about literature. We do so for three reasons. First, the term **argument** refers to a kind of talk as well as a kind of writing; thus, focusing on this term can help you relate your own written work to discussions in class. Second, you will read a work of literature with greater direction and purpose if you are working toward the goal of constructing arguments about it. Finally, when you argue, you learn a lot, because you have to ponder things you may have taken for granted as well as things unfamiliar to you.

Specifically, *arguing* is a process in which you identify a subject of current or possible debate; you take a position on that subject; you analyze why you view the subject the way you do; and you try to persuade others that your view is worth sharing or is at least reasonable. Often the process of arguing is not straightforward. Just when you think you have decided how you feel about a subject, class discussion may lead you to change your position or shift to a completely different topic. Whatever the case, to argue well means to engage in self-examination. Also, it means attending to the world around you: especially to the ways that other people think differently from you.

For many, *argument* is a negative term. Perhaps it makes you think of unpleasant shouting matches you have been in or witnessed—times when people have bitterly disagreed with one another and refused to compromise. Almost everyone has experienced arguments of this sort. Moreover, they are a kind of argument that the media promote. On talk radio, hosts as well as callers are often brutally argumentative, mixing strong opinion with outright insult. Similarly, television's political talk shows regularly become sheer quarrels; on *Crossfire, The McLaughlin Group,* and *The Capital Gang* panelists fall again and again into nasty, noisy debate. Spats are even more spectacular on daytime talk shows like Jerry Springer's, which invite friends and family members to clash in public on such high-voltage topics as "You Stole Him from Me and I Want Him Back!" On occasion, these shows actually get violent, the participants turning from words to fists. No wonder many people see argument as fierce competition, even as a form of war.

A WRITING EXERCISE

Although this book emphasizes written argument, a good way of starting to think about argument is to consider its oral forms. Recall a specific oral argument you recently observed or one in which you recently participated. Do not worry about whether your understanding of the term *argument* is correct; the aim of this exercise is for you to review what you associate with the term.

Write an informal account of the argument you recall. Who engaged in this argument? What did they argue about? What views did they express? What tones did they use? How willing were they to compromise? What were the stages of this argument? What was the outcome? Besides addressing these questions, evaluate the participants' thinking and behavior. To what extent was each person's position reasonable? In what ways, if any, might they have talked more productively?

ARGUMENT AS INQUIRY

Although many people view argument as war and have plenty of reasons to do so, we encourage you to argue in a more positive sense. In any meaning of the term, to *argue* is to disagree with others or to set forth a view that you suspect not everyone holds. But argument need not be a competition in which you aim to prove that only you are right. For one thing, at times you might collaborate with someone else in arguing a position. Also, in an argument you can concede that several views on the subject are possible, even as you develop your own position. Actually, you are more apt to persuade your audience if you treat fairly opinions other than yours. Furthermore, successful arguers establish common ground with their audience; they identify and honor at least some of the beliefs that their readers or listeners hold.

Keep in mind, too, that participants in an argument ought to learn from one another. If you take seriously other people's responses to your position, you will find yourself reexamining why and how you express that view. As we have already noted, you may even change your mind. Above all, we hope you will see argument as *inquiry*, a process in which you think hard about your beliefs rather than just declare them.

THE ELEMENTS OF ARGUMENT

When you argue, you attempt to *persuade* an *audience* to accept your *claims* regarding an *issue* by presenting *evidence* and relying on *warrants*. The italicized words are key to this book; we will bring them up often. Here we will explain what we mean by each, beginning with *issue* and then moving to *claims*, *persuasion*, *audience*, *evidence*, and *warrants*. As we discuss these terms, we will refer mostly to the process of arguing about literature. In particular, we will mention arguments that might be made about the three poems by Milton, Harper, and Piercy. Also, we will stress the usefulness of comparing these poems. Therefore, before going further, you may want to read them again.

Issues

An **issue** is something about which people have disagreed or might disagree. Even as you read a text, you can try to guess what features of it will lead to disagreements in class. You may sense that your own reaction to certain aspects of the text is heavily influenced by your background and values, which other students may not share. Some parts of the text may leave you with conflicting ideas or mixed feelings, as if half of you disagrees with the other half. At moments like these, you come to realize what are issues for you, and next you can urge the rest of your class to see them as issues, too.

An issue is best defined as a question with no obvious, immediate answer. Thus, you can start identifying issues by noting questions that occur to you as you read. Perhaps this question-posing approach to texts is new for you. Often readers demand that a text be clear, and they get annoyed if it leaves them puzzled. Of course, certain writing ought to be immediately clear in meaning; think of operating instructions on a plane's emergency doors. But the value of a literary work often lies in the work's complexities, which can lead readers to reexamine their own ways of perceiving the world. Also, your discussions and papers about literature are likely to be most useful when they go beyond the obvious to deal with more challenging matters. When your class begins talking about a work, you may feel obliged to stay quiet if you have no firm statements to make. But you can contribute a lot by bringing up questions that occurred to you as you read. Especially worth raising are questions that continue to haunt you.

In the case of "When I consider how my light is spent," one possible issue concerns its ending. Milton's speaker wonders how he can serve God now that he is blind. Specifically, the speaker asks, "Doth God exact day-labor, light denied?" But it is Patience, not God, who responds to the speaker's question, proclaiming in the last line that "they also serve who only stand and wait." Why does Milton have Patience, rather than God, reply to the speaker? This issue deserves to be raised because Milton does not thoroughly explain what he means by *patience*, a word that can be defined in various ways. When Piercy's speaker in "To be of use" celebrates those people "who pull like water buffalo, with massive patience," she may or may not be endorsing the kind of patience to which Milton refers.

A possible issue with Harper's "Free Labor" concerns the last two lines of the third stanza. There, the speaker denies hearing "some sad despairing cry." If you wish, you can accept her denial at face value, taking her to mean that slave labor has really ended and that an era of truly free labor has arrived. But this interpretation is not the only conceivable one. You may see the speaker's use of the words "sad despairing cry" as indicating that she still hears such a sound. Maybe she cannot forget slavery after all; maybe she believes African Americans remain slaves in some sense. Whatever you conclude, you can raise this issue: How should the lines be interpreted?

Similarly, Piercy's first stanza presents an apparent paradox. Like the whole poem, the stanza emphasizes work. Yet it ends with an image of play: "the black sleek heads of seals / bouncing like half-submerged balls." Therefore, a possible issue is, What should Piercy's readers conclude when the stanza brings work and play together?

You may feel that at present, you are far from able to answer questions like these. But again, you achieve much when you simply formulate questions and bring them up in class. Then, as other students help you ponder them, you will grow more able to explore issues through writing as well as through conversation.

You are more likely to come up with questions about a text if you do not assume that the text had to be written exactly the way it was. For every move the writer made, alternatives existed. Milton might have had God speak directly rather than having Patience speak. Harper might have let her speaker admit to hearing the cry. Piercy might have stuck entirely with images of work. When you bear in mind writers' options, you grow more inclined to explore why they made the choices they did and what the effects of those choices may be.

You will recognize writers' options more easily if you compare their texts with others. As we have said, we invite comparison throughout this book. Milton's reference to Patience is more apt to strike you as a calculated decision if you note Piercy's use of the word. Recall that she doesn't capitalize *patience* or treat it as a being who can speak. Also, whereas Milton associates the word with waiting, Piercy seems to associate it with hard labor, which is not necessarily the same thing. In light of Piercy's poem, then, Milton's reference to Patience comes across as thoroughly questionable. That is, it emerges as a strategy whose aims and effects are worth pondering.

Next we identify ten kinds of issues that come up in literature courses. Our list will help you detect the issues that arise in your class and discover ones to bring up in discussions or in your writing. The list does not include every kind of issue; you may think of others. Moreover, you may find that an issue can fit into more than one of the categories we name. But when you do have an issue that seems hard to classify, try nevertheless to assign it to a single category, if only for the time being. You will then have some initial guidance for your reading, class discussions, and writing. If you later feel that the issue belongs to another category, you can shift your focus.

1. *Issues of fact.* Rarely does a work of literature provide complete information about its characters and events. Rather, literature is usually marked by what literary theorist Wolfgang Iser calls "gaps," moments when certain facts are omitted or obscured. At such times, readers may give various answers to the question, What is happening in this text? Recall, for instance, Milton's first line: "When I consider how my light is spent." The word *when* is ambiguous, leaving unclear how often the speaker has brooded about his apparent uselessness. Is it just on this occasion that he worries about the effects of his blindness? Or does he repeatedly sink into despair and need Patience's response every time? Of course, readers tackle questions of fact only if they suspect that the answers will affect their overall view of the text. Imagine one reader who believes that Milton's *when* refers only to the present occasion, and a second reader who believes that the word refers to repeated brooding. How might they see the whole poem differently because of their different assumptions?

2. *Issues of theme.* You may be familiar with the term **theme** from other literature courses. By *theme* critics usually mean the main claim that an author seems to be making with his or her text. Sometimes a theme is defined in terms of a single word — for example, *work* or *love.* But such words are really mere topics. Identifying the topics addressed by a text can be a useful way of starting to analyze that text, and later in Part One we will list several topics that currently preoccupy

literary studies. A text's theme, however, is best seen as an assertion that you need at least one whole sentence to express.

With many texts, an issue of theme arises because readers can easily disagree over what the text's main idea is. In literature classes, such disagreements often occur, in part because literary works tend to express their themes indirectly. Readers of Harper's poem may give several different answers to the question, What is Harper ultimately saying about "free labor"? Some readers may accept the speaker's statements at face value, assuming that the speaker truly believes slavery is over and that an era of free labor has begun. Furthermore, these readers may figure that Harper, the author, holds the same belief. But other readers may feel the speaker is being ironic, since she continually refers to the horrors of slavery even as she vows to wear her garment "lightly." These readers may feel that the author, too, remains highly conscious of African Americans' servitude. Perhaps Harper assumes that African Americans' work should *never* be taken lightly, because it is connected with their history of pain. Maybe she is even criticizing the term *free labor*, fearing that it will obscure the past and the present suffering of her race. Or perhaps Harper does like the term but wants to point out that black freedom is a recent, fragile achievement, with slavery always threatening to return.

If you try to express a text's theme, avoid making it a statement so general that it could apply to an enormous number of works. Arguing that Milton's theme is "Have faith in God" hardly gets at the details of his poem. On the other hand, do not let the text's details restrict you so much that you wind up making the theme seem relevant only to a tiny group. If you argue that Milton's theme is "Blind poets shouldn't let their condition make them doubt God," then the many people who are *not* blind poets will wonder why they should care. In short, try to express themes as midlevel generalizations. With Milton's poem, one possibility is "Some people's conditions may prevent them from serving God in obvious ways, and they may therefore question His plan for them, but in the long run they may be able to maintain their faith and believe they are fulfilling His will." A statement like this seems both attentive to Milton's specific text and applicable to a fairly large portion of humanity. Of course, you are free to challenge this version of Milton's theme by proposing an alternative. Moreover, even if you do accept this statement as his theme, you are then free to decide whether it is a good principle to live by. Identifying a theme is one thing; evaluating it is another.

Sometimes an author will appear to state the theme explicitly in his or her text. Such moments are worth studying as you try to determine what the theme is. For instance, you may believe that Milton's theme is the concluding line of his poem: "They also serve who only stand and wait." Yet remember that a theme ties together various parts of a text. Focusing on a single passage, even if it seems "thematic," may lead you to ignore other passages that a statement of theme should encompass. With Milton's poem, someone may argue that the last line does *not* seem to state the theme. After all, much comes before that line: in particular, the speaker's extensive expression of doubt.

Often you will sense a work's theme but still have to decide whether to state it as an **observation** or as a **recommendation**. You would be doing the first if, for example, you said Piercy's theme is that "People need to feel that the work they do is real." You would be doing the second if you said Piercy's theme is that "People should look for work that they find real." Indeed, when they depict a theme as a recommendation, people often use a word like *should*. Neither way of expressing a theme is necessarily better than the other. But keep in mind that each way conjures up a particular image of the author. Reporting Piercy's theme as an observation suggests that she is writing as a psychologist, a philosopher, or some other analyst of human nature. Reporting her theme as a recommendation suggests that she is writing as a teacher, preacher, manager, or coach: someone who is telling her readers what to do. Your decision about how to phrase a theme will depend in part on which of these two images of the author you think appropriate.

You risk obscuring the intellectual, emotional, and stylistic richness of a text if you insist on reducing it to a single "message." Try stating the text's theme as a problem for which there is no easy solution. This way you will be suggesting that the text is, in fact, complex. For instance, you might state the theme of Harper's poem as follows: "It is important to value African Americans' new ability to engage in free labor, but such appreciation threatens to obscure their painful history of slave labor, a history that may come back to life if the gains of Reconstruction are reversed."

Also weigh the possibility that a text is conveying more than one theme. If you plan to associate the text with any theme at all, you might refer to *a* theme of the text rather than *the* theme of the text. To be sure, your use of the term *theme* would still have implications. Above all, you would still be suggesting that you have identified one of the text's major points. Subsequently, you might have to defend this claim, showing how the point you have identified is indeed central to the text.

Issues of theme have loomed large in literary studies. We hope that you will find them useful to pursue. But because references to theme are so common in literary studies, students sometimes forget that there are other kinds of issues. As you move through this list, you may find some that interest you more.

3. *Issues of definition.*   In arguments about literature, issues of **definition** arise most often when readers try to decide what the author means by a particular word. Look back at the last line of Milton's poem: "They also serve who only stand and wait." What, conceivably, does Milton mean by *wait*? Readers may express different notions of how Milton defines this activity. Perhaps he sees waiting as altogether passive; then again, perhaps he believes it can involve several actions, including the writing of poems. To address this issue of definition, readers would also have to consider what the poem's speaker is waiting *for*. Evidently, the speaker hopes for something from God, but what exactly might that something be?

An issue of definition may come up even when the author straightforwardly explains terms. For one thing, readers may argue about whether the author's definitions make sense. Think again of Piercy's poem, which suggests that work is "real" when people "submerge" themselves in it. Perhaps a number of readers would disagree with her, choosing to define "real" work differently. Moreover, even readers who like Piercy's definition may disagree with one another as they seek to apply it. They may have different opinions about what jobs are "real" in her sense.

Like all kinds of issues, those involving definition can emerge more clearly when you compare texts. Recall Milton's and Piercy's references to "patience." Looking at their different uses of the word will probably lead you to reflect at length on how each of them defines it.

4. *Issues of symbolism.* In literary studies, an issue of **symbolism** is often a question about the meaning and purpose of a particular image. A good example is Harper's use of the word *garment*. Readers may have different ideas about why she uses this image, her specific adjectives for it, the effects of her building the whole poem around it, and the exact kind of clothing this "garment" may be. An issue of symbolism is also involved if you find yourself wondering whether some element of a text is symbolic in the first place. Milton uses the word *light* as he describes his loss of vision. What various things can *light* symbolize?

5. *Issues of pattern.* With issues of **pattern**, you observe how a text is organized. More precisely, you try to determine how certain parts of the text are related to other parts of it. But in thinking about how elements of the text may be grouped together, keep in mind the meaning and purpose of any pattern you find, especially since readers may disagree about that pattern's significance.

Many poems exhibit patterns in their rhymes and stanza lengths. You may have noticed that Milton's poem rhymes, although you may not know the technical term for the structure he is using. His poem is an **Italian sonnet**, in his time a popular form of verse. Following the conventions of this form, Milton has written fourteen lines: eight lines with one pattern of rhyming followed by six lines that rhyme in a different way. (Try to identify each rhyme scheme.) Even if you already possess this information about Milton's poem, there is still the issue of how the poem's form relates to its content. Do the first eight lines differ from the last six in subject matter? If so, do these sections' different rhyme schemes affect your response to their subjects?

Another common pattern in literature is **repetition**. Perhaps you have noted already that Milton uses the word *serve* three times. Moreover, Harper uses *sigh* three times, *lightly* twice, and the phrase *too light* twice. Yet even when repetition is easy to detect, readers may have different ideas about its function. Again, the issue then becomes not so much whether the author is repeating words, but how this repetition contributes to the work as a whole. What might Milton and Harper be trying to achieve when they use certain words more than once?

Often a text's patterns are more elusive. In the words of literary theorist Kenneth Burke, readers must spend time figuring out "what goes with what," besides having to determine the significance of the patterns they find. With Milton's poem, you may not have realized immediately that the words *spent* and *account* can be linked. Both of these words come from the world of finance. Even if you do make this connection, you still face the task of deciding why economic terms appear in a poem about religious matters.

A text's apparent oppositions are also patterns to be debated. For instance, when Milton contrasts "my light" with "this dark world," readers may have different notions of what he associates with each phrase. And while some readers may readily point out Harper's contrast between free labor and slave labor, others may say she is implying that the two really should not be distinguished.

  6. *Issues of evaluation.*   Consciously or unconsciously, **evaluation** always plays a central role in reading. When you read a work of literature, you evaluate its ideas and the actions of its characters. You judge, too, the views you assume the author is promoting. Moreover, you gauge the artistic quality of the text.

  Specifically, you engage in three kinds of evaluation as you read. One kind is philosophical: You decide whether a particular idea or action is wise. Another kind is ethical: You decide whether an idea or action is morally good. The third kind is aesthetic: You decide whether parts of the text, or the work as a whole, succeed as art. Of course, another reader may disagree with your criteria for wisdom, morality, and art; people's standards often differ. It is not surprising, then, that in the study of literature issues of evaluation come up frequently.

  Philosophical differences may arise with Milton's ultimate willingness to serve God by "waiting." Some readers may feel that his attitude makes sense, others may accuse him of being too passive, and there may be both praise and criticism of his devotion to God in the first place. With Piercy's poem, different ethical judgments are possible regarding the final stanza. Like the poem's speaker, some readers may feel it wrong for museums to house objects intended for practical use. Other readers may praise this practice, believing that often such objects survive only because museums preserve them. Finally, different aesthetic judgments are possible as readers decide the artistic value of Piercy's poem. Some readers may be stirred by the poem's call for "real" work; some may feel the poem too much resembles a lecture; and other readers may have mixed feelings about the poem, appreciating certain lines but not others. These different assessments of the poem would probably reflect different conceptions of what poetry in general should be like.

  Sometimes you may have trouble distinguishing the three types of judgments from one another. Philosophical evaluation, ethical evaluation, and aesthetic evaluation can overlap. For example, return to Milton's endorsement of "waiting." You may conclude that his attitude is neither wise nor ethical, and for this reason you may also find it an artistic flaw in the poem. Keep in mind, however, that you can still like many aspects of a literary work even if you disagree with views you believe the author is promoting. Atheists may admire the craft of Milton's poem while refusing to share his belief in God.

  If you did dispute the artistic value of Milton's poem, you would be challenging countless admirers of it. Increasingly, though, the status of Milton's poem and other literary classics is being questioned. Many scholars argue that literary studies have focused too much on white male authors. They refuse to assume that Milton's works are great and universally relevant; they criticize the long neglect of women and minority authors. Yet even as these scholars call attention to writers such as Frances Harper, other people continue to prize more well-known writers such as Milton. The result is ongoing debate about whose works should be taught in the first place.

7. *Issues of historical and cultural context.*   Because works of literature are written by people living in particular times and places, issues of **historical** and **cultural context** arise. Eventually these works may engage a wide variety of readers, including members of much-later generations and inhabitants of distant cultures. Yet these works often continue to reflect the circumstances of their creation. You can tell by the content of Frances Harper's poem "Free Labor" that she wrote it soon after the American Civil War. You may recall that Milton wrote his poem soon after the seventeenth-century English Civil War. If you did not know that fact when you first read the poem, probably much of Milton's language nevertheless struck you as belonging to an era long past. Even the word *fondly*, which is still used, had a different definition in Milton's time: Whereas most of us would now take it to mean "affectionately," for Milton it meant "foolishly."

Since Marge Piercy's language is easily understood by many people today, her poem seems much closer to the present. All the same, you can examine from a historical perspective the specific aspects of twentieth-century life Piercy mentions. You might look for answers to questions like these: To what extent, and in what places, do workers today engage in the heavy field labor she depicts? How did modern museums acquire the kinds of objects she refers to? What are the various ways that museums have exhibited these artifacts?

We provide some background for each literary work we present, thereby helping you begin to situate it historically and culturally. In the appendix, we explain how to keep putting literature in context, especially by doing research in the library. For now, we want to emphasize that contextualizing a work involves more than just piling up facts about its origin. In the study of literature, often issues of historical and cultural context are issues of *relevance*. The question becomes, *Which* facts about a work's creation are important for contemporary readers to know? and *How* would awareness of these facts help them understand the work better? For instance, while readers can inform themselves about Frances Harper's career as a political activist, they may disagree about the extent to which her poem should be interpreted as autobiographical.

Perhaps you do like to connect a literary work with its author's own life. Since all three poems here use the first person ("I" or "we"), you may feel that they strongly invite you to make such a link. Yet you are almost always engaging in a debatable move when you assert that a work is thoroughly autobiographical. Among other things, you risk overlooking aspects of the text that depart significantly from the author's own experiences, impressions, and beliefs. Like Milton's poem about his blindness, certain texts do seem windows into the author's life. Nevertheless, some readers would argue that Milton's poem presents just one side of him and that he actually continued to do much more than "wait." Even in Milton's case, then, the work should be distinguished from the author's life. To be sure, we are not urging you to refrain from ever connecting the two. Rather, we are pointing out that whatever links you draw may be the subject of debate.

It is also important to note that the term *history* can be defined in various ways. When you refer to a work's historical context, you need to clarify what you have in mind. After all, you may be examining one or more of the following: (1) the life of the work's author; (2) the time period in which it was written;

(3) any time period mentioned within the text; (4) its subsequent reception, including responses to it by later generations; (5) the forms in which the work has been published, which may involve changes in its spelling, punctuation, wording, and overall appearance.

8. *Issues of genre.*   So far, we have been identifying categories of issues. Issues of **genre** are *about* categorization, for they involve efforts to determine what *kind* of text a particular work is. Nowadays, most people would say that the basic genres of literature are poetry, the short story, the novel, and drama. If you were asked to identify the genres of the works by Milton, Harper, and Piercy that we have been discussing, you might logically call each a poem. But you do not have to stop there. You can try to classify each poem more precisely, aiming for a term that better sums up its specific content and form. Issues of genre most often arise with such further classification. And as you come up with more exact labels for the poems, other readers may label them differently. Because Milton is obviously trying to soothe his distress over his blindness, you may see his poem as basically an act of self-consolation or therapy. Meanwhile, a number of readers may be more inclined to call his poem a sermon, believing that he is primarily concerned with strengthening his society's faith in God. Perhaps you feel that Milton's poem is both an act of self-consolation and a sermon. But even then, you must still decide whether these labels are equally appropriate. Does one convey the poem's overall drift better, or do they both convey it well? Much of the time, issues of genre are issues of priority. Readers debate not whether a certain label for a work is possible, but whether that label is the best.

9. *Issues of social policy.*   Many works of literature have been attempts at social reform, exposing defects of their cultures and encouraging specific cures. A famous example is Upton Sinclair's 1906 novel *The Jungle*; by vividly depicting horrible working conditions in Chicago's stockyards, it led the meat processing industry to adopt more humane practices. Even when a work of literature is not blatantly political or seems rooted in the distant past, it may make you conscious of your own society's problems and possible solutions to them. Yet you and your classmates may propose different solutions and even disagree about what is a problem in the first place. The result is what we call issues of **social policy**.

Sometimes your position on a current issue of social policy will affect how you read a certain work. For instance, your view on whether religion should play a central role in contemporary American society may affect your response to Milton's poem. Even if current issues of social policy do not influence your original reading of a work, you can still use the work to raise such issues in your writing or in class discussion. Take Harper's poem, for example. Although it seems closely linked to America's Reconstruction period, it can serve you as a springboard for plunging into debates about how contemporary "garments" are made. A few years ago, television personality Kathie Lee Gifford was criticized because her clothing line was produced by women and children toiling in sweatshops for just a few cents an hour. In essence, many people argued that these workers were slave labor, not free labor, although the manufacturers who employed them evidently thought otherwise. Eventually Gifford herself apologized for this exploitation and, in testimony before a congressional committee, proposed ways of ending it. But Americans still have not agreed on whether and how sweatshop conditions should be abolished. Imagine a paper in which, using Harper's poem as a point of departure, you elaborate your own perspective on the Gifford case.

10. *Issues of cause and effect.*   Issues of **causality** are common in literary studies. Often they arise as readers present different explanations for a certain character's behavior. Remember that even the speaker in a poem can be thought of as a character with motives worth analyzing. You can pursue questions like these: Why does the speaker of Milton's poem not hear Patience sooner? Why does Harper's speaker brood so much about slave labor in a poem titled "Free Labor"? Why does the "I" of Piercy's poem turn from describing physical activities (like harnessing, pulling, and straining) to identifying objects (Greek amphoras, Hopi vases, the pitcher)? You can also analyze characters' impact.

These questions can be rephrased to center on the author. For example, you can ask why Harper has her speaker brood about slave labor, and why Piercy has her poem shift from activities to objects. Actually, if you look back at all the questions we have brought up in discussing the various types of issues, you may see that most can be phrased as questions about the author's purposes. But keep in mind your options. You may not find it useful to focus on authorial intention in a given case. Often you will be better off sticking with one of the other types of issues we have mentioned. Or you may prefer to turn a question about authorial purpose into a question about authorial effect. For instance, how should readers react when Harper has her speaker brood about slave labor? What does Piercy accomplish when she shifts in her poem from activities to objects? You can address questions like these without sounding as if you know exactly what the author really intended.

Claims

You may not be used to calling things you say or write *claims*. But even when you utter a simple observation about the weather—for instance, "It's beginning to rain"—you are making a claim. Basically, a **claim** is a statement that is spoken or written in the hope that it will be considered true. With this definition in mind, you may start noticing claims everywhere. Most of us make lots of them every day. Furthermore, most of our claims are accepted as true by the people to whom we make them. Imagine how difficult life would be if the opposite were the case; human beings would be perpetually anxious if they distrusted almost everything they were told.

At times, though, claims do conflict with other claims. In a literature course, disagreements inevitably arise. Again, try not to let disagreements scare you. You can learn a lot from encountering views other than yours and from having to support your own. Moreover, exciting talk can occur as your class negotiates differences of opinion.

Recall that we defined an *issue* as a question with various debatable answers. *Claims*, as we will be using the term, are the debatable answers. For examples of claims in literary studies, look back at our explanations of various kinds of issues. Along the way, we mentioned a host of claims: for instance, that Milton's "when" represents a single occasion; that Harper's speaker does not actually distinguish between slave labor and free labor; and that Piercy's definition of *real* is misguided. These claims are debatable because in each case at least one other position is possible.

Not every claim is a firm, sweeping generalization. In some instances, you may want to *qualify* a claim of yours, which involves expressing the claim in words that make it less than absolute. The terms available for qualifying a claim are numerous. You might use words such as *perhaps, maybe, seems, appears, probably,* and *most likely* to indicate that you are not reporting a definite fact. Similarly, words such as *some, many, most,* and *several* allow you to acknowledge that your claim is limited in scope, applicable to just a portion of whatever you are discussing.

In literature classes, two types of claims are especially common. To criticize Piercy's definition of *real* is to engage in **evaluation**. To identify the main ideas of her poem is to engage in **interpretation**. Conventionally, interpretation is the kind of analysis that depends on hypotheses rather than simple observation of plain fact. Throughout this book, we will refer to the practice of interpreting a work or certain aspects of it. Admittedly, sometimes you may have trouble distinguishing interpretation from evaluation. When you evaluate some feature of a work or make an overall judgment of that work, probably you are operating with a certain interpretation as well, even if you do not make that interpretation explicit. Similarly, when you interpret part of a work or the text as a whole, probably you have already decided whether the text is worth figuring out. Nevertheless, the two types of claims differ in their emphases. When you attempt to interpret a work, you are mostly analyzing it; when you attempt to evaluate the work, you are mostly judging it.

In class discussions, other students may resist a claim you make about a literary work. Naturally, you may choose to defend your view at length. But remain open to the possibility of changing your mind, either by modifying your claim somehow or by shifting completely to another one. Also, entertain the possibility that a view different from yours is just as reasonable, even if you do not share it.

In much of your writing for your course, you will be identifying an issue and making one main claim about it, which can be called your **thesis**. Then, as you attempt to support your main claim, you will make a number of smaller claims. In drafts of your paper, welcome opportunities to test the claims you make in it. Review your claims with classmates to help you determine how persuasive your thinking is. You will be left with a stronger sense of what you must do to make your paper credible.

Persuasion

As we have noted, argument is often associated with arrogant insistence. Many assume that if two people are arguing, they are each demanding to be seen as correct. At its best, however, argument involves careful efforts to persuade. When you make such an effort, you indicate that you believe your claims, even if you remain open to revising them. You indicate as well that you would like others to agree with you. Yet to attempt **persuasion** is to concede that you must support your claims if others are to value them.

The art of persuasion has been studied for centuries under the name of **rhetoric**. Today, often the term *rhetoric* is used negatively: Politicians accuse one another of indulging in "mere rhetoric," as if the term meant deceptive exaggeration. But human beings habitually resort to persuasion; hence, rhetoric deserves more esteem. Besides, only in modern times has rhetoric not been regarded as a central part of education. In ancient Greece and Rome as well as in Renaissance Europe, rhetoric was an important academic subject. It was viewed, too, as a body of thought that people could actually put to use, especially in the realm of public affairs. Much of the advice we will give you about writing looks back to this history. Over and over, we will convey to you principles drawn from the rhetorical tradition.

As you have probably discovered on many occasions, it can be hard for you to sway people who hold views different from yours. Not always will you be able to change their minds. Yet you may still convince them that your claims are at least reasonable. Moreover, the process of trying to persuade others will force you to clarify your ideas, to review why you hold them, and to analyze the people you aim to affect.

Audience

When you hear the word **audience**, perhaps you think first of people attending plays, concerts, movies, or lectures. Yet *audience* also describes readers, including the people who read your writing. Not everything you write is for other people's eyes; in this course, you may produce notes, journal entries, and even full-length drafts that only you will see. From time to time in the course, however, you will do public writing. On these occasions, you will be trying to persuade your audience to accept whatever claims you make.

These occasions will require you to consider more than just your subject matter. If you are truly to persuade your readers, you must take them into account. Unfortunately, you will not be able to find out everything about your audience beforehand. Moreover, you will have to study the ways in which your readers differ from one another. Usually, though, you will be able to identify some of their common values, experiences, and assumptions. Having this knowledge will strengthen your ability to make a case they appreciate.

In analyzing a work of literature, you may try to identify its *implied reader*: that is, the type of person that the work seems to address. Remember, too, that people may have read the work in manuscript or when it was first published. Finally, the work may have had innumerable readers since. Often we will ask you to write about a text's effect on you, and to compare your reaction with your classmates'.

Evidence

Evidence is the support that you give your claims so that others will accept them. What sort of evidence you must provide depends on what your audience requires to be persuaded. When you make claims during class discussions, your classmates and instructor might ask you follow-up questions, thereby suggesting what you must do to convince them. As a writer, you might often find yourself having to guess your readers' standards of evidence. Naturally, your guesses will be influenced by any prior experiences you have had with your audience. Moreover, you may have opportunities to review drafts with some of its members.

When you make an argument about literature, the evidence most valued by your audience is likely to be details of the work itself. Direct quotations from the text are an especially powerful means of indicating that your claims are well grounded. But when you quote, you need to avoid seeming willfully selective. If you merely quote Milton's description of himself as "useless," without acknowledging his final line ("They also serve who only stand and wait"), you may come across as distorting his poem. In general, quoting from various parts of a text will help you give the impression that you are being accurate.

If you make claims about the historical or cultural context of a work, your evidence may include facts about its original circumstances. You may be drawn to the author's own experiences and statements, believing these shed light on the text. But again, use such materials cautiously, for not always will they seem strong evidence for your claims. Even if the author of a text explicitly declared what he or she was up to in writing it, people are not obliged to accept that declaration as a guide to the finished work. Some people may feel that the author's statement of intention was deliberately misleading, while others may claim that the author failed to understand his or her own achievement.

Another kind of evidence for your arguments about literature is your **ethos**. This is a traditional term in rhetoric; it refers to the image of you that your audience gets as you attempt to persuade. Actually, there are two kinds of ethos. One is the image of you that your audience holds even before you present your analysis. Often your audience will not know much about you beforehand. In general, this kind of ethos plays a role when the speaker or writer has a prior reputation. When retired army general Colin Powell gives a speech, he can expect much of his audience to start off trusting him, since millions of Americans admire him already.

Even if you are not well known, the second kind of ethos may greatly influence how people respond to your argument. This kind is the image of you that your audience develops in hearing or reading your actual words. To secure your audience's trust, you ought to give the impression that you are calmly and methodically laying out your claims as well as your reasons for them. Making concessions to views different from yours is also a good strategy, indicating that you aim to be fair. On the other hand, if your presentation is disorganized or your tone self-righteous, you may put your audience on guard. You may come across as someone not committed to serious inquiry.

Warrants

Of all the elements of argument, **warrants** may be the least familiar to you. You have heard of search warrants and arrest warrants, documents that indicate the police are justified in searching a place or jailing a person. More generally, warrants are the beliefs that lead people to call certain things evidence for their claims. Imagine that you have just made a claim to your classmates and are now trying to support it. Imagine further that your listeners are reluctant to call your supporting information *evidence*; they want you to explain why you do so. In effect, your audience is asking you to identify your warrants: that is, the assumptions that make you think the information you have given reinforces your case. Throughout this book, we use the terms *warrants* and *assumptions* interchangeably.

Let's say you claim that, despite her denial, the speaker in Harper's poem does hear the "sad despairing cry" of a slave even when she puts on the garment made by free labor. Asked to provide evidence for your claim, you might note two things: (1) The speaker refers repeatedly to slavery throughout the rest of the poem; (2) her mention of the phrase "sad despairing cry" suggests that this sound still haunts her. But then you may be asked for your warrants, the assumptions that lead you to see your evidence as support for your claim. Some of your assumptions might be about literature itself: for instance, that repetition in a poem is significant; that the speaker of a poem may contradict herself; and that literary works are most interesting when they undercut their apparent meaning. Some of your assumptions might be about human nature: for example, that people's denials can express their unconscious obsessions. Some of your assumptions might be about specific historical periods and cultures: for instance, that slavery could not have been easily forgotten by African Americans of the 1870s, especially when white Northerners as well as white Southerners were increasingly reluctant to aid black free labor. Often literature classes are most enlightening when students discuss with one another their assumptions about literature, about human nature, and about other times and places. If your classmates differ in their assumptions, that may be because they differ in the ways they grew up, the experiences they have had, the reading they have done, and the authorities that have influenced them.

Once you state your warrants for a claim you are making, your audience may go further, asking you to identify assumptions supporting the warrants themselves. But more frequently you will have to decide how much you should mention your warrants in the first place. In class discussion, usually your classmates' and instructor's responses to your claims will indicate how much you have to spell out your assumptions. When you write, you have to rely more on your own judgment of what your audience requires. If you suspect that your readers will find your evidence unusual, you should identify your warrants at length. If, however, your readers are bound to accept your evidence, then a presentation of warrants may simply distract them. Again, reviewing drafts of your paper with potential readers will help you determine what to do.

A WRITING EXERCISE

We have noted that when you argue, you attempt to *persuade* an *audience* to accept your *claims* regarding an *issue*, by presenting *evidence* and relying on *warrants*. In addition, we have explained the italicized terms. Now we would like you to write an analysis of an argument someone has made in print. Certainly it can be an argument about literature, but you need not restrict your-self to that subject. Perhaps you will look to another discipline, analyzing an argument made in one of that field's journals or books. Perhaps you will ana-lyze a political argument made by a newspaper or magazine columnist. Whatever the argument you choose, try to identify its issues, claims, evi-dence, warrants, and intended audience. State whether you find the argu-ment persuasive, and explain why you feel about it the way you do.

LITERATURE AS ARGUMENT

Much of this book concerns arguing *about* literature. But sometimes literary works can be said to present arguments themselves. In some of the works we have included, certain characters make claims, often in debate with one another, while other works give the impression that the author is arguing for a certain position. Admittedly, not all works of literature are best seen as containing or making argu-ments, but occasionally, you will find that associating a literary text with argument opens up productive lines of inquiry. Moreover, as you argue about literature, arguments *within* literature can help you see how you might persuade others.

For examples of arguments within literature, turn again to Milton's poem on page 11. The poem's initial speaker, presumably Milton himself, asks "'Doth God exact day-labor, light denied?'" Although technically these words form a question, they can also be considered a claim. With them, the speaker is evi-dently trying to persuade his audience that God is unfair, demanding hard work from him even though he is now blind. The speaker's preceding lines can be regarded as evidence that he is using to justify his despair. He notes that though his "one talent" is to write, and though he wants to serve God by writing, he has lost his sight before his life is half over.

The speaker does not actually spell out his warrants. Consider, however, his reference to Christ's parable of the talents (Luke 19:12–27). In the ancient Middle East, a *talent* was a unit of money. In the parable, a servant is scolded by his master for hoarding the one talent that his master had given him. By telling this story, Christ implies that people should make use of the gifts afforded them by God. For the speaker in Milton's poem, the parable has a lot of authority. Evi-dently he feels that he should carry out its lesson. In effect, then, the parable has indeed become a warrant for him: that is, a basis for finding his blindness cause for lament.

Who, exactly, is the speaker's audience? Perhaps he is not addressing anyone in particular. Or, perhaps the speaker's mind is divided and one side of it is addressing the other. Or, perhaps the speaker is addressing God, even though he refers to God in the third person. Given that the speaker is answered by Patience, perhaps he means to address *that* figure, although Patience may actually be just a part of him rather than an altogether separate being.

At any rate, Patience takes the speaker for an audience in responding. And while Patience does not provide evidence, let alone warrants, Patience does make claims about God and His followers. Furthermore, Milton as author seems to endorse Patience's claims; apparently he is using the poem to advance them.

Besides pointing out how God is served, Milton suggests that God ought to be served, even if God lets bad things happen to good people like Milton.

Every author can be considered an audience for his or her own writing, but some authors write expressly to engage in a dialogue with themselves. Perhaps Milton wrote his poem partly to convince himself that his religion was still valid and his life still worth living. Significantly, he did not publish the poem until about twenty years later. Yet, because he did publish it eventually, at some point he must have contemplated a larger audience for it. The first readers of the poem would have been a relatively small segment of the English population: those literate and prosperous enough to have access to books of poetry. In addition, a number of the poem's first readers would have shared Milton's religious beliefs. Perhaps, however, Milton felt that even the faith of this band had to be bolstered. For one thing, not every Protestant of the time would have shared Milton's enthusiasm for the Puritan government. Recall that this regime executed the king, supposedly replacing him with the rule of God. Milton's words "His state / is kingly" can be seen as an effort to persuade readers that the Puritans did put God on England's throne.

Most works of literature do not incorporate each element of argument we have discussed. Rarely do they feature arguments that do everything: acknowledge an audience, specify an issue, articulate claims, and carefully support these claims with substantial evidence and identified warrants. When characters argue, typically they do so in dramatic situations, not the sort of circumstances that permit elaborate debate. Also, traditionally literature has been a way for authors to make their own arguments indirectly: that is, to persuade with characterization, plot, and image rather than with straightforward development of claims. Do register the "gaps" as well as the strengths of any argument you find in a literary work. If the argument seems incomplete, however, a more drawn-out argument may have made the work less compelling.

Investigating Topics of Literary Criticism

To get ideas about a literary text, try considering how it deals with **topics** that have preoccupied literary studies as a profession. Some of these topics have interested the discipline for many years. One example is work, a common subject of the poems by Milton, Harper, and Piercy. Traditionally, literary studies has also been concerned with the chapter topics in Part Two: family relations, teaching and learning, love, insiders and outsiders, acts of judgment, and mortality. Moreover, the discipline has long called attention to topics that are essentially classic conflicts: for example, innocence versus experience; free will versus fate or determinism; the individual versus society; nature versus culture; and eternity versus the passing time.

Over the last few years, however, literary studies has turned to several new concerns. For instance, quite a few literary critics now consider the ways in which literary texts are often *about* reading, writing, interpretation, and evaluation. Some other subjects that critics increasingly refer to in their analysis of literature are:

- traits that significantly shape human identity, including gender, race, ethnic background, social class, sexual orientation, cultural background, nationality, and historical context;
- how groups are represented, including stereotypes held by others;
- how people acknowledge — or fail to acknowledge — differences among human beings;
- divisions, conflicts, and multiple forces *within* the self;
- boundaries, including the processes through which these are created, preserved, and challenged;
- politics and ideology, including the various forms that power and authority can take; acts of domination, oppression, exclusion, and appropriation; and acts of subversion, resistance, and parody;
- how carnivals and other festivities challenge or preserve social order;
- distinctions between what's universal and what's historically or culturally specific;
- relations between the public and the private; the social and the personal;
- relations between the apparently central and the apparently marginal;
- relations between what's supposedly normal and what's supposedly abnormal;
- relations between "high" culture and "low" (that is, mass or popular) culture;
- economic and technological developments, as well as their effects;
- the role of performance in everyday life;
- values — ethical, aesthetic, religious, professional, and institutional;
- desire and pleasure;
- the body;
- the unconscious;
- memory, including public commemorations as well as personal memory.

If you find that a literary text touches on one of these topics, try next to determine how the work specifically addresses that topic. Perhaps you will consider the topic an element of the text's theme. In any case, remember that by itself, a topic is not the same as a theme. While a topic can usually be expressed in a word or short phrase, a theme is a whole claim or assertion that you believe the text makes.

Actually, the topics we have identified may be most worth consulting when you have just begun analyzing a literary text and are far from establishing its theme. By using these topics, you can generate preliminary questions about the text, various issues you can then explore.

To demonstrate how these topics can stimulate inquiry, we will apply some of them to the following poem, "Night Waitress." It is from the 1986 book *Ghost Memory*, by the late American poet Lynda Hull (1954–1994). Hull had been developing an impressive career in literature when she died in a car accident. This poem is also about work, the speaker being the night waitress of the title.

LYNDA HULL

Night Waitress

Reflected in the plate glass, the pies
look like clouds drifting off my shoulder.
I'm telling myself my face has character,
not beauty. It's my mother's Slavic face.
She washed the floor on hands and knees   5
below the Black Madonna, praying
to her god of sorrows and visions
who's not here tonight when I lay out the plates,
small planets, the cups and moons of saucers.
At this hour the men all look   10
as if they'd never had mothers.
They do not see me. I bring the cups.
I bring the silver. There's the man
who leans over the jukebox nightly
pressing the combinations   15
of numbers. I would not stop him
if he touched me, but it's only songs
of risky love he leans into. The cook sings
with the jukebox, a moan and sizzle
into the grill. On his forehead   20
a tattooed cross furrows,
diminished when he frowns. He sings words
dragged up from the bottom of his lungs.
I want a song that rolls
through the night like a big Cadillac   25
past factories to the refineries
squatting on the bay, round and shiny
as the coffee urn warming my palm.
Sometimes when coffee cruises my mind
visiting the most remote way stations,   30
I think of my room as a calm arrival
each book and lamp in its place. The calendar
on my wall predicts no disaster
only another white square waiting
to be filled like the desire that fills   35
jail cells, the old arrest
that makes me stare out the window or want
to try every bar down the street.
When I walk out of here in the morning
my mouth is bitter with sleeplessness.   40
Men surge to the factories and I'm too tired
to look. Fingers grip lunch box handles,

> belt buckles gleam, wind riffles my uniform
> and it's not romantic when the sun unlids
> the end of the avenue. I'm fading   45
> in the morning's insinuations
> collecting in the crevices of buildings,
> in wrinkles, in every fault
> of this frail machinery.   [1986]

A WRITING EXERCISE

After you read "Night Waitress," do a ten-minute freewrite in which you try to identify how the poem relates to one or more of the topics mentioned on pages 32–33. You might also find it helpful to compare this poem about work to the poems by Milton, Harper, and Piercy on pages 11–13.

We think several of the topics now popular in literary studies are relevant to Hull's poem. Here are just a few possibilities, along with questions that these topics can generate:

Gender.   The speaker alludes to conventional roles through which men and women relate to each other. When the speaker declares that "at this hour the men all look / as if they'd never had mothers," she indicates that women have often played a maternal role for men. Furthermore, she implies that often women have been the primary caretaker of their sons. (Notice that she makes no reference to fathers.) What is the effect of this attention to women as mothers of men? In most of the poem, the speaker refers to men as potential lovers. Yet even as she suggests she would like a sexual relationship with a man, she suggests as well that she has had trouble establishing worthwhile attachments. Why has she had such difficulty, do you think? Does the problem seem due to her personality alone, or do you sense larger forces shaping her situation? Notice, too, that the poem refers to the factory workers as male, while the woman who speaks is a waitress. To what extent does American society perpetuate a gendered division of labor?

Ethnic background.   Near the start of the poem, the speaker refers to her mother's "Slavic face" and points out that her mother served "the Black Madonna," a religious icon popular in Central European countries like the Czech Republic and Poland. What is the effect of these particular ethnic references? To pursue this line of inquiry, probably you will need to do research into the Black Madonna, whether in a library or on the Internet.

Social class.   In part, considering social class means thinking about people's ability to obtain material goods. When the speaker compares her ideal song to "a big Cadillac," she implies that she doesn't currently possess such a luxurious car. At the same time, she is expressing her desire for the song, not the car. Why might the first item be more important to her right now? Social class is also a matter of how various workplaces are related to one another. This poem evokes a restaurant, factories, refineries, and bars. How are these settings connected as parts of American society? Think, too, about how you would label the social class of the various occupations the poem mentions. What would you say is the social class of a waitress? To what classes would you assign people who work in factories and refineries? Who, for the most part, are the social classes that have to work at night?

Sexual orientation.   The speaker of "Night Waitress" seems heterosexual, an orientation often regarded as the only legitimate one. Because almost all societies have made heterosexuality the norm, a lot of people forget that it is a particular orientation and that not everyone practices it. Within literary studies, gay and lesbian critics have pointed out that a literary work may seem to deal with sexuality in general but may actually refer just to heterosexuality. Perhaps "Night Waitress" is examining heterosexuality as a specific social force. If so, how might the speaker's discontent be related to heterosexuality's influence as a particular institution? Keep in mind that you don't have to assume anything about the author's sexuality as you pursue such a question. In fact, heterosexuality may be a more important topic in Hull's poem than she intended.

Divisions, conflicts, and multiple forces within the self.   The poem's beginning indicates that the speaker experiences herself as divided. The first four lines reveal that she feels pride and disappointment in her mirror image: "telling myself my face has character, / not beauty." Later she indicates that within her mind are "remote way stations" that she visits only on occasion. Furthermore, she seems to contradict herself. Although she initially refers to her room as "a calm arrival," she goes on to describe that place negatively, as empty and confined. Early in the evening, she seems sexually attracted to the man playing the jukebox ("I would not stop him / if he touched me"), but by morning her mood is "not romantic" and she is "too tired / to look" at the male factory workers. What may be the significance of these paradoxes?

Boundaries.   In the first line the speaker is apparently looking at a window, and later, she reveals that at times she feels driven to "stare out the window" of her room. What should a reader make of these two references to such a common boundary? When the speaker observes that the men in the restaurant "do not see me," she indicates that a boundary exists between them and her. Do you think she is merely being paranoid, or do you suspect that the men are indeed ignoring her? If they *are* oblivious to her, how do you explain their behavior? Still another boundary explored in the poem is the line between night and day. What happens when the speaker crosses this line? What can night, day, and the boundary between them signify? You might also consider what the author of a literary work does with its technical boundaries. Often a poem creates boundaries in its breaks between stanzas. Yet "Night Waitress" is a continuous, unbroken text; what is the effect of Hull's making it so? At the same time, Hull doesn't always respect sentence boundaries in her lines. At several points in the poem, sentences spill over from one line to another. This poetic technique is called **enjambment**; what is its effect here?

Politics and ideology.   When, in referring to the jukebox man, the speaker declares that "I would not stop him / if he touched me," she can be taken to imply that often male customers flirt with waitresses. How might flirtation be seen as involving power, authority, and even outright domination? Do you see the poem as commenting on such things? Earlier we raised issues of social class; these can be seen as political issues, too. How would you describe a society in which some people have "a big Cadillac" and others do not?

Carnivals and other festivities.   Although the poem does not refer to a "carnival" in any sense of that word, it does mention bars, which today are regarded by many people as places of festive retreat from work. What adjectives would you use to describe the speaker when she says that sometimes she wants "to try every bar down the street"?

Distinctions between what is universal and what is historically or culturally specific.   Try to identify anything that is historically or culturally specific about this poem's setting. Certainly the word *Slavic* and the reference to the Black Madonna indicate that the speaker has a particular background. You might also note her description of the restaurant, her use of the Cadillac as a metaphor, and her mention of the "factories" and the "refineries" that "are squatting on the bay." Although a wide range of places might fit these details, the poem's setting does not seem universal. Indeed, many readers are attracted to literature *because* it deals with specific landscapes, people, and plots. Nevertheless, these same readers usually expect to get some larger, more widely applicable meanings out of literature even as they are engaged by its specific details. Are you inclined to draw general conclusions from "Night Waitress"? If so, what general meanings do you find in it? What sorts of people do you think might learn something about themselves from reading this poem?

Relations between the public and the private, the social and the personal.   The speaker of "Night Waitress" works in a very public place, a restaurant. Yet she seems to feel isolated there, trapped in her own private world. How did she come to experience public life this way, do you think? Later, she initially seems to value her room as a private retreat, calling it a "calm arrival," but then she describes it as a place so lonely that it leads her to "stare out the window or want / to try every bar down the street." How, then, would you ultimately describe the relations between the speaker's public life and her private one? In addressing this issue, probably you need to consider whether the speaker's difficulties are merely personal or reflect a larger social disorder. When, at the end of the poem, she refers to "this frail machinery," is she referring just to herself or is she suggesting that this phrase applies to her society in general? If she is indeed making a social observation, what do you sense are the "faults" in her society? Who else might be "fading"?

Relations between "high" culture and "low" culture.   Although the speaker does not identify the "songs / of risky love" playing on the jukebox, surely they are examples of what is called low, mass, or popular culture. Just as a lot of us are moved by such music when we hear it, so the jukebox player and the cook are engaged by it. In contrast, the poem itself can be considered an example of high culture. Often poetry is regarded as a serious art even by people who don't read it. In what ways, if any, does this poem conceivably resemble the songs it mentions? Given that author Lynda Hull is in essence playing with combinations of words, can we compare her with "the man / who leans over the jukebox nightly / pressing the combinations / of numbers"? (Actually, *numbers* has been a poetic term; centuries ago, it was commonly used as a synonym for the rhythms of poems.)

The role of performance in everyday life. The most conspicuous "performer" in this poem is the cook, who "sings words / dragged up from the bottom of his lungs." But in everyday life, people often perform in the sense of taking on certain roles, even disguising their real personalities. Do you see such instances of performing in this poem? If so, where? Notice that the speaker wears a uniform; can that be considered a costume she wears while performing as a waitress?

Religious values. The speaker clearly refers to religion when she recalls her mother's devotion to the Black Madonna, behavior that involved "praying / to her god of sorrows and visions." And although that god is "not here tonight," the speaker's description of waitressing has ritualistic overtones reminiscent of religious ceremonies. When she says, "I bring the cups. / I bring the silver," she could almost be describing preparations for Communion. In fact, she depicts the cook as wearing a religious emblem: "On his forehead / a tattooed cross furrows, / diminished when he frowns." What do you make of all this religious imagery? Might the speaker be trying to pursue certain religious values? Can she be reasonably described as looking for salvation?

Desire and pleasure. The speaker explicitly mentions the word *desire* when she describes the emptiness she feels in her room, a feeling of desolation "that makes me stare out the window or want / to try every bar down the street." These lines may lead you to believe that her desire is basically sexual. Yet when the speaker uses the words *I want* earlier in the poem, she expresses her wish for "a song that rolls / through the night like a big Cadillac." Here, her longing does not appear sexual in nature. Is the speaker referring to at least two kinds of desire, then? Or do you see her as afflicted with basically one kind?

The body. A notable feature of this poem is its attention to body parts. The speaker mentions her "shoulder," her "face," her mother's "face," her mother's "hands and knees," the cook's "forehead," his "lungs," her "palm," the "way stations" of her "mind," her "mouth," the factory workers' "fingers," and their "belt buckles." At the same time, the speaker never describes any particular body as a whole. What is the effect of this emphasis on mere parts? Does it connect in any way to the speaker's ultimate "fading"?

Memory. Already we have noted the speaker's reference to her mother at the start of the poem. In what way, if any, is it significant that she engages in recollection? What circumstances in her life might have prompted the speaker to look back at the past?

A WRITING EXERCISE

We have applied several topics from our list to Lynda Hull's poem "Night Waitress." Now, see how you can apply topics from the list to another poem about work. Choose one of the following four poems and try to come up with several questions about it by referring to the topics on the list. Then, select one of the questions you have formulated and freewrite for ten minutes in response to it.

The first poem, William Blake's "The Chimney Sweeper," is the oldest of the set. It appeared in Blake's 1789 book *Songs of Innocence*, each poem of which was accompanied by an engraving done by Blake (1757–1827). The other three poems are by contemporary authors. "Blackberries" is by Yusef Komunyakaa (b. 1947), who has become known for exploring various dimensions of African American experience; the poem appeared in his 1992 book *Magic City*. Next is "Singapore," by Mary Oliver (b. 1935), a Pulitzer Prize–winning American poet. This poem appeared in her 1992 book *House of Light* and was subsequently included in her 1993 collection *New and Selected Poems*. The final poem, "The Machinist, Teaching His Daughter to Play the Piano," is from B. H. Fairchild's 1997 volume *The Art of the Lathe*, which won the Kingsley Tufts Poetry Award. Although Fairchild (b. 1942) has published several books of poetry, he has also worked in factories, and much of his writing concerns industrial life.

WILLIAM BLAKE
The Chimney Sweeper

When my mother died I was very young,
And my father sold me while yet my tongue
Could scarcely cry "'weep! 'weep! 'weep! 'weep!"
So your chimneys I sweep, and in soot I sleep.

There's little Tom Dacre, who cried when his head,   5
That curled like a lamb's back, was shaved: so I said
"Hush, Tom! never mind it, for when your head's bare
You know that the soot cannot spoil your white hair."

And so he was quiet, and that very night,
As Tom was a-sleeping, he had such a sight!   10
That thousands of sweepers, Dick, Joe, Ned, and Jack,
Were all of them locked up in coffins of black.

And by came an Angel who had a bright key,
And he opened the coffins and set them all free;
Then down a green plain leaping, laughing, they run,   15
And wash in the river, and shine in the sun.

♦ ♦ ♦

Then naked and white, all their bags left behind,
They rise upon clouds and sport in the wind;
And the Angel told Tom, if he'd be a good boy,
He'd have God for his father, and never want joy.   20

And so Tom awoke; and we rose in the dark,
And got with our bags and our brushes to work.
Though the morning was cold, Tom was happy and warm;
So if all do their duty they need not fear harm.   [1789]

YUSEF KOMUNYAKAA

Blackberries

They left my hands like a printer's
Or thief's before a police blotter
& pulled me into early morning's
Terrestrial sweetness, so thick
The damp ground was consecrated   5
Where they fell among a garland of thorns.

Although I could smell old lime-covered
History, at ten I'd still hold out my hands
& berries fell into them. Eating from one
& filling a half gallon with the other,   10
I ate the mythology & dreamt
Of pies & cobbler, almost

Needful as forgiveness. My bird dog Spot
Eyed blue jays & thrashers. The mud frogs
In rich blackness, hid from daylight.   15
An hour later, beside City Limits Road
I balanced a gleaming can in each hand,
Limboed between worlds, repeating *one dollar.*

The big blue car made me sweat.
Wintertime crawled out of the windows.   20
When I leaned closer I saw the boy
& girl my age, in the wide back seat
Smirking, & it was then I remembered my fingers
Burning with thorns among berries too ripe to touch.   [1992]

MARY OLIVER

Singapore

In Singapore, in the airport,
a darkness was ripped from my eyes.
In the women's restroom, one compartment stood open.
A woman knelt there, washing something
    in the white bowl.   5

Disgust argued in my stomach
and I felt, in my pocket, for my ticket.

A poem should always have birds in it.
Kingfishers, say, with their bold eyes and gaudy wings.
Rivers are pleasant, and of course trees.   10
A waterfall, or if that's not possible, a fountain
    rising and falling.
A person wants to stand in a happy place, in a poem.

When the woman turned I could not answer her face.
Her beauty and her embarrassment struggled together, and   15
    neither could win.
She smiled and I smiled. What kind of nonsense is this?
Everybody needs a job.

Yes, a person wants to stand in a happy place, in a poem.
But first we must watch her as she stares down at her labor,   20
    which is dull enough.
She is washing the tops of the airport ashtrays, as big as
    hubcaps, with a blue rag.
Her small hands turn the metal, scrubbing and rinsing.
She does not work slowly, nor quickly, but like a river.   25
Her dark hair is like the wing of a bird.

I don't doubt for a moment that she loves her life.
And I want her to rise up from the crust and the slop
    and fly down to the river.
This probably won't happen.   30
But maybe it will.
If the world were only pain and logic, who would want it?

Of course, it isn't.
Neither do I mean anything miraculous, but only
the light that can shine out of a life. I mean   35
the way she unfolded and refolded the blue cloth,
the way her smile was only for my sake; I mean
the way this poem is filled with trees, and birds.   [1992]

B. H. FAIRCHILD

The Machinist, Teaching His Daughter to Play the Piano

The brown wrist and hand with its raw knuckles and blue nails
    packed with dirt and oil, pause in mid-air,
the fingers arched delicately,

and she mimics him, hand held just so, the wrist loose,
    then swooping down to the wrong chord.   5
She lifts her hand and tries again.

Drill collars rumble, hammering the nubbin-posts.
    The helper lifts one, turning it slowly,
then lugs it into the lathe's chuck.

The bit shears the dull iron into new metal, falling   10
    into the steady chant of lathe work,
and the machinist lights a cigarette, holding

in his upturned palms the polonaise he learned at ten,
    then later the easiest waltzes,
etudes, impossible counterpoint   15

like the voice of his daughter he overhears one night
    standing in the backyard. She is speaking
to herself but not herself, as in prayer,

the listener is some version of herself,
    and the names are pronounced carefully,   20
self-consciously: Chopin, Mozart,

Scarlatti, . . . these gestures of voice and hands
    suspended over the keyboard
that move like the lathe in its turning

toward music, the wind dragging the hoist chain, the ring   25
    of iron on iron in the holding rack.
His daughter speaks to him one night,

but not to him, rather someone created between them,
    a listener, there and not there,
a master of lathes, a student of music.   [1997]   30

2

Writing

In Chapters 3 through 6, we will discuss how to write about each of the four literary genres featured in this book. At the moment, however, we will suggest how to write about a literary work of any genre. To make our advice concrete, we will trace what one student did as she worked on a writing assignment for a course much like yours. The assignment was given to a class that had been reading and discussing several poems about work, including the poems in Chapter 1 by John Milton, Frances Harper, Marge Piercy, and Lynda Hull. Each student chose a single poem from the syllabus and wrote a 600-word argument paper on it for a general audience. We will focus on the writing process of a student named Theresa Gardella.

Ultimately, Theresa chose to write about "What Work Is," the title poem from Philip Levine's 1991 book. Like Marge Piercy, Levine (b. 1928) grew up in Detroit. Although he has long been esteemed as a poet, much of his poetry continues to recall his youth in his native city, a world of automobile plants and other forms of heavy industry. Often Levine writes about his own hard work as a laborer in Detroit factories. Even when he is not being autobiographical, his poems often examine the difficulties faced by the American working class, both of his youth and of the present.

Before examining Theresa's writing process, read Levine's "What Work Is":

PHILIP LEVINE
What Work Is

We stand in the rain in a long line
waiting at Ford Highland Park. For work.
You know what work is—if you're
old enough to read this you know what
work is, although you may not do it.   5
Forget you. This is about waiting,
shifting from one foot to another.
Feeling the light rain falling like mist

43

into your hair, blurring your vision
until you think you see your own brother   10
ahead of you, maybe ten places.
You rub your glasses with your fingers,
and of course its someone else's brother,
narrower across the shoulders than
yours but with the same sad slouch, the grin   15
that does not hide the stubbornness,
the sad refusal to give in to
rain, to the hours wasted waiting,
to the knowledge that somewhere ahead
a man is waiting who will say, "No,   20
we're not hiring today," for any
reason he wants. You love your brother,
now suddenly you can hardly stand
the love flooding you for your brother,
who's not beside you or behind or   25
ahead because he's home trying to
sleep off a miserable night shift
at Cadillac so he can get up
before noon to study his German.
Works eight hours a night so he can sing   30
Wagner, the opera you hate most,
the worst music ever invented.
How long has it been since you told him
you loved him, held his wide shoulders,
opened your eyes wide and said those words,   35
and maybe kissed his cheek? You've never
done something so simple, so obvious,
not because you're too young or too dumb,
not because you're jealous or even mean
or incapable of crying in   40
the presence of another man, no,
just because you don't know what work is.   [1991]

Once she chose to write about Levine's poem for her paper, Theresa engaged
in four sorts of activities: (1) exploring, (2) planning, (3) composing, and (4) revising. As we describe each, keep in mind that these activities need not be consecutive. Theresa moved back and forth among them as she worked on her assignment.

Exploring

As you read a literary work, you are bound to interpret and judge it. Yet not
all reading is **critical reading**, which involves carefully and self-consciously analyzing various aspects of a text, including its meanings, its effects, and what it does

with typical elements of its genre. When you read a work critically, you also note questions it raises for you — issues you might explore further in class discussion and writing. Indeed, critical reading is a process of self-reflection. During this process, you monitor your own response to the text and try to identify why you see the text the way you do.

Perhaps you assume that literature contains hidden meanings that only an elite group of readers can spot. This is a common belief, but most people are quite capable of analyzing a literary work, especially if they know certain strategies for getting ideas about it. In rhetorical theory, these strategies are called methods of invention. Here we list some that Theresa used, including a few strategies that we have mentioned already. Try out any of them that are unfamiliar to you, even as you first read a text. Again, critical reading does not require divine inspiration. The following techniques have helped many a mortal:

1. *Make predictions as you read a text, guessing how it will turn out.* If you wind up being surprised, fine. You may gain several insights into the text, and yourself, as you reflect on the ways in which the text defies your expectations. Even if the text proceeds as you anticipated, making predictions about it is worthwhile, for at least you will have considered its possible lines of development.

2. *Read the text more than once.* You greatly increase your chances of getting ideas about it if you do. The first time around, you may be preoccupied with following the plot or with figuring out the text's basic meaning. Only by looking at the text repeatedly may you notice several of its other aspects, including features that really stir your thoughts. Given the busy schedule of a college student, you may be tempted to read a work just once before your class discusses it. But a single reading may leave you with relatively little to say, whereas multiple readings may give you several ideas to share.

3. *Note whatever changes of mind you go through as you read and reread the text.*

4. *Describe the audience that the author apparently had in mind, and note features of the text that support your image of its implied author.* At the same time, consider how real readers of the text — past, present, and future — might react to it, and why they might respond so. Also reflect on your own response to the text, noting anything in your own life that affects your reading of it.

5. *Read at least part of the text aloud, even if you are alone.* Doing this will give you a better sense of how the text manipulates language.

6. *Consciously focus on the text's content and on its form.* If you can focus on both content and form at the same time, fine, but many readers have trouble paying attention to the two simultaneously. In this case, deliberately alternate your focus first on content, then on form. This way you increase your chances of noticing things that the text is saying and doing.

7. *Consult a dictionary when you come across words in the text that you do not understand.* Keep in mind that a text may make a familiar word ambiguous,

leaving you with the impression that the author is attaching more than one meaning to it. An example might be Levine's use of the word *work*, which seems to take on various definitions as his poem proceeds. Furthermore, a text may define a commonly used word in a way unfamiliar to you. As we noted earlier, an example would be Milton's use of the word *fondly*, which in his time meant "foolishly," not "affectionately." If you suspect that a writer is using a common word in what for you is an uncommon way, turn to a dictionary to check the word's possible meanings.

8. *Note patterns within the text.* At the same time, pay attention to elements of the text that appear to threaten its unity, for instance, apparent contradictions or digressions.

9. *Try to identify the text's most important word, image, or scene.* At the same time, consider how to justify your choice.

10. *Identify moments where the text makes a significant shift in meaning, imagery, tone, plot, narrator, or point of view.* These moments may very well occur at typographic breaks in the text. In a poem, for example, significant changes may occur when one stanza ends and another begins. Similarly, a play may change significantly as it moves from scene to scene. Short stories and essays may also engage in important shifts as they go from paragraph to paragraph. But you may find turning points anywhere in the text, so do not look solely at its obvious moments of transition.

11. *Mark passages in the text that strike you as especially memorable.* These passages would include any that you might quote in a paper about the text.

12. *Aim to complicate the views you take of characters in the text.* If you tend to see a character as thoroughly mistaken, evil, or "sick," look for potentially redeeming qualities of that person. Similarly, if you tend to see a character as thoroughly good, look for qualities that suggest the person is less than perfect. Furthermore, consider whether you or the author are inclined to stereotype people. Note, too, any ways in which the characters fail to fit stereotypes.

13. *Raise questions about the text even as you read.* For help, you can turn to our list of ten different types of issues (pp. 19–26). In effect, the list indicates some aspects of the text that might be especially worth pondering. Recall that these include the following:

- facts obscured or absent in the text
- the text's theme
- possible definitions of key words in the text
- the symbols it employs
- its patterns
- evaluations that might be made in response to it
- its historical and cultural context
- its genre
- its relevance to current political debates
- causes and effects of its characters' behavior; the author's aims and effects

14. *Note whether and how the text addresses topics of particular interest to professional literary critics today.* (For a discussion of such topics, refer to the last section of Chapter 1, pp. 32–42.

15. *Think about the writer's alternatives: things the writer could have done and yet didn't do.* Then, imagine that the writer had pursued these alternatives. How would the effect of the text have been different?

16. *Consider whether and how the text itself features elements of argument.* (Refer back to pp. 17–30 in Chapter 1.)

17. *Compare the text with others on the same subject.* So far, we have encouraged you to compare various poems about work. Going beyond the world of literature, you might compare whatever text you are focusing on to certain films, television shows, songs, advertisements, and articles in newspapers and magazines.

18. *Discuss the text with your instructor, your classmates, and other people you know.* If differences emerge between their views and yours, try to identify the exact issues at hand, as well as the possible reasons for those differences. Perhaps you will talk about the text with people who have not read it at all. If so, note the questions these people have about the text. Note, too, what you find yourself emphasizing as you describe the text to them.

You can also develop and pull together your thoughts about a text by informally writing about it. And the sooner you plunge into the rhythms of composing, the more comfortable you will feel producing a full-fledged paper. Your informal, preliminary writing can take various shapes. The following are just some of the things you might do.

1. *Make notes in the text itself.* A common method is to mark key passages, either by underlining these passages or running a magic marker through them. Both ways of marking are popular because they help readers recall main features of the text. But use these techniques moderately if you use them at all, for marking lots of passages will leave you unable to distinguish the really important parts of the text. Also, try "talking back" to the text in its margins. Next to particular passages, you might jot down words of your own, indicating any feelings and questions you have about those parts. On any page of the text, you might circle related words and then draw lines between these words to emphasize their connection. If a word or an idea shows up on numerous pages, you might circle it each time. Furthermore, try cross-referencing, by listing on at least one page the numbers of all those pages where the word or idea appears.

2. *As you read the text, occasionally look away from it and jot down anything in it you recall.* This memory exercise lets you review your developing impressions of the text. When you turn back to its actual words, you may find that you have distorted or overlooked aspects of it that you should take into account.

3. *At various moments in your reading, freewrite about the text for ten minutes or so.* Spontaneously explore your preliminary thoughts and feelings about it, as

well as any personal experiences the text leads you to recall. One logical moment to do freewriting is when you have finished reading the text. But you do not have to wait until then; as you read, you might pause occasionally to freewrite. This way, you give yourself an opportunity to develop and review your thoughts about the text early on.

4. *Create what composition theorist Ann Berthoff calls a "dialectical note-book."* It involves using pages of your regular notebook in a particular way. On each page, draw a line down the middle to create two columns. In the left column, list various details of the text: specifically, words, images, characters, and events that strike you. Then, in the right column, jot down for each detail one or more sentences indicating *why* you were drawn to it. Take as many pages as you need to record and reflect on your observations. You can also use the two-column format to carry out a dialogue with yourself about the text. This is an especially good way to ponder aspects of the text that you find confusing, mysterious, or complex.

5. *Play with the text by revising it.* Doing so will make you more aware of options that the author rejected and give you a better sense of the moves that the author chose to make. Specifically, you might rearrange parts of the text, add to it, change some of its words, or shift its narrative point of view. After you revise the text, compare your alternative version with the original, considering especially differences in their effects.

A WRITING EXERCISE

Do at least ten minutes of freewriting about Levine's poem. Note questions you have about the poem that might be worth addressing in a more formal paper. Also compare Levine's poem on work to Milton's, Harper's, Piercy's, or Hull's poem on the subject. What similarities do you find? What differences?

The first time Theresa read Levine's poem, she started out predicting that it would define *work*. After all, its title is "What Work Is." Soon, though, she felt her expectation thwarted. For one thing, the speaker claims "you know what work is," as if the word does not need to be defined. Then, the speaker proceeds to declare that the poem is not even about work, but rather about "waiting." Theresa did not know how to interpret this change of subject. Her confusion was only heightened at the end of the poem, where the speaker contradicts the poem's beginning by asserting "you don't know what work is." After her first reading of the poem, Theresa came away from it puzzled.

At the same time, Theresa was excited because she felt that she had discovered at least one issue that she could write her paper about. As we noted, Theresa found herself grappling specifically with an issue of definition. She suspected that if she wrote her paper on this poem, she would analyze how it defines the word *work*, especially in relation to the word *waiting*.

Theresa realized, though, that first she had to pinpoint the text's patterns. Therefore, she began noting words that the poem uses more than once. After personal reflection, consultation with her teacher, and a meeting with a small group of classmates, Theresa had compiled a substantial list of words: *work, stand, know, waiting, rain, long, love, sad, ahead, man, wide, not,* and *because.* She also saw that the statement "you know what work is" occurs twice. Furthermore, Theresa noticed that certain words in the poem closely echo each other: *know / knowledge, say / said, shifting / shift.* Some of the poem's words represent related concepts: for instance, the "light rain falling like mist" can be connected to *flooding* and *crying.* A second example occurs in the last sentence, where the words *never, not, incapable, no,* and *don't* all emphasize negativity.

Not until she had read the poem aloud several times did Theresa become aware that it also features patterns of **alliteration**. In alliteration, certain words near one another begin with the same consonant. Here are some examples in Levine's poem:

forget, foot, feeling, falling, fingers

someone, shoulders, same sad slouch, stubbornness, sad

wasted, waiting (twice), wants (also: some*wh*ere)

brother, beside, behind

works, worst, wide, words

never, not (twice)

Yet Theresa knew that she had to do more than trace patterns. After all, she was thrown by the poem's shifts, its apparent discontinuities. So she also tried to pinpoint these breaks. As we reported, she was extremely conscious of the speaker's shift from the word *work* to *waiting* near the start. She was quite aware, too, that the poem's final line clashes with its earlier statement that "you know what work is." But upon reflection she felt that the biggest change occurs in the middle of the poem. There, with the words "you love your brother," the poem thoroughly departs from the scene of people waiting for a job, and it comes to focus instead on brotherly love.

As Theresa reread the poem several times, she looked for words that, in one way or another, helped connect its two halves. Again, she recognized as a form of connection the poem's imagery of falling water (*rain, flooding,* and *crying*), which runs throughout the text. She became aware that certain words in the poem have a dual frame of reference. They mean one thing in the context of the men's waiting in line and another, quite different thing when applied to the brothers' relationship. An example is the phrase "sad refusal." Clearly this phrase expresses the determination of the sleeping brother not to let life defeat him. Yet it could also apply to the statement made by the company's representative to the men waiting in line. By saying "'No, / we're not hiring today,'" the representative engages in a "sad refusal," though his listeners are the ones left sad. Similarly, while the word *stand* first appears as a label for what the men in line do, later it appears in connection with the brothers' bond ("now suddenly you can hardly stand / the love flooding you for your brother"). The same thing happens with the words *shifting* and *shift*: the first describes behavior in the line, but the second refers to the work of the sleeping brother. Note, too, what happens with the word *long*. At first it refers to the length of the line, but later it refers to the brothers' personal history ("How long has it been since you told him / you loved him").

Together, these double reference words led Theresa to consider what the poem is doing with the subject of time. She perceived the men waiting in line as oriented toward the future: They hope to be employed. But later the speaker accuses the brother in line of waiting too long to tell his brother he loves him. *This* waiting, Theresa saw, is not a matter of looking to the future. Rather, it is a failure to acknowledge the past: specifically, all the years that have passed before the brother in line can express fraternal affection.

Theresa was beginning to envision a paper in which she made claims about how the poem relates waiting to past, present, and future. As yet, though, she had not decided exactly what her main claim would be. Nor had she determined how her paper would examine the poem's references to work. In addition, Theresa still had some questions about the text itself. The following is an excerpt from freewriting she did at this point:

> I'm still not sure who the "you" is. In the fourth line, the "you" seems to be the reader. Then the speaker says "Forget you." But then the poem keeps referring to "you," and this "you" seems to be not the reader but someone waiting in the line. Maybe it's the speaker himself. Anyway, I'm confused.
>
> I also wonder if the poem is autobiographical. It might be about Levine's own experience of waiting in a job line and thinking about his relationship with his brother. The references to car factories make me think the city is Detroit, and that's where Levine grew up. He might be both the speaker and the "you" that the speaker addresses for most of the poem. But does this mean the poem takes place in the past? Levine is now a well-known poet, so I doubt that he's currently looking for a job. Since he was born in 1928, maybe the poem is set around 1950, when he would have been in his twenties.
>
> Of course, there are unemployed people today, so I don't have any trouble relating the poem to the present even if it does take place years ago. Plus I guess it doesn't really matter whether the poem is about Levine himself. Other people still have to relate to it if it's going to succeed as a poem. I can identify with the

"you." I've applied for lots of jobs, and I haven't always gotten them. And I've waited in lots of lines. Just a few weeks ago, I waited in a long line at this school to register for courses. Plus I know that sometimes I haven't thought about my family the way that I should have. It's true that I haven't been as desperate as the men in line in the poem seem to be. But I can still empathize with them pretty much.

In class, our instructor said that a lot of literary critics today see literary works as being about reading and writing. I hadn't looked at literature that way before, but the idea is interesting to me, and I've been thinking about it the more I read Levine's poem. I wonder if the poem is to some extent about Levine's experience in writing it, or our experience in reading it, or both. I mean, besides using the word "shifting," the poem itself shifts in focus. And the poem itself seems to me like a long line that I'm moving through, waiting to get the meaning. Maybe Levine wants me to think about the work I am doing in reading his poem. Maybe he wants me to see this work as involving reflection on human relationships, like the relationship between the brothers, instead of just being a matter of waiting for the meaning to emerge. Plus I think "foot" is a term in poetry. If I remember right, it's a unit of measurement. A line in a poem is a certain number of feet. But am I reading too much into Levine's poem at this point?

Freewriting enabled Theresa to raise several issues. At the same time, she wondered if she had to resolve them completely before writing her paper. She knew that the paper would have to address at least some of her questions about the poem, but she also knew that the paper could not deal with everything that puzzled her. When you first get an assignment like hers, you may fear that you will have nothing to say. But you will come up with a lot of material if, like Theresa, you take time for exploration. As we have suggested, it's a process of examining potential subjects through writing, discussion, and just plain thinking. One of your challenges will then be to choose among the various issues you have formulated. Like Theresa, you will need to decide which issues to pursue and which to drop.

Planning

Planning for an assignment like Theresa's involves five main activities:

1. choosing the text you will analyze;
2. identifying your audience;
3. identifying the main issue, claim, and evidence you will present;
4. identifying particular challenges you will face and warrants you will use; and
5. determining how you will organize your argument.

Theresa considered several poems before choosing one for her paper. She settled on Levine's for five reasons. First, it was a text that left her with plenty of questions. Second, she believed that these questions could be issues for other readers. Third, she felt increasingly able to *argue* about the poem — that is, to make and support claims about it. Fourth, she believed that she could adequately analyze the poem within the assignment's word limit. Finally, Levine's poem interested her the most, largely because she found it the most complex and thought-provoking.

Faced with the same assignment, you might choose another poem than Theresa did. Still, the principles that she followed are useful. Think about them whenever you are free to decide which texts you will write about. With some assignments, of course, you may need a while to decide which text is best for you. And later, after you have made your decision, you may want to make a switch. For example, you may find yourself changing your mind once you have done a complete draft. Frustrated by the text you have chosen, you may realize that another inspires you more. If so, consider making a substitution. Naturally, you will feel more able to switch if you have ample time left to write the paper, so avoid waiting to start your paper just before it is due.

To know what your readers will see as an issue, and to make your claims about it persuasive to them, you need to develop an audience profile. Perhaps your instructor will specify your audience, even invite you to write for classmates. Most often, though, instructors ask students to write for a "general" audience, the readership that Theresa was asked to address. Assume that a general audience is one that will want evidence for your claims. While this audience will obviously include your instructor, let it also include your classmates, since in class discussions they will be an audience for you whenever you speak. Besides, your class may engage in peer review, with students giving one another feedback on their drafts.

If your audience is indeed supposed to be a general group of readers, what can you assume about their prior knowledge? You may not be sure. Above all, you may wonder how familiar your readers already are with the text you are analyzing. Perhaps your teacher will resolve your uncertainty, telling you exactly how much your audience knows about the text. Then again, you may be left to guess. Should you presume that your audience is totally unfamiliar with the text? This approach is risky, for it may lead you to spend a lot of your paper merely summarizing the text rather than analyzing it. A better move is to write as if your audience is at least a bit more knowledgeable. Here is a good rule of thumb: Assume that your audience has, in fact, read the text, but that you need to recall for this group any features of the text that are crucial to your argument. Although probably your paper will still include summary, the amount you provide will be limited, and your own ideas will be more prominent.

Perhaps your instructor will ask you occasionally to write for a specific audience whom you have imagined. Even when not required, such an exercise can be fun and thought-provoking for you as you plan a paper. Think about how you might refer to Harper's poem "Free Labor" if, like Kathie Lee Gifford, you testified to Congress about the garment industry's current reliance on poorly paid sweatshop workers. Theresa's teacher asked her what she would say if she were giving a speech about Levine's poem to the United Auto Workers convention. This question left Theresa with mixed feelings. To her, Levine's poem chiefly concerns the work of preserving human relationships. But she suspected that auto workers would scoff if she emphasized this topic more than their jobs. Moreover, she sensed that Levine is not mocking people's wish to be employed. What he *is* doing, she concluded, is encouraging his readers to *extend* their usual definition of work so that it includes the labor involved in building human relationships.

When you have written papers for previous classes, you may have been most concerned with coming up with a thesis. Maybe you did not encounter the term *issue* at all. But good planning for a paper does entail identifying the main issue you will address. Once you have sensed what that issue is, try phrasing it as a question. If the answer would be obvious to your readers, be cautious, for you really do not have an issue if the problem you are raising can be easily resolved.

Also, try to identify what *kind* of issue you will focus on. For help, look at our list of the various types (pp. 19–26). Theresa realized that her main issue could be one of pattern. The question might be, Are the two halves of Levine's poem actually related, or is the second a definite break from the first? But Theresa felt more comfortable making the issue one of definition. Even then, however, she could think of at least three possible questions:

How does Levine's poem define *work*?

How does the poem define *waiting*?

How does the poem define *work* and *waiting* in relation to each other?

Ultimately, Theresa decided to write a paper that raised and addressed the third question. To her, it was the most stimulating, and just as important, she felt able to answer it well. Perhaps you have grown comfortable with the term *thesis* and want to keep using it. Fine. Bear in mind, though, that your thesis is your main *claim*. And when you put your main issue as a question, then your main claim is your answer to that question. Sometimes you will come up with question and answer simultaneously. Once in a while, you may even settle on your answer first, not being certain yet how to word the question. Whatever the case, planning for your paper involves articulating both the question (your issue) and the answer (your main claim). Try actually writing both down, making sure to phrase your main issue as a question and your main claim as the answer. Theresa's main issue was, How does the poem define *work* and *waiting* in relation to each other? After much thought, she expressed her main claim this way:

```
The poem first defines work as physical labor, and wait-
ing as the process of searching for a job. Eventually,
the poem defines work as emotional labor in human rela-
tionships, and it implies that often people unfortunately
"wait" in the sense of letting a lot of time pass before
they tell members of their family that they love them.
```

Audiences usually want evidence, and as we noted earlier, most arguments you make about literature will need to cite details of the work itself. In particular, direct quotation is usually an effective move. Theresa planned to elaborate her claim by bringing up several of Levine's own words, especially those that change meaning as the poem shifts from physical work to emotional work. Remember you need to avoid seeming willfully selective when you quote. Theresa knew that for her argument to be plausible, she would have to quote from both halves of Levine's text.

Theresa recognized that she would be facing other challenges. One of them involved the *you* of the poem. Although Theresa had decided that it does not matter exactly who this *you* is, she knew that some of her readers might feel otherwise. Therefore, she planned to include a paragraph that explained why they should not be concerned. Another challenge involved the key terms of Theresa's argument. She knew that the poem does not actually use the word *work* to describe emotional labor. Nor does the poem actually use the word *waiting* in referring to the *you*'s neglect of his brother. Basically, she would be arguing that the poem redefines these two words by *implication*. To make her view credible, she would have to refer extensively to the words that the poem does use.

Often, to think about particular challenges of your paper is to think about your warrants. Remember that warrants are assumptions; they are what lead you to call certain things evidence for your claims. Theresa knew that one of her warrants was an assumption about Levine himself: namely, that he was not just being crazy when he ended his poem by contradicting the statement "you know what work is." Rarely will your paper need to admit all the warrants you are relying on. Most of the time, your task will be to guess which warrants your readers do want stated. Theresa felt there was at least one warrant she would have to spell out: her belief that a poem may redefine terms implicitly rather than explicitly.

To make sure their texts seem organized, most writers first do an **outline**, a list of their key points in the order they will appear. Outlines are indeed a good idea, but bear in mind that there are various kinds. One popular type, which you may already know, is the **sentence outline**. As the name implies, it lists the writer's key points in sentence form. Its advantages are obvious: This kind of outline forces you to develop a detailed picture of your argument's major steps, and it leaves you with sentences you can then incorporate into your paper. Unfortunately, sentence outlines tend to discourage flexibility. Because they demand much thought and energy, you may hesitate to revise them, even if you come to feel your paper would work better with a new structure.

A second, equally familiar outline is the **topic outline**, a list in which the writer uses a few words to signify the main subjects that he or she will discuss. Because it is sketchy, this kind of outline allows writers to go back and change plans if necessary. Nevertheless, a topic outline may fail to provide all the guidance a writer needs.

We find a third type useful: a **rhetorical purpose outline**. As with the first two, you list the major sections of your paper. Next, you briefly indicate two things for each section: the effect you want it to have on your audience, and how you will achieve that effect. Here is the rhetorical purpose outline that Theresa devised for her paper.

INTRODUCTION

The audience needs to know the text I'll discusss.	I'll identify Levine's poem.
The audience must know my main issue.	I'll show how the poem is confusing about how it defines and relates work and waiting.
The audience must know my main claim.	I'll claim that although the poem first defines work as physical labor and waiting as the process of searching for a job, eventually it defines work as emotional labor in human relationships, and it implies that often people unfortunately wait in the sense of letting a lot of time pass before they tell their family that they love them.

CONCESSION

The audience must be reassured that it doesn't matter that I haven't figured out who the "you" is.	I'll admit that I'm not certain about the identity of the "you," but I'll point out that my issue and my main claim can be valid no matter who the "you" is.

ANALYSIS OF THE POEM'S FIRST HALF

The audience needs to be sure of how the poem defines work and waiting in its first half.

I'll briefly review how the first half defines these terms, perhaps quoting briefly but relying mostly on paraphrase.

ANALYSIS OF THE POEM'S SECOND HALF

The audience needs to see that the second half of the poem defines work and waiting differently from how the first half defines them.

I'll quote and paraphrase specific lines that point to work as emotional labor and waiting as a failure to acknowledge the family.

The audience needs to feel the poem is suggesting that people should take seriously these new definitions.

I'll point out that the whole movement of the poem is toward these definitions.

IDENTIFICATION OF RELATED WORDS
WHOSE MEANING IS TRANSFORMED

The audience may want further evidence that the poem transforms the meaning of work and waiting as it proceeds.

I'll show how related words also get redefined as the poem moves from its first half to its second. Specifically, I'll discuss the words standing, shifting, long, and sad refusal.

CONCLUSION

The audience may need to be clearer about how important the second definitions of work and waiting are in relation to the first.

I'll say that while Levine evidently feels that people haven't paid enough attention to the second set of meanings, he isn't necessarily calling for them to throw out the first set.

For your own rhetorical purpose outlines, you may want to use phrases rather than sentences. If you do use sentences, as Theresa did, you do not have to write all that many. Note that Theresa wrote relatively few as she stated the effects she would aim for and her strategies for achieving those effects. Thus, she was not tremendously invested in preserving her original outline. She felt free to change it if it failed to prove helpful.

Composing

Not always is **composing** distinguishable from exploring, planning, and revising. As you prepare for your paper, you may jot down words or whole sentences. Once you begin a draft, you may alter that draft in several ways before you complete it. You may be especially prone to making changes in drafts if you use a computer, for word processing enables you to jump around in your text, revisiting and revising what you have written.

Still, most writers feel that doing a draft is an activity in its own right, and a major one at that. The next four chapters present various tips for writing about specific genres, and the appendix discusses writing research papers. Meanwhile, here are some tips to help you with composing in general.

Title

You may be inclined to let your **title** be the same as that of the text you discuss. Were you to write about Levine's poem, then, you would be calling your own paper "What Work Is." But often such mimicry backfires. For one thing, it may lead your readers to think that you are unoriginal and perhaps even lazy. Also, you risk confusing your audience, since your paper would actually be about Levine's poem rather than being the poem itself. So, take the time to come up with a title of your own. Certainly it may announce the text you will focus on, but let it do more. In particular, use your title to indicate the main claim you will be making. With just a few words, you can preview the argument to come.

Style

Perhaps you have been told to "sound like yourself" when you write. Yet that can be a difficult demand (especially if you are not sure what your "self" is really like). Above all, the **style** you choose depends on your audience and purpose. In writing an argument for a general audience, probably you would do best to avoid the extremes of pomposity and breezy informality. Try to stick with words you know well, and if you do want to use some that are only hazily familiar to you, check their dictionary definitions first.

At some point in our lives, probably all of us have been warned not to use *I* in our writing. In the course you are taking, however, you may be asked to write about your experiences. If so, you will find *I* hard to avoid. Whether to use it does become a real question when you get assignments like Theresa's, which require you chiefly to make an argument about a text. Since you are supposed to focus on that text, your readers may be disconcerted if you keep referring to yourself. Even so, you need not assume that your personal life is irrelevant to the task. Your open-ing paragraph might refer to your personal encounters with the text, as a way of establishing the issue you will discuss. A personal anecdote might serve as a forceful conclusion to your paper. Moreover, before you reach the conclusion, you might orient your readers to the structure of your paper by using certain expressions that feature the word *I*: for example, *As I suggested earlier, As I have noted, As I will argue later*. In general, you may be justified in saying *I* at certain moments. When tempted to use this pronoun, though, consider whether it really is your best move.

In a paper, the expressions *I think* and *I feel* are rarely effective. Often writers resort to such phrasing because they sense they are offering nothing more than their own opinion. The audience may view such expressions as indications of a weak argument or limited evidence. You might make the claim more persuasive by avoiding *I think* and *I feel* and by qualifying it through words such as *probably, possibly, maybe,* and *perhaps*. If you believe that you have little evidence for a claim you want to make, take time out from writing and go back to exploring your ideas. If you can, come up with additional means of support.

Arguments about literature are most compelling when supported by quota-tions, but be careful not to quote excessively. If you constantly repeat other people's words, providing few of your own, your readers will hardly get a sense of you as an author. Moreover, a paper full of quotation marks is hard to read. Make sure to quote selectively, remembering that sometimes you can simply paraphrase. When you do quote, try to cite only the words you need. You do not have to repro-duce a whole line or sentence if one word is enough to support your point.

When summarizing what happens in a literary work, be careful not to shift tenses as you go along. Your reader may be confused if you shift back and forth between past and present. We suggest that you stick primarily to the present tense, which is the tense that literary critics customarily employ. For example, instead of saying that the men *waited* in line, say that they *wait* in line.

Introduction

Many writers aim to impress their audience right away. You may be tempted, then, to begin your paper with a grand philosophical statement, hoping your readers will find such an **introduction** profound. Often, however, this approach results in broad, obvious generalities. Here are some examples:

Society doesn't always appreciate the work that everyone does.

Over the centuries, there has been a lot of literature, and much of it has been about work.

Philip Levine is a great poet writing today.

As writing theorist William Coles points out, statements like these are mere "throat-clearing." They may lead your audience to think that you are delaying, not introducing, your real argument. Rather than beginning your paper with such statements, try mentioning the specific text you will analyze. Get started making assertions about that text.

Usually, your introduction will identify the main issue that you will discuss. Perhaps you will be able to assume that your audience is already aware of this issue and sees it as important. Theresa felt that her audience would wonder, as she did, how Levine relates *working* and *waiting*. Sometimes, however, your introduction will need to set out your issue at greater length. It will need to identify the issue as a significant question with no obvious answer.

A classic way to establish the importance of an issue is to show that other critics have grappled with it or wrongly ignored it. You may, however, get assignments in your course that do not push you to consider what previous critics have said. An alternative method of establishing your issue's significance is personal anecdote. By describing how the issue came to matter to you, you may persuade your readers to see it as mattering to them. If you do not want to be autobiographical, you have at least one other option. You can show that if your issue is left unaddressed, your readers will remain puzzled by other key aspects of the text you are discussing.

Development

When you write a paper, naturally you want the parts of each sentence to hang together. But make sure, too, that each sentence connects clearly to the one before and the one after. Smooth transitions from one paragraph to the next encourage your reader to follow the **development** of your argument. Certain words can help you signal relations between sentences. Here are just a few examples. Each could appear at the beginning of a sentence, where it would indicate how that sentence relates to the one before.

- Numerical order: *first, second, third*, etc.
- Temporal order: *then, next, earlier, previously, before, later, subsequently, afterward*
- Addition: *also, in addition to, furthermore, moreover, another*
- Degree: *more/less important, more/less often*
- Effect: *thus, therefore, as a result, consequently, hence, so*
- Opposition: *but, yet, however, nevertheless, still, even so, by contrast, on the contrary, conversely, on the other hand*
- Exemplarity: *for example, for instance*
- Emphasis: *indeed, in fact*
- Restatement: *that is, in other words*
- Specificity: *specifically, more precisely, in particular*

Do not fall into the habit of relying on *and* as a connective. As a means of linking sentences or of bridging ideas within them, *and* may seem a safe choice; besides being a common word, it looks too little to cause trouble. Nevertheless, as a connective *and* is often vague, failing to show how words actually relate. Note the following sentence:

The "you" has not shown enough brotherly love, and he does not really "know what work is."

The word *and* does little to fuse the sentence's two halves. A more precise way to connect the halves would be with language that shows their relation to be cause and effect:

> The "you" has not shown enough brotherly love; *therefore*, he does not really "know what work is."

Some people might disagree with this statement, claiming the relation is actually effect and cause:

> The "you" has not shown enough brotherly love, *because* he does not really "know what work is."

Whatever the merits of these two revisions, both are more coherent than the sentence using *and*, which hardly conveys relation at all. Also, if your paper constantly uses *and* or any other particular word, your prose may come across as monotonous.

The word *and* often becomes a prime means of transition in papers that mostly just summarize plots of texts. Presumably, though, your goal in a paper is to *analyze* whatever text you are discussing, not simply outline it. If you see that you are using *and* a lot in your writing, consider the possibility that you are, in fact, summarizing more than analyzing. In our experience, writers are most apt to lapse into plot summary toward the middle of their paper. At that point, they may grow tired of developing and keeping track of their own ideas. The easiest thing to do then is to coast, simply paraphrasing their chosen text line by line. Pause in your writing from time to time to see if you have lapsed into this practice. Remember that you can analyze details of a text without sticking to their original order.

How coherent a paper seems depends in part on the length of its paragraphs. Usually, a paragraph should be at least three sentences long. When readers confront one very short paragraph after another, they are apt to feel that they are seeing random, fragmented observations rather than a well-organized argument. Of course, paragraphs can also be too long. Readers have trouble following the structure of one that runs a full page. If you find yourself writing a lengthy paragraph, stop and check to see if there is any place in it where starting a new paragraph makes sense.

Emphasis

Many people assume that academic writing consists of long, dense statements. Furthermore, they assume that such prose is virtually unreadable. Whether or not they are right about the kind of writing favored in college, your own readers may get tired and lost if each of your sentences seems endless. On the other hand, your writing may strike your readers as choppy if each sentence contains just a few words. Usually, your papers will be most effective if you vary the lengths of your sentence for **emphasis**. In any paper you write for your course, aim for a mixture of sentence lengths, blending long, medium, and short.

But in any of your sentences, use only the amount of words you need to make your point. For example, do not resort to sixteen words when eight will suffice. Your readers are likely to become impatient, even bored, if your prose seems padded. Also, they may doubt your credibility, suspecting that you are pretending to have more ideas than you do.

Perhaps you fear that if you economize with your language, all your sentences will wind up short. But a concise sentence is not always brief; a sentence can be long and yet tightly edited, with every word in it deserving a place. Another possible fear has to do with writer's block. You may worry that you will have trouble getting words down if you must justify every single one of them. A good solution is to postpone editing for a while, perhaps even waiting until you have finished a draft. Simply remember that at some point you should review whatever you have written, looking for words you might trim.

Your sentences will have more impact if you use active rather than passive verbs. To grasp the difference, read the following two sentences:

At the end, the "you" is accused by the speaker of the poem of not knowing "what work is."

At the end, the speaker of the poem accuses the "you" of not knowing "what work is."

Certainly both sentences are grammatical. The second, however, is more concise and dynamic. That is because it uses the active form of the verb *to accuse* and indicates right away the agent performing the action. The first sentence uses the passive form, *is accused by*. The word *is* can serve as a tip-off: Passive verbs always feature some version of *to be*.

Passive verbs are not always bad. Sometimes a sentence will work better if it uses one. We can even envision a situation where our first sample sentence would perhaps make more sense. Imagine that up to this point, the writer has repeatedly referred to the "you." Imagine, too, that the writer had left off mentioning the speaker several paragraphs back. By making the "you" the grammatical subject of the sentence, the writer can maintain consistency, whereas suddenly switching to "the speaker" might throw readers off. Usually, however, passive verbs are unnecessary and counterproductive. Make them an exception, not the rule.

Usually, a sentence will seem better paced if you keep the main subject and verb close together. When several words come between subject and verb, readers may have trouble following along. This pair of sentences illustrates what we mean:

The word *long*, first brought up in the opening line, reappears with a different meaning in the poem's second half.

First brought up in the opening line, the word *long* reappears with a different meaning in the poem's second half.

Neither sentence is bad. But the first forces the reader to slow down right in the middle, since it puts several words between subject and verb. By keeping them together, the second sentence flows more.

Sentences are easier to read when they include at most one negative expression: words such as *not, never, don't,* and *won't.* On the other hand, a sentence is often hard to follow when it features several negatives. Look at the following pair of examples:

Not saying that physical work is never good, the speaker simply will not let
the "you" get away with not doing emotional work.

Not criticizing physical work, the speaker simply suggests that the "you"
should also do emotional work.

While the first sentence is grammatically correct and makes a logical point, its
blizzard of negatives will confuse many readers. The second sentence makes
basically the same point, but because it minimizes negatives, it is easier to read.

A point can have greater or less emphasis depending on where you place it. If
you want to call attention to a paragraph's main idea, try beginning the paragraph
with it. In any case, most likely your readers will assume that a paragraph's opening sentence is important. Usually they will pay special attention to its last sentence, too. Therefore, try not to fill either of these slots with relatively trivial
points. Also, remember that you may obscure an important idea if you put it in
the middle of a paragraph. There, the idea will have trouble getting the prominence it deserves.

Conclusion

You can always end your paper by summarizing the argument you have
made. In fact, many readers will welcome a recap. Yet a conclusion that merely
restates your argument risks boring your audience. Therefore, try to keep any
final summary brief, using your **conclusion** to do additional things.

For example, the conclusion is a good place to make concessions. Even if
you have already indicated ways in which people may reasonably disagree with
you, you may use the close of your paper to acknowledge that you have no
monopoly on truth. Your conclusion is also an opportunity for you to evaluate the
text you have been discussing or to identify questions that the text still leaves in
your mind. Consider as well the possibility of using your conclusion to bring up
some personal experience that relates to the text. Yet another option is to have
your conclusion identify implications of your argument that you have not so far
announced: How might people apply your method of analysis to other texts?
What, in effect, have you suggested about how people should live? What image
have you given of the author that you have been discussing?

You might also end your paper by indicating further research you would like
to do. Admittedly, this sort of conclusion is more typical of the sciences and social
sciences. Literary critics tend to conclude their arguments as if there is nothing
more they need to investigate. But if you do suggest you have more work to do,
your readers may admire you for remaining curious and ambitious.

Sample Student Paper: First Draft

The following is Theresa's first complete draft of her paper. Eventually she
revised this draft after a group of her classmates reviewed it, and she reflected further on it herself. For the moment, though, read this first version and decide what
you would have said to her about it.

Theresa Gardella

Professor Schwartz

English 102

10 March ----

The Shifting Definitions of <u>Work</u> and

<u>Waiting</u> in Philip Levine's "What Work Is"

The title of Philip Levine's poem "What Work Is" suggests that the poem will clearly define <u>work</u>. But as it
goes on, it gets confusing about this subject. Early on,
the speaker says, "You know what work is." By contrast,
at the end the speaker says, "You don't know what work
is." Another puzzling thing is that the speaker says
early on that despite the poem's title, "this is about
waiting." So, after I first read the poem, I wondered how
it was defining <u>work</u> and <u>waiting</u>. I also wondered how it
was relating these two words. After thinking a lot about
the poem, I want to claim now that it redefines both
words as it moves along. First, it refers to work as
physical labor and to waiting as the process of searching
for a job. Eventually it defines work as emotional labor
in human relationships, and it implies that often people
wait, in the sense of letting a lot of time pass, before
they tell members of their family that they love them.
The first kind of waiting looks to the future. The second
kind of waiting is in part a failure to take sufficient
account of someone else in the present, the "you"'s
brother sleeping at home. This second kind of waiting is
also a failure to acknowledge the past, the amount of
time that the "you" has let go by before telling his
brother that he loves him.

Before going further, I must confess that I am still
not sure who the "you" of the poem is. My first impression was that the "you" is the reader, since the speaker
says "if you're / old enough to read this you know what /
work is, although you may not do it." But pretty soon
after this statement, the "you" apparently becomes one of
the people waiting in line for work at Ford Highland

Park, "Feeling the light rain falling like mist / into your hair." As the poem goes on, the "you" seems to get even more specific. The speaker says things like "you love your brother" and "you've never / done something so simple, so obvious." In addition, the "you" has a brother who works at an auto plant, studies German, and sings opera. When the speaker concludes by saying "you don't know what work is," I am still left wondering if this is the same "you" who did know what work is back at the start. Moreover, I wonder if at least one of the "you"'s in the poem is really the speaker. Yet even though I still cannot decide the identity of the "you," the poem redefines <u>work</u> and <u>waiting</u> in any case, and that is what I will claim in this paper. My argument applies whether or not any of us can be sure who the "you" is.

In the first half of the poem, the speaker clearly refers to work as physical labor. The men being described are standing in line at an auto plant, Ford Highland Park, hoping to get a job there. The men's time in this line seems to be "hours wasted waiting," though, because the plant representative is probably going to say "'No, / we're not hiring today.'" Although that representative is himself "waiting" to make his response, the poem has so far been emphasizing the waiting process of the unemployed men who hope that the plant will hire them.

The second half of the poem does have an additional reference to work as physical labor. The "you"'s brother "works eight hours a night so he can sing / Wagner." But in this half the speaker tends to emphasize the work involved in expressing love for the rest of one's family. The speaker suggests that the "you" has let too much time go by before telling his brother "you loved him." The "you" apparently does love his brother. Moreover, expressing love for him would evidently be a "simple" and "obvious" thing to do. But the speaker says to the "you" that "you don't know what work is." In part, this could mean work as physical labor again. The speaker would thus be saying that the "you" hasn't expressed brotherly love because he hasn't thought enough about the physical hardships that his brother has endured. Nevertheless, the more important meaning of work here seems to be emotional labor. The speaker would thus be saying that the "you" doesn't understand that expressing love for his brother is a form of work he hasn't thought about and that he really should do, instead of concentrating on his own search for a job.

I admit that the second half of the poem does not actually mention the word waiting. But because the speaker has said earlier that "this is about waiting," the reader should feel encouraged to think that the word applies to the second half of the poem as much as to the first half. No longer does the speaker refer, though, to waiting in the sense of standing in line for a job. When the speaker asks the "how long has it been" question, it seems as if this question involves waiting in the sense of the "you"'s taking too long to show the brotherly love he feels.

The shifts in definition of work and waiting that I am talking about are reinforced by shifts in the meanings of other words as the poem moves from its first half to its second. In the first half, the people looking for physical labor "stand" in line for it. In the second half, emotional labor is suggested by the words "you can hardly stand / the love flooding you for your brother." Also, while in the first half the unemployed are "shifting" as they wait, the second half brings up feelings by mentioning the brother's "miserable night shift." Similarly, although it is the line of unemployed people that's "long" in the first half, the second half of the poem suggests a "long" time has gone by since the "you" last showed his love for his brother.

A clear switching point in the poem is the phrase
"sad refusal." This phrase could easily fit what the
plant's representative will probably say to the men waiting in line for a job. He will engage in a sad refusal in
the sense of denying them a job, though it is the men
rather than the representative who will be made sad by
this announcement. Yet as currently used in the poem, the
phrase "sad refusal" refers to the attitude of the
"you"'s brother. He is going to press on with his ambitions no matter what. As I have said, the second half of
the poem focuses on the emotional labor that the "you"
should engage in as far as his brother is concerned. The
speaker evidently wants the "you" to acknowledge more his
brother's spirit. So, the "you" too has engaged in a sad
refusal in the sense that he has been unwilling to show
his brother love.

Even though the poem comes to emphasize emotional
work, that does not mean it is saying people should forget about doing physical work and consider it pointless.
The speaker suggests that the "you" should pay more
attention to his brother in part because the brother
labors so hard. Overall, the poem is not telling us to
dismiss physical work. Instead, it is urging us to realize that emotional work is at least as important.

Revising

Most first drafts are far from perfect. Even experienced professional writers
often have to revise their work. Besides making changes on their own, many of
them solicit feedback from others. In various workplaces, writing is collaborative,
with coauthors exchanging ideas as they try to improve a piece. Remain open to
the possibility that your draft needs changes, perhaps several. Of course, you are
more apt to revise extensively if you have given yourself enough time. Conversely,
you will not feel able to change much of your paper if it is due the next day. You
will also limit your ability to revise if you work only with your original manuscript,
scribbling possible changes between the lines. This practice amounts to conservatism, for it encourages you to keep passages that really ought to be overhauled.

You may have trouble, however, improving a draft if you are checking many
things in it at once. Therefore, read the draft repeatedly, looking at a different
aspect of it each time. A good way to begin is to outline the paper you have writ-

ten and then compare that outline with your original one. If the two outlines differ, your draft may or may not need adjusting; perhaps you were wise to swerve from your original plan. In any case, you should ponder your departures from that plan, considering whether they were for the best.

If, like Theresa, you are writing an argument paper, here are some topics and questions you might apply as you review your first draft. Obviously some of these considerations overlap. Nevertheless, take them in turn rather than all at once.

Logic

+ Will my audience see that the issue I am focusing on is indeed an issue?
+ Will the audience be able to follow the logic of my argument?
+ Is the logic as persuasive as it might be? Is there more evidence I can provide? Do I need to identify more of my warrants?
+ Have I addressed all of my audience's potential concerns?

Organization

+ Does my introduction identify the issue that I will focus on? Does it state my main claim?
+ Will my audience be able to detect and follow the stages of my argument?
+ Does the order of my paragraphs seem purposeful rather than arbitrary?
+ Have I done all I can to signal connections within and between sentences? Within and between paragraphs?
+ Have I avoided getting bogged down in mere summary?
+ Will my conclusion satisfy readers? Does it leave any key questions dangling?

Clarity

+ Does my title offer a good preview of my argument?
+ Will each of my sentences be immediately clear?
+ Am I sure how to define each word that I have used?

Emphasis

+ Have I put key points in prominent places?
+ Have I worded each sentence for maximum impact? In particular, is each sentence as concise as possible? Do I use active verbs whenever I can?

Style

+ Are my tone and level of vocabulary appropriate?
+ Will my audience think me fair-minded? Should I make any more concessions?
+ Do I use any mannerisms that may distract my readers?

- Have I used any expressions that may annoy or offend?
- Is there anything else I can do to make my paper readable and
  interesting?

Grammar

- Is each of my sentences grammatically correct?
- Have I punctuated properly?

Physical Appearance

- Have I followed the proper format for quotations, notes, and
  bibliography?
- Are there any typographical errors?

We list these considerations from most to least important. When revising a draft,
think first about matters of logic, organization, and clarity. There is little point in
fixing the grammar of particular sentences if you are going to drop them later
because they fail to advance your argument.

As we noted, a group of Theresa's classmates discussed her draft. Most of
these students seemed to like her overall argument, including her main issue and
claim. Having been similarly confused by Levine's poem, they appreciated the
light that Theresa shed on it. They were especially impressed by her evidence,
since she repeatedly drew on Levine's actual text. Nevertheless, the group made
several comments about Theresa's paper that she took as suggestions for improvement. Ultimately, she decided that several changes were in order, the three main
ones being these:

- Many of her sentences could be more concise. This problem is common
  to first drafts; often writers cannot detect all the wordiness in a draft until
  they finish it and then review it. Theresa saw in particular that she could
  cut down on the number of self-references ("I") and that she did not
  have to mention "the speaker" as much as she had.
- She should move the material in her second paragraph to her conclusion, where her concession about not knowing the "you"'s identity
  would make for an appropriate ending. Several students in her group
  liked this concession but found it distracting in the second paragraph,
  for two reasons: (1) Its apologetic tone prevented Theresa from developing authority for her argument; (2) the first and second paragraphs
  together featured the first person ("I") so much that readers might feel
  their attention being taken away from Levine's poem.
- She could hint that some of the words in the poem also refer to what
  Levine is doing. In particular, Levine writes "lines" and makes "shifts" in
  meaning. Theresa had been reluctant to relate the poem to its author.
  While such connections interested her, she feared they would greatly
  complicate her paper, sending her reader off in all sorts of directions.
  Now she saw that she could add at least a brief reference to Levine's own
  "shifts" in the poem.

Sample Student Paper: Revised Draft

Here is the new version of her paper that Theresa wrote. Again, decide what you think of it.

```
Theresa Gardella
Professor Schwartz
English 102
21 April ----
```

The Shifting Definitions of <u>Work</u> and

<u>Waiting</u> in Philip Levine's "What Work Is"

```
     Philip Levine's title "What Work Is" suggests that
his poem will clearly define work. Yet it gets confusing
about this subject. Early on, the speaker says, "You know
what work is." But the poem concludes with the statement,
"You don't know what work is." Also puzzling is that the
speaker says early on that, despite the poem's title,
"this is about waiting." So, how does the poem define and
relate these two words, work and waiting? In fact, it
redefines both words as it moves along. First, it refers
to work as physical labor and to waiting as the process
of searching for a job. Eventually, though, it defines
work as emotional labor in human relationships. Moreover,
the poem implies that often people wait a long time to
tell members of their family that they love them. The
first kind of waiting looks to the future. The second
kind of waiting is in part a failure to acknowledge some-
one else in the present: the "you"'s brother sleeping at
home. This kind of waiting is also a failure to acknowl-
edge the past: the amount of time that the "you" has
allowed to pass before telling his brother he loves him.
     The first half of the poem refers to work as physical
labor as it describes the men standing in line. They hope
to get a job at an auto plant, Ford Highland Park. This
period of time seems to be "hours wasted waiting,"
though, because the plant representative is probably
going to say, "'No / we're not hiring today.'" Although
that representative is himself waiting to make his
```

response, the poem has so far emphasized the other men's waiting for employment.

The second half of the poem makes an additional reference to work as physical. The "you"'s brother "works eight hours a night so he can sing / Wagner." But in this half, the poem turns to emphasizing the work involved in expressing love of family. The speaker suggests that the "you" has let too much time go by before telling his brother "you loved him." The "you" apparently does love his brother. Moreover, expressing love for him would evidently be a "simple" and "obvious" thing to do. Nevertheless, the speaker says to the "you" that "you don't know what work is." In part, this could mean work as physical labor again. The speaker would thus be saying that the "you" has not expressed brotherly love because he's thought too little about his brother's physical hardships. Yet the more important meaning of work here seems to be emotional labor. The speaker would thus be saying that the "you" does not understand that expressing love for his brother is work. In addition, the speaker would be pushing the "you" to think more about this work and to do it, rather than just search for a job.

Admittedly, the second half of the poem does not mention the word <u>waiting</u>. But because the speaker has said earlier that "this is about waiting," we should see the word <u>waiting</u> as probably applying to the second half too. No longer does the poem refer, though, to waiting as standing in line for a job. The "how long has it been" question suggests that the word <u>waiting</u> now means taking too long to show love for one's family. In this case, the "you" has neglected his brother.

Other words in the poem change meaning, too, thus reinforcing what happens with <u>work</u> and <u>waiting</u>. Ironically, one of these shifts involves the word <u>shift</u> itself. While in the first half the unemployed are "shifting" as they wait for physical work, the second half brings in emotions by mentioning the brother's "miserable

night shift." Another change is with the word <u>stand</u>. In
the first half, the people looking for physical labor
"stand" in line for it. The second half brings up emotional labor as it mentions that "you can hardly stand /
the love flooding you for your brother." Similarly,
although "long" first describes the line of unemployed
people, in the second half it refers to the "you"'s emotional life, through the "how long has it been" question.

A clear switching point in the poem is "sad refusal."
This phrase could fit what the plant's representative will
probably say to the men waiting for a job. He will engage
in a sad refusal by denying them a job, though it is they
rather than he who will be made sad by this announcement.
As actually used in the poem, "sad refusal" describes the
attitude of the "you"'s brother, who is going to pursue
his goals despite his hardships. A third possible meaning
comes in the poem's second half, where the speaker evidently wants the "you" to acknowledge more his brother's
spirit. The "you," too, has engaged in a sad refusal in
the sense that he has been unwilling to show his brother
love.

I must confess that I am still not sure who the "you"
of the poem is. Perhaps he is the reader, since the
speaker says "if you're / old enough to read this you
know what / work is, although you may not do it." But
pretty soon after this statement, the "you" apparently
becomes one of the people waiting in line for work at
Ford Highland Park, "feeling the light rain falling like
mist / into your hair." As the poem goes on, the "you"
seems to get even more specific. The speaker says things
like "you love your brother" and "you've never / done
something so simple, so obvious." In addition, the "you"
has a brother who works at an auto plant, studies German,
and sings opera. When the speaker concludes by saying
"you don't know what work is," I am still left wondering
if this is the same "you" who did know what work is back
at the start. Moreover, I wonder if at least one of the

"you"'s in the poem is really the speaker. Yet whatever
the "you"'s identity, the poem redefines <u>work</u> and <u>waiting</u>
in the ways I have pointed out.

Even though the poem comes to emphasize emotional
work, the poem is not necessarily dismissing physical
work as pointless. The speaker even seems to admire the
brother because of the physical work he does. Overall,
the poem is not criticizing either kind of work, but
rather stressing that emotional work is at least as
important as the physical kind.

To us, Theresa's revision heightens the impact of her paper. In particular, she has trimmed several sentences while preserving their points. While some references to "I" remain, they do not prove distracting; rather, they end the paper on a warm personal note. All the same, we would hesitate to call this revision the definitive version of Theresa's paper. Maybe you have thought of things she could do to make it even more effective. In presenting her two drafts, we mainly want to emphasize the importance of revision. We hope, too, that you will remember our specific tips as you work on your own writing.

3

Writing about Stories

Short stories can be said to resemble novels. Above all, both are works of fiction. Yet the difference in length matters. As William Trevor, a veteran writer of short stories, has observed, short fiction is "the art of the glimpse; it deals in echoes and reverberations; craftily it withholds information. Novels tell all. Short stories tell as little as they dare." Maybe Trevor overstates the situation when he claims that novels reveal everything. All sorts of texts feature what literary theorist Wolfgang Iser calls "gaps." Still, Trevor is right to emphasize that short stories usually tell much less than novels do. They demand that you understand and evaluate characters on the basis of just a few details and events. In this respect, short stories resemble poems. Both tend to rely on compression rather than expansion, seeking to affect their audience with a sharply limited number of words.

Short stories' focused use of language can make the experience of reading them wonderfully intense. Furthermore, you may end up considering important human issues as you try to interpret the "glimpses" they provide. Precisely because short stories "tell as little as they dare," they offer you much to ponder as you proceed to write about them.

In discussing that writing process, we will refer often to the two stories that follow. Both stories tell of a healthy person's encounter with someone physically suffering. The first story, "A Visit of Charity," is by a pioneer of the modern American short story, Eudora Welty (b. 1909), who still lives in her hometown of Jackson, Mississippi. This particular piece appeared in Welty's first collection, *A Curtain of Green and Other Stories*, published in 1941. The second story, "The Gift of Sweat," is by a much younger American, Rebecca Brown (b. 1956). It is the lead-off piece of her 1994 book *The Gifts of the Body*, a sequence of short stories narrated by a woman who does housekeeping for people with AIDS — a kind of service work that Brown, too, has done.

EUDORA WELTY
A Visit of Charity

It was mid-morning—a very cold, bright day. Holding a potted plant before her, a girl of fourteen jumped off the bus in front of the Old Ladies' Home, on the outskirts of town. She wore a red coat, and her straight yellow hair was hanging down loose from the pointed white cap all the little girls were wearing that year. She stopped for a moment beside one of the prickly dark shrubs with which the city had beautified the Home, and then proceeded slowly toward the building, which was of whitewashed brick and reflected the winter sunlight like a block of ice. As she walked vaguely up the steps she shifted the small pot from hand to hand; then she had to set it down and remove her mittens before she could open the heavy door.

"I'm a Campfire Girl. . . . I have to pay a visit to some old lady," she told the nurse at the desk. This was a woman in a white uniform who looked as if she were cold; she had close-cut hair which stood up on the very top of her head exactly like a sea wave. Marian, the little girl, did not tell her that this visit would give her a minimum of only three points in her score.

"Acquainted with any of our residents?" asked the nurse. She lifted one eyebrow and spoke like a man.

"With any old ladies? No—but—that is, any of them will do," Marian stammered. With her free hand she pushed her hair behind her ears, as she did when it was time to study Science.

The nurse shrugged and rose. "You have a nice *multiflora cineraria*° there," she remarked as she walked ahead down the hall of closed doors to pick out an old lady. 5

There was loose, bulging linoleum on the floor. Marian felt as if she were walking on the waves, but the nurse paid no attention to it. There was a smell in the hall like the interior of a clock. Everything was silent until, behind one of the doors, an old lady of some kind cleared her throat like a sheep bleating. This decided the nurse. Stopping in her tracks, she first extended her arm, bent her elbow, and leaned forward from the hips—all to examine the watch strapped to her wrist; then she gave a loud double-rap on the door.

"There are two in each room," the nurse remarked over her shoulder.

"Two what?" asked Marian without thinking. The sound like a sheep's bleating almost made her turn around and run back.

One old woman was pulling the door open in short, gradual jerks, and when she saw the nurse a strange smile forced her old face dangerously awry. Marian, suddenly propelled by the strong, impatient arm of the nurse, saw next the side-face of another old woman, even older, who was lying flat in bed with a cap on and a counterpane° drawn up to her chin.

---

multiflora cineraria: A house plant with brightly colored flowers and heart-shaped leaves.
counterpane: Bedspread.

"Visitor," said the nurse, and after one more shove she was off up the hall.   10

Marian stood tongue-tied; both hands held the potted plant. The old woman, still with that terrible, square smile (which was a smile of welcome) stamped on her bony face, was waiting. . . . Perhaps she said something. The old woman in bed said nothing at all, and she did not look around.

Suddenly Marian saw a hand, quick as a bird claw, reach up in the air and pluck the white cap off her head. At the same time, another claw to match drew her all the way into the room, and the next moment the door closed behind her.

"My, my, my," said the old lady at her side.

Marian stood enclosed by a bed, a washstand and a chair; the tiny room had altogether too much furniture. Everything smelled wet—even the bare floor. She held on to the back of the chair, which was wicker and felt soft and damp. Her heart beat more and more slowly, her hands got colder and colder, and she could not hear whether the old women were saying anything or not. She could not see them very clearly. How dark it was! The window shade was down, and the only door was shut. Marian looked at the ceiling. . . . It was like being caught in a robbers' cave, just before one was murdered.

"Did you come to be our little girl for a while?" the first robber asked.   15

Then something was snatched from Marian's hand—the little potted plant.

"Flowers!" screamed the old woman. She stood holding the pot in an undecided way. "Pretty flowers," she added.

Then the old woman in bed cleared her throat and spoke. "They are not pretty," she said, still without looking around, but very distinctly.

Marian suddenly pitched against the chair and sat down in it.

"Pretty flowers," the first old woman insisted. "Pretty—pretty . . ."   20

Marian wished she had the little pot back for just a moment—she had forgotten to look at the plant herself before giving it away. What did it look like?

"Stinkweeds," said the other old woman sharply. She had a bunchy white forehead and red eyes like a sheep. Now she turned them toward Marian. The fogginess seemed to rise in her throat again, and she bleated, "Who—are—you?"

To her surprise, Marian could not remember her name. "I'm a Campfire Girl," she said finally.

"Watch out for the germs," said the old woman like a sheep, not addressing anyone.

"One came out last month to see us," said the first old woman.   25

A sheep or a germ? wondered Marian dreamily, holding on to the chair.

"Did not!" cried the other old woman.

"Did so! Read to us out of the Bible, and we enjoyed it!" screamed the first.

"Who enjoyed it!" said the woman in bed. Her mouth was unexpectedly small and sorrowful, like a pet's.

"We enjoyed it," insisted the other. "You enjoyed it—I enjoyed it."   30

"We all enjoyed it," said Marian, without realizing that she had said a word.

The first old woman had just finished putting the potted plant high, high on the top of the wardrobe, where it could hardly be seen from below. Marian wondered how she had ever succeeded in placing it there, how she could ever have reached so high.

"You mustn't pay any attention to old Addie," she now said to the little girl. "She's ailing today."

"Will you shut your mouth?" said the woman in bed. "I am not."

"You're a story." 35

"I can't stay but a minute — really, I can't," said Marian suddenly. She looked down at the wet floor and thought that if she were sick in here they would have to let her go.

With much to-do the first old woman sat down in a rocking chair — still another piece of furniture! — and began to rock. With the fingers of one hand she touched a very dirty cameo pin on her chest. "What do you do at school?" she asked.

"I don't know . . ." said Marian. She tried to think but she could not.

"Oh, but the flowers are beautiful," the old woman whispered. She seemed to rock faster and faster; Marian did not see how anyone could rock so fast.

"Ugly," said the woman in bed. 40

"If we bring flowers —" Marian began, and then fell silent. She had almost said that if Campfire Girls brought flowers to the Old Ladies' Home, the visit would count one extra point, and if they took a Bible with them on the bus and read it to the old ladies, it counted double. But the old woman had not listened, anyway; she was rocking and watching the other one, who watched back from the bed.

"Poor Addie is ailing. She has to take medicine — see?" she said, pointing a horny finger at a row of bottles on the table, and rocking so high that her black comfort shoes lifted off the floor like a little child's.

"I am no more sick than you are," said the woman in bed.

"Oh, yes you are!"

"I just got more sense than you have, that's all," said the other old woman, 45 nodding her head.

"That's only the contrary way she talks when *you all* come," said the first old lady with sudden intimacy. She stopped the rocker with a neat pat of her feet and leaned toward Marian. Her hand reached over — it felt like a petunia leaf, clinging and just a little sticky.

"Will you hush! Will you hush!" cried the other one.

Marian leaned back rigidly in her chair.

"When I was a little girl like you, I went to school and all," said the old woman in the same intimate, menacing voice. "Not here — another town . . ."

"Hush!" said the sick woman. "You never went to school. You never came 50 and you never went. You never were anything — only here. You never were born! You don't know anything. Your head is empty, your heart and hands and your old black purse are all empty, even that little old box that you brought with you you brought empty — you showed it to me. And yet you talk, talk, talk, talk, talk all the time until I think I'm losing my mind! Who are you? You're a stranger — a perfect stranger! Don't you know you're a stranger? Is it possible that they have actually done a thing like this to anyone — sent them in a stranger to talk, and rock, and tell away her whole long rigmarole? Do they seriously suppose that I'll be able to keep it up, day in, day out, night in, night out, living in the same room with a terrible old woman — forever?"

Marian saw the old woman's eyes grow bright and turn toward her. This old woman was looking at her with despair and calculation in her face. Her small lips suddenly dropped apart, and exposed a half circle of false teeth with tan gums.

"Come here, I want to tell you something," she whispered. "Come here!"

Marian was trembling, and her heart nearly stopped beating altogether for a moment.

"Now, now, Addie," said the first old woman. "That's not polite. Do you know what's really the matter with old Addie today?" She, too, looked at Marian; one of her eyelids dropped low.

"The matter?" the child repeated stupidly. "What's the matter with her?"   55

"Why, she's mad because it's her birthday!" said the first old woman, beginning to rock again and giving a little crow as though she had answered her own riddle.

"It is not, it is not!" screamed the old woman in bed. "It is not my birthday, no one knows when that is but myself, and will you please be quiet and say nothing more, or I'll go straight out of my mind!" She turned her eyes toward Marian again, and presently she said in the soft, foggy voice, "When the worst comes to the worst, I ring this bell, and the nurse comes." One of her hands was drawn out from under the patched counterpane — a thin little hand with enormous black freckles. With a finger which would not hold still she pointed to a little bell on the table among the bottles.

"How old are you?" Marian breathed. Now she could see the old woman in bed very closely and plainly, and very abruptly, from all sides, as in dreams. She wondered about her — she wondered for a moment as though there was nothing else in the world to wonder about. It was the first time such a thing had happened to Marian.

"I won't tell!"

The old face on the pillow, where Marian was bending over it, slowly gathered and collapsed. Soft whimpers came out of the small open mouth. It was a sheep that she sounded like — a little lamb. Marian's face drew very close, the yellow hair hung forward.   60

"She's crying!" She turned a bright, burning face up to the first old woman.

"That's Addie for you," the old woman said spitefully.

Marian jumped up and moved toward the door. For the second time, the claw almost touched her hair, but it was not quick enough. The little girl put her cap on.

"Well, it was a real visit," said the old woman, following Marian through the doorway and all the way out into the hall. Then from behind she suddenly clutched the child with her sharp little fingers. In an affected, high-pitched whine she cried, "Oh, little girl, have you a penny to spare for a poor old woman that's not got anything of her own? We don't have a thing in the world — not a penny for candy — not a thing! Little girl, just a nickel — a penny —"

Marian pulled violently against the old hands for a moment before she was free. Then she ran down the hall, without looking behind her and without looking at the nurse, who was reading *Field & Stream* at her desk. The nurse, after another triple motion to consult her wrist watch, asked automatically the question put to visitors in all institutions: "Won't you stay and have dinner with *us?*"   65

Marian never replied. She pushed the heavy door open into the cold air and ran down the steps.

Under the prickly shrub she stooped and quickly, without being seen, retrieved a red apple she had hidden there.

Her yellow hair under the white cap, her scarlet coat, her bare knees all flashed in the sunlight as she ran to meet the big bus rocketing through the street.

"Wait for me!" she shouted. As though at an imperial command, the bus ground to a stop.

She jumped on and took a big bite out of the apple.   [1941]   70

REBECCA BROWN
The Gift of Sweat

I went to Rick's every Tuesday and Thursday morning. I usually called before I went to see if he wanted me to pick up anything for him on the way. He never used to ask me for anything until once when I hadn't had breakfast and I stopped at this place a couple blocks from him, the Hostess with the Mostest, to get a cinnamon roll and I got two, one for him. I didn't really think he'd eat it because he was so organic. He had this incredible garden on the side of the apartment with tomatoes and zucchinis and carrots and he used to do all his own baking. I also got two large coffees with milk. I could have eaten it all if he didn't want his. But when I got to his place and asked him if he'd had breakfast and showed him what I'd brought, he squealed. He said those cinnamon rolls were his absolute favorite things in the world and he used to go to the Hostess on Sunday mornings. He said he'd try to be there when they were fresh out of the oven and get the best ones, the ones from the center of the pan, which are the stickiest and softest. It was something he used to do for himself on Sunday, which was not his favorite day.

So after that when I called him before I went over and asked if he wanted anything, he'd still say no thanks, and then I would say, "How about the usual," meaning the rolls and coffee, and he'd say he'd love it.

So one morning when I called and asked him if he wanted "the usual" and he said he didn't, I was surprised.

He said, "Not today!" He sounded really chirpy. "Just get your sweet self over here. I got a surprise for you."

I said OK and that I'd see him in a few. I made a quick cup of coffee and   5
downed the end of last night's pizza and went over. I was at his place in half an hour.

I always knocked on the door. When he was there he'd always shout, "Hello! Just a minute!" and come let me in. It took him a while to get to the door but he liked being able to answer it himself, he liked still living in his own place. If he wasn't at home I let myself in and read the note he would have left me — that he had an appointment or something, or if there was some special thing he wanted me to do. Then I would clean or do chores. I used to like being there alone some-times. I could do surprises for him, like leave him notes under his pillow or rearrange his wind-up toys so they were kissing or other silly things. Rick loved surprises.

But this one morning when I knocked on the door it took him a long time to answer. Then I heard him trying to shout, but he sounded small. "Can you let yourself in?"

I unlocked the door and went in. He was in the living room on the futon. It was usually up like a couch to sit on, but it was flat like a bed and he was lying on it.

I went over and sat on the floor by the futon. He was lying on his side, facing away from me, curled up. His knees were near his chest.

"Rick?" I said. I put my hand on his back.   10

He didn't move, but said, "Hi," very quietly.

"What's going on?" I said.

He made a noise like a little animal.

"You want me to call your doc?"

He swallowed a couple of times. Then he said, "I called UCS. Margaret is   15
coming over to take me to the hospital."

"Good," I said, "she'll be here soon."

"Yeah," he said. Then he made that animal noise again. He was holding his stomach. "I meant to call you back," he said, "to tell you you didn't need to come over today."

"That's OK, Rick. I'm glad I'm here. I'm glad I'm with you right now."

"I didn't feel bad when you called." He sounded apologetic. "It was so sudden."

"Your stomach?"   20

He tried to nod. "Uh-huh. But everywhere some."

He was holding the corner of his quilt, squeezing it.

"I was about to get in the shower. I wanted to be all clean before you came over. It was so sudden."

"Oh, Rick," I said, "I'm sorry you hurt so much."

"Thank you."   25

"Is there anything I can do before Margaret gets here?"

"No." He swallowed again. I could smell his breath. "No thank you."

Then his mouth got tight and he squeezed the quilt corner, then he was pulsing it, then more like stabs. He started to shake. "I'm cold," he said.

I pulled the quilt over most of him. It had a pattern of moon and stars. "I'm gonna go get another blanket," I said.

"Don't go," he said really fast. "Please don't go."   30

"OK," I said, "I'll stay here."

"I'm so cold," he said again.

I touched his back. It was sweaty and hot.

I got onto the futon. I slid on very carefully so I wouldn't jolt him. I lay on my side behind him. I could feel him shaking. I put my left arm around his middle. I slipped my right hand under his head and touched his forehead. It was wet and hot. I held my hand on his forehead a couple of seconds to cool it. Then I petted

his forehead and up through his hair. His hair was wet too. I combed my fingers
through his wet hair to his ponytail. I said, "Poor Rick. Poor Ricky."

He was still shaking. I pulled my body close to him so his butt was in my lap   35
and my breasts and stomach were against his back. I pressed against him to warm
him. He pulled my hand onto his stomach. I opened my hand so my palm was flat
across him, my fingers spread. He held his hand on top of mine, squeezing it like
the quilt. I could feel the sweat of his hand on the back of mine, and of his stomach,
through his shirt, against my palm. I could feel his pulse all through him; it was fast.

I tightened my arms around him as if I could press the sickness out.

After a while he started to shake less. He was still sweating and I could feel
more wet on the side of his face from crying.

When Margaret came we wrapped his coat around him and helped him,
one on either side of him, to the car. Rick hunched and kept making noises. I
helped him get in and closed the door behind him while Margaret got in the
driver's side. While she was fumbling for her keys I ran around to her and asked
her, "You want me to come with you?"

She said, "You don't need to. We'll be OK."

Rick didn't say anything.   40

I leaned in and said, "Your place will be all clean when you come back
home, Rick."

He tried to smile.

"I'll call you later," said Margaret. She put her hand up and touched the side
of my face. "You're wet," she told me.

I touched my face. It was wet. "I'll talk to you later," I said to her.

"I'll see you later, Rick," I said.   45

He nodded but didn't say anything. His face was splotched. Margaret found
her keys and started the car.

I went back into his apartment. When I closed the door behind me I could
smell it. It was a slight smell, sour, but also partly sweet. It was the smell of Rick's
sweat.

I started cleaning. I usually started in the kitchen, but as soon as I set foot in
there and saw the kitchen table I couldn't. I turned around and stood in the hall a
second and held my breath. After a while I let it out.

I did everything else first. I stripped the bed and put a load of laundry in. I
vacuumed and dusted. I dusted all his fairy gear, his stones and incense burners
and little statues and altars. I straightened clothes in his closet he hadn't worn in
ages. I untangled ties and necklaces. I put cassettes back in their cases and
reshelved them. I took out the trash. I did it all fast because I wanted to get
everything done, but I also wished I could stretch it out and still be doing it and
be here when he came home as if he would come home soon.

I cleaned the bathroom. I shook cleanser in the shower and sink and cleaned   50
them. I sprayed Windex on the mirror. When I was wiping it off I saw myself. My
face was splotched. My t-shirt had a dark spot. I put my hands to it and sniffed
them. They smelled like me, but also him. It was Rick's sweat. I put my hands up

to my face and I could smell him in my hands. I put my face in my hands and closed my eyes. I stood there like that a while then I went to the kitchen.

What was on the kitchen table was this: his two favorite coffee mugs, his and what used to be Barry's. There was a Melitta over one full of ground coffee, all ready to go. There were two dessert plates with a pair of cinnamon rolls from the Hostess, the soft sticky ones from the center of the pan.

I thought of Rick going down there, how long it took him to get down the street, how early he had to go to get the best ones. I thought of him planning a nice surprise, of him trying to do what he couldn't.

Rick told me once how one of the things he missed most was Sunday breakfast in bed. Every Saturday night he and Barry would watch a movie on the VCR in the living room. They'd pull the futon out like a bed and watch it from there and pretend they were at a bed-and-breakfast on vacation. Rick would make something fabulous and they'd eat it together. That was when he was still trying to help Barry eat. After Barry died Rick started going to the Hostess, especially on Sundays, because he had to get out of the apartment. He used to go to the Hostess all the time until it got to be too much for him. That's about the time I started coming over.

I sat at the table he'd laid for us. I put my elbows on the table and folded my hands. I closed my eyes and lowered my head and put my forehead in my hands. I tried to think how Rick would think, I tried to imagine Barry.

After a while I opened my eyes. He'd laid the table hopefully. I took the food   55
he meant for me, I ate.   [1994]

A WRITING EXERCISE

Once you have read the two stories, write your reaction to them off the top of your head, spending at least ten minutes on each. For each story, note any personal experience affecting your response as well as one or more questions that you have about the story even after you have finished reading it. Remember that question-posing is a good way to prepare for a formal paper on the story, enabling you to identify issues worth writing about at length.

A Student's Personal Response to the Stories

Monica Albertson was enrolled in a class that read and discussed both Welty's "A Visit of Charity" and Brown's "The Gift of Sweat." Here is some freewriting she did about each story:

I'm not sure which character I should be sympathizing with in Welty's story. Right away I disliked the girl because she wasn't really interested in seeing the old women. I don't know why the story is called "A Visit of Charity," since she just wanted to get more points. And yet I have to admit that when I was younger I was sort of like her. I remember one time that my church youth group

had to sing Christmas carols at an old folks' home, and I
was uneasy about having to meet all these ancient men and
women I didn't know, some of whom could barely walk or
talk. It's funny, because I was always comfortable around
my grandparents, but I have to confess that being around
all those old people at once spooked me a little. I
smiled a lot at them and joined in the singing and helped
hand out candy canes afterward. But I couldn't wait to
leave. Once I did, I felt proud of myself for going
there, but I guess I also felt a little guilty because I
didn't really want to be there at all. So, maybe I'm
being hypocritical when I criticize the girl in Welty's
story for insensitivity. Anyway, I expected that Welty
would present in a good light any old women that Marian
encountered, just to emphasize that Marian was being
unkind and that it's really sad for people to have to
live in a retirement home (or senior citizens center or
whatever they're calling such places nowadays). And yet
the two old women she meets are cranky and unpleasant.
Even the receptionist doesn't come off all that good. If
I were Marian, I probably would have left even sooner
than she did! Maybe Welty didn't want us to sympathize
with anyone in the story, and maybe that's OK. I tend to
want a story to make at least some of the characters sympathetic, but maybe it's unfair of me to demand that.
Still, I'm wondering if I'm not appreciating Welty's
characters enough. When the two old women argue, should
we side with one of them, or are we supposed to be bothered by them both? Are we supposed to think any better of
the girl by the time she leaves? The apple she eats immediately made me think of the Adam and Eve story, but I
don't know what I'm supposed to do with that parallel.

On the other hand, I was very moved by the scene in
Brown's story when the narrator holds the sick man like
she's his mother and she's comforting her child. It made
me think of times when I myself was sick in bed and my
mother would come in and put cold compresses on my

burning forehead and do other things like that. Also I really admire the narrator for being willing to do housework for someone with AIDS and for treasuring his sweat. I can imagine plenty of people would worry about catching AIDS from Rick that way. I have to admit that even I would be anxious about touching any of his bodily fluids. I guess Brown thinks that's an unreasonable fear. Maybe I would react to this story differently if I knew someone who had AIDS, but I don't, or I think I don't. I did know a couple of gay kids in high school but just to say hi to.

One question I found myself asking is why the narrator doesn't tell us right away what's in the kitchen. Why keep the breakfast a secret for a while? Instead of telling us about it, she takes a deep breath and goes and does the cleaning. She must have been having some important thoughts while cleaning but I couldn't figure out what they were. (I still admire her, though, for cleaning Rick's home when she probably didn't have to.) Not until later does she tell us about the breakfast and then she finally starts eating it. Is she at first just too depressed by his collapse to enjoy what he's prepared and tell us about it? Or, does she feel guilty because he exhausted himself doing all this for her? Another question I have concerns the title. The title is "The Gift of Sweat," and I can certainly see that the narrator values Rick's sweat, but the main gift in the story seems to be the breakfast he's prepared. So is the title misleading? By the way, I thought it interesting that the breakfast was basically just cinnamon rolls. Many people would consider those junk food. For me, rolls like that are too rich to eat at any time of day. In the morning I'm a Special K fan if I eat anything at all. But there seems to be something holy about Rick's breakfast. In fact, when the narrator eats it, I thought of Communion. But maybe that's just the Catholic in me. If I were in danger of dying maybe I would just go for junk food too!

Before Monica could produce a full-fledged paper on either Welty's story or Brown's, she had to do more writing and thinking. Yet, simply by jotting down some memories and questions that the stories raised for her, she provided herself with the seeds of a paper. Compare your thoughts to hers. To what extent did you react to these stories as Monica did? In what ways, if any, did your responses differ from hers? What would you say to her if she were your classmate, especially as she proceeded to write a more developed argument based on her first impressions?

The Elements of Short Fiction

Whether discussing them in class or writing about them, you will improve your ability to analyze stories like Welty's and Brown's if you grow familiar with typical elements of short fiction. These elements include plot and structure, point of view, characterization, setting, imagery, language, and theme.

Plot and Structure

For many readers, the most important element in any work of fiction is **plot**. As they turn the pages of a short story, their main question is, "What will happen next?" In reading Welty's story, quite possibly you wanted to know how Marian's visit to the rest home would turn out. In reading Brown's story, most likely you hoped to learn why Rick was unable to let the narrator into his home. Furthermore, if a friend unfamiliar with Welty's and Brown's stories asked you what each was about, probably you would begin by summarizing their plots.

A WRITING EXERCISE

In one or two sentences, summarize what you take to be the plot of Welty's story. Then, read the following three summaries of her plot, which were written by three other students. Finally, list a few similarities and differences you notice as you compare the three summaries with one another and with yours.

Jerry's summary: A girl visits an Old Ladies' Home just so she can add some points to her record as a Campfire Girl. Much to her dismay, she encounters two roommates who fight a lot with each other, and their unpleasantness eventually causes her to flee.

Carla's summary: A young girl named Marian who starts off basically interested in only herself is forced to consider the suffering of old people when she spends time with two old women at a retirement home. Eventually she leaves in fear and disgust, but as she leaves she eats an apple, which implies that she is no longer as innocent as she was and that she is maybe a little more prepared to acknowledge what goes on in the wider world.

Matt's summary: A really insensitive girl meets two old women, and though in many respects she is put off by both of them, she can't help being intrigued by the one who is sick in bed. Maybe she becomes more aware of mortality at this point, but if so she has trouble facing it, and in the end runs away.

To an extent, the students point out different things. For instance, only Carla mentions the apple, and only Matt observes that Marian is momentarily interested in the bedridden woman. Also, these two students are more willing than Jerry is to speculate about Marian's final state of mind. At the same time, Carla's summary ends on a slightly more upbeat note than Matt's. She emphasizes that Marian has perhaps become more open-minded, while Matt concludes by pointing out that Marian nevertheless flees.

Any summary of Welty's story will be somewhat personal. It is bound to reflect the reader's own sense of who the story's main characters are, which of their actions are significant, how these actions are connected, and what principles these actions illustrate. Were you to compare summaries with Jerry, Carla, and Matt in class, each of you might learn much from discussing experiences and beliefs that influenced your accounts.

Even so, you do not have to treat every summary of Welty's story as merely subjective. Probably some accounts of it are more attentive than others to actual details of Welty's text. If a reader declared that Marian loves visiting the Old Ladies' Home, many other readers would rightfully disagree, pointing out that Marian dashes off. If you discussed Welty's story with Jerry, Carla, and Matt, the four of you would probably consider which summary of it is best. Furthermore, probably each of you would argue for your respective candidates by pointing to specific passages in Welty's text. Ultimately, you might still prefer your own summary. On the other hand, you might wind up adopting someone else's, or you might want to combine aspects of various summaries you have read.

Jerry's, Carla's, and Matt's summaries do have some features in common, indicating that there are certain basic things for you to consider when you examine a short story's plot. For example, plots usually center on human beings, who can be seen as engaging in actions, as being acted upon, or both. In recounting the plot of Welty's story, each of the three students focuses on Marian. Furthermore, each describes her as acting (she "encounters," "flees," "spends time," "leaves," "eats," "meets," "runs away") *and* as being affected by other forces (the "unpleasantness" of the old women "causes her to flee"; she is "forced to consider" their pain; she is "put off" as well as "intrigued"). Also, most short stories put characters into a high-pressure situation, whether for dark or comic effect. To earn the merit points she desires, Marian has to contend with the feuding roommates.

Besides physical events, a short story may involve psychological developments. Each student here points to mental changes in Welty's heroine. According to Jerry, Marian experiences "dismay." According to Carla, she "starts off basically interested in only herself" but perhaps becomes "a little more prepared to acknowledge what goes on in the wider world." According to Matt, she starts off "really insensitive," perhaps grows "more aware of mortality," yet then "has trouble facing it." Many stories do show characters undergoing complete or partial conversions. Meanwhile, a number of stories include characters who stick to their beliefs but gain a new perspective on them.

Jerry, Carla, and Matt connect Marian's visit to the rest home with her subsequent behavior. Like most plot summaries, in other words, theirs bring up relations of cause and effect. The novelist and short-story writer E. M. Forster refers to cause and effect in his famous definition of plot. To Forster, a plot is not simply one incident after another, such as "the king died and then the queen died." Rather, it is a situation or a whole chain of events in which there are reasons *why* characters behave as they do. Forster's example: "The king died, and then the queen died of grief."

Writers of short stories do not always make cause and effect immediately clear. Another possible plot, Forster suggests, is "The queen died, no one knew why, until it was discovered that it was through grief at the death of the king." In this scenario, all of the characters lack information about the queen's true psychology for a while, and perhaps the reader is in the dark as well. Indeed, many short stories leave the reader ignorant for a spell. For instance, only near the conclusion of her story does Welty reveal that prior to entering the rest home, Marian had put an apple under the shrub. Why does the author withhold this key fact from you? Perhaps Welty was silent about the apple because, had she reported it right away, its echoes of Eve might have overshadowed your interpretation of the story as you read. Worth considering are issues of effect: what the characters' behavior makes you think of them and what impact the author's strategies have on you.

When you summarize a story's plot, you may be inclined to put events in chronological order. But remember that short stories are not always linear. Often they depart from strict chronology, moving back and forth in time. Consider the following opening sentences, both of which deal with a funeral ceremony. They come from two of the stories featured in this book, William Faulkner's "A Rose for Emily," reprinted in Chapter 9, and Andre Dubus's "Killings," reprinted in Chapter 11:

> When Miss Emily Grierson died, our whole town went to her funeral: the men through a sort of respectful affection for a fallen monument, the women mostly out of curiosity to see the inside of her house, which no one save an old manservant — a combined gardener and cook — had seen in at least ten years.

> On the August morning when Matt Fowler buried his youngest son, Frank, who had lived for twenty-one years, eight months, and four days, Matt's older son, Steve, turned to him as the family left the grave and walked between their friends, and said: "I should kill him."

Probably Faulkner's opening makes you wonder why Emily Grierson kept people out of her house. Probably Dubus's opening makes you wonder how Frank died and whom Steve means by "him." Eventually the authors do answer these questions by moving their stories back in time. Faulkner presents episodes in Emily's life, returning only at the end of the story to the time after her death. Dubus spends much of his story's first half on flashbacks that inform you about Frank's murder; then, Dubus returns to the present and shows Matt's effort to avenge his son. Many literary critics use the term **discourse** for a text's actual ordering of events. Chronologically, Emily Grierson's funeral comes near the end of Faulkner's short story. Yet it appears at the beginning of his discourse. Chronologically, Frank's funeral is sandwiched between several events. Yet it is the start of Dubus's discourse.

Alice Adams, author of many short stories, offers a more detailed outline of their typical **structure**. She has proposed the formula ABDCE: These letters stand for **action, background, development, climax,** and **ending**. More precisely, Adams has said that she sometimes begins a story with an action, follows that action with some background information, and then moves the plot forward in time through a major turning point and toward some sort of resolution. Not all writers of short stories follow this scheme. In fact, Adams does not always stick to it. Certainly a lot of short stories combine her background and development stages, moving the plot along while offering details of their characters' pasts. And sometimes a story will have several turning points rather than a single distinct climax. But if you keep Adams's formula in mind, if only as a common way to construct short stories, you will be better prepared to recognize how a story departs from chronological order.

The first paragraph of Welty's story seems to be centered on *action*. Marian arrives at the Old Ladies' Home and prepares to enter it. Even so, Welty provides some basic information in this paragraph, describing Marian and the rest home as if the reader is unfamiliar with both. Yet only in the second paragraph do you learn Marian's name and the purpose of her visit. Therefore, Welty can be said to obey Adams's formula, beginning with *action* and then moving to *background*. Note, however, that the second paragraph features *development* as well. By explaining to the receptionist who she is and why she is there, Marian takes a step closer to the central event, her meeting with the two roommates. The remainder of the story keeps moving forward in time.

Brown's story "The Gift of Sweat" begins with two paragraphs mostly devoted to background. They tell you about the arrangements between the narrator and Rick prior to the particular day that will be the story's focus. With the opening words of her third paragraph — "So one morning when I called" — Brown signals that she has spent the previous two on background material. Now, she implies, she will turn to developing the story's main situation.

What about *climax*, Adams's fourth term? Traditionally, the climax of a story has been defined as a peak moment of drama appearing near the end. Also, it is usually thought of as a point when at least one character commits a significant act, experiences a significant change, makes a significant discovery, learns a significant lesson, or perhaps does all these things. With Welty's story, you could argue that the climax is when Marian asks Addie her age, meets with refusal, sees Addie crying, and tries to bolt. Certainly this is a dramatic moment, involving intense display of emotion resulting in Marian's departure. But Welty indicates, too, that Marian here experiences inner change. When she looks on Addie "as though there was nothing else in the world to wonder about," this is "the first time such a thing had happened to Marian."

Adams's term *ending* may seem unnecessary. Why would anyone have to be reminded that stories end? Yet a story's climax may engage readers so much that they overlook whatever follows. If the climax of Welty's story is Marian's conversation with tearful Addie, then the ending is basically in four parts: the plea that Addie's roommate makes to Marian as she is leaving; Marian's final encounter with the receptionist; Marian's retrieval of the apple; and her escape on the bus, where she bites into the apple. Keep in mind that the ending of a story may relate somehow to its beginning. The ending of Welty's "A Visit of Charity," for instance, brings the story full circle. Whereas at the start Marian gets off a bus, hides the apple, and meets the receptionist, at the conclusion she rushes by the receptionist, recovers the apple, and boards another bus. However a story ends, ask yourself if any of the characters has changed at some point between start and finish. Does the conclusion of the story indicate that at least one person has developed in some way, or does it leave you with the feeling of lives frozen since the start? As Welty's story ends, readers may have various opinions about Marian. Some may find that she has not been changed all that much by her visit to the home, while others may feel that it has helped her mature.

A common organizational device in short stories is **repetition**. It takes various forms. First, a story may repeat certain words; in Brown's story, for example, the narrator repeatedly refers to sweat. Second, a story may involve repeated actions. In Welty's story, the two roommates repeatedly argue; Marian travels by bus at beginning and end; and the receptionist consults her wristwatch both when Marian arrives and when she leaves. Third, a story may echo previous events. In Brown's story, the narrator mentions her earlier visits to Rick and his past trips to the Hostess. Of course, in various ways a story's current situation will be new. In Brown's story, Rick's present condition makes his trek to the Hostess a big step for him, and he winds up in pain.

Point of View

A short story may be told from a particular character's perspective or **point of view**. Probably you have noticed that Brown's story is written in the **first person**; it is narrated by someone using the pronoun *I*. With every first-person story, you have to decide how much to accept the narrator's point of view, keeping in mind that the narrator may be psychologically complex. How objective does the narrator seem in depicting other people and events? In what ways, if any, do the narrator's perceptions seem influenced by his or her personal experiences, circumstances, feelings, values, and beliefs? Does the narrator seem to have changed in any way since the events recalled? How reasonable do the narrator's judgments seem? At what moments, if any, do you find yourself disagreeing with the narrator's view of things?

Not every short story is narrated by an identifiable person. Many of them are told by what has been traditionally called an **omniscient narrator**. The word *omniscient* means "all-knowing" and is often used as an adjective for God. An omniscient narrator is usually a seemingly all-knowing, objective voice. This is the kind of voice operating in the first paragraph of Welty's story. There, Marian is described in an authoritatively matter-of-fact tone that appears detached from her: "Holding a potted plant before her, a girl of fourteen jumped off the bus in front of the Old Ladies' Home." Keep in mind, though, that a story may primarily rely on an omniscient narrator and yet at some points seem immersed in a character's perspective. This, too, is the case with Welty's story. Consider the following passage about Marian:

Everything smelled wet — even the bare floor. She held on to the back of the chair, which was wicker and felt soft and damp. Her heart beat more and more slowly, her hands got colder and colder, and she could not hear whether the old women were saying anything or not. She could not see them very clearly. How dark it was! The window shade was down, and the only door was shut. Marian looked at the ceiling. . . . It was like being caught in a robbers' cave, just before one was murdered.

The passage remains in the third person, referring to "she" rather than to "I." Nevertheless, the passage seems intimately in touch with Marian's physical sensations. Indeed, the sentence "How dark it was!" seems something that Marian would say to herself. Similarly, the analogy to the robbers' cave may be Marian's own personal perception, and as such, the analogy may reveal more about her own state of mind than about the room. Many literary critics use the term **free indirect style** for moments like this, when a narrator otherwise omniscient conveys a particular character's viewpoint by resorting to the character's own language.

First-person singular narration and omniscient narration are not the only methods for telling a story. For instance, William Faulkner's "A Rose for Emily" (in Chapter 9) is narrated by "we," the first-person plural. Even more striking is the technique that Pam Houston uses in her short story "How to Talk to a Hunter" (Chapter 8). The story seems to be narrated from an unnamed woman's point of view, but she avoids the word *I* and instead consistently refers to *you*. While Houston's method is unusual, it serves as a reminder that short stories can be told in all sorts of ways.

Throughout this book, we encourage you to analyze an author's strategies by considering the options that he or she faced. You may better understand a short story's point of view if you think about the available alternatives. For example, how would you have reacted to Welty's story if it had focused on Addie's perceptions more than on Marian's? With Brown's story, how would you have felt if the narrator had been omniscient?

A WRITING EXERCISE

Choose a passage from Welty's or Brown's story and rewrite it from another point of view. Then exchange your rewritten passage with a classmate's response to this assignment. Finally, write a paragraph analyzing your classmate's revision. Specifically, compare the revision with the original passage that your classmate chose, noting any differences in effect.

Characters

Although we have been discussing plots, we have also referred to the people caught up in them. Any analysis you do of a short story will reflect your understanding and evaluation of its **characters**. Rarely does the author of a story provide you with extended, enormously detailed biographies. Rather, you see the story's characters at select moments of their lives. To quote William Trevor again, the short story is "the art of the glimpse."

A WRITING EXERCISE

Choose any character from the two stories featured here. Then, off the top of your head, jot down at least five adjectives you think apply to that character. Next, exchange lists with a classmate, even if the list you get in return deals with another character. When you look at your classmate's list, circle the adjective that surprises you most. Finally, write a brief essay in which you consider how applicable that adjective is. Do you agree with your classmate that it suits the character he or she chose? Why, or why not?

You may want to judge characters according to how easily you can identify with them. Yet there is little reason for you to read works that merely reinforce your prejudices. Furthermore, you may overlook the potential richness of a story if you insist that its characters fit your usual standards of behavior. An author can teach you much by introducing you to the complexity of people you might automatically praise or condemn in real life. If you tend to admire home-care providers, Brown's portrayal of one can be thought-provoking for you, since this particular provider is not sure what to do with the breakfast that Rick has set out in his kitchen. You may be tempted to dismiss the roommates in Welty's story as unpleasant, even "sick"; in any case, take the story as an opportunity to explore *why* women in a rest home may express discontent.

One thing to consider about the characters in a story is what each basically desires. At the beginning of Welty's story, for example, Marian is hardly visiting the Old Ladies' Home out of "charity," despite that word's presence in the story's title. Rather, Marian hopes to earn points as a Campfire Girl. Again, characters in a story may change, so consider whether the particular characters you are examining alter their thinking. Perhaps you feel that Marian's visit broadens her vision of life; then again, perhaps you conclude that she remains much the same.

Reading a short story involves relating its characters to one another. In part, you will be determining their relative importance in the story. When a particular character seems to be the story's focus, he or she is referred to as the story's **protagonist**. Many readers would say that Marian is the protagonist of Welty's story and that the home-care worker is the protagonist of Brown's. When a protagonist is in notable conflict with another character, the latter is referred to as the **antagonist**. Brown's story seems to lack an antagonist, unless you want to argue that the AIDS virus is one. What about Welty's story? Do you find any antagonists there?

Even a seemingly minor character can perform some noteworthy function in a story. Take Brown's character Margaret, who is apparently the narrator's supervisor. On the surface, Margaret seems much less important to the story than the narrator and Rick do. For one thing, Margaret's appearance is brief: She arrives, she exchanges some words with the narrator, and then she drives off with Rick. Before she goes, though, Margaret points out that the narrator is sweaty, and thus she makes the reader aware of this fact. Furthermore, Brown uses Margaret to put the narrator in a psychologically complex situation. Once Margaret takes Rick away, the narrator must figure out how to express her concern for him, which she ultimately does by thoroughly cleaning his home. On the whole, Margaret is more a plot device than a fully developed personality. Nevertheless, she merits study if only as an example of author Brown's craft.

In many short stories, characters are allies or enemies. But as the story proceeds, they may alter their relationships, forging new bonds or developing new conflicts. Although Welty's Marian initially finds both roommates unpleasant, she grows more conscious of the tension *between* them, and then for a moment she sympathizes with Addie. It is possible, too, for one character to be ambivalent about another, feeling both drawn and opposed to that person. One might argue, for example, that the two roommates in Welty's story have a love-hate relationship, needing each other's company even as they bicker. As perhaps you have found in your own experience, human relationships are often far from simple. Works of literature can prove especially interesting when they suggest as much.

What power and influence people can achieve have often depended on particular traits of theirs. These include their gender, social class, race, ethnic background, nationality, sexual orientation, and the kind of work they do. Because these attributes can greatly affect a person's life, pay attention to them if an author refers to them in describing a character. For instance, in Brown's story, the narrator indicates her gender as she recalls how she lay down with pain-stricken Rick: "I pulled my body close to him so his butt was in my lap and my breasts and stomach were against his back." But would the story be significantly different if she were a man? Perhaps. Certainly it is interesting that she has become a caretaker of what was formerly the home of a male couple. Also, note that the physical position described in the quoted passage is that of mother with fetus. In fact, just before the passage, the narrator addresses Rick as if he were her child, changing his name to "Ricky." Remember, too, that for many people, Mother is the original Hostess with the Mostest! Still, you may feel that we are making too much of gender here. If so, what would you point to in arguing that view?

Typically, characters express views of one another, and you have to decide how accurate these are. Some characters will seem wise observers of humanity. Others will strike you as making distorted statements about the world, revealing little more than their own biases and quirks. And some characters will seem to fall in the middle, coming across as partly objective and partly subjective. On occasion, you and your classmates may find yourselves debating which category a particular character fits. One interesting case is Welty's character Addie. Look again at the speech in which she berates her roommate:

> "Hush!" said the sick woman. "You never went to school. You never came and you never went. You never were anything—only here. You never were born! You don't know anything. Your head is empty, your heart and hands and your old black purse are all empty, even that little old box that you brought with you you brought empty—you showed it to me. And yet you talk, talk, talk, talk, talk all the time until I think I'm losing my mind! Who are you? You're a stranger—a perfect stranger! Don't you know you're a stranger? Is it possible that they have actually done a thing like this to

anyone—sent them in a stranger to talk, and rock, and tell away her whole long rigmarole? Do they seriously suppose that I'll be able to keep it up, day in, day out, night in, night out, living in the same room with a terrible old woman—forever?"

Some may argue that this speech is merely an unreasonable rant, indicating Addie's dour mood rather than her roommate's true nature. (For one thing, contrary to Addie's declaration, the roommate must have been born!) Yet it can also be argued that Addie shrewdly diagnoses her situation. Perhaps statements like "you never were born," "your head is empty," and "you're a stranger" are true in a metaphorical sense.

Setting

Usually a short story enables readers to examine how people behave in concrete circumstances. The characters are located in a particular place or **setting**. Moreover, they are shown at particular moments in their personal histories. Sometimes the story goes further, referring to them as living at a certain point in world history.

As the word *sometimes* implies, short stories do vary in the precision with which they identify their settings. At one extreme is Haruki Murakami's "Another Way to Die," featured in Chapter 11. This story's place and time are sharply defined: The action occurs in a Manchurian zoo in August 1945, when the Russian army was about to seize the region from its Japanese occupiers. On the other hand, the setting of Welty's "A Visit of Charity" is less exact. The story's main scene is clearly a nursing home for women, but the text does not refer explicitly to a particular region or era. Even when a story's setting is rather vague, however, certain details of the text may seem historically or geographically specific. Brown's story says rather little about Rick's apartment and events in the larger world, but since he has AIDS, the time frame is probably no earlier than the 1980s.

Short stories differ as well in the importance of their setting. Sometimes location serves as a mere backdrop to the plot, while at other times it is a looming presence. This second possibility is especially true of stories in which people journey to places they have not seen before. When Welty's character Marian visits the Old Ladies' Home, readers get her vivid impressions of it. Even when a story's setting is ordinary to the characters and to you, it may become filled with drama and meaning as the plot develops. For most people, kitchens are mundane places, but in Brown's story a kitchen becomes a scene of significant action. There, Brown's narrator must decide whether to accept the hospitality for which Rick has endangered his health.

Stories may focus on one site and yet show it changing over time. This is the case with Faulkner's "A Rose for Emily" (Chapter 9), in which Emily's town comes to view her differently over the years. Of course, a story may take place in more than one setting, and when it does, the differences between its various sites may be notable. In Katherine Mansfield's story "The Garden-Party" (Chapter 12) the young protagonist struggles to understand the sharp contrast between two events she witnesses: the garden party of the title, which is on her family's estate, and another family's mourning for a dead workman, which occurs in a nearby house. Even apparently minor shifts of location may prove important. Although Welty's story focuses chiefly on the Old Ladies' Home, it also shows you the world beyond that building when Marian eats her apple and flees. Perhaps Marian's escape is an illusion in the sense that old age awaits her, too. At the moment, though, Marian evidently sees this outside world as a refuge from the old and infirm.

One way of analyzing characters is to consider how they accommodate themselves — or fail to accommodate themselves — to their surroundings. The two roommates in Welty's story are evidently frustrated with living in the Old Ladies' Home, and they take out this frustration on each other. In Brown's story, the narrator's cleaning of Rick's home may leave you with mixed feelings. When, in his absence, she strips his bed, washes his laundry, vacuums his floor, dusts his objects, straightens his clothes, stores his cassettes, removes his garbage, and scrubs his bathroom, she is certainly caring for him. At the same time, her actions signify that he has lost all privacy. Though it is his own apartment, she has taken charge.

A WRITING EXERCISE

To become more aware of how setting may function in a short story, write a two- to three-page description of a setting you associate with someone you know. Choose a particular room, building, or landscape in which you have seen that person. In your description, use details of the setting to reveal something about his or her life.

Imagery

Just like poems, short stories often use **imagery** to convey meaning. Sometimes a character in the story may interpret a particular image just the way you do. Some stories, though, include images that you and the characters may analyze quite differently. One example is the apple in Welty's story. Whereas Marian probably views the apple as just something to eat, many readers would make other associations with it, thinking in particular of the apple that Adam and Eve ate from the Tree of Knowledge in Eden. By the end of Welty's story, perhaps Marian has indeed become like Adam and Eve, in that she has lost her innocence and grown more aware that human beings age. At any rate, many readers would call Marian's apple a **symbol**. Traditionally, that is the term for an image seen as representing some concept or concepts. Again, probably Marian herself does not view her apple as symbolic; indeed, characters within stories rarely use the word *symbol* at all.

Images may appear in the form of metaphors or other figures of speech. For example, when Marian enters the Old Ladies' Home, she experiences "a smell in the hall like the interior of a clock." Welty soon builds on the clock image as she describes the receptionist checking her wristwatch, an action that this character repeats near the end. Welty's whole story can be said to deal with time and its effects, both on the old and on the young.

Images in short stories usually appeal to the reader's visual sense. Most often, they are things you can picture in your mind. Yet stories are not limited to rendering visual impressions. They may refer and appeal to other senses, too. In Brown's story, the narrator is struck by how Rick's sweat smells. Similarly, Welty's young heroine notes the odor of the hall.

A WRITING EXERCISE

Write a brief essay in which you analyze how a particular advertisement uses imagery. The ad may come from any medium, including a newspaper, a magazine, television, or radio. What specific associations do you make with the ad's imagery? Why do you think the advertiser used it? Would you say that this use of imagery is successful? Why, or why not?

Language

Everything about short stories we have discussed so far concerns **language**. After all, works of literature are constructed entirely out of words. Here, however, we call your attention to three specific uses of language in stories: their title, their predominant style, and their dialogue.

A story's title may be just as important as any words in the text. Not always will the relevance of the title be immediately clear to you. Usually you have to read a story all the way through before you can sense fully how its title applies. In any case, play with the title in your mind, considering its various possible meanings and implications.

A WRITING EXERCISE

Write a brief essay in which you examine how Welty's title relates to her story or Brown's title relates to hers. Consider the writer's alternatives. If you choose to discuss Welty's "A Visit of Charity," you may find it helpful to think about this famous passage from the New Testament: "And now abideth faith, hope, charity, these three; but the greatest of these is charity" (I Corinthians 13:13). You may also want to look up the word *charity* in a dictionary.

Not all short stories have a uniform **style**. Some feature various tones, dialects, vocabularies, and levels of formality. Stories that do have a predominant style are often narrated in the first person, thus giving the impression of a presiding "voice." Brown's story "The Gift of Sweat," with its matter-of-fact, conversational tone, comes across as an anecdote that someone is relating to a friend.

Dialogue may serve more than one purpose in a short story. By reporting various things, characters may provide you with necessary background for the plot. In Welty's story, it's only from the roommates' fragmentary remarks that Marian — and the reader — can learn anything about their lives up until now. Also, by saying certain things to one another, characters may advance the plot. When, in Brown's story, suffering Rick says to the narrator "please don't go," she winds up in a physical intimacy with him that they may not have had together before. Actually, dialogue can be thought of as action in itself. Try to identify the particular kinds of acts that characters perform when they speak. For instance, Rick's "please don't go" can be labeled a plea. When Welty's character Addie addresses her roommate in the speech we quoted earlier, she makes accusations.

Dialogue may function as well to reveal shifts in characters' relations with one another. Through much of Welty's story, Addie's roommate is rather brusque with Marian; as Marian starts to leave, however, she acts like a beggar toward her: "Oh, little girl, have you a penny to spare for a poor old woman that's not got anything of her own?" Whether or not this performance is a mere pose, it suggests that the woman now hopes to get more out of Marian than she has gotten so far.

Theme

We have already discussed the term **theme** on pages 19–21. There, we identified issues of theme as one kind of issue that comes up in literary studies. At the same time, we suggested that term *theme* applies to various literary genres, not just short stories. Later, in Chapters 4, 5, and 6, we examine theme in connection with essays, poems, and plays. Here, though, we will consider theme as an element of short fiction. In doing so, we will be reviewing some points from our earlier discussion, applying them now to the two stories you have just read.

Recall that we defined the theme of a work as the main claim it seems to make. Furthermore, we identified it as an assertion, proposition, or statement rather than as a single word. "Charity" is obviously a *topic* of Welty's story, but because it is just one word, it is not an adequate expression of the story's *theme*. The following exercise invites you to consider just what that theme may be.

A WRITING EXERCISE

Here are several statements that readers have declared to be Welty's theme. Rank them, placing at the top the one you think most accurate and moving down to the one you think least accurate. Then, in two or three pages, explain your reasoning, referring to each statement at least once. Propose your own statement of the theme if none of these strike you as adequate.

1. Be nice to old people, for many of them have it tough.
2. None of us can escape the passage of time.
3. Searching for merit points is incompatible with a true spirit of charity.
4. Everyone has to give up dreams of innocence and paradise, just as Adam and Eve did.
5. Although we are tempted to repress our awareness of mortality, we should maintain that awareness.
6. We should all behave charitably toward one another.
7. We can tell how charitable we are by the way we treat people we find strange or irritable.

8. Old age homes need to be made more pleasant, both for the residents and for their visitors.

9. Whenever we become strongly aware of mortality, we tend to repress that awareness, thus robbing ourselves of any benefit we may gain from it.

10. Young people are capable of showing interest in others, if only for a moment, but for better or worse they're basically self-centered.

Think about the other points we made when we discussed theme in Chapter 1. To see how these apply to short fiction, we can start by relating each point to the stories by Welty and Brown.

1. Try to state a text's theme as a midlevel generalization. If you were to put it in very broad terms, your audience would see it as fitting a great many works besides the one you have read. If you went to the opposite extreme, tying the theme completely to specific details of the text, your audience might think the theme irrelevant to their own lives.

The phrase "the moral of the story" suggests that a story can usually be reduced to a single message, often a principle of ethics or religion. Plenty of examples can be cited to support this suggestion. In the New Testament, for instance, Christ tells stories — they are called *parables* — to convey some of His key ideas. In any number of cultures today, stories are used to teach children elements of good conduct. Moreover, people often determine the significance of a real-life event by building a story from it and by drawing a moral from it at the same time. These two processes conspicuously dovetailed when England's Princess Diana was killed in a car crash. Given that she died fleeing photographers, many people saw her entire life story as that of a woman hounded by media. The moral was simultaneous and clear: Thou shalt honor the right to privacy.

When you read short stories, you may be inclined to define their themes as broad generalizations, along the lines of "Thou shalt honor the right to privacy." For instance, the theme of Brown's "The Gift of Sweat" can probably be phrased as "We should do whatever we can for sick people." But that statement hardly conveys the specific flavor of Brown's text. After all, it can be used to sum up any number of stories, including Welty's. A story is often most interesting when it *complicates* some widely held idea that it seemed ready to endorse. As we have noted, it is possible to lose sight of a story's theme by placing too much emphasis on minor details in the text. Such would be the case if you declared Brown's theme to be "You're nice if you clean for a man with AIDS, but you show true sensitivity to him if you accept breakfast when he prepares it for you, even if that task makes him sicker." The more common temptation, however, is to turn a story's theme into an all-too-general cliché.

Therefore, a useful exercise is to start with a very general thematic statement but then make it increasingly specific. For a test case, refer again to our quite general version of Brown's theme: "We should do whatever we can for sick people." Your next step would be to identify the specific spin that Brown's story puts on this idea. How does her story differ from others on this theme? Note, for instance, that Brown's narrator evidently wants to help sick people right from the beginning of the story, whereas other stories might trace how a character gradually becomes committed to charity. Also, not every story about helping sick people would emphasize sweat and cleaning as Brown's does. With these two observations and others in mind, try now to restate our version of Brown's theme so that it seems more in touch with the specific details of her text.

2. *The theme of a text may be related to its title.* It may also be expressed by some statement made within the text. But often various parts of the text merit consideration as you try to determine its theme.

In our discussion of a short story's language, we called attention to the potential significance of its title. The title may serve as a guide to the story's theme. What clues, if any, do you find in Welty's title "A Visit of Charity" and Brown's title "The Gift of Sweat"? Of course, determining a story's theme entails going beyond the title. You have to read, and usually reread, the entire text. In doing so, you may come across a statement that seems a candidate for the theme because it is a philosophical generalization. Nevertheless, take the time to consider whether the story's essence is indeed captured by this statement alone.

3. *You can state a text's theme either as an observation or as a recommendation.* Each way of putting it evokes a certain image of the text's author. When you state the theme as an **observation**, you depict the author as a psychologist, a philosopher, or some other kind of analyst. When you state the theme as a **recommendation**—which often involves your using the word *should*—you depict the author as a teacher, preacher, manager, or coach. That is, the author comes across as telling readers what to do.

As we have noted, stories are often used to teach lessons. Moreover, often the lessons are recommendations for action, capable of being phrased as "Do X" or "Do not do X." The alternative is to make a generalization about some state of affairs. When you try to express a particular story's theme, which of these two options should you follow? There are several things to consider in making your decision. First is your personal comfort: Do you feel at ease with both ways of stating the theme, or is one of these ways more to your taste? Also worth pondering is the impression you want to give of the author. Do you want to portray this person as a maker of recommendations, or do you want to assign the author a more modest role? Because Brown has helped people with AIDS, you may want to state the theme of her story as a prescription for physical and spiritual health. Yet maybe Brown is out to remind her audience that health-care providers have human frailties; hence, expressing her theme as an observation may be the more appropriate move.

4. *Consider stating a text's theme as a problem.* That way, you are more apt to convey the complexity and drama of the text.

We have suggested that short stories often pivot around conflicts between people and conflicts within people. Perhaps the most interesting stories are ones that pose conflicts not easily resolved. Probably you will be more faithful to such a text if you phrase its theme as a problem. In the case of Brown's story, for example, you might state the theme as follows: "When we try to help people, we may find ourselves resisting the gifts they want to give us, because our guilt over their suffering interferes with our ability to accept things they do for us."

5. *Rather than refer to* the *theme of a text, you might refer to* a *theme of the text, implying that the text has more than one.*   You would still be suggesting that you have identified a central idea of the text. Subsequently, you might have to defend your claim.

Unlike the average novel, the typical short story pivots around only a few ideas. Yet you need not insist that the story you are analyzing has a single theme; in fact, even the shortest piece of short fiction may have a number of them. Besides, your audience is apt to think you nicely open-minded if you suggest that the theme you have discovered is not the only one. We believe, for example, that Brown's story has at least two themes. One is that people with AIDS deserve more understanding, appreciation, and attention than many of them now get. A second theme is that care of the ill may involve more than helping them keep their life "clean"; it may also mean sharing their "sweat," by making bodily contact with them and accepting whatever they achieve in their pain. Although we are label-ing each of these ideas *a* theme of Brown's story rather than *the* theme of it, we are still making strong claims. To use the term *theme* at all implies that we are identifying key principles of the text. You might disagree with our claims about Brown's themes, and if you did, we would have to support our position in order to change your mind.

Perhaps the biggest challenge you will face in writing about short stories is to avoid long stretches of plot summary. Selected details of the plot will often serve as key evidence for you. You will need to describe such moments from the story you are discussing, even if your audience has already read it. But your readers are apt to be frustrated if you just repeat plot at length. They will feel that they may as well turn back to the story itself rather than linger with your rehash. Your paper is worth your readers' time only if you provide insights of your own, *analyzing* the story rather than just *summarizing* it.

To understand what analysis of a short story involves, let's return to Monica Albertson, the student whose freewriting you read earlier. Monica was assigned to write an argument paper about Welty's or Brown's story for an audience consist-ing of her classmates as well as her instructor. Monica knew that she was more interested in writing about Brown's story. But she realized as well that for her paper to be effective, she had to come up with an issue worth addressing, a claim about that issue, and evidence for that claim. Moreover, she had to be prepared to identify the warrants or assumptions behind her evidence.

For most writing assignments, settling on an issue will be your most impor-tant preliminary step. Without a driving question, you will have difficulty produc-ing fresh, organized, and sustained analysis. To identify an issue concerning "The Gift of Sweat," Monica reviewed her freewriting, noting questions she had already raised there about Brown's text. She saw that her questions revolved around the story's narrator. Specifically, this character's behavior posed for Mon-ica issues of cause and effect. Monica wondered (1) why the narrator does not immediately reveal what is in the kitchen; (2) why the narrator cleans Rick's home instead of eating the breakfast right away; and (3) why the narrator's self-examination in the bathroom leads her finally to enter the kitchen, describe the breakfast, and eat it. In addition, Monica wondered about the significance of the story's title, "The Gift of Sweat," since the most important "gift" in the story seems to be food rather than sweat. This apparent contradiction can be phrased, too, as a cause-and-effect issue: Why does Brown call her story "The Gift of Sweat" if she ultimately emphasizes the gift of a breakfast? or, What is the effect of Brown's giving the story the title she does, especially when the story ultimately highlights a gift of breakfast? (Note that the second way of putting the question does not require Monica to determine the author's intentions, as the first does.)

Obviously Monica had several possible issues, as well as several possible ways of phrasing them. Therefore, she next considered whether any of these issues deserved priority. Looking at each issue she had raised, she thought about how much it interested her, how important it seemed to the story, and how easily she could address it within a 600-word paper. She also considered whether any of her issues could be combined. Ultimately, Monica settled on the following question as the focus of her analysis: Why does Rick's sweat lead the narrator to return to the kitchen and eat the breakfast that Rick has prepared? This question blended some of the issues that Monica had already raised, and again, it can be seen as an issue of cause and effect.

Monica chose to pursue this question after reviewing the options that Brown had in writing "The Gift of Sweat." In particular, Monica realized that Brown could have had something other than Rick's sweat be the catalyst for the narrator's ultimate acceptance of Rick's breakfast. Indeed, as Monica's class had discussed, many people fear the sweat of someone with AIDS, for they unreasonably believe they can catch the virus through superficial contact with an infected person. Given this widespread conviction, Brown's decision to have her narrator value Rick's sweat struck Monica as quite an intriguing move.

When you write a paper about a short story, your audience will expect a focused and coherent analysis. Therefore, you may have to be selective, omitting some of your ideas about the story as you emphasize others. As her freewriting reveals, Monica sensed religious symbolism in the meal that concludes "The Gift of Sweat." Yet she was not sure whether she had enough evidence to support this line of inquiry and felt it would seem a digression from her argument about the narrator's behavior. As you will see, Monica's final draft refers only slightly to religion, although she remained quite interested in this possible dimension of Brown's story.

A paper about a short story need not explicitly mention the elements of short fiction we have identified. Nevertheless, thinking of these elements can help you plan such a paper, providing you with some preliminary terms for your analysis. Monica came to see that her paper would be very much about a particular character in Brown's story, the home-care provider, who is both narrator and protagonist. Specifically, Monica's paper would be concerned with how this character behaves during the story's climax and ending. Clearly the paper would deal as well with imagery in the story: in particular, the image of Rick's sweat. Monica realized, too, that she would be touching on the story's theme, especially if she presented her main claim as a lesson that the story's narrator learns. But Monica was wary of reducing the story to one particular point, as thematic claims risk doing. Therefore, as you will see in the final version of her paper, Monica decided to make her main claim a cause-and-effect statement explaining the narrator's behavior.

When you plan a paper about a short story, keep in mind that you are more apt to persuade your readers if you include quotations from the text you discuss. Before you attempt a complete draft, copy down in your notebook any words from the story that might figure in your analysis. Monica, for example, was pretty sure that her paper analyzing the narrator's behavior in "The Gift of Sweat" would incorporate this statement made by the narrator just before the story ends: "I tried to think how Rick would think, I tried to imagine Barry." Yet, as with plot summary, quoting should be kept within limits, so that the paper seems an original argument about the story instead of a mere recycling of it. Monica was tempted to quote the three paragraphs from Brown's story that describe the narrator's cleaning of Rick's home. Eventually, though, Monica realized that so much quoting would seem excessive and that writing a brief reference to the cleaning in her own words would probably suffice.

Sample Student Paper: Final Draft

Here is Monica's final draft of her paper about "The Gift of Sweat." As you read it, keep in mind that it emerged only after she had done several preliminary drafts, in consultation with some of her classmates as well as her instructor. Although Monica's paper is a good example of how to write about a short story, most drafts can stand to be revised further. What do you think Monica has done well in her paper? If she planned to do yet another version, what suggestions would you make?

```
Monica Albertson

Professor Harvey

English 102

5 May ----

              "The Gift of Sweat" as a Story about
                      Learning to Identify

     The narrator of Rebecca Brown's story "The Gift of

Sweat" evidently does housekeeping for people with AIDS,

including Rick, the other major character. On one of her

regular Sunday visits to Rick's home, the narrator finds

him lying in pain. But basically all she can do is cuddle

him. After Rick is taken off to the hospital, the narra-

tor looks into his kitchen and sees that he has bought
```

cinnamon rolls for the two of them. At first she is unwilling to enter the kitchen, yet later she does decide to go there and eat the breakfast. The narrator reaches this decision when she becomes more aware of Rick's sweat on her. In fact, she actually seems to appreciate his sweat. But many readers may wonder why it is a positive influence on the narrator, especially since many people in real life would try to avoid the sweat of a person with AIDS, wrongly believing they might get infected. The narrator's thinking is not as puzzling, though, as it may first appear. Rick's sweat on her body enables her to identify with him, in the sense that it brings home to her the willpower he has shown despite his condition. Once his sweat reminds her that he is more than just a victim, she can more easily accept his offering of the breakfast.

For most of the story, the narrator seems mainly interested in helping. Probably this desire to help is what led her to become a caregiver for people with AIDS in the first place. When she discovers Rick in pain, she is frustrated that she can only do a little to relieve his suffering. As she cuddles him, she yearns to have something like the power of Christ, who could heal sick people just by touching them: "I tightened my arms around him as if I could press the sickness out." Probably the narrator feels frustrated, too, when her supervisor Margaret takes Rick off to the hospital without her. She needs to feel needed. In the words of a poem by Marge Piercy, she wants "to be of use."

The narrator's desire to help is a big influence on her when she first spots the breakfast that Rick has set up in his kitchen. Her response is avoidance: She backs away from the kitchen and doesn't even tell the reader what she has seen. Probably this response results in part from the guilt she feels over Rick's having risked his health to get the rolls. But the narrator's interest in helping Rick also seems to be a factor. Apparently she is so committed to assisting Rick that she has difficulty accepting what he has bought and prepared for her. Maybe she even prefers to look upon Rick as helpless and therefore in constant need of her help. You can tell that she is really into helping because instead of eating the breakfast, she throws herself into cleaning the rest of Rick's home.

The narrator's change of mind occurs after she has cleaned Rick's bathroom. At that point, she becomes very conscious of the sweat that Rick has left on her: "I put my hands up to my face and I could smell him in my hands. I put my face in my hands and closed my eyes." Here she is not just seeing his sweat but also inhaling it. Probably one reason she values it is that it provides her with a trace of Rick's presence even after he has gone off to the hospital. But in addition, the sweat enables her to identify with Rick. Most likely she has trouble distinguishing his sweat from hers in the first place. She seems, however, to be engaging in an even stronger identification with him when she reports that her hands "smelled like me, but also him."

Readers are still left with the question of what this identification really means as well as why it leads the narrator to accept Rick's breakfast at last. The nature of this identification becomes clearer once the narrator reenters Rick's kitchen. For the first time in the story, she makes a big effort to view his life from <u>his</u> perspective rather than from hers. In fact, near the very end of the story, she reports that "I tried to think how Rick would think, I tried to imagine Barry." Barry was Rick's companion, who is now dead (apparently from AIDS). In the story's last few pages, the narrator recalls how Rick tried to help Barry, just as she has tried to help Rick: "Rick would make something fabulous and they'd eat it together. That was when he was still trying to help Barry eat." The narrator also recognizes the effort that Rick showed that very morning in shopping for the cinnamon rolls: "I thought of Rick going down there, how long it took him to get down the street, how early he had to go to get the best ones." Although this shopping expedition does not really involve helping, it demonstrates that Rick wants to be more than just a receiver of help. When the narrator observes that his expedition is a case of "him trying to do what he couldn't," some readers may think that she still views him as basically helpless. But at this point she is clearly emphasizing the effort he has shown, rather than the pain that his effort has caused him.

Overall, Rick's sweat has changed the narrator's image of Rick. She is now able to imagine both Rick and her as helpers, or as people who try to be as active and generous as helpers are. Previously, the narrator's conception of Rick as helpless made her feel bad about eating his breakfast. When the scene in the bathroom changes her image of Rick, she is able to accept the breakfast, for she now sees it as indicating his generosity and determination.

It is significant that the narrator uses the same gesture on two occasions: when she notices Rick's sweat on her in the bathroom, and when she is finally about to eat his breakfast. Both times, she closes her eyes and puts her face in her hands. The repetition of this image encourages readers to connect the narrator's awareness of Rick's sweat with her decision to eat. One is cause and the other is effect. Furthermore, the gesture resembles the saying of grace before a meal. This impression is especially appropriate when the narrator accepts the gift of Rick's breakfast. But, as the title of the story indicates, Rick sweat is also a gift for the narrator, although not exactly in the same sense. The breakfast is a gift because it is something of value that Rick has offered the narrator free of charge. On the other hand, Rick's sweat is a gift because, through it, the narrator grows able to appreciate Rick's perspective and therefore his offer of the breakfast.

4

Writing about Poems

Some students are put off by poetry, perhaps because their early experiences with it were discouraging. They imagine poems have deep hidden meanings that they can't uncover. Maybe their high-school English teacher always had the right interpretation, and they rarely did. This need not be the case. Poetry can be accessible to all readers.

The problem is often a confusion about the nature of poetry, since poetry is more compressed than prose. It focuses more on connotative, emotional, or associative meanings and conveys meaning more through suggestion, indirection, and the use of metaphor, symbol, and imagery than prose does. Poetry seldom hands us a specific meaning. Poetic texts suggest certain possibilities, but the reader completes the transaction. Part of the meaning comes from the writer, part from the text itself, and part from the reader. Even if students are the same age, race, religion, and ethnicity, they are not exact duplicates of each other. All of them have their own experiences, their own family histories, their own emotional lives. If thirty people are reading a poem about conformity or responsibility, all thirty will have varying views about these concepts, even though there will probably be commonalities. (Our culture is so saturated with media images that it is nearly impossible to avoid some overlap in responses.)

In a good class discussion, then, we should be aware that even though we might be members of the same culture, each of us reads from a unique perspective, a perspective that might also shift from time to time. If a woman reads a poem about childbirth, her identity as a female will seem more relevant than if she were reading a poem about death, a more universal experience. In other words, how we read a poem and how significant and meaningful the poem is for us depends both on the content of the poem and our specific circumstances. Suppose you read a poem about dating at age fourteen; you would likely have very different responses rereading it at nineteen, twenty-five, and fifty. We read poems through our experiences. As we gain new experiences, our readings change.

That is one reason why it is important to respond in writing to your first reading. You want to be able to separate your first thoughts from those of your classmates; they too will be bringing their own experiences, values, and ideas to the discussion. In the give-and-take of open discussion, it may be difficult to remember what you first said. Of course, the point of a classroom discussion is not simply to defend your initial response, for then you would be denying yourself the benefit of other people's ideas. A good discussion should open up the poem, allow you to see it from multiple viewpoints, and enable you to expand your perspective, to see how others make sense of the world.

This rich mixture of the poet's text, the reader's response, and discussion among several readers can create new possibilities of meaning. Even more than fiction or drama, poetry encourages creative readings that can be simultaneously true to the text and to the reader. A lively class discussion can uncover a dozen or more plausible interpretations of a poem, each backed up with valid evidence both from the poem and the reader's experience. You may try to persuade others that your views about the poem are correct; others may do the same to you. This negotiation is at the heart of a liberal, democratic education. In fact, maybe the most respected and repeated notion about being well-educated is the ability to empathize with another's point of view, to see as another sees. Reading, discussing, and writing about poetry can help you become a person who can both create meaning and understand and appreciate how others do. This is one important way literature matters.

We have chosen three poems by Robert Frost (1874–1963) that have mattered to millions of readers. Frost writes beautiful, apparently simple poems, ones that rhyme, have compelling images, and tell accessible stories of American country life. Yet there is something deeper and more complex in these classics. The surface meaning of these poems seems clear enough, but below the surface they are tantalizing and purposefully ambiguous — "indeterminate" poems that seem to mean many things, depending on the values and experiences readers bring with them to their reading.

ROBERT FROST

Stopping by Woods on a Snowy Evening

Whose woods these are I think I know.
His house is in the village, though;
He will not see me stopping here
To watch his woods fill up with snow.

My little horse must think it queer   5
To stop without a farmhouse near
Between the woods and frozen lake
The darkest evening of the year.

He gives his harness bells a shake
To ask if there is some mistake.   10
The only other sound's the sweep
Of easy wind and downy flake.

♦ ♦ ♦

The woods are lovely, dark and deep,
But I have promises to keep,   15
And miles to go before I sleep,
And miles to go before I sleep.   [1923]

ROBERT FROST
The Road Not Taken

Two roads diverged in a yellow wood,
And sorry I could not travel both
And be one traveler, long I stood
And looked down one as far as I could
To where it bent in the undergrowth;   5

Then took the other, as just as fair,
And having perhaps the better claim,
Because it was grassy and wanted wear;
Though as for that the passing there
Had worn them really about the same,   10

And both that morning equally lay
In leaves no step had trodden black.
Oh, I kept the first for another day!
Yet knowing how way leads on to way,
I doubted if I should ever come back.   15

I shall be telling this with a sigh
Somewhere ages and ages hence:
Two roads diverged in a wood, and I–
I took the one less traveled by,
And that has made all the difference.   [1916]   20

ROBERT FROST
Mending Wall

Something there is that doesn't love a wall,
That sends the frozen-ground-swell under it,
And spills the upper boulders in the sun;
And makes gaps even two can pass abreast.
The work of hunters is another thing: 5
I have come after them and made repair
Where they have left not one stone on a stone,
But they would have the rabbit out of hiding,

To please the yelping dogs. The gaps I mean,
No one has seen them made or heard them made,   10
But at spring mending-time we find them there.
I let my neighbor know beyond the hill;
And on a day we meet to walk the line
And set the wall between us once again.
We keep the wall between us as we go.   15
To each the boulders that have fallen to each.
And some are loaves and some so nearly balls
We have to use a spell to make them balance:
"Stay where you are until our backs are turned!"
We wear our fingers rough with handling them.   20
Oh, just another kind of outdoor game,
One on a side. It comes to little more:
There where it is we do not need the wall:
He is all pine and I am apple orchard.
My apple trees will never get across   25
And eat the cones under his pines, I tell him.
He only says, "Good fences make good neighbors."
Spring is the mischief in me, and I wonder
If I could put a notion in his head:
"*Why* do they make good neighbors? Isn't it   30
Where there are cows? But here there are no cows.
Before I built a wall I'd ask to know
What I was walling in or walling out,
And to whom I was like to give offense.
Something there is that doesn't love a wall,   35
That wants it down." I could say "Elves" to him,
But it's not elves exactly, and I'd rather
He said it for himself. I see him there
Bringing a stone grasped firmly by the top
In each hand, like an old-stone savage armed.   40
He moves in darkness as it seems to me,
Not of woods only and the shade of trees.
He will not go behind his father's saying,
And he likes having thought of it so well
He says again, "Good fences make good neighbors."   [1914]   45

A WRITING EXERCISE

"Stopping by Woods on a Snowy Evening," "The Road Not Taken," and
"Mending Wall" are perhaps Frost's most popular poems. Read each selection
twice and then record your impression of what the poems seem to be about.
Include any personal associations that seem relevant. Are there noticeable

similarities and differences among the three? Try to freewrite steadily for about ten to twelve minutes. The exercise is an exploratory technique to help you plan an essay on these three poems. As with all exploring, being self-reflective, raising questions, and noting the context of the issues and their relevance to your life are all useful things to include.

Students' Personal Responses to the Poems

Here we have several students' responses to Frost's three poems. As a way to add different voices to the discussion, compare what you have written with what they have written.

Mary Ellen Chin, eighteen years old, writes:

    In "The Road Not Taken" Robert Frost is very pleased
    that he went down the road less traveled because that has
    made him much happier in his later life. He doesn't want
    to look back. He sighs out of relief that he doesn't have
    to worry about past decisions. In "Stopping by Woods on a
    Snowy Evening" Frost is also looking to the future and to
    his responsibilities and duties. He appreciates the
    beauty of nature but is not one to dillydally. He is a
    hard worker and doesn't require much sleep. In "Mending
    Wall" Frost is willing to help his old neighbor rebuild
    the wall but doesn't really care for it. He would rather
    it were down. The old man is fairly ignorant and just
    wants it up because his father did. As in the other two
    poems, Frost here is practical and not obsessed by the
    past.

Twenty-four-year-old Mitchell Ellerby writes:

    I see the speaker in "The Road Not Taken" as a sad
    man, one who has made a mistake, probably a big one like
    marrying the wrong person or maybe leaving the right one.
    This is a poem about bad choices and the regret that
    often follows in its wake. I think he really tried to
    judge what was the right thing to do --"and looked down
    one as far as I could"--but just blew it. Now it's too
    late and he sighs out of futility for taking the wrong
    road. "Stopping by Woods on a Snowy Evening" seems the

direct result of his sorrow. He says it's the "darkest evening of the year," which is a statement about his soul not the light. The whole wintry scene is the condition of his frozen heart. I think he is having such a bad time that he might walk into the woods and simply curl up and disappear from the pain. The woods are "lovely" because they offer an immediate way out of his life. But he can't go through with it. It seems he has made promises to somebody, maybe a wife or a young child. In a sad poem, this is his one saving grace. But even that doesn't improve his mood as he plods on, wearily hoping finally for sleep or death. "Mending Wall" is about the emotional barriers that people keep between them. The speaker knows this is a bad idea right away when he says "something there is that doesn't love a wall." Later on he demands to know why walls are good, but his neighbor just repeats a cliché about good fences making good neighbors. But because he calls him an "old-stone savage," I figure he really thinks such a saying is primitive. I don't know if Robert Frost wanted these poems to be read together, but if you put "Mending Wall" first, then the other two fol-low. What I'm saying is that if you build walls between people or if you cut yourself off from others, then you will feel depressed, you will think you have made bad choices, taken wrong turns. And if you really feel iso-lated, you might even contemplate suicide in the woods.

Tom Mason, age nineteen, writes:

I think "The Road Not Taken" describes something we all go through, making choices that will affect us later. I know I should have made another decision instead of going to college. Quite literally, I wanted to take the road less traveled and go on a bike tour through Europe. Everybody was going to college, even my friends who hated school--just because their parents wanted them to. Actually, I like school, but I have lived my whole life in this little town in southern Maryland. I've

never seen the world. I haven't even been to New York.
I wanted to take a year off, but I got so much grief that
I was forced to back down. And that has made all the
difference. What I wanted to do was sit by beautiful
spots in the Alps like the speaker in "Stopping by Woods
on a Snowy Evening." That must be very satisfying. He
feels one with nature, with the lovely woods. I think he
is ready to come back to civilization, just like I would
have been after my interlude in an exotic and far-off
land. In "Mending Wall" the speaker doesn't like walls. I
agree and one way to understand our neighbors is to
travel, to understand other cultures. How else can we
really understand each other? I'm afraid if I stay in my
little town, I'll become like that savage who can only
quote his father. Like the elves, I want the walls to
come down, but I'm surrounded by conformists.

Forty-year-old Sophia De Puy writes:

Robert Frost seems to be a confused person or maybe
just ambivalent about what he really wants to do or what
he thinks. In "The Road Not Taken," he wants to "travel
both" roads; he wants to have it both ways. The line "had
worn them really about the same" suggests to me there
really wasn't a big difference in the choice. He does say
both are equal, so what's the big deal? Why does he say
going down one path has made all the difference? Actually
when you think about it, that's an odd thing to say since
we never know what might have happened. Would I have been
happier or more satisfied if I had gone to college instead
of getting married to my high-school boyfriend? That made
a difference, but then all our thousands of decisions
make some kind of difference. I really wonder about that
"sigh." Is it regret, satisfaction, or resignation? Does
Frost know? He also seems confused in "Stopping by Woods
on a Snowy Evening." There seems to be a temptation to
retreat from the world on the one hand and a commitment
to participate in the world's duties and promises on the

other. I have sometimes felt like giving up too, but I
endured. I think he has mixed feelings. He thinks the
woods (which I see as death) are lovely but he weakly
decides to continue. In "Mending Wall" he is also not sure
if he wants the wall up or not. It looks like he wants it
down, but then why does he ask his neighbor to repair it
with him? Why does he mend the wall unless he thinks walls
really do work? Frost is like many of my friends: not too
sure which way to go, what position to take.

A WRITING EXERCISE

Choose one poem by Frost, and reread the responses by Mary Ellen, Mitchell, Tom, and Sophia. Next, write a brief paragraph or two comparing your response to theirs. You may want to list significant points of agreement and disagreement before attempting to write the comparison.

Out of dozens of students, we picked these four because they provide an interesting range of response to what at first appear to be three fairly straightforward poems. But poetry is so condensed and so energized that even seemingly simple poems allow readers to read between the lines and to fill in gaps in a variety of ways. More than likely, Frost did not specifically mean "The Road Not Taken" to refer to a bike trip to Europe as Mitchell Ellerby describes it. But this is fine. Mitchell filled in the gaps from his own experience. Unless you take the poem quite literally, Frost's two roads could be just about any choice we have to make.

What choices did the poem remind you of? How about the speaker's reason for stopping? To commune with nature, to take a break from a hard day's work, or to contemplate suicide? How would you fill in that gap? And what is the speaker of "Mending Wall" really interested in doing with the walls? Did you interpret that image as a literal wall or fence? As a less-tangible barrier like a border? Or did you, like Mitchell, figure the wall is a metaphor for our refusal to understand others and our tendency to avoid showing our private emotions, our deeper selves? These are questions to which there are no definitive answers. Definitive answers are not what poetry is about.

Each of the four students begins his or her understanding of these three poems with reasonable, often perceptive, observations. They move from these to write interesting explorations. To move ahead in the writing process from exploring to planning, it is useful to briefly review some elements of poetry. Of course, no element of poetry exists by itself; each works together. Our four students tended to focus on the thematic element of poetry. This is a good start since this anthology is arranged thematically, but the consideration of other elements can enhance their analysis.

The Elements of Poetry

Speaker and Tone

The voice we hear in a poem could be the poet's, but it is better to think of the **speaker** as a sort of poetic construction: perhaps a **persona** (mask) for the poet, or perhaps a complete fiction. The speaker's **tone** or attitude is sometimes difficult to discern. It could be ironic or sentimental, joyful or morose, or a combination. In "The Road Not Taken," for example, determining the speaker's tone hinges on how you hear certain words, especially an ambiguous word like *sigh*. We know of one critic who believes the speaker is closely aligned with Frost in complaining that most people want their poetry to have a catchy, bumper-sticker conclusion. Even though the poem doesn't really say one road is "less traveled by," the speaker resigns himself to telling people he did choose the unusual and "that has made all the difference." This is a different reading than most and suggests how a simple word like *sigh* can be interpreted in different ways. It also indicates how the theme of the poem is connected to the speaker's voice and tone. If you read this poem as a celebration of choice, then the tone of *sigh* is probably positive. If you think the speaker's attitude is negative, then you most likely hear a *sigh* of sadness.

A WRITING EXERCISE

Each of the poems has a first-person narrator, a speaker with whom a reader must reckon to make sense of the poems' meaning. Try to characterize the "I" of each poem. You may want to consider, for example, the attitude of the speaker in "Stopping by Woods on a Snowy Evening." What is the speaker's attitude toward the woods? Toward promises? How does the speaker in "The Road Not Taken" seem to feel about his decision? What is the attitude of the speaker in "Mending Wall" toward the neighbor? Toward the wall?

Diction and Syntax

In "Stopping by Woods on a Snowy Evening," the speaker uses ordinary concrete words, not the flowery and abstract poetic **diction** many people associate with poetry. Except perhaps for "downy flake," the words here are almost conversational. The same seems true for "The Road Not Taken." But these words gain power and grace in their simplicity. Arranging exact words in a meticulously constructed order is a most demanding aspect of poetry. Frost's genius is to do so with such apparent ease. It is his words that make a poem memorable, even more so than his ideas. The words in Frost's line "The woods are lovely, dark and deep" seem just right. The **denotations** (literal meanings) of these words work fine, but their **connotations** (associations, emotional overtones, suggestions) help create both a sense of serenity and the possibility of an ultimate withdrawal.

Frost's colloquial diction also helps to create the personality of the speaker (and the poet) as a country sage, one who does not need "highfalutin" diction to see clearly and deeply. But Frost's poems are crafted works of art. Like a professional basketball player driving to the hoop or a dancer executing a perfect leap, Frost makes it look gracefully easy. Take the first line of "Stopping by Woods," for example; Frost achieves added emphasis and rhythm here by inverting the usual **syntax**, or word order. By comparison, the usual subject/verb/object pattern ("I think I know whose woods these are") sounds flat. By inverting the usual word order, Frost subtly shifts our attention to the woods, not to the speaker's thinking.

A WRITING EXERCISE

All of these poems use simple language to denote apparently simple actions: stopping by woods at night, choosing a road, building a wall. Reread them with an eye to where connotations may take you or where unusual syntax might signal ambiguity or complexity. (In "Mending Wall," for example, what connotations do you associate with "savage," "darkness," and "good neighbors"?) List a few of these points and freewrite on them for ten minutes to see where your own free associations may take you.

Figures of Speech

When we use **figures of speech**, we mean something other than the words' literal meaning. In "Mending Wall" Frost writes that the stones from the wall are "loaves." This direct comparison is a **metaphor**. Had he said it more indirectly using *like* or *as*—for example, "like loaves"—it would be a **simile**. Aristotle claimed that metaphor is a poet's intuitive grasp of the way unlike things are similar. Is a simile a clearer, less suggestive way to imply sameness? Frost says his neighbor in "Mending Wall" is "like an old-stone savage armed." Might it have been too direct to claim that his neighbor is a savage? What do you think the difference is between "like a savage" and is "an old-stone savage"? Metaphors are suggestive, and it is still possible to read that line positively—if, for example, you (like the French Romantic philosopher Jean-Jacques Rousseau) believe in the dignity of "the noble savage." Frost's metaphor in the next line, "he moves in darkness," does, however, seem to suggest the conventional Western meaning of the savage as ignorant. Metaphors and similes enhance poetry's multiple possibilities.

A **symbol** is also a suggestive device. Symbols stand for more than themselves, for something beyond the specific words used. What, after all, does the wall stand for in "Mending Wall"? The context of its use in the poem helps the reader determine what the wall might stand for. The numerous details of Frost's poem suggest some kind of abstract barrier, but the specific possibilities are still open. Readers of "Mending Wall" mention that the wall could be anything from lack of intimacy to fear of strangers to the Berlin Wall. When Frost wrote "Mending Wall," he could have been thinking of novelist Henry James's claim that symbols cast long shadows.

Sometimes poets create more elaborate symbolic apparatus. In "The Road Not Taken," the road can be symbolic of conformity, but the idea of choice is played out in such detail that critics call this an **allegory**, or sustained symbolism. A popular film with clear allegorical implication is *Star Wars* (1977) where Luke Skywalker (goodness) triumphs over Darth Vader (evil) on his journey toward self-fulfillment. Using Obi-Wan (wisdom) to achieve the Force (morality), Luke rescues Princess Leia (purity), and so on. Both symbolism and allegory intimately extend and reinforce the meaning and significance of poetry.

A WRITING EXERCISE

Do you find any of these poems allegorical? (For example, how might the woods, the frozen lake, the darkest evening, the promises, and the miles be seen as allegorical in "Stopping by Woods on a Snowy Evening"?) Do the poems resist being read as allegories? In a couple of pages, make the case for whether any, or all, of the poems can be considered allegorical.

Sound

The English poet Alexander Pope hoped that poetry's **sound** could become "an echo to [its] sense," that what the ear hears would reinforce what the mind understands. To many people, **rhyme** is the most recognizable aspect of poetry. The matching of final vowel and consonant sounds can make a poem trite or interesting. The now-familiar rhyming of "moon" and "June" with "swoon" suggests a poet that will settle for a cliché rather than do the hard work of being fresh. Rhyme, of course, is pleasing to the ear and makes the poem easier to remember, but it also gives the poem psychological force.

In the first stanza of "Stopping by Woods," lines 1, 2, and 4 use **perfect rhyme**; they sound exactly alike. Note, too, that the unrhymed third line rhymes with the first line of the next stanza ("here" with "queer"). This is also true in the second stanza when "lake" rhymes with "shake" in the first line of stanza three. And later the "ee" sound in *sweet* rhymes with that in "deep." Such patterns, called **rhyme schemes**, are indicated with letters. The first **quatrain** (four-line stanza) would be marked *aaba*, the second *bbcb*, the third *ccdc*, the last *dddd*. Why do you think Frost ends with the repeated **couplet** (two lines)?

This is more than a clever way to interconnect the four stanzas because both ear and mind are pleased when they move forward to a new sound and then back for a moment to an old one. When we read "he gives his harness bells a *shake*," we remember "lake" from the previous stanza. When we hear "the woods are lovely, dark and *deep*," we also remember "sweep." Does such forward and backward movement suggest a tension, an ambivalence? In the student essay that follows this section, Sophia De Puy makes just this point, arguing that the speaker's anxiety is echoed in the poem.

The pleasure of reading "Stopping by Woods" is also enhanced by both **alliteration** and **assonance**. Alliteration is the repetition of consonant sounds; a closely related device, assonance repeats vowel sounds. Notice in the third stanza how Frost duplicates the "ee" sound in "sweep" in both "easy" and "downy." Can you find a duplicate for the "ow" in "downy"? Also notice the alliterative "s" sound in "some," "sound," and "sweep." Can you find other "s" sounds? Do these sounds help establish a mood?

A WRITING EXERCISE

One of the best ways to understand how a poem "works" is to rewrite it — or part of it — using a different rhyme scheme, or different rhyme words, while trying to keep the poem as close as possible to its original meaning. Try this with "Stopping by Woods on a Snowy Evening" or "The Road Not Taken." Or try to capture the meaning of "Mending Wall" in a short poem with a simple rhyme scheme.

Rhythm and Meter

Rhythm in poetry refers to the beat, a series of stresses, pauses, and accents. We are powerfully attuned to rhythm, whether it is our own heartbeat or the throb of the bass guitar in a rock band. When we pronounce a word, we give more **stress** (breath, emphasis) to some syllables than to others. When these stresses occur at a regular interval over, say, a line of poetry, we refer to it as **meter**. When we scan a line of poetry, we try to mark its stresses and pauses. We use ´ to indicate a stressed syllable and ˘ for an unstressed one. The basic measuring unit for these stressed and unstressed syllables in English is the **foot**. There are four usual feet: *iambic, trochaic, anapestic,* and *dactylic*. An **iamb** is an unstressed syllable followed by a stressed one, as in "the woods." Reversed we have a **trochee,** as in "tiger." An **anapest** contains three syllables that are unstressed, then unstressed, then stressed, as in "When the blue / wave rolls nightly / on deep Galilee." The reverse, the **dactyl,** can be heard in the Mother Goose rhyme, "Pussy cat, / pussy cat / where have you / been?" Look again at the last stanza of "Stopping by Woods on a Snowy Evening." When we read it out loud, we hear a fairly regular beat of iambs:

The woods / are love / ly, dark / and deep

But I / have pro / mises / to keep

And miles / to go / before / I sleep

And miles / to go / before / I sleep

Depending on the number of feet, we give lines various names. If a line contains one foot, it is a **monometer**; two is a **dimeter**; three a **trimeter**; four a **tetrameter**; five a **pentameter**; six a **hexameter**; seven a **heptameter**, and eight an **octometer**. So Frost's last stanza is mostly iambic tetrameter. (Line 14 is a variation.) Most lines in Shakespeare's sonnets are iambic pentameter, or five iambs.

Note how Frost alters line 14 slightly for variety. He also employs **end stops** and **enjambment** for emphasis. When a line ends with a period we are meant to pause (end stop), but in line 3, for example, we are supposed to pause only briefly, continuing on until we get to the period in line 4 (enjambment). These poetic techniques improve the sound and flow of the poem and enhance the thoughts and feelings that give poetry its depth and meaningfulness.

A WRITING EXERCISE

Right on the page, mark out the rhythm and meter of "The Road Not Taken," using the system of marks we just presented. Then describe the predominant rhythm and meter. Alternatively, map out the rhythm and meter of the poem you wrote for the preceding exercise.

Theme

Some readers are fond of extracting **theme statements** from poems, claiming, for example, that the theme of "Stopping by Woods" is about the need to struggle on or that "Mending Wall" champions nonconformity over tradition. In a sense these thematic observations are plausible enough, but they are limiting and misleading. "Stopping by Woods" certainly has something to do with the tension between retreat and responsibility, but the significance for each reader might be much more specific, having to do with drug addiction or suicidal impulses, with joyful acceptance of duty or a need for aesthetic beauty. Reducing a complex, ambiguous poem to a bald statement robs the poem of its evocative power, its mystery, and its art.

Some critics stress the response of readers; others care only for what the text itself says; still others are concerned with the social and cultural implications of the poem's meaning. There are psychoanalytic readers who see poems as reflections of the psychological health or illness of the poet; source-hunting or intertextual readers want to find references and hints of other literary works hidden deep within the poem. Feminist readers may find sexism, Marxists may find economic injustice, and gay and lesbian readers may find heterosexual bias. Readers can and will find in texts a whole range of issues. Perhaps we find what we are looking for, or we find what matters most to us.

This does not mean that we should think of committed readers as biased or as distorting the text to fulfill their own agenda, although biased or distorted readings are not rare. In a literature course, readers are entitled to read poems according to their own lights as long as they follow the general conventions of academic discourse. That is, if you can make a reasonable case that "Stopping by Woods" is about, say, the inability of animals ("My little horse must think it queer") to appreciate the aesthetic beauty of nature, then you should marshall your evidence both from the text and from your own experience and put your energy into writing an essay that is clear, informed, and persuasive.

A WRITING EXERCISE

State in sentence form two possible themes for each of the three poems. Then exchange your sentences with a classmate. Choose one of your classmate's sentences and freewrite on it for five minutes, exploring how the sentence captures the theme of the poem. Finally, exchange your freewriting and discuss. Did you find the same themes? What are significant differences?

Sample Student Paper: Revised Draft

After her initial response, Sophia De Puy planned her essay on Frost and wrote her first draft. When the class worked in small groups, she received feedback from her group about what she was doing well and how to improve her essay. She also met with her instructor, who made some suggestions about revising her focus.

Sophia wrote the following revision that combines her own subjective response with explication and analysis.

Sophia De Puy

Professor Frye

English 102

21 April ----

Robert Frost's Uncertainties:

A Reading of Three Poems

Hardly anything makes us feel better about life than to read a novel or see a film where good wins over evil, where the hero knows what he or she is doing, where the choices are clear and certain, the path cleared of ambiguity. Maybe it goes without saying that we draw comfort from these narratives because they are so unlike the stories we actually live. In my own life, I am well acquainted with uncertainty. I used to dream that when I entered my twenties--then my thirties--my decisions, indeed my life, would clarify itself. I was confused but thought that later on I would know which choice was right.

As a high-school senior, I was in love with the captain of the track team, a handsome and virile javelin thrower. He disliked school but was great at repairing foreign cars. He wanted us to get married, to open our own specialty garage, and to start a family. My parents wanted me to go to college and be a nurse. I was torn, confused, uncertain but finally did marry. That was twenty years ago. Today I have two sons in college. Unfortunately, my husband died two years ago; fortunately, he left us a good deal of money. So I have decided to go back and start again. I have been moderately happy, mostly. But did I make the right decision? I don't know. Do we ever know? Do we have the nerve to look back and admit our befuddlement at life's choices? I think some writers do.

I was particularly taken with this enigma of choice when I read Robert Frost's "The Road Not Taken."

Interesting, I thought, that he focuses on the mysterious, the unknowable road he doesn't take. Frost's speaker echoed my own thoughts about "what if." When I was twenty and nursing my first son on Saturday nights, I would fantasize about what I would be doing if I had gone to college with my girlfriends: Drinking at some wild frat party? Talking about our hopes and dreams or our anxieties and frustrations in a fashionable café with would-be poets? The path I didn't take seemed romantic and exciting. Like Frost's speaker, I was "sorry I could not travel both / And be one traveler." I too stood for a long time trying to decide if I had taken the best path. Only I could answer, but I didn't know. I was both in love and longing for the freedom of my youth. My husband had wanted real life to happen. I wanted to be two travelers.

Frost's speaker has a choice to make between "two roads." I could speculate about what they might be, but I think it's best to fill in that gap with my own experience. When he says he looked down one road "as far as [he] could," I was reminded that I too tried to imagine my future having children, married to a blue-collar man, staying in my neighborhood. Should I venture forth into the world, go away to college, delay marriage? I took "the other" road just like Frost's speaker. The usual interpretation of this poem seems to turn on a misreading of lines 9, 10, and 11. But Frost seems quite lucid here:

> Though as for that the passing there
> Had worn them really about the same,
> And both that morning equally lay . . .

Isn't it clear that both roads, both choices were equally attractive? This isn't a matter of being a conformist or a rebel, or a farmer or a poet, it's just one of life's many conundrums: Which choice is best? Should I go to school or get married? I didn't know, and neither did Frost. He says he "kept the first for another day,"

which is, of course, technically impossible. True, I am
now going to college--but at forty, not eighteen. You
can never go back, simply because you have changed, have
grown. Somehow I don't see myself pledging for Delta
whatever or worrying if I have a date for Saturday night.

This brings me to the mysterious and controversial
last stanza. I read the "sigh" as the speaker's resignation at having to imply in the last two lines that he is
contented that he made the right decision by taking the
"one less traveled by." But as I suggested, Frost's
speaker claims earlier both roads were worn "about the
same." Is he somehow going along with those people who
demand simple, clear answers, people who want poets to be
all wise? I know for a long while I used to say how glad
I was that I got married and had two great children. But
secretly I was never that sure. I think I gave people the
answer they wanted. I think the speaker feels he should,
too, like in Hollywood films where everything is clear,
where people live happily ever after. But here in a
subtle way, Frost is admitting that he doesn't have all
the answers.

Perhaps this kind of compromise is necessary in life.
Indeed, the speaker of "Stopping by Woods on a Snowy
Evening" seems equally conflicted. He stops to watch
"woods fill up with snow" even though from the response
of his horse this is not business as usual. Perhaps the
driver is a hard-working country doctor or a salesman
used to stopping only at houses. But he is doing more
than sightseeing: He is seriously questioning his life.
When he says it is "the darkest evening of the year," he
is referring to his mood. Everyone says the holidays are
the most joyful season of the year, but when my children
were two and three and wild with energy and my husband
was working overtime at the garage, I was not celebra-
tory. My old friends were home for Christmas vacation
and full of stories of trips to Florida and plans for

graduate school and jobs in New York and Atlanta. I was
morose, and I think Frost's speaker is, too. He needs a
long rest. He might even be suicidal. Everything around
him is peaceful, serene, restful. The lines "the only
other sound's the sweep / of easy wind and downy flake"
are more than pleasant alliteration; they are what his
mind longs for: stillness, pause. To me the line "the
woods are lovely, dark and deep" is a symbolic way of
saying death might be quite appealing. I know that tension between retreat and moving on, between sleep and
work, between the longing for rest and the necessity to
do your duty.

After reading this poem several times and studying
its rhyme scheme, I found that the rhyme moves us forward
but then takes us back. The last word in the third line
("here," "lake," "sweep") in each stanza becomes the
major repeated rhyme of the next. When we read each
stanza aloud, we can hear an echo of the previous one,
almost as if Frost is duplicating the choice between
movement and retreat the speaker is contemplating. But he
does go on; he does accept the harsh reality that a working life offers little real rest. If we are content or
not, we must endure. That is what I felt for years: that
"I have promises to keep." And I probably repeated words
like this too, droning them like a mantra I truly had to
believe in.

Does the speaker of "Mending Wall" truly believe that
"good fences make good neighbors"? At the very beginning
he does seem to suggest that there is almost a cosmic
presence that doesn't love a wall. And later he wants to
encourage his neighbor to question his conformist way of
thinking. The speaker claims he would be careful about
building a wall, but I notice that he doesn't say he
plans to take this one down, just that he might not want
another. The wall here seems symbolic of emotional
restraint or a psychological barrier. Might it also sug-

gest privacy or secrets of the heart? Could he be suggesting that emotional honesty (for example, "we tell
each other everything") is like living without walls?
This is too complex to say, and like the other two speakers, I think this one isn't so sure. True, he seems to
employ a negative connotation, calling his neighbor a
"savage armed," who "moves in darkness." But why then
does the speaker make repairs? Why does he invite his
neighbor to join him in mending the wall? He seems to
disagree with the neighbor's conformity but then he himself conforms with him. Why?

Because he wants it both ways; he wants to travel
both roads; he wants to retreat from the world and
embrace it. He wants to be close with his neighbor (or
perhaps his family and friends), but he also wants to
keep them at a safe distance. Since this has definitely
been a part of my personality for years, I have no
trouble understanding such contradictory thinking.
Even now, as I look forward to seeing my family during
the holidays, I know that after I have been there awhile,
I will be eager to return home to the serenity behind my
own wall.

Robert Frost is willing to suggest easy answers to
those who long for certainty. If you need to believe that
a choice you made years ago was the right one, then you
can get comfort from "The Road Not Taken." If you want to
plow ahead without doubting what you are doing, then
"Stopping by Woods" will confirm your certainty. If you
think honesty is always the best policy, then you will
think the speaker of "Mending Wall" wise. But if like me,
you face life with a certain tentativeness, if the past
is still a puzzle, if the future is an enigma, then
Frost's poetry will suggest that uncertainty is our lot
and that those who would have it otherwise are the real
"old-stone savage[s]," moving in the "darkness" of
illusions.

5

Writing about Plays

Most plays incorporate elements also found in short fiction, such as plot, characterization, dialogue, setting, and theme. But unlike short fiction and other literary genres, plays are typically enacted live, in front of an audience. Theater professionals distinguish between the written *script* of a play and its actual *performances*. When you write about a play, you may wind up saying little or nothing about performances of it. When you first read and analyze a play, however, try to imagine ways of staging it. You might even research past productions of the play, noting how scenery, costumes, and lighting—as well as particular actors—were used.

Because a play is usually meant to be staged, its readers are rarely its only interpreters. Theater audiences also ponder its meanings. So, too, do cast members; no doubt you have heard of actors "interpreting" their parts. When a play is put on, even members of the backstage team are involved in interpreting it. The technical designers' choices of sets, costumes, and lighting reflect their ideas about the play, while the director works with cast and crew to implement a particular vision of it. No matter what the author of the script intended, theater is a collaborative art: All of the key figures involved in a play's production are active interpreters of the play in that they influence the audience's understanding and experience of it. Therefore, you can develop good ideas when you read a play if you imagine yourself directing a production of it. More specifically, think what you would say to the actors as you guided them through their parts. As you engage in this thought experiment, you will see that you have options, for even directors keen on staying faithful to the script know it can be staged in any number of ways. Perhaps your course will give you and other students the chance to perform a scene together; if so, you will be deciding what interpretation of the scene to set forth.

To help you understand how to write about plays, we will refer often to the two one-act plays that follow. Both works explore relations between women. The first play, *The Stronger*, had its stage debut in 1889. Its author, the Swedish playwright August Strindberg (1849–1912), is widely acknowledged as a founder of modern drama. Throughout his career, Strindberg experimented with theatrical styles. For this particular play about an encounter between two actresses, he unconventionally chose to have one character speak and the other remain silent. The second play, Susan Glaspell's *Trifles*, premiered in 1916 with the author and her husband, the novelist George Cram Cook, in the cast. Glaspell (1876–1948) is best known for her association with the Provincetown Players, which was considered avant-garde in its day. Glaspell and Cook had founded the company a year earlier while vacationing in Provincetown, Massachusetts. Since its debut, the play has continued to be performed and read, in part because it is a compelling detective story as well as an analysis of female relations.

AUGUST STRINDBERG
The Stronger
Translated by Elizabeth Sprigge

CHARACTERS

MRS. X, *actress, married*
MISS Y, *actress, unmarried*
A WAITRESS

SCENE: *A corner of a ladies' café [in Stockholm in the eighteen eighties].° Two small wrought-iron tables, a red plush settee, and a few chairs.*

Miss Y is sitting with a half-empty bottle of beer on the table before her, reading an illustrated weekly which from time to time she exchanges for another.

Mrs. X enters, wearing a winter hat and coat and carrying a decorative Japanese basket.

MRS. X: Why, Millie, my dear, how are you? Sitting here all alone on Christmas Eve like some poor bachelor.

Miss Y looks up from her magazine, nods, and continues to read.

MRS. X: You know it makes me feel really sad to see you. Alone. Alone in a café and on Christmas Eve of all times. It makes me feel as sad as when once in Paris I saw a wedding party at a restaurant. The bride was reading a comic paper and the bridegroom playing billiards with the witnesses. Ah me, I said to myself, with such a beginning how will it go, and how will it end? He was playing billiards on his wedding day! And she, you were going to say, was reading a comic paper on hers. But that's not quite the same.

A waitress brings a cup of chocolate to Mrs. X and goes out.

MRS. X: Do you know, Amelia, I really believe now you would have done better to stick to him. Don't forget I was the first who told you to forgive him. Do you remember? Then you would be married now and have a home. Think how happy you were that Christmas when you stayed with your fiancé's

---

Addition to scene bracketed. First mention of Miss Y and Mrs. X reversed. [Translator's note]

people in the country. How warmly you spoke of domestic happiness! You really quite longed to be out of the theatre. Yes, Amelia dear, home is best — next best to the stage, and as for children — but you couldn't know anything about that.

Miss Y's expression is disdainful. Mrs. X sips a few spoonfuls of chocolate, then opens her basket and displays some Christmas presents.

MRS. X: Now you must see what I have bought for my little chicks. *(Takes out a doll.)* Look at this. That's for Lisa. Do you see how she can roll her eyes and turn her head. Isn't she lovely? And here's a toy pistol for Maja.° *(She loads the pistol and shoots it at Miss Y who appears frightened.)*

MRS. X: Were you scared? Did you think I was going to shoot you? Really, I didn't think you'd believe that of me. Now if *you* were to shoot *me* it wouldn't be so surprising, for after all I did get in your way, and I know you never forget it — although I was entirely innocent. You still think I intrigued to get you out of the Grand Theatre, but I didn't. I didn't, however much you think I did. Well, it's no good talking, you will believe it was me . . . *(Takes out a pair of embroidered slippers.)* And these are for my old man, with tulips on them that I embroidered myself. As a matter of fact I hate tulips, but he has to have tulips on everything.

Miss Y looks up, irony and curiosity in her face.

MRS. X *(putting one hand in each slipper)*:   Look what small feet Bob has, hasn't he? And you ought to see the charming way he walks — you've never seen him in slippers, have you?

Miss Y laughs.

MRS. X: Look, I'll show you. *(She makes the slippers walk across the table, and Miss Y laughs again.)*

MRS. X: But when he gets angry, look, he stamps his foot like this. "Those damn girls who can never learn how to make coffee! Blast! That silly idiot hasn't trimmed the lamp properly!" Then there's a draught under the door and his feet get cold. "Hell, it's freezing, and the damn fools can't even keep the stove going!" *(She rubs the sole of one slipper against the instep of the other. Miss Y roars with laughter.)*

MRS. X: And then he comes home and has to hunt for his slippers, which Mary has pushed under the bureau . . . Well, perhaps it's not right to make fun of one's husband like this. He's sweet anyhow, and a good, dear husband. You ought to have had a husband like him, Amelia. What are you laughing at? What is it? Eh? And, you see, I know he is faithful to me. Yes, I know it. He told me himself — what *are* you giggling at? — that while I was on tour in Norway that horrible Frederica came and tried to seduce him. Can you imagine anything more abominable? *(Pause.)* I'd have scratched her eyes out if she had come around while I was at home. *(Pause.)* I'm glad Bob told me about it himself, so I didn't just hear it from gossip. *(Pause.)* And, as a matter of fact,

Maja: Pronounced Maya.

Frederica wasn't the only one. I can't think why, but all the women in the Company° seem to be crazy about my husband. They must think his position gives him some say in who is engaged at the Theatre. Perhaps you have run after him yourself? I don't trust you very far, but I know he has never been attracted by you, and you always seemed to have some sort of grudge against him, or so I felt. *(Pause. They look at one another guardedly.)*

MRS. X: Do come and spend Christmas Eve with us tonight, Amelia — just to show that you're not offended with us, or anyhow not with me. I don't know why, but it seems specially unpleasant not to be friends with you. Perhaps it's because I did get in your way that time . . . *(slowly)* or — I don't know — really, I don't know at all why it is.

Pause. Miss Y gazes curiously at Mrs. X.

MRS. X *(thoughtfully)*:   It was so strange when we were getting to know one another. Do you know, when we first met, I was frightened of you, so frightened I didn't dare let you out of my sight. I arranged all my goings and comings to be near you. I dared not be your enemy, so I became your friend. But when you came to our home, I always had an uneasy feeling, because I saw my husband didn't like you, and that irritated me — like when a dress doesn't fit. I did all I could to make him be nice to you, but it was no good — until you went and got engaged. Then you became such tremendous friends that at first it looked as if you only dared show your real feelings then — when you were safe. And then, let me see, how was it after that? I wasn't jealous — that's queer. And I remember at the christening, when you were the godmother, I told him to kiss you. He did, and you were so upset . . . As a matter of fact I didn't notice that then . . . I didn't think about it afterwards either . . . I've never thought about it — until *now!* *(Rises abruptly.)* Why don't you say something? You haven't said a word all this time. You've just let me go on talking. You have sat there with your eyes drawing all these thoughts out of me — they were there in me like silk in a cocoon — thoughts . . . Mistaken thoughts? Let me think. Why did you break off your engagement? Why did you never come to our house after that? Why don't you want to come to us tonight?

Miss Y makes a motion, as if about to speak.

MRS. X: No. You don't need to say anything, for now I see it all. That was why — and why — and why. Yes. Yes, that's why it was. Yes, yes, all the pieces fit together now. That's it. I won't sit at the same table as you. *(Moves her things to the other table.)* That's why I have to embroider tulips, which I loathe, on his slippers — because you liked tulips. *(Throws the slippers on the floor.)* That's why we have to spend the summer on the lake — because you couldn't bear the seaside. That's why my son had to be called Eskil — because it was your father's name. That's why I had to wear your colours, read your books, eat the dishes you liked, drink your drinks — your chocolate, for instance. That's why — oh my God, it's terrible to think of, terrible! Everything, everything came to me from

in the Company: Translator's addition.

you — even your passions. Your soul bored into mine like a worm into an apple, and ate and ate and burrowed and burrowed, till nothing was left but the skin and a little black mould. I wanted to fly from you, but I couldn't. You were there like a snake, your black eyes fascinating me. When I spread my wings, they only dragged me down. I lay in the water with my feet tied together, and the harder I worked my arms, the deeper I sank — down, down, till I reached the bottom, where you lay in waiting like a giant crab to catch me in your claws — and now here I am. Oh how I hate you! I hate you, I hate you! And you just go on sitting there, silent, calm, indifferent, not caring whether the moon is new or full, if it's Christmas or New Year, if other people are happy or unhappy. You don't know how to hate or to love. You just sit there without moving — like a cat° at a mouse-hole. You can't drag your prey out, you can't chase it, but you can out-stay it. Here you sit in your corner — you know they call it the rat-trap after you — reading the papers to see if anyone's ruined or wretched or been thrown out of the Company. Here you sit sizing up your victims and weighing your chances — like a pilot his shipwrecks for the salvage. *(Pause.)* Poor Amelia! Do you know, I couldn't be more sorry for you. I know you are miserable, miserable like some wounded creature, and vicious because you are wounded. I can't be angry with you. I should like to be, but after all you are the small one — and as for your affair with Bob, that doesn't worry me in the least. Why should it matter to me? And if you, or somebody else taught me to drink chocolate, what's the difference? *(Drinks a spoonful. Smugly.)* Chocolate is very wholesome anyhow. And if I learnt from you how to dress, *tant mieux!*° — that only gave me a stronger hold over my husband, and you have lost what I gained. Yes, to judge from various signs, I think you have now lost him. Of course, you meant me to walk out, as you once did, and which you're now regretting. But I won't do that, you may be sure. One shouldn't be narrow-minded, you know. And why should nobody else want what I have? *(Pause.)* Perhaps, my dear, taking everything into consideration, at this moment it is I who am the stronger. You never got anything from me, you just gave away — from yourself. And now, like the thief in the night, when you woke up I had what you had lost. Why was it then that everything you touched became worthless and sterile? You couldn't keep a man's love — for all your tulips and your passions — but I could. You couldn't learn the art of living from your books — but I learnt it. You bore no little Eskil, although that was your father's name. *(Pause.)* And why is it you are silent — everywhere, always silent? Yes, I used to think this was strength, but perhaps it was because you hadn't anything to say, because you couldn't think of anything. *(Rises and picks up the slippers.)* Now I am going home, taking the tulips with me — *your* tulips. You couldn't learn from others, you couldn't bend, and so you broke like a dry stick. I did not. Thank you, Amelia, for all your good lessons. Thank you for teaching my husband how to love. Now I am going home — to love him.

Exit.   [1907]

---

cat: In Swedish, "stork."   ***tant mieux:*** French for "so much the better."

SUSAN GLASPELL
Trifles

CHARACTERS

GEORGE HENDERSON, *county attorney*
HENRY PETERS, *sheriff*
LEWIS HALE, *a neighboring farmer*
MRS. PETERS
MRS. HALE

SCENE: *The kitchen in the now abandoned farmhouse of John Wright, a gloomy kitchen, and left without having been put in order—the walls covered with a faded wall paper. Down right is a door leading to the parlor. On the right wall above this door is a built-in kitchen cupboard with shelves in the upper portion and drawers below. In the rear wall at right, up two steps is a door opening onto stairs leading to the second floor. In the rear wall at left is a door to the shed and from there to the outside. Between these two doors is an old-fashioned black iron stove. Running along the left wall from the shed door is an old iron sink and sink shelf, in which is set a hand pump. Downstage of the sink is an uncurtained window. Near the window is an old wooden rocker. Centerstage is an unpainted wooden kitchen table with straight chairs on either side. There is a small chair down right. Unwashed pans under the sink, a loaf of bread outside the breadbox, a dish towel on the table—other signs of incompleted work. At the rear the shed door opens and the Sheriff comes in followed by the County Attorney and Hale. The Sheriff and Hale are men in middle life, the County Attorney is a young man; all are much bundled up and go at once to the stove. They are followed by the two women—the Sheriff's wife, Mrs. Peters, first; she is a slight wiry woman, a thin nervous face. Mrs. Hale is larger and would ordinarily be called more comfortable looking, but she is disturbed now and looks fearfully about as she enters. The women have come in slowly, and stand close together near the door.*

COUNTY ATTORNEY (*at stove rubbing his hands*):   This feels good. Come up to the fire, ladies.

MRS. PETERS (*after taking a step forward*):   I'm not—cold.

SHERIFF (*unbuttoning his overcoat and stepping away from the stove to right of table as if to mark the beginning of official business*):   Now, Mr. Hale, before we move things about, you explain to Mr. Henderson just what you saw when you came here yesterday morning.

COUNTY ATTORNEY (*crossing down to left of the table*):   By the way, has anything been moved? Are things just as you left them yesterday?

SHERIFF (*looking about*):   It's just about the same. When it dropped below zero last night I thought I'd better send Frank out this morning to make a fire for us—(*sits right of center table*) no use getting pneumonia with a big case on, but I told him not to touch anything except the stove—and you know Frank.

COUNTY ATTORNEY: Somebody should have been left here yesterday.

SHERIFF: Oh—yesterday. When I had to send Frank to Morris Center for that man who went crazy—I want you to know I had my hands full yesterday. I knew you could get back from Omaha by today and as long as I went over everything here myself——

COUNTY ATTORNEY: Well, Mr. Hale, tell just what happened when you came here yesterday morning.

HALE *(crossing down to above table)*:   Harry and I had started to town with a load of potatoes. We came along the road from my place and as I got here I said, "I'm going to see if I can't get John Wright to go in with me on a party telephone." I spoke to Wright about it once before and he put me off, saying folks talked too much anyway, and all he asked was peace and quiet—I guess you know about how much he talked himself; but I thought maybe if I went to the house and talked about it before his wife, though I said to Harry that I didn't know as what his wife wanted made much difference to John——

COUNTY ATTORNEY: Let's talk about that later, Mr. Hale. I do want to talk about that, but tell now just what happened when you got to the house.

HALE: I didn't hear or see anything; I knocked at the door, and still it was all quiet inside. I knew they must be up, it was past eight o'clock. So I knocked again, and I thought I heard somebody say, "Come in." I wasn't sure, I'm not sure yet, but I opened the door—this door *(indicating the door by which the two women are still standing)* and there in that rocker—*(pointing to it)* sat Mrs. Wright. *(They all look at the rocker down left.)*

COUNTY ATTORNEY: What—was she doing?

HALE: She was rockin' back and forth. She had her apron in her hand and was kind of—pleating it.

COUNTY ATTORNEY: And how did she—look?

HALE: Well, she looked queer.

COUNTY ATTORNEY: How do you mean—queer?

HALE: Well, as if she didn't know what she was going to do next. And kind of done up.

COUNTY ATTORNEY *(takes out notebook and pencil and sits left of center table)*:   How did she seem to feel about your coming?

HALE: Why, I don't think she minded—one way or other. She didn't pay much attention. I said, "How do, Mrs. Wright, it's cold, ain't it?" And she said, "Is it?"—and went on kind of pleating at her apron. Well, I was surprised; she didn't ask me to come up to the stove, or to set down, but just sat there, not even looking at me, so I said, "I want to see John." And then she—laughed. I guess you would call it a laugh. I thought of Harry and the team outside, so I said a little sharp: "Can't I see John?" "No," she says, kind o' dull like. "Ain't he home?" says I. "Yes," says she, "he's home." "Then why can't I see him?" I asked her, out of patience. "'Cause he's dead," says she. *"Dead?"* says I. She just nodded her head, not getting a bit excited, but rockin' back and forth. "Why—where is he?" says I, not knowing what to say. She just pointed upstairs—like that. *(Himself pointing to the room above.)* I started for the stairs, with the idea of going up there. I walked from there to here—then I says, "Why, what did he die of?" "He died of a rope round his neck," says she, and just went on pleatin' at her apron. Well, I went out and called Harry. I thought I might—need help. We went upstairs and there he was lyin'——

COUNTY ATTORNEY: I think I'd rather have you go into that upstairs, where you can point it all out. Just go on now with the rest of the story.

HALE: Well, my first thought was to get that rope off. It looked . . . (*stops; his face twitches*) . . . but Harry, he went up to him, and he said, "No, he's dead all right, and we'd better not touch anything." So we went back downstairs. She was still sitting that same way. "Has anybody been notified?" I asked. "No," says she, unconcerned. "Who did this, Mrs. Wright?" said Harry. He said it businesslike—and she stopped pleatin' of her apron. "I don't know," she says. "You don't *know?*" says Harry. "No," says she. "Weren't you sleepin' in the bed with him?" says Harry. "Yes," says she, "but I was on the inside." "Somebody slipped a rope round his neck and strangled him and you didn't wake up?" says Harry. "I didn't wake up," she said after him. We must 'a' looked as if we didn't see how that could be, for after a minute she said, "I sleep sound." Harry was going to ask her more questions but I said maybe we ought to let her tell her story first to the coroner, or the sheriff, so Harry went fast as he could to Rivers' place, where there's a telephone.

COUNTY ATTORNEY: And what did Mrs. Wright do when she knew that you had gone for the coroner?

HALE: She moved from the rocker to that chair over there (*pointing to a small chair in the down right corner*) and just sat there with her hands held together and looking down. I got a feeling that I ought to make some conversation, so I said I had come in to see if John wanted to put in a telephone, and at that she started to laugh, and then she stopped and looked at me—scared. (*The County Attorney, who has had his notebook out, makes a note.*) I dunno, maybe it wasn't scared. I wouldn't like to say it was. Soon Harry got back, and then Dr. Lloyd came and you, Mr. Peters, and so I guess that's all I know that you don't.

COUNTY ATTORNEY (*rising and looking around*):   I guess we'll go upstairs first— and then out to the barn and around there. (*To the Sheriff.*) You're convinced that there was nothing important here—nothing that would point to any motive?

SHERIFF: Nothing here but kitchen things. (*The County Attorney, after again looking around the kitchen, opens the door of a cupboard closet in right wall. He brings a small chair from right—gets on it and looks on a shelf. Pulls his hand away, sticky.*)

COUNTY ATTORNEY: Here's a nice mess. (*The women draw nearer up center.*)

MRS. PETERS (*to the other woman*):   Oh, her fruit; it did freeze. (*To the Lawyer.*) She worried about that when it turned so cold. She said the fire'd go out and her jars would break.

SHERIFF (*rises*):   Well, can you beat the woman! Held for murder and worryin' about her preserves.

COUNTY ATTORNEY (*getting down from chair*):   I guess before we're through she may have something more serious than preserves to worry about. (*Crosses down right center.*)

HALE: Well, women are used to worrying over trifles. (*The two women move a little closer together.*)

COUNTY ATTORNEY (*with the gallantry of a young politician*):   And yet, for all their worries, what would we do without the ladies? (*The women do not unbend. He goes below the center table to the sink, takes a dipperful of water from the pail, and pouring it into a basin, washes his hands. While he is doing this the Sheriff and Hale cross to cupboard, which they inspect. The County Attorney starts to wipe his hands on the roller towel, turns it for a cleaner place.*) Dirty towels! (*Kicks his foot against the pans under the sink.*) Not much of a housekeeper, would you say, ladies?

MRS. HALE (*stiffly*):   There's a great deal of work to be done on a farm.

COUNTY ATTORNEY: To be sure. And yet (*with a little bow to her*) I know there are some Dickson County farmhouses which do not have such roller towels. (*He gives it a pull to expose its full-length again.*)

MRS. HALE: Those towels get dirty awful quick. Men's hands aren't always as clean as they might be.

COUNTY ATTORNEY: Ah, loyal to your sex, I see. But you and Mrs. Wright were neighbors. I suppose you were friends, too.

MRS. HALE (*shaking her head*):   I've not seen much of her of late years. I've not been in this house — it's more than a year.

COUNTY ATTORNEY (*crossing to women up center*):   And why was that? You didn't like her?

MRS. HALE: I liked her all well enough. Farmers' wives have their hands full, Mr. Henderson. And then——

COUNTY ATTORNEY: Yes——?

MRS. HALE (*looking about*):   It never seemed a very cheerful place.

COUNTY ATTORNEY: No — it's not cheerful. I shouldn't say she had the home-making instinct.

MRS. HALE: Well, I don't know as Wright had, either.

COUNTY ATTORNEY: You mean that they didn't get on very well?

MRS. HALE: No, I don't mean anything. But I don't think a place'd be any cheer-fuller for John Wright's being in it.

COUNTY ATTORNEY: I'd like to talk more of that a little later. I want to get the lay of things upstairs now. (*He goes past the women to up right where steps lead to a stair door.*)

SHERIFF: I suppose anything Mrs. Peters does'll be all right. She was to take in some clothes for her, you know, and a few little things. We left in such a hurry yesterday.

COUNTY ATTORNEY: Yes, but I would like to see what you take, Mrs. Peters, and keep an eye out for anything that might be of use to us.

MRS. PETERS: Yes, Mr. Henderson. (*The men leave by up right door to stairs. The women listen to the men's steps on the stairs, then look about the kitchen.*)

MRS. HALE (*crossing left to sink*):   I'd hate to have men coming into my kitchen, snooping around and criticizing. (*She arranges the pans under sink which the lawyer had shoved out of place.*)

MRS. PETERS: Of course it's no more than their duty. (*Crosses to cupboard up right.*)

MRS. HALE: Duty's all right, but I guess that deputy sheriff that came out to make the fire might have got a little of this on. (*Gives the roller towel a pull.*) Wish I'd thought of that sooner. Seems mean to talk about her for not having things slicked up when she had to come away in such a hurry. (*Crosses right to Mrs. Peters at cupboard.*)

MRS. PETERS (*who has been looking through cupboard, lifts one end of towel that covers a pan*): She had bread set. (*Stands still.*)

MRS. HALE (*eyes fixed on a loaf of bread beside the breadbox, which is on a low shelf of the cupboard*): She was going to put this in there. (*Picks up loaf, abruptly drops it. In a manner of returning to familiar things.*) It's a shame about her fruit. I wonder if it's all gone. (*Gets up on the chair and looks.*) I think there's some here that's all right, Mrs. Peters. Yes — here; (*holding it toward the window*) this is cherries, too. (*Looking again.*) I declare I believe that's the only one. (*Gets down, jar in her hand. Goes to the sink and wipes it off on the outside.*) She'll feel awful bad after all her hard work in the hot weather. I remember the afternoon I put up my cherries last summer. (*She puts the jar on the big kitchen table, center of the room. With a sigh, is about to sit down in the rocking chair. Before she is seated realizes what chair it is; with a slow look at it, steps back. The chair which she has touched rocks back and forth. Mrs. Peters moves to center table and they both watch the chair rock for a moment or two.*)

MRS. PETERS (*shaking off the mood which the empty rocking chair has evoked. Now in a businesslike manner she speaks*): Well I must get those things from the front room closet. (*She goes to the door at the right but, after looking into the other room, steps back.*) You coming with me, Mrs. Hale? You could help me carry them. (*They go in the other room; reappear, Mrs. Peters carrying a dress, petticoat, and skirt, Mrs. Hale following with a pair of shoes.*) My, it's cold in there. (*She puts the clothes on the big table and hurries to the stove.*)

MRS. HALE (*right of center table examining the skirt*): Wright was close. I think maybe that's why she kept so much to herself. She didn't even belong to the Ladies' Aid. I suppose she felt she couldn't do her part, and then you don't enjoy things when you feel shabby. I heard she used to wear pretty clothes and be lively, when she was Minnie Foster, one of the town girls singing in the choir. But that — oh, that was thirty years ago. This all you want to take in?

MRS. PETERS: She said she wanted an apron. Funny thing to want, for there isn't much to get you dirty in jail, goodness knows. But I suppose just to make her feel more natural. (*Crosses to cupboard.*) She said they was in the top drawer in this cupboard. Yes, here. And then her little shawl that always hung behind the door. (*Opens stair door and looks.*) Yes, here it is. (*Quickly shuts door leading upstairs.*)

MRS. HALE (*abruptly moving toward her*): Mrs. Peters?

MRS. PETERS: Yes, Mrs. Hale? (*At up right door.*)

MRS. HALE: Do you think she did it?

MRS. PETERS (*in a frightened voice*):   Oh, I don't know.

MRS. HALE: Well, I don't think she did. Asking for an apron and her little shawl. Worrying about her fruit.

MRS. PETERS (*starts to speak, glances up, where footsteps are heard in the room above. In a low voice*):   Mr. Peters says it looks bad for her. Mr. Henderson is awful sarcastic in a speech and he'll make fun of her sayin' she didn't wake up.

MRS. HALE: Well, I guess John Wright didn't wake when they was slipping that rope under his neck.

MRS. PETERS (*crossing slowly to table and placing shawl and apron on table with other clothing*):   No, it's strange. It must have been done awful crafty and still. They say it was such a — funny way to kill a man, rigging it all up like that.

MRS. HALE (*crossing to left of Mrs. Peters at table*):   That's just what Mr. Hale said. There was a gun in the house. He says that's what he can't understand.

MRS. PETERS: Mr. Henderson said coming out that what was needed for the case was a motive; something to show anger, or — sudden feeling.

MRS. HALE (*who is standing by the table*):   Well, I don't see any signs of anger around here. (*She puts her hand on the dish towel, which lies on the table, stands looking down at table, one-half of which is clean, the other half messy.*) It's wiped to here. (*Makes a move as if to finish work, then turns and looks at loaf of bread outside the breadbox. Drops towel. In that voice of coming back to familiar things.*) Wonder how they are finding things upstairs. (*Crossing below table to down right.*) I hope she had it a little more red-up up there. You know, it seems kind of *sneaking*. Locking her up in town and then coming out here and trying to get her own house to turn against her!

MRS. PETERS: But, Mrs. Hale, the law is the law.

MRS. HALE: I s'pose 'tis. (*Unbuttoning her coat.*) Better loosen up your things, Mrs. Peters. You won't feel them when you go out. (*Mrs. Peters takes off her fur tippet, goes to hang it on chair back left of table, stands looking at the work basket on floor near down left window.*)

MRS. PETERS: She was piecing a quilt. (*She brings the large sewing basket to the center table and they look at the bright pieces, Mrs. Hale above the table and Mrs. Peters left of it.*)

MRS. HALE: It's a log cabin pattern. Pretty, isn't it? I wonder if she was goin' to quilt it or just knot it? (*Footsteps have been heard coming down the stairs. The Sheriff enters followed by Hale and the County Attorney.*)

SHERIFF: They wonder if she was going to quilt it or just knot it! (*The men laugh, the women look abashed.*)

COUNTY ATTORNEY (*rubbing his hands over the stove*):   Frank's fire didn't do much up there, did it? Well, let's go out to the barn and get that cleared up. (*The men go outside by up left door.*)

MRS. HALE (*resentfully*):   I don't know as there's anything so strange, our takin' up our time with little things while we're waiting for them to get the evidence. (*She sits in chair right of table smoothing out a block with decision.*) I don't see as it's anything to laugh about.

MRS. PETERS *(apologetically):* Of course they've got awful important things on their minds. *(Pulls up a chair and joins Mrs. Hale at the left of the table.)*

MRS. HALE *(examining another block):* Mrs. Peters, look at this one. Here, this is the one she was working on, and look at the sewing! All the rest of it has been so nice and even. And look at this! It's all over the place! Why, it looks as if she didn't know what she was about! *(After she has said this they look at each other, then start to glance back at the door. After an instant Mrs. Hale has pulled at a knot and ripped the sewing.)*

MRS. PETERS: Oh, what are you doing, Mrs. Hale?

MRS. HALE *(mildly):* Just pulling out a stitch or two that's not sewed very good. *(Threading a needle.)* Bad sewing always made me fidgety.

MRS. PETERS *(with a glance at door, nervously):* I don't think we ought to touch things.

MRS. HALE: I'll just finish up this end. *(Suddenly stopping and leaning forward.)* Mrs. Peters?

MRS. PETERS: Yes, Mrs. Hale?

MRS. HALE: What do you suppose she was so nervous about?

MRS. PETERS: Oh—I don't know. I don't know as she was nervous. I sometimes sew awful queer when I'm just tired. *(Mrs. Hale starts to say something, looks at Mrs. Peters, then goes on sewing.)* Well, I must get these things wrapped up. They may be through sooner than we think. *(Putting apron and other things together.)* I wonder where I can find a piece of paper, and string. *(Rises.)*

MRS. HALE: In that cupboard, maybe.

MRS. PETERS *(crosses right looking in cupboard):* Why, here's a bird-cage. *(Holds it up.)* Did she have a bird, Mrs. Hale?

MRS. HALE: Why, I don't know whether she did or not—I've not been here for so long. There was a man around last year selling canaries cheap, but I don't know as she took one; maybe she did. She used to sing real pretty herself.

MRS. PETERS *(glancing around):* Seems funny to think of a bird here. But she must have had one, or why would she have a cage? I wonder what happened to it?

MRS. HALE: I s'pose maybe the cat got it.

MRS. PETERS: No, she didn't have a cat. She's got that feeling some people have about cats—being afraid of them. My cat got in her room and she was real upset and asked me to take it out.

MRS. HALE: My sister Bessie was like that. Queer, ain't it?

MRS. PETERS *(examining the cage):* Why, look at this door. It's broke. One hinge is pulled apart. *(Takes a step down to Mrs. Hale's right.)*

MRS. HALE *(looking too):* Looks as if someone must have been rough with it.

MRS. PETERS: Why, yes. *(She brings the cage forward and puts it on the table.)*

MRS. HALE *(glancing toward up left door):* I wish if they're going to find any evidence they'd be about it. I don't like this place.

MRS. PETERS: But I'm awful glad you came with me, Mrs. Hale. It would be lonesome for me sitting here alone.

MRS. HALE: It would, wouldn't it? *(Dropping her sewing.)* But I tell you what I
do wish, Mrs. Peters. I wish I had come over sometimes when *she* was here.
I—*(looking around the room)*—wish I had.

MRS. PETERS: But of course you were awful busy, Mrs. Hale—your house and
your children.

MRS. HALE *(rises and crosses left)*:   I could've come. I stayed away because it
weren't cheerful—and that's why I ought to have come. I—*(looking out left
window)*—I've never liked this place. Maybe because it's down in a hollow
and you don't see the road. I dunno what it is, but it's a lonesome place and
always was. I wish I had come over to see Minnie Foster sometimes. I can see
now—*(Shakes her head.)*

MRS. PETERS *(left of table and above it)*:   Well, you mustn't reproach yourself,
Mrs. Hale. Somehow we just don't see how it is with other folks until—something turns up.

MRS. HALE: Not having children makes less work—but it makes a quiet house,
and Wright out to work all day, and no company when he did come in.
(Turning from window.) Did you know John Wright, Mrs. Peters?

MRS. PETERS: Not to know him; I've seen him in town. They say he was a good
man.

MRS. HALE: Yes—good; he didn't drink, and kept his word as well as most, I
guess, and paid his debts. But he was a hard man, Mrs. Peters. Just to pass the
time of day with him—*(Shivers.)* Like a raw wind that gets to the bone.
(Pauses, her eye falling on the cage.) I should think she would 'a' wanted a
bird. But what do you suppose went with it?

MRS. PETERS: I don't know, unless it got sick and died. *(She reaches over and
swings the broken door, swings it again, both women watch it.)*

MRS. HALE: You weren't raised round here, were you? *(Mrs. Peters shakes her
head.)* You didn't know—her?

MRS. PETERS: Not till they brought her yesterday.

MRS. HALE: She—come to think of it, she was kind of like a bird herself—real
sweet and pretty, but kind of timid and—fluttery. How—she—did—change.
*(Silence: then as if struck by a happy thought and relieved to get back to
everyday things. Crosses right above Mrs. Peters to cupboard, replaces small
chair used to stand on to its original place down right.)* Tell you what, Mrs.
Peters, why don't you take the quilt in with you? It might take up her mind.

MRS. PETERS: Why, I think that's a real nice idea, Mrs. Hale. There couldn't
possibly be any objection to it could there? Now, just what would I take? I
wonder if her patches are in here—and her things. *(They look in the sewing
basket.)*

MRS. HALE *(crosses to right of table)*:   Here's some red. I expect this has got
sewing things in it. *(Brings out a fancy box.)* What a pretty box. Looks like
something somebody would give you. Maybe her scissors are in here. *(Opens
box. Suddenly puts her hand to her nose.)* Why——*(Mrs. Peters bends
nearer, then turns her face away.)* There's something wrapped up in this piece
of silk.

MRS. PETERS: Why, this isn't her scissors.

MRS. HALE *(lifting the silk):* Oh, Mrs. Peters—it's——*(Mrs. Peters bends closer.)*

MRS. PETERS: It's the bird.

MRS. HALE: But, Mrs. Peters—look at it! Its neck! Look at its neck! It's all—other side *to.*

MRS. PETERS: Somebody—wrung—its—neck. *(Their eyes meet. A look of growing comprehension, of horror. Steps are heard outside. Mrs. Hale slips box under quilt pieces, and sinks into her chair. Enter Sheriff and County Attorney. Mrs. Peters steps down left and stands looking out of window.)*

COUNTY ATTORNEY *(as one turning from serious things to little pleasantries):* Well, ladies, have you decided whether she was going to quilt it or knot it? *(Crosses to center above table.)*

MRS. PETERS: We think she was going to—knot it. *(Sheriff crosses to right of stove, lifts stove lid, and glances at fire, then stands warming hands at stove.)*

COUNTY ATTORNEY: Well, that's interesting, I'm sure. *(Seeing the bird-cage.)* Has the bird flown?

MRS. HALE *(putting more quilt pieces over the box):* We think the—cat got it.

COUNTY ATTORNEY *(preoccupied):* Is there a cat? *(Mrs. Hale glances in a quick covert way at Mrs. Peters.)*

MRS. PETERS *(turning from window takes a step in):* Well, not *now.* They're superstitious, you know. They leave.

COUNTY ATTORNEY *(to Sheriff Peters, continuing an interrupted conversation):* No sign at all of anyone having come from the outside. Their own rope. Now let's go up again and go over it piece by piece. *(They start upstairs.)* It would have to have been someone who knew just the——*(Mrs. Peters sits down left of table. The two women sit there not looking at one another, but as if peering into something and at the same time holding back. When they talk now it is in the manner of feeling their way over strange ground, as if afraid of what they are saying, but as if they cannot help saying it.)*

Mrs. Hale *(hesitatively and in hushed voice):* She liked the bird. She was going to bury it in that pretty box.

MRS. PETERS *(in a whisper):* When I was a girl—my kitten—there was a boy took a hatchet, and before my eyes—and before I could get there——*(Covers her face an instant.)* If they hadn't held me back I would have—*(catches herself, looks upstairs where steps are heard, falters weakly)*—hurt him.

MRS. HALE *(with a slow look around her):* I wonder how it would seem never to have had any children around. *(Pause.)* No, Wright wouldn't like the bird—a thing that sang. She used to sing. He killed that, too.

MRS. PETERS *(moving uneasily):* We don't know who killed the bird.

MRS. HALE: I knew John Wright.

MRS. PETERS: It was an awful thing was done in this house that night, Mrs. Hale. Killing a man while he slept, slipping a rope around his neck that choked the life out of him.

MRS. HALE: His neck. Choked the life out of him. *(Her hand goes out and rests on the bird-cage.)*

MRS. PETERS *(with rising voice):* We don't know who killed him. We don't *know.*

MRS. HALE (*her own feeling not interrupted*):   If there'd been years and years of nothing, then a bird to sing to you, it would be awful — still, after the bird was still.

MRS. PETERS (*something within her speaking*):   I know what stillness is. When we homesteaded in Dakota, and my first baby died — after he was two years old, and me with no other then ——

MRS. HALE (*moving*):   How soon do you suppose they'll be through looking for the evidence?

MRS. PETERS: I know what stillness is. (*Pulling herself back.*) The law has got to punish crime, Mrs. Hale.

MRS. HALE (*not as if answering that*):   I wish you'd seen Minnie Foster when she wore a white dress with blue ribbons and stood up there in the choir and sang. (*A look around the room.*) Oh, I *wish* I'd come over here once in a while! That was a crime! That was a crime! Who's going to punish that?

MRS. PETERS (*looking upstairs*):   We mustn't — take on.

MRS. HALE: I might have known she needed help! I know how things can be — for women. I tell you, it's queer, Mrs. Peters. We live close together and we live far apart. We all go through the same things — it's all just a different kind of the same thing. (*Brushes her eyes, noticing the jar of fruit, reaches out for it.*) If I was you I wouldn't tell her her fruit was gone. Tell her it *ain't*. Tell her it's all right. Take this in to prove it to her. She — she may never know whether it was broke or not.

MRS. PETERS (*takes the jar, looks about for something to wrap it in; takes petticoat from the clothes brought from the other room, very nervously begins winding this around the jar. In a false voice*):   My, it's a good thing the men couldn't hear us. Wouldn't they just laugh! Getting all stirred up over a little thing like a — dead canary. As if that could have anything to do with — with — wouldn't they *laugh*! (*The men are heard coming downstairs.*)

MRS. HALE (*under her breath*):   Maybe they would — maybe they wouldn't.

COUNTY ATTORNEY: No, Peters, it's all perfectly clear except a reason for doing it. But you know juries when it comes to women. If there was some definite thing. (*Crosses slowly to above table. Sheriff crosses down right. Mrs. Hale and Mrs. Peters remain seated at either side of table.*) Something to show — something to make a story about — a thing that would connect up with this strange way of doing it —— (*The women's eyes meet for an instant. Enter Hale from outer door.*)

HALE (*remaining by door*):   Well, I've got the team around. Pretty cold out there.

COUNTY ATTORNEY: I'm going to stay awhile by myself. (*To the Sheriff.*) You can send Frank out for me, can't you? I want to go over everything. I'm not satisfied that we can't do better.

SHERIFF: Do you want to see what Mrs. Peters is going to take in? (*The Lawyer picks up the apron, laughs.*)

COUNTY ATTORNEY: Oh, I guess they're not very dangerous things the ladies have picked out. (*Moves a few things about, disturbing the quilt pieces which cover the box. Steps back.*) No, Mrs. Peters doesn't need supervising. For that matter a sheriff's wife is married to the law. Ever think of it that way, Mrs. Peters?

MRS. PETERS: Not—just that way.

SHERIFF *(chuckling):*   Married to the law. *(Moves to down right door to the other room.)* I just want you to come in here a minute, George. We ought to take a look at these windows.

COUNTY ATTORNEY *(scoffingly):*   Oh, windows!

SHERIFF: We'll be right out, Mr. Hale. *(Hale goes outside. The Sheriff follows the County Attorney into the room. Then Mrs. Hale rises, hands tight together, looking intensely at Mrs. Peters, whose eyes make a slow turn, finally meeting Mrs. Hale's. A moment Mrs. Hale holds her, then her own eyes point the way to where the box is concealed. Suddenly Mrs. Peters throws back quilt pieces and tries to put the box in the bag she is carrying. It is too big. She opens box, starts to take bird out, cannot touch it, goes to pieces, stands there helpless. Sound of a knob turning in the other room. Mrs. Hale snatches the box and puts it in the pocket of her big coat. Enter County Attorney and Sheriff, who remains down right.)*

COUNTY ATTORNEY *(crosses to up left door facetiously):*   Well, Henry, at least we found out that she was not going to quilt it. She was going to—what is it you call it, ladies?

MRS. HALE *(standing center below table facing front, her hand against her pocket):* We call it—knot it, Mr. Henderson.

Curtain.   [1916]

A WRITING EXERCISE

Once you have read the two plays, write your reaction to them off the top of your head, spending at least ten minutes on each. Note any personal experiences affecting your response to each play. Note as well the questions you have about each, for one or more of these questions can serve as the basis for a paper of your own.

A Student's Personal Response to the Plays

Trish Carlisle was enrolled in a class that read and discussed both Strindberg's *The Stronger* and Glaspell's *Trifles*. Members of her class even performed these plays. Here is some freewriting that Trisha did about each of them:

> Near the end of Strindberg's play, Mrs. X says that
> "at this moment it is I who am the stronger." But is she?
> I guess that depends on what Strindberg meant by "the
> stronger" when he gave his play that title. As I was
> reading, I started to think that the stronger woman is

actually the silent one, Miss Y, because she seems to
have more self-control than Mrs. X does. I mean, Miss Y
doesn't apparently feel that she has to make long, loud
speeches in defense of her way of life. I can even
believe that with her silence she is manipulating Mrs. X
into getting fairly hysterical. Also, I guess we're to
think that Amelia has managed to lure away Mrs. X's husband, at least for a while. Furthermore, we don't have to
believe Mrs. X when at the end she claims that she has
triumphed over Miss Y. Maybe people who have really succeeded in life don't need to proclaim that they have, as
Mrs. X does.

Nevertheless, I can see why some students in this
class feel that Mrs. X is in fact the stronger. If she
has her husband back and wants her husband back, and if
Miss Y is really without companionship at the end and has
even lost her job at the theater, then probably Mrs. X is
entitled to crow. Was Strindberg being deliberately
unclear? Did he want his audience to make up their own
minds about who is stronger? Maybe neither of these women
is strong, because each of them seems dependent on a man,
and Mrs. X's husband may not even be such a great person
in the first place. If I were Mrs. X, maybe I wouldn't
even take him back. I guess someone could say that it's
Mrs. X's husband who is the stronger, since he has managed to make the two women fight over him while he enjoys
his creature comforts. Anyway, Strindberg makes us guess
what he is really like. Because he's offstage, he's just
as silent as Miss Y is, although his wife imitates his
voice at one point.

In a way, I feel that this play is too short. I want
it to go on longer so that I can be sure how to analyze
the two women and the man. But I realize that one of the
reasons the play is dramatic is that it's brief. I might
not be interested in it if it didn't leave me hanging.
And it's also theatrical because Miss Y is silent even as
Mrs. X lashes out at her. I wonder what the play would be

like if we could hear Miss Y's thoughts in a sort of
voice-over, like we find in some movies. It's interesting
to me that the play is <u>about</u> actresses. I wonder if these
characters are still "performing" with each other even if
they're not acting in a theater at the moment.

   <u>Trifles</u> is a clearer play to me because obviously I'm
supposed to agree with the two women that Minnie Wright
was justified in killing her husband. Glaspell steers all
our sympathies toward the two women onstage and Minnie.
I'm hazy about the offstage husband in Strindberg's play,
but Glaspell makes clear how we're to feel about the offstage Minnie. Meanwhile, the men in her play come across
as insensitive dummies. They're not really brutal or
mean, but they don't seem to understand or appreciate
women. Their wives seem a heck of a lot smarter about
women's daily lives than they are. Glaspell did keep me
guessing about how John Wright died. I figured early on
that his wife played a big role in his death, but I
didn't know exactly how she contributed to it. I liked
how slowly her motives were revealed; the use of the dead
bird as a prop must be very theatrical on a real stage.
At the end, I despised the men for thinking that their
wives were still just concerned with trivial things. A
lot of men I know would probably say that men today
aren't nearly as condescending as Glaspell's men are in
this play. But I think men today really are inclined to
consider women's interests as a bunch of trifles.

   I'm undecided, though, about whether women who kill
their husbands should go free if those husbands are
cruel. It's interesting to me that Minnie's husband evidently didn't beat her. Glaspell implies that Minnie is
more a victim of psychological abuse rather than physical
abuse. I realize that a woman out in the country couldn't
go to a counselor, but I think that she had more options
than Glaspell suggests. Why didn't Minnie just leave her
husband if he was so mean to her? Mrs. Hale seems to feel
guilty about not doing more to help Minnie, but can't we

```
expect Minnie to have tried to help herself? I guess I
wish that Minnie and her husband had been onstage so that
I could see better what they're really like. As things
stand, I feel that Glaspell is pushing me to accept Mrs.
Peters's and Mrs. Hale's interpretation and evaluation of
the marriage. I can imagine a second act to this play,
where we get to see Minnie thinking in her jail cell and
maybe even talking with some other prisoners about her
marriage. Of course, then I'd have to decide whether to
accept Minnie's own account of her marriage and her
explanation of why she killed her husband. In Glaspell's
play, there's some reference to the possibility that
Minnie has gone insane. If I saw Minnie and heard her
speak, I'd have to decide whether she's crazy and whether
her degree of sanity should even matter to me as I con-
sider whether she should go free.
```

Trish's freewriting will eventually help her develop ideas for one of her major class assignments, a paper in which she has to analyze either Strindberg's play or Glaspell's. Compare your responses to the plays with hers. Did the same issues come up for you? How do you feel about the two plays' women characters? What, if anything, do you wish the playwrights had made clearer? What would you advise Trish to think about as she moved from freewriting to drafting a paper?

The Elements of Drama

You will strengthen your ability to write about plays like Strindberg's and Glaspell's if you grow familiar with typical elements of drama. These elements include plot and structure, characterization, stage directions and setting, language, and theme.

Plot and Structure

Most plays, like most short stories, have a **plot**. When you read them, you find yourself following a **narrative**, a sequence of interrelated events. Even plays as short as *The Stronger* and *Trifles* feature plots, though in their cases the onstage action occurs in just one place and takes just a little while. As with short fiction, the reader of a play is often anxious to know how the events will turn out. The reader may especially feel this way when the play contains a mystery that characters are trying to solve. In Strindberg's play, for example, Mrs. X is apparently bent on discovering what relation her husband has had with her friend, while the two women onstage in Glaspell's play attempt to figure out the circumstances of John Wright's death.

In summarizing these two plays, you might choose to depict each plot as a detective story. Then again, you might prefer to emphasize the characters' emotional conflicts as you describe how these plays proceed. In fact, there are various ways you can describe Strindberg's and Glaspell's plots; just bear in mind that your accounts should be grounded in actual details of the texts. However you summarize a play's **structure** will reflect your sense of which characters are central to it. How prominent in Glaspell's plot is Minnie Wright, would you say? Is she as important as the two women onstage? More important than them? Less important? Your summary will also reflect your sense of which characters have power. Do you think the two women in Strindberg's drama equally influence that play's events? In addition, your summary ought to acknowledge the human motives that drive the play's action. Why, evidently, did Minnie Wright kill her husband?

Summarizing the plot of a play can mean arranging its events chronologically. Yet bear in mind that some of the play's important events may have occurred in the characters' pasts. In many plays, characters learn things about the past that they did not know and must now try to accept. For example, several of the important events in *Trifles* take place before the play begins. By the time the curtain rises, John Wright has already tormented his wife, and she has already killed him. Now, onstage, Mrs. Hale and Mrs. Peters proceed to investigate how John Wright died. A summary of Glaspell's play could begin with the sad state of the Wrights' marriage, then move to the murder, and then chronicle the subsequent investigation. But you can also summarize the play by starting with the investigation, which is what the audience first sees. Only later would you bring up the past events that Mrs. Hale and Mrs. Peter learn about through their detective work.

A WRITING EXERCISE

List in chronological order the events referred to and shown in *The Stronger*. Start with the earliest event that Mrs. X mentions; end with the event that concludes the play. Next, choose from this list an event that apparently occurred before the characters appear onstage. Then, write at least a paragraph analyzing the moment when the audience is made aware of this event. Most likely the audience learns of the event from Mrs. X. Why do you think Strindberg has her announce it at this particular moment?

In discussing the structure of short stories, we noted that many of them follow Alice Adams's formula ABDCE (**action, background, development, climax, and ending**). This scheme, however, does not fit many plays. In a sense, the average play is entirely action, for its performers are constantly engaged in physical movement of various sorts. Furthermore, as we have been suggesting, information about background can surface quite often as the play's characters talk. Yet the terms *development, climax,* and *ending* do seem appropriate for many plays. Certainly the plot of *The Stronger* develops, as Mrs. X becomes increasingly hostile to Miss Y. Certainly the play can be said to reach a climax, a moment of great significance and intensity, when Mrs. X moves to another table and declares her hatred for Miss Y. The term *ending* can also apply to this play, although readers may disagree about exactly when its climax turns into its ending. Certainly Mrs. X is in a different state of mind at the play's last moment; at that point, she stops haranguing Miss Y and leaves, declaring that she will save her own marriage.

Like short stories, plays often use repetition as an organizational device. The characters in a play may repeat certain words; for example, trace the multiple appearances of the word *knot* in *Trifles*. Also, a play may show repeated actions, as when the men in Glaspell's drama repeatedly interrupt the two women's conversation. In addition, a play may suggest that the onstage situation echoes previous events; when the men onstage in *Trifles* utter obnoxious comments about women, these remarks make Mrs. Hale and Mrs. Peters more aware of the abuse that Minnie Wright's husband inflicted on her.

The Stronger and *Trifles* are both short one-act plays. But many other plays are longer and divided conspicuously into subsections. The ancient Greek drama *Antigone*, which appears in Chapter 11, alternates choral sections with scenes involving only two characters. All of Shakespeare's plays, and most modern ones, are divided into acts, which are often further divided into scenes. Detecting various stages in the action is easier when the play is fairly lengthy, as is the case with Marsha Norman's *'night, Mother* (Chapter 12). But you can also break Strindberg's and Glaspell's one-act plays down into stages.

A WRITING EXERCISE

Outline either *The Stronger* or *Trifles*, breaking down its action into at least three stages. Write at least a couple of sentences describing each stage you have identified.

Characters

Many short stories have a narrator who reveals the characters' inner thoughts. Most plays, however, have no narrator. To figure out what the characters think, you must study what they say and how they move. Some characters say a great deal, leaving you with several clues to their psyche. Shakespeare's play *Hamlet*, for example, contains thousands of lines. Moreover, when Hamlet is alone onstage making long speeches to the audience, he seems to be baring his very soul. Yet despite such moments, Hamlet's mental state remains far from clear; scholars continue to debate his sanity. Thus, as a reader of *Hamlet* and other plays, you have much room for interpretation. Often you will have to decide whether to accept the judgments that characters express about one another. For example, how fair and accurate does Strindberg's Mrs. X seem to you as she berates Miss Y?

As with short stories, a good step toward analyzing a play's characters is to consider what each desires. The drama or comedy of many plays arises when the desires of one character conflict with those of another. Strindberg's Mrs. X feels that Miss Y has been a threat to her marriage, and while we cannot be sure of Miss Y's thoughts, evidently she is determined not to answer Mrs. X's charges. At the end of the play, the women's conflict seems to endure, even though Mrs. X proclaims victory. Many other plays end with characters managing to resolve conflict because one or more of them experiences a change of heart. Whatever play you are studying, consider whether any of its characters change. For example, is anyone's thinking transformed in *Trifles*? If so, whose?

The main character of a play is referred to as its **protagonist**, and a character who notably opposes this person is referred to as the **antagonist**. As you might guess without even reading Shakespeare's play, Hamlet is the protagonist of *Hamlet*; his uncle Claudius serves as his antagonist. Applying these terms may be tricky or impossible in some instances. The two women in *The Stronger* oppose each other, but each can be called the protagonist and each can be called the antagonist. *Trifles* also seems a challenging case. How, if at all, would you apply the two terms to Glaspell's characters?

In discussing the elements of short fiction, we referred to point of view, the perspective from which a story is told. Since very few plays are narrated, the term *point of view* fits this genre less well. While it is possible to claim that much of Shakespeare's *Hamlet* reflects the title character's point of view, he is offstage for stretches, and the audience may focus on other characters even when he appears. Also, think about the possible significance of characters who are not physically present. A character may be important even if he or she never appears onstage. In *The Stronger*, the two women's conflict is partly about Mrs. X's unseen husband. In *Trifles*, everyone onstage aims to discover what happened between two unseen people, Minnie and John Wright.

In most plays, characters' lives are influenced by their social standing, which in turn is influenced by particular traits of theirs. These may include their gender, social class, race, ethnic background, nationality, sexual orientation, and the kind of work they do. Obviously *Trifles* deals with gender relationships. Mrs. Peters and Mrs. Hale come to feel an affinity with Minnie Wright because they sense she has been an oppressed wife; meanwhile, their husbands scoff at women's obsession with "trifles."

A WRITING EXERCISE

Susan Glaspell's play *Trifles* depicts Mrs. Peters and Mrs. Hale covering up evidence to protect Minnie Wright. They seem to act out of loyalty to their gender. Do you feel that there are indeed times when you should be someone's ally because that person is of the same gender as you? What would you say to someone who is generally comfortable with alliances between women but less comfortable with alliances between men, since throughout history women have been oppressed by bands of men? Freewrite for fifteen minutes in response to these questions.

Stage Directions and Setting

When analyzing a script, pay attention to the **stage directions** it gives, and try to imagine additional ways that the actors might move around. Through a slight physical movement, performers can indicate important developments in their characters' thoughts. A good example is Glaspell's stage directions when Mr. Hale declares that "women are used to worrying over trifles." By having Mrs. Hale and Mrs. Peters "move a little closer together," Glaspell suggests that these two women *grow* closer because of Mr. Hale's scorn. As we have noted, Mrs. Hale and Mrs. Peters do seem to develop a kinship based on their common gender, and in turn they both seem increasingly sensitive to Minnie's plight.

You can get a better sense of how a play might be staged if you research its actual production history. Granted, finding out about its previous stagings may be difficult. But at the very least, you can discover some of the theatrical conventions that must have shaped presentations of the play, even one that is centuries old. Take the case of Sophocles' *Antigone* and Shakespeare's *Hamlet*, both of which appear in this book. While classical scholars would like to learn more about early performances of *Antigone*, they already know that it and other ancient Greek plays were staged in open-air arenas. They know, too, that, *Antigone's* Chorus turned in unison at particular moments, and that the whole cast wore large masks. Although the premiere of *Hamlet* was not videotaped, Shakespeare scholars are sure that, like other productions in Renaissance England, it made spare use of scenery and featured an all-male cast.

Most of the modern plays we include in this book were first staged in a style alien to Sophocles and Shakespeare, a style most often called **realism**. Realism marked, for example, the first production of Lorraine Hansberry's *A Raisin in the Sun*, reprinted in Chapter 7. When the curtain rose on that play's opening night in 1959, the audience saw a vivid re-creation of a shabby Chicago apartment. Indeed, when a production seems quite true to life, audiences may think it has no style at all. Nevertheless, even realism uses a set of identifiable conventions. That first production of Hansberry's play relied on what theater professionals call the *illusion of the fourth wall*. Although the actors pretended the "apartment" was completely enclosed, the set had just three walls, and the audience looked in. Similarly, an audience watching a production of *Trifles* is encouraged to think that it is peering into Minnie Wright's kitchen.

Some plays can be staged in any number of styles and still work well. Shakespeare wrote *Hamlet* back in Renaissance England, but quite a few successful productions of it have been set in later times, such as late-nineteenth-century England. Even modern plays that seem to call for realistic productions can be staged in a variety of ways. Note Strindberg's description of the setting for *The Stronger*: "A corner of a ladies' café [in Stockholm in the eighteen eighties]. Two small wrought-iron tables, a red plush settee, and a few chairs." Many productions of this play have remained within the conventions of realism, striving to make the audience believe that it is seeing a late-nineteenth-century Stockholm café. But a production of *The Stronger* may present the audience with only a few pieces of furniture that barely evoke the café. Furthermore, the production might have Mrs. X's husband physically hover in the background, as if he were a ghost haunting both women's minds. You may feel that such a production would horribly distort Strindberg's drama; a boldly experimental staging of a play can indeed become a virtual rewriting of it. Nevertheless, remember that productions of a play may be more diverse in style than the script would indicate.

A WRITING EXERCISE

A particular theater's architecture may affect a production team's decisions. Realism's illusion of the "fourth wall" works best on a proscenium stage, which is the kind probably most familiar to you. A **proscenium stage** is a boxlike space where the actors perform in front of the entire audience. In a proscenium production of *Trifles*, Minnie Wright's kitchen can be depicted in great detail. The performing spaces at some theaters, however, are "in the round": that is, the audience completely encircles the stage. What would have to be done with Minnie's kitchen then? List some items in the kitchen that an "in the round" staging could accommodate.

In referring to possible ways of staging a play, we inevitably refer as well to its setting. A play may not be all that precise in describing its setting; Strindberg provides set designers with few guidelines for creating his Stockholm café. More significant, perhaps, than the place of the action is its *timing*: Mrs. X finds Miss Y sitting alone on Christmas Eve. Yet a play may stress to its audience that its characters are located in particular places, at particular moments in their personal histories, or at a particular moment in *world* history. For example, *Trifles* repeatedly calls attention to the fact that it is set in a kitchen, traditionally a female domain. Furthermore, the audience is reminded that Minnie Wright's kitchen is in an isolated rural area, where a spouse's abuse and a neighbor's indifference can have devastating impact on a woman. Furthermore, as Mrs. Peters and Mrs. Hale explore Minnie's kitchen, they increasingly see its physical decline as a symptom of the Wrights' failing marriage.

You can learn much about a play's characters by studying how they accommodate themselves—or fail to accommodate themselves—to their settings. When Strindberg's Mrs. X can no longer bear sitting next to Miss Y, her shift to another table dramatically signifies her feelings. In *Trifles*, Mrs. Peters and Mrs. Hale are clearly interlopers in Minnie Wright's kitchen; they analyze its condition like detectives, or even like anthropologists. Increasingly they realize that they should have been more familiar with this kitchen—in other words, they should have been better neighbors for Minnie. Of course, much of the drama in Strindberg's and Glaspell's plays occurs because there is a single setting, which in both plays makes at least one character feel confined. Other plays employ a wider variety of settings to dramatize their characters' lives.

Imagery

When plays use images to convey meaning, sometimes they do so through **dialogue**. At the beginning of *The Stronger*, for instance, Mrs. X recalls "a wedding party at a restaurant," where "the bride was reading a comic paper and the bridegroom playing billiards with the witnesses." The play proceeds to become very much about divisions between husband and wife; moreover, the two women engage in a tense "game" that seems analogous to billiards. But just as often, a play's meaningful images are physically presented in the staging: through gestures, costumes, lighting, and props. For instance, perhaps the key image in *Trifles* is the dead bird wrapped in silk, which the audience is encouraged to associate with Minnie Wright. While Glaspell presents dialogue about the bird, the physical presence of the bird and cage props may make the audience more inclined to see the bird as a **symbol**, the term traditionally used for an image that represents some concept or concepts.

A WRITING EXERCISE

Imagine that you have been asked to stage a production of *The Stronger*. List the key props and gestures you would use to stress the meanings you find in the play. Then exchange lists with a classmate, and write a brief interpretation of each item on that classmate's list. Then, get your own list back and see whether the interpretations written there are what you wanted to convey.

Keep in mind that you may interpret an image differently than the characters within the play do. When Strindberg's Mrs. X refers to billiards, she may not think at all that she will be playing an analogous game with Miss Y. You, however, may make this connection, especially as the play proceeds.

Language

You can learn much about a play's meaning and impact from studying the **language** in its script. Start with the play's title. At the climax of Strindberg's play, for example, Mrs. X even refers to herself as "the stronger;" in Glaspell's play, the men and women express conflicting views about women's apparent concern with "trifles." Obviously both playwrights are encouraging audiences to think about their titles' implications. Yet not always will the meaning of a play's title be immediately clear. In her freewriting, Trish wonders how to define *stronger* and which of Strindberg's characters fits the term. Even if you think the title of a play is easily explainable, pause to see whether that title actually leads to an issue of definition.

In most plays, language is a matter of dialogue. The audience tries to figure out the play by focusing on how the characters address one another. At the beginning of Glaspell's play, the dialogue between Mrs. Peters and Mrs. Hale reveals that they do not completely agree about how to view Minnie Wright's situation:

MRS. PETERS: But, Mrs. Hale, the law is the law.
MRS. HALE: I s'pose 'tis. *(Unbuttoning her coat.)* Better loosen up your
   things, Mrs. Peters. You won't feel them when you go out.

Mrs. Hale's response seems half-hearted. Unlike Mrs. Peters, the wife of the county attorney, she seems more disposed to believe that Minnie's situation may justify sparing Minnie the force of the law. To bring up issues of definition again, you might say that Mrs. Hale subtly questions just what "the law" should be, whereas Mrs. Peters says only that "the law is the law." Furthermore, when Mrs. Hale advises Mrs. Peters to "loosen up your things," perhaps the playwright is suggesting that Mrs. Peters should also "loosen up" her moral code.

Remember that the pauses or silences within a play may be just as important as its dialogue. In fact, a director may add moments of silence that the script does not explicitly demand. In many plays, however, the author does specify moments when one or more characters significantly fail to speak. *The Stronger* is a prominent example: Miss Y is notably silent throughout the play, and as a reader you probably find yourself wondering why she is. Ironically, the play's absence of true dialogue serves to remind us that plays usually *depend* on dialogue.

A WRITING EXERCISE

Choose a moment in *The Stronger* when Miss Y notably fails to speak — perhaps one in which she makes a sound but does not utter words. Then, write a brief monologue for her in which you express what she may be thinking at that moment. Next, write a paragraph or two in which you identify what Strindberg conceivably gains by *not* having Miss Y speak at that moment.

Theme

We have already discussed **theme** in Part One, and here we will build on some points from our earlier discussion. A theme is the main claim — an assertion, proposition, or statement — that a work seems to make. As with other literary genres, try to state a play's theme as a midlevel generalization. If expressed in very broad terms, it will seem to fit many other works besides the one you have read; if narrowly tied to the play's characters and their particular situation, it will seem irrelevant to most other people's lives. With *The Stronger*, an example of a very broad theme would be "Women should not fight over a man." At the opposite extreme, a too-narrow theme would be "Women should behave well toward each other on Christmas Eve, even if one of them has slept with the other's husband." If you are formulating Strindberg's theme, you might start with the broad generalization we have cited and then try to narrow it down to a midlevel one. You might even think of ways that Strindberg's play *complicates* that broad generalization. What might, in fact, be a good midlevel generalization in Strindberg's case?

As we have noted, the titles of *The Stronger* and *Trifles* seem significant. Indeed, a play's theme may be related to its title. Nevertheless, be wary of couching the theme in terms drawn solely from the title. The play's theme may not be reducible to these words alone. Remember that the titles of Strindberg's and Glaspell's plays can give rise to issues of definition in the first place.

You can state a play's theme as an **observation** or as a **recommendation.** With Strindberg's play, an observation-type theme would be "Marriage and career may disrupt relations between women." A recommendation-type theme would be either the broad or narrow generalization that we cited earlier. Neither way of stating the theme is automatically preferable, but remain aware of the different tones and effects they may carry. Consider, too, the possibility of stating the theme as a problem, as in this example: "We may be inclined to defend our marriages when they seem threatened, but in our defense we may cling to illusions that can easily shatter." Furthermore, consider the possibility of referring to *a* theme of the play rather than *the* theme, thereby acknowledging the possibility that the play is making several important claims.

A WRITING EXERCISE

Write three different versions of the theme of *Trifles*: a version that is excessively broad, one that is a midlevel generalization, and one that is too narrow. Then, exchange sheets with several of your classmates. (Your instructor may have all the sheets circulated quickly through the entire class.) As a group, select the best midlevel generalization. Be prepared to say why it is the best.

When you write about a play, certainly you will refer to the text of it, its **script**. But probably the play was meant to be staged, and most likely it has been. Thus, you might refer to actual productions of it and to ways it can be performed. Remember, though, that different productions of the play may stress different meanings and create different effects. In your paper, you might discuss how much room for interpretation the script allows those who would stage it. For any paper you write about the play, look beyond the characters' dialogue and study whatever stage directions the script gives.

Undoubtedly your paper will have to offer some plot summary, even if your audience has already read the play. After all, certain details of the plot will be important support for your points. But, as with papers about short fiction, keep the amount of plot summary small, mentioning only events in the play that are crucial to your overall argument. Your reader should feel that you are analyzing the play rather than just recounting it.

To understand more what analysis of a play involves, let's return to Trish Carlisle, the student whose freewriting you read earlier. Trish was assigned to write a 600-word paper about Strindberg's *The Stronger* or Glaspell's *Trifles*. She was asked to imagine herself writing to a particular audience: performers rehearsing a production of the play she chose. More specifically, she was to identify and address some question that these performers might have, an issue that might be bothering them as they prepared to put on the play. Trish knew that, besides presenting an issue, her paper would have to make a main claim and support it with evidence. Moreover, the paper might have to spell out some of the warrants or assumptions behind her evidence.

Trish found both Strindberg's play and Glaspell's interesting, so she was not immediately sure which one to choose. Because finding an issue was such an important part of the assignment, she decided to review her freewriting about each play, noting questions she had raised there about them. Trish saw that the chief issue posed for her by *The Stronger* was, "Which character is the stronger?" She also saw that, for her, *Trifles* was a more clear-cut play, although it did leave her with the question, "Should women who kill their husbands go free if their husbands are cruel?" Eventually Trish decided to focus on Strindberg's play and the issue of how to apply its title. Much as she liked *Trifles*, she thought the issue she associated with it went far beyond the play itself, whereas the issue she associated with *The Stronger* would enable her to discuss many of that play's specific details. Also, she thought that performers of Strindberg's play would be anxious to clarify its title, whereas performers of *Trifles* need not be sure how to judge the Minnie Wrights of this world.

Nevertheless, Trish recognized that the issue "Which character is the stronger?" still left her with various decisions to make. For one thing, she had to decide what kind of an issue she would call it. Trish saw that it could be considered an issue of fact, an issue of evaluation, or an issue of definition. Although it could fit into all of these categories, Trish knew that the category she chose would influence the direction of her paper. Eventually she decided to treat "Which character is the stronger?" as primarily an issue of definition, because she figured that, no matter what, she would be devoting much of her paper to defining *stronger* as a term.

Of course, there are many different senses in which someone may be "stronger" than someone else. Your best friend may be a stronger tennis player than you, in the sense that he or she always beats you at that game. But you may be a stronger student than your friend, in the sense that you get better grades in school. In the case of Strindberg's play, Trish came to see that a paper focused on which character is *morally* stronger would differ from one focused on who is *emotionally* stronger, and these papers would differ in turn from one focused on which character is *politically* stronger, more able to impose his or her will. These reflections led Trish to revise her issue somewhat. She decided to address the question, "Which particular sense of the word 'stronger' is most relevant to Strindberg's play?" In part, Trish came up with this reformulation of her issue because she realized that the two women feuding in the play are actresses, and that they behave as actresses even when they are not professionally performing. Trish's answer to her revised question was that the play encourages the audience to consider which woman is the stronger *actress* — which woman is more able, that is, to convey her preferred version of reality.

When you write about a play, you may have to be selective, for your paper may not be able to accommodate all the ideas and issues that occur to you. Trish was not sure which woman in Strindberg's play is the stronger actress. She felt that a case can be made for Mrs. X or Miss Y; indeed, she suspected that Strindberg was letting his audience decide. But she decided that her paper was not obligated to resolve this matter; she could simply mention the various possible positions in her final paragraph. In the body of her paper, Trish felt she would contribute much if she focused on addressing her main issue with her main claim. Again, her main issue was, "Which particular sense of the word 'stronger' is most relevant to Strindberg's play?" Her main claim was that, "The play is chiefly concerned with which woman is the stronger actress, 'stronger' here meaning 'more able to convey one's version of reality.'"

Although a paper about a play need not explicitly mention the elements of plays we have identified, thinking about these elements can provide you with a good springboard for analysis. Trish saw that her paper would be very much concerned with the title of Strindberg's play, especially as that title applied to the characters. Also, she would have to refer to stage directions and imagery, because Miss Y's silence leaves the reader having to look at her physical movements and the play's props for clues to her thinking. The play does not really include dialogue, a term that implies people talking with each other. Nevertheless, Trish saw that there are utterances in the script she could refer to, especially as she made points about the play's lone speaker, Mrs. X. Indeed, a persuasive paper about a play is one that quotes from characters' lines and perhaps from the stage direc-tions, too. Yet the paper needs to quote selectively, for a paper chock full of quo-tations may obscure instead of enhance the writer's argument.

Sample Student Paper: Final Draft

Here is Trish's final draft of her paper about *The Stronger*. It emerged out of several drafts, and after Trish had consulted classmates and her instructor. As you read this version of her paper, note its strengths, but also think of any suggestions that might help Trish make the paper even better.

```
Trish Carlisle
Professor Zelinsky
English 102
28 April ----
                Which Is the Stronger Actress
                  in August Strindberg's Play?
        You have asked me to help you solve difficulties you
may be experiencing with August Strindberg's script for
The Stronger as you prepare to play the roles of Mrs. X
and Miss Y. These female characters seem harder to judge
than the three women who are the focus of Susan Glaspell's
play Trifles, the play you are performing next month.
Obviously Glaspell is pushing us to think well of Mrs.
Hale, Mrs. Peters, and Minnie Wright. The two women in
Strindberg's play are another matter; in particular, you
have probably been wondering which of these two women
Strindberg thinks of as "the stronger." If you knew which
character he had in mind with that term, you might play
the roles accordingly. As things stand, however, Strind-
berg's use of the term in his title is pretty ambiguous.
It is not even clear, at least not immediately, which
particular sense of the word stronger is most relevant to
the play. I suggest that the play is chiefly concerned
with which character is the stronger actress. In making
this claim, I am defining stronger as "more able to con-
vey one's version of reality."
        You may feel that Strindberg is clarifying his use of
the word stronger when he has Mrs. X bring up the word in
```

the long speech that ends the play. In that final speech,
she declares to Miss Y that "it is I who am the stronger"
and that Miss Y's silence is not the "strength" that Mrs.
X previously thought it was. At this point in the play,
Mrs. X is evidently defining stronger as "more able to
keep things, especially a man." She feels that she is the
stronger because she is going home to her husband, while
Miss Y is forced to be alone on Christmas Eve. Yet there
is little reason to believe that Mrs. X is using the word
stronger in the sense that the playwright has chiefly in
mind. Furthermore, there is little reason to believe that
Mrs. X is an accurate judge of the two women's situations. Perhaps she is telling herself that she is
stronger because she simply needs to believe that she is.
Similarly, perhaps she is telling herself that she now
has control over her husband when in actuality he may
still be emotionally attached to Miss Y. In addition,
because Miss Y does not speak and because Mrs. X sweeps
out without giving her any further opportunity to do so,
we don't know if Miss Y agrees with Mrs. X's last speech.

Since Mrs. X's final use of the word stronger is so
questionable, we are justified in thinking of other ways
that the term might be applied. In thinking about this
play, I have entertained the idea that the stronger character is actually Mrs. X's husband Bob, for he has two
women fighting over him and also apparently has the creature comforts that servants provide. But now I tend to
think that the term applies to one or both of the two
women. Unfortunately, we are not given many facts about
them, for it is a brief one-act play and one of the major
characters does not even speak. But as we try to figure
out how Strindberg is defining the term stronger, we
should notice one fact that we are indeed given: Each of
these women is an actress. Both of them have worked at
Stockholm's Grand Theater, although apparently Mrs. X got
Miss Y fired from the company. Furthermore, Mrs. X
engages in a bit of theatrical illusion when she scares

Miss Y by firing the toy pistol at her. Soon after, Mrs. X
plays the role of her own husband when she puts her hands
in the slippers she has bought for him and imitates not
only his walk but also the way he scolds his servants.
Miss Y even laughs at this "performance," as if she is
being an appreciative audience for it. In addition, if
Mrs. X is right about there being an adulterous affair
between her husband and Miss Y, then those two people
have basically been performing an act for Mrs. X. It is
possible, too, that Mrs. X has not been quite so naive;
perhaps she has deliberately come to the café in order to
confront Miss Y about the affair and to proclaim ultimate
victory over her. In that case, Mrs. X is performing as
someone more innocent than she really is. On the other
hand, Miss Y might be using her silences as an actress
would, manipulating her audience's feelings by behaving
in a theatrical way.

   Because we do know that these women are professional
actresses, and because Strindberg gives us several hints
that they are performing right there in the café, we
should feel encouraged to think that he is raising the
question of which is the stronger actress. Of course, we
would still have to decide how he is defining the term
stronger. But if he does have in mind the women's careers
and behavior as actresses, then he seems to be defining
stronger as "more able to convey one's version of reality." Obviously Mrs. X is putting forth her own version
of reality in her final speech, although we do not know
how close her version comes to the actual truth. Again,
we cannot be sure of Miss Y's thoughts because she does
not express them in words; nevertheless, she can be said
to work at influencing Mrs. X's version of reality by
making strategic use of silence.

   I realize that the claim I am making does not solve
every problem you might have with the play as you prepare
to perform it. Frankly, I am not sure who is the stronger
actress. I suspect that Strindberg is being deliberately

ambiguous; he wants the performers to act in a way that will let each member of the audience arrive at his or her own opinion. Still, if you accept my claim, each of you will think of yourself as playing the part of an actress who is trying to shape the other woman's sense of reality.

6

Writing about Essays

Many readers do not think of nonfiction as a literary genre. They believe dealing with information and facts, science and technology, history and biography, memories and arguments is too ordinary, too far from traditional literary works such as sonnets, short stories, and plays. But what counts as literature is often more a matter of tradition and perspective than content, language, or merit. Many contemporary critics have noticed that definitions of literature are quite subjective, even arbitrary. We are told that literature must move us emotionally; it must contain imaginative, extraordinary language; it must deal with profound, timeless, and universal themes. If all of these claims are true of poems, stories, and plays, they might also be true of essays, autobiographies, memoirs, and historical writing.

Essays demand as much of a reader's attention as fiction, drama, and poetry. They also demand a reader's active participation. And, as with more conventional literature, the intellectual, emotional, and aesthetic rewards of attentively reading essays are significant.

Writing about essays in college is best done as a process, one that begins with a first response and ends with editing and proofreading. Author Henry David Thoreau once noted that books should be read with the same care and deliberation with which they were written. This is as true for essays as it is for complex modern poetry. One's understanding is enhanced by careful reading and a composing process that calls for a cycle of reading, writing, and reflecting. Few people, even professionals, can read a text and write cogently about it the first time. Writing well about essays takes as much energy and discipline as writing about other genres. And the results are always worth it.

To begin practicing the process, read the following essays carefully, underlining interesting passages and jotting down brief comments in the margins. The three essays deal with revisiting an important place in one's past. It is something we have all done and, whether we have written about it or not, it would be unusual if the experience did not make us reflect about the effects the passage of time has on us all. The first essay, "Once More to the Lake," is a classic reprinted in scores of college anthologies. E. B. White's (1899–1985) reminiscence about his boyhood vacation in Maine is beautifully vivid and finally a bit unsettling. Joan Didion's

(b. 1934) brief essay is almost as popular, perhaps because most of us can remember the rush of conflicting feelings one has on going home after being away for a while. The last essay, written by Andrea Lee (b. 1953), appeared in a recent issue of *The New Yorker* and reflects our culture's contemporary focus on coming to terms with the inequalities of our racial past, especially in schooling.

E. B. WHITE
Once More to the Lake

One summer, along about 1904, my father rented a camp on a lake in Maine and took us all there for the month of August. We all got ringworm from some kittens and had to rub Pond's Extract on our arms and legs night and morning, and my father rolled over in a canoe with all his clothes on; but outside of that the vacation was a success and from then on none of us ever thought there was any place in the world like that lake in Maine. We returned summer after summer—always on August 1st for one month. I have since become a salt-water man, but sometimes in summer there are days when the restlessness of the tides and the fearful cold of the sea water and the incessant wind which blows across the afternoon and into the evening make me wish for the placidity of a lake in the woods. A few weeks ago this feeling got so strong I bought myself a couple of bass hooks and a spinner and returned to the lake where we used to go, for a week's fishing and to revisit old haunts.

I took along my son, who had never had any fresh water up his nose and who had seen lily pads only from train windows. On the journey over to the lake I began to wonder what it would be like. I wondered how time would have marred this unique, this holy spot—the coves and streams, the hills that the sun set behind, the camps and the paths behind the camps. I was sure that the tarred road would have found it out and I wondered in what other ways it would be desolated. It is strange how much you can remember about places like that once you allow your mind to return into the grooves which lead back. You remember one thing, and that suddenly reminds you of another thing. I guess I remembered clearest of all the early mornings, when the lake was cool and motionless, remembered how the bedroom smelled of the lumber it was made of and the wet woods whose scent entered through the screen. The partitions in the camp were thin and did not extend clear to the top of the rooms, and as I was always the first up I would dress softly so as not to wake the others, and sneak out into the sweet outdoors and start out in the canoe, keeping close along the shore in the long shadows of the pines. I remembered being very careful never to rub my paddle against the gunwale for fear of disturbing the stillness of the cathedral.

The lake had never been what you would call a wild lake. There were cottages sprinkled around the shores, and it was in farming country although the shores of the lake were quite heavily wooded. Some of the cottages were owned by nearby farmers, and you would live at the shore and eat your meals at the farmhouse. That's what our family did. But although it wasn't wild, it was a fairly large and undisturbed lake and there were places in it which, to a child at least, seemed infinitely remote and primeval.

I was right about the tar: it led to within half a mile of the shore. But when I got back there, with my boy, and we settled into a camp near a farmhouse and into the kind of summertime I had known, I could tell that it was going to be pretty much the same as it had been before—I knew it, lying in bed the first morning, smelling the bedroom, and hearing the boy sneak quietly out and go off along the shore in a boat. I began to sustain the illusion that he was I, and there-fore, by simple transposition, that I was my father. This sensation persisted, kept cropping up all the time we were there. It was not an entirely new feeling, but in this setting it grew much stronger. I seemed to be living a dual existence. I would be in the middle of some simple act, I would be picking up a bait box or laying down a table fork, or I would be saying something, and suddenly it would be not I but my father who was saying the words or making the gesture. It gave me a creepy sensation.

We went fishing the first morning. I felt the same damp moss covering the   5 worms in the bait can, and saw the dragonfly alight on the tip of my rod as it hov-ered a few inches from the surface of the water. It was the arrival of this fly that convinced me beyond any doubt that everything was as it always had been, that the years were a mirage and there had been no years. The small waves were the same, chucking the rowboat under the chin as we fished at anchor, and the boat was the same boat, the same color green and the ribs broken in the same places, and under the floor-boards the same freshwater leavings and débris—the dead helgramite, the wisps of moss, the rusty discarded fishhook, the dried blood from yesterday's catch. We stared silently at the tips of our rods, at the dragonflies that came and went. I lowered the tip of mine into the water, tentatively, pensively dis-lodging the fly, which darted two feet away, poised, darted two feet back, and came to rest again a little farther up the rod. There had been no years between the duck-ing of this dragonfly and the other one—the one that was part of memory. I looked at the boy, who was silently watching his fly, and it was my hands that held his rod, my eyes watching. I felt dizzy and didn't know which rod I was at the end of.

We caught two bass, hauling them in briskly as though they were mackerel, pulling them over the side of the boat in a businesslike manner without any land-ing net, and stunning them with a blow on the back of the head. When we got back for a swim before lunch, the lake was exactly where we had left it, the same number of inches from the dock, and there was only the merest suggestion of a breeze. This seemed an utterly enchanted sea, this lake you could leave to its own devices for a few hours and come back to, and find that it had not stirred, this con-stant and trustworthy body of water. In the shallows, the dark, water-soaked sticks and twigs, smooth and old, were undulating in clusters on the bottom against the clean ribbed sand, and the track of the mussel was plain. A school of minnows swam by, each minnow with its small individual shadow, doubling the atten-dance, so clear and sharp in the sunlight. Some of the other campers were in swimming, along the shore, one of them with a cake of soap, and the water felt thin and clear and unsubstantial. Over the years there had been this person with the cake of soap, this cultist, and here he was. There had been no years.

Up to the farmhouse to dinner through the teeming, dusty field, the road under our sneakers was only a two-track road. The middle track was missing, the one with the marks of the hooves and the splotches of dried, flaky manure. There had always been three tracks to choose from in choosing which track to walk in; now the choice was narrowed down to two. For a moment I missed terribly the middle alternative. But the way led past the tennis court, and something about the way it lay there in the sun reassured me; the tape had loosened along the backline, the alleys were green with plantains and other weeds, and the net (installed in June and removed in September) sagged in the dry noon, and the whole place steamed with midday heat and hunger and emptiness. There was a choice of pie for dessert, and one was blueberry and one was apple, and the waitresses were the same country girls, there having been no passage of time, only the illusion of it as in a dropped curtain—the waitresses were still fifteen; their hair had been washed, that was the only difference—they had been to the movies and seen the pretty girls with the clean hair.

Summertime, oh summertime, pattern of life indelible, the fade-proof lake, the woods unshatterable, the pasture with the sweetfern and the juniper forever and ever, summer without end; this was the background, and the life along the shore was the design, the cottages with their innocent and tranquil design, their tiny docks with the flagpole and the American flag floating against the white clouds in the blue sky, the little paths over the roots of the trees leading from camp to camp and the paths leading back to the outhouses and the can of lime for sprinkling, and at the souvenir counters at the store the miniature birch-bark canoes and the post cards that showed things looking a little better than they looked. This was the American family at play, escaping the city heat, wondering whether the newcomers in the camp at the head of the cove were "common" or "nice," wondering whether it was true that the people who drove up for Sunday dinner at the farmhouse were turned away because there wasn't enough chicken.

It seemed to me, as I kept remembering all this, that those times and those summers had been infinitely precious and worth saving. There had been jollity and peace and goodness. The arriving (at the beginning of August) had been so big a business in itself, at the railway station the farm wagon drawn up, the first smell of the pineladen air, the first glimpse of the smiling farmer, and the great importance of the trunks and your father's enormous authority in such matters, and the feel of the wagon under you for the long ten-mile haul, and at the top of the last long hill catching the first view of the lake after eleven months of not seeing this cherished body of water. The shouts and cries of the other campers when they saw you, and the trunks to be unpacked, to give up their rich burden. (Arriving was less exciting nowadays, when you sneaked up in your car and parked it under a tree near the camp and took out the bags and in five minutes it was all over, no fuss, no loud wonderful fuss about trunks.)

Peace and goodness and jollity. The only thing that was wrong now, really, was the sound of the place, an unfamiliar nervous sound of the outboard motors. This was the note that jarred, the one thing that would sometimes break the illusion and set the years moving. In those other summertimes all motors were inboard; and when they were at a little distance, the noise they made was a sedative, an

10

ingredient of summer sleep. They were one-cylinder and two-cylinder engines, and some were make-and-break and some were jump-spark, but they all made a sleepy sound across the lake. The one-lungers throbbed and fluttered, and the twin-cylinder ones purred and purred, and that was a quiet sound too. But now the campers all had outboards. In the daytime, in the hot mornings, these motors made a petulant, irritable sound; at night, in the still evening when the afterglow lit the water, they whined about one's ears like mosquitoes. My boy loved our rented outboard, and his great desire was to achieve singlehanded mastery over it, and authority, and he soon learned the trick of choking it a little (but not too much), and the adjustment of the needle valve. Watching him I would remember the things you could do with the old one-cylinder engine with the heavy flywheel, how you could have it eating out of your hand if you got really close to it spiritually. Motor boats in those days didn't have clutches, and you would make a landing by shutting off the motor at the proper time and coasting in with a dead rudder. But there was a way of reversing them, if you learned the trick, by cutting the switch and putting it on again exactly on the final dying revolution of the flywheel, so that it would kick back against compression and begin reversing. Approaching a dock in a strong following breeze, it was difficult to slow up sufficiently by the ordinary coasting method, and if a boy felt he had complete mastery over his motor, he was tempted to keep it running beyond its time and then reverse it a few feet from the dock. It took a cool nerve, because if you threw the switch a twentieth of a second too soon you could catch the flywheel when it still had speed enough to go up past center, and the boat would leap ahead, charging bull-fashion at the dock.

We had a good week at the camp. The bass were biting well and the sun shone endlessly, day after day. We would be tired at night and lie down in the accumulated heat of the little bedrooms after the long hot day and the breeze would stir almost imperceptibly outside and the smell of the swamp drift in through the rusty screens. Sleep would come easily and in the morning the red squirrel would be on the roof, tapping out his gay routine. I kept remembering everything, lying in bed in the mornings — the small steamboat that had a long rounded stern like the lip of a Ubangi,° how quietly she ran on the moonlight sails, when the older boys played their mandolins and the girls sang and we ate doughnuts dipped in sugar, and how sweet the music was on the water in the shining night, and what it had felt like to think about girls then. After breakfast we would go up to the store and the things were in the same place — the minnows in a bottle, the plugs and spinners disarranged and pawed over by the youngsters from the boys' camp, the fig newtons and the Beeman's gum. Outside, the road was tarred and cars stood in front of the store. Inside, all was just as it had always been, except there was more Coca-Cola and not so much Moxie and root beer and birch beer and sarsaparilla. We would walk out with a bottle of pop apiece and sometimes the pop would backfire up our noses and hurt. We explored the streams, quietly, where the turtles slid off the sunny logs and dug their way into

---

Ubangi: A member of an African tribe whose customary dress includes disk-shaped mouth ornaments that stretch the wearer's lips.

the soft bottom; and we lay on the town wharf and fed worms to the tame bass. Everywhere we went I had trouble making out which was I, the one walking at my side, the one walking in my pants.

One afternoon while we were there at that lake a thunderstorm came up. It was like the revival of an old melodrama that I had seen long ago with childish awe. The second-act climax of the drama of the electrical disturbance over a lake in America had not changed in any important respect. This was the big scene, still the big scene. The whole thing was so familiar, the first feeling of oppression and heat and a general air around camp of not wanting to go very far away. In midafternoon (it was all the same) a curious darkening of the sky, and a lull in everything that had made life tick; and then the way the boats suddenly swung the other way at their moorings with the coming of a breeze out of the new quarter, and the premonitory rumble. Then the kettle drum, then the snare, then the bass drum and cymbals, then crackling light against the dark, and the gods grinning and licking their chops in the hills. Afterward the calm, the rain steadily rustling in the calm lake, the return of light and hope and spirits, and the campers running out in joy and relief to go swimming in the rain, their bright cries perpetuating the deathless joke about how they were getting simply drenched, and the children screaming with delight at the new sensation of bathing in the rain, and the joke about getting drenched linking the generations in a strong indestructible chain. And the comedian who waded in carrying an umbrella.

When the others went swimming my son said he was going in too. He pulled his dripping trunks from the line where they had hung all through the shower, and wrung them out. Languidly, and with no thought of going in, I watched him, his hard little body, skinny and bare, saw him wince slightly as he pulled up around his vitals the small, soggy, icy garment. As he buckled the swollen belt suddenly my groin felt the chill of death.   [1914]

JOAN DIDION

On Going Home

I am home for my daughter's first birthday. By "home" I do not mean the house in Los Angeles where my husband and I and the baby live, but the place where my family is, in the Central Valley of California. It is a vital although troublesome distinction. My husband likes my family but is uneasy in their house, because once there I fall into their ways, which are difficult, oblique, deliberately inarticulate, not my husband's ways. We live in dusty houses ("D-U-S-T," he once wrote with his finger on surfaces all over the house, but no one noticed it) filled with mementos quite without value to him (what could the Canton dessert plates mean to him? how could he have known about the assay scales, why should he care if he did know?), and we appear to talk exclusively about people we know who have been committed to mental hospitals, about people we know who have been booked on drunk-driving charges, and about property, particularly about property, land, price per acre and C-2 zoning and assessments and freeway access. My brother does not understand my husband's inability to perceive the advantage in the rather common real-estate transaction known as "sale-leaseback," and my husband in turn does not understand why so many of the people he hears about in my father's house have recently been committed to mental hospitals or booked on drunk-driving charges. Nor does he understand that when we talk about sale-leasebacks and right-of-way condemnations we are talking in code about the things we like best, the yellow fields and the cotton-woods and the rivers rising and falling and the mountain roads closing when the heavy snow comes in. We miss each other's points, have another drink and regard the fire. My brother refers to my husband, in his presence, as "Joan's husband." Marriage is the classic betrayal.

Or perhaps it is not any more. Sometimes I think that those of us who are now in our thirties were born into the last generation to carry the burden of "home," to find in family life the source of all tension and drama. I had by all objective accounts a "normal" and a "happy" family situation, and yet I was almost thirty years old before I could talk to my family on the telephone without crying after I had hung up. We did not fight. Nothing was wrong. And yet some nameless anxiety colored the emotional charges between me and the place that I came from. The question of whether or not you could go home again was a very real part of the sentimental and largely literary baggage with which we left home in the fifties; I suspect that it is irrelevant to the children born of the frag-mentation after World War II. A few weeks ago in a San Francisco bar I saw a pretty young girl on crystal take off her clothes and dance for the cash prize in an "amateur-topless" contest. There was no particular sense of moment about this, none of the effect of romantic degradation, of "dark journey," for which my gen-eration strived so assiduously. What sense could that girl possibly make of, say, *Long Day's Journey into Night*? Who is beside the point?

That I am trapped in this particular irrelevancy is never more apparent to me than when I am home. Paralyzed by the neurotic lassitude engendered by meet-ing one's past at every turn, around every corner, inside every cupboard, I go aim-lessly from room to room. I decide to meet it head-on and clean out a drawer, and I spread the contents on the bed. A bathing suit I wore the summer I was seven-teen. A letter of rejection from *The Nation*, an aerial photograph of the site for a shopping center my father did not build in 1954. Three teacups hand-painted with cabbage roses and signed "E.M.," my grandmother's initials. There is no final solution for letters of rejection from *The Nation* and teacups hand-painted in 1900. Nor is there any answer to snapshots of one's grandfather as a young man on skis, surveying around Donner Pass in the year 1910. I smooth out the snap-shot and look into his face, and do and do not see my own. I close the drawer, and have another cup of coffee with my mother. We get along very well, veterans of a guerrilla war we never understood.

Days pass. I see no one. I come to dread my husband's evening call, not only because he is full of news of what by now seems to me our remote life in Los Angeles, people he has seen, letters which require attention, but because he asks what I have been doing, suggests uneasily that I get out, drive to San Francisco or

Berkeley. Instead I drive across the river to a family graveyard. It has been vandalized since my last visit and the monuments are broken, overturned in the dry grass. Because I once saw a rattlesnake in the grass I stay in the car and listen to a country-and-Western station. Later I drive with my father to a ranch he has in the foothills. The man who runs his cattle on it asks us to the roundup, a week from Sunday, and although I know that I will be in Los Angeles I say, in the oblique way my family talks, that I will come. Once home I mention the broken monuments in the graveyard. My mother shrugs.

I go to visit my great-aunts. A few of them think now that I am my cousin, or their daughter who died young. We recall an anecdote about a relative last seen in 1948, and they ask if I still like living in New York City. I have lived in Los Angeles for three years, but I say that I do. The baby is offered a horehound drop, and I am slipped a dollar bill "to buy a treat." Questions trail off, answers are abandoned, the baby plays with the dust motes in a shaft of afternoon sun.

It is time for the baby's birthday party: a white cake, strawberry-marshmallow ice cream, a bottle of champagne saved from another party. In the evening, after she has gone to sleep, I kneel beside the crib and touch her face, where it is pressed against the slats, with mine. She is an open and trusting child, unprepared for and unaccustomed to the ambushes of family life, and perhaps it is just as well that I can offer her little of that life. I would like to give her more. I would like to promise her that she will grow up with a sense of her cousins and of rivers and of her great-grandmother's teacups, would like to pledge her a picnic on a river with fried chicken and her hair uncombed, would like to give her *home* for her birthday, but we live differently now and I can promise her nothing like that. I give her a xylophone and a sundress from Madeira, and promise to tell her a funny story.   [1967]

ANDREA LEE
Back to School

A couple of weeks ago, I paid a visit to the girls' preparatory school outside Philadelphia where, about thirty years ago, I enrolled as one of the first two black students. It wasn't my first return trip, but it was one that had a peculiarly definitive feeling: this time, I was going back to look at classes with my daughter, who is eleven — exactly the age I was when I first put on a blue-and-white uniform and walked in the front entrance of an institution where black people had always used the back door. My daughter, who was born in Europe, and who views the civil-rights struggle of the sixties as an antique heroic cycle not much removed in drama and time frame from the Iliad, sees her mother's experience as a singularly tame example of integration. There were, after all no jeering mobs, no night riders, no police dogs or fire hoses — just a girl going to school and learning with quiet thoroughness the meaning of isolation.

The air inside the schoolhouse smelled exactly as it used to on rainy April days — that mysterious school essence of damp wood and ancient chalk dust and pent-up young flesh. For an instant, I relived precisely what it felt like to walk those halls with girls who never included me in a social event, with teachers and administrators who regarded me with bemused incomprehension—halls where the only other black faces I saw were those of maids and cooks, and where I never received the slightest hint that books had been written and discoveries made by people whose skin wasn't white. I remembered the defensive bravado that I once used as a cover for a constant and despairing sense of worthlessness, born and reinforced at school.

As I delivered my daughter to the sixth-grade classroom where she would spend the day, I saw that in the intervening time not only had the school sprouted a few glossy modern additions—an art wing, science and computer facilities, and a new lower school—but the faculty and the student body had also been transformed. Black and Asian girls mingled in the crowd of students rushing back and forth between classrooms and playing fields, giddy with excitement over the impending Easter and Passover weekend. A black teacher with braids strode out of the room where long ago I'd conjugated Latin verbs. Posters celebrating African-American artists and scientists hung on the walls, and the school's curriculum included dozens of works by black, Native American, and Hispanic writers. The director of the middle school was, miracle of miracles, a young black woman—a woman who combined an old-fashioned headmistress's unflappable good sense with a preternatural sensitivity to the psychology of culture and identity. She explained to me that she herself had once been a student at a mostly white East Coast prep school. When I asked who on her staff in particular, was responsible for the self-esteem of minority students, she said firmly, "Every person who works here."

That day, I finally forgave my old school. I'd held a touchy rancor toward it through much of my adult life, like someone heaping blame on a negligent parent, and had taken the institution rather churlishly to task during a Commencement address I gave there some years ago. The changes I saw now disarmed and delighted me. Watching my daughter run by with a group of girls, I realized with envy how different her experience would be from mine if she were enrolled there. "Just think, I used to dream of burning the place down," I remarked to her, as we drove away, along the school's winding drive. She looked at me impatiently. "Can't you just forget all that?" she asked. The sound of her voice—half childish and half adolescent—made it clear to me that I wouldn't do any such thing. Wounds that have healed bring a responsibility to avoid repeating the past. The important thing is to pardon, even with joy, when the time comes—but never, I thought, driving on in silence, to forget.   [1996]

A WRITING EXERCISE

Skim the essays, and jot down notes and comments in the margins. Consider your immediate reactions; don't ignore personal associations. Your experiences, age, gender, race, and so forth are as relevant as noting the voice, style, structure, and ideas in the text. "Meaning," as one critic put it, "exists in the margin of overlap between the writer's experience and the reader's." After skimming the three pieces and considering your comments, freewrite for fifteen minutes.

A Student's Personal Response to the Essays

Stevie Goronski, a college sophomore from Queens, New York, wrote the following response to the three essays:

I was surprised by the ending of "Once More to the Lake." I thought the father was enjoying the drama of the summer storm and the memories that he was having about when he was a boy at the lake in Maine with his father in 1904. When he mentioned the "chill of death," I thought that I probably missed his point. Almost forty years after his first visit he has returned with his son who I imagined was a preteen. I guess his own father is dead. He seems to enjoy being back at the camp, remembering the old sights and smells around the lake. I had somewhat of a hard time relating to this, since I never have been to a lake in the woods. I've been to the lake in Central Park which has trees and is nice, but I don't think it's anything like Maine. In fact, I've only been on vacation twice. Both times my father and mother, my twin sisters, and I went to the beach at Atlantic City for a long weekend. I remembered this when he says his son never had "fresh water up his nose." Since I never swam in Central Park, and since city pools certainly aren't fresh, then neither have I.

I was a little puzzled when they go fishing and he says "I felt dizzy and didn't know which rod I was at the end of." This must have something to do with remembering when he and his father were sitting there fishing forty years ago. Then he says there had been no years, as if everything was the same then as it is now. He must really want it to be that way. I guess there wasn't much development at this lake; it must be a lot more isolated than the lakes I've heard about. Later he does say that it is noisier now because of outboard motors. But he still seems to love it at the lake, especially when he says "summertime, oh, summertime," like in a song or a poem, but then a lot of the writing here reminds me of a poem. I noticed he says that

the people at the lake were "the American family" which is
a bit of an exaggeration since most of the people in my
neighborhood in Queens go to the beach just for the day and
can't afford vacations, especially not for a week or a
month in Maine, which probably costs a small fortune.

Toward the end he brings up the idea again that he is
confused if he is his son or himself. Since this seems
unlikely I guess it's just a way to say that everything
is the same as it was forty years ago when he and his
father were doing exactly what he is doing now with his
son. This seems to be an essay about memories that were
important and how we want to relive them or hold on to
them even though almost a lifetime has passed.

I can relate better to "On Going Home" since I have my
own apartment near campus which is about fifty miles from
my home in Queens. I haven't been away from home as long
as Didion seems to have been, but I don't live there anymore and probably never will again. Yet I still call it
home; and I say I'm going to my apartment. Like me, when
Didion goes home she has a lot of mixed feelings. This
happens to me especially if I bring my boyfriend home
with me; he grew up in a suburb of Charlotte and is
amazed at how differently my family lives in Queens. In
fact, Didion leaves her husband at their house because he
usually can't relate to their different ways. She says
that marriage is a classic betrayal which means that when
you get married, you have a new family and can't relate
like you once did to your birth family. But then she
talks about what I would call sociology and claims that
for her generation the family was everything, but not
anymore. I think there are a lot of Italian families (and
I'm half Italian) who see each other every week and are
always involved in each other's business. I know Irish
and Asian families where this is also true. But maybe
this is only true for ethnic families and Didion's sounds
more like an upper-middle-class family that has been in
America for generations.

She also talks about tension with her mother and uncomfortable conversations with her old aunts. My take on these events is that you get used to talking to people you live with but when you leave, that comfortable connection never comes back. Perhaps she goes home expecting the fond experiences of childhood but what she finds is awkwardness and paralysis. She does seem to get over these negative feelings in the last paragraph, however. At the party for her baby, she wonders if it really would be so great for her daughter to have the family life she had. I think this is a good point because the past is over anyhow, and wishing for the good old days is just a fantasy that leads to disappointment. My favorite line is "we live different now." I think it's fine to think of what Bruce Springsteen calls our "glory days," but the thing that is the most important is the present.

In "Back to School" the narrator also looks back to a former time through the eyes of her daughter, who is about E. B. White's son's age. She also remembers the sights and smells of her past, although I was puzzled by what "pent-up young flesh" might mean. She seemed to live in a segregated society, except for a few token minorities. I suspect the only reason she was allowed to go to this fancy school was because she was smart. Maybe it made the school look good. But even so, her self-esteem must have been damaged by the general atmosphere of white privilege. At the school, things have changed, unlike at the lake in Maine. Now there are lots of minorities, and their cultures are also being studied in English and history. In fact, the principal is a black woman. All of these changes make the narrator forgive the indignities she suffered in the past. She must be a fairly famous person because she gave the commencement address at some point. Her daughter can't relate to these past experiences and seems like she just wants to get on with her life, which is very healthy. But because she is young, the mother can't completely heed the daughter's advice to get over it. The mother decides to forgive but not forget, which seems reasonable to me since we should remember history for the lessons it might teach us.

In all three essays, people are confronted with their past. E. B. White seems to be a bit dazed by the experience of going back to a beloved place. He seems to imagine that everything stays the same. I think it does but only in his memories. When he comes to his senses after the storm, he realizes that he is a middle-aged man who will eventually die. Didion is also dazed by the past, but she is able to see that change is inevitable and, for better or worse, this fact needs to be accepted. Lee's memories of a white-only world were so negative that she doesn't want to forget out of a sense of social responsibility, like remembering the Holocaust. Lee could have been the one and only black camp counselor at White's lake and she wants to remember that kind of exclusion. But she does forgive the school and society, which makes sense to me because bitterness hurts you more than those you're angry with. Visiting our past is risky and you have to be mature enough to see what really happened, what is gone, and how to move on. If not, you could try to hold on to the past and that could be damaging.

A WRITING EXERCISE

An exceptional paper can grow out of probing, thoughtful, early responses like this one. Stevie seems to have several promising ideas that are worth pursuing. Which of Stevie's ideas seem interesting to you? Did she overlook any ideas that you noticed? Make note of what you admired in her response, and what you think she may have overlooked.

The Elements of Essays

First impressions are valuable, but writing intelligently about essays should not be completely spontaneous. We can be personal and insightful, but persuading others about the validity of our reading takes a more focused and textually informed presentation. The following discussion of the basic elements of the essay is meant to increase your ability to analyze and write about essays. The elements include voice, style, structure, and idea.

Voice

When we read the first few sentences of an essay, we usually hear the narrator's **voice**: We hear a person speaking to us, and we begin to notice if he or she sounds friendly or hostile, stuffy or casual, self-assured or tentative. The voice might be austere and technical or personal and flamboyant. The voice may be intimate or remote. It may be sincere, hectoring, hysterical, meditative, or ironic. The possibilities are endless.

We usually get a sense of the writer's voice from the **tone** the writer takes. In the first paragraph of "Once More to the Lake," E. B. White's voice is casual and folksy; it is filled with admiration for the lake and for the fun his family enjoyed there. As soon as he mentions fresh water up his son's nose, we suspect that White's tone is going to combine informality and seriousness. Indeed, we can see in the second paragraph that the narrator is filled with complex emotions on returning to his beloved childhood lake. He wonders if time has marred "this holy spot." Deeply nostalgic, White is probably worried that he might sound sentimental. The phrase about the "stillness of the cathedral" indeed sounds reverential, perhaps too reverential. He doesn't linger in reverence, however, quickly returning to more specific, less figurative details about the lake.

Just as White's voice approaches confusion and dreaminess — "I felt dizzy and didn't know which rod I was at the end of" — he suddenly grounds himself in the concrete reality of bass fishing. Just when his emotions seem to bubble to the surface with his rapturous "summertime, oh, summertime . . . summer without end," White returns to the specifics of arrival and a detailed paragraph about boats.

A WRITING EXERCISE

Make a list of details you can remember from the first several paragraphs of E. B. White's "Once More to the Lake." How do you react to a writer who notices and presents such concrete details? Now look at the last two paragraphs and try to describe White's voice, including his stance toward the drama of the storm. Did the last sentence surprise you? Look back through the essay to see how White might have set up the final sentence.

After assigning Joan Didion's "On Going Home," Stevie's instructor asked the class to freewrite on the voice they heard. Stevie wrote the following response:

```
Didion seems anxious to me, maybe a bit confused
about how she should behave on returning home. She claims
"marriage is the classic betrayal" and then says "perhaps
it is not." She is honest though, telling us how para-
lyzed she is at home and how strange she becomes around
her family. The last paragraph shows us that she finally
relaxes and faces things as they are.
```

Although Stevie's response is her subjective view of what she hears, Didion also seems to us to be tentative, hedging with her statements. Didion's attitude toward her home is certainly ambivalent, a mixture of nostalgia, resentment, and wariness. She is unwilling to delude herself; denial and repression will not do. Inappropriate optimism and sentimental nostalgia are to be avoided at all costs: better to see things as they are. The persona that emerges seems to face reality squarely and bravely. The past is over, and she will endure: no picnics on the river perhaps, but certainly music, and stories, and love. We find Didion's voice ultimately to be unsentimental, realistic, and yet hopeful.

A WRITING EXERCISE

Describe the voice you hear when you read Andrea Lee's "Back to School." Be specific about the tone, her attitude toward the school, toward her daughter, and toward the past.

Stevie hears some irony in Andrea Lee's first paragraph, and then notes in the second paragraph some of the same sensory alertness White felt when he returned to the lake. But, unlike White, Lee is negative about her previous experiences. Some sarcasm surfaces when she uses the phrase "miracle of miracles," but like Didion she seems willing to surrender bad feelings from the past, since there have been so many positive changes. Her voice also conveys honesty and a certain self-reflectiveness especially when she realizes that "envy" is influencing her. Like Didion, Lee speaks in an ambivalently optimistic voice when she notes that she is willing to forgive but not forget.

Style

We all have stylish friends. They look good. Their shoes and pants and shirts seem to complement each other perfectly. It's not that they are color-coordinated — that would be too obvious for them — it's something more subtle. They seem to make just the right choices. When they go to a party, to the movies, or to school, they have a personal style that is their own.

Writers also have **style**. They make specific choices in words, in syntax and sentence length, in diction, in metaphors, even in sentence beginnings and endings. Writers use parallelism, balance, formal diction, poetic language, even sentence fragments to create their own styles. Read again the opening paragraphs of each of the three essays with an eye to comparing the styles of White, Didion, and Lee.

This is what Stevie wrote about the differing styles:

```
I noticed that White's sentences are much longer than
mine. But Didion also has lengthy sentences and so does
Lee. Didion seems to write in a plainer style, especially
the first sentence (I guess each paragraph begins this
way). White uses the phrase "long about 1904" which
```

```
sounds informal, even countryish, but he also uses fancy
words like "placidity" and phrases like "the restlessness
of the tides and the fearful cold of the sea water and
the incessant wind." He seems both literary and conversa-
tional. Didion's style is clear and forceful and concrete
with lots of details. Lee's style is less literary and
more matter-of-fact, almost like a newspaper story.
```

Stevie's comments are perceptive. Indeed, White is famous for his skilled blending of the high and the low and for sensual details, focusing our attention on the sights, smells, and sounds of the lake, the woods, and the cabin. Look especially at paragraph 7 for visual details and paragraphs 10, 11, and 12 for sound and sense details. How does such rich stylistic detail affect you?

White's sentences can be elegant, filled with the rhythms of repeated words and phrases. Notice the use of *same* in the fourth sentence in paragraph 5. White repeats *jollity* and *good* in paragraphs 9 and 10 and alternates simple, compound, and complex sentences. Consider the various ways he begins sentences, sometimes using the usual subject/verb/object pattern, other times inverting this order. Find other examples of these stylistic variations. Notice also the sentence pattern called a **cumulative sentence** that begins with a brief direct statement and then adds parallel words, phrases, or clauses. The opening sentence of paragraph 6 is a good example. Notice that *hauling, pulling,* and *stunning* all end with *ing*.

A WRITING EXERCISE

Find other cumulative sentences in White's essay. Notice that you can actually invert the order by beginning with the phrases. Read some of White's cumulative sentences out loud, then invert them. Which order do you prefer? Why? Why do you think White uses cumulative sentences? Try to write several cumulative sentences yourself by simply describing the room you are in or the people surrounding you.

Didion also varies the length of her sentences and inverts normal word order. But mostly she writes in an unadorned, crisp, lean style with brief and direct assertions.

Stevie noted that Lee's style was journalistic. The piece did appear in *The New Yorker*, a weekly magazine, but her essay seems more polished than a simple news account. When you read the second paragraph aloud, notice the sensual details, the inverted sentence patterns, the repetition and rhythm of the elegant second sentence. Lee is also fond of the dash. Notice the ways in which she uses it. Is there a comparison with White's cumulative phrases? In the last paragraph she begins like Didion with a direct assertion, and then she ends with an interesting sentence. See how many ways you can rearrange the parts of this sentence. Which variation do you like best?

A WRITING EXERCISE

We've pointed out several different kinds of sentences, suggesting that variety of sentence structure is an essential element of style. Find an especially striking paragraph in one of the three essays, and characterize the tone (for example, ironic, pained, matter of fact, dreamy). Then, try to change the tone by rewriting it. Focus on changing sentence structure — simplifying compound sentences, complicating simple sentences, and so forth — rather than substantially changing diction.

Structure

The way essayists put their work together is not very mysterious. The best writers create a **structure** to fit their needs. Most do not have a prearranged structure in mind or feel the need to obey the composition rules many students think they have to follow: topic sentence first and three examples following. Writers of essays aren't so inclined to follow formulas. Essayists begin and end as they see fit; they give explicit topic sentences or create narratives that imply themes; they begin with an assertion and support it, or vice versa. Essayists are inventors of structures that fit the occasion and their own way of seeing the world. The thought of the essay significantly influences its structure. Like the relationship between mind and body, form and thought are inseparable.

A WRITING EXERCISE

Briefly respond to the following writing suggestions and then compare your answer to Stevie's. How would you map the structure of Didion's essay? Is there an introduction, a body, and a conclusion? Pick any two paragraphs and describe the relationship between them.

Here is Stevie's analysis of Didion's structure:

    The way Joan Didion put her six paragraphs together
    seems traditional, with an introduction, a body, and
    a conclusion. We first learn that Didion is going home
    and about the difficulty her husband has relating to
    her family in the opening paragraph. Then she talks about
    the tension that used to exist in families but doesn't
    much anymore. Then she realizes that she is still a kind
    of victim of this old way of thinking. Then she tells us
    about how she is spending her time, visiting aunts and
    such. In the last paragraph, she talks about the birthday
    party, realizes the past is gone and what she plans to
    give her daughter. I like the transition between the

first two paragraphs. The last sentence of the first
paragraph leads nicely into the next. Very smooth.

Didion likes to begin her essays concretely with lots of specific detail, allowing readers to draw conclusions; she does not begin with an abstraction that she must support, although her second paragraph is quite speculative. Mostly she grounds her ideas about the cultural change in families in her own experience. Her conclusion is concrete, as if she were too tentative or suspicious about the confident conclusions found in most academic essays.

White also divides his essays between speculation and narration, although the organizational frame for the thirteen paragraphs opens with White's planned trip to the Maine woods and then moves on by giving us many concrete details of the actual vacation. The simple introduction, body, and conclusion also works well. The lyrical description of the lake and the narrative of the father and son fishing, rowing, and swimming move the essay along nicely. Notice how effortlessly the narrator guides us from one paragraph to the next, acting like an attentive host who wants to be sure guests know where they're going next. It is bad manners to confuse guests or readers. The transition to the last paragraph, for example, is especially smooth. Here White simply uses "others" in the first sentence to connect the reader to the previous episode. And his last sentence nicely brings to a conclusion the connection between father and son that White has been playing with throughout the vacation.

Since Lee's essay is shorter, the structure of her piece is perhaps easier to see. But it is still quite efficient, giving us the usual who, what, when, where, why, and how in the first few sentences. Lee's walk through the school becomes the organizing center. She notices, she comments, she interacts. Her first-person point of view dominates and orchestrates the four paragraphs, ending with her thematic observation as she drives away.

Ideas

All writers have something on their minds when they write. That seems especially true when writers decide to put their **ideas** into a nonfictional form such as the essay. Of course, lots of ideas fill poems and short stories too, but they are usually expressed more indirectly. Although essays seem more idea-driven, this does not mean that as readers we have a responsibility to extract the precise idea or argument the writer had in mind. That may not even be possible since in the creative process of all writing, ideas get modified or changed. Sometimes a writer's original intention is significantly transformed; sometimes writers are not fully conscious of all their hidden intentions. Regardless, readers of essays are not simply miners unearthing hidden meanings; they are more like coproducers. And in creating that meaning, ideas are central. In responding to "Once More to the Lake," for example, Stevie was interested in several ideas, from the disparity between White's summer vacations and Stevie's more urban experience to White's concern for the past and his hope that things at the lake would not have changed. Stevie does not specifically mention what we considered an important idea—White's final realization of his inevitable death—perhaps because Stevie is a twenty-year-old student and the editors of this book are middle-aged professors. That is important to remember. Your perception of the ideas in an essay come partially from the author and partially from your own experiences, your opinions, your sense of what is important and what is not. It is a collaborative and creative process.

White does his part in providing food for thought. One way to think about "Once More to the Lake" is to focus on time. White wants to believe that little has changed at the lake as a way to avoid the fact that he has indeed changed, that he is no longer a boy but a middle-aged man, that death, while not around the corner, is no longer a remote possibility. The epiphany or sudden insight that White has in the last line deals with age and death, with White's mortality. Although it is reasonable to note that White also exhibits a love of nature, a nostalgia for the past, an affection for his son, and even a certain blindness about his privileged status, it seems to us that White's essay revolves around the idea that everything changes, that our eventual fate cannot be denied. It is this thought that animates the whole essay, that gives the piece its structure, its reason for being.

Indeed, it may be that Didion is playing with something like the same idea. Although she seems to have more mixed feelings about the past than White, she does seem attached to the tradition of the extended American family. She sees the good in that kind of rooted past, in small-town closeness and love of place, but she also understands that things change, that new family arrangements are replacing the old. The cliché "you can't go home again" is one way to characterize Didion's acceptance that the past is gone. She seems comfortable rather than pessimistic about her present life. Perhaps she is a realist, rejecting a false hope for a world that no longer exists (and perhaps never did). Although a "picnic on a river with fried chicken" sounds romantically nostalgic, she seems more committed to her nuclear family. If she cannot give her daughter the same kind of childhood she had, she can give her music, style, culture, and love.

Lee's "Back to School" also allows us to see a writer confronting her past and thinking her way through to a resolution. She certainly does not share White's sentimental view of the past since she was made to feel so different and alienated from mainstream culture. She also sees that her bad memories are in the past, that progress has been made. And so she forgives her old school. She comes to a separate peace with discrimination. She is delighted and disarmed by progress, but she cannot forget what was. She is healed but feels a responsibility to remember. This seems less like bitterness than a desire not to let the past repeat itself.

It is interesting to note that in all three essays the narrators confront and deal with the past through their children. The three children represent the future, a realization that each writer uses to establish a mature and healthy relationship with the past. All three writers move on, apparently wiser.

A WRITING EXERCISE

The essays by White, Didion, and Lee work against the notion that an essay should begin with a thesis statement that the rest of the essay supports.

Instead, all three writers capture us with their tone and gradually initiate us into their thought, into the direction their essays are headed. We propose two possible exercises. For the first, try to rewrite one of the essays as a traditional five-paragraph paper: thesis paragraph, supporting paragraphs, closing paragraphs. What, if anything, is gained? What is lost? For the second, if you have at hand a five-paragraph essay you have written recently, try rewriting it in the style of White, Didion, or Lee. Try to engage your reader with concrete details and fluent style, letting the thesis emerge as the essay builds.

Sample Student Paper: Final Draft

After writing journal entries and then a freewrite, Stevie planned her essay and then wrote a draft. After receiving responses from several students in a small-group workshop and from her instructor, she revised her essay, sharpening her focus and supporting her claims more explicitly. Here is Stevie's final version:

Stevie Goronski

Professor McLaughlin

English 102

21 April ----

The Return of the Past

In her essay "On Going Home," Joan Didion notes that when she returns home she wanders about her former home "meeting [her] past at every turn . . . I decide to meet it head-on." This is a courageous position to take, one that requires self-awareness, confidence, and the ability to deal realistically with life's disappointments. Didion works hard to deal with the challenge of letting the past go in order to face the present, to be ready for the future. In his essay "Once More to the Lake," E. B. White is not ready to face the reality that his youth is over until the last sentence when he is shocked into a sudden insight. Andrea Lee in "Back to School" also refuses to let the past go, but this time for good reason. When writers tell us stories about their past, part of their motivation is to come to a separate peace with unre-solved, troublesome memories. As Didion claimed in another essay, "The White Album," "we tell ourselves stories in order to live . . . we interpret what we see." Didion, White, and Lee do just this; they shape the past

to understand it. We also read these tales for understanding. But in the process, we also come to know ourselves better. I read these three essays as a warning
that the past never completely disappears; we can bump
into it unexpectedly. We should realize that and develop
mature strategies to deal with reality.

In her essay "On Going Home," Didion tells us of her
return to her childhood home for her daughter's first
birthday. She does so with understandably mixed feelings.
Returning to one's old home is psychologically unnerving,
as Didion suggests when she goes "aimlessly from room to
room." She examines such mementos from her adolescence as
a bathing suit, a photo, a letter of rejection. More
importantly she resumes the emotionally tense relationship with her mother that she refers to as a "nameless
anxiety." Didion has been living away from home for many
years and has become a productive writer in the larger
world. But at home, things are the same; at home the
present gets gobbled up by the past; at home Didion, the
famous writer, is seventeen again. As Didion says, "I
fall into their ways." Her husband can't take this
strange time warp and so stays at their home. He is used
to an independent adult Didion and cannot relate to her
psychological regression. This return to the past is evident when she visits her great-aunts who are so trapped
in the past they slip her a dollar bill as a gift.

But in the last paragraph Didion regains her sense of
reality when she kneels beside her daughter's crib. When
she contemplates her child's future, she realizes that
her past with her family is over. She writes that "it is
just as well that I can offer her a little of that life."
So Didion's return home only temporarily paralyzes her.
She is ambushed by her past ways but recovers nicely when
she realizes that the lifestyle of the large extended
family is no longer. Instead she promises her daughter
not the past but music, style, and stories: "a xylophone

and a sundress from Madeira, and promise to tell her a funny story."

Something like this also happens at the end of White's "Once More to the Lake." In this essay, White revisits a lake in the Maine woods where he and his father used to vacation some forty years ago. This time around, however, White is now a middle-aged man who has his own son. White visits this lake with great expectations and reverence, calling it a "holy spot" and "a cathedral." He obviously has fond memories of these long ago vacations, so much so that when White says that "we settled into . . . the kind of summertime I had known . . . it was going to be pretty much the same as it had been before." White actually starts to get the present and the past confused. The middle-aged White begins to imagine that he is his father and his son is himself as a boy ("he was I . . . I was my father"). This feeling continues throughout the essay. While they are both fishing, for example, White says:

> there had been no years . . . I looked at the boy, who
> was silently watching his fly, and it was my hands
> that held his rod, my eyes watching. I felt dizzy and
> didn't know which rod I was at the end of.

If Didion was a bit dazed by the past walking around her mother's home, White is in a hallucinatory trance. Over and over he says, "There had been no years." It is perhaps plausible that the lake would stay the same, but what about him? He has not stood still. But maybe that is just the point. White is in denial about growing old. Some men buy red sports cars in middle age; some dye their hair and date women half their age. White returns to a sacred spot from his youth and tries to convince himself everything is like it always was. But, as in Didion's essay, White does finally gain some self-awareness. After a thunderstorm at the lake during which the campers react with the same lighthearted behavior

they did years ago, White watches his son put on a pair
of cold, wet swim trunks. The last line is startling: "As
he buckled the swollen belt suddenly my groin felt the
chill of death." Reality finally sets in. White is not a
young boy cavorting in a summer storm; he is, instead,
some forty years closer to his death. That might be
regrettable, but it is reality and White is better off by
facing the truth: The past is irretrievable.

Lee's journey to her past in "Back to School" is to a
time thirty years ago when racial integration was still a
novelty. She returns to her former prep school with a
daughter who might be the same age as White's son. When
she attended school there, she was one of only two
African American pupils. She felt like an outsider, as if
the curriculum was culturally biased. But when she
returns to see if her own daughter might attend this
school, she finds a different place. Unlike White's lake
or Didion's home, her old school is now integrated and
multicultural with a young black woman in charge. Although she is also carried back in time by the school's
smells: "For an instant, I relived precisely what it felt
like to walk those halls." But she is not dazzled by the
past. She sees clearly that the atmosphere is more tolerant, more progressive. And so she decides to forgive the
school its previous insensitivity to her. Her daughter
responds to her mother's statement that she had wanted to
burn this place down by saying, "'Can't you just forget
all that?'" Like Didion and White, Lee comes to a sudden
realization: It is good to forgive but not to forget.
This seems quite mature. The past will not haunt us if it
is put to rest with understanding and tolerance. Lee is
now more interested in avoiding the mistakes of the past.

In all three essays, adults are confronted by a past
that keeps popping up around every corner. Didion and Lee
seem to have achieved a measure of peace by seeing that
the past cannot, and should not, be relived. White is
probably on the verge of accepting this insight, once he

comes to terms with his own mortality. In many ways, we are our past; consequently, it helps to face it straight-forwardly, to see what it was, what it can never be again, and finally to get beyond its staleness into the fresh air of the future.

Literature
and Its Issues

7

Living in Families

In the not-too-distant past, family life was the focal point of our emotional existence, the center of all our important psychological successes and failures. It was common for several generations to live together in the same town and even the same home. Grandparents, aunts, and uncles were an intimate part of daily life, not just relatives one saw during the holidays. Besides the usual emotional drama that always takes place between parents and children, there were the additional tensions that inevitably arise when the values of the old clash with those of the young. Of course, there was also the comforting emotional support available from more than just a mother and father as well as the sense of belonging and bonding with the many aunts, uncles, and cousins that usually lived nearby.

As extended families become less common, the emotional stakes of home life seem higher than ever. Since we rely on each other more in today's nuclear family, our sense of disappointment, our sense of rejection, and our sense of unworthiness can be more acute. During childhood, the drama of family life can stamp an indelible mark on our psyches, leaving psychological scars that make safe passage into adulthood difficult. Our status within the family can also offer us a sense of worth and confidence that leads to contentment and success later on. For all of us, however, family life is not composed of psychological and sociological generalities but, rather, of our one-to-one relationships with fathers, sisters, grandmothers. Writers often give us imaginative, honest, and illuminating charts of their successes and failures in negotiating both the calm and choppy waters of our family journeys. The following clusters do not hope to be complete or representative of your experiences. We do hope, however, that in reading and discussing these poems and stories, you will find them an interesting and provocative catalyst for you to delve into the joys and sorrows of your own life in a family.

The chapter opens with three famous folktales of family conflict (p. 182). Next three contemporary writers give autobiographical accounts of their childhood memories, and of people and events that taught them valuable lessons about life (p. 201). Fathers are the focus of the third cluster (p. 220) as four poets paint memorable but not always positive portraits of their fathers. The fourth cluster (p. 226) groups Sylvia Plath's "Daddy" with three critical commentaries on the poet's brilliant and haunting attempt to come to grips with her father's death when she was a girl. The next cluster (p. 240) examines the tensions between mothers and daughters as they try to work out questions of identity and responsibility. The sixth cluster (p. 256) sharply contrasts the relationship of brothers in different socioeconomic settings. In the next cluster (p. 293), two plays, *Hamlet* and *The Glass Menagerie*, become the occasion for an exploration of troubled families. Two writers reveal the difficulty and pain of raising disabled children in the eighth cluster (p. 448). In the ninth cluster (p. 467), five poets give us loving, humorous, and honest snapshots of their grandparents. The feelings of gays and lesbians within families are the concern of the poets in the tenth cluster (p. 476). The last cluster (p. 483) brings together Lorraine Hansberry's *A Raisin in the Sun* and three background documents that help us understand this powerful portrayal of a family's hopes and dreams in a racially conflicted society.

FAMILIES IN FOLKTALES:
A COLLECTION OF WRITINGS
BY THE BROTHERS GRIMM

JACOB AND WILHELM GRIMM, "Cinderella"
JACOB AND WILHELM GRIMM, "Hansel and Gretel"
JACOB AND WILHELM GRIMM, "Snow White"

Although many of us probably have pleasant childhood memories of being told the stories of "Cinderella," "Hansel and Gretel," and "Snow White," most people do not realize that filmmaker Walt Disney did not originate these tales. Indeed, most fairy tales are hundreds of years old and exist in several variations, some quite different from Disney's sanitized narratives. Americans tend to think that the animated versions are the original ones, but actually the Brothers Grimm collected these stories from oral traditions and published them in the early nineteenth century. The Brothers Grimm were serious scholars who understood the importance of keeping these tales alive so that listeners could better understand the values, assumptions, and concerns of past cultures. Today, the folktales may be aimed at children, but they also serve as mirrors of our cultural traditions.

Although the references to princes, balls, and magic associated with "Cinderella" might seem quite remote, the rivalry and animosity of the stepsisters will have a familiar ring to contemporary readers used to the difficulties of children growing up with siblings from different marriages. "Snow White" will certainly seem relevant to those dealing with a hostile family environment; psychologists tell us that the fears of Hansel and Gretel are shared by many normal children. A careful reading of these stories should reward the reader with insights about the biases, struggles, and fears that existed within families of the past. Stereotypes like the cruel stepmother, the vain queen, and the handsome prince may seem both foreign and familiar.

BEFORE YOU READ

Can you remember being lost as a child? Did you imagine harm would come to you without your parents? Did you ever feel envious or hostile toward your siblings? Do you know of situations where blended families have had difficulties? Do you think it reasonable to assume that people from widely different social classes could live "happily ever after"? Do you think that suddenly inheriting a fortune would let you live a life of the "utmost joy"?

JACOB AND WILHELM GRIMM

Jacob Grimm (1785–1863) and Wilhelm Grimm (1786–1859) were born in Hanau, Germany, and studied law at Marburg University. They began to collect folktales from various oral European traditions just for their friends, but later published their efforts for both children and adults. In 1812, they published their first edition of Kinder-und Hausmärchen (Children's and Household Tales); *the translations reprinted here are based on the seventh and final edition of 1857. To the brothers folktales expressed the eternal joys, sorrows, hopes, and dreams of humankind. Their methods became a model for the scientific collection of folk songs and folktales. The brothers also served as linguistics professors at Göttingen University and made major contributions to the historical study of language. They are buried in Berlin.*

Cinderella

Translated by Jack Zipes

The wife of a rich man fell ill, and as she felt her end approaching, she called her only daughter to her bedside and said, "Dear child, be good and pious. Then the dear Lord shall always assist you, and I shall look down from heaven and take care of you." She then closed her eyes and departed.

After her mother's death the maiden went every day to visit her grave and weep, and she remained good and pious. When winter came, snow covered the grave like a little white blanket, and by the time the sun had taken it off again in the spring, the rich man had a second wife, who brought along her two daughters. They had beautiful and fair features but nasty and wicked hearts. As a result a difficult time was ahead for the poor stepsister.

"Why should the stupid goose be allowed to sit in the parlor with us?" they said. "Whoever wants to eat bread must earn it. Out with this kitchen maid!"

They took away her beautiful clothes, dressed her in an old gray smock, and gave her wooden shoes.

"Just look at the proud princess and how decked out she is!" they exclaimed with laughter, and led her into the kitchen.   5

They expected her to work hard there from morning till night. She had to get up before dawn, carry the water into the house, make the fire, cook, and wash. Besides this, her sisters did everything imaginable to cause her grief and make her look ridiculous. For instance, they poured peas and lentils into the hearth ashes so she had to sit there and pick them out. In the evening, when she was exhausted from working, they took away her bed, and she had to lie next to the hearth in the ashes. This is why she always looked so dusty and dirty and why they all called her Cinderella.

One day it happened that her father was going to the fair and asked his two stepdaughters what he could bring them.

"Beautiful dresses," said one.

"Pearls and jewels," said the other.

"And you, Cinderella?" he asked. "What do you want?"   10

"Father," she said, "just break off the first twig that brushes against your hat on your way home and bring it to me."

So he bought beautiful dresses, pearls, and jewels for the two stepsisters, and as he was riding through some green bushes on his return journey, a hazel twig brushed against him and knocked off his hat. So he broke off that twig and took it with him. When he arrived home, he gave his stepdaughters what they had requested, and Cinderella received the twig from the hazel bush. She thanked him, went to her mother's grave, planted the twig on it, and wept so hard that the tears fell on the twig and watered it. Soon the twig grew and quickly became a beautiful tree. Three times every day Cinderella would go and sit beneath it and weep and pray, and each time, a little white bird would also come to the tree. Whenever Cinderella expressed a wish, the bird would throw her whatever she had requested.

In the meantime, the king had decided to sponsor a three-day festival, and all the beautiful young girls in the country were invited so that his son could choose a bride. When the two stepsisters learned that they too had been summoned to make an appearance, they were in good spirits and called Cinderella.

"Comb our hair, brush our shoes, and fasten our buckles!" they said. "We're going to the wedding at the king's castle."

Cinderella obeyed but wept, because she too would have liked to go to the   15
ball with them, and so she asked her stepmother for permission to go.

"You, Cinderella!" she said. "You're all dusty and dirty, and yet you want to go to the wedding? How can you go dancing when you've got no clothes or shoes?"

When Cinderella kept pleading, her stepmother finally said, "I've emptied a bowlful of lentils into the ashes. If you can pick out all the lentils in two hours, you may have my permission to go."

The maiden went through the back door into the garden and cried out, "Oh, you tame pigeons, you turtledoves, and all you birds under heaven, come and help me pick

the good ones for the little pot,
the bad ones for your little crop."

Two white pigeons came flying to the kitchen window, followed by the turtle-doves. Eventually, all the birds under heaven swooped down, swarmed into the kitchen, and settled around the ashes. The pigeons bobbed their heads and began to peck, peck, peck, peck, and all the other birds also began to peck, peck, peck, peck, and they put all the good lentils into the bowl. It did not take longer than an hour for the birds to finish the work, whereupon they flew away. Happy, because she thought she would now be allowed to go to the wedding, the maiden brought the bowl to her stepmother. But her stepmother said, "No, Cinderella. You don't have any clothes, nor do you know how to dance. Everyone would only laugh at you."

When Cinderella started crying, the stepmother said, "If you can pick two bowlfuls of lentils out of the ashes in one hour, I'll let you come along." But she thought, She'll never be able to do it. 20

Then the stepmother dumped two bowlfuls of lentils into the ashes, and the maiden went through the back door into the garden and cried out, "Oh, you tame pigeons, you turtledoves, and all you birds under heaven, come and help me pick

the good ones for the little pot,
the bad ones for your little crop."

Two white pigeons came flying to the kitchen window, followed by the turtledoves. Eventually, all the birds under heaven swooped down, swarmed into the kitchen, and settled around the ashes. The pigeons bobbed their heads and began to peck, peck, peck, peck, and all the other birds also began to peck, peck, peck, peck, and they put all the good lentils into the bowl. Before half an hour had passed, they finished their work and flew away. Happy, because she thought she would now be allowed to go to the wedding, the maiden carried the bowls to her stepmother. But her stepmother said, "Nothing can help you. I can't let you come with us because you don't have any clothes to wear and you don't know how to dance. We'd only be ashamed of you!"

Then she turned her back on Cinderella and hurried off with her two haughty daughters. When they had all departed, Cinderella went to her mother's grave beneath the hazel tree and cried out:

"Shake and wobble, little tree!
Let gold and silver fall all over me."

The bird responded by throwing her a gold and silver dress and silk slippers embroidered with silver. She hastily slipped into the dress and went to the wedding. She looked so beautiful in her golden dress that her sisters and stepmother did not recognize her and thought she must be a foreign princess. They never imagined it could be Cinderella; they thought she was sitting at home in the dirt picking lentils out of the ashes.

Now, the prince approached Cinderella, took her by the hand, and danced with her. Indeed, he would not dance with anyone else and would not let go of her hand. Whenever someone came and asked her to dance, he said, "She's my partner." 25

She danced well into the night, and when she wanted to go home, the prince said, "I'll go along and escort you," for he wanted to see whose daughter the beautiful maiden was. But she managed to slip away from him and got into her father's dovecote. Now the prince waited until her father came, and he told him that the unknown maiden had escaped into his dovecote. The old man thought, Could that be Cinderella? And he had an ax and pick brought to him so he could chop it down. However, no one was inside, and when they went into the house, Cinderella was lying in the ashes in her dirty clothes, and a dim little oil lamp was burning on the mantel of the chimney. Cinderella had swiftly jumped out the back of the dovecote and run to the hazel tree. There she had taken off the beautiful clothes and laid them on the grave. After the bird had taken them away, she had made her way into the kitchen, where she had seated herself in the gray ashes wearing her gray smock.

The next day when the festival had begun again and her parents and sisters had departed, Cinderella went to the hazel tree and cried out:

"Shake and wobble, little tree!
Let gold and silver fall all over me."

The bird responded by throwing her a dress that was even more splendid than the one before. And when she appeared at the wedding in this dress, everyone was amazed by her beauty. The prince had been waiting for her, and when she came, he took her hand right away and danced with no one but her. When others went up to her and asked her to dance, he said, "She's my partner."

When evening came and she wished to leave, the prince followed her, wanting to see which house she went into, but she ran away from him and disappeared into the garden behind the house. There she went to a beautiful tall tree covered with the most wonderful pears, and she climbed up into the branches as nimbly as a squirrel. The prince did not know where she had gone, so he waited until her father came and said, "The unknown maiden has slipped away from me, and I think she climbed the pear tree."

The father thought, Can that be Cinderella? And he had an ax brought to him and chopped the tree down, but there was no one in it. When they went into the kitchen, Cinderella was lying in the ashes as usual, for she had jumped down on the other side of the tree, brought the beautiful clothes back to the bird, and put on her gray smock.

On the third day, when her parents and sisters had departed, Cinderella went to her mother's grave again and cried out to the tree:

"Shake and wobble, little tree!
Let gold and silver fall all over me."

The bird responded by throwing her a dress that was more magnificent and radiant than all the others she had received, and the slippers were pure gold. When she appeared at the wedding in this dress, the people were so astounded they did not know what to say. The prince danced with no one but her, and whenever someone asked her to dance, he said, "She's my partner."

When it was evening and Cinderella wished to leave, the prince wanted to escort her, but she slipped away from him so swiftly that he could not follow her. However, the prince had prepared for this with a trick: he had all the stairs coated with pitch, and when Cinderella went running down the stairs, her left slipper got stuck there. After the prince picked it up, he saw it was small and dainty and made of pure gold.

Next morning he carried it to Cinderella's father and said, "No one else shall be my wife but the maiden whose foot fits this golden shoe."

The two sisters were glad to hear this because they had beautiful feet. The   35
oldest took the shoe into a room to try it on, and her mother stood by her side. However, the shoe was too small for her, and she could not get her big toe into it. So her mother handed her a knife and said, "Cut your toe off. Once you become queen, you won't have to walk anymore."

The maiden cut her toe off, forced her foot into the shoe, swallowed the pain, and went out to the prince. He took her on his horse as his bride and rode off. But they had to pass the grave where the two pigeons were sitting on the hazel tree, and they cried out:

"Looky, look, look
at the shoe that she took.
There's blood all over, and her foot's too small.
She's not the bride you met at the ball."

He looked down at her foot and saw the blood oozing out. So he turned his horse around, brought the false bride home again, and said that she was definitely not the right one and the other sister should try on the shoe. Then the second sister went into a room and was fortunate enough to get all her toes in, but her heel was too large. So her mother handed her a knife and said, "Cut off a piece of your heel. Once you become queen, you won't have to walk anymore."

The maiden cut off a piece of her heel, forced her foot into the shoe, swallowed the pain, and went out to the prince. He took her on his horse as his bride, and rode off with her. As they passed the hazel tree the two pigeons were sitting there, and they cried out:

"Looky, look, look
at the shoe that she took.
There's blood all over, and her foot's too small.
She's not the bride you met at the ball."

He looked down at her foot and saw the blood oozing out of the shoe and staining her white stockings all red. Then he turned his horse around and brought the false bride home again.

"She isn't the right one either," he said. "Don't you have any other daughters?"   40

"No," said the man. "There's only little Cinderella, my dead wife's daughter, who's deformed, but she can't possibly be the bride."

The prince told him to send the girl to him, but the mother responded, "Oh, she's much too dirty and really shouldn't be seen."

However, the prince demanded to see her, and Cinderella had to be called. First she washed her hands and face until they were clean, and then she went and curtsied before the prince, who handed her the golden shoe. She sat down on a stool, took her foot out of the heavy wooden shoe, and put it into the slipper that fit her perfectly. After she stood up and the prince looked her straight in the face, he recognized the beautiful maiden who had danced with him.

"This is my true bride!" he exclaimed.

The stepmother and the two sisters were horrified and turned pale with rage.   45
However, the prince took Cinderella on his horse and rode away with her. As they
passed the hazel tree the two white pigeons cried out:

"Looky, look, look
at the shoe that she took.
Her foot's just right, and there's no blood at all.
She's truly the bride you met at the ball."

After the pigeons had made this known, they both came flying down and
landed on Cinderella's shoulders, one on the right, the other on the left, and
there they stayed.

On the day that the wedding with the prince was to take place, the two false
sisters came to ingratiate themselves and to share in Cinderella's good fortune.
When the bridal couple set out for the church, the oldest sister was on the right,
the younger on the left. Suddenly the pigeons pecked out one eye from each of
them. And as they came back from the church later on the oldest was on the left
and the youngest on the right, and the pigeons pecked out the other eye from
each sister. Thus they were punished with blindness for the rest of their lives due
to their wickedness and malice.   [1857, 1987]

THINKING ABOUT THE TEXT

1. Do you think such triumphs actually happened several hundred years
   ago? Do they happen today? How might this story be updated today in,
   say, a movie?

2. What attracts the prince to Cinderella? Is this typical? Superficial? Does
   anything in this story suggest they will be "happy ever after"?

3. Might the prince have been happy if he married one of Cinderella's stepsisters? What happens to the father? Why does he not intervene?

4. Characters in folktales are clearly neither rounded nor complex. Why
   not? If Cinderella were more fully human, how might that be portrayed
   in a modern revision? How might the prince be portrayed with more
   complexity? What about the other characters?

5. Justice does seem to prevail here. Do you think the stepsisters' punishment matches their offenses? Or does it seem a bit severe? Why would an
   audience want such an ending? Because it reflects reality? Or because it
   does not? What might that say about the function of fiction?

Hansel and Gretel

Translated by Jack Zipes

A poor woodcutter lived with his wife and his two children on the edge of a
large forest. The boy was called Hansel and the girl Gretel. The woodcutter did
not have much food around the house, and when a great famine devastated the

entire country, he could no longer provide enough for his family's daily meals. One night, as he was lying in bed and thinking about his worries, he began tossing and turning. Then he sighed and said to his wife, "What's to become of us? How can we feed our poor children when we don't even have enough for ourselves?"

"I'll tell you what," answered his wife. "Early tomorrow morning we'll take the children out into the forest where it's most dense. We'll build a fire and give them each a piece of bread. Then we'll go about our work and leave them alone. They won't find their way back home, and we'll be rid of them."

"No, wife," the man said. "I won't do this. I don't have the heart to leave my children in the forest. The wild beasts would soon come and tear them apart."

"Oh, you fool!" she said. "Then all four of us will have to starve to death. You'd better start planing the boards for our coffins!" She continued to harp on this until he finally agreed to do what she suggested.

"But still, I feel sorry for the poor children," he said.   5

The two children had not been able to fall asleep that night either. Their hunger kept them awake, and when they heard what their stepmother said to their father, Gretel wept bitter tears and said to Hansel, "Now it's all over for us."

"Be quiet, Gretel," Hansel said. "Don't get upset. I'll soon find a way to help us."

When their parents had fallen asleep, Hansel put on his little jacket, opened the bottom half of the door, and crept outside. The moon was shining very brightly, and the white pebbles glittered in front of the house like pure silver coins. Hansel stooped down to the ground and stuffed his pocket with as many pebbles as he could fit in. Then he went back and said to Gretel, "Don't worry, my dear little sister. Just sleep in peace. God will not forsake us." And he lay down again in his bed.

At dawn, even before the sun began to rise, the woman came and woke the two children: "Get up, you lazybones! We're going into the forest to fetch some wood." Then she gave each one of them a piece of bread and said, "Now you have something for your noonday meal, but don't eat it before then because you're not getting anything else."

Gretel put the bread under her apron because Hansel had the pebbles in his   10
pocket. Then they all set out together toward the forest. After they had walked a while, Hansel stopped and looked back at the house. He did this time and again until his father said, "Hansel, what are you looking at there? Why are you dawdling? Pay attention, and don't forget how to use your legs!"

"Oh, Father," said Hansel, "I'm looking at my little white cat that's sitting up on the roof and wants to say good-bye to me."

"You fool," the mother said. "That's not a cat. It's the morning sun shining on the chimney."

But Hansel had not been looking at the cat. Instead, he had been taking the shiny pebbles from his pocket and constantly dropping them on the ground. When they reached the middle of the forest, the father said, "Children, I want you to gather some wood. I'm going to make a fire so you won't get cold."

Hansel and Gretel gathered together some brushwood and built quite a nice little pile. The brushwood was soon kindled, and when the fire was ablaze, the woman said, "Now, children, lie down by the fire, and rest yourselves. We're going into the forest to chop wood. When we're finished, we'll come back and get you."

Hansel and Gretel sat by the fire, and when noon came, they ate their pieces 15 of bread. Since they heard the sounds of the ax, they thought their father was nearby. But it was not the ax. Rather, it was a branch that he had tied to a dead tree, and the wind was banging it back and forth. After they had been sitting there for a long time, they became so weary that their eyes closed, and they fell sound asleep. By the time they finally awoke, it was already pitch black, and Gretel began to cry and said, "How are we going to get out of the forest?"

But Hansel comforted her by saying, "Just wait awhile until the moon has risen. Then we'll find the way."

And when the full moon had risen, Hansel took his little sister by the hand and followed the pebbles that glittered like newly minted silver coins and showed them the way. They walked the whole night long and arrived back at their father's house at break of day. They knocked at the door, and when the woman opened it and saw it was Hansel and Gretel, she said, "You wicked children, why did you sleep so long in the forest? We thought you'd never come back again."

But the father was delighted because he had been deeply troubled by the way he had abandoned them in the forest.

Not long after that the entire country was once again ravaged by famine, and one night the children heard their mother talking to their father in bed. "Everything's been eaten up again. We only have half a loaf of bread, but after it's gone, that will be the end of our food. The children must leave. This time we'll take them even farther into the forest so they won't find their way back home again. Otherwise, there's no hope for us."

All this saddened the father, and he thought, It'd be much better to share 20 your last bite to eat with your children. But the woman would not listen to anything he said. She just scolded and reproached him. Once you've given a hand, people will take your arm, and since he had given in the first time, he also had to yield a second time.

However, the children were still awake and had overheard their conversation. When their parents had fallen asleep, Hansel got up, intending to go out and gather pebbles as he had done the time before, but the woman had locked the door, and Hansel could not get out. Nevertheless, he comforted his little sister and said, "Don't cry, Gretel. Just sleep in peace. The dear Lord is bound to help us."

Early the next morning the woman came and got the children out of bed. They each received little pieces of bread, but they were smaller than the last time. On the way into the forest Hansel crumbled the bread in his pocket and stopped as often as he could to throw the crumbs on the ground.

"Hansel, why are you always stopping and looking around?" asked the father. "Keep going!"

"I'm looking at my little pigeon that's sitting on the roof and wants to say good-bye to me," Hansel answered.

"Fool!" the woman said. "That's not your little pigeon. It's the morning sun 25 shining on the chimney."

But little by little Hansel managed to scatter all the bread crumbs on the path. The woman led the children even deeper into the forest until they came to a spot they had never in their lives seen before. Once again a large fire was made, and the mother said, "Just keep sitting here, children. If you get tired, you can sleep a little. We're going into the forest to chop wood, and in the evening, when we're done, we'll come and get you."

When noon came, Gretel shared her bread with Hansel, who had scattered his along the way. Then they fell asleep, and evening passed, but no one came for the poor children. Only when it was pitch black did they finally wake up, and Hansel comforted his little sister by saying, "Just wait until the moon has risen, Gretel. Then we'll see the little bread crumbs that I scattered. They'll show us the way back home."

When the moon rose, they set out but could not find the crumbs, because the many thousands of birds that fly about in the forest and fields had devoured them.

"Don't worry, we'll find the way," Hansel said to Gretel, but they could not find it. They walked the entire night and all the next day as well, from morning till night, but they did not get out of the forest. They were now also very hungry, for they had had nothing to eat except some berries that they had found growing on the ground. Eventually they became so tired that their legs would no longer carry them, and they lay down beneath a tree and fell asleep.

It was now the third morning since they had left their father's house. They began walking again, and they kept going deeper and deeper into the forest. If help did not arrive soon, they were bound to perish of hunger and exhaustion. At noon they saw a beautiful bird as white as snow sitting on a branch. It sang with such a lovely voice that the children stood still and listened to it. When the bird finished its song, it flapped its wings and flew ahead of them. They followed it until they came to a little house that was made of bread. Moreover, it had cake for a roof and pure sugar for windows.

"What a blessed meal!" said Hansel. "Let's have a taste. I want to eat a piece of the roof. Gretel, you can have some of the window, since it's sweet."

Hansel reached up high and broke off a piece of the roof to see how it tasted, and Gretel leaned against the windowpanes and nibbled on them. Then they heard a shrill voice cry out from inside:

"Nibble, nibble, I hear a mouse.
Who's that nibbling at my house?"

The children answered:

"The wind, the wind; it's very mild,
blowing like the Heavenly Child."

And they did not bother to stop eating or let themselves be distracted. Since the roof tasted so good, Hansel ripped off a large piece and pulled it down, while Gretel pushed out a round piece of the windowpane, sat down, and ate it with great relish. Suddenly the door opened, and a very old woman leaning on a crutch came slinking out of the house. Hansel and Gretel were so tremendously

30

frightened that they dropped what they had in their hands. But the old woman wagged her head and said, "Well now, dear children, who brought you here? Just come inside and stay with me. Nobody's going to harm you."

She took them both by the hand and led them into her house. Then she served them a good meal of milk and pancakes with sugar and apples and nuts. Afterward she made up two little beds with white sheets, whereupon Hansel and Gretel lay down in them and thought they were in heaven.

The old woman, however, had only pretended to be friendly. She was really a wicked witch on the lookout for children, and had built the house made of bread only to lure them to her. As soon as she had any children in her power, she would kill, cook, and eat them. It would be like a feast day for her. Now, witches have red eyes and cannot see very far, but they have a keen sense of smell, like animals, and can detect when human beings are near them. Therefore, when Hansel and Gretel had come into her vicinity, she had laughed wickedly and scoffed, "They're mine! They'll never get away from me!"

Early the next morning, before the children were awake, she got up and looked at the two of them sleeping so sweetly with full rosy cheeks. Then she muttered to herself, "They'll certainly make for a tasty meal!"

She seized Hansel with her scrawny hands and carried him into a small pen, where she locked him up behind a grilled door. No matter how much he screamed, it did not help. Then she went back to Gretel, shook her until she woke up, and yelled, "Get up, you lazybones! I want you to fetch some water and cook your brother something nice. He's sitting outside in a pen, and we've got to fatten him up. Then, when he's fat enough, I'm going to eat him."

Gretel began to weep bitter tears, but they were all in vain. She had to do what the wicked witch demanded. So the very best food was cooked for poor Hansel, while Gretel got nothing but crab shells. Every morning the old woman went slinking to the little pen and called out, "Hansel, stick out your finger so I can feel how fat you are."

However, Hansel stuck out a little bone, and since the old woman had poor eyesight, she thought the bone was Hansel's finger. She was puzzled that Hansel did not get any fatter, and when a month had gone by and Hansel still seemed to be thin, she was overcome by her impatience and decided not to wait any longer.

"Hey there, Gretel!" she called to the little girl. "Get a move on and fetch some water! I don't care whether Hansel's fat or thin. He's going to be slaughtered tomorrow, and then I'll cook him."

Oh, how the poor little sister wailed as she was carrying the water, and how the tears streamed down her cheeks!

"Dear God, help us!" she exclaimed. "If only the wild beasts had eaten us in the forest, then we could have at least died together!"

Early the next morning Gretel had to go out, hang up a kettle full of water, and light the fire.

"First we'll bake," the old woman said. "I've already heated the oven and kneaded the dough." She pushed poor Gretel out to the oven, where the flames were leaping from the fire. "Crawl inside," said the witch, "and see if it's properly heated so we can slide the bread in."

The witch intended to close the oven door once Gretel had climbed inside, for the witch wanted to bake her and eat her too. But Gretel sensed what she had in mind and said, "I don't know how to do it. How do I get in?"

"You stupid goose," the old woman said. "The opening's large enough. Watch, even I can get in!"

She waddled up to the oven and stuck her head through the oven door. Then Gretel gave her a push that sent her flying inside and shut the iron door and bolted it. *Whew!* The witch began to howl dreadfully, but Gretel ran away, and the godless witch was miserably burned to death.

Meanwhile, Gretel ran straight to Hansel, opened the pen, and cried out, "Hansel, we're saved! The old witch is dead!"

Then Hansel jumped out of the pen like a bird that hops out of a cage when   50
the door is opened. My how happy they were! They hugged each other, danced around, and kissed. Since they no longer had anything to fear, they went into the witch's house, and there they found chests filled with pearls and jewels all over the place.

"They're certainly much better than pebbles," said Hansel, and he put whatever he could fit into his pockets, and Gretel said, "I'm going to carry some home too," and she filled her apron full of jewels and pearls.

"We'd better be on our way now," said Hansel, "so we can get out of the witch's forest."

When they had walked for a few hours, they reached a large river.

"We can't get across," said Hansel. "I don't see a bridge or any way over it."

"There are no boats either," Gretel responded, "but there's a white duck   55
swimming over there. It's bound to help us across if I ask it." Then she cried out:

> "Help us, help us, little duck!
> It's Hansel and Gretel, and we're really stuck.
> We can't get over, try as we may.
> Please take us across right away!"

The little duck came swimming up to them, and Hansel got on top of its back and told his sister to sit down beside him.

"No," Gretel answered. "That will be too heavy for the little duck. Let it carry us across one at a time."

The kind little duck did just that, and when they were safely across and had walked on for some time, the forest became more and more familiar to them, and finally they caught sight of their father's house from afar. They began to run at once, and soon rushed into the house and threw themselves around their father's neck. The man had not had a single happy hour since he had abandoned his children in the forest, and in the meantime his wife had died. Gretel opened and shook out her apron so that the pearls and jewels bounced about the room, and Hansel added to this by throwing one handful after another from his pocket. Now all their troubles were over, and they lived together in utmost joy.

My tale is done. See the mouse run. Catch it, whoever can, and then you can make a great big cap out of its fur.   [1857, 1987]

THINKING ABOUT THE TEXT

1. The wife's decision to get rid of the children is usually assumed to be evil. How might you argue her side?

2. How would you respond to the father in this story? Does your opinion of him change? Can you muster some sympathy for his plight?

3. Note the ways in which Hansel and Gretel are admirable. Do you think they represent certain values the culture was fond of?

4. The story closes with an excessively happy ending. Why do such endings exist? What is their purpose? What do they tell us about the intended audience?

5. Do you think children should be told a tale such as this? Do you think it would have a salubrious or a detrimental effect?

MAKING COMPARISONS

1. How would you compare the fathers in "Cinderella" and "Hansel and Gretel"? The mothers? How might you account for such differences?

2. What are the similarities and differences between Cinderella and Gretel?

3. Compare the two endings. What specific cultural values or fantasies do they suggest?

Snow White

Translated by Jack Zipes

Once upon a time, in the middle of winter, when snowflakes were falling like feathers from the sky, a queen was sitting and sewing at a window with a black ebony frame. And as she was sewing and looking out the window, she pricked her finger with the needle, and three drops of blood fell on the snow. The red looked so beautiful on the white snow that she thought to herself, If only I had a child as white as snow, as red as blood, and as black as the wood of the window frame!

Soon after she gave birth to a little daughter who was as white as snow, as red as blood, and her hair as black as ebony. Accordingly, the child was called Snow White, and right after she was born, the queen died. When a year had passed, the king married another woman, who was beautiful but proud and haughty, and she could not tolerate anyone else who might rival her beauty. She had a magic mirror and often she stood in front of it, looked at herself, and said:

"Mirror, mirror, on the wall,
who in this realm is the fairest of all?"

Then the mirror would answer:

"You, my queen, are the fairest of all."

That reply would make her content, for she knew the mirror always told the truth.

In the meantime, Snow White grew up and became more and more beautiful. By the time she was seven years old, she was as beautiful as the day is clear and more beautiful than the queen herself. One day when the queen asked her mirror:

"Mirror, mirror, on the wall,
who in this realm is the fairest of all?"

The mirror answered:

"You, my queen, may have a beauty quite rare,
but Snow White is a thousand times more fair."

The queen shuddered and became yellow and green with envy. From that hour on, her hate for the girl was so great that her heart throbbed and turned in her breast each time she saw Snow White. Like weeds, the envy and arrogance grew so dense in her heart that she no longer had any peace, day or night. Finally, she summoned a huntsman and said, "Take the child out into the forest. I never want to lay eyes on her again. You are to kill her and to bring me back her lungs and liver as proof of your deed."

The huntsman obeyed and led Snow White out into the forest, but when he drew his hunting knife and was about to stab Snow White's innocent heart, she began to weep and said, "Oh, dear huntsman, spare my life, and I'll run into the wild forest and never come home again."

Since she was so beautiful, the huntsman took pity on her and said, "You're free to go, my poor child!" Then he thought, The wild beasts will soon eat you up. Nevertheless, he felt as if a great weight had been lifted off his mind, because he did not have to kill her. Just then a young boar came dashing by, and the huntsman stabbed it to death. He took out the lungs and liver and brought them to the queen as proof that the child was dead. The cook was ordered to boil them in salt, and the wicked woman ate them and thought that she had eaten Snow White's lungs and liver.

Meanwhile, the poor child was all alone in the huge forest. When she looked at all the leaves on the trees, she was petrified and did not know what to do. Then she began to run, and she ran over sharp stones and through thornbushes. Wild beasts darted by her at times, but they did not harm her. She ran as long as her legs could carry her, and it was almost evening when she saw a little cottage and went inside to rest. Everything was tiny in the cottage and indescribably dainty and neat. There was a little table with a white tablecloth, and on it were seven little plates. Each plate had a tiny spoon next to it, and there were also seven tiny knives and forks and seven tiny cups. In a row against the wall stood seven little beds covered with sheets as white as snow. Since she was so hungry and thirsty, Snow White ate some vegetables and bread from each of the little plates and had a drop of wine to drink out of each of the tiny cups, for she did not

5

want to take everything from just one place. After that she was tired and began trying out the beds, but none of them suited her at first: one was too long, another too short, but at last, she found that the seventh one was just right. So she stayed in that bed, said her prayers, and fell asleep.

When it was completely dark outside, the owners of the cottage returned. They were seven dwarfs who searched in the mountains for minerals with their picks and shovels. They lit their seven little candles, and when it became light in the house, they saw that someone had been there, for none of their things was in the exact same spot in which it had been left.

"Who's been sitting in my chair?" said the first dwarf.

"Who's been eating off my plate?" said the second.

"Who's been eating my bread?" said the third.   10

"Who's been eating my vegetables?" said the fourth.

"Who's been using my fork?" said the fifth.

"Who's been cutting with my knife?" said the sixth.

"Who's been drinking from my cup?" said the seventh.

Then the first dwarf looked around and noticed that his bed had been   15
wrinkled and said, "Who's been sleeping in my bed?"

The others ran over to their beds and cried out, "Someone's been sleeping in my bed too!"

But when the seventh dwarf looked at his bed, he saw Snow White lying there asleep. So he called the others over to him, and when they came, they were so astounded that they fetched their seven little candles to allow more light to shine on Snow White.

"Oh, my Lord! Oh, my Lord!" they exclaimed. "What a beautiful child!"

They were so delirious with joy that they did not wake her up. Instead, they let her sleep in the bed, while the seventh dwarf spent an hour in each one of his companions' beds until the night had passed. In the morning Snow White awoke, and when she saw the seven dwarfs, she was frightened. But they were friendly and asked, "What's your name?"

"My name's Snow White," she replied.   20

"What's brought you to our house?" the dwarfs continued.

She told them how her stepmother had ordered her to be killed, how the huntsman had spared her life, and how she had run all day until she had eventually discovered their cottage.

Then the dwarfs said, "If you'll keep house for us, cook, make the beds, wash, sew, and knit, and if you'll keep everything neat and orderly, you can stay with us, and we'll provide you with everything you need."

"Yes," agreed Snow White, "with all my heart."

So she stayed with them and kept their house in order. In the morning they   25
went to the mountains to search for minerals and gold. In the evening they returned, and their dinner had to be ready. During the day Snow White was alone, and the good dwarfs made sure to caution her.

"Beware of your stepmother," they said. "She'll soon know that you're here. Don't let anybody in!"

Since the queen believed she had eaten Snow White's liver and lungs, she was totally convinced that she was again the most beautiful woman in the realm. And when she went to her mirror, she said:

"Mirror, mirror, on the wall,
    who in this realm is the fairest of all?"

The mirror answered:

"You, my queen, may have a beauty quite rare,
    but beyond the mountains, where the seven dwarfs dwell,
    Snow White is thriving, and this I must tell:
    Within this realm she's still a thousand times more fair."

The queen was horrified, for she knew that the mirror never lied, which meant that the huntsman had deceived her and Snow White was still alive. Once more she began plotting ways to kill her. As long as Snow White was the fairest in the realm, the queen's envy would leave her no peace. Finally, she thought up a plan. She painted her face and dressed as an old peddler woman so that nobody could recognize her. Then she crossed the seven mountains in this disguise and arrived at the cottage of the seven dwarfs, where she knocked at the door and cried out, "Pretty wares for sale! Pretty wares!"

Snow White looked out of the window and called out, "Good day, dear woman, what do you have for sale?"

"Nice and pretty things! Staylaces in all kinds of colors!" she replied and took out a lace woven from silk of many different colors.

I can certainly let this honest woman inside, Snow White thought. She   30
unbolted the door and bought the pretty lace.

"My goodness, child! What a sight you are!" said the old woman. "Come, I'll lace you up properly for once."

Snow White did not suspect anything, so she stood in front of the old woman and let herself be laced with the new staylace. However the old woman laced her so quickly and so tightly that Snow White lost her breath and fell down as if dead.

"Well, you used to be the fairest in the realm, but not now!" the old woman said and rushed off.

Not long after, at dinnertime, the dwarfs came home, and when they saw their dear Snow White lying on the ground, they were horrified. She neither stirred nor moved and seemed to be dead. They lifted her up, and when they saw that she was laced too tightly, they cut the staylace in two. At once she began to breathe a little, and after a while she had fully revived. When the dwarfs heard what had happened, they said, "The old peddler woman was none other than the wicked queen! Beware, don't let anyone in when we're not with you!"

When the evil woman returned home, she went to her mirror and asked: 35

"Mirror, mirror, on the wall,
    who in this realm is the fairest of all?"

Then the mirror answered as usual:

"You, my queen, may have a beauty quite rare,
    but beyond the mountains, where the seven dwarfs dwell,

Snow White is thriving, and this I must tell:
Within this realm she's still a thousand times more fair."

When the queen heard that, she was so upset that all her blood rushed to her heart, for she realized that Snow White had recovered.

"This time I'm going to think of something that will destroy her," she said, and by using all the witchcraft at her command, she made a poison comb. Then she again disguised herself as an old woman and crossed the seven mountains to the cottage of the seven dwarfs, where she knocked at the door and cried out, "Pretty wares for sale! Pretty wares!"

Snow White looked out the window and said, "Go away! I'm not allowed to let anyone in."

"But surely you're allowed to look," said the old woman, and she took out the poison comb and held it up in the air. The comb pleased the girl so much that she let herself be carried away and opened the door. After they agreed on the price, the old woman said, "Now I'll give your hair a proper combing for once."

Poor Snow White did not give this a second thought and let the old woman do as she wished. But no sooner did the comb touch her hair than the poison began to take effect, and the maiden fell to the ground and lay there unconscious.   40

"You paragon of beauty!" said the wicked woman. "Now you're finished!" And she went away.

Fortunately, it was nearly evening, the time when the seven dwarfs began heading home. And, when they arrived and saw Snow White lying on the ground as if she were dead, they immediately suspected the stepmother and began looking around. As soon as they found the poison comb, they took it out, and Snow White instantly regained consciousness. She told them what had happened, and they warned her again to be on her guard and not to open the door for anyone.

In the meantime, the queen returned home, went to the mirror, and said:

"Mirror, mirror, on the wall,
who in this realm is the fairest of all?"

Then the mirror answered as before:

"You, my queen, may have a beauty quite rare,
but beyond the mountains, where the seven dwarfs dwell,
Snow White is thriving, and this I must tell:
Within this realm she's still a thousand times more fair."

When she heard the mirror's words, she trembled and shook with rage.
"Snow White shall die!" she exclaimed. "Even if it costs me my own life!"   45

Then she went into a secret and solitary chamber where no one else ever went. Once inside she made a deadly poisonous apple. On the outside it looked beautiful—white with red cheeks. Anyone who saw it would be enticed, but whoever took a bite was bound to die. When the apple was ready, the queen painted her face and dressed herself up as a peasant woman and crossed the seven mountains to the cottage of the seven dwarfs. When she knocked at the door, Snow White stuck her head out of the window and said, "I'm not allowed to let anyone inside. The seven dwarfs have forbidden me."

"That's all right with me," answered the peasant woman. "I'll surely get rid of my apples in time. But let me give you one as a gift."

"No," said Snow White. "I'm not allowed to take anything."

"Are you afraid that it might be poisoned?" said the old woman. "Look, I'll cut the apple in two. You eat the red part, and I'll eat the white."

However, the apple had been made with such cunning that only the red part   50
was poisoned. Snow White was eager to eat the beautiful apple, and when she saw the peasant woman eating her half, she could no longer resist, stretched out her hand, and took the poisoned half. No sooner did she take a bite than she fell to the ground dead. The queen stared at her with a cruel look, then burst out laughing and said, "White as snow, red as blood, black as ebony! This time the dwarfs won't be able to bring you back to life!"

When she got home, she asked the mirror:

"Mirror, mirror, on the wall,
who in this realm is the fairest of all?"

Then the mirror finally answered, "You, my queen, are now the fairest of all." So her jealous heart was satisfied as much as a jealous heart can be satisfied.

When the dwarfs came home that evening, they found Snow White lying on the ground. There was no breath coming from her lips, and she was dead. They lifted her up and looked to see if they could find something poisonous. They unlaced her, combed her hair, washed her with water and wine, but it was to no avail. The dear child was dead and remained dead. They laid her on a bier, and all seven of them sat down beside it and mourned over her. They wept for three whole days, and then they intended to bury her, but she looked so alive and still had such pretty red cheeks that they said, "We can't possibly bury her in the dingy ground."

Instead, they made a transparent glass coffin so that she could be seen from all sides. Then they put her in it, wrote her name on it in gold letters, and added that she was a princess. They carried the coffin to the top of the mountain, and from then on one of them always stayed beside it and guarded it. Some animals came also and wept for Snow White. There was an owl, then a raven, and finally a dove. Snow White lay in the coffin, for many, many years and did not decay. Indeed, she seemed to be sleeping, for she was still as white as snow, as red as blood, and her hair as black as ebony.

Now it happened that a prince came to the forest one day, and when he   55
arrived at the dwarfs' cottage, he decided to spend the night. Then he went to the mountain and saw the coffin with beautiful Snow White inside. After he read what was written on the coffin in gold letters, he said to the dwarfs, "Let me have the coffin, and I'll pay you whatever you want."

But the dwarfs answered, "We won't give it up for all the gold in the world."

"Then give it to me as a gift," he said, "for I can't go on living without being able to see Snow White. I'll honor her and cherish her as my dearly beloved."

Since he spoke with such fervor, the good dwarfs took pity on him and gave him the coffin. The prince ordered his servants to carry the coffin on their shoulders, but they stumbled over some shrubs, and the jolt caused the poisoned piece of apple that Snow White had bitten off to be released from her throat. It was not long before she opened her eyes, lifted up the lid of the coffin, sat up, and was alive again.

"Oh, Lord! Where am I?" she exclaimed.

The prince rejoiced and said, "You're with me," and he told her what had   60
happened. Then he added, "I love you more than anything else in the world. Come with me to my father's castle. I want you to be my wife."

Snow White felt that he was sincere, so she went with him, and their wedding was celebrated with great pomp and splendor.

Now, Snow White's stepmother had also been invited to the wedding celebration, and after she had dressed herself in beautiful clothes, she went to the mirror and said:

"Mirror, mirror, on the wall,
who in this realm is the fairest of all?"

The mirror answered:

"You, my queen, may have a beauty quite rare,
but Snow White is a thousand times more fair."

The evil woman uttered a loud curse and became so terribly afraid that she did not know what to do. At first she did not want to go to the wedding celebration. But, she could not calm herself until she saw the young queen. When she entered the hall, she recognized Snow White. The evil queen was so petrified with fright that she could not budge. Iron slippers had already been heated over a fire, and they were brought over to her with tongs. Finally, she had to put on the red-hot slippers and dance until she fell down dead.   [1857, 1987]

THINKING ABOUT THE TEXT

1. Given the malevolence of the queen, could you argue that this is a sexist story?

2. As with Cinderella, Snow White's life deteriorates rapidly once her birth mother dies. Why is this? Do you get some sense of a Freudian rivalry for the father? What other explanations can you give for this pattern in folktales? Are there parallels in real life?

3. The queen, the dwarfs, and the prince place great emphasis on beauty. Why do you think this is so? Have our values changed since then?

4. How does this authentic tale jibe with the Disney version? How can you account for the specific differences?

5. Snow White finds safety in an atypical "family." Can you think of contemporary books, movies, or TV programs where characters find refuge from the world in unconventional adopted families?

MAKING COMPARISONS

1. Compare the queen in "Snow White" with the "bad mothers" in "Cinderella" and "Hansel and Gretel." How might these stories work with bad fathers?

2. Snow White is rescued by a prince; so is Cinderella. What might this say about a society that uses such a repeated plot device?

3. Compare the use of magic in these three stories. Is it good or bad, or does it depend on something else? What power does it have? What might this say about the beliefs of these societies?

WRITING ABOUT ISSUES

1. Have the Brothers Grimm captured something real about family life, either then or now? Write an essay analyzing these three stories for elements that offer insights into the positive and negative aspects of families.

2. Argue for or against the idea that these three stories represent a sexist view of women within the family.

3. Write a personal response to the idea that stories like these do more harm than good to young children.

4. Locate a copy of Bruno Bettelheim's *The Uses of Enchantment* (1976) and read his psychological analysis of our three stories. Write an essay in which you briefly summarize his interpretations and then agree or disagree with his theories.

MEMORIES OF FAMILY

BELL HOOKS, "Inspired Eccentricity"
BRENT STAPLES, "The Runaway Son"
N. SCOTT MOMADAY, "The Way to Rainy Mountain"

We all tell stories about our lives in families. Perhaps the first are those about our relationships with our parents and about our contradictory impulses for understanding and independence. When we tell these tales to others, we might be trying to give meaning to our experiences, perhaps trying to give narrative shape to what seemed confusing and random at the time. Because our childhood memories may seem a disparate series of anecdotes and snapshots, it is probably natural to order them into coherent narratives with definite beginnings and ends. But memories are puzzling. Do we really remember these events, or do we remember someone else telling us about them? Or, more mysteriously, are we remembering earlier memories? The three writers in this cluster create narratives out of their experience, giving a sense of meaning to their futures.

BEFORE YOU READ

Are there members of your immediate or extended family you want to forget? Are there family members you always want to remember? Do the stories you tell about family members have a recurring theme? Why do you tell these stories? How do you feel about the stories members of your family tell about you?

BELL HOOKS

Inspired Eccentricity

Writer, professor, and social critic, bell hooks, born Gloria Jean Watkins in 1952, adopted the name of her maternal great-grandmother, a woman known for speaking her mind. Her books reflect her position as a bold interpreter of contemporary culture in terms of race, class, and gender: Ain't I a Woman *(1981),* Talking Back: Thinking Feminist, Thinking Black *(1989),* Yearning: Race, Gender and Cultural Politics *(1990),* Outlaw Culture: Resisting Representation *(1994), among others. She most recently published a memoir,* Bone Black: Memories of Girlhood *(1996). She has taught literature, women's studies, and African American studies at Yale University, Oberlin College, and City College of New York and continues to teach and to write poetry and social criticism. The selection that follows is from* Family: American Writers Remember Their Own *(1996), edited by Sharon Sloan Fiffer and Steve Fiffer.*

There are family members you try to forget and ones that you always remember, that you can't stop talking about. They may be dead — long gone — but their presence lingers and you have to share who they were and who they still are with the world. You want everyone to know them as you did, to love them as you did.

All my life I have remained enchanted by the presence of my mother's parents, Sarah and Gus Oldham. When I was a child they were already old. I did not see that then, though. They were Baba and Daddy Gus, together for more than seventy years at the time of his death. Their marriage fascinated me. They were strangers and lovers — two eccentrics who created their own world.

More than any other family members, together they gave me a worldview that sustained me during a difficult and painful childhood. Reflecting on the eclectic writer I have become, I see in myself a mixture of these two very different but equally powerful figures from my childhood. Baba was tall, her skin so white and her hair so jet black and straight that she could have easily "passed" denying all traces of blackness. Yet the man she married was short and dark, and sometimes his skin looked like the color of soot from burning coal. In our childhood the fireplaces burned coal. It was bright heat, luminous and fierce. If you got too close it could burn you.

Together Baba and Daddy Gus generated a hot heat. He was a man of few words, deeply committed to silence — so much so that it was like a religion to

him. When he spoke you could hardly hear what he said. Baba was just the opposite. Smoking an abundance of cigarettes a day, she talked endlessly. She
preached. She yelled. She fussed. Often her vitriolic rage would heap itself on
Daddy Gus, who would sit calmly in his chair by the stove, as calm and still as the
Buddha sits. And when he had enough of her words, he would reach for his hat
and walk.

Neither Baba nor Daddy Gus drove cars. Rarely did they ride in them. They   5
preferred walking. And even then their styles were different. He moved slow, as
though carrying a great weight; she with her tall, lean, boyish frame moved
swiftly, as though there was never time to waste. Their one agreed-upon passion
was fishing. Though they did not do even that together. They lived close but they
created separate worlds.

In a big two-story wood frame house with lots of rooms they constructed a
world that could contain their separate and distinct personalities. As children one
of the first things we noticed about our grandparents was that they did not sleep in
the same room. This arrangement was contrary to everything we understood
about marriage. While Mama never wanted to talk about their separate worlds,
Baba would tell you in a minute that Daddy Gus was nasty, that he smelled like
tobacco juice, that he did not wash enough, that there was no way she would
want him in her bed. And while he would say nothing nasty about her, he would
merely say why would he want to share somebody else's bed when he could have
his own bed to himself, with no one to complain about anything.

I loved my granddaddy's smells. Always, they filled my nostrils with the scent
of happiness. It was sheer ecstasy for me to be allowed into his inner sanctum. His
room was a small Van Gogh–like space off from the living room. There was no
door. Old-fashioned curtains were the only attempt at privacy. Usually the curtains were closed. His room reeked of tobacco. There were treasures everywhere
in that small room. As a younger man Daddy Gus did odd jobs, and sometimes
even in his old age he would do a chore for some needy lady. As he went about
his work, he would pick up found objects, scraps. All these objects would lie
about his room, on the dresser, on the table near his bed. Unlike all other grown-
ups he never cared about children looking through his things. Anything we
wanted he gave to us.

Daddy Gus collected beautiful wooden cigar boxes. They held lots of the
important stuff—the treasures. He had tons of little diaries that he made notes in.
He gave me my first wallet, my first teeny little book to write in, my first beautiful
pen, which did not write for long, but it was still a found and shared treasure.
When I would lie on his bed or sit close to him, sometimes just standing near, I
would feel all the pain and anxiety of my troubled childhood leave me. His spirit
was calm. He gave me the unconditional love I longed for.

"Too calm," his grown-up children thought. That's why he had let this old
woman rule him, my cousin BoBo would say. Even as children we knew that
grown-ups felt sorry for Daddy Gus. At times his sons seemed to look upon him as
not a "real man." His refusal to fight in wars was another sign to them of weakness. It was my grandfather who taught me to oppose war. They saw him as a man
controlled by the whims of others, by this tall, strident, demanding woman he

had married. I saw him as a man of profound beliefs, a man of integrity. When he heard their put-downs — for they talked on and on about his laziness — he merely muttered that he had no use for them. He was not gonna let anybody tell him what to do with his life.

Daddy Gus was a devout believer, a deacon at his church; he was one of the right-hand men of God. At church, everyone admired his calmness. Baba had no use for church. She liked nothing better than to tell us all the ways it was one big hypocritical place: "Why, I can find God anywhere I want to — I do not need a church." Indeed, when my grandmother died, her funeral could not take place in a church, for she had never belonged. Her refusal to attend church bothered some of her daughters, for they thought she was sinning against God, setting a bad example for the children. We were not supposed to listen when she began to damn the church and everybody in it.

Baba loved to "cuss." There was no bad word she was not willing to say. The improvisational manner in which she would string those words together was awesome. It was the goddamn sons of bitches who thought that they could fuck with her when they could just kiss her black ass. A woman of strong words and powerful metaphors, she could not read or write. She lived in the power of language. Her favorite sayings were a prelude for storytelling. It was she who told me, "Play with a puppy, he'll lick you in the mouth." When I heard this saying, I knew what was coming — a long polemic about not letting folks get too close, 'cause they will mess with you.

Baba loved to tell her stories. And I loved to hear them. She called me Glory. And in the midst of her storytelling she would pause to say, "Glory, are ya listenin'. Do you understand what I'm telling ya." Sometimes I would have to repeat the lessons I had learned. Sometimes I was not able to get it right and she would start again. When Mama felt I was learning too much craziness "over home" (that is what we called Baba's house), my visits were curtailed. As I moved into my teens I learned to keep to myself all the wisdom of the old ways I picked up over home.

Baba was an incredible quilt maker, but by the time I was old enough to really understand her work, to see its beauty; she was already having difficulty with her eyesight. She could not sew as much as in the old days, when her work was on everybody's bed. Unwilling to throw anything away, she loved to make crazy quilts, 'cause they allowed every scrap to be used. Although she would one day order patterns and make perfect quilts with colors that went together, she always collected scraps.

Long before I read Virginia Woolf's *A Room of One's Own* I learned from Baba that a woman needed her own space to work. She had a huge room for her quilting. Like every other space in the private world she created upstairs, it had her treasures, an endless array of hatboxes, feathers, and trunks filled with old clothes she had held on to. In room after room there were feather tick mattresses; when they were pulled back, the wooden slats of the bed were revealed, lined with exquisite hand-sewn quilts.

In all these trunks, in crevices and drawers were braided tobacco leaves to keep away moths and other insects. A really hot summer could make cloth sweat, and stains from tobacco juice would end up on quilts no one had ever used. When I was a young child, a quilt my grandmother had made kept me warm, was my solace and comfort. Even though Mama protested when I dragged that old raggedy quilt from Kentucky to Stanford, I knew I needed that bit of the South, of Baba's world, to sustain me.

Like Daddy Gus, she was a woman of her word. She liked to declare with pride, "I mean what I say and I say what I mean." "Glory," she would tell me, "nobody is better than their word—if you can't keep ya word you ain't worth nothin' in this world." She would stop speaking to folk over the breaking of their word, over lies. Our mama was not given to loud speech or confrontation. I learned all those things from Baba—"to stand up and speak up" and not to "give a good goddamn" what folk who "ain't got a pot to pee in" think. My parents were concerned with their image in the world. It was pure blasphemy for Baba to teach that it did not matter what other folks thought— "Ya have to be right with yaself in ya own heart—that's all that matters." Baba taught me to listen to my heart—to follow it. From her we learned as small children to remember our dreams in the night and to share them when we awakened. They would be interpreted by her. She taught us to listen to the knowledge in dreams. Mama would say this was all nonsense, but she too was known to ask the meaning of a dream.

In their own way my grandparents were rebels, deeply committed to radical individualism. I learned how to be myself from them. Mama hated this. She thought it was important to be liked, to conform. She had hated growing up in such an eccentric, otherworldly household. This world where folks made their own wine, their own butter, their own soap; where chickens were raised, and huge gardens were grown for canning everything. This was the world Mama wanted to leave behind. She wanted store-bought things.

Baba lived in another time, a time when all things were produced in the individual household. Everything the family needed was made at home. She loved to tell me stories about learning to trap animals, to skin, to soak possum and coon in brine, to fry up a fresh rabbit. Though a total woman of the outdoors who could shoot and trap as good as any man, she still believed every woman should sew—she made her first quilt as a girl. In her world, women were as strong as men because they had to be. She had grown up in the country and knew that country ways were the best ways to live. Boasting about being able to do anything that a man could do and better, this woman who could not read or write was confident about her place in the universe.

My sense of aesthetics came from her. She taught me to really look at things, to see underneath the surface, to see the different shades of red in the peppers she had dried and hung in the kitchen sunlight. The beauty of the ordinary, the everyday, was her feast of light. While she had no use for the treasures in my granddaddy's world, he too taught me to look for the living spirit in things—the things that are cast away but still need to be touched and cared for. Picking up a found object he would tell me its story or tell me how he was planning to give it life again.

Connected in spirit but so far apart in the life of everydayness, Baba and Daddy Gus were rarely civil to each other. Every shared talk begun with goodwill

20

ended in disagreement and contestation. Everyone knew Baba just loved to fuss. She liked a good war of words. And she was comfortable using words to sting and hurt, to punish. When words would not do the job, she could reach for the strap, a long piece of black leather that would leave tiny imprints on the flesh.

There was no violence in Daddy Gus. Mama shared that he had always been that way, a calm and gentle man, full of tenderness. I remember clinging to his tenderness when nothing I did was right in my mother's eyes, when I was constantly punished. Baba was not an ally. She advocated harsh punishment. She had no use for children who would not obey. She was never ever affectionate. When we entered her house, we gave her a kiss in greeting and that was it. With Daddy Gus we could cuddle, linger in his arms, give as many kisses as desired. His arms and heart were always open.

In the back of their house were fruit trees, chicken coops, and gardens, and in the front were flowers. Baba could make anything grow. And she knew all about herbs and roots. Her home remedies healed our childhood sicknesses. Of course she thought it crazy for anyone to go to a doctor when she could tell them just what they needed. All these things she had learned from her mother, Bell Blair Hooks, whose name I would choose as my pen name. Everyone agreed that I had the temperament of this great-grandmother I would not remember. She was a sharp-tongued woman. Or so they said. And it was believed I had inherited my way with words from her.

Families do that. They chart psychic genealogies that often overlook what is right before our eyes. I may have inherited my great-grandmother Bell Hook's way with words, but I learned to use those words listening to my grandmother. I learned to be courageous by seeing her act without fear. I learned to risk because she was daring. Home and family were her world. While my grandfather journeyed downtown, visited at other folks' houses, went to church, and conducted affairs in the world, Baba rarely left home. There was nothing in the world she needed. Things out there violated her spirit.

As a child I had no sense of what it would mean to live a life, spanning so many generations, unable to read or write. To me Baba was a woman of power. That she would have been extraordinarily powerless in a world beyond 1200 Broad Street was a thought that never entered my mind. I believed that she stayed home because it was the place she liked best. Just as Daddy Gus seemed to need to walk — to roam.

After his death it was easier to see the ways that they complemented and   25
completed each other. For suddenly, without him as a silent backdrop, Baba's spirit was diminished. Something in her was forever lonely and could not find solace. When she died, tulips, her favorite flower, surrounded her. The preacher told us that her death was not an occasion for grief, for "it is hard to live in a world where your choicest friends are gone." Daddy Gus was the companion she missed most. His presence had always been the mirror of memory. Without it there was so much that could not be shared. There was no witness.

Seeing their life together, I learned that it was possible for women and men to fashion households arranged around their own needs. Power was shared. When there was an imbalance, Baba ruled the day. It seemed utterly alien to me to learn about black women and men not making families and homes together. I had not been raised in a world of absent men. One day I knew I would fashion a life using the patterns I inherited from Baba and Daddy Gus. I keep treasures in my cigar box, which still smells after all these years. The quilt that covered me as a child remains, full of ink stains and faded colors. In my trunks are braided tobacco leaves, taken from over home. They keep evil away—keep bad spirits from crossing the threshold, like the ancestors they guard and protect.   [1996]

THINKING ABOUT THE TEXT

1. Do you think hooks is right, that we learn specific life lessons from people in our families? What lessons were you explicitly taught? Are there other, more indirect lessons that you learned from members of your family?

2. Explain the title. What attitude does hooks take toward her grandparents? Does she convince you? What would you think if they were your grandparents?

3. Hooks begins her memoir with a generalization that Baba and Daddy Gus gave her a "worldview that sustained [her] during a difficult and painful childhood" (para. 3). Does she adequately support this idea? How?

4. Writers use specific details about their characters to make them come alive. What are some concrete details or images that you remember about Baba or Daddy Gus? Do these details seem authentic? Is that important?

5. Often a tension exists in families between the roles and personalities members present in their public lives and those they have in their families. Is that the case in this memoir? In what ways might these tensions be good or bad for individual family members? For our culture?

BRENT STAPLES
The Runaway Son

As an editorial writer for the New York Times, *Brent Staples (b. 1951) is an influential commentator on American politics and culture. A proponent of individual effort, Staples resists being reduced to a symbol of African American progress, remembering his childhood as economically stable until marred by his father's alcoholism. After a chaotic family life during his high-school years, he had such little hope of attending college that he did not take the SAT; however, a special program at Philadelphia Military College and Penn Morton College provided needed skills. He earned a B.A. with honors from Widener University (1973) and received a Danforth Fellowship for graduate study at the University of Chicago, where he earned a Ph.D. in psychology (1977). "The Runaway Son" comes from Staple's memoir,* Parallel Time: Growing Up in Black and White *(1994).*

The mother at the beach was supernaturally pale, speaking that blunt Canadian French with a couple on the next blanket. At the market, she wore a business suit and was lost in a dream at the cheese counter. At the museum, the mother was tan and grimly thin, wearing ink-black shades and hissing furiously into a pocket phone. I was watching when each of these women let a small child wander away. The events were years and cities apart, but basically the same each time. I shadowed the child and waited for its absence to hit home. A mother who loses her cub—even for a moment—displays a seizure of panic unique to itself. Those seizures of panic are a specialty of mine. I guess you could say I collect them.

This morning I am walking to the doctor's office, brooding about mortality and the yearly finger up the butt. Today's mother has flaming red hair and is standing on the steps, riffling her bag for keys. Her little girl is no more than four—with the same creamy face, trimmed in ringlets of red. The mother's hair is thick and shoulder length, blocking her view as she leans over the bag. The child drifts down the steps and stands on the sidewalk. Idling as children do, she crosses to the curb and stares dreamily into traffic. Three people pass her without breaking stride. A pair of teenagers with backpacks. A homeless man pushing a junk-laden shopping cart. A businessman, who glances up at the woman's legs and marches onward.

For some people a four-year-old beyond its mother's reach is invisible. For me that child is the axis of the world. Should I run to her, pull her back from the curb? Should I yell in crude Brooklynese, "Hey lady, look out for the friggin' kid!" Nearing the child, I croon in sweet falsetto, "Hey honey, let's wait for Mommy before you cross." The mention of Mommy freezes her. Up on the steps, the red mane of hair whips hysterically into the air. "Patty, get back here! I told you: Don't go near the street!" The woman thanks me and flushes with embarrassment. I smile—"No trouble at all"—and continue on my way.

Most men past forty dream of muscle tone and sex with exotic strangers. Mine is a constant fantasy of rescue, with a sobbing child as the star. What I tell now is how this came to be.

My parents were children when they married. She was eighteen. He was twenty-two. The ceremony was performed in the log house where my mother was born and where she, my grandmother Mae, and my great-grandmother Luella still lived, in the foothills of the Blue Ridge Mountains. I visited the house often as a small child. The only surviving picture shows a bewildered toddler sitting in the grass, staring fixedly at an unknown something in the distance. My great-grandmother Luella was a tall, raw-boned woman with a mane of hair so long she had to move it aside to sit down. Her daughter, my Grandma Mae, wore tight dresses that showed off her bosoms and a string of dead foxes that trailed from her shoulder. The beady eyes of the foxes were frightening when she bent to kiss me.

The log house had no running water, no electricity. At night I bathed in a metal washtub set near the big, wood-burning stove. Once washed, I got into my white dressing gown and prepared for the trip to the outhouse. My grandmother held a hurricane lamp out of the back door to light the way. The path was long and dark and went past the cornfield where all the monsters were. I could tell they were there, hidden behind the first row, by the way the corn squeaked and rustled as I passed. Most feared among them were the snakes that turned themselves into hoops and rolled after you at tremendous speed, thrashing through the corn as they came.

The outhouse itself was dank and musty. While sitting on the toilet I tried as much as possible to keep the lamp in view through cracks in the outhouse wall. The trip back to the log house was always the worst; the monsters gathered in the corn to ambush me, their groaning, growling reaching a crescendo as they prepared to spring. I ran for the light and landed in the kitchen panting and out of breath.

My father's clan, the Staples of Troutville, had an indoor toilet. My paternal great-grandparents, John Wesley and Eliza Staples, were people of substance in the Roanoke valley. In the 1920s, when folks still went about on horseback, John Wesley burst on the scene in a Model T Ford with all the extras—and let it be known that he paid for the car in cash. Though not an educated man, he could read and write. He was vain of his writing: he scribbled even grocery lists with flourish, pausing often to lick the pencil point. There was no school for black children at that time. And so John Wesley and his two immediate neighbors built one at the intersection of their three properties. Then they retained the teacher who worked in it.

The Pattersons were rich in love, but otherwise broke. This made my mother's marriage to a Staples man seem a fine idea. But domestic stability was not my father's experience, the role of husband and father not one that he could play. His own father, John Wesley's son Marshall, had routinely disappeared on payday and reappeared drunk and broke several days later. He abandoned the family at the start of the Depression, leaving Grandma Ada with four children in hand and one—my father—on the way. Ada had no choice but to place her children with relatives and go north, looking for work.

The luckiest of my uncles landed with John Wesley and Eliza. My father 10
came to rest in hell on earth: the home of Ada's father, Tom Perdue. Three wives preceded Tom into the grave and the family lore was that he worked them to death. He hired out his sons for farmwork and collected their pay, leaving them with nothing. My father was beaten for wetting the bed and forced to sleep on a pallet under the kitchen sink. He left school at third grade and became part of Tom's dark enterprise. Birthdays went by unnoted. Christmas meant a new pair of work boots—if that. Had it not been for my father and a younger cousin, Tom would have died with no one to note his passing.

This childhood left its mark. My father distrusted affection and what there was of it he pushed away. He looked suspicious when you hugged or kissed him—as though doubting that affection was real. The faculty for praising us was dead in him. I could choose any number of examples from childhood, but permit me to skip ahead to college. I was obsessed with achievement and made the dean's list nearly every semester. My father was mute on the subject—and never once said "good job." Finally, I achieved the perfect semester—an A in every subject—with still not a word from him. Years later, I found that he had carried my grades in his wallet and bragged on them to strangers at truck stops.

My father worked as a truck driver; he earned a handsome salary, then tried to drink it up. My mother mishandled what was left. How could she do otherwise when money was a mystery to her? She grew up in a barter economy, where one farmer's milk bought another's eggs and the man who butchered the hogs was paid in port. She stared at dollar bills as though awaiting divine instruction on how to spend them.

I grew up in a household on the verge of collapse, the threat of eviction ever present, the utilities subject to cutoff at any moment. Gas was cheap and therefore easy to regain. The water company had pity on us and relented when we made even token efforts to pay. But the electric company had no heart to harden. We lived in darkness for weeks at a time. While our neighbors' houses were blazing with light, we ate, played, and bathed in the sepia glow of hurricane lamps. My mother made the darkness into a game. Each night before bed, she assembled us in a circle on the floor, with a hurricane lamp at the center. First she told a story, then had each of us tell one. Those too young to tell stories sang songs. I looked forward to the circle and my brothers' and sisters' faces in the lamplight. The stories I told were the first stirrings of the writer in me.

On Saturday night my father raged through the house hurling things at the walls. Sunday morning would find him placid, freshly shaven, and in his favorite chair, the air around him singing with Mennon Speed Stick and Old Spice Cologne. At his feet were stacked the Sunday papers, *The Philadelphia Bulletin* and *The Philadelphia Inquirer*. I craved his attention but I was wary of him; it was never clear who he would be.

On a table nearby was a picture of him when he was in the navy and not yet   15 twenty years old. He was wearing dress whites, with his cap tilted snappily back on his head, his hand raised in a salute. He smiled a rich expansive smile that spread to every corner of his face. A hardness had undermined the smile and limited its radius. His lips — full and fleshy in the picture — were tense and narrow by comparison. The picture showed a carefree boy — free of terrible Tom — on the verge of a life filled with possibility. Ten years later those possibilities had all been exhausted. He was knee-deep in children, married to a woman he no longer loved but lacked the courage to leave. The children were coming fast. We were three, then five, then nine.

Our first neighborhood was called The Hill, a perfect place for a young mother with a large family and an unreliable husband. The men went to work at the shipyard and brought home hefty paychecks that easily supported an entire household. The women stayed home to watch and dote on the children. Not just their own, but all of us. Many of these women were no happier than my mother. They had husbands who beat them; husbands who took lovers within full view of their neighbors; husbands who drove them crazy in any number of ways. The women submerged their suffering in love for children. There was no traffic to speak of, and we played for hours in the streets. A child five years old passed easily from its mother's arms into the arms of the neighborhood. Eyes were on us at every moment. We'd be playing with broken glass when a voice rang out from nowhere: "Y'all stop that and play nice!" We'd be transfixed by the sight of wet cement, ripe for writing curse words, when the voice rang out again: "Y'all get away from that cement. Mr. Prince paid good money to have that done!" Women on errands patroled the sidewalks and made them unsafe for fighting. Every woman had license to discipline a child caught in the wrong. We feigned the deepest remorse, hopeful that the report would not reach our mothers.

Everyone on The Hill grew some kind of fruit; my gang was obsessed with stealing it. We prowled hungrily at people's fences, eyeing their apples, pears, and especially their peaches. We were crazed to get at them, even when they were tiny and bitter and green. We turned surly when there was no fruit at all. Then we raided gardens where people grew trumpet flowers, which gave a sweet nectar when you sucked them. The flowers were enormous and bright orange. When the raid was finished, the ground would be covered with them.

I lost The Hill when my family was evicted. We landed miles away in the Polish West End. The Poles and Ukrainians had once ruled much of the city. They had surrendered it street by street and were now confined to the westernmost neighborhood, their backs pressed to the city limits.

My family had crossed the color line. The people who lived in the house before us had been black as well. But they were all adults. After them, my brothers and sisters must have seemed an invading army.

The Polish and Ukrainian kids spelled their names exotically and ate unpronounceable foods. They were Catholics and on certain Wednesdays wore ashes on their foreheads. On Fridays they were forbidden to eat meat. When you walked by their churches you caught a glimpse of a priest swinging incense at the end of a chain. I wanted to know all there was to know about them. That I was their neighbor entitled me to it. 20

The Polish and Ukrainian boys did not agree. The first week was a series of fights, one after another. They despised us, as did their parents and grandparents. I gave up trying to know them and played alone. Deprived of friends, I retreated into comic books. My favorite hero was the Silver Surfer, bald and naked to his silver skin, riding a surfboard made of the same silver stuff. The comic's most perfect panels showed the seamless silver body flashing through space on the board. No words; just the long view of the Surfer hurtling past planets and stars.

My fantasies of escape centered on airplanes; I was drunk with the idea of flying. At home, I labored over model planes until the glue made me dizzy. At school, I made planes out of notebook paper and crammed them into my pockets and books. I was obsessed with movies about aerial aces and studied them carefully, prepping for the acehood that I'd been born to and that was destined to be mine. I planned to join the air force when I graduated from high school. The generals would already have heard of me; my jet would be warming up on the runway.

My favorite plane was a wooden Spitfire with British Air Force markings and a propeller powered by a rubber band. I was flying it one day when it landed in the yard of a Ukrainian boy whose nose I had bloodied. His grandfather was gardening when the plane touched down on the neatly kept lawn. He seized the plane, sputtered at me in Ukrainian, and disappeared into the house. A few minutes later one of his older grandsons delivered what was left of it. The old man had destroyed it with malevolent purpose. The wings and fuselage were broken the long way, twice. The pieces were the width of popsicle sticks and wrapped in the rubber band. This was the deepest cruelty I had known.

My mother suffered too. She missed her friends on The Hill, but we were too far west for them to reach us easily. She was learning how difficult it was to care for us on her own, especially since there were few safe places to play. The new house sat on a truck route. Forty-foot semis thundered by, spewing smoke and rattling windows. My mother lived in terror of the traffic and forbade us to roller-skate even on the sidewalk. On The Hill, she had swept off on errands confident that we would be fine. In the Polish West End, she herded us into the house and told us to stay there until she got back.

The house had become a prison. My eldest sister, Yvonne, was thirteen years   25
old—and the first to escape. She stayed out later and later and finally disappeared for days at a time. My mother strapped her. My father threatened her with the juvenile home. But Yvonne met their anger with steeliness. When they questioned her she went dumb and stared into space. I knew the look from prisoner-of-war movies; do your worst, it said, I will tell you nothing. She lied casually and with great skill. But I was an expert listener, determined to break the code. The lie had a strained lightness, the quality of cotton candy. I recognized that sound when she said, "Mom, I'll be right back, I'm going out to the store." I followed her. She passed the store and started across town just as I thought she would. I trotted after her, firing questions. "Where do you think you're going? What is on your mind? What are you trying to do to yourself?" I was my mother's son and accepted all she told me about the dangers of the night. Girls became sluts at night. Boys got into fights and went to jail. These hazards meant nothing to Yvonne; she ignored me and walked on. I yelled "Slut! Street dog!" She lunged at me, but I dodged out of reach. "Slut" I had gotten from my mother. But "street dog" was an original, I'd made it up on the spur of the moment. I had become the child parent. I could scold and insult—but I was too young and ill-formed to instruct. I relished the role; it licensed me to be judge and disparage people I envied but lacked the courage to imitate.

Yvonne was wild to get away. You turned your back and—POOF!—she was gone. Finally she stayed away for days that stretched into weeks and then months. There was no sign or word of her. My mother was beaten up with worry. By night she walked the floors, tilting at every sound in the street.

What is it like to be one of nine children, to be tangled in arms and legs in bed and at the dinner table? My brothers and sisters were part of my skin; you only notice your skin when something goes wrong with it. My youngest brother, Blake, got infections that dulled his hearing and closed his ears to the size of pin-holes. Bruce broke his arm—while playing in the safety of our treeless and boring backyard. Sherri began to sleepwalk, once leaping down a flight of stairs. Every illness and injury and visit to the hospital involved me. I was first assistant mother now, auxiliary parent in every emergency.

My five-year-old sister Christi was burned nearly to death. Her robe caught fire at the kitchen stove. I was upstairs in my room when it happened. First I heard the scream. Then came thunder of feet below me, and soon after the sound of the ambulance. The doctors did the best they could and gave the rest up to God.

The sign at the nurses' station said that no one under sixteen could visit. I was only eleven; with Yvonne missing, I was as close to sixteen as the children got. I knew that Christi had been brought back from the dead. What I saw the first day added mightily to that awareness. A domed frame had been built over the bed to keep the sheets from touching the burns. Peering under the dome, I saw her wrapped in gauze, round and round the torso, round and round each leg, like a mummy. Blood seeped through the bandages where the burns were deepest. The burns that I could see outside the bandages didn't look too bad. The skin was blackened, but bearable.

Eventually she was allowed to sit up. I would arrive to find her in her bright white gauze suit, sitting in a child's rocking chair. I got used to the gauze. Then they took it off to air out the wounds. Her body was raw from the breast to below the knee. The flesh was wet and bloody in places; I could see the blood pulsing beneath what had been her skin. The room wobbled, but I kept smiling and tried to be natural. I walked in a wide circle around her that day, afraid that I would brush against her. I got past even this, because Christi smiled interminably. The nerve endings were dead and she felt nothing. In time I grew accustomed to flesh without skin.

Christi's injuries were the worst on the ward. Next to the burns everything else was easy to look at. I was especially interested in the boy with the steel rods jutting out of his leg. He'd been hit by a car, and the bone was shattered. He didn't talk much, but the rods in his legs were fascinating. The skin clung to them like icing to the candies on a cake.

The children's ward was sparsely visited on weekdays. I cruised the room, cooing at toddlers and making jokes with frightened newcomers. On weekends the ward filled up with parents, highlighting the fact that I was eleven years old — and that my own parents were elsewhere. When real parents visited, I felt like a fraud. I clung to Christi's bedside and did not stray. I wished that the scene at Christi's bed was like the scene around the other beds: fathers, mothers, relatives. But that was not to be.

Christi's accident made the world dangerous. When left in charge, I gathered the children in the living room and imprisoned them there. Trips to the bathroom were timed and by permission only. Now and then I imagined the smell of gas and trotted into the kitchen to check the stove. I avoided looking out of windows for fear of daydreaming. Staring at the sky, I punched through it into space and roamed the galaxy with my hero, the Silver Surfer.

I was daydreaming one day when my brother Brian cried out in pain. He had taken a pee and gotten his foreskin snarled in his zipper. He had given a good yank, too, and pulled it nearly halfway up. Every step tugged at the zipper and caused him to scream. I cut off the pants and left just the zipper behind. To keep his mind off his troubles and kill time until my parents got home, I plunked out a tune on the piano. The longer they stayed away the more crazed I became.

The days were too full for an eleven-year-old who needed desperately to dream. The coal-fired boiler that heated our house was part of the reason. The fire went out at night, which meant that I built a new fire in the morning: chop kindling; haul ashes; shovel coal. Then it was up from the basement, to iron shirts, polish shoes, make sandwiches, and pack the school lunches. My mother tried to sweeten the jobs by describing them as "little": "Build a little fire to throw the chill off of the house." But there was no such thing as a "little" fire. Every fire required the same backbreaking work. Chop kindling. Chop wood. Shovel coal. Haul ashes. One morning she said, "Put a little polish on the toe of your brother's shoes." I dipped the applicator into the liquid polish and dabbed the tiniest spot on the top of each shoe. Yvonne's departure had left my mother brittle and on the edge of violence. I knew this but couldn't stop myself. She was making breakfast when I presented her with the shoes, which were still scuffed and unpolished. "I told you to polish those shoes," she said. "No, you didn't," I said, "you said 'put a little polish on the toe.'" She snapped at me. I snapped back. Then she lifted the serving platter and smashed it across my head.

My father was drinking more than ever. Debt mounted in the customary pattern. We pushed credit to the limit at one store, then abandoned the bills and moved on to the next. Mine was the face of the family's debt. I romanced the shop owners into giving us food and coal on time, then tiptoed past their windows to put the bite on the next guy. When gas and electricity were cut off, I traveled across town to plead with the utility companies. The account executives were mainly women with soft spots for little boys. I conned them, knowing we would never pay. We were behind in the rent and would soon be evicted. Once settled elsewhere, we would apply for gas and electricity, under a fictitious name.

The only way to get time to myself was to steal it. During the summer, I got up early, dressed with the stealth of a burglar, and tiptoed out of the house. The idea was to get in a full day's play unencumbered by errands or housework. Most days I escaped. On other days my mother's radar was just too good, and her rich contralto came soaring out of the bedroom. "Brent, make sure you're back here in time to . . ." to go shopping, to visit Christi at the hospital, to go a thousand places on a thousand errands.

Inevitably I thought of running away—to Florida. In Florida you could sleep outside, live on fruit from the orange groves, and never have to work. I decided to do it on a snowy Saturday at the start of a blizzard. Thought and impulse were one: I took an orange from the fruit bowl, grabbed my parka from the coat rack, and ran from the house.

I did not get to Florida. In my haste, I had grabbed the coat belonging to my younger brother Brian. It was the same color as mine but too small even to zip up. The freight train I planned to take never left the rail yard. The snow thickened and began to freeze. Numb and disheartened, I headed home.

Five years later I succeeded in running away—this time to college. Widener   40
University was two miles from where my family lived. For all that I visited them, two miles could have been two thousand. I lived at school year round—through holidays, semester breaks, and right through the summer. Alone in bed for the first time, I recognized how crowded my life had been. I enjoyed the campus most when it was deserted. I wandered the dormitory drinking in the space. At night I sat in the stadium, smoking pot and studying the constellations. I never slept with my brothers again.

Years later youngest sister, Yvette, accused me of abandoning the family. But the past is never really past; what we have lived is who we are. I am still the frightened ten-year-old tending babies and waiting for my parents. The sight of a child on its own excludes everything else from view. No reading. No idle conversation. No pretending not to see. I follow and watch and intervene because I have no choice. When next you see a child beyond its mother's reach, scan the crowd for me. I am there, watching you watch the child.   [1994]

THINKING ABOUT THE TEXT

1. "If you hadn't read the first and last sections (paras. 1–4, 41), what would you say Staples's theme is? What generalizations does his narrative evidence point to?

2. Race and class figure in this essay in varying degrees. Explain. Do they figure in your experiences? In those of your friends?

3. Staples begins with three anecdotes about mothers and children, then concludes his first section with his "fantasy of rescue" (para. 4). Is his last paragraph a satisfactory conclusion to this idea?

4. Re-creating the past in nonfiction often involves the same techniques as fiction writing: using the five senses. Find examples of creative touches that you think make the essay real.

5. Do you agree that "the past is never really past" (para. 41)? Are you still somehow a ten-year-old? Is Staples's idea of having "no choice" one you identify with? Since the last paragraph cannot be literally true, what is Staples driving at?

MAKING COMPARISONS

1. Is there something typically male or female about hooks's and Staples's memoirs? For example, how might Staples's childhood experiences have been different for a female?

2. Do you think hooks and Staples would have chosen their childhoods? Be specific about what each might keep or change.

3. What do you think is hooks's and Staples's sense of themselves in these first two essays? Do they seem secure? Happy? Defensive? Proud? Bitter?

N. SCOTT MOMADAY
The Way to Rainy Mountain

Born in 1934 into a Native American family in Oklahoma next to Rainy Mountain, Momaday grew up on a family farm and later on several reservations. Momaday graduated from the University of New Mexico and earned his Ph.D. at Stanford University. He has taught writing at the University of California at Berkeley, Stanford, and currently the University of Arizona. Momaday is a poet and

*novelist as well as an accomplished essayist and painter. He won the Pulitzer Prize
in 1969 for* House Made of Dawn. *Momaday's work celebrates his Native American heritage, about which he writes with reverence and artistic subtlety. The following essay appeared as the introduction to* The Way to Rainy Mountain *(1969), a
collection of Kiowa legends.*

A single knoll rises out of the plain in Oklahoma, north and west of the
Wichita range. For my people, the Kiowas, it is an old landmark, and they gave it
the name Rainy Mountain. The hardest weather in the world is there. Winter
brings blizzards, hot tornadic winds arise in the spring, and in summer the prairie
is an anvil's edge. The grass turns brittle and brown, and it cracks beneath your
feet. There are green belts along the rivers and creeks, linear groves of hickory
and pecan, willow and witch hazel. At a distance in July or August the steaming
foliage seems almost to writhe in fire. Great green and yellow grasshoppers are
everywhere in the tall grass, popping up like corn to sting the flesh, and tortoises
crawl about on the red earth, going nowhere in the plenty of time. Loneliness is
an aspect of the land. All things in the plain are isolate; there is no confusion of
objects in the eye, but *one* hill or *one* tree or *one* man. To look upon that landscape in the early morning, with the sun at your back, is to lose the sense of proportion. Your imagination comes to life, and this, you think, is where Creation
was begun.

I returned to Rainy Mountain in July. My grandmother had died in the
spring, and I wanted to be at her grave. She had lived to be very old and at last
infirm. Her only living daughter was with her when she died, and I was told that
in death her face was that of a child.

I like to think of her as a child. When she was born, the Kiowas were living
the last great moment of their history. For more than a hundred years they had
controlled the open range from the Smoky Hill River to the Red, from the head-
waters of the Canadian to the fork of the Arkansas and Cimarron. In alliance with
the Comanches, they had ruled the whole of the Southern Plains. War was their
sacred business, and they were the finest horsemen the world has ever known.
But warfare for the Kiowas was pre-eminently a matter of disposition rather than
of survival, and they never understood the grim, unrelenting advance of the U.S.
Cavalry. When at last, divided and ill provisioned, they were driven onto the
Staked Plains in the cold of autumn, they fell into panic. In Palo Duro Canyon
they abandoned their crucial stores to pillage and had nothing then but their
lives. In order to save themselves, they surrendered to the soldiers at Fort Sill and
were imprisoned in the old stone corral that now stands as a military museum.
My grandmother was spared the humiliation of those high gray walls by eight or
ten years, but she must have known from birth the affliction of defeat, the dark
brooding of old warriors.

Her name was Aho, and she belonged to the last culture to evolve in North
America. Her forebears came down from the high country in western Montana
nearly three centuries ago. They were a mountain people, a mysterious tribe of

hunters whose language has never been classified in any major group. In the late seventeenth century they began a long migration to the south and east. It was a journey toward the dawn, and it led to a golden age. Along the way the Kiowas were befriended by the Crows, who gave them the culture and religion of the Plains. They acquired horses, and their ancient nomadic spirit was suddenly free of the ground. They acquired Tai-me, the sacred sun-dance doll, from that moment the object and symbol of their worship, and so shared in the divinity of the sun. Not least, they acquired the sense of destiny, therefore courage and pride. When they entered upon the Southern Plains they had been transformed. No longer were they slaves to the simple necessity of survival; they were a lordly and dangerous society of fighters and thieves, hunters and priests of the sun. According to their origin myth, they entered the world through a hollow log. From one point of view, their migration was the fruit of an old prophecy, for indeed they emerged from a sunless world.

5 Though my grandmother lived out her long life in the shadow of Rainy Mountain, the immense landscape of the continental interior lay like memory in her blood. She could tell of the Crows, whom she had never seen, and of the Black Hills, where she had never been. I wanted to see in reality what she had seen more perfectly in the mind's eye, and drove fifteen hundred miles to begin my pilgrimage.

A dark mist lay over the Black Hills, and the land was like iron. At the top of a ridge I caught sight of Devil's Tower upthrust against the gray sky as if in the birth of time the core of the earth had broken through its crust and the motion of the world was begun. There are things in nature that engender an awful quiet in the heart of man; Devil's Tower is one of them. Two centuries ago, because of their need to explain it, the Kiowas made a legend at the base of the rock. My grandmother said:

"Eight children were there at play, seven sisters and their brother. Suddenly the boy was struck dumb; he trembled and began to run upon his hands and feet. His fingers became claws, and his body was covered with fur. There was a bear where the boy had been. The sisters were terrified; they ran, and the bear after them. They came to the stump of a great tree, and the tree spoke to them. It bade them climb upon it, and as they did so, it began to rise into the air. The bear came to kill them, but they were just beyond its reach. It reared against the tree and scored the bark all around with its claws. The seven sisters were borne into the sky, and they became the stars of the Big Dipper." From that moment, and so long as the legend lives, the Kiowas have kinsmen in the night sky. Whatever they were in the mountains, they could be no more. However tenuous their well-being, however much they had suffered and would suffer again, they had found a way out of the wilderness.

My grandmother had a reverence for the sun, a holy regard that now is all but gone out of mankind. There was a wariness in her, and an ancient awe. She was a Christian in her later years, but she had come a long way about, and she never forgot her birthright. As a child she had been to the sun dances; she had taken part in that annual rite, and by it she had learned the restoration of her people in the presence of Tai-me. She was about seven when the last Kiowa sun dance was held in 1887 on the Washita River above Rainy Mountain Creek. The buffalo were gone. In order to consummate the ancient sacrifice — to impale the head of a buffalo bull upon the Tai-me tree — a delegation of old men journeyed into Texas, there to beg and barter for an animal from the Goodnight herd. She was ten when the Kiowas came together for the last time as a living sun-dance culture. They could find no buffalo; they had to hang an old hide from the sacred tree. Before the dance could begin, a company of soldiers rode out from Fort Sill under orders to disperse the tribe. Forbidden without cause the essential act of their faith, having seen the wild herds slaughtered and left to rot upon the ground, the Kiowas backed away forever from the tree. That was July 20, 1890, at the great bend of the Washita. My grandmother was there. Without bitterness, and for as long as she lived, she bore a vision of deicide.

Now that I can have her only in memory, I see my grandmother in the several postures that were peculiar to her: standing at the wood stove on a winter morning and turning meat in a great iron skillet; sitting at the south window, bent above her beadwork, and afterwards, when her vision failed, looking down for a long time into the fold of her hands; going out upon a cane, very slowly as she did when the weight of age came upon her; praying. I remember her most often at prayer. She made long, rambling prayers out of suffering and hope, having seen many things. I was never sure that I had the right to hear, so exclusive were they of all mere custom and company. The last time I saw her she prayed standing by the side of the bed at night, naked to the waist, the light of a kerosene lamp moving upon her dark skin. Her long black hair, always drawn and braided in the day, lay upon her shoulders and against her breasts like a shawl. I do not speak Kiowa, and I never understood her prayers, but there was something inherently sad in the sound, some merest hesitation upon the syllables of sorrow. She began in a high and descending pitch, exhausting her breath to silence; then again and again — and always the same intensity of effort, of something that is, and is not, like urgency in the human voice. Transported so in the dancing light among the shadows of her room, she seemed beyond the reach of time. But that was illusion; I think I knew then that I should not see her again.

Houses are like sentinels in the plain, old keepers of the weather watch. There,   10
in a very little while, wood takes on the appearance of great age. All colors wear soon away in the wind and rain, and then the wood is burned gray and the grain appears and the nails turn red with rust. The window panes are black and opaque; you imagine there is nothing within, and indeed there are many ghosts, bones given up to the land. They stand here and there against the sky, and you approach them for a longer time than you expect. They belong in the distance; it is their domain.

Once there was a lot of sound in my grandmother's house, a lot of coming and going, feasting and talk. The summers there were full of excitement and reunion. The Kiowas are a summer people; they abide the cold and keep to themselves, but when the season turns and the land becomes warm and vital they cannot hold still; an old love of going returns upon them. The aged visitors who came to my grandmother's house when I was a child were made of lean and leather, and they bore themselves upright. They wore great black hats and bright ample shirts that shook in the wind. They rubbed fat upon their hair and wound their braids with strips of colored cloth. Some of them painted their faces and carried the scars of old and cherished enmities. They were an old council of warlords, come to remind and be reminded of who they were. Their wives and daughters served them well. The women might indulge themselves; gossip was at once the mark and compensation of their servitude. They made loud and elaborate talk among themselves, full of jest and gesture, fright and false alarm. They went abroad in fringed and flowered shawls, bright beadwork and German silver. They were at home in the kitchen, and they prepared meals that were banquets.

There were frequent prayer meetings, and nocturnal feasts. When I was a child I played with my cousins outside, where the lamplight fell upon the ground and the singing of the old people rose up around us and carried away into the darkness. There were a lot of good things to eat, a lot of laughter and surprise. And afterwards, when the quiet returned, I lay down with my grandmother and could hear the frogs away by the river and feel the motion of the air.

Now there is a funereal silence in the rooms, the endless wake of some final word. The walls have closed in upon my grandmother's house. When I returned to it in mourning, I saw for the first time in my life how small it was. It was late at night, and there was a white moon, nearly full. I sat for a long time on the stone steps by the kitchen door. From there I could see out across the land; I could see the long row of trees by the creek, the low light upon the rolling plains, and the stars of the Big Dipper. Once I looked at the moon and caught sight of a strange thing. A cricket had perched upon the handrail, only a few inches away. My line of vision was such that the creature filled the moon like a fossil. It had gone there, I thought to live and die, for there, of all places, was its small definition made whole and eternal. A warm wind rose up and purled like the longing within me.

The next morning, I awoke at dawn and went out on the dirt road to Rainy Mountain. It was already hot and the grasshoppers began to fill the air. Still, it was early in the morning, and birds sang out of the shadows. The long yellow grass on the mountain shone in the bright light, and a scissortail hied above the land. There, where it ought to be, at the end of a long and legendary way, was my grandmother's grave. She had at last succeeded to that holy ground. Here and there on the dark stones were ancestral names. Looking back once, I saw the mountain and came away.   [1969]

THINKING ABOUT THE TEXT

1. Momaday wants to "see in reality" the things his grandmother described, so he travels "fifteen hundred miles to begin [his] pilgrimage" (para. 5). Is he successful in this quest? What does it mean to see as someone else has seen? How would you know if you had succeeded?

2. Momaday mixes memoir, folklore, myth, history, and personal reflections in this essay. Does he successfully blend these genres? What is Momaday's aim in each? How does he achieve coherence?

3. Critics claim that Momaday treats his grandmother's memory with tenderness and reverence. Can you cite specific examples of this attitude?

4. What specific attitudes or values of his grandmother's world does Momaday seem to miss? Does he share some of these values? Would our culture benefit from adopting the attitudes of the Kiowas, or is that impossible now?

5. How would you describe Momaday's attitude in the beginning of the penultimate paragraph?

MAKING COMPARISONS

1. Momaday doesn't seem to reveal his own feeling as much as bell hooks and Brent Staples? Do you agree?

2. Make a brief list of what you think hooks, Staples, and Momaday learn from members of their families.

3. How would you characterize these three writers' attitudes toward the past? Does sentimentality play a role? Nostalgia? Resentment? Regret?

WRITING ABOUT ISSUES

1. Argue in a brief essay that one can or cannot get beyond the past. Use concrete examples.

2. Argue that difficulties in one's childhood are not necessarily a negative influence.

3. Write a personal essay that imitates the general structure of hooks's, Staples's, or Momaday's essay.

4. Find another essay by each of these writers and write a brief report about its concerns.

RECONCILING WITH FATHERS

LUCILLE CLIFTON, "forgiving my father"
ROBERT HAYDEN, "Those Winter Sundays"
THEODORE ROETHKE, "My Papa's Waltz"
SHIRLEY GEOK-LIN LIM, "Father from Asia"

In childhood, our emotions are often intense. Fears about life arise because we feel so powerless. For some of us, our fathers held all the power. Fathers may use their power in various ways, some to control or abuse, others to comfort and protect. We form perceptions about our fathers from these early memories. Often we become judgmental about their failures in the world or their failures as parents. As we grow older, we sometimes come to terms with our fathers and see them simply as human beings with strengths and weaknesses. But it is not always so simple;

some wounds may be too deep for us to reconcile. The four poets in this cluster approach memories of their fathers with different perspectives and purposes: Some want to forgive, others will not.

BEFORE YOU READ

Make a list of four strong memories about your father from your childhood. Are the memories positive or not? Can you remember how you felt then? Is it different from how you feel now? How can you explain the difference?

LUCILLE CLIFTON

forgiving my father

Born in 1936 in a small town near Buffalo, New York, Lucille Clifton attended Howard University and Fredonia State Teacher's College and has taught poetry at a number of universities. Her numerous awards for writing include two Creative Writing Fellowships from the National Endowment for the Arts (1970 and 1973), two Pulitzer Prize nominations (for Good Woman: Poems and a Memoir *and for* Next, *both in 1988), several major poetry awards, and an Emmy. The mother of six, Clifton's works include fifteen children's books. She is a former poet laureate of Maryland and has been the Distinguished Professor of Humanities at St. Mary's College since 1991. "Forgiving my father" is from her 1980 book* Two-Headed Woman.

it is friday. we have come
to the paying of the bills.
all week you have stood in my dreams
like a ghost, asking for more time
but today is payday, payday old man,   5
my mother's hand opens in her early grave
and i hold it out like a good daughter.

there is no more time for you. there will
never be time enough daddy daddy old lecher
old liar. i wish you were rich so i could take it all   10
and give the lady what she was due
but you were the son of a needy father,
the father of a needy son,
you gave her all you had
which was nothing. you have already given her   15
all you had.

you are the pocket that was going to open
and come up empty any friday.

you were each other's bad bargain, not mine.
daddy old pauper   old prisoner,   old dead man   20
what am i doing here collecting?
you like side by side in debtor's boxes
and no accounting will open them up.   [1980]

THINKING ABOUT THE TEXT

1. How might you answer the question in line 21? Are the last two lines of the poem a kind of answer? Is there some way we can "collect" from the dead?

2. Should we "bury the dead," that is, should we let the past go and let bygones be bygones? Or is it necessary to "settle old scores"? What do you think Clifton's answer would be?

3. How consistently does Clifton use the payday analogy? Make a list of words that reinforce her overall scheme.

4. Would you think differently about the speaker's father if Clifton had written "elderly one" instead of "old man" (line 5) or "old playboy / old fibber" instead of "old lecher / old liar" (lines 9–10)?

5. Some readers look for tensions or contradictions early in a poem, hoping they will be resolved at the end. Does this poem end in a resolution of paying up and forgiving?

ROBERT HAYDEN
Those Winter Sundays

Born in Detroit, Michigan, African American poet Robert Hayden (1913–1980) grew up in a poor neighborhood where he was left by his natural parents with family friends. He grew up with the Hayden name, not discovering his original name until he was forty. Hayden attended Detroit City College (now Wayne State University) from 1932 to 1936, worked in the Federal Writer's Project, and later earned his M.A. at the University of Michigan in 1944. He taught at Fisk University from 1946 to 1968 and at the University of Michigan from 1968 to 1980 and published several collections of poetry. Although his poems sometimes contain autobiographical elements, Hayden is primarily a formalist poet who preferred that his poems not be limited to personal or ethnic interpretations. "Those Winter Sundays" is from Angle of Ascent *(1966).*

Sundays too my father got up early
and put his clothes on in the blueblack cold,
then with cracked hands that ached
from labor in the weekday weather made
banked fires blaze. No one ever thanked him.   5

♦ ♦ ♦

I'd wake and hear the cold splintering, breaking.
When the rooms were warm, he'd call,
and slowly I would rise and dress,
fearing the chronic angers of that house,

Speaking indifferently to him,   10
who had driven out the cold
and polished my good shoes as well.
What did I know, what did I know
of love's austere and lonely offices?   [1962]

THINKING ABOUT THE TEXT

1. Is the concluding question meant rhetorically; that is, is the answer so obvious no real reply is expected? Write a response you think the son would give now.

2. Why did the children never thank their father? Is this common? What specific things might you thank your father (or mother) for? Do parents have some basic responsibilities to their children that do not warrant thanks?

3. Is there evidence that the son loves his father now? Did he then? Why did he speak "indifferently" to his father? Is it clear what the "chronic angers" are? Should it be?

4. How might you fill in the gaps here? For example, how old do you think the boy is? How old is the father? What kind of a job might he have? What else can you infer?

5. What is the speaker's tone? Is he hoping for your understanding? Your sympathy? Are we responsible for the things we do in childhood? Is this speaker repentant or simply explaining?

MAKING COMPARISONS

1. What degrees of forgiveness do you see in Clifton's and Hayden's poems?

2. Writing a poem for one's father seems different from writing a poem about him. Explain in reference to these poems.

3. Compare the purpose of the questions in each poem. How might each poet answer the other poet's questions?

THEODORE ROETHKE
My Papa's Waltz

Born in Saginaw, Michigan, Theodore Roethke (1908–1963) was strongly influenced by childhood experiences with his father, a usually stern man who sold plants and flowers and who kept a large greenhouse, the setting for many of Roethke's poems. Theodore Roethke was educated at the University of Michigan, took courses at Harvard, and taught at several universities before becoming poet-in-residence at the University of Washington in 1948. Roethke's books include The Lost Son and Other Poems *(1949), the source for "My Papa's Waltz,"* The Waking *(1953), which won a Pulitzer Prize, and* Words for the Wind *(1958), which won the National Book Award. Roethke's intensely personal style insures his place among the most influential postmodern American poets.*

The whiskey on your breath
Could make a small boy dizzy;
But I hung on like death:
Such waltzing was not easy.

We romped until the pans   5
Slid from the kitchen shelf;
My mother's countenance
Could not unfrown itself.

The hand that held my wrist
Was battered on one knuckle;   10
At every step you missed
My right ear scraped a buckle.

You beat time on my head
With a palm caked hard by dirt,
Then waltzed me off to bed   15
Still clinging to your shirt.   [1948]

THINKING ABOUT THE TEXT

1. Is the narrator looking back at his father with fondness? Bitterness?

2. Would the poem make a different impression if we changed "romped" to "fought" and "waltz" to "danced"?

3. Why did the boy hang on and cling to his father? From fear? From affection?

4. What is the mother's role here? How would you characterize her frown?

5. Readers often have a negative view of the relationship represented here, but many change their minds, seeing some positive aspects to the father and son's waltz. How might you account for this revision?

MAKING COMPARISONS

1. Would you have read this poem differently if the poet had used Clifton's title "forgiving my father"?

2. How would you compare the tone of Roethke's poem with that of Hayden's? Do they miss their fathers?

3. Would you say that Roethke has more complex feelings about his father, whereas Clifton and Hayden seem clearer?

SHIRLEY GEOK-LIN LIM
Father from Asia

Born in 1944 in Malacca, Malaysia, Shirley Geok-lin Lim attended the University of Malaysia and came to study in the United States in the 1960s; she earned a Ph.D. from Brandeis University in 1971. Of her four published books of poetry, Crossing the Peninsula *won the Commonwealth Poetry Prize in 1980, a first both for an Asian and for a woman. Her published works include two short-story collections and several editions of critical studies and anthologies focusing on gender and Asian American issues, including* The Forbidden Stitch: An Asian American Women's Anthology *(1989), which won an American Book Award. She is a professor of English at the University of California at Santa Barbara. The poem that follows is from* Crossing the Peninsula.

Father, you turn your hands toward me.
Large hollow bowls, they are empty
stigmata of poverty. Light pours
through them, and I back away,
for you are dangerous, father   5
of poverty, father of ten children,
father of nothing, from whose life
I have learned nothing for myself.
You are the father of childhood,
father from Asia, father of sacrifice.   10
I renounce you, keep you in my sleep,
keep you two oceans away, ghost
who eats his own children,
Asia who loved his children,
who didn't know abandonment,   15
father who lived at the center of the world,
whose life I dare not remember,
for memory is a wheel that crushes,
and Asia is dust, is dust.   [1980]

THINKING ABOUT THE TEXT

1. What does "I renounce you" (line 11) mean? If the speaker renounces her father, why does the line end with "keep you in my sleep"?

2. If you were to write a poem about your father, would it be for you? For him? For someone else? Do you think poets write for a specific audience or only for themselves? Which does Lim do?

3. "Father of nothing" (line 7) seems harsh. Does Lim mean it to be? Is "ghost who eats his own children" (lines 12–13) hyperbolic, that is, a deliberate overstatement?

4. Why does Lim compare the father's hands to bowls? What other metaphors does she use? Rewrite the last line, being explicit about what you think she means.

5. Lim's speaker says she "learned nothing" from her father's life. Is this possible? Is memory "a wheel that crushes" (line 18)? Is this poem a remembrance? Can we escape the past? Should we? Does the speaker?

MAKING COMPARISONS

1. Is Lim's speaker angrier than Clifton's, Hayden's, or Roethke's? Is there a resolution in Lim's poem? Is there in the other three poems?

2. Clifton's speaker seems to be forgiving her father for something. Is Lim's forgiving her father? Is Hayden's? Roethke's?

3. Which speaker's attitude seems the healthiest? Which the least?

WRITING ABOUT ISSUES

1. Choose one of the four preceding poems to argue that our feelings for our fathers are complex, not simple.

2. Jean-Paul Sartre writes in *Words* (1964) that "there is no good father, that is the rule." Use examples from the four poems to argue that this is, or is not, the case.

3. Do you think all children leave childhood or adolescence with unresolved tensions in their relationships with their fathers? Write a personal narrative that confronts this idea.

4. Locate at least six more poems that deal with memories of fathers. Write a brief report, noting the similarities to the four poems given here.

EXORCISING THE DEAD:
CRITICAL COMMENTARIES ON SYLVIA PLATH'S "DADDY"

SYLVIA PLATH, "Daddy"

CRITICAL COMMENTARIES:
MARY LYNN BROE, From *Protean Poetic: The Poetry of Sylvia Plath*
LYNDA K. BUNDTZEN, From *Plath's Incarnations*
STEVEN GOULD AXELROD, From *Sylvia Plath: The Wound and the Cure of Words*

As contradictory as it might seem, we sometimes get angry when someone close to us dies. Psychologists tell us that anger is a healthy emotion in the mourning process, following sorrow and preceding acceptance: It is painful to miss loved ones, and we resent it. We might even direct the anger at them, feeling as if they are responsible for depriving us of their love. Sometimes, however, this anger lingers on long after the normal grieving process is over. Perhaps the attachment was abnormally strong, or the person's own life is too unstable to follow through to reach the final acceptance stage.

In the following poem, Sylvia Plath writes about her dead father as if he were a terrible person, even though as a young girl she seems to have adored him. Perhaps she is trying to expel his memory so she can find peace; perhaps she is using the poem as an occasion to express a deeper meaning about authority or influence from the past. Regardless, the poem is a powerful, strange, and passionate work of art.

BEFORE YOU READ

Does it make sense to you that we might get angry at those who die because they have somehow deserted us? Do you think we have to "work out" the tensions between us and our parents before we can move into adulthood? Might it be healthy to exaggerate the difficulties of our childhood in poems and stories?

SYLVIA PLATH
Daddy

Born to middle-class parents in suburban New York, Sylvia Plath (1932–1963) became known as an intensely emotional "confessional" poet whose work is primarily autobiographical. Her father, a professor of biology and German, died when she was eight, the year her first poem was published. She graduated with honors from Smith College in 1950, after an internship at Mademoiselle *and a suicide attempt in her junior year, experiences described in her novel* The Bell Jar *(1963). She won a Fulbright Scholarship to study at Cambridge, England, where she met and married poet Ted Hughes. The couple had two children; the marriage ended the year before her suicide in 1963. "Daddy" is from* Ariel, *published posthumously in 1965.*

You do not do, you do not do
Any more, black shoe
In which I have lived like a foot
For thirty years, poor and white,
Barely daring to breathe or Achoo.   5

Daddy, I have had to kill you.
You died before I had time —
Marble-heavy, a bag full of God,
Ghastly statue with one gray toe
Big as a Frisco seal   10

◆ ◆ ◆

And a head in the freakish Atlantic
Where it pours bean green over blue
In the waters off beautiful Nauset.°   *Cape Cod inlet*
I used to pray to recover you.
Ach, du.°   *Oh, you*   15

In the German tongue, in the Polish Town°
Scraped flat by the roller
Of wars, wars, wars.
But the name of the town is common.
My Polack friend   20

Says there are a dozen or two.
So I never could tell where you
Put your foot, your root,
I never could talk to you.
The tongue stuck in my jaw.   25

It stuck in a barb wire snare.
Ich, ich, ich, ich,°   *I, I, I, I*
I could hardly speak.
I thought every German was you.
And the language obscene   30

An engine, an engine
Chuffing me off like a Jew.
A Jew to Dachau, Auschwitz, Belsen.°
I began to talk like a Jew.
I think I may well be a Jew.   35

The snows of the Tyrol, the clear beer of Vienna
Are not very pure or true.
With my gypsy-ancestress and my weird luck
And my Taroc° pack and my Taroc pack
I may be a bit of a Jew.   40

I have always been scared of *you*,
With your Luftwaffe,° your gobbledygoo.
And your neat mustache
And your Aryan eye, bright blue.
Panzer-man, panzer-man,° O You —   45

Not God but a swastika
So black no sky could squeak through.

---

16 Polish town: Plath's father was born in Granbow, Poland.   **33 Dachau . . . Belsen:** Nazi
death camps in World War II.   **39 Taroc:** Tarot cards used to tell fortunes. The practice may
have originated among the early Jewish Cabalists and then widely adopted by European Gyp-
sies during the Middle Ages.   **42 Luftwaffe:** World War II German air force.   **45 panzer-
man:** A member of the German armored vehicle division.

Every woman adores a Fascist,
The boot in the face, the brute
Brute heart of a brute like you.   50

You stand at the blackboard, daddy,
In the picture I have of you,
A cleft in your chin instead of your foot
But no less a devil for that, no not
Any less the black man who   55

Bit my pretty red heart in two.
I was ten when they buried you.
At twenty I tried to die
And get back, back, back to you.
I thought even the bones would do   60

But they pulled me out of the sack,
And they stuck me together with glue.
And then I knew what to do.
I made a model of you,
A man in black with a Meinkampf° look   65

And a love of the rack and the screw.
And I said I do, I do.
So daddy, I'm finally through.
The black telephone's off at the root,
The voices just can't worm through.   70

If I've killed one man, I've killed two—
The vampire who said he was you
And drank my blood for a year,
Seven years, if you want to know.
Daddy, you can lie back now.   75

There's a stake in your fat black heart
And the villagers never liked you.
They are dancing and stamping on you.
They always *knew* it was you.
Daddy, daddy, you bastard, I'm through.   [1962]   80

65 **Meinkampf:** Hitler's autobiography (*My Struggle*).

THINKING ABOUT THE TEXT

1. Can this poem be seen as a series of arguments for why Plath has to forget her father? What complaints does the speaker seem to have against her father?

2. Some psychologists claim that we all have a love-hate relationship with our parents. Do you agree? Would Plath's speaker agree?

3. How effective is it for the speaker to compare herself to a Jew in Hitler's Germany? What other similes and metaphors are used to refer to her father? Do they work, or are they too extreme? Perhaps Plath wants them to be outrageous. Why might she?

4. Plath combines childhood rhymes and words with brutal images. What effect does this have on you? Why do you think Plath does this? What odd stylistic features can you point to here?

5. Why do you think it is necessary for the speaker to be finally "through" with her father? Is it normal young adult rebelliousness? What else might it be?

MARY LYNN BROE

From *Protean Poetic: The Poetry of Sylvia Plath*

Mary Lynn Broe (b. 1946) was educated at St. Louis University, where she received her B.A. in 1967, and the University of Connecticut, where she earned an M.A. in 1970 and a Ph.D. in 1976. She currently teaches English at the State University of New York at Binghamton. She publishes and travels extensively and is an international voice in the fields of women's studies and modern literature.

Among the other poems that display the performing self, "Daddy" and "Lady Lazarus" are two of the most often quoted, but most frequently misunderstood, poems in the Plath canon. The speaker in "Daddy" performs a mock poetic exorcism of an event that has already happened—the death of her father who she feels withdrew his love from her by dying prematurely: "Daddy, I have had to kill you. / You died before I had time—."

The speaker attempts to exorcise not just the memory of her father but her own *Mein Kampf* model of him as well as her inherited behavioral traits that lead her graveward under the Freudian banner of death instinct or Thanatos's libido. But her ritual reenactment simply does not take. The event comically backfires as pure self-parody: the metaphorical murder of the father dwindles into Hollywood spectacle, while the poet is lost in the clutter of the collective unconscious.

Early in the poem, the ritual gets off on the wrong foot both literally and figuratively. A sudden rhythmic break midway through the first stanza interrupts the insistent and mesmeric chant of the poet's own freedom:

You do not do, you do not do
Any more, black shoe
In which I have lived like a foot
For thirty years, poor and white,
Barely daring to breathe or Achoo.

The break suggests, on the one hand, that the nursery-rhyme world of contained terror is here abandoned; on the other, that the poet-exorcist's mesmeric control is superficial, founded in a shaky faith and an unsure heart — the worst possible state for the strong, disciplined exorcist.

At first, she kills her father succinctly with her own words, demythologizing him to a ludicrous piece of statuary that is hardly a Poseidon or the Colossus of Rhodes:

> Marble-heavy, a bag full of God,
> Ghastly statue with one grey toe
> Big as a Frisco seal
>
> And a head in the freakish Atlantic
> Where it pours bean green over blue
> In the waters off beautiful Nauset.
> I used to pray to recover you.
> Ach, du.

Then as she tries to patch together the narrative of him, his tribal myth (the "common" town, the "German tongue," the war-scraped culture), she begins to lose her own powers of description to a senseless Germanic prattle ("The tongue stuck in my jaw. / It stuck in a barb wire snare. / Ich, ich, ich, ich"). The individual man is absorbed by his inhuman archetype, the "panzer-man," "an engine / Chuffing me off like a Jew." Losing the exorcist's power that binds the spirit and then casts out the demon, she is the classic helpless victim of the swastika man. As she culls up her own picture of him as a devil, he refuses to adopt this stereotype. Instead he jumbles his trademark:

> A cleft in your chin instead of your foot
> But no less a devil for that, no not
> Any less the black man who
>
> Bit my pretty red heart in two.

The overt Nazi-Jew allegory throughout the poem suggests that, by a simple inversion of power, father and daughter grow more alike. But when she tries to imitate his action of dying, making all the appropriate grand gestures, she once again fails: "But they pulled me out of the sack, / And they stuck me together with glue." She retreats to a safe world of icons and replicas, but even the doll image she constructs turns out to be "the vampire who said he was you." At last, she abandons her father to the collective unconscious where it is *he* who is finally recognized ("They always *knew* it was you"). *She* is lost, impersonally absorbed by his irate persecutors, bereft of both her power and her conjurer's discipline, and possessed by the incensed villagers. The exorcist's ritual, one of purifying, cleansing, commanding silence, and then ordering the evil spirit's departure, has dwindled to a comic picture from the heart of darkness. Mad villagers stamp on the devil-vampire creation.

In the course of performing the imaginative "killing," the speaker moves through a variety of emotions, from viciousness ("a stake in your fat black heart"), to vengefulness ("you bastard, I'm through"), finally to silence ("The black telephone's off at the root"). It would seem that the real victim is the poet-performer who, despite her straining toward identification with the public events of holocaust and destruction of World War II, becomes more murderously persecuting

than the "panzer-man" who smothered her, and who abandoned her with a paradoxical love, guilt, and fear. Unlike him, she kills three times: the original subject,
the model to whom she said "I do, I do," and herself, the imitating victim. But
each of these killings is comically inverted. Each backfires. Instead of successfully
binding the spirits, commanding them to remain silent and cease doing harm, and
then ordering them to an appointed place, the speaker herself is stricken dumb.

The failure of the exorcism and the emotional ambivalence are echoed in
the curious rhythm. The incantatory safety of the nursery-rhyme thump (seemingly one of controlled, familiar terrors) also suggests some sinister brooding by its
repetition. The poem opens with a suspiciously emphatic protest, a kind of psychological whistling-in-the-dark. As it proceeds, "Daddy"'s continuous life-rhythms—
the assonance, consonance, and especially the sustained *oo* sounds—triumph over
either the personal or the cultural-historical imagery. The sheer sense of organic
life in the interwoven sounds carries the verse forward in boisterous spirit and
communicates an underlying feeling of comedy that is also echoed in the
repeated failure of the speaker to perform her exorcism.

Ultimately, "Daddy" is like an emotional, psychological, and historical
autopsy, a final report. There is no real progress. The poet is in the same place in
the beginning as in the end. She begins the poem as a hesitant but familiar fairytale daughter who parodies her attempt to reconstruct the myth of her father. Suffocating in her shoe house, she is unable to do much with that "bag full of God."
She ends as a murderous member of a mythical community enacting the ritual or
vampire killing, but only for a surrogate vampire, not the real thing ("The vampire who said he was you"). Although it seems that the speaker has moved from
identification with the persecuted to identify as persecutor, Jew to vampire-killer,
powerless to powerful, she has simply enacted a performance that allows her to
live with what is unchangeable. She has used her art to stave off suffocation and
performs her self-contempt with a degree of bravado.   [1980]

LYNDA K. BUNDTZEN
From *Plath's Incarnations*

*Educated at the University of Minnesota, where she earned a B.A. in 1968, and the
University of Chicago, where she earned a Ph.D. in 1972, Lynda Bundtzen (b.
1947) teaches at Williams College. A Renaissance scholar with a strong interest in
women's issues, she teaches and writes on subjects that range from Shakespeare to
Thelma and Louise. Plath's Incarnations was published in 1983.*

In "Daddy," Plath is conscious of her complicity in creating and worshiping
a father-colossus.

You stand at the blackboard, daddy,
In the picture I have of you,

A cleft in your chin instead of your foot
But no less a devil for that, no not
Any less the black man who

Bit my pretty red heart in two.
I was ten when they buried you.
At twenty I tried to die
And get back, back, back to you.
I thought even the bones would do.

The photograph is of an ordinary man, a teacher, with a cleft chin. She imaginatively transforms him into a devil who broke her heart, and she tells her audience precisely what she is doing. As Plath describes "Daddy," it is "spoken by a girl with an Electra complex. Her father died while she thought he was God. Her case is complicated by the fact that her father was also a Nazi and her mother very possibly part Jewish. In the daughter the two strains marry and paralyze each other — she has to act out the awful little allegory once over before she is free of it." The poem is a figurative drama about mourning — about the human impulse to keep a dead loved one alive emotionally. And it is about mourning gone haywire — a morbid inability to let go of the dead. The child was unready for her father's death, which is why, she says, she must kill him a second time. She resurrected Daddy and sustained his unnatural existence in her psyche as a vampire, sacrificing her own life's blood, her vitality, to a dead man. The worship of this father-god, she now realizes, is self-destructive.

There is nothing unconscious about the poem; instead it seems to force into consciousness the child's dread and love for the father, so that these feelings may be resolved. Plath skillfully evokes the child's world with her own versions of Mother Goose rhymes. Like the "old woman who lived in a shoe and had so many children she didn't know what to do," she has tried to live in the confines of the black shoe that is Daddy. Like Chicken Little, waiting for the sky to fall in, she lives under an omnipresent swastika "So black no sky could squeak through." And Daddy is a fallen giant toppled over and smothering, it seems, the entire United States. He has one grey toe (recalling Otto Plath's gangrened appendage) dangling like a Frisco seal in the Pacific and his head lies in the Atlantic.

The Mother Goose rhythms gradually build to a goose step march as the mourning process turns inward. She feels more than sorrow, now guilt, for Daddy's death and this guilt leads to feelings of inadequacy, acts of self-abasement, and finally self-murder. Nothing she can do will appease the guilt: she tries to learn his language; she tries to kill herself; she marries a man in his image. It will not do.

The self-hatred must be turned outward again into "*You* do not do" by a very self-conscious transformation of a mild-mannered professor into an active oppressor. Her emotional paralysis is acted out as a struggle between Nazi man and Jewess, and, I would argue, the Jewess wins. The poem builds toward the imaginary stake driving, the dancing and stamping and "Daddy, daddy, you bastard, I'm through." Not necessarily through with life, as many critics have read this line, but through with the paralysis, powerlessness, guilt. At last Daddy — the Nazi Daddy she frightened herself with, and not the real one, the professor — is at rest.

Plath's control over ambivalent feelings toward her father is probably the   5
result of their availability for conscious artistic manipulation. She had already
written several poems about her dead father when she composed "Daddy," and
we also know from a conversation recorded by Steiner that she had "worked
through" her emotions in therapy. "She talked freely about her father's death
when she was nine and her reactions to it. 'He was an autocrat,' she recalled. 'I
adored and despised him, and I probably wished many times that he were dead.
When he obliged me and died, I imagined that I had killed him.'" The result in
"Daddy" is a powerful and remarkably accessible allegory about her adoration
and dread, which ends in emotional catharsis.

STEVEN GOULD AXELROD
From *Sylvia Plath: The Wound and the Cure of Words*

An expert in nineteenth- and twentieth-century American poetry, Steven Gould
Axelrod (b. 1944) was educated at the University of California at Los Angeles and
currently serves as chair of the English Department at the University of California
at Riverside, where he received a Distinguished Teaching Award in 1989. His pub-
lications include book-length works on modern and contemporary poets. Sylvia
Plath: The Wound and the Cure of Words *was published in 1990.*

The covert protest of "The Colossus" eventually transformed itself into the
overt rebellion of "Daddy." Although this poem too has traditionally been read as
"personal" or "confessional," Margaret Homans has more recently suggested that
it concerns a woman's dislocated relations to speech. Plath herself introduced it
on the BBC as the opposite of confession, as a constructed fiction: "Here is a poem
spoken by a girl with an Electra complex. Her father died while she thought he
was God. Her case is complicated by the fact that her father was also a Nazi and
her mother very possibly part Jewish. In the daughter the two strains marry and
paralyze each other—she has to act out the awful little allegory once over before
she is free of it." We might interpret this preface as an accurate retelling of the
poem; or we might regard it as a case of an author's estrangement from her text, on
the order of Coleridge's preface to "Kubla Khan" in which he claims to be unable
to finish the poem, having forgotten what it was about. However we interpret
Plath's preface, we must agree that "Daddy" is dramatic and allegorical, since its
details depart freely from the facts of her biography. In this poem she again figures
her unresolved conflicts with paternal authority as a textual issue. Significantly,
her father was a published writer, and his successor, her husband, was also a
writer. Her preface asserts that the poem concerns a young woman's paralyzing
self-division, which she can defeat only through allegorical representation. Recalling that paralysis was one of Plath's main tropes for literary incapacity, we begin to
see that the poem evokes the female poet's anxiety of authorship and specifically

Plath's strategy of delivering herself from that anxiety by making it the topic of her discourse. Viewed from this perspective, "Daddy" enacts the woman poet's struggle with "daddy-poetry." It represents her effort to eject the "buried male muse" from her invention process and the "jealous gods" from her audience.

Plath wrote "Daddy" several months after Hughes left her, on the day she learned that he had agreed to a divorce. George Brown and Tirril Harris have shown that early loss makes one especially vulnerable to subsequent loss, and Plath seems to have defended against depression by almost literally throwing herself into her poetry. She followed "Daddy" with a host of poems that she considered her greatest achievement to date: "Medusa," "The Jailer," "Lady Lazarus," "Ariel," the bee sequence, and others. The letters she wrote to her mother and brother on the day of "Daddy," and then again four days later, brim with a sense of artistic self-discovery: "Writing like mad. . . . Terrific stuff, as if domesticity had choked me." Composing at the "still blue, almost eternal hour before the baby's cry, before the glassy music of the milkman, settling his bottles," she experienced an "enormous surge in creative energy. Yet she also expressed feelings of misery: "The half year ahead seems like a lifetime, and the half behind an endless hell." She was again contemplating things German: a trip to the Austrian Alps, a renewed effort to learn the language. If "German" was Randall Jarrell's "favorite country," it was not hers, yet it returned to her discourse like clockwork at times of psychic distress. Clearly Plath was attempting to find and to evoke in her art what she could not find or communicate in her life. She wished to compensate for her fragmenting social existence by investing herself in her texts: "Hope, when free, to write myself out of this hole." Desperately eager to sacrifice her "flesh," which was "wasted," to her "mind and spirit," which were "fine," she wrote "Daddy" to demonstrate the existence of her voice, which had been silent or subservient for so long. She wrote it to prove her "genius."

Plath projected her struggle for textual identity onto the figure of a partly Jewish young woman who learns to express her anger at the patriarch and at his language of male mastery, which is as foreign to her as German, as "obscene" as murder, and as meaningless as "gobbledygoo." The patriarch's death "off beautiful Nauset" recalls Plath's journal entry in which she associated the "green seaweeded water" at "Nauset Light" with "the deadness of a being . . . who no longer creates." Daddy's deadness — suggesting Plath's unwillingness to let her father, her education, her library, or her husband inhibit her any longer — inspires the poem's speaker to her moment of illumination. At a basic level, "Daddy" concerns its own violent, transgressive birth as a text, its origin in a culture that regards it as illegitimate — a judgment the speaker hurls back on the patriarch himself when she labels *him* a bastard. Plath's unaccommodating worldview, which was validated by much in her childhood and adult experience, led her to understand literary tradition not as an expanding universe of beneficial influence . . . but as a closed universe in which every addition required a corresponding subtraction — a Spencerian agon in which only the fittest survived. If Plath's speaker was to be born as a poet, a patriarch must die.

As in "The Colossus," the father here appears as a force or an object rather than as a person. Initially he takes the form of an immense "black shoe," capable of stamping on his victim. Immediately thereafter he becomes a marble "statue," cousin to the monolith of the earlier poem. He then transforms into Nazi Germany, the archetypal totalitarian state. When the protagonist mentions Daddy's "boot in the face," she may be alluding to Orwell's comment in *1984*, "If you want a picture of the future, imagine a boot stomping on a human face — forever." Eventually the father declines in stature from God to a devil to a dying vampire. Perhaps he shrinks under the force of his victim's denunciation, which de-creates him as a power as it creates him as figure. But whatever his size, he never assumes human dimensions, aspirations, and relations — except when posing as a teacher in a photograph. Like the colossus, he remains figurative and symbolic, not individual.

Nevertheless, the male figure of "Daddy" does differ significantly from that   5
of "The Colossus." In the earlier poem, which emphasizes his lips, mouth, throat, tongue, and voice, the colossus allegorically represents the power of speech, however fragmented and resistant to the protagonist's ministrations. In the later poem Daddy remains silent, apart from the gobbledygoo attributed to him once. He uses his mouth primarily for biting and for drinking blood. The poem emphasizes his feet and, implicitly, his phallus. He is a "black shoe," a statue with "one gray toe," a "boot." The speaker, estranged from him by fear, could never tell where he put his "foot," his "root." Furthermore, she is herself silenced by his shoe: "I never could talk to you." Daddy is no "male muse," not even one in ruins, but frankly a male censor. His boot in the face of "every woman" is presumably lodged in her mouth. He stands for all the elements in the literary situation and in the female ephebe's internalization of it, that prevent her from producing any words at all, even copied or subservient ones. Appropriately, Daddy can be killed only by being stamped on: he lives and dies by force, not language. If "The Colossus" tells a tale of the patriarch's speech, his grunts and brays, "Daddy" tells a tale of the daughter's effort to speak.

Thus we are led to another important difference between the two poems. The "I" of "The Colossus" acquires her identity only through serving her "father," whereas the "I" of "Daddy" actuates her gift only through opposition to him. The latter poem precisely inscribes the plot of Plath's dream novel of 1958: "a girl's search for her dead father — for an outside authority which must be developed, instead, from the inside." As the child of a Nazi, the girl could "hardly speak," but as a Jew she begins "to talk" and to acquire an identity. In Plath's allegory, the outsider Jew corresponds to "the rebel, the artist, the odd," and particularly to the woman artist. Otto Rank's *Beyond Psychology*, which had a lasting influence on her, explicitly compares women to Jews, since "woman . . . has suffered from the very beginning a fate similar to that of the Jew, namely, suppression, slavery, confinement, and subsequent persecution." Rank, whose discourse I would consider tainted by anti-Semitism, argues that Jews speak a language of pessimistic "self-hatred" that differs essentially from the language of the majority cultures in which they find themselves. He analogously, though more sympathetically, argues that woman speaks in a language different from man's, and that as a result of man's denial of woman's world, "woman's 'native tongue' has hitherto been unknown or at least unheard." Although Rank's essentializing of woman's "nature" lapses into the sexist clichés of his time ("intuitive," "irrational"), his idea of linguistic difference based on gender and his analogy between Jewish and female speech seem to have embedded themselves in the substructure of "Daddy" (and in many of Plath's other texts as well). For Plath, as later for Adrienne Rich, the Holocaust and the patriarchy's silencing of women were linked outcomes of the masculinist interpretation of the world. Political insurrection and female self-assertion also interlaced symbolically. In "Daddy," Plath's speaker finds her voice and motive by identifying herself as antithetical to her Fascist father. Rather than getting the colossus "glued" and properly jointed, she wishes to stick herself "together with glue," an act that seems to require her father's dismemberment. Previously devoted to the patriarch—both in "The Colossus" and in memories evoked in "Daddy" of trying to "get back" to him—she now seeks only to escape from him and to see him destroyed.

Plath has unleashed the anger, normal in mourning as well as in revolt, that she suppressed in the earlier poem. But she has done so at a cost. Let us consider her childlike speaking voice. The language of "Daddy," beginning with its title, is often regressive. The "I" articulates herself by moving backward in time, using the language of nursery rhymes and fairy tales (the little old woman who lived in a shoe, the black man of the forest). Such language accords with a child's conception of the world, not an adult's. Plath's assault on the language of "daddy-poetry" has turned inward, on the language of her own poem, which teeters precariously on the edge of a preverbal abyss—represented by the eerie, keening "oo" sound with which a majority of the verses end. And then let us consider the play on "through" at the poem's conclusion. Although that last line allows for multiple readings, one interpretation is that the "I" has unconsciously carried out her father's wish: her discourse, by transforming itself into cathartic oversimplifications, has undone itself.

Yet the poem does contain its verbal violence by means more productive than silence. In a letter to her brother, Plath referred to "Daddy" as "gruesome," while on almost the same day she described it to A. Alvarez as a piece of "light verse." She later read it on the BBC in a highly ironic tone of voice. The poem's unique spell derives from its rhetorical complexity: its variegated and perhaps bizarre fusion of the horrendous and the comic. . . . [I]t both shares and remains detached from the fixation of its protagonist. The protagonist herself seems detached from her own fixation. She is "split in the most complex fashion," as Plath wrote of Ivan Karamazov in her Smith College honors thesis. Plath's speaker uses potentially self-mocking melodramatic terms to describe both her opponent ("so black no sky could squeak through") and herself ("poor and white"). While this aboriginal speaker quite literally expresses black-and-white thinking, her civilized double possesses a sensibility sophisticated enough to subject such thinking to irony. Thus the poem expresses feelings that it simultaneously parodies—it may be parodying the very idea of feeling. The tension between erudition and simplicity in the speaker's voice appears in her pairings that juxtapose adult with childlike diction: "breathe or Achoo," "your Luftewaffe, your gobbledygoo." She can expound such adult topics as Taroc packs, Viennese beer, and Tyrolean snowfall; can specify death camps by name; and can employ an adult vocabulary of "recover," "ancestress," "Aryan," "*Meinkampf,*" "obscene," and "bastard." Yet she also has recourse to a more primitive lexicon that includes "chuffing," "your fat black heart," and "my pretty red heart." She proves herself capable of careful intellectual discriminations ("so I never could tell"), conventionalized description ("beautiful Nauset"), and moral analogy ("if I've killed one man, I've killed two"), while also exhibiting regressive fantasies (vampires), repetitions ("wars, wars, wars"), and inarticulateness ("panzer-man, panzer-man, O You—"). She oscillates between calm reflection ("You stand at the blackboard, daddy, / In the picture I have of you") and mad incoherence ("Ich, ich, ich, ich"). Her sophisticated language puts her wild language in an ironic perspective, removing the discourse from the control of the archaic self who understands experience only in extreme terms.

The ironies in "Daddy" proliferate in unexpected ways, however. When the speaker proclaims categorically that "every woman adores a Fascist," she is subjecting her victimization to irony by suggesting that sufferers choose, or at least accommodate themselves to, their suffering. But she is also subjecting her authority to irony, since her claim about "every woman" is transparently false. It simply parodies patriarchal commonplaces, such as those advanced . . . concerning "feminine masochism." The adult, sophisticated self seems to be speaking here: Who else would have the confidence to make a sociological generalization? Yet the content of the assertion, if taken straightforwardly, returns us to the regressive self who is dominated by extravagant emotions she cannot begin to understand. Plath's mother wished that Plath would write about "decent, courageous people," and she herself heard an inner voice demanding that she be a perfect "paragon" in her language and feeling. But in the speaker of "Daddy," she inscribed the opposite of such a paragon: a divided self whose veneer of civilization is breached and infected by unhealthy instincts.

Plath's irony cuts both ways. At the same time that the speaker's sophisticated voice undercuts her childish voice, reducing its melodrama to comedy, the childish or maddened voice undercuts the pretensions of the sophisticated voice, revealing the extremity of suffering masked by its ironies. While demonstrating the inadequacy of thinking and feeling in opposites, the poem implies that such a mode can locate truths denied more complex cognitive and affective systems. The very moderation of the normal adult intelligence, its tolerance of ambiguity, its defenses against the primal energies of the id, results in falsification. Reflecting Schiller's idea that the creative artist experiences a "momentary and passing madness" (quoted by Freud in a passage of *The Interpretation of Dreams* that Plath underscored), "Daddy" gives voice to that madness. Yet the poem's sophisticated awareness, its comic vision, probably wins out in the end, since the poem concludes by curtailing the power of its extreme discourse. . . . Furthermore, Plath distanced herself from the poem's aboriginal voice by introducing her text as "a poem spoken by a girl with an Electra complex"—that is, as a study of the *girl's* pathology rather than her father's—and as an allegory that will "free" her from that pathology. She also distanced herself by reading the poem in a tone that emphasized its irony. And finally, she distanced herself by laying the poem's wild voice permanently to rest after October. The aboriginal vision was indeed

10

purged. "Daddy" represents not Dickinson's madness that is divinest sense, but rather an entry into a style of discourse and a mastery of it. The poem realizes the trope of suffering by means of an inherent irony that both questions and validates the trope in the same gestures, and that finally allows the speaker to conclude the discourse and to remove herself from the trope with a sense of completion rather than wrenching, since the irony was present from the very beginning.

Plath's poetic revolt in "Daddy" liberated her pent-up creativity, but the momentary success sustained her little more than self-sacrifice had done. "Daddy" became another stage in her development, an unrepeatable experiment, a vocal opening that closed itself at once. The poem is not only an elegy for the power of "daddy-poetry" but for the powers of speech Plath discovered in composing it.

When we consider "Daddy" generically, a further range of implications presents itself. Although we could profitably consider the poem as the dramatic monologue Plath called it in her BBC broadcast, let us regard it instead as the kind of poem most readers have taken it to be: a domestic poem. I have chosen this term, rather than M. L. Rosenthal's better-known "confessional poem" or the more neutral "autobiographical poem," because "confessional poem" implies a confession rather than a making (though Steven Hoffman and Lawrence Kramer have recently indicated the mode's conventions) and because "autobiographical poem" is too general for our purpose. I shall define the domestic poem as one that represents and comments on a protagonist's relationship to one or more family members, usually a parent, child, or spouse. To focus our discussion even further, I shall emphasize poetry that specifically concerns a father.   [1990]

MAKING COMPARISONS

1. "Daddy" seems to be a protest, but some critics see it as more than that. Which of the three commentaries makes the best case that it is more than a revolt against the speaker's father?

2. Which critic seems to answer most of the perplexing questions of this poem, for example, the father as Nazi, the father as vampire, the childlike rhythms, the speaker's vengefulness, her viciousness?

3. Do these critics make any similar points? How might you describe them? What is their most striking difference?

WRITING ABOUT ISSUES

1. Argue that the textual evidence Axelrod provides for his assertions is, or is not, adequate.

2. Imagine you are Sylvia Plath. After reading these three essays, write a letter to a literary journal either attacking or praising these critics.

3. Write an essay arguing that your own reading of "Daddy" makes more sense than those of Broe, Bundtzen, and Axelrod. Assume that the audience for the criticism is your class.

4. There are dozens of critical commentaries on Plath's "Daddy." Some were written soon after the poem's publication; others are quite recent. Locate an early piece of criticism and compare it to one published in the past two years. Do these critics make similar or different points? Is one more concerned with the text, with gender issues, with cultural concerns, or with what other critics say? Write a brief comparison of the two, explaining your evidence.

MOTHERS AND DAUGHTERS

TILLIE OLSEN, "I Stand Here Ironing"
AMY TAN, "Two Kinds"

We all know stories of parents who want to mold their children, mothers and fathers who push their reluctant children to be fashion models or beauty queens or little league stars. Some studies of adults playing musical instruments in orchestras say the biggest factor in their success was the commitment of their parents. But we also hear about tennis prodigies who burn out at sixteen because of parental pressure. Mothers and daughters have always struggled with each other over life goals and identity. How much guidance is enough? How much is too much? What is a reasonable balance between preparing a child for life's challenges and shaping a child to act out the mother's fantasy or her internal vision of what the good life is? And no matter where parents fall on this continuum, are there childhood events so powerful that we cannot get beyond them? The following two stories chart the difficulties mothers and daughters have with each other and with the social and cultural forces that influence our destiny.

BEFORE YOU READ

Are your parents responsible for your successes? Your failures? Do you wish that your parents had pushed you to succeed more insistently? Are you annoyed that your parents set unreasonable standards for you?

TILLIE OLSEN
I Stand Here Ironing

Born in Omaha, Nebraska, to Russian immigrants of Jewish descent and socialist views, Tillie Olsen (b. 1913) has been an activist in social and political causes all of her life, often choosing family, work, union, feminist, or other political causes over writing. Although her publishing record is short, its quality is greatly admired. In addition to critically respected short stories, Olsen has written a novel, Yonnondio *(1974), which paints a vivid picture of a coal-mining family during the Depression. Her essay collection,* Silences *(1978), stimulated debate about class and gender as factors in the creation of literature and led both directly and indirectly to the revived interest in works by women writers. The mother of four daughters, Olsen often writes about generational relationships within families. "I Stand Here Ironing" is from her 1961 collection of stories,* Tell Me a Riddle.

I stand here ironing, and what you asked me moves tormented back and forth with the iron.

"I wish you would manage the time to come in and talk with me about your daughter. I'm sure you can help me understand her. She's a youngster who needs help and whom I'm deeply interested in helping."

"Who needs help." . . . Even if I came, what good would it do? You think because I am her mother I have a key, or that in some way you could use me as a key? She has lived for nineteen years. There is all that life that has happened outside of me, beyond me.

And when is there time to remember, to sift, to weigh, to estimate, to total? I will start and there will be an interruption and I will have to gather it all together again. Or I will become engulfed with all I did or did not do, with what should have been and what cannot be helped.

She was a beautiful baby. The first and only one of our five that was beautiful at birth. You do not guess how new and uneasy her tenancy in her now-loveliness. You did not know her all those years she was thought homely, or see her poring over her baby pictures, making me tell her over and over how beautiful she had been — and would be, I would tell her — and was now, to the seeing eye. But the seeing eyes were few or nonexistent. Including mine.

I nursed her. They feel that's important nowadays, I nursed all the children, but with her, with all the fierce rigidity of first motherhood, I did like the books then said. Though her cries battered me to trembling and my breasts ached with swollenness, I waited till the clock decreed.

Why do I put that first? I do not even know if it matters, or if it explains anything.

She was a beautiful baby. She blew shining bubbles of sound. She loved motion, loved light, loved color and music and textures. She would lie on the floor in her blue overalls patting the surface so hard in ecstasy her hands and feet would blur. She was a miracle to me, but when she was eight months old I had to leave her daytimes with the woman downstairs to whom she was no miracle at all, for I worked or looked for work and for Emily's father, who "could no longer endure" (he wrote in his good-bye note) "sharing want with us."

I was nineteen. It was the pre-relief, pre-WPA world of the depression. I would start running as soon as I got off the streetcar, running up the stairs, the place smelling sour, and awake or asleep to startle awake, when she saw me she would break into a clogged weeping that could not be comforted, a weeping I can hear yet.

5

After a while I found a job hashing at night so I could be with her days, and it   10
was better. But it came to where I had to bring her to his family and leave her.

It took a long time to raise the money for her fare back. Then she got chicken
pox and I had to wait longer. When she finally came, I hardly knew her, walking
quick and nervous like her father, looking like her father, thin, and dressed in a
shoddy red that yellowed her skin and glared at the pockmarks. All the baby loveliness gone.

She was two. Old enough for nursery school they said, and I did not know
then what I know now — the fatigue of the long day, and the lacerations of group
life in the kinds of nurseries that are only parking places for children.

Except that it would have made no difference if I had known. It was the only
place there was. It was the only way we could be together, the only way I could
hold a job.

And even without knowing, I knew. I knew the teacher that was evil because
all these years it has curdled into my memory, the little boy hunched in the corner, her rasp, "why aren't you outside, because Alvin hits you? that's no reason, go
out, scaredy." I knew Emily hated it even if she did not clutch and implore "don't
go Mommy" like the other children, mornings.

She always had a reason why we should stay home. Momma, you look sick.   15
Momma, I feel sick. Momma, the teachers aren't there today, they're sick.
Momma, we can't go, there was a fire there last night. Momma, it's a holiday
today, no school, they told me.

But never a direct protest, never rebellion. I think of our others in their three-,
four-year-oldness — the explosions, the tempers, the denunciations, the demands —
and I feel suddenly ill. I put the iron down. What in me demanded that goodness
in her? And what was the cost, the cost to her of such goodness?

The old man living in the back once said in his gentle way: "You should
smile at Emily more when you look at her." What *was* in my face when I looked
at her? I loved her. There were all the acts of love.

It was only with the others I remembered what he said, and it was the face of
joy, and not of care or tightness or worry I turned to them — too late for Emily. She
does not smile easily, let alone almost always as her brothers and sisters do. Her face
is closed and sombre, but when she wants, how fluid. You must have seen it in her
pantomimes, you spoke of her rare gift for comedy on the stage that rouses laughter
out of the audience so dear they applaud and applaud and do not want to let her go.

Where does it come from, that comedy? There was none of it in her when
she came back to me that second time, after I had to send her away again. She
had a new daddy now to learn to love, and I think perhaps it was a better time.

Except when we left her alone nights, telling ourselves she was old enough.   20
"Can't you go some other time, Mommy, like tomorrow?" she would ask.
"Will it be just a little while you'll be gone? Do you promise?"

The time we came back, the front door open, the clock on the floor in the
hall. She rigid awake. "It wasn't just a little while. I didn't cry. Three times I called
you, just three times, and then I ran downstairs to open the door so you could
come faster. The clock talked loud. I threw it away, it scared me what it talked."

She said the clock talked loud again that night I went to the hospital to have

Susan. She was delirious with the fever that comes before red measles, but she was fully conscious all the week I was gone and the week after we were home when she could not come near the new baby or me.

She did not get well. She stayed skeleton thin, not wanting to eat, and night after night she had nightmares. She would call for me, and I would rouse from exhaustion to sleepily call back: "You're all right, darling, go to sleep, it's just a dream," and if she still called, in a sterner voice, "now go to sleep, Emily, there's nothing to hurt you." Twice, only twice, when I had to get up for Susan anyhow, I went in to sit with her.

Now when it is too late (as if she would let me hold her and comfort her like   25
I do the others) I get up and go to her at once at her moan or restless stirring. "Are you awake, Emily? Can I get you something?" And the answer is always the same: "No, I'm all right, go back to sleep, Mother."

They persuaded me at the clinic to send her away to a convalescent home in the country where "she can have the kind of food and care you can't manage for her, and you'll be free to concentrate on the new baby." They still send children to that place. I see pictures on the society page of sleek young women planning affairs to raise money for it, or dancing at the affairs, or decorating Easter eggs or filling Christmas stockings for the children.

They never have a picture of the children so I do not know if the girls still wear those gigantic red bows and the ravaged looks on the every other Sunday when parents can come to visit "unless otherwise notified" — as we were notified the first six weeks.

Oh it is a handsome place, green lawns and tall trees and fluted flower beds. High up on the balconies of each cottage the children stand, the girls in their red bows and white dresses, the boys in white suits and giant red ties. The parents stand below shrieking up to be heard and the children shriek down to be heard, and between them the invisible wall "Not To Be Contaminated by Parental Germs or Physical Affection."

There was a tiny girl who always stood hand in hand with Emily. Her parents never came. One visit she was gone. "They moved her to Rose Cottage," Emily shouted in explanation. "They don't like you to love anybody here."

She wrote once a week, the labored writing of a seven-year-old. "I am fine.   30
How is the baby. If I write my leter nicly I will have a star. Love." There never was a star. We wrote every other day, letters she could never hold or keep but only hear read — once. "We simply do not have room for children to keep any personal possessions," they patiently explained when we pieced one Sunday's shrieking together to plead how much it would mean to Emily, who loved so to keep things, to be allowed to keep her letters and cards.

Each visit she looked frailer. "She isn't eating," they told us.

(They had runny eggs for breakfast or mush with lumps, Emily said later, I'd hold it in my mouth and not swallow. Nothing ever tasted good, just when they had chicken.)

It took us eight months to get her released home, and only the fact that she gained back so little of her seven lost pounds convinced the social worker.

I used to try to hold and love her after she came back, but her body would stay stiff, and after a while she'd push away. She ate little. Food sickened her, and I think much of life too. Oh she had physical lightness and brightness, twinkling by on skates, bouncing like a ball up and down up and down over the jump rope, skimming over the hill; but these were momentary.

She fretted about her appearance, thin and dark and foreign-looking at a   35
time when every little girl was supposed to look or thought she should look a chubby blonde replica of Shirley Temple. The doorbell sometimes rang for her, but no one seemed to come and play in the house or to be a best friend. Maybe because we moved so much.

There was a boy she loved painfully through two school semesters. Months later she told me how she had taken pennies from my purse to buy him candy. "Licorice was his favorite and I brought him some every day, but he still liked Jennifer better'n me. Why, Mommy?" The kind of question for which there is no answer.

School was a worry for her. She was not glib or quick in a world where glibness and quickness were easily confused with ability to learn. To her overworked and exasperated teachers she was an overconscientious "slow learner" who kept trying to catch up and was absent entirely too often.

I let her be absent, though sometimes the illness was imaginary. How different from my now-strictness about attendance with the others. I wasn't working. We had a new baby. I was home anyhow. Sometimes, after Susan grew old enough, I would keep her home from school, too, to have them all together.

Mostly Emily had asthma, and her breathing, harsh and labored, would fill the house with a curiously tranquil sound. I would bring the two old dresser mirrors and her boxes of collections to her bed. She would select beads and single earrings, bottle tops and shells, dried flowers and pebbles, old postcards and scraps, all sorts of oddments; then she and Susan would play Kingdom, setting up landscapes and furniture, peopling them with action.

Those were the only times of peaceful companionship between her and   40
Susan. I have edged away from it, that poisonous feeling between them, that terrible balancing of hurts and needs I had to do between the two, and did so badly, those earlier years.

Oh there were conflicts between the others too, each one human, needing, demanding, hurting, taking—but only between Emily and Susan, no, Emily toward Susan that corroding resentment. It seems so obvious on the surface, yet it is not obvious; Susan, the second child, Susan, golden- and curly-haired and chubby, quick and articulate and assured, everything in appearance and manner Emily was not; Susan, not able to resist Emily's precious things, losing or sometimes clumsily breaking them; Susan telling jokes and riddles to company for applause while Emily sat silent (to say to me later: that was *my* riddle, Mother, I told it to Susan); Susan, who for all the five years' difference in age was just a year behind Emily in developing physically.

I am glad for that slow physical development that widened the difference between her and her contemporaries, though she suffered over it. She was too vulnerable for that terrible world of youthful competition, of preening and parading, of constant measuring of yourself against every other, of envy, "If I had that copper hair," "If I had that skin. . . ." She tormented herself enough about not looking like the others, there was enough of unsureness, the having to be conscious of words before you speak, the constant caring—what are they thinking of me? without having it all magnified by the merciless physical drives.

Ronnie is calling. He is wet and I change him. It is rare there is such a cry now. That time of motherhood is almost behind me when the ear is not one's own but must always be racked and listening for the child cry, the child call. We sit for a while and I hold him, looking out over the city spread in charcoal with its soft aisles of light. "*Shoogily*," he breathes and curls closer. I carry him back to bed, asleep. *Shoogily*. A funny word, a family word, inherited from Emily, invented by her to say: *comfort*.

In this and other ways she leaves her seal, I say aloud. And startle at my saying it. What do I mean? What did I start to gather together, to try and make coherent? I was at the terrible, growing years. War years. I do not remember them well. I was working, there were four smaller ones now, there was not time for her. She had to help be a mother, and housekeeper, and shopper. She had to get her seal. Mornings of crisis and near hysteria trying to get lunches packed, hair combed, coats and shoes found, everyone to school or Child Care on time, the baby ready for transportation. And always the paper scribbled on by a smaller one, the book looked at by Susan then mislaid, the homework not done. Running out to that huge school where she was one, she was lost, she was a drop; suffering over the unpreparedness, stammering and unsure in her classes.

There was so little time left at night after the kids were bedded down. She would struggle over books, always eating (it was in those years she developed her enormous appetite that is legendary in our family) and I would be ironing, or preparing food for the next day, or writing V-mail to Bill, or tending the baby. Sometimes, to make me laugh, or out of her despair, she would imitate happenings or types at school.

I think I said once: "Why don't you do something like this in the school amateur show?" One morning she phoned me at work, hardly understandable through the weeping: "Mother, I did it. I won, I won; they gave me first prize; they clapped and clapped and wouldn't let me go."

Now suddenly she was Somebody, and as imprisoned in her difference as she had been in anonymity.

She began to be asked to perform at other high schools, even in colleges, then at city and statewide affairs. The first one we went to, I only recognized her that first moment when thin, shy, she almost drowned herself into the curtains. Then: Was this Emily? The control, the command, the convulsing and deadly clowning, the spell, then the roaring, stamping audience, unwilling to let this rare and precious laughter out of their lives.

Afterwards: You ought to do something about her with a gift like that—but without money or knowing how, what does one do? We have left it all to her, and the gift has so often eddied inside, clogged and clotted, as been used and growing.

She is coming. She runs up the stairs two at a time with her light graceful step, and I know she is happy tonight. Whatever it was that occasioned your call did not happen today.

"Aren't you ever going to finish the ironing, Mother? Whistler painted his mother in a rocker. I'd have to paint mine standing over an ironing board." This is one of her communicative nights and she tells me everything and nothing as she fixes herself a plate of food out of the icebox.

She is so lovely. Why did you want me to come in at all? Why were you concerned? She will find her way.

She starts up the stairs to bed. "Don't get me up with the rest in the morning." "But I thought you were having midterms." "Oh, those," she comes back in, kisses me, and says quite lightly, "in a couple of years when we'll all be atom-dead they won't matter a bit."

She has said it before. She *believes* it. But because I have been dredging the past, and all that compounds a human being is so heavy and meaningful in me, I cannot endure it tonight.

I will never total it all. I will never come in to say: She was a child seldom   55
smiled at. Her father left me before she was a year old. I had to work her first six years when there was work, or I sent her home and to his relatives. There were years she had care she hated. She was dark and thin and foreign-looking in a world where the prestige went to blondeness and curly hair and dimples, she was slow where glibness was prized. She was a child of anxious, not proud, love. We were poor and could not afford for her the soil of easy growth. I was a young mother, I was a distracted mother. There were other children pushing up, demanding. Her younger sister seemed all that she was not. There were years she did not want me to touch her. She kept too much in herself, her life was such she had to keep too much in herself. My wisdom came too late. She has much to her and probably little will come of it. She is a child of her age, of depression, of war, of fear.

Let her be. So all that is in her will not bloom—but in how many does it? There is still enough left to live by. Only help her to know—help make it so there is cause for her to know—that she is more than this dress on the ironing board, helpless before the iron.   [1961]

THINKING ABOUT THE TEXT

1. Is Olsen's last paragraph optimistic or pessimistic about personal destiny? Is there some support in the story for both perspectives?

2. There is an old expression: "To know all is to forgive all." Do you agree in regards to "I Stand Here Ironing"? Some critics want to privilege personal responsibility, others social conditions. Do you blame Emily's mother? Or is she just a victim?

3. How might this story be different if told from Emily's perspective? From Susan's? From Emily's teacher's? What are the advantages and disadvantages of writing a story from one character's point of view?

4. How would you describe the voice or voices we hear in the story? What qualities, dimensions, or emotions can you infer? Does one dominate? Are you sympathetic to this voice? Is that what Olsen wanted?

5. Do you agree with the mother's decision not to visit the school for a conference? What are her reasons? Are they sound? What do you think the teacher wants to discuss? How involved in a child's life should a teacher be?

AMY TAN
Two Kinds

Born to Chinese immigrants in Oakland, California, Amy Tan (b. 1952) weaves intricate stories about generational and intercultural relationships among women in families, basing much of her writing on her own family history. She earned a B.A. in English and an M.A. in linguistics at San Jose State University. Her novels dealing with mother-daughter relationships, The Joy Luck Club *(1989) and* The Kitchen God's Wife *(1991), have received awards and critical acclaim. Her latest novel,* The Hundred Secret Senses *(1996), explores the relationship between sisters who grew up in different cultures. At the age of twenty-six, Tan learned that she had three half-sisters in China. "Two Kinds" is excerpted from* The Joy Luck Club.

My mother believed you could be anything you wanted to be in America. You could open a restaurant. You could work for the government and get good retirement. You could buy a house with almost no money down. You could become rich. You could become instantly famous.

"Of course you can be prodigy, too," my mother told me when I was nine. "You can be best anything. What does Auntie Lindo know? Her daughter, she is only best tricky."

America was where all my mother's hopes lay. She had come here in 1949 after losing everything in China: her mother and father, her family home, her first husband, and two daughters, twin baby girls. But she never looked back with regret. There were so many ways for things to get better.

We didn't immediately pick the right kind of prodigy. At first my mother thought I could be a Chinese Shirley Temple. We'd watch Shirley's old movies on TV as though they were training films. My mother would poke my arm and say, "*Ni kan*" — You watch. And I would see Shirley tapping her feet, or singing a sailor song, or pursing her lips into a very round O while saying, "Oh my goodness."

"*Ni kan*," said my mother as Shirley's eyes flooded with tears. "You already know how. Don't need talent for crying!"   5

Soon after my mother got this idea about Shirley Temple, she took me to a beauty training school in the Mission district and put me in the hands of a student who could barely hold the scissors without shaking. Instead of getting big fat curls, I emerged with an uneven mass of crinkly black fuzz. My mother dragged me off to the bathroom and tried to wet down my hair.

"You look like Negro Chinese," she lamented, as if I had done this on purpose.

The instructor of the beauty training school had to lop off these soggy clumps to make my hair even again. "Peter Pan is very popular these days," the instructor assured my mother. I now had hair the length of a boy's, with straight-across bangs that hung at a slant two inches above my eyebrows. I liked the haircut and it made me actually look forward to my future fame.

In fact, in the beginning, I was just as excited as my mother, maybe even more so. I pictured this prodigy part of me as many different images, trying each one on for size. I was a dainty ballerina girl standing by the curtains, waiting to hear the right music that would send me floating on my tiptoes. I was like the Christ child lifted out of the straw manger, crying with holy indignity. I was Cinderella stepping from her pumpkin carriage with sparkly cartoon music filling the air.

In all of my imaginings, I was filled with a sense that I would soon become   10
perfect. My mother and father would adore me. I would be beyond reproach. I would never feel the need to sulk for anything.

But sometimes the prodigy in me became impatient. "If you don't hurry up and get me out of here, I'm disappearing for good," it warned. "And then you'll always be nothing."

Every night after dinner, my mother and I would sit at the Formica kitchen table. She would present new tests, taking her examples from stories of amazing children she had read in *Ripley's Believe It or Not*, or *Good Housekeeping*, *Reader's Digest*, and a dozen other magazines she kept in a pile in our bathroom. My mother got these magazines from people whose houses she cleaned. And since she cleaned many houses each week, we had a great assortment. She would look through them all, searching for stories about remarkable children.

The first night she brought out a story about a three-year-old boy who knew the capitals of all the states and even most of the European countries. A teacher was quoted as saying the little boy could also pronounce the names of the foreign cities correctly.

"What's the capital of Finland?" my mother asked me, looking at the magazine story.

All I knew was the capital of California, because Sacramento was the name   15
of the street we lived on in Chinatown. "Nairobi!" I guessed, saying the most foreign word I could think of. She checked to see if that was possibly one way to pronounce "Helsinki" before showing me the answer.

The tests got harder — multiplying numbers in my head, finding the queen of hearts in a deck of cards, trying to stand on my head without using my hands, predicting the daily temperatures in Los Angeles, New York, and London.

One night I had to look at a page from the Bible for three minutes and then report everything I could remember. "Now Jehoshaphat had riches and honor in abundance and . . . that's all I remember, Ma," I said.

And after seeing my mother's disappointed face once again, something inside of me began to die. I hated the tests, the raised hopes and failed expectations. Before going to bed that night, I looked in the mirror above the bathroom sink and when I saw only my face staring back — and that it would always be this ordinary face — I began to cry. Such a sad, ugly girl! I made high-pitched noises like a crazed animal, trying to scratch out the face in the mirror.

And then I saw what seemed to be the prodigy side of me — because I had never seen that face before. I looked at my reflection, blinking so I could see more clearly. The girl staring back at me was angry, powerful. This girl and I were the same. I had new thoughts, willful thoughts, or rather thoughts filled with lots of won'ts. I won't let her change me, I promised myself. I won't be what I'm not.

So now on nights when my mother presented her tests, I performed listlessly,   20
my head propped on one arm. I pretended to be bored. And I was. I got so bored I started counting the bellows of the foghorns out on the bay while my mother drilled me in other areas. The sound was comforting and reminded me of the cow jumping over the moon. And the next day, I played a game with myself, seeing if my mother would give up on me before eight bellows. After a while I usually counted only one, maybe two bellows at most. At last she was beginning to give up hope.

Two or three months had gone by without any mention of my being a prodigy again. And then one day my mother was watching *The Ed Sullivan Show* on TV. The TV was old and the sound kept shorting out. Every time my mother got halfway up from the sofa to adjust the set, the sound would go back on and Ed would be talking. As soon as she sat down, Ed would go silent again. She got up, the TV broke into loud piano music. She sat down. Silence. Up and down, back and forth, quiet and loud. It was like a stiff embraceless dance between her and the TV set. Finally she stood by the set with her hand on the sound dial.

She seemed entranced by the music, a little frenzied piano piece with this mesmerizing quality, sort of quick passages and then teasing lilting ones before it returned to the quick playful parts.

"*Ni kan*," my mother said, calling me over with hurried hand gestures. "Look here."

I could see why my mother was fascinated by the music. It was being pounded out by a little Chinese girl, about nine years old, with a Peter Pan haircut. The girl had the sauciness of a Shirley Temple. She was proudly modest like a proper Chinese child. And she also did this fancy sweep of a curtsy, so that the fluffy skirt of her white dress cascaded slowly to the floor like the petals of a large carnation.

In spite of these warning signs, I wasn't worried. Our family had no piano   25
and we couldn't afford to buy one, let alone reams of sheet music and piano lessons. So I could be generous in my comments when my mother bad-mouthed the little girl on TV.

"Play note right, but doesn't sound good! No singing sound," complained my mother.

"What are you picking on her for?" I said carelessly. "She's pretty good. Maybe she's not the best, but she's trying hard." I knew almost immediately I would be sorry I said that.

"Just like you," she said. "Not the best. Because you not trying." She gave a little huff as she let go of the sound dial and sat down on the sofa.

The little Chinese girl sat down also to play an encore of "Anitra's Dance" by Grieg. I remember the song, because later on I had to learn how to play it.

Three days after watching *The Ed Sullivan Show*, my mother told me what   30
my schedule would be for piano lessons and piano practice. She had talked to

Mr. Chong, who lived on the first floor of our apartment building. Mr. Chong was a retired piano teacher and my mother had traded housecleaning services for weekly lessons and a piano for me to practice on every day, two hours a day, from four until six.

When my mother told me this, I felt as though I had been sent to hell. I whined and then kicked my foot a little when I couldn't stand it anymore.

"Why don't you like me the way I am? I'm *not* a genius! I can't play the piano. And even if I could, I wouldn't go on TV if you paid me a million dollars!" I cried.

My mother slapped me. "Who ask you be genius?" she shouted. "Only ask you be your best. For you sake. You think I want you be genius? Hnnh! What for! Who ask you!"

"So ungrateful," I heard her mutter in Chinese. "If she had as much talent as she has temper, she would be famous now."

Mr. Chong, whom I secretly nicknamed Old Chong, was very strange,   35 always tapping his fingers to the silent music of an invisible orchestra. He looked ancient in my eyes. He had lost most of the hair on top of his head and he wore thick glasses and had eyes that always looked tired and sleepy. But he must have been younger than I thought, since he lived with his mother and was not yet married.

I met Old Lady Chong once and that was enough. She had this peculiar smell like a baby that had done something in its pants. And her fingers felt like a dead person's, like an old peach I once found in the back of the refrigerator; the skin just slid off the meat when I picked it up.

I soon found out why Old Chong had retired from teaching piano. He was deaf. "Like Beethoven!" he shouted to me. "We're both listening only in our head!" And he would start to conduct his frantic silent sonatas.

Our lessons went like this. He would open the book and point to different things, explaining their purpose: "Key! Treble! Bass! No sharps or flats! So this is C major! Listen now and play after me!"

And then he would play the C scale a few times, a simple chord, and then, as if inspired by an old, unreachable itch, he gradually added more notes and running trills and a pounding bass until the music was really something quite grand.

I would play after him, the simple scale, the simple chord, and then I just   40 played some nonsense that sounded like a cat running up and down on top of garbage cans. Old Chong smiled and applauded and then said, "Very good! But now you must learn to keep time!"

So that's how I discovered that Old Chong's eyes were too slow to keep up with the wrong notes I was playing. He went through the motions in half-time. To help me keep rhythm, he stood behind me, pushing down on my right shoulder for every beat. He balanced pennies on top of my wrists so I would keep them still as I slowly played scales and arpeggios. He had me curve my hand around an apple and keep that shape when playing chords. He marched stiffly to show me how to make each finger dance up and down, staccato like an obedient little soldier.

He taught me all these things, and that was how I also learned I could be lazy and get away with mistakes, lots of mistakes. If I hit the wrong notes because I hadn't practiced enough, I never corrected myself. I just kept playing in rhythm. And Old Chong kept conducting his own private reverie.

So maybe I never really gave myself a fair chance. I did pick up the basics pretty quickly, and I might have become a good pianist at that young age. But I was so determined not to try, not to be anybody different that I learned to play only the most ear-splitting preludes, the most discordant hymns.

Over the next year, I practiced like this, dutifully in my own way. And then one day I heard my mother and her friend Lindo Jong both talking in a loud bragging tone of voice so others could hear. It was after church, and I was leaning against the brick wall wearing a dress with stiff white petticoats. Auntie Lindo's daughter, Waverly, who was about my age, was standing farther down the wall about five feet away. We had grown up together and shared all the closeness of two sisters squabbling over crayons and dolls. In other words, for the most part, we hated each other. I thought she was snotty. Waverly Jong had gained a certain amount of fame as "Chinatown's Littlest Chinese Chess Champion."

"She bring home too many trophy," lamented Auntie Lindo that Sunday. 45 "All day she play chess. All day I have no time do nothing but dust off her winnings." She threw a scolding look at Waverly, who pretended not to see her.

"You lucky you don't have this problem," said Auntie Lindo with a sigh to my mother.

And my mother squared her shoulders and bragged: "Our problem worser than yours. If we ask Jing-mei wash dish, she hear nothing but music. It's like you can't stop this natural talent."

And right then, I was determined to put a stop to her foolish pride.

A few weeks later, Old Chong and my mother conspired to have me play in a talent show which would be held in the church hall. By then, my parents had saved up enough to buy me a secondhand piano, a black Wurlitzer spinet with a scarred bench. It was the showpiece of our living room.

For the talent show, I was to play a piece called "Pleading Child" from 50 Schumann's *Scenes from Childhood.* It was a simple, moody piece that sounded more difficult than it was. I was supposed to memorize the whole thing, playing the repeat parts twice to make the piece sound longer. But I dawdled over it, playing a few bars and then cheating, looking up to see what notes followed. I never really listened to what I was playing. I daydreamed about being somewhere else, about being someone else.

The part I liked to practice best was the fancy curtsy: right foot out, touch the rose on the carpet with a pointed foot, sweep to the side, left leg bends, look up and smile.

My parents invited all the couples from the Joy Luck Club to witness my debut. Auntie Lindo and Uncle Tin were there. Waverly and her two older brothers had also come. The first two rows were filled with children both younger and older than I was. The littlest ones got to go first. They recited simple nursery rhymes, squawked out tunes on miniature violins, twirled Hula Hoops, pranced in pink ballet tutus, and when they bowed or curtsied, the audience would sigh in unison, "Awww," and then clap enthusiastically.

When my turn came, I was very confident. I remember my childish excitement. It was as if I knew, without a doubt, that the prodigy side of me really did
exist. I had no fear whatsoever, no nervousness. I remember thinking to myself,
This is it! This is it! I looked out over the audience, at my mother's blank face, my
father's yawn, Auntie Lindo's stiff-lipped smile, Waverly's sulky expression. I had
on a white dress layered with sheets of lace, and a pink bow in my Peter Pan haircut. As I sat down I envisioned people jumping to their feet and Ed Sullivan rushing up to introduce me to everyone on TV.

And I started to play. It was so beautiful. I was so caught up in how lovely I
looked that at first I didn't worry how I would sound. So it was a surprise to me
when I hit the first wrong note and I realized something didn't sound quite right.
And then I hit another and another followed that. A chill started at the top of my
head and began to trickle down. Yet I couldn't stop playing, as though my hands
were bewitched. I kept thinking my fingers would adjust themselves back, like a
train switching to the right track. I played this strange jumble through two
repeats, the sour notes staying with me all the way to the end.

When I stood up, I discovered my legs were shaking. Maybe I had just been   55
nervous and the audience, like Old Chong, had seen me go through the right
motions and had not heard anything wrong at all. I swept my right foot out, went
down on my knee, looked up and smiled. The room was quiet, except for Old
Chong, who was beaming and shouting, "Bravo! Bravo! Well done!" But then I
saw my mother's face, her stricken face. The audience clapped weakly, and as
I walked back to my chair, with my whole face quivering as I tried not to cry, I
heard a little boy whisper loudly to his mother, "That was awful," and the mother
whispered back, "Well, she certainly tried."

And now I realized how many people were in the audience, the whole world
it seemed. I was aware of eyes burning into my back. I felt the shame of my
mother and father as they sat stiffly throughout the rest of the show.

We could have escaped during intermission. Pride and some strange sense
of honor must have anchored my parents to their chairs. And so we watched it
all: the eighteen-year-old boy with a fake mustache who did a magic show and
juggled flaming hoops while riding a unicycle. The breasted girl with white
makeup who sang from *Madama Butterfly* and got honorable mention. And the
eleven-year-old boy who won first prize playing a tricky violin song that sounded
like a busy bee.

After the show, the Hsus, the Jongs, and the St. Clairs from the Joy Luck
Club came up to my mother and father.

"Lots of talented kids," Auntie Lindo said vaguely, smiling broadly.

"That was somethin' else," said my father, and I wondered if he was referring   60
to me in a humorous way, or whether he even remembered what I had done.

Waverly looked at me and shrugged her shoulders. "You aren't a genius like
me," she said matter-of-factly. And if I hadn't felt so bad, I would have pulled her
braids and punched her stomach.

But my mother's expression was what devastated me: a quiet, blank look that
said she had lost everything. I felt the same way, and it seemed as if everybody
were now coming up, like gawkers at the scene of an accident, to see what parts

were actually missing. When we got on the bus to go home, my father was humming the busy-bee tune and my mother was silent. I kept thinking she wanted to wait until we got home before shouting at me. But when my father unlocked the door to our apartment, my mother walked in and then went to the back, into the bedroom. No accusations. No blame. And in a way, I felt disappointed. I had been waiting for her to start shouting, so I could shout back and cry and blame her for all my misery.

I assumed my talent-show fiasco meant I never had to play the piano again. But two days later, after school, my mother came out of the kitchen and saw me watching TV.

"Four clock," she reminded me as if it were any other day. I was stunned, as though she were asking me to go through the talent-show torture again. I wedged myself more tightly in front of the TV.

"Turn off TV," she called from the kitchen five minutes later.   65

I didn't budge. And then I decided. I didn't have to do what my mother said anymore. I wasn't her slave. This wasn't China. I had listened to her before and look what happened. She was the stupid one.

She came out from the kitchen and stood in the arched entryway of the living room. "Four clock," she said once again, louder.

"I'm not going to play anymore," I said nonchalantly. "Why should I? I'm not a genius."

She walked over and stood in front of the TV. I saw her chest was heaving up and down in an angry way.

"No!" I said, and I now felt stronger, as if my true self had finally emerged. So   70
this was what had been inside me all along.

"No! I won't!" I screamed.

She yanked me by the arm, pulled me off the floor, snapped off the TV. She was frighteningly strong, half pulling, half carrying me toward the piano as I kicked the throw rugs under my feet. She lifted me up and onto the hard bench. I was sobbing by now, looking at her bitterly. Her chest was heaving even more and her mouth was open, smiling crazily as if she were pleased I was crying.

"You want me to be someone that I'm not!" I sobbed. "I'll never be the kind of daughter you want me to be!"

"Only two kinds of daughters," she shouted in Chinese. "Those who are obedient and those who follow their own mind! Only one kind of daughter can live in this house. Obedient daughter!"

"Then I wish I wasn't your daughter. I wish you weren't my mother," I   75
shouted. As I said these things I got scared. I felt like worms and toads and slimy things were crawling out of my chest, but it also felt good, as if this awful side of me had surfaced, at last.

"Too late change this," said my mother shrilly.

And I could sense her anger rising to its breaking point. I wanted to see it spill over. And that's when I remembered the babies she had lost in China, the ones we never talked about. "Then I wish I'd never been born!" I shouted. "I wish I were dead! Like them."

It was as if I had said the magic words, Alakazam!—and her face went blank, her mouth closed, her arms went slack, and she backed out of the room, stunned, as if she were blowing away like a small brown leaf, thin, brittle, lifeless.

It was not the only disappointment my mother felt in me. In the years that followed, I failed her so many times, each time asserting my own will, my right to fall short of expectations. I didn't get straight As. I didn't become class president. I didn't get into Stanford. I dropped out of college.

For unlike my mother, I did not believe I could be anything I wanted to be. I   80
could only be me.

And for all those years, we never talked about the disaster at the recital or my terrible accusations afterward at the piano bench. All that remained unchecked, like a betrayal that was now unspeakable. So I never found a way to ask her why she had hoped for something so large that failure was inevitable.

And even worse, I never asked her what frightened me the most: Why had she given up hope?

For after our struggle at the piano, she never mentioned my playing again. The lessons stopped, the lid to the piano was closed, shutting out the dust, my misery, and her dreams.

So she surprised me. A few years ago, she offered to give me the piano, for my thirtieth birthday. I had not played in all those years. I saw the offer as a sign of forgiveness, a tremendous burden removed.

"Are you sure?" I asked shyly. "I mean, won't you and Dad miss it?"   85

"No, this your piano," she said firmly. "Always your piano. You only one can play."

"Well, I probably can't play anymore," I said. "It's been years."

"You pick up fast," said my mother, as if she knew this was certain. "You have natural talent. You could been genius if you want to."

"No I couldn't."

"You just not trying," said my mother. And she was neither angry nor sad.   90
She said it as if to announce a fact that could never be disproved. "Take it," she said.

But I didn't at first. It was enough that she had offered it to me. And after that, every time I saw it in my parents' living room, standing in front of the bay windows, it made me feel proud, as if it were a shiny trophy I had won back.

Last week I sent a tuner over to my parents' apartment and had the piano reconditioned, for purely sentimental reasons. My mother had died a few months before and I had been getting things in order for my father, a little bit at a time. I put the jewelry in special silk pouches. The sweaters she had knitted in yellow, pink, bright orange—all the colors I hated—I put those in moth-proof boxes. I found some old Chinese silk dresses, the kind with little slits up the sides. I rubbed the old silk against my skin, then wrapped them in tissue and decided to take them home with me.

After I had the piano tuned, I opened the lid and touched the keys. It sounded even richer than I remembered. Really, it was a very good piano. Inside

the bench were the same exercise notes with handwritten scales, the same secondhand music books with their covers held together with yellow tape.

I opened up the Schumann book to the dark little piece I had played at the
recital. It was on the left-hand side of the page, "Pleading Child." It looked more
difficult than I remembered. I played a few bars, surprised at how easily the notes
came back to me.

And for the first time, or so it seemed, I noticed the piece on the right-hand   95
side. It was called "Perfectly Contented." I tried to play this one as well. It had a
lighter melody but the same flowing rhythm and turned out to be quite easy.
"Pleading Child" was shorter but slower; "Perfectly Contented" was longer but
faster. And after I played them both a few times, I realized they were two halves of
the same song.   [1989]

THINKING ABOUT THE TEXT

1. Most sons and daughters struggle to establish their own identities. Does
   this seem true in "Two Kinds"? Does the cultural difference between the
   immigrant mother and americanized daughter intensify their struggle?
   Do you think you have different goals in life than your parents do?

2. Do you agree with the mother's belief that "you could be anything you
   wanted to be in America" (para. 1)? Does race matter? Gender? Ethnicity? Religion? Sexual orientation?

3. What do you believe each character learned from the argument at the
   piano bench the day after the recital?

4. How does Tan establish the differing personalities of her characters?
   Through details? Dialogue? Anecdotes? Do the main characters change
   significantly? Does she tell us or show us?

5. Do you sympathize with the mother or the daughter? Should parents
   channel their children toward selected activities? Or should parents let
   their children choose their own paths? Can parents push their children
   too much? Why would they do this?

MAKING COMPARISONS

1. Do you think Emily's mother in Olsen's story would want to be like the
   Chinese mother if given the opportunity? Which mother would you prefer to have? Why?

2. One mother seems to do too little, one too much. Is this your reading
   of the two stories? Is the lesson of Olsen's and Tan's stories that mothers
   can't win no matter what they do? Or do you have a more optimistic interpretation?

3. Which daughter's life seems more difficult? How possible is it to say from
   the outside looking in?

WRITING ABOUT ISSUES

1. As Emily's teacher, write a letter to Emily's mother persuading her that she should still come in for a conference. Acknowledge her excuses and her side of the issue but offer objections.

2. Write a brief essay arguing that each of the mothers presented in Olsen's and Tan's stories is either a good or bad model for parenting.

3. Write a personal experience narrative about a time when your parents pushed you too hard, or too little, or wanted you to be someone you thought you were not. Conclude with your present view of the consequences of their action.

4. Ask six males and six females if they feel their parents tried to shape their personalities, behavior, choice of friends, and so forth. Were the parents' efforts successful? Do the sons and daughters resent it now? Conclude your brief report with some generalizations, including how relevant gender is.

SIBLINGS IN CONFLICT

TOBIAS WOLFF, "The Rich Brother"
JAMES BALDWIN, "Sonny's Blues"

Although the expression "blood is thicker than water" suggests that brothers and sisters should support each other, the reality is often more complex. Children growing up together share intense emotional ties, but affection and loyalty sometimes conflict with hostility and jealousy. Children often feel they are competing for their parents' attention and love, a rivalry often played out over a lifetime and intensified as siblings choose different lifestyles. Well into adulthood, brothers and sisters often find their relationships with each other conflicted by unresolved issues of mutual responsibility and disparities in values as well as individual issues of financial success, self-esteem, and guilt. The siblings in the following two stories, separated by age and disparate occupations, engage in a psychologically complex dance that ebbs and flows over their lives. They struggle to understand each other and ultimately themselves, for, as with all of us, healthy relationships with siblings start with a healthy relationship with oneself.

BEFORE YOU READ

How would you describe your relationship with your siblings? Did rivalry ever play a part? Does it now? Do you consider your siblings' futures as similar to yours? Is it important for brothers and sisters to look after each other? Or might that create more problems than it solves?

TOBIAS WOLFF
The Rich Brother

Tobias Wolff (b. 1945) is known chiefly for his short stories. The following piece comes from his second collection, Back in the World *(1985). He has produced two other volumes of stories,* In the Garden of the North American Martyrs *(1981) and* The Night in Question *(1996), and a short novel,* The Barracks Thief *(1984). Wolff is also the author of two memoirs. In the first,* This Boy's Life *(1989), he recalls his parents' divorce and subsequent family dramas. These include wanderings with his mother through the West and Northwest; arguments with his abusive stepfather; occasional contact with his real father, who was a habitual liar later imprisoned for fraud; and years of separation from his brother Geoffrey, who eventually became a writer himself.* This Boy's Life *won the* Los Angeles Times *Book Award for Biography and later became a movie starring Robert De Niro as the stepfather and Leonardo DiCaprio as the young Toby. Wolff's second memoir,* In Pharaoh's Army: Memories of the Lost War *(1994), mostly deals with his military service in Vietnam. Today, Wolff teaches creative writing at Syracuse University.*

There were two brothers, Pete and Donald.

Pete, the older brother, was in real estate. He and his wife had a Century 21 franchise in Santa Cruz. Pete worked hard and made a lot of money, but not any more than he thought he deserved. He had two daughters, a sailboat, a house from which he could see a thin slice of the ocean, and friends doing well enough in their own lives not to wish bad luck on him. Donald, the younger brother, was still single. He lived alone, painted houses when he found the work, and got deeper in debt to Pete when he didn't.

No one would have taken them for brothers. Where Pete was stout and hearty and at home in the world, Donald was bony, grave, and obsessed with the fate of his soul. Over the years Donald had worn the images of two different Perfect Masters around his neck. Out of devotion to the second of these he entered an ashram in Berkeley, where he nearly died of undiagnosed hepatitis. By the time Pete finished paying the medical bills Donald had become a Christian. He drifted from church to church, then joined a pentecostal community that met somewhere in the Mission District to sing in tongues and swap prophecies.

Pete couldn't make sense of it. Their parents were both dead, but while they were alive neither of them had found it necessary to believe in anything. They managed to be decent people without making fools of themselves, and Pete had the same ambition. He thought that the whole thing was an excuse for Donald to take himself seriously.

The trouble was that Donald couldn't content himself with worrying about his own soul. He had to worry about everyone else's, and especially Pete's. He handed down his judgments in ways that he seemed to consider subtle: through significant silence, innuendo, looks of mild despair that said, *Brother, what have*

5

you come to? What Pete had come to, as far as he could tell, was prosperity. That was the real issue between them. Pete prospered and Donald did not prosper.

At the age of forty Pete took up sky diving. He made his first jump with two friends who'd started only a few months earlier and were already doing stunts. He never would have used the word *mystical*, but that was how Pete felt about the experience. Later he made the mistake of trying to describe it to Donald, who kept asking how much it cost and then acted appalled when Pete told him.

"At least I'm trying something new," Pete said. "At least I'm breaking the pattern."

Not long after that conversation Donald also broke the pattern, by going to live on a farm outside Paso Robles. The farm was owned by several members of Donald's community, who had bought it and moved there with the idea of forming a family of faith. That was how Donald explained it in the first letter he sent. Every week Pete heard how happy Donald was, how "in the Lord." He told Pete that he was praying for him, he and the rest of Pete's brothers and sisters on the farm.

"I only have one brother," Pete wanted to answer, "and that's enough." But he kept this thought to himself.

In November the letters stopped. Pete didn't worry about this at first, but   10
when he called Donald at Thanksgiving Donald was grim. He tried to sound upbeat but he didn't try hard enough to make it convincing. "Now listen," Pete said, "you don't have to stay in that place if you don't want to."

"I'll be all right," Donald answered.

"That's not the point. Being all right is not the point. If you don't like what's going on up there, then get out."

"I'm all right," Donald said again, more firmly. "I'm doing fine."

But he called Pete a week later and said that he was quitting the farm. When Pete asked him where he intended to go, Donald admitted that he had no plan. His car had been repossessed just before he left the city, and he was flat broke.

"I guess you'll have to stay with us," Pete said.   15

Donald put up a show of resistance. Then he gave in. "Just until I get my feet on the ground," he said.

"Right," Pete said. "Check out your options." He told Donald he'd send him money for a bus ticket, but as they were about to hang up Pete changed his mind. He knew that Donald would try hitchhiking to save the fare. Pete didn't want him out on the road all alone where some head case would pick him up, where anything could happen to him.

"Better yet," he said, "I'll come and get you."

"You don't have to do that. I didn't expect you to do that," Donald said. He added, "It's a pretty long drive."

"Just tell me how to get there."   20

But Donald wouldn't give him directions. He said that the farm was too depressing, that Pete wouldn't like it. Instead, he insisted on meeting Pete at a service station called Jonathan's Mechanical Emporium.

"You must be kidding," Pete said.

"It's close to the highway," Donald said. "I didn't name it."

"That's one for the collection," Pete said.

The day before he left to bring Donald home, Pete received a letter from a 25
man who described himself as "head of household" at the farm where Donald
had been living. From this letter Pete learned that Donald had not quit the farm,
but had been asked to leave. The letter was written on the back of a mimeo-
graphed survey form asking people to record their response to a ceremony of
some kind. The last question said:

> What did you feel during the liturgy?
> a) Being
> b) Becoming
> c) Being and Becoming
> d) None of the Above
> e) All of the Above

Pete tried to forget the letter. But of course he couldn't. Each time he
thought of it he felt crowded and breathless, a feeling that came over him again
when he drove into the service station and saw Donald sitting against a wall with
his head on his knees. It was late afternoon. A paper cup tumbled slowly past
Donald's feet, pushed by the damp wind.

Pete honked and Donald raised his head. He smiled at Pete, then stood and
stretched. His arms were long and thin and white. He wore a red bandanna across
his forehead, a T-shirt with a couple of words on the front. Pete couldn't read
them because the letters were inverted.

"Grow up," Pete yelled. "Get a Mercedes."

Donald came up to the window. He bent down and said, "Thanks for coming. You must be totally whipped."

"I'll make it." Pete pointed at Donald's T-shirt. "What's that supposed to say?" 30

Donald looked down at his shirt front. "Try God. I guess I put it on backwards. Pete, could I borrow a couple of dollars? I owe these people for coffee and
sandwiches."

Pete took five twenties from his wallet and held them out the window.

Donald stepped back as if horrified. "I don't need that much."

"I can't keep track of all these nickels and dimes," Pete said. "Just pay me
back when your ship comes in." He waved the bills impatiently. "Go on—
take it."

"Only for now." Donald took the money and went into the service station 35
office. He came out carrying two orange sodas, one of which he gave to Pete as he
got into the car. "My treat," he said.

"No bags?"

"Wow, thanks for reminding me." Donald balanced his drink on the dashboard, but the slight rocking of the car as he got out tipped it onto the passenger's
seat, where half its contents foamed over before Pete could snatch it up again.
Donald looked on while Pete held the bottle out the window, soda running down
his fingers.

"Wipe it up," Pete told him. "Quick!"

"With what?"

Pete stared at Donald. "That shirt. Use the shirt."

Donald pulled a long face but did as he was told, his pale skin puckering against the wind.

"Great, just great," Pete said. "We haven't even left the gas station yet."

Afterwards, on the highway, Donald said, "This is a new car, isn't it?"

"Yes. This is a new car."

"Is that why you're so upset about the seat?"

"Forget it, okay? Let's just forget about it."

"I said I was sorry."

Pete said, "I just wish you'd be more careful. These seats are made of leather. That stain won't come out, not to mention the smell. I don't see why I can't have leather seats that smell like leather instead of orange pop."

"What was wrong with the other car?"

Pete glanced over at Donald. Donald had raised the hood of the blue sweat-shirt he'd put on. The peaked hood above his gaunt, watchful face gave him the look of an inquisitor.

"There wasn't anything wrong with it," Pete said. "I just happened to like this one better."

Donald nodded.

There was a long silence between them as Pete drove on and the day dark-ened toward evening. On either side of the road lay stubble-covered fields. A line of low hills ran along the horizon, topped here and there with trees black against the grey sky. In the approaching line of cars a driver turned on his headlights. Pete did the same.

"So what happened?" he asked. "Farm life not your bag?"

Donald took some time to answer, and at last he said, simply, "It was my fault."

"What was your fault?"

"The whole thing. Don't play dumb, Pete. I know they wrote to you." Donald looked at Pete, then stared out the windshield again.

"I'm not playing dumb."

Donald shrugged.

"All I really know is they asked you to leave," Pete went on. "I don't know any of the particulars."

"I blew it," Donald said. "Believe me, you don't want to hear the gory details."

"Sure I do," Pete said. He added, "Everybody likes the gory details."

"You mean everybody likes to hear how someone messed up."

"Right," Pete said. "That's the way it is here on Spaceship Earth."

Donald bent one knee onto the front seat and leaned against the door so that he was facing Pete instead of the windshield. Pete was aware of Donald's scrutiny. He waited. Night was coming on in a rush now, filling the hollows of the land. Donald's long cheeks and deep-set eyes were dark with shadow. His brow was white. "Do you ever dream about me?" Donald asked.

"Do I ever dream about you? What kind of a question is that? Of course I don't dream about you," Pete said, untruthfully.

"What do you dream about?"

"Sex and money. Mostly money. A nightmare is when I dream I don't have any."

"You're just making that up," Donald said.

Pete smiled.

"Sometimes I wake up at night," Donald went on, "and I can tell you're dreaming about me."

"We were talking about the farm," Pete said. "Let's finish that conversation and then we can talk about our various out-of-body experiences and the interesting things we did during previous incarnations."

For a moment Donald looked like a grinning skull; then he turned serious again. "There's not much to tell," he said. "I just didn't do anything right."

"That's a little vague," Pete said.

"Well, like the groceries. Whenever it was my turn to get the groceries I'd blow it somehow. I'd bring the groceries home and half of them would be missing, or I'd have all the wrong things, the wrong kind of flour or the wrong kind of chocolate or whatever. One time I gave them away. It's not funny, Pete."

Pete said, "Who did you give the groceries to?"

"Just some people I picked up on the way home. Some fieldworkers. They had about eight kids with them and they didn't even speak English — just nodded their heads. Still, I shouldn't have given away the groceries. Not all of them, anyway. I really learned my lesson about that. You have to be practical. You have to be fair to yourself." Donald leaned forward, and Pete could sense his excitement. "There's nothing actually wrong with being in business," he said. "As long as you're fair to other people you can still be fair to yourself. I'm thinking of going into business, Pete."

"We'll talk about it," Pete said. "So, that's the story? There isn't any more to it than that?"

"What did they tell you?" Donald asked.

"Nothing."

"They must have told you something."

Pete shook his head.

"They didn't tell you about the fire?" When Pete shook his head again Donald regarded him for a time, then folded his arms across his chest and slumped back into the corner. "Everybody had to take turns cooking dinner. I usually did tuna casserole or spaghetti with garlic bread. But this one night I thought I'd do something different, something really interesting." Donald looked sharply at Pete. "It's all a big laugh to you, isn't it?"

"I'm sorry," Pete said.

"You don't know when to quit. You just keep hitting away."

"Tell me about the fire, Donald."

Donald kept watching him. "You have this compulsion to make me look foolish."

"Come off it, Donald. Don't make a big thing out of this."

"I know why you do it. It's because you don't have any purpose in life. You're afraid to relate to people who do, so you make fun of them."

"Relate," Pete said.

"You're basically a very frightened individual," Donald said. "Very threatened. You've always been like that. Do you remember when you used to try to kill me?"

"I don't have any compulsion to make you look foolish, Donald—you do it yourself. You're doing it right now."

"You can't tell me you don't remember," Donald said. "It was after my operation. You remember that?"

"Sort of." Pete shrugged. "Not really."

"Oh yes," Donald said. "Do you want to see the scar?"

"I remember you had an operation. I don't remember the specifics, that's all. And I sure as hell don't remember trying to kill you."

"Oh yes," Donald repeated, maddeningly. "You bet your life you did. All the time. The thing was, I couldn't have anything happen to me where they sewed me up because then my intestines would come apart again and poison me. That was a big issue, Pete. Mom was always in a state about me climbing trees and so on. And you used to hit me there every chance you got."

"Mom was in a state every time you burped," Pete said. "I don't know. Maybe I bumped into you accidentally once or twice. I never did it deliberately."

"Every chance you got," Donald said. "Like when the folks went out at night and left you to baby-sit. I'd hear them say good night, and then I'd hear the car start up, and when they were gone I'd lie there and listen. After a while I would hear you coming down the hall, and I would close my eyes and pretend to be asleep. There were nights when you would stand outside the door, just stand there, and then go away again. But most nights you'd open the door and I would hear you in the room with me, breathing. You'd come over and sit next to me on the bed—you remember, Pete, you have to—you'd sit next to me on the bed and pull the sheets back. If I was on my stomach you'd roll me over. Then you would lift up my pajama shirt and start hitting me on my stitches. You'd hit me as hard as you could, over and over. I was afraid that you'd get mad if you knew I was awake. Is that strange or what? I was afraid that you'd get mad if you found out that I knew you were trying to kill me." Donald laughed. "Come on, you can't tell me you don't remember that."

"It might have happened once or twice. Kids do those things. I can't get all excited about something I maybe did twenty-five years ago."

"No maybe about it. You did it."

Pete said, "You're wearing me out with this stuff. We've got a long drive ahead of us and if you don't back off pretty soon we aren't going to make it. You aren't, anyway."

Donald turned away.

"I'm doing my best," Pete said. The self-pity in his own voice made the words sound like a lie. But they weren't a lie! He was doing his best.

The car topped a rise. In the distance Pete saw a cluster of lights that blinked out when he started downhill. There was no moon. The sky was low and black.

"Come to think of it," Pete said, "I did have a dream about you the other night." Then he added, impatiently, as if Donald were badgering him, "A couple of other nights, too. I'm getting hungry," he said.

"The same dream?"

"Different dreams. I only remember one of them. There was something wrong with me, and you were helping out. Taking care of me. Just the two of us. I don't know where everyone else was supposed to be."

Pete left it at that. He didn't tell Donald that in this dream he was blind.

"I wonder if that was when I woke up," Donald said. He added, "I'm sorry I   110
got into that thing about my scar. I keep trying to forget it but I guess I never will. Not really. It was pretty strange, having someone around all the time who wanted to get rid of me."

"Kid stuff," Pete said. "Ancient history."

They ate dinner at a Denny's on the other side of King City. As Pete was paying the check he heard a man behind him say, "Excuse me, but I wonder if I might ask which way you're going?" and Donald answer, "Santa Cruz."

"Perfect," the man said.

Pete could see him in the fish-eye mirror above the cash register: a red blazer with some kind of crest on the pocket, little black moustache, glossy black hair combed down on his forehead like a Roman emperor's. A rug. Pete thought. Definitely a rug.

Pete got his change and turned. "Why is that perfect?" he asked.   115

The man looked at Pete. He had a soft, ruddy face that was doing its best to express pleasant surprise, as if this new wrinkle were all he could have wished for, but the eyes behind the aviator glasses showed signs of regret. His lips were moist and shiny. "I take it you're together," he said.

"You got it," Pete told him.

"All the better, then," the man went on. "It so happens I'm going to Santa Cruz myself. Had a spot of car trouble down the road. The old Caddy let me down."

"What kind of trouble?" Pete asked.

"Engine trouble," the man said. "I'm afraid it's a bit urgent. My daughter is sick.   120
Urgently sick. I've got a telegram here." He patted the breast pocket of his blazer.

Before Pete could say anything Donald got into the act again. "No problem," Donald said. "We've got tons of room."

"Not that much room," Pete said.

Donald nodded. "I'll put my things in the trunk."

"The trunk's full," Pete told him.

"It so happens I'm traveling light," the man said. "This leg of the trip anyway.   125
In fact, I don't have any luggage at this particular time."

Pete said, "Left it in the old Caddy, did you?"

"Exactly," the man said.

"No problem," Donald repeated. He walked outside and the man went with him. Together they strolled across the parking lot, Pete following at a distance. When they reached Pete's car Donald raised his face to the sky, and the man did the same. They stood there looking up. "Dark night," Donald said.

"Stygian," the man said.

Pete still had it in his mind to brush him off, but he didn't do that. Instead he   130
unlocked the door for him. He wanted to see what would happen. It was an
adventure, but not a dangerous adventure. The man might steal Pete's ashtrays
but he wouldn't kill him. If Pete got killed on the road it would be by some spiritual person in a sweatsuit, someone with his eyes on the far horizon and a wet Try
God T-shirt in his duffel bag.

As soon as they left the parking lot the man lit a cigar. He blew a cloud of
smoke over Pete's shoulder and sighed with pleasure. "Put it out," Pete told him.

"Of course," the man said. Pete looked in the rearview mirror and saw the
man take another long puff before dropping the cigar out the window. "Forgive
me," he said. "I should have asked. Name's Webster, by the way."

Donald turned and looked back at him. "First name or last?"

The man hesitated. "Last," he said finally.

"I know a Webster," Donald said. "Mick Webster."   135

"There are many of us," Webster said.

"Big fellow, wooden leg," Pete said.

Donald gave Pete a look.

Webster shook his head. "Doesn't ring a bell. Still, I wouldn't deny the connection. Might be one of the cousinry."

"What's your daughter got?" Pete asked.   140

"That isn't clear," Webster answered. "It appears to be a female complaint of
some nature. Then again it may be tropical." He was quiet for a moment, and
added: "If indeed it *is* tropical, I will have to assume some of the blame myself. It
was my own vaulting ambition that first led us to the tropics and kept us in the
tropics all those many years, exposed to every evil. Truly I have much to answer
for. I left my wife there."

Donald said quietly, "You mean she died?"

"I buried her with these hands. The earth will be repaid, gold for gold."

"Which tropics?" Pete asked.

"The tropics of Peru."   145

"What part of Peru are they in?"

"The lowlands," Webster said.

"What's it like down there? In the lowlands."

"Another world," Webster said. His tone was sepulchral. "A world better
imagined than described."

"Far out," Pete said.   150

The three men rode in silence for a time. A line of trucks went past in the
other direction, trailers festooned with running lights, engines roaring.

"Yes," Webster said at last, "I have much to answer for."

Pete smiled at Donald, but Donald had turned in his seat again and was gazing at Webster. "I'm sorry about your wife," Donald said.

"What did she die of?" Pete asked.

"A wasting illness," Webster said. "The doctors have no name for it, but I do."   155
He leaned forward and said, fiercely, "*Greed*. My greed, not hers. She wanted no
part of it."

Pete bit his lip. Webster was a find and Pete didn't want to scare him off by hooting at him. In a voice low and innocent of knowingness, he asked, "What took you there?"

"It's difficult for me to talk about."

"Try," Pete told him.

"A cigar would make it easier."

Donald turned to Pete and said, "It's okay with me."   160

"All right," Pete said. "Go ahead. Just keep the window rolled down."

"Much obliged." A match flared. There were eager sucking sounds.

"Let's hear it," Pete said.

"I am by training an engineer," Webster began. "My work has exposed me to all but one of the continents, to desert and alp and forest, to every terrain and season of the earth. Some years ago I was hired by the Peruvian government to search for tungsten in the tropics. My wife and daughter accompanied me. We were the only white people for a thousand miles in any direction, and we had no choice but to live as the Indians lived—to share their food and drink and even their culture."

Pete said, "You knew the lingo, did you?"   165

"We picked it up." The ember of the cigar bobbed up and down. "We were used to learning as necessity decreed. At any rate, it became evident after a couple of years that there was no tungsten to be found. My wife had fallen ill and was pleading to be taken home. But I was deaf to her pleas, because by then I was on the trail of another metal—a metal far more valuable than tungsten."

"Let me guess," Pete said. "Gold?"

Donald looked at Pete, then back at Webster.

"Gold," Webster said. "A vein of gold greater than the Mother Lode itself. After I found the first traces of it nothing could tear me away from my search—not the sickness of my wife or anything else. I was determined to uncover the vein, and so I did—but not before I laid my wife to rest. As I say, the earth will be repaid."

Webster was quiet. Then he said, "But life must go on. In the years since my   170
wife's death I have been making the arrangements necessary to open the mine. I could have done it immediately, of course, enriching myself beyond measure, but I knew what that would mean—the exploitation of our beloved Indians, the brutal destruction of their environment. I felt I had too much to atone for already." Webster paused, and when he spoke again his voice was dull and rushed, as if he had used up all the interest he had in his own words. "Instead I drew up a program for returning the bulk of the wealth to the Indians themselves. A kind of trust fund. The interest alone will allow them to secure their ancient lands and rights in perpetuity. At the same time, our investors will be rewarded a thousandfold. Two-thousandfold. Everyone will prosper together."

"That's great," said Donald. "That's the way it ought to be."

Pete said, "I'm willing to bet that you just happen to have a few shares left. Am I right?"

Webster made no reply.

"Well?" Pete knew that Webster was on to him now, but he didn't care. The story had bored him. He'd expected something different, something original, and

Webster had let him down. He hadn't even tried. Pete felt sour and stale. His eyes
burned from cigar smoke and the high beams of road-hogging truckers. "Douse
the stogie," he said to Webster. "I told you to keep the window down."

"Got a little nippy back here."   175

Donald said, "Hey, Pete. Lighten up."

"Douse it!"

Webster sighed. He got rid of the cigar.

"I'm a wreck," Pete said to Donald. "You want to drive for a while?"

Donald nodded.   180

Pete pulled over and they changed places.

Webster kept his counsel in the back seat. Donald hummed while he drove,
until Pete told him to stop. Then everything was quiet.

Donald was humming again when Pete woke up. Pete stared sullenly at the
road, at the white lines sliding past the car. After a few moments of this he turned
and said, "How long have I been out?"

Donald glanced at him. "Twenty, twenty-five minutes."

Pete looked behind him and saw that Webster was gone. "Where's our   185
friend?"

"You just missed him. He got out in Soledad. He told me to say thanks and
good-bye."

"Soledad? What about his sick daughter? How did he explain her away?"

"He has a brother living there. He's going to borrow a car from him and drive
the rest of the way in the morning."

"I'll bet his brother's living there," Pete said. "Doing fifty concurrent life sentences. His brother and his sister and his mom and his dad."

"I kind of liked him," Donald said.   190

"I'm sure you did," Pete said wearily.

"He was interesting. He's been places."

"His cigars had been places, I'll give you that."

"Come on, Pete."

"Come on yourself. What a phony."   195

"You don't know that."

"Sure I do."

"How? How do you know?"

Pete stretched. "Brother, there are some things you're just born knowing.
What's the gas situation?"

"We're a little low."   200

"Then why didn't you get some more?"

"I wish you wouldn't snap at me like that," Donald said.

"Then why don't you use your head? What if we run out?"

"We'll make it," Donald said. "I'm pretty sure we've got enough to make it.
You didn't have to be so rude to him," Donald added.

Pete took a deep breath. "I don't feel like running out of gas tonight, okay?"   205

Donald pulled in at the next station they came to and filled the tank while
Pete went to the men's room. When Pete came back, Donald was sitting in the

passenger's seat. The attendant came up to the driver's window as Pete got in behind the wheel. He bent down and said, "Twelve fifty-five."

"You heard the man," Pete said to Donald.

Donald looked straight ahead. He didn't move.

"Cough up," Pete said. "This trip's on you."

"I can't."   210

"Sure you can. Break out that wad."

Donald glanced up at the attendant, then at Pete. "Please," he said, "Pete, I don't have it anymore."

Pete took this in. He nodded, and paid the attendant.

Donald began to speak when they left the station but Pete cut him off. He said, "I don't want to hear from you right now. You just keep quiet or I swear to God I won't be responsible."

They left the fields and entered a tunnel of tall trees. The trees went on and   215 on. "Let me get this straight," Pete said at last. "You don't have the money I gave you."

"You treated him like a bug or something," Donald said.

"You don't have the money," Pete said again.

Donald shook his head.

"Since I bought dinner, and since we didn't stop anywhere in between, I assume you gave it to Webster. Is that right? Is that what you did with it?"

"Yes."   220

Pete looked at Donald. His face was dark under the hood but he still managed to convey a sense of remove, as if none of this had anything to do with him.

"Why?" Pete asked. "Why did you give it to him?" When Donald didn't answer, Pete said, "A hundred dollars. Gone. Just like that. I *worked* for that money, Donald."

"I know, I know," Donald said.

"You don't know! How could you? You get money by holding out your hand."

"I work too," Donald said.   225

"You work too. Don't kid yourself, brother."

Donald leaned toward Pete, about to say something, but Pete cut him off again.

"You're not the only one on the payroll, Donald. I don't think you understand that. I have a family."

"Pete, I'll pay you back."

"Like hell you will. A hundred dollars!" Pete hit the steering wheel with the   230 palm of his hand. "Just because you think I hurt some goofball's feelings. Jesus, Donald."

"That's not the reason," Donald said. "And I didn't just *give* him the money."

"What do you call it, then? What do you call what you did?"

"I *invested* it. I wanted a share, Pete." When Pete looked over at him Donald nodded and said again, "I wanted a share."

Pete said, "I take it you're referring to the gold mine in Peru."

"Yes," Donald said.   235

"You believe that such a gold mine exists?"

Donald looked at Pete, and Pete could see him just beginning to catch on. "You'll believe anything," Pete said. "Won't you? You really will believe anything at all."

"I'm sorry," Donald said, and turned away.

Pete drove on between the trees and considered the truth of what he had just said—that Donald would believe anything at all. And it came to him that it would be just like this unfair life for Donald to come out ahead in the end, by believing in some outrageous promise that would turn out to be true and that he, Pete, would reject out of hand because he was too wised up to listen to anybody's pitch anymore except for laughs. What a joke. What a joke if there really was a blessing to be had, and the blessing didn't come to the one who deserved it, the one who did all the work, but to the other.

And as if this had already happened Pete felt a shadow move upon him, dark-   240
ening his thoughts. After a time he said, "I can see where all this is going, Donald."

"I'll pay you back," Donald said.

"No," Pete said. "You won't pay me back. You can't. You don't know how. All you've ever done is take. All your life."

Donald shook his head.

"I see exactly where this is going," Pete went on. "You can't work, you can't take care of yourself, you believe anything anyone tells you. I'm stuck with you, aren't I?" He looked over at Donald. "I've got you on my hands for good."

Donald pressed his fingers against the dashboard as if to brace himself. "I'll   245
get out," he said.

Pete kept driving.

"Let me out," Donald said. "I mean it, Pete."

"Do you?"

Donald hesitated. "Yes," he said.

"Be sure," Pete told him. "This is it. This is for keeps."   250

"I mean it."

"All right. You made the choice." Pete braked the car sharply and swung it to the shoulder of the road. He turned off the engine and got out. Trees loomed on both sides, shutting out the sky. The air was cold and musty. Pete took Donald's duffel bag from the back seat and set it down behind the car. He stood there, facing Donald in the red glow of the taillights. "It's better this way," Pete said.

Donald just looked at him.

"Better for you," Pete said.

Donald hugged himself. He was shaking. "You don't have to say all that," he   255
told Pete. "I don't blame you."

"Blame me? What the hell are you talking about? Blame me for what?"

"For anything," Donald said.

"I want to know what you mean by blame me."

"Nothing. Nothing, Pete. You'd better get going. God bless you."

"That's it," Pete said. He dropped to one knee, searching the packed dirt with   260
his hands. He didn't know what he was looking for, his hands would know when
they found it.

Donald touched Pete's shoulder. "You'd better go," he said.

Somewhere in the trees Pete heard a branch snap. He stood up. He looked at
Donald, then went back to the car and drove away. He drove fast, hunched over
the wheel, conscious of the way he was hunched and the shallowness of his
breathing, refusing to look in the mirror above his head until there was nothing
behind him but darkness.

Then he said, "A hundred dollars," as if there were someone to hear.

The trees gave way to fields. Metal fences ran beside the road, plastered with
windblown scraps of paper. Tule fog hung above the ditches, spilling into the
road, dimming the ghostly halogen lights that burned in the yards of the farms
Pete passed. The fog left beads of water rolling up the windshield.

Pete rummaged among his cassettes. He found Pachelbel's Canon and   265
pushed it into the tape deck. When the violins began to play he leaned back and
assumed an attentive expression as if he were really listening to them. He smiled
to himself like a man at liberty to enjoy music, a man who has finished his work
and settled his debts, done all things meet and due.

And in this way, smiling, nodding to the music, he went another mile or so
and pretended that he was not already slowing down, that he was not going to
turn back, that he would be able to drive on like this, alone, and have the right
answer when his wife stood before him in the doorway of his home and asked,
Where is he? Where is your brother?   [1985]

THINKING ABOUT THE TEXT

1. Are you more sympathetic to Donald's side or to Pete's side in this story?
   Do you agree with the comment that "everybody likes to hear how someone messed up" (para. 63)? Does Donald get conned by Webster? Would
   you be angry with Donald for giving Webster your money? Does Pete
   want Donald to look foolish? Is Donald foolish?

2. How do you interpret Donald's story about Pete hitting his stitches? Is
   Pete trying to get rid of Donald? What could his reason be?

3. Why doesn't Pete tell Donald he was blind in his dream? How do you
   interpret this dream? Is the heart of their dispute "prosperity" or is it something else?

4. Your response to the Webster episode might say something about your
   own level of credulity. Were you skeptical of Webster from the first?
   Would you have given him a ride? Will Donald believe "anything"? Is it
   sometimes a good thing to be skeptical? Is it sometimes a good thing to
   believe in "some outrageous promise"?

5. Why would Pete turn around to get Donald? Why would he keep going?
   What would you do? Why?

JAMES BALDWIN
Sonny's Blues

James Baldwin (1924–1987) wanted to be a writer since he was a boy growing up in Harlem. He continued his writing through high school while also following in his foster father's footsteps by doing some preaching. On his own since he was eighteen, Baldwin left Greenwich Village in 1948 and moved to Paris. He lived in France for eight years before returning to New York, where he wrote widely about the civil rights movement. Indeed, passionate and eloquent essays like those in Notes of a Native Son *(1955) and* The Fire Next Time *(1963) exploring the place of African Americans in contemporary society are considered among the best nonfiction of Baldwin's generation.*

Being an artist and an African American were lifelong central issues for Baldwin. His fiction confronts the psychological challenges that were inevitable for black writers searching for identity in America. Themes of responsibility, pain, identity, frustration, and bitterness are woven into his fiction along with understanding, equanimity, love, and tolerance. "Sonny's Blues," from Going to Meet the Man *(1965), is one of his strongest dramatizations of the struggles and achievements of black artists.*

I read about it in the paper, in the subway, on my way to work. I read it, and I couldn't believe it, and I read it again. Then perhaps I just stared at it, at the newsprint spelling out his name, spelling out the story. I stared at it in the swinging lights of the subway car, and in the faces and bodies of the people, and in my own face, trapped in the darkness which roared outside.

It was not to be believed and I kept telling myself that, as I walked from the subway station to the high school. And at the same time I couldn't doubt it. I was scared, scared for Sonny. He became real to me again. A great block of ice got settled in my belly and kept melting there slowly all day long, while I taught my classes algebra. It was a special kind of ice. It kept melting, sending trickles of ice water all up and down my veins, but it never got less. Sometimes it hardened and seemed to expand until I felt my guts were going to come spilling out or that I was going to choke or scream. This would always be at a moment when I was remembering some specific thing Sonny had once said or done.

When he was about as old as the boys in my classes his face had been bright and open, there was a lot of copper in it; and he'd had wonderfully direct brown eyes, and great gentleness and privacy. I wondered what he looked like now. He had been picked up, the evening before, in a raid on an apartment downtown, for peddling and using heroin.

I couldn't believe it: but what I mean by that is that I couldn't find any room for it anywhere inside me. I had kept it outside me for a long time. I hadn't wanted to know. I had had suspicions, but I didn't name them, I kept putting them away. I told myself that Sonny was wild, but he wasn't crazy. And he'd always been a good boy, he hadn't ever turned hard or evil or disrespectful, the way kids can, so quick, so quick, especially in Harlem. I didn't want to believe that I'd ever see my brother going down, coming to nothing, all that light in his face gone out, in the condition I'd already seen so many others. Yet it had happened and here I was, talking about algebra to a lot of boys who might, every one of them for all I knew, be popping off needles every time they went to the head. Maybe it did more for them than algebra could.

I was sure that the first time Sonny had ever had horse, he couldn't have   5
been much older than these boys were now. These boys, now, were living as we'd been living then, they were growing up with a rush and their heads bumped abruptly against the low ceiling of their actual possibilities. They were filled with rage. All they really knew were two darknesses, the darkness of their lives, which was now closing in on them, and the darkness of the movies, which had blinded them to that other darkness, and in which they now, vindictively, dreamed, at once more together than they were at any other time, and more alone.

When the last bell rang, the last class ended, I let out my breath. It seemed I'd been holding it for all that time. My clothes were wet—I may have looked as though I'd been sitting in a steam bath, all dressed up, all afternoon. I sat alone in the classroom a long time. I listened to the boys outside, downstairs, shouting and cursing and laughing. Their laughter struck me for perhaps the first time. It was not the joyous laughter which—God knows why—one associates with children. It was mocking and insular, its intent to denigrate. It was disenchanted, and in this, also, lay the authority of their curses. Perhaps I was listening to them because I was thinking about my brother and in them I heard my brother. And myself.

One boy was whistling a tune, at once very complicated and very simple, it seemed to be pouring out of him as though he were a bird, and it sounded very cool and moving through all that harsh, bright air, only just holding its own through all those other sounds.

I stood up and walked over to the window and looked down into the courtyard. It was the beginning of the spring and the sap was rising in the boys. A teacher passed through them every now and again, quickly, as though he or she couldn't wait to get out of that courtyard, to get those boys out of their sight and off their minds. I started collecting my stuff. I thought I'd better get home and talk to Isabel.

The courtyard was almost deserted by the time I got downstairs. I saw this boy standing in the shadow of a doorway, looking just like Sonny. I almost called his name. Then I saw that it wasn't Sonny, but somebody we used to know, a boy from around our block. He'd been Sonny's friend. He'd never been mine, having been too young for me, and, anyway, I'd never liked him. And now, even though he was a grown-up man, he still hung around that block, still spent hours on the street corners, was always high and raggy. I used to run into him from time to time and he'd often work around to asking me for a quarter or fifty cents. He always had some real good excuse, too, and I always gave it to him, I don't know why.

But now, abruptly, I hated him. I couldn't stand the way he looked at me,   10
partly like a dog, partly like a cunning child. I wanted to ask him what the hell he was doing in the school courtyard.

He sort of shuffled over to me, and he said, "I see you got the papers. So you already know about it."

"You mean about Sonny? Yes, I already know about it. How come they didn't get you?"

He grinned. It made him repulsive and it also brought to mind what he'd looked like as a kid. "I wasn't there. I stay away from them people."

"Good for you." I offered him a cigarette and I watched him through the smoke. "You come all the way down here just to tell me about Sonny?"

"That's right." He was sort of shaking his head and his eyes looked strange, as   15
though they were about to cross. The bright sun deadened his damp dark brown skin and it made his eyes look yellow and showed up the dirt in his kinked hair. He smelled funky. I moved a little away from him and I said, "Well, thanks. But I already know about it and I got to get home."

"I'll walk you a little ways," he said. We started walking. There were a couple of kids still loitering in the courtyard and one of them said goodnight to me and looked strangely at the boy beside me.

"What're you going to do?" he asked me. "I mean, about Sonny?"

"Look. I haven't seen Sonny for over a year. I'm not sure I'm going to do anything. Anyway, what the hell *can* I do?"

"That's right," he said quickly, "ain't nothing you can do. Can't much help old Sonny no more, I guess."

It was what I was thinking and so it seemed to me he had no right to say it.   20

"I'm surprised at Sonny, though," he went on — he had a funny way of talking, he looked straight ahead as though he were talking to himself — "I thought Sonny was a smart boy, I thought he was too smart to get hung."

"I guess he thought so too," I said sharply, "and that's how he got hung. And now about you? You're pretty goddamn smart, I bet."

Then he looked directly at me, just for a minute. "I ain't smart," he said. "If I was smart, I'd have reached for a pistol a long time ago."

"Look. Don't tell *me* your sad story, if it was up to me, I'd give you one." Then I felt guilty — guilty, probably, for never having supposed that the poor bastard *had* a story of his own, much less a sad one, and I asked, quickly, "What's going to happen to him now?"

He didn't answer this. He was off by himself some place. "Funny thing," he   25
said, and from his tone we might have been discussing the quickest way to get to Brooklyn, "when I saw the papers this morning, the first thing I asked myself was if I had anything to do with it. I felt sort of responsible."

I began to listen more carefully. The subway station was on the corner, just before us, and I stopped. He stopped, too. We were in front of a bar and he ducked slightly, peering in, but whoever he was looking for didn't seem to be there. The juke box was blasting away with something black and bouncy and I half watched the barmaid as she danced her way from the juke box to her place behind the bar. And I watched her face as she laughingly responded to something someone said to her, still keeping time to the music. When she smiled one saw the little girl, one sensed the doomed, still-struggling woman beneath the battered face of the semi-whore.

"I never *give* Sonny nothing," the boy said finally, "but a long time ago I come to school high and Sonny asked me how it felt." He paused, I couldn't bear to watch

him, I watched the barmaid, and I listened to the music which seemed to be causing the pavement to shake. "I told him it felt great." The music stopped, the barmaid paused and watched the juke box until the music began again. "It did."

All this was carrying me some place I didn't want to go. I certainly didn't
want to know how it felt. It filled everything, the people, the houses, the music,
the dark, quicksilver barmaid, with menace; and this menace was their reality.

"What's going to happen to him now?" I asked again.

"They'll send him away some place and they'll try to cure him." He shook his   30
head. "Maybe he'll even think he's kicked the habit. Then they'll let him
loose" — he gestured, throwing his cigarette into the gutter. "That's all."

"What do you mean, that's *all*?"

But I knew what he meant.

"I *mean*, that's *all*." He turned his head and looked at me, pulling down the
corners of his mouth. "Don't you know what I mean?" he asked, softly.

"How the hell *would* I know what you mean?" I almost whispered it, I don't
know why.

"That's right," he said to the air, "how would *he* know what I mean?" He   35
turned toward me again, patient and calm, and yet I somehow felt him shaking,
shaking as though he were going to fall apart. I felt that ice in my guts again, the
dread I'd felt all afternoon; and again I watched the barmaid, moving about the
bar, washing glasses, and singing. "Listen. They'll let him out and then it'll just
start all over again. That's what I mean."

"You mean — they'll let him out. And then he'll just start working his way
back in again. You mean he'll never kick the habit. Is that what you mean?"

"That's right," he said, cheerfully. "*You* see what I mean."

"Tell me," I said at last, "why does he want to die? He must want to die, he's
killing himself, why does he want to die?"

He looked at me in surprise. He licked his lips. "He don't want to die. He
wants to live. Don't nobody want to die, ever."

Then I wanted to ask him — too many things. He could not have answered,   40
or if he had, I could not have borne the answers. I started walking. "Well, I guess
it's none of my business."

"It's going to be rough on old Sonny," he said. We reached the subway station. "This is your station?" he asked. I nodded. I took one step down. "Damn!"
he said, suddenly. I looked up at him. He grinned again. "Damn it if I didn't
leave all my money home. You ain't got a dollar on you, have you? Just for a
couple of days, is all."

All at once something inside gave and threatened to come pouring out of
me. I didn't hate him any more. I felt that in another moment I'd start crying like
a child.

"Sure," I said. "Don't sweat." I looked in my wallet and didn't have a dollar, I
only had a five. "Here," I said. "That hold you?"

He didn't look at it — he didn't want to look at it. A terrible closed look came
over his face, as though he were keeping the number on the bill a secret from
him and me. "Thanks," he said, and now he was dying to see me go. "Don't worry
about Sonny. Maybe I'll write him or something."

"Sure," I said. "You do that. So long."   45
"Be seeing you," he said. I went on down the steps.

And I didn't write Sonny or send him anything for a long time. When I finally did, it was just after my little girl died, he wrote me back a letter which made me feel like a bastard.

Here's what he said:

> Dear brother,
> You don't know how much I needed to hear from you. I wanted to write you many a time but I dug how much I must have hurt you and so I didn't write. But now I feel like a man who's been trying to climb up out of some deep, real deep and funky hole and just saw the sun up there, outside. I got to get outside.
> I can't tell you much about how I got here. I mean I don't know how to tell you. I guess I was afraid of something or I was trying to escape from something and you know I have never been very strong in the head (smile). I'm glad Mama and Daddy are dead and can't see what's happened to their son and I swear if I'd known what I was doing I would never have hurt you so, you and a lot of other fine people who were nice to me and who believed in me.
> I don't want you to think it had anything to do with me being a musician. It's more than that. Or maybe less than that. I can't get anything straight in my head down here and I try not to think about what's going to happen to me when I get outside again. Sometime I think I'm going to flip and *never* get outside and sometime I think I'll come straight back. I tell you one thing, though, I'd rather blow my brains out than go through this again. But that's what they all say, so they tell me. If I tell you when I'm coming to New York and if you could meet me, I sure would appreciate it. Give my love to Isabel and the kids and I was sure sorry to hear about little Gracie. I wish I could be like Mama and say the Lord's will be done, but I don't know it seems to me that trouble is the one thing that never does get stopped and I don't know what good it does to blame it on the Lord. But maybe it does some good if you believe it.
>
> Your brother,
> Sonny

Then I kept in constant touch with him and I sent him whatever I could and I went to meet him when he came back to New York. When I saw him many things I thought I had forgotten came flooding back to me. This was because I had begun, finally, to wonder about Sonny, about the life that Sonny lived inside. This life, whatever it was, had made him older and thinner and it had deepened the distant stillness in which he had always moved. He looked very unlike my baby brother. Yet, when he smiled, when we shook hands, the baby brother I'd never known looked out from the depths of his private life, like an animal waiting to be coaxed into the light.

"How you been keeping?" he asked me.   50
"All right. And you?"
"Just fine." He was smiling all over his face. "It's good to see you again."

"It's good to see you."

The seven years' difference in our ages lay between us like a chasm: I wondered if these years would ever operate between us as a bridge. I was remembering, and it made it hard to catch my breath, that I had been there when he was born; and I had heard the first words he had ever spoken. When he started to walk, he walked from our mother straight to me. I caught him just before he fell when he took the first steps he ever took in this world.

"How's Isabel?" 55

"Just fine. She's dying to see you."

"And the boys?"

"They're fine, too. They're anxious to see their uncle."

"Oh, come on. You know they don't remember me."

"Are you kidding? Of course they remember you." 60

He grinned again. We got into a taxi. We had a lot to say to each other, far too much to know how to begin.

As the taxi began to move, I asked, "You still want to go to India?"

He laughed. "You still remember that. Hell, no. This place is Indian enough for me."

"It used to belong to them," I said.

And he laughed again. "They damn sure knew what they were doing when 65 they got rid of it."

Years ago, when he was around fourteen, he'd been all hipped on the idea of going to India. He read books about people sitting on rocks, naked, in all kinds of weather, but mostly bad, naturally, and walking barefoot through hot coals and arriving at wisdom. I used to say that it sounded to me as though they were getting away from wisdom as fast as they could. I think he sort of looked down on me for that.

"Do you mind," he asked, "if we have the driver drive alongside the park? On the west side — I haven't seen the city in so long."

"Of course not," I said. I was afraid that I might sound as though I were humoring him, but I hoped he wouldn't take it that way.

So we drove along, between the green of the park and the stony, lifeless elegance of hotels and apartment buildings, toward the vivid, killing streets of our childhood. These streets hadn't changed, though housing projects jutted up out of them now like rocks in the middle of a boiling sea. Most of the houses in which we had grown up had vanished, as had the stores from which we had stolen, the basements in which we had first tried sex, the rooftops from which we had hurled tin cans and bricks. But houses exactly like the houses of our past yet dominated the landscape, boys exactly like the boys we once had been found themselves smothering in these houses, came down into the streets for light and air and found themselves encircled by disaster. Some escaped the trap, most didn't. Those who got out always left something of themselves behind, as some animals amputate a leg and leave it in the trap. It might be said, perhaps, that I had escaped, after all, I was a school teacher; or that Sonny had, he hadn't lived in Harlem for years. Yet, as the cab moved uptown through streets which seemed, with a rush, to darken with dark people, and as I covertly studied Sonny's face, it came to me that what we both were seeking through our separate cab windows was that part of ourselves which had been left behind. It's always at the hour of trouble and confrontation that the missing member aches.

We hit 110th Street and started rolling up Lenox Avenue. And I'd known this avenue all my life, but it seemed to me again, as it had seemed on the day I'd first heard about Sonny's trouble, filled with a hidden menace which was its very breath of life.

"We almost there," said Sonny.

"Almost." We were both too nervous to say anything more.

We live in a housing project. It hasn't been up long. A few days after it was up it seemed uninhabitably new, now, of course, it's already rundown. It looks like a parody of the good, clean, faceless life — God knows the people who live in it do their best to make it a parody. The beat-looking grass lying around isn't enough to make their lives green, the hedges will never hold out the streets, and they know it. The big windows fool no one, they aren't big enough to make space out of no space. They don't bother with the windows, they watch the TV screen instead. The playground is most popular with the children who don't play at jacks, or skip rope, or roller skate, or swing, and they can be found in it after dark. We moved in partly because it's not too far from where I teach, and partly for the kids; but it's really just like the houses in which Sonny and I grew up. The same things happen, they'll have the same things to remember. The moment Sonny and I started into the house I had the feeling that I was simply bringing him back into the danger he had almost died trying to escape.

Sonny has never been talkative. So I don't know why I was sure he'd be dying to talk to me when supper was over the first night. Everything went fine, the oldest boy remembered him, and the youngest boy liked him, and Sonny had remembered to bring something for each of them; and Isabel, who is really much nicer than I am, more open and giving, had gone to a lot of trouble about dinner and was genuinely glad to see him. And she's always been able to tease Sonny in a way that I haven't. It was nice to see her face so vivid again and to hear her laugh and watch her make Sonny laugh. She wasn't, or, anyway, she didn't seem to be, at all uneasy or embarrassed. She chatted as though there were no subject which had to be avoided and she got Sonny past his first, faint stiffness. And thank God she was there, for I was filled with that icy dread again. Everything I did seemed awkward to me, and everything I said sounded freighted with hidden meaning. I was trying to remember everything I'd heard about dope addiction and I couldn't help watching Sonny for signs. I wasn't doing it out of malice. I was trying to find out something about my brother. I was dying to hear him tell me he was safe.

"Safe!" my father grunted, whenever Mama suggested trying to move to a neighborhood which might be safer for children. "Safe, hell! Ain't no place safe for kids, nor nobody."

He always went on like this, but he wasn't, ever, really as bad as he sounded, not even on weekends, when he got drunk. As a matter of fact, he was always on the lookout for "something a little better," but he died before he found it. He died suddenly, during a drunken weekend in the middle of the war, when Sonny was fifteen. He and Sonny hadn't ever got on too well. And this was partly because

70

75

Sonny was the apple of his father's eye. It was because he loved Sonny so much and was frightened for him, that he was always fighting with him. It doesn't do any good to fight with Sonny. Sonny just moves back, inside himself, where he can't be reached. But the principal reason that they never hit it off is that they were so much alike. Daddy was big and rough and loud-talking, just the opposite of Sonny, but they both had — that same privacy.

Mama tried to tell me something about this, just after Daddy died. I was home on leave from the army.

This was the last time I ever saw my mother alive. Just the same, this picture gets all mixed up in my mind with pictures I had of her when she was younger. The way I always see her is the way she used to be on a Sunday afternoon, say, when the old folks were talking after the big Sunday dinner. I always see her wearing pale blue. She'd be sitting on the sofa. And my father would be sitting in the easy chair, not far from her. And the living room would be full of church folks and relatives. There they sit, in chairs all around the living room, and the night is creeping up outside, but nobody knows it yet. You can see the darkness growing against the windowpanes and you hear the street noises every now and again, or maybe the jangling beat of a tambourine from one of the churches close by, but it's real quiet in the room. For a moment nobody's talking, but every face looks darkening, like the sky outside. And my mother rocks a little from the waist, and my father's eyes are closed. Everyone is looking at something a child can't see. For a minute they've forgotten the children. Maybe a kid is lying on the rug, half asleep. Maybe somebody's got a kid in his lap and is absent-mindedly stroking the kid's head. Maybe there's a kid, quiet and big-eyed, curled up in a big chair in the corner. The silence, the darkness coming, and the darkness in the faces frightens the child obscurely. He hopes that the hand which strokes his forehead will never stop — will never die. He hopes that there will never come a time when the old folks won't be sitting around the living room, talking about where they've come from, and what they've seen, and what's happened to them and their kinfolk.

But something deep and watchful in the child knows that this is bound to end, is already ending. In a moment someone will get up and turn on the light. Then the old folks will remember the children and they won't talk any more that day. And when light fills the room, the child is filled with darkness. He knows that every time this happens he's moved just a little closer to that darkness outside. The darkness outside is what the old folks have been talking about. It's what they've come from. It's what they endure. The child knows that they won't talk any more because if he knows too much about what's happened to *them*, he'll know too much too soon, about what's going to happen to *him*.

The last time I talked to my mother, I remember I was restless. I wanted to get out and see Isabel. We weren't married then and we had a lot to straighten out between us.

There Mama sat, in black, by the window. She was humming an old church song, *Lord, you brought me from a long ways off.* Sonny was out somewhere. Mama kept watching the streets.

"I don't know," she said, "if I'll ever see you again, after you go off from here. But I hope you'll remember the things I tried to teach you."

80

"Don't talk like that," I said, and smiled. "You'll be here a long time yet."

She smiled, too, but she said nothing. She was quiet for a long time. And I said, "Mama, don't you worry about nothing. I'll be writing all the time, and you be getting the checks. . . ."

"I want to talk to you about your brother," she said, suddenly. "If anything   85
happens to me he ain't going to have nobody to look out for him."

"Mama," I said, "ain't nothing going to happen to you *or* Sonny. Sonny's all right. He's a good boy and he's got good sense."

"It ain't a question of his being a good boy," Mama said, "nor of his having good sense. It ain't only the bad ones, nor yet the dumb ones that gets sucked under." She stopped, looking at me. "Your Daddy once had a brother," she said, and she smiled in a way that made me feel she was in pain. "You didn't never know that, did you?"

"No," I said, "I never knew that," and I watched her face.

"Oh, yes," she said, "your Daddy had a brother." She looked out of the window again. "I know you never saw your Daddy cry. But *I* did—many a time, through all these years."

I asked her, "What happened to his brother? How come nobody's ever talked   90
about him?"

This was the first time I ever saw my mother look old.

"His brother got killed," she said, "when he was just a little younger than you are now. I knew him. He was a fine boy. He was maybe a little full of the devil, but he didn't mean nobody no harm."

Then she stopped and the room was silent, exactly as it had sometimes been on those Sunday afternoons. Mama kept looking out into the streets.

"He used to have a job in the mill," she said, "and, like all young folks, he just liked to perform on Saturday nights. Saturday nights, him and your father would drift around to different places, go to dances and things like that, or just sit around with people they knew, and your father's brother would sing, he had a fine voice, and play along with himself on his guitar. Well, this particular Saturday night, him and your father was coming home from some place, and they were both a little drunk and there was a moon that night, it was bright like day. Your father's brother was feeling kind of good, and he was whistling to himself, and he had his guitar slung over his shoulder. They was coming down a hill and beneath them was a road that turned off from the highway. Well, your father's brother, being always kind of frisky, decided to run down this hill, and he did, with that guitar banging and clanging behind him, and he ran across the road, and he was making water behind a tree. And your father was sort of amused at him and he was still coming down the hill, kind of slow. Then he heard a car motor and that same minute his brother stepped from behind the tree, into the road, in the moonlight. And he started to cross the road. And your father started to run down the hill, he says he don't know why. This car was full of white men. They was all drunk, and when they seen your father's brother they let out a great whoop and holler and they aimed the car straight at him. They was having fun, they just wanted to scare him, the way they do sometimes, you know. But they was drunk. And I guess the boy, being drunk, too, and scared, kind of lost his head. By the time he jumped it was too late. Your father says he heard his brother scream when the car rolled over him, and he heard the wood of that guitar when it give, and he heard them strings go flying, and he heard them white men shouting, and the car kept on a-going and it ain't stopped till this day. And, time your father got down the hill, his brother weren't nothing but blood and pulp."

Tears were gleaming on my mother's face. There wasn't anything I could say.   95

"He never mentioned it," she said, "because I never let him mention it before you children. Your Daddy was like a crazy man that night and for many a night thereafter. He says he never in his life seen anything as dark as that road after the lights of that car had gone away. Weren't nothing, weren't nobody on that road, just your Daddy and his brother and that busted guitar. Oh, yes. Your Daddy never did really get right again. Till the day he died he weren't sure but that every white man he saw was the man that killed his brother."

She stopped and took out her handkerchief and dried her eyes and looked at me.

"I ain't telling you all this," she said, "to make you scared or bitter or to make you hate nobody. I'm telling you this because you got a brother. And the world ain't changed."

I guess I didn't want to believe this. I guess she saw this in my face. She turned away from me, toward the window again, searching those streets.

"But I praise my Redeemer," she said at last, "that He called your Daddy   100 home before me. I ain't saying it to throw no flowers at myself, but, I declare, it keeps me from feeling too cast down to know I helped your father get safely through this world. Your father always acted like he was the roughest, strongest man on earth. And everybody took him to be like that. But if he hadn't had *me* there—to see his tears!"

She was crying again. Still, I couldn't move. I said, "Lord, Lord, Mama, I didn't know it was like that."

"Oh, honey," she said, "there's a lot that you don't know. But you are going to find it out." She stood up from the window and came over to me. "You got to hold on to your brother," she said, "and don't let him fall, no matter what it looks like is happening to him and no matter how evil you gets with him. You going to be evil with him many a time. But don't you forget what I told you, you hear?"

"I won't forget," I said. "Don't you worry, I won't forget. I won't let nothing happen to Sonny."

My mother smiled as though she were amused at something she saw in my face. Then, "You may not be able to stop nothing from happening. But you got to let him know you's *there*."

Two days later I was married, and then I was gone. And I had a lot of things   105 on my mind and I pretty well forgot my promise to Mama until I got shipped home on a special furlough for her funeral.

And, after the funeral, with just Sonny and me alone in the empty kitchen, I tried to find out something about him.

"What do you want to do?" I asked him.

"I'm going to be a musician," he said.

For he had graduated, in the time I had been away, from dancing to the juke box to finding out who was playing what, and what they were doing with it, and he had bought himself a set of drums.

"You mean, you want to be a drummer?" I somehow had the feeling that   110 being a drummer might be all right for other people but not for my brother Sonny.

"I don't think," he said, looking at me very gravely, "that I'll ever be a good drummer. But I think I can play a piano."

I frowned. I'd never played the role of the older brother quite so seriously before, had scarcely ever, in fact, *asked* Sonny a damn thing. I sensed myself in the presence of something I didn't really know how to handle, didn't understand. So I made my frown a little deeper as I asked: "What kind of musician do you want to be?"

He grinned. "How many kinds do you think there are?"

"Be *serious*," I said.

He laughed, throwing his head back, and then looked at me. "I *am* serious."   115

"Well, then, for Christ's sake, stop kidding around and answer a serious question. I mean, do you want to be a concert pianist, you want to play classical music and all that, or—or what?" Long before I finished he was laughing again. "For Christ's *sake*, Sonny!"

He sobered, but with difficulty. "I'm sorry. But you sound so—*scared!*" and he was off again.

"Well, you may think it's funny now, baby, but it's not going to be so funny when you have to make your living at it, let me tell you *that*." I was furious because I knew he was laughing at me and I didn't know why.

"No," he said, very sober now, and afraid, perhaps, that he'd hurt me, "I don't want to be a classical pianist. That isn't what interests me. I mean"—he paused, looking hard at me, as though his eyes would help me to understand, and then gestured helplessly, as though perhaps his hand would help—"I mean, I'll have a lot of studying to do, and I'll have to study *everything*, but, I mean, I want to play *with*—jazz musicians." He stopped. "I want to play jazz," he said.

Well, the word had never before sounded as heavy, as real, as it sounded that   120 afternoon in Sonny's mouth. I just looked at him and I was probably frowning a real frown by this time. I simply couldn't see why on earth he'd want to spend his time hanging around nightclubs, clowning around on bandstands, while people pushed each other around a dance floor. It seemed—beneath him, somehow. I had never thought about it before, had never been forced to, but I suppose I had always put jazz musicians in a class with what Daddy called "good-time people."

"Are you *serious*?"

"Hell, *yes*, I'm serious."

He looked more helpless than ever, and annoyed, and deeply hurt.

I suggested, helpfully: "You mean—like Louis Armstrong?"

His face closed as though I'd struck him. "No. I'm not talking about none of   125 that old-time, down home crap."

"Well, look, Sonny, I'm sorry, don't get mad. I just don't altogether get it, that's all. Name somebody—you know, a jazz musician you admire."

"Bird."

"Who?"

"Bird! Charlie Parker! Don't they teach you nothing in the goddamn army?"

I lit a cigarette. I was surprised and then a little amused to discover that I was   130
trembling. "I've been out of touch," I said. "You'll have to be patient with me.
Now. Who's this Parker character?"

"He's just one of the greatest jazz musicians alive," said Sonny, sullenly, his
hands in his pockets, his back to me. "Maybe *the* greatest," he added, bitterly,
"that's probably why *you* never heard of him."

"All right," I said, "I'm ignorant. I'm sorry. I'll go out and buy all the cat's
records right away, all right?"

"It don't," said Sonny, with dignity, "make any difference to me. I don't care
what you listen to. Don't do me no favors."

I was beginning to realize that I'd never seen him so upset before. With
another part of my mind I was thinking that this would probably turn out to be
one of those things kids go through and that I shouldn't make it seem important
by pushing it too hard. Still, I didn't think it would do any harm to ask: "Doesn't
all this take a lot of time? Can you make a living at it?"

He turned back to me and half leaned, half sat, on the kitchen table. "Every-   135
thing takes time," he said, "and — well, yes, sure, I can make a living at it. But
what I don't seem to be able to make you understand is that it's the only thing I
want to do."

"Well, Sonny," I said, gently, "you know people can't always do exactly what
they *want* to do —"

"No, I don't know that," said Sonny, surprising me. "I think people *ought* to
do what they want to do, what else are they alive for?"

"You getting to be a big boy," I said desperately, "it's time you started thinking
about your future."

"I'm thinking about my future," said Sonny, grimly. "I think about it all the
time."

I gave up. I decided, if he didn't change his mind, that we could always talk   140
about it later. "In the meantime," I said, "you got to finish school." We had
already decided that he'd have to move in with Isabel and her folks. I knew this
wasn't the ideal arrangement because Isabel's folks are inclined to be dicty and
they hadn't especially wanted Isabel to marry me. But I didn't know what else to
do. "And we have to get you fixed up at Isabel's."

There was a long silence. He moved from the kitchen table to the window.
"That's a terrible idea. You know it yourself."

"Do you have a *better* idea?"

He just walked up and down the kitchen for a minute. He was as tall as I
was. He had started to shave. I suddenly had the feeling that I didn't know him
at all.

He stopped at the kitchen table and picked up my cigarettes. Looking at me
with a kind of mocking, amused defiance, he put one between his lips. "You
mind?"

"You smoking already?"   145

He lit the cigarette and nodded, watching me through the smoke. "I just wanted to see if I'd have the courage to smoke in front of you." He grinned and blew a great cloud of smoke to the ceiling. "It was easy." He looked at my face. "Come on, now. I bet you was smoking at my age, tell the truth."

I didn't say anything but the truth was on my face, and he laughed. But now there was something very strained in his laugh. "Sure. And I bet that ain't all you was doing."

He was frightening me a little. "Cut the crap," I said. "We already decided that you was going to go and live at Isabel's. Now what's got into you all of a sudden?"

"*You* decided it," he pointed out. "*I* didn't decide nothing." He stopped in front of me, leaning against the stove, arms loosely folded. "Look, brother. I don't want to stay in Harlem no more, I really don't." He was very earnest. He looked at me, then over toward the kitchen window. There was something in his eyes I'd never seen before, some thoughtfulness, some worry all his own. He rubbed the muscle of one arm. "It's time I was getting out of here."

"Where do you want to *go*, Sonny?"   150

"I want to join the army. Or the navy, I don't care. If I say I'm old enough, they'll believe me."

Then I got mad. It was because I was so scared. "You must be crazy. You god-damn fool, what the hell do you want to go and join the *army* for?"

"I just told you. To get out of Harlem."

"Sonny, you haven't even finished *school*. And if you really want to be a musician, how do you expect to study if you're in the *army*?"

He looked at me, trapped, and in anguish. "There's ways. I might be able to   155
work out some kind of deal. Anyway, I'll have the G.I. Bill when I come out."

"*If* you come out." We stared at each other. "Sonny, please. Be reasonable. I know the setup is far from perfect. But we got to do the best we can."

"I ain't learning nothing in school," he said. "Even when I go." He turned away from me and opened the window and threw his cigarette out into the narrow alley. I watched his back. "At least, I ain't learning nothing you'd want me to learn." He slammed the window so hard I thought the glass would fly out, and turned back to me. "And I'm sick of the stink of these garbage cans!"

"Sonny," I said, "I know how you feel. But if you don't finish school now, you're going to be sorry later that you didn't." I grabbed him by the shoulders. "And you only got another year. It ain't so bad. And I'll come back and I swear I'll help you do *whatever* you want to do. Just try to put up with it till I come back. Will you please do that? For me?"

He didn't answer and he wouldn't look at me.

"Sonny. You hear me?"   160

He pulled away. "I hear you. But you never hear anything *I* say."

I didn't know what to say to that. He looked out of the window and then back at me. "OK," he said, and sighed. "I'll try."

Then I said, trying to cheer him up a little, "They got a piano at Isabel's. You can practice on it."

And as a matter of fact, it did cheer him up for a minute. "That's right," he said to himself. "I forgot that." His face relaxed a little. But the worry, the thoughtfulness, played on it still, the way shadows play on a face which is staring into the fire.

But I thought I'd never hear the end of that piano. At first, Isabel would write me, saying how nice it was that Sonny was so serious about his music and how, as soon as he came in from school, or wherever he had been when he was supposed to be at school, he went straight to that piano and stayed there until suppertime. And, after supper, he went back to that piano and stayed there until everybody went to bed. He was at the piano all day Saturday and all day Sunday. Then he bought a record player and started playing records. He'd play one record over and over again, all day long sometimes, and he'd improvise along with it on the piano. Or he'd play one section of the record, one chord, one change, one progression, then he'd do it on the piano. Then back to the record. Then back to the piano.

Well, I really don't know how they stood it. Isabel finally confessed that it wasn't like living with a person at all, it was like living with sound. And the sound didn't make any sense to her, didn't make any sense to any of them — naturally. They began, in a way, to be afflicted by this presence that was living in their home. It was as though Sonny were some sort of god, or monster. He moved in an atmosphere which wasn't like theirs at all. They fed him and he ate, he washed himself, he walked in and out of their door; he certainly wasn't nasty or unpleasant or rude, Sonny isn't any of those things; but it was as though he were all wrapped up in some cloud, some fire, some vision all his own; and there wasn't any way to reach him.

At the same time, he wasn't really a man yet, he was still a child, and they had to watch out for him in all kinds of ways. They certainly couldn't throw him out. Neither did they dare to make a great scene about that piano because even they dimly sensed, as I sensed, from so many thousands of miles away, that Sonny was at that piano playing for his life.

But he hadn't been going to school. One day a letter came from the school board and Isabel's mother got it — there had, apparently, been other letters but Sonny had torn them up. This day, when Sonny came in, Isabel's mother showed him the letter and asked where he'd been spending his time. And she finally got it out of him that he'd been down in Greenwich Village, with musicians and other characters, in a white girl's apartment. And this scared her and she started to scream at him and what came up, once she began — though she denies it to this day — was what sacrifices they were making to give Sonny a decent home and how little he appreciated it.

Sonny didn't play the piano that day. By evening, Isabel's mother had calmed down but then there was the old man to deal with, and Isabel herself. Isabel says she did her best to be calm but she broke down and started crying. She says she just watched Sonny's face. She could tell, by watching him, what was happening with him. And what was happening was that they penetrated his cloud, they had reached him. Even if their fingers had been a thousand times more gentle than human fingers ever are, he could hardly help feeling that they

165

had stripped him naked and were spitting on that nakedness. For he also had to see that his presence, that music, which was life or death to him, had been torture for them and that they had endured it, not at all for his sake, but only for mine. And Sonny couldn't take that. He can take it a little better today than he could then but he's still not very good at it and, frankly, I don't know anybody who is.

The silence of the next few days must have been louder than the sound of all 170 the music ever played since time began. One morning, before she went to work, Isabel was in his room for something and she suddenly realized that all of his records were gone. And she knew for certain that he was gone. And he was. He went as far as the navy would carry him. He finally sent me a postcard from some place in Greece and that was the first I knew that Sonny was still alive. I didn't see him any more until we were both back in New York and the war had long been over.

He was a man by then, of course, but I wasn't willing to see it. He came by the house from time to time, but we fought almost every time we met. I didn't like the way he carried himself, loose and dreamlike all the time, and I didn't like his friends, and his music seemed to be merely an excuse for the life he led. It sounded just that weird and disordered.

Then we had a fight, a pretty awful fight, and I didn't see him for months. By and by I looked him up, where he was living, in a furnished room in the Village, and I tried to make it up. But there were lots of people in the room and Sonny just lay on his bed, and he wouldn't come downstairs with me, and he treated these other people as though they were his family and I weren't. So I got mad and then he got mad, and then I told him that he might just as well be dead as live the way he was living. Then he stood up and he told me not to worry about him any more in life, that he *was* dead as far as I was concerned. Then he pushed me to the door and the other people looked on as though nothing were happening, and he slammed the door behind me. I stood in the hallway, staring at the door. I heard somebody laugh in the room and then the tears came to my eyes. I started down the steps, whistling to keep from crying, I kept whistling to myself, *You going to need me, baby, one of these cold, rainy days.*

I read about Sonny's trouble in the spring. Little Grace died in the fall. She was a beautiful little girl. But she only lived a little over two years. She died of polio and she suffered. She had a slight fever for a couple of days, but it didn't seem like anything and we just kept her in bed. And we would certainly have called the doctor, but the fever dropped, she seemed to be all right. So we thought it had just been a cold. Then, one day, she was up, playing, Isabel was in the kitchen fixing lunch for the two boys when they'd come in from school, and she heard Grace fall down in the living room. When you have a lot of children you don't always start running when one of them falls, unless they start screaming or something. And, this time, Grace was quiet. Yet, Isabel says that when she heard that *thump* and then that silence, something happened in her to make her afraid. And she ran to the living room and there was little Grace on the floor, all twisted up, and the reason she hadn't screamed was that she couldn't get her breath. And when she did scream, it was the worst sound, Isabel says, that she'd ever heard in all her life, and she still hears it sometimes in her dreams. Isabel will sometimes wake me up with a low, moaning, strangled sound and I have to be quick to awaken her and hold her to me and where Isabel is weeping against me seems a mortal wound.

I think I may have written Sonny the very day that little Grace was buried. I was sitting in the living room in the dark, by myself, and I suddenly thought of Sonny. My trouble made his real.

One Saturday afternoon, when Sonny had been living with us, or, anyway, been in our house, for nearly two weeks, I found myself wandering aimlessly about the living room, drinking from a can of beer, and trying to work up the courage to search Sonny's room. He was out, he was usually out whenever I was home, and Isabel had taken the children to see their grandparents. Suddenly I was standing still in front of the living room window, watching Seventh Avenue. The idea of searching Sonny's room made me still. I scarcely dared to admit to myself what I'd be searching for. I didn't know what I'd do if I found it. Or if I didn't. 175

On the sidewalk across from me, near the entrance to a barbecue joint, some people were holding an old-fashioned revival meeting. The barbecue cook, wearing a dirty white apron, his conked hair reddish and metallic in the pale sun, and a cigarette between his lips, stood in the doorway, watching them. Kids and older people paused in their errands and stood there, along with some older men and a couple of very tough-looking women who watched everything that happened on the avenue, as though they owned it, or were maybe owned by it. Well, they were watching this, too. The revival was being carried on by three sisters in black, and a brother. All they had were their voices and their Bibles and a tambourine. The brother was testifying and while he testified two of the sisters stood together, seeming to say, amen, and the third sister walked around with the tambourine outstretched and a couple of people dropped coins into it. Then the brother's testimony ended and the sister who had been taking up the collection dumped the coins into her palm and transferred them to the pocket of her long black robe. Then she raised both hands, striking the tambourine against the air, and then against one hand, and she started to sing. And the two other sisters and the brother joined in.

It was strange, suddenly, to watch, though I had been seeing these street meetings all my life. So, of course, had everybody else down there. Yet, they paused and watched and listened and I stood still at the window. *"Tis the old ship of Zion,"* they sang, and the sister with the tambourine kept a steady, jangling beat, *"it has rescued many a thousand!"* Not a soul under the sound of their voices was hearing this song for the first time, not one of them had been rescued. Nor had they seen much in the way of rescue work being done around them. Neither did they especially believe in the holiness of the three sisters and the brother, they knew too much about them, knew where they lived, and how. The woman with the tambourine, whose voice dominated the air, whose face was bright with joy, was divided by very little from the woman who stood watching her, a cigarette between her heavy, chapped lips, her hair a cuckoo's nest, her face scarred and swollen from many beatings, and her black eyes glittering like coal. Perhaps they both knew this, which was why, when, as rarely, they addressed each other, they addressed each other as Sister. As the singing filled the air the watching, listening faces underwent a change, the eyes focusing on something within; the music seemed to soothe a poison out of them; and time seemed, nearly, to fall away from the sullen, belligerent, battered faces, as though they were fleeing back to their first condition, while dreaming of their last. The barbecue cook half shook his head and smiled, and dropped his cigarette and disappeared into his joint. A man fumbled in his pockets for change and stood holding it in his hand impatiently, as though he had just remembered a pressing appointment further up the avenue. He looked furious. Then I saw Sonny, standing on the edge of the crowd. He was carrying a wide, flat notebook with a green cover, and it made him look, from where I was standing, almost like a schoolboy. The coppery sun brought out the copper in his skin, he was very faintly smiling, standing very still. Then the singing stopped, the tambourine turned into a collection plate again. The furious man dropped in his coins and vanished, so did a couple of the women, and Sonny dropped some change in the plate, looking directly at the woman with a little smile. He started across the avenue, toward the house. He has a slow, loping walk, something like the way Harlem hipsters walk, only he's imposed on this his own half-beat. I had never really noticed it before.

I stayed at the window, both relieved and apprehensive. As Sonny disappeared from my sight, they began singing again. And they were still singing when his key turned in the lock.

"Hey," he said.

"Hey, yourself. You want some beer?"   180

"No. Well, maybe." But he came up to the window and stood beside me, looking out. "What a warm voice," he said.

They were singing *If I could only hear my mother pray again!*

"Yes," I said, "and she can sure beat that tambourine."

"But what a terrible song," he said, and laughed. He dropped his notebook on the sofa and disappeared into the kitchen. "Where's Isabel and the kids?"

"I think they went to see their grandparents. You hungry?"   185

"No." He came back into the living room with his can of beer. "You want to come some place with me tonight?"

I sensed, I don't know how, that I couldn't possibly say no. "Sure. Where?"

He sat down on the sofa and picked up his notebook and started leafing through it. "I'm going to sit in with some fellows in a joint in the Village."

"You mean, you're going to play, tonight?"

"That's right." He took a swallow of his beer and moved back to the window.   190
He gave me a sidelong look. "If you can stand it."

"I'll try," I said.

He smiled to himself and we both watched as the meeting across the way broke up. The three sisters and the brother, heads bowed, were singing *God be with you till we meet again.* The faces around them were very quiet. Then the song ended. The small crowd dispersed. We watched the three women and the lone man walk slowly up the avenue.

"When she was singing before," said Sonny, abruptly, "her voice reminded me for a minute of what heroin feels like sometimes — when it's in your veins. It makes you feel sort of warm and cool at the same time. And distant. And—and sure." He sipped his beer, very deliberately not looking at me. I watched his face. "It makes you feel—in control. Sometimes you've got to have that feeling."

"Do you?" I sat down slowly in the easy chair.

"Sometimes." He went to the sofa and picked up his notebook again. "Some people do." 195

"In order," I asked, "to play?" And my voice was very ugly, full of contempt and anger.

"Well"—he looked at me with great, troubled eyes, as though, in fact, he hoped his eyes would tell me things he could never otherwise say—"they *think* so. And *if* they think so—!"

"And what do *you* think?" I asked.

He sat on the sofa and put his can of beer on the floor. "I don't know," he said, and I couldn't be sure if he were answering my question or pursuing his thoughts. His face didn't tell me. "It's not so much to *play*. It's to *stand* it, to be able to make it at all. On any level." He frowned and smiled: "In order to keep from shaking to pieces."

"But these friends of yours," I said, "they seem to shake themselves to pieces 200 pretty goddamn fast."

"Maybe." He played with the notebook. And something told me that I should curb my tongue, that Sonny was doing his best to talk, that I should listen. "But of course you only know the ones that've gone to pieces. Some don't—or at least they haven't *yet* and that's just about all *any* of us can say." He paused. "And then there are some who just live, really, in hell, and they know it and they see what's happening and they go right on. I don't know." He sighed, dropped the notebook, folded his arms. "Some guys, you can tell from the way they play, they on something *all* the time. And you can see that, well, it makes something real for them. But of course," he picked up his beer from the floor and sipped it and put the can down again, "they *want* to, too, you've got to see that. Even some of them that say they don't—*some*, not all."

"And what about you?" I asked—I couldn't help it. "What about you? Do *you* want to?"

He stood up and walked to the window and remained silent for a long time. Then he sighed. "Me," he said. Then: "While I was downstairs before, on my way here, listening to that woman sing, it struck me all of a sudden how much suffering she must have had to go through—to sing like that. It's *repulsive* to think you have to suffer that much."

I said: "But there's no way not to suffer—is there, Sonny?"

"I believe not," he said and smiled, "but that's never stopped anyone from 205 trying." He looked at me. "Has it?" I realized, with this mocking look, that there stood between us, forever, beyond the power of time or forgiveness, the fact that I had held silence—so long!—when he had needed human speech to help him. He turned back to the window. "No, there's no way not to suffer. But you try all kinds of ways to keep from drowning in it, to keep on top of it, and to make it seem—well, like *you*. Like you did something, all right, and now you're suffering for it. You know?" I said nothing. "Well you know," he said, impatiently, "why *do* people suffer? Maybe it's better to do something to give it a reason, *any* reason."

"But we just agreed," I said, "that there's no way not to suffer. Isn't it better, then, just to — take it?"

"But nobody just takes it," Sonny cried, "that's what I'm telling you! *Every-body* tries not to. You're just hung up on the *way* some people try — it's not *your* way!"

The hair on my face began to itch, my face felt wet. "That's not true," I said, "that's not true. I don't give a damn what other people do, I don't even care how they suffer. I just care how *you* suffer." And he looked at me. "Please believe me," I said, "I don't want to see you — die — trying not to suffer."

"I won't," he said, flatly, "die trying not to suffer. At least, not any faster than anybody else."

"But there's no need," I said, trying to laugh, "is there? in killing yourself."   210

I wanted to say more, but I couldn't. I wanted to talk about will power and how life could be — well, beautiful. I wanted to say that it was all within; but was it? or, rather, wasn't that exactly the trouble? And I wanted to promise that I would never fail him again. But it would all have sounded — empty words and lies.

So I made the promise to myself and prayed that I would keep it.

"It's terrible sometimes, inside," he said, "that's what's the trouble. You walk these streets, black and funky and cold, and there's not really a living ass to talk to, and there's nothing shaking, and there's no way of getting it out — that storm inside. You can't talk it and you can't make love with it, and when you finally try to get with it and play it, you realize *nobody's* listening. So *you've* got to listen. You got to find a way to listen."

And then he walked away from the window and sat on the sofa again, as though all the wind had suddenly been knocked out of him. "Sometimes you'll do *anything* to play, even cut your mother's throat." He laughed and looked at me. "Or your brother's." Then he sobered. "Or your own." Then: "Don't worry. I'm all right now and I think I'll *be* all right. But I can't forget — where I've been. I don't mean just the physical place I've been, I mean where I've *been*. And *what* I've been."

"What have you been, Sonny?" I asked.   215

He smiled — but sat sideways on the sofa, his elbow resting on the back, his fingers playing with his mouth and chin, not looking at me. "I've been something I didn't recognize, didn't know I could be. Didn't know anybody could be." He stopped, looking inward, looking helplessly young, looking old. "I'm not talking about it now because I feel *guilty* or anything like that — maybe it would be better if I did, I don't know. Anyway, I can't really talk about it. Not to you, not to anybody," and now he turned and faced me. "Sometimes, you know, and it was actually when I was most *out* of the world, I felt that I was in it, that I was *with* it, really, and I could play or I didn't really have to *play*, it just came out of me, it was there. And I don't know how I played, thinking about it now, but I know I did awful things, those times, sometimes, to people. Or it wasn't that I *did* anything to them — it was that they weren't real." He picked up the beer can; it was empty; he rolled it between his palms: "And other times—well, I needed a fix, I needed to find a place to lean, I needed to clear a space to *listen*—and I couldn't find it, and I—went crazy, I did terrible things to *me*, I was terrible *for* me." He began pressing the beer can between his hands, I watched the metal begin to give. It glittered, as he played with it, like a knife, and I was afraid he would cut himself, but I said nothing. "Oh well. I can never tell you. I was all by myself at the bottom of something, stinking and sweating and crying and shaking, and I smelled it, you know? *my* stink, and I thought I'd die if I couldn't get away from it and yet, all the same, I knew that everything I was doing was just locking me in with it. And I didn't know," he paused, still flattening the beer can, "I didn't know, I still *don't* know, something kept telling me that maybe it was good to smell your own stink, but I didn't think that *that* was what I'd been trying to do—and—who can stand it?" and he abruptly dropped the ruined beer can, looking at me with a small, still smile, and then rose, walking to the window as though it were the lodestone rock. I watched his face, he watched the avenue. "I couldn't tell you when Mama died—but the reason I wanted to leave Harlem so bad was to get away from drugs. And then, when I ran away, that's what I was running from—really. When I came back, nothing had changed, *I* hadn't changed, I was just—older." And he stopped, drumming with his fingers on the windowpane. The sun had vanished, soon darkness would fall. I watched his face. "It can come again," he said, almost as though speaking to himself. Then he turned to me. "It can come again," he repeated. "I just want you to know that."

"All right," I said, at last. "So it can come again, All right."

He smiled, but the smile was sorrowful. "I had to try to tell you," he said.

"Yes," I said. "I understand that."

"You're my brother," he said, looking straight at me, and not smiling at all.   220

"Yes," I repeated, "yes. I understand that."

He turned back to the window, looking out. "All that hatred down there," he said, "all that hatred and misery and love. It's a wonder it doesn't blow the avenue apart."

We went to the only nightclub on a short, dark street, downtown. We squeezed through the narrow, chattering, jam-packed bar to the entrance of the big room, where the bandstand was. And we stood there for a moment, for the lights were very dim in this room and we couldn't see. Then, "Hello, boy," said a voice and an enormous black man, much older than Sonny or myself, erupted out of all that atmospheric lighting and put an arm around Sonny's shoulder. "I been sitting right here," he said, "waiting for you."

He had a big voice, too, and heads in the darkness turned toward us.

Sonny grinned and pulled a little away, and said, "Creole, this is my brother.   225
I told you about him."

Creole shook my hand. "I'm glad to meet you, son," he said, and it was clear that he was glad to meet me *there*, for Sonny's sake. And he smiled, "You got a real musician in *your* family," and he took his arm from Sonny's shoulder and slapped him, lightly, affectionately, with the back of his hand.

"Well. Now I've heard it all," said a voice behind us. This was another musician, and a friend of Sonny's, a coal-black, cheerful-looking man, built close to the ground. He immediately began confiding to me, at the top of his lungs, the most terrible things about Sonny, his teeth gleaming like a lighthouse and his laugh coming up out of him like the beginning of an earthquake. And it turned out that everyone at the bar knew Sonny, or almost everyone; some were musicians, working there, or nearby, or not working, some were simply hangers-on, and some were there to hear Sonny play. I was introduced to all of them and they were all very polite to me. Yet, it was clear that, for them, I was only Sonny's brother. Here, I was in Sonny's world. Or, rather: his kingdom. Here, it was not even a question that his veins bore royal blood.

They were going to play soon and Creole installed me, by myself, at a table in a dark corner. Then I watched them, Creole, and the little black man, and Sonny, and the others, while they horsed around, standing just below the bandstand. The light from the bandstand spilled just a little short of them and, watching them laughing and gesturing and moving about, I had the feeling that they, nevertheless, were being most careful not to step into that circle of light too suddenly: that if they moved into the light too suddenly, without thinking, they would perish in flame. Then, while I watched, one of them, the small, black man, moved into the light and crossed the bandstand and started fooling around with his drums. Then — being funny and being, also, extremely ceremonious — Creole took Sonny by the arm and led him to the piano. A woman's voice called Sonny's name and a few hands started clapping. And Sonny, also being funny and being ceremonious, and so touched, I think, that he could have cried, but neither hiding it nor showing it, riding it like a man, grinned, and put both hands to his heart and bowed from the waist.

Creole then went to the bass fiddle and a lean, very bright-skinned brown man jumped up on the bandstand and picked up his horn. So there they were, and the atmosphere on the bandstand and in the room began to change and tighten. Someone stepped up to the microphone and announced them. Then there were all kinds of murmurs. Some people at the bar shushed others. The waitress ran around, frantically getting in the last orders, guys and chicks got closer to each other, and the lights on the bandstand, on the quartet, turned to a kind of indigo. Then they all looked different there. Creole looked about him for the last time, as though he were making certain that all his chickens were in the coop, and then he — jumped and struck the fiddle. And there they were.

All I know about music is that not many people ever really hear it. And even then, on the rare occasions when something opens within, and the music enters, what we mainly hear, or hear corroborated, are personal, private, vanishing evocations. But the man who creates the music is hearing something else, is dealing with the roar rising from the void and imposing order on it as it hits the air. What is evoked in him, then, is of another order, more terrible because it has no words, and triumphant, too, for that same reason. And his triumph, when he triumphs, is ours. I just watched Sonny's face. His face was troubled, he was working hard, but he wasn't with it. And I had the feeling that, in a way, everyone on the bandstand was waiting for him, both waiting for him and pushing him along. But as I began to watch Creole, I realized that it was Creole who held them all back. He had them on a short rein. Up there, keeping the beat with his whole body, wailing

230

on the fiddle, with his eyes half closed, he was listening to everything, but he was listening to Sonny. He was having a dialogue with Sonny. He wanted Sonny to leave the shoreline and strike out for the deep water. He was Sonny's witness that deep water and drowning were not the same thing — he had been there, and he knew. And he wanted Sonny to know. He was waiting for Sonny to do the things on the keys which would let Creole know that Sonny was in the water.

And, while Creole listened, Sonny moved, deep within, exactly like someone in torment. I had never before thought of how awful the relationship must be between the musician and his instrument. He has to fill it, this instrument, with the breath of life, his own. He has to make it do what he wants it to do. And a piano is just a piano. It's made out of so much wood and wires and little hammers and big ones, and ivory. While there's only so much you can do with it, the only way to find this out is to try; to try and make it do everything.

And Sonny hadn't been near a piano for over a year. And he wasn't on much better terms with his life, not the life that stretched before him now. He and the piano stammered, started one way, got scared, stopped; started another way, panicked, marked time, started again; then seemed to have found a direction, panicked again, got stuck. And the face I saw on Sonny I'd never seen before. Everything had been burned out of it, and, at the same time, things usually hidden were being burned in, by the fire and fury of the battle which was occurring in him up there.

Yet, watching Creole's face as they neared the end of the first set, I had the feeling that something had happened, something I hadn't heard. Then they finished, there was scattered applause, and then, without an instant's warning, Creole started into something else, it was almost sardonic, it was *Am I Blue*. And, as though he commanded, Sonny began to play. Something began to happen. And Creole let out the reins. The dry, low, black man said something awful on the drums, Creole answered, and the drums talked back. Then the horn insisted, sweet and high, slightly detached perhaps, and Creole listened, commenting now and then, dry, and driving, beautiful and calm and old. Then they all came together again, and Sonny was part of the family again. I could tell this from his face. He seemed to have found, right there beneath his fingers, a damn brand-new piano. It seemed that he couldn't get over it. Then, for awhile, just being happy with Sonny, they seemed to be agreeing with him that brand-new pianos certainly were a gas.

Then Creole stepped forward to remind them that what they were playing was the blues. He hit something in all of them, he hit something in me, myself, and the music tightened and deepened, apprehension began to beat the air. Creole began to tell us what the blues were all about. They were not about anything very new. He and his boys up there were keeping it new, at the risk of ruin, destruction, madness, and death, in order to find new ways to make us listen. For, while the tale of how we suffer, and how we are delighted, and how we may triumph is never new, it always must be heard. There isn't any other tale to tell, it's the only light we've got in all this darkness.

And this tale, according to that face, that body, those strong hands on those strings, has another aspect in every country, and a new depth in every generation. Listen, Creole seemed to be saying, listen. Now these are Sonny's blues. He made the little black man on the drums know it, and the bright, brown man on

235

the horn. Creole wasn't trying any longer to get Sonny in the water. He was wishing him Godspeed. Then he stepped back, very slowly, filling the air with the immense suggestion that Sonny speak for himself.

Then they all gathered around Sonny and Sonny played. Every now and again one of them seemed to say, amen. Sonny's fingers filled the air with life, his life. But that life contained so many others. And Sonny went all the way back, he really began with the spare, flat statement of the opening phrase of the song. Then he began to make it his. It was very beautiful because it wasn't hurried and it was no longer a lament. I seemed to hear with what burning he had made it his, with what burning we had yet to make it ours, how we could cease lamenting. Freedom lurked around us and I understood, at last, that he could help us to be free if we would listen, that he would never be free until we did. Yet, there was no battle in his face now. I heard what he had gone through, and would continue to go through until he came to rest in earth. He had made it his: that long line, of which we knew only Mama and Daddy. And he was giving it back, as everything must be given back, so that, passing through death, it can live forever. I saw my mother's face again, and felt, for the first time, how the stones of the road she had walked on must have bruised her feet. I saw the moonlit road where my father's brother died. And it brought something else back to me, and carried me past it. I saw my little girl again and felt Isabel's tears again, and I felt my own tears begin to rise. And I was yet aware that this was only a moment, that the world waited outside, as hungry as a tiger, and that trouble stretched above us, longer than the sky.

Then it was over. Creole and Sonny let out their breath, both soaking wet, and grinning. There was a lot of applause and some of it was real. In the dark, the girl came by and I asked her to take drinks to the bandstand. There was a long pause, while they talked up there in the indigo light and after awhile I saw the girl put a Scotch and milk on top of the piano for Sonny. He didn't seem to notice it, but just before they started playing again, he sipped from it and looked toward me, and nodded. Then he put it back on top of the piano. For me, then, as they began to play again, it glowed and shook above my brother's head like the very cup of trembling.   [1957]

THINKING ABOUT THE TEXT

1. Were you sympathetic to the older brother in the beginning of the story? Did this become more so or less so as the story progressed? Is Sonny a sympathetic character in the beginning? At the end?

2. In real life, what do you believe is the role of an older brother? Do you have a responsibility to the members of your family regardless of their behavior? Explain. What is Sonny's mother's view of this?

3. Baldwin refers to the "darkness outside" several times. What do you think this means for Sonny? For Sonny's mother and father? For the older brother?

4. Listening seems to play an important function for Sonny and his brother. Cite specific examples of how they do or do not listen to each other. What might be some definitions of "listening" in this context?

5. One might think that brothers would understand each other better than outsiders. But is that the case here? In your experience? In other stories or movies? How might you account for this difficulty?

MAKING COMPARISONS

1. The older brothers in "The Rich Brother" and "Sonny's Blues" struggle to understand their younger brothers. Which one seems more successful? Why?

2. Both younger brothers in these two stories seem to march to different drummers. How would you describe their variations from the norm?

3. Some critics claim that these two stories are about responsibility; others claim they are about tolerance; still others see sibling rivalry, blind faith, or ego as the focus. What do you think, and why?

WRITING ABOUT ISSUES

1. Baldwin shows us the letter Sonny writes to his older brother, but we do not see any of the older brother's letters to Sonny. Based on the older brother's insights about Sonny in the closing scene, write a letter to Sonny from the older brother's point of view, explaining the substance of his new understanding of Sonny's life and music.

2. Write an essay that compares the relationship between Pete and Donald to the one between Sonny and his brother. Be sure to comment on similarities and differences.

3. Write a personal essay based on a conflict you had with a sibling, explaining how the relationship evolved. Use at least two specific incidents and describe how they fit into a larger pattern.

4. Do some library research on birth order as it affects sibling rivalry, especially between brothers. Write a report comparing your findings to the relationships depicted in these two stories.

DYSFUNCTIONAL FAMILIES

WILLIAM SHAKESPEARE, *Hamlet, Prince of Denmark*
TENNESSEE WILLIAMS, *The Glass Menagerie*

Families can sustain us through life's difficulties, offering a safe harbor against the inevitable emotional storms of the outside world. They can also be the source of our pain, drawing us into a whirlpool of obligations and moral decisions we would never choose on our own. Families can provide a solid psychological center for our encounters with others, but they can sometimes destabilize our sense of who we are and what we need to do in the world. Sometimes families are broken, dysfunctional, or aberrant, and drastic action is required to get the family back on course. At other times that is not possible, and heartbreak and tragedy ensue.

In both *Hamlet* and *The Glass Menagerie* we enter worlds sorely offcenter. Upon his return from his university studies, Prince Hamlet is asked by his father's ghost to avenge his murder by the present king, his brother Claudius. Hamlet agonizes that his mother has too quickly married the new king. The family's psychology is complex and disturbing. Hamlet wants to honor his dead father's wishes, but to do so would be a great crime—regicide. And there are other complications. Hamlet seems especially attached to his mother; some critics even see hints of sexual jealousy. He seems embroiled in a family drama beyond his (or perhaps anyone's) abilities. And so he forges ahead, but perhaps not wisely or well.

Tom's family in *The Glass Menagerie* is less violently troubled, but its demands are nevertheless suffocating him. His mother wants Tom to be the absent father, to financially support her and Tom's sister Laura, and to find a husband for Laura. Tom knows that he has to be selfish to survive. Although both Tom and Hamlet are deeply divided over the claims of self and family, duty weighs more heavily, and fatally, on the prince. It is a tragic burden that eventually destroys his entire family. Tom avoids such a fate by abandoning his family, but he is still wracked with guilt.

BEFORE YOU READ

Have you ever felt pressure from your family to behave contrary to your interest? Do you know friends who live in troubled families? How do they cope? Are there higher responsibilities than family? Should one sacrifice all for the family? What if the family is maladjusted?

WILLIAM SHAKESPEARE
Hamlet, Prince of Denmark

William Shakespeare's reputation as the greatest dramatist in the English language is built on his five major tragedies: Romeo and Juliet *(1594),* Hamlet *(1600),* Othello *(1604),* Macbeth *(1605), and* King Lear *(1605). But he was also a master in other genres, including comedies* (As You Like It *in 1599), histories* (Henry IV *in 1597), and romances* (The Tempest *in 1611). And his collection of sonnets is considered art of the highest order.*

Very little is known about Shakespeare's personal life. He attended the grammar school at Stratford-upon-Avon where he was born in 1564. He married Anne Hathaway in 1582 and had three children. Around 1590 he moved to London where he became an actor and began writing plays. He was an astute businessperson, becoming a shareholder in the famous Globe Theatre. After having written thirty-seven plays, he retired to Stratford in 1611. When he died in 1616, he left behind the most respected body of work in literature. Shakespeare's ability to use artistic language to convey a wide range of humor and emotion is perhaps unsurpassed.

[DRAMATIS PERSONAE

CLAUDIUS, *King of Denmark*
HAMLET, *son to the late and nephew to the present king*
POLONIUS, *lord chamberlain*
HORATIO, *friend to Hamlet*
LAERTES, *son to Polonius*
VOLTIMAND
CORNELIUS
ROSENCRANTZ   } *courtiers*
GUILDENSTERN
OSRIC
A GENTLEMAN
A PRIEST
MARCELLUS   } *officers*
BERNARDO
FRANCISCO, *a soldier*
REYNALDO, *servant to Polonius*
PLAYERS
TWO CLOWNS, *grave-diggers*
FORTINBRAS, *Prince of Norway*
A CAPTAIN
ENGLISH AMBASSADORS
GERTRUDE, *Queen of Denmark, and mother to Hamlet*
OPHELIA, *daughter to Polonius*
LORDS, LADIES, OFFICERS, SOLDIERS, SAILORS, MESSENGERS, AND OTHER
     ATTENDANTS
GHOST *of Hamlet's Father*

SCENE: *Denmark.*]

[ACT 1, Scene 1]

[Elsinore. A platform° before the castle.]
     Enter Bernardo and Francisco, two sentinels.
BERNARDO: Who's there?
FRANCISCO: Nay, answer me:° stand, and unfold yourself.

ACT 1, SCENE 1. **platform:** A level space on the battlements of the royal castle at Elsinore, a Danish seaport; now Helsingör.   **2 me:** This is emphatic, since Francisco is the sentry.

BERNARDO: Long live the king!°
FRANCISCO: Bernardo?
BERNARDO: He.   5
FRANCISCO: You come most carefully upon your hour.
BERNARDO: 'Tis now struck twelve; get thee to bed, Francisco.
FRANCISCO: For this relief much thanks: 'tis bitter cold,
And I am sick at heart.
BERNARDO: Have you had quiet guard?
FRANCISCO: Not a mouse stirring.   10
BERNARDO: Well, good night.
If you do meet Horatio and Marcellus,
The rivals° of my watch, bid them make haste.

Enter Horatio and Marcellus.

FRANCISCO: I think I hear them. Stand, ho! Who is there?
HORATIO: Friends to this ground.
MARCELLUS: And liegemen to the Dane.   15
FRANCISCO: Give you° good night.
MARCELLUS: O, farewell, honest soldier:
Who hath reliev'd you?
FRANCISCO: Bernardo hath my place.
Give you good night.   *Exit Francisco.*
MARCELLUS: Holla! Bernardo!
BERNARDO: Say,
What, is Horatio there?
HORATIO: A piece of him.
BERNARDO: Welcome, Horatio: welcome, good Marcellus.   20
MARCELLUS: What, has this thing appear'd again to-night?
BERNARDO: I have seen nothing.
MARCELLUS: Horatio says 'tis but our fantasy,
And will not let belief take hold of him
Touching this dreaded sight, twice seen of us: 25
Therefore I have entreated him along
With us to watch the minutes of this night;
That if again this apparition come,
He may approve° our eyes and speak to it.
HORATIO: Tush, tush, 'twill not appear.
BERNARDO: Sit down awhile;   30
And let us once again assail your ears,
That are so fortified against our story
What we have two nights seen.
HORATIO: Well, sit we down,
And let us hear Bernardo speak of this.

---

3 **Long live the king**: Either a password or greeting; Horatio and Marcellus use a different one in line 15. **13 rivals**: Partners. **16 Give you**: God give you. **29 approve**: Corroborate.

BERNARDO: Last night of all,   35
    When yond same star that's westward from the pole°
    Had made his course t' illume that part of heaven
    Where now it burns, Marcellus and myself,
    The bell then beating one, —

Enter Ghost.

MARCELLUS: Peace, break thee off; look, where it comes again!   40
BERNARDO: In the same figure, like the king that's dead.
MARCELLUS: Thou art a scholar;° speak to it, Horatio.
BERNARDO: Looks 'a not like the king? mark it, Horatio.
HORATIO: Most like: it harrows° me with fear and wonder.
BERNARDO: It would be spoke to.°
MARCELLUS: Speak to it, Horatio.   45
HORATIO: What art thou that usurp'st this time of night,
    Together with that fair and warlike form
    In which the majesty of buried Denmark°
    Did sometimes march? by heaven I charge thee, speak!
MARCELLUS: It is offended.
BERNARDO: See it stalks away!   50
HORATIO: Stay! speak, speak! I charge thee, speak!   *Exit Ghost.*
MARCELLUS: 'Tis gone, and will not answer.
BERNARDO: How now, Horatio! you tremble and look pale:
    Is not this something more than fantasy?
    What think you on 't?   55
HORATIO: Before my God, I might not this believe
    Without the sensible and true avouch
    Of mine own eyes.
MARCELLUS: Is it not like the king?
HORATIO: As thou art to thyself:
    Such was the very armour he had on   60
    When he the ambitious Norway combated;
    So frown'd he once, when, in an angry parle,
    He smote° the sledded Polacks° on the ice.
    'Tis strange.
MARCELLUS: Thus twice before, and jump° at this dead hour,   65
    With martial stalk hath he gone by our watch.
HORATIO: In what particular thought to work I know not;
    But in the gross and scope° of my opinion,
    This bodes some strange eruption to our state.
MARCELLUS: Good now,° sit down, and tell me, he that knows,   70

---

36 pole: Polestar.   **42 scholar:** Exorcisms were performed in Latin, which Horatio as an educated man would be able to speak.   **44 harrows:** Lacerates the feelings.   **45 It . . . to:** A ghost could not speak until spoken to.   **48 buried Denmark:** The buried king of Denmark.   **63 smote:** Defeated;   **sledded Polacks:** Polanders using sledges.   **65 jump:** Exactly.   **68 gross and scope:** General drift.   **70 Good now:** An expression denoting entreaty or expostulation.

Why this same strict and most observant watch
So nightly toils° the subject° of the land,
And why such daily cast° of brazen cannon,
And foreign mart° for implements of war;
Why such impress° of shipwrights, whose sore task   75
Does not divide the Sunday from the week;
What might be toward, that this sweaty haste
Doth make the night joint-labourer with the day:
Who is't that can inform me?

HORATIO: That can I;
    At least, the whisper goes so. Our last king,   80
    Whose image even but now appear'd to us,
    Was, as you know, by Fortinbras of Norway,
    Thereto prick'd on° by a most emulate° pride,
    Dar'd to the combat; in which our valiant Hamlet—
    For so this side of our known world esteem'd him—   85
    Did slay this Fortinbras; who, by a seal'd compact,
    Well ratified by law and heraldry,°
    Did forfeit, with his life, all those his lands
    Which he stood seiz'd° of, to the conqueror:
    Against the which, a moiety competent°   90
    Was gaged by our king; which had return'd
    To the inheritance of Fortinbras,
    Had he been vanquisher; as, by the same comart,°
    And carriage° of the article design'd,
    His fell to Hamlet. Now, sir, young Fortinbras,   95
    Of unimproved° mettle hot and full,°
    Hath in the skirts of Norway here and there
    Shark'd up° a list of lawless resolutes,°
    For food and diet,° to some enterprise
    That hath a stomach in't; which is no other—   100
    As it doth well appear unto our state—
    But to recover of us, by strong hand
    And terms compulsatory, those foresaid lands
    So by his father lost: and this, I take it,
    Is the main motive of our preparations,   105
    The source of this our watch and the chief head
    Of this post-haste and romage° in the land.

---

72 **toils:** Causes or makes to toil;   **subject:** People, subjects.   73 **cast:** Casting, founding.
74 **mart:** Buying and selling, traffic.   75 **impress:** Impressment.   83 **prick'd on:** Incited;
emulate: Rivaling.   87 **law and heraldry:** Heraldic law, governing combat.   89 **seiz'd:** Possessed.   90 **moiety competent:** Adequate or sufficient portion.   93 **comart:** Joint bargain.
94 **carriage:** Import, bearing.   96 **unimproved:** Not turned to account;   **hot and full:** Full
of fight.   98 **Shark'd up:** Got together in haphazard fashion;   **resolutes:** Desperadoes.
99 **food and diet:** No pay but their keep.   107 **romage:** Bustle, commotion.

BERNARDO: I think it be no other but e'en so:
    Well may it sort° that this portentous figure
    Comes armed through our watch; so like the king   110
    That was and is the question of these wars.
HORATIO: A mote° it is to trouble the mind's eye.
    In the most high and palmy state° of Rome,
    A little ere the mightiest Julius fell,
    The graves stood tenantless and the sheeted dead   115
    Did squeak and gibber in the Roman streets:
    As stars with trains of fire° and dews of blood,
    Disasters° in the sun; and the moist star°
    Upon whose influence Neptune's empire° stands
    Was sick almost to doomsday with eclipse: 120
    And even the like precurse° of fear'd events,
    As harbingers preceding still the fates
    And prologue to the omen coming on,
    Have heaven and earth together demonstrated
    Unto our climatures and countrymen. —   125

Enter Ghost.

    But soft, behold! lo, where it comes again!
    I'll cross° it, though it blast me. Stay, illusion!
    If thou hast any sound, or use of voice,
    Speak to me!   *It° spreads his arms.*
    If there be any good thing to be done,   130
    That may to thee do ease and grace to me,
    Speak to me!
    If thou art privy to thy country's fate,
    Which, happily, foreknowing may avoid,
    O, speak!   135
    Or if thou hast uphoarded in thy life
    Extorted treasure in the womb of earth,
    For which, they say, you spirits oft walk in death,   *The cock crows.*
    Speak of it:° stay, and speak! Stop it, Marcellus.
MARCELLUS: Shall I strike at it with my partisan?°   140
HORATIO: Do, if it will not stand.
BERNARDO: 'Tis here!
HORATIO: 'Tis here!
MARCELLUS: 'Tis gone!   *[Exit Ghost.]*
    We do it wrong, being so majestical,

---

109 **sort:** Suit.   112 **mote:** Speck of dust.   113 **palmy state:** Triumphant sovereignty.
117 **stars . . . fire:** I.e., comets.   118 **Disasters:** Unfavorable aspects;   **moist star:** The moon,
governing tides.   119 **Neptune's empire:** The sea.   121 **precurse:** Heralding.   127 **cross:**
Meet, face, thus bringing down the evil influence on the person who crosses it.   129 **It:** The
Ghost, or perhaps Horatio.   133–139 **If . . . it:** Horatio recites the traditional reasons why
ghosts might walk.   140 **partisan:** Long-handled spear with a blade having lateral projections.

To offer it the show of violence;
For it is, as the air, invulnerable,   145
And our vain blows malicious mockery.
BERNARDO: It was about to speak, when the cock crew.°
HORATIO: And then it started like a guilty thing
    Upon a fearful summons. I have heard,
    The cock, that is the trumpet to the morn,   150
    Doth with his lofty and shrill-sounding throat
    Awake the god of day; and, at his warning,
    Whether in sea or fire, in earth or air,
    Th' extravagant and erring° spirit hies
    To his confine:° and of the truth herein   155
    This present object made probation.°
MARCELLUS: It faded on the crowing of the cock.
    Some say that ever 'gainst° that season comes
    Wherein our Saviour's birth is celebrated,
    The bird of dawning singeth all night long: 160
    And then, they say, no spirit dare stir abroad;
    The nights are wholesome; then no planets strike,°
    No fairy takes, nor witch hath power to charm,
    So hallow'd and so gracious° is that time.
HORATIO: So have I heard and do in part believe it.   165
    But, look, the morn, in russet mantle clad,
    Walks o'er the dew of yon high eastward hill:
    Break we our watch up; and by my advice,
    Let us impart what we have seen to-night
    Unto young Hamlet; for, upon my life,   170
    This spirit, dumb to us, will speak to him.
    Do you consent we shall acquaint him with it,
    As needful in our loves, fitting our duty?
MARCELLUS: Let's do 't, I pray; and I this morning know
    Where we shall find him most conveniently.   *Exeunt.*   175

[Scene 2]

[A room of state in the castle.]
    Flourish. Enter Claudius, King of Denmark, Gertrude the Queen, Coun-
cilors, Polonius and his son Laertes, Hamlet, cum aliis° [including Voltimand and
Cornelius].

KING: Though yet of Hamlet our dear brother's death
    The memory be green, and that it us befitted

---

147 **cock crew:** According to traditional ghost lore, spirits returned to their confines at cock-
crow.   154 **extravagant and erring:** Wandering. Both words mean the same thing.
155 **confine:** Place of confinement.   156 **probation:** Proof, trial.   158 **'gainst:** Just before.
162 **planets strike:** It was thought that planets were malignant and might strike travelers by
night.   164 **gracious:** Full of goodness.   SCENE 2. **cum aliis:** With others.

To bear our hearts in grief and our whole kingdom
To be contracted in one brow of woe,
Yet so far hath discretion fought with nature   5
That we with wisest sorrow think on him,
Together with remembrance of ourselves.
Therefore our sometime sister, now our queen,
Th' imperial jointress° to this warlike state,
Have we, as 'twere with a defeated joy,—   10
With an auspicious and a dropping eye,
With mirth in funeral and with dirge in marriage,
In equal scale weighing delight and dole,—
Taken to wife: nor have we herein barr'd
Your better wisdoms, which have freely gone   15
With this affair along. For all, our thanks.
Now follows, that° you know, young Fortinbras,
Holding a weak supposal° of our worth,
Or thinking by our late dear brother's death
Our state to be disjoint° and out of frame,°   20
Colleagued° with this dream of his advantage,°
He hath not fail'd to pester us with message,
Importing° the surrender of those lands
Lost by his father, with all bands of law,
To our most valiant brother. So much for him.   25
Now for ourself and for this time of meeting:
Thus much the business is: we have here writ
To Norway, uncle of young Fortinbras,—
Who, impotent and bed-rid, scarcely hears
Of this his nephew's purpose,—to suppress   30
His further gait° herein; in that the levies,
The lists and full proportions, are all made
Out of his subject:° and we here dispatch
You, good Cornelius, and you, Voltimand,
For bearers of this greeting to old Norway;   35
Giving to you no further personal power
To business with the king, more than the scope
Of these delated° articles allow.
Farewell, and let your haste commend your duty.

CORNELIUS: ⎫
                ⎬ In that and all things will we show our duty.   40
VOLTIMAND: ⎭

KING: We doubt it nothing: heartily farewell.

[Exeunt Voltimand and Cornelius.]

9 jointress: Woman possessed of a jointure, or, joint tenancy of an estate.   **17 that:** That
which.   **18 weak supposal:** Low estimate.   **20 disjoint:** Distracted, out of joint;   **frame:**
Order.   **21 Colleagued:** Added to;   **dream . . . advantage:** Visionary hope of success.
23 Importing: Purporting, pertaining to.   **31 gait:** Proceeding.   **33 Out of his subject:** At
the expense of Norway's subjects (collectively).   **38 delated:** Expressly stated.

And now, Laertes, what's the news with you?
You told us of some suit; what is 't, Laertes?
You cannot speak of reason to the Dane,°
And lose your voice:° what wouldst thou beg, Laertes, 45
That shall not be my offer, not thy asking?
The head is not more native° to the heart,
The hand more instrumental° to the mouth,
Than is the throne of Denmark to thy father.
What wouldst thou have, Laertes?

LAERTES: My dread lord, 50
Your leave and favour to return to France;
From whence though willingly I came to Denmark,
To show my duty in your coronation,
Yet now, I must confess, that duty done,
My thoughts and wishes bend again toward France 55
And bow them to your gracious leave and pardon.°

KING: Have you your father's leave? What says Polonius?

POLONIUS: He hath, my lord, wrung from me my slow leave
By laboursome petition, and at last
Upon his will I seal'd my hard consent: 60
I do beseech you, give him leave to go.

KING: Take thy fair hour, Laertes; time be thine,
And thy best graces spend it at thy will!
But now, my cousin° Hamlet, and my son, —

HAMLET [aside]:   A little more than kin, and less than kind!° 65

KING: How is it that the clouds still hang on you?

HAMLET: Not so, my lord; I am too much in the sun.°

QUEEN: Good Hamlet, cast thy nighted colour off,
And let thine eye look like a friend on Denmark.
Do not for ever with thy vailed lids 70
Seek for thy noble father in the dust:
Thou know'st 'tis common; all that lives must die,
Passing through nature to eternity.

HAMLET: Ay, madam, it is common.°

QUEEN: If it be,
Why seems it so particular with thee? 75

---

44 the Dane: Danish king.   **45 lose your voice:** Speak in vain.   **47 native:** Closely connected, related.   **48 instrumental:** Serviceable.   **56 leave and pardon:** Permission to depart.   **64 cousin:** Any kin not of the immediate family.   **65 A little . . . kind:** My relation to you has become more than kinship warrants; it has also become unnatural.   **67 I am . . . sun:** (1) I am too much out of doors, (2) I am too much in the sun of your grace (ironical), (3) I am too much of a son to you. Possibly an allusion to the proverb "Out of heaven's blessing into the warm sun"; i.e., Hamlet is out of house and home in being deprived of the kingship. **74 Ay . . . common:** It is common, but it hurts nevertheless; possibly a reference to the commonplace quality of the queen's remark.

HAMLET: Seems, madam! nay, it is; I know not "seems."
    'Tis not alone my inky cloak, good mother,
    Nor customary suits° of solemn black,
    Nor windy suspiration° of forc'd breath,
    No, nor the fruitful river in the eye,   80
    Nor the dejected 'haviour of the visage,
    Together with all forms, moods, shapes of grief,
    That can denote me truly: these indeed seem,
    For they are actions that a man might play:
    But I have that within which passeth show;   85
    These but the trappings and the suits of woe.
KING: 'Tis sweet and commendable in your nature, Hamlet,
    To give these mourning duties to your father:
    But, you must know, your father lost a father;
    That father lost, lost his, and the survivor bound   90
    In filial obligation for some term
    To do obsequious° sorrow: but to persever
    In obstinate condolement° is a course
    Of impious stubbornness; 'tis unmanly grief;
    It shows a will most incorrect° to heaven,   95
    A heart unfortified, a mind impatient,
    An understanding simple and unschool'd:
    For what we know must be and is as common
    As any the most vulgar thing° to sense,
    Why should we in our peevish opposition   100
    Take it to heart? Fie! 'tis a fault to heaven,
    A fault against the dead, a fault to nature,
    To reason most absurd; whose common theme
    Is death of fathers, and who still hath cried,
    From the first corse till he that died to-day,   105
    "This must be so." We pray you, throw to earth
    This unprevailing° woe, and think of us
    As of a father: for let the world take note,
    You are the most immediate° to our throne;
    And with no less nobility° of love   110
    Than that which dearest father bears his son,
    Do I impart° toward you. For your intent
    In going back to school in Wittenberg,°
    It is most retrograde° to our desire:
    And we beseech you, bend you° to remain   115

---

78 **customary suits:** Suits prescribed by custom for mourning.   79 **windy suspiration:** Heavy sighing.   92 **obsequious:** Dutiful.   93 **condolement:** Sorrowing.   95 **incorrect:** Untrained, uncorrected.   99 **vulgar thing:** Common experience.   107 **unprevailing:** Unavailing. 109 **most immediate:** Next in succession.   110 **nobility:** High degree.   112 **impart:** The object is apparently *love* (line 110).   113 **Wittenberg:** Famous German university founded in 1502.   114 **retrograde:** Contrary.   115 **bend you:** Incline yourself; imperative.

Here, in the cheer and comfort of our eye,
Our chiefest courtier, cousin, and our son.
QUEEN: Let not thy mother lose her prayers, Hamlet:
I pray thee, stay with us; go not to Wittenberg.
HAMLET: I shall in all my best obey you, madam.   120
KING: Why, 'tis a loving and a fair reply:
Be as ourself in Denmark. Madam, come;
This gentle and unforc'd accord of Hamlet
Sits smiling to my heart: in grace whereof,
No jocund health that Denmark drinks to-day,   125
But the great cannon to the clouds shall tell,
And the king's rouse° the heaven shall bruit again,°
Re-speaking earthly thunder. Come away.

> *Flourish. Exeunt all but Hamlet.*

HAMLET: O, that this too too sullied flesh would melt,
Thaw and resolve itself into a dew!   130
Or that the Everlasting had not fix'd
His canon 'gainst self-slaughter! O God! God!
How weary, stale, flat and unprofitable,
Seem to me all the uses of this world!
Fie on't! ah fie! 'tis an unweeded garden,   135
That grows to seed; things rank and gross in nature
Possess it merely.° That it should come to this!
But two months dead: nay, not so much, not two:
So excellent a king; that was, to this,
Hyperion° to a satyr; so loving to my mother   140
That he might not beteem° the winds of heaven
Visit her face too roughly. Heaven and earth!
Must I remember? why, she would hang on him,
As if increase of appetite had grown
By what it fed on: and yet, within a month —   145
Let me not think on't — Frailty, thy name is woman! —
A little month, or ere those shoes were old
With which she followed my poor father's body,
Like Niobe,° all tears: — why she, even she —
O God! a beast, that wants discourse of reason,°   150
Would have mourn'd longer — married with my uncle,
My father's brother, but no more like my father
Than I to Hercules: within a month:

---

127 rouse: Draft of liquor; **bruit again:** Echo.   **137 merely:** Completely, entirely.
140 Hyperion: God of the sun in the older regime of ancient gods.   **141 beteem:** Allow.
149 Niobe: Tantalus's daughter, who boasted that she had more sons and daughters than Leto;
for this Apollo and Artemis slew her children. She was turned into stone by Zeus on Mount
Sipylus.   **150 discourse of reason:** Process or faculty of reason.

Ere yet the salt of most unrighteous tears
Had left the flushing in her galled° eyes, 155
She married. O, most wicked speed, to post
With such dexterity° to incestuous sheets!
It is not nor it cannot come to good:
But break, my heart; for I must hold my tongue.

Enter Horatio, Marcellus, and Bernardo.

HORATIO: Hail to your lordship!
HAMLET: I am glad to see you well: 160
Horatio! — or I do forget myself.
HORATIO: The same, my lord, and your poor servant ever.
HAMLET: Sir, my good friend; I'll change that name with you:°
And what make you from Wittenberg, Horatio?
Marcellus? 165
MARCELLUS: My good lord—
HAMLET: I am very glad to see you. Good even, sir.
But what, in faith, make you from Wittenberg?
HORATIO: A truant disposition, good my lord.
HAMLET: I would not hear your enemy say so, 170
Nor shall you do my ear that violence,
To make it truster of your own report
Against yourself: I know you are no truant.
But what is your affair in Elsinore?
We'll teach you to drink deep ere you depart. 175
HORATIO: My lord, I came to see your father's funeral.
HAMLET: I prithee, do not mock me, fellow-student;
I think it was to see my mother's wedding.
HORATIO: Indeed, my lord, it follow'd hard° upon.
HAMLET: Thrift, thrift, Horatio! the funeral bak'd meats° 180
Did coldly furnish forth the marriage tables.
Would I had met my dearest° foe in heaven
Or ever I had seen that day, Horatio!
My father! — methinks I see my father.
HORATIO: Where, my lord!
HAMLET: In my mind's eye, Horatio. 185
HORATIO: I saw him once; 'a° was a goodly king.
HAMLET: 'A was a man, take him for all in all,
I shall not look upon his like again.
HORATIO: My lord, I think I saw him yesternight.
HAMLET: Saw? who? 190

---

155 galled: Irritated.   **157 dexterity:** Facility.   **163 I'll . . . you:** I'll be your servant, you shall be my friend; also explained as "I'll exchange the name of friend with you."   **179 hard:** Close.   **180 bak'd meats:** Meat pies.   **182 dearest:** Direst. The adjective *dear* in Shakespeare has two different origins: O.E. *deore,* "beloved," and O.E. *deor,* "fierce." *Dearest* is the superlative of the second.   **186 'a:** He.

HORATIO: My lord, the king your father.
HAMLET: The king my father!
HORATIO: Season your admiration° for a while
    With an attent ear, till I may deliver,
    Upon the witness of these gentlemen,
    This marvel to you.
HAMLET: For God's love, let me hear.   195
HORATIO: Two nights together had these gentlemen,
    Marcellus and Bernardo, on their watch,
    In the dead waste and middle of the night,
    Been thus encount'red. A figure like your father,
    Armed at point exactly, cap-a-pe,°   200
    Appears before them, and with solemn march
    Goes slow and stately by them: thrice he walk'd
    By their oppress'd° and fear-surprised eyes,
    Within his truncheon's° length; whilst they, distill'd°
    Almost to jelly with the act° of fear,   205
    Stand dumb and speak not to him. This to me
    In dreadful secrecy impart they did;
    And I with them the third night kept the watch:
    Where, as they had deliver'd, both in time,
    Form of the thing, each word made true and good,   210
    The apparition comes: I knew your father;
    These hands are not more like.
HAMLET: But where was this?
MARCELLUS: My lord, upon the platform where we watch'd.
HAMLET: Did you not speak to it?
HORATIO: My lord, I did;
    But answer made it none: yet once methought   215
    It lifted up it° head and did address
    Itself to motion, like as it would speak;
    But even then the morning cock crew loud,
    And at the sound it shrunk in haste away,
    And vanish'd from our sight.
HAMLET: 'Tis very strange.   220
HORATIO: As I do live, my honour'd lord, 'tis true;
    And we did think it writ down in our duty
    To let you know of it.
HAMLET: Indeed, indeed, sirs, but this troubles me.
    Hold you the watch to-night?
MARCELLUS: ⎫
BERNARDO: ⎭   We do, my lord.   225

---

192 **Season your admiration:** Restrain your astonishment.   200 **cap-a-pe:** From head to foot.
203 **oppress'd:** Distressed.   204 **truncheon:** Officer's staff;   **distill'd:** Softened, weakened.
205 **act:** Action.   216 **it:** Its.

HAMLET: Arm'd, say you?

MARCELLUS: }
BERNARDO: }   Arm'd, my lord.

HAMLET: From top to toe?

MARCELLUS: }
BERNARDO: }   My lord, from head to foot.

HAMLET: Then saw you not his face?

HORATIO: O, yes, my lord; he wore his beaver° up.

HAMLET: What, look'd he frowningly?

HORATIO: A countenance more   230
In sorrow than in anger.

HAMLET: Pale or red?

HORATIO: Nay, very pale.

HAMLET: And fix'd his eyes upon you?

HORATIO: Most constantly.

HAMLET: I would I had been there.

HORATIO: It would have much amaz'd you.

HAMLET: Very like, very like. Stay'd it long?   235

HORATIO: While one with moderate haste might tell a hundred.

MARCELLUS: }
BERNARDO: }   Longer, longer.

HORATIO: Not when I saw't.

HAMLET: His beard was grizzled,—no?

HORATIO: It was, as I have seen it in his life,
A sable° silver'd.

HAMLET: I will watch to-night;   240
Perchance 'twill walk again.

HORATIO: I warr'nt it will.

HAMLET: If it assume my noble father's person,
I'll speak to it, though hell itself should gape
And bid me hold my peace. I pray you all,
If you have hitherto conceal'd this sight,   245
Let it be tenable in your silence still;
And whatsoever else shall hap to-night,
Give it an understanding, but no tongue:
I will requite your loves. So, fare you well:
Upon the platform, 'twixt eleven and twelve,   250
I'll visit you.

ALL: Our duty to your honour.

HAMLET: Your loves, as mine to you: farewell.   *Exeunt [all but Hamlet].*
My father's spirit in arms! all is not well;
I doubt° some foul play: would the night were come!
Till then sit still, my soul: foul deeds will rise,   255
Though all the earth o'erwhelm them, to men's eyes.   *Exit.*

---

229 beaver: Visor on the helmet.   **239 sable:** Black color.   **254 doubt:** Fear.

[Scene 3]

[A room in Polonius's house.]
　　Enter Laertes and Ophelia, his Sister.

LAERTES:　My necessaries are embark'd: farewell:
　　And, sister, as the winds give benefit
　　And convoy is assistant,° do not sleep,
　　But let me hear from you.
OPHELIA:　　　　　　　　　Do you doubt that?
LAERTES:　For Hamlet and the trifling of his favour,　　　　　　　　5
　　Hold it a fashion° and a toy in blood,°
　　A violet in the youth of primy° nature,
　　Forward,° not permanent, sweet, not lasting,
　　The perfume and suppliance of a minute;°
　　No more.
OPHELIA:　　No more but so?
LAERTES:　　　　　　　　　　Think it no more:　　　　　　　　10
　　For nature, crescent,° does not grow alone
　　In thews° and bulk, but, as this temple° waxes,
　　The inward service of the mind and soul
　　Grows wide withal. Perhaps he loves you now,
　　And now no soil° nor cautel° doth besmirch　　　　　　　　15
　　The virtue of his will: but you must fear,
　　His greatness weigh'd,° his will is not his own;
　　For he himself is subject to his birth:
　　He may not, as unvalued persons do,
　　Carve for himself; for on his choice depends　　　　　　　　20
　　The safety and health of this whole state;
　　And therefore must his choice be circumscrib'd
　　Unto the voice and yielding° of that body
　　Whereof he is the head. Then if he says he loves you,
　　It fits your wisdom so far to believe it　　　　　　　　25
　　As he in his particular act and place
　　May give his saying deed;° which is no further
　　Than the main voice of Denmark goes withal.
　　Then weigh what loss your honour may sustain,
　　If with too credent° ear you list his songs,　　　　　　　　30
　　Or lose your heart, or your chaste treasure open
　　To his unmast'red° importunity.

SCENE 3. **3 convoy is assistant:** Means of conveyance are available. **6 fashion:** Custom, prevailing usage; **toy in blood:** Passing amorous fancy. **7 primy:** In its prime. **8 Forward:** Precocious. **9 suppliance of a minute:** Diversion to fill up a minute. **11 crescent:** Growing, waxing. **12 thews:** Bodily strength; **temple:** Body. **15 soil:** Blemish; **cautel:** Crafty device. **17 greatness weigh'd:** High position considered. **23 voice and yielding:** Assent, approval. **27 deed:** Effect. **30 credent:** Credulous. **32 unmast'red:** Unrestrained.

Fear it, Ophelia, fear it, my dear sister,
And keep you in the rear of your affection,
Out of the shot and danger of desire.   35
The chariest° maid is prodigal enough,
If she unmask her beauty to the moon:
Virtue itself 'scapes not calumnious strokes:
The canker galls the infants of the spring,°
Too oft before their buttons° be disclos'd,°   40
And in the morn and liquid dew° of youth
Contagious blastments° are most imminent.
Be wary then; best safety lies in fear:
Youth to itself rebels, though none else near.

OPHELIA: I shall the effect of this good lesson keep,   45
As watchman to my heart. But, good my brother,
Do not, as some ungracious° pastors do,
Show me the steep and thorny way to heaven;
Whiles, like a puff'd° and reckless libertine,
Himself the primrose path of dalliance treads,   50
And recks° not his own rede.°

Enter Polonius.

LAERTES: O, fear me not.
I stay too long: but here my father comes.
A double° blessing is a double grace;
Occasion° smiles upon a second leave.
POLONIUS: Yet here, Laertes? aboard, aboard, for shame!   55
The wind sits in the shoulder of your sail,
And you are stay'd for. There; my blessing with thee!
And these few precepts° in thy memory
Look thou character.° Give thy thoughts no tongue,
Nor any unproportion'd° thought his act.   60
Be thou familiar, but by no means vulgar.°
Those friends thou hast, and their adoption tried,
Grapple them to thy soul with hoops of steel;
But do not dull thy palm with entertainment
Of each new-hatch'd, unfledg'd° comrade. Beware   65
Of entrance to a quarrel, but being in,
Bear't that th' opposed may beware of thee.
Give every man thy ear, but few thy voice;

---

36 **chariest:** Most scrupulously modest.   39 **The canker . . . spring:** The cankerworm destroys
the young plants of spring.   40 **buttons:** Buds;   **disclos'd:** Opened.   41 **liquid dew:** I.e., time
when dew is fresh.   42 **blastments:** Blights.   47 **ungracious:** Graceless.   49 **puff'd:** Bloated.
51 **recks:** Heeds;   **rede:** Counsel.   53 **double:** I.e., Laertes has already bade his father good-by.
54 **Occasion:** Opportunity.   58 **precepts:** Many parallels have been found to the series of
maxims which follows, one of the closer being that in Lyly's *Euphues.*   59 **character:** Inscribe.
60 **unproportion'd:** Inordinate.   61 **vulgar:** Common.   65 **unfledg'd:** Immature.

Take each man's censure, but reserve thy judgement.
Costly thy habit as thy purse can buy,   70
But not express'd in fancy;° rich, not gaudy;
For the apparel oft proclaims the man,
And they in France of the best rank and station
Are of a most select and generous chief in that.°
Neither a borrower nor a lender be;   75
For loan oft loses both itself and friend,
And borrowing dulleth edge of husbandry.°
This above all: to thine own self be true,
And it must follow, as the night the day,
Thou canst not then be false to any man.   80
Farewell: my blessing season° this in thee!

LAERTES: Most humbly do I take my leave, my lord.
POLONIUS: The time invites you; go; your servants tend.
LAERTES: Farewell, Ophelia; and remember well
    What I have said to you.
OPHELIA: 'Tis in my memory lock'd,   85
    And you yourself shall keep the key of it.
LAERTES: Farewell.   *Exit Laertes.*
POLONIUS: What is 't, Ophelia, he hath said to you?
OPHELIA: So please you, something touching the Lord Hamlet.
POLONIUS: Marry, well bethought: 90
    'Tis told me, he hath very oft of late
    Given private time to you; and you yourself
    Have of your audience been most free and bounteous:
    If it be so, as so 'tis put on° me,
    And that in way of caution, I must tell you,   95
    You do not understand yourself so clearly
    As it behooves my daughter and your honour.
    What is between you? give me up the truth.
OPHELIA: He hath, my lord, of late made many tenders°
    Of his affection to me.   100
POLONIUS: Affection! pooh! you speak like a green girl,
    Unsifted° in such perilous circumstance.
    Do you believe his tenders, as you call them?
OPHELIA: I do not know, my lord, what I should think.
POLONIUS: Marry, I will teach you: think yourself a baby;   105
    That you have ta'en these tenders° for true pay,
    Which are not sterling.° Tender° yourself more dearly;

---

71 **express'd in fancy:** Fantastical in design.   74 **Are ... that:** *Chief* is usually taken as a
substantive meaning "head," "eminence."   77 **husbandry:** Thrift.   81 **season:** Mature.
94 **put on:** Impressed on.   99, 103 **tenders:** Offers.   102 **Unsifted:** Untried.   106 **ten-**
ders: Promises to pay.   107 **sterling:** Legal currency;   **Tender:** Hold.

Or — not to crack the wind° of the poor phrase,
Running it thus — you'll tender me a fool.°

OPHELIA: My lord, he hath importun'd me with love   110
In honourable fashion.

POLONIUS: Ay, fashion° you may call it; go to, go to.

OPHELIA: And hath given countenance° to his speech, my lord,
With almost all the holy vows of heaven.

POLONIUS: Ay, springes° to catch woodcocks.° I do know,   115
When the blood burns, how prodigal the soul
Lends the tongue vows: these blazes, daughter,
Giving more light than heat, extinct in both,
Even in their promise, as it is a-making,
You must not take for fire. From this time   120
Be somewhat scanter of your maiden presence;
Set your entreatments° at a higher rate
Than a command to parley.° For Lord Hamlet,
Believe so much in him,° that he is young,
And with a larger tether may he walk   125
Than may be given you: in few,° Ophelia,
Do not believe his vows; for they are brokers;°
Not of that dye° which their investments° show,
But mere implorators of° unholy suits,
Breathing° like sanctified and pious bawds,   130
The better to beguile. This is for all:
I would not, in plain terms, from this time forth,
Have you so slander° any moment leisure,
As to give words or talk with the Lord Hamlet.
Look to 't, I charge you: come your ways.   135

OPHELIA: I shall obey, my lord.   *Exeunt.*

[Scene 4]

[The platform.]
Enter Hamlet, Horatio, and Marcellus.

HAMLET: The air bites shrewdly; it is very cold.

HORATIO: It is a nipping and an eager air.

HAMLET: What hour now?

HORATIO: I think it lacks of twelve.

MARCELLUS: No, it is struck.

---

108 **crack the wind:** I.e., run it until it is broken-winded.   109 **tender . . . fool:** Show me a fool
(for a daughter).   112 **fashion:** Mere form, pretense.   113 **countenance:** Credit, support.
115 **springes:** Snares;   **woodcocks:** Birds easily caught, type of stupidity.   122 **entreatments:**
Conversations, interviews.   123 **command to parley:** Mere invitation to talk.   124 **so . . .
him:** This much concerning him.   126 **in few:** Briefly.   127 **brokers:** Go-betweens, pro-
curers.   128 **dye:** Color or sort;   **investments:** Clothes.   129 **implorators of:** Solicitors of.
130 **Breathing:** Speaking.   133 **slander:** Bring disgrace or reproach upon.

HORATIO: Indeed? I heard it not: then it draws near the season   5
Wherein the spirit held his wont to walk.

A flourish of trumpets, and two pieces go off.

What does this mean, my lord?

HAMLET: The king doth wake° to-night and takes his rouse,°
Keeps wassail,° and the swagg'ring up-spring° reels;°
And, as he drains his draughts of Rhenish° down,   10
The kettle-drum and trumpet thus bray out
The triumph of his pledge.°

HORATIO: Is it a custom?

HAMLET: Ay, marry, is 't:
But to my mind, though I am native here
And to the manner born,° it is a custom   15
More honour'd in the breach than the observance.
This heavy-headed revel east and west
Makes us traduc'd and tax'd of other nations:
They clepe° us drunkards, and with swinish phrase°
Soil our addition;° and indeed it takes   20
From our achievements, though perform'd at height,
The pith and marrow of our attribute.°
So, oft it chances in particular men,
That for some vicious mole of nature° in them,
As, in their birth — wherein they are not guilty,   25
Since nature cannot choose his origin —
By the o'ergrowth of some complexion,
Oft breaking down the pales° and forts of reason,
Or by some habit that too much o'er-leavens°
The form of plausive° manners, that these men,   30
Carrying, I say, the stamp of one defect,
Being nature's livery,° or fortune's star,° —
Their virtues else — be they as pure as grace,
As infinite as man may undergo —
Shall in the general censure take corruption   35
From that particular fault: the dram of eale°

SCENE 4. 8 **wake:** Stay awake, hold revel;   **rouse:** Carouse, drinking bout.   9 **wassail:** Carousal;
up-spring: Last and wildest dance at German merry-makings;   **reels:** Reels through.   10 **Rhen-**
ish: Rhine wine.   12 **triumph . . . pledge:** His glorious achievement as a drinker.   15 **to . . .**
born: Destined by birth to be subject to the custom in question.   19 **clepe:** Call;   **with swinish**
phrase: By calling us swine.   20 **addition:** Reputation.   22 **attribute:** Reputation.   24 **mole**
of nature: Natural blemish in one's constitution.   28 **pales:** Palings (as of a fortification).
29 **o'er-leavens:** Induces a change throughout (as yeast works in bread).   30 **plausive:** Pleasing.
32 **nature's livery:** Endowment from nature;   **fortune's star:** The position in which one is
placed by fortune, a reference to astrology. The two phrases are aspects of the same thing.
36–38 **the dram . . . scandal:** A famous crux: *dram of eale* has had various interpretations, the
preferred one being probably, "a dram of evil."

Doth all the noble substance of a doubt
To his own scandal.°

Enter Ghost.

HORATIO: Look, my lord, it comes!
HAMLET: Angels and ministers of grace° defend us!
Be thou a spirit of health or goblin damn'd,   40
Bring with thee airs from heaven or blasts from hell,
Be thy intents wicked or charitable,
Thou com'st in such a questionable° shape
That I will speak to thee: I'll call thee Hamlet,
King, father, royal Dane: O, answer me!   45
Let me not burst in ignorance; but tell
Why thy canoniz'd° bones, hearsed° in death,
Have burst their cerements;° why the sepulchre,
Wherein we saw thee quietly interr'd,
Hath op'd his ponderous and marble jaws,   50
To cast thee up again. What may this mean,
That thou, dead corse, again in complete steel
Revisits thus the glimpses of the moon,°
Making night hideous; and we fools of nature°
So horridly to shake our disposition   55
With thoughts beyond the reaches of our souls?
Say, why is this? wherefore? what should we do?

[Ghost] beckons [Hamlet].

HORATIO: It beckons you to go away with it,
As if it some impartment° did desire
To you alone.
MARCELLUS: Look, with what courteous action   60
It waves you to a more removed° ground:
But do not go with it.
HORATIO: No, by no means.
HAMLET: It will not speak; then I will follow it.
HORATIO: Do not, my lord!
HAMLET: Why, what should be the fear?
I do not set my life at a pin's fee;   65
And for my soul, what can it do to that,
Being a thing immortal as itself?
It waves me forth again: I'll follow it.
HORATIO: What if it tempt you toward the flood, my lord,
Or to the dreadful summit of the cliff   70

---

39 ministers of grace: Messengers of God.   **43 questionable:** Inviting question or conversation.   **47 canoniz'd:** Buried according to the canons of the church;   **hearsed:** Coffined.   **48 cerements:** Grave-clothes.   **53 glimpses of the moon:** The earth by night.   **54 fools of nature:** Mere men, limited to natural knowledge.   **59 impartment:** Communication.   **61 removed:** Remote.

That beetles o'er° his base into the sea,
And there assume some other horrible form,
Which might deprive your sovereignty of reason°
And draw you into madness? think of it:
The very place puts toys of desperation,°   75
Without more motive, into every brain
That looks so many fathoms to the sea
And hears it roar beneath.
HAMLET: It waves me still.
      Go on; I'll follow thee.
MARCELLUS: You shall not go, my lord.
HAMLET: Hold off your hands!   80
HORATIO: Be rul'd; you shall not go.
HAMLET: My fate cries out,
      And makes each petty artere° in this body
      As hardy as the Nemean lion's° nerve.°
      Still am I call'd. Unhand me, gentlemen.
      By heaven, I'll make a ghost of him that lets° me!   85
      I say, away! Go on; I'll follow thee.   *Exeunt Ghost and Hamlet.*
HORATIO: He waxes desperate with imagination.
MARCELLUS: Let's follow; 'tis not fit thus to obey him.
HORATIO: Have after. To what issue° will this come?
MARCELLUS: Something is rotten in the state of Denmark.   90
HORATIO: Heaven will direct it.°
MARCELLUS: Nay, let's follow him.   *Exeunt.*

[Scene 5]

[Another part of the platform.]
      Enter Ghost and Hamlet.

HAMLET: Whither wilt thou lead me? speak; I'll go no further.
GHOST: Mark me.
HAMLET: I will.
GHOST: My hour is almost come,
      When I to sulphurous and tormenting flames
      Must render up myself.
HAMLET: Alas, poor ghost!

---

71 **beetles o'er:** Overhangs threateningly.   73 **deprive . . . reason:** Take away the sovereignty of your reason. It was thought that evil spirits would sometimes assume the form of departed spirits in order to work madness in a human creature.   75 **toys of desperation:** Freakish notions of suicide.   82 **artere:** Artery.   83 **Nemean lion's:** The Nemean lion was one of the monsters slain by Hercules;   **nerve:** Sinew, tendon. The point is that the arteries which were carrying the spirits out into the body were functioning and were as stiff and hard as the sinews of the lion.   85 **lets:** Hinders.   89 **issue:** Outcome.   91 **it:** I.e., the outcome.

GHOST: Pity me not, but lend thy serious hearing   5
    To what I shall unfold.
HAMLET: Speak; I am bound to hear.
GHOST: So art thou to revenge, when thou shalt hear.
HAMLET: What?
GHOST: I am thy father's spirit,
    Doom'd for a certain term to walk the night,   10
    And for the day confin'd to fast° in fires,
    Till the foul crimes done in my days of nature
    Are burnt and purg'd away. But that I am forbid
    To tell the secrets of my prison-house,
    I could a tale unfold whose lightest word   15
    Would harrow up thy soul, freeze thy young blood,
    Make thy two eyes, like stars, start from their spheres,°
    Thy knotted° and combined° locks to part
    And each particular hair to stand an end,
    Like quills upon the fretful porpentine:°   20
    But this eternal blazon° must not be
    To ears of flesh and blood. List, list, O, list!
    If thou didst ever thy dear father love —
HAMLET: O God!
GHOST: Revenge his foul and most unnatural° murder.   25
HAMLET: Murder!
GHOST: Murder most foul, as in the best it is;
    But this most foul, strange and unnatural.
HAMLET: Haste me to know't, that I, with wings as swift
    As meditation or the thoughts of love,   30
    May sweep to my revenge.
GHOST: I find thee apt;
    And duller shouldst thou be than the fat weed°
    That roots itself in ease on Lethe wharf,°
    Wouldst thou not stir in this. Now, Hamlet, hear:
    'Tis given out that, sleeping in my orchard,   35
    A serpent stung me; so the whole ear of Denmark
    Is by a forged process of my death
    Rankly abus'd: but know, thou noble youth,
    The serpent that did sting thy father's life
    Now wears his crown.

SCENE 5. 11 **fast:** Probably, do without food. It has been sometimes taken in the sense of doing general penance.   17 **spheres:** Orbits.   18 **knotted:** Perhaps intricately arranged; **combined:** Tied, bound.   20 **porpentine:** Porcupine.   21 **eternal blazon:** Promulgation or proclamation of eternity, revelation of the hereafter.   25 **unnatural:** I.e., pertaining to fratricide.   32 **fat weed:** Many suggestions have been offered as to the particular plant intended, including asphodel; probably a general figure for plants growing along rotting wharves and piles.   33 **Lethe wharf:** Bank of the river of forgetfulness in Hades.

HAMLET: O my prophetic soul!   40
    My uncle!
GHOST: Ay, that incestuous, that adulterate° beast,
    With witchcraft of his wit, with traitorous gifts, —
    O wicked wit and gifts, that have the power
    So to seduce! — won to his shameful lust   45
    The will of my most seeming-virtuous queen:
    O Hamlet, what a falling-off was there!
    From me, whose love was of that dignity
    That it went hand in hand even with the vow
    I made to her in marriage, and to decline   50
    Upon a wretch whose natural gifts were poor
    To those of mine!
    But virtue, as it never will be moved,
    Though lewdness court it in a shape of heaven,
    So lust, though to a radiant angel link'd,   55
    Will sate itself in a celestial bed,
    And prey on garbage.
    But, soft! methinks I scent the morning air;
    Brief let me be. Sleeping within my orchard,
    My custom always of the afternoon,   60
    Upon my secure° hour thy uncle stole,
    With juice of cursed hebona° in a vial,
    And in the porches of my ears did pour
    The leperous° distilment; whose effect
    Holds such an enmity with blood of man   65
    That swift as quicksilver it courses through
    The natural gates and alleys of the body,
    And with a sudden vigour it doth posset°
    And curd, like eager° droppings into milk,
    The thin and wholesome blood: so did it mine;   70
    And a most instant tetter bark'd about,
    Most lazar-like,° with vile and loathsome crust,
    All my smooth body.
    Thus was I, sleeping, by a brother's hand
    Of life, of crown, of queen, at once dispatch'd:°   75
    Cut off even in the blossoms of my sin,
    Unhous'led,° disappointed,° unanel'd,°
    No reck'ning made, but sent to my account
    With all my imperfections on my head:

---

42 adulterate: Adulterous. **61 secure:** Confident, unsuspicious. **62 hebona:** Generally supposed to mean henbane, conjectured *hemlock*; *ebenus*, meaning "yew." **64 leperous:** Causing leprosy. **68 posset:** Coagulate, curdle. **69 eager:** Sour, acid. **72 lazar-like:** Leperlike. **75 dispatch'd:** Suddenly bereft. **77 Unhous'led:** Without having received the sacrament; **disappointed:** Unready, without equipment for the last journey; **unanel'd:** Without having received extreme unction.

O, horrible! O, horrible! most horrible!°   80
If thou hast nature in thee, bear it not;
Let not the royal bed of Denmark be
A couch for luxury° and damned incest.
But, howsomever thou pursues this act,
Taint not thy mind,° nor let thy soul contrive   85
Against thy mother aught: leave her to heaven
And to those thorns that in her bosom lodge,
To prick and sting her. Fare thee well at once!
The glow-worm shows the matin° to be near,
And 'gins to pale his uneffectual fire:°   90
Adieu, adieu, adieu! remember me.   *[Exit.]*
HAMLET: O all you host of heaven! O earth! what else?
And shall I couple° hell? O, fie! Hold, hold, my heart;
And you, my sinews, grow not instant old,
But bear me stiffly up. Remember thee!   95
Ay, thou poor ghost, whiles memory holds a seat
In this distracted globe.° Remember thee!
Yea, from the table of my memory
I'll wipe away all trivial fond records,
All saws° of books, all forms, all pressures° past,   100
That youth and observation copied there;
And thy commandment all alone shall live
Within the book and volume of my brain,
Unmix'd with baser matter: yes, by heaven!
O most pernicious woman!   105
O villain, villain, smiling, damned villain!
My tables,° — meet it is I set it down,
That one may smile, and smile, and be a villain;
At least I am sure it may be so in Denmark: *[Writing.]*
So, uncle, there you are. Now to my word;°   110
It is "Adieu, adieu! remember me,"
I have sworn't.

Enter Horatio and Marcellus.

HORATIO: My lord, my lord —
MARCELLUS: Lord Hamlet, —
HORATIO: Heavens secure him!
HAMLET: So be it!
MARCELLUS: Hillo, ho, ho,° my lord!   115

---

80 **O . . . horrible:** Many editors give this line to Hamlet; Garrick and Sir Henry Irving spoke it in
that part.   83 **luxury:** Lechery.   85 **Taint . . . mind:** Probably, deprave not thy character, do
nothing except in the pursuit of a natural revenge.   89 **matin:** Morning.   90 **uneffectual fire:**
Cold light.   93 **couple:** Add.   97 **distracted globe:** Confused head.   100 **saws:** Wise sayings;
pressures: Impressions stamped.   107 **tables:** Probably a small portable writing-tablet carried at
the belt.   110 **word:** Watchword.   115 **Hillo, ho, ho:** A falconer's call to a hawk in air.

HAMLET: Hillo, ho, ho, boy! come, bird, come.

MARCELLUS: How is't, my noble lord?

HORATIO: What news, my lord?

HAMLET: O, wonderful!

HORATIO: Good my lord, tell it.

HAMLET: No; you will reveal it.

HORATIO: Not I, my lord, by heaven.

MARCELLUS: Nor I, my lord.   120

HAMLET: How say you, then; would heart of man once think it?
    But you'll be secret?

HORATIO: ⎫
         ⎬   Ay, by heaven, my lord.
MARCELLUS: ⎭

HAMLET: There's ne'er a villain dwelling in all Denmark
    But he's an arrant° knave.

HORATIO: There needs no ghost, my lord, come from the grave   125
    To tell us this.

HAMLET: Why, right; you are in the right;
    And so, without more circumstance at all,
    I hold it fit that we shake hands and part:
    You, as your business and desire shall point you;
    For every man has business and desire,   130
    Such as it is; and for my own poor part,
    Look you, I'll go pray.

HORATIO: These are but wild and whirling words, my lord.

HAMLET: I am sorry they offend you, heartily;
    Yes, 'faith, heartily.

HORATIO: There's no offence, my lord.   135

HAMLET: Yes, by Saint Patrick,° but there is, Horatio,
    And much offence too. Touching this vision here,
    It is an honest° ghost, that let me tell you:
    For your desire to know what is between us,
    O'ermaster 't as you may. And now, good friends,   140
    As you are friends, scholars and soldiers,
    Give me one poor request.

HORATIO: What is 't, my lord? we will.

HAMLET: Never make known what you have seen to-night.

HORATIO: ⎫
         ⎬   My lord, we will not.
MARCELLUS: ⎭

HAMLET: Nay, but swear 't.

HORATIO: In faith,   145
    My lord, not I.

MARCELLUS: Nor I, my lord, in faith.

---

124 arrant: Thoroughgoing.   **136 Saint Patrick:** St. Patrick was keeper of Purgatory and patron saint of all blunders and confusion.   **138 honest:** I.e., a real ghost and not an evil spirit.

HAMLET: Upon my sword.°
MARCELLUS: We have sworn, my lord, already.
HAMLET: Indeed, upon my sword, indeed.   *Ghost cries under the stage.*
GHOST: Swear.
HAMLET: Ah, ha, boy! say'st thou so? art thou there, truepenny?°   150
     Come on—you hear this fellow in the cellarage—
     Consent to swear.
HORATIO: Propose the oath, my lord.
HAMLET: Never to speak of this that you have seen,
     Swear by my sword.
GHOST *[beneath]*:   Swear.   155
HAMLET: Hic et ubique?° then we'll shift our ground.
     Come hither, gentlemen,
     And lay your hands again upon my sword:
     Swear by my sword,
     Never to speak of this that you have heard.   160
GHOST *[beneath]*:   Swear by his sword.
HAMLET: Well said, old mole! canst work i' th' earth so fast?
     A worthy pioner!° Once more remove, good friends.
HORATIO: O day and night, but this is wondrous strange!
HAMLET: And therefore as a stranger give it welcome.   165
     There are more things in heaven and earth, Horatio,
     Than are dreamt of in your philosophy.
     But come;
     Here, as before, never, so help you mercy,
     How strange or odd soe'er I bear myself,   170
     As I perchance hereafter shall think meet
     To put an antic° disposition on,
     That you, at such times seeing me, never shall,
     With arms encumb'red° thus, or this head-shake,
     Or by pronouncing of some doubtful phrase,   175
     As "Well, well, we know," or "We could, an if we would,"
     Or "If we list to speak," or "There be, an if they might,"
     Or such ambiguous giving out,° to note°
     That you know aught of me: this not to do,
     So grace and mercy at your most need help you,   180
     Swear.
GHOST *[beneath]*:   Swear.
HAMLET: Rest, rest, perturbed spirit! *[They swear.]* So, gentlemen,
     With all my love I do commend me to you:
     And what so poor a man as Hamlet is   185
     May do, t' express his love and friending° to you,

---

147 sword: I.e., the hilt in the form of a cross.   **150 truepenny:** Good old boy, or the like.
156 Hic et ubique?: Here and everywhere?   **163 pioner:** Digger, miner.   **172 antic:** Fantastic.   **174 encumb'red:** Folded or entwined.   **178 giving out:** Profession of knowledge;
to note: To give a sign.   **186 friending:** Friendliness.

God willing, shall not lack. Let us go in together;
And still your fingers on your lips, I pray.
The time is out of joint: O cursed spite,
That ever I was born to set it right!   190
Nay, come, let's go together.   *Exeunt.*

[ACT 2, Scene 1]

[A room in Polonius's house.]
   Enter old Polonius with his man [Reynaldo].

POLONIUS: Give him this money and these notes, Reynaldo.
REYNALDO: I will, my lord.
POLONIUS: You shall do marvellous wisely, good Reynaldo,
   Before you visit him, to make inquire
   Of his behaviour.
REYNALDO: My lord, I did intend it.   5
POLONIUS: Marry, well said; very well said. Look you, sir,
   Inquire me first what Danskers° are in Paris;
   And how, and who, what means, and where they keep,°
   What company, at what expense; and finding
   By this encompassment° and drift° of question   10
   That they do know my son, come you more nearer
   Than your particular demands will touch it:°
   Take° you as 'twere, some distant knowledge of him;
   As thus, "I know his father and his friends,
   And in part him": do you mark this, Reynaldo?   15
REYNALDO: Ay, very well, my lord.
POLONIUS: "And in part him; but" you may say "not well:
   But, if 't be he I mean, he's very wild;
   Addicted so and so": and there put on° him
   What forgeries° you please; marry, none so rank   20
   As may dishonour him; take heed of that;
   But, sir, such wanton,° wild and usual slips
   As are companions noted and most known
   To youth and liberty.
REYNALDO: As gaming, my lord.
POLONIUS: Ay, or drinking, fencing,° swearing, quarrelling,   25
   Drabbing;° you may go so far.
REYNALDO: My lord, that would dishonour him.

ACT 2, SCENE 1.   **7 Danskers:** Danke was a common variant for "Denmark"; hence "Dane."
8 keep: Dwell.   **10 encompassment:** Roundabout talking;   **drift:** Gradual approach or course.
11–12 come . . . it: I.e., you will find out more this way than by asking pointed questions.
13 Take: Assume, pretend.   **19 put on:** Impute to.   **20 forgeries:** Invented tales.   **22 wanton:** Sportive, unrestrained.   **25 fencing:** Indicative of the ill repute of professional fencers and
fencing schools in Elizabethan times.   **26 Drabbing:** Associating with immoral women.

POLONIUS: 'Faith, no; as you may season it in the charge.
　　You must not put another scandal on him,
　　That he is open to incontinency;°   30
　　That's not my meaning: but breathe his faults so quaintly°
　　That they may seem the taints of liberty,°
　　The flash and outbreak of a fiery mind,
　　A savageness in unreclaimed° blood,
　　Of general assault.°
REYNALDO: But, my good lord,—   35
POLONIUS: Wherefore should you do this?
REYNALDO: Ay, my lord,
　　I would know that.
POLONIUS: Marry, sir, here's my drift;
　　And, I believe, it is a fetch of wit:°
　　You laying these slight sullies on my son,
　　As 'twere a thing a little soil'd i' th' working,   40
　　Mark you,
　　Your party in converse, him you would sound,
　　Having ever° seen in the prenominate° crimes
　　The youth you breathe of guilty, be assur'd
　　He closes with you in this consequence;°   45
　　"Good sir," or so, or "friend," or "gentleman,"
　　According to the phrase or the addition
　　Of man and country.
REYNALDO: Very good, my lord.
POLONIUS: And then, sir, does 'a this—'a does—what was I about to say? By the
　　mass, I was about to say something: where did I leave?   50
REYNALDO: At "closes in the consequence," at "friend or so," and "gentle-
　　man."
POLONIUS: At "closes in the consequence," ay, marry;
　　He closes thus: "I know the gentleman;
　　I saw him yesterday, or t' other day,
　　Or then, or then; with such, or such; and, as you say,   55
　　There was 'a gaming; there o'ertook in 's rouse;°
　　There falling out at tennis": or perchance,
　　"I saw him enter such a house of sale,"
　　Videlicet,° a brothel, or so forth.   60
　　See you now;
　　Your bait of falsehood takes this carp of truth:
　　And thus do we of wisdom and of reach,°

---

30 incontinency: Habitual loose behavior. **31 quaintly:** Delicately, ingeniously. **32 taints of liberty:** Blemishes due to freedom. **34 unreclaimed:** Untamed. **35 general assault:** Tendency that assails all untrained youth. **38 fetch of wit:** Clever trick. **43 ever:** At any time; **prenominate:** Before-mentioned. **45 closes . . . consequence:** Agrees with you in this conclusion. **57 o'ertook in 's rouse:** Overcome by drink. **60 Videlicet:** Namely. **63 reach:** Capacity, ability.

With windlasses° and with assays of bias,°
By indirections° find directions° out: 65
So by my former lecture° and advice,
Shall you my son. You have me, have you not?

REYNALDO: My lord, I have.

POLONIUS: God bye ye;° fare ye well.

REYNALDO: Good my lord!

POLONIUS: Observe his inclination in yourself.°   70

REYNALDO: I shall, my lord.

POLONIUS: And let him ply his music.°

REYNALDO: Well, my lord.

POLONIUS: Farewell!   *Exit Reynaldo.*

Enter Ophelia.

                How now, Ophelia! what's the matter?

OPHELIA: O, my lord, my lord, I have been so affrighted!

POLONIUS: With what, i' th' name of God?   75

OPHELIA: My lord, as I was sewing in my closet,°
Lord Hamlet, with his doublet° all unbrac'd;°
No hat upon his head; his stockings foul'd,
Ungart'red, and down-gyved° to his ankle;
Pale as his shirt; his knees knocking each other;   80
And with a look so piteous in purport
As if he had been loosed out of hell
To speak of horrors, — he comes before me.

POLONIUS: Mad for thy love?

OPHELIA: My lord, I do not know;
But truly, I do fear it.

POLONIUS: What said he?   85

OPHELIA: He took me by the wrist and held me hard;
Then goes he to the length of all his arm;
And, with his other hand thus o'er his brow,
He falls to such perusal of my face
As 'a would draw it. Long stay'd he so;   90
At last, a little shaking of mine arm
And thrice his head thus waving up and down,
He rais'd a sigh so piteous and profound
As it did seem to shatter all his bulk°
And end his being: that done, he lets me go: 95

---

64 windlasses: I.e., circuitous paths;   **assays of bias:** Attempts that resemble the course of the bowl, which, being weighted on one side, has a curving motion.   **65 indirections:** Devious courses;   **directions:** Straight courses, i.e., the truth.   **66 lecture:** Admonition.   **68 bye ye:** Be with you.   **70 Observe . . . yourself:** In your own person, not by spies; or conform your own conduct to his inclination; or test him by studying yourself.   **72 ply his music:** Probably to be taken literally.   **76 closet:** Private chamber.   **77 doublet:** Close-fitting coat;   **unbrac'd:** Unfastened.   **79 down-gyved:** Fallen to the ankles (like gyves or fetters).   **94 bulk:** Body.

And, with his head over his shoulder turn'd,
He seem'd to find his way without his eyes;
For out o' doors he went without their helps,
And, to the last, bended their light on me.
POLONIUS: Come, go with me: I will go seek the king.   100
This is the very ecstasy of love,
Whose violent property° fordoes° itself
And leads the will to desperate undertakings
As oft as any passion under heaven
That does afflict our natures. I am sorry.   105
What, have you given him any hard words of late?
OPHELIA: No, my good lord, but, as you did command,
I did repel his letters and denied
His access to me.
POLONIUS: That hath made him mad.
I am sorry that with better heed and judgement   110
I had not quoted° him: I fear'd he did but trifle,
And meant to wrack thee; but, beshrew my jealousy!°
By heaven, it is as proper to our age
To cast beyond° ourselves in our opinions
As it is common for the younger sort   115
To lack discretion. Come, go we to the king:
This must be known; which, being kept close, might move
More grief to hide than hate to utter love.°
Come.   *Exeunt.*

[Scene 2]

[A room in the castle.]
Flourish. Enter King and Queen, Rosencrantz, and Guildenstern [with others].

KING: Welcome, dear Rosencrantz and Guildenstern!
Moreover that° we much did long to see you,
The need we have to use you did provoke
Our hasty sending. Something have you heard
Of Hamlet's transformation; so call it,   5
Sith° nor th' exterior nor the inward man
Resembles that it was. What it should be,
More than his father's death, that thus hath put him
So much from th' understanding of himself,
I cannot dream of: I entreat you both,   10

---

102 **property:** Nature; **fordoes:** Destroys.   111 **quoted:** Observed.   112 **beshrew my jealousy:** Curse my suspicions.   114 **cast beyond:** Overshoot, miscalculate.   117–118 **might . . . love:** I.e., I might cause more grief to others by hiding the knowledge of Hamlet's love to Ophelia than hatred to me and mine by telling of it.   SCENE 2.   2 **Moreover that:** Besides the fact that.   6 **Sith:** Since.

That, being of so young days° brought up with him,
And sith so neighbour'd to his youth and haviour,
That you vouchsafe your rest° here in our court
Some little time: so by your companies
To draw him on to pleasures, and to gather,   15
So much as from occasion you may glean,
Whether aught, to us unknown, afflicts him thus,
That, open'd, lies within our remedy.
QUEEN: Good gentlemen, he hath much talk'd of you;
And sure I am two men there are not living   20
To whom he more adheres. If it will please you
To show us so much gentry° and good will
As to expend your time with us awhile,
For the supply and profit° of our hope,
Your visitation shall receive such thanks   25
As fits a king's remembrance.
ROSENCRANTZ: Both your majesties
Might, by the sovereign power you have of us,
Put your dread pleasures more into command
Than to entreaty.
GUILDENSTERN: But we both obey,
And here give up ourselves, in the full bent°   30
To lay our service freely at your feet,
To be commanded.
KING: Thanks, Rosencrantz and gentle Guildenstern.
QUEEN: Thanks, Guildenstern and gentle Rosencrantz:
And I beseech you instantly to visit   35
My too much changed son. Go, some of you,
And bring these gentlemen where Hamlet is.
GUILDENSTERN: Heavens make our presence and our practices
Pleasant and helpful to him!
QUEEN: Ay, amen!
          Exeunt Rosencrantz and Guildenstern [with some Attendants].
Enter Polonius.
POLONIUS: Th' ambassadors from Norway, my good lord,   40
Are joyfully return'd.
KING: Thou still hast been the father of good news.
POLONIUS: Have I, my lord? I assure my good liege,
I hold my duty, as I hold my soul,
Both to my God and to my gracious king: 45
And I do think, or else this brain of mine

---

11 **of . . . days:** From such early youth.   13 **vouchsafe your rest:** Please to stay.   22 **gentry:**
Courtesy.   24 **supply and profit:** Aid and successful outcome.   30 **in . . . bent:** To the
utmost degree of our mental capacity.

Hunts not the trail of policy so sure
As it hath us'd to do, that I have found
The very cause of Hamlet's lunacy.
KING: O, speak of that; that do I long to hear.   50
POLONIUS: Give first admittance to th' ambassadors;
My news shall be the fruit to that great feast.
KING: Thyself do grace to them, and bring them in.   *[Exit Polonius.]*
He tells me, my dear Gertrude, he hath found
The head and source of all your son's distemper.   55
QUEEN: I doubt° it is no other but the main;°
His father's death, and our o'erhasty marriage.
KING: Well, we shall sift him.

Enter Ambassadors [Voltimand and Cornelius, with Polonius.]

                    Welcome, my good friends!
Say, Voltimand, what from our brother Norway?
VOLTIMAND: Most fair return of greetings and desires.   60
Upon our first, he sent out to suppress
His nephew's levies; which to him appear'd
To be a preparation 'gainst the Polack;
But, better look'd into, he truly found
It was against your highness: whereat griev'd,   65
That so his sickness, age and impotence
Was falsely borne in hand,° sends out arrests
On Fortinbras; which he, in brief, obeys;
Receives rebuke from Norway, and in fine°
Makes vow before his uncle never more   70
To give th' assay° of arms against your majesty.
Whereon old Norway, overcome with joy,
Gives him three score thousand crowns in annual fee,
And his commission to employ those soldiers,
So levied as before, against the Polack: 75
With an entreaty, herein further shown,   *[Giving a paper.]*
That it might please you to give quiet pass
Through your dominions for this enterprise,
On such regards of safety and allowance°
As therein are set down.
KING: It likes° us well;   80
And at our more consider'd° time we'll read,
Answer, and think upon this business.
Meantime we thank you for your well-took labour:
Go to your rest; at night we'll feast together:

---

56 doubt: Fear;   **main:** Chief point, principal concern.   **67 borne in hand:** Deluded.
69 in fine: In the end.   **71 assay:** Assault, trial (of arms).   **79 safety and allowance:** Pledges
of safety to the country and terms of permission for the troops to pass.   **80 likes:** Pleases.
81 consider'd: Suitable for deliberation.

Most welcome home!   *Exeunt Ambassadors.*

POLONIUS: This business is well ended.   85
  My liege, and madam, to expostulate
  What majesty should be, what duty is,
  Why day is day, night night, and time is time,
  Were nothing but to waste night, day and time.
  Therefore, since brevity is the soul of wit,°   90
  And tediousness the limbs and outward flourishes,°
  I will be brief: your noble son is mad:
  Mad call I it; for, to define true madness
  What is 't but to be nothing else but mad?
  But let that go.
QUEEN: More matter, with less art.   95
POLONIUS: Madam, I swear I use no art at all.
  That he is mad, 'tis true: 'tis true 'tis pity;
  And pity 'tis 'tis true: a foolish figure;°
  But farewell it, for I will use no art.
  Mad let us grant him, then: and now remains   100
  That we find out the cause of this effect,
  Or rather say, the cause of this defect,
  For this effect defective comes by cause:
  Thus it remains, and the remainder thus.
  Perpend.°   105
  I have a daughter — have while she is mine —
  Who, in her duty and obedience, mark,
  Hath given me this: now gather, and surmise.
  [*Reads the letter.*] "To the celestial and my soul's idol, the most beautified
  Ophelia," —   110
  That's an ill phrase, a vile phrase; "beautified" is a vile phrase: but you shall
  hear. Thus: [*Reads.*]
  "In her excellent white bosom, these, & c."
QUEEN: Came this from Hamlet to her?
POLONIUS: Good madam, stay awhile; I will be faithful.   [*Reads.*]   115
          "Doubt thou the stars are fire;
              Doubt that the sun doth move;
          "Doubt truth to be a liar;
              But never doubt I love.
  "O dear Ophelia, I am ill at these numbers;° I have not art to reckon°   120
  my groans: but that I love thee best, O most best, believe it. Adieu.
      "Thine evermore, most dear lady, whilst this machine° is to him,
                                                        HAMLET."

---

90 **wit:** Sound sense or judgment.   91 **flourishes:** Ostentation, embellishments.   98 **figure:**
Figure of speech.   105 **Perpend:** Consider.   120 **ill . . . numbers:** Unskilled at writing
verses;   **reckon:** Number metrically, scan.   122 **machine:** Bodily frame.

This, in obedience, hath my daughter shown me,
And more above,° hath his solicitings,   125
As they fell out° by time, by means° and place,
All given to mine ear.
KING: But how hath she
Receiv'd his love?
POLONIUS: What do you think of me?
KING: As of a man faithful and honourable.
POLONIUS: I would fain prove so. But what might you think,   130
When I had seen this hot love on the wing—
As I perceiv'd it, I must tell you that,
Before my daughter told me—what might you,
Or my dear majesty your queen here, think,
If I had play'd the desk or table-book,°   135
Or given my heart a winking,° mute and dumb,
Or look'd upon this love with idle sight;
What might you think? No, I went round to work,
And my young mistress thus I did bespeak:°
"Lord Hamlet is a prince, out of thy star;°   140
This must not be": and then I prescripts gave her,
That she should lock herself from his resort,
Admit no messengers, receive no tokens.
Which done, she took the fruits of my advice;
And he, repelled—a short tale to make—   145
Fell into a sadness, then into a fast,
Thence to a watch,° thence into a weakness,
Thence to a lightness,° and, by this declension,°
Into the madness wherein now he raves,
And all we mourn for.
KING: Do you think 'tis this?   150
QUEEN: It may be, very like.
POLONIUS: Hath there been such a time—I would fain know that—
That I have positively said " 'Tis so,"
When it prov'd otherwise?
KING: Not that I know.
POLONIUS [*pointing to his head and shoulder*]:   Take this from this, if this be
        otherwise: 155
If circumstances lead me, I will find
Where truth is hid, though it were hid indeed
Within the centre.°
KING: How may we try it further?

125 **more above:** Moreover.   126 **fell out:** Occurred;   **means:** Opportunities (of access).
135 **play'd . . . table-book:** I.e., remained shut up, concealed this information.   136 **given . . .
winking:** Given my heart a signal to keep silent.   139 **bespeak:** Address.   140 **out . . . star:**
Above thee in position.   147 **watch:** State of sleeplessness.   148 **lightness:** Lightheadedness;
declension: Decline, deterioration.   158 **centre:** Middle point of the earth.

POLONIUS: You know, sometimes he walks four hours together
 Here in the lobby.
QUEEN: So he does indeed.   160
POLONIUS: At such a time I'll loose my daughter to him:
 Be you and I behind an arras° then;
 Mark the encounter: if he love her not
 And be not from his reason fall'n thereon,°
 Let me be no assistant for a state,   165
 But keep a farm and carters.
KING: We will try it.

Enter Hamlet [reading on a book].

QUEEN: But, look, where sadly the poor wretch comes reading.
POLONIUS: Away, I do beseech you both, away:

        Exeunt King and Queen [with Attendants].

 I'll board° him presently. O, give me leave.
 How does my good Lord Hamlet?   170
HAMLET: Well, God-a-mercy.
POLONIUS: Do you know me, my lord?
HAMLET: Excellent well; you are a fishmonger.°
POLONIUS: Not I, my lord.
HAMLET: Then I would you were so honest a man.   175
POLONIUS: Honest, my lord!
HAMLET: Ay, sir; to be honest, as this world goes, is to be one man picked out of
 ten thousand.
POLONIUS: That's very true, my lord.
HAMLET: For if the sun breed maggots in a dead dog, being a good kissing 180
 carrion,° — Have you a daughter?
POLONIUS: I have, my lord.
HAMLET: Let her not walk i' the sun:° conception° is a blessing: but as your
 daughter may conceive — Friend, look to 't.
POLONIUS *[aside]:*   How say you by° that? Still harping on my daughter: yet he 185
 knew me not at first; 'a said I was a fishmonger: 'a is far gone, far gone: and
 truly in my youth I suffered much extremity for love; very near this. I'll speak
 to him again. What do you read, my lord?
HAMLET: Words, words, words.
POLONIUS: What is the matter,° my lord?   190
HAMLET: Between who?°
POLONIUS: I mean, the matter that you read, my lord.

---

162 arras: Hanging, tapestry. **164 thereon:** On that account. **169 board:** Accost. **173 fish-monger:** An opprobrious expression meaning "bawd," "procurer." **180–181 good kissing carrion:** I.e., a good piece of flesh for kissing (?). **183 i' the sun:** In the sunshine of princely favors; **conception:** Quibble on "understanding" and "pregnancy." **185 by:** Concerning.
190 matter: Substance. **191 Between who:** Hamlet deliberately takes *matter* as meaning "basis of dispute."

HAMLET: Slanders, sir: for the satirical rogue says here that old men have grey
beards, that their faces are wrinkled, their eyes purging° thick amber and
plum-tree gum and that they have a plentiful lack of wit, together with most   195
weak hams: all which, sir, though I most powerfully and potently believe, yet
I hold it not honesty° to have it thus set down, for yourself, sir, should be old
as I am, if like a crab you could go backward.

POLONIUS [aside]: Though this be madness, yet there is method in 't.—Will
you walk out of the air, my lord?   200

HAMLET: Into my grave.

POLONIUS: Indeed, that's out of the air. (Aside.) How pregnant sometimes his
replies are! a happiness° that often madness hits on, which reason and sanity
could not so prosperously° be delivered of. I will leave him, and suddenly
contrive the means of meeting between him and my daughter.—My hon-   205
ourable lord, I will most humbly take my leave of you.

HAMLET: You cannot, sir, take from me any thing that I will more willingly part
withal: except my life, except my life, except my life.

Enter Guildenstern and Rosencrantz.

POLONIUS: Fare you well, my lord.

HAMLET: These tedious old fools!   210

POLONIUS: You go to seek the Lord Hamlet; there he is.

ROSENCRANTZ [to Polonius]: God save you, sir!   [Exit Polonius.]

GUILDENSTERN: My honoured lord!

ROSENCRANTZ: My most dear lord!

HAMLET: My excellent good friends! How dost thou, Guildenstern? Ah, Rosen-   215
crantz! Good lads, how do ye both?

ROSENCRANTZ: As the indifferent° children of the earth.

GUILDENSTERN: Happy, in that we are not over-happy;
On Fortune's cap we are not the very button.

HAMLET: Nor the soles of her shoe?   220

ROSENCRANTZ: Neither, my lord.

HAMLET: Then you live about her waist, or in the middle of her favours?

GUILDENSTERN: 'Faith, her privates° we.

HAMLET: In the secret parts of Fortune? O, most true; she is a strumpet. What's
the news?   225

ROSENCRANTZ: None, my lord, but that the world's grown honest.

HAMLET: Then is doomsday near: but your news is not true. Let me question
more in particular: what have you, my good friends, deserved at the hands of
Fortune, that she sends you to prison hither?

GUILDENSTERN: Prison, my lord!   230

HAMLET: Denmark's a prison.

ROSENCRANTZ: Then is the world one.

---

194 purging: discharging.   **197 honesty:** Decency.   **203 happiness:** Felicity of expression.
204 prosperously: Successfully.   **217 indifferent:** Ordinary.   **223 privates:** I.e., ordinary
men (sexual pun on *private parts*).

HAMLET: A goodly one; in which there are many confines,° wards and dungeons, Denmark being one o' the worst.

ROSENCRANTZ: We think not so, my lord.   235

HAMLET: Why, then, 'tis none to you; for there is nothing either good or bad, but thinking makes it so: to me it is a prison.

ROSENCRANTZ: Why then, your ambition makes it one; 'tis too narrow for your mind.

HAMLET: O God, I could be bounded in a nutshell and count myself a king of   240
infinite space, were it not that I have bad dreams.

GUILDENSTERN: Which dreams indeed are ambition, for the very substance of the ambitious° is merely the shadow of a dream.

HAMLET: A dream itself is but a shadow.

ROSENCRANTZ: Truly, and I hold ambition of so airy and light a quality that it is   245
but a shadow's shadow.

HAMLET: Then are our beggars bodies, and our monarchs and outstretched heroes the beggars' shadows. Shall we to the court? for, by my fay,° I cannot reason.°

ROSENCRANTZ: ⎱
GUILDENSTERN: ⎰ We'll wait upon° you.   250

HAMLET: No such matter: I will not sort° you with the rest of my servants, for, to speak to you like an honest man, I am most dreadfully attended.° But, in the beaten way of friendship,° what make you at Elsinore?

ROSENCRANTZ: To visit you, my lord: no other occasion.

HAMLET: Beggar that I am, I am ever poor in thanks; but I thank you: and sure,   255
dear friends, my thanks are too dear a° halfpenny. Were you not sent for? Is it your own inclining? Is it a free visitation? Come, come, deal justly with me: come, come; nay, speak.

GUILDENSTERN: What should we say, my lord?

HAMLET: Why, any thing, but to the purpose. You were sent for; and there is a   260
kind of confession in your looks which your modesties have not craft enough to colour: I know the good king and queen have sent for you.

ROSENCRANTZ: To what end, my lord?

HAMLET: That you must teach me. But let me conjure° you, by the rights of our fellowship, by the consonancy of our youth,° by the obligation of our ever-   265
preserved love, and by what more dear a better proposer° could charge you withal, be even and direct with me, whether you were sent for, or no?

ROSENCRANTZ [aside to Guildenstern]:   What say you?

HAMLET [aside]:   Nay, then, I have an eye of you. — If you love me, hold not off.

GUILDENSTERN: My lord, we were sent for.   270

---

233 confines: Places of confinement.   **242–243 very . . . ambitious:** That seemingly most substantial thing which the ambitious pursue.   **248 fay:** Faith.   **249 reason:** Argue.   **250 wait upon:** Accompany.   **251 sort:** Class.   **252 dreadfully attended:** Poorly provided with servants.   **252–253 in the . . . friendship:** As a matter of course among friends.   **256 a:** I.e., at a.   **264 conjure:** Adjure, entreat.   **265 consonancy of our youth:** The fact that we are of the same age.   **266 better proposer:** One more skillful in finding proposals.

HAMLET: I will tell you why; so shall my anticipation prevent your discovery,°
and your secrecy to the king and queen moult no feather. I have of late — but
wherefore I know not — lost all my mirth, forgone all custom of exercises;
and indeed it goes so heavily with my disposition that this goodly frame, the
earth, seems to me a sterile promontory, this most excellent canopy, the air,   275
look you, this brave o'erhanging firmament, this majestical roof fretted° with
golden fire, why, it appeareth nothing to me but a foul and pestilent congregation of vapours. What a piece of work is a man! how noble in reason! how
infinite in faculties!° in form and moving how express° and admirable! in
action how like an angel! in apprehension° how like a god! the beauty of the   280
world! the paragon of animals! And yet, to me, what is this quintessence° of
dust? man delights not me: no, nor woman neither, though by your smiling
you seem to say so.

ROSENCRANTZ: My lord, there was no such stuff in my thoughts.

HAMLET: Why did you laugh then, when I said "man delights not me"?   285

ROSENCRANTZ: To think, my lord, if you delight not in man, what lenten° entertainment the players shall receive from you: we coted° them on the way; and
hither are they coming, to offer you service.

HAMLET: He that plays the king shall be welcome; his majesty shall have tribute
of me; the adventurous knight shall use his foil and target;° the lover shall   290
not sigh gratis; the humorous man° shall end his part in peace; the clown
shall make those laugh whose lungs are tickle o' the sere;° and the lady shall
say her mind freely, or the blank verse shall halt for 't.° What players are
they?

ROSENCRANTZ: Even those you were wont to take delight in, the tragedians of   295
the city.

HAMLET: How chances it they travel? their residence,° both in reputation and
profit, was better both ways.

ROSENCRANTZ: I think their inhibition° comes by the means of the late innovation.°   300

HAMLET: Do they hold the same estimation they did when I was in the city? are
they so followed?

ROSENCRANTZ: No, indeed, are they not.

HAMLET: How° comes it? do they grow rusty?

---

271 **prevent your discovery:** Forestall your disclosure.   276 **fretted:** Adorned.   279 **faculties:** Capacity; **express:** Well-framed (?), exact (?).   280 **apprehension:** Understanding.
281 **quintessence:** The fifth essence of ancient philosophy, supposed to be the substance of
the heavenly bodies and to be latent in all things.   286 **lenten:** Meager.   287 **coted:** Overtook and passed beyond.   290 **foil and target:** Sword and shield.   291 **humorous man:**
Actor who takes the part of the humor characters.   292 **tickle o' the sere:** Easy on the trigger.
292–293 **the lady . . . for 't:** The lady (fond of talking) shall have opportunity to talk, blank
verse or no blank verse.   297 **residence:** Remaining in one place.   299 **inhibition:** Formal
prohibition (from acting plays in the city or, possibly, at court).   299–300 **innovation:** The
new fashion in satirical plays performed by boy actors in the "private" theaters.   304–322
How . . . load: The passage is the famous one dealing with the War of the Theatres (1599–1602);
namely, the rivalry between the children's companies and the adult actors.

ROSENCRANTZ: Nay, their endeavour keeps in the wonted pace: but there is,   305
    sir, an aery° of children, little eyases,° that cry out on the top of question,°
    and are most tyrannically° clapped for 't: these are now the fashion, and so
    berattle° the common stages°—so they call them—that many wearing
    rapiers° are afraid of goose-quills° and dare scarce come thither.

HAMLET: What, are they children? who maintains 'em? how are they escoted?°   310
    Will they pursue the quality° no longer than they can sing?° will they not say
    afterwards, if they should grow themselves to common° players—as it is most
    like, if their means are no better—their writers do them wrong, to make
    them exclaim against their own succession?°

ROSENCRANTZ: 'Faith, there has been much to do on both sides; and the nation   315
    holds it no sin to tarre° them to controversy: there was, for a while, no money
    bid for argument,° unless the poet and the player went to cuffs° in the
    question.°

HAMLET: Is 't possible?

GUILDENSTERN: O, there has been much throwing about of brains.   320

HAMLET: Do the boys carry it away?°

ROSENCRANTZ: Ay, that they do, my lord; Hercules and his load° too.

HAMLET: It is not very strange; for my uncle is king of Denmark, and those that
    would make mows° at him while my father lived, give twenty, forty, fifty, a
    hundred ducats° a-piece for his picture in little.° 'Sblood, there is something   325
    in this more than natural, if philosophy could find it out.

                                        A flourish [of trumpets within].

GUILDENSTERN: There are the players.

HAMLET: Gentlemen, you are welcome to Elsinore. Your hands, come then:
    the appurtenance of welcome is fashion and ceremony: let me comply° with
    you in this garb,° lest my extent° to the players, which, I tell you, must show   330
    fairly outwards, should more appear like entertainment than yours. You are
    welcome: but my uncle-father and aunt-mother are deceived.

GUILDENSTERN: In what, my dear lord?

HAMLET: I am but mad north-north-west:° when the wind is southerly I know a
    hawk from a handsaw.°   335

---

306 aery: Nest; **eyases:** Young hawks; **cry . . . question:** Speak in a high key dominating conversation; clamor forth the height of controversy; probably "excel"; perhaps intended to decry leaders of the dramatic profession. **307 tyrannically:** Outrageously. **308 berattle:** Berate; **common stages:** Public theaters. **308–309 many wearing rapiers:** Many men of fashion, who were afraid to patronize the common players for fear of being satirized by the poets who wrote for the children. **309 goose-quills:** I.e., pens of satirists. **310 escoted:** Maintained. **311 quality:** Acting profession; **no longer . . . sing:** I.e., until their voices change. **312 common:** Regular, adult. **314 succession:** Future careers. **316 tarre:** Set on (as dogs). **317 argument:** Probably, plot for a play; **went to cuffs:** Came to blows. **318 question:** Controversy. **321 carry it away:** Win the day. **322 Hercules . . . load:** Regarded as an allusion to the sign of the Globe Theatre, which was Hercules bearing the world on his shoulder. **324 mows:** Grimaces. **325 ducats:** Gold coins worth 9s. 4d; **in little:** In miniature. **329 comply:** Observe the formalities of courtesy. **330 garb:** Manner; **extent:** Showing of kindness. **334 I am . . . north-north-west:** I am only partly mad, i.e., in only one point of the compass. **335 handsaw:** A proposed reading of *hernshaw* would mean "heron"; *handsaw* may be an early corruption of *hernshaw*. Another view regards *hawk* as the variant of *hack*, a tool of the pickax type, and *handsaw* as a saw operated by hand.

Enter Polonius.

POLONIUS: Well be with you, gentlemen!

HAMLET: Hark you, Guildenstern; and you too: at each ear a hearer: that great
baby you see there is not yet out of his swaddling-clouts.°

ROSENCRANTZ: Happily he is the second time come to them; for they say an old
man is twice a child.   340

HAMLET: I will prophesy he comes to tell me of the players; mark it. — You say
right, sir: o' Monday morning;° 'twas then indeed.

POLONIUS: My lord, I have news to tell you.

HAMLET: My lord, I have news to tell you. When Roscius° was an actor in
Rome, —   345

POLONIUS: The actors are come hither, my lord.

HAMLET: Buz, buz!°

POLONIUS: Upon my honour, —

HAMLET: Then came each actor on his ass, —

POLONIUS: The best actors in the world, either for tragedy, comedy, history,   350
pastoral, pastoral-comical, historical-pastoral, tragical-historical, tragical-
comical-historical-pastoral, scene individable,° or poem unlimited:° Seneca°
cannot be too heavy, nor Plautus° too light. For the law of writ and the
liberty,° these are the only men.

HAMLET: O Jephthah, judge of Israel,° what a treasure hadst thou!   355

POLONIUS: What a treasure had he, my lord?

HAMLET: Why,
"One fair daughter, and no more,
   The which he loved passing well."

POLONIUS [*aside*]:   Still on my daughter.   360

HAMLET: Am I not i' the right, old Jephthah?

POLONIUS: If you call me Jephthah, my lord, I have a daughter that I love
passing° well.

HAMLET: Nay, that follows not.

POLONIUS: What follows, then, my lord?   365

HAMLET: Why,
"As by lot, God wot,"
and then, you know,
"It came to pass, as most like° it was," —
the first row° of the pious chanson° will show you more; for look, where my   370
abridgement comes.°

338 **swaddling-clouts:** Cloths in which to wrap a newborn baby.   342 **o' Monday morning:**
Said to mislead Polonius.   344 **Roscius:** A famous Roman actor.   347 **Buz, buz:** An interjec-
tion used at Oxford to denote stale news.   352 **scene individable:** A play observing the unity of
place;   **poem unlimited:** A play disregarding the unities of time and place;   **Seneca:** Writer of
Latin tragedies, model of early Elizabethan writers of tragedy.   353 **Plautus:** Writer of Latin comedy.   353–354 **law . . . liberty:** Pieces written according to rules and without rules, i.e., "classical"
and "romantic" dramas.   355 **Jephthah . . . Israel:** Jephthah had to sacrifice his daughter; see
Judges 11.   363 **passing:** Surpassingly.   369 **like:** Probable.   370 **row:** Stanza;   **chanson:**
Ballad.   371 **abridgement comes:** Opportunity comes for cutting short the conversation.

Enter the Players.

You are welcome, masters; welcome, all. I am glad to see thee well. Welcome, good friends. O, old friend! why, thy face is valanced° since I saw thee last: comest thou to beard me in Denmark? What, my young lady and mistress! By'r lady, your ladyship is nearer to heaven than when I saw you last, by the   375
altitude of a chopine.° Pray God, your voice, like a piece of uncurrent° gold, be not cracked within the ring.° Masters, you are all welcome. We'll e'en to 't like French falconers, fly at any thing we see: we'll have a speech straight: come, give us a taste of your quality; come, a passionate speech.

FIRST PLAYER: What speech, my good lord?   380

HAMLET: I heard thee speak me a speech once, but it was never acted; or, if it was, not above once; for the play, I remember, pleased not the million; 'twas caviary to the general:° but it was — as I received it, and others, whose judgements in such matters cried in the top of° mine — an excellent play, well digested in the scenes, set down with as much modesty as cunning.° I remem-   385
ber, one said there were no sallets° in the lines to make the matter savoury, nor no matter in the phrase that might indict° the author of affectation; but called it an honest method, as wholesome as sweet, and by very much more handsome than fine.° One speech in 't I chiefly loved: 'twas Æneas' tale to Dido;° and thereabout of it especially, where he speaks of Priam's slaughter: if   390
it live in your memory, begin at this line: let me see, let me see —
"The rugged Pyrrhus,° like th' Hyrcanian beast,"° —
'tis not so: — it begins with Pyrrhus: —
"The rugged Pyrrhus, he whose sable arms,
Black as his purpose, did the night resemble   395
When he lay couched in the ominous horse,°
Hath now this dread and black complexion smear'd
With heraldry more dismal; head to foot
Now is he total gules;° horridly trick'd°
With blood of fathers, mothers, daughters, sons,   400
Bak'd and impasted° with the parching streets,
That lend a tyrannous and a damned light
To their lord's murder: roasted in wrath and fire,

---

373 **valanced:** Fringed (with a beard).   376 **chopine:** Kind of shoe raised by the thickness of the heel; worn in Italy, particularly at Venice;   **uncurrent:** Not passable as lawful coinage. 377 **cracked within the ring:** In the center of coins were rings enclosing the sovereign's head; if the coin was cracked within this ring, it was unfit for currency.   383 **caviary to the general:** Not relished by the multitude.   384 **cried in the top of:** Spoke with greater authority than. 385 **cunning:** Skill.   386 **sallets:** Salads: here, spicy improprieties.   387 **indict:** Convict. 388–389 **as wholesome . . . fine:** Its beauty was not that of elaborate ornament, but that of order and proportion.   389–390 **Æneas' tale to Dido:** The lines recited by the player are imitated from Marlowe and Nashe's *Dido Queen of Carthage* (2.1.214 ff.). They are written in such a way that the conventionality of the play within a play is raised above that of ordinary drama. 392 **Pyrrhus:** A Greek hero in the Trojan War;   **Hyrcanian beast:** The tiger; see Virgil, *Aeneid*, 4.266.   396 **ominous horse:** Trojan horse.   399 **gules:** Red, a heraldic term; **trick'd:** Spotted, smeared.   401 **impasted:** Made into a paste.

And thus o'er-sized° with coagulate gore,
With eyes like carbuncles, the hellish Pyrrhus   405
Old grandsire Priam seeks."
So, proceed you.

POLONIUS: 'Fore God, my lord, well spoken, with good accent and good discretion.

FIRST PLAYER: "Anon he finds him   410
Striking too short at Greeks; his antique sword,
Rebellious to his arm, lies where it falls,
Repugnant° to command: unequal match'd,
Pyrrhus at Priam drives; in rage strikes wide;
But with the whiff and wind of his fell sword   415
Th' unnerved father falls. Then senseless Ilium,°
Seeming to feel this blow, with flaming top
Stoops to his base, and with a hideous crash
Takes prisoner Pyrrhus' ear: for, lo! his sword
Which was declining on the milky head   420
Of reverend Priam, seem'd i' th' air to stick:
So, as a painted tyrant,° Pyrrhus stood,
And like a neutral to his will and matter,°
Did nothing.
But, as we often see, against° some storm,   425
A silence in the heavens, the rack° stand still,
The bold winds speechless and the orb below
As hush as death, anon the dreadful thunder
Doth rend the region,° so, after Pyrrhus' pause,
Aroused vengeance sets him new a-work;   430
And never did the Cyclops' hammers fall
On Mars's armour forg'd for proof eterne°
With less remorse than Pyrrhus' bleeding sword
Now falls on Priam.
Out, out, thou strumpet, Fortune! All you gods,   435
In general synod,° take away her power;
Break all the spokes and fellies° from her wheel,
And bowl the round nave° down the hill of heaven,
As low as to the fiends!"

POLONIUS: This is too long.   440

HAMLET: It shall to the barber's, with your beard. Prithee, say on: he's for a jig°
or a tale of bawdry,° or he sleeps: say on: come to Hecuba.°

FIRST PLAYER: "But who, ah woe! had seen the mobled° queen—"

---

404 o'er-sized: Covered as with size or glue.   **413 Repugnant:** Disobedient.   **416 Then senseless Ilium:** Insensate Troy.   **422 painted tyrant:** Tyrant in a picture.   **423 matter:** Task.   **425
against:** Before.   **426 rack:** Mass of clouds.   **429 region:** Assembly.   **432 proof eterne:** External resistance to assault.   **436 synod:** Assembly.   **437 fellies:** Pieces of wood forming the rim of
a wheel.   **438 nave:** Hub.   **441 jig:** Comic performance given at the end or in an interval of a
play.   **442 bawdry:** Indecency;   **Hecuba:** Wife of Priam, king of Troy.   **443 mobled:** Muffled.

HAMLET: "The mobled queen?"

POLONIUS: That's good; "mobled queen" is good.   445

FIRST PLAYER: "Run barefoot up and down, threat'ning the flames
 With bisson rheum;° a clout° upon that head
 Where late the diadem stood, and for a robe,
 About her lank and all o'er-teemed° loins,
 A blanket, in the alarm of fear caught up;   450
 Who this had seen, with tongue in venom steep'd,
 'Gainst Fortune's state would treason have pronounc'd:°
 But if the gods themselves did see her then
 When she saw Pyrrhus make malicious sport
 In mincing with his sword her husband's limbs,   455
 The instant burst of clamour that she made,
 Unless things mortal move them not at all,
 Would have made milch° the burning eyes of heaven,
 And passion in the gods."

POLONIUS: Look, whe'r he has not turned° his colour and has tears in 's eyes.   460
Prithee, no more.

HAMLET: 'Tis well; I'll have thee speak out the rest soon. Good my lord, will you
see the players well bestowed? Do you hear, let them be well used; for they
are the abstract° and brief chronicles of the time: after your death you were
better have a bad epitaph than their ill report while you live.   465

POLONIUS: My lord, I will use them according to their desert.

HAMLET: God's bodykins,° man, much better: use every man after his desert,
and who shall 'scape whipping? Use them after your own honour and dignity: the less they deserve, the more merit is in your bounty. Take them in.

POLONIUS: Come, sirs.   470

HAMLET: Follow him, friends: we'll hear a play tomorrow.   *[Aside to First Player.]*
Dost thou hear me, old friend; can you play the Murder of Gonzago?

FIRST PLAYER: Ay, my lord.

HAMLET: We'll ha 't to-morrow night. You could, for a need, study a speech of
some dozen or sixteen lines,° which I would set down and insert in 't, could   475
you not?

FIRST PLAYER: Ay, my lord.

HAMLET: Very well. Follow that lord; and look you mock him not. — My good
friends, I'll leave you till night: you are welcome to Elsinore.
Exeunt Polonius and Players.

ROSENCRANTZ: Good my lord!   *Exeunt [Rosencrantz and Guildenstern.]*   480

HAMLET: Ay, so, God bye to you. — Now I am alone.
O, what a rogue and peasant° slave am I!

---

447 bisson rheum: Blinding tears;   **clout:** Piece of cloth.   **449 o'er-teemed:** Worn out with
bearing children.   **452 pronounc'd:** Proclaimed.   **458 milch:** Moist with tears.   **460 turned:**
Changed.   **464 abstract:** Summary account.   **467 bodykins:** Diminutive form of the oath
"by God's body."   **475 dozen or sixteen lines:** Critics have amused themselves by trying to
locate Hamlet's lines. Lucianus's speech 3.2.222–227 is the best guess.   **482 peasant:** Base.

Is it not monstrous that this player here,
But in a fiction, in a dream of passion,
Could force his soul so to his own conceit   485
That from her working all his visage wann'd,°
Tears in his eyes, distraction in 's aspect,
A broken voice, and his whole function suiting
With forms to his conceit?° and all for nothing!
For Hecuba!   490
What's Hecuba to him, or he to Hecuba,
That he should weep for her? What would he do,
Had he the motive and the cue for passion
That I have? He would drown the stage with tears
And cleave the general ear with horrid speech,   495
Make mad the guilty and appall the free,
Confound the ignorant, and amaze indeed
The very faculties of eyes and ears.
Yet I,
A dull and muddy-mettled° rascal, peak,°   500
Like John-a-dreams,° unpregnant of° my cause,
And can say nothing; no, not for a king.
Upon whose property° and most dear life
A damn'd defeat was made. Am I a coward?
Who calls me villain? breaks my pate across?   505
Plucks off my beard, and blows it in my face?
Tweaks me by the nose? gives me the lie i' th' throat,
As deep as to the lungs? who does me this?
Ha!
'Swounds, I should take it: for it cannot be   510
But I am pigeon-liver'd° and lack gall
To make oppression bitter, or ere this
I should have fatted all the region kites°
With this slave's offal: bloody, bawdy villain!
Remorseless, treacherous, lecherous, kindless° villain!   515
O, vengeance!
Why, what an ass am I! This is most brave,
That I, the son of a dear father murder'd,
Prompted to my revenge by heaven and hell,
Must, like a whore, unpack my heart with words,   520

---

486 **wann'd:** Grew pale. **488–489 his whole . . . conceit:** His whole being responded
with forms to suit his thought. **500 muddy-mettled:** Dull-spirited; **peak:** Mope, pine.
501 John-a-dreams: An expression occurring elsewhere in Elizabethan literature to indicate a
dreamer; **unpregnant of:** Not quickened by. **503 property:** Proprietorship (of crown and
life). **511 pigeon-liver'd:** The pigeon was supposed to secrete no gall; if Hamlet, so he says,
had had gall, he would have felt the bitterness of oppression, and avenged it. **513 region
kites:** Kites of the air. **515 kindless:** Unnatural.

And fall a-cursing, like a very drab,°
A stallion!°
Fie upon 't! foh! About,° my brains! Hum, I have heard
That guilty creatures sitting at a play
Have by the very cunning of the scene   525
Been struck so to the soul that presently
They have proclaim'd their malefactions;
For murder, though it have no tongue, will speak
With most miraculous organ. I'll have these players
Play something like the murder of my father   530
Before mine uncle: I'll observe his looks:
I'll tent° him to the quick: if 'a do blench,°
I know my course. The spirit that I have seen
May be the devil:° and the devil hath power
T' assume a pleasing shape; yea, and perhaps   535
Out of my weakness and my melancholy,
As he is very potent with such spirits,°
Abuses me to damn me: I'll have grounds
More relative° than this:° the play's the thing
Wherein I'll catch the conscience of the king.   *Exit.*   540

[ACT 3, Scene 1]

[A room in the castle.]
   Enter King, Queen, Polonius, Ophelia, Rosencrantz, Guildenstern, Lords.

KING: And can you, by no drift of conference,°
   Get from him why he puts on this confusion,
   Grating so harshly all his days of quiet
   With turbulent and dangerous lunacy?
ROSENCRANTZ: He does confess he feels himself distracted;   5
   But from what cause 'a will by no means speak.
GUILDENSTERN: Nor do we find him forward° to be sounded,
   But, with a crafty madness, keeps aloof,
   When we would bring him on to some confession
   Of his true state.
QUEEN: Did he receive you well?   10
ROSENCRANTZ: Most like a gentleman.
GUILDENSTERN: But with much forcing of his disposition.°

---

521 drab: Prostitute. **522 stallion:** Prostitute (male or female). **523 About:** About it, or turn thou right about. **532 tent:** Probe; **blench:** Quail, flinch. **534 May be the devil:** Hamlet's suspicion is properly grounded in the belief of the time. **537 spirits:** Humors. **539 relative:** Closely related, definite; **this:** I.e., the ghost's story. **ACT 3, SCENE 1. 1 drift of conference:** Device of conversation. **7 forward:** Willing. **12 forcing of his disposition:** I.e., against his will.

ROSENCRANTZ: Niggard of question;° but, of our demands,
    Most free in his reply.
QUEEN: Did you assay° him
    To any pastime?   15
ROSENCRANTZ: Madam, it so fell out, that certain players
    We o'er-raught° on the way: of these we told him;
    And there did seem in him a kind of joy
    To hear of it: they are here about the court,
    And, as I think, they have already order   20
    This night to play before him.
POLONIUS: 'Tis most true:
    And he beseech'd me to entreat your majesties
    To hear and see the matter.
KING: With all my heart; and it doth much content me
    To hear him so inclin'd.   25
    Good gentlemen, give him a further edge,°
    And drive his purpose into these delights.
ROSENCRANTZ: We shall, my lord.   *Exeunt Rosencrantz and Guildenstern.*
KING: Sweet Gertrude, leave us too;
    For we have closely° sent for Hamlet hither,
    That he, as 'twere by accident, may here   30
    Affront° Ophelia:
    Her father and myself, lawful espials,°
    Will so bestow ourselves that, seeing, unseen,
    We may of their encounter frankly judge,
    And gather by him, as he is behav'd,   35
    If 't be th' affliction of his love or no
    That thus he suffers for.
QUEEN: I shall obey you.
    And for your part, Ophelia, I do wish
    That your good beauties be the happy cause
    Of Hamlet's wildness:° so shall I hope your virtues   40
    Will bring him to his wonted way again,
    To both your honours.
OPHELIA: Madam, I wish it may.   *[Exit Queen.]*
POLONIUS: Ophelia, walk you here. Gracious,° so please you,
    We will bestow ourselves. *[To Ophelia.]* Read on this book;
    That show of such an exercise° may colour°   45
    Your loneliness. We are oft to blame in this, —
    'Tis too much prov'd — that with devotion's visage

---

13 Niggard of question: Sparing of conversation.   **14 assay:** Try to win.   **17 o'er-raught:**
Overtook.   **26 edge:** Incitement.   **29 closely:** Secretly.   **31 Affront:** Confront.   **32 lawful espials:** Legitimate spies.   **40 wildness:** Madness.   **43 Gracious:** Your grace (addressed
to the king).   **45 exercise:** Act of devotion (the book she reads is one of devotion);   **colour:**
Give a plausible appearance to.

And pious action we do sugar o'er
The devil himself.

KING: *[aside]* O, 'tis too true!   50
How smart a lash that speech doth give my conscience!
The harlot's cheek, beautied with plast'ring art,
Is not more ugly to° the thing° that helps it
Than is my deed to my most painted word:
O heavy burthen!

POLONIUS: I hear him coming: let's withdraw, my lord.   55

[Exeunt King and Polonius.]

Enter Hamlet.

HAMLET: To be, or not to be: that is the question:
Whether 'tis nobler in the mind to suffer
The slings and arrows of outrageous fortune,
Or to take arms against a sea° of troubles,
And by opposing end them? To die: to sleep;   60
No more; and by a sleep to say we end
The heart-ache and the thousand natural shocks
That flesh is heir to, 'tis a consummation
Devoutly to be wish'd. To die, to sleep;
To sleep: perchance to dream: ay, there's the rub;   65
For in that sleep of death what dreams may come
When we have shuffled° off this mortal coil,°
Must give us pause: there's the respect°
That makes calamity of so long life;°
For who would bear the whips and scorns of time,°   70
Th' oppressor's wrong, the proud man's contumely,
The pangs of despis'd° love, the law's delay,
The insolence of office° and the spurns°
That patient merit of th' unworthy takes,
When he himself might his quietus° make   75
With a bare bodkin?° who would fardels° bear,
To grunt and sweat under a weary life,
But that the dread of something after death,
The undiscover'd country from whose bourn°
No traveller returns, puzzles the will   80
And makes us rather bear those ills we have

---

52 to: Compared to; **thing:** I.e., the cosmetic. **59 sea:** The mixed metaphor of this speech
has often been commented on; a later emendation *siege* has sometimes been spoken on the
stage. **67 shuffled:** Sloughed, cast; **coil:** Usually means "turmoil"; here, possibly "body"
(conceived of as wound about the soul like rope); *clay, soil, veil,* have been suggested as emen-
dations. **68 respect:** Consideration. **69 of . . . life:** So long-lived. **70 time:** The world.
72 despis'd: Rejected. **73 office:** Office-holders; **spurns:** Insults. **75 quietus:** Acquittance; here, death. **76 bare bodkin:** Mere dagger; *bare* is sometimes understood as
"unsheathed"; **fardels:** Burdens. **79 bourn:** Boundary.

Than fly to others that we know not of?
Thus conscience° does make cowards of us all;
And thus the native hue° of resolution
Is sicklied o'er° with the pale cast° of thought,   85
And enterprises of great pitch° and moment°
With this regard° their currents° turn awry,
And lose the name of action — Soft you now!
The fair Ophelia! Nymph, in thy orisons°
Be all my sins rememb'red.

OPHELIA: Good my lord,   90
How does your honour for this many a day?

HAMLET: I humbly thank you; well, well, well.

OPHELIA: My lord, I have remembrances of yours,
That I have longed long to re-deliver;
I pray you, now receive them.

HAMLET: No, not I;   95
I never gave you aught.

OPHELIA: My honour'd lord, you know right well you did;
And, with them, words of so sweet breath compos'd
As made the things more rich: their perfume lost,
Take these again; for to the noble mind   100
Rich gifts wax poor when givers prove unkind.
There, my lord.

HAMLET: Ha, ha! are you honest?°

OPHELIA: My lord?

HAMLET: Are you fair?   105

OPHELIA: What means your lordship?

HAMLET: That if you be honest and fair, your honesty° should admit no discourse to° your beauty.

OPHELIA: Could beauty, my lord, have better commerce° than with honesty?

HAMLET: Ay, truly; for the power of beauty will sooner transform honesty from   110
what it is to a bawd than the force of honesty can translate beauty into his
likeness: this was sometime a paradox, but now the time° gives it proof. I did
love you once.

OPHELIA: Indeed, my lord, you made me believe so.

HAMLET: You should not have believed me; for virtue cannot so inoculate° our   115
old stock but we shall relish of it:° I loved you not.

83 **conscience:** Probably, inhibition by the faculty of reason restraining the will from doing
wrong.   84 **native hue:** Natural color; metaphor derived from the color of the face.   85 **sicklied o'er:** Given a sickly tinge;   **cast:** Shade of color.   86 **pitch:** Height (as of a falcon's flight);
moment: Importance.   87 **regard:** Respect, consideration;   **currents:** Courses.   89 **orisons:**
Prayers.   103–108 **are you honest . . . beauty:** *Honest* meaning "truthful" and "chaste" and
fair meaning "just, honorable" (line 105) and "beautiful" (line 107) are not mere quibbles; the
speech has the irony of a *double entendre*.   107 **your honesty:** Your chastity.   107–108 **discourse to:** Familiar intercourse with.   109 **commerce:** Intercourse.   112 **the time:** The present age.   115 **inoculate:** Graft (metaphorical).   116 **but . . . it:** I.e., that we do not still
have about us a taste of the old stock; i.e., retain our sinfulness.

OPHELIA: I was the more deceived.

HAMLET: Get thee to a nunnery: why wouldst thou be a breeder of sinners? I am
myself indifferent honest;° but yet I could accuse me of such things that it
were better my mother had not borne me: I am very proud, revengeful,   120
ambitious, with more offences at my beck° than I have thoughts to put them
in, imagination to give them shape, or time to act them in. What should
such fellows as I do crawling between earth and heaven? We are arrant
knaves, all; believe none of us. Go thy ways to a nunnery. Where's your
father?   125

OPHELIA: At home, my lord.

HAMLET: Let the doors be shut upon him, that he may play the fool no where
but in 's own house. Farewell.

OPHELIA: O, help him, you sweet heavens!

HAMLET: If thou dost marry, I'll give thee this plague for thy dowry: be thou as   130
chaste as ice, as pure as snow, thou shalt not escape calumny. Get thee to a
nunnery, go: farewell. Or, if thou wilt needs marry, marry a fool; for wise
men know well enough what monsters° you make of them. To a nunnery, go,
and quickly too. Farewell.

OPHELIA: O heavenly powers, restore him!   135

HAMLET: I have heard of your° paintings too, well enough; God hath given you
one face, and you make yourselves another: you jig,° you amble, and you
lisp; you nick-name God's creatures, and make your wantonness your ignorance.° Go to, I'll no more on 't; it hath made me mad. I say, we will have no
moe marriage: those that are married already, all but one,° shall live; the rest   140
shall keep as they are. To a nunnery, go.   *Exit.*

OPHELIA: O, what a noble mind is here o'er-thrown!
The courtier's, soldier's, scholar's, eye, tongue, sword;
Th' expectancy and rose° of the fair state,
The glass of fashion and the mould of form,°   145
Th' observ'd of all observers,° quite, quite down!
And I, of ladies most deject and wretched,
That suck'd the honey of his music vows,
Now see that noble and most sovereign reason,
Like sweet bells jangled, out of time and harsh;   150
That unmatch'd form and feature of blown° youth
Blasted with ecstasy:° O, woe is me,
T' have seen what I have seen, see what I see!

---

119 **indifferent honest:** Moderately virtuous.   121 **beck:** Command.   133 **monsters:** An allusion to the horns of a cuckold.   136 **your:** Indefinite use.   137 **jig:** Move with jerky motion;
probably allusion to the *jig*, or song and dance, of the current stage.   138–139 **make . . . ignorance:** I.e., excuse your wantonness on the ground of your ignorance.   140 **one:** I.e., the king.
144 **expectancy and rose:** Source of hope.   145 **The glass . . . form:** The mirror of fashion
and the pattern of courtly behavior.   146 **observ'd . . . observers:** I.e., the center of attention
in the court.   151 **blown:** Blooming.   152 **ecstasy:** Madness.

Enter King and Polonius.

KING: Love! his affections do not that way tend;
          Nor what he spake, though it lack'd form a little,   155
          Was not like madness. There's something in his soul,
          O'er which his melancholy sits on brood;
          And I do doubt° the hatch and the disclose°
          Will be some danger: which for to prevent,
          I have in quick determination   160
          Thus set it down: he shall with speed to England,
          For the demand of our neglected tribute:
          Haply the seas and countries different
          With variable° objects shall expel
          This something-settled° matter in his heart,   165
          Whereon his brains still beating puts him thus
          From fashion of himself.° What think you on 't?
POLONIUS: It shall do well: but yet do I believe
          The origin and commencement of his grief
          Sprung from neglected love. How now, Ophelia!   170
          You need not tell us what Lord Hamlet said;
          We heard it all. My lord, do as you please;
          But, if you hold it fit, after the play
          Let his queen mother all alone entreat him
          To show his grief: let her be round° with him;   175
          And I'll be plac'd, so please you, in the ear
          Of all their conference. If she find him not,
          To England send him, or confine him where
          Your wisdom best shall think.
KING: It shall be so: 180
          Madness in great ones must not unwatch'd go.   *Exeunt.*

[Scene 2]

[A hall in the castle.]
Enter Hamlet and three of the Players.

HAMLET: Speak the speech, I pray you, as I pronounced it to you, trippingly on
      the tongue: but if you mouth it, as many of your° players do, I had as lief the
      town-crier spoke my lines. Nor do not saw the air too much with your hand,
      thus, but use all gently; for in the very torrent, tempest, and, as I may say,
      whirlwind of your passion, you must acquire and beget a temperance that   5
      may give it smoothness. O, it offends me to the soul to hear a robustious°
      periwig-pated° fellow tear a passion to tatters, to very rags, to split the ears of

---

158 doubt: Fear; **disclose:** Disclosure or revelation (by chipping of the shell). **164 variable:** Various. **165 something-settled:** Somewhat settled. **167 From . . . himself:** Out of his natural manner. **175 round:** Blunt. **SCENE 2. 2 your:** Indefinite use. **6 robustious:** Violent, boisterous. **7 periwig-pated:** Wearing a wig.

the groundlings,° who for the most part are capable of° nothing but inexplic-
able° dumb-shows and noise: I would have such a fellow whipped for o'er-
doing Termagant;° it out-herods Herod:° pray you, avoid it.   10
FIRST PLAYER: I warrant your honour.
HAMLET: Be not too tame neither, but let your own discretion be your tutor: suit
the action to the word, the word to the action; with this special observance,
that you o'er-step not the modesty of nature: for any thing so overdone is
from the purpose of playing, whose end, both at the first and now, was and is,   15
to hold, as 't were, the mirror up to nature; to show virtue her own feature,
scorn her own image, and the very age and body of the time his form and
pressure.° Now this overdone, or come tardy off,° though it make the unskil-
ful laugh, cannot but make the judicious grieve; the censure of the which
one° must in your allowance o'erweigh a whole theatre of others. O, there be   20
players that I have seen play, and heard others praise, and that highly, not to
speak it profanely, that, neither having the accent of Christians nor the gait
of Christian, pagan, nor man, have so strutted and bellowed that I have
thought some of nature's journeymen° had made men and not made them
well, they imitated humanity so abominably.   25
FIRST PLAYER: I hope we have reformed that indifferently° with us, sir.
HAMLET: O, reform it altogether. And let those that play your clowns speak no
more than is set down for them; for there be of° them that will themselves
laugh, to set on some quantity of barren° spectators to laugh too; though, in
the mean time, some necessary question of the play be then to be consid-   30
ered: that's villanous, and shows a most pitiful ambition in the fool that uses
it. Go, make you ready.   *[Exeunt Players.]*

Enter Polonius, Guildenstern, and Rosencrantz.

How now, my lord! will the king hear this piece of work?
POLONIUS: And the queen too, and that presently.
HAMLET: Bid the players make haste.   *[Exit Polonius.]*   35
Will you two help to hasten them?
ROSENCRANTZ: ⎫
                         ⎬   We will, my lord.   *Exeunt they two.*
GUILDENSTERN: ⎭
HAMLET: What ho! Horatio!

Enter Horatio.

HORATIO: Here, sweet lord, at your service.

---

8 **groundlings:** Those who stood in the yard of the theater;   **capable of:** Susceptible of being
influenced by.   8–9 **inexplicable:** Of no significance worth explaining.   10 **Termagant:** A
god of the Saracens; a character in the St. Nicholas play, where one of his worshipers, leaving
him in charge of goods, returns to find them stolen; whereupon he beats the god (or idol), which
howls vociferously;   **Herod:** Herod of Jewry; a character in *The Slaughter of the Innocents* and
other cycle plays. The part was played with great noise and fury.   18 **pressure:** Stamp,
impressed character;   **come tardy off:** Inadequately done.   19–20 **the censure . . . one:** The
judgment of even one of whom.   24 **journeymen:** Laborers not yet masters in their trade.
26 **indifferently:** Fairly, tolerably.   28 **of:** I.e., some among them.   29 **barren:** I.e., of wit.

HAMLET: Horatio, thou art e'en as just° a man
    As e'er my conversation cop'd withal.   40
HORATIO: O, my dear lord, —
HAMLET: Nay, do not think I flatter;
    For what advancement may I hope from thee
    That no revenue hast but thy good spirits,
    To feed and clothe thee? Why should the poor be flatter'd?
    No, let the candied tongue lick absurd pomp,   45
    And crook the pregnant° hinges of the knee
    Where thrift° may follow fawning. Dost thou hear?
    Since my dear soul was mistress of her choice
    And could of men distinguish her election,
    S' hath seal'd thee for herself; for thou hast been   50
    As one, in suff'ring all, that suffers nothing,
    A man that fortune's buffets and rewards
    Hast ta'en with equal thanks: and blest are those
    Whose blood and judgement are so well commeddled,
    That they are not a pipe for fortune's finger   55
    To sound what stop° she please. Give me that man
    That is not passion's slave, and I will wear him
    In my heart's core, ay, in my heart of heart,
    As I do thee. — Something too much of this. —
    There is a play to-night before the king;   60
    One scene of it comes near the circumstance
    Which I have told thee of my father's death:
    I prithee, when thou seest that act afoot,
    Even with the very comment of thy soul°
    Observe my uncle: if his occulted° guilt   65
    Do not itself unkennel in one speech,
    It is a damned° ghost that we have seen,
    And my imaginations are as foul
    As Vulcan's stithy.° Give him heedful note;
    For I mine eyes will rivet to his face,   70
    And after we will both our judgements join
    In censure of his seeming.°
HORATIO: Well, my lord:
    If 'a steal aught the whilst this play is playing,
    And 'scape detecting, I will pay the theft.

Enter trumpets and kettledrums, King, Queen, Polonius, Ophelia, [Rosencrantz, Guildenstern, and others].

---

39 just: Honest, honorable.   **46 pregnant:** Pliant.   **47 thrift:** Profit.   **56 stop:** Hole in a wind instrument for controlling the sound.   **64 very . . . soul:** Inward and sagacious criticism. **65 occulted:** Hidden.   **67 damned:** In league with Satan.   **69 stithy:** Smithy, place of *stiths* (anvils).   **72 censure . . . seeming:** Judgment of his appearance or behavior.

HAMLET: They are coming to the play; I must be idle:° Get you a place.   75
KING: How fares our cousin Hamlet?
HAMLET: Excellent, i' faith; of the chameleon's dish:° I eat the air, promise-crammed: you cannot feed capons so.
KING: I have nothing with° this answer, Hamlet; these words are not mine.°
HAMLET: No, nor mine now. *[To Polonius.]* My lord, you played once i' the uni-   80
versity, you say?
POLONIUS: That did I, my lord; and was accounted a good actor.
HAMLET: What did you enact?
POLONIUS: I did enact Julius Cæsar: I was killed i' the Capitol; Brutus killed me.
HAMLET: It was a brute part of him to kill so capital a calf there. Be the players   85
ready?
ROSENCRANTZ: Ay, my lord; they stay upon your patience.
QUEEN: Come hither, my dear Hamlet, sit by me.
HAMLET: No, good mother, here's metal more attractive.
POLONIUS *[to the king]*:   O, ho! do you mark that?   90
HAMLET: Lady, shall I lie in your lap?   *[Lying down at Ophelia's feet.]*
OPHELIA: No, my lord.
HAMLET: I mean, my head upon your lap?
OPHELIA: Ay, my lord.
HAMLET: Do you think I meant country° matters?   95
OPHELIA: I think nothing, my lord.
HAMLET: That's a fair thought to lie between maids' legs.
OPHELIA: What is, my lord?
HAMLET: Nothing.
OPHELIA: You are merry, my lord.   100
HAMLET: Who, I?
OPHELIA: Ay, my lord.
HAMLET: O God, your only° jig-maker.° What should a man do but be merry?
for, look you, how cheerfully my mother looks, and my father died within's
two hours.   105
OPHELIA: Nay, 'tis twice two months, my lord.
HAMLET: So long? Nay then, let the devil wear black, for I'll have a suit of
sables.° O heavens! die two months ago, and not forgotten yet? Then there's
hope a great man's memory may outlive his life half a year: but, by 'r lady, 'a
must build churches, then; or else shall 'a suffer not thinking on,° with the   110
hobbyhorse, whose epitaph is "For, O, for, O, the hobbyhorse is forgot."°

The trumpets sound. Dumb show follows.

75 **idle:** Crazy, or not attending to anything serious.   77 **chameleon's dish:** Chameleons were supposed to feed on air. (Hamlet deliberately misinterprets the king's "fares" as "feeds.")
79 **have . . . with:** Make nothing of;   **are not mine:** Do not respond to what I ask.   95 **country:** With a bawdy pun.   103 **your only:** Only your;   **jig-maker:** Composer of jigs (song and dance).   107–108 **suit of sables:** Garments trimmed with the fur of the sable, with a quibble on *sable* meaning "black."   110 **suffer . . . on:** Undergo oblivion.   111 **"For . . . forgot":** Verse of a song occurring also in *Love's Labour's Lost*, 3.1.30. The hobbyhorse was a character in the Morris Dance.

Enter a King and a Queen [very lovingly]; the Queen embracing him, and he her. [She kneels, and makes show of protestation unto him.] He takes her up, and declines his head upon her neck: he lies him down upon a bank of flowers: she, seeing him asleep, leaves him. Anon comes in another man, takes off his crown, kisses it, pours poison in the sleeper's ears, and leaves him. The Queen returns; finds the King dead, makes passionate action. The Poisoner, with some three or four come in again, seem to condole with her. The dead body is carried away. The Poisoner woos the Queen with gifts: she seems harsh awhile, but in the end accepts love. [Exeunt.]

OPHELIA: What means this, my lord?

HAMLET: Marry, this is miching mallecho;° it means mischief.

OPHELIA: Belike this show imports the argument of the play.

Enter Prologue.

HAMLET: We shall know by this fellow: the players cannot keep counsel; they'll   115
tell all.

OPHELIA: Will 'a tell us what this show meant?

HAMLET: Ay, or any show that you'll show him: be not you ashamed to show,
he'll not shame to tell you what it means.

OPHELIA: You are naught, you are naught:° I'll mark the play.   120

PROLOGUE: For us, and for our tragedy,
Here stooping° to your clemency,
We beg your hearing patiently.   *[Exit.]*

HAMLET: Is this a prologue, or the posy° of a ring?

OPHELIA: 'Tis brief, my lord.   125

HAMLET: As woman's love.

Enter [two Players as] King and Queen.

PLAYER KING: Full thirty times hath Phoebus' cart gone round
Neptune's salt wash° and Tellus'° orbed ground,
And thirty dozen moons with borrowed° sheen
About the world have times twelve thirties been,   130
Since love our hearts and Hymen° did our hands
Unite commutual° in most sacred bands.

PLAYER QUEEN: So many journeys may the sun and moon
Make us again count o'er ere love be done!
But, woe is me, you are so sick of late,   135
So far from cheer and from your former state,
That I distrust° you. Yet, though I distrust,
Discomfort you, my lord, it nothing must:
For women's fear and love holds quantity;°

---

113 **miching mallecho:** Sneaking mischief.   120 **naught:** Indecent.   122 **stooping:** Bowing.   124 **posy:** Motto.   128 **salt wash:** The sea;   **Tellus:** Goddess of the earth (*orbed ground*).   129 **borrowed:** I.e., reflected.   131 **Hymen:** God of matrimony.   132 **commutual:** Mutually.   137 **distrust:** Am anxious about.   139 **holds quantity:** Keeps proportion between.

In neither aught, or in extremity.   140
Now, what my love is, proof hath made you know;
And as my love is siz'd, my fear is so:
Where love is great, the littlest doubts are fear;
Where little fears grow great, great love grows there.
PLAYER KING: 'Faith, I must leave thee, love, and shortly too;   145
My operant° powers their functions leave° to do:
And thou shalt live in this fair world behind,
Honour'd, belov'd; and haply one as kind
For husband shalt thou—
PLAYER QUEEN: O, confound the rest!
Such love must needs be treason in my breast: 150
In second husband let me be accurst!
None wed the second but who kill'd the first.
HAMLET *(aside)*:   Wormwood, wormwood.
PLAYER QUEEN: The instances that second marriage move
Are base respects of thrift, but none of love: 155
A second time I kill my husband dead,
When second husband kisses me in bed.
PLAYER KING: I do believe you think what now you speak;
But what we do determine oft we break.
Purpose is but the slave to memory,   160
Of violent birth, but poor validity:
Which now, like fruit unripe, sticks on the tree;
But fall, unshaken, when they mellow be.
Most necessary 'tis that we forget
To pay ourselves what to ourselves is debt: 165
What to ourselves in passion we propose,
The passion ending, doth the purpose lose.
The violence of either grief or joy
Their own enactures° with themselves destroy:
Where joy most revels, grief doth most lament;   170
Grief joys, joy grieves, on slender accident.
This world is not for aye,° nor 'tis not strange
That even our loves should with our fortunes change;
For 'tis a question left us yet to prove,
Whether love lead fortune, or else fortune love.   175
The great man down, you mark his favourite flies;
The poor advanc'd makes friends of enemies.
And hitherto doth love on fortune tend;
For who° not needs shall never lack a friend,
And who in want a hollow friend doth try,   180

---

146 **operant**: Active; **leave**: Cease. 169 **enactures**: Fulfillments. 172 **aye**: Ever. 179 **who**:
Whoever.

Directly seasons° him his enemy.
But, orderly to end where I begun,
Our wills and fates do so contrary run
That our devices still are overthrown;
Our thoughts are ours, their ends° none of our own: 185
So think thou wilt no second husband wed;
But die thy thoughts when thy first lord is dead.

PLAYER QUEEN: Nor earth to me give food, nor heaven light!
Sport and repose lock from me day and night!
To desperation turn my trust and hope!   190
An anchor's° cheer° in prison be my scope!
Each opposite° that blanks° the face of joy
Meet what I would have well and it destroy!
Both here and hence pursue me lasting strife,
If, once a widow, ever I be wife!   195

HAMLET: If she should break it now!

PLAYER KING: 'Tis deeply sworn. Sweet, leave me here awhile;
My spirits grow dull, and fain I would beguile
The tedious day with sleep.   *[Sleeps.]*

PLAYER QUEEN: Sleep rock thy brain;
And never come mischance between us twain!   *Exit.*   200

HAMLET: Madam, how like you this play?

QUEEN: The lady doth protest too much, methinks.

HAMLET: O, but she'll keep her word.

KING: Have you heard the argument? Is there no offence in 't?

HAMLET: No, no, they do but jest, poison in jest; no offence i' the world.   205

KING: What do you call the play?

HAMLET: The Mouse-trap. Marry, how? Tropically.° This play is the image of a
murder done in Vienna: Gonzago° is the duke's name; his wife, Baptista:
you shall see anon; 't is a knavish piece of work: but what o' that? your
majesty and we that have free souls, it touches us not: let the galled jade°   210
winch,° our withers° are unwrung.°

Enter Lucianus.

This is one Lucianus, nephew to the king.

OPHELIA: You are as good as a chorus,° my lord.

---

181 seasons: Matures, ripens.   **185 ends:** Results.   **191 An anchor's:** An anchorite's;
cheer: Fare; sometimes printed as *chair.*   **192 opposite:** Adverse thing;   **blanks:** Causes to
blanch or grow pale.   **207 Tropically:** Figuratively, *trapically* suggests a pun on *trap* in *Mouse-
trap* (line 207).   **208 Gonzago:** In 1538 Luigi Gonzago murdered the Duke of Urbano by
pouring poisoned lotion in his ears.   **210 galled jade:** Horse whose hide is rubbed by saddle
or harness.   **211 winch:** Wince;   **withers:** The part between the horse's shoulder blades;
unwrung: Not wrung or twisted.   **213 chorus:** In many Elizabethan plays the action was
explained by an actor known as the "chorus"; at a puppet show the actor who explained the
action was known as an "interpreter," as indicated by the lines following.

HAMLET: I could interpret between you and your love, if I could see the puppets
dallying.°   215

OPHELIA: You are keen, my lord, you are keen.

HAMLET: It would cost you a groaning to take off my edge.

OPHELIA: Still better, and worse.°

HAMLET: So you mistake° your husbands. Begin, murderer; pox,° leave thy
damnable faces, and begin. Come: the croaking raven doth bellow for   220
revenge.

LUCIANUS: Thoughts black, hands apt, drugs fit, and time agreeing;
Confederate° season, else no creature seeing;
Thou mixture rank, of midnight weeds collected,
With Hecate's° ban° thrice blasted, thrice infected,   225
Thy natural magic and dire property,
On wholesome life usurp immediately.

> *[Pours the poison into the sleeper's ears.]*

HAMLET: 'A poisons him i' the garden for his estate. His name's Gonzago: the
story is extant, and written in very choice Italian: you shall see anon how the
murderer gets the love of Gonzago's wife.   230

OPHELIA: The king rises.

HAMLET: What, frighted with false fire!°

QUEEN: How fares my lord?

POLONIUS: Give o'er the play.

KING: Give me some light: away!   235

POLONIUS: Lights, lights, lights!   *Exeunt all but Hamlet and Horatio.*

HAMLET: Why, let the strucken deer go weep,
The hart ungalled play;
For some must watch, while some must sleep:
Thus runs the world away.°   240
Would not this,° sir, and a forest of feathers° — if the rest of my fortunes turn
Turk with° me — with two Provincial roses° on my razed° shoes, get me a
fellowship in a cry° of players,° sir?

HORATIO: Half a share.°

HAMLET: A whole one, I.   245

---

215 dallying: With sexual suggestion, continued in *keen* (sexually aroused), *groaning*
(i.e., in pregnancy), and *edge* (i.e., sexual desire or impetuosity).   **218 Still . . . worse:** More
keen, less decorous.   **219 mistake:** Err in taking; **pox:** An imprecation.   **223 Confederate:**
Conspiring (to assist the murderer).   **225 Hecate:** The goddess of witchcraft; **ban:**
Curse.   **232 false fire:** Fireworks, or a blank discharge.   **237–240 Why . . . away:** Probably
from an old ballad, with allusion to the popular belief that a wounded deer retires to weep and
die. Cf. *As You Like It*, 2.1.66.   **241 this:** I.e., the play; **feathers:** Allusion to the plumes
which Elizabethan actors were fond of wearing.   **241–242 turn Turk with:** Go back on; **two
Provincial roses:** Rosettes of ribbon like the roses of Provins near Paris, or else the roses of
Provence; **razed:** Cut, slashed (by way of ornament).   **243 cry:** Pack (as of hounds); **fellowship . . . players:** Partnership in a theatrical company.   **244 Half a share:** Allusion to the
custom in dramatic companies of dividing the ownership into a number of shares among the
householders.

> For thou dost know, O Damon dear,
>> This realm dismantled° was
> Of Jove himself; and now reigns here
>> A very, very° — pajock.°

HORATIO: You might have rhymed.   250
HAMLET: O good Horatio, I'll take the ghost's word for a thousand pound. Didst
   perceive?
HORATIO: Very well, my lord.
HAMLET: Upon the talk of the poisoning?
HORATIO: I did very well note him.   255
HAMLET: Ah, ha! Come, some music! come, the recorders!°
> For if the king like not the comedy,
> Why then, belike, he likes it not, perdy.°
> Come, some music!

Enter Rosencrantz and Guildenstern.

GUILDENSTERN: Good my lord, vouchsafe me a word with you.   260
HAMLET: Sir, a whole history.
GUILDENSTERN: The king, sir, —
HAMLET: Ay, sir, what of him?
GUILDENSTERN: Is in his retirement marvellous distempered.
HAMLET: With drink, sir?   265
GUILDENSTERN: No, my lord, rather with choler.°
HAMLET: Your wisdom should show itself more richer to signify this to his doc-
   tor; for, for me to put him to his purgation would perhaps plunge him into
   far more choler.
GUILDENSTERN: Good my lord, put your discourse into some frame° and start   270
   not so wildly from my affair.
HAMLET: I am tame, sir: pronounce.
GUILDENSTERN: The queen, your mother, in most great affliction of spirit, hath
   sent me to you.
HAMLET: You are welcome.   275
GUILDENSTERN: Nay, good my lord, this courtesy is not of the right breed. If it
   shall please you to make me a wholesome° answer, I will do your mother's
   commandment; if not, your pardon and my return shall be the end of my
   business.
HAMLET: Sir, I cannot.   280
GUILDENSTERN: What, my lord?
HAMLET: Make you a wholesome answer; my wit's diseased: but, sir, such
   answer as I can make, you shall command; or, rather, as you say, my mother:
   therefore no more, but to the matter:° my mother, you say, —

---

247 **dismantled:** Stripped, divested.   246–249 **For . . . very:** Probably from an old ballad having
to do with Damon and Pythias.   249 **pajock:** Peacock (a bird with a bad reputation). Possibly the
word was *patchock*, diminutive of *patch*, clown.   256 **recorders:** Wind instruments of the flute
kind.   258 **perdy:** Corruption of *par dieu*.   266 **choler:** Bilious disorder, with quibble on the
sense "anger."   270 **frame:** Order.   277 **wholesome:** Sensible.   284 **matter:** Matter in hand.

ROSENCRANTZ: Then thus she says; your behaviour hath struck her into amaze-   285
ment and admiration.

HAMLET: O wonderful son, that can so 'stonish a mother! But is there no sequel
at the heels of this mother's admiration? Impart.

ROSENCRANTZ: She desires to speak with you in her closet, ere you go to bed.

HAMLET: We shall obey, were she ten times our mother. Have you any further   290
trade with us?

ROSENCRANTZ: My lord, you once did love me.

HAMLET: And do still, by these pickers and stealers.°

ROSENCRANTZ: Good my lord, what is your cause of distemper? you do, surely,
bar the door upon your own liberty, if you deny your griefs to your friend.   295

HAMLET: Sir, I lack advancement.

ROSENCRANTZ: How can that be, when you have the voice° of the king himself
for your succession in Denmark?

HAMLET: Ay, sir, but "While the grass grows,"° — the proverb is something
musty.   300

Enter the Players with recorders.

O, the recorders! let me see one. To withdraw° with you: — why do you go
about to recover the wind° of me, as if you would drive me into a toil?°

GUILDENSTERN: O, my lord, if my duty be too bold, my love is too unmannerly.°

HAMLET: I do not well understand that. Will you play upon this pipe?   305

GUILDENSTERN: My lord, I cannot.

HAMLET: I pray you.

GUILDENSTERN: Believe me, I cannot.

HAMLET: I beseech you.

GUILDENSTERN: I know no touch of it, my lord.   310

HAMLET: 'Tis as easy as lying: govern these ventages° with your fingers and
thumb, give it breath with your mouth, and it will discourse most eloquent
music. Look you, these are the stops.

GUILDENSTERN: But these cannot I command to any utterance of harmony; I
have not the skill.   315

HAMLET: Why, look you now, how unworthy a thing you make of me! You
would play upon me; you would seem to know my stops; you would pluck
out the heart of my mystery; you would sound me from my lowest note to the
top of my compass:° and there is much music, excellent voice, in this little
organ;° yet cannot you make it speak. 'Sblood, do you think I am easier to be   320

---

293 pickers and stealers: Hands, so called from the catechism "to keep my hands from picking
and stealing."   **297 voice:** Support.   **299 "While . . . grows":** The rest of the proverb is "the
silly horse starves." Hamlet may be destroyed while he is waiting for the succession to the kingdom.   **301 withdraw:** Speak in private.   **302 recover the wind:** Get to the windward side;
toil: Snare.   **303–304 if . . . unmannerly:** If I am using an unmannerly boldness, it is my love
which occasions it.   **311 ventages:** Stops of the recorders.   **319 compass:** Range of voice.
320 organ: Musical instrument, i.e., the pipe.

played on than a pipe? Call me what instrument you will, though you can fret° me, you cannot play upon me.

Enter Polonius.

God bless you, sir!

POLONIUS: My lord, the queen would speak with you, and presently.

HAMLET: Do you see yonder cloud that's almost in shape of a camel?   325

POLONIUS: By the mass, and 'tis like a camel, indeed.

HAMLET: Methinks it is like a weasel.

POLONIUS: It is backed like a weasel.

HAMLET: Or like a whale?

POLONIUS: Very like a whale.   330

HAMLET: Then I will come to my mother by and by. *[Aside.]* They fool me to the top of my bent.° — I will come by and by.°

POLONIUS: I will say so.   *[Exit.]*

HAMLET: By and by is easily said.

Leave me, friends.   *[Exeunt all but Hamlet.]*   335

'Tis now the very witching time° of night,

When churchyards yawn and hell itself breathes out

Contagion to this world: now could I drink hot blood,

And do such bitter business as the day

Would quake to look on. Soft! now to my mother.   340

O heart, lose not thy nature; let not ever

The soul of Nero° enter this firm bosom:

Let me be cruel, not unnatural:

I will speak daggers to her, but use none;

My tongue and soul in this be hypocrites;   345

How in my words somever she be shent,°

To give them seals° never, my soul, consent!   *Exit.*

[Scene 3]

[A room in the castle.]

Enter King, Rosencrantz, and Guildenstern.

KING: I like him not, nor stands it safe with us

To let his madness range. Therefore prepare you;

I your commission will forthwith dispatch,°

And he to England shall along with you:

The terms° of our estate° may not endure   5

Hazard so near us as doth hourly grow

---

322 fret: Quibble on meaning "irritate" and the piece of wood, gut, or metal which regulates the fingering.   **332 top of my bent:** Limit of endurance, i.e., extent to which a bow may be bent; **by and by:** Immediately.   **336 witching time:** I.e., time when spells are cast. **342 Nero:** Murderer of his mother, Agrippina.   **346 shent:** Rebuked.   **347 give them seals:** Confirm with deeds.   **SCENE 3. 3 dispatch:** Prepare.   **5 terms:** Condition, circumstances; **estate:** State.

Out of his brows.°
GUILDENSTERN: We will ourselves provide:
Most holy and religious fear it is
To keep those many many bodies safe
That live and feed upon your majesty.   10
ROSENCRANTZ: The single and peculiar° life is bound,
With all the strength and armour of the mind,
To keep itself from noyance;° but much more
That spirit upon whose weal depend and rest
The lives of many. The cess° of majesty   15
Dies not alone; but, like a gulf,° doth draw
What's near it with it: it is a massy wheel,
Fix'd on the summit of the highest mount,
To whose huge spokes ten thousand lesser things
Are mortis'd and adjoin'd; which, when it falls,   20
Each small annexment, petty consequence,
Attends° the boist'rous ruin. Never alone
Did the king sigh, but with a general groan.
KING: Arm° you, I pray you, to this speedy voyage;
For we will fetters put about this fear,   25
Which now goes too free-footed.
ROSENCRANTZ: We will haste us.
          Exeunt Gentlemen [Rosencrantz and Guildenstern].

Enter Polonius.

POLONIUS: My lord, he's going to his mother's closet:
Behind the arras° I'll convey° myself,
To hear the process;° I'll warrant she'll tax him home:°
And, as you said, and wisely was it said,   30
'Tis meet that some more audience than a mother,
Since nature makes them partial, should o'erhear
The speech, of vantage.° Fare you well, my liege:
I'll call upon you ere you go to bed,
And tell you what I know.
KING: Thanks, dear my lord.   *Exit [Polonius].*   35
O, my offence is rank, it smells to heaven;
It hath the primal eldest curse° upon't,
A brother's murder. Pray can I not,
Though inclination be as sharp as will:°

---

7 **brows:** Effronteries.   11 **single and peculiar:** Individual and private.   13 **noyance:** Harm.
15 **cess:** Decease.   16 **gulf:** Whirlpool.   22 **Attends:** Participates in.   24 **Arm:** Prepare.
28 **arras:** Screen of tapestry placed around the walls of household apartments;   **convey:** Implication of secrecy, *convey* was often used to mean "steal."   29 **process:** Proceedings;   **tax him
home:** Reprove him severely.   33 **of vantage:** From an advantageous place.   37 **primal
eldest curse:** The curse of Cain, the first to kill his brother.   39 **sharp as will:** I.e., his desire is
as strong as his determination.

My stronger guilt defeats my strong intent;   40
And, like a man to double business bound,
I stand in pause where I shall first begin,
And both neglect. What if this cursed hand
Were thicker than itself with brother's blood,
Is there not rain enough in the sweet heavens   45
To wash it white as snow? Whereto serves mercy
But to confront° the visage of offence?
And what's in prayer but this two-fold force,
To be forestalled° ere we come to fall,
Or pardon'd being down? Then I'll look up;   50
My fault is past. But, O, what form of prayer
Can serve my turn? "Forgive me my foul murder"?
That cannot be: since I am still possess'd
Of those effects for which I did the murder,
My crown, mine own ambition° and my queen.   55
May one be pardon'd and retain th' offence?°
In the corrupted currents° of this world
Offence's gilded hand° may shove by justice,
And oft 'tis seen the wicked prize° itself
Buys out the law: but 'tis not so above;   60
There is no shuffling,° there the action lies°
In his true nature; and we ourselves compell'd,
Even to the teeth and forehead° of our faults,
To give in evidence. What then? what rests?°
Try what repentance can: what can it not?   65
Yet what can it when one can not repent?
O wretched state! O bosom black as death!
O limed° soul, that, struggling to be free,
Art more engag'd!° Help, angels! Make assay!°
Bow, stubborn knees; and, heart with strings of steel,   70
Be soft as sinews of the new-born babe!
All may be well.   *[He kneels.]*

Enter Hamlet.

HAMLET: Now might I do it pat,° now he is praying;
And now I'll do't. And so 'a goes to heaven;
And so am I reveng'd. That would be scann'd:°   75
A villain kills my father; and for that,

---

47 **confront:** Oppose directly.   49 **forestalled:** Prevented.   55 **ambition:** I.e., realization of
ambition.   56 **offence:** Benefit accruing from offense.   57 **currents:** Courses.   58 **gilded
hand:** Hand offering gold as a bribe.   59 **wicked prize:** Prize won by wickedness.   61 **shuffling:** Escape by trickery;   **lies:** Is sustainable.   63 **teeth and forehead:** Very face.   64 **rests:**
Remains.   68 **limed:** Caught as with birdlime.   69 **engag'd:** Embedded;   **assay:** Trial.
73 **pat:** Opportunely.   75 **would be scann'd:** Needs to be looked into.

I, his sole son, do this same villain send
To heaven.
Why, this is hire and salary, not revenge.
'A took my father grossly, full of bread;°   80
With all his crimes broad blown,° as flush° as May;
And how his audit stands who knows save heaven?
But in our circumstance and course° of thought,
'Tis heavy with him: and am I then reveng'd,
To take him in the purging of his soul,   85
When he is fit and season'd for his passage?°
No!
Up, sword; and know thou a more horrid hent:°
When he is drunk asleep,° or in his rage,
Or in th' incestuous pleasure of his bed;   90
At game, a-swearing, or about some act
That has no relish of salvation in 't;
Then trip him, that his heels may kick at heaven,
And that his soul may be as damn'd and black
As hell, whereto it goes. My mother stays: 95
This physic° but prolongs thy sickly days.   *Exit.*

KING: *[Rising]* My words fly up, my thoughts remain below:
Words without thoughts never to heaven go.   *Exit.*

[Scene 4]

[The Queen's closet.]
Enter [Queen] Gertrude and Polonius.

POLONIUS: 'A will come straight. Look you lay° home to him:
Tell him his pranks have been too broad° to bear with,
And that your grace hath screen'd and stood between
Much heat° and him. I'll sconce° me even here.
Pray you, be round° with him.   5

HAMLET *(within):*   Mother, mother, mother!

QUEEN: I'll warrant you,
Fear me not: withdraw, I hear him coming.
                            [Polonius hides behind the arras.]

Enter Hamlet.

HAMLET: Now, mother, what's the matter?

QUEEN: Hamlet, thou hast thy father much offended.

---

80 full of bread: Enjoying his worldly pleasures (see Ezekiel 16:49).   **81 broad blown:** In full bloom; **flush:** Lusty.   **83 in . . . course:** As we see it in our mortal situation.   **86 fit . . . passage:** I.e., reconciled to heaven by forgiveness of his sins.   **88 hent:** Seizing; or more probably, occasion of seizure.   **89 drunk asleep:** In a drunken sleep.   **96 physic:** Purging (by prayer).
SCENE 4. 1 lay: Thrust.   **2 broad:** Unrestrained.   **4 Much heat:** I.e., the king's anger; **sconce:** Hide.   **5 round:** Blunt.   **9–10 thy father, my father:** I.e., Claudius, the elder Hamlet.

HAMLET: Mother, you have my father° much offended.   10
QUEEN: Come, come, you answer with an idle tongue.
HAMLET: Go, go, you question with a wicked tongue.
QUEEN: Why, how now, Hamlet!
HAMLET: What's the matter now?
QUEEN: Have you forgot me?
HAMLET: No, by the rood,° not so:
    You are the queen, your husband's brother's wife;   15
    And — would it were not so! — you are my mother.
QUEEN: Nay, then, I'll set those to you that can speak.
HAMLET: Come, come, and sit you down; you shall not budge;
    You go not till I set you up a glass
    Where you may see the inmost part of you.   20
QUEEN: What wilt thou do? thou wilt not murder me?
    Help, help, ho!
POLONIUS *[behind]*:   What, ho! help, help; help!
HAMLET *[drawing]*:   How now! a rat? Dead, for a ducat, dead!
                                          [Makes a pass through the arras.]
POLONIUS *[behind]*:   O, I am slain!   *[Falls and dies.]*   25
QUEEN: O me, what hast thou done?
HAMLET: Nay, I know not:
    Is it the king?
QUEEN: O, what a rash and bloody deed is this!
HAMLET: A bloody deed! almost as bad, good mother,
    As kill a king, and marry with his brother.   30
QUEEN: As kill a king!
HAMLET: Ay, lady, it was my word.
                              [Lifts up the arras and discovers Polonius.]
    Thou wretched, rash, intruding fool, farewell!
    I took thee for thy better: take thy fortune;
    Thou find'st to be too busy is some danger.
    Leave wringing of your hands: peace! sit you down,   35
    And let me wring your heart; for so I shall,
    If it be made of penetrable stuff,
    If damned custom have not braz'd° it so
    That it be proof and bulwark against sense.
QUEEN: What have I done, that thou dar'st wag thy tongue   40
    In noise so rude against me?
HAMLET: Such an act
    That blurs the grace and blush of modesty,
    Calls virtue hypocrite, takes off the rose
    From the fair forehead of an innocent love
    And sets a blister° there, makes marriage-vows   45

---

14 rood: Cross.   **38 braz'd:** Brazened, hardened.   **45 sets a blister:** Brands as a harlot.

As false as dicers' oaths: O, such a deed
As from the body of contraction° plucks
The very soul, and sweet religion° makes
A rhapsody° of words: heaven's face does glow
O'er this solidity and compound mass   50
With heated visage, as against the doom
Is thought-sick at the act.°

QUEEN: Ay me, what act,
That roars so loud, and thunders in the index?°

HAMLET: Look here, upon this picture, and on this.
The counterfeit presentment° of two brothers.   55
See, what a grace was seated on this brow;
Hyperion's° curls; the front° of Jove himself;
An eye like Mars, to threaten and command;
A station° like the herald Mercury
New-lighted on a heaven-kissing hill;   60
A combination and a form indeed,
Where every god did seem to set his seal,
To give the world assurance° of a man:
This was your husband. Look you now, what follows:
Here is your husband; like a mildew'd ear,°   65
Blasting his wholesome brother. Have you eyes?
Could you on this fair mountain leave to feed,
And batten° on this moor?° Ha! have you eyes?
You cannot call it love; for at your age
The hey-day° in the blood is tame, it's humble,   70
And waits upon the judgement: and what judgement
Would step from this to this? Sense, sure, you have,
Else could you not have motion;° but sure, that sense
Is apoplex'd;° for madness would not err,
Nor sense to ecstasy was ne'er so thrall'd°   75
But it reserv'd some quantity of choice,°
To serve in such a difference. What devil was't
That thus hath cozen'd° you at hoodman-blind?°
Eyes without feeling, feeling without sight,
Ears without hands or eyes, smelling sans° all,   80

47 **contraction**: The marriage contract.   48 **religion**: Religious vows.   49 **rhapsody**: Sense-
less string.   49–52 **heaven's . . . act**: Heaven's face blushes to look down on this world, and
Gertrude's marriage makes heaven feel as sick as though the day of doom were near.   53 **index**:
Prelude or preface.   55 **counterfeit presentment**: Portrayed representation.   57 **Hyperion's**:
The sun god's; **front**: Brow.   59 **station**: Manner of standing.   63 **assurance**: Pledge, guarantee.   65 **mildew'd ear**: See Genesis 41:5–7.   68 **batten**: Grow fat; **moor**: Barren upland.
70 **hey-day**: State of excitement.   72–73 **Sense . . . motion**: Sense and motion are functions
of the middle or sensible soul, the possession of sense being the basis of motion.   74 **apoplex'd**:
Paralyzed. Mental derangement was thus of three sorts: apoplexy, ecstasy, and diabolic possession.   75 **thrall'd**: Enslaved.   76 **quantity of choice**: Fragment of the power to choose.
78 **cozen'd**: Tricked, cheated; **hoodman-blind**: Blindman's buff.   80 **sans**: Without.

Or but a sickly part of one true sense
Could not so mope.°
O shame! where is thy blush? Rebellious hell,
If thou canst mutine° in a matron's bones,
To flaming youth let virtue be as wax,   85
And melt in her own fire: proclaim no shame
When the compulsive ardour gives the charge,°
Since frost itself as actively doth burn
And reason pandars will.°

QUEEN: O Hamlet, speak no more:
Thou turn'st mine eyes into my very soul;   90
And there I see such black and grained° spots
As will not leave their tinct.

HAMLET: Nay, but to live
In the rank sweat of an enseamed° bed,
Stew'd in corruption, honeying and making love
Over the nasty sty, —

QUEEN: O, speak to me no more;   95
These words, like daggers, enter in mine ears;
No more, sweet Hamlet!

HAMLET: A murderer and a villain;
A slave that is not twentieth part the tithe
Of your precedent lord;° a vice of kings;°
A cutpurse of the empire and the rule,   100
That from a shelf the precious diadem stole,
And put it in his pocket!

QUEEN: No more!

Enter Ghost.

HAMLET: A king of shreds and patches,° —
Save me, and hover o'er me with your wings,
You heavenly guards! What would your gracious figure?   105

QUEEN: Alas, he's mad!

HAMLET: Do you not come your tardy son to chide,
That, laps'd in time and passion,° lets go by
Th' important° acting of your dread command?
O, say!   110

---

82 mope: Be in a depressed, spiritless state, act aimlessly.   **84 mutine:** Mutiny, rebel.
87 gives the charge: Delivers the attack.   **89 reason pandars will:** The normal and proper situation was one in which reason guided the will in the direction of good; here, reason is perverted and leads in the direction of evil.   **91 grained:** Dyed in grain.   **93 enseamed:** Loaded
with grease, greased.   **99 precedent lord:** I.e., the elder Hamlet;   **vice of kings:** Buffoon of
kings; a reference to the Vice, or clown, of the morality plays and interludes.   **103 shreds and
patches:** I.e., motley, the traditional costume of the Vice.   **108 laps'd . . . passion:** Having
suffered time to slip and passion to cool; also explained as "engrossed in casual events and
lapsed into mere fruitless passion, so that he no longer entertains a rational purpose."
109 important: Urgent.

GHOST: Do not forget: this visitation
    Is but to whet thy almost blunted purpose.
    But, look, amazement° on thy mother sits:
    O, step between her and her fighting soul:
    Conceit in weakest bodies strongest works: 115
    Speak to her, Hamlet.
HAMLET: How is it with you, lady?
QUEEN: Alas, how is 't with you,
    That you do bend your eye on vacancy
    And with th' incorporal° air do hold discourse?
    Forth at your eyes your spirits wildly peep;   120
    And, as the sleeping soldiers in th' alarm,
    Your bedded° hair, like life in excrements,°
    Start up, and stand an° end. O gentle son,
    Upon the heat and flame of thy distemper
    Sprinkle cool patience. Whereon do you look?   125
HAMLET: On him, on him! Look you, how pale he glares!
    His form and cause conjoin'd,° preaching to stones,
    Would make them capable. — Do not look upon me;
    Lest with this piteous action you convert
    My stern effects:° then what I have to do   130
    Will want true colour;° tears perchance for blood.
QUEEN: To whom do you speak this?
HAMLET: Do you see nothing there?
QUEEN: Nothing at all; yet all that is I see.
HAMLET: Nor did you nothing hear?
QUEEN: No, nothing but ourselves.
HAMLET: Why, look you there! look, how it steals away!   135
    My father, in his habit as he liv'd!
    Look, where he goes, even now, out at the portal!   *Exit Ghost.*
QUEEN: This is the very coinage of your brain:
    This bodiless creation ecstasy
    Is very cunning in.
HAMLET: Ecstasy!   140
    My pulse, as yours, doth temperately keep time,
    And makes as healthful music: it is not madness
    That I have utt'red: bring me to the test,
    And I the matter will re-word,° which madness
    Would gambol° from. Mother, for love of grace,   145

---

113 amazement: Frenzy, distraction.   **119 incorporal:** Immaterial.   **122 bedded:** Laid in
smooth layers;   **excrements:** The hair was considered an excrement or voided part of the body.
123 an: On.   **127 conjoin'd:** United.   **129–130 convert . . . effects:** Divert me from my
stern duty. For *effects*, possibly *affects* (affections of the mind).   **131 want true colour:** Lack
good reason so that (with a play on the normal sense of *colour*) I shall shed tears instead of
blood.   **144 re-word:** Repeat in words.   **145 gambol:** Skip away.

Lay not that flattering unction° to your soul,
That not your trespass, but my madness speaks:
It will but skin and film the ulcerous place,
Whiles rank corruption, mining° all within,
Infects unseen. Confess yourself to heaven;　　　　　　150
Repent what's past; avoid what is to come;°
And do not spread the compost° on the weeds,
To make them ranker. Forgive me this my virtue;°
For in the fatness° of these pursy° times
Virtue itself of vice must pardon beg,　　　　　　　155
Yea, curb° and woo for leave to do him good.

QUEEN: O Hamlet, thou hast cleft my heart in twain.

HAMLET: O, throw away the worser part of it,
　And live the purer with the other half.
　Good night: but go not to my uncle's bed;　　　　160
　Assume a virtue, if you have it not.
　That monster, custom, who all sense doth eat,
　Of habits devil, is angel yet in this,
　That to the use of actions fair and good
　He likewise gives a frock or livery,　　　　　　165
　That aptly is put on. Refrain to-night,
　And that shall lend a kind of easiness
　To the next abstinence: the next more easy;
　For use almost can change the stamp of nature,
　And either . . . the devil, or throw him out°　　　170
　With wondrous potency. Once more, good night:
　And when you are desirous to be bless'd,°
　I'll blessing beg of you. For this same lord,　　　*[Pointing to Polonius.]*
　I do repent: but heaven hath pleas'd it so,
　To punish me with this and this with me,　　　　175
　That I must be their scourge and minister.
　I will bestow him, and will answer well
　The death I gave him. So, again, good night.
　I must be cruel, only to be kind:
　Thus bad begins and worse remains behind.　　　180
　One word more, good lady.

QUEEN:　　　　　　　　What shall I do?

HAMLET: Not this, by no means, that I bid you do:
　Let the bloat° king tempt you again to bed;
　Pinch wanton on your cheek; call you his mouse;

---

146 **unction:** Ointment used medicinally or as a rite; suggestion that forgiveness for sin may
not be so easily achieved.　149 **mining:** Working under the surface.　151 **what is to come:**
I.e., the sins of the future.　152 **compost:** Manure.　153 **this my virtue:** My virtuous talk in
reproving you.　154 **fatness:** Grossness; **pursy:** Short-winded, corpulent.　156 **curb:** Bow,
bend the knee.　170 Defective line usually emended by inserting *master* after *either*.　172 **be
bless'd:** Become blessed, i.e., repentant.　183 **bloat:** Bloated.

And let him, for a pair of reechy° kisses,   185
Or paddling in your neck with his damn'd fingers,
Make you to ravel all this matter out,
That I essentially° am not in madness,
But mad in craft. 'Twere good you let him know;
For who, that's but a queen, fair, sober, wise,   190
Would from a paddock,° from a bat, a gib,°
Such dear concernings° hide? who would do so?
No, in despite of sense and secrecy,
Unpeg the basket on the house's top,
Let the birds fly, and, like the famous ape,°   195
To try conclusions,° in the basket creep,
And break your own neck down.

QUEEN: Be thou assur'd, if words be made of breath,
And breath of life, I have no life to breathe
What thou hast said to me.   200

HAMLET: I must to England; you know that?

QUEEN: Alack,
I had forgot: 'tis so concluded on.

HAMLET: There's letters seal'd: and my two schoolfellows,
Whom I will trust as I will adders fang'd,
They bear the mandate; they must sweep my way,°   205
And marshal me to knavery. Let it work;
For 'tis the sport to have the enginer°
Hoist° with his own petar:° and 't shall go hard
But I will delve one yard below their mines,
And blow them at the moon: O, 'tis most sweet,   210
When in one line two crafts° directly meet.
This man shall set me packing:°
I'll lug the guts into the neighbour room.
Mother, good night. Indeed this counsellor
Is now most still, most secret and most grave,   215
Who was in life a foolish prating knave.
Come, sir, to draw° toward an end with you.
Good night, mother.   *Exeunt [severally; Hamlet dragging in Polonius.]*

---

185 **reechy:** Dirty, filthy.   188 **essentially:** In my essential nature.   191 **paddock:** Toad;
gib: Tomcat.   192 **dear concernings:** Important affairs.   195 **the famous ape:** A letter from
Sir John Suckling seems to supply other details of the story, otherwise not identified: "It is the
story of the jackanapes and the partridges; thou starest after a beauty till it be lost to thee, then
let'st out another, and starest after that till it is gone too."   196 **conclusions:** Experiments.
205 **sweep my way:** Clear my path.   207 **enginer:** Constructor of military works, or possibly,
artilleryman.   208 **Hoist:** Blown up;   **petar:** Defined as a small engine of war used to blow in
a door or make a breach, and as a case filled with explosive materials.   211 **two crafts:** Two
acts of guile, with quibble on the sense of "two ships."   212 **set me packing:** Set me to making
schemes, and set me to lugging (him), and, also, send me off in a hurry.   217 **draw:** Come,
with quibble on literal sense.

[ACT 4, Scene 1]

[A room in the castle.]
    Enter King and Queen, with Rosencrantz and Guildenstern.

KING: There's matter in these sighs, these profound heaves:
    You must translate: 'tis fit we understand them.
    Where is your son?
QUEEN: Bestow this place on us a little while.
                     [Exeunt Rosencrantz and Guildenstern.]
    Ah, mine own lord, what have I seen to-night!   5
KING: What, Gertrude? How does Hamlet?
QUEEN: Mad as the sea and wind, when both contend
    Which is the mightier: in his lawless fit,
    Behind the arras hearing something stir,
    Whips out his rapier, cries, "A rat, a rat!"   10
    And, in this brainish° apprehension,° kills
    The unseen good old man.
KING: O heavy deed!
    It had been so with us, had we been there:
    His liberty is full of threats to all;
    To you yourself, to us, to every one.   15
    Alas, how shall this bloody deed be answer'd?
    It will be laid to us, whose providence°
    Should have kept short,° restrain'd and out of haunt,°
    This mad young man: but so much was our love,
    We would not understand what was most fit;   20
    But, like the owner of a foul disease,
    To keep it from divulging,° let it feed
    Even on the pith of life. Where is he gone?
QUEEN: To draw apart the body he hath kill'd:
    O'er whom his very madness, like some ore   25
    Among a mineral° of metals base,
    Shows itself pure; 'a weeps for what is done.
KING: O Gertrude, come away!
    The sun no sooner shall the mountains touch,
    But we will ship him hence: and this vile deed   30
    We must, with all our majesty and skill,
    Both countenance and excuse. Ho, Guildenstern!
Enter Rosencrantz and Guildenstern.

    Friends both, go join you with some further aid:
    Hamlet in madness hath Polonius slain,

ACT 4, SCENE 1. **11 brainish:** Headstrong, passionate;   **apprehension:** Conception, imagination.   **17 providence:** Foresight.   **18 short:** I.e., on a short tether;   **out of haunt:** Secluded. **22 divulging:** Becoming evident.   **26 mineral:** Mine.

And from his mother's closet hath he dragg'd him: 35
Go seek him out; speak fair, and bring the body
Into the chapel. I pray you, haste in this.
                          [Exeunt Rosencrantz and Guildenstern.]
Come, Gertrude, we'll call up our wisest friends;
And let them know, both what we mean to do,
And what's untimely done . . .°   40
Whose whisper o'er the world's diameter,°
As level° as the cannon to his blank,°
Transports his pois'ned shot, may miss our name,
And hit the woundless° air. O, come away!
My soul is full of discord and dismay.   *Exeunt.*   45

[Scene 2]

[Another room in the castle.]
    Enter Hamlet.

HAMLET: Safely stowed.

ROSENCRANTZ:
                    (within) Hamlet! Lord Hamlet!
GUILDENSTERN:

HAMLET: But soft, what noise? who calls on Hamlet? O, here they come.

Enter Rosencrantz and Guildenstern.

ROSENCRANTZ: What have you done, my lord, with the dead body?
HAMLET: Compounded it with dust, whereto 'tis kin.
ROSENCRANTZ: Tell us where 'tis, that we may take it thence   5
    And bear it to the chapel.
HAMLET: Do not believe it.
ROSENCRANTZ: Believe what?
HAMLET: That I can keep your counsel° and not mine own. Besides, to be
    demanded of a sponge! what replication° should be made by the son of a king?   10
ROSENCRANTZ: Take you me for a sponge, my lord?
HAMLET: Ay, sir, that soaks up the king's countenance, his rewards, his authori-
    ties.° But such officers do the king best service in the end: he keeps them,
    like an ape an apple, in the corner of his jaw; first mouthed, to be last swal-
    lowed: when he needs what you have gleaned, it is but squeezing you, and,   15
    sponge, you shall be dry again.
ROSENCRANTZ: I understand you not, my lord.
HAMLET: I am glad of it: a knavish speech sleeps in a foolish ear.
ROSENCRANTZ: My lord, you must tell us where the body is, and go with us to
    the king.   20

---

40 Defective line; some editors add: *so, haply, slander*; others add: *for, haply, slander*; other
conjectures.   **41 diameter:** Extent from side to side.   **42 level:** Straight;   **blank:** White spot
in the center of a target.   **44 woundless:** Invulnerable.   **SCENE 2. 9 keep your counsel:**
Hamlet is aware of their treachery but says nothing about it.   **10 replication:** Reply.
12–13 authorities: Authoritative backing.

HAMLET: The body is with the king, but the king is not with the body.° The king
is a thing —
GUILDENSTERN: A thing, my lord!
HAMLET: Of nothing: bring me to him. Hide fox, and all after.°   *Exeunt.*

[Scene 3]

[Another room in the castle.]
Enter King, and two or three.

KING: I have sent to seek him, and to find the body.
How dangerous is it that this man goes loose!
Yet must not we put the strong law on him:
He's lov'd of the distracted° multitude,
Who like not in their judgement, but their eyes;   5
And where 'tis so, th' offender's scourge° is weigh'd,°
But never the offence. To bear all smooth and even,
This sudden sending him away must seem
Deliberate pause:° diseases desperate grown
By desperate appliance are reliev'd,   10
Or not at all.

Enter Rosencrantz, [Guildenstern,] and all the rest.

    How now! what hath befall'n?
ROSENCRANTZ: Where the dead body is bestow'd, my lord,
We cannot get from him.
KING: But where is he?
ROSENCRANTZ: Without, my lord; guarded, to know your pleasure.
KING: Bring him before us.   15
ROSENCRANTZ: Ho! bring in the lord.

They enter [with Hamlet].

KING: Now, Hamlet, where's Polonius?
HAMLET: At supper.
KING: At supper! where?
HAMLET: Not where he eats, but where 'a is eaten: a certain convocation of   20
politic° worms° are e'en at him. Your worm is your only emperor for diet: we
fat all creatures else to fat us, and we fat ourselves for maggots: your fat king
and your lean beggar is but variable service,° two dishes, but to one table:
that's the end.
KING: Alas, alas!   25

---

21 **The body . . . body:** There are many interpretations; possibly, "The body lies in death with
the king, my father; but my father walks disembodied"; or "Claudius has the bodily possession of
kingship, but kingliness, or justice of inheritance, is not with him."   24 **Hide . . . after:** An old
signal cry in the game of hide-and-seek.   SCENE 3.   4 **distracted:** I.e., without power of forming logical judgments.   6 **scourge:** Punishment;   **weigh'd:** Taken into consideration.
9 **Deliberate pause:** Considered action.   20–21 **convocation . . . worms:** Allusion to the
Diet of Worms (1521).   21 **politic:** Crafty.   23 **variable service:** A variety of dishes.

HAMLET: A man may fish with the worm that hath eat of a king, and eat of the
fish that hath fed of that worm.

KING: What dost thou mean by this?

HAMLET: Nothing but to show you how a king may go a progress° through the
guts of a beggar.   30

KING: Where is Polonius?

HAMLET: In heaven; send thither to see: if your messenger find him not there,
seek him i' the other place yourself. But if indeed you find him not within
this month, you shall nose him as you go up the stairs into the lobby.

KING [*to some Attendants*]:   Go seek him there.   35

HAMLET: 'A will stay till you come.   [*Exeunt Attendants.*]

KING: Hamlet, this deed, for thine especial safety, —
Which we do tender,° as we dearly grieve
For that which thou hast done, — must send thee hence
With fiery quickness: therefore prepare thyself;   40
The bark is ready, and the wind at help,
Th' associates tend, and everything is bent
For England.

HAMLET: For England!

KING: Ay, Hamlet.

HAMLET: Good.

KING: So is it, if thou knew'st our purposes.

HAMLET: I see a cherub° that sees them. But, come; for England! Farewell, dear   45
mother.

KING: Thy loving father, Hamlet.

HAMLET: My mother: father and mother is man and wife; man and wife is one
flesh; and so, my mother. Come, for England!   *Exit.*

KING: Follow him at foot;° tempt him with speed aboard;   50
Delay it not; I'll have him hence to-night:
Away! for every thing is seal'd and done
That else leans on th' affair: pray you, make haste.

                                                       [*Exeunt all but the King.*]

And, England, if my love thou hold'st at aught —
As my great power thereof may give thee sense,   55
Since yet thy cicatrice° looks raw and red
After the Danish sword, and thy free awe°
Pays homage to us — thou mayst not coldly set
Our sovereign process; which imports at full,
By letters congruing to that effect,   60
The present death of Hamlet. Do it, England;
For like the hectic° in my blood he rages,
And thou must cure me: till I know 'tis done,
Howe'er my haps,° my joys were ne'er begun.   *Exit.*

---

29 progress: Royal journey of state.   **38 tender:** Regard, hold dear.   **45 cherub:** Cherubim
are angels of knowledge.   **50 at foot:** Close behind, at heel.   **56 cicatrice:** Scar.   **57 free
awe:** Voluntary show of respect.   **62 hectic:** Fever.   **64 haps:** Fortunes.

[Scene 4]

[A plain in Denmark.]
    Enter Fortinbras with his Army over the stage.

FORTINBRAS: Go, captain, from me greet the Danish king;
        Tell him that, by his license,° Fortinbras
        Craves the conveyance° of a promis'd march
        Over his kingdom. You know the rendezvous.
        If that his majesty would aught with us,   5
        We shall express our duty in his eye;°
        And let him know so.
CAPTAIN: I will do't, my lord.
FORTINBRAS: Go softly° on.   *[Exeunt all but Captain.]*

Enter Hamlet, Rosencrantz, [Guildenstern,] &c.

HAMLET: Good sir, whose powers are these?
CAPTAIN: They are of Norway, sir.   10
HAMLET: How purpos'd, sir, I pray you?
CAPTAIN: Against some part of Poland.
HAMLET: Who commands them, sir?
CAPTAIN: The nephew to old Norway, Fortinbras.
HAMLET: Goes it against the main° of Poland, sir,   15
    Or for some frontier?
CAPTAIN: Truly to speak, and with no addition,
    We go to gain a little patch of ground
    That hath in it no profit but the name.
    To pay five ducats, five, I would not farm it;°   20
    Nor will it yield to Norway or the Pole
    A ranker rate, should it be sold in fee.°
HAMLET: Why, then the Polack never will defend it.
CAPTAIN: Yes, it is already garrison'd.
HAMLET: Two thousand souls and twenty thousand ducats   25
    Will not debate the question of this straw:°
    This is th' imposthume° of much wealth and peace,
    That inward breaks, and shows no cause without
    Why the man dies. I humbly thank you, sir.
CAPTAIN: God be wi' you, sir.   *[Exit.]*
ROSENCRANTZ: Will 't please you go, my lord?   30
HAMLET: I'll be with you straight. Go a little before.
                        [Exeunt all except Hamlet.]
    How all occasions° do inform against° me,
    And spur my dull revenge! What is a man,

SCENE 4.   **2 license:** Leave.   **3 conveyance:** Escort, convoy.   **6 in his eye:** In his presence.
8 softly: Slowly.   **15 main:** Country itself.   **20 farm it:** Take a lease of it.   **22 fee:** Fee simple.   **26 debate . . . straw:** Settle this trifling matter.   **27 imposthume:** Purulent abscess or
swelling.   **32 occasions:** Incidents, events;   **inform against:** Generally defined as "show,"
"betray" (i.e., his tardiness); more probably *inform* means "take shape," as in *Macbeth*, 2.1.48.

If his chief good and market of his time°
Be but to sleep and feed? a beast, no more.   35
Sure, he that made us with such large discourse,
Looking before and after, gave us not
That capability and god-like reason
To fust° in us unus'd. Now, whether it be
Bestial oblivion, or some craven scruple   40
Of thinking too precisely on th' event,
A thought which, quarter'd, hath but one part wisdom
And ever three parts coward, I do not know
Why yet I live to say "This thing 's to do";
Sith I have cause and will and strength and means   45
To do 't. Examples gross as earth exhort me:
Witness this army of such mass and charge
Led by a delicate and tender prince,
Whose spirit with divine ambition puff'd
Makes mouths at the invisible event,   50
Exposing what is mortal and unsure
To all that fortune, death and danger dare,
Even for an egg-shell. Rightly to be great
Is not to stir without great argument,
But greatly to find quarrel in a straw   55
When honour's at the stake. How stand I then,
That have a father kill'd, a mother stain'd,
Excitements of° my reason and my blood,
And let all sleep? while, to my shame, I see
The imminent death of twenty thousand men,   60
That, for a fantasy and trick° of fame,
Go to their graves like beds, fight for a plot°
Whereon the numbers cannot try the cause,
Which is not tomb enough and continent
To hide the slain? O, from this time forth,   65
My thoughts be bloody, or be nothing worth!   *Exit.*

[Scene 5]

[Elsinore. A room in the castle.]
   Enter Horatio, [Queen] Gertrude, and a Gentleman.

QUEEN: I will not speak with her.
GENTLEMAN: She is importunate, indeed distract:
   Her mood will needs be pitied.
QUEEN: What would she have?

---

34 **market of his time:** The best use he makes of his time, or, that for which he sells his time.
39 **fust:** Grow moldy.   58 **Excitements of:** Incentives to.   61 **trick:** Toy, trifle.   62 **plot:**
Piece of ground.

GENTLEMAN: She speaks much of her father; says she hears
  There's tricks° i' th' world; and hems, and beats her heart;°   5
  Spurns enviously at straws;° speaks things in doubt,
  That carry but half sense: her speech is nothing,
  Yet the unshaped° use of it doth move
  The hearers to collection;° they yawn° at it,
  And botch° the words up fit to their own thoughts;   10
  Which, as her winks, and nods, and gestures yield° them,
  Indeed would make one think there might be thought,
  Though nothing sure, yet much unhappily.°
HORATIO: 'Twere good she were spoken with: for she may strew
  Dangerous conjectures in ill-breeding minds.°   15
QUEEN: Let her come in.   *[Exit Gentleman.]*
  [Aside.] To my sick soul, as sin's true nature is,
  Each toy seems prologue to some great amiss:°
  So full of artless jealousy is guilt,
  It spills itself in fearing to be spilt.°   20

Enter Ophelia [distracted].

OPHELIA: Where is the beauteous majesty of Denmark?
QUEEN: How now, Ophelia!
OPHELIA *(she sings):*   How should I your true love know
    From another one?
  By his cockle hat° and staff,   25
    And his sandal shoon.°
QUEEN: Alas, sweet lady, what imports this song?
OPHELIA: Say you? nay, pray you mark.
    (Song) He is dead and gone, lady,
    He is dead and gone;   30
  At his head a grass-green turf,
    At his heels a stone.
  O, ho!
QUEEN: Nay, but, Ophelia—
OPHELIA: Pray you, mark   35
    [Sings.] White his shroud as the mountain snow,—

Enter King.

QUEEN: Alas, look here, my lord.

SCENE 5.   **5 tricks:** Deceptions;   **heart:** I.e., breast.   **6 Spurns . . . straws:** Kicks spitefully at small objects in her path.   **8 unshaped:** Unformed, artless.   **9 collection:** Inference, a guess at some sort of meaning;   **yawn:** Wonder.   **10 botch:** Patch.   **11 yield:** Deliver, bring forth (her words).   **13 much unhappily:** Expressive of much unhappiness.   **15 ill-breeding minds:** Minds bent on mischief.   **18 great amiss:** Calamity, disaster.   **19–20 So . . . spilt:** Guilt is so full of suspicion that it unskillfully betrays itself in fearing to be betrayed.   **25 cockle hat:** Hat with cockleshell stuck in it as a sign that the wearer has been a pilgrim to the shrine of St. James of Compostella. The pilgrim's garb was a conventional disguise for lovers.   **26 shoon:** Shoes.

OPHELIA *(Song)*:   Larded° all with flowers;
   Which bewept to the grave did not go
     With true-love showers.   40
KING: How do you, pretty lady?
OPHELIA: Well, God 'ild° you! They say the owl° was a baker's daughter.
Lord, we know what we are, but know not what we may be. God be at your
table!
KING: Conceit upon her father.   45
OPHELIA: Pray let's have no words of this; but when they ask you what it means,
say you this:
  (Song) To-morrow is Saint Valentine's day,
   All in the morning betime,
  And I a maid at your window,   50
   To be your Valentine.°
  Then up he rose, and donn'd his clothes,
   And dupp'd° the chamber-door;
  Let in the maid, that out a maid
   Never departed more.   55
KING: Pretty Ophelia!
OPHELIA: Indeed, la, without an oath, I'll make an end on 't:
  [Sings.] By Gis° and by Saint Charity,
   Alack, and fie for shame!
  Young men will do 't, if they come to 't;   60
   By cock,° they are to blame.
  Quoth she, before you tumbled me,
   You promis'd me to wed.
  So would I ha' done, by yonder sun,
   An thou hadst not come to my bed.   65
KING: How long hath she been thus?
OPHELIA: I hope all will be well. We must be patient: but I cannot choose
but weep, to think they would lay him i' the cold ground. My brother
shall know of it: and so I thank you for your good counsel. Come, my
coach! Good night, ladies; good night, sweet ladies; good night, good   70
night.   *[Exit.]*
KING: Follow her close; give her good watch, I pray you.   *[Exit Horatio.]*
  O, this is the poison of deep grief; it springs
All from her father's death. O Gertrude, Gertrude,
When sorrows come, they come not single spies,   75
But in battalions. First, her father slain:
Next your son gone; and he most violent author
Of his own just remove: the people muddied,

---

38 Larded: Decorated.   **42 God 'ild:** God yield or reward;   **owl:** Reference to a monkish
legend that a baker's daughter was turned into an owl for refusing bread to the Savior.
51 Valentine: This song alludes to the belief that the first girl seen by a man on the morning of
this day was his valentine or true love.   **53 dupp'd:** Opened.   **58 Gis:** Jesus.   **61 cock:** Perversion of "God" in oaths.

Thick and unwholesome in their thoughts and whispers,
For good Polonius' death; and we have done but greenly,°   80
In hugger-mugger° to inter him: poor Ophelia
Divided from herself and her fair judgement,
Without the which we are pictures, or mere beasts:
Last, and as much containing as all these,
Her brother is in secret come from France;   85
Feeds on his wonder, keeps himself in clouds,°
And wants not buzzers° to infect his ear
With pestilent speeches of his father's death;
Wherein necessity, of matter beggar'd,°
Will nothing stick° our person to arraign   90
In ear and ear.° O my dear Gertrude, this,
Like to a murd'ring-piece,° in many places
Gives me superfluous death.   *A noise within.*

QUEEN: Alack, what noise is this?

KING: Where are my Switzers?° Let them guard the door.

Enter a Messenger.

What is the matter?

MESSENGER: Save yourself, my lord: 95
The ocean, overpeering° of his list,°
Eats not the flats with more impiteous haste
Than young Laertes, in a riotous head,
O'erbears your officers. The rabble call him lord;
And, as the world were now but to begin,   100
Antiquity forgot, custom not known,
The ratifiers and props of every word,°
They cry "Choose we: Laertes shall be king":
Caps, hands, and tongues, applaud it to the clouds:
"Laertes shall be king, Laertes king!"   *A noise within.*   105

QUEEN: How cheerfully on the false trail they cry!
O, this is counter,° you false Danish dogs!

KING: The doors are broke.

Enter Laertes with others.

LAERTES: Where is this king? Sirs, stand you all without.

DANES: No, let's come in.

LAERTES: I pray you, give me leave.   110

DANES: We will, we will.   *[They retire without the door.]*

LAERTES: I thank you: keep the door. O thou vile king,

---

80 greenly: Foolishly.   **81 hugger-mugger:** Secret haste.   **86 in clouds:** Invisible.
87 buzzers: Gossipers.   **89 of matter beggar'd:** Unprovided with facts.   **90 nothing stick:**
Not hesitate.   **91 In ear and ear:** In everybody's ears.   **92 murd'ring-piece:** Small cannon or
mortar; suggestion of numerous missiles fired.   **94 Switzers:** Swiss guards, mercenaries.
96 overpeering: Overflowing;   **list:** Shore.   **102 word:** Promise.   **107 counter:** A hunting
term meaning to follow the trail in a direction opposite to that which the game has taken.

Give me my father!

QUEEN: Calmly, good Laertes.

LAERTES: That drop of blood that's calm proclaims me bastard,
　　Cries cuckold to my father, brands the harlot   115
　　Even here, between the chaste unsmirched brow
　　Of my true mother.

KING: What is the cause, Laertes,
　　That thy rebellion looks so giant-like?
　　Let him go, Gertrude; do not fear our person:
　　There's such divinity doth hedge a king,   120
　　That treason can but peep to° what it would,°
　　Acts little of his will. Tell me, Laertes,
　　Why thou art thus incens'd. Let him go, Gertrude.
　　Speak, man.

LAERTES: Where is my father?

KING: Dead.

QUEEN: But not by him.   125

KING: Let him demand his fill.

LAERTES: How came he dead? I'll not be juggled with:
　　To hell, allegiance! vows, to the blackest devil!
　　Conscience and grace, to the profoundest pit!
　　I dare damnation. To this point I stand,   130
　　That both the worlds I give to negligence,°
　　Let come what comes; only I'll be reveng'd
　　Most throughly° for my father.

KING: Who shall stay you?

LAERTES: My will,° not all the world's:
　　And for my means, I'll husband them so well,   135
　　They shall go far with little.

KING: Good Laertes,
　　If you desire to know the certainty
　　Of your dear father, is 't writ in your revenge,
　　That, swoopstake,° you will draw both friend and foe,
　　Winner and loser?   140

LAERTES: None but his enemies.

KING: Will you know them then?

LAERTES: To his good friends thus wide I'll ope my arms;
　　And like the kind life-rend'ring pelican,°
　　Repast° them with my blood.

KING: Why, now you speak
　　Like a good child and a true gentleman.   145

121 **peep to:** I.e., look at from afar off;   **would:** Wishes to do.   131 **give to negligence:** He
despises both the here and the hereafter.   133 **throughly:** thoroughly.   134 **My will:** He will
not be stopped except by his own will.   139 **swoopstake:** Literally, drawing the whole stake at
once, i.e., indiscriminately.   143 **pelican:** Reference to the belief that the pelican feeds its
young with its own blood.   144 **Repast:** Feed.

That I am guiltless of your father's death,
And am most sensibly in grief for it,
It shall as level to your judgement 'pear
As day does to your eye.   *A noise within: "Let her come in."*

LAERTES: How now! what noise is that?   150

Enter Ophelia.

O heat,° dry up my brains! tears seven times salt,
Burn out the sense and virtue of mine eye!
By heaven, thy madness shall be paid with weight,
Till our scale turn the beam. O rose of May!
Dear maid, kind sister, sweet Ophelia!   155
O heavens! is 't possible, a young maid's wits
Should be as mortal as an old man's life?
Nature is fine in love, and where 'tis fine,
It sends some precious instance of itself
After the thing it loves.   160

OPHELIA *(Song):*   They bore him barefac'd on the bier;
          Hey non nonny, nonny, hey nonny;
          And in his grave rain'd many a tear: —
Fare you well, my dove!

LAERTES: Hadst thou thy wits, and didst persuade revenge,   165
It could not move thus.

OPHELIA *[sings]:*   You must sing a-down a-down,
          An you call him a-down-a.
O, how the wheel° becomes it! It is the false steward,° that stole his master's
daughter.   170

LAERTES: This nothing's more than matter.

OPHELIA: There's rosemary,° that's for remembrance; pray you, love, remember: and there is pansies,° that's for thoughts.

LAERTES: A document° in madness, thoughts and remembrance fitted.

OPHELIA: There's fennel° for you, and columbines:° there's rue° for you; and   175
here's some for me: we may call it herb of grace o' Sundays: O, you must
wear your rue with a difference. There's a daisy:° I would give you some
violets,° but they withered all when my father died: they say 'a made a
good end, —
[Sings.] For bonny sweet Robin is all my joy.°   180

---

151 heat: Probably the heat generated by the passion of grief.   **169 wheel:** Spinning wheel as accompaniment to the song refrain;   **false steward:** The story is unknown.   **172 rosemary:** Used as a symbol of remembrance both at weddings and at funerals.   **173 pansies:** Emblems of love and courtship (from the French *pensée*).   **174 document:** Piece of instruction or lesson.   **175 fennel:** Emblem of flattery;   **columbines:** Emblem of unchastity (?) or ingratitude (?);   **rue:** Emblem of repentance. It was usually mingled with holy water and then known as *herb of grace.* Ophelia is probably playing on the two meanings of *rue*, "repentant" and "even for ruth (pity)"; the former signification is for the queen, the latter for herself.   **177 daisy:** Emblem of dissembling, faithlessness.   **178 violets:** Emblems of faithfulness.   **180 For . . . joy:** Probably a line from a Robin Hood ballad.

LAERTES: Thought° and affliction, passion, hell itself,
    She turns to favour and to prettiness.
OPHELIA *(Song):*   And will 'a not come again?°
    And will 'a not come again?
        No, no, he is dead: 185
        Go to thy death-bed:
    He never will come again.

    His beard was as white as snow,
    All flaxen was his poll:°
        He is gone, he is gone,   190
        And we cast away° moan:
    God ha' mercy on his soul!
    And of all Christian souls, I pray God. God be wi' you.   *[Exit.]*
LAERTES: Do you see this, O God?
KING: Laertes, I must commune with your grief,   195
    Or you deny me right.° Go but apart,
    Make choice of whom your wisest friends you will,
    And they shall hear and judge 'twixt you and me:
    If by direct or by collateral° hand
    They find us touch'd,° we will our kingdom give,   200
    Our crown, our life, and all that we call ours,
    To you in satisfaction; but if not,
    Be you content to lend your patience to us,
    And we shall jointly labour with your soul
    To give it due content.
LAERTES: Let this be so;   205
    His means of death, his obscure funeral —
    No trophy, sword, nor hatchment° o'er his bones,
    No noble rite nor formal ostentation —
    Cry to be heard, as 'twere from heaven to earth,
    That I must call 't in question.
KING: So you shall;   210
    And where th' offence is let the great axe fall.
    I pray you, go with me.   *Exeunt.*

[Scene 6]

[Another room in the castle.]
    Enter Horatio and others.

HORATIO: What are they that would speak with me?
GENTLEMAN: Sea-faring men, sir: they say they have letters for you.

---

181 Thought: Melancholy thought.   **183 And . . . again:** This song appeared in the song-books as "The Merry Milkmaids' Dumps."   **189 poll:** Head.   **191 cast away:** Shipwrecked.
196 right: My rights.   **199 collateral:** Indirect.   **200 touch'd:** Implicated.   **207 hatch-ment:** Tablet displaying the armorial bearings of a deceased person.

HORATIO: Let them come in.   *[Exit Gentleman.]*
   I do not know from what part of the world
   I should be greeted, if not from lord Hamlet.   5

Enter Sailors.

FIRST SAILOR: God bless you, sir.
HORATIO: Let him bless thee too.
FIRST SAILOR: 'A shall sir, an 't please him. There's a letter for you, sir; it comes
   from the ambassador that was bound for England; if your name be Horatio,
   as I am let to know it is.   10
HORATIO *[reads]*:   "Horatio, when thou shalt have overlooked this, give these fellows some means° to the king: they have letters for him. Ere we were two
   days old at sea, a pirate of very warlike appointment gave us chase. Finding
   ourselves too slow of sail, we put on a compelled valour, and in the grapple I
   boarded them: on the instant they got clear of our ship; so I alone became   15
   their prisoner. They have dealt with me like thieves of mercy:° but they knew
   what they did; I am to do a good turn for them. Let the king have the letters I
   have sent; and repair thou to me with as much speed as thou wouldest fly
   death. I have words to speak in thine ear will make thee dumb; yet are they
   much too light for the bore° of the matter. These good fellows will bring thee   20
   where I am. Rosencrantz and Guildenstern hold their course for England: of
   them I have much to tell thee. Farewell.
                  "He that thou knowest thine, HAMLET."
   Come, I will give you way for these your letters;
   And do 't the speedier, that you may direct me
   To him from whom you brought them.   *Exeunt.*   25

[Scene 7]

[Another room in the castle.]
Enter King and Laertes.

KING: Now must your conscience° my acquittance seal,
   And you must put me in your heart for friend,
   Sith you have heard, and with a knowing ear,
   That he which hath your noble father slain
   Pursued my life.
LAERTES: It well appears: but tell me   5
   Why you proceeded not against these feats,
   So criminal and so capital° in nature,
   As by your safety, wisdom, all things else,
   You mainly° were stirr'd up.
KING: O, for two special reasons;
   Which may to you, perhaps, seem much unsinew'd,°   10

SCENE 6. **12 means:** Means of access.   **16 thieves of mercy:** Merciful thieves.   **20 bore:**
Caliber, importance.   SCENE 7. **1 conscience:** Knowledge that this is true.   **7 capital:** Punishable by death.   **9 mainly:** Greatly.   **10 unsinew'd:** Weak.

But yet to me th' are strong. The queen his mother
Lives almost by his looks; and for myself—
My virtue or my plague, be it either which—
She's so conjunctive° to my life and soul,
That, as the star moves not but in his sphere,°   15
I could not but by her. The other motive,
Why to a public count° I might not go,
Is the great love the general gender° bear him;
Who, dipping all his faults in their affection,
Would, like the spring° that turneth wood to stone,   20
Convert his gyves° to graces; so that my arrows,
Too slightly timber'd° for so loud° a wind,
Would have reverted to my bow again,
And not where I had aim'd them.

LAERTES: And so have I a noble father lost;   25
A sister driven into desp'rate terms,°
Whose worth, if praises may go back° again,
Stood challenger on mount° of all the age°
For her perfections: but my revenge will come.

KING: Break not your sleeps for that: you must not think   30
That we are made of stuff so flat and dull
That we can let our beard be shook with danger
And think it pastime. You shortly shall hear more:
I lov'd your father, and we love ourself;
And that, I hope, will teach you to imagine—   35

Enter a Messenger with letters.

How now! what news?

MESSENGER: Letters, my lord, from Hamlet:
These to your majesty; this to the queen.°

KING: From Hamlet! who brought them?

MESSENGER: Sailors, my lord, they say; I saw them not:
They were given me by Claudio;° he receiv'd them   40
Of him that brought them.

KING: Laertes, you shall hear them.
Leave us.   *[Exit Messenger.]*
[Reads.] "High and mighty, You shall know I am set naked° on your king-
dom. Tomorrow shall I beg leave to see your kingly eyes: when I shall, first

14 **conjunctive:** Conformable (the next line suggesting planetary conjunction). 15 **sphere:**
The hollow sphere in which, according to Ptolemaic astronomy, the planets were supposed to
move. 17 **count:** Account, reckoning. 18 **general gender:** Common people. 20 **spring:**
I.e., one heavily charged with lime. 21 **gyves:** Fetters; here, faults, or possibly, punishments
inflicted (on him). 22 **slightly timber'd:** Light; **loud:** Strong. 26 **terms:** State, condition.
27 **go back:** Return to Ophelia's former virtues. 28 **on mount:** Set up on high; **mounted**
(on horseback); **of all the age:** Qualifies *challenger* and not *mount.* 37 **to the queen:** One
hears no more of the letter to the queen. 40 **Claudio:** This character does not appear in the
play. 43 **naked:** Unprovided (with retinue).

asking your pardon thereunto, recount the occasion of my sudden and   45
more strange return.   "HAMLET."
What should this mean? Are all the rest come back?
Or is it some abuse, and no such thing?

LAERTES: Know you the hand?

KING: 'Tis Hamlet's character. "Naked!"
And in a postscript here, he says "alone."   50
Can you devise° me?

LAERTES: I'm lost in it, my lord. But let him come;
It warms the very sickness in my heart,
That I shall live and tell him to his teeth,
"Thus didst thou."

KING: If it be so, Laertes —   55
As how should it be so? how otherwise?° —
Will you be rul'd by me?

LAERTES: Ay, my lord;
So you will not o'errule me to a peace.

KING: To thine own peace. If he be now return'd,
As checking at° his voyage, and that he means   60
No more to undertake it, I will work him
To an exploit, now ripe in my device,
Under the which he shall not choose but fall:
And for his death no wind of blame shall breathe,
But even his mother shall uncharge the practice°   65
And call it accident.

LAERTES: My lord, I will be rul'd;
The rather, if you could devise it so
That I might be the organ.°

KING: It falls right.
You have been talk'd of since your travel much,
And that in Hamlet's hearing, for a quality   70
Wherein, they say, you shine: your sum of parts
Did not together pluck such envy from him
As did that one, and that, in my regard,
Of the unworthiest siege.°

LAERTES: What part is that, my lord?

KING: A very riband in the cap of youth,   75
Yet needful too; for youth no less becomes
The light and careless livery that it wears
Than settled age his sables° and his weeds,

51 **devise:** Explain to.   56 **As . . . otherwise?** How can this (Hamlet's return) be true? (yet) how otherwise than true (since we have the evidence of his letter)? Some editors read *How should it not be so*, etc., making the words refer to Laertes's desire to meet with Hamlet. 60 **checking at:** Used in falconry of a hawk's leaving the quarry to fly at a chance bird; turn aside.   65 **uncharge the practice:** Acquit the stratagem of being a plot.   68 **organ:** Agent, instrument.   74 **siege:** Rank.   78 **sables:** Rich garments.

Importing health and graveness. Two months since,
Here was a gentleman of Normandy: —   80
I have seen myself, and serv'd against, the French,
And they can well° on horseback: but this gallant
Had witchcraft in 't; he grew unto his seat;
And to such wondrous doing brought his horse,
As had he been incorps'd and demi-natur'd°   85
With the brave beast: so far he topp'd° my thought,
That I, in forgery° of shapes and tricks,
Come short of what he did.

LAERTES: A Norman was 't?
KING: A Norman.
LAERTES: Upon my life, Lamord.°
KING: The very same.   90
LAERTES: I know him well: he is the brooch indeed
And gem of all the nation.
KING: He made confession° of you,
And gave you such a masterly report
For art and exercise° in your defence°   95
And for your rapier most especial,
That he cried out, 'twould be a sight indeed,
If one could match you: the scrimers° of their nation,
He swore, had neither motion, guard, nor eye,
If you oppos'd them. Sir, this report of his   100
Did Hamlet so envenom with his envy
That he could nothing do but wish and beg
Your sudden coming o'er, to play° with you.
Now, out of this, —
LAERTES: What out of this, my lord?
KING: Laertes, was your father dear to you?   105
Or are you like the painting of a sorrow,
A face without a heart?
LAERTES: Why ask you this?
KING: Not that I think you did not love your father;
But that I know love is begun by time;
And that I see, in passages of proof,°   110
Time qualifies the spark and fire of it.
There lives within the very flame of love
A kind of wick or snuff that will abate it;
And nothing is at a like goodness still;

---

82 **can well**: Are skilled.   85 **incorps'd and demi-natur'd**: Of one body and nearly of one
nature (like the centaur).   86 **topp'd**: Surpassed.   87 **forgery**: Invention.   90 **Lamord**:
This refers possibly to Pietro Monte, instructor to Louis XII's master of the horse.   93 **confession**: Grudging admission of superiority.   95 **art and exercise**: Skillful exercise; **defence**:
Science of defense in sword practice.   98 **scrimers**: Fencers.   103 **play**: Fence.   110 **passages of proof**: Proved instances.

For goodness, growing to a plurisy,°   115
Dies in his own too much:° that we would do,
We should do when we would; for this "would" changes
And hath abatements° and delays as many
As there are tongues, are hands, are accidents;°
And then this "should" is like a spendthrift° sigh,   120
That hurts by easing. But, to the quick o' th' ulcer:° —
Hamlet comes back: what would you undertake,
To show yourself your father's son in deed
More than in words?
LAERTES: To cut his throat i' th' church.
KING: No place, indeed, should murder sanctuarize;°   125
Revenge should have no bounds. But, good Laertes,
Will you do this, keep close within your chamber.
Hamlet return'd shall know you are come home:
We'll put on those shall praise your excellence
And set a double varnish on the fame   130
The Frenchman gave you, bring you in fine together
And wager on your heads: he, being remiss,
Most generous and free from all contriving,
Will not peruse the foils; so that, with ease,
Or with a little shuffling, you may choose   135
A sword unbated,° and in a pass of practice°
Requite him for your father.
LAERTES: I will do 't:
And, for that purpose, I'll anoint my sword.
I bought an unction of a mountebank,°
So mortal that, but dip a knife in it,   140
Where it draws blood no cataplasm° so rare,
Collected from all simples° that have virtue
Under the moon,° can save the thing from death
That is but scratch'd withal: I'll touch my point
With this contagion, that, if I gall° him slightly,   145
It may be death.
KING: Let's further think of this;
Weigh what convenience both of time and means
May fit us to our shape:° if this should fail,

---

115 **plurisy:** Excess, plethora.   116 **in his own too much:** Of its own excess.   118 **abatements:** Diminutions.   119 **accidents:** Occurrences, incidents.   120 **spendthrift:** An allusion to the belief that each sigh cost the heart a drop of blood.   121 **quick o' th' ulcer:** Heart of the difficulty.   125 **sanctuarize:** Protect from punishment; allusion to the right of sanctuary with which certain religious places were invested.   136 **unbated:** Not blunted, having no button; **pass of practice:** Treacherous thrust.   139 **mountebank:** Quack doctor.   141 **cataplasm:** Plaster or poultice.   142 **simples:** Herbs.   143 **Under the moon:** I.e., when collected by moonlight to add to their medicinal value.   145 **gall:** Graze, wound.   148 **shape:** Part we propose to act.

And that our drift look through our bad performance,°
'Twere better not assay'd: therefore this project   150
Should have a back or second, that might hold,
If this should blast in proof.° Soft! let me see:
We'll make a solemn wager on your cunnings:°
I ha 't:
When in your motion you are hot and dry—   155
As make your bouts more violent to that end—
And that he calls for drink, I'll have prepar'd him
A chalice° for the nonce, whereon but sipping,
If he by chance escape your venom'd stuck,°
Our purpose may hold there. But stay, what noise?   160

Enter Queen.

QUEEN: One woe doth tread upon another's heel,
    So fast they follow: your sister's drown'd, Laertes.
LAERTES: Drown'd! O, where?
QUEEN: There is a willow° grows askant° the brook,
    That shows his hoar° leaves in the glassy stream;   165
    There with fantastic garlands did she make
    Of crow-flowers,° nettles, daisies, and long purples°
    That liberal° shepherds give a grosser name,
    But our cold maids do dead men's fingers call them:
    There, on the pendent boughs her crownet° weeds   170
    Clamb'ring to hang, an envious sliver° broke;
    When down her weedy° trophies and herself
    Fell in the weeping brook. Her clothes spread wide;
    And, mermaid-like, awhile they bore her up:
    Which time she chanted snatches of old lauds;°   175
    As one incapable° of her own distress,
    Or like a creature native and indued°
    Upon that element: but long it could not be
    Till that her garments, heavy with their drink,
    Pull'd the poor wretch from her melodious lay   180
    To muddy death.
LAERTES: Alas, then, she is drown'd?
QUEEN: Drown'd, drown'd.
LAERTES: Too much of water hast thou, poor Ophelia,

---

149 **drift . . . performance**: Intention be disclosed by our bungling.   152 **blast in proof**: Burst in the test (like a cannon).   153 **cunnings**: Skills.   158 **chalice**: Cup.   159 **stuck**: Thrust (from *stoccado*).   164 **willow**: For its significance of forsaken love;   **askant**: Aslant.   165 **hoar**: White (i.e., on the underside).   167 **crow-flowers**: Buttercups;   **long purples**: Early purple orchids.   168 **liberal**: Probably, free-spoken.   170 **crownet**: Coronet; made into a chaplet.   171 **sliver**: Branch.   172 **weedy**: I.e., of plants.   175 **lauds**: Hymns. 176 **incapable**: Lacking capacity to apprehend.   177 **indued**: Endowed with qualities fitting her for living in water.

And therefore I forbid my tears: but yet
It is our trick;° nature her custom holds,   185
Let shame say what it will: when these are gone,
The woman will be out.° Adieu, my lord:
I have a speech of fire, that fain would blaze,
But that this folly drowns it.   *Exit.*

KING: Let's follow, Gertrude:
How much I had to do to calm his rage!   190
Now fear I this will give it start again;
Therefore let 's follow.   *Exeunt.*

[ACT 5, Scene 1]

[A churchyard.]
Enter two Clowns° [with spades, &c.].

FIRST CLOWN: Is she to be buried in Christian burial when she wilfully seeks
   her own salvation?

SECOND CLOWN: I tell thee she is; therefore make her grave straight:° the
   crowner° hath sat on her, and finds it Christian burial.

FIRST CLOWN: How can that be, unless she drowned herself in her own   5
   defence?

SECOND CLOWN: Why, 'tis found so.

FIRST CLOWN: It must be "se offendendo";° it cannot be else. For here lies the
   point: if I drown myself wittingly,° it argues an act: and an act hath three
   branches;° it is, to act, to do, and to perform: argal,° she drowned herself   10
   wittingly.

SECOND CLOWN: Nay, but hear you, goodman delver,° —

FIRST CLOWN: Give me leave. Here lies the water; good: here stands the man;
   good: if the man go to this water, and drown himself, it is, will he, nill he, he
   goes, — mark you that; but if the water come to him and drown him, he   15
   drowns not himself: argal, he that is not guilty of his own death shortens not
   his own life.

SECOND CLOWN: But is this law?

FIRST CLOWN: Ay, marry, is 't; crowner's quest° law.

SECOND CLOWN: Will you ha' the truth on 't? If this had not been a gentle-   20
   woman, she should have been buried out o' Christian burial.

---

185 **trick:** Way.   186–187 **when . . . out:** When my tears are all shed, the woman in me will
be satisfied.   **ACT 5, SCENE 1. Clowns:** The word *clown* was used to denote peasants as well as
humorous characters; here applied to the rustic type of clown.   **3 straight:** Straightway, immediately; some interpret "from east to west in a direct line, parallel with the church."
4 crowner: Coroner.   **8 "se offendendo":** For *se defendendo*, term used in verdicts of justifiable homicide.   **9 wittingly:** Intentionally.   **10 three branches:** Parody of legal phraseology;
argal: Corruption of *ergo*, therefore.   **12 delver:** Digger.   **19 quest:** Inquest.

FIRST CLOWN: Why, there thou say'st:° and the more pity that great folk
should have countenance° in this world to drown or hang themselves, more
than their even° Christian. Come, my spade. There is no ancient gentlemen but gardeners, ditchers, and grave-makers: they hold up° Adam's   25
profession.

SECOND CLOWN: Was he a gentleman?

FIRST CLOWN: 'A was the first that ever bore arms.

SECOND CLOWN: Why, he had none.

FIRST CLOWN: What, art a heathen? How dost thou understand the Scripture?   30
The Scripture says "Adam digged": could he dig without arms? I'll put
another question to thee: if thou answerest me not to the purpose, confess
thyself° —

SECOND CLOWN: Go to.°

FIRST CLOWN: What is he that builds stronger than either the mason, the ship-   35
wright, or the carpenter?

SECOND CLOWN: The gallows-maker; for that frame outlives a thousand tenants.

FIRST CLOWN: I like thy wit well, in good faith: the gallows does well; but how
does it well? it does well to those that do ill: now thou dost ill to say the gal-   40
lows is built stronger than the church: argal, the gallows may do well to thee.
To 't again, come.

SECOND CLOWN: "Who builds stronger than a mason, a shipwright, or a carpenter?"

FIRST CLOWN: Ay, tell me that, and unyoke.°   45

SECOND CLOWN: Marry, now I can tell.

FIRST CLOWN: To 't.

SECOND CLOWN: Mass,° I cannot tell.

Enter Hamlet and Horatio [at a distance].

FIRST CLOWN: Cudgel thy brains no more about it, for your dull ass will not
mend his pace with beating; and, when you are asked this question next, say   50
"a grave-maker": the houses he makes lasts till doomsday. Go, get thee in,
and fetch me a stoup° of liquor.   *[Exit Second Clown.] Song. [He digs.]*

In youth, when I did love, did love,
     Methought it was very sweet,
To contract — O — the time, for — a — my behove,°   55
     O, methought, there — a — was nothing — a — meet.

HAMLET: Has this fellow no feeling of his business, that 'a sings at grave-
making?

HORATIO: Custom hath made it in him a property of easiness.°

---

22 **there thou say'st**: That's right.   23 **countenance**: Privilege.   24 **even**: Fellow.   25 **hold
up**: Maintain, continue.   32–33 **confess thyself**: "And be hanged" completes the proverb.
34 **Go to**: Perhaps, "begin," or some other form of concession.   45 **unyoke**: After this great
effort you may unharness the team of your wits.   48 **Mass**: By the Mass.   52 **stoup**: Two-
quart measure.   55 **behove**: Benefit.   59 **property of easiness**: A peculiarity that now is easy.

HAMLET: 'Tis e'en so: the hand of little employment hath the daintier sense.   60
FIRST CLOWN: *(Song.)* But age, with his stealing steps,
    Hath claw'd me in his clutch,
And hath shipped me into the land
    As if I had never been such.   *[Throws up a skull.]*
HAMLET: That skull had a tongue in it, and could sing once: how the knave   65
jowls° it to the ground, as if 'twere Cain's jaw-bone,° that did the first murder!
This might be the pate of a politician,° which this ass now o'er-reaches;° one
that would circumvent God, might it not?
HORATIO: It might, my lord.
HAMLET: Or of a courtier; which could say "Good morrow, sweet lord! How   70
dost thou, sweet lord?" This might be my lord such-a-one, that praised my
lord such-a-one's horse, when he meant to beg it; might it not?
HORATIO: Ay, my lord.
HAMLET: Why, e'en so: and now my Lady Worm's; chapless,° and knocked
about the mazzard° with a sexton's spade: here's fine revolution, an we had   75
the trick to see 't. Did these bones cost no more the breeding, but to play at
loggats° with 'em? mine ache to think on 't.
FIRST CLOWN: *(Song.)* A pick-axe, and a spade, a spade,
    For and° a shrouding sheet:
O, a pit of clay for to be made   80
    For such a guest is meet.   *[Throws up another skull.]*
HAMLET: There's another: why may not that be the skull of a lawyer? Where be
his quiddities° now, his quillities,° his cases, his tenures,° and his tricks? why
does he suffer this mad knave now to knock him about the sconce° with a
dirty shovel, and will not tell him of his action of battery? Hum! This fellow   85
might be in 's time a great buyer of land, with his statutes, his recognizances,° his fines, his double vouchers,° his recoveries:° is this the fine° of
his fines, and the recovery of his recoveries, to have his fine pate full of fine
dirt? will his vouchers vouch him no more of his purchases, and double ones
too, than the length and breadth of a pair of indentures?° The very con-   90
veyances of his lands will scarcely lie in this box; and must the inheritor°
himself have no more, ha?
HORATIO: Not a jot more, my lord.
HAMLET: Is not parchment made of sheep-skins?
HORATIO: Ay, my lord, and of calf-skins° too.   95

---

66 jowls: Dashes;   **Cain's jaw-bone:** Allusion to the old tradition that Cain slew Abel with the jawbone of an ass.   **67 politician:** Schemer, plotter;   **o'er-reaches:** Quibble on the literal sense and the sense "circumvent."   **74 chapless:** Having no lower jaw.   **75 mazzard:** Head.   **77 loggats:** A game in which six sticks are thrown to lie as near as possible to a stake fixed in the ground, or block of wood on a floor.   **79 For and:** And moreover.   **83 quiddities:** Subtleties, quibbles; **quillities:** Verbal niceties, subtle distinctions;   **tenures:** The holding of a piece of property or office or the conditions or period of such holding.   **84 sconce:** Head.   **86–87 statutes, recognizances:** Legal terms connected with the transfer of land.   **87 vouchers:** Persons called on to warrant a tenant's title;   **recoveries:** Process for transfer of entailed estate;   **fine:** The four uses of this word are as follows: (1) end, (2) legal process, (3) elegant, (4) small.   **90 indentures:** Conveyances or contracts.   **91 inheritor:** Possessor, owner.   **95 calf-skins:** Parchments.

HAMLET: They are sheep and calves which seek out assurance in that.° I will
speak to this fellow. Whose grave's this, sirrah?

FIRST CLOWN: Mine, sir.

[Sings.] O, a pit of clay for to be made
    For such a guest is meet.   100

HAMLET: I think it be thine, indeed; for thou liest in 't.

FIRST CLOWN: You lie out on 't, sir, and therefore 't is not yours: for my part, I do
not lie in 't, yet it is mine.

HAMLET: Thou dost lie in 't, to be in 't and say it is thine: 'tis for the dead, not for
the quick; therefore thou liest.   105

FIRST CLOWN: 'Tis a quick lie, sir; 'twill away again, from me to you.

HAMLET: What man dost thou dig it for?

FIRST CLOWN: For no man, sir.

HAMLET: What woman, then?

FIRST CLOWN: For none, neither.   110

HAMLET: Who is to be buried in 't?

FIRST CLOWN: One that was a woman, sir; but, rest her soul, she's dead.

HAMLET: How absolute° the knave is! we must speak by the card,° or equivoca-
tion° will undo us. By the Lord, Horatio, these three years I have taken note
of it; the age is grown so picked° that the toe of the peasant comes so near the   115
heel of the courtier, he galls° his kibe.° How long hast thou been a grave-
maker?

FIRST CLOWN: Of all the day i' the year, I came to 't that day that our last king
Hamlet overcame Fortinbras.

HAMLET: How long is that since?   120

FIRST CLOWN: Cannot you tell that? every fool can tell that: it was the very day
that young Hamlet was born; he that is mad, and sent into England.

HAMLET: Ay, marry, why was he sent into England?

FIRST CLOWN: Why, because 'a was mad: 'a shall recover his wits there; or, if 'a
do not, 'tis no great matter there.   125

HAMLET: Why?

FIRST CLOWN: 'Twill not be seen in him there; there the men are as mad as he.

HAMLET: How came he mad?

FIRST CLOWN: Very strangely, they say.

HAMLET: How strangely?   130

FIRST CLOWN: Faith, e'en with losing his wits.

HAMLET: Upon what ground?

FIRST CLOWN: Why, here in Denmark: I have been sexton here, man and boy,
thirty years.°

HAMLET: How long will a man lie i' the earth ere he rot?   135

---

96 assurance in that: Safety in legal parchments.   **113 absolute:** Positive, decided;   **by the
card:** With precision, i.e., by the mariner's card on which the points of the compass were
marked.   **113–114 equivocation:** Ambiguity in the use of terms.   **115 picked:** Refined, fastidious.   **116 galls:** Chafes;   **kibe:** Chilblain.   **134 thirty years:** This statement with that in
line 122 shows Hamlet's age to be thirty years.

FIRST CLOWN: Faith, if 'a be not rotten before 'a die — as we have many pocky°
  corses now-a-days, that will scarce hold the laying in — 'a will last you some
  eight year or nine year: a tanner will last you nine year.

HAMLET: Why he more than another?

FIRST CLOWN: Why, sir, his hide is so tanned with his trade, that 'a will keep out   140
  water a great while; and your water is a sore decayer of your whoreson dead
  body. Here's a skull now hath lain you i' th' earth three and twenty years.

HAMLET: Whose was it?

FIRST CLOWN: A whoreson mad fellow's it was: whose do you think it was?

HAMLET: Nay, I know not.   145

FIRST CLOWN: A pestilence on him for a mad rogue! 'a poured a flagon of Rhen-
  ish on my head once. This same skull, sir, was Yorick's skull, the king's jester.

HAMLET: This?

FIRST CLOWN: E'en that.

HAMLET: Let me see. [*Takes the skull.*] Alas, poor Yorick! I knew him, Horatio: a   150
  fellow of infinite jest, of most excellent fancy: he hath borne me on his back
  a thousand times; and now, how abhorred in my imagination it is! my gorge
  rises at it. Here hung those lips that I have kissed I know not how oft. Where
  be your gibes now? your gambols? your songs? your flashes of merriment,
  that were wont to set the table on a roar? Not one now, to mock your own   155
  grinning? quite chap-fallen? Now get you to my lady's chamber, and tell her,
  let her paint an inch thick, to this favour she must come; make her laugh at
  that. Prithee, Horatio, tell me one thing.

HORATIO: What's that, my lord?

HAMLET: Dost thou think Alexander looked o' this fashion i' the earth?   160

HORATIO: E'en so.

HAMLET: And smelt so? pah!   [*Puts down the skull.*]

HORATIO: E'en so, my lord.

HAMLET: To what base uses we may return, Horatio! Why may not imagination
  trace the noble dust of Alexander, till 'a find it stopping a bung-hole?   165

HORATIO: 'Twere to consider too curiously,° to consider so.

HAMLET: No, faith, not a jot; but to follow him thither with modesty enough,
  and likelihood to lead it: as thus: Alexander died, Alexander was buried,
  Alexander returneth into dust; the dust is earth; of earth we make loam;° and
  why of that loam, whereto he was converted, might they not stop a beer-   170
  barrel?

  Imperious° Cæsar, dead and turn'd to clay,
  Might stop a hole to keep the wind away:
  O, that that earth, which kept the world in awe,
  Should patch a wall t'expel the winter's flaw!°   175
  But soft! but soft awhile! here comes the king,

*Enter King, Queen, Laertes, and the Corse of [Ophelia, in procession, with Priest,
Lords, etc.].*

---

136 pocky: Rotten, diseased.   **166 curiously:** Minutely.   **169 loam:** Clay paste for brick-
making.   **172 Imperious:** Imperial.   **175 flaw:** Gust of wind.

The queen, the courtiers: who is this they follow?
And with such maimed rites? This doth betoken
The corse they follow did with desp'rate hand
Fordo° it° own life: 'twas of some estate.   180
Couch° we awhile, and mark.   *[Retiring with Horatio.]*
LAERTES: What ceremony else?
HAMLET: That is Laertes,
   A very noble youth: mark.
LAERTES: What ceremony else?
FIRST PRIEST: Her obsequies have been as far enlarg'd°   185
   As we have warranty: her death was doubtful;
   And, but that great command o'ersways the order,
   She should in ground unsanctified have lodg'd
   Till the last trumpet; for charitable prayers,
   Shards,° flints and pebbles should be thrown on her: 190
   Yet here she is allow'd her virgin crants,°
   Her maiden strewments° and the bringing home
   Of bell and burial.°
LAERTES: Must there no more be done?
FIRST PRIEST: No more be done:
   We should profane the service of the dead   195
   To sing a requiem and such rest to her
   As to peace-parted° souls.
LAERTES: Lay her i' th' earth:
   And from her fair and unpolluted flesh
   May violets spring! I tell thee, churlish priest,
   A minist'ring angel shall my sister be,   200
   When thou liest howling.°
HAMLET: What, the fair Ophelia!
QUEEN: Sweets to the sweet: farewell!   *[Scattering flowers.]*
   I hop'd thou shouldst have been my Hamlet's wife;
   I thought thy bride-bed to have deck'd, sweet maid,
   And not have strew'd thy grave.
LAERTES: O, treble woe   205
   Fall ten times treble on that cursed head,
   Whose wicked deed thy most ingenious sense°
   Depriv'd thee of! Hold off the earth awhile,
   Till I have caught her once more in mine arms: *[Leaps into the grave.]*
   Now pile your dust upon the quick and dead,   210
   Till of this flat a mountain you have made,

---

180 **Fordo:** Destroy;   **it:** Its.   181 **Couch:** Hide, lurk.   185 **enlarg'd:** Extended, referring to the fact that suicides are not given full burial rites.   190 **Shards:** Broken bits of pottery.   191 **crants:** Garlands customarily hung upon the biers of unmarried women.   192 **strewments:** Traditional strewing of flowers.   192–193 **bringing . . . burial:** The laying to rest of the body, to the sound of the bell.   197 **peace-parted:** Allusion to the text "Lord, now lettest thou thy servant depart in peace."   201 **howling:** I.e., in hell.   207 **ingenious sense:** Mind endowed with finest qualities.

T' o'ertop old Pelion,° or the skyish head
Of blue Olympus.
HAMLET: [*Advancing*] What is he whose grief
    Bears such an emphasis? whose phrase of sorrow
    Conjures the wand'ring stars,° and makes them stand   215
    Like wonder-wounded hearers? This is I,
    Hamlet the Dane.   [*Leaps into the grave.*]
LAERTES: The devil take thy soul!   [*Grappling with him.*]
HAMLET: Thou pray'st not well.
    I prithee, take thy fingers from my throat;
    For, though I am not splenitive° and rash,   220
    Yet have I in me something dangerous,
    Which let thy wisdom fear: hold off thy hand.
KING: Pluck them asunder.
QUEEN: Hamlet, Hamlet!
ALL: Gentlemen,—
HORATIO: Good my lord, be quiet.

[*The Attendants part them, and they come out of the grave.*]

HAMLET: Why, I will fight with him upon this theme   225
    Until my eyelids will no longer wag.°
QUEEN: O my son, what theme?
HAMLET: I lov'd Ophelia: forty thousand brothers
    Could not, with all their quantity° of love,
    Make up my sum. What wilt thou do for her?   230
KING: O, he is mad, Laertes.
QUEEN: For love of God, forbear° him.
HAMLET: 'Swounds,° show me what thou 'lt do:
    Woo 't° weep? woo 't fight? woo 't fast? woo 't tear thyself?
    Woo 't drink up eisel?° eat a crocodile?   235
    I'll do 't. Dost thou come here to whine?
    To outface me with leaping in her grave?
    Be buried quick with her, and so will I:
    And, if thou prate of mountains, let them throw
    Millions of acres on us, till our ground,   240
    Singeing his pate against the burning zone,°
    Make Ossa like a wart! Nay, an thou 'lt mouth,
    I'll rant as well as thou.
QUEEN: This is mere madness:
    And thus awhile the fit will work on him;

---

212 **Pelion:** Olympus, Pelion, and Ossa are mountains in the north of Thessaly.   215 **wand'ring stars:** Planets.   220 **splenitive:** Quick-tempered.   226 **wag:** Move (not used ludicrously).   229 **quantity:** Some suggest that the word is used in a deprecatory sense (little bits, fragments).   232 **forbear:** Leave alone.   233 **'Swounds:** Oath, "God's wounds."   234 **Woo 't:** Wilt thou.   235 **eisel:** Vinegar. Some editors have taken this to be the name of a river, such as the Yssel, the Weissel, and the Nile.   241 **burning zone:** Sun's orbit.

Anon, as patient as the female dove. 245
When that her golden couplets° are disclos'd,
His silence will sit drooping.

HAMLET: Hear you, sir;
What is the reason that you use me thus?
I lov'd you ever: but it is no matter;
Let Hercules himself do what he may, 250
The cat will mew and dog will have his day.

KING: I pray thee, good Horatio, wait upon him. *Exit Hamlet and Horatio.*
[*To Laertes.*] Strengthen your patience in° our last night's speech;
We'll put the matter to the present push.°
Good Gertrude, set some watch over your son. 255
This grave shall have a living° monument:
An hour of quiet shortly shall we see;
Till then, in patience our proceeding be. *Exeunt.*

[Scene 2]

[*A hall in the castle.*]
Enter Hamlet and Horatio.

HAMLET: So much for this, sir: now shall you see the other;
You do remember all the circumstance?

HORATIO: Remember it, my lord!

HAMLET: Sir, in my heart there was a kind of fighting,
That would not let me sleep: methought I lay 5
Worse than the mutines in the bilboes.° Rashly,°
And prais'd be rashness for it, let us know,
Our indiscretion sometime serves us well,
When our deep plots do pall:° and that should learn us
There's a divinity that shapes our ends, 10
Rough-hew° them how we will, —

HORATIO: That is most certain.

HAMLET: Up from my cabin,
My sea-gown° scarf'd about me, in the dark
Grop'd I to find out them; had my desire,
Finger'd° their packet, and in fine° withdrew 15
To mine own room again; making so bold,
My fears forgetting manners, to unseal
Their grand commission; where I found, Horatio, —

---

246 **golden couplets:** The pigeon lays two eggs; the young when hatched are covered with golden down. 253 **in:** By recalling. 254 **present push:** Immediate test. 256 **living:** Lasting; also refers (for Laertes's benefit) to the plot against Hamlet. SCENE 2. 6 **mutines in the bilboes:** Mutineers in shackles; **Rashly:** Goes with line 12. 9 **pall:** Fail. 11 **Rough-hew:** Shape roughly; it may mean "bungle." 13 **sea-gown:** "A sea-gown, or a coarse, high-collered, and short-sleeved gowne, reaching down to the mid-leg, and used most by seamen and saylors" (Cotgrave, quoted by Singer). 15 **Finger'd:** Pilfered, filched; **in fine:** Finally.

O royal knavery!—an exact command,
Larded° with many several sorts of reasons   20
Importing Denmark's health and England's too,
With, ho! such bugs° and goblins in my life,°
That, on the supervise,° no leisure bated,°
No, not to stay the grinding of the axe,
My head should be struck off.
HORATIO: Is 't possible?   25
HAMLET: Here's the commission: read it at more leisure.
  But wilt thou hear me how I did proceed?
HORATIO: I beseech you.
HAMLET: Being thus be-netted round with villanies,—
  Ere I could make a prologue to my brains,   30
  They had begun the play°—I sat me down,
  Devis'd a new commission, wrote it fair:
  I once did hold it, as our statists° do,
  A baseness to write fair° and labour'd much
  How to forget that learning, but, sir, now   35
  It did me yeoman's° service: wilt thou know
  Th' effect of what I wrote?
HORATIO: Ay, good my lord.
HAMLET: An earnest conjuration from the king,
  As England was his faithful tributary,
  As love between them like the palm might flourish,   40
  As peace should still her wheaten garland° wear
  And stand a comma° 'tween their amities,
  And many such-like 'As'es° of great charge,°
  That, on the view and knowing of these contents,
  Without debatement further, more or less,   45
  He should the bearers put to sudden death,
  Not shriving-time° allow'd.
HORATIO: How was this seal'd?
HAMLET: Why, even in that was heaven ordinant.°
  I had my father's signet in my purse,
  Which was the model of that Danish seal;   50
  Folded the writ up in the form of th' other,
  Subscrib'd it, gave 't th' impression, plac'd it safely,
  The changeling never known. Now, the next day

---

20 Larded: Enriched.   **22 bugs:** Bugbears;   **such . . . life:** Such imaginary dangers if I were allowed to live.   **23 supervise:** Perusal;   **leisure bated:** Delay allowed.   **30–31 prologue . . . play:** I.e., before I could begin to think, my mind had made its decision.   **33 statists:** Statesmen.   **34 fair:** In a clear hand.   **36 yeoman's:** I.e., faithful.   **41 wheaten garland:** Symbol of peace.   **42 comma:** Smallest break or separation. Here *amity* begins and *amity* ends the period, and *peace* stands between like a dependent clause. The comma indicates continuity, link.   **43 'As'es:** The "whereases" of a formal document, with play on the word *ass;*   **charge:** Import, and burden.   **47 shriving-time:** Time for absolution.   **48 ordinant:** Directing.

Was our sea-fight; and what to this was sequent°
Thou know'st already.   55
HORATIO: So Guildenstern and Rosencrantz go to 't.
HAMLET: Why, man, they did make love to this employment;
They are not near my conscience; their defeat
Does by their own insinuation° grow:
'Tis dangerous when the baser nature comes   60
Between the pass° and fell incensed° points
Of mighty opposites.
HORATIO: Why, what a king is this!
HAMLET: Does it not, think thee, stand° me now upon —
He that hath kill'd my king and whor'd my mother,
Popp'd in between th' election° and my hopes,   65
Thrown out his angle° for my proper life,
And with such coz'nage° — is 't not perfect conscience,
To quit° him with this arm? and is 't not to be damn'd,
To let this canker° of our nature come
In further evil?   70
HORATIO: It must be shortly known to him from England
What is the issue of the business there.
HAMLET: It will be short: the interim is mine;
And a man's life's no more than to say "One."
But I am very sorry, good Horatio,   75
That to Laertes I forgot myself;
For, by the image of my cause, I see
The portraiture of his: I'll court his favours:
But, sure, the bravery° of his grief did put me
Into a tow'ring passion.
HORATIO: Peace! who comes here?   80

Enter a Courtier [Osric].

OSRIC: Your lordship is right welcome back to Denmark.
HAMLET: I humbly thank you, sir. *[To Horatio.]* Dost know this water-fly?°
HORATIO: No, my good lord.
HAMLET: Thy state is the more gracious; for 'tis a vice to know him. He hath
much land, and fertile: let a beast be lord of beasts,° and his crib shall stand   85
at the king's mess:° 'tis a chough;° but, as I say, spacious in the possession of
dirt.

---

54 **sequent:** Subsequent.   59 **insinuation:** Interference.   61 **pass:** Thrust;   **fell incensed:**
Fiercely angered.   63 **stand:** Become incumbent.   65 **election:** The Danish throne was
filled by election.   66 **angle:** Fishing line.   67 **coz'nage:** Trickery.   68 **quit:** Repay.
69 **canker:** Ulcer, or possibly the worm which destroys buds and leaves.   79 **bravery:**
Bravado.   82 **water-fly:** Vain or busily idle person.   85 **lord of beasts:** See Genesis 1:26, 28.
85–86 **his crib . . . mess:** He shall eat at the king's table and be one of the group of persons
(usually four) constituting a *mess* at a banquet.   86 **chough:** Probably, chattering jackdaw;
also explained as *chuff*, provincial boor or churl.

OSRIC: Sweet lord, if your lordship were at leisure, I should impart a thing to you from his majesty.

HAMLET: I will receive it, sir, with all diligence of spirit. Put your bonnet to his   90
right use; 'tis for the head.

OSRIC: I thank you lordship, it is very hot.

HAMLET: No, believe me, 'tis very cold; the wind is northerly.

OSRIC: It is indifferent° cold, my lord, indeed.

HAMLET: But yet methinks it is very sultry and hot for my complexion.   95

OSRIC: Exceedingly, my lord; it is very sultry, — as 'twere, — I cannot tell how.
But, my lord, his majesty bade me signify to you that 'a has laid a great wager
on your head: sir, this is the matter, —

HAMLET: I beseech you, remember° —   [*Hamlet moves him to put on his hat.*]

OSRIC: Nay, good my lord; for mine ease,° in good faith. Sir, here is newly come   100
to court Laertes; believe me, an absolute gentleman, full of most excellent
differences, of very soft° society and great showing:° indeed, to speak
feelingly° of him, he is the card° or calendar of gentry,° for you shall find in
him the continent of what part a gentleman would see.

HAMLET: Sir, his definement° suffers no perdition° in you; though, I know, to   105
divide him inventorially° would dozy° the arithmetic of memory, and yet but
yaw° neither, in respect of his quick sail. But, in the verity of extolment, I
take him to be a soul of great article;° and his infusion° of such dearth and
rareness,° as, to make true diction of him, his semblable° is his mirror; and
who else would trace° him, his umbrage,° nothing more.   110

OSRIC: Your lordship speaks most infallibly of him.

HAMLET: The concernancy,° sir? why do we wrap the gentleman in our more
rawer breath?°

OSRIC: Sir?

HORATIO [*aside to Hamlet*]:   Is 't not possible to understand in another tongue?°   115
You will do 't, sir, really.

HAMLET: What imports the nomination° of this gentleman?

OSRIC: Of Laertes?

Horatio [*aside to Hamlet*]:   His purse is empty already; all 's golden words are
spent.   120

HAMLET: Of him, sir.

---

94 **indifferent:** Somewhat.   99 **remember:** I.e., remember thy courtesy; conventional phrase
for "Be covered."   100 **mine ease:** Conventional reply declining the invitation of "Remember
thy courtesy."   102 **soft:** Gentle;   **showing:** Distinguished appearance.   103 **feelingly:**
With just perception;   **card:** Chart, map;   **gentry:** Good breeding.   105 **definement:** Definition;   **perdition:** Loss, diminution.   106 **divide him inventorially:** I.e., enumerate his
graces;   **dozy:** Dizzy.   107 **yaw:** To move unsteadily (of a ship).   108 **article:** Moment or
importance;   **infusion:** Infused temperament, character imparted by nature.
108–109 **dearth and rareness:** Rarity.   109 **semblable:** True likeness.   110 **trace:** Follow;
umbrage: Shadow.   112 **concernancy:** Import.   113 **breath:** Speech.   115 **Is 't . . . tongue?:**
I.e., can one converse with Osric only in this outlandish jargon?   117 **nomination:** Naming.

OSRIC: I know you are not ignorant—

HAMLET: I would you did, sir; yet, in faith, if you did, it would not much
approve° me. Well, sir?

OSRIC: You are not ignorant of what excellence Laertes is—   125

HAMLET: I dare not confess that, lest I should compare with him in excellence;
but, to know a man well, were to know himself.°

OSRIC: I mean, sir, for his weapon; but in the imputation° laid on him by
them, in his meed° he's unfellowed.

HAMLET: What's his weapon?   130

OSRIC: Rapier and dagger.

HAMLET: That's two of his weapons: but, well.

OSRIC: The king, sir, hath wagered with him six Barbary horses: against the
which he has impawned,° as I take it, six French rapiers and poniards, with
their assigns, as girdle, hangers,° and so: three of the carriages, in faith, are   135
very dear to fancy,° very responsive° to the hilts, most delicate° carriages, and
of very liberal conceit.°

HAMLET: What call you the carriages?

HORATIO *[aside to Hamlet]:*   I knew you must be edified by the margent° ere you
had done.   140

OSRIC: The carriages, sir, are the hangers.

HAMLET: The phrase would be more german° to the matter, if we could carry
cannon by our sides: I would it might be hangers till then. But, on: six Barbary horses against six French swords, their assigns, and three liberal-
conceited carriages; that's the French bet against the Danish. Why is this   145
"impawned," as you call it?

OSRIC: The king, sir, hath laid, that in a dozen passes between yourself and
him, he shall not exceed you three hits: he hath laid on twelve for nine; and
it would come to immediate trial, if your lordship would vouchsafe the
answer.   150

HAMLET: How if I answer "no"?

OSRIC: I mean, my lord, the opposition of your person in trial.

HAMLET: Sir, I will walk here in the hall: if it please his majesty, it is the breathing time° of day with me; let the foils be brought, the gentleman willing, and
the king hold his purpose, I will win for him as I can; if not, I will gain noth-   155
ing but my shame and the odd hits.

OSRIC: Shall I re-deliver you e'en so?

HAMLET: To this effect, sir; after what flourish your nature will.

OSRIC: I commend my duty to your lordship.

---

124 approve: Command.   **127 but . . . himself:** But to know a man as excellent were to
know Laertes.   **128 imputation:** Reputation.   **129 meed:** Merit.   **134 he has impawned:**
He has wagered.   **135 hangers:** Straps on the sword belt from which the sword hung.
136 dear to fancy: Fancifully made;   **responsive:** Probably, well balanced, corresponding
closely;   **delicate:** Fine in workmanship.   **137 liberal conceit:** Elaborate design.   **139 mar-
gent:** Margin of a book, place for explanatory notes.   **142 german:** Germane, appropriate.
153–154 breathing time: Exercise period.

HAMLET: Yours, yours. *[Exit Osric.]* He does well to commend it himself; there   160
are no tongues else for 's turn.

HORATIO: This lapwing° runs away with the shell on his head.

HAMLET: 'A did comply, sir, with his dug,° before 'a sucked it. Thus has hey—
and many more of the same breed that I know the drossy° age dotes on—
only got the tune° of the time and out of an habit of encounter;° a kind of   165
yesty° collection, which carries them through and through the most fann'd
and winnowed° opinions; and do but blow them to their trial, the bubbles
are out.°

Enter a Lord.

LORD: My lord, his majesty commended him to you by young Osric, who
brings back to him, that you attend him in the hall: he sends to know if your   170
pleasure hold to play with Laertes, or that you will take longer time.

HAMLET: I am constant to my purposes; they follow the king's pleasure: if his fit-
ness speaks, mine is ready; now or whensoever, provided I be so able as now.

LORD: The king and queen and all are coming down.

HAMLET: In happy time.°   175

LORD: The queen desires you to use some gentle entertainment to Laertes
before you fall to play.

HAMLET: She well instructs me.   *[Exit Lord.]*

HORATIO: You will lose this wager, my lord.

HAMLET: I do not think so; since he went into France, I have been in continual   180
practice; I shall win at the odds. But thou wouldst not think how ill all 's here
about my heart: but it is no matter.

HORATIO: Nay, good my lord,—

HAMLET: It is but foolery; but it is such a kind of gain-giving,° as would perhaps
trouble a woman.   185

HORATIO: If your mind dislike any thing, obey it: I will forestall their repair
hither, and say you are not fit.

HAMLET: Not a whit, we defy augury: there's a special providence in the fall of a
sparrow. If it be now, 'tis not to come; if it be not to come, it will be now; if it
be not now, yet it will come: the readiness is all:° since no man of aught he   190
leaves knows, what is 't to leave betimes? Let be.

*A table prepared. [Enter] Trumpets, Drums, and Officers with cushions; King,
Queen, [Osric,] and all the State; foils, daggers, [and wine borne in;] and Laertes.*

KING: Come, Hamlet, come, and take this hand from me.

[The King puts Laertes' hand into Hamlet's.]

---

162 **lapwing:** Peewit; noted for its wiliness in drawing a visitor away from its nest and its
supposed habit of running about when newly hatched with its head in the shell; possibly
an allusion to Osric's hat.   163 **did comply . . . dug:** Paid compliments to his mother's
breast.   164 **drossy:** Frivolous.   165 **tune:** Temper, mood; **habit of encounter:** Demeanor
of social intercourse.   166 **yesty:** Frothy.   166–167 **fann'd and winnowed:** Select and refined.
167–168 **blow . . . out:** I.e., put them to the test, and their ignorance is exposed.   175 **In happy
time:** A phrase of courtesy.   184 **gain-giving:** Misgiving.   190 **all:** All that matters.

HAMLET: Give me your pardon, sir: I have done you wrong;
    But pardon 't as you are a gentleman.
    This presence° knows,   195
    And you must needs have heard, how I am punish'd
    With a sore distraction. What I have done,
    That might your nature, honour and exception°
    Roughly awake, I here proclaim was madness.
    Was 't Hamlet wrong'd Laertes? Never Hamlet: 200
    If Hamlet from himself be ta'en away,
    And when he's not himself does wrong Laertes,
    Then Hamlet does it not, Hamlet denies it.
    Who does it, then? His madness: if 't be so,
    Hamlet is of the faction that is wrong'd;   205
    His madness is poor Hamlet's enemy.
    Sir, in this audience,
    Let my disclaiming from a purpos'd evil
    Free me so far in your most generous thoughts,
    That I have shot mine arrow o'er the house,   210
    And hurt my brother.

LAERTES: I am satisfied in nature,°
    Whose motive, in this case, should stir me most
    To my revenge: but in my terms of honour
    I stand aloof; and will no reconcilement,
    Till by some elder masters, of known honour,   215
    I have a voice° and precedent of peace,
    To keep my name ungor'd. But till that time,
    I do receive your offer'd love like love,
    And will not wrong it.

HAMLET: I embrace it freely;
    And will this brother's wager frankly play.   220
    Give us the foils. Come on.

LAERTES: Come, one for me.

HAMLET: I'll be your foil,° Laertes: in mine ignorance
    Your skill shall, like a star i' th' darkest night,
    Stick fiery off° indeed.

LAERTES: You mock me, sir.

HAMLET: No, by this hand.   225

KING: Give them the foils, young Osric. Cousin Hamlet,
    You know the wager?

HAMLET: Very well, my lord;
    Your grace has laid the odds o' th' weaker side.

---

195 presence: Royal assembly.   **198 exception:** Disapproval.   **211 nature:** I.e., he is personally satisfied, but his honor must be satisfied by the rules of the code of honor.   **216 voice:** Authoritative pronouncement.   **222 foil:** Quibble on the two senses: "background which sets something off," and "blunted rapier for fencing."   **224 Stick fiery off:** Stand out brilliantly.

KING: I do not fear it; I have seen you both:
    But since he is better'd, we have therefore odds.   230
LAERTES: This is too heavy, let me see another.
HAMLET: This likes me well. These foils have all a length?

[They prepare to play.]

OSRIC: Ay, my good lord.
KING: Set me the stoups of wine upon that table.
    If Hamlet give the first or second hit,   235
    Or quit in answer of the third exchange,
    Let all the battlements their ordnance fire;
    The king shall drink to Hamlet's better breath;
    And in the cup an union° shall he throw,
    Richer than that which four successive kings   240
    In Denmark's crown have worn. Give me the cups;
    And let the kettle° to the trumpet speak,
    The trumpet to the cannoneer without,
    The cannons to the heavens, the heavens to earth,
    "Now the king drinks to Hamlet." Come begin: *Trumpets the while.* 245
    And you, the judges, bear a wary eye.
HAMLET: Come on, sir.
LAERTES: Come, my lord.   *[They play.]*
HAMLET: One.
LAERTES: No.
HAMLET: Judgement.
OSRIC: A hit, a very palpable hit.

Drum, trumpets, and shot. Flourish. A piece goes off.

LAERTES: Well; again.
KING: Stay; give me drink. Hamlet, this pearl° is thine;
    Here's to thy health. Give him the cup.   250
HAMLET: I'll play this bout first; set it by awhile.
    Come. *[They play.]* Another hit; what say you?
LAERTES: A touch, a touch, I do confess 't.
KING: Our son shall win.
QUEEN: He's fat,° and scant of breath.
    Here, Hamlet, take my napkin, rub thy brows: 255
    The queen carouses° to thy fortune, Hamlet.
HAMLET: Good madam!
KING: Gertrude, do not drink.
QUEEN: I will, my lord; I pray you, pardon me.   *[Drinks.]*
KING *[aside]*:   It is the poison'd cup: it is too late.

---

239 union: Pearl.   **242 kettle:** Kettledrum.   **249 pearl:** I.e., the poison.   **254 fat:** Not physically fit, out of training. Some earlier editors speculated that the term applied to the corpulence of Richard Burbage, who originally played the part, but the allusion now appears unlikely. *Fat* may also suggest "sweaty."   **256 carouses:** Drinks a toast.

HAMLET: I dare not drink yet, madam; by and by.   260
QUEEN: Come, let me wipe thy face.
LAERTES: My lord, I'll hit him now.
KING: I do not think 't.
LAERTES [*aside*]:   And yet 'tis almost 'gainst my conscience.
HAMLET: Come, for the third, Laertes: you but dally;
    I pray you, pass with your best violence;   265
    I am afeard you make a wanton° of me.
LAERTES: Say you so? come on.   [*They play.*]
OSRIC: Nothing, neither way.
LAERTES: Have at you now!

[*Laertes wounds Hamlet; then, in scuffling, they change rapiers,° and Hamlet
wounds Laertes.*]

KING: Part them; they are incens'd.
HAMLET: Nay, come again.   [*The Queen falls.*]
OSRIC: Look to the queen there, ho!   270
HORATIO: They bleed on both sides. How is it, my lord?
OSRIC: How is 't, Laertes?
LAERTES: Why, as a woodcock° to mine own springe,° Osric;
    I am justly kill'd with mine own treachery.
HAMLET: How does the queen?
KING: She swounds° to see them bleed.   275
QUEEN: No, no, the drink, the drink, — O my dear Hamlet, —
    The drink, the drink! I am poison'd.   [*Dies.*]
HAMLET: O villany! Ho! let the door be lock'd:
    Treachery! Seek it out.   [*Laertes falls.*]
LAERTES: It is here, Hamlet: Hamlet, thou art slain;   280
    No med'cine in the world can do thee good;
    In thee there is not half an hour of life;
    The treacherous instrument is in thy hand,
    Unbated° and envenom'd: the foul practice
    Hath turn'd itself on me; lo, here I lie,   285
    Never to rise again: thy mother's poison'd:
    I can no more: the king, the king's to blame.
HAMLET: The point envenom'd too!
    Then, venom, to thy work.   [*Stabs the King.*]
ALL: Treason! treason!   290
KING: O, yet defend me, friends; I am but hurt.
HAMLET: Here, thou incestuous, murd'rous, damned Dane,
    Drink off this potion. Is thy union here?
    Follow my mother.   [*King dies.*]

---

266 **wanton:** Spoiled child;   **in scuffling, they change rapiers:** According to a widespread
stage tradition, Hamlet receives a scratch, realizes that Laertes's sword is unbated, and accordingly forces an exchange.   273 **woodcock:** As type of stupidity or as decoy;   **springe:** Trap,
snare.   275 **swounds:** Swoons.   284 **Unbated:** Not blunted with a button.

LAERTES: He is justly serv'd;
   It is a poison temper'd° by himself.   295
   Exchange forgiveness with me, noble Hamlet:
   Mine and my father's death come not upon thee,
   Nor thine on me!   *[Dies.]*
HAMLET: Heaven make thee free of it! I follow thee.
   I am dead, Horatio. Wretched queen, adieu!   300
   You that look pale and tremble at this chance,
   That are but mutes° or audience to this act,
   Had I but time — as this fell sergeant,° Death,
   Is strict in his arrest — O, I could tell you —
   But let it be. Horatio, I am dead;   305
   Thou livest; report me and my cause aright
   To the unsatisfied.
HORATIO: Never believe it:
   I am more an antique Roman° than a Dane:
   Here 's yet some liquor left.
HAMLET: As th' art a man,
   Give me the cup: let go, by heaven, I'll ha 't.   310
   O God! Horatio, what a wounded name,
   Things standing thus unknown, shall live behind me!
   If thou didst ever hold me in thy heart,
   Absent thee from felicity awhile,
   And in this harsh world draw thy breath in pain,   315
   To tell my story.   *A march afar off.*
        What warlike noise is this?
OSRIC: Young Fortinbras, with conquest come from Poland,
   To the ambassadors of England gives
   This warlike volley.
HAMLET: O, I die, Horatio;
   The potent poison quite o'er-crows° my spirit: 320
   I cannot live to hear the news from England;
   But I do prophesy th' election lights
   On Fortinbras: he has my dying voice;
   So tell him, with th' occurrents,° more and less,
   Which have solicited.° The rest is silence.   *[Dies.]* 325
HORATIO: Now cracks a noble heart. Good night, sweet prince;
   And flights of angels sing thee to thy rest!
   Why does the drum come hither?   *[March within.]*

Enter Fortinbras, with the [English] Ambassadors [and others].

FORTINBRAS: Where is this sight?

---

295 temper'd: Mixed.   **302 mutes:** Performers in a play who speak no words.   **303 sergeant:** Sheriff's officer.   **308 Roman:** It was the Roman custom to follow masters in death.   **320 o'er-crows:** Triumphs over.   **324 occurrents:** Events, incidents.   **325 solicited:** Moved, urged.

HORATIO: What is it you would see?
  If aught of woe or wonder, cease your search.   330
FORTINBRAS: This quarry° cries on havoc.° O proud Death,
  What feast is toward in thine eternal cell,
  That thou so many princes at a shot
  So bloodily hast struck?
FIRST AMBASSADOR: The sight is dismal;
  And our affairs from England come too late: 335
  The ears are senseless that should give us hearing,
  To tell him his commandment is fulfill'd,
  That Rosencrantz and Guildenstern are dead:
  Where should we have our thanks?
HORATIO: Not from his mouth,°
  Had it th' ability of life to thank you: 340
  He never gave commandment for their death.
  But since, so jump° upon this bloody question,°
  You from the Polack wars, and you from England,
  Are here arriv'd, give order that these bodies
  High on a stage° be placed to the view;   345
  And let me speak to th' yet unknowing world
  How these things came about: so shall you hear
  Of carnal, bloody, and unnatural acts,
  Of accidental judgements, casual slaughters,
  Of deaths put on by cunning and forc'd cause,   350
  And, in this upshot, purposes mistook
  Fall'n on th' inventors' heads: all this can I
  Truly deliver.
FORTINBRAS: Let us haste to hear it,
  And call the noblest to the audience.
  For me, with sorrow I embrace my fortune: 355
  I have some rights of memory° in this kingdom,
  Which now to claim my vantage doth invite me.
HORATIO: Of that I shall have also cause to speak,
  And from his mouth whose voice will draw on more:°
  But let this same be presently perform'd,   360
  Even while men's minds are wild; lest more mischance,
  On° plots and errors, happen.
FORTINBRAS: Let four captains
  Bear Hamlet, like a soldier, to the stage;
  For he was likely, had he been put on,
  To have prov'd most royal: and, for his passage,°   365

---

331 **quarry:** Heap of dead;   **cries on havoc:** Proclaims a general slaughter.   339 **his mouth:** I.e.,
the king's.   342 **jump:** Precisely;   **question:** Dispute.   345 **stage:** Platform.   356 **of memory:**
Traditional, remembered.   359 **voice . . . more:** Vote will influence still others.   362 **On:** On
account of, or possibly, on top of, in addition to.   365 **passage:** Death.

The soldiers' music and the rites of war
Speak loudly for him.
Take up the bodies: such a sight as this
Becomes the field,° but here shows much amiss.
Go, bid the soldiers shoot.   370

Exeunt [marching, bearing off the dead bodies; after which a peal of ordnance is shot off].   [c. 1600]

369 **field:** I.e., of battle.

THINKING ABOUT THE TEXT

1. Hamlet takes a long time to act on his father's request. Why does he delay? Should he have acted sooner, for example, when Claudius is praying?

2. In act 3, scene 4, Hamlet confronts his mother. After rereading this scene, what is your view of Hamlet's feelings toward his mother? Why do you think he uses such lurid imagery?

3. Contrast the relationship of Laertes and Polonius with that of Hamlet and his father. Is Laertes a more loyal son? Is Hamlet less devoted?

4. Some critics think that Hamlet idealizes his father's memory because he unconsciously resents his father. They also suggest that he cannot attach himself emotionally to Ophelia because he has not fully transferred his affection from his mother. Do you agree with these psychological interpretations? Why, or why not?

5. Make a list of all the family relationships in the play and characterize them as positive or negative, as healthy or troubled. Which relationship seems to you to be the most modern? The most ambiguous?

TENNESSEE WILLIAMS
The Glass Menagerie

Thomas Lanier "Tennessee" Williams (1911–1983) wrote some of the most famous plays of the American stage. The Glass Menagerie (1945), A Streetcar Named Desire (1948), Cat on a Hot Tin Roof (1955), Suddenly Last Summer (1958), and The Night of the Iguana (1961) all were made into popular and acclaimed films. His plays were considered shocking at the time since they dealt frankly with adultery, mental illness, homosexuality, and incest. His childhood was "lonely and miserable" largely because of his domineering, alcoholic father and because he was taunted for being small, sickly, and bookish. After many difficulties, he graduated from the University of Iowa in 1939 and immediately began writing fiction and drama. The Glass Menagerie is inspired by Williams's own troubled family situation. Laura is based on his, sister, Rose, who had numerous mental problems. Tom, of course, is modeled on

Williams and reflects his desire to escape the responsibilities of his family and live a life of adventure. Williams noted that leaving Rose was the most traumatic event of his life, one from which, like Tom, he never fully recovered.

> nobody,not even the rain,has such small hands
> —e. e. cummings

LIST OF CHARACTERS

AMANDA WINGFIELD, *the mother. A little woman of great but confused vitality clinging frantically to another time and place. Her characterization must be carefully created, not copied from type. She is not paranoiac, but her life is paranoia. There is much to admire in Amanda, and as much to love and pity as there is to laugh at. Certainly she has endurance and a kind of heroism, and though her foolishness makes her unwittingly cruel at times, there is tenderness in her slight person.*

LAURA WINGFIELD, *her daughter. Amanda, having failed to establish contact with reality, continues to live vitally in her illusions, but Laura's situation is even graver. A childhood illness has left her crippled, one leg slightly shorter than the other, and held in a brace. This defect need not be more than suggested on the stage. Stemming from this, Laura's separation increases till she is like a piece of her own glass collection, too exquisitely fragile to move from the shelf.*

TOM WINGFIELD, *her son. And the narrator of the play. A poet with a job in a warehouse. His nature is not remorseless, but to escape from a trap he has to act without pity.*

JIM O'CONNOR, *the gentleman caller. A nice, ordinary, young man.*

SCENE: *An alley in St. Louis.*
PART I: *Preparation for a Gentleman Caller.*
PART II: *The Gentleman Calls.*
TIME: *Now and the Past.*

Scene 1

The Wingfield apartment is in the rear of the building, one of those vast hivelike conglomerations of cellular living-units that flower as warty growths in overcrowded urban centers of lower middle-class population and are symptomatic of the impulse of this largest and fundamentally enslaved section of American society to avoid fluidity and differentiation and to exist and function as one interfused mass of automatism.

The apartment faces an alley and is entered by a fire-escape, a structure whose name is a touch of accidental poetic truth, for all of these huge buildings are always burning with the slow and implacable fires of human desperation. The fire-escape is included in the set—that is, the landing of it and steps descending from it.

The scene is memory and is therefore nonrealistic. Memory takes a lot of poetic license. It omits some details; others are exaggerated, according to the emotional value of the articles it touches, for memory is seated predominantly in the heart. The interior is therefore rather dim and poetic.

At the rise of the curtain, the audience is faced with the dark, grim rear wall of the Wingfield tenement. This building, which runs parallel to the footlights, is flanked on both sides by dark, narrow alleys which run into murky canyons of tangled clotheslines, garbage cans, and the sinister latticework of neighboring fire-escapes. It is up and down these side alleys that exterior entrances and exits are made, during the play. At the end of Tom's opening commentary, the dark tenement wall slowly reveals (by means of a transparency) the interior of the ground floor Wingfield apartment.

Downstage is the living room, which also serves as a sleeping room for Laura, the sofa unfolding to make her bed. Upstage, center, and divided by a wide arch or second proscenium with transparent faded portieres (or second curtain), is the din-ing room. In an old-fashioned what-not in the living room are seen scores of trans-parent glass animals. A blown-up photograph of the father hangs on the wall of the living room, facing the audience, to the left of the archway. It is the face of a very handsome young man in a doughboy's First World War cap. He is gallantly smil-ing, ineluctably smiling, as if to say, "I will be smiling forever."

The audience hears and sees the opening scene in the dining room through both the transparent fourth wall of the building and the transparent gauze portieres of the dining-room arch. It is during this revealing scene that the fourth wall slowly ascends, out of sight. This transparent exterior wall is not brought down again until the very end of the play, during Tom's final speech.

The narrator is an undisguised convention of the play. He takes whatever license with dramatic convention as is convenient to his purposes.

Tom enters dressed as a merchant sailor from alley, stage left, and strolls across the front of the stage to the fire-escape. There he stops and lights a cigarette. He addresses the audience.

TOM: Yes, I have tricks in my pocket, I have things up my sleeve. But I am the opposite of a stage magician. He gives you illusion that has the appearance of truth. I give you truth in the pleasant disguise of illusion. To begin with, I turn back time. I reverse it to that quaint period, the thirties, when the huge middle class of America was matriculating in a school for the blind. Their eyes had failed them, or they had failed their eyes, and so they were having their fingers pressed forcibly down on the fiery Braille alphabet of a dissolving economy. In Spain there was revolution. Here there was only shouting and confusion. In Spain there was Guernica.° Here there were disturbances of labor, sometimes pretty violent, in otherwise peaceful cities such as Chicago, Cleveland, Saint Louis. . . . This is the social background of the play.

(Music.)

The play is memory. Being a memory play, it is dimly lighted, it is senti-mental, it is not realistic. In memory everything seems to happen to music. That explains the fiddle in the wings. I am the narrator of the play, and also a character in it. The other characters are my mother, Amanda, my sister,

---

Guernica: A town in northern Spain destroyed by German bombers in 1937 during the Span-ish Civil War.

Laura, and a gentleman caller who appears in the final scenes. He is the most realistic character in the play, being an emissary from a world of reality that we were somehow set apart from. But since I have a poet's weakness for symbols, I am using this character also as a symbol; he is the long delayed but always expected something that we live for. There is a fifth character in the play who doesn't appear except in this larger-than-life photograph over the mantel. This is our father who left us a long time ago. He was a telephone man who fell in love with long distances; he gave up his job with the telephone company and skipped the light fantastic out of town. . . . The last we heard of him was a picture post-card from Mazatlán, on the Pacific coast of Mexico, containing a message of two words — "Hello — Good-bye!" and no address. I think the rest of the play will explain itself. . . .

Amanda's voice becomes audible through the portieres.

(*Legend on screen: "Où sont les neiges."°*)

> *He divides the portieres and enters the upstage area.*
> *Amanda and Laura are seated at a drop-leaf table. Eating is indicated by gestures without food or utensils. Amanda faces the audience.*
> *Tom and Laura are seated in profile.*
> *The interior has lit up softly and through the scrim we see Amanda and Laura seated at the table in the upstage area.*

AMANDA (*calling*):   Tom?

TOM: Yes, Mother.

AMANDA: We can't say grace until you come to the table!

TOM: Coming, Mother. (*He bows slightly and withdraws, reappearing a few moments later in his place at the table.*)

AMANDA (*to her son*):   Honey, don't *push* with your *fingers*. If you have to push with something, the thing to push with is a crust of bread. And chew — chew! Animals have sections in their stomachs which enable them to digest food without mastication, but human beings are supposed to chew their food before they swallow it down. Eat food leisurely, son, and really enjoy it. A well-cooked meal has lots of delicate flavors that have to be held in the mouth for appreciation. So chew your food and give your salivary glands a chance to function!

Tom deliberately lays his imaginary fork down and pushes his chair back from the table.

TOM: I haven't enjoyed one bite of this dinner because of your constant directions on how to eat it. It's you that makes me rush through meals with your hawklike attention to every bite I take. Sickening — spoils my appetite — all this discussion of animals' secretion — salivary glands — mastication!

AMANDA (*lightly*):   Temperament like a Metropolitan star! (*He rises and crosses downstage.*) You're not excused from the table.

TOM: I am getting a cigarette.

Où sont les neiges: Part of a line from a poem by the French medieval writer François Villon; the full line translates, "Where are the snows of yesteryear?"

AMANDA: You smoke too much.

Laura rises.

LAURA: I'll bring in the blanc mange.

He remains standing with his cigarette by the portieres during the following.

AMANDA *(rising):* No, sister, no, sister — you be the lady this time and I'll be the darky.

LAURA: I'm already up.

AMANDA: Resume your seat, little sister — I want you to stay fresh and pretty — for gentlemen callers!

LAURA: I'm not expecting any gentlemen callers.

AMANDA *(crossing out to kitchenette. Airily):* Sometimes they come when they are least expected! Why, I remember one Sunday afternoon in Blue Mountain — *(Enters kitchenette.)*

TOM: I know what's coming!

LAURA: Yes. But let her tell it.

TOM: Again?

LAURA: She loves to tell it.

Amanda returns with bowl of dessert.

AMANDA: One Sunday afternoon in Blue Mountain — your mother received — seventeen! — gentlemen callers! Why, sometimes there weren't chairs enough to accommodate them all. We had to send the nigger over to bring in folding chairs from the parish house.

TOM *(remaining at portieres):* How did you entertain those gentlemen callers?

AMANDA: I understood the art of conversation!

TOM: I bet you could talk.

AMANDA: Girls in those days knew how to talk, I can tell you.

TOM: Yes?

(Image: Amanda as a girl on a porch greeting callers.)

AMANDA: They knew how to entertain their gentlemen callers. It wasn't enough for a girl to be possessed of a pretty face and a graceful figure — although I wasn't slighted in either respect. She also needed to have a nimble wit and a tongue to meet all occasions.

TOM: What did you talk about?

AMANDA: Things of importance going on in the world! Never anything coarse or common or vulgar. *(She addresses Tom as though he were seated in the vacant chair at the table though he remains by portieres. He plays this scene as though he held the book.)* My callers were gentlemen — all! Among my callers were some of the most prominent young planters of the Mississippi Delta — planters and sons of planters!

Tom motions for music and a spot of light on Amanda.
Her eyes lift, her face glows, her voice becomes rich and elegiac.
(Screen legend: "Où sont les neiges.")

There was young Champ Laughlin who later became vice-president of the Delta Planters Bank. Hadley Stevenson who was drowned in Moon Lake and left his widow one hundred and fifty thousand in Government bonds. There were the Cutrere brothers, Wesley and Bates. Bates was one of my bright particular beaux! He got in a quarrel with that wild Wainright boy. They shot it out on the floor of Moon Lake Casino. Bates was shot through the stomach. Died in the ambulance on his way to Memphis. His widow was also well-provided for, came into eight or ten thousand acres, that's all. She married him on the rebound—never loved her—carried my picture on him the night he died! And there was that boy that every girl in the Delta had set her cap for! That beautiful, brilliant young Fitzhugh boy from Green County!

TOM: What did he leave his widow?

AMANDA: He never married! Gracious, you talk as though all of my old admirers had turned up their toes to the daisies!

TOM: Isn't this the first you mentioned that still survives?

AMANDA: That Fitzhugh boy went North and made a fortune—came to be known as the Wolf of Wall Street! He had the Midas touch, whatever he touched turned to gold! And I could have been Mrs. Duncan J. Fitzhugh, mind you! But—I picked your *father!*

LAURA *(rising):*   Mother, let me clear the table.

AMANDA: No dear, you go in front and study your typewriter chart. Or practice your shorthand a little. Stay fresh and pretty!—It's almost time for our gentlemen callers to start arriving. *(She flounces girlishly toward the kitchenette.)* How many do you suppose we're going to entertain this afternoon?

Tom throws down the paper and jumps up with a groan.

LAURA *(alone in the dining room):*   I don't believe we're going to receive any, Mother.

AMANDA *(reappearing, airily):*   What? No one—not one? You must be joking! *(Laura nervously echoes her laugh. She slips in a fugitive manner through the half-open portieres and draws them gently behind her. A shaft of very clear light is thrown on her face against the faded tapestry of the curtains.) (Music: "The Glass Menagerie" under faintly.) (Lightly.)* Not one gentleman caller? It can't be true! There must be a flood, there must have been a tornado!

LAURA: It isn't a flood, it's not a tornado, Mother. I'm just not popular like you were in Blue Mountain. . . . *(Tom utters another groan. Laura glances at him with a faint, apologetic smile. Her voice catching a little.)* Mother's afraid I'm going to be an old maid.

(The scene dims out with "Glass Menagerie" music.)

Scene 2

"Laura, Haven't You Ever Liked Some Boy?"

On the dark stage the screen is lighted with the image of blue roses.
    Gradually Laura's figure becomes apparent and the screen goes out.

The music subsides.

Laura is seated in the delicate ivory chair at the small clawfoot table.

She wears a dress of soft violet material for a kimono — her hair tied back from her forehead with a ribbon.

She is washing and polishing her collection of glass.

Amanda appears on the fire-escape steps. At the sound of her ascent, Laura catches her breath, thrusts the bowl of ornaments away, and seats herself stiffly before the diagram of the typewriter keyboard as though it held her spellbound. Something has happened to Amanda. It is written in her face as she climbs to the landing: a look that is grim and hopeless and a little absurd.

She has on one of those cheap or imitation velvety-looking cloth coats with imitation fur collar. Her hat is five or six years old, one of those dreadful cloche hats that were worn in the late twenties, and she is clasping an enormous black patent-leather pocketbook with nickel clasp and initials. This is her full-dress outfit, the one she usually wears to the D.A.R.°

Before entering she looks through the door.

She purses her lips, opens her eyes wide, rolls them upward, and shakes her head.

Then she slowly lets herself in the door. Seeing her mother's expression Laura touches her lips with a nervous gesture.

LAURA: Hello, Mother, I was — *(She makes a nervous gesture toward the chart on the wall. Amanda leans against the shut door and stares at Laura with a martyred look.)*

AMANDA: Deception? Deception? *(She slowly removes her hat and gloves, continuing the swift suffering stare. She lets the hat and gloves fall on the floor — a bit of acting.)*

LAURA *(shakily):*   How was the D.A.R. meeting? *(Amanda slowly opens her purse and removes a dainty white handkerchief, which she shakes out delicately and delicately touches to her lips and nostrils.)* Didn't you go to the D.A.R. meeting, Mother?

AMANDA *(faintly, almost inaudibly):*   — No. — No. *(Then more forcibly.)* I did not have the strength — to go to the D.A.R. In fact, I did not have the courage! I wanted to find a hole in the ground and hide myself in it forever! *(She crosses slowly to the wall and removes the diagram of the typewriter keyboard. She holds it in front of her for a second, staring at it sweetly and sorrowfully — then bites her lips and tears it in two pieces.)*

LAURA *(faintly):*   Why did you do that, Mother? *(Amanda repeats the same procedure with the chart of the Gregg Alphabet.°)* Why are you —

AMANDA: Why? Why? How old are you, Laura?

LAURA: Mother, you know my age.

D.A.R.: Daughters of the American Revolution; members must document that they have ancestors who served the patriots' cause in the Revolutionary War.
Gregg Alphabet: System of shorthand symbols invented by John Robert Gregg.

AMANDA: I thought that you were an adult; it seems that I was mistaken. *(She crosses slowly to the sofa and sinks down and stares at Laura.)*

LAURA: Please don't stare at me, Mother.

Amanda closes her eyes and lowers her head. Count ten.

AMANDA: What are we going to do, what is going to become of us, what is the future?

Count ten.

LAURA: Has something happened, Mother? *(Amanda draws a long breath and takes out the handkerchief again. Dabbing process.)* Mother, has—something happened?

AMANDA: I'll be all right in a minute. I'm just bewildered—*(count five)*—by life. . . .

LAURA: Mother, I wish that you would tell me what's happened.

AMANDA: As you know, I was supposed to be inducted into my office at the D.A.R. this afternoon. *(Image: A swarm of typewriters.)* But I stopped off at Rubicam's Business College to speak to your teachers about your having a cold and ask them what progress they thought you were making down there.

LAURA: Oh. . . .

AMANDA: I went to the typing instructor and introduced myself as your mother. She didn't know who you were. Wingfield, she said. We don't have any such student enrolled at the school! I assured her she did, that you had been going to classes since early in January. "I wonder," she said, "if you could be talking about that terribly shy little girl who dropped out of school after only a few days' attendance?" "No," I said, "Laura, my daughter, has been going to school every day for the past six weeks!" "Excuse me," she said. She took the attendance book out and there was your name, unmistakably printed, and all the dates you were absent until they decided that you had dropped out of school. I still said, "No, there must have been some mistake! There must have been some mix-up in the records!" And she said, "No—I remember her perfectly now. Her hand shook so that she couldn't hit the right keys! The first time we gave a speed-test, she broke down completely—was sick at the stomach and almost had to be carried into the wash-room! After that morning she never showed up any more. We phoned the house but never got any answer"—while I was working at Famous and Barr, I suppose, demonstrating those—Oh! I felt so weak I could barely keep on my feet. I had to sit down while they got me a glass of water! Fifty dollars' tuition, all of our plans—my hopes and ambitions for you—just gone up the spout, just gone up the spout like that. *(Laura draws a long breath and gets awkwardly to her feet. She crosses to the Victrola, and winds it up.)* What are you doing?

LAURA: Oh! *(She releases the handle and returns to her seat.)*

AMANDA: Laura, where have you been going when you've gone out pretending that you were going to business college?

LAURA: I've just been going out walking.

AMANDA: That's not true.

LAURA: It is. I just went walking.

AMANDA: Walking? Walking? In winter? Deliberately courting pneumonia in that light coat? Where did you walk to, Laura?

LAURA: It was the lesser of two evils, Mother. *(Image: Winter scene in park.)* I couldn't go back up. I—threw up—on the floor!

AMANDA: From half past seven till after five every day you mean to tell me you walked around in the park, because you wanted to make me think that you were still going to Rubicam's Business College?

LAURA: It wasn't as bad as it sounds. I went inside places to get warmed up.

AMANDA: Inside where?

LAURA: I went in the art museum and the bird-houses at the Zoo. I visited the penguins every day! Sometimes I did without lunch and went to the movies. Lately I've been spending most of my afternoons in the Jewel-box, that big glass house where they raise the tropical flowers.

AMANDA: You did all this to deceive me, just for the deception? *(Laura looks down.)* Why?

LAURA: Mother, when you're disappointed, you get that awful suffering look on your face, like the picture of Jesus' mother in the museum!

AMANDA: Hush!

LAURA: I couldn't face it.

Pause. A whisper of strings.
(Legend: "The Crust of Humility.")

AMANDA *(hopelessly fingering the huge pocketbook):*   So what are we going to do the rest of our lives? Stay home and watch the parades go by? Amuse ourselves with the glass menagerie, darling? Eternally play those worn-out phonograph records your father left as a painful reminder of him? We won't have a business career—we've given that up because it gave us nervous indigestion! *(Laughs wearily.)* What is there left but dependency all our lives? I know so well what becomes of unmarried women who aren't prepared to occupy a position. I've seen such pitiful cases in the South—barely tolerated spinsters living upon the grudging patronage of sister's husband or brother's wife!—stuck away in some little mousetrap of a room—encouraged by one in-law to visit another—little birdlike women without any nest—eating the crust of humility all their life! Is that the future that we've mapped out for ourselves? I swear it's the only alternative I can think of! It isn't a very pleasant alternative, is it? Of course—some girls *do marry. (Laura twists her hands nervously.)* Haven't you ever liked some boy?

LAURA: Yes. I liked one once. *(Rises.)* I came across his picture a while ago.

AMANDA *(with some interest):*   He gave you his picture?

LAURA: No, it's in the year-book.

AMANDA *(disappointed):*   Oh—a high-school boy.

(Screen image: Jim as a high-school hero bearing a silver cup.)

LAURA: Yes. His name was Jim. *(Laura lifts the heavy annual from the clawfoot table.)* Here he is in *The Pirates of Penzance.*

AMANDA (*absently*):   The what?

LAURA: The operetta the senior class put on. He had a wonderful voice and we sat across the aisle from each other Mondays, Wednesdays, and Fridays in the Aud. Here he is with the silver cup for debating! See his grin?

AMANDA (*absently*):   He must have had a jolly disposition.

LAURA: He used to call me — Blue Roses.

(*Image: Blue roses.*)

AMANDA: Why did he call you such a name as that?

LAURA: When I had that attack of pleurosis — he asked me what was the matter when I came back. I said pleurosis — he thought that I said Blue Roses! So that's what he always called me after that. Whenever he saw me, he'd holler, "Hello, Blue Roses!" I didn't care for the girl that he went out with. Emily Meisenbach. Emily was the best-dressed girl at Soldan. She never struck me, though, as being sincere. . . . It says in the Personal Section — they're engaged. That's — six years ago! They must be married by now.

AMANDA: Girls that aren't cut out for business careers usually wind up married to some nice man. (*Gets up with a spark of revival.*) Sister, that's what you'll do!

Laura utters a startled, doubtful laugh. She reaches quickly for a piece of glass.

LAURA: But, Mother —

AMANDA: Yes? (*Crossing to photograph.*)

LAURA (*in a tone of frightened apology*):   I'm — crippled!

(*Image: Screen.*)

AMANDA: Nonsense! Laura, I've told you never, never to use that word. Why, you're not crippled, you just have a little defect — hardly noticeable, even! When people have some slight disadvantage like that, they cultivate other things to make up for it — develop charm — and vivacity — and — *charm*! That's all you have to do! (*She turns again to the photograph.*) One thing your father had *plenty of* — was *charm*!

Tom motions to the fiddle in the wings.

(*The scene fades out with music.*)

Scene 3

(*Legend on the screen: "After the Fiasco —"*)
Tom speaks from the fire-escape landing.

TOM: After the fiasco at Rubicam's Business College, the idea of getting a gentleman caller for Laura began to play a more important part in Mother's calculations. It became an obsession. Like some archetype of the universal unconscious, the image of the gentleman caller haunted our small apartment. . . . (*Image: Young man at door with flowers.*) An evening at home rarely passed without some allusion to this image, this specter, this hope. . . . Even when he wasn't mentioned, his presence hung in Mother's preoccupied look and in my sister's frightened, apologetic manner — hung like a sentence passed upon the Wingfields! Mother was a woman of action as well as words. She began to take logical steps in the planned direction. Late that winter and in the early spring—realizing that extra money would be needed to properly feather the nest and plume the bird—she conducted a vigorous campaign on the telephone, roping in subscribers to one of those magazines for matrons called *The Home-maker's Companion*, the type of journal that features the serialized sublimations of ladies of letters who think in terms of delicate cuplike breasts, slim, tapering waists, rich, creamy thighs, eyes like wood-smoke in autumn, fingers that soothe and caress like strains of music, bodies as powerful as Etruscan sculpture.

(Screen image: Glamour *magazine cover.)*
Amanda enters with phone on long extension cord. She is spotted in the dim stage.

AMANDA: Ida Scott? This is Amanda Wingfield! We *missed* you at the D.A.R. last Monday! I said to myself: She's probably suffering with that sinus condition! How is that sinus condition? Horrors! Heaven have mercy!—You're a Christian martyr, yes, that's what you are, a Christian martyr! Well, I just now happened to notice that your subscription to the *Companion's* about to expire! Yes, it expires with the next issue, honey!—just when that wonderful new serial by Bessie Mae Hopper is getting off to such an exciting start. Oh, honey, it's something that you can't miss! You remember how *Gone with the Wind* took everybody by storm? You simply couldn't go out if you hadn't read it. All everybody *talked* was Scarlett O'Hara. Well, this is a book that critics already compare to *Gone with the Wind*. It's the *Gone with the Wind* of the post–World War generation!—What?—Burning?—Oh, honey, don't let them burn, go take a look in the oven and I'll hold the wire! Heavens—I think she's hung up!

(Dim out.)
(Legend on screen: "You think I'm in love with Continental Shoemakers?")
Before the stage is lighted, the violent voices of Tom and Amanda are heard. They are quarreling behind the portieres. In front of them stands Laura with clenched hands and panicky expression.
A clear pool of light on her figure throughout this scene.

TOM: What in Christ's name am I—
AMANDA *(shrilly):*   Don't you use that—
TOM: Supposed to do!
AMANDA: Expression! Not in my—
TOM: Ohhh!
AMANDA: Presence! Have you gone out of your senses?
TOM: I have, that's true, *driven* out!
AMANDA: What is the matter with you, you—big—big—IDIOT!
TOM: Look—I've got *no thing*, no single thing—
AMANDA: Lower your voice!
TOM: In my life here that I can call my own! Everything is—
AMANDA: Stop that shouting!

TOM: Yesterday you confiscated my books! You had the nerve to—

AMANDA: I took that horrible novel back to the library—yes! That hideous book by that insane Mr. Lawrence.° *(Tom laughs wildly.)* I cannot control the output of diseased minds or people who cater to them—*(Tom laughs still more wildly.)* BUT I WON'T ALLOW SUCH FILTH BROUGHT INTO MY HOUSE! No, no, no, no, no!

TOM: House, house! Who pays rent on it, who makes a slave of himself to—

AMANDA *(fairly screeching):* Don't you DARE to—

TOM: No, no, I mustn't say things! *I've* got to just—

AMANDA: Let me tell you—

TOM: I don't want to hear any more! *(He tears the portieres open. The upstage area is lit with a turgid smoky red glow.)*

Amanda's hair is in metal curlers and she wears a very old bathrobe, much too large for her slight figure, a relic of the faithless Mr. Wingfield.

An upright typewriter and a wild disarray of manuscripts are on the drop-leaf table. The quarrel was probably precipitated by Amanda's interruption of his creative labor. A chair lying overthrown on the floor.

Their gesticulating shadows are cast on the ceiling by the fiery glow.

AMANDA: You *will* hear more, you—

TOM: No, I won't hear more, I'm going out!

AMANDA: You come right back in—

TOM: Out, out, out! Because I'm—

AMANDA: Come back here, Tom Wingfield! I'm not through talking to you!

TOM: Oh, go—

LAURA *(desperately):* Tom!

AMANDA: You're going to listen, and no more insolence from you! I'm at the end of my patience! *(He comes back toward her.)*

TOM: What do you think I'm at? Aren't I supposed to have any patience to reach the end of, Mother? I know, I know. It seems unimportant to you, what I'm *doing*—what I *want* to do—having a little *difference* between them! You don't think that—

AMANDA: I think you've been doing things that you're ashamed of. That's why you act like this. I don't believe that you go every night to the movies. Nobody goes to the movies night after night. Nobody in their right minds goes to the movies as often as you pretend to. People don't go to the movies at nearly midnight, and movies don't let out at two A.M. Come in stumbling. Muttering to yourself like a maniac! You get three hours' sleep and then go to work. Oh, I can picture the way you're doing down there. Moping, doping, because you're in no condition.

TOM *(wildly):* No, I'm in no condition!

AMANDA: What right have you got to jeopardize your job? Jeopardize the security of us all? How do you think we'd manage if you were—

Mr. Lawrence: D. H. Lawrence (1885–1930), English poet and novelist who advocated sexual freedom.

TOM: Listen! You think I'm crazy *about* the *warehouse! (He bends fiercely toward her slight figure.)* You think I'm in love with the Continental Shoemakers? You think I want to spend fifty-five *years* down there in that—*celotex interior!* with—*fluorescent*—*tubes!* Look! I'd rather somebody picked up a crowbar and battered out my brains—than go back mornings! I *go!* Every time you come in yelling that God damn *"Rise and Shine!" "Rise and Shine!"* I say to myself "How *lucky dead* people are!" But I get up. I *go!* For sixty-five dollars a month I give up all that I dream of doing and being *ever!* And you say self—*self's* all I ever think of. Why, listen, if self is what I thought of, Mother, I'd be where he is—! *(Pointing to father's picture.)* As far as the system of transportation reaches! *(He starts past her. She grabs his arm.)* Don't grab at me, Mother!

AMANDA: Where are you going?

TOM: I'm going to the *movies!*

AMANDA: I don't believe that lie!

TOM *(crouching toward her, overtowering her tiny figure. She backs away, gasping):* I'm going to opium dens! Yes, opium dens, dens of vice and criminals' hang-outs, Mother. I've joined the Hogan gang, I'm a hired assassin, I carry a tommy-gun in a violin case! I run a string of cat-houses in the Valley! They call me Killer, Killer Wingfield, I'm leading a double-life, a simple, honest ware-house worker by day, by night a dynamic *czar* of the *underworld, Mother.* I go to gambling casinos, I spin away fortunes on the roulette table! I wear a patch over one eye and a false mustache, sometimes I put on green whiskers. On those occasions they call me—*El Diablo!°* Oh, I could tell you things to make you sleepless! My enemies plan to dynamite this place. They're going to blow us all sky-high some night! I'll be glad, very happy, and so will you! You'll go up, up on a broomstick, over Blue Mountain with seventeen gentlemen callers! You ugly—babbling old—*witch.* . . . *(He goes through a series of violent, clumsy movements, seizing his overcoat, lunging to the door, pulling it fiercely open. The women watch him, aghast. His arm catches in the sleeve of the coat as he struggles to pull it on. For a moment he is pinioned by the bulky garment. With an outraged groan he tears the coat off again, splitting the shoulders of it, and hurls it across the room. It strikes against the shelf of Laura's glass collection, there is a tinkle of shattering glass. Laura cries out as if wounded.)*

(Music legend: "The Glass Menagerie.")

LAURA *(shrilly):*   My glass!—menagerie. . . . *(She covers her face and turns away.)*

But Amanda is still stunned and stupefied by the "ugly witch" so that she barely notices this occurrence. Now she recovers her speech.

AMANDA *(in an awful voice):*   I won't speak to you—until you apologize! *(She crosses through portieres and draws them together behind her. Tom is left with Laura. Laura clings weakly to the mantel with her face averted. Tom stares at her stupidly for a moment. Then he crosses to shelf. Drops awkwardly to his knees to collect the fallen glass, glancing at Laura as if he would speak but couldn't.)*

El Diablo: The devil (Spanish).

"The Glass Menagerie" steals in as
(The scene dims out.)

Scene 4

The interior is dark. Faint light in the alley.

A deep-voiced bell in a church is tolling the hour of five as the scene commences.

Tom appears at the top of the alley. After each solemn boom of the bell in the tower, he shakes a little noise-maker or rattle as if to express the tiny spasm of man in contrast to the sustained power and dignity of the Almighty. This and the unsteadiness of his advance make it evident that he has been drinking.

As he climbs the few steps to the fire-escape landing light steals up inside. Laura appears in night-dress, observing Tom's empty bed in the front room.

Tom fishes in his pockets for the door-key, removing a motley assortment of articles in the search, including a perfect shower of movie-ticket stubs and an empty bottle. At last he finds the key, but just as he is about to insert it, it slips from his fingers. He strikes a match and crouches below the door.

TOM (*bitterly*):   One crack—and it falls through!

Laura opens the door.

LAURA: Tom! Tom, what are you doing?

TOM: Looking for a door-key.

LAURA: Where have you been all this time?

TOM: I have been to the movies.

LAURA: All this time at the movies?

TOM: There was a very long program. There was a Garbo picture and a Mickey Mouse and a travelogue and a newsreel and a preview of coming attractions. And there was an organ solo and a collection for the milk-fund—simultaneously—which ended up in a terrible fight between a fat lady and an usher!

LAURA (*innocently*):   Did you have to stay through everything?

TOM: Of course! And, oh, I forgot! There was a big stage show! The headliner on this stage show was Malvolio the Magician. He performed wonderful tricks, many of them, such as pouring water back and forth between pitchers. First it turned to wine and then it turned to beer and then it turned to whiskey. I know it was whiskey it finally turned into because he needed somebody to come up out of the audience to help him, and I came up— both shows! It was Kentucky Straight Bourbon. A very generous fellow, he gave souvenirs. (*He pulls from his back pocket a shimmering rainbow-colored scarf.*) He gave me this. This is his magic scarf. You can have it, Laura. You wave it over a canary cage and you get a bowl of gold-fish. You wave it over the gold-fish bowl and they fly away canaries. . . . But the wonderfullest trick of all was the coffin trick. We nailed him into a coffin and he got out of the coffin without removing one nail. (*He has come inside.*) There is a trick that would come in handy for me—get me out of this 2 by 4 situation! *(Flops onto bed and starts removing shoes.)*

LAURA: Tom—Shhh!

TOM: What you shushing me for?

LAURA: You'll wake up Mother.

TOM: Goody, goody! Pay 'er back for all those "Rise an' Shines." *(Lies down, groaning.)* You know it don't take much intelligence to get yourself into a nailed-up coffin, Laura. But who in hell ever got himself out of one without removing one nail?

As if in answer, the father's grinning photograph lights up.

(Scene dims out.)

Immediately following: The church bell is heard striking six. At the sixth stroke the alarm clock goes off in Amanda's room, and after a few moments we hear her calling: "Rise and Shine! Rise and Shine! Laura, go tell your brother to rise and shine!"

TOM *(sitting up slowly)*: I'll rise—but I won't shine.

The light increases.

AMANDA: Laura, tell your brother his coffee is ready.

Laura slips into front room.

LAURA: Tom! it's nearly seven. Don't make Mother nervous. *(He stares at her stupidly. Beseechingly.)* Tom, speak to Mother this morning. Make up with her, apologize, speak to her!

TOM: She won't to me. It's her that started not speaking.

LAURA: If you just say you're sorry she'll start speaking.

TOM: Her not speaking—is that such a tragedy?

LAURA: Please—please!

AMANDA *(calling from kitchenette)*: Laura, are you going to do what I asked you to do, or do I have to get dressed and go out myself?

LAURA: Going, going—soon as I get on my coat! *(She pulls on a shapeless felt hat with nervous, jerky movement, pleadingly glancing at Tom. Rushes awkwardly for coat. The coat is one of Amanda's, inaccurately made-over, the sleeves too short for Laura.)* Butter and what else?

AMANDA *(entering upstage)*: Just butter. Tell them to charge it.

LAURA: Mother, they make such faces when I do that.

AMANDA: Sticks and stones may break my bones, but the expression on Mr. Garfinkel's face won't harm us! Tell your brother his coffee is getting cold.

LAURA *(at door)*: Do what I asked you, will you, will you, Tom?

He looks sullenly away.

AMANDA: Laura, go now or just don't go at all!

LAURA *(rushing out)*: Going—going! *(A second later she cries out. Tom springs up and crosses to the door. Amanda rushes anxiously in. Tom opens the door.)*

TOM: Laura?

LAURA: I'm all right. I slipped, but I'm all right.

AMANDA *(peering anxiously after her)*:   If anyone breaks a leg on those fire-escape steps, the landlord ought to be sued for every cent he possesses! *(She shuts door. Remembers she isn't speaking and returns to other room.)*

As Tom enters listlessly for his coffee, she turns her back to him and stands rigidly facing the window on the gloomy gray vault of the areaway. Its light on her face with its aged but childish features is cruelly sharp, satirical as a Daumier° print. *(Music under: "Ave Maria.")*

Tom glances sheepishly but sullenly at her averted figure and slumps at the table. The coffee is scalding hot; he sips it and gasps and spits it back in the cup. At his gasp, Amanda catches her breath and half turns. Then catches herself and turns back to window.

Tom blows on his coffee, glancing sidewise at his mother. She clears her throat. Tom clears his. He starts to rise. Sinks back down again, scratches his head, clears his throat again. Amanda coughs. Tom raises his cup in both hands to blow on it, his eyes staring over the rim of it at his mother for several moments. Then he slowly sets the cup down and awkwardly and hesitantly rises from the chair.

TOM *(hoarsely)*:   Mother. I—I apologize. Mother. *(Amanda draws a quick, shuddering breath. Her face works grotesquely. She breaks into childlike tears.)* I'm sorry for what I said, for everything that I said, I didn't mean it.

AMANDA *(sobbingly)*:   My devotion has made me a witch and so I make myself hateful to my children!

TOM: No, you *don't.*

AMANDA: I worry so much, don't sleep, it makes me nervous!

TOM *(gently)*:   I understand that.

AMANDA: I've had to put up a solitary battle all these years. But you're my right-hand bower! Don't fall down, don't fail!

TOM *(gently)*:   I try, Mother.

AMANDA *(with great enthusiasm)*:   Try and you will SUCCEED! *(The notion makes her breathless.)* Why, you—you're just *full* of natural endowments! Both of my children—they're *unusual* children! Don't you think I know it? I'm so— proud! Happy and—feel I've—so much to be thankful for but—Promise me one thing, son!

TOM: What, Mother?

AMANDA: Promise, son, you'll—never be a drunkard!

TOM *(turns to her grinning)*:   I will never be a drunkard, Mother.

AMANDA: That's what frightened me so, that you'd be drinking! Eat a bowl of Purina!

TOM: Just coffee, Mother.

AMANDA: Shredded wheat biscuit?

TOM: No. No, Mother, just coffee.

Daumier: Honoré Daumier (1808–1879), French caricaturist, lithographer, and painter who mercilessly satirized bourgeois society.

AMANDA: You can't put in a day's work on an empty stomach. You've got ten minutes — don't gulp! Drinking too-hot liquids makes cancer of the stomach. . . . Put cream in.

TOM: No, thank you.

AMANDA: To cool it.

TOM: No! No, thank you, I want it black.

AMANDA: I know, but it's not good for you. We have to do all that we can to build ourselves up. In these trying times we live in, all that we have to cling to is — each other. . . . That's why it's so important to — Tom, I — I sent out your sister so I could discuss something with you. If you hadn't spoken I would have spoken to you. *(Sits down.)*

TOM *(gently):*   What is it, Mother, that you want to discuss?

AMANDA: Laura!

Tom puts his cup down slowly.
  (Legend on screen: "Laura.")
  (Music: "The Glass Menagerie.")

TOM: — Oh. — Laura . . .

AMANDA *(touching his sleeve):*   You know how Laura is. So quiet but — still water runs deep! She notices things and I think she — broods about them. *(Tom looks up.)* A few days ago I came in and she was crying.

TOM: What about?

AMANDA: You.

TOM: Me?

AMANDA: She has an idea that you're not happy here.

TOM: What gave her that idea?

AMANDA: What gives her any idea? However, you do act strangely. I — I'm not criticizing, understand *that!* I know your ambitions do not lie in the warehouse, that like everybody in the whole wide world — you've had to — make sacrifices, but — Tom — Tom — life's not easy, it calls for — Spartan endurance! There's so many things in my heart that I cannot describe to you! I've never told you but I — *loved* your father. . . .

TOM *(gently):*   I know that, Mother.

AMANDA: And you — when I see you taking after his ways! Staying out late — and — well, you *had* been drinking the night you were in that — terrifying condition! Laura says that you hate the apartment and that you go out nights to get away from it! Is that true, Tom?

TOM: No. You say there's so much in your heart that you can't describe to me. That's true of me, too. There's so much in my heart that I can't describe to *you!* So let's respect each other's —

AMANDA: But, why — *why,* Tom — are you always so *restless?* Where do you go to, nights?

TOM: I — go to the movies.

AMANDA: Why do you go to the movies so much, Tom?

TOM: I go to the movies because — I like adventure. Adventure is something I don't have much of at work, so I go to the movies.

AMANDA: But, Tom, you go to the movies *entirely too much!*
TOM: I like a lot of adventure.

Amanda looks baffled, then hurt. As the familiar inquisition resumes he becomes hard and impatient again. Amanda slips back into her querulous attitude toward him.
    (Image on screen: Sailing vessel with Jolly Roger.)

AMANDA: Most young men find adventure in their careers.
TOM: Then most young men are not employed in a warehouse.
AMANDA: The world is full of young men employed in warehouses and offices and factories.
TOM: Do all of them find adventure in their careers?
AMANDA: They do or they do without it! Not everybody has a craze for adventure.
TOM: Man is by instinct a lover, a hunter, a fighter, and none of those instincts are given much play at the warehouse!
AMANDA: Man is by instinct! Don't quote instinct to me! Instinct is something that people have got away from! It belongs to animals! Christian adults don't want it!
TOM: What do Christian adults want, then, Mother?
AMANDA: Superior things! Things of the mind and the spirit! Only animals have to satisfy instincts! Surely your aims are somewhat higher than theirs! Than monkeys — pigs —
TOM: I reckon they're not.
AMANDA: You're joking. However, that isn't what I wanted to discuss.
TOM *(rising):*   I haven't much time.
AMANDA *(pushing his shoulders):*   Sit down.
TOM: You want me to punch in red° at the warehouse, Mother?
AMANDA: You have five minutes. I want to talk about Laura.

(Legend: "Plans and Provisions.")

TOM: All right! What about Laura?
AMANDA: We have to be making plans and provisions for her. She's older than you, two years, and nothing has happened. She just drifts along doing nothing. It frightens me terribly how she just drifts along.
TOM: I guess she's the type that people call home girls.
AMANDA: There's no such type, and if there is, it's a pity! That is unless the home is hers, with a husband!
TOM: What?
AMANDA: Oh, I can see the handwriting on the wall as plain as I see the nose in front of my face! It's terrifying! More and more you remind me of your father! He was out all hours without explanation — Then *left! Good-bye!* And me with the bag to hold. I saw that letter you got from the Merchant Marine. I know what you're dreaming of. I'm not standing here blindfolded. Very well, then. Then *do* it! But not till there's somebody to take your place.
TOM: What do you mean?

punch in red: Be late for work.

AMANDA: I mean that as soon as Laura has got somebody to take care of her, married, a home of her own, independent — why, then you'll be free to go wherever you please, on land, on sea, whichever way the wind blows! But until that time you've got to look out for your sister. I don't say me because I'm old and don't matter! I say for your sister because she's young and dependent. I put her in business college — a dismal failure! Frightened her so it made her sick to her stomach. I took her over to the Young People's League at the church. Another fiasco. She spoke to nobody, nobody spoke to her. Now all she does is fool with those pieces of glass and play those worn-out records. What kind of a life is that for a girl to lead!

TOM: What can I do about it?

AMANDA: Overcome selfishness! Self, self, self is all that you ever think of! *(Tom springs up and crosses to get his coat. It is ugly and bulky. He pulls on a cap with earmuffs.)* Where is your muffler? Put your wool muffler on! *(He snatches it angrily from the closet and tosses it around his neck and pulls both ends tight.)* Tom! I haven't said what I had in mind to ask you.

TOM: I'm too late to —

AMANDA *(catching his arms — very importunately. Then shyly.):*   Down at the warehouse, aren't there some — nice young men?

TOM: No!

AMANDA: There *must* be — *some.*

TOM: Mother —

Gesture.

AMANDA: Find out one that's clean-living — doesn't drink and — ask him out for sister!

TOM: What?

AMANDA: For *sister!* To *meet!* Get *acquainted!*

TOM *(stamping to door):*   Oh, my go-osh!

AMANDA: Will you? *(He opens door. Imploringly.)* Will you? *(He starts down.)* Will you? *Will* you, dear?

TOM *(calling back):*   YES!

Amanda closes the door hesitantly and with a troubled but faintly hopeful expression.
(Screen image: Glamour *magazine cover.)*
Spot Amanda at phone.

AMANDA: Ella Cartwright? This is Amanda Wingfield! How are you, honey? How is that kidney condition? *(Count five.)* Horrors! *(Count five.)* You're a Christian martyr, yes, honey, that's what you are, a Christian martyr! Well, I just happened to notice in my little red book that your subscription to the *Companion* has just run out! I knew that you wouldn't want to miss out on the wonderful serial starting in this new issue. It's by Bessie Mae Hopper, the first thing she's written since *Honeymoon for Three.* Wasn't that a strange and interesting story? Well, this one is even lovelier, I believe. It has a sophisticated society background. It's all about the horsey set on Long Island!

(Fade out.)

Scene 5

(Legend on screen: "Annunciation.") Fade with music.

It is early dusk of a spring evening. Supper has just been finished in the Wing-field apartment. Amanda and Laura in light-colored dresses are removing dishes from the table, in the upstage area, which is shadowy, their movements formalized almost as a dance or ritual, their moving forms as pale and silent as moths.

Tom, in white shirt and trousers, rises from the table and crosses toward the fire-escape.

AMANDA *(as he passes her):*   Son, will you do me a favor?

TOM: What?

AMANDA: Comb your hair! You look so pretty when your hair is combed! *(Tom slouches on sofa with evening paper. Enormous caption "Franco Triumphs."°)* There is only one respect in which I would like you to emulate your father.

TOM: What respect is that?

AMANDA: The care he always took of his appearance. He never allowed himself to look untidy. *(He throws down the paper and crosses to fire-escape.)* Where are you going?

TOM: I'm going out to smoke.

AMANDA: You smoke too much. A pack a day at fifteen cents a pack. How much would that amount to in a month? Thirty times fifteen is how much, Tom? Figure it out and you will be astounded at what you could save. Enough to give you a night-school course in accounting at Washington U! Just think what a wonderful thing that would be for you, son!

Tom is unmoved by the thought.

TOM: I'd rather smoke. *(He steps out on landing, letting the screen door slam.)*

AMANDA *(sharply):*   I know! That's the tragedy of it. . . . *(Alone, she turns to look at her husband's picture.)*

(Dance music: "All the World Is Waiting for the Sunrise!")

TOM *(to the audience):*   Across the alley from us was the Paradise Dance Hall. On evenings in spring the windows and doors were open and the music came outdoors. Sometimes the lights were turned out except for a large glass sphere that hung from the ceiling. It would turn slowly about and filter the dusk with delicate rainbow colors. Then the orchestra played a waltz or a tango, something that had a slow and sensuous rhythm. Couples would come outside, to the relative privacy of the alley. You could see them kissing behind ash-pits and telephone poles. This was the compensation for lives that passed like mine, without any change or adventure. Adventure and change were imminent in this year. They were waiting around the corner for all these kids. Suspended in the mist over the Berchtesgaden,° caught in the

---

"Franco Triumphs": In January 1939 the Republican forces of Francisco Franco (1892–1975) defeated the Loyalists, ending the Spanish Civil War.
Berchtesgaden: A resort in the German Alps where Adolf Hitler had a heavily protected villa.

folds of Chamberlain's° umbrella—In Spain there was Guernica! But here there was only hot swing music and liquor, dance halls, bars, and movies, and sex that hung in the gloom like a chandelier and flooded the world with brief, deceptive rainbows. . . . All the world was waiting for bombardments!

Amanda turns from the picture and comes outside.

AMANDA *(sighing):* A fire-escape landing's a poor excuse for a porch. *(She spreads a newspaper on a step and sits down, gracefully and demurely as if she were settling into a swing on a Mississippi veranda.)* What are you looking at?

TOM: The moon.

AMANDA: Is there a moon this evening?

TOM: It's rising over Garfinkel's Delicatessen.

AMANDA: So it is! A little silver slipper of a moon. Have you made a wish on it yet?

TOM: Um-hum.

AMANDA: What did you wish for?

TOM: That's a secret.

AMANDA: A secret, huh? Well, I won't tell mine either. I will be just as mysterious as you.

TOM: I bet I can guess what yours is.

AMANDA: Is my head so transparent?

TOM: You're not a sphinx.

AMANDA: No, I don't have secrets. I'll tell you what I wished for on the moon. Success and happiness for my precious children! I wish for that whenever there's a moon, and when there isn't a moon, I wish for it, too.

TOM: I thought perhaps you wished for a gentleman caller.

AMANDA: Why do you say that?

TOM: Don't you remember asking me to fetch one?

AMANDA: I remember suggesting that it would be nice for your sister if you brought home some nice young man from the warehouse. I think I've made that suggestion more than once.

TOM: Yes, you have made it repeatedly.

AMANDA: Well?

TOM: We are going to have one.

AMANDA: *What?*

TOM: A gentleman caller!

(The Annunciation is celebrated with music.)
    Amanda rises.
    (Image on screen: Caller with bouquet.)

AMANDA: You mean you have asked some nice young man to come over?

TOM: Yep. I've asked him to dinner.

AMANDA: You really did?

TOM: I did!

Chamberlain: Neville Chamberlain (1869–1940), British prime minister who sought to avoid war with Hitler through a policy of appeasement.

AMANDA: You did, and did he—*accept?*

TOM: He did!

AMANDA: Well, well—well, well! That's—lovely!

TOM: I thought that you would be pleased.

AMANDA: It's definite, then?

TOM: Very definite.

AMANDA: Soon?

TOM: Very soon.

AMANDA: For heaven's sake, stop putting on and tell me some things, will you?

TOM: What things do you want me to tell you?

AMANDA: Naturally I would like to know when he's *coming!*

TOM: He's coming tomorrow.

AMANDA: *Tomorrow?*

TOM: Yep. Tomorrow.

AMANDA: But, Tom!

TOM: Yes, Mother?

AMANDA: Tomorrow gives me no time!

TOM: Time for what?

AMANDA: Preparations! Why didn't you phone me at once, as soon as you asked him, the minute that he accepted? Then, don't you see, I could have been getting ready!

TOM: You don't have to make any fuss.

AMANDA: Oh, Tom, Tom, Tom, of course I have to make a fuss! I want things nice, not sloppy! Not thrown together. I'll certainly have to do some fast thinking, won't I?

TOM: I don't see why you have to think at all.

AMANDA: You just don't know. We can't have a gentleman caller in a pig-sty! All my wedding silver has to be polished, the monogrammed table linen ought to be laundered! The windows have to be washed and fresh curtains put up. And how about clothes? We have to *wear* something, don't we?

TOM: Mother, this boy is no one to make a fuss over!

AMANDA: Do you realize he's the first young man we've introduced to your sister? It's terrible, dreadful, disgraceful that poor little sister has never received a single gentleman caller! Tom, come inside! *(She opens the screen door.)*

TOM: What for?

AMANDA: I want to ask you some things.

TOM: If you're going to make such a fuss, I'll call it off, I'll tell him not to come.

AMANDA: You certainly won't do anything of the kind. Nothing offends people worse than broken engagements. It simply means I'll have to work like a Turk! We won't be brilliant, but we'll pass inspection. Come on inside. *(Tom follows, groaning.)* Sit down.

TOM: Any particular place you would like me to sit?

AMANDA: Thank heavens I've got that new sofa! I'm also making payments on a floor lamp I'll have sent out! And put the chintz covers on, they'll brighten things up! Of course I'd hoped to have these walls re-papered. . . . What is the young man's name?

TOM: His name is O'Connor.

AMANDA: That, of course, means fish — tomorrow is Friday! I'll have that salmon loaf — with Durkee's dressing! What does he do? He works at the warehouse?

TOM: Of course! How else would I —

AMANDA: Tom, he — doesn't drink?

TOM: Why do you ask me that?

AMANDA: Your father *did!*

TOM: Don't get started on that!

AMANDA: He *does* drink, then?

TOM: Not that I know of!

AMANDA: Make sure, be certain! The last thing I want for my daughter's a boy who drinks!

TOM: Aren't you being a little premature? Mr. O'Connor has not yet appeared on the scene!

AMANDA: But will tomorrow. To meet your sister, and what do I know about his character? Nothing! Old maids are better off than wives of drunkards!

TOM: Oh, my God!

AMANDA: Be still!

TOM (*leaning forward to whisper*):   Lots of fellows meet girls whom they don't marry!

AMANDA: Oh, talk sensibly, Tom — and don't be sarcastic! (*She has gotten a hairbrush.*)

TOM: What are you doing?

AMANDA: I'm brushing that cow-lick down! What is this young man's position at the warehouse?

TOM (*submitting grimly to the brush and the interrogation*):   This young man's position is that of a shipping clerk, Mother.

AMANDA: Sounds to me like a fairly responsible job, the sort of a job *you* would be in if you just had more *get-up*. What is his salary? Have you got any idea?

TOM: I would judge it to be approximately eighty-five dollars a month.

AMANDA: Well — not princely, but —

TOM: Twenty more than I make.

AMANDA: Yes, how well I know! But for a family man, eighty-five dollars a month is not much more than you can just get by on. . . .

TOM: Yes, but Mr. O'Connor is not a family man.

AMANDA: He might be, mightn't he? Some time in the future?

TOM: I see. Plans and provisions.

AMANDA: You are the only young man that I know of who ignores the fact that the future becomes the present, the present the past, and the past turns into everlasting regret if you don't plan for it!

TOM: I will think that over and see what I can make of it.

AMANDA: Don't be supercilious with your mother! Tell me some more about this — what do you call him?

TOM: James D. O'Connor. The D. is for Delaney.

AMANDA: Irish on *both* sides! *Gracious!* And doesn't drink?

TOM: Shall I call him up and ask him right this minute?

AMANDA: The only way to find out about those things is to make discreet inquiries at the proper moment. When I was a girl in Blue Mountain and it was suspected that a young man drank, the girl whose attentions he had been receiving, if any girl *was*, would sometimes speak to the minister of his church, or rather her father would if her father was living, and sort of feel him out on the young man's character. That is the way such things are discreetly handled to keep a young woman from making a tragic mistake!

TOM: Then how did you happen to make a tragic mistake?

AMANDA: That innocent look of your father's had everyone fooled! He *smiled* — the world was *enchanted*! No girl can do worse than put herself at the mercy of a handsome appearance! I hope that Mr. O'Connor is not too good-looking.

TOM: No, he's not too good-looking. He's covered with freckles and hasn't too much of a nose.

AMANDA: He's not right-down homely, though?

TOM: Not right-down homely. Just medium homely, I'd say.

AMANDA: Character's what to look for in a man.

TOM: That's what I've always said, Mother.

AMANDA: You've never said anything of the kind and I suspect you would never give it a thought.

TOM: Don't be suspicious of me.

AMANDA: At least I hope he's the type that's up and coming.

TOM: I think he really goes in for self-improvement.

AMANDA: What reason have you to think so?

TOM: He goes to night school.

AMANDA *(beaming)*:   Splendid! What does he do, I mean study?

TOM: Radio engineering and public speaking!

AMANDA: Then he has visions of being advanced in the world! Any young man who studies public speaking is aiming to have an executive job some day! And radio engineering? A thing for the future! Both of these facts are very illuminating. Those are the sort of things that a mother should know concerning any young man who comes to call on her daughter. Seriously or — not.

TOM: One little warning. He doesn't know about Laura. I didn't let on that we had dark ulterior motives. I just said, why don't you come have dinner with us? He said okay and that was the whole conversation.

AMANDA: I bet it was! You're eloquent as an oyster. However, he'll know about Laura when he gets here. When he sees how lovely and sweet and pretty she is, he'll thank his lucky stars he was asked to dinner.

TOM: Mother, you mustn't expect too much of Laura.

AMANDA: What do you mean?

TOM: Laura seems all those things to you and me because she's ours and we love her. We don't even notice she's crippled any more.

AMANDA: Don't say crippled! You know that I never allow that word to be used!

TOM: But face facts, Mother. She is and — that's not all —

AMANDA: What do you mean "not all"?

TOM: Laura is very different from other girls.

AMANDA: I think the difference is all to her advantage.

TOM: Not quite all—in the eyes of others—strangers—she's terribly shy and lives in a world of her own and those things make her seem a little peculiar to people outside the house.

AMANDA: Don't say peculiar.

TOM: Face the facts. She is.

(The dance-hall music changes to a tango that has a minor and somewhat ominous tone.)

AMANDA: In what way is she peculiar—may I ask?

TOM *(gently)*:   She lives in a world of her own—a world of—little glass orna-ments, Mother. . . . *(Gets up. Amanda remains holding brush, looking at him, troubled.)* She plays old phonograph records and—that's about all—*(He glances at himself in the mirror and crosses to door.)*

AMANDA *(sharply)*:   Where are you going?

TOM: I'm going to the movies. *(Out screen door.)*

AMANDA: Not to the movies, every night to the movies! *(Follows quickly to screen door.)* I don't believe you always go to the movies! *(He is gone. Amanda looks worriedly after him for a moment. Then vitality and optimism return and she turns from the door. Crossing to portieres.)* Laura! Laura! *(Laura answers from kitchenette.)*

LAURA: Yes, Mother.

AMANDA: Let those dishes go and come in front! *(Laura appears with dish towel. Gaily.)* Laura, come here and make a wish on the moon!

LAURA *(entering)*:   Moon—moon?

AMANDA: A little silver slipper of a moon. Look over your left shoulder, Laura, and make a wish! *(Laura looks faintly puzzled as if called out of sleep. Amanda seizes her shoulders and turns her at angle by the door.)* Now! Now, darling, *wish!*

LAURA: What shall I wish for, Mother?

AMANDA *(her voice trembling and her eyes suddenly filling with tears)*:   Happi-ness! Good Fortune!

The violin rises and the stage dims out.

Scene 6

(Image: High-school hero.)

TOM: And so the following evening I brought Jim home to dinner. I had known Jim slightly in high school. In high school Jim was a hero. He had tremen-dous Irish good nature and vitality with the scrubbed and polished look of white chinaware. He seemed to move in a continual spotlight. He was a star in basketball, captain of the debating club, president of the senior class and the glee club and he sang the male lead in the annual light operas. He was always running or bounding, never just walking. He seemed always at the point of defeating the law of gravity. He was shooting with such velocity through his adolescence that you would logically expect him to arrive at nothing short of the White House by the time he was thirty. But Jim apparently ran into more interference after his graduation from Soldan. His speed had definitely slowed. Six years after he left high school he was holding a job that wasn't much better than mine.

(Image: Clerk.)

He was the only one at the warehouse with whom I was on friendly terms. I was valuable to him as someone who could remember his former glory, who had seen him win basketball games and the silver cup in debating. He knew of my secret practice of retiring to a cabinet of the washroom to work on poems when business was slack in the warehouse. He called me Shakespeare. And while the other boys in the warehouse regarded me with suspicious hostility, Jim took a humorous attitude toward me. Gradually his attitude affected the others, their hostility wore off, and they also began to smile at me as people smile at an oddly fashioned dog who trots across their paths at some distance.

I knew that Jim and Laura had known each other at Soldan, and I had heard Laura speak admiringly of his voice. I didn't know if Jim remembered her or not. In high school Laura had been as unobtrusive as Jim had been astonishing. If he did remember Laura, it was not as my sister, for when I asked him to dinner, he grinned and said, "You know, Shakespeare, I never thought of you as having folks!"

He was about to discover that I did. . . .

(Light upstage.)
(Legend on screen: "The Accent of a Coming Foot.")
Friday evening. It is about five o'clock of a late spring evening which comes "scattering poems in the sky."
A delicate lemony light is in the Wingfield apartment.
Amanda has worked like a Turk in preparation for the gentleman caller. The results are astonishing. The new floor lamp with its rose-silk shade is in place, a colored paper lantern conceals the broken light fixture in the ceiling, new billowing white curtains are at the windows, chintz covers are on chairs and sofa, a pair of new sofa pillows make their initial appearance.
Open boxes and tissue paper are scattered on the floor.
Laura stands in the middle with lifted arms while Amanda crouches before her, adjusting the hem of the new dress, devout and ritualistic. The dress is colored and designed by memory. The arrangement of Laura's hair is changed; it is softer and more becoming. A fragile, unearthly prettiness has come out in Laura: she is like a piece of translucent glass touched by light, given a momentary radiance, not actual, not lasting.

AMANDA *(impatiently):*   Why are you trembling?
LAURA: Mother, you've made me so nervous!
AMANDA: How have I made you nervous?
LAURA: By all this fuss! You make it seem so important!

AMANDA: I don't understand you, Laura. You couldn't be satisfied with just sitting home, and yet whenever I try to arrange something for you, you seem to
resist it. *(She gets up.)* Now take a look at yourself. No, wait! Wait just a
moment—I have an idea!

LAURA: What is it now?

*Amanda produces two powder puffs which she wraps in handkerchiefs and stuffs in
Laura's bosom.*

LAURA: Mother, what are you doing?

AMANDA: They call them "Gay Deceivers"!

LAURA: I won't wear them!

AMANDA: You will!

LAURA: Why should I?

AMANDA: Because, to be painfully honest, your chest is flat.

LAURA: You make it seem like we were setting a trap.

AMANDA: All pretty girls are a trap, a pretty trap, and men expect them to be.
(Legend: "A Pretty Trap.") Now look at yourself, young lady. This is the prettiest you will ever be! I've got to fix myself now! You're going to be surprised
by your mother's appearance! *(She crosses through portieres, humming gaily.)*

Laura moves slowly to the long mirror and stares solemnly at herself.

   *A wind blows the white curtains inward in a slow, graceful motion and with a
faint, sorrowful sighing.*

AMANDA *(offstage)*:   It isn't dark enough yet. *(She turns slowly before the mirror
with a troubled look).*

(Legend on screen: "This Is My Sister: Celebrate Her with Strings!" Music.)

AMANDA *(laughing, off)*:   I'm going to show you something. I'm going to make a
spectacular appearance!

LAURA: What is it, Mother?

AMANDA: Possess your soul in patience—you will see! Something I've resurrected
from that old trunk! Styles haven't changed so terribly much after all. . . . *(She
parts the portieres.)* Now just look at your mother! *(She wears a girlish frock of
yellowed voile with a blue silk sash. She carries a bunch of jonquils—the legend
of her youth is nearly revived. Feverishly.)* This is the dress in which I led the
cotillion. Won the cakewalk twice at Sunset Hill, wore one spring to the Governor's ball in Jackson! See how I sashayed around the ballroom, Laura? *(She
raises her skirt and does a mincing step around the room.)* I wore it on Sundays
for my gentlemen callers! I had it on the day I met your father—I had malaria
fever all that spring. The change of climate from East Tennessee to the
Delta—weakened resistance—I had a little temperature all the time—not
enough to be serious—just enough to make me restless and giddy! Invitations
poured in—parties all over the Delta!—"Stay in bed," said Mother, "you have
fever!"—but I just wouldn't.—I took quinine but kept on going, going!—
Evenings, dances!—Afternoons, long, long rides! Picnics—lovely!—So lovely,
that country in May.—All lacy with dogwood, literally flooded with jonquils!—That was the spring I had the craze for jonquils. Jonquils became an

absolute obsession. Mother said, "Honey, there's no more room for jonquils." And still I kept bringing in more jonquils. Whenever, wherever I saw them, I'd say, "Stop! Stop! I see jonquils!" I made the young men help me gather the jonquils! It was a joke, Amanda and her jonquils! Finally there were no more vases to hold them, every available space was filled with jonquils. No vases to hold them? All right, I'll hold them myself! And then I—*(She stops in front of the picture.) (Music.)* met your father! Malaria fever and jonquils and then—this—boy. . . . *(She switches on the rose-colored lamp.)* I hope they get here before it starts to rain. *(She crosses upstage and places the jonquils in bowl on table.)* I gave your brother a little extra change so he and Mr. O'Connor could take the service car home.

LAURA *(with altered look):* What did you say his name was?

AMANDA: O'Connor.

LAURA: What is his first name?

AMANDA: I don't remember. Oh, yes, I do. It was—Jim!

Laura sways slightly and catches hold of a chair.
  (Legend on screen: "Not Jim!")

LAURA *(faintly):* Not—Jim!

AMANDA: Yes, that was it, it was Jim! I've never known a Jim that wasn't nice!

(Music: Ominous.)

LAURA: Are you sure his name is Jim O'Connor?

AMANDA: Yes. Why?

LAURA: Is he the one that Tom used to know in high school?

AMANDA: He didn't say so. I think he just got to know him at the warehouse.

LAURA: There was a Jim O'Connor we both knew in high school—*(Then, with effort.)* If that is the one that Tom is bringing to dinner—you'll have to excuse me, I won't come to the table.

AMANDA: What sort of nonsense is this?

LAURA: You asked me once if I'd ever liked a boy. Don't you remember I showed you this boy's picture?

AMANDA: You mean the boy you showed me in the year-book?

LAURA: Yes, that boy.

AMANDA: Laura, Laura, were you in love with that boy?

LAURA: I don't know, Mother. All I know is I couldn't sit at the table if it was him!

AMANDA: It won't be him! It isn't the least bit likely. But whether it is or not, you will come to the table. You will not be excused.

LAURA: I'll have to be, Mother.

AMANDA: I don't intend to humor your silliness, Laura. I've had too much from you and your brother, both! So just sit down and compose yourself till they come. Tom has forgotten his key so you'll have to let them in, when they arrive.

LAURA *(panicky):* Oh, Mother—*you* answer the door!

AMANDA *(lightly):* I'll be in the kitchen—busy!

LAURA: Oh, Mother, please answer the door, don't make me do it!

AMANDA *(crossing into kitchenette):* I've got to fix the dressing for the salmon. Fuss, fuss—silliness!—over a gentleman caller!

Door swings shut. Laura is left alone.
> *(Legend: "Terror!")*
She utters a low moan and turns off the lamp — sits stiffly on the edge of the sofa, knotting her fingers together.
> *(Legend on screen: "The Opening of a Door!")*
Tom and Jim appear on the fire-escape steps and climb to landing. Hearing their approach, Laura rises with a panicky gesture. She retreats to the portieres. The doorbell. Laura catches her breath and touches her throat. Low drums.

AMANDA *(calling):*   Laura, sweetheart! The door!

Laura stares at it without moving.

JIM: I think we just beat the rain.

TOM: Uh-huh. *(He rings again, nervously. Jim whistles and fishes for a cigarette.)*

AMANDA *(very, very gaily):*   Laura, that is your brother and Mr. O'Connor! Will you let them in, darling?

Laura crosses toward kitchenette door.

LAURA *(breathlessly):*   Mother — you go to the door!

Amanda steps out of kitchenette and stares furiously at Laura. She points imperiously at the door.

LAURA: Please, please!

AMANDA *(in a fierce whisper):*   What is the matter with you, you silly thing?

LAURA *(desperately):*   Please, you answer it, *please!*

AMANDA: I told you I wasn't going to humor you, Laura. Why have you chosen this moment to lose your mind?

LAURA: Please, please, please, you go!

AMANDA: You'll have to go to the door because I can't!

LAURA *(despairingly):*   I can't either!

AMANDA: Why?

LAURA: I'm *sick!*

AMANDA: I'm sick, too — of your nonsense! Why can't you and your brother be normal people? Fantastic whims and behavior! *(Tom gives a long ring.)* Preposterous goings on! Can you give me one reason — *(Calls out lyrically.)* COMING! JUST ONE SECOND! — why should you be afraid to open a door? Now you answer it, Laura!

LAURA: Oh, oh, oh . . . *(She returns through the portieres. Darts to the Victrola and winds it frantically and turns it on.)*

AMANDA: Laura Wingfield, you march right to that door!

LAURA: Yes — yes, Mother!

A faraway, scratchy rendition of "Dardanella" softens the air and gives her strength to move through it. She slips to the door and draws it cautiously open.
> *Tom enters with the caller, Jim O'Connor.*

TOM: Laura, this is Jim. Jim, this is my sister, Laura.

JIM *(stepping inside):*   I didn't know that Shakespeare had a sister!

LAURA *(retreating stiff and trembling from the door):*   How — how do you do?

JIM (*heartily extending his hand*):   Okay!

Laura touches it hesitantly with hers.

JIM: Your hand's *cold*, Laura!

LAURA: Yes, well — I've been playing the Victrola . . .

JIM: Must have been playing classical music on it! You ought to play a little hot swing music to warm you up!

LAURA: Excuse me — I haven't finished playing the Victrola . . .

She turns awkwardly and hurries into the front room. She pauses a second by the Victrola. Then catches her breath and darts through the portieres like a frightened deer.

JIM (*grinning*):   What was the matter?

TOM: Oh — with Laura? Laura is — terribly shy.

JIM: Shy, huh? It's unusual to meet a shy girl nowadays. I don't believe you ever mentioned you had a sister.

TOM: Well, now you know. I have one. Here is the *Post Dispatch*. You want a piece of it?

JIM: Uh-huh.

TOM: What piece? The comics?

JIM: Sports! (*Glances at it.*) Ole Dizzy Dean is on his bad behavior.

TOM (*disinterest*):   Yeah? (*Lights cigarette and crosses back to fire-escape door.*)

JIM: Where are *you* going?

TOM: I'm going out on the terrace.

JIM (*goes after him*):   You know, Shakespeare — I'm going to sell you a bill of goods!

TOM: What goods?

JIM: A course I'm taking.

TOM: Huh?

JIM: In public speaking! You and me, we're not the warehouse type.

TOM: Thanks — that's good news. But what has public speaking got to do with it?

JIM: It fits you for — executive positions!

TOM: Awww.

JIM: I tell you it's done a helluva lot for me.

(*Image: Executive at desk.*)

TOM: In what respect?

JIM: In every! Ask yourself what is the difference between you an' me and men in the office down front? Brains? — No! — Ability? — No! Then what? Just one little thing —

TOM: What is that one little thing?

JIM: Primarily it amounts to — social poise! Being able to square up to people and hold your own on any social level!

AMANDA (*offstage*):   Tom?

TOM: Yes, Mother?

AMANDA: Is that you and Mr. O'Connor?

TOM: Yes, Mother.

AMANDA: Well, you just make yourselves comfortable in there.

TOM: Yes, Mother.

AMANDA: Ask Mr. O'Connor if he would like to wash his hands.

JIM: Aw—no—no—thank you—I took care of that at the warehouse. Tom—

TOM: Yes?

JIM: Mr. Mendoza was speaking to me about you.

TOM: Favorably?

JIM: What do you think?

TOM: Well—

JIM: You're going to be out of a job if you don't wake up.

TOM: I am waking up—

JIM: You show no signs.

TOM: The signs are interior.

(Image on screen: The sailing vessel with Jolly Roger again.)

TOM: I'm planning to change. *(He leans over the rail speaking with quiet exhilaration. The incandescent marquees and signs of the first-run movie houses light his face from across the alley. He looks like a voyager.)* I'm right at the point of committing myself to a future that doesn't include the warehouse and Mr. Mendoza or even a night-school course in public speaking.

JIM: What are you gassing about?

TOM: I'm tired of the movies.

JIM: Movies!

TOM: Yes, movies! Look at them — *(A wave toward the marvels of Grand Avenue.)* All of those glamorous people — having adventures — hogging it all, gobbling the whole thing up! You know what happens? People go to the *movies* instead of *moving!* Hollywood characters are supposed to have all the adventures for everybody in America, while everybody in America sits in a dark room and watches them have them! Yes, until there's a war. That's when adventure becomes available to the masses! *Everyone's* dish, not only Gable's! Then the people in the dark room come out of the dark room to have some adventures themselves — Goody, goody — It's our turn now, to go to the South Sea Island — to make a safari — to be exotic, far-off — But I'm not patient. I don't want to wait till then. I'm tired of the *movies* and I am *about* to *move!*

JIM *(incredulously):*   Move?

TOM: Yes.

JIM: When?

TOM: Soon!

JIM: Where? Where?

(Theme three: Music seems to answer the question, while Tom thinks it over. He searches among his pockets.)

TOM: I'm starting to boil inside. I know I seem dreamy, but inside — well, I'm boiling! Whenever I pick up a shoe, I shudder a little thinking how short life is and what I am doing! — Whatever that means. I know it doesn't mean shoes — except as something to wear on a traveler's feet! *(Finds paper.)* Look —

JIM: What?

TOM: I'm a member.

JIM (*reading*): The Union of Merchant Seamen.

TOM: I paid my dues this month, instead of the light bill.

JIM: You will regret it when they turn the lights off.

TOM: I won't be here.

JIM: How about your mother?

TOM: I'm like my father. The bastard son of a bastard! See how he grins? And he's been absent going on sixteen years!

JIM: You're just talking, you drip. How does your mother feel about it?

TOM: Shhh—Here comes Mother! Mother is not acquainted with my plans!

AMANDA (*enters portieres*): Where are you all?

TOM: On the terrace, Mother.

They start inside. She advances to them. Tom is distinctly shocked at her appearance. Even Jim blinks a little. He is making his first contact with girlish Southern vivacity and in spite of the night-school course in public speaking is somewhat thrown off the beam by the unexpected outlay of social charm.

Certain responses are attempted by Jim but are swept aside by Amanda's gay laughter and chatter. Tom is embarrassed but after the first shock Jim reacts very warmly. Grins and chuckles, is altogether won over.

(Image: Amanda as a girl.)

AMANDA (*coyly smiling, shaking her girlish ringlets*): Well, well, well, so this is Mr. O'Connor. Introductions entirely unnecessary. I've heard so much about you from my boy. I finally said to him, Tom—good gracious!—why don't you bring this paragon to supper? I'd like to meet this nice young man at the warehouse!—Instead of just hearing him sing your praises so much! I don't know why my son is so stand-offish—that's not Southern behavior! Let's sit down and—I think we could stand a little more air in here! Tom, leave the door open. I felt a nice fresh breeze a moment ago. Where has it gone? Mmm, so warm already! And not quite summer, even. We're going to burn up when summer really gets started. However, we're having—we're having a very light supper. I think light things are better fo' this time of year. The same as light clothes are. Light clothes an' light food are what warm weather calls fo'. You know our blood gets so thick during th' winter—it takes a while fo' us to *adjust* ou'selves!—when the season changes. . . . It's come so quick this year. I wasn't prepared. All of a sudden—heavens! Already summer!—I ran to the trunk an' pulled out this light dress—Terribly old! Historical almost! But feels so good—so good an' co-ol, y'know. . . .

TOM: Mother—

AMANDA: Yes, honey?

TOM: How about—supper?

AMANDA: Honey, you go ask Sister if supper is ready! You know that Sister is in full charge of supper! Tell her you hungry boys are waiting for it. (*To Jim.*) Have you met Laura?

JIM: She—

AMANDA: Let you in? Oh, good, you've met already! It's rare for a girl as sweet
an' pretty as Laura to be domestic! But Laura is, thank heavens, not only
pretty but also very domestic. I'm not at all. I never was a bit. I never could
make a thing but angel-food cake. Well, in the South we had so many servants. Gone, gone, gone. All vestiges of gracious living! Gone completely! I
wasn't prepared for what the future brought me. All of my gentlemen callers
were sons of planters and so of course I assumed that I would be married to
one and raise my family on a large piece of land with plenty of servants. But
man proposes — and woman accepts the proposal! — To vary that old, old saying a little bit — I married no planter! I married a man who worked for the
telephone company! — that gallantly smiling gentleman over there! *(Points
to the picture.)* A telephone man who — fell in love with long distance! —
Now he travels and I don't even know where! — But what am I going on for
about my — tribulations! Tell me yours — I hope you don't have any! Tom?

TOM *(returning)*:   Yes, Mother?

AMANDA: Is supper nearly ready?

TOM: It looks to me like supper is on the table.

AMANDA: Let me look — *(She rises prettily and looks through portieres.)* Oh,
lovely — But where is Sister?

TOM: Laura is not feeling well and she says that she thinks she'd better not come
to the table.

AMANDA: What? — Nonsense! — Laura? Oh, Laura!

LAURA *(offstage, faintly)*:   Yes, Mother.

AMANDA: You really must come to the table. We won't be seated until you come
to the table! Come in, Mr. O'Connor. You sit over there and I'll — Laura?
Laura Wingfield! You're keeping us waiting, honey! We can't say grace until
you come to the table!

*The back door is pushed weakly open and Laura comes in. She is obviously quite
faint, her lips trembling, her eyes wide and staring. She moves unsteadily toward
the table.*
    (Legend: "Terror!")
    *Outside a summer storm is coming abruptly. The white curtains billow inward
at the windows and there is a sorrowful murmur and deep blue dusk.*
    Laura suddenly stumbles — She catches at a chair with a faint moan.

TOM: Laura!

AMANDA: Laura! *(There is a clap of thunder.)* *(Legend: "Ah!")* *(Despairingly.)*
Why, Laura, you *are* sick, darling! Tom, help your sister into the living room,
dear! Sit in the living room, Laura — rest on the sofa. Well! *(To the gentleman
caller.)* Standing over the hot stove made her ill! — I told her that it was just
too warm this evening, but — *(Tom comes back in. Laura is on the sofa.)* Is
Laura all right now?

TOM: Yes.

AMANDA: What *is* that? Rain? A nice cool rain has come up! *(She gives the
gentleman caller a frightened look.)* I think we may — have grace — now . . .
(Tom looks at her stupidly.) Tom, honey — you say grace!

TOM: Oh . . . "For these and all thy mercies—" *(They bow their heads, Amanda stealing a nervous glance at Jim. In the living room Laura, stretched on the sofa, clenches her hand to her lips, to hold back a shuddering sob.)* God's Holy Name be praised—

(The scene dims out.)

Scene 7

A Souvenir

  Half an hour later. Dinner is just being finished in the upstage area, which is concealed by the drawn portieres.

  As the curtain rises Laura is still huddled upon the sofa, her feet drawn under her, her head resting on a pale blue pillow, her eyes wide and mysteriously watchful. The new floor lamp with its shade of rose-colored silk gives a soft, becoming light to her face, bringing out the fragile, unearthly prettiness which usually escapes attention. There is a steady murmur of rain, but it is slackening and stops soon after the scene begins; the air outside becomes pale and luminous as the moon breaks out.

  A moment after the curtain rises, the lights in both rooms flicker and go out.

JIM: Hey, there, Mr. Light Bulb!

Amanda laughs nervously.

  (Legend: "Suspension of a Public Service.")

AMANDA: Where was Moses when the lights went out? Ha-ha. Do you know the answer to that one, Mr. O'Connor?

JIM: No, Ma'am, what's the answer?

AMANDA: In the dark! *(Jim laughs appreciatively.)* Everybody sit still. I'll light the candles. Isn't it lucky we have them on the table? Where's a match? Which of you gentlemen can provide a match?

JIM: Here.

AMANDA: Thank you, sir.

JIM: Not at all, Ma'am!

AMANDA: I guess the fuse has burnt out. Mr. O'Connor, can you tell a burnt-out fuse? I know I can't and Tom is a total loss when it comes to mechanics. *(Sound: Getting up: Voices recede a little to kitchenette.)* Oh, be careful you don't bump into something. We don't want our gentleman caller to break his neck. Now wouldn't that be a fine howdy-do?

JIM: Ha-ha! Where is the fuse-box?

AMANDA: Right here next to the stove. Can you see anything?

JIM: Just a minute.

AMANDA: Isn't electricity a mysterious thing? Wasn't it Benjamin Franklin who tied a key to a kite? We live in such a mysterious universe, don't we? Some people say that science clears up all the mysteries for us. In my opinion it only creates more! Have you found it yet?

JIM: No, Ma'am. All these fuses look okay to me.

AMANDA: Tom!

TOM: Yes, Mother?

AMANDA: That light bill I gave you several days ago. The one I told you we got the notices about?

TOM: Oh.—Yeah.

(Legend: "Ha!")

AMANDA: You didn't neglect to pay it by any chance?

TOM: Why, I—

AMANDA: Didn't! I might have known it!

JIM: Shakespeare probably wrote a poem on that light bill, Mrs. Wingfield.

AMANDA: I might have known better than to trust him with it! There's such a high price for negligence in this world!

JIM: Maybe the poem will win a ten-dollar prize.

AMANDA: We'll just have to spend the remainder of the evening in the nineteenth century, before Mr. Edison made the Mazda lamp!

JIM: Candlelight is my favorite kind of light.

AMANDA: That shows you're romantic! But that's no excuse for Tom. Well, we got through dinner. Very considerate of them to let us get through dinner before they plunged us into everlasting darkness, wasn't it, Mr. O'Connor?

JIM: Ha-ha!

AMANDA: Tom, as a penalty for your carelessness you can help me with the dishes.

JIM: Let me give you a hand.

AMANDA: Indeed you will not!

JIM: I ought to be good for something.

AMANDA: Good for something? *(Her tone is rhapsodic.)* You? Why, Mr. O'Connor, nobody, *nobody's* given me this much entertainment in years—as you have!

JIM: Aw, now, Mrs. Wingfield!

AMANDA: I'm not exaggerating, not one bit! But Sister is all by her lonesome. You go keep her company in the parlor! I'll give you this lovely old candelabrum that used to be on the altar at the church of the Heavenly Rest. It was melted a little out of shape when the church burnt down. Lightning struck it one spring. Gypsy Jones was holding a revival at the time and he intimated that the church was destroyed because the Episcopalians gave card parties.

JIM: Ha-ha.

AMANDA: And how about coaxing Sister to drink a little wine? I think it would be good for her! Can you carry both at once?

JIM: Sure. I'm Superman!

AMANDA: Now, Thomas, get into this apron!

The door of kitchenette swings closed on Amanda's gay laughter; the flickering light approaches the portieres.

Laura sits up nervously as he enters. Her speech at first is low and breathless from the almost intolerable strain of being alone with a stranger.

(Legend: "I Don't Suppose You Remember Me at All!")

In her first speeches in this scene, before Jim's warmth overcomes her paralyzing shyness, Laura's voice is thin and breathless as though she has run up a steep flight of stairs.

Jim's attitude is gently humorous. In playing this scene it should be stressed that while the incident is apparently unimportant, it is to Laura the climax of her secret life.

JIM: Hello, there, Laura.

LAURA *(faintly)*:   Hello. *(She clears her throat.)*

JIM: How are you feeling now? Better?

LAURA: Yes. Yes, thank you.

JIM: This is for you. A little dandelion wine. *(He extends it toward her with extravagant gallantry.)*

LAURA: Thank you.

JIM: Drink it—but don't get drunk! *(He laughs heartily. Laura takes the glass uncertainly; laughs shyly.)* Where shall I set the candles?

LAURA: Oh—oh, anywhere . . .

JIM: How about here on the floor? Any objections?

LAURA: No.

JIM: I'll spread a newspaper under to catch the drippings. I like to sit on the floor. Mind if I do?

LAURA: Oh, no.

JIM: Give me a pillow?

LAURA: What?

JIM: A pillow!

LAURA: Oh . . . *(Hands him one quickly.)*

JIM: How about you? Don't you like to sit on the floor?

LAURA: Oh—yes.

JIM: Why don't you, then?

LAURA: I—will.

JIM: Take a pillow! *(Laura does. Sits on the other side of the candelabrum. Jim crosses his legs and smiles engagingly at her.)* I can't hardly see you sitting way over there.

LAURA: I can—see you.

JIM: I know, but that's not fair, I'm in the limelight. *(Laura moves her pillow closer.)* Good! Now I can see you! Comfortable?

LAURA: Yes.

JIM: So am I. Comfortable as a cow. Will you have some gum?

LAURA: No, thank you.

JIM: I think that I will indulge, with your permission. *(Musingly unwraps it and holds it up.)* Think of the fortune made by the guy that invented the first piece of chewing gum. Amazing, huh? The Wrigley Building is one of the sights of Chicago.—I saw it summer before last when I went up to the Century of Progress. Did you take in the Century of Progress?

LAURA: No, I didn't.

JIM: Well, it was quite a wonderful exposition. What impressed me most was the Hall of Science. Gives you an idea of what the future will be in America, even more wonderful than the present time is! *(Pause. Smiling at her.)* Your brother tells me you're shy. Is that right, Laura?

LAURA: I—don't know.

JIM: I judge you to be an old-fashioned type of girl. Well, I think that's a pretty good type to be. Hope you don't think I'm being too personal—do you?

LAURA *(hastily, out of embarrassment):*   I believe I *will* take a piece of gum, if you—don't mind. *(Clearing her throat.)* Mr. O'Connor, have you—kept up with your singing?

JIM: Singing? Me?

LAURA: Yes. I remember what a beautiful voice you had.

JIM: When did you hear me sing?

(Voice offstage in the pause.)

VOICE *(offstage):*   O blow, ye winds, heigh-ho,
　　　　　　　　　　A-roving I will go!
　　　　　　　　　　I'm off to my love
　　　　　　　　　　With a boxing glove—
　　　　　　　　　　Ten thousand miles away!

JIM: You say you've heard me sing?

LAURA: Oh, yes! Yes, very often . . . I—don't suppose you remember me—at all?

JIM *(smiling doubtfully):*   You know I have an idea I've seen you before. I had that idea soon as you opened the door. It seemed almost like I was about to remember your name. But the name that I started to call you—wasn't a name! And so I stopped myself before I said it.

LAURA: Wasn't it—Blue Roses?

JIM *(springs up, grinning):*   Blue Roses! My gosh, yes—Blue Roses! That's what I had on my tongue when you opened the door! Isn't it funny what tricks your memory plays? I didn't connect you with the high school somehow or other. But that's where it was; it was high school. I didn't even know you were Shakespeare's sister! Gosh, I'm sorry.

LAURA: I didn't expect you to. You—barely knew me!

JIM: But we did have a speaking acquaintance, huh?

LAURA: Yes, we—spoke to each other.

JIM: When did you recognize me?

LAURA: Oh, right away!

JIM: Soon as I came in the door?

LAURA: When I heard your name I thought it was probably you. I knew that Tom used to know you a little in high school. So when you came in the door—Well, then I was—sure.

JIM: Why didn't you *say* something, then?

LAURA *(breathlessly):*   I didn't know what to say, I was—too surprised!

JIM: For goodness' sakes! You know, this sure is funny!

LAURA: Yes! Yes, isn't it, though . . .

JIM: Didn't we have a class in something together?

LAURA: Yes, we did.

JIM: What class was that?

LAURA: It was—singing—Chorus!

JIM: Aw!

LAURA: I sat across the aisle from you in the Aud.

JIM: Aw.

LAURA: Mondays, Wednesdays, and Fridays.

JIM: Now I remember—you always came in late.

LAURA: Yes, it was so hard for me, getting upstairs. I had that brace on my leg—it clumped so loud!

JIM: I never heard any clumping.

LAURA (*wincing in the recollection*):   To me it sounded like—thunder!

JIM: Well, well, well. I never even noticed.

LAURA: And everybody was seated before I came in. I had to walk in front of all those people. My seat was in the back row. I had to go clumping all the way up the aisle with everyone watching!

JIM: You shouldn't have been self-conscious.

LAURA: I know, but I was. It was always such a relief when the singing started.

JIM: Aw, yes, I've placed you now! I used to call you Blue Roses. How was it that I got started calling you that?

LAURA: I was out of school a little while with pleurosis. When I came back you asked me what was the matter. I said I had pleurosis—you thought I said Blue Roses. That's what you always called me after that!

JIM: I hope you didn't mind.

LAURA: Oh, no—I liked it. You see, I wasn't acquainted with many—people. . . .

JIM: As I remember you sort of stuck by yourself.

LAURA: I—I—never had much luck at—making friends.

JIM: I don't see why you wouldn't.

LAURA: Well, I—started out badly.

JIM: You mean being—

LAURA: Yes, it sort of—stood between me—

JIM: You shouldn't have let it!

LAURA: I know, but it did, and—

JIM: You were shy with people!

LAURA: I tried not to be but never could—

JIM: Overcome it?

LAURA: No, I—I never could!

JIM: I guess being shy is something you have to work out of kind of gradually.

LAURA (*sorrowfully*):   Yes—I guess it—

JIM: Takes time!

LAURA: Yes—

JIM: People are not so dreadful when you know them. That's what you have to remember! And everybody has problems, not just you, but practically everybody has got some problems. You think of yourself as having the only problems, as being the only one who is disappointed. But just look around you and you will see lots of people as disappointed as you are. For instance, I hoped when I was going to high school that I would be further along at this time, six years later, than I am now — You remember that wonderful write-up I had in *The Torch?*

LAURA: Yes! *(She rises and crosses to table.)*

JIM: It said I was bound to succeed in anything I went into! *(Laura returns with the annual.)* Holy Jeez! *The Torch!* *(He accepts it reverently. They smile across it with mutual wonder. Laura crouches beside him and they begin to turn through it. Laura's shyness is dissolving in his warmth.)*

LAURA: Here you are in *Pirates of Penzance!*

JIM *(wistfully):* I sang the baritone lead in that operetta.

LAURA *(rapidly):* So — *beautifully!*

JIM *(protesting):* Aw —

LAURA: Yes, yes — beautifully — beautifully!

JIM: You heard me?

LAURA: All three times!

JIM: No!

LAURA: Yes!

JIM: All three performances?

LAURA *(looking down):* Yes.

JIM: Why?

LAURA: I — wanted to ask you to — autograph my program.

JIM: Why didn't you ask me to?

LAURA: You were always surrounded by your own friends so much that I never had a chance to.

JIM: You should have just —

LAURA: Well, I — thought you might think I was —

JIM: Thought I might think you was — what?

LAURA: Oh —

JIM *(with reflective relish):* I was beleaguered by females in those days.

LAURA: You were terribly popular!

JIM: Yeah —

LAURA: You had such a — friendly way —

JIM: I was spoiled in high school.

LAURA: Everybody — liked you!

JIM: Including you?

LAURA: I — yes, I — I did, too — *(She gently closes the book in her lap.)*

JIM: Well, well, well! — Give me that program, Laura. *(She hands it to him. He signs it with a flourish.)* There you are — better late than never!

LAURA: Oh, I — what a — surprise!

JIM: My signature isn't worth very much right now. But some day — maybe — it will increase in value! Being disappointed is one thing and being discouraged is something else. I am disappointed but I'm not discouraged. I'm twenty-three years old. How old are you?

LAURA: I'll be twenty-four in June.

JIM: That's not old age.

LAURA: No, but—

JIM: You finished high school?

LAURA *(with difficulty)*:   I didn't go back.

JIM: You mean you dropped out?

LAURA: I made bad grades in my final examinations. *(She rises and replaces the book and the program. Her voice strained.)* How is—Emily Meisenbach getting along?

JIM: Oh, that kraut-head!

LAURA: Why do you call her that?

JIM: That's what she was.

LAURA: You're not still—going with her?

JIM: I never see her.

LAURA: It said in the Personal Section that you were—engaged!

JIM: I know, but I wasn't impressed by that—propaganda!

LAURA: It wasn't—the truth?

JIM: Only in Emily's optimistic opinion!

LAURA: Oh—

(Legend: "What Have You Done Since High School?")

Jim lights a cigarette and leans indolently back on his elbows smiling at Laura with a warmth and charm which light her inwardly with altar candles. She remains by the table and turns in her hands a piece of glass to cover her tumult.

JIM *(after several reflective puffs on a cigarette)*:   What have you done since high school? *(She seems not to hear him.)* Huh? *(Laura looks up.)* I said what have you done since high school, Laura?

LAURA: Nothing much.

JIM: You must have been doing something these six long years.

LAURA: Yes.

JIM: Well, then, such as what?

LAURA: I took a business course at business college—

JIM: How did that work out?

LAURA: Well, not very—well—I had to drop out, it gave me—indigestion—

Jim laughs gently.

JIM: What are you doing now?

LAURA: I don't do anything—much. Oh, please don't think I sit around doing nothing! My glass collection takes up a good deal of my time. Glass is something you have to take good care of.

JIM: What did you say—about glass?

LAURA: Collection I said—I have one—*(She clears her throat and turns away again, acutely shy.)*

JIM *(abruptly)*:   You know what I judge to be the trouble with you? Inferiority complex! Know what that is? That's what they call it when someone low-rates himself! I understand it because I had it, too. Although my case was not so aggravated as yours seems to be. I had it until I took up public speaking, developed my voice, and learned that I had an aptitude for science. Before that time I never thought of myself as being outstanding in any way whatsoever! Now I've never made a regular study of it, but I have a friend who says I can analyze people better than doctors that make a profession of it. I don't claim that to be necessarily true, but I can sure guess a person's psychology, Laura! *(Takes out his gum.)* Excuse me, Laura. I always take it out when the flavor is gone. I'll use this scrap of paper to wrap it in. I know how it is to get it stuck on a shoe. Yep—that's what I judge to be your principal trouble. A lack of confidence in yourself as a person. You don't have the proper amount of faith in yourself. I'm basing that fact on a number of your remarks and also on certain observations I've made. For instance that clumping you thought was so awful in high school. You say that you even dreaded to walk into class. You see what you did? You dropped out of school, you gave up an education because of a clump, which as far as I know was practically nonexistent! A little physical defect is what you have. Hardly noticeable even! Magnified thousands of times by imagination! You know what my strong advice to you is? Think of yourself as *superior* in some way!

LAURA: In what way would I think?

JIM: Why, man alive, Laura! Just look about you a little. What do you see? A world full of common people! All of 'em born and all of 'em going to die! Which of them has one-tenth of your good points! Or mine! Or anyone else's, as far as that goes—Gosh! Everybody excels in some one thing. Some in many! *(Unconsciously glances at himself in the mirror.)* All you've got to do is discover in *what!* Take me, for instance. *(He adjusts his tie at the mirror.)* My interest happened to lie in electrodynamics. I'm taking a course in radio engineering at night school, Laura, on top of a fairly responsible job at the warehouse. I'm taking that course and studying public speaking.

LAURA: Ohhhh.

JIM: Because I believe in the future of television! *(Turning back to her.)* I wish to be ready to go up right along with it. Therefore I'm planning to get in on the ground floor. In fact, I've already made the right connections and all that remains is for the industry itself to get under way! Full steam—*(His eyes are starry.) Knowledge*—Zzzzzp! *Money*—Zzzzzzp!—*Power!* That's the cycle democracy is built on! *(His attitude is convincingly dynamic. Laura stares at him, even her shyness eclipsed in her absolute wonder. He suddenly grins.)* I guess you think I think a lot of myself!

LAURA: No—o-o-o, I—

JIM: Now how about you? Isn't there something you take more interest in than anything else?

LAURA: Well, I do—as I said—have my—glass collection—

A peal of girlish laughter from the kitchen.

JIM: I'm not right sure I know what you're talking about. What kind of glass is it?

LAURA: Little articles of it, they're ornaments mostly! Most of them are little animals made out of glass, the tiniest little animals in the world. Mother calls them a glass menagerie! Here's an example of one, if you'd like to see it! This one is one of the oldest. It's nearly thirteen. *(He stretches out his hand.) (Music: "The Glass Menagerie.")* Oh, be careful—if you breathe, it breaks!

JIM: I'd better not take it. I'm pretty clumsy with things.

LAURA: Go on, I trust you with him! *(Places it in his palm.)* There now—you're holding him gently! Hold him over the light, he loves the light! You see how the light shines through him?

JIM: It sure does shine!

LAURA: I shouldn't be partial, but he is my favorite one.

JIM: What kind of thing is this one supposed to be?

LAURA: Haven't you noticed the single horn on his forehead?

JIM: A unicorn, huh?

LAURA: Mmm-hmmm!

JIM: Unicorns, aren't they extinct in the modern world?

LAURA: I know!

JIM: Poor little fellow, he must feel sort of lonesome.

LAURA *(smiling)*:   Well, if he does he doesn't complain about it. He stays on a shelf with some horses that don't have horns and all of them seem to get along nicely together.

JIM: How do you know?

LAURA *(lightly)*:   I haven't heard any arguments among them!

JIM *(grinning)*:   No arguments, huh? Well, that's a pretty good sign! Where shall I set him?

LAURA: Put him on the table. They all like a change of scenery once in a while!

JIM *(stretching)*:   Well, well, well, well—Look how big my shadow is when I stretch!

LAURA: Oh, oh, yes—it stretches across the ceiling!

JIM *(crossing to door)*:   I think it's stopped raining. *(Opens fire-escape door.)* Where does the music come from?

LAURA: From the Paradise Dance Hall across the alley.

JIM: How about cutting the rug a little, Miss Wingfield?

LAURA: Oh, I—

JIM: Or is your program filled up? Let me have a look at it. *(Grasps imaginary card.)* Why, every dance is taken! I'll have to scratch some out. *(Waltz music: "La Golondrina.")* Ahhh, a waltz! *(He executes some sweeping turns by himself then holds his arms toward Laura.)*

LAURA *(breathlessly)*:   I—can't dance!

JIM: There you go, that inferiority stuff!

LAURA: I've never danced in my life!

JIM: Come on, try!

LAURA: Oh, but I'd step on you!

JIM: I'm not made out of glass.

LAURA: How—how—how do we start?

JIM: Just leave it to me. You hold your arms out a little.

LAURA: Like this?

JIM:　A little bit higher. Right. Now don't tighten up, that's the main thing about it — relax.

LAURA *(laughing breathlessly)*:　It's hard not to.

JIM:　Okay.

LAURA:　I'm afraid you can't budge me.

JIM:　What do you bet I can't? *(He swings her into motion.)*

LAURA:　Goodness, yes, you can!

JIM:　Let yourself go, now, Laura, just let yourself go.

LAURA:　I'm —

JIM:　Come on!

LAURA:　Trying.

JIM:　Not so stiff — Easy does it!

LAURA:　I know but I'm —

JIM:　Loosen th' backbone! There now, that's a lot better.

LAURA:　Am I?

JIM:　Lots, lots better! *(He moves her about the room in a clumsy waltz.)*

LAURA:　Oh, my!

JIM:　Ha-ha!

LAURA:　Goodness, yes you can!

JIM:　Ha-ha-ha! *(They suddenly bump into the table. Jim stops.)* What did we hit on?

LAURA:　Table.

JIM:　Did something fall off it? I think —

LAURA:　Yes.

JIM:　I hope it wasn't the little glass horse with the horn!

LAURA:　Yes.

JIM:　Aw, aw, aw. Is it broken?

LAURA:　Now it is just like all the other horses.

JIM:　It's lost its —

LAURA:　Horn! It doesn't matter. Maybe it's a blessing in disguise.

JIM:　You'll never forgive me. I bet that that was your favorite piece of glass.

LAURA:　I don't have favorites much. It's no tragedy, Freckles. Glass breaks so easily. No matter how careful you are. The traffic jars the shelves and things fall off them.

JIM:　Still I'm awfully sorry that I was the cause.

LAURA *(smiling)*:　I'll just imagine he had an operation. The horn was removed to make him feel less — freakish! *(They both laugh.)* Now he will feel more at home with the other horses, the ones that don't have horns . . .

JIM:　Ha-ha, that's very funny! *(Suddenly serious.)* I'm glad to see that you have a sense of humor. You know — you're — well — very different! Surprisingly different from anyone else I know! *(His voice becomes soft and hesitant with a genuine feeling.)* Do you mind me telling you that? *(Laura is abashed beyond speech.)* You make me feel sort of — I don't know how to put it! I'm usually pretty good at expressing things, but — This is something that I don't know how to say! *(Laura touches her throat and clears it — turns the broken unicorn in her hands.)* *(Even softer.)* Has anyone ever told you that you were pretty?

Pause: Music.

> *(Laura looks up slowly, with wonder, and shakes her head.)* Well, you are! In a very different way from anyone else. And all the nicer because of the difference, too. *(His voice becomes low and husky. Laura turns away, nearly faint with the novelty of her emotions.)* I wish that you were my sister. I'd teach you to have some confidence in yourself. The different people are not like other people, but being different is nothing to be ashamed of. Because other people are not such wonderful people. They're one hundred times one thousand. You're one times one! They walk all over the earth. You just stay here. They're common as — weeds, but — you — well, you're — *Blue Roses!*

(Image on screen: Blue Roses.)
(Music changes.)

LAURA: But blue is wrong for — roses . . .

JIM: It's right for you — You're — pretty!

LAURA: In what respect am I pretty?

JIM: In all respects — believe me! Your eyes — your hair — are pretty! Your hands are pretty! *(He catches hold of her hand.)* You think I'm making this up because I'm invited to dinner and have to be nice. Oh, I could do that! I could put on an act for you, Laura, and say lots of things without being very sincere. But this time I am. I'm talking to you sincerely. I happened to notice you had this inferiority complex that keeps you from feeling comfortable with people. Somebody needs to build your confidence up and make you proud instead of shy and turning away and — blushing — Somebody ought to — ought to — kiss you, Laura! *(His hand slips slowly up her arm to her shoulder.)* *(Music swells tumultuously.)* *(He suddenly turns her about and kisses her on the lips. When he releases her Laura sinks on the sofa with a bright, dazed look. Jim backs away and fishes in his pocket for a cigarette.)* *(Legend on screen: "Souvenir.")* Stumble-john! *(He lights the cigarette, avoiding her look. There is a peal of girlish laughter from Amanda in the kitchen. Laura slowly raises and opens her hand. It still contains the little broken glass animal. She looks at it with a tender, bewildered expression.)* Stumble-john! I shouldn't have done that — That was way off the beam. You don't smoke, do you? *(She looks up, smiling, not hearing the question. He sits beside her a little gingerly. She looks at him speechlessly — waiting. He coughs decorously and moves a little farther aside as he considers the situation and senses her feelings, dimly, with perturbation. Gently.)* Would you — care for a — mint? *(She doesn't seem to hear him but her look grows brighter even.)* Peppermint — Life Saver? My pocket's a regular drug store — wherever I go . . . *(He pops a mint in his mouth. Then gulps and decides to make a clean breast of it. He speaks slowly and gingerly.)* Laura, you know, if I had a sister like you, I'd do the same thing as Tom. I'd bring out fellows — introduce her to them. The right type of boys of a type to — appreciate her. Only — well — he made a mistake about me. Maybe I've got no call to be saying this. That may not have been the idea in having me over. But what if it was? There's nothing wrong about that. The only trouble is that in my case — I'm not in a situation to — do the right thing.

I can't take down your number and say I'll phone. I can't call up next week and — ask for a date. I thought I had better explain the situation in case you misunderstood it and — hurt your feelings. . . . *(Pause. Slowly, very slowly, Laura's look changes, her eyes returning slowly from his to the ornament in her palm.)*

Amanda utters another gay laugh in the kitchen.

LAURA *(faintly)*:   You — won't — call again?

JIM: No, Laura, I can't. *(He rises from the sofa.)* As I was just explaining, I've — got strings on me, Laura, I've — been going steady! I go out all the time with a girl named Betty. She's a home-girl like you, and Catholic, and Irish, and in a great many ways we — get along fine. I met her last summer on a moonlight boat trip up the river to Alton, on the *Majestic*. Well — right away from the start it was — love! *(Legend: Love!)* *(Laura sways slightly forward and grips the arm of the sofa. He fails to notice, now enrapt in his own comfortable being.)* Being in love has made a new man of me! *(Leaning stiffly forward, clutching the arm of the sofa, Laura struggles visibly with her storm. But Jim is oblivious, she is a long way off.)* The power of love is really pretty tremendous! Love is something that — changes the whole world, Laura! *(The storm abates a little and Laura leans back. He notices her again.)* It happened that Betty's aunt took sick, she got a wire and had to go to Centralia. So Tom — when he asked me to dinner — I naturally just accepted the invitation, not knowing that you — that he — that I — *(He stops awkwardly.)* Huh — I'm a stumble-john! *(He flops back on the sofa. The holy candles in the altar of Laura's face have been snuffed out! There is a look of almost infinite desolation. Jim glances at her uneasily.)* I wish that you would — say something. *(She bites her lip which was trembling and then bravely smiles. She opens her hand again on the broken glass ornament. Then she gently takes his hand and raises it level with her own. She carefully places the unicorn in the palm of his hand, then pushes his fingers closed upon it.)* What are you — doing that for? You want me to have him? — Laura? *(She nods.)* What for?

LAURA: A — souvenir . . .

She rises unsteadily and crouches beside the Victrola to wind it up.

(Legend on screen: "Things Have a Way of Turning Out So Badly.")

(Or image: "Gentleman caller waving good-bye! — Gaily.")

At this moment Amanda rushes brightly back in the front room. She bears a pitcher of fruit punch in an old-fashioned cut-glass pitcher and a plate of macaroons. The plate has a gold border and poppies painted on it.

AMANDA: Well, well, well! Isn't the air delightful after the shower? I've made you children a little liquid refreshment. *(Turns gaily to the gentleman caller.)* Jim, do you know that song about lemonade?

"Lemonade, lemonade

Made in the shade and stirred with a spade —

Good enough for any old maid!"

JIM *(uneasily)*:   Ha-ha! No — I never heard it.

AMANDA: Why, Laura! You look so serious!

JIM: We were having a serious conversation.

AMANDA: Good! Now you're better acquainted!

JIM *(uncertainly)*:   Ha-ha! Yes.

AMANDA: You modern young people are much more serious-minded than my generation. I was so gay as a girl!

JIM: You haven't changed, Mrs. Wingfield.

AMANDA: Tonight I'm rejuvenated! The gaiety of the occasion, Mr. O'Connor! *(She tosses her head with a peal of laughter. Spills lemonade.)* Oooo! I'm baptizing myself!

JIM: Here—let me—

AMANDA *(setting the pitcher down)*:   There now. I discovered we had some maraschino cherries. I dumped them in, juice and all!

JIM: You shouldn't have gone to that trouble, Mrs. Wingfield.

AMANDA: Trouble, trouble? Why it was loads of fun! Didn't you hear me cutting up in the kitchen? I bet your ears were burning! I told Tom how outdone with him I was for keeping you to himself so long a time! He should have brought you over much, much sooner! Well, now that you've found your way, I want you to be a very frequent caller! Not just occasional but all the time. Oh, we're going to have a lot of gay times together! I see them coming! Mmm, just breathe that air! So fresh, and the moon's so pretty! I'll skip back out—I know where my place is when young folks are having a—serious conversation!

JIM: Oh, don't go out, Mrs. Wingfield. The fact of the matter is I've got to be going.

AMANDA: Going, now? You're joking! Why, it's only the shank of the evening, Mr. O'Connor!

JIM: Well, you know how it is.

AMANDA: You mean you're a young workingman and have to keep workingmen's hours. We'll let you off early tonight. But only on the condition that next time you stay later. What's the best night for you? Isn't Saturday night the best night for you workingmen?

JIM: I have a couple of time-clocks to punch, Mrs. Wingfield. One at morning, another one at night!

AMANDA: My, but you *are* ambitious! You work at night, too?

JIM: No, Ma'am, not work but—Betty! *(He crosses deliberately to pick up his hat. The band at the Paradise Dance Hall goes into a tender waltz.)*

AMANDA: Betty? Betty? Who's—Betty! *(There is an ominous cracking sound in the sky.)*

JIM: Oh, just a girl. The girl I go steady with! *(He smiles charmingly. The sky falls.)*

(Legend: "The Sky Falls.")

AMANDA *(a long-drawn exhalation)*:   Ohhhh . . . Is it a serious romance, Mr. O'Connor?

JIM: We're going to be married the second Sunday in June.

AMANDA: Ohhhh—how nice! Tom didn't mention that you were engaged to be married.

JIM: The cat's not out of the bag at the warehouse yet. You know how they are. They call you Romeo and stuff like that. *(He stops at the oval mirror to put on his hat. He carefully shapes the brim and the crown to give a discreetly dashing effect.)* It's been a wonderful evening, Mrs. Wingfield. I guess this is what they mean by Southern hospitality.

AMANDA: It really wasn't anything at all.

JIM: I hope it don't seem like I'm rushing off. But I promised Betty I'd pick her up at the Wabash depot, an' by the time I get my jalopy down there her train'll be in. Some women are pretty upset if you keep 'em waiting.

AMANDA: Yes, I know — The tyranny of women! *(Extends her hand.)* Good-bye, Mr. O'Connor. I wish you luck — and happiness — and success! All three of them, and so does Laura — Don't you, Laura?

LAURA: Yes!

JIM *(taking her hand)*:   Good-bye, Laura. I'm certainly going to treasure that souvenir. And don't you forget the good advice I gave you. *(Raises his voice to a cheery shout.)* So long, Shakespeare! Thanks again, ladies — Good night!

He grins and ducks jauntily out.

  Still bravely grimacing, Amanda closes the door on the gentleman caller. Then she turns back to the room with a puzzled expression. She and Laura don't dare to face each other. Laura crouches beside the Victrola to wind it.

AMANDA *(faintly)*:   Things have a way of turning out so badly. I don't believe that I would play the Victrola. Well, well — well — Our gentleman caller was engaged to be married! Tom!

TOM *(from back)*:   Yes, Mother?

AMANDA: Come in here a minute. I want to tell you something awfully funny.

TOM *(enters with macaroon and a glass of the lemonade)*:   Has the gentleman caller gotten away already?

AMANDA: The gentleman caller has made an early departure. What a wonderful joke you played on us!

TOM: How do you mean?

AMANDA: You didn't mention that he was engaged to be married.

TOM: Jim? Engaged?

AMANDA: That's what he just informed us.

TOM: I'll be jiggered! I didn't know about that.

AMANDA: That seems very peculiar.

TOM: What's peculiar about it?

AMANDA: Didn't you call him your best friend down at the warehouse?

TOM: He is, but how did I know?

AMANDA: It seems extremely peculiar that you wouldn't know your best friend was going to be married!

TOM: The warehouse is where I work, not where I know things about people!

AMANDA: You don't know things anywhere! You live in a dream; you manufacture illusions! *(He crosses to door.)* Where are you going?

TOM: I'm going to the movies.

AMANDA: That's right, now that you've had us make such fools of ourselves. The effort, the preparations, all the expense! The new floor lamp, the rug, the clothes for Laura! All for what? To entertain some other girl's fiancé! Go to the movies, go! Don't think about us, a mother deserted, an unmarried sister who's crippled and has no job! Don't let anything interfere with your selfish pleasure! Just go, go, go — to the movies!

TOM: All right, I will! The more you shout about my selfishness to me the quicker I'll go, and I won't go to the movies!

AMANDA: Go, then! Then go to the moon — you selfish dreamer!

Tom smashes his glass on the floor. He plunges out on the fire-escape, slamming the door. Laura screams — cut by door.

Dance-hall music up. Tom goes to the rail and grips it desperately, lifting his face in the chill white moonlight penetrating the narrow abyss of the alley.

(Legend on screen: "And So Good-Bye . . .")

Tom's closing speech is timed with the interior pantomime. The interior scene is played as though viewed through sound-proof glass. Amanda appears to be making a comforting speech to Laura who is huddled upon the sofa. Now that we cannot hear the mother's speech, her silliness is gone and she has dignity and tragic beauty. Laura's dark hair hides her face until at the end of the speech she lifts it to smile at her mother. Amanda's gestures are slow and graceful, almost dancelike, as she comforts the daughter. At the end of her speech she glances a moment at the father's picture — then withdraws through the portieres. At close of Tom's speech, Laura blows out the candles, ending the play.

TOM: I didn't go to the moon, I went much further — for time is the longest distance between two places — Not long after that I was fired for writing a poem on the lid of a shoe-box. I left Saint Louis. I descended the steps of this fire-escape for a last time and followed, from then on, in my father's footsteps, attempting to find in motion what was lost in space — I traveled around a great deal. The cities swept about me like dead leaves, leaves that were brightly colored but torn away from the branches. I would have stopped, but I was pursued by something. It always came upon me unawares, taking me altogether by surprise. Perhaps it was a familiar bit of music. Perhaps it was only a piece of transparent glass — Perhaps I am walking along a street at night, in some strange city, before I have found companions. I pass the lighted window of a shop where perfume is sold. The window is filled with pieces of colored glass, tiny transparent bottles in delicate colors, like bits of a shattered rainbow. Then all at once my sister touches my shoulder. I turn around and look into her eyes. . . . Oh, Laura, Laura, I tried to leave you behind me, but I am more faithful than I intended to be! I reach for a cigarette, I cross the street, I run into the movies or a bar, I buy a drink, I speak to the nearest stranger — anything that can blow your candles out! *(Laura bends over the candles)* — for nowadays the world is lit by lightning! Blow out your candles, Laura — and so good-bye . . .

She blows the candles out.

(The Scene Dissolves.)   [1945]

THINKING ABOUT THE TEXT

1. Is Amanda just overprotective, or is there something seriously wrong with her devotion to Laura's eventual marriage? If you were a close friend of Amanda, how would you advise her to behave toward Laura?

2. Why does Laura keep the glass menagerie? Why does she give Jim her broken unicorn? Is this a positive sign?

3. This is a play about love, guilt, pity, regret, cruelty, and self-loathing. Can you cite concrete examples of these emotions in this play? Are there other emotions that you noticed? Is this a realistic portrait of family life, or is it an exaggeration?

4. Critics are divided over Williams's motivation in this play. Is he trying to get rid of Laura's memory (based on his sister Rose who went mad and whom Williams deserted), or is he replaying the traumatic leaving? Which makes the most sense to you? How do you read the last line, "Blow out your candles, Laura — and so good-bye . . ."?

5. Do you blame Tom for leaving? Does he abandon his responsibilities? What do you think of Tom's priorities? Does he have a duty to take the place of his absent father? What would have happened if Tom had stayed? What would you do?

MAKING COMPARISONS

1. Williams claims that there is "much to admire in Amanda, and as much to love and pity." Do you agree with his assessment? Do you think the same could be said for Hamlet's mother, Gertrude?

2. What do you consider a proper relationship between children and parents? How well do Laertes and Ophelia embody this ideal? How well does Hamlet? Tom? Laura?

3. Compare Hamlet and Tom Wingfield as men of action, as sensitive and poetic thinkers, as loyal children, as moral citizens, as psychologically healthy individuals.

WRITING ABOUT ISSUES

1. Locate Hamlet's two great soliloquies ("too too sullied flesh" [1.2.129–59] and "To be, or not to be" [3.1.56–89]) and write a comparison between them and Tom's opening and closing monologues.

2. Argue that the catastrophes in *Hamlet* are either Claudius's or Hamlet's responsibility.

3. What is your view of Ophelia and Laura? Are they victims of an insensitive male culture? Are they responsible for their own situation? Write a

personal response that compares these two characters to friends or relatives you think are similar.

4. Write an essay that compares Hamlet's and Tom's behavior, making reference to their specific situations, their differing sense of duty and obligations, and the impact such behavior might have on society.

DIFFERENT CHILDREN

JOYCE CAROL OATES, "Wednesday's Child"
KATHERINE ANNE PORTER, "He"

While being a parent is difficult, being a parent of a mentally disabled child is a special challenge. Many of us would have difficulty finding the strength, patience, and commitment to raise a child who may not return our attention or love. The bond between a parent and a child grows strong because it is a give-and-take relationship. Parents give care, love, and support in innumerable ways, usually receiving back the child's respect and affection. Without that, it is difficult to sustain unilateral giving. For a family that is financially strapped as well, lavishing attention on a disabled child becomes an additional burden.

The following stories present the painful situation of two families, one affluent and the other poor. One child suffers from autism, the other from mental retardation. Both families struggle to do the right thing. Both fail to connect with their distant children. These stories do not offer easy answers or sentimental resolutions. They do, however, capture our compassion and make us wonder how we would respond as members of these families.

BEFORE YOU READ

Think back to a childhood encounter with someone mentally, emotionally, or physically different. How did you react? Are children cruel to the disabled? To what extent is society responsible for caring for the disabled?

JOYCE CAROL OATES
Wednesday's Child

Born as part of an Irish-Catholic family in Lockport, New York, Joyce Carol Oates (b. 1938) grew up in the sort of rural, working-class setting in which she sets much of her fiction. After earning a B.A. from Syracuse University in 1960 and an M.A. from the University of Wisconsin in 1961, she went on to teach at the

University of Detroit and the University of Windsor, Ontario. A prolific writer who has produced at least a volume of work a year since 1965, Oates has published poetry, drama, novels, short stories, and essays on diverse topics. Her many honors include the National Book Award for them (1969). She is currently writer-in-residence and the Roger S. Berlind Distinguished Professor in the Humanities at Princeton University. "Wednesday's Child" is from her book Marriage and Infidelities *(1972).*

Around the high handsome roof of the house birds flew in the first hours of daylight, calling out, so that their small shadows fell against the bedroom curtains harmless as flowers thrown by anonymous admirers. Squirrels ran along the gutters. At some distance the horns of river freighters sounded, melancholy and exciting. Today he was not going to work; today he woke slowly, with a sense of luxury, aware of these sounds and their lovely softness, thinking that sound itself seemed a kind of touch.

His wife lay sleeping beside him. She was a dark-haired woman of thirty-five, attractive, exhausted even in sleep, wounded by small impatient lines in her forehead; he did not quite believe in those lines. He always expected them to be gone. Even in sleep his wife seemed to him thoughtful, thinking, sensitive to his feeling of luxury—so she lay perfectly still, not waking. She would not join him in it.

Several shadows fell against the curtains—the weightless shadows of birds. He watched. Everything was still. This house, thirty years old, had stood firm and wonderfully solid among its more contemporary neighbors, a high brick colonial home with white shutters, quite perfect. It was not his idea of a final home. It was his idea of a home for himself and his wife and daughter in this decade, just as this famous suburb was his idea of a way of preparing for a distant, delightful, aristocratic life in another part of the country. He was an architect and worked for an excellent firm. Only thirty-seven, he was successful in the eyes of his parents and even in the eyes of his friends, who were themselves scampering like squirrels with their tiny shrewd toe-nails pulling them, pulling them up, always up, their cheeks rosy with the exhilaration of success. He was one of them. He was not his parents' son any longer; his father had been a high-school teacher, a good, deferential, exploited man.

So he woke on Wednesday morning, very early. The day would be a long one. His wife was evidently not going to wake, but lay frowning and severe in sleep, as if giving up to him the burden of this day. Already he could hear his daughter. Coming out of her room . . . in the hall . . . now on her way downstairs. He listened closely. He could hear, or could imagine, her pulling the piano bench away from the piano, down in the living room. Yes, she must be there. The bench was white—a white grand piano, very beautiful—and she sat at it, seriously, frowning like her mother, staring down at the keys. White and black keys. Even the cracks arrested her attention. He lay in bed on the second floor of his house, imagining his daughter almost directly below him, sitting at the piano. He heard the first note. His face went rigid.

He got dressed quickly. He put on a tie his mother had given him, a very con-   5
servative tie, dark green. His secret was a dark, serious, grimly green soul—he
liked to hide it behind smiles, enthusiasm for football, hearty compliments to his
wife. . . . She had turned over in bed, she was still asleep or pretending to sleep.
The other day she had told him she would not remain herself much longer. "I
can't live like this much longer," she had said. It was not a threat or a warning,
only a curious, exploratory remark. They had come in late from a dinner party,
from a marvelous evening, and she had told him suddenly that she was failing,
giving up, being conquered, defeated . . . all she had accomplished as a mother
was failure. Failure.

Why should she wake up to see him off?

Downstairs he saw with a slight shock Brenda at the piano, seated just as he
had imagined her. She was running her fingers gently over the keyboard. The
sound was gentle, soft. It would not shatter any crystal; there was no power
behind it. Down at the far end of the living room the wide French windows were
seared with light, the filmy curtains glowing. He appreciated that; he appreciated
beauty. The living room had been decorated in white and gold. His daughter's
face was pale, not quite white, and her legs pale, limp, motionless. She had put
her little white socks on perfectly. She wore a yellow dress, perfectly ironed by the
laundry that did her father's shirts so meticulously, and her hair was a fine, dull
gold, very neat. Everything matched. He appreciated that.

She was playing the "Moonlight Sonata" with a numb, feverish, heavy
rhythm, leaning too hard on the more emphatic passages, too breathy and rushed
with the delicate ones. She played like a sixteen-year-old girl who had taken
lessons dutifully for years, mediocre and competent, with a firm failure of imagination underlying every note. Brenda was only six and had never had any music
lessons, did not even listen in any evident way to music, and yet she could play for
hours with this mysterious sub-competence—why? He stood staring at her. She
was oblivious to him. Why, if his daughter must be insane, why not brilliantly
insane? Why not a genius?

Instead, she was extraordinary but not astonishing. She might be written up
in someone's textbook someday, but the case history would not be important;
there wasn't enough to her. "Good morning, honey," he said. He came to her and
put his arms gently around her. She stopped playing the piano but did not seem
to notice him. Instead, as if paralyzed by a thought that had nothing to do with
him, she sat rigid, intense, staring at her fingers on the keyboard.

"You're all ready, are you? Scrubbed and clean and ready for the trip?"   10

She did not appear to have heard him. She did hear him, of course, every
word, and some words hardly audible—they had discovered that when she was
hardly a year old, her uncanny animal-like omnipotence. She heard what was
breathed into his ear by his wife, up in their secret bed, she heard the secret date
of her next appointment with the Dreaded Doctor, she knew instinctively when
an innocent drive would take her to the dentist, she knew everything. . . . Today,
Wednesday, was not a fearful day. She was not afraid of school. She gave no indication of liking it, or of anticipating it, but she was not afraid and she would not
go limp, forcing them to carry her out to the car.

"I'll have some coffee, then we'll leave. Mommy's staying home today and I'm taking you. I thought we'd have a nice drive to school, then come back through the park. . . . I took the whole day off today. I hope the sun stays out."

He was aware of the paragraphs of his speech. Talking to his silent, frowning daughter, a child of six with an ageless look, he understood how silence mocks words; her blocks of silence, like terrible monstrous blocks of stone, fell heavily on either side of his words. What he said was never quite accurate. He was speaking to a child when, perhaps, he should have been speaking to an adult. Brenda's intelligence had never been measured. She might be ten years old, or eighteen, or two. It was a mystery, an abyss. As soon as he entered the kitchen he heard her begin to play where she had left off, the "Moonlight Sonata" in that sun-filled living room. . . .

He made instant coffee. His hands had begun to tremble. The harmonic green and brown of the kitchen did not soothe him, he could not sit down. When he came home from the office each day he always came out to the kitchen to talk to his wife, and he talked energetically about his work. His wife always appeared to listen with sympathy. His paragraphs of words, tossed against her appreciative silence, were attempts to keep her quiet; he realized that now. She made dinner and listened to him, flattering him with her complete attention. He hinted of trouble at work, maybe a union threatening to strike, or the federal government again raising mortgage interest rates . . . tricks to keep his wife from talking about Brenda. He realized that now.

When he returned to the living room Brenda slid dutifully off the bench.   15
She never resisted physically; her body was not really her own. She was quite small for her age, with knobby white knees. He loved her knees. Her hair was thin and straight, cut off to show her delicate ears. Her face was a pretty face, though too thin, unnaturally pale; her eyes were a light green. Seeing her was always a shock; you expected to see a dull, squat child, a kind of dwarf. Not at all. Everyone, especially the two sets of grandparents, remarked on her beauty. "She's so pretty! It will all work itself out!" both grandmothers said constantly. They were anxious to share in her mythical progress and contributed toward the tuition charged by the private, expensive school she went to, though Arthur resented this. He made enough money to send his own child to school. But the grandparents wanted to get as close as possible, nudging their beautiful prodigy into life, breathing the mysterious breath of normal life into her. Why, why was she not normal, when it was so obviously easier to be normal than to be Brenda? Perfectly stupid children were normal, ugly children were normal, and this golden-haired little lady, with her perfect face and ears and limbs, was somehow not . . . not "normal." It was an abyss, the fact of her.

Drawing slightly away from him, with a woman's coolness, she put on her own coat. He knelt to check her, to see if the buttons were lined up correctly. Of course. It had been years since she'd buttoned them wrong. "All set? Great! We're on our way!" Arthur said heartily. She did not look at him. She never met his eye, that was part of her strangeness — she would not look anyone in the eye, as if some secret shame or hatred forced her away, like the invisible force of like magnets.

And so . . . they were on their way. No backing out. His wife had driven Brenda to school ever since Brenda had begun, and today he was driving her, a generous act. Minutes flew by. It was a surprise how quickly time had passed, getting him up out of bed and on his way, drawing him to the ride. The minutes had passed as if flying toward an execution. . . . He had tried to think of this day as a gift, a day off from work, but it had been nothing but pretense. He was afraid of the long trip and afraid of his daughter.

Between his wife and himself was the fact of their daughter. They had created her together, somehow they had brought her into the world. It was a mystery that jarred the soul; better not to think of it. His wife had accused him more than once of blaming her for the child. "You hate me unconsciously. You can't control it," she had said. Her wisdom was sour and impregnable. "You hate failure," she said. Didn't he hate, in his cheerful secretive way, his own father because his own father was something of a failure? "Jesus Christ, what are you saying?" he had shouted. He denied everything.

The school was experimental and chancy, very expensive. Was it really quite professional? The several doctors they'd taken Brenda to were not enthusiastic; they expressed their opinion of the school with a neutral shrug of the shoulders. Why not try? And so, desperate, they had driven fifty miles to talk with the director, a long-nosed, urgent female with grimy fingernails and great excitement, and she had agreed to take Brenda on. "But we make no promises. Everything is exploratory," she had said. "Nothing is given a form, no theories are allowed to be hardened into dogma, no theories are rejected without trial, no emotions are stifled. . . ." Why not try? After several months Brenda showed no signs of improvement, and no signs of degeneration. If she showed any "signs" at all, they were private and indecipherable. But Wednesday had become the center of the week. He and his wife looked to Wednesday, that magic day, as a kind of Sabbath; on that day he drove to work with a sense of anticipation, and his wife drove Brenda fifty miles to school and fifty miles back again, hoping. This was the usual procedure. Then, when he came home, he would always ask, "How do you think it went today?" and she would always reply, "The director is still hopeful . . . I think it's going well . . . yes, I think it's going well."

In the car Brenda seated herself as far from him as possible. No use to urge her to move over. She was not stubborn, not exactly. It was rather as if no one inhabited her body, as if her spirit had abandoned it. "A great day for a ride!" he said. He chatted with her, or toward her. His voice sounded nervous. He disliked silence because of its emptiness, the possibility of anything happening inside it — no warning, no form to it. He was amorous of forms, solid forms. He distrusted shapelessness. In his daydreams he had always wanted to force action into a shape, to freeze explosions into art, into the forms in which beauty is made bearable. He lived in one of those forms. The style of his living was one of them. Why not? The work he did was professional in every way, geared to a market, imagination within certain limiting forms. He was not a genius, he would not revolutionize architecture. Like his daughter, he was extraordinary but not astonishing.

Brenda took a piece of spaghetti out of her coat pocket. It was uncooked, broken in half. She began to chew on it. Except for random, unlikely things — fish

20

sticks, bits of cardboard, cucumber, grapes with seeds—she ate nothing but uncooked spaghetti. She bit pieces off slowly, solemnly, chewing them with precision. Her green eyes were very serious. Every day she stuffed her pockets with pieces of spaghetti, broken in pieces. Bits of spaghetti were all over the house. His wife vacuumed every day, with great patience. It wasn't that Brenda seemed to like spaghetti, or that she had any concept of "liking" food at all. Perhaps she could not taste it. But she would not eat anything else. Arthur had long ago stopped snatching it away from her. He had stopped pleading with her. For what had seemed a decade she had sat at the table with them, listless and stony-eyed, refusing to eat. She did not quite *refuse*—nothing so emphatic. But she would not eat. She had no obvious conception of "eating." What she did was nibble slowly at pieces of spaghetti, all day long, or chew cardboard and shape it into little balls, or suck at grapes and very carefully extract the seeds. She walked around the house or out in the back yard as if in a trance, slow, precise, unhurried, spiritless. Demurely she turned aside when someone approached her. She went dead. The only life she showed was her piano playing, which was monotonous and predictable, the same pieces over and over again for months. . . . Her silence was immense as a mountain neither Arthur nor his wife could climb. And when the silence came to an end—when Brenda cried, which was infrequent—they heard to their horror the sobs of a six-year-old child, breathy and helpless. But how to help her? She could not be embraced, even by a distraught parent. A bump on the head, a bleeding scratch, would not soften her. The jolly mindlessness of Christmas would not give any grandparent the right to hug her. No nonsense. No touching. When his wife took Brenda for her monthly checkup, at which time the doctor gave her vitamin shots, she always asked the doctor how Brenda was "doing"; and the doctor always said, with a special serious smile to show how sorry he was about all this, "She's surprisingly healthy, considering her diet. You should be thankful."

It was a long drive. Arthur began to think longingly of his office—an older associate of his whom he admired and imitated, the naïveté of a secretary he could almost have loved, in another dimension. Elevators, high buildings. Occasional long lunches. He thought of his office, of his working space. He liked to work. He liked problems. They came to him in the shape of lines with three dimensions. It was remarkable how they were then transferred into shapes that were solid, into buildings. He was working on a shopping plaza. A shopping "mall." With love he dreamed of the proper shapes of banks, the proper shapes of supermarkets, of hardware stores—seductive as music! Their lines had to be gentle, seductive, attractive as the face of his secretary, who was only twenty-three. He wanted to love them. Certainly he had enough love in him . . . love for his work, for his wife, his secretary, his parents, his friends, his daughter. . . . Why did he feel so exhausted though it was early morning?

He entered the expressway in silence. Brenda was awake but silent. It was worse than being truly alone, for a swerving of the car would knock her around; if he slammed on the brakes she would fly forward and crack her skull. A limp weight. No true shape to her, because she was so empty. What was she thinking? He glanced sideways at her, smiling in case she noticed him. He and his wife

believed that their daughter was thinking constantly. Her silence was not peaceful. It seemed to them nervous, jumpy, alert, but alert to invisible shapes. Something unseen would move in the corner of her eye and she would shiver, almost
imperceptibly. What did she see? What did she think? Idiot children who giggle
and squirm happily in their mothers' embraces make more sense, being only
defective of intelligence. It would be possible to love them.

"Look at the cows!" he said, pointing. "Do you see the cows?"

No response. No cows.   25

"Look at the big truck up ahead . . . all those new cars on it. . . ." He felt the
need to talk. He wanted to keep a sense of terror at some distance; her silence, her
terrifying silence! He stared at the carrier with its double row of shining cars, cars of
all colors, very handsome. He was preparing to pass the truck. What if, at the crucial
moment, the truck wobbled and the cars came loose? They seemed precariously
fastened to the carrier. He imagined metal shearing through metal, slicing off the
top of his skull. The steering wheel would cut him in two. And his daughter would
be crushed in an instant, pressed into her essential silence. The end.

"Like to hear some music, Brenda?" He turned on the radio. Strange, how he
felt the need to talk to her in spurts, as if offering her a choice of remarks. Like his
wife, he somehow thought that a magic moment would arrive and Brenda would
wake up, a fairy princess awakened by the right incantation. . . . If only she would
let them kiss her, perhaps the perfect kiss would awaken her. But she did not hear
the words, did not hear the love and yearning behind them, would not suffer the
kiss, nothing. She did not need them. She was a delicate weight in the corner of
his eye, not a threat, not really a burden because she wanted nothing — unlike
other children, she wanted nothing. And so there was nothing to give her.

She ate uncooked spaghetti for the rest of the drive.

The school was housed in a one-story building, previously a small-parts shop.
On the walk he noticed a bit of drool about Brenda's mouth — should he wipe it
off? He wanted to wipe it off, not because he was anxious for her to look neat for
school but because he was her father and had the right to touch her.

"Do you have a handkerchief, honey?"   30

This was too mild. She sensed his weakness. She wiped her own mouth with
her hand, blankly and efficiently. A college-age girl with a suntanned face took
Brenda from him, all popeyed charm and enthusiasm. He watched Brenda walk
away. It pained him to see how easily she left him, how unconnected they were.
There was nothing between them. She did not glance back, did not notice that
he was remaining behind. Nothing.

He drove around for a while, feeling sorry for himself, then stopped to have
some coffee. Then he walked around the university, browsing in bookstores, wondering if he could remain sane — he had several hours to get through. What did
his wife do on these holy Wednesdays? At noon he went to a good restaurant for
lunch. Two cocktails first, then a steak sandwich. Women shoppers surrounded
him. He admired their leisure, their rings, their gloves; women who had the air of
being successes. They seemed happy. Once at a party he had noticed his wife in
deep conversation with a stranger, and something in his wife's strained, rapt face

had frightened him. When he asked her about it later she had said, "With him I felt anonymous, I could have begun everything again. He doesn't know about me. About Brenda." Like those bizarre unshaped pieces of sculpture that are placed around new buildings to suggest their important ties with the future, he and his wife had lost their ability to maintain a permanent shape; they were always being distorted. Too many false smiles, false enthusiasm and fear covered over. . . . The very passage of days had tugged at their faces and bodies, aging them. They were no longer able to touch each other and to recognize a human form. But he had seen her touch that man's arm, unconsciously, wanting from him the gift of a sane perspective, an anonymous freedom, that Arthur could no longer give her.

He wandered into another bookstore. In a mirror he caught sight of himself and was surprised, though pleasantly—so much worry and yet he was a fairly young man, still handsome, with light hair and light, friendly eyes, a good face. The necktie looked good. He wandered along the aisles, looking at textbooks. These manuals for beginning lives, for starting out fresh. . . . Engineering texts, medical texts. French dictionaries. A crunching sound at the back of the store put him in mind of his daughter eating. Spaghetti being bitten, snapped, crunched, chewed . . . an eternity of spaghetti. . . . He wandered to another part of the store and picked up a paperback book, *Forbidden Classics.* An Egyptian woman, heavily made up, beckoned to him from the cover. He picked up another book, *Bizarre Customs of the World;* on this cover a child beckoned to him, dressed in an outlandish outfit of feathers and furs. . . . He leafed through the book, paused at a few pages, then let the book fall. Garbage. He was insulted. A sense of disorder threatened. Better for him to leave.

He strolled through the campus but its buildings had no interest for him. They were dead, they were tombs. The sidewalks were newer, wide, functional. The university's landscaping was impressive. Students sat on the grass, reading. A girl caught his attention—she wore soiled white slacks, sat with her legs apart, her head flung back so that the sun might shine flatly onto her face. Her long brown hair hung down behind her. She was immobile, alone. Distracted, he nearly collided with someone. He stared at the girl and wondered why she frowned so, why her face was lined though she could not have been more than twenty—what strange intensity was in her?

He walked in another direction. There were too many young girls, all in a hurry. Their faces were impatient. Their hair swung around their eyes impatiently, irritably. His blood seemed to return to his heart alert and jumpy, as if infected by their intensity, by the mystery of their secret selves. He felt panic. A metallic taste rose to his mouth, as if staining his mouth. He felt that something was coming loose in him, something dangerous.

What did his wife do on these long hateful days?

He went to the periodical room of the university's undergraduate library. He leafed through magazines. World affairs; nothing of interest. Domestic affairs: no, nothing. What about medicine, what new miracles? What about architecture? He could not concentrate. He tried to daydream about his work, his problems, about

35

the proper shapes of banks and stores. . . . Nothing. He thought of his salary, his impressive salary, and tried to feel satisfaction; but nothing. His brain was dazzled as if with sparks. Suddenly he saw the girl on the grass, in a blaze of light, her white slacks glowing. An anonymous girl. Beginning again with an anonymous girl. The girl shivered in his brain, wanting more from the sun than the sun could give her.

He wanted to leave the library and find her, but he did not move. He remained with the magazines on his lap. He waited. After a while, when he thought it was safe, he went to a campus bar and had a drink. Two drinks. Around him were music, noise; young people who were not youthful. People jostled his chair all the time, as if seeking him out, contemptuous of his age. A slight fever had begun in his veins. Around him the boys and girls hung over one another, arguing, stabbing the air with their fingers, scraping their chairs angrily on the floor. "I am not defensive!" a girl cried. Now and then a girl passed by him who was striking as a poster—lovely face, lovely eyes. Why didn't she glance at Arthur? It was as if she sensed the failure of his genes, the quiet catastrophe of his chromosomes. He heard beneath the noise in the bar a terrible silence, violent as the withheld violence of great boulders.

When he picked Brenda up he felt a sense of levity rising in him, as if he had survived an ordeal. "How was it today, honey? What is that you've got—a paper flower?" He took it from her buttonhole, the buttonhole indifferent as her face. Yes, a paper flower. A red rose. "It's great. Did you make it yourself, honey?" He put it in his own buttonhole, as if his daughter had made it for him. She did not glance up. In the car she sat as far from him as possible, while he chattered wildly, feeling his grin slip out of control. Around him boulders precarious on mountainsides were beginning their long fall, soundlessly.

"We'll stop in the park for a few minutes. You should get out in the sun." He   40
tried to sound festive. Parks meant fun; children knew that. The park was large, mostly trees, with a few swings and tennis courts. It was nearly empty. He walked alongside her on one of the paths, not touching her, the two of them together but wonderfully independent. "Look at the birds. Blue jays," he said. He wanted to take her hand but feared her rejection. Only by force could anyone take her hand. She took a stick of spaghetti out of her pocket and bit into it, munching slowly and solemnly. "Look at the squirrels, aren't they cute? There's a chipmunk," he said. He felt that he was in charge of all these animals and that he must point them out to his daughter, as if he had to inform her of their names. What terror, not to know the names of animals, of objects, of the world! What if his daughter woke someday to a world of total blankness, terror? He was responsible for her. He had created her.

"Stay nearby, honey. Stay on the path," he said. He was suddenly exhausted; he sat on a bench. Brenda walked along the path in her precise, spiritless baby steps, munching spaghetti. She seemed not to have noticed that he was sitting, weary. He put his hands to his head and heard the notes of the "Moonlight Sonata." Brenda walked on slowly, not looking around. She could walk like this for hours in the back yard of their house, circling the yard in a certain space of time. A safe child, predictable. She might have been walking on a ledge, high above a street. She might have been stepping through poisonous foam on a shore. . . . The shadows of leaves moved about her and on her, silently. Birds flew overhead. She saw nothing. Arthur thought suddenly of his father sitting on the steps of the back porch of their old house, his head in his hands, weeping. Why had his father wept?

It seemed suddenly important for him to know why his father had wept, and why Brenda so rarely wept.

And then something happened—afterward Arthur was never able to remember it clearly. Brenda was on the path not far from him, no one was in sight, the park was ordinary and unsurprising, and yet out of nowhere a man appeared, running. He was middle-aged. In spite of the mild September day he wore an overcoat that flapped around his knees; his face was very red; his hair was gray and spiky; he ran bent over, stooped as if about to snatch up something from the ground. Arthur was watching Brenda and then, in the next instant, this outlandish running figure appeared, colliding with her, knocking her down. The man began to scream. He seized Brenda's arm and shook her, screaming down into her face in a high, waspish, womanish voice, screaming words Arthur could not make out. "What are you doing—what are you doing?" Arthur cried. He ran to Brenda and the man jumped back. His mouth worked. He was crouching, foolishly alert, his face very red—he began to back up slowly, cunningly. Arthur picked Brenda up. "Are you all right? Are you hurt?" He stared into her face and saw the same face, unchanged. He wondered if he was going out of his mind. Now, as if released, the man in the overcoat turned and began walking quickly away. He was headed back into the woods. "You'd better get out of here before I call the police!" Arthur yelled. His voice was shrill. He was terribly agitated, he could not control the sickening fear in his body.

The man was nearly gone. He was escaping. Arthur's heart pounded, he looked down at Brenda and back up, at the woods, and suddenly decided to run after the man. "You, hey wait! You'd better wait!" he yelled. He left Brenda behind and ran after the man. "Come back here, you dirty bastard, dirty filthy pervert bastard!" The man crashed into something. He stumbled in a thicket. Arthur caught up with him and could hear his panicked breathing. The back of the man's neck was dirty and reddened, blushing fiercely. He turned away from the thicket and tried to run in another direction, but his knees seemed broken. He was sobbing. Panicked, defeated, stumbling, he turned suddenly toward Arthur as if to push past him—Arthur swung his fist around and struck the man on the side of the neck. One hard blow. The man cried out sharply, nearly fell. Arthur struck him again. "Dirty bastard! Filth!" Arthur cried. His third blow knocked the man down, and then he found himself standing over him, kicking him—his heel into the jawbone, into the nose, crunching the nose, splattering blood onto the grass, onto his shoe. He could actually feel the nose break! Something gave way, he felt even the vibrations of the man's screams, his stifled screams. Arthur bent over him, pounding with his fists. *I'll kill you, I'll tear you into pieces!* The man rolled over wildly onto his stomach, hiding his face in his hands. Arthur kicked viciously at his back. He kicked the back of his head. "I'm going to call the police—throw you in jail—you can rot—you dirty pervert, dirty bastard—" Arthur kicked at the body until he could not recall what he was doing; the paper rose fell out of his buttonhole and onto the man's back, and onto the ground. "You'd better get the hell out of here because I'm going to call the police. You'd better not be here when I come back," he said, backing away.

And he had forgotten . . . about Brenda. . . . What was wrong with him? He 45 ran back to her and there she was, safe. Only her leg was a little dirty. A small scratch, small dots of blood. Nothing serious! Greatly relieved, panting with relief, Arthur bent to dab at her knee with a Kleenex. She stepped away. "There, there, it's just a tiny scratch . . ." he said. He was very hot, sweating. He could feel sweat everywhere on his body. Hardly able to bear the pounding of his heart, he made another attempt to blot the blood, but Brenda side-stepped him. He looked sharply up at her and saw her look away from him. Just in that instant she had been looking at him . . . and then she looked away, at once. Their eyes had almost met.

He took her back to the car. They were safe, nothing had happened. Safe. No one had seen. His clothes were rumpled, his breathing hoarse, but still they were safe. He was alarmed at the pounding of his heart. Excitement still rose in him in waves, overwhelming his heart. . . . Wait, he should wait for a few minutes. Sit quietly. The two of them sat in the front seat of the car, in silence. Arthur wiped his face. He looked over at his daughter and saw that her coat was perfectly buttoned, her hair was not even mussed, her face was once again composed and secret. His panting alarmed him. Did she notice? Of course she noticed, she noticed everything, understood everything, and yet would never inform on him; what gratitude he felt for her silence!

After a few minutes he felt well enough to drive. He was a little nauseous with excitement. A little lightheaded. He turned on the radio, heard static and loud music, then turned it off again, not knowing what he was doing. He headed for the expressway and saw with burning eyes the signs pointing toward home; everything had been composed in a perfect design, no one could get lost. It was impossible to get lost in this country. Beside him, in the far corner of the seat, his daughter took out a small piece of spaghetti and began to chew on it. They were safe. He glanced at her now and then as if to check her — had that man really collided with her? Knocked her down and shaken her, screamed into her face? Or had he imagined it all — no man, no smashed nose, no blood? There was blood on his shoes. Good. He drove home at a leisurely pace, being in no hurry. Brenda said nothing.   [1972]

THINKING ABOUT THE TEXT

1. Why does Arthur chase after the man? Why doesn't he just let him go? Does he accomplish something? Prove something? Does Arthur love Brenda? Can you love someone who never responds to you?

2. What indications can you point to in Oates's story that suggest the mother's attitude toward Brenda? What effect does Brenda have on the parents' relationship? Why? How would you respond if Brenda were your daughter? Your sister? An acquaintance?

3. Would you have preferred Brenda to smile at her father? Would that be appropriate? Were you disappointed that "their eyes had almost met" (para. 45)? How do you read the line "what gratitude he felt for her silence" (para. 46)?

4. The line "it was impossible to get lost in this country" (para. 47) is literally untrue. What is Oates trying to say? Is the ending optimistic, or is everything the same as before? Why isn't Oates clearer on this point?

5. Some autistic children are placed in special facilities. Is this appropriate, or should parents be given the necessary support to provide for them at home? How would this story be different if Brenda's parents were poor? What, then, would be the community's responsibility?

KATHERINE ANNE PORTER

He

Born in Indian Creek, Texas, Katherine Anne Porter (1890–1980) was brought up by her father and her paternal grandmother after her mother's early death. She was educated privately and did not begin to have her fiction published until after she was thirty; however, when Flowering Judas and Other Stories *appeared in 1930, she soon began to receive honorary degrees and awards, including two Guggenheim Fellowships (1931, 1938). Her stories received an O. Henry Award (1962) and a Pulitzer Prize (1966). Her novel* Ship of Fools *(1962) was made into a movie. "He" originally appeared in* Flowering Judas.

Life was very hard for the Whipples. It was hard to feed all the hungry mouths, it was hard to keep the children in flannels during the winter, short as it was: "God knows what would become of us if we lived north," they would say: keeping them decently clean was hard. "It looks like our luck won't never let up on us," said Mr. Whipple, but Mrs. Whipple was all for taking what was sent and calling it good, anyhow when the neighbors were in earshot. "Don't ever let a soul hear us complain," she kept saying to her husband. She couldn't stand to be pitied. "No, not if it comes to it that we have to live in a wagon and pick cotton around the country," she said, "nobody's going to get a chance to look down on us."

Mrs. Whipple loved her second son, the simple-minded one, better than she loved the other two children put together. She was forever saying so, and when she talked with certain of her neighbors, she would even throw in her husband and her mother for good measure.

"You needn't keep on saying it around," said Mr. Whipple, "you'll make people think nobody else has any feelings about Him but you."

"It's natural for a mother," Mrs. Whipple would remind him. "You know yourself it's more natural for a mother to be that way. People don't expect so much of fathers, some way."

This didn't keep the neighbors from talking plainly among themselves. "A 5
Lord's pure mercy if He should die," they said. "It's the sins of the fathers," they
agreed among themselves. "There's bad blood and bad doings somewhere, you
can bet on that." This behind the Whipples' backs. To their faces everybody said,
"He's not so bad off. He'll be all right yet. Look how He grows!"

Mrs. Whipple hated to talk about it, she tried to keep her mind off it, but
every time anybody set foot in the house, the subject always came up, and she
had to talk about Him first, before she could get on to anything else. It seemed to
ease her mind. "I wouldn't have anything happen to Him for all the world, but it
just looks like I can't keep Him out of mischief. He's so strong and active, He's
always into everything; He was like that since He could walk. It's actually funny
sometimes, the way He can do anything; it's laughable to see Him up to His
tricks. Emly has more accidents; I'm forever tying up her bruises, and Adna can't
fall a foot without cracking a bone. But He can do anything and not get a scratch.
The preacher said such a nice thing once when he was here. He said, and I'll
remember it to my dying day, 'The innocent walk with God—that's why He don't
get hurt.'" Whenever Mrs. Whipple repeated these words, she always felt a warm
pool spread in her breast, and the tears would fill her eyes, and then she could
talk about something else.

He did grow and He never got hurt. A plank blew off the chicken house and
struck Him on the head and He never seemed to know it. He had learned a few
words, and after this He forgot them. He didn't whine for food as the other children did, but waited until it was given Him; He ate squatting in the corner, smacking and mumbling. Rolls of fat covered Him like an overcoat, and He could carry
twice as much wood and water as Adna. Emly had a cold in the head most of the
time—"she takes that after me," said Mrs. Whipple—so in bad weather they gave
her the extra blanket off His cot. He never seemed to mind the cold.

Just the same, Mrs. Whipple's life was a torment for fear something might
happen to Him. He climbed the peach trees much better than Adna and went
skittering along the branches like a monkey, just a regular monkey. "Oh, Mrs.
Whipple, you hadn't ought to let Him do that. He'll lose His balance sometime.
He can't rightly know what He's doing."

Mrs. Whipple almost screamed out at the neighbor. "He *does* know what
He's doing! He's as able as any other child! Come down out of there, you!" When
He finally reached the ground she could hardly keep her hands off Him for act-
ing like that before people, a grin all over His face and her worried sick about
Him all the time.

"It's the neighbors," said Mrs. Whipple to her husband. "Oh, I do mortally 10
wish they would keep out of our business. I can't afford to let Him do anything for
fear they'll come nosing around about it. Look at the bees, now. Adna can't
handle them, they sting him up so; I haven't got time to do everything, and now I
don't dare let Him. But if He gets a sting He don't really mind."

"It's just because He ain't got sense enough to be scared of anything," said
Mr. Whipple.

"You ought to be ashamed of yourself," said Mrs. Whipple, "talking that way
about your own child. Who's to take up for Him if we don't, I'd like to know? He

sees a lot that goes on, He listens to things all the time. And anything I tell Him to do He does it. Don't never let anybody hear you say such things. They'd think you favored the other children over Him."

"Well, now I don't, and you know it, and what's the use of getting all worked up about it? You always think the worst of everything. Just let Him alone, He'll get along somehow. He gets plenty to eat and wear, don't He?" Mr. Whipple suddenly felt tired out. "Anyhow, it can't be helped now."

Mrs. Whipple felt tired too, she complained in a tired voice. "What's done can't never be undone, I know that as good as anybody; but He's my child, and I'm not going to have people say anything. I get sick of people coming around saying things all the time."

In the early fall Mrs. Whipple got a letter from her brother saying he and his wife and two children were coming over for a little visit next Sunday week. "Put the big pot in the little one," he wrote at the end. Mrs. Whipple read this part out loud twice, she was so pleased. Her brother was a great one for saying funny things. "We'll just show him that's no joke," she said, "we'll just butcher one of the sucking pigs."

"It's a waste and I don't hold with waste the way we are now," said Mr. Whipple. "That pig'll be worth money by Christmas."

"It's a shame and a pity we can't have a decent meal's vittles once in a while when my own family comes to see us," said Mrs. Whipple. "I'd hate for his wife to go back and say there wasn't a thing in the house to eat. My God, it's better than buying up a great chance of meat in town. There's where you'd spend the money!"

"All right, do it yourself then," said Mr. Whipple. "Christamighty, no wonder we can't get ahead!"

The question was how to get the little pig away from his ma, a great fighter, worse than a Jersey cow. Adna wouldn't try it: "That sow'd rip my insides out all over the pen." "All right, old fraidy," said Mrs. Whipple, "*He's* not scared. Watch *Him* do it." And she laughed as though it was all a good joke and gave Him a little push towards the pen. He sneaked up and snatched the pig right away from the teat and galloped back and was over the fence with the sow raging at His heels. The little black squirming thing was screeching like a baby in a tantrum, stiffening its back and stretching its mouth to the ears. Mrs. Whipple took the pig with her face stiff and sliced its throat with one stroke. When He saw the blood He gave a great jolting breath and ran away. "But He'll forget and eat plenty, just the same," thought Mrs. Whipple. Whenever she was thinking, her lips moved making words. "He'd eat it all if I didn't stop Him. He'd eat up every mouthful from the other two if I'd let Him."

She felt badly about it. He was ten years old now and a third again as large as Adna, who was going on fourteen. "It's a shame, a shame," she kept saying under her breath, "and Adna with so much brains!"

She kept on feeling badly about all sorts of things. In the first place it was the man's work to butcher; the sight of the pig scraped pink and naked made her sick. He was too fat and soft and pitiful-looking. It was simply a shame the way things had to happen. By the time she had finished it up, she almost wished her brother would stay at home.

15

20

Early Sunday morning Mrs. Whipple dropped everything to get Him all cleaned up. In an hour He was dirty again, with crawling under fences after a possum, and straddling along the rafters of the barn looking for eggs in the hayloft. "My Lord, look at you now after all my trying! And here's Adna and Emly staying so quiet. I get tired trying to keep you decent. Get off that shirt and put on another, people will say I don't half dress you!" And she boxed Him on the ears, hard. He blinked and blinked and rubbed His head, and His face hurt Mrs. Whipple's feelings. Her knees began to tremble, she had to sit down while she buttoned His shirt. "I'm just all gone before the day starts."

The brother came with his plump healthy wife and two great roaring hungry boys. They had a grand dinner, with the pig roasted to a crackling in the middle of the table, full of dressing, a pickled peach in his mouth and plenty of gravy for the sweet potatoes.

"This looks like prosperity all right," said the brother; "you're going to have to roll me home like I was a barrel when I'm done."

Everybody laughed out loud; it was fine to hear them laughing all at once   25
around the table. Mrs. Whipple felt warm and good about it. "Oh, we've got six more of these; I say it's as little as we can do when you come to see us so seldom."

He wouldn't come into the dining room, and Mrs. Whipple passed it off very well. "He's timider than my other two," she said, "He'll just have to get used to you. There isn't everybody He'll make up with, you know how it is with some children, even cousins." Nobody said anything out of the way.

"Just like my Alfy here," said the brother's wife. "I sometimes got to lick him to make him shake hands with his own grandmammy."

So that was over, and Mrs. Whipple loaded up a big plate for Him first, before everybody. "I always say He ain't to be slighted, no matter who else goes without," she said, and carried it to Him herself.

"He can chin Himself on the top of the door," said Emly, helping along.

"That's fine, He's getting along fine," said the brother.   30

They went away after supper. Mrs. Whipple rounded up the dishes, and sent the children to bed and sat down and unlaced her shoes. "You see?" she said to Mr. Whipple. "That's the way my whole family is. Nice and considerate about everything. No out-of-the-way remarks—they *have* got refinement. I get awfully sick of people's remarks. Wasn't that pig good?"

Mr. Whipple said, "Yes, we're out three hundred pounds of pork, that's all. It's easy to be polite when you come to eat. Who knows what they had in their minds all along?"

"Yes, that's like you," said Mrs. Whipple. "I don't expect anything else from you. You'll be telling me next that my own brother will be saying around that we made Him eat in the kitchen! Oh, my God!" She rocked her head in her hands, a hard pain started in the very middle of her forehead. "Now it's all spoiled, and everything was so nice and easy. All right, you don't like them and you never did—all right, they'll not come here again soon, never you mind! But they *can't* say He wasn't dressed every lick as good as Adna—oh, honest, sometimes I wish I was dead!"

"I wish you'd let up," said Mr. Whipple. "It's bad enough as it is."

◆ ◆ ◆

It was a hard winter. It seemed to Mrs. Whipple that they hadn't ever known   35
anything but hard times, and now to cap it all a winter like this. The crops were
about half of what they had a right to expect; after the cotton was in it didn't do
much more than cover the grocery bill. They swapped off one of the plow horses,
and got cheated, for the new one died of the heaves. Mrs. Whipple kept thinking
all the time it was terrible to have a man you couldn't depend on not to get
cheated. They cut down on everything, but Mrs. Whipple kept saying there are
things you can't cut down on, and they cost money. It took a lot of warm clothes
for Adna and Emly, who walked four miles to school during the three-months session. "He sets around the fire a lot, He won't need so much," said Mr. Whipple.
"That's so," said Mrs. Whipple, "and when He does the outdoor chores He can
wear your tarpaullion coat. I can't do no better, that's all."

In February He was taken sick, and lay curled up under His blanket looking
very blue in the face and acting as if He would choke. Mr. and Mrs. Whipple did
everything they could for Him for two days, and then they were scared and sent
for the doctor. The doctor told them they must keep Him warm and give Him
plenty of milk and eggs. "He isn't as stout as He looks, I'm afraid," said the doctor.
"You've got to watch them when they're like that. You must put more cover onto
Him, too."

"I just took off His big blanket to wash," said Mrs. Whipple, ashamed. "I
can't stand dirt."

"Well, you'd better put it back on the minute it's dry," said the doctor, "or
He'll have pneumonia."

Mr. and Mrs. Whipple took a blanket off their own bed and put His cot in by
the fire. "They can't say we didn't do everything for Him," she said, "even to
sleeping cold ourselves on His account."

When the winter broke He seemed to be well again, but He walked as if His   40
feet hurt Him. He was able to run a cotton planter during the season.

"I got it all fixed up with Jim Ferguson about breeding the cow next time,"
said Mr. Whipple. "I'll pasture the bull this summer and give Jim some fodder in
the fall. That's better than paying out money when you haven't got it."

"I hope you didn't say such a thing before Jim Ferguson," said Mrs. Whipple.
"You oughtn't to let him know we're so down as all that."

"Godamighty, that ain't saying we're down. A man is got to look ahead sometimes. He can lead the bull over today. I need Adna on the place."

At first Mrs. Whipple felt easy in her mind about sending Him for the bull.
Adna was too jumpy and couldn't be trusted. You've got to be steady around animals. After He was gone she started thinking, and after a while she could hardly
bear it any longer. She stood in the lane and watched for Him. It was nearly three
miles to go and a hot day, but He oughtn't to be so long about it. She shaded her
eyes and stared until colored bubbles floated in her eyeballs. It was just like
everything else in life, she must always worry and never know a moment's peace
about anything. After a long time she saw Him turn into the side lane, limping.
He came on very slowly, leading the big hulk of an animal by a ring in the nose,
twirling a little stick in His hand, never looking back or sideways, but coming on
like a sleepwalker with His eyes half shut.

Mrs. Whipple was scared sick of bulls; she had heard awful stories about how   45
they followed on quietly enough, and then suddenly pitched on with a bellow
and pawed and gored a body to pieces. Any second now that black monster would
come down on Him, my God, He'd never have sense enough to run.

She mustn't make a sound nor a move; she mustn't get the bull started. The
bull heaved his head aside and horned the air at a fly. Her voice burst out of her
in a shriek, and she screamed at Him to come on, for God's sake. He didn't seem
to hear her clamor, but kept on twirling His switch and limping on, and the bull
lumbered along behind him as gently as a calf. Mrs. Whipple stopped calling and
ran towards the house, praying under her breath: "Lord, don't let anything happen to Him. Lord, you *know* people will say we oughtn't to have sent Him. You
know they'll say we didn't take care of Him. Oh, get Him home, safe home, safe
home, and I'll look out for Him better! Amen."

She watched from the window while He led the beast in, and tied him up in
the barn. It was no use trying to keep up, Mrs. Whipple couldn't bear another
thing. She sat down and rocked and cried with her apron over her head.

From year to year the Whipples were growing poorer and poorer. The place
just seemed to run down of itself, no matter how hard they worked. "We're losing
our hold," said Mrs. Whipple. "Why can't we do like other people and watch for
our best chances? They'll be calling us poor white trash next."

"When I get to be sixteen I'm going to leave," said Adna. "I'm going to get a
job in Powell's grocery store. There's money in that. No more farm for me."

"I'm going to be a schoolteacher," said Emly. "But I've got to finish the   50
eighth grade, anyhow. Then I can live in town. I don't see any chances here."

"Emly takes after my family," said Mrs. Whipple. "Ambitious every last one
of them, and they don't take second place for anybody."

When fall came Emly got a chance to wait on table in the railroad eating-
house in the town near by, and it seemed such a shame not to take it when the
wages were good and she could get her food too, that Mrs. Whipple decided to let
her take it, and not bother with school until the next session. "You've got plenty of
time," she said. "You're young and smart as a whip."

With Adna gone too, Mr. Whipple tried to run the farm with just Him to
help. He seemed to get along fine, doing His work and part of Adna's without
noticing it. They did well enough until Christmas time, when one morning He
slipped on the ice coming up from the barn. Instead of getting up He thrashed
round and round, and when Mr. Whipple got to Him, He was having some sort
of fit.

They brought Him inside and tried to make Him sit up, but He blubbered
and rolled, so they put Him to bed and Mr. Whipple rode to town for the doctor.
All the way there and back he worried about where the money was to come from:
it sure did look like he had about all the troubles he could carry.

From then on He stayed in bed. His legs swelled up double their size, and   55
the fits kept coming back. After four months, the doctor said, "It's no use, I think
you'd better put Him in the County Home for treatment right away. I'll see about
it for you. He'll have good care there and be off your hands."

"We don't begrudge Him any care, and I won't let Him out of my sight," said Mrs. Whipple. "I won't have it said I sent my sick child off among strangers."

"I know how you feel," said the doctor. "You can't tell me anything about that, Mrs. Whipple. I've got a boy of my own. But you'd better listen to me. I can't do anything more for Him, that's the truth."

Mr. and Mrs. Whipple talked it over a long time that night after they went to bed. "It's just charity," said Mrs. Whipple, "that's what we've come to, charity! I certainly never looked for this."

"We pay taxes to help support the place just like everybody else," said Mr. Whipple, "and I don't call that taking charity. I think it would be fine to have Him where He'd get the best of everything . . . and besides, I can't keep up with these doctor bills any longer."

"Maybe that's why the doctor wants us to send Him — he's scared he won't get his money," said Mrs. Whipple.

"Don't talk like that," said Mr. Whipple, feeling pretty sick, "or we won't be able to send Him."

"Oh, but we won't keep Him there long," said Mrs. Whipple. "Soon's He's better, we'll bring Him right back home."

"The doctor has told you and told you time and again He can't ever get better, and you might as well stop talking," said Mr. Whipple.

"Doctors don't know everything," said Mrs. Whipple, feeling almost happy. "But anyhow, in the summer Emly can come home for a vacation, and Adna can get down for Sundays: we'll all work together and get on our feet again, and the children will feel they've got a place to come to."

All at once she saw it full summer again, with the garden going fine, and new white roller shades up all over the house, and Adna and Emly home, so full of life, all of them happy together. Oh, it could happen, things would ease up on them.

They didn't talk before Him much, but they never knew just how much He understood. Finally the doctor set the day and a neighbor who owned a double-seated carryall offered to drive them over. The hospital would have sent an ambulance, but Mrs. Whipple couldn't stand to see Him going away looking so sick as all that. They wrapped Him in blankets, and the neighbor and Mr. Whipple lifted Him into the back seat of the carryall beside Mrs. Whipple, who had on her black shirt waist. She couldn't stand to go looking like charity.

"You'll be all right, I guess I'll stay behind," said Mr. Whipple. "It don't look like everybody ought to leave the place at once."

"Besides, it ain't as if He was going to stay forever," said Mrs. Whipple to the neighbor. "This is only for a little while."

They started away, Mrs. Whipple holding to the edges of the blankets to keep Him from sagging sideways. He sat there blinking and blinking. He worked His hands out and began rubbing His nose with His knuckles, and then with the end of the blanket. Mrs. Whipple couldn't believe what she saw; He was scrubbing away big tears that rolled out of the corners of His eyes. He sniveled and made a gulping noise. Mrs. Whipple kept saying, "Oh, honey, you don't feel so bad, do you? You don't feel so bad, do you?" for He seemed to be accusing her of some-

60

65

thing. Maybe He remembered that time she boxed His ears, maybe He had been scared that day with the bull, maybe He had slept cold and couldn't tell her about it; maybe He knew they were sending Him away for good and all because they were too poor to keep Him. Whatever it was, Mrs. Whipple couldn't bear to think of it. She began to cry, frightfully, and wrapped her arms tight around Him. His head rolled on her shoulder: she had loved Him as much as she possibly could, there were Adna and Emly who had to be thought of too, there was nothing she could do to make up to Him for His life. Oh, what a mortal pity He was ever born.

They came in sight of the hospital, with the neighbor driving very fast, not   70
daring to look behind him.   [1930]

THINKING ABOUT THE TEXT

1. Within the context of the story, do the Whipples do all they can for Him? What details might cast some doubt on this?

2. Would you make the same decision as the Whipples? Why? What rights does He have?

3. Explain your reading of the last two paragraphs. How do you account for the tears? If He is sensitive and aware of what is about to happen to him, does that reflect badly on the Whipples?

4. Can you point to any "editorializing" on Porter's part? Is it possible the pig episode is symbolic? Explain why you think the neighbor responds in the last paragraph as he does?

5. Who should be responsible for the care of the disabled? The family? The community? The state? Are we all responsible for the less fortunate? This story seems fairly objective. Do you think so? Should writers be activists or reporters?

MAKING COMPARISONS

1. Compare the response of the family in Oates's story with that in Porter's. Would the Whipples do what Brenda's parents do if they had the money?

2. Both He and Brenda seem removed from their families. Are they? How does this affect each family?

3. Compare Brenda's mother with Mrs. Whipple.

WRITING ABOUT ISSUES

1. Write a brief analysis of the pig dinner in "He." Include the response of the Whipples, He, and Mrs. Whipple's brother.

2. Write a personal account about any contact you have had with people treated as Other. Narrate the experience and explain your response.

3. Argue that the community does (or does not) have an ethical obligation to provide support for the disabled.

4. Do some research on either autism or mental retardation. Write a brief report on our current understanding of either.

GRANDPARENTS AND LEGACIES

NIKKI GIOVANNI, "Legacies"
WILLIAM CARLOS WILLIAMS, "The Last Words of My English Grandmother"
GRACE CAVALIERI, "Grandmother"
LINDA HOGAN, "Heritage"
GARY SOTO, "Behind Grandma's House"

In contemporary middle-class America the influence, even the presence, of our grandparents has waned. They often live elsewhere, perhaps in retirement communities or nursing homes. But this was not always the case. Grandparents in the past, and in traditional households even today, were very active members of the family, exerting influence on the daily decisions of everyday life, from diet to childrearing. Some of this was beneficial: Grandparents gave children a personal understanding of their cultural traditions as well as the benefit of their accumulated wisdom. But they could also create tension in families where change and progress conflict with the habits and attitudes of the past. The following five poets present us with different perspectives on their grandparents, some loving and proud, others less positive, and one quite funny.

BEFORE YOU READ

What specific memories do you have of your grandparents? What role do you think they should play in a family's life? What effects might the segregation of the elderly have on a society?

NIKKI GIOVANNI

Legacies

Raised near Cincinnati, Ohio, Nikki Giovanni (b. 1943) returned as a teenager to her birthplace and "spiritual" home in Knoxville, Tennessee, where she experienced the strong influence of her grandmother, Louvenia Watson. She studied at the University of Cincinnati from 1961–1963 and earned a B.A. at Fisk University in 1967. She also attended the University of Pennsylvania School of Social Work (1967) and Columbia University School of the Arts (1968). She has taught at a number of universities, since 1987 at Virginia Polytechnic Institute where she is a professor of English. Her poetry, essays, and works for children reflect her commitment to African American community, family, and womanhood. "Legacies" is from Giovanni's 1972 book My House.

her grandmother called her from the playground
    "yes, ma'am"
    "i want chu to learn how to make rolls," said the old
woman proudly
but the little girl didn't want
to learn how because she knew   5
even if she couldn't say it that
that would mean when the old one died she would be less
dependent on her spirit so
she said
    "i don't want to know how to make no rolls"   10
with her lips poked out
and the old woman wiped her hands on
her apron saying "lord
    these children"
and neither of them ever   15
said what they meant
and i guess nobody ever does   [1972]

THINKING ABOUT THE TEXT

1. Does the dialogue in Giovanni's poem reveal the true feelings of the grandmother and the girl? Be explicit about what is really going on in their minds. Is the girl superstitious?

2. Is it true that "nobody" says what they really mean? Do you? Is this an indication of honesty or something else, say, tact or convention? Are poets more likely to tell the truth?

3. What makes this piece a poem? Would you prefer more metaphors or similes, allusions, or flowery language? Is "proudly" (line 4) an important word here?

4. Change the grandmother's words to those that reflect more of what is in her heart. Might the girl respond differently if the grandmother were more forthright?

5. The title is only referred to obliquely. Why? What does it refer to? Is contemporary society concerned with legacies? Are you? Are they important or irrelevant?

WILLIAM CARLOS WILLIAMS

The Last Words of My English Grandmother

For most of his eighty years, William Carlos Williams (1883–1963) lived and practiced medicine in Rutherford, New Jersey, his birthplace, and in the nearby city of Paterson, the setting for his influential poetry sequence. He earned his medical degree at the University of Pennsylvania in 1906 and studied pediatrics in Germany. An important voice among modernist poets of the early twentieth century, Williams focused his theoretical prose on ideas and experiences that he saw as distinctly American and incorporated the rhythms and color of American speech into his poetry. Deceptively simple, his poems are crafted with deliberate precision. This poem appears in The Collected Poems of William Carlos Williams, 1909–1939.

There were some dirty plates
and a glass of milk
beside her on a small table
near the rank, disheveled bed —

Wrinkled and nearly blind   5
she lay and snored
rousing with anger in her tones
to cry for food,

Gimme something to eat —
They're starving me —   10
I'm all right I won't go
to the hospital. No, no, no

Give me something to eat
Let me take you
to the hospital, I said   15
and after you are well

you can do as you please.
She smiled, Yes
you do what you please first
then I can do what I please —   20

Oh, oh, oh! she cried
as the ambulance men lifted
her to the stretcher —
Is this what you call

making me comfortable?   25
By now her mind was clear —
Oh you think you're smart
you young people,

◆ ◆ ◆

she said, but I'll tell you
you don't know anything.   30
Then we started.
On the way

we passed a long row
of elms. She looked at them
awhile out of   35
the ambulance window and said,

What are all those
fuzzy-looking things out there?
Trees? Well, I'm tired
of them and rolled her head away.   [1924]   40

THINKING ABOUT THE TEXT

1. What is the speaker's attitude toward his grandmother? What is yours? Could you argue that the grandmother is brave and independent? Frightened and bitter?

2. What does she mean by saying young people "don't know anything" (line 30)? Do thirteen-year-olds "know anything" in your view?

3. Poets sometimes like to present concrete images that carry emotional weight instead of telling the reader what they intend. How do you respond to some of Williams's specific images? What do they suggest?

4. Rewrite "Well, I'm tired / of them" (lines 39–40) to something else and explain how your change alters the meaning of the poem.

5. Should the grandmother's requests be honored? Is the speaker right to intervene? Are we responsible for how our grandparents want to act?

MAKING COMPARISONS

1. How would you describe the attitude of Giovanni's grandmother toward the young? Of Williams's grandmother?

2. How might the speaker in Williams's poem react if he had the grandmother of the first poem?

3. Would these two grandmothers get along?

GRACE CAVALIERI

Grandmother

A resident of Washington, D.C., since 1966, Grace Cavalieri (b. 1932) worked for the Public Broadcasting System and the National Endowment for the Humanities before beginning a twenty-year career at radio station WPFW, where she conducted the weekly reading and interview program The Poet and the Poem. *She received the PEN/Syndicated Award in 1985 and the Allen Ginsberg Award in 1992 and has edited a poetry anthology. She has four daughters. "Grandmother" is from her 1990 collection titled* Trenton.

For Graziella Zoda

What is the purpose of visits to me twice since you've died?

Downstairs near a woodstove I hear you
in motion, always working,
a long silken dress —
tight sleeves at your wrist, soft above the elbow,   5
wide top at your shoulder for free movement.

When we were young you didn't visit —
You never baked a cake that I remember
or babysat or held me in your lap,
You were in the men's part of town running a man's business   10
calling the world to order
six children behind you
raised singlehanded in your large house. You were
moving, always moving.

When I kept losing things like my parents, my children, money,   15
my time and health,
why did you appear in my room with gifts painted
red, yellow, blue,
brilliant colored toys. What
essential fact did you want me to know,   20
that the body is the essence of the spirit and so
must be in motion?

Now that I've lost my foothold, my direction, my way,
what is your message, strong spirit,
strong Grandmother,   25
What is the meaning of your dream-present,
a bright clock shaped like a train —
                    simply that it moves?   [1990]

THINKING ABOUT THE TEXT

1. What do you think is a plausible answer to the opening question? Is the speaker chiding her grandmother in the third stanza or just being factual? How do you know?

2. Why does the grandmother visit in the fourth stanza? Does the grandmother have a secret intention? Is the poet reading too much into her gifts?

3. Would Cavalieri's poem be more effective if it had fewer questions? Would it be more effective if the speaker tried to analyze the dream and give possible interpretations?

4. Imagine you are the poet's editor. What suggestions would you make if you wanted her to be more concrete? Focus on the words *foothold, direction,* and *way* (line 23).

5. It seems the poet has had a dream. What might it have been? What meaning do you think such dreams have? Are poems like dreams? Why are readers so intent on discussing a poem's meaning?

MAKING COMPARISONS

1. Cavalieri's poem seems more indirect than Giovanni's or Williams's. Do you agree? Which poet's approach do you like better?

2. Cavalieri's speaker seems positive about her grandmother's influence. Are Giovanni's and Williams's speakers more ambivalent? Say why.

3. Which poem of the three contains the most interesting images? Why?

LINDA HOGAN
Heritage

Born in 1947 in Denver, Colorado, Linda Hogan is a contemporary Native American poet who calls on her Chickasaw heritage to interpret environmental, anti-nuclear, and other spiritual and societal issues. Her published works include poems, stories, screenplays, essays, and novels. Her most recent book is the novel Solar Storms *(1995). Her many honors include an American Book Award for* Seeing Through the Sun *(1985), a Colorado Book Award and a Pulitzer nomination for* The Book of Medicines *(1993), and fellowships from the Guggenheim Foundation and the National Endowment for the Arts, and a Lannan Award. Hogan received her M.A. from the University of Colorado at Boulder, where she currently teaches creative writing. "Heritage" is from her 1978 book titled* Calling Myself Home.

From my mother, the antique mirror
where I watch my face take on her lines.
She left me the smell of baking bread
to warm fine hairs in my nostrils,
she left the large white breasts that weigh down   5
my body.

From my father I take his brown eyes,
the plague of locusts that leveled our crops,
they flew in formation like buzzards.

◆ ◆ ◆

From my uncle the whittled wood   10
that rattles like bones
and is white
and smells like all our old houses
that are no longer there. He was the man
who sang old chants to me, the words   15
my father was told not to remember.

From my grandfather who never spoke
I learned to fear silence.
I learned to kill a snake
when you're begging for rain.   20

And Grandmother, blue-eyed woman
whose skin was brown,
she used snuff.
When her coffee can full of black saliva
spilled on me   25
it was like the brown cloud of grasshoppers
that leveled her fields.
It was the brown stain
that covered my white shirt,
my whiteness a shame.   30
That sweet black liquid like the food
she chewed up and spit into my father's mouth
when he was an infant.
It was the brown earth of Oklahoma
stained with oil.   35
She said tobacco would purge your body of poisons.
It has more medicine than stones and knives
against your enemies.
That tobacco is the dark night that covers me.

She said it is wise to eat the flesh of deer   40
so you will be swift and travel over many miles.
She told me how our tribe has always followed a stick
that pointed west
that pointed east.
From my family I have learned the secrets   45
of never having a home.   [1978]

THINKING ABOUT THE TEXT

1. The last sentence seems to contain a contradiction. "From my family I
   have learned the secrets" might lead you to expect something positive.
   But maybe the last phrase is meant to be positive. What is your reading of
   Hogan's conclusion?

2. What does the narrator learn from her mother? Her father? Her uncle? Her grandfather? Her grandmother? What kinds of things did you learn from your family members? Use concrete images.

3. Why does she say, "my whiteness a shame" (line 30)? Is this a racial comment?

4. Examine the "black saliva" section in lines 21–39. Does it start off negatively? Does it change? Explain.

5. We all learn things from our families, both positive and negative. Is Hogan giving a balanced account? Should she? Would you? Do poets have any responsibility to the larger culture? Or should they just follow their own inner vision?

MAKING COMPARISONS

1. Does Hogan's poem seem more complex than those by Giovanni, Williams, and Cavalieri? Explain how.

2. The last two stanzas in "Heritage" seem nonjudgmental, their tone flat. Do you think so? Describe the tone of the previous three poems.

3. Traditionally, characters in fiction grow, they learn something from their interactions with others. How would you characterize the speakers in these four poems? Do they learn something?

GARY SOTO

Behind Grandma's House

Born in 1952 in Fresno, California, Gary Soto gives voice to San Joaquín Valley agricultural workers whose deprivations have been part of his experience and social awareness from an early age. After graduating with honors from California State University in 1974, Soto went on to earn an M.F.A. in creative writing from the University of California at Irvine in 1976 and to teach in the university system. He has received numerous writing awards, including the distinction of being the first writer identifying himself as Chicano to be nominated for a Pulitzer Prize. His Mexican American heritage continues to be central to his work. The poem reprinted here is from Soto's 1985 book, Black Hair.

At ten I wanted fame. I had a comb
And two Coke bottles, a tube of Bryl-creem.
I borrowed a dog, one with
Mismatched eyes and a happy tongue,
And wanted to prove I was tough   5

In the alley, kicking over trash cans,
A dull chime of tuna cans falling.
I hurled light bulbs like grenades
And men teachers held their heads,
Fingers of blood lengthening   10
On the ground. I flicked rocks at cats,
Their goofy faces spurred with foxtails.
I kicked fences. I shooed pigeons.
I broke a branch from a flowering peach
And frightened ants with a stream of spit.   15
I said "Shit," "Fuck you," and "No way
Daddy-O" to an imaginary priest
Until grandma came into the alley,
Her apron flapping in a breeze,
Her hair mussed, and said, "Let me help you,"   20
And punched me between the eyes.   [1985]

THINKING ABOUT THE TEXT

1. Were you glad or disturbed when the narrator's grandmother hit him? Does he deserve it? Are you angry or sympathetic to his attempts to be tough? Do you understand why he wants to appear older? Is this normal?

2. What did you want at ten? Did your grandparents know your desires? Did they support you? Did they ever set you straight? Are our grandparents' values too dated to matter?

3. Are the concrete details meaningful to you? Does the profanity help Soto achieve authenticity, or is it unnecessary?

4. Does the speaker learn something here, or is this just a snapshot of an event?

5. How would you describe our culture's ideas of the different roles of parents and grandparents? Do grandparents in today's culture have less influence than in the past? Is this a good thing or not?

MAKING COMPARISONS

1. Compare Soto's attitude here with that of the previous four poets. Is Soto less respectful or more?

2. Is this a gendered poem? That is, is it about male experience only, or could a female reader see herself in this or a comparable situation? Do any of the other four preceding poems seem gendered?

3. Do any of the five encounters with grandparents seem ideal to you? Which relationship comes closest to the one you would want?

WRITING ABOUT ISSUES

1. Pick one of the five preceding poems and argue that it offers an appropriate view of grandparents.

2. Pick two of these poems and argue that something of value is learned in each.

3. Which poem comes closest to your own experiences? Write a narrative that demonstrates this.

4. Do some research on retirement homes from a sociological point of view. Write a report about your findings. Include the import of such places on the family and on the larger culture. Do you think they are a positive development or not?

GAYS AND LESBIANS IN FAMILIES

ESSEX HEMPHILL, "Commitments"
KITTY TSUI, "A Chinese Banquet"
MINNIE BRUCE PRATT, "Two Small-Sized Girls"

The late Essex Hemphill was gay; Kitty Tsui and Minnie Bruce Pratt are lesbian. All three writers in this cluster remind their audience that families may have gay or lesbian members. Usually the media give a different impression. The families depicted in most literature, films, television shows, and songs are heterosexual. Indeed, much of American society prefers this image. Families that do have gay or lesbian members may refuse to admit the fact, let alone accept it. Throughout history, of course, plenty of gays and lesbians have concealed their sexual identities from their families in the first place, fearing rejection.

Nowadays, though, increasing numbers of gays and lesbians are not only "coming out of the closet" but are also publicly claiming the term *family*. Many of them seek acceptance by the families they were raised in. Many also seek the right to form and raise families of their own. Some are working to get same-sex marriage legalized. Note that in all these efforts, they have quite a few heterosexual allies. Obviously they face a lot of heterosexual resistance too. As demonstrated in the 1990s' case of lesbian mother Sharon Bottoms, a parent who is not heterosexual can still lose custody of his or her children for that reason. Also, gays and lesbians are far from winning a universal right to adopt. When Hawaii seemed on the verge of permitting same-sex marriage, arguments about it raged throughout the United States, and the federal government sought to discourage it by passing the Defense of Marriage Act in 1996. Consider your own position on these matters as you read the following poems. Each refers to American society's widespread assumption that families are heterosexual; each also points out the suffering that can result from this belief.

BEFORE YOU READ

What, at present, is your attitude toward gays and lesbians? Try to identify specific people, experiences, and institutions that have shaped your view. If it has changed over the years, explain how. Finally, describe an occasion that made you quite conscious of the attitude you now hold.

ESSEX HEMPHILL
Commitments

Before his untimely death from AIDS-related complications, Essex Hemphill (1957–1995) explored through prose, poetry, and film what it meant to live as a black gay man. The following poem comes from his 1992 book Ceremonies: Prose and Poetry. *His other books include a collection he edited,* Brother to Brother: New Writings by Black Gay Men *(1991). Hemphill also appeared in the documentaries* Looking for Langston *and* Tongues Untied.

I will always be there.
When the silence is exhumed.
When the photographs are examined
I will be pictured smiling
among siblings, parents,   5
nieces and nephews.

In the background of the photographs
the hazy smoke of barbecue,
a checkered red-and-white tablecloth
laden with blackened chicken,   10
glistening ribs, paper plates,
bottles of beer, and pop.

In the photos
the smallest children
are held by their parents.   15
My arms are empty, or around
the shoulders of unsuspecting aunts
expecting to throw rice at me someday.

Or picture tinsel, candles,
ornamented, imitation trees,   20
or another table, this one
set for Thanksgiving,
a turkey steaming the lens.

My arms are empty
in those photos, too,   25

so empty they would break
around a lover.

I am always there
for critical emergencies,
graduations,   30
the middle of the night.

I am the invisible son.
In the family photos
nothing appears out of character.
I smile as I serve my duty.   [1992]   35

THINKING ABOUT THE TEXT

1. The speaker begins with the announcement "I will always be there," and
   yet later he says "I am the invisible son" (line 32). How can these two
   statements be reconciled? In the second line, he uses the word *exhumed.*
   Look up this word in a dictionary. What do you infer from the speaker's
   use of it?

2. Unlike the other stanzas, the second lacks verbs. Should Hemphill have
   included at least one verb there for the sake of consistency? Why or why
   not? Is the scene described in the second stanza characteristic of your
   own family? Note similarities and differences.

3. What do you think the speaker means when he describes his arms in the
   photographs as "so empty they would break / around a lover" (lines
   26–27)?

4. In line 34, the speaker refers to "character." How does he seem to define
   the term? He concludes the poem by noting, "I smile as I serve my duty."
   Should this line be taken as an indication of how he really feels about his
   family "commitments"? Why or why not?

5. List some commitments that you think the speaker's family should be
   making toward him. What overall attitude of yours toward the family does
   your list suggest? What is your overall attitude toward the speaker?

KITTY TSUI

A Chinese Banquet

*Born in Hong Kong in 1953, Kitty Tsui grew up there and in England before mov-
ing to the United States in 1969. Besides being a writer, she is an artist, an actor,
and a bodybuilder. The following comes from her 1983 volume of poetry* The
Words of a Woman Who Breathes Fire. *Her latest book is* Breathless *(1996), a collection of stories.*

for the one who was not invited

it was not a very formal affair but
all the women over twelve
wore long gowns and a corsage,
except for me.

it was not a very formal affair, just   5
the family getting together,
poa poa,° *kuw fu*° without *kuw mow*°
(her excuse this year is a headache).

aunts and uncles and cousins,
the grandson who is a dentist,   10
the one who drives a mercedes benz,
sitting down for shark's fin soup.

they talk about buying a house and
taking a two week vacation in beijing.
i suck on shrimp and squab,   15
dreaming of the cloudscape in your eyes.

my mother, her voice beaded with sarcasm;
you're twenty six and not getting younger.
it's about time you got a decent job.
she no longer asks when i'm getting married.   20

you're twenty six and not getting younger.
what are you doing with your life?
you've got to make a living.
why don't you study computer programming?

she no longer asks when i'm getting married.   25
one day, wanting desperately to
bridge the boundaries that separate us,
wanting desperately to touch her,

tell her: mother, i'm gay,
mother i'm gay and so happy with her.   30
but she will not listen,
she shakes her head.

she sits across from me,
emotions invading her face.
her eyes are wet but   35
she will not let tears fall.

mother, i say,
you love a man.

7. *poa poa:* Maternal grandmother; *kuw fu:* Uncle; *kuw mow:* Aunt.

i love a woman.
it is not what she wants to hear.   40

aunts and uncles and cousins,
very much a family affair.
but you are not invited,
being neither my husband nor my wife.

aunts and uncles and cousins   45
eating longevity noodles
fragrant with ham inquire:
sold that old car of yours yet?

i want to tell them: my back is healing,
i dream of dragons and water.   50
my home is in her arms,
our bedroom ceiling the wide open sky.

                                                                        [1983]

THINKING ABOUT THE TEXT

1. How would you describe the speaker's relationship with her mother? Do you think the mother is wrong not to invite her daughter's lover? Identify specific values, principles, and experiences of yours that influence your answer.

2. How would you describe the conversations at the banquet? How familiar are such conversations to you? Where does the speaker contrast them with another kind of talk?

3. How helpful is the poem's title? Where specifically does the poem refer to Chinese culture? To what extent does ethnicity seem to matter in this text?

4. Note repetitions in the poem. What is their effect?

5. Tsui doesn't use capitalization. What is the effect of this move?

MAKING COMPARISONS

1. Do you sense that Hemphill's speaker, like Tsui's, is "wanting desperately to / bridge the boundaries that separate us"? Support your answer by referring to specific words in Hemphill's poem.

2. By focusing so much on photographs, Hemphill's poem emphasizes sight. Does Tsui's poem emphasize sight, or does it give at least as much attention to another sense? Support your answer by referring to details of the poem.

3. Tsui's poem addresses someone in particular; Hemphill's does not. Does this difference make for a significant difference in effect? Why, or why not?

MINNIE BRUCE PRATT
Two Small-Sized Girls

Minnie Bruce Pratt (b. 1946) has long been active in the women's movement. Her prose writings include Rebellion: Essays, 1980–1991 *(1991) and a 1995 volume of short pieces titled* S/HE. *As a poet, she has published* The Sound of One Fork *(1981);* Crime Against Nature *(1990), which won the prestigious Lamont Prize of the American Academy of Poets; and* We Say We Love Each Other *(1992). In divorce proceedings, Pratt lost custody of her two sons because she is a lesbian. Many of the poems in* Crime Against Nature, *including the following, refer to this experience.*

1.

Two small-sized girls, hunched in the corn crib,
skin prickly with heat and dust.   We rustle
in the corn husks and grab rough cobs gnawed
empty as bone.   We twist them with papery shreds.
Anyone passing would say we're making our dolls.   5

Almost sisters, like our mothers, we turn and shake
the shriveled beings.   We are not playing at babies.
We are doing, single-minded, what we've been watching
our grandmother do.   We are making someone.   We hunker
on splintered grey planks older than our mothers,   10
and ignore how the sun blazes across us, the straw husks,
the old door swung open for the new corn of the summer.

2.

Here's the cherry spool bed from her old room,
the white bedspread crocheted by Grandma,
rough straw baskets hanging on the blank wall,   15
snapshots from her last trip home, ramshackle
houses eaten up by kudzu.   The same past
haunts us.   We have ended up in the same present

where I sit crosslegged with advice on how to keep
her children from being seized by their father   20
ten years after I lost my own.   The charge then:
crime against nature, going too far with women,
and not going back to men.   And hers?   Wanting
to have her small garden the way she wanted it,
and wanting to go her own way.   The memory: 25

Her father's garden, immense rows of corn,
cantaloupe and melon squiggling, us squatting,

late afternoon, cool in the four o'clocks;
waiting for them to open, making up stories,
anything might happen, waiting in the garden.   30

3.

So much for the power of my ideas about oppression
and her disinterest in them.   In fact we've ended
in the same place.   Made wrong, knowing we've done
nothing wrong:
                    Like the afternoon we burned up   35
the backyard, wanting to see some fire.
The match's seed opened into straw, paper,
then bushes, like enormous red and orange
lantana flowers.   We chased the abrupt power
blooming around us down to charred straw,   40
and Grandma bathed us, scorched and ashy,
never saying a word.

                    Despite our raw hearts,
guilt from men who used our going to take our children,
we know we've done nothing wrong, to twist and search   45
for the kernels of fire deep in the body's shaken husk.   [1990]

THINKING ABOUT THE TEXT

1. Do you think any behavior deserves to be called a "crime against nature" (line 22)? Explain your reasoning.

2. Ironically, one pattern in Pratt's poem is nature imagery. Do you consider some or all of this imagery to be symbolic, or do you accept the images simply as details of a physical scene? Refer to specific examples.

3. Compare the three sections of the poem. What are their common elements? How do they significantly differ from one another? Why does the speaker believe that she and her cousin have "ended / in the same place" (lines 32–33)?

4. How would you describe the two girls' relationship to their grandmother? Support your answer with specific details from the text.

5. Do you think this poem is an affirmation of family ties? A criticism of them? Both? Again, refer to specific details.

MAKING COMPARISONS

1. Both Tsui's speaker and Pratt's address another woman. In Tsui's poem, it is the "one who was not invited"; in Pratt's, it is the speaker's cousin. Are the speakers expressing pretty much the same message to these women? Support your answer with specific details from both poems.

2. Do you get the impression that all three speakers in this cluster are searching for Pratt's "kernels of fire deep in the body's shaken husk" (line 46)? Show how these words are or are not relevant in each case.

3. Do you sympathize with any of the three speakers more than the others? Why, or why not?

WRITING ABOUT ISSUES

1. Choose Hemphill's, Tsui's, or Pratt's poem and write an essay arguing for, or against, a position held by someone in the poem. The person can be the speaker. Support your argument with specific details and examples.

2. Choose two of the poems in this cluster and write an essay comparing how commitments figure in them. Be sure to cite specific words of each poem.

3. In the next week, observe and jot down things on your campus that you think might disturb a gay or lesbian student. (If you are a gay or lesbian student, you may have already thought about such matters.) Then write an essay addressing the issue of whether your campus is "inviting" to gay and lesbian students. In arguing for your position on this issue, refer to some of the observations you made. If you wish, refer as well to one or more of the poems in this cluster.

4. Increasingly, the United States is grappling with whether same-sex marriage should be legalized. Another debate is whether gays and lesbians should lose child custody rights because of their sexual orientation. Choose one of these issues and read at least three articles about it. Then write an essay in which you not only put forth and support your own position on the issue, but also state whether and how the articles affected your thinking. If you wish, you may refer as well to one or more of the poems in this cluster.

A FAMILY'S DREAMS: CULTURAL CONTEXTS FOR LORRAINE HANSBERRY'S *A RAISIN IN THE SUN*

LORRAINE HANSBERRY, *A Raisin in the Sun*

CULTURAL CONTEXTS:
THE CRISIS, "The Hansberrys of Chicago: They Join Business Acumen with Social Vision"
LORRAINE HANSBERRY, April 23, 1964, Letter to the *New York Times*
ALAN EHRENHALT, From *The Lost City: Discovering the Forgotten Virtues of Community in the Chicago of the 1950s*

It is common for members of a family to dream of a better future for them all as a group. Yet what specifically should they strive to achieve? From time to time, this question may emerge as a burning issue for them, with family members disagreeing over goals. In her 1959 play *A Raisin in the Sun*, Lorraine Hansberry dramatized such a conflict, through the eyes of an African American family living in a Chicago ghetto. Hansberry's title comes from African American poet Langston Hughes's 1951 poem "Harlem," which begins by asking "What happens to a dream deferred? / Does it dry up / Like a raisin in the sun?" Hughes had in mind white America's continued thwarting of his own race's hopes for true freedom, equality, and prosperity, a situation painfully familiar to the family in Hansberry's play. Moreover, each member is tired of living in near poverty. Throughout the play, however, they argue over what specific dreams to pursue, revealing different values in the process.

Following the play are three texts to help place it in historical context. The first, a short article about Hansberry's own family, comes from a 1941 issue of *The Crisis*, the journal of the National Association for the Advancement of Colored People (NAACP). Next is an excerpt from a letter to the *New York Times* that Hansberry wrote in 1964 when the civil rights movement was gaining momentum. Last we feature a set of excerpts from Alan Ehrenhalt's recent book, *The Lost City: Discovering the Forgotten Virtues of Community in the Chicago of the 1950s* (1995). In these specific passages, Ehrenhalt describes Bronzeville, the segregated community where Hansberry grew up and the setting of her play.

BEFORE YOU READ

Think of your own family or another you know well. For outsiders to get a sense of this family, what do they have to know about its social and historical background? Do you think the phrase *a dream deferred* applies to this family? Why, or why not?

LORRAINE HANSBERRY
A Raisin in the Sun

The life of Lorraine Hansberry (1930–1965) was brief. She died of cancer the day that her second play, The Sign in Sidney Brustein's Window *(1964), closed on Broadway. But even by then, she had been immensely productive as a writer and gained a considerable reputation for her work. In 1959, her first play,* A Raisin in the Sun, *was the first by an African American woman to be produced on Broadway. Later that year, it became the first play by an African American to win the New York Drama Critics Circle Award. In part, the play was based on an experience that Hansberry's own family endured while she was growing up in Chicago. Her father, Carl Hansberry, a prominent realtor and banker, made history in 1938 when he moved his family to an all-white section of Chicago's Hyde Park neighborhood. After encountering white resistance there, he fought a series of legal battles that went all the way to the Supreme Court. In 1940, the Court ruled in his favor, but its decision largely was not enforced; housing remained basically segregated in Chicago and in most of the* country. Embittered, Carl Hansberry considered moving his family permanently to Mexico, but before he could he died of a cerebral hemorrhage there in 1946.

After attending the University of Wisconsin, Lorraine Hansberry moved to New York City. Besides plays, she wrote essays, articles, and pieces of journalism on a variety of subjects, including homophobia and racism. She also wrote the screenplay for the 1961 film version of A Raisin in the Sun, which featured the original Broadway cast (including Sidney Poitier as Walter Lee Younger). In 1969, her husband Robert Nemiroff combined various writings of hers into a play called To Be Young, Gifted, and Black. In 1970, a book version of it was published, and that same year there was a Broadway production of Hansberry's final play, Les Blancs.

Harlem (A Dream Deferred)

What happens to a dream deferred?

Does it dry up
Like a raisin in the sun?
Or fester like a sore —
And then run?
Does it stink like rotten meat?
Or crust and sugar over —
Like a syrupy sweet?

Maybe it just sags
Like a heavy load.

Or does it explode?
— Langston Hughes

CHARACTERS (in order of appearance)

RUTH YOUNGER
TRAVIS YOUNGER
WALTER LEE YOUNGER, *brother*
BENEATHA YOUNGER
LENA YOUNGER, MAMA
JOSEPH ASAGAI
GEORGE MURCHISON
MRS. JOHNSON
KARL LINDNER
BOBO
MOVING MEN

The action of the play is set in Chicago's Southside, sometime between World War II and the present.

ACT 1, Scene 1

[*Friday morning.*]

The Younger living room would be a comfortable and well-ordered room if it were not for a number of indestructible contradictions to this state of being. Its furnishings are typical and undistinguished and their primary feature now is that they have clearly had to accommodate the living of too many people for too many years — and they are tired. Still, we can see that at some time, a time probably no longer remembered by the family (except perhaps for Mama), the furnishings of this room were actually selected with care and love and even hope — and brought to this apartment and arranged with taste and pride.

That was a long time ago. Now the once loved pattern of the couch upholstery has to fight to show itself from under acres of crocheted doilies and couch covers which have themselves finally come to be more important than the upholstery. And here a table or a chair has been moved to disguise the worn places in the carpet; but the carpet has fought back by showing its weariness, with depressing uniformity, elsewhere on its surface.

Weariness has, in fact, won in this room. Everything has been polished, washed, sat on, used, scrubbed too often. All pretenses but living itself have long since vanished from the very atmosphere of this room.

Moreover, a section of this room, for it is not really a room unto itself, though the landlord's lease would make it seem so, slopes backward to provide a small kitchen area, where the family prepares the meals that are eaten in the living room proper, which must also serve as dining room. The single window that has been provided for these "two" rooms is located in this kitchen area. The sole natural light the family may enjoy in the course of a day is only that which fights its way through this little window.

At left, a door leads to a bedroom which is shared by Mama and her daughter, Beneatha. At right, opposite, is a second room (which in the beginning of the life of this apartment was probably a breakfast room) which serves as a bedroom for Walter and his wife, Ruth.

Time: Sometime between World War II and the present.

Place: Chicago's Southside.

At Rise: It is morning dark in the living room. Travis is asleep on the makedown bed at center. An alarm clock sounds from within the bedroom at right, and presently Ruth enters from that room and closes the door behind her. She crosses sleepily toward the window. As she passes her sleeping son she reaches down and shakes him a little. At the window she raises the shade and a dusky Southside morning light comes in feebly. She fills a pot with water and puts it on to boil. She calls to the boy, between yawns, in a slightly muffled voice.

Ruth is about thirty. We can see that she was a pretty girl, even exceptionally so, but now it is apparent that life has been little that she expected, and disappointment has already begun to hang in her face. In a few years, before thirty-five even, she will be known among her people as a "settled woman."

She crosses to her son and gives him a good, final, rousing shake.

RUTH: Come on now, boy, it's seven thirty! *(Her son sits up at last, in a stupor of sleepiness.)* I say hurry up, Travis! You ain't the only person in the world got to use a bathroom! *(The child, a sturdy, handsome little boy of ten or eleven, drags himself out of the bed and almost blindly takes his towels and "today's clothes" from drawers and a closet and goes out to the bathroom, which is in an outside hall and which is shared by another family or families on the same floor. Ruth crosses to the bedroom door at right and opens it and calls in to her husband.)* Walter Lee! . . . It's after seven thirty! Lemme see you do some waking up in there now! *(She waits.)* You better get up from there, man! It's after seven thirty I tell you. *(She waits again.)* All right, you just go ahead and lay there and next thing you know Travis be finished and Mr. Johnson'll be in there and you'll be fussing and cussing round here like a madman! And be late too! *(She waits, at the end of patience.)* Walter Lee — it's time for you to GET UP!

She waits another second and then starts to go into the bedroom, but is apparently satisfied that her husband has begun to get up. She stops, pulls the door to, and returns to the kitchen area. She wipes her face with a moist cloth and runs her fingers through her sleep-disheveled hair in a vain effort and ties an apron around her housecoat. The bedroom door at right opens and her husband stands in the doorway in his pajamas, which are rumpled and mismated. He is a lean, intense young man in his middle thirties, inclined to quick nervous movements and erratic speech habits — and always in his voice there is a quality of indictment.

WALTER: Is he out yet?

RUTH: What you mean *out?* He ain't hardly got in there good yet.

WALTER *(wandering in, still more oriented to sleep than to a new day)*:   Well, what was you doing all that yelling for if I can't even get in there yet? *(Stopping and thinking.)* Check coming today?

RUTH: They *said* Saturday and this is just Friday and I hopes to God you ain't going to get up here first thing this morning and start talking to me 'bout no money — 'cause I 'bout don't want to hear it.

WALTER: Something the matter with you this morning?

RUTH: No — I'm just sleepy as the devil. What kind of eggs you want?

WALTER: Not scrambled. *(Ruth starts to scramble eggs.)* Paper come? *(Ruth points impatiently to the rolled up Tribune on the table, and he gets it and spreads it out and vaguely reads the front page.)* Set off another bomb yesterday.

RUTH *(maximum indifference)*:   Did they?

WALTER *(looking up)*:   What's the matter with you?

RUTH: Ain't nothing the matter with me. And don't keep asking me that this morning.

WALTER: Ain't nobody bothering you. *(Reading the news of the day absently again.)* Say Colonel McCormick is sick.

RUTH *(affecting tea-party interest)*:   Is he now? Poor thing.

WALTER *(sighing and looking at his watch)*:   Oh, me. *(He waits.)* Now what is that boy doing in that bathroom all this time? He just going to have to start getting up earlier. I can't be being late to work on account of him fooling around in there.

RUTH *(turning on him):*   Oh, no he ain't going to be getting up no earlier no such thing! It ain't his fault that he can't get to bed no earlier nights 'cause he got a bunch of crazy good-for-nothing clowns sitting up running their mouths in what is supposed to be his bedroom after ten o'clock at night . . .

WALTER: That's what you mad about, ain't it? The things I want to talk about with my friends just couldn't be important in your mind, could they?

He rises and finds a cigarette in her handbag on the table and crosses to the little window and looks out, smoking and deeply enjoying this first one.

RUTH *(almost matter of factly, a complaint too automatic to deserve emphasis):*   Why you always got to smoke before you eat in the morning?

WALTER *(at the window):*   Just look at 'em down there . . . Running and racing to work . . . *(He turns and faces his wife and watches her a moment at the stove, and then, suddenly.)* You look young this morning, baby.

RUTH *(indifferently):*   Yeah?

WALTER: Just for a second—stirring them eggs. Just for a second it was—you looked real young again. *(He reaches for her; she crosses away. Then, drily.)* It's gone now—you look like yourself again!

RUTH: Man, if you don't shut up and leave me alone.

WALTER *(looking out to the street again):*   First thing a man ought to learn in life is not to make love to no colored woman first thing in the morning. You all some eeeevil people at eight o'clock in the morning.

Travis appears in the hall doorway, almost fully dressed and quite wide awake now, his towels and pajamas across his shoulders. He opens the door and signals for his father to make the bathroom in a hurry.

TRAVIS *(watching the bathroom):*   Daddy, come on!

Walter gets his bathroom utensils and flies out to the bathroom.

RUTH: Sit down and have your breakfast, Travis.

TRAVIS: Mama, this is Friday. *(Gleefully.)* Check coming tomorrow, huh?

RUTH: You get your mind off money and eat your breakfast.

TRAVIS *(eating):*   This is the morning we supposed to bring the fifty cents to school.

RUTH: Well, I ain't got no fifty cents this morning.

TRAVIS: Teacher say we have to.

RUTH: I don't care what teacher say. I ain't got it. Eat your breakfast, Travis.

TRAVIS: I *am* eating.

RUTH: Hush up now and just eat!

The boy gives her an exasperated look for her lack of understanding, and eats grudgingly.

TRAVIS: You think Grandmama would have it?

RUTH: No! And I want you to stop asking your grandmother for money, you hear me?

TRAVIS *(outraged):*   Gaaaleee! I don't ask her, she just gimme it sometimes!

RUTH: Travis Willard Younger — I got too much on me this morning to be —

TRAVIS: Maybe Daddy —

RUTH: *Travis!*

The boy hushes abruptly. They are both quiet and tense for several seconds.

TRAVIS *(presently):*   Could I maybe go carry some groceries in front of the super-market for a little while after school then?

RUTH: Just hush, I said. *(Travis jabs his spoon into his cereal bowl viciously, and rests his head in anger upon his fists.)* If you through eating, you can get over there and make up your bed.

The boy obeys stiffly and crosses the room, almost mechanically, to the bed and more or less folds the bedding into a heap, then angrily gets his books and cap.

TRAVIS *(sulking and standing apart from her unnaturally):*   I'm gone.

RUTH *(looking up from the stove to inspect him automatically):*   Come here. *(He crosses to her and she studies his head.)* If you don't take this comb and fix this here head, you better! *(Travis puts down his books with a great sigh of oppression, and crosses to the mirror. His mother mutters under her breath about his "slubbornness.")* 'Bout to march out of here with that head looking just like chickens slept in it! I just don't know where you get your slubborn ways . . . And get your jacket, too. Looks chilly out this morning.

TRAVIS *(with conspicuously brushed hair and jacket):*   I'm gone.

RUTH: Get carfare and milk money — *(Waving one finger.)* — and not a single penny for no caps, you hear me?

TRAVIS *(with sullen politeness):*   Yes'm.

He turns in outrage to leave. His mother watches after him as in his frustration he approaches the door almost comically. When she speaks to him, her voice has become a very gentle tease.

RUTH *(mocking; as she thinks he would say it):*   Oh, Mama makes me so mad sometimes, I don't know what to do! *(She waits and continues to his back as he stands stock-still in front of the door.)* I wouldn't kiss that woman good-bye for nothing in this world this morning! *(The boy finally turns around and rolls his eyes at her, knowing the mood has changed and he is vindicated; he does not, however, move toward her yet.)* Not for nothing in this world! *(She finally laughs aloud at him and holds out her arms to him and we see that it is a way between them, very old and practiced. He crosses to her and allows her to embrace him warmly but keeps his face fixed with masculine rigidity. She holds him back from her presently and looks at him and runs her fingers over the features of his face. With utter gentleness —.)* Now — whose little old angry man are you?

TRAVIS *(the masculinity and gruffness start to fade at last):*   Aw gaalee — Mama . . .

RUTH *(mimicking):*   Aw — gaaaaalleeeee, Mama! *(She pushes him, with rough playfulness and finality, toward the door.)* Get on out of here or you going to be late.

TRAVIS *(in the face of love, new aggressiveness):*   Mama, could I *please* go carry groceries?

RUTH: Honey, it's starting to get so cold evenings.

WALTER (*coming in from the bathroom and drawing a make-believe gun from a make-believe holster and shooting at his son*):   What is it he wants to do?

RUTH: Go carry groceries after school at the supermarket.

WALTER: Well, let him go . . .

TRAVIS (*quickly, to the ally*):   I *have* to—she won't gimme the fifty cents . . .

WALTER (*to his wife only*):   Why not?

RUTH (*simply, and with flavor*):   'Cause we don't have it.

WALTER (*to Ruth only*):   What you tell the boy things like that for? (*Reaching down into his pants with a rather important gesture.*) Here, son—

He hands the boy the coin, but his eyes are directed to his wife's. Travis takes the money happily.

TRAVIS: Thanks, Daddy.

He starts out. Ruth watches both of them with murder in her eyes. Walter stands and stares back at her with defiance, and suddenly reaches into his pocket again on an afterthought.

WALTER (*without even looking at his son, still staring hard at his wife*):   In fact, here's another fifty cents . . . Buy yourself some fruit today—or take a taxicab to school or something!

TRAVIS: Whoopee—

He leaps up and clasps his father around the middle with his legs, and they face each other in mutual appreciation; slowly Walter Lee peeks around the boy to catch the violent rays from his wife's eyes and draws his head back as if shot.

WALTER: You better get down now—and get to school, man.

TRAVIS (*at the door*):   O.K. Good-bye.

He exits.

WALTER (*after him, pointing with pride*):   That's *my* boy. (*She looks at him in disgust and turns back to her work.*) You know what I was thinking 'bout in the bathroom this morning?

RUTH: No.

WALTER: How come you always try to be so pleasant!

RUTH: What is there to be pleasant 'bout!

WALTER: You want to know what I was thinking 'bout in the bathroom or not!

RUTH: I know what you thinking 'bout.

WALTER (*ignoring her*):   'Bout what me and Willy Harris was talking about last night.

RUTH (*immediately—a refrain*):   Willy Harris is a good-for-nothing loudmouth.

WALTER: Anybody who talks to me has got to be a good-for-nothing loudmouth, ain't he? And what you know about who is just a good-for-nothing loudmouth? Charlie Atkins was just a "good-for-nothing loudmouth" too, wasn't he! When he wanted me to go in the dry-cleaning business with him. And now—he's grossing a hundred thousand a year. A hundred thousand dollars a year! You still call *him* a loudmouth!

RUTH (*bitterly*):   Oh, Walter Lee . . .

She folds her head on her arms over the table.

WALTER (*rising and coming to her and standing over her*):   You tired, ain't you?
Tired of everything. Me, the boy, the way we live—this beat-up hole—
everything. Ain't you? (*She doesn't look up, doesn't answer.*) So tired—moaning and groaning all the time, but you wouldn't do nothing to help, would
you? You couldn't be on my side that long for nothing, could you?

RUTH: Walter, please leave me alone.

WALTER: A man needs for a woman to back him up . . .

RUTH: Walter—

WALTER: Mama would listen to you. You know she listen to you more than she
do me and Bennie. She think more of you. All you have to do is just sit down
with her when you drinking your coffee one morning and talking 'bout
things like you do and—(*He sits down beside her and demonstrates graphi-
cally what he thinks her methods and tone should be.*)—you just sip your coffee, see, and say easy like that you been thinking 'bout that deal Walter Lee is
so interested in, 'bout the store and all, and sip some more coffee, like what
you saying ain't really that important to you—And the next thing you know,
she be listening good and asking you questions and when I come home—I
can tell her the details. This ain't no fly-by-night proposition, baby. I mean
we figured it out, me and Willy and Bobo.

RUTH (*with a frown*):   Bobo?

WALTER: Yeah. You see, this little liquor store we got in mind cost seventy-five
thousand and we figured the initial investment on the place be 'bout thirty
thousand, see. That be ten thousand each. Course, there's a couple of hundred you got to pay so's you don't spend your life just waiting for them clowns
to let your license get approved—

RUTH: You mean graft?

WALTER (*frowning impatiently*):   Don't call it that. See there, that just goes to
show you what women understand about the world. Baby, don't *nothing*
happen for you in the world 'less you pay *somebody* off!

RUTH: Walter, leave me alone! (*She raises her head and stares at him vigorously—then says, more quietly.*) Eat your eggs, they gonna be cold.

WALTER (*straightening up from her and looking off*):   That's it. There you are.
Man say to his woman: I got me a dream. His woman say: Eat your eggs.
(*Sadly, but gaining in power.*) Man say: I got to take hold of this here world,
baby! And a woman will say: Eat your eggs and go to work. (*Passionately
now.*) Man say: I got to change my life, I'm choking to death, baby! And his
woman say—(*In utter anguish as he brings his fists down on his thighs.*)—
Your eggs is getting cold!

RUTH (*softly*):   Walter, that ain't none of our money.

WALTER (*not listening at all or even looking at her*):   This morning, I was lookin'
in the mirror and thinking about it . . . I'm thirty-five years old; I been married eleven years and I got a boy who sleeps in the living room—(*Very, very*

quietly.) — and all I got to give him is stories about how rich white people live . . .

RUTH: Eat your eggs, Walter.

WALTER *(slams the table and jumps up)*:   —DAMN MY EGGS—DAMN ALL THE EGGS THAT EVER WAS!

RUTH: Then go to work.

WALTER *(looking up at her)*:   See—I'm trying to talk to you 'bout myself— *(Shaking his head with the repetition.)* — and all you can say is eat them eggs and go to work.

RUTH *(wearily)*:   Honey, you never say nothing new. I listen to you every day, every night and every morning, and you never say nothing new. *(Shrugging.)* So you would rather *be* Mr. Arnold than be his chauffeur. So—I would *rather* be living in Buckingham Palace.

WALTER: That is just what is wrong with the colored woman in this world . . . Don't understand about building their men up and making 'em feel like they somebody. Like they can do something.

RUTH *(drily, but to hurt)*:   There *are* colored men who do things.

WALTER: No thanks to the colored woman.

RUTH: Well, being a colored woman, I guess I can't help myself none.

She rises and gets the ironing board and sets it up and attacks a huge pile of rough-dried clothes, sprinkling them in preparation for the ironing and then rolling them into tight fat balls.

WALTER *(mumbling)*:   We one group of men tied to a race of women with small minds!

His sister Beneatha enters. She is about twenty, as slim and intense as her brother. She is not as pretty as her sister-in-law, but her lean, almost intellectual face has a handsomeness of its own. She wears a bright-red flannel nightie, and her thick hair stands wildly about her head. Her speech is a mixture of many things; it is different from the rest of the family's insofar as education has permeated her sense of English—and perhaps the Midwest rather than the South has finally—at last—won out in her inflection; but not altogether, because over all of it is a soft slurring and transformed use of vowels which is the decided influence of the Southside. She passes through the room without looking at either Ruth or Walter and goes to the outside door and looks, a little blindly, out to the bathroom. She sees that it has been lost to the Johnsons. She closes the door with a sleepy vengeance and crosses to the table and sits down a little defeated.

BENEATHA: I am going to start timing those people.

WALTER: You should get up earlier.

BENEATHA *(her face in her hands. She is still fighting the urge to go back to bed)*:   Really—would you suggest dawn? Where's the paper?

WALTER *(pushing the paper across the table to her as he studies her almost clinically, as though he has never seen her before)*:   You a horrible-looking chick at this hour.

BENEATHA *(drily)*:   Good morning, everybody.

WALTER *(senselessly):*   How is school coming?

BENEATHA *(in the same spirit):*   Lovely. Lovely. And you know, biology is the greatest. *(Looking up at him.)* I dissected something that looked just like you yesterday.

WALTER: I just wondered if you've made up your mind and everything.

BENEATHA *(gaining in sharpness and impatience):*   And what did I answer yesterday morning—and the day before that?

RUTH *(from the ironing board, like someone disinterested and old):*   Don't be so nasty, Bennie.

BENEATHA *(still to her brother):*   And the day before that and the day before that!

WALTER *(defensively):*   I'm interested in you. Something wrong with that? Ain't many girls who decide—

WALTER AND BENEATHA *(in unison):*   —"to be a doctor."

Silence.

WALTER: Have we figured out yet just exactly how much medical school is going to cost?

RUTH: Walter Lee, why don't you leave that girl alone and get out of here to work?

BENEATHA *(exits to the bathroom and bangs on the door):*   Come on out of there, please!

She comes back into the room.

WALTER *(looking at his sister intently):*   You know the check is coming tomorrow.

BENEATHA *(turning on him with a sharpness all her own):*   That money belongs to Mama, Walter, and it's for her to decide how she wants to use it. I don't care if she wants to buy a house or a rocket ship or just nail it up somewhere and look at it. It's hers. Not ours—*hers.*

WALTER *(bitterly):*   Now ain't that fine! You just got your mother's interest at heart, ain't you, girl? You such a nice girl—but if Mama got that money she can always take a few thousand and help you through school too—can't she?

BENEATHA: I have never asked anyone around here to do anything for me!

WALTER: No! And the line between asking and just accepting when the time comes is big and wide—ain't it!

BENEATHA *(with fury):*   What do you want from me, Brother—that I quit school or just drop dead, which!

WALTER: I don't want nothing but for you to stop acting holy 'round here. Me and Ruth done made some sacrifices for you—why can't you do something for the family?

RUTH: Walter, don't be dragging me in it.

WALTER: You are in it—Don't you get up and go work in somebody's kitchen for the last three years to help put clothes on her back?

RUTH: Oh, Walter—that's not fair . . .

WALTER: It ain't that nobody expects you to get on your knees and say thank you, Brother; thank you, Ruth; thank you, Mama—and thank you, Travis, for wearing the same pair of shoes for two semesters—

BENEATHA (*dropping to her knees*):   Well—I *do*—all right?—thank everybody! And forgive me for ever wanting to be anything at all! (*Pursuing him on her knees across the floor.*) FORGIVE ME, FORGIVE ME, FORGIVE ME!

RUTH: Please stop it! Your mama'll hear you.

WALTER: Who the hell told you you had to be a doctor? If you so crazy 'bout messing 'round with sick people—then go be a nurse like other women—or just get married and be quiet . . .

BENEATHA: Well—you finally got it said . . . It took you three years but you finally got it said. Walter, give up; leave me alone—it's Mama's money.

WALTER: *He was my father, too!*

BENEATHA: So what? He was mine, too—and Travis' grandfather—but the insurance money belongs to Mama. Picking on me is not going to make her give it to you to invest in any liquor stores—(*Under breath, dropping into a chair.*)—and I for one say, God bless Mama for that!

WALTER (*to Ruth*):   See—did you hear? Did you hear!

RUTH: Honey, please go to work.

WALTER: Nobody in this house is ever going to understand me.

BENEATHA: Because you're a nut.

WALTER: Who's a nut?

BENEATHA: You—you are a nut. Thee is mad, boy.

WALTER (*looking at his wife and his sister from the door, very sadly*):   The world's most backward race of people, and that's a fact.

BENEATHA (*turning slowly in her chair*):   And then there are all those prophets who would lead us out of the wilderness—(*Walter slams out of the house.*)—into the swamps!

RUTH: Bennie, why you always gotta be pickin' on your brother? Can't you be a little sweeter sometimes? (*Door opens. Walter walks in. He fumbles with his cap, starts to speak, clears throat, looks everywhere but at Ruth. Finally:*)

WALTER (*to Ruth*):   I need some money for carfare.

RUTH (*looks at him, then warms; teasing, but tenderly*):   Fifty cents? (*She goes to her bag and gets money.*) Here—take a taxi!

Walter exits. Mama enters. She is a woman in her early sixties, full-bodied and strong. She is one of those women of a certain grace and beauty who wear it so unobtrusively that it takes a while to notice. Her dark-brown face is surrounded by the total whiteness of her hair, and, being a woman who has adjusted to many things in life and overcome many more, her face is full of strength. She has, we can see, wit and faith of a kind that keep her eyes lit and full of interest and expectancy. She is, in a word, a beautiful woman. Her bearing is perhaps most like the noble bearing of the women of the Hereros of Southwest Africa—rather as if she imagines that as she walks she still bears a basket or a vessel upon her head. Her speech, on the other hand, is as careless as her carriage is precise—she is inclined to slur everything—but her voice is perhaps not so much quiet as simply soft.

MAMA: Who that 'round here slamming doors at this hour?

She crosses through the room, goes to the window, opens it, and brings in a feeble little plant growing doggedly in a small pot on the window sill. She feels the dirt and puts it back out.

RUTH: That was Walter Lee. He and Bennie was at it again.

MAMA: My children and they tempers. Lord, if this little old plant don't get more sun than it's been getting it ain't never going to see spring again. *(She turns from the window.)* What's the matter with you this morning, Ruth? You looks right peaked. You aiming to iron all them things? Leave some for me. I'll get to 'em this afternoon. Bennie honey, it's too drafty for you to be sitting 'round half dressed. Where's your robe?

BENEATHA: In the cleaners.

MAMA: Well, go get mine and put it on.

BENEATHA: I'm not cold, Mama, honest.

MAMA: I know—but you so thin . . .

BENEATHA *(irritably)*:   Mama, I'm not cold.

MAMA *(seeing the make-down bed as Travis has left it)*:   Lord have mercy, look at that poor bed. Bless his heart—he tries, don't he?

She moves to the bed Travis has sloppily made up.

RUTH: No—he don't half try at all 'cause he knows you going to come along behind him and fix everything. That's just how come he don't know how to do nothing right now—you done spoiled that boy so.

MAMA *(folding bedding)*:   Well—he's a little boy. Ain't supposed to know 'bout housekeeping. My baby, that's what he is. What you fix for his breakfast this morning?

RUTH *(angrily)*:   I feed my son, Lena!

MAMA: I ain't meddling—*(Under breath; busy-bodyish.)* I just noticed all last week he had cold cereal, and when it starts getting this chilly in the fall a child ought to have some hot grits or something when he goes out in the cold—

RUTH *(furious)*:   I gave him hot oats—is that all right!

MAMA: I ain't meddling. *(Pause.)* Put a lot of nice butter on it? *(Ruth shoots her an angry look and does not reply.)* He likes lots of butter.

RUTH *(exasperated)*:   Lena—

MAMA *(to Beneatha. Mama is inclined to wander conversationally sometimes)*:   What was you and your brother fussing 'bout this morning?

BENEATHA: It's not important, Mama.

She gets up and goes to look out at the bathroom, which is apparently free, and she picks up her towels and rushes out.

MAMA: What was they fighting about?

RUTH: Now you know as well as I do.

MAMA *(shaking her head)*:   Brother still worrying hisself sick about that money?

RUTH: You know he is.

MAMA: You had breakfast?

RUTH: Some coffee.

MAMA: Girl, you better start eating and looking after yourself better. You almost thin as Travis.

RUTH: Lena —

MAMA: Un-hunh?

RUTH: What are you going to do with it?

MAMA: Now don't you start, child. It's too early in the morning to be talking about money. It ain't Christian.

RUTH: It's just that he got his heart set on that store —

MAMA: You mean that liquor store that Willy Harris want him to invest in?

RUTH: Yes —

MAMA: We ain't no business people, Ruth. We just plain working folks.

RUTH: Ain't nobody business people till they go into business. Walter Lee say colored people ain't never going to start getting ahead till they start gambling on some different kinds of things in the world — investments and things.

MAMA: What done got into you, girl? Walter Lee done finally sold you on investing.

RUTH: No. Mama, something is happening between Walter and me. I don't know what it is — but he needs something — something I can't give him any more. He needs this chance, Lena.

MAMA *(frowning deeply)*:   But liquor, honey —

RUTH: Well — like Walter say — I spec people going to always be drinking themselves some liquor.

MAMA: Well — whether they drinks it or not ain't none of my business. But whether I go into business selling it to 'em *is*, and I don't want that on my ledger this late in life. *(Stopping suddenly and studying her daughter-in-law.)* Ruth Younger, what's the matter with you today? You look like you could fall over right there.

RUTH: I'm tired.

MAMA: Then you better stay home from work today.

RUTH: I can't stay home. She'd be calling up the agency and screaming at them, "My girl didn't come in today — send me somebody! My girl didn't come in!" Oh, she just have a fit . . .

MAMA: Well, let her have it. I'll just call her up and say you got the flu —

RUTH *(laughing)*:   Why the flu?

MAMA: 'Cause it sounds respectable to 'em. Something white people get, too. They know 'bout the flu. Otherwise they think you been cut up or something when you tell 'em you sick.

RUTH: I got to go in. We need the money.

MAMA: Somebody would of thought my children done all but starved to death the way they talk about money here late. Child, we got a great big old check coming tomorrow.

RUTH *(sincerely, but also self-righteously)*:   Now that's your money. It ain't got nothing to do with me. We all feel like that — Walter and Bennie and me — even Travis.

MAMA *(thoughtfully, and suddenly very far away)*:   Ten thousand dollars —

RUTH: Sure is wonderful.

MAMA: Ten thousand dollars.

RUTH: You know what you should do, Miss Lena? You should take yourself a trip somewhere. To Europe or South America or someplace —

MAMA *(throwing up her hands at the thought)*:   Oh, child!

RUTH: I'm serious. Just pack up and leave! Go on away and enjoy yourself some. Forget about the family and have yourself a ball for once in your life —

MAMA *(drily)*:   You sound like I'm just about ready to die. Who'd go with me? What I look like wandering 'round Europe by myself?

RUTH: Shoot — these here rich white women do it all the time. They don't think nothing of packing up they suitcases and piling on one of them big steamships and — swoosh! — they gone, child.

MAMA: Something always told me I wasn't no rich white woman.

RUTH: Well — what are you going to do with it then?

MAMA: I ain't rightly decided. *(Thinking. She speaks now with emphasis.)* Some of it got to be put away for Beneatha and her schoolin' — and ain't nothing going to touch that part of it. Nothing. *(She waits several seconds, trying to make up her mind about something, and looks at Ruth a little tentatively before going on.)* Been thinking that we maybe could meet the notes on a little old two-story somewhere, with a yard where Travis could play in the summer-time, if we use part of the insurance for a down payment and everybody kind of pitch in. I could maybe take on a little day work again, few days a week —

RUTH *(studying her mother-in-law furtively and concentrating on her ironing, anxious to encourage without seeming to)*:   Well, Lord knows, we've put enough rent into this here rat trap to pay for four houses by now . . .

MAMA *(looking up at the words "rat trap" and then looking around and leaning back and sighing — in a suddenly reflective mood —)*:   "Rat trap" — yes, that's all it is. *(Smiling.)* I remember just as well the day me and Big Walter moved in here. Hadn't been married but two weeks and wasn't planning on living here no more than a year. *(She shakes her head at the dissolved dream.)* We was going to set away, little by little, don't you know, and buy a little place out in Morgan Park. We had even picked out the house. *(Chuckling a little.)* Looks right dumpy today. But Lord, child, you should know all the dreams I had 'bout buying that house and fixing it up and making me a little garden in the back — *(She waits and stops smiling.)* And didn't none of it happen.

Dropping her hands in a futile gesture.

RUTH *(keeps her head down, ironing)*:   Yes, life can be a barrel of disappoint-ments, sometimes.

MAMA: Honey, Big Walter would come in here some nights back then and slump down on that couch there and just look at the rug, and look at me and look at the rug and then back at me — and I'd know he was down then . . . really down. *(After a second very long and thoughtful pause; she is seeing back to times that only she can see.)* And then, Lord, when I lost that baby — little Claude — I almost thought I was going to lose Big Walter too. Oh, that man grieved hisself! He was one man to love his children.

RUTH: Ain't nothin' can tear at you like losin' your baby.

MAMA: I guess that's how come that man finally worked hisself to death like he done. Like he was fighting his own war with this here world that took his baby from him.

RUTH: He sure was a fine man, all right. I always liked Mr. Younger.

MAMA: Crazy 'bout his children! God knows there was plenty wrong with Walter Younger—hard-headed, mean, kind of wild with women—plenty wrong with him. But he sure loved his children. Always wanted them to have something—be something. That's where Brother gets all these notions, I reckon. Big Walter used to say, he'd get right wet in the eyes sometimes, lean his head back with the water standing in his eyes and say, "Seem like God didn't see fit to give the black man nothing but dreams—but He did give us children to make them dreams seem worthwhile." *(She smiles.)* He could talk like that, don't you know.

RUTH: Yes, he sure could. He was a good man, Mr. Younger.

MAMA: Yes, a fine man—just couldn't never catch up with his dreams, that's all.

Beneatha comes in, brushing her hair and looking up to the ceiling, where the sound of a vacuum cleaner has started up.

BENEATHA: What could be so dirty on that woman's rugs that she has to vacuum them every single day?

RUTH: I wish certain young women 'round here who I could name would take inspiration about certain rugs in a certain apartment I could also mention.

BENEATHA *(shrugging)*:   How much cleaning can a house need, for Christ's sakes.

MAMA *(not liking the Lord's name used thus)*:   Bennie!

RUTH: Just listen to her—just listen!

BENEATHA: Oh, God!

MAMA: If you use the Lord's name just one more time—

BENEATHA *(a bit of a whine)*:   Oh, Mama—

RUTH: Fresh—just fresh as salt, this girl!

BENEATHA *(drily)*:   Well—if the salt loses its savor—

MAMA: Now that will do. I just ain't going to have you 'round here reciting the scriptures in vain—you hear me?

BENEATHA: How did I manage to get on everybody's wrong side by just walking into a room?

RUTH: If you weren't so fresh—

BENEATHA: Ruth, I'm twenty years old.

MAMA: What time you be home from school today?

BENEATHA: Kind of late. *(With enthusiasm.)* Madeline is going to start my guitar lessons today.

Mama and Ruth look up with the same expression.

MAMA: Your *what* kind of lessons?

BENEATHA: Guitar.

RUTH: Oh, Father!

MAMA: How come you done taken it in your mind to learn to play the guitar?

BENEATHA: I just want to, that's all.

MAMA *(smiling):*   Lord, child, don't you know what to do with yourself? How long it going to be before you get tired of this now — like you got tired of that little play-acting group you joined last year? *(Looking at Ruth.)* And what was it the year before that?

RUTH: The horseback-riding club for which she bought that fifty-five-dollar riding habit that's been hanging in the closet ever since!

MAMA *(to Beneatha):*   Why you got to flit so from one thing to another, baby?

BENEATHA *(sharply):*   I just want to learn to play the guitar. Is there anything wrong with that?

MAMA: Ain't nobody trying to stop you. I just wonders sometimes why you has to flit so from one thing to another all the time. You ain't never done nothing with all that camera equipment you brought home —

BENEATHA: I don't flit! I — I experiment with different forms of expression —

RUTH: Like riding a horse?

BENEATHA: — People have to express themselves one way or another.

MAMA: What is it you want to express?

BENEATHA *(angrily):*   Me! *(Mama and Ruth look at each other and burst into raucous laughter.)* Don't worry — I don't expect you to understand.

MAMA *(to change the subject):*   Who you going out with tomorrow night?

BENEATHA *(with displeasure):*   George Murchison again.

MAMA *(pleased):*   Oh — you getting a little sweet on him?

RUTH: You ask me, this child ain't sweet on nobody but herself — *(Under breath.)* Express herself!

They laugh.

BENEATHA: Oh — I like George all right, Mama. I mean I like him enough to go out with him and stuff, but —

RUTH *(for devilment):*   What does *and stuff* mean?

BENEATHA: Mind your own business.

MAMA: Stop picking at her now, Ruth. *(She chuckles — then a suspicious sudden look at her daughter as she turns in her chair for emphasis.)* What DOES it mean?

BENEATHA *(wearily):*   Oh, I just mean I couldn't ever really be serious about George. He's — he's so shallow.

RUTH: Shallow — what do you mean he's shallow? He's *rich!*

MAMA: Hush, Ruth.

BENEATHA: I know he's rich. He knows he's rich, too.

RUTH: Well — what other qualities a man got to have to satisfy you, little girl?

BENEATHA: You wouldn't even begin to understand. Anybody who married Walter could not possibly understand.

MAMA *(outraged):*   What kind of way is that to talk about your brother?

BENEATHA: Brother is a flip — let's face it.

MAMA *(to Ruth, helplessly):*   What's a flip?

RUTH *(glad to add kindling)*:   She's saying he's crazy.

BENEATHA: Not crazy. Brother isn't really crazy yet—he—he's an elaborate neurotic.

MAMA: Hush your mouth!

BENEATHA: As for George. Well. George looks good—he's got a beautiful car and he takes me to nice places and, as my sister-in-law says, he is probably the richest boy I will ever get to know and I even like him sometimes—but if the Youngers are sitting around waiting to see if their little Bennie is going to tie up the family with the Murchisons, they are wasting their time.

RUTH: You mean you wouldn't marry George Murchison if he asked you some-day? That pretty, rich thing? Honey, I knew you was odd—

BENEATHA: No I would not marry him if all I felt for him was what I feel now. Besides, George's family wouldn't really like it.

MAMA: Why not?

BENEATHA: Oh, Mama—The Murchisons are honest-to-God-real-*live*-rich col-ored people, and the only people in the world who are more snobbish than rich white people are rich colored people. I thought everybody knew that. I've met Mrs. Murchison. She's a scene!

MAMA: You must not dislike people 'cause they well off, honey.

BENEATHA: Why not? It makes just as much sense as disliking people 'cause they are poor, and lots of people do that.

RUTH *(a wisdom-of-the-ages manner. To Mama)*:   Well, she'll get over some of this—

BENEATHA: Get over it? What are you talking about, Ruth? Listen, I'm going to be a doctor. I'm not worried about who I'm going to marry yet—if I ever get married.

MAMA and RUTH: *If!*

MAMA: Now, Bennie—

BENEATHA: Oh, I probably will . . . but first I'm going to be a doctor, and George, for one, still thinks that's pretty funny. I couldn't be bothered with that. I am going to be a doctor and everybody around here better understand that!

MAMA *(kindly)*:   'Course you going to be a doctor, honey, God willing.

BENEATHA *(drily)*:   God hasn't got a thing to do with it.

MAMA: Beneatha—that just wasn't necessary.

BENEATHA: Well—neither is God. I get sick of hearing about God.

MAMA: Beneatha!

BENEATHA: I mean it! I'm just tired of hearing about God all the time. What has He got to do with anything? Does He pay tuition?

MAMA: You 'bout to get your fresh little jaw slapped!

RUTH: That's just what she needs, all right!

BENEATHA: Why? Why can't I say what I want to around here, like everybody else?

MAMA: It don't sound nice for a young girl to say things like that—you wasn't brought up that way. Me and your father went to trouble to get you and Brother to church every Sunday.

BENEATHA: Mama, you don't understand. It's all a matter of ideas, and God is just one idea I don't accept. It's not important. I am not going out and be immoral or commit crimes because I don't believe in God. I don't even think about it. It's just that I get tired of Him getting credit for all the things the human race achieves through its own stubborn effort. There simply is no blasted God — there is only man and it is *He* who makes miracles!

Mama absorbs this speech, studies her daughter, and rises slowly and crosses to Beneatha and slaps her powerfully across the face. After, there is only silence and the daughter drops her eyes from her mother's face, and Mama is very tall before her.

MAMA: Now — you say after me, in my mother's house there is still God. *(There is a long pause and Beneatha stares at the floor wordlessly. Mama repeats the phrase with precision and cool emotion.)* In my mother's house there is still God.

BENEATHA: In my mother's house there is still God.

A long pause.

MAMA *(walking away from Beneatha, too disturbed for triumphant posture. Stopping and turning back to her daughter):* There are some ideas we ain't going to have in this house. Not long as I am at the head of this family.

BENEATHA: Yes, ma'am.

Mama walks out of the room.

RUTH *(almost gently, with profound understanding):* You think you a woman, Bennie — but you still a little girl. What you did was childish — so you got treated like a child.

BENEATHA: I see. *(Quietly.)* I also see that everybody thinks it's all right for Mama to be a tyrant. But all the tyranny in the world will never put a God in the heavens!

She picks up her books and goes out. Pause.

RUTH *(goes to Mama's door):* She said she was sorry.

MAMA *(coming out, going to her plant):* They frightens me, Ruth. My children.

RUTH: You got good children, Lena. They just a little off sometimes — but they're good.

MAMA: No — there's something come down between me and them that don't let us understand each other and I don't know what it is. One done almost lost his mind thinking 'bout money all the time and the other done commence to talk about things I can't seem to understand in no form or fashion. What is it that's changing, Ruth.

RUTH *(soothingly, older than her years):* Now . . . you taking it all too seriously. You just got strong-willed children and it takes a strong woman like you to keep 'em in hand.

MAMA *(looking at her plant and sprinkling a little water on it):* They spirited all right, my children. Got to admit they got spirit — Bennie and Walter. Like this little old plant that ain't never had enough sunshine or nothing — and look at it . . .

She has her back to Ruth, who has had to stop ironing and lean against something and put the back of her hand to her forehead.

RUTH (*trying to keep Mama from noticing*):   You . . . sure . . . loves that little old thing, don't you? . . .

MAMA: Well, I always wanted me a garden like I used to see sometimes at the back of the houses down home. This plant is close as I ever got to having one. (*She looks out of the window as she replaces the plant.*) Lord, ain't nothing as dreary as the view from this window on a dreary day, is there? Why ain't you singing this morning, Ruth? Sing that "No Ways Tired." That song always lifts me up so — (*She turns at last to see that Ruth has slipped quietly to the floor, in a state of semiconsciousness.*) Ruth! Ruth honey — what's the matter with you . . . Ruth!

Curtain.

Scene 2

It is the following morning; a Saturday morning, and house cleaning is in progress at the Youngers'. Furniture has been shoved hither and yon and Mama is giving the kitchen-area walls a washing down. Beneatha, in dungarees, with a handkerchief tied around her face, is spraying insecticide into the cracks in the walls. As they work, the radio is on and a Southside disk-jockey program is inappropriately filling the house with a rather exotic saxophone blues. Travis, the sole idle one, is leaning on his arms, looking out of the window.

TRAVIS: Grandmama, that stuff Bennie is using smells awful. Can I go downstairs, please?

MAMA: Did you get all them chores done already? I ain't seen you doing much.

TRAVIS: Yes'm — finished early. Where did Mama go this morning?

MAMA (*looking at Beneatha*):   She had to go on a little errand.

The phone rings. Beneatha runs to answer it and reaches it before Walter, who has entered from bedroom.

TRAVIS: Where?

MAMA: To tend to her business.

BENEATHA: Haylo . . . (*Disappointed.*) Yes, he is. (*She tosses the phone to Walter, who barely catches it.*) It's Willie Harris again.

WALTER (*as privately as possible under Mama's gaze*):   Hello, Willie. Did you get the papers from the lawyer? . . . No, not yet. I told you the mailman doesn't get here till ten-thirty . . . No, I'll come there . . . Yeah! Right away. (*He hangs up and goes for his coat.*)

BENEATHA: Brother, where did Ruth go?

WALTER (*as he exits*):   How should I know!

TRAVIS: Aw come on, Grandma. Can I go outside?

MAMA: Oh, I guess so. You stay right in front of the house, though, and keep a good lookout for the postman.

TRAVIS: Yes'm. (*He darts into bedroom for stickball and bat, reenters, and sees Beneatha on her knees spraying under sofa with behind upraised. He edges closer to the target, takes aim, and lets her have it. She screams.*) Leave them poor little cockroaches alone, they ain't bothering you none! (*He runs as she swings the spraygun at him viciously and playfully.*) Grandma! Grandma!

MAMA: Look out there, girl, before you be spilling some of that stuff on that child!

TRAVIS (*safely behind the bastion of Mama*):   That's right—look out, now! (*He exits.*)

BENEATHA (*drily*):   I can't imagine that it would hurt him—it has never hurt the roaches.

MAMA: Well, little boys' hides ain't as tough as Southside roaches. You better get over there behind the bureau. I seen one marching out of there like Napoleon yesterday.

BENEATHA: There's really only one way to get rid of them, Mama—

MAMA: How?

BENEATHA: Set fire to this building! Mama, where did Ruth go?

MAMA (*looking at her with meaning*):   To the doctor, I think.

BENEATHA: The doctor? What's the matter? (*They exchange glances.*) You don't think—

MAMA (*with her sense of drama*):   Now I ain't saying what I think. But I ain't never been wrong 'bout a woman neither.

The phone rings.

BENEATHA (*at the phone*):   Hay-lo . . . (*Pause, and a moment of recognition.*) Well—when did you get back! . . . And how was it? . . . Of course I've missed you—in my way . . . This morning? No . . . house cleaning and all that and Mama hates it if I let people come over when the house is like this . . . You *have?* Well, that's different . . . What is it—Oh, what the hell, come on over . . . Right, see you then. *Arrividerci.*

She hangs up.

MAMA (*who has listened vigorously, as is her habit*):   Who is that you inviting over here with this house looking like this? You ain't got the pride you was born with!

BENEATHA: Asagai doesn't care how houses look, Mama—he's an intellectual.

MAMA: *Who?*

BENEATHA: Asagai—Joseph Asagai. He's an African boy I met on campus. He's been studying in Canada all summer.

MAMA: What's his name?

BENEATHA: Asagai, Joseph. Ah-sah-guy . . . He's from Nigeria.

MAMA: Oh, that's the little country that was founded by slaves way back . . .

BENEATHA: No, Mama—that's Liberia.

MAMA: I don't think I never met no African before.

BENEATHA: Well, do me a favor and don't ask him a whole lot of ignorant questions about Africans. I mean, do they wear clothes and all that—

MAMA: Well, now, I guess if you think we so ignorant 'round here maybe you shouldn't bring your friends here —

BENEATHA: It's just that people ask such crazy things. All anyone seems to know about when it comes to Africa is Tarzan —

MAMA *(indignantly)*:   Why should I know anything about Africa?

BENEATHA: Why do you give money at church for the missionary work?

MAMA: Well, that's to help save people.

BENEATHA: You mean save them from *heathenism* —

MAMA *(innocently)*:   Yes.

BENEATHA: I'm afraid they need more salvation from the British and the French.

Ruth comes in forlornly and pulls off her coat with dejection. They both turn to look at her.

RUTH *(dispiritedly)*:   Well, I guess from all the happy faces — everybody knows.

BENEATHA: You pregnant?

MAMA: Lord have mercy, I sure hope it's a little old girl. Travis ought to have a sister.

Beneatha and Ruth give her a hopeless look for this grandmotherly enthusiasm.

BENEATHA: How far along are you?

RUTH: Two months.

BENEATHA: Did you mean to? I mean did you plan it or was it an accident?

MAMA: What do you know about planning or not planning?

BENEATHA: Oh, Mama.

RUTH *(wearily)*:   She's twenty years old, Lena.

BENEATHA: Did you plan it, Ruth?

RUTH: Mind your own business.

BENEATHA: It is my business — where is he going to live, on the *roof*? *(There is silence following the remark as the three women react to the sense of it.)* Gee — I didn't mean that, Ruth, honest. Gee, I don't feel like that at all. I — I think it is wonderful.

RUTH *(dully)*:   Wonderful.

BENEATHA: Yes — really.

MAMA *(looking at Ruth, worried)*:   Doctor say everything going to be all right?

RUTH *(far away)*:   Yes — she says everything is going to be fine . . .

MAMA *(immediately suspicious)*:   "She" — What doctor you went to?

Ruth folds over, near hysteria.

MAMA *(worriedly hovering over Ruth)*:   Ruth honey — what's the matter with you — you sick?

Ruth has her fists clenched on her thighs and is fighting hard to suppress a scream that seems to be rising in her.

BENEATHA: What's the matter with her, Mama?

MAMA *(working her fingers in Ruth's shoulders to relax her)*:   She be all right. Women gets right depressed sometimes when they get her way. *(Speaking softly, expertly, rapidly.)* Now you just relax. That's right . . . just lean back, don't think 'bout nothing at all . . . nothing at all —

RUTH: I'm all right . . .

The glassy-eyed look melts and then she collapses into a fit of heavy sobbing. The bell rings.

BENEATHA: Oh, my God — that must be Asagai.

MAMA *(to Ruth):*   Come on now, honey. You need to lie down and rest awhile . . . then have some nice hot food.

They exit, Ruth's weight on her mother-in-law. Beneatha, herself profoundly disturbed, opens the door to admit a rather dramatic-looking young man with a large package.

ASAGAI: Hello, Alaiyo —

BENEATHA *(holding the door open and regarding him with pleasure):*   Hello . . . *(Long pause.)* Well — come in. And please excuse everything. My mother was very upset about my letting anyone come here with the place like this.

ASAGAI *(coming into the room):*   You look disturbed too . . . Is something wrong?

BENEATHA *(still at the door, absently):*   Yes . . . we've all got acute ghetto-itus. *(She smiles and comes toward him, finding a cigarette and sitting.)* So — sit down! No! Wait! *(She whips the spraygun off sofa where she had left it and puts the cushions back. At last perches on arm of sofa. He sits.)* So, how was Canada?

ASAGAI *(a sophisticate):*   Canadian.

BENEATHA *(looking at him):*   Asagai, I'm very glad you are back.

ASAGAI *(looking back at her in turn):*   Are you really?

BENEATHA: Yes — very.

ASAGAI: Why? — you were quite glad when I went away. What happened?

BENEATHA: You went away.

ASAGAI: Ahhhhhhhh.

BENEATHA: Before — you wanted to be so serious before there was time.

ASAGAI: How much time must there be before one knows what one feels?

BENEATHA *(stalling this particular conversation. Her hands pressed together, in a deliberately childish gesture):*   What did you bring me?

ASAGAI *(handing her the package):*   Open it and see.

BENEATHA *(eagerly opening the package and drawing out some records and the colorful robes of a Nigerian woman):*   Oh Asagai! . . . You got them for me! . . . How beautiful . . . and the records too! *(She lifts out the robes and runs to the mirror with them and holds the drapery up in front of herself.)*

ASAGAI *(coming to her at the mirror):*   I shall have to teach you how to drape it properly. *(He flings the material about her for the moment and stands back to look at her.)* Ah — Oh-pay-gay-day, oh-gbah-mu-shay. *(A Yoruba exclamation for admiration.)* You wear it well . . . very well . . . mutilated hair and all.

BENEATHA *(turning suddenly):*   My hair — what's wrong with my hair?

ASAGAI *(shrugging):*   Were you born with it like that?

BENEATHA *(reaching up to touch it):*   No . . . of course not.

She looks back to the mirror, disturbed.

ASAGAI *(smiling):*   How then?

BENEATHA: You know perfectly well how . . . as crinkly as yours . . . that's how.

ASAGAI: And it is ugly to you that way?

BENEATHA *(quickly):*   Oh, no — not ugly . . . *(More slowly, apologetically.)* But it's so hard to manage when it's, well — raw.

ASAGAI: And so to accommodate that — you mutilate it every week?

BENEATHA: It's not mutilation!

ASAGAI *(laughing aloud at her seriousness):*   Oh . . . please! I am only teasing you because you are so very serious about these things. *(He stands back from her and folds his arms across his chest as he watches her pulling at her hair and frowning in the mirror.)* Do you remember the first time you met me at school? . . . *(He laughs.)* You came up to me and you said — and I thought you were the most serious little thing I had ever seen — you said: *(He imitates her.)* "Mr. Asagai — I want very much to talk with you. About Africa. You see, Mr. Asagai, I am looking for my *identity!*"

He laughs.

BENEATHA *(turning to him, not laughing):*   Yes —

Her face is quizzical, profoundly disturbed.

ASAGAI *(still teasing and reaching out and taking her face in his hands and turning her profile to him):*   Well . . . it is true that this is not so much a profile of a Hollywood queen as perhaps a queen of the Nile — *(A mock dismissal of the importance of the question.)* But what does it matter? Assimilationism is so popular in your country.

BENEATHA *(wheeling, passionately, sharply):*   I am not an assimilationist!

ASAGAI *(the protest hangs in the room for a moment and Asagai studies her, his laughter fading):*   Such a serious one. *(There is a pause.)* So — you like the robes? You must take excellent care of them — they are from my sister's personal wardrobe.

BENEATHA *(with incredulity):*   You — you sent all the way home — for me?

ASAGAI *(with charm):*   For you — I would do much more . . . Well, that is what I came for. I must go.

BENEATHA: Will you call me Monday?

ASAGAI: Yes . . . We have a great deal to talk about. I mean about identity and time and all that.

BENEATHA: Time?

ASAGAI: Yes. About how much time one needs to know what one feels.

BENEATHA: You see! You never understood that there is more than one kind of feeling which can exist between a man and a woman — or, at least, there should be.

ASAGAI *(shaking his head negatively but gently):*   No. Between a man and a woman there need be only one kind of feeling. I have that for you . . . Now even . . . right this moment . . .

BENEATHA: I know — and by itself — it won't do. I can find that anywhere.

ASAGAI: For a woman it should be enough.

BENEATHA: I know—because that's what it says in all the novels that men write. But it isn't. Go ahead and laugh—but I'm not interested in being someone's little episode in America or—*(With feminine vengeance.)*—one of them! *(Asagai has burst into laughter again.)* That's funny as hell, huh!

ASAGAI: It's just that every American girl I have known has said that to me. White—black—in this you are all the same. And the same speech, too!

BENEATHA *(angrily):*   Yuk, yuk, yuk!

ASAGAI: It's how you can be sure that the world's most liberated women are not liberated at all. You all talk about it too much!

Mama enters and is immediately all social charm because of the presence of a guest.

BENEATHA: Oh—Mama—this is Mr. Asagai.

MAMA: How do you do?

ASAGAI *(total politeness to an elder):*   How do you do, Mrs. Younger. Please forgive me for coming at such an outrageous hour on a Saturday.

MAMA: Well, you are quite welcome. I just hope you understand that our house don't always look like this. *(Chatterish.)* You must come again. I would love to hear all about—*(Not sure of the name.)*—your country. I think it's so sad the way our American Negroes don't know nothing about Africa 'cept Tarzan and all that. And all that money they pour into these churches when they ought to be helping you people over there drive out them French and Englishmen done taken away your land.

The mother flashes a slightly superior look at her daughter upon completion of the recitation.

ASAGAI *(taken aback by this sudden and acutely unrelated expression of sympathy):*   Yes . . . yes . . .

MAMA *(smiling at him suddenly and relaxing and looking him over):*   How many miles is it from here to where you come from?

ASAGAI: Many thousands.

MAMA *(looking at him as she would Walter):*   I bet you don't half look after yourself, being away from your mama either. I spec you better come 'round here from time to time to get yourself some decent homecooked meals . . .

ASAGAI *(moved):*   Thank you. Thank you very much. *(They are all quiet, then—)* Well . . . I must go. I will call you Monday, Alaiyo.

MAMA: What's that he call you?

ASAGAI: Oh—"Alaiyo." I hope you don't mind. It is what you would call a nickname, I think. It is a Yoruba word. I am a Yoruba.

MAMA *(looking at Beneatha):*   I—I thought he was from—*(Uncertain.)*

ASAGAI *(understanding):*   Nigeria is my country. Yoruba is my tribal origin—

BENEATHA: You didn't tell us what Alaiyo means . . . for all I know, you might be calling me Little Idiot or something . . .

ASAGAI: Well . . . let me see . . . I do not know how just to explain it . . . The sense of a thing can be so different when it changes languages.

BENEATHA: You're evading.

ASAGAI: No — really it is difficult . . . *(Thinking.)* It means . . . it means One for
Whom Bread — Food — Is Not Enough. *(He looks at her.)* Is that all right?

BENEATHA *(understanding, softly)*:   Thank you.

MAMA *(looking from one to the other and not understanding any of it)*:   Well . . .
that's nice . . . You must come see us again — Mr. —

ASAGAI: Ah-sah-guy . . .

MAMA: Yes . . . Do come again.

ASAGAI: Good-bye.

He exits.

MAMA *(after him)*:   Lord, that's a pretty thing just went out here! *(Insinuatingly,
to her daughter.)* Yes, I guess I see why we done commence to get so interested in Africa 'round here. Missionaries my aunt Jenny!

She exits.

BENEATHA: Oh, Mama! . . .

*She picks up the Nigerian dress and holds it up to her in front of the mirror again.
She sets the headdress on haphazardly and then notices her hair again and
clutches at it and then replaces the headdress and frowns at herself. Then she starts
to wriggle in front of the mirror as she thinks a Nigerian woman might. Travis
enters and stands regarding her.*

TRAVIS: What's the matter, girl, you cracking up?

BENEATHA: Shut up.

*She pulls the headdress off and looks at herself in the mirror and clutches at her
hair again and squinches her eyes as if trying to imagine something. Then, suddenly, she gets her raincoat and kerchief and hurriedly prepares for going out.*

MAMA *(coming back into the room)*:   She's resting now. Travis, baby, run next
door and ask Miss Johnson to please let me have a little kitchen cleanser.
This here can is empty as Jacob's kettle.

TRAVIS: I just came in.

MAMA: Do as you told. *(He exits and she looks at her daughter.)* Where you
going?

BENEATHA *(halting at the door)*:   To become a queen of the Nile!

She exits in a breathless blaze of glory. Ruth appears in the bedroom doorway.

MAMA: Who told you to get up?

RUTH: Ain't nothing wrong with me to be lying in no bed for. Where did Bennie go?

MAMA *(drumming her fingers)*:   Far as I could make out — to Egypt. *(Ruth just
looks at her.)* What time is it getting to?

RUTH: Ten twenty. And the mailman going to ring that bell this morning just
like he done every morning for the last umpteen years.

Travis comes in with the cleanser can.

TRAVIS: She say to tell you that she don't have much.

MAMA (*angrily*):   Lord, some people I could name sure is tight-fisted! (*Directing her grandson.*) Mark two cans of cleanser on the list there. If she that hard up for kitchen cleanser, I sure don't want to forget to get her none!

RUTH: Lena—maybe the woman is just short on cleanser—

MAMA (*not listening*):   —Much baking powder as she done borrowed from me all these years, she could of done gone into the baking business!

The bell sounds suddenly and sharply and all three are stunned—serious and silent—midspeech. In spite of all the other conversations and distractions of the morning, this is what they have been waiting for, even Travis, who looks helplessly from his mother to his grandmother. Ruth is the first to come to life again.

RUTH (*to Travis*):   Get down them steps, boy!

Travis snaps to life and flies out to get the mail.

MAMA (*her eyes wide, her hand to her breast*):   You mean it done really come?

RUTH (*excited*):   Oh, Miss Lena!

MAMA (*collecting herself*):   Well . . . I don't know what we all so excited about 'round here for. We known it was coming for months.

RUTH: That's a whole lot different from having it come and being able to hold it in your hands . . . a piece of paper worth ten thousand dollars . . . (*Travis bursts back into the room. He holds the envelope high above his head, like a little dancer, his face is radiant and he is breathless. He moves to his grandmother with sudden slow ceremony and puts the envelope into her hands. She accepts it, and then merely holds it and looks at it.*) Come on! Open it . . . Lord have mercy, I wish Walter Lee was here!

TRAVIS: Open it, Grandmama!

MAMA (*staring at it*):   Now you all be quiet. It's just a check.

RUTH: Open it . . .

MAMA (*still staring at it*):   Now don't act silly . . . We ain't never been no people to act silly 'bout no money—

RUTH (*swiftly*):   We ain't never had none before—OPEN IT!

Mama finally makes a good strong tear and pulls out the thin blue slice of paper and inspects it closely. The boy and his mother study it raptly over Mama's shoulders.

MAMA: Travis! (*She is counting off with doubt.*) Is that the right number of zeros?

TRAVIS: Yes'm . . . ten thousand dollars. Gaalee, grandmama, you rich.

MAMA (*She holds the check away from her, still looking at it. Slowly her face sobers into a mask of unhappiness*):   Ten thousand dollars. (*She hands it to Ruth.*) Put it away somewhere, Ruth. (*She does not look at Ruth; her eyes seem to be seeing something somewhere very far off.*) Ten thousand dollars they give you. Ten thousand dollars.

TRAVIS (*to his mother, sincerely*):   What's the matter with Grandmama—don't she want to be rich?

RUTH (*distractedly*):   You go on out and play now, baby. (*Travis exits. Mama starts wiping dishes absently, humming intently to herself. Ruth turns to her, with kind exasperation.*) You've gone and got yourself upset.

MAMA (*not looking at her*):   I spec if it wasn't for you all . . . I would just put that
money away or give it to the church or something.

RUTH: Now what kind of talk is that. Mr. Younger would just be plain mad if he
could hear you talking foolish like that.

MAMA (*stopping and staring off*):   Yes . . . he sure would. (*Sighing.*) We got
enough to do with that money, all right. (*She halts then, and turns and looks
at her daughter-in-law hard; Ruth avoids her eyes and Mama wipes her hands
with finality and starts to speak firmly to Ruth.*) Where did you go today, girl?

RUTH: To the doctor.

MAMA (*impatiently*):   Now, Ruth . . . you know better than that. Old Doctor
Jones is strange enough in his way but there ain't nothing 'bout him make
somebody slip and call him "she"—like you done this morning.

RUTH: Well, that's what happened—my tongue slipped.

MAMA: You went to see that woman, didn't you?

RUTH (*defensively, giving herself away*):   What woman you talking about?

MAMA (*angrily*):   That woman who—

Walter enters in great excitement.

WALTER: Did it come?

MAMA (*quietly*):   Can't you give people a Christian greeting before you start asking about money?

WALTER (*to Ruth*):   Did it come? (*Ruth unfolds the check and lays it quietly
before him, watching him intently with thoughts of her own. Walter sits down
and grasps it close and counts off the zeros.*) Ten thousand dollars—(*He turns
suddenly, frantically to his mother and draws some papers out of his breast
pocket.*) Mama—look. Old Willy Harris put everything on paper—

MAMA: Son—I think you ought to talk to your wife . . . I'll go on out and leave
you alone if you want—

WALTER: I can talk to her later—Mama, look—

MAMA: Son—

WALTER: WILL SOMEBODY PLEASE LISTEN TO ME TODAY!

MAMA (*quietly*):   I don't 'low no yellin' in this house, Walter Lee, and you know
it—(*Walter stares at them in frustration and starts to speak several times.*) And
there ain't going to be no investing in no liquor stores.

WALTER: But, Mama, you ain't even looked at it.

MAMA: I don't aim to have to speak on that again.

A long pause.

WALTER: You ain't looked at it and you don't aim to have to speak on that again?
You ain't even looked at it and *you* have decided—(*Crumpling his papers.*)
Well, *you* tell that to my boy tonight when you put him to sleep on the living-
room couch . . . (*Turning to Mama and speaking directly to her.*) Yeah—and
tell it to my wife, Mama, tomorrow when she has to go out of here to look
after somebody else's kids. And tell it to *me*, Mama, every time we need a
new pair of curtains and I have to watch *you* go out and work in somebody's
kitchen. Yeah, you tell me then!

Walter starts out.

RUTH: Where you going?

WALTER: I'm going out!

RUTH: Where?

WALTER: Just out of this house somewhere —

RUTH *(getting her coat)*:   I'll come too.

WALTER: I don't want you to come!

RUTH: I got something to talk to you about, Walter.

WALTER: That's too bad.

MAMA *(still quietly)*:   Walter Lee — *(She waits and he finally turns and looks at her.)* Sit down.

WALTER: I'm a grown man, Mama.

MAMA: Ain't nobody said you wasn't grown. But you still in my house and my presence. And as long as you are — you'll talk to your wife civil. Now sit down.

RUTH *(suddenly)*:   Oh, let him go on out and drink himself to death! He makes me sick to my stomach! *(She flings her coat against him and exits to bedroom.)*

WALTER *(violently flinging the coat after her)*:   And you turn mine too, baby! *(The door slams behind her.)* That was my biggest mistake —

MAMA *(still quietly)*:   Walter, what is the matter with you?

WALTER: Matter with me? Ain't nothing the matter with *me!*

MAMA: Yes there is. Something eating you up like a crazy man. Something more than me not giving you this money. The past few years I been watching it happen to you. You get all nervous acting and kind of wild in the eyes — *(Walter jumps up impatiently at her words.)* I said sit there now, I'm talking to you!

WALTER: Mama — I don't need no nagging at me today.

MAMA: Seem like you getting to a place where you always tied up in some kind of knot about something. But if anybody ask you 'bout it you just yell at 'em and bust out the house and go out and drink somewheres. Walter Lee, people can't live with that. Ruth's a good, patient girl in her way — but you getting to be too much. Boy, don't make the mistake of driving that girl away from you.

WALTER: Why — what she do for me?

MAMA: She loves you.

WALTER: Mama — I'm going out. I want to go off somewhere and be by myself for a while.

MAMA: I'm sorry 'bout your liquor store, son. It just wasn't the thing for us to do. That's what I want to tell you about —

WALTER: I got to go out, Mama —

He rises.

MAMA: It's dangerous, son.

WALTER: What's dangerous?

MAMA: When a man goes outside his home to look for peace.

WALTER *(beseechingly)*:   Then why can't there never be no peace in this house then?

MAMA: You done found it in some other house?

WALTER: No—there ain't no woman! Why do women always think there's a woman somewhere when a man gets restless. *(Picks up the check.)* Do you know what this money means to me? Do you know what this money can do for us? *(Puts it back.)* Mama—Mama—I want so many things . . .

MAMA: Yes, son—

WALTER: I want so many things that they are driving me kind of crazy . . . Mama—look at me.

MAMA: I'm looking at you. You a good-looking boy. You got a job, a nice wife, a fine boy, and—

WALTER: A job. *(Looks at her.)* Mama, a job? I open and close car doors all day long. I drive a man around in his limousine and I say, "Yes, sir; no, sir; very good, sir; shall I take the Drive, sir?" Mama, that ain't no kind of job . . . that ain't nothing at all. *(Very quietly.)* Mama, I don't know if I can make you understand.

MAMA: Understand what, baby?

WALTER *(quietly)*:   Sometimes it's like I can see the future stretched out in front of me—just plain as day. The future, Mama. Hanging over there at the edge of my days. Just waiting for me—a big, looming blank space—full of *nothing*. Just waiting for *me*. But it don't have to be. *(Pause. Kneeling beside her chair.)* Mama—sometimes when I'm downtown and I pass them cool, quiet-looking restaurants where them white boys are sitting back and talking 'bout things . . . sitting there turning deals worth millions of dollars . . . sometimes I see guys don't look much older than me—

MAMA: Son—how come you talk so much 'bout money?

WALTER *(with immense passion)*:   Because it is life, Mama!

MAMA *(quietly)*:   Oh—*(Very quietly.)* So now it's life. Money is life. Once upon a time freedom used to be life—now it's money. I guess the world really do change . . .

WALTER: No—it was always money, Mama. We just didn't know about it.

MAMA: No . . . something has changed. *(She looks at him.)* You something new, boy. In my time we was worried about not being lynched and getting to the North if we could and how to stay alive and still have a pinch of dignity too . . . Now here come you and Beneatha—talking 'bout things we ain't never even thought about hardly, me and your daddy. You ain't satisfied or proud of nothing we done. I mean that you had a home; that we kept you out of trouble till you was grown; that you don't have to ride to work on the back of nobody's streetcar—You my children—but how different we done become.

WALTER *(a long beat. He pats her hand and gets up)*:   You just don't understand, Mama, you just don't understand.

MAMA: Son—do you know your wife is expecting another baby? *(Walter stands, stunned, and absorbs what his mother has said.)* That's what she wanted to talk to you about. *(Walter sinks down into a chair.)* This ain't for me to be telling—but you ought to know. *(She waits.)* I think Ruth is thinking 'bout getting rid of that child.

WALTER *(slowly understanding):* —No—no—Ruth wouldn't do that.

MAMA: When the world gets ugly enough—a woman will do anything for her family. *The part that's already living.*

WALTER: You don't know Ruth, Mama, if you think she would do that.

Ruth opens the bedroom door and stands there a little limp.

RUTH *(beaten):*   Yes I would too, Walter. *(Pause.)* I gave her a five-dollar down payment.

There is total silence as the man stares at his wife and the mother stares at her son.

MAMA *(presently):*   Well—*(Tightly.)* Well—son, I'm waiting to hear you say something . . . *(She waits.)* I'm waiting to hear how you be your father's son. Be the man he was . . . *(Pause. The silence shouts.)* Your wife say she going to destroy your child. And I'm waiting to hear you talk like him and say we a people who give children life, not who destroys them—*(She rises.)* I'm waiting to see you stand up and look like your daddy and say we done give up one baby to poverty and that we ain't going to give up nary another one . . . I'm waiting.

WALTER: Ruth—*(He can say nothing.)*

MAMA: If you a son of mine, tell her! *(Walter picks up his keys and his coat and walks out. She continues, bitterly.)* You . . . you are a disgrace to your father's memory. Somebody get me my hat!

Curtain.

ACT 2, Scene 1

Time: Later the same day.

   At rise: Ruth is ironing again. She has the radio going. Presently Beneatha's bedroom door opens and Ruth's mouth falls and she puts down the iron in fascination.

RUTH: What have we got on tonight!

BENEATHA *(emerging grandly from the doorway so that we can see her thoroughly robed in the costume Asagai brought):*   You are looking at what a well-dressed Nigerian woman wears—*(She parades for Ruth, her hair completely hidden by the headdress; she is coquettishly fanning herself with an ornate oriental fan, mistakenly more like Butterfly than any Nigerian that ever was.)* Isn't it beautiful? *(She promenades to the radio and, with an arrogant flourish, turns off the good loud blues that is playing.)* Enough of this assimilationist junk! *(Ruth follows her with her eyes as she goes to the phonograph and puts on a record and turns and waits ceremoniously for the music to come up. Then, with a shout—)* OCOMOGOSIAY!

Ruth jumps. The music comes up, a lovely Nigerian melody. Beneatha listens, enraptured, her eyes far way—"back to the past." She begins to dance. Ruth is dumfounded.

RUTH: What kind of dance is that?

BENEATHA: A folk dance.

RUTH *(Pearl Bailey)*: What kind of folks do that, honey?

BENEATHA: It's from Nigeria. It's a dance of welcome.

RUTH: Who you welcoming?

BENEATHA: The men back to the village.

RUTH: Where they been?

BENEATHA: How should I know—out hunting or something. Anyway, they are coming back now . . .

RUTH: Well, that's good.

BENEATHA *(with the record)*:

Alundi, alundi
Alundi alunya
Jop pu a jeepua
Ang gu sooooooooooo
Ai yai yae . . .
Ayehaye—alundi . . .

Walter comes in during this performance; he has obviously been drinking. He leans against the door heavily and watches his sister, at first with distaste. Then his eyes look off—"back to the past"—as he lifts both his fists to the roof, screaming.

WALTER: YEAH . . . AND ETHIOPIA STRETCH FORTH HER HANDS AGAIN! . . .

RUTH *(drily, looking at him)*: Yes—and Africa sure is claiming her own tonight. *(She gives them both up and starts ironing again.)*

WALTER *(all in a drunken, dramatic shout)*: Shut up! . . . I'm diggin them drums . . . them drums move me! . . . *(He makes his weaving way to his wife's face and leans in close to her.)* In my *heart of hearts*—*(He thumps his chest.)*—I am much warrior!

RUTH *(without even looking up)*: In your heart of hearts you are much drunkard.

WALTER *(coming away from her and starting to wander around the room, shouting)*: Me and Jomo . . . *(Intently, in his sister's face. She has stopped dancing to watch him in this unknown mood.)* That's my man, Kenyatta. *(Shouting and thumping his chest.)* FLAMING SPEAR! HOT DAMN! *(He is suddenly in possession of an imaginary spear and actively spearing enemies all over the room.)* OCOMOGOSIAY . . .

BENEATHA *(to encourage Walter, thoroughly caught up with this side of him)*: OCOMOGOSIAY, FLAMING SPEAR!

WALTER: THE LION IS WAKING . . . OWIMOWEH!

He pulls his shirt open and leaps up on the table and gestures with his spear.

BENEATHA: OWIMOWEH!

WALTER *(on the table, very far gone, his eyes pure glass sheets. He sees what we cannot, that he is a leader of his people, a great chief, a descendant of Chaka, and that the hour to march has come)*: Listen, my black brothers—

BENEATHA: OCOMOGOSIAY!

WALTER: —Do you hear the waters rushing against the shores of the coastlands—

BENEATHA: OCOMOGOSIAY!

WALTER: —Do you hear the screeching of the cocks in yonder hills beyond where the chiefs meet in council for the coming of the mighty war—

BENEATHA: OCOMOGOSIAY!

And now the lighting shifts subtly to suggest the world of Walter's imagination, and the mood shifts from pure comedy. It is the inner Walter speaking: the Southside chauffeur has assumed an unexpected majesty.

WALTER: —Do you hear the beating of the wings of the birds flying low over the mountains and the low places of our land—

BENEATHA: OCOMOGOSIAY!

WALTER: —Do you hear the singing of the women, singing the war songs of our fathers to the babies in the great houses? Singing the sweet war songs! *(The doorbell rings.)* OH, DO YOU HEAR, MY *BLACK* BROTHERS!

BENEATHA *(completely gone):*   We hear you, Flaming Spear—

Ruth shuts off the phonograph and opens the door. George Murchison enters.

WALTER: Telling us to prepare for the GREATNESS OF THE TIME! *(Lights back to normal. He turns and sees George.)* Black Brother!

He extends his hand for the fraternal clasp.

GEORGE: Black Brother, hell!

RUTH *(having had enough, and embarrassed for the family):*   Beneatha, you got company—what's the matter with you? Walter Lee Younger, get down off that table and stop acting like a fool . . .

Walter comes down off the table suddenly and makes a quick exit to the bathroom.

RUTH: He's had a little to drink . . . I don't know what her excuse is.

GEORGE *(to Beneatha):*   Look honey, we're going to the theater—we're not going to be *in* it . . . so go change, huh?

Beneatha looks at him and slowly, ceremoniously, lifts her hands and pulls off the headdress. Her hair is close-cropped and unstraightened. George freezes midsentence and Ruth's eyes all but fall out of her head.

GEORGE: What in the name of—

RUTH *(touching Beneatha's hair):*   Girl, you done lost your natural mind? Look at your head!

GEORGE: What have you done to your head—I mean your hair!

BENEATHA: Nothing—except cut it off.

RUTH: Now that's the truth—it's what ain't been done to it! You expect this boy to go out with you with your head all nappy like that?

BENEATHA *(looking at George):*   That's up to George. If he's ashamed of his heritage—

GEORGE: Oh, don't be so proud of yourself, Bennie—just because you look eccentric.

BENEATHA: How can something that's natural be eccentric?

GEORGE: That's what being eccentric means — being natural. Get dressed.

BENEATHA: I don't like that, George.

RUTH: Why must you and your brother make an argument out of everything people say?

BENEATHA: Because I hate assimilationist Negroes!

RUTH: Will somebody please tell me what assimila-whoever means!

GEORGE: Oh, it's just a college girl's way of calling people Uncle Toms — but that isn't what it means at all.

RUTH: Well, what does it mean?

BENEATHA *(cutting George off and staring at him as she replies to Ruth)*:   It means someone who is willing to give up his own culture and submerge himself completely in the dominant, and in this case *oppressive* culture!

GEORGE: Oh, dear, dear, dear! Here we go! A lecture on the African past! On our Great West African Heritage! In one second we will hear all about the great Ashanti empires; the great Songhay civilizations; and the great sculpture of Bénin — and then some poetry in the Bantu — and the whole monologue will end with the word *heritage! (Nastily.)* Let's face it, baby, your heritage is nothing but a bunch of raggedy-assed spirituals and some grass huts!

BENEATHA: GRASS HUTS! *(Ruth crosses to her and forcibly pushes her toward the bedroom.)* See there . . . you are standing there in your splendid ignorance talking about people who were the first to smelt iron on the face of the earth! *(Ruth is pushing her through the door.)* The Ashanti were performing surgical operations when the English — *(Ruth pulls the door to, with Beneatha on the other side, and smiles graciously at George. Beneatha opens the door and shouts the end of the sentence defiantly at George.)* — were still tatooing themselves with blue dragons! *(She goes back inside.)*

RUTH: Have a seat, George. *(They both sit. Ruth folds her hands rather primly on her lap, determined to demonstrate the civilization of the family.)* Warm, ain't it? I mean for September. *(Pause.)* Just like they always say about Chicago weather: if it's too hot or cold for you, just wait a minute and it'll change. *(She smiles happily at this cliché of clichés.)* Everybody say it's got to do with them bombs and things they keep setting off. *(Pause.)* Would you like a nice cold beer?

GEORGE: No, thank you. I don't care for beer. *(He looks at his watch.)* I hope she hurries up.

RUTH: What time is the show?

GEORGE: It's an eight-thirty curtain. That's just Chicago, though. In New York standard curtain time is eight forty.

He is rather proud of this knowledge.

RUTH *(properly appreciating it)*:   You get to New York a lot?

GEORGE *(offhand)*:   Few times a year.

RUTH: Oh — that's nice. I've never been to New York.

Walter enters. We feel he has relieved himself, but the edge of unreality is still with him.

WALTER: New York ain't got nothing Chicago ain't. Just a bunch of hustling people all squeezed up together — being "Eastern."

He turns his face into a screw of displeasure.

GEORGE: Oh — you've been?

WALTER: *Plenty* of times.

RUTH *(shocked at the lie):* Walter Lee Younger!

WALTER *(staring her down):* Plenty! *(Pause.)* What we got to drink in this house? Why don't you offer this man some refreshment. *(To George.)* They don't know how to entertain people in this house, man.

GEORGE: Thank you — I don't really care for anything.

WALTER *(feeling his head; sobriety coming):* Where's Mama?

RUTH: She ain't come back yet.

WALTER *(looking Murchison over from head to toe, scrutinizing his carefully casual tweed sports jacket over cashmere V-neck sweater over soft eyelet shirt and tie, and soft slacks, finished off with white buckskin shoes):* Why all you college boys wear them faggoty-looking white shoes?

RUTH: Walter Lee!

George Murchison ignores the remark.

WALTER *(to Ruth):* Well, they look crazy as hell — white shoes, cold as it is.

RUTH *(crushed):* You have to excuse him —

WALTER: No he don't! Excuse me for what? What you always excusing me for! I'll excuse myself when I needs to be excused! *(A pause.)* They look as funny as them black knee socks Beneatha wears out of here all the time.

RUTH: It's the college *style*, Walter.

WALTER: Style, hell. She looks like she got burnt legs or something!

RUTH: Oh, Walter —

WALTER *(an irritable mimic):* Oh, Walter! Oh, Walter! *(To Murchison.)* How's your old man making out? I understand you all going to buy that big hotel on the Drive? *(He finds a beer in the refrigerator, wanders over to Murchison, sipping and wiping his lips with the back of his hand, and straddling a chair backwards to talk to the other man.)* Shrewd move. Your old man is all right, man. *(Tapping his head and half winking for emphasis.)* I mean he knows how to operate. I mean he thinks *big*, you know what I mean, I mean for a *home*, you know? But I think he's kind of running out of ideas now. I'd like to talk to him. Listen, man, I got some plans that could turn this city upside down. I mean think like he does. *Big.* Invest big, gamble big, hell, lose *big* if you have to, you know what I mean. It's hard to find a man on this whole Southside who understands my kind of thinking — you dig? *(He scrutinizes Murchison again, drinks his beer, squints his eyes and leans in close, confidential, man to man.)* Me and you ought to sit down and talk sometimes, man. Man, I got me some ideas . . .

MURCHISON *(with boredom):* Yeah — sometimes we'll have to do that, Walter.

WALTER *(understanding the indifference, and offended):* Yeah — well, when you get the time, man. I know you a busy little boy.

RUTH: Walter, please —

WALTER (*bitterly, hurt*):   I know ain't nothing in this world as busy as you colored college boys with your fraternity pins and white shoes . . .

RUTH (*covering her face with humiliation*):   Oh, Walter Lee—

WALTER: I see you all all the time—with the books tucked under your arms—going to your (*British A—a mimic.*) "clahsses." And for what! What the hell you learning over there? Filling up your heads—(*Counting off on his fingers.*)—with the sociology and the psychology—but they teaching you how to be a man? How to take over and run the world? They teaching you how to run a rubber plantation or a steel mill? Naw—just to talk proper and read books and wear them faggoty-looking white shoes . . .

GEORGE (*looking at him with distaste, a little above it all*):   You're all wacked up with bitterness, man.

WALTER (*intently, almost quietly, between the teeth, glaring at the boy*):   And you—ain't you bitter, man? Ain't you just about had it yet? Don't you see no stars gleaming that you can't reach out and grab? You happy?—You contented son-of-a-bitch—you happy? You got it made? Bitter? Man, I'm a volcano. Bitter? Here I am a giant—surrounded by ants! Ants who can't even understand what it is the giant is talking about.

RUTH (*passionately and suddenly*):   Oh, Walter—ain't you with nobody!

WALTER (*violently*):   No! 'Cause ain't nobody with me! Not even my own mother!

RUTH: Walter, that's a terrible thing to say!

Beneatha enters, dressed for the evening in a cocktail dress and earrings, hair natural.

GEORGE: Well—hey—(*Crosses to Beneatha; thoughtful, with emphasis, since this is a reversal.*) You look great!

WALTER (*seeing his sister's hair for the first time*):   What's the matter with your head?

BENEATHA (*tired of the jokes now*):   I cut it off, Brother.

WALTER (*coming close to inspect it and walking around her*):   Well, I'll be damned. So that's what they mean by the African bush . . .

BENEATHA: Ha ha. Let's go, George.

GEORGE (*looking at her*):   You know something? I like it. It's sharp. I mean it really is. (*Helps her into her wrap.*)

RUTH: Yes—I think so, too. (*She goes to the mirror and starts to clutch at her hair.*)

WALTER: Oh no! You leave yours alone, baby. You might turn out to have a pin-shaped head or something!

BENEATHA: See you all later.

RUTH: Have a nice time.

GEORGE: Thanks. Good night. (*Half out the door, he reopens it. To Walter.*) Good night, Prometheus!

Beneatha and George exit.

WALTER (*to Ruth*):   Who is Prometheus?

RUTH: I don't know. Don't worry about it.

WALTER (*in fury, pointing after George*):   See there—they get to a point where they can't insult you man to man — they got to go talk about something ain't nobody never heard of!

RUTH: How do you know it was an insult? *(To humor him.)* Maybe Prometheus is a nice fellow.

WALTER: Prometheus! I bet there ain't even no such thing! I bet that simple-minded clown —

RUTH: Walter —

She stops what she is doing and looks at him.

WALTER *(yelling):*   Don't start!

RUTH: Start what?

WALTER: Your nagging! Where was I? Who was I with? How much money did I spend?

RUTH *(plaintively):*   Walter Lee — why don't we just try to talk about it . . .

WALTER *(not listening):*   I been out talking with people who understand me. People who care about the things I got on my mind.

RUTH *(wearily):*   I guess that means people like Willy Harris.

WALTER: Yes, people like Willy Harris.

RUTH *(with a sudden flash of impatience):*   Why don't you all just hurry up and go into the banking business and stop talking about it!

WALTER: Why? You want to know why? 'Cause we all tied up in a race of people that don't know how to do nothing but moan, pray and have babies!

The line is too bitter even for him and he looks at her and sits down.

RUTH: Oh, Walter . . . *(Softly.)* Honey, why can't you stop fighting me?

WALTER *(without thinking):*   Who's fighting you? Who even cares about you?

This line begins the retardation of his mood.

RUTH: Well — *(She waits a long time, and then with resignation starts to put away her things.)* I guess I might as well go on to bed . . . *(More or less to herself.)* I don't know where we lost it . . . but we have . . . *(Then, to him.)* I — I'm sorry about this new baby, Walter. I guess maybe I better go on and do what I started . . . I guess I just didn't realize how bad things was with us . . . I guess I just didn't really realize — *(She starts out to the bedroom and stops.)* You want some hot milk?

WALTER: Hot milk?

RUTH: Yes — hot milk.

WALTER: Why hot milk?

RUTH: 'Cause after all that liquor you come home with you ought to have something hot in your stomach.

WALTER: I don't want no milk.

RUTH: You want some coffee then?

WALTER: No, I don't want no coffee. I don't want nothing hot to drink. *(Almost plaintively.)* Why you always trying to give me something to eat?

RUTH *(standing and looking at him helplessly):*   What *else* can I give you, Walter Lee Younger?

She stands and looks at him and presently turns to go out again. He lifts his head and watches her going away from him in a new mood which began to emerge when he asked her "Who cares about you?"

WALTER: It's been rough, ain't it, baby? (*She hears and stops but does not turn around and he continues to her back.*) I guess between two people there ain't never as much understood as folks generally thinks there is. I mean like between me and you—(*She turns to face him.*) How we gets to the place where we scared to talk softness to each other. (*He waits, thinking hard himself.*) Why you think it got to be like that? (*He is thoughtful, almost as a child would be.*) Ruth, what is it gets into people ought to be close?

RUTH: I don't know, honey. I think about it a lot.

WALTER: On account of you and me, you mean? The way things are with us. The way something done come down between us.

RUTH: There ain't so much between us, Walter . . . Not when you come to me and try to talk to me. Try to be with me . . . a little even.

WALTER (*total honesty*): Sometimes . . . sometimes . . . I don't even know how to try.

RUTH: Walter—

WALTER: Yes?

RUTH (*coming to him, gently and with misgiving, but coming to him*): Honey . . . life don't have to be like this. I mean sometimes people can do things so that things are better . . . You remember how we used to talk when Travis was born . . . about the way we were going to live . . . the kind of house . . . (*She is stroking his head.*) Well, it's all starting to slip away from us . . .

He turns her to him and they look at each other and kiss, tenderly and hungrily. The door opens and Mama enters—Walter breaks away and jumps up. A beat.

WALTER: Mama, where have you been?

MAMA: My—them steps is longer than they used to be. Whew! (*She sits down and ignores him.*) How you feeling this evening, Ruth?

Ruth shrugs, disturbed at having been interrupted and watching her husband knowingly.

WALTER: Mama, where have you been all day?

MAMA (*still ignoring him and leaning on the table and changing to more comfortable shoes*): Where's Travis?

RUTH: I let him go out earlier and he ain't come back yet. Boy, is he going to get it!

WALTER: Mama!

MAMA (*as if she has heard him for the first time*): Yes, son?

WALTER: Where did you go this afternoon?

MAMA: I went downtown to tend to some business that I had to tend to.

WALTER: What kind of business?

MAMA: You know better than to question me like a child, Brother.

WALTER (*rising and bending over the table*): Where were you, Mama? (*Bringing his fists down and shouting.*) Mama, you didn't go do something with that insurance money, something crazy?

The front door opens slowly, interrupting him, and Travis peeks his head in, less than hopefully.

TRAVIS *(to his mother):*   Mama, I —

RUTH: "Mama I" nothing! You're going to get it, boy! Get on in that bedroom and get yourself ready!

TRAVIS: But I —

MAMA: Why don't you all never let the child explain hisself.

RUTH: Keep out of it now, Lena.

Mama clamps her lips together, and Ruth advances toward her son menacingly.

RUTH: A thousand times I have told you not to go off like that —

MAMA *(holding out her arms to her grandson):*   Well — at least let me tell him something. I want him to be the first one to hear . . . Come here, Travis. *(The boy obeys, gladly.)* Travis — *(She takes him by the shoulder and looks into his face.)* — you know that money we got in the mail this morning?

TRAVIS: Yes'm —

MAMA: Well — what you think your grandmama gone and done with that money?

TRAVIS: I don't know, Grandmama.

MAMA *(putting her finger on his nose for emphasis):*   She went out and she bought you a house! *(The explosion comes from Walter at the end of the revelation and he jumps up and turns away from all of them in a fury. Mama continues, to Travis.)* You glad about the house? It's going to be yours when you get to be a man.

TRAVIS: Yeah — I always wanted to live in a house.

MAMA: All right, gimme some sugar then — *(Travis puts his arms around her neck as she watches her son over the boy's shoulder. Then, to Travis, after the embrace.)* Now when you say your prayers tonight, you thank God and your grandfather — 'cause it was him who give you the house — in his way.

RUTH *(taking the boy from Mama and pushing him toward the bedroom):*   Now you get out of here and get ready for your beating.

TRAVIS: Aw, Mama —

RUTH: Get on in there — *(Closing the door behind him and turning radiantly to her mother-in-law.)* So you went and did it!

MAMA *(quietly, looking at her son with pain):*   Yes, I did.

RUTH *(raising both arms classically):*   PRAISE GOD! *(Looks at Walter a moment, who says nothing. She crosses rapidly to her husband.)* Please, honey — let me be glad . . . you be glad too. *(She has laid her hands on his shoulders, but he shakes himself free of her roughly, without turning to face her.)* Oh, Walter . . . a home . . . a home. *(She comes back to Mama.)* Well — where is it? How big is it? How much it going to cost?

MAMA: Well —

RUTH: When we moving?

MAMA *(smiling at her):*   First of the month.

RUTH *(throwing back her head with jubilance):*   Praise God!

MAMA *(tentatively, still looking at her son's back turned against her and Ruth):* It's — it's a nice house too . . . *(She cannot help speaking directly to him. An*

imploring quality in her voice, her manner, makes her almost like a girl now.)
Three bedrooms — nice big one for you and Ruth . . . Me and Beneatha still
have to share our room, but Travis have one of his own — and *(With difficulty.)* I figure if the — new baby — is a boy, we could get one of them double-
decker outfits . . . And there's a yard with a little patch of dirt where I could
maybe get to grow me a few flowers . . . And a nice big basement . . .

RUTH: Walter honey, be glad —

MAMA *(still to his back, fingering things on the table):*   'Course I don't want to
make it sound fancier than it is . . . It's just a plain little old house — but it's
made good and solid — and it will be *ours*. Walter Lee — it makes a difference
in a man when he can walk on floors that belong to *him* . . .

RUTH: Where is it?

MAMA *(frightened at this telling):*   Well — well — it's out there in Clybourne Park —

*Ruth's radiance fades abruptly, and Walter finally turns slowly to face his mother
with incredulity and hostility.*

RUTH: Where?

MAMA *(matter-of-factly):*   Four o six Clybourne Street, Clybourne Park.

RUTH: Clybourne Park? Mama, there ain't no colored people living in
Clybourne Park.

MAMA *(almost idiotically):*   Well, I guess there's going to be some now.

WALTER *(bitterly):*   So that's the peace and comfort you went out and bought for
us today!

MAMA *(raising her eyes to meet his finally):*   Son — I just tried to find the nicest
place for the least amount of money for my family.

RUTH *(trying to recover from the shock):*   Well — well — 'course I ain't one never
been 'fraid of no crackers, mind you — but — well, wasn't there no other
houses nowhere?

MAMA: Them houses they put up for colored in them areas way out all seem to
cost twice as much as other houses. I did the best I could.

RUTH *(struck senseless with the news, in its various degrees of goodness and trouble,
she sits a moment, her fists propping her chin in thought, and then she starts to
rise, bringing her fists down with vigor, the radiance spreading from cheek to
cheek again):*   Well — well — All I can say is — if this is my time in life — MY
TIME — to say good-bye — (And she builds with momentum as she starts to
circle the room with an exuberant, almost tearfully happy release.) — to these
Goddamned cracking walls! — (She pounds the walls.) — and these marching
roaches! — (She wipes at an imaginary army of marching roaches.) — and this
cramped little closet which ain't now or never was no kitchen! . . . then I say
it loud and good, HALLELUJAH! AND GOOD-BYE MISERY . . . I
DON'T NEVER WANT TO SEE YOUR UGLY FACE AGAIN! (She
laughs joyously, having practically destroyed the apartment, and flings her
arms up and lets them come down happily, slowly, reflectively, over her
abdomen, aware for the first time perhaps that the life therein pulses with happiness and not despair.) Lena?

MAMA *(moved, watching her happiness):*   Yes, honey?

RUTH (*looking off*):   Is there — is there a whole lot of sunlight?

MAMA (*understanding*):   Yes, child, there's a whole lot of sunlight.

Long pause.

Ruth (*collecting herself and going to the door of the room Travis is in*):   Well — I guess I better see 'bout Travis. (*To Mama.*) Lord, I sure don't feel like whipping nobody today!

She exits.

Mama (*the mother and son are left alone now and the mother waits a long time, considering deeply, before she speaks*):   Son — you — you understand what I done, don't you? (*Walter is silent and sullen.*) I — I just seen my family falling apart today . . . just falling to pieces in front of my eyes . . . We couldn't of gone on like we was today. We was going backwards 'stead of forwards — talking 'bout killing babies and wishing each other was dead . . . When it gets like that in life — you just got to do something different, push on out and do something bigger . . . (*She waits.*) I wish you say something, son . . . I wish you'd say how deep inside you you think I done the right thing —

WALTER (*crossing slowly to his bedroom door and finally turning there and speaking measuredly*):   What you need me to say you done right for? You the head of this family. You run our lives like you want to. It was your money and you did what you wanted with it. So what you need for me to say it was all right for? (*Bitterly, to hurt her as deeply as he knows is possible.*) So you butchered up a dream of mine — you — who always talking 'bout your children's dreams . . .

MAMA: Walter Lee —

He just closes the door behind him. Mama sits alone, thinking heavily.

Curtain.

Scene 2

Time: Friday night, a few weeks later.

   At rise: Packing crates mark the intention of the family to move. Beneatha and George come in, presumably from an evening out again.

GEORGE: O.K. . . . O.K., whatever you say . . . (*They both sit on the couch. He tries to kiss her. She moves away.*) Look, we've had a nice evening; let's not spoil it, huh? . . .

He again turns her head and tries to nuzzle in and she turns away from him, not with distaste but with momentary lack of interest; in a mood to pursue what they were talking about.

BENEATHA: I'm *trying* to talk to you.

GEORGE: We always talk.

BENEATHA: Yes — and I love to talk.

GEORGE (*exasperated; rising*):   I know it and I don't mind it sometimes . . . I want you to cut it out, see — The moody stuff, I mean. I don't like it. You're a nice-looking girl . . . all over. That's all you need, honey, forget the atmosphere. Guys aren't going to go for the atmosphere—they're going to go for what they see. Be glad for that. Drop the Garbo routine. It doesn't go with you. As for myself, I want a nice—*(Groping.)*—simple *(Thoughtfully.)*—sophisticated girl . . . not a poet—O.K.?

He starts to kiss her, she rebuffs him again and he jumps up.

BENEATHA: Why are you angry, George?

GEORGE: Because this is stupid! I don't go out with you to discuss the nature of "quiet desperation" or to hear all about your thoughts—because the world will go on thinking what it thinks regardless—

BENEATHA: Then why read books? Why go to school?

GEORGE *(with artificial patience, counting on his fingers)*:   It's simple. You read books—to learn facts—to get grades—to pass the course—to get a degree. That's all—it has nothing to do with thoughts.

A long pause.

BENEATHA: I see. *(He starts to sit.)* Good night, George.

George looks at her a little oddly, and starts to exit. He meets Mama coming in.

GEORGE: Oh—hello, Mrs. Younger.

MAMA: Hello, George, how you feeling?

GEORGE: Fine—fine, how are you?

MAMA: Oh, a little tired. You know them steps can get you after a day's work. You all have a nice time tonight?

GEORGE: Yes—a fine time. A fine time.

MAMA: Well, good night.

GEORGE: Good night. *(He exits. Mama closes the door behind her.)* Hello, honey. What you sitting like that for?

BENEATHA: I'm just sitting.

MAMA: Didn't you have a nice time?

BENEATHA: No.

MAMA: No? What's the matter?

BENEATHA: Mama, George is a fool—honest. *(She rises.)*

MAMA *(hustling around unloading the packages she has entered with. She stops)*: Is he, baby?

BENEATHA: Yes.

Beneatha makes up Travis's bed as she talks.

MAMA: You sure?

BENEATHA: Yes.

MAMA: Well—I guess you better not waste your time with no fools.

Beneatha looks up at her mother, watching her put groceries in the refrigerator. Finally she gathers up her things and starts into the bedroom. At the door she stops and looks back at her mother.

BENEATHA: Mama—

MAMA: Yes, baby—

BENEATHA: Thank you.

MAMA: For what?

BENEATHA: For understanding me this time.

She exits quickly and the mother stands, smiling a little, looking at the place where Beneatha just stood. Ruth enters.

RUTH: Now don't you fool with any of this stuff, Lena —

MAMA: Oh, I just thought I'd sort a few things out. Is Brother here?

RUTH: Yes.

MAMA *(with concern):*   Is he —

RUTH *(reading her eyes):*   Yes.

Mama is silent and someone knocks on the door. Mama and Ruth exchange weary and knowing glances and Ruth opens it to admit the neighbor, Mrs. Johnson,° who is a rather squeaky wide-eyed lady of no particular age, with a newspaper under her arm.

MAMA *(changing her expression to acute delight and a ringing cheerful greeting):*   Oh — hello there, Johnson.

JOHNSON *(this is a woman who decided long ago to be enthusiastic about EVERY-THING in life and she is inclined to wave her wrist vigorously at the height of her exclamatory comments):*   Hello there, yourself! H'you this evening, Ruth?

RUTH *(not much of a deceptive type):*   Fine, Mis' Johnson, h'you?

JOHNSON: Fine. *(Reaching out quickly, playfully, and patting Ruth's stomach.)* Ain't you starting to poke out none yet! *(She mugs with delight at the over familiar remark and her eyes dart around looking at the crates and packing preparation; Mama's face is a cold sheet of endurance.)* Oh, ain't we getting ready round here, though! Yessir! Lookathere! I'm telling you the Youngers is really getting ready to "move on up a little higher!" — Bless God!

MAMA *(a little drily, doubting the total sincerity of the Blesser):*   Bless God.

JOHNSON: He's good, ain't He?

MAMA: Oh yes, He's good.

JOHNSON: I mean sometimes He works in mysterious ways . . . but He works, don't He!

MAMA *(the same):*   Yes, he does.

JOHNSON: I'm just soooooo happy for y'all. And this here child — *(About Ruth.)* looks like she could just pop open with happiness, don't she. Where's all the rest of the family?

MAMA: Bennie's gone to bed —

JOHNSON: Ain't no . . . *(The implication is pregnancy.)* sickness done hit you — I hope . . . ?

MAMA: No — she just tired. She was out this evening.

JOHNSON *(all is a coo, an emphatic coo):*   Aw — ain't that lovely. She still going out with the little Murchison boy?

MAMA *(drily):*   Ummmm huh.

Mrs. Johnson: This character and the scene of her visit were cut from the original production and early editions of the play.

JOHNSON: That's lovely. You sure got lovely children, Younger. Me and Isaiah talks all the time 'bout what fine children you was blessed with. We sure do.

MAMA: Ruth, give Mis' Johnson a piece of sweet potato pie and some milk.

JOHNSON: Oh honey, I can't stay hardly a minute — I just dropped in to see if there was anything I could do. *(Accepting the food easily.)* I guess y'all seen the news what's all over the colored paper this week . . .

MAMA: No — didn't get mine yet this week.

JOHNSON *(lifting her head and blinking with the spirit of catastrophe):* You mean you ain't read 'bout them colored people that was bombed out their place out there?

Ruth straightens with concern and takes the paper and reads it. Johnson notices her and feeds commentary.

JOHNSON: Ain't it something how bad these here white folks is getting here in Chicago! Lord, getting so you think you right down in Mississippi! *(With a tremendous and rather insincere sense of melodrama.)* 'Course I thinks it's wonderful how our folk keeps on pushing out. You hear some of these Negroes round here talking 'bout how they don't go where they ain't wanted and all that — but not me, honey! *(This is a lie.)* Wilhemenia Othella Johnson goes anywhere, any time she feels like it! *(With head movement for emphasis.)* Yes I do! Why if we left it up to these here crackers, the poor niggers wouldn't have nothing — *(She clasps her hand over her mouth.)* Oh, I always forgets you don't 'low that word in your house.

MAMA *(quietly, looking at her):* No — I don't 'low it.

JOHNSON *(vigorously again):* Me neither! I was just telling Isaiah yesterday when he come using it in front of me — I said, "Isaiah, it's just like Mis' Younger says all the time —"

MAMA: Don't you want some more pie?

JOHNSON: No — no thank you; this was lovely. I got to get on over home and have my midnight coffee. I hear some people say it don't let them sleep but I finds I can't close my eyes right lessen I done had that laaaast cup of coffee . . . *(She waits. A beat. Undaunted.)* My Goodnight coffee, I calls it!

MAMA *(with much eye-rolling and communication between herself and Ruth):* Ruth, why don't you give Mis' Johnson some coffee.

Ruth gives Mama an unpleasant look for her kindness.

JOHNSON *(accepting the coffee):* Where's Brother tonight?

MAMA: He's lying down.

JOHNSON: MMmmmmm, he sure gets his beauty rest, don't he? Good-looking man. Sure is a good-looking man! *(Reaching out to pat Ruth's stomach again.)* I guess that's how come we keep on having babies around here. *(She winks at Mama.)* One thing 'bout Brother, he always know how to have a *good* time. And soooooo ambitious! I bet it was his idea y'all moving out to Clybourne Park. Lord — I bet this time next month y'all's names will have been in the papers plenty — *(Holding up her hands to mark off each word of the headline she can see in front of her.)* "NEGROES INVADE CLYBOURNE PARK — BOMBED!"

MAMA *(she and Ruth look at the woman in amazement):* We ain't exactly moving out there to get bombed.

JOHNSON: Oh honey—you know I'm praying to God every day that don't nothing like that happen! But you have to think of life like it is—and these here Chicago peckerwoods is some baaaad peckerwoods.

MAMA *(wearily):* We done thought about all that Mis' Johnson.

Beneatha comes out of the bedroom in her robe and passes through to the bathroom. Mrs. Johnson turns.

JOHNSON: Hello there, Bennie!

BENEATHA *(crisply):* Hello, Mrs. Johnson.

JOHNSON: How is school?

BENEATHA *(crisply):* Fine, thank you. *(She goes out.)*

JOHNSON *(insulted):* Getting so she don't have much to say to nobody.

MAMA: The child was on her way to the bathroom.

JOHNSON: I know—but sometimes she act like ain't got time to pass the time of day with nobody ain't been to college. Oh—I ain't criticizing her none. It's just—you know how some of our young people gets when they get a little education. *(Mama and Ruth say nothing, just look at her.)* Yes—well. Well, I guess I better get on home. *(Unmoving.)* 'Course I can understand how she must be proud and everything—being the only one in the family to make something of herself. I know just being a chauffeur ain't never satisfied Brother none. He shouldn't feel like that, though. Ain't nothing wrong with being a chauffeur.

MAMA: There's plenty wrong with it.

JOHNSON: What?

MAMA: Plenty. My husband always said being any kind of a servant wasn't a fit thing for a man to have to be. He always said a man's hands was made to make things, or to turn the earth with—not to drive nobody's car for 'em— or—*(She looks at her own hands.)* carry they slop jars. And my boy is just like him—he wasn't meant to wait on nobody.

JOHNSON *(rising, somewhat offended):* Mmmmmmmmm. The Youngers is too much for me! *(She looks around.)* You sure one proud-acting bunch of colored folks. Well—I always thinks like Booker T. Washington said that time— "Education has spoiled many a good plow hand"—

MAMA: Is that what old Booker T. said?

JOHNSON: He sure did.

MAMA: Well, it sounds just like him. The fool.

JOHNSON *(indignantly):* Well—he was one of our great men.

MAMA: Who said so?

JOHNSON *(nonplussed):* You know, me and you ain't never agreed about some things, Lena Younger. I guess I better be going—

RUTH *(quickly):* Good night.

JOHNSON: Good night. Oh—*(Thrusting it at her.)* You can keep the paper! *(With a trill.)* 'Night.

MAMA: Good night, Mis' Johnson.

Mrs. Johnson exits.

RUTH: If ignorance was gold . . .

MAMA: Shush. Don't talk about folks behind their backs.

RUTH: You do.

MAMA: I'm old and corrupted. *(Beneatha enters.)* You was rude to Mis' Johnson, Beneatha, and I don't like it at all.

BENEATHA *(at her door):*   Mama, if there are two things we, as a people, have got to overcome, one is the Klu Klux Klan—and the other is Mrs. Johnson. *(She exits.)*

MAMA: Smart aleck.

The phone rings.

RUTH: I'll get it.

MAMA: Lord, ain't this a popular place tonight.

RUTH *(at the phone):*   Hello—Just a minute. *(Goes to door.)* Walter, it's Mrs. Arnold. *(Waits. Goes back to the phone. Tense.)* Hello. Yes, this is his wife speaking . . . He's lying down now. Yes . . . well, he'll be in tomorrow. He's been very sick. Yes—I know we should have called, but we were so sure he'd be able to come in today. Yes—yes, I'm very sorry. Yes . . . Thank you very much. *(She hangs up. Walter is standing in the doorway of the bedroom behind her.)* That was Mrs. Arnold.

WALTER *(indifferently):*   Was it?

RUTH: She said if you don't come in tomorrow that they are getting a new man . . .

WALTER: Ain't that sad—ain't that crying sad.

RUTH: She said Mr. Arnold has had to take a cab for three days . . . Walter, you ain't been to work for three days! *(This is a revelation to her.)* Where you been, Walter Lee Younger? *(Walter looks at her and starts to laugh.)* You're going to lose your job.

WALTER: That's right . . . *(He turns on the radio.)*

RUTH: Oh, Walter, and with your mother working like a dog every day—

A steamy, deep blues pours into the room.

WALTER: That's sad too—Everything is sad.

MAMA: What you been doing for these three days, son?

WALTER: Mama—you don't know all the things a man what got leisure can find to do in this city . . . What's this—Friday night? Well—Wednesday I borrowed Willy Harris' car and I went for a drive . . . just me and myself and I drove and drove . . . Way out . . . way past South Chicago, and I parked the car and I sat and looked at the steel mills all day long. I just sat in the car and looked at them big black chimneys for hours. Then I drove back and I went to the Green Hat. *(Pause.)* And Thursday—Thursday I borrowed the car again and I got in it and I pointed it the other way and I drove the other way—for hours—way, way up to Wisconsin, and I looked at the farms. I just drove and looked at the farms. Then I drove back and I went to the Green Hat. *(Pause.)* And today—today I didn't get the car. Today I just walked. All over the South-side. And I looked at the Negroes and they looked at me and finally I just sat down on the curb at Thirty-ninth and South Parkway and I just sat there and watched the Negroes go by. And then I went to the Green Hat. You all sad? You all depressed? And you know where I am going right now—

Ruth goes out quietly.

MAMA: Oh, Big Walter, is this the harvest of our days?

WALTER: You know what I like about the Green Hat? I like this little cat they got there who blows a sax . . . He blows. He talks to me. He ain't but 'bout five feet tall and he's got a conked head and his eyes is always closed and he's all music—

MAMA *(rising and getting some papers out of her handbag)*:   Walter—

WALTER: And there's this other guy who plays the piano . . . and they got a sound. I mean they can work on some music . . . They got the best little combo in the world in the Green Hat . . . You can just sit there and drink and listen to them three men play and you realize that don't nothing matter worth a damn, but just being there—

MAMA: I've helped do it to you, haven't I, son? Walter, I been wrong.

WALTER: Naw—you ain't never been wrong about nothing, Mama.

MAMA: Listen to me, now. I say I been wrong, son. That I been doing to you what the rest of the world been doing to you. *(She turns off the radio.)* Walter— *(She stops and he looks up slowly at her and she meets his eyes pleadingly.)* What you ain't never understood is that I ain't got nothing, don't own nothing, ain't never really wanted nothing that wasn't for you. There ain't nothing as precious to me . . . There ain't nothing worth holding on to, money, dreams, nothing else—if it means—if it means it's going to destroy my boy. *(She takes an envelope out of her handbag and puts it in front of him and he watches her without speaking or moving.)* I paid the man thirty-five hundred dollars down on the house. That leaves sixty-five hundred dollars. Monday morning I want you to take this money and take three thousand dollars and put it in a savings account for Beneatha's medical schooling. The rest you put in a checking account—with your name on it. And from now on any penny that come out of it or that go in it is for you to look after. For you to decide. *(She drops her hands a little helplessly.)* It ain't much, but it's all I got in the world and I'm putting it in your hands. I'm telling you to be the head of this family from now on like you supposed to be.

WALTER *(stares at the money)*:   You trust me like that, Mama?

MAMA: I ain't never stop trusting you. Like I ain't never stop loving you.

She goes out, and Walter sits looking at the money on the table. Finally, in a decisive gesture, he gets up, and, in mingled joy and desperation, picks up the money. At the same moment, Travis enters for bed.

TRAVIS: What's the matter, Daddy? You drunk?

WALTER *(sweetly, more sweetly than we have ever known him)*:   No, Daddy ain't drunk. Daddy ain't going to never be drunk again . . .

TRAVIS: Well, good night, Daddy.

The father has come from behind the couch and leans over, embracing his son.

WALTER: Son, I feel like talking to you tonight.

TRAVIS: About what?

WALTER: Oh, about a lot of things. About you and what kind of man you going to be when you grow up . . . Son—son, what do you want to be when you grow up?

TRAVIS: A bus driver.

WALTER *(laughing a little):*   A what? Man, that ain't nothing to want to be!

TRAVIS: Why not?

WALTER: 'Cause, man—it ain't big enough—you know what I mean.

TRAVIS: I don't know then. I can't make up my mind. Sometimes Mama asks me that too. And sometimes when I tell her I just want to be like you—she says she don't want me to be like that and sometimes she says she does. . . .

WALTER *(gathering him up in his arms):*   You know what, Travis? In seven years you going to be seventeen years old. And things is going to be very different with us in seven years, Travis. . . . One day when you are seventeen I'll come home—home from my office downtown somewhere—

TRAVIS: You don't work in no office, Daddy.

WALTER: No—but after tonight. After what your daddy gonna do tonight, there's going to be offices—a whole lot of offices. . . .

TRAVIS: What you gonna do tonight, Daddy?

WALTER: You wouldn't understand yet, son, but your daddy's gonna make a transaction . . . a business transaction that's going to change our lives. . . . That's how come one day when you 'bout seventeen years old I'll come home and I'll be pretty tired, you know what I mean, after a day of conferences and secretaries getting things wrong the way they do . . .'cause an executive's life is hell, man—*(The more he talks the farther away he gets.)* And I'll pull the car up on the driveway . . . just a plain black Chrysler, I think, with white walls—no—black tires. More elegant. Rich people don't have to be flashy . . . though I'll have to get something a little sportier for Ruth—maybe a Cadillac convertible to do her shopping in. . . . And I'll come up the steps to the house and the gardener will be clipping away at the hedges and he'll say, "Good evening, Mr. Younger." And I'll say, "Hello, Jefferson, how are you this evening?" And I'll go inside and Ruth will come downstairs and meet me at the door and we'll kiss each other and she'll take my arm and we'll go up to your room to see you sitting on the floor with the catalogues of all the great schools in America around you. . . . All the great schools in the world! And—and I'll say, all right son—it's your seventeenth birthday, what is it you've decided? . . . Just tell me where you want to go to school and you'll go. Just tell me, what it is you want to be—and you'll *be* it. . . . Whatever you want to be—Yessir! *(He holds his arms open for Travis.)* You just name it, son . . . *(Travis leaps into them.)* and I hand you the world!

Walter's voice has risen in pitch and hysterical promise and on the last line he lifts Travis high.

Blackout.

Scene 3

Time: Saturday, moving day, one week later.

Before the curtain rises, Ruth's voice, a strident, dramatic church alto, cuts through the silence.

It is, in the darkness, a triumphant surge, a penetrating statement of expectation: "Oh, Lord, I don't feel no ways tired! Children, oh, glory hallelujah!"

As the curtain rises we see that Ruth is alone in the living room, finishing up the family's packing. It is moving day. She is nailing crates and tying cartons. Beneatha enters, carrying a guitar case, and watches her exuberant sister-in-law.

RUTH: Hey!

BENEATHA *(putting away the case)*: Hi.

RUTH *(pointing at a package)*: Honey—look in that package there and see what I found on sale this morning at the South Center. *(Ruth gets up and moves to the package and draws out some curtains.)* Lookahere—hand-turned hems!

BENEATHA: How do you know the window size out there?

RUTH *(who hadn't thought of that)*: Oh—Well, they bound to fit something in the whole house. Anyhow, they was too good a bargain to pass up. *(Ruth slaps her head, suddenly remembering something.)* Oh, Bennie—I meant to put a special note on that carton over there. That's your mama's good china and she wants 'em to be very careful with it.

BENEATHA: I'll do it.

Beneatha finds a piece of paper and starts to draw large letters on it.

RUTH: You know what I'm going to do soon as I get in that new house?

BENEATHA: What?

RUTH: Honey—I'm going to run me a tub of water up to here . . . *(With her fingers practically up to her nostrils.)* And I'm going to get in it—and I am going to sit . . . and sit . . . and sit in that hot water and the first person who knocks to tell *me* to hurry up and come out—

BENEATHA: Gets shot at sunrise.

RUTH *(laughing happily)*: You said it, sister! *(Noticing how large Beneatha is absent-mindedly making the note)*: Honey, they ain't going to read that from no airplane.

BENEATHA *(laughing herself)*: I guess I always think things have more emphasis if they are big, somehow.

RUTH *(looking up at her and smiling)*: You and your brother seem to have that as a philosophy of life. Lord, that man—done changed so 'round here. You know—you know what we did last night? Me and Walter Lee?

BENEATHA: What?

RUTH *(smiling to herself)*: We went to the movies. *(Looking at Beneatha to see if she understands.)* We went to the movies. You know the last time me and Walter went to the movies together?

BENEATHA: No.

RUTH: Me neither. That's how long it been. *(Smiling again.)* But we went last night. The picture wasn't much good, but that didn't seem to matter. We went—and we held hands.

BENEATHA: Oh, Lord!

RUTH: We held hands—and you know what?

BENEATHA: What?

RUTH: When we come out of the show it was late and dark and all the stores and things was closed up . . . and it was kind of chilly and there wasn't many people on the streets . . . and we was still holding hands, me and Walter.

BENEATHA: You're killing me.

Walter enters with a large package. His happiness is deep in him; he cannot keep still with his newfound exuberance. He is singing and wiggling and snapping his fingers. He puts his package in a corner and puts a phonograph record, which he has brought in with him, on the record player. As the music, soulful and sensuous, comes up he dances over to Ruth and tries to get her to dance with him. She gives in at last to his raunchiness and in a fit of giggling allows herself to be drawn into his mood. They dip and she melts into his arms in a classic, body-melting "slow drag."

BENEATHA *(regarding them a long time as they dance, then drawing in her breath for a deeply exaggerated comment which she does not particularly mean):* Talk about—oldddddddddd-fashioneddddddd—Negroes!

WALTER *(stopping momentarily):*   What kind of Negroes?

He says this in fun. He is not angry with her today, nor with anyone. He starts to dance with his wife again.

BENEATHA: Old-fashioned.

WALTER *(as he dances with Ruth):*   You know, when these *New Negroes* have their convention—*(Pointing at his sister.)*—that is going to be the chairman of the Committee on Unending Agitation. *(He goes on dancing, then stops.)* Race, race, race! . . . Girl, I do believe you are the first person in the history of the entire human race to successfully brainwash yourself. *(Beneatha breaks up and he goes on dancing. He stops again, enjoying his tease.)* Damn, even the N double A C P takes a holiday sometimes! *(Beneatha and Ruth laugh. He dances with Ruth some more and starts to laugh and stops and pantomimes someone over an operating table.)* I can just see that chick someday looking down at some poor cat on an operating table and before she starts to slice him, she says . . . *(Pulling his sleeves back maliciously.)* "By the way, what are your views on civil rights down there? . . ."

He laughs at her again and starts to dance happily. The bell sounds.

BENEATHA: Sticks and stones may break my bones but . . . words will never hurt me!

Beneatha goes to the door and opens it as Walter and Ruth go on with the clowning. Beneatha is somewhat surprised to see a quiet-looking middle-aged white man in a business suit holding his hat and a briefcase in his hand and consulting a small piece of paper.

MAN: Uh—how do you do, miss. I am looking for a Mrs.—*(He looks at the slip of paper.)* Mrs. Lena Younger? *(He stops short, struck dumb at the sight of the oblivious Walter and Ruth.)*

BENEATHA *(smoothing her hair with slight embarrassment)*:   Oh—yes, that's my mother. Excuse me. *(She closes the door and turns to quiet the other two.)* Ruth! Brother! *(Enunciating precisely but soundlessly: "There's a white man at the door!" They stop dancing, Ruth cuts off the phonograph, Beneatha opens the door. The man casts a curious quick glance at all of them.)* Uh—come in please.

MAN *(coming in)*:   Thank you.

BENEATHA: My mother isn't here just now. Is it business?

MAN: Yes . . . well, of a sort.

WALTER *(freely, the Man of the House)*:   Have a seat. I'm Mrs. Younger's son. I look after most of her business matters.

Ruth and Beneatha exchange amused glances.

MAN *(regarding Walter, and sitting)*:   Well—My name is Karl Lindner . . .

WALTER *(stretching out his hand)*:   Walter Younger. This is my wife—*(Ruth nods politely.)*—and my sister.

LINDNER: How do you do.

WALTER *(amiably, as he sits himself easily on a chair, leaning forward on his knees with interest and looking expectantly into the newcomer's face)*:   What can we do for you, Mr. Lindner!

LINDNER *(some minor shuffling of the hat and briefcase on his knees)*:   Well—I am a representative of the Clybourne Park Improvement Association—

WALTER *(pointing)*:   Why don't you sit your things on the floor?

LINDNER: Oh—yes. Thank you. *(He slides the briefcase and hat under the chair.)* And as I was saying—I am from the Clybourne Park Improvement Association and we have had it brought to our attention at the last meeting that you people—or at least your mother—has bought a piece of residential property at—*(He digs for the slip of paper again.)*—four o six Clybourne Street . . .

WALTER: That's right. Care for something to drink? Ruth, get Mr. Lindner a beer.

LINDNER *(upset for some reason)*:   Oh—no, really. I mean thank you very much, but no thank you.

RUTH *(innocently)*:   Some coffee?

LINDNER: Thank you, nothing at all.

Beneatha is watching the man carefully.

LINDNER: Well, I don't know how much you folks know about our organization. *(He is a gentle man; thoughtful and somewhat labored in his manner.)* It is one of these community organizations set up to look after—oh, you know, things like block upkeep and special projects and we also have what we call our New Neighbors Orientation Committee . . .

BENEATHA *(drily)*:   Yes—and what do they do?

LINDNER *(turning a little to her and then returning the main force to Walter)*:   Well—it's what you might call a sort of welcoming committee, I guess. I mean they, we — I'm the chairman of the committee — go around and see the new people who move into the neighborhood and sort of give them the low-down on the way we do things out in Clybourne Park.

BENEATHA *(with appreciation of the two meanings, which escape Ruth and Walter):* Un-huh.

LINDNER: And we also have the category of what the association calls — *(He looks elsewhere.)* — uh — special community problems . . .

BENEATHA: Yes — and what are some of those?

WALTER: Girl, let the man talk.

LINDNER *(with understated relief):* Thank you. I would sort of like to explain this thing in my own way. I mean I want to explain to you in a certain way.

WALTER: Go ahead.

LINDNER: Yes. Well. I'm going to try to get right to the point. I'm sure we'll all appreciate that in the long run.

BENEATHA: Yes.

WALTER: Be still now!

LINDNER: Well —

RUTH *(still innocently):* Would you like another chair — you don't look comfortable.

LINDNER *(more frustrated than annoyed):* No, thank you very much. Please. Well — to get right to the point, I — *(A great breath, and he is off at last.)* I am sure you people must be aware of some of the incidents which have happened in various parts of the city when colored people have moved into certain areas — *(Beneatha exhales heavily and starts tossing a piece of fruit up and down in the air.)* Well — because we have what I think is going to be a unique type of organization in American community life — not only do we deplore that kind of thing — but we are trying to do something about it. *(Beneatha stops tossing and turns with a new and quizzical interest to the man.)* We feel — *(gaining confidence in his mission because of the interest in the faces of the people he is talking to.)* — we feel that most of the trouble in this world, when you come right down to it — *(He hits his knee for emphasis.)* — most of the trouble exists because people just don't sit down and talk to each other.

RUTH *(nodding as she might in church, pleased with the remark):* You can say that again, mister.

LINDNER *(more encouraged by such affirmation):* That we don't try hard enough in this world to understand the other fellow's problem. The other guy's point of view.

RUTH: Now that's right.

Beneatha and Walter merely watch and listen with genuine interest.

LINDNER: Yes — that's the way we feel out in Clybourne Park. And that's why I was elected to come here this afternoon and talk to you people. Friendly like, you know, the way people should talk to each other and see if we couldn't find some way to work this thing out. As I say, the whole business is a matter of *caring* about the other fellow. Anybody can see that you are a nice family of folks, hard working and honest I'm sure. *(Beneatha frowns slightly, quizzically, her head tilted regarding him.*) Today everybody knows what it means to be on the outside of *something*. And of course, there is always somebody who is out to take advantage of people who don't always understand.

WALTER: What do you mean?

LINDNER: Well—you see our community is made up of people who've worked hard as the dickens for years to build up that little community. They're not rich and fancy people; just hard-working, honest people who don't really have much but those little homes and a dream of the kind of community they want to raise their children in. Now, I don't say we are perfect and there is a lot wrong in some of the things they want. But you've got to admit that a man, right or wrong, has the right to want to have the neighborhood he lives in a certain kind of way. And at the moment the overwhelming majority of our people out there feel that people get along better, take more of a common interest in the life of the community, when they share a common background. I want you to believe me when I tell you that race prejudice simply doesn't enter into it. It is a matter of the people of Clybourne Park believing, rightly or wrongly, as I say, that for the happiness of all concerned that our Negro families are happier when they live in their *own* communities.

BENEATHA (*with a grand and bitter gesture*):   This, friends, is the Welcoming Committee!

WALTER (*dumfounded, looking at Lindner*):   Is this what you came marching all the way over here to tell us?

LINDNER: Well, now we've been having a fine conversation. I hope you'll hear me all the way through.

WALTER (*tightly*):   Go ahead, man.

LINDNER: You see—in the face of all the things I have said, we are prepared to make your family a very generous offer . . .

BENEATHA: Thirty pieces and not a coin less!

WALTER: Yeah?

LINDNER (*putting on his glasses drawing a form out of the briefcase*):   Our association is prepared, through the collective effort of our people, to buy the house from you at a financial gain to your family.

RUTH: Lord have mercy, ain't this the living gall!

WALTER: All right, you through?

LINDNER: Well, I want to give you the exact terms of the financial arrangement—

WALTER: We don't want to hear no exact terms of no arrangements. I want to know if you got any more to tell us 'bout getting together?

LINDNER (*taking off his glasses*):   Well—I don't suppose that you feel . . .

WALTER: Never mind how I feel—you got any more to say 'bout how people ought to sit down and talk to each other? . . . Get out of my house, man.

He turns his back and walks to the door.

LINDNER (*looking around at the hostile faces and reaching and assembling his hat and briefcase*):   Well—I don't understand why you people are reacting this way. What do you think you are going to gain by moving into a

neighborhood where you just aren't wanted and where some elements—
well—people can get awful worked up when they feel that their whole way
of life and everything they've ever worked for is threatened.

WALTER: Get out.

LINDNER *(at the door, holding a small card)*:   Well—I'm sorry it went like this.

WALTER: Get out.

LINDNER *(almost sadly regarding Walter)*:   You just can't force people to change
their hearts, son.

*He turns and puts his card on a table and exits. Walter pushes the door to with
stinging hatred, and stands looking at it. Ruth just sits and Beneatha just stands.
They say nothing. Mama and Travis enter.*

MAMA: Well—this all the packing got done since I left out of here this morning.
I testify before God that my children got all the energy of the *dead!* What
time the moving men due?

BENEATHA: Four o'clock. You had a caller, Mama.

She is smiling, teasingly.

MAMA: Sure enough—who?

BENEATHA *(her arms folded saucily)*:   The Welcoming Committee.

Walter and Ruth giggle.

MAMA *(innocently)*:   Who?

BENEATHA: The Welcoming Committee. They said they're sure going to be
glad to see you when you get there.

WALTER *(devilishly)*:   Yeah, they said they can't hardly wait to see your face.

Laughter.

MAMA *(sensing their facetiousness)*:   What's the matter with you all?

WALTER: Ain't nothing the matter with us. We just telling you 'bout the gentleman who came to see you this afternoon. From the Clybourne Park Improvement Association.

MAMA: What he want?

RUTH *(in the same mood as Beneatha and Walter)*:   To welcome you, honey.

WALTER: He said they can't hardly wait. He said the one thing they don't have,
that they just *dying* to have out there is a fine family of fine colored people!
(To Ruth and Beneatha.) Ain't that right!

RUTH *(mockingly)*:   Yeah! He left his card—

BENEATHA *(handing card to Mama)*:   In case.

*Mama reads and throws it on the floor—understanding and looking off as she
draws her chair up to the table on which she has put her plant and some sticks and
some cord.*

MAMA: Father, give us strength. *(Knowingly—and without fun.)* Did he
threaten us?

BENEATHA: Oh—Mama—they don't do it like that any more. He talked Brotherhood. He said everybody ought to learn how to sit down and hate each
other with good Christian fellowship.

She and Walter shake hands to ridicule the remark.

MAMA *(sadly)*:   Lord, protect us . . .

RUTH: You should hear the money those folks raised to buy the house from us. All we paid and then some.

BENEATHA: What they think we going to do — eat 'em?

RUTH: No, honey, marry 'em.

MAMA *(shaking her head)*:   Lord, Lord, Lord . . .

RUTH: Well — that's the way the crackers crumble. *(A beat.)* Joke.

BENEATHA *(laughingly noticing what her mother is doing)*:   Mama, what are you doing?

MAMA: Fixing my plant so it won't get hurt none on the way . . .

BENEATHA: Mama, you going to take *that* to the new house?

MAMA: Un-huh —

BENEATHA: That raggedy-looking old thing?

MAMA *(stopping and looking at her)*:   It expresses ME!

RUTH *(with delight, to Beneatha)*:   So there, Miss Thing!

Walter comes to Mama suddenly and bends down behind her and squeezes her in his arms with all his strength. She is overwhelmed by the suddenness of it and, though delighted, her manner is like that of Ruth and Travis.

MAMA: Look out now, boy! You make me mess up my thing here!

WALTER *(his face lit, he slips down on his knees beside her, his arms still about her)*:   Mama . . . you know what it means to climb up in the chariot?

MAMA *(gruffly, very happy)*:   Get on away from me now . . .

RUTH *(near the gift-wrapped package, trying to catch Walter's eye)*:   Psst —

WALTER: What the old song say, Mama . . .

RUTH: Walter — Now?

She is pointing at the package.

WALTER *(speaking the lines, sweetly, playfully, in his mother's face)*:
     I got wings . . . you got wings . . .
     All God's children got wings . . .

MAMA: Boy — get out of my face and do some work . . .

WALTER:
     When I get to heaven gonna put on my wings,
     Gonna fly all over God's heaven . . .

BENEATHA *(teasingly, from across the room)*:   Everybody talking 'bout heaven ain't going there!

WALTER *(to Ruth, who is carrying the box across to them)*:   I don't know, you think we ought to give her that . . . Seems to me she ain't been very appreciative around here.

MAMA *(eying the box, which is obviously a gift)*:   What is that?

WALTER *(taking it from Ruth and putting it on the table in front of Mama)*:   Well — what you all think? Should we give it to her?

RUTH: Oh — she was pretty good today.

MAMA: I'll good you —

She turns her eyes to the box again.

BENEATHA: Open it, Mama.

She stands up, looks at it, turns and looks at all of them, and then presses her hands together and does not open the package.

WALTER *(sweetly)*:   Open it, Mama. It's for you. *(Mama looks in his eyes. It is the first present in her life without its being Christmas. Slowly she opens her package and lifts out, one by one, a brand-new sparkling set of gardening tools. Walter continues, prodding.)* Ruth made up the note—read it . . .

MAMA *(picking up the card and adjusting her glasses)*:   "To our own Mrs. Miniver—Love from Brother, Ruth, and Beneatha." Ain't that lovely . . .

TRAVIS *(tugging at his father's sleeve)*:   Daddy, can I give her mine now?

WALTER: All right, son. *(Travis flies to get his gift.)*

MAMA: Now I don't have to use my knives and forks no more . . .

WALTER: Travis didn't want to go in with the rest of us, Mama. He got his own. *(Somewhat amused.)* We don't know what it is . . .

TRAVIS *(racing back in the room with a large hatbox and putting it in front of his grandmother)*:   Here!

MAMA: Lord have mercy, baby. You done gone and bought your grandmother a hat?

TRAVIS *(very proud)*:   Open it!

She does and lifts out an elaborate, but very elaborate, wide gardening hat, and all the adults break up at the sight of it.

RUTH: Travis, honey, what is that?

TRAVIS *(who thinks it is beautiful and appropriate)*:   It's a gardening hat! Like the ladies always have on in the magazines when they work in their gardens.

BENEATHA *(giggling fiercely)*:   Travis—we were trying to make Mama Mrs. Miniver—not Scarlett O'Hara!

MAMA *(indignantly)*:   What's the matter with you all! This here is a beautiful hat! *(Absurdly.)* I always wanted me one just like it!

She pops it on her head to prove it to her grandson, and the hat is ludicrous and considerably oversized.

RUTH: Hot dog! Go, Mama!

WALTER *(doubled over with laughter)*:   I'm sorry, Mama—but you look like you ready to go out and chop you some cotton sure enough!

They all laugh except Mama, out of deference to Travis's feelings.

MAMA *(gathering the boy up to her)*:   Bless your heart—this is the prettiest hat I ever owned—*(Walter, Ruth, and Beneatha chime in—noisily, festively, and insincerely congratulating Travis on his gift.)* What are we all standing around here for? We ain't finished packin' yet. Bennie, you ain't packed one book.

The bell rings.

BENEATHA: That couldn't be the movers . . . it's not hardly two good yet —

Beneatha goes into her room. Mama starts for door.

WALTER (*turning, stiffening*):   Wait—wait—I'll get it.

He stands and looks at the door.

MAMA: You expecting company, son?

WALTER (*just looking at the door*):   Yeah—yeah . . .

Mama looks at Ruth, and they exchange innocent and unfrightened glances.

MAMA (*not understanding*):   Well, let them in, son.

BENEATHA (*from her room*):   We need some more string.

MAMA: Travis—you run to the hardware and get me some string cord.

Mama goes out and Walter turns and looks at Ruth. Travis goes to a dish for money.

RUTH: Why don't you answer the door, man?

WALTER (*suddenly bounding across the floor to embrace her*):   'Cause sometimes it hard to let the future begin! (*Stooping down in her face.*)

> I got wings! You got wings!
> All God's children got wings!

He crosses to the door and throws it open. Standing there is a very slight little man in a not-too-prosperous business suit and with haunted frightened eyes and a hat pulled down tightly, brim up, around his forehead. Travis passes between the men and exits. Walter leans deep in the man's face, still in his jubilance.

> When I get to heaven gonna put on my wings,
> Gonna fly all over God's heaven . . .

The little man just stares at him.

> Heaven—

Suddenly he stops and looks past the little man into the empty hallway.

> Where's Willy, man?

BOBO: He ain't with me.

WALTER (*not disturbed*):   Oh—come on in. You know my wife.

BOBO (*dumbly, taking off his hat*):   Yes—h'you, Miss Ruth.

RUTH (*quietly, a mood apart from her husband already, seeing Bobo*):   Hello, Bobo.

WALTER: You right on time today . . . Right on time. That's the way! (*He slaps Bobo on his back.*) Sit down . . . lemme hear.

Ruth stands stiffly and quietly in back of them, as though somehow she senses death, her eyes fixed on her husband.

BOBO (*his frightened eyes on the floor, his hat in his hands*):   Could I please get a drink of water, before I tell you about it, Walter Lee?

Walter does not take his eyes off the man. Ruth goes blindly to the tap and gets a glass of water and brings it to Bobo.

WALTER: There ain't nothing wrong, is there?

BOBO: Lemme tell you—

WALTER: Man—didn't nothing go wrong?

BOBO: Lemme tell you—Walter Lee. (*Looking at Ruth and talking to her more than to Walter.*) You know how it was. I got to tell you how it was. I mean first

I got to tell you how it was all the way . . . I mean about the money I put in, Walter Lee . . .

WALTER *(with taut agitation now):* What about the money you put in?

BOBO: Well—it wasn't much as we told you—me and Willy—*(He stops.)* I'm sorry, Walter. I got a bad feeling about it. I got a real bad feeling about it . . .

WALTER: Man, what you telling me about all this for? . . . Tell me what happened in Springfield . . .

BOBO: Springfield.

RUTH *(like a dead woman):* What was supposed to happen in Springfield?

BOBO *(to her):* This deal that me and Walter went into with Willy—Me and Willy was going to go down to Springfield and spread some money 'round so's we wouldn't have to wait so long for the liquor license . . . That's what we were going to do. Everybody said that was the way you had to do, you understand, Miss Ruth?

WALTER: Man—what happened down there?

BOBO *(a pitiful man, near tears):* I'm trying to tell you, Walter.

WALTER *(screaming at him suddenly):* THEN TELL ME, GODDAMMIT . . . WHAT'S THE MATTER WITH YOU?

BOBO: Man . . . I didn't go to no Springfield, yesterday.

WALTER *(halted, life hanging in the moment):* Why not?

BOBO *(the long way, the hard way to tell):* 'Cause I didn't have no reasons to . . .

WALTER: Man, what are you talking about!

BOBO: I'm talking about the fact that when I got to the train station yesterday morning—eight o'clock like we planned . . . Man—*Willy didn't never show up.*

WALTER: Why . . . where was he . . . where is he?

BOBO: That's what I'm trying to tell you . . . I don't know . . . I waited six hours . . . I called his house . . . and I waited . . . six hours . . . I waited in that train station six hours . . . *(Breaking into tears.)* That was all the extra money I had in the world . . . *(Looking up at Walter with the tears running down his face.)* Man, *Willy is gone.*

WALTER: Gone, what you mean Willy is gone? Gone where? You mean he went by himself. You mean he went off to Springfield by himself—to take care of getting the license—*(Turns and looks anxiously at Ruth.)* You mean maybe he didn't want too many people in on the business down there? *(Looks to Ruth again, as before.)* You know Willy got his own ways. *(Looks back to Bobo.)* Maybe you was late yesterday and he just went on down there without you. Maybe—maybe—he's been callin' you at home tryin' to tell you what happened or something. Maybe—maybe—he just got sick. He's somewhere—he's got to be somewhere. We just got to find him—me and you got to find him. *(Grabs Bobo senselessly by the collar and starts to shake him.)* We got to!

BOBO *(in sudden angry, frightened agony):* What's the matter with you, Walter! When a cat take off with your money he don't leave you no road maps!

WALTER *(turning madly, as though he is looking for Willy in the very room):* Willy! . . . Willy . . . don't do it . . . Please don't do it . . . Man, not with that money . . . Man, please, not with that money . . . Oh, God . . . Don't let it be true . . . *(He is wandering around, crying out for Willy and looking for him or perhaps for help from God.)* Man . . . I trusted you . . . Man, I put my life in your hands . . . *(He starts to crumple down on the floor as Ruth just covers her face in horror. Mama opens the door and comes into the room, with Beneatha behind her.)* Man . . . *(He starts to pound the floor with his fists, sobbing wildly.)* THAT MONEY IS MADE OUT OF MY FATHER'S FLESH —

BOBO *(standing over him helplessly)*: I'm sorry, Walter . . . *(only Walter's sobs reply. Bobo puts on his hat.)* I had my life staked on this deal, too . . .

He exits.

MAMA *(to Walter)*: Son — *(She goes to him, bends down to him, talks to his bent head.)* Son . . . Is it gone? Son, I gave you sixty-five hundred dollars. Is it gone? All of it? Beneatha's money too?

WALTER *(lifting his head slowly)*: Mama . . . I never . . . went to the bank at all . . .

MAMA *(not wanting to believe him)*: You mean . . . your sister's school money . . . you used that too . . . Walter? . . .

WALTER: Yessss! All of it . . . It's all gone . . .

There is total silence. Ruth stands with her face covered with her hands; Beneatha leans forlornly against a wall, fingering a piece of red ribbon from the mother's gift. Mama stops and looks at her son without recognition and then, quite without thinking about it, starts to beat him senselessly in the face. Beneatha goes to them and stops it.

BENEATHA: Mama!

Mama stops and looks at both of her children and rises slowly and wanders vaguely, aimlessly away from them.

MAMA: I seen . . . him . . . night after night . . . come in . . . and look at that rug . . . and then look at me . . . the red showing in his eyes . . . the veins moving in his head . . . I seen him grow thin and old before he was forty . . . working and working and working like somebody's old horse . . . killing himself . . . and you — you give it all away in a day — *(She raises her arms to strike him again.)*

BENEATHA: Mama —

MAMA: Oh, God . . . *(She looks up to Him.)* Look down here — and show me the strength.

BENEATHA: Mama —

MAMA *(folding over)*: Strength . . .

BENEATHA *(plaintively)*: Mama . . .

MAMA: Strength!

Curtain.

ACT 3

Time: An hour later.

    At curtain, there is a sullen light of gloom in the living room, gray light not unlike that which began the first scene of Act 1. At left we can see Walter within his room, alone with himself. He is stretched out on the bed, his shirt out and open, his arms under his head. He does not smoke, he does not cry out, he merely lies there, looking up at the ceiling, much as if he were alone in the world.

In the living room Beneatha sits at the table, still surrounded by the now almost ominous packing crates. She sits looking off. We feel that this is a mood struck perhaps an hour before, and it lingers now, full of the empty sound of profound disappointment. We see on a line from her brother's bedroom the sameness of their attitudes. Presently the bell rings and Beneatha rises without ambition or interest in answering. It is Asagai, smiling broadly, striding into the room with energy and happy expectation and conversation.

ASAGAI: I came over . . . I had some free time. I thought I might help with the packing. Ah, I like the look of packing crates! A household in preparation for a journey! It depresses some people . . . but for me . . . it is another feeling. Something full of the flow of life, do you understand? Movement, progress . . . It makes me think of Africa.

BENEATHA: Africa!

ASAGAI: What kind of a mood is this? Have I told you how deeply you move me?

BENEATHA: He gave away the money, Asagai . . .

ASAGAI: Who gave away what money?

BENEATHA: The insurance money. My brother gave it away.

ASAGAI: Gave it away?

BENEATHA: He made an investment! With a man even Travis wouldn't have trusted with his most worn-out marbles.

ASAGAI: And it's gone?

BENEATHA: Gone!

ASAGAI: I'm very sorry . . . And you, now?

BENEATHA: Me? . . . Me? . . . Me, I'm nothing . . . Me. When I was very small . . . we used to take our sleds out in the wintertime and the only hills we had were the ice-covered stone steps of some houses down the street. And we used to fill them in with snow and make them smooth and slide down them all day . . . and it was very dangerous, you know . . . far too steep . . . and sure enough one day a kid named Rufus came down too fast and hit the sidewalk and we saw his face just split open right there in front of us . . . And I remember standing there looking at his bloody open face thinking that was the end of Rufus. But the ambulance came and they took him to the hospital and they fixed the broken bones and they sewed it all up . . . and the next time I saw Rufus he just had a little line down the middle of his face . . . I never got over that . . .

ASAGAI: What?

BENEATHA: That that was what one person could do for another, fix him up— sew up the problem, make him all right again. That was the most marvelous thing in the world . . . I wanted to do that. I always thought it was the one concrete thing in the world that a human being could do. Fix up the sick, you know—and make them whole again. This was truly being God . . .

ASAGAI: You wanted to be God?

BENEATHA: No—I wanted to cure. It used to be so important to me. I wanted to cure. It used to matter. I used to care. I mean about people and how their bodies hurt . . .

ASAGAI: And you've stopped caring?

BENEATHA: Yes—I think so.

ASAGAI: Why?

BENEATHA *(bitterly):* Because it doesn't seem deep enough, close enough to what ails mankind! It was a child's way of seeing things—or an idealist's.

ASAGAI: Children see things very well sometimes—and idealists even better.

BENEATHA: I know that's what you think. Because you are still where I left off. You with all your talk and dreams about Africa! You still think you can patch up the world. Cure the Great Sore of Colonialism—*(Loftily, mocking it.)* with the Penicillin of Independence—!

ASAGAI: Yes!

BENEATHA: Independence *and then what?* What about all the crooks and thieves and just plain idiots who will come into power and steal and plunder the same as before—only now they will be black and do it in the name of the new Independence—WHAT ABOUT THEM?!

ASAGAI: That will be the problem for another time. First we must get there.

BENEATHA: And where does it end?

ASAGAI: End? Who even spoke of an end? To life? To living?

BENEATHA: An end to misery! To stupidity! Don't you see there isn't any real progress, Asagai, there is only one large circle that we march in, around and around, each of us with our own little picture in front of us—our own little mirage that we think is the future.

ASAGAI: That is the mistake.

BENEATHA: What?

ASAGAI: What you just said—about the circle. It isn't a circle—it is simply a long line—as in geometry, you know, one that reaches into infinity. And because we cannot see the end—we also cannot see how it changes. And it is very odd but those who see the changes—who dream, who will not give up—are called idealists . . . and those who see only the circle—we call *them* the "realists"!

BENEATHA: Asagai, while I was sleeping in that bed in there, people went out and took the future right out of my hands! And nobody asked me, nobody consulted me—they just went out and changed my life!

ASAGAI: Was it your money?

BENEATHA: What?

ASAGAI: Was it your money he gave away?

BENEATHA: It belonged to all of us.

ASAGAI: But did you earn it? Would you have had it at all if your father had not died?

BENEATHA: No.

ASAGAI: Then isn't there something wrong in a house—in a world—where all dreams, good or bad, must depend on the death of a man? I never thought to see *you* like this, Alaiyo. You! Your brother made a mistake and you are grateful to him so that now you can give up the ailing human race on account of it! You talk about what good is struggle, what good is anything! Where are we all going and why are we bothering!

BENEATHA: AND YOU CANNOT ANSWER IT!

ASAGAI (*shouting over her*): I LIVE THE ANSWER! (*Pause.*) In my village at home it is the exceptional man who can even read a newspaper . . . or who ever sees a book at all. I will go home and much of what I will have to say will seem strange to the people of my village. But I will teach and work and things will happen, slowly and swiftly. At times it will seem that nothing changes at all . . . and then again the sudden dramatic events which make history leap into the future. And then quiet again. Retrogression even. Guns, murder, revolution. And I even will have moments when I wonder if the quiet was not better than all that death and hatred. But I will look about my village at the illiteracy and disease and ignorance and I will not wonder long. And perhaps . . . perhaps I will be a great man . . . I mean perhaps I will hold on to the substance of truth and find my way always with the right course . . . and perhaps for it I will be butchered in my bed some night by the servants of empire . . .

BENEATHA: *The martyr!*

ASAGAI (*he smiles*): . . . or perhaps I shall live to be a very old man, respected and esteemed in my new nation . . . And perhaps I shall hold office and this is what I'm trying to tell you, Alaiyo: perhaps the things I believe now for my country will be wrong and outmoded, and I will not understand and do terrible things to have things my way or merely to keep my power. Don't you see that there will be young men and women — not British soldiers then, but my own black countrymen — to step out of the shadows some evening and slit my then useless throat? Don't you see they have always been there . . . that they always will be. And that such a thing as my own death will be an advance? They who might kill me even . . . actually replenish all that I was.

BENEATHA: Oh, Asagai, I know all that.

ASAGAI: Good! Then stop moaning and groaning and tell me what you plan to do.

BENEATHA: Do?

ASAGAI: I have a bit of a suggestion.

BENEATHA: What?

ASAGAI (*rather quietly for him*): That when it is all over — that you come home with me —

BENEATHA (*staring at him and crossing away with exasperation*): Oh — Asagai — at this moment you decide to be romantic!

ASAGAI (*quickly understanding the misunderstanding*): My dear, young creature of the New World — I do not mean across the city — I mean across the ocean: home — to Africa.

BENEATHA (*slowly understanding and turning to him with murmured amazement*): To Africa?

ASAGAI: Yes! . . . (*smiling and lifting his arms playfully.*) Three hundred years later the African Prince rose up out of the seas and swept the maiden back across the middle passage over which her ancestors had come —

BENEATHA *(unable to play)*: To—to Nigeria?

ASAGAI: Nigeria. Home. *(Coming to her with genuine romantic flippancy.)* I will show you our mountains and our stars; and give you cool drinks from gourds and teach you the old songs and the ways of our people—and, in time, we will pretend that—*(Very softly.)*—you have only been away for a day. Say that you'll come—*(He swings her around and takes her full in his arms in a kiss which proceeds to passion.)*

BENEATHA *(pulling away suddenly)*: You're getting me all mixed up—

ASAGAI: Why?

BENEATHA: Too many things—too many things have happened today. I must sit down and think. I don't know what I feel about anything right this minute.

She promptly sits down and props her chin on her fist.

ASAGAI *(charmed)*: All right, I shall leave you. No—don't get up. *(Touching her, gently, sweetly.)* Just sit awhile and think . . . Never be afraid to sit awhile and think. *(He goes to door and looks at her.)* How often I have looked at you and said, "Ah—so this is what the New World hath finally wrought . . ."

He exits. Beneatha sits on alone. Presently Walter enters from his room and starts to rummage through things, feverishly looking for something. She looks up and turns in her seat.

BENEATHA *(hissingly)*: Yes—just look at what the New World hath wrought! . . . Just look! *(She gestures with bitter disgust.)* There he is! *Monsieur le petit bourgeois noir*°—himself! There he is—Symbol of a Rising Class! Entrepreneur! Titan of the system! *(Walter ignores her completely and continues frantically and destructively looking for something and hurling things to floor and tearing things out of their place in his search. Beneatha ignores the eccentricity of his actions and goes on with the monologue of insult.)* Did you dream of yachts on Lake Michigan, Brother? Did you see yourself on that Great Day sitting down at the Conference Table, surrounded by all the mighty bald-headed men in America? All halted, waiting, breathless, waiting for your pronouncements on industry? Waiting for you—Chairman of the Board! *(Walter finds what he is looking for—a small piece of white paper—and pushes it in his pocket and puts on his coat and rushes out without ever having looked at her. She shouts after him.)* I look at you and I see the final triumph of stupidity in the world!

The door slams and she returns to just sitting again. Ruth comes quickly out of Mama's room.

RUTH: Who was that?

BENEATHA: Your husband.

RUTH: Where did he go?

BENEATHA: Who knows—maybe he has an appointment at U.S. Steel.

RUTH *(anxiously, with frightened eyes)*: You didn't say nothing bad to him, did you?

Monsieur le petit bourgeois noir: Mr. Black Bourgoisie (French).

BENEATHA: Bad? Say anything bad to him? No—I told him he was a sweet boy and full of dreams and everything is strictly peachy keen, as the ofay kids say!

Mama enters from her bedroom. She is lost, vague, trying to catch hold, to make some sense of her former command of the world, but it still eludes her. A sense of waste overwhelms her gait; a measure of apology rides on her shoulders. She goes to her plant, which has remained on the table, looks at it, picks it up and takes it to the window sill and sits it outside, and she stands and looks at it a long moment. Then she closes the window, straightens her body with effort and turns around to her children.

MAMA: Well—ain't it a mess in here, though? (*A false cheerfulness, a beginning of something.*) I guess we all better stop moping around and get some work done. All this unpacking and everything we got to do. (*Ruth raises her head slowly in response to the sense of the line; and Beneatha in similar manner turns very slowly to look at her mother.*) One of you all better call the moving people and tell 'em not to come.

RUTH: Tell 'em not to come?

MAMA: Of course, baby. Ain't no need in 'em coming all the way here and having to go back. They charges for that too. (*She sits down, fingers to her brow, thinking.*) Lord, ever since I was a little girl, I always remembers people saying, "Lena—Lena Eggleston, you aims too high all the time. You needs to slow down and see life a little more like it is. Just slow down some." That's what they always used to say down home—"Lord, that Lena Eggleston is a high-minded thing. She'll get her due one day!"

RUTH: No, Lena . . .

MAMA: Me and Big Walter just didn't never learn right.

RUTH: Lena, no! We gotta go. Bennie—tell her . . .

She rises and crosses to Beneatha with her arms outstretched. Beneatha doesn't respond.

Tell her we can still move . . . the notes ain't but a hundred and twenty-five a month. We got four grown people in this house—we can work . . .

MAMA (*to herself*):   Just aimed too high all the time—

RUTH (*turning and going to Mama fast—the words pouring out with urgency and desperation*):   Lena—I'll work . . . I'll work twenty hours a day in all the kitchens in Chicago . . . I'll strap my baby on my back if I have to and scrub all the floors in America and wash all the sheets in America if I have to—but we got to MOVE! We got to get OUT OF HERE!!

Mama reaches out absently and pats Ruth's hand.

MAMA: No—I sees things differently now. Been thinking 'bout some of the things we could do to fix this place up some. I seen a second-hand bureau over on Maxwell Street just the other day that could fit right there. (*She points to where the new furniture might go. Ruth wanders away from her.*) Would need some new handles on it and then a little varnish and it look like something brand-new. And—we can put up them new curtains in the kitchen . . . Why this place be looking fine. Cheer us all up so that we forget trouble ever come . . . (*To Ruth.*) And you could get some nice screens to put up in your room round the baby's bassinet . . . *(She looks at both of them pleadingly.)* Sometimes you just got to know when to give up some things . . . and hold on to what you got . . .

Walter enters from the outside, looking spent and leaning against the door, his coat hanging from him.

MAMA: Where you been, son?

WALTER *(breathing hard)*: Made a call.

MAMA: To who, son?

WALTER: To The Man. *(He heads for his room.)*

MAMA: What man, baby?

WALTER *(stops in the door)*: The Man, Mama. Don't you know who The Man is?

RUTH: Walter Lee?

WALTER: *The Man*. Like the guys in the streets say — The Man. Captain Boss — Mistuh Charley . . . Old Cap'n Please Mr. Bossman . . .

BENEATHA *(suddenly)*: Lindner!

WALTER: That's right! That's good. I told him to come right over.

BENEATHA *(fiercely, understanding)*: For what? What do you want to see him for!

WALTER *(looking at his sister)*: We going to do business with him.

MAMA: What you talking 'bout, son?

WALTER: Talking 'bout life, Mama. You all always telling me to see life like it is. Well — I laid in there on my back today . . . and I figured it out. Life just like it is. Who gets and who don't get. *(He sits down with his coat on and laughs.)* Mama, you know it's all divided up. Life is. Sure enough. Between the takers and the "tooken." *(He laughs.)* I've figured it out finally. *(He looks around at them.)* Yeah. Some of us always getting "tooken." *(He laughs.)* People like Willy Harris, they don't never get "tooken." And you know why the rest of us do? 'Cause we all mixed up. Mixed up bad. We get to looking 'round for the right and the wrong; and we worry about it and cry about it and stay up nights trying to figure out 'bout the wrong and the right of things all the time . . . And all the time, man, them takers is out there operating, just taking and taking. Willy Harris? Shoot — Willy Harris don't even count. He don't even count in the big scheme of things. But I'll say one thing for old Willy Harris . . . he's taught me something. He's taught me to keep my eye on what counts in this world. Yeah — *(Shouting out a little.)* Thanks, Willy!

RUTH: What did you call that man for, Walter Lee?

WALTER: Called him to tell him to come on over to the show. Gonna put on a show for the man. Just what he wants to see. You see, Mama, the man came here today and he told us that them people out there where you want us to move — well they so upset they willing to pay us *not* to move! *(He laughs again.)* And — and oh, Mama — you would of been proud of the way me and Ruth and Bennie acted. We told him to get out . . . Lord have mercy! We told the man to get out! Oh, we was some proud folks this afternoon, yeah. *(He lights a cigarette.)* We were still full of that old-time stuff . . .

RUTH *(coming toward him slowly)*: You talking 'bout taking them people's money to keep us from moving in that house?

WALTER: I ain't just talking 'bout it, baby — I'm telling you that's what's going to happen!

BENEATHA: Oh, God! Where is the bottom! Where is the real honest-to-God bottom so he can't go any farther!

WALTER: See — that's the old stuff. You and that boy that was here today. You all want everybody to carry a flag and a spear and sing some marching songs, huh? You wanna spend your life looking into things and trying to find the right and the wrong part, huh? Yeah. You know what's going to happen to that boy someday — he'll find himself sitting in a dungeon, locked in forever — and the takers will have the key! Forget it, baby! There ain't no causes — there ain't nothing but taking in this world, and he who takes most is smartest — and it don't make a damn bit of difference *how*.

MAMA: You making something inside me cry, son. Some awful pain inside me.

WALTER: Don't cry, Mama. Understand. That white man is going to walk in that door able to write checks for more money than we ever had. It's important to him and I'm going to help him . . . I'm going to put on the show, Mama.

MAMA: Son — I come from five generations of people who was slaves and share-croppers — but ain't nobody in my family never let nobody pay 'em no money that was a way of telling us we wasn't fit to walk the earth. We ain't never been that poor. (*Raising her eyes and looking at him.*) We ain't never been that — dead inside.

BENEATHA: Well — we are dead now. All the talk about dreams and sunlight that goes on in this house. It's all dead now.

WALTER: What's the matter with you all! I didn't make this world! It was give to me this way! Hell, yes, I want me some yachts someday! Yes, I want to hang some real pearls 'round my wife's neck. Ain't she supposed to wear no pearls? Somebody tell me — tell me, who decides which women is suppose to wear pearls in this world. I tell you I am a *man* — and I think my wife should wear some pearls in this world!

This last line hangs a good while and Walter begins to move about the room. The word "Man" has penetrated his consciousness; he mumbles it to himself repeatedly between strange agitated pauses as he moves about.

MAMA: Baby, how you going to feel on the inside?

WALTER: Fine! . . . Going to feel fine . . . a man . . .

MAMA: You won't have nothing left then, Walter Lee.

WALTER (*coming to her*): I'm going to feel fine, Mama. I'm going to look that son-of-a-bitch in the eyes and say — (*He falters.*) — and say, "All right, Mr. Lindner — (*He falters even more.*) — that's *your* neighborhood out there! You got the right to keep it like you want! You got the right to have it like you want! Just write the check and — the house is yours." And — and I am going to say — (*His voice almost breaks.*) "And you — you people just put the money in my hand and you won't have to live next to this bunch of stinking niggers! . . ." (*He straightens up and moves away from his mother, walking around the room.*) And maybe — maybe I'll just get down on my black knees . . . (*He does so; Ruth and Bennie and Mama watch him in frozen horror.)* "Captain, Mistuh, Bossman — *(Groveling and grinning and wringing his hands in profoundly anguished imitation of the slow-witted movie stereotype.)* A-hee-hee-hee! Oh, yassuh boss! Yasssssuh! Great white — *(Voice breaking, he forces himself to go on.)* — Father, just gi' ussen de money, fo' God's sake, and we's — we's ain't gwine come out deh and dirty up yo' white folks neighborhood . . ." *(He breaks down completely.)* And I'll feel fine! Fine! FINE! *(He gets up and goes into the bedroom.)*

BENEATHA: That is not a man. That is nothing but a toothless rat.

MAMA: Yes — death done come in this here house. *(She is nodding, slowly, reflectively.)* Done come walking in my house on the lips of my children. You what supposed to be my beginning again. You — what supposed to be my harvest. *(To Beneatha.)* You — you mourning your brother?

BENEATHA: He's no brother of mine.

MAMA: What you say?

BENEATHA: I said that that individual in that room is no brother of mine.

MAMA: That's what I thought you said. You feeling like you better than he is today? *(Beneatha does not answer.)* Yes? What you tell him a minute ago? That he wasn't a man? Yes? You give him up for me? You done wrote his epitaph too — like the rest of the world? Well, who give you the privilege?

BENEATHA: Be on my side for once! You saw what he just did, Mama! You saw him — down on his knees. Wasn't it you who taught me to despise any man who would do that? Do what he's going to do?

MAMA: Yes — I taught you that. Me and your daddy. But I thought I taught you something else too . . . I thought I taught you to love him.

BENEATHA: Love him? There is nothing left to love.

MAMA: There is *always* something left to love. And if you ain't learned that, you ain't learned nothing. *(Looking at her.)* Have you cried for that boy today? I don't mean for yourself and for the family 'cause we lost the money. I mean for him: what he been through and what it done to him. Child, when do you think is the time to love somebody the most? When they done good and made things easy for everybody? Well then, you ain't through learning — because that ain't the time at all. It's when he's at his lowest and can't believe in hisself 'cause the world done whipped him so! When you starts measuring somebody, measure him right, child, measure him right. Make sure you done taken into account what hills and valleys he come through before he got to wherever he is.

Travis bursts into the room at the end of the speech, leaving the door open.

TRAVIS: Grandmama — the moving men are downstairs! The truck just pulled up.

MAMA *(turning and looking at him)*: Are they, baby? They downstairs?

She sighs and sits. Lindner appears in the doorway. He peers in and knocks lightly, to gain attention, and comes in. All turn to look at him.

LINDNER *(hat and briefcase in hand)*: Uh — hello . . .

Ruth crosses mechanically to the bedroom door and opens it and lets it swing open freely and slowly as the lights come up on Walter within, still in his coat, sitting at the far corner of the room. He looks up and out through the room to Lindner.

RUTH: He's here.

A long minute passes and Walter slowly gets up.

LINDNER *(coming to the table with efficiency, putting his briefcase on the table and starting to unfold papers and unscrew fountain pens):*   Well, I certainly was glad to hear from you people. *(Walter has begun the trek out of the room, slowly and awkwardly, rather like a small boy, passing the back of his sleeve across his mouth from time to time.)* Life can really be so much simpler than people let it be most of the time. Well—with whom do I negotiate? You, Mrs. Younger, or your son here? *(Mama sits with her hands folded on her lap and her eyes closed as Walter advances. Travis goes closer to Lindner and looks at the papers curiously.)* Just some official papers, sonny.

RUTH: Travis, you go downstairs—

MAMA *(opening her eyes and looking into Walter's):*   No. Travis, you stay right here. And you make him understand what you doing, Walter Lee. You teach him good. Like Willy Harris taught you. You show where our five genera-tions done come to. *(Walter looks from her to the boy, who grins at him inno-cently.)* Go ahead, son—*(She folds her hands and closes her eyes.)* Go ahead.

WALTER *(at last crosses to Lindner, who is reviewing the contract):*   Well, Mr. Lindner. *(Beneatha turns away.)* We called you—*(There is a profound, simple groping quality in his speech.)*—because, well, me and my family *(He looks around and shifts from one foot to the other.)* Well—we are very plain people . . .

LINDNER: Yes—

WALTER: I mean—I have worked as a chauffeur most of my life—and my wife here, she does domestic work in people's kitchens. So does my mother. I mean—we are plain people . . .

LINDNER: Yes, Mr. Younger—

WALTER *(really like a small boy, looking down at his shoes and then up at the man):*   And—uh—well, my father, well, he was a laborer most of his life. . . .

LINDNER *(absolutely confused):*   Uh, yes—yes, I understand. *(He turns back to the contract.)*

WALTER *(a beat; staring at him):*   And my father—*(With sudden intensity.)* My father almost *beat a man to death* once because this man called him a bad name or something, you know what I mean?

LINDNER *(looking up, frozen):*   No, no, I'm afraid I don't—

WALTER *(a beat. The tension hangs; then Walter steps back from it):*   Yeah. Well—what I mean is that we come from people who had a lot of *pride.* I mean—we are very proud people. And that's my sister over there and she's going to be a doctor—and we are very proud—

LINDNER: Well—I am sure that is very nice, but—

WALTER: What I am telling you is that we called you over here to tell you that we are very proud and that this—*(Signaling to Travis.)* Travis, come here. *(Travis crosses and Walter draws him before him facing the man.)* This is my son, and he makes the sixth generation our family in this country. And we have all thought about your offer—

LINDNER: Well, good . . . good—

WALTER: And we have decided to move into our house because my father—my father—he earned it for us brick by brick. *(Mama has her eyes closed and is rocking back and forth as though she were in church, with her head nodding the Amen yes.)* We don't want to make no trouble for nobody or fight no causes, and we will try to be good neighbors. And that's *all* we got to say about that. *(He looks the man absolutely in the eyes.)* We don't want your money. *(He turns and walks away.)*

LINDNER *(looking around at all of them):* I take it then—that you have decided to occupy . . .

BENEATHA: That's what the man said.

LINDNER *(to Mama in her reverie):* Then I would like to appeal to you, Mrs. Younger. You are older and wiser and understand things better I am sure . . .

MAMA: I am afraid you don't understand. My son said we was going to move and there ain't nothing left for me to say. *(Briskly.)* You know how these young folks is nowadays, mister. Can't do a thing with 'em! *(As he opens his mouth, she rises.)* Good-bye.

LINDNER *(folding up his materials):* Well—if you are that final about it . . . there is nothing left for me to say. *(He finishes, almost ignored by the family, who are concentrating on Walter Lee. At the door Lindner halts and looks around.)* I sure hope you people know what you're getting into.

He shakes his head and exits.

RUTH *(looking around and coming to life):* Well, for God's sake—if the moving men are here—LET'S GET THE HELL OUT OF HERE!

MAMA *(into action):* Ain't it the truth! Look at all this here mess. Ruth, put Travis' good jacket on him . . . Walter Lee, fix your tie and tuck your shirt in, you look like somebody's hoodlum! Lord have mercy, where is my plant? *(She flies to get it amid the general bustling of the family, who are deliberately trying to ignore the nobility of the past moment.)* You all start on down . . . Travis child, don't go empty-handed . . . Ruth, where did I put that box with my skillets in it? I want to be in charge of it myself . . . I'm going to make us the biggest dinner we ever ate tonight . . . Beneatha, what's the matter with them stockings? Pull them things up, girl . . .

The family starts to file out as two moving men appear and begin to carry out the heavier pieces of furniture, bumping into the family as they move about.

BENEATHA: Mama, Asagai asked me to marry him today and go to Africa—

MAMA *(in the middle of her getting-ready activity):* He did? You ain't old enough to marry nobody—*(Seeing the moving men lifting one of her chairs precariously.)* Darling, that ain't no bale of cotton, please handle it so we can sit in it again! I had that chair twenty-five years . . .

The movers sigh with exasperation and go on with their work.

BENEATHA *(girlishly and unreasonably trying to pursue the conversation):* To go to Africa, Mama—be a doctor in Africa . . .

MAMA *(distracted):* Yes, baby—

WALTER: *Africa!* What he want you to go to Africa for?

BENEATHA: To practice there . . .

WALTER: Girl, if you don't get all them silly ideas out your head! You better marry yourself a man with some loot . . .

BENEATHA *(angrily, precisely as in the first scene of the play):* What have you got to do with who I marry!

WALTER: Plenty. Now I think George Murchison —

BENEATHA: *George Murchison!* I wouldn't marry him if he was Adam and I was Eve!

Walter and Beneatha go out yelling at each other vigorously and the anger is loud and real till their voices diminish. Ruth stands at the door and turns to Mama and smiles knowingly.

MAMA *(fixing her hat at last):* Yeah — they something all right, my children . . .

RUTH: Yeah — they're something. Let's go, Lena.

MAMA *(stalling, starting to look around at the house):* Yes — I'm coming. Ruth —

RUTH: Yes?

MAMA *(quietly, woman to woman):* He finally come into his manhood today, didn't he? Kind of like a rainbow after the rain . . .

RUTH *(biting her lip lest her own pride explode in front of Mama):* Yes, Lena.

Walter's voice calls for them raucously.

WALTER *(offstage):* Y'all come on! These people charges by the hour, you know!

MAMA *(waving Ruth out vaguely):* All right, honey — go on down. I be down directly.

Ruth hesitates, then exits. Mama stands, at last alone in the living room, her plant on the table before her as the lights start to come down. She looks around at all the walls and ceilings and suddenly, despite herself, while the children call below, a great heaving thing rises in her and she puts her fist to her mouth to stifle it, takes a final desperate look, pulls her coat about her, pats her hat, and goes out. The lights dim down. The door opens and she comes back in, grabs her plant, and goes out for the last time.

Curtain.   [1959]

THINKING ABOUT THE TEXT

1. The play's main characters are Walter Lee, Mama, Ruth, and Beneatha. List three or more adjectives to describe each of these characters. What basic values does each character seem to express during the arguments that occur in their family? Do you sympathize with them equally? Why, or why not? What, evidently, was Walter Lee's father like?

2. At the end of the play, speaking to Ruth about Walter Lee, Mama says "He finally come into his manhood today, didn't he"? How does Mama appear to be defining *manhood*? What other possible definitions of *manhood* come up directly or indirectly in the play? Identify places where

characteristics of *womanhood* are brought up. In general, would you say that gender is at least as important in this play as race is? Why, or why not?

3. Analyze Asagai's conversations with Beneatha and the rest of her family. What does Hansberry suggest about the relations of Africans and African Americans in the late 1950s?

4. Although there is a white character, he makes only two relatively brief appearances, and no other white characters are shown. Why do you suppose Hansberry keeps the presence of whites minimal?

5. Do you think this play is universal in its truths and concerns, or are you more inclined to see it as specifically about African Americans? Explain. In what ways is this 1959 play relevant to life in the United States today?

THE CRISIS

The Hansberrys of Chicago: They Join Business Acumen with Social Vision

The following article appeared in the April 1941 issue of The Crisis, *the journal of the National Association for the Advancement of Colored People (NAACP). The photographs to which the article refers are omitted. The NAACP was established in 1909 and* The Crisis *a year later, its founder and first editor being the noted African American intellectual W. E. B. Du Bois. This article pays tribute to Lorraine Hansberry's parents; it notes their successful real estate business, the foundation they established to get civil rights laws enforced, and their 1940 Supreme Court victory. The Court's decision was meant to erode at least some racial covenants, policies by which white neighborhoods kept out blacks. However, the decision lacked enforcement and very little changed.*

Mr. and Mrs. Carl A. Hansberry of Chicago, Ill., have the distinction not only of conducting one of the largest real estate enterprises in the country operated by Negroes but they are unique business people because they are spending much of their wealth to safeguard the civil rights of colored citizens in their city, state, and nation.

The properties shown on these pages are a part of the $250,000.00 worth of Chicago real estate from which The Hansberry Enterprises and The Hansberry Foundation receive a gross annual income of $100,000.00. The real estate firm makes available to Negroes with limited income apartments within their economic reach, while the profits from this enterprise are used to safeguard the Negro's civil rights and to make additional housing available to him. The Hansberrys played a very significant role in the recent Chicago restrictive covenant case before the United States Supreme Court whose decision opened blocks of houses and apartment buildings from which Negroes formerly had been excluded.

THE HANSBERRY ENTERPRISES

The Hansberry Enterprises is a real estate syndicate founded by Mr. Hansberry in 1929. From a very modest beginning, the business has grown to be one of the largest in the Mid-West. The property owned and controlled by the company is in excess of $250,000 in value and accommodates four hundred families. During the past ten years the payroll and commissions have aggregated more than $350,000.00.

The offices of the Hansberry Enterprises are located at 4247 Indiana Avenue, Chicago, Ill.

THE HANSBERRY FOUNDATION

The Hansberry Foundation was established in 1936 by Mrs. N. Louise   5
Hansberry, and her husband, Carl A. Hansberry, with substantial grants of the interest from the Hansberry Enterprises. Mr. Hansberry is the Director. The Foundation was set up as a Trust Fund and only the members of the immediate Hansberry family may contribute to this Fund. A provision of the Trust provides "That during the first ten (10) years only 60 percent of the income of the trust may be used, thereafter, both the income and the principal may be used, but at no time shall the principal be reduced to less than Ten Thousand ($10,000.00) dollars."

The purpose of the Foundation is to encourage and promote respect for all laws, and especially those laws as related to the Civil Rights of American citizens. The following paragraph taken from a letter to the Cook County Bar Association under date of April 27, 1937, gives a precise statement of the purpose and scope of the Hansberry Foundation:

> The Creators of the Hansberry Foundation believe that the Illinois Civil Rights Law represents the crystallized views of the best citizens of Illinois and were made in the best interest of the whole people of Illinois. They therefore believed, that the Civil Rights Code should be enforced; that the passiveness of any citizen should cease. Because of and in view of the foregoing premises, the Hansberry Foundation was created and now therefore announces its desire to cooperate with sympathetic public officials, associations, or organizations, likewise interested in the active enforcement of the Civil Rights Laws of Illinois and throughout the Nation. The Foundation will assume (at its discretion) a part, or all of the costs of prosecuting violations of the law wherever, and/or whenever, the authorities willfully neglect or refuse to act; and where the victims are financially unable to protect themselves.

[1941]

THINKING ABOUT THE TEXT

1. What do you sense is the main rhetorical purpose of *The Crisis* in publishing this article? Does anyone in *A Raisin in the Sun* share the values expressed by the article? To what extent do you aim to "join business acumen with social vision"?

2. Much of the article consists of quotations from legal documents associated with the Hansberry Foundation. What do you think of this rhetorical strategy?

3. The article makes clear that when Lorraine Hansberry's family sought to live in an all-white part of Chicago, they were wealthier than the Youngers. What would you say to someone who argued that it would have been more honest of Hansberry to focus her play on a family as well-off as hers?

LORRAINE HANSBERRY
April 23, 1964, *Letter to the* New York Times

Here is part of a letter by Lorraine Hansberry written five years after A Raisin in the Sun. *Once again, she quotes the poem by Langston Hughes containing her play's title. Now, however, she is expressing approval of civil rights activists' aggressive tactics, including attempts by the Congress of Racial Equality (CORE) to block traffic. In her letter, Hansberry also recalls her family's fight against racial covenants and her father's subsequent death in Mexico. Although the* New York Times *never published Hansberry's letter, some of it was included by her husband Robert Nemiroff in his 1969 compilation of her writings* To Be Young, Gifted, and Black.

April 23, 1964

To the Editor,
The New York Times:

. . . My father was typical of a generation of Negroes who believed that the "American way" could successfully be made to work to democratize the United States. Thus, twenty-five years ago, he spent a small personal fortune, his considerable talents, and many years of his life fighting, in association with NAACP attorneys, Chicago's "restrictive covenants" in one of this nation's ugliest ghettoes.

That fight also required that our family occupy the disputed property in a hellishly hostile "white neighborhood" in which, literally, howling mobs surrounded our house. One of their missiles almost took the life of the then eight-year-old signer of this letter. My memories of this "correct" way of fighting white supremacy in America include being spat at, cursed and pummeled in the daily trek to and from school. And I also remember my desperate and courageous mother, patrolling our house all night with a loaded German luger, doggedly guarding her four children, while my father fought the respectable part of the battle in the Washington court.

The fact that my father and the NAACP "won" a Supreme Court decision, in a now famous case which bears his name in the lawbooks, is — ironically — the sort of "progress" our satisfied friends allude to when they presume to deride the more radical means of struggle. The cost, in emotional turmoil, time and money, which led to my father's early death as a permanently embittered exile in a foreign country when he saw that after such sacrificial efforts the Negroes of Chicago were as ghetto-locked as ever, does not seem to figure in their calculations.

That is the reality that I am faced with when I now read that some Negroes my own age and younger say that we must now lie down in the streets, tie up traffic, do whatever we can — take to the hills with guns if necessary — and fight back. Fatuous people remark these days on our "bitterness." Why, of course we are bitter. The entire situation suggests that the nation be reminded of the too little noted final lines of Langston Hughes' mighty poem:

> *What happens to a dream deferred?*
>
> > Does it dry up
> > Like a raisin in the sun?
> > Or fester like a sore —
> > And then run?
> > Does it stink like rotten meat?
> > Or crust and sugar over —
> > Like a syrupy sweet?
>
> > Maybe it just sags
> > Like a heavy load.
>
> *Or does it explode?*

Sincerely,
Lorraine Hansberry
[1964]

THINKING ABOUT THE TEXT

1. Hansberry indicates that she is "bitter." Is *bitter* a word that you associate with the author of *A Raisin in the Sun*? Why, or why not? Do you get the sense that the bitterness she refers to in her letter is justified? Why, or why not?

2. Does Hansberry's play give you the impression that the family in it will suffer the same kinds of things described in the second paragraph of Hansberry's letter? Support your answer with details from the play.

3. In the letter, Hansberry seems to condone acts of civil disobedience. In what kinds of cases, if any, do you think people are justified in breaking the law?

ALAN EHRENHALT

From *The Lost City: Discovering the Forgotten Virtues of Community in the Chicago of the 1950s*

Alan Ehrenhalt (b. 1947) is the executive editor of Governing *magazine and was formerly political editor of* Congressional Quarterly. *In much of his writing, he argues that Americans will achieve true democracy only if they regain the sense of community they once had. This is the basic claim of Ehrenhalt's first book,* The

United States of Ambition: Politicians, Power, and the Pursuit of Office *(1991)*. *In his second,* The Lost City: Discovering the Forgotten Virtues of Community in the Chicago of the 1950s *(1995), he extends his concern with community spirit by focusing on the role it played in Chicago during the 1950s. The following excerpts deal with Bronzeville, the South Side ghetto where Lorraine Hansberry grew up and where her 1959 play* A Raisin in the Sun *takes place.*

    If St. Nick's parish° was a world of limited choices, a far more limited world existed five miles further east, where the bulk of Chicago's black community—hundreds of thousands of people—lived together in Bronzeville, a neighborhood they were all but prohibited from escaping.

    Any discussion of the city we have lost during the past generation must eventually confront the issue of Bronzeville, and the question that may be most troublesome of all: Have we lost something important that existed even in the worst place that the Chicago of the 1950s had to offer?

    Anybody who did not live in a black ghetto is bound to be leery of asking the question, with its implied assumption that segregation hid its good points. But the fact remains, long after Bronzeville's disappearance from the map, that a remarkable number of people who did live there find themselves asking it.

    "Fifty-first and Dearborn was a bunch of shacks," Alice Blair wrote thirty years later, after she had become Chicago's deputy superintendent of education. "We didn't have hot water—and the houses were torn down for slum clearance to build Robert Taylor Homes. But in those shacks, there was something different from what is there now."

    What was it, exactly? Several things. "People took a great deal of pride in just being where they were," says John Stroger, the first black president of the Cook County Board of Commissioners. "It was economically poor, but spiritually and socially rich. People had hope that things would be better." Stroger echoes what Vernon Jarrett, the longtime Chicago newspaper columnist, said rather hauntingly a few years ago. "The ghetto used to have something going for it. It had a beat, it had a certain rhythm, and it was all hope. I don't care how rough things were."   5

    Then there is the bluntness of Timuel Black, a lifelong civil rights activist, looking back at age seventy-five on the South Side as it used to be and as it has become: "I would say," he declares at the end of a long conversation, "at this point in my life and experience, that we made a mistake leaving the ghetto."

    These fragments prove nothing. To many who read them, they will suggest merely that nostalgia is not only powerful but dangerous, that late in life it can generate a fondness for times and places that should be properly remembered with nothing more than relief that they are gone. And yet something valuable did die with Bronzeville, and we can learn something about community and authority, faith and hope, by tracing their presence even in what was, by common agreement, an unjust and constricted corner of the world.

St. Nick's parish: St. Nicholas of Tolentine parish, a post-immigrant, working-class neighborhood of Chicago.

What Bronzeville had, and so many of its graduates continue to mourn, was a sense of posterity—a feeling that, however difficult the present might be, the future was worth thinking about and planning for in some detail. Most of the inhabitants of Bronzeville were farsighted people, able to focus on events and ideas whose outlines were hazy and whose arrival might still be very far away. They were looking forward to a time in which it would be possible to break free of the constrictions and indignities of the moment.

Forty years later, in a time-shortened world hooked on fax machines, microwave popcorn, and MTV, the word *posterity* carries far less meaning than it once did. Its gradual disappearance is one of the genuine losses of modern life. To find the concept so vibrant and well entrenched in a place as deprived as Bronzeville in the 1950s seems to mock the freer but far less anchored world that most of us inhabit today.

The indignities of life for a black person on the South Side in the 1950s are   10
unlikely to come as news to very many readers of any race, but some details are worth dredging up. They reveal the triumphs and comforts of Bronzeville society to have been that much more impressive.

It was, for example, uncommonly dangerous for a black Chicagoan to get sick. Of the seventy-seven hospitals in the metropolitan area, only six would accept black patients at all, and five of those had quotas, so that once a certain small number of beds were occupied by blacks, the next black patient would be turned away, no matter how ill he or she was. It was not unusual for blacks who could perfectly well afford private hospital care to be taken to Cook County Hospital, the spartan and overcrowded charity institution on the West Side.

Most of the time, though, even in an emergency, they would be rushed to Provident, the city's only "black" hospital, sometimes speeding past one white facility after another to get to the Provident emergency room. In 1956, Provident saw an emergency patient every nineteen minutes, five times the average for the city's other hospitals. And it was, of course, the only place where a black doctor could aspire to practice; the other hospitals did their hiring on a strict Jim Crow basis.

Getting stopped for a traffic ticket on the South Side was not the same experience for blacks that it was for whites. Until 1958, all traffic tickets in Chicago mentioned the race of the driver. The police maintained a special task force, known to just about everybody as the "flying squad," which was supposed to zero in on high-crime neighborhoods but in fact spent a good deal of its time harassing black citizens, middle-class as well as poor. It was standard practice for flying squad officers to stop black motorists for traffic violations, frisk them, and search their cars before writing the ticket, often abusing them verbally and physically in the process. The abuses nearly always took place when someone was driving alone, so there were rarely any witnesses.

The force that patrolled these neighborhoods was still mostly white, and the supervisors were essentially all white. There were 1,200 black police officers in Chicago in 1957, but only one black captain, and no lieutenants. In the Englewood district, where many of the new recruits were sent, black patrolmen were nearly always given the most tedious assignments: guard duty night after night, or a motorcycle beat in the depths of winter. The two-man teams were all segregated; blacks and whites were not allowed to work together.

Meanwhile, the public schools were not only segregated but demonstrably   15
unequal. Most of the white elementary schools on the South Side were underused, while the black ones were jammed far beyond capacity. Some black schools in Bronzeville were handling more than 2,000 pupils a day on a double-shift basis, with one set of children in attendance from 8 A.M. to noon and another from noon to 4 P.M. At the same time, there were nearly 300 vacant classrooms elsewhere in the city and more than 1,000 classrooms being used for nonessential activities of one sort or another. But the school board did not want to adjust the district lines to permit black kids to take advantage of the space that existed beyond the racial borders.

The incidents of hospital bias, police harassment, and school inequity pointed up just how indifferent Jim Crow was to class distinctions in the 1950s: having money was simply no help in these situations. There was a fourth indignity that somehow makes this point even clearer, and it had to do with travel and vacations.

For $20 a year in 1957, a black family could join an organization called the Tourist Motor Club. What they received in return was a list of hotels and restaurants where blacks would be allowed inside the door, and a guarantee of $500 in bond money in case they found themselves being arrested for making the wrong choice. "Are you ready for any traveling emergency — even in a hostile town?" the Tourist Motor Club asked in its ads, and not unreasonably. "What would you do if you were involved in a highway accident in a hostile town — far away from home. You could lose your life savings — you could be kept in jail without adequate reason. You could lose your entire vacation fighting unjust prejudice."

Vacations were for those who could afford them. The problem that united everyone in the black community — wealthy, working class, and poor — was housing. Unlike St. Nick's or any other white community in Chicago, the ghetto was almost impossible to move out of. The rules of segregation simply made it difficult for a black family to live anywhere else, whether it could afford to or not.

By 1957, that had begun to change. Chicago's South Side black population was expanding, block by block, into what had been white working-class territory on its southern and western borders, and a new, separate black enclave had emerged a few miles west of downtown. But as a practical matter, the number of decent housing opportunities opening up for blacks was far smaller than the number needed. Thus, most of the city's black community remained where it had been since the 1920s: in a narrow strip south of Twenty-third Street, roughly eight miles long and still no more than two or three miles wide.

This ghetto had been badly overcrowded by the time of World War II, and in   20
the years since then it had grown more crowded still. The number of black people in Chicago had increased nearly 40 percent between 1950 and 1956, while the white population was declining. And the newcomers were simply stacking up on top of one another. The Kenwood-Oakland neighborhood, centered around Forty-seventh Street, had gone from 13,000 white residents to 80,000 blacks in a matter of

a few years. "A new Negro reaches this sprawling city every fifteen minutes," the young black journalist Carl Rowan wrote in 1957, seeming a little overwhelmed himself. Parts of the South Side that had once been relatively spacious and comfortable now held more people than anyone had imagined possible.

The physical world that those migrants confronted was the world of the infamous "kitchenette" — a one-room flat with an icebox, a bed, and a hotplate, typically in an ancient building that once held a few spacious apartments but had been cut up into the tiniest possible pieces to bring the landlord more money. The bathroom and stove were shared with neighbors, a dozen or more people taking turns with the same meager facilities. . . .

In Bronzeville, hope and authority tended to come out of the same package. If the ultimate authority figures were wealthy white people somewhere far away, the most familiar and important ones were right there, inside the community. They were people who had maneuvered their way through the currents of segregated life, made careers and often fortunes for themselves, and remained in the neighborhood, hammering home the message that there were victories to strive for. They were employers and entrepreneurs of all sorts: businessmen, politicians, and entertainers, gambling czars and preachers of the Gospel. They were people whose moral flaws and weaknesses were no secret to those around them, and those weaknesses were a frequent topic of discussion in the community. But they were leaders nevertheless. They led by command, sometimes rather crudely, and they also led by example.

It is easy to forget, forty years later, just how many successful black-owned businesses there were in Chicago. There were black entrepreneurs all up and down the commercial streets in the 1950s, able to stay afloat because they were guaranteed a clientele. They provided services that white businesses simply did not want to provide to blacks. They ran barber shops and beauty parlors, restaurants and taverns, photography studios and small hotels. Many of them were mom-and-pop operations but quite a few evolved into sizable corporations. "Business," as Dempsey Travis says, "was the pillar of optimism."

The nation's largest black-owned bank was at Forty-seventh Street and Cottage Grove Avenue. Parker House Sausage Company, at Forty-sixth and State, called itself the "Jackie Robinson of meat-packing." At Twenty-seventh and Wabash, S. B. Fuller operated a giant cosmetics business that touted three hundred different products, maintained thirty-one branches all over the country, and employed five thousand salesmen. "Anyone can succeed," Fuller used to say, "if he has the desire."

But the great symbols of the entrepreneurial spirit in Bronzeville were the   25
funeral parlors and the insurance companies. In many cases they were related businesses, a legacy of the burial insurance associations that had existed among black sharecroppers in Mississippi and Arkansas early in the century. Undertakers were the largest single source of advertising in the *Defender*; they were also, like their white counterparts elsewhere in the city, mainstays of every community organization: lodges, churches, social clubs.

The opening of a new funeral parlor was a community event in itself. In the spring of 1957, the Jackson funeral home opened a state-of-the art facility on Cottage Grove Avenue, complete, with three large chapels, slumber rooms, a powder room, and a smoking lounge. On the first day, three thousand people came to see it. The Jackson family also owned Jackson Mutual, the fifth largest insurance company in Bronzeville, employing one hundred and twenty people and writing nearly $2 million worth of policies every year.

Insurance actually was a service that white corporations were willing to provide to black customers. Thousands of Bronzeville residents had policies with Metropolitan Life, paying a dollar or two every month to an agent who came by door-to-door to collect. But this was one case where black firms could compete fairly easily. Met Life charged black families more than it charged whites for the same policies, its agents didn't like to come at night when customers were home, and they often seemed to resent having to be there at all. There were billboards all over the neighborhood urging people to buy their insurance from a Negro company.

The result was that by the mid-1950s, the five largest black-owned insurance companies in Chicago had nearly $50 million in assets and more than two thousand employees among them. "Negro life insurance companies," said Walter Lowe, one of the leading agents, "represent the core of Negro economic life. It is the axis upon which are revolved the basic financial activities of a world constricted by the overpowering forces of discrimination."

But it was more than that. It was the underwriter of the extended time horizons that made life in Bronzeville tolerable in the first place. It was the primary symbol of hope for people burdened with a difficult present but unwilling to abandon their focus on the future. In 1954, *Ebony* magazine, published in Chicago, took a survey of its black readership and found that 42 percent owned washing machines, 44 percent owned cars, and 60 percent owned television sets. But 86 percent said they carried life insurance.

The *Defender*'s tribute to the life insurance companies was reprinted every year to coincide with National Negro Insurance Week: "I am the destroyer of poverty and the enemy of crime," it said. "I bring sunshine and happiness wherever I am given half the welcome I deserve. I do not live for the day nor for the morrow but for the unfathomable future. I am your best friend—I am life insurance." . . .   30

Overcoming evil was a job at which most of Bronzeville worked very hard every Sunday, in congregations that ranged in size from tiny to immense. There were five churches whose sanctuary had a seating capacity of two thousand or more, and at least two churches had more than ten thousand people on their membership rolls. But a majority of the churches in the community, even in the late 1950s, were basically storefront operations—often a couple of dozen worshipers or even fewer than that.

In the bigger churches, Sunday worship was an all-day affair: Sunday school at nine in the morning and the main service at eleven; an evening musicale later on, with the full choir and Gospel chorus; and then, for many of the faithful, a radio sermon from one of the big-name Bronzeville preachers before retiring for the night. Music was at the heart of the experience. Most churches had choirs that accompanied the pastor when he preached as a guest in another pulpit, which all of them did. Some choirs spent considerable time traveling outside the city.

Between Sundays, the odds were that a larger congregation would be busy with some social activity every single night. All these churches had a wide variety of auxiliary organizations — youth groups, missionary societies, sewing circles — and some had as many as two dozen different ones in existence at the same time. Of all the Bronzeville social institutions of the 1950s, the churches were the most uniformly successful and self-reliant. "In their own churches in their own denominational structures," the historian C. Eric Lincoln was to write in retrospect, "black Christians had become accustomed to a sense of dignity and self-fulfillment impossible even to contemplate in the white church in America. . . . To be able to say that 'I belong to Mount Nebo Baptist' or 'We go to Mason's Chapel Methodist' was the accepted way of establishing identity and status."

The storefront churches had to make do without the elaborate network of groups and social involvement. But the key distinction was not the size of the facility; it was the style of worship and particularly the level of emotion. Many of the storefronts, perhaps most, were Holiness or Pentecostal churches — Holy Rollers, as the outside world had already come to know them. The service combined shouting, faith healing, and speaking in tongues; as much as three hours of singing, accompanied by guitar, drum, and tambourine; and vivid story-telling sermons about such things as the fiery furnace or the prodigal son. Some churches employed attendants in white uniforms to calm the shouting worshipers when they became too excited. In a liturgy that devoted a great deal of its time to discussing the nature and consequences of sin — and the specific sins of alcohol, tobacco, profanity, gambling, and adultery — there was intense joy as well. "I have known the sisters and the brothers to become so happy," one woman told Horace Cayton and St. Clair Drake in *Black Metropolis*, "that persons around them are in actual danger of getting knocked in the face."

The popularity of these storefronts was something of a problem for the main-line Baptist and African Methodist Episcopal (AME) congregations that aimed for what they saw as a higher level of decorum and dignity. Some ministers used to upbraid their worshipers for becoming too emotional during the service. By the mid-1950s, however, the liturgical distinction between the storefronts and the mainline institutions was blurring. Dozens of preachers who had begun with nothing had built their churches into successful operations, all without departing significantly from the Holiness or Pentecostal script.

The mid-1950s were an exciting time for Bronzeville churches of all varieties. Congregations were growing, debts were being paid, and churches everywhere seemed to be moving into larger, more elaborate facilities: the shouters as well as the elite. . . .

Bronzeville no longer exists. That is not merely because no one would use such a name anymore, but because most of the buildings that comprised the neighborhood have long since been leveled. With the completion in 1962 of Robert Taylor Homes, the nation's largest public housing project and quite possibly its most squalid, the area once called Bronzeville ceased to run the gamut from worn-out but respectable apartment buildings to gruesome kitchenettes. It became a much more uniform high-rise slum, punctuated every half-mile or so by decrepit commercial strips, hosting intermittent taverns, barbecues, and convenience stores and suggesting only a remnant of the much more thriving business streets that once existed.

Bronzeville is long gone not only physically but socially; it passed out of existence as a community as soon as the middle class left, which was as soon as it was permitted to leave with the lifting of segregation. By 1960, the middle-class exodus had already begun, and by 1970, it was virtually complete. Thousands of families who had been the pillars of Bronzeville society returned at most once a week, for church on Sunday.

So much his been written about the impact of middle-class departure on the life of the ghetto that it seems unnecessary to belabor the point. Perhaps it is sufficient to say that Bronzeville was a community unique in America, that its uniqueness depended on the presence of people from all classes and with all sorts of values, living and struggling together, and that with the disappearance of that diversity, the community could not have continued to exist, even if there had been no physical changes at all.

In thinking about what has disappeared, however, there is no shortage of ironies to ponder. The policy racket is legal now, run neither by local black gamblers nor by the Mafia but by the state of Illinois, which calls it a lottery. The game that was once considered an emblem of sin by much of white Chicago is now depended upon as a contributor to the financing of public education. Policy is merely a business now, managed by a colorless bureaucracy far away — it is no longer a cult or a neighborhood institution. There is no demand for dream books anymore on the South Side, no circus-like drawings in crowded basements with a light over the entrance. People play the legal numbers game with a humorless compulsiveness that has little in common with the old-fashioned emotional experience. 40

Legal businesses have fared almost as badly as illegal ones. Notwithstanding Earl Dickerson's prediction that Supreme Liberty Life would thrive under integration to become a billion-dollar insurance business by the end of the century, the company was simply absorbed into United of America, becoming a piece of a gigantic white institution, and a rather small and inconspicuous piece at that. Not that there was anything racist about such a consolidation; plenty of smaller white-owned insurance companies suffered the same fate. But the cumulative effect on black economic life was powerful: the old life insurance companies were the one significant engine of capital in Chicago's black community, and by 1990, not a single firm was left.

The *Chicago Defender* remains in business at the same location it occupied in the 1950s, published by the same man, John Sengstacke. But it never really found a coherent role to play as a voice of its people in an integrated city. Once the white newspapers began printing news about blacks on the South Side, the paper lost its franchise as virtually the sole source of information within the community. It played a surprisingly passive role in the civil rights confrontations of the 1960s, serving neither as a conspicuous engine of militant activism nor as a persistent critic. By the 1970s, the *Defender* had essentially been superseded as a forum for political debate by the plethora of black radio stations that had sprung up on the South Side. The Bud Billiken parade is still held each summer in Washington Park, attracting a huge contingent of Chicago politicians, white as well as black, but it is no longer the signature event of a powerful black journalistic institution: it is a reminder of the influence that institution once had.

Of all the fixtures of Bronzeville life, the churches come the closest to having survived in recognizable form. Olivet Baptist stands as an impressive edifice at Thirty-first Street and King Drive, its front lawn dominated by a statue of the Reverend J. H. Jackson, pugnacious in stone as he was in life, along with quotations from some of his sermons and praise for him from around the world. Olivet, South Park Baptist, and some of the other Bronzeville churches still turn out crowds at services on Sunday morning, attracting families who return from the far South Side and the suburbs, senior citizens who have remained in the neighborhood, and a sprinkling of children and adults from the projects nearby.

Some of the churches still maintain choirs, Sunday schools, Bible study groups, and social outreach programs, struggling rather heroically against the social disorganization that is all around them. But they have ceased to be voices of clear authority. No preacher can deliver instruction and expect compliance in the way that J. H. Jackson could in his prime. And while sin remains a familiar topic in the South Side black churches on Sundays—a more important topic than at St. Nick's or Elmhurst Presbyterian—the subject no longer has the hold over its listeners that it had a generation ago.

Only in politics can one really argue that Bronzeville has gained more than   45
it has lost. William L. Dawson was a power broker and even a role model of sorts, but he was a leader whose rewards from the white machine were disappointingly meager, somehow not commensurate with the job he did in guaranteeing the election of Richard J. Daley and other white politicians. Dawson's machine yielded in the 1980s to something truly remarkable—a citywide coalition that made possible the election of Harold Washington as the city's first black mayor. Washington's victory in 1983, in a campaign with "Our Turn" as its most conspicuous slogan, was a psychological triumph far beyond anything the old Dawson organization could possibly accomplish, perhaps beyond anything blacks had experienced in any American city. And while the extent of Washington's tangible achievements in office can be debated, the fact that he died in 1987 with his heroic status in the black community intact, and his respect growing even among whites, represented a victory comparable in its way to the first one.

Black political power in Chicago, however, seemed to disappear almost as suddenly as it emerged. Ten years after Washington's first election, Chicago was again being governed by a white mayor, Richard M. Daley, son of the old boss, and by a majority coalition in which Hispanics, not blacks, were the significant minority partner. Meanwhile, the black community was deeply divided over whom to follow and how to proceed, seemingly years away from the level of influence it had had in city politics in the mid-1980s.

In the black community, unlike the white working-class neighborhoods or white suburbia, it may seem perverse — or at least misleading — to dwell on the losses of the past generation. At the individual level, there have been so many gains — in personal freedom, in job opportunities, in income. Today's black middle class is far larger in proportional terms than the one that existed in Bronzeville in the 1950s, much of it living comfortably in neighborhoods scattered all across the Chicago metropolitan area.

When it comes to community institutions, however, the losses are no less real for Chicago's blacks than for white ethnics or for the split-level suburbanites of the 1950s generation. If anything, they are more real. Nearly all of the things that gave texture and coherence to life in Bronzeville, demeaning as that life often was, are simply not reproducible in the freer, more individualistic, more bewildering world of the 1990s. [1995]

THINKING ABOUT THE TEXT

1. Does reading these passages from Ehrenhalt's book make you think differently about any of the events and characters in *A Raisin in the Sun?* Why, or why not?

2. To what extent does the neighborhood described by Ehrenhalt resemble where you grew up? Identify specific similarities and differences.

3. Note Ehrenhalt's last sentence. While he recognizes that Bronzeville was segregated, evidently he feels some regret over its passing, mourning in particular what he sees as the death of its community spirit. Does his attitude make sense to you? Explain your reasoning. What do you think he might say about the Younger family's decision to leave the neighborhood? How much does it matter to you that this historian of Bronzeville is white?

WRITING ABOUT ISSUES

1. Choose a particular moment in *A Raisin in the Sun* when characters disagree. Then, write an essay analyzing their disagreement. More specifically, identify the different positions they take, the warrants or assumptions that seem to underlie their positions, the outcome of their disagreement, your own evaluation of their views, and the relationship of this moment to the rest of the play. Be sure to quote from the text.

2. Imagine that Hansberry's play is being republished and that you are asked to edit it. Imagine further that the publisher asks you to introduce the play with one of the three background documents in this cluster. Write an essay stating which document you would choose and why.

3. Choose a family you know well and write an essay comparing it with the Younger family. Above all, consider whether your chosen family, too, has conflicting dreams.

4. Spend time in the library examining newspapers and magazines from 1959, the year *A Raisin in the Sun* opened on Broadway. In particular, try to identify a variety of events and trends that might have affected an American family that year. Next, imagine a specific American family living in 1959. Finally, write an essay describing a play that might be written about your imagined family's reaction to a specific event or trend back then. Give details of the plot, the family's social background, and its members' personalities. If you wish, present some dialogue.

8

Teaching and Learning

Probably you are thinking a lot about teaching and learning as you read selections from this book because you are encountering it in a college course. But even if you were delving into the book entirely on your own, it might bring issues of teaching and learning to mind. Countless readers turn to literature hoping to learn things from it, and many writers see literature as a way to teach others their insights. In addition, a vast number of literary works depict situations of teaching and learning, sometimes explicitly labeling them as such. But these are not the only reasons we feature a chapter on teaching and learning. We do so also because teaching and learning involve many of the same *rhetorical* considerations you face as a writer of arguments. Much of the time, the student is an audience, and the student's teacher aims to persuade him or her to accept a certain idea, to try a certain line of inquiry, or to see a certain subject as interesting. Naturally, roles can wind up reversed, with the teacher learning things from the student. As you may find in this class, students also wind up teaching one another.

Teaching and learning can occur outside of officially designated classrooms. Indeed, teaching and learning are an integral part of everyday life. To emphasize this point, we begin with a cluster of poems by Cathy Song, Julia Alvarez, and Forrest Hamer in which the speakers recall lessons they learned elsewhere (p. 567). In the second cluster (p. 574), stories by James Agee and Toni Cade Bambara remind us that, whether inside or outside a classroom, adults must decide when, what, and how to teach young children about society. Of course, for better or worse, few adults manage to exert total control over a child's fate. In quite a few literary works, grown-ups mourn the loss of a young person's life or innocence. The third cluster (p. 597), a trio of poems by Louise Glück, Toi Derricotte, and Philip Levine, features speakers, presumably adults, who brood over constraints faced by schoolchildren they observe.

Of course, rarely do students comply like robots with those teaching them. The poems by Langston Hughes, Linda Pastan, Henry Reed, and Walt Whitman that comprise the fourth cluster (p. 603) present speakers who resist, or at least carefully weigh, a specific instructor's demands. In David Mamet's play *Oleanna*, the centerpiece of the next cluster (p. 610), a college student even charges her professor with sexual harassment. To help you examine their conflict and put it in a larger context, we include three background documents: a university pamphlet on sexual harassment, the case study of a college student who used informal mediation to deal with a teacher who had harassed her, and an article proposing changes in the way that many colleges deal with sexual harassment charges.

The next two clusters encourage you to consider how education and culture may relate. In the first (p. 656), Richard Rodriguez recalls the painful process he went through as he moved from the Mexican American heritage of his parents to the Anglo-American world of school. Rodriguez does conclude that this shift was ultimately necessary and desirable; we follow his essay, though, with comments from Hispanic Americans who disagree. The next cluster (p. 672) consists of two short stories and an essay by Jamaica Kincaid. Although she lives now in the United States, Kincaid was born and raised on the island of Antigua when it was a colony of England. Her short story "Girl" suggests the training in Antiguan gender roles she received within her family, while the other two works show how the island's schools tried to indoctrinate its children in British lore.

The next-to-last cluster (p. 690) reminds you that literature itself has served as a means of educating. The three poems we feature, by David Wagoner, Theodore Roethke, and Elizabeth Bishop, provide lessons on how to live one's life, but that is not to say you must simply accept whatever an author or character tries to teach. Consider, for example, how much you should trust the advice-giving narrators of Jonathan Swift's "A Modest Proposal," Daniel Orozco's "Orientation," and Pam Houston's "How to Talk to a Hunter." We conclude this chapter with these three pieces (p. 696) precisely because they force you to consider just how reliable a would-be teacher is.

RECALLING LESSONS OF CHILDHOOD

CATHY SONG, "The Grammar of Silk"
JULIA ALVAREZ, "How I Learned to Sweep"
FORREST HAMER, "Lesson"

Many people recall learning significant childhood lessons in settings other than school. Such is the case with the following three poems. In the first, the speaker values the time she spent in a Saturday sewing school. The speaker in the second poem recalls how she learned to sweep her home, although the reader is plainly encouraged to think about sweeping as a metaphor for other, more troubling acts. In the third poem, an African American man describes a family trip through Mississippi in the early 1960s, an experience that gave him certain ideas about his relationship with his father. As you read these poems, observe how each depicts a parent-child relationship. Consider whether each parent consciously intends the lesson emphasized in the poem. Furthermore, compare the adult speaker of each poem with his or her younger self. To what extent do they seem similar? In what ways might their perspectives differ?

BEFORE YOU READ

What are some things that your parents or other people who raised you intentionally taught you? What are some things that they unintentionally taught you?

CATHY SONG
The Grammar of Silk

Cathy Song (b. 1955) was born and raised in Honolulu, Hawaii, and currently teaches at the University of Hawaii at Manoa. Her first volume of poetry, Picture Bride, *won the 1982 Yale Series of Younger Poets Award and was nominated for the National Book Critics Circle Award. She has published two others:* Frameless Windows, Available Light *(1988) and* School Figures *(1994), which includes the following poem.*

On Saturdays in the morning
my mother sent me to Mrs. Umemoto's sewing school.
It was cool and airy in her basement,
pleasant—a word I choose
to use years later to describe   5
the long tables where we sat
and cut, pinned, and stitched,
the Singer's companionable whirr,
the crisp, clever bite of scissors
parting like silver fish a river of calico.   10

The school was in walking distance
to Kaimuki Dry Goods
where my mother purchased my supplies—
small cards of buttons,
zippers and rickrack packaged like licorice,   15
lifesaver rolls of thread
in fifty-yard lengths,
spun from spools, tough as tackle.
Seamstresses waited at the counters
like librarians to be consulted.   20
Pens and scissors dangled like awkward pendants
across flat chests,
a scarf of measuring tape flung across a shoulder,
time as a pincushion bristled at the wrist.
They deciphered a dress's blueprints   25
with an architect's keen eye.

◆   ◆   ◆

This evidently was a sanctuary,
a place where women confined with children
conferred, consulted the oracle,
the stone tablets of the latest pattern books.   30
Here mothers and daughters paused in symmetry,
offered the proper reverence —
hushed murmurings for the shantung silk
which required a certain sigh,
as if it were a piece from the Ming Dynasty.   35

My mother knew there would be no shortcuts
and headed for the remnants,
the leftover bundles with yardage
enough for a heart-shaped pillow,
a child's dirndl, a blouse without darts.   40
Along the aisles
my fingertips touched the titles —
satin, tulle, velvet,
peach, lavender, pistachio,
sherbet-colored linings —   45
and settled for the plain brown-and-white composition
of polka dots on kettle cloth
my mother held up in triumph.

She was determined that I should sew
as if she knew what she herself was missing,   50
a moment when she could have come up for air —
the children asleep,
the dishes drying on the rack —
and turned on the lamp
and pulled back the curtain of sleep.   55
To inhabit the night,
the night as a black cloth, white paper,
a sheet of music in which she might find herself singing.

On Saturdays at Mrs. Umemoto's sewing school,
when I took my place beside the other girls,   60
bent my head and went to work,
my foot keeping time on the pedal,
it was to learn the charitable oblivion
of hand and mind as one —
a refuge such music affords the maker —   65
the pleasure of notes in perfectly measured time.   [1994]

THINKING ABOUT THE TEXT

1. How do you think Song defines the word *grammar*? Note that the word
   appears only in the poem's title and is not usually applied to silk. Why,

then, do you think Song calls her poem "The Grammar of Silk"? Which lines seem related to this title?

2. Even as she uses the word *pleasant* to describe Mrs. Umemoto's basement, the speaker admits that it is "a word I choose / to use years later" (lines 4–5). What other lines seem to reflect the adult's perspective more than the child's?

3. Only the first and last stanzas describe the sewing school itself. What might Song's purpose be in including the four middle stanzas? How important do they seem compared with the first and last stanzas?

4. Describe the speaker's mother with three adjectives of your own. What, in your own words, does she seem to have been "missing"? Do you mainly think of her as missing something, or are you more conscious of what she had?

5. Does the culture evoked in this poem seem different from your own? What specific aspects of the poem's culture and your own come to mind as you try to answer this question?

JULIA ALVAREZ
How I Learned to Sweep

Although born in New York City, Julia Alvarez (b. 1950) was raised in the Dominican Republic until she was ten. Her first novel, How the Garcia Girls Lost Their Accents *(1991), concerns Dominican immigrants living in Manhattan. Her second,* In the Time of the Butterflies *(1994), is based on real-life women who were murdered by the regime of the Dominican dictator Rafael Leonidas Trujillo. Her third novel,* Yo! *(1996), centers on a writer much like Alvarez herself. Alvarez has also published volumes of poetry, including* Homecoming *(1984; revised edition, 1996) and* The Other Side/El Otro Lado *(1995). The following poem appears in* Homecoming *as one of a series of thirteen poems collectively entitled "Housekeeping."*

My mother never taught me sweeping. . . .
One afternoon she found me watching
t.v. She eyed the dusty floor
boldly, and put a broom before
me, and said she'd like to be able   5
to eat her dinner off that table,
and nodded at my feet, then left.
I knew right off what she expected
and went at it. I stepped and swept;
the t.v. blared the news; I kept   10
my mind on what I had to do,
until in minutes, I was through.

Her floor was as immaculate
as a just-washed dinner plate.
I waited for her to return   15
and turned to watch the President,
live from the White House, talk of war:
in the Far East our soldiers were
landing in their helicopters
into jungles their propellers   20
swept like weeds seen underwater
while perplexing shots were fired
from those beautiful green gardens
into which these dragonflies
filled with little men descended.   25
I got up and swept again
as they fell out of the sky.
I swept all the harder when
I watched a dozen of them die . . .
as if their dust fell through the screen   30
upon the floor I had just cleaned.
She came back and turned the dial;
the screen went dark. *That's beautiful,*
she said, and ran her clean hand through
my hair, and on, over the window-   35
sill, coffee table, rocker, desk,
and held it up — I held my breath —
That's beautiful, she said, impressed,
she hadn't found a speck of death.   [1984]

THINKING ABOUT THE TEXT

1. In line 1 the speaker begins by announcing "My mother never taught me
   sweeping. . . ." How is it, then, that the speaker "knew right off what she
   [the mother] expected" (line 8)?

2. Identify rhyming patterns in this poem. What is their effect? Identify sections where there is no rhyme. What is their effect?

3. How old do you think the speaker was when she learned how to sweep?
   Why do you think the sight of dying soldiers made her sweep "all the
   harder" (line 28)? What response to the war might reasonably have been
   expected of her?

4. What do you conclude about the speaker's mother from the last two lines?

5. What other things do children or parents like to "sweep" away?

MAKING COMPARISONS

1. Whereas Alvarez uses rhyme at various points, Song does not. Does this
   difference lead to a difference in the two poems' overall effect? Explain.

2. Song uses the words *sanctuary* and *oblivion*. Look these up in a dictionary. How might they be applied to Alvarez's poem? Do you think Alvarez would attach the same connotations to them as Song does? Why, or why not?

3. Compare the mothers in Alvarez's and Song's poems. Do you sympathize with one mother more than the other? Why, or why not?

FORREST HAMER
Lesson

Besides being a poet, Forrest Hamer (b. 1956) is a psychologist, a lecturer in psychology at the University of California at Berkeley, and a candidate at the San Francisco Psychoanalytic Institute. As a poet, he has published in several journals. "Lesson" appears in his first book of poems, Call & Response *(1996), much of which deals with his experiences growing up African American.*

It was 1963 or 4, summer,
and my father was driving our family
from Ft. Hood to North Carolina in our 56 Buick.
We'd been hearing about Klan attacks, and we knew

Mississippi to be more dangerous than usual.   5
Dark lay hanging from trees the way moss did,
and when it moaned light against the windows
that night, my father pulled off the road to sleep.

                    Noises
that usually woke me from rest afraid of monsters   10
kept my father awake that night, too,
and I lay in the quiet noticing him listen, learning
that he might not be able always to protect us

from everything and the creatures besides;
perhaps not even from the fury suddenly loud   15
through my body about this trip from Texas
to settle us home before he would go away

to a place no place in the world
he named Viet Nam. A boy needs a father
with him, I kept thinking, fixed against noise   20
from the dark.   [1996]

THINKING ABOUT THE TEXT

1. Hamer's title suggests there was only one lesson, yet there seem to be two. On the one hand, the child seems to have learned that his father "might

not be able always to protect us/from everything and the creatures besides" (lines 13–14). On the other hand, the child seems to have learned that "A boy needs a father/with him" (lines 19–20). Consider whether these two lessons are compatible. Do you believe that the title applies to both? Why, or why not?

2. The speaker begins with "It was 1963 or 4, summer." What do you conclude from his uncertainty about the year his journey through Mississippi took place? How does it affect you? What was going on in Mississippi from 1963 to 1964? (You may need to research this in the library.)

3. What is the effect of Hamer's visually isolating the word *Noises* in line 9? What other words in the poem can be linked to this one?

4. Was the child justified in resenting his father's departure for Vietnam? Should the father not have gone? Your answers to these questions are, in effect, claims. With what evidence and assumptions do you make them?

5. In the United States today, many children are raised without their fathers. This fact has led to much debate over social policy. People argue about whether and how fathers should be pushed to participate in their children's upbringing. At the same time, some feel that women should be discouraged from becoming single mothers, in part because sons need to have fathers around. What would you think if they used Hamer's claim "A boy needs a father / with him" (lines 19–20) in arguing for their position?

MAKING COMPARISONS

1. Think of the father in Hamer's poem and the mothers in Song's and Alvarez's poems. Do any of these parents seem like *intentional* teachers who consciously aim to impart certain lessons to their children? Support your answer by referring to specific details in each poem.

2. What might each of these poems have looked like if written by the parent involved? More specifically, what sorts of things might the parent have said?

3. Hamer's poem and Alvarez's share a historical context in that they both refer to the Vietnam war. What do you associate with this war? Compare how the children in these two poems think about it. Do they each regard the war in much the same way? Refer to specific lines in each text to support your answer. How historically specific is Song's poem in comparison?

WRITING ABOUT ISSUES

1. Choose Song's, Alvarez's, or Hamer's poem and write an essay discussing the role gender plays in it. Does the poem focus on one gender? In what ways? How is the poem relevant to both men and women? Be sure to support your claim with specific details of the text.

2. Write an essay comparing the speakers in two of the poems in this cluster. Consider not only how the speakers thought and acted as youths, but also what they may be like now as adults, including the attitudes they may have toward their younger selves. Refer to specific details of both texts.

3. Write a dialogue between your present self and the person you were at a particular age. Focus this dialogue on a specific historical event or development that your younger self was struggling to understand. Then write at least three paragraphs comparing the two perspectives that emerged in your dialogue. What turned out to be the similarities and differences between your present and younger selves?

4. Think of a school you attended and a skill or principle that the school didn't teach but should have. Taking as your audience the school's current administrators, write an essay arguing for including this skill or principle in the school's curriculum now. While you may cite experiences of your own as evidence for your position, be sure to give additional reasons for adopting it.

TEACHING CHILDREN ABOUT SOCIETY

JAMES AGEE, "A Mother's Tale"
TONI CADE BAMBARA, "The Lesson"

In the first story here, a cow tells a group of calves about the horrors of the slaughterhouse. In the second story, an African American woman tries to convince some children of her race that whites unfairly control their society's wealth. In effect, both stories remind us that whether in or out of school, adults often try to teach young children about the society they are entering.

What specific aspects of their society, though, should young children learn about? What overall view of their society should they be taught to adopt? People give different answers to these questions. Often their responses vary because they have in mind their own social circumstances, including the treatment given their specific class, race, gender, religion, ethnic group, and sexual orientation. Furthermore, even people who respond similarly may disagree about other matters: in particular, about *how* and *when* a child should be taught whatever vision of society they think appropriate. The two stories here encourage you to ponder all these issues.

BEFORE YOU READ

In his memoir *Fatheralong* (1994), John Edgar Wideman notes that his father's attitude toward society differs from that of his late mother. "The first rule of my father's world," Wideman writes, "is that you stand alone. Alone,

alone, alone. . . . Accept the bottom line, icy clarity, of the one thing you can rely on: nothing" (50). On the other hand, "My mother's first rule was love. She refused to believe she was alone. *Be not dismayed, what e'er betides / God will take care of you*" (51). What were you taught about society as you were growing up. What specific messages were you given about it by your parents or the people who raised you? How did they convey these messages to you?

JAMES AGEE
A Mother's Tale

Today, James Agee (1909–1955) is probably best known for his journalistic 1941 book Let Us Now Praise Famous Men, *in which he and photographer Walker Evans documented the hardships of sharecroppers during the Great Depression. Agee is also known for his Pulitzer Prize–winning novel* A Death in the Family *(1957), a fictionalized account of his father's death that was published posthumously. Agee wrote in several other genres, including short fiction, poetry, screenplays, and film criticism. "A Mother's Tale" was published in* Harper's Bazaar *magazine in 1951. Agee wrote it shortly after he had suffered a series of heart attacks; it was his last work of fiction published while he was alive.*

The calf ran up the little hill as fast as he could and stopped sharp.

"Mama!" he cried, all out of breath. "What *is* it! What are they *doing!* Where are they *going!*"

Other spring calves came galloping too.

They all were looking up at her and awaiting her explanation, but she looked out over their excited eyes. As she watched the mysterious and majestic thing they had never seen before, her own eyes became even more than ordinarily still, and during the considerable moment before she answered, she scarcely heard their urgent questioning.

Far out along the autumn plain, beneath the sloping light, an immense drove of cattle moved eastward. They went at a walk, not very fast, but faster than they could imaginably enjoy. Those in front were compelled by those behind; those at the rear, with few exceptions, did their best to keep up; those who were locked within the herd could no more help moving than the particles inside a falling rock. Men on horses rode ahead, and alongside, and behind, or spurred their horses intensely back and forth, keeping the pace steady, and the herd in shape; and from man to man a dog sped back and forth incessantly as a shuttle, barking, incessantly, in a hysterical voice. Now and then one of the men shouted fiercely, and this like the shrieking of the dog was tinily audible above a low and awesome sound which seemed to come not from the multitude of hooves but from the center of the world, and above the sporadic bawlings and bellowings of the herd.

From the hillside this tumult was so distant that it only made more delicate the prodigious silence in which the earth and sky were held; and, from the hill, the sight was as modest as its sound. The herd was virtually hidden in the dust it raised, and could be known, in general, only by the horns, which pricked this flat sunlit dust like little briars. In one place a twist of the air revealed the trembling fabric of many backs; but it was only along the near edge of the mass that individual animals were discernible, small in a driven frieze, walking fast, stumbling and recovering, tossing their armed heads, or opening their skulls heavenward in one of those cries which searched the hillside long after the jaws were shut.

From where she watched, the mother could not be sure whether there were any she recognized. She knew that among them there must be a son of hers; she had not seen him since some previous spring, and she would not be seeing him again. Then the cries of the young ones impinged on her bemusement: "Where are they going?"

She looked into their ignorant eyes.

"Away," she said.

"Where?" they cried. "Where? Where?" her own son cried again.   10

She wondered what to say.

"On a long journey."

"But where *to?*" they shouted. "Yes, where *to?*" her son exclaimed, and she could see that he was losing his patience with her, as he always did when he felt she was evasive.

"I'm not sure," she said.

Their silence was so cold that she was unable to avoid their eyes for long.   15

"Well, not *really* sure. Because, you see," she said in her most reasonable tone, "I've never seen it with my own eyes, and that's the only way to *be* sure; isn't it."

They just kept looking at her. She could see no way out.

"But I've *heard* about it," she said with shallow cheerfulness, "from those who *have* seen it, and I don't suppose there's any good reason to doubt them."

She looked away over them again, and for all their interest in what she was about to tell them, her eyes so changed that they turned and looked, too.

The herd, which had been moving broadside to them, was being turned   20 away, so slowly that like the turning of stars it could not quite be seen from one moment to the next; yet soon it was moving directly away from them, and even during the little while she spoke and they all watched after it, it steadily and very noticeably diminished, and the sounds of it as well.

"It happens always about this time of year," she said quietly while they watched. "Nearly all the men and horses leave, and go into the North and the West."

"Out on the range," her son said, and by his voice she knew what enchantment the idea already held for him.

"Yes," she said, "out on the range." And trying, impossibly, to imagine the range, they were touched by the breath of grandeur.

"And then before long," she continued, "everyone has been found, and brought into one place; and then . . . what you see, happens. All of them.

"Sometimes when the wind is right," she said more quietly, "you can hear   25
them coming long before you can see them. It isn't even like a sound, at first. It's
more as if something were moving far under the ground. It makes you uneasy.
You wonder, why, what in the world can *that* be! Then you remember what it is
and then you can really hear it. And then, finally, there they all are."

She could see this did not interest them at all.

"But where are they *going?*" one asked, a little impatiently.

"I'm coming to that," she said; and she let them wait. Then she spoke slowly
but casually.

"They are on their way to a railroad."

There, she thought; that's for that look you all gave me when I said I wasn't   30
sure. She waited for them to ask; they waited for her to explain.

"A railroad," she told them, "is great hard bars of metal lying side by side, or
so they tell me, and they go on and on over the ground as far as the eye can see.
And great wagons run on the metal bars on wheels, like wagon wheels but
smaller, and these wheels are made of solid metal too. The wagons are much bigger than any wagon you've ever seen, as big as, big as sheds, they say, and they are
pulled along on the iron bars by a terrible huge dark machine, with a loud
scream."

"Big as *sheds?*" one of the calves said skeptically.

"Big *enough*, anyway," the mother said. "I told you I've never seen it myself.
But those wagons are so big that several of us can get inside at once. And that's
exactly what happens."

Suddenly she became very quiet, for she felt that somehow, she could not
imagine just how, she had said altogether too much.

"Well, *what* happens," her son wanted to know. "What do you mean,   35
happens."

She always tried hard to be a reasonably modern mother. It was probably better, she felt, to go on, than to leave them all full of imaginings and mystification.
Besides, there was really nothing at all awful about what happened . . . if only one
could know *why*.

"Well," she said, "it's nothing much, really. They just—why, when they all
finally *get* there, why there are all the great cars waiting in a long line, and the big
dark machine is up ahead . . . smoke comes out of it, they say . . . and . . . well,
then, they just put us into the wagons, just as many as will fit in each wagon, and
when everybody is in, why . . ." She hesitated, for again, though she couldn't be
sure why, she was uneasy.

"Why then," her son said, "the train takes them away."

Hearing that word, she felt a flinching of the heart. Where had he picked it
up, she wondered, and she gave him a shy and curious glance. Oh dear, she
thought. I should never have even *begun* to explain. "Yes," she said, "when
everybody is safely in, they slide the doors shut."

They were all silent for a little while. Then one of them asked thoughtfully,   40
"Are they taking them somewhere they don't want to go?"

"Oh, I don't think so," the mother said. "I imagine it's very nice."

"*I* want to go," she heard her son say with ardor. "I want to go right now," he cried. "Can I, Mama? *Can* I? *Please?*" And looking into his eyes, she was overwhelmed by sadness.

"Silly thing," she said, "there'll be time enough for that when you're grown up. But what I very much hope," she went on, "is that instead of being chosen to go out on the range and to make the long journey, you will grow up to be very strong and bright so they will decide that you may stay here at home with Mother. And you, too," she added, speaking to the other little males; but she could not honestly wish this for any but her own, least of all for the eldest, strongest and most proud, for she knew how few are chosen.

She could see that what she said was not received with enthusiasm.

"But I want to go," her son said.   45

"Why?" she asked. "I don't think any of you realize that it's a great *honor* to be chosen to stay. A great privilege. Why, it's just the most ordinary ones are taken out onto the range. But only the very pick are chosen to stay here at home. If you want to go out on the range," she said in hurried and happy inspiration, "all you have to do is be ordinary and careless and silly. If you want to have even a chance to be chosen to stay, you have to try to be stronger and bigger and braver and brighter than anyone else, and that takes *hard work. Every day.* Do you see?" And she looked happily and hopefully from one to another. "Besides," she added, aware that they were not won over, "I'm told it's a very rough life out there, and the men are unkind."

"Don't you see," she said again; and she pretended to speak to all of them, but it was only to her son.

But he only looked at her. "Why do you want me to stay home?" he asked flatly; in their silence she knew the others were asking the same question.

"Because it's safe here," she said before she knew better, and realized she had put it in the most unfortunate way possible. "Not safe, not just that," she fumbled. "I mean . . . because here we *know* what happens, and what's going to happen, and there's never any doubt about it, never any reason to wonder, to worry. Don't you see? It's just *Home*," and she put a smile on the word, "where we all know each other and are happy and well."

They were so merely quiet, looking back at her, that she felt they were nei-   50 ther won over nor alienated. Then she knew of her son that he, anyhow, was most certainly not persuaded, for he asked the question she most dreaded: "Where do they go on the train?" And hearing him, she knew that she would stop at nothing to bring that curiosity and eagerness, and that tendency toward skepticism, within safe bounds.

"Nobody knows," she said, and she added, in just the tone she knew would most sharply engage them, "Not for sure, anyway."

"What do you mean, *not for sure*," her son cried. And the oldest, biggest calf repeated the question, his voice cracking.

The mother deliberately kept silence as she gazed out over the plain, and while she was silent they all heard the last they would ever hear of all those who were going away: one last great cry, as faint almost as a breath; the infinitesimal jabbing vituperation of the dog; the solemn muttering of the earth.

"Well," she said, after even this sound was entirely lost, "there was one who came back." Their instant, trustful eyes were too much for her. She added, "Or so they say."

They gathered a little more closely around her, for now she spoke very 55 quietly.

"It was my great-grandmother who told me," she said. "She was told it by *her* great-grandmother, who claimed she saw it with her own eyes, though of course I can't vouch for that. Because of course I wasn't even dreamed of then, and Great-grandmother was so very, very old, you see, that you couldn't always be sure she knew quite *what* she was saying."

Now that she began to remember it more clearly, she was sorry she had committed herself to telling it.

"Yes," she said, "the story is, there was one, *just* one, who ever came back, and he told what happened on the train, and where the train went and what happened after. He told it all in a rush, they say, the last things first and every which way, but as it was finally sorted out and gotten into order by those who heard it and those they told it to, this is more or less what happened:

"He said that after the men had gotten just as many of us as they could into the car he was in, so that their sides pressed tightly together and nobody could lie down, they slid the door shut with a startling rattle and a bang, and then there was a sudden jerk, so strong they might have fallen except that they were packed so closely together, and the car began to move. But after it had moved only a little way, it stopped as suddenly as it had started, so that they all nearly fell down again. You see, they were just moving up the next car that was joined on behind, to put more of us into it. He could see it all between the boards of the car, because the boards were built a little apart from each other, to let in air."

Car, her son said again to himself. Now he would never forget the word. 60

"He said that then, for the first time in his life, he became very badly frightened, he didn't know why. But he was sure, at that moment, that there was something dreadfully to be afraid of. The others felt this same great fear. They called out loudly to those who were being put into the car behind, and the others called back, but it was no use; those who were getting aboard were between narrow white fences and then were walking up a narrow slope and the man kept jabbing them as they do when they are in an unkind humor, and there was no way to go but on into the car. There was no way to get out of the car, either: he tried, with all his might, and he was the one nearest the door.

"After the next car behind was full, and the door was shut, the train jerked forward again, and stopped again, and they put more of us into still another car, and so on, and on, until all the starting and stopping no longer frightened anybody; it was just something uncomfortable that was never going to stop, and they began instead to realize how hungry and thirsty they were. But there was no food and no water, so they had to put up with this; and about the time they became resigned to going without their suppers (for by now it was almost dark), they heard a sudden and terrible scream which frightened them even more deeply than anything had frightened them before, and the train began to move again, and they braced their legs once more for the jolt when it would stop, but this time, instead of stopping, it began to go fast, and then even faster, so fast that the ground nearby slid past like a flooded creek and the whole country, he claimed, began to move too, turning slowly around a far mountain as if it were on one great wheel. And then there was a strange kind of disturbance inside the car, he said, or even inside his very bones. He felt as if everything in him was *falling*, as if he had been filled full of a heavy liquid that all wanted to flow one way, and all the others were leaning as he was leaning, away from this queer heaviness that was trying to pull them over, and then just as suddenly this leaning heaviness was gone and they nearly fell again before they could stop leaning against it. He could never understand what this was, but it too happened so many times that they all got used to it, just as they got used to seeing the country turn like a slow wheel, and just as they got used to the long cruel screams of the engine, and the steady iron noise beneath them which made the cold darkness so fearsome, and the hunger and the thirst and the continual standing up, and the moving on and on and on as if they would never stop."

"*Didn't* they ever stop?" one asked.

"Once in a great while," she replied. "Each time they did," she said, "he thought, Oh, now *at last! At last* we can get out and stretch our tired legs and lie down! *At last* we'll be given food and water! But they never let them out. And they never gave them food or water They never even cleaned up under them. They had to stand in their manure and in the water they made."

"Why did the train stop?" her son asked, and with somber gratification; she saw that he was taking all this very much to heart.

"He could never understand why," she said. "Sometimes men would walk up and down alongside the cars, and the more nervous and the more trustful of us would call out; but they were only looking around, they never seemed to do anything. Sometimes he could see many houses and bigger buildings together where people lived. Sometimes it was far out in the country and after they had stood still for a long time they would hear a little noise which quickly became louder, and then became suddenly a noise so loud it stopped their breathing and during this noise something black would go by, very close, and so fast it couldn't be seen. And then it was gone as suddenly as it had appeared, and the noise became small, and then in the silence their train would start up again.

"Once, he tells us, something very strange happened. They were standing still, and cars of a very different kind began to move slowly past. These cars were not red, but black, with many glass windows like those in a house; and he says they were as full of human beings as the car he was in was full of our kind. And one of these people looked into his eyes and smiled, as if he liked him, or as if he knew only too well how hard the journey was.

"So by his account it happens to them, too," she said, with a certain pleased vindictiveness. "Only they were sitting down at their ease, not standing. And the one who smiled was eating."

She was still, trying to think of something; she couldn't quite grasp the thought.

"But didn't they *ever* let them out?" her son asked.

65

70

The oldest calf jeered. "Of *course* they did. He came back, didn't he? How would he ever come back if he didn't get out?"

"They didn't let them out," she said, "for a long, long time."

"How long?"

"So long, and he was so tired, he could never quite be sure. But he said that it turned from night to day and from day to night and back again several times over, with the train moving nearly all of this time, and that when it finally stopped, early one morning, they were all so tired and so discouraged that they hardly even noticed any longer, let alone felt any hope that anything would change for them, ever again; and then all of a sudden men came up and put up a wide walk and unbarred the door and slid it open, and it was the most wonderful and happy moment of his life when he saw the door open, and walked into the open air with all his joints trembling, and drank the water and ate the delicious food they had ready for him; it was worth the whole terrible journey."

Now that these scenes came clear before her, there was a faraway shining in her eyes, and her voice, too, had something in it of the faraway.

75

"When they had eaten and drunk all they could hold they lifted up their heads and looked around, and everything they saw made them happy. Even the trains made them cheerful now, for now they were no longer afraid of them. And though these trains were forever breaking to pieces and joining again with other broken pieces, with shufflings and clashings and rude cries, they hardly paid them attention any more, they were so pleased to be in their new home, and so surprised and delighted to find they were among thousands upon thousands of strangers of their own kind, all lifting up their voices in peacefulness and thanksgiving, and they were so wonderstruck by all they could see, it was so beautiful and so grand.

"For he has told us that now they lived among fences as white as bone, so many, and so spiderishly complicated, and shining so pure, that there's no use trying even to hint at the beauty and the splendor of it to anyone who knows only the pitiful little outfittings of a ranch. Beyond these mazy fences, through the dark and bright smoke which continually turned along the sunlight, dark buildings stood shoulder to shoulder in a wall as huge and proud as mountains. All through the air, all the time, there was an iron humming like the humming of the iron bar after it has been struck to tell the men it is time to eat, and in all the air, all the time, there was that same strange kind of iron strength which makes the silence before lightning so different from all other silence.

"Once for a little while the wind shifted and blew over them straight from the great buildings, and it brought a strange and very powerful smell which confused and disturbed them. He could never quite describe this smell, but he has told us it was unlike anything he had ever known before. It smelled like old fire, he said, and old blood and fear and darkness and sorrow and most terrible and brutal force and something else, something in it that made him want to run away. This sudden uneasiness and this wish to run away swept through every one of them, he tells us, so that they were all moved at once as restlessly as so many leaves in a wind, and there was great worry in their voices. But soon the leaders among them concluded that it was simply the way men must smell when there are a great many of them living together. Those dark buildings must be crowded very full of men, they decided, probably as many thousands of them, indoors, as there were of us, outdoors; so it was no wonder their smell was so strong and, to our kind, so unpleasant. Besides, it was so clear now in every other way that men were not as we had always supposed, but were doing everything they knew how to make us comfortable and happy, that we ought to just put up with their smell, which after all they couldn't help, any more than we could help our own. Very likely men didn't like the way we smelled, any more than we liked theirs. They passed along these ideas to the others, and soon everyone felt more calm, and then the wind changed again, and the fierce smell no longer came to them, and the smell of their own kind was back again, very strong of course, in such a crowd, but ever so homey and comforting, and everyone felt easy again.

"They were fed and watered so generously, and treated so well, and the majesty and the loveliness of this place where they had all come to rest was so far beyond anything they had ever known or dreamed of, that many of the simple and ignorant, whose memories were short, began to wonder whether that whole difficult journey, or even their whole lives up to now, had ever really been. Hadn't it all been just shadows, they murmured, just a bad dream?

"Even the sharp ones, who knew very well it had all really happened, began to figure that everything up to now had been made so full of pain only so that all they had come to now might seem all the sweeter and the more glorious. Some of the oldest and deepest were even of a mind that all the puzzle and tribulation of the journey had been sent us as a kind of harsh trying or proving of our worthiness; and that it was entirely fitting and proper that we could earn our way through to such rewards as these, only through suffering, and through being patient under pain which was beyond our understanding; and that now at the last, to those who had borne all things well, all things were made known: for the mystery of suffering stood revealed in joy. And now as they looked back over all that was past, all their sorrows and bewilderments seemed so little and so fleeting that, from the simplest among them even to the most wise, they could feel only the kind of amused pity we feel toward the very young when, with the first thing that hurts them or they are forbidden, they are sure there is nothing kind or fair in all creation, and carry on accordingly, raving and grieving as if their hearts would break."

She glanced among them with an indulgent smile, hoping the little lesson would sink home. They seemed interested but somewhat dazed. I'm talking way over their heads, she realized. But by now she herself was too deeply absorbed in her story to modify it much. *Let* it be, she thought, a little impatient; it's over *my* head, for that matter.

"They had hardly before this even wondered that they were alive," she went on, "and now all of a sudden they felt they understood *why* they were. This made them very happy, but they were still only beginning to enjoy this new wisdom when quite a new and different kind of restiveness ran among them. Before they quite knew it they were all moving once again, and now they realized that they were being moved, once more, by men, toward still some other place and purpose they could not know. But during these last hours they had been so well that

80

now they felt no uneasiness, but all moved forward calm and sure toward better things still to come; he has told us that he no longer felt as if he were being driven, even as it became clear that they were going toward the shade of those great buildings; but guided.

"He was guided between fences which stood ever more and more narrowly near each other among companions who were pressed ever more and more closely against one another; and now as he felt their warmth against him it was not uncomfortable, and his pleasure in it was not through any need to be close among others through anxiousness, but was a new kind of strong and gentle delight, at being so very close, so deeply of his own kind that it seemed as if the very breath and heartbeat of each one were being exchanged through all that multitude, and each was another, and others were each, and each was a multitude, and the multitude was one. And quieted and made mild within this melting, they now entered the cold shadow cast by the buildings, and now with every step the smell of the buildings grew stronger, and in the darkening air the glittering of the fences was ever more queer.

"And now as they were pressed ever more intimately together he could see ahead of him a narrow gate, and he was strongly pressed upon from either side and from behind, and went in eagerly, and now he was between two fences so narrowly set that he brushed either fence with either flank, and walked alone, seeing just one other ahead of him, and knowing of just one other behind him, and for a moment the strange thought came to him, that the one ahead was his father, and that the one behind was the son he had never begotten.

"And now the light was so changed that he knew he must have come inside one of the gloomy and enormous buildings, and the smell was so much stronger that it seemed almost to burn his nostrils, and the smell and the somber new light blended together and became some other thing again, beyond his describing to us except to say that the whole air beat with it like one immense heart and it was as if the beating of this heart were pure violence infinitely manifolded upon violence: so that the uneasy feeling stirred in him again that it would be wise to turn around and run out of this place just as fast and as far as ever he could go. This he heard, as if he were telling it to himself at the top of his voice, but it came from somewhere so deep and so dark inside him that he could only hear the shouting of it as less than a whisper, as just a hot and chilling breath, and he scarcely heeded it, there was so much else to attend to.

"For as he walked along in this sudden and complete loneliness, he tells us, this wonderful knowledge of being one with all his race meant less and less to him, and in its place came something still more wonderful: he knew what it was to be himself alone, a creature separate and different from any other, who had never been before, and would never be again. He could feel this in his whole weight as he walked, and in each foot as he put it down and gave his weight to it and moved above it, and in every muscle as he moved, and it was a pride which lifted him up and made him feel large, and a pleasure which pierced him through. And as he began with such wondering delight to be aware of his own exact singleness in this world, he also began to understand (or so he thought) just why these fences were set so very narrow, and just why he was walking all by himself. It stole over him, he

85

tells us, like the feeling of a slow cool wind, that he was being guided toward some still more wonderful reward or revealing, up ahead, which he could not of course imagine, but he was sure it was being held in store for him alone.

"Just then the one ahead of him fell down with a great sigh, and was so quickly taken out of the way that he did not even have to shift the order of his hooves as he walked on. The sudden fall and the sound of that sigh dismayed him, though, and something within him told him that it would be wise to look up: and there he saw Him.

"A little bridge ran crosswise above the fences. He stood on this bridge with His feet as wide apart as He could set them. He wore spattered trousers but from the belt up He was naked and as wet as rain. Both arms were raised high above His head and in both hands He held an enormous Hammer. With a grunt which was hardly like the voice of a human being, and with all His strength, He brought this Hammer down onto the forehead of our friend: who, in a blinding blazing, heard from his own mouth the beginning of a gasping sigh; then there was only darkness."

Oh, this is *enough!* it's *enough!* she cried out within herself, seeing their terrible young eyes. How *could* she have been so foolish as to tell so much!

"What happened then?" she heard, in the voice of the oldest calf, and she   90
was horrified. This shining in their eyes: was it only excitement? no pity? no fear?

"What happened?" two others asked.

Very well, she said to herself. I've gone so far; now I'll go the rest of the way. She decided not to soften it, either. She'd teach them a lesson they wouldn't forget in a hurry.

"Very well," she was surprised to hear herself say aloud.

"How long he lay in this darkness he couldn't know, but when he began to come out of it, all he knew was the most unspeakably dreadful pain. He was upside down and very slowly swinging and turning, for he was hanging by the tendons of his heels from great frightful hooks, and he has told us that the feeling was as if his hide were being torn from him inch by inch, in one piece. And then as he became more clearly aware he found that this was exactly what was happening. Knives would sliver and slice along both flanks, between the hide and the living flesh; then there was a moment of most precious relief; then red hands seized his hide and there was a jerking of the hide and a tearing of tissue which it was almost as terrible to hear as to feel, turning his whole body and the poor head at the bottom of it; and then the knives again.

"It was so far beyond anything he had ever known unnatural and amazing   95
that he hung there through several more such slicings and jerkings and tearings before he was fully able to take it all in: then, with a scream, and a supreme straining of all his strength, he tore himself from the hooks and collapsed sprawling to the floor and, scrambling right to his feet, charged the men with the knives. For just a moment they were so astonished and so terrified they could not move. Then they moved faster than he had ever known men could — and so did all the other men who chanced to be in his way. He ran down a glowing floor of blood and down endless corridors which were hung with the bleeding carcasses of our kind and with bleeding fragments of carcasses, among blood-clothed men who

carried bleeding weapons, and out of that vast room into the open, and over and through one fence after another, shoving aside many an astounded stranger and shouting out warnings as he ran, and away up the railroad toward the West.

"How he ever managed to get away, and how he ever found his way home, we can only try to guess. It's told that he scarcely knew, himself, by the time he came to this part of his story. He was impatient with those who interrupted him to ask about that, he had so much more important things to tell them, and by then he was so exhausted and so far gone that he could say nothing very clear about the little he did know. But we can realize that he must have had really tremendous strength, otherwise he couldn't have outlived the Hammer; and that strength such as his—which we simply don't see these days, it's of the olden time—is capable of things our own strongest and bravest would sicken to dream of. But there was something even stronger than his strength. There was his righteous fury, which nothing could stand up against, which brought him out of that fearful place. And there was his high and burning and heroic purpose, to keep him safe along the way, and to guide him home, and to keep the breath of life in him until he could warn us. He did manage to tell us that he just followed the railroad, but how he chose one among the many which branched out from that place, he couldn't say. He told us, too, that from time to time he recognized shapes of mountains and other landmarks, from his journey by train, all reappearing backward and with a changed look and hard to see, too (for he was shrewd enough to travel mostly at night), but still recognizable. But that isn't enough to account for it. For he has told us, too, that he simply *knew* the way; that he didn't hesitate one moment in choosing the right line of railroad, or even think of it as choosing; and that the landmarks didn't really guide him, but just made him the more sure of what he was already sure of; and that whenever he *did* encounter human beings—and during the later stages of his journey, when he began to doubt he would live to tell us, he traveled day and night—they never so much as moved to make him trouble, but stopped dead in their tracks, and their jaws fell open.

"And surely we can't wonder that their jaws fell open. I'm sure yours would, if you had seen him as he arrived, and I'm very glad I wasn't there to see it, either, even though it is said to be the greatest and most momentous day of all the days that ever were or shall be. For we have the testimony of eyewitnesses, how he looked, and it is only too vivid, even to hear of. He came up out of the East as much staggering as galloping (for by now he was so worn out by pain and exertion and loss of blood that he could hardly stay upright), and his heels were so piteously torn by the hooks that his hooves doubled under more often than not, and in his broken forehead the mark of the Hammer was like the socket for a third eye.

"He came to the meadow where the great trees made shade over the water. 'Bring them all together!' he cried out, as soon as he could find breath. 'All!' Then he drank; and then he began to speak to those who were already there: for as soon as he saw himself in the water it was as clear to him as it was to those who watched him that there was no time left to send for the others. His hide was all gone from his head and his neck and his forelegs and his chest and most of one side and a part of the other side. It was flung backward from his naked muscles by the wind of his running and now it lay around him in the dust like a ragged garment. They say there is no imagining how terrible and in some way how grand the eyeball is when the skin has been taken entirely from around it: his eyes, which were bare in this way, also burned with pain, and with the final energies of his life, and with his desperate concern to warn us while he could: and he rolled his eyes wildly while he talked, or looked piercingly from one to another of the listeners, interrupting himself to cry out, '*Believe* me! Oh, *believe* me!' For it had evidently never occurred to him that he might not be believed, and must make this last great effort, in addition to all he had gone through for us, to *make* himself believed; so that he groaned with sorrow and with rage and railed at them without tact or mercy for their slowness to believe. He had scarcely what you could call a voice left, but with this relic of a voice he shouted and bellowed and bullied us and insulted us, in the agony of his concern. While he talked he bled from the mouth, and the mingled blood and saliva hung from his chin like the beard of a goat.

"Some say that with his naked face, and his savage eyes, and that beard and the hide lying off his bare shoulders like shabby clothing, he looked almost human. But others feel this is an irreverence even to think; and others, that it is a poor compliment to pay the one who told us, at such cost to himself, the true ultimate purpose of Man. Some did not believe he had ever come from our ranch in the first place, and of course he was so different from us in appearance and even in his voice, and so changed from what he might ever have looked or sounded like before, that nobody could recognize him for sure, though some were sure they did. Others suspected that he had been sent among us with his story for some mischievous and cruel purpose, and the fact that they could not imagine what this purpose might be, made them, naturally, all the more suspicious. Some believed he was actually a man, trying — and none too successfully, they said — to disguise himself as one of us; and again the fact that they could not imagine why a man would do this, made them all the more uneasy. There were quite a few who doubted that anyone who could get into such bad condition as he was in, was fit even to give reliable information, let alone advice, to those in good health. And some whispered, even while he spoke, that he had turned lunatic; and many came to believe this. It wasn't only that his story was so fantastic; there was good reason to wonder, many felt, whether anybody in his right mind would go to such trouble for others. But even those who did not believe him listened intently, out of curiosity to hear so wild a tale, and out of the respect it is only proper to show any creature who is in the last agony.

"What he told, was what I have just told you. But his purpose was away 100 beyond just the telling. When they asked questions, no matter how curious or suspicious or idle or foolish, he learned, toward the last, to answer them with all the patience he could and in all the detail he could remember. He even invited them to examine his wounded heels and the pulsing wound in his head as closely as they pleased. He even begged them to, for he knew that before everything else, he must be believed. For unless we could believe him, wherever could we find any reason, or enough courage, to do the hard and dreadful things he told us we must do!

"It was only these things, he cared about. Only for these, he came back."

Now clearly remembering what these things were, she felt her whole being quail. She looked at the young ones quickly and as quickly looked away.

"While he talked," she went on, "and our ancestors listened, men came quietly among us; one of them shot him. Whether he was shot in kindness or to silence him is an endlessly disputed question which will probably never be settled. Whether, even, he died of the shot, or through his own great pain and weariness (for his eyes, they say, were glazing for some time before the men came), we will never be sure. Some suppose even that he may have died of his sorrow and his concern for us. Others feel that he had quite enough to die of, without that. All these things are tangled and lost in the disputes of those who love to theorize and to argue. There is no arguing about his dying words, though; they were very clearly remembered:

"*'Tell them! Believe!'*"

After a while her son asked, "What did he tell them to do?"   105

She avoided his eyes. "There's a great deal of disagreement about that, too," she said after a moment. "You see, he was so very tired."

They were silent.

"So tired," she said, "some think that toward the end, he really *must* have been out of his mind."

"Why?" asked her son.

"Because he was so tired out and so badly hurt."   110

They looked at her mistrustfully.

"And because of what he told us to do."

"What did he tell us to do?" her son asked again.

Her throat felt dry. "Just . . . things you can hardly bear even to think of. That's all."

They waited. "Well, *what?*" her son asked in a cold, accusing voice.   115

"*'Each one is himself,'*" she said shyly. "*'Not of the herd. Himself alone.'* That's one."

"What else?"

"*'Obey nobody. Depend on none.'*"

"What else?"

She found that she was moved. "*'Break down the fences,'*" she said less shyly.   120 "*'Tell everybody, everywhere.'*"

"Where?"

"Everywhere. You see, he thought there must be ever so many more of us than we had ever known."

They were silent. "What else?" her son asked.

"*'For if even a few do not hear me, or disbelieve me, we are all betrayed.'*"

"Betrayed?"   125

"He meant, doing as men want us to. Not for ourselves, or the good of each other."

They were puzzled.

"Because, you see, he felt there was no other way." Again her voice altered: "*'All who are put on the range are put onto trains. All who are put onto trains meet*

The Man With The Hammer. All who stay home are kept there to breed others to go onto the range, and so betray themselves and their kind and their children forever.

"'We are brought into this life only to be victims; and there is no other way for us unless we save ourselves.'

"Do you understand?"   130

Still they were puzzled, she saw; and no wonder, poor things. But now the ancient lines rang in her memory, terrible and brave. They made her somehow proud. She began actually to want to say them.

"'Never be taken,'" she said. "'Never be driven. Let those who can, kill Man. Let those who cannot, avoid him.'"

She looked around at them.

"What else?" her son asked, and in his voice there was a rising valor.

She looked straight into his eyes. "'Kill the yearlings,'" she said very gently.   135
"'Kill the calves.'"

She saw the valor leave his eyes.

"Kill us?"

She nodded. "'So long as Man holds dominion over us,'" she said. And in dread and amazement she heard herself add, "'Bear no young.'"

With this they all looked at her at once in such a way that she loved her child, and all these others, as never before; and there dilated within her such a sorrowful and marveling grandeur that for a moment she saw nothing, and heard nothing except her own inward whisper, "Why, I am one alone. And of the herd, too. Both at once. All one."

Her son's voice brought her back: "Did they do what he told them to?"   140

The oldest one scoffed, "Would we be here, if they had?"

"They say some did," the mother replied. "Some tried. Not all."

"What did the men do to them?" another asked.

"I don't know," she said. "It was such a very long time ago."

"Do you believe it?" asked the oldest calf.   145

"There are some who believe it," she said.

"Do *you*?"

"I'm told that far back in the wildest corners of the range there are some of us, mostly very, very old ones, who have never been taken. It's said that they meet, every so often, to talk and just to think together about the heroism and the terror of two sublime Beings, The One Who Came Back, and The Man With The Hammer. Even here at home, some of the old ones, and some of us who are just old-fashioned, believe it, or parts of it anyway. I know there are some who say that a hollow at the center of the forehead — a sort of shadow of the Hammer's blow — is a sign of very special ability. And I remember how Great-grandmother used to sing an old, pious song, let's see now, yes, 'Be not like dumb-driven cattle, be a hero in the strife.' But there aren't many. Not any more."

"Do *you* believe it?" the oldest calf insisted; and now she was touched to realize that every one of them, from the oldest to the youngest, needed very badly to be sure about that.

"Of course not, silly," she said; and all at once she was overcome by a curious   150
shyness, for it occurred to her that in the course of time, this young thing might

be bred to her. "It's just an old, old legend." With a tender little laugh she added, lightly, "We use it to frighten children with."

By now the light was long on the plain and the herd was only a fume of gold near the horizon. Behind it, dung steamed, and dust sank gently to the shattered ground. She looked far away for a moment, wondering. Something — it was like a forgotten word on the tip of the tongue. She felt the sudden chill of the late afternoon and she wondered what she had been wondering about. "Come, children," she said briskly, "it's high time for supper." And she turned away; they followed.

The trouble was, her son was thinking, you could never trust her. If she said a thing was so, she was probably just trying to get her way with you. If she said a thing wasn't so, it probably was so. But you never could be sure. Not without seeing for yourself. I'm going to go, he told himself; I don't care *what* she wants. And if it isn't so, why then I'll live on the range and make a great journey and find out what *is* so. And if what she told was true, why then I'll know ahead of time and the one I will charge is The Man With The Hammer. I'll put Him and His Hammer out of the way forever, and that will make me an even better hero than The One Who Came Back.

So, when his mother glanced at him in concern, not quite daring to ask her question, he gave her his most docile smile, and snuggled his head against her, and she was comforted.

The littlest and youngest of them was doing double skips in his effort to keep up with her. Now that he wouldn't be interrupting her, and none of the big ones would hear and make fun of him, he shyly whispered his question, so warmly moistly ticklish that she felt as if he were licking her ear.

"What is it, darling?" she asked, bending down. 155

"What's a train?" [1951]

THINKING ABOUT THE TEXT

1. In one sense, Agee's is not a realistic story. After all, it features animals that talk and engage in philosophical reflection. Do you find the story plausible in any respect, or is your reaction to it complete disbelief? Develop your response by referring to particular details of the text.

2. What historical events resemble the fictional events in this story — in particular, the transport and slaughter of the cows? Whom, if anyone, do you think of as you read about The One Who Came Back?

3. What are the mother cow's changing thoughts and feelings as she tells the story? How does her audience influence her way of telling it? Refer to specific passages.

4. Although she recounts the experiences of The One Who Came Back, the mother cow does not directly witness them. Moreover, the story that she tells about him has been passed down through the years; she is only the latest teller of it. What might have been Agee's purpose in having her lack direct evidence for the history she recalls?

5. What lessons does The One Who Came Back draw from his experiences?
What does the mother cow seem to think of his views? What do you think
of them?

TONI CADE BAMBARA
The Lesson

Toni Cade Bambara (1939–1995) taught at various colleges and worked as a community activist. She edited The Black Woman *(1970), a collection of essays that became a landmark of contemporary black feminism. Also a fiction writer, she received the American Book Award for her 1980 novel* The Salt Eaters *and has produced several collections of short stories. "The Lesson" comes from her first short-story collection,* Gorilla, My Love *(1972).*

Back in the days when everyone was old and stupid or young and foolish and me and Sugar were the only ones just right, this lady moved on our block with nappy hair and proper speech and no makeup. And quite naturally we laughed at her, laughed the way we did at the junk man who went about his business like he was some big-time president and his sorry-ass horse his secretary. And we kinda hated her too, hated the way we did the winos who cluttered up our parks and pissed on our handball walls and stank up our hallways and stairs so you couldn't halfway play hide-and-seek without a goddamn gas mask. Miss Moore was her name. The only woman on the block with no first name. And she was black as hell, cept for her feet, which were fish-white and spooky. And she was always planning these boring-ass things for us to do, us being my cousin, mostly, who lived on the block cause we all moved North the same time and to the same apartment then spread out gradual to breathe. And our parents would yank our heads into some kinda shape and crisp up our clothes so we'd be presentable for travel with Miss Moore, who always looked like she was going to church, though she never did. Which is just one of the things the grownups talked about when they talked behind her back like a dog. But when she came calling with some sachet she'd sewed up or some gingerbread she'd made or some book, why then they'd all be too embarrassed to turn her down and we'd get handed over all spruced up. She'd been to college and said it was only right that she should take responsibility for the young ones' education, and she not even related by marriage or blood. So they'd go for it. Specially Aunt Gretchen. She was the main gofer in the family. You got some ole dumb shit foolishness you want somebody to go for, you send for Aunt Gretchen. She been screwed into the go-along for so long, it's a blood-deep natural thing with her. Which is how she got saddled with me and Sugar and Junior in the first place while our mothers were in a la-de-da apartment up the block having a good ole time.

So this one day, Miss Moore rounds us all up at the mailbox and it's puredee hot and she's knockin herself out about arithmetic. And school suppose to let up in summer I heard, but she don't never let up. And the starch in my pinafore scratching the shit outta me and I'm really hating this nappy-head bitch and her goddamn college degree. I'd much rather go to the pool or to the show where it's cool. So me and Sugar leaning on the mailbox being surly, which is a Miss Moore word. And Flyboy checking out what everybody brought for lunch. And Fat Butt already wasting his peanut-butter-and-jelly sandwich like the pig he is. And Junebug punchin on Q.T.'s arm for potato chips. And Rosie Giraffe shifting from one hip to the other waiting for somebody to step on her foot or ask her if she from Georgia so she can kick ass, preferably Mercedes'. And Miss Moore asking us do we know what money is, like we a bunch of retards. I mean real money, she say, like it's only poker chips or monopoly papers we lay on the grocer. So right away I'm tired of this and say so. And would much rather snatch Sugar and go to the Sunset and terrorize the West Indian kids and take their hair ribbons and their money too. And Miss Moore files that remark away for next week's lesson on brotherhood, I can tell. And finally I say we oughta get to the subway cause it's cooler and besides we might meet some cute boys. Sugar done swiped her mama's lipstick, so we ready.

So we heading down the street and she's boring us silly about what things cost and what our parents make and how much goes for rent and how money ain't divided up right in this country. And then she gets to the part about we all poor and live in the slums, which I don't feature. And I'm ready to speak on that, but she steps out in the street and hails two cabs just like that. Then she hustles half the crew in with her and hands me a five-dollar bill and tells me to calculate 10 percent tip for the driver. And we're off. Me and Sugar and Junebug and Flyboy hangin out the window and hollering to everybody, putting lipstick on each other cause Flyboy a faggot anyway, and making farts with our sweaty armpits. But I'm mostly trying to figure how to spend this money. But they all fascinated with the meter ticking and Junebug starts laying bets as to how much it'll read when Flyboy can't hold his breath no more. Then Sugar lays bets as to how much it'll be when we get there. So I'm stuck. Don't nobody want to go for my plan, which is to jump out at the next light and run off to the first bar-b-que we can find. Then the driver tells us to get the hell out cause we there already. And the meter reads eighty-five cents. And I'm stalling to figure out the tip and Sugar say give him a dime. And I decide he don't need it bad as I do, so later for him. But then he tries to take off with Junebug foot still in the door so we talk about his mama something ferocious. Then we check out that we on Fifth Avenue and everybody dressed up in stockings. One lady in a fur coat, hot as it is. White folks crazy.

"This is the place," Miss Moore say, presenting it to us in the voice she uses at the museum. "Let's look in the windows before we go in."

"Can we steal?" Sugar asks very serious like she's getting the ground rules squared away before she plays. "I beg your pardon," say Miss Moore, and we fall out. So she leads us around the windows of the toy store and me and Sugar screamin, "This is mine, that's mine, I gotta have that, that was made for me, I was born for that," till Big Butt drowns us out.

"Hey, I'm goin to buy that there."

5

"That there? You don't even know what it is, stupid."

"I do so," he say punchin on Rosie Giraffe. "It's a microscope."

"Whatcha gonna do with a microscope, fool?"

"Look at things."   10

"Like what, Ronald?" ask Miss Moore. And Big Butt ain't got the first notion. So here go Miss Moore gabbing about the thousands of bacteria in a drop of water and the somethinorother in a speck of blood and the million and one living things in the air around us is invisible to the naked eye. And what she say that for? Junebug go to town on that "naked" and we rolling. Then Miss Moore ask what it cost. So we all jam into the window smudgin it up and the price tag say $300. So then she ask how long'd take for Big Butt and Junebug to save up their allowances. "Too long," I say. "Yeh," adds Sugar, "outgrown it by that time." And Miss Moore say no, you never outgrow learning instruments. "Why, even medical students and interns and," blah, blah, blah. And we ready to choke Big Butt for bringing it up in the first damn place.

"This here costs four hundred eighty dollars," says Rosie Giraffe. So we pile up all over her to see what she pointin out. My eyes tell me it's a chunk of glass cracked with something heavy, and different-color inks dripped into the splits, then the whole thing put into a oven or something. But for $480 it don't make sense.

"That's a paperweight made of semi-precious stones fused together under tremendous pressure," she explains slowly, with her hands doing the mining and all the factory work.

"So what's a paperweight?" asks Rosie Giraffe.

"To weigh paper with, dumbbell," say Flyboy, the wise man from the East.   15

"Not exactly," say Miss Moore, which is what she say when you warm or way off too. "It's to weigh paper down so it won't scatter and make your desk untidy." So right away me and Sugar curtsy to each other and then to Mercedes who is more the tidy type.

"We don't keep paper on top of the desk in my class," say Junebug, figuring Miss Moore crazy or lyin one.

"At home, then," she say. "Don't you have a calendar and pencil case and a blotter and a letter-opener on your desk at home where you do your homework?" And she know damn well what our homes look like cause she nosys around in them every chance she gets.

"I don't even have a desk," say Junebug. "Do we?"

"No. And I don't get no homework neither," says Big Butt.   20

"And I don't even have a home," say Flyboy like he do at school to keep the white folks off his back and sorry for him. Send this poor kid to camp posters, is his specialty.

"I do," says Mercedes. "I have a box of stationery on my desk and a picture of my cat. My godmother bought the stationery and the desk. There's a big rose on each sheet and the envelopes smell like roses."

"Who wants to know about your smelly-ass stationery," say Rosie Giraffe fore I can get my two cents in.

"It's important to have a work area all your own so that . . ."

"Will you look at this sailboat, please," say Flyboy, cuttin her off and pointin   25
to the thing like it was his. So once again we tumble all over each other to gaze at
this magnificent thing in the toy store which is just big enough to maybe sail two
kittens across the pond if you strap them to the posts tight. We all start reciting the
price tag like we in assembly. "Handcrafted sailboat of fiberglass at one thousand
one hundred ninety-five dollars."

"Unbelievable," I hear myself say and am really stunned. I read it again for
myself just in case the group recitation put me in a trance. Same thing. For some
reason this pisses me off. We look at Miss Moore and she lookin at us, waiting for
I dunno what.

"Who'd pay all that when you can buy a sailboat set for a quarter at Pop's, a
tube of glue for a dime, and a ball of string for eight cents? It must have a motor
and a whole lot else besides," I say. "My sailboat cost me about fifty cents."

"But will it take water?" say Mercedes with her smart ass.

"Took mine to Alley Pond Park once," say Flyboy. "String broke. Lost it. Pity."

"Sailed mine in Central Park and it keeled over and sank. Had to ask my   30
father for another dollar."

"And you got the strap," laugh Big Butt. "The jerk didn't even have a string
on it. My old man wailed on his behind."

Little Q.T. was staring hard at the sailboat and you could see he wanted it
bad. But he too little and somebody'd just take it from him. So what the hell.
"This boat for kids, Miss Moore?"

"Parents silly to buy something like that just to get all broke up," say Rosie
Giraffe.

"That much money it should last forever," I figure.

"My father'd buy it for me if I wanted it."   35

"Your father, my ass," say Rosie Giraffe getting a chance to finally push Mercedes.

"Must be rich people shop here," say Q.T.

"You are a very bright boy," say Flyboy. "What was your first clue?" And he
rap him on the head with the back of his knuckles, since Q.T. the only one he
could get away with. Though Q.T. liable to come up behind you years later and
get his licks in when you half expect it.

"What I want to know is," I says to Miss Moore though I never talk to her, I
wouldn't give the bitch that satisfaction, "is how much a real boat costs? I figure a
thousand'd get you a yacht any day."

"Why don't you check that out," she says, "and report back to the group?"   40
Which really pains my ass. If you gonna mess up a perfectly good swim day least
you could do is have some answers. "Let's go in," she say like she got something
up her sleeve. Only she don't lead the way. So me and Sugar turn the corner to
where the entrance is, but when we get there I kinda hang back. Not that I'm
scared, what's there to be afraid of, just a toy store. But I feel funny, shame. But
what I got to be shamed about? Got as much right to go in as anybody. But somehow I can't seem to get hold of the door, so I step away from Sugar to lead. But
she hangs back too. And I look at her and she looks at me and this is ridiculous. I
mean, damn, I have never ever been shy about doing nothing or going nowhere.

But then Mercedes steps up and then Rosie Giraffe and Big Butt crowd in behind and shove, and next thing we all stuffed into the doorway with only Mercedes squeezing past us, smoothing out her jumper and walking right down the aisle. Then the rest of us tumble in like a glued-together jigsaw done all wrong. And people lookin at us. And it's like the time me and Sugar crashed into the Catholic church on a dare. But once we got in there and everything so hushed and holy and the candles and the bowin and the handkerchiefs on all the drooping heads, I just couldn't go through with the plan. Which was for me to run up to the altar and do a tap dance while Sugar played the nose flute and messed around in the holy water. And Sugar kept givin me the elbow. Then later teased me so bad I tied her up in the shower and turned it on and locked her in. And she'd be there till this day if Aunt Gretchen hadn't finally figured I was lying about the boarder takin a shower.

Same thing in the store. We all walkin on tiptoe and hardly touchin the games and puzzles and things. And I watched Miss Moore who is steady watchin us like she waitin for a sign. Like Mama Drewery watches the sky and sniffs the air and takes note of just how much slant is in the bird formation. Then me and Sugar bump smack into each other, so busy gazing at the toys, 'specially the sailboat. But we don't laugh and go into our fat-lady bump-stomach routine. We just stare at that price tag. Then Sugar run a finger over the whole boat. And I'm jealous and want to hit her. Maybe not her, but I sure want to punch somebody in the mouth.

"Watcha bring us here for, Miss Moore?"

"You sound angry, Sylvia. Are you mad about something?" Givin me one of them grins like she tellin a grown-up joke that never turns out to be funny. And she's lookin very closely at me like maybe she plannin to do my portrait from memory. I'm mad, but I won't give her that satisfaction. So I slouch around the store bein very bored and say, "Let's go."

Me and Sugar at the back of the train watchin the tracks whizzin by large then small then getting gobbled up in the dark. I'm thinkin about this tricky toy I saw in the store. A clown that somersaults on a bar then does chin-ups just cause you yank lightly at his leg. Cost $35. I could see me askin my mother for a $35 birthday clown. "You wanna who that costs what?" she'd say, cocking her head to the side to get a better view of the hole in my head. Thirty-five dollars could buy new bunk beds for Junior and Gretchen's boy. Thirty-five dollars and the whole household could go visit Grand-daddy Nelson in the country. Thirty-five dollars would pay for the rent and the piano bill too. Who are these people that spend that much for performing clowns and $1000 for toy sailboats? What kinda work they do and how they live and how come we ain't in on it? Where we are is who we are, Miss Moore always pointin out. But it don't necessarily have to be that way, she always adds then waits for somebody to say that poor people have to wake up and demand their share of the pie and don't none of us know what kind of pie she talking about in the first damn place. But she ain't so smart cause I still got her four dollars from the taxi and she sure ain't gettin it. Messin up my day with this shit. Sugar nudges me in my pocket and winks.

Miss Moore lines us up in front of the mailbox where we started from, seem   45
like years ago, and I got a headache for thinkin so hard. And we lean all over each
other so we can hold up under the draggy-ass lecture she always finishes us off
with at the end before we thank her for borin us to tears. But she just looks at us
like she readin tea leaves. Finally she say, "Well, what did you think of F. A. O.
Schwarz?"

Rosie Giraffe mumbles, "White folks crazy."

"I'd like to go there again when I get my birthday money," says Mercedes,
and we shove her out the pack so she has to lean on the mailbox by herself.

"I'd like a shower. Tiring day," say Flyboy.

Then Sugar surprises me by sayin, "You know, Miss Moore, I don't think all
of us here put together eat in a year what that sailboat costs." And Miss Moore
lights up like somebody goosed her. "And?" she say, urging Sugar on. Only I'm
standin on her foot so she don't continue.

"Imagine for a minute what kind of society it is in which some people can   50
spend on a toy what it would cost to feed a family of six or seven. What do you
think?"

"I think," say Sugar pushing me off her feet like she never done before, cause
I whip her ass in a minute, "that this is not much of a democracy if you ask me.
Equal chance to pursue happiness means an equal crack at the dough, don't it?"
Miss Moore is beside herself and I am disgusted with Sugar's treachery. So I stand
on her foot one more time to see if she'll shove me. She shuts up, and Miss
Moore looks at me, sorrowfully I'm thinkin. And somethin weird is goin on, I can
feel it in my chest.

"Anybody else learn anything today?" lookin dead at me. I walk away and
Sugar has to run to catch up and don't even seem to notice when I shrug her arm
off my shoulder.

"Well, we got four dollars anyway," she says.

"Uh hunh."

"We could go to Hascombs and get half a chocolate layer and then go to the   55
Sunset and still have plenty money for potato chips and ice cream sodas."

"Un hunh."

"Race you to Hascombs," she say.

We start down the block and she gets ahead which is O.K. by me cause I'm
going to the West End and then over to the Drive to think this day through. She
can run if she want to and even run faster. But ain't nobody gonna beat me at
nuthin.   [1972]

THINKING ABOUT THE TEXT

1. Bambara's story begins with "Back in the days," which suggests that Sylvia
   is significantly older now than she was then. How much time do you
   think has passed since the events she recalls? Does it matter to you how
   old she is now? Why, or why not?

2. Miss Moore is not officially a teacher. Nor is she a relative of the children she instructs. Is it right, then, for her to "take responsibility for the young ones' education" (para. 1)? Make arguments for and against her doing so.

3. Consider Miss Moore herself as making an argument. What are her claims? Which of her strategies, if any, seem effective in persuading her audience? Which, if any, seem ineffective?

4. What statements by the children articulate the lesson that Miss Moore teaches? Are all these statements saying pretty much the same thing? At the end of the story is Sylvia ready to agree with all of them? Explain.

5. Do class and race seem equally important in this story, or does one seem more important than the other? Elaborate your reasoning.

MAKING COMPARISONS

1. In paragraph 92 of "A Mother's Tale," Agee writes, "Very well, she said to herself. I've gone so far; now I'll go the rest of the way. She decided not to soften it, either. She'd teach them a lesson they wouldn't forget in a hurry." Can this passage about the mother cow be applied to Miss Moore as well? Why, or why not? What would you think if a teacher of yours had this attitude?

2. Compare the lessons that the mother cow and Miss Moore teach. Do the lessons seem similar, or are you more struck by their differences?

3. Rewrite a paragraph of Agee's story as narrated by one of the young cows using a voice like Sylvia's. What does this exercise tell you about Agee's story? About Bambara's?

WRITING ABOUT ISSUES

1. Choose either "A Mother's Tale" or "The Lesson" and write an essay explaining how the story depicts children as learners. Refer to specific statements made by and about them. Whichever story you choose, feel free to make distinctions among its children.

2. At the end of Agee's story, the mother cow's son distrusts her account. Furthermore, he plans to "make the great journey" despite her wishes. At the end of Bambara's story, however, Sylvia evidently comes closer to sharing Miss Moore's view of society. Should we conclude that Miss Moore is a better teacher than the mother cow? Write an essay arguing your position on this issue of evaluation.

3. Write an essay explaining how a certain occasion changed, or came close to changing, your view of society. Give details of the occasion itself, identifying any "teachers" involved. Be specific, too, about the view you held before the occasion, why you had thought of your society that way, and how the occasion provided you with evidence for another view.

4. Today, cattle are still slaughtered for meat, and some people can afford expensive toys while others don't have much money at all. Think of eight-year-olds in your neighborhood. Choose one of these situations and write an essay identifying what and how you would teach the children about it. Be sure to justify the goals and methods you would adopt.

OBSERVING SCHOOLCHILDREN

LOUISE GLÜCK, "The School Children"
TOI DERRICOTTE, "Fears of the Eighth Grade"
PHILIP LEVINE, "Among Children"

Even writers who no longer attend school make schoolchildren a subject of their work. Indeed, many poems depict schoolchildren as symbols of innocence. Several of these suggest that such innocence is doomed to fade with adulthood, while others find that particular social trends threaten it. Of course, to decide whether a poem takes either position, you must first think about what you mean by *innocence*. As you read the following poems by Louise Glück, Toi Derricotte, and Philip Levine, consider your own definition of the term as well as the specific comments each poem makes about the schoolchildren it describes.

BEFORE YOU READ

Recall a class that you were part of in school. Imagine an older person observing that class in preparation for writing a poem about it. What are some specific aspects of the class that he or she might have observed? If you wish, try writing a poem about the class.

LOUISE GLÜCK

The School Children

For many years, Louise Glück (b. 1943) has taught creative writing at Goddard College in Vermont. She has also published several volumes of poetry, winning the Pulitzer Prize for The Wild Iris *(1992). In her poetry, Glück often deals with domestic life, though with mythic references that make it seem more mysterious than familiar. The following poem comes from her 1975 book* The House on Marshland.

The children go forward with their little satchels.
And all morning the mothers have labored
to gather the late apples, red and gold,
like words of another language.

◆ ◆ ◆

And on the other shore   5
are those who wait behind great desks
to receive these offerings.

How orderly they are — the nails
on which the children hang
their overcoats of blue or yellow wool.   10

And the teachers shall instruct them in silence
and the mothers shall scour the orchards for a way out,
drawing to themselves the gray limbs of the fruit trees
bearing so little ammunition.   [1975]

THINKING ABOUT THE TEXT

1. Do you think Glück is commenting on a very particular group of school-children or on schoolchildren in general? Explain your reasoning.

2. The words "How orderly they are" (line 8) appear before Glück identifies the "they." Only afterward does she indicate that "they" refers to "the nails." Why do you think she delays? What is the effect?

3. Although the poem's title suggests that it will focus on the schoolchildren, the poem also refers to mothers and teachers. After reading it, do you think the schoolchildren are indeed its focus? Support your claim by referring to specific lines.

4. What roles do colors play in this poem? Identify each color mentioned and some things that a reader might associate with each.

5. What are some specific ways in which a teacher might instruct children "in silence" (line 11)? Has a teacher of yours ever done so? In what sense might the mothers of schoolchildren need "a way out" (line 12) and "ammunition" (line 14)?

TOI DERRICOTTE
Fears of the Eighth Grade

Toi Derricotte (b. 1941) is an associate professor of English at Old Dominion University in Virginia. She has published poetry in several journals and written three books of it. The following poem appears in her 1989 volume Captivity.

When I ask what things they fear,
their arms raise like soldiers volunteering for battle:
Fear of going into a dark room, my murderer is waiting.
Fear of taking a shower, someone will stab me.
Fear of being kidnapped, raped.   5

Fear of dying in war.
When I ask how many fear this,
all the children raise their hands.

I think of this little box of consecrated land,
the bombs somewhere else,   10
the dead children in their mothers' arms,
women crying at the gates of the bamboo palace.

How thin the veneer!
The paper towels, napkins, toilet paper — everything
burned up in a day.   15

These children see the city after Armageddon°
The demons stand visible in the air
between their friends talking.
They see fire in a spring day
the instant before conflagration.   20
They feel blood through closed faucets,
the dead rising from boiling seas.   [1989]

16 Armageddon: In the Bible (Rev. 16:16), Armageddon is associated with the end of the world; specifically, it is the place where the forces of good and evil fight their final battle.

THINKING ABOUT THE TEXT

1. Evidently the speaker is referring to a particular group of eighth graders whom she has interviewed. Do you think many other eighth graders would have the same fears? What else might the speaker have asked these children to learn how they view the world?

2. Does Derricotte's speaker seem to express a particular attitude toward the children's statements? Or do you see her as leaving you free to make your own judgment of them? Refer to specific lines.

3. Where, specifically, might the "somewhere else" in line 10 be? Think of particular countries.

4. Does the reference to Armageddon in line 16 make sense? Do you assume that the last stanza truly conveys what "these children see"? Again, support your answers by referring to specific lines.

5. What would you say to these children? In what ways would you address their fears if you were their teacher? In your view, to what extent does the typical eighth-grade curriculum address their concerns?

MAKING COMPARISONS

1. Both Glück's and Derricotte's poems end with images of violence. Glück refers to "ammunition" and Derricotte evokes Armageddon. Does the emphasis on violence seem appropriate in each case?

2. Both Glück's and Derricotte's poems are four stanzas long, with the middle two stanzas being shorter than the first and the last. Is the effect of this structure the same in each case?

3. While Glück's poem refers to teachers, Derricotte's doesn't. Is this a significant difference? Why, or why not?

PHILIP LEVINE

Among Children

Philip Levine (b. 1928) is a leading contemporary American poet. Much of his writing deals with his youth in the industrial city of Detroit, especially his work in various factories there. He won the National Book Award for his 1991 volume What Work Is. *We featured its title poem in Chapter 2, and the following poem comes from the same book.*

I walk among the rows of bowed heads —
the children are sleeping through fourth grade
so as to be ready for what is ahead,
the monumental boredom of junior high
and the rush forward tearing their wings   5
loose and turning their eyes forever inward.
These are the children of Flint, their fathers
work at the spark plug factory or truck
bottled water in 5 gallon sea-blue jugs
to the widows of the suburbs. You can see   10
already how their backs have thickened,
how their small hands, soiled by pig iron,
leap and stutter even in dreams. I would like
to sit down among them and read slowly
from *The Book of Job*° until the windows   15

15 *The Book of Job*: In the Old Testament, Job is a virtuous man whose faith in God is tested when God allows horrible suffering to be inflicted on him. In Chapter 39, God speaks to Job about the vast differences in their knowledge and power. A particular passage from this speech seems especially pertinent to Levine's poem (Job 39:19–25, King James Version):

> Hast thou given the horse strength? Hast thou clothed his neck with thunder?
> Canst thou make him afraid as a grasshopper? The glory of his nostrils *is* terrible.
> He paweth in the valley, and rejoiceth in *his* strength; he goeth on to meet the armed men.
> He mocketh at fear, and is not affrighted; neither turneth he back from the sword.
> The quiver rattleth against him, the glittering spear and the shield.
> He swalloweth the ground with fierceness and rage; neither believeth he that *it* is the sound of the trumpet.
> He saith among the trumpets, Ha, ha; and he smelleth the battle afar off, the thunder of the captains, and the shouting.

pale and the teacher rises out of a milky sea
of industrial scum, her gowns streaming
with light, her foolish words transformed
into song, I would like to arm each one
with a quiver of arrows so that they might   20
rush like wind there where no battle rages
shouting among the trumpets, Ha! Ha!
How dear the gift of laughter in the face
of the 8 hour day, the cold winter mornings
without coffee and oranges, the long lines   25
of mothers in old coats waiting silently
where the gates have closed. Ten years ago
I went among these same children, just born,
in the bright ward of the Sacred Heart and leaned
down to hear their breaths delivered that day,   30
burning with joy. There was such wonder
in their sleep, such purpose in their eyes
closed against autumn, in their damp heads
blurred with the hair of ponds, and not one
turned against me or the light, not one   35
said, I am sick, I am tired, I will go home,
not one complained or drifted alone,
unloved, on the hardest day of their lives.
Eleven years from now they will become
the men and women of Flint or Paradise,   40
the majors of a minor town, and I
will be gone into smoke or memory,
so I bow to them here and whisper
all I know, all I will never know.   [1991]

THINKING ABOUT THE TEXT

1. Characterize the poem's speaker, using at least three adjectives of your own. What specific lines support your characterization?

2. The speaker describes these children at various stages in their lives. Besides discussing their present situation, he refers back to their births and forward to their adulthoods "eleven years from now" (line 39). Do you find his comments about each stage plausible? Why, or why not?

3. In line 7, the speaker specifically identifies his subjects as "the children of Flint," an industrial city in Michigan. In what ways does their situation resemble that of schoolchildren in other places?

4. Do you find Levine's reference to the Book of Job effective, or does it reduce your ability to understand and appreciate the poem? Explain.

5. At the end of the poem, the speaker reports that "I bow to them here and whisper / all I know, all I will never know" (lines 43–44). What would you

say to someone who doubts that the speaker actually bows to these children and whispers such things to them? What would you say to someone
who argues that the speaker should have taken more active steps to improve the children's lot?

MAKING COMPARISONS

1. Compared with Glück's and Derricotte's poems, Levine's more extensively uses "I." Does his reliance on it make his poem more or less effective than the other two? Why, or why not?

2. Of the three poems, Levine's most specifically identifies the schoolchildren it describes, announcing that they "are the children of Flint." Does
   Levine's poem therefore seem less universal in its implications than the
   other two poems do? Why, or why not?

3. In describing schoolchildren, Glück and Derricotte focus on the present.
   Levine, however, refers to three stages in his subjects' lives: infancy,
   youth, and adulthood. Does his broader perspective amount to a significant difference? Explain.

WRITING ABOUT ISSUES

1. Each of the poems in this cluster uses biblical allusions. Besides Derricotte's reference to Armageddon and Levine's to the Book of Job, Glück's
   mention of apples can be linked with events in the Garden of Eden.
   Choose one of these poems and write an essay explaining how echoes of
   the Bible function in it. How do these echoes contribute to the poem's
   overall meaning and effect?

2. Any of the poems in this cluster can be seen as being mainly about the
   schoolchildren it describes. But perhaps one or more of these poems
   should be seen as mainly about the speaker who does the describing.
   Then again, perhaps one or more of them should be seen as equally concerned with the schoolchildren and the speaker. Choose two of these
   poems and write an essay explaining how each should be seen. Support
   your claims by referring to specific lines.

3. Choose a person you have known since he or she was a child. Write an
   essay examining the extent to which this person was an "innocent" child,
   as well as the extent to which he or she is "innocent" now. (Obviously you
   will have to define what you mean by *innocent*.) Be sure to support your
   claims about the person with specific details of his or her life.

4. What are the fears of schoolchildren today? Ask a group of them, or ask at
   least two pre-college teachers, or read at least two articles on the subject.
   On the basis of your research, write an essay focusing on one of the fears
   you have discovered. Besides identifying the fear, propose and argue for
   one way of addressing it. (Feel free to admit that additional ways may be
   necessary.) If you wish, refer to one or more of the poems in this cluster.

RESPONDING TO TEACHERS

LANGSTON HUGHES, "Theme for English B"
LINDA PASTAN, "Ethics"
HENRY REED, "Naming of Parts"
WALT WHITMAN, "When I Heard the Learn'd Astronomer"

Each of the following poems features a student responding to someone given institutional authority to teach him or her. In the first poem, the speaker is an African American college student writing an essay assigned by his white instructor. The speaker in the second poem remembers ethics classes she took as a youth, recalling in particular how she treated a certain question the teacher liked to ask. The third poem seems to feature two speakers: While a military officer teaches recruits how to use a rifle, one student mentally plays with his instructor's words. In the final poem, the speaker chooses to observe the heavens by himself rather than hear a "learn'd astronomer" lecture about them.

By this point in your life, you have had many people officially designated as your teachers. Probably you have seen their lectures, questions, assignments, and overall behavior as reflecting their particular educational philosophy. At the same time, your reactions to them have said something about what you consider worth learning and how you think those subjects should be taught. In some cases, perhaps, your view of teaching and learning coincided with your teacher's. At other times, though, you may have suffered an unfortunate mismatch. With each poem here, identify the teacher's assumptions about teaching and learning. Also consider those expressed by the student in his or her response.

BEFORE YOU READ

Think of a past or present writing assignment that you have found especially challenging. What specifically was the assignment? What do you believe was the educational philosophy behind it? Why did you find it a challenge? Was it a worthwhile assignment? Why, or why not? In what ways, if any, would you have changed it?

LANGSTON HUGHES
Theme for English B

Langston Hughes (1902–1967) has long been regarded as a major African American writer. He is increasingly seen today as an important contributor to American literature in general. Hughes worked in a wide range of genres, including fiction, drama, and autobiography. Nevertheless, he is primarily known for his poems. He wrote "Theme for English B" in 1949, when he was twenty-five years older than the poem's speaker. He himself, though, had attended "a college on the hill above Harlem"—namely, Columbia University.

The instructor said,
> Go *home and write*
> *a page tonight.*
> *And let that page come out of you —*
> *Then, it will be true.*   5

I wonder if it's that simple?
I am twenty-two, colored, born in Winston-Salem.
I went to school there, then Durham, then here
to this college on the hill above Harlem.
I am the only colored student in my class.   10
The steps from the hill lead down into Harlem,
through a park, then I cross St. Nicholas,
Eighth Avenue, Seventh, and I come to the Y,
the Harlem Branch Y, where I take the elevator
up to my room, sit down, and write this page: 15

It's not easy to know what is true for you or me
at twenty-two, my age. But I guess I'm what
I feel and see and hear, Harlem, I hear you:
hear you, hear me — we two — you, me, talk on this page.
(I hear New York, too.) Me — who?   20
Well, I like to eat, sleep, drink, and be in love.
I like to work, read, learn, and understand life.
I like a pipe for a Christmas present,
or records — Bessie,° bop, or Bach.
I guess being colored doesn't make me *not* like   25
the same things other folks like who are other races.
So will my page be colored that I write?
Being me, it will not be white.
But it will be
a part of you, instructor.   30
You are white —
yet a part of me, as I am part of you.
That's American.
Sometimes perhaps you don't want to be a part of me.
Nor do I often want to be a part of you.   35
But we are, that's true!
As I learn from you,
I guess you learn from me —
although you're older — and white —
and somewhat more free.   40

This is my page for English B.   [1949]

---

24 **Bessie:** Bessie Smith (1898?–1937), the famous American blues singer.

THINKING ABOUT THE TEXT

1. Write a page in which you respond to the teacher's assignment. In what respects has your page "come out of you" (line 4)? In what respects is it "true" (line 5)? Do you find the assignment reasonable? Why, or why not?

2. What seems to be the speaker's evaluation of the assignment? To what extent does he critique or challenge the assignment rather than merely submit to it? Support your answer by referring to specific lines.

3. What does Hughes's speaker mean by "you are . . . a part of me, as I am part of you" (lines 31–32)? Do you think that in today's historical and cultural context any white teacher of a black student is "somewhat more free" (line 40) than that student? Why, or why not?

4. Identify where the poem rhymes. What is the effect of this rhyming?

5. What might be the teacher's reaction to the speaker's page? What would you like the teacher's reaction to be?

LINDA PASTAN
Ethics

Raised in New York City, Linda Pastan (b. 1932) now lives in Potomac, Maryland. She has published many books of poetry, including The Five Stages of Grief *(1981);* Waiting for My Life *(1981), where "Ethics" originally appeared; and* PM/AM: New and Selected Poems *(1982). Much of Pastan's poetry deals with her own family life. Increasingly, she has been concerned as well with issues of aging and mortality.*

In ethics class so many years ago
our teacher asked this question every fall:
if there were a fire in a museum
which would you save, a Rembrandt painting
or an old woman who hadn't many   5
years left anyhow? Restless on hard chairs
caring little for pictures or old age
we'd opt one year for life, the next for art
and always half-heartedly. Sometimes
the woman borrowed my grandmother's face   10
leaving her usual kitchen to wander
some drafty, half-imagined museum.
One year, feeling clever, I replied
why not let the woman decide herself?
Linda, the teacher would report, eschews   15
the burdens of responsibility.

This fall in a real museum I stand
before a real Rembrandt, old woman,
or nearly so, myself. The colors
within this frame are darker than autumn,   20
darker even than winter—the browns of earth,
though earth's most radiant elements burn
through the canvas. I know now that woman
and painting and season are almost one
and all beyond saving by children.   [1981]   25

THINKING ABOUT THE TEXT

1. What specific topics would you expect to see addressed in a college-level ethics class? Which do you think are appropriate for an ethics class at the high-school level? Should students be required to take such a class in earlier grades? Why, or why not? (You may want to consult a dictionary definition of the word *ethics*.)

2. How would you respond to the teacher's question? Do you think it an appropriate one to ask? Why, or why not? Judging by Linda's behavior in the poem, what do you think the teacher should have said about her?

3. What do you usually associate with fall and winter? Does Pastan seem to encourage these associations? Explain.

4. Note the speaker's description of the actual Rembrandt painting. Do you find it an objective description? Why, or why not?

5. State in your own words the lesson articulated in the poem's last sentence. Do you agree with the argument made there against the teacher's question? Why, or why not? Do you think the speaker is rejecting the whole subject of ethics? Why, or why not?

MAKING COMPARISONS

1. Compare the teacher's question in Pastan's poem to the assignment given Hughes's speaker. Do you prefer one to the other? Explain.

2. Unlike Hughes's poem, Pastan's explicitly leaps to a later stage in the speaker's life. Is this a significant difference? Why, or why not?

3. Is it fair to say that Pastan's poem is pessimistic, while Hughes's is optimistic? Elaborate your reasoning.

HENRY REED

Naming of Parts

The English writer Henry Reed (1914–1986) was primarily known as an author and translator of plays for radio. But he also wrote two volumes of poetry, A Map of Verona: Poems (1946) and Lessons of the War (1970). The following poem, which appears in both volumes, is one in a series of poems collectively entitled "Naming of the Parts."

Today we have naming of parts. Yesterday,
We had daily cleaning. And tomorrow morning,
We shall have what to do after firing. But today,
Today we have naming of parts. Japonica
Glistens like coral in all of the neighboring gardens,   5
          And today we have naming of parts.

This is the lower sling swivel. And this
Is the upper sling swivel, whose use you will see,
When you are given your slings. And this is the piling swivel,
Which in your case you have not got. The branches   10
Hold in the gardens their silent, eloquent gestures,
          Which in our case we have not got.

This is the safety-catch, which is always released
With an easy flick of the thumb. And please do not let me
See anyone using his finger. You can do it quite easy   15
If you have any strength in your thumb. The blossoms
Are fragile and motionless, never letting anyone see
          Any of them using their finger.

And this you can see is the bolt. The purpose of this
Is to open the breech, as you see. We can slide it   20
Rapidly backwards and forwards: we call this
Easing the spring. And rapidly backwards and forwards
The early bees are assaulting and fumbling the flowers:
          They call it easing the Spring.

They call it easing the Spring: it is perfectly easy   25
If you have any strength in your thumb: like the bolt,
And the breech, and the cocking-piece, and the point of balance,
Which in our case we have not got; and the almond-blossom
Silent in all of the gardens and the bees going backwards and forwards,
          For today we have naming of parts.   [1946]   30

THINKING ABOUT THE TEXT

1. Reed's poem features two voices. Identify the lines where each appears. What adjectives would you use to describe each?

2. Does this poem progress in any way, or does the situation it presents remain unchanged at the end? Refer to specific lines in supporting your response.

3. Do you take the poem to be antimilitary? Why, or why not?

4. The author visually isolates the last line of each stanza. Why do you think he does so?

5. The poem features a lot of repetition. What is its effect?

MAKING COMPARISONS

1. Does the scene of instruction that Reed presents seem very different from the classes evoked by Hughes and Pastan? From classes that you have taken? Explain.

2. The instructor in "Naming of Parts" speaks a lot more than the instructors in "Theme for English B" and "Ethics." Does this difference matter? Why, or why not?

3. Reed's poem seems very much concerned with language — specifically, the act of "naming" various things. Do the other two poems show similar concerns, or do they deal with largely different topics? Refer to specific lines in each text.

WALT WHITMAN

When I Heard the Learn'd Astronomer

Walt Whitman (1819–1892) became one of the United States's most famous and influential poets. He was especially known for celebrating the human body and democracy. His most important volume of poetry was Leaves of Grass *(1855). Although it originally consisted of a dozen poems, Whitman added to it and revised its format as it went through several more editions, the final one appearing in 1892. Besides being a poet, Whitman worked as a printer, newspaper editor, journalist, and government clerk. During the Civil War, he tended wounded Union soldiers. He wrote the following poem in 1865.*

When I heard the learn'd astronomer,
When the proofs, the figures, were ranged in columns before me,
When I was shown the charts and diagrams, to add, divide, and measure them,
When I sitting heard the astronomer where he lectured with much applause in
     the lecture-room,

How soon unaccountable I became tired and sick,   5
Till rising and gliding out I wandered off by myself,
In the mystical moist night-air, and from time to time,
Looked up in perfect silence at the stars.   [1865]

THINKING ABOUT THE TEXT

1. How does Whitman's speaker seem to define *learn'd*? Do you think he would apply this term to himself? If so, what definition of it would he have in mind?

2. The first four lines all begin with the word *when*, a technique known as anaphora. What is its effect?

3. Describe how the lines change in length as the poem moves along. Do you think Whitman is justified in making the fourth line as long as it is? Explain your reasoning. Note that the poem is actually just one sentence; what does Whitman achieve by making it so?

4. What distinctions does the speaker make between his behavior in the first line and his behavior in the last? Do you see him as proposing another method of education than the astronomer's, or do you take him to be rejecting education altogether? Explain. How much do you think a person can learn by simply gazing at the stars?

5. The poem ends by apparently endorsing "perfect silence." Yet Whitman *is not* silent; after all, he wrote this poem. Do you think Whitman is contradicting himself? Why, or why not?

MAKING COMPARISONS

1. Of the poems in this cluster, only in Whitman's does a student walk out on a teacher. Does this action make you regard the student in Whitman's poem differently than you do the students in the other poems? Why, or why not?

2. In each of the other three poems, we see a teacher's words quoted. Whitman's poem, however, does not actually quote the astronomer. Is this a significant difference? Why, or why not?

3. In what ways, if any, does Whitman's word *unaccountable* apply to the other three poems?

WRITING ABOUT ISSUES

1. Choose any poem in this cluster and write an essay describing and evaluating the relationship between student and teacher. Use specific lines to support your claims.

2. Choose two of the teachers in these poems and write an essay comparing their educational philosophies. What do they think their students should

know and do? What method of instruction might they think works best? What do you think of their approaches to teaching?

3. Think of a teacher whose style disturbed you at first. Did you eventually regard this person as a good teacher, or did you reach a different conclusion? Write an essay answering this question, making sure to define what you mean by *good*. Refer to specific interactions you had with the teacher and specific things that influenced your reactions to him or her. You may find it useful to refer to one or more poems in this cluster.

4. Ask five or more students not in this class the following questions: What basic goals should teachers have when they respond to their students' writing? What sorts of things should they comment on? How should they word their comments? How many comments should they make? Then, write an essay presenting and arguing for your own answers to these questions, making reference to what your interviewees said.

Charging a Teacher with Sexual Harassment: Cultural Contexts for David Mamet's Oleanna

DAVID MAMET, *Oleanna*

Cultural Contexts:
UNIVERSITY OF MARYLAND AT COLLEGE PARK, Pamphlet on Sexual Harassment
HOWARD GADLIN, From "Mediating Sexual Harassment"
ROBERT M. O'NEIL, "Protecting Free Speech When the Issue Is Sexual Harassment"

Many would say that for a college to be a truly educational community, it must be a community whose members treat one another with respect. Yet no campus is free from abuses of power. Consider, for example, sexual harassment. The term is fairly new, dating to the early 1970s. But the forms of behavior it refers to have long occurred on campuses, even if only now prohibited by law. In the introduction to their 1997 book *Sexual Harassment on Campus: A Guide for Administrators, Faculty, and Students,* Bernice R. Sandler and Robert J. Shoop note that "most of the studies done at individual campuses document that 20 percent to 30 percent of undergraduate women have experienced some form of sexual harassment from faculty, administrators, or other staff" (13). In some cases, students have harassed faculty, other campus employees, and other students. Many people who experience sexual harassment fail to complain about it, often because their harassers are in positions of power and may very well proclaim innocence. Therefore, more and more colleges are developing means of encouraging victims of sexual harassment to report it. At the same time, these colleges need to define sexual harassment clearly for their communities and to decide what procedures to follow when someone is accused of it.

In the following play, a female student accuses a male professor of sexual harassment. As you might guess, this play incites controversy. While some audience members sympathize with the accuser, others sympathize with the accused. Debate also arises over how fair Mamet is to each character. To help you think about the play and the issues it raises, we add three background documents. One, produced by the University of Maryland at College Park and widely distributed there, is a pamphlet that defines sexual harassment and gives procedures for lodging complaints about it. The other two documents are reports of specific cases, each of which might be compared to the case that Mamet dramatizes. First, Howard Gadlin tells of a woman student who, feeling sexually harassed by one of her professors, chooses to confront him in an informal proceeding supervised by a mediator. Then, law professor Robert O'Neil uses the case of another professor charged with sexual harassment to argue for new ways of defining and handling it.

BEFORE YOU READ

Have you experienced or observed sexual harassment? How widespread do you think it is on your campus? What kinds of behavior come to mind as you consider these questions?

DAVID MAMET
Oleanna

For much of his career as a playwright, David Mamet (b. 1947) worked in the theater world of Chicago. He has written over twenty plays, including American Buffalo *(1975),* Glengarry Glen Ross *(1984),* Speed the Plow *(1988), and* The Cryptogram *(1994). He has also worked in film. Besides writing the screenplays for* The Verdict *(1982) and* The Untouchables *(1987), he wrote and directed the movies* House of Games *(1987),* Things Change *(1988), and* Homicide *(1991), as well as the film version of* Oleanna *(1994). The play premiered in Cambridge, Massachusetts, in May 1992 and then opened off Broadway the following October. Mamet directed both the Cambridge and the New York productions, with his wife Rebecca Pidgeon starring as Carol. You will notice that much of* Oleanna's *dialogue is fragmented with interrupted sentences. They are typical of Mamet's careerlong effort to reproduce the discontinuities of everyday speech. You may find the play easier to follow if you read at least some of it aloud, either by yourself or with others.*

The want of fresh air does not seem much to affect the happiness of children in a London alley: the greater part of them sing and play as though they were on a moor in Scotland. So the absence of a genial mental atmosphere is not commonly recognized by children who have never known it. Young people have a marvelous faculty of either dying or adapting themselves to circumstances. Even if they are unhappy—very unhappy—it is astonishing how

easily they can be prevented from finding it out, or at any rate from attribut-
ing it to any other cause than their own sinfulness.

— Samuel Butler, *The Way of All Flesh*

"Oh, to be in *Oleanna*,
That's where I would rather be.
Than be bound in Norway
And drag the chains of slavery."

— folk song

CHARACTERS

CAROL, *a woman of twenty*
JOHN, *a man in his forties*

The play takes place in John's office.

ONE

John is talking on the phone. Carol is seated across the desk from him.

JOHN (*on the phone*):   And what about the land. (*Pause*) The land. And what about
the land? (*Pause*) What about it? (*Pause*) No. I don't understand. Well, yes, I'm
I'm . . . no, I'm *sure* it's signif . . . I'm sure it's significant. (*Pause*) Because it's
significant to mmmmmm . . . did you call Jerry? (*Pause*) Because . . . no, no,
no, no, no. What did they say . . . ? Did you speak to the *real* estate . . . where *is*
she . . . ? Well, well, all right. Where are her notes? Where are the notes we
took with her. (*Pause*) I thought you were? No. No, I'm sorry, I didn't mean
that, I just thought that I saw you, when we were there . . . what . . . ? I thought
I saw you with a *pencil*. WHY NOW? is what I'm say . . . well, that's why I say
"call Jerry." Well, I can't right now, be . . . no, I *didn't* schedule any . . . Grace:
I *didn't* . . . I'm well aware . . . Look: Look. Did you call Jerry? Will you call
Jerry . . . ? Because I can't now. I'll be there, I'm sure I'll be there in fifteen, in
twenty. I intend to. No, we aren't *going* to lose the, we aren't *going* to lose the
house. Look: Look, I'm not minimizing it. The "easement." Did she say "easement"? (*Pause*) What did she *say; is* it a "term of art," are we *bound* by it . . . I'm
sorry . . . (*Pause*) are: we: yes. *Bound* by . . . Look: (*He checks his watch.*) before
the other side *goes home*, all right? "a term of art." Because: that's right (*Pause*)
The yard for the boy. Well, that's the whole . . . Look: I'm going to meet you
there . . . (*He checks his watch.*) Is the realtor there? All right, tell her to show
you the basement again. Look at the *this* because . . . Bec . . . I'm leaving in,
I'm leaving in ten or fifteen . . . Yes. No, no, I'll meet you at the new . . . That's
a good. If he thinks it's necc . . . you tell Jerry to meet . . . All right? We *aren't*
going to lose the deposit. All right? I'm sure it's going to be . . . (*Pause*) I hope
so. (*Pause*) I love you, too. (*Pause*) I love you, too. As soon as . . . I will.
     (*He hangs up.*) (*He bends over the desk and makes a note.*) (*He looks up.*)
(*To Carol:*) I'm sorry . . .

CAROL: (*Pause*) What is a "term of art"?

JOHN: *(Pause)* I'm sorry . . . ?

CAROL: *(Pause)* What is a "term of art"?

JOHN: Is that what you want to talk about?

CAROL: . . . to talk about . . . ?

JOHN: Let's take the mysticism out of it, shall we? Carol? *(Pause)* Don't you think? I'll tell you: when you have some "thing." Which must be broached. *(Pause)* Don't you think . . . ? *(Pause)*

CAROL: . . . don't I think . . . ?

JOHN: Mmm?

CAROL: . . . did I . . . ?

JOHN: . . . what?

CAROL: Did . . . did I . . . did I say something wr . . .

JOHN: *(Pause)* No. I'm sorry. No. You're right. I'm very sorry. I'm somewhat rushed. As you see. I'm sorry. You're right. *(Pause)* What is a "term of art"? It seems to mean a *term*, which has come, through its use, to mean something *more specific* than the words would, to someone *not acquainted* with them . . . indicate. That, I believe, is what a "term of art," would mean. *(Pause)*

CAROL: You don't know what it means . . . ?

JOHN: I'm not sure that I know what it means. It's one of those things, perhaps you've had them, that, you look them up, or have someone explain them to you, and you say "aha," and, you immediately *forget* what . . .

CAROL: You don't do that.

JOHN: . . . I . . . ?

CAROL: You don't do . . .

JOHN: . . . I don't, what . . . ?

CAROL: . . . for . . .

JOHN: . . . I don't for . . .

CAROL: . . . no . . .

JOHN: . . . forget things? Everybody does that.

CAROL: No, they don't.

JOHN: They don't . . .

CAROL: No.

JOHN: *(Pause)* No. Everybody does that.

CAROL: Why would they do that . . . ?

JOHN: Because. I don't know. Because it doesn't interest them.

CAROL: No.

JOHN: I think so, though. *(Pause)* I'm sorry that I was distracted.

CAROL: You don't have to say that to me.

JOHN: You paid me the compliment, or the "obeisance" — all right — of coming in here . . . All right. Carol. I find that I am at a *standstill*. I find that I . . .

CAROL: . . . what . . .

JOHN: . . . one moment. In regard to your . . . to your . . .

CAROL: Oh, oh. You're buying a new house!

JOHN: No, let's get on with it.

CAROL: "get on"? *(Pause)*

JOHN: I know how . . . *believe* me. I know how . . . potentially *humiliating* these . . . I have no desire to . . . I have no desire other than to help you. But: *(He picks up some papers on his desk.)* I won't even say "but." I'll say that as I go back over the . . .

CAROL: I'm just, I'm just trying to . . .

JOHN: . . . no, it will not do.

CAROL: . . . what? What will . . . ?

JOHN: No. I see, I see what you, it . . . *(He gestures to the papers.)* but your work . . .

CAROL: I'm just: I sit in class I . . . *(She holds up her notebook.)* I take notes . . .

JOHN *(simultaneously with* "notes"*)*:   Yes. I understand. What I am trying to *tell* you is that some, some basic . . .

CAROL: . . . I . . .

JOHN: . . . one moment: some basic miss communi . . .

CAROL: I'm doing what I'm told. I bought your book, I read your . . .

JOHN: No, I'm sure you . . .

CAROL: No, no, no. I'm doing what I'm told. It's *difficult* for me. It's *difficult* . . .

JOHN: . . . but . . .

CAROL: I don't . . . lots of the *language* . . .

JOHN: . . . please . . .

CAROL: The *language*, the "things" that you say . . .

JOHN: I'm sorry. No. I don't think that that's true.

CAROL: It *is* true. I . . .

JOHN: I think . . .

CAROL: It *is* true.

JOHN: . . . I . . .

CAROL: Why would I . . . ?

JOHN: I'll tell you why: you're an incredibly bright girl.

CAROL: . . . I . . .

JOHN: You're an incredibly . . . you have no problem with the . . . Who's kidding who?

CAROL: . . . I . . .

JOHN: No. No. I'll tell you why. I'll tell . . . I think you're *angry*, I . . .

CAROL: . . . why would I . . .

JOHN: . . . wait one moment. I . . .

CAROL: It *is* true. I have *problems* . . .

JOHN: . . . every . . .

CAROL: . . . I come from a different *social* . . .

JOHN: . . . ev . . .

CAROL: a different economic . . .

JOHN: . . . Look:

CAROL: No. I: when I *came* to this school:

JOHN: Yes. Quite . . . *(Pause)*

CAROL: . . . does that mean nothing . . . ?

JOHN: . . . but look: look . . .

CAROL: . . . I . . .

JOHN: *(Picks up paper.)* Here: Please: Sit down. *(Pause)* Sit down. *(Reads from her paper.)* "I think that the ideas contained in this work express the author's feelings in a way that he intended, based on his results." What can that mean? Do you see? What . . .

CAROL: I, the best that I . . .

JOHN: I'm saying, that perhaps this course . . .

CAROL: No, no, no, you can't, you can't . . . I have to . . .

JOHN: . . . how . . .

CAROL: . . . I have to pass it . . .

JOHN: Carol, I:

CAROL: I *have* to pass this course, I . . .

JOHN: Well.

CAROL: . . . don't you . . .

JOHN: Either the . . .

CAROL: . . . I . . .

JOHN: . . . either the, I . . . either the *criteria* for judging progress in the class are . . .

CAROL: No, no, no, no, I have to pass it.

JOHN: Now, look: I'm a human being, I . . .

CAROL: I did what you told me. I did, I did everything that, I read your *book,* you told me to buy your book and read it. Everything you *say* I . . . *(She gestures to her notebook.)* *(The phone rings.)* I do. . . . Ev . . .

JOHN: . . . look:

CAROL: . . . everything I'm told . . .

JOHN: Look. Look. I'm not your *father. (Pause)*

CAROL: What?

JOHN: I'm.

CAROL: Did I say you were my father?

JOHN: . . . no . . .

CAROL: Why did you say that . . . ?

JOHN: I . . .

CAROL: . . . why . . . ?

JOHN: . . . in class I . . . *(He picks up the phone.)* *(Into phone:)* Hello. I can't talk now. Jerry? Yes? I underst . . . I can't talk now. I know . . . I know . . . Jerry. I can't *talk* now. Yes, I. Call me back in . . . Thank you. *(He hangs up.)* *(To Carol:)* What do you want me to do? We are two people, all right? Both of whom have subscribed to . . .

CAROL: No, no . . .

JOHN: . . . certain arbitrary . . .

CAROL: No. You have to help me.

JOHN: Certain institutional . . . you tell me what you want me to do. . . . You tell me what you want me to . . .

CAROL: How can I go back and tell them the *grades* that I . . .

JOHN: . . . what can I do . . . ?

CAROL: *Teach* me. *Teach* me.

JOHN: . . . I'm trying to teach you.

CAROL: I read your book. I read it. I don't under . . .

JOHN: . . . you don't understand it.

CAROL: No.

JOHN: Well, perhaps it's not well *written* . . .

CAROL (*simultaneously with* "written"):   No. No. No. I want to *understand* it.

JOHN: What don't you understand? (*Pause*)

CAROL: *Any* of it. What you're trying to say. When you talk about . . .

JOHN: . . . yes . . . ? (*She consults her notes.*)

CAROL: "Virtual warehousing of the young" . . .

JOHN: "Virtual warehousing of the young." If we artificially prolong adolescence . . .

CAROL: . . . and about "The Curse of Modern Education."

JOHN: . . . well . . .

CAROL: I don't . . .

JOHN: Look. It's just a *course*, it's just a *book*, it's just a . . .

CAROL: No. No. There are *people* out there. People who came *here*. To know something they didn't *know*. Who *came* here. To be *helped*. To be *helped*. So someone would *help* them. To *do* something. To *know* something. To get, what do they say? "To get on in the world." How can I do that if I don't, if I fail? But I don't *understand*. I don't *understand*. I don't understand what anything means . . . and I walk around. From morning 'til night: with this one thought in my head. I'm *stupid*.

JOHN: No one thinks you're stupid.

CAROL: No? What am I . . . ?

JOHN: I . . .

CAROL: . . . what am I, then?

JOHN: I think you're angry. Many people are. I have a *telephone* call that I have to make. And an *appointment*, which is rather *pressing*; though I sympathize with your concerns, and though I wish I had the time, this was not a previously scheduled meeting and I . . .

CAROL: . . . you think I'm nothing . . .

JOHN: . . . have an appointment with a *realtor*, and with my wife and . . .

CAROL: You think that I'm stupid.

JOHN: No. I certainly don't.

CAROL: You said it.

JOHN: No. I did not.

CAROL: You did.

JOHN: When?

CAROL: . . . you . . .

JOHN: No. I never did, or never would say that to a student, and . . .

CAROL: You said, "What can that mean?" (*Pause*) "What can that mean?" . . . (*Pause*)

JOHN: . . . and what did that mean to you . . . ?

CAROL: That meant I'm stupid. And I'll never learn. That's what that meant. And you're right.

JOHN: . . . I . . .

CAROL: But then. But then, what am I doing here . . . ?

JOHN: . . . if you thought that I . . .

CAROL: . . . when nobody wants me, and . . .

JOHN: . . . if you interpreted . . .

CAROL: Nobody *tells* me anything. And I *sit* there . . . in the *corner*. In the *back*. And everybody's talking about "this" all the time. And "concepts," and "precepts" and, and, and, and, and, WHAT IN THE WORLD ARE YOU TALK-ING ABOUT? And I read your book. And they said, "Fine, go in that class." Because you talked about responsibility to the young. I DON'T KNOW WHAT IT MEANS AND I'M *FAILING* . . .

JOHN: May . . .

CAROL: No, you're right. "Oh, hell." I failed. Flunk me out of it. It's garbage. Everything I do. "The ideas contained in this work express the author's feelings." That's right. That's right. I know I'm stupid. I know what I am. *(Pause)* I know what I am, Professor. You don't have to tell me. *(Pause)* It's pathetic. Isn't it?

JOHN: . . . Aha . . . *(Pause)* Sit down. Sit down. Please. *(Pause)* Please sit down.

CAROL: Why?

JOHN: I want to talk to you.

CAROL: Why?

JOHN: Just sit down. *(Pause)* Please. Sit down. Will you, please . . . ? *(Pause. She does so.)* Thank you.

CAROL: What?

JOHN: I want to tell you something.

CAROL: *(Pause)* What?

JOHN: Well, I know what you're talking about.

CAROL: No. You don't.

JOHN: I think I do. *(Pause)*

CAROL: How can you?

JOHN: I'll tell you a story about myself. *(Pause)* Do you mind? *(Pause)* I was raised to think myself stupid. That's what I want to tell you. *(Pause)*

CAROL: What do you mean?

JOHN: Just what I said. I was brought up, and my earliest, and most persistent memories are of being told that I was stupid. "You have such *intelligence*. Why must you behave so *stupidly?*" Or, "Can't you *understand?* Can't you *understand?*" And I could *not* understand. I could *not* understand.

CAROL: What?

JOHN: The simplest problem. Was beyond me. It was a mystery.

CAROL: What was a mystery?

JOHN: How people learn. How *I* could learn. Which is what I've been speaking of in class. And of *course* you can't hear it. Carol. Of *course* you can't. *(Pause)* I used to speak of "real people," and wonder what the *real* people did. The *real* people. Who were they? *They* were the people other than myself. The *good* people. The *capable* people. The people who could do the things, *I* could not do: learn, study, retain . . . all that *garbage*—which is what I have been talking of in class, and that's *exactly* what I have been talking of—If you are told . . . Listen to this. If the young child is told he cannot understand. Then he takes it as a *description* of himself. What am I? I am *that which can not understand*. And I saw you out there, when we were speaking of the concepts of . . .

CAROL: I can't understand any of them.

JOHN: Well, then, that's *my* fault. That's not your fault. And that is not verbiage. That's what I firmly hold to be the truth. And I am sorry, and I owe you an apology.

CAROL: Why?

JOHN: And I suppose that I have had some *things* on my mind. . . . We're buying a *house*, and . . .

CAROL: People said that you were stupid . . . ?

JOHN: Yes.

CAROL: When?

JOHN: I'll tell you when. Through my life. In my childhood; and, perhaps, they stopped. But I heard them continue.

CAROL: And what did they say?

JOHN: They said I was incompetent. Do you see? And when I'm tested the, the, the *feelings* of my youth about the *very subject of learning* come up. And I . . . I become, I feel "unworthy," and "unprepared." . . .

CAROL: . . . yes.

JOHN: . . . eh?

CAROL: . . . yes.

JOHN: And I feel that I must fail. *(Pause)*

CAROL: . . . but then you *do* fail. *(Pause)* You have to. *(Pause)* Don't you?

JOHN: A *pilot*. Flying a plane. The pilot is flying the plane. He thinks: Oh, my God, my mind's been drifting! Oh, my God! What kind of a cursed imbecile am I, that I, with this so precious cargo of *Life* in my charge, would allow my attention to wander. Why was I born? How deluded are those who put their trust in me, . . . et cetera, so on, and he crashes the plane.

CAROL: *(Pause)* He could just . . .

JOHN: That's right.

CAROL: He could say:

JOHN: My attention *wandered* for a moment . . .

CAROL: . . . uh huh . . .

JOHN: I had a *thought* I did not like . . . but now:

CAROL: . . . but now it's . . .

JOHN: That's what I'm telling you. It's time to put my attention . . . see: it is not: this is what I learned. It is Not Magic. Yes. Yes. *You*. You are going to be frightened. When faced with what may or may not be but which you are going to perceive as a test. You will become frightened. And you will say: "I am incapable of . . ." and everything *in* you will think these two things. "I must. But I can't." And you will think: Why was I born to be the laughing-stock of a world in which everyone is better than I? In which I am entitled to nothing. Where I can not learn. *(Pause)*

CAROL: Is that . . . *(Pause)* Is that what I have . . . ?

JOHN: Well. I don't know if I'd put it that way. Listen: I'm talking to you as I'd talk to my son. Because that's what I'd like him to have that I never had. I'm talking to you the way I wish that someone had talked to me. I don't know how to do it, other than to be *personal*, . . . but . . .

CAROL: Why would you want to be personal with me?

JOHN:　Well, you see? That's what I'm saying. We can only interpret the behavior of others through the screen we . . . *(The phone rings.)* Through . . . *(To phone:)* Hello . . . ? *(To Carol:)* Through the screen we create. *(To phone:)* Hello. *(To Carol:)* Excuse me a moment. *(To phone:)* Hello? No, I can't talk nnn . . . I know I did. In a few . . . I'm . . . is he coming to the . . . yes. I talked to him. We'll meet you at the No, because I'm with a *student.* It's going to be fff . . . This is important, too. I'm with a *student,* Jerry's going to . . . Listen: the sooner I get off, the sooner I'll be down, all right. I love you. Listen, listen, I said "I love you," it's going to work *out* with the, because I feel that it is, I'll be right down. All right? Well, then it's going to take as long as it takes. *(He hangs up.)* *(To Carol:)* I'm sorry.

CAROL:　What was that?

JOHN:　There are some problems, as there usually are, about the final agreements for the new house.

CAROL:　You're buying a new house.

JOHN:　That's right.

CAROL:　Because of your promotion.

JOHN:　Well, I suppose that that's right.

CAROL:　Why did you stay here with me?

JOHN:　Stay here.

CAROL:　Yes. When you should have gone.

JOHN:　Because I like you.

CAROL:　You like me.

JOHN:　Yes.

CAROL:　Why?

JOHN:　Why? Well? Perhaps we're similar. *(Pause)* Yes. *(Pause)*

CAROL:　You said "everyone has problems."

JOHN:　Everyone has problems.

CAROL:　Do they?

JOHN:　Certainly.

CAROL:　You do?

JOHN:　Yes.

CAROL:　What are they?

JOHN:　Well. *(Pause)* Well, you're perfectly right. *(Pause)* If we're going to take off the Artificial *Stricture,* of "Teacher," and "Student," why should *my* problems be any more a mystery than your own? Of *course* I have problems. As you saw.

CAROL:　. . . with what?

JOHN:　With my *wife* . . . with *work* . . .

CAROL:　With work?

JOHN:　Yes. And, and, perhaps my problems are, do you see? *Similar* to yours.

CAROL:　Would you tell me?

JOHN:　All right. *(Pause)* I came *late* to teaching. And I found it Artificial. The notion of "I know and you do not"; and I saw an *exploitation* in the education process. I told you. I hated school, I hated teachers. I hated everyone who was in the position of a "boss" because I *knew*—I didn't *think,* mind

you, I *knew* I was going to fail. Because I was a fuckup. I was just no goddamned good. When I . . . late in life . . . *(Pause)* When I *got out from
under* . . . when I worked my way out of the need to fail. When I . . .

CAROL: How do you do that? *(Pause)*

JOHN: You have to look at what you are, and what you feel, and how you act.
And, finally, you have to look at how you act. And say: If that's what I *did*, that
must be how I think of myself.

CAROL: I don't understand.

JOHN: If I fail all the time, it must be that I think of myself as a failure. If I do not
want to think of myself as a failure, perhaps I should begin by *succeeding* now
and again. Look. The tests, you see, which you encounter, in school, in college, in life, were designed, in the most part, for idiots. *By* idiots. There is no
need to fail at them. They are not a test of your worth. They are a test of your
ability to retain and spout back misinformation. Of *course* you fail them.
They're *nonsense*. And I . . .

CAROL: . . . no . . .

JOHN: Yes. They're *garbage*. They're a *joke*. Look at me. Look at me. The
Tenure Committee. The Tenure Committee. Come to judge me. The Bad
Tenure Committee.

The "Test." Do you see? They put me to the test. Why, they had people voting on me I wouldn't employ to wax my car. And yet, I go before the Great
Tenure Committee, and I have an urge, to *vomit*, to, to, to puke my *badness*
on the table, to show them: "I'm no good. Why would you pick *me*?"

CAROL: They granted you tenure.

JOHN: Oh no, they announced it, but they haven't *signed*. Do you see? "At any
moment . . . "

CAROL: . . . mmm . . .

JOHN: "They might not *sign*" . . . I might not . . . the *house* might not go
through . . . Eh? Eh? They'll find out my "dark secret." *(Pause)*

CAROL: . . . what is it . . . ?

JOHN: There *isn't* one. But *they* will find an index of my badness . . .

CAROL: Index?

JOHN: A ". . . pointer." A "Pointer." You see? Do you see? I *understand* you. I.
Know. That. Feeling. Am I entitled to my job, and my nice *home*, and my
wife, and my *family*, and so on. This is what I'm saying: That theory of education which, that *theory*:

CAROL: I . . . I . . . *(Pause)*

JOHN: What?

CAROL: I . . .

JOHN: What?

CAROL: I want to know about my grade. *(Long pause)*

JOHN: Of course you do.

CAROL: Is that bad?

JOHN: No.

CAROL: Is it bad that I asked you that?

JOHN: No.

CAROL: Did I upset you?

JOHN: No. And I apologize. Of *course* you want to know about your grade. And, of course, you can't concentrate on anyth . . . *(The telephone starts to ring.)* Wait a moment.

CAROL: I should go.

JOHN: I'll make you a deal.

CAROL: No, you have to . . .

JOHN: Let it ring. I'll make you a deal. You stay here. We'll start the whole course over. I'm going to say it was not you, it was I who was not paying attention. We'll start the whole course over. Your grade is an "A." Your final grade is an "A." *(The phone stops ringing.)*

CAROL: But the class is only half over . . .

JOHN *(simultaneously with* "over"*)*:   Your grade for the whole term is an "A." If you will come back and meet with me. A few more times. Your grade's an "A." Forget about the paper. You didn't like it, you didn't like writing it. It's not important. What's important is that I awake your interest, if I can, and that I answer your questions. Let's start over. *(Pause)*

CAROL: Over. With what?

JOHN: Say this is the beginning.

CAROL: The beginning.

JOHN: Yes.

CAROL: Of what?

JOHN: Of the class.

CAROL: But we can't start over.

JOHN: I say we can. *(Pause)* I say we can.

CAROL: But I don't believe it.

JOHN: Yes, I know that. But it's true. What is The Class but you and me? *(Pause)*

CAROL: There are rules.

JOHN: Well. We'll break them.

CAROL: How can we?

JOHN: We won't tell anybody.

CAROL: Is that all right?

JOHN: I say that it's fine.

CAROL: Why would you do this for me?

JOHN: I like you. Is that so difficult for you to . . .

CAROL: Um . . .

JOHN: There's no one here but you and me. *(Pause)*

CAROL: All right. I did not understand. When you referred . . .

JOHN: All right, yes?

CAROL: When you referred to hazing.

JOHN: Hazing.

CAROL: You wrote, in your book. About the comparative . . . the comparative . . . *(She checks her notes.)*

JOHN: Are you checking your notes . . . ?

CAROL: Yes.

JOHN: Tell me in your own . . .

CAROL: I want to make sure that I have it right.

JOHN: No. Of course. You want to be exact.

CAROL: I want to know everything that went on.

JOHN: . . . that's good.

CAROL: . . . so I . . .

JOHN: That's very good. But I was suggesting, many times, that that which we wish to retain is retained oftentimes, I think, *better* with less expenditure of effort.

CAROL: *(Of notes)* Here it is: you wrote of *hazing*.

JOHN: . . . that's correct. Now: I said "hazing." It means ritualized annoyance. We shove this book at you, we say read it. Now, you say you've read it? I think that you're *lying*. I'll *grill* you, and when I find you've lied, you'll be disgraced, and your life will be ruined. It's a sick game. Why do we do it? Does it educate? In no sense. Well, then, what is higher education? It is something-other-than-useful.

CAROL: What is "something-other-than-useful?"

JOHN: It has become a ritual, it has become an article of faith. That all must be subjected to, or to put it differently, that all are entitled to Higher Education. And my point . . .

CAROL: You disagree with that?

JOHN: Well, let's address that. What do you think?

CAROL: I don't know.

JOHN: What do you think, though? *(Pause)*

CAROL: I don't know.

JOHN: I spoke of it in class. Do you remember my example?

CAROL: Justice.

JOHN: Yes. Can you repeat it to me? *(She looks down at her notebook.)* Without your notes? I ask you as a favor to me, so that I can see if my idea was interesting.

CAROL: You said "justice" . . .

JOHN: Yes?

CAROL: . . . that all are entitled . . . *(Pause)* I . . . I . . . I . . .

JOHN: Yes. To a speedy trial. To a fair trial. But they needn't be given a trial *at all* unless they stand accused. Eh? Justice is their right, should they choose to avail themselves of it, they should have a fair trial. It does not follow, of necessity, a person's life is incomplete without a trial in it. Do you see?

My point is a confusion between equity and *utility* arose. So we confound the *usefulness* of higher education with our, granted, right to equal access to the same. We, in effect, create a *prejudice* toward it, completely independent of . . .

CAROL: . . . that it is prejudice that we should go to school?

JOHN: Exactly. *(Pause)*

CAROL: How can you say that? How . . .

JOHN: Good. Good. *Good*. That's right! Speak up! What is a prejudice? An unreasoned belief. We are all subject to it. None of us is not. When it is threatened, or opposed, we feel anger, and feel, do we not? As you do now. Do you not? Good.

CAROL: . . . but how can you . . .

JOHN: . . . let us examine. Good.

CAROL: How . . .

JOHN: Good. Good. When . . .

CAROL: I'M SPEAKING . . . *(Pause)*

JOHN: I'm sorry.

CAROL: How can you . . .

JOHN: . . . I beg your pardon.

CAROL: That's all right.

JOHN: I beg your pardon.

CAROL: That's all right.

JOHN: I'm sorry I interrupted you.

CAROL: That's all right.

JOHN: You were saying?

CAROL: I was saying . . . I was saying . . . *(She checks her notes.)* How can you say in a class. Say in a college class, that college education is prejudice?

JOHN: I said that our predilection for it . . .

CAROL: Predilection . . .

JOHN: . . . you know what that means.

CAROL: Does it mean "liking"?

JOHN: Yes.

CAROL: But how can you say that? That College . . .

JOHN: . . . that's my *job*, don't you know.

CAROL: What is?

JOHN: To provoke you.

CAROL: No.

JOHN: Oh. Yes, though.

CAROL: To provoke me?

JOHN: That's right.

CAROL: To make me mad?

JOHN: That's right. To force you . . .

CAROL: . . . to make me mad is your job?

JOHN: To force you to . . . listen: *(Pause)* Ah. *(Pause)* When I was young somebody told me, are you ready, the rich copulate less often than the poor. But when they do, they take more of their clothes off. Years. Years, mind you, I would compare experiences of my own to this dictum, saying, aha, this fits the norm, or ah, this is a variation from it. What did it mean? Nothing. It was some jerk thing, some school kid told me that took up room inside my head. *(Pause)*

Somebody told *you*, and you hold it as an article of faith, that higher education is an unassailable good. This notion is so dear to you that when I question it you become angry. Good. Good, I say. Are not those the very things which we should question? I say college education, since the war, has become so a matter of course, and such a fashionable necessity, for those either of or aspiring *to* to the new vast middle class, that we *espouse* it, as a matter of right, and have ceased to ask, "What is it good for?" *(Pause)*

What might be some reasons for pursuit of higher education?
One: A love of learning.
Two: The wish for mastery of a skill.
Three: For economic betterment.
(Stops. Makes a note.)

CAROL: I'm keeping you.

JOHN: One moment. I have to make a note . . .

CAROL: It's something that I said?

JOHN: No, we're buying a house.

CAROL: You're buying the new house.

JOHN: To go with the tenure. That's right. Nice *house,* close to the *private school . . . (He continues making his note.) . . .* We were talking of economic betterment *(Carol writes in her notebook.) . . .* I was thinking of the School Tax. *(He continues writing.) (To himself:) . . . where is it written* that I have to send my child to public school. . . . Is it a law that I have to improve the City Schools at the expense of my own interest? And, is this not simply *The White Man's Burden?* Good. And *(Looks up to Carol) . . .* does this interest you?

CAROL: No. I'm taking notes . . .

JOHN: You don't have to take notes, you know, you can just listen.

CAROL: I want to make sure I remember it. *(Pause)*

JOHN: I'm not lecturing you, I'm just trying to tell you some things I think.

CAROL: What do you think?

JOHN: Should all kids go to college? Why . . .

CAROL: *(Pause)* To learn.

JOHN: But if he does not learn.

CAROL: If the child does not learn?

JOHN: Then why is he in college? Because he was told it was his "right"?

CAROL: Some might find college instructive.

JOHN: I would hope so.

CAROL: But how do they feel? Being told they are wasting their time?

JOHN: I don't think I'm telling them that.

CAROL: You said that education was "prolonged and systematic hazing."

JOHN: Yes. It can be so.

CAROL: . . . if education is so *bad,* why do you do it?

JOHN: I do it because I love it. *(Pause)* Let's. . . . I suggest you look at the demographics, wage-earning capacity, college- and non-college-educated men and women, 1855 to 1980, and let's see if we can wring some worth from the statistics. Eh? And . . .

CAROL: No.

JOHN: What?

CAROL: I can't understand them.

JOHN: . . . you . . . ?

CAROL: . . . the "charts." The *Concepts*, the . . .

JOHN: "Charts" are simply . . .

CAROL: When I leave here . . .

JOHN: Charts, do you see . . .

CAROL: No, I can't . . .

JOHN: You can, though.

CAROL: NO, NO—I DON'T UNDERSTAND. DO YOU SEE??? I DON'T
UNDERSTAND . . .

JOHN: What?

CAROL: Any of it. Any of it. I'm *smiling* in class, I'm *smiling*, the whole time.
What are you *talking* about? What is everyone *talking* about? I don't *under-*
stand. I don't know what it *means*. I don't know what it means to *be* here . . .
you tell me I'm intelligent, and then you tell me I should not be *here*, what
do you *want* with me? What does it *mean*? Who should I *listen* to . . . I . . .
(He goes over to her and puts his arm around her shoulder.)
NO! *(She walks away from him.)*

JOHN: Sshhhh.

CAROL: No, I don't under . . .

JOHN: Sshhhhh.

CAROL: I don't know what you're *saying* . . .

JOHN: Sshhhhh. It's all right.

CAROL: . . . I have to . . .

JOHN: Sshhhhh. Sshhhhh. Let it go a moment. *(Pause)* Sshhhhh . . . let it go.
(Pause) Just let it go. *(Pause)* Just let it go. It's all right. *(Pause)* Sshhhhh.
(Pause) I understand . . . *(Pause)* What do you feel?

CAROL: I feel bad.

JOHN: I know. It's all right.

CAROL: I . . . *(Pause)*

JOHN: What?

CAROL: I . . .

JOHN: What? Tell me.

CAROL: I don't understand you.

JOHN: I know. It's all right.

CAROL: I . . .

JOHN: What? *(Pause)* What? *Tell* me.

CAROL: I can't tell you.

JOHN: No, you must.

CAROL: I can't.

JOHN: No. Tell me. *(Pause)*

CAROL: I'm bad. *(Pause)* Oh, God. *(Pause)*

JOHN: It's all right.

CAROL: I'm . . .

JOHN: It's all right.

CAROL: I can't talk about this.

JOHN: It's all right. Tell me.

CAROL: Why do you want to know this?

JOHN: I don't want to know. I want to know whatever you . . .

CAROL: I always . . .

JOHN: . . . good . . .

CAROL: I always . . . all my life . . . I have never told anyone this . . .

JOHN: Yes. Go on. *(Pause)* Go on.

CAROL: All of my life . . . *(The phone rings.) (Pause. John goes to the phone and picks it up.)*

JOHN *(into phone):*   I can't talk now. *(Pause)* What? *(Pause)* Hmm. *(Pause)* All right, I . . . I. Can't. Talk. Now. No, no, no, I *Know* I did, but. . . . What? Hello. What? She *what?* She *can't,* she said the agreement is void? How, how is the agreement *void? That's Our House.*

I have the *paper;* when we come down, next week, with the payment, and the paper, that house is . . . wait, wait, wait, wait, wait, wait, wait: Did Jerry . . . is Jerry there? *(Pause)* Is *she* there . . . ? Does she have a *lawyer* . . . ? How the *hell,* how the *Hell.* That is . . . it's a question, you said, of the *easement.* I don't underst . . . it's not the *whole agreement.* It's just the *easement,* why would she? Put, put, put, *Jerry* on. *(Pause)* Jer, *Jerry:* What the *Hell* . . . that's my *house.* That's . . . Well, I'm no, no, no, I'm *not* coming ddd . . . List, *Listen, screw* her. You *tell* her. You, listen: I want you to take *Grace,* you take Grace, and get out of that house. You *leave* her there. Her and her lawyer, and you *tell* them, we'll see them in court next . . . no. No. Leave her there, leave her to *stew* in it: You tell her, we're *getting* that house, and we are going to . . . No. I'm *not* coming down. I'll be damned if I'll sit in the same rrr . . . the next, you tell her the next time I *see* her is in court . . . I . . . *(Pause)* What? *(Pause)* What? I don't understand. *(Pause)* Well, what about the house? *(Pause)* There isn't any problem with the hhh . . . *(Pause)* No, no, no, that's all right. All ri . . . All right . . . *(Pause)* Of course. Tha . . . Thank you. No, I will. Right away. *(He hangs up.) (Pause)*

CAROL: What is it? *(Pause)*

JOHN: It's a surprise party.

CAROL: It is.

JOHN: Yes.

CAROL: A party for you.

JOHN: Yes.

CAROL: Is it your birthday?

JOHN: No.

CAROL: What is it?

JOHN: The tenure announcement.

CAROL: The tenure announcement.

JOHN: They're throwing a party for us in our new house.

CAROL: Your new house.

JOHN: The house that we're buying.

CAROL: You have to go.

JOHN: It seems that I do.

CAROL: *(Pause)* They're proud of you.
JOHN: Well, there are those who would say it's a form of aggression.
CAROL: What is?
JOHN: A surprise.

TWO

John and Carol seated across the desk from each other.

JOHN: You see, *(pause)* I love to teach. And flatter myself I am *skilled* at it. And I love the, the aspect of *performance.* I think I must confess that.

When I found I loved to teach I swore that I would not become that cold, rigid automaton of an instructor which I had encountered as a child.

Now, I was not unconscious that it was given me to err upon the other side. And, so, I asked and *ask* myself if I engaged in heterodoxy, I will not say "gratuitously" for I do not care to posit orthodoxy as a given good—but, "to the detriment of, of my students." *(Pause)*

As I said. When the possibility of tenure opened, and, of course, I'd long pursued it, I was, of course *happy,* and *covetous* of it. I asked myself if I was wrong to covet it. And thought about it long, and, I hope, truthfully, and saw in myself several things in, I think, no particular order. *(Pause)*

That I *would* pursue it. That I *desired* it, that I was not pure of longing for security, and that that, perhaps, was not reprehensible in me. That I had duties *beyond* the school, and that my duty to my home, for instance, was, or should be, if it were not, of an equal weight. That tenure, and security, and yes, and *comfort,* were not, of themselves, to be scorned; and were even worthy of honorable pursuit. And that it was given me. Here, in this place, which I enjoy, and in which I find comfort, to assure myself of—as far as it rests in The Material—a continuation of that joy and comfort. In exchange for what? Teaching? Which I love.

What was the price of this security? To obtain *tenure.* Which tenure the committee is in the process of granting me. And on the basis of which I contracted to purchase a house. Now, as you don't have your own family, at this point, you may not know what that means. But to me it is important. A home. A Good Home. To raise my family. Now: The Tenure Committee will meet. This is the process, and a *good* process. Under which the school has functioned for quite a long time. They will meet, and hear your complaint— which you have the right to make; and they will dismiss it. They will *dismiss* your complaint; and, in the intervening period, I will lose my house. I will not be able to close on my house. I will lose my *deposit,* and the home I'd picked out for my wife and son will go by the boards. Now: I see I have angered you. I understand your anger at teachers. I was angry with mine. I felt hurt and humiliated by them. Which is one of the reasons that I went into education.

CAROL: What do you want of me?

JOHN: *(Pause)* I was hurt. When I received the report. Of the tenure committee. I was shocked. And I was hurt. No, I don't mean to subject you to my weak sensibilities. All right. Finally, I didn't understand. Then I thought: is it not always at those points at which we reckon ourselves unassailable that we are most vulnerable and . . . *(Pause)* Yes. All right. You find me pedantic. Yes. I am. By nature, by *birth*, by profession. I don't know . . . I'm always looking for a *paradigm* for . . .

CAROL: I don't know what a paradigm is.

JOHN: It's a model.

CAROL: Then why can't you use that word? *(Pause)*

JOHN: If it is important to you. Yes, all right. I was looking for a model. To continue: I feel that one point . . .

CAROL: I . . .

JOHN: One second . . . upon which I am unassailable is my unflinching concern for my students' dignity. I asked you here to . . . in the spirit of *investigation*, to ask you . . . to ask . . . *(Pause)* What have I done to you? *(Pause)* And, and, I suppose, how can I make amends. Can we not settle this now? It's pointless, really, and I want to know.

CAROL: What you can do to force me to retract?

JOHN: That is not what I meant at all.

CAROL: To bribe me, to convince me . . .

JOHN: . . . No.

CAROL: To retract . . .

JOHN: That is not what I meant at all. I think that you know it is not.

CAROL: That is not what I know. I *wish* I . . .

JOHN: I do not want to . . . you wish what?

CAROL: No, you said what amends can you make. To force me to retract.

JOHN: That is not what I said.

CAROL: I have my notes.

JOHN: Look. Look. The Stoics say . . .

CAROL: The Stoics?

JOHN: The Stoical Philosophers say if you remove the phrase "I have been injured," you have removed the injury. Now: Think: I know that you're upset. Just tell me. Literally. Literally: what wrong have I done you?

CAROL: Whatever you have done to me — to the extent that you've done it to *me*, do you know, rather than to me as a *student*, and, so, to the student body, is contained in my report. To the tenure committee.

JOHN: Well, all right. *(Pause)* Let's see. *(He reads.)* I find that I am sexist. That I am *elitist*. I'm not sure I know what that means, other than it's a derogatory word, meaning "bad." That I . . . That I insist on wasting time, in nonprescribed, in self-aggrandizing and theatrical *diversions* from the prescribed *text* . . . that these have taken both sexist and pornographic forms . . . here we find listed . . . *(Pause)* Here we find listed . . . instances ". . . closeted with a student" . . . "Told a rambling, sexually explicit story, in which the frequency and attitudes of fornication of the poor and rich are, it would seem, the central point . . . moved to *embrace* said student and . . . all part of a pattern . . ." *(Pause)*

(He reads.) That I used the phrase "The White Man's Burden" . . . that I told you how I'd asked you to my room because I quote like you. *(Pause)*

(He reads.) "He said he 'liked' me. That he 'liked being with me.' He'd let me write my examination paper over, if I could come back oftener to see him in his office." *(Pause) (To Carol:)* It's *ludicrous*. Don't you know that? It's not *necessary*. It's going to *humiliate* you, and it's going to cost me my *house*, and . . .

CAROL: It's "*ludicrous* . . ."?

John picks up the report and reads again.

JOHN: "He told me he had problems with his wife; and that he wanted to take off the artificial stricture of Teacher and Student. He put his arm around me . . ."

CAROL: Do you deny it? Can you deny it . . . ? Do you see? *(Pause)* Don't you see? You don't see, do you?

JOHN: I don't see . . .

CAROL: You think, you think you can deny that these things happened; or, if they *did*, if they *did*, that they meant what you *said* they meant. Don't you see? You drag me in here, you drag us, to listen to you "go on"; and "go on" about this, or that, or we don't "express" ourselves very well. We don't say what we mean. Don't we? Don't we? We *do* say what we mean. And you say that "I don't understand you . . .": Then *you* . . . *(Points.)*

JOHN: "Consult the Report"?

CAROL: . . . that's right.

JOHN: You see. You see. Can't you. . . . You see what I'm saying? Can't you tell me in your own words?

CAROL: Those are my own words. *(Pause)*

JOHN: *(He reads.)* "He told me that if I would stay alone with him in his office, he would change my grade to an A." *(To Carol:)* What have I done to you? Oh. My God, are you so hurt?

CAROL: What I "feel" is irrelevant. *(Pause)*

JOHN: Do you know that I tried to help you?

CAROL: What I know I have reported.

JOHN: I would like to help you now. I would. Before this escalates.

CAROL *(simultaneously with* "escalates"*)*:   You see. I don't think that I need your help. I don't think I need anything you have.

JOHN: I feel . . .

CAROL: I don't *care* what you feel. Do you see? DO YOU SEE? You can't *do* that anymore. You. Do. Not. Have. The. Power. Did you misuse it? *Someone* did. Are you part of that group? Yes. Yes. You Are. You've *done* these things. And to say, and to say, "Oh. Let me help you with your problem . . ."

JOHN: Yes. I understand. I understand. You're *hurt*. You're *angry*. Yes. I think your *anger* is *betraying* you. Down a path which helps no one.

CAROL: I don't *care* what you think.

JOHN: You don't? *(Pause)* But you talk of *rights*. Don't you see? *I* have rights too. Do you see? I have a *house* . . . part of the *real* world; and The Tenure Committee, Good Men and True . . .

CAROL: . . . Professor . . .

JOHN: . . . Please: *Also* part of that world: you understand? This is my *life*. I'm not a *bogeyman*. I don't "stand" for something, I . . .

CAROL: . . . Professor . . .

JOHN: . . . I . . .

CAROL: Professor. I came here as a *favor*. At your personal request. Perhaps I should not have done so. But I did. On my behalf, and on behalf of my group. And you speak of the tenure committee, one of whose members is a woman, as you know. And though you might call it Good Fun, or An Historical Phrase, or An Oversight, or, All of the Above, to refer to the committee as Good Men and True, it is a demeaning remark. It is a sexist remark, and to overlook it is to countenance continuation of that method of thought. It's a remark . . .

JOHN: OH COME ON. Come on. . . . Sufficient to deprive a family of . . .

CAROL: Sufficient? Sufficient? Sufficient? Yes. It is a *fact* . . . and that story, which I quote, is *vile* and *classist*, and *manipulative* and *pornographic*. It . . .

JOHN: . . . it's pornographic . . . ?

CAROL: What gives you the *right*. Yes. To speak to a *woman* in your private . . . Yes. Yes. I'm sorry. I'm sorry. You feel yourself empowered . . . you say so yourself. To *strut*. To *posture*. To "perform." To "Call me in here . . ." Eh? You say that higher education is a joke. And treat it as such, you *treat* it as such. And *confess* to a taste to play the *Patriarch* in your class. To grant *this*. To deny *that*. To embrace your students.

JOHN: How can you assert. How can you stand there and . . .

CAROL: How can you *deny* it. You did it to me. *Here*. You *did*. . . . You *confess*. You love the Power. To *deviate*. To *invent*, to transgress . . . to *transgress* whatever norms have been established for us. And you think it's charming to "question" in yourself this taste to mock and destroy. But you should question it. Professor. And you pick those things which you feel *advance* you: publication, *tenure*, and the steps to get them you call "harmless rituals." And you perform those steps. Although you say it is hypocrisy. But to the aspirations of your students. Of *hardworking students*, who come here, who *slave* to come here — you have no idea what it cost me to come to this school — you *mock* us. You call education "hazing," and from your so-protected, so-elitist seat you hold our confusion as a *joke*, and our hopes and efforts with it. Then you sit there and say "what have I done?" And ask me to understand that *you* have aspirations too. But I tell you. I tell you. That you are vile. And that you are exploitative. And if you possess one ounce of that inner honesty you describe in your book, you can look in yourself and see those things that

I see. And you can find revulsion equal to my own. Good day. *(She prepares to leave the room.)*

JOHN: Wait a second, will you, just one moment. *(Pause)* Nice day today.

CAROL: What?

JOHN: You said "Good day." I think that it is a nice day today.

CAROL: *Is* it?

JOHN: Yes, I think it is.

CAROL: And why is that important?

JOHN: Because it is the essence of all human communication. I say something conventional, you respond, and the information we exchange is not about the "weather," but that we both agree to converse. In effect, we agree that we are both human. *(Pause)*

I'm not a . . . "exploiter," and you're not a . . . "deranged," what? *Revolutionary* . . . that we may, that we may have . . . positions, and that we may have . . . desires, which are in *conflict*, but that we're just human. *(Pause)* That means that sometimes we're *imperfect*. *(Pause)* Often we're in conflict . . . *(Pause) Much* of what we do, you're right, in the name of "principles" is *self-serving* . . . much of what we do is *conventional*. *(Pause)* You're right. *(Pause)* You said you came in the class because you wanted to learn about *education*. I don't know that I can teach you about education. But I know that I can tell you what I *think* about education, and then *you* decide. And you don't have to fight with me. *I'm* not the subject. *(Pause)* And where I'm *wrong* . . . perhaps it's not your job to "fix" me. I don't want to fix *you*. I would like to tell you what I *think*, because that *is* my job, conventional as it is, and flawed as I may be. And then, if you can show me some better *form*, then we can proceed from there. But, just like "nice day, isn't it . . . ?" I don't think we can proceed until we accept that each of us is human. *(Pause)* And we still can have difficulties. We *will* have them . . . that's all right too. *(Pause)* Now:

CAROL: . . . wait . . .

JOHN: Yes. I want to hear it.

CAROL: . . . the . . .

JOHN: Yes. Tell me frankly.

CAROL: . . . my position . . .

JOHN: I want to hear it. In your own words. What you want. And what you feel.

CAROL: . . . I . . .

JOHN: . . . yes . . .

CAROL: My Group.

JOHN: Your "Group" . . . ? *(Pause)*

CAROL: The people I've been talking to . . .

JOHN: There's no shame in that. Everybody needs advisers. Everyone needs to expose themselves. To various points of view. It's not wrong. It's essential. Good. Good. Now: You and I . . . *(The phone rings.)*

You and I . . .

(*He hesitates for a moment, and then picks it up.*) (*Into phone*) Hello. (*Pause*) Um . . . no, I know they do. (*Pause*) I know she does. Tell her that I . . . can I call you back? . . . Then tell her that I think it's going to be fine. (*Pause*) Tell her just, just hold on, I'll . . . can I get back to you? . . . Well . . . no, no, no, we're *taking* the house . . . we're . . . no, no, nn . . . no, she will nnn, it's not a *question* of refunding the dep . . . no . . . it's not a *question* of the deposit . . . will you call Jerry? Babe, baby, will you just call Jerry? Tell him, nnn . . . tell him they, well, they're to keep the deposit, because the deal, be . . . because the deal is going to go *through* . . . because I know . . . be . . . will you please? Just *trust* me. Be . . . well, I'm dealing with the complaint. Yes. Right *Now*. Which is why I . . . yes, no, no, it's really, I can't *talk* about it now. Call Jerry, and I can't talk now. Ff . . . fine. Gg . . . good-bye. (*Hangs up.*) (*Pause*) I'm sorry we were interrupted.

CAROL: No . . .

JOHN: I . . . I was saying:

CAROL: You said that we should agree to talk about my complaint.

JOHN: That's correct.

CAROL: But we *are* talking about it.

JOHN: Well, that's correct too. You see? This is the *gist* of education.

CAROL: No, no. I mean, we're talking about it at the Tenure Committee Hearing. (*Pause*)

JOHN: Yes, but I'm saying: we can talk about it *now*, as easily as . . .

CAROL: No. I think that we should stick to the process . . .

JOHN: . . . wait a . . .

CAROL: . . . the "conventional" process. As you said. (*She gets up.*) And you're right, I'm sorry if I was, um, if I was "discourteous" to you. You're right.

JOHN: Wait, wait a . . .

CAROL: I really should go.

JOHN: Now, look, granted. I have an interest. In the status quo. All right? Everyone does. But what I'm saying is that the *committee* . . .

CAROL: Professor, you're right. Just don't impinge on me. We'll take our differences, and . . .

JOHN: You're going to make a . . . look, look, look, you're going to . . .

CAROL: I shouldn't have come here. They told me . . .

JOHN: One moment. No. No. There are *norms*, here, and there's no reason. Look: I'm trying to *save* you . . .

CAROL: No one *asked* you to . . . you're trying to save *me*? Do me the courtesy to . . .

JOHN: I *am* doing you the courtesy. I'm talking *straight* to you. We can settle this *now*. And I want you to sit *down* and . . .

CAROL: You must excuse me . . . (*She starts to leave the room.*)

JOHN: Sit down, it seems we each have a. . . . Wait one moment. Wait one moment . . . just do me the courtesy to . . .

He restrains her from leaving.

CAROL: LET ME GO.

JOHN: I have no desire to *hold* you, I just want to *talk* to you . . .

CAROL: LET ME GO. LET ME GO. WOULD SOMEBODY *HELP* ME? WOULD SOMEBODY *HELP* ME PLEASE . . . ?

THREE

At rise, Carol and John are seated.

JOHN: I have asked you here. *(Pause)* I have asked you here against, against my . . .

CAROL: I was most surprised you asked me.

JOHN: . . . against my better *judgment*, against . . .

CAROL: I was most surprised . . .

JOHN: . . . against the . . . yes. I'm sure.

CAROL: . . . If you would like me to leave, I'll leave. I'll go right now . . . *(She rises.)*

JOHN: Let us begin *correctly*, may we? I feel . . .

CAROL: That is what I wished to do. That's why I came here, but now . . .

JOHN: . . . I feel . . .

CAROL: But now perhaps you'd like me to leave . . .

JOHN: I don't want you to leave. I asked you to come . . .

CAROL: I didn't have to come here.

JOHN: No. *(Pause)* Thank you.

CAROL: All right. *(Pause) (She sits down.)*

JOHN: Although I feel that it *profits*, it would *profit* you something, to . . .

CAROL: . . . what I . . .

JOHN: If you would hear me out, if you would hear me out.

CAROL: I came here to, the court officers told me not to come.

JOHN: . . . the "court" officers . . . ?

CAROL: I was shocked that you asked.

JOHN: . . . wait . . .

CAROL: Yes. But I did *not* come here to hear what it "profits" me.

JOHN: The "court" officers . . .

CAROL: . . . no, no, perhaps I should leave . . . *(She gets up.)*

JOHN: Wait.

CAROL: No. I shouldn't have . . .

JOHN: . . . wait. Wait. Wait a moment.

CAROL: Yes? What is it you want? *(Pause)* What is it you want?

JOHN: I'd like you to stay.

CAROL: You want me to stay.

JOHN: Yes.

CAROL: You do.

JOHN: Yes. *(Pause)* Yes. I would like to have you hear me out. If you would. *(Pause)* Would you please? If you would do that I would be in your debt. *(Pause) (She sits.)* Thank you. *(Pause)*

CAROL: What is it you wish to tell me?

JOHN: All right. I cannot . . . *(Pause)* I cannot help but feel you are owed an apology. *(Pause)* *(Of papers in his hands)* I have read. *(Pause)* And reread these accusations.

CAROL: What "accusations"?

JOHN: The, the tenure comm . . . what other accusations . . . ?

CAROL: The tenure committee . . . ?

JOHN: Yes.

CAROL: Excuse me, but those are not accusations. They have been *proved.* They are facts.

JOHN: . . . I . . .

CAROL: No. Those are not "accusations."

JOHN: . . . those?

CAROL: . . . the committee *(The phone starts to ring.)* the committee has . . .

JOHN: . . . All right . . .

CAROL: . . . those are not accusations. The Tenure Committee.

JOHN: ALL RIGHT. ALL RIGHT. ALL RIGHT. *(He picks up the phone.)* Hello. Yes. No. I'm here. Tell Mister . . . No, I can't talk to him now . . . I'm sure he has, but I'm fff . . . I know . . . No, I have no time t . . . tell Mister . . . tell Mist . . . tell Jerry that I'm *fine* and that I'll call him right aw . . . *(Pause)* My wife . . . Yes. I'm sure she has. Yes, thank you. Yes, I'll call her too. I cannot talk to you now. *(He hangs up.)* *(Pause)* All right. It was good of you to come. Thank you. I have studied. I have spent some time studying the indictment.

CAROL: You will have to explain that word to me.

JOHN: An "indictment" . . .

CAROL: Yes.

JOHN: Is a "bill of particulars." A . . .

CAROL: All right. Yes.

JOHN: In which is alleged . . .

CAROL: No. I cannot allow that. I cannot allow that. Nothing is alleged. Everything is proved . . .

JOHN: Please, wait a sec . . .

CAROL: I cannot *come* to allow . . .

JOHN: If I may . . . If I may, from whatever you feel is "established," by . . .

CAROL: The issue here is not what I "feel." It is not my "feelings," but the feelings of women. And men. Your superiors, who've been "polled," do you see? To whom *evidence* has been presented, who have *ruled,* do you see? Who have weighed the testimony and the evidence, and have *ruled,* do you see? That you are *negligent.* That you are *guilty,* that you are found *wanting,* and in *error;* and are *not,* for the reasons so-told, to be given tenure. That you are to be disciplined. For facts. For *facts.* Not "alleged," what is the word? But *proved.* Do you see? *By your own actions.*

That is what the tenure committee has said. That is what my lawyer said. For what you did in class. For what you did *in this office.*

JOHN: They're going to discharge me.

CAROL: As full well they should. You don't understand? You're angry? What has *led* you to this place? Not your sex. Not your race. Not your class. YOUR OWN ACTIONS. And you're *angry*. You *ask* me here. What *do* you want? You want to "charm" me. You want to "convince" me. You want me to recant. I will *not* recant. Why should I . . . ? What I say is right. You tell me, you are going to tell me that you have a wife and child. You are going to say that you have a career and that you've worked for twenty years for this. Do you know what you've *worked* for? *Power*. For *power*. Do you understand? And you sit there, and you tell me *stories*. About your *house*, about all the private *schools*, and about *privilege*, and how you are entitled. To *buy*, to *spend*, to *mock*, to *summon*. All your stories. All your silly weak *guilt*, it's all about *privilege*; and you won't know it. Don't you see? You worked twenty years for the right to *insult* me. And you feel entitled to be *paid* for it. Your Home. Your Wife . . . Your sweet "deposit" on your house . . .

JOHN: Don't you have feelings?

CAROL: That's my point. You see? Don't you have feelings? Your final argument. What is it that has no feelings. *Animals*. I don't take your side, you question if I'm Human.

JOHN: Don't you have feelings?

CAROL: I have a responsibility. I . . .

JOHN: . . . to . . . ?

CAROL: To? This institution. To the *students*. To my *group*.

JOHN: . . . your "group." . . .

CAROL: Because I speak, yes, not for myself. But for the group; for those who suffer what I suffer. On behalf of whom, even if I, were, inclined, to what, forgive? Forget? What? Overlook your . . .

JOHN: . . . my behavior?

CAROL: . . . it would be wrong.

JOHN: Even if you were inclined to "forgive" me.

CAROL: It would be wrong.

JOHN: And what would transpire.

CAROL: Transpire?

JOHN: Yes.

CAROL: "Happen?"

JOHN: Yes.

CAROL: Then *say* it. For Christ's sake. Who the *hell* do you think that you are? You want a post. You want unlimited power. To do and to say what you want. As it pleases you — Testing, Questioning, Flirting . . .

JOHN: I never . . .

CAROL: Excuse me, one moment, will you?

(She reads from her notes.)

> The twelfth: "Have a good day, dear."
> The fifteenth: "Now, don't *you* look fetching . . ."
> April seventeenth: "If you girls would come over here . . ." I saw you. I

saw you, Professor. For two semesters sit there, stand there and exploit our, as you thought, "paternal prerogative," and what is that but rape; I swear to God. You asked me in here to explain something to me, as a child, that I did not understand. But I came to explain something to you. You Are Not God. You ask me why I came? I came here to instruct you.

(She produces his book.)

And your book? You think you're going to show me some "light"? You *"maverick."* Outside of tradition. No, no, *(She reads from the book's liner notes.)* "of that fine tradition of *inquiry*. Of Polite *skepticism"* . . . and you say you believe in free intellectual discourse. YOU BELIEVE IN NOTHING. YOU BELIEVE IN NOTHING AT ALL.

JOHN: I believe in freedom of thought.

CAROL: Isn't that fine. *Do* you?

JOHN: Yes. I do.

CAROL: Then why do you question, for one moment, the committee's decision refusing your tenure? Why do you question your suspension? You believe in what *you call* freedom of thought. Then, fine. *You* believe in freedom-of-thought *and* a home, and, *and* prerogatives for your kid, *and* tenure. And I'm going to tell you. You believe *not* in "freedom of thought," but in an elitist, in, in a protected hierarchy which rewards you. And for whom you are the clown. And you mock and exploit the system which pays your rent. You're wrong. I'm not wrong. You're wrong. You think that I'm full of hatred. I know what you think I am.

JOHN: Do you?

CAROL: You think I'm a, of course I do. You think I am a frightened, repressed, confused, I don't know, abandoned young thing of some doubtful sexuality, who wants, power and revenge. *(Pause) Don't* you? *(Pause)*

JOHN: Yes. I do. *(Pause)*

CAROL: Isn't that better? And I feel that that is the first moment which you've treated me with respect. For you told me the truth. *(Pause)* I did not come here, as you are assured, to gloat. Why would I want to gloat? I've profited nothing from your, your, as you say, your "misfortune." I came here, as you did me the honor to *ask* me here, I came here to *tell* you something.

(Pause) That I think . . . that I think you've been wrong. That I think you've been terribly wrong. Do you hate me now? *(Pause)*

JOHN: Yes.

CAROL: Why do you hate me? Because you think me wrong? No. Because I have, you think, *power* over you. Listen to me. Listen to me, Professor. *(Pause)* It is the power that you hate. So deeply that, that any atmosphere of free discussion is impossible. It's not "unlikely." It's *impossible.* Isn't it?

JOHN: Yes.

CAROL: *Isn't* it . . . ?

JOHN: Yes. I suppose.

CAROL: Now. The thing which you find so cruel is the self-same process of selection I, and my group, go through *every day of our lives.* In admittance to school. In our tests, in our class rankings. . . . Is it unfair? I can't tell you. But, if it is fair. Or even if it is "unfortunate but necessary" for us, then, by God, so must it be for you. *(Pause)* You write of your "responsibility to the young." Treat us with respect, and that will *show* you your responsibility. You write that education is just hazing. *(Pause)* But we worked to get to this school. *(Pause)* And some of us. *(Pause)* Overcame prejudices. Economic, sexual, you cannot begin to imagine. And endured humiliations I *pray* that you and those you love never will encounter. *(Pause)* To gain admittance here. To pursue that same dream of security *you* pursue. We, who, who are, at any moment, in danger of being deprived of it. By . . .

JOHN: . . . by . . . ?

CAROL: By the administration. By the teachers. By *you*. By, say, one low grade, that keeps us out of graduate school; by one, say, one capricious or inventive answer on our parts, which, perhaps, you don't find amusing. Now you *know*, do you see? What it is to be subject to that power. *(Pause)*

JOHN: I don't understand. *(Pause)*

CAROL: My charges are not trivial. You see that in the haste, I think, with which they were accepted. A *joke* you have told, with a sexist tinge. The language you use, a verbal or physical caress, yes, yes, I know, you say that it is meaningless. I understand. I differ from you. To lay a hand on someone's shoulder.

JOHN: It was devoid of sexual content.

CAROL: I say it was not. I SAY IT WAS NOT. Don't you begin to *see* . . . ? Don't you begin to understand? IT'S NOT FOR YOU TO SAY.

JOHN: I take your point, and I see there is much good in what you refer to.

CAROL: . . . do you think so . . . ?

JOHN: . . . but, and this is not to say that I cannot change, in those things in which I am deficient . . . But, the . . .

CAROL: Do you hold yourself harmless from the charges of sexual exploitativeness . . . ? *(Pause)*

JOHN: Well, I . . . I . . . I . . . You know I, as I said, I . . . think I am not too old to *learn*, and I *can* learn, I . . .

CAROL: Do you hold yourself innocent of the charge of . . .

JOHN: . . . wait, wait, wait . . . All right, let's go back to . . .

CAROL: YOU FOOL. Who do you think I am? To come here and be taken in by a *smile*. You little yapping fool. You think I want "revenge." I don't want revenge. I WANT UNDERSTANDING.

JOHN: . . . *do* you?

CAROL: I do. *(Pause)*

JOHN: What's the use. It's over.

CAROL: Is it? What is?

JOHN: My job.

CAROL: Oh. Your job. That's what you want to talk about. *(Pause) (She starts to leave the room. She steps and turns back to him.)* All right. *(Pause)* What if it were possible that my Group withdraws its complaint. *(Pause)*

JOHN: What?

CAROL: That's right. *(Pause)*
JOHN: Why.
CAROL: Well, let's say as an act of friendship.
JOHN: An act of friendship.
CAROL: Yes. *(Pause)*
JOHN: In exchange for what.
CAROL: Yes. But I don't think, "exchange." Not "in exchange." For what do we derive from it? *(Pause)*
JOHN: "Derive."
CAROL: Yes.
JOHN: *(Pause)* Nothing. *(Pause)*
CAROL: That's right. We derive nothing. *(Pause)* Do you see that?
JOHN: Yes.
CAROL: That is a little word, Professor. "Yes." "I see that." But you will.
JOHN: And you might speak to the committee . . . ?
CAROL: To the committee?
JOHN: Yes.
CAROL: Well. Of course. That's on your mind. We might.
JOHN: "If" what?
CAROL: "Given" what. Perhaps. I think that that is more friendly.
JOHN: GIVEN WHAT?
CAROL: And, believe me, I understand your rage. It is not that I don't feel it. But I do not see that it is deserved, so I do not resent it. . . . All right. I have a list.
JOHN: . . . a list.
CAROL: Here is a list of books, which we . . .
JOHN: . . . a list of books . . . ?
CAROL: That's right. Which we find questionable.
JOHN: What?
CAROL: Is this so bizarre . . . ?
JOHN: I can't believe . . .
CAROL: It's not necessary you believe it.
JOHN: Academic freedom . . .
CAROL: Someone chooses the books. If you can choose them, others can. What are you, "God"?
JOHN: . . . no, no, the "dangerous." . . .
CAROL: You have an agenda, we have an agenda. I am not interested in your feelings or your motivation, but your actions. If you would like me to speak to the Tenure Committee, here is my list. You are a Free Person, you decide. *(Pause)*
JOHN: Give me the list. *(She does so. He reads.)*
CAROL: I think you'll find . . .
JOHN: I'm capable of reading it. Thank you.
CAROL: We have a number of *texts* we need re . . .
JOHN: I see that.
CAROL: We're amenable to . . .

JOHN: Aha. Well, let me look over the . . . *(He reads.)*

CAROL: I think that . . .

JOHN: LOOK. I'm reading your demands. All right?! *(He reads) (Pause)* You want to ban my book?

CAROL: We do not . . .

JOHN *(Of list):*   It says here . . .

CAROL: . . . We want it removed from inclusion as a representative example of the university.

JOHN: Get out of here.

CAROL: If you put aside the issues of personalities.

JOHN: Get the fuck out of my office.

CAROL: No, I think I would reconsider.

JOHN: . . . you think you can.

CAROL: We can and we *will*. Do you want our support? That is the only quest . . .

JOHN: . . . to ban my *book* . . . ?

CAROL: . . . that is correct . . .

JOHN: . . . this . . . this is a *university* . . . we . . .

CAROL: . . . and we have a statement . . . which we need you to . . . *(She hands him a sheet of paper.)*

JOHN: No, no. It's out of the question. I'm sorry. I don't know what I was thinking of. I want to tell you something. I'm a teacher. I am a teacher. Eh? It's my *name* on the door, and *I* teach the class, and that's what I do. I've got a book with my name on it. And my son will *see* that *book* someday. And I have a respon . . . No, I'm sorry I have a *responsibility* . . . to *myself*, to my *son*, to my *profession.* . . . I haven't been *home* for two days, do you know that? Thinking this out.

CAROL: . . . you haven't?

JOHN: I've been, no. If it's of interest to you. I've been in a *hotel. Thinking. (The phone starts ringing.) Thinking* . . .

CAROL: . . . you haven't been home?

JOHN: . . . *thinking*, do you see?

CAROL: Oh.

JOHN: And, and, I owe you a debt, I see that now. *(Pause)* You're *dangerous*, you're *wrong* and it's my *job* . . . to say no to you. That's my job. You are absolutely right. You want to ban my book? Go to *hell*, and they can do whatever they want to me.

CAROL: . . . you haven't been home in two days . . .

JOHN: I think I told you that.

CAROL: . . . you'd better get that phone. *(Pause)* I think that you should pick up the phone. *(Pause)*

John picks up the phone.

JOHN *(on phone):*   Yes. *(Pause)* Yes. Wh . . . I. I. I had to be away. All ri . . . did they wor . . . did they worry ab . . . No. I'm all right, now, Jerry. I'm f . . . I got a little turned *around,* but I'm *sitting* here and . . . I've got it figured out. I'm fine. I'm fine don't worry about me. I got a little bit mixed up. But I am not sure that it's not a blessing. It cost me my job? Fine. Then the job was not worth having. Tell Grace that I'm coming home and everything is fff . . . *(Pause)* What? *(Pause)* What? *(Pause)* What do you *mean?* WHAT? Jerry . . . Jerry. They . . . Who, who, what can they do . . . ? *(Pause)* NO. *(Pause)* NO. They can't do th . . . What do you mean? *(Pause)* But how . . . *(Pause)* She's, she's, she's *here* with me. To . . . Jerry. I don't underst . . . *(Pause)* *(He hangs up.)* *(To Carol:)* What does this mean?

CAROL: I thought you knew.

JOHN: What. *(Pause)* What does it mean. *(Pause)*

CAROL: You tried to rape me. *(Pause)* According to the law. *(Pause)*

JOHN: . . . what . . . ?

CAROL: You tried to rape me. I was leaving this office, you "pressed" yourself into me. You "pressed" your body into me.

JOHN: . . . I . . .

CAROL: My Group has told your lawyer that we may pursue criminal charges.

JOHN: . . . no . . .

CAROL: . . . under the statute. I am told. It was battery.

JOHN: . . . no . . .

CAROL: Yes. And attempted rape. That's right. *(Pause)*

JOHN: I think that you should go.

CAROL: Of course. I thought you knew.

JOHN: I have to talk to my lawyer.

CAROL: Yes. Perhaps you should. *(The phone rings again.)* *(Pause)*

JOHN: *(Picks up phone. Into phone:)* Hello? I . . . Hello . . . ? I . . . Yes, he just called. No . . . I. I can't talk to you now, Baby. *(To Carol:)* Get out.

CAROL: . . . your wife . . . ?

JOHN: . . . who it is is no concern of yours. Get out. *(To phone:)* No, no, it's going to be all right. I. I can't talk now, Baby. *(To Carol:)* Get out of here.

CAROL: I'm going.

JOHN: Good.

CAROL *(exiting):*   . . . and don't call your wife "baby."

JOHN: What?

CAROL: Don't call your wife baby. You heard what I said.

Carol starts to leave the room. John grabs her and begins to beat her.

JOHN: You vicious little bitch. You think you can come in here with your political correctness and destroy my life?

He knocks her to the floor.

After how I treated you . . . ? You should be . . . *Rape you* . . . ? Are you kidding me . . . ?

He picks up a chair, raises it above his head, and advances on her.

I wouldn't touch you with a ten-foot pole. You little *cunt* . . .

She cowers on the floor below him. Pause. He looks down at her. He lowers the chair. He moves to his desk, and arranges the papers on it. Pause. He looks over at her.

. . . well . . .

Pause. She looks at him.

CAROL: Yes. That's right.

(She looks away from him, and lowers her head. To herself:) . . . yes. That's right.

End   [1992]

THINKING ABOUT THE TEXT

1. What are the main arguments that each character makes during the play? In particular, what are their respective views on education?

2. What should an audience consider in evaluating the characters' arguments? Do you sympathize with one character more than the other? When *Oleanna* was performed in Washington, D.C., the theater lobby featured a chalkboard on which audience members could "vote" for either John or Carol. Do you think Mamet encourages the audience to take sides? Why, or why not?

3. Near the end of the first scene, Carol says, "I have never told anyone this . . ." (p. 626). What might she have been about to tell John? What should an audience consider in trying to resolve this issue of fact?

4. In the second and third scenes, Carol refers several times to her "group." Identify some places where she strikes you as relying especially on language worked out in this group. Should the audience be critical of Carol's reliance on the group's language? Why, or why not? How individualistic does John's language seem?

5. Should Mamet have had his characters speak in complete sentences more often? Why, or why not? At numerous moments in the play, Mamet has John speaking on the phone. Why might Mamet have done this? How do John's phone conversations conceivably affect Carol? How do they affect you?

UNIVERSITY OF MARYLAND AT COLLEGE PARK
Pamphlet on Sexual Harassment

The following selection comes from a 1997 college pamphlet on sexual harassment. The Office of Human Relations Programs at the University of Maryland at College Park produced this pamphlet for distribution to the entire campus community. The pamphlet outlines key elements of the university's policy on sexual harassment, which is spelled out in its undergraduate and graduate catalogs.

Sexual harassment by University faculty, staff, and students is prohibited.

WHAT IS SEXUAL HARASSMENT?

Sexual harassment is defined as: (1) unwanted sexual advances; or (2) unwelcome requests for sexual favors; and (3) other behavior of a sexual nature where:

A. Submission to such conduct is made either explicitly or implicitly a term or condition of an individual's employment or participation in a University-sponsored educational program or activity; or

B. Submission to or rejection of such conduct by an individual is used as the basis for academic or employment decisions affecting that individual; or

C. Such conduct has the purpose or effect of unreasonably interfering with an individual's academic or work performance, or of creating an intimidating, hostile, or offensive educational or working environment.

Sexual harassment is a violation of federal and state law and may violate the civil and criminal laws of the State of Maryland. The University of Maryland, its agents, supervising employees, employees and students shall be held liable for their acts of sexual harassment and are subject to appropriate University disciplinary action and personal legal liability.

For a copy of the UMCP Sexual Harassment Policy, call: 405-2838

The University of Maryland at College Park is committed to maintaining a learning and working environment in which students, faculty, and staff can develop intellectually, professionally, personally, and socially. Sexual harassment impedes us from achieving such an environment and is, therefore, prohibited by University policy.

—William E. Kirwan, President

WHO ARE THE PARTICIPANTS?

Sexual harassment can involve:

- professor and professor
- professor and student
- teaching assistant and student
- supervisor and employee
- student and student
- other relationships among colleagues, peers, and co-workers

The following behavior may constitute sexual harassment:

- lewd remarks, whistles, or personal reference to one's anatomy
- unwanted physical contact such as patting, pinching, or constant brushing against a person's body
- subtle or overt pressure for sexual favors

5

- persistent and offensive sexual jokes and comments
- misuse or abuse of power or hierarchal authority

The consequences to a person responsible for sexual harassment may be:

- denial of a promotion
- termination or forced resignation
- negative evaluation or poor recommendations
- demotion

The effects upon the person harassed and their environment may be:

- diminished self-esteem
- self-blame
- decreased productivity
- increased absenteeism
- stress-related physical symptoms (e.g., stress, headaches, backaches, etc.)
- low morale

WHAT CAN THE UMCP COMMUNITY DO ABOUT SEXUAL HARASSMENT?

To effectively enforce sexual harassment guidelines the University strongly encourages anyone who believes they have been harassed to report all incidents.

If you believe you are being, or have been sexually harassed, you should take the following steps immediately:

1. Keep records—write a journal or record the facts on a tape recorder and tell a friend in confidence. Keep track of dates, places, times, witnesses, and the nature of the harassment. Save any letters, cards, or notes in a secure place, preferably at home.
2. Seek the advice of or report the incident of harassment to any of the individuals listed under the Informal Grievance Procedure (contained in this brochure). You may file an informal or formal complaint. You may also seek the assistance of the Counseling Center (314-7651) or the Faculty/Staff Assistance Program (314-8170).

You may also consider using the following strategies, although these actions are not required to pursue a complaint:

1. Say "no" to your harasser. Say it firmly, without smiling, and without apologizing.
2. Tell the harasser, in writing, that you object to this behavior. Describe the specific behaviors which are offensive or threatening. Treat this letter as a confidential piece of communication and keep a copy.

If you have been accused of sexual harassment you should seek the advice of any of the individuals listed under the section in Informal Complaints Section.

If you receive a report of sexual harassment, notify the President's Legal Office prior to taking any action to investigate or resolve the matter informally.

10

The Legal Office will normally coordinate all matters relating to sexual harassment complaints.

If your unit, department, or organization has not had a Sexual Harassment Prevention Workshop within the past two years, contact the Office of Human Relations Programs to schedule a workshop. All units, departments, or organizations are strongly encouraged to receive Sexual Harassment Prevention Training.

WHERE TO GO FOR HELP

Information and Educational Programs

Contact the Office of Human Relations Programs (405-2838) for further information or to schedule a Sexual Harassment Prevention Workshop.

Informal Complaints

Contact the following persons on campus for guidance, information, or informal resolution: 15

- ♦ Your supervisor, chair, director, or dean
- ♦ The Staff of the President's Legal Office (405-4945)
- ♦ The Campus Compliance Officer in the Office of Human Relations Programs (405-2838)
- ♦ The Equity Administrator in your College/Unit
- ♦ The Staff in Employee Relations of Personnel Services Department (405-5651)
- ♦ The Director of the Office of Judicial Programs (314-8204)
- ♦ Any UMCP official or faculty member

Formal Complaints

Formal grievance procedures for resolving complaints are available. For further information contact the Campus Compliance Officer in the Office of Human Relations Programs (405-2638) or the Staff of the President's Legal Office (405-4945).

Off-Campus Resources

- ♦ Equal Employment Opportunity Commission (410)962-3932 or (800)669-4000
- ♦ U.S. Department of Education Office for Civil Rights (215)596-6791
- ♦ The Maryland Commission on Human Relations (410)333-1700 or (800)637-6247   [1997]

THINKING ABOUT THE TEXT

1. Describe and evaluate the format of this pamphlet. In what ways does the pamphlet seem appropriate for its audience, that is, members of the

university community who may be unfamiliar with how the university defines and handles sexual harassment? In what ways might the pamphlet be more informative or better designed?

2. What specific parts of the University of Maryland's pamphlet might have drawn Carol's attention in *Oleanna* as she considered her experiences with John?

3. Compare this pamphlet to materials that your own college produces on the subject of sexual harassment. Are you aware of how your college defines and handles it? Why, or why not?

HOWARD GADLIN
From "Mediating Sexual Harassment"

Howard Gadlin (b. 1940) is university ombudsperson at the University of California at Los Angeles. He also codirects UCLA's Center for Inter-racial/Inter-ethnic Conflict Resolution. In both these capacities, he mediates disputes among members of the university community, including cases of sexual harassment. The following case study is an excerpt from Gadlin's essay "Mediating Sexual Harassment," which appears in Bernice R. Sandler and Robert J. Shoop's 1997 book Sexual Harassment on Campus: A Guide for Administrators, Faculty, and Students.

When Joanna first called the office, she only wanted the answers to a few questions about the university's sexual harassment policy. "What does one do if she has a sexual harassment complaint about a teacher?" At that point it wasn't clear if she was calling for a friend or for herself. After a brief explanation from the secretary "she" became "I." "Where do I go? Who do I talk to? What happens to me? How much time would it take?" You could almost feel her poised to hang up the phone if the conversation went the wrong way, but you couldn't tell immediately which way was the wrong way.

We knew only that she didn't want to bring a charge; she didn't want to get him in trouble. She preferred not to give her name and, no, she didn't want to talk with one of the ombudspersons. The secretary reminded her that the Ombuds Office keeps these matters confidential and pointed out that it is often helpful to someone who has been harassed to at least come in and talk with us about the situation—there is no obligation to pursue a charge, no one would take her complaint away from her and act on it without her knowledge and permission.

The secretary also acknowledged that it must be a difficult experience to cope with on one's own. She finally said, "Well, maybe I should come in." "Why don't we set up an appointment, and if you don't come in, that's no problem?" Tentatively, Joanna agreed to come in the next day and she was even willing to leave her name. At this point, we knew only that her complaint had to do with a teacher.

When Joanna arrived, although somewhat tentative about being in the office, she relaxed as I repeated our pledge of confidentiality and our reassurance that we would not act without her knowledge and permission. I asked if she would be more comfortable if another woman were present or even if she would prefer meeting alone with the associate ombudsperson, a woman. Without hesitation she assured me that wasn't necessary. She was very bright, quite relaxed with herself, and her friendliness was apparent even when she was being cautious. Joanna's story was pretty straightforward:

> After receiving notification of her admission to several graduate schools (she was accepted everywhere she applied, all of them excellent schools), she had gone to the office of one of her professors to let him know of her success and to thank him for his letters of recommendation. She had taken two courses with Professor Toma and done very well. The professor had supported her interest in graduate school and there had never been any indication that he had any interest in her except as a student. After talking about her acceptance letters and graduate school choices, he suddenly shifted the focus of their conversation and began talking about how he was attracted to her and suggested that they find some way to get together off campus. There was no physical contact and he was polite, even charming, but she was totally taken off guard, and repulsed. [If faculty knew how many students find their advances either humorous or repulsive, there would be much less sexual harassment.] Joanna had managed to extricate herself from the situation without giving any indication of how upset she was. The only person she told about the incident was her boyfriend, and if it had not been for his insistence, she probably would not have pursued the matter.

Once we began talking her anger and disappointment came quickly to the surface. We reviewed the full range of formal and informal options available to her; she dismissed everything that would involve formal charges or investigations. As we talked, Joanna returned over and over again to two main concerns: She wanted Professor Toma to understand how inappropriate his advance had been and how upsetting it was for her; and she wanted to know that he would learn enough from this that he wouldn't do the same to another student in the future. Of all the options, mediation seemed most appealing because it would allow her to speak for herself, but at the same time, mediation was daunting because she would have to meet with him face to face.

We talked about the concerns she had for a meeting — the ways in which he might be intimidating, his facility with language, the fact that he was the professor and she the student, and her uncertainty that she would be able to say the same things to his face that she was telling to me. I asked her to think about the kinds of things that could be done before and during the mediation to address these concerns so that it would not be a continuation of the harassment. From her perspective, she wanted a safe setting in which to confront him, one in which he could not intimidate her, throw around his status and power, or overwhelm her with smooth talk. Yet she felt very strongly that she wanted to be the person to confront him — shuttle diplomacy would not give her what she wanted from the process.

At that point we agreed that I would speak with him about her desire to address the incident in a nonadversarial manner, explain the process of mediation, and arrange for the three of us to meet. I urged her to approach the

5

Woman's Resource Center for support and advocacy, explaining again that, as ombudsperson and mediator, I could not serve as her advocate. I encouraged her to bring someone who could serve as a support person with her to the mediation. Although appreciative of my suggestions, she decided to forgo having an advocate. She did, however, decide to meet with someone from the Woman's Resource Center. Without using her name, I made those arrangements so that she only had to mention that I had referred her.

The next step was to contact Professor Toma. When I identified myself on the phone, he seemed curious that I was calling him; but as soon as I mentioned that a student had come to see me, he said, "Oh, you must be calling about. . . ." We met within an hour of my call. At our initial meeting, after I explained the role of my office and the nature of mediation, he gave me an account of the events that differed very little from the one given by the student. Professor Toma was both remorseful and defensive — acknowledging that he had acted foolishly and reassuring me that, as a matter of principle, he did not get involved with undergraduates. (This was said in such a way as to imply, or at least so I inferred, that graduate students were another matter.) I reviewed with him the various options for handling sexual harassment complaints against faculty, reminded him again of the student's preference to resolve this without filing a formal charge, and asked him to take some time to think about how he wanted to respond before we went ahead with arrangements for mediation. We agreed to talk again before proceeding.

Over the years I have learned to be suspicious when someone accused of wrongdoing does not react with some self-righteous anger. This is especially so for people with status and power in an institution, and I knew he needed time to react to the accusation before I would risk letting the student be in the same room with him. It is important to note that this reaction has nothing to do with disputing the accuracy of the story told by the accuser. Sure enough, when he called back two days later, he was angry and much less apologetic than he had been in our first meeting. At that point I knew there was a chance that mediation, when we got to it, could be successful; without engaging his self-justification, there would be no hope of meaningful interaction between them at the mediation. Of course, the first step was to work through this stage with him, in private. To bring them together at this point would only mean subjecting her to his self-righteousness and intimidation.

We met for an hour and a half. Toma alternated between expressing rage   10 about her making so much of so little and asserting that he had not violated the sexual harassment policy: It was a single occurrence, she was no longer his student, there had been no physical contact, and so on. I was pretty certain he had spoken with a lawyer. Given that he was a tenured faculty member, it is most likely he was right — Toma would probably be cleared if there were a formal grievance and investigation. Much of the meaning of what had transpired between him and the student was implicit. His inclination was to take a legalistic stance and deny that what he had done was sexual harassment: Although not quite saying it, he implied he was being victimized here.

My role, beyond the usual active-listening restatements of feelings and positions, was to help him develop a framework for comparing the relative merits of sticking to this legalistic approach versus opening himself up to a more genuine engagement with the student in mediation. Several factors brought him around to mediation. First was the fact that he was preparing a formal defense against a charge that was not being posed in a formal way. The student, in asking for mediation, was asking for interaction rather than investigation. He was someone who took his role as a teacher seriously, and I believe it was difficult for him actually to be as adversarial as he was saying he was. Mediation could allow him to interact as a committed faculty member who had, tempted by the student's attractiveness and deluded by his own misreading of her gratitude, made a serious mistake and abused the power of his position. To defend his innocence in a formal investigation he would have to play a very different role — that of the misunderstood professor. And, most likely he would have had to lie. Second was his concern to not have the matter become public. I think he was especially concerned about his wife, but he was also aware that despite promises of confidentiality, formal charges usually become known. Certainly it would be difficult to keep his wife from learning he was under formal investigation for a charge of sexual harassment. Although he could probably be cleared in any formal proceeding, it was his reluctance to be involved in a formal proceeding that provided incentive for him to enter the mediation.

Those who would prefer that all sexual harassment cases be referred to a formal process must keep in mind how significant a factor formal proceedings are in mediation. It looms as an option for the victim, thereby influencing the decisions harassers make about being cooperative with mediation, and it lurks in the mediation sessions: Most of the time the person accused of harassment has no idea about the willingness or unwillingness of the person harassed to pursue a formal charge should the outcome of mediation be unsatisfactory. The existence of the possibility of a formal charge influences the person harassed as well, in part by reminding her of a potential source of leverage should the harasser be unresponsive to her concerns in the mediation. Although she may not want to go the formal route, that option is always available, and an especially recalcitrant harasser might well push the person he harassed over the edge into a decision to pursue a formal charge after all.

Of course we must be alert to the analogous risks to the person bringing the complaint as well. No doubt the harasser, especially when he is a person of some influence within the institution and in his field, is in a position to do irreparable harm to the reputation and career of the person he harassed. Should she not be responsive to his concerns during the course of mediation, or should she be too vociferous in the pursuit of her goals, he could easily create considerable difficulty for her.

In any event, by the time we had explored all the options available to him and the implications of pursuing each one, Professor Toma committed himself to the mediation although he remained convinced that he would be exonerated if a formal charge were to be brought against him. This was a wonderful illustration of the way formal and informal avenues of complaint work together. Without a formal mechanism, there would have been no leverage to move him toward mediation. Without an informal mechanism, either the student would not have come forward or he would have prevailed.

We scheduled the mediation session. However, before bringing them   15
together, I met again with Joanna to report to her about the outcome of my session
with the faculty member, to explore further her concerns now that she had met
with a support person, and to prepare for the mediation itself. Despite my urging
but not surprisingly, her preference was still to meet with me without the support
person present and to attend the mediation session on her own as well. Acting
autonomously was very important to her, and she felt it was important to confront
him by herself, with only the mediator present. This is not to say that the support
person was unhelpful or unimportant. She had helped her prioritize her goals and
had given her an additional perspective from which to understand sexual harassment and its impact on those who are harassed. In my meeting with Joanna, we
identified the conditions she felt would facilitate her ability to speak for herself,
anticipated things he might say or do to throw her off, and clarified what she was
hoping for as an outcome of the mediation. She was both apprehensive and eager
for it to be over. We arranged to meet at the mediation session the next day.

The mediation itself was somewhat anticlimactic. Joanna spoke first and
quite eloquently described her disappointment in the way he had misinterpreted
her gratitude for his support. She pointed out that Professor Toma was older than
her father and made it clear how his actions had dissolved her respect for him.
She spoke about how her sense of academic accomplishment and achievement
had been undermined by his actions, introducing an element of uncertainty in
her response to other professors. She reviewed her actions to help him see what
her friendliness meant, perhaps, from my point of view, with a bit too much
implicit apology for what he might have imagined as her role in all this. Finally,
Joanna expressed her concerns about future students and how he might approach
them. While she reiterated her desire to not get him in trouble, she was unsure
about what he could do to reassure her that he would not repeat his behavior with
someone else.

I had been expecting Toma to put up some sort of defense, most likely in the
form of the sort of explanation that recontextualized the whole event and gave it a
different spin, making each statement and action more innocent than they probably were. I have heard such alternate accounts more times than I care to mention,
often having to swallow my skepticism and remind myself about the importance of
face-saving and the dynamics of embarrassment. But, he surprised me by beginning with an apology that was built around an acknowledgment of what he had
done. He took full responsibility for any misinterpretations of her friendliness and
made it clear that she had never given him reason to believe she was interested in
him. It was, he owned up, a construction grounded in his own desire. He was
defensive only when he tried to convince her that his support for her as a student
had been based on his respect for her academic ability and achievement and not a
strategy to flatter her. He insisted that until she returned to thank him, he had
never paid attention to her attractiveness and although she probably didn't believe
him completely he was specific enough in his praise of her work that she knew at
least he remembered more about her than her appearance.

It was more complicated when it came to her concerns about the safety of
other students. Although Toma attempted to assure her that he had never acted

this way with undergraduates, she remained, quite reasonably, skeptical. Still, Joanna did not want to go to the department chair, or as some who have been harassed do, ask for a sealed letter to be placed in his file, to be opened only should a subsequent harassment charge be raised. It was almost as if she was asking him to give her a reason to believe him, but his harassment of her had made it unlikely that he could offer her adequate reassurance that it would not be happen again.

In the end she was left with his promises. Throughout the process she had been unwilling to have anyone else learn about the harassment incident. Because his account of why he had come on to her hadn't really made sense to her, his explanation about why he could be trusted not to repeat his actions was equally implausible. But he had understood her enough, she felt, to bring the matter to a close. Although I am often quite skeptical of agreements that address the possibility of recidivism only with promises of clean living, both my private sessions with the faculty member and his conduct during the mediation gave me reasons to trust his word here. This trust was borne out several months later when he called asking for some additional readings on sexual harassment to distribute among members of a newly formed committee whose function it would be to address sexual harassment in the department.

Nonetheless, the resolution of this case does point to one of the dilemmas facing mediators of sexual harassment cases — how to ensure that the harasser does not use the confidentiality of a mediated agreement as a cover for continuing his harassment. Although it is true that most people who have been harassed mention a concern about other possible victims among the reasons they chose to come forward, addressing that concern while preserving confidentiality is a complicated matter. To be sure, an agreement can include a clause about the possibility of future harassment, but in most cases we need more than promises. Some agreements specify that the grievant would come forward to present a formal complaint should there be a later charge of harassment against the same person. Others involve depositing a sealed statement in a confidential file to be opened only should there be another harassment charge. Some policies protect the confidentiality of mediated agreements but allow the appropriate administrators to inquire of the ombudsperson about previous informally settled charges in the event of a later formal charge.

Although each of these options requires complex administrative manipulations, they can add teeth to clauses in agreements intended to protect others. My own preference is to conclude mediations with written agreements — they leave less room for differential recall about what exactly it was the parties agreed to. However, as is often the case with mediation, I am committed to tailoring the process to the needs and interests of the disputants. In circumstances where both parties prefer not to have a written agreement, I feel impelled, after exploring with them the implications of not having a written agreement, to honor their preferences. Of course, should they disagree about the form for expressing their agreement, then that too becomes an issue to be addressed in the mediation.

One of the ongoing debates among mediators is about whether and how to incorporate the interests of unrepresented parties in mediation. In the field of

20

environmental and public policy mediation, concerns have been raised that agreements can have significant and long-term effects on large numbers of people who are not parties to the formal dispute. Some mediators advocate a very active role for the mediator to ensure that larger public interests are considered and argued for during the negotiations. At the very least, we should pose an analogous set of questions to those who mediate sexual harassment cases. It is not enough to reassure oneself that both parties agreed to the process, attended "voluntarily," and achieved a resolution that met both of their needs. As an ombudsperson, I have a certain latitude for raising concerns about institutional and individual interests that must be addressed in an agreement. Clearly this is one area that challenges the advocates of mediation.

No doubt those who are opposed, in principle, to the use of mediation for settling sexual harassment charges will not be satisfied by the arguments presented and the proposed modifications of the mediation method. But even if they cannot be persuaded, the objections raised point in the direction mediators must go to ensure that their method does not serve purposes that are the opposite of those that made mediation attractive to begin with — a prompt, confidential, creative, effective, humane, educational, and empowering alternative to formal processes for those who cannot or will not use them.

Having worked with literally hundreds of sexual harassment allegations, I am convinced that framing mediation and formal procedures as antithetical to one another undercuts efforts to address the problem effectively. In a well-designed system the availability of each approach strengthens the effectiveness of the other. I would never argue for a system that required mediation for sexual harassment, nor for one that permitted no options other than mediation. At the same time, I would be equally wary of a system that did not allow for the informal settlement of harassment charges, and mediation is one of the most effective means to informal settlement.

Formal justice systems can offer only punishment, retribution, and stigmatization of the offender. Although there are circumstances in which these are appropriate responses to harassment, formal procedures also take a tremendous toll on those who have been harassed and the organizations in which harassment occurs. Even though we have all assumed that punishment can reduce the frequency of sexual harassment, there is no reason to believe there is a connection between punishment and the need for healing required by either the person harassed or the organization. Anyone who has worked, taught, or studied in a department that has endured a formal sexual harassment case can testify to the fact that many more people than the two protagonists are affected by such cases. Relationships are strained, allegiances are polarized, and trust is diminished. Formal procedures cannot address these dynamics. Mediation can, both for the protagonists and for all those who care about the climates in their institutions. Mediation allows differences to be addressed without waging war. The potential effectiveness of mediation resides in the respect it affords both parties, the control it gives them over the resolution of their dispute, and its ability to construct a non-adversarial space in which "a remedial imagination," as my colleague, Carrie Menkel-Meadow calls it, can flourish.   [1997]

25

THINKING ABOUT THE TEXT

1. Joanna chose to go through mediation rather than lodge a formal complaint against Professor Toma. When does Gadlin indicate that it is nevertheless important for students to have the option of formally accusing someone of sexual harassment? What things did Joanna have to consider before she decided on mediation as her course of action?

2. After reading this case study, what do you think are the potential advantages and disadvantages of mediation?

3. Imagine that you were asked to serve as a mediator between Carol and John. What might you have said and to whom at the beginning of scene 2? At the beginning of scene 3? If you wish, try actually rewriting the beginning of these scenes, putting yourself in as mediator.

ROBERT M. O'NEIL

Protecting Free Speech When the Issue Is Sexual Harassment

The following article appeared in the September 13, 1996, issue of the Chronicle of Higher Education, *a weekly newspaper for college administrators and faculty. Author Robert M. O'Neil (b. 1934), a professor of constitutional law at the University of Virginia, founded and still directs the Thomas Jefferson Center for the Protection of Free Expression. In his article, O'Neil refers to Dean Cohen, a teacher whose college found him guilty of sexual harassment. When Cohen sued the college for violating his freedom of speech, a federal district court ruled against him, but subsequently an appeals court found in his favor. Like the appeals court, O'Neil criticizes how the sexual harassment policy at Cohen's school was worded.*

If sexually harassing speech is the least tolerable form of professorial speech, it may also be the hardest to define and constrain. But now, in the first federal appellate ruling on purely verbal harassment, the U.S. Court of Appeals for the Ninth Circuit has provided some guidance to institutions that seek to curb such expression. The ruling also offered some implicit warnings about policies that contain excessively broad language.

The case arose at San Bernardino Valley College, when a grievance committee and the college's president found Dean Cohen, a longtime English teacher, guilty of sexual harassment. A female student in his remedial English class had complained that she found his teaching style and classroom materials offensive; he conceded that he could be "abrasive" and "confrontational." The facts were not in dispute: Mr. Cohen had used profanity and vulgarities, had occasionally read articles from *Playboy* and *Hustler* aloud in class, and had discussed such topics as obscenity, cannibalism, and consensual sex with children. The student had asked for an alternative exercise when Mr. Cohen assigned a paper asking students to "define pornography," but Mr. Cohen refused her request.

After he was found guilty of sexual harassment under San Bernardino Valley College's newly adopted harassment policy, Mr. Cohen sued the college in federal court, claiming that his rights to free speech had been violated. The college's policy included in its definition of sexual harassment speech or conduct that unreasonably interferes "with an individual's academic performance" or that creates "an intimidating, hostile, or offensive learning environment." A district court upheld the college's action, while recognizing that so broad a harassment policy might give "the most sensitive and easily offended students . . . a veto power over class content and methodology." The judge also upheld the college's order that Mr. Cohen be required to attend sexual-harassment seminars, to "become sensitive to the particular needs of his students" and to "modify his teaching strategy when it becomes apparent that his techniques create a climate which impedes the students' ability to learn." The college also told Mr. Cohen that further violation of the policy could result in discipline "up to and including suspension or termination."

The appeals court unanimously reversed the district judge, faulting the vagueness of the college's policy. What especially troubled the court was that a professor's "sexually oriented teaching methods" could be found to create a "hostile learning environment" and could lead to severe sanctions under the policy. Invoking such imprecise terms, the court warned, would "trap the innocent by not providing fair warning," and amounted to "legalistic ambush."

What does the Ninth Circuit's ruling mean for other harassment policies that proscribe conduct that creates an offensive "climate" or "environment"? The appeals court stopped short of declaring all "hostile environment" policies invalid.

The opinion left open, among other issues, whether classroom speech such as Mr. Cohen's might be punishable if a harassment policy, as the appeals court put it, "were more precisely construed by authoritative interpretive guidelines or if the College were to adopt a clearer and more precise policy."

Nonetheless, this judgment creates grave doubts about harassment policies that are aimed at classroom speech that produces an offensive environment. The court was concerned that such policies could penalize controversial or provocative pedagogical styles or the choice of teaching materials containing sexual themes — teaching styles and materials that might challenge or engage some students, even as they offended others. (Although the court stopped short of saying that Mr. Cohen's teaching constituted speech protected by the First Amendment, it did note that his style had long been deemed "pedagogically sound and within the bounds of teaching methodology permitted at the college.")

After the Cohen case, colleges should carefully review existing policies that attempt to deal with the presence of a hostile teaching environment. There are alternatives to the type of wording in San Bernardino's policy that would serve the same laudable goal — deterring unacceptable sexism in the college classroom — without falling afoul of the Constitution.

♦ ♦ ♦

Last year, for example, The American Association of University Professors suggested a sexual-harassment policy for institutions' consideration. Under the terms of that policy, before it may be punished as harassment, speech "of a sexual nature . . . directed against another" must be shown to be "abusive" or "severely humiliating" or to have persisted despite the objection of the person or persons against whom it was directed. Alternatively, it must be speech that is "reasonably regarded as offensive and substantially impairs the academic or work opportunity of students, colleagues, or co-workers."

The latter option includes a critical stipulation. If a complaint is lodged   10 against speech of a sexual nature uttered in the context of teaching, to be found to be sexual harassment the speech must also be "persistent, pervasive, and not germane to the subject matter." Therein lies the key to the dilemma posed by the Cohen case. A harassment policy that is limited and qualified in this way would almost certainly meet the court's wish for "a clearer and more precise policy." Such a policy would also minimize the risk of punishing professorial speech that might offend some students, but nonetheless is "pedagogically sound" — for example, because it helps hold the attention of marginal students.

At the same time, such a policy would effectively address unacceptable harassment or exploitation of sexual themes in the classroom. It would clearly proscribe sexually oriented jibes, jokes, taunts, and the like that are addressed to another person, when they are abusive or severely humiliating or persist despite objection from the person addressed.

But what about speech not directed at a particular individual? Even though it creates a hostile climate or environment, speech that is not accompanied by physical harassment and that is not targeted at an individual should not be the sole reason for getting rid of a teacher. Something more clearly detrimental to basic academic values should be required for so severe a penalty, and such a situation also can be covered by a carefully bounded harassment policy. If, for example, a professor (save possibly in a course on twentieth-century American humor) begins each class with a round of sexist jokes, the conditions of the A. A.U.P.'s or similarly worded policies would seem to be met: The speech would be "persistent, pervasive, and not germane to the subject matter."

One other issue is important. Fair procedures are as essential in dealing with sexual harassment as they are in any other area of professorial misconduct. The intolerability of sexual harassment does not justify diluting the rigorous standards and safeguards that apply to the handling of other charges of misconduct. Informal procedures may, of course, be used to gather evidence or to facilitate the mediation of complaints, but when formal charges are filed and heard by campus officials, a faculty member's right to due process of law must be protected. Consistent with past legal precedents, the Ninth Circuit noted in the Cohen ruling that "Cohen was simply without any notice that the Policy would be applied in such a way as to punish his long-standing teaching style."

If classroom language creates a hostile climate but does not fall within the bounds of what the courts allow to be proscribed, the language still cannot be ignored by institutions. Indeed, the cases that have ended up in court would never have got that far if the academic system had been working properly. College teachers who create a hostile classroom climate, however acceptable their teaching styles may be to some students, must be warned of the corrosive effects of their behavior. They need to be guided by deans, department heads, and other colleagues in the quest for teaching methods and materials that enliven classes without offending or demeaning their students.

The first indication of students' concern about a professor's use of sexually   15
sensitive material might, for example, warrant a classroom visit by someone designated by the department. Teaching-resource centers, which now exist on most campuses, should devote special attention to concerns about sexually sensitive material, so that faculty members become more aware of ways in which their teaching may unintentionally offend or alienate students. It also is clear that regular reviews of the classroom teaching of both tenured and non-tenured professors should include greater attention to practices that might impair the learning environment. It is such constructive approaches, not coercive sanctions or penalties, that constitute the most appropriate academic response.

While the Cohen decision leaves open many more issues than it settles or even addresses, it does, at the very least, warn us that in dealing with restrictions on speech in the classroom, vague and imprecise standards simply will not do. Precision of language and clarity of policy now are required in this realm, just as they have been for many years in policies dealing with other restraints on speech.

At the same time, the decision intensifies the need to make our campuses and classrooms more welcoming to all students. The issue is not whether sexual harassment in any form is tolerable, for surely it is not. Rather, the issue is how we define and address practices that we all agree have no place in the academy.

[1996]

THINKING ABOUT THE TEXT

1. In paragraph 17 O'Neil concludes his article by saying, "The issue is not whether sexual harassment in any form is tolerable, for surely it is not. Rather, the issue is how we define and address practices that we all agree have no place in the academy." Reread O'Neil's second paragraph, where he describes Dean Cohen's teaching methods. Would you grant Cohen's practices a place in the academy? Why, or why not? In reporting these practices, O'Neil states in the same paragraph that "the facts were not in dispute." Does he provide you with all the facts about Cohen's teaching that you would like to have? If not, what else would you like to know?

2. What are O'Neil's objections to the language that Cohen's college presently uses in its sexual harassment policy? What language would he like to see colleges use? Evaluate his recommendation.

3. In *Oleanna*, would Carol have a strong case against John if her college's policy on sexual harassment were phrased the way San Bernardino's policy was? Would she have a strong case against him if her college's policy used the language that O'Neil recommends? Explain your reasoning.

WRITING ABOUT ISSUES

1. At the end of *Oleanna*, argument degenerates into profanity and physical violence. Write an essay identifying at least three actions that, had they been taken well before then, might have prevented this outcome. Choose actions that you think would have been reasonable, productive, and fair. For each action you propose, identify who or what should have taken it. Throughout your essay, support your recommendations by referring to specific details of the actual text.

2. Write an essay comparing Carol with Joanna (the student in Gadlin's case study) or John with Dean Cohen (the professor that O'Neil discusses). Focus on whether the two people you discuss are equally justified in feeling wronged. Support your position by referring to specific details of both cases. If you wish, refer to language in the University of Maryland pamphlet.

3. Write an essay recalling a time when you were in conflict with a teacher and consulted another school official about it or considered doing so. Besides identifying the issue or issues involved in the conflict, explain why you considered bringing it to another official's attention and why you ultimately did, or did not, consult such an official. If you wish, compare your situation to Carol's.

4. Imagine that the Office of Student Life at your college is thinking about issuing a pamphlet similar to the University of Maryland's. Write a letter to that office stating and supporting your view of this plan. Identify specific features of the Maryland pamphlet that you like, specific features of it that you dislike, and the reasoning behind your position. If you wish, use Mamet's *Oleanna* as a case study.

COMPARING SCHOOL CULTURE WITH THE CULTURE OF HOME: CRITICAL COMMENTARIES ON RICHARD RODRIGUEZ'S "ARIA"

RICHARD RODRIGUEZ, "Aria"

CRITICAL COMMENTARIES:
RAMÓN SALDÍVAR, From *Chicano Narrative*
TOMÁS RIVERA, From "Richard Rodriguez's *Hunger of Memory* as Humanistic Antithesis"
VICTOR VILLANUEVA JR., From "Whose Voice Is It Anyway?"

For many American children, the culture of school differs greatly from the one they know at home. Children of immigrants to America may sense such a cultural divide, especially if their teachers insist on speaking English while their parents speak another language at home. In his 1982 memoir *Hunger of Memory*, Richard

Rodriguez recalls how he faced exactly this situation as the child of Mexican immigrants. Rodriguez uses his own experiences to argue that if the children of immigrants are to succeed in the United States, they must separate themselves from their home culture and immerse themselves in the English-oriented atmosphere of the American school. In making this argument, Rodriguez comes out against bilingual education and affirmative action. When it was first published, many people praised his book for its eloquence, honesty, and realism. Subsequently, however, the book received strong criticism, especially from Hispanic American educators. Several of them disagree with the positions it takes; moreover, they worry that Rodriguez will be seen as the authoritative guide to Hispanic American life. Here we include an excerpt from Rodriguez's book along with comments by three of his Hispanic critics. Although three of these texts are from the 1980s, the issues they examine are still very much alive. As the twentieth century draws to a close, people continue to debate how American immigrants and their children should be educated, arguing over such things as California's Proposition 209 (which outlawed racial preferences) and the English Only movement (which wants laws requiring government business to be conducted entirely in English).

BEFORE YOU READ

The following excerpt from Richard Rodriguez's *Hunger of Memory* ends with his claim that "the day I raised my hand in class and spoke loudly to an entire roomful of faces, my childhood started to end." When do you think your childhood started to end? Think of a particular moment or set of experiences.

RICHARD RODRIGUEZ
Aria

A native of San Francisco, California, Richard Rodriguez (b. 1944), is the son of Mexican immigrants. Until he entered school at the age of six, he primarily spoke Spanish. His 1982 memoir Hunger of Memory *describes how English language instruction distanced him from his parents' native culture. Rodriguez went on to attend Stanford University and the University of California at Berkeley, where he earned a doctorate in English Renaissance literature. He is also the author of* Days of Obligation: An Argument with My Mexican Father *(1992). Currently* Rodriguez is a contributing editor for Harper's magazine and a commentator on public television's News Hour.

1

I remember to start with that day in Sacramento — a California now nearly thirty years past — when I first entered a classroom, able to understand some fifty stray English words.

The third of four children, I had been preceded to a neighborhood Roman Catholic school by an older brother and sister. But neither of them had revealed very much about their classroom experiences. Each afternoon they returned, as they left in the morning, always together, speaking in Spanish as they climbed the five steps of the porch. And their mysterious books, wrapped in shopping-bag paper, remained on the table next to the door, closed firmly behind them.

An accident of geography sent me to a school where all my classmates were white, many the children of doctors and lawyers and business executives. All my classmates certainly must have been uneasy on that first day of school — as most children are uneasy — to find themselves apart from their families in the first institution of their lives. But I was astonished.

The nun said, in a friendly but oddly impersonal voice, "Boys and girls, this is Richard Rodriguez." (I heard her sound out: *Rich-heard Road-ree-guess.*) It was the first time I had heard anyone name me in English. "Richard," the nun repeated more slowly, writing my name down in her black leather book. Quickly I turned to see my mother's face dissolve in a watery blur behind the pebbled glass door.

Many years later there is something called bilingual education — a scheme proposed in the late 1960s by Hispanic-American social activists, later endorsed by a congressional vote. It is a program that seeks to permit non-English-speaking children, many from lower-class homes, to use their family language as the language of school. (Such is the goal its supporters announce.) I hear them and am forced to say no: It is not possible for a child — any child — ever to use his family's language in school. Not to understand this is to misunderstand the public uses of schooling and to trivialize the nature of intimate life — a family's "language." 5

Memory teaches me what I know of these matters; the boy reminds the adult. I was a bilingual child, a certain kind — socially disadvantaged — the son of working-class parents, both Mexican immigrants.

In the early years of my boyhood, my parents coped very well in America. My father had steady work. My mother managed at home. They were nobody's victims. Optimism and ambition led them to a house (our home) many blocks from the Mexican south side of town. We lived among *gringos* and only a block from the biggest, whitest houses. It never occurred to my parents that they couldn't live wherever they chose. Nor was the Sacramento of the fifties bent on teaching them a contrary lesson. My mother and father were more annoyed than intimidated by those two or three neighbors who tried initially to make us unwelcome. ("Keep your brats away from my sidewalk!") But despite all they achieved, perhaps because they had so much to achieve, any deep feeling of ease, the confidence of "belonging" in public was withheld from them both. They regarded the people at work, the faces in crowds, as very distant from us. They were the others, *los gringos*. That term was interchangeable in their speech with another, even more telling, *los americanos*.

I grew up in a house where the only regular guests were my relations. For one day, enormous families of relatives would visit and there would be so many people that the noise and the bodies would spill out to the backyard and front porch. Then, for weeks, no one came by. (It was usually a salesman who rang the doorbell.) Our house stood apart. A gaudy yellow in a row of white bungalows. We were the people with the noisy dog. The people who raised pigeons and chickens. We were the foreigners on the block. A few neighbors smiled and waved. We waved back. But no one in the family knew the names of the old couple who lived next door; until I was seven years old, I did not know the names of the kids who lived across the street.

In public, my father and mother spoke a hesitant, accented, not always grammatical English. And they would have to strain—their bodies tense—to catch the sense of what was rapidly said by *los gringos*. At home they spoke Spanish. The language of their Mexican past sounded in counterpoint to the English of public society. The words would come quickly, with ease. Conveyed through those sounds was the pleasing, soothing, consoling reminder of being at home.

During those years when I was first conscious of hearing, my mother and father addressed me only in Spanish; in Spanish I learned to reply. By contrast, English (*inglés*), rarely heard in the house, was the language I came to associate with *gringos*. I learned my first words of English overhearing my parents speak to strangers. At five years of age, I knew just enough English for my mother to trust me on errands to stores one block away. No more.

I was a listening child, careful to hear the very different sounds of Spanish and English. Wide-eyed with hearing, I'd listen to sounds more than words. First, there were English (*gringo*) sounds. So many words were still unknown that when the butcher or the lady at the drugstore said something to me, exotic polysyllabic sounds would bloom in the midst of their sentences. Often, the speech of people in public seemed to me very loud, booming with confidence. The man behind the counter would literally ask, "What can I do for you?" But by being so firm and so clear, the sound of his voice said that he was a *gringo*; he belonged in public society.

I would also hear then the high nasal notes of middle-class American speech. The air stirred with sound. Sometimes, even now, when I have been traveling abroad for several weeks, I will hear what I heard as a boy. In hotel lobbies or airports, in Turkey or Brazil, some Americans will pass, and suddenly I will hear it again—the high sound of American voices. For a few seconds I will hear it with pleasure, for it is now the sound of *my* society—a reminder of home. But inevitably—already on the flight headed for home—the sound fades with repetition. I will be unable to hear it anymore.

When I was a boy, things were different. The accent of *los gringos* was never pleasing nor was it hard to hear. Crowds at Safeway or at bus stops would be noisy with sound. And I would be forced to edge away from the chirping chatter above me.

I was unable to hear my own sounds, but I knew very well that I spoke English poorly. My words could not stretch far enough to form complete thoughts. And the words I did speak I didn't know well enough to make into distinct sounds. (Listeners would usually lower their heads, better to hear what I was trying to say.) But it was one thing for *me* to speak English with difficulty. It was more troubling for me to hear my parents speak in public: their high-whining vowels and guttural consonants; their sentences that got stuck with "eh" and "ah" sounds; the confused

10

syntax; the hesitant rhythm of sounds so different from the way *gringos* spoke. I'd notice, moreover, that my parents' voices were softer than those of *gringos* we'd meet.

I am tempted now to say that none of this mattered. In adulthood I am   15
embarrassed by childhood fears. And in a way, it didn't matter very much that my parents could not speak English with ease. Their linguistic difficulties had no serious consequences. My mother and father made themselves understood at the county hospital clinic and at government offices. And yet, in another way, it mattered very much—it was unsettling to hear my parents struggle with English. Hearing them, I'd grow nervous, my clutching trust in their protection and power weakened.

There were many times like the night at a brightly lit gasoline station (a blaring white memory) when I stood uneasily, hearing my father. He was talking to a teenaged attendant. I do not recall what they were saying, but I cannot forget the sounds my father made as he spoke. At one point his words slid together to form one word—sounds as confused as the threads of blue and green oil in the puddle next to my shoes. His voice rushed through what he had left to say. And, toward the end, reached falsetto notes, appealing to his listener's understanding. I looked away to the lights of passing automobiles. I tried not to hear anymore. But I heard only too well the calm, easy tones in the attendant's reply. Shortly afterward, walking toward home with my father, I shivered when he put his hand on my shoulder. The very first chance that I got, I evaded his grasp and ran on ahead into the dark, skipping with feigned boyish exuberance.

But then there was Spanish. *Español:* my family's language. *Español:* the language that seemed to me a private language. I'd hear strangers on the radio and in the Mexican Catholic church across town speaking in Spanish, but I couldn't really believe that Spanish was a public language, like English. Spanish speakers, rather, seemed related to me, for I sensed that we shared—through our language—the experience of feeling apart from *los gringos*. It was thus a ghetto Spanish that I heard and I spoke. Like those whose lives are bound by a barrio, I was reminded by Spanish of my separateness from *los otros, los gringos* in power. But more intensely than for most barrio children—because I did not live in a barrio—Spanish seemed to me the language of home. (Most days it was only at home that I'd hear it.) It became the language of joyful return.

A family member would say something to me and I would feel myself specially recognized. My parents would say something to me and I would feel embraced by the sounds of their words. Those sounds said: *I am speaking with ease in Spanish. I am addressing you in words I never use with* los gringos. *I recognize you as someone special, close, like no one outside. You belong with us. In the family.*
(*Ricardo.*)

At the age of five, six, well past the time when most other children no longer   20
easily notice the difference between sounds uttered at home and words spoken in public, I had a different experience. I lived in a world magically compounded of sounds. I remained a child longer than most; I lingered too long, poised at the edge of language—often frightened by the sounds of *los gringos*, delighted by the

sounds of Spanish at home. I shared with my family a language that was startlingly different from that used in the great city around us.

For me there were none of the gradations between public and private society so normal to a maturing child. Outside the house was public society; inside the house was private. Just opening or closing the screen door behind me was an important experience. I'd rarely leave home all alone or without reluctance. Walking down the sidewalk, under the canopy of tall trees, I'd warily notice the — suddenly — silent neighborhood kids who stood warily watching me. Nervously, I'd arrive at the grocery store to hear there the sounds of the *gringo* — foreign to me — reminding me that in this world so big, I was a foreigner. But then I'd return. Walking back toward our house, climbing the steps from the sidewalk, when the front door was open in summer, I'd hear voices beyond the screen door talking in Spanish. For a second or two, I'd stay, linger there, listening. Smiling, I'd hear my mother call out, saying in Spanish (words): "Is that you, Richard?" All the while her sounds would assure me: *You are home now; come closer; inside. With us.*

"*Sí*," I'd reply.

Once more inside the house I would resume (assume) my place in the family. The sounds would dim, grow harder to hear. Once more at home, I would grow less aware of that fact. It required, however, no more than the blurt of the doorbell to alert me to listen to sounds all over again. The house would turn instantly still while my mother went to the door. I'd hear her hard English sounds. I'd wait to hear her voice return to soft-sounding Spanish, which assured me, as surely as did the clicking tongue of the lock on the door, that the stranger was gone.

Plainly, it is not healthy to hear such sounds so often. It is not healthy to distinguish public words from private sounds so easily. I remained cloistered by sounds, timid and shy in public, too dependent on voices at home. And yet it needs to be emphasized: I was an extremely happy child at home. I remember many nights when my father would come back from work, and I'd hear him call out to my mother in Spanish, sounding relieved. In Spanish, he'd sound light and free notes he never could manage in English. Some nights I'd jump up just at hearing his voice. With *mis hermanos* I would come running into the room where he was with my mother. Our laughing (so deep was the pleasure!) became screaming. Like others who know the pain of public alienation, we transformed the knowledge of our public separateness and made it consoling — the reminder of intimacy. Excited, we joined our voices in a celebration of sounds. *We are speaking now the way we never speak out in public. We are alone — together,* voices sounded, surrounded to tell me. Some nights, no one seemed willing to loosen the hold sounds had on us. At dinner, we invented new words. (Ours sounded Spanish, but made sense only to us.) We pieced together new words by taking, say, an English verb and giving it Spanish endings. My mother's instructions at bedtime would be lacquered with mock-urgent tones. Or a word like *sí* would become, in several notes, able to convey added measures of feeling. Tongues explored the edges of words, especially the fat vowels. And we happily sounded that military drum roll, the twirling roar of the Spanish *r*. Family language: my family's sounds. The voices of my parents and sisters and brother. Their voices insisting: *You belong here. We are family members. Related. Special to one another. Listen!* Voices singing and sighing, rising, straining, then surging, teeming with pleasure that burst syllables into fragments of laughter. At times it seemed there was steady quiet only when, from another room, the rustling whispers of my parents faded and I moved closer to sleep.

2

Supporters of bilingual education today imply that students like me miss a   25
great deal by not being taught in their family's language. What they seem not to recognize is that, as a socially disadvantaged child, I considered Spanish to be a private language. What I needed to learn in school was that I had the right — and the obligation — to speak the public language of *los gringos.* The odd truth is that my first-grade classmates could have become bilingual, in the conventional sense of that word, more easily than I. Had they been taught (as upper-middle-class children are often taught early) a second language like Spanish or French, they could have regarded it simply as that: another public language. In my case such bilingualism could not have been so quickly achieved. What I did not believe was that I could speak a single public language.

Without question, it would have pleased me to hear my teachers address me in Spanish when I entered the classroom. I would have felt much less afraid. I would have trusted them and responded with ease. But I would have delayed — for how long postponed? — having to learn the language of public society. I would have evaded — and for how long could I have afforded to delay? — learning the great lesson of school, that I had a public identity.

Fortunately, my teachers were unsentimental about their responsibility. What they understood was that I needed to speak a public language. So their voices would search me out, asking me questions. Each time I'd hear them, I'd look up in surprise to see a nun's face frowning at me. I'd mumble, not really meaning to answer. The nun would persist, "Richard, stand up. Don't look at the floor. Speak up. Speak to the entire class, not just to me!" But I couldn't believe that the English language was mine to use. (In part, I did not want to believe it.) I continued to mumble. I resisted the teacher's demands. (Did I somehow suspect that once I learned public language my pleasing family life would be changed?) Silent, waiting for the bell to sound, I remained dazed, diffident, afraid.

Because I wrongly imagined that English was intrinsically a public language and Spanish an intrinsically private one, I easily noted the difference between classroom language and the language of home. At school, words were directed to a general audience of listeners. ("Boys and girls.") Words were meaningfully ordered. And the point was not self-expression alone but to make oneself understood by many others. The teacher quizzed: "Boys and girls, why do we use that word in this sentence? Could we think of a better word to use there? Would the sentence change its meaning if the words were differently arranged? And wasn't there a better way of saying much the same thing?" (I couldn't say. I wouldn't try to say.)

Three months, Five. Half a year passed. Unsmiling, ever watchful, my teachers noted my silence. They began to connect my behavior with the difficult progress my older sister and brother were making. Until one Saturday morning three nuns arrived at the house to talk to our parents. Stiffly, they sat on the blue living room sofa. From the doorway of another room, spying the visitors, I noted the incongruity — the clash of two worlds, the faces and voices of school intruding upon the familiar setting of home. I overheard one voice gently wondering, "Do your children speak only Spanish at home, Mrs. Rodriguez?" While another voice added, "That Richard especially seems so timid and shy."

That Rich-heard!   30

With great tact the visitors continued, "Is it possible for you and your husband to encourage your children to practice their English when they are home?" Of course, my parents complied. What would they not do for their children's well-being? And how could they have questioned the Church's authority which those women represented? In an instant, they agreed to give up the language (the sounds) that had revealed and accentuated our family's closeness. The moment after the visitors left, the change was observed. "*Ahora*, speak to us *en inglés*," my father and mother united to tell us.

At first, it seemed a kind of game. After dinner each night, the family gathered to practice "our" English. (It was still then *inglés*, a language foreign to us, so we felt drawn as strangers to it.) Laughing, we would try to define words we could not pronounce. We played with strange English sounds, often overanglicizing our pronunciations. And we filled the smiling gaps of our sentences with familiar Spanish sounds. But that was cheating, somebody shouted. Everyone laughed. In school, meanwhile, like my brother and sister, I was required to attend a daily tutoring session. I needed a full year of special attention. I also needed my teachers to keep my attention from straying in class by calling out, *Rich-heard* — their English voices slowly prying loose my ties to my other name, its three notes, *Ri-car-do*. Most of all I needed to hear my mother and father speak to me in a moment of seriousness in broken — suddenly heartbreaking — English. The scene was inevitable: One Saturday morning I entered the kitchen where my parents were talking in Spanish. I did not realize that they were talking in Spanish however until, at the moment they saw me, I heard their voices change to speak English. Those *gringo* sounds they uttered startled me. Pushed me away. In that moment of trivial misunderstanding and profound insight, I felt my throat twisted by unsounded grief. I turned quickly and left the room. But I had no place to escape to with Spanish. (The spell was broken.) My brother and sisters were speaking English in another part of the house.

Again and again in the days following, increasingly angry, I was obliged to hear my mother and father: "Speak to us *en inglés*." (*Speak.*) Only then did I determine to learn classroom English. Weeks after, it happened: One day in school I raised my hand to volunteer an answer. I spoke out in a loud voice. And I did not think it remarkable when the entire class understood. That day, I moved very far from the disadvantaged child I had been only days earlier. The belief, the calming assurance that I belonged in public, had at last taken hold.

Shortly after, I stopped hearing the high and loud sounds of *los gringos*. A more and more confident speaker of English, I didn't trouble to listen to *how* strangers sounded, speaking to me. And there simply were too many English-speaking people in my day for me to hear American accents anymore. Conversations quickened. Listening to persons who sounded eccentrically pitched voices, I usually noted their sounds for an initial few seconds before I concentrated on *what* they were saying. Conversations became content-full. Transparent. Hearing someone's *tone* of voice — angry or questioning or sarcastic or happy or sad — I didn't distinguish it from the words it expressed. Sound and word were thus tightly wedded. At the end of a day, I was often bemused, always relieved, to realize how "silent," though crowded with words, my day in public had been. (This public silence measured and quickened the change in my life.)

At last, seven years old, I came to believe what had been technically true   35
since my birth: I was an American citizen.

But the special feeling of closeness at home was diminished by then. Gone was the desperate, urgent, intense feeling of being at home; rare was the experience of feeling myself individualized by family intimates. We remained a loving family, but one greatly changed. No longer so close; no longer bound tight by the pleasing and troubling knowledge of our public separateness. Neither my older brother nor sister rushed home after school anymore. Nor did I. When I arrived home there would often be neighborhood kids in the house. Or the house would be empty of sounds.

Following the dramatic Americanization of their children, even my parents grew more publicly confident. Especially my mother. She learned the names of all the people on our block. And she decided we needed to have a telephone installed in the house. My father continued to use the word *gringo*. But it was no longer charged with the old bitterness or distrust. (Stripped of any emotional content, the word simply became a name for those Americans not of Hispanic descent.) Hearing him, sometimes, I wasn't sure if he was pronouncing the Spanish word *gringo* or saying gringo in English.

Matching the silence I started hearing in public was a new quiet at home. The family's quiet was partly due to the fact that, as we children learned more and more English, we shared fewer and fewer words with our parents. Sentences needed to be spoken slowly when a child addressed his mother or father. (Often the parent wouldn't understand.) The child would need to repeat himself. (Still the parent misunderstood.) The young voice, frustrated, would end up saying, "Never mind" — the subject was closed. Dinners would be noisy with the clinking of knives and forks against dishes. My mother would smile softly between her remarks; my father at the other end of the table would chew and chew at his food, while he stared over the heads of his children.

My *mother*! My *father*! After English became my primary language, I no longer knew what words to use in addressing my parents. The old Spanish words (those tender accents of sound) I had used earlier — *mamá* and *papá* — I couldn't use anymore. They would have been too painful reminders of how much had changed in my life. On the other hand, the words I heard neighborhood kids call *their* parents seemed equally unsatisfactory. *Mother* and *Father*; *Ma, Papa, Pa,*

Dad, Pop (how I hated the all-American sound of that last word especially) — all these terms I felt were unsuitable, not really terms of address for *my* parents. As a result, I never used them at home. Whenever I'd speak to my parents, I would try to get their attention with eye contact alone. In public conversations, I'd refer to "my parents" or "my mother and father."

My mother and father, for their part, responded differently, as their children spoke to them less. She grew restless, seemed troubled and anxious at the scarcity of words exchanged in the house. It was she who would question me about my day when I came home from school. She smiled at small talk. She pried at the edges of my sentences to get me to say something more. (What?) She'd join conversations she overheard, but her intrusions often stopped her children's talking. By contrast, my father seemed reconciled to the new quiet. Though his English improved somewhat, he retired into silence. At dinner he spoke very little. One night his children and even his wife helplessly giggled at his garbled English pronunciation of the Catholic Grace before Meals. Thereafter he made his wife recite the prayer at the start of each meal, even on formal occasions, when there were guests in the house. Hers became the public voice of the family. On official business, it was she, not my father, one would usually hear on the phone or in stores, talking to strangers. His children grew so accustomed to his silence that, years later, they would speak routinely of his shyness. (My mother would often try to explain: Both his parents died when he was eight. He was raised by an uncle who treated him like little more than a menial servant. He was never encouraged to speak. He grew up alone. A man of few words.) But my father was not shy, I realized, when I'd watch him speaking Spanish with relatives. Using Spanish, he was quickly effusive. Especially when talking with other men, his voice would spark, flicker, flare alive with sounds. In Spanish, he expressed ideas and feelings he rarely revealed in English. With firm Spanish sounds, he conveyed confidence and authority English would never allow him.

The silence at home, however, was finally more than a literal silence. Fewer words passed between parent and child, but more profound was the silence that resulted from my inattention to sounds. At about the time I no longer bothered to listen with care to the sounds of English in public, I grew careless about listening to the sounds family members made when they spoke. Most of the time I heard someone speaking at home and didn't distinguish his sounds from the words people uttered in public. I didn't even pay much attention to my parents' accented and ungrammatical speech. At least not at home. Only when I was with them in public would I grow alert to their accents. Though, even then, their sounds caused me less and less concern. For I was increasingly confident of my own public identity.

I would have been happier about my public success had I not sometimes recalled what it had been like earlier, when my family had conveyed its intimacy through a set of conveniently private sounds. Sometimes in public, hearing a stranger, I'd hark back to my past. A Mexican farmworker approached me downtown to ask directions to somewhere. "*¿Hijito . . . ?*" he said. And his voice summoned deep longing. Another time, standing beside my mother in the visiting room of a Carmelite convent, before the dense screen which rendered the nuns

40

shadowy figures, I heard several Spanish-speaking nuns—their busy, singsong overlapping voices—assure us that yes, yes, we were remembered, all our family was remembered in their prayers. (Their voices echoed faraway family sounds.) Another day, a dark-faced old woman—her hand light on my shoulder—steadied herself against me as she boarded a bus. She murmured something I couldn't quite comprehend. Her Spanish voice came near, like the face of a never-before-seen relative in the instant before I was kissed. Her voice, like so many of the Spanish voices I'd hear in public, recalled the golden age of my youth. Hearing Spanish then, I continued to be a careful, if sad, listener to sounds. Hearing a Spanish-speaking family walking behind me, I turned to look. I smiled for an instant, before my glance found the Hispanic-looking faces of strangers in the crowd going by.

Today I hear bilingual educators say that children lose a degree of "individuality" by becoming assimilated into public society. (Bilingual schooling was popularized in the seventies, that decade when middle-class ethnics began to resist the process of assimilation—the American melting pot.) But the bilingualists simplistically scorn the value and necessity of assimilation. They do not seem to realize that there are *two* ways a person is individualized. So they do not realize that while one suffers a diminished sense of *private* individuality by becoming assimilated into public society, such assimilation makes possible the achievement of *public* individuality.

The bilingualists insist that a student should be reminded of his difference from others in mass society, his heritage. But they equate mere separateness with individuality. The fact is that only in private—with intimates—is separateness from the crowd a prerequisite for individuality. (An intimate draws me apart, tells me that I am unique, unlike all others.) In public, by contrast, full individuality is achieved, paradoxically, by those who are able to consider themselves members of the crowd. Thus it happened for me: Only when I was able to think of myself as an American, no longer an alien in *gringo* society, could I seek the rights and opportunities necessary for full public individuality. The social and political advantages I enjoy as a man result from the day that I came to believe that my name, indeed, is *Rich-heard Road-ree-guess.* It is true that my public society today is often impersonal. (My public society is usually mass society.) Yet despite the anonymity of the crowd and despite the fact that the individuality I achieve in public is often tenuous—because it depends on my being one in a crowd—I celebrate the day I acquired my new name. Those middle-class ethnics who scorn assimilation seem to me filled with decadent self-pity, obsessed by the burden of public life. Dangerously, they romanticize public separateness and they trivialize the dilemma of the socially disadvantaged.

My awkward childhood does not prove the necessity of bilingual education.   45
My story discloses instead an essential myth of childhood—inevitable pain. If I rehearse here the changes in my private life after my Americanization, it is finally to emphasize the public gain. The loss implies the gain: The house I returned to each afternoon was quiet. Intimate sounds no longer rushed to the door to greet me. There were other noises inside. The telephone rang. Neighborhood kids ran

past the door of the bedroom where I was reading my schoolbooks — covered with shopping-bag paper. Once I learned public language, it would never again be easy for me to hear intimate family voices. More and more of my day was spent hearing words. But that may only be a way of saying that the day I raised my hand in class and spoke loudly to an entire roomful of faces, my childhood started to end. [1982]

THINKING ABOUT THE TEXT

1. What distinctions does Rodriguez make between the "private" and "public" worlds of his childhood? Ultimately, he brings up the possibility of "public individuality" (para. 43). What does he mean by this? Does this concept make sense to you?

2. What, according to Rodriguez, were the changes he experienced? With what tone does he recall these changes? Consider in particular the way he describes his changing relationship to his parents.

3. Do you agree with Rodriguez that the changes he went through were necessary? To what extent is your answer influenced by your own social position?

4. Rodriguez declares, "Those middle-class ethnics who scorn assimilation seem to me filled with decadent self-pity, obsessed by the burden of public life. Dangerously, they romanticize public separateness and they trivialize the dilemma of the socially disadvantaged" (para. 44). Evaluate this claim. Would you say that you are a "middle-class ethnic"? Why, or why not?

5. Rodriguez suggests that a student must speak up in class to succeed in school. Do you agree? Rodriguez indicates that matters of language play a crucial role in a child's education. Have you found this true? Be specific.

RAMÓN SALDÍVAR
From *Chicano Narrative*

Ramón Saldívar (b. 1949) is a professor of English and comparative literature at Stanford University. There, he is also associate dean in the School of Humanities and Sciences as well as vice provost for Undergraduate Education. The following remarks about Hunger of Memory *come from Saldívar's 1990 book* Chicano Narrative.

    Once Rodriguez learns a public language, he acquires a public identity. But he realizes that in his transformation from the private person of the home-centered Mexican culture to the public assimilated man of the Anglo society he has lost something. Each world's language brought out different emotions. Spanish radiated family intimacy but also provoked shame and embarrassment. English opened doors to society's networks, rewards, and recognitions, but also subverted the family's sense of intimacy. His life then becomes a tenuous attempt to hold off these contradictions, to accept the benefits of his Mexican-ness while rejecting its demands, until he must irrevocably choose between them.

And choose he does. He chooses with great anxiety and precious sadness to reject the duality of his working-class origins and his middle-class manners; he chooses to market his existential anguish to the most receptive audience imaginable: the right-wing establishment and the liberal academic intelligentsia. His writings against bilingual education [because it is a hindrance to the access to a "public" language] and against affirmative action [because it denigrates the achievements of those who have made it on their own merits] involve him, whether he admits it or not, in a political service to the Right. Rodriguez chooses to assimilate without ever considering whether he acted by will or merely submitted to an unquestioned grander scheme of political ideology.   [1990]

TOMÁS RIVERA

From "Richard Rodriguez's Hunger of Memory as Humanistic Antithesis"

Tomás Rivera (1935–1984) was chancellor of the University of California at the time he wrote the following comments. They appear in his article "Richard Rodriguez's Hunger of Memory *as Humanistic Antithesis," which was published posthumously in a 1984 issue of the journal* Melus.

[Rodriguez's] search for life and form in the literary form of autobiography has as a premise the basic core of family life. But then Richard Rodriguez struggles with the sense of dissociation from that basic culture. Clearly, he opts to dissociate, and, as a scholar, attempts to rationalize that only through dissociation from a native culture was he to gain and thus has gained the "other," that is, the "public" world. Without wisdom he almost forgets the original passions of human life. Is he well educated in literature? For literature above all gives and inculcates in the student and scholar the fundamental original elements of humanistic endeavor without regard to race or language, much less with regards to a public voice. The most important ideas that the study of the humanities relates are the fundamental values and elements of human beings, regardless of race and nationality. Ultimately, the study of the humanities teaches the idea that life is a relationship with the totality of people within its circumstance.

Then we come to the question of place and being. In Spanish there are two verbs meaning "to be," *ser* and *estar*. This is quite important to *Hunger of Memory*. Being born into a family is equal to being, *ser*. Education and instruction teaches us to be, *estar*. Both are fundamental verbs. *Ser* is an interior stage, and *estar* is an exterior one. To leave the *ser* only for the *estar* is a grievous error.

Richard Rodriguez implies, at times explicitly, that the authentic being is and can be only in the *estar* (public voice) and only there is he/she complete. And further, he states that authenticity can only come by being an exterior being in English in the English speaking world. In the Hispanic world, the interior world of *ser* is ultimately more important than the world of *estar*. *Honra*, honesty, emanates from and is important to the *ser*. Richard Rodriguez opts for the *estar* world as the more important and does not give due importance to the world of *ser*. He has problems, in short, with the world from which he came. Surely this is an antithesis to a humanistic development

As with memory, the centrality of language is a constant pattern in the book. For the Hispanic reader the struggle quickly becomes English versus Spanish. His parents do not know the grand development of the Spanish language and its importance beyond their immediate family. However, Richard Rodriguez should, as an educated person, recognize this grand development. Surely, he could have given credit to the development of a language that has existed over six hundred years, which has elaborated a world literature, which has mixed with the many languages of the American continents, which is perhaps the most analytical of the romance languages, and which will be of such importance in the twenty-first century. Instead Richard Rodriguez flees, as a young man, from this previous human achievement. This fleeing is understandable as a symbol of the pressures of the Americanization process. Yet, as a formally educated scholar, reflecting upon that flight, he does not dare to signal the importance that the language has. Instead he sees it as an activity that has no redeeming value. He gives no value to the Hispanic language, its culture, its arts. It is difficult to believe that as an educated humanist he doesn't recognize the most important element of Hispanic culture — the context of the development of the distinct religions in the Spanish peninsula — the Judaic, the Christian, and the Moorish. These distinct cultures reached their apogees and clearly influenced Spanish. As a humanist, surely he must know this. The Hispanic world has elaborated and developed much in the history of ideas. Richard Rodriguez seems to indicate that the personal Spanish voice lacks the intelligence and ability to communicate beyond the sensibilities of the personal interactions of personal family life. This is intolerable. Hispanic culture has a historical tradition of great intellectual development.

[1984]

VICTOR VILLANUEVA JR.
From "Whose Voice Is It Anyway?"

Of Puerto Rican descent, Victor Villanueva Jr. (b. 1948) grew up in New York City. Currently he is a professor of English at Washington State University in Pullman, Washington. In 1993 he published an autobiography entitled Bootstraps: The Autobiography of an Academic of Color. *The following remarks come from his article "Whose Voice Is It Anyway? Rodriguez' Speech in Retrospect," which appeared in a 1987 issue of* English Journal. *As its title implies, Villanueva's article concerns not only* Hunger of Memory *but also a speech that Richard Rodriguez gave at a convention of English teachers.*

[Rodriguez] is a fine writer; of that there can be no doubt. But it is his message that has brought him fame, a message that states that the minority is no different than any other immigrant who came to this country not knowing its culture or its language, leaving much of the old country behind to become part of this new one, and in becoming part of America subtly changing what it means to be American. . . .

But choice hardly entered into most minorities' decisions to become American. Most of us recognize this when it comes to Blacks or American Indians. Slavery, forcible displacement, and genocide are fairly clear-cut. Yet the circumstances by which most minorities became Americans are no less clear-cut. The minority became an American almost by default, as part of the goods in big-time real-estate deals or as some of the spoils of war. What is true for the Native American applies to the Alaska Native, the Pacific Islander (including the Asian), Mexican Americans, Puerto Ricans. Puerto Rico was part of Christopher Columbus's great discovery, Arawaks and Boriquens among his "Indians," a real-estate coup for the Queen of Spain. Then one day in 1898, the Puerto Ricans who had for nearly four hundred years been made proud to be the offspring of Spain, so much so that their native Arawak and Boricua languages and ways were virtually gone, found themselves the property of the United States, property without the rights and privileges of citizenship until — conveniently — World War I. But citizenship notwithstanding, Puerto Rico remains essentially a colony today.

One day in 1845 and in 1848 other descendants of Spain who had all but lost their Indian identities found themselves Americans. These were the longtime residents and landowners of the Republic of Texas and the California Republic: the area from Texas to New Mexico, Arizona, Utah, and California. Residents in the newly established U.S. territories were given the option to relocate to Mexico or to remain on their native lands, with the understanding that should they remain they would be guaranteed American Constitutional rights. Those who stayed home saw their rights not very scrupulously guarded, falling victim over time to displacement, dislocation, and forced expatriation. There is something tragic in losing a long-established birthright, tragic but not heroic — especially not heroic to those whose ancestors had fled their homelands rather than acknowledge external rule.

The immigrant gave up much in the name of freedom — and for the sake of dignity. For the Spanish-speaking minority in particular, the freedom to be American without once again relinquishing one's ancestry is also a matter of dignity. . . .

Today I sport a doctorate in English from a major university, study and teach rhetoric at another university, do research in and teach composition, continue to enjoy and teach English literature. I live in an all-American city in the heart of America. And I know I am not quite assimilated. In one weekend I was asked if I was Iranian one day and East Indian the next. "No," I said. "You have an accent,"   5

I was told. Yet tape recordings and passing comments throughout the years have told me that though there is a "Back East" quality to my voice, there isn't much of New York to it anymore, never mind the Black English of my younger years or the Spanish of my youngest. My "accent" was in my not sounding midwestern, which does have a discernible, though not usually a pronounced, regional quality. And my "accent," I would guess, was in my "foreign" features (which pale alongside the brown skin of Richard Rodriguez).

Friends think I make too much of such incidents. Minority hypersensitivity, they say. They desensitize me (and display their liberal attitudes) with playful jabs at Puerto Ricans: greasy-hair jokes, knife-in-pocket jokes, spicy-food jokes (and Puerto Ricans don't even eat hot foods, unless we're eating Mexican or East Indian foods). If language alone were the secret to assimilation, the rate of Puerto Rican and Mexican success would be greater, I think. So many Mexican Americans and Puerto Ricans remain in the barrios — even those who are monolingual, who have never known Spanish. If language alone were the secret, wouldn't the secret have gotten out long before Richard Rodriguez recorded his memoirs?

[1987]

MAKING COMPARISONS

1. Do you agree with Saldívar that Rodriguez's narrative serves the interests of political conservatives? Why, or why not?

2. To Rivera, Rodriguez fails to appreciate the rich cultural heritage behind Spanish as a language. Is it possible to value this heritage and yet still feel that the nuns were right to insist that his parents speak English at home? Explain.

3. How does Villanueva see minorities as different from immigrants? Does this distinction make sense to you? He argues that minorities need more than mastery of English if other Americans are to accept them. What do you think is required for such acceptance?

WRITING ABOUT ISSUES

1. Write an essay arguing for a particular characterization of the older Rodriguez, focusing on particular words that he uses as he recalls his childhood.

2. Should the young Rodriguez's school have been more respectful toward his home language and culture? Write an essay stating and arguing for your answer to this question. Refer to at least one of the critics quoted here. (Keep in mind that you don't have to agree with any of them.)

3. Write an essay recalling an experience that made you aware of the extent to which school had distanced you from the values and habits you knew at home. Perhaps you came to see the distance as vast; then again, perhaps you decided that it was minimal or nonexistent. Describe the

experience with specific details and identify the conclusions it led you to. Also indicate whether you feel the same way as you look back on the experience now.

4. Write an essay arguing for your position on bilingual education or the English Only movement. Refer to at least two articles, on your chosen topic. If you wish, refer to one or more of the selections in this cluster.

LEARNING IN A COLONIAL CONTEXT: A COLLECTION OF WRITINGS BY JAMAICA KINCAID

JAMAICA KINCAID, "Girl"
JAMAICA KINCAID, "Columbus in Chains"
JAMAICA KINCAID, "On Seeing England for the First Time"

American public education has long aimed to ensure that students are proud of the United States and committed to its basic principles. Inevitably, much debate centers around what exactly are America's basic principles and around how they are best realized. Many people accuse American public education of insisting too much on cultural uniformity, while others argue that it does not pursue this goal enough. Such disagreement is evident in the previous cluster, where various commentators take issue with Richard Rodriguez's willingness to exchange his parents' Hispanic culture for the Anglo-American one of school.

Of course, citizens in many countries are taught in school to honor their nation's present rulers along with a particular cultural heritage. Children in countries dominated by others from a different culture often experience school as a place where the oppressor's culture is reinforced. The link between colonialism and indoctrination is a recurring concern of the writer Jamaica Kincaid, three of whose works we include here. Kincaid was born on Antigua, an island in the West Indies long ruled by England. Through her fiction and her nonfiction, she repeatedly reflects on what it means for a young woman to be educated in this political context. In her short story "Girl," the title character, presumably an Antiguan girl, gets instructed by a parental voice (her mother's?) in the supposed responsibilities of her gender. In the next story, "Columbus in Chains," and in her essay "On Seeing England for the First Time," Kincaid confronts her readers more directly with the practices and prejudices of the British-dominated schooling she experienced growing up. As you read all three texts, think about the political contexts of your own education and consider the various ways in which schooling is used to control as well as to liberate people.

BEFORE YOU READ

In what ways have the schools you attended affirmed a particular nation or culture? Try to recall at least a few examples. Do you think schools should encourage students to love their country? Another country? All countries? Explain your reasoning.

JAMAICA KINCAID

Girl

Jamaica Kincaid was born on the island of Antigua in the West Indies in 1949. At the time, Antigua was a British colony. Kincaid lived there until she was seventeen, when she emigrated to the United States. Soon after she arrived in this country, she became a nanny for the family of Michael Arlen, television critic of The New Yorker. *Eventually, her own short stories were published in that magazine, and during the early 1990s she wrote gardening columns for it as well. Although she continues to live in the United States, residing for the last several years in Vermont, almost all of her writing deals with her native land. In particular, she has written about Antiguan women growing up under British domination. "Girl" appeared in* The New Yorker *in 1978 and was later reprinted in Kincaid's first book, a 1984 collection of short stories entitled* At the Bottom of the River. *She has since published a work of nonfiction about Antigua titled* A Small Place *(1988) and a memoir* My Brother *(1997), as well as the novels* Annie John *(1985),* Lucy *(1990), and* Autobiography of My Mother *(1996).*

Wash the white clothes on Monday and put them on the stone heap; wash the color clothes on Tuesday and put them on the clothesline to dry; don't walk barehead in the hot sun; cook pumpkin fritters in very hot sweet oil; soak your little cloths right after you take them off; when buying cotton to make yourself a nice blouse, be sure that it doesn't have gum on it, because that way it won't hold up well after a wash; soak salt fish overnight before you cook it; is it true that you sing benna° in Sunday school?; always eat your food in such a way that it won't turn someone else's stomach; on Sundays try to walk like a lady and not like the slut you are so bent on becoming; don't sing benna in Sunday school; you mustn't speak to wharf-rat boys, not even to give directions; don't eat fruits on the street — flies will follow you; *but I don't sing benna on Sundays at all and never in Sunday school*; this is how to sew on a button; this is how to make a button-hole for the button you have just sewed on; this is how to hem a dress when you see the hem coming down and so to prevent yourself from looking like the slut I know you are so bent on becoming; this is how you iron your father's khaki shirt so that it doesn't have a crease; this is how you iron your father's khaki pants so that they don't have a crease; this is how you grow okra — far from the house, because okra tree harbors red ants; when you are growing dasheen, make sure it gets plenty of water or else it makes your throat itch when you are eating it; this is how you sweep a corner; this is how you sweep a whole house; this is how you sweep a yard; this is how you

benna: Calypso music.

smile to someone you don't like too much; this is how you smile to someone you don't like at all; this is how you smile to someone you like completely; this is how you set a table for tea; this is how you set a table for dinner; this is how you set a table for dinner with an important guest; this is how you set a table for lunch; this is how you set a table for breakfast; this is how to behave in the presence of men who don't know you very well, and this way they won't recognize immediately the slut I have warned you against becoming; be sure to wash every day, even if it is with your own spit; don't squat down to play marbles—you are not a boy, you know; don't pick people's flowers—you might catch something; don't throw stones at blackbirds, because it might not be a blackbird at all; this is how to make a bread pudding; this is how to make doukona;° this is how to make pepper pot; this is how to make a good medicine for a cold; this is how to make a good medicine to throw away a child before it even becomes a child; this is how to catch a fish; this is how to throw back a fish you don't like, and that way something bad won't fall on you; this is how to bully a man; this is how a man bullies you; this is how to love a man, and if this doesn't work there are other ways, and if they don't work don't feel too bad about giving up; this is how to spit up in the air if you feel like it, and this is how to move quick so that it doesn't fall on you; this is how to make ends meet; always squeeze bread to make sure it's fresh; *but what if the baker won't let me feel the bread?*; you mean to say that after all you are really going to be the kind of woman who the baker won't let near the bread?   [1978]

doukona: A spicy plantain pudding.

THINKING ABOUT THE TEXT

1. Is "Girl" really a "story"? What characteristics of a story come to mind as you consider this issue?

2. Describe the culture depicted in "Girl" as well as the role of females in that culture. Is either the culture or the role of females in it different from what you are familiar with? Explain.

3. Do you think that the instructions to this girl are all given on the same occasion? Why, or why not? Who do you suppose is giving the instructions? Would you say that the instructor is oppressive or domineering? Identify some of the assumptions or warrants behind your position.

4. What effect does Kincaid achieve by making this text a single long sentence? By having the girl speak at only two brief moments?

5. At one point, the girl is shown "how to make a good medicine to throw away a child before it even becomes a child." What do you think of the instructor's willingness to give such advice? What do you conclude from its position in the text between "how to make a good medicine for a cold" and "how to catch a fish"? Does the order of the various pieces of advice matter? Could Kincaid have presented them in a different order without changing their effects?

JAMAICA KINCAID
Columbus in Chains

First published in The New Yorker *in 1983, the following short story later became a chapter in Jamaica Kincaid's 1985 novel* Annie John. *The book traces the early life of its title character, who is also the narrator. Like Kincaid, Annie John grows up on Antigua during its days as a British colony and ultimately leaves her native land. In "Columbus in Chains," which appears midway through the book, Annie recalls a day in her British-oriented education.*

Outside, as usual, the sun shone, the trade winds blew; on her way to put some starched clothes on the line, my mother shooed some hens out of her garden; Miss Dewberry baked the buns, some of which my mother would buy for my father and me to eat with our afternoon tea; Miss Henry brought the milk, a glass of which I would drink with my lunch, and another glass of which I would drink with the bun from Miss Dewberry; my mother prepared our lunch; my father noted some perfectly idiotic thing his partner in housebuilding, Mr. Oatie, had done, so that over lunch he and my mother could have a good laugh.

The Anglican church bell struck eleven o'clock—one hour to go before lunch. I was then sitting at my desk in my classroom. We were having a history lesson—the last lesson of the morning. For taking first place over all the other girls, I had been given a prize, a copy of a book called *Roman Britain*, and I was made prefect of my class. What a mistake the prefect part had been, for I was among the worst-behaved in my class and did not at all believe in setting myself up as a good example, the way a prefect was supposed to do. Now I had to sit in the prefect's seat—the first seat in the front row, the seat from which I could stand up and survey quite easily my classmates. From where I sat I could see out the window. Sometimes when I looked out, I could see the sexton going over to the minister's house. The sexton's daughter, Hilarene, a disgusting model of good behavior and keen attention to scholarship, sat next to me, since she took second place. The minister's daughter, Ruth, sat in the last row, the row reserved for all the dunce girls. Hilarene, of course, I could not stand. A girl that good would never do for me. I would probably not have cared so much for first place if I could be sure it would not go to her. Ruth I liked, because she was such a dunce and came from England and had yellow hair. When I first met her, I used to walk her home and sing bad songs to her just to see her turn pink, as if I had spilled hot water all over her.

Our books, *A History of the West Indies*, were open in front of us. Our day had begun with morning prayers, then a geometry lesson, then it was over to the science building for a lesson in "Introductory Physics" (not a subject we cared much for), taught by the most dingy-toothed Mr. Slacks, a teacher from Canada, then precious recess, and now this, our history lesson. Recess had the usual drama: this time, I coaxed Gwen out of her disappointment at not being allowed to join the junior choir. Her father—how many times had I wished he would become a leper and so

be banished to a leper colony for the rest of my long and happy life with Gwen—
had forbidden it, giving as his reason that she lived too far away from church, where
choir rehearsals were conducted, and that it would be dangerous for her, a young
girl, to walk home alone at night in the dark. Of course, all the streets had lamplight, but it was useless to point that out to him. Oh, how it would have pleased us to
press and rub our knees together as we sat in our pew while pretending to pay close
attention to Mr. Simmons, our choirmaster, as he waved his baton up and down
and across, and how it would have pleased us even more to walk home together,
alone in the "early dusk" (the way Gwen had phrased it, a ready phrase always on
her tongue), stopping, if there was a full moon, to lie down in a pasture and expose
our bosoms in the moonlight. We had heard that full moonlight would make our
breasts grow to a size we would like. Poor Gwen! When I first heard from her that
she was one of ten children, right on the spot I told her that I would love only her,
since her mother already had so many other people to love.

Our teacher, Miss Edward, paced up and down in front of the class in her
usual way. In front of her desk stood a small table, and on it stood the dunce cap.
The dunce cap was in the shape of a coronet, with an adjustable opening in the
back, so that it could fit any head. It was made of cardboard with a shiny gold
paper covering and the word "DUNCE" in shiny red paper on the front. When the
sun shone on it, the dunce cap was all aglitter, almost as if you were being tricked
into thinking it a desirable thing to wear. As Miss Edward paced up and down,
she would pass between us and the dunce cap like an eclipse. Each Friday morning, we were given a small test to see how well we had learned the things taught
to us all week. The girl who scored lowest was made to wear the dunce cap all day
the following Monday. On many Mondays, Ruth wore it—only, with her short
yellow hair, when the dunce cap was sitting on her head she looked like a girl
attending a birthday party in *The Schoolgirl's Own Annual*.

It was Miss Edward's way to ask one of us a question the answer to which she   5
was sure the girl would not know and then put the same question to another girl
who she was sure would know the answer. The girl who did not answer correctly
would then have to repeat the correct answer in the exact words of the other girl.
Many times, I had heard my exact words repeated over and over again, and I liked
it especially when the girl doing the repeating was one I didn't care about very
much. Pointing a finger at Ruth, Miss Edward asked a question the answer to
which was "On the third of November 1493, a Sunday morning, Christopher
Columbus discovered Dominica." Ruth, of course, did not know the answer, as
she did not know the answer to many questions about the West Indies. I could
hardly blame her. Ruth had come all the way from England. Perhaps she did not
want to be in the West Indies at all. Perhaps she wanted to be in England, where
no one would remind her constantly of the terrible things her ancestors had
done; perhaps she had felt even worse when her father was a missionary in Africa.
I could see how Ruth felt from looking at her face. Her ancestors had been the
masters, while ours had been the slaves. She had such a lot to be ashamed of, and
by being with us every day she was always being reminded. We could look
everybody in the eye, for our ancestors had done nothing wrong except just sit
somewhere, defenseless. Of course, sometimes, what with our teachers and our

books, it was hard for us to tell on which side we really now belonged — with the masters or the slaves — for it was all history, it was all in the past, and everybody behaved differently now; all of us celebrated Queen Victoria's birthday, even though she had been dead a long time. But we, the descendants of the slaves, knew quite well what had really happened, and I was sure that if the tables had been turned we would have acted differently; I was sure that if our ancestors had gone from Africa to Europe and come upon the people living there, they would have taken a proper interest in the Europeans on first seeing them, and said, "How nice," and then gone home to tell their friends about it.

I was sitting at my desk, having these thoughts to myself. I don't know how long it had been since I lost track of what was going on around me. I had not noticed that the girl who was asked the question after Ruth failed — a girl named Hyacinth — had only got a part of the answer correct. I had not noticed that after these two attempts Miss Edward had launched into a harangue about what a worthless bunch we were compared to girls of the past. In fact, I was no longer on the same chapter we were studying. I was way ahead, at the end of the chapter about Columbus's third voyage. In this chapter, there was a picture of Columbus that took up a whole page, and it was in color — one of only five color pictures in the book. In this picture, Columbus was seated in the bottom of a ship. He was wearing the usual three-quarter trousers and a shirt with enormous sleeves, both the trousers and shirt made of maroon-colored velvet. His hat, which was cocked up on one side of his head, had a gold feather in it, and his black shoes had huge gold buckles. His hands and feet were bound up in chains, and he was sitting there staring off into space, looking quite dejected and miserable. The picture had as a title "Columbus in Chains," printed at the bottom of the page. What had happened was that the usually quarrelsome Columbus had got into a disagreement with people who were even more quarrelsome, and a man named Bobadilla, representing King Ferdinand and Queen Isabella, had sent him back to Spain fettered in chains attached to the bottom of a ship. What just deserts, I thought, for I did not like Columbus. How I loved this picture — to see the usually triumphant Columbus, brought so low, seated at the bottom of a boat just watching things go by. Shortly after I first discovered it in my history book, I heard my mother read out loud to my father a letter she had received from her sister, who still lived with her mother and father in the very same Dominica, which is where my mother came from. Ma Chess was fine, wrote my aunt, but Pa Chess was not well. Pa Chess was having a bit of trouble with his limbs; he was not able to go about as he pleased; often he had to depend on someone else to do one thing or another for him. My mother read the letter in quite a state, her voice rising to a higher pitch with each sentence. After she read the part about Pa Chess's stiff limbs, she turned to my father and laughed as she said, "So the great man can no longer just get up and go. How I would love to see his face now!" When I next saw the picture of Columbus sitting there all locked up in his chains, I wrote under it the words "The Great Man Can No Longer Just Get Up and Go." I had written this out with my fountain pen, and in Old English lettering — a script I had recently mastered. As I sat there looking at the picture, I traced the words with my pen over and over, so that the letters grew big and you could read what I had written from not very far away. I don't know how long it was before I heard that my name, Annie John, was being said by this bellowing dragon in the form of Miss Edward bearing down on me.

I had never been a favorite of hers. Her favorite was Hilarene. It must have pained Miss Edward that I so often beat out Hilarene. Not that I liked Miss Edward and wanted her to like me back, but all my other teachers regarded me with much affection, would always tell my mother that I was the most charming student they had ever had, beamed at me when they saw me coming, and were very sorry when they had to write some version of this on my report card: "Annie is an unusually bright girl. She is well behaved in class, at least in the presence of her masters and mistresses, but behind their backs and outside the classroom quite the opposite is true." When my mother read this or something like it, she would burst into tears. She had hoped to display, with a great flourish, my report card to her friends, along with whatever prize I had won. Instead, the report card would have to take a place at the bottom of the old trunk in which she kept any important thing that had to do with me. I became not a favorite of Miss Edward's in the following way: Each Friday afternoon, the girls in the lower forms were given, instead of a last lesson period, an extra-long recess. We were to use this in ladylike recreation—walks, chats about the novels and poems we were reading, showing each other the new embroidery stitches we had learned to master in home class, or something just as seemly. Instead, some of the girls would play a game of cricket or rounders or stones, but most of us would go to the far end of the school grounds and play band. In this game, of which teachers and parents disapproved and which was sometimes absolutely forbidden, we would place our arms around each other's waist or shoulders, forming lines of ten or so girls, and then we would dance from one end of the school grounds to the other. As we danced, we would sometimes chant these words: "Tee la la la, come go. Tee la la la, come go." At other times we would sing a popular calypso song which usually had lots of unladylike words to it. Up and down the schoolyard, away from our teachers, we would dance and sing. At the end of recess—forty-five minutes—we were missing ribbons and other ornaments from our hair, the pleats of our linen tunics became unset, the collars of our blouses were pulled out, and we were soaking wet all the way down to our bloomers. When the school bell rang, we would make a whooping sound, as if in a great panic, and then we would throw ourselves on top of each other as we laughed and shrieked. We would then run back to our classes, where we prepared to file into the auditorium for evening prayers. After that, it was home for the weekend. But how could we go straight home after all that excitement? No sooner were we on the street than we would form little groups, depending on the direction we were headed in. I was never keen on joining them on the way home, because I was sure I would run into my mother. Instead, my friends and I would go to our usual place near the back of the churchyard and sit on the tombstones of people who had been buried there way before slavery was abolished, in 1833. We would sit and sing bad songs, use forbidden words, and, of course, show each other various parts of our bodies. While some of us watched, the others would walk up and down on the large tombstones showing off their legs. It was immediately a popular idea; everybody soon wanted to do it. It wasn't long before many girls—the ones whose mothers didn't pay strict attention to what they were doing—started to come to school on Fridays wearing not bloomers under their uniforms but underpants trimmed with lace and satin frills. It also wasn't long before an end came to all that. One Friday afternoon, Miss Edward, on her way home from school, took a shortcut through the churchyard. She must have heard the commotion we were making, because there she suddenly was, saying, "What is the meaning of this?"—just the very thing some-one like her would say if she came unexpectedly on something like us. It was obvi-ous that I was the ringleader. Oh, how I wished the ground would open up and take her in, but it did not. We all, shamefacedly, slunk home, I with Miss Edward at my side. Tears came to my mother's eyes when she heard what I had done. It was apparently such a bad thing that my mother couldn't bring herself to repeat my misdeed to my father in my presence. I got the usual punishment of dinner alone, outside under the breadfruit tree, but added on to that, I was not allowed to go to the library on Saturday, and on Sunday, after Sunday school and dinner, I was not allowed to take a stroll in the botanical gardens, where Gwen was waiting for me in the bamboo grove.

That happened when I was in the first form. Now here Miss Edward stood. Her whole face was on fire. Her eyes were bulging out of her head. I was sure that at any minute they would land at my feet and roll away. The small pimples on her face, already looking as if they were constantly irritated, now ballooned into huge, on-the-verge-of-exploding boils. Her head shook from side to side. Her strange bottom, which she carried high in the air, seemed to rise up so high that it almost touched the ceiling. Why did I not pay attention, she said. My imperti-nence was beyond endurance. She then found a hundred words for the different forms my impertinence took. On she went. I was just getting used to this amazing bellowing when suddenly she was speechless. In fact, everything stopped. Her eyes stopped, her bottom stopped, her pimples stopped. Yes, she had got close enough so that her eyes caught a glimpse of what I had done to my textbook. The glimpse soon led to closer inspection. It was bad enough that I had defaced my schoolbook by writing in it. That I should write under the picture of Columbus "The Great Man . . ." etc. was just too much. I had gone too far this time, defam-ing one of the great men in history, Christopher Columbus, discoverer of the island that was my home. And now look at me. I was not even hanging my head in remorse. Had my peers ever seen anyone so arrogant, so blasphemous?

I was sent to the headmistress, Miss Moore. As punishment, I was removed from my position as prefect, and my place was taken by the odious Hilarene. As an added punishment, I was ordered to copy Books I and II of *Paradise Lost*, by John Milton, and to have it done a week from that day. I then couldn't wait to get home to lunch and the comfort of my mother's kisses and arms. I had nothing to worry about there yet; it would be a while before my mother and father heard of my bad deeds. What a terrible morning! Seeing my mother would be such a tonic—something to pick me up.

When I got home, my mother kissed me absentmindedly. My father had got home ahead of me, and they were already deep in conversation, my father regaling 10 her with some unusually outlandish thing the oaf Mr. Oatie had done. I washed my hands and took my place at table. My mother brought me my lunch. I took one smell of it, and I could tell that it was the much hated breadfruit. My mother said not at all, it was a new kind of rice imported from Belgium, and not breadfruit, mashed and forced through a ricer, as I thought. She went back to talking to my father. My father could hardly get a few words out of his mouth before she was a jellyfish of laughter. I sat there, putting my food in my mouth. I could not believe that she couldn't see how miserable I was and so reach out a hand to comfort me and caress my cheek, the way she usually did when she sensed that something was amiss with me. I could not believe how she laughed at everything he said, and how bitter it made me feel to see how much she liked him. I ate my meal. The more I ate of it, the more I was sure that it was breadfruit. When I finished, my mother got up to remove my plate. As she started out the door, I said, "Tell me, really, the name of the thing I just ate."

My mother said, "You just ate some breadfruit. I made it look like rice so that you would eat it. It's very good for you, filled with lots of vitamins." As she said this, she laughed. She was standing half inside the door, half outside. Her body was in the shade of our house, but her head was in the sun. When she laughed, her mouth opened to show off big, shiny, sharp white teeth. It was as if my mother had suddenly turned into a crocodile.   [1983]

THINKING ABOUT THE TEXT

1. What adjectives would you use to describe Annie? List at least three. Do you trust her as a narrator? Why, or why not?

2. Evaluate the kind of education Annie is receiving. Would you say it is a "good" education? Why, or why not?

3. What do you make of the fact that Annie's caption for the picture of Columbus—"The Great Man Can No Longer Just Get Up and Go"— echoes what her mother said about Pa Chess? Do you admire Annie for writing this caption? Why, or why not? What image of Columbus do you think American children should be taught?

4. Although Miss Edward plays an important role in Kincaid's story, she speaks directly only once. What is the effect of this rarity?

5. At the end, Annie's mother lies to her. Given that so much of what comes before is about Annie's school relationships rather than about her relationship with her mother, how appropriate is this conclusion to the narrative? Explain your reasoning.

MAKING COMPARISONS

1. Considering what you know about Annie, how do you think she would react to the instructions given in "Girl"?

2. Compare the kinds of education presented in "Girl" and "Columbus in Chains." Does one kind seem better than the other? Support your reasoning by referring to specific details of each text.

3. Is gender equally important in "Girl" and "Columbus in Chains"? Again, refer to specific details of each.

JAMAICA KINCAID

On Seeing England for the First Time

In addition to her short stories and books, Jamaica Kincaid has written several essays, some of which have been gardening columns for The New Yorker. *Even in these, she has taken the opportunity to comment on England's political and cultural domination of her native island. But some of her essays very much focus on this subject. The following piece is an example. It was first published in a 1991 issue of* Transition, *a journal devoted to analyzing racial and ethnic relations around the world.*

When I saw England for the first time, I was a child in school sitting at a desk. The England I was looking at was laid out on a map gently, beautifully, delicately, a very special jewel; it lay on a bed of sky blue—the background of the map—its yellow form mysterious, because though it looked like a leg of mutton, it could not really look like anything so familiar as a leg of mutton because it was England—with shadings of pink and green, unlike any shadings of pink and green I had seen before, squiggly veins of red running in every direction. England was a special jewel all right, and only special people got to wear it. The people who got to wear England were English people. They wore it well and they wore it everywhere: in jungles, in deserts, on plains, on top of the highest mountains, on all the oceans, on all the seas, in places where they were not welcome, in places they should not have been. When my teacher had pinned this map up on the blackboard, she said, "This is England"—and she said it with authority, seriousness, and adoration, and we all sat up. It was as if she had said, "This is Jerusalem, the place you will go to when you die but only if you have been good." We understood then—we were meant to understand then—that England was to be our source of myth and the source from which we got our sense of reality, our sense of what was meaningful, our sense of what was meaningless—and much about our own lives and much about the very idea of us headed that last list.

At the time I was a child sitting at my desk seeing England for the first time, I was already very familiar with the greatness of it. Each morning before I left for school, I ate a breakfast of half a grapefruit, an egg, bread and butter and a slice of cheese, and a cup of cocoa; or half a grapefruit, a bowl of oat porridge, bread and butter and a slice of cheese, and a cup of cocoa. The can of cocoa was often left on the table in front of me. It had written on it the name of the company, the year the company was established, and the words "Made in England." Those words, "Made in England," were written on the box the oats came in too. They would also have been written on the box the shoes I was wearing came in; a bolt of gray linen cloth lying on the shelf of a store from which my mother had bought three yards to make the uniform that I was wearing had written along its edge those three words. The shoes I wore were made in England, so were my socks and cotton undergarments and the satin ribbons I wore tied at the end of two plaits of my hair. My father, who might have sat next to me at breakfast, was a carpenter and cabinet maker. The shoes he wore to work would have been made in England, as were his khaki shirt and trousers, his underpants and undershirt, his socks and brown felt hat. Felt was not the proper material from which a hat that was expected to provide shade from the hot sun should be made, but my father must have seen and admired a picture of an Englishman wearing such a hat in England, and this picture that he saw must have been so compelling that it caused him to wear the wrong hat for a hot climate most of his long life. And this hat—a brown felt hat—became so central to his character that it was the first thing he put on in the morning as he stepped out of bed and the last thing he took off before he stepped back into bed at night. As we sat at breakfast a car might go by. The car, a Hillman or a Zephyr, was made in England. The very idea of the meal itself, breakfast, and its substantial quality and quantity was an idea from England; we somehow knew that in England they began the day with this meal called breakfast and a proper breakfast was a big breakfast. No one I knew liked eating so much food so early in the day; it made us feel sleepy, tired. But this breakfast business was Made in England like almost everything else that surrounded us, the exceptions being the sea, the sky, and the air we breathed.

At the time I saw this map—seeing England for the first time—I did not say to myself, "Ah, so that's what it looks like," because there was no longing in me to put a shape to those three words that ran through every part of my life, no matter how small; for me to have had such a longing would have meant that I lived in a certain atmosphere, an atmosphere in which those three words were felt as a burden. But I did not live in such an atmosphere. My father's brown felt hat would develop a hole in its crown, the lining would separate from the hat itself, and six weeks before he thought that he could not be seen wearing it—he was a very vain man—he would order another hat from England. And my mother taught me to eat my food in the English way: the knife in the right hand, the fork in the left, my elbows held still close to my side, the food carefully balanced on my fork and then brought up to my mouth. When I had finally mastered it, I overheard her saying to a friend, "Did you see how nicely she can eat?" But I knew then that I enjoyed my food more when I ate it with my bare hands, and I continued to do so when she wasn't looking. And when my teacher showed us the map, she asked us to study it carefully, because no test we would ever take would be complete without this statement: "Draw a map of England."

I did not know then that the statement "Draw a map of England" was something far worse than a declaration of war, for in fact a flat-out declaration of war would have put me on alert, and again in fact, there was no need for war—I had long ago been conquered. I did not know then that this statement was part of a process that would result in my erasure, not my physical erasure, but my erasure all the same. I did not know then that this statement was meant to make me feel in awe and small whenever I heard the word "England": awe at its existence, small because I was not from it. I did not know very much of anything then — certainly not what a blessing it was that I was unable to draw a map of England correctly

After that there were many times of seeing England for the first time. I saw   5
England in history. I knew the names of all the kings of England. I knew the names of their children, their wives, their disappointments, their triumphs, the names of people who betrayed them, I knew the dates on which they were born and the dates they died. I knew their conquests and was made to feel glad if I figured in them; I knew their defeats. I knew the details of the year 1066 (the Battle of Hastings, the end of the reign of the Anglo-Saxon kings) before I knew the details of the year 1832 (the year slavery was abolished). It wasn't as bad as I make it sound now; it was worse. I did like so much hearing again and again how Alfred the Great, traveling in disguise, had been left to watch cakes, and because he wasn't used to this the cakes got burned, and Alfred burned his hands pulling them out of the fire, and the woman who had left him to watch the cakes screamed at him. I loved King Alfred. My grandfather was named after him; his son, my uncle, was named after King Alfred; my brother is named after King Alfred. And so there are three people in my family named after a man they have never met, a man who died over ten centuries ago. The first view I got of England then was not unlike the first view received by the man who named my grandfather.

This view, though — the naming of the kings, their deeds, their disappointments — was the vivid view, the forceful view. There were other ones, subtler ones, softer, almost not there — but these were the ones that made the most lasting impression on me, these were the ones that made me really feel like nothing. "When morning touched the sky" was one phrase, for no morning touched the sky where I lived. The mornings where I lived came on abruptly, with a shock of heat and loud noises. "Evening approaches" was another, but the evenings where I lived did not approach; in fact, I had no evening — I had night and I had day and they came and went in a mechanical way: on, off; on, off. And then there were gentle mountains and low blue skies and moors over which people took walks for nothing but pleasure, when where I lived a walk was an act of labor, a burden, something only death or the automobile could relieve. And there were things that a small turn of a head could convey — entire worlds, whole lives would depend on this thing, a certain turn of a head. Everyday life could be quite tiring, more tiring than anything I was told not to do. I was told not to gossip, but they did that all the time. And they ate so much food, violating another of those rules they taught me: Do not indulge in gluttony. And the foods they ate actually: If only sometime I could eat cold cuts after theater, cold cuts of lamb and mint sauce, and Yorkshire pudding and scones, and clotted cream, and sausages that came from up-country (imagine, "up-country"). And having troubling thoughts at twilight, a good time to have troubling thoughts, apparently; and servants who stole and left in the middle of a crisis, who were born with a limp or some other kind of deformity, not nourished properly in their mother's womb (that last part I figured out for myself; the point was, oh to have an untrustworthy servant); and wonderful cobbled streets onto which solid front doors opened; and people whose eyes were blue and who had fair skins and who smelled only of lavender, or sometimes sweet pea or primrose. And those flowers with those names: delphiniums, foxgloves, tulips, daffodils, floribunda, peonies: in bloom, a striking display, being cut and placed in large glass bowls, crystal, decorating rooms so large twenty families the size of mine could fit in comfortably but used only for passing through. And the weather was so remarkable because the rain fell gently always, only occasionally in deep gusts, and it colored the air various shades of gray, each an appealing shade for a dress to be worn when a portrait was being painted; and when it rained at twilight, wonderful things happened: People bumped into each other unexpectedly and that would lead to all sorts of turns of events — a plot, the mere weather caused plots. I saw that people rushed: They rushed to catch trains, they rushed toward each other and away from each other; they rushed and rushed and rushed. That word: rushed! I did not know what it was to do that. It was too hot to do that, and so I came to envy people who would rush, even though it had no meaning to me to do such a thing. But there they are again. They loved their children; their children were sent to their own rooms as a punishment, rooms larger than my entire house. They were special, everything about them said so, even their clothes; their clothes rustled, swished, soothed. The world was theirs, not mine; everything told me so.

If now as I speak of all this I give the impression of someone on the outside looking in, nose pressed up against a glass window, that is wrong. My nose was pressed up against a glass window all right, but there was an iron vise at the back of my neck forcing my head to stay in place. To avert my gaze was to fall back into something from which I had been rescued, a hole filled with nothing, and that was the word for everything about me, nothing. The reality of my life was conquests, subjugation, humiliation, enforced amnesia. I was forced to forget. Just for instance, this: I lived in a part of St. John's, Antigua, called Ovals. Ovals was made up of five streets, each of them named after a famous English seaman — to be quite frank, an officially sanctioned criminal: Rodney Street (after George Rodney), Nelson Street (after Horatio Nelson), Drake Street (after Francis Drake), Hood Street, and Hawkins Street (after John Hawkins). But John Hawkins was knighted after a trip he made to Africa, opening up a new trade, the slave trade. He was then entitled to wear as his crest a Negro bound with a cord. Every single person living on Hawkins Street was descended from a slave. John Hawkins's ship, the one in which he transported the people he had bought and kidnapped, was called *The Jesus*. He later became the treasurer of the Royal Navy and rear admiral.

Again, the reality of my life, the life I led at the time I was being shown these views of England for the first time, for the second time, for the one-hundred-millionth time, was this: The sun shone with what sometimes seemed to be a deliberate cruelty; we must have done something to deserve that. My dresses did not rustle in the evening air as I strolled to the theater (I had no evening, I had no theater; my dresses were made of a cheap cotton, the weave of which would give way after not too many washings). I got up in the morning, I did my chores (fetched water from the public pipe for my mother, swept the yard), I washed myself, I went to a woman to have my hair combed freshly every day (because before we were allowed into our classroom our teachers would inspect us, and children who had not bathed that day, or had dirt under their fingernails, or whose hair had not been combed anew that day, might not be allowed to attend class). I ate that breakfast. I walked to school. At school we gathered in an auditorium and sang a hymn, "All Things Bright and Beautiful," and looking down on us as we sang were portraits of the Queen of England and her husband; they wore jewels and medals and they smiled. I was a Brownie. At each meeting we would form a little group around a flagpole, and after raising the Union Jack, we would say, "I promise to do my best, to do my duty to God and the Queen, to help other people every day and obey the scouts' law."

Who were these people and why had I never seen them, I mean really seen them, in the place where they lived? I had never been to England. No one I knew had ever been to England, or I should say, no one I knew had ever been and returned to tell me about it. All the people I knew who had gone to England had stayed there. Sometimes they left behind them their small children, never to see them again. England! I had seen England's representatives. I had seen the governor general at the public grounds at a ceremony celebrating the Queen's birthday. I had seen an old princess and I had seen a young princess. They had both been extremely not beautiful, but who of us would have told them that? I had never seen England, really seen it, I had only met a representative, seen a picture, read books, memorized its history. I had never set foot, my own foot, in it.

The space between the idea of something and its reality is always wide and deep and dark. The longer they are kept apart—idea of thing, reality of thing—the wider the width, the deeper the depth, the thicker and darker the darkness. This space starts out empty, there is nothing in it, but it rapidly becomes filled up with obsession or desire or hatred or love—sometimes all of these things, sometimes some of these things, sometimes only one of these things. The existence of the world as I came to know it was a result of this: idea of thing over here, reality of thing way, way over there. There was Christopher Columbus, an unlikable man, an unpleasant man, a liar (and so, of course, a thief) surrounded by maps and schemes and plans, and there was the reality on the other side of that width, the depth, that darkness. He became obsessed, he became filled with desire, the hatred came later, love was never a part of it. Eventually, his idea met the longed-for reality. That the idea of something and its reality are often two completely different things is something no one ever remembers; and so when they meet and find that they are not compatible, the weaker of the two, idea or reality, dies. That idea Christopher Columbus had was more powerful than the reality he met, and so the reality he met died.

And so finally, when I was a grown-up woman, the mother of two children, the wife of someone, a person who resides in a powerful country that takes up more than its fair share of a continent, the owner of a house with many rooms in it and of two automobiles, with the desire and will (which I very much act upon) to take from the world more than I give back to it, more than I deserve, more than I need, finally then, I saw England, the real England, not a picture, not a painting,

10

not through a story in a book, but England, for the first time. In me, the space between the idea of it and its reality had become filled with hatred, and so when at last I saw it I wanted to take it into my hands and tear it into little pieces and then crumble it up as if it were clay, child's clay. That was impossible, and so I could only indulge in not-favorable opinions.

There were monuments everywhere; they commemorated victories, battles fought between them and the people who lived across the sea from them, all vile people, fought over which of them would have dominion over the people who looked like me. The monuments were useless to them now, people sat on them and ate their lunch. They were like markers on an old useless trail, like a piece of old string tied to a finger to jog the memory, like old decoration in an old house, dirty, useless, in the way. Their skins were so pale, it made them look so fragile, so weak, so ugly. What if I had the power to simply banish them from their land, send boat after boatload of them on a voyage that in fact had no destination, force them to live in a place where the sun's presence was a constant? This would rid them of their pale complexion and make them look more like me, make them look more like the people I love and treasure and hold dear, and more like the people who occupy the near and far reaches of my imagination, my history, my geography, and reduce them and everything they have ever known to figurines as evidence that I was in divine favor, what if all this was in my power? Could I resist it? No one ever has.

And they were rude, they were rude to each other. They didn't like each other very much. They didn't like each other in the way they didn't like me, and it occurred to me that their dislike for me was one of the few things they agreed on.

I was on a train in England with a friend, an English woman. Before we were in England she liked me very much. In England she didn't like me at all. She didn't like the claim I said I had on England, she didn't like the views I had of England. I didn't like England, she didn't like England, but she didn't like me not liking it too. She said, "I want to show you my England, I want to show you the England that I know and love." I had told her many times before that I knew England and I didn't want to love it anyway. She no longer lived in England; it was her own country, but it had not been kind to her, so she left. On the train, the conductor was rude to her; she asked something, and he responded in a rude way. She became ashamed. She was ashamed at the way he treated her; she was ashamed at the way he behaved. "This is the new England," she said. But I liked the conductor being rude; his behavior seemed quite appropriate. Earlier this had happened: We had gone to a store to buy a shirt for my husband; it was meant to be a special present, a special shirt to wear on special occasions. This was a store where the Prince of Wales has his shirts made, but the shirts sold in this store are beautiful all the same. I found a shirt I thought my husband would like and I wanted to buy him a tie to go with it. When I couldn't decide which one to choose, the salesman showed me a new set. He was very pleased with these, he said, because they bore the crest of the Prince of Wales, and the Prince of Wales had never allowed his crest to decorate an article of clothing before. There was something in the way he said it; his tone was slavish, reverential, awed. It made me feel angry; I wanted to hit him. I didn't do that. I said, my husband and I hate princes, my husband would never wear anything that had a prince's anything on it. My friend stiffened. The salesman stiffened. They both drew themselves in, away from me. My friend told me that the prince was a symbol of her Englishness, and I could see that I had caused offense. I looked at her. She was an English person, the sort of English person I used to know at home, the sort who was nobody in England but somebody when they came to live among the people like me. There were many people I could have seen England with; that I was seeing it with this particular person, a person who reminded me of the people who showed me England long ago as I sat in church or at my desk, made me feel silent and afraid, for I wondered if, all these years of our friendship, I had had a friend or had been in the thrall of a racial memory.

I went to Bath — we, my friend and I, did this, but though we were together, I   15
was no longer with her. The landscape was almost as familiar as my own hand, but I had never been in this place before, so how could that be again? And the streets of Bath were familiar, too, but I had never walked on them before. It was all those years of reading, starting with Roman Britain. Why did I have to know about Roman Britain? It was of no real use to me, a person living on a hot, drought-ridden island, and it is of no use to me now, and yet my head is filled with this nonsense, Roman Britain. In Bath, I drank tea in a room I had read about in a novel written in the eighteenth century. In this very same room, young women wearing those dresses that rustled and so on danced and flirted and sometimes disgraced themselves with young men, soldiers, sailors, who were on their way to Bristol or someplace like that, so many places like that where so many adventures, the outcome of which was not good for me, began. Bristol, England. A sentence that began "That night the ship sailed from Bristol, England" would end not so good for me. And then I was driving through the countryside in an English motorcar, on narrow winding roads, and they were so familiar, though I had never been on them before; and through little villages the names of which I somehow knew so well though I had never been there before. And the countryside did have all those hedges and hedges, fields hedged in. I was marveling at all the toil of it, the planting of the hedges to begin with and then the care of it, all that clipping, year after year of clipping, and I wondered at the lives of the people who would have to do this, because wherever I see and feel the hands that hold up the world, I see and feel myself and all the people who look like me. And I said, "Those hedges" and my friend said that someone, a woman named Mrs. Rothchild, worried that the hedges weren't being taken care of properly; the farmers couldn't afford or find the help to keep up the hedges, and often they replaced them with wire fencing. I might have said to that, well if Mrs. Rothchild doesn't like the wire fencing, why doesn't she take care of the hedges herself, but I didn't. And then in those fields that were now hemmed in by wire fencing that a privileged woman didn't like was planted a vile yellow flowering bush that produced an oil, and my friend said that Mrs. Rothchild didn't like this either; it ruined the English countryside, it ruined the traditional look of the English countryside.

It was not at that moment that I wished every sentence, everything I knew, that began with England would end with "and then it all died; we don't know how, it just all died." At that moment, I was thinking, who are these people who forced me to think of them all the time, who forced me to think that the world I knew was incomplete, or without substance, or did not measure up because it was not England; that I was incomplete, or without substance, and did not measure up because I was not English. Who were these people? The person sitting next to me couldn't give me a clue; no one person could. In any case, if I had said to her, I find England ugly, I hate England; the weather is like a jail sentence, the English are a very ugly people, the food in England is like a jail sentence, the hair of English people is so straight, so dead looking, the English have an unbearable smell so different from the smell of people I know, real people of course, she would have said that I was a person full of prejudice. Apart from the fact that it is I—that is, the people who look like me—who made her aware of the unpleasantness of such a thing, the idea of such a thing, prejudice, she would have been only partly right, sort of right: I may be capable of prejudice, but my prejudices have no weight to them, my prejudices have no force behind them, my prejudices remain opinions, my prejudices remain my personal opinion. And a great feeling of rage and disappointment came over me as I looked at England, my head full of personal opinions that could not have public, my public, approval. The people I come from are powerless to do evil on grand scale.

The moment I wished every sentence, everything I knew, that began with England would end with "and then it all died, we don't know how, it just all died" was when I saw the white cliffs of Dover. I had sung hymns and recited poems that were about a longing to see the white cliffs of Dover again. At the time I sang the hymns and recited the poems, I could really long to see them again because I had never seen them at all, nor had anyone around me at the time. But there we were, groups of people longing for something we had never seen. And so there they were, the white cliffs, but they were not that pearly majestic thing I used to sing about, that thing that created such a feeling in these people that when they died in the place where I lived they had themselves buried facing a direction that would allow them to see the white cliffs of Dover when they were resurrected, as surely they would be. The white cliffs of Dover, when finally I saw them, were cliffs, but they were not white; you would only call them that if the word "white" meant something special to you; they were dirty and they were steep; they were so steep, the correct height from which all my views of England, starting with the map before me in my classroom and ending with the trip I had just taken, should jump and die and disappear forever.   [1991]

THINKING ABOUT THE TEXT

1. Kincaid indicates that for her, "there were many times of seeing England for the first time" (para. 5). How does she develop this seemingly illogical claim?

2. What do you think Kincaid wants to make her audience believe and feel with this essay? Describe her tone. Is its effect on you the effect you think

Kincaid wants it to have? Describe her characterization of herself. Do you think it is rhetorically effective? Why, or why not?

3. From what did the young Kincaid get her images of England? Look in particular at the images she reports in paragraph 6.

4. In paragraph 14, Kincaid recalls the incident in the clothing store after she describes her train trip, even though the incident in the store took place before the train trip. What does she gain by violating chronological order?

5. Does Kincaid learn anything from her trip to England? What? What would you say to someone who argued that she ought to have been more open-minded as a tourist?

MAKING COMPARISONS

1. Kincaid presents "Girl" and "Columbus in Chains" as works of fiction. As a reader, do you approach "On Seeing England for the First Time" differently because it is labeled nonfiction? Explain.

2. Compare the remarks about Columbus in "On Seeing England for the First Time" with Annie John's treatment of his picture in "Columbus in Chains." Do you think the two narrators have the same ideas about him? Refer to specific sentences in both texts.

3. "Girl" seems less explicitly concerned with colonialism than do the other two works. Is the world evoked in "Girl" quite different from the worlds of "Columbus in Chains" and "On Seeing England for the First Time"? Why, or why not? Using words from either or both of those texts, add a few sentences to "Girl" that more clearly establish the setting as colonial.

WRITING ABOUT ISSUES

1. Each of the three selections in this cluster either repeats certain words, refers to certain repeated acts, or both. Choose one of these selections and write an essay explaining the role and function of repetition in it. Give specific examples of whatever repetitions you discuss.

2. Choose two of these selections and write an essay comparing the educational processes depicted in them. Do they depict the same kinds of teaching and learning or are there significant differences? Refer to specific details of both works.

3. Write your own version of "Girl," calling it either "Girl" or "Boy" and presenting in it advice that you were given as a youth. Exchange your version with a classmate's. After you read your classmate's version, add a paragraph or two to it in which you describe and evaluate the kind of education it depicts. Your classmate will do the same with your version. Return

your classmate's version and get yours back. Finally, read your classmate's comments on your version and write a paragraph or two in which you state what you have learned from this exercise.

4. Midway through "On Seeing England for the First Time," Kincaid states the following: "The space between the idea of something and its reality is always wide and deep and dark. The longer they are kept apart — idea of thing, reality of thing — the wider the width, the deeper the depth, the thicker and darker the darkness. This space starts out empty, there is nothing in it, but it rapidly becomes filled up with obsession or desire or hatred or love — sometimes all of these things, sometimes some of these things, sometimes only one of these things" (para. 10). In the rest of the paragraph, Kincaid gives the example of Columbus's relationship with the native inhabitants of the New World. Write an essay applying the passage quoted to another specific political situation, past or present. Focus on identifying who or what is responsible for "the space between the idea of something and its reality." Support your argument with facts drawn from library research.

Teaching through Literature

DAVID WAGONER, "The Singing Lesson"
THEODORE ROETHKE, "The Waking"
ELIZABETH BISHOP, "One Art"

Novelist and short-story writer Jane Smiley has observed that "every piece of fiction is in some degree also a how-to manual." Smiley could have said the same about any work of literature, not just fiction. Through the centuries many readers have turned to literature for guidance, believing that within its pages lie valuable lessons. Furthermore, many writers of literature have seen it as a way of teaching. They have followed a recommendation made by the ancient philosopher Horace: He pointed out that art should both delight and instruct. In this cluster, we present works that associate literature with education. David Wagoner's poem has the word *lesson* in its very title, and Theodore Roethke's poem explicitly suggests how to learn. Elizabeth Bishop's poem gives instructions in "the art of losing," which supposedly "isn't hard to master." Can a poem be "poetic" when it resembles a lecture? Consider that question as you read the following texts.

BEFORE YOU READ

If you were asked to declare in a poem certain principles of living you have come to adopt, what are some you might express? How controversial do you think each would be?

DAVID WAGONER
The Singing Lesson

David Wagoner (b. 1926) is a chancellor of the Academy of American Poets and editor of the journal Poetry Northwest. *The author of ten novels, he has also written many volumes of poetry, the latest of which is* Walt Whitman Bathing *(1996). The following poem appears in his 1974 book* Sleeping in the Woods.

You must stand erect but at your ease, a posture
Demanding a compromise
Between your spine and your head, your best face forward,
Your willful hands
Not beckoning or clenching or sweeping upward   5
But drawn in close:
A man with his arms spread wide is asking for it,
A martyred beggar,
A flightless bird on the nest dreaming of flying.
For your full resonance   10
You must keep your inspiring and expiring moments
Divided but equal,
Not locked like antagonists from breast to throat,
Choking toward silence.

If you have learned, with labor and luck, the measures   15
You were meant to complete,
You may find yourself before an audience
Singing into the light,
Transforming the air you breathe — that malleable wreckage,
That graveyard of shouts,   20
That inexhaustible pool of chatter and whimpers —
Into deathless music.
But remember, with your mouth wide open, eyes shut,
Some men will wonder,
When they look at you without listening, whether   25
You're singing or dying.
Take care to be heard. But even singing alone,
Singing for nothing,
Singing to empty space in no one's honor,
Keep time: it will tell   30
When you must give the final end-stopped movement
Your tacit approval.   [1974]

THINKING ABOUT THE TEXT

1. What words of Wagoner's poem might be used during an actual singing lesson? What words suggest that the poem is about more than singing? Does the poem do what the speaker is urging? In what ways?

2. Do you consider it significant that this singing lesson never uses rhyme? What do you think readers should conclude? What other verbal patterns does Wagoner use?

3. How might someone other than a singer or musician "keep time" (line 30) and produce "deathless music" (line 22)?

4. At various points, the speaker refers to the singer's possible audience. How does the speaker characterize this audience? Refer to specific lines.

5. Evaluate the poem's advice. In what ways, if any, do you currently do what the poem recommends?

THEODORE ROETHKE
The Waking

Theodore Roethke (1908–1963) is regarded as one of the great modern American poets. The following poem appeared in his 1953 Pulitzer Prize–winning book entitled The Waking. *The poem is a villanelle, a centuries-old French form that is quite technically challenging for a writer. A villanelle is a nineteen-line poem consisting of five tercets (three-line stanzas) followed by a quatrain (four-line stanza); the first and third lines of the first tercet are used alternately to conclude each succeeding tercet, and they are joined to form a rhyme at the poem's end.*

I wake to sleep, and take my waking slow.
I feel my fate in what I cannot fear.
I learn by going where I have to go.

We think by feeling. What is there to know?
I hear my being dance from ear to ear.   5
I wake to sleep, and take my waking slow.

Of those so close beside me, which are you?
God bless the Ground! I shall walk softly there,
And learn by going where I have to go.

Light takes the Tree; but who can tell us how?   10
The lowly worm climbs up a winding stair;
I wake to sleep, and take my waking slow.

◆   ◆   ◆

Great Nature has another thing to do
To you and me; so take the lively air,
And, lovely, learn by going where to go.   15

This shaking keeps me steady. I should know.
What falls away is always. And is near.
I wake to sleep, and take my waking slow.
I learn by going where I have to go.   [1953]

THINKING ABOUT THE TEXT

1. Explain how Roethke's poem is a villanelle, referring to the definition of this genre provided in the headnote about him. In Roethke's case, do you find the form effective? Why, or why not?

2. How would you respond to someone who is annoyed by the paradoxical phrase "I wake to sleep" (line 1)? Do you think the sentence "We think by feeling" (line 4) violates logic, too? Why, or why not?

3. At the end of the fourth tercet, Roethke departs a bit from the pattern of the villanelle by altering the line he is supposed to repeat. Instead of "I learn by going where I have to go" (line 3), he writes, "And, lovely, learn by going where to go" (line 15). Do you think this shift to explicit advice-giving is justifiable? Explain. Whom do you think "lovely" refers to? Is this fact important?

4. What philosophy of learning is expressed in this poem? Would you say that the line "I learn by going where I have to go" applies to you? What specific behavior do you think of in trying to answer this question? Do you believe the kind of learning described in the poem could take place in a college course? What assumptions are reflected in your answer to this question?

5. The first line of the fourth tercet seems to make "Great Nature" (line 13) an authority over human beings. What is your attitude toward this move? What does "take the lively air" (line 14) conceivably mean?

MAKING COMPARISONS

1. Because it is a villanelle, Roethke's poem can be described as highly formal. Is it much more formal than Wagoner's? Why, or why not?

2. Wagoner's is consistently a poem of advice or instruction. Is Roethke's? Support your answer by referring to specific lines of his.

3. Roethke's poem frequently uses the first person, but Wagoner's poem avoids it. Does this difference lead to a significant difference in the poems' effect?

ELIZABETH BISHOP
One Art

Although she also wrote short stories, Elizabeth Bishop (1911–1979) became known primarily for her poetry, winning both a Pulitzer Prize and a National Book Award for it. Born in Worcester, Massachusetts, she spent much of her youth in Nova Scotia. As an adult, she lived in various places, including New York City, Florida, Mexico, and Brazil. Much of her poetry observes and reflects on a particular object or figure. "One Art" appeared in Geography III *(1976), the last book that Bishop published during her lifetime. Like Roethke's "The Waking," this poem is a villanelle. (See the headnote to "The Waking" for a description of the form.)*

The art of losing isn't hard to master;
so many things seem filled with the intent
to be lost that their loss is no disaster.

Lose something every day. Accept the fluster
of lost door keys, the hour badly spent.   5
The art of losing isn't hard to master.

Then practice losing farther, losing faster:
places, and names, and where it was you meant
to travel. None of these will bring disaster.

I lost my mother's watch. And look! my last, or   10
next-to-last, of three loved houses went.
The art of losing isn't hard to master.

I lost two cities, lovely ones. And, vaster,
some realms I owned, two rivers, a continent.
I miss them, but it wasn't a disaster.   15

—Even losing you (the joking voice, a gesture
I love) I shan't have lied. It's evident
the art of losing's not too hard to master
though it may look like (*Write* it!) like disaster.   [1976]

THINKING ABOUT THE TEXT

1. What makes "One Art" a villanelle? Review the general definition of the form on page 692.

2. Describe the speaker's tone. Is it consistent? What do you conclude about the speaker's attitude toward "the art of losing"?

3. Look at the advice given in the third stanza. In what ways can it be considered useful? Would you argue that this advice shouldn't be heeded? Why, or why not?

4. In line 16, the word *you* is suddenly introduced. What is the effect?

5. The parenthetical expression "(*Write* it!)" in line 19 is a departure from the sheer repetition of lines characteristic of a villanelle. What do you make of this break? Do you think it appropriate, or do you find it merely jarring?

MAKING COMPARISONS

1. Compare Bishop's use of the villanelle form with Roethke's. Are you more aware of similarities or differences in their uses of it?

2. Both Wagoner and Bishop write about arts. For Wagoner, it's the art of singing; for Bishop, the art of losing. Do you see any resemblances between the two, judging by the poems? If so, what?

3. Does the implied listener seem equally important in all three poems? Explain.

WRITING ABOUT ISSUES

1. Choose Wagoner's, Roethke's, or Bishop's poem, and write an essay tracing how the poem develops. How, for instance, is the middle different from the beginning, and the end different from earlier parts? Don't let yourself get stuck in merely repeating lines. While you should quote from the poem, focus on identifying in your own words the key stages it moves through.

2. Write an essay comparing the philosophies you see expressed in two of the poems in this cluster. Do these two poems appear to put forth similar philosophies, or are there important differences? As you explain the philosophy of each poem, be sure to cite specific lines.

3. Wagoner's poem elaborates a philosophy of life by focusing on the activity of singing. Roethke's poem does so by focusing on the activity of waking. Bishop's poem is about the activity of losing. Write an essay or poem expressing a philosophy of your own by focusing on a familiar activity. Feel free to bring in actual experiences of your own to develop your ideas.

4. Ask at least three students not in this class to tell you about a specific learning experience each has had recently. Write an essay discussing the extent to which each student apparently assumes that one must "Take care to be heard" (Wagoner's words), or that "I learn by going where I have to go" (Roethke's words), or that "loss is no disaster" (Bishop's words). Support your claims about each student with specific details of the story he or she told you.

NARRATORS GIVING ADVICE

JONATHAN SWIFT, "A Modest Proposal"
DANIEL OROZCO, "Orientation"
PAM HOUSTON, "How to Talk to a Hunter"

The introduction to the previous cluster suggested that any work of literature can be considered a "how-to manual." Each of the three works in this cluster has a narrator who dispenses advice. Yet in each case, you will be trying to determine whom the narrator is addressing, what the situation exactly is, how to evaluate the narrator's advice, and how to describe the narrator overall. These works belong to a specific literary tradition: that of the unreliable narrator. The term *unreliable* applies when you find yourself unable to accept a narrator's vision of life right away. Eventually, you may like and trust the narrator, but part of the process of reading the work is deciding whether you should.

BEFORE YOU READ

Recall an orientation you experienced. What were its goals? Its main activities? The key terms used during it? What did the people in charge seem to assume about their audience? What did you think of this orientation at the time? Why? Did your evaluation of it ever change? In what respect?

JONATHAN SWIFT

A Modest Proposal

FOR PREVENTING THE CHILDREN OF POOR PEOPLE
IN IRELAND FROM BEING A BURDEN TO THEIR PARENTS
OR COUNTRY, AND FOR MAKING THEM
BENEFICIAL TO THE PUBLIC

Jonathan Swift (1667–1745) was an eminent clergyman in his native Ireland, rising to the position of dean of St. Patrick's Cathedral in Dublin. But he also wrote many essays, political pamphlets, poems, and works of fiction, his best-known text being his 1726 prose satire Gulliver's Travels. "A Modest Proposal," written in 1729, also continues to be widely read and much discussed. It reflects Swift's concern over the poverty and food shortages then afflicting Ireland. To him, the country suffered in part because of the narrow-minded policies of its ruler, England. Swift also faulted British owners of property in Ireland, many of whom were absentee landlords indifferent to their tenants' woes. Although "A Modest Proposal" is often classified as an essay, we think it can be called a short story because it contains a significant element of fiction: The real-life Swift hardly agreed with his narrator's remedy for Ireland. Indeed, this work is regarded as a classic example of irony. Through his narrator's absurd proposal, Swift aimed to shock readers into thinking about genuine solutions to his country's plight.

It is a melancholy object to those who walk through this great town or travel in the country, when they see the streets, the roads, and cabin doors, crowded with beggars of the female sex, followed by three, four, or six children, all in rags and importuning every passenger for an alms. These mothers, instead of being able to work for their honest livelihood, are forced to employ all their time in strolling to beg sustenance for their helpless infants: who as they grow up either turn thieves for want of work, or leave their dear native country to fight for the Pretender in Spain, or sell themselves to the Barbadoes.

I think it is agreed by all parties that this prodigious number of children in the arms, or on the backs, or at the heels of their mothers, and frequently of their fathers, is in the present deplorable state of the kingdom a very great additional grievance; and, therefore, whoever could find out a fair, cheap, and easy method of making these children sound, useful members of the commonwealth, would deserve so well of the public as to have his statue set up for a preserver of the nation.

But my intention is very far from being confined to provide only for the children of professed beggars; it is of a much greater extent, and shall take in the whole number of infants at a certain age who are born of parents in effect as little able to support them as those who demand our charity in the streets.

As to my own part, having turned my thoughts for many years upon this important subject, and maturely weighed the several schemes of our projectors,° have always found them grossly mistaken in their computation. It is true, a child just dropped from its dam may be supported by her milk for a solar year, with little other nourishment; at most not above the value of 2s.,° which the mother may certainly get, or the value in scraps, by her lawful occupation of begging; and it is exactly at one year old that I propose to provide for them in such a manner as instead of being a charge upon their parents or the parish, or wanting food and raiment for the rest of their lives, they shall on the contrary contribute to the feeding, and partly to the clothing, of many thousands.

There is likewise another great advantage in my scheme, that it will prevent those voluntary abortions, and that horrid practice of women murdering their bastard children, alas! too frequent among us! sacrificing the poor innocent babes I doubt more to avoid the expense than the shame, which would move tears and pity in the most savage and inhuman breast.

The number of souls in this kingdom being usually reckoned one million and a half, of these I calculate there may be about 200,000 couples whose wives are breeders; from which number I subtract 30,000 couples, who are able to maintain their own children (although I apprehend there cannot be so many, under the present distress of the kingdom); but this being granted, there will remain 170,000 breeders. I again subtract 50,000 for those women who miscarry, or whose

5

projectors: Those who devise plans.　**2s.:** Two shillings. In paragraph 7, "£" is an abbreviation for pounds sterling and "d" for pence.

children die by accident or disease within the year. There only remain 120,000 children of poor parents annually born. The question therefore is, how this number shall be reared and provided for? which, as I have already said, under the present situation of affairs, is utterly impossible by all the methods hitherto proposed. For we can neither employ them in handicraft or agriculture; we neither build houses (I mean in the country) nor cultivate land; they can very seldom pick up a livelihood by stealing, till they arrive at six years old, except where they are of towardly parts; although I confess they learn the rudiments much earlier; during which time they can, however, be properly looked upon only as probationers; as I have been informed by a principal gentleman in the county of Cavan, who protested to me that he never knew above one or two instances under the age of six, even in a part of the kingdom so renowned for the quickest proficiency in that art.

I am assured by our merchants, that a boy or a girl before twelve years old is no salable commodity; and even when they come to this age they will not yield above 3£. or 3£. 2s. 6d. at most on the exchange; which cannot turn to account either to the parents or kingdom, the charge of nutriment and rags having been at least four times that value.

I shall now therefore humbly propose my own thoughts, which I hope will not be liable to the least objection.

I have been assured by a very knowing American of my acquaintance in London, that a young healthy child well nursed is at a year old a most delicious, nourishing, and wholesome food, whether stewed, roasted, baked, or broiled; and I make no doubt that it will equally serve in a fricassee or a ragout.

I do therefore humbly offer it to public consideration that of the 120,000 children already computed, 20,000 may be reserved for breed, whereof only one-fourth part to be males; which is more than we allow to sheep, black cattle, or swine; and my reason is, that these children are seldom the fruits of marriage, a circumstance not much regarded by our savages; therefore one male will be sufficient to serve four females. That the remaining 100,000 may, at a year old, be offered in sale to the persons of quality and fortune through the kingdom; always advising the mother to let them suck plentifully in the last month, so as to render them plump and fat for a good table. A child will make two dishes at an entertainment for friends; and when the family dines alone, the fore or hind quarter will make a reasonable dish, and seasoned with a little pepper or salt will be very good boiled on the fourth day, especially in winter.

I have reckoned upon a medium that a child just born will weigh twelve pounds, and in a solar year, if tolerably nursed, will increase to twenty-eight pounds.

I grant this food will be somewhat dear, and therefore very proper for landlords, who, as they have already devoured most of the parents, seem to have the best title to the children.

Infant's flesh will be in season throughout the year, but more plentiful in March, and a little before and after: for we are told by a grave author, an eminent French physician, that fish being a prolific diet, there are more children born in Roman Catholic countries about nine months after Lent than at any other season; therefore, reckoning a year after Lent, the markets will be more glutted than usual, because the number of popish infants is at least three to one in this kingdom: and

10

therefore it will have one other collateral advantage, by lessening the number of papists among us.

I have already computed the charge of nursing a beggar's child (in which list I reckon all cottagers, laborers, and four-fifths of the farmers) to be about 2s. per annum, rags included; and I believe no gentleman would repine to give 10s. for the carcass of a good fat child, which, as I have said, will make four dishes of excellent nutritive meat, when he has only some particular friend or his own family to dine with him. Thus the squire will learn to be a good landlord, and grow popular among the tenants; the mother will have 8s. net profit, and be fit for work till she produces another child.

Those who are more thrifty (as I must confess the times require) may flay the   15
carcass; the skin of which artificially dressed will make admirable gloves for ladies, and summer boots for fine gentlemen.

As to our city of Dublin, shambles° may be appointed for this purpose in the most convenient parts of it, and butchers we may be assured will not be wanting: although I rather recommend buying the children alive, and dressing them hot from the knife as we do roasting pigs.

A very worthy person, a true lover of his country, and whose virtues I highly esteem, was lately pleased in discoursing on this matter to offer a refinement upon my scheme. He said that many gentlemen of this kingdom, having of late destroyed their deer, he conceived that the want of venison might be well supplied by the bodies of young lads and maidens, not exceeding fourteen years of age nor under twelve; so great a number of both sexes in every country being now ready to starve for want of work and service; and these to be disposed of by their parents, if alive, or otherwise by their nearest relations. But with due deference to so excellent a friend and so deserving a patriot, I cannot be altogether in his sentiments; for as to the males, my American acquaintance assured me from frequent experience that their flesh was generally tough and lean, like that of our schoolboys by continual exercise, and their taste disagreeable; and to fatten them would not answer the charge. Then as to the females, it would, I think, with humble submission be a loss to the public, because they soon would become breeders themselves: and besides, it is not improbable that some scrupulous people might be apt to censure such a practice (although indeed very unjustly), as a little bordering upon cruelty; which, I confess, has always been with me the strongest objection against any project, how well soever intended.

But in order to justify my friend, he confessed that this expedient was put into his head by the famous Psalmanazar° a native of the island Formosa, who came from thence to London about twenty years ago: and in conversation told my friend, that in his country when any young person happened to be put to death, the executioner sold the carcass to persons of quality as a prime dainty; and that in his time the body of a plump girl of fifteen, who was crucified for an attempt to poison the emperor, was sold to his imperial majesty's prime minister of state, and

shambles: Slaughterhouses.
Psalmanazar: In 1704, the Frenchman George Psalmanazar (c. 1679–1763) wrote *An Historical and Geographical Description of Formosa* (now Taiwan). He claimed to be a Formosan native, but his hoax was exposed soon after the book's publication.

other great mandarins of the court, in joints from the gibbet, at 400 crowns. Neither indeed, can I deny, that if the same use were made of several plump young girls in this town, who without one single groat to their fortunes cannot stir abroad without a chair, and appear at the playhouse and assemblies in foreign fineries which they never will pay for, the kingdom would not be the worse.

Some persons of a depending spirit are in great concern about the vast number of poor people, who are aged, diseased, or maimed, and I have been desired to employ my thoughts what course may be taken to ease the nation of so grievous an encumbrance. But I am not in the least pain upon that matter, because it is very well known that they are every day dying and rotting by cold and famine, and filth and vermin, as fast as can be reasonably expected. And as to the young laborers, they are now in as hopeful a condition: They cannot get work, and consequently pine away for want of nourishment, to a degree that if at any time they are accidentally hired to common labor, they have not strength to perform it; and thus the country and themselves are happily delivered from the evils to come.

I have too long digressed, and therefore shall return to my subject. I think the   20
advantages by the proposal which I have made are obvious and many, as well as of the highest importance.

For first, as I have already observed, it would greatly lessen the number of papists, with whom we are yearly overrun, being the principal breeders of the nation as well as our most dangerous enemies; and who stay at home on purpose to deliver the kingdom to the Pretender, hoping to take their advantage by the absence of so many good Protestants, who have chosen rather to leave their country than stay at home and pay tithes against their conscience to an Episcopal curate.

Secondly, The poor tenants will have something valuable of their own, which by law may be made liable to distress and help to pay their landlord's rent, their corn and cattle being already seized, and money a thing unknown.

Thirdly, Whereas the maintenance of 100,000 children from two years old and upward, cannot be computed at less than 10s. a-piece per annum, the nation's stock will be thereby increased £50,000 per annum, beside the profit of a new dish introduced to the tables of all gentlemen of fortune in the kingdom who have any refinement in taste. And the money will circulate among ourselves, the goods being entirely of our own growth and manufacture.

Fourthly, The constant breeders beside the gain of 8s. sterling per annum by the sale of their children, will be rid of the charge of maintaining them after the first year.

Fifthly, This food would likewise bring great custom to taverns, where the   25
vintners will certainly be so prudent as to procure the best receipts for dressing it to perfection, and consequently have their houses frequented by all the fine gentlemen, who justly value themselves upon their knowledge in good eating; and a skilful cook who understands how to oblige his guests, will contrive to make it as expensive as they please.

Sixthly, This would be a great inducement to marriage, which all wise nations have either encouraged by rewards or enforced by laws and penalties. It would increase the care and tenderness of mothers toward their children, when they were sure of a settlement for life to the poor babes, provided in some sort by the public, to their annual profit instead of expense. We should see an honest emulation among the married women, which of them would bring the fattest child to the market. Men would become as fond of their wives during the time of their pregnancy as they are now of their mares in foal, their cows in calf, their sows when they are ready to farrow; nor offer to beat or kick them (as is too frequent a practice) for fear of a miscarriage.

Many other advantages might be enumerated. For instance, the addition of some thousand carcasses in our exportation of barreled beef, the propagation of swine's flesh, and improvement in the art of making good bacon, so much wanted among us by the great destruction of pigs, too frequent at our table; which are no way comparable in taste or magnificence to a well-grown, fat, yearling child, which roasted whole will make a considerable figure at a lord mayor's feast or any other public entertainment. But this and many others I omit, being studious of brevity.

Supposing that 1,000 families in this city would be constant customers for infants' flesh, besides others who might have it at merry-meetings, particularly at weddings and christenings, I compute that Dublin would take off annually about 20,000 carcasses; and the rest of the kingdom (where probably they will be sold somewhat cheaper) the remaining 80,000.

I can think of no one objection that will possibly be raised against this proposal, unless it should be urged that the number of people will be thereby much lessened in the kingdom. This I freely own, and it was indeed one principal design in offering it to the world. I desire the reader will observe, that I calculate my remedy for this one individual kingdom of Ireland and for no other that ever was, is, or I think ever can be upon earth. Therefore let no man talk to me of other expedients: of taxing our absentees at 5s. a pound; of using neither clothes nor household furniture except what is of our own growth and manufacture; of utterly rejecting the materials and instruments that promote foreign luxury; of curing the expensiveness of pride, vanity, idleness, and gaming in our women; of introducing a vein of parsimony, prudence, and temperance; of learning to love our country, in the want of which we differ even from Laplanders and the inhabitants of Topinamboo; of quitting our animosities and factions, nor acting any longer like the Jews, who were murdering one another at the very moment their city was taken; of being a little cautious not to sell our country and conscience for nothing; of teaching landlords to have at least one degree of mercy toward their tenants; lastly, of putting a spirit of honesty, industry, and skill into our shopkeepers; who, if a resolution could now be taken to buy only our native goods, would immediately unite to cheat and exact upon us in the price the measure, and the goodness, nor could ever yet be brought to make one fair proposal of just dealing, though often and earnestly invited to it.

Therefore I repeat, let no man talk to me of these and the like expedients, till he has at least some glimpse of hope that there will be ever some hearty and sincere attempt to put them in practice. 30

But as to myself, having been wearied out for many years with offering vain, idle, visionary thoughts, and at length utterly despairing of success, I fortunately fell upon this proposal; which, as it is wholly new, so it has something solid and real, of no expense and little trouble, full in our own power, and whereby we can incur no danger in disobliging England. For this kind of commodity will not bear exportation, the flesh being of too tender a consistence to admit a long continuance in salt, although perhaps I could name a country which would be glad to eat up our whole nation without it.

After all, I am not so violently bent upon my own opinion as to reject any offer proposed by wise men, which shall be found equally innocent, cheap, easy, and effectual. But before something of that kind shall be advanced in contradiction to my scheme, and offering a better, I desire the author or authors will be pleased maturely to consider two points. First, as things now stand, how they will be able to find food and raiment for 100,000 useless mouths and backs. And secondly, there being a round million of creatures in human figure throughout this kingdom, whose subsistence put into a common stock would leave them in debt 2,000,000£. sterling, adding those who are beggars by profession to the bulk of farmers, cottagers, and laborers, with the wives and children who are beggars in effect; I desire those politicians who dislike my overture, and may perhaps be so bold as to attempt an answer, that they will first ask the parents of these mortals, whether they would not at this day think it a great happiness to have been sold for food at a year old in the manner I prescribe, and thereby have avoided such a perpetual scene of misfortunes as they have since gone through by the oppression of landlords, the impossibility of paying rent without money or trade, the want of common sustenance, with neither house nor clothes to cover them from the inclemencies of the weather, and the most inevitable prospect of entailing the like or greater miseries upon their breed for ever.

I profess, in the sincerity of my heart, that I have not the least personal interest in endeavoring to promote this necessary work, having no other motive than the public good of my country, by advancing our trade, providing for infants, relieving the poor, and giving some pleasure to the rich. I have no children by which I can propose to get a single penny; the youngest being nine years old, and my wife past childbearing.   [1729]

THINKING ABOUT THE TEXT

1. Analyze this essay as an argument that the narrator makes. What are his main claims? What support does he provide for them? What are some of his key warrants or assumptions?

2. What is the narrator's attitude toward the Irish poor? Identify various words he uses that indicate his judgments of them.

3. A word often associated with Swift's piece is *irony*. What are possible meanings of this term? What meaning of it seems most appropriate to Swift's work?

4. At what point in the piece do you realize that it is ironic? How would you describe the narrator's personality and tone before you get to this moment? List several adjectives for him.

5. Do you think Swift's piece would have succeeded in making many people more determined to solve Ireland's problems? Why, or why not?

DANIEL OROZCO
Orientation

Daniel Orozco (b. 1957) currently holds a writing fellowship at Stanford University. "Orientation" was selected for The Best American Short Stories 1995. *Originally, it appeared in a 1994 issue of* Seattle Review. *In a 1998 issue of the same journal, Orozco reports that since his story was published, "it has even been included in an employee orientation manual, which is either very funny or very disturbing."*

Those are the offices and these are the cubicles. That's my cubicle there, and this is your cubicle. This is your phone. Never answer your phone. Let the Voicemail System answer it. This is your Voicemail System Manual. There are no personal phone calls allowed. We do, however, allow for emergencies. If you must make an emergency phone call, ask your supervisor first. If you can't find your supervisor, ask Phillip Spiers, who sits over there. He'll check with Clarissa Nicks, who sits over there. If you make an emergency phone call without asking, you may be let go.

These are your IN and OUT boxes. All the forms in your IN box must be logged in by the date shown in the upper left-hand corner, initialed by you in the upper right-hand corner, and distributed to the Processing Analyst whose name is numerically coded in the lower left-hand corner. The lower right-hand corner is left blank. Here's your Processing Analyst Numerical Code Index. And here's your Forms Processing Procedures Manual.

You must pace your work. What do I mean? I'm glad you asked that. We pace our work according to the eight-hour workday. If you have twelve hours of work in your IN box, for example, you must compress that work into the eight-hour day. If you have one hour of work in your IN box, you must expand that work to fill the eight-hour day. That was a good question. Feel free to ask questions. Ask too many questions, however, and you may be let go.

That is our receptionist. She is a temp. We go through receptionists here. They quit with alarming frequency. Be polite and civil to the temps. Learn their names, and invite them to lunch occasionally. But don't get close to them, as it only makes it more difficult when they leave. And they always leave. You can be sure of that.

The men's room is over there. The women's room is over there. John LaFountaine, who sits over there, uses the women's room occasionally. He says it is accidental. We know better, but we let it pass. John LaFountaine is harmless, his forays into the forbidden territory of the women's room simply a benign thrill, a faint blip on the dull flat line of his life.

Russell Nash, who sits in the cubicle to your left, is in love with Amanda Pierce, who sits in the cubicle to your right. They ride the same bus together after work. For Amanda Pierce, it is just a tedious bus ride made less tedious by the idle nattering of Russell Nash. But for Russell Nash, it is the highlight of his day. It is the highlight of his life. Russell Nash has put on forty pounds, and grows fatter

5

with each passing month, nibbling on chips and cookies while peeking glumly over the partitions at Amanda Pierce, and gorging himself at home on cold pizza and ice cream while watching adult videos on TV.

Amanda Pierce, in the cubicle to your right, has a six-year-old son named Jamie, who is autistic. Her cubicle is plastered from top to bottom with the boy's crayon artwork—sheet after sheet of precisely drawn concentric circles and ellipses, in black and yellow. She rotates them every other Friday. Be sure to comment on them. Amanda Pierce also has a husband, who is a lawyer. He subjects her to an escalating array of painful and humiliating sex games, to which Amanda Pierce reluctantly submits. She comes to work exhausted and freshly wounded each morning, wincing from the abrasions on her breasts, or the bruises on her abdomen, or the second-degree burns on the backs of her thighs.

But we're not supposed to know any of this. Do not let on. If you let on, you may be let go.

Amanda Pierce, who tolerates Russell Nash, is in love with Albert Bosch, whose office is over there. Albert Bosch, who only dimly registers Amanda Pierce's existence, has eyes only for Ellie Tapper, who sits over there. Ellie Tapper, who hates Albert Bosch, would walk through fire for Curtis Lance. But Curtis Lance hates Ellie Tapper. Isn't the world a funny place? Not in the ha-ha sense, of course.

Anika Bloom sits in that cubicle. Last year, while reviewing quarterly reports in a meeting with Barry Hacker, Anika Bloom's left palm began to bleed. She fell into a trance, stared into her hand, and told Barry Hacker when and how his wife would die. We laughed it off. She was, after all, a new employee. But Barry Hacker's wife is dead. So unless you want to know exactly when and how you'll die, never talk to Anika Bloom.   10

Colin Heavey sits in that cubicle over there. He was new once, just like you. We warned him about Anika Bloom. But at last year's Christmas Potluck, he felt sorry for her when he saw that no one was talking to her. Colin Heavey brought her a drink. He hasn't been himself since. Colin Heavey is doomed. There's nothing he can do about it, and we are powerless to help him. Stay away from Colin Heavey. Never give any of your work to him. If he asks to do something, tell him you have to check with me. If he asks again, tell him I haven't gotten back to you.

This is the Fire Exit. There are several on this floor, and they are marked accordingly. We have a Floor Evacuation Review every three months, and an Escape Route Quiz once a month. We have our Biannual Fire Drill twice a year, and our Annual Earthquake Drill once a year. These are precautions only. These things never happen.

For your information, we have a comprehensive health plan. Any catastrophic illness, any unforeseen tragedy is completely covered. All dependents are completely covered. Larry Bagdikian, who sits over there, has six daughters. If anything were to happen to any of his girls, or to all of them, if all six were to simultaneously fall victim to illness or injury—stricken with a hideous degenerative muscle disease or some rare toxic blood disorder, sprayed with semiautomatic gunfire while on a class field trip, or attacked in their bunk beds by some prowling nocturnal lunatic—if any of this were to pass, Larry's girls would all be taken care of. Larry Bagdikian would not have to pay one dime. He would have nothing to worry about.

We also have a generous vacation and sick leave policy. We have an excellent disability insurance plan. We have a stable and profitable pension fund. We get group discounts for the symphony, and block seating at the ballpark. We get commuter ticket books for the bridge. We have Direct Deposit. We are all members of Costco.

This is our kitchenette. And this, this is our Mr. Coffee. We have a coffee 15 pool, into which we each pay two dollars a week for coffee, filters, sugar, and CoffeeMate. If you prefer Cremora or half-and-half to CoffeeMate, there is a special pool for three dollars a week. If you prefer Sweet 'n Low to sugar, there is a special pool for two-fifty a week. We do not do decaf. You are allowed to join the coffee pool of your choice, but you are not allowed to touch the Mr. Coffee.

This is the microwave oven. You are allowed to *heat* food in the microwave oven. You are not, however, allowed to *cook* food in the microwave oven.

We get one hour for lunch. We also get one fifteen-minute break in the morning, and one fifteen-minute break in the afternoon. Always take your breaks. **If you skip a break, it is gone forever. For your information, your break is a privilege, not a right. If you abuse the break policy, we are authorized to rescind your** breaks. Lunch, however, is a right, not a privilege. If you abuse the lunch policy, our hands will be tied, and we will be forced to look the other way. We will not enjoy that.

This is the refrigerator. You may put your lunch in it. Barry Hacker, who sits over there, steals food from this refrigerator. His petty theft is an outlet for his grief. Last New Year's Eve, while kissing his wife, a blood vessel burst in her brain. Barry Hacker's wife was two months pregnant at the time, and lingered in a coma for half a year before dying. It was a tragic loss for Barry Hacker. He hasn't been himself since. Barry Hacker's wife was a beautiful woman. She was also completely covered. Barry Hacker did not have to pay one dime. But his dead wife haunts him. She haunts all of us. We have seen her, reflected in the monitors of our computers, moving past our cubicles. We have seen the dim shadow of her face in our photocopies. She pencils herself in in the receptionist's appointment book, with the notation: To see Barry Hacker. She has left messages in the receptionist's Voicemail box, messages garbled by the electronic chirrups and buzzes in the phone line, her voice echoing from an immense distance within the ambient hum. But the voice is hers. And beneath her voice, beneath the tidal *whoosh* of static and hiss, the gurgling and crying of a baby can be heard.

In any case, if you bring a lunch, put a little something extra in the bag for Barry Hacker. We have four Barrys in this office. Isn't that a coincidence?

This is Matthew Payne's office. He is our Unit Manager, and his door is 20 always closed. We have never seen him, and you will never see him. But he is here. You can be sure of that. He is all around us.

This is the Custodian's Closet. You have no business in the Custodian's Closet.

And this, this is our Supplies Cabinet. If you need supplies, see Curtis Lance. He will log you in on the Supplies Cabinet Authorization Log, then give

you a Supplies Authorization Slip. Present your pink copy of the Supplies Authorization Slip to Ellie Tapper. She will log you in on the Supplies Cabinet Key Log,
then give you the key. Because the Supplies Cabinet is located outside the Unit
Manager's office, you must be very quiet. Gather your supplies quietly. The Supplies Cabinet is divided into four sections. Section One contains letterhead stationery, blank paper and envelopes, memo and note pads, and so on. Section
Two contains pens and pencils and typewriter and printer ribbons, and the like.
In Section Three we have erasers, correction fluids, transparent tapes, glue sticks,
et cetera. And in Section Four we have paper clips and push pins and scissors and
razor blades. And here are the spare blades for the shredder. Do not touch the
shredder, which is located over there. The shredder is of no concern to you.

Gwendolyn Stich sits in that office there. She is crazy about penguins, and
collects penguin knickknacks: penguin posters and coffee mugs and stationery,
penguin stuffed animals, penguin jewelry, penguin sweaters and T-shirts and
socks. She has a pair of penguin fuzzy slippers she wears when working late at the
office. She has a tape cassette of penguin sounds which she listens to for relaxation.
Her favorite colors are black and white. She has personalized license plates that
read PEN GWEN. Every morning, she passes through all the cubicles to wish each of
us a *good* morning. She brings Danish on Wednesdays for Hump Day morning
break, and doughnuts on Fridays for TGIF afternoon break. She organizes the
Annual Christmas Potluck, and is in charge of the Birthday List. Gwendolyn Stich's
door is always open to all of us. She will always lend an ear, and put in a good word
for you; she will always give you a hand, or the shirt off her back, or a shoulder to cry
on. Because her door is always open, she hides and cries in a stall in the women's
room. And John LaFountaine — who, enthralled when a woman enters, sits quietly
in his stall with his knees to his chest — John LaFountaine has heard her vomiting
in there. We have come upon Gwendolyn Stich huddled in the stairwell, shivering in the updraft, sipping a Diet Mr. Pibb and hugging her knees. She does not
let any of this interfere with her work. If it interfered with her work, she might
have to be let go.

Kevin Howard sits in that cubicle over there. He is a serial killer, the one
they call the Carpet Cutter, responsible for the mutilations across town. We're
not supposed to know that, so do not let on. Don't worry. His compulsion inflicts
itself on strangers only, and the routine established is elaborate and unwavering.
The victim must be a white male, a young adult no older than thirty, heavyset,
with dark hair and eyes, and the like. The victim must be chosen at random,
before sunset, from a public place; the victim is followed home, and must put up
a struggle; et cetera. The carnage inflicted is precise: the angle and direction of
the incisions; the layering of skin and muscle tissue; the rearrangement of the vis-
ceral organs; and so on. Kevin Howard does not let any of this interfere with his
work. He is, in fact, our fastest typist. He types as if he were on fire. He has a secret
crush on Gwendolyn Stich, and leaves a red-foil-wrapped Hershey's Kiss on her
desk every afternoon. But he hates Anika Bloom, and keeps well away from her.
In his presence, she has uncontrollable fits of shaking and trembling. Her left
palm does not stop bleeding.

In any case, when Kevin Howard gets caught, act surprised. Say that he 25 seemed like a nice person, a bit of a loner, perhaps, but always quiet and polite.

This is the photocopier room. And this, this is our view. It faces southwest. West is down there, toward the water. North is back there. Because we are on the seventeenth floor, we are afforded a magnificent view. Isn't it beautiful? It overlooks the park, where the tops of those trees are. You can see a segment of the bay between those two buildings there. You can see the sun set in the gap between those two buildings over there. You can see this building reflected in the glass panels of that building across the way. There. See? That's you, waving. And look there. There's Anika Bloom in the kitchenette, waving back.

Enjoy this view while photocopying. If you have problems with the photocopier, see Russell Nash. If you have any questions, ask your supervisor. If you can't find your supervisor, ask Phillip Spiers. He sits over there. He'll check with Clarissa Nicks. She sits over there. If you can't find them, feel free to ask me. That's my cubicle. I sit in there.   [1994]

THINKING ABOUT THE TEXT

1. Does this orientation resemble other orientations with which you are familiar? In what ways? Consider the kinds of advice and the language used.

2. Does the office described here resemble other offices with which you are familiar? In what ways? At what points in the story does this office seem unusual?

3. List at least three adjectives that describe Orozco's narrator. What influences your evaluation of this narrator? What would you say to someone who claims that the story is more about the narrator than about the office?

4. What assumptions do you make about the narrator's audience, that is, the listener being oriented? Write a page or two from this person's point of view, stating his or her response to the orientation.

5. Does the order of the narrator's statements matter? Explain.

MAKING COMPARISONS

1. Does Swift's piece become outlandish more quickly than Orozco's story does? Explain.

2. Swift's narrator seems to address many people, whereas Orozco's narrator is evidently talking to one person. Do the two works differ in effect because of this difference in audience? Why, or why not?

3. If Swift's narrator worked in the office described in Orozco's story, what might be his job? What comments do you imagine him making about his coworkers?

PAM HOUSTON
How to Talk to a Hunter

A graduate of Denison University, Pam Houston (b. 1962) is completing a doctorate in English at the University of Utah. She is not a hunter, though she is a hunting guide and has edited the book Women on Hunting (1994). *The following story was published in a 1989 issue of the journal* Quarterly West. *It was then included in* The Best American Short Stories 1990 *as well as in a 1992 volume of Houston's stories entitled* Cowboys Are My Weakness. *Her most recent book is another collection of her stories,* Waltzing the Cat (1998).

When he says "Skins or blankets?" it will take you a moment to realize that he's asking which you want to sleep under. And in your hesitation he'll decide that he wants to see your skin wrapped in the big black moose hide. He carried it, he'll say, soaking wet and heavier than a dead man, across the tundra for two — **was it hours or days or weeks? But the payoff, now, will be to see it fall across one of your white breasts. It's December, and your skin is never really warm, so you will pull the bulk** of it around you and pose for him, pose for his camera, without having to narrate this moose's death.

You will spend every night in this man's bed without asking yourself why he listens to top-forty country. Why he donated money to the Republican Party. Why he won't play back his messages while you are in the room. You are there so often the messages pile up. Once you noticed the bright green counter reading as high as fifteen.

He will have lured you here out of a careful independence that you spent months cultivating; though it will finally be winter, the dwindling daylight and the threat of Christmas, that makes you give in. Spending nights with this man means suffering the long face of your sheepdog, who likes to sleep on your bed, who worries when you don't come home. But the hunter's house is so much warmer than yours, and he'll give you a key, and just like a woman, you'll think that means something. It will snow hard for thirteen straight days. Then it will really get cold. When it is sixty below there will be no wind and no clouds, just still air and cold sunshine. The sun on the windows will lure you out of bed, but he'll pull you back under. The next two hours he'll devote to your body. With his hands, with his tongue, he'll express what will seem to you like the most eternal of loves. Like the house key, this is just another kind of lie. Even in bed; especially in bed, you and he cannot speak the same language. The machine will answer the incoming calls. From under an ocean of passion and hide and hair you'll hear a woman's muffled voice between the beeps.

Your best female friend will say, "So what did you think? That a man who sleeps under a dead moose is capable of commitment?"

This is what you learned in college: A man desires the satisfaction of his desire; a woman desires the condition of desiring.   5

♦ ♦ ♦

The hunter will talk about spring in Hawaii, summer in Alaska. The man who says he was always better at math will form the sentences so carefully it will be impossible to tell if you are included in these plans. When he asks you if you would like to open a small guest ranch way out in the country, understand that this is a rhetorical question. Label these conversations future perfect, but don't expect the present to catch up with them. Spring is an inconceivable distance from the December days that just keep getting shorter and gray.

He'll ask you if you've ever shot anything, if you'd like to, if you ever thought about teaching your dog to retrieve. Your dog will like him too much, will drop the stick at his feet every time, will roll over and let the hunter scratch his belly.

One day he'll leave you sleeping to go split wood or get the mail and his phone will ring again. You'll sit very still while a woman who calls herself something like Janie Coyote leaves a message on his machine: She's leaving work, she'll say, and the last thing she wanted to hear was the sound of his beautiful voice. Maybe she'll talk only in rhyme. Maybe the counter will change to sixteen. You'll look a question at the mule deer on the wall, and the dark spots on either side of his mouth will tell you he shares more with this hunter than you ever will. One night, drunk, the hunter told you he was sorry for taking that deer, that every now and then there's an animal that isn't meant to be taken, and he should have known that deer was one.

Your best male friend will say, "No one who needs to call herself Janie Coyote can hold a candle to you, but why not let him sleep alone a few nights, just to make sure?"

The hunter will fill your freezer with elk burger, venison sausage, organic   10
potatoes, fresh pecans. He'll tell you to wear your seat belt, to dress warmly, to drive safely. He'll say you are always on his mind, that you're the best thing that's ever happened to him, that you make him glad that he's a man.

Tell him it don't come easy, tell him freedom's just another word for nothing left to lose.

These are the things you'll know without asking: The coyote woman wears her hair in braids. She uses words like "howdy." She's man enough to shoot a deer.

A week before Christmas you'll rent *It's a Wonderful Life* and watch it together, curled on your couch, faces touching. Then you'll bring up the word "monogamy." He'll tell you how badly he was hurt by your predecessor. He'll tell you he couldn't be happier spending every night with you. He'll say there's just a few questions he doesn't have the answers for. He'll say he's just scared and confused. Of course this isn't exactly what he means. Tell him you understand. Tell him you are scared too. Tell him to take all the time he needs. Know that you could never shoot an animal; and be glad of it.

◆ ◆ ◆

Your best female friend will say, "You didn't tell him you loved him, did you?" Don't even tell her the truth. If you do you'll have to tell her that he said this: "I feel exactly the same way."

Your best male friend will say, "Didn't you know what would happen when   15
you said the word 'commitment'?"
But that isn't the word that you said.
He'll say, "Commitment, monogamy, it all means just one thing."

The coyote woman will come from Montana with the heavier snows. The hunter will call you on the day of the solstice to say he has a friend in town and can't see you. He'll leave you hanging your Christmas lights; he'll give new meaning to the phrase "longest night of the year." The man who has said he's not so good with words will manage to say eight things about his friend without using a gender-determining pronoun. Get out of the house quickly. Call the most understanding person you know who will let you sleep in his bed.

Your best female friend will say, "So what did you think? That he was capable of living outside his gender?"

When you get home in the morning there's a candy tin on your pillow.   20
Santa, obese and grotesque, fondles two small children on the lid. The card will say something like "From your not-so-secret admirer." Open it. Examine each carefully made truffle. Feed them, one at a time, to the dog. Call the hunter's machine. Tell him you don't speak chocolate.

Your best female friend will say, "At this point, what is it about him that you could possibly find appealing?"

Your best male friend will say, "Can't you understand that this is a good sign? Can't you understand that this proves how deep he's in with you?" Hug your best male friend. Give him the truffles the dog wouldn't eat.

Of course the weather will cooperate with the coyote woman. The highways will close, she will stay another night. He'll tell her he's going to work so he can come and see you. He'll even leave her your number and write "Me at Work" on the yellow pad of paper by his phone. Although you shouldn't, you'll have to be there. It will be you and your nauseous dog and your half-trimmed tree all waiting for him like a series of questions.

This is what you learned in graduate school: In every assumption is contained the possibility of its opposite.

In your kitchen he'll hug you like you might both die there. Sniff him for   25
coyote. Don't hug him back.

He will say whatever he needs to to win. He'll say it's just an old friend. He'll say the visit was all the friend's idea. He'll say the night away from you has given him time to think about how much you mean to him. Realize that nothing short of sleeping alone will ever make him realize how much you mean to him. He'll say that if you can just be a little patient, some good will come out of this for the two of you after all. He still won't use a gender-specific pronoun.

Put your head in your hands. Think about what it means to be patient. Think about the beautiful, smart, strong, clever woman you thought he saw when he looked at you. Pull on your hair. Rock your body back and forth. Don't cry.

He'll say that after holding you it doesn't feel right holding anyone else. For "holding," substitute "fucking." Then take it as a compliment.

He will get frustrated and rise to leave. He may, or may not be bluffing. Stall for time. Ask a question he can't immediately answer. Tell him you want to make love on the floor. When he tells you your body is beautiful say, "I feel exactly the same way." Don't, under any circumstances, stand in front of the door.

Your best female friend will say, "They lie to us, they cheat on us, and we love them more for it." She'll say, "It's our fault; we raise them to be like that." 30

Tell her it can't be your fault. You've never raised anything but dogs.

The hunter will say it's late and he has to go home to sleep. He'll emphasize the last word in the sentence. Give him one kiss that he'll remember while he's fucking the coyote woman. Give him one kiss that ought to make him cry if he's capable of it, but don't notice when he does. Tell him to have a good night.

Your best male friend will say, "We all do it. We can't help it. We're self-destructive. It's the old bad-boy routine. You have a male dog, don't you?"

The next day the sun will be out and the coyote woman will leave. Think about how easy it must be for a coyote woman and a man who listens to top-forty country. The coyote woman would never use a word like "monogamy"; the coyote woman will stay gentle on his mind.

If you can, let him sleep alone for at least one night. If you can't, invite him over to finish trimming your Christmas tree. When he asks how you are, tell him you think it's a good idea to keep your sense of humor during the holidays. 35

Plan to be breezy and aloof and full of interesting anecdotes about all the other men you've ever known. Plan to be hotter than ever before in bed, and a little cold out of it. Remember that necessity is the mother of invention. Be flexible.

First, he will find the faulty bulb that's been keeping all the others from lighting. He will explain, in great detail, the most elementary electrical principles. You will take turns placing the ornaments you and other men, he and other women, have spent years carefully choosing. Under the circumstances, try to let this be a comforting thought.

He will thin the clusters of tinsel you put on the tree. He'll say something ambiguous like "Next year you should string popcorn and cranberries." Finally, his arm will stretch just high enough to place the angel on the top of the tree.

Your best female friend will say, "Why can't you ever fall in love with a man who will be your friend?"

Your best male friend will say, "You ought to know this by now: Men always   40
cheat on the best women."

This is what you learned in the pop psychology book: Love means letting go of fear.

Play Willie Nelson's "Pretty Paper." He'll ask you to dance, and before you can answer he'll be spinning you around your wood stove, he'll be humming in your ear. Before the song ends he'll be taking off your clothes, setting you lightly under the tree, hovering above you with tinsel in his hair. Through the spread of the branches the all-white lights you insisted on will shudder and blur, outlining the ornaments he brought: a pheasant, a snow goose, a deer.

The record will end. Above the crackle of the wood stove and the rasp of the hunter's breathing you'll hear one long low howl break the quiet of the frozen night: your dog, chained and lonely and cold. You'll wonder if he knows enough to stay in his doghouse. You'll wonder if he knows that the nights are getting shorter now.   [1989]

THINKING ABOUT THE TEXT

1. Describe the narrator, listing at least three adjectives. What do you think of her? On what do you base your evaluation?

2. What would you say to someone who argued that this story engages in gender stereotypes? To someone who argued that it stereotypes hunters?

3. Do you think the "you" is the narrator herself? Why or why not? At any rate, Houston could have had the narrator dispense with references to "you" and just describe her own life. What are the possible purposes and effects of having the story be in the form of instructions? In what places does the narrator predict what the "you" will do rather than telling the "you" how to act?

4. Note the word *talk* in the title. In what ways does the story emphasize talking? What amount and kind of talk do you think should occur between the couple?

5. Would you say that the story has a happy ending? Why, or why not?

MAKING COMPARISONS

1. Both Orozco and Houston use humor, but do they use it in the same way? Does each of them use it to make a serious point? Support your answers

with specific details from both texts. Would you say "A Modest Proposal" is humorous? Why, or why not?

2. Does Houston's narrator seem more focused on her own particular situation than Swift's and Orozco's narrators do? Explain.

3. Would you call all three works in this cluster ironic? Why, or why not? Identify what meanings of the term *ironic* you are applying.

WRITING ABOUT ISSUES

1. To what extent do Orozco's and Houston's stories stress gender differences? Write an essay in which you answer this question by focusing on one of the stories. Identify not only how much the story emphasizes gender differences, but also the specific distinctions it seems to make. If you wish, you may also evaluate how the story treats gender differences, but provide support for your judgment.

2. Write an essay examining the extent to which Swift's, Orozco's, and Houston's narrators are independent people. How much do they serve others? How much individuality and freedom do they assert? In your essay, focus on comparing the three narrators. Does any one of them seem more independent than the others? Support your views by referring to specific details of the texts.

3. Imitating Swift, write a piece in which you calmly propose an outrageous solution to a current social problem. Or, imitating Orozco, write a piece in which you orient someone else to a group or community you know. Or, imitating Houston, write a piece in which you explain how to talk to a kind of person familiar to you. Whichever author you imitate, stick as much as possible to observations from your own experience.

4. Write an essay evaluating a proposal actually made to a group or community. Or write an essay evaluating a manual or other document meant to orient people. In either case, your audience is whoever produced what you are evaluating. Support your evaluation with specific details.

9

Loving

Our culture makes many claims about love: Stories of the rejected lover who dies of a broken heart abound. Modern kings give up the throne, ancient cities go to war — all for love. Love is thought to be such a powerful emotion that its loss may even make one want to die, or to kill. (In some countries, finding one's wife or husband in bed with a lover is a legal excuse for murder.) Men and women seem willing to radically change their lives to be near their beloved. These are but a few examples of love's powerful influence on our behavior and our understanding of who we are.

Yet a serious discussion about the nature of love is often frustratingly difficult. We can all make a list of things we love: a cold beer in summer, a great science-fiction film, a new car, a quiet dinner with a good friend, a walk in fresh snow, a football game when our favorite team comes from behind for a dramatic victory. We love our parents, our siblings, our best friends. How can one word cover such diversity?

When we try to generalize about love, we find ourselves relying on specific incidents because giving examples is easier than giving definitions. If clarifying the essence of love seems difficult, perhaps it is because our stories, myths, and songs are filled with contradictions. Love conquers all, we say, but doesn't love fade? We profess our undying love, but divorce statistics soar. Love is complex and frustrating to pin down. Our culture even identifies different types of love: true love, platonic love, maternal love, erotic love. Yet opinions about love are strong; we all have evidence for what it is and isn't that we find persuasive.

But the evidence we find so convincing is influenced by cultural assumptions, probably more than we know. It would be naive to claim otherwise when we are bombarded with so many movies, songs, and stories about love. Indeed, some critics argue that romantic love is only a socially constructed illusion, merely an elaborate rationalization for physical desire. Once the carnal attraction fades, we get restless. At least, this is one argument, and probably not a popular one among college students in search of love. Because we know what we feel about those we love, we often grow impatient with other people's perspectives. We are likely to ignore friends who say, "He wouldn't treat you like that if he really loved you." Perhaps nothing arouses our interest more than a discussion of our hopes and dreams about love.

Our engagement with stories and poems about love is equally complex and ambivalent. Although the stories in this chapter often illuminate the sometimes dark passageways we take in our romantic journeys, there will be no consensus about the final destination. Arguing about love stories engages us as much as it may also baffle us. As you read, rely on your own experience, ethical positions, and literary judgment in determining whether specific characters are indeed in love, whether they should continue their relationship, whether they need more commitment or less. The wise and the foolish seem equally perplexed in matters of the heart.

The first cluster (this page) deals with the poetic intensity of true love from three different perspectives. The next cluster (p. 720) focuses on three stories exploring the romantic illusions of dreams. Two essays comprise the next cluster (p. 738) as Diane Ackerman and Gore Vidal write frankly about the possibilities of finding one's soul mate. Four poems on courtship follow (p. 757); we then focus on three startling love stories by Kate Chopin (p. 768). The sixth cluster (p. 781) examines the illusions of love by placing David Henry Hwang's play *M. Butterfly* in a cultural context. Questions about the nature of love concern three modern fiction writers (p. 841). The last two clusters deal with, first, Ann Sexton's and Robert Lowell's poetic takes on troubled marriages (p. 866) and then Henrik Ibsen's popular and still controversial exploration of marriage and equality, *A Doll House* (p. 870).

TRUE LOVE

WILLIAM SHAKESPEARE, "Let me not to the marriage of true minds"
ANNE BRADSTREET, "To My Dear and Loving Husband"
E. E. CUMMINGS, "somewhere i have never travelled"

Think about the term *true love*. Why *true*? Does *love* need this modification? Isn't love supposed to be true? Is there a *false* love? Or is something else implied that *love* doesn't convey by itself? Might it be something like *the one-and-only*? Some writers seem committed to the idea that true love lasts forever, for better or worse, regardless of circumstances. Is this just a fantasy, something we hope will be true? Or is it a reality, delivered to those who are lucky or who work hard to make it true? See if you agree with the three poets in this cluster.

BEFORE YOU READ

Do you believe there is one perfect person in the world for you? Is it possible to love someone forever, even if both of you change over the years from young adulthood to retirement and beyond?

WILLIAM SHAKESPEARE
Let me not to the marriage of true minds

*William Shakespeare (1564–1616) is best known to modern readers as a dramatist;
however, there is evidence that both he and his contemporaries valued his poetry
above the plays. In 1598, for example, a writer praised Shakespeare's "sugared sonnets among his private friends." As with other aspects of his life and work, questions
about how much autobiographical significance to attach to Shakespeare's subject
matter continue to arise. Regardless of the discussion, there can be no doubt that
the sonnets attributed to Shakespeare, at times directed to a man and at others
directed to a woman, address the subject of love. Sonnet 116, which was written in
1609 and proposes a "marriage of true minds," is no exception.*

Let me not to the marriage of true minds,
Admit impediments. Love is not love
Which alters when it alteration finds,
Or bends with the remover to remove:
Oh, no! it is an ever-fixèd mark,   5
That looks on tempests and is never shaken;
It is the star to every wandering bark,
Whose worth's unknown, although his height be taken.
Love's not Time's fool, though rosy lips and cheeks
Within his bending sickle's compass come;   10
Love alters not with his brief hours and weeks,
But bears it out even to the edge of doom.
If this be error and upon me proved,
I never writ, nor no man ever loved.   [1609]

THINKING ABOUT THE TEXT

1. Would you be pleased if your beloved wrote you this sonnet? Is he pro-
   fessing his love or giving a definition of true love as unchanging?

2. What if love didn't last "even to the edge of doom" (line 12)? Would it
   then be ordinary?

3. Shakespeare uses images to describe true love. Which one strikes you as
   apt? Can you suggest an image of your own?

4. The concluding couplet seems to be saying something like, "I'm
   absolutely right." Do you think Shakespeare is? Can you think of a situation in which love should bend or alter?

5. The world seems to demonstrate that true love seldom lasts forever. Why
   then do writers of all kinds profess the opposite? If you really believe that true

love does not exist, would you still marry? If your beloved asked you if your love would last forever, would you truthfully answer, "Only time will tell"?

ANNE BRADSTREET
To My Dear and Loving Husband

Anne Bradstreet (1612?–1672), one of the earliest poets in the canon of American literature, was born in England and came to the Massachusetts Bay Colony as the daughter of a governor; later she married another of the colony's governors. Her writings include an autobiographical sketch, several religious works, and a collection of wise sayings written for her son's moral education. Her poems were published during her lifetime in The Tenth Muse Lately Sprang Up in America *(London, 1650), which has the distinction of being the first book of original verse written in what would become the United States. True to her Puritan milieu, her poems have their share of piety, but they also speak of married love.*

If ever two were one, then surely we.
If ever man were loved by wife, then thee;
If ever wife was happy in a man,
Compare with me, ye women, if you can.
I prize thy love more than whole mines of gold   5
Or all the riches that the East doth hold.
My love is such that rivers cannot quench,
Nor ought but love from thee, give recompense.
Thy love is such I can no way repay,
The heavens reward thee manifold, I pray.   10
Then while we live, in love let's so persevere
That when we live no more, we may live ever.   [1678]

THINKING ABOUT THE TEXT

1. Do you believe that the speaker means what she says? Why?
2. Do you agree that the goal of true love is to be one? What does this mean? Is there a danger in such a relationship?
3. Do you like Bradstreet's rhymes? Are they sophisticated? Subtle? Simple?
4. Why might she feel she has to repay her husband's love? Is true love based on reciprocity?
5. Does Bradstreet's concluding couplet suggest a link between persevering in love on earth and living forever in heaven? Does this connection make sense to you?

MAKING COMPARISONS

1. Would Bradstreet agree with Shakespeare's sonnet?
2. Compare Shakespeare's images with Bradstreet's. Which do you find more original? More appropriate? More sincere?
3. Why are these two poets so concerned with loving "forever"?

E. E. CUMMINGS
somewhere i have never travelled

Edward Estlin Cummings (1894–1962), who for many years preferred the lower-case e. e. cummings, was a highly innovative writer, willing to experiment with language on every level. Born in Cambridge, Massachusetts, and educated at Harvard, he tried his hand at essays, plays, and other types of prose; in fact, it was a novel based on a World War I concentration camp experience in France, The Enormous Room *(1922), that first brought cummings attention. It is his poetry, however, that most readers immediately recognize for its eccentric use of typography and punctuation, its wordplay and slang usage, its jazz rhythms, and its childlike foregrounding of the concrete above the abstract. Cummings hated pretension and would only agree to deliver the prestigious Eliot lectures at Harvard in 1953 if they were called* nonlectures. *His two large volumes of* The Complete Poems 1913–1962, *published in 1972, include humor, understated satire, and celebrations of love and sex.*

somewhere i have never travelled,gladly beyond
any experience,your eyes have their silence:
in your most frail gesture are things which enclose me,
or which i cannot touch because they are too near

your slightest look easily will unclose me   5
though i have closed myself as fingers,
you open always petal by petal myself as Spring opens
(touching skilfully,mysteriously)her first rose

or if your wish be to close me,i and
my life will shut very beautifully,suddenly,   10
as when the heart of this flower imagines
the snow carefully everywhere descending;

nothing which we are to perceive in this world equals
the power of your intense fragility:whose texture
compels me with the colour of its countries,   15
rendering death and forever with each breathing

♦ ♦ ♦

(i do not know what it is about you that closes
and opens;only something in me understands
the voice of your eyes is deeper than all roses)
nobody,not even the rain,has such small hands   [1931]   20

THINKING ABOUT THE TEXT

1. In your own words, what is cummings saying about the effect love has on him? Is this hyperbolic? Why?

2. Does love open us up? In what ways? Can you give a personal example of what a strong feeling did to you?

3. Is this a poem about love or obsession or romantic infatuation? What is the difference?

4. What do you think "the power of your intense fragility" (line 14) might mean? Is this a contradiction?

5. When cummings says "something in me understands" (line 18), what might he mean? Is love located inside us somewhere? In our hearts? Our brains?

MAKING COMPARISONS

1. Is cummings's flower imagery more effective than the images that Shakespeare and Bradstreet use?

2. All the poets here use *forever*. What do they intend?

3. What do you imagine Shakespeare and Bradstreet would think about cummings's sentence structure? His images?

WRITING ABOUT ISSUES

1. Translate the cummings poem into concrete prose. Try not to use images; just explain the individual lines as simply as you can.

2. Write a comparison of the effects Bradstreet's and cummings's poems had on you.

3. Write a position paper arguing for or against the reality of true love.

4. Look at a couple of love poems written at the same time as Shakespeare's sonnet (1609). Are there similarities? Differences? Do you think Shakespeare (or any great poet) can transcend his or her attitudes toward true love? Write an essay that tries to answer this question, using the poems you found.

ROMANTIC DREAMS

LESLIE MARMON SILKO, "Yellow Woman"
JAMES JOYCE, "Araby"
JOHN UPDIKE, "A & P"

Although centuries old, the cliché that the human heart is a mystery still seems valid. We still wonder if falling in love is natural: Is love our inborn impulse to seek romance, or is it simply a physical attraction spurred on by our evolutionary need to procreate? Perhaps Western culture has socialized us to believe in the power of romantic love and the often irrational behavior that follows. Might it serve some deep psychological need to find a substitute for a beloved parent? Is it a giving emotion? A selfish one? Is it a psychological malady or the one thing worth giving everything up for? Do we need to believe in it whether or not it exists? Since we are often driven to irrational behavior, delusions, and heartbreak might we be better off without romantic love? Or might life without it be intolerably flat?

In the following cluster, three fiction writers explore the ways romantic love can sometimes cloud judgment, encouraging us to act against our best interests.

Silko shows us a woman torn between myth and reality; Joyce shows us a boy in the throes of romantic idealism; and Updike gives us a memorable picture of how an indifferent world responds to romantic gestures.

BEFORE YOU READ

Can people be truly happy without being in love? Is there one person in the world who is your true love? Or are there only certain types of people you could love? If your love didn't make you "float on a cloud," would you be disappointed? Is true love unconditional? Have you ever been fooled by romantic dreams?

LESLIE MARMON SILKO
Yellow Woman

Leslie Marmon Silko (b. 1948) is a major figure in the American Indian Renaissance. Raised in "Old Laguna" on the Pueblo Reservation near Albuquerque, New Mexico, Silko weaves the mythology of her matrilineal society into stories that move freely through what she calls an "ocean of time." The Yellow Woman *character appears frequently in Silko's writing as both a traditional figure, closely connected with nature and heterosexuality, and as a female character awakening to her cultural and sexual identity. Silko writes both poetry and fiction, often synthesizing both genres into a single text. Her novels include* Storyteller *(1981), in which "Yellow Woman" appears;* Ceremony *(1977); and* Almanac of the Dead *(1991). She teaches at the University of Arizona at Tucson.*

1

My thigh clung to his with dampness, and I watched the sun rising up through the tamaracks and willows. The small brown water birds came to the river and hopped across the mud, leaving brown scratches in the alkali-white crust. They bathed in the river silently. I could hear the water, almost at our feet where the narrow fast channel bubbled and washed green ragged moss and fern leaves. I looked at him beside me, rolled in the red blanket on the white river sand. I cleaned the sand out of the cracks between my toes, squinting because the sun was above the willow trees. I looked at him for the last time, sleeping on the white river sand.

I felt hungry and followed the river south the way we had come the afternoon before, following our footprints that were already blurred by the lizard tracks and bug trails. The horses were still lying down, and the black one whinnied when he saw me but he did not get up—maybe it was because the corral was made out of thick cedar branches and the horses had not yet felt the sun like I had. I tried to look beyond the pale red mesas to the pueblo. I knew it was there, even if I could not see it, on the sand rock hill above the river, the same river that moved past me now and had reflected the moon last night.

The horse felt warm underneath me. He shook his head and pawed the sand. The bay whinnied and leaned against the gate trying to follow, and I remembered him asleep in the red blanket beside the river. I slid off the horse and tied him close to the other horse. I walked north with the river again, and the white sand broke loose in footprints over footprints.

"Wake up."

He moved in the blanket and turned his face to me with his eyes still closed.   5
I knelt down to touch him.

"I'm leaving."

He smiled now, eyes still closed. "You are coming with me, remember?" He sat up now with his bare dark chest and belly in the sun.

"Where?"

"To my place."

"And will I come back?"   10

He pulled his pants on. I walked away from him, feeling him behind me and smelling the willows.

"Yellow Woman," he said.

I turned to face him. "Who are you?" I asked.

He laughed and knelt on the low, sandy bank, washing his face in the river. "Last night you guessed my name, and you knew why I had come."

I stared past him at the shallow moving water and tried to remember the   15
night, but I could only see the moon in the water and remember his warmth around me.

"But I only said that you were him and that I was Yellow Woman—I'm not really her—I have my own name and I come from the pueblo on the other side of the mesa. Your name is Silva and you are a stranger I met by the river yesterday afternoon."

He laughed softly. "What happened yesterday has nothing to do with what you will do today, Yellow Woman."

"I know—that's what I'm saying—the old stories about the ka'tsina spirit° and Yellow Woman can't mean us."

My old grandpa liked to tell those stories best. There is one about Badger and Coyote who went hunting and were gone all day, and when the sun was going down they found a house. There was a girl living there alone, and she had light hair and eyes and she told them that they could sleep with her. Coyote wanted to be with her all night so he sent Badger into a prairie-dog hole, telling him he thought he saw something in it. As soon as Badger crawled in, Coyote blocked up the entrance with rocks and hurried back to Yellow Woman.

"Come here," he said gently.   20

He touched my neck and I moved close to him to feel his breathing and to hear his heart. I was wondering if Yellow Woman had known who she was—if she knew that she would become part of the stories. Maybe she'd had another name that her husband and relatives called her so that only the ka'tsina from the north and the storytellers would know her as Yellow Woman. But I didn't go on; I felt him all around me, pushing me down into the white river sand.

Yellow Woman went away with the spirit from the north and lived with him and his relatives. She was gone for a long time, but then one day she came back and she brought twin boys.

"Do you know the story?"

"What story?" He smiled and pulled me close to him as he said this. I was afraid lying there on the red blanket. All I could know was the way he felt, warm, damp, his body beside me. This is the way it happens in the stories, I was thinking, with no thought beyond the moment she meets the ka'tsina spirit and they go.

"I don't have to go. What they tell in stories was real only then, back in time   25
immemorial, like they say."

He stood up and pointed at my clothes tangled in the blanket. "Let's go," he said.

I walked beside him, breathing hard because he walked fast, his hand around my wrist. I had stopped trying to pull away from him, because his hand felt cool and the sun was high, drying the river bed into alkali. I will see someone, eventually I will see someone, and then I will be certain that he is only a man— some man from nearby—and I will be sure that I am not Yellow Woman. Because she is from out of time past and I live now and I've been to school and there are highways and pickup trucks that Yellow Woman never saw.

It was an easy ride north on horseback. I watched the change from the cottonwood trees along the river to the junipers that brushed past us in the foothills, and finally there were only piñons, and when I looked up at the rim of the mountain plateau I could see pine trees growing on the edge. Once I stopped to look down, but the pale sandstone had disappeared and the river was gone and the dark lava hills were all around. He touched my hand, not speaking, but always singing softly a mountain song and looking into my eyes.

ka'tsina spirit: A mountain spirit of the Laguna Pueblo Indians.

I felt hungry and wondered what they were doing at home now—my mother, my grandmother, my husband, and the baby. Cooking breakfast, saying, "Where did she go?—maybe kidnapped," and Al going to the tribal police with the details: "She went walking along the river."

The house was made with black lava rock and red mud. It was high above the spreading miles of arroyos and long mesas. I smelled a mountain smell of pitch and buck brush. I stood there beside the black horse, looking down on the small, dim country we had passed, and I shivered.

"Yellow Woman, come inside where it's warm." 30

2

He lit a fire in the stove. It was an old stove with a round belly and an enamel coffeepot on top. There was only the stove, some faded Navajo blankets, and a bedroll and cardboard box. The floor was made of smooth adobe plaster, and there was one small window facing east. He pointed at the box.

"There's some potatoes and the frying pan." He sat on the floor with his arms around his knees pulling them close to his chest and he watched me fry the potatoes. I didn't mind him watching me because he was always watching me—he had been watching me since I came upon him sitting on the river bank trimming leaves from a willow twig with his knife. We ate from the pan and he wiped the grease from his fingers on his Levis.

"Have you brought women here before?" He smiled and kept chewing, so I said, "Do you always use the same tricks?"

"What tricks?" He looked at me like he didn't understand. 35

"The story about being a ka'tsina from the mountains. The story about Yellow Woman."

Silva was silent; his face was calm.

"I don't believe it. Those stories couldn't happen now," I said.

He shook his head and said softly, "But someday they will talk about us, and they will say, 'Those two lived long ago when things like that happened.'"

He stood up and went out. I ate the rest of the potatoes and thought about things—about the noise the stove was making and the sound of the mountain wind outside. I remembered yesterday and the day before, and then I went outside. 40

I walked past the corral to the edge where the narrow trail cut through the black rim rock. I was standing in the sky with nothing around me but the wind that came down from the blue mountain peak behind me. I could see faint mountain images in the distance miles across the vast spread of mesas and valleys and plains. I wondered who was over there to feel the mountain wind on those sheer blue edges—who walks on the pine needles in those blue mountains.

"Can you see the pueblo?" Silva was standing behind me.

I shook my head. "We're too far away."

"From here I can see the world." He stepped out on the edge. "The Navajo reservation begins over there." He pointed to the east. "The Pueblo boundaries are over here." He looked below us to the south, where the narrow trail seemed to come from. "The Texans have their ranches over there, starting with that valley, the Concho Valley. The Mexicans run some cattle over there too."

"Do you ever work for them?" 45

"I steal from them," Silva answered. The sun was dropping behind us and shadows were filling the land below. I turned away from the edge that dropped forever into the valleys below.

"I'm cold," I said; "I'm going inside." I started wondering about this man who could speak the Pueblo language so well but who lived on a mountain and rustled cattle. I decided that this man Silva must be Navajo, because Pueblo men didn't do things like that.

"You must be a Navajo."

Silva shook his head gently. "Little Yellow Woman," he said, "you never give up, do you? I have told you who I am. The Navajo people know me, too." He knelt down and unrolled the bedroll and spread the extra blankets out on a piece of canvas. The sun was down, and the only light in the house came from out-side—the dim orange light from sundown.

I stood there and waited for him to crawl under the blankets. 50

"What are you waiting for?" he said, and I lay down beside him. He undressed me slowly like the night before beside the river—kissing my face gen-tly and running his hands up and down my belly and legs. He took off my pants and then he laughed.

"Why are you laughing?"

"You are breathing so hard."

I pulled away from him and turned my back to him.

He pulled me around and pinned me down with his arms and chest. "You 55 don't understand, do you, little Yellow Woman? You will do what I want."

And again he was all around me with his skin slippery against mine, and I was afraid because I understood that his strength could hurt me. I lay underneath him and I knew that he could destroy me. But later, while he slept beside me, I touched his face and I had a feeling—the kind of feeling for him that overcame me that morning along the river. I kissed him on the forehead and he reached out for me.

When I woke up in the morning he was gone. It gave me a strange feeling because for a long time I sat there on the blankets and looked around the little house for some object of his—some proof that he had been there or maybe that he was coming back. Only the blankets and the cardboard box remained. The .30–30° that had been leaning in the corner was gone, and so was the knife I had used the night before. He was gone, and I had my chance to go now. But first I had to eat, because I knew it would be a long walk home.

I found some dried apricots in the cardboard box, and I sat down on a rock at the edge of the plateau rim. There was no wind and the sun warmed me. I was surrounded by silence. I drowsed with apricots in my mouth, and I didn't believe that there were highways or railroads or cattle to steal.

When I woke up, I stared down at my feet in the black mountain dirt. Little black ants were swarming over the pine needles around my foot. They must have

.30–30: A rifle.

smelled the apricots. I thought about my family far below me. They would be
wondering about me, because this had never happened to me before. The tribal
police would file a report. But if old Grandpa weren't dead he would tell them
what happened — he would laugh and say, "Stolen by a ka'tsina, a mountain
spirit. She'll come home — they usually do." There are enough of them to handle
things. My mother and grandmother will raise the baby like they raised me. Al
will find someone else, and they will go on like before, except that there will be a
story about the day I disappeared while I was walking along the river. Silva had
come for me; he said he had. I did not decide to go. I just went. Moonflowers
blossom in the sand hills before dawn, just as I followed him. That's what I was
thinking as I wandered along the trail through the pine trees.

It was noon when I got back. When I saw the stone house I remembered that I   60
had meant to go home. But that didn't seem important any more, maybe because
there were little blue flowers growing in the meadow behind the stone house and
the gray squirrels were playing in the pines next to the house. The horses were
standing in the corral, and there was a beef carcass hanging on the shady side of a
big pine in front of the house. Flies buzzed around the clotted blood that hung
from the carcass. Silva was washing his hands in a bucket full of water. He must
have heard me coming because he spoke to me without turning to face me.

"I've been waiting for you."

"I went walking in the big pine trees."

I looked into the bucket full of bloody water with brown-and-white animal
hairs floating in it. Silva stood there letting his hand drip, examining me intently.

"Are you coming with me?"

"Where?" I asked him.   65

"To sell the meat in Marquez."

"If you're sure it's O.K."

"I wouldn't ask you if it wasn't," he answered.

He sloshed the water around in the bucket before he dumped it out and set
the bucket upside down near the door. I followed him to the corral and watched
him saddle the horses. Even beside the horses he looked tall, and I asked him
again if he wasn't Navajo. He didn't say anything; he just shook his head and kept
cinching up the saddle.

"But Navajos are tall."   70

"Get on the horse," he said, "and let's go."

The last thing he did before we started down the steep trail was to grab the
.30–30 from the corner. He slid the rifle into the scabbard that hung from his saddle.

"Do they ever try to catch you?" I asked.

"They don't know who I am."

"Then why did you bring the rifle?"   75

"Because we are going to Marquez where the Mexicans live."

3

The trail leveled out on a narrow ridge that was steep on both sides like an
animal spine. On one side I could see where the trail went around the rocky gray

hills and disappeared into the southeast where the pale sandrock mesas stood in the distance near my home. On the other side was a trail that went west, and as I looked far into the distance I thought I saw the little town. But Silva said no, that I was looking in the wrong place, that I just thought I saw houses. After that I quit looking off into the distance; it was hot and the wildflowers were closing up their deep-yellow petals. Only the waxy cactus flowers bloomed in the bright sun, and I saw every color that a cactus blossom can be; the white ones and the red ones were still buds, but the purple and the yellow were blossoms, open full and the most beautiful of all.

Silva saw him before I did. The white man was riding a big gray horse, coming up the trail toward us. He was traveling fast and the gray horse's feet sent rocks rolling off the trail into the dry tumbleweeds. Silva motioned for me to stop and we watched the white man. He didn't see us right away, but finally his horse whinnied at our horses and he stopped. He looked at us briefly before he loped the gray horse across the three hundred yards that separated us. He stopped his horse in front of Silva, and his young fat face was shadowed by the brim of his hat. He didn't look mad, but his small, pale eyes moved from the blood-soaked gunny sacks hanging from my saddle to Silva's face and then back to my face.

"Where did you get the fresh meat?" the white man asked.

"I've been hunting," Silva said, and when he shifted his weight in the saddle the leather creaked.　　　　　　　　　　　　　　　　　　　　　　　　80

"The hell you have, Indian. You've been rustling cattle. We've been looking for the thief for a long time."

The rancher was fat, and sweat began to soak through his white cowboy shirt and the wet cloth stuck to the thick rolls of belly fat. He almost seemed to be panting from the exertion of talking, and he smelled rancid, maybe because Silva scared him.

Silva turned to me and smiled. "Go back up the mountain, Yellow Woman."

The white man got angry when he heard Silva speak in a language he couldn't understand. "Don't try anything, Indian. Just keep riding to Marquez. We'll call the state police from there."

The rancher must have been unarmed because he was very frightened and if　　85 he had a gun he would have pulled it out then. I turned my horse around and the rancher yelled, "Stop!" I looked at Silva for an instant and there was something ancient and dark — something I could feel in my stomach — in his eyes, and when I glanced at his hand I saw his finger on the trigger of the .30–30 that was still in the saddle scabbard. I slapped my horse across the flank and the sacks of raw meat swung against my knees as the horse leaped up the trail. It was hard to keep my balance, and once I thought I felt the saddle slipping backward; it was because of this that I could not look back.

I didn't stop until I reached the ridge where the trail forked. The horse was breathing deep gasps and there was a dark film of sweat on its neck. I looked down in the direction I had come from, but I couldn't see the place. I waited. The wind came up and pushed warm air past me. I looked up at the sky, pale blue and full of thin clouds and fading vapor trails left by jets.

I think four shots were fired — I remember hearing four hollow explosions that reminded me of deer hunting. There could have been more shots after that, but I couldn't have heard them because my horse was running again and the loose rocks were making too much noise as they scattered around his feet.

Horses have a hard time running downhill, but I went that way instead of uphill to the mountain because I thought it was safer. I felt better with the horse running southeast past the round gray hills that were covered with cedar trees and black lava rock. When I got to the plain in the distance I could see the dark green patches of tamaracks that grew along the river; and beyond the river I could see the beginning of the pale sandrock mesas. I stopped the horse and looked back to see if anyone was coming; then I got off the horse and turned the horse around, wondering if it would go back to its corral under the pines on the mountain. It looked back at me for a moment and then plucked a mouthful of green tumbleweeds before it trotted back up the trail with its ears pointed forward, carrying its head daintily to one side to avoid stepping on the dragging reins. When the horse disappeared over the last hill, the gunny sacks full of meat were still swinging and bouncing.

4

I walked toward the river on a wood-hauler's road that I knew would eventually lead to the paved road. I was thinking about waiting beside the road for someone to drive by, but by the time I got to the pavement I had decided it wasn't very far to walk if I followed the river back the way Silva and I had come.

The river water tasted good, and I sat in the shade under a cluster of silvery willows. I thought about Silva, and I felt sad at leaving him; still, there was something strange about him, and I tried to figure it out all the way back home.

I came back to the place on the river bank where he had been sitting the first time I saw him. The green willow leaves that he had trimmed from the branch were still lying there, wilted in the sand. I saw the leaves and I wanted to go back to him—to kiss him and to touch him—but the mountains were too far away now. And I told myself, because I believe it, he will come back sometime and be waiting again by the river.

I followed the path up from the river into the village. The sun was getting low, and I could smell supper cooking when I got to the screen door of my house. I could hear their voices inside — my mother was telling my grandmother how to fix the Jell-O and my husband, Al, was playing with the baby. I decided to tell them that some Navajo had kidnapped me, but I was sorry that old Grandpa wasn't alive to hear my story because it was the Yellow Woman stories he liked to tell best.   [1974]

90

WRITING ABOUT THE TEXT

1. Why does Yellow Woman run away with Silva? Does it have something to do with the coyote stories? What stories in your own culture have persuaded you to trust in romantic love?

2. How do myths and stories differ? Are either based on reality or fantasy? What are the social or cultural purposes of stories about love?

3. Do you trust the narrator's judgment? Sincerity? On what textual evidence are you basing this evaluation? What bearing does her cultural heritage have on your analysis of her?

4. What specific details of Silko's story do you remember? Is the narrator a careful observer? Explain. What effect does the narrator's "noticing little things" have on you as a reader?

5. Has Yellow Woman learned her lesson? Do societies change their views of romantic love? How?

JAMES JOYCE
Araby

James Joyce (1882–1941) is regarded as one of the most innovative and influential writers of the modernist movement of the early twentieth century. His use of interior monologue, wordplay, complex allusions, and other techniques variously delighted, offended, or puzzled readers. Joyce's work demanded attention and often received censorship during his lifetime. A Portrait of the Artist as a Young Man *(1916), set in Joyce's native Dublin, is largely autobiographical. Like his hero at the end of the novel, Joyce left Ireland at the age of twenty to spend the remainder of his life in Paris and other European cities. His long, complex novel* Ulysses *(1922), also set in Dublin, takes the reader through one day in the life of its protagonist and his city. In "Araby," published in* Dubliners *(1914), as in other stories in the collection, Joyce pictures the limited life of his character and leads him toward a sudden insight, or epiphany.*

North Richmond Street, being blind, was a quiet street except at the hour when the Christian Brothers' School set the boys free. An uninhabited house of two storeys stood at the blind end, detached from its neighbours in a square ground. The other houses of the street, conscious of decent lives within them, gazed at one another with brown imperturbable faces.

The former tenant of our house, a priest, had died in the back drawing-room. Air, musty from having been long enclosed, hung in all the rooms, and the waste room behind the kitchen was littered with old useless papers. Among these I found a few paper-covered books, the pages of which were curled and damp: *The Abbot*, by Walter Scott, *The Devout Communicant*, and *The Memoirs of Vidocq*. I liked the last best because its leaves were yellow. The wild garden behind the house contained a central apple-tree and a few straggling bushes under one of which I found the late tenant's rusty bicycle-pump. He had been a very charitable priest; in his will he had left all his money to institutions and the furniture of his house to his sister.

When the short days of winter came dusk fell before we had well eaten our dinners. When we met in the street the houses had grown sombre. The space of sky above us was the colour of ever-changing violet and towards it the lamps of the street lifted their feeble lanterns. The cold air stung us and we played till our bodies glowed. Our shouts echoed in the silent street. The career of our play brought us through the dark muddy lanes behind the houses where we ran the gauntlet of the rough tribes from the cottages, to the back doors of the dark dripping gardens where odours arose from the ashpits, to the dark odorous stables where a coachman smoothed and combed the horse or shook music from the buckled harness. When we returned to the street light from the kitchen windows had filled the areas. If my uncle was seen turning the corner we hid in the shadow until we had seen him safely housed. Or if Mangan's sister came out on the doorstep to call her brother in to his tea we watched her from our shadow peer up and down the street. We waited to see whether she would remain or go in and, if she remained, we left our shadow and walked up to Mangan's steps resignedly. She was waiting for us, her figure defined by the light from the half-opened door. Her brother always teased her before he obeyed and I stood by the railings looking at her. Her dress swung as she moved her body and the soft rope of her hair tossed from side to side.

Every morning I lay on the floor in the front parlour watching her door. The blind was pulled down to within an inch of the sash so that I could not be seen. When she came out on the doorstep my heart leaped. I ran to the hall, seized my books, and followed her. I kept her brown figure always in my eye and, when we came near the point at which our ways diverged, I quickened my pace and passed her. This happened morning after morning. I had never spoken to her, except for a few casual words, and yet her name was like a summons to all my foolish blood.

Her image accompanied me even in places the most hostile to romance. On   5 Saturday evenings when my aunt went marketing I had to go to carry some of the parcels. We walked through the flaring streets, jostled by drunken men and bargaining women, amid the curses of labourers, the shrill litanies of shop-boys who stood on guard by the barrel of pigs' cheeks, the nasal chanting of street-singers, who sang a *come-all-you* about O'Donovan Rossa,° or a ballad about the troubles in our native land. These noises converged in a single sensation of life for me: I imagined that I bore my chalice safely through a throng of foes. Her name sprang to my lips at moments in strange prayers and praises which I myself did not understand. My eyes were often full of tears (I could not tell why) and at times a flood from my heart seemed to pour itself out into my bosom. I thought little of the future. I did not know whether I would ever speak to her or not or, if I spoke to her, how I could tell her of my confused adoration. But my body was like a harp and her words and gestures were like fingers running upon the wires.

One evening I went into the back drawing-room in which the priest had died. It was a dark rainy evening and there was no sound in the house. Through one of the broken panes I heard the rain impinge upon the earth, the fine incessant needles of water playing in the sodden beds. Some distant lamp or lighted window gleamed below me. I was thankful that I could see so little. All my senses seemed to desire to veil themselves and, feeling that I was about to slip from them, I pressed the palms of my hands together until they trembled, murmuring: "O love! O love!" many times.

O'Donovan Rossa: Jeremiah O'Donovan (1831–1915) was nicknamed "Dynamite Rossa" for advocating violent means to achieve Irish independence.

At last she spoke to me. When she addressed the first words to me I was so confused that I did not know what to answer. She asked me was I going to *Araby*. I forgot whether I answered yes or no. It would be a splendid bazaar, she said she would love to go.

"And why can't you?" I asked.

While she spoke she turned a silver bracelet round and round her wrist. She could not go, she said, because there would be a retreat that week in her convent. Her brother and two other boys were fighting for their caps and I was alone at the railings. She held one of the spikes, bowing her head towards me. The light from the lamp opposite our door caught the white curve of her neck, lit up her hair that rested there and, falling, lit up the hand upon the railing. It fell over one side of her dress and caught the white border of a petticoat, just visible as she stood at ease.

"It's well for you," she said.

"If I go," I said, "I will bring you something."

What innumerable follies laid waste my waking and sleeping thoughts after that evening! I wished to annihilate the tedious intervening days. I chafed against the work of school. At night in my bedroom and by day in the classroom her image came between me and the page I strove to read. The syllables of the word *Araby* were called to me through the silence in which my soul luxuriated and cast an Eastern enchantment over me. I asked for leave to go to the bazaar on Saturday night. My aunt was surprised and hoped it was not some Freemason affair. I answered few questions in class. I watched my master's face pass from amiability to sternness; he hoped I was not beginning to idle. I could not call my wandering thoughts together. I had hardly any patience with the serious work of life which, now that it stood between me and my desire, seemed to me child's play, ugly monotonous child's play.

On Saturday morning I reminded my uncle that I wished to go to the bazaar in the evening. He was fussing at the hallstand, looking for the hat-brush, and answered me curtly:

"Yes, boy, I know."

As he was in the hall I could not go into the front parlour and lie at the window. I left the house in bad humour and walked slowly towards the school. The air was pitilessly raw and already my heart misgave me.

When I came home to dinner my uncle had not yet been home. Still it was early. I sat staring at the clock for some time and, when its ticking began to irritate me, I left the room. I mounted the staircase and gained the upper part of the house. The high cold empty gloomy rooms liberated me and I went from room to room singing. From the front window I saw my companions playing below in the street. Their cries reached me weakened and indistinct and, leaning my forehead against the cool glass, I looked over at the dark house where she lived. I may have stood there for an hour, seeing nothing but the brown-clad figure cast by my imagination, touched discreetly by the lamplight at the curved neck, at the hand upon the railings and at the border below the dress.

When I came downstairs again I found Mrs. Mercer sitting at the fire. She was an old garrulous woman, a pawnbroker's widow, who collected used stamps for some pious purpose. I had to endure the gossip of the tea-table. The meal was prolonged beyond an hour and still my uncle did not come. Mrs. Mercer stood up to go: she was sorry she couldn't wait any longer, but it was after eight o'clock and she did not like to be out late, as the night air was bad for her. When she had gone I began to walk up and down the room, clenching my fists. My aunt said:

"I'm afraid you may put off your bazaar for this night of Our Lord."

At nine o'clock I heard my uncle's latchkey in the halldoor. I heard him talking to himself and heard the hallstand rocking when it had received the weight of his overcoat. I could interpret these signs. When he was midway through his dinner I asked him to give me the money to go to the bazaar. He had forgotten.

"The people are in bed and after their first sleep now," he said.   20

I did not smile. My aunt said to him energetically:

"Can't you give him the money and let him go? You've kept him late enough as it is."

My uncle said he was very sorry he had forgotten. He said he believed in the old saying: "All work and no play makes Jack a dull boy." He asked me where I was going and, when I had told him a second time he asked me did I know *The Arab's Farewell to his Steed*. When I left the kitchen he was about to recite the opening lines of the piece to my aunt.

I held a florin° tightly in my hand as I strode down Buckingham Street towards the station. The sight of the streets thronged with buyers and glaring with gas recalled to me the purpose of my journey. I took my seat in a third-class carriage of a deserted train. After an intolerable delay the train moved out of the station slowly. It crept onward among ruinous houses and over the twinkling river. At Westland Row Station a crowd of people pressed to the carriage doors; but the porters moved them back, saying that it was a special train for the bazaar. I remained alone in the bare carriage. In a few minutes the train drew up beside an improvised wooden platform. I passed out on to the road and saw by the lighted dial of a clock that it was ten minutes to ten. In front of me was a large building which displayed the magical name.

I could not find any sixpenny entrance and, fearing that the bazaar would   25
be closed, I passed in quickly through a turnstile, handing a shilling to a weary-looking man. I found myself in a big hall girdled at half its height by a gallery. Nearly all the stalls were closed and the greater part of the hall was in darkness. I recognised a silence like that which pervades a church after a service. I walked into the centre of the bazaar timidly. A few people were gathered about the stalls which were still open. Before a curtain, over which the words *Café Chantant* were written in coloured lamps, two men were counting money on a salver. I listened to the fall of the coins.

Remembering with difficulty why I had come I went over to one of the stalls and examined porcelain vases and flowered tea-sets. At the door of the stall a young lady was talking and laughing with two young gentlemen. I remarked their English accents and listened vaguely to their conversation.

florin: A silver coin worth two shillings.

"O, I never said such a thing!"

"O, but you did!"

"O, but I didn't!"

"Didn't she say that?"   30

"Yes. I heard her."

"O, there's a . . . fib!"

Observing me the young lady came over and asked me did I wish to buy anything. The tone of her voice was not encouraging; she seemed to have spoken to
me out of a sense of duty. I looked humbly at the great jars that stood like eastern
guards at either side of the dark entrance to the stall and murmured:

"No, thank you."

The young lady changed the position of one of the vases and went back to   35
the two young men. They began to talk of the same subject. Once or twice the
young lady glanced at me over her shoulder.

I lingered before her stall, though I knew my stay was useless, to make my
interest in her wares seem the more real. Then I turned away slowly and walked
down the middle of the bazaar. I allowed the two pennies to fall against the six-
pence in my pocket. I heard a voice call from one end of the gallery that the light
was out. The upper part of the hall was now completely dark.

Gazing up into the darkness I saw myself as a creature driven and derided by
vanity; and my eyes burned with anguish and anger.   [1914]

THINKING ABOUT THE TEXT

1. Why do the boy's eyes burn with anguish and anger? Has he learned
   something about romantic love? Was he in love with Mangan's sister?
   Give evidence.

2. If this story is partly autobiographical, what is Joyce's attitude toward this
   younger self? Are you sympathetic or critical of your own initiations into
   the complexities of relationships?

3. Reread the first and last paragraph. In what ways might they be connected?

4. Find examples of religious imagery. What do you think is its purpose?

5. Do you think the boy's quest has symbolic meaning? Do you think cultures can also search for something?

MAKING COMPARISONS

1. Compare the growth of the boy with the wife in "Yellow Woman."

2. Make explicit the insight or epiphany the boy comes to at the end. What
   would be a comparable epiphany for the wife in "Yellow Woman"?

3. Is one ending more realistic than the other? Explain.

JOHN UPDIKE
A & P

John Updike was born in 1932 in Shillington, Pennsylvania, an only child of a father who taught high-school algebra and a mother who wrote short stories and novels. After graduating from Harvard, Updike studied art in England and later joined the staff of The New Yorker. *In 1959 he published his first novel,* The Poorhouse Fair, *and moved to Massachusetts where he still lives. His many novels of contemporary American life are notable for their lyrical and accurate depiction of the details and concerns of modern America.* Rabbit Run *(1960) and the sequels* Rabbit Redux *(1971),* Rabbit Is Rich *(1981), and* Rabbit at Rest *(1990) are considered important and insightful records of American life. "A & P" comes from Updike's* Pigeon Feathers and Other Stories *(1962).*

In walks these three girls in nothing but bathing suits. I'm in the third checkout slot, with my back to the door, so I don't see them until they're over by the bread. The one that caught my eye first was the one in the plaid green two-piece. She was a chunky kid, with a good tan and a sweet broad soft-looking can with those two crescents of white just under it, where the sun never seems to hit, at the top of the backs of her legs. I stood there with my hand on a box of HiHo crackers trying to remember if I rang it up or not. I ring it up again and the customer starts giving me hell. She's one of these cash-register-watchers, a witch about fifty with rouge on her cheekbones and no eyebrows, and I know it made her day to trip me up. She'd been watching cash registers for fifty years and probably never seen a mistake before.

By the time I got her feathers smoothed and her goodies into a bag—she gives me a little snort in passing, if she'd been born at the right time they would have burned her over in Salem—by the time I get her on her way the girls had circled around the bread and were coming back, without a pushcart, back my way along the counters, in the aisle between the checkouts and the Special bins. They didn't even have shoes on. There was this chunky one, with the two-piece—it was bright green and the seams on the bra were still sharp and her belly was still pretty pale so I guessed she just got it (the suit) — there was this one, with one of those chubby berry-faces, the lips all bunched together under her nose, this one, and a tall one, with black hair that hadn't quite frizzed right, and one of these sunburns right across under the eyes, and a chin that was too long— you know, the kind of girl other girls think is very "striking" and "attractive" but never quite makes it, as they very well know, which is why they like her so much—and then the third one, that wasn't quite so tall. She was the queen. She kind of led them, the other two peeking around and making their shoulders round. She didn't look around, not this queen, she just walked straight on slowly, on these long white prima-donna legs. She came down a little hard on her heels, as if she didn't walk in her bare feet that much, putting down her heels and then letting the weight move along to her toes as if she was testing the floor with every step, putting a little deliberate extra action into it. You never know for sure how girls' minds work (do you really think it's a mind in there or just a little buzz like a bee in a glass jar?) but you got the idea she had talked the other two into coming in here with her, and now she was showing them how to do it, walk slow and hold yourself straight.

She had on a kind of dirty-pink — beige maybe, I don't know — bathing suit with a little nubble all over it, and what got me, the straps were down. They were off her shoulders looped loose around the cool tops of her arms, and I guess as a result the suit had slipped a little on her, so all around the top of the cloth there was this shining rim. If it hadn't been there you wouldn't have known there could have been anything whiter than those shoulders. With the straps pushed off, there was nothing between the top of the suit and the top of her head except just *her*, this clean bare plane of the top of her chest down from the shoulder bones like a dented sheet of metal tilted in the light. I mean, it was more than pretty.

She had sort of oaky hair that the sun and salt had bleached, done up in a bun that was unravelling, and a kind of prim face. Walking into the A & P with your straps down, I suppose it's the only kind of face you *can* have. She held her head so high her neck, coming up out of those white shoulders, looked kind of stretched, but I didn't mind. The longer her neck was, the more of her there was.

She must have felt in the corner of her eye me and over my shoulder Stoke-   5
sie in the second slot watching, but she didn't tip. Not this queen. She kept her eyes moving across the racks, and stopped, and turned so slow it made my stomach rub the inside of my apron, and buzzed to the other two, who kind of huddled against her for relief, and then they all three of them went up the cat-and-dog-food-breakfast-cereal-macaroni-rice-raisins-seasonings-spreads-spaghetti-soft-drinks-crackers-and-cookies aisle. From the third slot I look straight up this aisle to the meat counter, and I watched them all the way. The fat one with the tan sort of fumbled with the cookies, but on second thought she put the package back. The sheep pushing their carts down the aisle — the girls were walking against the usual traffic (not that we have one-way signs or anything) — were pretty hilarious. You could see them, when Queenie's white shoulders dawned on them, kind of jerk, or hop, or hiccup, but their eyes snapped back to their own baskets and on they pushed. I bet you could set off dynamite in an A & P and the people would by and large keep reaching and checking oatmeal off their lists and muttering "Let me see, there was a third thing, began with A, asparagus, no, ah, yes, applesauce!" or whatever it is they do mutter. But there was no doubt, this jiggled them. A few houseslaves in pin curlers even looked around after pushing their carts past to make sure what they had seen was correct.

You know, it's one thing to have a girl in a bathing suit down on the beach, where what with the glare nobody can look at each other much anyway, and another thing in the cool of the A & P, under the fluorescent lights, against all those stacked packages, with her feet paddling along naked over our checkboard green-and-cream rubber-tile floor.

"Oh Daddy," Stokesie said beside me. "I feel so faint."

"Darling," I said. "Hold me tight." Stokesie's married, with two babies chalked up on his fuselage already, but as far as I can tell that's the only difference. He's twenty-two, and I was nineteen this April.

"Is it done?" he asks, the responsible married man finding his voice. I forgot to say he thinks he's going to be manager some sunny day, maybe in 1990 when it's called the Great Alexandrov and Petrooshki Tea Company or something.

What he meant was, our town is five miles from a beach, with a big summer   10
colony out on the Point, but we're right in the middle of town, and the women generally put on a shirt or shorts or something before they get out of the car into the street. And anyway these are usually women with six children and varicose veins mapping their legs and nobody, including them, could care less. As I say, we're right in the middle of town, and if you stand at our front doors you can see two banks and the Congregational church and the newspaper store and three real-estate offices and about twenty-seven old freeloaders tearing up Central Street because the sewer broke again. It's not as if we're on the Cape; we're north of Boston and there's people in this town haven't seen the ocean for twenty years.

The girls had reached the meat counter and were asking McMahon something. He pointed, they pointed, and they shuffled out of sight behind a pyramid of Diet Delight peaches. All that was left for us to see was old McMahon patting his mouth and looking after them sizing up their joints. Poor kids, I began to feel sorry for them, they couldn't help it.

Now here comes the sad part of the story, at least my family says it's sad, but I don't think it's so sad myself. The store's pretty empty, it being Thursday afternoon, so there was nothing much to do except lean on the register and wait for the girls to show up again. The whole store was like a pinball machine and I didn't know which tunnel they'd come out of. After a while they come around out of the far aisle, around the light bulbs, records at discount of the Caribbean Six or Tony Martin Sings or some such gunk you wonder they waste the wax on, sixpacks of candy bars, and plastic toys done up in cellophane that fall apart when a kid looks at them anyway. Around they come, Queenie still leading the way, and holding a little gray jar in her hand. Slots Three through Seven are unmanned and I could see her wondering between Stokes and me, but Stokesie with his usual luck draws an old party in baggy gray pants who stumbles up with four giant cans of pineapple juice (what do these bums *do* with all that pineapple juice? I've often asked myself) so the girls come to me. Queenie puts down the jar and I take it into my fingers icy cold. Kingfish Fancy Herring Snacks in Pure Sour Cream: 49¢. Now her hands are empty, not a ring or a bracelet, bare as God made them, and I wonder where the money's coming from. Still with that prim look she lifts a folded dollar bill out of the hollow at the center of her nubbled pink top. The jar went heavy in my hand. Really, I thought that was so cute.

Then everybody's luck begins to run out. Lengel comes in from haggling with a truck full of cabbages on the lot and is about to scuttle into that door marked MANAGER behind which he hides all day when the girls touch his eye. Lengel's pretty dreary, teaches Sunday school and the rest, but he doesn't miss that much. He comes over and says, "Girls, this isn't the beach."

Queenie blushes, though maybe it's just a brush of sunburn I was noticing for the first time, now that she was so close. "My mother asked me to pick up a jar of herring snacks." Her voice kind of startled me, the way voices do when you see the people first, coming out so flat and dumb yet kind of tony, too, the way it ticked over "pick up" and "snacks." All of a sudden I slid right down her voice into her living room. Her father and the other men were standing around in ice-cream coats and bow ties and the women were in sandals picking up herring snacks on toothpicks off a big glass plate and they were all holding drinks the color of water with olives and sprigs of mint in them. When my parents have somebody over they get lemonade and if it's a real racy affair Schlitz in tall glasses with "They'll Do It Every Time" cartoons stencilled on.

"That's all right," Lengel said. "But this isn't the beach." His repeating this struck me as funny, as if it had just occurred to him, and he had been thinking all these years the A & P was a great big sand dune and he was the head lifeguard. He didn't like my smiling—as I say he doesn't miss much—but he concentrates on giving the girls that sad Sunday-school–superintendent stare.   15

Queenie's blush is no sunburn now, and the plump one in plaid, that I liked better from the back—a really sweet can—pipes up, "We weren't doing any shopping. We just came in for the one thing."

"That makes no difference," Lengel tells her, and I could see from the way his eyes went that he hadn't noticed she was wearing a two-piece before. "We want you decently dressed when you come in here."

"We *are* decent," Queenie says suddenly, her lower lip pushing, getting sore now that she remembers her place, a place from which the crowd that runs the A & P must look pretty crummy. Fancy Herring Snacks flashed in her very blue eyes.

"Girls, I don't want to argue with you. After this come in here with your shoulders covered. It's our policy." He turns his back. That's policy for you. Policy is what the kingpins want. What the others want is juvenile delinquency.

All this while, the customers had been showing up with their carts but, you know, sheep, seeing a scene, they had all bunched up on Stokesie, who shook open a paper bag as gently as peeling a peach, not wanting to miss a word. I could feel in the silence everybody getting nervous, most of all Lengel, who asks me, "Sammy, have you rung up their purchase?"   20

I thought and said "No" but it wasn't about that I was thinking. I go through the punches, 4, 9, GROC, TOT — it's more complicated than you think, and after you do it often enough, it begins to make a little song, that you hear words to, in my case "Hello (*bing*) there, you (*gung*) hap-py *pee*-pul (*splat*)!"—the *splat* being the drawer flying out. I uncrease the bill, tenderly as you may imagine, it just having come from between the two smoothest scoops of vanilla I had ever known were there, and pass a half and a penny into her narrow pink palm, and nestle the herrings in a bag and twist its neck and hand it over, all the time thinking.

The girls, and who'd blame them, are in a hurry to get out, so I say "I quit" to Lengel enough for them to hear, hoping they'll stop and watch me, their unsuspected hero. They keep right on going, into the electric eye; the door flies open and they flicker across the lot to their car, Queenie and Plaid and Big Tall Goony-Goony (not that as raw material she was so bad), leaving me with Lengel and a kink in his eyebrow.

"Did you say something, Sammy?"

"I said I quit."

"I thought you did."

"You didn't have to embarrass them."

"It was they who were embarrassing us."

I started to say something that came out "Fiddle-de-doo." It's a saying of my grandmother's, and I know she would have been pleased.

"I don't think you know what you're saying," Lengel said.

"I know you don't," I said. "But I do." I pull the bow at the back of my apron and start shrugging it off my shoulders. A couple customers that had been heading for my slot begin to knock against each other, like scared pigs in a chute.

Lengel sighs and begins to look very patient and old and gray. He's been a friend of my parents for years. "Sammy, you don't want to do this to your Mom and Dad," he tells me. It's true, I don't. But it seems to me that once you begin a gesture it's fatal not to go through with it. I fold the apron, "Sammy" stitched in red on the pocket, and put it on the counter, and drop the bow tie on top of it. The bow tie is theirs, if you've ever wondered. "You'll feel this for the rest of your life," Lengel says, and I know that's true, too, but remembering how he made that pretty girl blush makes me so scrunchy inside I punch the No Sale tab and the machine whirs "pee-pul" and the drawer splats out. One advantage to this scene taking place in summer, I can follow this up with a clean exit, there's no fumbling around getting your coat and galoshes, I just saunter into the electric eye in my white shirt that my mother ironed the night before, and the door heaves itself open, and outside the sunshine is skating around on the asphalt.

I look around for my girls, but they're gone, of course. There wasn't anybody but some young married screaming with her children about some candy they didn't get by the door of a powder-blue Falcon station wagon. Looking back in the big windows, over the bags of peat moss and aluminum lawn furniture stacked on the pavement, I could see Lengel in my place in the slot, checking the sheep through. His face was dark gray and his back stiff, as if he'd just had an injection of iron, and my stomach kind of fell as I felt how hard the world was going to be to me hereafter.   [1961]

THINKING ABOUT THE TEXT

1. Why do you think Sammy quits? Make a list of several plausible answers.

2. What would you do if you were in Sammy's position? What would your priorities be in this situation?

3. When Sammy hears Queenie's voice, he imagines an elegant cocktail party that he contrasts to his parents' "real racy affair" with lemonade and beer. What does this scene say about Sammy's attitude toward the girls? Toward his own social status?

4. Some critics have objected to Sammy's comment in the last sentence of paragraph 2 about "girls' minds." Is this a sexist observation? Does the time frame of the story figure in your opinion? Should it?

5. Comment on the last paragraph. What is the significance of the young couple? Why does Sammy mention "sheep"? Why does Sammy think the world will be hard on him? What does "hard" mean? Do you agree?

MAKING COMPARISONS

1. Are the three main characters here wiser at each story's end? Are they happier?

2. Which character's views about romance are most compatible with yours when you were, say, thirteen? With yours presently?

3. Compare the last paragraph of "Araby" and "A & P." What attitudes do they express?

WRITING ABOUT ISSUES

1. Choose either Yellow Woman, the boy in "Araby," or Sammy and argue that this character was or was not really in love. Support your argument with references to the text and your own cultural experience.

2. Write an essay that defends or denies the idea that romantic love is irrational. Use two of the stories.

3. Would any of the characters in this cluster have been comfortable in the cultural context you were raised in? (Consider movies, books, TV, family narratives, and so forth in analyzing your culture.) Write a brief analysis of how well one or more of these characters would "fit in."

4. Look up information about Native American culture and the coyote stories referred to in "Yellow Woman." Do they help to explain her attitudes? Do the same for the culture of Joyce's Ireland, especially religion and romance. How about the 1950s in middle America? In a brief essay argue that each story is understood more fully when the cultural context is filled out.

COMPLETING THE SELF THROUGH LOVE

DIANE ACKERMAN, "Plato: The Perfect Union"
GORE VIDAL, "The Desire and the Successful Pursuit of the Whole"

Sometimes when you meet someone and fall in love, you feel like you have known your beloved for a long time. The intellectual, emotional, and physical connections are so comfortable and authentic. You seem so compatible and seem to fit together so effortlessly that it feels almost mystical. Being in love is such a heady experience that few of those afflicted sit down to analyze the phenomenon. But some philosophers have. Several thousand years ago, Plato (c. 428–348 B.C.E.) wondered about the complexities of love. He wrote the *Symposium*, a version of drama called a *dialogue*, in which his mentor, Socrates, argues with various other philosophers. Socrates usually gets the best lines, and many critics think Plato's own thoughts are quite similar to those of Socrates. In the *Symposium*, Plato has Aristophanes tell an amazing story about the origins of the familiar, "I found my one true love." Diane Ackerman's essay explains the tale and gives some interesting explanations. Gore Vidal's essay recounts his one brief, teenage encounter with his other half, Jimmie Trimble, who was killed on Iwo Jima during World War II.

BEFORE YOU READ

Are some couples lucky in love and others not so? Do you think literature or science can offer us a better understanding of love? Do you think gay men and women experience love differently than straight men and women?

DIANE ACKERMAN

Plato: The Perfect Union

Diane Ackerman was born in 1948 in Waukegan, Illinois. She graduated from Pennsylvania State University and later received an M.F.A. and a Ph.D. from Cornell University. Ackerman has received the Academy of American Poets' Lavan Award as well as grants from the National Endowment for the Arts and the Rockefeller Foundation. Critics praised her book A Natural History of the Senses *(1990) for being wide-ranging, informed, and charming. Her latest poetry collection is* Jaguar of Sweet Laughter: New and Selected Poems *(1991).* A Natural History of Love *(1994), from which the following essay is taken, is her most recent nonfiction book. She has taught at Columbia University and Cornell and is currently a staff writer for* The New Yorker.

Proust's *Remembrance of Things Past* begins with a child waiting in bed for his mother to come and give him a good-night kiss. Sensitive and lonely, he grows anxious and unhinged, and the rest of the novel (more the mosaic of a life than a work of fiction) chronicles his attempts to bridge the gap between himself and the rest of humanity. He could not feel more separate, isolated, and alone. The passage shows the eternal quest of the child, who must learn to be separate from his mother even while he longs to reunite with her. One of the keystones of romantic love — and also of the ecstatic religion practiced by mystics — is the powerful desire to become one with the beloved.

This vision of love has its wellsprings in ancient Greek thought. To Plato, lovers are incomplete halves of a single puzzle, searching for each other in order to become whole. They are a strength forged by two weaknesses. At some point, all lovers wish to lose themselves, to merge, to become one entity. By giving up their autonomy, they find their true selves. In a world ruled by myth, Plato tried to be rational, often using myths as allegories to make a point. His investigations of love in the *Symposium* are the oldest surviving attempts to systematically understand love. In the *Symposium*, he advises people to bridle their sexual urges, and also their need to give and receive love. They should concentrate all that energy on higher goals. He understood perfectly well that people would have to struggle hard to redirect such powerful instincts; it would produce much inner warfare. When, almost 3,000 years later, Freud talks of the same struggle, using words like "sublimation" and "resistance," he is harking back to Plato, for whom love was a great predicament and a riddle. This was no doubt in part because Plato was confused about his own sexual identity; as a younger man, he wrote in praise of homosexual love, and as an older man he condemned it as an unnatural crime.

At the *Symposium*'s banquet staged in honor of Eros, Socrates — who was a teacher and companion of Plato — and his friends exchange ideas about love. Actually, Socrates' job is to poke holes in everyone else's ideas. The banqueters are not present just to praise love, but to fathom it, to dive through its waves and plumb its depths. One of their first home truths is that love is a universal human need. Not just a mythic god, or a whim, or madness, but something integral to each person's life. When it is Aristophanes' turn, he relates a fable — one that has influenced people for thousands of years since. He explains that originally there were three sexes: men, women, and a hermaphroditic combination of man and woman. These primitive beings had two heads, two arms, two sets of genitals, and so on. Threatened by their potential power, Zeus divided each one of them in half, making individual lesbians, homosexual men, and heterosexuals. But each person longed for its missing half, which it sought out, tracked down, and embraced, so that it could become one again — and thereby Aristophanes arrives at an astonishing definition of love:

> Each of us when separated, having one side only, like a flat fish, is but the indenture of a man, and he is always looking for his other half. . . . And when one of them meets with his other half, the actual half of himself, whether he be a lover of youth or a lover of another sort, the pair are lost in an amazement of love and friendship and intimacy, and will not be out of the other's sight, as I may say, even for a moment: these are the people who pass their whole lives together; yet they could not explain what they desire of one another. For the intense yearning which each of them has towards the other does not appear to be the desire of lover's intercourse, but of something else which the soul of either evidently desires and cannot tell, and of which she has only a dark and doubtful presentiment. Suppose Hephaestus,° with his instruments, were to come to the pair who are lying side by side and say to them, "What do you people want of one another?" They would be unable to explain. And suppose further, that when he saw their perplexity he said, "Do you desire to be wholly one; always day and night to

Hephaestus: Greek god of fire (also called Vulcan).

be in one another's company, for if this is what you desire, I am ready to melt you into one and let you grow together . . ." There is not a man of them who when he heard the proposal would deny or would acknowledge that this meeting and melting into one another, this becoming one instead of two, was the very expression of his ancient need. And the reason is that human nature was originally one and we were a whole, and the desire and pursuit of the whole is called love.

It is an amazing fable, saying, in effect, that each person has an ideal love waiting somewhere to be found. Not "There's a lid for every pot," as my mother has sometimes said, but that each of us has a one-and-only, and finding that person makes us whole. This romantic ideal of the perfect partner was invented by Plato. It appealed so strongly to hearts and minds that people believed it in all the following centuries, and many still believe it today. As Freud discovered, Plato took his fable from India, where some gods were bisexual. Indeed, the original human in the Upanishads° is as lonely as Adam in the Bible, and like Adam he asks for company and is pleased when a female is made from his own body. In each case, all the people of the earth are born from their union. Evolutionary biologists tell us that our ultimate ancestor almost certainly was hermaphroditic, and something about that news feels right, not just in our reason but in the part of us that yearns for the other. John Donne° wrote magnificently about this passion for oneness, which takes on a special piquancy in his poem "The Flea." One day, sweetly loitering with his mistress, he notices a flea sucking a little blood from her arm and then from his. Joyously, he observes that their blood is married inside the flea.

Why should the idea of oneness be so compelling? Love changes all the   5
physics in the known universe of one's emotions, and redraws the boundaries between what is real and what is possible. Children often believe in magic and miracles, and when they grow up they naturally believe in the miraculous power of love. Sometimes this is depicted in myths or legends by having the lovers drink a love potion, as Tristan and Isolde° do; be stung by Cupid's arrows; be enchanted by music as Eurydice° is; or receive a reviving kiss à la Sleeping Beauty.

In many eastern and western religions, the supplicants strive for a sense of unity with God. Although this is not supposed to be an erotic coupling, saints often describe it as if it were, dwelling in orgasmic detail on the sensuality of Christ's body. Religious ecstasy and the ecstasy of lovers have much in common — the sudden awareness, the taking of vows, the plighting of troths, the all-consuming fire in the heart and flesh, the rituals leading to bliss, and, for some Christians, a cannibalistic union with the godhead by symbolically drinking his blood and eating his flesh. Whether we fall in love with a human demigod or with a deity, we feel that they can return us to a primordial state of oneness, that then our inner electric can run its full circuit, that we can at last be whole.

Upanishads: Texts from circa 900 B.C.E. that form the basis of Hindu religion.
John Donne: British poet (1572–1631).
Tristan and Isolde: German opera (1865) by Richard Wagner celebrating romantic love.
Eurydice: In Greek mythology Orpheus tries in vain to rescue his wife, Eurydice, from Hades.

How bizarre it is to wish to blend blood and bones with someone. People cannot actually literally become one, of course; it's a physical impossibility. The idea is preposterous. We are separate organisms. Unless we are Siamese twins, we are not merged with another. Why should we feel incomplete, anyway? Why believe that uniting our body and thoughts and fate with another person's will cure our sense of loneliness? Wouldn't it make more sense to believe that when love brings two people together they are a community of two, not a compound of one? The idea of merging is so irrational, so contrary to common sense and observation, that its roots must strike deep into our psyche. Because a child is born of a mother, and lives as a separate entity, we think of the child as an individual. But in biological terms that is not precisely true. The child is an organic part of the mother that is expelled at birth, but it shares much of her biology, personality, even scent. The only and absolute perfect union of two is when a baby hangs suspended in its mother's womb, like a tiny madman in a padded cell, attached to her, feeling her blood and hormones and moods play through its body, feeling her feelings. After that perfect, pendent, dependent union, birth is an amputation, and the child like a limb looking to attach itself to the rest of its body. I am not saying this consciously occurs to anyone, but that it may explain the osmotic yearning we all feel, at one time or another, to blend our heart and body and fluids with someone else's. Only the thinnest rind of skin stands between us, only events slender as neurons. Only the fermenting mash of personality keeps us from crossing the boundary that organisms cherish to become one appetite, one struggle, one destiny. Then, when we finally reach that pinnacle, we feel more than whole: we feel limitless.   [1994]

THINKING ABOUT THE TEXT

1. Do you think Ackerman is making a claim about true love or the about the desire for wholeness? What support does she provide? Is there an opposition? Does she give it?

2. Ackerman suggests that the desire for wholeness is fairly common. Have you felt something similar to an "osmotic yearning" (para. 7)? Is it primarily physical or spiritual?

3. Ackerman begins with an anecdote from Marcel Proust's *Remembrance of Things Past*, which seems to describe something different from romantic love. Does she justify opening in this way?

4. Many of the essay's examples are from literature. Should Ackerman have given more factual examples? Should she have consulted scientists? Sociologists? Psychologists?

5. At the end, Ackerman suggests that the pinnacle can be, and is, reached. Do you agree? How can we account for so many failed relationships then? Should we keep trying to find our perfect mate no matter how disenchanted we are?

GORE VIDAL

The Desire and the Successful
Pursuit of the Whole

*Gore Vidal was born in 1925 at the U.S. military academy, West Point, into a thor-
oughly political family. As a boy he read to his blind grandfather, Senator T. P.
Gore. His father was an administrator for Franklin D. Roosevelt. His first novel,
Williwaw, was published in 1946 while he was in the army. Vidal's reputation was
assured with* Julian *(1964),* Washington, D.C. *(1967), and* Myra Breckinridge
(1968). His collection, United States: Essays 1952–1992 *won the National Book
Award. Vidal lives in Los Angeles and Ravello, Italy. The essay reprinted here
appeared in his 1995 book* Palimpsest.

Recently, I lectured at Harvard on how we are shaped by the movies we see
while growing up. In preparation for the lectures, I watched *The Prince and the
Pauper* for the first time since 1937. Like most of the movies that impress themselves on a child, the story is simple, but the subtexts are disturbingly complex if
one is the right age to be affected by them. The prince and the pauper were
played by Bobby and Billy Mauch, identical twins who were the same age as I—
twelve. So there was I, in surrogate, on the screen not once but twice, not only
prince but pauper, and the two of them—of us?—were so alike as to be interchangeable as well.

I do not know if a desire to be a twin is a common one or if such a longing
might run in families, psychically as well as genetically. My grandmother Gore
lost *her* twin at birth, and it required no uncanny knowledge of the human heart
for the family to figure out that when she took over the task of being not only wife
but eyes to a blind husband, she had found in him her long-lost twin. On the
other hand, I was quite pleased to be an only child. Later, I acquired various step-
and half brothers and sisters, but I never really knew any of them, since I was
gone for good at seventeen—into the army and to all those other worlds elsewhere.

When I watched *The Prince and the Pauper* the first time, I wanted to be not
one but two. Lonely children often have imaginary playmates, but I was never
lonely—I was solitary, and wanted no company at all other than books and
movies, and my own imagination.

A childhood desire to be a twin does not seem to me to be narcissistic in the
vulgar Freudian sense. After all, one is oneself; and the other, other. It is the sort
of likeness that makes for wholeness, and is it not that search for likeness, that
desire and pursuit of the whole—as Plato has Aristophanes remark—that is the
basis of all love? As no one has ever actually found perfect wholeness in another
human being, no matter of what sex, the twin is the closest that one can ever
come toward human wholeness with another; and—dare one invoke biology and
the origin of our species?—back of us mammals doomed to die once we have

procreated, there is always our sexless ancestor the amoeba, which never dies as it does not reproduce sexually but merely—serenely—breaks in two and identically replicates.

Anyway, I thought Billy and Bobby Mauch were cute as a pair of bug's ears, and I wished I were either one of them—one of them, mind you. I certainly did not want to be two of *me*, as one seemed more than enough to go around even in so exaggerated a family. Yet doubleness has always fascinated me, as mirrors do, as filmed images do. I have read that a recurring theme in my work is doubleness or duplicity. If this is the case, I see now where it might have—unconsciously, at least—begun.

In any case, it was after I saw the film that I saw my other half in Jimmie Trimble. It was thought best by Nina° that I board during the week at St. Albans, an all-boys' school near Washington's cathedral. I was allowed to come "home" on weekends. At midterm, Jimmie became a boarder. We were friends immediately. I was one week older than he. We were the same height and weight. He had pale blue eyes; mine were pale brown. He had the hunter-athlete's farsightedness; I had the writer-reader's myopic vision. I was blond, with straight hair. He was blond, with curly hair. His sweat smelled of honey, like that of Alexander the Great. At seventeen, when he graduated from St. Albans (I was doing the same at Exeter), he was offered contracts to play professional baseball with both the New York Giants and the Washington Senators; each club would have sent him to college and kept him out of the war. Loyal to his native city, he chose the Senators.

I had lunch with Jimmie's mother in Washington not long ago, our first meeting in fifty-five years. At ninety, Ruth Trimble Sewell is like a woman of fifty; she is alert, straight-backed, with blue eyes like Jimmie's, only just beginning to fade. Over lunch, we brought him back to life, briefly, each for his own purpose. She had been disturbed by the revelation in a magazine that the "JT" to whom I had dedicated *The City and the Pillar* (about one boy's love for another) was Jimmie Trimble; and the journalist made it as clear as he could, with no corroboration from me, that we had been schoolboy lovers. Of Jimmie's death at nineteen, on Iwo Jima, the journalist quoted me as saying, "He was the unfinished business of my life." A response as cryptic as it was accurate.

"Kind friends"—Mrs. Sewell emphasized the adjective in her Washington-Kentucky accent—"wrote me from all over to say how upset I must be. Perhaps I overreacted." She had given Jimmie's letters to a master at St. Albans, who was aware of my interest in . . . what? bringing him to life again? in order to . . . again, what? Discover who he was? As if I hadn't once known him as well as I knew myself. But since we had been separated by geography the last years of his short life, I suppose that I wanted—now—to fill in the details. "I shall but love thee better after death," as Mrs. Browning so stonily put it.

"Yes, perhaps I overreacted." She ordered a single vodka martini. She had been born in Washington, a belle of the town, one year older than my mother, whom she remembered. "So good-looking," she said tactfully.

Nina: Vidal's mother.

Ruth told me of Jimmie's first report home after a weekend in the great house   10
in Virginia where I was prince, he pauper. Of course, we were interchangeable, as
I was not really prince but only living for a time as princes do. Upon my mother's
divorce from Hughdie,° when I was sixteen, I, too, became pauper.

I had a very nice dog, Jimmie had reported, a toy Scottie named Wiggles. But
my mother would not let the dog in the house, so while I was away during the week
at boarding school, a thirty-minute drive from Merrywood, Wiggles was exiled to a
fenced-in area beside the garage, itself set over a squash court, where Hughdie
never played but Jimmie and I used to roller-skate, ruining the wood floor.

The dog was one of a thousand sore points between Nina and me. My father
had brought me the puppy, a present from Liz Whitney, whose numerous dogs
roamed her eighteenth-century Virginia house, Llangollen. Litters were constantly being produced beneath Chippendale consoles and allowed to grow up
on the spot. I often wished that Liz were my mother.

Nina promptly took the dog and said that Liz had given it to her. This was
followed by a flaming row of the sort that punctuated her life with me and,
indeed, with anyone that she knew well. In later, more reflective years, she
blamed her behavior on an agonizing menopause. But as of 1935 she was all set
to have two more children—ladled into her by silver spoon? — so she was also
obliged to note, for those who might be counting, that her periods had also been
more excruciating than those of any other woman in medical history.

At the beginning, Wiggles had slept in Nina's Art Deco bedroom. A fashionable word in those days was *neurasthenic,* which could mean practically anything. In Nina's case, it meant fearful hangovers combined with a morphine
habit. Once or twice a week one Dr. Huffman, wearing a Prince Albert,° would
arrive to administer a shot; then, if the company was not too grand, he would be
asked for lunch. "I am *upper*-middle-class," the drunken Auden° kept repeating at
our last meeting, "my father was a *doctor.*" To which I finally replied, "Well, he
would never have made the grade in my day, in my city." But with or without the
humble Dr. Huffman's drugs, the sound of the dog's claws at night on the bedroom floor gave Nina the jitters and so Wiggles was banished from the house.

On those weekends that I was allowed to come home—usually when Mr.   15
and Mrs. Auchincloss were on safari in Hobe Sound or places even more dangerous and farther to the south—Jimmie and I would join Wiggles in the enclosure
and tell her how sorry we were about her exile. Jimmie's mother had been much
struck by details of life in the great house: "'They also have silk sheets,' Jimmie
said to me, 'and the butler asks you at night what you want for breakfast!'" Mrs.
Sewell was beginning to remember a lot. So was—am—I.

I tried to recall, as I looked into what proved to be Jimmie's eyes across the
table from me, what it was that we had talked about when alone together. He was
an athlete; I played nothing except erratic tennis. I read everything that I could;
he read as little as possible. But I am intrigued by a letter he wrote his mother

Hughdie: Vidal's stepfather, Hugh D. Auchincloss.
Prince Albert: Queen Victoria's consort (husband).
W. H. Auden: British poet (1907–1973).

from Guam, in the South Pacific. Would she send him Whitman's *Leaves of Grass*? This set off a tremor. He and I had certainly lived out the Calamus idyll.° Now someone — a lover? — had suggested that he read Whitman. Is this to be a mystery story? Who was he, after all? Will I ever know now?

I remember him mostly in flashes. I'd go with him to hear Benny Goodman at the Capitol Theater. He loved jazz, swing; played saxophone. I liked "classical" music; played nothing. What we had entirely in common, aside from each other, was the fact that each was already what he would be when grown-up. He was professional athlete; I was writer. That was that. Neither was uncertain about what to do in the future because each was already doing it. This completeness set us off from our contemporaries. As a result, neither was much of a success as a schoolboy. Little of what we were offered in class was of the slightest use to either him or to me. I wanted to know far more history and literature than any school would ever have taught, while all he needed was a playing field to dominate. So, haphazardly, I educated myself, all the while resentful of the dullness and irrelevance of the classroom. Since learning then was mostly by rote, I developed a block against memorizing so great that now, when I occasionally act in films, dialogue must be glued to the backs of chairs or written on cards held out of camera range. Today, schools — for the rich, that is, there is nothing much for the rest — know better *how* to teach; their only problem is *what* to teach.

The differences between Jimmie and me were sometimes polar. I detested my mother; he adored his. I said as much to Mrs. Sewell. She smiled. "I remember when he was first brought to me, at the hospital. I had so much wanted a brunette, and there he was, all blond already. I must admit I was a little disappointed, to have two blonds, Jimmie and his sister." The smile vanished. "Tell me, did he ever talk to you about his father?"

I said that I couldn't remember. I had always assumed that his father was dead. I did know that there was a stepfather whom he disliked. She frowned. "Well, *he* and I were not married long. Then I married Mr. Sewell, and we lived happily ever after until last year, when he died. So you see," she said with no dramatic emphasis, "I am bereft."

I had been in her apartment earlier that morning. Over the mantel was a painting of Jimmie made in 1937. He is holding a model sailboat. Though he smiled a lot in life, in almost all his pictures he looks grave, eyes usually turned from painter or camera lens. I have a life-size reproduction of the painting on the wall beside my bed. Jimmie is looking to his right, to the west, to the approaching end, I morbidly think. Jimmie used to be excused from class so that he could go sit for his portrait. He was also excused, from time to time, for surgical enlargement of his urethra. I never knew what this condition was called medically, and I was not about to mention it to Mrs. Sewell. Jimmie said that it was a remarkably painful, slow business.

Mrs. Sewell described his first serious girlfriend, "She was absolutely beautiful, but she wasn't really. . . . Well, once I asked her to help with the punch bowl, to fill cups, you know? and she refused. She was . . ." But the word *common* did

20

Calamus idyll: A romantic, carefree episode. Calamus is a section of *Leaves of Grass*.

not pass her lips because, "I always tried to love anyone he loved. Then he met Chris White that last year and wanted to marry her."

"You mean Chris White the actress?"

She was surprised. "You know who she is? Yes, she *was* an actress on television, a long time ago. In the fifties, Chris White was a successful television actress who almost invariably got the parts that my friend Joanne Woodward wanted. When Joanne received the Academy Award, I wired her, "Where is Chris White tonight?" So here was Chris White yet again: Jimmie's final love except, perhaps, for whoever it was who got him to read Whitman.

"When they sent me Jimmie's footlocker, I burned all the letters to him from girls — hers too." But Chris, a Washington girl, continued to see Mrs. Sewell after the war. Then, some years ago, she dropped from view.

Mrs. Sewell laughed. "I remember Jimmie asked me, once, 'Did you ever tell a man that he was *beautiful?*'" Jimmie had been shocked at such a word applied to himself by a girl. But then, in those days before Tennessee Williams and Marlon Brando, males were taught to think of themselves as coarse and brutish Calibans, on a lower level of evolution than the fragile Ariels of the other sex.   25

Jimmie overflowed with animal energy, not to mention magnetism for both sexes. Even so, at twelve or thirteen, I was delighted to be able to report to him that I had had sex — if that is quite the phrase — with a girl before Jimmie did. He was riveted; wanted details. The event had taken place in the game room at Merrywood, an airless chamber in the cellar where game was hung and aged — game never shot by Hughdie, but often sent him by friends. I was showing a girl that I'd known for some time this scary room — scary because on the inside of the heavy metal door there was a rusty round knob that one had to push in order to open the door; if it failed to work, you would suffocate, unheard by anyone, since the room was soundproofed. On the floor, the girl and I fumbled about, and I was almost as interested in what I was going to tell Jimmie about the great mystery that I had at last — barely — penetrated as I was in the earthshaking event itself.

Rousseau° thought that Montaigne° should have told us more about his sex life. I think Montaigne told quite enough. But then I have never had much interest in the sexual lives of real people. I suspect that I was the only boy of that era to have read Frank Harris,° skipping the sex parts in order to get to the political and literary anecdotes. I do like pornography, but only when it is clearly fiction.

Mrs. Sewell picked at her elaborate lobster dish. The dining room at Willards, as we used to call the hotel, was half full. The hotel is not very like the original Willards, where Lincoln stayed; it was entirely rebuilt at the beginning of the century and, lately, rather well redone. I am at home with the result. Across Pennsylvania Avenue from the hotel is the Commerce Department, and from the windows of my room I can look into what had been my father's second-floor office when he was director of air commerce — a corner office at the west end of

---

Rousseau: French philosopher (1712–1778) who emphasized man's natural goodness.
Montaigne: French essayist (1533–1592).
Frank Harris: Controversial Irish writer (1856–1931), author of a sexually explicit memoir, *My Life and Loves* (1922–27).

the building, with windows shaded by a row of pillars set in a ledge, already darkened, even then, by the excrement of those multitudinous pigeons who were —
and are — almost as numerous as civil servants in our now imperial capital city.
Together, from the ledge, we watched Roosevelt's second inaugural parade, in
which Gene° took no part, since he was resigning his post.

"Before my children were born, I took a course in nutrition. I always made
the bread, and just about everything else, from scratch."

"Did they like it?"   30

"I never gave them any choice." She was serene. I wondered if her diet
explained Jimmie's odorless sweat. Anaïs Nin also prided herself on having no
odor, as I have just read in her latest posthumously published journal, *Incest.* I
remember otherwise. Yet too little is made of the importance of human odor
when it comes to sexual attraction. But then — is it the smell of a particular person whom we already like that attracts us? Or does a liking for a certain smell
draw us, bee to flower's pistil, to its owner?

Mrs. Sewell was a strong character. When the war turned bad for us, Jimmie
had wanted to enlist in the marines. He was seventeen, an age when one needed
parental consent. I got mine readily, but Ruth had refused to give hers and so he
had stayed at Duke University on a scholarship paid for by the Washington Senators. But then, when he came of age at eighteen, he enlisted. The last letters that
he wrote to her are more those of husband to wife than son to mother. I had also
not realized how much of an artist an athlete is until I read, again and
again, about "my arm," the pitcher's arm which he guarded with the same single-
mindedness that a dancer does his legs. Toward the end, he knows that he is not
going to survive and he tells her what to do about insurance and his effects, and
Chris. He is plainly in a rage at being killed before he could have his life.

"I think I'd like to make a little book about Jimmie, photographs, letters,
what people remember . . ."

Mrs. Sewell was on her guard, as well she should be after that magazine article. I told her of a similar book about Hobe Baker, a Princeton athlete much
admired by Scott Fitzgerald's generation. "Of course," she said, "I wouldn't want
anything said about his father and *his* problems." Jimmie's father had left Washington under a series of clouds. He was thought to be dead until he did indeed
die, years later, in California. I said that I had no interest in the father; after all,
the subject never came up between Jimmie and me. But then he was a boy who
could keep secrets, as I was about to learn.

I assured her that the book would be largely based on his letters to her.   35
Copies of several of them had been shown me by the master at St. Albans, who,
that morning, before my lunch with Mrs. Sewell, had also given me a tour of the
school. The gray Gothic-style stone of the original buildings still harmonizes
agreeably with the now-finished cathedral on its hill, separated from the school
by a green herb garden and tall trees. The Lower School dormitory of my day,
with its flimsy partitions and linoleum floor, has been replaced by a row of small
cell-like rooms. So all of our ghosts are gone. I did push open the swinging door

Gene: Vidal's father.

to the shower room to find that our communal Spartan shower was now modestly compartmentalized.

Boarders in the Lower School were divided between the aristocrats, who had pubic hair, and the plebes, who did not. I was part of the aristocracy. When Jimmie arrived, at midterm, he was much discussed. Did he or didn't he have pubic hair? He went for a shower, and I joined him: aristocratic, with bright gold curls. As I looked at him, he gave me a big grin and so it began, likeness drawn to likeness, soon to be made whole by desire minus the obligatory pursuit.

When I came to read the *Symposium*, I was amazed at how precisely Plato had anticipated two boys twenty-three hundred years later. The classical scholar M. I. Finley once told me that it was not he but one of his students who first noticed that Plato never speaks in his own voice at that famous dinner party; rather, he gives to others viewpoints that he may or may not have shared. So it is Aristophanes — not Plato — who explains to his dinner companions the nature of sexual desire.

To begin with, there were three sexes, each shaped like a globe — male, female, hermaphrodite. The three globes behaved offensively to the king of the gods, who chose to discipline them by slicing each in half. "Just as you or I might chop up sour apples for pickling," remarks Aristophanes, "or slice an egg with a hair." Apollo was then called in to tidy up the six creatures that had once been three. "Now when the work of bisection was complete it left each half with a desperate yearning for the other, and they ran together and flung their arms around each other's necks, and asked for nothing better than to be rolled into one."

This explains, according to Aristophanes, how the male half of the hermaphrodite is attracted to his female half, while the half of the woman sphere is drawn to woman and man to man. "And so when this boy-lover — or any lover, for that matter — is fortunate enough to meet his other half, they are both so intoxicated with affection, with friendship, and with love that they cannot bear to let each other out of sight for a single instant . . . although they may be hard put to say what they really want with one another, and indeed the purely sexual pleasure of their friendship could hardly account for the huge delight they take in one another's company. The fact is that both their souls are longing for something else — a something to which they can neither of them put a name. . . . And so all this to-do is a relic of that original state of ours, when we were whole . . ."

Parenthetically, I have just been reading Kenneth Dover's wonderfully self-confident memoirs. The author of *Greek Homosexuality* asks, "Why did Plato make Aristophanes the mouthpiece of the 'other half' doctrine? My own answer was (and is) that Plato recognizes it as a vulgar, uneducated idea, and therefore appropriate to a writer of comedies which are undeniably vulgar and populist." Dover then celebrates "those of us who are happily married . . ." One is pleased, of course, for the Dovers; even so, there are other equally successful unions. But I am hardly disinterested as I, too, have written vulgar and populist comedies.

I cannot think just how or why my coming together with Jimmie happened to take place on the white tile floor of the bathroom at Merrywood. I suppose that the butler was on the prowl at the time. But there we were, belly to belly, in the act of becoming one. As it turned out, Jimmie had been involved with another boy, while

40

I, despite wet dreams, had never even masturbated. As it was, mutual masturbation was impossible with Jimmie—too painful for me because his large callused hands gripped a cock like a baseball bat. So we simply came together, reconstituting the original male that Zeus had split in two. Yet "sexual pleasure could hardly account for the huge delight we took in one another's company." There was no guilt, no sense of taboo. But then we were in Arcadia, not diabolic Eden.

Suddenly, Mrs. Sewell turned to me. "I want to ask you a question," she said: our roles reversed. "What did Jimmie tell you about his step-father?"

"He said he didn't get on with him, and that was why he moved into the dormitory." Jimmie had not said much more than that. "I suppose they disliked each other."

"No, my husband didn't dislike Jimmie. I'm afraid he liked him altogether too much."

I could not believe what she was telling me. "He was German. A fine decora-   45
tor, a great horseman. Master of the Warrenton Hunt. A popular man, but he wanted to adopt Jimmie, and change his name, which I couldn't allow—I mean, the Trimbles would have been horrified. Jimmie was James Trimble the *third*." Then she looked very grim. "One day I found a letter written to my husband from a man who was . . . like *him*, in *green* ink," she added, the smoking gun, as it were, "and that was the end for me. We were divorced. Funny, I've only told two other people this story, the real story."

So Jimmie had become a boarder in order to escape from his stepfather. I am still startled by all the implications. Had anything happened between them? If so, what? As I replay the ancient tapes of memory, I begin to see the story from quite a new angle. I had always thought that I had been the seducer, as I was to prove to be for the rest of my life, and so it had never occurred to me that it might have been the other way around. Like me, Jimmie would have found repellent the idea of a sexual act with a grown man. But with another boy, an equal other half, it is the most natural business there is. Yet if *he* had made the first move . . .

If it were possible, I would like to reedit all the tapes, but they are now so fragile with age that they would probably turn to dust, as Jimmie has, in a box at Rock Creek Cemetery near the statue of the mysterious veiled youth that Henry Adams commissioned Saint-Gaudens to make as a memorial to his wife, Clover, and to—who knows what else?

Now there is a second startling mystery, along with the first one that I found in his letters to his mother.

I move to safer ground. "Did Jimmie go to Mrs. Shippen's?"

Ruth laughed. "Well, I used to aim him there, but I can't say if he ever   50
arrived. He thought the girls were a bit on the plain side." The upper-class youth of small-town Washington were sent to one of two dancing classes, Mrs. Shippen's or Miss Hawkes's. Boys and girls were taught not only to dance but to deport themselves in such a way that in due course they would either marry someone from the dancing class or someone very like someone from the dancing class, and settle down to a decorous life.

The last time I saw Jimmie was at one of these dances, held at the Sulgrave Club during the Christmas holiday of 1942, a year after the Japanese had attacked us at Pearl Harbor. I had not seen Jimmie since the fall of 1939, when I had been shipped off to the Los Alamos Ranch School in New Mexico, where one lived the vigorous life, much of it on horseback; the next year I moved on to Exeter. Nina wanted to keep me as far away from her field of operations as possible, and for once, we were in accord. The deterioration of her marriage with Hughdie was disagreeable for everyone.

Since Gene had remarried by then and moved to New York, I saw him only in the summers and so, as always, it was the Gores in Rock Creek Park who represented home during my exile, a life at whose emotional center was not my family but Jimmie; yet we never wrote each other. Of course, boys don't write boys, more or less on manly principle; even so, since I thought so much about him, I am surprised that I was so unenterprising. We had last seen each other as fourteen-year-old boys. Now we were seventeen-year-old men. Would we take up where we had left off in the spring of 1939, on a May day, in the woods above the Potomac River?

We met awkwardly in the ballroom. We wore "tuxedos"; girls wore long dresses. An orchestra played such novelties as "The Lambeth Walk" and "The Big Apple." Also slow fox-trots. "Night and Day." I could only turn right.

Now I erase a bit of Jimmie as Rosalind appears, demanding, if not equal, fair time. I had brought Rosalind to the dance. She was tall and dark and exuberant. We had known each other all our lives. We had been "a couple" for several years. We were used to each other in a low-key, comfortable way. Then the war came and everything changed. The desultory boy-girl relationship of our old life suddenly became urgent: The boy might soon be killed. We experienced what so many did in our time and place. We decided to get married between my graduation from Exeter in June and my enlistment in the army in July (a special army program for high school graduates was the army's siren song). Our announcement galvanized my usually casual family. My grandfather, Senator Gore ("I *never* give advice"), was suddenly Polonius; he also changed his usual line from "Never have children, only grandchildren" to "Be *not* fruitful, do *not* multiply." Certainly, his son and daughter had always been annoying to him and of little consequence to anyone else, while I, who read to him gladly, had been a treasure. But treasure no longer, since I seemed to be following both son and daughter into premature marriage, to be followed by certain failure in life's great adventure. Nina was concerned about the alcoholism in Rosalind's family.

Even my amiably offhand father came down to Washington to ask a significant question: "How much do you think you'll need to live on?" I said about five hundred dollars a month. Gene wondered where this would come from; an army private makes considerably less. I already knew that there would be nothing from my family, ever. It was a close contest who was meaner, T. P. Gore or Gene Vidal, two self-made men who had no intention of contributing one penny to the making of any other man, beyond the grim obligation to pay for a son's Education.

Education was the key to everything, as my uneducated mother knew when she approached Mr. True, head of the Lower School at St. Albans. My grades must improve "because," she said, "he is living in the lap of luxury now, but he's

55

never going to inherit anything! And he doesn't understand the *value of money* [a favorite refrain]." Mr. True said that my grades would probably improve if I could be persuaded to do more homework. She confessed defeat: "He locks himself in his room," she said sadly, "and *writes.*"

As it turned out, I did not go to college after the war, while my income during my first year of civilian life was about five hundred dollars a month. I could very easily have married and, conforming to every last one of the rules of the game, followed my grandfather into the Senate. Happily, life was to be more interesting than that. Unhappily, Rosalind, whom I did not marry, became an alcoholic—not on my account. Happily, in later life, Rosalind pulled herself together to become a commercial artist in London, where she had an affair with Churchill's attorney-general, John Foster, a large bearlike man of marvelous wit. I last saw the two of them in 1970 at the airport in Katmandu, where, on the tarmac, John gave a superb imitation of the judge in the Margaret Argyle divorce case. This featured a compromising Polaroid of the duchess sucking the cock of a man whose head is not visible in the Polaroid and whose pubic hair was not straight like the duke's (the valet's solemn testimony) but curly like—like an adulterer's.

"You are a jeweler, sir, by trade," said the judge. "I pray you, sir, note the ring on the hand that is holding the penis. Disregard the penis. Disregard the hand. Disregard the headless man. Concentrate your attention, sir, solely upon the ring. Is that your handiwork?"

But all this was far in the future that evening when I told Jimmie that I was going to marry Rosalind after I graduated from Exeter. "You're crazy," he said.

We went downstairs to the men's room with its tall marble urinals and large cubicles. I wondered what, if anything, he felt. After all, men are not boys. Fortunately, our bodies still fitted perfectly together, as we promptly discovered inside one of the cubicles, standing up, belly to belly, talking of girls and marriage and coming simultaneously.

Thus, we were whole for what proved to be the last time for the two of us—and for me, if not for him, for good. I not only never again encountered the other half, but by the time I was twenty-five, I had given up all pursuit, settling for a thousand brief anonymous adhesions, as Walt Whitman would put it, where wholeness *seems*, for an instant, to be achieved. Quite enough, I think, if the real thing has happened. At least, in Platonic terms, I had completed myself once. Jack Kennedy—a half of the hermaphrodite rather than the male—by his own admission never came close. I am lucky. He was not.

Why did Jimmie ask his mother to send him Whitman? Why am I jealous of a ghost—*two* ghosts? Did he find a lover in the marines, someone of a literary nature, who wanted him to read . . . I "knew too well the sick, sick dread lest the one he lov'd might secretly be indifferent to him . . ." So Whitman now resounds in these late, late reveries.

Two vivid images of Jimmie. One came back to me while I was smoking ganja in Katmandu, not an easy thing for a nonsmoker to do. But as I gasped my way into a sort of trance, Jimmie materialized beside me on the bed. He wore blue pajamas. He was asleep. He was completely present, as he had been in the bedroom at Merrywood. I tickled his foot. The callused sole was like sandpaper. It was a shock to touch him again. The simulacrum opened its blue eyes and smiled and yawned and put his hand alongside my neck; he was, for an instant, real in a hotel room in Katmandu. But only for an instant. Then he rejoined Achilles and all the other shadowy dead in war.

My second memory: I am lying on top of him, after sex, eyes shut; then I open them and see his eyes staring up into mine. The expression is like that of his sad-looking photographs rather than of the actual smiling boy whom I recall, or think that I do. In his last photographs, the marine private of nineteen looks to be a powerfully built man of thirty, in a rage because he knows that what's next is nothing.

After our final encounter at the Sulgrave, I knew that we would go on together until our business had finished itself in a natural way. I certainly never wanted to grow old with him. I just wanted to grow up with him. Each would marry in time; find wholeness elsewhere, if lucky. And so we went back to the dance upstairs, he as happy as I at being, if only briefly, rejoined.

In the light of all this it is puzzling to me now that I did not write him after he finally joined the marines in 1944, the worst year of the war. Of course, I was already in the army, and concerned with my own fate. So I left Jimmie to time and chance, as I left everything else. But then I hadn't much choice, while, a year later, he had none at all. I was stoic since, forever after, I was to be the surviving half of what had once been whole.

I realize that according to the School of Vienna (the Riding School), I should have become a lifelong pederast. But that did not happen. Naturally, like most men, I am attracted to adolescent males — this is, by the way, one of the best kept secrets of the male lodge, revealed in a study called *The Boys of Boise*, where most of the male establishment of that heartland Idaho city (each a *mature* married man) were revealed to be lovers of the high school football team. But I did not go prowling for fourteen-year-old athletes. After all, if the ideal is the other self, then that self would have had to age along with me, and attraction would have become affection, and lust would have then been diverted to . . . chance encounters or the other sex.

Montaigne is sharp about the Greek arrangement of young warrior and pubescent squire, the latter not enjoying — or supposed to enjoy — what the lustful other does with him. Although this relationship might produce excellent soldiers, it was not and could not be, in Montaigne's eyes, true love because man and boy were not equals and the relationship was grounded solely upon the passion of the older and more experienced male for the beauty of the younger. Only in equality can there be love, as Montaigne had uniquely experienced with his friend La Boétie's mind and character if not body. Montaigne thought that if a woman could ever be a man's equal in mind and education, then that relationship might be best of all, but since Montaigne is mildly misogynistic, he gives no examples.

Jimmie Trimble had applied for the navy V-12 program, where high school graduates of seventeen and eighteen were trained to be naval officers in Stateside universities. As of June 1943, I was in the army's equivalent, the Army Specialized Training Program at the Virginia Military Institute, to be trained as an engineer, for which I had no aptitude. After three months, I flunked out, more or less

65

deliberately, thus saving my life because, with the army's usual brutish haste and ill faith, the program was suddenly dissolved and my inadequately trained class-mates were shipped off to Europe as front-line infantrymen. Many were killed in the last German counteroffensive, the so-called Battle of the Bulge. But by then I was first mate of an army freight-supply ship in the Aleutians, more in danger of being killed by my own inadequacies as a navigator in the world's worst sea than from enemy fire. At least, unlike Jack Kennedy, I didn't get run over by a Japanese destroyer, the trick of the week, I always thought, though the latest biography makes more sense than usual of the harebrained fleet of PT boats to which the ailing Jack had been assigned, a thousand miles to the south of me.

Jimmie, according to a survivor from his unit, failed his physical for V-12, which seems impossible for a professional athlete. Yet, I now learn, he was indeed sickly, prey to a chronic form of pneumonia. But he had no problem in getting accepted, as cannon fodder, by the marines in January of 1944; his basic training was at Camp Lejeune; then, in August 1944, he became a member of a scout and observer group of the Third Marine Division in the South Pacific. He saw action until the end of October, when Guam was secured. 70

From October to February he seems to have had a quiet time on Guam. For one month he was again a baseball player, helping the division team win the local championship. On February 4, he played his last game for the division. He reports to his mother that he has sprained his ankle; meanwhile, "everything is once again wonderful with Chris and me." He remarks that his mother is a "worse procrastinator than I ever was" — she has not sent him a long-promised picture of herself, so "how about sending one while there is still a tomorrow?" He recalls the Sunday picnics that they used to have in the Virginia mountains. "I'll never forgive myself for refusing to follow your advice to stay in college. After the war we won't receive any credit for having been out here . . . Mom, please don't get the blues over what I am going to say, but some insurance should be taken just in case. Mom, you know if anything happens to me you are to have all I pos-sess but I would like to ask one favor. You know the gold ring with the diamonds set halfway around? Well, Mom, if (it won't) anything does happen, would you give it to Chris for me? Kind of a memorial the other way around." Finally, "Well, Mom, I'll write again in a couple of days . . . All my love to the swellest Mom in all the world. Your devoted son, Jimmie."

This letter could have been written in the Civil War. The tone is also that of Andy Hardy in an MGM movie, but there were once real boys like that, before the great sullenness spread over the land.

February 25, 1945, Jimmie arrived at Iwo Jima in what turned out to be one of the bloodiest engagements of the war. Twenty thousand Japanese were killed; 6,821 American troops were killed, mostly teenage marines. Jimmie was in the 4th Platoon, a member of what was called the Reconnaissance Company. A sur-vivor of the platoon recalls, "I was with the first observation team that went up there; we stayed three days, then they relieved us; I saw him [Jimmie] when they relieved us, and that was the last time. They relocated their position forward; lost contact with them. In the early morning hours."

There were eight men in Jimmie's squadron as of the night of February 28.

They were arranged, as far as I can tell from a news story, two to a foxhole "on a slope overlooking our infantry front line and the enemy's concrete placements beyond. As dawn broke at 4:45, March 1, 1945, all hell broke loose upon them. A Jap raiding party had infiltrated the front lines and attacked their post." Six of the eight were killed: "one . . . was dead in his foxhole. He had been bayoneted in his sleep. Another had been killed by a grenade, and a third by rifle fire. One burned poncho was found in the foxhole shared by the two missing men. . . . Sixty-three Jap bodies sprawled in the observation post's little battleground."

Jimmie was the scout who had been killed by a grenade. Another marine who was there bears witness: "We were all real proud of Jim Trimble, and everybody else was. He was a joy to be around. He had a good personality. He was always joking. I know he wanted to go back and go to school and play professional baseball. He was just a joy to be around. I remember that he went into the ship's store — because it was cold up in Iwo. Everybody thinks of it as the Pacific, but it was their winter up there, and it was only 700 miles from Tokyo. Jim went in and bought a black Navy watch sweater. He was the only guy that kept warm, before this happened. But then, you know, I'll never forget the way the grenade hit him in the back, and that sweater was just all wrapped up inside of him.

"You know, in circumstances like that, you're probably closer to those guys than you are your own brothers. Of course, for me now, we're talking about 50 years. You kind of forget. Like I said, the wars all kind of blend into each other.

"He was tall, blond curly hair. But I'll tell you, he was heavy, carrying back. I though I'd die. At that age, you know, I was 18, and I weighed about 145. He had to weigh 160. He felt like 2,000 pounds by the time I got back to the foxhole."

When the commanding general heard of Jimmie's death, he was, according to a witness, "moist-eyed" for one boy lost in all that carnage. The Third Division named its baseball field on Guam Trimble Field. That was that. End of Jimmie. Since then, "the wars all kind of blend into each other."

In the summer of 1945, I left Birmingham General Hospital, at Van Nuys, California, on leave to see my father in New York. I had acquired rheumatoid arthritis as a result of a modest freezing (hypothermia) in the Bering Sea; one knee was partly locked and the fingers of my left hand were like thumbs — yes, everything is a bit worse now. When I went before the hospital board, I was told that I could get a disability pension for life, but that would mean two years more of service. If I chose to forgo the pension, I would be let out in less than a year. The European war was over; the Japanese war nearly so. I let the pension go.

En route to New York, I stopped off in Jackson, Michigan, to see my father's sister. We were standing in a sunny garden when we were joined by a boy I had been at school with — which school? Even then Nina's educational enthusiasms had begun to blur: Potomac, Sidwell Friends, Landon, St. Albans, Los Alamos, Exeter. But since the boy spoke of Washington, it must have been one of the local schools — "You know," he said, "Jimmie Trimble's dead." By this time, I had pretty much distanced myself from these stark announcements. I think my first reaction must have been somewhat like that when I heard Jack Kennedy had been shot. I was in a Rome movie house, watching *David and Lisa*. News spread during the interval. I didn't believe it. There had been a mistake. That's not the

75

80

right plot. But, of course, finally, that was all that Jack was ever to be—a great media monster, now wreathed in garlands of paranoia of a most unpleasant sort. Jimmie was no media monster, but he was already vivid in his own right and, thus, no candidate for death. It took me some months to absorb the fact—or non-fact—of his being *not*-being.

To this day, in another world and almost another century, I have wondered what might have become of our so swiftly completed maleness. Is it only for a season that wholeness endures? On this matter Plato is silent. Experience suggests that desire of any kind is brief. In due course, I wrote a novel in which I described what *might* have happened had we met again years later. The conclusion was too harsh for many readers, but that is the way American society is and I was a realistic writer until, one day, I realized that there is no common reality beyond desire, the pursuit, and, in at least one case, the achievement of the whole. It would be greedy—not to say impractical—to expect a repetition of a lucky accident I was very much aware of my once perfect luck, and left it at that.

"Did you send Jimmie the copy of *Leaves of Grass* he asked for?"

Mrs. Sewell was vague. "If he asked me to, of course I did."

Will I ever know who got him to read Whitman on the island of Guam? No, I am not jealous, only sad I was never to be with him again. Actually, I hope that he did find someone. He was always lucky, except for his death—and maybe there was luck in that, too. Long life, finally, is nightmarish repetition while "Death is beautiful from you." Did he read that in Calamus? Did he read Whitman on "the brotherhood of lovers"? On "How together through life, through dangers, odium, unchanging, long and long, Through youth and through middle and old age, how unfaltering, how affectionate and faithful they were, Then I am pensive—I hastily walk away fill'd with bitterest envy." As who would not?

I have now lived a half century with a man, but sex has played no part in the relationship and so where there is no desire or pursuit, there is no wholeness. But there are satisfying lesser states, fragments.   85

[1995]

THINKING ABOUT THE TEXT

1. Vidal says of his encounter with Jimmie, "There was no guilt, no sense of taboo." Then he says they were in "Arcadia, not diabolic Eden" (para. 41). What might Vidal mean by this? Where do we get guilt from? Is it socially constructed or inborn?

2. Were you surprised that Vidal's possession of his other half occurred in the men's room at a dance (paras. 60–61)? Were you surprised by his casual reference to President Kennedy?

3. How would you describe Vidal's tone? Bitter? Sentimental? Nostalgic? Romantic?

4. Should writers be more or less explicit about the details of their intimate lives? How much would you choose to tell if you became a moderately famous person? On what would your judgment be based?

5. Vidal suggests that without desire there is no wholeness. Is desire something you can will into existence? Is it natural? Chemical? Psychological? Lucky? Does desire last? Does Vidal believe in Plato's myth?

MAKING COMPARISONS

1. Are there differences in Ackerman's and Vidal's telling of the *Symposium* tale? Explain.
2. According to Plato, heterosexuality and homosexuality have the same "natural" origin. Is this what you have been socialized to believe in America? What do you think Vidal and Ackerman think about this?
3. The down side of Plato's romantic fable is that there is only one person for each of us. Since Vidal's other dies early, he is never again whole. Does either Ackerman or Vidal suggest it is better to search or to find?

WRITING ABOUT ISSUES

1. Argue that there is (or is not) some validity to Plato's explanation of love in the *Symposium*.
2. Argue that the Vidal essay is the concrete example of Ackerman's generalization.
3. More gay and lesbian literature should be taught in high school or college to educate young people. Argue for or against.
4. Do library research on other gay writers. If they have written a memoir, write a brief report on how sexually explicit they are. How does the time period matter? Is being gay a prominent dynamic in their work? You might look at the work of Allen Ginsberg, Tennessee Williams, Jean Genet, W. H. Auden, and Walt Whitman.

COURTSHIP

CHRISTOPHER MARLOWE, "The Passionate Shepherd to His Love"
SIR WALTER RALEIGH, "The Nymph's Reply to the Shepherd"
ANDREW MARVELL, "To His Coy Mistress"
T. S. ELIOT, "The Love Song of J. Alfred Prufrock"

Our language and literature are filled with references to the smooth talker, the charming seducer, the insincere young man with a good line hoping to get "lucky." But our plays, poems, novels, songs, and films are also filled with images of truly passionate lovers, Romeos and Juliets who act impulsively and follow their heart's desire without heeding the consequences. In matters of the heart, we seem ambivalent about following emotion or reason, impulse or logic. While often suspicious of idealized romantic longing, we also seem to root for those who risk all for love.

Telling the difference between an honest plea and a dishonest ploy is not easy. Even when we can tell the difference, knowing whether to respond positively or not is usually problematic. The first three poems deal with lovers facing this dilemma. The passionate shepherd is asking a young woman to be his lover. Is he sincere? Is he practical? In Raleigh's poem, the young woman responds with a highly conditional answer. Has she thrown away a choice for happiness or has she been judicious? Is Marvell interested in love or sex? Does he expect her to treat his "arguments" seriously? Is he madly in love or an opportunist? The last poem is a kind of modern counterpoint to these traditional love poems. Prufrock seems to have had lovers, but is now wary and unsure of himself. He doesn't expect much, and, as a result, his heart will probably remain tentative.

BEFORE YOU READ

What decisions of the heart have you made that were not entirely logical? Do you feel that women are more susceptible to romantic promises than men, or is this just a stereotype?

CHRISTOPHER MARLOWE
The Passionate Shepherd to His Love

Best known for turning dramatic blank verse into high art in his play Doctor Faustus, *Marlowe (1564–1593) was also a major poet and one of the most learned and controversial writers of his time. He led a tempestuous and dangerous life and was often accused of being an atheist, a serious charge at the time. He was killed in a bar fight at the age of twenty-nine, the circumstances of which are still being debated. The official story that he was stabbed over the tavern bill is dubious given the informers, spies, and conspirators involved in the fight. Nevertheless, Marlowe's reputation as an Elizabethan dramatist is second only to Shakespeare's. The following poem is his only surviving lyric and suggests his impulsive attitude to live for the moment.*

Come live with me and be my love,
And we will all the pleasure prove
That valleys, groves, hills, and fields,
Woods, or steepy mountain yields.

And we will sit upon the rocks,   5
Seeing the shepherds feed their flocks,

By shallow rivers to whose falls
Melodious birds sing madrigals.

And I will make thee beds of roses
And a thousand fragrant posies,   10
A cap of flowers, and a kirtle°
Embroidered all with leaves of myrtle;

A gown made of the finest wool
Which from our pretty lambs we pull;
Fair lined slippers for the cold,   15
With buckles of the purest gold;

A belt of straw and ivy buds,
With coral clasps and amber studs:
And if these pleasures may thee move,
Come live with me, and be my love.   20

The shepherd swains shall dance and sing
For thy delight each May morning:
If these delights thy mind may move,
Then live with me and be my love.   [c. 1599]

11 **kirtle:** Dress or skirt.

THINKING ABOUT THE TEXT

1. As an argument, how persuasive do you think the shepherd's case is? Might his argument charm his listener? Might the speaker be more sophisticated than one would expect?

2. Marlowe is writing in the pastoral tradition, which highlights youth, optimism, and eternal love. Might Marlowe be dealing with a serious topic behind these idealized fancies?

3. What elements of reality or human nature does the speaker omit from his plea?

4. Carpe diem ("seize the day") was a popular attitude in Marlowe's day, as this poem suggests. Is it today? Can you give examples from popular culture? What are the advantages of adopting such an attitude? The disadvantages?

5. Do you think that love conquers all? Is sex a necessary prelude to love? Do you think love is more, or less, possible in certain settings, for example, at the beach, in the country, or perhaps in prison or a hospital? Does being in love depend on one's economic or psychological well-being?

SIR WALTER RALEIGH

The Nymph's Reply to the Shepherd

Sir Walter Raleigh (1554–1618) was an English soldier and explorer as well as a writer. He was a favorite of Elizabeth I, even though his outspokenness and interest in skeptical philosophy made him many enemies at court. In 1585, Raleigh sent the first of two groups of settlers to Roanoke Island, the second of which vanished without a trace by 1591. After he led an unsuccessful expedition to Guyana in search of gold, he was imprisoned in the Tower of London and eventually executed for trying to overthrow James I. The following poem exhibits his practical and skeptical bent.

If all the world and love were young,
And truth in every shepherd's tongue,
These pretty pleasures might me move
To live with thee and be thy love.

Time drives the flocks from field to fold   5
When rivers rage and rocks grow cold,
And Philomel° becometh dumb;
The rest complains of cares to come.

The flowers do fade, and wanton fields
To wayward winter reckoning yields;   10
A honey tongue, a heart of gall,
Is fancy's spring, but sorrow's fall.

Thy gowns, thy shoes, thy beds of roses,
Thy cap, thy kirtle, and thy posies
Soon break, soon wither, soon forgotten —   15
In folly ripe, in reason rotten.

Thy belt of straw and ivy buds,
Thy coral clasps and amber studs,
All these in me no means can move
To come to thee and be thy love.   20

But could youth last and love still breed,
Had joys no date° nor age no need,
Then these delights my mind might move
To live with thee and be thy love.   [1600]

7 **Philomel:** The nightingale.   22 **date:** End.

THINKING ABOUT THE TEXT

1. How might you consider this poem a refusal for a sexual affair? What arguments are put forth as a refutation?

2. Read between the lines, what might convince the speaker to be the Shepherd's Love? Or is that impossible?

3. What is the speaker's tone? Do you hear hostility or contempt?

4. What does Raleigh mean in line 16 by "In folly ripe, in reason rotten"?

5. What part does gender play in this poem? Is the speaker being stereotyped?

MAKING COMPARISONS

1. In what specific ways is Raleigh offering a refutation of Marlowe's poem? Is it effective?

2. What aspects of nature does Marlowe focus on? Raleigh?

3. How would you compare the attitudes of the two speakers in these poems? Is this a debate between man and woman? In what ways could this be both true and false?

ANDREW MARVELL

To His Coy Mistress

Andrew Marvell (1621–1678) was famous in his own time as an adroit politician and a writer of satire, but modern readers admire him for the style and content of his lyric, metaphysical poetry. Born into a Protestant family, Marvell was tolerant of Catholicism from a young age, and his willingness to somehow circumvent the religious prejudices of seventeenth-century England allowed his continued success. He traveled to Holland, France, Italy, and Spain—possibly to avoid the English civil war as a young man and undoubtedly to spy for England in later years. He tutored Cromwell's ward and later served on his Council of State, but was influential enough during the Restoration to get his fellow poet and mentor, John Milton, released from prison. Although admired by the Romantic poets of the early nineteenth century, Andrew Marvell's poetry was revived in the twentieth century by T. S. Eliot and has been widely read for its ironic approach to the conventions of love.

Had we but world enough, and time,
This coyness, lady, were no crime.
We would sit down, and think which way
To walk, and pass our long love's day.
Thou by the Indian Ganges'° side   5
Shouldst rubies find; I by the tide
Of Humber° would complain.° I would

---

5 Ganges: A river in India sacred to the Hindus.   **7 Humber:** An estuary that flows through Marvell's native town, Hull;   **complain:** sing love songs.

Love you ten years before the Flood,
And you should, if you please, refuse
Till the conversion of the Jews.
My vegetable love should grow°   10
Vaster than empires, and more slow;
An hundred years should go to praise
Thine eyes and on thy forehead gaze,
Two hundred to adore each breast,
But thirty thousand to the rest: 15
An age at least to every part,
And the last age should show your heart.
For, lady, you deserve this state,
Nor would I love at lower rate.   20
     But at my back I always hear
Time's wingèd chariot hurrying near;
And yonder all before us lie
Deserts of vast eternity.
Thy beauty shall no more be found,   25
Nor in thy marble vault shall sound
My echoing song; then worms shall try
That long preserved virginity,
And your quaint honor turn to dust,
And into ashes all my lust.   30
The grave's a fine and private place,
But none, I think, do there embrace.
     Now, therefore, while the youthful hue
Sits on thy skin like morning dew,
And while thy willing soul transpires°   35
At every pore with instant fires,
Now let us sport us while we may,
And now, like amorous birds of prey,
Rather at once our time devour
Than languish in his slow-chapped° power.   40
Let us roll all our strength and all
Our sweetness up into one ball,
And tear our pleasures with rough strife
Thorough° the iron gates of life.
Thus, though we cannot make our sun   45
Stand still, yet we will make him run.
                                          [1681]

---

11 **My vegetable love . . . grow:** A slow, insensible growth, like that of a vegetable.   35 **tran-**
spires: Breathes forth.   40 **slow-chapped:** Slow-jawed.   44 **Thorough:** Through.

THINKING ABOUT THE TEXT

1. Considered as both an intellectual and an emotional argument, what is the narrator's goal and what specific claims does he make? Are they convincing? Do you think they were in 1681? Do you think women three hundred years ago worried about virginity? Why?

2. What does this poem say about the needs of Marvell's audience? What assumptions about women does the poem make?

3. How many sections does this poem have? What is the purpose of each? How is the concluding couplet in each related to that section? Is the rhyme scheme related to the meaning of these couplets?

4. Is the speaker passionate? Sincere? How do you make such a decision? Do you look at his language or his message?

5. Some feminist readers see in the last ten lines a kind of indirect threat, a suggestion of force through the use of violent images. Is this a plausible reading? If this is the case, what do you now think of the narrator's pleading?

MAKING COMPARISONS

1. Which of the male speakers seems the most trustworthy to you?

2. Do Marlowe and Marvell have the same goal?

3. How do you think the nymph would answer Marvell?

T. S. ELIOT
The Love Song of J. Alfred Prufrock

*One of the most respected intellectuals of his time, Thomas Stearns Eliot (1888–1965) was a poet, playwright (*Murder in the Cathedral*), and critic (*The Sacred Wood*). His poem "The Waste Land" (1922), considered a modernist masterpiece, is perhaps this century's most influential poem. The long-running Broadway play* Cats *is based on some of Eliot's lighter poems. Born in America and educated at Harvard, Eliot lived his mature life in England. He was awarded the Nobel Prize for Literature in 1948.*

> *S'io credesse che mia risposta fosse*
> *A persona che mai tornasse al mondo,*
> *Questa fiamma staria senza più scosse.*
> *Ma perciocchè giammai di questo fondo*
> *Non tornò vivo alcun, s'i'odo il vero,*
> *Senza tema d'infamia ti rispondo.*°

EPIGRAPH: *S'io . . . rispondo:* In Dante's *Inferno*, a sufferer in hell says, "If I thought I was talking to someone who might return to earth, this flame would cease; but if what I have heard is true, no one does return; therefore, I can speak to you without fear of infamy."

Let us go then, you and I,
When the evening is spread out against the sky
Like a patient etherized upon a table;
Let us go, through certain half-deserted streets,
The muttering retreats   5
Of restless nights in one-night cheap hotels
And sawdust restaurants with oyster-shells:
Streets that follow like a tedious argument
Of insidious intent
To lead you to an overwhelming question . . .   10
Oh, do not ask, "What is it?"
Let us go and make our visit.

In the room the women come and go
Talking of Michelangelo.

    The yellow fog that rubs its back upon the window panes,   15
The yellow smoke that rubs its muzzle on the window panes
Licked its tongue into the corners of the evening,
Lingered upon the pools that stand in drains,
Let fall upon its back the soot that falls from chimneys,
Slipped by the terrace, made a sudden leap,   20
And seeing that it was a soft October night,
Curled once about the house, and fell asleep.

    And indeed there will be time°
For the yellow smoke that slides along the street,
Rubbing its back upon the window panes;   25
There will be time, there will be time
To prepare a face to meet the faces that you meet;
There will be time to murder and create,
And time for all the works and days° of hands
That lift and drop a question on your plate: 30
Time for you and time for me,
And time yet for a hundred indecisions,
And for a hundred visions and revisions,
Before the taking of a toast and tea.

In the room the women come and go   35
Talking of Michelangelo.

    And indeed there will be time
To wonder, "Do I dare?" and, "Do I dare?"—
Time to turn back and descend the stair,
With a bald spot in the middle of my hair—   40

---

23 **there will be time:** An allusion to Ecclesiastes 3:1–8: "To everything there is a season, and a time to every purpose under heaven. . . ." 29 **works and days:** Hesiod's eighth century B.C.E. poem gave practical advice.

(They will say: "How his hair is growing thin!")
My morning coat, my collar mounting firmly to the chin,
My necktie rich and modest, but asserted by a simple pin —
(They will say: "But how his arms and legs are thin!")
Do I dare   45
Disturb the universe?
In a minute there is time
For decisions and revisions which a minute will reverse.

    For I have known them all already, known them all:
Have known the evenings, mornings, afternoons,   50
I have measured out my life with coffee spoons;
I know the voices dying with a dying fall
Beneath the music from a farther room.
    So how should I presume?

    And I have known the eyes already, known them all —   55
The eyes that fix you in a formulated phrase.
And when I am formulated, sprawling on a pin,
When I am pinned and wriggling on the wall,
Then how should I begin
To spit out all the butt-ends of my days and ways?   60
    And how should I presume?

    And I have known the arms already, known them all —
Arms that are braceleted and white and bare
(But in the lamplight, downed with light brown hair!)
    Is it perfume from a dress   65
    That makes me so digress?
Arms that lie along a table, or wrap about a shawl.
    And should I then presume?
    And how should I begin?

    Shall I say, I have gone at dusk through narrow streets, 70
And watched the smoke that rises from the pipes
Of lonely men in shirtsleeves, leaning out of windows? . . .

I should have been a pair of ragged claws
Scuttling across the floors of silent seas.

    And the afternoon, the evening, sleeps so peacefully!   75
Smoothed by long fingers,
Asleep . . . tired . . . or it malingers,
Stretched on the floor, here beside you and me.
Should I, after tea and cakes and ices,
Have the strength to force the moment to its crisis?   80
But though I have wept and fasted, wept and prayed,
Though I have seen my head (grown slightly bald) brought in upon a platter,°

82 head . . . platter: Like John the Baptist (Matt. 14:1–12).

I am no prophet—and here's no great matter;
I have seen the moment of my greatness flicker,
And I have seen the eternal Footman hold my coat, and snicker,   85
    And in short, I was afraid.

    And would it have been worth it, after all,
After the cups, the marmalade, the tea,
Among the porcelain, among some talk of you and me,
Would it have been worth while   90
To have bitten off the matter with a smile,
To have squeezed the universe into a ball°
To roll it toward some overwhelming question,
To say: "I am Lazarus,° come from the dead,
Come back to tell you all, I shall tell you all"—   95
If one, settling a pillow by her head,
    Should say: "That is not what I meant at all;
    That is not it, at all."

    And would it have been worth it, after all,
Would it have been worth while,   100
After the sunsets and the dooryards and the sprinkled streets,
After the novels, after the teacups, after the skirts that trail along the floor—
And this, and so much more?—
It is impossible to say just what I mean!
But as if a magic lantern threw the nerves in patterns on a screen: 105
Would it have been worth while
If one, settling a pillow or throwing off a shawl,
And turning toward the window, should say:
    "That is not it at all,
    That is not what I meant, at all."   110

No! I am not Prince Hamlet, nor was meant to be;
Am an attendant lord,° one that will do
To swell a progress,° start a scene or two
Advise the prince: withal, an easy tool,
Deferential, glad to be of use,   115
Politic, cautious, and meticulous;
Full of high sentence, but a bit obtuse;
At times, indeed, almost ridiculous—
Almost, at times, the Fool.

I grow old . . . I grow old . . .   120
I shall wear the bottoms of my trowsers rolled.

    Shall I part my hair behind? Do I dare to eat a peach?

---

92 **squeezed . . . ball:** See lines 41–42 of Marvell's "To His Coy Mistress" (p. 762).   94 **I am Lazarus:** Raised from the dead by Jesus.   112 **attendant lord:** Like Polonius in Shakespeare's *Hamlet*.   113 **To swell or progress:** state procession.   121–122 **trowsers rolled . . . part my hair behind:** The latest fashion.

I shall wear white flannel trowsers, and walk upon the beach.
I have heard the mermaids singing, each to each.

I do not think that they will sing to me.   125

I have seen them riding seaward on the waves,
Combing the white hair of the waves blown back
When the wind blows the water white and black.

We have lingered in the chambers of the sea
By seagirls wreathed with seaweed red and brown,   130
Till human voices wake us, and we drown.   [1917]

THINKING ABOUT THE TEXT

1. To what is Prufrock referring when he says, "Do I dare?" (line 38)? How about "that is not it at all" (lines 98, 109)? What is Prufrock so anxious about?

2. Prufrock seems to characterize himself quite severely in lines 111–19. How would you describe him? Do you know people like him?

3. Do you think the imagery of the opening stanza sets the right tone for Prufrock's journey? How would you describe the tone? Ironic, self-mocking, depressed, overly cautious, too self-conscious?

4. Is Prufrock making an argument against getting involved in a romance? What evidence does he use to support his argument?

5. Critics have given widely different interpretations of the two couplets, "In the room the women come and go / Talking of Michelangelo" (lines 13–14) and "I should have been a pair of ragged claws / Scuttling across the floors of silent seas" (lines 73–74). What do you think these lines mean?

MAKING COMPARISONS

1. What would Prufrock think of Marlowe's and Marvell's poems?

2. Some critics suggest that line 92 of "Prufrock" is an allusion to lines 41–42 of "To His Coy Mistress." Some critics also claim that line 26 refers to "To His Coy Mistress." Do you think so? What might be the point of referring to this famous poem?

3. Do you think Eliot's poem is a kind of modern refutation of romantic love à la Marlowe and Marvell?

WRITING ABOUT ISSUES

1. Some critics see Marlowe's poem as a representation of idealistic romanticism and Raleigh's poem as one of realism and practicality. Write a brief thematic comparison of these two poems arguing for the position that is more like your own.

2. Argue either that the speaker in Marlowe's or Marvell's poem has the right approach or that Prufrock's attitude is more typical and realistic.

3. Write a personal narrative about a time when you were (or were not) susceptible to a "carpe diem" argument.

4. There have been other replies to Marlowe's poem. Locate William Carlos Williams's "Raleigh Was Right," for example, and write a brief analysis of his refutations.

THE APPEARANCE OF LOVE:
A COLLECTION OF WRITINGS BY KATE CHOPIN

KATE CHOPIN, "The Storm"
KATE CHOPIN, "The Story of an Hour"
KATE CHOPIN, "Désirée's Baby"

People at weddings often remark how happy and in love the bridal couple looks. But people can *appear* to be in love. Indeed, psychologists tell us that someone can play a loving role for years, at times actually believing the part he or she is playing. To a limited extent, this is true for all of us. We learn what it means to be in love from watching movies, reading books, and absorbing other clues from our culture. A man proposing marriage on one knee is just one cultural notion of how we should act when we are in love.

Suppose a woman acts lovingly toward her husband and then has a passionate sexual encounter with an old boyfriend. Which is her true self? Which is the appearance and which the reality? Sometimes a society's conventions about marriage are so strong that men and women have little choice but to conform. If we were to judge the behavior of a woman toward her husband a hundred years ago, we might not get an accurate reading of how much she loved him. Likewise, people can believe their lives to be quite harmonious until they find out that one of them has a surprising past. William Shakespeare wrote of love that would not change when difficulties arose, but such is not always the case. Does that mean that one's love is not deep enough? Or when a loved one does not live up to expectations, is it natural to readjust one's heart?

The following three stories take on controversial topics. Kate Chopin was not a conformist thinker, and her stories are filled with views of desire, love, and relationships meant to provoke her late-nineteenth-century readers. Indeed, they continue to provoke audiences today.

BEFORE YOU READ

Would you change your mind about loving someone if you found out he or she was having an affair? If they lied about their religion or their race? Is it possible to love someone and at the same time want to be free?

KATE CHOPIN
The Storm

Kate Chopin (1851–1904) is known for her evocations of the unique, multiethnic Creole and Cajun societies of late-nineteenth-century Louisiana; however, her characters transcend the limitation of regional genre writing, striking a particularly resonant note among feminist readers. Born Katherine O'Flaherty in St. Louis, Missouri, she married Oscar Chopin in 1870 and went to live with him in New Orleans and on his Mississippi River plantation. Her short stories were collected in Bayou Folk *(1894) and* A Night in Acadie *(1897). Chopin's last novel,* The Awakening, *scandalized readers at the time of its publication in 1899 because of its frank portrayal of female sexuality in the context of an extramarital affair. Long ignored by readers and critics, her work was revived in the 1960s and continues to provoke heated discussion of her female characters: Are they women who seek freedom in the only ways available to them, or are they willing participants in their own victimhood?*

"The Storm" was written about 1898, but because of its provocative content, Chopin probably did not even try to find a magazine that would risk the publicity.

1

The leaves were so still that even Bibi thought it was going to rain. Bobinôt, who was accustomed to converse on terms of perfect equality with his little son, called the child's attention to certain sombre clouds that were rolling with sinister intention from the west, accompanied by a sullen, threatening roar. They were at Friedheimer's store and decided to remain there till the storm had passed. They sat within the door on two empty kegs. Bibi was four years old and looked very wise.

"Mama'll be 'fraid, yes," he suggested with blinking eyes.

"She'll shut the house. Maybe she got Sylvie helpin' her this evenin'," Bobinôt responded reassuringly.

"No; she ent got Sylvie. Sylvie was helpin' her yistiday," piped Bibi.

Bobinôt arose and going across to the counter purchased a can of shrimps, of which Calixta was very fond. Then he returned to his perch on the keg and sat stolidly holding the can of shrimps while the storm burst. It shook the wooden store and seemed to be ripping great furrows in the distant field. Bibi laid his little hand on his father's knee and was not afraid.

2

Calixta, at home, felt no uneasiness for their safety. She sat at a side window sewing furiously on a sewing machine. She was greatly occupied and did not notice the approaching storm. But she felt very warm and often stopped to mop her face on which the perspiration gathered in beads. She unfastened her white sacque at the throat. It began to grow dark, and suddenly realizing the situation she got up hurriedly and went about closing windows and doors.

Out on the small front gallery she had hung Bobinôt's Sunday clothes to air and she hastened out to gather them before the rain fell. As she stepped outside, Alcée Laballière rode in at the gate. She had not seen him very often since her marriage, and never alone. She stood there with Bobinôt's coat in her hands, and the big rain drops began to fall. Alcée rode his horse under the shelter of a side projection where the chickens had huddled and there were plows and a harrow piled up in the corner.

"May I come and wait on your gallery till the storm is over, Calixta?" he asked.

"Come 'long in, M'sieur Alcée."

His voice and her own startled her as if from a trance, and she seized   10
Bobinôt's vest. Alcée, mounting to the porch, grabbed the trousers and snatched Bibi's braided jacket that was about to be carried away by a sudden gust of wind. He expressed an intention to remain outside, but it was soon apparent that he might as well have been out in the open: the water beat in upon the boards in driving sheets, and he went inside, closing the door after him. It was even necessary to put something beneath the door to keep the water out.

"My! what a rain! It's good two years sence it rain' like that," exclaimed Calixta as she rolled up a piece of bagging and Alcée helped her to thrust it beneath the crack.

She was a little fuller of figure than five years before when she married; but she had lost nothing of her vivacity. Her blue eyes still retained their melting quality; and her yellow hair, dishevelled by the wind and rain, kinked more stubbornly than ever about her ears and temples.

The rain beat upon the low, shingled roof with a force and clatter that threatened to break an entrance and deluge them there. They were in the dining room — the sitting room — the general utility room. Adjoining was her bed room, with Bibi's couch along side her own. The door stood open, and the room with its white, monumental bed, its closed shutters, looked dim and mysterious.

Alcée flung himself into a rocker and Calixta nervously began to gather up from the floor the lengths of a cotton sheet which she had been sewing.

"It this keeps up, *Dieu sait°* if the levees goin' to stan' it!" she exclaimed.   15

"What have you got to do with the levees?"

"I got enough to do! An' there's Bobinôt with Bibi out in that storm — if he only didn' left Friedheimer's!"

"Let us hope, Calixta, that Bobinôt's got sense enough to come in out of a cyclone."

She went and stood at the window with a greatly disturbed look on her face. She wiped the frame that was clouded with moisture. It was stiflingly hot. Alcée got up and joined her at the window, looking over her shoulder. The rain was coming down in sheets obscuring the view of far-off cabins and enveloping the distant wood in a gray mist. The playing of the lightning was incessant. A bolt

Dieu sait: God knows.

struck a tall chinaberry tree at the edge of the field. It filled all visible space with a blinding glare and the crash seemed to invade the very boards they stood upon.

Calixta put her hands to her eyes, and with a cry, staggered backward. Alcée's 20 arm encircled her, and for an instant he drew her close and spasmodically to him.

"*Bonté!*"° she cried, releasing herself from his encircling arm and retreating from the window, "the house'll go next! If I only knew w'ere Bibi was!" She would not compose herself; she would not be seated. Alcée clasped her shoulders and looked into her face. The contact of her warm, palpitating body when he had unthinkingly drawn her into his arm, had aroused all the old-time infatuation and desire for her flesh.

"Calixta," he said, "don't be frightened. Nothing can happen. The house is too low to be struck, with so many tall trees standing about. There! aren't you going to be quiet? say, aren't you?" He pushed her hair back from her face that was warm and steaming. Her lips were as red and moist as pomegranate seed. Her white neck and a glimpse of her full, firm bosom disturbed him powerfully. As she glanced up at him the fear in her liquid blue eyes had given place to a drowsy gleam that unconsciously betrayed a sensuous desire. He looked down into her eyes and there was nothing for him to do but to gather her lips in a kiss. It reminded him of Assumption.

"Do you remember — in Assumption, Calixta?" he asked in a low voice broken by passion. Oh! she remembered; for in Assumption he had kissed her and kissed and kissed her; until his senses would well nigh fail, and to save her he would resort to a desperate flight. If she was not an immaculate dove in those days, she was still inviolate; a passionate creature whose very defenselessness had made her defense, against which his honor forbade him to prevail. Now — well, now — her lips seemed in a manner free to be tasted, as well as her round, white throat and her whiter breasts.

They did not heed the crashing torrents, and the roar of the elements made her laugh as she lay in his arms. She was a revelation in that dim, mysterious chamber; as white as the couch she lay upon. Her firm, elastic flesh that was knowing for the first time its birthright, was like a creamy lily that the sun invites to contribute its breath and perfume to the undying life of the world.

The generous abundance of her passion, without guile or trickery, was like a 25 white flame which penetrated and found response in depths of his own sensuous nature that had never yet been reached.

When he touched her breasts they gave themselves up in quivering ecstasy, inviting his lips. Her mouth was a fountain of delight. And when he possessed her, they seemed to swoon together at the very borderland of life's mystery.

He stayed cushioned upon her, breathless, dazed, enervated, with his heart beating like a hammer upon her. With one hand she clasped his head, her lips lightly touching his forehead. The other hand stroked with a soothing rhythm his muscular shoulders.

Bonté: Goodness.

The growl of the thunder was distant and passing away. The rain beat softly upon the shingles, inviting them to drowsiness and sleep. But they dared not yield.

The rain was over; and the sun was turning the glistening green world into a palace of gems. Calixta, on the gallery, watched Alcée ride away. He turned and smiled at her with a beaming face; and she lifted her pretty chin in the air and laughed aloud.

3

Bobinôt and Bibi, trudging home, stopped without at the cistern to make   30
themselves presentable.

"My! Bibi, w'at will yo' mama say! You ought to be ashame'. You oughtn' put on those good pants. Look at 'em! An' that mud on yo' collar! How you got that mud on yo' collar, Bibi? I never saw such a boy!" Bibi was the picture of pathetic resignation. Bobinôt was the embodiment of serious solicitude as he strove to remove from his own person and his son's the signs of their tramp over heavy roads and through wet fields. He scraped the mud off Bibi's bare legs and feet with a stick and carefully removed all traces from his heavy brogans. Then, prepared for the worst — the meeting with an over-scrupulous housewife, they entered cautiously at the back door.

Calixta was preparing supper. She had set the table and was dripping coffee at the hearth. She sprang up as they came in.

"Oh, Bobinôt! You back! My! but I was uneasy. W'ere you been during the rain? An' Bibi? he ain't wet? he ain't hurt?" She had clasped Bibi and was kissing him effusively. Bobinôt's explanations and apologies which he had been composing all along the way, died on his lips as Calixta felt him to see if he were dry, and seemed to express nothing but satisfaction at their safe return.

"I brought you some shrimps, Calixta," offered Bobinôt, hauling the can from his ample side pocket and laying it on the table.

"Shrimps! Oh, Bobinôt! you too good fo' anything!" and she gave him a   35
smacking kiss on the cheek that resounded. "*J'vous réponds,*° we'll have a feas' to-night! umph-umph!"

Bobinôt and Bibi began to relax and enjoy themselves, and when the three seated themselves at table they laughed much and so loud that anyone might have heard them as far away as Laballière's.

4

Alcée Laballière wrote to his wife, Clarisse, that night. It was a loving letter, full of tender solicitude. He told her not to hurry back, but if she and the babies liked it at Biloxi, to stay a month longer. He was getting on nicely; and though he missed them, he was willing to bear the separation a while longer — realizing that their health and pleasure were the first things to be considered.

J'vous réponds: I'm telling you.

5

As for Clarisse, she was charmed upon receiving her husband's letter. She and the babies were doing well. The society was agreeable; many of her old friends and acquaintances were at the bay. And the first free breath since her marriage seemed to restore the pleasant liberty of her maiden days. Devoted as she was to her husband, their intimate conjugal life was something which she was more than willing to forego for a while.

So the storm passed and every one was happy.   [1898]

THINKING ABOUT THE TEXT

1. Does Calixta truly love Bobinôt? What explains the sudden passion of Calixta and Alcée? Are they in love?

2. Are you bothered by the happy ending? Are stories supposed to reinforce the dominant values of a society? What do you think would (or should) have happened in real life?

3. Can you recall other stories, novels, films, or television programs in which someone who is sexually transgressive is not punished?

4. Are the injured parties in this story really injured; that is, if they never find out, will they still suffer somehow?

5. Should extramarital affairs be illegal? Is Chopin suggesting that they are not so terrible, or is she simply saying something about passion?

KATE CHOPIN
The Story of an Hour

"The Story of an Hour" was first published in Bayou Folk *(1894). It is typical of Chopin's controversial works and caused a sensation among the reading public.*

Knowing that Mrs. Mallard was afflicted with a heart trouble, great care was taken to break to her as gently as possible the news of her husband's death.

It was her sister Josephine who told her, in broken sentences; veiled hints that revealed in half concealing. Her husband's friend Richards was there, too, near her. It was he who had been in the newspaper office when intelligence of the railroad disaster was received, with Brently Mallard's name leading the list of "killed." He had only taken the time to assure himself of its truth by a second telegram, and had hastened to forestall any less careful, less tender friend in bearing the sad message.

She did not hear the story as many women have heard the same, with a paralyzed inability to accept its significance. She wept at once, with sudden, wild abandonment, in her sister's arms. When the storm of grief had spent itself she went away to her room alone. She would have no one follow her.

There stood, facing the open window, a comfortable, roomy armchair. Into this she sank, pressed down by a physical exhaustion that haunted her body and seemed to reach into her soul.

She could see in the open square before her house the tops of trees that were   5
all aquiver with the new spring life. The delicious breath of rain was in the air. In the street below a peddler was crying his wares. The notes of a distant song which some one was singing reached her faintly, and countless sparrows were twittering in the eaves.

There were patches of blue sky showing here and there through the clouds that had met and piled one above the other in the west facing her window.

She sat with her head thrown back upon the cushion of the chair, quite motionless, except when a sob came up into her throat and shook her, as a child who had cried itself to sleep continues to sob in its dreams.

She was young, with a fair, calm face, whose lines bespoke repression and even a certain strength. But now there was a dull stare in her eyes, whose gaze was fixed away off yonder on one of those patches of blue sky. It was not a glance of reflection, but rather indicated a suspension of intelligent thought.

There was something coming to her and she was waiting for it, fearfully. What was it? She did not know; it was too subtle and elusive to name. But she felt it, creeping out of the sky, reaching toward her through the sounds, the scents, the color that filled the air.

Now her bosom rose and fell tumultuously. She was beginning to recognize   10
this thing that was approaching to possess her, and she was striving to beat it back with her will — as powerless as her two white slender hands would have been.

When she abandoned herself a little whispered word escaped her slightly parted lips. She said it over and over under her breath: "free, free, free!" The vacant stare and the look of terror that had followed it went from her eyes. They stayed keen and bright. Her pulses beat fast, and the coursing blood warmed and relaxed every inch of her body.

She did not stop to ask if it were or were not a monstrous joy that held her. A clear and exalted perception enabled her to dismiss the suggestion as trivial.

She knew that she would weep again when she saw the kind, tender hands folded in death; the face that had never looked save with love upon her, fixed and gray and dead. But she saw beyond that bitter moment a long procession of years to come that would belong to her absolutely. And she opened and spread her arms out to them in welcome.

There would be no one to live for her during those coming years: she would live for herself. There would be no powerful will bending hers in that blind persistence with which men and women believe they have a right to impose a private will upon a fellow-creature. A kind intention or a cruel intention made the act seem no less a crime as she looked upon it in that brief moment of illumination.

And yet she had loved him — sometimes. Often she had not. What did it mat-   15
ter! What could love, the unsolved mystery, count for in face of this possession of self-assertion which she suddenly recognized as the strongest impulse of her being!

"Free! Body and soul free!" she kept whispering.

Josephine was kneeling before the closed door with her lips to the keyhole, imploring for admission. "Louise, open the door! I beg; open the door — you will make yourself ill. What are you doing, Louise? For heaven's sake open the door."

"Go away. I am not making myself ill." No; she was drinking in a very elixir of life through that open window.

Her fancy was running riot along those days ahead of her. Spring days, and summer days, and all sorts of days that would be her own. She breathed a quick prayer that life might be long. It was only yesterday she had thought with a shudder that life might be long.

She arose at length and opened the door to her sister's importunities. There   20
was a feverish triumph in her eyes, and she carried herself unwittingly like a goddess of Victory. She clasped her sister's waist, and together they descended the stairs. Richards stood waiting for them at the bottom.

Some one was opening the front door with a latchkey. It was Brently Mallard who entered, a little travel-stained, composedly carrying his gripsack and umbrella. He had been far from the scene of accident, and did not even know there had been one. He stood amazed at Josephine's piercing cry; at Richards' quick motion to screen him from the view of his wife.

But Richards was too late.

When the doctors came they said she had died of heart disease — of joy that kills.   [1894]

THINKING ABOUT THE TEXT

1. Is Louise Mallard really in love with her husband? Regardless of your answer, would she ever leave him? Is it possible to confuse love with duty?

2. Is it possible to assign blame for this tragedy? To Mr. Mallard? Mrs. Mallard? The culture?

3. Why did Chopin keep the story so brief? What would you like to know more about?

4. What specifically do you think Mrs. Mallard was thinking about in the room?

5. Do you think this situation was common during Chopin's time? Today?

MAKING COMPARISONS

1. Compare Mrs. Mallard and Calixta. Do you think Mrs. Mallard would have an extramarital affair?

2. Is Chopin sympathetic to Mrs. Mallard and Calixta? Is she judgmental?

3. Calixta and Alcée seem to be on more equal terms than Mr. and Mrs. Mallard. Do you think this is the case? Explain why this might be so.

KATE CHOPIN
Désirée's Baby

"Désirée's Baby" was written in 1892 and published in Bayou Folk *(1894). The story reflects her experience among the French Creoles in Louisiana.*

As the day was pleasant, Madame Valmondé drove over to L'Abri to see Désirée and the baby.

It made her laugh to think of Désirée with a baby. Why, it seemed but yesterday that Désirée was little more than a baby herself; when Monsieur in riding through the gateway of Valmondé had found her lying asleep in the shadow of the big stone pillar.

The little one awoke in his arms and began to cry for "Dada." That was as much as she could do or say. Some people thought she might have strayed there of her own accord, for she was of the toddling age. The prevailing belief was that she had been purposely left by a party of Texans, whose canvas-covered wagon, late in the day, had crossed the ferry that Coton Maïs kept, just below the plantation. In time Madame Valmondé abandoned every speculation but the one that Désirée had been sent to her by a beneficent Providence to be the child of her affection, seeing that she was without child of the flesh. For the girl grew to be beautiful and gentle, affectionate and sincere, — the idol of Valmondé.

It was no wonder, when she stood one day against the stone pillar in whose shadow she had lain asleep, eighteen years before, that Armand Aubigny riding by and seeing her there, had fallen in love with her. That was the way all the Aubignys fell in love, as if struck by a pistol shot. The wonder was that he had not loved her before; for he had known her since his father brought him home from Paris, a boy of eight, after his mother died there. The passion that awoke in him that day, when he saw her at the gate, swept along like an avalanche, or like a prairie fire, or like anything that drives headlong over all obstacles.

Monsieur Valmondé grew practical and wanted things well considered: that is, the girl's obscure origin. Armand looked into her eyes and did not care. He was reminded that she was nameless. What did it matter about a name when he could give her one of the oldest and proudest in Louisiana? He ordered the *corbeille* from Paris, and contained himself with what patience he could until it arrived; then they were married.   5

Madame Valmondé had not seen Désirée and the baby for four weeks. When she reached L'Abri she shuddered at the first sight of it, as she always did. It was a sad looking place, which for many years had not known the gentle presence of a mistress, old Monsieur Aubigny having married and buried his wife in France, and she having loved her own land too well ever to leave it. The roof came down steep and black like a cowl, reaching out beyond the wide galleries that encircled the yellow stuccoed house. Big, solemn oaks grew close to it, and their thick-leaved, far-reaching branches shadowed it like a pall. Young Aubigny's rule was a strict one, too, and under it his negroes had forgotten how to be gay, as they had been during the old master's easy-going and indulgent lifetime.

The young mother was recovering slowly, and lay full length, in her white muslins and laces, upon a couch. The baby was beside her, upon her arm, where he had fallen sleep, at her breast. The yellow nurse woman sat beside a window fanning herself.

Madame Valmondé bent her portly figure over Désirée and kissed her, holding her an instant tenderly in her arms. Then she turned to the child.

"This is not the baby!" she exclaimed, in startled tones. French was the language spoken at Valmondé in those days.

"I knew you would be astonished," laughed Désirée, "at the way he has grown. The little *cochon de lait!*° Look at his legs, mamma, and his hands and fingernails,—real fingernails. Zandrine had to cut them this morning. Isn't it true, Zandrine?"

The woman bowed her turbaned head majestically, "Mais si, Madame."

"And the way he cries," went on Désirée, "is deafening. Armand heard him the other day as far away as La Blanche's cabin."

Madame Valmondé had never removed her eyes from the child. She lifted it and walked with it over to the window that was lightest. She scanned the baby narrowly, then looked as searchingly at Zandrine, whose face was turned to gaze across the fields.

"Yes, the child has grown, has changed," said Madame Valmondé, slowly, as she replaced it beside its mother. "What does Armand say?"

Désirée's face became suffused with a glow that was happiness itself.

"Oh, Armand is the proudest father in the parish, I believe, chiefly because it is a boy, to bear his name; though he says not,—that he would have loved a girl as well. But I know it isn't true. I know he says that to please me. And mamma," she added, drawing Madame Valmondé's head down to her and speaking in a whisper, "he hasn't punished one of them—not one of them—since baby is born. Even Négrillon, who pretended to have burnt his leg that he might rest from work—he only laughed, and said Négrillon was a great scamp. Oh, mamma, I'm so happy; it frightens me."

What Désirée said was true. Marriage, and later the birth of his son had softened Armand Aubigny's imperious and exacting nature greatly. This was what made the gentle Désirée so happy, for she loved him desperately. When he frowned she trembled, but loved him. When he smiled, she asked no greater blessing of God. But Armand's dark, handsome face had not often been disfigured by frowns since the day he fell in love with her.

When the baby was about three months old, Désirée awoke one day to the conviction that there was something in the air menacing her peace. It was at first too subtle to grasp. It had only been a disquieting suggestion; an air of mystery among the blacks; unexpected visits from far-off neighbors who could hardly account for their coming. Then a strange, an awful change in her husband's manner, which she dared not ask him to explain. When he spoke to her, it was with averted eyes, from which the old love-light seemed to have gone out. He absented himself from home; and when there, avoided her presence and

cochon de lait: French for "suckling pig"; an endearment.

that of her child, without excuse. And the very spirit of Satan seemed suddenly to take hold of him in his dealings with the slaves. Désirée was miserable enough to die.

She sat in her room, one hot afternoon, in her *peignoir*, listlessly drawing through her fingers the strands of her long, silky brown hair that hung about her shoulders. The baby, half naked, lay asleep upon her own great mahogany bed, that was like a sumptuous throne, with its satin-lined half-canopy. One of La Blanche's little quadroon boys — half naked too — stood fanning the child slowly with a fan of peacock feathers. Désirée's eyes had been fixed absently and sadly upon the baby, while she was striving to penetrate the threatening mist that she felt closing about her. She looked from her child to the boy who stood beside him, and back again; over and over. "Ah!" It was a cry that she could not help; which she was not conscious of having uttered. The blood turned like ice in her veins, and a clammy moisture gathered upon her face.

She tried to speak to the little quadroon boy; but no sound would come, at   20
first. When he heard his name uttered, he looked up, and his mistress was pointing to the door. He laid aside the great, soft fan, and obediently stole away, over the polished floor, on his bare tiptoes.

She stayed motionless, with gaze riveted upon her child, and her face the picture of fright.

Presently her husband entered the room, and without noticing her, went to a table and began to search among some papers which covered it.

"Armand," she called to him, in a voice which must have stabbed him, if he was human. But he did not notice. "Armand," she said again. Then she rose and tottered towards him. "Armand," she panted once more, clutching his arm, "look at our child. What does it mean? tell me."

He coldly but gently loosened her fingers from about his arm and thrust the hand away from him. "Tell me what it means!" she cried despairingly.

"It means," he answered lightly, "that the child is not white; it means that   25
you are not white."

A quick conception of all that this accusation meant for her nerved her with unwonted courage to deny it. "It is a lie; it is not true, I am white! Look at my hair, it is brown; and my eyes are gray, Armand, you know they are gray. And my skin is fair," seizing his wrist. "Look at my hand; whiter than yours, Armand," she laughed hysterically.

"As white as La Blanche's," he returned cruelly; and went away leaving her alone with their child.

When she could hold a pen in her hand, she sent a despairing letter to Madame Valmondé.

"My mother, they tell me I am not white. Armand has told me I am not white. For God's sake tell them it is not true. You must know it is not true. I shall die. I must die. I cannot be so unhappy, and live."

The answer that came was as brief: 30

"My own Désirée: Come home to Valmondé; back to your mother who loves you. Come with your child."

When the letter reached Désirée she went with it to her husband's study, and laid it open upon the desk before which he sat. She was like a stone image: silent, white, motionless after she placed it there.

In silence he ran his cold eyes over the written words. He said nothing. "Shall I go, Armand?" she asked in tones sharp with agonized suspense.

"Yes, go."

"Do you want me to go?"   35

"Yes, I want you to go."

He thought Almighty God had dealt cruelly and unjustly with him; and felt, somehow, that he was paying Him back in kind when he stabbed thus into his wife's soul. Moreover he no longer loved her, because of the unconscious injury she had brought upon his home and his name.

She turned away like one stunned by a blow, and walked slowly towards the door, hoping he would call her back.

"Good-by, Armand," she moaned.

He did not answer her. That was his last blow at fate.   40

Désirée went in search of her child. Zandrine was pacing the sombre gallery with it. She took the little one from the nurse's arms with no word of explanation, and descending the steps, walked away, under the live-oak branches.

It was an October afternoon; the sun was just sinking. Out in the still fields the negroes were picking cotton.

Désirée had not changed the thin white garment nor the slippers which she wore. Her hair was uncovered and the sun's rays brought a golden gleam from its brown meshes. She did not take the broad, beaten road which led to the far-off plantation of Valmondé. She walked across a deserted field, where the stubble bruised her tender feet, so delicately shod, and tore her thin gown to shreds.

She disappeared among the reeds and willows that grew thick along the banks of the deep, sluggish bayou; and she did not come back again.

Some weeks later there was a curious scene enacted at L'Abri. In the centre   45
of the smoothly swept back yard was a great bonfire. Armand Aubigny sat in the wide hallway that commanded a view of the spectacle; and it was he who dealt out to a half dozen negroes the material which kept this fire ablaze.

A graceful cradle of willow, with all its dainty furbishings, was laid upon the pyre, which had already been fed with the richness of a priceless *layette*. Then there were silk gowns, and velvet and satin ones added to these; laces, too, and embroideries; bonnets and gloves; for the *corbeille* had been of rare quality.

The last thing to go was a tiny bundle of letters; innocent little scribblings that Désirée had sent to him during the days of their espousal. There was the remnant of one back in the drawer from which he took them. But it was not Désirée's; it was part of an old letter from his mother to his father. He read it. She was thanking God for the blessing of her husband's love: —

"But, above all," she wrote, "night and day, I thank the good God for having so arranged our lives that our dear Armand will never know that his mother, who adores him, belongs to the race that is cursed with the brand of slavery."   [1892]

THINKING ABOUT THE TEXT

1. Does Armand really love Désirée? Explain.

2. Armand seems to have fallen in love "at first sight." Is this possible? Can love conquer all, even racial bias? Is Chopin skeptical?

3. What would you have done if you were Désirée? What will Armand do now that he knows?

4. Are we able to break free of our cultural heritage? What are the ways society tries to keep us in line? How do some people break free? Is there a danger in disregarding societal norms? Are there benefits?

5. Could this story happen this way today?

MAKING COMPARISONS

1. Which female character — Calixta, Louise, or Désirée — possesses true love for her husband? Do the husbands love their wives more? In different ways?

2. Which one of these marriages seems the strongest? Why?

3. Compare Chopin's attitude toward marriage in these three stories. Does she support all aspects of marriage? Since she wrote over a century ago, would she be pleased with the present state of marriage (including divorce)?

WRITING ABOUT ISSUES

1. Which ending seems more ethically questionable? Write a brief position paper suggesting that one of Chopin's endings should be changed (or remain the same) for moral reasons before junior high students read it.

2. Compare Alcée and Armand. Write a brief justification for or refutation of the behavior of one of them.

3. Do you think Louise Mallard should have admitted her feelings for her husband and left him? Would you? Why?

4. Chopin's works shocked American audiences. Research the ways sex, love, and relationships were dealt with in the 1880s in America. Write a brief explanation of why Chopin was ahead of her time.

Romantic Illusions: Cultural Contexts for David Henry Hwang's *M. Butterfly*

DAVID HENRY HWANG, *M. Butterfly*

CULTURAL CONTEXTS:
PAUL GRAY, "What Is Love?"
ANASTASIA TOUFEXIS, "The Right Chemistry"
NATHANIEL BRANDEN, "Immature Love"

Our cultural assumptions are so pervasive that we may find it hard to question "the obvious." The reality of romantic love is such an assumption. We see and hear about it so often in movies, books, television shows, and songs that the reality of romantic love seems beyond question. We may search for the all-consuming, magical, "spiritual-emotional-sexual attachment" we often see in contemporary films. But does this love exist? Perhaps romantic love is just an illusion that has more to do with physical attraction and passion than with true love. How do we know the difference, especially if we believe totally that such love exists? Can the belief create the illusion of reality? Or can it so blind us that we fall in love with someone who turns out to be someone else entirely? How deceived can we be by the belief in romantic love? Perhaps some people want to be deceived and fall in love with the "wrong" person on purpose. The mysteries of love never seem more puzzling and surprising than when we try to explain why some people choose implausible loves.

BEFORE YOU READ

In the film *The Crying Game* (1992) the main character, a former IRA fighter, falls in love with a man who he thinks is an attractive woman. He is shocked at the discovery. Can you imagine this happening to someone? To you?

DAVID HENRY HWANG

M. Butterfly

David Henry Hwang (b. 1957) characterizes himself as "interested in the dust that settles when two worlds collide." Born in Los Angeles into an affluent, ethnically Chinese family, Hwang's earliest influences were multicultural: His banker father was born in Shanghai, and his mother, a pianist and music teacher, spent her early years in the Philippines. Hwang attended the elite Harvard School in North Hollywood, California, and later majored in English literature at Stanford University, graduating in 1979 with honors and a Phi Beta Kappa award. The same year, his first play FOB *(for "fresh off the boat") was staged at the National Playwright's Conference. Hwang taught creative writing, studied playwriting at the Yale School of Drama, wrote television scripts, and saw several plays produced before achieving acclaim for* M. Butterfly *in 1988. The play, with John Lithgow and B. D. Wong in the principal roles, broke box-office records and gained numerous honors, including the 1988 Tony Award for best play of the year.*

THE CHARACTERS

RENE GALLIMARD
SONG LILING
MARC/MAN NO. 2/CONSUL SHARPLESS
RENEE/WOMAN AT PARTY/PINUP GIRL
COMRADE CHIN/SUZUKI/SHU-FANG
HELGA
TOULON/MAN NO. 1/JUDGE
DANCERS

TIME AND PLACE

The action of the play takes place in a Paris prison in the present, and, in recall, during the decade 1960–1970 in Beijing, and from 1966 to the present in Paris.

PLAYWRIGHT'S NOTES

A former French diplomat and a Chinese opera singer have been sentenced to six years in jail for spying for China after a two-day trial that traced a story of clandestine love and mistaken sexual identity. . . .

Mr. Boursicot was accused of passing information to China after he fell in love with Mr. Shi, whom he believed for twenty years to be a woman.
                                                              —The New York Times, *May 11, 1986*

This play was suggested by international newspaper accounts of a recent espionage trial. For purposes of dramatization, names have been changed, characters created, and incidents devised or altered, and this play does not purport to be a factual record of real events or real people.

> I could escape this feeling
> With my China girl . . .
> —David Bowie & Iggy Pop

ACT 1, Scene 1

M. *Gallimard's prison cell. Paris. 1988.*

Lights fade up to reveal Rene Gallimard, sixty-five, in a prison cell. He wears a comfortable bathrobe and looks old and tired. The sparsely furnished cell contains a wooden crate, upon which sits a hot plate with a kettle and a portable tape recorder. Gallimard sits on the crate staring at the recorder, a sad smile on his face.

Upstage Song, who appears as a beautiful woman in traditional Chinese garb, dances a traditional piece from the Peking Opera, surrounded by the percussive clatter of Chinese music.

Then, slowly, lights and sound cross-fade; the Chinese opera music dissolves into a Western opera, the "Love Duet" from Puccini's Madame Butterfly. *Song continues dancing, now to the Western accompaniment. Though her movements are the same, the difference in music now gives them a balletic quality.*

Gallimard rises, and turns upstage towards the figure of Song, who dances without acknowledging him.

GALLIMARD: Butterfly, Butterfly . . .

He forces himself to turn away, as the image of Song fades out, and talks to us.

GALLIMARD: The limits of my cell are as such: four-and-a-half meters by five. There's one window against the far wall; a door, very strong, to protect me from autograph hounds. I'm responsible for the tape recorder, the hot plate, and this charming coffee table.

When I want to eat, I'm marched off to the dining room — hot, steaming slop appears on my plate. When I want to sleep, the light bulb turns itself off — the work of fairies. It's an enchanted space I occupy. The French — we know how to run a prison.

But, to be honest, I'm not treated like an ordinary prisoner. Why? Because I'm a celebrity. You see, I make people laugh.

I never dreamed this day would arrive. I've never been considered witty or clever. In fact, as a young boy, in an informal poll among my grammar school classmates, I was voted "least likely to be invited to a party." It's a title I managed to hold on to for many years. Despite some stiff competition.

But now, how the tables turn! Look at me: the life of every social function in Paris. Paris? Why be modest: My fame has spread to Amsterdam, London, New York. Listen to them! In the world's smartest parlors. I'm the one who lifts their spirits!

With a flourish, Gallimard directs our attention to another part of the stage.

Scene 2

A party. 1988.

Lights go up on a chic-looking parlor, where a well-dressed trio, two men and one woman, make conversation. Gallimard also remains lit; he observes them from his cell.

WOMAN: And what of Gallimard?

MAN 1:   Gallimard?

MAN 2:   Gallimard!

GALLIMARD *(to us)*:   You see? They're all determined to say my name, as if it were some new dance.

WOMAN: He still claims not to believe the truth.

MAN 1:   What? Still? Even since the trial?

WOMAN: Yes. Isn't it mad?

MAN 2 *(laughing)*:   He says . . . it was dark . . . and she was very modest!

The trio break into laughter.

MAN 1:   So—what? He never touched her with his hands?

MAN 2:   Perhaps he did, and simply misidentified the equipment. A compelling case for sex education in the schools.

WOMAN: To protect the National Security—the Church can't argue with that.

MAN 1:   That's impossible! How could he not know?

MAN 2:   Simple ignorance.

MAN 1:   For twenty years?

MAN 2:   Time flies when you're being stupid.

WOMAN: Well, I thought the French were ladies' men.

MAN 2:   It seems Monsieur Gallimard was overly anxious to live up to his national reputation.

WOMAN: Well, he's not very good-looking.

MAN 1:   No, he's not.

MAN 2:   Certainly not.

WOMAN: Actually, I feel sorry for him.

MAN 2:   A toast! To Monsieur Gallimard!

WOMAN: Yes! To Gallimard!

MAN 1:   To Gallimard!

MAN 2:   *Vive la différence!*

They toast, laughing. Lights down on them.

Scene 3

M. Gallimard's cell.

GALLIMARD *(smiling):*   You see? They toast me. I've become a patron saint of the socially inept. Can they really be so foolish? Men like that—they should be scratching at my door, begging to learn my secrets! For I, Rene Gallimard, you see, I have known, and been loved by . . . the Perfect Woman.

    Alone in this cell, I sit night after night, watching our story play through my head, always searching for a new ending, one which redeems my honor, where she returns at last to my arms. And I imagine you—my ideal audience—who come to understand and even, perhaps just a little, to envy me.

He turns on his tape recorder. Over the house speakers, we hear the opening phrases of Madame Butterfly.

GALLIMARD: In order for you to understand what I did and why, I must introduce you to my favorite opera: *Madame Butterfly*. By Giacomo Puccini. First produced at La Scala, Milan, in 1904, it is now beloved throughout the Western world.

As Gallimard describes the opera, the tape segues in and out to sections he may be describing.

GALLIMARD: And why not? Its heroine, Cio-Cio-San, also known as Butterfly, is a feminine ideal, beautiful and brave. And its hero, the man for whom she gives up everything, is—*(He pulls out a naval officer's cap from under his crate, pops it on his head, and struts about.)* — not very good-looking, not too bright, and pretty much a wimp: Benjamin Franklin Pinkerton of the U.S. Navy. As the curtain rises, he's just closed on two great bargains: one on a house, the other on a woman — call it a package deal.

Pinkerton purchased the rights to Butterfly for one hundred yen — in modern currency, equivalent to about . . . sixty-six cents. So, he's feeling pretty pleased with himself as Sharpless, the American consul, arrives to witness the marriage.

Marc, wearing an official cap to designate Sharpless, enters and plays the character.

SHARPLESS/MARC: Pinkerton!

PINKERTON/GALLIMARD: Sharpless! How's it hangin'? It's a great day, just great. Between my house, my wife, and the rickshaw ride in from town, I've saved nineteen cents just this morning.

SHARPLESS: Wonderful. I can see the inscription on your tombstone already: "I saved a dollar, here I lie." *(He looks around.)* Nice house.

PINKERTON: It's artistic. Artistic, don't you think? Like the way the shoji screens slide open to reveal the wet bar and disco mirror ball? Classy, huh? Great for impressing the chicks.

SHARPLESS: "Chicks"? Pinkerton, you're going to be a married man!

PINKERTON: Well, sort of.

SHARPLESS: What do you mean?

PINKERTON: This country — Sharpless, it is okay. You got all these geisha girls running around —

SHARPLESS: I know! I live here!

PINKERTON: Then, you know the marriage laws, right? I split for one month, it's annulled!

SHARPLESS: Leave it to you to read the fine print. Who's the lucky girl?

PINKERTON: Cio-Cio-San. Her friends call her Butterfly. Sharpless, she eats out of my hand!

SHARPLESS: She's probably very hungry.

PINKERTON: Not like American girls. It's true what they say about Oriental girls. They want to be treated bad!

SHARPLESS: Oh, please!

PINKERTON: It's true!

SHARPLESS: Are you serious about this girl?

PINKERTON: I'm marrying her, aren't I?

SHARPLESS: Yes — with generous trade-in terms.

PINKERTON: When I leave, she'll know what it's like to have loved a real man. And I'll even buy her a few nylons.

SHARPLESS: You aren't planning to take her with you?

PINKERTON: Huh? Where?

SHARPLESS: Home!

PINKERTON: You mean, America? Are you crazy? Can you see her trying to buy rice in St. Louis?

SHARPLESS: So, you're not serious.

Pause.

PINKERTON/GALLIMARD *(as Pinkerton):* Consul, I am a sailor in port. *(As Galli-mard.)* They then proceed to sing the famous duet, "The Whole World Over."

The duet plays on the speakers. Gallimard, as Pinkerton, lip-syncs his lines from the opera.

GALLIMARD: To give a rough translation: "The whole world over, the Yankee travels, casting his anchor wherever he wants. Life's not worth living unless he can win the hearts of the fairest maidens, then hotfoot it off the premises ASAP." *(He turns towards Marc.)* In the preceding scene, I played Pinkerton, the womanizing cad, and my friend Marc from school . . . *(Marc bows grandly for our benefit.)* played Sharpless, the sensitive soul of reason. In life, however, our positions were usually — no, always — reversed.

Scene 4

École Nationale.° Aix-en-Provence. 1947.

GALLIMARD: No, Marc, I think I'd rather stay home.
MARC: Are you crazy?! We are going to Dad's condo in Marseilles! You know what happened last time?
GALLIMARD: Of course I do.
MARC: Of course you don't! You never know. . . . They stripped, Rene!
GALLIMARD: Who stripped?
MARC: The girls!
GALLIMARD: Girls? Who said anything about girls?
MARC: Rene, we're a buncha university guys goin' up to the woods. What are we gonna do — talk philosophy?
GALLIMARD: What girls? Where do you get them?
MARC: Who cares? The point is, they come. On trucks. Packed in like sardines. The back flips open, babes hop out, we're ready to roll.
GALLIMARD: You mean, they just — ?
MARC: Before you know it, every last one of them — they're stripped and splash-ing around my pool. There's no moon out, they can't see what's going on, their boobs are flapping, right? You close your eyes, reach out — it's grab bag, get it? Doesn't matter whose ass is between whose legs, whose teeth are sink-ing into who. You're just in there, going at it, eyes closed, on and on for as long as you can stand. *(Pause.)* Some fun, huh?
GALLIMARD: What happens in the morning?
MARC: In the morning, you're ready to talk some philosophy. *(Beat.)* So how 'bout it?
GALLIMARD: Marc, I can't . . . I'm afraid they'll say no — the girls. So I never ask.
MARC: You don't have to ask! That's the beauty — don't you see? They don't have to say yes. It's perfect for a guy like you, really.
GALLIMARD: You go ahead . . . I may come later.

École Nationale: National School.

MARC: Hey, Rene—it doesn't matter that you're clumsy and got zits—they're not looking!

GALLIMARD: Thank you very much.

MARC: Wimp.

Marc walks over to the other side of the stage, and starts waving and smiling at women in the audience.

GALLIMARD *(to us):*   We now return to my version of *Madame Butterfly* and the events leading to my recent conviction for treason.

Gallimard notices Marc making lewd gestures.

GALLIMARD: Marc, what are you doing?

MARC: Huh? *(Sotto voce.)* Rene, there're a lotta great babes out there. They're probably lookin' at me and thinking, "What a dangerous guy."

GALLIMARD: Yes—how could they help but be impressed by your cool sophistication?

Gallimard pops the Sharpless cap on Marc's head, and points him offstage. Marc exits, leering.

Scene 5

M. Gallimard's cell.

GALLIMARD: Next, Butterfly makes her entrance. We learn her age—fifteen . . . but very mature for her years.

Lights come up on the area where we saw Song dancing at the top of the play. She appears there again, now dressed as Madame Butterfly, moving to the "Love Duet." Gallimard turns upstage slightly to watch, transfixed.

GALLIMARD: But as she glides past him, beautiful, laughing softly behind her fan, don't we who are men sigh with hope? We, who are not handsome, nor brave, nor powerful, yet somehow believe, like Pinkerton, that we deserve a Butterfly. She arrives with all her possessions in the folds of her sleeves, lays them all out, for her man to do with as he pleases. Even her life itself—she bows her head as she whispers that she's not even worth the hundred yen he paid for her. He's already given too much, when we know he's really had to give nothing at all.

Music and lights on Song out. Gallimard sits at his crate.

GALLIMARD: In real life, women who put their total worth at less than sixty-six cents are quite hard to find. The closest we come is in the pages of these magazines. *(He reaches into his crate, pulls out a stack of girlie magazines, and begins flipping through them.)* Quite a necessity in prison. For three or four dollars, you get seven or eight women.

I first discovered these magazines at my uncle's house. One day, as a boy of twelve. The first time I saw them in his closet . . . all lined up—my body shook. Not with lust—no, with power. Here were women—a shelfful—who would do exactly as I wanted.

*The "Love Duet" creeps in over the speakers. Special comes up, revealing, not Song
this time, but a pinup girl in a sexy negligee, her back to us. Gallimard turns
upstage and looks at her.*

GIRL: I know you're watching me.

GALLIMARD: My throat . . . it's dry.

GIRL: I leave my blinds open every night before I go to bed.

GALLIMARD: I can't move.

GIRL: I leave my blinds open and the lights on.

GALLIMARD: I'm shaking. My skin is hot, but my penis is soft. Why?

GIRL: I stand in front of the window.

GALLIMARD: What is she going to do?

GIRL: I toss my hair, and I let my lips part . . . barely.

GALLIMARD: I shouldn't be seeing this. It's so dirty. I'm so bad.

GIRL: Then, slowly, I lift off my nightdress.

GALLIMARD: Oh, god. I can't believe it. I can't—

GIRL: I toss it to the ground.

GALLIMARD: Now, she's going to walk away. She's going to—

GIRL: I stand there, in the light, displaying myself.

GALLIMARD: No. She's—why is she naked?

GIRL: To you.

GALLIMARD: In front of a window? This is wrong. No—

GIRL: Without shame.

GALLIMARD: No, she must . . . like it.

GIRL: I like it.

GALLIMARD: She . . . she wants me to see.

GIRL: I want you to see.

GALLIMARD: I can't believe it! She's getting excited!

GIRL: I can't see you. You can do whatever you want.

GALLIMARD: I can't do a thing. Why?

GIRL: What would you like me to do . . . next?

*Lights go down on her. Music off. Silence, as Gallimard puts away his magazines.
Then he resumes talking to us.*

GALLIMARD: Act Two begins with Butterfly staring at the ocean. Pinkerton's been
    called back to the U.S., and he's given his wife a detailed schedule of his plans.
    In the column marked "return date," he's written "when the robins nest." This
    failed to ignite her suspicions. Now, three years have passed without a peep
    from him. Which brings a response from her faithful servant, Suzuki.

Comrade Chin enters, playing Suzuki.

SUZUKI: Girl, he's a loser. What'd he ever give you? Nineteen cents and those
    ugly Day-Glo stockings? Look, it's finished! Kaput! Done! And you should
    be glad! I mean, the guy was a woofer! He tried before, you know—before he
    met you, he went down to geisha central and plunked down his spare change
    in front of the usual candidates—everyone else gagged! These are hungry
    prostitutes, and they were not interested, get the picture? Now, stop slather-

ing when an American ship sails in, and let's make some bucks—I mean, yen! We are broke!

Now, what about Yamadori? Hey, hey—don't look away—the man is a prince—figuratively, and, what's even better, literally. He's rich, he's handsome, he says he'll die if you don't marry him—and he's even willing to overlook the little fact that you've been deflowered all over the place by a foreign devil. What do you mean, "But he's Japanese"? What do you think you are? You think you've been touched by the whitey god? He was a sailor with dirty hands!

Suzuki stalks offstage.

GALLIMARD: She's also visited by Consul Sharpless, sent by Pinkerton on a minor errand.

Marc enters, as Sharpless.

SHARPLESS: I hate this job.

GALLIMARD: This Pinkerton—he doesn't show up personally to tell his wife he's abandoning her. No, he sends a government diplomat . . . at taxpayers' expense.

SHARPLESS: Butterfly? Butterfly? I have some bad—I'm going to be ill. Butterfly, I came to tell you—

GALLIMARD: Butterfly says she knows he'll return and if he doesn't she'll kill herself rather than go back to her own people. *(Beat.)* This causes a lull in the conversation.

SHARPLESS: Let's put it this way . . .

GALLIMARD: Butterfly runs into the next room, and returns holding—

Sound cue: a baby crying. Sharpless, "seeing" this, backs away.

SHARPLESS: Well, good. Happy to see things going so well. I suppose I'll be going now. Ta ta. Ciao. *(He turns away. Sound cue out.)* I hate this job. *(He exits.)*

GALLIMARD: At that moment, Butterfly spots in the harbor an American ship— the *Abramo Lincoln!*

Music cue: "The Flower Duet." Song, still dressed as Butterfly, changes into a wedding kimono, moving to the music.

GALLIMARD: This is the moment that redeems her years of waiting. With Suzuki's help, they cover the room with flowers—

Chin, as Suzuki, trudges onstage and drops a lone flower without much enthusiasm.

GALLIMARD:—and she changes into her wedding dress to prepare for Pinkerton's arrival.

Suzuki helps Butterfly change. Helga enters, and helps Gallimard change into a tuxedo.

GALLIMARD: I married a woman older than myself—Helga.

HELGA: My father was ambassador to Australia. I grew up among criminals and kangaroos.

GALLIMARD: Hearing that brought me to the altar—

Helga exits.

GALLIMARD: —where I took a vow renouncing love. No fantasy woman would ever want me, so, yes, I would settle for a quick leap up the career ladder. Passion, I banish, and in its place—practicality!

But my vows had long since lost their charm by the time we arrived in China. The sad truth is that all men want a beautiful woman, and the uglier the man, the greater the want.

Suzuki makes final adjustments of Butterfly's costume, as does Gallimard of his tuxedo.

GALLIMARD: I married late, at age thirty-one. I was faithful to my marriage for eight years. Until the day when, as a junior-level diplomat in puritanical Peking, in a parlor at the German ambassador's house, during the "Reign of a Hundred Flowers,"° I first saw her . . . singing the death scene from *Madame Butterfly.*

Suzuki runs offstage.

Scene 6

German ambassador's house. Beijing. 1960.

The upstage special area now becomes a stage. Several chairs face upstage, representing seating for some twenty guests in the parlor. A few "diplomats"— Renee, Marc, Toulon—in formal dress enter and take seats.

Gallimard also sits down, but turns towards us and continues to talk. Orchestral accompaniment on the tape is now replaced by a simple piano. Song picks up the death scene from the point where Butterfly uncovers the hara-kiri knife.

GALLIMARD: The ending is pitiful. Pinkerton, in an act of great courage, stays home and sends his American wife to pick up Butterfly's child. The truth, long deferred, has come up to her door.

Song, playing Butterfly, sings the lines from the opera in her own voice—which, though not classical, should be decent.

SONG: "Con onor muore / chi non puo serbar / vita con onore."

GALLIMARD *(simultaneously):*   "Death with honor / Is better than life / Life with dishonor."

The stage is illuminated; we are now completely within an elegant diplomat's residence. Song proceeds to play out an abbreviated death scene. Everyone in the room applauds. Song, shyly, takes her bows. Others in the room rush to congratulate her. Gallimard remains with us.

GALLIMARD: They say in opera the voice is everything. That's probably why I'd never before enjoyed opera. Here . . . here was a Butterfly with little or no voice—but she had the grace, the delicacy . . . I believed this girl. I believed her suffering. I wanted to take her in my arms—so delicate, even I could protect her, take her home, pamper her until she smiled.

Reign of a Hundred Flowers: A brief period in 1957 when freedom of expression was allowed in China.

Over the course of the preceding speech, Song has broken from the upstage crowd and moved directly upstage of Gallimard.

SONG: Excuse me. Monsieur . . . ?

Gallimard turns upstage, shocked.

GALLIMARD: Oh! Gallimard. Mademoiselle . . . ? A beautiful . . .

SONG: Song Liling.

GALLIMARD: A beautiful performance.

SONG: Oh, please.

GALLIMARD: I usually —

SONG: You make me blush. I'm no opera singer at all.

GALLIMARD: I usually don't like *Butterfly*.

SONG: I can't blame you in the least.

GALLIMARD: I mean, the story —

SONG: Ridiculous.

GALLIMARD: I like the story, but . . . what?

SONG: Oh, you like it?

GALLIMARD: I . . . what I mean is, I've always seen it played by huge women in so much bad makeup.

SONG: Bad makeup is not unique to the West.

GALLIMARD: But, who can believe them?

SONG: And you believe me?

GALLIMARD: Absolutely. You were utterly convincing. It's the first time —

SONG: Convincing? As a Japanese woman? The Japanese used hundreds of our people for medical experiments during the war, you know. But I gather such an irony is lost on you.

GALLIMARD: No! I was about to say, it's the first time I've seen the beauty of the story.

SONG: Really?

GALLIMARD: Of her death. It's a . . . a pure sacrifice. He's unworthy, but what can she do? She loves him . . . so much. It's a very beautiful story.

SONG: Well, yes, to a Westerner.

GALLIMARD: Excuse me?

SONG: It's one of your favorite fantasies, isn't it? The submissive Oriental woman and the cruel white man.

GALLIMARD: Well, I didn't quite mean . . .

SONG: Consider it this way: what would you say if a blonde homecoming queen fell in love with a short Japanese businessman? He treats her cruelly, then goes home for three years, during which time she prays to his picture and turns down marriage from a young Kennedy. Then, when she learns he has remarried, she kills herself. Now, I believe you would consider this girl to be a deranged idiot, correct? But because it's an Oriental who kills herself for a Westerner — ah! — you find it beautiful.

Silence.

GALLIMARD: Yes . . . well . . . I see your point . . .

SONG: I will never do Butterfly again, Monsieur Gallimard. If you wish to see some real theater, come to the Peking Opera sometime. Expand your mind.

Song walks offstage. Other guests exit with her.

GALLIMARD *(to us):*   So much for protecting her in my big Western arms.

Scene 7

M. Gallimard's apartment. Beijing. 1960.
    Gallimard changes from his tux into a casual suit. Helga enters.

GALLIMARD: The Chinese are an incredibly arrogant people.

HELGA: They warned us about that in Paris, remember?

GALLIMARD: Even Parisians consider them arrogant. That's a switch.

HELGA: What is it that Madame Su says? "We are a very old civilization." I never know if she's talking about her country or herself.

GALLIMARD: I walk around here, all I hear every day, everywhere is how *old* this culture is. The fact that "old" may be synonymous with "senile" doesn't occur to them.

HELGA: You're not going to change them. "East is east, west is west, and . . ." whatever that guy said.

GALLIMARD: It's just that—silly. I met . . . at Ambassador Koening's tonight—you should've been there.

HELGA: Koening? Oh god, no. Did he enchant you all again with the history of Bavaria?

GALLIMARD: No. I met, I suppose, the Chinese equivalent of a diva. She's a singer in the Chinese opera.

HELGA: They have an opera, too? Do they sing in Chinese? Or maybe—in Italian?

GALLIMARD: Tonight, she did sing in Italian.

HELGA: How'd she manage that?

GALLIMARD: She must've been educated in the West before the Revolution. Her French is very good also. Anyway, she sang the death scene from *Madame Butterfly.*

HELGA: *Madame Butterfly!* Then I should have come. *(She begins humming, floating around the room as if dragging long kimono sleeves.)* Did she have a nice costume? I think it's a classic piece of music.

GALLIMARD: That's what *I* thought, too. Don't let her hear you say that.

HELGA: What's wrong?

GALLIMARD: Evidently the Chinese hate it.

HELGA: She hated it, but she performed it anyway? Is she perverse?

GALLIMARD: They hate it because the white man gets the girl. Sour grapes if you ask me.

HELGA: Politics again? Why can't they just hear it as a piece of beautiful music? So, what's in their opera?

GALLIMARD: I don't know. But, whatever it is, I'm sure it must be *old.*

Helga exits.

Scene 8

Chinese opera house and the streets of Beijing. 1960.
The sound of gongs clanging fills the stage.

GALLIMARD: My wife's innocent question kept ringing in my ears. I asked around, but no one knew anything about the Chinese opera. It took four weeks, but my curiosity overcame my cowardice. This Chinese diva—this unwilling Butterfly—what did she do to make her so proud?

     The room was hot, and full of smoke. Wrinkled faces, old women, teeth missing—a man with a growth on his neck, like a human toad. All smiling, pipes falling from their mouths, cracking nuts between their teeth, a live chicken pecking at my foot—all looking, screaming, gawking . . . at her.

The upstage area is suddenly hit with a harsh white light. It has become the stage for the Chinese opera performance. Two dancers enter, along with Song. Gallimard stands apart, watching. Song glides gracefully amidst the two dancers. Drums suddenly slam to a halt. Song strikes a pose, looking straight at Gallimard. Dancers exit. Light change. Pause, then Song walks right off the stage and straight up to Gallimard.

SONG: Yes. You. White man. I'm looking straight at you.

GALLIMARD: Me?

SONG: You see any other white men? It was too easy to spot you. How often does a man in my audience come in a tie?

Song starts to remove her costume. Underneath, she wears simple baggy clothes. They are now backstage. The show is over.

SONG: So, you are an adventurous imperialist?

GALLIMARD: I . . . thought it would further my education.

SONG: It took you four weeks. Why?

GALLIMARD: I've been busy.

SONG: Well, education has always been undervalued in the West, hasn't it?

GALLIMARD *(laughing):* I don't think that's true.

SONG: No, you wouldn't. You're a Westerner. How can you objectively judge your own values?

GALLIMARD: I think it's possible to achieve some distance.

SONG: Do you? *(Pause.)* It stinks in here. Let's go.

GALLIMARD: These are the smells of your loyal fans.

SONG: I love them for being my fans, I hate the smell they leave behind. I too can distance myself from my people. *(She looks around, then whispers in his ear.)* "Art for the masses" is a shitty excuse to keep artists poor. *(She pops a cigarette in her mouth.)* Be a gentleman, will you? And light my cigarette.

Gallimard fumbles for a match.

GALLIMARD: I don't . . . smoke.

SONG *(lighting her own):* Your loss. Had you lit my cigarette, I might have blown a puff of smoke right between your eyes. Come.

They start to walk about the stage. It is a summer night on the Beijing streets. Sounds of the city play on the house speakers.

SONG: How I wish there were even a tiny café to sit in. With cappuccinos, and men in tuxedos and bad expatriate jazz.

GALLIMARD: If my history serves me correctly, you weren't even allowed into the clubs in Shanghai before the Revolution.

SONG: Your history serves you poorly, Monsieur Gallimard. True, there were signs reading "No dogs and Chinamen." But a woman, especially a delicate Oriental woman — we always go where we please. Could you imagine it otherwise? Clubs in China filled with pasty, big-thighed white women, while thousands of slender lotus blossoms wait just outside the door? Never. The clubs would be empty. *(Beat.)* We have always held a certain fascination for you Caucasian men, have we not?

GALLIMARD: But . . . that fascination is imperialist, or so you tell me.

SONG: Do you believe everything I tell you? Yes. It is always imperialist. But sometimes . . . sometimes, it is also mutual. Oh — this is my flat.

GALLIMARD: I didn't even —

SONG: Thank you. Come another time and we will further expand your mind.

Song exits. Gallimard continues roaming the streets as he speaks to us.

GALLIMARD: What was that? What did she mean, "Sometimes . . . it is mutual"? Women do not flirt with me. And I normally can't talk to them. But tonight, I held up my end of the conversation.

Scene 9

Gallimard's bedroom. Beijing. 1960.
   Helga enters.

HELGA: You didn't tell me you'd be home late.

GALLIMARD: I didn't intend to. Something came up.

HELGA: Oh? Like what?

GALLIMARD: I went to the . . . to the Dutch ambassador's home.

HELGA: Again?

GALLIMARD: There was a reception for a visiting scholar. He's writing a six-volume treatise on the Chinese revolution. We all gathered that meant he'd have to live here long enough to actually write six volumes, and we all expressed our deepest sympathies.

HELGA: Well, I had a good night too. I went with the ladies to a martial arts demonstration. Some of those men — when they break those thick boards — *(she mimes fanning herself)* whoo-whoo!

Helga exits. Lights dim.

GALLIMARD: I lied to my wife. Why? I've never had any reason to lie before. But what reason did I have tonight? I didn't do anything wrong. That night, I had a dream. Other people, I've been told, have dreams when angels appear. Or dragons, or Sophia Loren in a towel. In my dream, Marc from school appeared.

Marc enters, in a nightshirt and cap.

MARC: Rene! You met a girl!

Gallimard and Marc stumble down the Beijing streets. Night sounds over the speakers.

GALLIMARD: It's not that amazing, thank you.

MARC: No! It's so monumental, I heard about it halfway around the world in my sleep!

GALLIMARD: I've met girls before, you know.

MARC: Name one. I've come across time and space to congratulate you. (*He hands Gallimard a bottle of wine.*)

GALLIMARD: Marc, this is expensive.

MARC: On those rare occasions when you become a formless spirit, why not steal the best?

Marc pops open the bottle, begins to share it with Gallimard.

GALLIMARD: You embarrass me. She . . . there's no reason to think she likes me.

MARC: "Sometimes, it is mutual"?

GALLIMARD: Oh.

MARC: "Mutual"? "Mutual"? What does that mean?

GALLIMARD: You heard?

MARC: It means the money is in the bank, you only have to write the check!

GALLIMARD: I am a married man!

MARC: And an excellent one too. I cheated after . . . six months. Then again and again, until now — three hundred girls in twelve years.

GALLIMARD: I don't think we should hold that up as a model.

MARC: Of course not! My life — it is disgusting! Phooey! Phooey! But, you — you are the model husband.

GALLIMARD: Anyway, it's impossible. I'm a foreigner.

MARC: Ah, yes. She cannot love you, it is taboo, but something deep inside her heart . . . she cannot help herself . . . she must surrender to you. It is her destiny.

GALLIMARD: How do you imagine all this?

MARC: The same way you do. It's an old story. It's in our blood. They fear us, Rene. Their women fear us. And their men — their men hate us. And, you know something? They are all correct.

They spot a light in a window.

MARC: There! There, Rene!

GALLIMARD: It's her window.

MARC: Late at night — it burns. The light — it burns for you.

GALLIMARD: I won't look. It's not respectful.

MARC: We don't have to be respectful. We're foreign devils.

Enter Song, in a sheer robe, her face completely swathed in black cloth. The "One Fine Day" aria creeps in over the speakers. With her back to us, Song mimes attending to her toilette. Her robe comes loose, revealing her white shoulders.

MARC: All your life you've waited for a beautiful girl who would lay down for you. All your life you've smiled like a saint when it's happened to every other man you know. And you see them in magazines and you see them in movies. And you wonder, what's wrong with me? Will anyone beautiful ever want me? As the years pass, your hair thins and you struggle to hold on to even your hopes. Stop struggling, Rene. The wait is over. *(He exits.)*

GALLIMARD: Marc? Marc?

At that moment, Song, her back still towards us, drops her robe. A second of her naked back, then a sound cue: a phone ringing, very loud. Blackout, followed in the next beat by a special up on the bedroom area, where a phone now sits. Gallimard stumbles across the stage and picks up the phone. Sound cue out. Over the course of his conversation, area lights fill in the vicinity of his bed. It is the following morning.

GALLIMARD: Yes? Hello?

SONG *(offstage)*: Is it very early?

GALLIMARD: Why, yes.

SONG *(offstage)*: How early?

GALLIMARD: It's . . . it's 5:30. Why are you — ?

SONG *(offstage)*: But it's light outside. Already.

GALLIMARD: It is. The sun must be in confusion today.

Over the course of Song's next speech, her upstage special comes up again. She sits in a chair, legs crossed, in a robe, telephone to her ear.

SONG: I waited until I saw the sun. That was as much discipline as I could manage for one night. Do you forgive me?

GALLIMARD: Of course . . . for what?

SONG: Then I'll ask you quickly. Are you really interested in the opera?

GALLIMARD: Why, yes. Yes I am.

SONG: Then come again next Thursday. I am playing *The Drunken Beauty.* May I count on you?

GALLIMARD: Yes. You may.

SONG: Perfect. Well, I must be getting to bed. I'm exhausted. It's been a very long night for me.

Song hangs up; special on her goes off. Gallimard begins to dress for work.

Scene 10

Song Liling's apartment. Beijing. 1960.

GALLIMARD: I returned to the opera that next week, and the week after that . . . she keeps our meetings so short — perhaps fifteen, twenty minutes at most. So I am left each week with a thirst which is intensified. In this way, fifteen weeks have gone by. I am starting to doubt the words of my friend Marc. But no, not really. In my heart, I know she has . . . an interest in me. I suspect this is her way. She is outwardly bold and outspoken, yet her heart is shy and afraid. It is the Oriental in her at war with her Western education.

SONG *(offstage)*: I will be out in an instant. Ask the servant for anything you want.

GALLIMARD: Tonight, I have finally been invited to enter her apartment. Though the idea is almost beyond belief, I believe she is afraid of me.

Gallimard looks around the room. He picks up a picture in a frame, studies it. Without his noticing, Song enters, dressed elegantly in a black gown from the twenties. She stands in the doorway looking like Anna May Wong.°

SONG: That is my father.

GALLIMARD *(surprised)*:   Mademoiselle Song . . .

She glides up to him, snatches away the picture.

SONG: It is very good that he did not live to see the Revolution. They would, no doubt, have made him kneel on broken glass. Not that he didn't deserve such a punishment. But he is my father. I would've hated to see it happen.

GALLIMARD: I'm very honored that you've allowed me to visit your home.

Song curtseys.

SONG: Thank you. Oh! Haven't you been poured any tea?

GALLIMARD: I'm really not—

SONG *(to her offstage servant)*:   Shu-Fang! Cha! Kwai-lah! *(To Gallimard.)* I'm sorry. You want everything to be perfect—

GALLIMARD: Please.

SONG: —and before the evening even begins—

GALLIMARD: I'm really not thirsty.

SONG: —it's ruined.

GALLIMARD *(sharply)*:   Mademoiselle Song!

Song sits down.

SONG: I'm sorry.

GALLIMARD: What are you apologizing for now?

Pause; Song starts to giggle.

SONG: I don't know!

Gallimard laughs.

GALLIMARD: Exactly my point.

SONG: Oh, I am silly. Light-headed. I promise not to apologize for anything else tonight, do you hear me?

GALLIMARD: That's a good girl.

Shu-Fang, a servant girl, comes out with a tea tray and starts to pour.

SONG *(to Shu-Fang)*:   No! I'll pour myself for the gentleman!

Shu-Fang, staring at Gallimard, exits.

GALLIMARD: You have a beautiful home.

SONG: No, I . . . I don't even know why I invited you up.

GALLIMARD: Well, I'm glad you did.

Song looks around the room.

Anna May Wong (1905–1961): Chinese American actor known for her exotic beauty and most often cast as a villain.

SONG: There is an element of danger to your presence.

GALLIMARD: Oh?

SONG: You must know.

GALLIMARD: It doesn't concern me. We both know why I'm here.

SONG: It doesn't concern me either. No . . . well perhaps . . .

GALLIMARD: What?

SONG: Perhaps I am slightly afraid of scandal.

GALLIMARD: What are we doing?

SONG: I'm entertaining you. In my parlor.

GALLIMARD: In France, that would hardly—

SONG: France. France is a country living in the modern era. Perhaps even ahead of it. China is a nation whose soul is firmly rooted two thousand years in the past. What I do, even pouring the tea for you now . . . it has . . . implications. The walls and windows say so. Even my own heart, strapped inside this Western dress . . . even it says things—things I don't care to hear.

Song hands Gallimard a cup of tea. Gallimard puts his hand over both the teacup and Song's hand.

GALLIMARD: This is a beautiful dress.

SONG: Don't.

GALLIMARD: What?

SONG: I don't even know if it looks right on me.

GALLIMARD: Believe me—

SONG: You are from France. You see so many beautiful women.

GALLIMARD: France? Since when are the European women—?

SONG: Oh! What am I trying to do, anyway?!

Song runs to the door, composes herself, then turns towards Gallimard.

SONG: Monsieur Gallimard, perhaps you should go.

GALLIMARD: But . . . why?

SONG: There's something wrong about this.

GALLIMARD: I don't see what.

SONG: I feel . . . I am not myself.

GALLIMARD: No. You're nervous.

SONG: Please. Hard as I try to be modern, to speak like a man, to hold a Western woman's strong face up to my own . . . in the end, I fail. A small, frightened heart beats too quickly and gives me away. Monsieur Gallimard, I'm a Chinese girl. I've never . . . never invited a man up to my flat before. The forwardness of my actions makes my skin burn.

GALLIMARD: What are you afraid of? Certainly not me, I hope.

SONG: I'm a modest girl.

GALLIMARD: I know. And very beautiful. *(He touches her hair.)*

SONG: Please—go now. The next time you see me, I shall again be myself.

GALLIMARD: I like you the way you are right now.

SONG: You are a cad.

GALLIMARD: What do you expect? I'm a foreign devil.

Gallimard walks downstage. Song exits.

GALLIMARD *(to us):*   Did you hear the way she talked about Western women? Much differently than the first night. She does — she feels inferior to them — and to me.

Scene 11

The French embassy. Beijing. 1960.
Gallimard moves towards a desk.

GALLIMARD: I determined to try an experiment. In *Madame Butterfly*, Cio-Cio-San fears that the Western man who catches a butterfly will pierce its heart with a needle, then leave it to perish. I began to wonder: had I, too, caught a butterfly who would writhe on a needle?

Marc enters, dressed as a bureaucrat, holding a stack of papers. As Gallimard speaks, Marc hands papers to him. He peruses, then signs, stamps, or rejects them.

GALLIMARD: Over the next five weeks, I worked like a dynamo. I stopped going to the opera, I didn't phone or write her. I knew this little flower was waiting for me to call, and, as I wickedly refused to do so, I felt for the first time that rush of power — the absolute power of a man.

Marc continues acting as the bureaucrat, but he now speaks as himself.

MARC: Rene! It's me.

GALLIMARD: Marc — I hear your voice everywhere now. Even in the midst of work.

MARC: That's because I'm watching you — all the time.

GALLIMARD: You were always the most popular guy in school.

MARC: Well, there's no guarantee of failure in life like happiness in high school. Somehow I knew I'd end up in the suburbs working for Renault and you'd be in the Orient picking exotic women off the trees. And they say there's no justice.

GALLIMARD: That's why you were my friend?

MARC: I gave you a little of my life, so that now you can give me some of yours. *(Pause.)* Remember Isabelle?

GALLIMARD: Of course I remember! She was my first experience.

MARC: We all wanted to ball her. But she only wanted me.

GALLIMARD: I had her.

MARC: Right. You balled her.

GALLIMARD: You were the only one who ever believed me.

MARC: Well, there's a good reason for that. *(Beat.)* C'mon. You must've guessed.

GALLIMARD: You told me to wait in the bushes by the cafeteria that night. The next thing I knew, she was on me. Dress up in the air.

MARC: She never wore underwear.

GALLIMARD: My arms were pinned to the dirt.

MARC: She loved the superior position. A girl ahead of her time.

GALLIMARD: I looked up, and there was this woman . . . bouncing up and down on my loins.

MARC: Screaming, right?

GALLIMARD: Screaming, and breaking off the branches all around me, and pounding my butt up and down into the dirt.

MARC: Huffing and puffing like a locomotive.

GALLIMARD: And in the middle of all this, the leaves were getting into my mouth, my legs were losing circulation, I thought, "God. So this is *it?*"

MARC: You thought that?

GALLIMARD: Well, I was worried about my legs falling off.

MARC: You didn't have a good time?

GALLIMARD: No, that's not what I — I had a great time!

MARC: You're sure?

GALLIMARD: Yeah. Really.

MARC: 'Cuz I wanted you to have a good time.

GALLIMARD: I did.

Pause.

MARC: Shit. (*Pause.*) When all is said and done, she was kind of a lousy lay, wasn't she? I mean, there was a lot of energy there, but you never knew what she was doing with it. Like when she yelled "I'm coming!" — hell, it was so loud, you wanted to go, "Look, it's not that big a deal."

GALLIMARD: I got scared. I thought she meant someone was actually coming. (*Pause.*) But, Marc?

MARC: What?

GALLIMARD: Thanks.

MARC: Oh, don't mention it.

GALLIMARD: It was my first experience.

MARC: Yeah. You got her.

GALLIMARD: I got her.

MARC: Wait! Look at that letter again!

Gallimard picks up one of the papers he's been stamping, and rereads it.

GALLIMARD (*to us*): After six weeks, they began to arrive. The letters.

Upstage special on Song, as Madame Butterfly. The scene is underscored by the "Love Duet."

SONG: Did we fight? I do not know. Is the opera no longer of interest to you? Please come — my audiences miss the white devil in their midst.

Gallimard looks up from the letter, towards us.

GALLIMARD (*to us*): A concession, but much too dignified. (*Beat; he discards the letter.*) I skipped the opera again that week to complete a position paper on trade.

The bureaucrat hands him another letter.

SONG: Six weeks have passed since last we met. Is this your practice — to leave friends in the lurch? Sometimes I hate you, sometimes I hate myself, but always I miss you.

GALLIMARD *(to us)*: Better, but I don't like the way she calls me "friend." When a woman calls a man her "friend," she's calling him a eunuch or a homosexual. *(Beat; he discards the letter.)* I was absent from the opera for the seventh week, feeling a sudden urge to clean out my files.

Bureaucrat hands him another letter.

SONG: Your rudeness is beyond belief. I don't deserve this cruelty. Don't bother to call. I'll have you turned away at the door.

GALLIMARD *(to us)*: I didn't. *(He discards the letter; bureaucrat hands him another.)* And then finally, the letter that concluded my experiment.

SONG: I am out of words. I can hide behind dignity no longer. What do you want? I have already given you my shame.

Gallimard gives the letter back to Marc, slowly. Special on Song fades out.

GALLIMARD *(to us)*: Reading it, I became suddenly ashamed. Yes, my experiment had been a success. She was turning on my needle. But the victory seemed hollow.

MARC: Hollow?! Are you crazy?

GALLIMARD: Nothing, Marc. Please go away.

MARC *(exiting, with papers)*: Haven't I taught you anything?

GALLIMARD: "I have already given you my shame." I had to attend a reception that evening. On the way, I felt sick. If there is a God, surely he would punish me now. I had finally gained power over a beautiful woman, only to abuse it cruelly. There must be justice in the world. I had the strange feeling that the ax would fall this very evening.

Scene 12

Ambassador Toulon's residence. Beijing. 1960.
Sound cue: party noises. Light change. We are now in a spacious residence.
Toulon, the French ambassador, enters and taps Gallimard on the shoulder.

TOULON: Gallimard? Can I have a word? Over here.

GALLIMARD *(to us)*: Manuel Toulon. French ambassador to China. He likes to think of us all as his children. Rather like God.

TOULON: Look, Gallimard, there's not much to say. I've liked you. From the day you walked in. You were no leader, but you were tidy and efficient.

GALLIMARD: Thank you, sir.

TOULON: Don't jump the gun. Okay, our needs in China are changing. It's embarrassing that we lost Indochina. Someone just wasn't on the ball there. I don't mean you personally, of course.

GALLIMARD: Thank you, sir.

TOULON: We're going to be doing a lot more information-gathering in the future. The nature of our work here is changing. Some people are just going to have to go. It's nothing personal.

GALLIMARD: Oh.

TOULON: Want to know a secret? Vice-Consul LeBon is being transferred.

GALLIMARD *(to us)*:   My immediate superior!

TOULON: And most of his department.

GALLIMARD *(to us)*:   Just as I feared! God has seen my evil heart—

TOULON: But not you.

GALLIMARD *(to us)*:   — and he's taking her away just as . . . *(To Toulon.)* Excuse me, sir?

TOULON: Scare you? I think I did. Cheer up, Gallimard. I want you to replace LeBon as vice-consul.

GALLIMARD: You—? Yes, well, thank you, sir.

TOULON: Anytime.

GALLIMARD: I . . . accept with great humility.

TOULON: Humility won't be part of the job. You're going to coordinate the revamped intelligence division. Want to know a secret? A year ago, you would've been out. But the past few months, I don't know how it happened, you've become this new aggressive confident . . . thing. And they also tell me you get along with the Chinese. So I think you're a lucky man, Gallimard. Congratulations.

They shake hands. Toulon exits. Party noises out. Gallimard stumbles across a darkened stage.

GALLIMARD: Vice-consul? Impossible! As I stumbled out of the party, I saw it written across the sky: There is no God. Or, no—say that there is a God. But that God . . . understands. Of course! God who creates Eve to serve Adam, who blesses Solomon with his harem but ties Jezebel to a burning bed° — that God is a man. And he understands! At age thirty-nine, I was suddenly initiated into the way of the world.

Scene 13

Song Liling's apartment. Beijing. 1960.
   Song enters, in a sheer dressing gown.

SONG: Are you crazy?

GALLIMARD: Mademoiselle Song—

SONG: To come here—at this hour? After . . . after eight weeks?

GALLIMARD: It's the most amazing—

SONG: You bang on my door? Scare my servants, scandalize the neighbors?

GALLIMARD: I've been promoted. To vice-consul.

Pause.

SONG: And what is that supposed to mean to me?

GALLIMARD: Are you my Butterfly?

SONG: What are you saying?

GALLIMARD: I've come tonight for an answer: are you my Butterfly?

God who creates Eve . . . burning bed: Eve, Adam, Solomon, and Jezebel are biblical characters. See Gen. 2:18–25; I Kings 11:1–8; and II Kings 9:11–37.

SONG: Don't you know already?

GALLIMARD: I want you to say it.

SONG: I don't want to say it.

GALLIMARD: So, that is your answer?

SONG: You know how I feel about —

GALLIMARD: I do remember one thing.

SONG: What?

GALLIMARD: In the letter I received today.

SONG: Don't.

GALLIMARD: "I have already given you my shame."

SONG: It's enough that I even wrote it.

GALLIMARD: Well, then —

SONG: I shouldn't have it splashed across my face.

GALLIMARD: — if that's all true —

SONG: Stop!

GALLIMARD: Then what is one more short answer?

SONG: I don't want to!

GALLIMARD: Are you my Butterfly? *(Silence; he crosses the room and begins to touch her hair.)* I want from you honesty. There should be nothing false between us. No false pride.

Pause.

SONG: Yes, I am. I am your Butterfly.

GALLIMARD: Then let me be honest with you. It is because of you that I was promoted tonight. You have changed my life forever. My little Butterfly, there should be no more secrets: I love you.

He starts to kiss her roughly. She resists slightly.

SONG: No . . . no . . . gently . . . please, I've never . . .

GALLIMARD: No?

SONG: I've tried to appear experienced, but . . . the truth is . . . no.

GALLIMARD: Are you cold?

SONG: Yes. Cold.

GALLIMARD: Then we will go very, very slowly.

He starts to caress her; her gown begins to open.

SONG: No . . . let me . . . keep my clothes . . .

GALLIMARD: But . . .

SONG: Please . . . it all frightens me. I'm a modest Chinese girl.

GALLIMARD: My poor little treasure.

SONG: I am your treasure. Though inexperienced, I am not . . . ignorant. They teach us things, our mothers, about pleasing a man.

GALLIMARD: Yes?

SONG: I'll do my best to make you happy. Turn off the lights.

Gallimard gets up and heads for a lamp. Song, propped up on one elbow, tosses her hair back and smiles.

SONG: Monsieur Gallimard?

GALLIMARD: Yes, Butterfly?

SONG: *"Vieni, vieni!"*

GALLIMARD: "Come, darling."

SONG: *"Ah! Dolce notte!"*

GALLIMARD: "Beautiful night."

SONG: *"Tutto estatico d'amor ride il ciel!"*

GALLIMARD: "All ecstatic with love, the heavens are filled with laughter."

He turns off the lamp. Blackout.

ACT 2, Scene 1

M. Gallimard's cell. Paris. 1988.
  Lights up on Gallimard. He sits in his cell, reading from a leaflet.

GALLIMARD: This, from a contemporary critic's commentary on *Madame Butterfly*: "Pinkerton suffers from . . . being an obnoxious bounder whom every man in the audience itches to kick." Bully for us men in the audience! Then, in the same note: "Butterfly is the most irresistibly appealing of Puccini's 'Little Women.' Watching the succession of her humiliations is like watching a child under torture." *(He tosses the pamphlet over his shoulder.)* I suggest that, while we men may all want to kick Pinkerton, very few of us would pass up the opportunity to *be* Pinkerton.

Gallimard moves out of his cell.

Scene 2

Gallimard and Butterfly's flat. Beijing. 1960.
  We are in a simple but well-decorated parlor. Gallimard moves to sit on a sofa, while Song, dressed in a cheongsam,° enters and curls up at his feet.

GALLIMARD *(to us)*:   We secured a flat on the outskirts of Peking. Butterfly, as I was calling her now, decorated our "home" with Western furniture and Chinese antiques. And there, on a few stolen afternoons or evenings each week, Butterfly commenced her education.

SONG: The Chinese men — they keep us down.

GALLIMARD: Even in the "New Society"?

SONG: In the "New Society," we are all kept ignorant equally. That's one of the exciting things about loving a Western man. I know you are not threatened by a woman's education.

GALLIMARD: I'm no saint, Butterfly.

SONG: But you come from a progressive society.

GALLIMARD: We're not always reminding each other how "old" we are, if that's what you mean.

---

cheongsam: A fitted dress with side slits in the skirt.

SONG: Exactly. We Chinese—once, I suppose, it is true, we ruled the world. But so what? How much more exciting to be part of the society ruling the world today. Tell me—what's happening in Vietnam?

GALLIMARD: Oh, Butterfly—you want me to bring my work home?

SONG: I want to know what you know. To be impressed by my man. It's not the particulars so much as the fact that you're making decisions which change the shape of the world.

GALLIMARD: Not the world. At best, a small corner.

Toulon enters, and sits at a desk upstage.

Scene 3

French embassy. Beijing. 1961.
  Gallimard moves downstage, to Toulon's desk. Song remains upstage, watching.

TOULON: And a more troublesome corner is hard to imagine.

GALLIMARD: So, the Americans plan to begin bombing?

TOULON: This is very secret, Gallimard: yes. The Americans don't have an embassy here. They're asking us to be their eyes and ears. Say Jack Kennedy signed an order to bomb North Vietnam, Laos. How would the Chinese react?

GALLIMARD: I think the Chinese will squawk—

TOULON: Uh-huh.

GALLIMARD: —but, in their hearts, they don't even like Ho Chi Minh.°

Pause.

TOULON: What a bunch of jerks. Vietnam was *our* colony. Not only didn't the Americans help us fight to keep them, but now, seven years later, they've come back to grab the territory for themselves. It's very irritating.

GALLIMARD: With all due respect, sir, why should the Americans have won our war for us back in fifty-four if we didn't have the will to win it ourselves?

TOULON: You're kidding, aren't you?

Pause.

GALLIMARD: The Orientals simply want to be associated with whoever shows the most strength and power. You live with the Chinese, sir. Do you think they like Communism?

TOULON: I live in China. Not with the Chinese.

GALLIMARD: Well, I—

TOULON: *You* live with the Chinese.

GALLIMARD: Excuse me?

TOULON: I can't keep a secret.

GALLIMARD: What are you saying?

Ho Chi Minh (1890–1969): First president of North Vietnam (1945–1969).

TOULON: Only that I'm not immune to gossip. So, you're keeping a native mistress? Don't answer. It's none of my business. *(Pause.)* I'm sure she must be gorgeous.

GALLIMARD: Well . . .

TOULON: I'm impressed. You had the stamina to go out into the streets and hunt one down. Some of us have to be content with the wives of the expatriate community.

GALLIMARD: I do feel . . . fortunate.

TOULON: So, Gallimard, you've got the inside knowledge—what *do* the Chinese think?

GALLIMARD: Deep down, they miss the old days. You know, cappuccinos, men in tuxedos—

TOULON: So what do we tell the Americans about Vietnam?

GALLIMARD: Tell them there's a natural affinity between the West and the Orient.

TOULON: And that you speak from experience?

GALLIMARD: The Orientals are people too. They want the good things we can give them. If the Americans demonstrate the will to win, the Vietnamese will welcome them into a mutually beneficial union.

TOULON: I don't see how the Vietnamese can stand up to American firepower.

GALLIMARD: Orientals will always submit to a greater force.

TOULON: I'll note your opinions in my report. The Americans always love to hear how "welcome" they'll be. *(He starts to exit.)*

GALLIMARD: Sir?

TOULON: Mmmm?

GALLIMARD: This . . . rumor you've heard.

TOULON: Uh-huh?

GALLIMARD: How . . . widespread do you think it is?

TOULON: It's only widespread within this embassy. Where nobody talks because everybody is guilty. We were worried about you, Gallimard. We thought you were the only one here without a secret. Now you go and find a lotus blossom . . . and top us all. *(He exits.)*

GALLIMARD *(to us)*:   Toulon knows! And he approves! I was learning the benefits of being a man. We form our own clubs, sit behind thick doors, smoke—and celebrate the fact that we're still boys. *(He starts to move downstage, towards Song.)* So, over the—

Suddenly Comrade Chin enters. Gallimard backs away.

GALLIMARD *(to Song)*:   No! Why does she have to come in?

SONG: Rene, be sensible. How can they understand the story without her? Now, don't embarrass yourself.

Gallimard moves down center.

GALLIMARD *(to us)*:   Now, you will see why my story is so amusing to so many people. Why they snicker at parties in disbelief. Please—try to understand it from my point of view. We are all prisoners of our time and place. *(He exits.)*

Scene 4

Gallimard and Butterfly's flat. Beijing. 1961.

SONG *(to us):*   1961. The flat Monsieur Gallimard rented for us. An evening after he has gone.

CHIN: Okay, see if you can find out when the Americans plan to start bombing Vietnam. If you can find out what cities, even better.

SONG: I'll do my best, but I don't want to arouse his suspicions.

CHIN: Yeah, sure, of course. So, what else?

SONG: The Americans will increase troops in Vietnam to 170,000 soldiers with 120,000 militia and 11,000 American advisors.

CHIN *(writing):*   Wait, wait, 120,000 militia and —

SONG: — 11,000 American —

CHIN: — American advisors. *(Beat.)* How do you remember so much?

SONG: I'm an actor.

CHIN: Yeah. *(Beat.)* Is that how come you dress like that?

SONG: Like what, Miss Chin?

CHIN: Like that dress! You're wearing a dress. And every time I come here, you're wearing a dress. Is that because you're an actor? Or what?

SONG: It's a . . . disguise, Miss Chin.

CHIN: Actors, I think they're all weirdos. My mother tells me actors are like gamblers or prostitutes or —

SONG: It helps me in my assignment.

Pause.

CHIN: You're not gathering information in any way that violates Communist Party principles, are you?

SONG: Why would I do that?

CHIN: Just checking. Remember: when working for the Great Proletarian State, you represent our Chairman Mao in every position you take.

SONG: I'll try to imagine the Chairman taking my positions.

CHIN: We all think of him this way. Good-bye, comrade. *(She starts to exit.)* Comrade?

SONG: Yes?

CHIN: Don't forget: there is no homosexuality in China!

SONG: Yes, I've heard.

CHIN: Just checking. *(She exits.)*

SONG *(to us):*   What passes for a woman in modern China.

Gallimard sticks his head out from the wings.

GALLIMARD: Is she gone?

SONG: Yes, Rene. Please continue in your own fashion.

Scene 5

Beijing. 1961–1963.

Gallimard moves to the couch where Song still sits. He lies down in her lap, and she strokes his forehead.

GALLIMARD *(to us):*   And so, over the years 1961, '62, '63, we settled into our routine, Butterfly and I. She would always have prepared a light snack and then, ever so delicately, and only if I agreed, she would start to pleasure me. With her hands, her mouth . . . too many ways to explain, and too sad, given my present situation. But mostly we would talk. About my life. Perhaps there is nothing more rare than to find a woman who passionately listens.

Song remains upstage, listening, as Helga enters and plays a scene downstage with Gallimard.

HELGA: Rene, I visited Dr. Bolleart this morning.

GALLIMARD: Why? Are you ill?

HELGA: No, no. You see, I wanted to ask him . . . that question we've been discussing.

GALLIMARD: And I told you, it's only a matter of time. Why did you bring a doctor into this? We just have to keep trying—like a crapshoot, actually.

HELGA: I went, I'm sorry. But listen: he says there's nothing wrong with me.

GALLIMARD: You see? Now, will you stop—?

HELGA: Rene, he says he'd like you to go in and take some tests.

GALLIMARD: Why? So he can find there's nothing wrong with both of us?

HELGA: Rene, I don't ask for much. One trip! One visit! And then, whatever you want to do about it—you decide.

GALLIMARD: You're assuming he'll find something defective!

HELGA: No! Of course not! Whatever he finds—if he finds nothing, we decide what to do about nothing! But go!

GALLIMARD: If he finds nothing, we keep trying. Just like we do now.

HELGA: But at least we'll know! *(Pause.)* I'm sorry. *(She starts to exit.)*

GALLIMARD: Do you really want me to see Dr. Bolleart?

HELGA: Only if you want a child, Rene. We have to face the fact that time is running out. Only if you want a child. *(She exits.)*

GALLIMARD *(to Song):*   I'm a modern man, Butterfly. And yet, I don't want to go. It's the same old voodoo. I feel like God himself is laughing at me if I can't produce a child.

SONG: You men of the West—you're obsessed by your odd desire for equality. Your wife can't give you a child, and *you're* going to the doctor?

GALLIMARD: Well, you see, she's already gone.

SONG: And because this incompetent can't find the defect, you now have to subject yourself to him? It's unnatural.

GALLIMARD: Well, what is the "natural" solution?

SONG: In Imperial China, when a man found that one wife was inadequate, he turned to another—to give him his son.

GALLIMARD: What do you—? I can't . . . marry you, yet.

SONG: Please. I'm not asking you to be my husband. But I am already your wife.

GALLIMARD: Do you want to . . . have my child?

SONG: I thought you'd never ask.

GALLIMARD: But, your career . . . your—

SONG: Phooey on my career! That's your Western mind, twisting itself into strange shapes again. Of course I love my career. But what would I love most of all? To feel something inside me—day and night—something I know is yours. *(Pause.)* Promise me . . . you won't go to this doctor. Who is this Western quack to set himself as judge over the man I love? I know who is a man, and who is not. *(She exits.)*

GALLIMARD *(to us):*   Dr. Bolleart? Of course I didn't go. What man would?

Scene 6

Beijing. 1963.

Party noises over the house speakers. Renee enters, wearing a revealing gown.

GALLIMARD: 1963. A party at the Austrian embassy. None of us could remember the Austrian ambassador's name, which seemed somehow appropriate. *(To Renee.)* So, I tell the Americans, Diem° must go. The U.S. wants to be respected by the Vietnamese, and yet they're propping up this nobody seminarian as her president. A man whose claim to fame is his sister-in-law imposing fanatic "moral order" campaigns? Oriental women—when they're good, they're very good, but when they're bad, they're Christians.

RENEE: Yeah.

GALLIMARD: And what do you do?

RENEE: I'm a student. My father exports a lot of useless stuff to the Third World.

GALLIMARD: How useless?

RENEE: You know. Squirt guns, confectioner's sugar, Hula Hoops . . .

GALLIMARD: I'm sure they appreciate the sugar.

RENEE: I'm here for two years to study Chinese.

GALLIMARD: Two years!

RENEE: That's what everybody says.

GALLIMARD: When did you arrive?

RENEE: Three weeks ago.

GALLIMARD: And?

RENEE: I like it. It's primitive, but . . . well, this is the place to learn Chinese, so here I am.

GALLIMARD: Why Chinese?

RENEE: I think it'll be important someday.

GALLIMARD: You do?

RENEE: Don't ask me when, but . . . that's what I think.

GALLIMARD: Well, I agree with you. One hundred percent. That's very farsighted.

Diem: Ngo Dinh Diem (1901–1963), president of South Vietnam (1955–1963), assassinated in a coup d'état supported by the United States.

RENEE: Yeah. Well of course, my father thinks I'm a complete weirdo.

GALLIMARD: He'll thank you someday.

RENEE: Like when the Chinese start buying Hula Hoops?

GALLIMARD: There're a billion bellies out there.

RENEE: And if they end up taking over the world—well, then I'll be lucky to know Chinese too, right?

Pause.

GALLIMARD: At this point, I don't see how the Chinese can possibly take—

RENEE: You know what I *don't* like about China?

GALLIMARD: Excuse me? No—what?

RENEE: Nothing to do at night.

GALLIMARD: You come to parties at embassies like everyone else.

RENEE: Yeah, but they get out at ten. And then what?

GALLIMARD: I'm afraid the Chinese idea of a dance hall is a dirt floor and a man with a flute.

RENEE: Are you married?

GALLIMARD: Yes. Why?

RENEE: You wanna . . . fool around?

Pause.

GALLIMARD: Sure.

RENEE: I'll wait for you outside. What's your name?

GALLIMARD: Gallimard. Rene.

RENEE: Weird. I'm Renee too. *(She exits.)*

GALLIMARD *(to us):*   And so, I embarked on my first extra-extramarital affair. Renee was picture perfect. With a body like those girls in the magazines. If I put a tissue paper over my eyes, I wouldn't have been able to tell the difference. And it was exciting to be with someone who wasn't afraid to be seen completely naked. But is it possible for a woman to be *too* uninhibited, *too* willing, so as to seem almost too . . . masculine?

Chuck Berry° blares from the house speakers, then comes down in volume as Renee enters, toweling her hair.

RENEE: You have a nice weenie.

GALLIMARD: What?

RENEE: Penis. You have a nice penis.

GALLIMARD: Oh. Well, thank you. That's very . . .

RENEE: What—can't take a compliment?

GALLIMARD: No, it's very . . . reassuring.

RENEE: But most girls don't come out and say it, huh?

GALLIMARD: And also . . . what did you call it?

RENEE: Oh. Most girls don't call it a "weenie," huh?

GALLIMARD: It sounds very—

RENEE: Small, I know.

Chuck Berry: Influential American rock 'n' roll musician whose first recording came out in 1955.

GALLIMARD: I was going to say, "young."

RENEE: Yeah. Young, small, same thing. Most guys are pretty, uh, sensitive about that. Like, you know, I had a boyfriend back home in Denmark. I got mad at him once and called him a little weeniehead. He got so mad! He said at least I should call him a great big weeniehead.

GALLIMARD: I suppose I just say "penis."

RENEE: Yeah. That's pretty clinical. There's "cock," but that sounds like a chicken. And "prick" is painful, and "dick" is like you're talking about some-one who's not in the room.

GALLIMARD: Yes. It's a . . . bigger problem than I imagined.

RENEE: I—I think maybe it's because I really don't know what to do with them—that's why I call them "weenies."

GALLIMARD: Well, you did quite well with . . . mine.

RENEE: Thanks, but I mean, really *do* with them. Like, okay, have you ever looked at one? I mean, really?

GALLIMARD: No, I suppose when it's part of you, you sort of take it for granted.

RENEE: I guess. But, like, it just hangs there. This little . . . flap of flesh. And there's so much fuss that we make about it. Like, I think the reason we fight wars is because we wear clothes. Because no one knows—between the men, I mean—who has the biggest . . . weenie. So, if I'm a guy with a small one, I'm going to build a really big building or take over a really big piece of land or write a really long book so the other men don't know, right? But, see, it never really works, that's the problem. I mean, you conquer the country, or whatever, but you're still wearing clothes, so there's no way to prove absolutely whose is bigger or smaller. And that's what we call a civilized soci-ety. The whole world run by a bunch of men with pricks the size of pins. *(She exits.)*

GALLIMARD *(to us)*:   This was simply not acceptable.

A high-pitched chime rings through the air. Song, dressed as Butterfly, appears in the upstage special. She is obviously distressed. Her body swoons as she attempts to clip the stems of flowers she's arranging in a vase.

GALLIMARD: But I kept up our affair, wildly, for several months. Why? I believe because of Butterfly. She knew the secret I was trying to hide. But, unlike a Western woman, she didn't confront me, threaten, even pout. I remembered the words of Puccini's *Butterfly*:

SONG: "*Noi siamo gente avvezza / alle piccole cose / umili e silenziose.*"

GALLIMARD: "I come from a people / Who are accustomed to little / Humble and silent." I saw Pinkerton and Butterfly, and what she would say if he were unfaithful . . . nothing. She would cry, alone, into those wildly soft sleeves, once full of possessions, now empty to collect her tears. It was her tears and her silence that excited me, every time I visited Renee.

TOULON *(offstage)*:   Gallimard!

Toulon enters. Gallimard turns towards him. During the next section, Song, up center, begins to dance with the flowers. It is a drunken, reckless dance, where she breaks small pieces off the stems.

TOULON: They're killing him.

GALLIMARD: Who? I'm sorry? What?

TOULON: Bother you to come over at this late hour?

GALLIMARD: No . . . of course not.

TOULON: Not after you hear my secret. Champagne?

GALLIMARD: Um . . . thank you.

TOULON: You're surprised. There's something that you've wanted, Gallimard.
No, not a promotion. Next time. Something in the world. You're not aware
of this, but there's an informal gossip circle among intelligence agents. And
some of ours heard from some of the Americans —

GALLIMARD: Yes?

TOULON: That the U.S. will allow the Vietnamese generals to stage a coup . . .
and assassinate President Diem.

The chime rings again. Toulon freezes. Gallimard turns upstage and looks at But-
terfly, who slowly and deliberately clips a flower off its stem. Gallimard turns back
towards Toulon.

GALLIMARD: I think . . . that's a very wise move!

Toulon unfreezes.

TOULON: It's what you've been advocating. A toast?

GALLIMARD: Sure. I consider this a vindication.

TOULON: Not exactly. "To the test. Let's hope you pass."

They drink. The chime rings again. Toulon freezes. Gallimard turns upstage, and
Song clips another flower.

GALLIMARD *(to Toulon):*   The test?

TOULON *(unfreezing):*   It's a test of everything you've been saying. I personally
think the generals probably will stop the Communists. And you'll be a hero.
But if anything goes wrong, then your opinions won't be worth a pig's ear.
I'm sure that won't happen. But sometimes it's easier when they don't listen
to you.

GALLIMARD: They're your opinions too, aren't they?

TOULON: Personally, yes.

GALLIMARD: So we agree.

TOULON: But my opinions aren't on that report. Yours are. Cheers.

Toulon turns away from Gallimard and raises his glass. At that instant Song picks
up the vase and hurls it to the ground. It shatters. Song sinks down amidst the
shards of the vase, in a calm, childlike trance. She sings softly, as if reciting a child's
nursery rhyme.

SONG *(repeat as necessary):*   "The whole world over, the white man travels, setting anchor, wherever he likes. Life's not worth living, unless he finds, the
finest maidens, of every land . . ."

Gallimard turns downstage towards us. Song continues singing.

GALLIMARD: I shook as I left his house. That coward! That worm! To put the
burden for his decisions on my shoulders!

I started for Renee's. But no, that was all I needed. A schoolgirl who would question the role of the penis in modern society. What I wanted was revenge. A vessel to contain my humiliation. Though I hadn't seen her in several weeks, I headed for Butterfly's.

Gallimard enters Song's apartment.

SONG: Oh! Rene . . . I was dreaming!

GALLIMARD: You've been drinking?

SONG: If I can't sleep, then yes, I drink. But then, it gives me these dreams which—Rene, it's been almost three weeks since you visited me last.

GALLIMARD: I know. There's been a lot going on in the world.

SONG: Fortunately I am drunk. So I can speak freely. It's not the world, it's you and me. And an old problem. Even the softest skin becomes like leather to a man who's touched it too often. I confess I don't know how to stop it. I don't know how to become another woman.

GALLIMARD: I have a request.

SONG: Is this a solution? Or are you ready to give up the flat?

GALLIMARD: It may be a solution. But I'm sure you won't like it.

SONG: Oh well, that's very important. "Like it?" Do you think I "like" lying here alone, waiting, always waiting for your return? Please—don't worry about what I may not "like."

GALLIMARD: I want to see you . . . naked.

Silence.

SONG: I thought you understood my modesty. So you want me to—what—strip? Like a big cowboy girl? Shiny pasties on my breasts? Shall I fling my kimono over my head and yell "ya-hoo" in the process? I thought you respected my shame!

GALLIMARD: I believe you gave me your shame many years ago.

SONG: Yes—and it is just like a white devil to use it against me. I can't believe it. I thought myself so repulsed by the passive Oriental and the cruel white man. Now I see—we are always most revolted by the things hidden within us.

GALLIMARD: I just mean—

SONG: Yes?

GALLIMARD: —that it will remove the only barrier left between us.

SONG: No, Rene. Don't couch your request in sweet words. Be yourself—a cad—and know that my love is enough, that I submit—submit to the worst you can give me. *(Pause.)* Well, come. Strip me. Whatever happens, know that you have willed it. Our love, in your hands. I'm helpless before my man.

Gallimard starts to cross the room.

GALLIMARD: Did I not undress her because I knew, somewhere deep down, what I would find? Perhaps. Happiness is so rare that our mind can turn somersaults to protect it.

At the time, I only knew that I was seeing Pinkerton stalking towards his Butterfly, ready to reward her love with his lecherous hands. The image sickened me, pulled me to my knees, so I was crawling towards her like a worm.

By the time I reached her, Pinkerton . . . had vanished from my heart. To be replaced by something new, something unnatural, that flew in the face of all I'd learned in the world — something very close to love.

He grabs her around the waist; she strokes his hair.

GALLIMARD: Butterfly, forgive me.

SONG: Rene . . .

GALLIMARD: For everything. From the start.

SONG: I'm . . .

GALLIMARD: I want to —

SONG: I'm pregnant. *(Beat.)* I'm pregnant. *(Beat.)* I'm pregnant.

Beat.

GALLIMARD: I want to marry you!

Scene 7

Gallimard and Butterfly's flat. Beijing. 1963.

Downstage, Song paces as Comrade Chin reads from her notepad. Upstage, Gallimard is still kneeling. He remains on his knees throughout the scene, watching it.

SONG: I need a baby.

CHIN *(from pad):*   He's been spotted going to a dorm.

SONG: I need a baby.

CHIN: At the Foreign Language Institute.

SONG: I need a baby.

CHIN: The room of a Danish girl. . . . What do you mean, you need a baby?!

SONG: Tell Comrade Kang — last night, the entire mission, it could've ended.

CHIN: What do you mean?

SONG: Tell Kang — he told me to strip.

CHIN: Strip?!

SONG: Write!

CHIN: I tell you, I don't understand nothing about this case anymore. Nothing.

SONG: He told me to strip, and I took a chance. Oh, we Chinese, we know how to gamble.

CHIN *(writing):*   ". . . told him to strip."

SONG: My palms were wet, I had to make a split-second decision.

CHIN: Hey! Can you slow down?!

Pause.

SONG: You write faster, I'm the artist here. Suddenly, it hit me — "All he wants is for her to submit. Once a woman submits, a man is always ready to become 'generous.'"

CHIN: You're just gonna end up with rough notes.

SONG: And it worked! He gave in! Now, if I can just present him with a baby. A Chinese baby with blond hair — he'll be mine for life!

CHIN: Kang will never agree! The trading of babies has to be a counterrevolutionary act!

SONG: Sometimes, a counterrevolutionary act is necessary to counter a counterrevolutionary act.

Pause.

CHIN: Wait.

SONG: I need one . . . in seven months. Make sure it's a boy.

CHIN: This doesn't sound like something the Chairman would do. Maybe you'd better talk to Comrade Kang yourself.

SONG: Good. I will.

Chin gets up to leave.

SONG: Miss Chin? Why, in the Peking Opera, are women's roles played by men?

CHIN: I don't know. Maybe, a reactionary remnant of male —

SONG: No. *(Beat.)* Because only a man knows how a woman is supposed to act.

Chin exits. Song turns upstage, towards Gallimard.

GALLIMARD *(calling after Chin):*   Good riddance! *(To Song.)* I could forget all that betrayal in an instant, you know. If you'd just come back and become Butterfly again.

SONG: Fat chance. You're here in prison, rotting in a cell. And I'm on a plane, winging my way back to China. Your President pardoned me of our treason, you know.

GALLIMARD: Yes, I read about that.

SONG: Must make you feel . . . lower than shit.

GALLIMARD: But don't you, even a little bit, wish you were here with me?

SONG: I'm an artist, Rene. You were my greatest . . . acting challenge. *(She laughs.)* It doesn't matter how rotten I answer, does it? You still adore me. That's why I love you, Rene. *(She points to us.)* So — you were telling your audience about the night I announced I was pregnant.

Gallimard puts his arms around Song's waist. He and Song are in the positions they were in at the end of Scene 6.

Scene 8

Same.

GALLIMARD: I'll divorce my wife. We'll live together here, and then later in France.

SONG: I feel so . . . ashamed.

GALLIMARD: Why?

SONG: I had begun to lose faith. And now, you shame me with your generosity.

GALLIMARD: Generosity? No, I'm proposing for very selfish reasons.

SONG: Your apologies only make me feel more ashamed. My outburst a moment ago!

GALLIMARD: Your outburst? What about my request?!

SONG: You've been very patient dealing with my . . . eccentricities. A Western man, used to women freer with their bodies—

GALLIMARD: It was sick! Don't make excuses for me.

SONG: I have to. You don't seem willing to make them for yourself.

Pause.

GALLIMARD: You're crazy.

SONG: I'm happy. Which often looks like crazy.

GALLIMARD: Then make me crazy. Marry me.

Pause.

SONG: No.

GALLIMARD: What?

SONG: Do I sound silly, a slave, if I say I'm not worthy?

GALLIMARD: Yes. In fact you do. No one has loved me like you.

SONG: Thank you. And no one ever will. I'll see to that.

GALLIMARD: So what is the problem?

SONG: Rene, we Chinese are realists. We understand rice, gold, and guns. You are a diplomat. Your career is skyrocketing. Now, what would happen if you divorced your wife to marry a Communist Chinese actress?

GALLIMARD: That's not being realistic. That's defeating yourself before you begin.

SONG: We conserve our strength for the battles we can win.

GALLIMARD: That sounds like a fortune cookie!

SONG: Where do you think fortune cookies come from!

GALLIMARD: I don't care.

SONG: You do. So do I. And we should. That is why I say I'm not worthy. I'm worthy to love and even to be loved by you. But I am not worthy to end the career of one of the West's most promising diplomats.

GALLIMARD: It's not that great a career! I made it sound like more than it is!

SONG: Modesty will get you nowhere. Flatter yourself, and you flatter me. I'm flattered to decline your offer. (*She exits.*)

GALLIMARD (*to us*):   Butterfly and I argued all night. And, in the end, I left, knowing I would never be her husband. She went away for several months— to the countryside, like a small animal. Until the night I received her call.

A baby's cry from offstage. Song enters, carrying a child.

SONG: He looks like you.

GALLIMARD: Oh! (*Beat; he approaches the baby.*) Well, babies are never very attractive at birth.

SONG: Stop!

GALLIMARD: I'm sure he'll grow more beautiful with age. More like his mother.

SONG: "*Chi vide mai / a bimbo del Giappon . . .*"

GALLIMARD: "What baby, I wonder, was ever born in Japan" — or China, for that matter—

SONG: "*. . . occhi azzurrini?*"

GALLIMARD: "With azure eyes" — they're actually sort of brown, wouldn't you say?

SONG: "*E il labbro.*"

GALLIMARD: "And such lips!" *(He kisses Song.)* And such lips.

SONG: "*E i ricciolini d'oro schietto?*"

GALLIMARD: "And such a head of golden"—if slightly patchy—"curls?"

SONG: I'm going to call him "Peepee."

GALLIMARD: Darling, could you repeat that because I'm sure a rickshaw just flew by overhead.

SONG: You heard me.

GALLIMARD: "Song Peepee"? May I suggest Michael, or Stephan, or Adolph?

SONG: You may, but I won't listen.

GALLIMARD: You can't be serious. Can you imagine the time this child will have in school?

SONG: In the West, yes.

GALLIMARD: It's worse than naming him Ping Pong or Long Dong or—

SONG: But he's never going to live in the West, is he?

Pause.

GALLIMARD: That wasn't my choice.

SONG: It is mine. And this is my promise to you: I will raise him, he will be our child, but he will never burden you outside of China.

GALLIMARD: Why do you make these promises? I want to be burdened! I want a scandal to cover the papers!

SONG *(to us):*   Prophetic.

GALLIMARD: I'm serious.

SONG: So am I. His name is as I registered it. And he will never live in the West.

Song exits with the child.

GALLIMARD *(to us):*   Is it possible that her stubbornness only made me want her more? That drawing back at the moment of my capitulation was the most brilliant strategy she could have chosen? It is possible. But it is also possible that by this point she could have said, could have done . . . anything, and I would have adored her still.

Scene 9

Beijing. 1966.
A driving rhythm of Chinese percussion fills the stage.

GALLIMARD: And then, China began to change. Mao became very old, and his cult became very strong. And, like many old men, he entered his second childhood. So he handed over the reins of state to those with minds like his own. And children ruled the Middle Kingdom° with complete caprice. The doctrine of the Cultural Revolution° implied continuous anarchy. Contact

---

Middle Kingdom: The royal domain of China during its feudal period.   **Cultural Revolution:** The reform campaign of 1965–1967 to purge counterrevolutionary thought in China, that challenged Mao Zedong.

between Chinese and foreigners became impossible. Our flat was confiscated. Her fame and my money now counted against us.

Two dancers in Mao suits and red-starred caps enter, and begin crudely mimicking revolutionary violence, in an agitprop fashion.

GALLIMARD: And somehow the American war went wrong too. Four hundred thousand dollars were being spent for every Viet Cong° killed; so General Westmoreland's° remark that the Oriental does not value life the way Americans do was oddly accurate. Why weren't the Vietnamese people giving in? Why were they content instead to die and die and die again?

Toulon enters. Percussion and dancers continue upstage.

TOULON: Congratulations, Gallimard.

GALLIMARD: Excuse me, sir?

TOULON: Not a promotion. That was last time. You're going home.

GALLIMARD: What?

TOULON: Don't say I didn't warn you.

GALLIMARD: I'm being transferred . . . because I was wrong about the American war?

TOULON: Of course not. We don't care about the Americans. We care about your mind. The quality of your analysis. In general, everything you've predicted here in the Orient . . . just hasn't happened.

GALLIMARD: I think that's premature.

TOULON: Don't force me to be blunt. Okay, you said China was ready to open to Western trade. The only thing they're trading out there are Western heads. And, yes, you said the Americans would succeed in Indochina. You were kidding, right?

GALLIMARD: I think the end is in sight.

TOULON: Don't be pathetic. And don't take this personally. You were wrong. It's not your fault.

GALLIMARD: But I'm going home.

TOULON: Right. Could I have the number of your mistress? *(Beat.)* Joke! Joke! Eat a croissant for me.

Toulon exits. Song, wearing a Mao suit, is dragged in from the wings as part of the upstage dance. They "beat" her, then lampoon the acrobatics of the Chinese opera, as she is made to kneel onstage.

GALLIMARD *(simultaneously)*:   I don't care to recall how Butterfly and I said our hurried farewell. Perhaps it was better to end our affair before it killed her.

Gallimard exits. Percussion rises in volume. The lampooning becomes faster, more frenetic. At its height, Comrade Chin walks across the stage with a banner reading: "The Actor Renounces His Decadent Profession!" She reaches the kneeling Song. At the moment Chin touches Song's chin, percussion stops with a thud. Dancers strike poses.

Viet Cong: Member of the National Liberation Front of South Vietnam, against which U.S. forces were fighting.   **General Westmoreland:** William Westmoreland (b. 1914), commander of American troops in Vietnam from 1964 to 1968.

CHIN: Actor-oppressor, for years you have lived above the common people and looked down on their labor. While the farmer ate millet—

SONG: I ate pastries from France and sweetmeats from silver trays.

CHIN: And how did you come to live in such an exalted position?

SONG: I was a plaything for the imperialists!

CHIN: What did you do?

SONG: I shamed China by allowing myself to be corrupted by a foreigner . . .

CHIN: What does this mean? The People demand a full confession!

SONG: I engaged in the lowest perversions with China's enemies!

CHIN: What perversions? Be more clear!

SONG: I let him put it up my ass!

Dancers look over, disgusted.

CHIN: Aaaa-ya! How can you use such sickening language?!

SONG: My language . . . is only as foul as the crimes I committed . . .

CHIN: Yeah. That's better. So—what do you want to do . . . now?

SONG: I want to serve the people!

Percussion starts up, with Chinese strings.

CHIN: What?

SONG: I want to serve the people!

Dancers regain their revolutionary smiles, and begin a dance of victory.

CHIN: What?!

SONG: I want to serve the people!!

Dancers unveil a banner: "The Actor Is Re-Habilitated!" Song remains kneeling before Chin, as the dancers bounce around them, then exit. Music out.

Scene 10

A commune. Hunan Province. 1970.

CHIN: How you planning to do that?

SONG: I've already worked four years in the fields of Hunan, Comrade Chin.

CHIN: So? Farmers work all their lives. Let me see your hands.

Song holds them out for her inspection.

CHIN: Goddamn! Still so smooth! How long does it take to turn you actors into good anythings? Hunh. You've just spent too many years in luxury to be any good to the Revolution.

SONG: I served the Revolution.

CHIN: Serve the Revolution? Bullshit! You wore dresses! Don't tell me—I was there. I saw you! You and your white vice-consul! Stuck up there in your flat, living off the People's Treasury! Yeah, I knew what was going on! You two . . . homos! Homos! Homos! (*Pause; she composes herself.*) Ah! Well . . . you will serve the people, all right. But not with the Revolution's money. This time, you use your own money.

SONG: I have no money.

CHIN: Shut up! And you won't stink up China anymore with your pervert stuff. You'll pollute the place where pollution begins — the West.

SONG: What do you mean?

CHIN: Shut up! You're going to France. Without a cent in your pocket. You find your consul's house, you make him pay your expenses —

SONG: No.

CHIN: And you give us weekly reports! Useful information!

SONG: That's crazy. It's been four years.

CHIN: Either that, or back to rehabilitation center!

SONG: Comrade Chin, he's not going to support me! Not in France! He's a white man! I was just his plaything —

CHIN: Oh yuck! Again with the sickening language? Where's my stick?

SONG: You don't understand the mind of a man.

Pause.

CHIN: Oh no? No I don't? Then how come I'm married, huh? How come I got a man? Five, six years ago, you always tell me those kind of things, I felt very bad. But not now! Because what does the Chairman say? He tells us *I'm* now the smart one, you're now the nincompoop! *You're* the blockhead, the hare-brain, the nitwit! You think you're so smart? You understand "The Mind of a Man"? Good! Then *you* go to France and be a pervert for Chairman Mao!

Chin and Song exit in opposite directions.

Scene 11

Paris. 1968–1970.
   Gallimard enters.

GALLIMARD: And what was waiting for me back in Paris? Well, better Chinese food than I'd eaten in China. Friends and relatives. A little accounting, regular schedule, keeping track of traffic violations in the suburbs. . . . And the indignity of students shouting the slogans of Chairman Mao at me — in French.

HELGA: Rene? Rene? *(She enters, soaking wet.)* I've had a . . . problem.

(She sneezes.)

GALLIMARD: You're wet.

HELGA: Yes, I . . . coming back from the grocer's. A group of students, waving red flags, they —

Gallimard fetches a towel.

HELGA: — they ran by, I was caught up along with them. Before I knew what was happening —

Gallimard gives her the towel.

HELGA: Thank you. The police started firing water cannons at us. I tried to shout, to tell them I was the wife of a diplomat, but — you know how it is . . . *(Pause.)* Needless to say, I lost the groceries. Rene, what's happening to France?

GALLIMARD: What's—? Well, nothing, really.

HELGA: Nothing?! The storefronts are in flames, there's glass in the streets, buildings are toppling—and I'm wet!

GALLIMARD: Nothing! . . . that I care to think about.

HELGA: And is that why you stay in this room?

GALLIMARD: Yes, in fact.

HELGA: With the incense burning? You know something? I hate incense. It smells so sickly sweet.

GALLIMARD: Well, I hate the French. Who just smell—period!

HELGA: And the Chinese were better?

GALLIMARD: Please—don't start.

HELGA: When we left, this exact same thing, the riots—

GALLIMARD: No, no . . .

HELGA: Students screaming slogans, smashing down doors—

GALLIMARD: Helga—

HELGA: It was all going on in China, too. Don't you remember?!

GALLIMARD: Helga! Please! *(Pause.)* You have never understood China, have you? You walk in here with these ridiculous ideas, that the West is falling apart, that China was spitting in our faces. You come in, dripping of the streets, and you leave water all over my floor. *(He grabs Helga's towel, begins mopping up the floor.)*

HELGA: But it's the truth!

GALLIMARD: Helga, I want a divorce.

Pause; Gallimard continues mopping the floor.

HELGA: I take it back. China is . . . beautiful. Incense, I like incense.

GALLIMARD: I've had a mistress.

HELGA: So?

GALLIMARD: For eight years.

HELGA: I knew you would. I knew you would the day I married you. And now what? You want to marry her?

GALLIMARD: I can't. She's in China.

HELGA: I see. You know that no one else is ever going to marry me, right?

GALLIMARD: I'm sorry.

HELGA: And you want to leave. For someone who's not here, is that right?

GALLIMARD: That's right.

HELGA: You can't live with her, but still you don't want to live with me.

GALLIMARD: That's right.

Pause.

HELGA: Shit. How terrible that I can figure that out. *(Pause.)* I never thought I'd say it. But, in China, I was happy. I knew, in my own way, I knew that you were not everything you pretended to be. But the pretense—going on your arm to the embassy ball, visiting your office and the guards saying, "Good morning, good morning, Madame Gallimard" — the pretense . . . was very good indeed. *(Pause.)* I hope everyone is mean to you for the rest of your life. *(She exits.)*

GALLIMARD *(to us):*   Prophetic.

Marc enters with two drinks.

GALLIMARD *(to Marc):*   In China, I was different from all other men.
MARC: Sure. You were white. Here's your drink.
GALLIMARD: I felt . . . touched.
MARC: In the head? Rene, I don't want to hear about the Oriental love goddess. Okay? One night — can we just drink and throw up without a lot of conversation?
GALLIMARD: You still don't believe me, do you?
MARC: Sure I do. She was the most beautiful, et cetera, et cetera, blasé, blasé.

Pause.

GALLIMARD: My life in the West has been such a disappointment.
MARC: Life in the West is like that. You'll get used to it. Look, you're driving me away. I'm leaving. Happy, now? *(He exits, then returns.)* Look, I have a date tomorrow night. You wanna come? I can fix you up with —
GALLIMARD: Of course. I would love to come.

Pause.

MARC: Uh — on second thought, no. You'd better get ahold of yourself first.

He exits; Gallimard nurses his drink.

GALLIMARD *(to us):*   This is the ultimate cruelty, isn't it? That I can talk and talk and to anyone listening, it's only air — too rich a diet to be swallowed by a mundane world. Why can't anyone understand? That in China, I once loved, and was loved by, very simply, the Perfect Woman.

Song enters, dressed as Butterfly in wedding dress.

GALLIMARD *(to Song):*   Not again. My imagination is hell. Am I asleep this time? Or did I drink too much?
SONG: Rene!
GALLIMARD: God, it's too painful! That you speak?
SONG: What are you talking about? Rene — touch me.
GALLIMARD: Why?
SONG: I'm real. Take my hand.
GALLIMARD: Why? So you can disappear again and leave me clutching at the air? For the entertainment of my neighbors who — ?

Song touches Gallimard.

SONG: Rene?

Gallimard takes Song's hand. Silence.

GALLIMARD: Butterfly? I never doubted you'd return.
SONG: You hadn't . . . forgotten — ?
GALLIMARD: Yes, actually, I've forgotten everything. My mind, you see — there wasn't enough room in this hard head — not for the world *and* for you. No, there was only room for one. *(Beat.)* Come, look. See? Your bed has been

waiting, with the Klimt° poster you like, and—see? The *xiang lu*° you gave me?

SONG: I . . . I don't know what to say.

GALLIMARD: There's nothing to say. Not at the end of a long trip. Can I make you some tea?

SONG: But where's your wife?

GALLIMARD: She's by my side. She's by my side at last.

Gallimard reaches to embrace Song. Song sidesteps, dodging him.

GALLIMARD: Why?!

SONG *(to us):*   So I did return to Rene in Paris. Where I found—

GALLIMARD: Why do you run away? Can't we show them how we embraced that evening?

SONG: Please. I'm talking.

GALLIMARD: You have to do what I say! I'm conjuring you up in *my* mind!

SONG: Rene, I've never done what you've said. Why should it be any different in your mind? Now split—the story moves on, and I must change.

GALLIMARD: I welcomed you into my home! I didn't have to, you know! I could've left you penniless on the streets of Paris! But I took you in!

SONG: Thank you.

GALLIMARD: So . . . please . . . don't change.

SONG: You know I have to. You know I will. And anyway, what difference does it make? No matter what your eyes tell you, you can't ignore the truth. You already know too much.

Gallimard exits. Song turns to us.

SONG: The change I'm going to make requires about five minutes. So I thought you might want to take this opportunity to stretch your legs, enjoy a drink, or listen to the musicians. I'll be here, when you return, right where you left me.

Song goes to a mirror in front of which is a wash basin of water. She starts to remove her makeup as stagelights go to half and houselights come up.

ACT 3, Scene 1

A courthouse in Paris. 1986.

As he promised, Song has completed the bulk of his transformation onstage by the time the houselights go down and the stagelights come up full. As he speaks to us, he removes his wig and kimono, leaving them on the floor. Underneath, he wears a well-cut suit.

SONG: So I'd done my job better than I had a right to expect. Well, give him some credit, too. He's right—I was in a fix when I arrived in Paris. I walked from the airport into town, then I located, by blind groping, the Chinatown

---

Klimt: Gustav Klimt (1863–1918), Austrian painter in the art nouveau style, whose most famous painting is *The Kiss.*   **xiang lu:** Incense burner.

district. Let me make one thing clear: whatever else may be said about the Chinese, they are stingy! I slept in doorways three days until I could find a tailor who would make me this kimono on credit. As it turns out, maybe I didn't even need it. Maybe he would've been happy to see me in a simple shift and mascara. But . . . better safe than sorry.

That was 1970, when I arrived in Paris. For the next fifteen years, yes, I lived a very comfy life. Some relief, believe me, after four years on a fucking commune in Nowheresville, China. Rene supported the boy and me, and I did some demonstrations around the country as part of my "cultural exchange" cover. And then there was the spying.

Song moves upstage, to a chair. Toulon enters as a judge, wearing the appropriate wig and robes. He sits near Song. It's 1986, and Song is testifying in a courtroom.

SONG: Not much at first. Rene had lost all his high-level contacts. Comrade Chin wasn't very interested in parking-ticket statistics. But finally, at my urging, Rene got a job as a courier, handling sensitive documents. He'd photograph them for me, and I'd pass them on to the Chinese embassy.

JUDGE: Did he understand the extent of his activity?

SONG: He didn't ask. He knew that I needed those documents, and that was enough.

JUDGE: But he must've known he was passing classified information.

SONG: I can't say.

JUDGE: He never asked what you were going to do with them?

SONG: Nope.

Pause.

JUDGE: There is one thing that the court—indeed, that all of France—would like to know.

SONG: Fire away.

JUDGE: Did Monsieur Gallimard know you were a man?

SONG: Well, he never saw me completely naked. Ever.

JUDGE: But surely, he must've . . . how can I put this?

SONG: Put it however you like. I'm not shy. He must've felt around?

JUDGE: Mmmmm.

SONG: Not really. I did all the work. He just laid back. Of course we did enjoy more . . . complete union, and I suppose he *might* have wondered why I was always on my stomach, but. . . . But what you're thinking is, "Of course a wrist must've brushed . . . a hand hit . . . over twenty years!" Yeah. Well, Your Honor, it was my job to make him think I was a woman. And chew on this: it wasn't all that hard. See, my mother was a prostitute along the Bundt before the Revolution. And, uh, I think it's fair to say she learned a few things about Western men. So I borrowed her knowledge. In service to my country.

JUDGE: Would you care to enlighten the court with this secret knowledge? I'm sure we're all very curious.

SONG: I'm sure you are. *(Pause.)* Okay, Rule One is: Men always believe what they want to hear. So a girl can tell the most obnoxious lies and the guys will believe them every time—"This is my first time"—"That's the biggest I've ever seen" — or *both,* which, if you really think about it, is not possible in a single lifetime. You've maybe heard those phrases a few times in your own life, yes, Your Honor?

JUDGE: It's not my life, Monsieur Song, which is on trial today.

SONG: Okay, okay, just trying to lighten up the proceedings. Tough room.

JUDGE: Go on.

SONG: Rule Two: As soon as a Western man comes into contact with the East — he's already confused. The West has sort of an international rape mentality towards the East. Do you know rape mentality?

JUDGE: Give us your definition, please.

SONG: Basically, "Her mouth says no, but her eyes say yes."

The West thinks of itself as masculine — big guns, big industry, big money — so the East is feminine — weak, delicate, poor . . . but good at art, and full of inscrutable wisdom — the feminine mystique.

Her mouth says no, but her eyes say yes. The West believes the East, deep down, *wants* to be dominated — because a woman can't think for herself.

JUDGE: What does this have to do with my question?

SONG: You expect Oriental countries to submit to your guns, and you expect Oriental women to be submissive to your men. That's why you say they make the best wives.

JUDGE: But why would that make it possible for you to fool Monsieur Gallimard? Please — get to the point.

SONG: One, because when he finally met his fantasy woman, he wanted more than anything to believe that she was, in fact, a woman. And second, I am an Oriental. And being an Oriental, I could never be completely a man.

Pause.

JUDGE: Your armchair political theory is tenuous, Monsieur Song.

SONG: You think so? That's why you'll lose in all your dealings with the East.

JUDGE: Just answer my question: did he know you were a man?

Pause.

SONG: You know, Your Honor, I never asked.

Scene 2

Same.

Music from the "Death Scene" from Butterfly blares over the house speakers. It is the loudest thing we've heard in this play.

Gallimard enters, crawling towards Song's wig and kimono.

GALLIMARD: Butterfly? Butterfly?

Song remains a man, in the witness box, delivering a testimony we do not hear.

GALLIMARD *(to us):*   In my moment of greatest shame, here, in this courtroom — with that . . . person up there, telling the world. . . . What strikes me especially is how shallow he is, how glib and obsequious . . . completely . . .

without substance! The type that prowls around discos with a gold medallion stinking of garlic. So little like my Butterfly.

Yet even in this moment my mind remains agile, flip-flopping like a man on a trampoline. Even now, my picture dissolves, and I see that . . . witness . . . talking to me.

Song suddenly stands straight up in his witness box, and looks at Gallimard.

SONG: Yes. You. White man.

Song steps out of the witness box, and moves downstage towards Gallimard. Light change.

GALLIMARD *(to Song)*:   Who? Me?
SONG: Do you see any other white men?
GALLIMARD: Yes. There're white men all around. This is a French courtroom.
SONG: So you are an adventurous imperialist. Tell me, why did it take you so long? To come back to this place?
GALLIMARD: What place?
SONG: This theater in China. Where we met many years ago.
GALLIMARD *(to us)*:   And once again, against my will, I am transported.

Chinese opera music comes up on the speakers. Song begins to do opera moves, as he did the night they met.

SONG: Do you remember? The night you gave your heart?
GALLIMARD: It was a long time ago.
SONG: Not long enough. A night that turned your world upside down.
GALLIMARD: Perhaps.
SONG: Oh, be honest with me. What's another bit of flattery when you've already given me twenty years' worth? It's a wonder my head hasn't swollen to the size of China.
GALLIMARD: Who's to say it hasn't?
SONG: Who's to say? And what's the shame? In pride? You think I could've pulled this off if I wasn't already full of pride when we met? No, not just pride. Arrogance. It takes arrogance, really — to believe you can will, with your eyes and your lips, the destiny of another. *(He dances.)* C'mon. Admit it. You still want me. Even in slacks and a button-down collar.
GALLIMARD: I don't see what the point of —
SONG: You don't? Well maybe, Rene, just maybe — I want you.
GALLIMARD: You do?
SONG: Then again, maybe I'm just playing with you. How can you tell? *(Reprising his feminine character, he sidles up to Gallimard.)* "How I wish there were even a small café to sit in. With men in tuxedos, and cappuccinos, and bad expatriate jazz." Now you want to kiss me, don't you?
GALLIMARD *(pulling away)*:   What makes you — ?
SONG: — so sure? See? I take the words from your mouth. Then I wait for you to come and retrieve them. *(He reclines on the floor.)*
GALLIMARD: Why?! Why do you treat me so cruelly?

SONG: Perhaps I *was* treating you cruelly. But now — I'm being nice. Come here, my little one.

GALLIMARD: I'm not your little one!

SONG: My mistake. It's I who am *your* little one, right?

GALLIMARD: Yes, I —

SONG: So come get your little one. If you like, I may even let you strip me.

GALLIMARD: I mean, you were! Before . . . but not like this!

SONG: I was? Then perhaps I still am. If you look hard enough. (*He starts to remove his clothes.*)

GALLIMARD: What — what are you doing?

SONG: Helping you to see through my act.

GALLIMARD: Stop that! I don't want to! I don't —

SONG: Oh, but you asked me to strip, remember?

GALLIMARD: What? That was years ago! And I took it back!

SONG: No. You postponed it. Postponed the inevitable. Today, the inevitable has come calling.

From the speakers, cacophony: Butterfly mixed in with Chinese gongs.

GALLIMARD: No! Stop! I don't want to see!

SONG: Then look away.

GALLIMARD: You're only in my mind! All this is in my mind! I order you! To stop!

SONG: To what? To strip? That's just what I'm —

GALLIMARD: No! Stop! I want you — !

SONG: You want me?

GALLIMARD: To stop!

SONG: You know something, Rene? Your mouth says no, but your eyes say yes. Turn them away. I dare you.

GALLIMARD: I don't have to! Every night, you say you're going to strip, but then I beg you and you stop!

SONG: I guess tonight is different.

GALLIMARD: Why? Why should that be?

SONG: Maybe I've become frustrated. Maybe I'm saying "Look at me, you fool!" Or maybe I'm just feeling . . . sexy. (*He is down to his briefs.*)

GALLIMARD: Please. This is unnecessary. I know what you are.

SONG: You do? What am I?

GALLIMARD: A — a man.

SONG: You don't really believe that.

GALLIMARD: Yes I do! I knew all the time somewhere that my happiness was temporary, my love a deception. But my mind kept the knowledge at bay. To make the wait bearable.

SONG: Monsieur Gallimard — the wait is over.

Song drops his briefs. He is naked. Sound cue out. Slowly, we and Song come to the realization that what we had thought to be Gallimard's sobbing is actually his laughter.

GALLIMARD: Oh god! What an idiot! Of course!

SONG: Rene — what?

GALLIMARD: Look at you! You're a man! (*He bursts into laughter again.*)

SONG: I fail to see what's so funny!

GALLIMARD: "You fail to see —!" I mean, you never did have much of a sense of humor, did you? I just think it's ridiculously funny that I've wasted so much time on just a man!

SONG: Wait. I'm not "just a man."

GALLIMARD: No? Isn't that what you've been trying to convince me of?

SONG: Yes, but what I mean —

GALLIMARD: And now, I finally believe you, and you tell me it's not true? I think you must have some kind of identity problem.

SONG: Will you listen to me?

GALLIMARD: Why?! I've been listening to you for twenty years. Don't I deserve a vacation?

SONG: I'm not just any man!

GALLIMARD: Then, what exactly are you?

SONG: Rene, how can you ask —? Okay, what about this?

He picks up Butterfly's robes, starts to dance around. No music.

GALLIMARD: Yes, that's very nice. I have to admit.

Song holds out his arm to Gallimard.

SONG: It's the same skin you've worshipped for years. Touch it.

GALLIMARD: Yes, it does feel the same.

SONG: Now — close your eyes.

Song covers Gallimard's eyes with one hand. With the other, Song draws Galli- mard's hand up to his face. Gallimard, like a blind man, lets his hands run over Song's face.

GALLIMARD: This skin, I remember. The curve of her face, the softness of her cheek, her hair against the back of my hand . . .

SONG: I'm your Butterfly. Under the robes, beneath everything, it was always me. Now, open your eyes and admit it — you adore me. (*He removes his hand from Gallimard's eyes.*)

GALLIMARD: You, who knew every inch of my desires — how could you, of all people, have made such a mistake?

SONG: What?

GALLIMARD: You showed me your true self. When all I loved was the lie. A per- fect lie, which you let fall to the ground — and now, it's old and soiled.

SONG: So — you never really loved me? Only when I was playing a part?

GALLIMARD: I'm a man who loved a woman created by a man. Everything else — simply falls short.

Pause.

SONG: What am I supposed to do now?

GALLIMARD: You were a fine spy, Monsieur Song, with an even finer accom- plice. But now I believe you should go. Get out of my life!

SONG: Go where? Rene, you can't live without me. Not after twenty years.

GALLIMARD: I certainly can't live with you — not after twenty years of betrayal.

SONG: Don't be stubborn! Where will you go?

GALLIMARD: I have a date . . . with my Butterfly.

SONG: So, throw away your pride. And come . . .

GALLIMARD: Get away from me! Tonight, I've finally learned to tell fantasy from reality. And, knowing the difference, I choose fantasy.

SONG: *I'm* your fantasy!

GALLIMARD: You? You're as real as hamburger. Now get out! I have a date with my Butterfly and I don't want your body polluting the room! *(He tosses Song's suit at him.)* Look at these — you dress like a pimp.

SONG: Hey! These are Armani slacks and — ! *(He puts on his briefs and slacks.)* Let's just say . . . I'm disappointed in you, Rene. In the crush of your adoration, I thought you'd become something more. More like . . . a woman.

But no. Men. You're like the rest of them. It's all in the way we dress, and make up our faces, and bat our eyelashes. You really have so little imagination!

GALLIMARD: You, Monsieur Song? Accuse me of too little imagination? You, if anyone, should know — I am pure imagination. And in imagination I will remain. Now get out!

Gallimard bodily removes Song from the stage, taking his kimono.

SONG: Rene! I'll never put on those robes again! You'll be sorry!

GALLIMARD *(to Song):*   I'm already sorry! *(Looking at the kimono in his hands.)* Exactly as sorry . . . as a Butterfly.

Scene 3

M. Gallimard's prison cell. Paris. 1988.

GALLIMARD: I've played out the events of my life night after night, always searching for a new ending to my story, one where I leave this cell and return forever to my Butterfly's arms.

Tonight I realize my search is over. That I've looked all along in the wrong place. And now, to you, I will prove that my love was not in vain — by returning to the world of fantasy where I first met her.

He picks up the kimono; dancers enter.

GALLIMARD: There is a vision of the Orient that I have. Of slender women in cheongsams and kimonos who die for the love of unworthy foreign devils. Who are born and raised to be the perfect women. Who take whatever punishment we give them, and bounce back, strengthened by love, unconditionally. It is a vision that has become my life.

Dancers bring the washbasin to him and help him make up his face.

GALLIMARD: In public, I have continued to deny that Song Liling is a man. This brings me headlines, and is a source of great embarrassment to my French colleagues, who can now be sent into a coughing fit by the mere mention of Chinese food. But alone, in my cell, I have long since faced the truth.

And the truth demands a sacrifice. For mistakes made over the course of a lifetime. My mistakes were simple and absolute — the man I loved was a cad, a bounder. He deserved nothing but a kick in the behind, and instead I gave him . . . all my love.

Yes—love. Why not admit it all? That was my undoing, wasn't it? Love warped my judgment, blinded my eyes, rearranged the very lines on my face . . . until I could look in the mirror and see nothing but . . . a woman.

Dancers help him put on the Butterfly wig.

GALLIMARD: I have a vision. Of the Orient. That, deep within its almond eyes, there are still women. Women willing to sacrifice themselves for the love of a man. Even a man whose love is completely without worth.

Dancers assist Gallimard in donning the kimono. They hand him a knife.

GALLIMARD: Death with honor is better than life . . . life with dishonor. *(He sets himself center stage, in a seppuku position.)* The love of a Butterfly can withstand many things—unfaithfulness, loss, even abandonment. But how can it face the one sin that implies all others? The devastating knowledge that, underneath it all, the object of her love was nothing more, nothing less than . . . a man. *(He sets the tip of the knife against his body.)* It is 1988. And I have found her at last. In a prison on the outskirts of Paris. My name is Rene Gallimard—also known as Madame Butterfly.

Gallimard turns upstage and plunges the knife into his body, as music from the "Love Duet" blares over the speakers. He collapses into the arms of the dancers, who lay him reverently on the floor. The image holds for several beats. Then a tight special up on Song, who stands as a man, staring at the dead Gallimard. He smokes a cigarette; the smoke filters up through the lights. Two words leave his lips.

SONG: Butterfly? Butterfly?

Smoke rises as lights fade slowly to black.   [1988]

THINKING ABOUT THE TEXT

1. Gallimard says near the end of act 1, scene 5 that he married Helga for practicality. When he sees *Madame Butterfly*, he is changed. Does this make sense to you?

2. Is it hard to imagine falling in love with a person you think is one sex but is really another? How does the play try to explain Gallimard's mistake? Does it have something to do with his statement, "Happiness is so rare that our mind can turn somersaults to protect it" (act 2, scene 6)?

3. Why does Hwang tell this story mostly in flashback through Gallimard's eyes? Why not just do a straight play in linear time?

4. Look again at the court scene (act 3, scene 1). What do you think of Song's ideas about a fantasy woman? Is Gallimard any wiser at the end of the play, or does he still want the illusion?

5. Some critics also see a political allegory here concerning the West's view of the East. Does this make sense to you?

PAUL GRAY

What Is Love?

Paul Gray, a senior writer and book reviewer for Time, *joined the magazine in 1972 after an academic career, teaching at Princeton University through the 1960s. Currently, he reads five books a week and writes articles on a great variety of subjects, many of which appear as cover stories. "What Is Love?" was* Time's *lead article in the February 15, 1993, issue.*

> What is this thing called love? What? Is this thing called love? What is this thing called? Love.

However punctuated, Cole Porter's simple question begs an answer. Love's symptoms are familiar enough: a drifting mooniness in thought and behavior, the mad conceit that the entire universe has rolled itself up into the person of the beloved, a conviction that no one on earth has ever felt so torrentially about a fellow creature before. Love is ecstasy and torment, freedom and slavery. Poets and songwriters would be in a fine mess without it. Plus, it makes the world go round.

Until recently, scientists wanted no part of it.

The reason for this avoidance, this reluctance to study what is probably life's most intense emotion, is not difficult to track down. Love is mushy; science is hard. Anger and fear, feelings that have been considerably researched in the field and the lab, can be quantified through measurements: pulse and breathing rates, muscle contractions, a whole spider web of involuntary responses. Love does not register as definitively on the instruments; it leaves a blurred fingerprint that could be mistaken for anything from indigestion to a manic attack. Anger and fear have direct roles — fighting or running — in the survival of the species. Since it is possible (a cynic would say commonplace) for humans to mate and reproduce without love, all the attendant sighing and swooning and sonnet writing have struck many pragmatic investigators as beside the evolutionary point.

So biologists and anthropologists assumed that it would be fruitless, even frivolous, to study love's evolutionary origins, the way it was encoded in our genes or imprinted in our brains. Serious scientists simply assumed that love — and especially Romantic Love — was really all in the head, put there five or six centuries ago when civilized societies first found enough spare time to indulge in flowery prose. The task of writing the book of love was ceded to playwrights, poets and pulp novelists.

But during the past decade, scientists across a broad range of disciplines have had a change of heart about love. The amount of research expended on the tender passion has never been more intense. Explanations for this rise in interest vary. Some cite the spreading threat of AIDS; with casual sex carrying mortal risks, it seems important to know more about a force that binds couples faithfully together. Others point to the growing number of women scientists and suggest that they may be more willing than their male colleagues to take love seriously. Says Elaine Hatfield, the author of *Love, Sex, and Intimacy: Their Psychology,*   5

Biology, and History, "When I was back at Stanford in the 1960s, they said study-ing love and human relationships was a quick way to ruin my career. Why not go where the real work was being done: on how fast rats could run?" Whatever the reasons, science seems to have come around to a view that nearly everyone else has always taken for granted: romance is real. It is not merely a conceit; it is bred into our biology.

Getting to this point logically is harder than it sounds. The love-as-cultural-delusion argument has long seemed unassailable. What actually accounts for the emotion, according to this scenario, is that people long ago made the mistake of taking fanciful literary tropes seriously. Ovid's *Ars Amatoria* is often cited as a major source of misreadings, its instructions followed, its ironies ignored. Other prime suspects include the twelfth-century troubadours in Provence who more or less invented the Art of Courtly Love, an elaborate, etiolated ritual for idle noblewomen and aspiring swains that would have been broken to bits by any hint of physical consummation.

Ever since then, the injunction to love and to be loved has hummed nonstop through popular culture; it is a dominant theme in music, films, novels, maga-zines and nearly everything shown on TV. Love is a formidable and thoroughly proved commercial engine; people will buy and do almost anything that promises them a chance at the bliss of romance.

But does all this mean that love is merely a phony emotion that we picked up because our culture celebrates it? Psychologist Lawrence Casler, author of *Is Marriage Necessary?*, forcefully thinks so, at least at first: "I don't believe love is part of human nature, not for a minute. There are social pressures at work." Then falls a shadow over this certainty. "Even if it is a part of human nature, like crime or violence, it's not necessarily desirable."

Well, love either is or is not intrinsic to our species; having it both ways leads nowhere. And the contention that romance is an entirely acquired trait—overly imaginative troubadours' revenge on muddled literalists—has always rested on some teetery premises.

For one thing, there is the chicken/egg dilemma. Which came first, sex or 10 love? If the reproductive imperative was as dominant as Darwinians maintain, sex probably led the way. But why was love hatched in the process, since it was presum-ably unnecessary to get things started in the first place? Furthermore, what has sus-tained romance—that odd collection of tics and impulses—over the centuries? Most mass hallucinations, such as the seventeenth-century tulip mania in Holland, flame out fairly rapidly when people realize the absurdity of what they have been doing and, as the common saying goes, come to their senses. When people in love come to their senses, they tend to orbit with added energy around each other and look more helplessly loopy and self-besotted. If romance were purely a figment, unsupported by any rational or sensible evidence, then surely most folks would be immune to it by now. Look around. It hasn't happened. Love is still in the air.

And it may be far more widespread than even romantics imagined. Those who argue that love is a cultural fantasy have tended to do so from a Eurocentric and class-driven point of view. Romance, they say, arose thanks to amenities peculiar to the West: leisure time, a modicum of creature comforts, a certain level of refinement in the arts and letters. When these trappings are absent, so is romance. Peasants mated; aristocrats fell in love.

But last year a study conducted by anthropologists William Jankowiak of the University of Nevada–Las Vegas and Edward Fischer of Tulane University found evidence of romantic love in at least 147 of the 166 cultures they studied. This discovery, if borne out, should pretty well wipe out the idea that love is an invention of the Western mind rather than a biological fact. Says Jankowiak: "It is, instead, a universal phenomenon, a panhuman characteristic that stretches across cultures. Societies like ours have the resources to show love through candy and flowers, but that does not mean that the lack of resources in other cultures indicates the absence of love."

Some scientists are not startled by this contention. One of them is anthropologist Helen Fisher, a research associate at the American Museum of Natural History and the author of *Anatomy of Love: The Natural History of Monogamy, Adultery and Divorce*, a recent book that is making waves among scientists and the general reading public. Says Fisher: "I've never *not* thought that love was a very primitive, basic human emotion, as basic as fear, anger or joy. It is so evident. I guess anthropologists have just been busy doing other things."

Among the things anthropologists—often knobby-kneed gents in safari shorts—tended to do in the past was ask questions about courtship and marriage rituals. This now seems a classic example, as the old song has it, of looking for love in all the wrong places. In many cultures, love and marriage do not go together. Weddings can have all the romance of corporate mergers, signed and sealed for family or territorial interests. This does not mean, Jankowiak insists, that love does not exist in such cultures; it erupts in clandestine forms, "a phenomenon to be dealt with."

Somewhere about this point, the specter of determinism begins once again   15
to flap and cackle. If science is going to probe and prod and then announce that we are all scientifically fated to love—and to love preprogrammed types—by our genes and chemicals, then a lot of people would just as soon not know. If there truly is a biological predisposition to love, as more and more scientists are coming to believe, what follows is a recognition of the amazing diversity in the ways humans have chosen to express the feeling. The cartoon images of cavemen bopping cavewomen over the head and dragging them home by their hair? Love. Helen of Troy, subjecting her adopted city to ten years of ruinous siege? Love. Romeo and Juliet? Ditto. Joe in Accounting making a fool of himself around the water cooler over Susan in Sales? Love. Like the universe, the more we learn about love, the more preposterous and mysterious it is likely to appear.   [1993]

THINKING ABOUT THE TEXT

1. Gray suggests that people will "do almost anything" that promises romance. Is this true of the people you know?

2. Gray claims scientists were looking for love in all the wrong places. Where were they looking, and why did they not find what they were looking for? Where should they have looked?

3. Does Gray's last sentence say something about the implausibility of *M. Butterfly*?

ANASTASIA TOUFEXIS
The Right Chemistry

Anastasia Toufexis received a bachelor's degree in premedicine from Smith College in 1967. After several years as a writer for medical and pharmaceutical publications, she began writing for Time *magazine, where she has been an associate editor since 1978. This essay appeared in the February 15, 1993, issue.*

O.K., let's cut out all this nonsense about romantic love. Let's bring some scientific precision to the party. Let's put love under a microscope.

When rigorous people with Ph.D.s after their names do that, what they see is not some silly, senseless thing. No, their probe reveals that love rests firmly on the foundations of evolution, biology and chemistry. What seems on the surface to be irrational, intoxicated behavior is in fact part of nature's master strategy—a vital force that has helped humans survive, thrive and multiply through thousands of years. Says Michael Mills, a psychology professor at Loyola Marymount University in Los Angeles: "Love is our ancestors whispering in our ears."

It was on the plains of Africa about 4 million years ago, in the early days of the human species, that the notion of romantic love probably first began to blossom—or at least that the first cascades of neurochemicals began flowing from the brain to the bloodstream to produce goofy grins and sweaty palms as men and women gazed deeply into each other's eyes. When mankind graduated from scuttling around on all fours to walking on two legs, this change made the whole person visible to fellow human beings for the first time. Sexual organs were in full display, as were other characteristics, from the color of eyes to the span of shoulders. As never before, each individual had a unique allure.

When the sparks flew, new ways of making love enabled sex to become a romantic encounter, not just a reproductive act. Although mounting mates from the rear was, and still is, the method favored among most animals, humans began to enjoy face-to-face couplings; both looks and personal attraction became a much greater part of the equation.

Romance served the evolutionary purpose of pulling males and females into   5
long-term partnership, which was essential to child rearing. On open grasslands, one parent would have a hard,—and dangerous—time handling a child while foraging for food. "If a woman was carrying the equivalent of a twenty-pound bowling ball in one arm and a pile of sticks in the other, it was ecologically critical to pair up with a mate to rear the young," explains anthropologist Helen Fisher, author of *Anatomy of Love*.

While Western culture holds fast to the idea that true love flames forever (the movie *Bram Stoker's Dracula* has the Count carrying the torch beyond the grave), nature apparently meant passions to sputter out in something like four years. Primitive pairs stayed together just "long enough to rear one child through infancy," says Fisher. Then each would find a new partner and start all over again.

What Fisher calls the "four-year itch" shows up unmistakably in today's divorce statistics. In most of the sixty-two cultures she has studied, divorce rates peak around the fourth year of marriage. Additional youngsters help keep pairs together longer. If, say, a couple have another child three years after the first, as often occurs, then their union can be expected to last about four more years. That makes them ripe for the more familiar phenomenon portrayed in the Marilyn Monroe classic *The Seven-Year Itch.*

If, in nature's design, romantic love is not eternal, neither is it exclusive. Less than 5 percent of mammals form rigorously faithful pairs. From the earliest days, contends Fisher, the human pattern has been "monogamy with clandestine adultery." Occasional flings upped the chances that new combinations of genes would be passed on to the next generation. Men who sought new partners had more children. Contrary to common assumptions, women were just as likely to stray. "As long as prehistoric females were secretive about their extramarital affairs," argues Fisher, "they could garner extra resources, life insurance, better genes and more varied DNA for their biological futures. Hence those who sneaked into the bushes with secret lovers lived on — unconsciously passing on through the centuries whatever it is in female spirit that motivates modern women to philander."

> Love is a romantic designation for a most ordinary biological — or, shall we say, chemical? — process. A lot of nonsense is talked and written about it.
> — Greta Garbo to Melvyn Douglas in *Ninotchka*

Lovers often claim that they feel as if they are being swept away. They're not mistaken; they are literally flooded by chemicals, research suggests. A meeting of eyes, a touch of hands or a whiff of scent sets off a flood that starts in the brain and races along the nerves and through the blood. The results are familiar: flushed skin, sweaty palms, heavy breathing. If love looks suspiciously like stress, the reason is simple: the chemical pathways are identical.

Above all, there is the sheer euphoria of falling in love — a not-so-surprising   10 reaction, considering that many of the substances swamping the newly smitten are chemical cousins of amphetamines. They include dopamine, norepinephrine and especially phenylethylamine (PEA). Cole Porter knew what he was talking about when he wrote "I get a kick out of you." "Love is a natural high," observes Anthony Walsh, author of *The Science of Love: Understanding Love and Its Effects on Mind and Body.* "PEA gives you that silly smile that you flash at strangers. When we meet someone who is attractive to us, the whistle blows at the PEA factory."

But phenylethylamine highs don't last forever, a fact that lends support to arguments that passionate romantic love is short-lived. As with any amphetamine, the body builds up a tolerance to PEA; thus it takes more and more of the substance to produce love's special kick. After two to three years, the body simply can't crank up the needed amount of PEA. And chewing on chocolate doesn't help, despite popular belief. The candy is high in PEA, but it fails to boost the body's supply.

Fizzling chemicals spell the end of delirious passion; for many people that marks the end of the liaison as well. It is particularly true for those whom Dr. Michael Liebowitz of the New York State Psychiatric Institute terms "attraction junkies." They crave the intoxication of falling in love so much that they move frantically from affair to affair just as soon as the first rush of infatuation fades.

Still, many romances clearly endure beyond the first years. What accounts for that? Another set of chemicals, of course. The continued presence of a partner gradually steps up production in the brain of endorphins. Unlike the fizzy amphet-amines, these are soothing substances. Natural painkillers, they give lovers a sense of security, peace and calm. "That is one reason why it feels so horrible when we're abandoned or a lover dies," notes Fisher. "We don't have our daily hit of narcotics."

Researchers see a contrast between the heated infatuation induced by PEA, along with other amphetamine-like chemicals, and the more intimate attach-ment fostered and prolonged by endorphins. "Early love is when you love the way the other person makes you feel," explains psychiatrist Mark Goulston of the University of California, Los Angeles. "Mature love is when you love the person as he or she is." It is the difference between passionate and compassionate love, observes Walsh, a psychobiologist at Boise State University in Idaho. "It's Bon Jovi vs. Beethoven."

Oxytocin is another chemical that has recently been implicated in love. Pro-duced by the brain, it sensitizes nerves and stimulates muscle contraction. In women it helps uterine contractions during childbirth as well as production of breast milk, and seems to inspire mothers to nuzzle their infants. Scientists specu-late that oxytocin might encourage similar cuddling between adult women and men. The versatile chemical may also enhance orgasms. In one study of men, oxytocin increased to three to five times its normal level during climax, and it may soar even higher in women.

One mystery is the prevalence of homosexual love. Although it would seem to have no evolutionary purpose, since no children are produced, there is no denying that gays and lesbians can be as romantic as anyone else. Some researchers speculate that homosexuality results from a biochemical anomaly that occurs during fetal development. But that doesn't make romance among gays any less real. "That they direct this love toward their own sex," says Walsh, "does not diminish the value of that love one iota."

> A certain smile, a certain face.
> — Johnny Mathis

Chemicals may help explain (at least to scientists) the feelings of passion and compassion, but why do people tend to fall in love with one partner rather than a myriad of others? Once again, it's partly a function of evolution and biology. "Men are looking for maximal fertility in a mate," says Loyola Marymount's Mills. "That is in large part why females in the prime childbearing ages of seventeen to twenty-eight are so desirable." Men can size up youth and vitality in a glance, and studies indeed show that men fall in love quite rapidly. Women tumble more slowly, to a large degree because their requirements are more complex; they need more time to, check the guy out. "Age is not vital," notes Mills, "but the ability to provide security, father children, share resources, and hold a high status in society are all key factors."

Still, that does not explain why the way Mary walks and laughs makes Bill dizzy with desire while Marcia's gait and giggle leave him cold. "Nature has wired us for one special person," suggests Walsh, romantically. He rejects the idea that a woman or a man can be in love with two people at the same time. Each person carries in his or her mind a unique subliminal guide to the ideal partner, a "love map," to borrow a term coined by sexologist John Money of Johns Hopkins University.

Drawn from the people and experiences of childhood, the map is a record of whatever we found enticing and exciting—or disturbing and disgusting. Small feet, curly hair. The way our mothers patted our head or how our fathers told a joke. A fireman's uniform, a doctor's stethoscope. All the information gathered while growing up is imprinted in the brain's circuitry by adolescence. Partners never meet each and every requirement, but a sufficient number of matches can light up the wires and signal, "It's love." Not every partner will be like the last one, since lovers may have different combinations of the characteristics favored by the map.

O.K., that's the scientific point of view. Satisfied? Probably not. To most people—with or without Ph.D.s—love will always be more than the sum of its natural parts. It's a commingling of body and soul, reality and imagination, poetry and phenylethylamine. In our deepest hearts, most of us harbor the hope that love will never fully yield up its secrets, that it will always elude our grasp.   [1993]

20

THINKING ABOUT THE TEXT

1. Toufexis concludes the last paragraph by asking, "Satisfied?" Were you impressed by these scientific claims?

2. Examine the last line carefully. Do you agree? Is this a possible "explanation" of what happens to Gallimard in M. *Butterfly?*

3. The author quotes Greta Garbo as saying "A lot of nonsense is talked and written about [romantic love.]" Do you agree? Give some examples from popular culture (movies, TV, MTV, and so forth).

NATHANIEL BRANDEN
Immature Love

Nathaniel Branden (b. 1930), a psychologist closely connected with the controversial novelist and philosopher Ayn Rand until 1968, conducts workshops and writes extensively on the subject of self-esteem. The following excerpt is taken from The Psychology of Romantic Love *(1980).*

"Maturity" and "immaturity" are concepts that refer to the success or failure of an individual's biological, intellectual, and psychological evolution to an adult stage of development.

In mature love relationships, "complementary differences" refers, predominately, to complementary *strengths*. In immature relationships, "complementary differences" tends to refer to complementary *weaknesses*. These weaknesses include needs, wants, and other personality traits that reflect some failure of healthy development, some failure of psychological maturation. As we shall see, we deal here, most essentially, with the issue of separation and individuation, with an individual's success or failure at the task of reaching an adult level of autonomy.

Many a person faces life with an attitude that, if translated into explicit speech, which it almost never is, would amount to the declaration, "When I was five years old, important needs of mine were not met—and until they are, I'm not moving on to six!" On a basic level these people are very passive, even though, on more superficial levels, they may sometimes appear active and "aggressive." At bottom, they are waiting, waiting to be rescued, waiting to be told they are good boys or good girls, waiting to be validated or confirmed by some outside source.

So their whole lives may be organized around the desire to please, to be taken care of, or, alternatively, to control and dominate, to manipulate and *coerce* the satisfaction of their needs and wants, because they don't trust the authenticity of anyone's love or caring. They have no confidence that what they are, without their facades and manipulations, is *enough*.

Whether their act is to be helpless and dependent, or to be controlling, over-protective, "responsible," "grown-up," there is an underlying sense of inadequacy, of nameless deficiency, that they feel only other human beings can correct. They are alienated from their own internal sources of strength and support; they are alienated from their own powers.

Whether they seek completion and fulfillment through domination or sub-mission, through controlling or being controlled, through ordering or obeying, there is the same fundamental sense of emptiness, a void in the center of their being, a screaming hole where an autonomous self failed to develop. They have never assimilated and integrated the basic fact of human aloneness, individuation has not been attained to a level appropriate to their chronological development.

They have failed to transfer the source of their approval from others to self. They have failed to evolve into a state of self-responsibility. They have failed to make peace with the immutable fact of their ultimate aloneness—therefore they are crippled in their efforts to relate.

They view other human beings with suspicion, hostility, and feelings of alienation, or else see them as life belts by which they can stay afloat in the stormy sea of their own anxiety and insecurity. There is a tendency for immature persons to view others primarily, if not exclusively, as sources for the gratification of their own wants and needs, not as human beings in their own right, much as an infant views a parent. So their relationships tend to be dependent and manipula-tive, not the encounter of two autonomous selves who feel free to express them-selves honestly and are able to appreciate and enjoy each other's being, but the

5

encounter of two incomplete beings who look to love to solve the problem of their internal deficiencies, to finish magically the unfinished business of childhood, to fill up the holes in their personality, to make of "love" a substitute for evolution to maturity and self-responsibility.

These are some of the "basic similarities" shared by immature persons who fall in love. To understand why immature love is born is also to understand why it generally dies so swiftly.

An immature woman looks at her lover and, deep in her psyche, there is the thought, "My father made me feel rejected, you will take his place and give me what he failed to give me. I will create a house for you, and cook your meals, and bear your children—I will be your good little girl."

Or a woman experiences herself as unloved or rejected by one or both parents. She fails to acknowledge the magnitude of her hurt and self-deprecatory feelings, and she passes into the *semblance* of adulthood. But the sense of unfinished business, the sense of incompleteness as a person, remains and continues to play a role in her motivation, beneath the surface of awareness. She "falls in love" with a man who, whatever his other virtues, shares important characteristics with her rejecting parent(s). Perhaps he is cold, unemotional, unable or unwilling to express love. Like a losing gambler who cannot resist returning to the table where past defeats were suffered, she feels compulsively drawn to him. *This time she will not lose.* She will melt him. She will find a way to melt him. She will find a way to inspire in him all the responses she longed for and failed to receive as a child. And in so doing, she feels, she will redeem her childhood—she will win the victory over her past.

What she does not realize is that, unless other factors intervene to generate a positive change in her psychology, the man is useful to her, is serviceable to her, in the drama she is playing only so long as he remains somewhat aloof, somewhat uncaring, somewhat distant from her. If he would become warm and loving, he no longer would be a suitable understudy for Mother or Father; he would no longer be appropriate for the role in which she has cast him. So at the same time that she cries for love, she takes careful measures to maintain the distance between them to prevent him from giving her the very things she asks for. If, somehow, in spite of her efforts, he does become loving and caring, the likelihood is that she will feel disoriented and will withdraw; probably she will fall out of love with him. "Why?" she cries to her psychotherapist, "do I always fall for men who don't know how to love?"

A man looks at his bride and there is the thought, "Now I am a married man; I am grown up; I have responsibilities—just like Father. I will work hard, I will be your protector, I will take care of you—just as Father did with Mother. Then he—and you—and everyone—will see that I am a good boy."

Or, when a man is a little boy his mother deserts her family to go off with her lover. The little boy feels betrayed and abandoned; it is *he* Mother has left, not Father. (This is the natural egocentricity of childhood.) He tells himself—perhaps with Father's help and encouragement—that "women are like that, not to be trusted." He resolves never to be vulnerable to such pain again. No woman will ever be allowed to make him suffer as Mother did. But years later he knows only two kinds of relationships with women; those in which he cares a good deal less than the woman, and it is he who hurts and betrays her; and those in which he has selected a woman who inevitably will not remain true to him, inevitably will make him suffer. Sooner or later, he almost always ends up with the second kind of woman—to complete the unfinished business of childhood (which he can never complete successfully in this manner, *because the woman is not his mother*, she is only a symbolic substitute). When the woman "lets him down," he professes to be shocked and bewildered. The intense "love affairs" of his life are of this second kind. He is disconnected from the original pain, from the source of the problem, from the feelings he disowned long ago; therefore he is powerless to deal with them effectively and to resolve them; he is the prisoner of that which he has failed to confront; but deep in his psyche, without a solution's ever being found, the drama continues. *Next* time he will beat the table. Meanwhile, for consolation, for rest, for recreation, for revenge, let him hurt as many women as he can. He asks, "Is romantic love a delusion? It never seems to work for me." . . .

On one level, it is true enough to say that a characteristic of immature love is   15
that the man or woman does not perceive his or her partner realistically; fantasies and projections take the place of clear vision. And yet, on a deeper level, on a level not ordinarily acknowledged, there is awareness, there is recognition, there is knowledge of whom they have chosen. They are not, in fact, blind, but the game in which they are engaged may require that they pretend, to themselves, to be blind. This allows them to go through the motions of being bewildered, hurt, outraged, shocked, when their partner behaves precisely as their own life scenario requires. Evidence for this lies in the consistency with which immature persons find precisely those immature other persons whose problems and style of being will complement and mesh with their own.   [1980]

THINKING ABOUT THE TEXT

1. Branden claims that some lovers are "waiting to be rescued" (para. 3). What does he mean by this? Might it apply to Gallimard?

2. According to Branden, the immature are dependent and manipulative and are trying "to finish magically the unfinished business of childhood" (para. 8). Explain.

3. Branden says that the immature often find compatible lovers. Is this true in your experience? In *M. Butterfly*?

WRITING ABOUT ISSUES

1. Argue that Gallimard's romantic attachment is either plausible or not. Use ideas from Gray, Toufexis, or Branden to enhance your claim.

2. Is Gallimard immature? Write an essay using your own experiences to support your claim.

3. Write a personal narrative about a strong attraction you had to someone who later turned out to be quite different than you imagined.

4.   Research romantic love. Find experts who argue that it is simply a cul-
     tural illusion and write a position paper agreeing or disagreeing with
     them.

Is This Love?

ANN PETRY, "Like a Winding Sheet"
WILLIAM FAULKNER, "A Rose for Emily"
RAYMOND CARVER, "What We Talk About When We Talk About Love"

Although stories about those who die for love are not unknown, those about killing for love are much rarer. Can "killing for love" still be considered love, or is it something quite different, something dark and perverse? Can the world be so stressful, so unjust and cruel that someone batters a beloved in frustration? What if that person is looking to someone else to relieve the disappointments of the world? Is that love or just physical need? What if someone harbors violent fantasies about a person loved years before? These are not simple questions. Trying to understand our emotional contradictions and paradoxes never is. The following three writers grapple with these issues in creative and sometimes painful ways: Petry's story explores the disturbing connections between self-esteem, violence, and love; Faulkner's focuses on the interaction of tradition, madness, and love; and Carver's looks at the complexity of discussing love. See if you can decide if the characters in these stories are motivated by love or something more dangerous.

BEFORE YOU READ

Have you ever hurt somebody you love? Did you mean to? Has a loved one ever hurt you? Is it possible for an emotionally disturbed person to love?

ANN PETRY
Like a Winding Sheet

Ann Lane Petry consciously writes in a long tradition of African American story-tellers; for this she has been recognized by writers like Toni Morrison, Alice Walker, and Gloria Naylor. Unlike most of her literary ancestors, however, she grew up with the advantages of the middle class, including access to education. Born in 1908 in Old Saybrook, Connecticut, she earned a degree from the University of Connecticut in 1934 and worked in the family drugstore until her marriage in 1938. Petry then became a journalist for Harlem newspapers and began to see her short stories pub-lished in magazines. In 1945, she won a fellowship for work on her first novel, The

Street, *which was published the next year. In 1946, the short story "Like a Winding Sheet" was included in the annual anthology* The Best American Short Stories, *which was also dedicated to Ann Petry. Her* Miss Muriel and Other Stories (1971) *was the first collection of short stories by a black woman published in the United States. In addition to her novels and stories, she has written children's literature.*

He had planned to get up before Mae did and surprise her by fixing break-fast. Instead he went back to sleep and she got out of bed so quietly he didn't know she wasn't there beside him until he woke up and heard the queer soft gurgle of water running out of the sink in the bathroom.

He knew he ought to get up but instead he put his arms across his forehead to shut the afternoon sunlight out of his eyes, pulled his legs up close to his body, testing them to see if the ache was still in them.

Mae had finished in the bathroom. He could tell because she never closed the door when she was in there and now the sweet smell of talcum powder was drifting down the hall and into the bedroom. Then he heard her coming down the hall.

"Hi, babe," she said affectionately.

"Hum," he grunted, and moved his arms away from his head, opened one eye. 5

"It's a nice morning."

"Yeah." He rolled over and the sheet twisted around him, outlining his thighs, his chest. "You mean afternoon, don't ya?"

Mae looked at the twisted sheet and giggled. "Looks like a winding sheet," she said. "A shroud —" Laughter tangled with her words and she had to pause for a moment before she could continue. "You look like a huckleberry — in a wind-ing sheet —"

"That's no way to talk. Early in the day like this," he protested.

He looked at his arms silhouetted against the white of the sheets. They were 10 inky black by contrast and he had to smile in spite of himself and he lay there smiling and savoring the sweet sound of Mae's giggling.

"Early?" She pointed a finger at the alarm clock on the table near the bed and giggled again. "It's almost four o'clock. And if you don't spring up out of there, you're going to be late again."

"What do you mean 'again'?"

"Twice last week. Three times the week before. And once the week before and —"

"I can't get used to sleeping in the daytime," he said fretfully. He pushed his legs out from under the covers experimentally. Some of the ache had gone out of them but they weren't really rested yet. "It's too light for good sleeping. And all that standing beats the hell out of my legs."

"After two years you oughta be used to it," Mae said. 15

He watched her as she fixed her hair, powdered her face, slipped into a pair of blue denim overalls. She moved quickly and yet she didn't seem to hurry.

"You look like you'd had plenty of sleep," he said lazily. He had to get up but he kept putting the moment off, not wanting to move, yet he didn't dare let his legs go completely limp because if he did he'd go back to sleep. It was getting later and later but the thought of putting his weight on his legs kept him lying there.

When he finally got up he had to hurry, and he gulped his breakfast so fast that he wondered if his stomach could possibly use food thrown at it at such a rate of speed. He was still wondering about it as he and Mae were putting their coats on in the hall.

Mae paused to look at the calendar. "It's the thirteenth," she said. Then a faint excitement in her voice, "Why, it's Friday the thirteenth." She had one arm in her coat sleeve and she held it there while she stared at the calendar. "I oughta stay home," she said. "I shouldn't go outa the house."

"Aw, don't be a fool," he said. "Today's payday. And payday is a good luck day   20
everywhere, any way you look at it." And as she stood hesitating he said, "Aw, come on."

And he was late for work again because they spent fifteen minutes arguing before he could convince her she ought to go to work just the same. He had to talk persuasively, urging her gently, and it took time. But he couldn't bring himself to talk to her roughly or threaten to strike her like a lot of men might have done. He wasn't made that way.

So when he reached the plant he was late and he had to wait to punch the time clock because the day-shift workers were streaming out in long lines, in groups and bunches that impeded his progress.

Even now just starting his workday his legs ached. He had to force himself to struggle past the outgoing workers, punch the time clock, and get the little cart he pushed around all night, because he kept toying with the idea of going home and getting back in bed.

He pushed the cart out on the concrete floor, thinking that if this was his plant he'd make a lot of changes in it. There were too many standing-up jobs for one thing. He'd figure out some way most of 'em could be done sitting down and he'd put a lot more benches around. And this job he had — this job that forced him to walk ten hours a night, pushing this little cart, well, he'd turn it into a sitting-down job. One of those little trucks they used around railroad stations would be good for a job like this. Guys sat on a seat and the thing moved easily, taking up little room and turning in hardly any space at all, like on a dime.

He pushed the cart near the foreman. He never could remember to refer to   25
her as the forelady even in his mind. It was funny to have a white woman for a boss in a plant like this one.

She was sore about something. He could tell by the way her face was red and her eyes were half-shut until they were slits. Probably been out late and didn't get enough sleep. He avoided looking at her and hurried a little, head down, as he passed her though he couldn't resist stealing a glance at her out of the corner of his eye. He saw the edge of the light-colored slacks she wore and the tip end of a big tan shoe.

"Hey, Johnson!" the woman said.

The machines had started full blast. The whirr and the grinding made the building shake, made it impossible to hear conversations. The men and women at the machines talked to each other but looking at them from just a little distance away, they appeared to be simply moving their lips because you couldn't hear what they were saying. Yet the woman's voice cut across the machine sounds — harsh, angry.

He turned his head slowly. "Good evenin', Mrs. Scott," he said, and waited.

"You're late again." 30

"That's right. My legs were bothering me."

The woman's face grew redder, angrier looking. "Half this shift comes in late," she said. "And you're the worst one of all. You're always late. Whatsa matter with ya?"

"It's my legs," he said. "Somehow they don't ever get rested. I don't seem to get used to sleeping days. And I just can't get started."

"Excuses. You guys always got excuses," her anger grew and spread. "Every guy comes in here late always has an excuse. His wife's sick or his grandmother died or somebody in the family had to go to the hospital," she paused, drew a deep breath. "And the niggers is the worse. I don't care what's wrong with your legs. You get in here on time. I'm sick of you niggers —"

"You got the right to get mad," he interrupted softly. "You got the right to cuss 35 me four ways to Sunday but I ain't letting nobody call me a nigger."

He stepped closer to her. His fists were doubled. His lips were drawn back in a thin narrow line. A vein in his forehead stood out swollen, thick.

And the woman backed away from him, not hurriedly but slowly — two, three steps back.

"Aw, forget it," she said. "I didn't mean nothing by it. It slipped out. It was an accident." The red of her face deepened until the small blood vessels in her cheeks were purple. "Go on and get to work," she urged. And she took three more slow backward steps.

He stood motionless for a moment and then turned away from the sight of the red lipstick on her mouth that made him remember that the foreman was a woman. And he couldn't bring himself to hit a woman. He felt a curious tingling in his fingers and he looked down at his hands. They were clenched tight, hard, ready to smash some of those small purple veins in her face.

He pushed the cart ahead of him, walking slowly. When he turned his head, 40 she was staring in his direction, mopping her forehead with a dark blue handkerchief. Their eyes met and then they both looked away.

He didn't glance in her direction again but moved past the long work benches, carefully collecting the finished parts, going slowly and steadily up and down, and back and forth the length of the building, and as he walked he forced himself to swallow his anger, get rid of it.

And he succeeded so that he was able to think about what had happened without getting upset about it. An hour went by but the tension stayed in his hands. They were clenched and knotted on the handles of the cart as though ready to aim a blow.

And he thought he should have hit her anyway, smacked her hard in the face, felt the soft flesh of her face give under the hardness of his hands. He tried to make his hands relax by offering them a description of what it would have been like to strike her because he had the queer feeling that his hands were not exactly a part of him anymore — they had developed a separate life of their own over which he had no control. So he dwelt on the pleasure his hands would have felt — both of them cracking at her, first one and then the other. If he had done that his hands would have felt good now — relaxed, rested.

And he decided that even if he'd lost his job for it, he should have let her have it and it would have been a long time, maybe the rest of her life, before she called anybody else a nigger.

The only trouble was he couldn't hit a woman. A woman couldn't hit   45
back the same way a man did. But it would have been a deeply satisfying thing to have cracked her narrow lips wide open with just one blow, beautifully timed and with all his weight in back of it. That way he would have gotten rid of all the energy and tension his anger had created in him. He kept remembering how his heart had started pumping blood so fast he had felt it tingle even in the tips of his fingers.

With the approach of night, fatigue nibbled at him. The corners of his mouth drooped, the frown between his eyes deepened, his shoulders sagged; but his hands stayed tight and tense. As the hours dragged by he noticed that the women workers had started to snap and snarl at each other. He couldn't hear what they said because of the sound of machines but he could see the quick lip movements that sent words tumbling from the sides of their mouths. They gestured irritably with their hands and scowled as their mouths moved.

Their violent jerky motions told him that it was getting close on to quitting time but somehow he felt that the night still stretched ahead of him, composed of endless hours of steady walking on his aching legs. When the whistle finally blew he went on pushing the cart, unable to believe that it had sounded. The whirring of the machines died away to a murmur and he knew then that he'd really heard the whistle. He stood still for a moment, filled with a relief that made him sigh.

Then he moved briskly, putting the cart in the storeroom, hurrying to take his place in the line forming before the paymaster. That was another thing he'd change, he thought. He'd have the pay envelopes handed to the people right at their benches so there wouldn't be ten or fifteen minutes lost waiting for the pay. He always got home about fifteen minutes late on payday. They did it better in the plant where Mae worked, brought the money right to them at their benches.

He stuck his pay envelope in his pants' pocket and followed the line of workers heading for the subway in a slow-moving stream. He glanced up at the sky. It was a nice night, the sky looked packed full to running over with stars. And he thought if he and Mae would go right to bed when they got home from work they'd catch a few hours of darkness for sleeping. But they never did. They fooled around — cooking and eating and listening to the radio and he always stayed in a big chair in the living room and went almost but not quite to sleep and when they finally got to bed it was five or six in the morning and daylight was already seeping around the edges of the sky.

He walked slowly, putting off the moment when he would have to plunge   50
into the crowd hurrying toward the subway. It was a long ride to Harlem and tonight the thought of it appalled him. He paused outside an all-night restaurant

to kill time, so that some of the first rush of workers would be gone when he reached the subway.

The lights in the restaurant were brilliant, enticing. There was life and motion inside. And as he looked through the window he thought that everything within range of his eyes gleamed—the long imitation marble counter, the tall stools, the white porcelain-topped tables and especially the big metal coffee urn right near the window. Steam issued from its top and a gas flame flickered under it—a lively, dancing, blue flame.

A lot of the workers from his shift—men and women—were lining up near the coffee urn. He watched them walk to the porcelain-topped tables carrying steaming cups of coffee and he saw that just the smell of the coffee lessened the fatigue lines in their faces. After the first sip their faces softened, they smiled, they began to talk and laugh.

On a sudden impulse he shoved the door open and joined the line in front of the coffee urn. The line moved slowly. And as he stood there the smell of the coffee, the sound of the laughter and of the voices, helped dull the sharp ache in his legs.

He didn't pay any attention to the white girl who was serving the coffee at the urn. He kept looking at the cups in the hands of the men who had been ahead of him. Each time a man stepped out of the line with one of the thick white cups the fragrant steam got in his nostrils. He saw that they walked carefully so as not to spill a single drop. There was a froth of bubbles at the top of each cup and he thought about how he would let the bubbles break against his lips before he actually took a big deep swallow.

Then it was his turn. "A cup of coffee," he said, just as he had heard the oth-   55
ers say.

The white girl looked past him, put her hands up to her head and gently lifted her hair away from the back of her neck, tossing her head back a little. "No more coffee for a while," she said.

He wasn't certain he'd heard her correctly and he said "What?" blankly.

"No more coffee for a while," she repeated.

There was silence behind him and then uneasy movement. He thought someone would say something, ask why or protest, but there was only silence and then a faint shuffling sound as though the men standing behind him had simultaneously shifted their weight from one foot to the other.

He looked at the girl without saying anything. He felt his hands begin to   60
tingle and the tingling went all the way down to his finger tips so that he glanced down at them. They were clenched tight, hard, into fists. Then he looked at the girl again. What he wanted to do was hit her so hard that the scarlet lipstick on her mouth would smear and spread over her nose, her chin, out toward her cheeks, so hard that she would never toss her head again and refuse a man a cup of coffee because he was black.

He estimated the distance across the counter and reached forward, balancing his weight on the balls of his feet, ready to let the blow go. And then his hands fell back down to his sides because he forced himself to lower them, to unclench them and make them dangle loose. The effort took his breath away because his hands fought against him. But he couldn't hit her. He couldn't even now bring himself to hit a woman, not even this one, who had refused him a cup of coffee with a toss of her head. He kept seeing the gesture with which she had lifted the length of her blond hair from the back of her neck as expressive of her contempt for him.

When he went out the door he didn't look back. If he had he would have seen the flickering blue flame under the shiny coffee urn being extinguished. The line of men who had stood behind him lingered a moment to watch the people drinking coffee at the tables and then they left just as he had without having had the coffee they wanted so badly. The girl behind the counter poured water in the urn and swabbed it out and as she waited for the water to run out, she lifted her hair gently from the back of her neck and tossed her head before she began making a fresh lot of coffee.

But he had walked away without a backward look, his head down, his hands in his pockets, raging at himself and whatever it was inside of him that had forced him to stand quiet and still when he wanted to strike out.

The subway was crowded and he had to stand. He tried grasping an overhead strap and his hands were too tense to grip it. So he moved near the train door and stood there swaying back and forth with the rocking of the train. The roar of the train beat inside his head, making it ache and throb, and the pain in his legs clawed up into his groin so that he seemed to be bursting with pain and he told himself that it was due to all that anger-born energy that had piled up in him and not been used and so it had spread through him like a poison — from his feet and legs all the way up to his head.

Mae was in the house before he was. He knew she was home before he put   65
the key in the door of the apartment. The radio was going. She had it tuned up loud and she was singing along with it.

"Hello, babe," she called out, as soon as he opened the door.

He tried to say "hello" and it came out half grunt and half sigh.

"You sure sound cheerful," she said.

She was in the bedroom and he went and leaned against the doorjamb. The denim overalls she wore to work were carefully draped over the back of a chair by the bed. She was standing in front of the dresser, tying the sash of a yellow housecoat around her waist and chewing gum vigorously as she admired her reflection in the mirror over the dresser.

"Whatsa matter?" she said. "You get bawled out by the boss or somep'n?"   70

"Just tired," he said slowly. "For God's sake, do you have to crack that gum like that?"

"You don't have to lissen to me," she said complacently. She patted a curl in place near the side of her head and then lifted her hair away from the back of her neck, ducking her head forward and then back.

He winced away from the gesture. "What you got to be always fooling with your hair for?" he protested.

"Say, what's the matter with you anyway?" She turned away from the mirror to face him, put her hands on her hips. "You ain't been in the house two minutes and you're picking on me."

He didn't answer her because her eyes were angry and he didn't want to   75
quarrel with her. They'd been married too long and got along too well and so he
walked all the way into the room and sat down in the chair by the bed and
stretched his legs out in front of him, putting his weight on the heels of his shoes,
leaning way back in the chair, not saying anything.

"Lissen," she said sharply. "I've got to wear those overalls again tomorrow.
You're going to get them all wrinkled up leaning against them like that."

He didn't move. He was too tired and his legs were throbbing now that he
had sat down. Besides the overalls were already wrinkled and dirty, he thought.
They couldn't help but be for she'd worn them all week. He leaned farther back
in the chair.

"Come on, get up," she ordered.

"Oh, what the hell," he said wearily, and got up from the chair. "I'd just as
soon live in a subway. There'd be just as much place to sit down."

He saw that her sense of humor was struggling with her anger. But her sense   80
of humor won because she giggled.

"Aw, come on and eat," she said. There was a coaxing note in her voice.
"You're nothing but an old hungry nigger trying to act tough and—" she paused
to giggle and then continued, "You—"

He had always found her giggling pleasant and deliberately said things that
might amuse her and then waited, listening for the delicate sound to emerge
from her throat. This time he didn't even hear the giggle. He didn't let her finish
what she was saying. She was standing close to him and that funny tingling
started in his finger tips, went fast up his arms and sent his fist shooting straight
for her face.

There was the smacking sound of soft flesh being struck by a hard object and
it wasn't until she screamed that he realized he had hit her in the mouth—so
hard that the dark red lipstick had blurred and spread over her full lips, reaching
up toward the tip of her nose, down toward her chin, out toward her cheeks.

The knowledge that he had struck her seeped through him slowly and he
was appalled but he couldn't drag his hands away from her face. He kept striking
her and he thought with horror that something inside him was holding him,
binding him to this act, wrapping and twisting about him so that he had to continue it. He had lost all control over his hands. And he groped for a phrase, a
word, something to describe what this thing was like that was happening to him
and he thought it was like being enmeshed in a winding sheet—that was it—like
a winding sheet. And even as the thought formed in his mind, his hands reached
for her face again and yet again.   [1946]

THINKING ABOUT THE TEXT

1. Early in the story Petry tells us that the husband "couldn't bring himself
    to talk to her roughly or threaten to strike her" (para. 21). Why does she
    tell us this?

2. Do you think it's possible to lose control? What has to happen? Can love be an antidote for a personal problem? Is this how you understand the husband? Explain.

3. Is Petry trying to build sympathy for the husband? Does she succeed? Can you hurt someone you love?

4. What specific insights into the life of the working poor does this story provide? Did you know these things before? What, if anything, can be done about these things?

5. An old expression claims, "to understand all is to forgive all." Is this true? Is it true for this story, or are you unwilling to forgive the husband? Explain.

WILLIAM FAULKNER
A Rose for Emily

William Faulkner (1897–1962) is recognized not only as one of the greatest American novelists and storytellers, but as one of the major figures of world literature, having won the Nobel Prize in 1949. This acclaim failed to impress the people of his hometown, however, where his genteel poverty and peculiar ways earned him the title "Count No Count." Born in New Albany, Mississippi, and raised in Oxford, the home of the University of Mississippi, Faulkner briefly attended college there after World War I but was reduced to working odd jobs while continuing his writing. His fiction is most often set in Yoknapatawpha County, a created world whose history, geography, and complex genealogies parallel those of the American South. His many novels and stories blend the grotesquely comic with the appallingly tragic. The Sound and the Fury (1929) is often considered his finest work. In later years, Faulkner's "odd jobs" included scriptwriting for Hollywood movies, speaking at universities, and writing magazine articles. "A Rose for Emily," first published in Forum, *presents a story of love as told by citizens of Yoknapatawpha County.*

1

When Miss Emily Grierson died, our whole town went to her funeral: the men through a sort of respectful affection for a fallen monument, the women mostly out of curiosity to see the inside of her house, which no one save an old manservant—a combined gardener and cook—had seen in at least ten years.

It was a big, squarish frame house that had once been white, decorated with cupolas and spires and scrolled balconies in the heavily lightsome style of the seventies, set on what had once been our most select street. But garages and cotton gins had encroached and obliterated even the august names of that neighborhood;

only Miss Emily's house was left, lifting its stubborn and coquettish decay above the cotton wagons and the gasoline pumps—an eyesore among eyesores. And now Miss Emily had gone to join the representatives of those august names where they lay in the cedar-bemused cemetery among the ranked and anonymous graves of Union and Confederate soldiers who fell at the battle of Jefferson.

Alive, Miss Emily had been a tradition, a duty, and a care; a sort of hereditary obligation upon the town, dating from that day in 1894 when Colonel Sartoris, the mayor—he who fathered the edict that no Negro woman should appear on the streets without an apron—remitted her taxes, the dispensation dating from the death of her father on into perpetuity. Not that Miss Emily would have accepted charity. Colonel Sartoris invented an involved tale to the effect that Miss Emily's father had loaned money to the town, which the town, as a matter of business, preferred this way of repaying. Only a man of Colonel Sartoris' generation and thought could have invented it, and only a woman could have believed it.

When the next generation, with its more modern ideas, became mayors and aldermen, this arrangement created some little dissatisfaction. On the first of the year they mailed her a tax notice. February came, and there was no reply. They wrote her a formal letter, asking her to call at the sheriff's office at her convenience. A week later the mayor wrote her himself, offering to call or to send his car for her, and received in reply a note on paper of an archaic shape, in a thin, flowing calligraphy in faded ink, to the effect that she no longer went out at all. The tax notice was also enclosed, without comment.

They called a special meeting of the Board of Aldermen. A deputation waited upon her, knocked at the door through which no visitor had passed since she ceased giving china-painting lessons eight or ten years earlier. They were admitted by the old Negro into a dim hall from which a stairway mounted into still more shadow. It smelled of dust and disuse—a close, dank smell. The Negro led them into the parlor. It was furnished in heavy, leather-covered furniture. When the Negro opened the blinds of one window, they could see that the leather was cracked; and when they sat down, a faint dust rose sluggishly about their thighs, spinning with slow motes in the single sun-ray. On a tarnished gilt easel before the fireplace stood a crayon portrait of Miss Emily's father.

They rose when she entered—a small, fat woman in black, with a thin gold chain descending to her waist and vanishing into her belt, leaning on an ebony cane with a tarnished gold head. Her skeleton was small and spare; perhaps that was why what would have been merely plumpness in another was obesity in her. She looked bloated, like a body long submerged in motionless water, and of that pallid hue. Her eyes, lost in the fatty ridges of her face, looked like two small pieces of coal pressed into a lump of dough as they moved from one face to another while the visitors stated their errand.

She did not ask them to sit. She just stood in the door and listened quietly until the spokesman came to a stumbling halt. Then they could hear the invisible watch ticking at the end of the gold chain.

Her voice was dry and cold. "I have no taxes in Jefferson. Colonel Sartoris explained it to me. Perhaps one of you can gain access to the city records and satisfy yourselves."

5

"But we have. We are the city authorities, Miss Emily. Didn't you get a notice from the sheriff, signed by him?"

"I received a paper, yes," Miss Emily said. "Perhaps he considers himself the sheriff. . . . I have no taxes in Jefferson."

"But there is nothing on the books to show that, you see. We must go by the—"

"See Colonel Sartoris. I have no taxes in Jefferson."

"But, Miss Emily—"

"See Colonel Sartoris." (Colonel Sartoris had been dead almost ten years.) "I have no taxes in Jefferson. Tobe!" The Negro appeared. "Show these gentlemen out."

2

So she vanquished them, horse and foot, just as she had vanquished their fathers thirty years before about the smell. That was two years after her father's death and a short time after her sweetheart—the one we believed would marry her—had deserted her. After her father's death she went out very little; after her sweetheart went away, people hardly saw her at all. A few of the ladies had the temerity to call, but were not received, and the only sign of life about the place was the Negro man—a young man then—going in and out with a market basket.

"Just as if a man—any man—could keep a kitchen properly," the ladies said; so they were not surprised when the smell developed. It was another link between the gross, teeming world and the high and mighty Griersons.

A neighbor, a woman, complained to the mayor, Judge Stevens, eighty years old.

"But what will you have me do about it, madam?" he said.

"Why, send her word to stop it," the woman said. "Isn't there a law?"

"I'm sure that won't be necessary," Judge Stevens said. "It's probably just a snake or a rat that nigger of hers killed in the yard. I'll speak to him about it."

The next day he received two more complaints, one from a man who came in diffident deprecation. "We really must do something about it, Judge. I'd be the last one in the world to bother Miss Emily, but we've got to do something." That night the Board of Aldermen met—three graybeards and one younger man, a member of the rising generation.

"It's simple enough," he said. "Send her word to have her place cleaned up. Give her a certain time to do it in, and if she don't. . . ."

"Dammit, sir," Judge Stevens said, "will you accuse a lady to her face of smelling bad?"

So the next night, after midnight, four men crossed Miss Emily's lawn and slunk about the house like burglars, sniffing along the base of the brickwork and at the cellar openings while one of them performed a regular sowing motion with his hand out of a sack slung from his shoulder. They broke open the cellar door and sprinkled lime there, and in all the outbuildings. As they recrossed the lawn, a window that had been dark was lighted and Miss Emily sat in it, the light behind her, and her upright torso motionless as that of an idol. They crept quietly

across the lawn and into the shadow of the locusts that lined the street. After a
week or two the smell went away.

That was when people had begun to feel really sorry for her. People in our   25
town, remembering how old lady Wyatt, her great-aunt, had gone completely
crazy at last, believed that the Griersons held themselves a little too high for what
they really were. None of the young men were quite good enough for Miss Emily
and such. We had long thought of them as a tableau, Miss Emily a slender figure
in white in the background, her father a spraddled silhouette in the foreground,
his back to her and clutching a horsewhip, the two of them framed by the back-
flung front door. So when she got to be thirty and was still single, we were not
pleased exactly, but vindicated; even with insanity in the family she wouldn't
have turned down all of her chances if they had really materialized.

When her father died, it got about that the house was all that was left to her;
and in a way, people were glad. At last they could pity Miss Emily. Being left
alone, and a pauper, she had become humanized. Now she too would know the
old thrill and the old despair of a penny more or less.

The day after his death all the ladies prepared to call at the house and offer
condolence and aid, as is our custom. Miss Emily met them at the door, dressed
as usual and with no trace of grief on her face. She told them that her father was
not dead. She did that for three days, with the ministers calling on her, and the
doctors, trying to persuade her to let them dispose of the body. Just as they were
about to resort to law and force, she broke down, and they buried her father
quickly.

We did not say she was crazy then. We believed she had to do that. We
remembered all the young men her father had driven away, and we knew that
with nothing left, she would have to cling to that which had robbed her, as
people will.

3

She was sick for a long time. When we saw her again, her hair was cut short,
making her look like a girl, with a vague resemblance to those angels in colored
church windows — sort of tragic and serene.

The town had just let the contracts for paving the sidewalks, and in the sum-   30
mer after her father's death they began the work. The construction company
came with niggers and mules and machinery, and a foreman named Homer Barron, a Yankee — a big, dark, ready man, with a big voice and eyes lighter than his
face. The little boys would follow in groups to hear him cuss the niggers, and the
niggers singing in time to the rise and fall of picks. Pretty soon he knew everybody
in town. Whenever you heard a lot of laughing anywhere about the square,
Homer Barron would be in the center of the group. Presently, we began to see
him and Miss Emily on Sunday afternoons driving in the yellow-wheeled buggy
and the matched team of bays from the livery stable.

At first we were glad that Miss Emily would have an interest, because the
ladies all said, "Of course a Grierson would not think seriously of a Northerner, a
day laborer." But there were still others, older people, who said that even grief

could not cause a real lady to forget *noblesse oblige* — without calling it *noblesse oblige*. They just said, "Poor Emily. Her kinsfolk should come to her." She had some kin in Alabama; but years ago her father had fallen out with them over the estate of old lady Wyatt, the crazy woman, and there was no communication between the two families. They had not even been represented at the funeral.

And as soon as the old people said, "Poor Emily," the whispering began. "Do you suppose it's really so?" they said to one another. "Of course it is. What else could. . . ." This behind their hands; rustling of craned silk and satin behind jalousies closed upon the sun of Sunday afternoon as the thin, swift clop-clop-clop of the matched team passed: "Poor Emily."

She carried her head high enough — even when we believed that she was fallen. It was as if she demanded more than ever the recognition of her dignity as the last Grierson; as if it had wanted that touch of earthiness to reaffirm her imperviousness. Like when she bought the rat poison, the arsenic. That was over a year after they had begun to say "Poor Emily," and while the two female cousins were visiting her.

"I want some poison," she said to the druggist. She was over thirty then, still a slight woman, though thinner than usual, with cold, haughty black eyes in a face the flesh of which was strained across the temples and about the eyesockets as you imagine a lighthouse-keeper's face ought to look. "I want some poison," she said.

"Yes, Miss Emily. What kind? For rats and such? I'd recom ——"   35

"I want the best you have. I don't care what kind."

The druggist named several. "They'll kill anything up to an elephant. But what you want is ——"

"Arsenic," Miss Emily said. "Is that a good one?"

"Is . . . arsenic? Yes, ma'am. But what you want ——"

"I want arsenic."   40

The druggist looked down at her. She looked back at him, erect, her face like a strained flag. "Why, of course," the druggist said. "If that's what you want. But the law requires you to tell what you are going to use it for."

Miss Emily just stared at him, her head tilted back in order to look him eye for eye, until he looked away and went and got the arsenic and wrapped it up. The Negro delivery boy brought her the package; the druggist didn't come back. When she opened the package at home there was written on the box, under the skull and bones: "For rats."

4

So the next day we all said, "She will kill herself"; and we said it would be the best thing. When she had first begun to be seen with Homer Barron, we had said, "She will marry him." Then we said, "She will persuade him yet," because Homer himself had remarked — he liked men, and it was known that he drank with the younger men in the Elks' Club — that he was not a marrying man. Later we said, "Poor Emily" behind the jalousies as they passed on Sunday afternoon in the glittering buggy, Miss Emily with her head high and Homer Barron with his hat cocked and a cigar in his teeth, reins and whip in a yellow glove.

Then some of the ladies began to say that it was a disgrace to the town and a bad example to the young people. The men did not want to interfere, but at last the ladies forced the Baptist minister—Miss Emily's people were Episcopal—to call upon her. He would never divulge what happened during that interview, but he refused to go back again. The next Sunday they again drove about the streets, and the following day the minister's wife wrote to Miss Emily's relations in Alabama.

So she had blood-kin under her roof again and we sat back to watch develop-   45
ments. At first nothing happened. Then we were sure that they were to be married. We learned that Miss Emily had been to the jeweler's and ordered a man's toilet set in silver, with the letters H.B. on each piece. Two days later we learned that she had bought a complete outfit of men's clothing, including a nightshirt, and we said, "They are married." We were really glad. We were glad because the two female cousins were even more Grierson than Miss Emily had ever been.

So we were not surprised when Homer Barron—the streets had been finished some time since—was gone. We were a little disappointed that there was not a public blowing-off, but we believed that he had gone on to prepare for Miss Emily's coming, or to give her a chance to get rid of the cousins. (By that time it was a cabal, and we were all Miss Emily's allies to help circumvent the cousins.) Sure enough, after another week they departed. And, as we had expected all along, within three days Homer Barron was back in town. A neighbor saw the Negro man admit him at the kitchen door at dusk one evening.

And that was the last we saw of Homer Barron. And of Miss Emily for some time. The Negro man went in and out with the market basket, but the front door remained closed. Now and then we would see her at the window for a moment, as the men did that night when they sprinkled the lime, but for almost six months she did not appear on the streets. Then we knew that this was to be expected too; as if that quality of her father which had thwarted her woman's life so many times had been too virulent and too furious to die.

When we next saw Miss Emily, she had grown fat and her hair was turning gray. During the next few years it grew grayer and grayer until it attained an even pepper-and-salt iron-gray, when it ceased turning. Up to the day of her death at seventy-four it was still that vigorous iron-gray, like the hair of an active man.

From that time on her front door remained closed, save during a period of six or seven years, when she was about forty, during which she gave lessons in china-painting. She fitted up a studio in one of the downstairs rooms, where the daughters and granddaughters of Colonel Sartoris' contemporaries were sent to her with the same regularity and in the same spirit that they were sent to church on Sundays with a twenty-five-cent piece for the collection plate. Meanwhile her taxes had been remitted.

Then the newer generation became the backbone and the spirit of the town,   50
and the painting pupils grew up and fell away and did not send their children to her with boxes of color and tedious brushes and pictures cut from the ladies' magazines. The front door closed upon the last one and remained closed for good. When the town got free postal delivery, Miss Emily alone refused to let them fasten the metal numbers above her door and attach a mailbox to it. She would not listen to them.

Daily, monthly, yearly we watched the Negro grow grayer and more stooped, going in and out with the market basket. Each December we sent her a tax notice, which would be returned by the post office a week later, unclaimed. Now and then we would see her in one of the downstairs windows—she had evidently shut up the top floor of the house—like the carven torso of an idol in a niche, looking or not looking at us, we could never tell which. Thus she passed from generation to generation—dear, inescapable, impervious, tranquil, and perverse.

And so she died. Fell ill in the house filled with dust and shadows, with only a doddering Negro man to wait on her. We did not even know she was sick; we had long since given up trying to get any information from the Negro. He talked to no one, probably not even to her, for his voice had grown harsh and rusty, as if from disuse.

She died in one of the downstairs rooms, in a heavy walnut bed with a curtain, her gray head propped on a pillow yellow and moldy with age and lack of sunlight.

5

The Negro met the first of the ladies at the front door and let them in, with their hushed, sibilant voices and their quick, curious glances, and then he disappeared. He walked right through the house and out the back and was not seen again.

The two female cousins came at once. They held the funeral on the second day, with the town coming to look at Miss Emily beneath a mass of bought flowers, with the crayon face of her father musing profoundly above the bier and the ladies sibilant and macabre; and the very old men—some in their brushed Confederate uniforms—on the porch and the lawn, talking of Miss Emily as if she had been a contemporary of theirs, believing that they had danced with her and courted her perhaps, confusing time with its mathematical progression, as the old do, to whom all the past is not a diminishing road but, instead, a huge meadow which no winter ever quite touches, divided from them now by the narrow bottleneck of the most recent decade of years.

Already we knew that there was one room in that region above stairs which no one had seen in forty years, and which would have to be forced. They waited until Miss Emily was decently in the ground before they opened it.

The violence of breaking down the door seemed to fill this room with pervading dust. A thin, acrid pall as of the tomb seemed to lie everywhere upon this room decked and furnished as for a bridal: upon the valance curtains of faded rose color, upon the rose-shaded lights, upon the dressing table, upon the delicate array of crystal and the man's toilet things backed with tarnished silver, silver so tarnished that the monogram was obscured. Among them lay a collar and tie, as if they had just been removed, which, lifted, left upon the surface a pale crescent in the dust. Upon a chair hung the suit, carefully folded; beneath it the two mute shoes and the discarded socks.

The man himself lay in the bed.

For a long while we just stood there, looking down at the profound and fleshless grin. The body had apparently once lain in the attitude of an embrace, but

55

now the long sleep that outlasts love, that conquers even the grimace of love, had cuckolded him. What was left of him, rotted beneath what was left of the night-shirt, had become inextricable from the bed in which he lay; and upon him and upon the pillow beside him lay that even coating of the patient and biding dust.

Then we noticed that in the second pillow was the indentation of a head.   60 One of us lifted something from it, and leaning forward, that faint and invisible dust dry and acrid in the nostrils, we saw a long strand of iron-gray hair.   [1931]

THINKING ABOUT THE TEXT

1. Do you think someone can love another so much they simply cannot bear for them to leave? Is it possible Emily was like this?

2. Can a disturbed person be in love? Does love have to be "healthy"? Is sanity culturally defined? Can you imagine a society that would accept Emily's behavior?

3. Who do you think the narrator of "A Rose for Emily" is? Why would Faulkner tell the story from this perspective? Why not from Emily's?

4. Look at the last sentence of paragraph 51. What do you make of the five adjectives used? Are they understandable in terms of the story?

5. Some critics think this story is not a love story but a political allegory about the South. Does this make sense to you? What else does the story suggest to you?

MAKING COMPARISONS

1. Johnson and Emily each face a stressful challenge; each deals with it in his or her own way. Explain.

2. Emily kills Homer. Is Johnson going to kill Mae? If you were on a jury, which would you deal with most harshly?

3. Is either of these couples in love? Explain.

RAYMOND CARVER
What We Talk About When We Talk About Love

Raymond Carver (1938–1988) re-creates in what has been called a "stripped-down and muscular prose style" the minutiae of everyday life in mid-twentieth-century America. Brought up in the Pacific Northwest in a working-class family, Carver began writing in high school and married early. While both he and his young wife worked at low-paying jobs, Carver took college courses and struggled to find time to write. In 1958, he studied fiction writing with John Gardner and graduated from what is now the California State University at Humboldt in 1963. He received national recognition in 1967 when a story was included in the Best American Short Stories *annual anthology. Although Carver was a National Endowment for the Arts fellow in poetry in 1971, fiction has remained his primary genre, earning him numerous awards and fellowships, including O. Henry awards in 1974, 1975, and 1980. Despite his success as a writer, alcoholism plagued Carver for most of his life until with the help of Alcoholics Anonymous he stopped drinking in 1982, soon after his divorce. "What We Talk About When We Talk About Love" was the title story in his 1981 collection.*

My friend Mel McGinnis was talking. Mel McGinnis is a cardiologist, and sometimes that gives him the right.

The four of us were sitting around his kitchen table drinking gin. Sunlight filled the kitchen from the big window behind the sink. There were Mel and me and his second wife, Teresa—Terri, we called her—and my wife, Laura. We lived in Albuquerque then. But we were all from somewhere else.

There was an ice bucket on the table. The gin and the tonic water kept going around, and we somehow got on the subject of love. Mel thought real love was nothing less than spiritual love. He said he'd spent five years in a seminary before quitting to go to medical school. He said he still looked back on those years in the seminary as the most important years in his life.

Terri said the man she lived with before she lived with Mel loved her so much he tried to kill her. Then Terri said, "He beat me up one night. He dragged me around the living room by my ankles. He kept saying, 'I love you, I love you, you bitch.' He went on dragging me around the living room. My head kept knocking on things." Terri looked around the table. "What do you do with love like that?"

She was a bone-thin woman with a pretty face, dark eyes, and brown hair that   5
hung down her back. She liked necklaces made of turquoise, and long pendant earrings.

"My God, don't be silly. That's not love, and you know it," Mel said. "I don't know what you'd call it, but I sure know you wouldn't call it love."

"Say what you want to, but I know it was," Terri said. "It may sound crazy to you, but it's true just the same. People are different, Mel. Sure, sometimes he may have acted crazy. Okay. But he loved me. In his own way maybe, but he loved me. There was love there, Mel. Don't say there wasn't."

Mel let out his breath. He held his glass and turned to Laura and me. "The man threatened to kill me," Mel said. He finished his drink and reached for the gin bottle. "Terri's a romantic. Terri's of the kick-me-so-I'll-know-you-love-me school. Terri, hon, don't look that way." Mel reached across the table and touched Terri's cheek with his fingers. He grinned at her.

"Now he wants to make up," Terri said.

"Make up what?" Mel said. "What is there to make up? I know what I know.   10
That's all."

"How'd we get started on this subject, anyway?" Terri said. She raised her glass and drank from it. "Mel always has love on his mind," she said. "Don't you, honey?" She smiled, and I thought that was the last of it.

"I just wouldn't call Ed's behavior love. That's all I'm saying, honey," Mel said. "What about you guys?" Mel said to Laura and me. "Does that sound like love to you?"

"I'm the wrong person to ask," I said. "I didn't even know the man. I've only heard his name mentioned in passing. I wouldn't know. You'd have to know the particulars. But I think what you're saying is that love is an absolute."

Mel said, "The kind of love I'm talking about is. The kind of love I'm talking about, you don't try to kill people."

Laura said, "I don't know anything about Ed, or anything about the situa-   15
tion. But who can judge anyone else's situation?"

I touched the back of Laura's hand. She gave me a quick smile. I picked up Laura's hand. It was warm, the nails polished, perfectly manicured. I encircled the broad wrist with my fingers, and I held her.

"When I left, he drank rat poison," Terri said. She clasped her arms with her hands. "They took him to the hospital in Sante Fe. That's where we lived then, about ten miles out. They saved his life. But his gums went crazy from it. I mean they pulled away from his teeth. After that, his teeth stood out like fangs. My God," Terri said. She waited a minute, then let go of her arms and picked up her glass.

"What people won't do!" Laura said.

"He's out of the action now," Mel said. "He's dead."

Mel handed me the saucer of limes. I took a section, squeezed it over my   20
drink, and stirred the ice cubes with my finger.

"It gets worse," Terri said. "He shot himself in the mouth. But he bungled that too. Poor Ed," she said. Terri shook her head.

"Poor Ed nothing," Mel said. "He was dangerous."

Mel was forty-five years old. He was tall and rangy with curly soft hair. His face and arms were brown from the tennis he played. When he was sober, his gestures, all his movements, were precise, very careful.

"He did love me though, Mel. Grant me that," Terri said. "That's all I'm asking. He didn't love me the way you love me. I'm not saying that. But he loved me. You can grant me that, can't you?"

"What do you mean, he bungled it?" I said.   25

Laura leaned forward with her glass. She put her elbows on the table and held her glass in both hands. She glanced from Mel to Terri and waited with a look of bewilderment on her open face, as if amazed that such things happened to people you were friendly with.

"How'd he bungle it when he killed himself?" I said.

"I'll tell you what happened," Mel said. "He took this twenty-two pistol he'd bought to threaten Terri and me with. Oh, I'm serious, the man was always threatening. You should have seen the way we lived in those days. Like fugitives. I even bought a gun myself. Can you believe it? A guy like me? But I did. I bought one for self-defense and carried it in the glove compartment. Sometimes I'd have to leave the apartment in the middle of the night. To go to the hospital, you know? Terri and I weren't married then, and my first wife had the house and kids, the dog, everything, and Terri and I were living in this apartment here. Sometimes, as I say,

I'd get a call in the middle of the night and have to go in to the hospital at two or three in the morning. It'd be dark out there in the parking lot, and I'd break into a sweat before I could even get to my car. I never knew if he was going to come up out of the shrubbery or from behind a car and start shooting. I mean, the man was crazy. He was capable of wiring a bomb, anything. He used to call my service at all hours and say he needed to talk to the doctor, and when I'd return the call, he'd say, 'Son of a bitch, your days are numbered.' Little things like that. It was scary, I'm telling you."

"I still feel sorry for him," Terri said.

"It sounds like a nightmare," Laura said. "But what exactly happened after he   30
shot himself?"

Laura is a legal secretary. We'd met in a professional capacity. Before we knew it, it was a courtship. She's thirty-five, three years younger than I am. In addition to being in love, we like each other and enjoy one another's company. She's easy to be with.

"What happened?" Laura said.

Mel said, "He shot himself in the mouth in his room. Someone heard the shot and told the manager. They came in with a passkey, saw what had happened, and called an ambulance. I happened to be there when they brought him in, alive but past recall. The man lived for three days. His head swelled up to twice the size of a normal head. I'd never seen anything like it, and I hope I never do again. Terri wanted to go in and sit with him when she found out about it. We had a fight over it. I didn't think she should see him like that. I didn't think she should see him, and I still don't."

"Who won the fight?" Laura said.

"I was in the room with him when he died," Terri said. "He never came up   35
out of it. But I sat with him. He didn't have anyone else."

"He was dangerous," Mel said. "If you call that love, you can have it."

"It was love," Terri said. "Sure, it's abnormal in most people's eyes. But he was willing to die for it. He did die for it."

"I sure as hell wouldn't call it love," Mel said. "I mean, no one knows what he did it for. I've seen a lot of suicides, and I couldn't say anyone ever knew what they did it for."

Mel put his hands behind his neck and tilted his chair back. "I'm not interested in that kind of love," he said. "If that's love, you can have it."

Terri said, "We were afraid. Mel even made a will out and wrote to his   40
brother in California who used to be a Green Beret. Mel told him who to look for if something happened to him."

Terri drank from her glass. She said, "But Mel's right—we lived like fugitives. We were afraid. Mel was, weren't you, honey? I even called the police at one point, but they were no help. They said they couldn't do anything until Ed actually did something. Isn't that a laugh?" Terri said.

She poured the last of the gin into her glass and waggled the bottle. Mel got up from the table and went to the cupboard. He took down another bottle.

◆ ◆ ◆

"Well, Nick and I know what love is," Laura said. "For us, I mean," Laura said. She bumped my knee with her knee. "You're supposed to say something now," Laura said, and turned her smile on me.

For an answer, I took Laura's hand and raised it to my lips. I made a big production out of kissing her hand. Everyone was amused.

"We're lucky," I said.   45

"You guys," Terri said. "Stop that now. You're making me sick. You're still on the honeymoon, for God's sake. You're still gaga, for crying out loud. Just wait. How long have you been together now? How long has it been? A year? Longer than a year?"

"Going on a year and a half," Laura said, flushed and smiling.

"Oh, now," Terri said. "Wait awhile."

She held her drink and gazed at Laura.

"I'm only kidding," Terri said.   50

Mel opened the gin and went around the table with the bottle.

"Here, you guys," he said. "Let's have a toast. I want to propose a toast. A toast to love. To true love," Mel said.

We touched glasses.

"To love," we said.

Outside in the backyard, one of the dogs began to bark. The leaves of the   55
aspen that leaned past the window ticked against the glass. The afternoon sun was like a presence in this room, the spacious light of ease and generosity. We could have been anywhere, somewhere enchanted. We raised our glasses again and grinned at each other like children who had agreed on something forbidden.

"I'll tell you what real love is," Mel said. "I mean, I'll give you a good example. And then you can draw your own conclusions." He poured more gin into his glass. He added an ice cube and a sliver of lime. We waited and sipped our drinks. Laura and I touched knees again. I put a hand on her warm thigh and left it there.

"What do any of us really know about love?" Mel said. "It seems to me we're just beginners at love. We say we love each other and we do, I don't doubt it. I love Terri and Terri loves me, and you guys love each other too. You know the kind of love I'm talking about now. Physical love, that impulse that drives you to someone special, as well as love of the other person's being, his or her essence, as it were. Carnal love and, well, call it sentimental love, the day-to-day caring about the other person. But sometimes I have a hard time accounting for the fact that I must have loved my first wife too. But I did, I know I did. So I suppose I am like Terri in that regard. Terri and Ed." He thought about it and then he went on. "There was a time when I thought I loved my first wife more than life itself. But now I hate her guts. I do. How do you explain that? What happened to that love? What happened to it, is what I'd like to know. I wish someone could tell me. Then there's Ed. Okay, we're back to Ed. He loves Terri so much he tries to kill her and he winds up killing himself." Mel stopped talking and swallowed from his glass. "You guys have been together eighteen months and you love each other. It shows all over you. You glow with it. But you both loved other people before you met each other. You've both been married before, just like us. And you probably loved other people before that too, even. Terri and I have been together five years, been married for four. And the terrible thing, the terrible thing is, but the good thing too, the saving grace, you might say, is that if something happened to one of us — excuse me for saying this — but if something happened to one of us tomorrow I think the other one, the other person, would grieve for a while, you know, but then the surviving party would go out and love again, have someone else soon enough. All this, all of this love we're talking about, it would just be a memory. Maybe not even a memory. Am I wrong? Am I way off base? Because I want you to set me straight if you think I'm wrong. I want to know. I mean, I don't know anything, and I'm the first one to admit it."

"Mel, for God's sake," Terri said. She reached out and took hold of his wrist. "Are you getting drunk? Honey? Are you drunk?"

"Honey, I'm just talking," Mel said. "All right? I don't have to be drunk to say what I think. I mean, we're all just talking, right?" Mel said. He fixed his eyes on her.

"Sweetie, I'm not criticizing," Terri said.   60

She picked up her glass.

"I'm not on call today," Mel said. "Let me remind you of that. I am not on call," he said.

"Mel, we love you," Laura said.

Mel looked at Laura. He looked at her as if he could not place her, as if she was not the woman she was.

"Love you too, Laura," Mel said. "And you, Nick, love you too. You know   65 something?" Mel said. "You guys are our pals," Mel said.

He picked up his glass.

Mel said, "I was going to tell you about something. I mean, I was going to prove a point. You see, this happened a few months ago, but it's still going on right now, and it ought to make us feel ashamed when we talk like we know what we're talking about when we talk above love."

"Come on now," Terri said. "Don't talk like you're drunk if you're not drunk."

"Just shut up for once in your life," Mel said very quietly. "Will you do me a favor and do that for a minute? So as I was saying, there's this old couple who had this car wreck out on the interstate. A kid hit them and they were all torn to shit and nobody was giving them much chance to pull through."

Terri looked at us and then back at Mel. She seemed anxious, or maybe that's   70 too strong a word.

Mel was handing the bottle around the table.

"I was on call that night," Mel said. "It was May or maybe it was June. Terri and I had just sat down to dinner when the hospital called. There'd been this thing out on the interstate. Drunk kid, teenager, plowed his dad's pickup into this camper with this old couple in it. They were up in their mid-seventies, that couple. The kid — eighteen, nineteen, something — he was DOA. Taken the steering wheel through his sternum. The old couple, they were alive, you understand. I mean, just barely. But they had everything. Multiple fractures, internal injuries, hemorrhaging, contusions, lacerations, the works, and they each of them had themselves concussions. They were in a bad way, believe me. And, of course, their age was two strikes against them. I'd say she was worse off than he was. Ruptured spleen along with everything else. Both kneecaps broken. But they'd been wearing their seatbelts and, God knows, that's what saved them for the time being."

"Folks, this is an advertisement for the National Safety Council," Terri said. "This is your spokesman, Dr. Melvin R. McGinnis, talking." Terri laughed. "Mel," she said, "sometimes you're just too much. But I love you, hon," she said.

"Honey, I love you," Mel said.

He leaned across the table. Terri met him halfway. They kissed. 75

"Terri's right," Mel said as he settled himself again. "Get those seatbelts on. But seriously, they were in some shape, those oldsters. By the time I got down there, the kid was dead, as I said. He was off in a corner, laid out on a gurney. I took one look at the old couple and told the ER nurse to get me a neurologist and an orthopedic man and a couple of surgeons down there right away."

He drank from his glass. "I'll try to keep this short," he said. "So we took the two of them up to the OR and worked like fuck on them most of the night. They had these incredible reserves, those two. You see that once in a while. So we did everything that could be done, and toward morning we're giving them a fifty-fifty chance, maybe less than that for her. So here they are, still alive the next morning. So, okay, we move them into the ICU, which is where they both kept plugging away at it for two weeks, hitting it better and better on all the scopes. So we transfer them out to their own room."

Mel stopped talking. "Here," he said, "let's drink this cheapo gin the hell up. Then we're going to dinner, right? Terri and I know a new place. That's where we'll go, to this new place we know about. But we're not going until we finish up this cut-rate, lousy gin."

Terri said, "We haven't actually eaten there yet. But it looks good. From the outside, you know."

"I like food," Mel said. "If I had it to do all over again, I'd be a chef, you 80 know? Right, Terri?" Mel said.

He laughed. He fingered the ice in his glass.

"Terri knows," he said. "Terri can tell you. But let me say this. If I could come back again in a different life, a different time and all, you know what? I'd like to come back as a knight. You were pretty safe wearing all that armor. It was all right being a knight until gunpowder and muskets and pistols came along."

"Mel would like to ride a horse and carry a lance," Terri said.

"Carry a woman's scarf with you everywhere," Laura said.

"Or just a woman," Mel said. 85

"Shame on you," Laura said.

Terri said, "Suppose you came back as a serf. The serfs didn't have it so good in those days," Terri said.

"The serfs never had it good," Mel said. "But I guess even the knights were vessels to someone. Isn't that the way it worked? But then everyone is always a vessel to someone. Isn't that right? Terri? But what I liked about knights, besides their ladies, was that they had that suit of armor, you know, and they couldn't get hurt very easy. No cars in those days, you know? No drunk teenagers to tear into your ass."

"Vassals," Terri said.

"What?" Mel said.   90

"Vassals," Terri said. "They were called vassals, not vessels."

"Vassals, vessels," Mel said, "what the fuck's the difference? You knew what I meant anyway. All right," Mel said. "So I'm not educated. I learned my stuff. I'm a heart surgeon, sure, but I'm just a mechanic. I go in and I fuck around and I fix things. Shit," Mel said.

"Modesty doesn't become you," Terri said.

"He's just a humble sawbones," I said. "But sometimes they suffocated in all that armor, Mel. They'd even have heart attacks if it got too hot and they were too tired and worn out. I read somewhere that they'd fall off their horses and not be able to get up because they were too tired to stand with all that armor on them. They got trampled by their own horses sometimes."

"That's terrible," Mel said. "That's a terrible thing, Nicky. I guess they'd just   95
lay there and wait until somebody came along and made a shish kebab out of them."

"Some other vessel," Terri said.

"That's right," Mel said. "Some vassal would come along and spear the bastard in the name of love. Or whatever the fuck it was they fought over in those days."

"Same things we fight over these days," Terri said.

Laura said, "Nothing's changed."

The color was still high in Laura's cheeks. Her eyes were bright. She brought   100
her glass to her lips.

Mel poured himself another drink. He looked at the label closely as if studying a long row of numbers. Then he slowly put the bottle down on the table and slowly reached for the tonic water.

"What about the old couple?" Laura said. "You didn't finish that story you started."

Laura was having a hard time lighting her cigarette. Her matches kept going out.

The sunshine inside the room was different now, changing, getting thinner. But the leaves outside the window were still shimmering, and I stared at the pattern they made on the panes and on the Formica counter. They weren't the same patterns, of course.

"What about the old couple?" I said.   105

"Older but wiser," Terri said.

Mel stared at her.

Terri said, "Go on with your story, hon. I was only kidding. Then what happened?"

"Terri, sometimes," Mel said.

"Please, Mel," Terri said. "Don't always be so serious, sweetie. Can't you take   110
a joke?"

"Where's the joke?" Mel said.

He held his glass and gazed steadily at his wife.

"What happened?" Laura said.

Mel fastened his eyes on Laura. He said, "Laura, if I didn't have Terri and if I
didn't love her so much, and if Nick wasn't my best friend, I'd fall in love with
you, I'd carry you off, honey," he said.

"Tell your story," Terri said. "Then we'll go to that new place, okay?"   115

"Okay," Mel said. "Where was I?" he said. He stared at the table and then he
began again.

"I dropped in to see each of them every day, sometimes twice a day if I was
up doing other calls anyway. Casts and bandages, head to foot, the both of them.
You know, you've seen it in the movies. That's just the way they looked, just like
in the movies. Little eye-holes and nose-holes and mouth-holes. And she had to
have her legs slung up on top of it. Well, the husband was very depressed for the
longest while. Even after he found out that his wife was going to pull through, he
was still very depressed. Not about the accident, though. I mean, the accident was
one thing, but it wasn't everything. I'd get up to his mouth-hole, you know, and
he'd say no, it wasn't the accident exactly but it was because he couldn't see her
through his eye-holes. He said that was what was making him feel so bad. Can
you imagine? I'm telling you, the man's heart was breaking because he couldn't
turn his goddamn head and *see* his goddamn wife."

Mel looked around the table and shook his head at what he was going to say.

"I mean, it was killing the old fart just because he couldn't *look* at the fucking
woman."

We all looked at Mel.   120

"Do you see what I'm saying?" he said.

Maybe we were a little drunk by then. I know it was hard keeping things in
focus. The light was draining out of the room, going back through the window
where it had come from. Yet nobody made a move to get up from the table to
turn on the overhead light.

"Listen," Mel said. "Let's finish this fucking gin. There's about enough left
here for one shooter all around. Then let's go eat. Let's go to the new place."

"He's depressed," Terri said. "Mel, why don't you take a pill?"

Mel shook his head. "I've taken everything there is."   125

"We all need a pill now and then," I said.

"Some people are born needing them," Terri said.

She was using her finger to rub at something on the table. Then she stopped
rubbing.

"I think I want to call my kids," Mel said. "Is that all right with everybody? I'll
call my kids," he said.

Terri said, "What if Marjorie answers the phone? You guys, you've heard us   130
on the subject of Marjorie? Honey, you know you don't want to talk to Marjorie.
It'll make you feel even worse."

"I don't want to talk to Marjorie," Mel said. "But I want to talk to my kids."

"There isn't a day goes by that Mel doesn't say he wishes she'd get married again. Or else die," Terri said. "For one thing," Terri said, "she's bankrupting us. Mel says it's just to spite him that she won't get married again. She has a boyfriend who lives with her and the kids, so Mel is supporting the boyfriend too."

"She's allergic to bees," Mel said. "If I'm not praying she'll get married again, I'm praying she'll get herself stung to death by a swarm of fucking bees."

"Shame on you," Laura said.

"Bzzzzzzz," Mel said, turning his fingers into bees and buzzing them at   135
Terri's throat. Then he let his hands drop all the way to his sides.

"She's vicious," Mel said. "Sometimes I think I'll go up there dressed like a beekeeper. You know, that hat that's like a helmet with the plate that comes down over your face, the big gloves, and the padded coat? I'll knock on the door and let loose a hive of bees in the house. But first I'd make sure the kids were out, of course."

He crossed one leg over the other. It seemed to take him a lot of time to do it. Then he put both feet on the floor and leaned forward, elbows on the table, his chin cupped in his hands.

"Maybe I won't call the kids, after all. Maybe it isn't such a hot idea. Maybe we'll just go eat. How does that sound?"

"Sounds fine to me," I said. "Eat or not eat. Or keep drinking. I could head right on out into the sunset."

"What does that mean, honey?" Laura said.   140

"It just means what I said," I said. "It means I could just keep going. That's all it means."

"I could eat something myself," Laura said. "I don't think I've ever been so hungry in my life. Is there something to nibble on?"

"I'll put out some cheese and crackers," Terri said.

But Terri just sat there. She did not get up to get anything.

Mel turned his glass over. He spilled it out on the table.   145

"Gin's gone," Mel said.

Terri said, "Now what?"

I could hear my heart beating. I could hear everyone's heart. I could hear the human noise we sat there making, not one of us moving, not even when the room went dark.   [1981]

THINKING ABOUT THE TEXT

1. The argument between the couples seems to be about the nature of love. Which character's ideas make the most sense to you? What kinds of love are discussed? Are these demonstrated in the story? Do you think true love is an illusion?

2. Do you see similarities between Mel and Ed? Do any of the characters seem aware of any similarities? Is Mel a perceptive person? What are his

problems? Is he in love with Terri? How do you interpret his fantasy with the bees and Marjorie?

3. Why does Mel seem so interested in knights? Is this symbolic? Are there other symbols here (light? dark? cardiologist?)? What do you make of the last paragraph? Why does it end with beating hearts and silence?

4. Is this story optimistic or pessimistic about true love? Is the old couple a positive or a negative example of true love? How about Laura? What about Ed? Could you argue that he was in love?

5. What does the title mean? Be specific, especially about the first word. Do you tell stories about love? Have you heard some recently? What lessons or information do they give about love?

MAKING COMPARISONS

1. Compare Ed to Emily and Mae's husband. What similarities do you see in their behavior?

2. Have these stories complicated your idea of love?

3. Do you see Terri, Homer, and Mae as victims of love? Did they do something wrong?

WRITING ABOUT ISSUES

1. Love often faces societal pressure. Write an analysis of how well love holds up in all these stories. Include your own view of love's resiliency.

2. Based on your own experiences, give examples of relationships that you think qualify as loving and ones that don't. Come to some conclusion, using your examples as evidence.

3. Argue that romantic love is, or is not, socially constructed.

4. Is there a class or gender difference in domestic violence? Write a brief report after researching this issue.

TROUBLED MARRIAGES

ANNE SEXTON, "The Farmer's Wife"
ROBERT LOWELL, "To Speak of the Woe That Is in Marriage"

Through wedding vows, lovers pledge their everlasting devotion to each other. When they utter the words "until death do us part" most of them believe this will be true; others hope it will be. But the words or even the intensity of feeling does not guarantee longevity. Relations go sour, love fades, marriages fail. No one intends for this to happen. Most people want to be in a supportive, loving relationship. So why doesn't married love last? And what is to be done when a marriage is sliding fast into an emotional wasteland or coming to a standstill? As divorce rates indicate, the contemporary answer is to leave. That was not always possible, of course, and experts are wondering if that solution is best. The following two texts offer painful glimpses of marriages in trouble. How do such things happen, and what, if anything, can be done?

BEFORE YOU READ

Do you think a marriage should last forever? What should couples do in a bad marriage? Is open communication always a solution to problems in a relationship?

ANNE SEXTON
The Farmer's Wife

Anne Sexton (1928–1974) began writing poetry as therapy for repeated mental breakdowns and suicide attempts following the birth of her first child in 1951. Among the writers Robert Lowell, Sylvia Plath, Maxine Kumin, W. D. Snodgrass, and others often grouped as confessional poets, Sexton learned to use the intense, intimate materials of personal life in her poetry, maintaining little distance between herself and her readers. Her first collection of poetry, To Bedlam and Part Way Back *(1960), reflects this intensely confessional, female perspective, as do the later collections* All My Pretty Ones *(1962) and* Live or Die *(1966), which won the Pulitzer Prize. In the poems of* Transformations *(1971) Sexton retells Grimm fairy tales with a wry, bitter, feminist twist. Anne Sexton committed suicide in 1974. "The Farmer's Wife" is from* To Bedlam and Part Way Back.

From the hodge porridge
of their country lust,
their local life in Illinois,
where all their acres look
like a sprouting broom factory,   5
they name just ten years now
that she has been his habit;
as again tonight he'll say
honey bunch let's go
and she will not say how there   10
must be more to living
than this brief bright bridge
of the raucous bed or even

the slow braille touch of him
like a heavy god grown light, 15
that old pantomime of love
that she wants although
it leaves her still alone,
built back again at last,
minds apart from him, living 20
her own self in her own words
and hating the sweat of the house
they keep when they finally lie
each in separate dreams
and then how she watches him, 25
still strong in the blowzy bag
of his usual sleep while
her young years bungle past
their same marriage bed
and she wishes him cripple, or poet, 30
or even lonely, or sometimes,
better, my lover, dead.   [1960]

THINKING ABOUT THE TEXT

1. The last line seems to move in two directions. She calls him "my lover" but then says she sometimes wishes him dead. Does this make sense?

2. How can making love with her husband leave the farmer's wife "still alone" (line 18)? Is this her fault? His? Their fault? No one's fault?

3. Is the wife dissatisfied with sex? With her husband? With marriage itself? What do you think of her "solution"? What would you do?

4. Describe what you think the connotation of "his habit" is in line 7. How about "honey bunch" (line 9) and the "old pantomime of love" (line 16)?

5. Does Sexton's poem reflect marriages in general or only those in rural areas? Only ten-year-old marriages? Just this particular relationship?

ROBERT LOWELL
To Speak of the Woe That Is in Marriage

Robert Lowell (1917–1977) spent much of his life as a poet reacting to cultural and historical influences that threatened to define him and to define American litera-ture as well. As the descendant of Mayflower New Englanders and the relative of poets James Russell Lowell and Amy Lowell, he struggled toward an individualistic vision and voice that greatly influenced his contemporaries in the 1950s and 1960s.

Beginning at Harvard as a student of English literature, he moved to Kenyon College and later to Louisiana State University to study with various New Critics, thus placing himself in the midst of intellectual debates about literature. Lowell also found himself in conflict with tradition when he protested both World War II and the Vietnam War and as he wrestled with the place of religion in poetry, with the morality of capitalism, and with the vicissitudes of three marriages. Although the more formal verse of Lord Weary's Castle *(1946) won the Pulitzer Prize, he is best known for the confessional tone of* Life Studies *(1959), from which "To Speak of the Woe That Is in Marriage" is taken.*

It is the future generation that presses into being by means of these exuberant feelings and supersensible soap bubbles of ours.

— Schopenhauer

"The hot night makes us keep our bedroom windows open.
Our magnolia blossoms. Life begins to happen.
My hopped up husband drops his home disputes,
and hits the streets to cruise for prostitutes,
free-lancing out along the razor's edge.   5
This screwball might kill his wife, then take the pledge.
Oh the monotonous meanness of his lust. . . .
It's the injustice . . . he is so unjust—
whiskey-blind, swaggering home at five.
My only thought is how to keep alive.   10
What makes him tick? Each night now I tie
ten dollars and his car key to my thigh. . . .
Gored by the climacteric of his want,
he stalls above me like an elephant."   [1959]

THINKING ABOUT THE TEXT

1. What do you think the "home disputes" in line 3 are about? Why does he go to look for paid sex? Is the husband at fault here? Could he be the victim instead of the wife?

2. The ten dollars tied to the wife's thigh seems symbolic and confusing. Is the money meant to provide him with an escape? Her with an escape? Is it meant to entice him? Is it possible to know?

3. The poem and its language are conversational in tone. What effect does this wife's monologue have on you? Is this intentional?

4. *Climacteric* has a specific meaning. Please look it up. Does this definition change your attitude toward the husband?

5. Since this poem was written in 1959, divorce has become quite common in America. Would Lowell be pleased? Are you?

MAKING COMPARISONS

1. Which poem seems the most pessimistic about the couple's future together, Sexton's or Lowell's?

2. The wives in these two poems seem trapped. Do you agree? Why might this be so? Should they have other options? Such as?

3. Would you give these poems to a friend considering marriage? Why, or why not?

WRITING ABOUT ISSUES

1. Imagine you are the farmer's wife. Compose a letter to your husband explaining your feelings about your marriage.

2. Write an essay arguing that the liberalization of the divorce laws in the 1960s was good or bad for American culture.

3. Write a personal essay narrating a relationship that began well but turned sour. Explain what went wrong. What is your present view about your decision to continue or end that relationship?

4. Try researching whether women in the 1940s were more satisfied in marriages than they are today.

A Marriage Worth Saving?: Critical Commentaries on Henrik Ibsen's *A Doll House*

HENRIK IBSEN, *A Doll House*

CRITICAL COMMENTARIES:
HENRIETTA FRANCES LORD, From "The Life of Henrik Ibsen"
CLEMENT SCOTT, "Ibsen's Unlovely Creed"
HERMANN J. WEIGAND, From *The Modern Ibsen*
KATHERINE M. ROGERS, From "Feminism and *A Doll House*"
JOAN TEMPLETON, From "The *Doll House* Backlash:
Criticism, Feminism, and Ibsen"

The writer and scientist Loren Eiseley notes that "to grow is a gain, an enlargement of life. . . . Yet it is also a departure." Eiseley's seems a more sophisticated idea than one portraying personal and social progress as only positive. Life is more complicated than that. Most of us eagerly anticipate becoming adults and embracing adult responsibilities and privileges. But our literature is filled with nostalgia for the innocence and wonder of childhood. We have a sense that we have lost something as our culture, technology, and lifestyles have advanced. There is no going back, but to some the old ways sometimes seem simpler. Our grandparents longed to leave the limitations of small-town life, but fifty years later their urban grandchildren idealize small communities. Women agonized over the legal and personal restrictions of Victorian marriages, but contemporary women understand that divorce is often painful and difficult. No reasonable thinker would want women to return to the childlike position that wives were expected to inhabit a hundred years ago, but that does not mean we cannot acknowledge that divorce often comes with a steep emotional and practical price.

It appears that Henrik Ibsen understood this when he wrote *A Doll House* in 1879. It was an era of great political and social change, and Ibsen believed that writers could be instrumental in affecting the way people thought about the great issues of the day. His realistic problem plays confronted topical and controversial issues. Among the most debated was the status of women in society, especially their legal and emotional subjugation within marriage. To a contemporary audience, Nora, the main character of *A Doll House*, is treated like a child. Although that disturbs most women today, Ibsen's female audience tended not to sympathize with Nora. The play's unsettling conclusion outraged most men. Changes in accepted thinking are always contested. But although most critics today see Ibsen as a social visionary who championed equality in marriage, he was not naive enough to think that great sacrifice and pain would not also accompany freedom and equality. The solution of one problem often creates new problems. When Nora begins to question the old ways, her future starts to grow uncertain. Knowing what she knows, can she remain in her marriage?

BEFORE YOU READ

Do you think a woman is justified in leaving her children? Do you think absolute equality is necessary for love to exist in a marriage?

HENRIK IBSEN

A Doll House

Translated by Rolf Fjelde

Henrik Ibsen (1828–1906) was born into a family with money in a small town in Norway, but his parents soon went bankrupt. Ibsen later remembered this genteel poverty by writing about issues of social injustice that he experienced firsthand. At fifteen Ibsen was apprenticed to a pharmacist, a profession he had no interest in. He soon was drawn to the theater, working to establish a Norwegian national theater. But this led to frustration, and Ibsen spent almost thirty years in a self-imposed exile in Italy and Germany where he wrote some of his most famous plays. Ibsen's plays are often performed today and still provoke controversy. They include Ghosts *(1881),* An Enemy of the People *(1882),* Hedda Gabler *(1890), and* When We Dead Awaken *(1899).*

THE CHARACTERS

TORVALD HELMER, *a lawyer*

NORA, *his wife*

DR. RANK

MRS. LINDE

NILS KROGSTAD, *a bank clerk*

THE HELMERS' THREE SMALL CHILDREN

ANNE-MARIE, *their nurse*

HELENE, *a maid*

A DELIVERY BOY

SCENE: *The action takes place in Helmer's residence.*

ACT 1

A comfortable room, tastefully but not expensively furnished. A door to the right in the back wall leads to the entryway; another to the left leads to Helmer's study. Between these doors, a piano. Midway in the left-hand wall a door, and further back a window. Near the window a round table with an armchair and a small sofa. In the right-hand wall, toward the rear, a door, and nearer the foreground a porcelain stove with two armchairs and a rocking chair beside it. Between the stove and the side door, a small table. Engravings on the walls. An etagère with china figures and other small art objects; a small bookcase with richly bound books; the floor carpeted; a fire burning in the stove. It is a winter day.

A bell rings in the entryway; shortly after we hear the door being unlocked. Nora comes into the room, humming happily to herself; she is wearing street clothes and carries an armload of packages, which she puts down on the table to the right. She has left the hall door open; and through it a Delivery Boy is seen, holding a Christmas tree and a basket, which he gives to the Maid who let them in.

NORA: Hide the tree well, Helene. The children mustn't get a glimpse of it till this evening, after it's trimmed. *(To the Delivery Boy, taking out her purse.)* How much?

DELIVERY BOY: Fifty, ma'am.

NORA: There's a crown. No, keep the change. *(The Boy thanks her and leaves. Nora shuts the door. She laughs softly to herself while taking off her street things. Drawing a bag of macaroons from her pocket, she eats a couple, then steals over and listens at her husband's study door.)* Yes, he's home. *(Hums again as she moves to the table right.)*

HELMER *(from the study)*: Is that my little lark twittering out there?

NORA *(busy opening some packages)*: Yes, it is.

HELMER: Is that my squirrel rummaging around?

NORA: Yes!

HELMER: When did my squirrel get in?

NORA: Just now. *(Putting the macaroon bag in her pocket and wiping her mouth.)* Do come in, Torvald, and see what I've bought.

HELMER: Can't be disturbed. *(After a moment he opens the door and peers in, pen in hand.)* Bought, you say? All that there? Has the little spendthrift been out throwing money around again?

NORA: Oh, but Torvald, this year we really should let ourselves go a bit. It's the first Christmas we haven't had to economize.

HELMER: But you know we can't go squandering.

NORA: Oh yes, Torvald, we can squander a little now. Can't we? Just a tiny, wee bit. Now that you've got a big salary and are going to make piles and piles of money.

HELMER: Yes — starting New Year's. But then it's a full three months till the raise comes through.

NORA: Pooh! We can borrow that long.

HELMER: Nora! *(Goes over and playfully takes her by the ear.)* Are your scatter-brains off again? What if today I borrowed a thousand crowns, and you squandered them over Christmas week, and then on New Year's Eve a roof tile fell on my head and I lay there —

NORA *(putting her hand on his mouth)*:   Oh! Don't say such things!

HELMER: Yes, but what if it happened — then what?

NORA: If anything so awful happened, then it just wouldn't matter if I had debts or not.

HELMER: Well, but the people I'd borrowed from?

NORA: Them? Who cares about them! They're strangers.

HELMER: Nora, Nora, how like a woman! No, but seriously, Nora, you know what I think about that. No debts! Never borrow! Something of freedom's lost — and something of beauty, too — from a home that's founded on bor-rowing and debt. We've made a brave stand up to now, the two of us; and we'll go right on like that the little while we have to.

NORA *(going toward the stove)*:   Yes, whatever you say, Torvald.

HELMER *(following her)*:   Now, now, the little lark's wings mustn't droop. Come on, don't be a sulky squirrel. *(Taking out his wallet.)* Nora, guess what I have here.

NORA *(turning quickly)*:   Money!

HELMER: There, see. *(Hands her some notes.)* Good grief, I know how costs go up in a house at Christmastime.

NORA: Ten — twenty — thirty — forty. Oh, thank you, Torvald; I can manage no end on this.

HELMER: You really will have to.

NORA: Oh yes, I promise I will! But come here so I can show you everything I bought. And so cheap! Look, new clothes for Ivar here — and a sword. Here a horse and a trumpet for Bob. And a doll and a doll's bed here for Emmy; they're nothing much, but she'll tear them to bits in no time anyway. And here I have dress material and handkerchiefs for the maids. Old Anne-Marie really deserves something more.

HELMER: And what's in that package there?

NORA *(with a cry)*:   Torvald, no! You can't see that till tonight!

HELMER: I see. But tell me now, you little prodigal, what have you thought of for yourself?

NORA: For myself? Oh, I don't want anything at all.

HELMER: Of course you do. Tell me just what — within reason — you'd most like to have.

NORA: I honestly don't know. Oh, listen, Torvald —

HELMER: Well?

NORA *(fumbling at his coat buttons, without looking at him)*:   If you want to give me something, then maybe you could — you could —

HELMER: Come on, out with it.

NORA *(hurriedly)*:   You could give me money, Torvald. No more than you think you can spare; then one of these days I'll buy something with it.

HELMER: But Nora —

NORA: Oh please, Torvald darling, do that! I beg you, please. Then I could hang the bills in pretty gilt paper on the Christmas tree. Wouldn't that be fun?

HELMER: What are those little birds called that always fly through their fortunes?

NORA: Oh yes, spendthrifts: I know all that. But let's do as I say, Torvald; then I'll have time to decide what I really need most. That's very sensible, isn't it?

HELMER *(smiling)*:   Yes, very — that is, if you actually hung onto the money I give you, and you actually used it to buy yourself something. But it goes for the house and for all sorts of foolish things, and then I only have to lay out some more.

NORA: Oh, but Torvald —

HELMER: Don't deny it, my dear little Nora. *(Putting his arm around her waist.)* Spendthrifts are sweet, but they use up a frightful amount of money. It's incredible what it costs a man to feed such birds.

NORA: Oh, how can you say that! Really, I save everything I can.

HELMER *(laughing)*:   Yes, that's the truth. Everything you can. But that's nothing at all.

NORA *(humming, with a smile of quiet satisfaction)*:   Hm, if you only knew what expenses we larks and squirrels have, Torvald.

HELMER: You're an odd little one. Exactly the way your father was. You're never at a loss for scaring up money; but the moment you have it, it runs right out through your fingers; you never know what you've done with it. Well, one takes you as you are. It's deep in your blood. Yes, these things are hereditary, Nora.

NORA: Ah, I could wish I'd inherited many of Papa's qualities.

HELMER: And I couldn't wish you anything but just what you are, my sweet little lark. But wait; it seems to me you have a very — what should I call it? — a very suspicious look today —

NORA: I do?

HELMER: You certainly do. Look me straight in the eye.

NORA *(looking at him)*:   Well?

HELMER *(shaking an admonitory finger)*:   Surely my sweet tooth hasn't been running riot in town today, has she?

NORA: No. Why do you imagine that?

HELMER: My sweet tooth really didn't make a little detour through the confectioner's?

NORA: No, I assure you, Torvald —

HELMER: Hasn't nibbled some pastry?

NORA: No, not at all.

HELMER: Not even munched a macaroon or two?

NORA: No, Torvald, I assure you, really—

HELMER: There, there now. Of course I'm only joking.

NORA *(going to the table, right)*:   You know I could never think of going against you.

HELMER: No, I understand that; and you *have* given me your word. *(Going over to her.)* Well, you keep your little Christmas secrets to yourself, Nora darling. I expect they'll come to light this evening, when the tree is lit.

NORA: Did you remember to ask Dr. Rank?

HELMER: No. But there's no need for that: it's assumed he'll be dining with us. All the same, I'll ask him when he stops by here this morning. I've ordered some fine wine. Nora, you can't imagine how I'm looking forward to this evening.

NORA: So am I. And what fun for the children, Torvald!

HELMER: Ah, it's so gratifying to know that one's gotten a safe, secure job, and with a comfortable salary. It's a great satisfaction, isn't it?

NORA: Oh, it's wonderful!

HELMER: Remember last Christmas? Three whole weeks before, you shut yourself in every evening till long after midnight, making flowers for the Christmas tree, and all the other decorations to surprise us. Ugh, that was the dullest time I've ever lived through.

NORA: It wasn't at all dull for me.

HELMER *(smiling)*:   But the outcome *was* pretty sorry, Nora.

NORA: Oh, don't tease me with that again. How could I help it that the cat came in and tore everything to shreds.

HELMER: No, poor thing, you certainly couldn't. You wanted so much to please us all, and that's what counts. But it's just as well that the hard times are past.

NORA: Yes, it's really wonderful.

HELMER: Now I don't have to sit here alone, boring myself, and you don't have to tire your precious eyes and your fair little delicate hands—

NORA *(clapping her hands)*:   No, is it really true, Torvald, I don't have to? Oh, how wonderfully lovely to hear! *(Taking his arm.)* Now I'll tell you just how I've thought we should plan things. Right after Christmas—*(The doorbell rings.)* Oh, the bell. *(Straightening the room up a bit.)* Somebody would have to come. What a bore!

HELMER: I'm not home to visitors, don't forget.

MAID *(from the hall doorway)*:   Ma'am, a lady to see you—

NORA: All right, let her come in.

MAID *(to Helmer)*:   And the doctor's just come too.

HELMER: Did he go right to my study?

MAID: Yes, he did.

Helmer goes into his room. The Maid shows in Mrs. Linde, dressed in traveling clothes, and shuts the door after her.

MRS. LINDE *(in a dispirited and somewhat hesitant voice)*:   Hello, Nora.

NORA *(uncertain)*:   Hello—

MRS. LINDE: You don't recognize me.

NORA: No, I don't know — but wait, I think — *(Exclaiming.)* What! Kristine! Is it really you?

MRS. LINDE: Yes, it's me.

NORA: Kristine! To think I didn't recognize you. But then, how could I? *(More quietly.)* How you've changed, Kristine!

MRS. LINDE: Yes, no doubt I have. In nine — ten long years.

NORA: Is it so long since we met! Yes, it's all of that. Oh, these last eight years have been a happy time, believe me. And so now you've come in to town, too. Made the long trip in the winter. That took courage.

MRS. LINDE: I just got here by ship this morning.

NORA: To enjoy yourself over Christmas, of course. Oh, how lovely! Yes, enjoy ourselves, we'll do that. But take your coat off. You're not still cold? *(Helping her.)* There now, let's get cozy here by the stove. No, the easy chair there! I'll take the rocker here. *(Seizing her hands.)* Yes, now you have your old look again; it was only in that first moment. You're a bit more pale, Kristine — and maybe a bit thinner.

MRS. LINDE: And much, much older, Nora.

NORA: Yes, perhaps a bit older: a tiny, tiny bit; not much at all. *(Stopping short; suddenly serious.)* Oh, but thoughtless me, to sit here, chattering away. Sweet, good Kristine, can you forgive me?

MRS. LINDE: What do you mean, Nora?

NORA *(softly):*   Poor Kristine, you've become a widow.

MRS. LINDE: Yes, three years ago.

NORA: Oh, I knew it, of course: I read it in the papers. Oh, Kristine, you must believe me; I often thought of writing you then, but I kept postponing it, and something always interfered.

MRS. LINDE: Nora dear, I understand completely.

NORA: No, it was awful of me, Kristine. You poor thing, how much you must have gone through. And he left you nothing?

MRS. LINDE: No.

NORA: And no children?

MRS. LINDE: No.

NORA: Nothing at all, then?

MRS. LINDE: Not even a sense of loss to feed on.

NORA *(looking incredulously at her):*   But Kristine, how could that be?

MRS. LINDE *(smiling wearily and smoothing her hair):*   Oh, sometimes it happens, Nora.

NORA: So completely alone. How terribly hard that must be for you. I have three lovely children. You can't see them now; they're out with the maid. But now you must tell me everything —

MRS. LINDE: No, no, no, tell me about yourself.

NORA: No, you begin. Today I don't want to be selfish. I want to think only of you today. But there *is* something I must tell you. Did you hear of the wonderful luck we had recently?

MRS. LINDE: No, what's that?

NORA: My husband's been made manager in the bank, just think!

MRS. LINDE: Your husband? How marvelous!

NORA: Isn't it? Being a lawyer is such an uncertain living, you know, especially if one won't touch any cases that aren't clean and decent. And of course Torvald would never do that, and I'm with him completely there. Oh, we're simply delighted, believe me! He'll join the bank right after New Year's and start getting a huge salary and lots of commissions. From now on we can live quite differently — just as we want. Oh, Kristine, I feel so light and happy! Won't it be lovely to have stacks of money and not a care in the world?

MRS. LINDE: Well, anyway, it would be lovely to have enough for necessities.

NORA: No, not just for necessities, but stacks and stacks of money!

MRS. LINDE *(smiling)*: Nora, Nora, aren't you sensible yet? Back in school you were such a free spender.

NORA *(with a quiet laugh)*: Yes, that's what Torvald still says. *(Shaking her finger.)* But "Nora, Nora" isn't as silly as you all think. Really, we've been in no position for me to go squandering. We've had to work, both of us.

MRS. LINDE: You too?

NORA: Yes, at odd jobs — needlework, crocheting, embroidery, and such — *(Casually.)* and other things too. You remember that Torvald left the department when we were married? There was no chance of promotion in his office, and of course he needed to earn more money. But that first year he drove himself terribly. He took on all kinds of extra work that kept him going morning and night. It wore him down, and then he fell deathly ill. The doctors said it was essential for him to travel south.

MRS. LINDE: Yes, didn't you spend a whole year in Italy?

NORA: That's right. It wasn't easy to get away, you know. Ivar had just been born. But of course we had to go. Oh, that was a beautiful trip, and it saved Torvald's life. But it cost a frightful sum, Kristine.

MRS. LINDE: I can well imagine.

NORA: Four thousand, eight hundred crowns it cost. That's really a lot of money.

MRS. LINDE: But it's lucky you had it when you needed it.

NORA: Well, as it was, we got it from Papa.

MRS. LINDE: I see. It was just about the time your father died.

NORA: Yes, just about then. And, you know, I couldn't make that trip out to nurse him. I had to stay here, expecting Ivar any moment, and with my poor sick Torvald to care for. Dearest Papa, I never saw him again, Kristine. Oh, that was the worst time I've known in all my marriage.

MRS. LINDE: I know how you loved him. And then you went off to Italy?

NORA: Yes. We had the means now, and the doctors urged us. So we left a month after.

MRS. LINDE: And your husband came back completely cured?

NORA: Sound as a drum!

MRS. LINDE: But — the doctor?

NORA: Who?

MRS. LINDE: I thought the maid said he was a doctor, the man who came in with me.

NORA: Yes, that was Dr. Rank—but he's not making a sick call. He's our closest friend, and he stops by at least once a day. No, Torvald hasn't had a sick moment since, and the children are fit and strong, and I am, too. *(Jumping up and clapping her hands.)* Oh, dear God, Kristine, what a lovely thing to live and be happy! But how disgusting of me—I'm talking of nothing but my own affairs. *(Sits on a stool close by Kristine, arms resting across her knees.)* Oh, don't be angry with me! Tell me, is it really true that you weren't in love with your husband? Why did you marry him, then?

MRS. LINDE: My mother was still alive, but bedridden and helpless—and I had my two younger brothers to look after. In all conscience, I didn't think I could turn him down.

NORA: No, you were right there. But was he rich at the time?

MRS. LINDE: He was very well off, I'd say. But the business was shaky, Nora. When he died, it all fell apart, and nothing was left.

NORA: And then—?

MRS. LINDE: Yes, so I had to scrape up a living with a little shop and a little teaching and whatever else I could find. The last three years have been like one endless workday without a rest for me. Now it's over, Nora. My poor mother doesn't need me, for she's passed on. Nor the boys, either; they're working now and can take care of themselves.

NORA: How free you must feel—

MRS. LINDE: No—only unspeakably empty. Nothing to live for now. *(Standing up anxiously.)* That's why I couldn't take it any longer out in that desolate hole. Maybe here it'll be easier to find something to do and keep my mind occupied. If I could only be lucky enough to get a steady job, some office work—

NORA: Oh, but Kristine, that's so dreadfully tiring, and you already look so tired. It would be much better for you if you could go off to a bathing resort.

MRS. LINDE *(going toward the window)*:   I have no father to give me travel money, Nora.

NORA *(rising)*:   Oh, don't be angry with me.

MRS. LINDE *(going to her)*:   Nora dear, don't you be angry with me. The worst of my kind of situation is all the bitterness that's stored away. No one to work for, and yet you're always having to snap up your opportunities. You have to live; and so you grow selfish. When you told me the happy change in your lot, do you know I was delighted less for your sakes than for mine?

NORA: How so? Oh, I see. You think maybe Torvald could do something for you.

MRS. LINDE: Yes, that's what I thought.

NORA: And he will, Kristine! Just leave it to me; I'll bring it up so delicately— find something attractive to humor him with. Oh, I'm so eager to help you.

MRS. LINDE: How very kind of you, Nora, to be so concerned over me—doubly kind, considering you really know so little of life's burdens yourself.

NORA: I—? I know so little—?

MRS. LINDE *(smiling)*:   Well, my heavens—a little needlework and such—Nora, you're just a child.

NORA *(tossing her head and pacing the floor)*:   You don't have to act so superior.

MRS. LINDE: Oh?

NORA: You're just like the others. You all think I'm incapable of anything serious —

MRS. LINDE: Come now —

NORA: That I've never had to face the raw world.

MRS. LINDE: Nora dear, you've just been telling me all your troubles.

NORA: Hm! Trivia! *(Quietly.)* I haven't told you the big thing.

MRS. LINDE: Big thing? What do you mean?

NORA: You look down on me so, Kristine, but you shouldn't. You're proud that
you worked so long and hard for your mother.

MRS. LINDE: I don't look down on a soul. But it *is* true: I'm proud — and happy,
too — to think it was given to me to make my mother's last days almost free of
care.

NORA: And you're also proud thinking of what you've done for your brothers.

MRS. LINDE: I feel I've a right to be.

NORA: I agree. But listen to this, Kristine — I've also got something to be proud
and happy for.

MRS. LINDE: I don't doubt it. But whatever do you mean?

NORA: Not so loud. What if Torvald heard! He mustn't, not for anything in the
world. Nobody must know, Kristine. No one but you.

MRS. LINDE: But what is it, then?

NORA: Come here. *(Drawing her down beside her on the sofa.)* It's true — I've
also got something to be proud and happy for. I'm the one who saved Torvald's life.

MRS. LINDE: Saved —? Saved how?

NORA: I told you about the trip to Italy. Torvald never would have lived if he
hadn't gone south —

MRS. LINDE: Of course; your father gave you the means —

NORA *(smiling)*:   That's what Torvald and all the rest think, but —

MRS. LINDE: But —?

NORA: Papa didn't give us a pin. I was the one who raised the money.

MRS. LINDE: You? That whole amount?

NORA: Four thousand, eight hundred crowns. What do you say to that?

MRS. LINDE: But Nora, how was it possible? Did you win the lottery?

NORA *(disdainfully)*:   The lottery? Pooh! No art to that.

MRS. LINDE: But where did you get it from then?

NORA *(humming, with a mysterious smile)*:   Hmm, tra-la-la-la.

MRS. LINDE: Because you couldn't have borrowed it.

NORA: No? Why not?

MRS. LINDE: A wife can't borrow without her husband's consent.

NORA *(tossing her head)*:   Oh, but a wife with a little business sense, a wife who
knows how to manage —

MRS. LINDE: Nora, I simply don't understand —

NORA: You don't have to. Whoever said I *borrowed* the money? I could have gotten it other ways. *(Throwing herself back on the sofa.)* I could have gotten it
from some admirer or other. After all, a girl with my ravishing appeal —

MRS. LINDE: You lunatic.

NORA: I'll bet you're eaten up with curiosity, Kristine.

MRS. LINDE: Now listen here, Nora—you haven't done something indiscreet?

NORA *(sitting up again)*:   Is it indiscreet to save your husband's life?

MRS. LINDE: I think it's indiscreet that without his knowledge you—

NORA: But that's the point: he mustn't know! My Lord, can't you understand? He mustn't ever know the close call he had. It was to *me* the doctors came to say his life was in danger—that nothing could save him but a stay in the south. Didn't I try strategy then! I began talking about how lovely it would be for me to travel abroad like other young wives; I begged and I cried; I told him please to remember my condition, to be kind and indulge me; and then I dropped a hint that he could easily take out a loan. But at that, Kristine, he nearly exploded. He said I was frivolous, and it was his duty as man of the house not to indulge me in whims and fancies—as I think he called them. Aha, I thought, now you'll just have to be saved—and that's when I saw my chance.

MRS. LINDE: And your father never told Torvald the money wasn't from him?

NORA: No, never. Papa died right about then. I'd considered bringing him into my secret and begging him never to tell. But he was too sick at the time— and then, sadly, it didn't matter.

MRS. LINDE: And you've never confided in your husband since?

NORA: For heaven's sake, no! Are you serious? He's so strict on that subject. Besides—Torvald, with all his masculine pride—how painfully humiliating for him if he ever found out he was in debt to me. That would just ruin our relationship. Our beautiful, happy home would never be the same.

MRS. LINDE: Won't you ever tell him?

NORA *(thoughtfully, half smiling)*:   Yes—maybe sometime, years from now, when I'm no longer so attractive. Don't laugh! I only mean when Torvald loves me less than now, when he stops enjoying my dancing and dressing up and reciting for him. Then it might be wise to have something in reserve— *(Breaking off.)* How ridiculous! That'll never happen—Well, Kristine, what do you think of my big secret? I'm capable of something too, hm? You can imagine, of course, how this thing hangs over me. It really hasn't been easy meeting the payments on time. In the business world there's what they call quarterly interest and what they call amortization, and these are always so terribly hard to manage. I've had to skimp a little here and there, wherever I could, you know. I could hardly spare anything from my house allowance, because Torvald has to live well. I couldn't let the children go poorly dressed; whatever I got for them, I felt I had to use up completely—the darlings!

MRS. LINDE: Poor Nora, so it had to come out of your own budget, then?

NORA: Yes, of course. But I was the one most responsible, too. Every time Torvald gave me money for new clothes and such, I never used more than half; always bought the simplest, cheapest outfits. It was a godsend that everything looks so well on me that Torvald never noticed. But it did weigh me down at times, Kristine. It *is* such a joy to wear fine things. You understand.

MRS. LINDE: Oh, of course.

NORA: And then I found other ways of making money. Last winter I was lucky enough to get a lot of copying to do. I locked myself in and sat writing every evening till late in the night. Ah, I was tired so often, dead tired. But still it was wonderful fun, sitting and working like that, earning money. It was almost like being a man.

MRS. LINDE: But how much have you paid off this way so far?

NORA: That's hard to say, exactly. These accounts, you know, aren't easy to figure. I only know that I've paid out all I could scrape together. Time and again I haven't known where to turn. (*Smiling.*) Then I'd sit here dreaming of a rich old gentleman who had fallen in love with me —

MRS. LINDE: What! Who is he?

NORA: Oh, really! And that he'd died, and when his will was opened, there in big letters it said, "All my fortune shall be paid over in cash, immediately, to that enchanting Mrs. Nora Helmer."

MRS. LINDE: But Nora dear — who *was* this gentleman?

NORA: Good grief, can't you understand? The old man never existed; that was only something I'd dream up time and again whenever I was at my wits' end for money. But it makes no difference now; the old fossil can go where he pleases for all I care; I don't need him or his will — because now I'm free. (*Jumping up.*) Oh, how lovely to think of that, Kristine! Carefree! To know you're carefree, utterly carefree; to be able to romp and play with the children, and to keep up a beautiful, charming home — everything just the way Torvald likes it! And think, spring is coming, with big blue skies. Maybe we can travel a little then. Maybe I'll see the ocean again. Oh yes, it *is* so marvelous to live and be happy!

The front doorbell rings.

MRS. LINDE (*rising*): There's the bell. It's probably best that I go.

NORA: No, stay. No one's expected. It must be for Torvald.

MAID (*from the hall doorway*): Excuse me, ma'am — there's a gentleman here to see Mr. Helmer, but I didn't know — since the doctor's with him —

NORA: Who is the gentleman?

KROGSTAD (*from the doorway*): It's me, Mrs. Helmer.

Mrs. Linde starts and turns away toward the window.

NORA (*stepping toward him, tense, her voice a whisper*): You? What is it? Why do you want to speak to my husband?

KROGSTAD: Bank business — after a fashion. I have a small job in the investment bank, and I hear now your husband is going to be our chief —

NORA: In other words, it's —

KROGSTAD: Just dry business, Mrs. Helmer. Nothing but that.

NORA: Yes, then please be good enough to step into the study. (*She nods indifferently as she sees him out by the hall door, then returns and begins stirring up the stove.*)

MRS. LINDE: Nora — who was that man?

NORA: That was a Mr. Krogstad — a lawyer.

MRS. LINDE: Then it really was him.

NORA: Do you know that person?

MRS. LINDE: I did once—many years ago. For a time he was a law clerk in our town.

NORA: Yes, he's been that.

MRS. LINDE: How he's changed.

NORA: I understand he had a very unhappy marriage.

MRS. LINDE: He's a widower now.

NORA: With a number of children. There now, it's burning. *(She closes the stove door and moves the rocker a bit to one side.)*

MRS. LINDE: They say he has a hand in all kinds of business.

NORA: Oh? That may be true; I wouldn't know. But let's not think about business. It's so dull.

Dr. Rank enters from Helmer's study.

RANK *(still in the doorway)*:   No, no really—I don't want to intrude, I'd just as soon talk a little while with your wife. *(Shuts the door, then notices Mrs. Linde.)* Oh, beg pardon. I'm intruding here too.

NORA: No, not at all. *(Introducing him.)* Dr. Rank, Mrs. Linde.

RANK: Well now, that's a name much heard in this house. I believe I passed the lady on the stairs as I came.

MRS. LINDE: Yes, I take the stairs very slowly. They're rather hard on me.

RANK: Uh-hm, some touch of internal weakness?

MRS. LINDE: More overexertion, I'd say.

RANK: Nothing else? Then you're probably here in town to rest up in a round of parties?

MRS. LINDE: I'm here to look for work.

RANK: Is that the best cure for overexertion?

MRS. LINDE: One has to live, Doctor.

RANK: Yes, there's a common prejudice to that effect.

NORA: Oh, come on, Dr. Rank—you really do want to live yourself.

RANK: Yes, I really do. Wretched as I am, I'll gladly prolong my torment indefinitely. All my patients feel like that. And it's quite the same, too, with the morally sick. Right at this moment there's one of those moral invalids in there with Helmer—

MRS. LINDE *(softly)*:   Ah!

NORA: Who do you mean?

RANK: Oh, it's a lawyer, Krogstad, a type you wouldn't know. His character is rotten to the root—but even he began chattering all-importantly about how he had to *live.*

NORA: Oh? What did he want to talk to Torvald about?

RANK: I really don't know. I only heard something about the bank.

NORA: I didn't know that Krog—that this man Krogstad had anything to do with the bank.

RANK: Yes, he's gotten some kind of berth down there. *(To Mrs. Linde.)* I don't know if you also have, in your neck of the woods, a type of person who scuttles about breathlessly, sniffing out hints of moral corruption, and then maneuvers his victim into some sort of key position where he can keep an eye on him. It's the healthy these days that are out in the cold.

MRS. LINDE: All the same, it's the sick who most need to be taken in.

RANK *(with a shrug)*:   Yes, there we have it. That's the concept that's turning society into a sanatorium.

Nora, lost in her thoughts, breaks out into quiet laughter and claps her hands.

RANK: Why do you laugh at that? Do you have any real idea of what society is?

NORA: What do I care about dreary old society? I was laughing at something quite different—something terribly funny. Tell me, Doctor—is everyone who works in the bank dependent now on Torvald?

RANK: Is that what you find so terribly funny?

NORA *(smiling and humming)*:   Never mind, never mind! *(Pacing the floor.)* Yes, that's really immensely amusing: that we—that Torvald has so much power now over all those people. *(Taking the bag out of her pocket.)* Dr. Rank, a little macaroon on that?

RANK: See here, macaroons! I thought they were contraband here.

NORA: Yes, but these are some that Kristine gave me.

MRS. LINDE: What? I—?

NORA: Now, now, don't be afraid. You couldn't possibly know that Torvald had forbidden them. You see, he's worried they'll ruin my teeth. But hmp! Just this once! Isn't that so, Dr. Rank? Help yourself! *(Puts a macaroon in his mouth.)* And you too, Kristine. And I'll also have one, only a little one—or two, at the most. *(Walking about again.)* Now I'm really tremendously happy. Now there's just one last thing in the world that I have an enormous desire to do.

RANK: Well! And what's that?

NORA: It's something I have such a consuming desire to say so Torvald could hear.

RANK: And why can't you say it?

NORA: I don't dare. It's quite shocking.

MRS. LINDE: Shocking?

RANK: Well, then it isn't advisable. But in front of us you certainly can. What do you have such a desire to say so Torvald could hear?

NORA: I have such a huge desire to say—to hell and be damned!

RANK: Are you crazy?

MRS. LINDE: My goodness, Nora!

RANK: Go on, say it. Here he is.

NORA *(hiding the macaroon bag)*:   Shh, shh, shh!

Helmer comes in from his study, hat in hand, overcoat over his arm.

NORA *(going toward him)*:   Well, Torvald dear, are you through with him?

HELMER: Yes, he just left.

NORA: Let me introduce you—this is Kristine, who's arrived here in town.

HELMER: Kristine—? I'm sorry, but I don't know—

NORA: Mrs. Linde, Torvald dear. Mrs. Kristine Linde.

HELMER: Of course. A childhood friend of my wife's, no doubt?

MRS. LINDE: Yes, we knew each other in those days.

NORA: And just think, she made the long trip down here in order to talk with you.

HELMER: What's this?

MRS. LINDE: Well, not exactly —

NORA: You see, Kristine is remarkably clever in office work, and so she's terribly eager to come under a capable man's supervision and add more to what she already knows —

HELMER: Very wise, Mrs. Linde.

NORA: And then when she heard that you'd become a bank manager — the story was wired out to the papers — then she came in as fast as she could and — Really, Torvald, for my sake you can do a little something for Kristine, can't you?

HELMER: Yes, it's not at all impossible. Mrs. Linde, I suppose you're a widow?

MRS. LINDE: Yes.

HELMER: Any experience in office work?

MRS. LINDE: Yes, a good deal.

HELMER: Well, it's quite likely that I can make an opening for you —

NORA (*clapping her hands*):   You see, you see!

HELMER: You've come at a lucky moment, Mrs. Linde.

MRS. LINDE: Oh, how can I thank you?

HELMER: Not necessary. (*Putting his overcoat on.*) But today you'll have to excuse me —

RANK: Wait, I'll go with you. (*He fetches his coat from the hall and warms it at the stove.*)

NORA: Don't stay out long, dear.

HELMER: An hour; no more.

NORA: Are you going too, Kristine?

MRS. LINDE (*putting on her winter garments*):   Yes, I have to see about a room now.

HELMER: Then perhaps we can all walk together.

NORA (*helping her*):   What a shame we're so cramped here, but it's quite impossible for us to —

MRS. LINDE: Oh, don't even think of it! Good-bye, Nora dear, and thanks for everything.

NORA: Good-bye for now. Of course you'll be back this evening. And you too, Dr. Rank. What? If you're well enough? Oh, you've got to be! Wrap up tight now.

In a ripple of small talk the company moves out into the hall; children's voices are heard outside on the steps.

NORA: There they are! There they are! (*She runs to open the door. The children come in with their nurse, Anne-Marie.*) Come in, come in! (*Bends down and kisses them.*) Oh, you darlings — ! Look at them, Kristine. Aren't they lovely!

RANK: No loitering in the draft here.

HELMER: Come, Mrs. Linde — this place is unbearable now for anyone but mothers.

Dr. Rank, Helmer, and Mrs. Linde go down the stairs. Anne-Marie goes into the living room with the children. Nora follows, after closing the hall door.

NORA: How fresh and strong you look. Oh, such red cheeks you have! Like apples and roses. *(The children interrupt her throughout the following.)* And it was so much fun? That's wonderful. Really? You pulled both Emmy and Bob on the sled? Imagine, all together! Yes, you're a clever boy, Ivar. Oh, let me hold her a bit, Anne-Marie. My sweet little doll baby! *(Takes the smallest from the nurse and dances with her.)* Yes, yes, Mama will dance with Bob as well. What? Did you throw snowballs? Oh, if I'd only been there! No, don't bother, Anne-Marie — I'll undress them myself. Oh yes, let me. It's such fun. Go in and rest; you look half frozen. There's hot coffee waiting for you on the stove. *(The nurse goes into the room to the left. Nora takes the children's winter things off, throwing them about, while the children talk to her all at once.)* Is that so? A big dog chased you? But it didn't bite? No, dogs never bite little, lovely doll babies. Don't peek in the packages, Ivar! What is it? Yes, wouldn't you like to know. No, no, it's an ugly something. Well? Shall we play? What shall we play? Hide-and-seek? Yes, let's play hide-and-seek. Bob must hide first. I must? Yes, let me hide first. *(Laughing and shouting, she and the children play in and out of the living room and the adjoining room to the right. At last Nora hides under the table. The children come storming in, search, but cannot find her, then hear her muffled laughter, dash over to the table, lift the cloth up and find her. Wild shouting. She creeps forward as if to scare them. More shouts. Meanwhile, a knock at the hall door; no one has noticed it. Now the door half opens, and Krogstad appears. He waits a moment; the game goes on.)*

KROGSTAD: Beg pardon, Mrs. Helmer —

NORA *(with a strangled cry, turning and scrambling to her knees)*: Oh! What do you want?

KROGSTAD: Excuse me. The outer door was ajar; it must be someone forgot to shut it —

NORA *(rising)*: My husband isn't home, Mr. Krogstad.

KROGSTAD: I know that.

NORA: Yes — then what do you want here?

KROGSTAD: A word with you.

NORA: With —? *(To the children, quietly.)* Go in to Anne-Marie. What? No, the strange man won't hurt Mama. When he's gone, we'll play some more. *(She leads the children into the room to the left and shuts the door after them. Then, tense and nervous:)* You want to speak to me?

KROGSTAD: Yes, I want to.

NORA: Today? But it's not yet the first of the month —

KROGSTAD: No, it's Christmas Eve. It's going to be up to you how merry a Christmas you have.

NORA: What is it you want? Today I absolutely can't —

KROGSTAD: We won't talk about that till later. This is something else. You do have a moment to spare, I suppose?

NORA: Oh yes, of course — I do, except —

KROGSTAD: Good. I was sitting over at Olsen's Restaurant when I saw your husband go down the street —

NORA: Yes?

KROGSTAD: With a lady.

NORA: Yes. So?

KROGSTAD: If you'll pardon my asking: wasn't that lady a Mrs. Linde?

NORA: Yes.

KROGSTAD: Just now come into town?

NORA: Yes, today.

KROGSTAD: She's a good friend of yours?

NORA: Yes, she is. But I don't see —

KROGSTAD: I also knew her once.

NORA: I'm aware of that.

KROGSTAD: Oh? You know all about it. I thought so. Well, then let me ask you short and sweet: is Mrs. Linde getting a job in the bank?

NORA: What makes you think you can cross-examine me, Mr. Krogstad — you, one of my husband's employees? But since you ask, you might as well know — yes, Mrs. Linde's going to be taken on at the bank. And I'm the one who spoke for her, Mr. Krogstad. Now you know.

KROGSTAD: So I guessed right.

NORA *(pacing up and down)*:   Oh, one does have a tiny bit of influence, I should hope. Just because I am a woman, don't think it means that — When one has a subordinate position, Mr. Krogstad, one really ought to be careful about pushing somebody who — hm —

KROGSTAD: Who has influence?

NORA: That's right.

KROGSTAD *(in a different tone)*:   Mrs. Helmer, would you be good enough to use your influence on my behalf?

NORA: What? What do you mean?

KROGSTAD: Would you please make sure that I keep my subordinate position in the bank?

NORA: What does that mean? Who's thinking of taking away your position?

KROGSTAD: Oh, don't play the innocent with me. I'm quite aware that your friend would hardly relish the chance of running into me again; and I'm also aware now whom I can thank for being turned out.

NORA: But I promise you —

KROGSTAD: Yes, yes, yes, to the point: there's still time, and I'm advising you to use your influence to prevent it.

NORA: But Mr. Krogstad, I have absolutely no influence.

KROGSTAD: You haven't? I thought you were just saying —

NORA: You shouldn't take me so literally. I! How can you believe that I have any such influence over my husband?

KROGSTAD: Oh, I've known your husband from our student days. I don't think the great bank manager's more steadfast than any other married man.

NORA: You speak insolently about my husband, and I'll show you the door.

KROGSTAD: The lady has spirit.

NORA: I'm not afraid of you any longer. After New Year's, I'll soon be done with the whole business.

KROGSTAD *(restraining himself)*: Now listen to me, Mrs. Helmer. If necessary, I'll fight for my little job in the bank as if it were life itself.

NORA: Yes, so it seems.

KROGSTAD: It's not just a matter of income; that's the least of it. It's something else—All right, out with it! Look, this is the thing. You know, just like all the others, of course, that once, a good many years ago, I did something rather rash.

NORA: I've heard rumors to that effect.

KROGSTAD: The case never got into court; but all the same, every door was closed in my face from then on. So I took up those various activities you know about. I had to grab hold somewhere; and I dare say I haven't been among the worst. But now I want to drop all that. My boys are growing up. For their sakes, I'll have to win back as much respect as possible here in town. That job in the bank was like the first rung in my ladder. And now your husband wants to kick me right back down in the mud again.

NORA: But for heaven's sake, Mr. Krogstad, it's simply not in my power to help you.

KROGSTAD: That's because you haven't the will to—but I have the means to make you.

NORA: You certainly won't tell my husband that I owe you money?

KROGSTAD: Hm—what if I told him that?

NORA: That would be shameful of you. *(Nearly in tears.)* This secret—my joy and my pride—that he should learn it in such a crude and disgusting way—learn it from you. You'd expose me to the most horrible unpleasantness—

KROGSTAD: Only unpleasantness?

NORA *(vehemently)*: But go on and try. It'll turn out the worse for you, because then my husband will really see what a crook you are, and then you'll *never* be able to hold your job.

KROGSTAD: I asked if it was just domestic unpleasantness you were afraid of?

NORA: If my husband finds out, then of course he'll pay what I owe at once, and then we'd be through with you for good.

KROGSTAD *(a step closer)*: Listen, Mrs. Helmer—you've either got a very bad memory, or else no head at all for business. I'd better put you a little more in touch with the facts.

NORA: What do you mean?

KROGSTAD: When your husband was sick, you came to me for a loan of four thousand, eight hundred crowns.

NORA: Where else could I go?

KROGSTAD: I promised to get you that sum—

NORA: And you got it.

KROGSTAD: I promised to get you that sum, on certain conditions. You were so involved in your husband's illness, and so eager to finance your trip, that I guess you didn't think out all the details. It might just be a good idea to remind you. I promised you the money on the strength of a note I drew up.

NORA: Yes, and that I signed.

KROGSTAD: Right. But at the bottom I added some lines for your father to guarantee the loan. He was supposed to sign down there.

NORA: Supposed to? He did sign.

KROGSTAD: I left the date blank. In other words, your father would have dated his signature himself. Do you remember that?

NORA: Yes, I think —

KROGSTAD: Then I gave you the note for you to mail to your father. Isn't that so?

NORA: Yes.

KROGSTAD: And naturally you sent it at once — because only some five, six days later you brought me the note, properly signed. And with that, the money was yours.

NORA: Well, then; I've made my payments regularly, haven't I?

KROGSTAD: More or less. But — getting back to the point — those were hard times for you then, Mrs. Helmer.

NORA: Yes, they were.

KROGSTAD: Your father was very ill, I believe.

NORA: He was near the end.

KROGSTAD: He died soon after?

NORA: Yes.

KROGSTAD: Tell me, Mrs. Helmer, do you happen to recall the date of your father's death? The day of the month, I mean.

NORA: Papa died the twenty-ninth of September.

KROGSTAD: That's quite correct; I've already looked into that. And now we come to a curious thing — *(Taking out a paper.)* which I simply cannot comprehend.

NORA: Curious thing? I don't know —

KROGSTAD: This is the curious thing: that your father co-signed the note for your loan three days after his death.

NORA: How —? I don't understand.

KROGSTAD: Your father died the twenty-ninth of September. But look. Here your father dated his signature October second. Isn't that curious, Mrs. Helmer? *(Nora is silent.)* Can you explain it to me? *(Nora remains silent.)* It's also remarkable that the words "October second" and the year aren't written in your father's hand, but rather in one that I think I know. Well, it's easy to understand. Your father forgot perhaps to date his signature, and then someone or other added it, a bit sloppily, before anyone knew of his death. There's nothing wrong in that. It all comes down to the signature. And there's no question about *that*, Mrs. Helmer. It really *was* your father who signed his own name here, wasn't it?

NORA *(after a short silence, throwing her head back and looking squarely at him)*: No, it wasn't. *I* signed Papa's name.

KROGSTAD: Wait, now — are you fully aware that this is a dangerous confession?

NORA: Why? You'll soon get your money.

KROGSTAD: Let me ask you a question — why didn't you send the paper to your father?

NORA: That was impossible. Papa was so sick. If I'd asked him for his signature, I also would have had to tell him what the money was for. But I couldn't tell him, sick as he was, that my husband's life was in danger. That was just impossible.

KROGSTAD: Then it would have been better if you'd given up the trip abroad.

NORA: I couldn't possibly. The trip was to save my husband's life. I couldn't give that up.

KROGSTAD: But didn't you ever consider that this was a fraud against me?

NORA: I couldn't let myself be bothered by that. You weren't any concern of mine. I couldn't stand you, with all those cold complications you made, even though you knew how badly off my husband was.

KROGSTAD: Mrs. Helmer, obviously you haven't the vaguest idea of what you've involved yourself in. But I can tell you this: it was nothing more and nothing worse that I once did — and it wrecked my whole reputation.

NORA: You? Do you expect me to believe that you ever acted bravely to save your wife's life?

KROGSTAD: Laws don't inquire into motives.

NORA: Then they must be very poor laws.

KROGSTAD: Poor or not — if I introduce this paper in court, you'll be judged according to law.

NORA: This I refuse to believe. A daughter hasn't a right to protect her dying father from anxiety and care? A wife hasn't a right to save her husband's life? I don't know much about laws, but I'm sure that somewhere in the books these things are allowed. And you don't know anything about it — you who practice the law? You must be an awful lawyer, Mr. Krogstad.

KROGSTAD: Could be. But business — the kind of business we two are mixed up in — don't you think I know about that? All right. Do what you want now. But I'm telling you *this*: if I get shoved down a second time, you're going to keep me company. (*He bows and goes out through the hall.*)

NORA (*pensive for a moment, then tossing her head*):   Oh, really! Trying to frighten me! I'm not so silly as all that. (*Begins gathering up the children's clothes, but soon stops.*) But — ? No, but that's impossible! I did it out of love.

THE CHILDREN (*in the doorway, left*):   Mama, that strange man's gone out the door.

NORA: Yes, yes, I know it. But don't tell anyone about the strange man. Do you hear? Not even Papa!

THE CHILDREN: No, Mama. But now will you play again?

NORA: No, not now.

THE CHILDREN: Oh, but Mama, you promised.

NORA: Yes, but I can't now. Go inside; I have too much to do. Go in, go in, my sweet darlings. (*She herds them gently back in the room and shuts the door after them. Settling on the sofa, she takes up a piece of embroidery and makes some stitches, but soon stops abruptly.*) No! (*Throws the work aside, rises, goes to the hall door and calls out.*) Helene! Let me have the tree in here. (*Goes to the table, left, opens the table drawer, and stops again.*) No, but that's utterly impossible!

MAID (*with the Christmas tree*):   Where should I put it, ma'am?

NORA: There. The middle of the floor.

MAID: Should I bring anything else?

NORA: No, thanks. I have what I need.

The Maid, who has set the tree down, goes out.

NORA *(absorbed in trimming the tree)*:   Candles here—and flowers here. That
    terrible creature! Talk, talk, talk! There's nothing to it at all. The tree's going
    to be lovely. I'll do anything to please you, Torvald. I'll sing for you, dance for
    you—

Helmer comes in from the hall, with a sheaf of papers under his arm.

NORA: Oh! You're back so soon?

HELMER: Yes. Has anyone been here?

NORA: Here? No.

HELMER: That's odd. I saw Krogstad leaving the front door.

NORA: So? Oh yes, that's true. Krogstad was here a moment.

HELMER: Nora, I can see by your face that he's been here, begging you to put in
    a good word for him.

NORA: Yes.

HELMER: And it was supposed to seem like your own idea? You were to hide it
    from me that he'd been here. He asked you that, too, didn't he?

NORA: Yes, Torvald, but—

HELMER: Nora, Nora, and you could fall for that? Talk with that sort of person
    and promise him anything? And then in the bargain, tell me an untruth.

NORA: An untruth—?

HELMER: Didn't you say that no one had been here? *(Wagging his finger.)* My
    little songbird must never do that again. A songbird needs a clean beak to
    warble with. No false notes. *(Putting his arm about her waist.)* That's the way
    it should be, isn't it? Yes, I'm sure of it. *(Releasing her.)* And so, enough of
    that. *(Sitting by the stove.)* Ah, how snug and cozy it is here. *(Leafing among
    his papers.)*

NORA *(busy with the tree, after a short pause)*:   Torvald!

HELMER: Yes.

NORA: I'm so much looking forward to the Stenborgs' costume party, day after
    tomorrow.

HELMER: And I can't wait to see what you'll surprise me with.

NORA: Oh, that stupid business!

HELMER: What?

NORA: I can't find anything that's right. Everything seems so ridiculous, so
    inane.

HELMER: So my little Nora's come to *that* recognition?

NORA *(going behind his chair, her arms resting on its back)*:   Are you very busy,
    Torvald?

HELMER: Oh—

NORA: What papers are those?

HELMER: Bank matters.

NORA: Already?

HELMER: I've gotten full authority from the retiring management to make all necessary changes in personnel and procedure. I'll need Christmas week for that. I want to have everything in order by New Year's.

NORA: So that was the reason this poor Krogstad —

HELMER: Hm.

NORA (*still leaning on the chair and slowly stroking the nape of his neck*): If you weren't so very busy, I would have asked you an enormous favor, Torvald.

HELMER: Let's hear. What is it?

NORA: You know, there isn't anyone who has your good taste — and I want so much to look well at the costume party. Torvald, couldn't you take over and decide what I should be and plan my costume?

HELMER: Ah, is my stubborn little creature calling for a lifeguard?

NORA: Yes, Torvald, I can't get anywhere without your help.

HELMER: All right — I'll think it over. We'll hit on something.

NORA: Oh, how sweet of you. (*Goes to the tree again. Pause.*) Aren't the red flowers pretty — ? But tell me, was it really such a crime that this Krogstad committed?

HELMER: Forgery. Do you have any idea what that means?

NORA: Couldn't he have done it out of need?

HELMER: Yes, or thoughtlessness, like so many others. I'm not so heartless that I'd condemn a man categorically for just one mistake.

NORA: No, of course not, Torvald!

HELMER: Plenty of men have redeemed themselves by openly confessing their crimes and taking their punishment.

NORA: Punishment — ?

HELMER: But now Krogstad didn't go that way. He got himself out by sharp practices, and that's the real cause of his moral breakdown.

NORA: Do you really think that would — ?

HELMER: Just imagine how a man with that sort of guilt in him has to lie and cheat and deceive on all sides, has to wear a mask even with the nearest and dearest he has, even with his own wife and children. And with the children, Nora — that's where it's most horrible.

NORA: Why?

HELMER: Because that kind of atmosphere of lies infects the whole life of a home. Every breath the children take in is filled with the germs of something degenerate.

NORA (*coming closer behind him*): Are you sure of that?

HELMER: Oh, I've seen it often enough as a lawyer. Almost everyone who goes bad early in life has a mother who's a chronic liar.

NORA: Why just — the mother?

HELMER: It's usually the mother's influence that's dominant, but the father's works in the same way, of course. Every lawyer is quite familiar with it. And still this Krogstad's been going home year in, year out, poisoning his own children with lies and pretense; that's why I call him morally lost. (*Reaching*

his hands out toward her.) So my sweet little Nora must promise me never to
plead his cause. Your hand on it. Come, come, what's this? Give me your
hand. There, now. All settled. I can tell you it'd be impossible for me to work
alongside of him. I literally feel physically revolted when I'm anywhere near
such a person.

NORA *(withdraws her hand and goes to the other side of the Christmas tree):* How
hot it is here! And I've got so much to do.

HELMER *(getting up and gathering his papers):* Yes, and I have to think about
getting some of these read through before dinner. I'll think about your costume, too. And something to hang on the tree in gilt paper, I may even see
about that. *(Putting his hand on her head.)* Oh you, my darling little songbird. *(He goes into his study and closes the door after him.)*

NORA *(softly, after a silence):* Oh, really! It isn't so. It's impossible. It must be
impossible.

ANNE-MARIE *(in the doorway, left):* The children are begging so hard to come in
to Mama.

NORA: No, no, no, don't let them in to me! You stay with them, Anne-Marie.

ANNE-MARIE: Of course, ma'am. *(Closes the door.)*

NORA *(pale with terror):* Hurt my children—! Poison my home? *(A moment's
pause; then she tosses her head.)* That's not true. Never. Never in all the world.

ACT 2

*Same room. Beside the piano the Christmas tree now stands stripped of ornament,
burned-down candle stubs on its ragged branches. Nora's street clothes lie on the
sofa. Nora, alone in the room, moves restlessly about; at last she stops at the sofa
and picks up her coat.*

NORA *(dropping the coat again):* Someone's coming! *(Goes toward the door, listens.)* No—there's no one. Of course—nobody's coming today, Christmas
Day—or tomorrow, either. But maybe—*(Opens the door and looks out.)* No,
nothing in the mailbox. Quite empty. *(Coming forward.)* What nonsense! He
won't do anything serious. Nothing terrible could happen. It's impossible.
Why, I have three small children.

Anne-Marie, with a large carton, comes in from the room to the left.

ANNE-MARIE: Well, at last I found the box with the masquerade clothes.

NORA: Thanks. Put it on the table.

ANNE-MARIE *(does so):* But they're all pretty much of a mess.

NORA: Ahh! I'd love to rip them in a million pieces!

ANNE-MARIE: Oh, mercy, they can be fixed right up. Just a little patience.

NORA: Yes, I'll go get Mrs. Linde to help me.

ANNE-MARIE: Out again now? In this nasty weather? Miss Nora will catch
cold—get sick.

NORA: Oh, worse things could happen. How are the children?

ANNE-MARIE: The poor mites are playing with their Christmas presents, but—

NORA: Do they ask for me much?

ANNE-MARIE: They're so used to having Mama around, you know.

NORA: Yes, but Anne-Marie, I *can't* be together with them as much as I was.

ANNE-MARIE: Well, small children get used to anything.

NORA: You think so? Do you think they'd forget their mother if she was gone for good?

ANNE-MARIE: Oh, mercy — gone for good!

NORA: Wait, tell me, Anne-Marie — I've wondered so often — how could you ever have the heart to give your child over to strangers?

ANNE-MARIE: But I had to, you know, to become little Nora's nurse.

NORA: Yes, but how could you *do* it?

ANNE-MARIE: When I could get such a good place? A girl who's poor and who's gotten in trouble is glad enough for that. Because that slippery fish, he didn't do a thing for me, you know.

NORA: But your daughter's surely forgotten you.

ANNE-MARIE: Oh, she certainly has not. She's written to me, both when she was confirmed and when she was married.

NORA *(clasping her about the neck)*:   You old Anne-Marie, you were a good mother for me when I was little.

ANNE-MARIE: Poor little Nora, with no other mother but me.

NORA: And if the babies didn't have one, then I know that you'd — What silly talk! *(Opening the carton.)* Go in to them. Now I'll have to — Tomorrow you can see how lovely I'll look.

ANNE-MARIE: Oh, there won't be anyone at the party as lovely as Miss Nora. *(She goes off into the room, left.)*

NORA *(begins unpacking the box, but soon throws it aside)*:   Oh, if I dared to go out. If only nobody would come. If only nothing would happen here while I'm out. What craziness — nobody's coming. Just don't think. This muff — needs a brushing. Beautiful gloves, beautiful gloves. Let it go. Let it go! One, two, three, four, five, six — *(With a cry.)* Oh, there they are! *(Poises to move toward the door, but remains irresolutely standing. Mrs. Linde enters from the hall, where she has removed her street clothes.)*

NORA: Oh, it's you, Kristine. There's no one else out there? How good that you've come.

MRS. LINDE: I hear you were up asking for me.

NORA: Yes, I just stopped by. There's something you really can help me with. Let's get settled on the sofa. Look, there's going to be a costume party tomorrow evening at the Stenborgs' right above us, and now Torvald wants me to go as a Neapolitan peasant girl and dance the tarantella that I learned in Capri.

MRS. LINDE: Really, are you giving a whole performance?

NORA: Torvald says yes, I should. See, here's the dress. Torvald had it made for me down there; but now it's all so tattered that I just don't know —

MRS. LINDE: Oh, we'll fix that up in no time. It's nothing more than the trimmings — they're a bit loose here and there. Needle and thread? Good, now we have what we need.

NORA: Oh, how sweet of you!

MRS. LINDE *(sewing):*   So you'll be in disguise tomorrow, Nora. You know what? I'll stop by then for a moment and have a look at you all dressed up. But listen, I've absolutely forgotten to thank you for that pleasant evening yesterday.

NORA *(getting up and walking about):*   I don't think it was as pleasant as usual yesterday. You should have come to town a bit sooner, Kristine—Yes, Torvald really knows how to give a home elegance and charm.

MRS. LINDE: And you do, too, if you ask me. You're not your father's daughter for nothing. But tell me, is Dr. Rank always so down in the mouth as yesterday?

NORA: No, that was quite an exception. But he goes around critically ill all the time—tuberculosis of the spine, poor man. You know, his father was a disgusting thing who kept mistresses and so on—and that's why the son's been sickly from birth.

MRS. LINDE *(lets her sewing fall to her lap):*   But my dearest Nora, how do you know about such things?

NORA *(walking more jauntily):*   Hmp! When you've had three children, then you've had a few visits from—from women who know something of medicine, and they tell you this and that.

MRS. LINDE *(resumes sewing; a short pause):*   Does Dr. Rank come here every day?

NORA: Every blessed day. He's Torvald's best friend from childhood, and *my* good friend, too. Dr. Rank almost belongs to this house.

MRS. LINDE: But tell me—is he quite sincere? I mean, doesn't he rather enjoy flattering people?

NORA: Just the opposite. Why do you think that?

MRS. LINDE: When you introduced us yesterday, he was proclaiming that he'd often heard my name in this house; but later I noticed that your husband hadn't the slightest idea who I really was. So how could Dr. Rank—?

NORA: But it's all true, Kristine. You see, Torvald loves me beyond words, and, as he puts it, he'd like to keep me all to himself. For a long time he'd almost be jealous if I even mentioned any of my old friends back home. So of course I dropped that. But with Dr. Rank I talk a lot about such things, because he likes hearing about them.

MRS. LINDE: Now listen, Nora; in many ways you're still like a child. I'm a good deal older than you, with a little more experience. I'll tell you something: you ought to put an end to all this with Dr. Rank.

NORA: What should I put an end to?

MRS. LINDE: Both parts of it, I think. Yesterday you said something about a rich admirer who'd provide you with money—

NORA: Yes, one who doesn't exist—worse luck. So?

MRS. LINDE: Is Dr. Rank well off?

NORA: Yes, he is.

MRS. LINDE: With no dependents?

NORA: No, no one. But—

MRS. LINDE: And he's over here every day?

NORA: Yes, I told you that.

MRS. LINDE: How can a man of such refinement be so grasping?

NORA: I don't follow you at all.

MRS. LINDE: Now don't try to hide it, Nora. You think I can't guess who loaned you the forty-eight hundred crowns?

NORA: Are you out of your mind? How could you think such a thing! A friend of ours, who comes here every single day. What an intolerable situation that would have been!

MRS. LINDE: Then it really wasn't him.

NORA: No, absolutely not. It never even crossed my mind for a moment—And he had nothing to lend in those days; his inheritance came later.

MRS. LINDE: Well, I think that was a stroke of luck for you, Nora dear.

NORA: No, it never would have occurred to me to ask Dr. Rank—Still, I'm quite sure that if I had asked him—

MRS. LINDE: Which you won't, of course.

NORA: No, of course not. I can't see that I'd ever need to. But I'm quite positive that if I talked to Dr. Rank—

MRS. LINDE: Behind your husband's back?

NORA: I've got to clear up this other thing; *that's* also behind his back. I've *got* to clear it all up.

MRS. LINDE: Yes, I was saying that yesterday, but—

NORA (*pacing up and down*):   A man handles these problems so much better than a woman—

MRS. LINDE: One's husband does, yes.

NORA: Nonsense. (*Stopping.*) When you pay everything you owe, then you get your note back, right?

MRS. LINDE: Yes, naturally.

NORA: And can rip it into a million pieces and burn it up—that filthy scrap of paper!

MRS. LINDE (*looking hard at her, laying her sewing aside, and rising slowly*):   Nora, you're hiding something from me.

NORA: You can see it in my face?

MRS. LINDE: Something's happened to you since yesterday morning. Nora, what is it?

NORA (*hurrying toward her*):   Kristine! (*Listening.*) Shh! Torvald's home. Look, go in with the children a while. Torvald can't bear all this snipping and stitching. Let Anne-Marie help you.

MRS. LINDE (*gathering up some of the things*):   All right, but I'm not leaving here until we've talked this out. (*She disappears into the room, left, as Torvald enters from the hall.*)

NORA: Oh, how I've been waiting for you, Torvald dear.

HELMER: Was that the dressmaker?

NORA: No, that was Kristine. She's helping me fix up my costume. You know, it's going to be quite attractive.

HELMER: Yes, wasn't that a bright idea I had?

NORA: Brilliant! But then wasn't I good as well to give in to you?

HELMER: Good—because you give in to your husband's judgment? All right, you little goose, I know you didn't mean it like that. But I won't disturb you. You'll want to have a fitting, I suppose.

NORA: And you'll be working?

HELMER: Yes. (*Indicating a bundle of papers.*) See. I've been down to the bank. (*Starts toward his study.*)

NORA: Torvald.

HELMER (*stops*):   Yes.

NORA: If your little squirrel begged you, with all her heart and soul, for something—?

HELMER: What's that?

NORA: Then would you do it?

HELMER: First, naturally, I'd have to know what it was.

NORA: Your squirrel would scamper about and do tricks, if you'd only be sweet and give in.

HELMER: Out with it.

NORA: Your lark would be singing high and low in every room—

HELMER: Come on, she does that anyway.

NORA: I'd be a wood nymph and dance for you in the moonlight.

HELMER: Nora—don't tell me it's that same business from this morning?

NORA (*coming closer*):   Yes, Torvald, I beg you, please!

HELMER: And you actually have the nerve to drag that up again?

NORA: Yes, yes, you've got to give in to me; you *have* to let Krogstad keep his job in the bank.

HELMER: My dear Nora, I've slated his job for Mrs. Linde.

NORA: That's awfully kind of you. But you could just fire another clerk instead of Krogstad.

HELMER: This is the most incredible stubbornness! Because you go and give an impulsive promise to speak up for him, I'm expected to—

NORA: That's not the reason, Torvald. It's for your own sake. That man does writing for the worst papers; you said it yourself. He could do you any amount of harm. I'm scared to death of him—

HELMER: Ah, I understand. It's the old memories haunting you.

NORA: What do you mean by that?

HELMER: Of course, you're thinking about your father.

NORA: Yes, all right. Just remember how those nasty gossips wrote in the papers about Papa and slandered him so cruelly. I think they'd have had him dismissed if the department hadn't sent you up to investigate, and if you hadn't been so kind and open-minded toward him.

HELMER: My dear Nora, there's a notable difference between your father and me. Your father's official career was hardly above reproach. But mine is; and I hope it'll stay that way as long as I hold my position.

NORA: Oh, who can ever tell what vicious minds can invent? We could be so snug and happy now in our quiet, carefree home—you and I and the children, Torvald! That's why I'm pleading with you so—

HELMER: And just by pleading for him you make it impossible for me to keep
        him on. It's already known at the bank that I'm firing Krogstad. What if it's
        rumored around now that the new bank manager was vetoed by his wife —

NORA: Yes, what then — ?

HELMER: Oh yes — as long as our little bundle of stubbornness gets her way — ! I
        should go and make myself ridiculous in front of the whole office — give
        people the idea I can be swayed by all kinds of outside pressure. Oh, you can
        bet I'd feel the effects of that soon enough! Besides — there's something that
        rules Krogstad right out at the bank as long as I'm the manager.

NORA: What's that?

HELMER: His moral failings I could maybe overlook if I had to —

NORA: Yes, Torvald, why not?

HELMER: And I hear he's quite efficient on the job. But he was a crony of mine
        back in my teens — one of those rash friendships that crop up again and
        again to embarrass you later in life. Well, I might as well say it straight out:
        we're on a first-name basis. And that tactless fool makes no effort at all to hide
        it in front of others. Quite the contrary — he thinks that entitles him to take a
        familiar air around me, and so every other second he comes booming out
        with his "Yes, Torvald!" and "Sure thing, Torvald!" I tell you, it's been excru-
        ciating for me. He's out to make my place in the bank unbearable.

NORA: Torvald, you can't be serious about all this.

HELMER: Oh no? Why not?

NORA: Because these are such petty considerations.

HELMER: What are you saying? Petty? You think I'm petty!

NORA: No, just the opposite, Torvald dear. That's exactly why —

HELMER: Never mind. You call my motives petty; then I might as well be just
        that. Petty! All right! We'll put a stop to this for good. (*Goes to the hall door
        and calls.*) Helene!

NORA: What do you want?

HELMER (*searching among his papers*):   A decision. (*The maid comes in.*) Look
        here; take this letter; go out with it at once. Get hold of a messenger and have
        him deliver it. Quick now. It's already addressed. Wait, here's some money.

MAID: Yes, sir. (*She leaves with the letter.*)

HELMER (*straightening his papers*):   There, now, little Miss Willful.

NORA (*breathlessly*):   Torvald, what was that letter?

HELMER: Krogstad's notice.

NORA: Call it back, Torvald! There's still time. Oh, Torvald, call it back! Do it
        for my sake — for your sake, for the children's sake! Do you hear, Torvald; do
        it! You don't know how this can harm us.

HELMER: Too late.

NORA: Yes, too late.

HELMER: Nora dear, I can forgive you this panic, even though basically you're
        insulting me. Yes, you are! Or isn't it an insult to think that *I* should be afraid
        of a courtroom hack's revenge? But I forgive you anyway, because this shows
        so beautifully how much you love me. (*Takes her in his arms.*) This is the way

it should be, my darling Nora. Whatever comes, you'll see; when it really counts, I have strength and courage enough as a man to take on the whole weight myself.

NORA *(terrified)*:   What do you mean by that?

HELMER: The whole weight, I said.

NORA *(resolutely)*:   No, never in all the world.

HELMER: Good. So we'll share it, Nora, as man and wife. That's as it should be. *(Fondling her.)* Are you happy now? There, there, there—not these frightened dove's eyes. It's nothing at all but empty fantasies—Now you should run through your tarantella and practice your tambourine. I'll go to the inner office and shut both doors, so I won't hear a thing; you can make all the noise you like. *(Turning in the doorway.)* And when Rank comes, just tell him where he can find me. *(He nods to her and goes with his papers into the study, closing the door.)*

NORA *(standing as though rooted, dazed with fright, in a whisper)*:   He really could do it. He will do it. He'll do it in spite of everything. No, not that, never, never! Anything but that! Escape! A way out—*(The doorbell rings.)* Dr. Rank! Anything but that! *Anything*, whatever it is! *(Her hands pass over her face, smoothing it; she pulls herself together, goes over and opens the hall door. Dr. Rank stands outside, hanging his fur coat up. During the following scene, it begins getting dark.)*

NORA: Hello, Dr. Rank. I recognized your ring. But you mustn't go in to Torvald yet; I believe he's working.

RANK: And you?

NORA: For you, I always have an hour to spare—you know that. *(He has entered, and she shuts the door after him.)*

RANK: Many thanks. I'll make use of these hours while I can.

NORA: What do you mean by that? While you can?

RANK: Does that disturb you?

NORA: Well, it's such an odd phrase. Is anything going to happen?

RANK: What's going to happen is what I've been expecting so long—but I honestly didn't think it would come so soon.

NORA *(gripping his arm)*:   What is it you've found out? Dr. Rank, you have to tell me!

RANK *(sitting by the stove)*:   It's all over for me. There's nothing to be done about it.

NORA *(breathing easier)*:   Is it you—then—?

RANK: Who else? There's no point in lying to one's self. I'm the most miserable of all my patients, Mrs. Helmer. These past few days I've been auditing my internal accounts. Bankrupt! Within a month I'll probably be laid out and rotting in the churchyard.

NORA: Oh, what a horrible thing to say.

RANK: The thing itself is horrible. But the worst of it is all the other horror before it's over. There's only one final examination left; when I'm finished with that, I'll know about when my disintegration will begin. There's something I want to say. Helmer with his sensitivity has such a sharp distaste for anything ugly. I don't want him near my sickroom.

NORA: Oh, but Dr. Rank —

RANK: I won't have him in there. Under no condition. I'll lock my door to him — As soon as I'm completely sure of the worst, I'll send you my calling card marked with a black cross, and you'll know then the wreck has started to come apart.

NORA: No, today you're completely unreasonable. And I wanted you so much to be in a really good humor.

RANK: With death up my sleeve? And then to suffer this way for somebody else's sins. Is there any justice in that? And in every single family, in some way or another, this inevitable retribution of nature goes on —

NORA *(her hands pressed over her ears)*: Oh, stuff! Cheer up! Please — be gay!

RANK: Yes, I'd just as soon laugh at it all. My poor, innocent spine, serving time for my father's gay army days.

NORA *(by the table, left)*: He was so infatuated with asparagus tips and pâté de foie gras, wasn't that it?

RANK: Yes — and with truffles.

NORA: Truffles, yes. And then with oysters, I suppose?

RANK: Yes, tons of oysters, naturally.

NORA: And then the port and champagne to go with it. It's so sad that all these delectable things have to strike at our bones.

RANK: Especially when they strike at the unhappy bones that never shared in the fun.

NORA: Ah, that's the saddest of all.

RANK *(looks searchingly at her)*: Hm.

NORA *(after a moment)*: Why did you smile?

RANK: No, it was you who laughed.

NORA: No, it was you who smiled, Dr. Rank!

RANK *(getting up)*: You're even a bigger tease than I'd thought.

NORA: I'm full of wild ideas today.

RANK: That's obvious.

NORA *(putting both hands on his shoulders)*: Dear, dear Dr. Rank, you'll never die for Torvald and me.

RANK: Oh, that loss you'll easily get over. Those who go away are soon forgotten.

NORA *(looks fearfully at him)*: You believe that?

RANK: One makes new connections, and then —

NORA: Who makes new connections?

RANK: Both you and Torvald will when I'm gone. I'd say you're well under way already. What was that Mrs. Linde doing here last evening?

NORA: Oh, come — you can't be jealous of poor Kristine?

RANK: Oh yes, I am. She'll be my successor here in the house. When I'm down under, that woman will probably —

NORA: Shh! Not so loud. She's right in there.

RANK: Today as well. So you see.

NORA: Only to sew on my dress. Good gracious, how unreasonable you are. *(Sitting on the sofa.)* Be nice now, Dr. Rank. Tomorrow you'll see how beautifully I'll dance; and you can imagine then that I'm dancing only for you—yes, and of course for Torvald, too—that's understood. (*Takes various items out of the carton.*) Dr. Rank, sit over here and I'll show you something.

RANK (*sitting*):   What's that?

NORA: Look here. Look.

RANK: Silk Stockings.

NORA: Flesh-colored. Aren't they lovely? Now it's so dark here, but tomorrow— No, no, no, just look at the feet. Oh well, you might as well look at the rest.

RANK: Hm—

NORA: Why do you look so critical? Don't you believe they'll fit?

RANK: I've never had any chance to form an opinion on that.

NORA (*glancing at him a moment*):   Shame on you. (*Hits him lightly on the ear with the stockings.*) That's for you. (*Puts them away again.*)

RANK: And what other splendors am I going to see now?

NORA: Not the least bit more, because you've been naughty. (*She hums a little and rummages among her things.*)

RANK (*after a short silence*):   When I sit here together with you like this, completely easy and open, then I don't know—I simply can't imagine—whatever would have become of me if I'd never come into this house.

NORA (*smiling*):   Yes, I really think you feel completely at ease with us.

RANK (*more quietly, staring straight ahead*):   And then to have to go away from it all—

NORA: Nonsense, you're not going away.

RANK (*his voice unchanged*):   — and not even be able to leave some poor show of gratitude behind, scarcely a fleeting regret—no more than a vacant place that anyone can fill.

NORA: And if I asked you now for—? No—

RANK: For what?

NORA: For a great proof of your friendship—

RANK: Yes, yes?

NORA: No, I mean—for an exceptionally big favor—

RANK: Would you really, for once, make me so happy?

NORA: Oh, you haven't the vaguest idea what it is.

RANK: All right, then tell me.

NORA: No, but I can't, Dr. Rank—it's all out of reason. It's advice and help, too—and a favor—

RANK: So much the better. I can't fathom what you're hinting at. Just speak out. Don't you trust me?

NORA: Of course. More than anyone else. You're my best and truest friend, I'm sure. That's why I want to talk to you. All right, then, Dr. Rank: there's something you can help me prevent. You know how deeply, how inexpressibly dearly Torvald loves me; he'd never hesitate a second to give up his life for me.

RANK (*leaning close to her*):   Nora—do you think he's the only one—

NORA (*with a slight start*):   Who—?

RANK: Who'd gladly give up his life for you.

NORA (*heavily*):   I see.

RANK: I swore to myself you should know this before I'm gone. I'll never find a better chance. Yes, Nora, now you know. And also you know now that you can trust me beyond anyone else.

NORA (*rising, natural and calm*): Let me by.

RANK (*making room for her, but still sitting*): Nora—

NORA (*in the hall doorway*): Helene, bring the lamp in. (*Goes over to the stove.*) Ah, dear Dr. Rank, that was really mean of you.

RANK (*getting up*): That I've loved you just as deeply as somebody else? Was *that* mean?

NORA: No, but that you came out and told me. That was quite unnecessary—

RANK: What do you mean? Have you known—?

The Maid comes in with the lamp, sets it on the table, and goes out again.

RANK: Nora—Mrs. Helmer—I'm asking you: have you known about it?

NORA: Oh, how can I tell what I know or don't know? Really, I don't know what to say—Why did you have to be so clumsy, Dr. Rank! Everything was so good.

RANK: Well, in any case, you now have the knowledge that my body and soul are at your command. So won't you speak out?

NORA (*looking at him*): After that?

RANK: Please, just let me know what it is.

NORA: You can't know anything now.

RANK: I have to. You mustn't punish me like this. Give me the chance to do whatever is humanly possible for you.

NORA: Now there's nothing you can do for me. Besides, actually, I don't need any help. You'll see—it's only my fantasies. That's what it is. Of course! (*Sits in the rocker, looks at him, and smiles.*) What a nice one you are, Dr. Rank. Aren't you a little bit ashamed, now that the lamp is here?

RANK: No, not exactly. But perhaps I'd better go—for good?

NORA: No, you certainly can't do that. You must come here just as you always have. You know Torvald can't do without you.

RANK: Yes, but *you*?

NORA: You know how much I enjoy it when you're here.

RANK: That's precisely what threw me off. You're a mystery to me. So many times I've felt you'd almost rather be with me than with Helmer.

NORA: Yes—you see, there are some people that one loves most and other people that one would almost prefer being with.

RANK: Yes, there's something to that.

NORA: When I was back home, of course I loved Papa most. But I always thought it was so much fun when I could sneak down to the maids' quarters, because they never tried to improve me, and it was always so amusing, the way they talked to each other.

RANK: Aha, so it's *their* place that I've filled.

NORA (*jumping up and going to him*): Oh, dear, sweet Dr. Rank, that's not what I meant at all. But you can understand that with Torvald it's just the same as with Papa—

The Maid enters from the hall.

MAID: Ma'am — please! *(She whispers to Nora and hands her a calling card.)*

NORA *(glancing at the card):*   Ah! *(Slips it into her pocket.)*

RANK: Anything wrong?

NORA: No, no, not at all. It's only some — it's my new dress —

RANK: Really? But — there's your dress.

NORA: Oh, that. But this is another one — I ordered it — Torvald mustn't know —

RANK: Ah, now we have the big secret.

NORA: That's right. Just go in with him — he's back in the inner study. Keep him there as long as —

RANK: Don't worry. He won't get away. *(Goes into the study.)*

NORA *(to the Maid):*   And he's standing waiting in the kitchen?

MAID: Yes, he came up by the back stairs.

NORA: But didn't you tell him somebody was here?

MAID: Yes, but that didn't do any good.

NORA: He won't leave?

MAID: No, he won't go till he's talked with you, ma'am.

NORA: Let him come in, then — but quietly. Helene, don't breathe a word about this. It's a surprise for my husband.

MAID: Yes, yes, I understand — *(Goes out.)*

NORA: This horror — it's going to happen. No, no, no, it can't happen, it mustn't. *(She goes and bolts Helmer's door. The Maid opens the hall door for Krogstad and shuts it behind him. He is dressed for travel in a fur coat, boots, and a fur cap.)*

NORA *(going toward him):*   Talk softly. My husband's home.

KROGSTAD: Well, good for him.

NORA: What do you want?

KROGSTAD: Some information.

NORA: Hurry up, then. What is it?

KROGSTAD: You know, of course, that I got my notice.

NORA: I couldn't prevent it, Mr. Krogstad. I fought for you to the bitter end, but nothing worked.

KROGSTAD: Does your husband's love for you run so thin? He knows everything I can expose you to, and all the same he dares to —

NORA: How can you imagine he knows anything about this?

KROGSTAD: Ah, no — I can't imagine it either, now. It's not at all like my fine Torvald Helmer to have so much guts —

NORA: Mr. Krogstad, I demand respect for my husband!

KROGSTAD: Why, of course — all due respect. But since the lady's keeping it so carefully hidden, may I presume to ask if you're also a bit better informed than yesterday about what you've actually done?

NORA: More than you could ever teach me.

KROGSTAD: Yes, I *am* such an awful lawyer.

NORA: What is it you want from me?

KROGSTAD: Just a glimpse of how you are, Mrs. Helmer. I've been thinking about you all day long. A cashier, a night-court scribbler, a — well, a type like me also has a little of what they call a heart, you know.

NORA: Then show it. Think of my children.

KROGSTAD: Did you or your husband ever think of mine? But never mind. I simply wanted to tell you that you don't need to take this thing too seriously. For the present, I'm not proceeding with any action.

NORA: Oh no, really! Well — I knew that.

KROGSTAD: Everything can be settled in a friendly spirit. It doesn't have to get around town at all; it can stay just among us three.

NORA: My husband must never know anything of this.

KROGSTAD: How can you manage that? Perhaps you can pay me the balance?

NORA: No, not right now.

KROGSTAD: Or you know some way of raising the money in a day or two?

NORA: No way that I'm willing to use.

KROGSTAD: Well, it wouldn't have done you any good, anyway. If you stood in front of me with a fistful of bills, you still couldn't buy your signature back.

NORA: Then tell me what you're going to do with it.

KROGSTAD: I'll just hold onto it — keep it on file. There's no outsider who'll even get wind of it. So if you've been thinking of taking some desperate step —

NORA: I have.

KROGSTAD: Been thinking of running away from home —

NORA: I have!

KROGSTAD: Or even of something worse —

NORA: How could you guess that?

KROGSTAD: You can drop those thoughts.

NORA: How could you guess I was thinking of *that*?

KROGSTAD: Most of us think about *that* at first. I thought about it too, but I discovered I hadn't the courage —

NORA *(lifelessly)*:   I don't either.

KROGSTAD *(relieved)*:   That's true, you haven't the courage? You too?

NORA: I don't have it — I don't have it.

KROGSTAD: It would be terribly stupid, anyway. After that first storm at home blows out, why, then — I have here in my pocket a letter for your husband —

NORA: Telling everything?

KROGSTAD: As charitably as possible.

NORA *(quickly)*:   He mustn't ever get that letter. Tear it up. I'll find some way to get money.

KROGSTAD: Beg pardon, Mrs. Helmer, but I think I just told you —

NORA: Oh, I don't mean the money I owe you. Let me know how much you want from my husband, and I'll manage it.

KROGSTAD: I don't want money from your husband.

NORA: What do you want, then?

KROGSTAD: I'll tell you what. I want to recoup, Mrs. Helmer; I want to get on in the world — and there's where your husband can help me. For a year and a half I've kept myself clean of anything disreputable — all that time struggling with the worst conditions; but I was satisfied, working my way up step by step. Now I've been written right off, and I'm just not in the mood to come crawling back. I tell you, I want to move on. I want to get back in the bank—in a better position. Your husband can set up a job for me—

NORA: He'll never do that!

KROGSTAD: He'll do it. I know him. He won't dare breathe a word of protest. And once I'm in there together with him, you just wait and see! Inside of a year, I'll be the manager's right-hand man. It'll be Nils Krogstad, not Torvald Helmer, who runs the bank.

NORA: You'll never see the day!

KROGSTAD: Maybe you think you can—

NORA: I have the courage now—for *that*.

KROGSTAD: Oh, you don't scare me. A smart, spoiled lady like you—

NORA: You'll see; you'll see!

KROGSTAD: Under the ice, maybe? Down in the freezing coal-black water? There, till you float up in the spring, ugly, unrecognizable, with your hair falling out—

NORA: You don't frighten me.

KROGSTAD: Nor do you frighten me. One doesn't do these things, Mrs. Helmer. Besides, what good would it be? I'd still have him safe in my pocket.

NORA: Afterwards? When I'm no longer—?

KROGSTAD: Are you forgetting that *I'll* be in control then over your final reputation? *(Nora stands speechless, staring at him.)* Good; now I've warned you. Don't do anything stupid. When Helmer's read my letter, I'll be waiting for his reply. And bear in mind that it's your husband himself who's forced me back to my old ways. I'll never forgive him for that. Good-bye, Mrs. Helmer. *(He goes out through the hall.)*

NORA *(goes to the hall door, opens it a crack, and listens):*   He's gone. Didn't leave the letter. Oh no, no, that's impossible too! *(Opening the door more and more.)* What's that? He's standing outside—not going downstairs. He's thinking it over? Maybe he'll—? *(A letter falls in the mailbox; then Krogstad's footsteps are heard, dying away down a flight of stairs. Nora gives a muffled cry and runs over toward the sofa table. A short pause.)* In the mailbox. *(Slips warily over to the hall door.)* It's lying there. Torvald, Torvald—now we're lost!

MRS. LINDE *(entering with costume from the room, left):*   There now, I can't see anything else to mend. Perhaps you'd like to try—

NORA *(in a hoarse whisper):*   Kristine, come here.

MRS. LINDE *(tossing the dress on the sofa):*   What's wrong? You look upset.

NORA: Come here. See that letter? *There!* Look—through the glass in the mailbox.

MRS. LINDE: Yes, yes, I see it.

NORA: That letter's from Krogstad—

MRS. LINDE: Nora—it's Krogstad who loaned you the money!

NORA: Yes, and now Torvald will find out everything.

MRS. LINDE: Believe me, Nora, it's best for both of you.

NORA: There's more you don't know. I forged a name.

MRS. LINDE: But for heaven's sake—?

NORA: I only want to tell you that, Kristine, so that you can be my witness.

MRS. LINDE: Witness? Why should I—?

NORA: If I should go out of my mind — it could easily happen —

MRS. LINDE: Nora!

NORA: Or anything else occurred — so I couldn't be present here —

MRS. LINDE: Nora, Nora, you aren't yourself at all!

NORA: And someone should try to take on the whole weight, all of the guilt, you follow me —

MRS. LINDE: Yes, of course, but why do you think — ?

NORA: Then you're the witness that it isn't true, Kristine. I'm very much myself; my mind right now is perfectly clear; and I'm telling you: nobody else has known about this; I alone did everything. Remember that.

MRS. LINDE: I will. But I don't understand all this.

NORA: Oh, how could you ever understand it? It's the miracle now that's going to take place.

MRS. LINDE: The miracle?

NORA: Yes, the miracle. But it's so awful, Kristine. It mustn't take place, not for anything in the world.

MRS. LINDE: I'm going right over and talk with Krogstad.

NORA: Don't go near him; he'll do you some terrible harm!

MRS. LINDE: There was a time once when he'd gladly have done anything for me.

NORA: He?

MRS. LINDE: Where does he live?

NORA: Oh, how do I know? Yes. (*Searches in her pocket.*) Here's his card. But the letter, the letter — !

HELMER (*from the study, knocking on the door*):   Nora!

NORA (*with a cry of fear*):   Oh! What is it? What do you want?

HELMER: Now, now, don't be so frightened. We're not coming in. You locked the door — are you trying on the dress?

NORA: Yes, I'm trying it. I'll look just beautiful, Torvald.

MRS. LINDE (*who has read the card*):   He's living right around the corner.

NORA: Yes, but what's the use? We're lost. The letter's in the box.

MRS. LINDE: And your husband has the key?

NORA: Yes, always.

MRS. LINDE: Krogstad can ask for his letter back unread; he can find some excuse —

NORA: But it's just this time that Torvald usually —

MRS. LINDE: Stall him. Keep him in there. I'll be back as quick as I can. (*She hurries out through the hall entrance.*)

NORA (*goes to Helmer's door, opens it, and peers in*):   Torvald!

HELMER (*from the inner study*):   Well — does one dare set foot in one's own living room at last? Come on, Rank, now we'll get a look — (*In the doorway.*) But what's this?

NORA: What, Torvald dear?

HELMER: Rank had me expecting some grand masquerade.

RANK (*in the doorway*):   That was my impression, but I must have been wrong.

NORA: No one can admire me in my splendor — not till tomorrow.

HELMER: But Nora dear, you look so exhausted. Have you practiced too hard?

NORA: No, I haven't practiced at all yet.

HELMER: You know, it's necessary—

NORA: Oh, it's absolutely necessary, Torvald. But I can't get anywhere without your help. I've forgotten the whole thing completely.

HELMER: Ah, we'll soon take care of that.

NORA: Yes, take care of me, Torvald, please! Promise me that? Oh, I'm so nervous. That big party—You must give up everything this evening for me. No business—don't even touch your pen. Yes? Dear Torvald, promise?

HELMER: It's a promise. Tonight I'm totally at your service—you little helpless thing. Hm—but first there's one thing I want to—*(Goes toward the hall door.)*

NORA: What are you looking for?

HELMER: Just to see if there's any mail.

NORA: No, no, don't do that, Torvald!

HELMER: Now what?

NORA: Torvald, please. There isn't any.

HELMER: Let me look, though. *(Starts out. Nora, at the piano, strikes the first notes of the tarantella. Helmer, at the door, stops.)* Aha!

NORA: I can't dance tomorrow if I don't practice with you.

HELMER *(going over to her):*   Nora dear, are you really so frightened?

NORA: Yes, so terribly frightened. Let me practice right now; there's still time before dinner. Oh, sit down and play for me, Torvald. Direct me. Teach me, the way you always have.

HELMER: Gladly, if it's what you want. *(Sits at the piano.)*

NORA *(snatches the tambourine up from the box, then a long, varicolored shawl, which she throws around herself, whereupon she springs forward and cries out):* Play for me now! Now I'll dance!

Helmer plays and Nora dances. Rank stands behind Helmer at the piano and looks on.

HELMER *(as he plays):*   Slower. Slow down.

NORA: Can't change it.

HELMER: Not so violent, Nora!

NORA: Has to be just like this.

HELMER *(stopping):*   No, no, that won't do at all.

NORA *(laughing and swinging her tambourine):*   Isn't that what I told you?

RANK: Let me play for her.

HELMER *(getting up):*   Yes, go on. I can teach her more easily then.

Rank sits at the piano and plays; Nora dances more and more wildly. Helmer has stationed himself by the stove and repeatedly gives her directions; she seems not to hear them; her hair loosens and falls over her shoulders; she does not notice, but goes on dancing. Mrs. Linde enters.

MRS. LINDE *(standing dumbfounded at the door):*   Ah—!

NORA *(still dancing):*   See what fun, Kristine!

HELMER: But Nora darling, you dance as if your life were at stake.

NORA: And it is.

HELMER: Rank, stop! This is pure madness. Stop it, I say!

Rank breaks off playing, and Nora halts abruptly.

HELMER *(going over to her):*   I never would have believed it. You've forgotten everything I taught you.

NORA *(throwing away the tambourine):*   You see for yourself.

HELMER: Well, there's certainly room for instruction here.

NORA: Yes, you see how important it is. You've got to teach me to the very last minute. Promise me that, Torvald?

HELMER: You can bet on it.

NORA: You mustn't, either today or tomorrow, think about anything else but me; you mustn't open any letters—or the mailbox—

HELMER: Ah, it's still the fear of that man—

NORA: Oh yes, yes, that too.

HELMER: Nora, it's written all over you—there's already a letter from him out there.

NORA: I don't know. I guess so. But you mustn't read such things now; there mustn't be anything ugly between us before it's all over.

RANK *(quietly to Helmer):*   You shouldn't deny her.

HELMER *(putting his arms around her):*   The child can have her way. But tomorrow night, after you've danced—

NORA: Then you'll be free.

MAID *(in the doorway, right):*   Ma'am, dinner is served.

NORA: We'll be wanting champagne, Helene.

MAID: Very good, ma'am. *(Goes out.)*

HELMER: So—a regular banquet, hm?

NORA: Yes, a banquet—champagne till daybreak! *(Calling out.)* And some macaroons, Helene. Heaps of them—just this once.

HELMER *(taking her hands):*   Now, now, now—no hysterics. Be my own little lark again.

NORA: Oh, I will soon enough. But go on in—and you, Dr. Rank. Kristine, help me put up my hair.

RANK *(whispering, as they go):*   There's nothing wrong—really wrong, is there?

HELMER: Oh, of course not. It's nothing more than this childish anxiety I was telling you about. *(They go out, right.)*

NORA: Well?

MRS. LINDE: Left town.

NORA: I could see by your face.

MRS. LINDE: He'll be home tomorrow evening. I wrote him a note.

NORA: You shouldn't have. Don't try to stop anything now. After all, it's a wonderful joy, this waiting here for the miracle.

MRS. LINDE: What is it you're waiting for?

NORA: Oh, you can't understand that. Go in to them; I'll be along in a moment.

Mrs. Linde goes into the dining room. Nora stands a short while as if composing herself; then she looks at her watch.

NORA: Five. Seven hours to midnight. Twenty-four hours to the midnight after, and then the tarantella's done. Seven and twenty-four? Thirty-one hours to live.

HELMER *(in the doorway, right):*   What's become of the little lark?
NORA *(going toward him with open arms):*   Here's your lark!

ACT 3

Same scene. The table, with chairs around it, has been moved to the center of the room. A lamp on the table is lit. The hall door stands open. Dance music drifts down from the floor above. Mrs. Linde sits at the table, absently paging through a book, trying to read, but apparently unable to focus her thoughts. Once or twice she pauses, tensely listening for a sound at the outer entrance.

MRS. LINDE *(glancing at her watch):*   Not yet—and there's hardly any time left. If only he's not—*(Listening again.)* Ah, there he is. *(She goes out in the hall and cautiously opens the outer door. Quiet footsteps are heard on the stairs. She whispers:)* Come in. Nobody's here.

KROGSTAD *(in the doorway):*   I found a note from you at home. What's back of all this?

MRS. LINDE: I just *had* to talk to you.

KROGSTAD: Oh? And it just *had* to be here in this house?

MRS. LINDE: At my place it was impossible; my room hasn't a private entrance. Come in; we're all alone. The maid's asleep, and the Helmers are at the dance upstairs.

KROGSTAD *(entering the room):*   Well, well, the Helmers are dancing tonight? Really?

MRS. LINDE: Yes, why not?

KROGSTAD: How true—why not?

MRS. LINDE: All right, Krogstad, let's talk.

KROGSTAD: Do we two have anything more to talk about?

MRS. LINDE: We have a great deal to talk about.

KROGSTAD: I wouldn't have thought so.

MRS. LINDE: No, because you've never understood me, really.

KROGSTAD: Was there anything more to understand—except what's all too common in life? A calculating woman throws over a man the moment a better catch comes by.

MRS. LINDE: You think I'm so thoroughly calculating? You think I broke it off lightly?

KROGSTAD: Didn't you?

MRS. LINDE: Nils—is that what you really thought?

KROGSTAD: If you cared, then why did you write me the way you did?

MRS. LINDE: What else could I do? If I had to break off with you, then it was my job as well to root out everything you felt for me.

KROGSTAD *(wringing his hands):*   So that was it. And this—all this, simply for money!

MRS. LINDE: Don't forget I had a helpless mother and two small brothers. We couldn't wait for you, Nils; you had such a long road ahead of you then.

KROGSTAD: That may be; but you still hadn't the right to abandon me for somebody else's sake.

MRS. LINDE: Yes—I don't know. So many, many times I've asked myself if I did have that right.

KROGSTAD *(more softly)*: When I lost you, it was as if all the solid ground dissolved from under my feet. Look at me; I'm a half-drowned man now, hanging onto a wreck.

MRS. LINDE: Help may be near.

KROGSTAD: It was near—but then you came and blocked it off.

MRS. LINDE: Without my knowing it, Nils. Today for the first time I learned that it's you I'm replacing at the bank.

KROGSTAD: All right—I believe you. But now that you know, will you step aside?

MRS. LINDE: No, because that wouldn't benefit you in the slightest.

KROGSTAD: Not "benefit" me, hm! I'd step aside anyway.

MRS. LINDE: I've learned to be realistic. Life and hard, bitter necessity have taught me that.

KROGSTAD: And life's taught me never to trust fine phrases.

MRS. LINDE: Then life's taught you a very sound thing. But you do have to trust in actions, don't you?

KROGSTAD: What does that mean?

MRS. LINDE: You said you were hanging on like a half-drowned man to a wreck.

KROGSTAD: I've good reason to say that.

MRS. LINDE: I'm also like a half-drowned woman on a wreck. No one to suffer with; no one to care for.

KROGSTAD: You made your choice.

MRS. LINDE: There wasn't any choice then.

KROGSTAD: So—what of it?

MRS. LINDE: Nils, if only we two shipwrecked people could reach across to each other.

KROGSTAD: What are you saying?

MRS. LINDE: Two on one wreck are at least better off than each on his own.

KROGSTAD: Kristine!

MRS. LINDE: Why do you think I came into town?

KROGSTAD: Did you really have some thought of me?

MRS. LINDE: I have to work to go on living. All my born days, as long as I can remember, I've worked, and it's been my best and my only joy. But now I'm completely alone in the world; it frightens me to be so empty and lost. To work for yourself—there's no joy in that. Nils, give me something—someone to work for.

KROGSTAD: I don't believe all this. It's just some hysterical feminine urge to go out and make a noble sacrifice.

MRS. LINDE: Have you ever found me to be hysterical?

KROGSTAD: Can you honestly mean this? Tell me—do you know everything about my past?

MRS. LINDE: Yes.

KROGSTAD: And you know what they think I'm worth around here.

MRS. LINDE: From what you were saying before, it would seem that with me you could have been another person.

KROGSTAD: I'm positive of that.

MRS. LINDE: Couldn't it happen still?

KROGSTAD: Kristine—you're saying this in all seriousness? Yes, you are! I can see it in you. And do you really have the courage, then—?

MRS. LINDE: I need to have someone to care for; and your children need a mother. We both need each other. Nils, I have faith that you're good at heart—I'll risk everything together with you.

KROGSTAD *(gripping her hands)*:   Kristine, thank you, thank you—Now I know I can win back a place in their eyes. Yes—but I forgot—

MRS. LINDE *(listening)*:   Shh! The tarantella. Go now! Go on!

KROGSTAD: Why? What is it?

MRS. LINDE: Hear the dance up there? When that's over, they'll be coming down.

KROGSTAD: Oh, then I'll go. But—it's all pointless. Of course, you don't know the move I made against the Helmers.

MRS. LINDE: Yes, Nils, I know.

KROGSTAD: And all the same, you have the courage to—?

MRS. LINDE: I know how far despair can drive a man like you.

KROGSTAD: Oh, if I only could take it all back.

MRS. LINDE: You easily could—your letter's still lying in the mailbox.

KROGSTAD: Are you sure of that?

MRS. LINDE: Positive. But—

KROGSTAD *(looks at her searchingly)*:   Is that the meaning of it, then? You'll save your friend at any price. Tell me straight out. Is that it?

MRS. LINDE: Nils—anyone who's sold herself for somebody else once isn't going to do it again.

KROGSTAD: I'll demand my letter back.

MRS. LINDE: No, no.

KROGSTAD: Yes, of course. I'll stay here till Helmer comes down; I'll tell him to give me my letter again—that it only involves my dismissal—that he shouldn't read it—

MRS. LINDE: No, Nils, don't call the letter back.

KROGSTAD: But wasn't that exactly why you wrote me to come here?

MRS. LINDE: Yes, in that first panic. But it's been a whole day and night since then, and in that time I've seen such incredible things in this house. Helmer's got to learn everything; this dreadful secret has to be aired; those two have to come to a full understanding; all these lies and evasions can't go on.

KROGSTAD: Well, then, if you want to chance it. But at least there's one thing I can do, and do right away—

MRS. LINDE *(listening)*:   Go now, go quick! The dance is over. We're not safe another second.

KROGSTAD: I'll wait for you downstairs.

MRS. LINDE: Yes, please do; take me home.

KROGSTAD: I can't believe it; I've never been so happy. *(He leaves by way of the outer door; the door between the room and the hall stays open.)*

MRS. LINDE *(straightening up a bit and getting together her street clothes)*: How different now! How different! Someone to work for, to live for — a home to build. Well, it is worth the try! Oh, if they'd only come! *(Listening.)* Ah, there they are. Bundle up. *(She picks up her hat and coat. Nora's and Helmer's voices can be heard outside; a key turns in the lock, and Helmer brings Nora into the hall almost by force. She is wearing the Italian costume with a large black shawl about her; he has on evening dress, with a black domino open over it.)*

NORA *(struggling in the doorway)*:   No, no, no, not inside! I'm going up again. I don't want to leave so soon.

HELMER: But Nora dear —

NORA: Oh, I beg you, please, Torvald. From the bottom of my heart, *please* — only an hour more!

HELMER: Not a single minute, Nora darling. You know our agreement. Come on, in we go; you'll catch cold out here. *(In spite of her resistance, he gently draws her into the room.)*

MRS. LINDE: Good evening.

NORA: Kristine!

HELMER: Why, Mrs. Linde — are you here so late?

MRS. LINDE: Yes, I'm sorry, but I did want to see Nora in costume.

NORA: Have you been sitting here, waiting for me?

MRS. LINDE: Yes. I didn't come early enough; you were all upstairs; and then I thought I really couldn't leave without seeing you.

HELMER *(removing Nora's shawl)*:   Yes, take a good look. She's worth looking at, I can tell you that, Mrs. Linde. Isn't she lovely?

MRS. LINDE: Yes, I should say —

HELMER: A dream of loveliness, isn't she? That's what everyone thought at the party, too. But she's horribly stubborn — this sweet little thing. What's to be done with her? Can you imagine, I almost had to use force to pry her away.

NORA: Oh, Torvald, you're going to regret you didn't indulge me, even for just a half hour more.

HELMER: There, you see. She danced her tarantella and got a tumultuous hand — which was well earned, although the performance may have been a bit too naturalistic — I mean it rather overstepped the proprieties of art. But never mind — what's important is, she made a success, an overwhelming success. You think I could let her stay on after that and spoil the effect? Oh no; I took my lovely little Capri girl — my capricious little Capri girl, I should say — took her under my arm; one quick tour of the ballroom, a curtsy to every side, and then — as they say in novels — the beautiful vision disappeared. An exit should always be effective, Mrs. Linde, but that's what I can't get Nora to grasp. Phew, it's hot in here. *(Flings the domino on a chair and opens the door to his room.)* Why's it dark in here? Oh yes, of course. Excuse me. *(He goes in and lights a couple of candles.)*

NORA *(in a sharp, breathless whisper)*:   So?

MRS. LINDE *(quietly)*:   I talked with him.

NORA: And—?

MRS. LINDE: Nora—you must tell your husband everything.

NORA *(dully)*: I knew it.

MRS. LINDE: You've got nothing to fear from Krogstad, but you have to speak out.

NORA: I won't tell.

MRS. LINDE: Then the letter will.

NORA: Thanks, Kristine. I know now what's to be done. Shh!

HELMER *(reentering)*: Well, then, Mrs. Linde—have you admired her?

MRS. LINDE: Yes, and now I'll say good night.

HELMER: Oh, come, so soon? Is this yours, this knitting?

MRS. LINDE: Yes, thanks. I nearly forgot it.

HELMER: Do you knit, then?

MRS. LINDE: Oh yes.

HELMER: You know what? You should embroider instead.

MRS. LINDE: Really? Why?

HELMER: Yes, because it's a lot prettier. See here, one holds the embroidery so, in the left hand, and then one guides the needle with the right—so—in an easy, sweeping curve—right?

MRS. LINDE: Yes, I guess that's—

HELMER: But, on the other hand, knitting—it can never be anything but ugly. Look, see here, the arms tucked in, the knitting needles going up and down—there's something Chinese about it. Ah, that was really a glorious champagne they served.

MRS. LINDE: Yes, good night, Nora, and don't be stubborn anymore.

HELMER: Well put, Mrs. Linde!

MRS. LINDE: Good night, Mr. Helmer.

HELMER *(accompanying her to the door)*: Good night, good night. I hope you get home all right. I'd be very happy to—but you don't have far to go. Good night, good night. *(She leaves. He shuts the door after her and returns.)* There, now, at last we got her out the door. She's a deadly bore, that creature.

NORA: Aren't you pretty tired, Torvald?

HELMER: No, not a bit.

NORA: You're not sleepy?

HELMER: Not at all. On the contrary, I'm feeling quite exhilarated. But you? Yes, you really look tired and sleepy.

NORA: Yes, I'm very tired. Soon now I'll sleep.

HELMER: See! You see! I was right all along that we shouldn't stay longer.

NORA: Whatever you do is always right.

HELMER *(kissing her brow)*: Now my little lark talks sense. Say, did you notice what a time Rank was having tonight?

NORA: Oh, was he? I didn't get to speak with him.

HELMER: I scarcely did either, but it's a long time since I've seen him in such high spirits. *(Gazes at her a moment, then comes nearer her.)* Hm—it's marvelous, though, to be back home again—to be completely alone with you. Oh, you bewitchingly lovely young woman!

NORA: Torvald, don't look at me like that!

HELMER: Can't I look at my richest treasure? At all that beauty that's mine, mine alone — completely and utterly.

NORA (*moving around to the other side of the table*):   You mustn't talk to me that way tonight.

HELMER (*following her*):   The tarantella is still in your blood, I can see — and it makes you even more enticing. Listen. The guests are beginning to go. (*Dropping his voice.*) Nora — it'll soon be quiet through this whole house.

NORA: Yes, I hope so.

HELMER: You do, don't you, my love? Do you realize — when I'm out at a party like this with you — do you know why I talk to you so little, and keep such a distance away; just send you a stolen look now and then — you know why I do it? It's because I'm imagining then that you're my secret darling, my secret bride-to-be, and that no one suspects there's anything between us.

NORA: Yes, yes; oh, yes, I know you're always thinking of me.

HELMER: And then when we leave and I place the shawl over those fine young rounded shoulders — over that wonderful curving neck — then I pretend that you're my young bride, that we're just coming from the wedding, that for the first time I'm bringing you into my house — that for the first time I'm alone with you — completely alone with you, your trembling young beauty! All this evening I've longed for nothing but you. When I saw you turn and sway in the tarantella — my blood was pounding till I couldn't stand it — that's why I brought you down here so early —

NORA: Go away, Torvald! Leave me alone. I don't want all this.

HELMER: What do you mean? Nora, you're teasing me. You will, won't you? Aren't I your husband — ?

A knock at the outside door.

NORA (*startled*):   What's that?

HELMER (*going toward the hall*):   Who is it?

RANK (*outside*):   It's me. May I come in a moment?

HELMER (*with quiet irritation*):   Oh, what does he want now? (*Aloud.*) Hold on. (*Goes and opens the door.*) Oh, how nice that you didn't just pass us by!

RANK: I thought I heard your voice, and then I wanted so badly to have a look in. (*Lightly glancing about.*) Ah, me, these old familiar haunts. You have it snug and cozy in here, you two.

HELMER: You seemed to be having it pretty cozy upstairs, too.

RANK: Absolutely. Why shouldn't I? Why not take in everything in life? As much as you can, anyway, and as long as you can. The wine was superb —

HELMER: The champagne especially.

RANK: You noticed that too? It's amazing how much I could guzzle down.

NORA: Torvald also drank a lot of champagne this evening.

RANK: Oh?

NORA: Yes, and that always makes him so entertaining.

RANK: Well, why shouldn't one have a pleasant evening after a well-spent day?

HELMER: Well spent? I'm afraid I can't claim that.

RANK (*slapping him on the back*):   But I can, you see!

NORA: Dr. Rank, you must have done some scientific research today.

RANK: Quite so.

HELMER: Come now — little Nora talking about scientific research!

NORA: And can I congratulate you on the results?

RANK: Indeed you may.

NORA: Then they were good?

RANK: The best possible for both doctor and patient — certainty.

NORA (*quickly and searchingly*):   Certainty?

RANK: Complete certainty. So don't I owe myself a gay evening afterwards?

NORA: Yes, you're right, Dr. Rank.

HELMER: I'm with you — just so long as you don't have to suffer for it in the morning.

RANK: Well, one never gets something for nothing in life.

NORA: Dr. Rank — are you very fond of masquerade parties?

RANK: Yes, if there's a good array of odd disguises —

NORA: Tell me, what should we two go as at the next masquerade?

HELMER: You little featherhead — already thinking of the next!

RANK: We two? I'll tell you what: you must go as Charmed Life —

HELMER: Yes, but find a costume for *that*!

RANK: Your wife can appear just as she looks every day.

HELMER: That was nicely put. But don't you know what you're going to be?

RANK: Yes, Helmer, I've made up my mind.

HELMER: Well?

RANK: At the next masquerade I'm going to be invisible.

HELMER: That's a funny idea.

RANK: They say there's a hat — black, huge — have you never heard of the hat that makes you invisible? You put it on, and then no one on earth can see you.

HELMER (*suppressing a smile*):   Ah, of course.

RANK: But I'm quite forgetting what I came for. Helmer, give me a cigar, one of the dark Havanas.

HELMER: With the greatest pleasure. (*Holds out his case.*)

RANK: Thanks. (*Takes one and cuts off the tip.*)

NORA (*striking a match*):   Let me give you a light.

RANK: Thank you. (*She holds the match for him; he lights the cigar.*) And now good-bye.

HELMER: Good-bye, good-bye, old friend.

NORA: Sleep well, Doctor.

RANK: Thanks for that wish.

NORA: Wish me the same.

RANK: You? All right, if you like — Sleep well. And thanks for the light. (*He nods to them both and leaves.*)

HELMER (*his voice subdued*):   He's been drinking heavily.

NORA (*absently*):   Could be. (*Helmer takes his keys from his pocket and goes out in the hall.*) Torvald — what are you after?

HELMER: Got to empty the mailbox; it's nearly full. There won't be room for the morning papers.

NORA: Are you working tonight?

HELMER: You know I'm not. Why—what's this? Someone's been at the lock.

NORA: At the lock—?

HELMER: Yes, I'm positive. What do you suppose—? I can't imagine one of the maids—? Here's a broken hairpin. Nora, it's yours—

NORA *(quickly)*:   Then it must be the children—

HELMER: You'd better break them of that. Hm, hm—well, opened it after all. *(Takes the contents out and calls into the kitchen.)* Helene! Helene, would you put out the lamp in the hall. *(He returns to the room shutting the hall door, then displays the handful of mail.)* Look how it's piled up. *(Sorting through them.)* Now what's this?

NORA *(at the window)*:   The letter! Oh, Torvald, no!

HELMER: Two calling cards—from Rank.

NORA: From Dr. Rank?

HELMER *(examining them)*:   "Dr. Rank, Consulting Physician." They were on top. He must have dropped them in as he left.

NORA: Is there anything on them?

HELMER: There's a black cross over the name. See? That's a gruesome notion. He could almost be announcing his own death.

NORA: That's just what he's doing.

HELMER: What! You've heard something? Something he's told you?

NORA: Yes. That when those cards came, he'd be taking his leave of us. He'll shut himself in now and die.

HELMER: Ah, my poor friend! Of course I knew he wouldn't be here much longer. But so soon—And then to hide himself away like a wounded animal.

NORA: If it has to happen, then it's best it happens in silence—don't you think so, Torvald?

HELMER *(pacing up and down)*:   He'd grown right into our lives. I simply can't imagine him gone. He with his suffering and loneliness—like a dark cloud setting off our sunlit happiness. Well, maybe it's best this way. For him, at least. *(Standing still.)* And maybe for us too, Nora. Now we're thrown back on each other, completely. *(Embracing her.)* Oh you, my darling wife, how can I hold you close enough? You know what, Nora—time and again I've wished you were in some terrible danger, just so I could stake my life and soul and everything, for your sake.

NORA *(tearing herself away, her voice firm and decisive)*:   Now you must read your mail, Torvald.

HELMER: No, no, not tonight. I want to stay with you, dearest.

NORA: With a dying friend on your mind?

HELMER: You're right. We've both had a shock. There's ugliness between us—these thoughts of death and corruption. We'll have to get free of them first. Until then—we'll stay apart.

NORA *(clinging about his neck)*:   Torvald—good night! Good night!

HELMER *(kissing her on the cheek)*:   Good night, little songbird. Sleep well, Nora. I'll be reading my mail now. *(He takes the letters into his room and shuts the door after him.)*

NORA *(with bewildered glances, groping about, seizing Helmer's domino, throwing it around her, and speaking in short, hoarse, broken whispers)*:   Never see him again. Never, never. *(Putting her shawl over her head.)* Never see the children either — them, too. Never, never. Oh, the freezing black water! The depths — down — Oh, I wish it were over — He has it now; he's reading it — now. Oh no, no, not yet. Torvald, good-bye, you and the children — *(She starts for the hall; as she does, Helmer throws open his door and stands with an open letter in his hand.)*

HELMER: Nora!

NORA *(screams)*:   Oh — !

HELMER: What is this? You know what's in this letter?

NORA: Yes, I know. Let me go! Let me out!

HELMER *(holding her back)*:   Where are you going?

NORA *(struggling to break loose)*:   You can't save me, Torvald!

HELMER *(slumping back)*:   True! Then it's true what he writes? How horrible! No, no, it's impossible — it can't be true.

NORA: It *is* true. I've loved you more than all this world.

HELMER: Ah, none of your slippery tricks.

NORA *(taking one step toward him)*:   Torvald — !

HELMER: What *is* this you've blundered into!

NORA: Just let me loose. You're not going to suffer for my sake. You're not going to take on my guilt.

HELMER: No more play-acting. *(Locks the hall door.)* You stay right here and give me a reckoning. You understand what you've done? Answer! You understand?

NORA *(looking squarely at him, her face hardening)*:   Yes. I'm beginning to understand everything now.

HELMER *(striding about)*:   Oh, what an awful awakening! In all these eight years — she who was my pride and joy — a hypocrite, a liar — worse, worse — a criminal! How infinitely disgusting it all is! The shame! *(Nora says nothing and goes on looking straight at him. He stops in front of her.)* I should have suspected something of the kind. I should have known. All your father's flimsy values — Be still! All your father's flimsy values have come out in you. No religion, no morals, no sense of duty — Oh, how I'm punished for letting him off! I did it for your sake, and you repay me like this.

NORA: Yes, like this.

HELMER: Now you've wrecked all my happiness — ruined my whole future. Oh, it's awful to think of. I'm in a cheap little grafter's hands; he can do anything he wants with me, ask for anything, play with me like a puppet — and I can't breathe a word. I'll be swept down miserably into the depths on account of a featherbrained woman.

NORA: When I'm gone from this world, you'll be free.

HELMER: Oh, quit posing. Your father had a mess of those speeches too. What good would that ever do me if you were gone from this world, as you say? Not the slightest. He can still make the whole thing known; and if he does, I could be falsely suspected as your accomplice. They might even think that I was behind it—that I put you up to it. And all that I can thank you for—you that I've coddled the whole of our marriage. Can you see now what you've done to me?

NORA *(icily calm):*   Yes.

HELMER: It's so incredible, I just can't grasp it. But we'll have to patch up whatever we can. Take off the shawl. I said, take if off! I've got to appease him somehow or other. The thing has to be hushed up at any cost. And as for you and me, it's got to seem like everything between us is just as it was—to the outside world, that is. You'll go right on living in this house, of course. But you can't be allowed to bring up the children; I don't dare trust you with them— Oh, to have to say this to someone I've loved so much! Well, that's done with. From now on happiness doesn't matter; all that matters is saving the bits and pieces, the appearance—*(The doorbell rings. Helmer starts.)* What's that? And so late. Maybe the worst—? You think he'd—? Hide, Nora! Say you're sick. *(Nora remains standing motionless. Helmer goes and opens the door.)*

MAID *(half dressed, in the hall):*   A letter for Mrs. Helmer.

HELMER: I'll take it. *(Snatches the letter and shuts the door.)* Yes, it's from him. You don't get it; I'm reading it myself.

NORA: Then read it.

HELMER *(by the lamp):*   I hardly dare. We may be ruined, you and I. But—I've got to know. *(Rips open the letter, skims through a few lines, glances at an enclosure, then cries out joyfully.)* Nora! *(Nora looks inquiringly at him.)* Nora! Wait—better check it again—Yes, yes, it's true. I'm saved. Nora, I'm saved!

NORA: And I?

HELMER: You too, of course. We're both saved, both of us. Look. He's sent back your note. He says he's sorry and ashamed—that a happy development in his life—oh, who cares what he says! Nora, we're saved! No one can hurt you. Oh, Nora, Nora—but first, this ugliness all has to go. Let me see—*(Takes a look at the note.)* No, I don't want to see it; I want the whole thing to fade like a dream. *(Tears the note and both letters to pieces, throws them into the stove and watches them burn.)* There—now there's nothing left—He wrote that since Christmas Eve you—Oh, they must have been three terrible days for you, Nora.

NORA: I fought a hard fight.

HELMER: And suffered pain and saw no escape but—No, we're not going to dwell on anything unpleasant. We'll just be grateful and keep on repeating: it's over now, it's over! You hear me, Nora? You don't seem to realize—it's over. What's it mean—that frozen look? Oh, poor little Nora, I understand. You can't believe I've forgiven you. But I have, Nora; I swear I have. I know that what you did, you did out of love for me.

NORA: That's true.

HELMER: You loved me the way a wife ought to love her husband. It's simply the means that you couldn't judge. But you think I love you any the less for not knowing how to handle your affairs? No, no — just lean on me; I'll guide you and teach you. I wouldn't be a man if this feminine helplessness didn't make you twice as attractive to me. You mustn't mind those sharp words I said — that was all in the first confusion of thinking my world had collapsed. I've forgiven you, Nora; I swear I've forgiven you.

NORA: My thanks for your forgiveness. *(She goes out through the door, right.)*

HELMER: No, wait — *(Peers in.)* What are you doing in there?

NORA *(inside)*:   Getting out of my costume.

HELMER *(by the open door)*:   Yes, do that. Try to calm yourself and collect your thoughts again, my frightened little songbird. You can rest easy now; I've got wide wings to shelter you with. *(Walking about close by the door.)* How snug and nice our home is, Nora. You're safe here; I'll keep you like a hunted dove I've rescued out of a hawk's claws. I'll bring peace to your poor, shuddering heart. Gradually it'll happen, Nora; you'll see. Tomorrow all this will look different to you; then everything will be as it was. I won't have to go on repeating I forgive you; you'll feel it for yourself. How can you imagine I'd ever conceivably want to disown you — or even blame you in any way? Ah, you don't know a man's heart, Nora. For a man there's something indescribably sweet and satisfying in knowing he's forgiven his wife — and forgiven her out of a full and open heart. It's as if she belongs to him in two ways now: in a sense he's given her fresh into the world again, and she's become his wife and his child as well. From now on that's what you'll be to me — you little, bewildered, helpless thing. Don't be afraid of anything, Nora; just open your heart to me, and I'll be conscience and will to you both — *(Nora enters in her regular clothes.)* What's this? Not in bed? You've changed your dress?

NORA: Yes, Torvald, I've changed my dress.

HELMER: But why now, so late?

NORA: Tonight I'm not sleeping.

HELMER: But Nora dear —

NORA *(looking at her watch)*:   It's still not so very late. Sit down, Torvald; we have a lot to talk over. *(She sits at one side of the table.)*

HELMER: Nora — what is this? That hard expression —

NORA: Sit down. This'll take some time. I have a lot to say.

HELMER *(sitting at the table directly opposite her)*:   You worry me, Nora. And I don't understand you.

NORA: No, that's exactly it. You don't understand me. And I've never understood you either — until tonight. No, don't interrupt. You can just listen to what I say. We're closing out accounts, Torvald.

HELMER: How do you mean that?

NORA *(after a short pause)*:   Doesn't anything strike you about our sitting here like this?

HELMER: What's that?

NORA: We've been married now eight years. Doesn't it occur to you that this is the first time we two, you and I, man and wife, have ever talked seriously together?

HELMER: What do you mean — seriously?

NORA: In eight whole years — longer even — right from our first acquaintance, we've never exchanged a serious word on any serious thing.

HELMER: You mean I should constantly go and involve you in problems you couldn't possibly help me with?

NORA: I'm not talking of problems. I'm saying that we've never sat down seriously together and tried to get to the bottom of anything.

HELMER: But dearest, what good would that ever do you?

NORA: That's the point right there: you've never understood me. I've been wronged greatly, Torvald — first by Papa, and then by you.

HELMER: What! By us — the two people who've loved you more than anyone else?

NORA *(shaking her head)*:   You never loved me. You've thought it fun to be in love with me, that's all.

HELMER: Nora, what a thing to say!

NORA: Yes, it's true now, Torvald. When I lived at home with Papa, he told me all his opinions, so I had the same ones too; or if they were different I hid them, since he wouldn't have cared for that. He used to call me his doll-child, and he played with me the way I played with my dolls. Then I came into your house —

HELMER: How can you speak of our marriage like that?

NORA *(unperturbed)*:   I mean, then I went from Papa's hands into yours. You arranged everything to your own taste, and so I got the same taste as you — or I pretended to; I can't remember. I guess a little of both, first one, then the other. Now when I look back, it seems as if I'd lived here like a beggar — just from hand to mouth. I've lived by doing tricks for you, Torvald. But that's the way you wanted it. It's a great sin what you and Papa did to me. You're to blame that nothing's become of me.

HELMER: Nora, how unfair and ungrateful you are! Haven't you been happy here?

NORA: No, never. I thought so — but I never have.

HELMER: Not — not happy!

NORA: No, only lighthearted. And you've always been so kind to me. But our home's been nothing but a playpen. I've been your doll-wife here, just as at home I was Papa's doll-child. And in turn the children have been my dolls. I thought it was fun when you played with me, just as they thought it fun when I played with them. That's been our marriage, Torvald.

HELMER: There's some truth in what you're saying — under all the raving exaggeration. But it'll all be different after this. Playtime's over; now for the schooling.

NORA: Whose schooling — mine or the children's?

HELMER: Both yours and the children's, dearest.

NORA: Oh, Torvald, you're not the man to teach me to be a good wife to you.

HELMER: And you can say that?

NORA: And I — how am I equipped to bring up children?

HELMER: Nora!

NORA: Didn't you say a moment ago that that was no job to trust me with?

HELMER: In a flare of temper! Why fasten on that?

NORA: Yes, but you were so very right. I'm not up to the job. There's another job I have to do first. I have to try to educate myself. You can't help me with that. I've got to do it alone. And that's why I'm leaving you now.

HELMER *(jumping up)*:   What's that?

NORA: I have to stand completely alone, if I'm ever going to discover myself and the world out there. So I can't go on living with you.

HELMER: Nora, Nora!

NORA: I want to leave right away. Kristine should put me up for the night —

HELMER: You're insane! You've no right! I forbid you!

NORA: From here on, there's no use forbidding me anything. I'll take with me whatever is mine. I don't want a thing from you, either now or later.

HELMER: What kind of madness is this!

NORA: Tomorrow I'm going home — I mean, home where I came from. It'll be easier up there to find something to do.

HELMER: Oh, you blind, incompetent child!

NORA: I must learn to be competent, Torvald.

HELMER: Abandon your home, your husband, your children! And you're not even thinking what people will say.

NORA: I can't be concerned about that. I only know how essential this is.

HELMER: Oh, it's outrageous. So you'll run out like this on your most sacred vows.

NORA: What do you think are my most sacred vows?

HELMER: And I have to tell you that! Aren't they your duties to your husband and children?

NORA: I have other duties equally sacred.

HELMER: That isn't true. What duties are they?

NORA: Duties to myself.

HELMER: Before all else, you're a wife and mother.

NORA: I don't believe in that anymore. I believe that, before all else, I'm a human being, no less than you — or anyway, I ought to try to become one. I know the majority thinks you're right, Torvald, and plenty of books agree with you, too. But I can't go on believing what the majority says, or what's written in books. I have to think over these things myself and try to understand them.

HELMER: Why can't you understand your place in your own home? On a point like that, isn't there one everlasting guide you can turn to? Where's your religion?

NORA: Oh, Torvald, I'm really not sure what religion is.

HELMER: What —?

NORA: I only know what the minister said when I was confirmed. He told me religion was this thing and that. When I get clear and away by myself, I'll go into that problem too. I'll see if what the minister said was right, or, in any case, if it's right for me.

HELMER: A young woman your age shouldn't talk like that. If religion can't move you, I can try to rouse your conscience. You do have some moral feeling? Or, tell me — has that gone too?

NORA: It's not easy to answer that, Torvald. I simply don't know. I'm all confused about these things. I just know I see them so differently from you. I find out, for one thing, that the law's not at all what I'd thought—but I can't get it through my head that the law is fair. A woman hasn't a right to protect her dying father or save her husband's life! I can't believe that.

HELMER: You talk like a child. You don't know anything of the world you live in.

NORA: No, I don't. But now I'll begin to learn for myself. I'll try to discover who's right, the world or I.

HELMER: Nora, you're sick; you've got a fever. I almost think you're out of your head.

NORA: I've never felt more clearheaded and sure in my life.

HELMER: And—clearheaded and sure—you're leaving your husband and children?

NORA: Yes.

HELMER: Then there's only one possible reason.

NORA: What?

HELMER: You no longer love me.

NORA: No. That's exactly it.

HELMER: Nora! You can't be serious!

NORA: Oh, this is so hard, Torvald—you've been so kind to me always. But I can't help it. I don't love you anymore.

HELMER (*struggling for composure*): Are you also clearheaded and sure about that?

NORA: Yes, completely. That's why I can't go on staying here.

HELMER: Can you tell me what I did to lose your love?

NORA: Yes, I can tell you. It was this evening when the miraculous thing didn't come—then I knew you weren't the man I'd imagined.

HELMER: Be more explicit; I don't follow you.

NORA: I've waited now so patiently eight long years—for, my Lord, I know miracles don't come every day. Then this crisis broke over me, and such a certainty filled me: *now* the miraculous event would occur. While Krogstad's letter was lying out there, I never for an instant dreamed that you could give in to his terms. I was so utterly sure you'd say to him: go on, tell your tale to the whole wide world. And when he'd done that—

HELMER: Yes, what then? When I'd delivered my own wife into shame and disgrace—

NORA: When he'd done that, I was so utterly sure that you'd step forward, take the blame on yourself and say: I am the guilty one.

HELMER: Nora—!

NORA: You're thinking I'd never accept such a sacrifice from you? No, of course not. But what good would my protests be against you? That was the miracle I was waiting for, in terror and hope. And to stave that off, I would have taken my life.

HELMER: I'd gladly work for you day and night, Nora—and take on pain and deprivation. But there's no one who gives up honor for love.

NORA: Millions of women have done just that.

HELMER: Oh, you think and talk like a silly child.

NORA: Perhaps. But you neither think nor talk like the man I could join myself to. When your big fright was over — and it wasn't from any threat against me, only for what might damage you — when all the danger was past, for you it was just as if nothing had happened. I was exactly the same, your little lark, your doll, that you'd have to handle with double care now that I'd turned out so brittle and frail. *(Gets up.)* Torvald — in that instant it dawned on me that for eight years I've been living here with a stranger, and that I've even conceived three children — oh, I can't stand the thought of it! I could tear myself to bits.

HELMER *(heavily):*   I see. There a gulf that's opened between us — that's clear. Oh, but Nora, can't we bridge it somehow?

NORA: The way I am now, I'm no wife for you.

HELMER: I have the strength to make myself over.

NORA: Maybe — if your doll gets taken away.

HELMER: But to part! To part from you! No, Nora no — I can't imagine it.

NORA *(going out, right):*   All the more reason why it has to be. *(She reenters with her coat and a small overnight bag, which she puts on a chair by the table.)*

HELMER: Nora, Nora, not now! Wait till tomorrow.

NORA: I can't spend the night in a strange man's room.

HELMER: But couldn't we live here like brother and sister —

NORA: You know very well how long that would last. *(Throws her shawl about her.)* Good-bye, Torvald. I won't look in on the children. I know they're in better hands than mine. The way I am now, I'm no use to them.

HELMER: But someday, Nora — someday — ?

NORA: How can I tell? I haven't the least idea what'll become of me.

HELMER: But you're my wife, now and wherever you go.

NORA: Listen, Torvald — I've heard that when a wife deserts her husband's house just as I'm doing, then the law frees him from all responsibility. In any case, I'm freeing you from being responsible. Don't feel yourself bound, any more than I will. There has to be absolute freedom for us both. Here, take your ring back. Give me mine.

HELMER: That too?

NORA: That too.

HELMER: There it is.

NORA: Good. Well, now it's all over. I'm putting the keys here. The maids know all about keeping up the house — better than I do. Tomorrow, after I've left town, Kristine will stop by to pack up everything that's mine from home. I'd like those things shipped up to me.

HELMER: Over! All over! Nora, won't you ever think about me?

NORA: I'm sure I'll think of you often, and about the children and the house here.

HELMER: May I write you?

NORA: No — never. You're not to do that.

HELMER: Oh, but let me send you —

NORA: Nothing. Nothing.

HELMER: Or help you if you need it.

NORA: No. I accept nothing from strangers.

HELMER: Nora — can I never be more than a stranger to you?

NORA *(picking up her overnight bag):*   Ah, Torvald — it would take the greatest miracle of all —

HELMER: Tell me the greatest miracle!

NORA: You and I both would have to transform ourselves to the point that — Oh, Torvald, I've stopped believing in miracles.

HELMER: But I'll believe. Tell me! Transform ourselves to the point that — ?

NORA: That our living together could be a true marriage. *(She goes out down the hall.)*

HELMER *(sinks down on a chair by the door, face buried in his hands):*   Nora! Nora! *(Looking about and rising.)* Empty. She's gone. *(A sudden hope leaps in him.)* The greatest miracle — ?

From below, the sound of a door slamming shut.   [1879]

THINKING ABOUT THE TEXT

1. Critics disagree about the necessity for Nora's leaving. What would your advice to her be? One critic thinks she has to because Torvald is impossible. What do you think?

2. Do you find credible the change in Nora's character from the first scene to the last? Do you know people who have transformed themselves?

3. Is Torvald in love with Nora in the first act? Explain. Is Nora in love with him in the first act? What is your idea of love in a marriage?

4. An early critic of the play claims that it is a comedy. Is this possible? How would you characterize it? Is it an optimistic or a pessimistic play? Is it tragic?

5. A few critics think Nora will return. Do you think this is possible? Under what conditions would you counsel her to do so? Do you think the "door heard 'round the world" had a positive or negative effect on marriage?

HENRIETTA FRANCES LORD
From "The Life of Henrik Ibsen"

Henrietta Frances Lord was the first English translator of Ibsen's A Doll House. *The following excerpt is from the introductory essay to her 1882 translation, which she titled* Nora.

Some of the clearest light Ibsen has so far shed on marriage we get from *Nora*. The problem is set in its purest form; no unfavourable circumstances hinder the working out of marriage; nor does the temper of Nora or Helmer; both are well fitted for married life, and everything points to their being naturally suited to each other. The hindrance lies exclusively in the application of a false view of life, or — if some insist it once contained truth — a view that Western peoples have out-lived. When Helmer said he would work night and day for his wife, his were no empty words. He had done it, he meant to do it; he had been faithfully working for eight years, and there is no sign that he meant to cease. His happiness lay in Nora's being unruffled. Nor would he dream of curtailing what *he* considers her wife's freedom, *i.e.* the happy play of her imagination. He would deprive her but of one thing — reality. How could he claim to be a "real man," he would say, if he gave it to her? And he so far succeeds in unfitting her for action, that when she takes upon herself to meddle in realities, she immediately commits a crime. He gives her everything but his confidence; not because he has anything to conceal, but because she is a woman. . . .

The idea in *Nora* is: the object of marriage is to make each human personality free. However incontrovertible this may be when laid down as an axiom, does that confer the power of giving it expression in real life, steering one's way among all the difficulties of deceit, inexperience, etc.? Doubtless not; but the poet's work tells us, until the relation between man and woman turns in this direction, the relation is not yet Love. This is the idea in *Nora*, freed from all side issues, and no other key will unlock it.   [1882]

CLEMENT SCOTT
"Ibsen's Unlovely Creed"

Clement Scott (1841–1904), the editor of the journal Theatre, *published "A Doll's House" in the July 1889 issue. This article was a lengthy attack on Ibsen's ten-year-old play.*

It is an unlovely, selfish creed — but let women hear it. Nora, when she finds her husband is not the ideal hero she imagined, determines to cap his egotism with her selfishness. It is to be an eye for an eye, a tooth for a tooth. Pardon she cannot grant, humiliation she will not recognise. The frivolous butterfly, the Swedish Frou-Frou, the spoiled plaything has mysteriously become an Ibsenite revivalist. There were no previous signs of her conversion, but she has exchanged playfulness for preaching. She, a loving, affectionate woman, forgets about the eight years' happy married life, forgets the nest of the little bird, forgets her duty, her very instinct as a mother, forgets the three innocent children who are asleep in the next room, forgets her responsibilities, and does a thing that one of the lower animals would not do. A cat or dog would tear any one who separated it from its offspring, but the socialistic Nora, the apostle of the new creed of humanity, leaves her children almost without a pang. She has determined to leave her home. . . .

It is all self, self, self! This is the ideal woman of the new creed; not a woman who is the fountain of love and forgiveness and charity, not the pattern woman we have admired in our mothers and our sisters, not the model of unselfishness and charity, but a mass of aggregate conceit and self-sufficiency, who leaves her home and deserts her friendless children because she has *herself* to look after. The "strange man" who is the father of her children has dared to misunderstand her; she will scorn his regrets and punish him. Why should the men have it all their own way, and why should women be bored with the love of their children when they have themselves to study? And so Nora goes out, delivers up her wedding-ring without a sigh, quits her children without a kiss, and bangs the door! And the husband cries, "A miracle! a miracle!" and well he may. It would be a miracle, if he could ever live again with so unnatural a creature.   [1889]

HERMANN J. WEIGAND
From *The Modern Ibsen*

Hermann J. Weigand (1892–1985) wrote one of the first full-length studies of Ibsen, The Modern Ibsen *(1925). To contemporary readers, Weigand's thesis that Ibsen wrote* A Doll House *as a comedy seems odd indeed. But in the 1920s, Weigand was a respected academic critic and his ideas were influential.*

If I have been successful in showing "A Doll's House" to be high comedy of the subtlest order up to this point, our vision will not be put to any particular strain to see the genius of comedy hovering over the scene of the settlement. If we see Torvald as neither a cad nor a villain, but as a worthy, honest citizen as citizens go, a careful provider, a doting husband, unimaginative, but scarcely a shade less so than the average male, self-complacent and addicted to heroic stage-play—a habit fostered by the uncritical adoration of his mate; if Nora is to us not the tragic heroine as which she is commonly pictured, but an irresistibly bewitching piece of femininity, an extravagant poet and romancer, utterly lacking in sense of fact, and endowed with a natural gift for play-acting which makes her instinctively dramatize her experiences:—how can the settlement fail of a fundamentally comic appeal? We can follow Nora's indictment of Torvald and conventional man-governed society with the most alert sympathy; we can be thrilled by her spirited gesture of emancipation; we can applaud her bravery; we can enjoy watching Torvald's bluffed expression turn gradually into a hangdog look of contrition as he winces under her trouncing and gets worsted in every phase of the argument: and we will be aware at the same time that Nora is enjoying the greatest moment of her life—the supreme thrill that is tantamount, in fact, to a fulfillment of her hunger for the miracle!

Not the least among the items contributing to the comedy is the fact that Nora scores with even the most questionable of her accusations, thanks to the dash of her unexpected invective. "You have never understood me," she charges. Nothing could be truer; but how was he to understand her, when she played the lark and the squirrel with such spontaneous zest? How was he to divine her capacity for devotion, when she delighted in acting the incorrigible spendthrift, when it amused her to make him believe that the money he gave her simply melted between her fingers, when she played a perpetual game of hide-and-seek—and played it so effectively because play-acting was second nature to her? Now she blames him for not having treated her as a serious, responsible person, whereas all her efforts had heretofore been bent on appearing charmingly irresponsible. Past master of the arts of feminine coquetry, she is fully persuaded that she has cultivated these little tricks only under the pressure of male egotism, as if they were not a fundamental part of her instinctive endowment. And she gravely distributes the blame for having made the desire to please the supreme rule of her conduct, between Torvald and her father. Incidentally, her charge that in all the years of their marriage they have never exchanged one serious word about serious things, is incorrect: she has quite forgotten how seriously Torvald lectured her on the subjects of forgery and lying less than three days ago. If what she means is rather that they have never discussed any of their domestic problems in the spirit of serious partnership, it would seem that she were at least as much to blame for this as Torvald. Similarly, when she claims that her tastes in all matters are nothing but a reflection of those of her husband, she is certainly deluding herself. She very cleverly inculcated the idea in Torvald that she was dependent on his counsel even in such matters as choosing a fancy dress costume; but to be convinced that it is in reality her taste which is reflected in the cozy interior of their flat, scarcely requires so direct a hint as her chatter in the first scene, where she says: "And now I'll tell you how I think we ought to plan things, Torvald. As soon as Christmas is over . . ." The ring at the door cuts her short, but we can wager that she had a whole bagful of suggestions on refurnishing and redecorating the apartment on a scale in keeping with their enlarged income; and Torvald would not be the man he is, if he did not follow the lead of his little charmer.

She has never been happy, she now discovers. She had thought herself happy for eight years, but now it appears that she has been only merry. You are mistaken, dear Nora, we are obliged to reply. If your happiness now turns out to have been based on an illusion, its present collapse can not touch feelings that have become part of the irrevocable past. As we see, Nora brings the same intense will-to-believe to the reinterpretation of her past, as had supported her so recently in her expectation of the miracle. She is the same play-acting, hysterical Nora she always was, only: she has now changed her dress.

There is melodrama in Nora's calm announcement that she is going to leave her husband. She extracts all the thrills she possibly can from the situation. She has lived with a strange man for eight years, and borne three children to a stranger; she will not stay another night under a stranger's roof; she will not take a cent of Torvald's money, for she accepts no gifts from strangers; he must not even write to her; she returns his ring and demands her own, as a symbol of the total severance of their relations. Even the thought of her children, to whom she is devotedly attached, can not budge her from her determination. "I know they are in better hands than mine," she says, referring evidently to the old nursemaid of whose educative talent Nora is herself the most striking product.

One miracle Nora has undeniably accomplished. She has seen her husband, strutting lately in a pose of self-complacent heroism, wilt under the withering fire of her words. She has seen his conceited pride shrink and dwindle and disappear altogether. She has seen his face register shame, contrition and abject humility.

5

The suggestive power of the words in which she voiced her sense of injury has been so intense as to turn his initial resistance into a complete rout. Succumbing to the hypnotic spell of her personality, he accepts her version of the facts as the truth. (And there is not a reader of "A Doll's House," I daresay, who has not equally succumbed to that spell at one time or other.) When Nora makes her dramatic exit, she is conscious of having scored a complete psychological victory. Torvald's final gesture is one of unconditional surrender.

The conclusion is skillfully timed. The drop of the curtain finds us in a state of comic elation; for, whatever we think of the logic of Nora's arguments, we enjoy the victory of the superior, if erratic individual over the representative of commonplace respectability. And we are the less inclined to begrudge Nora the completeness of her triumph, as our imagination leaps ahead to speculate on the reaction that is bound to set in on the next day.

I would not predict with dogmatic certainty what is going to happen. It is barely possible that not even Christina's sober counsels will succeed in dissuading Nora from leaving her home. In that case, granted that she succeeds in finding employment, will she find the tedium of the daily routine endurable? Working in earnest for a living will not provide any of the thrills of those nights of secret copy-work that made her remark to Christina: "Sometimes I was so tired, so tired. And yet it was so awfully amusing to work in that way and earn money. I almost felt as if I were a man." It is hard to picture Nora as a bank clerk or a telephone operator, but it is harder to think of her playing the part for more than three days at a time. Other possibilities come to mind, too. One can choose to think of Nora taking to the lecture platform, agitating for the emancipation of woman. Or, again, she may find a lover and weave new romances about a new hero.

But personally I am convinced that after putting Torvald through a sufficiently protracted ordeal of suspense, Nora will yield to his entreaties and return home — on her own terms. She will not bear the separation from her children very long, and her love for Torvald, which is not as dead as she thinks, will reassert itself. For a time the tables will be reversed: a meek and chastened husband will eat out of the hand of his squirrel; and Nora, hoping to make up by a sudden spurt of zeal for twenty-eight years of lost time, will be trying desperately hard to grow up. I doubt, however, whether her volatile enthusiasm will even carry her beyond the stage of resolutions. The charm of novelty worn off, she will tire of the new game very rapidly and revert, imperceptibly, to her role of song-bird and charmer, as affording an unlimited range to the exercise of her inborn talents of coquetry and play-acting. [1925]

KATHERINE M. ROGERS
From "Feminism and A Doll House"

The following excerpt is from "Feminism and A Doll House," *an essay by Katherine M. Rogers (b. 1932) that was included in the collection* Approaches to Teaching Ibsen's A Doll House *(1985).*

. . . In the context of a women's studies course, the critical opinion that Ibsen was not concerned specifically with women's freedom in *A Doll House* has no credibility. Nevertheless, at some point we consider his famous declaration, in his "Speech at the Banquet of the Norwegian League for Women's Rights" (1898), that he never "consciously worked for the women's rights movement" and was "not even quite clear as to just what this women's rights movement really is." This statement can easily be explained by Ibsen's dislike for party affiliation, his objection to being reduced from an artist to a propagandist, and his belief that the important thing is human development rather than specific political rights. It is valuable to make this point in women's studies courses, which tend to become overpoliticized. Our students should also be reminded of the differences between their attitudes and those of the original audience of 1879, who would not have considered the Helmer marriage so obviously bad or Torvald's complacency self-evidently ludicrous. In fact, Ibsen was concerned lest the audience sympathize entirely with Torvald, and he therefore purposely overwrote Torvald's lines — with the result that Torvald seems a caricature today and Nora's admiration for him seems fatuous. Similarly, we must not let contemporary enthusiasm for liberation lead us to oversimplify the ending into a happy triumph. Thinking of Nora's painful disillusionment, her parting from her children, and the uncertainties of her future independent career, Ibsen called his play "the tragedy of modern times."

But most of our class time is spent exploring the major feminist issues raised in the play, first analyzing what Ibsen says about them and then evaluating his presentation in terms of our own experience. Looking beyond the differences in property laws and modes of speech between Ibsen's time and our own, we see how the economic dependency, patriarchal rationalizations, and chivalric illusions that Ibsen so brilliantly anatomized in the nineteenth-century Helmer marriage continue to influence men's and women's attitudes today.

Immediately in the opening dialogue, Torvald lectures Nora about squandering his money and doles out to her the amount he thinks proper; and Nora petitions and excuses her expenditures — just like the beggar she ultimately recognizes herself to be. Thus Ibsen shows us how economic dependence degrades women in a society where respect is based on earning power, where unpaid work in the home is not considered work. Ibsen goes on to slow the exhilarating freedom, traditionally denied women, of having one's own money — when Nora asks for money as a Christmas present (and Torvald would rather give her anything else) or when she confides that she enjoyed the copying work she did at night because it made her feel like a man. Kristine, who was forced to marry to support her family, and Anne-Marie, who was forced to give up her child to support herself, round out the picture of women's economic helplessness. Having explored what Ibsen said about economic oppression, we ask ourselves whether the conditions he exposed still prevail: To what extent do men still control money in the home and in society at large? Are women still thought to be doing nothing when they merely run their households? Are such women generally considered parasitic and extravagant? How many men are still more comfortable with dependent wives than with independent ones?

We then analyze the patriarchal rationalizations that govern Torvald's treatment of Nora—his assumption that logic and responsibility pertain to men, his
belief that male honor is supremely important while female honor is too negligible to mention, his self-congratulation on the heroism with which he would
defend her should the need arise. We note that he appreciates Nora's real or supposed deficiencies because he needs something to belittle her for. We proceed
from there to the destructive interplay between Torvald and Nora—for of course
he could not be what he is if she did not constantly feed his self-importance.
When he orders her not to eat macaroons, she meekly agrees, then disobeys and
lies to him like a naughty child (thus behaving in a way that would reinforce his
feelings of superiority, if he should find out). When she wants something from
him, she flatters and manipulates instead of asking directly, as an equal. She
proves his charge that she does not understand the society she lives in when she
declares her indifference to the well-being of anyone outside her family and defiantly asserts that the law would never prosecute the mother of three little children. Concealing her competence and strength, Nora makes every effort to
appear the twittering lark Torvald believes and wants her to be.

Their relationship leads us to consider how couples reinforce each other's   5
destructive behavior patterns and whether an oppressive or exploitative situation
is possible without mutual connivance. We decide how much Nora's limitations
are merely assumed by those who wish to patronize her (Torvald's assurance that
she cannot deal with serious problems) and how much they are real (her blind
confidence in her husband's strength and wisdom). To the extent that they are
real, we look into their social causes—for example, limited education and experience confine one's sympathies; lack of authority encourages one to resort to lies
and tricks to gain one's ends. We may contrast Nora with Kristine, a woman who
has been forced to live in a hard world (and who also starts out patronizing Nora).

What my students find hardest to accept in Nora is her romantic illusion that
Torvald will assume responsibility for her forgery; it strikes them as a ridiculously
unwarranted expectation, as well as a humiliating admission of feminine weakness. We must recognize that Ibsen's deflation of romantic chivalry, which seems
far-fetched and pointless now, was necessary in the nineteenth century, when
chivalry was pervasively used to conceal the domination and exploitation of
women. Having implied from the beginning the falsities of nineteenth-century
patriarchal marriage, in which the husband protects his wife from life in return
for her uncritical admiration and dependence, Ibsen clinches his point by subjecting masculine heroism to a test and showing that a woman cannot in fact trust
it to protect her. Nora's longing for a romantic hero who will save her is not only
demeaning; it cannot be fulfilled because it is false. Once required to sacrifice
something to his grandiose ideals, Torvald dismisses love and heroics as irrelevant
and chides Nora for her faith in them. Men teach women that love is all-important
and pretend to believe it themselves, but they soon enough reveal their disbelief
when put to the test. Nora, confined to private life, has simply taken at face value
the myths she has been taught about romantic love. While the ideal of chivalry
may no longer be sufficiently credited to be worth attacking. we can profitably
discuss other aspects of idealized romantic love. What is the difference between

loving and being in love with? Must traditional romantic expectations be changed if marriage is to become egalitarian?

Having accounted for Nora's romantic illusions about her breach of the law, we concentrate on those aspects of her behavior that persist in ourselves. This can be a useful exercise in self-knowledge. I confess that on seeing A *Doll House* for the first time I was actually filled with rage — it must have been because I saw too much of myself in Nora, being patronized and acquiescing in that patronage. We would like to believe that we have nothing in common with the little lark, but how many of us are altogether liberated from traditional sexual role-playing? How effectively do we deal with men's assumptions of superiority? Don't we, in fact, sometimes confirm those assumptions by acting cute or use them to flatter men into giving us what we want? Do we always react appropriately to belittlement if the tone is playful? Are we not occasionally tempted to forgo equality for sexual tributes and chivalrous protectiveness, even though we are more aware than Nora of the diminution these imply?

Finally, our class discusses two general moral issues important to feminists. First, do we agree with Ibsen's opinion, stated in his preliminary notes and dramatized in the play, that women and men have completely different concepts of law and conscience? Or should we attribute it to sexual stereotyping, based on the fact that most of the women he knew were confined to private life? If there are differences, are they natural or acquired? Have the increased education and experience of women since Nora's day changed their concepts of justice? Men have defined justice in abstract and sociological terms, ignoring the values important to women and then finding women wanting. Should women disprove masculine sneers by proving they can understand abstract justice as clearly as men can? Or should they strive to realize a new standard where consideration for a sick husband or a dying father outweighs the letter of the law? Do women naturally respond more to the concrete, the personal, the familial? And if so, should they use this sensitivity to modify society's concept of justice?

Second, there is the even more fundamental issue of duty to oneself, an issue that becomes ever more acute as women become increasingly unwilling to sacrifice themselves to the family. If women put their self-realization first, as men have traditionally done, what will happen to dependent others? The conflict between Nora's duty to herself and her duty to her children (if not to Torvald) must not be minimized. Can women take care of their duty to their children by redividing responsibilities in the home? Is everyone's first duty, as Nora comes to feel, to think out his or her own values and face reality without illusions? Is this self-development, in fact, necessary for adequacy as a parent? Can a woman who is not a mature human being be a good mother? (In this connection I mention Ibsen's suggestion, in his notes for A *Doll House*, that many nineteenth-century mothers might well go away and die, like insects, once they had completed the work of physical propagation.) How can one reconcile necessary self-realization with fulfilling the obligations of conventional social roles? (Torvald, Nora says, must learn to live independently of her as she must of him.) How can one be independent in marriage? How is it that Kristine will apparently find fulfillment in the relationship that Nora must reject in order to find herself? What is the difference between the

Helmer marriage (and Kristine's first one, where she "sold herself" for her dependent mother and brothers) and the one she will make with Krogstad, since there too she will be working for him and his children?

In short, I try to make my students see how Ibsen illuminates the way women   10
and men still interact, raises questions that still need to be asked, and suggests answers that still apply. *A Doll House* continues to remind us that we are not as liberated as we would like to believe.   [1985]

JOAN TEMPLETON

From "The Doll House *Backlash: Criticism, Feminism, and Ibsen"*

Joan Templeton (b. 1940), a professor and critic, published "The Doll House *Backlash: Criticism, Feminism, and Ibsen," in the academic journal* PMLA *in January 1989. The following is an excerpt from that essay.*

The a priori dismissal of women's rights as the subject of *A Doll House* is a gentlemanly backlash, a refusal to acknowledge the existence of a tiresome reality, "the hoary problem of women's rights," as Michael Meyer has it; the issue is decidedly *vieux jeu,*° and its importance has been greatly exaggerated. In Ibsen's timeless world of Everyman, questions of gender can only be tedious intrusions.

But for over a hundred years, Nora has been under direct siege as exhibiting the most perfidious characteristics of her sex; the original outcry of the 1880s is swollen now to a mighty chorus of blame. She is denounced as an irrational and frivolous narcissist; an "abnormal" woman, a "hysteric"; a vain, unloving egoist who abandons her family in a paroxysm of selfishness. The proponents of the last view would seem to think Ibsen had in mind a housewife Medea, whose cruelty to husband and children he tailored down to fit the framed, domestic world of realist drama.

The first attacks were launched against Nora on moral grounds and against Ibsen, ostensibly, on "literary" ones. The outraged reviewers of the premiere claimed that *A Doll House* did not have to be taken as a serious statement about women's rights because the heroine of Act III is an incomprehensible transformation of the heroine of Acts I and II. This reasoning provided an ideal way to dismiss Nora altogether; nothing she said needed to be taken seriously, and her door slamming could be written off as silly theatrics.

The argument for the two Noras, which still remains popular, has had its most determined defender in the Norwegian scholar Else Høst, who argues that Ibsen's carefree, charming "lark" could never have become the "newly fledged, feminist." In any case it is the "childish, expectant, ecstatic, broken-hearted Nora" who makes *A Doll House* immortal; the other one, the unfeeling woman

vieux jeu: Old hat.

of Act III who coldly analyzes the flaws in her marriage, is psychologically unconvincing and wholly unsympathetic.

The most unrelenting attempt on record to trivialize Ibsen's protagonist, and   5
a favorite source for Nora's later detractors, is Hermann Weigand's. In a classic 1925 study, Weigand labors through forty-nine pages to demonstrate that Ibsen conceived of Nora as a silly, lovable female. At the beginning, Weigand confesses, he was, like all men, momentarily shaken by the play: "Having had the misfortune to be born of the male sex, we slink away in shame, vowing to mend our ways." The chastened critic's remorse is short-lived, however, as a "clear male voice, irreverently breaking the silence," stuns with its critical acumen: "'The meaning of the final scene,' the voice says, 'is epitomized by Nora's remark: "Yes, Torvald. Now I have changed my dress."'" With this epiphany as guide, Weigand spends the night poring over the "little volume." Dawn arrives, bringing with it the return of "masculine self-respect." For there is only one explanation for the revolt of "this winsome little woman" and her childish door slamming: Ibsen meant *A Doll House* as comedy. Nora's erratic behavior at the curtain's fall leaves us laughing heartily, for there is no doubt that she will return home to "revert, imperceptibly, to her role of songbird and charmer," After all, since Nora is

> an irresistibly bewitching piece of femininity, an extravagant poet and romancer, utterly lacking in sense of fact, and endowed with a natural gift for play-acting which makes her instinctively dramatize her experiences: how can the settlement fail of a fundamentally comic appeal?

The most popular way to render Nora inconsequential has been to attack her morality; whatever the vocabulary used, the arguments have remained much the same for over a century. Oswald Crawford, writing in the *Fortnightly Review* in 1891, scolded that while Nora may be "charming as doll-women may be charming," she is "unprincipled." A half century later, after Freudianism had produced a widely accepted "clinical" language of disapproval, Nora could be called "abnormal." Mary McCarthy lists Nora as one of the "neurotic" women whom Ibsen, she curiously claims, was the first playwright to put on stage. For Maurice Valency, Nora is a case study of female hysteria, a willful, unwomanly woman: "Nora is a carefully studied example of what we have come to know as the hysterical personality—bright, unstable, impulsive, romantic, quite immune from feelings of guilt, and, at bottom, not especially feminine."

More recent assaults on Nora have argued that her forgery to obtain the money to save her husband's life proves her irresponsibility and egotism. Brian Johnston condemns Nora's love as "unintelligent" and her crime as "a trivial act which nevertheless turns to evil because it refused to take the universal ethical realm into consideration at all"; Ibsen uses Torvald's famous pet names for Nora—lark, squirrel—to give her a "strong 'animal' identity" and to underscore her inability to understand the ethical issues faced by human beings. Evert Sprinchorn argues that Nora had only to ask her husband's kindly friends (entirely missing from the play) for the necessary money: ". . . any other woman would have done so. But Nora knew that if she turned to one of Torvald's friends for help, she would have had to share her role of savior with someone else."

Even Nora's sweet tooth is evidence of her unworthiness, as we see her "surreptitiously devouring the forbidden [by her husband] macaroons," even "brazenly offer[ing] macaroons to Doctor Rank, and finally lying in her denial that the macaroons are hers"; eating macaroons in secret suggests that "Nora is deceitful and manipulative from the start" and that her exit thus "reflects only a petulant woman's irresponsibility." As she eats the cookies, Nora adds insult to injury by declaring her hidden wish to say "death and damnation" in front of her husband, thus revealing, according to Brian Downs, of Christ's College, Cambridge, "something a trifle febrile and morbid" in her nature.

Much has been made of Nora's relationship with Doctor Rank, the surest proof, it is argued, of her dishonesty. Nora is revealed as *la belle dame sans merci°* when she "suggestively queries Rank whether a pair of silk stockings will fit her"; she "flirts cruelly with [him] and toys with his affection for her, drawing him on to find out how strong her hold over him actually is."

Nora's detractors have often been, from the first, her husband's defenders. In an argument that claims to rescue Nora and Torvald from "the campaign for the liberation of women" so that they "become vivid and disturbingly real," Evert Sprinchorn pleads that Torvald "has given Nora all the material things and all the sexual attention that any young wife could reasonably desire. He loves beautiful things, and not least his pretty wife." Nora is incapable of appreciating her husband because she "is not a normal woman. She is compulsive, highly imaginative, and very much inclined to go to extremes." Since it is she who has acquired the money to save his life, Torvald, and not Nora, is really the "wife in the family," although he "has regarded himself as the breadwinner . . . the main support of his wife and children, as any decent husband would like to regard himself." In another defense, John Chamberlain argues that Torvald deserves our sympathy because he is no "mere common or garden chauvinist." If Nora were less the actress Weigand has proved her to be, "the woman in her might observe what the embarrassingly naive feminist overlooks or ignores, namely, the indications that Torvald, for all his faults, is taking her at least as seriously as he can — and perhaps even as seriously as she deserves." [1989]

la belle dame sans merci: The beautiful lady without mercy.

MAKING COMPARISONS

1. Lord argues that the purpose of marriage "is to make each human personality free." Without this axiom, she believes, there cannot be real love in a marriage. Would Templeton agree?

2. How did you respond to Weigand's last sentence about "inborn talents of coquetry and play-acting"? How do you think Rogers would respond?

3. Which comments from these five critics do you find the most useful in understanding Nora and Torvald? Which are the least useful? Outline a brief position paper citing the comments and explaining your reasoning.

WRITING ABOUT ISSUES

1. Argue that Nora will, or will not, return. Be specific about the implications of either decision. Refer to at least one of the critics.

2. Write a brief comparison of Weigand and Rogers, pointing out their basic disagreement about Nora, women, the purpose of the play, and anything else that seems relevant.

3. What is your idea of a "real marriage"? Write an essay in which you explain the elements of such a relationship.

4. Ibsen was practically forced to change his ending when the play was produced in other countries. In Germany, for example, Nora's last line is "Ah, though it is a sin against myself, I cannot leave them!" Do you like this ending better? Write an essay in which you rewrite the ending for a current audience. Explain your choice, noting both what you think the function of the writer should be in our culture and what the nature of a marriage should be.

10

Considering Outsiders

America has historically thought of itself as an open society and a democratic culture, an inclusive land where the persecuted, the tired, and the homeless could find refuge. America's rewards are based on achievement and hard work, not royal blood, class affiliation, race, religion, or country of origin. This, at least, is the dream, the rhetoric of heterogeneity and tolerance. In many ways it is wonderfully true. Millions of Irish, Italians, Asians, and Russian Jews who came here during the last hundred years have been assimilated into a prosperous middle class. Most of them are treated as and feel like insiders. And there are probably more different religions in America than anywhere else.

But that is not the whole story. Generations of those Irish, Jewish, and Italian immigrants were very much outside the mainstream, openly discriminated against in employment, housing, and schools. Although the analogy of the melting pot is often used to describe the blending of ethnicities in America, perhaps a quilt is more apt since many ethnic groups such as African Americans, Native Americans, Japanese Americans, and Hispanics are often seen as separate panels of the American fabric. Many still live in homogeneous neighborhoods that suffer economically. Many still feel like outsiders as they watch television programs and movies in which being white and middle class is the norm and in which others are judged to be less or inferior.

Of course, there are many other ways to be an outsider besides ethnicity, race, and religion. Sometimes even those on the inside do not feel psychologically accepted because of some aspect of their identity. They may be alienated from conventional life because they have a different sexual or philosophical orientation, or perhaps they have strayed from the norm and incurred their communities' censure. It seems as if all societies create outsiders, perhaps to protect those on the inside from real or imagined threats. As the following nine clusters demonstrate, being on the outside often provides writers with a powerful perspective that is difficult to obtain on the inside. Outsiders help us to see more clearly and to understand our attitudes more acutely. Some outsiders are literally in mortal danger, while others are simply living in a self-created universe. All give a compelling testament to our ability to create art and wisdom out of pain.

935

The first cluster (below) focuses on Ralph Ellison's startling story of segregation and humiliation, "Battle Royal." It is followed by three stories from a master of the surreal, Franz Kafka, whose stories seem to be about another world but actually are accurate portraits of the frustration and alienation some people feel in the modern world (p. 961). The horror of the Holocaust is captured by the five poets in the next cluster (p. 1005). Five poets also examine the difficulties of being an ethnic outsider in America in the next cluster (p. 1014). Maxine Hong Kingston's and Naomi Wolf's essays in the fifth cluster (p. 1025) deal with the problems that beset women who violate a society's sexual conventions. The sixth cluster (p. 1042) brings into focus several critical essays revolving around the mysterious tale of Bartleby, who one day simply refuses to work. Next, two short stories (p. 1085) portray the consequences as individuals drift away from the human community and its ethical conventions. The last two clusters deal first with stories about the difficulties of foreigners in America (p. 1108) and finally two plays about insiders and outsiders (p. 1138). The first of these plays is William Shakespeare's *The Tempest*, whose setting is possibly America. The second, Aimé Césaire's *A Tempest*, gives us an interesting take on Shakespeare's play from someone on the outside of the colonial experience, one whose people have been colonized. As you read, write, and argue about these selections, it is not hard to see that the challenge of an inclusive democracy continues in America.

PASSIVE RESISTANCE: CULTURAL CONTEXTS FOR RALPH ELLISON'S "BATTLE ROYAL"

RALPH ELLISON, "Battle Royal"

CULTURAL CONTEXTS:
BOOKER T. WASHINGTON, "Atlanta Exposition Address"
W. E. B. DU BOIS, "Of Mr. Booker T. Washington"
GUNNAR MYRDAL, "Social Equality"
AFRICAN AMERICAN FOLK SONG, "Run, Nigger, Run"

Some thirty years after the civil rights movement of the 1960s, our national awareness of how brutal discrimination was against African Americans is diminished. While discrimination has not been completely eradicated, progress has been made, especially in eliminating official policies and gestures of bias. Before World War II, however, overt discrimination was common, especially in the small towns of the segregated South and the rural Midwest. African Americans were rarely allowed anything more than menial jobs in small towns. Most middle class whites knew African Americans only as maids, gardeners, and servants. African Americans were completely outside the established power structure and rarely able to complain or obtain justice for their many grievances. Public protest was out of the question. Many African Americans were wary of even private protest against their outsider status, fearing that their situation would get worse. Among both African American intellectuals and ordinary citizens debates raged about which strategy to pursue: to cooperate with the white establishment hoping to modify hostility or to agitate for change. Generations of blacks followed the first course until the 1960s, when sit-ins of the civil rights movement ushered in the public protests that ended state-sanctioned segregation. Ralph Ellison's story takes place in the era of segregation and gives a graphic picture of how marginalized African Americans were and how difficult it was to decide on an effective strategy for progress.

BEFORE YOU READ

Have you ever been in a situation where you felt discriminated against because of your race, religion, gender, sexual orientation, or age? Did you ever see someone else suffer discrimination? Did you feel powerless? What was your strategy for dealing with this feeling?

RALPH ELLISON
Battle Royal

Born in Oklahoma to an activist mother and an intellectual father, Ralph Ellison (1914–1994) was well grounded in literary and social matters by the time he entered Tuskegee Institute to study music in 1933. Finding the conservatism and accommodationism of Tuskegee limiting, Ellison read modernist poets like T. S. Eliot and soon moved to New York in 1936, where he met writers Langston Hughes and Richard Wright. Inspired by Wright and by the works of Conrad, Dostoyevsky, and other writers of fiction, Ellison began drafting his novel Invisible Man *(1952) while serving in the merchant marine during World War II. Published as a short story in 1947, "Battle Royal" became the first chapter of this National Book Award–winning novel.*

It goes a long way back, some twenty years. All my life I had been looking for something, and everywhere I turned someone tried to tell me what it was. I accepted their answers too, though they were often in contradiction and even self-contradictory. I was naive. I was looking for myself and asking everyone except myself questions which I, and only I, could answer. It took me a long time and much painful boomeranging of my expectations to achieve a realization everyone else appears to have been born with: That I am nobody but myself. But first I had to discover that I am an invisible man!

And yet I am no freak of nature, nor of history. I was in the cards, other things having been equal (or unequal) eighty-five years ago. I am not ashamed of my grandparents for having been slaves. I am only ashamed of myself for having at one time been ashamed. About eighty-five years ago they were told that they were free, united with others of our country in everything pertaining to the common good, and, in everything social, separate like the fingers of the hand. And they believed it. They exulted in it. They stayed in their place, worked hard, and brought up my father to do the same. But my grandfather is the one. He was an odd old guy, my grandfather, and I am told I take after him. It was he who caused the trouble. On his deathbed he called my father to him and said, "Son, after I'm gone I want you to keep up the good fight. I never told you, but our life is a war and I have been a traitor all my born days, a spy in the enemy's country ever since I give up my gun back in the Reconstruction. Live with your head in the lion's mouth. I want you to overcome 'em with yeses, undermine 'em with grins, agree 'em to death and destruction, let 'em swoller you till they vomit or bust wide open." They thought the old man had gone out of his mind. He had been the meekest of men. The younger children were rushed from the room, the shades drawn and the flame of the lamp turned so low that it sputtered on the wick like the old man's breathing. "Learn it to the younguns," he whispered fiercely; then he died.

But my folks were more alarmed over his last words than over his dying. It was as though he had not died at all, his words caused so much anxiety. I was warned emphatically to forget what he had said and, indeed, this is the first time it has been mentioned outside the family circle. It had a tremendous effect upon me, however. I could never be sure of what he meant. Grandfather had been a quiet old man who never made any trouble, yet on his deathbed he had called himself a traitor and a spy, and he had spoken of his meekness as a dangerous activity. It became a constant puzzle which lay unanswered in the back of my mind. And whenever things went well for me I remembered my grandfather and felt guilty and uncomfortable. It was as though I was carrying out his advice in spite of myself. And to make it worse, everyone loved me for it. I was praised by the most lily-white men of the town. I was considered an example of desirable conduct—just as my grandfather had been. And what puzzled me was that the old man had defined it as *treachery*. When I was praised for my conduct I felt a guilt that in some way I was doing something that was really against the wishes of the white folks, that if they had understood they would have desired me to act just the opposite, that I should have been sulky and mean, and that that really would have been what they wanted, even though they were fooled and thought they wanted me to act as I did. It made me afraid that some day they would look upon me as a traitor and I would be lost. Still I was more afraid to act any other way because they didn't like that at all. The old man's words were like a curse. On my graduation day I delivered an oration in which I showed that humility was the secret, indeed, the very essence of progress. (Not that I believed this—how could I, remembering my grandfather?—I only believed that it worked.) It was a great success. Everyone praised me and I was invited to give the speech at a gathering of the town's leading white citizens. It was a triumph for our whole community.

It was in the main ballroom of the leading hotel. When I got there I discovered that it was on the occasion of a smoker, and I was told that since I was to be there anyway I might as well take part in the battle royal to be fought by some of my schoolmates as part of the entertainment. The battle royal came first.

All of the town's big shots were there in their tuxedoes, wolfing down the buffet foods, drinking beer and whiskey and smoking black cigars. It was a large room with a high ceiling. Chairs were arranged in neat rows around three sides of a portable boxing ring. The fourth side was clear, revealing a gleaming space of polished floor. I had some misgivings over the battle royal, by the way. Not from a distaste for fighting, but because I didn't care too much for the other fellows who were to take part. They were tough guys who seemed to have no grandfather's curse worrying their minds. No one could mistake their toughness. And besides, I suspected that fighting a battle royal might detract from the dignity of my speech. In those pre-invisible days I visualized myself as a potential Booker T. Washington. But the other fellows didn't care too much for me either, and there were nine of them. I felt superior to them in my way, and I didn't like the manner in which we were all crowded together into the servants' elevator. Nor did they like my being there. In fact, as the warmly lighted floors flashed past the elevator we had words over the fact that I, by taking part in the fight, had knocked one of their friends out of a night's work.

We were led out of the elevator through a rococo hall into an anteroom and told to get into our fighting togs. Each of us was issued a pair of boxing gloves and ushered out into the big mirrored hall, which we entered looking cautiously about us and whispering, lest we might accidentally be heard above the noise of the room. It was foggy with cigar smoke. And already the whiskey was taking effect. I was shocked to see some of the most important men of the town quite tipsy. They were all there — bankers, lawyers, judges, doctors, fire chiefs, teachers, merchants. Even one of the more fashionable pastors. Something we could not see was going on up front. A clarinet was vibrating sensuously and the men were standing up and moving eagerly forward. We were a small tight group, clustered together, our bare upper bodies touching and shining with anticipatory sweat; while up front the big shots were becoming increasingly excited over something we still could not see. Suddenly I heard the school superintendent, who had told me to come, yell, "Bring up the shines, gentlemen! Bring up the little shines!"

We were rushed up to the front of the ballroom, where it smelled even more strongly of tobacco and whiskey. Then we were pushed into place. I almost wet my pants. A sea of faces, some hostile, some amused, ringed around us, and in the center, facing us, stood a magnificent blonde — stark naked. There was dead silence. I felt a blast of cold air chill me. I tried to back away, but they were behind me and around me. Some of the boys stood with lowered heads, trembling. I felt a wave of irrational guilt and fear. My teeth chattered, my skin turned to goose flesh, my knees knocked. Yet I was strongly attracted and looked in spite of myself. Had the price of looking been blindness, I would have looked. The hair was yellow like that of a circus kewpie doll, the face heavily powdered and rouged, as though to form an abstract mask, the eyes hollow and smeared a cool blue, the color of a baboon's butt. I felt a desire to spit upon her as my eyes brushed slowly over her body. Her breasts were firm and round as the domes of East Indian temples, and I stood so close as to see the fine skin texture and beads of pearly perspiration glistening like dew around the pink and erected buds of her nipples. I wanted at one and the same time to run from the room, to sink through the floor, or go to her and cover her from my eyes and the eyes of the others with my body; to feel the soft thighs, to caress her and destroy her, to love her and murder her, to hide from her, and yet to stroke where below the small American flag tattooed upon her belly her thighs formed a capital V. I had a notion that of all in the room she saw only me with her impersonal eyes.

And then she began to dance, a slow sensuous movement; the smoke of a hundred cigars clinging to her like the thinnest of veils. She seemed like a fair bird-girl girdled in veils calling to me from the angry surface of some gray and threatening sea. I was transported. Then I became aware of the clarinet playing and the big shots yelling at us. Some threatened us if we looked and others if we did not. On my right I saw one boy faint. And now a man grabbed a silver pitcher from a table and stepped close as he dashed ice water upon him and stood him up and forced two of us to support him as his head hung and moans issued from his thick bluish lips. Another boy began to plead to go home. He was the largest of the group, wearing dark red fighting trunks much too small to conceal the erection which projected from him as though in answer to the insinuating low-registered moaning of the clarinet. He tried to hide himself with his boxing gloves.

And all the while the blonde continued dancing, smiling faintly at the big shots who watched her with fascination, and faintly smiling at our fear. I noticed a certain merchant who followed her hungrily, his lips loose and drooling. He was a large man who wore diamond studs in a shirtfront which swelled with the ample paunch underneath, and each time the blonde swayed her undulating hips he ran his hand through the thin hair of his bald head and, with his arms upheld, his posture clumsy like that of an intoxicated panda, wound his belly in a slow and obscene grind. This creature was completely hypnotized. The music had quickened. As the dancer flung herself about with a detached expression on her face, the men began reaching out to touch her. I could see their beefy fingers sink into the soft flesh. Some of the others tried to stop them as she began to move around the floor in graceful circles, as they gave chase, slipping and sliding over the polished floor. It was mad. Chairs went crashing, drinks were spilt, as they ran laughing and howling after her. They caught her just as she reached a door, raised her from the floor, and tossed her as college boys are tossed at a hazing, and above her red, fixed-smiling lips I saw the terror and disgust in her eyes, almost like my own terror and that which I saw in some of the other boys. As I watched, they tossed her twice and her soft breasts seemed to flatten against the air and her legs flung wildly as she spun. Some of the more sober ones helped her to escape. And I started off the floor, heading for the anteroom with the rest of the boys.

Some were still crying in hysteria. But as we tried to leave we were stopped and ordered to get into the ring. There was nothing to do but what we were told. All ten of us climbed under the ropes and allowed ourselves to be blindfolded with broad bands of white cloth. One of the men seemed to feel a bit sympathetic and tried to cheer us up as we stood with our backs against the ropes. Some of us tried to grin. "See that boy over there?" one of the men said. "I want you to run across at the bell and give it to him right in the belly. If you don't get him, I'm

10

going to get you. I don't like his looks." Each of us was told the same. The blindfolds were put on. Yet even then I had been going over my speech. In my mind each word was as bright as flame. I felt the cloth pressed into place, and frowned so that it would be loosened when I relaxed.

But now I felt a sudden fit of blind terror. I was unused to darkness. It was as though I had suddenly found myself in a dark room filled with poisonous cottonmouths. I could hear the bleary voices yelling insistently for the battle royal to begin.

"Get going in there!"

"Let me at that big nigger!"

I strained to pick up the school superintendent's voice, as though to squeeze some security out of that slightly more familiar sound.

"Let me at those black sonsabitches!" someone yelled.   15

"No, Jackson, no!" another voice yelled. "Here, somebody, help me hold Jack."

"I want to get at that ginger-colored nigger. Tear him limb from limb," the first voice yelled.

I stood against the ropes trembling. For in those days I was what they called ginger-colored, and he sounded as though he might crunch me between his teeth like a crisp ginger cookie.

Quite a struggle was going on. Chairs were being kicked about and I could hear voices grunting as with a terrific effort. I wanted to see, to see more desperately than ever before. But the blindfold was tight as a thick skin-puckering scab and when I raised my gloved hands to push the layers of white aside a voice yelled, "Oh, no you don't, black bastard! Leave that alone!"

"Ring the bell before Jackson kills him a coon!" someone boomed in the   20 sudden silence. And I heard the bell clang and the sound of the feet scuffling forward.

A glove smacked against my head. I pivoted, striking out stiffly as someone went past, and felt the jar ripple along the length of my arm to my shoulder. Then it seemed as though all nine of the boys had turned upon me at once. Blows pounded me from all sides while I struck out as best I could. So many blows landed upon me that I wondered if I were not the only blindfolded fighter in the ring, or if the man called Jackson hadn't succeeded in getting me after all.

Blindfolded, I could no longer control my motions. I had no dignity. I stumbled about like a baby or a drunken man. The smoke had become thicker and with each new blow it seemed to sear and further restrict my lungs. My saliva became like hot bitter glue. A glove connected with my head, filling my mouth with warm blood. It was everywhere. I could not tell if the moisture I felt upon my body was sweat or blood. A blow landed hard against the nape of my neck. I felt myself going over, my head hitting the floor. Streaks of blue light filled the black world behind the blindfold. I lay prone, pretending that I was knocked out, but felt myself seized by hands and yanked to my feet. "Get going, black boy! Mix it up!" My arms were like lead, my head smarting from blows. I managed to feel my way to the ropes and held on, trying to catch my breath. A glove landed in my mid-section and I went over again, feeling as though the smoke had become a knife jabbed into my guts. Pushed this way and that by the legs milling around me, I finally pulled erect and discovered that I could see the black, sweat-washed forms weaving in the smoky-blue atmosphere like drunken dancers weaving to the rapid drumlike thuds of blows.

Everyone fought hysterically. It was complete anarchy. Everybody fought everybody else. No group fought together for long. Two, three, four, fought one, then turned to fight each other, were themselves attacked. Blows landed below the belt and in the kidney, with the gloves open as well as closed, and with my eye partly opened now there was not so much terror. I moved carefully, avoiding blows, although not too many to attract attention, fighting from group to group. The boys groped about like blind, cautious crabs crouching to protect their mid-sections, their heads pulled in short against their shoulders, their arms stretched nervously before them, with their fists testing the smoke-filled air like the knobbed feelers of hypersensitive snails. In one corner I glimpsed a boy violently punching the air and heard him scream in pain as he smashed his hand against a ring post. For a second I saw him bent over holding his hand, then going down as a blow caught his unprotected head. I played one group against the other, slipping in and throwing a punch then stepping out of range while pushing the others into the melee to take the blows blindly aimed at me. The smoke was agonizing and there were no rounds, no bells at three minute intervals to relieve our exhaustion. The room spun round me, a swirl of lights, smoke, sweating bodies surrounded by tense white faces. I bled from both nose and mouth, the blood spattering upon my chest.

The men kept yelling, "Slug him, black boy! Knock his guts out!"

"Uppercut him! Kill him! Kill that big boy!"   25

Taking a fake fall, I saw a boy going down heavily beside me as though we were felled by a single blow, saw a sneaker-clad foot shoot into his groin as the two who had knocked him down stumbled upon him. I rolled out of range, feeling a twinge of nausea.

The harder we fought the more threatening the men became. And yet, I had begun to worry about my speech again. How would it go? Would they recognize my ability? What would they give me?

I was fighting automatically when suddenly I noticed that one after another of the boys was leaving the ring. I was surprised, filled with panic, as though I had been left alone with an unknown danger. Then I understood. The boys had arranged it among themselves. It was the custom for the two men left in the ring to slug it out for the winner's prize. I discovered this too late. When the bell sounded two men in tuxedoes leaped into the ring and removed the blindfold. I found myself facing Tatlock, the biggest of the gang. I felt sick at my stomach. Hardly had the bell stopped ringing in my ears than it clanged again and I saw him moving swiftly toward me. Thinking of nothing else to do I hit him smash on the nose. He kept coming, bringing the rank sharp violence of stale sweat. His face was a black blank of a face, only his eyes alive — with hate of me and aglow with a feverish terror from what had happened to us all. I became anxious. I wanted to deliver my speech and he came at me as though he meant to beat it out of me. I smashed him again and again, taking his blows as they came. Then on a sudden impulse I struck him lightly and as we clinched, I whispered, "Fake like I knocked you out, you can have the prize."

"I'll break your behind," he whispered hoarsely.

"For *them?*" 30

"For *me*, sonofabitch!"

They were yelling for us to break it up and Tatlock spun me half around with a blow, and as a joggled camera sweeps in a reeling scene, I saw the howling red faces crouching tense beneath the cloud of blue-gray smoke. For a moment the world wavered, unraveled, flowed, then my head cleared and Tatlock bounced before me. That fluttering shadow before my eyes was his jabbing left hand. Then falling forward, my head against his damp shoulder, I whispered,

"I'll make it five dollars more."

"Go to hell!"

But his muscles relaxed a trifle beneath my pressure and I breathed, "Seven?" 35

"Give it to your ma," he said, ripping me beneath the heart.

And while I still held him I butted him and moved away. I felt myself bombarded with punches. I fought back with hopeless desperation. I wanted to deliver my speech more than anything else in the world, because I felt that only these men could judge truly my ability, and now this stupid clown was ruining my chances. I began fighting carefully now, moving in to punch him and out again with my greater speed. A lucky blow to his chin and I had him going too — until I heard a loud voice yell, "I got my money on the big boy."

Hearing this, I almost dropped my guard. I was confused: Should I try to win against the voice out there? Would not this go against my speech, and was not this a moment for humility, for nonresistance? A blow to my head as I danced about sent my right eye popping like a jack-in-the-box and settled my dilemma. The room went red as I fell. It was a dream fall, my body languid and fastidious as to where to land, until the floor became impatient and smashed up to meet me. A moment later I came to. An hypnotic voice said FIVE emphatically. And I lay there, hazily watching a dark red spot of my own blood shaping itself into a butterfly, glistening and soaking into the soiled gray world of the canvas.

When the voice drawled TEN I was lifted up and dragged to a chair. I sat dazed. My eye pained and swelled with each throb of my pounding heart and I wondered if now I would be allowed to speak. I was wringing wet, my mouth still bleeding. We were grouped along the wall now. The other boys ignored me as they congratulated Tatlock and speculated as to how much they would be paid. One boy whimpered over his smashed hand. Looking up front, I saw attendants in white jackets rolling the portable ring away and placing a small square rug in the vacant space surrounded by chairs. Perhaps, I thought, I will stand on the rug to deliver my speech.

Then the M.C. called to us, "Come on up here boys and get your money." 40
We ran forward to where the men laughed and talked in their chairs, waiting. Everyone seemed friendly now.

"There it is on the rug," the man said. I saw the rug covered with coins of all dimensions and a few crumpled bills. But what excited me, scattered here and there, were the gold pieces.

"Boys, it's all yours," the man said. "You get all you grab."

"That's right, Sambo," a blond man said, winking at me confidentially.

I trembled with excitement, forgetting my pain. I would get the gold and the bills, I thought. I would use both hands. I would throw my body against the boys nearest me to block them from the gold.

"Get down around the rug now," the man commanded, "and don't anyone   45
touch it until I give the signal."

"This ought to be good," I heard.

As told, we got around the square rug on our knees. Slowly the man raised his freckled hand as we followed it upward with our eyes.

I heard, "These niggers look like they're about to pray!"

Then, "Ready," the man said. "Go!"

I lunged for a yellow coin lying on the blue design of the carpet, touching it   50
and sending a surprised shriek to join those rising around me. I tried frantically to remove my hand but could not let go. A hot, violent force tore through my body, shaking me like a wet rat. The rug was electrified. The hair bristled up on my head as I shook myself free. My muscles jumped, my nerves jangled, writhed. But I saw that this was not stopping the other boys. Laughing in fear and embarrassment, some were holding back and scooping up the coins knocked off by the painful contortions of the others. The men roared above us as we struggled.

"Pick it up, goddamnit, pick it up!" someone called like a bass-voiced parrot. "Go on, get it!"

I crawled rapidly around the floor, picking up the coins, trying to avoid the coppers and to get greenbacks and the gold. Ignoring the shock by laughing, as I brushed the coins off quickly, I discovered that I could contain the electricity—a contradiction, but it works. Then the men began to push us onto the rug. Laughing embarrassedly, we struggled out of their hands and kept after the coins. We were all wet and slippery and hard to hold. Suddenly I saw a boy lifted into the air, glistening with sweat like a circus seal, and dropped, his wet back landing flush upon the charged rug, heard him yell and saw him literally dance upon his back, his elbows beating a frenzied tattoo upon the floor, his muscles twitching like the flesh of a horse stung by many flies. When he finally rolled off, his face was gray and no one stopped him when he ran from the floor amid booming laughter.

"Get the money," the M.C. called. "That's good hard American cash!"

And we snatched and grabbed, snatched and grabbed. I was careful not to come too close to the rug now, and when I felt the hot whiskey breath descend upon me like a cloud of foul air I reached out and grabbed the leg of a chair. It was occupied and I held on desperately.

"Leggo, nigger! Leggo!"   55

The huge face wavered down to mine as he tried to push me free. But my body was slippery and he was too drunk. It was Mr. Colcord, who owned a chain of movie houses and "entertainment palaces." Each time he grabbed me I slipped out of his hands. It became a real struggle. I feared the rug more than I did the drunk, so I held on, surprising myself for a moment by trying to topple *him* upon the rug. It was such an enormous idea that I found myself actually carrying it out. I tried not to be obvious, yet when I grabbed his leg, trying to tumble him out of the chair, he raised up roaring with laughter, and, looking at me with soberness dead in the eye, kicked me viciously in the chest. The chair leg flew out of my hand and I felt myself going and rolled. It was as though I had rolled through a bed of hot coals. It seemed a whole century would pass before I would roll free, a century in which I was seared through the deepest levels of my body to the fearful breath within me and the breath seared and heated to the point of explosion. It'll all be over in a flash, I thought as I rolled clear. It'll all be over in a flash.

But not yet, the men on the other side were waiting, red faces swollen as though from apoplexy as they bent forward in their chairs. Seeing their fingers coming toward me I rolled away as a fumbled football rolls off the receiver's fingertips, back into the coals. That time I luckily sent the rug sliding out of place and heard the coins ringing against the floor and the boys scuffling to pick them up and the M.C. calling, "All right, boys, that's all. Go get dressed and get your money."

I was limp as a dish rag. My back felt as though it had been beaten with wires.

When we had dressed the M.C. came in and gave us each five dollars, except Tatlock, who got ten for being last in the ring. Then he told us to leave. I was not to get a chance to deliver my speech, I thought. I was going out into the dim alley in despair when I was stopped and told to go back. I returned to the ballroom, where the men were pushing back their chairs and gathering in groups to talk.

The M.C. knocked on a table for quiet. "Gentlemen," he said, "we almost 60 forgot an important part of the program. A most serious part, gentlemen. This boy was brought here to deliver a speech which he made at his graduation yesterday . . ."

"Bravo!"

"I'm told that he is the smartest boy we've got out there in Greenwood. I'm told that he knows more big words than a pocket-sized dictionary."

Much applause and laughter.

"So now, gentlemen, I want you to give him your attention."

There was still laughter as I faced them, my mouth dry, my eye throbbing. I 65 began slowly, but evidently my throat was tense, because they began shouting, "Louder! Louder!"

"We of the younger generation extol the wisdom of that great leader and educator," I shouted, "who first spoke these flaming words of wisdom: 'A ship lost at sea for many days suddenly sighted a friendly vessel. From the mast of the unfortunate vessel was seen a signal: "Water, water; we die of thirst!" The answer from the friendly vessel came back: "Cast down your bucket where you are." The captain of the distressed vessel, at last heeding the injunction, cast down his bucket, and it came up full of fresh sparkling water from the mouth of the Amazon River.' And like him I say, and in his words, 'To those of my race who depend upon bettering their condition in a foreign land, or who underestimate the importance of cultivating friendly relations with the Southern white man, who is his next-door neighbor, I would say: "Cast down your bucket where you are" — cast it down in making friends in every manly way of the people of all races by whom we are surrounded . . .'"

I spoke automatically and with such fervor that I did not realize that the men were still talking and laughing until my dry mouth, filling up with blood from the cut, almost strangled me. I coughed, wanting to stop and go to one of the tall brass, sand-filled spittoons to relieve myself, but a few of the men, especially the superintendent, were listening and I was afraid. So I gulped it down, blood, saliva, and all, and continued. (What powers of endurance I had during those days! What enthusiasm! What a belief in the rightness of things!) I spoke even louder in spite of the pain. But still they talked and still they laughed, as though deaf with cotton in dirty ears. So I spoke with greater emotional emphasis. I closed my ears and swallowed blood until I was nauseated. The speech seemed a hundred times as long as before, but I could not leave out a single word. All had to be said, each memorized nuance considered, rendered. Nor was that all. Whenever I uttered a word of three or more syllables a group of voices would yell for me to repeat it. I used the phrase "social responsibility" and they yelled:

"What's that word you say, boy?"

"Social responsibility," I said.

"What?"   70

"Social . . ."

"Louder."

". . . responsibility."

"More!"

"Respon—"   75

"Repeat!"

"— sibility."

The room filled with the uproar of laughter until, no doubt, distracted by having to gulp down my blood, I made a mistake and yelled a phrase I had often seen denounced in newspaper editorials, heard debated in private.

"Social . . ."

"What?" they yelled.   80

". . . equality—"

The laughter hung smokelike in the sudden stillness. I opened my eyes, puzzled. Sounds of displeasure filled the room. The M.C. rushed forward. They shouted hostile phrases at me. But I did not understand.

A small dry mustached man in the front row blared out, "Say that slowly, son!"

"What, sir?"

"What you just said!"   85

"Social responsibility, sir," I said.

"You weren't being smart, were you, boy?" he said, not unkindly.

"No, sir!"

"You sure that about 'equality' was a mistake?"

"Oh, yes, sir," I said. "I was swallowing blood." 90

"Well, you had better speak more slowly so we can understand. We mean to do right by you, but you've got to know your place at all times. All right, now, go on with your speech."

I was afraid. I wanted to leave but I wanted also to speak and I was afraid they'd snatch me down.

"Thank you, sir," I said, beginning where I had left off, and having them ignore me as before.

Yet when I finished there was a thunderous applause. I was surprised to see the superintendent come forth with a package wrapped in white tissue paper, and, gesturing for quiet, address the men.

"Gentlemen, you see that I did not overpraise this boy. He makes a good 95 speech and some day he'll lead his people in the proper paths. And I don't have to tell you that that is important in these days and times. This is a good, smart boy, and so to encourage him in the right direction, in the name of the Board of Education I wish to present him a prize in the form of this . . . "

He paused, removing the tissue paper and revealing a gleaming calfskin brief case.

". . . in the form of this first-class article from Shad Whitmore's shop."

"Boy," he said, addressing me, "take this prize and keep it well. Consider it a badge of office. Prize it. Keep developing as you are and some day it will be filled with important papers that will help shape the destiny of your people."

I was so moved that I could hardly express my thanks. A rope of bloody saliva forming a shape like an undiscovered continent drooled upon the leather and I wiped it quickly away. I felt an importance that I had never dreamed.

"Open it and see what's inside," I was told. 100

My fingers a-tremble, I complied, smelling the fresh leather and finding an official-looking document inside. It was a scholarship to the state college for Negroes. My eyes filled with tears and I ran awkwardly off the floor.

I was overjoyed; I did not even mind when I discovered that the gold pieces I had scrambled for were brass pocket tokens advertising a certain make of automobile.

When I reached home everyone was excited. Next day the neighbors came to congratulate me. I even felt safe from grandfather, whose deathbed curse usually spoiled my triumphs. I stood beneath his photograph with my brief case in hand and smiled triumphantly into his stolid black peasant's face. It was a face that fascinated me. The eyes seemed to follow everywhere I went.

That night I dreamed I was at a circus with him and that he refused to laugh at the clowns no matter what they did. Then later he told me to open my brief case and read what was inside and I did, finding an official envelope stamped with the state seal; and inside the envelope I found another and another, endlessly, and I thought I would fall of weariness. "Them's years," he said. "Now open that one." And I did and in it I found an engraved document containing a short message in letters of gold. "Read it," my grandfather said. "Out loud!"

"To Whom It May Concern," I intoned. "Keep This Nigger-Boy Running." 105

I awoke with the old man's laughter ringing in my ears.

(It was a dream I was to remember and dream again for many years after. But at that time I had no insight into its meaning. First I had to attend college.)

[1947]

THINKING ABOUT THE TEXT

1. Some critics have seen the events at the smoker as symbolic or perhaps as an allegory of the plight of African Americans in the segregated South. Pick at least two specific events from the story. How are they meant to explain certain aspects of the African American experience before the civil rights movement of the 1960s?

2. Some readers are surprised by the bizarre and cruel behavior of the town's leaders. Are you? How do you explain what goes on there?

3. How do you interpret the narrator's dream (paras. 104–06)? Why would his grandfather be laughing?

4. Reread paragraphs 1–4. How is this opening section connected to the story? To the last paragraph? What might Ellison's narrator mean when he says in paragraph 1 that he is an invisible man?

5. The grandfather's deathbed advice in paragraph 2 causes quite a stir. In your own words, what is his advice? Why are his relatives surprised? What might be some alternatives for dealing with oppression? Which "solution" sounds like the one you would have promoted for our society during Ellison's boyhood?

BOOKER T. WASHINGTON
Atlanta Exposition Address

Recognized in his time as the major spokesman for his race, Booker T. Washington (1856–1915) is often seen today as an accommodationist whose insistence on gradual progress and vocational rather than intellectual education played into the hands of the white power structure, delaying racial equality. He founded and served as president of Tuskegee Institute, wrote twelve books (including the autobiographical Up From Slavery *in 1901), controlled much of the Negro press, and spoke all over the nation. His speech at the Atlanta Cotton States and International Exposition in 1895 in which he praised the South, condoned segregation and the glory of "common labour" for his race, and called for harmony and cooperation between the races is often called "The Atlanta Compromise."*

One-third of the population of the South is of the Negro race. No enterprise seeking the material, civil, or moral welfare of this section can disregard this element of our population and reach the highest success. I but convey to you, Mr. President and Directors, the sentiment of the masses of my race when I say that in no way have the value and manhood of the American Negro been more fittingly and generously recognized than by the managers of this magnificent Exposition at every stage of its progress. It is a recognition that will do more to cement the friendship of the two races than any occurrence since the dawn of our freedom.

Not only this, but the opportunity here afforded will awaken among us a new era of industrial progress. Ignorant and inexperienced, it is not strange that in the first years of our new life we began at the top instead of at the bottom; that a seat in Congress or the state legislature was more sought than real estate or industrial skill; that the political convention or stump speaking had more attractions than starting a dairy farm or truck garden.

A ship lost at sea for many days suddenly sighted a friendly vessel. From the mast of the unfortunate vessel was seen a signal, "Water, water; we die of thirst!" The answer from the friendly vessel at once came back, "Cast down your bucket where you are." A second time the signal, "Water, water, send us water!" ran up from the distressed vessel, and was answered, "Cast down your bucket where you are." And a third and fourth signal for water was answered, "Cast down your bucket where you are." The captain of the distressed vessel, at last heeding the injunction, cast down his bucket, and it came up full of fresh, sparkling water from the mouth of the Amazon River. To those of my race who depend on bettering their condition in a foreign land or who underestimate the importance of cultivating friendly relations with the Southern white man, who is their next-door neighbour, I would say: "Cast down your bucket where you are" — cast it down in making friends in every manly way of the people of all races by whom we are surrounded.

Cast it down in agriculture, mechanics, in commerce, in domestic service, and in the professions. And in this connection it is well to bear in mind that whatever other sins the South may be called to bear, when it comes to business, pure and simple, it is in the South that the Negro is given a man's chance in the commercial world, and in nothing is this Exposition more eloquent than in emphasizing this chance. Our greatest danger is that in the great leap from slavery to freedom we may overlook the fact that the masses of us are to live by the productions of our hands, and fail to keep in mind that we shall prosper in proportion as we learn to dignify and glorify common labour and put brains and skill into the common occupations of life; shall prosper in proportion as we learn to draw the line between the superficial and the substantial, the ornamental gewgaws of life and the useful. No race can prosper till it learns that there is as much dignity in tilling a field as in writing a poem. It is at the bottom of life we must begin, and not at the top. Nor should we permit our grievances to overshadow our opportunities.

To those of the white race who look to the incoming of those of foreign birth and strange tongue and habits for the prosperity of the South, were I permitted I would repeat what I say to my own race, "Cast down your bucket where you are." Cast it down among the eight millions of Negroes whose habits you know, whose

5

fidelity and love you have tested in days when to have proved treacherous meant the ruin of your firesides. Cast down your bucket among these people who have, without strikes and labour wars, tilled your fields, cleared your forests, builded your railroads and cities, and brought forth treasures from the bowels of the earth, and helped make possible this magnificent representation of the progress of the South. Casting down your bucket among my people, helping and encouraging them as you are doing on these grounds, and to education of head, hand, and heart, you will find that they will buy your surplus land, make blossom the waste places in your fields, and run your factories. While doing this, you can be sure in the future, as in the past, that you and your families will be surrounded by the most patient, faithful, law-abiding, and unresentful people that the world has seen. As we have proved our loyalty to you in the past, in nursing your children, watching by the sick-bed of your mothers and fathers, and often following them with tear-dimmed eyes to their graves, so in the future, in our humble way, we shall stand by you with a devotion that no foreigner can approach, ready to lay down our lives, if need be, in defence of yours, interlacing our industrial, commercial, civil, and religious life with yours in a way that shall make the interests of both races one. In all things that are purely social we can be as separate as the fingers, yet one as the hand in all things essential to mutual progress.

There is no defence or security for any of us except in the highest intelligence and development of all. If anywhere there are efforts tending to curtail the fullest growth of the Negro, let these efforts be turned into stimulating, encouraging, and making him the most useful and intelligent citizen. Effort or means so invested will pay a thousand per cent interest. These efforts will be twice blessed — "blessing him that gives and him that takes."

There is no escape through law of man or God from the inevitable: —

> The laws of changeless justice bind
> Oppressor with oppressed;
> And close as sin and suffering joined
> We march to fate abreast.

Nearly sixteen millions of hands will aid you in pulling the load upward, or they will pull against you the load downward. We shall constitute one-third and more of the ignorance and crime of the South, or one-third its intelligence and progress; we shall contribute one-third to the business and industrial prosperity of the South, or we shall prove a veritable body of death, stagnating, depressing, retarding every effort to advance the body politic.

Gentlemen of the Exposition, as we present to you our humble effort at an exhibition of our progress, you must not expect overmuch. Starting thirty years ago with ownership here and there in a few quilts and pumpkins and chickens (gathered from miscellaneous sources), remember the path that has led from these to the inventions and production of agricultural implements, buggies, steam-engines, newspapers, books, statuary, carving, paintings, the management of drug-stores and banks, has not been trodden without contact with thorns and thistles. While we take pride in what we exhibit as a result of our independent efforts, we do not for a moment forget that our part in this exhibition would fall far short of your expectations but for the constant help that has come to our educational life, not only from the Southern states, but especially from Northern philanthropists who have made their gifts a constant stream of blessing and encouragement.

The wisest among my race understand that the agitation of questions of   10 social equality is the extremest folly, and that progress in the enjoyment of all the privileges that will come to us must be the result of severe and constant struggle rather than of artificial forcing. No race that has anything to contribute to the markets of the world is long in any degree ostracized. It is important and right that all privileges of the law be ours, but it is vastly more important that we be prepared for the exercises of these privileges. The opportunity to earn a dollar in a factory just now is worth infinitely more than the opportunity to spend a dollar in an opera-house.

In conclusion, may I repeat that nothing in thirty years has given us more hope and encouragement, and drawn us so near to you of the white race, as this opportunity offered by the Exposition; and here bending, as it were, over the altar that represents the results of the struggles of your race and mine, both starting practically empty-handed three decades ago, I pledge that in your effort to work out the great and intricate problem which God has laid at the doors of the South, you shall have at all times the patient, sympathetic help of my race; only let this be constantly in mind, that, while from representations in these buildings of the product of field, of forest, of mine, of factory, letters, and art, much good will come, yet far above and beyond material benefits will be that higher good, that, let us pray God, will come, in a blotting out of sectional differences and racial animosities and suspicions, in a determination to administer absolute justice, in a willing obedience among all classes to the mandates of law. This, this, coupled with our material prosperity, will bring into our beloved South a new heaven and a new earth.   [1895]

THINKING ABOUT THE TEXT

1. Cite two specific passages from Washington that would probably have had an impact on the African American characters in "Battle Royal."

2. Do you think Washington is right in saying, "No race can prosper till it learns that there is as much dignity in tilling a field as in writing a poem" (para. 4)?

3. Are you surprised that Washington pledges the "patient, sympathetic help of my race" as those whites in power "work out the great and intricate problem which God has laid at the doors of the South" (para. 11)? What might contemporary black leaders think of this attitude?

W. E. B. DU BOIS
Of Mr. Booker T. Washington

W. E. B. Du Bois (1868–1963) was a driving force in the movement for equality for people of color in America and throughout the world well into his nineties. He was born in Massachusetts soon after the Civil War, and his death in Africa coincided with the March on Washington in 1963. Du Bois was educated at Fisk, Berlin, and Harvard Universities, receiving a Ph.D. from Harvard in 1895 for his dissertation on the history of the slave trade. He is best known for his work with the National Association for the Advancement of Colored People (NAACP), serving as editor of The Crisis *from 1910 to 1932. As a scholar, writer, and intellectual, Du Bois openly opposed policies such as those supported by Booker T. Washington that kept social, political, and educational opportunities from most African Americans. The* Souls of Black Folk *(1903), from which our reading is taken, is perhaps the most influential of his many writings.*

Easily the most striking thing in the history of the American Negro since 1876 is the ascendancy of Mr. Booker T. Washington. It began at the time when war memories and ideals were rapidly passing; a day of astonishing commercial development was dawning; a sense of doubt and hesitation overtook the freedmen's sons, — then it was that his leading began. Mr. Washington came, with a simple definite programme, at the psychological moment when the nation was a little ashamed of having bestowed so much sentiment on Negroes, and was concentrating its energies on Dollars. His programme of industrial education, conciliation of the South, and submission and silence as to civil and political rights, was not wholly original; the Free Negroes from 1830 up to wartime had striven to build industrial schools, and the American Missionary Association had from the first taught various trades; and Price° and others had sought a way of honorable alliance with the best of the Southerners. But Mr. Washington first indissolubly linked these things; he put enthusiasm, unlimited energy, and perfect faith into this programme, and changed it from a by-path into a veritable Way of Life. And the tale of the methods by which he did this is a fascinating study of human life.

It startled the nation to hear a Negro advocating such a programme after many decades of bitter complaint; it startled and won the applause of the South, it interested and won the admiration of the North; and after a confused murmur of protest, it silenced if it did not convert the Negroes themselves.

To gain the sympathy and coöperation of the various elements comprising the white South was Mr. Washington's first task; and this, at the time Tuskegee was founded, seemed, for a black man, well-nigh impossible. And yet ten years later it was done in the word spoken at Atlanta: "In all things purely social we can be as separate as the five fingers, and yet one as the hand in all things essential to

Price: Joseph C. Price (1854–1893), founder of Zion Wesley College and Livingstone College, was a prominent black educator and championed liberal arts education.

mutual progress." This "Atlanta Compromise" is by all odds the most notable thing in Mr. Washington's career. The South interpreted it in different ways: the radicals received it as a complete surrender of the demand for civil and political equality; the conservatives, as a generously conceived working basis for mutual understanding. So both approved it, and to-day its author is certainly the most distinguished Southerner since Jefferson Davis, and the one with the largest personal following. . . .

Mr. Washington represents in Negro thought the old attitude of adjustment and submission; but adjustment at such a peculiar time as to make his programme unique. This is an age of unusual economic development, and Mr. Washington's programme naturally takes an economic cast, becoming a gospel of Work and Money to such an extent as apparently almost completely to overshadow the higher aims of life. Moreover, this is an age when the more advanced races are coming in closer contact with the less developed races, and the race-feeling is therefore intensified; and Mr. Washington's programme practically accepts the alleged inferiority of the Negro races. Again, in our own land, the reaction from the sentiment of war time has given impetus to race-prejudice against Negroes, and Mr. Washington withdraws many of the high demands of Negroes as men and American citizens. In other periods of intensified prejudice all the Negro's tendency to self-assertion has been called forth; at this period a policy of submission is advocated. In the history of nearly all other races and people the doctrine preached at such crises has been that manly self-respect is worth more than lands and houses, and that a people who voluntarily surrender such respect, or cease striving for it, are not worth civilizing.

In answer to this, it has been claimed that the Negro can survive only through submission. Mr. Washington distinctly asks that black people give up, at least for the present, three things — 5

> First, political power,
> Second, insistence on civil rights,
> Third, higher education of Negro youth, —

and concentrate all their energies on industrial education, the accumulation of wealth, and the conciliation of the South. This policy has been courageously and insistently advocated for over fifteen years, and has been triumphant for perhaps ten years. As a result of this tender of the palm-branch, what has been the return? In these years there have occurred:

1. The disfranchisement of the Negro.
2. The legal creation of a distinct status of civil inferiority for the Negro.
3. The steady withdrawal of aid from institutions for the higher training of the Negro.

These movements are not, to be sure, direct results of Mr. Washington's teachings; but his propaganda has, without a shadow of doubt, helped their speedier accomplishment. The question then comes: Is it possible, and probable, that nine millions of men can make effective progress in economic lines if they are deprived of political rights, made a servile caste, and allowed only the most meagre chance for developing their exceptional men? If history and reason give any distinct answer to these questions, it is an emphatic No. . . .

In failing thus to state plainly and unequivocally the legitimate demands of their people, even at the cost of opposing an honored leader the thinking classes of American Negroes would shirk a heavy responsibility, — a responsibility to themselves, a responsibility to struggling masses, a responsibility to the darker races of men whose future depends so largely on this American experiment, but especially a responsibility to this nation, — this common Fatherland. It is wrong to encourage a man or a people in evil-doing; it is wrong to aid and abet a national crime simply because it is unpopular not to do so. The growing spirit of kindliness and reconciliation between the North and South after the frightful differences of a generation ago ought to be a source of deep congratulation to all, and especially to those whose mistreatment caused the war; but if that reconciliation is to be marked by the industrial slavery and civic death of those same black men, with permanent legislation into a position of inferiority, then those black men, if they are really men, are called upon by every consideration of patriotism and loyalty to oppose such a course by all civilized methods, even though such opposition involves disagreement with Mr. Booker T. Washington. We have no right to sit silently by while the inevitable seeds are sown for a harvest of disaster to our children, black and white.

First, it is the duty of black men to judge the South discriminatingly. The present generation of Southerners are not responsible for the past, and they should not be blindly hated or blamed for it. Furthermore, to no class is the indiscriminate endorsement of the recent course of the South toward Negroes more nauseating than to the best thought of the South. The South is not "solid"; it is a land in the ferment of social change, wherein forces of all kinds are fighting for supremacy; and to praise the ill the South is to-day perpetrating is just as wrong as to condemn the good. Discriminating and broad-minded criticism is what the South needs, — needs it for the sake of her own white sons and daughters, and for the insurance of robust, healthy mental and moral development.

To-day even the attitude of the Southern whites toward the blacks is not, as so many assume, in all cases the same; the ignorant Southerner hates the Negro, the workingmen fear his competition, the money-makers wish to use him as a laborer, some of the educated see a menace in his upward development, while others, — usually the sons of the masters — wish to help him to rise. National opinion has enabled this last class to maintain the Negro common schools, and to protect the Negro partially in property, life, and limb. Through the pressure of the money-makers, the Negro is in danger of being reduced to semi-slavery, especially in the country districts; the workingmen, and those of the educated who fear the Negro, have united to disfranchise him, and some have urged his deportation; while the passions of the ignorant are easily aroused to lynch and abuse any black man. To praise this intricate whirl of thought and prejudice is nonsense; to inveigh indiscriminately against "the South" is unjust; but to use the same breath in praising Governor Aycock, exposing Senator Morgan, arguing with Mr. Thomas Nelson Page, and denouncing Senator Ben Tillman, is not only sane, but the imperative duty of thinking black men.

It would be unjust to Mr. Washington not to acknowledge that in several instances he has opposed movements in the South which were unjust to the Negro; he sent memorials to the Louisiana and Alabama constitutional conventions, he has spoken against lynching, and in other ways has openly or silently set his influence against sinister schemes and unfortunate happenings. Notwithstanding this, it is equally true to assert that on the whole the distinct impression left by Mr. Washington's propaganda is, first, that the South is justified in its present attitude toward the Negro because of the Negro's degradation; secondly, that the prime cause of the Negro's failure to rise more quickly is his wrong education in the past; and, thirdly, that his future rise depends primarily on his own efforts. Each of these propositions is a dangerous half-truth. The supplementary truths must never be lost sight of: first, slavery and race-prejudice are potent if not sufficient causes of the Negro's position; second, industrial and common-school training were necessarily slow in planting because they had to await the black teachers trained by higher institutions, — it being extremely doubtful if any essentially different development was possible, and certainly a Tuskegee was unthinkable before 1880; and, third, while it is a great truth to say that the Negro must strive and strive mightily to help himself, it is equally true that unless his striving be not simply seconded, but rather aroused and encouraged, by the initiative of the richer and wiser environing group, he cannot hope for great success.

In his failure to realize and impress this last point, Mr. Washington is especially to be criticised. His doctrine has tended to make the whites, North and South, shift the burden of the Negro problem to the Negro's shoulders and stand aside as critical and rather pessimistic spectators; when in fact the burden belongs to the nation, and the hands of none of us are clean if we bend not our energies to righting these great wrongs.

The South ought to be led, by candid and honest criticism, to assert her better self and do her full duty to the race she has cruelly wronged and is still wronging. The North — her copartner in guilt — cannot salve her conscience by plastering it with gold. We cannot settle this problem by diplomacy and suaveness, by "policy" alone. If worse come to worst, can the moral fibre of this country survive the slow throttling and murder of nine millions of men?

The black men of America have a duty to perform, a duty stern and delicate, — a forward movement to oppose a part of the work of their greatest leader. So far as Mr. Washington preaches Thrift, Patience, and Industrial Training for the masses, we must hold up his hands and strive with him, rejoicing in his honors and glorying in the strength of this Joshua called of God and of man to lead the headless host. But so far as Mr. Washington apologizes for injustice, North or South, does not rightly value the privilege and duty of voting, belittles the emasculating effects of caste distinctions, and opposes the higher training and ambition of our brighter minds, — so far as he, the South, or the Nation, does this, — we must unceasingly and firmly oppose them. By every civilized and peaceful method we must strive for the rights which the world accords to men, clinging unwaveringly to those great words which the sons of the Fathers would fain forget: "We hold these truths to be self-evident: That all men are created equal; that they are endowed by their Creator with certain unalienable rights; that among these are life, liberty, and the pursuit of happiness." [1903]

THINKING ABOUT THE TEXT

1. Du Bois is clearly upset with Washington. What is his main objection to the Atlanta Compromise? Do you agree with him?
2. Is the narrator of "Battle Royal" still under Washington's influence or has the thinking of Du Bois made some inroads?
3. What might the grandfather in "Battle Royal" think of Du Bois's last paragraph?

GUNNAR MYRDAL
Social Equality

A Swedish economist who with wife Alva Myrdal (winner of the 1982 Nobel Peace Prize) established a model social-welfare system for Sweden in the 1930s, Gunnar Myrdal (1898–1987) was asked by the Carnegie Foundation in 1938 to study racism in the United States. "Social Equality" is an excerpt from the book that elaborated on the results of his study, An American Dilemma: The Negro Problem and Modern Democracy *(1944). In* Cultural Contexts for Ralph Ellison's "Invisible Man," *historian Eric Sundquist points out that the white men in "Battle Royal" would have understood the term* social equality *to include sexual relations and marriage between black men and white women, an idea that would have been unconscionable to them in a great many ways.*

In his first encounter with the American Negro problem, perhaps nothing perplexes the outside observer more than the popular term and the popular theory of "no social equality." He will be made to feel from the start that it has concrete implications and a central importance for the Negro problem in America. But, nevertheless, the term is kept vague and elusive, and the theory loose and ambiguous. One moment it will be stretched to cover and justify every form of social segregation and discrimination, and, in addition, all the inequalities in justice, politics, and breadwinning. The next moment it will be narrowed to express only the denial of close personal intimacies and intermarriage. The very lack of precision allows the notion of "no social equality" to rationalize the rather illogical and wavering system of color caste in America.

The kernel of the popular theory of "no social equality" will, when pursued, be presented as a firm determination on the part of the whites to block amalgamation and preserve "the purity of the white race." The white man identifies himself with "the white race" and feels that he has a stake in resisting the dissipation of its racial identity. Important in this identification is the notion of "the absolute and unchangeable superiority of the white race." From this racial dogma will often be drawn the *direct* inference that the white man shall dominate in all spheres. But when the logic of this inference is inquired about, the inference will be made *indirect* and will be made to lead over to the danger of amalgamation, or, as it is popularly expressed, "intermarriage."

It is further found that the ban on intermarriage is focused on white women. For them it covers both formal marriage and illicit intercourse. In regard to white men it is taken more or less for granted that they would not stoop to marry Negro women, and that illicit intercourse does not fall under the same intense taboo. Their offspring, under the popular doctrine that maternity is more certain than paternity, become Negroes anyway, and the white race easily avoids pollution with Negro blood. To prevent "intermarriage" in this specific sense of sex relations between white women and Negro men, it is not enough to apply legal and social sanctions against it—so the popular theory runs. In using the danger of intermarriage as a defense for the whole caste system, it is assumed both that Negro men have a strong desire for "intermarriage," and that white women would be open to proposals from Negro men, *if* they are not guarded from even meeting them on an equal plane. The latter assumption, of course, is never openly expressed, but is logically implicit in the popular theory. The conclusion follows that the whole system of segregation and discrimination is justified. Every single measure is defended as necessary to block "social equality" which in its turn is held necessary to prevent "intermarriage."

The basic role of the fear of amalgamation in white attitudes to the race problem is indicated by the popular magical concept of "blood." Educated white Southerners, who know everything about modern genetic and biological research, confess readily that they actually feel an irrational or "instinctive" repugnance in thinking of "intermarriage." These measures of segregation and discrimination are often of the type found in the true taboos, and in the notion "not to be touched" of primitive religion. The specific taboos are characterized, further, by a different degree of excitement which attends their violation and a different degree of punishment to the violator: the closer the act to sexual association, the more furious is the public reaction. Sexual association itself is punished by death and is accompanied by tremendous public excitement; the other social relations meet decreasing degrees of public fury. Sex becomes in this popular theory the principle around which the whole structure of segregation of the Negroes—down to disfranchisement and denial of equal opportunities on the labor market—is organized. The reasoning is this: "For, say what we will, may not all the equalities be ultimately based on potential social equality, and that in turn on intermarriage? Here we reach the real *crux* of the question." In cruder language, but with the same logic, the Southern man on the street responds to any plea for social equality: "Would you like to have your daughter marry a Negro?"

This theory of color caste centering around the aversion to amalgamation determines, as we have just observed, the white man's rather definite rank order of the various measures of segregation and discrimination against Negroes. The

5

relative significance attached to each of those measures is dependent upon their degree of expediency or necessity—in the view of white people—as means of upholding the ban on "intermarriage." In this rank order, (1) the ban on intermarriage and other sex relations involving white women and colored men takes precedence before everything else. It is the end for which the other restrictions are arranged as means. Thereafter follow: (2) all sorts of taboos and etiquettes in personal contacts; (3) segregation in schools and churches; (4) segregation in hotels, restaurants, and theaters, and other public places where people meet socially; (5) segregation in public conveyances; (6) discrimination in public services; and, finally, inequality in (7) politics, (8) justice, and (9) breadwinning and relief.

The degree of liberalism on racial matters in the white South can be designated mainly by the point on this rank order where a man stops because he believes further segregation and discrimination are not necessary to prevent "intermarriage." We have seen that white liberals in the South of the present day, as a matter of principle, rather unanimously stand up against inequality in breadwinning, relief, justice, and politics. These fields of discrimination form the chief battleground and considerable changes in them are, as we have seen, on the way. When we ascend to the higher ranks which concern social relations in the narrow sense, we find the Southern liberals less prepared to split off from the majority opinion of the region. Hardly anybody in the South is prepared to go the whole way and argue that even the ban on intermarriage should be lifted. Practically all agree, not only upon the high desirability of preventing "intermarriage," but also that a certain amount of separation between the two groups is expedient and necessary to prevent it. Even the one who has his philosophical doubts on the point must, if he is reasonable, abstain from ever voicing them. The social pressure is so strong that it would be foolish not to conform. Conformity is a political necessity for having any hope of influence; it is, in addition, a personal necessity for not meeting social ostracism. . . .

The fixation on the purity of white womanhood, and also part of the intensity of emotion surrounding the whole sphere of segregation and discrimination, are to be understood as the backwashes of the sore conscience on the part of white men for their own or their compeers' relations with, or desires for, Negro women. These psychological effects are greatly magnified because of the puritan *milieu* of America and especially of the South. The upper class men in a less puritanical people could probably have indulged in sex relations with, and sexual daydreams of, lower caste women in a more matter-of-course way and without generating so much pathos about white womanhood. The Negro people have to carry the burden not only of the white men's sins but also of their virtues. The virtues of the honest, democratic, puritan white Americans in the South are great, and the burden upon the Negroes becomes ponderous.

Our practical conclusion is that it would have cleansing effects on race relations in America, and particularly in the South, to have an open and sober discussion in rational terms of this ever present popular theory of "intermarriage" and "social equality," giving matters their factual ground, true proportions and logical relations. Because it is, to a great extent, an opportunistic rationalization, and because it refers directly and indirectly to the most touchy spots in American life and American morals, tremendous inhibitions have been built up against a detached and critical discussion of this theory. But such inhibitions are gradually overcome when, in the course of secularized education, people become rational about their life problems. It must never be forgotten that in our increasingly intellectualized civilization even the plain citizen feels an urge for truth and objectivity, and that this rationalistic urge is increasingly competing with the opportunistic demands for rationalization and escape.

There are reasons to believe that a slow but steady cleansing of the American mind is proceeding as the cultural level is raised. The basic racial inferiority doctrine is being undermined by research and education. For a white man to have illicit relations with Negro women is increasingly meeting disapproval. Negroes themselves are more and more frowning upon such relations. This all must tend to dampen the emotional fires around "social equality." Sex and race fears are, however, even today the main defense for segregation and, in fact, for the whole caste order. The question shot at the interviewer touching any point of this order is still: "Would you like to have your daughter (sister) marry a Negro?"   [1944]

THINKING ABOUT THE TEXT

1. Look back at the smoker section in "Battle Royal," especially when the narrator during his speech says "social equality" instead of "social responsibility." Why do you think there was a "sudden stillness" in the room?

2. Based on his ideas about white sexual fears, how might Myrdal read the part at the smoker dealing with the naked dancer?

3. Myrdal writes that "conformity is a political necessity for having any hope of influence; it is, in addition, a personal necessity for not meeting social ostracism." Does this insight help your understanding of the world of the smoker?

AFRICAN AMERICAN FOLK SONG

Run, Nigger, Run

Like all true folk creations, this song is not attributed to a particular writer but is one of many that grew out of a community. First printed in 1867 but certainly much older, "Run, Nigger, Run" expresses the desire for freedom in the face of injustice, disappointment, and broken promises that runs through African American literature from the earliest slave narratives to the poetic novels of Toni Morrison. The calaboose *refers to jail, often in the form of a "workhouse" where cruel punishments were meted out to errant slaves; the* patter-roller *is the "patrol" made up of mounted men and hunting dogs formed to track down and capture those who actually ran. Imprisoned in a racist culture, Ralph Ellison's protagonist is not simply an* invisible man—*he is a* running man *as well.*

Do, please, marster, don't ketch me,
Ketch dat nigger behin' dat tree;
He stole money en I stole none,
Put him in the calaboose des for fun!

Chorus:
    Oh, run, nigger, run! de patter-roller ketch you.   5
    Run, nigger, run! hit's almos' day!
    Oh, run, nigger, run! de patter-roller ketch you.
    Run, nigger run! hit's almos' day!

Some folks say dat a nigger won't steal,
But I kotch one in my corn-fiel';   10
He run ter de eas', he run ter de wes',
He run he head in a hornet nes'!

De sun am set, dis nigger am free;
De yaller gals he goes to see;
I heard a man cry, "Run, doggone you,"   15
Run, nigger, run, patter-roller ketch you.

Wid eyes wide open and head hangin' down,
Like de rabbit before de houn',
Dis nigger streak it for de pasture;
Nigger run fast, white man run faster.   20

And ober de fence as slick as a eel
Dis nigger jumped all but his heel;
De white man ketch dat fast, you see,
And tied it tight aroun' de tree.

Dis nigger heard dat old whip crack,   25
But nebber stopped fur to look back;
I started home as straight as a bee
And left my heel tied aroun' de tree.

My ol' Miss, she prommus me
Dat when she die, she set me free;   30
But she done dead dis many year ago,
En yer I'm hoein' de same ol' row!

I'm a-hoein' across, I'm a-hoein' aroun',
I'm a-cleanin' up some mo' new groun'.
Whar I lif' so hard, I lif' so free,   35
Dat my sins rise up in front er me!

But some er dese days my time will come,
I'll year dat bugle, I'll year dat drum,
I'll see dem armies a-marchin' along,

I'll lif' my head en jine der song— [40]
I'll dine no mo' behin' dat tree,
W'en de angels flock fer to wait on me!   [1867]

THINKING ABOUT THE TEXT

1. Does the folk song help explain the attitudes of the African Americans in "Battle Royal"?
2. Explain how this song can be seen as mixing fantasy and realism.
3. What specific elements of "slave culture" does the song illustrate?

WRITING ABOUT ISSUES

1. Argue that the episode at the smoker is, or is not, evidence that the grand-father's advice to "overcome 'em with yeses, undermine 'em with grins, agree 'em to death and destruction" (para. 2) will not work.
2. Analyze the arguments of Washington and Du Bois in terms of the claims they both make, the assumptions these are based on, the evidence they use as support, and their effectiveness in relation to the intended audience. Which writer do you find more persuasive?
3. Write a personal narrative detailing an experience when you were either the victim of bias because of your race, gender, age, religion, ethnicity, sexual preference, or any other personal dynamic or when you were part of a group that held biased views. Be specific about what happened, how you felt then, how you feel now, and what you learned from the experience.

THE OUTSIDER IN A DREAMLIKE WORLD:
A COLLECTION OF WRITINGS BY FRANZ KAFKA

FRANZ KAFKA, "The Metamorphosis"
FRANZ KAFKA, "A Hunger Artist"
FRANZ KAFKA, "Before the Law"

Many readers prefer fiction with recognizable characters and familiar events that correspond to the logic of the world. Perhaps all of us are more comfortable with fictional characters we can relate to or with situations we have experienced ourselves. For that reason, reading the work of Franz Kafka can be disorienting. A bizarre logic animates his fictional world: People change into insects, wait for years outside a gate, or starve themselves as entertainment. *Enigmatic* and *surreal* are terms that come to mind; *puzzling* and *dreamlike* are others. But for many readers, his stories are profound, penetrating, and personal. Even though the surface details are almost hallucinatory, readers feel Kafka is writing about the world they experience. They sometimes feel cut off from other humans, confused, or alienated from the values they find at work or at home. If you have ever felt as if you were an outsider, at odds with the insiders at school, home, or work, then perhaps Kafka will seem relevant to you. Some critics think he captures the displacement and disconnectedness of modern life, especially the power of bureaucracies to crush the innocent. The following three stories, told in a disarmingly matter-of-fact tone, are darkly serious and comic at the same time. *Kafkaesque* is now a term used to describe the world you are about to enter, a world so mysterious as to both intrigue and baffle.

BEFORE YOU READ

Do you ever discuss your dreams with friends? Are there alternative views about their meaning? Do you ever feel disconnected? Alienated from a group? An outsider? How would it be if you felt like this all the time?

FRANZ KAFKA

The Metamorphosis

Translated by Willa and Edwin Muir

Born and raised in the German-Jewish ghetto in Prague, Czechoslovakia, Franz Kafka (1883–1924) faced prejudice and alienation as a Jew, as an Austrian in a predominately Czech city, and as the son of a comparatively rich businessman in a place where many were poor. After earning a law degree, Kafka worked in a boring and limiting bureaucratic job and lived with his autocratic father, writing and struggling with religious questions late into the night. After he died of tuberculosis, a friend published several of his novels, including The Trial *(1925) and* The Castle *(1930), disobeying Kafka's request that they be burned. "The Metamorphosis," published in 1915, is one of Kafka's best-known works and contains one of the most memorable first sentences in literature. Many critics see this symbolic work as part autobiography and part fiction.*

1

As Gregor Samsa awoke one morning from uneasy dreams he found himself transformed in his bed into a gigantic insect. He was lying on his hard, as it were armor-plated, back and when he lifted his head a little he could see his dome-like brown belly divided into stiff arched segments on top of which the bed quilt could hardly keep in position and was about to slide off completely. His numerous legs, which were pitifully thin compared to the rest of his bulk, waved helplessly before his eyes.

What has happened to me? he thought. It was no dream. His room, a regular human bedroom, only rather too small, lay quiet between the four familiar walls. Above the table on which a collection of cloth samples was unpacked and spread out — Samsa was a commercial traveler — hung the picture which he had recently cut out of an illustrated magazine and put into a pretty gilt frame. It showed a lady, with a fur cap on and a fur stole, sitting upright and holding out to the spectator a huge fur muff into which the whole of her forearm had vanished!

Gregor's eyes turned next to the window, and the overcast sky — one could hear rain drops beating on the window gutter — made him quite melancholy. What about sleeping a little longer and forgetting all this nonsense, he thought, but it could not be done, for he was accustomed to sleep on his right side and in his present condition he could not turn himself over. However violently he forced himself towards his right side he always rolled on to his back again. He tried it at least a hundred times, shutting his eyes to keep from seeing his struggling legs, and only desisted when he began to feel in his side a faint dull ache he had never experienced before.

Oh God, he thought, what an exhausting job I've picked on! Traveling about day in, day out. It's much more irritating work than doing the actual business in the office, and on top of that there's the trouble of constant traveling, of worrying about train connections, the bed and irregular meals, casual acquaintances that are always new and never become intimate friends. The devil take it all! He felt a slight itching up on his belly; slowly pushed himself on his back nearer to the top of the bed so that he could lift his head more easily; identified the itching place which was surrounded by many small white spots the nature of which he could not understand and made to touch it with a leg, but drew the leg back immediately, for the contact made a cold shiver run through him.

He slid down again into his former position. This getting up early, he thought, makes one quite stupid. A man needs his sleep. Other commercials live like harem women. For instance, when I come back to the hotel of a morning to write up the orders I've got, these others are only sitting down to breakfast. Let me just try that with my chief; I'd be sacked on the spot. Anyhow, that might be quite a good thing for me, who can tell? If I didn't have to hold my hand because of my parents I'd have given notice long ago, I'd have gone to the chief and told him exactly what I think of him. That would knock him endways from his desk! It's a queer way of doing, too, this sitting on high at a desk and talking down to employees, especially when they have to come quite near because the chief is hard of hearing. Well, there's still hope; once I've saved enough money to pay back my parents' debts to him — that should take another five or six years — I'll do it without fail. I'll cut myself completely loose then. For the moment, though, I'd better get up, since my train goes at five.

He looked at the alarm clock ticking on the chest. Heavenly Father! he thought. It was half-past six o'clock and the hands were quietly moving on, it was even past the half-hour, it was getting on toward a quarter to seven. Had the alarm clock not gone off? From the bed one could see that it had been properly set for

5

four o'clock; of course it must have gone off. Yes, but was it possible to sleep quietly through that ear-splitting noise? Well, he had not slept quietly, yet apparently all the more soundly for that. But what was he to do now? The next train went at seven o'clock; to catch that he would need to hurry like mad and his samples weren't even packed up, and he himself wasn't feeling particularly fresh and active. And even if he did catch the train he wouldn't avoid a row with the chief, since the firm's porter would have been waiting for the five o'clock train and would have long since reported his failure to turn up. The porter was a creature of the chief's, spineless and stupid. Well, supposing he were to say he was sick? But that would be most unpleasant and would look suspicious, since during his five years' employment he had not been ill once. The chief himself would be sure to come with the sick-insurance doctor, would reproach his parents with their son's laziness and would cut all excuses short by referring to the insurance doctor, who of course regarded all mankind as perfectly healthy malingerers. And would he be so far wrong on this occasion? Gregor really felt quite well, apart from a drowsiness that was utterly superfluous after such a long sleep, and he was even unusually hungry.

As all this was running through his mind at top speed without his being able to decide to leave his bed — the alarm clock had just struck a quarter to seven — there came a cautious tap at the door behind the head of his bed. "Gregor," said a voice — it was his mother's — "it's a quarter to seven. Hadn't you a train to catch?" That gentle voice! Gregor had a shock as he heard his own voice answering hers, unmistakably his own voice, it was true, but with a persistent horrible twittering squeak behind it like an undertone, that left the words in their clear shape only for the first moment and then rose up reverberating round them to destroy their sense, so that one could not be sure one had heard them rightly. Gregor wanted to answer at length and explain everything, but in the circumstances he confined himself to saying: "Yes, yes, thank you, Mother, I'm getting up now." The wooden door between them must have kept the change in his voice from being noticeable outside, for his mother contented herself with this statement and shuffled away. Yet this brief exchange of words had made the other members of the family aware that Gregor was still in the house, as they had not expected, and at one of the side doors his father was already knocking, gently, yet with his fist. "Gregor, Gregor," he called, "what's the matter with you?" And after a little while he called again in a deeper voice: "Gregor! Gregor!" At the other side door his sister was saying in a low, plaintive tone: "Gregor? Aren't you well? Are you needing anything?" He answered them both at once: "I'm just ready," and did his best to make his voice sound as normal as possible by enunciating the words very clearly and leaving long pauses between them. So his father went back to his breakfast, but his sister whispered: "Gregor, open the door, do." However, he was not thinking of opening the door, and felt thankful for the prudent habit he had acquired in traveling of locking all doors during the night, even at home.

His immediate intention was to get up quietly without being disturbed, to put on his clothes and above all eat his breakfast, and only then to consider what else was to be done, since in bed, he was well aware, his meditations would come to no sensible conclusion. He remembered that often enough in bed he had felt small aches and pains, probably caused by awkward postures, which had proved purely imaginary once he got up, and he looked forward eagerly to seeing this morning's delusions gradually fall away. That the change in his voice was nothing but the precursor of a severe chill, a standing ailment of commercial travelers, he had not the least possible doubt.

To get rid of the quilt was quite easy; he had only to inflate himself a little and it fell off by itself. But the next move was difficult, especially because he was so uncommonly broad. He would have needed arms and hands to hoist himself up; instead he had only the numerous little legs which never stopped waving in all directions and which he could not control in the least. When he tried to bend one of them it was the first to stretch itself straight; and did he succeed at last in making it do what he wanted, all the other legs meanwhile waved the more wildly in a high degree of unpleasant agitation. "But what's the use of lying idle in bed," said Gregor to himself.

He thought that he might get out of bed with the lower part of his body first, but this lower part, which he had not yet seen and of which he could form no clear conception, proved too difficult to move; it shifted so slowly; and when finally, almost wild with annoyance, he gathered his forces together and thrust out recklessly, he had miscalculated the direction and bumped heavily against the lower end of the bed, and the stinging pain he felt informed him that precisely this lower part of his body was at the moment probably the most sensitive. 10

So he tried to get the top part of himself out first, and cautiously moved his head towards the edge of the bed. That proved easy enough, and despite its breadth and mass the bulk of his body at last slowly followed the movement of his head. Still, when he finally got his head free over the edge of the bed he felt too scared to go on advancing, for after all if he let himself fall in this way it would take a miracle to keep his head from being injured. And at all costs he must not lose consciousness now, precisely now; he would rather stay in bed.

But when after a repetition of the same efforts he lay in his former position again, sighing, and watched his little legs struggling against each other more wildly than ever, if that were possible, and saw no way of bringing any order into this arbitrary confusion, he told himself again that it was impossible to stay in bed and that the most sensible course was to risk everything for the smallest hope of getting away from it. At the same time he did not forget meanwhile to remind himself that cool reflection, the coolest possible, was much better than desperate resolves. In such moments he focused his eyes as sharply as possible on the window, but, unfortunately, the prospect of the morning fog, which muffled even the other side of the narrow street, brought him little encouragement and comfort. "Seven o'clock already," he said to himself when the alarm clock chimed again, "seven o'clock already and still such a thick fog." And for a little while he lay quiet, breathing lightly, as if perhaps expecting such complete repose to restore all things to their real and normal condition.

But then he said to himself: "Before it strikes a quarter past seven I must be quite out of this bed, without fail. Anyhow, by that time someone will have come from the office to ask for me, since it opens before seven." And he set himself to rocking his whole body at once in a regular rhythm, with the idea of swinging it out of the bed. If he tipped himself out in that way he could keep his head from injury by lifting it at an acute angle when he fell. His back seemed to be hard and was not likely to suffer from a fall on the carpet. His biggest worry was the loud crash he would not be able to help making, which would probably cause anxiety, if not terror, behind all the doors. Still, he must take the risk.

When he was already half out of the bed — the new method was more a game than an effort, for he needed only to hitch himself across by rocking to and fro — it struck him how simple it would be if he could get help. Two strong people — he thought of his father and the servant girl — would be amply sufficient; they would only have to thrust their arms under his convex back, lever him out of the bed, bend down with their burden and then be patient enough to let him turn himself right over on to the floor, where it was to be hoped his legs would then find their proper function. Well, ignoring the fact that the doors were all locked, ought he really to call for help? In spite of his misery he could not suppress a smile at the very idea of it.

He had got so far that he could barely keep his equilibrium when he rocked   15
himself strongly, and he would have to nerve himself very soon for the final decision since in five minutes' time it would be a quarter past seven — when the front doorbell rang. "That's someone from the office," he said to himself, and grew almost rigid, while his little legs only jigged about all the faster. For a moment everything stayed quiet. "They're not going to open the door," said Gregor to himself, catching at some kind of irrational hope. But then of course the servant girl went as usual to the door with her heavy tread and opened it. Gregor needed only to hear the first good morning of the visitor to know immediately who it was — the chief clerk himself. What a fate, to be condemned to work for a firm where the smallest omission at once gave rise to the gravest suspicion! Were all employees in a body nothing but scoundrels, was there not among them one single loyal devoted man who, had he wasted only an hour or so of the firm's time in a morning, was so tormented by conscience as to be driven out of his mind and actually incapable of leaving his bed? Wouldn't it really have been sufficient to send an apprentice to inquire — if any inquiry were necessary at all — did the chief clerk himself have to come and thus indicate to the entire family, an innocent family, that this suspicious circumstance could be investigated by no one less versed in affairs than himself? And more through the agitation caused by these reflections than through any act of will Gregor swung himself out of bed with all his strength. There was a loud thump, but it was not really a crash. His fall was broken to some extent by the carpet, his back, too, was less stiff than he thought, and so there was merely a dull thud, not so very startling. Only he had not lifted his head carefully enough and had hit it; he turned it and rubbed it on the carpet in pain and irritation.

"That was something falling down in there," said the chief clerk in the next room to the left. Gregor tried to suppose to himself that something like what had happened to him today might some day happen to the chief clerk; one really could not deny that it was possible. But as if in brusque reply to this supposition the chief clerk took a couple of firm steps in the next-door room and his patent leather boots creaked. From the right-hand room his sister was whispering to inform him of the situation: "Gregor, the chief clerk's here." "I know," muttered Gregor to himself; but he didn't dare to make his voice loud enough for his sister to hear it.

"Gregor," said his father now from the left-hand room, "the chief clerk has come and wants to know why you didn't catch the early train. We don't know what to say to him. Besides, he wants to talk to you in person. So open the door, please. He will be good enough to excuse the untidiness of your room." "Good morning, Mr. Samsa," the chief clerk was calling amiably meanwhile. "He's not well," said his mother to the visitor, while his father was still speaking through the door, "he's not well, sir, believe me. What else would make him miss a train! The boy thinks about nothing but his work. It makes me almost cross the way he never goes out in the evenings; he's been here the last eight days and has stayed at home every single evening. He just sits there quietly at the table reading a newspaper or looking through railway timetables. The only amusement he gets is doing fret-work. For instance, he spent two or three evenings cutting out a little picture frame; you would be surprised to see how pretty it is; it's hanging in his room; you'll see it in a minute when Gregor opens the door. I must say I'm glad you've come, sir; we should never have got him to unlock the door by ourselves; he's so obstinate; and I'm sure he's unwell, though he wouldn't have it to be so this morning." "I'm just coming," said Gregor slowly and carefully, not moving an inch for fear of losing one word of the conversation. "I can't think of any other explanation, madam," said the chief clerk, "I hope it's nothing serious. Although on the other hand I must say that we men of business—fortunately or unfortunately—very often simply have to ignore any slight indisposition, since business must be attended to." "Well, can the chief clerk come in now?" asked Gregor's father impatiently, again knocking on the door. "No," said Gregor. In the left-hand room a painful silence followed this refusal, in the right-hand room his sister began to sob.

Why didn't his sister join the others? She was probably newly out of bed and hadn't even begun to put on her clothes yet. Well, why was she crying? Because he wouldn't get up and let the chief clerk in, because he was in danger of losing his job, and because the chief would begin dunning his parents again for the old debts? Surely these were things one didn't need to worry about for the present. Gregor was still at home and not in the least thinking of deserting the family. At the moment, true, he was lying on the carpet and no one who knew the condition he was in could seriously expect him to admit the chief clerk. But for such a small discourtesy, which could plausibly be explained away somehow later on, Gregor could hardly be dismissed on the spot. And it seemed to Gregor that it would be much more sensible to leave him in peace for the present than to trouble him with tears and entreaties. Still, of course, their uncertainty bewildered them all and excused their behavior.

"Mr. Samsa," the chief clerk called now in a louder voice, "what's the matter with you? Here you are, barricading yourself in your room, giving only 'yes' and 'no' for answers, causing your parents a lot of unnecessary trouble and neglecting—I mention this only in passing—neglecting your business duties in an incredible fashion. I am speaking here in the name of your parents and of your chief, and I beg you quite seriously to give me an immediate and precise explanation. You amaze me, you amaze me. I thought you were a quiet, dependable person, and now all at once you seem bent on making a disgraceful exhibition of yourself. The chief did hint to me early this morning a possible explanation for your disappearance—with reference to the cash payments that were entrusted to you recently—but I almost pledged my solemn word of honor that this could not be so. But now that I see how incredibly obstinate you are, I no longer have the slightest desire to take your part at all. And your position in the firm is not so unassailable. I came with the intention of telling you all this in private, but since you are wasting my time so needlessly I don't see why your parents shouldn't hear it too. For some time past your work has been most unsatisfactory; this is not the season of the year for a business boom, of course, we admit that, but a season of the year for doing no business at all, that does not exist, Mr. Samsa, must not exist."

"But, sir," cried Gregor, beside himself and in his agitation forgetting everything else, "I'm just going to open the door this very minute. A slight illness, an attack of giddiness, has kept me from getting up. I'm still lying in bed. But I feel all right again. I'm getting out of bed now. Just give me a moment or two longer! I'm not quite so well as I thought. But I'm all right, really. How a thing like that can suddenly strike one down! Only last night I was quite well, my parents can tell you, or rather I did have a slight presentiment. I must have showed some sign of it. Why didn't I report it at the office! But one always thinks that an indisposition can be got over without staying in the house. Oh sir, do spare my parents! All that you're reproaching me with now has no foundation; no one has ever said a word to me about it. Perhaps you haven't looked at the last orders I sent in. Anyhow, I can still catch the eight o'clock train, I'm much the better for my few hours' rest. Don't let me detain you here, sir; I'll be attending to business very soon, and do be good enough to tell the chief so and to make my excuses to him!"

And while all this was tumbling out pell-mell and Gregor hardly knew what he was saying, he had reached the chest quite easily, perhaps because of the practice he had had in bed, and was now trying to lever himself upright by means of it. He meant actually to open the door, actually to show himself and speak to the chief clerk; he was eager to find out what the others, after all their insistence, would say at the sight of him. If they were horrified then the responsibility was no longer his and he could stay quiet. But if they took it calmly, then he had no reason either to be upset, and could really get to the station for the eight o'clock train if he hurried. At first he slipped down a few times from the polished surface of the chest, but at length with a last heave he stood upright; he paid no more attention to the pains in the lower part of his body, however they smarted. Then he let himself fall against the back of a near-by chair, and clung with his little legs to the edges of it. That brought him into control of himself again and he stopped speaking, for now he could listen to what the chief clerk was saying.

"Did you understand a word of it?" the chief clerk was asking; "surely he can't be trying to make fools of us?" "Oh dear," cried his mother, in tears, "per-

20

haps he's terribly ill and we're tormenting him. Grete! Grete!" she called out then. "Yes, Mother?" called his sister from the other side. They were calling to each other across Gregor's room. "You must go this minute for the doctor. Gregor is ill. Go for the doctor, quick. Did you hear how he was speaking?" "That was no human voice," said the chief clerk in a voice noticeably low beside the shrillness of the mother's. "Anna! Anna!" his father was calling through the hall to the kitchen, clapping his hands, "get a locksmith at once!" And the two girls were already running through the hall with a swish of skirts—how could his sister have got dressed so quickly?—and were tearing the front door open. There was no sound of its closing again; they had evidently left it open, as one does in houses where some great misfortune has happened.

But Gregor was now much calmer. The words he uttered were no longer understandable, apparently, although they seemed clear enough to him, even clearer than before, perhaps because his ear had grown accustomed to the sound of them. Yet at any rate people now believed that something was wrong with him, and were ready to help him. The positive certainty with which these first measures had been taken comforted him. He felt himself drawn once more into the human circle and hoped for great and remarkable results from both the doctor and the locksmith, without really distinguishing precisely between them. To make his voice as clear as possible for the decisive conversation that was now imminent he coughed a little, as quietly as he could, of course, since this noise too might not sound like a human cough for all he was able to judge. In the next room meanwhile there was complete silence. Perhaps his parents were sitting at the table with the chief clerk, whispering, perhaps they were all leaning against the door and listening.

Slowly Gregor pushed the chair towards the door, then let go of it, caught hold of the door for support—the soles at the end of his little legs were somewhat sticky—and rested against it for a moment after his efforts. Then he set himself to turning the key in the lock with his mouth. It seemed, unhappily, that he hadn't really any teeth—what could he grip the key with?—but on the other hand his jaws were certainly very strong; with their help he did manage to set the key in motion, heedless of the fact that he was undoubtedly damaging them somewhere, since a brown fluid issued from his mouth, flowed over the key and dripped on the floor. "Just listen to that," said the chief clerk next door; "he's turning the key." That was a great encouragement to Gregor; but they should all have shouted encouragement to him, his father and mother too: "Go on, Gregor," they should have called out, "keep going, hold on to that key!" And in the belief that they were all following his efforts intently, he clenched his jaws recklessly on the key with all the force at his command. As the turning of the key progressed he circled round the lock, holding on now only with his mouth, pushing on the key, as required, or pulling it down again with all the weight of his body. The louder click of the finally yielding lock literally quickened Gregor. With a deep breath of relief he said to himself: "So I didn't need the locksmith," and laid his head on the handle to open the door wide.

Since he had to pull the door towards him, he was still invisible when it was really wide open. He had to edge himself slowly round the near half of the double   25 door, and to do it very carefully if he was not to fall plump upon his back just on the threshold. He was still carrying out this difficult manoeuvre, with no time to observe anything else, when he heard the chief clerk utter a loud "Oh!" — it sounded like a gust of wind — and now he could see the man, standing as he was nearest to the door, clapping one hand before his open mouth and slowly backing away as if driven by some invisible steady pressure. His mother — in spite of the chief clerk's being there her hair was still undone and sticking up in all directions — first clasped her hands and looked at his father, then took two steps towards Gregor and fell on the floor among her outspread skirts, her face hidden on her breast. His father knotted his fist with a fierce expression on his face as if he meant to knock Gregor back into his room, then looked uncertainly round the living room, covered his eyes with his hands and wept till his great chest heaved.

Gregor did not go now into the living room, but leaned against the inside of the firmly shut wing of the door, so that only half his body was visible and his head above it bending sideways to look at the others. The light had meanwhile strengthened; on the other side of the street one could see clearly a section of the endlessly long, dark gray building opposite — it was a hospital — abruptly punctuated by its row of regular windows; the rain was still falling, but only in large singly discernible and literally singly splashing drops. The breakfast dishes were set out on the table lavishly, for breakfast was the most important meal of the day to Gregor's father, who lingered it out for hours over various newspapers. Right opposite Gregor on the wall hung a photograph of himself on military service, as a lieutenant, hand on sword, a carefree smile on his face, inviting one to respect his uniform and military bearing. The door leading to the hall was open, and one could see that the front door stood open too, showing the landing beyond and the beginning of the stairs going down.

"Well," said Gregor, knowing perfectly that he was the only one who had retained any composure, "I'll put my clothes on at once, pack up my samples and start off. Will you only let me go? You see, sir, I'm not obstinate, and I'm willing to work; traveling is a hard life, but I couldn't live without it. Where are you going, sir? To the office? Yes? Will you give a true account of all this? One can be temporarily incapacitated, but that's just the moment for remembering former services and bearing in mind that later on, when the incapacity has been got over, one will certainly work with all the more industry and concentration. I'm loyally bound to serve the chief, you know that very well. Besides, I have to provide for my parents and my sister. I'm in great difficulties, but I'll get out of them again. Don't make things any worse for me than they are. Stand up for me in the firm. Travelers are not popular there, I know. People think they earn sacks of money and just have a good time. A prejudice there's no particular reason for revising. But you, sir, have a more comprehensive view of affairs than the rest of the staff, yes, let me tell you in confidence, a more comprehensive view than the chief himself, who, being the owner, lets his judgment easily be swayed against one of his employees. And you know very well that the traveler, who is never seen in the office almost the whole year round, can so easily fall a victim to gossip and ill luck and unfounded complaints, which he mostly knows nothing about, except when he comes back exhausted from his rounds, and only then suffers in person from their evil consequences, which he can no longer trace back to the original causes. Sir, sir, don't go away without a word to me to show that you think me in the right at least to some extent!"

But at Gregor's very first words the chief clerk had already backed away and only stared at him with parted lips over one twitching shoulder. And while Gregor was speaking he did not stand still one moment but stole away towards the door, without taking his eyes off Gregor, yet only an inch at a time, as if obeying some secret injunction to leave the room. He was already at the hall, and the suddenness with which he took his last step out of the living room would have made one believe he had burned the sole of his foot. Once in the hall he stretched his right arm before him towards the staircase, as if some supernatural power were waiting there to deliver him.

Gregor perceived that the chief clerk must on no account be allowed to go away in this frame of mind if his position in the firm were not to be endangered to the utmost. His parents did not understand this so well; they had convinced themselves in the course of years that Gregor was settled for life in this firm, and besides they were so occupied with their immediate troubles that all foresight had forsaken them. Yet Gregor had this foresight. The chief clerk must be detained, soothed, persuaded and finally won over; the whole future of Gregor and his family depended on it! If only his sister had been there! She was intelligent; she had begun to cry while Gregor was still lying quietly on his back. And no doubt the chief clerk, so partial to ladies, would have been guided by her; she would have shut the door of the flat and in the hall talked him out of his horror. But she was not there, and Gregor would have to handle the situation himself. And without remembering that he was still unaware what powers of movement he possessed, without even remembering that his words in all possibility, indeed in all likelihood, would again be unintelligible, he let go the wing of the door, pushed himself through the opening, started to walk towards the chief clerk, who was already ridiculously clinging with both hands to the railing on the landing; but immediately, as he was feeling for a support, he fell down with a little cry upon all his numerous legs. Hardly was he down when he experienced for the first time this morning a sense of physical comfort; his legs had firm ground under them; they were completely obedient, as he noted with joy; they even strove to carry him forward in whatever direction he chose; and he was inclined to believe that a final relief from all his sufferings was at hand. But in the same moment as he found himself on the floor, rocking with suppressed eagerness to move, not far from his mother, indeed just in front of her, she, who had seemed so completely crushed, sprang all at once to her feet, her arms and fingers outspread, cried: "Help, for God's sake, help!" bent her head down as if to see Gregor better, yet on the contrary kept backing senselessly away; had quite forgotten that the laden table stood behind her; sat upon it hastily, as if in absence of mind, when she bumped into it; and seemed altogether unaware that the big coffee pot beside her was upset and pouring coffee in a flood over the carpet.

"Mother, Mother," said Gregor in a low voice, and looked up at her. The chief clerk, for the moment, had quite slipped from his mind; instead, he could not resist snapping his jaws together at the sight of the streaming coffee. That made his mother scream again, she fled from the table and fell into the arms of his father, who hastened to catch her. But Gregor had now no time to spare for his parents; the chief clerk was already on the stairs; with his chin on the banisters he was taking one last backward look. Gregor made a spring, to be as sure as possible of overtaking him; the chief clerk must have divined his intention, for he leaped down several steps and vanished; he was still yelling "Ugh!" and it echoed through the whole staircase.

Unfortunately, the flight of the chief clerk seemed completely to upset Gregor's father, who had remained relatively calm until now, for instead of running after the man himself, or at least not hindering Gregor in his pursuit, he seized in his right hand the walking stick which the chief clerk had left behind on a chair, together with a hat and greatcoat, snatched in his left hand a large newspaper from the table and began stamping his feet and flourishing the stick and the newspaper to drive Gregor back into his room. No entreaty of Gregor's availed, indeed no entreaty was even understood, however humbly he bent his head his father only stamped on the floor the more loudly. Behind his father his mother had torn open a window, despite the cold weather, and was leaning far out of it with her face in her hands. A strong draught set in from the street to the staircase, the window curtains blew in, the newspapers on the table fluttered, stray pages whisked over the floor. Pitilessly Gregor's father drove him back, hissing and crying "Shoo!" like a savage. But Gregor was quite unpracticed in walking backwards, it really was a slow business. If he only had a chance to turn round he could get back to his room at once, but he was afraid of exasperating his father by the slowness of such a rotation and at any moment the stick in his father's hand might hit him a fatal blow on the back or on the head. In the end, however, nothing else was left for him to do since to his horror he observed that in moving backwards he could not even control the direction he took; and so, keeping an anxious eye on his father all the time over his shoulder, he began to turn round as quickly as he could, which was in reality very slowly. Perhaps his father noted his good intentions, for he did not interfere except every now and then to help him in the manoeuvre from a distance with the point of the stick. If only he would have stopped making that unbearable hissing noise! It made Gregor quite lose his head. He had turned almost completely round when the hissing noise so distracted him that he even turned a little the wrong way again. But when at last his head was fortunately right in front of the doorway, it appeared that his body was too broad simply to get through the opening. His father, of course, in his present mood was far from thinking of such a thing as opening the other half of the door, to let Gregor have enough space. He had merely the fixed idea of driving Gregor back into his room as quickly as possible. He would never have suffered Gregor to make the circumstantial preparations for standing up on end and perhaps slipping his way through the door. Maybe he was now making more noise than ever to urge Gregor forward, as if no obstacle impeded him; to Gregor, anyhow, the noise in his rear sounded no longer like the voice of one single father; this was really no joke, and Gregor thrust himself—come what might—into the doorway. One side of his body rose up, he was tilted at an angle in the doorway, his flank was quite bruised, horrid blotches stained the white door, soon he was stuck fast and, left to himself, could not have moved at all, his legs on one side fluttered trembling to the air, those on the other were crushed painfully to the floor—when from behind his father gave him a strong push which was literally a deliverance and he flew far into the room, bleeding freely. The door was slammed behind him with the stick, and then at last there was silence.

2

Not until it was twilight did Gregor awake out of a deep sleep, more like a swoon than a sleep. He would certainly have waked up of his own accord not much later, for he felt himself sufficiently rested and well-slept, but it seemed to him as if a fleeting step and a cautious shutting of the door leading into the hall had aroused him. The electric lights in the street cast a pale sheen here and there on the ceiling and the upper surfaces of the furniture, but down below, where he lay, it was dark. Slowly, awkwardly trying out his feelers, which he now first learned to appreciate, he pushed his way to the door to see what had been happening there. His left side felt like one single long, unpleasant tense scar, and he had actually to limp on his two rows of legs. One little leg, moreover, had been severely damaged in the course of that morning's events—it was almost a miracle that only one had been damaged—and trailed uselessly behind him.

He had reached the door before he discovered what had really drawn him to it: the smell of food. For there stood a basin filled with fresh milk in which floated little sops of white bread. He could almost have laughed with joy, since he was now still hungrier than in the morning, and he dipped his head almost over the eyes straight into the milk. But soon in disappointment he withdrew it again; not only did he find it difficult to feed because of his tender left side—and he could only feed with the palpitating collaboration of his whole body—he did not like the milk either, although milk had been his favorite drink and that was certainly why his sister had set it there for him, indeed it was almost with repulsion that he turned away from the basin and crawled back to the middle of the room.

He could see through the crack of the door that the gas was turned on in the living room, but while usually at this time his father made a habit of reading the afternoon newspaper in a loud voice to his mother and occasionally to his sister as well, not a sound was now to be heard. Well, perhaps his father had recently given up this habit of reading aloud, which his sister had mentioned so often in conversation and in her letters. But there was the same silence all around, although the flat was certainly not empty of occupants. "What a quiet life our family has been leading," said Gregor to himself, and as he sat there motionless staring into the darkness he felt great pride in the fact that he had been able to provide such a life for his parents and sister in such a fine flat. But what if all the quiet, the comfort, the contentment were now to end in horror? To keep himself from being lost in such thoughts Gregor took refuge in movement and crawled up and down the room.

Once during the long evening one of the side doors was opened a little and quickly shut again, later the other side door too; someone had apparently wanted to come in and then thought better of it. Gregor now stationed himself immediately before the living room door, determined to persuade any hesitating visitor to come in or at least to discover who it might be; but the door was not opened again

35

and he waited in vain. In the early morning, when the doors were locked, they had all wanted to come in, now that he had opened one door and the other had apparently been opened during the day, no one came in and even the keys were on the other side of the doors.

It was late at night before the gas went out in the living room, and Gregor could easily tell that his parents and his sister had all stayed awake until then, for he could clearly hear the three of them stealing away on tiptoe. No one was likely to visit him, not until the morning, that was certain; so he had plenty of time to meditate at his leisure on how he was to arrange his life afresh. But the lofty, empty room in which he had to lie flat on the floor filled him with an apprehension he could not account for, since it had been his very own room for the past five years—and with a half-unconscious action, not without a slight feeling of shame, he scuttled under the sofa, where he felt comfortable at once, although his back was a little cramped and he could not lift his head up, and his only regret was that his body was too broad to get the whole of it under the sofa.

He stayed there all night, spending the time partly in a light slumber, from which his hunger kept waking him up with a start, and partly in worrying and sketching vague hopes, which all led to the same conclusion, that he must lie low for the present and, by exercising patience, and the utmost consideration, help the family to bear the inconvenience he was bound to cause them in his present condition.

Very early in the morning, it was still almost night, Gregor had the chance to test the strength of his new resolutions, for his sister, nearly fully dressed, opened the door from the hall and peered in. She did not see him at once, yet when she caught sight of him under the sofa—well, he had to be somewhere, he couldn't have flown away, could he?—she was so startled that without being able to help it she slammed the door shut again. But as if regretting her behavior she opened the door again immediately and came in on tiptoe, as if she were visiting an invalid or even a stranger. Gregor had pushed his head forward to the very edge of the sofa and watched her. Would she notice that he had left the milk standing, and not for lack of hunger, and would she bring in some other kind of food more to his taste? If she did not do it of her own accord, he would rather starve than draw her attention to the fact, although he felt a wild impulse to dart out from under the sofa, throw himself at her feet and beg her for something to eat. But his sister at once noticed, with surprise, that the basin was still full, except for a little milk that had been spilt all around it, she lifted it immediately, not with her bare hands, true, but with a cloth and carried it away. Gregor was wildly curious to know what she would bring instead, and made various speculations about it. Yet what she actually did next, in the goodness of her heart, he could never have guessed at. To find out what he liked she brought him a whole selection of food, all set out on an old newspaper. There were old, half-decayed vegetables, bones from last night's supper covered with a white sauce that had thickened; some raisins and almonds; a piece of cheese that Gregor would have called uneatable two days ago; a dry roll of bread, a buttered roll, and a roll both buttered and salted. Besides all that, she set down again the same basin, into which she had poured some water, and which was apparently to be reserved for his exclusive use. And with fine tact, knowing that Gregor would not eat in her presence, she withdrew quickly and even turned the key, to let him understand that he could take his ease as much as he liked. Gregor's legs all whizzed towards the food. His wounds must have healed completely, moreover, for he felt no disability, which amazed him and made him reflect how more than a month ago he had cut one finger a little with a knife and had still suffered pain from the wound only the day before yesterday. Am I less sensitive now? he thought, and sucked greedily at the cheese, which above all the other edibles attracted him at once and strongly. One after another and with tears of satisfaction in his eyes he quickly devoured the cheese, the vegetables and the sauce; the fresh food, on the other hand, had no charms for him, he could not even stand the smell of it and actually dragged away to some little distance the things he could eat. He had long finished his meal and was only lying lazily on the same spot when his sister turned the key slowly as a sign for him to retreat. That roused him at once, although he was nearly asleep, and he hurried under the sofa again. But it took considerable self-control for him to stay under the sofa, even for the short time his sister was in the room, since the large meal had swollen his body somewhat and he was so cramped he could hardly breathe. Slight attacks of breathlessness afflicted him and his eyes were starting a little out of his head as he watched his unsuspecting sister sweeping together with a broom not only the remains of what he had eaten but even the things he had not touched, as if these were now of no use to anyone, and hastily shoveling it all into a bucket, which she covered with a wooden lid and carried away. Hardly had she turned her back when Gregor came from under the sofa and stretched and puffed himself out.

In this manner Gregor was fed, once in the early morning while his parents and the servant girl were still asleep, and a second time after they had all had their midday dinner, for then his parents took a short nap and the servant girl could be sent out on some errand or other by his sister. Not that they would have wanted him to starve, of course, but perhaps they could not have borne to know more about his feeding than from hearsay, perhaps too his sister wanted to spare them such little anxieties wherever possible, since they had quite enough to bear as it was.

Under what pretext the doctor and the locksmith had been got rid of on that first morning Gregor could not discover, for since what he had said was not understood by the others it never struck any of them, not even his sister, that he could understand what they said, and so whenever his sister came into his room he had to content himself with hearing her utter only a sigh now and then and an occasional appeal to the saints. Later on, when she had got a little used to the situation — of course she could never get completely used to it — she sometimes threw out a remark which was kindly meant or could be so interpreted. "Well, he liked his dinner today," she would say when Gregor had made a good clearance of his food; and when he had not eaten, which gradually happened more and more often, she would say almost sadly: "Everything's been left standing again."

But although Gregor could get no news directly, he overheard a lot from the neighboring rooms, and as soon as voices were audible, he would run to the door of the room concerned and press his whole body against it. In the first few days

40

especially there was no conversation that did not refer to him somehow, even if only indirectly. For two whole days there were family consultations at every meal-time about what should be done; but also between meals the same subject was discussed, for there were always at least two members of the family at home, since no one wanted to be alone in the flat and to leave it quite empty was unthinkable. And on the very first of these days the household cook—it was not quite clear what and how much she knew of the situation—went down on her knees to his mother and begged leave to go, and when she departed, a quarter of an hour later, gave thanks for her dismissal with tears in her eyes as if for the greatest benefit that could have been conferred on her, and without any prompting swore a solemn oath that she would never say a single word to anyone about what had happened.

Now Gregor's sister had to cook too, helping her mother; true, the cooking did not amount to much, for they ate scarcely anything. Gregor was always hearing one of the family vainly urging another to eat and getting no answer but: "Thanks, I've had all I want," or something similar. Perhaps they drank nothing either. Time and again his sister kept asking his father if he wouldn't like some beer and offered kindly to go and fetch it herself, and when he made no answer suggested that she could ask the concierge to fetch it, so that he need feel no sense of obligation, but then a round "No" came from his father and no more was said about it.

In the course of that very first day Gregor's father explained the family's financial position and prospects to both his mother and his sister. Now and then he rose from the table to get some voucher or memorandum out of the small safe he had rescued from the collapse of his business five years earlier. One could hear him opening the complicated lock and rustling papers out and shutting it again. This statement made by his father was the first cheerful information Gregor had heard since his imprisonment. He had been of the opinion that nothing at all was left over from his father's business, at least his father had never said anything to the contrary, and of course he had not asked him directly. At the time Gregor's sole desire was to do his utmost to help the family to forget as soon as possible the catastrophe which had overwhelmed the business and thrown them all into a state of complete despair. And so he had set to work with unusual ardor and almost overnight had become a commercial traveler instead of a little clerk, with of course much greater chances of earning money, and his success was immediately translated into good round coin which he could lay on the table for his amazed and happy family. These had been fine times, and they had never recurred, at least not with the same sense of glory, although later on Gregor had earned so much money that he was able to meet the expenses of the whole household and did so. They had simply got used to it, both the family and Gregor; the money was gratefully accepted and gladly given, but there was no special uprush of warm feeling. With his sister alone had he remained intimate, and it was a secret plan of his that she, who loved music, unlike himself, and could play movingly on the violin, should be sent next year to study at the Conservatorium, despite the great expense that would entail, which must be made up in some other way. During his brief visits home the Conservatorium was often mentioned in the talks he had with his sister, but always merely as a beautiful dream which could never come true, and his parents discouraged even these innocent references to it; yet Gregor had made up his mind firmly about it and meant to announce the fact with due solemnity on Christmas Day.

Such were the thoughts, completely futile in his present condition, that went through his head as he stood clinging upright to the door and listening. Sometimes out of sheer weariness he had to give up listening and let his head fall negligently against the door, but he always had to pull himself together again at once, for even the slight sound his head made was audible next door and brought all conversation to a stop. "What can he be doing now?" his father would say after a while, obviously turning towards the door, and only then would the interrupted conversation gradually be set going again.

Gregor was now informed as amply as he could wish—for his father tended   45 to repeat himself in his explanations, partly because it was a long time since he had handled such matters and partly because his mother could not always grasp things at once—that a certain amount of investments, a very small amount it was true, had survived the wreck of their fortunes and had even increased a little because the dividends had not been touched meanwhile. And besides that, the money Gregor brought home every month—he had kept only a few dollars for himself—had never been quite used up and now amounted to a small capital sum. Behind the door Gregor nodded his head eagerly, rejoiced at this evidence of unexpected thrift and foresight. True, he could really have paid off some more of his father's debts to the chief with his extra money, and so brought much nearer the day on which he could quit his job, but doubtless it was better the way his father had arranged it.

Yet this capital was by no means sufficient to let the family live on the interest of it; for one year, perhaps, or at the most two, they could live on the principal, that was all. It was simply a sum that ought not to be touched and should be kept for a rainy day; money for living expenses would have to be earned. Now his father was still hale enough but an old man, and he had done no work for the past five years and could not be expected to do much; during these five years, the first years of leisure in his laborious though unsuccessful life, he had grown rather fat and become sluggish. And Gregor's old mother, how was she to earn a living with her asthma, which troubled her even when she walked through the flat and kept her lying on a sofa every other day panting for breath beside an open window? And was his sister to earn her bread, she who was still a child of seventeen and whose life hitherto had been so pleasant, consisting as it did in dressing herself nicely, sleeping long, helping in the housekeeping, going out to a few modest entertainments and above all playing the violin? At first whenever the need for earning money was mentioned Gregor let go his hold on the door and threw himself down on the cool leather sofa beside it, he felt so hot with shame and grief.

Often he just lay there the long nights through without sleeping at all, scrabbling for hours on the leather. Or he nerved himself to the great effort of pushing an armchair to the window, then crawled up over the window sill and, braced against the chair, leaned against the windowpanes, obviously in some recollection of the sense of freedom that looking out of a window always used to give him. For in reality day by day things that were even a little way off were growing dimmer to his sight; the hospital across the street, which he used to execrate for being all too often before his eyes, was now quite beyond his range of vision, and if he had not known that he lived in Charlotte Street, a quiet street but still a city street, he might have believed that his window gave on a desert waste where gray sky and gray land blended indistinguishably into each other. His quick-witted sister only needed to observe twice that the armchair stood by the window; after that whenever she had tidied the room she always pushed the chair back to the same place at the window and even left the inner casements open.

If he could have spoken to her and thanked her for all she had to do for him, he could have borne her ministrations better; as it was, they oppressed him. She certainly tried to make as light as possible of whatever was disagreeable in her task, and as time went on she succeeded, of course, more and more, but time brought more enlightenment to Gregor too. The very way she came in distressed him. Hardly was she in the room when she rushed to the window, without even taking time to shut the door, careful as she was usually to shield the sight of Gregor's room from the others, and as if she were almost suffocating tore the casements open with hasty fingers, standing then in the open draught for a while even in the bitterest cold and drawing deep breaths. This noisy scurry of hers upset Gregor twice a day; he would crouch trembling under the sofa all the time, knowing quite well that she would certainly have spared him such a disturbance had she found it at all possible to stay in his presence without opening a window.

On one occasion, about a month after Gregor's metamorphosis, when there was surely no reason for her to be still startled at his appearance, she came a little earlier than usual and found him gazing out of the window, quite motionless, and thus well placed to look like a bogey. Gregor would not have been surprised had she not come in at all, for she could not immediately open the window while he was there, but not only did she retreat, she jumped back as if in alarm and banged the door shut; a stranger might well have thought that he had been lying in wait for her there meaning to bite her. Of course he hid himself under the sofa at once, but he had to wait until midday before she came again, and she seemed more ill at ease than usual. This made him realize how repulsive the sight of him still was to her, and that it was bound to go on being repulsive, and what an effort it must cost her not to run away even from the sight of the small portion of his body that stuck out from under the sofa. In order to spare her that, therefore, one day he carried a sheet on his back to the sofa—it cost him four hours' labor—and arranged it there in such a way as to hide him completely, so that even if she were to bend down she could not see him. Had she considered the sheet unnecessary, she would certainly have stripped it off the sofa again, for it was clear enough that this curtaining and confining of himself was not likely to conduce Gregor's comfort, but she left it where it was, and Gregor even fancied that he caught a thankful glance from her eye when he lifted the sheet carefully a very little with his head to see how she was taking the new arrangement.

For the first fortnight his parents could not bring themselves to the point of entering his room, and he often heard them expressing their appreciation of his sister's activities, whereas formerly they had frequently scolded her for being as

50

they thought a somewhat useless daughter. But now, both of them often waited outside the door, his father and his mother, while his sister tidied his room, and as soon as she came out she had to tell them exactly how things were in the room, what Gregor had eaten, how he had conducted himself this time and whether there was not perhaps some slight improvement in his condition. His mother, moreover, began relatively soon to want to visit him, but his father and sister dissuaded her at first with arguments which Gregor listened to very attentively and altogether approved. Later, however, she had to be held back by main force, and when she cried out: "Do let me in to Gregor, he is my unfortunate son! Can't you understand that I must go to him?" Gregor thought that it might be well to have her come in, not every day, of course, but perhaps once a week; she understood things, after all, much better than his sister, who was only a child despite the efforts she was making and had perhaps taken on so difficult a task merely out of childish thoughtlessness.

Gregor's desire to see his mother was soon fulfilled. During the daytime he did not want to show himself at the window, out of consideration for his parents, but he could not crawl very far around the few square yards of floor space he had, nor could he bear lying quietly at rest all during the night, while he was fast losing any interest he had ever taken in food, so that for mere recreation he had formed the habit of crawling crisscross over the walls and ceiling. He especially enjoyed hanging suspended from the ceiling; it was much better than lying on the floor; one could breathe more freely; one's body swung and rocked lightly; and in the almost blissful absorption induced by this suspension it could happen to his own surprise that he let go and fell plump on the floor. Yet he now had his body much better under control than formerly, and even such a big fall did him no harm. His sister at once remarked the new distraction Gregor had found for himself—he left traces behind him of the sticky stuff on his soles wherever he crawled—and she got the idea in her head of giving him as wide a field as possible to crawl in and of removing the pieces of furniture that hindered him, above all the chest of drawers and the writing desk. But that was more than she could manage all by herself; she did not dare ask her father to help her; and as for the servant girl, a young creature of sixteen who had had the courage to stay on after the cook's departure, she could not be asked to help, for she had begged as an especial favor that she might keep the kitchen door locked and open it only on a definite summons; so there was nothing left but to apply to her mother at an hour when her father was out. And the old lady did come, with exclamations of joyful eagerness, which, however, died away at the door of Gregor's room. Gregor's sister, of course, went in first, to see that everything was in order before letting his mother enter. In great haste Gregor pulled the sheet lower and rucked it more in folds so that it really looked as if it had been thrown accidentally over the sofa. And this time he did not peer out from under it; he renounced the pleasure of seeing his mother on this occasion and was only glad that she had come at all. "Come in, he's out of sight," said his sister, obviously leading her mother in by the hand. Gregor could now hear the two women struggling to shift the heavy old chest from its place, and his sister claiming the greater part of the labor for herself, without listening to the admonitions of her mother who feared she might overstrain herself. It took a long time. After at least a quarter of an hour's tugging his mother objected that the chest had better be left where it was, for in the first place it was too heavy and could never be got out before his father came home, and standing in the middle of the room like that it would only hamper Gregor's movements, while in the second place it was not at all certain that removing the furniture would be doing a service to Gregor. She was inclined to think to the contrary; the sight of the naked walls made her own heart heavy, and why shouldn't Gregor have the same feeling, considering that he had been used to his furniture for so long and might feel forlorn without it. "And doesn't it look," she concluded in a low voice — in fact she had been almost whispering all the time as if to avoid letting Gregor, whose exact whereabouts she did not know, hear even the tones of her voice, for she was convinced that he could not understand her words — "doesn't it look as if we were showing him, by taking away his furniture, that we have given up hope of his ever getting better and are just leaving him coldly to himself? I think it would be best to keep his room exactly as it has always been, so that when he comes back to us he will find everything unchanged and be able all the more easily to forget what has happened in between."

On hearing these words from his mother Gregor realized that the lack of all direct human speech for the past two months together with the monotony of family life must have confused his mind, otherwise he could not account for the fact that he had quite earnestly looked forward to having his room emptied of furnishing. Did he really want his warm room, so comfortably fitted with old family furniture, to be turned into a naked den in which he would certainly be able to crawl unhampered in all directions but at the price of shedding simultaneously all recollection of his human background? He had indeed been so near the brink of forgetfulness that only the voice of his mother, which he had not heard for so long, had drawn him back from it. Nothing should be taken out of his room; everything must stay as it was; he could not dispense with the good influence of the furniture on his state of mind; and even if the furniture did hamper him in his senseless crawling round and round, that was no drawback but a great advantage.

Unfortunately his sister was of the contrary opinion; she had grown accustomed, and not without reason, to consider herself an expert in Gregor's affairs as against her parents, and so her mother's advice was now enough to make her determined on the removal not only of the chest and the writing desk, which had been her first intention, but of all the furniture except the indispensable sofa. This determination was not, of course, merely the outcome of childish recalcitrance and of the self-confidence she had recently developed so unexpectedly and at such cost; she had in fact perceived that Gregor needed a lot of space to crawl about in, while on the other hand he never used the furniture at all, so far as could be seen. Another factor might have been also the enthusiastic temperament of an adolescent girl, which seeks to indulge itself on every opportunity and which now tempted Grete to exaggerate the horror of her brother's circumstances in order that she might do all the more for him. In a room where Gregor lorded it all alone over empty walls no one save herself was likely ever to set foot.

And so she was not to be moved from her resolve by her mother who seemed moreover to be ill at ease in Gregor's room and therefore unsure of herself, was soon reduced to silence and helped her daughter as best she could to push the chest outside. Now, Gregor could do without the chest, if need be, but the writing desk he must retain. As soon as the two women had got the chest out of his room, groaning as they pushed it, Gregor stuck his head out from under the sofa to see how he might intervene as kindly and cautiously as possible. But as bad luck would have it, his mother was the first to return, leaving Grete clasping the chest in the room next door where she was trying to shift it all by herself, without of course moving it from the spot. His mother however was not accustomed to the sight of him, it might sicken her and so in alarm Gregor backed quickly to the other end of the sofa, yet could not prevent the sheet from swaying a little in front. That was enough to put her on the alert. She paused, stood still for a moment and then went back to Grete.

Although Gregor kept reassuring himself that nothing out of the way was happening, but only a few bits of furniture were being changed round, he soon had to admit that all this trotting to and fro of the two women, their little ejaculations and the scraping of furniture along the floor affected him like a vast disturbance coming from all sides at once, and however much he tucked in his head and legs and cowered to the very floor he was bound to confess that he would not be able to stand it for long. They were clearing his room out; taking away everything he loved; the chest in which he kept his fret saw and other tools was already dragged off; they were now loosening the writing desk which had almost sunk into the floor, the desk at which he had done all his homework when he was at the commercial academy, at the grammar school before that, and, yes, even at the primary school—he had no more time to waste in weighing the good intentions of the two women, whose existence he had by now almost forgotten, for they were so exhausted that they were laboring in silence and nothing could be heard but the heavy scuffling of their feet.

And so he rushed out—the women were just leaning against the writing desk in the next room to give themselves a breather—and four times changed his direction, since he really did not know what to rescue first, then on the wall opposite, which was already otherwise cleared, he was struck by the picture of the lady muffled in so much fur and quickly crawled up to it and pressed himself to the glass, which was a good surface to hold on to and comforted his hot belly. This picture at least, which was entirely hidden beneath him, was going to be removed by nobody. He turned his head towards the door of the living room so as to observe the women when they came back.

They had not allowed themselves much of a rest and were already coming; Grete had twined her arm round her mother and was almost supporting her. "Well, what shall we take now?" said Grete, looking round. Her eyes met Gregor's from the wall. She kept her composure, presumably because of her mother, bent her head down to her mother, to keep her from looking up, and said, although in a fluttering, unpremeditated voice: "Come, hadn't we better go back to the living room for a moment?" Her intentions were clear enough to Gregor, she wanted to bestow her mother in safety and then chase him down from the wall. Well, just let her try it! He clung to his picture and would not give it up. He would rather fly in Grete's face.

55

But Grete's words had succeeded in disquieting her mother, who took a step to one side, caught sight of the huge brown mass on the flowered wallpaper, and before she was really conscious that what she saw was Gregor screamed in a loud, hoarse voice: "Oh God, oh God!" fell with outspread arms over the sofa as if giving up and did not move. "Gregor!" cried his sister, shaking her fist and glaring at him. This was the first time she had directly addressed him since his metamorphosis. She ran into the next room for some aromatic essence with which to rouse her mother from her fainting fit. Gregor wanted to help too — there was still time to rescue the picture — but he was stuck fast to the glass and had to tear himself loose; he then ran after his sister into the next room as if he could advise her, as he used to do; but then had to stand helplessly behind her; she meanwhile searched among various small bottles and when she turned round started in alarm at the sight of him; one bottle fell on the floor and broke; a splinter of glass cut Gregor's face and some kind of corrosive medicine splashed him; without pausing a moment longer Grete gathered up all the bottles she could carry and ran to her mother with them; she banged the door shut with her foot. Gregor was now cut off from his mother, who was perhaps nearly dying because of him; he dared not open the door for fear of frightening away his sister, who had to stay with her mother; there was nothing he could do but wait; and harassed by self-reproach and worry he began now to crawl to and fro, over everything, walls, furniture and ceiling, and finally in his despair, when the whole room seemed to be reeling round him, fell down on to the middle of the big table.

A little while elapsed, Gregor was still lying there feebly and all around was quiet, perhaps that was a good omen. Then the doorbell rang. The servant girl was of course locked in her kitchen, and Grete would have to open the door. It was his father. "What's been happening?" were his first words; Grete's face must have told him everything. Grete answered in a muffled voice, apparently hiding her head on his breast: "Mother has been fainting, but she's better now. Gregor's broken loose." "Just what I expected," said his father, "just what I've been telling you, but you women would never listen." It was clear to Gregor that his father had taken the worst interpretation of Grete's all too brief statement and was assuming that Gregor had been guilty of some violent act. Therefore Gregor must now try to propitiate his father, since he had neither time nor means for an explanation. And so he fled to the door of his own room and crouched against it, to let his father see as soon as he came in from the hall that his son had the good intention of getting back into his room immediately and that it was not necessary to drive him there, but that if only the door were opened he would disappear at once.

Yet his father was not in the mood to perceive such fine distinctions. "Ah!" he cried as soon as he appeared, in a tone which sounded at once angry and exultant. Gregor drew his head back from the door and lifted it to look at his father. Truly, this was not the father he had imagined to himself; admittedly he had been too absorbed of late in his new recreation of crawling over the ceiling to take the same interest as before in what was happening elsewhere in the flat, and he ought really to be prepared for some changes. And yet, and yet, could that be his father? The man who used to lie wearily sunk in bed whenever Gregor set out on a busi- 60 ness journey; who welcomed him back of an evening lying in a long chair in a dressing gown; who could not really rise to his feet but only lifted his arms in greeting, and on the rare occasions when he did go out with his family, on one or two Sundays a year and on high holidays, walked between Gregor and his mother, who were slow walkers anyhow, even more slowly than they did, muffled in his old greatcoat, shuffling laboriously forward with the help of his crook-handled stick which he set down most cautiously at every step and, whenever he wanted to say anything, nearly always came to a full stop and gathered his escort around him? Now he was standing there in fine shape; dressed in a smart blue uniform with gold buttons, such as bank messengers wear; his strong double chin bulged over the stiff high collar of his jacket; from under his bushy eyebrows his black eyes darted fresh and penetrating glances; his onetime tangled white hair had been combed flat on either side of a shining and carefully exact parting. He pitched his cap, which bore a gold monogram, probably the badge of some bank, in a wide sweep across the whole room on to a sofa and with the tail-ends of his jacket thrown back, his hands in his trouser pockets, advanced with a grim visage towards Gregor. Likely enough he did not himself know what he meant to do; at any rate he lifted his feet uncommonly high, and Gregor was dumbfounded at the enormous size of his shoe soles. But Gregor could not risk standing up to him, aware as he had been from the very first day of his new life that his father believed only the severest measures suitable for dealing with him. And so he ran before his father, stopping when he stopped and scuttling forward again when his father made any kind of move. In this way they circled the room several times without anything decisive happening; indeed the whole operation did not even look like a pursuit because it was carried out so slowly. And so Gregor did not leave the floor, for he feared that his father might take as a piece of peculiar wickedness any excursion of his over the walls or the ceiling. All the same, he could not stay this course much longer, for while his father took one step he had to carry out a whole series of movements. He was already beginning to feel breathless, just as in his former life his lungs had not been very dependable. As he was staggering along, trying to concentrate his energy on running, hardly keeping his eyes open; in his dazed state never even thinking of any other escape than simply going forward; and having almost forgotten that the walls were free to him, which in this room were well provided with finely carved pieces of furniture full of knobs and crevices—suddenly something lightly flung landed close behind him and rolled before him. It was an apple; a second apple followed immediately; Gregor came to a stop in alarm; there was no point in running on, for his father was determined to bombard him. He had filled his pockets with fruit from the dish on the sideboard and was now shying apple after apple, without taking particularly good aim for the moment. The small red apples rolled about the floor as if magnetized and cannoned into each other. An apple thrown without much force grazed Gregor's back and glanced off harmlessly. But another following immediately landed right on his back and sank in; Gregor wanted to drag himself forward, as if this startling, incredible pain could be left behind him: but he felt as if nailed to the spot and flattened himself out in a complete derangement of all his senses. With his last conscious look he saw the door of his room being torn open and his mother rushing out ahead of his screaming sister, in her underbodice, for her daughter had loosened her clothing to let her breathe more freely and recover from her swoon, he saw his mother rushing towards his father, leaving one after another behind her on the floor her loosened petticoats, stumbling over her petticoats straight to his father and embracing him, in complete union with him—but here Gregor's sight began to fail—with her hands clasped round his father's neck as she begged for her son's life.

3

The serious injury done to Gregor, which disabled him for more than a month—the apple went on sticking in his body as a visible reminder, since no one ventured to remove it—seemed to have made even his father recollect that Gregor was a member of the family, despite his present unfortunate and repulsive shape, and ought not to be treated as an enemy, that, on the contrary, family duty required the suppression of disgust and the exercise of patience, nothing but patience.

And although his injury had impaired, probably forever, his power of movement, and for the time being it took him long, long minutes to creep across his room like an old invalid—there was no question now of crawling up the wall—yet in his own opinion he was sufficiently compensated for this worsening of his condition by the fact that towards evening the living-room door, which he used to watch intently for an hour or two beforehand, was always thrown open, so that lying in the darkness of his room, invisible to the family, he could see them all at the lamp-lit table and listen to their talk, by general consent as it were, very different from his earlier eavesdropping.

True, their intercourse lacked the lively character of former times, which he had always called to mind with a certain wistfulness in the small hotel bedrooms where he had been wont to throw himself down, tired out, on damp bedding. They were now mostly very silent. Soon after supper his father would fall asleep in his armchair; his mother and sister would admonish each other to be silent; his mother, bending low over the lamp, stitched at fine sewing for an underwear firm; his sister, who had taken a job as a salesgirl, was learning shorthand and French in the evenings on the chance of bettering herself. Sometimes his father woke up, and as if quite unaware that he had been sleeping said to his mother: "What a lot of sewing you're doing today!" and at once fell asleep again, while the two women exchanged a tired smile.

With a kind of mulishness his father persisted in keeping his uniform on even in the house; his dressing gown hung uselessly on its peg and he slept fully dressed where he sat, as if he were ready for service at any moment and even here only at the beck and call of his superior. As a result, his uniform, which was not brand-new to start with, began to look dirty, despite all the loving care of the mother and sister to keep it clean, and Gregor often spent whole evenings gazing at the many greasy spots on the garment, gleaming with gold buttons always in a high state of polish, in which the old man sat sleeping in extreme discomfort and yet quite peacefully.

As soon as the clock struck ten his mother tried to rouse his father with gentle   65
words and to persuade him after that to get into bed, for sitting there he could not
have a proper sleep and that was what he needed most, since he had to go to duty
at six. But with the mulishness that had obsessed him since he became a bank
messenger he always insisted on staying longer at the table, although he regularly
fell asleep again and in the end only with the greatest trouble could be got out of
his armchair and into his bed. However insistently Gregor's mother and sister
kept urging him with gentle reminders, he would go on slowly shaking his head
for a quarter of an hour, keeping his eyes shut, and refuse to get to his feet. The
mother plucked at his sleeve, whispering endearments in his ear, the sister left
her lessons to come to her mother's help, but Gregor's father was not to be
caught. He would only sink down deeper in his chair. Not until the two women
hoisted him up by the armpits did he open his eyes and look at them both, one
after the other, usually with the remark: "This is a life. This is the peace and quiet
of my old age." And leaning on the two of them he would heave himself up, with
difficulty, as if he were a great burden to himself, suffer them to lead him as far
as the door and then wave them off and go on alone, while the mother abandoned her needlework and the sister her pen in order to run after him and help
him farther.

Who could find time, in this overworked and tired-out family, to bother
about Gregor more than was absolutely needful? The household was reduced
more and more; the servant girl was turned off; a gigantic bony charwoman with
white hair flying round her head came in morning and evening to do the rough
work; everything else was done by Gregor's mother, as well as great piles of
sewing. Even various family ornaments, which his mother and sister used to wear
with pride at parties and celebrations, had to be sold, as Gregor discovered of an
evening from hearing them all discuss the prices obtained. But what they
lamented most was the fact that they could not leave the flat which was much too
big for their present circumstances, because they could not think of any way to
shift Gregor. Yet Gregor saw well enough that consideration for him was not the
main difficulty preventing the removal, for they could have easily shifted him in
some suitable box with a few air holes in it; what really kept them from moving
into another flat was rather their own complete hopelessness and the belief that
they had been singled out for a misfortune such as had never happened to any of
their relations or acquaintances. They fulfilled to the uttermost all that the world
demands of poor people, the father fetched breakfast for the small clerks in the
bank, the mother devoted her energy to making underwear for strangers, the sister trotted to and fro behind the counter at the behest of customers, but more
than this they had not the strength to do. And the wound in Gregor's back began
to nag at him afresh when his mother and sister, after getting his father into bed,
came back again, left their work lying, drew close to each other and sat cheek by
cheek; when his mother, pointing towards his room, said: "Shut that door now,
Grete," and he was left again in darkness, while next door the women mingled
their tears or perhaps sat dry-eyed staring at the table.

Gregor hardly slept at all by night or by day. He was often haunted by the
idea that next time the door opened he would take the family's affairs in hand

again just as he used to do; once more, after this long interval, there appeared in his thoughts the figures of the chief and the chief clerk, the commercial travelers and the apprentices, the porter who was so dull-witted, two or three friends in other firms, a chambermaid in one of the rural hotels, a sweet and fleeting memory, a cashier in a milliner's shop, whom he had wooed earnestly but too slowly— they all appeared, together with strangers or people he had quite forgotten, but instead of helping him and his family they were one and all unapproachable and he was glad when they vanished. At other times he would not be in the mood to bother about his family, he was only filled with rage at the way they were neglecting him, and although he had no clear idea of what he might care to eat he would make plans for getting into the larder to take the food that was after all his due, even if he were not hungry. His sister no longer took thought to bring him what might especially please him, but in the morning and at noon before she went to business hurriedly pushed into his room with her foot any food that was available, and in the evening cleared it out again with one sweep of the broom, heedless of whether it had been merely tasted, or—as most frequently happened—left untouched. The cleaning of his room, which she now did always in the evenings, could not have been more hastily done. Streaks of dirt stretched along the walls, here and there lay balls of dust and filth. At first Gregor used to station himself in some particularly filthy corner when his sister arrived, in order to reproach her with it, so to speak. But he could have sat there for weeks without getting her to make any improvements; she could see the dirt as well as he did, but she had simply made up her mind to leave it alone. And yet, with a touchiness that was new to her, which seemed anyhow to have infected the whole family, she jealously guarded her claim to be the sole caretaker of Gregor's room. His mother once subjected his room to a thorough cleaning, which was achieved only by means of several buckets of water—all this dampness of course upset Gregor too and he lay widespread, sulky and motionless on the sofa—but she was well punished for it. Hardly had his sister noticed the changed aspect of his room than she rushed in high dudgeon into the living room and, despite the imploringly raised hands of her mother, burst into a storm of weeping, while her parents—her father had of course been startled out of his chair—looked on at first in helpless amazement; then they too began to go into action; the father reproached the mother on his right for not having left the cleaning of Gregor's room to his sister; shrieked at the sister on his left that never again was she to be allowed to clean Gregor's room; while the mother tried to pull the father into his bedroom, since he was beyond himself with agitation; the sister, shaken with sobs, then beat upon the table with her small fists; and Gregor hissed loudly with rage because not one of them thought of shutting the door to spare him such a spectacle and so much noise.

Still, even if the sister, exhausted by her daily work, had grown tired of looking after Gregor as she did formerly, there was no need for his mother's intervention or for Gregor's being neglected at all. The charwoman was there. This old widow, whose strong bony frame had enabled her to survive the worst a long life could offer, by no means recoiled from Gregor. Without being in the least curious she had once by chance opened the door of his room and at the sight of Gregor, who, taken by surprise, began to rush to and fro although no one was chasing him, merely stood there with her arms folded. From that time she never failed to open his door a little for a moment, morning and evening, to have a look at him. At first she even used to call him to her, with words which apparently she took to be friendly, such as: "Come along, then, you old dung beetle!" or "Look at the old dung beetle, then!" To such allocutions Gregor made no answer, but stayed motionless where he was, as if the door had never been opened. Instead of being allowed to disturb him so senselessly whenever the whim took her, she should rather have been ordered to clean out his room daily, that charwoman! Once, early in the morning—heavy rain was lashing on the windowpanes, perhaps a sign that spring was on the way—Gregor was so exasperated when she began addressing him again that he ran at her, as if to attack her, although slowly and feebly enough. But the charwoman instead of showing fright merely lifted high a chair that happened to be beside the door, and as she stood there with her mouth wide open it was clear that she meant to shut it only when she brought the chair down on Gregor's back. "So you're not coming any nearer?" she asked, as Gregor turned away again, and quietly put the chair back into the corner.

Gregor was now eating hardly anything. Only when he happened to pass the food laid out for him did he take a bit of something in his mouth as a pastime, kept it there for an hour at a time and usually spat it out again. At first he thought it was chagrin over the state of his room that prevented him from eating, yet he soon got used to the various changes in his room. It had become a habit in the family to push into his room things there was no room for elsewhere, and there were plenty of these now, since one of the rooms had been let to three lodgers. These serious gentlemen—all three of them with full beards, as Gregor once observed through a crack in the door—had a passion for order, not only in their own room but, since they were now members of the household, in all its arrangements, especially in the kitchen. Superfluous, not to say dirty, objects they could not bear. Besides, they had brought with them most of the furnishings they needed. For this reason many things could be dispensed with that it was no use trying to sell but that should not be thrown away either. All of them found their way into Gregor's room. The ash can likewise and the kitchen garbage can. Anything that was not needed for the moment was simply flung into Gregor's room by the charwoman, who did everything in a hurry; fortunately Gregor usually saw only the object, whatever it was, and the hand that held it. Perhaps she intended to take the things away again as time and opportunity offered, or to collect them until she could throw them all out in a heap, but in fact they just lay wherever she happened to throw them, except when Gregor pushed his way through the junk heap and shifted it somewhat, at first out of necessity, because he had not room enough to crawl, but later with increasing enjoyment, although after such excursions, being sad and weary to death, he would lie motionless for hours. And since the lodgers often ate their supper at home in the common living room, the living room door stayed shut many an evening, yet Gregor reconciled himself quite easily to the shutting of the door, for often enough on evenings when it was opened he had disregarded it entirely and lain in the darkest corner of his room, quite unnoticed by the family. But on one occasion the charwoman left the door open a little and it stayed ajar even when the lodgers came in for supper and the lamp was lit. They set themselves at the top end of the table where formerly Gregor and his father and mother had eaten their meals, unfolded their napkins and took knife and fork in hand. At once his mother appeared in the other doorway with a dish of meat and close behind her his sister with a dish of potatoes piled high. The food steamed with a thick vapor. The lodgers bent over the food set before them as if to scrutinize it before eating, in fact the man in the middle, who seemed to pass for an authority with the other two, cut a piece of meat as it lay on the dish, obviously to discover if it were tender or should be sent back to the kitchen. He showed satisfaction, and Gregor's mother and sister, who had been watching anxiously, breathed freely and began to smile.

The family itself took its meals in the kitchen. Nonetheless, Gregor's father   70
came into the living room before going in to the kitchen and with one prolonged bow, cap in hand, made a round of the table. The lodgers all stood up and murmured something in their beards. When they were alone again they ate their food in almost complete silence. It seemed remarkable to Gregor that among the various noises coming from the table he could always distinguish the sound of their masticating teeth, as if this were a sign to Gregor that one needed teeth in order to eat, and that with toothless jaws even of the finest make one could do nothing. "I'm hungry enough," said Gregor sadly to himself, "but not for that kind of food. How these lodgers are stuffing themselves, and here am I dying of starvation!"

On that very evening—during the whole of his time there Gregor could not remember ever having heard the violin—the sound of violin-playing came from the kitchen. The lodgers had already finished their supper, the one in the middle had brought out a newspaper and given the other two a page apiece, and now they were leaning back at ease reading and smoking. When the violin began to play they pricked up their ears, got to their feet, and went on tiptoe to the hall door where they stood huddled together. Their movements must have been heard in the kitchen, for Gregor's father called out: "Is the violin-playing disturbing you, gentlemen? It can be stopped at once." "On the contrary," said the middle lodger, "could not Fräulein Samsa come and play in this room, beside us, where it is much more convenient and comfortable?" "Oh certainly," cried Gregor's father, as if he were the violin-player. The lodgers came back into the living room and waited. Presently Gregor's father arrived with the music stand, his mother carrying the music and his sister with the violin. His sister quietly made everything ready to start playing; his parents, who had never let rooms before and so had an exaggerated idea of the courtesy due to lodgers, did not venture to sit down on their own chairs; his father leaned against the door, the right hand thrust between two buttons of his livery coat, which was formally buttoned up; but his mother was offered a chair by one of the lodgers and, since she left the chair just where he had happened to put it, sat down in a corner to one side.

Gregor's sister began to play; the father and mother, from either side, intently watched the movements of her hands. Gregor, attracted by the playing, ventured to move forward a little until his head was actually inside the living room. He felt hardly any surprise at his growing lack of consideration for the others; there had been a time when he prided himself on being considerate. And yet just on this occasion he had more reason than ever to hide himself, since owing to the amount of dust which lay thick in his room and rose into the air at the slightest movement, he too was covered with dust; fluff and hair and remnants of food trailed with him, caught on his back and along his sides; his indifference to everything was much too great for him to turn on his back and scrape himself clean on the carpet, as once he had done several times a day. And in spite of his condition, no shame deterred him from advancing a little over the spotless floor of the living room.

To be sure, no one was aware of him. The family was entirely absorbed in the violin-playing; the lodgers, however, who first of all had stationed themselves, hands in pockets, much too close behind the music stand so that they could all have read the music, which must have bothered his sister, had soon retreated to the window, half-whispering with downbent heads, and stayed there while his father turned an anxious eye on them. Indeed, they were making it more than obvious that they had been disappointed in their expectation of hearing good or enjoyable violin-playing, that they had had more than enough of the performance and only out of courtesy suffered a continued disturbance of their peace. From the way they all kept blowing the smoke of their cigars high in the air through nose and mouth one could divine their irritation. And yet Gregor's sister was playing so beautifully. Her face leaned sideways, intently and sadly her eyes followed the notes of music. Gregor crawled a little farther forward and lowered his head to the ground so that it might be possible for his eyes to meet hers. Was he an animal, that music had such an effect upon him? He felt as if the way were opening before him to the unknown nourishment he craved. He was determined to push forward till he reached his sister, to pull at her skirt and so let her know that she was to come into his room with her violin, for no one here appreciated her playing as he would appreciate it. He would never let her out of his room, at least, not so long as he lived; his frightful appearance would become, for the first time, useful to him; he would watch all the doors of his room at once and spit at intruders; but his sister should need no constraint, she should stay with him of her own free will; she should sit beside him on the sofa, bend down her ear to him and hear him confide that he had had the firm intention of sending her to the Conservatorium, and that, but for his mishap, last Christmas — surely Christmas was long past? — he would have announced it to everybody without allowing a single objection. After this confession his sister would be so touched that she would burst into tears, and Gregor would then raise himself to her shoulder and kiss her on the neck, which, now that she went to business, she kept free of any ribbon or collar.

"Mr. Samsa!" cried the middle lodger, to Gregor's father, and pointed, without wasting any more words, at Gregor, now working himself slowly forwards. The violin fell silent, the middle lodger first smiled to his friends with a shake of the head and then looked at Gregor again. Instead of driving Gregor out, his father seemed to think it more needful to begin by soothing down the lodgers, although they were not at all agitated and apparently found Gregor more entertaining than the violin-playing. He hurried toward them and, spreading out his arms, tried to urge them back into their own room and at the same time to block their view of Gregor. They now began to be really a little angry, one could not tell whether because of the old man's behavior or because it had just dawned on them that all unwittingly they had such a neighbor as Gregor next door. They demanded explanations of his father, they waved their arms like him, tugged uneasily at their beards, and only with reluctance backed towards their room. Meanwhile Gregor's sister, who stood there as if lost when her playing was so abruptly broken off, came to life again, pulled herself together all at once after standing for a while holding violin and bow in nervelessly hanging hands and staring at her music, pushed her violin into the lap of her mother, who was still sitting in her chair fighting asthmatically for breath, and ran into the lodgers' room to which they were now being shepherded by her father rather more quickly than before. One could see the pillows and blankets on the beds flying under her accustomed fingers and being laid in order. Before the lodgers had actually reached their room she had finished making the beds and slipped out.

The old man seemed once more to be so possessed by his mulish self-assertiveness that he was forgetting all the respect he should show to his lodgers. He kept driving them on and driving them on until in the very door of the bedroom the middle lodger stamped his foot loudly on the floor and so brought him to a halt. "I beg to announce," said the lodger, lifting one hand and looking also at Gregor's mother and sister, "that because of the disgusting conditions prevailing in this household and family"—here he spat on the floor with emphatic brevity—"I give you notice on the spot. Naturally I won't pay you a penny for the days I have lived here, on the contrary I shall consider bringing an action for damages against you, based on claims—believe me—that will be easily susceptible of proof." He ceased and stared straight in front of him, as if he expected something. In fact his two friends at once rushed into the breach with these words: "And we too give notice on the spot." On that he seized the door-handle and shut the door with a slam. 75

Gregor's father, groping with his hands, staggered forward and fell into his chair; it looked as if he were stretching himself there for his ordinary evening nap, but the marked jerkings of his head, which was as if uncontrollable, showed that he was far from asleep. Gregor had simply stayed quietly all the time on the spot where the lodgers had espied him. Disappointment at the failure of his plan, perhaps also the weakness arising from extreme hunger, made it impossible for him to move. He feared, with a fair degree of certainty, that at any moment the general tension would discharge itself in a combined attack upon him, and he lay waiting. He did not react even to the noise made by the violin as it fell off his mother's lap from under her trembling fingers and gave out a resonant note.

"My dear parents," said his sister, slapping her hand on the table by way of introduction, "things can't go on like this. Perhaps you don't realize that, but I do. I won't utter my brother's name in the presence of this creature, and so all I say is: we must try to get rid of it. We've tried to look after it and to put up with it as far as is humanly possible, and I don't think anyone could reproach us in the slightest."

"She is more than right," said Gregor's father to himself. His mother, who was still choking for lack of breath, began to cough hollowly into her hand with a wild look in her eyes.

His sister rushed over to her and held her forehead. His father's thoughts seemed to have lost their vagueness at Grete's words, he sat more upright, fingering his service cap that lay among the plates still lying on the table from the lodgers' supper, and from time to time looked at the still form of Gregor.

"We must try to get rid of it," his sister now said explicitly to her father, since   80
her mother was coughing too much to hear a word, "it will be the death of both of you, I can see that coming. When one has to work as hard as we do, all of us, one can't stand this continual torment at home on top of it. At least I can't stand it any longer." And she burst into such a passion of sobbing that her tears dropped on her mother's face, where she wiped them off mechanically.

"My dear," said the old man sympathetically, and with evident understanding, "but what can we do?"

Gregor's sister merely shrugged her shoulders to indicate the feeling of helplessness that had now overmastered her during her weeping fit, in contrast to her former confidence.

"If he could understand us," said her father, half questioningly; Grete, still sobbing, vehemently waved a hand to show how unthinkable that was.

"If he could understand us," repeated the old man, shutting his eyes to consider his daughter's conviction that understanding was impossible, "then perhaps we might come to some agreement with him. But as it is—"

"He must go," cried Gregor's sister. "That's the only solution, Father. You   85
must just try to get rid of the idea that this is Gregor. The fact that we've believed it for so long is the root of all our trouble. But how can it be Gregor? If this were Gregor, he would have realized long ago that human beings can't live with such a creature, and he'd have gone away on his own accord. Then we wouldn't have any brother, but we'd be able to go on living and keep his memory in honor. As it is, this creature persecutes us, drives away our lodgers, obviously wants the whole apartment to himself and would have us all sleep in the gutter. Just look, Father," she shrieked all at once, "he's at it again!" And in an access of panic that was quite incomprehensible to Gregor she even quitted her mother, literally thrusting the chair from her as if she would rather sacrifice her mother than stay so near to Gregor, and rushed behind her father, who also rose up, being simply upset by her agitation, and half-spread his arms out as if to protect her.

Yet Gregor had not the slightest intention of frightening anyone, far less his sister. He had only begun to turn round in order to crawl back to his room, but it was certainly a startling operation to watch, since because of his disabled condition he could not execute the difficult turning movements except by lifting his head and then bracing it against the floor over and over again. He paused and looked round. His good intentions seemed to have been recognized; the alarm had only been momentary. Now they were all watching him in melancholy silence. His mother lay in her chair, her legs stiffly outstretched and pressed together, her eyes almost closing for sheer weariness; his father and his sister were sitting beside each other, his sister's arm around the old man's neck.

Perhaps I can go on turning round now, thought Gregor, and began his labors again. He could not stop himself from panting with the effort, and had to pause now and then to take breath. Nor did anyone harass him, he was left entirely to himself. When he had completed the turn-round he began at once to crawl straight back. He was amazed at the distance separating him from his room and could not understand how in his weak state he had managed to accomplish the same journey so recently, almost without remarking it. Intent on crawling as fast as possible, he barely noticed that not a single word, not an ejaculation from his family, interfered with his progress. Only when he was already in the doorway did he turn his head round, not completely, for his neck muscles were getting stiff, but enough to see that nothing had changed behind him except that his sister had risen to her feet. His last glance fell on his mother, who was not quite overcome by sleep.

Hardly was he well inside his room when the door was hastily pushed shut, bolted, and locked. The sudden noise in his rear startled him so much that his little legs gave beneath him. It was his sister who had shown such haste. She had been standing ready waiting and had made a light spring forward, Gregor had not even heard her coming, and she cried "At last!" to her parents as she turned the key in the lock.

"And what now?" said Gregor to himself, looking round in the darkness. Soon he made the discovery that he was now unable to stir a limb. This did not surprise him, rather it seemed unnatural that he should ever actually have been able to move on these feeble little legs. Otherwise he felt relatively comfortable. True, his whole body was aching, but it seemed that the pain was gradually growing less and would finally pass away. The rotting apple in his back and the inflamed area around it, all covered with soft dust, already hardly troubled him. He thought of his family with tenderness and love. The decision that he must disappear was one that he held to even more strongly than his sister, if that were possible. In this state of vacant and peaceful meditation he remained until the tower clock struck three in the morning. The first broadening of light in the world outside the window entered his consciousness once more. Then his head sank to the floor of its own accord and from his nostrils came the last faint flicker of his breath.

When the charwoman arrived early in the morning—what between her strength and her impatience she slammed all the doors so loudly, never mind how often she had been begged not to do so, that no one in the whole apartment could enjoy any quiet sleep after her arrival—she noticed nothing unusual as she took her customary peep into Gregor's room. She thought he was lying motionless on purpose, pretending to be in the sulks; she credited him with every kind of intelligence. Since she happened to have the long-handled broom in her hand she tried to tickle him up with it from the doorway. When that too produced no reaction she felt provoked and poked at him a little harder, and only when she had pushed him along the floor without meeting any resistance was her attention aroused. It did not take her long to establish the truth of the matter, and her eyes widened, she let out a whistle, yet did not waste much time over it but tore open the door of the Samsas' bedroom and yelled into the darkness at the top of her voice: "Just look at this, it's dead; it's lying here dead and done for!"

Mr. and Mrs. Samsa started up in their double bed and before they realized the nature of the charwoman's announcement had some difficulty in overcom-

90

ing the shock of it. But then they got out of bed quickly, one on either side, Mr. Samsa throwing a blanket over his shoulders, Mrs. Samsa in nothing but her nightgown; in this array they entered Gregor's room. Meanwhile the door of the living room opened, too, where Grete had been sleeping since the advent of the lodgers; she was completely dressed as if she had not been to bed, which seemed to be confirmed also by the paleness of her face. "Dead?" said Mrs. Samsa, looking questioningly at the charwoman, although she could have investigated for herself, and the fact was obvious enough without investigation. "I should say so," said the charwoman, proving her words by pushing Gregor's corpse a long way to one side with her broomstick. Mrs. Samsa made a movement as if to stop her, but checked it. "Well," said Mr. Samsa, "now thanks be to God." He crossed himself, and the three women followed his example. Grete, whose eyes never left the corpse, said: "Just see how thin he was. It's such a long time since he's eaten anything. The food came out again just as it went in." Indeed, Gregor's body was completely flat and dry, as could only now be seen when it was no longer supported by the legs and nothing prevented one from looking closely at it.

"Come in beside us, Grete, for a little while," said Mrs. Samsa with a tremulous smile, and Grete, not without looking back at the corpse, followed her parents into their bedroom. The charwoman shut the door and opened the window wide. Although it was so early in the morning a certain softness was perceptible in the fresh air. After all, it was already the end of March.

The three lodgers emerged from their room and were surprised to see no breakfast; they had been forgotten. "Where's our breakfast?" said the middle lodger peevishly to the charwoman. But she put her finger to her lips and hastily, without a word, indicated by gestures that they should go into Gregor's room. They did so and stood, their hands in the pockets of their somewhat shabby coats, around Gregor's corpse in the room where it was now fully light.

At that the door of the Samsas' bedroom opened and Mr. Samsa appeared in his uniform, his wife on one arm, his daughter on the other. They all looked a little as if they had been crying; from time to time Grete hid her face on her father's arm.

"Leave my house at once!" said Mr. Samsa, and pointed to the door without disengaging himself from the women. "What do you mean by that?" said the middle lodger, taken somewhat aback, with a feeble smile. The two others put their hands behind them and kept rubbing them together, as if in gleeful expectation of a fine set-to in which they were bound to come off the winners. "I mean just what I say," answered Mr. Samsa, and advanced in a straight line with his two companions towards the lodger. He stood his ground at first quietly, looking at the floor as if his thoughts were taking a new pattern in his head. "Then let us go, by all means," he said, and looked up at Mr. Samsa as if in a sudden access of humility he were expecting some renewed sanction for this decision. Mr. Samsa merely nodded briefly once or twice with meaning eyes. Upon that the lodger really did go with long strides into the hall, his two friends had been listening and had quite stopped rubbing their hands for some moments and now went scuttling after him as if afraid that Mr. Samsa might get into the hall before them and cut them off from their leader. In the hall they all three took their hats from the rack,

95

their sticks from the umbrella stand, bowed in silence and quitted the apartment. With a suspiciousness which proved quite unfounded Mr. Samsa and the two women followed them out to the landing; leaning over the banister they watched the three figures slowly but surely going down the long stairs, vanishing from sight at a certain turn of the staircase on every floor and coming into view again after a moment or so; the more they dwindled, the more the Samsa family's interest in them dwindled, and when a butcher's boy met them and passed them on the stairs coming up proudly with a tray on his head, Mr. Samsa and the two women soon left the landing and as if a burden had been lifted from them went back into their apartment.

They decided to spend this day in resting and going for a stroll; they had not only deserved such a respite from work but absolutely needed it. And so they sat down at the table and wrote three notes of excuse, Mr. Samsa to his board of management, Mrs. Samsa to her employer and Grete to the head of her firm. While they were writing, the charwoman came in to say that she was going now, since her morning's work was finished. At first they only nodded without looking up, but as she kept hovering there they eyed her irritably. "Well?" said Mr. Samsa. The charwoman stood grinning in the doorway as if she had good news to impart to the family but meant not to say a word unless properly questioned. The small ostrich feather standing upright on her hat, which had annoyed Mr. Samsa ever since she was engaged, was waving gaily in all directions. "Well, what is it then?" asked Mrs. Samsa, who obtained more respect from the charwoman than the others. "Oh," said the charwoman, giggling so amiably that she could not at once continue, "just this, you don't need to bother about how to get rid of the thing next door. It's been seen to already." Mrs. Samsa and Grete bent over their letters again, as if preoccupied; Mr. Samsa, who perceived that she was eager to begin describing it all in detail, stopped her with a decisive hand. But since she was not allowed to tell her story, she remembered the great hurry she was in, being obviously deeply huffed: "Bye, everybody," she said, whirling off violently, and departed with a frightful slamming of doors.

"She'll be given notice tonight," said Mr. Samsa, but neither from his wife nor his daughter did he get any answer, for the charwoman seemed to have shattered again the composure they had barely achieved. They rose, went to the window and stayed there, clasping each other tight. Mr. Samsa turned in his chair to look at them and quietly observed them for a little. Then he called out: "Come along, now, do. Let bygones be bygones. And you might have some consideration for me." The two of them complied at once, hastened to him, caressed him and quickly finished their letters.

Then they all three left the apartment together, which was more than they had done for months, and went by tram into the open country outside the town. The tram, in which they were the only passengers, was filled with warm sunshine. Leaning comfortably back in their seats they canvassed their prospects for the future, and it appeared on closer inspection that these were not at all bad, for the jobs they had got, which so far they had never really discussed with each other, were all three admirable and likely to lead to better things later on. The greatest immediate improvement in their condition would of course arise from moving to another house; they wanted to take a smaller and cheaper but also better situated and more easily run apartment than the one they had, which Gregor had selected. While they were thus conversing, it struck both Mr. and Mrs. Samsa, almost at the same moment, as they became aware of their daughter's increasing vivacity, that in spite of all the sorrow of recent times, which had made her cheeks pale, she had bloomed into a pretty girl with a good figure. They grew quieter and half unconsciously exchanged glances of complete agreement, having come to the conclusion that it would soon be time to find a good husband for her. And it was like a confirmation of their new dreams and excellent intentions that at the end of their journey their daughter sprang to her feet first and stretched her young body. [1915]

THINKING ABOUT THE TEXT

1. Some readers think Gregor literally turns into an insect; others interpret the transformation as a metaphorical change, symbolic of how he feels. Make a case for one of these positions by pointing to evidence in the text. Take into consideration the opposition.

2. Does your opinion of Gregor change over the course of the story? For example, are you more or less sympathetic to him at the end? Does your opinion of the rest of the family change?

3. Make a list of all the possible "metamorphoses" in the story. Might Gregor's initial change not be the most significant?

4. Were you surprised by the matter-of-fact tone with which Kafka announces Gregor's metamorphosis? What effect does this have on you? Can you point to other "flat" assertions of amazing events?

5. The father seems to regain authority as the story progresses, while Gregor becomes more the outsider. Do you think Gregor deserves his fate? Might Kafka be saying something about rightful authority?

FRANZ KAFKA

A Hunger Artist

Translated by Willa and Edwin Muir

"The Hunger Artist" was published in 1924. It is often thought of as a parable of alienation. Kafka read the proofs for this story a few days before he died.

During these last decades the interest in professional fasting has markedly diminished. It used to pay very well to stage such great performances under one's own management, but today that is quite impossible. We live in a different world now. At one time the whole town took a lively interest in the hunger artist; from day to day of his fast the excitement mounted; everybody wanted to see him at least once a day; there were people who bought season tickets for the last few days and sat from morning till night in front of his small barred cage; even in the nighttime there were visiting hours, when the whole effect was heightened by torch flares; on fine days the cage was set out in the open air, and then it was the children's special treat to see the hunger artist; for their elders he was often just a joke that happened to be in fashion, but the children stood openmouthed, holding each other's hands for greater security, marveling at him as he sat there pallid in black tights, with his ribs sticking out so prominently, not even on a seat but down among straw on the ground, sometimes giving a courteous nod, answering questions with a constrained smile, or perhaps stretching an arm through the bars so that one might feel how thin it was, and then again withdrawing deep into himself, paying no attention to anyone or anything, not even to the all-important striking of the clock that was the only piece of furniture in his cage, but merely staring into vacancy with half-shut eyes, now and then taking a sip from a tiny glass of water to moisten his lips.

Besides casual onlookers there were also relays of permanent watchers selected by the public, usually butchers, strangely enough, and it was their task to watch the hunger artist day and night, three of them at a time, in case he should have some secret recourse to nourishment. This was nothing but a formality, instituted to reassure the masses, for the initiates knew well enough that during his fast the artist would never in any circumstances, not even under forcible compulsion, swallow the smallest morsel of food; the honor of his profession forbade it. Not every watcher, of course, was capable of understanding this, there were often groups of night watchers who were very lax in carrying out their duties and deliberately huddled together in a retired corner to play cards with great absorption, obviously intending to give the hunger artist the chance of a little refreshment, which they supposed he could draw from some private hoard. Nothing annoyed the artist more than such watchers; they made him miserable; they made his fast seem unendurable; sometimes he mastered his feebleness sufficiently to sing during their watch for as long as he could keep going, to show them how unjust their suspicions were. But that was of little use; they only wondered at his cleverness in being able to fill his mouth even while singing. Much more to his taste were the watchers who sat close up to the bars, who were not content with the dim night lighting of the hall but focused him in the full glare of the electric pocket torch given them by the impresario. The harsh light did not trouble him at all, in any case he could never sleep properly, and he could always drowse a little, whatever the light, at any hour, even when the hall was thronged with noisy onlookers. He was quite happy at the prospect of spending a sleepless night with such watchers; he was ready to exchange jokes with them, to tell them stories out of his nomadic life, anything at all to keep them awake and demonstrate to them again that he had no eatables in his cage and that he was fasting as not one of them could fast. But his happiest moment was when the morning came and an enormous breakfast was brought them, at his expense, on which they flung themselves with the keen appetite of healthy men after a weary night of wakefulness. Of course there were people who argued that this breakfast was an unfair attempt to bribe the watchers, but that was going rather too far, and when they were invited to take on a night's vigil without a breakfast, merely for the sake of the cause, they made themselves scarce, although they stuck stubbornly to their suspicions.

Such suspicions, anyhow, were a necessary accompaniment to the profession of fasting. No one could possibly watch the hunger artist continuously, day and night, and so no one could produce first-hand evidence that the fast had really been rigorous and continuous; only the artist himself could know that, he was therefore bound to be the sole completely satisfied spectator of his own fast. Yet for other reasons he was never satisfied; it was not perhaps mere fasting that had brought him to such skeleton thinness that many people had regretfully to keep away from his exhibitions, because the sight of him was too much for them, perhaps it was dissatisfaction with himself that had worn him down. For he alone knew, what no other initiate knew, how easy it was to fast. It was the easiest thing in the world. He made no secret of this, yet people did not believe him, at the best they set him down as modest, most of them, however, thought he was out for publicity or else was some kind of cheat who found it easy to fast because he had discovered a way of making it easy, and then had the impudence to admit the fact, more or less. He had to put up with all that, and in the course of time had got used to it, but his inner dissatisfaction always rankled, and never yet, after any term of fasting — this must be granted to his credit — had he left the cage of his own free will. The longest period of fasting was fixed by his impresario at forty days, beyond that term he was not allowed to go, not even in great cities, and there was good reason for it, too. Experience had proved that for about forty days the interest of the public could be stimulated by a steadily increasing pressure of advertisement, but after that the town began to lose interest, sympathetic support began notably to fall off; there were of course local variations as between one town and another or one country and another, but as a general rule forty days marked the limit. So on the fortieth day the flower-bedecked cage was opened, enthusiastic spectators filled the hall, a military band played, two doctors entered the cage to measure the results of the fast, which were announced through a megaphone, and finally two young ladies appeared blissful at having been selected for the honor, to help the hunger artist down the few steps leading to a small table on which was spread a carefully chosen invalid repast. And at this very moment the artist always turned stubborn. True, he would entrust his bony arms to the outstretched helping hands of the ladies bending over him, but stand up he would not. Why stop fasting at this particular moment, after forty days of it? He had held out for a long time, an illimitably long time; why stop now, when he was in his best fasting form, or rather, not yet quite in his best fasting form? Why should he be cheated of the fame he would get for fasting longer, for being not only the record hunger artist of all time, which presumably he was already, but for beating his own record by a performance beyond human imagination, since he felt that there were no limits to his capacity for fasting? His public pretended to admire him so much, why should it have so little patience with him; if he could endure fasting longer, why shouldn't the public endure it? Besides, he was tired, he was comfortable sitting in the straw, and now he was supposed to lift himself to his full height and go down to a meal the very thought of which gave him a nausea that only the presence of the ladies kept him from betraying, and even that with an effort. And he looked up into the eyes of the ladies who were apparently so friendly and in reality so cruel, and shook his head, which felt too heavy on its strengthless neck. But then there happened yet again what always happened. The impresario came forward, without a word—for the band made speech impossible—lifted his arms in the air above the artist, as if inviting Heaven to look down upon its creature here in the straw, this suffering martyr, which indeed he was, although in quite another sense; grasped him around the emaciated waist, with exaggerated caution, so that the frail condition he was in might be appreciated; and committed him to the care of the blenching ladies, not without secretly giving him a shaking so that his legs and body tottered and swayed. The artist now submitted completely; his head lolled on his breast as if it had landed there by chance; his body was hollowed out; his legs in a spasm of self-preservation clung close to each other at the knees, yet scraped on the ground as if it were not really solid ground, as if they were only trying to find solid ground; and the whole weight of his body, a featherweight after all, relapsed onto one of the ladies, who, looking around for help and panting a little—this post of honor was not at all what she had expected it to be—first stretched her neck as far as she could to keep her face at least free from contact with the artist, then finding this impossible, and her more fortunate companion not coming to her aid but merely holding extended in her own trembling hand the little bunch of knuckle-bones that was the artist's, to the great delight of the spectators burst into tears and had to be replaced by an attendant who had long been stationed in readiness. Then came the food, a little of which the impresario managed to get between the artist's lips, while he sat in a kind of half-fainting trance, to the accompaniment of cheerful patter designed to distract the public's attention from the artist's condition; after that, a toast was drunk to the public, supposedly prompted by a whisper from the artist in the impresario's ear; the band confirmed it with a mighty flourish, the spectators melted away, and no one had any cause to be dissatisfied with the proceedings, no one except the hunger artist himself, he only, as always.

So he lived for many years, with small regular intervals of recuperation, in visible glory, honored by the world, yet in spite of that troubled in spirit, and all the more troubled because no one would take his trouble seriously. What comfort could he possibly need? What more could he possibly wish for? And if some good-natured person, feeling sorry for him, tried to console him by pointing out that his melancholy was probably caused by fasting, it could happen, especially when he had been fasting for some time, that he reacted with an outburst of fury and to the general alarm began to shake the bars of his cage like a wild animal. Yet the impresario had a way of punishing these outbreaks which he rather enjoyed putting into operation. He would apologize publicly for the artist's behavior, which was only to be excused, he admitted, because of the irritability caused by fasting; a condition hardly to be understood by well-fed people; then by natural transition he went on to mention the artist's equally incomprehensible boast that he could fast for much longer than he was doing; he praised the high ambition, the good will, the great self-denial undoubtedly implicit in such a statement; and then quite simply countered it by bringing out photographs, which were also on sale to the public, showing the artist on the fortieth day of a fast lying in bed almost dead from exhaustion. This perversion of the truth, familiar to the artist though it was, always unnerved him afresh and proved too much for him. What was a consequence of the premature ending of his fast was here presented as the cause of it! To fight against this lack of understanding, against a whole world of nonunderstanding, was impossible. Time and again in good faith he stood by the bars listening to the impresario, but as soon as the photographs appeared he always let go and sank with a groan back onto his straw, and the reassured public could once more come close and gaze at him.

A few years later when the witnesses of such scenes called them to mind, they often failed to understand themselves at all. For meanwhile the aforementioned change in public interest had set in; it seemed to happen almost overnight; there may have been profound causes for it, but who was going to bother about that; at any rate the pampered hunger artist suddenly found himself deserted one fine day by the amusement-seekers, who went streaming past him to other more-favored attractions. For the last time the impresario hurried him over half Europe to discover whether the old interest might still survive here and there; all in vain; everywhere, as if by secret agreement, a positive revulsion from professional fasting was in evidence. Of course it could not really have sprung up so suddenly as all that, and many premonitory symptoms which had not been sufficiently remarked or suppressed during the rush and glitter of success now came retrospectively to mind, but it was now too late to take any countermeasures. Fasting would surely come into fashion again at some future date, yet that was no comfort for those living in the present. What, then, was the hunger artist to do? He had been applauded by thousands in his time and could hardly come down to showing himself in a street booth at village fairs, and as for adopting another profession, he was not only too old for that but too fanatically devoted to fasting. So he took leave of the impresario, his partner in an unparalleled career, and hired himself to a large circus; in order to spare his own feelings he avoided reading the conditions of his contract.

A large circus with its enormous traffic in replacing and recruiting men, animals, and apparatus can always find a use for people at any time, even for a hunger artist, provided of course that he does not ask too much, and in this particular case anyhow it was not only the artist who was taken on but his famous and long-known name as well, indeed considering the peculiar nature of his performance, which was not impaired by advancing age, it could not be objected that here was an artist past his prime, no longer at the height of his professional skill, seeking a refuge in some quiet corner of a circus; on the contrary, the hunger artist averred that he could fast as well as ever, which was entirely credible, he even alleged that if he were allowed to fast as he liked and this was at once promised him without more ado, he could astound the world by establishing a record never yet achieved, a statement that certainly provoked a smile among the other professionals, since it left out of account the change in public opinion, which the hunger artist in his zeal conveniently forgot.

He had not, however, actually lost his sense of the real situation and took it as a matter of course that he and his cage should be stationed, not in the middle of the ring as a main attraction, but outside, near the animal cages, on a site that was after all easily accessible. Large and gaily painted placards made a frame for the cage and announced what was to be seen inside it. When the public came thronging out in the intervals to see the animals, they could hardly avoid passing the hunger artist's cage and stopping there for a moment, perhaps they might even have stayed longer had not those pressing behind them in the narrow gangway, who did not understand why they should be held up on their way toward the excitements of the menagerie, made it impossible for anyone to stand gazing quietly for any length of time. And that was the reason why the hunger artist, who had of course been looking forward to these visiting hours as the main achievement of his life, began instead to shrink from them. At first he could hardly wait for the intervals; it was exhilarating to watch the crowds come streaming his way, until only too soon—not even the most obstinate self-deception, clung to almost consciously, could hold out against the fact—the conviction was borne in upon him that these people, most of them, to judge from their actions, again and again, without exception, were all on their way to the menagerie. And the first sight of them from the distance remained the best. For when they reached his cage he was at once deafened by the storm of shouting and abuse that arose from the two contending factions, which renewed themselves continuously, of those who wanted to stop and stare at him—he soon began to dislike them more than the others—not out of real interest but only out of obstinate self-assertiveness, and those who wanted to go straight on to the animals. When the first great rush was past, the stragglers came along, and these, whom nothing could have prevented from stopping to look at him as long as they had breath, raced past with long strides, hardly even glancing at him, in their haste to get to the menagerie in time. And all too rarely did it happen that he had a stroke of luck, when some father of a family fetched up before him with his children, pointed a finger at the hunger artist, and explained at length what the phenomenon meant, telling stories of earlier years when he himself had watched similar but much more thrilling performances, and the children, still rather uncomprehending, since neither inside nor outside school had they been sufficiently prepared for this lesson—what did they care about fasting?—yet showed by the brightness of their intent eyes that new and better times might be coming. Perhaps, said the hunger artist to himself many a time, things would be a little better if his cage were set not quite so near the menagerie. That made it too easy for people to make their choice, to say nothing of what he suffered from the stench of the menagerie, the animals' restlessness by night, the carrying past of raw lumps of flesh for the beasts of prey, the roaring at feeding times, which depressed him continually. But he did not dare to lodge a complaint with the management; after all, he had the animals to thank for the troops of people who passed his cage, among whom there might always be one here and there to take an interest in him, and who could tell where they might seclude him if he called attention to his existence and thereby to the fact that, strictly speaking, he was only an impediment on the way to the menagerie.

A small impediment, to be sure, one that grew steadily less. People grew familiar with the strange idea that they could be expected, in times like these, to take an interest in a hunger artist, and with this familiarity the verdict went out against him. He might fast as much as he could, and he did so; but nothing could save him now, people passed him by. Just try to explain to anyone the art of fasting! Anyone who has no feeling for it cannot be made to understand it. The fine placards grew dirty and illegible, they were torn down; the little notice board telling the number of fast days achieved, which at first was changed carefully every day, had long stayed at the same figure, for after the first few weeks even this small task seemed pointless to the staff; and so the artist simply fasted on and on, as he had once dreamed of doing, and it was no trouble to him, just as he had always foretold, but no one counted the days, no one, not even the artist himself, knew what records he was already breaking and his heart grew heavy. And when once in a while some leisurely passer-by stopped, made merry over the old figure on the board, and spoke of swindling, that was in its way the stupidest lie ever invented by indifference and inborn malice, since it was not the hunger artist who was cheating, he was working honestly, but the world was cheating him of his reward.

Many more days went by, however, and that too came to an end. An overseer's eye fell on the cage one day and he asked the attendants why this perfectly good cage should be left standing there unused with dirty straw inside it; nobody knew, until one man, helped out by the notice board, remembered about the hunger artist. They poked into the straw with sticks and found him in it. "Are you still fasting?" asked the overseer, "when on earth do you mean to stop?" "Forgive me, everybody," whispered the hunger artist; only the overseer, who had his ear to the bars, understood him. "Of course," said the overseer, and tapped his forehead with a finger to let the attendants know what state the man was in, "we forgive you." "I always wanted you to admire my fasting," said the hunger artist. "We do admire it," said the overseer, affably. "But you shouldn't admire it," said the hunger artist. "Well then we don't admire it," said the overseer, "but why shouldn't we admire it?" "Because I have to fast, I can't help it," said the hunger artist. "What a fellow you are," said the overseer, "and why can't you help it?" "Because," said the hunger artist, lifting his head a little and speaking, with his lips pursed, as if for a kiss, right into the overseer's ear, so that no syllable might be lost, "because I couldn't find the food I liked. If I had found it, believe me, I should have made no fuss and stuffed myself like you or anyone else." These were his last words, but in his dimming eyes remained the firm though no longer proud persuasion that he was still continuing to fast.

"Well, clear this out now!" said the overseer, and they buried the hunger artist, straw and all. Into the cage they put a young panther. Even the most insensitive felt it refreshing to see this wild creature leaping around the cage that had so long been dreary. The panther was all right. The food he liked was brought him without hesitation by the attendants; he seemed not even to miss his freedom; his noble body, furnished almost to the bursting point with all that it needed, seemed to carry freedom around with it too; somewhere in his jaws it seemed to lurk; and the joy of life streamed with such ardent passion from his throat that for the onlookers it was not easy to stand the shock of it. But they braced themselves, crowded around the cage, and did not want ever to move away.   [1924]

10

THINKING ABOUT THE TEXT

1. This mysterious story sounds symbolic, as if Kafka wanted the hunger artist to represent certain kinds of people, perhaps those who deny themselves something important. Who might fit this category? Might Kafka be trying to praise? Satirize? Parody? Condemn?

2. Do you think the hunger artist deserves our admiration? Why? What if it were artists (writers, painters, musicians) he were describing? Priests or saints? Do you feel sympathy for him during his decline? Is he making a choice?

3. How would the story change in significance if the hunger artist saw that his time had passed and quit that profession for another?

4. Does the conversation with the overseer in the penultimate paragraph change your mind about the hunger artist's sacrifices? Is he more admirable or less? More normal or less? More pathetic or less?

5. Do contemporary performers sacrifice? Why do they? Would they continue to if their public did not show any interest?

MAKING COMPARISONS

1. How would you compare the thinking process of Gregor and the hunger artist in terms of their grasp on reality?

2. Both main characters seem to be insiders who become outsiders. How come?

3. Does Gregor's or the hunger artist's death seem more grotesque? What do you think Kafka is trying to do with such haunting images?

FRANZ KAFKA

Before the Law

Translated by Willa and Edwin Muir

"Before the Law" is an excerpt from Kafka's 1925 novel The Trial, *which is often read as a chilling parable of how helpless we are before the power of the law.*

Before the law stands a doorkeeper. To this doorkeeper there comes a man from the country and prays for admittance to the Law. But the doorkeeper says that he cannot grant admittance at the moment. The man thinks it over and then asks if he will be allowed in later. "It is possible," says the doorkeeper, "but not at the moment." Since the gate stands open, as usual, and the doorkeeper steps to one side, the man stoops to peer through the gateway into the interior. Observing that, the doorkeeper laughs and says: "If you are so drawn to it, just try to go in despite my veto. But take note: I am powerful. And I am only the least of the doorkeepers. From hall to hall there is one doorkeeper after another, each more powerful than the last. The third doorkeeper is already so terrible that even I cannot bear to look at him." These are difficulties the man from the country has not expected; the Law, he thinks, should surely be accessible at all times and to everyone, but as he now takes a closer look at the doorkeeper in his fur coat, with his big sharp nose and long, thin, black Tartar beard, he decides that it is better to wait until he gets permission to enter. The doorkeeper gives him a stool and lets him sit down, at one side of the door. There he sits for days and years. He makes many attempts to be admitted, and wearies the doorkeeper by his importunity. The doorkeeper frequently has little interviews with him, asking him questions about his home and many other things, but the questions are put indifferently, as great lords put them, and always finish with the statement that he cannot be let in yet. The man, who has furnished himself with many things for his journey, sacrifices all he has, however valuable, to bribe the doorkeeper. The doorkeeper accepts everything, but always with the remark: "I am only taking it to keep you from thinking you have omitted anything." During these many years the man fixes his attention almost continuously on the doorkeeper. He forgets the other doorkeepers, and this first one seems to him the sole obstacle preventing access to the Law. He curses his bad luck, in his early years boldly and loudly, later, as he grows old, he only grumbles to himself. He becomes childish, and since in his yearlong contemplation of the doorkeeper he has come to know even the fleas in his fur collar, he begs the fleas as well to help him and to change the doorkeeper's mind. At length his eyesight begins to fail, and he does not know whether the world is really darker or whether his eyes are only deceiving him. Yet in his darkness he is now aware of a radiance that streams inextinguishably from the gateway of the Law. Now he has not very long to live. Before he dies, all his experiences in these long years gather themselves in his head to one point, a question he has not yet asked the doorkeeper. He waves him nearer, since he can no longer raise his stiffening body. The doorkeeper has to bend low towards him, for the difference in height between them has altered much to the man's disadvantage. "What do you want to know now?" asks the doorkeeper; "you are insatiable." "Everyone strives to reach the Law," says the man, "so how does it happen that for all these many years no one but myself has ever begged for admittance?" The doorkeeper recognizes that the man has reached his end, and to let his failing senses catch the words roars in his ear: "No one else could ever be admitted here, since this gate was made only for you. I am now going to shut it." [1925]

THINKING ABOUT THE TEXT

1. This brief text seems more a parable than a story. What is it a parable of? What does the man want? How would you make that concrete in today's world? Is the man's quest reasonable? Why is he unsuccessful?

2. Do you see this tale as cynical, pessimistic, or simply realistic? Is your answer based on your experience, your opinion of the law, or some other idea?

3. What do you think would have happened if the man forced his way in? Write three or four sentences that fit the tone and narrative of this story.

4. As a literal narration, the events here are not realistic. No one would actually sit outside a gate for years staring at the gatekeeper. What other details are less than plausible? What is gained by telling such a surreal or absurd narrative?

5. Do you think this story of an outsider is relevant to contexts other than Kafka's Prague? Which ones? Might some in our culture find that this piece speaks to them?

MAKING COMPARISONS

1. Kafka believed he lived in an irrational universe. Which of these stories seems the most incredible or lacking in reason? Or do you disagree? Are all three quite rational beneath the surface?

2. Can you relate to the motivations of Gregor, the hunger artist, or the man before the gate? Are they like anyone you know, or maybe exaggerations of them?

3. Which story seems the most dreamlike? The most enigmatic? The most understandable?

WRITING ABOUT ISSUES

1. Kafka once wrote that he viewed writing as "an axe to break up the frozen sea within us." Choose one of his stories and argue that this quotation applies.

2. Argue that Gregor and the hunger artist are, or are not, more sinned against than sinning.

3. Because Kafka is such a suggestive, minimalist writer, readers find many possible meanings in his work. Write a personal response agreeing or disagreeing that Kafka captures something important about modern life.

4. Locate two or three pieces of Kafka criticism and write a review essay that incorporates explanations of some of the following terms: *absurd, alienation, angst, bureaucratic domination, enigmatic, exile, hallucinatory dreamlike reality, nihilism, surreal.*

Persecuting Outsiders: Poetry of the Holocaust

MARTIN NIEMÖLLER, "First They Came for the Jews"
NELLY SACHS, "A Dead Child Speaks"
YEVGENY YEVTUSHENKO, "Babii Yar"
KAREN GERSHON, "Race"
ANNE SEXTON, "After Auschwitz"

Being shunned by neighbors because of religion, race, gender, or ethnicity creates painful psychological alienation for victims of such treatment. But what if being the Other were part of official government policy? What if your religion, cultural heritage, or sexual orientation were deemed dangerous to the well-being of your country? What if the powerful so dehumanized you that you were thought of as vermin to be disposed of? This would be more than alienation; this would be putting respect for human life beyond normal moral restraints. As in war, the outsider now becomes the enemy who is less than human and who can be destroyed with impunity.

Of course, this describes exactly what happened during the Holocaust when the Nazis exterminated millions of Jews. Thousands of eyewitness accounts of this tragedy are written, but writers who were not there feel equally compelled to write about the events of the Holocaust. It is impossible to adequately represent such horrors: Some writers are furious; others are disciplined and controlled. It is one of a writer's challenges to express in words what is truly beyond description.

BEFORE YOU READ

Have you seen photographs of Holocaust survivors? Have you seem films, read books, or heard stories about these events? What are your feelings? Can you explain how systematic genocide is possible? Do such things still happen in the world?

MARTIN NIEMÖLLER

First They Came for the Jews

A German Protestant theologian and pastor, Martin Niemöller (1892–1984), who won the Iron Cross as a submarine commander in World War I, is best known as an outspoken critic of Adolf Hitler and Nazism during and preceding World War II. As the pastor of the Berlin congregation of the Evangelical Church from 1931, Niemöller led a group of clergy working to counter Nazism and earned Hitler's hatred. From 1937 to 1945, he was interned at the Dachau and Sachsenhausen concentration camps. After the war he concentrated his efforts on international disarmament and the recovery of the German church. He served as president of the World Council of Churches from 1961 to 1968.

First they came for the Jews
and I did not speak out
because I was not a Jew.
Then they came for the Communists
and I did not speak out   5
because I was not a Communist.
Then they came for the trade unionists
and I did not speak out
because I was not a trade unionist.
Then they came for me   10
and there was no one left
to speak out for me.

                                                     [1945]

THINKING ABOUT THE TEXT

1. The poem seems to merely narrate a sequence of events, but is there an implicit argument here? Should the writer have been more explicit?

2. As you read this poem do you think, "He's talking to me"? Do you think that might be Niemöller's intention?

3. Many poems are lyrical, filled with beautiful images and imaginative phrases. Would this poem be improved by moving in this direction?

4. Often in poetry, people and situations can be taken both literally and as symbols for something else. Do you think that is the case here with the Jews and Communists?

5. Most societies, even democracies, have insiders and outsiders, those with power and privilege and those with no influence. In your experience, does literature relate the feelings and experiences of both equally? Should this anthology balance the poems in this cluster with the experience of insiders?

NELLY SACHS
A Dead Child Speaks
Translated by Ruth and Matthew Mead

A poet and playwright born in Berlin of Jewish parents, Nelly Sachs (1891–1970) escaped from Nazi Germany in 1940 to Stockholm, where she became a Swedish citizen, and eventually won the Nobel Prize for Literature in 1966. First published as a poet in Germany in 1921, she later used biblical forms and motifs and empathized with the millions who suffered in the Holocaust. Her best-known play, Eli: A Mystery Play of the Sufferings of Israel, epitomizes this style, as does the following poem which uses pathos to evoke sympathy.

My mother held me by my hand
Then someone raised the knife of parting:
So that it should not strike me,
My mother loosed her hand from mine,
But she lightly touched my thighs once more   5
And her hand was bleeding —

After that the knife of parting
Cut in two each bite I swallowed —
It rose before me with the sun at dawn
And began to sharpen itself in my eyes —   10
Wind and water ground in my ear
And every voice of comfort pierced my heart —

As I was led to death
I still felt in the last moment
The unsheathing of the great knife of parting.   [1971]   15

THINKING ABOUT THE TEXT

1. The Nazis often separated children from their parents on arrival at the concentration camps. How does Sachs represent the brutality of such a sorting?

2. Do you find it effective that Sachs's child narrator dies? What is gained by this point of view? Is anything lost?

3. Should Sachs have been more emotional? Less? When writing poetry about horrific events, is it better to underplay the horror or to be explicit?

4. What does the metaphor "the knife of parting" imply? Can you suggest another metaphor or simile that is less dramatic?

5. Do you think the poem suggests that parting is more painful than death? In what ways might this be true?

MAKING COMPARISONS

1. Even though both Niemöller's and Sachs's poems are about the Holocaust, are you able to relate to them from your own experiences?

2. With its central metaphor, Sachs's poem seems more typically poetic. Would Niemöller's poem have been improved with more poetic devices? Might Sachs's poem have been improved with less?

3. One might argue that these two poems are causally connected. Explain.

YEVGENY YEVTUSHENKO
Babii Yar

Translated by George Reavey

Born in Siberia near Lake Baikal in 1933, Yevgeny Yevtushenko is Russia's best-known living poet, attracting huge stadium audiences (30,000 at one reading). He has also written essays and toured the world as a speaker, currently spending half of the year teaching at Tulsa University in Oklahoma. His most recent work is a novel, Don't Die Before You're Dead (1991), which follows the Soviet Union from the end of World War II through the early 1990s. Although he was sometimes held in disfavor during the Soviet years (once labeled "the head of the intellectual juvenile delinquents" whose poems were "pygmy spittle"), Yevtushenko has been immensely popular from the early 1960s until the present. A poem from the early 1960s, "Babii Yar" responds to the refusal of anti-Semites in the Ukraine to place a monument on the spot of a Nazi massacre of the Jews.

No monument stands over Babii Yar.
A drop sheer as a crude gravestone.
I am afraid.
        Today I am as old in years
as all the Jewish people.   5
Now I seem to be
        a Jew.
Here I plod through ancient Egypt.
Here I perish crucified, on the cross,
and to this day I bear the scars of nails.   10
I seem to be
        Dreyfus.°
The Philistine
        is both informer and judge.
I am behind bars.   15
        Beset on every side.
Hounded,
      spat on,
        slandered.
Squealing, dainty ladies in flounced Brussels lace   20
stick their parasols into my face.
I seem to be then
        a young boy in Byelostok.
Blood runs, spilling over the floors.

12 Dreyfus: A French army officer accused of spying for Germany around 1894. His trial caused a political crisis. Many feel that he was accused because he was Jewish.

The barroom rabble-rousers   25
give off a stench of vodka and onion.
A boot kicks me aside, helpless.
In vain I plead with these pogrom bullies.
While they jeer and shout,
                'Beat the Yids. Save Russia!'   30
Some grain-marketeer beats up my mother.
O my Russian people!
          I know
              you
are international to the core.   35
But those with unclean hands
have often made a jingle of your purest name.
I know the goodness of my land.
How vile these anti-Semites —
                without a qualm   40
they pompously called themselves
the Union of the Russian People!

I seem to be
        Anne Frank°
transparent   45
        as a branch in April.
And I love.
        And have no need of phrases.
My need
        is that we gaze into each other.   50
How little we can see
        or smell!
We are denied the leaves,
        we are denied the sky.
Yet we can do so much —   55
        tenderly
embrace each other in a darkened room.
They're coming here?
        Be not afraid. Those are the booming
sounds of spring: 60
        spring is coming here.
Come then to me.
        Quick, give me your lips.
Are they smashing down the door?
        No, it's the ice breaking . . .   65
The wild grasses rustle over Babii Yar.

---

44 Anne Frank: A fourteen-year-old Jewish girl captured by the Nazis after hiding in an attic
for months; she died in a concentration camp. Her diary was published posthumously.

The trees look ominous,
               like judges.
Here all things scream silently,
                    and, baring my head,   70
slowly I feel myself
             turning grey.
And I myself
          am one massive, soundless scream
above the thousand thousand buried here.   75
I am
    each old man
            here shot dead.
I am
    every child
            here shot dead.   80
Nothing in me
          shall ever forget!
The 'Internationale,'° let it
            thunder   85
when the last anti-Semite on earth
is buried for ever.
In my blood there is no Jewish blood.
In their callous rage, all anti-Semites
must hate me now as a Jew.   90
For that reason
         I am a true Russian!   [c. 1960]

84 **The 'Internationale'**: The hymn of an international federation of workers influential in liberal causes.

THINKING ABOUT THE TEXT

1. Yevtushenko identifies with the Jews, claiming he is crucified, is Dreyfus, is Anne Frank. Why do you think he is so moved? Who is the target audience for this poem? Explain.

2. Do you think this is a poem of nationalist feelings? Are you proud of our American history? Are there episodes in our history that do not reflect our "real nature" as Americans?

3. What might "We are denied the leaves, / we are denied the sky" (lines 53–54) mean? Why would "The trees look ominous, / like judges" (lines 67–68)?

4. Make a list of the poetic devices used in the poem. How might you change some to convey a different feeling?

5. In line 88, Yevtushenko says he has "no Jewish blood." Does this contradict his earlier identification? What do you guess is his defini-

tion of "a true Russian" (line 92)? Could you extend his idea to "a true American"?

MAKING COMPARISONS

1. Sachs is a literal Jew; Yevtushenko is one metaphorically. Does this make sense to you?

2. Niemöller and Yevtushenko manage to speak specifically of the Holocaust, but their themes also seem more universal. How might you explain this?

3. Is it effective for Sachs and Yevtushenko to identify with the dead? Why, or why not?

KAREN GERSHON

Race

Later known by her married name, Karen Tripp, Gershon (1923–1993) escaped from Nazi Germany in 1939 as a teenager. Sent to England without her family, she wrote in her poetry of this experience and the loss of her parents, who died in the Holocaust. Gershon published eight books, contributed to numerous periodicals, and won much recognition, including the British Arts Council Award in 1967. Her poetry was widely read in the 1960s and later, perhaps influencing contemporaries Anne Sexton and Sylvia Plath, who borrowed the imagery of Holocaust survivors to describe family conflict and inner turmoil. "Race" is from Selected Poems *(1966).*

When I returned to my home town
believing that no one would care
who I was and what I thought
it was as if the people caught
an echo of me everywhere   5
they knew my story by my face
and I who am always alone
became a symbol of my race

Like every living Jew I have
in imagination seen   10
the gas-chamber the mass-grave
the unknown body which was mine
and found in every German face
behind the mask the mark of Cain
I will not make their thoughts my own   15
by hating people for their race.

[1966]

THINKING ABOUT THE TEXT

1. Is Gershon imagining or actually describing her reception? How can we tell?

2. Do you mind the poet speaking for "every living Jew" (line 9)? Do you think this is accurate? Can someone be a symbol of their race?

3. Does the title refer to Jews or Germans? Why is neither group mentioned in the title?

4. Gershon writes fairly straightforward poetry, letting her content speak for itself. What specific poetic devices does she employ? Should she use more?

5. Do you find the last four lines ambiguous? Does she see Germans as murderers, or does she reject such invidious generalizations? Should Germans be held accountable for the Holocaust? Should Americans be held accountable for slavery? Are only the people who specifically partake in evil deeds responsible, or is the whole culture that "allowed" it guilty as well?

MAKING COMPARISONS

1. Both Gershon and Yevtushenko revisit Holocaust sites. Describe their different perspectives.

2. Do you think Sachs could have written "Race"? Explain.

3. Which of the four poets finds something positive out of the horrors of the Holocaust?

ANNE SEXTON
After Auschwitz

Growing up in New England and attending elite boarding and finishing schools during the years of World War II, Anne Sexton (1928–1974) had an emotional connection with the Holocaust rather than a firsthand one: Her obsession with images of death and degradation and her "confessional" poetic stance blend seamlessly with such a theme. Additional biographical information appears on page 867. "After Auschwitz" is from The Awful Rowing Toward God *(1977).*

Anger,
as black as a hook,
overtakes me.
Each day,
each Nazi   5

took, at 8.00 a.m., a baby
and sautéed him for breakfast
in his frying pan.

And death looks on with a casual eye
and picks at the dirt under his fingernail.   10

Man is evil,
I say aloud.
Man is a flower
that should be burnt,
I say aloud.   15
Man
is a bird full of mud,
I say aloud.

And death looks on with a casual eye
and scratches his anus.   20

Man with his small pink toes,
with his miraculous fingers
is not a temple
but an outhouse,
I say aloud.   25
Let man never again raise his teacup.
Let man never again write a book.
Let man never again put on his shoe.
Let man never again raise his eyes,
on a soft July night.   30
Never. Never. Never. Never. Never.
I say these things aloud.

I beg the Lord not to hear.   [1977]

THINKING ABOUT THE TEXT

1. What is Sexton's purpose here if she really does not want God to listen?

2. What is your response to the image of Nazi cannibalism in lines 4–8? What about her inclusive accusation that "Man is evil" (line 11)?

3. As Sexton's editor, would you suggest that she change any specific words or phrases? Should she control the generally angry tone?

4. Sexton personifies death. Why? Why do you think she refers to man's "pink toes" and "miraculous fingers" in lines 21 and 22?

5. Sexton sees the Holocaust as an indictment of everyone. Do you agree with her?

MAKING COMPARISONS

1. Compare the ambivalence at the end of Sexton's poem to that of Gershon's poem.

2. Do you think Sachs's poem would be improved by Sexton's explicit anger? Would Sexton's poem be improved by Sachs's control?

3. Which of these five poets comes closest to expressing your feelings about the Holocaust?

WRITING ABOUT ISSUES

1. Argue that Sexton's indictment of humankind is either hyperbolic or accurate.

2. Make a case in a brief essay that "First They Came for the Jews" leads to "A Dead Child Speaks."

3. Write a brief personal response explaining your feelings about the Holocaust or suggesting what such an event tells us about human nature, if anything.

4. Rent Steven Spielberg's film about the Holocaust, *Schindler's List*. Write a review expressing your feelings and thoughts about its contents and its representation of the Holocaust. Include a comparison to the poems you read.

ETHNIC OUTSIDERS

CHRYSTOS, "Today Was a Bad Day Like TB"
LOUISE ERDRICH, "Dear John Wayne"
DWIGHT OKITA, "Response to Executive Order 9066"
JANICE MIRIKITANI, "Doreen"
DAVID HERNANDEZ, "Pigeons"

America's history and cultural identity has long included her status as the "land of opportunity," a place where merit and hard work carry more weight than one's birthplace. Except for Native Americans, all U.S. settlers have ethnic roots that originated elsewhere, thus giving America her nickname as the great melting pot of innumerable cultures. But the reality is a little more complicated. Being Irish or Italian in early twentieth-century America was often a distinct disadvantage, as well as being Eastern European Jewish, Polish, Slavic, or Asian. These ethnic groups were often not welcomed by established Americans who no longer thought of themselves as ethnic. Many of these former outcast groups now think of themselves as the insiders and worry that new ethnic groups might diminish the American dream. There seems to be an unfortunate cycle of insiders discriminating against outsiders who then become discriminating insiders. Some groups, however, never seem to have gained insider status. Many Native Americans still live on the fringes of American society, physically and economically; some Asians still feel as if they are looked at as non-American; and many Hispanics still live in the large urban ghettoes that the Irish and Jews passed through almost three generations ago. Writers from these groups try to give voice to their feelings as they struggle with their minority identity in the vastly more powerful American culture. The following five poets express anger, resentment, and sadness at the insensitive way America often treats its ethnic minorities.

BEFORE YOU READ

Do you think of yourself as an ethnic American? Have you ever seen the term *English American* or *Dutch American*? What's the difference between those terms and *African American* or *Irish American*? Do you think ethnic traditions should be preserved, or should they be replaced with American traditions? Can these traditions coexist?

CHRYSTOS
Today Was a Bad Day Like TB

Born in San Francisco of a Lithuanian/Alsace-Lorraine mother and a Native American father of the Menominee tribe, Chrystos (b. 1946) writes in the outsider traditions of her ancestry, her lesbian perspective, and her geographical position on Bainbridge Island off the coast of the Pacific Northwest. She is a women's and native rights advocate, a working artist, and a poet. Her poetry collections include Not Vanishing *(1988),* Dream On *(1991),* In Her I Am *(1993),* Fire Power *(1995), and the 1994 winner of the Audre Lorde International Poetry Competition,* Fugitive Colors. *She is a Lannan Foundation fellow and the 1995 recipient of the Sappho Award of Distinction. The poem reprinted here is from* Not Vanishing.

    For Amanda White

Saw whites clap during a sacred dance
Saw young blond hippie boy with a red stone pipe
    My eyes burned him up
He smiled   *This is a Sioux pipe* he said from his sportscar
    Yes   I hiss   *I'm wondering how you got it*   5
    & the name is Lakota not Sioux
I'll tell you he said all friendly & liberal as only
    those with no pain can be
    I turned away   Can't charm me   can't bear to know
thinking of the medicine bundle I saw opened up in a glass case   10
    with a small white card beside it
    naming the rich whites who say they
    "own" it

Maybe they have an old Indian grandma back in time
    to excuse themselves   15
Today was a day I wanted to beat up the smirking man wearing
a pack with a Haida design from Moe's bookstore
Listen Moe's   How many Indians do you have working there?
How much money are you sending the Haida people
to use their sacred Raven design?   20
    You probably have an Indian grandma too
    whose name you don't know
    Today was a day like TB
    you cough & cough trying to get it out
           all that comes   25
                is blood & spit   [1988]

THINKING ABOUT THE TEXT

1. What argument about the ways whites relate to Native Americans is Chrystos making? What assumptions about whites does Chrystos seem to have?

2. Might you have clapped during a Lakota dance? During a Catholic Mass? What is the "it" in line 24 that the poet is trying to get out? Do you think she is angry with her readers?

3. Why does the poet use so little punctuation? What reasons could Chrystos have for the shape of the poem? Would another form (couplets, sonnet, prose poem) have worked better?

4. Is the ending too stark or perhaps too crude? Might the language have been more indirect and subtle, or is it appropriate to the theme?

5. Americans who are part of the mainstream—that is, white, male, middle class, or heterosexual—sometimes get annoyed when those who are not complain about bias, probably because the offense was inadvertent. (Think of Atlanta Braves fans doing "the tomahawk chop.") The young man in this poem, for example, seems quite oblivious of giving offense. Does that make the clapping innocent? Who determines who is right in these situations?

LOUISE ERDRICH
Dear John Wayne

Born in Little Falls, Minnesota, Louise Erdrich (b. 1954) is a member of the Turtle Mountain Band of the Chippewa Tribe. Her parents taught at the Bureau of Indian Affairs Boarding School in North Dakota, where Erdrich worked as a beet

weeder, waitress, and teacher. She earned a B.A. from Dartmouth College in 1976
and an M.A. from the Writing Program at Johns Hopkins University in 1979, and
went on to win many awards and fellowships for her writing, including the
National Book Critics Circle Award in 1984 for her first novel, Love Medicine.
Although she writes both poetry and nonfiction, she has received the most acclaim
for her novels, which include The Beet Queen *(1986),* Tracks *(1988),* The Bingo
Palace *(1994), and* Tales of Burning Love *(1996). "Dear John Wayne" is taken*
from Jacklight, *her 1984 collection of poems.*

August and the drive-in picture is packed.
We lounge on the hood of the Pontiac
surrounded by the slow-burning spirals they sell
at the window, to vanquish the hordes of mosquitoes.
Nothing works. They break through the smoke-screen for blood.   5

Always the look-out spots the Indians first,
spread north to south, barring progress.
The Sioux, or Cheyenne, or some bunch
in spectacular columns, arranged like SAC missiles,
their feathers bristling in the meaningful sunset.   10

The drum breaks. There will be no parlance.
Only the arrows whining, a death-cloud of nerves
swarming down on the settlers
who die beautifully, tumbling like dust weeds
into the history that brought us all here   15
together: this wide screen beneath the sign of the bear.

The sky fills, acres of blue squint and eye
that the crowd cheers. His face moves over us,
a thick cloud of vengeance, pitted
like the land that was once flesh. Each rut,   20
each scar makes a promise: *It is*
not over, this fight, not as long as you resist.

Everything we see belongs to us.
A few laughing Indians fall over the hood
slipping in the hot spilled butter.   25
The eye sees a lot, John, but the heart is so blind.
How will you know what you own?
He smiles, a horizon of teeth
the credits reel over, and then the white fields
again blowing in the true-to-life dark.   30
The dark films over everything.
We get into the car
scratching our mosquito bites, speechless and small

as people are when the movie is done.
We are back in ourselves.   35

How can we help but keep hearing his voice,
the flip side of the sound-track, still playing:
Come on, boys, we've got them
where we want them, drunk, running.
They will give us what we want, what we need: 40
The heart is a strange wood inside of everything
we see, burning, doubling, splitting out of its skin.   [1984]

THINKING ABOUT THE TEXT

1. While watching John Wayne fighting the Sioux or Cheyenne, Erdrich realizes she is not the intended audience for this traditional "cowboys and Indians" movie. Why not? Who is? What are the traditional assumptions about the Native Americans in these movies?

2. When John Wayne and other movie heroes defeat "our" enemies, do you ever doubt that you are on the same side? Would Native Americans see these films differently than a mainstream audience? Have you seen recent films about Native Americans where the conventional us-versus-them plot was disrupted in some way?

3. What do you think of Erdrich's transition from "hordes of mosquitoes" (line 4) to "Always the look-out spots the Indians first" (line 6)? What does "laughing Indians" mean in line 24?

4. Why does Erdrich say that "the heart is so blind" (line 26)? What does "They will give us what we want, what we need" refer to in line 40? Is that what John Wayne actually thought?

5. Movies give us a powerful sense of our history and our identity as Americans. Historical films about wars and heroes seem especially influential. Do you think Erdrich is overly sensitive? Do you think filmmakers have a responsibility to give a positive portrayal of the ethnic diversity of America?

MAKING COMPARISONS

1. If Chrystos's tone is bitter and angry, how might you characterize Erdrich's?

2. Compare the arguments both poets make about the perception whites have of Native Americans? Which is more persuasive? Why?

3. How do you imagine Chrystos would respond to the movie? Erdrich to the dance?

DWIGHT OKITA
In Response to Executive Order 9066

ALL AMERICANS OF JAPANESE DESCENT
MUST REPORT TO RELOCATION CENTERS

A third-generation Japanese American, poet and playwright Dwight Okita (b. 1958) won an Illinois Art Council Fellowship for poetry in 1988. Although Crossing with the Light *(1992), from which this poem is taken, is his first book of poetry, Okita has been more active in promoting the performance of poetry than the printing of it, and he is well known as a "slam" poet at open-mike readings in Chicago. A member of the large Japanese American community that developed in Chicago as a result of the migration from the West after the bitter experience of the internment camps during World War II, Okita expresses his family history in his poetry and plays. His dramas include* The Rainy Season *(1992) and* The Salad Bowl Dance *(1993).*

Dear Sirs:
Of course I'll come. I've packed my galoshes
and three packets of tomato seeds. Denise calls them
love apples. My father says where we're going
they won't grow.   5

I am a fourteen-year-old girl with bad spelling
and a messy room. If it helps any, I will tell you
I have always felt funny using chopsticks
and my favorite food is hot dogs.
My best friend is a white girl named Denise —   10
we look at boys together. She sat in front of me
all through grade school because of our names:
O'Connor, Ozawa. I know the back of Denise's head very well.

I tell her she's going bald. She tells me I copy on tests.
We're best friends.   15

I saw Denise today in Geography class.
She was sitting on the other side of the room.
"You're trying to start a war," she said, "giving secrets
away to the Enemy. Why can't you keep your big
mouth shut?"   20

I didn't know what to say.
I gave her a packet of tomato seeds
and asked her to plant them for me, told her
when the first tomato ripened
she'd miss me.   [1992]   25

THINKING ABOUT THE TEXT

1. What claim is Okita making in the last stanza? On what assumption about friendship is it based?

2. During the U.S. government's internment of Japanese American citizens, thousands were told to leave their homes to live in relocation centers for the duration of the war. To represent this complex historical event, do you think it effective to have a young girl writing a letter about being shunned by her best friend?

3. Explain Okita's use of the tomato seeds throughout the poem. What about other concrete words: *galoshes, chopsticks, hot dogs?*

4. Since there was no evidence that Japanese citizens ever gave any "secrets" away to the "Enemy" during World War II, why do you think Denise and millions of other Americans made that assumption?

MAKING COMPARISONS

1. Compare the tone of Okita's poem to that of Chrystos's. What emotions do you see in each?

2. Okita creates a young female narrator to speak for him. Does this make his poem less direct than Chrystos's and Erdrich's? Who might be appropriate narrators in their poems?

3. Is the alienation described by Okita more or less painful than that described by Chrystos and Erdrich?

JANICE MIRIKITANI
Doreen

A third-generation Japanese American, Janice Mirikitani (b. 1942) is like Dwight Okita in her desire to deal with the wartime experiences of her parents. Too young to remember internment camps, Mirikitani confronts the historical event in her poetry, writing not only from the ethnic awareness of a generation coming of age in the 1960s, but from the perspective of the Civil Liberties Act of 1988, which calls for official apologies and monetary reparations for internees. Mirikitani's books of poetry and prose include Awake in the River *(1982) and* Shedding Silence *(1987), from which "Doreen" is taken. This poem explores a later, more personal dilemma of societal definitions of beauty, gender, and identity, but images of war and demonization of the enemy continue to resonate from the Japanese American experiences of the 1940s.*

Doreen had a round face.
She tried to change it.

Everybody made fun
of her in school.

Her eyes so narrow   5
they asked if she could see,

called her Moonface and
Slits.

Doreen frost tipped her hair,
ratted it five inches high,   10
painted her eyes round,
glittering blue shadow up to her brow.

Made her look sad
even when she smiled.

She cut gym all the time   15
because the white powder on her neck
and face would streak
when she sweat.

But Doreen had boobs
more than most of us Japanese girls   20
so she wore tight sweaters
and low cut dresses
even in winter.

She didn't hang
with us,   25
since she put so much time
into changing her face.

White boys
would snicker when she passed by
and word got around   30
that Doreen
went all the way,
smoked and drank beer.

She told us
She met a veteran   35
fresh back from Korea.
Fresh back
his leg
still puckered pink
from landmines.   40

She told us
it was a kick
to listen to his stories

about how they'd torture
the gooks   45
hang them from trees
by their feet
grenades
in their crotch
and watch   50
them sweat.

I asked her
why she didn't dig brothers.

And her eyes
would disappear   55
laughing
so loud
she couldn't hear herself.

One day,
Doreen riding fast   60
with her friend
went through the windshield
and tore off
her skin
from scalp to chin.   65

And we were sad.

Because
no one could remember
Doreen's face.   [1987]

THINKING ABOUT THE TEXT

1. Why is Doreen so intent on "changing her face" (line 27)? Doesn't she realize she's "obvious"? Does she care? Is Doreen a rebel? Against what? Why?

2. Are most students in junior high school cruel to each other? Why are they so conformist? So cliquish? Is Doreen trying to fit in? With whom?

3. What would be the effect of having Doreen narrate this poem?

4. Why does Doreen get a kick out of the veteran's stories? Why does she laugh so loud at the narrator's question in lines 52–53?

5. Is it natural for excluded minorities to want to imitate those with higher social status? Can you give examples from American culture? Can you also give examples of outsiders consciously rebelling against American cultural norms?

MAKING COMPARISONS

1. Mirikitani seems to put the "blame" on Doreen. Do you agree? Would Chrystos write a poem from this perspective?

2. Are whites portrayed in a less positive way in Mirikitani's poem than in those by Chrystos, Erdrich, and Okita?

3. Mirikitani's poem seems sad. Which of the other three poems comes closest to this emotion?

DAVID HERNANDEZ
Pigeons

An active member of Chicago's arts community, David Hernandez (b. 1946) has published several books of poetry, including Despertando/Waking Up *(1991),* Satin City Lullaby *(1986), and* Rooftop Piper *(1991), from which this poem is taken. He has written, recited, and taught poetry for thirty years and was commissioned to write a poem for Chicago's one-hundred-and-fiftieth anniversary in 1987. In addition to his own publications, Hernandez has edited three poetry anthologies.*

Pigeons are the spiks of Birdland.
   They are survivors of blood, fire and stone.
      They can't afford to fly south
        or a Florida winter home.
Most everybody passing up a pigeon pack   5
tries to break it up because they move funny
and seem to be dancing like young street thugs
with an 18-foot, 10-speaker Sanyo book box radio
on a 2-foot red shoulder strap.
            Pigeons have feathers of a different color.   10
            They are too bright to be dull
            and too dull to be bright
            so they are not accepted anywhere.

        Nobody wants to give pigeons a job.
        Parakeets, canaries and parrots   15
        have the market sewn up as far as that goes.
        They live in fancy cages, get 3 meals a day
        for a song and dance routine.
        When was the last time you saw a pigeon

        in someone's home?   20
        Unless they bleach their feathers white

and try to pass off as doves,
you will never see pet pigeons.
Besides, their accents give them away
when they start cooing.   25

Once in a while, some creature will treat them decent.
    They are known as pigeon ladies, renegades,
        or bleeding-heart Liberals.
                          What they do is build these wooden cages
                                on rooftops that look like huge   30
                          pigeon housing projects
                      where they freeze during the winters
                  and get their little claws stuck in tar
              on hot summer days
No wonder they are pigeon-toed.   35
I tell you,
        Pigeons are the spiks of Birdland.   [1991]

THINKING ABOUT THE TEXT

1. Hernandez uses the pigeon simile to comment on the place of Latinos in
   Birdland/America. What specific comparisons does he make? What is his
   larger argument?

2. Is this poem a complaint or an accusation of Birdland/America? Do you
   see some validity in what Hernandez says?

3. Does he press the bird comparison too far? Not far enough? What about
   attempts to eradicate pigeons or their reputation as disease carriers? How
   far should a poet carry such similes or metaphors? How far should the
   reader?

4. Is *spiks* an appropriate word to use in a poem? What if a white person (a
   dove?) used the term? What does Hernandez mean by "pigeon-toed"?

5. Is the poet being ironic about those who try to treat the pigeons decently?
   What would he have preferred?

MAKING COMPARISONS

1. How would you compare Hernandez's complaint against the liberals with
   Chrystos's against the hippie?

2. Hernandez's poem seems more ambitious than some of the other poems.
   Do you think he is trying to paint a fuller picture of discrimination?

3. Which of the poetic devices in these five poems strikes you as the most
   effective? The least? Why?

WRITING ABOUT ISSUES

1. Write a letter back to the narrator of "In Response to Executive Order 9066" from Denise's point of view or to Chrystos's from the hippie's point of view.

2. Compare "In Response to Executive Order 9066" to "Dear John Wayne." Which approach to discrimination do you find more effective?

3. Write a personal response to these poems. Do you feel the speakers make unfair accusations? Are these examples of discrimination extreme or typical?

4. After doing research on an ethnic group not represented here, locate a poet from that group and write a brief report on his or her work.

Sexual Transgression

MAXINE HONG KINGSTON, "No Name Woman"
NAOMI WOLF, "The Making of a Slut"

Women have always run the risk in breaking their cultures' sexual norms. The historic punishment for sexual transgression has ranged from ostracism, to public humiliation, to death. Men generally have not been subject to the same strictures, perhaps because they have been the ones making up the rules. In traditional rural societies, sexual freedom for women was almost never allowed. (Of course, women were constrained in other ways too, so it is not really surprising that their sexual activities were severely circumscribed.) Some women did violate these rules, but they paid a price in doing so, either in overt punishment or in guilt. Women willing to flaunt conventional morality have usually become societal outsiders. Even in contemporary America, where many assume a sexual revolution has occurred, women are often labeled *sluts* for behavior that wins young men the admiration of their peers. The following writers both tell stories of women who transgress mores and try to understand how cultures can allow men sexual freedom while making women outcasts.

BEFORE YOU READ

How does a girl get the reputation of being a "slut"? What was your view of such girls in high school? Did you experience strong peer pressure to judge them in certain ways?

MAXINE HONG KINGSTON
No Name Woman

Born in Stockton, California, to Chinese immigrants, Maxine Hong Kingston's (b. 1940) first language was Say Yup, a dialect of Cantonese. As a member of a close-knit community, many of whose members came from the same village in China, she was immersed in the storytelling tradition of her particular Chinese culture and soon became a gifted writer in her second language, English. Winning eleven scholarships, Kingston began her education at the University of California at Berkeley as an engineering major but soon moved into English literature, receiving her B.A. in 1962 and her teaching certificate in 1965. After teaching in Hawaii for ten years, Kingston published her first book in 1976. The Woman Warrior: Memoirs of a Girlhood Among Ghosts, *the book from which our selection comes, won the National Book Critics Circle Award for nonfiction. This reinterpretation of oral traditions is continued in Kingston's later books, including* Tripmaster Monkey: His Fake Book *(1989). Her most recent work is a collection of critical essays,* Hawai'i One Summer *(1998).*

"You must not tell anyone," my mother said, "what I am about to tell you. In China your father had a sister who killed herself. She jumped into the family well. We say that your father has all brothers because it is as if she had never been born.

"In 1924 just a few days after our village celebrated seventeen hurry-up weddings—to make sure that every young man who went 'out on the road' would responsibly come home—your father and his brothers and your grandfather and his brothers and your aunt's new husband sailed for America, the Gold Mountain. It was your grandfather's last trip. Those lucky enough to get contracts waved good-bye from the decks. They fed and guarded the stowaways and helped them off in Cuba, New York, Bali, Hawaii. 'We'll meet in California next year,' they said. All of them sent money home.

"I remember looking at your aunt one day when she and I were dressing; I had not noticed before that she had such a protruding melon of a stomach. But I did not think, 'She's pregnant,' until she began to look like other pregnant women, her shirt pulling and the white tops of her black pants showing. She could not have been pregnant, you see, because her husband had been gone for years. No one said anything. We did not discuss it. In early summer she was ready to have the child, long after the time when it could have been possible.

"The village had also been counting. On the night the baby was to be born the villagers raided our house. Some were crying. Like a great saw, teeth strung with lights, files of people walked zigzag across our land, tearing the rice. Their lanterns doubled in the disturbed black water, which drained away through the broken bunds. As the villagers closed in, we could see that some of them, probably men and women we knew well, wore white masks. The people with long hair hung it over their faces. Women with short hair made it stand up on end. Some had tied white bands around their foreheads, arms, and legs.

"At first they threw mud and rocks at the house. Then they threw eggs and   5
began slaughtering our stock. We could hear the animals scream their deaths—the roosters, the pigs, a last great roar from the ox. Familiar wild heads flared in our night windows; the villagers encircled us. Some of the faces stopped to peer at us, their eyes rushing like searchlights. The hands flattened against the panes, framed heads, and left red prints.

"The villagers broke in the front and the back doors at the same time, even though we had not locked the doors against them. Their knives dripped with the blood of our animals. They smeared blood on the doors and walls. One woman swung a chicken, whose throat she had slit, splattering blood in red arcs about her. We stood together in the middle of our house, in the family hall with the pictures and tables of the ancestors around us, and looked straight ahead.

"At that time the house had only two wings. When the men came back, we would build two more to enclose our courtyard and a third one to begin a second courtyard. The villagers pushed through both wings, even your grandparents' rooms, to find your aunt's, which was also mine until the men returned. From this room a new wing for one of the younger families would grow. They ripped up her clothes and shoes and broke her combs, grinding them underfoot. They tore her work from the loom. They scattered the cooking fire and rolled the new weaving in it. We could hear them in the kitchen breaking our bowls and banging the pots. They overturned the great waist-high earthenware jugs; duck eggs, pickled fruits, vegetables burst out and mixed in acrid torrents. The old woman from the next field swept a broom through the air and loosed the spirits-of-the-broom over our heads. 'Pig.' 'Ghost.' 'Pig,' they sobbed and scolded while they ruined our house.

"When they left, they took sugar and oranges to bless themselves. They cut pieces from the dead animals. Some of them took bowls that were not broken and clothes that were not torn. Afterward we swept up the rice and sewed it back up into sacks. But the smells from the spilled preserves lasted. Your aunt gave birth in the pigsty that night. The next morning when I went for the water, I found her and the baby plugging up the family well.

"Don't let your father know that I told you. He denies her. Now that you have started to menstruate, what happened to her could happen to you. Don't humiliate us. You wouldn't like to be forgotten as if you had never been born. The villagers are watchful."

Whenever she had to warn us about life, my mother told stories that ran like   10
this one, a story to grow up on. She tested our strength to establish realities. Those in the emigrant generations who could not reassert brute survival died young and far from home. Those of us in the first American generations have had to figure out how the invisible world the emigrants built around our childhoods fits in solid America.

The emigrants confused the gods by diverting their curses, misleading them with crooked streets and false names. They must try to confuse their offspring as well, who, I suppose, threaten them in similar ways—always trying to get things straight, always trying to name the unspeakable. The Chinese I know hide their names; sojourners take new names when their lives change and guard their real names with silence.

Chinese-Americans, when you try to understand what things in you are Chinese, how do you separate what is peculiar to childhood, to poverty, insanities, one family, your mother who marked your growing with stories, from what is Chinese? What is Chinese tradition and what is the movies?

If I want to learn what clothes my aunt wore, whether flashy or ordinary, I would have to begin, "Remember Father's drowned-in-the-well sister?" I cannot ask that. My mother has told me once and for all the useful parts. She will add nothing unless powered by Necessity, a riverbank that guides her life. She plants vegetable gardens rather than lawns; she carries the odd-shaped tomatoes home from the fields and eats food left for the gods.

Whenever we did frivolous things, we used up energy; we flew high kites. We children came up off the ground over the melting cones our parents brought home from work and the American movie on New Year's Day — *Oh, You Beautiful Doll* with Betty Grable one year, and *She Wore a Yellow Ribbon* with John Wayne another year. After the one carnival ride each, we paid in guilt; our tired father counted his change on the dark walk home.

Adultery is extravagance. Could people who hatch their own chicks and eat   15 the embryos and the heads for delicacies and boil the feet in vinegar for party food, leaving only the gravel, eating even the gizzard lining — could such people engender a prodigal aunt? To be a woman, to have a daughter in starvation time was a waste enough. My aunt could not have been the lone romantic who gave up everything for sex. Women in the old China did not choose. Some man had commanded her to lie with him and be his secret evil. I wonder whether he masked himself when he joined the raid on her family.

Perhaps she had encountered him in the fields or on the mountain where the daughters-in-law collected fuel. Or perhaps he first noticed her in the marketplace. He was not a stranger because the village housed no strangers. She had to have dealings with him other than sex. Perhaps he worked an adjoining field, or he sold her the cloth for the dress she sewed and wore. His demand must have surprised, then terrified her. She obeyed him; she always did as she was told.

When the family found a young man in the next village to be her husband, she had stood tractably beside the best rooster, his proxy, and promised before they met that she would be his forever. She was lucky that he was her age and she would be the first wife, an advantage secure now. The night she first saw him, he had sex with her. Then he left for America. She had almost forgotten what he looked like. When she tried to envision him, she only saw the black and white face in the group photograph the men had had taken before leaving.

The other man was not, after all, much different from her husband. They both gave orders: she followed. "If you tell your family, I'll beat you. I'll kill you. Be here again next week." No one talked sex, ever. And she might have separated the rapes from the rest of living if only she did not have to buy her oil from him or gather wood in the same forest. I want her fear to have lasted just as long as rape lasted so that the fear could have been contained. No drawn-out fear. But women at sex hazarded birth and hence lifetimes. The fear did not stop but permeated everywhere. She told the man, "I think I'm pregnant." He organized the raid against her.

On nights when my mother and father talked about their life back home, sometimes they mentioned an "outcast table" whose business they still seemed to be settling, their voices tight. In a commensal tradition, where food is precious, the powerful older people made wrongdoers eat alone. Instead of letting them start separate new lives like the Japanese, who could become samurais and geishas, the Chinese family, faces averted but eyes glowering sideways, hung on to the offenders and fed them leftovers. My aunt must have lived in the same house as my parents and eaten at an outcast table. My mother spoke about the raid as if she had seen it, when she and my aunt, a daughter-in-law to a different household, should not have been living together at all. Daughters-in-law lived with their husbands' parents, not their own; a synonym for marriage in Chinese is "taking a daughter-in-law." Her husband's parents could have sold her, mortgaged her, stoned her. But they had sent her back to her own mother and father, a mysterious act hinting at disgraces not told me. Perhaps they had thrown her out to deflect the avengers.

She was the only daughter; her four brothers went with her father, husband, and uncles "out on the road" and for some years became western men. When the goods were divided among the family, three of the brothers took land, and the youngest, my father, chose an education. After my grandparents gave their daughter away to her husband's family, they had dispensed all the adventure and all the property. They expected her alone to keep the traditional ways, which her brothers, now among the barbarians, could fumble without detection. The heavy, deep-rooted women were to maintain the past against the flood, safe for returning. But the rare urge west had fixed upon our family, and so my aunt crossed boundaries not delineated in space.

The work of preservation demands that the feelings playing about in one's guts not be turned into action. Just watch their passing like cherry blossoms. But perhaps my aunt, my forerunner, caught in a slow life, let dreams grow and fade and after some months or years went toward what persisted. Fear at the enormities of the forbidden kept her desires delicate, wire and bone. She looked at a man because she liked the way the hair was tucked behind his ears, or she liked the question-mark line of a long torso curving at the shoulder and straight at the hip. For warm eyes or a soft voice or a slow walk — that's all — a few hairs, a line, a brightness, a sound, a pace, she gave up family. She offered us up for a charm that vanished with tiredness, a pigtail that didn't toss when the wind died. Why, the wrong lighting could erase the dearest thing about him.

It could very well have been, however, that my aunt did not take subtle enjoyment of her friend, but, a wild woman, kept rollicking company. Imagining her free with sex doesn't fit, though. I don't know any women like that, or men either. Unless I see her life branching into mine, she gives me no ancestral help.

To sustain her being in love, she often worked at herself in the mirror, guessing at the colors and shapes that would interest him, changing them frequently in order to hit on the right combination. She wanted him to look back.

20

On a farm near the sea, a woman who tended her appearance reaped a reputation for eccentricity. All the married women blunt-cut their hair in flaps about their ears or pulled it back in tight buns. No nonsense. Neither style blew easily into heart-catching tangles. And at their weddings they displayed themselves in their long hair for the last time. "It brushed the backs of my knees," my mother tells me. "It was braided, and even so, it brushed the backs of my knees."

At the mirror my aunt combined individuality into her bob. A bun could have been contrived to escape into black streamers blowing in the wind or in quiet wisps about her face, but only the older women in our picture album wear buns. She brushed her hair back from her forehead, tucking the flaps behind her ears. She looped a piece of thread, knotted into a circle between her index fingers and thumbs, and ran the double strand across her forehead. When she closed her fingers as if she were making a pair of shadow geese bite, the string twisted together catching the little hairs. Then she pulled the thread away from her skin, ripping the hairs out neatly, her eyes watering from the needles of pain. Opening her fingers, she cleaned the thread, then rolled it along her hairline and the tops of her eyebrows. My mother did the same to me and my sisters and herself. I used to believe that the expression "caught by the short hairs" meant a captive held with a depilatory string. It especially hurt at the temples, but my mother said we were lucky we didn't have to have our feet bound when we were seven. Sisters used to sit on their beds and cry together, she said, as their mothers or their slave removed the bandages for a few minutes each night and let the blood gush back into their veins. I hope that the man my aunt loved appreciated a smooth brow, that he wasn't just a tits-and-ass man.

Once my aunt found a freckle on her chin, at a spot that the almanac said predestined her for unhappiness. She dug it out with a hot needle and washed the wound with peroxide.

More attention to her looks than these pullings of hairs and pickings at spots would have caused gossip among the villagers. They owned work clothes and good clothes, and they wore good clothes for feasting the new seasons. But since a woman combing her hair hexes beginnings, my aunt rarely found an occasion to look her best. Women looked like great sea snails—the corded wood, babies, and laundry they carried were the whorls on their backs. The Chinese did not admire a bent back; goddesses and warriors stood straight. Still there must have been a marvelous freeing of beauty when a worker laid down her burden and stretched and arched.

Such commonplace loveliness, however, was not enough for my aunt. She dreamed of a lover for the fifteen days of New Year's, the time for families to exchange visits, money, and food. She plied her secret comb. And sure enough she cursed the year, the family, the village, and herself.

Even as her hair lured her imminent lover, many other men looked at her. Uncles, cousins, nephews, brothers would have looked, too, had they been home between journeys. Perhaps they had already been restraining their curiosity, and they left, fearful that their glances, like a field of nesting birds, might be startled and caught. Poverty hurt, and that was their first reason for leaving. But another, final reason for leaving the crowded house was the never-said.

25

She may have been unusually beloved, the precious only daughter, spoiled   30
and mirror gazing because of the affection the family lavished on her. When her
husband left, they welcomed the chance to take her back from the in-laws; she
could live like the little daughter for just a while longer. There are stories that my
grandfather was different from other people, "crazy ever since the little Jap bayoneted him in the head." He used to put his naked penis on the dinner table,
laughing. And one day he brought home a baby girl, wrapped up inside his
brown western-style greatcoat. He had traded one of his sons, probably my father,
the youngest, for her. My grandmother made him trade back. When he finally
got a daughter of his own, he doted on her. They must have all loved her, except
perhaps my father, the only brother who never went back to China, having once
been traded for a girl.

Brothers and sisters, newly men and women, had to efface their sexual color
and present plain miens. Disturbing hair and eyes, a smile like no other, threatened the ideal of five generations living under one roof. To focus blurs, people
shouted face to face and yelled from room to room. The immigrants I know
have loud voices, unmodulated to American tones even after years away from
the village where they called their friendships out across the fields. I have not
been able to stop my mother's screams in public libraries or over telephones.
Walking erect (knees straight, toes pointed forward, not pigeon-toed, which is
Chinese-feminine) and speaking in an inaudible voice, I have tried to turn myself
American-feminine. Chinese communication was loud, public. Only sick people
had to whisper. But at the dinner table, where the family members came nearest
one another, no one could talk, not the outcasts nor any eaters. Every word that
falls from the mouth is a coin lost. Silently they gave and accepted food with both
hands. A preoccupied child who took his bowl with one hand got a sideways
glare. A complete moment of total attention is due everyone alike. Children and
lovers have no singularity here, but my aunt used a secret voice, a separate atten-
tiveness.

She kept the man's name to herself throughout her labor and dying; she did
not accuse him that he be punished with her. To save her inseminator's name she
gave silent birth.

He may have been somebody in her own household, but intercourse with
a man outside the family would have been no less abhorrent. All the village
were kinsmen, and the titles shouted in loud country voices never let kinship be
forgotten. Any man within visiting distance would have been neutralized as a
lover — "brother," "younger brother," "older brother" — one hundred and fifteen
relationship titles. Parents researched birth charts probably not so much to assure
good fortune as to circumvent incest in a population that has but one hundred
surnames. Everybody has eight million relatives. How useless then sexual mannerisms, how dangerous.

As if it came from an atavism deeper than fear, I used to add "brother" silently
to boys' names. It hexed the boys, who would or would not ask me to dance, and
made them less scary and as familiar and deserving of benevolence as girls.

But, of course, I hexed myself also — no dates. I should have stood up, both   35
arms waving, and shouted out across libraries, "Hey, you! Love me back." I had

no idea, though, how to make attraction selective, how to control its direction and magnitude. If I made myself American-pretty so that the five or six Chinese boys in the class fell in love with me, everyone else — the Caucasian, Negro, and Japanese boys — would too. Sisterliness, dignified and honorable, made much more sense.

Attraction eludes control so stubbornly that whole societies designed to organize relationships among people cannot keep order, not even when they bind people to one another from childhood and raise them together. Among the very poor and the wealthy, brothers married their adopted sisters, like doves. Our family allowed some romance, paying adult brides' prices and providing dowries so that their sons and daughters could marry strangers. Marriage promises to turn strangers into friendly relatives — a nation of siblings.

In the village structure, spirits shimmered among the live creatures, balanced and held in equilibrium by time and land. But one human being flaring up into violence could open up a black hole, a maelstrom that pulled in the sky. The frightened villagers, who depended on one another to maintain the real, went to my aunt to show her a personal, physical representation of the break she had made in the "roundness." Misallying couples snapped off the future, which was to be embodied in true offspring. The villagers punished her for acting as if she could have a private life, secret and apart from them.

If my aunt had betrayed the family at a time of large grain yields and peace, when many boys were born, and wings were being built on many houses, perhaps, she might have escaped such severe punishment. But the men — hungry, greedy, tired of planting in dry soil — had been forced to leave the village in order to send food-money home. There were ghost plagues, bandit plagues, wars with the Japanese, floods. My Chinese brother and sister had died of an unknown sickness. Adultery, perhaps only a mistake during good times, became a crime when the village needed food.

The round moon cakes and round doorways, the round tables of graduated size that fit one roundness inside another, round windows and rice bowls — these talismans had lost their power to warn this family of the law: a family must be whole, faithfully keeping the descent line by having sons to feed the old and the dead, who in turn look after the family. The villagers came to show my aunt and her lover-in-hiding a broken house. The villagers were speeding up the circling of events because she was too shortsighted to see that her infidelity had already harmed the village, that waves of consequences would return unpredictably, sometimes in disguise, as now, to hurt her. This roundness had to be made coin-sized so that she would see its circumference: punish her at the birth of her baby. Awaken her to the inexorable. People who refused fatalism because they could invent small resources insisted on culpability. Deny accidents and wrest fault from the stars.

After the villagers left, their lanterns now scattering in various directions toward home, the family broke their silence and cursed her. "Aiaa, we're going to die. Death is coming. Death is coming. Look what you've done. You've killed us. Ghost! Dead ghost! Ghost! You've never been born." She ran out into the fields,

40

far enough from the house so that she could no longer hear their voices, and pressed herself against the earth, her own land no more. When she felt the birth coming, she thought that she had been hurt. Her body seized together. "They've hurt me too much," she thought. "This is gall, and it will kill me." With forehead and knees against the earth, her body convulsed and then relaxed. She turned on her back, lay on the ground. The black well of sky and stars went out and out and out forever; her body and her complexity seemed to disappear. She was one of the stars, a bright dot in blackness, without home, without a companion, in eternal cold and silence. An agoraphobia rose in her, speeding higher and higher, bigger and bigger; she would not be able to contain it; there would be no end to fear.

Flayed, unprotected against space, she felt pain return, focusing her body. This pain chilled her — a cold, steady kind of surface pain. Inside, spasmodically, the other pain, the pain of the child, heated her. For hours she lay on the ground, alternately body and space. Sometimes a vision of normal comfort obliterated reality: she saw the family in the evening gambling at the dinner table, the young people massaging their elders' backs. She saw them congratulating one another, high joy on the mornings the rice shoots came up. When these pictures burst, the stars drew yet further apart. Black space opened.

She got to her feet to fight better and remembered that old-fashioned women gave birth in their pigsties to fool the jealous, pain-dealing gods, who do not snatch piglets. Before the next spasms could stop her, she ran to the pigsty, each step a rushing out into emptiness. She climbed over the fence and knelt in the dirt. It was good to have a fence enclosing her, a tribal person alone.

Laboring, this woman who had carried her child as a foreign growth that sickened her every day, expelled it at last. She reached down to touch the hot, wet, moving mass, surely smaller than anything human, and could feel that it was human after all — fingers, toes, nails, nose. She pulled it up on to her belly, and it lay curled there, butt in the air, feet precisely tucked one under the other. She opened her loose shirt and buttoned the child inside. After resting, it squirmed and thrashed and she pushed it up to her breast. It turned its head this way and that until it found her nipple. There, it made little snuffling noises. She clenched her teeth at its preciousness, lovely as a young calf, a piglet, a little dog.

She may have gone to the pigsty as a last act of responsibility: she would protect this child as she had protected its father. It would look after her soul, leaving supplies on her grave. But how would this tiny child without family find her grave when there would be no marker for her anywhere, neither in the earth nor the family hall? No one would give her a family hall name. She had taken the child with her into the wastes. At its birth the two of them had felt the same raw pain of separation, a wound that only the family pressing tight could close. A child with no descent line would not soften her life but only trail after her, ghostlike, begging her to give it purpose. At dawn the villagers on their way to the fields would stand around the fence and look.

Full of milk, the little ghost slept. When it awoke, she hardened her breasts against the milk that crying loosens. Toward morning she picked up the baby and walked to the well.   45

Carrying the baby to the well shows loving. Otherwise abandon it. Turn its face into the mud. Mothers who love their children take them along. It was probably a girl; there is some hope of forgiveness for boys.

"Don't tell anyone you had an aunt. Your father does not want to hear her name. She has never been born." I have believed that sex was unspeakable and words so strong and fathers so frail that "aunt" would do my father mysterious harm. I have thought that my family, having settled among immigrants who had also been their neighbors in the ancestral land, needed to clean their name, and a wrong word would incite the kinspeople even here. But there is more to this silence: they want me to participate in her punishment. And I have.

In the twenty years since I heard this story I have not asked for details nor said my aunt's name; I do not know it. People who can comfort the dead can also chase after them to hurt them further—a reverse ancestor worship. The real punishment was not the raid swiftly inflicted by the villagers, but the family's deliberately forgetting her. Her betrayal so maddened them, they saw to it that she would suffer forever, even after death. Always hungry, always needing, she would have to beg food from other ghosts, snatch and steal it from those whose living descendants give them gifts. She would have to fight the ghosts massed at crossroads for the buns a few thoughtful citizens leave to decoy her away from village and home so that the ancestral spirits could feast unharassed. At peace, they could act like gods, not ghosts, their descent lines providing them with paper suits and dresses, spirit money, paper houses, paper automobiles, chicken, meat, and rice into eternity—essences delivered up in smoke and flames, steam and incense rising from each rice bowl. In an attempt to make the Chinese care for people outside the family, Chairman Mao encourages us now to give our paper replicas to the spirits of outstanding soldiers and workers, no matter whose ancestors they may be. My aunt remains forever hungry. Goods are not distributed evenly among the dead.

My aunt haunts me—her ghost drawn to me because now, after fifty years of neglect, I alone devote pages of paper to her, though not origamied into houses and clothes. I do not think she always means me well. I am telling on her, and she was a spite suicide, drowning herself in the drinking water. The Chinese are always very frightened of the drowned one, whose weeping ghost, wet hair hanging and skin bloated, waits silently by the water to pull down a substitute. [1976]

THINKING ABOUT THE TEXT

1. This cautionary tale is meant to persuade Kingston to conform to her parents' values. What is the argument behind the narrative the mother tells? Does it make sense to you? What might be a contemporary argument in a middle-class American family?

2. Were you ever put at an "outcast table" (para. 19) or anything comparable in your house or school? Did you ever hear of such a ritual? What did happen when you were punished? What kinds of things were you punished for? Why do you think these specific things were chosen?

3. Is this also a tale about gender inequality? How does Kingston suggest this? How are relations between men and women portrayed here?

4. Kingston talks a good deal about spirits and ghosts. How do they function in this essay? Which parts of this piece seem true to you? Which seem fictional? Why does she blend these elements together?

5. Sexual mores change over time and from country to country. What specifically about the aunt's context made her transgression so severe? How would her "crime" be viewed in contemporary America? Why? What do you think an ideal response would be?

NAOMI WOLF

The Making of a Slut

A Rhodes scholar and Yale University graduate, Naomi Wolf (b. 1962) is a provocative writer and speaker on women's issues. Her successful 1991 book The Beauty Myth *elaborates on how society uses beauty ideals to maintain the power structure controlling women's social behavior and status. Her 1993 book* Fire with Fire *drew some criticism from feminists who objected to her celebration of heterosexuality and her insistence that women had accepted a "victim feminism." They were further alienated by Wolf's conventional wedding, her "Culture Babes" women's group, and her apparent attack on the pro-choice position in a* New Republic *article (her husband is a former executive editor of the magazine) soon after the birth of her daughter in 1995. In the following essay from the March/April 1997 edition of* Ms., *Wolf reprises her theme of conventional definitions and social control of women.*

So much of the debate over issues relating to women and sexuality today is stereotypical, grinding together false dualisms of good and evil, saints and villains. All too often we discuss important issues such as teen pregnancy and date rape with a lot of name-calling but with too little real-life experience providing a background against which to measure myths and distortions.

Because sexual awakening for girls and sexuality for women are almost always complex, contextual and nuanced, I felt a need to "unpack" the statistics and the polemics. As a writer, I have faith in the power of stories to get at truths that numbers and political screeds can't reach. So this is my effort to tell some of the stories that statistics can't and that polemics won't.

Many women of my mother's generation told their stories of sexual coming-of-age in the shadow of the repressive hypocrisy of the fifties, and of "finding themselves" by casting off that era's inhibitions. For a quarter century, their conclusions have shaped our discussions of sex, women, and freedom. Those conclusions no longer fit the experiences of the two generations that have grown into womanhood during and after the sexual and feminist revolutions—generations whose experiences are sometimes so very different from those of their mothers that in some ways their stories are harder to tell, and, consequently, harder to learn from.

It is still more difficult to lay claim to the personal experiences of the slut than to those of the virgin. Women's sexual past is still materially used against them. This can happen in a court of law, a place of business, a congressional hearing, or an intimate negotiation. When someone's past "catches up with her," that woman is scapegoated and separated from the "good girls." But the punishment aimed at her inhibits all of us, and can keep us from actions ranging from charging a supervisor with sexual harassment to running for school board office to fighting for custody of children. And, in the wake of the sexual revolution, the line between "good" and "bad" girls is always shifting, keeping us unsteady, as it is meant to do.

It will not be safe for us to live comfortably in our skins until we say: "You can   5
no longer separate us out one from another. We are all 'bad' girls."

In any group of girls, someone has to be the slut.

In our group, Dinah became the slut. She found that role — or rather, it found her — and she did not deign to fight it. She put it on with dignity.

We were fourteen and a half; it was our eighth-grade year at our junior high. After school, before she became an outcast, I used to go over to Dinah's house in the Fillmore District almost every day.

She had the gift not only of inventing a more alluring world, but of extending it to others so they could see it too. When the two of us were alone, a glamour would descend on us. Dinah had a chewed-up collection of records of musicals, and for her these created an alternative world. Singing along with them, her pointed chin would lift upward as she sang, and her red-rimmed eyes would light up, and she would lose her tough scrapper quality. The headache-tight Lee jeans, the hair darkened with henna streaks, the pookah shell necklaces, the run-down hiking boots, would all disappear. She became Mary Martin in the South Seas or Auntie Mame loose on Manhattan.

But Dinah was the slut. She became the slut because of conditions so tan-   10
gential that they could almost never have been, or could as easily have slipped the designation to someone else. She was poor; that is, poorer than the other white kids. And her body changed faster than many of the other girls'. Her breasts were large and high by seventh grade — but that visitation had come to other girls, too. It was how she decided to carry it that did her in.

She refused the good-girl slump, the binder held crosswise across her chest. She would not back down and rest her weight on her pelvis and ruin her line. Instead she flagrantly kept walking with her spine extended to her full height, her back slightly swayed. I understood what she was doing with her tailbone tucked under and her torso supple and erect like a figure on the prow of a ship, and her feet turned carefully out: she was being a star. She was thinking of the technique of stage movement that she was reading about in the books on drama, and trying always to imagine a fine filament connecting the top of her talented head to the heavens. She was walking always out to her public, graciously, for an encore. But there was no visual language in our world for a poor girl with big breasts walking tall except "slut."

By watching what happened to Dinah, we discovered that sex—for girls at least—was a game of musical chairs. It was very important to stay in the game, if always nervously moving; but finding yourself suddenly singled out was nothing short of fatal. And—just like that game—the rules that isolated one or another of us were arbitrary and capricious. One thing was certain: if you were targeted, no matter how randomly, whether you had moved not fast enough or too fast for the music, in some sure way your exclusion was your own fault.

Dinah was a spectacular dancer. On late afternoons, she could usually be found practicing steps alone in our school's shabby music room, head up, facing solemnly into the wall-length mirror. Dinah's kicks were higher and her splits deeper than those of any of the other girls over whom she towered in our class. She was more than disciplined with herself—she was almost brutal in the service of what she thought of, very levelly, as her art. There was a genre of teenage-girl novel in which a hardworking and usually orphaned ballet student pits her all to attain the great performance and accolades, and then a life of grace and ease. Dinah devoured these books.

It was no surprise that, when the call for cheerleader auditions went out, it provoked her competitive spirit. We were not the kind of girls to approach the cheerleading squad with straight faces. But the idea of a test—even more compellingly, a test of skill and charm—seduced us. Cheerleading was sexy, but for once it was a sexuality that was also absolutely safe for us.

The junior high school cheerleading squad would be chosen not by P.E. or drama teachers on the basis of physical skill, but rather, by a panel of regular subject teachers. These teachers thought of themselves as the conscience of the school. ("And," as one was overheard to say, "the cheerleaders represent the school.") They saw a heavily made-up girl, in her short red-leather jacket and midriff cropped T-shirt, leaning against a graffiti-stained wall every afternoon with the guys in the band, smoking; and they thought they knew all about Dinah.

For weeks, Dinah prepared. She believed in merit. In the try-out red plush outfit that she had sewn herself, she played the role of "wholesome cheerleader"—the only jarring note being the crease of metallic blue eye shadow that, against the dictates of *Seventeen* magazine, she insisted on applying daily. On the afternoon of the tryout, Dinah was tense. But her performance of the two cheers was, insofar as such a crude and bouncy set piece could be, a star turn. She held out her arms to the dark and silent auditorium seats, pom-poms lifted in an exuberant V, and then swooped them low.

The panel of teachers sat in the center of the pit, in the otherwise empty auditorium, their faces impassive.

Then the other girls and I tried out, sheepishly, in jeans. None of us were any better than pedestrian in contrast to Dinah. We went back outside to wait for the panel's decision.

A secretary posted a typewritten list outside the gym door. She avoided our eyes. All the new members of the team consisted of commonly acknowledged

15

"popular" older girls. And me. In a mostly poor and working-class school, almost all of the chosen were daughters of the middle class. And — in a student population that was mostly Chinese, Japanese, Filipino, or African American — almost all were white. Dinah was not even an alternate.

I felt sick.   20

Dinah looked at the list on the door. She made her Judy Garland chin-out "struggling" face, then laughed at herself. "You," she said, "don't know what to say."

She shrugged her shoulders under her leather jacket. "It's that I hang out with the wrong group, that's all," she said. She looked past me to the hills above the playground, and assumed the ironic detachment she was so good at. "Well," she said crisply, lighting a Marlboro and then making one perfect French curl of smoke, "it can't be because they think I don't know how to dance."

We filed to the bus stop together in silence. We had been classified differently and we knew it. Our companionship was never exactly the same again.

The girl named head cheerleader, called "the cutest girl in ninth grade" and a paragon of her church group, was no angel. But her parents were "nice" and her clothes were good. The popular girls whom the teachers approved of often conducted their sexual experiences after sneaking away from their parents' cabanas on the white-sand beaches of family vacations. Dinah went out with nineteen-year-old store clerk motorcycle rockers and lay around on foam mattresses in garages.

Dinah got called a slut because she was too poor and she was too proud of   25
her body, and, by implication, she was too proud of her sexuality.

By the time we reached high school, Dinah had found a new gang. They were mostly guys, the rough kind of guys. Class considerations, which were like an invisible, undeniable hand moving us over a school-sized chessboard, directed Dinah to a whole new group of girls. The whole school spread rumors that girls in that gang had mastered every technique in *The Sensuous Woman*.

Years later, another woman who as a girl was familiar with what was becoming Dinah's world, said that fellatio was the first genuine adult skill she ever mastered except driving, and that it made her feel just as powerful, just as valuable and free of her childhood helplessness. She spoke about the feeling among the girls in that subculture that sex was a performance for the benefit of boys.

Dinah's reputation worsened as we got older. But I also guess from having known her that during the same time in her life that her name became a fixture on the boys' bathroom walls, she was probably studying and trying to keep her family life together. According to the junior high and high school grapevine, when she heard about the graffiti in the bathrooms that talked about her blow jobs, she thought it was funny. At least, I heard she laughed. I believed it. She liked to shock the world that had repudiated her.

By our junior year in high school, her clothes tighter and her makeup heavier than ever, Dinah still seemed proud, and she still carried herself with that head-held-high, fuck-you regalness. I don't know for sure what she was thinking because I stopped "knowing" her — the result of that adolescent social dynamic, when class or race or gender pulls friends apart, that is so irrevocable. Class had declared her a slut by fourteen, while she was still technically a virgin, and kept her there, and kept me and my other wild little middle-class friends safe. As she passed us in the halls, her face grew more and more impassive with every year. That still haunts me.

From her story, and the stories of so many others, I knew that "keeping control" of my desire was the only key to keeping myself and my emerging identity safe. So much depended on my taking the careful, balanced paces of a tightrope walker. Go — but DON'T JUMP!!! Go, but go slow, and keep watching. Yet part of me wanted above all else the experience of shutting my eyes and falling through the air.

I knew I was dangerous to myself the day that I let a boy walk me home from school and drew me into the overgrown alley that ran alongside the stone staircase up the hill to my house. He pushed the hair away from my forehead and then kissed my forehead, as if to make everything all right. He kissed down the side of my face to the corner of my mouth, too shy to look me in the eyes, but moving always closer to my lips. All I had to do was turn my face up toward him, and hold perfectly still. It was the easiest important thing I had ever done.

I knew that arching my neck just a little meant, "That's all right; go on." His hand lay against my clavicle and then against my chest above my collar. Finally, he slid just the tips of his fingers not even to my breast but to the skin between that lay just inside the line of my clothing. Through my closed eyes, the light went red. He withdrew his hand and watched my face. Even as the cold air rippled my shirt, his fingerprints were still burning.

He was watching to see if it was all right. It wasn't all right. I was capable of anything. I was capable of being Dinah.

Almost every society punishes its sluts in its own ways. It's just that right now, our own sometimes pretends it does not. The summer that I went back home to ask my friends about our girlhoods, there was a rash of sex industry films coming out of Hollywood. *Striptease* and *Showgirls* were following their predecessor, *Pretty Woman.* Teenage girls were reading about how Demi Moore worked out for hours each day to play a stripper; how she would go to the strip joints and hang with the dancers to "get it right."

As we drove through the hills above Marin, I asked a friend who had grown up with us what she thought about those films. Her opinion was better informed than most of ours was, for she had spent time as a stripper, and later as a professional mistress. She embodied the contradiction we live under: a college-educated, happily married, community-minded woman with curly black hair, a hip way of wearing her tailored clothes, a timid grin — indistinguishable from any of the rest of our tribe. But by the standards of the culture she had been a real whore, a true, dyed-in-the-wool, no-argument, verifiable slut. She had gone all the way. The bad girl, the good girl — the dimorphism was a fantasy. They were both here in the car; in her, in myself, in us all.

As she drove, the carefree mood of two women in their early thirties thinking about girlhood in an open car, feet on the dashboard and reggae on the radio, evaporated. "Here is all I have to say about how they are glamorizing those images for girls, who are just sucking it in," she said. Her words became slow and deliberate. "When men think a woman is a whore, it's open . . . season . . . on her. They can say anything to her they want, they can do anything they want, they can be absolutely as crass and vile and violent and cruel and uncaring as the darkest part of their personality wants to be. And it's okay. They don't have to afford the woman one ounce of respect for being a human being. She's not a human being. She's a thing.

"Since the sexual revolution, there's a license, and there's terror, and we're living under . . . both."

Then the words came out in a torrent. "I was shocked. I was shocked. I thought that because of the progress that women have made in our society men would have a clue that prostitutes are human beings and that they don't deserve to be treated so poorly, but they don't. It's almost as if now they see sex workers as the only women that they can be so aggressive and cruel to. They can't get away with it in their jobs anymore, they can't get away with it in their marriages, but with sex workers, it's okay. That's what they're paid for! They're paid to be sexually harassed, they're paid to be assaulted. Women outside the sex industry won't put up with it anymore."

I was quiet. I was thinking: if all women, even nice women, can do what only whores used to do, but you can no longer treat all women who do such things like whores—that is, if feminism is succeeding at breaking down some of the penalties that used to be directed at nonprofessional, sexually licentious women—then society will all the more rigidly professionalize and demarcate the bad girl for sale, to whom anything can be done. My friend was explaining that "real" prostitutes used to bear the burden of the fact that nice girls had a limited repertoire; now they bear the burden of the fact that nice girls have gotten wild.

The feeling of foreboding that had hung over the word "slut" in my sexually libertine girlhood became clearer. The culture had said: Take it off. Take it all off. The culture had also said, of the raped girl, of the hitchhiker, of the dead girl: She was in the wrong place at the wrong time, doing the wrong thing.

Suddenly, as the soft round hills sped by, I saw flash before my eyes a photograph from one of the social histories I had been reading. It was of the nearly intact, mummified remains, dating from the first century A.D., of a fourteen-year-old German girl. Her long, shapely legs and slender feet were intact, and her right arm still clutched the garrote that had been used to twist the rope around her neck. Her lips were still in an O of surprise or pain, and a twisted rag was still securely bound against her eyes. At fourteen, the girl had been blindfolded, strangled, and drowned, most likely as retribution for "adultery"—for what we would call a teenage love affair.

Given these origins, it is no wonder that even today fourteen-year-old girls who notice, let alone act upon, desire have the heart-racing sense that they are doing something obscurely, but surely, dangerous. It is also in part because of this inheritance that a contemporary woman wakes up after a night of being erotically

40

"out of control" feeling sure, on some primal level, that something punitive is bound to happen to her — and that if it doesn't, it should. [1997]

THINKING ABOUT THE TEXT

1. Wolf argues that sexual rules are "arbitrary and capricious" (para. 12). Do her anecdotes support this assertion? Is "'keeping control'" (para. 30) contextual, depending on class, gender, race, or time period?

2. In paragraph 6 Wolf makes the provocative statement, "In any group of girls, someone has to be the slut." In your experience is this true? Why? Is it true for males also? Why? Is the slut an outcast? From whom?

3. Wolf makes sexual assertions and then supports them with concrete examples. Which ones seem especially illuminating? Which ones the least?

4. When Wolf says "We are all 'bad' girls" (para. 5), is it clear what she means by *bad*?

5. Wolf claims that every society punishes sluts differently. What does this mean? She seems to give a historical reason for guilt. Do you agree with her?

MAKING COMPARISONS

1. Explain how economics plays a part in both Kingston's and Wolf's essays, especially in constructing sexual rules.

2. In both essays, compare the influence the following play in setting the sexual agenda for females: mothers, social class, boys, peer groups.

3. Imagine a conversation between Dinah and Kingston's aunt on the night of the villagers' attack. What might Dinah tell her?

WRITING ABOUT ISSUES

1. Argue that Kingston's aunt should, or should not, have killed herself and her baby.

2. Write an explanation for why Kingston's aunt and Dinah are both considered sluts.

3. From your own experiences and those of friends, argue that Wolf is correct (or incorrect) in saying that it is still dangerous for young girls to notice or act on desire.

4. Interview at least six males for their definition of what a slut is and for their opinions about them. Ask them if they would marry one, and why. Write a report of your findings with a brief analysis.

THE MYSTERIOUS EXILE: CRITICAL COMMENTARIES ON HERMAN MELVILLE'S "BARTLEBY, THE SCRIVENER"

HERMAN MELVILLE, "Bartleby, the Scrivener"

CRITICAL COMMENTARIES:
MICHAEL PAUL ROGIN, From "Class Struggles in America"
LEO MARX, From "Melville's Parable of the Walls"
MAURICE FRIEDMAN, From "Bartleby and the Modern Exile"
ALFRED KAZIN, From "Ishmael in His Academic Heaven"

Something haunts us about Herman Melville's most anthologized short story, a tale of a man who baffles his boss by refusing to work. Readers see in Bartleby's rebellion meanings of all kinds, from a retelling of Christ's persecution to a Marxist condemnation of capitalism, from a satire on Henry David Thoreau to praise for Thoreau, from a case study of schizophrenia to statements of nihilism, Buddhism, Hinduism, and pragmatic Christianity. Some readers think of Bartleby as an existential hero whose "passive resistance" made him a modern exile, abandoned by God and his fellow man. Others see Bartleby as renouncing the world, as a person so alienated that he cannot be reached and cannot be saved. Bartleby seems to insist on his destiny, even if that leads to his destruction. But finally what is most interesting about Bartleby is what Melville does not tell us, what we do not know about a person who speaks very little, who seems to live in a universe of his own. His mysterious life has charmed and puzzled critics who have read the story dozens of times as well as those who are encountering for the first time the man who would prefer not to work.

BEFORE YOU READ

Have you ever refused to do something you were expected to do? Did you accept the consequences? What if you simply said, "No, I will not" to any request? What would eventually happen to you? Can you remember being shocked by someone else's refusal?

HERMAN MELVILLE
Bartleby, the Scrivener

A STORY OF WALL STREET

Born in New York to a family that had slipped from well-to-do circumstances, Herman Melville (1819–1891) earned a living as a teacher, a sailor, and a bank clerk. His early writing was influenced by his acquaintance with Nathaniel Hawthorne, and he drew on his sailing experiences to write several novels, including Moby-

Dick *(1851), considered to be a masterpiece of American literature. He wrote short stories, often for magazines, and poetry, a volume of which was published after his death, and a novella,* Billy Budd. *"Bartleby, the Scrivener" was written for magazine publication, probably from financial necessity to support his family.*

I am a rather elderly man. The nature of my avocations, for the last thirty years, has brought me into more than ordinary contact with what would seem an interesting and somewhat singular set of men, of whom, as yet, nothing, that I know of, has ever been written — I mean, the law-copyists, or scriveners. I have known very many of them, professionally and privately, and, if I pleased, could relate divers histories, at which good-natured gentlemen might smile, and sentimental souls might weep. But I waive the biographies of all other scriveners, for a few passages in the life of Bartleby, who was a scrivener, the strangest I ever saw, or heard of. While, of other law-copyists, I might write the complete life, of Bartleby nothing of that sort can be done. I believe that no materials exist, for a full and satisfactory biography of this man. It is an irreparable loss to literature. Bartleby was one of those beings of whom nothing is ascertainable, except from the original sources, and, in his case, those are very small. What my own astonished eyes saw of Bartleby, *that* is all I know of him, except, indeed, one vague report, which will appear in the sequel.

Ere introducing the scrivener, as he first appeared to me, it is fit I make some mention of myself, my *employés,* my business, my chambers, and general surroundings, because some such description is indispensable to an adequate understanding of the chief character about to be presented. Imprimis:° I am a man who, from his youth upwards, has been filled with a profound conviction that the easiest way of life is the best. Hence, though I belong to a profession proverbially energetic and nervous, even to turbulence, at times, yet nothing of that sort have I ever suffered to invade my peace. I am one of those unambitious lawyers who never address a jury, or in any way draw down public applause; but, in the cool tranquillity of a snug retreat, do a snug business among rich men's bonds, and mortgages, and title-deeds. All who know me, consider me an eminently *safe* man. The late John Jacob Astor, a personage little given to poetic enthusiasm, had no hesitation in pronouncing my first grand point to be prudence; my next, method. I do not speak it in vanity, but simply record the fact, that I was not unemployed in my profession by the late John Jacob Astor; a name which, I admit, I love to repeat; for it hath a rounded and orbicular sound to it, and rings like unto bullion. I will freely add, that I was not insensible to the late John Jacob Astor's good opinion.

Some time prior to the period at which this little history begins, my avocations had been largely increased. The good old office, now extinct in the State of New York, of a Master in Chancery, had been conferred upon me. It was not a very arduous office, but very pleasantly remunerative. I seldom lose my temper;

Imprimis: In the first place (Latin).

much more seldom indulge in dangerous indignation at wrongs and outrages; but I must be permitted to be rash here and declare, that I consider the sudden and violent abrogation of the office of Master in Chancery, by the new Constitution, as a——premature act; inasmuch as I had counted upon a life-lease of the profits, whereas I only received those of a few short years. But this is by the way.

My chambers were up stairs, at No.—Wall Street. At one end, they looked upon the white wall of the interior of a spacious skylight shaft, penetrating the building from top to bottom.

This view might have been considered rather tame than otherwise, deficient   5
in what landscape painters call "life." But, if so, the view from the other end of my chambers offered, at least, a contrast, if nothing more. In that direction, my windows commanded an unobstructed view of a lofty brick wall, black by age and everlasting shade; which wall required no spy-glass to bring out its lurking beauties, but, for the benefit of all near-sighted spectators, was pushed up to within ten feet of my window-panes. Owing to the great height of the surrounding buildings, and my chambers being on the second floor, the interval between this wall and mine not a little resembled a huge square cistern.

At the period just preceding the advent of Bartleby, I had two persons as copyists in my employment, and a promising lad as an office-boy. First, Turkey; second, Nippers; third, Ginger Nut. These may seem names, the like of which are not usually found in the Directory. In truth, they were nicknames, mutually conferred upon each other by my three clerks, and were deemed expressive of their respective persons or characters. Turkey was a short, pursy Englishman, of about my own age—that is, somewhere not far from sixty. In the morning, one might say, his face was of a fine florid hue, but after twelve o'clock, meridian— his dinner hour—it blazed like a grate full of Christmas coals; and continued blazing—but, as it were, with a gradual wane—till six o'clock, P.M., or thereabouts; after which, I saw no more of the proprietor of the face, which, gaining its meridian with the sun, seemed to set with it, to rise, culminate, and decline the following day, with the like regularity and undiminished glory. There are many singular coincidences I have known in the course of my life, not the least among which was the fact, that, exactly when Turkey displayed his fullest beams from his red and radiant countenance, just then, too, at that critical moment, began the daily period when I considered his business capacities as seriously disturbed for the remainder of the twenty-four hours. Not that he was absolutely idle, or averse to business then; far from it. The difficulty was, he was apt to be altogether too energetic. There was a strange, inflamed, flurried, flighty recklessness of activity about him. He would be incautious in dipping his pen into his inkstand. All his blots upon my documents were dropped there after twelve o'clock, meridian. Indeed, not only would he be reckless, and sadly given to making blots in the afternoon, but, some days, he went further, and was rather noisy. At such times, too, his face flamed with augmented blazonry, as if cannel coal had been heaped on anthracite. He made an unpleasant racket with his chair; spilled his sand-box; in mending his pens, impatiently split them all to pieces, and threw them on the floor in a sudden passion; stood up, and leaned over his table, boxing his papers about in a most indecorous manner, very sad to behold in an elderly man like him. Nevertheless, as he was in many ways a most valuable person to me, and all the time before twelve o'clock, meridian, was the quickest, steadiest creature, too, accomplishing a great deal of work in a style not easily to be matched—for these reasons, I was willing to overlook his eccentricities, though, indeed, occasionally, I remonstrated with him. I did this very gently, however, because, though the civilest, nay, the blandest and most reverential of men in the morning, yet, in the afternoon, he was disposed, upon provocation, to be slightly rash with his tongue—in fact, insolent. Now, valuing his morning services as I did, and resolved not to lose them—yet, at the same time, made uncomfortable by his inflamed ways after twelve o'clock—and being a man of peace, unwilling by my admonitions to call forth unseemly retorts from him, I took upon me, one Saturday noon (he was always worse on Saturdays) to hint to him, very kindly, that, perhaps, now that he was growing old, it might be well to abridge his labors; in short, he need not come to my chambers after twelve o'clock, but, dinner over, had best go home to his lodgings, and rest himself till tea-time. But no; he insisted upon his afternoon devotions. His countenance became intolerably fervid, as he oratorically assured me—gesticulating with a long ruler at the other end of the room— that if his services in the morning were useful, how indispensable, then, in the afternoon?

"With submission, sir," said Turkey, on this occasion, "I consider myself your right-hand man. In the morning I but marshal and deploy my columns; but in the afternoon I put myself at their head, and gallantly charge the foe, thus"—and he made a violent thrust with the ruler.

"But the blots, Turkey," intimated I.

"True; but, with submission, sir, behold these hairs! I am getting old. Surely, sir, a blot or two of a warm afternoon is not to be severely urged against gray hairs. Old age—even if it blot the page—is honorable. With submission, sir, we *both* are getting old."

This appeal to my fellow-feeling was hardly to be resisted. At all events, I saw   10 that go he would not. So, I made up my mind to let him stay, resolving, nevertheless, to see to it that, during the afternoon, he had to do with my less important papers.

Nippers, the second on my list, was a whiskered, sallow, and, upon the whole, rather piratical-looking young man, of about five-and-twenty. I always deemed him the victim of two evil powers—ambition and indigestion. The ambition was evinced by a certain impatience of the duties of a mere copyist, an unwarrantable usurpation of strictly professional affairs such as the original drawing up of legal documents. The indigestion seemed betokened in an occasional nervous testiness and grinning irritability, causing the teeth to audibly grind together over mistakes committed in copying; unnecessary maledictions, hissed, rather than spoken, in the heat of business; and especially by a continual discontent with the height of the table where he worked. Though of a very ingenious mechanical turn, Nippers could never get this table to suit him. He put chips under it, blocks of various sorts, bits of pasteboard, and at last went so far as to attempt an exquisite adjustment, by final pieces of folded blotting paper. But no invention would answer. If, for the sake of easing his back, he brought the table-lid at a sharp angle well up towards his chin, and wrote there like a man using the steep roof of a Dutch house for his desk, then he declared that it stopped the circulation in his arms. If now he lowered the table to his waistbands, and stooped over it in writing, then there was a sore aching in his back. In short, the truth of the matter was, Nippers knew not what he wanted. Or, if he wanted anything, it was to be rid of a scrivener's table altogether. Among the manifestations of his diseased ambition was a fondness he had for receiving visits from certain ambiguous-looking fellows in seedy coats, whom he called his clients. Indeed, I was aware that not only was he, at times, considerable of a ward-politician, but he occasionally did a little business at the justices' courts, and was not unknown on the steps of the Tombs.° I have good reason to believe, however, that one individual who called upon him at my chambers, and who, with a grand air, he insisted was his client, was no other than a dun, and the alleged title-deed, a bill. But, with all his failings, and the annoyances he caused me, Nippers, like his compatriot Turkey, was a very useful man to me; wrote a neat, swift hand; and, when he chose, was not deficient in a gentlemanly sort of deportment. Added to this, he always dressed in a gentlemanly sort of way; and so, incidentally, reflected credit upon my chambers. Whereas, with respect to Turkey, I had much ado to keep him from being a reproach to me. His clothes were apt to look oily, and smell of eating-houses. He wore his pantaloons very loose and baggy in summer. His coats were execrable, his hat not to be handled. But while the hat was a thing of indifference to me, inasmuch as his natural civility and deference, as a dependent Englishman, always led him to doff it the moment he entered the room, yet his coat was another matter. Concerning his coats, I reasoned with him; but with no effect. The truth was, I suppose, that a man with so small an income could not afford to sport such a lustrous face and a lustrous coat at one and the same time. As Nippers once observed, Turkey's money went chiefly for red ink. One winter day, I presented Turkey with a highly respectable-looking coat of my own—a padded gray coat, of a most comfortable warmth, and which buttoned straight up from the knee to the neck. I thought Turkey would appreciate the favor, and abate his rashness and obstreperousness of afternoons. But no; I verily believe that buttoning himself up in so downy and blanket-like a coat had a pernicious effect upon him upon the same principle that too much oats are bad for horses. In fact, precisely as a rash, restive horse is said to feel his oats, so Turkey felt his coat. It made him insolent. He was a man whom prosperity harmed.

Though, concerning the self-indulgent habits of Turkey, I had my own private surmises, yet, touching Nippers, I was well persuaded that, whatever might be his faults in other respects, he was, at least, a temperate young man. But, indeed, nature herself seemed to have been his vintner, and, at his birth, charged him so thoroughly with an irritable, brandy-like disposition, that all subsequent potations were needless. When I consider how, amid the stillness of my chambers, Nippers would sometimes impatiently rise from his seat, and stooping over his table, spread his arms wide apart, seize the whole desk, and move it, and jerk it, with a grim, grinding motion on the floor, as if the table were a perverse volun-

---

the Tombs: A prison in New York City.

tary agent, intent on thwarting and vexing him, I plainly perceive that, for Nippers, brandy-and-water were altogether superfluous.

It was fortunate for me that, owing to its peculiar cause — indigestion — the irritability and consequent nervousness of Nippers were mainly observable in the morning, while in the afternoon he was comparatively mild. So that, Turkey's paroxysms only coming on about twelve o'clock, I never had to do with their eccentricities at one time. Their fits relieved each other, like guards. When Nippers' was on, Turkey's was off; and *vice versa*. This was a good natural arrangement, under the circumstances.

Ginger Nut, the third on my list, was a lad, some twelve years old. His father was a carman, ambitious of seeing his son on the bench instead of a cart, before he died. So he sent him to my office, as student at law, errand-boy, cleaner, and sweeper, at the rate of one dollar a week. He had a little desk to himself, but he did not use it much. Upon inspection, the drawer exhibited a great array of the shells of various sorts of nuts. Indeed, to this quick-witted youth, the whole noble science of the law was contained in a nutshell. Not the least among the employments of Ginger Nut, as well as one which he discharged with the most alacrity, was his duty as cake and apple purveyor for Turkey and Nippers. Copying lawpapers being proverbially a dry, husky sort of business, my two scriveners were fain to moisten their mouths very often with Spitzenbergs, to be had at the numerous stalls nigh the Custom House and Post Office. Also, they sent Ginger Nut very frequently for that peculiar cake — small, flat, round, and very spicy — after which he had been named by them. Of a cold morning, when business was but dull, Turkey would gobble up scores of these cakes, as if they were mere wafers — indeed, they sell them at the rate of six or eight for a penny — the scrape of his pen blending with the crunching of the crisp particles in his mouth. Of all the fiery afternoon blunders and flurried rashness of Turkey, was his once moistening a ginger-cake between his lips, and clapping it on to a mortgage, for a seal. I came within an ace of dismissing him then. But he mollified me by making an oriental bow, and saying —

"With submission, sir, it was generous of me to find you in stationery on my own account."   15

Now my original business — that of a conveyancer and title hunter, and drawer-up of recondite documents of all sorts — was considerably increased by receiving the Master's office. There was now great work for scriveners. Not only must I push the clerks already with me, but I must have additional help.

In answer to my advertisement, a motionless young man one morning stood upon my office threshold, the door being open, for it was summer. I can see that figure now — pallidly neat, pitiably respectable, incurably forlorn! It was Bartleby.

After a few words touching his qualifications, I engaged him, glad to have among my corps of copyists a man of so singularly sedate an aspect, which I thought might operate beneficially upon the flighty temper of Turkey, and the fiery one of Nippers.

I should have stated before that ground-glass folding-doors divided my premises into two parts, one of which was occupied by my scriveners, the other by myself. According to my humor, I threw open these doors, or closed them. I resolved to assign Bartleby a corner by the folding-doors, but on my side of them, so as to have this quiet man within easy call, in case any trifling thing was to be done. I placed his desk close up to a small side-window in that part of the room, a window which originally had afforded a lateral view of certain grimy brickyards and bricks, but which, owing to subsequent erections, commanded at present no view at all, though it gave some light. Within three feet of the panes was a wall, and the light came down from far above, between two lofty buildings, as from a very small opening in a dome. Still further to a satisfactory arrangement, I procured a high green folding screen, which might entirely isolate Bartleby from my sight, though not remove him from my voice. And thus, in a manner, privacy and society were conjoined.

At first, Bartleby did an extraordinary quantity of writing. As if long famishing 20 for something to copy, he seemed to gorge himself on my documents. There was no pause for digestion. He ran a day and night line, copying by sunlight and by candle-light. I should have been quite delighted with his application, had he been cheerfully industrious. But he wrote on silently, palely, mechanically.

It is, of course, an indispensable part of a scrivener's business to verify the accuracy of his copy, word by word. Where there are two or more scriveners in an office, they assist each other in this examination, one reading from the copy, the other holding the original. It is a very dull, wearisome, and lethargic affair. I can readily imagine that, to some sanguine temperaments, it would be altogether intolerable. For example, I cannot credit that the mettlesome poet, Byron, would have contentedly sat down with Bartleby to examine a law document of, say five hundred pages, closely written in a crimpy hand.

Now and then, in the haste of business, it had been my habit to assist in comparing some brief document myself, calling Turkey or Nippers for this purpose. One object I had, in placing Bartleby so handy to me behind the screen, was, to avail myself of his services on such trivial occasions. It was on the third day, I think, of his being with me, and before any necessity had arisen for having his own writing examined, that, being much hurried to complete a small affair I had in hand, I abruptly called to Bartleby. In my haste and natural expectancy of instant compliance, I sat with my head bent over the original on my desk, and my right hand sideways, and somewhat nervously extended with the copy, so that, immediately upon emerging from his retreat, Bartleby might snatch it and proceed to business without the least delay.

In this very attitude did I sit when I called to him, rapidly stating what it was I wanted him to do — namely, to examine a small paper with me. Imagine my surprise, nay, my consternation, when, without moving from his privacy, Bartleby, in a singularly mild, firm voice, replied, "I would prefer not to."

I sat awhile in perfect silence, rallying my stunned faculties. Immediately it occurred to me that my ears had deceived me, or Bartleby had entirely misunderstood my meaning. I repeated my request in the clearest tone I could assume; but in quite as clear a one came the previous reply, "I would prefer not to."

"Prefer not to," echoed I, rising in high excitement, and crossing the room 25 with a stride. "What do you mean? Are you moonstruck? I want you to help me compare this sheet here — take it," and I thrust it towards him.

"I would prefer not to," said he.

I looked at him steadfastly. His face was leanly composed; his gray eye dimly calm. Not a wrinkle of agitation rippled him. Had there been the least uneasiness, anger, impatience, or impertinence in his manner; in other words, had there been anything ordinarily human about him, doubtless I should have violently dismissed him from the premises. But as it was, I should have as soon thought of turning my pale plaster-of-paris bust of Cicero out of doors. I stood gazing at him awhile, as he went on with his own writing, and then reseated myself at my desk. This is very strange, thought I. What had one best do? But my business hurried me. I concluded to forget the matter for the present, reserving it for my future leisure. So, calling Nippers from the other room, the paper was speedily examined.

A few days after this, Bartleby concluded four lengthy documents, being quadruplicates of a week's testimony taken before me in my High Court of Chancery. It became necessary to examine them. It was an important suit, and great accuracy was imperative. Having all things arranged, I called Turkey, Nippers, and Ginger Nut, from the next room, meaning to place the four copies in the hands of my four clerks, while I should read from the original. Accordingly, Turkey, Nippers, and Ginger Nut had taken their seats in a row, each with his document in his hand, when I called to Bartleby to join this interesting group.

"Bartleby! quick, I am waiting."

I heard a slow scrape of his chair legs on the uncarpeted floor, and soon he 30
appeared standing at the entrance of his hermitage.

"What is wanted?" said he, mildly.

"The copies, the copies," said I, hurriedly. "We are going to examine them. There"—and I held towards him the fourth quadruplicate.

"I would prefer not to," he said, and gently disappeared behind the screen.

For a few moments I was turned into a pillar of salt, standing at the head of my seated column of clerks. Recovering myself, I advanced towards the screen, and demanded the reason for such extraordinary conduct.

"*Why* do you refuse?" 35

"I would prefer not to."

With any other man I should have flown outright into a dreadful passion, scorned all further words, and thrust him ignominiously from my presence. But there was something about Bartleby that not only strangely disarmed me, but, in a wonderful manner, touched and disconcerted me. I began to reason with him.

"These are your own copies we are about to examine. It is labor saving to you, because one examination will answer for your four papers. It is common usage. Every copyist is bound to help examine his copy. Is it not so? Will you not speak? Answer!"

"I prefer not to," he replied in a flute-like tone. It seemed to me that, while I had been addressing him, he carefully revolved every statement that I made; fully comprehended the meaning; could not gainsay the irresistible conclusion; but, at the same time, some paramount consideration prevailed with him to reply as he did.

"You are decided, then, not to comply with my request—a request made   40
according to common usage and common sense?"

He briefly gave me to understand, that on that point my judgment was
sound. Yes: his decision was irreversible.

It is not seldom the case that, when a man is browbeaten in some unprecedented and violently unreasonable way, he begins to stagger in his own plainest
faith. He begins, as it were, vaguely to surmise that, wonderful as it may be, all the
justice and all the reason is on the other side. Accordingly, if any disinterested
persons are present, he turns to them for some reinforcement for his own falter-
ing mind.

"Turkey," said I, "what do you think of this? Am I not right?"

"With submission, sir," said Turkey, in his blandest tone, "I think that you
are."

"Nippers," said I, "what do *you* think of it?"   45

"I think I should kick him out of the office."

(The reader of nice perceptions will have perceived that, it being morning,
Turkey's answer is couched in polite and tranquil terms, but Nippers replies in
ill-tempered ones. Or, to repeat a previous sentence, Nippers' ugly mood was on
duty, and Turkey's off.)

"Ginger Nut," said I, willing to enlist the smallest suffrage in my behalf,
"what do *you* think of it?"

"I think, sir, he's a little *luny*," replied Ginger Nut, with a grin.

"You hear what they say," said I, turning towards the screen, "come forth and   50
do your duty."

But he vouchsafed no reply. I pondered a moment in sore perplexity. But
once more business hurried me. I determined again to postpone the consideration of this dilemma to my future leisure. With a little trouble we made out to
examine the papers without Bartleby, though at every page or two Turkey deferentially dropped his opinion, that this proceeding was quite out of the common;
while Nippers, twitching in his chair with a dyspeptic nervousness, ground out,
between his set teeth, occasional hissing maledictions against the stubborn oaf
behind the screen. And for his (Nippers') part, this was the first and the last time
he would do another man's business without pay.

Meanwhile Bartleby sat in his hermitage, oblivious to everything but his own
peculiar business there.

Some days passed, the scrivener being employed upon another lengthy
work. His late remarkable conduct led me to regard his ways narrowly. I observed
that he never went to dinner; indeed, that he never went anywhere. As yet I had
never, of my personal knowledge, known him to be outside of my office. He was a
perpetual sentry in the corner. At about eleven o'clock though, in the morning, I
noticed that Ginger Nut would advance towards the opening in Bartleby's screen,
as if silently beckoned thither by a gesture invisible to me where I sat. The boy
would then leave the office, jingling a few pence, and reappear with a handful of
ginger-nuts, which he delivered in the hermitage, receiving two of the cakes for
his trouble.

He lives, then, on ginger-nuts, thought I; never eats a dinner, properly speaking; he must be a vegetarian, then, but no; he never eats even vegetables, he eats nothing but ginger-nuts. My mind then ran on in reveries concerning the probable effects upon the human constitution of living entirely on ginger-nuts. Ginger-nuts are so called, because they contain ginger as one of their peculiar constituents, and the final flavoring one. Now, what was ginger? A hot, spicy thing. Was Bartleby hot and spicy? Not at all. Ginger, then, had no effect upon Bartleby. Probably he preferred it should have none.

Nothing so aggravates an earnest person as a passive resistance. If the individual so resisted be of a not inhumane temper, and the resisting one perfectly harmless in his passivity, then, in the better moods of the former, he will endeavor charitably to construe to his imagination what proves impossible to be solved by his judgment. Even so, for the most part, I regarded Bartleby and his ways. Poor fellow! thought I, he means no mischief; it is plain he intends no insolence; his aspect sufficiently evinces that his eccentricities are involuntary. He is useful to me. I can get along with him. If I turn him away, the chances are he will fall in with some less indulgent employer, and then he will be rudely treated, and perhaps driven forth miserably to starve. Yes. Here I can cheaply purchase a delicious self-approval. To befriend Bartleby; to humor him in his strange wilfulness, will cost me little or nothing, while I lay up in my soul what will eventually prove a sweet morsel for my conscience. But this mood was not invariable with me. The passiveness of Bartleby sometimes irritated me. I felt strangely goaded on to encounter him in new opposition—to elicit some angry spark from him answerable to my own. But, indeed, I might as well have essayed to strike fire with my knuckles against a bit of Windsor soap. But one afternoon the evil impulse in me mastered me, and the following little scene ensued: 55

"Bartleby," said I, "when those papers are all copied, I will compare them with you."

"I would prefer not to."

"How? Surely you do not mean to persist in that mulish vagary?"

No answer.

I threw open the folding-doors nearby, and turning upon Turkey and Nippers, exclaimed: 60

"Bartleby a second time says, he won't examine his papers. What do you think of it, Turkey?"

It was afternoon, be it remembered. Turkey sat glowing like a brass boiler; his bald head steaming; his hands reeling among his blotted papers.

"Think of it?" roared Turkey. "I think I'll just step behind his screen, and black his eyes for him!"

So saying, Turkey rose to his feet and threw his arms into a pugilistic position. He was hurrying away to make good his promise, when I detained him, alarmed at the effect of incautiously rousing Turkey's combativeness after dinner.

"Sit down, Turkey," said I, "and hear what Nippers has to say. What do you think of it, Nippers? Would I not be justified in immediately dismissing Bartleby?" 65

"Excuse me, that is for you to decide, sir. I think his conduct quite unusual, and, indeed, unjust, as regards Turkey and myself. But it may only be a passing whim."

"Ah," exclaimed I, "you have strangely changed your mind, then—you speak very gently of him now."

"All beer," cried Turkey; "gentleness is effects of beer—Nippers and I dined together to-day. You see how gentle *I* am, sir. Shall I go and black his eyes?"

"You refer to Bartleby, I suppose. No, not to-day, Turkey," I replied; "pray, put up your fists."

I closed the doors, and again advanced towards Bartleby. I felt additional   70
incentives tempting me to my fate. I burned to be rebelled against again. I
remembered that Bartleby never left the office.

"Bartleby," said I, "Ginger Nut is away; just step around to the Post Office,
won't you?" (it was but a three minutes' walk) "and see if there is anything
for me."

"I would prefer not to."

"You *will* not?"

"I *prefer* not."

I staggered to my desk, and sat there in a deep study. My blind inveteracy   75
returned. Was there any other thing in which I could procure myself to be ignominiously repulsed by this lean, penniless wight? my hired clerk? What added
thing is there, perfectly reasonable, that he will be sure to refuse to do?

"Bartleby!"

No answer.

"Bartleby," in a louder tone.

No answer.

"Bartleby," I roared.   80

Like a very ghost, agreeably to the laws of magical invocation, at the third
summons, he appeared at the entrance of his hermitage.

"Go to the next room, and tell Nippers to come to me."

"I would prefer not to," he respectfully and slowly said, and mildly disappeared.

"Very good, Bartleby," said I, in a quiet sort of serenely-severe self-possessed
tone, intimating the unalterable purpose of some terrible retribution very close at
hand. At the moment I half intended something of the kind. But upon the whole,
as it was drawing towards my dinner-hour, I thought it best to put on my hat and
walk home for the day, suffering much from perplexity and distress of mind.

Shall I acknowledge it? The conclusion of this whole business was, that it   85
soon became a fixed fact of my chambers, that a pale young scrivener, by the
name of Bartleby, had a desk there; that he copied for me at the usual rate of four
cents a folio (one hundred words); but he was permanently exempt from examining the work done by him, that duty being transferred to Turkey and Nippers, out
of compliment, doubtless, to their superior acuteness; moreover, said Bartleby was
never, on any account, to be dispatched on the most trivial errand of any sort; and
that even if entreated to take upon him such a matter, it was generally understood
that he would "prefer not to"—in other words, that he would refuse point blank.

As days passed on, I became considerably reconciled to Bartleby. His steadiness, his freedom from all dissipation, his incessant industry (except when he chose to throw himself into a standing revery behind his screen), his great stillness, his unalterableness of demeanor under all circumstances, made him a valuable acquisition. One prime thing was this — *he was always there* — first in the morning, continually through the day, and the last at night. I had a singular confidence in his honesty. I felt my most precious papers perfectly safe in his hands. Sometimes, to be sure, I could not, for the very soul of me, avoid falling into sudden spasmodic passions with him. For it was exceeding difficult to bear in mind all the time those strange peculiarities, privileges, and unheard-of exemptions, forming the tacit stipulations on Bartleby's part under which he remained in my office. Now and then, in the eagerness of dispatching pressing business, I would inadvertently summon Bartleby, in a short, rapid tone, to put his finger, say, on the incipient tie of a bit of red tape with which I was about compressing some papers. Of course, from behind the screen the usual answer, "I prefer not to," was sure to come; and then, how could a human creature, with the common infirmities of our nature, refrain from bitterly exclaiming upon such perverseness — such unreasonableness? However, every added repulse of this sort which I received only tended to lessen the probability of my repeating the inadvertence.

Here it must be said, that, according to the custom of most legal gentlemen occupying chambers in densely populated law buildings, there were several keys to my door. One was kept by a woman residing in the attic, which person weekly scrubbed and daily swept and dusted my apartments. Another was kept by Turkey for convenience sake. The third I sometimes carried in my own pocket. The fourth I knew not who had.

Now, one Sunday morning I happened to go to Trinity Church, to hear a celebrated preacher, and finding myself rather early on the ground I thought I would walk round to my chambers for a while. Luckily I had my key with me; but upon applying it to the lock, I found it resisted by something inserted from the inside. Quite surprised, I called out; when to my consternation a key was turned from within; and thrusting his lean visage at me, and holding the door ajar, the apparition of Bartleby appeared, in his shirt-sleeves, and otherwise in a strangely tattered *deshabille*, saying quietly that he was sorry, but he was deeply engaged just then, and preferred not admitting me at present. In a brief word or two, he moreover added, that perhaps I had better walk round the block two or three times, and by that time he would probably have concluded his affairs.

Now, the utterly unsurmised appearance of Bartleby, tenanting my law-chambers of a Sunday morning, with his cadaverously gentlemanly *nonchalance*, yet withal firm and self-possessed, had such a strange effect upon me, that incontinently I slunk away from my own door, and did as desired. But not without sundry twinges of impotent rebellion against the mild effrontery of this unaccountable scrivener. Indeed, it was his wonderful mildness chiefly, which not only disarmed me, but unmanned me, as it were. For I consider that one, for the time, is sort of unmanned when he tranquilly permits his hired clerk to dictate to him, and order him away from his own premises. Furthermore, I was full of uneasiness as to what Bartleby could possibly be doing in my office in his shirt-sleeves, and in an otherwise dismantled condition on a Sunday morning. Was anything amiss going on? Nay, that was out of the question. It was not to be thought of for a moment that Bartleby was an immoral person. But what could he be doing there?—copying? Nay again, whatever might be his eccentricities, Bartleby was an eminently decorous person. He would be the last man to sit down to his desk in any state approaching to nudity. Besides, it was Sunday; and there was something about Bartleby that forbade the supposition that he would by any secular occupation violate the proprieties of the day.

Nevertheless, my mind was not pacified; and full of a restless curiosity, at last I returned to the door. Without hindrance I inserted my key, opened it, and entered. Bartleby was not to be seen. I looked round anxiously, peeped behind his screen; but it was very plain that he was gone. Upon more closely examining the place, I surmised that for an indefinite period Bartleby must have ate, dressed, and slept in my office, and that too without plate, mirror, or bed. The cushioned seat of a rickety old sofa in one corner bore the faint impress of a lean, reclining form. Rolled away under his desk, I found a blanket; under the empty grate, a blacking box and brush; on a chair, a tin basin, with soap and a ragged towel; in a newspaper a few crumbs of ginger-nuts and a morsel of cheese. Yes, thought I, it is evident enough that Bartleby has been making his home here, keeping bachelor's hall all by himself. Immediately then the thought came sweeping across me, what miserable friendlessness and loneliness are here revealed! His poverty is great; but his solitude, how horrible! Think of it. Of a Sunday, Wall Street is deserted as Petra;° and every night of every day it is an emptiness. This building, too, which of week-days hums with industry and life, at nightfall echoes with sheer vacancy, and all through Sunday is forlorn. And here Bartleby makes his home; sole spectator of a solitude which he has seen all populous—a sort of innocent and transformed Marius° brooding among the ruins of Carthage!

For the first time in my life a feeling of overpowering stinging melancholy seized me. Before, I had never experienced aught but a not unpleasing sadness. The bond of a common humanity now drew me irresistibly to gloom. A fraternal melancholy! For both I and Bartleby were sons of Adam. I remembered the bright silks and sparkling faces I had seen that day, in gala trim, swan-like sailing down the Mississippi of Broadway; and I contrasted them with the pallid copyist, and thought to myself, Ah, happiness courts the light, so we deem the world is gay; but misery hides aloof, so we deem that misery there is none. These sad fancyings—chimeras, doubtless, of a sick and silly brain—led on to other and more special thoughts, concerning the eccentricities of Bartleby. Presentiments of

90

Petra: Once the center of an ancient Arab kingdom, the city of Petra lay deserted for more than ten centuries, until its rediscovery by explorers in 1812.
Marius: Gaius Marius (157?–86 B.C.E.), a Roman General and elected consul. Marius achieved great military successes in the Jugurthine War, in Africa. Later, when his opponents gained power and he was banished, he fled to Africa. Carthage was a city in North Africa.

strange discoveries hovered round me. The scrivener's pale form appeared to me laid out, among uncaring strangers, in its shivering winding-sheet.

Suddenly I was attracted by Bartleby's closed desk, the key in open sight left in the lock.

I mean no mischief, seek the gratification of no heartless curiosity, thought I; besides, the desk is mine, and its contents, too, so I will make bold to look within. Everything was methodically arranged, the papers smoothly placed. The pigeon-holes were deep, and removing the files of documents, I groped into their recesses. Presently I felt something there, and dragged it out. It was an old bandanna hand-kerchief, heavy and knotted. I opened it, and saw it was a saving's bank.

I now recalled all the quiet mysteries which I had noted in the man. I remembered that he never spoke but to answer; that, though at intervals he had considerable time to himself, yet I had never seen him reading — no, not even a newspaper; that for long periods he would stand looking out, at his pale window behind the screen, upon the dead brick wall; I was quite sure he never visited any refectory or eating-house; while his pale face clearly indicated that he never drank beer like Turkey; or tea and coffee even, like other men; that he never went anywhere in particular that I could learn; never went out for a walk, unless, indeed, that was the case at present; that he had declined telling who he was, or whence he came, or whether he had any relatives in the world; that though so thin and pale, he never complained of ill-health. And more than all, I remembered a certain unconscious air of pallid — how shall I call it? — of pallid haughtiness, say, or rather an austere reserve about him, which has positively awed me into my tame compliance with his eccentricities, when I had feared to ask him to do the slightest incidental thing for me, even though I might know, from his long-continued motionlessness, that behind his screen he must be standing in one of those dead-wall reveries of his.

Revolving all these things, and coupling them with the recently discovered fact, that he made my office his constant abiding place and home, and not forget-ful of his morbid moodiness; revolving all these things, a prudential feeling began to steal over me. My first emotions had been those of pure melancholy and sin-cerest pity; but just in proportion as the forlornness of Bartleby grew and grew to my imagination, did that same melancholy merge into fear, that pity into repul-sion. So true it is, and so terrible, too, that up to a certain point the thought or sight of misery enlists our best affections; but, in certain special cases, beyond that point it does not. They err who would assert that invariably this is owing to the inherent selfishness of the human heart. It rather proceeds from a certain hopelessness of remedying excessive and organic ill. To a sensitive being, pity is not seldom pain. And when at last it is perceived that such pity cannot lead to effectual succor, common sense bids the soul be rid of it. What I saw that morn-ing persuaded me that the scrivener was the victim of innate and incurable disor-der. I might give alms to his body; but his body did not pain him; it was his soul that suffered, and his soul I could not reach.

I did not accomplish the purpose of going to Trinity Church that morning. Somehow, the things I had seen disqualified me for the time from church-going. I

95

walked homeward, thinking what I would do with Bartleby. Finally, I resolved upon this — I would put certain calm questions to him the next morning, touching his history, etc., and if he declined to answer them openly and unreservedly (and I supposed he would prefer not), then to give him a twenty dollar bill over and above whatever I might owe him, and tell him his services were no longer required; but that if in any other way I could assist him, I would be happy to do so, especially if he desired to return to his native place, wherever that might be, I would willingly help to defray the expenses. Moreover, if, after reaching home, he found himself at any time in want of aid, a letter from him would be sure of a reply.

The next morning came.

"Bartleby," said I, gently calling to him behind his screen.

No reply.

"Bartleby," said I, in a still gentler tone, "come here; I am not going to ask you to do anything you would prefer not to do — I simply wish to speak to you."

Upon this he noiselessly slid into view.

"Will you tell me, Bartleby, where you were born?"

"I would prefer not to."

"Will you tell me *anything* about yourself?"

"I would prefer not to."

"But what reasonable objection can you have to speak to me? I feel friendly towards you."

He did not look at me while I spoke, but kept his glance fixed upon my bust of Cicero, which, as I then sat, was directly behind me, some six inches above my head.

"What is your answer, Bartleby?" said I, after waiting a considerable time for a reply, during which his countenance remained immovable, only there was the faintest conceivable tremor of the white attenuated mouth.

"At present I prefer to give no answer," he said, and retired into his hermitage.

It was rather weak in me I confess, but his manner, on this occasion, nettled me. Not only did there seem to lurk in it a certain calm disdain, but his perverseness seemed ungrateful, considering the undeniable good usage and indulgence he had received from me.

Again I sat ruminating what I should do. Mortified as I was at his behavior, and resolved as I had been to dismiss him when I entered my office, nevertheless I strangely felt something superstitious knocking at my heart, and forbidding me to carry out my purpose, and denouncing me for a villain if I dared to breathe one bitter word against this forlornest of mankind. At last, familiarly drawing my chair behind his screen, I sat down and said: "Bartleby, never mind, then, about revealing your history; but let me entreat you, as a friend, to comply as far as may be with the usages of this office. Say now, you will help to examine papers tomorrow or next day: in short, say now, that in a day or two you will begin to be a little reasonable: — say so, Bartleby."

"At present I would prefer not to be a little reasonable," was his mildly cadaverous reply.

Just then the folding-doors opened, and Nippers approached. He seemed suffering from an unusually bad night's rest, induced by severer indigestion than common. He overheard those final words of Bartleby.

"*Prefer not*, eh?" gritted Nippers — "I'd *prefer* him, if I were you, sir," addressing me — "I'd *prefer* him; I'd give him preferences, the stubborn mule! What is it, sir, pray, that he *prefers* not to do now?"

Bartleby moved not a limb.   115

"Mr. Nippers," said I, "I'd prefer that you would withdraw for the present."

Somehow, of late, I had got into the way of involuntarily using this word "prefer" upon all sorts of not exactly suitable occasions. And I trembled to think that my contact with the scrivener had already and seriously affected me in a mental way. And what further and deeper aberration might it not yet produce? This apprehension had not been without efficacy in determining me to summary measures.

As Nippers, looking very sour and sulky, was departing, Turkey blandly and deferentially approached.

"With submission, sir," said he, "yesterday I was thinking about Bartleby here, and I think that if he would but prefer to take a quart of good ale every day, it would do much towards mending him, and enabling him to assist in examining his papers."

"So you have got the word, too," said I, slightly excited.   120

"With submission, what word, sir?" asked Turkey, respectfully crowding himself into the contracted space behind the screen, and by so doing, making me jostle the scrivener. "What word, sir?"

"I would prefer to be left alone here," said Bartleby, as if offended at being mobbed in his privacy.

"*That's* the word, Turkey," said I — "*that's* it."

"Oh, *prefer*? oh yes — queer word. I never use it myself. But, sir, as I was saying, if he would but prefer — "

"Turkey," interrupted I, "you will please withdraw."   125

"Oh certainly, sir, if you prefer that I should."

As he opened the folding-door to retire, Nippers at his desk caught a glimpse of me, and asked whether I would prefer to have a certain paper copied on blue paper or white. He did not in the least roguishly accent the word "prefer." It was plain that it involuntarily rolled from his tongue. I thought to myself, surely I must get rid of a demented man, who already has in some degree turned the tongues, if not the heads of myself and clerks. But I thought it prudent not to break the dismission at once.

The next day I noticed that Bartleby did nothing but stand at his window in his dead-wall revery. Upon asking him why he did not write, he said that he had decided upon doing no more writing.

"Why, how now? what next?" exclaimed I, "do no more writing?"

"No more."   130

"And what is the reason?"

"Do you not see the reason for yourself?" he indifferently replied.

I looked steadfastly at him, and perceived that his eyes looked dull and glazed. Instantly it occurred to me, that his unexampled diligence in copying by his dim window for the first few weeks of his stay with me might have temporarily impaired his vision.

I was touched. I said something in condolence with him. I hinted that of course he did wisely in abstaining from writing for a while; and urged him to embrace that opportunity of taking wholesome exercise in the open air. This, however, he did not do. A few days after this, my other clerks being absent, and being in a great hurry to dispatch certain letters by the mail, I thought that, having nothing else earthly to do, Bartleby would surely be less inflexible than usual, and carry these letters to the Post Office. But he blankly declined. So, much to my inconvenience, I went myself.

Still added days went by. Whether Bartleby's eyes improved or not, I could   135
not say. To all appearance, I thought they did. But when I asked him if they did he vouchsafed no answer. At all events, he would do no copying. At last, in replying to my urgings, he informed me that he had permanently given up copying.

"What!" exclaimed I; "suppose your eyes should get entirely well—better than ever before—would you not copy then?"

"I have given up copying," he answered, and slid aside.

He remained as ever, a fixture in my chamber. Nay—if that were possible—he became still more of a fixture than before. What was to be done? He would do nothing in the office; why should he stay there? In plain fact, he had now become a millstone to me, not only useless as a necklace, but afflictive to bear. Yet I was sorry for him. I speak less than truth when I say that, on his own account, he occasioned me uneasiness. If he would but have named a single relative or friend, I would instantly have written, and urged their taking the poor fellow away to some convenient retreat. But he seemed alone, absolutely alone in the universe. A bit of wreck in the mid-Atlantic. At length, necessities connected with my business tyrannized over all other considerations. Decently as I could, I told Bartleby that in six days' time he must unconditionally leave the office. I warned him to take measures, in the interval, for procuring some other abode. I offered to assist him in this endeavor, if he himself would but take the first step towards a removal. "And when you finally quit me, Bartleby," added I, "I shall see that you go not away entirely unprovided. Six days from this hour, remember."

At the expiration of that period, I peeped behind the screen, and lo! Bartleby was there.

I buttoned up my coat, balanced myself; advanced slowly towards him,   140
touched his shoulder, and said, "The time has come; you must quit this place; I am sorry for you; here is money; but you must go."

"I would prefer not," he replied, with his back still towards me.

"You *must*."

He remained silent.

Now I had an unbounded confidence in this man's common honesty. He had frequently restored to me sixpences and shillings carelessly dropped upon the floor, for I am apt to be very reckless in such shirt-button affairs. The proceeding, then, which followed will not be deemed extraordinary.

"Bartleby," said I, "I owe you twelve dollars on account; here are thirty-two; 145 the odd twenty are yours—Will you take it?" and I handed the bills towards him.

But he made no motion.

"I will leave them here, then," putting them under a weight on the table. Then taking my hat and cane and going to the door, I tranquilly turned and added—"After you have removed your things from these offices, Bartleby, you will of course lock the door—since every one is now gone for the day but you—and if you please, slip your key underneath the mat, so that I may have it in the morning. I shall not see you again; so good-bye to you. If, hereafter, in your new place of abode, I can be of any service to you, do not fail to advise me by letter. Good-bye, Bartleby, and fare you well."

But he answered not a word; like the last column of some ruined temple, he remained standing mute and solitary in the middle of the otherwise deserted room.

As I walked home in a pensive mood, my vanity got the better of my pity. I could not but highly plume myself on my masterly management in getting rid of Bartleby. Masterly I call it, and such it must appear to any dispassionate thinker. The beauty of my procedure seemed to consist in its perfect quietness. There was no vulgar bullying, no bravado of any sort, no choleric hectoring, and striding to and fro across the apartment, jerking out vehement commands for Bartleby to bundle himself off with his beggarly traps. Nothing of the kind. Without loudly bidding Bartleby depart—as an inferior genius might have done—I *assumed* the ground that depart he must; and upon that assumption built all I had to say. The more I thought over my procedure, the more I was charmed with it. Nevertheless, next morning, upon awakening, I had my doubts—I had somehow slept off the fumes of vanity. One of the coolest and wisest hours a man has, is just after he awakes in the morning. My procedure seemed as sagacious as ever—but only in theory. How it would prove in practice—there was the rub. It was truly a beautiful thought to have assumed Bartleby's departure; but, after all, that assumption was simply my own, and none of Bartleby's. The great point was, not whether I had assumed that he would quit me, but whether he would prefer to do so. He was more a man of preferences than assumptions.

After breakfast, I walked down town, arguing the probabilities *pro* and *con*. 150 One moment I thought it would prove a miserable failure, and Bartleby would be found all alive at my office as usual; the next moment it seemed certain that I should find his chair empty. And so I kept veering about. At the corner of Broadway and Canal Street, I saw quite an excited group of people standing in earnest conversation.

"I'll take odds he doesn't," said a voice as I passed.

"Doesn't go?—done!" said I, "put up your money."

I was instinctively putting my hand in my pocket to produce my own, when I remembered that this was an election day. The words I had overheard bore no reference to Bartleby, but to the success or non-success of some candidate for the mayoralty. In my intent frame of mind, I had, as it were, imagined that all Broadway shared in my excitement, and were debating the same question with me. I passed on, very thankful that the uproar of the street screened my momentary absent-mindedness.

As I had intended, I was earlier than usual at my office door. I stood listening for a moment. All was still. He must be gone. I tried the knob. The door was locked. Yes, my procedure had worked to a charm; he indeed must be vanished. Yet a certain melancholy mixed with this: I was almost sorry for my brilliant success. I was fumbling under the door mat for the key, which Bartleby was to have left there for me, when accidentally my knee knocked against a panel, producing a summoning sound, and in response a voice came to me from within — "Not yet; I am occupied."

It was Bartleby.

155

I was thunderstruck. For an instant I stood like the man who, pipe in mouth, was killed one cloudless afternoon long ago in Virginia, by summer lightning; at his own warm open window he was killed, and remained leaning out there upon the dreamy afternoon, till someone touched him, when he fell.

"Not gone!" I murmured at last. But again obeying that wondrous ascendancy which the inscrutable scrivener had over me, and from which ascendancy, for all my chafing, I could not completely escape, I slowly went down stairs and out into the street, and while walking round the block, considered what I should next do in this unheard-of perplexity. Turn the man out by an actual thrusting I could not; to drive him away by calling him hard names would not do; calling in the police was an unpleasant idea; and yet, permit him to enjoy his cadaverous triumph over me — this, too, I could not think of. What was to be done? or, if nothing could be done, was there anything further that I could *assume* in the matter? Yes, as before I had prospectively assumed that Bartleby would depart, so now I might retrospectively assume that departed he was. In the legitimate carrying out of this assumption, I might enter my office in a great hurry, and pretending not to see Bartleby at all, walk straight against him as if he were air. Such a proceeding would in a singular degree have the appearance of a home-thrust. It was hardly possible that Bartleby could withstand such an application of the doctrine of assumption. But upon second thoughts the success of the plan seemed rather dubious. I resolved to argue the matter over with him again.

"Bartleby," said I, entering the office, with a quietly severe expression, "I am seriously displeased. I am pained, Bartleby. I had thought better of you. I had imagined you of such a gentlemanly organization, that in any delicate dilemma a slight hint would suffice — in short, an assumption. But it appears I am deceived. Why," I added, unaffectedly starting, "you have not even touched that money yet," pointing to it, just where I had left it the evening previous.

He answered nothing.

"Will you, or will you not, quit me?" I now demanded in a sudden passion, advancing close to him.

160

"I would prefer *not* to quit you," he replied, gently emphasizing the *not*.

"What earthly right have you to stay here? Do you pay any rent? Do you pay my taxes? Or is this property yours?"

He answered nothing.

"Are you ready to go on and write now? Are your eyes recovered? Could you copy a small paper for me this morning? or help examine a few lines? or step round to the Post Office? In a word, will you do anything at all, to give a coloring to your refusal to depart the premises?"

He silently retired into his hermitage.

165

I was now in such a state of nervous resentment that I thought it but prudent to check myself at present from further demonstrations. Bartleby and I were alone. I remembered the tragedy of the unfortunate Adams and the still more unfortunate Colt in the solitary office of the latter; and how poor Colt, being dreadfully incensed by Adams, and imprudently permitting himself to get wildly excited, was at unawares hurried into his fatal act—an act which certainly no man could possibly deplore more than the actor himself.° Often it had occurred to me in my ponderings upon the subject that had that altercation taken place in the public street, or at a private residence, it would not have terminated as it did. It was the circumstance of being alone in a solitary office, up stairs, of a building entirely unhallowed by humanizing domestic associations— an uncarpeted office, doubtless, of a dusty, haggard sort of appearance—this it must have been, which greatly helped to enhance the irritable desperation of the hapless Colt.

But when this old Adam of resentment rose in me and tempted me concerning Bartleby, I grappled him and threw him. How? Why, simply by recalling the divine injunction: "A new commandment give I unto you, that ye love one another." Yes, this it was that saved me. Aside from higher considerations, charity often operates as a vastly wise and prudent principle—a great safeguard to its possessor. Men have committed murder for jealousy's sake, and anger's sake, and hatred's sake, and selfishness' sake, and spiritual pride's sake; but no man, that ever I heard of, ever committed a diabolical murder for sweet charity's sake. Mere self-interest, then, if no better motive can be enlisted, should, especially with high-tempered men, prompt all beings to charity and philanthropy. At any rate, upon the occasion in question, I strove to drown my exasperated feelings towards the scrivener by benevolently construing his conduct. Poor fellow, poor fellow! thought I, he don't mean anything; and besides, he has seen hard times, and ought to be indulged.

I endeavored, also, immediately to occupy myself, and at the same time to comfort my despondency. I tried to fancy, that in the course of the morning, at such time as might prove agreeable to him, Bartleby, of his own free accord, would emerge from his hermitage and take up some decided line of march in the direction of the door. But no. Half-past twelve o'clock came; Turkey began to glow in the face, overturn his inkstand, and become generally obstreperous; Nippers abated down into quietude and courtesy; Ginger Nut munched his noon apple; and Bartleby remained standing at his window in one of his profoundest

I remembered . . . actor himself: John C. Colt murdered Samuel Adams in January 1842. Later that year, after his conviction, Colt committed suicide a half-hour before he was to be hanged. The case received wide and sensationalistic press coverage at the time.

dead-wall reveries. Will it be credited? Ought I to acknowledge it? That after-noon I left the office without saying one further word to him.

Some days now passed, during which, at leisure intervals I looked a little into "Edwards° on the Will," and "Priestley° on Necessity." Under the circumstances, those books induced a salutary feeling. Gradually I slid into the persuasion that these troubles of mine, touching the scrivener, had been all predestined from eternity, and Bartleby was billeted upon me for some mysterious purpose of an all-wise Providence, which it was not for a mere mortal like me to fathom. Yes, Bartleby, stay there behind your screen, thought I; I shall persecute you no more; you are harmless and noiseless as any of these old chairs; in short, I never feel so private as when I know you are here. At last I see it, I feel it; I penetrate to the pre-destined purpose of my life. I am content. Others may have loftier parts to enact; but my mission in this world, Bartleby, is to furnish you with office-room for such period as you may see fit to remain.

I believe that this wise and blessed frame of mind would have continued with   170
me, had it not been for the unsolicited and uncharitable remarks obtruded upon me by my professional friends who visited the rooms. But thus it often is, that the constant friction of illiberal minds wears out at last the best resolves of the more generous. Though to be sure, when I reflected upon it, it was not strange that people entering my office should be struck by the peculiar aspect of the unac-countable Bartleby, and so be tempted to throw out some sinister observations concerning him. Sometimes an attorney, having business with me, and calling at my office, and finding no one but the scrivener there, would undertake to ob-tain some sort of precise information from him touching my whereabouts; but without heeding his idle talk, Bartleby would remain standing immovable in the middle of the room. So after contemplating him in that position for a time, the attorney would depart, no wiser than he came.

Also, when a reference was going on, and the room full of lawyers and wit-nesses, and business driving fast, some deeply-occupied legal gentleman present, seeing Bartleby wholly unemployed, would request him to run round to his (the legal gentleman's) office and fetch some papers for him. Thereupon, Bartleby would tranquilly decline, and yet remain idle as before. Then the lawyer would give a great stare, and turn to me. And what could I say? At last I was made aware that all through the circle of my professional acquaintance, a whisper of wonder was running round, having reference to the strange creature I kept at my office. This worried me very much. And as the idea came upon me of his possibly turn-ing out a long-lived man, and keeping occupying my chambers, and denying my

---

Edwards: Jonathan Edwards, *Freedom of the Will* (1754). Edwards was an important American theologian, a rigidly orthodox Calvinist who believed in the doctrine of predestination and a leader of the Great Awakening, the religious revival that swept the North American colonies in the 1740s.
Priestley: Joseph Priestley (1733–1803), English scientist and clergyman. Priestley began as a Unitarian but developed his own radical ideas on "natural determinism." As a scientist, he did early experiments with electricity and was one of the first to discover the existence of oxygen. As a political philosopher, he championed the French Revolution — a cause so unpopular in En-gland that he had to flee that country and spend the last decade of his life in the United States.

authority; and perplexing my visitors; and scandalizing my professional reputation; and casting a general gloom over the premises; keeping soul and body together to the last upon his savings (for doubtless he spent but half a dime a day), and in the end perhaps outlive me, and claim possession of my office by right of his perpetual occupancy: as all these dark anticipations crowded upon me more and more, and my friends continually intruded their relentless remarks upon the apparition in my room; a great change was wrought in me. I resolved to gather all my faculties together, and forever rid me of this intolerable incubus.

Ere revolving any complicated project, however, adapted to this end, I first simply suggested to Bartleby the propriety of his permanent departure. In a calm and serious tone, I commended the idea to his careful and mature consideration. But, having taken three days to meditate upon it, he apprised me, that his original determination remained the same; in short, that he still preferred to abide with me.

What shall I do? I now said to myself, buttoning up my coat to the last button. What shall I do? what ought I to do? what does conscience say I *should* do with this man, or, rather, ghost. Rid myself of him, I must; go, he shall. But how? You will not thrust him, the poor, pale, passive mortal you will not thrust such a helpless creature out of your door? you will not dishonor yourself by such cruelty? No, I will not, I cannot do that. Rather would I let him live and die here, and then mason up his remains in the wall. What, then, will you do? For all your coaxing, he will not budge. Bribes he leaves under your own paper-weight on your table; in short, it is quite plain that he prefers to cling to you.

Then something severe, something unusual must be done. What! surely you will not have him collared by a constable, and commit his innocent pallor to the common jail? And upon what ground could you procure such a thing to be done? — a vagrant, is he? What! he a vagrant, a wanderer, who refuses to budge? It is because he will not be a vagrant, then, that you seek to count him *as* a vagrant. That is too absurd. No visible means of support: there I have him. Wrong again: for indubitably he *does* support himself, and that is the only unanswerable proof that any man can show of his possessing the means so to do. No more, then. Since he will not quit me, I must quit him. I will change my offices; I will move elsewhere, and give him fair notice, that if I find him on my new premises I will then proceed against him as a common trespasser.

Acting accordingly, next day I thus addressed him: "I find these chambers   175 too far from the City Hall; the air is unwholesome. In a word, I propose to remove my offices next week, and shall no longer require your services. I tell you this now, in order that you may seek another place."

He made no reply, and nothing more was said.

On the appointed day I engaged carts and men, proceeded to my chambers, and, having but little furniture, everything was removed in a few hours. Throughout, the scrivener remained standing behind the screen, which I directed to be removed the last thing. It was withdrawn; and, being folded up like a huge folio, left him the motionless occupant of a naked room. I stood in the entry watching him a moment, while something from within me upbraided me.

I re-entered, with my hand in my pocket — and — and my heart in my mouth.

"Good-bye, Bartleby; I am going — good-bye, and God some way bless you; and take that," slipping something in his hand. But it dropped upon the floor, and then — strange to say — I tore myself from him whom I had so longed to be rid of.

Established in my new quarters, for a day or two I kept the door locked, started at every footfall in the passages. When I returned to my rooms, after any little absence, I would pause at the threshold for an instant, and attentively listen, ere applying my key. But these fears were needless. Bartleby never came nigh me.   180

I thought all was going well, when a perturbed-looking stranger visited me, inquiring whether I was the person who had recently occupied rooms at No. — Wall Street.

Full of forebodings, I replied that I was.

"Then, sir," said the stranger, who proved a lawyer, "you are responsible for the man you left there. He refuses to do any copying; he refuses to do anything; he says he prefers not to; and he refuses to quit the premises."

"I am very sorry, sir," said I, with assumed tranquillity, but an inward tremor, "but, really, the man you allude to is nothing to me — he is no relation or apprentice of mine, that you should hold me responsible for him."

"In mercy's name, who is he?"   185

"I certainly cannot inform you. I know nothing about him. Formerly I employed him as a copyist; but he has done nothing for me now for some time past."

"I shall settle him, then — good morning, sir."

Several days passed, and I heard nothing more; and, though I often felt a charitable prompting to call at the place and see poor Bartleby, yet a certain squeamishness, of I know not what, withheld me.

All is over with him, by this time, thought I, at last, when, through another week, no further intelligence reached me. But, coming to my room the day after, I found several persons waiting at my door in a high state of nervous excitement.

"That's the man here — he comes," cried the foremost one, whom I recognized as the lawyer who had previously called upon me alone.   190

"You must take him away, sir, at once," cried a portly person among them, advancing upon me, and whom I knew to be the landlord of No. — Wall Street. "These gentlemen, my tenants, cannot stand it any longer; Mr. B——" pointing to the lawyer, "has turned him out of his room, and he now persists in haunting the building generally, sitting upon the banisters of the stairs by day, and sleeping in the entry by night. Everybody is concerned; clients are leaving the offices; some fears are entertained of a mob; something you must do, and that without delay."

Aghast at this torrent, I fell back before it, and would fain have locked myself in my new quarters. In vain I persisted that Bartleby was nothing to me — no more than to any one else. In vain — I was the last person known to have anything to do with him, and they held me to the terrible account. Fearful, then, of being exposed in the papers (as one person present obscurely threatened), I considered the matter, and, at length, said, that if the lawyer would give me a confidential interview with the scrivener, in his (the lawyer's) own room, I would, that afternoon, strive my best to rid them of the nuisance they complained of.

Going up stairs to my old haunt, there was Bartleby silently sitting upon the banister at the landing.

"What are you doing here, Bartleby?" said I.

"Sitting upon the banister," he mildly replied.   195

I motioned him into the lawyer's room, who then left us.

"Bartleby," said I, "are you aware that you are the cause of great tribulation to me, by persisting in occupying the entry after being dismissed from the office?" No answer.

"Now one of two things must take place. Either you must do something, or something must be done to you. Now what sort of business would you like to engage in? Would you like to re-engage in copying for some one?"

"No; I would prefer not to make any change."   200

"Would you like a clerkship in a dry-goods store?"

"There is too much confinement about that. No, I would not like a clerkship; but I am not particular."

"Too much confinement," I cried, "why, you keep yourself confined all the time!"

"I would prefer not to take a clerkship," he rejoined, as if to settle that little item at once.

"How would a bar-tender's business suit you? There is no trying of the eye-   205
sight in that."

"I would not like it at all; though, as I said before, I am not particular."

His unwonted wordiness inspirited me. I returned to the charge.

"Well, then, would you like to travel through the country collecting bills for the merchants? That would improve your health."

"No, I would prefer to be doing something else."

"How, then, would going as a companion to Europe, to entertain some   210
young gentleman with your conversation — how would that suit you?"

"Not at all. It does not strike me that there is anything definite about that. I like to be stationary. But I am not particular."

"Stationary you shall be, then," I cried, now losing all patience, and, for the first time in all my exasperating connections with him, fairly flying into a passion. "If you do not go away from these premises before night, I shall feel bound — indeed, I *am* bound — to — to — to quit the premises myself!" I rather absurdly concluded, knowing not with what possible threat to try to frighten his immobility into compliance. Despairing of all further efforts, I was precipitately leaving him, when a final thought occurred to me — one which had not been wholly unindulged before.

"Bartleby," said I, in the kindest tone I could assume under such exciting circumstances, "will you go home with me now not to my office, but my dwelling — and remain there till we can conclude upon some convenient arrangement for you at our leisure? Come, let us start now, right away."

"No: at present I would prefer not to make any change at all."

I answered nothing; but, effectually dodging every one by the suddenness   215
and rapidity of my flight, rushed from the building, ran up Wall Street towards
Broadway, and, jumping into the first omnibus, was soon removed from pursuit.
As soon as tranquillity returned, I distinctly perceived that I had now done all that
I possibly could, both in respect to the demands of the landlord and his tenants,
and with regard to my own desire and sense of duty, to benefit Bartleby, and
shield him from rude persecution. I now strove to be entirely care-free and quies-
cent; and my conscience justified me in the attempt; though, indeed, it was not
so successful as I could have wished. So fearful was I of being again hunted out by
the incensed landlord and his exasperated tenants, that, surrendering my business to Nippers, for a few days, I drove about the upper part of the town and
through the suburbs, in my rockaway; crossed over to Jersey City and Hoboken,
and paid fugitive visits to Manhattanville and Astoria. In fact, I almost lived in my
rockaway for the time.

When again I entered my office, lo, a note from the landlord lay upon the
desk. I opened it with trembling hands. It informed me that the writer had sent to
the police, and had Bartleby removed to the Tombs as a vagrant. Moreover, since
I knew more about him than any one else, he wished me to appear at that place,
and make a suitable statement of the facts. These tidings had a conflicting effect
upon me. At first I was indignant; but, at last, almost approved. The landlord's
energetic, summary disposition, had led him to adopt a procedure which I do not
think I would have decided upon myself; and yet, as a last resort, under such
peculiar circumstances, it seemed the only plan.

As I afterwards learned, the poor scrivener, when told that he must be conducted to the Tombs, offered not the slightest obstacle, but, in his pale, unmoving way, silently acquiesced.

Some of the compassionate and curious by-standers joined the party; and
headed by one of the constables arm-in-arm with Bartleby, the silent procession
filed its way through all the noise, and heat, and joy of the roaring thoroughfares
at noon.

The same day I received the note, I went to the Tombs, or, to speak more
properly, the Halls of Justice. Seeking the right officer, I stated the purpose of my
call, and was informed that the individual I described was, indeed, within. I then
assured the functionary that Bartleby was a perfectly honest man, and greatly to
be compassionated, however unaccountably eccentric. I narrated all I knew, and
closed by suggesting the idea of letting him remain in as indulgent confinement
as possible, till something less harsh might be done—though, indeed, I hardly
knew what. At all events, if nothing else could be decided upon, the alms-house
must receive him. I then begged to have an interview.

Being under no disgraceful charge, and quite serene and harmless in all his   220
ways, they had permitted him freely to wander about the prison, and, especially,
in the inclosed grass-platted yards thereof. And so I found him there, standing all
alone in the quietest of the yards, his face towards a high wall, while all around,
from the narrow slits of the jail windows, I thought I saw peering out upon him
the eyes of murderers and thieves.

"Bartleby!"

"I know you," he said, without looking round — "and I want nothing to say to you."

"It was not I that brought you here, Bartleby," said I, keenly pained at his implied suspicion. "And to you, this should not be so vile a place. Nothing reproachful attaches to you by being here. And see, it is not so sad a place as one might think. Look, there is the sky, and here is the grass."

"I know where I am," he replied, but would say nothing more, and so I left him.

As I entered the corridor again, a broad meat-like man, in an apron, accosted me, and, jerking his thumb over my shoulder, said "Is that your friend?" 225

"Yes."

"Does he want to starve? If he does, let him live on the prison fare, that's all."

"Who are you?" asked I, not knowing what to make of such an unofficially speaking person in such a place.

"I am the grub-man. Such gentlemen as have friends here, hire me to provide them with something good to eat."

"Is this so?" said I, turning to the turnkey. 230

He said it was.

"Well, then," said I, slipping some silver into the grub-man's hands (for so they called him), "I want you to give particular attention to my friend there; let him have the best dinner you can get. And you must be as polite to him as possible."

"Introduce me, will you?" said the grub-man, looking at me with an expression which seemed to say he was all impatience for an opportunity to give a specimen of his breeding.

Thinking it would prove of benefit to the scrivener, I acquiesced; and, asking the grub-man his name, went up with him to Bartleby.

"Bartleby, this is a friend; you will find him very useful to you." 235

"Your sarvant, sir, your sarvant," said the grub-man, making a low salutation behind his apron. "Hope you find it pleasant here, sir; nice grounds — cool apartments — hope you'll stay with us some time — try to make it agreeable. What will you have for dinner to-day?"

"I prefer not to dine to-day," said Bartleby, turning away. "It would disagree with me; I am unused to dinners." So saying, he slowly moved to the other side of the inclosure, and took up a position fronting the dead-wall.

"How's this?" said the grub-man, addressing me with a stare of astonishment. "He's odd, ain't he?"

"I think he is a little deranged," said I, sadly.

"Deranged? deranged is it? Well, now, upon my word, I thought that friend 240 of yourn was a gentleman forger; they are always pale and genteel-like, them forgers. I can't help pity 'em — can't help it, sir. Did you know Monroe Edwards?" he added, touchingly, and paused. Then, laying his hand piteously on my shoulder, sighed, "he died of consumption at Sing-Sing. So you weren't acquainted with Monroe?"

"No, I was never socially acquainted with any forgers. But I cannot stop longer. Look to my friend yonder. You will not lose by it. I will see you again."

Some few days after this, I again obtained admission to the Tombs, and went through the corridors in quest of Bartleby; but without finding him.

"I saw him coming from his cell not long ago," said a turnkey, "may be he's gone to loiter in the yards."

So I went in that direction.

"Are you looking for the silent man?" said another turnkey, passing me.   245
"Yonder he lies—sleeping in the yard there. 'Tis not twenty minutes since I saw him lie down."

The yard was entirely quiet. It was not accessible to the common prisoners. The surrounding walls, of amazing thickness, kept off all sounds behind them. The Egyptian character of the masonry weighed upon me with its gloom. But a soft imprisoned turf grew under foot. The heart of the eternal pyramids, it seemed, wherein, by some strange magic, through the clefts, grass-seed, dropped by birds, had sprung.

Strangely huddled at the base of the wall, his knees drawn up, and lying on his side, his head touching the cold stones, I saw the wasted Bartleby. But nothing stirred. I paused; then went close up to him; stooped over, and saw that his dim eyes were open; otherwise he seemed profoundly sleeping. Something prompted me to touch him. I felt his hand, when a tingling shiver ran up my arm and down my spine to my feet.

The round face of the grub-man peered upon me now. "His dinner is ready. Won't he dine to-day, either? Or does he live without dining?"

"Lives without dining," said I, and closed the eyes.

"Eh!—He's asleep, ain't he?"   250

"With kings and counselors,"° murmured I.

There would seem little need for proceeding further in this history. Imagination will readily supply the meagre recital of poor Bartleby's interment. But, ere parting with the reader, let me say, that if this little narrative has sufficiently interested him, to awaken curiosity as to who Bartleby was, and what manner of life he led prior to the present narrator's making his acquaintance, I can only reply, that in such curiosity I fully share, but am wholly unable to gratify it. Yet here I hardly know whether I should divulge one little item of rumor, which came to my ear a few months after the scrivener's decease. Upon what basis it rested, I could never ascertain; and hence, how true it is I cannot now tell. But, inasmuch as this vague report has not been without a certain suggestive interest to me, however sad, it may prove the same with some others; and so I will briefly mention it. The report was this: that Bartleby had been a subordinate clerk in the Dead Letter Office at Washington, from which he had been suddenly removed by a change in the administration. When I think over this rumor, hardly can I express the emotions which seize me. Dead letters! does it not sound like dead men? Conceive a man by nature and misfortune prone to a pallid hopelessness, can any business seem

---

"With kings and counselors": A reference to Job 3:14. Job, who has lost his family and all his property and been stricken by a terrible disease, wishes he had never been born: "then had I been at rest with kings and counselors of the earth, which built desolate places for themselves."

more fitted to heighten it than that of continually handling these dead letters, and assorting them for the flames? For by the cart-load they are annually burned. Sometimes from out the folded paper the pale clerk takes a ring the finger it was meant for, perhaps, moulders in the grave; a bank-note sent in swiftest charity he whom it would relieve, nor eats nor hungers any more; pardon for those who died despairing; hope for those who died unhoping; good tidings for those who died stifled by unrelieved calamities. On errands of life, these letters speed to death.

Ah, Bartleby! Ah, humanity!   [1853]

THINKING ABOUT THE TEXT

1. Some readers see this story as an allegory for the plight of serious writers in a commercial world (like the case of Melville and his novel *Moby-Dick*). How might you support this view?

2. Do you think Bartleby is a rebel-hero or a loser? Could "I prefer not to" be a negative or a positive statement? Is there a way both interpretations might be correct? Is the impulse to resist or rebel one you can relate to? What prevents you from following Bartleby's path?

3. Describe the narrator's personality. Be specific about what he does, how he treats his staff, his goals, and so on. How might your view of Bartleby be colored by his perspective? How might the story change if Bartleby himself told the tale? What about the third-person point of view? What if Ginger Nut or Nippers told the tale?

4. Does the ending add to the story, or should Melville have ended with "with kings and counselors"? Do you learn something more about Bartleby? What do you think the penultimate line means?

5. How do you read the last line? Has the narrator learned something about us all? What if Bartleby refused to cooperate in a terrible undertaking, say, the Holocaust—would your view of him change? Is it his act of refusal that defines him or what he rebels against? How do societies prevent serious mass refusals? Should they?

MICHAEL PAUL ROGIN
From "Class Struggles in America"

Educated at Harvard University (B.A., 1958) and the University of Chicago (M.A., 1959; Ph.D., 1962), Michael Paul Rogin (b. 1937) teaches in the Department of Political Science at the University of California at Berkeley. He writes on political and sociological topics for both academic journals and popular magazines, and his books approach literature and history from this perspective. The following excerpt is from Subversive Genealogy: The Politics and Art of Herman Melville *(1983).*

Bartleby seemed a "dependable and willing worker," to recall David Brion Davis's words, in an office bounded by a "white wall" at one end and a "lofty brick wall" at the other. This "pallidly neat, pitiably respectable" young man, working at first with mechanical intensity, is a welcome contrast to the erratic scriveners his employer cannot control. "As if long famishing for something to copy, he seemed to gorge himself on my documents," the lawyer remembers. Deprivation seems to have reformed Bartleby; the documents are his medicated milk. He soon withdraws from legal copying into "dead-wall reveries," however, and his "passive resistance" gives him a mysterious hold on the lawyer. . . .

. . . "Confined within the limits of his own experience," as Georg Lukács says of the modern hero, Bartleby "is without personal history." Like the protagonist of a modernist fiction, he is existentially alone. "Beyond significant human relationship," in Lukács's words, Bartleby is "unable to enter into relationships with other human beings." "He does not develop through contact with the world; he neither forms nor is formed by it." Bartleby inhabits, beneath tangible appearance, "the ghostly aspect of reality." Outside of history, he is given no specific social fate. Bartleby's absence of qualities, however, does place him historically. Bartleby inhabits the mass society that Tocqueville feared would triumph in America if meaningful, free, political action decayed. The power of Melville's short story comes from its abstractness. By resituating *Bartleby* historically, we can see it as comment on the historical triumph of abstraction.

The failure of political reform, alluded to in *Bartleby*, confines the scrivener and his employer in the office they share. Economic relations replace political dreams. Unlike realistic fiction, however, *Bartleby* is not brought to life by a move from the spiritual to the concrete. It neither places egotistic man in the social complexity of rooted relationships, nor does it chart the breakdown of those relationships. It does allude to them, however. The lawyer's title, Master in Chancery, evokes the personal ties of dependence between master and apprentice. It recalls a time when apprentices, slowly learning the skills of their trade, looked forward to becoming masters in turn. Major Melvill, for example, had learned his trade as a merchant's clerk. When Allan Melvill and John Adams praised the passion for emulation as the source of personal achievement in America, they were speaking from a setting of masters and apprentices, of personal models and family-connected avenues of mobility. Maria Melville, deploring her nephew Peter Gansevoort's lack of ambition, complained that he was "devoid of emulation, which urges so many on to exertion." Registering the shift from paternal models to maternal love, Maria blamed Mary Ann Gansevoort for her son's failure. But she, too, still inhabited a personal network of imitation and advancement. Melville's Master in Chancery, alluding to the traditional household organization of work, underlines by contrast the anonymity of the modern office.

Bartleby's employer does not preside over apprentices, bound to him by learning a craft. He is master over a refractory slave, who first copies him "mechanically" and then withdraws his labor. Bartleby could imitate the lawyer forever without acquiring either his employer's competence or his status. The "degraded . . . drill" of the unskilled worker, the drill in which Bartleby engages, is "sealed off from experience; practice counts for nothing there." Bartleby's "I have given up copying" speaks to the changing character of work, the growing distance between master and employee, and the chasm separating imitation from maturity. Bartleby's jailer thought he was a "forger," appropriating another's identity through imitating his handwriting. Bartleby actually does the opposite. He appropriates the lawyer's identity by refusing to copy him. The lawyer recognizes the "wondrous ascendancy which the inscrutable scrivener had over me." How account for his "cadaverous triumph"?

Bartleby protests, with "passive resistance," against his condition. In refusing   5
to copy, he is copying Thoreau. "I simply wish to refuse allegiance," announced Thoreau, "to withdraw." Bartleby's "I prefer not to" is an echo of "Civil Disobedience." But just as Bartleby appropriates the lawyer to discredit him, so he undermines the Thoreauvian alternative. The intent of passive resistance was to save the adversary as well as to triumph over him. It avoided the costs of direct aggression. Richard Lebeaux suggests that Thoreau's father's weakness and his brother's death influenced Thoreau to choose a nonviolent form of rebellion. Melville had a weak, dead father and a dead brother, and he also stepped back from straightforward, aggressive triumphs. But *Bartleby* exposed the passive aggression which lies behind nonviolent resistance. Bartleby punishes the lawyer by punishing himself. He avoids a straightforward triumph, as Thoreau does, but in a way that inverts Thoreau's project. Bartleby undermines his adversary and destroys himself.

Already pale and "motionless" when he appears at the office, Bartleby successively detaches himself from each of his (already meager) social connections. He prefers not to read copy, prefers not to copy, prefers not to leave the office, haunts the office after the lawyer abandons it, and finally refuses to eat in jail. Turning aggression against himself, Bartleby refuses (by attacking the lawyer directly) to sanction the lawyer's anger at him. Bartleby exercises the power of weakness. The "young man" taught obedience by the withdrawal of love (instead of by physical violence) is turning that lesson against this "elderly man."

Bartleby is formed solely from within the walls by which he is confined. Emptiness without means emptiness within. There is no transcendent flight from Wall Street routine either to nature or to the interior. Thoreau's speech embodies the feelings with which he resists appropriation. Bartleby's silence at once creates a wall between interior state and external appearance, and suggests that the former is merely a pale reflection of the latter. Thoreau "was not born to be forced"; Bartleby was. Nevertheless, by refusing to explain himself, he protects himself from colonization. Bartleby has the power of negativity. He drains his surroundings of the humanity in which the lawyer would like to believe.

Bartleby is Tocqueville's democratic individual, cut off from family, class, and community. He is "locked in the solitude of his own heart." He is the man, "himself alone," "not tied to time or place," that Tocqueville imagined as the subject of democratic art. Bartleby is alone not in nature, as Tocqueville predicted the hero of American poetry would be, but in the lonely crowd. Melville uses the paltry details of American life, which Tocqueville thought were artistically refractory, to make an aesthetic form.

The lawyer introduces his office by calling "spacious" the skylight shaft between his window and the white wall. "What landscape painters call 'life,'" he remarks, is visible through the opposing window, in the "lofty brick wall, black by age and everlasting shade; which wall required no spy-glass to bring out its lurking beauties." No spyglass is needed because that wall "was pushed up to within ten feet of my window panes." As the narrator finds life and variety in the view from his office, the words Melville puts into his mouth call that space a "cistern." The narrator's feeble, novelistic efforts, Melville is pointing out, are false to reality on Wall Street.

The lawyer's attempt to humanize his environment gives Bartleby his negative power. It is not so much the scrivener's withdrawal from life that needs explaining, as the way in which he draws in the narrator, the other employees, and the reader. The story hints at a social explanation for Bartleby's influence, and insists on a psychological one.

The routinization of work undermined the familiarity based set of master-apprentice relations. Employers and reformers claimed, in response, that their social institutions reproduced among strangers those shattered familial and communal bonds. As wage labor replaced household production, the employer insisted he was united to his workers by deeper ties than those of legal contract and market interest. Employers and their defenders spoke of workplaces as families. Reformers proposed asylums, modeled on the family, to reclaim the dangerous classes for useful work. . . .

When Bartleby also proves difficult, the lawyer seeks to reach him with understanding. . . . He tries, in turn, the various liberal strategies for overcoming the resistance of society's "dangerous" and "perishing classes." First he hopes that his benevolent paternalism will "purchase a delicious self-approval." That reform effort fails, as it generally did in Indian relations; it gives way (as in Indian policy) to cruder strategies. The lawyer tries to provoke Bartleby's active resistance, so he can justify aggression on his own. He tries to bribe him. He pretends that Bartleby does not exist. Finally he contemplates murder. But the lawyer draws back from these direct forms of aggression. Invoking Christ's injunction that "ye love one another" to stop himself from doing violence to Bartleby, he cites "self-interest" as a motive for "charity." The lawyer's interest is in preserving his self; for that purpose he needs to feel he has not done violence to Bartleby.

Thoreau voices the question Bartleby puts to the lawyer, "How shall he ever know well what he is and does as an officer of the government, or as a man, until he is obliged to consider whether he shall treat me . . . as a neighbor and well-disposed man, or as a maniac and disturber of the peace." Bartleby disturbs the lawyer's peace, but the lawyer tries not to treat him as a maniac. He wants to nurture Bartleby, but his charity reveals the failure of his office to sustain human life. At every step the lawyer takes toward Bartleby, Bartleby withdraws more deeply into himself. "Formerly tyranny used the clumsy weapons of chains and hangmen," wrote Tocqueville. "Despotism, to reach the soul, clumsily struck at the body, and the soul, escaping from such blows, rose gloriously above it; but in democratic republics . . . tyranny . . . leaves the body alone and goes straight for

10

the soul." The lawyer "might give alms to [Bartleby's] body; but his body did not pain him; it was his soul that suffered, and his soul I could not reach."

Bartleby's withdrawals discredit the lawyer; they expose his bad faith. Unwilling to commit himself fully to the scrivener, he tries to set boundaries to the relationship. Those boundaries become Bartleby's targets. Contractual arrangements in the traditional workshop operated in a setting of tangible, specific, and customary reciprocal obligations. As persons and contracts separated, the bonds that would structure and limit Bartleby's expectations disappear. The lawyer needs to erect boundaries, for Bartleby is boundaryless and insatiable.

The lawyer is nothing but his office, and he needs to have Bartleby in it. He experiences Bartleby as an "incubus" clinging to him, but he cannot let him go. Their intimacy goes beneath that of paternal employer and prodigal son; it extends beyond class and ideology to personality. *Bartleby* is not just a parable of capitalist trying to reclaim worker, or father seeking forgiveness from son. Though set in the workplace, *Bartleby* offers the barest description of white-collar, working-class life. *Bartleby* is social critique not as realistic story but as psychological parable. It gains its power from the virtual disappearance of society, swallowed up in a psychological symbiosis. Bartleby (who has neither history nor speech) and the lawyer (who has neither name nor interior) are two halves of a single, divided self.

Folding doors divide the lawyer's office in two. His scriveners are on one side, and he is on the other. The lawyer places Bartleby on his side of the folding doors, however, behind a screen and by a window facing a wall. The narrator is drawing "this quiet man" into his private space, and at the same time placing a division between them. He wants to "isolate Bartleby from my sight, though not removing him from my voice." He wants Bartleby to do his bidding without having to look at him face-to-face.

The lawyer is drawn to this "pitiably respectable, incurably forlorn" young man. Bartleby seems at once needier and more tractable than his other scriveners. Because Bartleby has almost no self of his own, the lawyer thinks he can more easily absorb him. But the very absence of self, which allows Bartleby and the lawyer to merge, also introduces the withdrawal from life in which Bartleby will implicate the narrator. The symbiosis between Bartleby and his employer is a residue of that which twinned Isabel and Pierre. Pierre and the lawyer both engage in rescue operations to reclaim a lost interior. But the passion which seduces Pierre, because it is secretly present within him, is absent in the lawyer. Bartleby is the "ghost" left behind after the battle is over. He is the lawyer's interior, impoverished by a lifetime in contracts and deeds.

The lawyer is "an eminently *safe* man." He lives by avoiding risks; his "first grand point" is "prudence." "The lawyer's truth is not Truth, but . . . a consistent expediency," Thoreau protested. "His quality is not wisdom, but prudence." Thoreau was attacking Daniel Webster. He was calling for civil disobedience against the federal law that legalized slavery and made war on Mexico. Like Webster, Bartleby's lawyer stands "so completely within the institution" that he "never distinctly and nakedly behold[s] it." The lawyer lacks heroic stature, or interior,

15

personal authority. He is a "title-hunter" without a title of his own. He abdicates authority to the walls on the outside and to Bartleby within. Bartleby forces him to behold his institution by withdrawing even further within it.

The lawyer's lack of authority makes him long for Bartleby's approval. To find a place for Bartleby would redeem his own impoverished life. The very internal emptiness which makes him fear Bartleby, however, makes him fear public opinion more. Rumors that Bartleby is "denying my authority" make him decide to evict the scrivener. "Buttoning up my coat to the last button," the lawyer emphasizes his physical separation from Bartleby. Still, he cannot "thrust him, the poor, pale, passive mortal" away. "Rather would I let him live and die here, and then mason up his remains in the wall." Theodore Parker had imagined that the outcast, once a "rejected stone," would find his "place on the wall, and his use." The lawyer would allow Bartleby his place, even if he had no use. In naming Parker's desire, however, the lawyer reveals it as a wish for death.

Public opinion forces the lawyer to abandon Bartleby; unwilling to use force and throw Bartleby out of his office, he "tore myself from him" instead. The lawyer changes offices, but public opinion still connects him to the ghost that haunts his old quarters. "Fearful . . . of being exposed in the papers," he takes what seems the final step toward intimacy, and invites Bartleby home. Bartleby prefers not to go.   20

The lawyer hopes that "humanizing domestic associations" will nurture Bartleby. Bartleby prefers to underline the absence of those associations at work. The lawyer has fallen back on the separation of office from home; by making the office his home, Bartleby discredits that boundary, too. Like Andrew Jackson, Bartleby retreats to his "hermitage" for privacy, to escape being "mobbed" in the metropolis. But Bartleby's "hermitage," as the narrator calls it half a dozen times, is in his office; the lawyer's screen has located it there. Unlike the home in Nashville where Gansevoort Melville stayed, Bartleby's hermitage is no escape from society.

Finally, Bartleby is taken off to jail. There he might have joined Thomas Melvill, whose "sensibility" became "morbid," he wrote his brother, from being consigned to debtor's prison by his family. Bartleby was, as Thomas Melvill wrote, secluded "within these walls." His keeper might have been Leonard Gansevoort (Guert and Stanwix's father), who served as sheriff of Albany. He might have been confined by Peter Gansevoort, when he was Albany county court judge, or by Lemuel Shaw. Peter Gansevoort, who served as chairman of the committee on prisons in the New York state assembly, might have investigated Bartleby's condition. Lawyers, judges, and prison-keepers were everywhere in Melville's family. Melville, in negative identification, gained the capability of imagining a prisoner whom their authority could not reclaim.

"Under a government which imprisons men unjustly, the true place for a just man is also a prison," wrote Thoreau. Thoreau chose prison to declare his freedom from society. "I saw that, if there was a wall of stone between me and my townsmen, there was a still more difficult one to climb to break through before they could be as free as I was. I did not for a moment feel confined." Prison confirmed Thoreau's freedom; it confirms Bartleby's confinement. "Removed to the Tombs as a vagrant," Bartleby turns his face to the wall. "Look, there is the sky, and here is the grass," the lawyer tells him. "I know where I am," Bartleby replies.

Bartleby is within the "walls of amazing thickness" that surround the prison yard. There the lawyer's wish to mason up his remains in a wall is fulfilled. The lawyer visits Bartleby one last time. He finds him "huddled at the base of the wall, his knees drawn up, and lying on his side." Assuming the foetal position, Bartleby has starved himself to death. The lawyer, however, finds rebirth even there. Within these "eternal pyramids," he observes, "through the clefts, grass-seed, dropped by birds, had sprung." Melville had imagined himself a seed, which had bloomed when it was taken from an Egyptian pyramid, and then fallen to mold. He puts Bartleby back to die within the Egyptian tomb. The seed dropped "through the clefts," like the "fertilizations" of Mount Greylock, does not generate human life.

As Thoreau imagined castles on the Rhine from within his prison cell, so Bartleby is "asleep . . . with kings and counselors." The narrator's reference is to Job. "Why died I not from the womb?" cries Job. "Why did the knees prevent me? Or why the breasts that I should suck? For now . . . I should have slept: then had been at rest, with kings and counsellors . . . as infants which never saw light." "There the prisoners rest together," Job thinks, ". . . which long for death." Job's outcry, with its references to knees and to refusing suck, describers the prisoner Bartleby. Bartleby has had Job's wish, and died in the womb. The lawyer's language betrays him to the end, however, for his invocation of Job undercuts his sentimentalizing of Bartleby's death.

The lawyer makes one last effort to circumscribe the meaning of his scrivener's fate. He reports the rumor that Bartleby was fired from the Dead Letter Office in Washington. It is too late to explain Bartleby away by his specific historical origins. The formal economy and self-sufficiency of this story, by freeing the text from its historical referents, free Bartleby from his textual confines. He haunts the reader forever.   [1983]

25

LEO MARX
From "Melville's Parable of the Walls"

Receiving his education at Harvard University (Ph.D., 1950), Leo Marx (b. 1919) has been a distinguished professor of English and American studies at a number of universities, including the Massachusetts Institute of Technology, where he has served as the W. R. Kenan, Jr., Professor of American Cultural History from 1977 to the present. Marx's critical writings often focus on the place of technology in American culture and arts, including literature, exemplified by his coining of the term The Machine in the Garden *as a book title (1964) up to his participation in a recent "colloquium on advanced information technology" (1996). "Melville's Parable of the Walls" was originally published in the* Sewanee Review *(October 1953).*

Dead,

> 25. Of a wall . . . : Unbroken, unrelieved by breaks or interruptions; absolutely uniform and continuous.
>
> — *New English Dictionary*

In the spring of 1851, while still at work on *Moby Dick*, Herman Melville wrote his celebrated "dollars damn me" letter to Hawthorne:

> In a week or so, I go to New York, to bury myself in a third-story room, and work and slave on my "Whale" while it is driving through the press. *That* is the only way I can finish it now—I am so pulled hither and thither by circumstances. The calm, the coolness, the silent grass-growing mood in which a man *ought* always to compose,—that, I fear, can seldom be mine. Dollars damn me. . . . My dear Sir, a presentiment is on me,—I shall at last be worn out and perish. . . . What I feel most moved to write, that is banned—it will not pay. Yet, altogether, write the *other* way I cannot.

He went on and wrote the "Whale" as he felt moved to write it; the public was apathetic and most critics were cool. Nevertheless Melville stubbornly refused to return to the *other* way, to his more successful earlier modes, the South Sea romance and the travel narrative. In 1852 he published *Pierre*, a novel even more certain not to be popular. And this time the critics were vehemently hostile. Then, the following year, Melville turned to shorter fiction. "Bartleby, the Scrivener," the first of his stories, dealt with a problem unmistakably like the one Melville had described to Hawthorne.

There are excellent reasons for reading "Bartleby" as a parable having to do with Melville's own fate as a writer. To begin with, the story *is* about a kind of writer, a "copyist" in a Wall Street lawyer's office. Furthermore, the copyist is a man who obstinately refuses to go on doing the sort of writing demanded of him. Under the circumstances there can be little doubt about the connection between Bartleby's dilemma and Melville's own. Although some critics have noted the autobiographical relevance of this facet of the story, a close examination of the parable reveals a more detailed parallel with Melville's situation than has been suggested. In fact the theme itself can be described in a way which at once establishes a more precise relation. "Bartleby" is not only about a writer who refuses to conform the demands of society, but it is, more relevantly, about a writer who foresakes conventional modes because of an irresistible preoccupation with the most baffling philosophical questions. This shift of Bartleby's attention is the symbolic equivalent of Melville's own shift of interest between *Typee* and *Moby Dick*. And it is significant that Melville's story, read in this light, does not by any means proclaim the desirability of the change. It was written in a time of deep hopelessness, and as I shall attempt to show, it reflects Melville's doubts about the value of his recent work.

Indeed, if I am correct about what this parable means, it has immense importance, for it provides the most explicit and mercilessly self-critical statement of his own dilemma that Melville has left us. Perhaps it is because "Bartleby" reveals so much of his situation that Melville took such extraordinary pains to mask its meaning. This may explain why he chose to rely upon symbols which derive from his earlier work, and to handle them with so light a touch that only the reader who comes to the story after an immersion in the other novels can be expected to see how much is being said here. Whatever Melville's motive may have been, I believe it may legitimately be accounted a grave defect of the parable that we must go back to *Typee* and *Moby Dick* and *Pierre* for the clues to its meaning. It is as if Melville had decided that the only adequate test of a reader's qualifications for sharing so damaging a self-revelation was a thorough reading of his own work.

"Bartleby, the Scrivener" is a parable about a particular kind of writer's relations to a particular kind of society. The subtitle, "A Story of Wall Street," provides the first clue about the nature of the society. It is a commercial society, dominated by a concern with property and finance. Most of the action takes place in Wall Street. But the designation has a further meaning: as Melville describes the street it literally becomes a walled street. The walls are the controlling symbols of the story, and in fact it may be said that this is a parable of walls, the walls which hem in the meditative artist and for that matter every reflective man. Melville also explicitly tells us that certain prosaic facts are "indispensable" to an understanding of the story. These facts fall into two categories: first, details concerning the personality and profession of the narrator, the center of consciousness in this tale, and more important, the actual floor-plan of his chambers.

The narrator is a Wall Street lawyer. One can easily surmise that at this   5 unhappy turning point in his life Melville was fascinated by the problem of seeing what his sort of writer looked like to a representative American. For his narrator he therefore chose, as he did in "Benito Cereno," which belongs to the same period, a man of middling status with a propensity for getting along with people, but a man of distinctly limited perception. Speaking in lucid, matter-of-fact language, this observer of Bartleby's strange behavior describes himself as comfortable, methodical and prudent. He has prospered; he unabashedly tells of the praise with which John Jacob Astor has spoken of him. Naturally, he is a conservative, or as he says, an "eminently *safe*" man, proud of his snug traffic in rich men's bonds, mortgages and deeds. As he tells the story we are made to feel his mildness, his good humor, his satisfaction with himself and his way of life. He is the sort who prefers the remunerative though avowedly obsolete sinecure of the Mastership of Chancery, which has just been bestowed upon him when the action starts, to the exciting notoriety of the courtroom. He wants only to be left alone; nothing disturbs his complacency until Bartleby appears. As a spokesman for the society he is well chosen; he stands at its center and performs a critical role, unravelling and retying the invisible cords of property and equity which intertwine in Wall Street and bind the social system.

The lawyer describes his chambers with great care, and only when the plan of the office is clearly in mind can we find the key to the parable. Although the chambers are on the second floor, the surrounding buildings rise above them, and as a result only very limited vistas are presented to those inside the office. At each end the windows look out upon a wall. One of the walls, which is part of a sky-light shaft, is *white*. It provides the best light available, but even from the windows which open upon the white wall the sky is invisible. No direct rays of the sun penetrate the legal sanctum. The wall at the other end gives us what seems at first to be a sharply contrasting view of the outside world. It is a lofty brick structure within ten feet of the lawyer's window. It stands in an everlasting shade and is *black* with age; the space it encloses reminds the lawyer of a huge black cistern. But we are not encouraged to take this extreme black and white, earthward and skyward contrast at face value (readers of *Moby Dick* will recall how illusory colors can be), for the lawyer tells us that the two views," in spite of their colors, have something very important in common: they are equally "deficient in what landscape painters call 'life'." The difference in color is less important than the fact that what we see through each window is only a wall.

This is all we are told about the arrangement of the chambers until Bartleby is hired. When the lawyer is appointed Master in Chancery he requires the services of another copyist. He places an advertisement, Bartleby appears, and the lawyer hastily checks his qualifications and hires him. Clearly the lawyer cares little about Bartleby's previous experience; the kind of writer wanted in Wall Street need merely be one of the great interchangeable white-collar labor force. It is true that Bartleby seems to him peculiarly pitiable and forlorn, but on the other hand the lawyer is favorably impressed by his neat, respectable appearance. So sedate does he seem that the boss decides to place Bartleby's desk close to his own. This is his first mistake; he thinks it will be useful to have so quiet and apparently tractable a man within easy call. He does not understand Bartleby then or at any point until their difficult relationship ends.

When Bartleby arrives we discover that there is also a kind of wall inside the office. It consists of the ground-glass folding-doors which separate the lawyer's desk, and now Bartleby's, from the desks of the other employees, the copyists and the office boy. Unlike the walls outside the windows, however, this is a social barrier men can cross, and the lawyer makes a point of telling us that he opens and shuts these doors according to *his* humor. Even when they are shut, it should be noted, the ground glass provides at least an illusion of penetrability quite different from the opaqueness of the walls outside.

So far we have been told of only two possible views of the external world which are to be had from the office, one black and the other white. It is fitting that the coming of a writer like Bartleby is what makes us aware of another view, one neither black nor white, but a quite distinct third view which is now added to the topography of the Wall Street microcosm.

> I placed his desk close up to a small side-window in that part of the room [a corner near the folding-doors]—a window which originally had afforded a lateral view of certain grimy back yards and bricks, but which, owing to subsequent erections, commanded at present no view at all, though it gave some light. Within three feet of the panes was a wall, and the light came down from far above, between two lofty buildings, as from a very small opening in a dome. Still further to a satisfactory arrangement, I procured a high green folding screen, which might entirely isolate Bartleby from my sight, though not remove him from my voice. And thus, in a manner, privacy and society were conjoined.

Notice that of all the people in the office Bartleby is to be in the best possible position to make a close scrutiny of a wall. His is only three feet away. And although the narrator mentions that the new writer's window offers "no view at all," we recall that he has, paradoxically, used the word "view" a moment before to describe the walled vista to be had through the other windows. Actually every window in the office looks out upon some sort of wall; the important difference between Bartleby and the others is that he is closest to a wall. Another notable difference is implied by the lawyer's failure to specify the color of Bartleby's wall. Apparently it is almost colorless, or blank. This also enhances the new man's ability to scrutinize and know the wall which limits his vision; he does not have to contend with the illusion of blackness or whiteness. Only Bartleby faces the stark problem of perception presented by the walls. For him external reality thus takes on some of the character it had for Ishmael, who knew that color did not reside in objects, and therefore saw beyond the deceptive whiteness of the whale to "a colorless, all-color of atheism." As we shall see, only the nature of the wall with which the enigmatic Bartleby is confronted can account for his strange behavior later.

What follows (and it is necessary to remember that all the impressions we   10
receive are the lawyer's) takes place in three consecutive movements: Bartleby's gradually stiffening resistance to the Wall Street routine, then a series of attempts by the lawyer to enforce the scrivener's conformity, and finally, society's punishment of the recalcitrant writer.   [1953]

MAURICE FRIEDMAN
From "Bartleby and the Modern Exile"

Currently professor of religious studies at San Diego State University, Maurice Friedman (b. 1921) was educated at Harvard University (B.S., 1940), Ohio State University (M.A., 1947), and the University of Chicago (Ph.D., 1950). He has taught at a number of universities, written twenty books, and has received many fellowships and awards, including the 1985 National Jewish Book Award. He is a translator, critic, and acknowledged expert on the life and work of German theologian Martin Buber. His most recent work is Religion and Psychology: A Dialogical Approach *(1992).*

In Bartleby, Melville carries the Modern Exile a stage beyond his representation in Ishmael in *Moby Dick*. It is this that led me to write in *Problematic Rebel: An Image of Modern Man:* "In its paradoxical strangeness and its portrayal of a condition of alienation utterly devoid of romantic pathos, 'Bartleby' is a remarkable anticipation of Kafka° and Camus.° Bartleby himself bears an amazing

Kafka: Franz Kafka (1883–1924), German novelist.
Camus: Albert Camus (1913–1960), French existential writer and philosopher.

resemblance to many of Kafka's heroes in the sense that he gives of being afforded existence only on the narrowest and most restricted terms."

Bartleby is a Modern Exile. He does not merely represent that exile of man from paradise which has characterized the human condition from earliest times. He also represents that special intensification of exile that arises from the "death of God" and the alienation of modern man. The "death of God," as that phrase has been used from Nietzsche° down, is not a statement about God but about man's alienation itself.

> The "death of God" does not mean that modern man does not "believe" in God, any more than it means that God himself has actually died. Whether or not one holds with Sartre° that God never existed at all or with Buber that God is in "eclipse" and that it is we, the "slayers of God," who dwell in the darkness, the "death of God" means the awareness of a basic crisis in modern history—the crisis that comes when man no longer knows what it means to be human and becomes aware that he does not know this. This is not just a question of the relativization of "values" and the absence of universally accepted mores. It is the absence of an image of meaningful human existence, the absence of the ground that enabled Greek, Biblical, and Renaissance man to move with some sureness even in the midst of tragedy.

This may seem like a great metaphysical weight to make poor Bartleby carry, but he does not carry it by himself. The true story is not Bartleby in himself but his employer's relation to him. The employer is not only the narrator of the story and the point of view; he is also in himself the representative of that humanity on which Bartleby impinges through his uncommon yet "common" humanity. The employer, by his own confession, is a man filled from his youth upwards "with a profound conviction that the easiest way of life is the best." His grand point was prudence, his second method, according to John Jacob Astor, who but confirmed thereby the general opinion that he was "an eminently safe man." This complete unwillingness to venture is reflected in his practice which never calls him forth to address a jury but leaves him "in the cool tranquillity of a snug retreat," to "do a snug business among rich men's bonds, and mortgages, and title-deeds." Even his law chambers of Wall Street offer a tame view, deficient in "life," namely the soot-blackened square cistern made by the walls of the surrounding high buildings. In similar fashion, he exploits his law clerks, or scriveners, to the fullest, but, "being a man of peace," does not insist when they refuse to take off work during their "fits." Since Nippers's fit is on when Turkey's is off and vice versa, the narrator accepts this as "a good natural arrangement, under the circumstances."

It is against this background that we first meet Bartleby, who comes in answer to an advertisement and stands, "a motionless young man," upon his office threshold—"pallidly neat, pitiably respectable, incurably forlorn!" At the same time he is described as "so singularly sedate" in aspect that the employer is

---

Nietzsche: Friedrich Nietzsche (1844–1900), German philosopher who rejected Christian values in favor of a superman and his heroic ethic, achieved by a will to power.
Sartre: Jean-Paul Sartre (1905–1980), French philosopher, novelist, and founder of existentialism; he believed humankind is condemned to be free.

glad to have him among his corps of copyists. Instead of placing him with the others assigns him a corner on his side of the folding doors, "so as to have this quiet man within easy call, in case any trifling thing was to be done." Bartleby presents all the aspect of an efficient office machine which the employer is glad to take advantage of without troubling over the eclipsed humanity that this quiet efficiency purports. Bartleby's window commands no view at all, though it gives some light through a small opening between buildings. To make his enclosure more complete still, the employer put up a high green folding screen which entirely isolates Bartleby from his sight while not removing him from his commanding voice. Bartleby fits into this "satisfactory arrangement" with machine-like compliance, writing by sunlight and candlelight. The only thing that mars the employer's delight in Bartleby's application is the fact that he is not "cheerfully industrious" but writes on "silently, palely, mechanically."

Even so, one may imagine that this arrangement would have gone on indefinitely had not Bartleby one day surprised his employer by the quiet words "I prefer not to" when asked to compare a copy sheet. Without anger, impatience, or impertinence, Bartleby sets a limit to the employer's ready willingness to relate to him as a non-human machine. At the outermost margins of personal existence without active rebellion or "anything ordinarily human," Bartleby asserts through his passive resistance that he does after all exist as a self, even if only in this entirely negative form.

The employer is flabbergasted, to say the least. In the face of this mild but unmovable wall, he feels helpless and unable to act. "I should have as soon thought of turning my pale plaster-of-paris bust of Cicero out of doors," he confesses. With any other man he would have flown into a rage and thrust him ignominiously away, but Bartleby not only strangely disarms him, "in a wonderful manner" he touches and disconcerts him. What touches and disconcerts the employer? The curious mixture of the human and the inhuman. The ordinary picture of the exploiter is that of a ruthless man. The narrator of our story, in contrast, is an "easy-going" man who combines exploitation with truth. The very nature of his exploitation, in fact, is his willingness to take advantage of Bartleby's eccentricities without raising too much fuss or demanding for Bartleby what he can or will not demand for himself. After his surprise at Bartleby's failure to fulfill duties which are customary for copyists, the employer quickly becomes reconciled to the new situation, again on the basis of his own advantage.

> His steadiness, his freedom from all dissipation, his incessant industry (except when he chose to throw himself into a standing reverie behind his screen), his great stillness, his unalterableness of demeanour under all circumstances, made him a valuable acquisition. One prime thing was this — *he was always there* — first in the morning, continually through the day, and the last at night. I had a singular confidence in his honesty.

This adjustment on the part of the employer to what is so manifestly his own best interests does not prevent him from "falling into sudden spasmodic passions" with Bartleby. But the passion is not so much anger as it is irritation at something that troubles routine and makes it necessary for him to think in unaccustomed

ways. "It was exceedingly difficult to bear in mind all the time those strange peculiarities, privileges, and unheard-of exemptions, forming the tacit stipulations on
Bartleby's part under which he remained in my office."

It is a strange reversal of situation that allows the employee rather than the
employer to stipulate the terms of work, especially when this stipulation is not
based on any contractual agreement or mutual bargaining but upon an entirely
unexplained and undefended "I prefer not to." That the employer puts up with
such a fiat from his employee seems to be due to the fact that Bartleby's paleness
and lack of life "touch" him while his "wonderful mildness" disarms and unmans
him. The employer confesses to a strange and superstitious knocking at his heart,
threatening to denounce him for a villain if he dares "to breathe one bitter word
against this forlornest of mankind."

This still does not adequately explain why Bartleby so disconcerts the
employer. He is continually at a loss as to what response he can make to
Bartleby's quiet setting of limits, which finally extends to preferring not to do any
work at all at the same time preferring not to quit the office. This rupture of the
climate of social expectation catapults the nineteenth-century Bartleby into the
absurd world of Camus's *The Stranger* and Kafka's "The Judgment." If Bartleby
had sought to justify his refusal to comply with some rational or emotional argument, if he had even add I *will* not instead of I *prefer* not, the employer would
have known how to respond. As it is, Bartleby destroys the common world of
mutual expectation within which the easy-going employer exploits and indulges
his employees.

> It is not seldom the case that, when a man is browbeaten in some unprece-
> dentedly and violently unreasonable way, he begins to stagger in his plainest
> faith. He begins, as it were, vaguely to surmise that, wonderful as it may be,
> all the justice and all the reason is on the other side.

The language that the employer uses here is entirely inappropriate. Bartleby
browbeats nobody, and there is nothing violent even about his unreasonableness.
Nor is there any reason to suppose that what is in question here is whether reason
and justice are on one side or the other, since these terms are utterly irrelevant to
the situation. But the situation *is* an unprecedented one, and the employer does
stagger in his plainest faith — the faith that rests on a common social world, a
common social expectation that Bartleby no longer shares. . . .

It is the inability to trust in existence that lies at the core of the remarkable
resemblance between Bartleby and Kafka's "Hunger Artist." Bartleby eats almost
nothing except ginger-nuts when he is in the office, and in the Tombs he
declares, "I prefer not to dine to-day . . . It would disagree with me; I am unused
to dinners." On the employer's second visit, the grub-man asks him whether
Bartleby will dine today or whether he lives without dining. The employer
replies, "Lives without dining," and closes the eyes of "the wasted Bartleby," who
though apparently sleeping is actually dead. This brings to mind the death of
Kafka's Gregor Samsa, the routine-bound traveling salesman who, after his metamorphosis into a gigantic insect, starves to death because he cannot find any food
that he can eat or any confirmation from his family that could lead him to want to

eat. But the parallels with "A Hunger Artist" are more striking still. "A Hunger Artist" is the story of a man whose self-imposed fasts are of such spectacular length that an impresario is able to exploit this talent to draw huge crowds into a coliseum to watch as, against his will, he breaks his fast after forty days. Later he ceases to attract great crowds and is sold to a circus as a minor side show. At last he is entirely forgotten, and an overseer discovers him dying in the straw of his cage. The hunger artist whispers, "Forgive me everybody," and confesses that although he has always wanted everybody to admire his fasting, they should not admire him since at bottom his fasting is not an art but an inescapable necessity.

> "I have to fast, I can't help it," said the hunger artist. "What a fellow you are," said the overseer, "and why can't you help it?" "Because . . . I couldn't find the food I liked. If I had found it, believe me, I should have made no fuss and stuffed myself like you or anyone else."

The hunger artist would have "stuffed" himself had he only found "food" he liked—had he found some way open to a meaningful existence. This coincides exactly with the prophetic first question which the grub-man puts to the employer concerning Bartleby: "Does he want to starve?" Bartleby *wants* to starve because he can find no way to live, no access to real life, to authentic existence. In him the exile of modern man has become absolute and irrevocable. The only way that remains open to him is death.

It is death, and death in the peculiarly modern emphasis that Freud and Heidegger give to it, that is the focus of the epilogue of this novella. In this epilogue Bartleby's exile is broadened into the exile of modern man, whose hyperintensive awareness of death is the exact corollary of the alienation and rootlessness of his existence and the tenuousness of his sense of self. Although no certain facts about Bartleby ever come to light, a rumor does reach the ear of the narrator that Bartleby had once "been a subordinate clerk in the Dead Letter Office at Washington, from which he had been suddenly removed by a change in the administration." The impersonality of the Dead Letter Office, combined with the attempts at personal communication which come to nought there, make Bartleby's derangement understandable to the narrator, if not very convincingly so to us. "By nature and misfortune prone to a pallid hopelessness," Bartleby became permanently disordered through working where he had to consign such letters to the flames by the cartload. 10

Must we conclude that if there is no way of man for Bartleby, then all possibility of authentic humanity goes under with him? Bartleby's "I prefer not to" is not only negative. It is also positive—the last effort of the drowning self to preserve its existence as a self. In this sense, even his defeat and death may be for us an image of the outermost limit of a common human condition—a condition which forces us to go through the anguish of the Modern Exile but need not leave us there. This condition is the inescapable but nonetheless genuine personal struggle of each one of us. Each of us, in his unique tension of compulsion and responsibility, must try to find a way forward which will be true—true both to ourselves and to the situation to which we must respond. In this struggle, and in it alone, there remains a possibility of authenticating our humanity. [1965]

ALFRED KAZIN
From "Ishmael in His Academic Heaven"

Alfred Kazin (b. 1915) studied at what is now City College of the City University of New York and at Columbia University, where he received his Ph.D. in 1938. For over fifty years, he has been a literary critic, teacher, and nonfiction writer. Among his many publications, his most recent is A Lifetime Burning in Every Moment *(1997), a collection of journal writings dating from 1938. In 1997, he received a Lifetime Achievement Award in Literary Criticism. The excerpt reprinted here is from the February 12, 1949, issue of* The New Yorker *magazine.*

. . . I do not know who Bartleby was. I have always thought he was the stranger in the city, in an extreme condition of loneliness, and the story a fable of how we detach ourselves from others to gain a deeper liberty and then find ourselves so walled up by our own pride that we can no longer accept the love that is offered us. While there is "irony" in the story, it is directed not against Bartleby but against the good-hearted, mediocre, ineffectual narrator, Bartleby's employer, who admits, "I might give alms to his body; but his body did not pain him; it was his soul that suffered, and his soul I could not reach." "Bartleby" is a story of the ultimate difficulty human beings have in reaching each other, and I do not think Melville was writing *about* anyone, except as he drew (How could he help it? Where else would he have learned it?) on his own situation and his bitter understanding of himself. Surely a little less bookish source-hunting, a little more awareness of what attracts us to Melville, would make it impossible for us to be so "scientific" about his intentions, when they can still be found in the life around us.   [1949]

MAKING COMPARISONS

1. Kazin's view seems clear and commonsensical. How do you rank the plausibility of the other critical pieces? Do any strike you as too "far out"?

2. Do any of the excerpts give good explanations for why Bartleby haunts critics and other readers? What are they?

3. Marx sees the story as being about Melville himself. In what ways do the other three critics agree?

WRITING ABOUT ISSUES

1. Argue that Kazin oversimplifies Bartleby and that there is more to the story than he asserts.

2. Compare the arguments of Marx and Rogin. What are their central claims? What evidence do they deploy in support? Do they note the opposition? Which do you find the more convincing? Why?

3. Write your own explanation for Bartleby's behavior, supporting your view by reference to your own experience.

4. Locate three additional pieces of criticism on "Bartleby, the Scrivener" and write a review essay that explains their perspective while also providing a context that includes our four excerpts.

MISFITS

NATHANIEL HAWTHORNE, "Young Goodman Brown"
FLANNERY O'CONNOR, "A Good Man Is Hard to Find"

We are social beings who long to fit in. The communities we form sustain us and give us our moral compasses and our psychological bearings. It is difficult to imagine how much a physical separation from our various communities would impair our emotional health. It is this physical isolation that makes prison such a severe punishment.

But sometimes people voluntarily remove themselves from all traditional communities. Our literature is filled with such outsiders and misfits. Their decisions intrigue us but also perplex and trouble us, perhaps because they represent antisocial impulses in all of us. While occasionally feeling alienated and demanding a period of isolation is natural, the two misfits in the following stories are extreme cases of such impulses. One becomes a killer of innocent people, the other lives a solitary and lonely life in the midst of family and friends. While such actions are disturbing, they often are illuminating.

BEFORE YOU READ

Have you ever felt threatened by violence? What was your response? Do you know of anyone who has been the victim of random violence? What was their reaction? How do you think you would act if you knew you were about to be killed?

NATHANIEL HAWTHORNE
Young Goodman Brown

Nathaniel Hawthorne (1804–1864) was born in Salem, Massachusetts, into a family that could be traced back to the Puritans. This lineage troubled Hawthorne because two of his ancestors were harsh judges involved in persecuting Quakers and in burning witches. After graduating from Bowdoin College in 1825, Hawthorne returned to live in his mother's house in Salem, developing his ability as a writer for twelve years.

After he married, he moved to Concord where Ralph Waldo Emerson and Henry David Thoreau were his neighbors. Unlike them, however, his ideas about human nature were rarely optimistic. In The Scarlet Letter *(1850) and* The House of the Seven Gables *(1851), Hawthorne wrote of conflicted characters, with hearts and souls torn by guilt, sin, pride, and isolation. Indeed, his good friend Herman Melville praised "the power of blackness" found in Hawthorne's fiction. "Young Goodman Brown" is a typical allegorical story where the moral absolutism of the Puritans contributes to the suffering of a man because he cannot accept the flawed complexity of the human condition.*

Young Goodman Brown came forth at sunset into the street at Salem village; but put his head back, after crossing the threshold, to exchange a parting kiss with his young wife. And Faith, as the wife was aptly named, thrust her own pretty head into the street, letting the wind play with the pink ribbons of her cap while she called to Goodman Brown.

"Dearest heart," whispered she, softly and rather sadly, when her lips were close to his ear, "prithee put off your journey until sunrise and sleep in your own bed to-night. A lone woman is troubled with such dreams and such thoughts that she's afeared of herself sometimes. Pray tarry with me this night, dear husband, of all nights in the year."

"My love and my Faith," replied young Goodman Brown, "of all nights in the year, this one night must I tarry away from thee. My journey, as thou callest it, forth and back again, must needs be done 'twixt now and sunrise. What, my sweet, pretty wife, dost thou doubt me already, and we but three months married?"

"Then God bless you!" said Faith, with the pink ribbons; "and may you find all well when you come back."

"Amen!" cried Goodman Brown. "Say thy prayers, dear Faith, and go to bed at dusk, and no harm will come to thee."   5

So they parted; and the young man pursued his way until, being about to turn the corner by the meeting-house, he looked back and saw the head of Faith still peeping after him with a melancholy air, in spite of her pink ribbons.

"Poor little Faith!" thought he, for his heart smote him. "What a wretch am I to leave her on such an errand! She talks of dreams, too. Methought as she spoke there was trouble in her face, as if a dream had warned her what work is to be done to-night. But no, no; 't would kill her to think it. Well, she's a blessed angel on earth, and after this one night I'll cling to her skirts and follow her to heaven."

With this excellent resolve for the future, Goodman Brown felt himself justified in making more haste on his present evil purpose. He had taken a dreary road, darkened by all the gloomiest trees of the forest, which barely stood aside to let the narrow path creep through, and closed immediately behind. It was all as lonely as could be; and there is this peculiarity in such a solitude, that the traveller knows not who may be concealed by the innumerable trunks and the thick boughs overhead; so that with lonely footsteps he may yet be passing through an unseen multitude.

"There may be a devilish Indian behind every tree," said Goodman Brown to himself; and he glanced fearfully behind him as he added, "What if the devil himself should be at my very elbow!"

His head being turned back, he passed a crook of the road, and, looking for-　　10
ward again, beheld the figure of a man, in grave and decent attire, seated at the foot of an old tree. He arose at Goodman Brown's approach and walked onward side by side with him.

"You are late, Goodman Brown," said he. "The clock of the Old South was striking as I came through Boston, and that is full fifteen minutes agone."

"Faith kept me back a while," replied the young man, with a tremor in his voice, caused by the sudden appearance of his companion, though not wholly unexpected.

It was now deep dusk in the forest, and deepest in that part of it where these two were journeying. As nearly as could be discerned, the second traveller was about fifty years old, apparently in the same rank of life as Goodman Brown, and bearing a considerable resemblance to him, though perhaps more in expression than features. Still they might have been taken for father and son. And yet, though the elder person was as simply clad as the younger, and as simple in man-ner too, he had an indescribable air of one who knew the world, and who would not have felt abashed at the governor's dinner table or in King William's court, were it possible that his affairs should call him thither. But the only thing about him that could be fixed upon as remarkable was his staff, which bore the likeness of a great black snake, so curiously wrought that it might almost be seen to twist and wriggle itself like a living serpent. This, of course, must have been an ocular deception, assisted by the uncertain light.

"Come, Goodman Brown," cried his fellow-traveller, "this is a dull pace for the beginning of a journey. Take my staff, if you are so soon weary."

"Friend," said the other, exchanging his slow pace for a full stop, "having　　15
kept covenant by meeting thee here, it is my purpose now to return whence I came. I have scruples touching the matter thou wot'st of."

"Sayest thou so?" replied he of the serpent, smiling apart. "Let us walk on, nevertheless, reasoning as we go; and if I convince thee not thou shalt turn back. We are but a little way in the forest yet."

"Too far! too far!" exclaimed the goodman, unconsciously resuming his walk. "My father never went into the woods on such an errand, nor his father before him. We have been a race of honest men and good Christians since the days of the martyrs; and shall I be the first of the name of Brown that ever took this path and kept" —

"Such company, thou wouldst say," observed the elder person, interpreting his pause. "Well said, Goodman Brown! I have been as well acquainted with your family as with ever a one among the Puritans; and that's no trifle to say. I helped your grandfather, the constable, when he lashed the Quaker woman so smartly through the streets of Salem; and it was I that brought your father a pitch-pine knot, kindled at my own hearth, to set fire to an Indian village, in King Philip's war.° They were my good friends, both; and many a pleasant walk have we had along this path, and returned merrily after midnight. I would fain be friends with you for their sake."

"If it be as thou sayest," replied Goodman Brown, "I marvel they never spoke of these matters; or, verily, I marvel not, seeing that the least rumor of the sort would have driven them from New England. We are a people of prayer, and good works to boot, and abide no such wickedness."

"Wickedness or not," said the traveller with the twisted staff, "I have a very   20
general acquaintance here in New England. The deacons of many a church have drunk the communion wine with me; the selectmen of divers towns make me their chairman; and a majority of the Great and General Court are firm supporters of my interest. The governor and I, too — But these are state secrets."

"Can this be so?" cried Goodman Brown, with a stare of amazement at his undisturbed companion. "Howbeit, I have nothing to do with the governor and council; they have their own ways, and are no rule for a simple husbandman like me. But, were I to go on with thee, how should I meet the eye of that good old man, our minister, at Salem village? Oh, his voice would make me tremble both Sabbath day and lecture day."

Thus far the elder traveller had listened with due gravity; but now burst into a fit of irrepressible mirth, shaking himself so violently that his snake-like staff actually seemed to wriggle in sympathy.

"Ha! ha! ha!" shouted he again and again; then composing himself, "Well, go on, Goodman Brown, go on; but, prithee, don't kill me with laughing."

"Well, then, to end the matter at once," said Goodman Brown, considerably nettled, "there is my wife, Faith. It would break her dear little heart; and I'd rather break my own."

"Nay, if that be the case," answered the other, "e'en go thy ways, Goodman   25
Brown. I would not for twenty old women like the one hobbling before us that Faith should come to any harm."

As he spoke he pointed his staff at a female figure on the path, in whom Goodman Brown recognized a very pious and exemplary dame, who had taught him his catechism in youth, and was still his moral and spiritual adviser, jointly with the minister and Deacon Gookin.

"A marvel, truly that Goody Cloyse should be so far in the wilderness at nightfall," said he. "But with your leave, friend, I shall take a cut through the woods until we have left this Christian woman behind. Being a stranger to you, she might ask whom I was consorting with and whither I was going."

"Be it so," said his fellow-traveller. "Betake you to the woods, and let me keep the path."

Accordingly the young man turned aside, but took care to watch his companion, who advanced softly along the road until he had come within a staff's length of the old dame. She, meanwhile, was making the best of her way, with

---

King Philip's war: King Philip, a Wampanoag chief, waged a bloody war against the New England colonists from 1675 to 1676.

singular speed for so aged a woman, and mumbling some indistinct words — a prayer, doubtless — as she went. The traveller put forth his staff and touched her withered neck with what seemed the serpent's tail.

"The devil!" screamed the pious old lady.   30

"Then Goody Cloyse knows her old friend?" observed the traveller, confronting her and leaning on his writhing stick.

"Ah, forsooth, and is it your worship indeed?" cried the good dame. "Yea, truly is it, and in the very image of my old gossip, Goodman Brown, the grandfather of the silly fellow that now is. But — would your worship believe it? — my broomstick hath strangely disappeared, stolen, as I suspect, by that unhanged witch, Goody Cory, and that, too, when I was all anointed with the juice of smallage, and cinquefoil, and wolf's bane" —

"Mingled with fine wheat and the fat of a new-born babe," said the shape of old Goodman Brown.

"Ah, your worship knows the recipe," cried the old lady, cackling aloud. "So, as I was saying, being all ready for the meeting, and no horse to ride on, I made up my mind to foot it; for they tell me there is a nice young man to be taken into communion to-night. But now your good worship will lend me your arm, and we shall be there in a twinkling."

"That can hardly be," answered her friend. "I may not spare you my arm,   35
Goody Cloyse; but here is my staff, if you will."

So saying, he threw it down at her feet, where, perhaps, it assumed life, being one of the rods which its owner had formerly lent to the Egyptian magi. Of this fact, however, Goodman Brown could not take cognizance. He had cast up his eyes in astonishment, and, looking down again, beheld neither Goody Cloyse nor the serpentine staff, but his fellow-traveller alone, who waited for him as calmly as if nothing had happened.

"That old woman taught me my catechism," said the young man; and there was a world of meaning in this simple comment.

They continued to walk onward, while the elder traveller exhorted his companion to make good speed and persevere in the path, discoursing so aptly that his arguments seemed rather to spring up in the bosom of his auditor than to be suggested by himself. As they went, he plucked a branch of maple to serve for a walking stick, and began to strip it of the twigs and little boughs, which were wet with evening dew. The moment his fingers touched them they became strangely withered and dried up as with a week's sunshine. Thus the pair proceeded, at a good free pace, until suddenly, in a gloomy hollow of the road, Goodman Brown sat himself down on the stump of a tree and refused to go any farther.

"Friend," he said, stubbornly, "my mind is made up. Not another step will I budge on this errand. What if a wretched old woman do choose to go to the devil when I thought she was going to heaven: is that any reason why I should quit my dear Faith and go after her?"

"You will think better of this by and by," said his acquaintance, composedly.   40
"Sit here and rest yourself a while; and when you feel like moving again, there is my staff to help you along."

Without more words, he threw his companion the maple stick, and was as speedily out of sight as if he had vanished into the deepening gloom. The young man sat a few moments by the roadside, applauding himself greatly, and thinking with how clear a conscience he should meet the minister in his morning walk, nor shrink from the eye of good old Deacon Gookin. And what calm sleep would be his that very night, which was to have been spent so wickedly, but so purely and sweetly now, in the arms of Faith! Amidst these pleasant and praiseworthy meditations, Goodman Brown heard the tramp of horses along the road, and deemed it advisable to conceal himself within the verge of the forest, conscious of the guilty purpose that had brought him thither, though now so happily turned from it.

On came the hoof tramps and the voices of the riders, two grave old voices, conversing soberly as they drew near. These mingled sounds appeared to pass along the road, within a few yards of the young man's hiding-place; but, owing doubtless to the depth of the gloom at that particular spot, neither the travellers nor their steeds were visible. Though their figures brushed the small boughs by the wayside, it could not be seen that they intercepted, even for a moment, the faint gleam from the strip of bright sky athwart which they must have passed. Goodman Brown alternately crouched and stood on tiptoe, pulling aside the branches and thrusting forth his head as far as he durst without discerning so much as a shadow. It vexed him the more, because he could have sworn, were such a thing possible, that he recognized the voices of the minister and Deacon Gookin, jogging along quietly, as they were wont to do, when bound to some ordination or ecclesiastical council. While yet within hearing, one of the riders stopped to pluck a switch.

"Of the two, reverend sir," said the voice like the deacon's, "I had rather miss an ordination dinner than to-night's meeting. They tell me that some of our community are to be here from Falmouth and beyond, and others from Connecticut and Rhode Island, besides several of the Indian powwows, who, after their fashion, know almost as much deviltry as the best of us. Moreover, there is a goodly young woman to be taken into communion."

"Mighty well, Deacon Gookin!" replied the solemn old tones of the minister. "Spur up, or we shall be late. Nothing can be done, you know, until I get on the ground."

The hoofs clattered again; and the voices, talking so strangely in the empty air, passed on through the forest, where no church had ever been gathered or solitary Christian prayed. Whither, then, could these holy men be journeying so deep into the heathen wilderness? Young Goodman Brown caught hold of a tree for support, being ready to sink down on the ground, faint and overburdened with the heavy sickness of his heart. He looked up to the sky, doubting whether there really was a heaven above him. Yet there was the blue arch, and the stars brightening in it.   45

"With heaven above and Faith below, I will yet stand firm against the devil!" cried Goodman Brown.

While he still gazed upward into the deep arch of the firmament and had lifted his hands to pray, a cloud, though no wind was stirring, hurried across the zenith and hid the brightening stars. The blue sky was still visible, except directly overhead, where this black mass of cloud was sweeping swiftly northward. Aloft in the air, as if from the depths of the cloud, came a confused and doubtful sound of voices. Once the listener fancied that he could distinguish the accents of towns-people of his own, men and women, both pious and ungodly, many of whom he had met at the communion table, and had seen others rioting at the tavern. The next moment, so indistinct were the sounds, he doubted whether he had heard aught but the murmur of the old forest, whispering without a wind. Then came a stronger swell of those familiar tones, heard daily in the sunshine at Salem village, but never until now from a cloud of night. There was one voice, of a young woman, uttering lamentations, yet with an uncertain sorrow, and entreating for some favor, which, perhaps, it would grieve her to obtain; and all the unseen multitude, both saints and sinners, seemed to encourage her onward.

"Faith!" shouted Goodman Brown, in a voice of agony and desperation; and the echoes of the forest mocked him, crying, "Faith! Faith!" as if bewildered wretches were seeking her all through the wilderness.

The cry of grief, rage, and terror was yet piercing the night, when the unhappy husband held his breath for a response. There was a scream, drowned immediately in a louder murmur of voices, fading into far-off laughter, as the dark cloud swept away, leaving the clear and silent sky above Goodman Brown. But something fluttered lightly down through the air and caught on the branch of a tree. The young man seized it, and beheld a pink ribbon.

"My Faith is gone!" cried he after one stupefied moment. "There is no good 50 on earth; and sin is but a name. Come, devil; for to thee is this world given."

And, maddened with despair, so that he laughed loud and long, did Goodman Brown grasp his staff and set forth again, at such a rate that he seemed to fly along the forest path rather than to walk or run. The road grew wilder and drearier and more faintly traced, and vanished at length, leaving him in the heart of the dark wilderness, still rushing onward with the instinct that guides mortal man to evil. The whole forest was peopled with frightful sounds—the creaking of the trees, the howling of wild beasts, and the yell of Indians; while sometimes the wind tolled like a distant church bell, and sometimes gave a broad roar around the traveller, as if all Nature were laughing him to scorn. But he was himself the chief horror of the scene, and shrank not from its other horrors.

"Ha! ha! ha!" roared Goodman Brown when the wind laughed at him. "Let us hear which will laugh loudest. Think not to frighten me with your deviltry. Come witch, come wizard, come Indian powwow, come devil himself, and here comes Goodman Brown. You may as well fear him as he fear you."

In truth, all through the haunted forest there could be nothing more frightful than the figure of Goodman Brown. On he flew among the black pines, brandishing his staff with frenzied gestures, now giving vent to an inspiration of horrid blasphemy, and now shouting forth such laughter as set all the echoes of the forest laughing like demons around him. The fiend in his own shape is less hideous than when he rages in the breast of man. Thus sped the demoniac on his course, until, quivering among the trees, he saw a red light before him, as when the felled trunks and branches of a clearing have been set on fire, and throw up their lurid blaze against the sky, at the hour of midnight. He paused, in a lull of the tempest that had driven him onward, and heard the swell of what seemed a hymn, rolling solemnly from a distance with the weight of many voices. He knew the tune; it was a familiar one in the choir of the village meeting-house. The verse died heavily away, and was lengthened by a chorus, not of human voices, but of all the sounds of the benighted wilderness pealing in awful harmony together. Goodman Brown cried out, and his cry was lost to his own ear by its unison with the cry of the desert.

In the interval of silence he stole forward until the light glared full upon his eyes. At one extremity of an open space, hemmed in by the dark wall of the forest, arose a rock, bearing some rude, natural resemblance either to an altar or a pulpit, and surrounded by four blazing pines, their tops aflame, their stems untouched, like candles at an evening meeting. The mass of foliage that had overgrown the summit of the rock was all on fire, blazing high into the night and fitfully illuminating the whole field. Each pendent twig and leafy festoon was in a blaze. As the red light arose and fell, a numerous congregation alternately shone forth, then disappeared in shadow, and again grew, as it were, out of the darkness, peopling the heart of the solitary woods at once.

"A grave and dark-clad company," quoth Goodman Brown. 55

In truth they were such. Among them, quivering to and fro between gloom and splendor, appeared faces that would be seen next day at the council board of the province, and others which, Sabbath after Sabbath, looked devoutly heavenward, and benignantly over the crowded pews, from the holiest pulpits in the land. Some affirm that the lady of the governor was there. At least there were high dames well known to her, and wives of honored husbands, and widows, a great multitude, and ancient maidens, all of excellent repute, and fair young girls, who trembled lest their mothers should espy them. Either the sudden gleams of light flashing over the obscure field bedazzled Goodman Brown, or he recognized a score of the church members of Salem village famous for their especial sanctity. Good old Deacon Gookin had arrived, and waited at the skirts of that venerable saint, his revered pastor. But, irreverently consorting with these grave, reputable, and pious people, these elders of the church, these chaste dames and dewy virgins, there were men of dissolute lives and women of spotted fame, wretches given over to all mean and filthy vice, and suspected even of horrid crimes. It was strange to see that the good shrank not from the wicked, nor were the sinners abashed by the saints. Scattered also among their pale-faced enemies were the Indian priests, or powwows, who had often scared their native forest with more hideous incantations than any known to English witchcraft.

"But where is Faith?" thought Goodman Brown; and, as hope came into his heart, he trembled.

Another verse of the hymn arose, a slow and mournful strain, such as the pious love, but joined to words which expressed all that our nature can conceive of sin, and darkly hinted at far more. Unfathomable to mere mortals is the lore of fiends. Verse after verse was sung; and still the chorus of the desert swelled between like the deepest tone of a mighty organ; and with the final peal of that dreadful anthem there came a sound, as if the roaring wind, the rushing streams, the howling beasts, and every other voice of the unconcerted wilderness were mingling and according with the voice of guilty man in homage to the prince of all. The four blazing pines threw up a loftier flame, and obscurely discovered shapes and visages of horror on the smoke wreaths above the impious assembly. At the same moment the fire on the rock shot redly forth and formed a flowing arch above its base, where now appeared a figure. With reverence be it spoken, the figure bore no slight similitude, both in garb and manner, to some grave divine of the New England churches.

"Bring forth the converts!" cried a voice that echoed through the field and rolled into the forest.

At the word, Goodman Brown stepped forth from the shadow of the trees   60 and approached the congregation, with whom he felt a loathful brotherhood by the sympathy of all that was wicked in his heart. He could have well-nigh sworn that the shape of his own dead father beckoned him to advance, looking downward from a smoke wreath, while a woman, with dim features of despair, threw out her hand to warn him back. Was it his mother? But he had no power to retreat one step, nor to resist, even in thought, when the minister and good old Deacon Gookin seized his arms and led him to the blazing rock. Thither came also the slender form of a veiled female, led between Goody Cloyse, that pious teacher of the catechism, and Martha Carrier, who had received the devil's promise to be queen of hell. A rampant hag was she. And there stood the proselytes beneath the canopy of fire.

"Welcome, my children," said the dark figure, "to the communion of your race. Ye have found thus young your nature and your destiny. My children, look behind you!"

They turned; and flashing forth, as it were, in a sheet of flame, the fiend worshippers were seen; the smile of welcome gleamed darkly on every visage.

"There," resumed the sable form, "are all whom ye have reverenced from youth. Ye deemed them holier than yourselves and shrank from your own sin, contrasting it with their lives of righteousness and prayerful aspirations heavenward. Yet here are they all in my worshipping assembly. This night it shall be granted you to know their secret deeds: how hoary-bearded elders of the church have whispered wanton words to the young maids of their households; how many a woman, eager for widows' weeds, has given her husband a drink at bedtime and let him sleep his last sleep in her bosom; how beardless youths have made haste to inherit their fathers' wealth; and how fair damsels—blush not, sweet ones— have dug little graves in the garden, and bidden me, the sole guest, to an infant's funeral. By the sympathy of your human hearts for sin ye shall scent out all the places—whether in church, bedchamber, street, field, or forest—where crime has been committed, and shall exult to behold the whole earth one stain of guilt, one mighty blood spot. Far more than this. It shall be yours to penetrate, in every bosom, the deep mystery of sin, the fountain of all wicked arts, and which inexhaustibly supplies more evil impulses than human power—than my power at its utmost—can make manifest in deeds. And now, my children, look upon each other."

They did so; and, by the blaze of the hell-kindled torches, the wretched man beheld his Faith, and the wife her husband, trembling before that unhallowed altar.

"Lo, there ye stand, my children," said the figure, in a deep and solemn tone, almost sad with its despairing awfulness, as if his once angelic nature could yet mourn for our miserable race. "Depending upon one another's hearts, ye had still hoped that virtue were not all a dream. Now are ye undeceived. Evil is the nature of mankind. Evil must be your only happiness. Welcome again, my children, to the communion of your race." 65

"Welcome," repeated the fiend worshippers, in one cry of despair and triumph.

And there they stood, the only pair, as it seemed, who were yet hesitating on the verge of wickedness in this dark world. A basin was hallowed, naturally, in the rock. Did it contain water, reddened by the lurid light? or was it blood? or, perchance, a liquid flame? Herein did the shape of evil dip his hand and prepare to lay the mark of baptism upon their foreheads, that they might be partakers of the mystery of sin, more conscious of the secret guilt of others, both in deed and thought, than they could now be of their own. The husband cast one look at his pale wife, and Faith at him. What polluted wretches would the next glance show them to each other, shuddering alike at what they disclosed and what they saw!

"Faith! Faith!" cried the husband, "look up to heaven, and resist the wicked one."

Whether Faith obeyed he knew not. Hardly had he spoken when he found himself amid calm night and solitude, listening to a roar of the wind which died heavily away through the forest. He staggered against the rock, and felt it chill and damp; while a hanging twig, that had been all on fire, besprinkled his cheek with the coldest dew.

The next morning young Goodman Brown came slowly into the street of Salem village, staring around him like a bewildered man. The good old minister was taking a walk along the graveyard to get an appetite for breakfast and meditate his sermon, and bestowed a blessing, as he passed, on Goodman Brown. He shrank from the venerable saint as if to avoid an anathema. Old Deacon Gookin was at domestic worship, and the holy words of his prayer were heard through the open window. "What God doth the wizard pray to?" quoth Goodman Brown. Goody Cloyse, that excellent old Christian, stood in the early sunshine at her own lattice, catechizing a little girl who had brought her a pint of morning's milk. Goodman Brown snatched away the child as from the grasp of the fiend himself. Turning the corner by the meeting-house, he spied the head of Faith, with the pink ribbons, gazing anxiously forth, and bursting into such joy at sight of him that she skipped along the street and almost kissed her husband before the whole village. But Goodman Brown looked sternly and sadly into her face, and passed on without a greeting. 70

Had Goodman Brown fallen asleep in the forest and only dreamed a wild dream of a witch-meeting?

Be it so if you will; but, alas! it was a dream of evil omen for young Goodman Brown. A stern, a sad, a darkly meditative, a distrustful, if not a desperate man did he become from the night of that fearful dream. On the Sabbath day, when the congregation were singing a holy psalm, he could not listen because an anthem of sin rushed loudly upon his ear and drowned all the blessed strain. When the minister spoke from the pulpit with power and fervid eloquence, and, with his hand on the open Bible, of the sacred truths of our religion, and of saint-like lives and triumphant deaths, and of future bliss or misery unutterable, then did Goodman Brown turn pale, dreading lest the roof should thunder down upon the gray blasphemer and his hearers. Often, awaking suddenly at midnight, he shrank from the bosom of Faith; and at morning or eventide, when the family knelt down at prayer, he scowled and muttered to himself, and gazed sternly at his wife, and turned away. And when he had lived long, and was borne to his grave a hoary corpse, followed by Faith, an aged woman, and children and grandchildren, a goodly procession, besides neighbors not a few, they carved no hopeful verse upon his tombstone, for his dying hour was gloom. [1835]

THINKING ABOUT THE TEXT

1. "Young Goodman Brown" seems quite allegorical with journeys in the night woods and statements like "my Faith is gone." How would you explain this allegorical story? What is Brown looking for? What does he find out? How does he deal with his discoveries?

2. If you were a good friend of Brown's, what might you tell him to try to save him from a life of gloom?

3. The devil suggests that there is more evil in the human heart "than my power at its utmost." Do you agree? If so, is this a message to despair about?

4. The devil says he is well acquainted with Brown's family. What has his family done? Is Brown innocent and naive, or perhaps stubborn and arrogant, in his refusal to admit that evil exists all around us?

5. Are you surprised when famous people like rock stars, athletes, actors, business executives, politicians, and preachers are caught in immoral or criminal activities? Should such public figures be role models? Are such people different from you?

FLANNERY O'CONNOR
A Good Man Is Hard to Find

Born in Savannah, Flannery O'Connor (1925–1964) spent most of her life in Milledgeville, Georgia, where she died of lupus at age thirty-nine. Her early stories won her a scholarship to the University of Iowa, where she received her M.F.A. Her collections, A Good Man Is Hard to Find *(1955) and* Everything That Rises Must Converge *(1965), are considered to be among the very best stories in American fiction. O'Connor's Roman Catholic faith and her Southern heritage are crucial elements in her work. Critics have sometimes seen in her work Christian parables of grace and redemption in the face of random violence. Like her fellow Southerners William Faulkner and Carson McCullers, she uses grotesque characters to suggest our own morally flawed humanity. The following story is typical of her fiction in that it transcends both theology and regionalism. As O'Connor herself noted, "it hangs on and expands in the mind."*

> The dragon is by the side of the road, watching those who pass. Beware lest he devour you. We go to the Father of Souls, but it is necessary to pass by the dragon.
>
> — St. Cyril of Jerusalem

The grandmother didn't want to go to Florida. She wanted to visit some of her connections in east Tennessee and she was seizing at every chance to change Bailey's mind. Bailey was the son she lived with, her only boy. He was sitting on the edge of his chair at the table, bent over the orange sports section of the *Journal*. "Now look here, Bailey," she said, "see here, read this," and she stood with one hand on her thin hip and the other rattling the newspaper at his bald head. "Here this fellow that calls himself The Misfit is aloose from the Federal Pen and headed toward Florida and you read here what it says he did to these people. Just you read it. I wouldn't take my children in any direction with a criminal like that aloose in it. I couldn't answer to my conscience if I did."

Bailey didn't look up from his reading so she wheeled around then and faced the children's mother, a young woman in slacks, whose face was as broad and innocent as a cabbage and was tied around with a green head-kerchief that had two points on the top like rabbit's ears. She was sitting on the sofa, feeding the baby his apricots out of a jar. "The children have been to Florida before," the old lady said. "You all ought to take them somewhere else for a change so they would see different parts of the world and be broad. They never have been to east Tennessee."

The children's mother didn't seem to hear her but the eight-year-old boy, John Wesley, a stocky child with glasses, said, "If you don't want to go to Florida, why dontcha stay at home?" He and the little girl, June Star, were reading the funny papers on the floor.

"She wouldn't stay at home to be queen for a day," June Star said without raising her yellow head.

"Yes and what would you do if this fellow, The Misfit, caught you?" the   5
grandmother asked.

"I'd smack his face," John Wesley said.

"She wouldn't stay at home for a million bucks," June Star said. "Afraid she'd miss something. She has to go everywhere we go."

"All right, Miss," the grandmother said. "Just remember that the next time you want me to curl your hair."

June Star said her hair was naturally curly.

The next morning the grandmother was the first one in the car, ready to go.   10
She had her big black valise that looked like the head of a hippopotamus in one corner, and underneath it she was hiding a basket with Pitty Sing, the cat, in it.

She didn't intend for the cat to be left alone in the house for three days because he would miss her too much and she was afraid he might brush against one of the gas burners and accidentally asphyxiate himself. Her son, Bailey, didn't like to arrive at a motel with a cat.

She sat in the middle of the back seat with John Wesley and June Star on either side of her. Bailey and the children's mother and the baby sat in front and they left Atlanta at eight forty-five with the mileage on the car at 55890. The grandmother wrote this down because she thought it would be interesting to say how many miles they had been when they got back. It took them twenty minutes to reach the outskirts of the city.

The old lady settled herself comfortably, removing her white cotton gloves and putting them up with her purse on the shelf in front of the back window. The children's mother still had on slacks and still had her head tied up in a green kerchief, but the grandmother had on a navy blue straw sailor hat with a bunch of white violets on the brim and a navy blue dress with a small white dot in the print. Her collars and cuffs were white organdy trimmed with lace and at her neckline she had pinned a purple spray of cloth violets containing a sachet. In case of an accident, anyone seeing her dead on the highway would know at once that she was a lady.

She said she thought it was going to be a good day for driving, neither too hot nor too cold, and she cautioned Bailey that the speed limit was fifty-five miles an hour and that the patrolmen hid themselves behind billboards and small clumps of trees and sped out after you before you had a chance to slow down. She pointed out interesting details of the scenery: Stone Mountain; the blue granite that in some places came up to both sides of the highway; the brilliant red clay banks slightly streaked with purple; and the various crops that made rows of green lace-work on the ground. The trees were full of silver-white sunlight and the meanest of them sparkled. The children were reading comic magazines and their mother had gone back to sleep.

"Let's go through Georgia fast so we won't have to look at it much," John Wesley said.

"If I were a little boy," said the grandmother, "I wouldn't talk about my native state that way. Tennessee has the mountains and Georgia has the hills."   15

"Tennessee is just a hillbilly dumping ground," John Wesley said, "and Georgia is a lousy state too."

"You said it," June Star said.

"In my time," said the grandmother, folding her thin veined fingers, "children were more respectful of their native states and their parents and everything else. People did right then. Oh look at the cute little pickaninny!" she said and pointed to a Negro child standing in the door of a shack. "Wouldn't that make a picture, now?" she asked and they all turned and looked at the little Negro out of the back window. He waved.

"He didn't have any britches on," June Star said.

"He probably didn't have any," the grandmother explained. "Little niggers in   20
the country don't have things like we do. If I could paint, I'd paint that picture," she said.

The children exchanged comic books.

The grandmother offered to hold the baby and the children's mother passed him over the front seat to her. She set him on her knee and bounced him and told him about the things they were passing. She rolled her eyes and screwed up her mouth and stuck her leathery thin face into his smooth bland one. Occasionally he gave her a faraway smile. They passed a large cotton field with five or six graves fenced in the middle of it, like a small island. "Look at the graveyard!" the grandmother said, pointing it out. "That was the old family burying ground. That belonged to the plantation."

"Where's the plantation?" John Wesley asked.

"Gone with the Wind," said the grandmother. "Ha. Ha."

When the children finished all the comic books they had brought, they opened the lunch and ate it. The grandmother ate a peanut butter sandwich and an olive and would not let the children throw the box and the paper napkins out the window. When there was nothing else to do they played a game by choosing a cloud and making the other two guess what shape it suggested. John Wesley took one the shape of a cow and June Star guessed a cow and John Wesley said, no, an automobile, and June Star said he didn't play fair, and they began to slap each other over the grandmother.

The grandmother said she would tell them a story if they would keep quiet. When she told a story, she rolled her eyes and waved her head and was very dramatic. She said once when she was a maiden lady she had been courted by a Mr. Edgar Atkins Teagarden from Jasper, Georgia. She said he was a very good-looking man and a gentleman and that he brought her a watermelon every Saturday afternoon with his initials cut in it, E. A. T. Well, one Saturday, she said, Mr. Teagarden brought the watermelon and there was nobody at home and he left it on the front porch and returned in his buggy to Jasper, but she never got the watermelon, she said, because a nigger boy ate it when he saw the initials, E. A. T.! This story tickled John Wesley's funny bone and he giggled and giggled but June Star didn't think it was any good. She said she wouldn't marry a man that just brought her a watermelon on Saturday. The grandmother said she would have done well to marry Mr. Teagarden because he was a gentleman and had bought Coca-Cola stock when it first came out and that he had died only a few years ago, a very wealthy man.

They stopped at The Tower for barbecued sandwiches. The Tower was a part stucco and part wood filling station and dance hall set in a clearing outside of Timothy. A fat man named Red Sammy Butts ran it and there were signs stuck here and there on the building and for miles up and down the highway saying, TRY RED SAMMY'S FAMOUS BARBECUE. NONE LIKE FAMOUS RED SAMMY'S! RED SAM! THE FAT BOY WITH THE HAPPY LAUGH. A VETERAN! RED SAMMY'S YOUR MAN!

Red Sammy was lying on the bare ground outside The Tower with his head under a truck while a gray monkey about a foot high, chained to a small china-berry tree, chattered nearby. The monkey sprang back into the tree and got on the highest limb as soon as he saw the children jump out of the car and run toward him.

25

Inside, The Tower was a long dark room with a counter at one end and tables at the other and dancing space in the middle. They all sat down at a board table next to the nickelodeon and Red Sam's wife, a tall burnt-brown woman with hair and eyes lighter than her skin, came and took their order. The children's mother put a dime in the machine and played "The Tennessee Waltz," and the grandmother said that tune always made her want to dance. She asked Bailey if he would like to dance but he only glared at her. He didn't have a naturally sunny disposition like she did and trips made him nervous. The grandmother's brown eyes were very bright. She swayed her head from side to side and pretended she was dancing in her chair. June Star said play something she could tap to so the children's mother put in another dime and played a fast number and June Star stepped out onto the dance floor and did her tap routine.

"Ain't she cute?" Red Sam's wife said, leaning over the counter. "Would you   30
like to come be my little girl?"

"No I certainly wouldn't," June Star said. "I wouldn't live in a broken-down place like this for a million bucks!" and she ran back to the table.

"Ain't she cute?" the woman repeated, stretching her mouth politely.

"Aren't you ashamed?" hissed the grandmother.

Red Sam came in and told his wife to quit lounging on the counter and hurry up with these people's order. His khaki trousers reached just to his hip bones and his stomach hung over them like a sack of meal swaying under his shirt. He came over and sat down at a table nearby and let out a combination sigh and yodel. "You can't win," he said. "You can't win," and he wiped his sweating red face off with a gray handkerchief. "These days you don't know who to trust," he said. "Ain't that the truth?"

"People are certainly not nice like they used to be," said the grandmother.   35

"Two fellers come in here last week," Red Sammy said, "driving a Chrysler. It was a old beat-up car but it was a good one and these boys looked all right to me. Said they worked at the mill and you know I let them fellers charge the gas they bought? Now why did I do that?"

"Because you're a good man!" the grandmother said at once.

"Yes'm, I suppose so," Red Sam said as if he were struck with this answer.

His wife brought the orders, carrying the five plates all at once without a tray, two in each hand and one balanced on her arm. "It isn't a soul in this green world of God's that you can trust," she said. "And I don't count nobody out of that, not nobody," she repeated, looking at Red Sammy.

"Did you read about that criminal, The Misfit, that's escaped?" asked the   40
grandmother.

"I wouldn't be a bit surprised if he didn't attact this place right here," said the woman. "If he hears about it being here, I wouldn't be none surprised to see him. If he hears it's two cent in the cash register, I wouldn't be a tall surprised if he . . ."

"That'll do," Red Sam said. "Go bring these people their Co'-Colas," and the woman went off to get the rest of the order.

"A good man is hard to find," Red Sammy said. "Everything is getting terrible. I remember the day you could go off and leave your screen door unlatched. Not no more."

He and the grandmother discussed better times. The old lady said that in her opinion Europe was entirely to blame for the way things were now. She said the way Europe acted you would think we were made of money and Red Sam said it was no use talking about it, she was exactly right. The children ran outside into the white sunlight and looked at the monkey in the lacy chinaberry tree. He was busy catching fleas on himself and biting each one carefully between his teeth as if it were a delicacy.

They drove off again into the hot afternoon. The grandmother took cat naps   45
and woke up every few minutes with her own snoring. Outside of Toombsboro she woke up and recalled an old plantation that she had visited in this neighborhood once when she was a young lady. She said the house had six white columns across the front and that there was an avenue of oaks leading up to it and two little wooden trellis arbors on either side in front where you sat down with your suitor after a stroll in the garden. She recalled exactly which road to turn off to get to it. She knew that Bailey would not be willing to lose any time looking at an old house, but the more she talked about it, the more she wanted to see it once again and find out if the little twin arbors were still standing. "There was a secret panel in this house," she said craftily, not telling the truth but wishing that she were, "and the story went that all the family silver was hidden in it when Sherman came through but it was never found . . ."

"Hey!" John Wesley said. "Let's go see it! We'll find it! We'll poke all the woodwork and find it! Who lives there? Where do you turn off at? Hey Pop, can't we turn off there?"

"We never have seen a house with a secret panel!" June Star shrieked. "Let's go to the house with the secret panel! Hey Pop, can't we go see the house with the secret panel!"

"It's not far from here, I know," the grandmother said. "It wouldn't take over twenty minutes."

Bailey was looking straight ahead. His jaw was as rigid as a horseshoe. "No," he said.

The children began to yell and scream that they wanted to see the house   50
with the secret panel. John Wesley kicked the back of the front seat and June Star hung over her mother's shoulder and whined desperately into her ear that they never had any fun even on their vacation, that they could never do what THEY wanted to do. The baby began to scream and John Wesley kicked the back of the seat so hard that his father could feel the blows in his kidney.

"All right!" he shouted and drew the car to a stop at the side of the road. "Will you all shut up? Will you all just shut up for one second? If you don't shut up, we won't go anywhere."

"It would be very educational for them," the grandmother murmured.

"All right," Bailey said, "but get this: this is the only time we're going to stop for anything like this. This is the one and only time."

"The dirt road that you have to turn down is about a mile back," the grandmother directed. "I marked it when we passed."

"A dirt road," Bailey groaned.   55

After they had turned around and were headed toward the dirt road, the grandmother recalled other points about the house, the beautiful glass over the front doorway and the candle-lamp in the hall. John Wesley said that the secret panel was probably in the fireplace.

"You can't go inside this house," Bailey said. "You don't know who lives there."

"While you all talk to the people in front, I'll run around behind and get in a window," John Wesley suggested.

"We'll all stay in the car," his mother said.

They turned onto the dirt road and the car raced roughly along in a swirl of pink dust. The grandmother recalled the times when there were no paved roads and thirty miles was a day's journey. The dirt road was hilly and there were sudden washes in it and sharp curves on dangerous embankments. All at once they would be on a hill, looking down over the blue tops of trees for miles around, then the next minute, they would be in a red depression with the dust-coated trees looking down on them. 60

"This place had better turn up in a minute," Bailey said, "or I'm going to turn around."

The road looked as if no one had traveled on it in months.

"It's not much farther," the grandmother said and just as she said it, a horrible thought came to her. The thought was so embarrassing that she turned red in the face and her eyes dilated and her feet jumped up, upsetting her valise in the corner. The instant the valise moved, the newspaper top she had over the basket under it rose with a snarl and Pitty Sing, the cat, sprang onto Bailey's shoulder.

The children were thrown to the floor and their mother, clutching the baby, was thrown out the door onto the ground; the old lady was thrown into the front seat. The car turned over once and landed right-side-up in a gulch off the side of the road. Bailey remained in the driver's seat with the cat—gray-striped with a broad white face and an orange nose—clinging to his neck like a caterpillar.

As soon as the children saw they could move their arms and legs, they scrambled out of the car, shouting, "We've had an ACCIDENT!" The grandmother was curled up under the dashboard, hoping she was injured so that Bailey's wrath would not come down on her all at once. The horrible thought she had had before the accident was that the house she had remembered so vividly was not in Georgia but in Tennessee. 65

Bailey removed the cat from his neck with both hands and flung it out the window against the side of a pine tree. Then he got out of the car and started looking for the children's mother. She was sitting against the side of the red gutted ditch, holding the screaming baby, but she only had a cut down her face and a broken shoulder. "We've had an ACCIDENT!" the children screamed in a frenzy of delight.

"But nobody's killed," June Star said with disappointment as the grandmother limped out of the car, her hat still pinned to her head but the broken front brim standing up at a jaunty angle and the violet spray hanging off the side. They all sat down in the ditch, except the children, to recover from the shock. They were all shaking.

"Maybe a car will come along," said the children's mother hoarsely.

"I believe I have injured an organ," said the grandmother, pressing her side, but no one answered her. Bailey's teeth were clattering. He had on a yellow sport shirt with bright blue parrots designed in it and his face was as yellow as the shirt. The grandmother decided that she would not mention that the house was in Tennessee.

The road was about ten feet above and they could only see the tops of the trees on the other side of it. Behind the ditch they were sitting in there were more woods, tall and dark and deep. In a few minutes they saw a car some distance away on top of a hill, coming slowly as if the occupants were watching them. The grandmother stood up and waved both arms dramatically to attract their attention. The car continued to come on slowly, disappeared around a bend and appeared again, moving even slower, on top of the hill they had gone over. It was a big black battered hearse-like automobile. There were three men in it.

It came to a stop just over them and for some minutes, the driver looked down with a steady expressionless gaze to where they were sitting, and didn't speak. Then he turned his head and muttered something to the other two and they got out. One was a fat boy in black trousers and a red sweat shirt with a silver stallion embossed on the front of it. He moved around on the right side of them and stood staring, his mouth partly open in a kind of loose grin. The other had on khaki pants and a blue striped coat and a gray hat pulled very low, hiding most of his face. He came around slowly on the left side. Neither spoke.

The driver got out of the car and stood by the side of it, looking down at them. He was an older man than the other two. His hair was just beginning to gray and he wore silver-rimmed spectacles that gave him a scholarly look. He had a long creased face and didn't have on any shirt or undershirt. He had on blue jeans that were too tight for him and was holding a black hat and a gun. The two boys also had guns.

"We've had an ACCIDENT!" the children screamed.

The grandmother had the peculiar feeling that the bespectacled man was someone she knew. His face was as familiar to her as if she had known him all her life but she could not recall who he was. He moved away from the car and began to come down the embankment, placing his feet carefully so that he wouldn't slip. He had on tan and white shoes and no socks, and his ankles were red and thin. "Good afternoon," he said. "I see you all had you a little spill."

"We turned over twice!" said the grandmother.

"Oncet," he corrected. "We seen it happen. Try their car and see will it run, Hiram," he said quietly to the boy with the gray hat.

"What you got that gun for?" John Wesley asked. "Whatcha gonna do with that gun?"

"Lady," the man said to the children's mother, "would you mind calling them children to sit down by you? Children make me nervous. I want all you all to sit down right together there where you're at."

"What are you telling US what to do for?" June Star asked.

Behind them the line of woods gaped like a dark open mouth. "Come here," said the mother.

70

75

80

"Look here now," Bailey began suddenly, "we're in a predicament! We're in . . ."

The grandmother shrieked. She scrambled to her feet and stood staring. "You're The Misfit!" she said. "I recognized you at once!"

"Yes'm," the man said, smiling slightly as if he were pleased in spite of himself to be known, "but it would have been better for all of you, lady, if you hadn't of reckernized me."

Bailey turned his head sharply and said something to his mother that shocked even the children. The old lady began to cry and The Misfit reddened.

"Lady," he said, "don't you get upset. Sometimes a man says things he don't   85
mean. I don't reckon he meant to talk to you thataway."

"You wouldn't shoot a lady, would you?" the grandmother said and removed a clean handkerchief from her cuff and began to slap at her eyes with it.

The Misfit pointed the toe of his shoe into the ground and made a little hole and then covered it up again. "I would hate to have to," he said.

"Listen," the grandmother almost screamed, "I know you're a good man. You don't look a bit like you have common blood. I know you must come from nice people!"

"Yes mam," he said, "finest people in the world." When he smiled he showed a row of strong white teeth. "God never made a finer woman than my mother and my daddy's heart was pure gold," he said. The boy with the red sweat shirt had come around behind them and was standing with his gun at his hip. The Misfit squatted down on the ground. "Watch them children, Bobby Lee," he said. "You know they make me nervous." He looked at the six of them huddled together in front of him and he seemed to be embarrassed as if he couldn't think of anything to say. "Ain't a cloud in the sky," he remarked, looking up at it. "Don't see no sun but don't see no cloud neither."

"Yes, it's a beautiful day," said the grandmother. "Listen," she said, "you   90
shouldn't call yourself The Misfit because I know you're a good man at heart. I can just look at you and tell."

"Hush!" Bailey yelled. "Hush! Everybody shut up and let me handle this!" He was squatting in the position of a runner about to sprint forward but he didn't move.

"I pre-chate that, lady," The Misfit said and drew a little circle in the ground with the butt of his gun.

"It'll take a half a hour to fix this here car," Hiram called, looking over the raised hood of it.

"Well, first you and Bobby Lee get him and that little boy to step over yonder with you," The Misfit said, pointing to Bailey and John Wesley. "The boys want to ast you something," he said to Bailey. "Would you mind stepping back in them woods there with them?"

"Listen," Bailey began, "we're in a terrible predicament! Nobody realizes   95
what this is," and his voice cracked. His eyes were as blue and intense as the parrots in his shirt and he remained perfectly still.

The grandmother reached up to adjust her hat brim as if she were going to the woods with him but it came off in her hand. She stood staring at it and after a second she let it fall on the ground. Hiram pulled Bailey up by the arm as if he were assisting an old man. John Wesley caught hold of his father's hand and Bobby Lee followed. They went off toward the woods and just as they reached the dark edge, Bailey turned and supporting himself against a gray naked pine trunk, he shouted, "I'll be back in a minute, Mamma, wait on me!"

"Come back this instant!" his mother shrilled but they all disappeared into the woods.

"Bailey Boy!" the grandmother called in a tragic voice but she found she was looking at The Misfit squatting on the ground in front of her. "I just know you're a good man," she said desperately. "You're not a bit common!"

"Nome, I ain't a good man," The Misfit said after a second as if he had considered her statement carefully, "but I ain't the worst in the world neither. My daddy said I was a different breed of dog from my brothers and sisters. 'You know,' Daddy said, 'it's some that can live their whole life out without asking about it and it's others has to know why it is, and this boy is one of the latters. He's going to be into everything!'" He put on his black hat and looked up suddenly and then away deep into the woods as if he were embarrassed again. "I'm sorry I don't have on a shirt before you ladies," he said, hunching his shoulders slightly. "We buried our clothes that we had on when we escaped and we're just making do until we can get better. We borrowed these from some folks we met," he explained.

"That's perfectly all right," the grandmother said. "Maybe Bailey has an extra shirt in his suitcase."   100

"I'll look and see terrectly," The Misfit said.

"Where are they taking him?" the children's mother screamed.

"Daddy was a card himself," The Misfit said. "You couldn't put anything over on him. He never got in trouble with the Authorities though. Just had the knack of handling them."

"You could be honest too if you'd only try," said the grandmother. "Think how wonderful it would be to settle down and live a comfortable life and not have to think about somebody chasing you all the time."

The Misfit kept scratching in the ground with the butt of his gun as if he were thinking about it. "Yes'm, somebody is always after you," he murmured.   105

The grandmother noticed how thin his shoulder blades were just behind his hat because she was standing up looking down at him. "Do you ever pray?" she asked.

He shook his head. All she saw was the black hat wiggle between his shoulder blades. "Nome," he said.

There was a pistol shot from the woods, followed closely by another. Then silence. The old lady's head jerked around. She could hear the wind move through the tree tops like a long satisfied insuck of breath. "Bailey Boy!" she called.

"I was a gospel singer for a while," The Misfit said. "I been most everything. Been in the arm service, both land and sea, at home and abroad, been twict married, been an undertaker, been with the railroads, plowed Mother Earth, been in a tornado, seen a man burnt alive oncet," and he looked up at the children's mother and the little girl who were sitting close together, their faces white and their eyes glassy; "I even seen a woman flogged," he said.

"Pray, pray," the grandmother began, "pray, pray . . ." 110

"I never was a bad boy that I remember of," The Misfit said in an almost dreamy voice, "but somewheres along the line I done something wrong and got sent to the penitentiary. I was buried alive," and he looked up and held her attention to him by a steady stare.

"That's when you should have started to pray," she said. "What did you do to get sent to the penitentiary, that first time?"

"Turn to the right, it was a wall," The Misfit said, looking up again at the cloudless sky. "Turn to the left, it was a wall. Look up it was a ceiling, look down it was a floor. I forgot what I done, lady. I set there and set there, trying to remember what it was I done and I ain't recalled it to this day. Oncet in a while, I would think it was coming to me, but it never come."

"Maybe they put you in by mistake," the old lady said vaguely.

"Nome," he said. "It wasn't no mistake. They had the papers on me." 115

"You must have stolen something," she said.

The Misfit sneered slightly. "Nobody had nothing I wanted," he said. "It was a head-doctor at the penitentiary said what I had done was kill my daddy but I known that for a lie. My daddy died in nineteen ought nineteen of the epidemic flu and I never had a thing to do with it. He was buried in the Mount Hopewell Baptist churchyard and you can go there and see for yourself."

"If you would pray," the old lady said, "Jesus would help you."

"That's right," The Misfit said.

"Well then, why don't you pray?" she asked trembling with delight suddenly. 120

"I don't want no hep," he said. "I'm doing all right by myself."

Bobby Lee and Hiram came ambling back from the woods. Bobby Lee was dragging a yellow shirt with bright blue parrots in it.

"Thow me that shirt, Bobby Lee," The Misfit said. The shirt came flying at him and landed on his shoulder and he put it on. The grandmother couldn't name what the shirt reminded her of. "No, lady," The Misfit said while he was buttoning it up, "I found out the crime don't matter. You can do one thing or you can do another, kill a man or take a tire off his car, because sooner or later you're going to forget what it was you done and just be punished for it."

The children's mother had begun to make heaving noises as if she couldn't get her breath. "Lady," he asked, "would you and that little girl like to step off yonder with Bobby Lee and Hiram and join your husband?"

"Yes, thank you," the mother said faintly. Her left arm dangled helplessly and 125 she was holding the baby, who had gone to sleep, in the other. "Hep that lady up, Hiram," The Misfit said as she struggled to climb out of the ditch, "and Bobby Lee, you hold onto that little girl's hand."

"I don't want to hold hands with him," June Star said. "He reminds me of a pig."

The fat boy blushed and laughed and caught her by the arm and pulled her off into the woods after Hiram and her mother.

Alone with The Misfit, the grandmother found that she had lost her voice. There was not a cloud in the sky nor any sun. There was nothing around her but woods. She wanted to tell him that he must pray. She opened and closed her mouth several times before anything came out. Finally she found herself saying, "Jesus. Jesus," meaning, Jesus will help you, but the way she was saying it, it sounded as if she might be cursing.

"Yes'm," The Misfit said as if he agreed. "Jesus thown everything off balance. It was the same case with Him as with me except He hadn't committed any crime and they could prove I had committed one because they had the papers on me. Of course," he said, "they never shown me my papers. That's why I sign myself now. I said long ago, you get you a signature and sign everything you do and keep a copy of it. Then you'll know what you done and you can hold up the crime to the punishment and see do they match and in the end you'll have something to prove you ain't been treated right. I call myself The Misfit," he said, "because I can't make what all I done wrong fit what all I gone through in punishment."

There was a piercing scream from the woods, followed closely by a pistol   130
report. "Does it seem right to you, lady, that one is punished a heap and another ain't punished at all?"

"Jesus!" the old lady cried. "You've got good blood! I know you wouldn't shoot a lady! I know you come from nice people! Pray! Jesus, you ought not to shoot a lady. I'll give you all the money I've got!"

"Lady," The Misfit said, looking beyond her far into the woods, "there never was a body that give the undertaker a tip."

There were two more pistol reports and the grandmother raised her head like a parched old turkey hen crying for water and called, "Bailey Boy, Bailey Boy!" as if her heart would break.

"Jesus was the only One that ever raised the dead," The Misfit continued, "and He shouldn't have done it. He thown everything off balance. If He did what He said, then it's nothing for you to do but thow away everything and follow Him, and if He didn't, then it's nothing for you to do but enjoy the few minutes you got left the best you can—by killing somebody or burning down his house or doing some other meanness to him. No pleasure but meanness," he said and his voice had become almost a snarl.

"Maybe He didn't raise the dead," the old lady mumbled, not knowing what   135
she was saying and feeling so dizzy that she sank down in the ditch with her legs twisted under her.

"I wasn't there so I can't say He didn't," The Misfit said. "I wisht I had of been there," he said, hitting the ground with his fist. "It ain't right I wasn't there because if I had of been there I would of known. Listen lady," he said in a high voice, "if I had of been there I would of known and I wouldn't be like I am now." His voice seemed about to crack and the grandmother's head cleared for an instant. She saw the man's face twisted close to her own as if he were going to cry and she murmured, "Why you're one of my babies. You're one of my own children!" She reached out and touched him on the shoulder. The Misfit sprang back as if a snake had bitten him and shot her three times through the chest. Then he put his gun down on the ground and took off his glasses and began to clean them.

Hiram and Bobby Lee returned from the woods and stood over the ditch, looking down at the grandmother who half sat and half lay in a puddle of blood with her legs crossed under her like a child's and her face smiling up at the cloudless sky.

Without his glasses, The Misfit's eyes were red-rimmed and pale and defenseless-looking. "Take her off and thow her where you thown the others," he said, picking up the cat that was rubbing itself against his leg.

"She was a talker, wasn't she?" Bobby Lee said, sliding down the ditch with a yodel.

"She would of been a good woman," The Misfit said, "if it had been some-   140
body there to shoot her every minute of her life."

"Some fun!" Bobby Lee said.

"Shut up, Bobby Lee," The Misfit said. "It's no real pleasure in life."   [1955]

THINKING ABOUT THE TEXT

1. The Misfit seems to justify his murderous violence by claiming he was "punished a heap." Can you point to other examples of such rationalizing? Do these explanations make sense to you? Have you heard of or read about characters similar to The Misfit? How would you describe him?

2. What do you think the grandmother means when she says to The Misfit, "Why you're one of my babies. You're one of my own children!"?

3. Critics note that O'Connor's religious belief often plays a role in her stories. Certainly there is a good deal of discussion at the end of this story of prayer and Jesus. Is The Misfit blaming Jesus for something? Is redemption a factor here? What religious ideas here seem the most interesting to you?

4. The Misfit's comment that the grandmother would have been a good woman if somebody was "there to shoot her every minute of her life" has intrigued critics who have offered up a variety of interpretations. How do you read this line?

5. Provocative stories often make us think how we would respond if faced with a similar situation. Describe the grandmother's strategy in confronting The Misfit. Was it wise? What were some alternatives? How might you deal with him?

MAKING COMPARISONS

1. Have both Goodman Brown and The Misfit lost faith in something? Explain.

2. Goodman Brown emotionally removes himself from the warmth and love of his family and community. How can you account for this choice? How can you account for The Misfit's choice to remove himself from the laws and compassion of the human community?

3. To some, the supernatural atmosphere and occurrences in Hawthorne's story make it seem unrealistic. Do you think so? Is "A Good Man Is Hard to Find" more realistic or less so? How would you define realism in fiction? Is it important?

WRITING ABOUT ISSUES

1. Read carefully what happens in the woods in "Young Goodman Brown." Look especially at the scene described in paragraphs 55–68. Argue that Brown responds appropriately to these events or that he overreacts.

2. The Misfit seems to embrace evil; Brown seems to reject anyone connected to evil. Both end up isolated. Write brief analyses of the two, suggesting where each went astray and if salvation is possible for either.

3. Write a personal essay that recounts a time in your life when you were surprised by violence or evil or when someone seemed to be quite different than you thought.

4. Do some research and write a brief comparative report on what several major religions say about some of the themes these two stories deal with: salvation, grace, redemption, the source of evil, the power of faith, and so on.

ENCOUNTERS WITH FOREIGNERS

GISH JEN, "What Means Switch"
MARGARET ATWOOD, "The Man from Mars"

If you grew up in a country other than this one, probably you have learned a lot about the culture since moving here. If you have lived all your life in this country, perhaps you have traveled beyond its borders and been given a new perspective on your own culture as well as new exposure to others. Perhaps you have learned much about other people — and about yourself — simply through conversations with immigrants or visitors to this country. Gish Jen's and Margaret Atwood's heroines are spurred to self-reflection by their encounters with foreign students. In Jen's story, Chinese American eighth grader Mona Chang finds herself considering her own heritage, identity, and goals as she develops a relationship with Sherman, a student from Japan. In Atwood's story, set in Canada, a college student named Christine finds her life increasingly affected by a mysterious stranger from a distant land. At the end of each story, readers are faced with an issue of evaluation: Do we approve of how the heroine treats the foreigner? The stories present an occasion for reflecting on our real-life encounters with people foreign to us and for discovering our native customs, values, and beliefs.

In your view, how are foreign students treated at your present school, and how have they been treated at other schools you have attended? Identify specific things that come to mind as you consider these questions.

GISH JEN
What Means Switch

Gish Jen (b. 1956) grew up in Scarsdale, New York, where this story is set. Educated at Harvard University, Stanford University, and the Writers Workshop at the University of Iowa, she has taught writing at such institutions as Tufts University and the University of Massachusetts. Jen is known for her humorous yet incisive short stories and novels about Chinese American life. The following story about Mona Chang first appeared in the May 1990 issue of The Atlantic. *Subsequently, Jen published two novels about the Chang family. The first centers mostly on Mona's father, Ralph, and is titled* Typical American (1991). *The second,* Mona in the Promised Land (1996), *focuses on Mona and begins with a revised version of "What Means Switch."*

There we are, nice Chinese family—father, mother, two born-here girls. Where should we live next? My parents slide the question back and forth like a cup of ginseng neither one wants to drink. Until finally it comes to them, what they really want is a milkshake (chocolate) and to go with it a house in Scarsdale. What else? The broker tries to hint: the neighborhood, she says. Moneyed. Many delis. Meaning rich and Jewish. But someone has sent my parents a list of the top ten schools nation-wide (based on the opinion of selected educators and others) and so *many-deli* or not we nestle into a Dutch colonial on the Bronx River Parkway. The road's windy where we are, very charming; drivers miss their turns, plough up our flower beds, then want to use our telephone. "Of course," my mom tells them, like it's no big deal, we can replant. We're the type to adjust. You know—the lady drivers weep, my mom gets out the Kleenex for them. We're a bit down the hill from the private plane set, in other words. Only in our dreams do our jacket zippers jam, what with all the lift tickets we have stapled to them, Killington on top of Sugarbush on top of Stowe, and we don't even know where the Virgin Islands are—although certain of us do know that virgins are like priests and nuns, which there were a lot more of in Yonkers, where we just moved from, than there are here.

This is my first understanding of class. In our old neighborhood everybody knew everything about virgins and nonvirgins, not to say the technicalities of staying in-between. Or almost everybody, I should say; in Yonkers I was the laugh-along type. Here I'm an expert.

"You mean the man . . . ?" Pig-tailed Barbara Gugelstein spits a mouthful of Coke back into her can. "That is *so* gross!"

Pretty soon I'm getting popular for a new girl, the only problem is Danielle Meyers, who wears blue mascara and has gone steady with two boys. "How do *you* know," she starts to ask, proceeding to edify us all with how she French-kissed one boyfriend and just regular kissed another. ("Because, you know, he had braces.") We hear about his rubber bands, how once one popped right into her mouth. I begin to realize I need to find somebody to kiss too. But how?

Luckily, I just about then happen to tell Barbara Gugelstein I know karate. I don't know why I tell her this. My sister Callie's the liar in the family; ask anybody. I'm the one who doesn't see why we should have to hold our heads up. But for some reason I tell Barbara Gugelstein I can make my hands like steel by thinking hard. "I'm not supposed to tell anyone," I say.

The way she backs away, blinking, I could be the burning bush.

"I can't do bricks," I say—a bit of expectation management. "But I can do your arm if you want." I set my hand in chop position.

"Uhh, it's okay," she says. "I know you can, I saw it on TV last night."

That's when I recall that I too saw it on TV last night—in fact, at her house. I rush on to tell her I know how to get pregnant with tea.

"With *tea?*"

"That's how they do it in China."

She agrees that China is an ancient and great civilization that ought to be known for more than spaghetti and gunpowder. I tell her I know Chinese. "*Be-yeh fa-foon*," I say. "*Shee-veh. Ji nu.*" Meaning, "Stop acting crazy. Rice gruel. Soy sauce." She's impressed. At lunch the next day, Danielle Meyers and Amy Weinstein and Barbara's crush, Andy Kaplan, are all impressed too. Scarsdale is a liberal town, not like Yonkers, where the Whitman Road Gang used to throw crabapple mash at my sister Callie and me and tell us it would make our eyes stick shut. Here we're like permanent exchange students. In another ten years, there'll be so many Orientals we'll turn into Asians; a Japanese grocery will buy out that one deli too many. But for now, the mid-sixties, what with civil rights on TV, we're not so much accepted as embraced. Especially by the Jewish part of town—which, it turns out, is not all of town at all. That's just an idea people have, Callie says, and lots of them could take us or leave us same as the Christians, who are nice too; I shouldn't generalize. So let me not generalize except to say that pretty soon I've been to so many bar and bas mitzvahs, I can almost say myself whether the kid chants like an angel or like a train conductor, maybe they could use him on the commuter line. At seder I know to forget the bricks, get a good pile of that mortar. Also I know what is schmaltz. I know that I am a goy. This is not why people like me, though. People like me because I do not need to use deodorant, as I demonstrate in the locker room before and after gym. Also, I can explain to them, for example, what is tofu (*der-voo*, we say at home). Their mothers invite me to taste-test their Chinese cooking.

"Very authentic." I try to be reassuring. After all, they're nice people, I like them. "De-lish." I have seconds. On the question of what we eat, though, I have to admit, "Well, no, it's different than that." I have thirds. "What my mom makes is home style, it's not in the cookbooks."

Not in the cookbooks! Everyone's jealous. Meanwhile, the big deal at home is when we have turkey pot pie. My sister Callie's the one introduced them — Mrs. Wilder's, they come in this green-and-brown box — and when we have them, we both get suddenly interested in helping out in the kitchen. You know, we stand in front of the oven and help them bake. Twenty-five minutes. She and I have a deal, though, to keep it secret from school, as everybody else thinks they're gross. We think they're a big improvement over authentic Chinese home cooking. Ox-tail soup — now that's gross. Stir-fried beef with tomatoes. One day I say, "You know Ma, I have never seen a stir-fried tomato in any Chinese restaurant we have ever been in, ever."

"In China," she says, real lofty, "we consider tomatoes are a delicacy."   15

"Ma," I say. "Tomatoes are *Italian*."

"No respect for elders." She wags her finger at me, but I can tell it's just to try and shame me into believing her. "I'm tell you, tomatoes *invented* in China."

"*Ma*."

"Is true. Like noodles. Invented in China."

"That's not what they said in *school*."   20

"In *China*," my mother counters, "we also eat tomatoes uncooked, like apple. And in summertime we slice them, and put some sugar on top."

"Are you sure?"

My mom says of course she's sure, and in the end I give in, even though she once told me that China was such a long time ago, a lot of things she can hardly remember. She said sometimes she has trouble remembering her characters, that sometimes she'll be writing a letter, just writing along, and all of a sudden she won't be sure if she should put four dots or three.

"So what do you do then?"

"Oh, I just make a little sloppy."   25

"You mean you *fudge*?"

She laughed then, but another time, when she was showing me how to write my name, and I said, just kidding, "Are you sure that's the right number of dots now?" she was hurt.

"I mean, of course you know," I said. "I mean, *oy*."

Meanwhile, what *I* know is that in the eighth grade, what people want to hear does not include how Chinese people eat sliced tomatoes with sugar on top. For a gross fact, it just isn't gross enough. On the other hand, the fact that somewhere in China somebody eats or has eaten or once ate living monkey brains — now that's conversation.

"They have these special tables," I say, "kind of like a giant collar. With a   30
hole in the middle, for the monkey's neck. They put the monkey in the collar, and then they cut off the top of its head."

"Whadda they use for cutting?"

I think. "Scalpels."

"*Scalpels?*" says Andy Kaplan.

"Kaplan, don't be dense," Barbara Gugelstein says. "The Chinese *invented* scalpels."

Once a friend said to me, You know, everybody is valued for something. She   35
explained how some people resented being valued for their looks; others resented being valued for their money. Wasn't it still better to be beautiful and rich than

ugly and poor, though? You should be just glad, she said, that you have something people value. It's like having a special talent, like being good at ice-skating,
or opera-singing. She said, You could probably make a career out of it.

Here's the irony: I am.

Anyway. I am ad-libbing my way through eighth grade, as I've described.
Until one bloomy spring day, I come in late to homeroom, and to my chagrin discover there's a new kid in class.

Chinese.

So what should I do, pretend to have to go to the girls' room, like Barbara
Gugelstein the day Andy Kaplan took his ID back? I sit down; I am so cool I
remind myself of Paul Newman. First thing I realize, though, is that no one looking at me is thinking of Paul Newman. The notes fly:

"I think he's cute."   40

"Who?" I write back. (I am still at an age, understand, when I believe a person can be saved by aplomb.)

"I don't think he talks English too good. Writes it either."

"Who?"

"They might have to put him behind a grade, so don't worry."

"He has a crush on you already, you could tell as soon as you walked in, he   45
turned kind of orangish."

I hope I'm not turning orangish as I deal with my mail, I could use a secretary. The second round starts:

"What do you mean who? Don't be weird. Didn't you *see* him??? Straight
back over your right shoulder!!!!"

I have to look; what else can I do? I think of certain tips I learned in Girl
Scouts about poise. I cross my ankles. I hold a pen in my hand. I sit up as though
I have a crown on my head. I swivel my head slowly, repeating to myself, *I could
be Miss America.*

"Miss Mona Chang."

Horror raises its hoary head.   50

"Notes, please."

Mrs. Mandeville's policy is to read all notes aloud.

I try to consider what Miss America would do, and see myself, back straight,
knees together, crying. Some inspiration. Cool Hand Luke, on the other hand,
would, quick, eat the evidence. And why not? I should yawn as I stand up and
boom, the notes are gone. All that's left is to explain is that it's an old Chinese reflex.

I shuffle up to the front of the room.

"One minute please," Mrs. Mandeville says.   55

I wait, noticing how large and plastic her mouth is.

She unfolds a piece of paper.

And I, Miss Mona Chang, who got almost straight A's her whole life except
in math and conduct, am about to start crying in front of everyone.

I am delivered out of hot Egypt by the bell. General pandemonium. Mrs.
Mandeville still has her hand clamped on my shoulder, though. And the next

thing I know, I'm holding the new boy's schedule. He's standing next to me like a big blank piece of paper. "This is Sherman," Mrs. Mandeville says.

"Hello," I say.   60

"*Non how a,*" I say.

I'm glad Barbara Gugelstein isn't there to see my Chinese in action.

"*Ji nu,*" I say. "*Shee veh.*"

Later I find out that his mother asked if there were any other Orientals in our grade. She had him put in my class on purpose. For now, though, he looks at me as though I'm much stranger than anything else he's seen so far. Is this because he understands I'm saying "soy sauce rice gruel" to him or because he doesn't?

"Sher-man," he says finally.   65

I look at his schedule card. Sherman Matsumoto. What kind of name is that for a nice Chinese boy?

(Later on, people ask me how I can tell Chinese from Japanese. I shrug. You just kind of know, I say. *Oy!*)

Sherman's got the sort of looks I think of as pretty-boy. Monsignor-black hair (not monk brown like mine), bouncy. Crayola eyebrows, one with a round bald spot in the middle of it, like a golf hole. I don't know how anybody can think of him as orangish; his skin looks white to me, with pink triangles hanging down the front of his cheeks like flags. Kind of delicate-looking, but the only truly uncool thing about him is that his spiral notebook has a picture of a kitty cat on it. A big white fluffy one, with a blue ribbon above each perky little ear. I get much opportunity to view this, as all the poor kid understands about life in junior high school is that he should follow me everywhere. It's embarrassing. On the other hand, he's obviously even more miserable than I am, so I try not to say anything. Give him a chance to adjust. We communicate by sign language, and by drawing pictures, which he's better at than I am; he puts in every last detail, even if it takes forever. I try to be patient.

A week of this. Finally I enlighten him. "You should get a new notebook."

His cheeks turn a shade of pink you mostly only see in hyacinths.   70

"Notebook." I point to his. I show him mine, which is psychedelic, with big purple and yellow stick-on flowers. I try to explain he should have one like this, only without the flowers. He nods enigmatically, and the next day brings me a notebook just like his, except that this cat sports pink bows instead of blue.

"Pret-ty," he says. "You."

He speaks English! I'm dumbfounded. Has he spoken it all this time? I consider: Pretty. You. What does that mean? Plus actually, he's said *plit-ty*, much as my parents would; I'm assuming he means pretty, but maybe he means pity. Pity. You.

"Jeez," I say finally.

"You are wel-come," he says.   75

I decorate the back of the notebook with stick-on flowers, and hold it so that these show when I walk through the halls. In class I mostly keep my book open. After all, the kid's so new; I think I really ought to have a heart. And for a live-long day nobody notices.

Then Barbara Gugelstein sidles up. "Matching notebooks, huh?"

I'm speechless.

"First comes love, then comes marriage, and then come chappies in a baby carriage."

"Barbara!"

"Get it?" she says. "Chinese Japs."   80

"Bar-*bra*," I say to get even.

"Just make sure he doesn't give you any *tea*," she says.

Are Sherman and I in love? Three days later, I hazard that we are. My thinking proceeds this way: I think he's cute, and I think he thinks I'm cute. On the other hand, we don't kiss and we don't exactly have fantastic conversations. Our talks *are* getting better, though. We started out, "This is a book." "Book." "This is a chair." "Chair." Advancing to, "What is this?" "This is a book." Now, for fun, he tests me.

"What is this?" he says.   85

"This is a book," I say, as if I'm the one who has to learn how to talk.

He claps. "Good!"

Meanwhile, people ask me all about him, I could be his press agent.

"No, he doesn't eat raw fish."

"No, his father wasn't a kamikaze pilot."   90

"No, he can't do karate."

"Are you sure?" somebody asks.

Indeed he doesn't know karate, but judo he does. I am hurt I'm not the one to find this out; the guys know from gym class. They line up to be flipped, he flips them all onto the floor, and after that he doesn't eat lunch at the girls' table with me anymore. I'm more or less glad. Meaning, when he was there, I never knew what to say. Now that he's gone, though, I seem to be stuck at the "This is a chair" level of conversation. Ancient Chinese eating habits have lost their cachet; all I get are more and more questions about me and Sherman. "I dunno," I'm saying all the time. *Are* we going out? We do stuff, it's true. For example, I take him to the department stores, explain to him who shops in Alexander's, who shops in Saks. I tell him my family's the type that shops in Alexander's. He says he's sorry. In Saks he gets lost; either that, or else I'm the lost one. (It's true I find him calmly waiting at the front door, hands behind his back, like a guard.) I take him to the candy store. I take him to the bagel store. Sherman is crazy about bagels. I explain to him that Lender's is gross, he should get his bagels from the bagel store. He says thank you.

"Are you going steady?" people want to know.

How can we go steady when he doesn't have an ID bracelet? On the other   95
hand, he brings me more presents than I think any girl's ever gotten before. Oranges. Flowers. A little bag of bagels. But what do they mean? Do they mean thank you, I enjoyed our trip; do they mean I like you; do they mean I decided I liked the Lender's better even if they are gross, you can have these? Sometimes I think he's acting on his mother's instructions. Also I know at least a couple of the

presents were supposed to go to our teachers. He told me that once and turned red. I figured it still might mean something that he didn't throw them out.

More and more now, we joke. Like, instead of "I'm thinking," he always says, "I'm sinking," which we both think is so funny, that all either one of us has to do is pretend to be drowning and the other one cracks up. And he tells me things — for example, that there are electric lights everywhere in Tokyo now.

"You mean you didn't have them before?"

"Everywhere now!" He's amazed too. "Since Olympics!"

"Olympics?"

"1960," he says proudly, and as proof, hums for me the Olympic theme song.   100
"You know?"

"Sure," I say, and hum with him happily. We could be a picture on a UNICEF poster. The only problem is that I don't really understand what the Olympics have to do with the modernization of Japan, any more than I get this other story he tells me, about that hole in his left eyebrow, which is from some time his father accidentally hit him with a lit cigarette. When Sherman was a baby. His father was drunk, having been out carousing; his mother was very mad but didn't say anything, just cleaned the whole house. Then his father was so ashamed he bowed to ask her forgiveness.

"Your mother cleaned the house?"

Sherman nods solemnly.

"And your father *bowed*?" I find this more astounding than anything I ever thought to make up. "That is so weird," I tell him.

"Weird," he agrees. "This I no forget, forever. *Father* bow to *mother*!"   105
We shake our heads.

As for the things he asks me, they're not topics I ever discussed before. Do I like it here? Of course I like it here, I was born here, I say. Am I Jewish? Jewish! I laugh. *Oy!* Am I American? "Sure I'm American," I say. "Everybody who's born here is American, and also some people who convert from what they were before. You could become American." But he says no, he could never. "Sure you could," I say. "You only have to learn some rules and speeches."

"But I Japanese," he says.

"You could become American anyway," I say. "Like I *could* become Jewish, if I wanted to. I'd just have to switch, that's all."

"But you Catholic," he says.   110

I think maybe he doesn't get what means switch.

I introduce him to Mrs. Wilder's turkey pot pies. "Gross?" he asks. I say they are, but we like them anyway. "Don't tell anybody." He promises. We bake them, eat them. While we're eating, he's drawing me pictures.

"This American," he says, and he draws something that looks like John Wayne. "This Jewish," he says, and draws something that looks like the Wicked Witch of the West, only male.

"I don't think so," I say.

He's undeterred. "This Japanese," he says, and draws a fair rendition of himself.   115
"This Chinese," he says, and draws what looks to be another fair rendition of himself.

"How can you tell them apart?"

"This way," he says, and he puts the picture of the Chinese so that it is look-ing at the pictures of the American and the Jew. The Japanese faces the wall. Then he draws another picture, of a Japanese flag, so that the Japanese has that to contemplate. "Chinese lost in department store," he says. "Japanese know how go." For fun, he then takes the Japanese flag and fastens it to the refrigerator door with magnets. "In school, in ceremony, we this way," he explains, and bows to the picture.

When my mother comes in, her face is so red that with the white wall behind her she looks a bit like the Japanese flag herself. Yet I get the feeling I bet-ter not say so. First she doesn't move. Then she snatches the flag off the refrigera-tor, so fast the magnets go flying. Two of them land on the stove. She crumples up the paper. She hisses at Sherman, *This is the U.S. of A., do you hear me!"*

Sherman hears her.

"You call your mother right now, tell her come pick you up."   120

He understands perfectly. *I,* on the other hand, am stymied. How can two people who don't really speak English understand each other better than I can understand them? "But Ma," I say.

"Don't *Ma* me," she says.

Later on she explains that World War II was in China, too. "Hitler," I say. "Nazis. Volkswagens." I know the Japanese were on the wrong side, because they bombed Pearl Harbor. My mother explains about before that. The Napkin Mas-sacre. "*Nan*-king," she corrects me.

"Are you sure?" I say. "In school, they said the war was about putting the Jews in ovens."

"Also about ovens."   125

"About both?"

"Both."

"That's not what they said in school."

"Just forget about school."

Forget about school? "I thought we moved here for the schools."   130

"We moved here," she says, "for your education."

Sometimes I have no idea what she's talking about.

"I like Sherman," I say after a while.

"He's nice boy," she agrees.

Meaning what? I would ask, except that my dad's just come home, which   135
means it's time to start talking about whether we should build a brick wall across the front of the lawn. Recently a car made it almost into our living room, which was so scary, the driver fainted and an ambulance had to come. "We should have discussion," my dad said after that. And so for about a week, every night we do.

"Are you just friends, or more than just friends?" Barbara Gugelstein is giving me the cross-ex.

"Maybe," I say.

"Come on," she says, "I told you *everything* about me and Andy."

I actually *am* trying to tell Barbara everything about Sherman, but everything turns out to be nothing. Meaning, I can't locate the conversation in what I have to say. Sherman and I go places, we talk, one time my mother threw him out of the house because of World War II.

"I think we're just friends," I say.   140

"You think or you're sure?"

Now that I do less of the talking at lunch, I notice more what other people talk about — cheerleading, who likes who, this place in White Plains to get earrings. On none of these topics am I an expert. Of course, I'm still friends with Barbara Gugelstein, but I notice Danielle Meyers has spun away to other groups.

Barbara's analysis goes this way: To be popular, you have to have big boobs, a note from your mother that lets you use her Lord and Taylor credit card, and a boyfriend. On the other hand, what's so wrong with being unpopular? "We'll get them in the end," she says. It's what her dad tells her. "Like they'll turn out too dumb to do their own investing, and then they'll get killed in fees and then they'll have to move to towns where the schools stink. And my dad should know," she winds up. "He's a broker."

"I guess," I say.

But the next thing I know, I have a true crush on Sherman Matsumoto. *Mis-*   145
ter Judo, the guys call him now, with real respect; and the more they call him that, the more I don't care that he carries a notebook with a cat on it.

I sigh. "Sherman."

"I thought you were just friends," says Barbara Gugelstein.

"We were," I say mysteriously. This, I've noticed, is how Danielle Meyers talks; everything's secret, she only lets out so much, it's like she didn't grow up with everybody telling her she had to share.

And here's the funny thing: The more I intimate that Sherman and I are more than just friends, the more it seems we actually are. It's the old imagination giving reality a nudge. When I start to blush, he starts to blush; we reach a point where we can hardly talk at all.

"Well, there's first base with tongue, and first base without," I tell Barbara   150
Gugelstein.

In fact, Sherman and I have brushed shoulders, which was equivalent to first base I was sure, maybe even second. I felt as though I'd turned into one huge shoulder; that's all I was, one huge shoulder. We not only didn't talk, we didn't breathe. But how can I tell Barbara Gugelstein that? So instead I say, "Well there's second base and second base."

Danielle Meyers is my friend again. She says, "I know exactly what you mean," just to make Barbara Gugelstein feel bad.

"Like *what* do I mean?" I say.

Danielle Meyers can't answer.

"You know what I think?" I tell Barbara the next day. "I think Danielle's giv-   155
ing us a line."

Barbara pulls thoughtfully on one of her pigtails.

If Sherman Matsumoto is never going to give me an ID to wear, he should at least get up the nerve to hold my hand. I don't think he sees this. I think of the story he told me about his parents, and in a synaptic firestorm realize we don't see the same things at all.

So one day, when we happen to brush shoulders again, I don't move away. He doesn't move away either. There we are. Like a pair of bleachers, pushed together but not quite matched up. After a while, I have to breathe, I can't help it. I breathe in such a way that our elbows start to touch too. We are in a crowd, waiting for a bus. I crane my neck to look at the sign that says where the bus is going; now our wrists are touching. Then it happens: He links his pinky around mine.

Is that holding hands? Later, in bed, I wonder all night. One finger, and not even the biggest one.

Sherman is leaving in a month. Already! I think, well, I suppose he will leave and we'll never even kiss. I guess that's all right. Just when I've resigned myself to it, though, we hold hands all five fingers. Once when we are at the bagel shop, then again in my parents' kitchen. Then, when we are at the playground, he kisses the back of my hand. 160

He does it again not too long after that, in White Plains.

I invest in a bottle of mouthwash.

Instead of moving on, though, he kisses the back of my hand again. And again. I try raising my hand, hoping he'll make the jump from my hand to my cheek. It's like trying to wheedle an inchworm out the window. You know, *This way, this way.*

All over the world, people have their own cultures. That's what we learned in social studies.

If we never kiss, I'm not going to take it personally. 165

It is the end of the school year. We've had parties. We've turned in our textbooks. Hooray! Outside the asphalt already steams if you spit on it. Sherman isn't leaving for another couple of days, though, and he comes to visit every morning, staying until the afternoon, when Callie comes home from her big-deal job as a bank teller. We drink Kool-Aid in the backyard and hold hands until they are sweaty and make smacking noises coming apart. He tells me how busy his parents are, getting ready for the move. His mother, particularly, is very tired. Mostly we are mournful.

The very last day we hold hands and do not let go. Our palms fill up with water like a blister. We do not care. We talk more than usual. How much airmail is to Japan, that kind of thing. Then suddenly he asks, will I marry him?

I'm only thirteen.

But when old? Sixteen? 170

If you come back to get me.

I come. Or you can come to Japan, be Japanese.

How can I be Japanese?

Like you become American. Switch.

He kisses me on the cheek, again and again and again.

His mother calls to say she's coming to get him. I cry. I tell him how I've 175 saved every present he's ever given me—the ruler, the pencils, the bags from the bagels, all the flower petals. I even have the orange peels from the oranges.

All?

I put them in a jar.

I'd show him, except that we're not allowed to go upstairs to my room. Anyway, something about the orange peels seems to choke him up too. *Mister* Judo, but I've gotten him in a soft spot. We are going together to the bathroom to get some toilet paper to wipe our eyes when poor tired Mrs. Matsumoto, driving a shiny new station wagon, skids up onto our lawn.

"Very sorry!"

We race outside.   180

"Very sorry!"

Mrs. Matsumoto is so short that about all we can see of her is a green cotton sun hat, with a big brim. It's tied on. The brim is trembling.

I hope my mom's not going to start yelling about World War II.

"Is all right, no trouble," she says, materializing on the steps behind me and Sherman. She's propped the screen door wide open; when I turn I see she's waving. "No trouble, no trouble!"

"No trouble, no trouble!" I echo, twirling a few times with relief.   185

Mrs. Matsumoto keeps apologizing; my mom keeps insisting she shouldn't feel bad, it was only some grass and a small tree. Crossing the lawn, she insists Mrs. Matsumoto get out of the car, even though it means trampling some lilies-of-the-valley. She insists that Mrs. Matsumoto come in for a cup of tea. Then she will not talk about anything unless Mrs. Matsumoto sits down, and unless she lets my mom prepare her a small snack. The coming in and the tea and the sitting down are settled pretty quickly, but they negotiate ferociously over the small snack, which Mrs. Matsumoto will not eat unless she can call Mr. Matsumoto. She makes the mistake of linking Mr. Matsumoto with a reparation of some sort, which my mom will not hear of.

"Please!"

"No no no no."

Back and forth it goes: "No no no no." "No no no no." "No no no no." What kind of conversation is that? I look at Sherman, who shrugs. Finally Mr. Matsumoto calls on his own, wondering where his wife is. He comes over in a taxi. He's a heavy-browed businessman, friendly but brisk—not at all a type you could imagine bowing to a lady with a taste for tie-on sunhats. My mom invites him in as if it's an idea she just this moment thought of. And would he maybe have some tea and a small snack?

Sherman and I sneak back outside for another farewell, by the side of the   190
house, behind the forsythia bushes. We hold hands. He kisses me on the cheek again, and then—just when I think he's finally going to kiss me on the lips—he kisses me on the neck.

Is this first base?

He does it more. Up and down, up and down. First it tickles, and then it doesn't. He has his eyes closed. I close my eyes too. He's hugging me. Up and down. Then down.

He's at my collarbone.

Still at my collarbone. Now his hand's on my ribs. So much for first base. More ribs. The idea of second base would probably make me nervous if he weren't on his way back to Japan and if I really thought we were going to get there. As it is, though, I'm not in much danger of wrecking my life on the shoals of passion; his unmoving hand feels more like a growth than a boyfriend. He has his whole face pressed to my neck skin so I can't tell his mouth from his nose. I think he may be licking me.

From indoors, a burst of adult laughter. My eyelids flutter. I start to try and   195
wiggle such that his hand will maybe budge upward.

Do I mean for my top blouse button to come accidentally undone?

He clenches his jaw, and when he opens his eyes, they're fixed on that button like it's a gnat that's been bothering him for far too long. He mutters in Japanese. If later in life he were to describe this as a pivotal moment in his youth, I would not be surprised. Holding the material as far from my body as possible, he buttons the button. Somehow we've landed up too close to the bushes.

What to tell Barbara Gugelstein? She says, "Tell me what were his last words. He must have said something last."

"I don't want to talk about it."

"Maybe he said, Good-bye?" she suggests. "Sayonara?" She means well.   200

"I don't want to talk about it."

"Aw, come on, I told you everything about . . ."

I say, "Because it's private, excuse me."

She stops, squints at me as though at a far-off face she's trying to make out. Then she nods and very lightly places her hand on my forearm.

The forsythia seemed to be stabbing us in the eyes. Sherman said, more or   205
less, *You will need to study how to switch.*

And I said, *I think you should switch. The way you do everything is weird.*

And he said, *You just want to tell everything to your friends. You just want to have boyfriend to become popular.*

Then he flipped me. Two swift moves, and I went sprawling through the air, a flailing confusion of soft human parts such as had no idea where the ground was.

It is the fall, and I am in high school, and still he hasn't written, so finally I write him.

I still have all your gifts, I write. *I don't talk so much as I used to. Although*   210
I am not exactly a mouse either. I don't care about being popular anymore. I swear. Are you happy to be back in Japan? I know I ruined everything. I was just try-ing to be entertaining. I miss you with all my heart, and hope I didn't ruin everything.

He writes back, *You will never be Japanese.*

I throw all the orange peels out that day. Some of them, it turns out, were moldy anyway. I tell my mother I want to move to Chinatown.

"Chinatown!" she says.

I don't know why I suggested it.

"What's the matter?" she says. "Still boy-crazy? That Sherman?"   215

"No."

"Too much homework?"

I don't answer.

"Forget about school."

Later she tells me if I don't like school, I don't have to go everyday. Some   220
days I can stay home.

"Stay home?" In Yonkers, Callie and I used to stay home all the time, but
that was because the schools there were *waste of time*.

"No good for a girl be too smart anyway."

For a long time I think about Sherman. But after a while I don't think about
him so much as I just keep seeing myself flipped onto the ground, lying there
shocked as the Matsumotos get ready to leave. My head has hit a rock; my brain
aches as though it's been shoved to some new place in my skull. Otherwise I am
okay. I see the forsythia, all those whippy branches, and can't believe how many
leaves there are on a bush — every one green and perky and durably itself. And
past them, real sky. I try to remember about why the sky's blue, even though this
one's gone the kind of indescribable grey you associate with the insides of old
shoes. I smell grass. Probably I have grass stains all over my back. I hear my
mother calling through the back door, "Mon-a! Everyone leaving now," and "Not
coming to say good-bye?" I hear Mr. and Mrs. Matsumoto bowing as they leave —
or at least I hear the embarrassment in my mother's voice as they bow. I hear their
car start. I hear Mrs. Matsumoto directing Mr. Matsumoto how to back off the
lawn so as not to rip any more of it up. I feel the back of my head for blood — just
a little. I hear their chug-chug grow fainter and fainter, until it has faded into the
whuzz-whuzz of all the other cars. I hear my mom singing, "*Mon*-a! *Mon*-a!"
until my dad comes home. Doors open and shut. I see myself standing up, brushing myself off so I'll have less explaining to do if she comes out to look for me.
Grass stains — just like I thought. I see myself walking around the house, going
over to have a look at our churned-up yard. It looks pretty sad, two big brown
tracks, right through the irises and the lilies of the valley, and that was a new dogwood we'd just planted. Lying there like that. I hear myself thinking about my
father, having to go dig it up all over again. Adjusting. I think how we probably
ought to put up that brick wall. And sure enough, when I go inside, no one's
thinking about me, or that little bit of blood at the back of my head, or the grass
stains. That's what they're talking about — that wall. Again. My mom doesn't
think it'll do any good, but my dad thinks we should give it a try. Should we or
shouldn't we? How high? How thick? What will the neighbors say? I plop myself
down on a hard chair. And all I can think is, we are the complete only family that
has to worry about this. If I could, I'd switch everything to be different. But since I
can't, I might as well sit here at the table for a while, discussing what I know how
to discuss. I nod and listen to the rest.   [1990]

THINKING ABOUT THE TEXT

1. Discuss how Jen's title can be applied to her story. Where in the story do you find instances of *switching*, efforts toward it, or failures of it? Do you come away believing that people can *switch*? Note how you are defining the term as you consider this question.

2. Going by what Mona reports about her school community, what are its main values and practices? What does someone have to do to fit in? How much cultural diversity does it allow? Compare it with those you have known as a student.

3. Mona doesn't always tell the truth about herself to others. Do you therefore consider her morally flawed? Why, or why not?

4. Although much of this story is comic, the ending is pretty serious: Mona and Sherman apparently break up forever. Do you accept this "switch" in tone, or do you think Jen should have kept a comic one? What does the ending lead you to conclude about Mona? About Sherman?

5. When she used this story for the first chapter of her novel *Mona in the Promised Land*, Jen made one major change in it. Whereas Mona narrates the story, the chapter (and the entire novel) uses third-person narration: References to "I" become references to "Mona." Would this change significantly affect your reaction to the story? Explain.

MARGARET ATWOOD
The Man from Mars

Born in Ottawa, Ontario, in 1939, Margaret Atwood graduated from the University of Toronto. Later, she pursued further education at Radcliffe College and Harvard University. For most of her life, though, she has lived in Canada and currently is a resident of Toronto. The author of over twenty-five books, Atwood has been especially acclaimed for her novels about the struggles of women, including Surfacing *(1972),* Life Before Man *(1979),* The Handmaid's Tale *(1986),* Cat's Eye *(1989),* The Robber Bride *(1993), and* Alias Grace *(1996). She has long been active in the women's movement as well as in campaigns for human rights. Besides her novels, Atwood has published several collections of poetry and short fiction. The following story first appeared in a 1977 issue of* Ontario Review; *Atwood then included it in her 1982 book* Dancing Girls and Other Stories.

A long time ago Christine was walking through the park. She was still wearing her tennis dress; she hadn't had time to shower and change, and her hair was held back with an elastic band. Her chunky reddish face, exposed with no softening fringe, looked like a Russian peasant's, but without the elastic band the hair got in her eyes. The afternoon was too hot for April; the indoor courts had been steaming, her skin felt poached.

The sun had brought the old men out from wherever they spent the winter: she had read a story recently about one who lived for three years in a manhole. They sat weedily on the benches or lay on the grass with their heads on squares of used newspaper. As she passed, their wrinkled toadstool faces drifted towards her, drawn by the movement of her body, then floated away again, uninterested.

The squirrels were out, too, foraging; two or three of them moved towards her in darts and pauses, eyes fixed on her expectantly, mouths with the ratlike receding chins open to show the yellowed front teeth. Christine walked faster, she had nothing to give them. People shouldn't feed them, she thought; it makes them anxious and they get mangy.

Halfway across the park she stopped to take off her cardigan. As she bent over to pick up her tennis racquet again someone touched her on her freshly bared arm. Christine seldom screamed; she straightened up suddenly, gripping the handle of her racquet. It was not one of the old men, however: it was a dark-haired boy of twelve or so.

"Excuse me," he said, "I search for Economics Building. Is it there?" He   5
motioned towards the west.

Christine looked at him more closely. She had been mistaken: he was not young, just short. He came a little above her shoulder, but then, she was above the average height; "statuesque," her mother called it when she was straining. He was also what was referred to in their family as "a person from another culture": oriental without a doubt, though perhaps not Chinese. Christine judged he must be a foreign student and gave him her official welcoming smile. In high school she had been president of the United Nations Club; that year her school had been picked to represent the Egyptian delegation at the Mock Assembly. It had been an unpopular assignment — nobody wanted to be the Arabs — but she had seen it through. She had made rather a good speech about the Palestinian refugees.

"Yes," she said, "that's it over there. The one with the flat roof. See it?"

The man had been smiling nervously at her the whole time. He was wearing glasses with transparent plastic rims, through which his eyes bulged up at her as though through a goldfish bowl. He had not followed where she was pointing. Instead he thrust towards her a small pad of green paper and a ball-point pen.

"You make map," he said.

Christine set down her tennis racquet and drew a careful map. "We are   10
here," she said, pronouncing distinctly. "You go this way. The building is here." She indicated the route with a dotted line and an X. The man leaned close to her, watching the progress of the map attentively; he smelled of cooked cauliflower and an unfamiliar brand of hair grease. When she had finished Christine handed the paper and pen back to him with a terminal smile.

"Wait," the man said. He tore the piece of paper with the map off the pad, folded it carefully and put it in his jacket pocket; the jacket sleeves came down over his wrists and had threads at the edges. He began to write something; she noticed with a slight feeling of revulsion that his nails and the ends of his fingers were so badly bitten they seemed almost deformed. Several of his fingers were blue from the leaky ball-point.

"Here is my name," he said, holding the pad out to her.

Christine read an odd assemblage of Gs, Ys and Ns, neatly printed in block letters. "Thank you," she said.

"You now write *your* name," he said, extending the pen.

Christine hesitated. If this had been a person from her own culture she   15 would have thought he was trying to pick her up. But then, people from her own culture never tried to pick her up, she was too big. The only one who had made the attempt was the Moroccan waiter at the beer parlour where they sometimes went after meetings, and he had been direct. He had just intercepted her on the way to the Ladies' Room and asked and she said no; that had been that. This man was not a waiter though, but a student; she didn't want to offend him. In his culture, whatever it was, this exchange of names on pieces of paper was probably a formal politeness, like saying thank you. She took the pen from him.

"That is a very pleasant name," he said. He folded the paper and placed it in his jacket pocket with the map.

Christine felt she had done her duty. "Well, goodbye," she said. "It was nice to have met you." She bent for her tennis racquet but he had already stooped and retrieved it and was holding it with both hands in front of him, like a captured banner.

"I carry this for you."

"Oh no, please. Don't bother, I am in a hurry," she said, articulating clearly. Deprived of her tennis racquet she felt weaponless. He started to saunter along the path; he was not nervous at all now, he seemed completely at ease.

"*Vous parlez français?*" he asked conversationally.   20

"*Oui, un petit peu,*" she said. "Not very well." How am I going to get my racquet away from him without being rude? she was wondering.

"*Mais vous avez un bel accent.*" His eyes goggled at her through the glasses: was he being flirtatious? She was well aware that her accent was wretched.

"Look," she said, for the first time letting her impatience show, "I really have to go. Give me my racquet, please."

He quickened his pace but gave no sign of returning the racquet. "Where you are going?"

"Home," she said. "My house."   25

"I go with you now," he said hopefully.

"No," she said: she would have to be firm with him. She made a lunge and got a grip on her racquet; after a brief tug of war it came free.

"Goodbye," she said, turning away from his puzzled face and setting off at what she hoped was a discouraging jog-trot. It was like walking away from a growling dog: you shouldn't let on you were frightened. Why should she be frightened anyway? He was only half her size and she had the tennis racquet, there was nothing he could do to her.

Although she did not look back she could tell he was still following. Let there be a streetcar, she thought, and there was one, but it was far down the line, stuck behind a red light. He appeared at her side, breathing audibly, a moment after she reached the stop. She gazed ahead, rigid.

"You are my friend," he said tentatively.   30

Christine relented: he hadn't been trying to pick her up after all, he was a stranger, he just wanted to meet some of the local people; in his place she would have wanted the same thing.

"Yes," she said, doling him out a smile.

"That is good," he said. "My country is very far."

Christine couldn't think of an apt reply. "That's interesting," she said. *"Trés interessant."* The streetcar was coming at last; she opened her purse and got out a ticket.

"I go with you now," he said. His hand clamped on her arm above the elbow.   35

"You . . . stay . . . *here,*" Christine said, resisting the impulse to shout but pausing between each word as though for a deaf person. She detached his hand—his hold was quite feeble and could not compete with her tennis biceps— and leapt off the curb and up the streetcar steps, hearing with relief the doors grind shut behind her. Inside the car and a block away she permitted herself a glance out a side window. He was standing where she had left him; he seemed to be writing something on his little pad of paper.

When she reached home she had only time for a snack, and even then she was almost late for the Debating Society. The topic was, "Resolved: That War Is Obsolete." Her team took the affirmative and won.

Christine came out of her last examination feeling depressed. It was not the exam that depressed her but the fact that it was the last one: it meant the end of the school year. She dropped into the coffee shop as usual, then went home early because there didn't seem to be anything else to do.

"Is that you, dear?" her mother called from the living room. She must have heard the front door close. Christine went in and flopped on the sofa, disturbing the neat pattern of cushions.

"How was your exam, dear?" her mother asked.   40

"Fine," said Christine flatly. It had been fine; she had passed. She was not a brilliant student, she knew that, but she was conscientious. Her professors always wrote things like "A serious attempt" and "Well thought out but perhaps lacking in élan" on her term papers; they gave her Bs, the occasional B+. She was taking Political Science and Economics, and hoped for a job with the Government after she graduated; with her father's connections she had a good chance.

"That's nice."

Christine felt, resentfully, that her mother had only a hazy idea of what an exam was. She was arranging gladioli in a vase; she had rubber gloves on to protect her hands as she always did when engaged in what she called "housework." As far as Christine could tell her housework consisted of arranging flowers in vases: daffodils and tulips and hyacinths through gladioli, irises and roses, all the way to asters and mums. Sometimes she cooked, elegantly and with chafing-dishes, but she thought of it as a hobby. The girl did everything else. Christine thought it faintly sinful to have a girl. The only ones available now were either foreign or pregnant; their expressions usually suggested they were being taken advantage of somehow. But her mother asked what they would do otherwise; they'd either have to go into a Home or stay in their own countries, and Christine had to agree this was probably true. It was hard, anyway, to argue with her mother. She was so delicate, so preserved-looking, a harsh breath would scratch the finish.

"An interesting young man phoned today," her mother said. She had finished the gladioli and was taking off her rubber gloves. "He asked to speak with you and when I said you weren't in we had quite a little chat. You didn't tell me about him, dear." She put on the glasses which she wore on a decorative chain around her neck, a signal that she was in her modern, intelligent mood rather than her old-fashioned whimsical one.

"Did he leave his name?" Christine asked. She knew a lot of young men but 45 they didn't often call her; they conducted their business with her in the coffee shop or after meetings.

"He's a person from another culture. He said he would call back later."

Christine had to think a moment. She was vaguely acquainted with several people from other cultures, Britain mostly; they belonged to the Debating Society.

"He's studying Philosophy in Montreal," her mother prompted. "He sounded French."

Christine began to remember the man in the park. "I don't think he's French, exactly," she said.

Her mother had taken off her glasses again and was poking absentmindedly 50 at a bent gladiolus. "Well, he sounded French." She meditated, flowery sceptre in hand. "I think it would be nice if you had him to tea."

Christine's mother did her best. She had two other daughters, both of whom took after her. They were beautiful; one was well married already and the other would clearly have no trouble. Her friends consoled her about Christine by saying, "She's not fat, she's just big-boned, it's the father's side," and "Christine is so healthy." Her other daughters had never gotten involved in activities when they were at school, but since Christine could not possibly ever be beautiful even if she took off weight, it was just as well she was so athletic and political, it was a good thing she had interests. Christine's mother tried to encourage her interests whenever possible. Christine could tell when she was making an extra effort, there was a reproachful edge to her voice.

She knew her mother expected enthusiasm but she could not supply it. "I don't know, I'll have to see," she said dubiously.

"You look tired, darling," said her mother. "Perhaps you'd like a glass of milk."

Christine was in the bathtub when the phone rang. She was not prone to fantasy but when she was in the bathtub she often pretended she was a dolphin, a game left over from one of the girls who used to bathe her when she was small. Her mother was being bell-voiced and gracious in the hall; then there was a tap at the door.

"It's that nice young French student, Christine," her mother said.   55

"Tell him I'm in the bathtub," Christine said, louder than necessary. "He isn't French."

She could hear her mother frowning. "That wouldn't be very polite, Christine. I don't think he'd understand."

"Oh, all right," Christine said. She heaved herself out of the bathtub, swathed her pink bulk in a towel and splattered to the phone.

"Hello," she said gruffly. At a distance he was not pathetic, he was a nuisance. She could not imagine how he had tracked her down: most likely he went through the phone book, calling all the numbers with her last name until he hit on the right one.

"It is your friend."   60

"I know," she said. "How are you?"

"I am very fine." There was a long pause, during which Christine had a vicious urge to say, "Well goodbye then," and hang up; but she was aware of her mother poised figurine-like in her bedroom doorway. Then he said, "I hope you also are very fine."

"Yes," said Christine. She wasn't going to participate.

"I come to tea," he said.

This took Christine by surprise. "You do?"   65

"Your pleasant mother ask me. I come Thursday, four o'clock."

"Oh," Christine said, ungraciously.

"See you then," he said, with the conscious pride of one who has mastered a difficult idiom.

Christine set down the phone and went along the hall. Her mother was in her study, sitting innocently at her writing desk.

"Did you ask him to tea on Thursday?"   70

"Not exactly, dear," her mother said. "I did mention he might come round to tea *some*time, though."

"Well, he's coming Thursday. Four o'clock."

"What's wrong with that?" her mother said serenely. "I think it's a very nice gesture for us to make. I do think you might try to be a little more co-operative." She was pleased with herself.

"Since you invited him," said Christine, "you can bloody well stick around and help me entertain him. I don't want to be left making nice gestures all by myself."

"Christine, *dear*," her mother said, above being shocked. "You ought to put   75
on your dressing gown, you'll catch a chill."

After sulking for an hour Christine tried to think of the tea as a cross between an examination and an executive meeting: not enjoyable, certainly, but to be got through as tactfully as possible. And it *was* a nice gesture. When the cakes her mother had ordered arrived from The Patisserie on Thursday morning she began to feel slightly festive; she even resolved to put on a dress, a good one, instead of a skirt and blouse. After all, she had nothing against him, except the memory of the way he had grabbed her tennis racquet and then her arm. She suppressed a quick impossible vision of herself pursued around the living room, fending him off with thrown sofa cushions and vases of gladioli; nevertheless she told the girl they would have tea in the garden. It would be a treat for him, and there was more space outdoors.

She had suspected her mother would dodge the tea, would contrive to be going out just as he was arriving: that way she could size him up and then leave them alone together. She had done things like that to Christine before; the excuse this time was the Symphony Committee. Sure enough, her mother carefully mislaid her gloves and located them with a faked murmur of joy when the doorbell rang. Christine relished for weeks afterwards the image of her mother's dropped jaw and flawless recovery when he was introduced: he wasn't quite the foreign potentate her optimistic, veil-fragile mind had concocted.

He was prepared for celebration. He had slicked on so much hair cream that his head seemed to be covered with a tight black patent-leather cap, and he had cut the threads off his jacket sleeves. His orange tie was overpoweringly splendid. Christine noticed, however, as he shook her mother's suddenly braced white glove that the ball-point ink on his fingers was indelible. His face had broken out, possibly in anticipation of the delights in store for him; he had a tiny camera slung over his shoulder and was smoking an exotic-smelling cigarette.

Christine led him through the cool flowery softly padded living room and out by the French doors into the garden. "You sit here," she said. "I will have the girl bring tea."

This girl was from the West Indies: Christine's parents had been enraptured   80
with her when they were down at Christmas and had brought her back with them. Since that time she had become pregnant, but Christine's mother had not dismissed her. She said she was slightly disappointed but what could you expect, and she didn't see any real difference between a girl who was pregnant before you hired her and one who got that way afterwards. She prided herself on her tolerance; also there was a scarcity of girls. Strangely enough, the girl became progressively less easy to get along with. Either she did not share Christine's mother's view of her own generosity, or she felt she had gotten away with something and was therefore free to indulge in contempt. At first Christine had tried to treat her as an equal. "Don't call me 'Miss Christine,'" she had said with an imitation of light, comradely laughter. "What you want me to call you then?" the girl had said, scowling. They had begun to have brief, surly arguments in the kitchen, which Christine decided were like the arguments between one servant and another: her mother's attitude towards each of them was similar, they were not altogether satisfactory but they would have to do.

The cakes, glossy with icing, were set out on a plate and the teapot was standing ready; on the counter the electric kettle boiled. Christine headed for it, but the girl, till then sitting with her elbows on the kitchen table and watching her expressionlessly, made a dash and intercepted her. Christine waited until she had poured the water into the pot. Then, "I'll carry it out, Elvira," she said. She had just decided she didn't want the girl to see her visitor's orange tie; already, she knew, her position in the girl's eyes had suffered because no one had yet attempted to get *her* pregnant.

"What you think they pay me for, Miss Christine?" the girl said insolently. She swung towards the garden with the tray; Christine trailed her, feeling lumpish and awkward. The girl was at least as big as she was but in a different way.

"Thank you, Elvira," Christine said when the tray was in place. The girl departed without a word, casting a disdainful backward glance at the frayed jacket sleeves, the stained fingers. Christine was now determined to be especially kind to him.

"You are very rich," he said.

"No," Christine protested, shaking her bead, "we're not." She had never   85
thought of her family as rich; it was one of her father's sayings that nobody made any money with the Government.

"Yes," he repeated, "You are very rich." He sat back in his lawn chair, gazing about him as though dazed.

Christine set his cup of tea in front of him. She wasn't in the habit of paying much attention to the house or the garden; they were nothing special, far from being the largest on the street; other people took care of them. But now she looked where he was looking, seeing it all as though from a different height: the long expanses, the border flowers blazing in the early-summer sunlight, the flagged patio and walks, the high walls and the silence.

He came back to her face, sighing a little. "My English is not good," he said, "but I improve."

"You do," Christine said, nodding encouragement.

He took sips of his tea, quickly and tenderly, as though afraid of injuring the   90
cup. "I like to stay here."

Christine passed him the cakes. He took only one, making a slight face as he ate it; but he had several more cups of tea while she finished the cakes. She managed to find out from him that he had come over on a church fellowship—she could not decode the denomination—and was studying Philosophy or Theology, or possibly both. She was feeling well-disposed towards him: he had behaved himself, he had caused her no inconvenience.

The teapot was at last empty. He sat up straight in his chair, as though alerted by a soundless gong. "You look this way, please," he said. Christine saw that he had placed his miniature camera on the stone sundial her mother had shipped back from England two years before. He wanted to take her picture. She was flattered, and settled herself to pose, smiling evenly.

He took off his glasses and laid them beside his plate. For a moment she saw his myopic, unprotected eyes turned towards her, with something tremulous and confiding in them she wanted to close herself off from knowing about. Then he went over and did something to the camera, his back to her. The next instant he was crouched beside her, his arm around her waist as far as it could reach, his other hand covering her own hands which she had folded in her lap, his cheek jammed up against hers. She was too startled to move. The camera clicked.

He stood up at once and replaced his glasses, which glittered now with a sad triumph. "Thank you, miss," he said to her. "I go now." He slung the camera back over his shoulder, keeping his hand on it as though to hold the lid on and prevent escape. "I send to my family; they will like."

He was out the gate and gone before Christine had recovered; then she   95
laughed. She had been afraid he would attack her, she could admit it now, and
he had; but not in the usual way. He had raped, *rapeo, rapere, rapui, to seize and
carry off*, not herself but her celluloid image, and incidentally that of the silver tea
service, which glinted mockingly at her as the girl bore it away, carrying it regally,
the insignia, the official jewels.

Christine spent the summer as she had for the past three years: she was the
sailing instructress at an expensive all-girls camp near Algonquin Park. She had
been a camper there, everything was familiar to her; she sailed almost better than
she played tennis.

The second week she got a letter from him, postmarked Montreal and for-
warded from her home address. It was printed in block letters on a piece of
the green paper, two or three sentences. It began, "I hope you are well," then
described the weather in monosyllables and ended, "I am fine." It was signed,
"Your friend." Each week she got another of these letters, more or less identical.
In one of them a colour print was enclosed: himself, slightly cross-eyed and grinning hilariously, even more spindly than she remembered him against her billowing draperies, flowers exploding around them like firecrackers, one of his
hands an equivocal blur in her lap, the other out of sight; on her own face, astonishment and outrage, as though he was sticking her in the behind with his hidden
thumb.

She answered the first letter, but after that the seniors were in training for the
races. At the end of the summer, packing to go home, she threw all the letters
away.

When she had been back for several weeks she received another of the green
letters. This time there was a return address printed at the top which Christine
noted with foreboding was in her own city. Every day she waited for the phone to
ring; she was so certain his first attempt at contact would be a disembodied voice
that when he came upon her abruptly in midcampus she was unprepared.

"How are you?"   100

His smile was the same, but everything else about him had deteriorated. He
was, if possible, thinner; his jacket sleeves had sprouted a lush new crop of
threads, as though to conceal hands now so badly bitten they appeared to have
been gnawed by rodents. His hair fell over his eyes, uncut, ungreased; his eyes in
the hollowed face, a delicate triangle of skin stretched on bone, jumped behind
his glasses like hooded fish. He had the end of a cigarette in the corner of his
mouth, and as they walked he lit a new one from it.

"I'm fine," Christine said. She was thinking, I'm not going to get involved
again, enough is enough, I've done my bit for internationalism. "How are you?"

"I live here now," he said. "Maybe I study Economics."

"That's nice." He didn't sound as though he was enrolled anywhere.

"I come to see you."   105

Christine didn't know whether he meant he had left Montreal in order to be
near her or just wanted to visit her at her house as he had done in the spring;

either way she refused to be implicated. They were outside the Political Science Building. "I have a class here," she said. "Goodbye." She was being callous, she realized that, but a quick chop was more merciful in the long run, that was what her beautiful sisters used to say.

Afterwards she decided it had been stupid of her to let him find out where her class was. Though a timetable was posted in each of the colleges: all he had to do was look her up and record her every probable movement in block letters on his green notepad. After that day he never left her alone.

Initially he waited outside the lecture rooms for her to come out. She said hello to him curtly at first and kept on going, but this didn't work; he followed her at a distance, smiling his changeless smile. Then she stopped speaking altogether and pretended to ignore him, but it made no difference, he followed her anyway. The fact that she was in some way afraid of him—or was it just embarrassment?—seemed only to encourage him. Her friends started to notice, asking her who he was and why he was tagging along behind her; she could hardly answer because she hardly knew.

As the weekdays passed and he showed no signs of letting up, she began to jog-trot between classes, finally to run. He was tireless, and had an amazing wind for one who smoked so heavily: he would speed along behind her, keeping the distance between them the same, as though he were a pull-toy attached to her by a string. She was aware of the ridiculous spectacle they must make, galloping across campus, something out of a cartoon short, a lumbering elephant stampeded by a smiling, emaciated mouse, both of them locked in the classic pattern of comic pursuit and flight; but she found that to race made her less nervous than to walk sedately, the skin on the back of her neck crawling with the feel of his eyes on it. At least she could use her muscles. She worked out routines, escapes: she would dash in the front door of the Ladies' Room in the coffee shop and out the back door, and he would lose the trail, until he discovered the other entrance. She would try to shake him by detours through baffling archways and corridors, but he seemed as familiar with the architectural mazes as she was herself. As a last refuge she could head for the women's dormitory and watch from safety as he was skidded to a halt by the receptionist's austere voice: men were not allowed past the entrance.

Lunch became difficult. She would be sitting, usually with other members   110
of the Debating Society, just digging nicely into a sandwich, when he would appear suddenly as though he'd come up through an unseen manhole. She then had the choice of barging out through the crowded cafeteria, sandwich half-eaten, or finishing her lunch with him standing behind her chair, everyone at the table acutely aware of him, the conversation stilting and dwindling. Her friends learned to spot him from a distance; they posted lookouts. "Here he comes," they would whisper, helping her collect her belongings for the sprint they knew would follow.

Several times she got tired of running and turned to confront him. "What do you want?" she would ask, glowering belligerently down at him, almost clenching her fists; she felt like shaking him, hitting him.

"I wish to talk with you."

"Well, here I am," she would say. "What do you want to talk about?"

But he would say nothing; he would stand in front of her, shifting his feet, smiling perhaps apologetically (though she could never pinpoint the exact tone of that smile, chewed lips stretched apart over the nicotine-yellowed teeth, rising at the corners, flesh held stiffly in place for an invisible photographer), his eyes jerking from one part of her face to another as though he saw her in fragments.

Annoying and tedious though it was, his pursuit of her had an odd result: 115
mysterious in itself, it rendered her equally mysterious. No one had ever found Christine mysterious before. To her parents she was a beefy heavyweight, a plodder, lacking in flair, ordinary as bread. To her sisters she was the plain one, treated with an indulgence they did not give to each other: they did not fear her as a rival. To her male friends she was the one who could be relied on. She was helpful and a hard worker, always good for a game of tennis with the athletes among them. They invited her along to drink beer with them so they could get into the cleaner, more desirable Ladies and Escorts side of the beer parlour, taking it for granted she would buy her share of the rounds. In moments of stress they confided to her their problems with women. There was nothing devious about her and nothing interesting.

Christine had always agreed with these estimates of herself. In childhood she had identified with the false bride or the ugly sister; whenever a story had begun, "Once there was a maiden as beautiful as she was good," she had known it wasn't her. That was just how it was, but it wasn't so bad. Her parents never expected her to be a brilliant social success and weren't overly disappointed when she wasn't. She was spared the manoeuvring and anxiety she witnessed among others her age, and she even had a kind of special position among men: she was an exception, she fitted none of the categories they commonly used when talking about girls; she wasn't a cock-teaser, a cold fish, an easy lay or a snarky bitch; she was an honorary person. She had grown to share their contempt for most women.

Now, however, there was something about her that could not be explained. A man was chasing her, a peculiar sort of man, granted, but still a man, and he was without doubt attracted to her, he couldn't leave her alone. Other men examined her more closely than they ever had, appraising her, trying to find out what it was those twitching bespectacled eyes saw in her. They started to ask her out, though they returned from these excursions with their curiosity unsatisfied, the secret of her charm still intact. Her opaque dumpling face, her solid bear-shaped body became for them parts of a riddle no one could solve. Christine sensed this. In the bathtub she no longer imagined she was a dolphin; instead she imagined she was an elusive water-nixie, or sometimes, in moments of audacity, Marilyn Monroe. The daily chase was becoming a habit; she even looked forward to it. In addition to its other benefits she was losing weight.

All these weeks he had never phoned her or turned up at the house. He must have decided however that his tactics were not having the desired result, or perhaps he sensed she was becoming bored. The phone began to ring in the early morning or late at night when he could be sure she would be there. Sometimes he would simply breathe (she could recognize, or thought she could, the quality of his breathing), in which case she would hang up. Occasionally he would say

again that he wanted to talk to her, but even when she gave him lots of time nothing else would follow. Then he extended his range: she would see him on her
streetcar, smiling at her silently from a seat never closer than three away; she
could feel him tracking her down her own street, though when she would break
her resolve to pay no attention and would glance back he would be invisible or in
the act of hiding behind a tree or hedge.

Among crowds of people and in daylight she had not really been afraid of
him; she was stronger than he was and he had made no recent attempt to touch
her. But the days were growing shorter and colder, it was almost November.
Often she was arriving home in twilight or a darkness broken only by the feeble
orange streetlamps. She brooded over the possibility of razors, knives, guns; by
acquiring a weapon he could quickly turn the odds against her. She avoided
wearing scarves, remembering the newspaper stories about girls who had been
strangled by them. Putting on her nylons in the morning gave her a funny feeling. Her body seemed to have diminished, to have become smaller than his.

Was he deranged, was he a sex maniac? He seemed so harmless, yet it was   120
that kind who often went berserk in the end. She pictured those ragged fingers at
her throat, tearing at her clothes, though she could not think of herself as screaming. Parked cars, the shrubberies near her house, the driveways on either side of
it, changed as she passed them from unnoticed background to sinister shadowed
foreground, every detail distinct and harsh: they were places a man might
crouch, leap out from. Yet every time she saw him in the clear light of morning or
afternoon (for he still continued his old methods of pursuit), his aging jacket and
jittery eyes convinced her that it was she herself who was the tormentor, the persecutor. She was in some sense responsible; from the folds and crevices of the
body she had treated for so long as a reliable machine was emanating, against her
will, some potent invisible odour, like a dog's in heat or a female moth's, that
made him unable to stop following her.

Her mother, who had been too preoccupied with the unavoidable fall entertaining to pay much attention to the number of phone calls Christine was getting
or to the hired girl's complaints of a man who hung up without speaking,
announced that she was flying down to New York for the weekend; her father
decided to go too. Christine panicked: she saw herself in the bathtub with her
throat slit, the blood drooling out of her neck and running in a little spiral down
the drain (for by this time she believed he could walk through walls, could be
everywhere at once). The girl would do nothing to help; she might even stand in
the bathroom door with her arms folded, watching. Christine arranged to spend
the weekend at her married sister's.

When she arrived back Sunday evening she found the girl close to hysterics.
She said that on Saturday she had gone to pull the curtains across the French
doors at dusk and had found a strangely contorted face, a man's face, pressed
against the glass, staring in at her from the garden. She claimed she had fainted
and had almost had her baby a month too early right there on the living-room
carpet. Then she had called the police. He was gone by the time they got there
but she had recognized him from the afternoon of the tea; she had informed
them he was a friend of Christine's.

They called Monday evening to investigate, two of them. They were very polite, they knew who Christine's father was. Her father greeted them heartily; her mother hovered in the background, fidgeting with her porcelain hands, letting them see how frail and worried she was. She didn't like having them in the living room but they were necessary.

Christine had to admit he'd been following her around. She was relieved he'd been discovered, relieved also that she hadn't been the one to tell, though if he'd been a citizen of the country she would have called the police a long time ago. She insisted he was not dangerous, he had never hurt her.

"That kind don't hurt you," one of the policemen said. "They just kill you.   125
You're lucky you aren't dead."

"Nut cases," the other one said.

Her mother volunteered that the thing about people from another culture was that you could never tell whether they were insane or not because their ways were so different. The policemen agreed with her, deferential but also condescending, as though she was a royal halfwit who had to be humoured.

"You know where he lives?" the first policeman asked. Christine had long ago torn up the letter with his address on it; she shook her head.

"We'll have to pick him up tomorrow then," he said. "Think you can keep him talking outside your class if he's waiting for you?"

After questioning her they held a murmured conversation with her father in   130
the front hall. The girl, clearing away the coffee cups, said if they didn't lock him up she was leaving, she wasn't going to be scared half out of her skin like that again.

Next day when Christine came out of her Modern History lecture he was there, right on schedule. He seemed puzzled when she did not begin to run. She approached him, her heart thumping with treachery and the prospect of freedom. Her body was back to its usual size; she felt herself a giantess, self-controlled, invulnerable.

"How are you?" she asked, smiling brightly.

He looked at her with distrust.

"How have you been?" she ventured again. His own perennial smile faded; he took a step back from her.

"This the one?" said the policeman, popping out from behind a notice board   135
like a Keystone Cop and laying a competent hand on the worn jacket shoulder. The other policeman lounged in the background; force would not be required.

"Don't *do* anything to him," she pleaded as they took him away. They nodded and grinned, respectful, scornful. He seemed to know perfectly well who they were and what they wanted.

The first policeman phoned that evening to make his report. Her father talked with him, jovial and managing. She herself was now out of the picture; she had been protected, her function was over.

"What did they *do* to him?" she asked anxiously as he came back into the living room. She was not sure what went on in police stations.

"They didn't do anything to him," he said, amused by her concern. "They could have booked him for Watching and Besetting, they wanted to know if I'd like to press charges. But it's not worth a court case: he's got a visa that says he's only allowed in the country as long as he studies in Montreal, so I told them to just ship him down there. If he turns up here again they'll deport him. They went around to his rooming house, his rent's two weeks overdue; the landlady said she was on the point of kicking him out. He seems happy enough to be getting his back rent paid and a free train ticket to Montreal." He paused. "They couldn't get anything out of him though."

"*Out* of him?" Christine asked. 140

"They tried to find out why he was doing it; following you, I mean." Her father's eyes swept her as though it was a riddle to him also. "They said when they asked him about that he just clammed up. Pretended he didn't understand English. He understood well enough, but he wasn't answering."

Christine thought this would be the end, but somehow between his arrest and the departure of the train he managed to elude his escort long enough for one more phone call.

"I see you again," he said. He didn't wait for her to hang up.

Now that he was no longer an embarrassing present reality, he could be talked about, he could become an amusing story. In fact, he was the only amusing story Christine had to tell, and telling it preserved both for herself and for others the aura of her strange allure. Her friends and the men who continued to ask her out speculated about his motives. One suggested he had wanted to marry her so he could remain in the country; another said that oriental men were fond of well-built women: "It's your Rubens quality."

Christine thought about him a lot. She had not been attracted to him, rather 145 the reverse, but as an idea only he was a romantic figure, the one man who had found her irresistible; though she often wondered, inspecting her unchanged pink face and hefty body in her full-length mirror, just what it was about her that had done it. She avoided whenever it was proposed the theory of his insanity: it was only that there was more than one way of being sane.

But a new acquaintance, hearing the story for the first time, had a different explanation. "So he got you, too," he said, laughing. "That has to be the same guy who was hanging around our day camp a year ago this summer. He followed all the girls like that, a short guy, Japanese or something, glasses, smiling all the time."

"Maybe it was another one," Christine said.

"There couldn't be two of them, everything fits. This was a pretty weird guy."

"What . . . *kind* of girls did he follow?" Christine asked.

"Oh, just anyone who happened to be around. But if they paid any attention 150 to him at first, if they were nice to him or anything, he was unshakeable. He was a bit of a pest, but harmless."

Christine ceased to tell her amusing story. She had been one among many, then. She went back to playing tennis, she had been neglecting her game.

A few months later the policeman who had been in charge of the case telephoned her again.

"Like you to know, miss, that fellow you were having the trouble with was sent back to his own country. Deported."

"What for?" Christine asked. "Did he try to come back here?" Maybe she had been special after all, maybe he had dared everything for her.

"Nothing like it," the policeman said. "He was up to the same tricks in Montreal but he really picked the wrong woman this time—a Mother Superior of a convent. They don't stand for things like that in Quebec—had him out of here before he knew what happened. I guess he'll be better off in his own place."   155

"How old was she?" Christine asked, after a silence.

"Oh, around sixty, I guess."

"Thank you very much for letting me know," Christine said in her best official manner. "It's such a relief." She wondered if the policeman had called to make fun of her.

She was almost crying when she put down the phone. What *had* he wanted from her then? A Mother Superior. Did she really look sixty, did she look like a mother? What did convents mean? Comfort, charity? Refuge? Was it that something had happened to him, some intolerable strain just from being in this country; her tennis dress and exposed legs too much for him, flesh and money seemingly available everywhere but withheld from him wherever he turned, the nun the symbol of some final distortion, the robe and veil reminiscent to his nearsighted eyes of the women of his homeland, the ones he was able to understand? But he was back in his own country, remote from her as another planet; she would never know.

He hadn't forgotten her though. In the spring she got a postcard with a foreign stamp and the familiar block-letter writing. On the front was a picture of a temple. He was fine, he hoped she was fine also, he was her friend. A month later another print of the picture he had taken in the garden arrived, in a sealed manila envelope otherwise empty.   160

Christine's aura of mystery soon faded; anyway, she herself no longer believed in it. Life became again what she had always expected. She graduated with mediocre grades and went into the Department of Health and Welfare; she did a good job, and was seldom discriminated against for being a woman because nobody thought of her as one. She could afford a pleasant-sized apartment, though she did not put much energy into decorating it. She played less and less tennis; what had been muscle with a light coating of fat turned gradually into fat with a thin substratum of muscle. She began to get headaches.

As the years were used up and the war began to fill the newspapers and magazines, she realized which Eastern country he had actually been from. She had known the name but it hadn't registered at the time, it was such a minor place; she could never keep them separate in her mind.

But though she tried, she couldn't remember the name of the city, and the postcard was long gone—had he been from the North or the South, was he near the battle zone or safely far from it? Obsessively she bought magazines and pored over the available photographs, dead villagers, soldiers on the march, colour blowups of frightened or angry faces, spies being executed; she studied maps, she watched the late-night newscasts, the distant country and terrain becoming almost more familiar to her than her own. Once or twice she thought she could recognize him but it was no use, they all looked like him.

Finally she had to stop looking at the pictures. It bothered her too much, it was bad for her; she was beginning to have nightmares in which he was coming through the French doors of her mother's house in his shabby jacket, carrying a packsack and a rifle and a huge bouquet of richly coloured flowers. He was smiling in the same way but with blood streaked over his face, partly blotting out the features. She gave her television set away and took to reading nineteenth-century novels instead; Trollope and Galsworthy were her favourites. When, despite herself, she would think about him, she would tell herself that he had been crafty and agile-minded enough to survive, more or less, in her country, so surely he would be able to do it in his own, where he knew the language. She could not see him in the army, on either side; he wasn't the type, and to her knowledge he had not believed in any particular ideology. He would be something nondescript, something in the background, like herself; perhaps he had become an interpreter.　　　　　　　　　　　　　　　　　　　　　[1977]

THINKING ABOUT THE TEXT

1. What specific elements of the text especially influence how you view Christine's life?

2. As you read the story, did your attitude toward the man remain much the same, or did it change? Explain.

3. Since Atwood first published the story, there has been greater public attention to the phenomenon of men stalking women, with many people seeing this as a crime that society should severely punish and do more to prevent. What would you say to someone who argued that the man in Atwood's story is a stalker and as such deserves no sympathy? Imagine that this story was about a woman always following a man. Would you respond differently to the story?

4. Describe in your own words Christine's reaction when, in later years, she learns of the war engulfing the man's country. How did you respond to this news?

5. The story ends with the word *interpreter* as well as with the suggestion that this word applies to both Christine and the man. How might each of these characters be considered an interpreter? What specific acts of interpretation do they engage in? Of course, the word *interpreter* can also apply to you as a reader. As an interpreter, do you think you are very different from Christine and the man? Why, or why not?

MAKING COMPARISONS

1. Whereas Jen tells you Sherman's name and the country he is from, Atwood doesn't identify the name and country of "the man from Mars." To what extent does this difference figure in your responses to the two characters?

2. Whereas Jen's story is narrated in the first person, Atwood's story has a third-person narrator. Does this difference in technique lead you to view Christine differently from the way you view Mona, or is it not relevant at all? Explain.

3. Jen's story deals with junior-high-school students, Atwood's story with college students. How much should a reader bear in mind the characters' specific level of school?

WRITING ABOUT ISSUES

1. Write an essay explaining either how Jen's title could apply to Atwood's story or how Atwood's title could prove suitable for Jen's story. Refer to specific elements of the story that would make the new title appropriate.

2. Write an essay comparing Mona with Christine. Consider above all whether you think more highly of one than the other, and what leads you to evaluate each as you do. Refer to specific details of both texts.

3. Imagine that you are asked to lead an orientation for new foreign students at your college. You have them read one of the stories in this cluster. Write an essay identifying the story you choose and why you think they would find it useful. If you wish, put your essay in the form of a letter that they receive with other orientation materials.

4. Get information about an organization on campus that is geared to helping foreigners or people with some sort of tie to a particular country. You might learn about the organization by interviewing its officers and other members as well as by looking at written materials it has produced. Try to find out about the organization's specific goals, activities, history, and level of financial support from your college. Then, write a letter to the president of your college requesting that it maintain, increase, or decrease the amount of funds it currently gives the organization. Back up your request by drawing on your research. If you wish, refer in your letter to either or both of the stories in this cluster.

Colonial Insiders and Outsiders

WILLIAM SHAKESPEARE, *The Tempest*
AIMÉ CÉSAIRE, *A Tempest*

Many people continue to live under colonial governments, while others live in countries previously dominated by foreigners. South Africa is an example of the latter. Such people may very well look upon their current or former conquerors as an "outside" force and consider natives such as themselves to be "insiders." On the other hand, they may think just the opposite. After all, once foreign powers seize a region, they become central to its government and culture. In this sense, *they* turn into "insiders," with natives being left "outside" the institutions controlling their society. Australia is one modern-day example of this. Moreover, even when countries manage to shake off foreign domination, they may still feel "outside" the rest of the world. Struggling to overcome their legacy of colonialism and develop a workable government of their own, they may find themselves looking to other nations for advice, trade, and financial support.

The first work in this cluster is William Shakespeare's seventeenth-century play *The Tempest*. It was written at a time when England and other European countries were very much engaged in colonizing the New World and so, to some extent, has always been seen as a study of colonialism. Today, a growing number of scholars, directors, and critics are inclined to explore *The Tempest* in this context, in part because many texts both reflect and comment on tensions and insider-outsider relationships that colonial politics may involve.

Of course, even when people choose to focus on elements of colonialism in Shakespeare's play, they must still decide how he treats those elements. Does he scorn colonialism? Endorse it? Express mixed feelings about it? To further explore this issue, we also include a modern adaptation of *The Tempest* by the West Indian writer Aimé Césaire. Having grown up on the French-controlled island of Martinique, Césaire is well acquainted with colonial life. Moreover, as a black man, he is keenly aware that the lust for power shown by Western countries has involved racism as well. In various ways, Césaire's approach to literary classics like Shakespeare's is that of both an "insider" and an "outsider." Think about how his dual perspective affects his version of *The Tempest*. To what extent does he seem to applaud Shakespeare? To what extent does he seem to accuse Shakespeare of sympathizing with colonialism?

BEFORE YOU READ

What do you associate with Shakespeare? Jot down some memories of your previous experiences with his plays. If you have not read or seen any of them, note anything you have heard about Shakespeare, and list some things you are curious to know about his work as you prepare to read *The Tempest*.

WILLIAM SHAKESPEARE

The Tempest

William Shakespeare (1564–1616) is generally regarded as the greatest English writer of all time. Even today, however, not much is known about his life. He was born in the English village of Stratford-upon-Avon and eventually retired there. His career as a writer, which he pursued in London, began with poetry. Besides his Sonnets, which he first circulated privately and then published in 1609, he wrote long narrative poems, including Venus and Adonis (1593) *and* The Rape of Lucrece (1593). *But Shakespeare remains best known for his roughly thirty-seven plays. He wrote them for a company of players first called the Lord Chamberlain's Men (during Queen Elizabeth's reign) and then, in 1603, renamed the King's Men (since James I had succeeded to the throne). The company had two theaters, the more famous of which was the open-air Globe. It burned down in 1613, but recently it has been reconstructed, and Shakespeare's plays are again being staged at the site.*

The Tempest *was first produced in 1611. Eventually, it was performed at King James's court as well as the Globe. One court performance took place during celebrations of the marriage of the king's daughter Elizabeth, which apparently Shakespeare was alluding to when he had his characters Miranda and Ferdinand wed. Within the play, their betrothal is the occasion for a masque, which would have been an appropriate spectacle at Elizabeth's nuptials. A masque was a typical kind of theater piece in the English Renaissance; basically, it was a spectacle of dance and music that featured characters drawn from mythology and classical literature. Shakespeare himself has long been associated with the character of Prospero, whose speech renouncing magic is often seen as the playwright's own farewell to the stage.*

Departing from his usual practice, Shakespeare completely invented the plot of The Tempest, *rather than deriving the play from other sources. As we pointed out in the introduction to this cluster, nowadays the play is often analyzed in the context of colonialism. In this regard, it seems important to note that while writing the play, Shakespeare was well aware of what had happened to an English fleet bound for Virginia in 1609, two years before* The Tempest *premiered. These ships were representing the Virginia Company, a commercial enterprise in which Shakespeare had invested. The flagship, with the new governor of Virginia aboard, was wrecked in a storm. The crew and passengers made their way to the island of Bermuda, then thought to be a sinister place. (The present-day notoriety of the Bermuda Triangle is a parallel.) Eventually, they did reach Jamestown in Virginia, joining in the European conquest of the New World.*

NAMES OF THE ACTORS

ALONSO, *King of Naples*
SEBASTIAN, *his brother*
PROSPERO, *the right Duke of Milan*
ANTONIO, *his brother, the usurping Duke of Milan*
FERDINAND, *son to the King of Naples*
GONZALO, *an honest old councillor*
ADRIAN *and* ⎫
⎬ *lords*
FRANCISCO, ⎭
CALIBAN, *a savage and deformed slave*
TRINCULO, *a jester*
STEPHANO, *a drunken butler*
MASTER *of a ship*

BOATSWAIN
MARINERS

MIRANDA, *daughter to Prospero*

ARIEL, *an airy spirit*
IRIS,
CERES,
JUNO,   } *[presented by] spirits*
NYMPHS,
REAPERS,
[OTHER SPIRITS ATTENDING ON PROSPERO]

THE SCENE: *An uninhabited island*

[ACT 1, Scene 1]

[On board ship, off the island's coast.]

A tempestuous noise of thunder and lightning heard. Enter a Shipmaster and a Boatswain.

MASTER: Boatswain!

BOATSWAIN: Here, Master. What cheer?

MASTER: Good,° speak to the mariners. Fall to 't yarely,° or we run ourselves
   aground. Bestir, bestir!   *Exit.*

Enter Mariners.

BOATSWAIN: Heigh, my hearts! Cheerly, cheerly, my hearts! Yare, yare! Take in   5
   the topsail. Tend° to the Master's whistle. — Blow° till thou burst thy wind,
   if room enough!°

Enter Alonso, Sebastian, Antonio, Ferdinand, Gonzalo, and others.

ALONSO: Good Boatswain, have care. Where's the Master? Play the men.°

BOATSWAIN: I pray now, keep below.

ANTONIO: Where is the Master, Boatswain?   10

BOATSWAIN: Do you not hear him? You mar our labor. Keep° your cabins! You
   do assist the storm.

GONZALO: Nay, good,° be patient.

BOATSWAIN: When the sea is. Hence! What cares these roarers° for the name of
   king? To cabin! Silence! Trouble us not.   15

GONZALO: Good, yet remember whom thou hast aboard.

ACT 1, SCENE 1.   **3 Good:** I.e., it's good you've come, or, my good fellow;   **yarely:** Nimbly.
6 Tend: Attend;   **Blow:** (Addressed to the wind.)   **7 if room enough:** As long as we have sea
room enough.   **8 Play the men:** Act like men (?) ply, urge the men to exert themselves (?).
11 Keep: Remain in.   **13 good:** Good fellow.   **14 roarers:** Waves or winds, or both; spoken
to as though they were "bullies" or "blusterers."

BOATSWAIN: None that I more love than myself. You are a councillor; if you can command these elements to silence and work the peace of the present,° we will not hand° a rope more. Use your authority. If you cannot, give thanks you have lived so long and make yourself ready in your cabin for the mis- 20 chance of the hours, if it so hap° — Cheerly, good hearts! — Out of our way, I say.   *Exit.*

GONZALO: I have great comfort from this fellow. Methinks he hath no drowning mark upon him; his complexion is perfect gallows.° Stand fast, good Fate, to his hanging! Make the rope of his destiny our cable, for our 25 own doth little advantage.° If he be not born to be hanged, our case is miserable.°   *Exeunt [courtiers].*

Enter Boatswain.

BOATSWAIN: Down with the topmast! Yare! Lower, lower! Bring her to try wi' the main course.° (*A cry within.*) A plague upon this howling! They are louder than the weather or our office.°   30

Enter Sebastian, Antonio, and Gonzalo.

Yet again? What do you hear? Shall we give o'er° and drown? Have you a mind to sink?

SEBASTIAN: A pox o' your throat, you bawling, blasphemous, incharitable dog!

BOATSWAIN: Work you, then.   35

ANTONIO: Hang, cur! Hang, you whoreson, insolent noisemaker! We are less afraid to be drowned than thou art.

GONZALO: I'll warrant him for drowning,° though the ship were no stronger than a nutshell and as leaky as an unstanched° wench.

BOATSWAIN: Lay her ahold, ahold!° Set her two courses.° Off to sea again! Lay 40 her off!

Enter Mariners, wet.

MARINERS: All lost! To prayers, to prayers! All lost!
                    [The Mariners run about in confusion, exiting at random.]

BOATSWAIN: What, must our mouths be cold?°

GONZALO: The King and Prince at prayers! Let's assist them,
        For our case is as theirs.

SEBASTIAN: I am out of patience.   45

---

18 work . . . present: Bring calm to our present circumstances.   **19 hand:** Handle.
21 hap: Happen.   **24 complexion . . . gallows:** Appearance shows he was born to be hanged (and therefore, according to the proverb, in no danger of drowning).   **25–26 our . . . advantage:** Our own cable is of little benefit.   **26–27 case is miserable:** Circumstances are desperate.   **28–29 Bring . . . course:** Sail her close to the wind by means of the mainsail.
30 our office: I.e., the noise we make at our work.   **31 give o'er:** Give up.   **38 warrant him for drowning:** Guarantee that he will never be drowned.   **39 unstanched:** Insatiable, loose, unrestrained (suggesting also "incontinent" and "menstrual").   **40 ahold:** Ahull, close to the wind;   **courses:** Sails, i.e., foresail as well as mainsail, set in an attempt to get the ship back out into open water.   **43 must . . . cold:** I.e., must we drown in the cold sea, or, let us heat up our mouths with liquor.

ANTONIO: We are merely° cheated of our lives by drunkards.
        This wide-chapped° rascal! Would thou mightst lie drowning
        The washing of ten tides!°
GONZALO: He'll be hanged yet,
        Though every drop of water swear against it
        And gape at wid'st° to glut° him.
        (*A confused noise within:*)   "Mercy on us!"—   50
        "We split, we split!"°—"Farewell my wife and children!"—
        "Farewell, brother!"—"We split, we split, we split!"   [*Exit Boatswain.*]
ANTONIO: Let's all sink wi' the King.
SEBASTIAN: Let's take leave of him.   *Exit* [*with Antonio*].
GONZALO: Now would I give a thousand furlongs of sea for an acre of barren   55
        ground: long heath,° brown furze,° anything. The wills above be done! But I
        would fain° die a dry death.   *Exit.*

[Scene 2]

*[The island, near Prospero's cell. On the Elizabethan stage, this cell is implicitly at
hand throughout the play, although in some scenes the convention of flexible distance allows us to imagine characters in other parts of the island.]*

Enter Prospero [in his magic cloak] and Miranda.

MIRANDA: If by your art,° my dearest father, you have
        Put the wild waters in this roar, allay° them.
        The sky, it seems, would pour down stinking pitch,
        But that the sea, mounting to th' welkin's cheek,°
        Dashes the fire out. O, I have suffered   5
        With those that I saw suffer! A brave° vessel,
        Who had, no doubt, some noble creature in her,
        Dashed all to pieces. O, the cry did knock
        Against my very heart! Poor souls, they perished.
        Had I been any god of power, I would   10
        Have sunk the sea within the earth or ere°
        It should the good ship so have swallowed and
        The freighting° souls within her.
PROSPERO: Be collected.°
        No more amazement.° Tell your piteous° heart
        There's no harm done.
MIRANDA: O, woe the day!
PROSPERO: No harm.   15

46 **merely:** Utterly.   47 **wide-chapped:** With mouth wide open.   47–48 **lie . . . tides:** (Pirates
were hanged on the shore and left until three tides had come in.)   50 **at wid'st:** Wide open;
glut: Swallow.   51 **split:** Break apart.   56 **heath:** Heather;   **furze:** Gorse, a weed growing on
wasteland.   57 **fain:** Rather.   SCENE 2. 1 **art:** Magic.   2 **allay:** Pacify.   4 **welkin's cheek:**
Sky's face.   6 **brave:** Gallant, splendid.   11 **or ere:** Before.   13 **freighting:** Forming the cargo;
collected: Calm, composed.   14 **amazement:** Consternation;   **piteous:** Pitying.

I have done nothing but° in care of thee,
Of thee, my dear one, thee, my daughter, who
Art ignorant of what thou art, naught knowing
Of whence I am, nor that I am more better°
Than Prospero, master of a full° poor cell,   20
And thy no greater father.
MIRANDA: More to know
Did never meddle° with my thoughts.
PROSPERO: 'Tis time
I should inform thee farther. Lend thy hand
And pluck my magic garment from me. So,
                          [*laying down his magic cloak and staff*]
Lie there, my art.—Wipe thou thine eyes. Have comfort.   25
The direful spectacle of the wreck,° which touched
The very virtue° of compassion in thee,
I have with such provision° in mine art
So safely ordered that there is no soul—
No, not so much perdition° as an hair   30
Betid° to any creature in the vessel
Which° thou heard'st cry, which thou saw'st sink. Sit down,
For thou must now know farther.
MIRANDA [*sitting*]:   You have often
Begun to tell me what I am, but stopped
And left me to a bootless inquisition,°   35
Concluding, "Stay, not yet."
PROSPERO: The hour's now come;
The very minute bids thee ope thine ear.
Obey, and be attentive. Canst thou remember
A time before we came unto this cell?
I do not think thou canst, for then thou wast not   40
Out° three years old.
MIRANDA: Certainly, sir, I can.
PROSPERO: By what? By any other house or person?
Of anything the image, tell me, that
Hath kept with thy remembrance.
MIRANDA: 'Tis far off,
And rather like a dream than an assurance   45
That my remembrance warrants.° Had I not
Four or five women once that tended me?
PROSPERO: Thou hadst, and more, Miranda. But how is it
That this lives in thy mind? What seest thou else

16 **but**: Except.   19 **more better**: Of higher rank.   20 **full**: Very.   22 **meddle**: Mingle.
26 **wreck**: Shipwreck.   27 **virtue**: Essence.   28 **provision**: Foresight.   30 **perdition**: Loss.
31 **Betid**: Happened.   32 **Which**: Whom.   35 **bootless inquisition**: Profitless inquiry.
41 **Out**: Fully.   45–46 **assurance . . . warrants**: Certainty that my memory guarantees.

In the dark backward and abysm of time?°   50
If thou rememberest aught° ere thou cam'st here,
How thou cam'st here thou mayst.
MIRANDA: But that I do not.
PROSPERO: Twelve year since, Miranda, twelve year since,
Thy father was the Duke of Milan and
A prince of power.
MIRANDA: Sir, are not you my father?   55
PROSPERO: Thy mother was a piece° of virtue, and
She said thou wast my daughter; and thy father
Was Duke of Milan, and his only heir
And princess no worse issued.°
MIRANDA: O the heavens!
What foul play had we, that we came from thence?   60
Or blessèd was't we did?
PROSPERO: Both, both, my girl.
By foul play, as thou sayst, were we heaved thence,
But blessedly holp° hither.
MIRANDA: O, my heart bleeds
To think o' the teen that I have turned you to,°
Which is from° my remembrance! Please you, farther.   65
PROSPERO: My brother and thy uncle, called Antonio—
I pray thee mark me—that a brother should
Be so perfidious!—he whom next° thyself
Of all the world I loved, and to him put
The manage° of my state, as at that time   70
Through all the seigniories° it was the first,
And Prospero the prime° duke, being so reputed
In dignity, and for the liberal arts
Without a parallel; those being all my study,
The government I cast upon my brother   75
And to my state grew stranger,° being transported°
And rapt in secret studies. Thy false uncle—
Dost thou attend me?
MIRANDA: Sir, most heedfully.
PROSPERO: Being once perfected° how to grant suits,
How to deny them, who t' advance and who   80
To trash° for overtopping,° new created

---

50 backward . . . time: Abyss of the past.   **51 aught:** Anything.   **56 piece:** Masterpiece, exemplar.   **59 no worse issued:** No less nobly born, descended.   **63 holp:** Helped.   **64 teen . . . to:** Trouble I've caused you to remember or put you to.   **65 from:** Out of.   **68 next:** Next to.   **70 manage:** Management, administration.   **71 seigniories:** I.e., city-states of northern Italy.   **72 prime:** First in rank and importance.   **76 to . . . stranger:** I.e., withdrew from my responsibilities as duke;   **transported:** Carried away.   **79 perfected:** Grown skillful.   **81 trash:** Check a hound by tying a cord or weight to its neck;   **overtopping:** Running too far ahead of the pack; surmounting, exceeding one's authority.

The creatures° that were mine, I say, or changed 'em,
Or else new formed 'em;° having both the key°
Of officer and office, set all hearts i' the state
To what tune pleased his ear, that° now he was   85
The ivy which had hid my princely trunk
And sucked my verdure° out on 't.° Thou attend'st not.

MIRANDA: O, good sir, I do.

PROSPERO: I pray thee, mark me.
I, thus neglecting worldly ends, all dedicated
To closeness° and the bettering of my mind   90
With that which, but by being so retired, ·
O'erprized all popular rate,° in my false brother
Awaked an evil nature; and my trust,
Like a good parent,° did beget of° him
A falsehood in its contrary as great   95
As my trust was, which had indeed no limit,
A confidence sans° bound. He being thus lorded°
Not only with what my revenue yielded
But what my power might else° exact, like one
Who, having into° truth by telling of it,   100
Made such a sinner of his memory
To° credit his own lie,° he did believe
He was indeed the Duke, out o'° the substitution
And executing th' outward face of royalty°
With all prerogative. Hence his ambition growing—   105
Dost thou hear?

MIRANDA: Your tale, sir, would cure deafness.

PROSPERO: To have no screen between this part he played
And him he played it for,° he needs will be°
Absolute Milan.° Me, poor man, my library
Was dukedom large enough. Of temporal royalties°   110

---

82 creatures: Dependents.   **82–83 or changed . . . formed 'em:** I.e., either changed their
loyalties and duties or else created new ones.   **83 key:** (1) Key for unlocking (2) tool for tuning
stringed instruments.   **85 that:** So that.   **87 verdure:** Vitality;   **on 't:** Of it.   **90 closeness:**
Retirement, seclusion.   **91–92 but . . . rate:** I.e., were it not that its private nature caused me
to neglect my public responsibilities, had a value far beyond what public opinion could appreciate, or, simply because it was done in such seclusion, had a value not appreciated by popular
opinion.   **94 good parent:** (Alludes to the proverb that good parents often bear bad children;
see also line 120);   **of:** In.   **97 sans:** Without;   **lorded:** Raised to lordship, with power and
wealth.   **99 else:** Otherwise, additionally.   **100–102 Who . . . lie:** I.e., who, by repeatedly
telling the lie (that he was indeed Duke of Milan), made his memory such a confirmed sinner
against truth that he began to believe his own lie;   **into:** Unto, against;   **To:** So as to.
103 out o': As a result of.   **104 And . . . royalty:** And (as a result of) his carrying out all the
visible functions of royalty.   **107–108 To have . . . it for:** To have no separation or barrier
between his role and himself. (Antonio wanted to act in his own person, not as substitute.)
108 needs will be: Insisted on becoming.   **109 Absolute Milan:** Unconditional Duke of
Milan.   **110 temporal royalties:** Practical prerogatives and responsibilities of a sovereign.

He thinks me now incapable; confederates°—
So dry° he was for sway°—wi' the King of Naples
To give him annual tribute, do him° homage,
Subject his coronet to his° crown, and bend°
The dukedom yet° unbowed—alas, poor Milan!—   115
To most ignoble stooping.

MIRANDA: O the heavens!

PROSPERO: Mark his condition° and th' event,° then tell me
    If this might be a brother.

MIRANDA: I should sin
    To think but° nobly of my grandmother.
    Good wombs have borne bad sons.

PROSPERO: Now the condition.   120
    This King of Naples, being an enemy
    To me inveterate, hearkens° my brother's suit,
    Which was that he,° in lieu o' the premises°
    Of homage and I know not how much tribute,
    Should presently extirpate° me and mine   125
    Out of the dukedom and confer fair Milan,
    With all the honors, on my brother. Whereon,
    A treacherous army levied, one midnight
    Fated to th' purpose did Antonio open
    The gates of Milan, and, i' the dead of darkness,   130
    The ministers for the purpose° hurried thence°
    Me and thy crying self.

MIRANDA: Alack, for pity!
    I, not remembering how I cried out then,
    Will cry it o'er again. It is a hint°
    That wrings° mine eyes to 't.

PROSPERO: Hear a little further,   135
    And then I'll bring thee to the present business
    Which now's upon's, without the which this story
    Were most impertinent.°

MIRANDA: Wherefore° did they not
    That hour destroy us?

PROSPERO: Well demanded,° wench.°
    My tale provokes that question. Dear, they durst not,   140

---

111 confederates: Conspires, allies himself.   **112 dry:** Thirsty;   **sway:** Power.   **113 him:**
I.e., the King of Naples.   **114 his . . . his:** Antonio's . . . the King of Naples';   **bend:** Make bow
down.   **115 yet:** Hitherto.   **117 condition:** Pact;   **event:** Outcome.   **119 but:** Other than.
122 hearkens: Listens to.   **123 he:** The King of Naples;   **in . . . premises:** In return for the
stipulation.   **125 presently extirpate:** At once remove.   **131 ministers . . . purpose:** Agents
employed to do this;   **thence:** From there.   **134 hint:** Occasion.   **135 wrings:** (1) Con-
strains (2) wrings tears from.   **138 impertinent:** Irrelevant;   **Wherefore:** Why.   **139 demanded:** Asked;   **wench:** (Here a term of endearment.)

So dear the love my people bore me, nor set
A mark so bloody° on the business, but
With colors fairer° painted their foul ends.
In few,° they hurried us aboard a bark,°
Bore us some leagues to sea, where they prepared   145
A rotten carcass of a butt,° not rigged,
Nor tackle,° sail, nor mast; the very rats
Instinctively have quit° it. There they hoist us,
To cry to th' sea that roared to us, to sigh
To th' winds whose pity, sighing back again,   150
Did us but loving wrong.°
MIRANDA: Alack, what trouble
Was I then to you!
PROSPERO: O, a cherubin
Thou wast that did preserve me. Thou didst smile,
Infusèd with a fortitude from heaven,
When I have decked° the sea with drops full salt,   155
Under my burden groaned, which° raised in me
An undergoing stomach,° to bear up
Against what should ensue.
MIRANDA: How came we ashore?
PROSPERO: By Providence divine.   160
Some food we had, and some fresh water, that
A noble Neapolitan, Gonzalo,
Out of his charity, who being then appointed
Master of this design, did give us, with
Rich garments, linens, stuffs,° and necessaries,   165
Which since have steaded much.° So, of° his gentleness,
Knowing I loved my books, he furnished me
From mine own library with volumes that
I prize above my dukedom.
MIRANDA: Would° I might
But ever° see that man!
PROSPERO: Now I arise.   *[He puts on his magic cloak.]*   170
Sit still, and hear the last of our sea sorrow.°
Here in this island we arrived; and here
Have I, thy schoolmaster, made thee more profit°

141–142 set . . . bloody: I.e., make obvious their murderous intent (from the practice of marking with the blood of the prey those who have participated in a successful hunt).   **143 fairer:** Apparently more attractive.   **144 few:** Few words;   **bark:** Ship.   **146 butt:** Cask, tub.   **147 Nor tackle:** Neither rigging.   **148 quit:** Abandoned.   **151 Did . . . wrong:** (I.e., the winds pitied Prospero and Miranda, though of necessity they blew them from shore.)   **155 decked:** Covered (with salt tears), adorned.   **156 which:** I.e., the smile.   **157 undergoing stomach:** Courage to go on.   **165 stuffs:** Supplies.   **166 steaded much:** Been of much use;   **So, of:** Similarly, out of.   **169 Would:** I wish.   **170 But ever:** I.e., someday.   **171 sea sorrow:** Sorrowful adventure at sea.   **173 more profit:** Profit more.

Than other princess'° can, that have more time
For vainer° hours and tutors not so careful.   175
MIRANDA: Heavens thank you for 't! And now, I pray you, sir—
For still 'tis beating in my mind—your reason
For raising this sea storm?
PROSPERO: Know thus far forth:
By accident most strange, bountiful Fortune,
Now my dear lady,° hath mine enemies   180
Brought to this shore; and by my prescience
I find my zenith° doth depend upon
A most auspicious star, whose influence°
If now I court not, but omit,° my fortunes
Will ever after droop. Here cease more questions.   185
Thou art inclined to sleep. 'Tis a good dullness,°
And give it way.° I know thou canst not choose.   *[Miranda sleeps.]*
Come away,° servant, come! I am ready now.
Approach, my Ariel, come.

Enter Ariel.

ARIEL: All hail, great master, grave sir, hail! I come   190
To answer thy best pleasure; be 't to fly,
To swim, to dive into the fire, to ride
On the curled clouds, to thy strong bidding task°
Ariel and all his quality.°
PROSPERO: Hast thou, spirit,
Performed to point° the tempest that I bade thee?   195
ARIEL: To every article.
I boarded the King's ship. Now on the beak,°
Now in the waist,° the deck,° in every cabin,
I flamed amazement.° Sometimes I'd divide
And burn in many places; on the topmast,   200
The yards, and bowsprit would I flame distinctly,°
Then meet and join. Jove's lightning, the precursors
O' the dreadful thunderclaps, more momentary
And sight-outrunning° were not.° The fire and cracks
Of sulfurous roaring the most mighty Neptune°   205

---

174 **princess':** Princesses (or the word may be *princes*, referring to royal children both male and female).   175 **vainer:** More foolishly spent.   180 **my dear lady:** (Refers to Fortune, not Miranda.)   182 **zenith:** Height of fortune (astrological term).   183 **influence:** Astrological power.   184 **omit:** Ignore.   186 **dullness:** Drowsiness.   187 **give it way:** Let it happen (i.e., don't fight it).   188 **Come away:** Come.   193 **task:** Make demands upon.   194 **quality:** (1) Fellow spirits (2) abilities.   195 **to point:** To the smallest detail.   197 **beak:** Prow.   198 **waist:** Midships;   **deck:** Poop deck at the stern.   199 **flamed amazement:** Struck terror in the guise of fire, i.e., Saint Elmo's fire.   201 **distinctly:** In different places.   204 **sight-outrunning:** Swifter than sight;   **were not:** Could not have been.   205 **Neptune:** Roman god of the sea.

Seem to besiege and make his bold waves tremble,
Yea, his dread trident shake.

PROSPERO: My brave spirit!
Who was so firm, so constant, that this coil°
Would not infect his reason?

ARIEL: Not a soul
But felt a fever of the mad° and played   210
Some tricks of desperation. All but mariners
Plunged in the foaming brine and quit the vessel,
Then all afire with me. The King's son, Ferdinand,
With hair up-staring° — then like reeds, not hair —
Was the first man that leapt; cried, "Hell is empty,   215
And all the devils are here!"

PROSPERO: Why, that's my spirit!
But was not this nigh shore?

ARIEL: Close by, my master.

PROSPERO: But are they, Ariel, safe?

ARIEL: Not a hair perished.
On their sustaining garments° not a blemish,
But fresher than before; and, as thou bad'st° me,   220
In troops° I have dispersed them, 'bout the isle.
The King's son have I landed by himself,
Whom I left cooling of° the air with sighs
In an odd angle° of the isle, and sitting,
His arms in this sad knot.°   *[He folds his arms.]*

PROSPERO: Of the King's ship,   225
The mariners, say how thou hast disposed,
And all the rest o' the fleet.

ARIEL: Safely in harbor
Is the King's ship; in the deep nook,° where once
Thou called'st me up at midnight to fetch dew°
From the still-vexed Bermudas,° there she's hid;   230
The mariners all under hatches stowed,
Who, with a charm joined to their suffered labor,°
I have left asleep. And for the rest o' the fleet,
Which I dispersed, they all have met again
And are upon the Mediterranean float°   235
Bound sadly home for Naples,

---

208 coil: Tumult.   **210 of the mad:** I.e., such as madmen feel.   **214 up-staring:** Standing on end.   **219 sustaining garments:** Garments that buoyed them up in the sea.   **220 bad'st:** Ordered.   **221 troops:** Groups.   **223 cooling of:** Cooling.   **224 angle:** Corner.   **225 sad knot:** (Folded arms are indicative of melancholy.)   **228 nook:** Bay.   **229 dew:** (Collected at midnight for magical purposes; compare with line 325.)   **230 still-vexed Bermudas:** Ever stormy Bermudas.   **232 with . . . labor:** By means of a spell added to all the labor they have undergone.   **235 float:** Sea.

Supposing that they saw the King's ship wrecked
And his great person perish.
PROSPERO: Ariel, thy charge
Exactly is performed. But there's more work.
What is the time o' the day?
ARIEL: Past the mid season.°   240
PROSPERO: At least two glasses.° The time twixt six and now
Must by us both be spent most preciously.
ARIEL: Is there more toil? Since thou dost give me pains,°
Let me remember° thee what thou hast promised,
Which is not yet performed me.
PROSPERO: How now? Moody?   245
What is 't thou canst demand?
ARIEL: My liberty.
PROSPERO: Before the time be out? No more!
ARIEL: I prithee,
Remember I have done thee worthy service,
Told thee no lies, made thee no mistakings, served
Without or grudge or grumblings. Thou did promise   250
To bate° me a full year.
PROSPERO: Dost thou forget
From what a torment I did free thee?
ARIEL: No.
PROSPERO: Thou dost, and think'st it much to tread the ooze
Of the salt deep,
To run upon the sharp wind of the north,   255
To do me° business in the veins° o' the earth
When it is baked° with frost.
ARIEL: I do not, sir.
PROSPERO: Thou liest, malignant thing! Hast thou forgot
The foul witch Sycorax, who with age and envy°
Was grown into a hoop?° Hast thou forgot her?   260
ARIEL: No, sir.
PROSPERO: Thou hast. Where was she born? Speak. Tell me.
ARIEL: Sir, in Argier.°
PROSPERO: O, was she so? I must
Once in a month recount what thou hast been,
Which thou forgett'st. This damned witch Sycorax,   265
For mischiefs manifold and sorceries terrible
To enter human hearing, from Argier,

---

240 mid season: Noon.   **241 glasses:** Hourglasses.   **243 pains:** Labors.   **244 remember:**
Remind.   **251 bate:** Remit, deduct.   **256 do me:** Do for me;   **veins:** Veins of minerals, or,
underground streams, thought to be analogous to the veins of the human body.   **257 baked:**
Hardened.   **259 envy:** Malice.   **260 grown into a hoop:** I.e., so bent over with age as to
resemble a hoop.   **263 Argier:** Algiers.

Thou know'st, was banished. For one thing she did°
They would not take her life. Is not this true?
ARIEL: Ay, sir.   270
PROSPERO: This blue-eyed° hag was hither brought with child°
And here was left by the sailors. Thou, my slave,
As thou report'st thyself, was then her servant;
And, for° thou wast a spirit too delicate
To act her earthy and abhorred commands,   275
Refusing her grand hests,° she did confine thee,
By help of her more potent ministers
And in her most unmitigable rage,
Into a cloven pine, within which rift
Imprisoned thou didst painfully remain   280
A dozen years; within which space she died
And left thee there, where thou didst vent thy groans
As fast as mill wheels strike.° Then was this island —
Save° for the son that she did litter° here,
A freckled whelp,° hag-born° — not honored with   285
A human shape.
ARIEL: Yes, Caliban her son.°
PROSPERO: Dull thing, I say so:° he, that Caliban
Whom now I keep in service. Thou best know'st
What torment I did find thee in. Thy groans
Did make wolves howl, and penetrate the breasts   290
Of ever-angry bears. It was a torment
To lay upon the damned, which Sycorax
Could not gain undo. It was mine art,
When I arrived and heard thee, that made gape°
The pine and let thee out.
ARIEL: I thank thee, master.   295
PROSPERO: If thou more murmur'st, I will rend an oak
And peg thee in his° knotty entrails till
Thou hast howled away twelve winters.
ARIEL: Pardon, master.
I will be correspondent° to command
And do my spriting° gently.°   300

---

268 **one . . . did:** (Perhaps a reference to her pregnancy, for which her life would be spared.)
271 **blue-eyed:** With dark circles under the eyes or with blue eyelids, implying pregnancy;
with child: Pregnant.   274 **for:** Because.   276 **hests:** Commands.   283 **as mill wheels
strike:** As the blades of a mill wheel strike the water.   284 **Save:** Except;   **litter:** Give birth to.
285 **whelp:** Offspring (used of animals);   **hag-born:** Born of a female demon.   286 **Yes . . .
son:** (Ariel is probably concurring with Prospero's comment about a "freckled whelp," not contradicting the point about "A human shape.")   287 **Dull . . . so:** I.e., exactly, that's what I said,
you dullard.   294 **gape:** Open wide.   297 **his:** Its.   299 **correspondent:** Responsive, submissive.   300 **spriting:** Duties as a spirit;   **gently:** Willingly, ungrudgingly.

PROSPERO: Do so, and after two days
     I will discharge thee.
ARIEL: That's my noble master!
     What shall I do? Say what? What shall I do?
PROSPERO: Go make thyself like a nymph o' the sea. Be subject
     To no sight but thine and mine, invisible   305
     To every eyeball else. Go take this shape
     And hither come in 't. Go, hence with diligence!   *Exit [Ariel].*
     Awake, dear heart, awake! Thou hast slept well.
     Awake!
MIRANDA: The strangeness of your story put   310
     Heaviness° in me.
PROSPERO: Shake it off. Come on,
     We'll visit Caliban, my slave, who never
     Yields us kind answer.
MIRANDA: 'Tis a villain, sir,
     I do not love to look on.
PROSPERO: But, as 'tis,
     We cannot miss° him. He does make our fire,   315
     Fetch in our wood, and serves in offices°
     That profit us.—What ho! Slave! Caliban!
     Thou earth, thou! Speak.
CALIBAN *(within):*   There's wood enough within.
PROSPERO: Come forth, I say! There's other business for thee.
     Come, thou tortoise! When?°   320

Enter Ariel like a water nymph.

     Fine apparition! My quaint° Ariel,
     Hark in thine ear.   *[He whispers.]*
ARIEL: My lord, it shall be done.   *Exit.*
PROSPERO: Thou poisonous slave, got° by the devil himself
     Upon thy wicked dam,° come forth!

Enter Caliban.

CALIBAN: As wicked° dew as e'er my mother brushed   325
     With raven's feather from unwholesome fen°
     Drop on you both! A southwest° blow on ye
     And blister you all o'er!
PROSPERO: For this, be sure, tonight thou shalt have cramps,
     Side-stitches that shall pen thy breath up. Urchins°   330

---

311 Heaviness: Drowsiness.   **315 miss:** Do without.   **316 offices:** Functions, duties.
320 When: (An exclamation of impatience.)   **321 quaint:** Ingenious.   **323 got:** Begotten,
sired.   **324 dam:** Mother (used of animals).   **325 wicked:** Mischievous, harmful.   **326 fen:**
Marsh, bog.   **327 southwest:** I.e., wind thought to bring disease.   **330 Urchins:** Hedgehogs;
here, suggesting goblins in the guise of hedgehogs.

Shall forth at vast° of night that they may work
All exercise on thee. Thou shalt be pinched
As thick as honeycomb,° each pinch more stinging
Than bees that made 'em.°

CALIBAN: I must eat my dinner.
This island's mine, by Sycorax my mother,   335
Which thou tak'st from me. When thou cam'st first,
Thou strok'st me and made much of me, wouldst give me
Water with berries in 't, and teach me how
To name the bigger light, and how the less,°
That burn by day and night. And then I loved thee   340
And showed thee all the qualities o' th' isle,
The fresh springs, brine pits, barren place and fertile.
Cursed be I that did so! All the charms°
Of Sycorax, toads, beetles, bats, light on you!
For I am all the subjects that you have,   345
Which first was mine own king; and here you sty° me
In this hard rock, whiles you do keep from me
The rest o' th' island.

PROSPERO: Thou most lying slave,
Whom stripes° may move, not kindness! I have used thee,
Filth as thou art, with humane° care, and lodged thee   350
In mine own cell, till thou didst seek to violate
The honor of my child.

CALIBAN: Oho, oho! Would 't had been done!
Thou didst prevent me; I had peopled else°
This isle with Calibans.

MIRANDA: Abhorrèd° slave,   355
Which any print° of goodness wilt not take,
Being capable of all ill! I pitied thee,
Took pains to make thee speak, taught thee each hour
One thing or other. When thou didst not, savage,
Know thine own meaning, but wouldst gabble like   360
A thing most brutish, I endowed thy purposes°
With words that made them known. But thy vile race,°
Though thou didst learn, had that in 't which good natures
Could not abide to be with; therefore wast thou

---

331 vast: Lengthy, desolate time. (Malignant spirits were thought to be restricted to the hours of darkness.)   **333 As thick as honeycomb:** I.e., all over, with as many pinches as a honeycomb has cells.   **334 'em:** I.e., the honeycomb.   **339 the bigger . . . less:** I.e., the sun and the moon (see Genesis 1:16: "God then made two great lights: the greater light to rule the day, and the less light to rule the night").   **343 charms:** Spells.   **346 sty:** Confine as in a sty.   **349 stripes:** Lashes.   **350 humane:** (Not distinguished as word from *human*.)   **354 peopled else:** Otherwise populated.   **355–366 Abhorrèd . . . prison:** (Sometimes assigned by editors to Prospero.)   **356 print:** Imprint, impression.   **361 purposes:** Meanings, desires.   **362 race:** Natural disposition; species, nature.

Deservedly confined into this rock,   365
Who hadst deserved more than a prison.
CALIBAN: You taught me language, and my profit on 't
   Is I know how to curse. The red plague° rid° you
   For learning° me your language!
PROSPERO: Hagseed,° hence!
   Fetch us in fuel, and be quick, thou'rt best,°   370
   To answer other business.° Shrugg'st thou, malice?
   If thou neglect'st or dost unwillingly
   What I command, I'll rack thee with old° cramps,
   Fill all thy bones with aches,° make thee roar
   That beasts shall tremble at thy din.
CALIBAN: No, pray thee.   375
   [Aside.] I must obey. His art is of such power
   It would control my dam's god, Setebos,°
   And make a vassal of him.
PROSPERO: So, slave, hence!   *Exit Caliban.*

*Enter Ferdinand; and Ariel, invisible,° playing and singing. [Ferdinand does not
see Prospero and Miranda.]*

   Ariel's Song.

ARIEL: Come unto these yellow sands,
     And then take hands;   380
   Curtsied when you have,° and kissed
     The wild waves whist,°
   Foot it featly° here and there,
     And, sweet sprites,° bear
   The burden.° Hark, hark!

              Burden, dispersedly° [within]. Bow-wow.   385
   The watchdogs bark.

              [Burden, dispersedly within.] Bow-wow.

   Hark, hark! I hear
   The strain of strutting chanticleer
     Cry Cock-a-diddle-dow.
FERDINAND: Where should this music be? I' th' air or th' earth?   390
   It sounds no more; and sure it waits upon°
   Some god o' th' island. Sitting on a bank,°

---

368 red plague: Plague characterized by red sores and evacuation of blood; **rid:** Destroy.
369 learning: Teaching; **Hagseed:** Offspring of a female demon.   **370 thou'rt best:** You'd
be well advised.   **371 answer other business:** Perform other tasks.   **373 old:** Such as old
people suffer, or, plenty of.   **374 aches:** (Pronounced "aitches.")   **377 Setebos:** (A god of the
Patagonians, named in Robert Eden's *History of Travel*, 1577.)   **Ariel, invisible:** (Ariel wears a
garment that by convention indicates he is invisible to the other characters.)   **381 Curtsied . . .
have:** When you have curtsied.   **381–382 kissed . . . whist:** Kissed the waves into silence, or,
kissed while the waves are being hushed.   **383 Foot it featly:** Dance nimbly.   **384 sprites:**
Spirits.   **385 burden:** Refrain, undersong; **dispersedly:** I.e., from all directions, not in unison.   **391 waits upon:** Serves, attends.   **392 bank:** Sandbank.

Weeping again the King my father's wreck,
This music crept by me upon the waters,
Allaying both their fury and my passion°   395
With its sweet air. Thence° I have followed it,
Or it hath drawn me rather. But 'tis gone.
No, it begins again.

    Ariel's Song.

ARIEL: Full fathom five thy father lies.
     Of his bones are coral made.   400
    Those are pearls that were his eyes.
     Nothing of him that doth fade
    But doth suffer a sea change
    Into something rich and strange.
    Sea nymphs hourly ring his knell.°

                Burden [within]. Ding dong.   405
Hark, now I hear them, ding dong bell.
FERDINAND: The ditty does remember° my drowned father.
This is no mortal business, nor no sound
That the earth owes.° I hear it now above me.
PROSPERO *[to Miranda]:*   The fringèd curtains of thine eye advance°   410
And say what thou seest yond.
MIRANDA: What is 't? A spirit?
Lord, how it looks about! Believe me, sir,
It carries a brave° form. But 'tis a spirit.
PROSPERO: No, wench, it eats and sleeps and hath such senses
As we have, such. This gallant which thou seest   415
Was in the wreck; and, but° he's something stained°
With grief, that's beauty's canker,° thou mightst call him
A goodly person. He hath lost his fellows
And strays about to find 'em.
MIRANDA: I might call him
A thing divine, for nothing natural   420
I ever saw so noble.
PROSPERO *[aside]:*   It goes on,° I see,
As my soul prompts it. — Spirit, fine spirit, I'll free thee
Within two days for this.
FERDINAND *[seeing Miranda]:*   Most sure, the goddess
On whom these airs° attend! — Vouchsafe° my prayer   425
May know° if you remain° upon this island,

---

395 passion: Grief. **396 Thence:** I.e., from the bank on which I sat. **405 knell:** Announcement of a death by the tolling of a bell. **407 remember:** Commemorate. **409 owes:** Owns. **410 advance:** Raise. **413 brave:** Excellent. **416 but:** Except that; **something stained:** Somewhat disfigured. **417 canker:** Cankerworm (feeding on buds and leaves). **421 It goes on:** I.e., my plan works. **425 airs:** Songs; **Vouchsafe:** Grant. **426 May know:** I.e., that I may know; **remain:** Dwell.

And that you will some good instruction give
How I may bear me° here. My prime° request,
Which I do last pronounce, is—O you wonder!°—
If you be maid or no?°

MIRANDA: No wonder, sir,   430
But certainly a maid.

FERDINAND: My language? Heavens!
I am the best° of them that speak this speech,
Were I but where 'tis spoken.

PROSPERO *[coming forward]*:   How? The best?
What wert thou if the King of Naples heard thee?

FERDINAND: A single° thing, as I am now, that wonders   435
To hear thee speak of Naples.° He does hear me,°
And that he does I weep.° Myself am Naples,°
Who with mine eyes, never since at ebb,° beheld
The King my father wrecked.

MIRANDA: Alack, for mercy!

FERDINAND: Yes, faith, and all his lords, the Duke of Milan   440
And his brave son° being twain.

PROSPERO *[aside]*:   The Duke of Milan
And his more braver° daughter could control° thee,
If now 'twere fit to do 't. At the first sight
They have changed eyes.°—Delicate Ariel,
I'll set thee free for this. *[To Ferdinand.]* A word, good sir.   445
I fear you have done yourself some wrong.° A word!

MIRANDA *[aside]*:   Why speaks my father so urgently? This
Is the third man that e'er I saw, the first
That e'er I sighed for. Pity move my father
To be inclined my way!

FERDINAND: O, if a virgin,   450
And your affection not gone forth, I'll make you
The Queen of Naples.

PROSPERO: Soft, sir! One word more.
[Aside.] They are both in either's° powers; but this swift business
I must uneasy° make, lest too light winning
Make the prize light.° *[To Ferdinand.]* One word more: I charge thee   455

---

428 bear me: Conduct myself;   **prime:** Chief.   **429 wonder:** (Miranda's name means "to be wondered at.")   **430 maid or no:** I.e., a human maiden as opposed to a goddess or married woman.   **432 best:** I.e., in birth.   **435 single:** (1) Solitary, being at once King of Naples and myself (2) feeble.   **436, 437 Naples:** The King of Naples.   **436 He does hear me:** I.e., the King of Naples does hear my words, for I am King of Naples.   **437 And . . . weep:** I.e., and I weep at this reminder that my father is seemingly dead, leaving me heir.   **438 at ebb:** I.e., dry, not weeping.   **441 son:** (The only reference in the play to a son of Antonio.)   **442 more braver:** More splendid;   **control:** Refute.   **444 changed eyes:** Exchanged amorous glances.   **446 done . . . wrong:** I.e., spoken falsely.   **453 both in either's:** Each in the other's.   **454 uneasy:** Difficult.   **454–455 light . . . light:** Easy . . . cheap.

That thou attend° me. Thou dost here usurp
The name thou ow'st° not, and hast put thyself
Upon this island as a spy, to win it
From me, the lord on 't.°
FERDINAND: No, as I am a man.
MIRANDA: There's nothing ill can dwell in such a temple.   460
If the ill spirit have so fair a house,
Good things will strive to dwell with 't.°
PROSPERO: Follow me. —
Speak not you for him; he's a traitor. — Come,
I'll manacle thy neck and feet together.
Seawater shalt thou drink; thy food shall be   465
The fresh-brook mussels, withered roots, and husks
Wherein the acorn cradled. Follow.
FERDINAND: No!
I will resist such entertainment° till
Mine enemy has more power.   *He draws, and is charmed° from moving.*
MIRANDA: O dear father,
Make not too rash° a trial of him, for   470
He's gentle,° and not fearful.°
PROSPERO: What, I say,
My foot° my tutor? — Put thy sword up, traitor,
Who mak'st a show but dar'st not strike, thy conscience
Is so possessed with guilt. Come, from thy ward,°
For I can here disarm thee with this stick   475
And make thy weapon drop.   *[He brandishes his staff.]*
MIRANDA *[trying to hinder him]:*   Beseech you, father!
PROSPERO: Hence! Hang not on my garments.
MIRANDA: Sir, have pity!
I'll be his surety.°
PROSPERO: Silence! One word more
Shall make me chide thee, if not hate thee. What,   480
An advocate for an impostor? Hush!
Thou think'st there is no more such shapes as he,
Having seen but him and Caliban. Foolish wench,
To° the most of men this is a Caliban,
And they to him are angels.
MIRANDA: My affections   485
Are then most humble; I have no ambition
To see a goodlier man.

---

456 attend: Follow, obey.   **457 ow'st:** Ownest.   **459 on 't:** Of it.   **462 strive . . . with 't:**
I.e., expel the evil and occupy the *temple*, the body.   **468 entertainment:** Treatment.
charmed: Magically prevented.   **470 rash:** Harsh.   **471   gentle:** Wellborn;   **fearful:**
Frightening, dangerous, or perhaps, cowardly.   **472 foot:** Subordinate (Miranda, the foot, pre-
sumes to instruct Prospero, the head).   **474 ward:** Defensive posture (in fencing).   **479 surety:**
Guarantee.   **484 To:** Compared to.

PROSPERO *[to Ferdinand]*:   Come on, obey.
  Thy nerves° are in their infancy again
  And have no vigor in them.
FERDINAND: So they are.
  My spirits,° as in a dream, are all bound up.   490
  My father's loss, the weakness which I feel,
  The wreck of all my friends, nor this man's threats
  To whom I am subdued, are but light° to me,
  Might I but through my prison once a day
  Behold this maid. All corners else° o' th' earth   495
  Let liberty make use of; space enough
  Have I in such a prison.
PROSPERO *[aside]*:   It works. *[To Ferdinand.]* Come on. — *[To Ariel]*
  Thou hast done well, fine Ariel! *[To Ferdinand.]* Follow me.
  [To Ariel.] Hark what thou else shalt do me.°
MIRANDA *[to Ferdinand]*:   Be of comfort.   500
  My father's of a better nature, sir,
  Than he appears by speech. This is unwonted°
  Which now came from him.
PROSPERO *[to Ariel]*:   Thou shalt be as free
  As mountain winds; but then° exactly do
  All points of my command.
ARIEL: To th' syllable.   505
PROSPERO *[to Ferdinand]*:   Come, follow. *[To Miranda.]* Speak not for him.
                                                            Exeunt.

[ACT 2, Scene 1]

[Another part of the island.]

Enter Alonso, Sebastian, Antonio, Gonzalo, Adrian, Francisco, and others.

GONZALO *[to Alonso]*:   Beseech you, sir, be merry. You have cause,
  So have we all, of joy, for our escape
  Is much beyond our loss. Our hint° of woe
  Is common; every day some sailor's wife,
  The masters of some merchant, and the merchant,°   5
  Have just our theme of woe. But for the miracle,
  I mean our preservation, few in millions
  Can speak like us. Then wisely, good sir, weigh
  Our sorrow with° our comfort.
ALONSO: Prithee, peace.

---

488 nerves: Sinews.   **490 spirits:** Vital powers.   **493 light:** Unimportant.   **495 corners else:** Other corners, regions.   **500 me:** For me.   **502 unwonted:** Unusual.   **504 then:** Until then, or, if that is to be so.   **ACT 2, SCENE 1. 3 hint:** Occasion.   **5 masters . . . the merchant:** Officers of some merchant vessel and the merchant himself, the owner.   **9 with:** Against.

SEBASTIAN [*aside to Antonio*]:   He receives comfort like cold porridge.°   10
ANTONIO [*aside to Sebastian*]:   The visitor° will not give him o'er° so.
SEBASTIAN: Look, he's winding up the watch of his wit; by and by it will strike.
GONZALO [*to Alonso*]:   Sir—
SEBASTIAN [*aside to Antonio*]:   One. Tell.°
GONZALO: When every grief is entertained   15
   That's offered, comes to th' entertainer°—
SEBASTIAN: A dollar.°
GONZALO: Dolor comes to him, indeed. You have spoken truer than you pur-
   posed.
SEBASTIAN: You have taken it wiselier than I meant you should.   20
GONZALO [*to Alonso*]:   Therefore, my lord—
ANTONIO: Fie, what a spendthrift is he of his tongue!
ALONSO [*to Gonzalo*]:   I prithee, spare.°
GONZALO: Well, I have done. But yet—
SEBASTIAN [*aside to Antonio*]:   He will be talking.   25
ANTONIO [*aside to Sebastian*]:   Which, of he or Adrian, for a good wager, first
   begins to crow?°
SEBASTIAN: The old cock.°
ANTONIO: The cockerel.°
SEBASTIAN: Done. The wager?   30
ANTONIO: A laughter.°
SEBASTIAN: A match!°
ADRIAN: Though this island seem to be desert°—
ANTONIO: Ha, ha, ha!
SEBASTIAN: So, you're paid.°   35
ADRIAN: Uninhabitable and almost inaccessible—
SEBASTIAN: Yet—
ADRIAN: Yet—
ANTONIO: He could not miss 't.°
ADRIAN: It must needs be° of subtle, tender, and delicate temperance.°   40
ANTONIO: Temperance° was a delicate° wench.

---

10 porridge: Pun suggested by *peace* for "peas" or "pease," a common ingredient of porridge.
11 visitor: One taking nourishment and comfort to the sick, as Gonzalo is doing;   **give him
o'er:** Abandon him.   **14 Tell:** Keep count.   **15–16 When . . . entertainer:** When every sorrow that presents itself is accepted without resistance, there comes to the recipient.   **17 dollar:**
Widely circulated coin, the German thaler and the Spanish piece of eight (Sebastian puns on
entertainer in the sense of innkeeper; to Gonzalo, *dollar* suggests "dolor," grief).   **23 spare:**
Forbear, cease.   **26–27 Which . . . crow:** Which of the two, Gonzalo or Adrian, do you bet
will speak (crow) first?   **28 old cock:** I.e., Gonzalo.   **29 cockerel:** I.e., Adrian.   **31 laughter:**
(1) Burst of laughter (2) sitting of eggs. (When Adrian, the *cockerel*, begins to speak two lines
later, Sebastian loses the bet. . . .)   **32 A match:** A bargain; agreed.   **33 desert:** Uninhabited.
35 you're paid: I.e., you've had your laugh.   **39 miss 't:** (1) Avoid saying "Yet" (2) miss the island.
40 must needs be: Has to be;   **temperance:** Mildness of climate.   **41 Temperance:** A girl's
name;   **delicate:** (Here it means "given to pleasure, voluptuous"; in line 40, "pleasant." Antonio is evidently suggesting that *tender, and delicate temperance* sounds like a Puritan phrase,
which Antonio then mocks by applying the words to a woman rather than an island. He began
this bawdy comparison with a double entendre on *inaccessible*, line 36.)

SEBASTIAN: Ay, and a subtle,° as he most learnedly delivered.°

ADRIAN: The air breathes upon us here most sweetly.

SEBASTIAN: As if it had lungs, and rotten ones.

ANTONIO: Or as 'twere perfumed by a fen.   45

GONZALO: Here is everything advantageous to life.

ANTONIO: True, save° means to live.

SEBASTIAN: Of that there's none, or little.

GONZALO: How lush and lusty° the grass looks! How green!

ANTONIO: The ground indeed is tawny.°   50

SEBASTIAN: With an eye° of green in 't.

ANTONIO: He misses not much.

SEBASTIAN: No. He doth but° mistake the truth totally.

GONZALO: But the rarity of it is—which is indeed almost beyond credit—

SEBASTIAN: As many vouched rarities° are.   55

GONZALO: That our garments, being, as they were, drenched in the sea, hold
notwithstanding their freshness and glosses, being rather new-dyed than
stained with salt water.

ANTONIO: If but one of his pockets° could speak, would it not say he lies?

SEBASTIAN: Ay, or very falsely pocket up° his report.°   60

GONZALO: Methinks our garments are now as fresh as when we put them on first
in Afric, at the marriage of the King's fair daughter Claribel to the King of
Tunis.

SEBASTIAN: 'Twas a sweet marriage, and we prosper well in our return.

ADRIAN: Tunis was never graced before with such a paragon to° their   65
queen.

GONZALO: Not since widow Dido's° time.

ANTONIO [*aside to Sebastian*]:   Widow? A pox o' that! How came that "widow"
in? Widow Dido!

SEBASTIAN: What if he had said "widower Aeneas" too? Good Lord, how you   70
take° it!

ADRIAN [*to Gonzalo*]:   "Widow Dido" said you? You make me study of° that.
She was of Carthage, not of Tunis.

GONZALO: This Tunis, sir, was Carthage.

ADRIAN: Carthage?   75

---

42 subtle: (Here it means "tricky, sexually crafty"; in line 40, "delicate"); **delivered:**
Uttered. (Sebastian joins Antonio in baiting the Puritans with his use of the pious cant
phrase *learnedly delivered*.)   **47 save:** Except.   **49 lusty:** Healthy.   **50 tawny:** Dull brown,
yellowish.   **51 eye:** Tinge, or spot (perhaps with reference to Gonzalo's eye or judgment).
53 but: Merely.   **55 vouched rarities:** Allegedly real though strange sights.   **59 pockets:**
I.e., because they are muddy.   **60 pocket up:** I.e., conceal, suppress; often used in the sense
of "receive unprotestingly, fail to respond to a challenge"; **his report:** (Sebastian's jest is
that the evidence of Gonzalo's soggy and sea-stained pockets would confute Gonzalo's
speech and his reputation for truth telling.)   **65 to:** For.   **67 widow Dido:** Queen of
Carthage, deserted by Aeneas. (She was, in fact, a widow when Aeneas, a widower, met her, but
Antonio may be amused at Gonzalo's prudish use of the term *widow* to describe a woman
deserted by her lover.)   **71 take:** Understand, respond to, interpret.   **72 study of:** Think
about.

GONZALO: I assure you, Carthage.

ANTONIO: His word is more than the miraculous harp.°

SEBASTIAN: He hath raised the wall, and houses too.

ANTONIO: What impossible matter will he make easy next?

SEBASTIAN: I think he will carry this island home in his pocket and give it his   80
son for an apple.

ANTONIO: And, sowing the kernels° of it in the sea, bring forth more islands.

GONZALO: Ay.°

ANTONIO: Why, in good time.°

GONZALO [*to Alonso*]:   Sir, we were talking° that our garments seem now as   85
fresh as when we were at Tunis at the marriage of your daughter, who is now
queen.

ANTONIO: And the rarest° that e'er came there.

SEBASTIAN: Bate,° I beseech you, widow Dido.

ANTONIO: O, widow Dido! Ay, widow Dido.   90

GONZALO: Is not, sir, my doublet° as fresh as the first day I wore it? I mean, in a
sort.°

ANTONIO: That "sort"° was well wished for.

GONZALO: When I wore it at your daughter's marriage.

ALONSO: You cram these words into mine ears against   95
The stomach of my sense.° Would I had never
Married° my daughter there! For, coming thence,
My son is lost and, in my rate,° she too,
Who is so far from Italy removed
I ne'er again shall see her. O thou mine heir   100
Of Naples and of Milan, what strange fish
Hath made his meal on thee?

FRANCISCO: Sir, he may live.
I saw him beat the surges° under him
And ride upon their backs. He trod the water,
Whose enmity he flung aside, and breasted   105
The surge most swoll'n that met him. His bold head
'Bove the contentious waves he kept, and oared
Himself with his good arms in lusty° stroke

---

77 miraculous harp: (Alludes to Amphion's harp, with which he raised the walls of Thebes;
Gonzalo has exceeded that deed by recreating ancient Carthage — *wall and houses* — mistakenly on the site of modern-day Tunis. Some Renaissance commentators believed, like Gonzalo,
that the two sites were near each other.)   **82 kernels:** Seeds.   **83 Ay:** (Gonzalo may be
reasserting his point about Carthage, or he may be responding ironically to Antonio, who, in
turn, answers sarcastically.)   **84 in good time:** (An expression of ironical acquiescence or
amazement, i.e., "sure, right away.")   **85 talking:** Saying.   **88 rarest:** Most remarkable, beautiful.   **89 Bate:** Abate, except, leave out (Sebastian says sardonically, surely you should allow
widow Dido to be an exception).   **91 doublet:** Close-fitting jacket.   **91–92 in a sort:** In a
way.   **93 "sort":** (Antonio plays on the idea of drawing lots and on "fishing" for something to
say.)   **96 The stomach . . . sense:** My appetite for hearing them.   **97 Married:** Given in
marriage.   **98 rate:** Estimation, opinion.   **103 surges:** Waves.   **108 lusty:** Vigorous.

To th' shore, that o'er his° wave-worn basis bowed,°
As° stooping to relieve him. I not doubt   110
He came alive to land.

ALONSO: No, no, he's gone.

SEBASTIAN *[to Alonso]:*   Sir, you may thank yourself for this great loss,
That° would not bless our Europe with your daughter,
But rather° loose° her to an African,
Where she at least is banished from your eye,°   115
Who hath cause to wet the grief on 't.°

ALONSO: Prithee, peace.

SEBASTIAN: You were kneeled to and importuned° otherwise
By all of us, and the fair soul herself
Weighed between loathness and obedience at
Which end o' the beam should bow.° We have lost your son,   120
I fear, forever. Milan and Naples have
More widows in them of this business' making°
Than we bring men to comfort them.
The fault's your own.

ALONSO: So is the dear'st° o' the loss.   125

GONZALO: My lord Sebastian,
The truth you speak doth lack some gentleness
And time° to speak it in. You rub the sore
When you should bring the plaster.°

SEBASTIAN: Very well.

ANTONIO: And most chirurgeonly.°   130

GONZALO *[to Alonso]:*   It is foul weather in us all, good sir,
When you are cloudy.

SEBASTIAN *[to Antonio]:*   Fowl° weather?

ANTONIO *[to Sebastian]:*   Very foul.

GONZALO: Had I plantation° of this isle, my lord—

ANTONIO *[to Sebastian]:*   He'd sow 't with nettle seed.

SEBASTIAN: Or docks, or mallows.°

---

109 that . . . bowed: I.e., that projected out over the base of the cliff that had been eroded by the surf, thus seeming to bend down toward the sea; **his:** Its. **110 As:** As if. **113 That:** You who. **114 rather:** Would rather; **loose:** (1) Release, let loose (2) lose. **115 is banished from your eye:** Is not constantly before your eye to serve as a reproachful reminder of what you have done. **116 Who . . . on 't:** I.e., your eye, which has good reason to weep because of this, or, Claribel, who has good reason to weep for it. **117 importuned:** Urged, implored. **118–120 the fair . . . bow:** Claribel herself was poised uncertainly between unwillingness to marry and obedience to her father as to which end of the scales should sink, which should prevail. **122 of . . . making:** On account of this marriage and subsequent shipwreck. **125 dear'st:** Heaviest, most costly. **128 time:** Appropriate time. **129 plaster:** (A medical application.) **130 chirurgeonly:** Like a skilled surgeon. (Antonio mocks Gonzalo's medical analogy of a *plaster* applied curatively to a wound.) **132 Fowl:** (With a pun on *foul*, returning to the imagery of lines 26–29.) **133 plantation:** Colonization (with subsequent wordplay on the literal meaning, "planting"). **134 docks, mallows:** (Weeds used as antidotes for nettle stings.)

GONZALO: And were the king on 't, what would I do?   135
SEBASTIAN: Scape° being drunk for want° of wine.
GONZALO: I' the commonwealth I would by contraries°
    Execute all things; for no kind of traffic,°
    Would I admit; no name of magistrate,
    Letters° should not be known; riches, poverty,   140
    And use of service,° none; contract, succession,°
    Bourn, bound of land, tilth,° vineyard, none;
    No use of metal, corn,° or wine, or oil;
    No occupation; all men idle, all,
    And women too, but innocent and pure;   145
    No sovereignty—
SEBASTIAN: Yet he would be king on 't.
ANTONIO: The latter end of his commonwealth forgets the beginning.
GONZALO: All things in common nature should produce
    Without sweat or endeavor. Treason, felony,
    Sword, pike,° knife, gun, or need of any engine°   150
    Would I not have; but nature should bring forth,
    Of its own kind, all foison,° all abundance,
    To feed my innocent people.
SEBASTIAN: No marrying 'mong his subjects?
ANTONIO: None, man, all idle—whores and knaves.   155
GONZALO: I would with such perfection govern, sir,
    T' excel the Golden Age.°
SEBASTIAN: 'Save° His Majesty!
ANTONIO: Long live Gonzalo!
GONZALO: And—do you mark me, sir?
ALONSO: Prithee, no more. Thou dost talk nothing to me.
GONZALO: I do well believe Your Highness, and did it to minister occasion° to   160
    these gentlemen, who are of such sensible° and nimble lungs that they always
    use° to laugh at nothing.
ANTONIO: 'Twas you we laughed at.
GONZALO: Who in this kind of merry fooling am nothing to you; so you may
    continue, and laugh at nothing still.   165
ANTONIO: What a blow was there given!
SEBASTIAN: An° it had not fallen flat-long.°

---

136 Scape: Escape; **want:** Lack. (Sebastian jokes sarcastically that this hypothetical ruler would be saved from dissipation only by the barrenness of the island.)   **137 contraries:** By what is directly opposite to usual custom.   **138 traffic:** Trade.   **140 Letters:** Learning.   **141 use of service:** Custom of employing servants;   **succession:** Holding of property by right of inheritance.   **142 Bourn . . . tilth:** Boundaries, property limits, tillage of soil.   **143 corn:** Grain.   **150 pike:** Lance;   **engine:** Instrument of warfare.   **152 foison:** Plenty.   **157 the Golden Age:** The age, according to Hesiod, when Cronus, or Saturn, ruled the world; an age of innocence and abundance;   **'Save:** God save.   **160 minister occasion:** Furnish opportunity. **161 sensible:** Sensitive.   **162 use:** Are accustomed.   **167 An:** If;   **flat-long:** With the flat of the sword, i.e., ineffectually. (Compare with "fallen flat.")

GONZALO: You are gentlemen of brave mettle;° you would lift the moon
out of her sphere° if she would continue in it five weeks without
changing.   170

Enter Ariel [invisible] playing solemn music.

SEBASTIAN: We would so, and then go a-batfowling.°
ANTONIO: Nay, good my lord, be not angry.
GONZALO: No, I warrant you, I will not adventure my discretion so weakly.°
Will you laugh me asleep? For I am very heavy.°
ANTONIO: Go sleep, and hear us.°   175

[All sleep except Alonso, Sebastian, and Antonio.]

ALONSO: What, all so soon asleep? I wish mine eyes
Would, with themselves, shut up my thoughts.° I find
They are inclined to do so.
SEBASTIAN: Please you, sir,
Do not omit° the heavy° offer of it.
It seldom visits sorrow; when it doth,   180
It is a comforter.
ANTONIO: We two, my lord,
Will guard your person while you take your rest,
And watch your safety.
ALONSO: Thank you. Wondrous heavy.

[Alonso sleeps. Exit Ariel.]

SEBASTIAN: What a strange drowsiness possesses them!
ANTONIO: It is the quality o' the climate.
SEBASTIAN: Why   185
Doth it not then our eyelids sink? I find not
Myself disposed to sleep.
ANTONIO: Nor I. My spirits are nimble.
They° fell together all, as by consent;°
They dropped, as by a thunderstroke. What might,
Worthy Sebastian, O, what might—? No more.   190
And yet methinks I see it in thy face,
What thou shouldst be. Th' occasion speaks thee,° and

---

168 mettle: Temperament, courage. (The sense of *metal*, indistinguishable as a form from
mettle, continues the metaphor of the sword.)   **169 sphere:** Orbit (literally, one of the concentric zones occupied by planets in Ptolemaic astronomy).   **171 a-batfowling:** Hunting birds at
night with lantern and *bat*, or "stick"; also, gulling a simpleton (Gonzalo is the simpleton, or
fowl, and Sebastian will use the moon as his lantern).   **173 adventure . . . weakly:** Risk
my reputation for discretion for so trivial a cause (by getting angry at these sarcastic fellows).
174 heavy: Sleepy.   **175 Go . . . us:** I.e., get ready for sleep, and we'll do our part by laughing.   **177 Would . . . thoughts:** Would shut off my melancholy brooding when they close
themselves in sleep.   **179 omit:** Neglect;   **heavy:** Drowsy.   **188 They:** The sleepers;   **consent:** Common agreement.   **192 occasion speaks thee:** Opportunity of the moment calls
upon you, i.e., proclaims you usurper of Alonso's crown.

My strong imagination sees a crown
Dropping upon thy head.

SEBASTIAN: What, art thou waking?

ANTONIO: Do you not hear me speak?

SEBASTIAN: I do, and surely   195
It is a sleepy° language, and thou speak'st
Out of thy sleep. What is it thou didst say?
This is a strange repose, to be asleep
With eyes wide open—standing, speaking, moving—
And yet so fast asleep.

ANTONIO: Noble Sebastian,   200
Thou lett'st thy fortune sleep—die, rather; wink'st°
Whiles thou art waking.

SEBASTIAN: Thou dost snore distinctly;°
There's meaning in thy snores.

ANTONIO: I am more serious than my custom. You
Must be so too if heed° me, which to do   205
Trebles thee o'er.°

SEBASTIAN: Well, I am standing water.°

ANTONIO: I'll teach you how to flow.

SEBASTIAN: Do so. To ebb°
Hereditary sloth° instructs me.

ANTONIO: O,
If you but knew how you the purpose cherish
Whiles thus you mock it!° How, in stripping it,   210
You more invest° it!° Ebbing men, indeed,
Most often do so near the bottom° run
By their own fear or sloth.

SEBASTIAN: Prithee, say on.
The setting° of thine eye and cheek proclaim
A matter° from thee, and a birth indeed   215
Which throes° thee much to yield.°

ANTONIO: Thus, sir:
Although this lord° of weak remembrance,° this

---

196 **sleepy:** Dreamlike, fantastic.   201 **wink'st:** (You) shut your eyes.   202 **distinctly:** Artic-
ulately.   205 **if heed:** If you heed.   206 **Trebles thee o'er:** Makes you three times as great
and rich;   **standing water:** Water that neither ebbs nor flows, at a standstill.   207 **ebb:**
Recede, decline.   208 **Hereditary sloth:** Natural laziness and the position of younger brother,
one who cannot inherit.   209–210 **If . . . mock it:** If you only knew how much you really
enhance the value of ambition even while your words mock your purpose.   210–211 **How . . .
invest it:** I.e., how the more you speak flippantly of ambition, the more you, in effect, affirm it;
invest: Clothe (Antonio's paradox is that, by skeptically stripping away illusions, Sebastian can
see the essence of a situation and the opportunity it presents or that, by disclaiming and deriding
his purpose, Sebastian shows how valuable it really is).   212 **the bottom:** I.e., on which unad-
venturous men may go aground and miss the tide of fortune.   214 **setting:** Set expression (of
earnestness).   215 **matter:** Matter of importance.   216 **throes:** Causes pain, as in giving birth;
yield: Give forth, speak about.   217 **this lord:** I.e., Gonzalo;   **remembrance:** (1) Power of
remembering (2) being remembered after his death.

Who shall be of as little memory
When he is earthed,° hath here almost persuaded—
For he's a spirit of persuasion, only   220
Professes to persuade°—the King his son's alive,
'Tis as impossible that he's undrowned
As he that sleeps here swims.

SEBASTIAN: I have no hope
That he's undrowned.

ANTONIO: O, out of that "no hope"
What great hope have you! No hope that way° is   225
Another way so high a hope that even
Ambition cannot pierce a wink° beyond,
But doubt discovery there.° Will you grant with me
That Ferdinand is drowned?

SEBASTIAN: He's gone.

ANTONIO: Then tell me,   230
Who's the next heir of Naples?

SEBASTIAN: Claribel.

ANTONIO: She that is Queen of Tunis; she that dwells
Ten leagues beyond man's life;° she that from Naples
Can have no note,° unless the sun were post°—
The Man i' the Moon's too slow—till newborn chins   235
Be rough and razorable;° she that from° whom
We all were sea-swallowed, though some cast° again,
And by that destiny to perform an act
Whereof what's past is prologue, what to come
In yours and my discharge.°   240

SEBASTIAN: What stuff is this? How say you?
'Tis true my brother's daughter's Queen of Tunis,
So is she heir of Naples, twixt which regions
There is some space.

ANTONIO: A space whose every cubit°
Seems to cry out, "How shall that Claribel   245
Measure us° back to Naples? Keep° in Tunis,
And let Sebastian wake."° Say this were death
That now hath seized them, why, they were no worse
Than now they are. There be° that can rule Naples

---

219 earthed: Buried.   **220–221 only . . . persuade:** Whose whole function (as a privy councillor) is to persuade.   **225 that way:** I.e., in regard to Ferdinand's being saved.   **227 wink:**
Glimpse.   **227–228 Ambition . . . there:** Ambition itself cannot see any further than that hope
(of the crown), is unsure of finding anything to achieve beyond it or even there.   **233 Ten . . .
life:** I.e., further than the journey of a lifetime.   **234 note:** News, intimation;   **post:** Messenger.   **236 razorable:** Ready for shaving;   **from:** On our voyage from.   **237 cast:** Were dis-
gorged (with a pun on *casting* of parts for a play).   **240 discharge:** Performance.   **244 cubit:**
Ancient measure of length of about twenty inches.   **246 Measure us:** I.e., traverse the cubits,
find her way;   **Keep:** Stay (addressed to Claribel).   **247 wake:** I.e., to his good fortune.
249 There be: There are those.

As well as he that sleeps, lords that can prate°   250
As amply and unnecessarily
As this Gonzalo. I myself could make
A chough of as deep chat.° O, that you bore
The mind that I do! What a sleep were this
For your advancement! Do you understand me?   255
SEBASTIAN: Methinks I do.
ANTONIO: And how does your content°
Tender° your own good fortune?
SEBASTIAN: I remember
You did supplant your brother Prospero.
ANTONIO: True.
And look how well my garments sit upon me,
Much feater° than before. My brother's servants   260
Were then my fellows. Now they are my men.
SEBASTIAN: But, for your conscience?
ANTONIO: Ay, sir, where lies that? If 'twere a kibe,°
'Twould put me to° my slipper; but I feel not
This deity in my bosom. Twenty consciences   265
That stand twixt me and Milan,° candied° be they°
And melt ere they molest!° Here lies your brother,
No better than the earth he lies upon,
If he were that which now he's like — that's dead,
Whom I, with this obedient steel, three inches of it,   270
Can lay to bed forever; whiles you, doing thus,°
To the perpetual wink° for aye° might put
This ancient morsel, this Sir Prudence, who
Should not° upbraid our course. For all the rest,
They'll take suggestion° as a cat laps milk;   275
They'll tell the clock° to any business that
We say befits the hour.
SEBASTIAN: Thy case, dear friend,
Shall be my precedent. As thou gott'st Milan,
I'll come by Naples. Draw thy sword. One stroke
Shall free thee from the tribute° which thou payest,   280
And I the king shall love thee.
ANTONIO: Draw together;

---

250 **prate:** Speak foolishly.   252–253 **I . . . chat:** I could teach a jackdaw to talk as wisely, or, be
such a garrulous talker myself.   256 **content:** Desire, inclination.   257 **Tender:** Regard, look
after.   260 **feater:** More becomingly, fittingly.   263 **kibe:** Chilblain, here a sore on the heel.
264 **put me to:** Oblige me to wear.   266 **Milan:** The dukedom of Milan;   **candied:** Frozen,
congealed in crystalline form;   **be they:** May they be.   267 **molest:** Interfere.   271 **thus:**
Similarly. (The actor makes a stabbing gesture.)   272 **wink:** Sleep, closing of eyes;   **aye:** Ever.
274 **Should not:** Would not then be able to.   275 **take suggestion:** Respond to prompting.
276 **tell the clock:** I.e., agree, answer appropriately, chime.   280 **tribute:** (See I.ii.113, 124.)

And when I rear my hand, do you the like
To fall it° on Gonzalo.   *[They draw.]*
SEBASTIAN: O, but one word.   *[They talk apart.]*

Enter Ariel [invisible], with music and song.

ARIEL *[to Gonzalo]*:   My master through his art foresees the danger
    That you, his friend, are in, and sends me forth —   285
    For else his project dies — to keep them living.   *Sings in Gonzalo's ear.*
        While you here do snoring lie,
        Open-eyed conspiracy
            His time° doth take.
        If of life you keep a care,   290
        Shake off slumber, and beware.
            Awake, awake!
ANTONIO: Then let us both be sudden.°
GONZALO *[waking]*:   Now, good angels preserve the King!   *[The others wake.]*
ALONSO: Why, how now, ho, awake? Why are you drawn?   295
    Wherefore this ghastly looking?
GONZALO: What's the matter?
SEBASTIAN: Whiles we stood here securing° your repose,
    Even now, we heard a hollow burst of bellowing
    Like bulls, or rather lions. Did 't not wake you?
    It struck mine ear most terribly.
ALONSO: I heard nothing.   300
ANTONIO: O, 'twas a din to fright a monster's ear,
    To make an earthquake! Sure it was the roar
    Of a whole herd of lions.
ALONSO: Heard you this, Gonzalo?
GONZALO: Upon mine honor, sir. I heard a humming,   305
    And that a strange one too, which did awake me.
    I shaked you, sir, and cried.° As mine eyes opened,
    I saw their weapons drawn. There was a noise,
    That's verily.° 'Tis best we stand upon our guard,
    Or that we quit this place. Let's draw our weapons.   310
ALONSO: Lead off this ground, and let's make further search
    For my poor son.
GONZALO: Heavens keep him from these beasts!
    For he is, sure, i' th' island.
ALONSO: Lead away.
ARIEL *[aside]*:   Prospero my lord shall know what I have done.
    So, King, go safely on to seek thy son.   *Exeunt [separately].*   315

---

283 fall it: Let it fall.   **289 time:** Opportunity.   **293 sudden:** Quick.   **297 securing:**
Standing guard over.   **307 cried:** Called out.   **309 verily:** True.

[Scene 2]

[Another part of the island.]

Enter Caliban with a burden of wood. A noise of thunder heard.

CALIBAN: All the infections that the sun sucks up
From bogs, fens, flats,° on Prosper fall, and make him
By inchmeal° a disease! His spirits hear me,
And yet I needs must° curse. But they'll nor° pinch,
Fright me with urchin shows,° pitch me i' the mire,   5
Nor lead me, like a firebrand,° in the dark
Out of my way, unless he bid 'em. But
For every trifle are they set upon me,
Sometimes like apes, that mow° and chatter at me
And after bite me; then like hedgehogs, which   10
Lie tumbling in my barefoot way and mount
Their pricks at my footfall. Sometimes am I
All wound with° adders, who with cloven tongues
Do hiss me into madness.

Enter Trinculo.

                Lo, now, lo!
Here comes a spirit of his, and to torment me   15
For bringing wood in slowly. I'll fall flat.
Perchance he will not mind° me.   *[He lies down.]*

TRINCULO: Here's neither bush nor shrub to bear off° any weather at all. And another storm brewing; I hear it sing i' the wind. Yond same black cloud, yond huge one, looks like a foul bombard° that would shed his° liquor. If it   20 should thunder as it did before, I know not where to hide my head. Yond same cloud cannot choose but fall by pailfuls. *[Seeing Caliban.]* What have we here, a man or a fish? Dead or alive? A fish, he smells like a fish; a very ancient and fishlike smell; a kind of not-of-the-newest Poor John.° A strange fish! Were I in England now, as once I was, and had but this fish painted,°   25 not a holiday fool there but would give a piece of silver. There would this monster make a man.° Any strange beast there makes a man. When they will not give a doit° to relieve a lame beggar, they will lay out ten to see a dead Indian. Legged like a man, and his fins like arms! Warm, o' my troth!° I do now let loose my opinion, hold it° no longer: this is no fish, but an islander,   30 that hath lately suffered° by a thunderbolt. *[Thunder.]* Alas, the storm is

---

SCENE 2. **2 flats:** Swamps. **3 By inchmeal:** Inch by inch. **4 needs must:** Have to; **nor:** Neither. **5 urchin shows:** Elvish apparitions shaped like hedgehogs. **6 like a firebrand:** They in the guise of a will-o'-the-wisp. **9 mow:** Make faces. **13 wound with:** Entwined by. **17 mind:** Notice. **18 bear off:** Keep off. **20 foul bombard:** Dirty leather jug; **his:** Its. **24 Poor John:** Salted fish, type of poor fare. **25 painted:** I.e., painted on a sign set up outside a booth or tent at a fair. **27 make a man:** (1) Make one's fortune (2) be indistinguishable from an Englishman. **28 doit:** Small coin. **29 o' my troth:** By my faith. **30 hold it:** Hold it in. **31 suffered:** I.e., died.

come again! My best way is to creep under his gaberdine.° There is no other
shelter hereabout. Misery acquaints a man with strange bedfellows. I will
here shroud° till the dregs° of the storm be past.

[He creeps under Caliban's garment.]

Enter Stephano, singing, [a bottle in his hand].

STEPHANO: "I shall no more to sea, to sea,   35
     Here shall I die ashore —"
This is a very scurvy tune to sing at a man's funeral.
Well, here's my comfort.   *Drinks.*
(Sings.)
    "The master, the swabber,° the boatswain, and I,
     The gunner and his mate,   40
    Loved Mall, Meg, and Marian, and Margery,
     But none of us cared for Kate.
      For she had a tongue with a tang,°
      Would cry to a sailor, 'Go hang!'
    She loved not the savor of tar nor of pitch,   45
    Yet a tailor might scratch her where'er she did itch.°
      Then to sea, boys, and let her go hang!"
This is a scurvy tune too. But here's my comfort.   *Drinks.*
CALIBAN: Do not torment me!° O!
STEPHANO: What's the matter?° Have we devils here? Do you put tricks upon 's°   50
with savages and men of Ind,° ha? I have not scaped drowning to be afeard
now of your four legs. For it hath been said, "As proper° a man as ever went
on four legs° cannot make him give ground"; and it shall be said so again
while Stephano breathes at'° nostrils.
CALIBAN: This spirit torments me! O!   55
STEPHANO: This is some monster of the isle with four legs, who hath got, as I
take it, an ague.° Where the devil should he learn° our language? I will give
him some relief, if it be but for that.° If I can recover° him and keep him
tame and get to Naples with him, he's a present for any emperor that ever
trod on neat's leather.°   60
CALIBAN: Do not torment me, prithee. I'll bring my wood home faster.
STEPHANO: He's in his fit now and does not talk after the wisest.° He shall taste
of my bottle. If he have never drunk wine afore,° it will go near to° remove

---

32 **gaberdine:** Cloak, loose upper garment.   34 **shroud:** Take shelter;   **dregs:** I.e., last remains (as in a *bombard* or jug, line 20).   39 **swabber:** Crew member whose job is to wash the
decks.   43 **tang:** Sting.   46 **tailor . . . itch:** (A dig at tailors for their supposed effeminacy and a
bawdy suggestion of satisfying a sexual craving.)   49 **Do . . . me:** (Caliban assumes that one of
Prospero's spirits has come to punish him.)   50 **What's the matter?:** What's going on here?
put tricks upon 's: Trick us with conjuring shows.   51 **Ind:** India.   52 **proper:** Handsome.
53 **four legs:** (The conventional phrase would supply *two* legs, but the creature Stephano thinks
he sees has four.)   54 **at':** At the.   57 **ague:** Fever. (Probably both Caliban and Trinculo are
quaking; see lines 49 and 66–67.);   **should he learn:** Could he have learned.   58 **for that:** I.e.,
for knowing our language;   **recover:** Restore.   60 **neat's leather:** Cowhide.   62 **after the wisest:** In the wisest fashion.   63 **afore:** Before;   **go near to:** Be in a fair way to.

his fit. If I can recover° him and keep him tame, I will not take too much° for
him. He shall pay for him that hath° him,° and that soundly.   65

CALIBAN: Thou dost me yet but little hurt; thou wilt anon,° I know it by thy
trembling. Now Prosper works upon thee.

STEPHANO: Come on your ways. Open your mouth. Here is that which will give
language to you, cat. Open your mouth.° This will shake your shaking, I can
tell you, and that soundly. *[Giving Caliban a drink.]* You cannot tell who's   70
your friend. Open your chaps° again.

TRINCULO: I should know that voice. It should be—but he is drowned, and
these are devils. O, defend me!

STEPHANO: Four legs and two voices—a most delicate° monster! His forward
voice now is to speak well of his friend; his backward voice° is to utter foul   75
speeches and to detract. If all the wine in my bottle will recover him,° I will
help° his ague. Come. *[Giving a drink.]* Amen! I will pour some in thy other
mouth.

TRINCULO: Stephano!

STEPHANO: Doth thy other mouth call me?° Mercy, mercy! This is a devil, and   80
no monster. I will leave him. I have no long spoon.°

TRINCULO: Stephano! If thou beest Stephano, touch me and speak to me, for I
am Trinculo—be not afeard—thy good friend Trinculo.

STEPHANO: If thou beest Trinculo, come forth. I'll pull thee by the lesser legs. If
any be Trinculo's legs, these are they. *[Pulling him out.]* Thou art very Trin-   85
culo indeed! How cam'st thou to be the siege° of this mooncalf?° Can he
vent° Trinculos?

TRINCULO: I took him to be killed with a thunderstroke. But art thou not
drowned, Stephano? I hope now thou art not drowned. Is the storm overblown?° I hid me under the dead mooncalf's gaberdine for fear of the storm.   90
And art thou living, Stephano? O Stephano, two Neapolitans scaped!

                                            [He capers with Stephano.]

STEPHANO: Prithee, do not turn me about. My stomach is not constant.°

CALIBAN: These be fine things, an if° they be not spirits.
That's a brave° god, and bears° celestial liquor.
I will kneel to him.   95

---

64 recover: Restore;   **I will . . . much:** I.e., no sum can be too much.   **65 He shall . . .**
hath him: I.e., anyone who wants him will have to pay dearly for him;   **hath:** Possesses,
receives.   **66 anon:** Presently.   **69 cat . . . mouth:** (Allusion to the proverb "Good liquor
will make a cat speak.")   **71 chaps:** Jaws.   **74 delicate:** Ingenious.   **75 backward voice:**
(Trinculo and Caliban are facing in opposite directions. Stephano supposes the monster to
have a rear end that can emit *foul speeches* or foul-smelling wind at the monster's *other mouth*,
line 80.)   **76 If . . . him:** Even if it takes all the wine in my bottle to cure him.   **77 help:**
Cure.   **80 call me:** I.e., call me by name, know supernaturally who I am.   **81 long spoon:**
(Allusion to the proverb "He that sups with the devil has need of a long spoon.")   **86 siege:**
Excrement;   **mooncalf:** Monstrous or misshapen creature (whose deformity is caused by the
malignant influence of the moon).   **87 vent:** Excrete, defecate.   **89–90 overblown:** Blown
over.   **92 not constant:** Unsteady.   **93 an if:** If.   **94 brave:** Fine, magnificent;   **bears:** He
carries.

STEPHANO: How didst thou scape? How cam'st thou hither? Swear by this bottle how thou cam'st hither. I escaped upon a butt of sack° which the sailors heaved o'erboard—by this bottle,° which I made of the bark of a tree with mine own hands since° I was cast ashore.

CALIBAN *[kneeling]*:   I'll swear upon that bottle to be thy true subject, for the   100
liquor is not earthly.

STEPHANO: Here. Swear then how thou escapedst.

TRINCULO: Swum ashore, man, like a duck. I can swim like a duck, I'll be sworn.

STEPHANO: Here, kiss the book.° Though thou canst swim like a duck, thou art   105
made like a goose.   *[Giving him a drink.]*

TRINCULO: O Stephano, hast any more of this?

STEPHANO: The whole butt, man. My cellar is in a rock by the seaside, where my wine is hid.—How now, mooncalf? How does thine ague?

CALIBAN: Hast thou not dropped from heaven?   110

STEPHANO: Out o' the moon, I do assure thee. I was the Man i' the Moon when time was.°

CALIBAN: I have seen thee in her, and I do adore thee. My mistress showed me thee, and thy dog, and thy bush.°

STEPHANO: Come, swear to that. Kiss the book. I will furnish it anon with new   115
contents. Swear.   *[Giving him a drink.]*

TRINCULO: By this good light,° this is a very shallow monster! I afeard of him? A very weak monster! The Man i' the Moon? A most poor credulous monster! Well drawn,° monster, in good sooth!°

CALIBAN *[to Stephano]*:   I'll show thee every fertile inch o' th' island, And I will   120
kiss thy foot. I prithee, be my god.

TRINCULO: By this light, a most perfidious and drunken monster! When 's god's asleep, he'll rob his bottle.°

CALIBAN: I'll kiss thy foot. I'll swear myself thy subject.

STEPHANO: Come on then. Down, and swear.   *[Caliban kneels.]*   125

TRINCULO: I shall laugh myself to death at this puppy-headed monster. A most scurvy monster! I could find in my heart to beat him—

STEPHANO: Come, kiss.

TRINCULO: But that the poor monster's in drink.° An abominable monster!

CALIBAN: I'll show thee the best springs. I'll pluck thee berries.   130
I'll fish for thee and get thee wood enough.
A plague upon the tyrant that I serve!

---

97 butt of sack: Barrel of Canary wine.   **98 by this bottle:** I.e., I swear by this bottle.
99 since: After.   **105 book:** I.e., bottle (but with ironic reference to the practice of kissing the
Bible in swearing an oath; see *I'll be sworn* in lines 103–104).   **111–112 when time was:** Once
upon a time.   **114 dog . . . bush:** (The Man in the Moon was popularly imagined to have
with him a dog and a bush of thorn.)   **117 By . . . light:** By God's light, by this good light from
heaven.   **119 Well drawn:** Well pulled (on the bottle); **in good sooth:** Truly, indeed.
122–123 When . . . bottle: I.e., Caliban wouldn't even stop at robbing his god of his bottle if
he could catch him asleep.   **129 in drink:** Drunk.

I'll bear him no more sticks, but follow thee,
Thou wondrous man.

TRINCULO: A most ridiculous monster, to make a   135
    wonder of a poor drunkard!

CALIBAN: I prithee, let me bring thee where crabs° grow,
    And I with my long nails will dig thee pignuts,°
    Show thee a jay's nest, and instruct thee how
    To snare the nimble marmoset.° I'll bring thee   140
    To clustering filberts, and sometimes I'll get thee
    Young scamels° from the rock. Wilt thou go with me?

STEPHANO: I prithee now, lead the way without any more talking. — Trinculo,
    the King and all our company else° being drowned, we will inherit° here. —
    Here, bear my bottle. — Fellow Trinculo, we'll fill him by and by again.   145

CALIBAN (*sings drunkenly*):   Farewell, master, farewell, farewell!

TRINCULO: A howling monster; a drunken monster!

CALIBAN: No more dams I'll make for fish,
        Nor fetch in firing°
        At requiring,   150
    Nor scrape trenchering,° nor wash dish.
        'Ban, 'Ban, Ca–Caliban
        Has a new master. Get a new man!°
    Freedom, high-day!° High-day, freedom! Freedom, high-day, freedom!

STEPHANO: O brave monster! Lead the way.   *Exeunt.*   155

[ACT 3, Scene 1]

[Before Prospero's cell.]

Enter Ferdinand, bearing a log.

FERDINAND: There be some sports are painful, and their labor
    Delight in them sets off.° Some kinds of baseness°
    Are nobly undergone,° and most poor° matters
    Point to rich ends. This my mean° task
    Would be as heavy to me as odious, but°   5

---

137 crabs: Crab apples, or perhaps crabs.   **138 pignuts:** Earthnuts, edible tuberous roots.
140 marmoset: Small monkey.   **142 scamels:** (Possibly *seamews*, mentioned in Strachey's
letter, or shellfish, or perhaps from *squamelle*, "furnished with little scales." Contemporary
French and Italian travel accounts report that the natives of Patagonia in South America ate
small fish described as *fort scameux* and *squame*.)   **144 else:** In addition, besides ourselves;
inherit: Take possession.   **149 firing:** Firewood.   **151 trenchering:** Trenchers, wooden plates.
153 Get a new man: (Addressed to Prospero.)   **154 high-day:** Holiday.   ACT 3, SCENE 1.
1–2 There . . . sets off: Some pastimes are laborious, but the pleasure we get from them com-
pensates for the effort. (Pleasure is *set off* by labor as a jewel is set off by its foil.)
2 baseness: Menial activity.   **3 undergone:** Undertaken;   **most poor:** Poorest.   **4 mean:**
Lowly.   **5 but:** Were it not that.

The mistress which I serve quickens° what's dead
And makes my labors pleasures. O, she is
Ten times more gentle than her father's crabbed,
And he's composed of harshness. I must remove
Some thousands of these logs and pile them up,   10
Upon a sore injunction.° My sweet mistress
Weeps when she sees me work and says such baseness
Had never like executor.° I forget;°
But these sweet thoughts do even refresh my labors,
Most busy lest when I do it.°

Enter Miranda; and Prospero [at a distance, unseen].

MIRANDA: Alas now, pray you,   15
　　Work not so hard. I would the lightning had
　　Burnt up those logs that you are enjoined° to pile!
　　Pray, set it down and rest you. When this° burns,
　　'Twill weep° for having wearied you. My father
　　Is hard at study. Pray now, rest yourself.   20
　　He's safe for these° three hours.
FERDINAND: O most dear mistress,
　　The sun will set before I shall discharge°
　　What I must strive to do.
MIRANDA: If you'll sit down,
　　I'll bear your logs the while. Pray, give me that.
　　I'll carry it to the pile.
FERDINAND: No, precious creature,   25
　　I had rather crack my sinews, break my back,
　　Than you should such dishonor undergo
　　While I sit lazy by.
MIRANDA: It would become me
　　As well as it does you; and I should do it
　　With much more ease, for my good will is to it,   30
　　And yours it is against.
PROSPERO *[aside]*:   Poor worm, thou art infected!
　　This visitation° shows it.
MIRANDA: You look wearily.
FERDINAND: No, noble mistress, 'tis fresh morning with me
　　When you are by° at night. I do beseech you—

---

6 quickens: Gives life to.   **11 sore injunction:** Severe command.   **13 Had . . . executor:**
I.e., was never before undertaken by so noble a being;   **I forget:** I.e., I forget that I'm supposed
to be working, or, I forget my happiness, oppressed by my labor.   **15 Most . . . it:** I.e., busy at
my labor but with my mind on other things (?) (the line may be in need of emendation).
17 enjoined: Commanded.   **18 this:** I.e., the log.   **19 weep:** I.e., exude resin.   **21 these:**
The next.   **22 discharge:** Complete.   **32 visitation:** (1) Miranda's visit to Ferdinand (2) visitation of the plague, i.e., infection of love.   **34 by:** Nearby.

Chiefly that I might set it in my prayers—   35
What is your name?

MIRANDA: Miranda.—O my father,
I have broke your hest° to say so.

FERDINAND: Admired Miranda!°
Indeed the top of admiration, worth
What's dearest° to the world! Full many a lady
I have eyed with best regard,° and many a time   40
The harmony of their tongues hath into bondage
Brought my too diligent° ear. For several° virtues
Have I liked several women, never any
With so full soul but some defect in her
Did quarrel with the noblest grace she owed°   45
And put it to the foil.° But you, O you,
So perfect and so peerless, are created
Of° every creature's best!

MIRANDA: I do not know
One of my sex; no woman's face remember,
Save, from my glass, mine own. Nor have I seen   50
More that I may call men than you, good friend,
And my dear father. How features are abroad°
I am skilless° of; but, by my modesty,°
The jewel in my dower, I would not wish
Any companion in the world but you;   55
Nor can imagination form a shape,
Besides yourself, to like of.° But I prattle
Something° too wildly, and my father's precepts
I therein do forget.

FERDINAND: I am in my condition°
A prince, Miranda; I do think, a king—   60
I would, not so!—and would° no more endure
This wooden slavery° than to suffer
The flesh-fly° blow° my mouth. Hear my soul speak:
The very instant that I saw you did
My heart fly to your service, there resides   65
To make me slave to it, and for your sake
Am I this patient long-man.

MIRANDA: Do you love me?

---

37 hest: Command; **Admired Miranda:** (Her name means "to be admired or wondered at.") **39 dearest:** Most treasured. **40 best regard:** Thoughtful and approving attention. **42 diligent:** Attentive; **several:** Various (also on line 43). **45 owed:** Owned. **46 put . . . foil:** (1) Overthrew it (as in wrestling) (2) served as a *foil*, or "contrast," to set it off. **48 Of:** Out of. **52 How . . . abroad:** What people look like in other places. **53 skilless:** Ignorant; **modesty:** Virginity. **57 like of:** Be pleased with, be fond of. **58 Something:** Somewhat. **59 condition:** Rank. **61 would:** Wish (it were). **62 wooden slavery:** Being compelled to carry wood. **63 flesh-fly:** Insect that deposits its eggs in dead flesh; **blow:** Befoul with fly eggs.

FERDINAND: O heaven, O earth, bear witness to this sound,
    And crown what I profess with kind event°
    If I speak true! If hollowly,° invert°   70
    What best is boded° me to mischief!° I
    Beyond all limit of what° else i' the world
    Do love, prize, honor you.
MIRANDA *[weeping]:*   I am a fool
    To weep at what I am glad of.
PROSPERO *[aside]:*   Fair encounter
    Of two most rare affections! Heavens rain grace   75
    On that which breeds between 'em!
FERDINAND: Wherefore weep you?
MIRANDA: At mine unworthiness, that dare not offer
    What I desire to give, and much less take
    What I shall die° to want.° But this is trifling,
    And all the more it seeks to hide itself   80
    The bigger bulk it shows. Hence, bashful cunning,°
    And prompt me, plain and holy innocence!
    I am your wife, if you will marry me;
    If not, I'll die your maid.° To be your fellow°
    You may deny me, but I'll be your servant   85
    Whether you will° or no.
FERDINAND: My mistress,° dearest,
    And I thus humble ever.
MIRANDA: My husband, then?
FERDINAND: Ay, with a heart as willing°
    As bondage e'er of freedom. Here's my hand.   90
MIRANDA *[clasping his hand]:*   And mine, with my heart in 't. And now farewell
    Till half an hour hence.
FERDINAND: A thousand thousand!°
                Exeunt [Ferdinand and Miranda, separately].
PROSPERO: So glad of this as they I cannot be,
    Who are surprised with all;° but my rejoicing
    At nothing can be more. I'll to my book,
    For yet ere suppertime must I perform   95
    Much business appertaining.°   *Exit.*

---

69 kind event: Favorable outcome. **70 hollowly:** Insincerely, falsely; **invert:** Turn. **71 boded:** In store for; **mischief:** Harm. **72 what:** Whatever. **79 die:** (Probably with an unconscious sexual meaning that underlies all of lines 77–81.); **to want:** Through lacking. **81 bashful cunning:** Coyness. **84 maid:** Handmaiden, servant; **fellow:** Mate, equal. **86 will:** Desire it; **My mistress:** I.e., the woman I adore and serve (not an illicit sexual partner). **89 willing:** Desirous. **92 A thousand thousand:** I.e., a thousand thousand farewells. **94 with all:** By everything that has happened, or, *withal,* "with it." **97 appertaining:** Related to this.

[Scene 2]

[Another part of the island.]

Enter Caliban, Stephano, and Trinculo.

STEPHANO: Tell not me. When the butt is out,° we will drink water, not a drop
before. Therefore bear up and board 'em.° Servant monster, drink to me.

TRINCULO: Servant monster? The folly of° this island! They say there's but five
upon this isle. We are three of them; if th' other two be brained° like us, the
state totters.   5

STEPHANO: Drink, servant monster, when I bid thee. Thy eyes are almost set° in
thy head.   *[Giving a drink.]*

TRINCULO: Where should they be set° else? He were a brave° monster indeed if
they were set in his tail.

STEPHANO: My man-monster hath drowned his tongue in sack. For my part, the   10
sea cannot drown me. I swam, ere I could recover° the shore, five and thirty
leagues° off and on.° By this light,° thou shalt be my lieutenant, monster, or
my standard.°

TRINCULO: Your lieutenant, if you list;° he's no standard.°

STEPHANO: We'll not run,° Monsieur Monster.   15

TRINCULO: Nor go° neither, but you'll lie° like dogs and yet say nothing
neither.

STEPHANO: Mooncalf, speak once in thy life, if thou beest a good mooncalf.

CALIBAN: How does thy honor? Let me lick thy shoe. I'll not serve him. He is
not valiant.   20

TRINCULO: Thou liest, most ignorant monster, I am in case to jostle a constable.° Why, thou debauched° fish, thou, was there ever man a coward that
hath drunk so much sack° as I today? Wilt thou tell a monstrous lie, being
but half a fish and half a monster?

CALIBAN: Lo, how he mocks me! Wilt thou let him, my lord?   25

TRINCULO: "Lord," quoth he? That a monster should be such a natural!°

CALIBAN: Lo, lo, again! Bite him to death, I prithee.

STEPHANO: Trinculo, keep a good tongue in your head. If you prove a mu-

---

SCENE 2. **1 out:** Empty.   **2 bear . . . 'em:** (Stephano uses the terminology of maneuvering
at sea and boarding a vessel under attack as a way of urging an assault on the liquor supply.)
3 folly of: I.e., stupidity found on.   **4 be brained:** Are endowed with intelligence.   **6 set:**
Fixed in a drunken stare, or, sunk, like the sun.   **8 set:** Placed;   **brave:** Fine, splendid.   **11 recover:** Gain, reach.   **12 leagues:** Units of distance, each equaling about three miles;   **off**
and on: Intermittently;   **By this light:** (An oath: by the light of the sun.).   **13 standard:**
Standard-bearer, ensign (as distinguished from *lieutenant*, lines 12, 14).   **14 list:** Prefer;   **no**
standard: I.e., not able to stand up.   **15 run:** (1) Retreat (2) urinate (taking Trinculo's *standard*, line 14, in the old sense of "conduit").   **16 go:** Walk;   **lie:** (1) Tell lies, (2) lie prostrate,
(3) excrete.   **21–22 in case . . . constable:** I.e., in fit condition, made valiant by drink, to taunt
or challenge the police.   **22 debauched:** (1) Seduced away from proper service and allegiance (2) depraved.   **23 sack:** Spanish white wine.   **26 natural:** (1) Idiot (2) natural as
opposed to unnatural, monsterlike.

tineer—the next tree!° The poor monster's my subject, and he shall not suf-
fer indignity.   30
CALIBAN: I thank my noble lord. Wilt thou be pleased
To hearken once again to the suit I made to thee?
STEPHANO: Marry,° will I. Kneel and repeat it. I will stand, and so shall
Trinculo.   *[Caliban kneels.]*

Enter Ariel, invisible.°

CALIBAN: As I told thee before, I am subject to a tyrant,   35
A sorcerer, that by his cunning hath
Cheated me of the island.
ARIEL *[mimicking Trinculo]*:   Thou liest.
CALIBAN: Thou liest, thou jesting monkey, thou!
I would my valiant master would destroy thee.
I do not lie.
STEPHANO: Trinculo, if you trouble him any more in 's tale, by this hand, I will   40
supplant° some of your teeth.
TRINCULO: Why, I said nothing.
STEPHANO: Mum, then, and no more. — Proceed.
CALIBAN: I say by sorcery he got this isle;
From me he got it. If thy greatness will   45
Revenge it on him—for I know thou dar'st,
But this thing° dare not—
STEPHANO: That's most certain.
CALIBAN: Thou shalt be lord of it, and I'll serve thee.
STEPHANO: How now shall this be compassed?° Canst thou bring me to the   50
party?
CALIBAN: Yea, yea, my lord. I'll yield him thee asleep,
Where thou mayst knock a nail into his head.
ARIEL: Thou liest; thou canst not.
CALIBAN: What a pied ninny's° this! Thou scurvy patch!° —   55
I do beseech thy greatness, give him blows
And take his bottle from him. When that's gone
He shall drink naught but brine, for I'll not show him
Where the quick freshes° are.
STEPHANO: Trinculo, run into no further danger. Interrupt the monster one   60
word further° and, by this hand, I'll turn my mercy out o' doors° and make a
stockfish° of thee.
TRINCULO: Why, what did I? I did nothing. I'll go farther off.°

---

29 the next tree: I.e., you'll hang.   **33 Marry:** I.e., indeed (originally an oath, "by the Virgin
Mary").   **invisible:** I.e., wearing a garment to connote invisibility, as at I.ii.378.   **41 supplant:** Uproot, displace.   **47 this thing:** I.e., Trinculo.   **50 compassed:** Achieved.   **55 pied
ninny:** Fool in motley;   **patch:** Fool.   **59 quick freshes:** Running springs.   **60–61 one word
further:** I.e., one more time.   **62 turn . . . doors:** I.e., forget about being merciful.   **62 stock-
fish:** Dried cod beaten before cooking.   **63 off:** Away.

STEPHANO: Didst thou not say he lied?

ARIEL: Thou liest.   65

STEPHANO: Do I so? Take thou that. *[He beats Trinculo.]* As you like this, give
      me the lie° another time.

TRINCULO: I did not give the lie. Out o' your wits and hearing too? A pox o' your
      bottle! This can sack and drinking do. A murrain° on your monster, and the
      devil take your fingers!   70

CALIBAN: Ha, ha, ha!

STEPHANO: Now, forward with your tale. *[To Trinculo.]* Prithee, stand further
      off.

CALIBAN: Beat him enough. After a little time
      I'll beat him too.   75

STEPHANO: Stand farther.—Come, proceed.

CALIBAN: Why, as I told thee, 'tis a custom with him
      I' th' afternoon to sleep. There thou mayst brain him,
      Having first seized his books; or with a log
      Batter his skull, or paunch° him with a stake,   80
      Or cut his weasand° with thy knife. Remember
      First to possess his books, for without them
      He's but a sot,° as I am, nor hath not
      One spirit to command. They all do hate him
      As rootedly as I. Burn but his books.   85
      He has brave utensils° — for so he calls them —
      Which, when he has a house, he'll deck withal.°
      And that most deeply to consider is
      The beauty of his daughter. He himself
      Calls her a nonpareil. I never saw a woman   90
      But only Sycorax my dam and she;
      But she as far surpasseth Sycorax
      As great'st does least.

STEPHANO: Is it so brave° a lass?

CALIBAN: Ay, lord. She will become° thy bed, I warrant,   95
      And bring thee forth brave brood.

STEPHANO: Monster, I will kill this man. His daughter and I will be king and
      queen — save Our Graces! — and Trinculo and thyself shall be viceroys. Dost
      thou like the plot, Trinculo?

TRINCULO: Excellent.   100

STEPHANO: Give me thy hand. I am sorry I beat thee; but, while thou liv'st, keep
      a good tongue in thy head.

CALIBAN: Within this half hour will he be asleep.

66–67 give me the lie: Call me a liar to my face.   **69 murrain:** Plague (literally, a cattle disease).   **80 paunch:** Stab in the belly.   **81 weasand:** Windpipe.   **83 sot:** Fool.   **86 brave utensils:** Fine furnishings.   **87 deck withal:** Furnish it with.   **94 brave:** Splendid, attractive. **95 become:** Suit (sexually).

Wilt thou destroy him then?

STEPHANO: Ay, on mine honor.   105

ARIEL [*aside*]:   This will I tell my master.

CALIBAN: Thou mak'st me merry; I am full of pleasure.
Let us be jocund.° Will you troll the catch°
You taught me but whilere?°

STEPHANO: At thy request, monster, I will do reason, any reason.° — Come on,   110
Trinculo, let us sing.   *Sings.*
    "Flout° 'em and scout° 'em
    And scout 'em and flout em!
        Thought is free."

CALIBAN: That's not the tune.   *Ariel plays the tune on a tabor° and pipe.*   115

STEPHANO: What is this same?

TRINCULO: This is the tune of our catch, played by the picture of Nobody.°

STEPHANO: If thou beest a man, show thyself in thy likeness. If thou beest a
devil, take 't as thou list.°

TRINCULO: O, forgive me my sins!   120

STEPHANO: He that dies pays all debts.° I defy thee. Mercy upon us!

CALIBAN: Art thou afeard?

STEPHANO: No, monster, not I.

CALIBAN: Be not afeard. The isle is full of noises,
Sounds, and sweet airs, that give delight and hurt not.   125
Sometimes a thousand twanging instruments
Will hum about mine ears, and sometimes voices
That, if I then had waked after long sleep,
Will make me sleep again; and then, in dreaming,
The clouds methought would open and show riches   130
Ready to drop upon me, that when I waked
I cried to dream° again.

STEPHANO: This will prove a brave kingdom to me, where I shall have my music
for nothing.

CALIBAN: When Prospero is destroyed.   135

STEPHANO: That shall be by and by.° I remember the story.

TRINCULO: The sound is going away. Let's follow it, and after do our work.

STEPHANO: Lead, monster; we'll follow. I would I could see this taborer! He lays
it on.°

TRINCULO: Wilt come? I'll follow, Stephano.   *Exeunt [following Ariel's music].*   140

---

108 jocund: Jovial, merry;   **troll the catch:** Sing the round.   **109 but whilere:** Only a short
time ago.   **110 reason, any reason:** Anything reasonable.   **112 Flout:** Scoff at;   **scout:**
Deride.   **115 tabor:** Small drum.   **117 picture of Nobody:** (Refers to a familiar figure with
head, arms, and legs but no trunk.)   **119 take 't . . . list:** I.e., take my defiance as you please, as
best you can.   **121 He . . . debts:** I.e., if I have to die, at least that will be the end of all my
woes and obligations.   **132 to dream:** Desirous of dreaming.   **136 by and by:** Very soon.
138–139 lays it on: I.e., plays the drum vigorously.

[Scene 3]

[Another part of the island.]

Enter Alonso, Sebastian, Antonio, Gonzalo, Adrian, Francisco, etc.

GONZALO: By 'r lakin,° I can go no further, sir.
    My old bones aches. Here's a maze trod indeed
    Through forthrights and meanders!° By your patience,
    I needs must° rest me.

ALONSO: Old lord, I cannot blame thee,
    Who am myself attached° with weariness,   5
    To th' dulling of my spirits.° Sit down and rest.
    Even here I will put off my hope, and keep it
    No longer for° my flatterer. He is drowned
    Whom thus we stray to find, and the sea mocks
    Our frustrate° search on land. Well, let him go.   *[Alonso and Gonzalo sit.]*   10

ANTONIO *[aside to Sebastian]:*   I am right° glad that he's so out of hope.
    Do not, for° one repulse, forgo the purpose
    That you resolved t' effect.

SEBASTIAN *[to Antonio]:*   The next advantage
    Will we take throughly.°

ANTONIO *[to Sebastian]:*   Let it be tonight,
    For, now° they are oppressed with travel,° they   15
    Will not, nor cannot, use° such vigilance
    As when they are fresh.

SEBASTIAN *[to Antonio]:*   I say tonight. No more.

Solemn and strange music; and Prospero on the top,° invisible.

ALONSO: What harmony is this? My good friends, hark!

GONZALO: Marvelous sweet music!

*Enter several strange shapes, bringing in a banquet, and dance about it with gentle
actions of salutations; and, inviting the King, etc., to eat, they depart.*

ALONSO: Give us kind keepers,° heavens! What were these?   20

SEBASTIAN: A living° drollery.° Now I will believe
    That there are unicorns; that in Arabia
    There is one tree, the phoenix' throne, one phoenix°

SCENE 3.   **1 By 'r lakin:** By our Ladykin, by our Lady.   **3 forthrights and meanders:** Paths
straight and crooked.   **4 needs must:** Have to.   **5 attached:** Seized.   **6 To . . . spirits:**
To the point of being dull-spirited.   **8 for:** As.   **10 frustrate:** Frustrated.   **11 right:** Very.
12 for: Because of.   **14 throughly:** Thoroughly.   **15 now:** Now that;   **travel:** Carrying the
sense of labor as well as traveling.   **16 use:** Apply;   **on the top:** At some high point of the
tiring-house or the theater, on a third level above the gallery.   **20 kind keepers:** Guardian
angels.   **21 living:** With live actors;   **drollery:** Comic entertainment, caricature, puppet
show.   **23 phoenix:** Mythical bird consumed to ashes every five hundred to six hundred years,
only to be renewed into another cycle.

At this hour reigning there.
ANTONIO: I'll believe both;
And what does else want credit,° come to me   25
And I'll be sworn 'tis true. Travelers ne'er did lie,
Though fools at home condemn 'em.
GONZALO: If in Naples
I should report this now, would they believe me
If I should say I saw such islanders?
For, certes,° these are people of the island,   30
Who, though they are of monstrous° shape, yet note,
Their manners are more gentle, kind, than of
Our human generation you shall find
Many, nay, almost any.
PROSPERO [*aside*]:   Honest lord,
Thou hast said well, for some of you there present   35
Are worse than devils.
ALONSO: I cannot too much muse°
Such shapes, such gesture, and such sound, expressing—
Although they want° the use of tongue—a kind
Of excellent dumb discourse.
PROSPERO [*aside*]:   Praise in departing.°
FRANCISCO: They vanished strangely.
SEBASTIAN: No matter, since   40
They have left their viands° behind, for we have stomachs.°
Will 't please you taste of what is here?
ALONSO: Not I.
GONZALO: Faith, sir, you need not fear. When we were boys,
Who would believe that there were mountaineers°
Dewlapped° like bulls, whose throats had hanging at 'em   45
Wallets° of flesh? Or that there were such men
Whose heads stood in their breasts? Which now we find
Each putter-out of five for one° will bring us
Good warrant° of.
ALONSO: I will stand to° and feed,
Although my last°—no matter, since I feel   50

---

25 want credit: Lack credence.   **30 certes:** Certainly.   **31 monstrous:** Unnatural.   **36 muse:**
Wonder at.   **38 want:** Lack.   **39 Praise in departing:** I.e., save your praise until the end of
the performance (proverbial).   **41 viands:** Provisions;   **stomachs:** Appetites.   **44 mountaineers:** Mountain dwellers.   **45 Dewlapped:** Having a dewlap, or fold of skin hanging from
the neck, like cattle.   **46 Wallets:** Pendent folds of skin, wattles.   **48 putter-out . . . one:**
One who invests money or gambles on the risks of travel on the condition that the traveler who
returns safely is to receive five times the amount deposited; hence, any traveler.   **49 Good warrant:** Assurance;   **stand to:** Fall to, take the risk.   **50 Although my last:** Even if this were to
be my last meal.

The best° is past. Brother, my lord the Duke,
Stand to, and do as we.   *[They approach the table.]*

Thunder and lightning. Enter Ariel, like a harpy,° claps his wings upon the table,
and with a quaint device° the banquet vanishes.°

ARIEL: You are three men of sin, whom Destiny —
 That hath to instrument this lower world
 And what is in 't — the never-surfeited sea   55
 Hath caused to belch up you,° and on this island
 Where man doth not inhabit, you 'mongst men
 Being most unfit to life. I have made you mad;
 And even with suchlike valor° men hang and drown
 Their proper° selves.   *[Alonso, Sebastian, and Antonio draw their swords.]*
                       You fools! I and my fellows   60
 Are ministers of Fate. The elements
 Of whom° your swords are tempered° may as well
 Wound the loud winds, or with bemocked-at° stabs
 Kill the still-closing° waters, as diminish
 One dowl° that's in my plume. My fellow ministers   65
 Are like° invulnerable. If° you could hurt,
 Your swords are now too massy° for your strengths
 And will not be uplifted. But remember —
 For that's my business to you — that you three
 From Milan did supplant good Prospero;   70
 Exposed unto the sea, which hath requit° it,
 Him and his innocent child; for which foul deed
 The powers, delaying, not forgetting, have
 Incensed the seas and shores, yea, all the creatures,
 Against your peace. Thee of thy son, Alonso,   75
 They have bereft; and to pronounce by me
 Ling'ring perdition,° worse than any death
 Can be at once, shall step by step attend
 You and your ways; whose° wraths to guard you from —
 Which here, in this most desolate isle, else° falls   80
 Upon your heads — is nothing° but heart's sorrow
 And a clear° life ensuing.

---

51 best: Best part of life.   **harpy:** A fabulous monster with a woman's face and breasts and a
vulture's body, supposed to be a minister of divine vengeance;   **quaint device:** Ingenious stage
contrivance;   **the banquet vanishes:** I.e., the food vanishes; the table remains until line 82.
53–56 whom . . . up you: You whom Destiny, controller of the sublunary world as its instrument, has caused the ever hungry sea to belch up.   **59 suchlike valor:** I.e., the reckless valor
derived from madness.   **60 proper:** Own.   **62 whom:** Which; **tempered:** Composed and
hardened.   **63 bemocked-at:** Scorned.   **64 still-closing:** Always closing again when parted.
65 dowl: Soft, fine feather.   **66 like:** Likewise, similarly; **If:** Even if.   **67 massy:** Heavy.
71 requit: Requited, avenged.   **77 perdition:** Ruin, destruction.   **79 whose:** (Refers to the
heavenly powers.)   **80 else:** Otherwise.   **81 is nothing:** There is no way.   **82 clear:** Unspot-
ted, innocent.

He vanishes in thunder; then, to soft music, enter the shapes again, and dance,
with mocks and mows,° and carrying out the table.

PROSPERO: Bravely° the figure of this harpy hast thou
        Performed, my Ariel; a grace it had devouring.°
        Of my instruction hast thou nothing bated°   85
        In what thou hadst to say. So,° with good life°
        And observation strange,° my meaner° ministers
        Their several kinds° have done. My high charms work,
        And these mine enemies are all knit up
        In their distractions.° They now are in my power;   90
        And in these fits I leave them, while I visit
        Young Ferdinand, whom they suppose is drowned,
        And his and mine loved darling.   *[Exit above.]*
GONZALO: I' the name of something holy, sir, why° stand you
        In this strange stare?
ALONSO: O, it° is monstrous, monstrous!   95
        Methought the billows° spoke and told me of it;
        The winds did sing it to me, and the thunder,
        That deep and dreadful organ pipe, pronounced
        The name of Prosper; it did bass my trespass.°
        Therefor° my son i' th' ooze is bedded; and   100
        I'll seek him deeper than e'er plummet° sounded,°
        And with him there lie mudded.   *Exit.*
SEBASTIAN: But one fiend at a time,
        I'll fight their legions o'er.°
ANTONIO: I'll be thy second.
                        Exeunt [Sebastian and Antonio].
GONZALO: All three of them are desperate.° Their great guilt,   105
        Like poison given to work a great time after,
        Now 'gins to bite the spirits.° I do beseech you,
        That are of suppler joints, follow them swiftly
        And hinder them from what this ecstasy°
        May now provoke them to.
ADRIAN: Follow, I pray you.   *Exeunt omnes.*   110

mocks and mows: Mocking gestures and grimaces. **83 Bravely:** Finely, dashingly. **84 a grace . . . devouring:** I.e., you gracefully caused the banquet to disappear as if you had consumed it (with puns on *grace*, meaning "gracefulness" and "a blessing on the meal," and on *devouring*, meaning "a literal eating" and "an all-consuming or ravishing grace"). **85 bated:** Abated, omitted. **86 So:** In the same fashion; **good life:** Faithful reproduction. **87 observation strange:** Exceptional attention to detail; **meaner:** I.e., subordinate to Ariel. **88 several kinds:** Individual parts. **90 distractions:** Trancelike state. **94 why:** (Gonzalo was not addressed in Ariel's speech to the *three men of sin*, line 53, and is not, as they are, in a maddened state; see lines 105–107.) **95 it:** I.e., my sin (also in line 96). **96 billows:** Waves. **99 bass my trespass:** Proclaim my trespass like a bass note in music. **100 Therefor:** In consequence of that. **101 plummet:** A lead weight attached to a line for testing depth; **sounded:** Probed, tested the depth of. **104 o'er:** One after another. **105 desperate:** Despairing and reckless. **107 bite the spirits:** Sap their vital powers through anguish. **109 ecstasy:** Mad frenzy.

[ACT 4, Scene 1]

[Before Prospero's cell.]

Enter Prospero, Ferdinand, and Miranda.

PROSPERO: If I have too austerely punished you,
    Your companion makes amends, for I
    Have given you here a third° of mine own life,
    Or that for which I live; who once again
    I tender° to thy hand. All thy vexations   5
    Were but my trials of thy love, and thou
    Hast strangely° stood the test. Here, afore heaven,
    I ratify this my rich gift. O Ferdinand,
    Do not smile at me that I boast her off,°
    For thou shalt find she will outstrip all praise   10
    And make it halt° behind her.

FERDINAND: I do believe it.
    Against an oracle.°

PROSPERO: Then, as my gift and thine own acquisition
    Worthily purchased, take my daughter. But
    If thou dost break her virgin-knot before   15
    All sanctimonious° ceremonies may
    With full and holy rite be ministered,
    No sweet aspersion° shall the heavens let fall
    To make this contract grow; but barren hate,
    Sour-eyed disdain, and discord shall bestrew   20
    The union of your bed with weeds° so loathly
    That you shall hate it both. Therefore take heed,
    As Hymen's lamps shall light you.°

FERDINAND: As I hope
    For quiet days, fair issue,° and long life,
    With such love as 'tis now, the murkiest den,   25
    The most opportune place, the strong'st suggestion°
    Our worser genius° can,° shall never melt
    Mine honor into lust, to° take away

ACT 4, SCENE 1. **3 a third:** I.e., Miranda, into whose education Prospero has put a third of his life (?) or who represents a large part of what he cares about, along with his dukedom and his learned study (?).   **5 tender:** Offer.   **7 strangely:** Extraordinarily.   **9 boast her off:** I.e., praise her so, or, perhaps an error for "boast of her."   **11 halt:** Limp.   **12 Against an oracle:** Even if an oracle should declare otherwise.   **16 sanctimonious:** Sacred.   **18 aspersion:** Dew, shower.   **21 weeds:** (In place of the flowers customarily strewn on the marriage bed.) **23 As . . . you:** I.e., as you long for happiness and concord in your marriage. (Hymen was the Greek and Roman god of marriage; his symbolic torches, the wedding torches, were supposed to burn brightly for a happy marriage and smokily for a troubled one.)   **24 issue:** Offspring. **26 suggestion:** Temptation.   **27 worser genius:** Evil genius, or, evil attendant spirit;   **can:** Is capable of.   **28 to:** So as to.

The edge° of that day's celebration
When I shall think or° Phoebus' steeds are foundered°   30
Or Night kept chained below.
PROSPERO: Fairly spoke.
Sit then and talk with her. She is thine own.
                    [Ferdinand and Miranda sit and talk together.]
What,° Ariel! My industrious servant, Ariel!

Enter Ariel.

ARIEL: What would my potent master? Here I am.
PROSPERO: Thou and thy meaner fellows° your last service   35
Did worthily perform, and I must use you
In such another trick.° Go bring the rabble,°
O'er whom I give thee power, here to this place.
Incite them to quick motion, for I must
Bestow upon the eyes of this young couple   40
Some vanity° of mine art. It is my promise,
And they expect it from me.
ARIEL: Presently?°
PROSPERO: Ay, with a twink.°
ARIEL: Before you can say "Come" and "Go,"
        And breathe twice, and cry "So, so,"   45
        Each one, tripping on his toe,
        Will be here with mop and mow.°
        Do you love me, master? No?
PROSPERO: Dearly, my delicate Ariel. Do not approach
Till thou dost hear me call.
ARIEL: Well; I conceive.°   *Exit.*   50
PROSPERO: Look thou be true;° do not give dalliance
Too much the rein. The strongest oaths are straw
To the fire i' the blood. Be more abstemious,
Or else good night° your vow!
FERDINAND: I warrant° you, sir,
The white cold virgin snow upon my heart°   55
Abates the ardor of my liver.°
PROSPERO: Well.

---

29 edge: Keen enjoyment, sexual ardor.   **30 or:** Either;   **foundered:** Broken down, made lame. (Ferdinand will wait impatiently for the bridal night.)   **33 What:** Now then.   **35 meaner fellows:** Subordinates.   **37 trick:** Device;   **rabble:** Band, i.e., the *meaner fellows* of line 35. **41 vanity:** (1) Illusion, (2) trifle, (3) desire for admiration, conceit.   **42 Presently:** Immediately.   **43 with a twink:** In the twinkling of an eye.   **47 mop and mow:** Gestures and grimaces.   **50 conceive:** Understand.   **51 true:** True to your promise.   **54 good night:** I.e., say good-bye to;   **warrant:** Guarantee.   **55 The white ... heart:** I.e., the ideal of chastity and consciousness of Miranda's chaste innocence enshrined in my heart.   **56 liver:** (As the presumed seat of the passions.)

Now come, my Ariel! Bring a corollary,°
Rather than want° a spirit. Appear, and pertly!° —
No tongue!° All eyes! Be silent.   *Soft music.*

Enter Iris.°

IRIS: Ceres,° most bounteous lady, thy rich leas°   60
        Of wheat, rye, barley, vetches,° oats, and peas;
        Thy turfy mountains, where live nibbling sheep,
        And flat meads° thatched with stover,° them to keep;
        Thy banks with pionèd and twillèd° brims,
        Which spongy° April at thy hest° betrims   65
        To make cold nymphs chaste crowns; and thy broom groves,°
        Whose shadow the dismissèd bachelor° loves,
        Being lass-lorn; thy poll-clipped° vineyard;
        And thy sea marge,° sterile and rocky hard,
        Where thou thyself dost air:° the queen o' the sky,°   70
        Whose watery arch° and messenger am I,
        Bids thee leave these, and with her sovereign grace,

Juno descends° *[slowly in her car].*

        Here on this grass plot, in this very place,
        To come and sport. Her peacocks° fly amain.°
        Approach, rich Ceres, her to entertain.°   75

Enter Ceres.

CERES: Hail, many-colored messenger, that ne'er
         Dost disobey the wife of Jupiter,
         Who with thy saffron° wings upon my flowers
         Diffusest honeydrops, refreshing showers,
         And with each end of thy blue bow° dost crown   80
         My bosky° acres and my unshrubbed down,°
         Rich scarf° to my proud earth. Why hath thy queen
         Summoned me hither to this short-grassed green?

---

57 corollary: Surplus, extra supply.   **58 want:** Lack; **pertly:** Briskly.   **59 No tongue:** All the beholders are to be silent (lest the spirits vanish).   **Iris:** Goddess of the rainbow and Juno's messenger.   **60 Ceres:** Goddess of the generative power of nature;   **leas:** Meadows. **61 vetches:** Plants for forage, fodder.   **63 meads:** Meadows;   **stover:** Winter fodder for cattle.   **64 pionèd and twillèd:** Undercut by the swift current and protected by roots and branches that tangle to form a barricade.   **65 spongy:** Wet;   **hest:** Command.   **66 broom groves:** Clumps of broom, gorse, yellow-flowered shrub.   **67 dismissèd bachelor:** Rejected male lover.   **68 poll-clipped:** Pruned, lopped at the top, or *pole-clipped*, "hedged in with poles."   **69 sea marge:** Shore.   **70 thou . . . air:** You take the air, go for walks;   **queen o' the sky:** I.e., Juno.   **71 watery arch:** Rainbow.   **Juno descends:** I.e., starts her descent from the "heavens" above the stage (?).   **74 peacocks:** Birds sacred to Juno and used to pull her chariot; **amain:** With full speed.   **75 entertain:** Receive.   **78 saffron:** Yellow.   **80 bow:** I.e., rainbow.   **81 bosky:** Wooded;   **unshrubbed down:** Open upland.   **82 scarf:** (The rainbow is like a colored silk band adorning the earth.)

IRIS: A contract of true love to celebrate,
    And some donation freely to estate°   85
    On the blest lovers.
CERES: Tell me, heavenly bow,
    If Venus or her son,° as° thou dost know,
    Do now attend the Queen? Since they did plot
    The means that° dusky° Dis my daughter got,°
    Her° and her blind boy's scandaled° company   90
    I have forsworn.
IRIS: Of her society°
    Be not afraid. I met her deity°
    Cutting the clouds towards Paphos,° and her son
    Dove-drawn° with her. Here thought they to have done°
    Some wanton charm° upon this man and maid,   95
    Whose vows are that no bed-right shall be paid
    Till Hymen's torch be lighted; but in vain.
    Mars's hot minion° is returned° again;
    Her waspish-headed° son has broke his arrows,
    Swears he will shoot no more, but play with sparrows°   100
    And be a boy right out.°

[Juno alights.]

CERES: Highest Queen of state,°
    Great Juno, comes; I know her by her gait.°
JUNO: How does my bounteous sister?° Go with me
    To bless this twain, that they may prosperous be,
    And honored in their issue.°   *They sing:* 105
JUNO: Honor, riches, marriage blessing,
    Long continuance, and increasing,
    Hourly joys be still° upon you!
    Juno sings her blessings on you.
CERES: Earth's increase, foison plenty,°   110
    Barns and garners° never empty,

---

85 **estate:** Bestow.   87 **son:** I.e., Cupid; **as:** As far as.   89 **that:** Whereby; **dusky:** Dark;
Dis . . . got: (Pluto, or *Dis*, god of the infernal regions, carried off Proserpina, daughter of
Ceres, to be his bride in Hades.)   90 **Her:** I.e., Venus's; **scandaled:** Scandalous.   91 **society:** Company.   92 **her deity:** I.e., Her Highness.   93 **Paphos:** Place on the island of Cyprus,
sacred to Venus.   94 **Dove-drawn:** (Venus's chariot was drawn by doves); **done:** Placed.
95 **wanton charm:** Lustful spell.   98 **Mars's hot minion:** I.e., Venus, the beloved of Mars;
returned: I.e., returned to Paphos.   99 **waspish-headed:** Hotheaded, peevish.   100 **sparrows:** (Supposed lustful, and sacred to Venus.)   101 **right out:** Outright.   101 **Highest . . .
state:** Most majestic Queen.   102 **gait:** I.e., majestic bearing.   103 **sister:** I.e., fellow goddess (?).   105 **issue:** Offspring.   108 **still:** Always.   110 **foison plenty:** Plentiful harvest.
111 **garners:** Granaries.

Vines with clustering bunches growing,
Plants with goodly burden bowing;

Spring come to you at the farthest
In the very end of harvest!°   115
Scarcity and want shall shun you;
Ceres' blessing so is on you.
FERDINAND: This is a most majestic vision, and
Harmonious charmingly.° May I be bold
To think these spirits?
PROSPERO: Spirits, which by mine art   120
I have from their confines called to enact
My present fancies.
FERDINAND: Let me live here ever!
So rare a wondered° father and a wife
Makes this place Paradise.

                 Juno and Ceres whisper, and send Iris on employment.
PROSPERO: Sweet now, silence!
Juno and Ceres whisper seriously;   125
There's something else to do. Hush and be mute,
Or else our spell is marred.
IRIS *[calling offstage]:*   You nymphs, called naiads,° of the windring° brooks,
With your sedged° crowns and ever-harmless° looks,
Leave your crisp° channels, and on this green land   130
Answer your summons; Juno does command.
Come, temperate° nymphs, and help to celebrate
A contract of true love. Be not too late.

Enter certain nymphs.

You sunburned sicklemen,° of August weary,°
Come hither from the furrow° and be merry.   135
Make holiday; your rye-straw hats put on,
And these fresh nymphs encounter° every one
In country footing.°

*Enter certain reapers, properly° habited. They join with the nymphs in a graceful
dance, towards the end whereof Prospero starts suddenly, and speaks; after which, to
a strange, hollow, and confused noise, they heavily° vanish.*

---

115 In . . . harvest: I.e., with no winter in between. **119 charmingly:** Enchantingly.
123 wondered: Wonder-performing, wondrous. **128 naiads:** Nymphs of springs, rivers, or
lakes; **windring:** Wandering, winding (?). **129 sedged:** Made of reeds; **ever-harmless:**
Ever innocent. **130 crisp:** Curled, rippled. **132 temperate:** Chaste. **134 sicklemen:** Har-
vesters, field workers who cut down grain and grass; **of August weary:** I.e., weary of the hard
work of the harvest. **135 furrow:** I.e., plowed fields. **137 encounter:** Join. **138 country
footing:** Country dancing. **properly:** Suitably; **heavily:** Slowly, dejectedly.

PROSPERO [*aside*]:   I had forgot that foul conspiracy
Of the beast Caliban and his confederates   140
Against my life. The minute of their plot
Is almost come. [*To the Spirits.*] Well done! Avoid;° no more!
FERDINAND [*to Miranda*]:   This is strange. Your father's in some passion
That works° him strongly.
MIRANDA: Never till this day
Saw I him touched with anger so distempered.   145
PROSPERO: You do look, my son, in a moved sort,°
As if you were dismayed. Be cheerful, sir.
Our revels° now are ended. These our actors,
As I foretold you, were all spirits and
Are melted into air, into thin air;   150
And, like the baseless fabric° of this vision,
The cloud-capped towers, the gorgeous palaces,
The solemn temples, the great globe° itself,
Yea, all which it inherit,° shall dissolve,
And, like this insubstantial pageant faded,   155
Leave not a rack° behind. We are such stuff
As dreams are made on,° and our little life
Is rounded° with a sleep. Sir, I am vexed.
Bear with my weakness. My old brain is troubled.
Be not disturbed with° my infirmity.   160
If you be pleased, retire° into my cell
And there repose. A turn or two I'll walk
To still my beating° mind.
FERDINAND, MIRANDA: We wish your peace.
                                                    Exeunt [Ferdinand and Miranda].
PROSPERO: Come with a thought!° I thank thee, Ariel. Come.
Enter Ariel.
ARIEL: Thy thoughts I cleave° to. What's thy pleasure?
PROSPERO: Spirit,   165
We must prepare to meet with Caliban.
ARIEL: Ay, my commander. When I presented° Ceres,
I thought to have told thee of it, but I feared
Lest I might anger thee.

142 **Avoid:** Withdraw.   144 **works:** Affects, agitates.   146 **moved sort:** Troubled state,
condition.   148 **revels:** Entertainment, pageant.   151 **baseless fabric:** Unsubstantial theatrical edifice or contrivance.   153 **great globe:** (With a glance at the Globe Theatre.)
154 **which it inherit:** Who subsequently occupy it.   156 **rack:** Wisp of cloud.   157 **on:**
Of.   158 **rounded:** Surrounded (before birth and after death), or crowned, rounded off.
160 **with:** By.   161 **retire:** Withdraw, go.   163 **beating:** Agitated.   164 **with a thought:** I.e.,
on the instant, or, summoned by my thought, no sooner thought of than here.   165 **cleave:**
Cling, adhere.   167 **presented:** Acted the part of, or, introduced.

PROSPERO: Say again, where didst thou leave these varlets?   170
ARIEL: I told you, sir, they were red-hot with drinking;
    So full of valor that they smote the air
    For breathing in their faces, beat the ground
    For kissing of their feet; yet always bending°
    Towards their project. Then I beat my tabor,   175
    At which, like unbacked° colts, they pricked their ears,
    Advanced° their eyelids, lifted up their noses
    As° they smelt music. So I charmed their ears
    That calflike they my lowing° followed through
    Toothed briers, sharp furzes, pricking gorse,° and thorns,   180
    Which entered their frail shins. At last I left them
    I' the filthy-mantled° pool beyond your cell,
    There dancing up to the chins, that the foul lake
    O'erstunk° their feet.
PROSPERO: This was well done, my bird.
    Thy shape invisible retain thou still.   185
    The trumpery° in my house, go bring it hither,
    For stale° to catch these thieves.
ARIEL: I go, I go.   *Exit.*
PROSPERO: A devil, a born devil, on whose nature
    Nurture can never stick; on whom my pains,
    Humanely taken, all, all lost, quite lost!   190
    And as with age his body uglier grows,
    So his mind cankers.° I will plague them all,
    Even to roaring.

Enter Ariel, loaden with glistering apparel, etc.

              Come, hang them on this line.°

[Ariel hangs up the showy finery; Prospero and Ariel remain,° invisible.] Enter Caliban, Stephano, and Trinculo, all wet.

CALIBAN: Pray you, tread softly, that the blind mole may
    Not hear a foot fall. We now are near his cell.   195
STEPHANO: Monster, your fairy, which you say is a harmless fairy, has done little
    better than played the jack° with us.
TRINCULO: Monster, I do smell all horse piss, at which my nose is in great indignation.

---

174 bending: Aiming.   **176 unbacked:** Unbroken, unridden.   **177 Advanced:** Lifted up.
178 As: As if.   **179 lowing:** Mooing.   **180 furzes, gorse:** Prickly shrubs.   **182 filthy-mantled:**
Covered with a slimy coating.   **184 O'erstunk:** Smelled worse than, or, caused to stink terribly.   **186 trumpery:** Cheap goods, the *glistering apparel* mentioned in the following stage
direction.   **187 stale:** (1) Decoy (2) out-of-fashion garments (with possible further suggestions
of "horse piss," as in line 198, and "steal," pronounced like *stale*). *For stale* could also mean "fit
for a prostitute."   **192 cankers:** Festers, grows malignant.   **193 line:** Lime tree or linden.
Prospero and Ariel remain: (The staging is uncertain. They may instead exit here and return
with the spirits at line 248.)   **197 jack:** (1) Knave (2) will-o'-the-wisp.

STEPHANO: So is mine. Do you hear, monster? If I should take a displeasure   200
   against you, look you —
TRINCULO: Thou wert but a lost monster.
CALIBAN: Good my lord, give me thy favor still.
   Be patient, for the prize I'll bring thee to
   Shall hoodwink this mischance.° Therefore speak softly.   205
   All's hushed as midnight yet.
TRINCULO: Ay, but to lose our bottles in the pool —
STEPHANO: There is not only disgrace and dishonor in that, monster, but an
   infinite loss.
TRINCULO: That's more to me than my wetting. Yet this is your harmless fairy,   210
   monster!
STEPHANO: I will fetch off my bottle, though I be o'er ears° for my labor.
CALIBAN: Prithee, my king, be quiet. Seest thou here,
   This is the mouth o' the cell. No noise, and enter.
   Do that good mischief which may make this island   215
   Thine own forever, and I thy Caliban
   For aye thy footlicker.
STEPHANO: Give me thy hand. I do begin to have bloody thoughts.
TRINCULO [*seeing the finery*]:   O King Stephano! O peer!° O worthy Stephano!
   Look what a wardrobe here is for thee!   220
CALIBAN: Let it alone, thou fool, it is but trash.
TRINCULO: Oho, monster! We know what belongs to a frippery.° O King
   Stephano!   [*He puts on a gown.*]
STEPHANO: Put off° that gown, Trinculo. By this hand, I'll have that gown.
TRINCULO: Thy Grace shall have it.   225
CALIBAN: The dropsy° drown this fool! What do you mean
   To dote thus on such luggage?° Let 't alone
   And do the murder first. If he awake,
   From toe to crown° he'll fill our skins with pinches,
   Make us strange stuff.   230
STEPHANO: Be you quiet, monster. — Mistress line,° is not this my jerkin?° [*He
   takes it down.*] Now is the jerkin under the line.° Now, jerkin, you are like° to
   lose your hair and prove a bald° jerkin.

---

205 hoodwink this mischance: (Misfortune is to be prevented from doing further harm by
being hooded like a hawk and also put out of remembrance.)   **212 o'er ears:** I.e., totally submerged and perhaps drowned.   **219 King . . . peer:** (Alludes to the old ballad beginning, "King
Stephen was a worthy peer.")   **222 frippery:** Place where cast-off clothes are sold.   **224 Put
off:** Put down, or, take off.   **226 dropsy:** Disease characterized by the accumulation of fluid
in the connective tissue of the body.   **227 luggage:** Cumbersome trash.   **229 crown:** Head.
231 Mistress line: (Addressed to the linden or lime tree upon which, at line 193, Ariel hung
the *glistering apparel*);   **jerkin:** Jacket made of leather.   **232 under the line:** Under the lime
tree (with punning sense of being south of the equinoctial line or equator; sailors on long voyages to the southern regions were popularly supposed to lose their hair from scurvy or other diseases. Stephano also quibbles bawdily on losing hair through syphilis, and in *Mistress* and
jerkin);   **like:** Likely.   **233 bald:** (1) Hairless, napless (2) meager.

TRINCULO: Do, do!° We steal by line and level,° an 't like° Your Grace.

STEPHANO: I thank thee for that jest. Here's a garment for 't. *[He gives a gar-*   235
ment.] Wit shall not go unrewarded while I am king of this country. "Steal
by line and level" is an excellent pass of pate.° There's another garment
for 't.

TRINCULO: Monster, come, put some lime° upon your fingers, and away with
the rest.   240

CALIBAN: I will have none on 't. We shall lose our time,
And all be turned to barnacles,° or to apes
With foreheads villainous° low.

STEPHANO: Monster, lay to° your fingers. Help to bear this° away where my
hogshead° of wine is, or I'll turn you out of my kingdom. Go to,° carry   245
this.

TRINCULO: And this.

STEPHANO: Ay, and this.   *[They load Caliban with more and more garments.]*

*A noise of hunters heard. Enter divers spirits, in shape of dogs and hounds, hunting
them about, Prospero and Ariel setting them on.*

PROSPERO: Hey, Mountain, hey!

ARIEL: Silver! There it goes, Silver!   250

PROSPERO: Fury, Fury! There, Tyrant, there! Hark! Hark!
            [Caliban, Stephano, and Trinculo are driven out.]
Go, charge my goblins that they grind their joints
With dry° convulsions,° shorten up their sinews
With agèd° cramps, and more pinch-spotted make them
Than pard° or cat o' mountain.°

ARIEL: Hark, they roar!   255

PROSPERO: Let them be hunted soundly.° At this hour
Lies at my mercy all mine enemies.
Shortly shall all my labors end, and thou
Shalt have the air at freedom. For a little°
Follow, and do me service.   *Exeunt.*   260

---

234 Do, do: I.e., bravo (said in response to the jesting or to the taking of the jerkin, or
both);   **by line and level:** I.e., by means of plumb line and carpenter's level, methodically
(with pun on *line,* "lime tree," line 232, and *steal,* pronounced like *stale,* i.e., prostitute, continuing Stephano's bawdy quibble);   **an 't like:** If it please.   **237 pass of pate:** Sally of wit.
(The metaphor is from fencing.)   **239 lime:** Birdlime, sticky substance (to give Caliban
sticky fingers).   **242 barnacles:** Barnacle geese, formerly supposed to be hatched from
barnacles attached to trees or to rotting timber; here, evidently used, like *apes,* as types of
simpletons.   **243 villainous:** Miserably.   **244 lay to:** Start using;   **this:** I.e., the *glistering
apparel.*   **245 hogshead:** Large cask;   **Go to:** (An expression of exhortation or remon-
strance.)   **253 dry:** Associated with age, arthritic (?);   **convulsions:** Cramps.   **254 agèd:**
Characteristic of old age.   **255 pard:** Panther or leopard;   **cat o' mountain:** Wildcat.
256 soundly: Thoroughly (and suggesting the sounds of the hunt).   **259 little:** Little while
longer.

[ACT 5, Scene 1]

[Before Prospero's cell.]

Enter Prospero in his magic robes, [with his staff,] and Ariel.

PROSPERO: Now does my project gather to a head.
　　My charms crack° not, my spirits obey, and Time
　　Goes upright with his carriage.° How's the day?
ARIEL: On° the sixth hour, at which time, my lord,
　　You said our work should cease.
PROSPERO:　　　　　　　　　　I did say so,   5
　　When first I raised the tempest. Say, my spirit,
　　How fares the King and 's followers?
ARIEL:　　　　　　　　　　　Confined together
　　In the same fashion as you gave in charge,
　　Just as you left them; all prisoners, sir,
　　In the line grove° which weather-fends° your cell.   10
　　They cannot budge till your release.° The King,
　　His brother, and yours abide all three distracted,°
　　And the remainder mourning over them,
　　Brim full of sorrow and dismay; but chiefly
　　Him that you termed, sir, the good old lord, Gonzalo.   15
　　His tears runs down his beard like winter's drops
　　From eaves of reeds.° Your charm so strongly works 'em
　　That if you now beheld them your affections°
　　Would become tender.
PROSPERO:　　　　　　　Dost thou think so, spirit?
ARIEL: Mine would, sir, were I human.°
PROSPERO:　　　　　　　　　　And mine shall.   20
　　Hast thou, which art but air, a touch,° a feeling
　　Of their afflictions, and shall not myself,
　　One of their kind, that relish all as sharply
　　Passion as they,° be kindlier° moved than thou art?
　　Though with their high wrongs I am struck to the quick,   25
　　Yet with my nobler reason 'gainst my fury
　　Do I take part. The rarer° action is

ACT 5, SCENE 1. 2 crack: Collapse, fail. (The metaphor is probably alchemical, as in *project* and *gather to a head,* line 1.)   **3 his carriage:** Its burden (time is no longer heavily burdened and so can go *upright,* "standing straight and unimpeded").   **4 On:** Approaching.   **10 line grove:** Grove of lime trees;   **weather-fends:** Protects from the weather.   **11 your release:** You release them.   **12 distracted:** Out of their wits.   **17 eaves of reeds:** Thatched roofs. **18 affections:** Disposition, feelings.   **20 human:** Humane [as well as human].   **21 touch:** Sense, apprehension.   **23–24 that . . . they:** I who experience human passions as acutely as they.   **24 kindlier:** (1) More sympathetically (2) more naturally, humanly.   **27 rarer:** Nobler.

In virtue than in vengeance. They being penitent,
The sole drift of my purpose doth extend
Not a frown further. Go release them, Ariel.   30
My charms I'll break, their senses I'll restore,
And they shall be themselves.

ARIEL: I'll fetch them, sir.   *Exit.*
                 [Prospero traces a charmed circle with his staff.]
PROSPERO: Ye elves of hills, brooks, standing lakes, and groves,
   And ye that on the sands with printless foot
   Do chase the ebbing Neptune, and do fly him   35
   When he comes back; you demi-puppets° that
   By moonshine do the green sour ringlets° make,
   Whereof the ewe not bites; and you whose pastime
   Is to make midnight mushrooms,° that rejoice
   To hear the solemn curfew;° by whose aid,   40
   Weak masters° though ye be, I have bedimmed
   The noontide sun, called forth the mutinous winds,
   And twixt the green sea and the azured vault°
   Set roaring war; to the dread rattling thunder
   Have I given fire,° and rifted° Jove's stout oak°   45
   With his own bolt;° the strong-based promontory
   Have I made shake, and by the spurs° plucked up
   The pine and cedar; graves at my command
   Have waked their sleepers, oped, and let 'em forth
   By my so potent art. But this rough° magic   50
   I here abjure, and when I have required°
   Some heavenly music — which even now I do —
   To work mine end upon their senses that°
   This airy charm° is for, I'll break my staff,
   Bury it certain fathoms in the earth,   55
   And deeper than did ever plummet sound
   I'll drown my book.   *Solemn music.*

Here enters Ariel before; then Alonso, with a frantic gesture, attended by Gonzalo;
Sebastian and Antonio in like manner, attended by Adrian and Francisco. They all
enter the circle which Prospero had made, and there stand charmed; which Prospero
observing, speaks:

33–50 Ye . . . art: (This famous passage is an embellished paraphrase of Golding's translation
of Ovid's *Metamorphoses*, Book VII, lines 197–219.)   **36 demi-puppets:** Puppets of half size,
i.e., elves and fairies.   **37 green sour ringlets:** Fairy rings, circles in grass (actually produced
by mushrooms).   **39 midnight mushrooms:** Mushrooms appearing overnight.   **40 curfew:**
Evening bell, usually rung at nine o'clock, ushering in the time when spirits are abroad.
41 Weak masters: I.e., subordinate spirits, as in IV.i.35 (?).   **43 the azured vault:** I.e., the sky.
44–45 to . . . fire: I have discharged the dread rattling thunderbolt.   **45 rifted:** Riven, split;
oak: A tree that was sacred to Jove.   **46 bolt:** Lightning bolt.   **47 spurs:** Roots.   **50 rough:**
Violent.   **51 required:** Requested.   **53 their senses that:** The senses of those whom.   **54 airy
charm:** I.e., music.

[To Alonso.] A solemn air,° and° the best comforter
To an unsettled fancy,° cure thy brains,
Now useless, boiled° within thy skull!   *[To Sebastian and Antonio.]*
   There stand,   60
For you are spell-stopped. —
Holy Gonzalo, honorable man,
Mine eyes, e'en sociable° to the show° of thine,
Fall° fellowly drops. *[Aside.]* The charm dissolves apace,
And as the morning steals upon the night,   65
Melting the darkness, so their rising senses
Begin to chase the ignorant fumes° that mantle°
Their clearer° reason. — O good Gonzalo,
My true preserver, and a loyal sir
To him thou follow'st! I will pay thy graces°   70
Home° both in word and deed. — Most cruelly
Didst thou, Alonso, use me and my daughter.
Thy brother was a furtherer° in the act. —
Thou art pinched° for 't now, Sebastian. *[To Antonio.]* Flesh and blood,
You, brother mine, that entertained ambition,   75
Expelled remorse° and nature,° whom,° with Sebastian,
Whose inward pinches therefore are most strong,
Would here have killed your king, I do forgive thee,
Unnatural though thou art. — Their understanding
Begins to swell, and the approaching tide   80
Will shortly fill the reasonable shore°
That now lies foul and muddy. Not one of them
That yet looks on me, or would know me. — Ariel,
Fetch me the hat and rapier in my cell.
          [Ariel goes to the cell and returns immediately.]
I will disease° me and myself present   85
As I was sometime Milan.° Quickly, spirit!
Thou shalt ere long be free.   *Ariel sings and helps to attire him.*
ARIEL: Where the bee sucks, there suck I.
          In a cowslip's bell I lie;
          There I couch° when owls do cry.   90
          On the bat's back I do fly
          After° summer merrily.

---

58 air: Song; **and:** I.e., which is. **59 fancy:** Imagination. **60 boiled:** I.e., extremely agitated. **63 sociable:** Sympathetic; **show:** Appearance. **64 Fall:** Let fall. **67 ignorant
fumes:** Fumes that render them incapable of comprehension; **mantle:** Envelop. **68 clearer:**
Growing clearer. **70 pay thy graces:** Requite your favors and virtues. **71 Home:** Fully.
73 furtherer: Accomplice. **74 pinched:** Punished, afflicted. **76 remorse:** Pity; **nature:**
Natural feeling; **whom:** I.e., who. **81 reasonable shore:** Shores of reason, i.e., minds (their
reason returns, like the incoming tide). **85 disease:** Disrobe. **86 As . . . Milan:** In my former appearance as Duke of Milan. **90 couch:** Lie. **92 After:** I.e., pursuing.

Merrily, merrily shall I live now
Under the blossom that hangs on the bough.
PROSPERO: Why, that's my dainty Ariel! I shall miss thee,   95
But yet thou shalt have freedom. So, so, so.°
To the King's ship, invisible as thou art!
There shalt thou find the mariners asleep
Under the hatches. The Master and the Boatswain
Being awake, enforce them to this place,   100
And presently,° I prithee.
ARIEL: I drink the air before me and return
Or ere° your pulse twice beat.   *Exit.*
GONZALO: All torment, trouble, wonder, and amazement
Inhabits here. Some heavenly power guide us   105
Out of this fearful° country!
PROSPERO: Behold, sir King,
The wrongèd Duke of Milan, Prospero.
For more assurance that a living prince
Does now speak to thee, I embrace thy body;
And to thee and thy company I bid   110
A hearty welcome.   *[Embracing him.]*
ALONSO: Whe'er thou be'st he or no,
Or some enchanted trifle° to abuse° me,
As late° I have been, I not know. Thy pulse
Beats as of flesh and blood; and, since I saw thee,
Th' affliction of my mind amends, with which   115
I fear a madness held me. This must crave° —
An if this be at all° — a most strange story.°
Thy dukedom I resign,° and do entreat
Thou pardon me my wrongs.° But how should Prospero
Be living, and be here?
PROSPERO *[to Gonzalo]:*   First, noble friend,   120
Let me embrace thine age,° whose honor cannot
Be measured or confined.   *[Embracing him.]*
GONZALO: Whether this be
Or be not, I'll not swear.
PROSPERO: You do yet taste
Some subtleties° o' th' isle, that will not let you

96 **So, so, so:** (Expresses approval of Ariel's help as valet.)   101 **presently:** Immediately.
103 **Or ere:** Before.   106 **fearful:** Frightening.   112 **trifle:** Trick of magic; **abuse:** Deceive.   113 **late:** Lately.   116 **crave:** Require.   117 **An . . . all:** If this is actually happening;
story: I.e., explanation.   118 **Thy . . . resign:** (Alonso made arrangements with Antonio at the
time of Prospero's banishment for Milan to pay tribute to Naples; see I.ii.113–127.)
119 **wrongs:** Wrongdoings.   121 **thine age:** Your venerable self.   124 **subtleties:** Illusions,
magical powers (playing on the idea of "pastries, concoctions").

Believe things certain. Welcome, my friends all!   125
[Aside to Sebastian and Antonio.] But you, my brace° of lords, were I so
   minded,
I here could pluck His Highness' frown upon you
And justify you° traitors. At this time
I will tell no tales.
SEBASTIAN: The devil speaks in him.
PROSPERO: No.
[To Antonio.] For you, most wicked sir, whom to call brother   130
Would even infect my mouth, I do forgive
Thy rankest fault—all of them; and require
My dukedom of thee, which perforce° I know
Thou must restore.
ALONSO: If thou be'st Prospero,
Give us particulars of thy preservation,   135
How thou hast met us here, whom° three hours since
Were wrecked upon this shore, where I have lost—
How sharp the point of this remembrance is!—
My dear son Ferdinand.
PROSPERO: I am woe° for 't, sir.
ALONSO: Irreparable is the loss, and Patience   140
Says it is past her cure.
PROSPERO: I rather think
You have not sought her help, of whose soft grace°
For the like loss I have her sovereign° aid
And rest myself content.
ALONSO: You the like loss?
PROSPERO: As great to me as late,° and supportable   145
To make the dear loss, have I° means much weaker
Than you may call to comfort you; for I
Have lost my daughter.
ALONSO: A daughter?
O heavens, that they were living both in Naples,   150
The king and queen there! That° they were, I wish
Myself were mudded° in that oozy bed
Where my son lies. When did you lose your daughter?
PROSPERO: In this last tempest. I perceive these lords
At this encounter do so much admire°   155

---

126 brace: Pair.   **128 justify you:** Prove you to be.   **133 perforce:** Necessarily.   **136 whom:**
I.e., who.   **139 woe:** Sorry.   **142 of . . . grace:** By whose mercy.   **143 sovereign:** Effica-
cious.   **145 late:** Recent.   **145–146 supportable . . . have I:** To make the deeply felt loss
bearable, I have.   **151 That:** So that.   **152 mudded:** Buried in the mud.   **155 admire:**
Wonder.

That they devour their reason° and scarce think
Their eyes do offices of truth, their words
Are natural breath.° But, howsoever you have
Been jostled from your senses, know for certain
That I am Prospero and that very duke   160
Which was thrust forth of° Milan, who most strangely
Upon this shore, where you were wrecked, was landed
To be the lord on 't. No more yet of this,
For 'tis a chronicle of day by day,°
Not a relation for a breakfast nor   165
Befitting this first meeting. Welcome, sir.
This cell's my court. Here have I few attendants,
And subjects none abroad.° Pray you, look in.
My dukedom since you have given me again,
I will requite° you with as good a thing,   170
At least bring forth a wonder to content ye
As much as me my dukedom.

Here Prospero discovers° Ferdinand and Miranda, playing at chess.

MIRANDA: Sweet lord, you play me false.°
FERDINAND: No, my dearest love,
I would not for the world.   175
MIRANDA: Yes, for a score of kingdoms you should wrangle,
And I would call it fair play.°
ALONSO: If this prove
A vision° of the island, one dear son
Shall I twice lose.
SEBASTIAN: A most high miracle!
FERDINAND [*approaching his father*]:
Though the seas threaten, they are merciful;   180
I have cursed them without cause.   [*He kneels.*]
ALONSO: Now all the blessings
Of a glad father compass° thee about!
Arise, and say how thou cam'st here.   [*Ferdinand rises.*]
MIRANDA: O, wonder!
How many goodly creatures are there here!

---

156 **devour their reason:** I.e., are openmouthed, dumbfounded.   156–158 **scarce . . . breath:**
Scarcely believe that their eyes inform them accurately as to what they see or that their
words are naturally spoken.   161 **of:** From.   164 **of day by day:** Requiring days to tell.
168 **abroad:** Away from here, anywhere else.   170 **requite:** Repay;   **discovers:** I.e., by
opening a curtain, presumably rearstage.   173 **play me false:** I.e., press your advantage.
176–177 **Yes . . . play:** Yes, even if we were playing for only twenty kingdoms, you would still
press your advantage against me, and I would lovingly let you do it as though it were fair play, or
if you were to play not just for stakes but literally for kingdoms, my complaint would be out of
order in that your "wrangling" would be proper.   178 **vision:** Illusion.   182 **compass:**
Encompass, embrace.

How beauteous mankind is! O brave° new world   185
That has such people in 't!
PROSPERO: 'Tis new to thee.
ALONSO: What is this maid with whom thou wast at play?
Your eld'st° acquaintance cannot be three hours.
Is she the goddess that hath severed us,
And brought us thus together?
FERDINAND: Sir, she is mortal;   190
But by immortal Providence she's mine.
I chose her when I could not ask my father
For his advice, nor thought I had one. She
Is daughter to this famous Duke of Milan,
Of whom so often I have heard renown,   195
But never saw before; of whom I have
Received a second life; and second father
This lady makes him to me.
ALONSO: I am hers.
But O, how oddly will it sound that I
Must ask my child forgiveness!
PROSPERO: There, sir, stop.   200
Let us not burden our remembrances with
A heaviness° that's gone.
GONZALO: I have inly° wept,
Or should have spoke ere this. Look down, you gods,
And on this couple drop a blessèd crown!
For it is you that have chalked forth the way°   205
Which brought us hither.
ALONSO: I say amen, Gonzalo!
GONZALO: Was Milan° thrust from Milan, that his issue
Should become kings of Naples? O, rejoice
Beyond a common joy, and set it down
With gold on lasting pillars: In one voyage   210
Did Claribel her husband find at Tunis,
And Ferdinand, her brother, found a wife
Where he himself was lost; Prospero his dukedom
In a poor isle; and all of us ourselves
When no man was his own.°
ALONSO [*to Ferdinand and Miranda*]:   Give me your hands.   215
Let grief and sorrow still° embrace his° heart
That° doth not wish you joy!
GONZALO: Be it so! Amen!

185 **brave:** Splendid, gorgeously appareled, handsome.   188 **eld'st:** Longest.   202 **heaviness:** Sadness; **inly:** Inwardly.   205 **chalked . . . way:** Marked as with a piece of chalk the pathway.   207 **Was Milan:** Was the Duke of Milan.   214–215 **all . . . own:** All of us have found ourselves and our sanity when we all had lost our senses.   216 **still:** Always;   **his:** That person's.   217 **That:** Who.

Enter Ariel, with the Master and Boatswain amazedly following.

    O, look, sir, look, sir! Here is more of us.
    I prophesied, if a gallows were on land,
    This fellow could not drown. — Now, blasphemy,°   220
    That swear'st grace o'erboard,° not an oath° on shore?
    Hast thou no mouth by land? What is the news?
BOATSWAIN: The best news is that we have safely found
    Our King and company; the next, our ship —
    Which, but three glasses° since, we gave out° split —   225
    Is tight and yare° and bravely° rigged as when
    We first put out to sea.
ARIEL *[aside to Prospero]:*   Sir, all this service
    Have I done since I went.
PROSPERO *[aside to Ariel]:*   My tricksy° spirit!
ALONSO: These are not natural events; they strengthen°
    From strange to stranger. Say, how came you hither?   230
BOATSWAIN: If I did think, sir, I were well awake,
    I'd strive to tell you. We were dead of sleep,°
    And — how we know not — all clapped under hatches,
    Where but even now, with strange and several° noises
    Of roaring, shrieking, howling, jingling chains,   235
    And more diversity of sounds, all horrible,
    We were awaked; straightway at liberty;
    Where we, in all her trim, freshly beheld
    Our royal, good, and gallant ship, our Master
    Cap'ring to eye° her. On a trice,° so please you,   240
    Even in a dream, were we divided from them°
    And were brought moping° hither.
ARIEL *[aside to Prospero]:*   Was 't well done?
PROSPERO *[aside to Ariel]:*   Bravely, my diligence. Thou shalt be free.
ALONSO: This is as strange a maze as e'er men trod,
    And there is in this business more than nature   245
    Was ever conduct° of. Some oracle
    Must rectify our knowledge.
PROSPERO: Sir, my liege,
    Do not infest° your mind with beating on°
    The strangeness of this business. At picked° leisure,

---

220 blasphemy: I.e., blasphemer.   **221 That swear'st grace o'erboard:** I.e., you who banish heavenly grace from the ship by your blasphemies;   **not an oath:** Aren't you going to swear an oath.   **225 glasses:** I.e., hours;   **gave out:** Reported, professed to be.   **226 yare:** Ready; **bravely:** Splendidly.   **228 tricksy:** Ingenious, sportive.   **229 strengthen:** Increase.   **232 dead of sleep:** Deep in sleep.   **234 several:** Diverse.   **240 Cap'ring to eye:** Dancing for joy to see;   **On a trice:** In an instant.   **241 them:** I.e., the other crew members.   **242 moping:** In a daze.   **246 conduct:** Guide.   **248 infest:** Harass, disturb;   **beating on:** Worrying about. **249 picked:** Chosen, convenient.

Which shall be shortly, single° I'll resolve° you, 250
Which to you shall seem probable,° of every
These° happened accidents;° till when, be cheerful
And think of each thing well.° *[Aside to Ariel.]* Come hither, spirit.
Set Caliban and his companions free.
Untie the spell. *[Exit Ariel.]* How fares my gracious sir? 255
There are yet missing of your company
Some few odd° lads that you remember not.

Enter Ariel, driving in Caliban, Stephano, and Trinculo, in their stolen apparel.

STEPHANO: Every man shift° for all the rest,° and let no man take care for himself; for all is but fortune. Coragio,° bully monster,° coragio!

TRINCULO: If these be true spies° which I wear in my head, here's a goodly 260
sight.

CALIBAN: O Setebos, these be brave° spirits indeed!
How fine° my master is! I am afraid
He will chastise me.

SEBASTIAN: Ha, ha! 265
What things are these, my lord Antonio?
Will money buy 'em?

ANTONIO: Very like. One of them
Is a plain fish, and no doubt marketable.

PROSPERO: Mark but the badges° of these men, my lords,
Then say if they be true.° This misshapen knave, 270
His mother was a witch, and one so strong
That could control the moon, make flows and ebbs,
And deal in her command without her power.°
These three have robbed me, and this demidevil—
For he's a bastard° one—had plotted with them 275
To take my life. Two of these fellows you
Must know and own.° This thing of darkness I
Acknowledge mine.

CALIBAN: I shall be pinched to death.

ALONSO: Is not this Stephano, my drunken butler?

SEBASTIAN: He is drunk now. Where had he wine? 280

ALONSO: And Trinculo is reeling ripe.° Where should they

---

250 single: Privately, by my own human powers; **resolve:** Satisfy, explain to. **251 probable:**
Plausible. **251–252 of every These:** About every one of these. **252 accidents:** Occurrences. **253 well:** Favorably. **257 odd:** Unaccounted for. **258 shift:** Provide; **for all
the rest:** (Stephano drunkenly gets wrong the saying "Every man for himself.") **259 Coragio:**
Courage; **bully monster:** Gallant monster (ironical). **260 true spies:** Accurate observers
(i.e., sharp eyes). **262 brave:** Handsome. **263 fine:** Splendidly attired. **269 badges:**
Emblems of cloth or silver worn by retainers to indicate whom they serve. (Prospero refers here
to the stolen clothes as emblems of their villainy.) **270 true:** Honest. **273 deal . . . power:**
Wield the moon's power, either without her authority or beyond her influence, or, even though
to do so was beyond Sycorax's own power. **275 bastard:** Counterfeit. **277 own:** Recognize,
admit as belonging to you. **281 reeling ripe:** Stumbling drunk.

Find this grand liquor that hath gilded° em?
[To Trinculo.] How cam'st thou in this pickle?°
TRINCULO: I have been in such a pickle since I saw you last that, I fear me, will
    never out of my bones. I shall not fear flyblowing.°   285
SEBASTIAN: Why, how now, Stephano?
STEPHANO: O, touch me not! I am not Stephano, but a cramp.
PROSPERO: You'd be king o' the isle, sirrah?°
STEPHANO: I should have been a sore° one, then.
ALONSO *[pointing to Caliban]*:   This is a strange thing as e'er I looked on.   290
PROSPERO: He is as disproportioned in his manners
    As in his shape. — Go, sirrah, to my cell.
    Take with you your companions. As you look
    To have my pardon, trim° it handsomely.
CALIBAN: Ay, that I will; and I'll be wise hereafter   295
    And seek for grace.° What a thrice-double ass
    Was I to take this drunkard for a god
    And worship this dull fool!
PROSPERO: Go to. Away!
ALONSO: Hence, and bestow your luggage where you found it.
SEBASTIAN: Or stole it, rather.   *[Exeunt Caliban, Stephano, and Trinculo.]*   300
PROSPERO: Sir, I invite Your Highness and your train
    To my poor cell, where you shall take your rest
    For this one night; which, part of it, I'll waste°
    With such discourse as, I not doubt, shall make it
    Go quick away: the story of my life,   305
    And the particular accidents° gone by
    Since I came to this isle. And in the morn
    I'll bring you to your ship, and so to Naples,
    Where I have hope to see the nuptial
    Of these our dear-belovèd solemnized;   310
    And thence retire me° to my Milan, where
    Every third thought shall be my grave.
ALONSO: I long
    To hear the story of your life, which must
    Take° the ear strangely.
PROSPERO: I'll deliver° all;
    And promise you calm seas, auspicious gales,   315
    And sail so expeditious that shall catch

---

282 gilded: (1) Flushed, made drunk (2) covered with gilt (suggesting the horse urine).
283 pickle: (1) Fix, predicament (2) pickling brine (in this case, horse urine).   **285 flyblow-
ing:** I.e., being fouled by fly eggs (from which he is saved by being pickled).   **288 sirrah:**
(Standard form of address to an inferior, here expressing reprimand.)   **289 sore:** (1) Tyrannical
(2) sorry, inept (3) wracked by pain.   **294 trim:** Prepare, decorate.   **296 grace:** Pardon, favor.
303 waste: Spend.   **306 accidents:** Occurrences.   **311 retire me:** Return.   **314 Take:**
Take effect upon, enchant;   **deliver:** Declare, relate.

Your royal fleet far off.° *[Aside to Ariel.]* My Ariel, chick,
That is thy charge. Then to the elements
Be free, and fare thou well! — Please you, draw near.°

                                        Exeunt omnes [except Prospero].

EPILOGUE

Spoken by Prospero.

Now my charms are all o'erthrown,
And what strength I have 's mine own,
Which is most faint. Now, 'tis true,
I must be here confined by you
Or sent to Naples. Let me not,   5
Since I have my dukedom got
And pardoned the deceiver, dwell
In this bare island by your spell,
But release me from my bands°
With the help of your good hands.°   10
Gentle breath° of yours my sails
Must fill, or else my project fails,
Which was to please. Now I want°
Spirits to enforce,° art to enchant,
And my ending is despair,   15
Unless I be relieved by prayer,°
Which pierces so that it assaults°
Mercy itself, and frees° all faults.
As you from crimes° would pardoned be,
Let your indulgence° set me free.   *Exit.*   20

                                                          [c. 1611]

316–317 catch . . . far off: Enable you to catch up with the main part of your royal fleet, now afar off en route to Naples (see I.ii.233–236). **319 draw near:** I.e., enter my cell. **EPI-LOGUE. 9 bands:** Bonds. **10 hands:** I.e., applause (the noise of which would break the spell of silence). **11 Gentle breath:** Favorable breeze (produced by hands clapping or favorable comment). **13 want:** Lack. **14 enforce:** Control. **16 prayer:** I.e., Prospero's petition to the audience. **17 assaults:** Rightfully gains the attention of. **18 frees:** Obtains forgiveness for. **19 crimes:** Sins. **20 indulgence:** (1) Humoring, lenient approval (2) remission of punishment for sin.

THINKING ABOUT THE TEXT

1. What seem to be the advantages for the playwright in setting his play on an island? What, if any, are the disadvantages?

2. Once they are stranded on the island, the ship's crew and passengers divide into several groups. Identify and compare these groups. (It might be helpful for you to make a chart of them.) To what extent do they go

through similar experiences on the island? In what ways do their experiences differ?

3. Describe and evaluate the character of Prospero. What lines of his strike you as especially important as you try to determine what to think of him? To what extent, and in what ways, does he change over the course of the play? Note the different tones with which he addresses other characters, such as Miranda, Caliban, and Ariel. Suppose Shakespeare did have himself in mind in creating Prospero; in what ways does this character resemble a theater artist?

4. Contrast Caliban with other key characters, especially Prospero, Miranda, and Ariel. Do you sympathize at all with him? Why, or why not? Near the end of the play, Prospero refers to Caliban by saying "This thing of darkness I / Acknowledge mine" (5.1.277–78). What do you suppose Prospero means by this statement?

5. What kind of play is *The Tempest*? It has often been referred to as one of Shakespeare's "romances"; it has been called a "tragicomedy" as well. In specifying the kind of play you think it is, define either or both of these terms for yourself. Then again, you may believe some other term is more appropriate. In any case, refer to elements of the play that support whatever label you give it.

AIMÉ CÉSAIRE
A Tempest

Translated by Richard Miller

Aimé Césaire was born in 1913 on the French-controlled island of Martinique in the West Indies. At eighteen, he left it to attend school in Paris. In 1939 he returned to his native island and has made it his home ever since. He has been quite active in the island's politics, serving for many years as mayor of his native town. During the 1930s while in France, Césaire pioneered the literary movement known as negritude, which associated black people with a particular racial consciousness and called for black writers to embody it in their work. Césaire's first use of the word negritude *came in his influential 1939 poem* Return to My Native Land. *Written when he was about to go home from France, the poem reflects Césaire's interest in surrealism, a movement begun by white European writers that he harnessed to his own ends. In the 1950s, after years of writing poetry, Césaire turned to playwriting in an effort to reach a broader audience. He wrote his adaptation of Shakespeare's* The Tempest *in 1969. Like all of his work, it was originally in French; the English translation reprinted here was published in 1986. Césaire has explicitly indicated that his version of Shakespeare's play is "for a Black Theatre." As you read it, note his departures from the play as well as elements of it that he chooses to emphasize.*

Keep in mind, too, that Césaire's Tempest *is written by a black man who grew up under colonialism.*

CHARACTERS

As in Shakespeare

Two alterations: ARIEL, *a mulatto slave*
                      CALIBAN, *a black slave*

An addition: ESHU, *a black devil-god*

Ambiance of a psychodrama. The actors enter singly, at random, and each chooses for himself a mask at his leisure.

MASTER OF CEREMONIES: Come gentlemen, help yourselves. To each his charac-
    ter, to each character his mask. You, Prospero? Why not? He has reserves of
    willpower he's not even aware of himself. You want Caliban? Well, that's
    revealing. Ariel? Fine with me. And what about Stephano, Trinculo? No tak-
    ers? Ah, just in time! It takes all kinds to make a world.
        And after all, they aren't the worst characters. No problem about the juve-
    nile leads, Miranda and Ferdinand. You, okay. And there's no problem about
    the villains either: you, Antonio; you, Alonso, perfect! Oh, Christ! I was for-
    getting the Gods. Eshu will fit you like a glove. As for the other parts, just
    take what you want and work it out among yourselves. But make up your
    minds . . . Now, there's one part I have to pick out myself: you! It's for the
    part of the Tempest, and I need a storm to end all storms . . . I need a really
    big guy to do the wind. Will you do that? Fine! And then someone strong for
    Captain of the ship. Good, now let's go. Ready? Begin. Blow, winds! Rain
    and lightning *ad lib!*

ACT 1, Scene 1

GONZALO: Of course, we're only straws tossed on the raging sea . . . but all's not
    lost, Gentlemen. We just have to try to get to the eye of the storm.
ANTONIO: We might have known this old fool would nag us to death!
SEBASTIAN: To the bitter end!
GONZALO: Try to understand what I'm telling you: imagine a huge cylinder like
    the chimney of a lamp, fast as a galloping horse, but in the center as still and
    unmoving as Cyclop's eye. That's what we're talking about when we say "the
    eye of the storm" and that's where we have to get.
ANTONIO: Oh, great! Do you really mean that the cyclone or Cyclops, if he can't
    see the beam in his own eye, will let us escape! Oh, that's very illuminating!
GONZALO: It's a clever way of putting it, at any rate. Literally false, but yet quite
    true. But what's the fuss going on up there? The Captain seems worried.
    (*Calling.*) Captain!

CAPTAIN *(with a shrug):*   Boatswain!

BOATSWAIN: Aye, sir!

CAPTAIN: We're coming round windward of the island. At this speed we'll run aground. We've got to turn her around. Heave to! *(Exits.)*

BOATSWAIN: Come on, men! Heave to! To the topsail; man the ropes. Pull! Heave ho, heave ho!

ALONSO *(approaching):*   Well, Boatswain, how are things going? Where are we?

BOATSWAIN: If you ask me, you'd all be better off below, in your cabins.

ANTONIO: *He* doesn't seem too happy. We'd better ask the Captain. Where's the Captain, Boatswain? He was here just a moment ago, and now he's gone off.

BOATSWAIN: Get back below where you belong! We've got work to do!

GONZALO: My dear fellow, I can quite understand your being nervous, but a man should be able to control himself in any situation, even the most upsetting.

BOATSWAIN: Shove it! If you want to save your skins, you'd better get yourselves back down below to those first-class cabins of yours.

GONZALO: Now, now, my good fellow, you don't seem to know to whom you're speaking. *(Making introductions.)* The King's brother, the King's son and myself, the King's counsellor.

BOATSWAIN: King! King! Well, there's someone who doesn't give a fuck more about the king than he does about you or me, and he's called the Gale. His Majesty the Gale! And right now, he's in control and we're all his subjects.

GONZALO: He might just as well be pilot on the ferry to hell . . . his mouth's foul enough!

ANTONIO: In a sense, the fellow *regales* me, as you might say. We'll pull through, you'll see, because he looks to me more like someone who'll end up on the gallows, not beneath the billows.

SEBASTIAN: The end result is the same. The fish will get us and the crows will get him.

GONZALO: He did irritate me, rather. However, I take the attenuating circumstances into account . . . and, you must admit, he lacks neither courage nor wit.

BOATSWAIN *(returning):*   Pull in the stud sails. Helmsman, into the wind! Into the wind!

Enter Sebastian, Antonio, Gonzalo.

BOATSWAIN: You again! If you keep bothering us and don't get below and say your prayers, I'll give up and let you sail the ship! You can't expect me to be the go-between for your souls and Beelzebub!

ANTONIO: It's really too much! The fellow is taking advantage of the situation . . .

BOATSWAIN: Windward! Windward! Heave into the wind!

Thunder, lightning.

SEBASTIAN: Ho! Ho!

GONZALO: Did you see that? There, at the top of the masts, in the rigging, that glitter of blue fire, flashing, flashing? They're right when they call these magic lands, so different from our homes in Europe . . . Look, even the lightning is different!

ANTONIO: Maybe it's a foretaste of the hell that awaits us.

GONZALO: You're too pessimistic. Anyway, I've always kept myself in a state of grace, ready to meet my maker.

Sailors enter.

SAILORS: Shit! We're sinking!

The passengers can be heard singing "Nearer, my God, to Thee . . ."

BOATSWAIN: To leeward! To leeward!

FERDINAND *(entering)*:   Alas! There's no one in hell . . . all the devils are here!

The ship sinks.

Scene 2

MIRANDA: Oh God! Oh God! A sinking ship! Father, help!

PROSPERO *(enters hurriedly carrying a megaphone)*:   Come daughter, calm your-self! It's only a play. There's really nothing wrong. Anyway, everything that happens is for our own good. Trust me, I won't say any more.

MIRANDA: But such a fine ship, and so many fine, brave lives sunk, drowned, laid waste to wrack and ruin . . . A person would have to have a heart of stone not to be moved . . .

PROSPERO: Drowned . . . hmmm. That remains to be seen. But draw near, dear Princess. The time has come.

MIRANDA: You're making fun of me, father. Wild as I am, you know I am happy — like a queen of the wildflowers, of the streams and paths, running barefoot through thorns and flowers, spared by one, caressed by the other.

PROSPERO: But you are a Princess . . . for how else does one address the daugh-ter of a Prince? I cannot leave you in ignorance any longer. Milan is the city of your birth, and the city where for many years I was the Duke.

MIRANDA: Then how did we come here? And tell me, too, by what ill fortune did a prince turn into the reclusive hermit you are now, here, on this desert isle? Was it because you found the world distasteful, or through the perfidy of some enemy? Is our island a prison or a hermitage? You've hinted at some mystery so many times and aroused my curiosity, and today you shall tell me all.

PROSPERO: In a way, it is because of all the things you mention. First, it is because of political disagreements, because of the intrigues of my ambitious younger brother. Antonio is his name, your uncle, and Alonso the name of the envious King of Naples. How their ambitions were joined, how my brother became the accomplice of my rival, how the latter promised the for-mer his protection and my throne . . . the devil alone knows how all that came about. In any event, when they learned that through my studies and experiments I had managed to discover the exact location of these lands for which many had sought for centuries and that I was making preparations to set forth to take possession of them, they hatched a scheme to steal my as-yet-unborn empire from me. They bribed my people, they stole my charts and documents and, to get rid of me, they denounced me to the Inquisition as a magician and sorcerer. To be brief, one day I saw arriving at the palace men to whom I had never granted audience: the priests of the Holy Office.

Flashback: Standing before Prospero, who is wearing his ducal robes, we see a friar reading from a parchment scroll.

THE FRIAR: The Holy Inquisition for the preservation and integrity of the Faith and the pursuit of heretical perversion, acting through the special powers entrusted to it by the Holy Apostolic See, informed of the errors you profess, insinuate and publish against God and his Creation with regard to the shape of the Earth and the possibility of discovering other lands, notwithstanding the fact that the Prophet Isaiah stated and taught that the Lord God is seated upon the circle of the Earth and in its center is Jerusalem and that around the world lies inaccessible Paradise, convinced that it is through wickedness that to support your heresy you quote Strabus, Ptolemy and the tragic author Seneca, thereby lending credence to the notion that profane writings can aspire to an authority equal to that of the most profound of the Holy Scriptures, given your notorious use by both night and day of Arabic calculations and scribblings in Hebrew, Syrian and other demonic tongues and, lastly, given that you have hitherto escaped punishment owing to your temporal authority and have, if not usurped, then transformed that authority and made it into a tyranny, doth hereby strip you of your titles, positions and honors in order that it may then proceed against you according to due process through a full and thorough examination, under which authority we require that you accompany us.

PROSPERO *(back in the present):*   And yet, the trial they said they were going to hold never took place. Such creatures of darkness are too much afraid of the light. To be brief: instead of killing me they chose — even worse — to maroon me here with you on this desert island.

MIRANDA: How terrible, and how wicked the world is! How you must have suffered!

PROSPERO: In all this tale of treason and felony there is but one honorable name: Gonzalo, counsellor to the King of Naples and fit to serve a better master. By furnishing me with food and clothing, by supplying me with my books and instruments, he has done all in his power to make my exile in this disgusting place bearable. And now, through a singular turn, Fortune has brought to these shores the very men involved in the plot against me. My prophetic science had of course already informed me that they would not be content merely with seizing my lands in Europe and that their greed would win out over their cowardice, that they would confront the sea and set out for those lands my genius had discovered. I couldn't let them get away with that, and since I was able to stop them, I did so, with the help of Ariel. We brewed up the storm you have just witnessed, thereby saving my possessions overseas and bringing the scoundrels into my power at the same time.

Enter Ariel.

PROSPERO: Well, Ariel?

ARIEL: Mission accomplished.

PROSPERO: Bravo; good work! But what seems to be the matter? I give you a compliment and you don't seem pleased? Are you tired?

ARIEL: Not tired; disgusted. I obeyed you but—well, why not come out with it?—I did so most unwillingly. It was a real pity to see that great ship go down, so full of life.

PROSPERO: Oh, so you're upset, are you! It's always like that with you intellectuals! Who cares! What interests me is not your moods, but your deeds. Let's split: I'll take the zeal and you can keep your doubts. Agreed?

ARIEL: Master, I must beg you to spare me this kind of labour.

PROSPERO (*shouting*):   Listen, and listen good! There's a task to be performed, and I don't care how it gets done!

ARIEL: You've promised me my freedom a thousand times, and I'm still waiting.

PROSPERO: Ingrate! And who freed you from Sycorax, may I ask? Who rent the pine in which you had been imprisoned and brought you forth?

ARIEL: Sometimes I almost regret it . . . After all, I might have turned into a real tree in the end . . . Tree: that's a word that really gives me a thrill! It often springs to mind: palm tree—springing into the sky like a fountain ending in nonchalant, squid-like elegance. The baobab—twisted like the soft entrails of some monster. Ask the calao bird that lives a cloistered season in its branches. Or the Ceiba tree—spread out beneath the proud sun. O bird, o green mansions set in the living earth!

PROSPERO: Stuff it! I don't like talking trees. As for your freedom, you'll have it when I'm good and ready. In the meanwhile, see to the ship. I'm going to have a few words with Master Caliban. I've been keeping my eye on him, and he's getting a little too emancipated. (*Calling*) Caliban! Caliban! (*He sighs.*)

Enter Caliban.

CALIBAN: Uhuru!

PROSPERO: What did you say?

CALIBAN: I said, Uhuru!

PROSPERO: Mumbling your native language again! I've already told you, I don't like it. You could be polite, at least; a simple "hello" wouldn't kill you.

CALIBAN: Oh, I forgot . . . But make that as froggy, waspish, pustular and dung-filled "hello" as possible. May today hasten by a decade the day when all the birds of the sky and beasts of the earth will feast upon your corpse!

PROSPERO: Gracious as always, you ugly ape! How can anyone be so ugly?

CALIBAN: You think I'm ugly . . . well, I don't think you're so handsome yourself. With that big hooked nose, you look just like some old vulture. (*Laughing*) An old vulture with a scrawny neck!

PROSPERO: Since you're so fond of invective, you could at least thank me for having taught you to speak at all. You, a savage . . . a dumb animal, a beast I educated, trained, dragged up from the bestiality that still clings to you.

CALIBAN: In the first place, that's not true. You didn't teach me a thing! Except to jabber in your own language so that I could understand your orders: chop the wood, wash the dishes, fish for food, plant vegetables, all because you're too lazy to do it yourself. And as for your learning, did you ever impart any of *that* to me? No, you took care not to. All your science you keep for yourself alone, shut up in those big books.

PROSPERO: What would you be without me?

CALIBAN: Without you? I'd be the king, that's what I'd be, the King of the Island. The king of the island given me by my mother, Sycorax.

PROSPERO: There are some family trees it's better not to climb! She's a ghoul! A witch from whom—and may God be praised—death has delivered us.

CALIBAN: Dead or alive, she was my mother, and I won't deny her! Anyhow, you only think she's dead because you think the earth itself is dead . . . It's so much simpler that way! Dead, you can walk on it, pollute it, you can tread upon it with the steps of a conqueror. I respect the earth, because I know that it is alive, and I know that Sycorax is alive.

Sycorax. Mother.

Serpent, rain, lightning.

And I see thee everywhere!

In the eye of the stagnant pool which stares back at me,

through the rushes,

in the gesture made by twisted root and its awaiting thrust.

In the night, the all-seeing blinded night,

the nostril-less all-smelling night!

. . . Often, in my dreams, she speaks to me and warns me . . . Yesterday, even, when I was lying by the stream on my belly lapping at the muddy water, when the Beast was about to spring upon me with that huge stone in his hand . . .

PROSPERO: If you keep on like that even your magic won't save you from punishment!

CALIBAN: That's right, that's right! In the beginning, the gentleman was all sweet talk: dear Caliban here, my little Caliban there! And what do you think you'd have done without me in this strange land? Ingrate! I taught you the trees, fruits, birds, the seasons, and now you don't give a damn . . . Caliban the animal, Caliban the slave! I know that story! Once you've squeezed the juice from the orange, you toss the rind away!

PROSPERO: Oh!

CALIBAN: Do I lie? Isn't it true that you threw me out of your house and made me live in a filthy cave? The ghetto!

PROSPERO: It's easy to say "ghetto"! It wouldn't be such a ghetto if you took the trouble to keep it clean! And there's something you forgot, which is that what forced me to get rid of you was your lust. Good God, you tried to rape my daughter!

CALIBAN: Rape! Rape! Listen, you old goat, you're the one that put those dirty thoughts in my head. Let me tell you something: I couldn't care less about your daughter, or about your cave, for that matter. If I gripe, it's on principle, because I didn't like living with you at all, as a matter of fact. Your feet stink!

PROSPERO: I did not summon you here to argue. Out! Back to work! Wood, water, and lots of both! I'm expecting company today.

CALIBAN: I've had just about enough. There's already a pile of wood that high . . .

PROSPERO: Enough! Careful, Caliban! If you keep grumbling you'll be whipped. And if you don't step lively, if you keep dragging your feet or try to strike or sabotage things, I'll beat you. Beating is the only language you really understand. So much the worse for you: I'll speak it, loud and clear. Get a move on!

CALIBAN: All right, I'm going . . . but this is the last time. It's the last time, do you hear me? Oh . . . I forgot: I've got something important to tell you.

PROSPERO: Important? Well, out with it.

CALIBAN: It's this: I've decided I don't want to be called Caliban any longer.

PROSPERO: What kind of rot is that? I don't understand.

CALIBAN: Put it this way: I'm *telling* you that from now on I won't answer to the name Caliban.

PROSPERO: Where did you get that idea?

CALIBAN: Well, because Caliban *isn't* my name. It's as simple as that.

PROSPERO: Oh, I suppose it's mine!

CALIBAN: It's the name given me by your hatred, and every time it's spoken it's an insult.

PROSPERO: My, aren't we getting sensitive! All right, suggest something else . . . I've got to call you something. What will it be? Cannibal would suit you, but I'm sure you wouldn't like that, would you? Let's see . . . what about Hanni-bal? That fits. And why not . . . they all seem to like historical names.

CALIBAN: Call me X. That would be best. Like a man without a name. Or, to be more precise, a man whose name has been stolen. You talk about history . . . well, that's history, and everyone knows it! Every time you summon me it reminds me of a basic fact, the fact that you've stolen everything from me, even my identity! Uhuru! *(He exits.)*

Enter Ariel as a sea-nymph.

PROSPERO: My dear Ariel, did you see how he looked at me, that glint in his eye? That's something new. Well, let me tell you, Caliban is the enemy. As for those people on the boat, I've changed my mind about them. Give them a scare, but for God's sake don't touch a hair of their heads! You'll answer to me if you do.

ARIEL: I've suffered too much myself for having made them suffer not to be pleased at your mercy. You can count on me, Master.

PROSPERO: Yes, however great their crimes, if they repent you can assure them of my forgiveness. They are men of my race, and of high rank. As for me, at my age one must rise above disputes and quarrels and think about the future. I have a daughter. Alonso has a son. If they were to fall in love, I would give my consent. Let Ferdinand marry Miranda, and may their marriage bring us harmony and peace. That is my plan. I want it executed. As for Caliban, does it matter what that villain plots against me? All the nobility of Italy, Naples and Milan henceforth combined, will protect me bodily. Go!

ARIEL: Yes, Master. Your orders will be fully carried out.

Ariel sings:

> Sandy seashore, deep blue sky,
> Surf is rising, sea birds fly
> Here the lover finds delight,
> Sun at noontime, moon at night.
> Join hands lovers, join the dance,
> Find contentment, find romance.
>
> Sandy seashore, deep blue sky,
> Cares will vanish . . . so can I . . .

FERDINAND: What is this music? It has led me here and now it stops . . . No, there it is again . . .

ARIEL *(singing):*

> Waters move, the ocean flows,
> Nothing comes and nothing goes . . .
> Strange days are upon us . . .
>
> Oysters stare through pearly eyes
> Heart-shaped corals gently beat
> In the crystal undersea
>
> Waters move and ocean flows,
> Nothing comes and nothing goes . . .
> Strange days are upon us . . .

FERDINAND: What is this that I see before me? A goddess? A mortal?

MIRANDA: I know what *I'm* seeing: a flatterer. Young man, your ability to pay compliments in the situation in which you find yourself at least proves your courage. Who are you?

FERDINAND: As you see, a poor shipwrecked soul.

MIRANDA: But one of high degree!

FERDINAND: In other surroundings I might be called "Prince," "son of the King" . . . But, no, I was forgetting . . . not "Prince" but "King," alas . . . "King" because my father has just perished in the shipwreck.

MIRANDA: Poor young man! Here, you'll be received with hospitality and we'll support you in your misfortune.

FERDINAND: Alas, my father . . . Can it be that I am an unnatural son? Your pity would make the greatest of sorrows seem sweet.

MIRANDA: I hope you'll like it here with us. The island is pretty. I'll show you the beaches and the forests, I'll tell you the names of fruits and flowers, I'll introduce you to a whole world of insects, of lizards of every hue, of birds . . . Oh, you cannot imagine! The birds! . . .

PROSPERO: That's enough, daughter! I find your chatter irritating . . . and let me assure you, it's not at all fitting. You are doing too much honor to an impostor. Young man, you are a traitor, a spy, and a woman-chaser to boot! No sooner has he escaped the perils of the sea than he's sweet-talking the first girl he meets! You won't get round me that way. Your arrival is convenient, because I need more manpower: you shall be my house servant.

FERDINAND: Seeing the young lady, more beautiful than any wood-nymph, I might have been Ulysses on Nausicaa's isle. But hearing you, Sir, I now understand my fate a little, better . . . I see I have come ashore on the Barbary Coast and am in the hands of a cruel pirate. (*Drawing his sword*) However, a gentleman prefers death to dishonor. I shall defend my life with my freedom!

PROSPERO: Poor fool: your arm is growing weak, your knees are trembling! Traitor! I could kill you now . . . but I need the manpower. Follow me.

ARIEL: It's no use trying to resist, young man. My master is a sorcerer: neither your passion nor your youth can prevail against him. Your best course would be to follow and obey him.

FERDINAND: Oh God! What sorcery is this? Vanquished, a captive—yet far from rebelling against my fate, I am finding my servitude sweet. Oh, I would be imprisoned for life, if only heaven will grant me a glimpse of my sun each day, the face of my own sun. Farewell, Nausicaa.

They exit.

ACT 2, Scene 1

Caliban's cave. Caliban is singing as he works when Ariel enters. He listens to him for a moment.

CALIBAN (*singing*):
> May he who eats his corn heedless of Shango
> Be accursed! May Shango creep beneath
> His nails and eat into his flesh!
> Shango, Shango ho!
>
> Forget to give him room if you dare!
> He will make himself at home on your nose!
>
> Refuse to have him under your roof at your own risk!
> He'll tear off your roof and wear it as a hat!
> Whoever tries to mislead Shango
> Will suffer for it!
> Shango, Shango ho!

ARIEL: Greetings, Caliban. I know you don't think much of me, but after all we *are* brothers, brothers in suffering and slavery, but brothers in hope as well. We both want our freedom. We just have different methods.

CALIBAN: Greetings to you. But you didn't come to see me just to make that profession of faith. Come on, Alastor! The old man sent you, didn't he? A great job: carrying out the Master's fine ideas, his great plans.

ARIEL: No, I've come on my own. I came to warn you. Prospero is planning horrible acts of revenge against you. I thought it my duty to alert you.

CALIBAN: I'm ready for him.

ARIEL: Poor Caliban, you're doomed. You know that you aren't the stronger, you'll never be the stronger. What good will it do you to struggle?

CALIBAN: And what about you? What good has your obedience done you, your Uncle Tom patience and your sucking up to him. The man's just getting more demanding and despotic day by day.

ARIEL: Well, I've at least achieved one thing: he's promised me my freedom. In the distant future, of course, but it's the first time he's actually committed himself.

CALIBAN: Talk's cheap! He'll promise you a thousand times and take it back a thousand times. Anyway, tomorrow doesn't interest me. What I want is (*shouting*) "Freedom now!"

ARIEL: Okay. But you know you're not going to get it out of him "now," and that he's stronger than you are. I'm in a good position to know just what he's got in his arsenal.

CALIBAN: The stronger? How do you know that? Weakness always has a thousand means and cowardice is all that keeps us from listing them.

ARIEL: I don't believe in violence.

CALIBAN: What *do* you believe in, then? In cowardice? In giving up? In kneeling and groveling? That's it, someone strikes you on the right cheek and you offer the left. Someone kicks you on the left buttock and you turn the right . . . that way there's no jealousy. Well, that's not Caliban's way . . .

ARIEL: You know very well that that's not what I mean. No violence, no submission either. Listen to me: Prospero is the one we've got to change. Destroy his serenity so that he's finally forced to acknowledge his own injustice and put an end to it.

CALIBAN: Oh sure . . . that's a good one! Prospero's conscience! Prospero is an old scoundrel who has no conscience.

ARIEL: Exactly—that's why it's up to us to give him one. I'm not fighting just for *my* freedom, for *our* freedom, but for Prospero too, so that Prospero can acquire a conscience. Help me, Caliban.

CALIBAN: Listen, kid, sometimes I wonder if you aren't a little bit nuts. So that Prospero can acquire a conscience? You might as well ask a stone to grow flowers.

ARIEL: I don't know what to do with you. I've often had this inspiring, uplifting dream that one day Prospero, you, me, we would all three set out, like brothers, to build a wonderful world, each one contributing his own special thing: patience, vitality, love, willpower too, and rigor, not to mention the dreams without which mankind would perish.

CALIBAN: You don't understand a thing about Prospero. He's not the collaborating type. He's a guy who only feels something when he's wiped someone out. A crusher, a pulveriser, that's what he is! And you talk about brotherhood!

ARIEL: So then what's left? War? And you know that when it comes to that, Prospero is invincible.

CALIBAN: Better death than humiliation and injustice. Anyhow, I'm going to have the last word. Unless nothingness has it. The day when I begin to feel that everything's lost, just let me get hold of a few barrels of your infernal powder and as you fly around up there in your blue skies you'll see this island, my inheritance, my work, all blown to smithereens . . . and, I trust, Prospero and me with it. I hope you'll like the fireworks display—it'll be signed Caliban.

ARIEL: Each of us marches to his own drum. You follow yours. I follow the beat of mine. I wish you courage, brother.

CALIBAN: Farewell, Ariel, my brother, and good luck.

Scene 2

GONZALO: A magnificent country! Bread hangs from the trees and the apricots are bigger than a woman's full breast.

SEBASTIAN: A pity that it's so wild and uncultivated . . . here and there.

GONZALO: Oh, that's nothing. If there were anything poisonous, an antidote would never be far away, for nature is intrinsically harmonious. I've even read somewhere that guano is excellent compost for sterile ground.

SEBASTIAN: Guano? What kind of animal is that? Are you sure you don't mean iguana?

GONZALO: Young man, if I say guano, I mean guano. Guano is the name for bird-droppings that build up over centuries, and it is by far the best fertilizer known. You dig it out of caves . . . If you want my opinion, I think we should investigate all the caves on this island one by one to see if we find any, and if we do, this island, if wisely exploited, will be richer than Egypt with its Nile.

ANTONIO: Let me understand: your guano cave contains a river of dried bird-shit.

GONZALO: To pick up your image, all we need to do is channel that river, use it to irrigate, if I may use the term, the fields with this wonderful fecal matter, and everything will bloom.

SEBASTIAN: But we'll still need manpower to farm it. Is the island even inhabited?

GONZALO: That's the problem, of course. But if it is, it must be by wonderful people. It's obvious: it wondrous land can only contain wonderful creatures.

ANTONIO: Yes!
Men whose bodies are wiry and strong
And women whose eyes are open and frank . . .
creatures in it! . . .

GONZALO: Something like that! I see you know your literature. But in that case, watch out: it will all mean new responsibilities for us!

SEBASTIAN: How do you get that?

GONZALO: I mean that if the island is inhabited, as I believe, and if we colonize it, as is my hope, then we have to take every precaution not to import our shortcomings, yes, what we call civilization. They must stay as they are: savages, noble and good savages, free, without any complexes or complications. Something like a pool granting eternal youth where we periodically come to restore our aging, citified souls.

ALONSO: Sir Gonzalo, when will you shut up?

GONZALO: Ah, Your Majesty, if I am boring you, I apologize. I was only speaking as I did to distract you and to turn our sad thoughts to something more pleasant. There, I'll be silent. Indeed, these old bones have had it. Oof! Let me sit down . . . with your permission, of course.

ALONSO: Noble Old Man, even though younger than you, we are all in the same fix.

GONZALO: In other words, dead tired and dying of hunger.

ALONSO: I have never pretended to be above the human condition.

A strange, solemn music is heard.

   . . . Listen, listen! Did you hear that?

GONZALO: Yes, it's an odd melody!

Prospero enters, invisible. Other strange figures enter as well, bearing a laden table. They dance and graciously invite the King and his company to eat, then they disappear.

ALONSO: Heaven protect us! Live marionettes!

GONZALO: Such grace! Such music! Hum. The whole thing is most peculiar.

SEBASTIAN: Gone! Faded away! But what does that matter, since they've left their food behind! No meal was ever more welcome. Gentlemen, to table!

ALONSO: Yes, let us partake of this feast, even though it may be our last.

They prepare to eat, but Elves enter and, with much grimacing and many contortions, carry off the table.

GONZALO: Ah! that's a fine way to behave!

ALONSO: I have the distinct feeling that we have fallen under the sway of powers that are playing at cat and mouse with us. It's a cruel way to make us aware of our dependent status.

GONZALO: The way things have been going it's not surprising, and it will do us no good to protest.

The Elves return, bringing the food with them.

ALONSO: Oh no, this time I won't bite!

SEBASTIAN: I'm so hungry that I don't care, I'll abandon my scruples.

GONZALO *(to Alonso)*:   Why not try? Perhaps the Powers controlling us saw how disappointed we were and took pity on us. After all, even though disappointed a hundred times, Tantalus still tried a hundred times.

ALONSO: That was also his torture. I won't touch that food.

PROSPERO *(invisible)*:   Ariel, I don't like his refusing. Harass them until they eat.

ARIEL: Why should we go to any trouble for them? If they won't eat, they can die of hunger.

PROSPERO: No, I *want* them to eat.

ARIEL: That's despotism. A while ago you made me snatch it away, just when they were about to gobble it up, and now that they don't want it you are ready to force feed them.

PROSPERO: Enough hairsplitting! My mood has changed! They insult me by not eating. They must be made to eat out of my hand like chicks. That is a sign of submission I insist they give me.

ARIEL: It's evil to play with their hunger as you do with their anxieties and their hopes.

PROSPERO: That is how power is measured. I am Power.

Alonso and his group eat.

ALONSO: Alas, when I think . . .

GONZALO: That's your trouble, Sire: you think too much.

ALONSO: And thus I should not even think of my lost son! My throne! My country!

GONZALO *(eating)*:   Your son! What's to say we won't find him again! As for the rest of it . . . Look, Sire, this filthy hole is now our entire world. Why seek further? If your thoughts are too vast, cut them down to size.

They eat.

ALONSO: So be it! But I would prefer to sleep. To sleep and to forget.

GONZALO: Good idea! Let's put up our hammocks!

They sleep.

Scene 3

ANTONIO: Look at those leeches, those slugs! Wallowing in their slime and their snot: Idiots, slime — they're like beached jellyfish.

SEBASTIAN: Shhh! It's the King. And that old graybeard is his venerable counsellor.

ANTONIO: The King is he who watches over his flock when they sleep. That one isn't watching over anything. Ergo, he's not the King. *(Brusquely)* You're really a bloodless lily-liver if you can see a king asleep without getting certain ideas . . .

SEBASTIAN: I mustn't have any blood, only water.

ANTONIO: Don't insult water. Every time I look at myself I think I'm more handsome, more *there*. My inner juices have always given me my greatness, my true greatness . . . not the greatness men grant me.

SEBASTIAN: All right, so I'm stagnant water.

ANTONIO: Water is never stagnant. It works, it works in us. It is what gives man his dimension, his true one. Believe me, you're mistaken if you don't grab the opportunity when it's offered you. It may never come again.

SEBASTIAN: What are you getting at? I have a feeling I can guess.

ANTONIO: Guess, guess! Look at that tree swaying in the wind. It's called a coconut palm. My dear Sebastian, in my opinion it's time to shake the coconut palm.

SEBASTIAN: Now I really don't understand.

ANTONIO: What a dope! Consider my position: I'm Duke of Milan. Well, I wasn't always . . . I had an older brother. That was Duke Prospero. And if I'm now Duke Antonio, it's because I knew when to shake the coconut palm.

SEBASTIAN: And Prospero?

ANTONIO: What do you mean by that? When you shake a tree, someone is bound to fall. And obviously it wasn't me who fell, because here I am: to assist and serve you, Majesty!

SEBASTIAN: Enough! He's my brother! My scruples won't allow me to . . . You take care of him while I deal with the old Counsellor.

They draw their swords.

ARIEL: Stop, ruffians! Resistance is futile: your swords are enchanted and falling from your hands!

ANTONIO, SEBASTIAN: Alas! Alas!

ARIEL: Sleepers, awake! Awake, I say! Your life depends on it. With these fine fellows with their long teeth and swords around, anyone who sleeps too soundly risks sleeping forever.

Alonso and Gonzalo awaken.

ALONSO *(rubbing his eyes):*   What's happening? I was asleep, and I was having a terrible dream!

ARIEL: No, you were not dreaming. These fine lords here are criminals who were about to perpetrate the most odious of crimes upon you. Yes, Alonso, you may well marvel that a god should fly to your aid. Were to heaven you deserved it more!

ALONSO: I have never been wanting in respect for the divinity . . .

ARIEL: I don't know what effect my next piece of news will have on you: The name of him who has sent me to you is Prospero.

ALONSO: Prospero! God save us! *(He falls to his knees.)*

ARIEL: I understand your feelings. He lives. It is he who reigns over this isle, as he reigns over the spirits of the air you breathe . . . But rise . . . You need fear no longer. He has not saved your lives to destroy them. Your repentance will suffice, for I can see that it is deep and sincere. *(To Antonio and Sebastian)* As for you, Gentlemen, my master's pardon extends to you as well, on the condition that you renounce your plans, knowing them to be vain.

SEBASTIAN *(to Antonio):*   We could have got worse!

ANTONIO: If it were men we were up against, no one could make me withdraw, but when it's demons and magic there's no shame in giving in. *(To Ariel)* . . . We are the Duke's most humble and obedient servants. Please beg him to accept our thanks.

GONZALO: Oh, how ignoble! How good of you to just wipe the slate clean! No surface repentance . . . not only do you want attrition, you want contrition as well! Why look at me as though you didn't know what I was talking about? *Attrition:* A selfish regret for offending God, caused by a fear of punishment. *Contrition:* An unselfish regret growing out of sorrow at displeasing God.

ARIEL: Honest Gonzalo, thank you for your clarification. Your eloquence has eased my mission and your pedagogical skill has abbreviated it, for in a few short words you have expressed my master's thought. May your words be heard! Therefore, let us turn the page. To terminate this episode, I need only convoke you all, on my master's behalf, to the celebrations that this very day will mark the engagement of his daughter, Miranda. Alonso, that's good news for you . . .

ALONSO: What—my son?

ARIEL: Correct. Saved by my master from the fury of the waves.

ALONSO *(falling to his knees)*:   God be praised for this blessing more than all the rest. Rank, fortune, throne, I am prepared to forgo all if my son is returned to me . . .

ARIEL: Come, Gentlemen, follow me.

ACT 3, Scene 1

FERDINAND *(hoeing and singing)*:
>   *How life has changed*
>   *Now, hoe in hand*
>   *I work away all day . . .*

>   *Hoeing all the day,*
>   *I go my weary way . . .*

CALIBAN: Poor kid! What would he say if he was Caliban! He works night and day, and when he sings, it's
>   *Oo-en-day, Oo-en-day, Oo-en-day, Macaya . . .*

And no pretty girl to console him! *(Sees Miranda approaching.)* Aha! Let's listen to this!

FERDINAND *(singing)*:
>   *How life has changed*
>   *Now, hoe in hand*
>   *I work away all day . . .*

MIRANDA: Poor young man! Can I help you? You don't look like you were cut out for this kind of work!

FERDINAND: One word from you would be more help to me than anything in the world.

MIRANDA: One word? From me? I must say, I . . .

FERDINAND: Your name—that's all: What is your name?

MIRANDA: That, I cannot do! It's impossible. My father has expressly forbidden it!

FERDINAND: It is the only thing I long for.

MIRANDA: But I can't, I tell you; it's forbidden!

CALIBAN *(taking advantage of Miranda's momentary distraction, he whispers her name to Ferdinand)*:   Mi-ran-da!

FERDINAND: All right then, I shall christen you with a name of my own. I will call you Miranda.

MIRANDA: That's too much! What a low trick! You must have heard my father calling me . . . Unless it was that awful Caliban who keeps pursuing me and calling out my name in his stupid dreams!

FERDINAND: No, Miranda . . . I had only to allow my eyes to speak, as you your face.

MIRANDA: Sssh! My father's coming! He'd better not catch you trying to sweet talk me.

FERDINAND *(goes back to work, singing)*:
> But times have changed
> Now, hoeing all the day,
> I go my weary way . . .

PROSPERO: That's fine, young man! You've managed to accomplish a good deal for a beginning! I see I've misjudged you. But you won't be the loser if you serve me well. Listen, my young friend, there are three things in life: Work, Patience, Continence, and the world is yours . . . Hey, Caliban, I'm taking this boy away with me. He's done enough for one day. But since the job is urgent, see that it gets finished.

CALIBAN: Me?

PROSPERO: Yes, you! You've cheated me enough with your loafing and fiddling around, so you can work a double shift for once!

CALIBAN: I don't see why I should do someone else's job!

PROSPERO: Who's the boss here? You or me? Listen, monster: if you don't like work, I'll see to it you change your mind!

Prospero and Ferdinand move away.

CALIBAN: Go on, go on . . . I'll get you one day, you bastard! *(He sets to work, singing.)*
> "Oo-en-day, Oo-en-day, Oo-en-day, Macaya . . ."

Shit, now it's raining! As if things weren't bad enough . . . *(Suddenly, at the sound of a voice, Caliban stiffens.)* Do you hear that, boy? That voice through the storm. Bah! It's Ariel. No, that's not his voice. Whose, then? With an old coot like Prospero . . . One of his cops, probably. Oh, fine! Now, I'm for it. Men and the elements both against me. Well, the hell with it . . . I'm used to it. Patience! I'll get them yet. In the meantime better make myself scarce! Let Prospero and his storm and his cops go by . . . let the seven maws of Malediction bay!

Scene 2

Enter Trinculo.

TRINCULO *(singing)*:
> Oh Susannah . . . oh don't you cry for me . . . *(Etc.)*

You can say that again! My dearest Susannah . . . trust Trinculo, we've had all the roaring storms we need, and more! I swear: the whole crew wiped out, liquidated . . . Nothing! Nothing left . . . ! Nothing but poor wandering and wailing Trinculo! No question about it, it'll be a while before anyone persuades me to depart from affectionate women and friendly towns to go off to brave roaring storms! How it's raining! *(Notices Caliban underneath the wheelbarrow.)* Ah, an Indian! Dead or alive? You never know with these tricky races. Yukkk! Anyhow, this will do me fine. If he's dead, I can use his clothes for shelter, for a coat, a tent, a covering. If he's alive I'll make him my prisoner and take him back to Europe and then, by golly, my fortune will be made! I'll sell him to a carnival. No! I'll show him myself at fairs! What a stroke of luck! I'll just settle in here where it's warm and let the storm rage! *(He crawls under cover, back to back with Caliban.)*

Enter Stephano.

STEPHANO *(singing):*
> Blow the man down, hearties
> Blow the man down . . . *(Etc.)*

(Takes a swig of his bottle and continues.)

> Blow, blow, blow the man down . . . *(Etc.)*

Fortunately, there's still a little wine left in this bottle . . . enough to give me courage! Be of good cheer, Stephano, where there's life there's thirst . . . and vice versa! *(Suddenly spies Caliban's head sticking out of the covers.)* My God, on Stephano's word, it looks like a Nindian! *(Comes nearer)* And that's just what it is! A Nindian. That's neat. I really am lucky. There's money to be made from a Nindian like that. If you showed him at a carnival . . . along with the bearded lady and the flea circus, a real Nindian! An authentic Nindian from the Caribbean! That means real dough, or I'm the last of the idiots! *(Touching Caliban)* But he's ice cold! I don't know what the body temperature of a Nindian is, but this one seems pretty cold to me! Let's hope he's not going to croak! How's that for bad luck: You find a Nindian and he dies on you! A fortune slips through your fingers! But wait, I've got an idea . . . a good swig of this booze between his lips, that'll warm him up. *(He gives Caliban a drink.)* Look . . . he's better already. The little glutton even wants some more! Just a second, just a second! *(He walks around the wheelbarrow and sees Trinculo's head sticking out from under the covering.)* Jeez! I must be seeing things! A Nindian with two heads! Shit! If I have to pour drink down *two* gullets I won't have much left for myself! Well, never mind. It's incredible . . . your everyday Nindian is already something, but one with two heads . . . a Siamese-twin Nindian, a Nindian with two heads and eight paws, that's really something! My fortune is made. Come on, you wonderful monster, you . . . let's get a look at your other head! *(He draws nearer to Trinculo.)* Hello! That face reminds me of something! That nose that shines like a lighthouse . . .

TRINCULO: That gut . . .

STEPHANO: That nose looks familiar . . .

TRINCULO: That gut — there can't be two of them in this lousy world!

STEPHANO: Oh-my-gawd, oh-my-gawd, oh-my-gawd . . . *that's* it . . . it's that crook Trinculo!

TRINCULO: Good lord! It's Stephano!

STEPHANO: So, Trinculo, you were saved too . . . It almost makes you believe God looks after drunks . . .

TRINCULO: Huh! God . . . Bacchus, maybe. As a matter of fact, I reached these welcoming shores by floating on a barrel . . .

STEPHANO: And I by floating on my stomach . . . it's nearly the same thing. But what kind of creature is this? Isn't it a Nindian?

TRINCULO: That's just what I was thinking . . . Yes, by God, it's a Nindian. That's a piece of luck . . . he'll be our guide.

STEPHANO: Judging from the way he can swill it down, he doesn't seem to be stupid. I'll try to civilize him. Oh . . . not too much, of course. But enough so that he can be of some use.

TRINCULO: Civilize him! Shee-it! Does he even know how to talk?

STEPHANO: I couldn't get a word out of him, but I know a way to loosen his tongue. *(He takes a bottle from his pocket.)*

TRINCULO *(stopping him)*:   Look here, you're not going to waste that nectar on the first savage that comes along, are you?

STEPHANO: Selfish! Back off! Let me perform my civilizing mission. *(Offering the bottle to Caliban.)* Of course, if he was cleaned up a bit he'd be worth more to both of us. Okay? We'll exploit him together? It's a deal? *(To Caliban)* Drink up, pal. You. Drink . . . Yum-yum botty botty! *(Caliban drinks.)* You, drink more. *(Caliban refuses.)* You no more thirsty? *(Stephano drinks.)* Me always thirsty! *(Stephano and Trinculo drink.)*

STEPHANO: Trinculo, you know I used to be prejudiced against shipwrecks, but I was wrong. They're not bad at all.

TRINCULO: That's true. It seems to make things taste better afterwards . . .

STEPHANO: Not to mention the fact that it's got rid of a lot of old farts that were always keeping the world down! May they rest in peace! But then, you liked them, didn't you, all those kings and dukes, all those noblemen! Oh, I served them well enough, you've got to earn your drink somehow . . . But I could never stand them, ever — understand? Never. Trinculo, my friend, I'm a longtime believer in the republic . . . you might as well say it: I'm a dyed-in-the-wool believer in the people first, a republican in my guts! Down with tyrants!

TRINCULO: Which reminds me . . . If, as it would seem, the King and the Duke are dead, there's a crown and a throne up for grabs around here . . .

STEPHANO: By God, you're right! Smart thinking, Trinculo! So, I appoint myself heir . . . I crown myself king of the island.

TRINCULO *(sarcastically)*:   Sure you do! And why you, may I ask? I'm the one who thought of it first, that crown!

STEPHANO: Look, Trinculo, don't be silly! I mean, really: just take a look at yourself! What's the first thing a king needs? Bearing. Presence. And if I've got anything, it's that. Which isn't true for everyone. So, I am the King!

CALIBAN: Long live the King!

STEPHANO: It's a miracle . . . he can talk! And what's more, he talks sense! O brave savage! *(He embraces Caliban.)* You see, my dear Trinculo, the people has spoken! Vox populi, vox Dei . . . But please, don't be upset. Stephano is magnanimous and will never abandon his friend Trinculo, the friend who stood by him in his trials. Trinculo, we've eaten rough bread together, we've drunk rot-gut wine together. I want to do something for you. I shall appoint you Marshal. But we're forgetting our brave savage . . . It's a scientific miracle! He can talk!

CALIBAN: Yes, Sire. My enthusiasm has restored my speech. Long live the King! But beware the usurper!

STEPHANO: Usurper? Who? Trinculo?

CALIBAN: No, the other one . . . Prospero!

STEPHANO: Prospero? Don't know him.

CALIBAN: Well, you see, this island used to belong to me, except that a man named Prospero cheated me of it. I'm perfectly willing to give you my right to it, but the only thing is, you'll have to fight Prospero for it.

STEPHANO: That is of no matter, brave savage. It's a bargain! I'll get rid of this Prospero for you in two shakes.

CALIBAN: Watch out, he's powerful.

STEPHANO: My dear savage, I eat a dozen Prosperos like that for breakfast every day. But say no more, say no more! Trinculo, take command of the troops! Let us march upon the foe!

TRINCULO: Yes, forward march! But first, a drink. We will need all our strength and vigor.

CALIBAN: Let's drink, my new-found friends, and let us sing. Let us sing of winning the day and of an end to tyranny.

(Singing)

> Black pecking creature of the savannas
> The quetzal measures out the new day
> solid and lively
> in its haughty armor.
> Zing! the determined hummingbird
> revels in the flower's depths,
> going crazy, getting drunk,
> a lyrebird gathers up our ravings,
> Freedom hi-day! Freedom hi-day!

STEPHANO, TRINCULO (together):   Freedom hi-day! Freedom hi-day!

CALIBAN:

> The ringdove dallies amid the trees,
> wandering the islands, here it rests —
> The white blossoms of the miconia
> Mingle with the violet blood of ripe berries
> And blood stains your plumage,
> traveller!
> Lying here after a weary day
> We listen to it:
> Freedom hi-day! Freedom hi-day!

STEPHANO: Okay, monster . . . enough crooning. Singing makes a man thirsty. Let's drink instead. Here, have some more . . . spirits create higher spirits . . . (Filling a glass.) Lead the way, O bountiful wine! Soldiers, forward march!

Or rather . . . no: At ease! Night is failing, the fireflies twinkle, the crickets chirp, all nature makes its brek-ke-ke-kek! And since night has fallen, let us take advantage of it to gather our forces and regain our strength, which has been sorely tried by the unusually . . . copious emotions of the day. And tomorrow, at dawn, with a new spring in our step, we'll have the tyrant's hide. Good night, gentlemen. *(He falls asleep and begins to snore.)*

Scene 3

Prospero's cave.

PROSPERO: So then, Ariel! Where are the gods and goddesses? They'd better get a move on! And all of them! I want all of them to take part in the entertainment I have planned for our dear children. Why do I say "entertainment"? Because starting today I want to inculcate in them the spectacle of tomorrow's world: logic, beauty, harmony, the foundations for which I have laid down by my own willpower. Unfortunately, alas, at my age it's time to stop thinking of deeds and to begin thinking of passing on . . . Enter, then!

Gods and Goddesses enter.

JUNO: Honor and riches to you! Long continuance and increasing long life and honored issue! Juno sings to you her blessings!

CERES: May scarcity and want shun you! That is Ceres' blessing on you.

IRIS *(beckoning to the Nymphs)*: Nymphs, come help to celebrate here a contact of true love.

Nymphs enter and dance.

PROSPERO: My thanks, Goddesses, and my thanks to you, Iris. Thank you for your good wishes.

Gods and Goddesses continue their dance.

FERDINAND: What a splendid and majestic vision! May I be so bold to think these spirits?

PROSPERO: Yes, spirits which by my art I have from their confines called to greet you and to bless you.

Enter Eshu.

MIRANDA: But who is that? He doesn't look very benevolent! If I weren't afraid of blaspheming, I'd say he was a devil rather than a god.

ESHU *(laughing)*: You are not mistaken, fair lady. God to my friends, the Devil to my enemies! And lots of laughs for all!

PROSPERO *(softly)*: Ariel must have made a mistake. Is my magic getting rusty? *(Aloud)* What are you doing here? Who invited you? I don't like such loose behavior, even from a god!

ESHU: But that's just the point . . . no one invited me . . . And that wasn't very nice! Nobody remembered poor Eshu! So poor Eshu came anyway. Hihihi! So how about something to drink? *(Without waiting for a reply, he pours a drink.*) . . . Your liquor's not bad. However, I must say I prefer dogs! (*Looking at Iris*) I see that shocks the little lady, but to each his own. Some prefer chickens, others prefer goats. I'm not too fond of chickens, myself. But if you're talking about a black dog . . . think of poor Eshu!

PROSPERO: Get out! Go away! We will have none of your grimaces and buffoonery in this noble assembly. (*He makes a magic sign.*)

ESHU: I'm going, boss, I'm going . . . But not without a little song in honor of the bride and the noble company, as you say.

> *Eshu can play many tricks,*
> *Give him twenty dogs!*
> *You will see his dirty tricks.*

> *Eshu plays a trick on the Queen*
> *And makes her so upset that she runs*
> *Naked into the street*

> *Eshu plays a trick on a bride,*
> *And on the day of the wedding*
> *She gets into the wrong bed!*

> *Eshu can throw a stone yesterday*
> *And kill a bird today.*
> *He can make a mess out of order and vice-versa.*
> *Ah, Eshu is a wonderful bad joke.*
> *Eshu is not the man to carry a heavy load.*
> *His head comes to a point. When he dances*
> *He doesn't move his shoulders . . .*
> *Oh, Eshu is a merry elf!*

> *Eshu is a merry elf,*
> *And he can whip you with his dick,*
> *He can whip you,*
> *He can whip you . . .*

CERES: My dear Iris, don't you find that song quite obscene?

JUNO: It's disgusting! It's quite intolerable . . . if he keeps on, I'm leaving!

IRIS: It's like Liber, or Priapus!

JUNO: Don't mention that name in my presence!

ESHU (*continuing to sing*):
> *. . . with his dick*
> *He can whip you, whip you . . .*

JUNO: Oh! Can't someone get rid of him? I'm not staying here!

ESHU: Okay, okay . . . Eshu will go. Farewell, my dear colleagues!

Gods and Goddesses exit.

PROSPERO: He's gone . . . what a relief! But alas, the harm is done! I am perturbed . . . My old brain is confused. Power! Power! Alas! All this will one day fade, like foam, like a cloud, like all the world. And what is power, if I cannot calm my own fears? But come! My power has gone cold. (*Calling*) Ariel!

ARIEL *(runs in):* What is it, Sire?

PROSPERO: Caliban is alive, he is plotting, he is getting a guerrilla force together and you—you don't say a word! Well, take care of him. Snakes, scorpions, porcupines, all stinging poisonous creatures, he is to be spared nothing! His punishment must be exemplary. Oh, and don't forget the mud and mosquitoes!

ARIEL: Master, let me intercede for him and beg your indulgence. You've got to understand: he's a rebel.

PROSPERO: By his insubordination he's calling into question the whole order of the world. Maybe the Divinity can afford to let him get away with it, but I have a sense of responsibility!

ARIEL: Very well, Master.

PROSPERO: But a thought: arrange some glass trinkets, some trumpery and some second-hand clothes too . . . but colorful ones . . . by the side of the road along which General Caliban and his troops are travelling. Savages adore loud, gaudy clothes . . .

ARIEL: Master . . .

PROSPERO: You're going to make me angry. There's nothing to understand. There is a punishment to be meted out. I will not compromise with evil. Hurry! Unless you want to be the next to feel my wrath.

Scene 4

In the wild; night is drawing to a close; the murmurings of the spirits of the tropical forest are heard.

VOICE 1: Fly!

VOICE 2: Here!

VOICE 1: Ant!

VOICE 2: Here.

VOICE 1: Vulture!

VOICE 2: Here.

VOICE 1: Soft-shelled crab, calao, crab, hummingbird!

VOICES: Here. Here. Here.

VOICE 1: Cramp, crime, fang, opossum!

VOICE 2: Kra. Kra. Kra.

VOICE 1: Huge hedgehog, you will be our sun today. Shaggy, taloned, stubborn. May it burn! Moon, my fat spider, my big dreamcat, go to sleep, my velvet one.

VOICES *(singing):*

> King-ay
> King-ay
> Von-von
> Maloto
> Vloom-vloom!

The sun rises. Ariel's band vanishes. Caliban stands for a moment, rubbing his eyes.

CALIBAN (*rises and searches the bushes*):   Have to think about getting going again. Away, snakes, scorpions, porcupines! All stinging, biting, sticking beasts! Sting, fever, venom, away, Or if you really want to lick me, do it with a gentle tongue, like the toad whose pure drool soothes me with sweet dreams of the future. For it is for you, for all of us, that I go forth today to face the common enemy. Yes, hereditary and common. Look, a hedgehog! Sweet little thing . . . How can any animal — any natural animal, if I may put it that way — go against me on the day I'm setting forth to conquer Prospero! Unimaginable! Prospero is the Anti-Nature! And I say, down with Anti-Nature! And does the porcupine bristle his spines at that? No, he smoothes them down! That's nature! It's kind and gentle, in a word. You've just got to know how to deal with it. So come on, the way is clear! Off we go!

The band sets out. Caliban marches forward singing his battle song:

> *Shango carries a big stick,*
> *He strikes and money expires!*
> *He strikes and lies expire!*
> *He strikes and larceny expires!*
> *Shango, Shango ho!*
>
> *Shango is the gatherer of the rain,*
> *He passes, wrapped in his fiery cloak,*
> *His horse's hoofs strike lightning*
> *On the pavements of the sky!*
> *Shango is a great knight!*
> *Shango, Shango ho!*

The roar of the sea can be heard.

STEPHANO: Tell me, brave savage, what is that noise? It sounds like the roaring of a beast at bay.

CALIBAN: Not at bay . . . more like on the prowl . . . Don't worry, it's a pal of mine.

STEPHANO: You are very closemouthed about the company you keep.

CALIBAN: And yet it helps me breathe. That's why I call it a pal. Sometimes it sneezes, and a drop falls on my forehead and cools me with its salt, or blesses me . . .

STEPHANO: I don't understand. You aren't drunk, are you?

CALIBAN: Come on! It's that howling impatient thing that suddenly appears in a clap of thunder like some God and hits you in the face, that rises up out of the very depths of the abyss and smites you with its fury! It's the sea!

STEPHANO: Odd country! And an odd baptism!

CALIBAN: But the best is still the wind and the songs it sings . . . its dirty sigh when it rustles through the bushes, or its triumphant chant when it passes by breaking trees, remnants of their terror in its beard.

STEPHANO: The savage is delirious, he's raving mad! Tough luck, Trinculo, our savage is playing without a full deck!

TRINCULO: I'm kind of shuffling myself . . . In other words, I'm exhausted. I never knew such hard going! Savage, even your mud is muddier.

CALIBAN: That isn't mud . . . it's something Prospero's dreamed up.

TRINCULO: There's a savage for you . . . everything's always caused by someone. The sun is Prospero's smile. The rain is the tear in Prospero's eye . . . And I suppose the mud is Prospero's shit. And what about the mosquitoes? What are they, may I ask? Zzzzzz, Zzzzz . . . do you hear them? My face is being eaten off!

CALIBAN: Those aren't mosquitoes. It's some kind of gas that stings your nose and throat and makes you itch. It's another of Prospero's tricks. It's part of his arsenal.

STEPHANO: What do you mean by that?

CALIBAN: I mean his anti-riot arsenal! He's got a lot of gadgets like these . . . gadgets to make you deaf, to blind you, to make you sneeze, to make you cry . . .

TRINCULO: And to make you slip! Shit! This is some fix you've got us in! I can't take anymore . . . I'm going to sit down!

STEPHANO: Come on, Trinculo, show a little courage! We're engaged in a mobile ground manoeuvre here, and you know what that means: drive, initiatives, split-second decisions to meet new eventualities, and — above all — mobility. Let's go! Up you get! Mobility!

TRINCULO: But my feet are bleeding!

STEPHANO: Get up or I'll knock you down! *(Trinculo begins to walk again.)* But tell me, my good savage, this usurper of yours seems very well protected. It might be dangerous to attack him!

CALIBAN: You mustn't underestimate him. You mustn't overestimate him, either . . . he's showing his power, but he's doing it mostly to impress us.

STEPHANO: No matter. Trinculo, we must take precautions. Axiom: never underestimate the enemy. Here, pass me that bottle. I can always use it as a club.

Highly colored clothing is seen, hanging from a rope.

TRINCULO: Right, Stephano. On with the battle. Victory means loot. And there's a foretaste of it . . . look at that fine wardrobe! Trinculo, my friend, methinks you are going to put on those britches . . . they'll replace your torn trousers.

STEPHANO: Look out, Trinculo . . . one move and I'll knock you down. As your lord and master I have the first pick, and with those britches I'm exercising my feudal rights . . .

TRINCULO: I saw them first!

STEPHANO: The King gets first pick in every country in the world.

TRINCULO: That's tyranny, Stephano. I'm not going to let you get away with it.

They fight.

CALIBAN: Let it alone, fool. I tell you about winning your dignity, and you start fighting over hand-me-downs! *(To himself)* To think I'm stuck with these jokers! What an idiot I am! How could I ever have thought I could create the Revolution with swollen guts and fat faces! Oh well! History won't blame me for not having been able to win my freedom all by myself. It's you and me, Prospero! *(Weapon in hand, he advances on Prospero who has just appeared.)*

PROSPERO *(bares his chest to him):*   Strike! Go on, strike! Strike your Master, your benefactor! Don't tell me you're going to spare him!

Caliban raises his arm, but hesitates.

Go on! You don't dare! See, you're nothing but an animal . . . you don't know how to kill.

CALIBAN: Defend yourself! I'm not a murderer.

PROSPERO *(very calm):*   The worse for you. You've lost your chance. Stupid as a slave! And now, enough of this farce. *(Calling)* Ariel! *(to Ariel)* Ariel, take charge of the prisoners!

Caliban, Trinculo and Stephano are taken prisoners.

Scene 5

Prospero's cave. Miranda and Ferdinand are playing chess.

MIRANDA: Sir, I think you're cheating.

FERDINAND: And what if I told you that I would not do so for twenty kingdoms?

MIRANDA: I would not believe a word of it, but I would forgive you. Now, be honest . . . you did cheat!

FERDINAND: I'm pleased that you were able to tell. *(Laughing)* That makes me less worried at the thought that soon you will be leaving your innocent flowery kingdom for my less-innocent world of men.

MIRANDA: Oh, you know that, hitched to your star, I would brave the demons of hell!

The Nobles enter.

ALONSO: My son! This marriage! The thrill of it has struck me dumb! The thrill and the joy!

GONZALO: A happy ending to a most opportune shipwreck!

ALONSO: A unique one, indeed, for it can legitimately be described as such.

GONZALO: Look at them! Isn't it wonderful! I've been too choked up to speak, or I would have already told these children all the joy my old heart feels at seeing them living love's young dream and cherishing each other so tenderly.

ALONSO *(to Ferdinand and Miranda):*   My children, give me your hands. May the Lord bless you.

GONZALO: Amen! Amen!

Enter Prospero.

PROSPERO: Thank you, Gentlemen, for having agreed to join in this little family party. Your presence has brought us comfort and joy. However, you must now think of getting some rest. Tomorrow morning, you will recover your vessels — they are undamaged — and your men, who I can guarantee are safe, hale and hearty. I shall return with you to Europe, and I can promise you — I should say: promise us — a rapid sail and propitious winds.

GONZALO: God be praised! We are delighted . . . delighted and overcome!

What a happy, what a memorable day! With one voyage Antonio has found a brother, his brother has found a dukedom, his daughter has found a husband. Alonso has regained his son and gained a daughter. And what else? . . . Anyway, I am the only one whose emotion prevents him from knowing what he's saying . . .

PROSPERO: The proof of that, my fine Gonzalo, is that you are forgetting someone: Ariel, my loyal servant. *(Turning to Ariel)* Yes, Ariel, today you will be free. Go, my sweet. I hope you will not be bored.

ARIEL: Bored! I fear that the days will seem all too short!
There, where the Cecropia gloves its impatient hands with silver,
Where the ferns free the stubborn black stumps
from their scored bodies with a green cry—
There where the intoxicating berry ripens the visit
of the wild ring-dove
through the throat of that musical bird
I shall let fall
one by one,
each more pleasing than the last
four notes so sweet that the last
will give rise to a yearning
in the heart of the most forgetful slaves
yearning for freedom!

PROSPERO: Come, come. All the same, you are not going to set my world on fire with your music, I trust!

ARIEL *(with intoxication)*:
Or on some stony plane
perched on an agave stalk
I shall be the thrush that launches
its mocking cry
to the benighted field-hand
"Dig, nigger! Dig, nigger!"
and the lightened agave will
straighten from my flight,
a solemn flag.

PROSPERO: That is a very unsettling agenda! Go! Scram! Before I change my mind!

Enter Stephano, Trinculo, Caliban.

GONZALO: Sire, here are your people.

PROSPERO: Oh no, not all of them! Some are yours.

ALONSO: True. There's that fool Trinculo and that unspeakable Stephano.

STEPHANO: The very ones, Sire, in person. We throw ourselves at your merciful feet.

ALONSO: What became of you?

STEPHANO: Sire, we were walking in the forest—no, it was in the fields—when we saw some perfectly respectable clothing blowing in the wind. We thought

it only right to collect them and we were returning them to their rightful
owner when a frightful adventure befell us . . .

TRINCULO: Yes, we were mistaken for thieves and treated accordingly.

STEPHANO: Yes, Sire, it is the most dreadful thing that could happen to an honest man: victims of a judicial error, a miscarriage of justice!

PROSPERO: Enough! Today is a day to be benevolent, and it will do no good to
try to talk sense to you in the state you're in . . . Leave us. Go sleep it off,
drunkards. We raise sail tomorrow.

TRINCULO: Raise sail! But that's what we do all the time, Sire, Stephano and
I . . . at least, we raise our glasses, from dawn till dusk till dawn. The hard
part is putting them down, landing, as you might say.

PROSPERO: Scoundrels! If only life could bring you to the safe harbors of Temperance and Sobriety!

ALONSO *(indicating Caliban):*   That is the strangest creature I've ever seen!

PROSPERO: And the most devilish too!

GONZALO: What's that? Devilish! You've reprimanded him, preached at him,
you've ordered and made him obey and you say he is still indomitable!

PROSPERO: Honest Gonzalo, it is as I have said.

GONZALO: Well — and forgive me, Counsellor, if I give counsel — on the basis of
my long experience the only thing left is exorcism. "Begone, unclean spirit,
in the name of the Father, of the Son and of the Holy Ghost." That's all there
is to it!

Caliban bursts out laughing.

GONZALO: You were absolutely right! And more so than you thought . . . He's
not just a rebel, he's a real tough customer! *(To Caliban)* So much the worse
for you, my friend. I have tried to save you. I give up. I leave you to the secular arm!

PROSPERO: Come here, Caliban. Have you got anything to say in your own
defence? Take advantage of my good humor. I'm in a forgiving mood today.

CALIBAN: I'm not interested in defending myself. My only regret is that I've
failed.

PROSPERO: What were you hoping for?

CALIBAN: To get back my island and regain my freedom.

PROSPERO: And what would you do all alone here on this island, haunted by the
devil, tempest-tossed?

CALIBAN: First of all, I'd get rid of you! I'd spit you out, all your works and
pomps! Your "white" magic!

PROSPERO: That's a fairly negative program . . .

CALIBAN: You don't understand it . . . I say I'm going to spit you out, and that's
very positive . . .

PROSPERO: Well, the world is really upside down . . . We've seen everything
now: Caliban as a dialectician! However, in spite of everything I'm fond of
you, Caliban. Come, let's make peace. We've lived together for ten years and
worked side by side! Ten years count for something, after all! We've ended
up by becoming compatriots!

CALIBAN: You know very well that I'm not interested in peace. I'm interested in
     being free! Free, you hear?
PROSPERO: It's odd . . . no matter what you do, you won't succeed in making me
     believe that I'm a tyrant!
CALIBAN: Understand what I say, Prospero:
     For years I bowed my head
     for years I took it, all of it —
     your insults, your ingratitude . . .
     and worst of all, more degrading than all the rest,
     your condescension.
     But now, it's over!
     Over, do you hear?
     Of course, at the moment
     You're still stronger than I am.
     But I don't give a damn for your power
     or for your dogs or your police or your inventions!
     And do you know why?
     It's because I know I'll get you.
     I'll impale you! And on a stake that you've sharpened yourself!
     You'll have impaled yourself!
     Prospero, you're a great magician:
     you're an old hand at deception.
     And you lied to me so much,
     about the world, about myself,
     that you ended up by imposing on me
     an image of myself:
     underdeveloped, in your words, undercompetent
     that's how you made me see myself!
     And I hate that image . . . and it's false!
     But now I know you, you old cancer,
     And I also know myself!
     And I know that one day
     my bare fist, just that,
     will be enough to crush your world!
     The old world is crumbling down!

     Isn't it true? Just look!
     It even bores you to death.
     And by the way . . . you have a chance to get it over with:
     You can pick up and leave.
     You can go back to Europe.
     But the hell you will!
     I'm sure you won't leave.
     You make me laugh with your "mission"!
     Your "vocation"!
     Your vocation is to hassle me.

And that's why you'll stay,
> just like those guys who founded the colonies
> and who now can't live anywhere else.
> You're just an old addict, that's what you are!

PROSPERO: Poor Caliban! You know that you're headed towards your own ruin.
> You're sliding towards suicide! You know I will be the stronger, and stronger
> all the time. I pity you!

CALIBAN: And I hate you!

PROSPERO: Beware! My generosity has its limits.

CALIBAN *(shouting)*:

> *Shango marches with strength*
> *along his path, the sky!*
> *Shango is a fire-bearer,*
> *his steps shake the heavens*
> *and the earth*
> *Shango, Shango, ho!*

PROSPERO: I have uprooted the oak and raised the sea,
> I have caused the mountain to tremble and have bared my
> chest to adversity.
> With Jove I have traded thunderbolt for thunderbolt.
> Better yet—from a brutish monster I have made man!
> But ah! To have failed to find the path to man's heart . . .
> if that be where man is.

(to Caliban)

> Well, I hate you as well!
> For it is you who have made me
> doubt myself for the first time.

(to the Nobles)

> . . . My friends, come near. We must say farewell . . . I shall not be going with
> you. My fate is here: I shall not run from it.

ANTONIO: What, Sire?

PROSPERO: Hear me well.
> I am not in any ordinary sense a master,
> as this savage thinks,
> but rather the conductor of a boundless score:
> this isle,
> summoning voices, I alone,
> and mingling them at my pleasure,
> arranging out of confusion
> one intelligible line.
> Without me, who would be able to draw music from all that?
> This isle is mute without me.
> My duty, thus, is here,
> and here I shall stay.

GONZALO: Oh day full rich in miracles!

PROSPERO: Do not be distressed. Antonio, be you the lieutenant of my goods and make use of them as procurator until that time when Ferdinand and Miranda may take effective possession of them, joining them with the Kingdom of Naples. Nothing of that which has been set for them must be postponed: Let their marriage be celebrated at Naples with all royal splendor. Honest Gonzalo, I place my trust in your word. You shall stand as father to our princess at this ceremony.

GONZALO: Count on me, Sire.

PROSPERO: Gentlemen, farewell.

They exit.

> And now, Caliban, it's you and me!
> What I have to tell you will be brief.
> Ten times, a hundred times, I've tried to save you,
> above all from yourself.
> But you have always answered me with wrath
> and venom,
> like the opossum that pulls itself up by its own tail
> the better to bite the hand that tears it from the darkness.
> Well, my boy, I shall set aside my indulgent nature
> and henceforth I will answer your violence
> with violence!

Time passes, symbolized by the curtain's being lowered halfway and reraised. In semidarkness Prospero appears, aged and weary. His gestures are jerky and automatic, his speech weak, toneless, trite.

PROSPERO: Odd, but for some time now we seem to be overrun with opossums. They're everywhere. Peccarys, wild boar, all this unclean nature! But mainly opossums. Those eyes! The vile grins they have! It's as though the jungle was laying siege to the cave . . . But I shall stand firm . . . I shall not let my work perish! *(Shouting)* I shall protect civilization! *(He fires in all directions.)* They're done for! Now, this way I'll be able to have some peace and quiet for a while. But it's cold. Odd how the climate's changed. Cold on this island . . . Have to think about making a fire . . . Well, Caliban, old fellow, it's just us two now, here on the island . . . only you and me. You and me. You-me . . . me-you! What in the hell is he up to? *(Shouting)* Caliban!

In the distance, above the sound of the surf and the chirping of birds, we hear snatches of Caliban's song:

FREEDOM HI-DAY, FREEDOM HI-DAY!   [1969]

THINKING ABOUT THE TEXT

1. What is the effect on you of Césaire's prologue as an introduction to his version of Shakespeare's play? Note that Césaire's version of the play uses

masks. What are the potential advantages and disadvantages of this device?

2. Césaire has made Ariel a mulatto slave and Caliban a black slave. In what ways do these identities matter in his play? Analyze the early scene in which they discuss their relationship to Prospero. How would you describe the different ideologies they express? What, if anything, do the two characters have in common or agree on?

3. Césaire has added the character of Eshu. To what effects?

4. What does Césaire emphasize about Prospero? What is the effect of his adding the scene featuring a representative of the Inquisition denouncing Prospero?

5. In this version of the play, Prospero remains on the island with Caliban. Why do you think Prospero decides to stay? What do you think Césaire is up to in having him stay?

6. Do you suppose that black audiences and white audiences would react differently to Césaire's play? Why, or why not?

MAKING COMPARISONS

1. In what ways is Césaire's play faithful to Shakespeare's? What strikes you as its most significant departures?

2. Even in a production of Shakespeare's play, Ariel and Caliban might be played by black actors. Do you think such casting would bring Shakespeare's *The Tempest* significantly closer to what Césaire's play is doing? Explain.

3. Evaluate the two plays in comparison with each other. Do you respond more positively to one? Why, or why not?

WRITING ABOUT ISSUES

1. Choose either Shakespeare's or Césaire's play and write an essay showing how it illustrates colonialism. (Obviously you will need to define the term, and you might even wish to consult one or more dictionary definitions of it.) Be sure to cite specific details of the play you discuss.

2. Write an essay comparing Shakespeare's and Césaire's treatments of the Prospero-Caliban relationship. Does this relationship seem much the same in both plays? Do the two authors handle it very differently? Something in between? Be sure to quote specific lines from each text.

3. Racially "recast" a play or movie you have seen by imagining that at least one key role played by a white person was actually played by a black person. Then write an essay discussing whether and how your recasting

would change the meaning and effect of the piece. If you wish, refer to Césaire's adaptation of Shakespeare's play.

4. Through library research, find out details about a particular production of Shakespeare's *The Tempest*. Then write an essay discussing how you might have reacted to this production, comparing it to your "ideal" one. If you wish, you may develop your analysis by referring to Césaire's version of the play.

11

Making Judgments

Thinking about literature involves people making judgments about other people's views. Throughout your course, you have been making judgments as you interpret and evaluate written works, including the texts in this book and those produced by the class. You have been deciding also how you feel about positions expressed by your teacher and classmates. In all these acts of judgment, you have considered where you stand on general issues of aesthetics, ethics, politics, religion, and law.

Outside school, you judge things all the time, though you may not always be aware that you are doing so. You may be more conscious of your judgments when other people disagree with you, when you face multiple options, when you are trying to understand something complex, when your decisions will have significant consequences, or when you must review an act you have already committed. Some people are quite conscious that they make judgments because they have the political, professional, or institutional authority to enforce their will. Of course, these people may wind up being judged by whomever they dominate, and they may even face active revolt.

The first cluster (p. 1240) in this chapter is a group of poems, each of which features a speaker deciding how to treat a certain animal. The second cluster (p. 1250) is also a group of poems, this time concerning judgments about an always controversial subject, abortion. In the third cluster (p. 1257), a pair of short stories, characters make judgments about duty as they decide whether and how to keep serving their military organizations. Often such judgments involve a tension between one's conscience and certain laws, rules, or regulations.

Then come several clusters that focus on judgments about crime and punishment. In a pair of essays (p. 1279), Scott Russell Sanders and Joyce Carol Oates recall their experiences as jurors and contemplate the ways in which social class and race may influence a jury's thinking. The next cluster (p. 1305) centers on a classic conflict of moral law and human law, Sophocles' play *Antigone*, whose title heroine feels moved by her conscience to defy an order forbidding burial of her brother. Following the play, we include three critical commentaries on it. The cluster on Charlotte Perkins Gilman's "The Yellow Wallpaper"

(p. 1351) concerns judgments about sanity; through her 1892 short story, Gilman points out that women diagnosed as mad may actually be exhibiting the trauma of patriarchal domination. Besides Gilman's story, we include three documents that shed light on the era in which she wrote. Next is a set of four poems (p. 1376), all dealing with specific punishments and the responsibilities of people who witness or learn about them. In the following cluster (p. 1388), which consists of three stories, characters avenge what they see as wrongdoing, leaving you to decide whether they are right to take justice into their own hands.

The next two clusters center on aesthetic judgments: decisions about the worth of art and other artifacts. In two stories and an essay, Alice Walker considers how African American culture is to be valued (p. 1419). In the three poems that follow, the speakers respond to someone else's writing, providing you with an opportunity to review your judgments about the writing you and your classmates have done in this course (p. 1447).

The last two clusters in this chapter deal with judgments about broader concerns. The first presents four poems in which the speaker negatively judges society (p. 1454). The final cluster, another quartet of poems, presents judgments about a particular person's life (p. 1462). As you read this last pair of clusters, think about how you would evaluate your own society as well as your life so far.

Judgments about Animals

MAXINE KUMIN, "Woodchucks"

D. H. LAWRENCE, "Snake"

ELIZABETH BISHOP, "The Fish"

WILLIAM STAFFORD, "Traveling through the Dark"

You live in an age of nearly constant debate over environmental policy, hunting, and animal rights. Literary works can serve to dramatize and illuminate issues involved in these controversies. Consider the following poems. In each, the speaker must judge how to treat a certain animal. As you read, compare not only the speakers' decisions but also the values that their judgments reflect. Think, too, about the judgments you have made regarding animals, your general attitude toward nature, and the forces influencing your view.

BEFORE YOU READ

Describe at least one encounter you have had with wildlife, noting how you behaved at the time and what influenced your conduct. What is your attitude toward people who like to hunt or fish? What forms of wildlife, if any, do you think people are justified in fearing or despising? Do you think the notion of animal rights has merit? Identify particular values of yours that your answers reflect.

MAXINE KUMIN
Woodchucks

Maxine Kumin (b. 1925) is a Pulitzer Prize–winning poet. She writes in a range of genres, however; her work includes four novels, a short-story collection, two volumes of essays, and several children's books. "Woodchucks" comes from her 1971 collection of poems Our Ground Time Here Will Be Brief. *Like much of Kumin's writing, this poem deals with the world of nature. Kumin lives on a farm in New Hampshire, where she raises horses.*

Gassing the woodchucks didn't turn out right.
The knockout bomb from the Feed and Grain Exchange
was featured as merciful, quick at the bone
and the case we had against them was airtight,
both exits shoehorned shut with puddingstone,°   5
but they had a sub-sub-basement out of range.

Next morning they turned up again, no worse
for the cyanide than we for our cigarettes
and state-store Scotch, all of us up to scratch.
They brought down the marigolds as a matter of course   10
and then took over the vegetable patch
nipping the broccoli shoots, beheading the carrots.

The food from our mouths, I said, righteously thrilling
to the feel of the .22, the bullets' neat noses.
I, a lapsed pacifist fallen from grace   15
puffed with Darwinian° pieties for killing,
now drew a bead on the littlest woodchuck's face.
He died down in the everbearing roses.

Ten minutes later I dropped the mother. She
flipflopped in the air and fell, her needle teeth   20
still hooked in a leaf of early Swiss chard.
Another baby next. O one-two-three
the murderer inside me rose up hard,
the hawkeye killer came on stage forthwith.

There's one chuck left. Old wily fellow, he keeps   25
me cocked and ready day after day after day.
All night I hunt his humped-up form. I dream
I sight along the barrel in my sleep.
If only they'd all consented to die unseen
gassed underground the quiet Nazi way.   [1972]   30

5 puddingstone: Cement mixed with pebbles.   **16 Darwinian:** Charles Darwin (1809–1882), an English naturalist who first theorized ideas about evolution and natural selection.

THINKING ABOUT THE TEXT

1. In line 4, the word *case* evidently refers to a method of entrapping the woodchucks, but probably it refers as well to the speaker's reasons for hunting them. Does the speaker have a good "case" for going after them? What is important to consider in evaluating her behavior? In what ways does your experience with farms and gardens affect your view of her?

2. Identify the stages in the speaker's campaign to get rid of the woodchucks. What psychological changes does she go through? In particular, what attitude toward her behavior does she express in the third and fourth stanzas? Support your answer by referring to specific words of hers.

3. Rewrite stanzas 3, 4, or 5 using the third person rather than the first. What is the effect of such a change? What advantages, if any, does the poet gain by resorting to the first person?

4. Trace the poem's rhyme pattern. Where does Kumin use alliteration as well? What effect do her technical choices have?

5. Presumably the last line alludes to the mass exterminations of the Holocaust. What would you say to someone who argues that this is an inappropriate, even tasteless, way to end a poem about woodchucks?

D. H. LAWRENCE

Snake

David Herbert Lawrence (1885–1930) was a leading novelist and short-story writer in the first half of the twentieth century. The son of a coal miner and a former schoolteacher, he describes his English working-class upbringing in his autobiographical novel Sons and Lovers *(1913). Probably he remains best known for his 1928 novel* Lady Chatterley's Lover. *For many years, it was banned in England and the United States because it explicitly described the sexual relationship between an aristocratic woman and her husband's gamekeeper. In most of his work, Lawrence endorses human passion, although he argued that people needed to exist in harmony with nature as well as with one another. Besides writing fiction, he painted and wrote poetry.* "Snake," *published in 1913, is based on Lawrence's stay in Sicily, one of the many places he went as he searched for a land friendly to his ideals.*

A snake came to my water-trough
On a hot, hot day, and I in pyjamas for the heat,
To drink there.

In the deep, strange-scented shade of the great dark carob-tree
I came down the steps with my pitcher
And must wait, must stand and wait, for there he was at the trough before me.

♦ ♦ ♦

5

He reached down from a fissure in the earth-wall in the gloom
And trailed his yellow-brown slackness soft-bellied down, over the edge of the
       stone trough
And rested his throat upon the stone bottom,
And where the water had dripped from the tap, in a small clearness,   10
He sipped with his straight mouth,
Softly drank through his straight gums, into his slack long body,
Silently.

Someone was before me at my water-trough,
And I, like a second comer, waiting.   15

He lifted his head from his drinking, as cattle do,
And looked at me vaguely, as drinking cattle do,
And flickered his two-forked tongue from his lips, and mused a moment,
And stooped and drank a little more,
Being earth-brown, earth-golden from the burning bowels of the earth   20
On the day of Sicilian July, with Etna smoking.

The voice of my education said to me
He must be killed,
For in Sicily the black, black snakes are innocent, the gold are venomous.

And voices in me said, If you were a man   25
You would take a stick and break him now, and finish him off.

But must I confess how I liked him,
How glad I was he had come like a guest in quiet, to drink at my water-trough
And depart peaceful, pacified, and thankless,
Into the burning bowels of this earth?   30

Was it cowardice, that I dared not kill him?
Was it perversity, that I longed to talk to him?
Was it humility, to feel so honoured?
I felt so honoured.

And yet those voices: 35
If you were not afraid, you would kill him!

And truly I was afraid, I was most afraid,
But even so, honoured still more
That he should seek my hospitality
From out the dark door of the secret earth.   40

He drank enough
And lifted his head, dreamily, as one who has drunken,
And flickered his tongue like a forked night on the air, so black;
Seeming to lick his lips,
And looked around like a god, unseeing, into the air,   45
And slowly turned his head,

And slowly, very slowly, as if thrice adream,
Proceeded to draw his slow length curving round
And climb again the broken bank of my wall-face.

And as he put his head into that dreadful hole,   50
And as he slowly drew up, snake-easing his shoulders, and entered farther,
A sort of horror, a sort of protest against his withdrawing into that horrid black
        hole,
Deliberately going into the blackness, and slowly drawing himself after,
Overcame me now his back was turned.

I looked round, I put down my pitcher,   55
I picked up a clumsy log
And threw it at the water-trough with a clatter.

I think it did not hit him,
But suddenly that part of him that was left behind convulsed in undignified
        haste,
Writhed like lightning, and was gone   60
Into the black hole, the earth-lipped fissure in the wall-front,
At which, in the intense still noon, I stared with fascination.

And immediately I regretted it.
I thought how paltry, how vulgar, what a mean act!
I despised myself and the voices of my accursed human education.   65

And I thought of the albatross,°
And I wished he would come back, my snake.

For he seemed to me again like a king,
Like a king in exile, uncrowned in the underworld,
Now due to be crowned again.   70

And so, I missed my chance with one of the lords
Of life.
And I have something to expiate;
A pettiness.   [1913]

66 **albatross:** In Samuel Taylor Coleridge's "Rime of the Ancient Mariner," a seaman brings misfortune to the crew of his ship by killing an albatross, an ocean bird.

THINKING ABOUT THE TEXT

1. What did you associate with snakes before reading this poem? Does Lawrence push you to look at snakes differently, or does his poem endorse the view you already had? Develop your answer by referring to specific lines.

2. Discuss the poem as an argument involving various "voices." How do you think you would have reacted to the snake if you had been the speaker?

What "voices" might you have heard inside your own mind? What people or institutions would these "voices" have come from?

3. Why does the speaker throw the log just as the snake is leaving? Note the explanation the speaker gives as well as the judgment he then makes about his act. Do both make sense to you? Why, or why not?

4. Lawrence begins many lines with the word *and*. What is the effect of his doing so?

5. In "Snake," Lawrence writes positively about an animal that is often feared. Think of a similar poem that you might write. What often-feared animal would you choose? What positive qualities would you point out or suggest in describing this animal? If you wish, try actually writing such a poem.

MAKING COMPARISONS

1. Here is an issue of evaluation: Do Kumin's and Lawrence's speakers seem equally guilty of pettiness? Consult a dictionary definition of the word.

2. Does one of these speakers seem more self-divided than the other? Explain.

3. Do Kumin's and Lawrence's poems seem equally "poetic"? What features of poetry do you have in mind as you address this issue of genre?

ELIZABETH BISHOP
The Fish

Although she also wrote short stories, Elizabeth Bishop (1911–1979) is primarily known for her poetry, winning both the Pulitzer Prize and the National Book Award for it. Born in Worcester, Massachusetts, she spent much of her youth in Nova Scotia. As an adult, she lived in various places, including New York City, Florida, Mexico, and Brazil. Much of her poetry observes and reflects on a particular object or figure. Such is the case with "The Fish," which Bishop wrote in 1940 and then included in her 1946 book North and South.

I caught a tremendous fish
and held him beside the boat
half out of water, with my hook
fast in a corner of his mouth.
He didn't fight.
He hadn't fought at all.
He hung a grunting weight,
battered and venerable

5

and homely. Here and there
his brown skin hung in strips   10
like ancient wall-paper,
and its pattern of darker brown
was like wall-paper:
shapes like full-blown roses
stained and lost through age.   15
He was speckled with barnacles,
fine rosettes of lime,
and infested
with tiny white sea-lice,
and underneath two or three   20
rags of green weed hung down.
While his gills were breathing in
the terrible oxygen
— the frightening gills,
fresh and crisp with blood,   25
that can cut so badly—
I thought of the coarse white flesh
packed in like feathers,
the big bones and the little bones,
the dramatic reds and blacks   30
of his shiny entrails,
and the pink swim-bladder
like a big peony.
I looked into his eyes
which were far larger than mine   35
but shallower, and yellowed,
the irises backed and packed
with tarnished tinfoil
seen through the lenses
of old scratched isinglass.   40
They shifted a little, but not
to return my stare.
— It was more like the tipping
of an object toward the light.
I admired his sullen face,   45
the mechanism of his jaw,
and then I saw
that from his lower lip
— if you could call it a lip—
grim, wet, and weapon-like,   50
hung five old pieces of fish-line,
or four and a wire leader
with the swivel still attached,
with all their five big hooks

grown firmly in his mouth.   55
A green line, frayed at the end
where he broke it, two heavier lines,
and a fine black thread
still crimped from the strain and snap
when it broke and he got away.   60
Like medals with their ribbons
frayed and wavering,
a five-haired beard of wisdom
trailing from his aching jaw.
I stared and stared   65
and victory filled up
the little rented boat,
from the pool of bilge
where oil had spread a rainbow
around the rusted engine   70
to the bailer rusted orange,
the sun-cracked thwarts,
the oarlocks on their strings,
the gunnels — until everything
was rainbow, rainbow, rainbow!   75
And I let the fish go.   [1946]

THINKING ABOUT THE TEXT

1. Does the speaker change her attitude toward the fish, or does it stay pretty much the same? Support your reasoning by referring to specific lines. Are you surprised that the speaker lets the fish go? Why, or why not? How effective a conclusion is her release of the fish?

2. To what extent is the speaker describing the fish objectively? In what ways, if any, does her description of him seem to reflect her own particular values? Refer to specific lines.

3. The speaker reports that "victory filled up / the little rented boat" (lines 66–67). Whose victory might she have in mind? Why might she use this word? Often, a victory for one is a defeat for another. Is that the case here?

4. Where does the poem refer to acts and instruments of seeing? What conclusions might be drawn from these references?

5. How significant is it that the fish is male?

MAKING COMPARISONS

1. What would you say to someone who argues that Bishop's speaker is more admirable than Kumin's and Lawrence's speakers because she lets the animal go in peace?

2. With each of these three poems, consider what you learn about the speaker's own state of mind. Does one of these poems tell you more about its speaker's thoughts than the other poems do? Support your answer by referring to specific lines.

3. Bishop's poem is one long, continuous stanza, whereas Kumin and Lawrence divide theirs into several stanzas. Does this difference in strategy lead to a significant difference in effect? Do you consider one of these strategies better than the other? Explain your reasoning.

WILLIAM STAFFORD
Traveling through the Dark

Besides being a poet himself, William Stafford (1914–1995) was a mentor to many others. During World War II, he was a conscientious objector. Later, he wrote and taught poetry at a variety of places in the United States, eventually settling in Oregon. The following poem was written in 1960 and subsequently appeared in a 1962 collection of Stafford's poems, also entitled Traveling through the Dark.

Traveling through the dark I found a deer
dead on the edge of the Wilson River road.
It is usually best to roll them into the canyon:
that road is narrow; to swerve might make more dead.

By glow of the tail-light I stumbled back of the car   5
and stood by the heap, a doe, a recent killing;
she had stiffened already, almost cold.
I dragged her off; she was large in the belly.

My fingers touching her side brought me the reason —
her side was warm; her fawn lay there waiting,   10
alive, still, never to be born.
Beside that mountain road I hesitated.

The car aimed ahead its lowered parking lights;
under the hood purred the steady engine.
I stood in the glare of the warm exhaust turning red;   15
around our group I could hear the wilderness listen.

I thought hard for us all — my only swerving —
then pushed her over the edge into the river.   [1962]

THINKING ABOUT THE TEXT

1. At the end of the poem, the speaker says "I thought hard for us all." Who does "us" refer to? What might the speaker have said to defend what he did? What might be an argument against his act? What would you have done, and why?

2. "To swerve" appears in the first stanza, "swerving" in the last. How would you define these words as they appear in the poem? What does Stafford achieve by using them to frame it?

3. Note in the fourth stanza what verbs the speaker associates with the car and the engine. What is the effect of these verbs on you?

4. Note, too, the last line of the fourth stanza. What would you say to someone who criticized this line because it is impossible for someone to "hear" someone else "listen"?

5. Though Stafford begins his poem with the phrase "Traveling through the dark," the rest of the poem deals with what happened when the speaker stopped traveling for a moment. How appropriate, then, is the poem's title?

MAKING COMPARISONS

1. Do you believe that the four authors in this cluster are all making the same point about human beings' relationship to nature? Why, or why not?

2. Could the words "I thought hard for us all" apply to all four speakers in this cluster? Support your answer by referring to specific lines of each text.

3. Rank the four poems in this cluster according to their degree of artistic success, moving down from your most favorite to your least favorite. Then rank them according to their degree of clarity, moving down from the poem you find most clear to the one you find least clear. Looking over your rankings, would you say that your evaluation of each poem is influenced by its degree of clarity? Explain. What other things affect how you judge these poems?

WRITING ABOUT ISSUES

1. Choose one of the poems in this cluster and write an essay describing and evaluating its speaker. As you develop your judgment, acknowledge and address at least one other possible way of looking at this person: that is, a different judgment that someone might make of him or her.

2. Write an essay suggesting what one of the speakers in these poems might say about another. What, for example, might Bishop's speaker say about Lawrence's? Support your conjecture with details from both texts.

3. Write an essay arguing for or against how you treated a certain animal in a certain situation. Choose a situation in which you did, in fact, consider

acting differently at the time. If you wish, you can draw analogies between your experience and any of those depicted in this cluster.

4. Should hunting and fishing be encouraged? Should society recognize animal rights, even to the extent of disallowing the use of animals in scientific and medical experiments? Choose one of these issues, read at least two articles on it, and then write an essay presenting and supporting your position. At some point in your essay, tell whether and how the articles you read taught you something you hadn't known. As you make your case, you may also want to mention one or more of the poems in this cluster.

JUDGMENTS ABOUT ABORTION

ANNE SEXTON, "The Abortion"
GWENDOLYN BROOKS, "The Mother"
MARGE PIERCY, "Right to Life"

In each of the following poems, the speaker makes a judgment about abortion. Even after the Supreme Court decision legalizing it, many Americans continue to oppose it, while many others strongly believe in keeping it legal. At the same time, plenty of Americans have mixed feelings about it. Taken together, the poems in this cluster express a range of attitudes toward abortion. With each poem, consider how your own position on the subject affects your reading. Think, too, about whether and how the poem is capable of altering your view. Finally, consider whether you can appreciate a poem about abortion even if it expresses a view different from yours. Is your aesthetic judgment of each poem here inevitably determined by your ethical beliefs?

BEFORE YOU READ

What is your present position on abortion? What has influenced your view? In this cluster, you will read what three women poets have to say about the subject. What are the various perspectives on it that they might express?

ANNE SEXTON
The Abortion

Anne Sexton (1928–1974) is recognized as one of the "confessional" poets of the 1960s. With Sylvia Plath, she took Robert Lowell's poetry writing seminar at Boston University, and all three writers became known for intensely autobiographical work that alluded, among other things, to their psychological problems. In fact, Sexton began writing poetry on the recommendation of a psychiatrist she saw after she became suicidal in 1955. Ultimately, she did kill herself in 1974; still, as her biographer Diane Middlebrook points out, she might have done so much earlier had she not found value in the act of writing. The following poem comes from Sexton's book All My Pretty Ones *(1963). She published many other volumes, including the Pulitzer Prize–winning* Live or Die *(1966) and an adaptation of fairy tales entitled* Transformations *(1971).*

Somebody who should have been born
is gone

Just as the earth puckered its mouth,
each bud puffing out from its knot,
I changed my shoes, and then drove south.   5

Up past the Blue Mountains, where
Pennsylvania humps on endlessly,
wearing, like a crayoned cat, its green hair,

its roads sunken in like a gray washboard;
where, in truth, the ground cracks evilly,   10
a dark socket from which the coal has poured,

Somebody who should have been born
is gone

the grass as bristly and stout as chives,
and me wondering when the ground would break,   15
and me wondering how anything fragile survives;

up in Pennsylvania, I met a little man,
not Rumpelstiltskin, at all, at all . . .
he took the fullness that love began.

Returning north, even the sky grew thin   20
like a high window looking nowhere.
The road was as flat as a sheet of tin.

Somebody who should have been born
is gone

Yes, woman, such logic will lead   25
to loss without death. Or say what you meant,
you coward . . . this baby that I bleed.   [1963]

THINKING ABOUT THE TEXT

1. Describe the overall tone of the poem. What words in it especially support your description?

2. Note the italicized refrain: "*Somebody who should have been born / is gone.*" What is the effect of repeating these words? Of having a line break within them? Do you take the refrain to be the moral or theme of the poem? Why, or why not?

3. Who is speaking in the last stanza? What audience is being addressed? What is the effect of ending the poem this way?

4. Do you know who Rumpelstiltskin is? If so, identify him and consider why he is mentioned in the poem. If you don't know who he is, should Sexton have told you more about him or not referred to him?

5. Sexton's biographer Diane Middlebrook reports that Sexton wrote the poem soon after she had an abortion, which would have been illegal at the time. In what ways, if any, does this biographical fact affect your attitude toward Sexton and your interpretation of the poem?

GWENDOLYN BROOKS
The Mother

Gwendolyn Brooks (b. 1917) became the first African American to win the Pulitzer Prize, receiving it in 1950 for a book of poems entitled Annie Allen. *Since then, she has garnered many other awards for her poetry, besides serving as poet laureate of Illinois and poetry consultant to the Library of Congress. In most of her work, Brooks has been concerned with the lives of African Americans, including issues of civil rights. "The Mother" appeared in her first book of poetry,* A Street in Bronzeville *(1945). Other collections of her verse include* Selected Poems *(1963, 1999),* Blacks *(1987), and* Children Coming Home *(1992). Brooks has also published a novel,* Maud Martha *(1953), and an autobiography,* Report from Part One *(1972).*

Abortions will not let you forget.
You remember the children you got that you did not get,
The damp small pulps with a little or with no hair,
The singers and workers that never handled the air.
You will never neglect or beat   5
Them, or silence or buy with a sweet.
You will never wind up the sucking-thumb
Or scuttle off ghosts that come.
You will never leave them, controlling your luscious sigh,
Return for a snack of them, with gobbling mother-eye.   10

I have heard in the voices of the wind the voices of my dim killed children
I have contracted. I have eased
My dim dears at the breasts they could never suck.
I have said, Sweets, if I sinned, if I seized

Your luck   15
And your lives from your unfinished reach,
If I stole your births and your names,
Your straight baby tears and your games,
Your stilted or lovely loves, your tumults, your marriages, aches, and your deaths,
If I poisoned the beginnings of your breaths,   20
Believe that even in my deliberateness I was not deliberate.
Though why should I whine,
Whine that the crime was other than mine? —
Since anyhow you are dead.
Or rather, or instead,   25
You were never made.
But that too, I am afraid,
Is faulty: oh, what shall I say, how is the truth to be said?
You were born, you had body, you died.
It is just that you never giggled or planned or cried.   30

Believe me, I loved you all.
Believe me, I knew you, though faintly, and I loved, I loved you
All.   [1945]

THINKING ABOUT THE TEXT

1. Describe the speaker using at least three adjectives of your own. What are
   her chief claims? Does this poem argue against abortion? For it? Explain.

2. In what ways do the three stanzas differ?

3. Three times the speaker uses the word *believe*. What does this pattern
   lead you to conclude about her? Also, three times she uses the word *loved*.
   Again, what do you conclude?

4. What would you say to someone who argues that Brooks shouldn't have
   called her poem "The Mother" because it deals with the killing of the
   unborn?

5. Imagine that Brooks had called her poem "The Father." What words
   would need to change for this title to make sense? Would your response to
   this poem differ from your response to "The Mother"? Explain.

MAKING COMPARISONS

1. Do the speakers in Sexton's and Brooks's poems feel equally guilty? Support your answer by referring to specific words in each text.

2. Note where each poem refers to the act of "saying." What is each suggesting about this act, especially when the subject is abortion?

3. Sexton's poem has ten stanzas, while Brooks's has three. What is the effect
   of this difference?

MARGE PIERCY
Right to Life

Marge Piercy (b. 1936) is a novelist and political activist as well as a poet. Born to a working-class family in Detroit, she has often used her writing to address issues of gender and class. Piercy's novels include a classic of contemporary science fiction, Woman on the Edge of Time *(1976), as well as* Small Changes *(1973),* Vida *(1979),* Braided Lives *(1982), and* Gone to Soldiers *(1987). "Right to Life" appeared in a collection of her poetry entitled* The Moon Is Always Female *(1980) and was later reprinted in* Circles on the Water: Selected Poems by Marge Piercy *(1979).*

A woman is not a pear tree
thrusting her fruit in mindless fecundity
into the world. Even pear trees bear
heavily one year and rest and grow the next.
An orchard gone wild drops few warm rotting   5
fruit in the grass but the trees stretch
high and wiry gifting the birds forty
feet up among inch long thorns
broken atavistically from the smooth wood.

A woman is not a basket you place   10
your buns in to keep them warm. Not a brood
hen you can slip duck eggs under.
Not a purse holding the coins of your
descendants till you spend them in wars.
Not a bank where your genes gather interest   15
and interesting mutations in the tainted
rain, any more than you are.

You plant corn and you harvest
it to eat or sell. You put the lamb
in the pasture to fatten and haul it in   20
to butcher for chops. You slice
the mountain in two for a road and gouge
the high plains for coal and the waters
run muddy for miles and years.
Fish die but you do not call them yours   25
unless you wished to eat them.

Now you legislate mineral rights in a woman.
You lay claim to her pastures for grazing,
fields for growing babies like iceberg
lettuce. You value children so dearly   30

that none ever go hungry, none weep
with no one to tend them when mothers
work, none lack fresh fruit,
none chew lead or cough to death and your
orphanages are empty. Every noon the best   35
restaurants serve poor children steaks.

At this moment at nine o'clock a *partera*
is performing a table top abortion on an
unwed mother in Texas who can't get Medicaid
any longer. In five days she will die   40
of tetanus and her little daughter will cry
and be taken away. Next door a husband
and wife are sticking pins in the son
they did not want. They will explain
for hours how wicked he is,   45
how he wants discipline.

We are all born of woman, in the rose
of the womb we suckled our mother's blood
and every baby born has a right to love
like a seedling to sun. Every baby born   50
unloved, unwanted is a bill that will come
due in twenty years with interest, an anger
that must find a target, a pain that will
beget pain. A decade downstream a child
screams, a woman falls, a synagogue is torched,   55
a firing squad is summoned, a button
is pushed and the world burns.

I will choose what enters me, what becomes
flesh of my flesh. Without choice, no politics,
no ethics lives. I am not your cornfield,   60
not your uranium mine, not your calf
for fattening, not your cow for milking.
You may not use me as your factory.
Priests and legislators do not hold
shares in my womb or my mind.   65
This is my body. If I give it to you
I want it back. My life
is a non-negotiable demand.   [1980]

THINKING ABOUT THE TEXT

1. Obviously Piercy is arguing for a woman's right to an abortion. What are
   the main stages in her argument? What reasons does she give for her position? Evaluate them.

2. Piercy's title is a phrase usually used by people who oppose abortion. Do you approve of her use of it? Why, or why not?

3. What sorts of images does Piercy use? Identify some general types. Do you find her imagery effective? Support your answer by referring to specific examples.

4. The poem concludes, "My life / is a non-negotiable demand." What do you think of this declaration as a philosophy? In what circumstances, if any, have you made or might you make the same statement? To whom?

5. Do you think it is possible for someone who opposes abortion to appreciate this poem? Elaborate your reasoning.

MAKING COMPARISONS

1. Compare the references to "I" and "you" in the three poems. In each, what meanings do these pronouns take on?

2. Compare the tones used in these poems. In each case, how much does the poem's tone influence your attitude toward it?

3. Would you say that all three poems are political? Define how you are using the term.

WRITING ABOUT ISSUES

1. Choose one of the poems in this cluster and write an essay discussing the extent to which the speaker is consistent. Does her thinking appear pretty much the same, or does she express multiple, perhaps even conflicting thoughts? Refer to the poem's actual words.

2. Write an essay considering how the speaker in Sexton's or in Brooks's poem would respond to the ideas expressed in Piercy's. Quote actual words of Piercy's poem and the other poem you discuss.

3. Write an essay about an occasion when you argued (with others or with yourself) about whether something had a "right to life." The specific subject may or may not have been abortion. Besides defining what you mean by "right to life," identify the specific values that were in conflict at the time, how the debate turned out, and how you feel about it looking back. If you wish, refer to any of the poems in this cluster.

4. Write an essay examining a recent nationally publicized event that has concerned abortion, motherhood, or the "right to life" (however you choose to define that term). In your essay, identify at least one issue involved, express your position on it, and support that position. Refer to at least one article, broadcast, or advertisement about the event. Feel free to refer as well to any of the poems in this cluster.

JUDGMENTS ABOUT DUTY

FRANK O'CONNOR, "Guests of the Nation"
HARUKI MURAKAMI, "Another Way to Die"

The following stories differ in setting. Frank O'Connor's focuses on the Irish-British conflict in the first decades of the twentieth century, while Haruki Murakami's deals with the Japanese occupation of Manchuria near the end of World War II. In both stories, however, characters must decide whether and how they will fulfill duties assigned them by the armies they serve. The decision is not easy because their duty requires them to assist in the destruction of people who have done them no personal harm. As you read, consider the conflicts you have felt between your "official" duty and other obligations.

BEFORE YOU READ

Think of an occasion when you were assigned a certain duty or task but were reluctant to perform it because you knew it would harm someone else. Identify the specific values that were in conflict, what you ultimately did, and why you decided to act that way. Do you think it is ever all right for soldiers to disobey orders or ignore rules they are supposed to enforce? Explain your reasoning.

FRANK O'CONNOR

Guests of the Nation

During the 1920s, Ireland was torn by various levels of armed conflict. The main opponents were England, who had been ruling the country, and Irish militants seeking to free it. Early in the decade, the southern part of Ireland did become semi-independent. Yet in many ways it remained under England's control, and Northern Ireland gained no freedom at all. Therefore, the Irish Republican Army and other groups initially fought against the new state as well as against the English government. One of the rebels was a clerk from Cork named Michael Donovan (1903–1955), who was eventually captured and sentenced to prison. After his release, he launched what became a long and distinguished career as a fiction writer, taking the pen name Frank O'Connor. Today, he is chiefly known for his short stories. The following one appeared in his first published collection, also entitled Guests of the Nation *(1931).*

1

At dusk the big Englishman, Belcher, would shift his long legs out of the ashes and say "Well, chums, what about it?" and Noble or me would say "All right, chum" (for we had picked up some of their curious expressions), and the little Englishman, Hawkins, would light the lamp and bring out the cards. Sometimes Jeremiah Donovan would come up and supervise the game and get excited over Hawkins's cards, which he always played badly, and shout at him as if he was one of our own "Ah, you divil, you, why didn't you play the tray?"

But ordinarily Jeremiah was a sober and contented poor devil like the big Englishman, Belcher, and was looked up to only because he was a fair hand at documents, though he was slow enough even with them. He wore a small cloth hat and big gaiters over his long pants, and you seldom saw him with his hands out of his pockets. He reddened when you talked to him, tilting from toe to heel and back, and looking down all the time at his big farmer's feet. Noble and me used to make fun of his broad accent, because we were from the town.

I couldn't at the time see the point of me and Noble guarding Belcher and Hawkins at all, for it was my belief that you could have planted that pair down anywhere from this to Claregalway and they'd have taken root there like a native weed. I never in my short experience seen two men to take to the country as they did.

They were handed on to us by the Second Battalion when the search for them became too hot, and Noble and myself, being young, took over with a natural feeling of responsibility, but Hawkins made us look like fools when he showed that he knew the country better than we did.

"You're the bloke they calls Bonaparte," he says to me. "Mary Brigid O'Con-   5
nell told me to ask you what you done with the pair of her brother's socks you borrowed."

For it seemed, as they explained it, that the Second used to have little evenings, and some of the girls of the neighborhood turned in, and, seeing they were such decent chaps, our fellows couldn't leave the two Englishmen out of them. Hawkins learned to dance "The Walls of Limerick," "The Siege of Ennis," and "The Waves of Tory" as well as any of them, though, naturally, he couldn't return the compliment, because our lads at that time did not dance foreign dances on principle.

So whatever privileges Belcher and Hawkins had with the Second they just naturally took with us, and after the first day or two we gave up all pretense of keeping a close eye on them. Not that they could have got far, for they had accents you could cut with a knife and wore khaki tunics and overcoats with civilian pants and boots. But it's my belief that they never had any idea of escaping and were quite content to be where they were.

It was a treat to see how Belcher got off with the old woman of the house where we were staying. She was a great warrant to scold, and cranky even with us, but before ever she had a chance of giving our guests, as I may call them, a lick of her tongue, Belcher had made her his friend for life. She was breaking sticks, and Belcher, who hadn't been more than ten minutes in the house, jumped up from his seat and went over to her.

"Allow me, madam," he says, smiling his queer little smile, "please allow me"; and he takes the bloody hatchet. She was struck too paralytic to speak, and after that, Belcher would be at her heels, carrying a bucket, a basket, or a load of turf, as the case might be. As Noble said, he got into looking before she leapt, and hot water, or any little thing she wanted, Belcher would have it ready for her. For such a huge man (and though I am five foot ten myself I had to look up at him) he had an uncommon shortness or should I say lack? of speech. It took us some time to get used to him, walking in and out, like a ghost, without a word. Especially because Hawkins talked enough for a platoon, it was strange to hear big Belcher with his toes in the ashes come out with a solitary "Excuse me, chum" or "That's right, chum." His one and only passion was cards, and I will say for him that he was a good card-player. He could have fleeced myself and Noble, but whatever we lost to him Hawkins lost to us, and Hawkins played with the money Belcher gave him.

Hawkins lost to us because he had too much old gab, and we probably lost to   10
Belcher for the same reason. Hawkins and Noble would spit at one another about religion into the early hours of the morning, and Hawkins worried the soul out of Noble, whose brother was a priest, with a string of questions that would puzzle a cardinal. To make it worse even in treating of holy subjects, Hawkins had a deplorable tongue. I never in all my career met a man who could mix such a variety of cursing and bad language into an argument. He was a terrible man, and a fright to argue. He never did a stroke of work, and when he had no one else to talk to, he got stuck in the old woman.

He met his match in her, for one day when he tried to get her to complain profanely of the drought, she gave him a great come-down by blaming it entirely on Jupiter Pluvius (a deity neither Hawkins nor I have ever heard of, though Noble said that among the pagans it was believed that he had something to do with the rain). Another day he was swearing at the capitalists for starting the German war when the old lady laid down her iron, puckered up her little crab's mouth, and said: "Mr. Hawkins, you can say what you like about the war, and think you'll deceive me because I'm only a simple poor countrywoman, but I know what started the war. It was the Italian Count that stole the heathen divinity out of the temple in Japan. Believe me, Mr. Hawkins, nothing but sorrow and want can follow the people that disturb the hidden powers."

A queer old girl, all right.

2

We had our tea one evening, and Hawkins lit the lamp and we all sat into cards. Jeremiah Donovan came in too, and sat down and watched us for a while, and it suddenly struck me that he had no great love for the two Englishmen. It came as a great surprise to me, because I hadn't noticed anything about him before.

Late in the evening a really terrible argument blew up between Hawkins and Noble, about capitalists and priests and love of your country.

"The capitalists," says Hawkins with an angry gulp, "pays the priests to tell you   15
about the next world so as you won't notice what the bastards are up to in this."

"Nonsense, man!" says Noble, losing his temper. "Before ever a capitalist was thought of, people believed in the next world."

Hawkins stood up as though he was preaching a sermon.

"Oh, they did, did they?" he says with a sneer. "They believed all the things you believe, isn't that what you mean? And you believe that God created Adam, and Adam created Shem, and Shem created Jehoshophat. You believe all that silly old fairytale about Eve and Eden and the apple. Well, listen to me, chum. If you're entitled to hold a silly belief—like that, I'm entitled to hold my silly belief which is that the first thing your God created was a bleeding capitalist, with morality and Rolls-Royce complete. Am I right, chum?" he says to Belcher.

"You're right, chum," says Belcher with his amused smile, and got up from the table to stretch his long legs into the fire and stroke his moustache. So, seeing that Jeremiah Donovan was going, and that there was no knowing when the argument about religion would be over, I went out with him. We strolled down to the village together, and then he stopped and started blushing and mumbling and saying I ought to be behind, keeping guard on the prisoners. I didn't like the tone he took with me, and anyway I was bored with life in the cottage, so I replied by asking him what the hell we wanted guarding them at all for. I told him I'd talked it over with Noble, and that we'd both rather be out with a fighting column.

"What use are those fellows to us?" says I.   20

He looked at me in surprise and said: "I thought you knew we were keeping them as hostages."

"Hostages?" I said.

"The enemy have prisoners belonging to us," he says, "and now they're talking of shooting them. If they shoot our prisoners, we'll shoot theirs."

"Shoot them?" I said.

"What else did you think we were keeping them for?" he says.   25

"Wasn't it very unforeseen of you not to warn Noble and myself of that in the beginning?" I said.

"How was it?" says he. "You might have known it."

"We couldn't know it, Jeremiah Donovan," says I. "How could we when they were on our hands so long?"

"The enemy have our prisoners as long and longer," says he.

"That's not the same thing at all," says I.   30

"What difference is there?" says he.

I couldn't tell him, because I knew he wouldn't understand. If it was only an old dog that was going to the vet's, you'd try and not get too fond of him, but Jeremiah Donovan wasn't a man that would ever be in danger of that.

"And when is this thing going to be decided?" says I.

"We might hear tonight," he says. "Or tomorrow or the next day at latest. So if it's only hanging round here that's a trouble to you, you'll be free soon enough."

It wasn't the hanging round that was a trouble to me at all by this time. I had   35
worse things to worry about. When I got back to the cottage the argument was still on. Hawkins was holding forth in his best style, maintaining that there was no next world, and Noble was maintaining that there was; but I could see that Hawkins had had the best of it.

"Do you know what, chum?" he was saying with a saucy smile. "I think you're just as big a bleeding unbeliever as I am. You say you believe in the next world, and you know just as much about the next world as I do, which is sweet damn-all. What's heaven? You don't know. Where's heaven? You don't know. You know sweet damn-all! I ask you again, do they wear wings?"

"Very well, then," says Noble, "they do. Is that enough for you? They do wear wings."

"Where do they get them, then? Who makes them? Have they a factory for wings? Have they a sort of store where you hands in your chit and takes your bleeding wings?"

"You're an impossible man to argue with," says Noble. "Now, listen to me —" And they were off again.

It was long after midnight when we locked up and went to bed. As I blew out the candle I told Noble what Jeremiah Donovan was after telling me. Noble took it very quietly. When we'd been in bed about an hour he asked me did I think we ought to tell the Englishmen. I didn't think we should, because it was more than likely that the English wouldn't shoot our men, and even if they did, the brigade officers, who were always up and down with the Second Battalion and knew the Englishmen well, wouldn't be likely to want them plugged. "I think so too," says Noble. "It would be great cruelty to put the wind up them now."

"It was very unforeseen of Jeremiah Donovan anyhow," says I.

It was next morning that we found it so hard to face Belcher and Hawkins. We went about the house all day scarcely saying a word. Belcher didn't seem to notice; he was stretched into the ashes as usual, with his usual look of waiting in quietness for something unforeseen to happen, but Hawkins noticed and put it down to Noble's being beaten in the argument of the night before.

"Why can't you take a discussion in the proper spirit?" he says severely. "You and your Adam and Eve! I'm a Communist, that's what I am. Communist or anarchist, it all comes to much the same thing." And for hours he went round the house, muttering when the fit took him. "Adam and Eve! Adam and Eve! Nothing better to do with their time than picking bleeding apples!"

3

I don't know how we got through that day, but I was very glad when it was over, the tea things were cleared away, and Belcher said in his peaceable way: "Well, chums, what about it?" We sat round the table and Hawkins took out the cards, and just then I heard Jeremiah Donovan's footstep on the path and a dark presentiment crossed my mind. I rose from the table and caught him before he reached the door.

"What do you want?" I asked.

"I want those two soldier friends of yours," he says, getting red.

"Is that the way, Jeremiah Donovan?" I asked.

"That's the way. There were four of our lads shot this morning, one of them a boy of sixteen."

40

45

"That's bad," I said.

At that moment Noble followed me out, and the three of us walked down   50
the path together, talking in whispers. Feeney, the local intelligence officer, was
standing by the gate.

"What are you going to do about it?" I asked Jeremiah Donovan.

"I want you and Noble to get them out; tell them they're being shifted again;
that'll be the quietest way."

"Leave me out of that," says Noble under his breath.

Jeremiah Donovan looks at him hard.

"All right," he says. "You and Feeney get a few tools from the shed and dig a   55
hole by the far end of the bog. Bonaparte and myself will be after you. Don't let
anyone see you with the tools. I wouldn't like it to go beyond ourselves."

We saw Feeney and Noble go round to the shed and went in ourselves. I left
Jeremiah Donovan to do the explanations. He told them that he had orders to
send them back to the Second Battalion. Hawkins let out a mouthful of curses,
and you could see that though Belcher didn't say anything, he was a bit upset too.
The old woman was for having them stay in spite of us, and she didn't stop advising them until Jeremiah Donovan lost his temper and turned on her. He had a
nasty temper, I noticed. It was pitch-dark in the cottage by this time, but no one
thought of lighting the lamp, and in the darkness the two Englishmen fetched
their topcoats and said good-bye to the old woman.

"Just as a man makes a home of a bleeding place, some bastard at headquarters thinks you're too cushy and shunts you off," says Hawkins, shaking her hand.

"A thousand thanks, madam," says Belcher. "A thousand thanks for everything"—as though he'd made it up.

We went round to the back of the house and down towards the bog. It was
only then that Jeremiah Donovan told them. He was shaking with excitement.

"There were four of our fellows shot in Cork this morning and now you're to   60
be shot as a reprisal."

"What are you talking about?" snaps Hawkins. "It's bad enough being mucked
about as we are without having to put up with your funny jokes."

"It isn't a joke," says Donovan. "I'm sorry, Hawkins, but it's true," and begins
on the usual rigmarole about duty and how unpleasant it is.

I never noticed that people who talk a lot about duty find it much of a
trouble to them.

"Oh, cut it out!" says Hawkins.

"Ask Bonaparte," says Donovan, seeing that Hawkins isn't taking him seri-   65
ously. "Isn't it true, Bonaparte?"

"It is," I say, and Hawkins stops.

"Ah, for Christ's sake, chum!"

"I mean it, chum," I say.

"You don't sound as if you mean it."

"If he doesn't mean it, I do," says Donovan, working himself up.   70

"What have you against me, Jeremiah Donovan?"

"I never said I had anything against you. But why did your people take out
four of our prisoners and shoot them in cold blood?"

He took Hawkins by the arm and dragged him on, but it was impossible to make him understand that we were in earnest. I had the Smith and Wesson in my pocket and I kept fingering it and wondering what I'd do if they put up a fight for it or ran, and wishing to God they'd do one or the other. I knew if they did run for it, that I'd never fire on them. Hawkins wanted to know was Noble in it, and when we said yes, he asked us why Noble wanted to plug him. Why did any of us want to plug him? What had he done to us? Weren't we all chums? Didn't we understand him and didn't he understand us? Did we imagine for an instant that he'd shoot us for all the so-and-so officers in the so-and-so British Army?

By this time we'd reached the bog, and I was so sick I couldn't even answer him. We walked along the edge of it in the darkness, and every now and then Hawkins would call a halt and begin all over again, as if he was wound up, about our being chums, and I knew that nothing but the sight of the grave would convince him that we had to do it. And all the time I was hoping that something would happen; that they'd run for it or that Noble would take over the responsibility from me. I had the feeling that it was worse on Noble than on me.

4

At last we saw the lantern in the distance and made towards it. Noble was carrying it, and Feeney was standing somewhere in the darkness behind him, and the picture of them so still and silent in the bogland brought it home to me that we were in earnest, and banished the last bit of hope I had.

Belcher, on recognizing Noble, said: "Hallo, chum," in his quiet way, but Hawkins flew at him at once, and the argument began all over again, only this time Noble had nothing to say for himself and stood with his head down, holding the lantern between his legs.

It was Jeremiah Donovan who did the answering. For the twentieth time, as though it was haunting his mind, Hawkins asked if anybody thought he'd shoot Noble.

"Yes, you would," says Jeremiah Donovan.

"No, I wouldn't, damn you!"

"You would, because you'd know you'd be shot for not doing it."

"I wouldn't, not if I was to be shot twenty times over. I wouldn't shoot a pal. And Belcher wouldn't—isn't that right, Belcher?"

"That's right, chum," Belcher said, but more by way of answering the question than of joining in the argument. Belcher sounded as though whatever unforeseen thing he'd always been waiting for had come at last.

"Anyway, who says Noble would be shot if I wasn't? What do you think I'd do if I was in his place, out in the middle of a blasted bog?"

"What would you do?" asks Donovan.

"I'd go with him wherever he was going, of course. Share my last bob with him and stick by him through thick and thin. No one can ever say of me that I let down a pal."

"We had enough of this," says Jeremiah Donovan, cocking his revolver. "Is there any message you want to send?"

"No, there isn't."

"Do you want to say your prayers?"

Hawkins came out with a cold-blooded remark that even shocked me and turned on Noble again.

"Listen to me, Noble," he says. "You and me are chums. You can't come over to my side, so I'll come over to your side. That show you I mean what I say? Give me a rifle and I'll go along with you and the other lads." 90

Nobody answered him. We knew that was no way out.

"Hear what I'm saying?" he says. "I'm through with it. I'm a deserter or anything else you like. I don't believe in your stuff, but it's no worse than mine. That satisfy you?"

Noble raised his head, but Donovan began to speak and he lowered it again without replying.

"For the last time, have you any messages to send?" says Donovan in a cool, excited sort of voice.

"Shut up, Donovan! You don't understand me, but these lads do. They're not the sort to make a pal and kill a pal. They're not the tools of any capitalist." 95

I alone of the crowd saw Donovan raise his Webley to the back of Hawkins's neck, and as he did so I shut my eyes and tried to pray. Hawkins had begun to say something else when Donovan fired, and as I opened my eyes at the bang, I saw Hawkins stagger at the knees and lie out flat at Noble's feet, slowly and as quiet as a kid falling asleep, with the lantern-light on his lean legs and bright farmer's boots. We all stood very still, watching him settle out in the last agony.

Then Belcher took out a handkerchief and began to tie it about his own eyes (in our excitement we'd forgotten to do the same for Hawkins), and, seeing it wasn't big enough, turned and asked for the loan of mine. I gave it to him and he knotted the two together and pointed with his foot at Hawkins. "He's not quite dead," he says. "Better give him another."

Sure enough, Hawkins's left knee is beginning to rise. I bend down and put my gun to his head; then, recollecting myself, I get up again. Belcher understands what's in my mind.

"Give him his first," he says. "I don't mind. Poor bastard, we don't know what's happening to him now." 100

I knelt and fired. By this time I didn't seem to know what I was doing. Belcher, who was fumbling a bit awkwardly with the handkerchiefs, came out with a laugh as he heard the shot. It was the first time I heard him laugh and it sent a shudder down my back; it sounded so unnatural.

"Poor bugger!" he said quietly. "And last night he was so curious about it all. It's very queer, chums, I always think. Now he knows as much about it as they'll ever let him know, and last night he was all in the dark."

Donovan helped him to tie the handkerchiefs about his eyes. "Thanks, chum," he said. Donovan asked if there were any messages he wanted sent.

"No, chum," he says, "not for me. If any of you would like to write to Hawkins's mother, you'll find a letter from her in his pocket. He and his mother were great chums. But my missus left me eight years ago. Went away with another fellow and took the kid with her. I like the feeling of a home, as you may have noticed, but I couldn't start again after that."

It was an extraordinary thing, but in those few minutes Belcher said more than in all the weeks before. It was just as if the sound of the shot had started a flood of talk in him and he could go on the whole night like that, quite happily, talking about himself. We stood round like fools now that he couldn't see us any longer. Donovan looked at Noble, and Noble shook his head. Then Donovan raised his Webley, and at that moment Belcher gives his queer laugh again. He may have thought we were talking about him, or perhaps he noticed the same thing I'd noticed and couldn't understand it.

"Excuse me, chums," he says. "I feel I'm talking the hell of a lot, and so silly, about my being so handy about a house and things like that. But this thing came on me suddenly. You'll forgive me, I'm sure."

"You don't want to say a prayer?" asks Donovan.

"No, chum," he says. "I don't think it would help. I'm ready, and you boys want to get it over."

"You understand that we're only doing our duty?" says Donovan.

Belcher's head was raised like a blind man's, so that you could only see his chin and the tip of his nose in the lantern-light.

"I never could make out what duty was myself," he said. "I think you're all good lads, if that's what you mean. I'm not complaining."

Noble, just as if he couldn't bear any more of it, raised his fist at Donovan, and in a flash Donovan raised his gun and fired. The big man went over like a sack of meal, and this time there was no need of a second shot.

I don't remember much about the burying, but that it was worse than all the rest because we had to carry them to the grave. It was all mad lonely with nothing but a patch of lantern-light between ourselves and the dark, and birds hooting and screeching all round, disturbed by the guns. Noble went through Hawkins's belongings to find the letter from his mother, and then joined his hands together. He did the same with Belcher. Then, when we'd filled the grave, we separated from Jeremiah Donovan and Feeney and took our tools back to the shed. All the way we didn't speak a word. The kitchen was dark and cold as we'd left it, and the old woman was sitting over the hearth, saying her beads. We walked past her into the room, and Noble struck a match to light the lamp. She rose quietly and came to the doorway with all her cantankerousness gone.

"What did ye do with them?" she asked in a whisper, and Noble started so that the match went out in his hand.

"What's that?" he asked without turning around.

"I heard ye," she said.

"What did you hear?" asked Noble.

"I heard ye. Do ye think I didn't hear ye, putting the spade back in the houseen?"

Noble struck another match and this time the lamp lit for him.

"Was that what ye did to them?" she asked.

Then, by God, in the very doorway, she fell on her knees and began praying, and after looking at her for a minute or two Noble did the same by the fireplace. I pushed my way out past her and left them at it. I stood at the door, watching the stars and listening to the shrieking of the birds dying out over the bogs. It is so strange what you feel at times like that that you can't describe it. Noble says he saw everything ten times the size, as though there were nothing in the whole world but that little patch of bog with the two Englishmen stiffening into it, but with me it was as if the patch of bog where the Englishmen were was a million miles away, and even Noble and the old woman, mumbling behind me, and the birds and the bloody stars were all far away, and I was somehow very small and very lost and lonely like a child astray in the snow. And anything that happened to me afterwards, I never felt the same about again.   [1931, 1954]

THINKING ABOUT THE TEXT

1. What thoughts are expressed about duty in this story? What do these thoughts indicate to you about the characters who express them? Does the story lead you to conclude that *any* duty is worthwhile? If so, what specific duty or duties do you see it is as endorsing?

2. Do you think there is anything Bonaparte can and should have done that he didn't do? Explain. How does his response to the executions differ from Noble's and the woman's? State the difference in your own words.

3. Identify references to the "unforeseen." Which characters were surprised by the execution order? Which, if any, foresaw it? Did the ending surprise you? Why, or why not?

4. Through much of the story, Hawkins argues against religion and capitalism. What do you think of his arguments? Near the end, he argues against his own execution. Should readers agree with the case he makes? Why, or why not? Compare Hawkins and Belcher. Which ultimately strikes you more, their similarities or their differences?

5. Before you read the story, what did you know about conflicts between the English and the Irish? Does O'Connor provide enough historical background for you? If not, what additional sorts of details should he have incorporated into his story? Where in the world are there conflicts today that could produce situations like the one O'Connor depicts?

HARUKI MURAKAMI
Another Way to Die

Translated by Jay Rubin

Haruki Murakami (b. 1949) was born in Kobe, Japan, and for many Japanese readers, he is now their country's leading fiction writer. Because his novels and short stories are increasingly translated, he is becoming better known in the United States and other countries. Murakami has translated into Japanese the works of several

American writers, and during the first half of the 1990s he taught at Princeton University. The following text first appeared in English as a short story in a 1997 issue of The New Yorker. *But it is actually a chapter from Murakami's most recent novel,* The Wind-Up Bird Chronicle, *the English version of which was also published in 1997. The novel deals with the Japanese occupation of Manchuria, an area of China. Beginning in the 1930s, this takeover involved the establishment of a nation called Manchukuo, which was headed by the former emperor of China but was actually under Japanese control. Japan's conquest of Manchuria ceased in 1945, when Russian forces moved in and World War II ended overall. "Another Way to Die" takes place during this period.*

The Japanese veterinarian woke before 6 A.M. Most of the animals in the Hsin-ching zoo were already awake. The open window let in their cries and the breeze that carried their smells, which told him the weather without his having to look outside. This was part of his routine here in Manchuria: he would listen, then inhale the morning air, and so ready himself for each new day.

Today, however, should have been different from the day before. It *had* to be different. So many voices and smells had been lost! The tigers, the leopards, the wolves, the bears: all had been liquidated — eliminated — by a Japanese squad the previous afternoon to avoid the animals' escaping as the city came under Russian attack. Now, after some hours of sleep, those events seemed to him like part of a sluggish nightmare he had had long ago. But he knew they had actually happened. His ears still felt a dull ache from the roar of the soldiers' rifles; that could not be a dream. It was August now, the year 1945, and he was here in the city of Hsin-ching, in Japanese-held Manchuria; Soviet troops had burst across the border and were pressing closer every hour. This was reality — as real as the sink and toothbrush he saw in front of him.

The sound of the elephants' trumpeting gave him some sense of relief. Ah, yes — the elephants had survived. Fortunately, the young lieutenant in charge of yesterday's action had had enough normal human sensitivity to remove the elephants from the list, the veterinarian thought as he washed his face. Since coming to Manchuria, he had met any number of stiff-necked, fanatical young officers from his homeland, and the experience always left him shaken. Most of them were farmers' sons who had spent their youthful years in the depressed nineteen-thirties, steeped in the tragedies of poverty while a megalomaniac nationalism was hammered into their skulls. They would follow the orders of a superior without a second thought, no matter how outlandish. If they were commanded, in the name of the Emperor, to dig a hole through the earth to Brazil, they would grab a shovel and set to work. Some people called this "purity," but the veterinarian had other words for it. As an urban doctor's son, educated in the relatively liberal atmosphere of Japan in the twenties, the veterinarian could never understand those young officers. Shooting a couple of elephants should have been a simpler assignment than digging through the earth to Brazil, but yesterday's lieutenant, though he spoke with a slight country accent, seemed to be a more normal human being than other officers were — better educated and more reasonable. The veterinarian could sense this from the way the young man spoke and handled himself.

In any case, the elephants had not been killed, and the veterinarian told himself that he should probably be grateful. The soldiers, too, must have been glad to be spared the task. The Chinese workers may have regretted the omission — they had missed out on a lot of meat and ivory.

The veterinarian boiled water in a kettle, soaked his beard in a hot towel, and   5
shaved. Then he ate breakfast alone: tea, toast, and butter. The food rations in Manchuria were far from sufficient, but compared with those elsewhere they were still fairly generous. This was good news both for him and for the animals. The animals showed resentment at their reduced allotments of feed, but the situation here was better than in zoos back in the Japanese homeland, where food supplies had already bottomed out. No one could predict the future, but for now, at least, both animals and humans were spared the pain of extreme hunger.

He wondered how his wife and daughter were doing. They had left for Japan a few days earlier, and if all went according to plan their train should have reached the Korean coast by now. There they would board the transport ship that would carry them home to Japan. The doctor missed seeing them when he woke up in the morning. He missed hearing their lively voices as they prepared breakfast. A hollow quiet ruled the house. This was no longer the home he loved, the place where he belonged. And yet, at the same time, he could not help feeling a certain strange joy at being left alone in this empty official residence; now he was able to sense the implacable power of fate in his very bones and flesh.

Fate itself was the veterinarian's own fatal disease. From his youngest days, he had had a weirdly lucid awareness that "I, as an individual, am living under the control of some outside force." Most of the time, the power of fate played on like a quiet and monotonous ground bass, coloring only the edges of his life. Rarely was he reminded of its existence. But every once in a while the balance would shift and the force would increase, plunging him into a state of near-paralytic resignation. He knew from experience that nothing he could do or think would ever change the situation.

Not that he was a passive creature; indeed, he was more decisive than most, and he always saw his decisions through. In his profession, too, he was outstanding: a veterinarian of exceptional skill, a tireless educator. He was certainly no fatalist, as most people use the word. And yet never had he experienced the unshakable certainty that he had arrived at a decision entirely on his own. He always had the sense that fate had forced him to decide things to suit its own convenience. On occasion, after the momentary satisfaction of having decided something of his own free will, he would see that things had been decided beforehand by an external power cleverly camouflaged as free will, mere bait thrown in his path to lure him into behaving as he was meant to. He felt like a titular head of state who did nothing more than impress the royal seal on documents at the behest of a regent who wielded all true power in the realm — like the Emperor of this puppet empire of Manchukuo.

Now, left behind in his residence at the zoo, the veterinarian was alone with his fate. And it was fate above all, the gigantic power of fate, that held sway here — not the Kwantung Army, not the Soviet Army, not the troops of the Chinese Communists or of the Kuomintang.° Anyone could see that fate was the ruler here, and that individual will counted for nothing. It was fate that had spared the elephants and buried the tigers and leopards and wolves and bears the day before. What would it bury now, and what would it spare? These were questions that no one could answer.

The veterinarian left his residence to prepare for the morning feeding. He　10 assumed that no one would show up for work anymore, but he found two Chinese boys waiting for him in his office. He did not know them. They were thirteen or fourteen years old, dark-complexioned and skinny, with roving animal eyes. "They told us to help you," one boy said. The doctor nodded. He asked their names, but they made no reply. Their faces remained blank, as if they had not heard the question. These boys had obviously been sent by the Chinese people who had worked here until the day before. Those people had probably ended all contact with the Japanese now, in anticipation of a new regime, but assumed that children would not be held accountable. The boys had been sent as a sign of good will — the workers knew that he could not care for the animals alone.

The veterinarian gave each boy two cookies, then put them to work helping him feed the animals. They led a mule-drawn cart from cage to cage, providing each animal with its particular feed and changing its water. Cleaning the cages was out of the question. The best they could manage was a quick hose-down, to wash away the droppings.

They started the work at eight o'clock and finished after ten. The boys then disappeared without a word. The veterinarian felt exhausted from the hard physical labor. He went back to the office and reported to the zoo director that the animals had been fed.

Just before noon, the young lieutenant came back to the zoo leading the same eight soldiers he had brought the day before. Fully armed again, they walked with a metallic clinking that could be heard far in advance of their arrival. Their shirts were blackened with sweat. Cicadas were screaming in the trees, as they had been yesterday. Today, however, the soldiers had not come to kill animals. The lieutenant saluted the director and said, "We need to know the current status of the zoo's usable carts and draft animals." The director informed him that the zoo had exactly one mule and one wagon. "We contributed our only truck and two horses two weeks ago," he noted. The lieutenant nodded and announced that he would immediately commandeer the mule and wagon, as per orders of Kwantung Army Headquarters.

---

not the . . . the Kuomintang: The Kwantung Army was the Japanese-controlled military force in Manchukuo. In August 1945, when Murakami's story takes place, the Soviet Army was on the verge of defeating this force. The Kuomintang, led by General Chiang Kai-shek, was the controlling party in the overall Chinese government. Although the Chinese Communists were out of power in 1945, they managed to take over China in 1948, forcing Chiang Kai-shek and his allies to flee to Taiwan.

"Wait just a minute," the veterinarian interjected. "We need those to feed the animals twice a day. All our local people have disappeared. Without that mule and wagon, our animals will starve to death. Even with them, we can barely keep up."

"We're all just barely keeping up, sir," said the lieutenant, whose eyes were   15
red and whose face was covered with stubble. "Our first priority is to defend the city. You can always let the animals out of their cages if need be. We've taken care of the dangerous carnivores. The others pose no security risk. These are military orders, sir. You'll just have to manage as you see fit."

Cutting the discussion short, the lieutenant had his men take the mule and wagon. When they were gone, the veterinarian and the director looked at each other. The director sipped his tea, shook his head, and said nothing.

Four hours later, the soldiers were back with the mule and wagon, a filthy canvas tarpaulin covering the mounded contents of the wagon. The mule was panting, its hide foaming with the afternoon heat and the weight of the load. The eight soldiers marched four Chinese men ahead of them at bayonet point— young men, perhaps twenty years old, wearing baseball uniforms and with their hands tied behind their backs. Black-and-blue marks on their faces made it obvious that they had been severely beaten. The right eye of one man was swollen almost shut, and the bleeding lips of another had stained his baseball shirt bright red. The shirtfronts had nothing written on them, but there were small rectangles where the name patches had been torn off. The numbers on their backs were 1, 4, 7, and 9. The veterinarian could not begin to imagine why, at such a time of crisis, four young Chinese men would be wearing baseball uniforms or why they had been so badly beaten and dragged here by Japanese troops. The scene looked like something not of this world— a painting by a mental patient.

The lieutenant asked the zoo director if he had any picks and shovels he could let them use. The young officer looked even more pale and haggard than he had before. The veterinarian led him and his men to a toolshed behind the office. The lieutenant chose two picks and two shovels for his men. Then he asked the veterinarian to come with him and, leaving his men there, walked into a thicket beyond the road. The veterinarian followed. Wherever the lieutenant walked, huge grasshoppers scattered. The smell of summer grass hung in the air. Mixed in with the deafening screams of cicadas, the sharp trumpeting of elephants now and then seemed to sound a distant warning.

The lieutenant went on among the trees without speaking, until he found a kind of opening in the woods. The area had been slated for construction of a plaza for small animals that children could play with. The plan had been postponed indefinitely, however, when the worsening military situation made construction materials scarce. The trees had been cleared away to make a circle of bare ground, and the sun illuminated this one part of the woods like stage lighting. The lieutenant stood in the center of the circle and scanned the area. Then he dug at the ground with the heel of his boot.

"We're going to bivouac here for a while," he said, kneeling down and scoop-   20
ing up a handful of dirt.

The veterinarian nodded in response. He had no idea why they had to bivouac in a zoo, but he decided not to ask. Here in Hsin-ching, experience had taught him never to question military men. Questions did nothing but make them angry, and they never gave you a straight answer in any case.

"First we dig a big hole here," the lieutenant said, speaking as if to himself. He stood up and took a pack of cigarettes from his shirt pocket. Putting a cigarette between his lips, he offered one to the doctor, then lit both with a match. The two concentrated on their smoking to fill the silence. Again the lieutenant began digging at the ground with his boot. He drew a kind of diagram in the earth, then rubbed it out. Finally, he asked the veterinarian, "Where were you born?"

"In Kanagawa," the doctor said. "In a town called Ofuna, near the sea, an hour or two from Tokyo."

The lieutenant nodded.

"And where were you born?" the veterinarian asked.

Instead of answering, the lieutenant narrowed his eyes and watched the smoke rising from between his fingers. No, it never pays to ask a military man questions, the veterinarian told himself again. They like to ask questions, but they'll never give you an answer. They wouldn't give you the time of day — literally.

"There's a movie studio there," the lieutenant said.

It took the veterinarian a few seconds to realize the lieutenant was talking about Ofuna. "That's right. A big studio. I've never been inside, though."

The lieutenant dropped what was left of his cigarette on the ground and crushed it out. "I hope you make it back there," he said. "Of course, there's an ocean to cross between here and Japan. We'll probably all die over here." He kept his eyes on the ground as he spoke. "Tell me, Doctor, are you afraid of death?"

"I guess it depends on how you die," the veterinarian said after a moment's thought.

The lieutenant raised his eyes and looked at the veterinarian as if his curiosity had been aroused. He had apparently been expecting another answer. "You're right," he said. "It does depend on how you die."

The two remained silent for a time. The lieutenant looked as if he might just fall asleep there standing up. He was obviously exhausted. An especially large grasshopper flew over them like a bird and disappeared into a distant clump of grass with a noisy beating of wings. The lieutenant glanced at his watch.

"Time to get started," he said to no one in particular. Then he spoke to the veterinarian. "I'd like you to stay around for a while. I might have to ask you to do me a favor."

The veterinarian nodded.

The soldiers led the Chinese prisoners to the opening in the woods and untied their hands. The corporal drew a large circle on the ground using a baseball bat — why a soldier would have a bat the veterinarian found another mystery — and ordered the prisoners, in Japanese, to dig a deep hole the size of the circle. With the picks and shovels, the four men in baseball uniforms started digging in silence. Half the Japanese squad stood guard over them while the other half stretched out beneath the trees. They seemed to be in desperate need of sleep; no sooner had they hit the ground in full gear than they began snoring. The four soldiers who remained awake kept watch over the digging nearby, rifles resting on their hips, bayonets fixed, ready for immediate use. The lieutenant and the corporal took turns overseeing the work and napping under the trees.

It took less than an hour for the four Chinese prisoners to dig a hole some twelve feet across and deep enough to come up to their necks. One of the men asked for water, speaking in Japanese. The lieutenant nodded, and a soldier brought a bucket full of water. The four Chinese took turns ladling water from the bucket and gulping it down with obvious relish. They drank almost the entire bucketful. Their uniforms were smeared black with blood, mud, and sweat.

The lieutenant had two of the soldiers pull the wagon over to the hole. The corporal yanked the tarpaulin off, to reveal four dead men piled in the wagon. They wore the same baseball uniforms as the prisoners, and they, too, were obviously Chinese. They appeared to have been shot, and their uniforms were covered with black bloodstains. Large flies were beginning to swarm over the corpses. Judging from the way the blood had dried, the doctor guessed that they had been dead for close to twenty-four hours.

The lieutenant ordered the four Chinese who had dug the hole to throw the bodies into it. Without a word, faces blank, the men took the bodies out of the wagon and threw them, one at a time, into the hole. Each corpse landed with a dull thud. The numbers on the dead men's uniforms were 2, 5, 6, and 8. The veterinarian committed them to memory.

When the four Chinese had finished throwing the bodies into the hole, the soldiers tied each man to a nearby tree. The lieutenant held up his wrist and studied his watch with a grim expression. Then he looked up toward a spot in the sky for a while, as if searching for something there. He looked like a stationmaster standing on the platform and waiting for a hopelessly overdue train. But in fact he was looking at nothing at all. He was just allowing a certain amount of time to go by. Once he had accomplished that, he turned to the corporal and gave him curt orders to bayonet three of the four prisoners — Nos. 1, 7, and 9.

Three soldiers were chosen and took up their positions in front of the three   40
Chinese. The soldiers looked paler than the men they were about to kill. The Chinese looked too tired to hope for anything. The corporal offered each of them a smoke, but they refused. He put his cigarettes back into his shirt pocket.

Taking the veterinarian with him, the lieutenant went to stand somewhat apart from the other soldiers. "You'd better watch this," he said. "This is another way to die."

The veterinarian nodded. The lieutenant is not saying this to me, he thought. He's saying it to himself.

In a gentle voice, the lieutenant explained, "Shooting them would be the simplest and most efficient way to kill them, but we have orders not to waste a single bullet — and certainly not to waste bullets killing Chinese. We're supposed to save our ammunition for the Russians. We'll just bayonet them, I suppose, but that's not as easy as it sounds. By the way, Doctor, did they teach you how to use a bayonet in the Army?"

The doctor explained that, as a cavalry veterinarian, he had not been trained to use a bayonet.

"Well, the proper way to kill a man with a bayonet is this: First, you thrust it in under the ribs—here." The lieutenant pointed to his own torso just above the stomach. "Then you drag the point in a big, deep circle inside him to scramble the organs. Then you thrust upward to puncture the heart. You can't just stick it in and expect him to die. We soldiers have this drummed into us. Hand-to-hand combat using bayonets ranks right up there along with night assaults as the pride of the Imperial Army—though mainly it's a lot cheaper than tanks and planes and cannons. Of course, you can train all you want, but finally what you're stabbing is a straw doll, not a live human being. It doesn't bleed or scream or spill its guts on the ground. These soldiers have never actually killed a human being that way. And neither have I." 45

The lieutenant looked at the corporal and gave him a nod. The corporal barked his order to the three soldiers, who snapped to attention. Then they took a half step back and thrust out their bayonets, each man aiming his blade at his prisoner. One of the young men (No. 7) growled something in Chinese that sounded like a curse and gave a defiant spit—which never reached the ground but dribbled down the front of his baseball uniform.

At the sound of the next order, the three soldiers thrust their bayonets into the Chinese men with tremendous force. Then, as the lieutenant had said, they twisted the blades so as to rip the men's internal organs, and thrust the tips upward. The cries of the Chinese men were not very loud—more like deep sobs than like screams, as if they were heaving out the breath left in their bodies all at once through a single opening. The soldiers pulled out their bayonets and stepped back. The corporal barked his order again, and the men repeated the procedure exactly as before—stabbing, twisting, thrusting upward, withdrawing. The veterinarian watched in numbed silence, overtaken by the sense that he was beginning to split in two. He became simultaneously the stabber and the stabbed. He could feel both the impact of the bayonet as it entered his victim's body and the pain of having his internal organs slashed to bits.

It took much longer than he would have imagined for the Chinese men to die. Their sliced-up bodies poured prodigious amounts of blood on the ground, but, even with their organs shredded, they went on twitching slightly for quite some time. The corporal used his own bayonet to cut the ropes that bound the men to the trees, and then he had the soldiers who had not participated in the killing help drag the fallen bodies to the hole and throw them in. These corpses also made a dull thud on impact, but the doctor couldn't help feeling that the sound was different from that made by the earlier corpses—probably because these were not entirely dead yet.

Now only the young Chinese prisoner with the number 4 on his shirt was left. The three pale-faced soldiers tore broad leaves from plants at their feet and proceeded to wipe their bloody bayonets. Not only blood but strange-colored body fluids and chunks of flesh adhered to the blades. The men had to use many leaves to return the bayonets to their original bare-metal shine.

The veterinarian wondered why only the one man, No. 4, had been left 50 alive, but he was not going to ask questions. The lieutenant took out another cigarette and lit up. He then offered a smoke to the veterinarian, who accepted it in silence and, after putting it between his lips, struck his own match. His hand did not tremble, but it seemed to have lost all feeling, as if he were wearing thick gloves.

"These men were cadets in the Manchukuo Army Officer Candidate School," the lieutenant said. "They refused to participate in the defense of Hsin-ching. They killed two of their Japanese instructors last night and tried to run away. We caught them during night patrol, killed four of them on the spot, and captured the other four. Two more escaped in the dark." The lieutenant rubbed his beard with the palm of his hand. "They were trying to make their getaway in baseball uniforms. I guess they figured they'd be arrested as deserters if they wore their military uniforms. Or maybe they were afraid of what Communist troops would do to them if they were caught in their Manchukuo uniforms. Anyway, all they had in their barracks to wear besides their cadet outfits were uniforms of the O.C.S. baseball team. So they tore off the names and tried to get away wearing these. I don't know if you know, but the school had a great team. They used to go to Taiwan and Korea for friendship games. That guy" — and here the lieutenant motioned toward the man tied to the tree — "was captain of the team and batted cleanup. We think he was the one who organized the getaway, too. He killed the two instructors with a bat. The instructors knew there was trouble in the barracks and weren't going to distribute weapons to the cadets until it was an absolute emergency. But they forgot about the baseball bats. Both of them had their skulls cracked open. They probably died instantly. Two perfect home runs. This is the bat."

The lieutenant had the corporal bring the bat to him. He passed the bat to the veterinarian. The doctor took it in both hands and held it up in front of his face, the way a player stepping into the batter's box does. It was just an ordinary bat, not very well made, with a rough finish and an uneven grain. It was heavy, though, and well broken in. The handle was black with sweat. It didn't look like a bat that had been used recently to kill two human beings. After getting a feel for its weight, the veterinarian handed it back to the lieutenant, who gave it a few easy swings, handling it like an expert.

"Do you play baseball?" the lieutenant asked the veterinarian.

"All the time when I was a kid."

"Too grown up now?"   55

"No more baseball for me," the veterinarian said, and he was on the verge of asking "How about you, lieutenant?" but he swallowed the words.

"I've been ordered to beat this guy to death with the same bat he used," the lieutenant said in a dry voice as he tapped the ground with the tip of the bat. "An eye for an eye, a tooth for a tooth. Just between you and me, I think the order stinks. What the hell good is it going to do to kill these guys? We don't have any planes left, we don't have any warships, our best troops are dead. Just the other day some kind of special new bomb wiped out the whole city of Hiroshima in a split second. Either we're going to be swept out of Manchuria or we'll all be killed, and China will belong to the Chinese again. We've already killed a lot of Chinese, and adding a few bodies to the count isn't going to make any difference. But orders are orders. I'm a soldier and I have to follow orders. We killed the tigers and leopards yesterday, and today we have to kill these guys. So take a good look, Doctor. This is another way for people to die. You're a doctor, so you're probably used to knives and blood and guts, but you've probably never seen anyone beaten to death with a baseball bat."

The lieutenant ordered the corporal to bring player No. 4, the cleanup batter, to the edge of the hole. Once again they tied his hands behind his back, then blindfolded him and had him kneel down on the ground. He was a tall, strongly built young man with massive arms the size of most people's thighs. The lieutenant called over one young soldier and handed him the bat. "Kill him with this," he said. The young soldier stood at attention and saluted before taking the bat, but having taken it in his hands he just went on standing there as if stupefied. He seemed unable to grasp the concept of beating a Chinese man to death with a baseball bat.

"Have you ever played baseball?" the lieutenant asked the young soldier.

"No, sir, never," the soldier replied in a loud voice. Both the village in   60
Hokkaido where he was born and the village in Manchuria where he grew up had been so poor that no family in either place could have afforded the luxury of a baseball or a bat. He had spent his boyhood running around the fields, catching dragonflies and playing at sword fighting with sticks. He had never in his life played baseball, or even seen a game. This was the first time he had ever held a bat.

The lieutenant showed him how to hold the bat and taught him the basics of the swing, demonstrating a few times himself. "See? It's all in the hips," he grunted through clenched teeth. "Starting from the backswing, you twist from the waist down. The tip of the bat follows through naturally. Understand? If you concentrate too much on swinging the bat, your arms do all the work and you lose power. Swing from the hips."

The soldier didn't seem fully to comprehend the lieutenant's instructions, but he took off his heavy gear as ordered and practiced his swing for a while. Everyone was watching him. The lieutenant placed his hands over the soldier's to help him adjust his grip. He was a good teacher. Before long, the soldier's swing, though somewhat awkward, was swishing through the air. What the young soldier lacked in skill he made up for in muscle power, having spent his days working on the farm.

"That's good enough," the lieutenant said, using his hat to wipe the sweat from his brow. "O.K., now try to do it in one good, clean swing. Don't let him suffer."

What he really wanted to say was "I don't want to do this any more than you do. Who the hell could have thought of anything so stupid? Killing a guy with a baseball bat . . ." But an officer could never say such a thing to an enlisted man.

The soldier stepped up behind the blindfolded Chinese man where he knelt   65
on the ground. When the soldier raised the bat, the strong rays of the setting

sun cast its long, thick shadow on the earth. This is so weird, the veterinarian thought. The lieutenant's right: I've never seen a man killed with a baseball bat. The young soldier held the bat aloft for a long time. The veterinarian saw its tip shaking.

The lieutenant nodded to the soldier. With a deep breath, the soldier took a backswing, then smashed the bat with all his strength into the back of the Chinese cadet's head. He did it amazingly well. He swung his hips exactly as the lieutenant had taught him to, the brand of the bat made a direct hit behind the man's ear, and the bat followed through perfectly. There was a dull crushing sound as the skull shattered. The man himself made no sound. His body hung in the air for a moment in a strange pose, then flopped forward. He lay with his cheek on the ground, blood flowing from one ear. He did not move. The lieutenant looked at his watch. Still gripping the bat, the young soldier stared off into space, his mouth agape.

The lieutenant was a person who did things with great care. He waited for a full minute. When he was certain that the Chinese man was not moving at all, he said to the veterinarian, "Could you do me a favor and check to see that he's really dead?"

The veterinarian nodded, walked over to where the young Chinese lay, and knelt down and removed his blindfold. The man's eyes were open wide, the pupils turned upward, and bright-red blood was flowing from his ear. His half-opened mouth revealed the tongue lying tangled inside. The impact had left his neck twisted at a strange angle. The man's nostrils had expelled thick gobs of blood, making black stains on the dry ground. One particularly alert—and large—fly had already burrowed its way into a nostril to lay eggs. Just to make sure, the veterinarian took the man's wrist and felt for a pulse. There was no pulse—certainly not where there was supposed to be one. The young soldier had ended this burly man's life with a single swing of a bat—indeed, his first-ever swing of a bat. The veterinarian glanced toward the lieutenant and nodded, to signal that the man was, without a doubt, dead. Having completed his assigned task, he was beginning slowly to rise to his full height when it seemed to him that the sun shining on his back suddenly increased in intensity.

At that very moment, the young Chinese batter in uniform No. 4 rose up into a sitting position as if he had just come fully awake. Without the slightest uncertainty or hesitation—or so it seemed to those watching—he grabbed the doctor's wrist. It all happened in a split second. The veterinarian could not understand; this man was dead, he was sure of it. But now, thanks to one last drop of life that seemed to well up out of nowhere, the man was gripping the veterinarian's wrist with the strength of a steel vise. Eyelids stretched open to the limit, pupils still glaring upward, the man fell forward into the hole, dragging the doctor in after him. The doctor fell in on top of him and heard the man's ribs crack as his weight came down. Still the Chinese ballplayer continued to grip his wrist. The soldiers saw all this happening, but they were too stunned to do anything more than stand and watch. The lieutenant recovered first and leaped into the hole. He drew his pistol from his holster, set the muzzle against the Chi-

nese man's head, and pulled the trigger twice. Two sharp, overlapping cracks
rang out, and a large black hole opened in the man's temple. Now his life was
completely gone, but still he refused to release the doctor's wrist. The lieutenant
knelt down and, pistol in one hand, began the painstaking process of prying open
the corpse's fingers one at a time. The veterinarian lay there in the hole, surrounded by eight silent Chinese corpses in baseball uniforms. Down in the hole,
the screeching of cicadas sounded very different from the way it sounded above
ground.

Once the veterinarian had been freed from the dead man's grasp, the soldiers   70
pulled him and the lieutenant out of the grave. The veterinarian squatted down
on the grass and took several deep breaths. Then he looked at his wrist. The
man's fingers had left five bright-red marks. On this hot August afternoon, the veterinarian felt chilled to the core of his body. I'll never get rid of this coldness
again, he thought. That man was truly, seriously trying to take me with him wherever he was going.

The lieutenant reset the pistol's safety and carefully slipped the gun into its
holster. This was the first time he had ever fired a gun at a human being. But he
tried not to think about it. The war would continue for a little while at least, and
people would continue to die. He could leave the deep thinking for later. He
wiped his sweaty right palm on his pants, then ordered the soldiers who had not
participated in the execution to fill in the hole. A huge swarm of flies had already
taken custody of the pile of corpses.

The young soldier went on standing where he was, stupefied, gripping the
bat. He couldn't seem to make his hands let go. The lieutenant and the corporal
left him alone. He had seemed to be watching the whole bizarre series of
events—the "dead" Chinese suddenly grabbing the veterinarian by the wrist,
their falling into the grave, the lieutenant's leaping in and finishing him off, and
now the other soldiers' filling in the hole. But in fact he had not been watching
any of it. He had been listening to a bird in a tree somewhere making a *"Creeeak!
Creeeak!"* sound as if winding a spring. The soldier looked up, trying to pinpoint
the direction of the cries, but he could see no sign of the windup bird. He felt a
slight sense of nausea at the back of his throat.

As he listened to the winding of the spring, the young soldier saw one fragmentary image after another rise up before him and fade away. After the Japanese
were disarmed by the Soviets, the lieutenant would be handed over to the Chinese and hanged for his responsibility in these executions. The corporal would
die of the plague in a Siberian concentration camp: he would be thrown into a
quarantine shed and left there until dead, though in fact he had merely collapsed
from malnutrition and had not contracted the plague—not, at least, until he was
thrown into the shed. The veterinarian would die in an accident a year later: a
civilian, he would be taken by the Soviets for cooperating with the military and
sent to another Siberian camp to do hard labor; he would be working in a deep
shaft of a Siberian coal mine when a flood would drown him along with many
soldiers. And I, thought the young soldier with the bat in his hands—but he
could not see his own future. He could not even see as real the events that were

happening before his very eyes. He closed his eyes now and listened to the call of the windup bird.

Then, all at once, he thought of the ocean—the ocean he had seen from the deck of the ship bringing him from Japan to Manchuria eight years earlier. He had never seen the ocean before, nor had he seen it since. He could still remember the smell of the salt air. The ocean was one of the greatest things he had ever seen in his life—bigger and deeper than anything he had imagined. It changed its color and shape and expression according to time and place and weather. It aroused a deep sadness in his heart, and at the same time it brought his heart peace and comfort. Would he ever see it again? He loosened his grip and let the bat fall to the ground. It made a dry sound as it struck the earth. After the bat left his hands, he felt a slight increase in his nausea.

The windup bird went on crying, but no one else could hear its call. [1997]   75

THINKING ABOUT THE TEXT

1. This story gets pretty violent. What would you say to someone who argues that it is too violent?

2. Review the veterinarian's reflections on fate in paragraphs 7 and 8. As the story proceeds, is it reasonable of him to believe that "as an individual, [he is] living under the control of some outside force"? Evaluate his behavior. Do you believe he could and should have done something other than what he actually does?

3. What is the effect of setting this story in and near a zoo? What is the effect of making baseball equipment an important feature of the story?

4. At the end, the story shifts to the young soldier's point of view. Do you find this move effective, or do you consider it unreasonably jarring? Explain. Should readers assume that the soldier is correctly predicting what will happen to other characters? Why, or why not?

5. Do you expect a Japanese audience to look at this story much differently than an American audience would? Identify some of the warrants or assumptions behind your answer. Do you think there have ever been Americans capable of behaving as the Japanese characters in this story do? Again, identify some of your warrants or assumptions.

MAKING COMPARISONS

1. O'Connor's story is told in the first person, but Murakami's is told in the third person. O'Connor gives names to most of the characters in his story, but Murakami does not name any of the characters in his. Do you react to the stories differently for these reasons? Why, or why not?

2. In O'Connor's story, the prisoners become friends with their guards. This does not happen in Murakami's story, though. Is one of the stories more horrifying than the other because of this difference? Explain.

3. "And anything that happened to me afterwards," Bonaparte reports, "I never felt the same about again." After being freed from the clutch of the dead man, the veterinarian in Murakami's story thinks, "I'll never get rid of this coldness again." Are these statements signs that Bonaparte and the veterinarian are quite similar people? Why, or why not?

WRITING ABOUT ISSUES

1. Choose O'Connor's or Murakami's story and write an essay comparing two of the characters in the story. Above all, consider whether they are more alike than different, and identify what their author conceivably accomplishes with the relationship he draws between them.

2. Do you consider the behavior of the Irish soldiers and the Japanese soldiers to be equally justifiable? Write an essay that addresses this question by focusing on both stories. Support your argument with specific details from both texts.

3. Choose a character from these stories who resembles you in some important way. Write a letter to this character that not only acknowledges the resemblance but also argues for or against the character's behavior. Be sure to give reasons for your position.

4. Throughout modern history, military personnel and revolutionary movements have either wrestled with moral dilemmas or engaged in morally debatable actions: examples include the behavior of Nazi and Japanese officers in World War II; the United States's dropping of the atomic bomb on Hiroshima and Nagasaki; the My Lai massacre during the Vietnam War; Irish Republican Army bombings in London; the U.S. Navy Tailhook scandal; and the treatment of gays and lesbians in the U.S. armed forces. Research one such case and write an essay stating and defending the principles you think should apply to it. In making your argument, you can refer to stories in this cluster and other reading you have done.

BEING ON A JURY

SCOTT RUSSELL SANDERS, "Doing Time in the Thirteenth Chair"
JOYCE CAROL OATES, "I, the Juror"

Jurors must collectively agree on a legal judgment. In criminal cases, they are charged with determining whether the defendant is guilty, and sometimes they have to decide the sentence as well. In civil cases, they consider whether the defendant is liable as well as the amount to be paid if their answer is yes. During their deliberations, jurors may find themselves also making other kinds of judgments, including ones about human nature. Furthermore, they may argue considerably about their individual judgments as they attempt to reach a verdict. Ideally, a jury is objective and impartial, its members refusing to let bias sway their view of a case. In recent years, however, the behavior of many juries has been controversial. When the white police officers who beat African American motorist Rodney King were initially acquitted by a jury from a predominantly white suburb, many people accused the jurors of racial prejudice. The criminal and civil trials of O. J. Simpson also produced quite divided opinions about how fair his juries were.

The following essays encourage you to consider whether race and class play a role in how juries judge defendants. Scott Russell Sanders and Joyce Carol Oates pointedly recall their own experiences as jurors (or, in Sanders's case, as an alternate juror). Sanders evidently feels that the white middle-class people he served with fairly decided the fate of a working-class man. Oates, on the other hand, believes that race seriously influenced her jury's thinking.

BEFORE YOU READ

Have you ever served on a jury? If so, what was the experience like? If not, would you like to be on a jury? Why, or why not? In general, do you have faith in the jury system? What specifically comes to mind as you consider this question?

SCOTT RUSSELL SANDERS
Doing Time in the Thirteenth Chair

Scott Russell Sanders (b. 1945) spent much of his youth at a military munitions base, where his father worked. He describes this experience in the title essay of his 1987 book The Paradise of Bombs, *which also includes the following piece. Today, Sanders is a professor of English at Indiana University. Besides essays, he has published fiction, a study of the writer D. H. Lawrence, and book-length nonfictional works including* Staying Put: Making a Home in a Restless World *(1993) and* Hunting for Hope: A Father's Journeys *(1998).*

The courtroom is filled with the ticking of a clock and the smell of mold. Listening to the minutes click away, I imagine bombs or mechanical hearts sealed behind the limestone walls. Forty of us have been yanked out of our usual orbits and called to appear for jury duty in this ominous room, beneath the stained-glass dome of the county courthouse. We sit in rows like strangers in a theater, coats rumpled in our laps, crossing and uncrossing our legs, waiting for the show to start.

I feel sulky and rebellious, the way I used to feel when a grade-school teacher made me stay inside during recess. This was supposed to have been the first day of my Christmas vacation, and the plain, uncitizenly fact is that I don't want to be here. I want to be home hammering together some bookshelves for my wife. I want to be out tromping the shores of Lake Monroe with my eye cocked skyward for bald eagles and sharp-shinned hawks.

But the computer-printed letter said to report today for jury duty, and so here I sit. The judge beams down at us from his bench. Tortoise-shell glasses, twenty-dollar haircut, square boyish face: although probably in his early forties, he could pass for a student-body president. He reminds me of an owlish television know-it-all named Mr. Wizard who used to conduct scientific experiments (Magnetism! Litmus tests! Sulphur dioxide!) on a kids' show in the 1950s. Like Mr. Wizard, he lectures us in slow, pedantic speech: trial by one's peers, tradition stretching back centuries to England, defendant innocent until proven guilty beyond a reasonable doubt, and so abundantly on. I spy around for the clock. It must be overhead, I figure, up in the cupola above the dome, raining its ticktocks down on us.

When the lecture is finished, the judge orders us to rise, lift our hands, and swear to uphold the truth. There is a cracking of winter-stiff knees as we stand and again as we sit down. Then he introduces the principal actors: the sleek young prosecutor, who peacocks around like a politician on the hustings; the married pair of brooding, elegantly dressed defense lawyers; and the defendant. I don't want to look at this man who is charged with crimes against the "peace and dignity" of the State of Indiana. I don't want anything to do with his troubles. But I grab an image anyway, of a squat, slit-eyed man about my age, mid-thirties, stringy black hair parted in the middle and dangling like curtains across his face, sparse black beard. The chin whiskers and squinted-up eyes make him look faintly Chinese, and faintly grimacing.

Next the judge reads a list of twelve names, none of them mine, and twelve　　5 sworn citizens shuffle into the jury box. The lawyers have at them, darting questions. How do you feel about drugs? Would you say the defendant there looks guilty because he has a beard? Are you related to any police officers? Are you pregnant? When these twelve have finished answering, the attorneys scribble names on sheets of paper which they hand to the judge, and eight of the first bunch are sent packing. The judge reads eight more names, the jury box fills up with fresh bodies, the questioning resumes. Six of these get the heave-ho. And so the lawyers cull through the potential jurors, testing and chucking them like two men picking over apples in the supermarket. At length they agree on a dozen, and still my name has not been called. Hooray, I think. I can build those bookshelves after all, can watch those hawks.

Before setting the rest of us free, however, the judge consults his list. "I am calling alternate juror number one," he says, and then he pronounces my name.

Groans echo down my inmost corridors. For the first time I notice a thirteenth chair beside the jury box, and that is where the judge orders me to go.

"Yours is the most frustrating job," the judge advises me soothingly. "Unless someone else falls ill or gets called away, you will have to listen to all the proceedings without taking part in the jury's final deliberations or decisions."

I feel as though I have been invited to watch the first four acts of a five-act play. Never mind, I console myself: the lawyers will throw me out. I'm the only one in the courtroom besides the defendant who sports a beard or long hair. A backpack decorated with NO NUKES and PEACE NOW and SAVE THE WHALES but-tons leans against my boots. How can they expect me, a fiction writer, to confine myself to facts? I am unreliable, a confessed fabulist, a marginal Quaker and Wobbly socialist, a man so out of phase with my community that I am thrown into fits of rage by the local newspaper. The lawyers will take a good look at me and race one another to the bench for the privilege of having the judge boot me out.

But neither Mr. Defense nor Mr. Prosecution quite brings himself to focus   10
on my shady features. Each asks me a perfunctory question, the way vacationers will press a casual thumb against the spare tire before hopping into the car for a trip. If there's air in the tire, you don't bother about blemishes. And that is all I am, a spare juror stashed away in the trunk of the court, in case one of the twelve originals gives out during the trial.

Ticktock. The judge assures us that we should be finished in five days, just in time for Christmas. The real jurors exchange forlorn glances. Here I sit, number thirteen, and nobody looks my way. Knowing I am stuck here for the duration, I perk up, blink my eyes. Like the bear going over the mountain, I might as well see what I can see.

What I see is a parade of mangled souls. Some of them sit on the witness stand and reveal their wounds; some of them remain offstage, summoned up only by the words of those who testify. The case has to do with the alleged sale, earlier this year, of hashish and cocaine to a confidential informer. First the pros-ecutor stands at a podium in front of the jury and tells us how it all happened, detail by criminal detail, and promises to prove every fact to our utter satisfaction. Next, one of the defense attorneys has a fling at us. It is the husband of the Mr.-and-Mrs. team, a melancholy-looking man with bald pate and mutton-chop sideburns, deep creases in the chocolate skin of his forehead. Leaning on the podium, he vows that he will raise a flock of doubts in our minds—grave doubts, reasonable doubts—particularly regarding the seedy character of the confiden-tial informer. They both speak well, without hemming and hawing, without stumbling over syntactic cliffs, better than senators at a press conference. Thus, like rival suitors, they begin to woo the jury.

At mid-morning, before hearing from the first witness, we take a recess. (It sounds more and more like school.) Thirteen of us with peel-away JUROR tags stuck to our shirts and sweaters retreat to the jury room. We drink coffee and make polite chat. Since the only thing we have in common is this trial, and since the judge has just forbidden us to talk about that, we grind our gears trying to get a conversation started. I find out what everybody does in the way of work: a bar waitress, a TV repairman (losing customers while he sits here), a department store security guard, a dentist's assistant, an accountant, a nursing home nurse, a cleaning woman, a caterer, a mason, a boisterous old lady retired from rearing children (and married, she tells us, to a school-crossing guard), a meek college student with the demeanor of a groundhog, a teacher. Three of them right now are unemployed. Six men, six women, with ages ranging from twenty-one to somewhere above seventy. Chaucer could gather this bunch together for a literary pilgrimage, and he would not have a bad sampling of smalltown America.

Presently the bailiff looks in to see what we're up to. She is a jowly woman, fiftyish, with short hair the color and texture of buffed aluminum. She wears silvery half-glasses of the sort favored by librarians; in the courtroom she peers at us above the frames with a librarian's skeptical glance, as if to make sure we are awake. To each of us she now gives a small yellow pad and a ballpoint pen. We are to write our names on the back, take notes on them during the trial, and surrender them to her whenever we leave the courtroom. (School again.) Without saying so directly, she lets us know that we are her flock and she is our shepherd. Anything we need, any yen we get for traveling, we should let her know.

I ask her whether I can go downstairs for a breath of air, and the bailiff   15
answers "sure." On the stairway I pass a teenage boy who is listlessly polishing with a rag the wrought-iron filigree that supports the banister. Old men sheltering from December slouch on benches just inside the ground-floor entrance of the courthouse. Their faces have been caved in by disappointment and the loss of teeth. Two-dollar cotton work gloves, the cheapest winter hand-covers, stick out of their back pockets. They are veterans of this place; so when they see me coming with the blue JUROR label pasted on my chest, they look away. Don't tamper with jurors, especially under the very nose of the law. I want to tell them I'm not a real juror, only a spare, number thirteen. I want to pry old stories out of them, gossip about hunting and dogs, about their favorite pickup trucks, their worst jobs. I want to ask them when and how it all started to go wrong for them. Did they hear a snap when the seams of their life began to come apart? But they will not be fooled into looking at me, not these wily old men with the crumpled faces. They believe the label on my chest and stare down at their unlaced shoes.

I stick my head out the door and swallow some air. The lighted thermometer on the bank reads twenty-eight degrees. Schmaltzy Christmas organ music rebounds from the brick-and-limestone shopfronts of the town square. The Salvation Army bell rings and rings. Delivery trucks hustling through yellow lights blare their horns at jaywalkers.

The bailiff must finally come fetch me, and I feel like a wayward sheep. On my way back upstairs, I notice the boy dusting the same square foot of iron filigree, and realize that he is doing this as a penance. Some judge ordered him to clean the metalwork. I'd like to ask the kid what mischief he's done, but the bailiff, looking very dour, is at my heels.

In the hallway she lines us up in our proper order, me last. Everybody stands up when we enter the courtroom, and then, as if we have rehearsed these routines, we all sit down at once. Now come the facts.

The facts are a mess. They are full of gaps, chuckholes, switchbacks, and dead ends — just like life.

At the outset we are shown three small plastic bags. Inside the first is a wad of   20
aluminum foil about the size of an earlobe; the second contains two white pills; the third holds a pair of stamp-sized, squarish packets of folded brown paper. A chemist from the state police lab testifies that he examined these items and found

cocaine inside the brown packets, hashish inside the wad of aluminum foil. As for the white pills, they are counterfeits of a popular barbiturate, one favored by politicians and movie stars. They're depressants — downers — but they contain no "controlled substances."

There follows half a day's worth of testimony about how the bags were sealed, who locked them in the narcotics safe at the Bloomington police station, which officer drove them up to the lab in Indianapolis and which drove them back again, who carried them in his coat pocket and who carried them in his briefcase. Even the judge grows bored during this tedious business. He yawns, tips back in his chair, sips coffee from a mug, folds and unfolds with deft thumbs a square of paper about the size of the cocaine packets. The wheels of justice grind slowly. We hear from police officers in uniform, their handcuffs clanking, and from mustachioed officers in civvies, revolvers bulging under their suitcoats. From across the courtroom, the bailiff glares at us above her librarian's glasses, alert to catch us napping. She must be an expert at judging the degrees of tedium.

"Do you have to go back and be in the jail again tomorrow?" my little boy asks me at supper.

"Not jail," I correct him. "*Jury.* I'm in the jury."

"With real police?"

"Yes."

"And guns?"   25

"Yes, real guns."

On the second day there is much shifting of limbs in the jury box when the confidential informer, whom the police call I90, takes the stand. Curly-haired, thirty-three years old, bear-built and muscular like a middle-range wrestler, slow of eye, calm under the crossfire of questions, I90 works — when he works — as a drywall finisher. (In other words, he gets plasterboard ready for painting. It's a dusty, blinding job; you go home powdered white as a ghost, and you taste the joint-filler all night.) Like roughly one-quarter of the construction workers in the county, right now he's unemployed.

The story he tells is essentially this: Just under a year ago, two cops showed up at his house. They'd been tipped off that he had a mess of stolen goods in his basement, stuff he'd swiped from over in a neighboring county. "Now look here," the cops said to him, "you help us out with some cases we've got going, and we'll see what we can do to help you when this here burglary business comes to court." "Like how?" he said. "Like tell us what you know about hot property, and maybe finger a drug dealer or so." He said yes to that, with the two cops sitting at his kitchen table, and — zap! — he was transformed into I90. (Hearing of this miraculous conversion, I am reminded of Saul on the road to Damascus, the devil's agent suddenly seeing the light and joining the angels.) In this new guise he gave information that led to several arrests and some prison terms, including one for his cousin and two or three for other buddies.

In this particular case, his story goes on, he asked a good friend of his where a   30
guy could buy some, you know, drugs. The friend's brother led him to Bennie's

trailer, where Bennie offered to sell I90 about any kind of drug a man's heart could desire. "All I want's some hash," I90 told him, "but I got to go get some money off my old lady first." "Then go get it," said Bennie.

Where I90 went was to the police station. There they fixed him up to make a "controlled buy": searched him, searched his car; strapped a radio transmitter around his waist; took his money and gave him twenty police dollars to make the deal. Back I90 drove to Bennie's place, and on his tail in an unmarked police car drove Officer B., listening over the radio to every burp and glitch sent out by I90's secret transmitter. On the way, I90 picked up a six-pack of Budweiser. ("If you walk into a suspect's house drinking a can of beer," Officer B. later tells us, "usually nobody'll guess you're working for the police.") Inside the trailer, the woman Bennie lives with was now fixing supper, and her three young daughters were playing cards on the linoleum floor. I90 bought a gram of blond Lebanese hashish from Bennie for six dollars. Then I90 said that his old lady was on him bad to get her some downers, and Bennie obliged by selling him a couple of 714's (the white pills favored by movie stars and politicians) at seven dollars for the pair. They shot the bull awhile, Bennie bragging about how big a dealer he used to be (ten pounds of hash and five hundred hits of acid a week), I90 jawing along like an old customer. After about twenty minutes in the trailer, I90 drove to a secluded spot near the L & N railroad depot, and there he handed over the hash and pills to Officer B., who milked the details out of him.

Four days later, I90 went through the same routine, this time buying two packets of cocaine — two "dimes'" worth — from Bennie for twenty dollars. Inside the trailer were half a dozen or so of Bennie's friends, drinking whiskey and smoking pot and watching TV and playing backgammon and generally getting the most out of a Friday night. Again Officer B. tailed I90, listened to the secret radio transmission, and took it all down in a debriefing afterwards behind the Colonial Bakery.

The lawyers burn up a full day leading I90 through this story, dropping questions like breadcrumbs to lure him on, Mr. Prosecutor trying to guide him out of the labyrinth of memory and Mr. Defense trying to get him lost. I90 refuses to get lost. He tells and retells his story without stumbling, intent as a wrestler on a dangerous hold.

On the radio news I hear that U.S. ships have intercepted freighters bound out from Beirut carrying tons and tons of Lebanese hashish, the very same prize strain of hash that I90 claims he bought from Bennie. Not wanting to irk the Lebanese government, the radio says, our ships let the freighters through. Tons and tons sailing across the Mediterranean — into how many one-gram slugs could that cargo be divided?

Out of jail the defense lawyers subpoena one of I90's brothers, who is awaiting his own trial on felony charges. He has a rabbity look about him, face pinched with fear, ready to bolt for the nearest exit. His canary yellow T-shirt is emblazoned with a scarlet silhouette of the Golden Gate Bridge. The shirt and the fear make looking at him painful. He is one of seven brothers and four sisters.

Hearing that total of eleven children—the same number as in my father's family—I wonder if the parents were ever booked for burglary or other gestures of despair.

This skittish gent tells us that he always buys his drugs from his brother, good old 190. And good old 190, he tells us further, has a special fondness for snorting cocaine. Glowing there on the witness stand in his yellow shirt, dear brother gives the lie to one after another of 190's claims. But just when I'm about ready, hearing all of this fraternal gossip, to consign 190 to the level of hell reserved by Dante for liars, the prosecutor takes over the questioning. He soon draws out a confession that there has been a bitter feud recently between the two brothers. "And haven't you been found on three occasions to be mentally incompetent to stand trial?" the prosecutor demands.

"Yessir," mutters the brother.

"And haven't you spent most of the past year in and out of mental institutions?"

"Yessir."

This second admission is so faint, like a wheeze, that I must lean forward to   40
hear it, even though I am less than two yards away. While the prosecutor lets this damning confession sink into the jury, the rabbity brother just sits there, as if exposed on a rock while the hawks dive, his eyes pinched closed.

By day three of the trial, we jurors are no longer strangers to one another. Awaiting our entry into court, we exhibit wallet photos of our children, of nieces and nephews. We moan in chorus about our Christmas shopping lists. The caterer tells about serving 3,000 people at a basketball banquet. The boisterous old lady, to whom we have all taken a liking, explains how the long hairs on her white cats used to get on her husband's black suit pants until she put the cats out in the garage with heating pads in their boxes.

"Where do you leave your car?" the accountant asks.

"On the street," explains the lady. "I don't want to crowd those cats. They're particular as all get-out."

People compare their bowling scores, their insurance rates, their diets. The mason, who now weighs about 300 pounds, recounts how he once lost 129 pounds in nine months. His blood pressure got so bad he had to give up dieting, and inside of a year he'd gained all his weight back and then some. The nurse, who wrestles the bloated or shriveled bodies of elderly paupers at the city's old folks' home, complains about her leg joints, and we all sympathize. The security guard entertains us with sagas about shoplifters. We compare notes on car wrecks, on where to get a transmission overhauled, on the outgoing college football coach and the incoming city mayor. We talk, in fact, about everything under the sun except the trial.

In the hall, where we line up for our reentry into the courtroom, a sullen boy   45
sits at a table scrawling on a legal pad. Line after line he copies the same sentence: "I never will steal anything ever again." More penance. He's balancing on the first rung of a ladder that leads up—or down—to the electric chair. Some-

where in the middle of the ladder is a good long prison sentence, and that, I calculate, is what is at stake in our little drug-dealing case.

On the third day of testimony, we learn that I90 has been hidden away overnight by police. After he stepped down from the witness stand yesterday, Bennie's mate, Rebecca, greeted the informant outside in the lobby and threatened to pull a bread knife out of her purse and carve him into mincemeat. I look with new interest at the stolid, bulky, black-haired woman who has been sitting since the beginning of the trial right behind the defendant. From time to time she has leaned forward, touched Bennie on the shoulder, and bent close to whisper something in his good ear. She reminds me of the Amish farm wives of my Ohio childhood — stern, unpainted, built stoutly for heavy chores, her face a fortress against outsiders.

When Rebecca takes the stand, just half a dozen feet from where I sit in chair thirteen, I sense a tigerish fierceness beneath her numb surface. She plods along behind the prosecutor's questions until he asks her, rhetorically, whether she would like to see Bennie X put in jail; then she lashes out. God no, she doesn't want him locked away. Didn't he take her in when she had two kids already and a third in the oven, and her first husband run off, and the cupboards empty? And haven't they been living together just as good as married for eight years, except while he was in jail, and don't her three little girls call him Daddy? And hasn't he been working on the city garbage trucks, getting up at four in the morning, coming home smelling like other people's trash, and hasn't she been bagging groceries at the supermarket, her hands slashed with paper cuts, and her mother looking after the girls, all so they can keep off the welfare? Damn right she doesn't want him going to any prison.

What's more, Rebecca declares, Bennie don't deserve prison because he's clean. Ever since he got out of the slammer a year ago, he's quit dealing. He's done his time and he's mended his ways and he's gone straight. What about that sale of cocaine? the prosecutor wants to know. It never happened, Rebecca vows. She was there in the trailer the whole blessed night, and she never saw Bennie sell nobody nothing, least of all cocaine, which he never used because it's too expensive — it'll run you seventy-five dollars a day — and which he never sold even when he was dealing. The prosecutor needles her: How can she remember that particular night so confidently? She can remember, she flares at him, because early that evening she got a call saying her sister's ten-year-old crippled boy was fixing to die, and all the family was going to the children's hospital in Indianapolis to watch him pass away. That was a night she'll never forget as long as she lives.

When I was a boy, my friends and I believed that if you killed a snake, the mate would hunt you out in your very bed and strangle or gnaw or smother you. We held a similar belief regarding bears, wolves, and mountain lions, although we were much less likely to run into any of those particular beasts. I have gone years without remembering that bit of child's lore, until today, when Rebecca's tigerish turn on the witness stand revives it. I can well imagine her stashing a bread knife in her purse. And if she loses her man for years and stony years, and has to rear those three girls alone, the cupboards empty again, she might well jerk that knife out of her purse one night and use it on something other than bread.

During recess, we thirteen sit in the jury room and pointedly avoid talking   50
about the bread knife. The mason tells how a neighbor kid's Ford Pinto skidded across his lawn and onto his front porch, blocking the door and nosing against the picture window. "I took the wheels off and chained the bumper to my maple tree until his daddy paid for fixing my porch."

Everyone, it seems, has been assaulted by a car or truck. Our vehicular yarns wind closer and closer about the courthouse. Finally, two of the women jurors — the cigarillo-smoking caterer and the elderly cat lady — laugh nervously. The two of them were standing just inside the plate-glass door of the courthouse last night, the caterer says, when along came a pickup truck, out poked an arm from the window, up flew a smoking beer can, and then BAM! the can exploded. "We jumped a yard in the air!" cries the old woman. "We thought it was some of Bennie's mean-looking friends," the caterer admits. Everybody laughs at the tableau of speeding truck, smoking can, exploding cherry bomb, leaping jurors. Then we choke into sudden silence, as if someone has grabbed each of us by the throat.

Four of Bennie's friends — looking not so much mean as broken, like shell-shocked refugees — testify on his behalf during the afternoon of day three. Two of them are out-of-work men in their twenties, with greasy hair to their shoulders, fatigue jackets, and clodhopper boots: their outfits and world-weary expressions are borrowed from record jackets. They are younger versions of the old men with caved-in faces who crouch on benches downstairs, sheltering from December. The other two witnesses are young women with reputations to keep up, neater than the scruffy men; gold crosses dangle over their sweaters, and gum cracks between crooked teeth. All four speak in muttered monosyllables and orphaned phrases, as if they are breaking a long vow of silence and must fetch bits and pieces of language from the archives of memory. They were all at Bennie's place on the night of the alleged cocaine sale, and they swear in unison that no such sale took place.

Officer B., the puppetmaster who pulled the strings on I90, swears just as adamantly that both the sales, of cocaine and of hash, *did* take place, for he listened to the proceedings over the radio in his unmarked blue Buick. He is a sleepy-eyed man in his mid-thirties, about the age of the informant and the defendant, a law-upholding alter ego for those skewed souls.

Double-chinned, padded with the considerable paunch that seems to be issued along with the police badge, Officer B. answers Mr. Prosecutor and Mr. Defense in a flat, walkie-talkie drawl, consulting a sheaf of notes in his lap, never contradicting himself. Yes, he neglected to tape the opening few minutes of the first buy, the minutes when the exchange of hashish and money actually took place. Why? "I had a suspicion my batteries were weak, and I wanted to hold off." And, yes, he did erase the tape of the debriefing that followed buy number one. Why? "It's policy to reuse the old cassettes. Saves the taxpayers' money." And, yes, the tape of the second buy is raw, indecipherable noise, because a blaring TV in the background drowns out all human voices. (Listening to the tape, we can understand nothing in the scrawking except an ad for the American Express Card.) The tapes, in other words, don't prove a thing. What it all boils down to is the word of the law and of the unsavory informer versus the word of the many-times-convicted defendant, his mate, and his friends.

Toward the end of Officer B.'s testimony, there is a resounding clunk, like a   55
muffled explosion, at the base of the witness stand. We all jump—witness, judge, jury, onlookers—and only relax when the prosecutor squats down and discovers that a pair of handcuffs has fallen out of Officer B.'s belt. Just a little reminder of the law's muscle. All of us were envisioning bombs. When Officer B. steps down, the tail of his sportcoat is hitched up over the butt of his gun.

The arrest: A squad car pulls up to the front of the trailer, and out the trailer's back door jumps Bennie, barefooted, wearing T-shirt and cut-off jeans. He dashes away between tarpaper shacks, through dog yards, over a stubbled field (his bare feet bleeding), through a patch of woods to a railroad cut. Behind him puffs a skinny cop (who recounts this scene in court), shouting, "Halt! Police!" But Bennie never slows down until he reaches that railroad cut, where he stumbles, falls, rolls down to the tracks like the sorriest hobo. The officer draws his gun. Bennie lifts his hands for the familiar steel cuffs. The two of them trudge back to the squad car, where Officer B. reads the arrest warrant and Bennie blisters everybody with curses.

The judge later instructs us that flight from arrest may be regarded as evidence, not of guilt but of *consciousness* of guilt. Oh ho! A fine distinction! Guilt for what! Selling drugs? Playing hooky? Original sin? Losing his job at Coca-Cola? I think of those bleeding feet, the sad chase. I remember a drunken uncle who stumbled down a railroad cut, fell asleep between the tracks, and died of fear when a train passed over.

On day four of the trial, Bennie himself takes the stand. He is shorter than I thought, and fatter—too many months of starchy jail food and no exercise. With exceedingly long thumbnails he scratches his jaw. When asked a question, he rolls his eyes, stares at the ceiling, then answers in a gravelly country voice, the voice of a late-night disk jockey. At first he is gruffly polite, brief in his replies, but soon he gets cranked up and rants in a grating monologue about his painful history.

He graduated from high school in 1968, worked eight months at RCA and Coca-Cola, had a good start, had a sweetheart, then the Army got him, made him a cook, shipped him to Vietnam. After a few weeks in the kitchen, he was transferred to the infantry because the fodder-machine was short of foot soldiers. "Hey, listen, man, I ain't nothing but a cook," he told them. "I ain't been trained for combat." And they said, "Don't you worry; you'll get on-the-job training. Learn or die." The artillery ruined his hearing. (Throughout the trial he has held a hand cupped behind one ear, and has followed the proceedings like a grandfather.) Some of his buddies got shot up. He learned to kill people. "We didn't even know what we was there for." To relieve his constant terror, he started doing drugs: marijuana, opium, just about anything that would ease a man's mind. Came home from Vietnam in 1971 a wreck, got treated like dirt, like a babykiller, like a murdering scumbag, and found no jobs. His sweetheart married an insurance salesman.

Within a year after his return he was convicted of shoplifting and burglary.   60
He was framed on the second charge by a friend, but couldn't use his only alibi because he had spent the day of the robbery in bed with a sixteen-year-old girl, whose father would have put him away for statutory rape. As it was, he paid out two years in the pen, where he sank deeper into drugs than ever before. "If you got anything to buy or trade with, you can score more stuff in the state prisons than on the streets of Indianapolis." After prison, he still couldn't find work, couldn't get any help for his drug-thing from the Veterans' Administration, moved in with Rebecca and her three girls, eventually started selling marijuana and LSD. "Everytime I went to somebody for drugs, I got ripped off. That's how I got into dealing. If you're a user, you're always looking for a better deal."

In 1979 he was busted for selling hash, in 1980 for possessing acid, betrayed in both cases by the man from whom he had bought his stock. "He's a snitch, just a filthy snitch. You can't trust nobody." Back to prison for a year, back out again in December 1981. No jobs, no jobs, no damn jobs; then part-time on the city garbage truck, up at four in the morning, minus five degrees and the wind blowing and the streets so cold his gloves stuck to the trash cans. Then March came, and this I90 guy showed up, wanted to buy some drugs, and "I told him I wasn't dealing any more. I done my time and gone straight. I told him he didn't have enough money to pay me for no thirty years in the can." (The prosecutor bristles, the judge leans meaningfully forward: we jurors are not supposed to have any notion of the sentence that might follow a conviction on this drug charge.)

In his disk-jockey voice, Bennie denies ever selling anything to this I90 snitch. (He keeps using the word "snitch": I think of tattle-tales, not this adult betrayal.) It was I90, he swears, who tried to sell *him* the hash. Now the pills, why, those he had lying around for a friend who never picked them up, and so he just gave them to I90. "They was give to me, and so I couldn't charge him nothing. They wasn't for me anyway. Downers I do not use. To me, life is a downer. Just to cope with every day, that is way down low enough for me." And as for the cocaine, he never laid eyes on it until the man produced that little plastic bag in court. "I don't use coke. It's too expensive. That's for the bigwigs and the upstanding citizens, as got the money."

Sure, he admits, he ran when the police showed up at his trailer. "I'm flat scared of cops. I don't like talking to them about anything. Since I got back from Vietnam, every time they cross my path they put bracelets on me." (He holds up his wrists. They are bare now, but earlier this morning, when I saw a deputy escorting him into the courthouse, they were handcuffed.) He refuses to concede that he is a drug addict, but agrees he has a terrible habit, "a gift from my country in exchange for me going overseas and killing a bunch of strangers."

After the arrest, forced to go cold turkey on his dope, he begged the jail doctor — "He's no kind of doctor, just one of them that fixes babies" — to zonk him out on something. And so, until the trial, he has spent eight months drowsing under Valium and Thorazine. "You can look down your nose at me for that if you want, but last month another vet hung himself two cells down from me." (The other guy was a scoutmaster, awaiting trial for sexually molesting one of his boys. He had a record of severe depression dating from the war, and used his belt for the suicide.)

"The problem with my life," says Bennie, "is Vietnam." For awhile after   65 coming home, he slept with a knife under his pillow. Once, wakened suddenly, thinking he was still in Vietnam, he nearly killed his best friend. During the week of our trial, another Vietnam vet up in Indianapolis shot his wife in the head, imagining she was a gook. Neighbors got to him before he could pull out her teeth, as he used to pull out the teeth of the enemies he bagged over in Vietnam.

When I look at Bennie, I see a double image. He was drafted during the same month in which I, studying in England, gave Uncle Sam the slip. I hated that war, and feared it, for exactly the reasons he describes — because it was foul slaughter, shameful, sinful, pointless butchery. While he was over there killing and dodging, sinking into the quicksand of drugs, losing his hearing, storing up a lifetime's worth of nightmares, I was snug in England, filling my head with words. We both came home to America in the same year, I to job and family, he to nothing. Ten years after that homecoming, we stare across the courtroom at one another as into a funhouse mirror.

As the twelve jurors file past me into the room where they will decide on Bennie's guilt or innocence, three of them pat my arm in a comradely way. They withdraw beyond a brass-barred gate; I sit down to wait on a deacon's bench in the hallway outside the courtroom. I feel stymied, as if I have rocketed to the moon only to be left riding the ship round and round in idle orbit while my fellow astronauts descend to the moon's surface. At the same time I feel profoundly relieved, because, after the four days of testimony, I still cannot decide whether Bennie truly sold those drugs, or whether I90, to cut down on his own prison time, set up this ill-starred Bennie for yet another fall. Time, time — it always comes down to time: in jail, job, and jury box we are spending and hoarding our only wealth, the currency of days.

Even through the closed door of the courtroom, I still hear the ticking of the clock. The sound reminds me of listening to my daughter's pulse through a stethoscope when she was still riding, curled up like a stowaway, in my wife's womb. Ask not for whom this heart ticks, whispered my unborn daughter through the stethoscope: it ticks for thee. So does the courtroom clock. It grabs me by the ear and makes me fret about time — about how little there is of it, about how we are forever bumming it from one another as if it were cups of sugar or pints of blood ("You got a minute?" "Sorry, have to run, not a second to spare"). Seize the day, we shout, to cheer ourselves; but the day has seized us and flings us forward pell-mell toward the end of all days.

Now and again there is a burst of laughter from the jury room, but it is always squelched in a hurry. They are tense, and laugh to relieve the tension, and then feel ashamed of their giddiness. Lawyers traipse past me — the men smoking, striking poses, their faces like lollipops atop their ties; the women teetering on high heels. The bailiff walks into our judge's office carrying a bread knife. To slice her lunch? As evidence against Rebecca? A moment later she emerges bearing a piece of cake and licking her fingers. Christmas parties are breaking out all over the courthouse.

Rebecca herself paces back and forth at the far end of my hallway, her steps   70
as regular as the clock's tick, killing time. Her bearded and cross-wearing friends sidle up to comfort her, but she shrugs them away. Once she paces down my way, glances at the barred door of the jury room, hears muffled shouts. This she must take for good news, because she throws me a rueful smile before turning back.

Evidently the other twelve are as muddled by the blurred and contradictory "facts" of the case as I am, for they spend from noon until five reaching their decision. They ask for lunch. They ask for a dictionary. They listen again to the tapes. Sullen teenagers, following in the footsteps of Bennie and 190, slouch into the misdemeanor office across the hall from me; by and by they slouch back out again, looking unrepentant. At length the 300-pound mason lumbers up to the gate of the jury room and calls the bailiff. "We're ready as we're going to be." He looks bone-weary, unhappy, and dignified. Raising his eyebrows at me, he shrugs. Comrades in uncertainty.

The cast reassembles in the courtroom, the judge asks the jury for its decision, and the mason stands up to pronounce Bennie guilty. I stare at my boots. Finally I glance up, not at Bennie or Rebecca or the lawyers, but at my fellow jurors. They look distraught, wrung-out and despairing, as if they have just crawled out of a mine after an explosion and have left some of their buddies behind. Before quitting the jury room, they composed and signed a letter to the judge pleading with him to get some help — drug help, mind help, any help — for Bennie.

The ticking of the clock sounds louder in my ears than the judge's closing recital. But I do, with astonishment, hear him say that we must all come back tomorrow for one last piece of business. He is sorry, he knows we are worn out, but the law has prevented him from warning us ahead of time that we might have to decide on one more question of guilt.

The legal question posed for us on the morning of day five is simple: Has Bennie been convicted, prior to this case, of two or more unrelated felonies? If so, then he is defined by Indiana state law as a "habitual offender," and we must declare him to be such. We are shown affidavits for those earlier convictions — burglary, sale of marijuana, possession of LSD — and so the answer to the legal question is clear.

But the moral and psychological questions are tangled, and they occupy the   75
jury for nearly five more hours on this last day of the trial. Is it fair to sentence a person again, after he has already served time for his earlier offenses? How does the prosecutor decide when to apply the habitual offender statute, and does its use in this case have anything to do with the political ambitions of the sleek young attorney? Did Bennie really steal that $150 stereo, for which he was convicted a decade ago, or did he really spend the day in bed with his sixteen-year-old girlfriend? Did Vietnam poison his mind and blight his life?

Two sheriff's deputies guard the jury today; another guards me in my own little cell. The bailiff would not let me stay out on the deacon's bench in the hall, and so, while a plainclothes detective occupies my old seat, I sit in a room lined with file cabinets and stare out like a prisoner through the glass door. "I have concluded," wrote Pascal, "that the whole misfortune of men comes from a single thing, and that is their inability to remain at rest in a room." I agree with him; nothing but that cruising deputy would keep me here.

This time, when the verdict is announced, Rebecca has her daughters with her, three little girls frightened into unchildlike stillness by the courtroom. Their lank hair and washed-out eyes remind me of my childhood playmates, the children of dead-end, used-up West Virginia coalminers who'd moved to Ohio in search of work. The mother and daughter are surrounded by half a dozen rough customers, guys my age with hair down over their shoulders and rings in their ears, with flannel shirts, unfocused eyes. Doubtless they are the reason so many holstered deputies and upholstered detectives are patrolling the courthouse, and the reason I was locked safely away in a cell while the jury deliberated.

When the mason stands to pronounce another verdict of guilty, I glimpse what I do not want to glimpse: Bennie flinging his head back, Rebecca snapping hers forward into her palms, the girls wailing.

The judge accompanies all thirteen of us into the jury room, where he keeps us for an hour while the deputies clear the rough customers from the courthouse. We are not to be alarmed, he reassures us; he is simply being cautious, since so much was at stake for the defendant. "How much?" the mason asks. "Up to twenty-four years for the drug convictions, plus a mandatory thirty years for the habitual offender charges," the judge replies. The cleaning woman, the nurse, and the TV repairman begin crying. I swallow carefully. For whatever it's worth, the judge declares comfortingly, he agrees with our decisions. If we knew as much about this Bennie as he knows, we would not be troubled. And that is just the splinter in the brain, the fact that we know so little — about Bennie, about Vietnam, about drugs, about ourselves — and yet we must grope along in our ignorance, pronouncing people guilty or innocent, squeezing out of one another that precious fluid, time.

And so I do my five days in the thirteenth chair. Bennie may do as many as   80
fifty-four years in prison, buying his drugs from meaner dealers, dreaming of land mines and of his adopted girls, checking the date on his watch, wondering at what precise moment the hinges of his future slammed shut.   [1987]

THINKING ABOUT THE TEXT

1. Trace the references to time in this essay. In what ways does Sanders make it a central subject? Note his references to bombs. What is the effect of his emphasis on them?

2. On the whole, is your impression of the jury positive? Negative? Somewhere in between? Identify some things that influence your opinion. Is there any other information about the jury that you wish Sanders had provided? If so, what sort of information?

3. Rather than being a full-fledged juror, Sanders was an alternate, occupying the thirteenth chair. What, if any, were the advantages of his position for him as an observer? What, if any, were the disadvantages?

4. At one point in his essay, Sanders compares himself to Bennie. Does this comparison make sense to you? Why, or why not? Throughout the essay, Sanders emphasizes the sense of community that developed among the jurors. To what extent does he call attention to Bennie's community — that is, Bennie's friends and family? Does he treat this community in a way you think appropriate? Explain.

5. Are you inclined to believe that justice was served in Bennie's case? Why, or why not? What additional sort of information, if any, would you need to be sure?

JOYCE CAROL OATES
I, the Juror

Since the early 1960s, Joyce Carol Oates (b. 1938) has been an extremely prolific writer, regularly publishing in all the genres represented in this book. In the 1990s alone, she wrote several well-regarded novels, including Because It Is Bitter, and Because It Is My Heart *(1990),* Black Water *(1992),* Foxfire *(1993),* What I Lived For *(1994), and* We Were the Mulvaneys *(1996). In the genre of the essay, she is probably best known for her book* On Boxing *(1987), whose subject has long fascinated her. At present, Oates teaches at Princeton University. The following essay was first published in a 1995 issue of the literary journal* Witness.

In pursuit of an abstract principle of Justice. In pursuit of that sense of community of which Justice is both the consequence and the catalyst. In pursuit of some wavering, insubstantial, indefinable expression of one's heart's desire — that, as citizens of a country, and not mere "individuals," we participate in an action that is unbiased, fair, equitable, *right*.

Yet — "Judge not, lest ye be judged." As if the very action through which Justice might be realized brings with it mortal risk.

When the pink, smudgily computer-printed summons from the Sheriff's Office, County of Mercer, Trenton, New Jersey, arrived in the mail for SMITH, JOYCE C., notifying that I was scheduled to serve as a petit juror for no less than five days in late August, in the Mercer County Courthouse, my feelings were ambivalent. Throughout adulthood I had always hoped to be called for jury duty — while living in Detroit, and more recently in Princeton — but I had never been selected; I did not think of it as a "duty" so much as a privilege, very likely an adventure. To live out one's life as an American citizen without having once served as a juror, no matter how minor the trial, would be a pity — wouldn't it?

Like not being caught up, at least once, in the romance of a Presidential campaign; indeed, like never having voted. We who oscillate between idealism and skepticism, with the quicksilver instability of those sub-atomic particles that are now one thing and now its opposite, begin after all as idealists.

The very *impersonality* of the summons had an air of romance for me — for it was "Joyce C. Smith" and not "Joyce Carol Oates" who had been called. Rare for me now, thus the more precious, any public experience in which I can be invisible, as if bodiless: that fundamental necessity for the writer.

Strictly speaking, "Joyce C. Smith" has no existence except as a legal entity: a 5 husband's wife in a patriarchal society. (One day, will the acquisition of a husband's name, and the eradication of one's maiden name, come to seem as curious a custom as its reverse would seem now?) This legal entity is duly registered as a property (co-)owner and voter. There are no publications indexed under "Joyce C. Smith" in any library, and there is no one on the faculty of Princeton University, where I teach, bearing that name. Since there was no provision in the questionnaire accompanying the summons for the explanation of a "career" name, and I feared a punitive misfiring in the unimaginative computer brain in Trenton, I thought it most pragmatic to identify "Joyce C. Smith" as a housewife and teacher. (Some years ago, in Detroit and Windsor, Ontario, "Joyce C. Smith" had in fact taught college.) This seemed to me to conform to the letter of the law, and to give me a fair chance to get onto a jury.

(I should explain that the local consensus is that Princeton residents are routinely dismissed from juries in Trenton, no matter our hope to serve. Prosecutors don't want us because we are collectively perceived as "liberals" likely to interpret crime in terms of societal pressures; defense attorneys don't want us because we are perceived as "intellectuals" likely to resist rhetorical manipulation.)

Any relationship with the law, as with any governmental bureaucracy, is qualified by a certain air of menace and threat; and so I did, for all my theoretical enthusiasm, feel ambivalent about the summons. To serve as a juror is not a volitional option: names are randomly selected from a merged list of registered voters and licensed drivers, and once your name is on such a list, stored in the computer, it is virtually impossible to get it off. And there is, in the New Jersey Statute, this inhospitable warning: *Every person summoned as a Grand or Petit Juror who shall either fail to appear or refuse, without reasonable excuse, to serve or be sworn, shall be fined by the Court and may be punished as for Contempt of Court.* (Meaning, bluntly, that you can be sent to jail for declining to participate in an action that may send another person to jail.)

Though, as a novelist, I have done extensive research into criminal law and into courtroom procedure, I had attended only a single trial in my life, and that not on a daily basis, long ago, in the 1950s, when I was a junior high school student in Lockport, New York. Two young men were being tried on charges of first-degree murder in a robbery slaying. Vivid as certain memories of that experience are — the old courthouse, the airlessness, the stiff, resigned postures of the accused men seated at the defense table, the elderly judge on his raised platform, in his somber judicial gown — I seem not to remember the verdict. (Probably I was not there for the verdict.) My general sense of the trial was its deliberate snail's pace, its lethargy. Its public display of an adult, and therefore an impenetrable ritual of which I had no clearer comprehension than an observer, say, of a gigantic grinding machine would have of its inner workings, seen from without. Your instinct is to know that you don't ever want to get caught in it.

One afternoon, during an interlude of fatiguing, seemingly pointless repetition, I must have surreptitiously opened a book to read, and a sheriff's deputy leaned toward me, to say in an undertone, "Better close that book. The judge will kick you out of the courtroom if he sees you reading." How startled I was, and how struck by the fact that in a courtroom, this highest expression of adult ritual, the judge, the emblem of all patriarchy, has the authority to determine where an individual's eyes might rest!

Fortunately, they can't see into our skulls.   10

The Mercer County Courthouse, built in 1903 in the generic American courthouse style, still exudes, from the street, a weatherworn dignity; its dank, antiquated interior exudes what might be called "atmosphere." We prospective jurors descended in a rambling herd into the basement, promptly at 8:30 A.M. on August 26, 1991, where we were crowded together in two low-ceilinged rooms, where we would sit on folding chairs while we waited to be called up to a courtroom on the fifth floor.

A prophetic sign was posted on a wall: *They also serve who only stand and wait.*—*John Milton.* The sign was yellowed with age.

And so we waited. Some of us tried to read or work, until the blaring television sets (game shows, soap operas) became too distracting; a few of us, the more restless, began to pace in the corridor immediately outside the jury assembly room, which was allowed by our overseers so long as it appeared, or could be made to appear, that we were really going to or coming from the restrooms. Other areas of the courthouse were forbidden to us (we were wearing white jurors' badges), and doors at the far end of two long corridors, opening to the outside, were conspicuously posted EMERGENCY ONLY—ALARM SET OFF IF OPENED. Already, by 11:00 A.M., I was tracing elongated figure eights in the corridors, with a hope of forestalling early glimmerings of panic.

I learned that, of the 599 citizens of Mercer County who had been summoned for jury duty that week, 500 had managed to exempt themselves. This in itself was certainly deflating; yet more deflating was it to be warned, by one of the assembly room overseers (they were all women, with a look of being prison matrons in disguise as office workers), that, should any of us leave the courthouse without authorization, an officer from the Mercer County Sheriff's Department was empowered to follow after us and arrest us—"This has been known to happen." Indeed, the bulletin boards in the assembly room were festooned with clippings celebrating the power of the state to arrest, fine, and confine: accounts of citizens who, having failed to comply with the summons to jury duty, were surprised and arrested in their homes or in their places of work, fined hundreds of dollars, jailed for three days and/or sentenced to one hundred hours of "community service."

I asked one of the administrators how long we might wait to be called up to a 15
courtroom, and the woman answered, curtly, "Until you're called." Was it possible, I asked, that we would not be called at all that day? "Yes, it's possible," she
said. I approached another administrator, a woman of my approximate age, to ask
why the system was so punitive, and so inefficient; and the woman stared at me
with a hurt, swimming look, and said, "I'm sorry you find it so!" "But don't *you*
find it so?" I asked reasonably, indicating the dreary room of glassy-eyed men and
women, and the woman said angrily, "The way it used to be done, two hundred
people were here for two solid weeks — and that was that." When I expressed dismay, she repeated, with an air of threat, "The way it used to be done, two hundred people were here for two solid weeks — *and that was that.*"

"I see," I said.

At last, shortly before noon, a panel of fifty men and women, including
"Joyce C. Smith, Juror 552," was summoned to a courtroom on the fifth floor.
Though I'd been warned that this part of the jury selection can be deadly — no
reading material is allowed in the courtroom, and, of course, no pacing is permitted — it was impossible not to feel a hopeful anticipation.

We were welcomed to her courtroom by Judge Judith A. Yaskin, an attractive,
highly articulate woman in her mid- or late forties, who presented the case to be
tried and explained the jury selection process. The case was aggravated assault;
the defendant, a thirty-year-old black man, and his attorney, and the prosecuting
attorney, were in the room. Selecting the jury begins with sheer chance: pellets
with numbers corresponding to jurors' numbers are shuffled and drawn by an
officer of the court, as in a bingo game. In theory, the jury of fourteen (including
two alternates) could be drawn from the first fourteen pellets, but during the voir
dire jurors are exempted for various reasons (admitted prejudices, prior knowledge of the case to be tried, connections with the defendant, law enforcement
officials, etc., as well as the peremptory challenge dismissals by the prosecuting
and defense attorneys) and new jurors have to be selected and questioned. The
procedure involves numberless repetitions and can be protracted for weeks in a
trial of major proportions; the case to be tried , here, fortunately, was a minor one,
and a jury was constituted by early afternoon.

To my surprise, number 552 was drawn from the lottery, and I took my seat in
the jury box as Juror Number Eleven. When Judge Yaskin questioned me I identified myself as a housewife and teacher, with the intention of explaining my professional career in more detail if required; but the judge had no further questions.
(As it would turn out at the trial's end, Judge Yaskin had recognized me as a
writer, but seemed to have thought that my writing career was not relevant to the
procedure. Neither the defense counsel nor the prosecuting attorney took the
slightest interest in me, except perhaps as a malleable presence on the jury. What
good fortune: I'd had a nightmare fantasy of being forced to explain to a gathering
of quizzical, bemused strangers that I was a "writer," of whom no one would have
heard — like the tragic Dorothy Richardson, in a nursing home at the end of her
life, believed delusional because she insisted she'd been a novelist.) The focus of
the voir dire was on jurors who had been victims of crimes: could they be impartial in judging a criminal case? How sobering to learn that so many jurors, most of

them residents of Trenton, were victims of multiple crimes. Burglary, vandalism, assault. One woman had been burglarized five times in recent years, but insisted she would be impartial as a juror. In each case Judge Yaskin asked if the criminals had been apprehended, and in each case, remarkably, the answer was "No." A message rippled through our midst: *Crime goes largely unpunished in Trenton;* and, a variant, *Criminals lead charmed lives in certain regions of America.*

But here we were gathered, in a solemn ritual, to isolate, contemplate, and pass judgment on a crime. One had to conclude that the defendant was sheerly unlucky to have been caught. [20]

Of course most of the crime victims were summarily rejected by the defense counsel, as if their insistences upon being impartial were handily recognized as lies. The defense counsel also rejected the only juror in the box to have acknowledged living in Princeton (I had not been asked where I lived), and the single man, of the approximately fifty male prospective jurors in the courthouse that day, to be wearing a suit.

(What of courtroom attire? To my surprise, the majority of my fellow jurors were dressed extremely casually. Here and there a man conspicuous in sport coat and tie, a few women in high heels and stockings, but, overall, the tide of prospective jurors looked as if they'd wandered off from a tour bus, in quintessentially American play clothes for adults. Blue jeans, slacks, T-shirts, shorts were in colorful abundance, contrasting with the more formal, subdued attire of the officers of the court. One youngish man made a comical sight as, in brief nylon-blue running shorts and T-shirt cut high on the shoulders, he came from the rear of the courtroom when his number was called to enter the jury box, passing close below the judge in her black robe. The death penalty is still on the statute in New Jersey: I couldn't help but wonder if jurors in Mickey Mouse sweatshirts vote to send defendants to their deaths.)

Another startling development, for those of us new to courtroom procedure, was the mechanical rejection of certain jurors on the basis of skin pigmentation. Overt racial prejudice has become so anachronistic, we like to think, or, in any case, associated with marginal renegade behavior, it is both shocking and puzzling to encounter it in a public place; still more, in the churchy atmosphere of a courtroom. Since the defendant to be tried was black, however, the prosecuting attorney exercised his right of peremptory challenge to reject as many persons of color as possible. Here was the most crude, the most brainless, racial discrimination in action, entirely countenanced by law: "Your Honor, please thank and excuse Juror Number Two," the attorney said, and a light-skinned black, startled, was urged to leave the box. Another juror was called, a young Chinese-American woman, and again the attorney said, "Your Honor, please thank and excuse Juror Number Two," and she too left the box. Another lottery draw, another juror, everyone stared as another black man came forward, and again — "Your Honor, please thank and excuse Juror Number Two." And he too left. Was this a comic routine? The next juror, as an oddity of luck would have it (by far the majority of the prospective jurors were Caucasian), was also a black man — an undergraduate, as it would turn out, at Middlebury College; hardly was he seated when the prosecuting attorney said, in a flat, inflectionless voice, "Your Honor, please thank and excuse Juror Number Two." And the young man too was ushered out, with a look of surprise, disappointment, hurt, embarrassment. Perhaps he had never before experienced such crude racial discrimination so personally? so publicly? in a gathering of elders?

Finally, and ironically, Juror Number Two was in fact a black man. The prosecuting attorney must have run out of options.

There is a mystique, homey and comforting as Norman Rockwell paintings, of trial-by-jury in America. Trial-by-jury-of-one's-peers.

A mystique predicated upon not having contemplated one's peers very closely in a while.

There is a mystique, too, accruing to the dignity, the sanctity of the court, which is meant to resemble a church. Were we not all obliged to swear, on the Holy Bible, to truthfulness? (In fact, there were not enough Bibles for fourteen jurors, so we had to share them, awkwardly. I wondered at my integrity as, an atheist, I murmured with the others, "I do swear." Perhaps my fingers were not exactly touching the simulated-leather hide of the Holy Book?) Somewhere in our judicial tradition the separation of church and state, surely one of the great principles of American society, seems to have been overlooked.

The trial was not a complex one, though with interruptions and delays it stretched out over several days. There were only five witnesses, four for the prosecution, and the defendant himself, who testified last. The charge of aggravated assault had been brought against a thirty-year-old black man apparently involved in the drug trade who had beaten a young black woman who he believed had informed on him to the police after a drug raid in January 1990; one had the sense (as a juror, denied virtually any contextual information, and made, from time to time, to leave the courtroom, one is absorbed in trying to figure out what *really* happened, what the *real* story is) that the defendant was someone the Trenton police and the prosecutor's office hoped to send to prison since, perhaps, they had not succeeded in sending him away on other charges. Otherwise the case, in crime-afflicted Trenton, seemed an anomaly.

"I am the judge of the law," Judge Yaskin told the jury several times, with the patience of a grade school teacher, " — and you are the judge of the facts." Hearing witnesses' testimonies that often conflicted, forced to sift through such "facts" as are proffered by such testimony, and having to remember everything (jurors may not take notes in the courtroom), one quickly becomes bedazzled, confused. Why take the word of one witness over another, when all sound sincere and plausible? Is there a singular truth that *must* exist, and can be brought to bear against the exactitude of the New Jersey criminal statute? (We jurors were to decide whether aggravated assault had been committed — whether the defendant "knowingly, purposefully, and recklessly intended to inflict serious physical injury, or did inflict serious physical injury." As if there were no significant difference between act and intention.) The witnesses' testimonies gave us, all but one of us Caucasian, a painfully intimate look at the black Trenton underclass; I found myself close to tears during the victim's testimony, hearing of her life, her activities as a crack addict, forced to examine, with the other jurors, her slightly disfigured left eyelid—the claim of the prosecution being that the woman had suffered permanent damage as a result of the beating. And what irony—the woman had her right arm in a sling, and a badly bruised face, from what was apparently a very recent beating, unrelated to the case being tried. (Of course, the woman's present condition was never explained.)

There was much sorrow here, and sordidness; and hopelessness; yet an air 30 now and then of the farcical as well. As in a ghetto version of "Rashomon," witnesses supplied wildly varying details, each convinced he or she was remembering correctly. Did the alleged assault take place at noon of January 21, 1990? at 4:30 P.M.? at 7:30 P.M.? Was the defendant, charged with kicking the victim in the head, wearing yellow steel-toed boots, as the victim swore, or black leather boots, as his cousin swore, or, as the defendant swore, black sneakers? One eyewitness saw only kicks, not punches; another saw punches, but no kicks. All of the prosecution witnesses, it developed through cross-examination, had criminal records; yet, because of legal protocol, we were never told if the defendant had a criminal record. (Later, during the jury's deliberation, some of the jurors seemed actually to have thought that the defendant was "clean.") How frustrating the testimonies were, how tediously protracted by the defense counsel's cross-examination, how repetitive, stupefyingly dull—as we traced and retraced the same narrow terrain, like a snail with a motor imbalance. I wondered if, my eyes open, I might begin to hallucinate.

And then, of course, as in fictionalized trials, the attorneys quickly called out, "Your Honor, I object!" when questioning got interesting; when crucial matters arose, as often they did, the judge and the attorneys conferred out of earshot, while we jurors looked on deaf and mute; at any time court might be recessed, and we would be sent out to the jury room, forbidden to discuss the case, and with no knowledge of when we might be summoned back, or if we would be summoned back at all. (Trials often end abruptly, and jurors, to that moment flattered into believing themselves essential to the execution of justice, are summarily dismissed and sent home.) To experience the legal system as a layman is to discover yourself on a playing field in the midst of a bizarre, intricately structured game with unknown rules and a private language; the jury itself, though the fabled glory of our American criminal justice system, resembles nothing so much as a large, ungainly, anachronistic beast with one eye patched over, a gag in its mouth, cotton stuffed in an ear, a leg shackled. Yet the delusion persists, the jury judges "facts."

> "She was fidgeting all the time, she was nervous."
> "She said she was going *down* the stairs, not *up*."
> "How can you believe her—she's a crack addict."
> "People like that, Walnut Street, Trenton—that's how they live."   35
> "Her eye didn't look like it was hurt that bad."
> "I'd almost believe the defendant, over her."
> "They're all a pack of liars."

So often, in recent years, has the reflex of blaming the victim been exposed by the media, some of us have been led to think it no longer presents much of a danger to impartial judgment in cases of assault and rape, especially cases of male defendant and female victims. Certainly, feminists would like to think that this is so, that some progress has been made. Yet, clearly, human instinct is conservative, even primitive: if you are a female victim pleading your case, and others can discover a way to blame you for your misfortune, they will do so. (After the St. John's University trial, in which white defendants were found not guilty of sexual assault against a young black woman, a commentator asked, "When have white men ever been found guilty of raping black women?") As if the victim, and not the defendant, were on trial. And especially, as in our case, if the victim is of another class and race, a self-confessed, if former, drug addict . . . The unvoiced judgment is: *She got what she deserved.*

The jury on which I served was very likely a representative cross-section of   40
area citizens, equally divided in gender, middle to lower-middle class incomes, eleven Caucasians and one black; and my experience in their midst left me shaken and depressed for days. So this is what a jury thinks, says, does! So this is the mystique in action! Certainly these men and women were not evil, nor even malicious. I am not suggesting that. I believe that most of them were well-intentioned and not racist, at least not consciously racist. But they were not thoughtful people; they were not, in a way, serious people. Among them, I was the only one to take notes during our recesses from the court; I was the only one, as it would turn out, who seemed to have considered the black witnesses, and especially the victim, as human beings like myself. (How vain this sounds! I wish there were some other way to express it.) When we were sequestered in our jury room and might have used the time to think quietly about the case (discussions are forbidden until a trial is over), most of the jurors chatted and laughed as if there were nothing of much import going on. Testimony that seemed to me self-evidently painful, heartrending in what it suggested of the profound distance between our worlds and theirs, slid off them as if uttered in a foreign language: a language that had nothing to do with them. (What of the single black juror? He was an older man, and probably said about five words during the discussion. Younger and possibly more assertive blacks had been bumped from the jury.) White jurors, reflecting the bias of their society, are notorious for not taking very seriously crimes by blacks committed against blacks, and this bias was borne out by our jury; if the victim had been, not black, but a young white woman, they would surely have seen the charge differently.

As it was, I was astonished by the ferocity of my fellow jurors' attack on the victim's testimony, which was not only pitiless but derisive, contemptuous. Men led the attack immediately, before we were even seated around the table — the most vociferous was, in fact, the man who had showed up on the first day in running shorts — but women joined in, too. Hours of earnest testimony were discounted by a wave of the hand, a "gut-level" opinion; inconsistencies in testimony were interpreted as evidence of falsehood even as the jurors themselves misremembered facts. There was no effort on the part of the jury foreman to assure an orderly discussion, and very likely this would not have made much of a difference in the quality of the discourse, which was on about the level of a group of people discussing where to go to eat.

Perhaps human beings have only a measure of sympathy for others, and little to spare. Perhaps there is a human instinct, a gene for survival, that shuts down identification with men and women in distress who are different from ourselves, and without power. I am trying to separate my own biases from those of my fellow jurors, who of course have a right to bias, and, as sworn jurors, the privilege of voting as intuition urged: they reacted swiftly, and they reacted without subtlety or ambiguity, and they reacted in near-unanimity in rejecting the prosecution's charge against the defendant. They simply did not take it, nor the world from which it sprang, seriously.

After deliberation, the twelve of us agreed upon a verdict of "guilty" for the lesser charge of simple assault. (Even the defense counsel acknowledged that something had been done to the victim to account for her injuries.) How many hours we jurors spent together, how many hours the protracted ceremony of the trial consumed, like an antique machine clanking and grinding and laboring to bring forth a verdict any Trenton judge might have handed down after a few hours' review of the case — multiply this by thousands, hundreds of thousands, adding in such cases as the child molestation trial in Los Angeles a few years ago that took two years — two years! — and you have a criminal justice system that not only fails to guarantee "justice" but is cumbersome, inefficient, outmoded. If jurors were really possessed of unique qualities of divination conferred upon them when they are sworn in, the archaic system might justify itself; but, as my personal experience suggests, this is not the case.

Moreover, verdicts of "guilty" handed down by petit juries are frequently of little real consequence. Judges do the actual sentencing, which might be a fine, or probation, or community service, or months in prison, or years; if years, the prison parole board determines the sentence. This is as it should be, since the idea of juries also determining sentences would be a nightmare.

In retrospect, I am grateful for my experience as a juror in Trenton, New Jersey, though it is not one I am eager to repeat. I came into contact with an estimable, indeed judicious judge; I experienced the procedure of a small, circumscribed criminal case; I was disabused, by my fellow jurors, of certain romantic illusions. And I was paid $5 a day by the State of New Jersey—which, considering the contribution we made, seems about right.

45

Afterword

I wrote this essay immediately after the conclusion of the trial. Months later, I am still haunted by the experience. What most distressed me was the assumption, so unexamined as to be chilling, on the part of the white jurors, that they belonged to a world, if not to a species, wholly distinct from the blacks of Trenton's underclass whom they were empowered to judge. There is *we*, and there is *they* — and an unbridgeable distance between.

In Richard Wright's classic novel *Native Son* (1940), the tragic argument is made that white racist America has so dehumanized Negro Americans that, like Bigger Thomas, the eponymous hero of the novel, some of the more aggressive are in danger of becoming primitive, brutalized, unfeeling killers (of Negroes as well as Caucasians: Bigger Thomas murders a young black woman as viciously and as gratuitously as he murders the white millionaire's daughter); these very Negroes are then loathed, repudiated, and sentenced to death, for being dehumanized. Bigger Thomas can have no "feeling" for his victims because he has been made incapable of human feeling.

Yet, as Wright says in his memoir *Black Boy* (1944):

> After I had learned other ways of life I used to brood upon the unconscious irony of those who felt that Negroes led so passional an existence! I saw that what had been taken as our emotional strength was our negative confusions, our flights, our frenzy under pressure.

In judging others, the burden is ours to transcend the limits of self; in terms of race, the limits, and blindnesses, of race. How is this possible? Who is qualified? Is the concept of human Justice a commonly held delusion, as readily served by, say, a lottery, as by human effort and collaboration? After so many weeks, I am still preoccupied with the experience of having been a juror, serving on that particular jury, in a representative American city of the present time. I hear again the smug assertions of certain of my fellow jurors; I see several faces with unwanted oneiric clarity; obsessively, I see the purse-lipped white-haired retiree who had denounced the blacks in the trial as a "pack of liars" sitting reading the New Testament, as he had done somewhat conspicuously during some of our sequestered time together. Though I am Caucasian, thus one of their own, the proposition unnerved me: *What if these people were entrusted with my life? What sympathy would they have for me?—or for one another?*

The shadow that falls upon us at such sobering moments is nothing less than   50
our estrangement from humanity, and surely there is no estrangement more profound and more corrosive. For juries too should submit to judgment. But in what court—and who to preside?   [1995]

THINKING ABOUT THE TEXT

1. What images do you get of Oates as you read her essay? Refer to details of the text that influence your impression of her. Overall, to what extent do you trust and respect her as a reporter?

2. In the second half of her essay, Oates focuses on the trial itself and the jury's subsequent deliberations. What do you sense her basically doing in the first half?

3. Oates seems to have been surprised by the behavior of the other jurors. Does the conduct she describes surprise you? Identify aspects of your past experiences that affect your answer. After Oates published her essay, the U.S. Supreme Court ruled that attorneys cannot exclude a potential juror on racial grounds. Evidently Oates believes that her jury would have behaved more responsibly if it had, in fact, included more African Americans. Do you agree? Why, or why not?

4. How do you think the jurors should have acted? Identify things you wish they had done.

5. Oates suggests that her experience as a juror reveals problems with the American criminal justice system as a whole. Do you think it is reasonable of her to generalize in this way? Explain.

MAKING COMPARISONS

1. Evidently Sanders believes that his jury behaved well, even though its members' social class apparently differed from the defendant's. Oates, on the other hand, suggests that her jurors were guilty of racism toward people involved in the case they judged. Are you convinced that the Indiana jury was, in fact, much better than the New Jersey one? Does Sanders lead you to think that the American criminal justice system is better than Oates suggests? Identify some of the warrants or assumptions behind your answers.

2. For the most part, Sanders and Oates use different tenses. He recounts his trial in present tense, while she uses the past. Do you like one of these rhetorical strategies more than the other? Why, or why not?

3. Is time as important a subject in Oates's essay as it is in Sanders's? Refer to specific details of both.

WRITING ABOUT ISSUES

1. In effect, Sanders and Oates invite you to judge the juries they describe. Think of the questions you would ask in your effort to evaluate a jury's behavior. Then, write an essay in which you state whether and how Sanders or Oates addresses these questions.

2. Write an essay comparing what Sanders and Oates tell you about themselves. Do you get pretty much the same impression of both, or do the images they project of themselves strike you as significantly different? Refer to specific details of their texts.

3. In 1991, four white police officers went on trial for various offenses related to their beating of an African American man, Rodney King. The judge felt that the officers could not receive a fair trial in southeast Los Angeles, where the beating occurred. Therefore, the trial was moved to a suburb, Simi Valley. Reflecting the predominantly white middle-class makeup of the town, the jury comprised ten whites, a Hispanic, and an Asian; critics argued that a Los Angeles jury probably would have been partially or even predominantly black. The Simi Valley jurors proceeded to acquit the officers of almost every charge. Many Americans protested the outcome, believing that a more racially diverse jury would have reached more responsible verdicts and that the trial should have taken

place at its original site. In the *Washington Post*, however, a letter writer disagreed: "As for the change of venue, the Constitution guarantees us a jury of our peers. The Simi Valley jury was surely more representative of the officers' peers than a southeast Los Angeles jury would have been." Write an essay in which you identify and defend what you think should be meant by the phrase "a jury of one's peers." In arguing for your definition, refer to at least one actual case. Possibilities include the King case, the case described by Sanders, the one described by Oates, the O. J. Simpson trials, and cases in your local community.

4. Write an essay analyzing and evaluating the behavior of a particular jury. It might be a jury that you sat on or observed. Then again, it might be a jury that someone told you about or that you read about. Possibilities include juries in the cases referred to at the end of assignment 3.

MORAL LAW VERSUS HUMAN LAW:
CRITICAL COMMENTARIES ON SOPHOCLES' ANTIGONE

SOPHOCLES, *Antigone*

CRITICAL COMMENTARIES:
BERNARD KNOX, From *The Heroic Temper*
MARTHA NUSSBAUM, From *The Fragility of Goodness*
CHARLES SEGAL, From *Interpreting Greek Tragedy*

Usually we obey laws, judging them to be appropriate. Even hardened criminals rarely argue that the laws they have broken shouldn't exist. From time to time you probably do find a particular law unfair to you or others. Every day there are organized groups campaigning against such laws, seeking to get them repealed or at least interpreted in new ways. Less commonly, though, do people engage in civil disobedience — that is, openly violate laws they find unjust. Such behavior is hardly foreign to this country. It has occurred throughout American history: recall, for example, the Boston Tea Party, the Underground Railroad, lunch counter sit-ins during the civil rights movement, the burning of draft cards in the Vietnam era, and Operation Rescue's current attempts to block women from abortion clinics. While these acts have expressed various political beliefs, the protesters have all claimed to be driven by conscience. To them, moral law has made them defy human law.

But deciding when and how these two kinds of law clash is itself an act of judgment. Moreover, when they do conflict, which of them should have priority? In which circumstances should conscience reign, and in which should you obey a law despite being offended by it? Finally, how should a society respond to civil

disobedience in its midst? All of these issues come up in the play you are about to
read, Sophocles' ancient Greek tragedy *Antigone*. They are touched on as well by
the critical commentaries that follow.

BEFORE YOU READ

Think of an occasion when you considered defying a law, rule, or regulation
you felt at odds with your conscience. What specific values were in conflict?
What did you ultimately decide to do, and why? What were the consequences? If later you changed your mind about your behavior, state how.

SOPHOCLES
Antigone
Translated by Robert Fagles

*Along with Aeschylus and Euripides, Sophocles (496? B.C.E.–406? B.C.E.) is con-
sidered one of the greatest writers of tragedy in ancient Athens. During his lifetime,
he was much respected in the city, often winning its dramatic competitions. Evidently he wrote over a hundred plays, but the only ones to survive complete are*
Antigone *and six other tragedies. As a practitioner of tragedy, Sophocles was innovative. Among other things, he increased the number of actors on stage from two to
three, while reducing the chorus from fifty to fifteen. Productions of his plays did
remain traditional in having the performers wear masks and be exclusively male.*
Antigone *continues to be much performed today; moreover, through the centuries
there have been numerous adaptations of it. The most notable of these was Jean
Anouilh's 1944 version, a challenge to the Nazi occupiers of Paris.*

*The original play was first produced in 441 B.C.E., and it was the first of three
interrelated plays by Sophocles now known as his Oedipus cycle. The other two are*
Oedipus Rex, *produced between 430 and 427 B.C.E., and* Oedipus at Colonus,
*posthumously produced in 401 B.C.E.. Scholars know that the plots of these other
two plays were familiar to Sophocles' audience. Less clear is whether that audience
was familiar with the story of* Antigone, *which comes last in terms of plot chronology. The title character of* Oedipus Rex *is Antigone's father, the ruler of Thebes. In
the play, Oedipus blinds himself and leaves Thebes when he discovers that he has
unknowingly fulfilled a terrible prophecy: that he would kill his own father and
marry his mother.* Oedipus at Colonus *focuses on his death. Just before the action
of* Antigone *begins, the heroine's two brothers have killed each other in battle. One,
Eteocles, was defending Thebes; the other, Polynices, was leading an army against
it. The current ruler of Thebes, Antigone's uncle Creon, now forbids burial of Polynices — a command that Antigone will defy.*

CHARACTERS

ANTIGONE, *daughter of Oedipus and Jocasta*
ISMENE, *sister of Antigone*
A CHORUS *of old Theban citizens and their* LEADER
CREON, *king of Thebes, uncle of Antigone and Ismene*
A SENTRY
HAEMON, *son of Creon and Eurydice*
TIRESIAS, *a blind prophet*
A MESSENGER
EURYDICE, *wife of Creon*
GUARDS, ATTENDANTS, AND A BOY

TIME AND SCENE: *The royal house of Thebes. It is still night, and the invading armies of Argos have just been driven from the city. Fighting on opposite sides, the sons of Oedipus, Eteocles and Polynices, have killed each other in combat. Their uncle, Creon, is now king of Thebes.*

    Enter Antigone, slipping through the central doors of the palace. She motions to her sister, Ismene, who follows her cautiously toward an altar at the center of the stage.

ANTIGONE: My own flesh and blood—dear sister, dear Ismene,
     how many griefs our father Oedipus handed down!
     Do you know one, I ask you, one grief
     that Zeus° will not perfect for the two of us
     while we still live and breathe? There's nothing,   5
     no pain—our lives are pain—no private shame,
     no public disgrace, nothing I haven't seen
     in your griefs and mine. And now this:
     an emergency decree, they say, the Commander
     has just declared for all of Thebes.   10
     What, haven't you heard? Don't you see?
     The doom reserved for enemies
     marches on the ones we love the most.
ISMENE: Not I, I haven't heard a word, Antigone.
     Nothing of loved ones,   15
     no joy or pain has come my way, not since
     the two of us were robbed of our two brothers,
     both gone in a day, a double blow—
     not since the armies of Argos vanished,
     just this very night. I know nothing more,   20
     whether our luck's improved or ruin's still to come.
ANTIGONE: I thought so. That's why I brought you out here,
     past the gates, so you could hear in private.

---

4 Zeus: The highest Olympian deity.

ISMENE: What's the matter? Trouble, clearly . . .
            you sound so dark, so grim.   25
ANTIGONE: Why not? Our own brothers' burial!
            Hasn't Creon graced one with all the rites,
            disgraced the other? Eteocles, they say,
            has been given full military honors,
            rightly so—Creon's laid him in the earth   30
            and he goes with glory down among the dead.
            But the body of Polynices, who died miserably—
            why, a city-wide proclamation, rumor has it,
            forbids anyone to bury him, even mourn him.
            He's to be left unwept, unburied, a lovely treasure   35
            for birds that scan the field and feast to their heart's content.

            Such, I hear, is the martial law our good Creon
            lays down for you and me—yes, me, I tell you—
            and he's coming here to alert the uninformed
            in no uncertain terms,   40
            and he won't treat the matter lightly. Whoever
            disobeys in the least will die, his doom is sealed:
            stoning to death inside the city walls!

            There you have it. You'll soon show what you are,
            worth your breeding, Ismene, or a coward—   45
            for all your royal blood.
ISMENE: My poor sister, if things have come to this,
            who am I to make or mend them, tell me,
            what good am I to you?
ANTIGONE: Decide.
            Will you share the labor, share the work?   50
ISMENE: What work, what's the risk? What do you mean?
ANTIGONE:

Raising her hands.

            Will you lift up his body with these bare hands
            and lower it with me?
ISMENE: What? You'd bury him—
            when a law forbids the city?
ANTIGONE: Yes!
            He is my brother and—deny it as you will—   55
            your brother too.
            No one will ever convict me for a traitor.
ISMENE: So desperate, and Creon has expressly—
ANTIGONE: No,
            he has no right to keep me from my own.
ISMENE: Oh my sister, think—   60
            think how our own father died, hated,

his reputation in ruins, driven on
by the crimes he brought to light himself
to gouge out his eyes with his own hands —
then mother . . . his mother and wife, both in one,   65
mutilating her life in the twisted noose —
and last, our two brothers dead in a single day,
both shedding their own blood, poor suffering boys,
battling out their common destiny hand-to-hand.

Now look at the two of us, left so alone . . .   70
think what a death we'll die, the worst of all
if we violate the laws and override
the fixed decree of the throne, its power —
we must be sensible. Remember we are women,
we're not born to contend with men. Then too,   75
we're underlings, ruled by much stronger hands,
so we must submit in this, and things still worse.

I, for one, I'll beg the dead to forgive me —
I'm forced, I have no choice — I must obey
the ones who stand in power. Why rush to extremes?   80
It's madness, madness.
ANTIGONE: I won't insist,
no, even if you should have a change of heart,
I'd never welcome you in the labor, not with me.
So, do as you like, whatever suits you best —
I'll bury him myself.   85
And even if I die in the act, that death will be a glory.
I'll lie with the one I love and loved by him —
an outrage sacred to the gods! I have longer
to please the dead than please the living here:
in the kingdom down below I'll lie forever.   90
Do as you like, dishonor the laws
the gods hold in honor.
ISMENE: I'd do them no dishonor . . .
but defy the city? I have no strength for that.
ANTIGONE: You have your excuses. I am on my way,
I'll raise a mound for him, for my dear brother.   95
ISMENE: Oh Antigone, you're so rash — I'm so afraid for you!
ANTIGONE: Don't fear for me. Set your own life in order.
ISMENE: Then don't, at least, blurt this out to anyone.
Keep it a secret. I'll join you in that, I promise.
ANTIGONE: Dear god, shout it from the rooftops. I'll hate you   100
all the more for silence — tell the world!
ISMENE: So fiery — and it ought to chill your heart.
ANTIGONE: I know I please where I must please the most.
ISMENE: Yes, if you can, but you're in love with impossibility.

ANTIGONE: Very well then, once my strength gives out   105
    I will be done at last.
ISMENE: You're wrong from the start,
    you're off on a hopeless quest.
ANTIGONE: If you say so, you will make me hate you,
    and the hatred of the dead, by all rights,
    will haunt you night and day.   110
    But leave me to my own absurdity, leave me
    to suffer this — dreadful thing. I'll suffer
    nothing as great as death without glory.

Exit to the side.

ISMENE: Then go if you must, but rest assured,
    wild, irrational as you are, my sister,   115
    you are truly dear to the ones who love you.

*Withdrawing to the palace. Enter a Chorus, the old citizens of Thebes, chanting as
the sun begins to rise.*

CHORUS: Glory! — great beam of sun, brightest of all
    that ever rose on the seven gates of Thebes,
            you burn through night at last!
                    Great eye of the golden day,   120
    mounting the Dirce's° banks you throw him back —
    the enemy out of Argos, the white shield, the man of bronze —
    he's flying headlong now
            the bridle of fate stampeding him with pain!

            And he had driven against our borders,   125
            launched by the warring claims of Polynices —
            like an eagle screaming, winging havoc
            over the land, wings of armor
            shielded white as snow,
            a huge army massing,   130
            crested helmets bristling for assault.

    He hovered above our roofs, his vast maw gaping
    closing down around our seven gates,
            his spears thirsting for the kill
                    but now he's gone, look,   135
    before he could glut his jaws with Theban blood
    or the god of fire put our crown of towers to the torch.
    He grappled the Dragon none can master — Thebes —
            the clang of our arms like thunder at his back!

            Zeus hates with a vengeance all bravado,   140
            the mighty boasts of men. He watched them

---

121 **the Dirce:** A river near Thebes.

coming on in a rising flood, the pride
of their golden armor ringing shrill —
and brandishing his lightning
blasted the fighter just at the goal,   145
rushing to shout his triumph from our walls.

Down from the heights he crashed, pounding down on the earth!
And a moment ago, blazing torch in hand —
      mad for attack, ecstatic
he breathed his rage, the storm   150
   of his fury hurling at our heads!
But now his high hopes have laid him low
and down the enemy ranks the iron god of war
    deals his rewards, his stunning blows — Ares°
rapture of battle, our right arm in the crisis.   155

    Seven captains marshaled at seven gates
seven against their equals, gave
their brazen trophies up to Zeus,
god of the breaking rout of battle,
all but two: those blood brothers,   160
one father, one mother — matched in rage,
spears matched for the twin conquest —
clashed and won the common prize of death.

But now for Victory! Glorious in the morning,
joy in her eyes to meet our joy   165
   she is winging down to Thebes,
our fleets of chariots wheeling in her wake —
   Now let us win oblivion from the wars,
thronging the temples of the gods
in singing, dancing choirs through the night!   170
   Lord Dionysus,° god of the dance
that shakes the land of Thebes, now lead the way!

Enter Creon from the palace, attended by his guard.

    But look, the king of the realm is coming,
Creon, the new man for the new day,
whatever the gods are sending now . . .   175
what new plan will he launch?
Why this, this special session?
Why this sudden call to the old men
summoned at one command?
CREON: My countrymen,
   the ship of state is safe. The gods who rocked her,   180

---

154 Ares: God of war.   **171 Dionysus:** God of fertility and wine.

after a long, merciless pounding in the storm,
have righted her once more.
                         Out of the whole city
I have called you here alone. Well I know,
first, your undeviating respect
for the throne and royal power of King Laius.   185
Next, while Oedipus steered the land of Thebes,
and even after he died, your loyalty was unshakable,
you still stood by their children. Now then,
since the two sons are dead—two blows of fate
in the same day, cut down by each other's hands,   190
both killers, both brothers stained with blood—
as I am next in kin to the dead,
I now possess the throne and all its powers.

Of course you cannot know a man completely,
his character, his principles, sense of judgment,   195
not till he's shown his colors, ruling the people,
making laws. Experience, there's the test.
As I see it, whoever assumes the task,
the awesome task of setting the city's course,
and refuses to adopt the soundest policies   200
but fearing someone, keeps his lips locked tight,
he's utterly worthless. So I rate him now,
I always have. And whoever places a friend
above the good of his own country, he is nothing:
I have no use for him. Zeus my witness,   205
Zeus who sees all things, always—
I could never stand by silent, watching destruction
march against our city, putting safety to rout,
nor could I ever make that man a friend of mine
who menaces our country. Remember this: 210
our country *is* our safety.
Only while she voyages true on course
can we establish friendships, truer than blood itself.
Such are my standards. They make our city great.

Closely akin to them I have proclaimed,   215
just now, the following decree to our people
concerning the two sons of Oedipus.
Eteocles, who died fighting for Thebes,
excelling all in arms: he shall be buried,
crowned with a hero's honors, the cups we pour   220
to soak the earth and reach the famous dead.

But as for his blood brother, Polynices,
who returned from exile, home to his father-city

and the gods of his race, consumed with one desire—
to burn them roof to roots—who thirsted to drink　　　　　225
his kinsmen's blood and sell the rest to slavery:
that man—a proclamation has forbidden the city
to dignify him with burial, mourn him at all.
No, he must be left unburied, his corpse
carrion for the birds and dogs to tear,　　　　　　　　230
an obscenity for the citizens to behold!

These are my principles. Never at my hands
will the traitor be honored above the patriot.
But whoever proves his loyalty to the state:
I'll prize that man in death as well as life.　　　　　235

LEADER:　　If this is your pleasure, Creon, treating
　　our city's enemy and our friend this way . . .
　　The power is yours, I suppose, to enforce it
　　with the laws, both for the dead and all of us,
　　the living.

CREON:　　　　Follow my orders closely then,　　　　240
　　be on your guard.

LEADER:　　　　　　　We're too old.
　　Lay that burden on younger shoulders.

CREON:　　　　　　　　　　　No, no,
　　I don't mean the body—I've posted guards already.

LEADER:　　What commands for us then? What other service?

CREON:　　See that you never side with those who break my orders.　　245

LEADER:　　Never. Only a fool could be in love with death.

CREON:　　Death is the price—you're right. But all too often
　　the mere hope of money has ruined many men.

A Sentry enters from the side.

SENTRY:　　　　　　　　　　　　　　　My lord,
　　I can't say I'm winded from running, or set out
　　with any spring in my legs either—no sir,　　　　250
　　I was lost in thought, and it made me stop, often,
　　dead in my tracks, wheeling, turning back,
　　and all the time a voice inside me muttering,
　　"Idiot, why? You're going straight to your death."
　　Then muttering, "Stopped again, poor fool?　　　　255
　　If somebody gets the news to Creon first,
　　what's to save your neck?"
　　　　　　　　　　And so,
　　mulling it over, on I trudged, dragging my feet,
　　you can make a short road take forever . . .
　　but at last, look, common sense won out,　　　　260
　　I'm here, and I'm all yours,
　　and even though I come empty-handed

I'll tell my story just the same, because
I've come with a good grip on one hope,
what will come will come, whatever fate— 265
CREON: Come to the point!
What's wrong—why so afraid?
SENTRY: First, myself, I've got to tell you,
I didn't do it, didn't see who did—
Be fair, don't take it out on me. 270
CREON: You're playing it safe, soldier,
barricading yourself from any trouble.
It's obvious, you've something strange to tell.
SENTRY: Dangerous too, and danger makes you delay
for all you're worth. 275
CREON: Out with it—then dismiss!
SENTRY: All right, here it comes. The body—
someone's just buried it, then run off . . .
sprinkled some dry dust on the flesh,
given it proper rites.
CREON: What? 280
What man alive would dare—
SENTRY: I've no idea, I swear it.
There was no mark of a spade, no pickaxe there,
no earth turned up, the ground packed hard and dry,
unbroken, no tracks, no wheelruts, nothing,
the workman left no trace. Just at sunup 285
the first watch of the day points it out—
it was a wonder! We were stunned . . .
a terrific burden too, for all of us, listen:
you can't see the corpse, not that it's buried,
really, just a light cover of road-dust on it, 290
as if someone meant to lay the dead to rest
and keep from getting cursed.
Not a sign in sight that dogs or wild beasts
had worried the body, even torn the skin.

But what came next! Rough talk flew thick and fast, 295
guard grilling guard—we'd have come to blows
at last, nothing to stop it; each man for himself
and each the culprit, no one caught red-handed,
all of us pleading ignorance, dodging the charges,
ready to take up red-hot iron in our fists, 300
go through fire, swear oaths to the gods—
"I didn't do it, I had no hand in it either,
not in the plotting, not in the work itself!"

Finally, after all this wrangling came to nothing,
one man spoke out and made us stare at the ground, 305

hanging our heads in fear. No way to counter him,
no way to take his advice and come through
safe and sound. Here's what he said:
"Look, we've got to report the facts to Creon,
we can't keep this hidden." Well, that won out,   310
and the lot fell on me, condemned me,
unlucky as ever, I got the prize. So here I am,
against my will and yours too, well I know—
no one wants the man who brings bad news.

LEADER: My king,
ever since he began I've been debating in my mind,   315
could this possibly be the work of the gods?

CREON: Stop—
before you make me choke with anger—the gods!
You, you're senile, must you be insane?
You say—why it's intolerable—say the gods
could have the slightest concern for that corpse?   320
Tell me, was it for meritorious service
they proceeded to bury him, prized him so? The hero
who came to burn their temples ringed with pillars,
their golden treasures—scorch their hallowed earth
and fling their laws to the winds.   325
Exactly when did you last see the gods
celebrating traitors? Inconceivable!

No, from the first there were certain citizens
who could hardly stand the spirit of my regime,
grumbling against me in the dark, heads together,   330
tossing wildly, never keeping their necks beneath
the yoke, loyally submitting to their king.
These are the instigators, I'm convinced—
they've perverted my own guard, bribed them
to do their work.

                        Money! Nothing worse   335
in our lives, so current, rampant, so corrupting.
Money—you demolish cities, root men from their homes,
you train and twist good minds and set them on
to the most atrocious schemes. No limit,
you make them adept at every kind of outrage,   340
every godless crime—money!

                              Everyone—
the whole crew bribed to commit this crime,
they've made one thing sure at least:
sooner or later they will pay the price.

Wheeling on the Sentry.

    You—   345

I swear to Zeus as I still believe in Zeus,
if you don't find the man who buried that corpse,
the very man, and produce him before my eyes,
simple death won't be enough for you,
not till we string you up alive   350
and wring the immorality out of you.
Then you can steal the rest of your days,
better informed about where to make a killing.
You'll have learned, at last, it doesn't pay
to itch for rewards from every hand that beckons.   355
Filthy profits wreck most men, you'll see —
they'll never save your life.

SENTRY: Please,
may I say a word or two, or just turn and go?

CREON: Can't you tell? Everything you say offends me.

SENTRY: Where does it hurt you, in the ears or in the heart?   360

CREON: And who are you to pinpoint my displeasure?

SENTRY: The culprit grates on your feelings,
I just annoy your ears.

CREON: Still talking?
You talk too much! A born nuisance —

SENTRY: Maybe so,
but I never did this thing, so help me!

CREON: Yes you did —   365
what's more, you squandered your life for silver!

SENTRY: Oh it's terrible when the one who does the judging
judges things all wrong.

CREON: Well now,
you just be clever about your judgments —
if you fail to produce the criminals for me,   370
you'll swear your dirty money brought you pain.

Turning sharply, reentering the palace.

SENTRY: I hope he's found. Best thing by far.
But caught or not, that's in the lap of fortune;
I'll never come back, you've seen the last of me.
I'm saved, even now, and I never thought,   375
I never hoped —
dear gods, I owe you all my thanks!

Rushing out.

CHORUS: Numberless wonders
terrible wonders walk the world but none the match for man —
that great wonder crossing the heaving gray sea,
        driven on by the blasts of winter   380
on through breakers crashing left and right,
    holds his steady course

and the oldest of the gods he wears away —
the Earth, the immortal, the inexhaustible —
as his plows go back and forth, year in, year out   385
    with the breed of stallions turning up the furrows.

And the blithe, lightheaded race of birds he snares,
the tribes of savage beasts, the life that swarms the depths —
        with one fling of his nets
woven and coiled tight, he takes them all,   390
    man the skilled, the brilliant!
He conquers all, taming with his techniques
the prey that roams the cliffs and wild lairs,
training the stallion, clamping the yoke across
    his shaggy neck, and the tireless mountain bull.   395

And speech and thought, quick as the wind
and the mood and mind for law that rules the city —
    all these he has taught himself
and shelter from the arrows of the frost
when there's rough lodging under the cold clear sky   400
and the shafts of lashing rain —
        ready, resourceful man!
           Never without resources
never an impasse as he marches on the future —
only Death, from Death alone he will find no rescue   405
but from desperate plagues he has plotted his escapes.

Man the master, ingenious past all measure
past all dreams, the skills within his grasp —
    he forges on, now to destruction
now again to greatness. When he weaves in   410
the laws of the land, and the justice of the gods
that binds his oaths together
    he and his city rise high —
        but the city casts out
that man who weds himself to inhumanity   415
thanks to reckless daring. Never share my hearth
never think my thoughts, whoever does such things.

Enter Antigone from the side, accompanied by the Sentry.

    Here is a dark sign from the gods —
    what to make of this? I know her,
    how can I deny it? That young girl's Antigone!   420
    Wretched, child of a wretched father,
    Oedipus. Look, is it possible?
    They bring you in like a prisoner —
    why? did you break the king's laws?
    Did they take you in some act of mad defiance?   425

SENTRY: She's the one, she did it single-handed —
      we caught her burying the body. Where's Creon?

Enter Creon from the palace.

LEADER: Back again, just in time when you need him.
CREON: In time for what? What is it?
SENTRY: My king,
      there's nothing you can swear you'll never do —   430
      second thoughts make liars of us all.
      I could have sworn I wouldn't hurry back
      (what with your threats, the buffeting I just took),
      but a stroke of luck beyond our wildest hopes,
      what a joy, there's nothing like it. So,   435
      back I've come, breaking my oath, who cares?
      I'm bringing in our prisoner — this young girl —
      we took her giving the dead the last rites.
      But no casting lots this time; this is *my* luck,
      my prize, no one else's.
                                    Now, my lord,   440
      here she is. Take her, question her,
      cross-examine her to your heart's content.
      But set me free, it's only right —
      I'm rid of this dreadful business once for all.
CREON: Prisoner! Her? You took her — where, doing what?   445
SENTRY: Burying the man. That's the whole story.
CREON: What?
      You mean what you say, you're telling me the truth?
SENTRY: She's the one. With my own eyes I saw her
      bury the body, just what you've forbidden.
      There. Is that plain and clear?   450
CREON: What did you see? Did you catch her in the act?
SENTRY: Here's what happened. We went back to our post,
      those threats of yours breathing down our necks —
      we brushed the corpse clean of the dust that covered it,
      stripped it bare . . . it was slimy, going soft,   455
      and we took to high ground, backs to the wind
      so the stink of him couldn't hit us;
      jostling, baiting each other to keep awake,
      shouting back and forth — no napping on the job,
      not this time. And so the hours dragged by   460
      until the sun stood dead above our heads,
      a huge white ball in the noon sky, beating,
      blazing down, and then it happened —
      suddenly, a whirlwind!
      Twisting a great dust-storm up from the earth,   465
      a black plague of the heavens, filling the plain,

ripping the leaves off every tree in sight,
choking the air and sky. We squinted hard
and took our whipping from the gods.

And after the storm passed — it seemed endless —   470
there, we saw the girl!
And she cried out a sharp, piercing cry,
like a bird come back to an empty nest,
peering into its bed, and all the babies gone . . .
Just so, when she sees the corpse bare   475
she bursts into a long, shattering wail
and calls down withering curses on the heads
of all who did the work. And she scoops up dry dust,
handfuls, quickly, and lifting a fine bronze urn,
lifting it high and pouring, she crowns the dead   480
with three full libations.
                Soon as we saw
we rushed her, closed on the kill like hunters,
and she, she didn't flinch. We interrogated her,
charging her with offenses past and present —
she stood up to it all, denied nothing. I tell you,   485
it made me ache and laugh in the same breath.
It's pure joy to escape the worst yourself,
it hurts a man to bring down his friends.
But all that, I'm afraid, means less to me
than my own skin. That's the way I'm made.
CREON:

Wheeling on Antigone.

                               You,   490
with your eyes fixed on the ground — speak up.
Do you deny you did this, yes or no?
ANTIGONE: I did it. I don't deny a thing.
CREON:

To the Sentry.

You, get out, wherever you please —
you're clear of a very heavy charge.   495

He leaves; Creon turns back to Antigone.

You, tell me briefly, no long speeches —
were you aware a decree had forbidden this?
ANTIGONE: Well aware. How could I avoid it? It was public.
CREON: And still you had the gall to break this law?
ANTIGONE: Of course I did. It wasn't Zeus, not in the least,   500
who made this proclamation — not to me.
Nor did that Justice, dwelling with the gods
beneath the earth, ordain such laws for men.

Nor did I think your edict had such force
that you, a mere mortal, could override the gods,   505
the great unwritten, unshakable traditions.
They are alive, not just today or yesterday:
they live forever, from the first time,
and no one knows when they first saw the light.

These laws — I was not about to break them,   510
not out of fear of some man's wounded pride,
and face the retribution of the gods.
Die I must, I've known it all my life —
how could I keep from knowing? — even without
your death-sentence ringing in my ears.   515
And if I am to die before my time
I consider that a gain. Who on earth,
alive in the midst of so much grief as I,
could fail to find his death a rich reward?
So for me, at least, to meet this doom of yours   520
is precious little pain. But if I had allowed
my own mother's son to rot, an unburied corpse —
that would have been an agony! This is nothing.
And if my present actions strike you as foolish,
let's just say I've been accused of folly   525
by a fool.

LEADER: Like father like daughter,
passionate, wild . . .
she hasn't learned to bend before adversity.

CREON: No? Believe me, the stiffest stubborn wills
fall the hardest; the toughest iron,   530
tempered strong in the white-hot fire,
you'll see it crack and shatter first of all.
And I've known spirited horses you can break
with a light bit — proud, rebellious horses.
There's no room for pride, not in a slave,   535
not with the lord and master standing by.

This girl was an old hand at insolence
when she overrode the edicts we made public.
But once she'd done it — the insolence,
twice over — to glory in it, laughing,   540
mocking us to our face with what she'd done.
I'm not the man, not now: she is the man
if this victory goes to her and she goes free.

Never! Sister's child or closer in blood
than all my family clustered at my altar   545
worshiping Guardian Zeus — she'll never escape,

she and her blood sister, the most barbaric death.
Yes, I accuse her sister of an equal part
in scheming this, this burial.

To his attendants.

                             Bring her here!
I just saw her inside, hysterical, gone to pieces.   550
It never fails: the mind convicts itself
in advance, when scoundrels are up to no good,
plotting in the dark. Oh but I hate it more
when a traitor, caught red-handed,
tries to glorify his crimes.   555
ANTIGONE: Creon, what more do you want
than my arrest and execution?
CREON: Nothing. Then I have it all.
ANTIGONE: Then why delay? Your moralizing repels me,
every word you say — pray god it always will.   560
So naturally all I say repels you too.
                            Enough.
Give me glory! What greater glory could I win
than to give my own brother decent burial?
These citizens here would all agree,

To the Chorus.

they'd praise me too   565
if their lips weren't locked in fear.

Pointing to Creon.

Lucky tyrants — the perquisites of power!
Ruthless power to do and say whatever pleases *them*.
CREON: You alone, of all the people in Thebes,
see things that way.
ANTIGONE: They see it just that way   570
but defer to you and keep their tongues in leash.
CREON: And you, aren't you ashamed to differ so from them?
So disloyal!
ANTIGONE: Not ashamed for a moment,
not to honor my brother, my own flesh and blood.
CREON: Wasn't Eteocles a brother too — cut down, facing him?   575
ANTIGONE: Brother, yes, by the same mother, the same father.
CREON: Then how can you render his enemy such honors,
such impieties in his eyes?
ANTIGONE: He'll never testify to that,
Eteocles dead and buried.
CREON: He will —   580
if you honor the traitor just as much as him.

ANTIGONE: But it was his brother, not some slave that died —
CREON: Ravaging our country! —
but Eteocles died fighting in our behalf.
ANTIGONE: No matter — Death longs for the same rites for all.   585
CREON: Never the same for the patriot and the traitor.
ANTIGONE: Who, Creon, who on earth can say the ones below
don't find this pure and uncorrupt?
CREON: Never. Once an enemy, never a friend,
not even after death.   590
ANTIGONE: I was born to join in love, not hate —
that is my nature.
CREON: Go down below and love,
if love you must — love the dead! While I'm alive,
no woman is going to lord it over me.

Enter Ismene from the palace, under guard.

CHORUS: Look,
Ismene's coming, weeping a sister's tears,   595
loving sister, under a cloud . . .
her face is flushed, her cheeks streaming.
Sorrow puts her lovely radiance in the dark.
CREON: You —
in my house, you viper, slinking undetected,
sucking my life-blood! I never knew   600
I was breeding twin disasters, the two of you
rising up against my throne. Come, tell me,
will you confess your part in the crime or not?
Answer me. Swear to me.
ISMENE: I did it, yes —
if only she consents — I share the guilt,   605
the consequences too.
ANTIGONE: No,
Justice will never suffer that — not you,
you were unwilling. I never brought you in.
ISMENE: But now you face such dangers . . . I'm not ashamed
to sail through trouble with you,   610
make your troubles mine.
ANTIGONE: Who did the work?
Let the dead and the god of death bear witness!
I've no love for a friend who loves in words alone.
ISMENE: Oh no, my sister, don't reject me, please,
let me die beside you, consecrating   615
the dead together.
ANTIGONE: Never share my dying,
don't lay claim to what you never touched.
My death will be enough.

ISMENE: What do I care for life, cut off from you?
ANTIGONE: Ask Creon. Your concern is all for him.   620
ISMENE: Why abuse me so? It doesn't help you now.
ANTIGONE: You're right—
    if I mock you, I get no pleasure from it,
    only pain.
ISMENE: Tell me, dear one,
    what can I do to help you, even now?
ANTIGONE: Save yourself. I don't grudge you your survival.   625
ISMENE: Oh no, no, denied my portion in your death?
ANTIGONE: You chose to live, I chose to die.
ISMENE: Not, at least,
    without every kind of caution I could voice.
ANTIGONE: Your wisdom appealed to one world—mine, another.
ISMENE: But look, we're both guilty, both condemned to death.   630
ANTIGONE: Courage! Live your life. I gave myself to death,
    long ago, so I might serve the dead.
CREON: They're both mad, I tell you, the two of them.
    One's just shown it, the other's been that way
    since she was born.
ISMENE: True, my king,   635
    the sense we were born with cannot last forever . . .
    commit cruelty on a person long enough
    and the mind begins to go.
CREON: Yours did,
    when you chose to commit your crimes with her.
ISMENE: How can I live alone, without her?
CREON: Her?   640
    Don't even mention her—she no longer exists.
ISMENE: What? You'd kill your own son's bride?
CREON: Absolutely:
    there are other fields for him to plow.
ISMENE: Perhaps,
    but never as true, as close a bond as theirs.
CREON: A worthless woman for my son? It repels me.   645
ISMENE: Dearest Haemon, your father wrongs you so!
CREON: Enough, enough—you and your talk of marriage!
ISMENE: Creon—you're really going to rob your son of Antigone?
CREON: Death will do it for me—break their marriage off.
LEADER: So, it's settled then? Antigone must die?   650
CREON: Settled, yes—we both know that.

To the guards.

    Stop wasting time. Take them in.
    From now on they'll act like women.
    Tie them up, no more running loose;

even the bravest will cut and run,   655
once they see Death coming for their lives.

*The guards escort Antigone and Ismene into the palace. Creon remains while the
old citizens form their chorus.*

CHORUS: Blest, they are the truly blest who all their lives
        have never tasted devastation. For others, once
        the gods have rocked a house to its foundations
            the ruin will never cease, cresting on and on   660
        from one generation on throughout the race —
        like a great mounting tide
        driven on by savage northern gales,
                    surging over the dead black depths
        roiling up from the bottom dark heaves of sand   665
        and the headlands, taking the storm's onslaught full-force,
        roar, and the low moaning
                            echoes on and on
                                    and now
        as in ancient times I see the sorrows of the house,
        the living heirs of the old ancestral kings,
        piling on the sorrows of the dead   670
            and one generation cannot free the next —
        some god will bring them crashing down,
        the race finds no release.
        And now the light, the hope
                springing up from the late last root   675
        in the house of Oedipus, that hope's cut down in turn
        by the long, bloody knife swung by the gods of death
        by a senseless word
                    by fury at the heart.
                                Zeus,
        yours is the power, Zeus, what man on earth
        can override it, who can hold it back?   680
        Power that neither Sleep, the all-ensnaring
            no, nor the tireless months of heaven
        can ever overmaster — young through all time,
        mighty lord of power, you hold fast
            the dazzling crystal mansions of Olympus.   685
        And throughout the future, late and soon
        as through the past, your law prevails:
        no towering form of greatness
                enters into the lives of mortals
                        free and clear of ruin.
                                    True,   690
        our dreams, our high hopes voyaging far and wide
        bring sheer delight to many, to many others
            delusion, blithe, mindless lusts

and the fraud steals on one slowly . . . unaware
till he trips and puts his foot into the fire.   695
    He was a wise old man who coined
the famous saying: "Sooner or later
foul is fair, fair is foul
to the man the gods will ruin"—
    He goes his way for a moment only   700
            free of blinding ruin.

Enter Haemon from the palace.

    Here's Haemon now, the last of all your sons.
    Does he come in tears for his bride,
    his doomed bride, Antigone—
    bitter at being cheated of their marriage?   705
CREON: We'll soon know, better than seers could tell us.

Turning to Haemon.

    Son, you've heard the final verdict on your bride?
    Are you coming now, raving against your father?
    Or do you love me, no matter what I do?
HAEMON: Father, I'm your *son* . . . you in your wisdom   710
set my bearings for me—I obey you.
No marriage could ever mean more to me than you,
whatever good direction you may offer.
CREON: Fine, Haemon.
That's how you ought to feel within your heart,
subordinate to your father's will in every way.   715
That's what a man prays for: to produce good sons—
households full of them, dutiful and attentive,
so they can pay his enemy back with interest
and match the respect their father shows his friend.
But the man who rears a brood of useless children,   720
what has he brought into the world, I ask you?
Nothing but trouble for himself, and mockery
from his enemies laughing in his face.
                            Oh Haemon,
never lose your sense of judgment over a woman.
The warmth, the rush of pleasure, it all goes cold   725
in your arms, I warn you . . . a worthless woman
in your house, a misery in your bed.
What wound cuts deeper than a loved one
turned against you? Spit her out,
like a mortal enemy—let the girl go.   730
Let her find a husband down among the dead.

Imagine it: I caught her in naked rebellion,
the traitor, the only one in the whole city.

I'm not about to prove myself a liar,
not to my people, no, I'm going to kill her!   735
That's right—so let her cry for mercy, sing her hymns
to Zeus who defends all bonds of kindred blood.
Why, if I bring up my own kin to be rebels,
think what I'd suffer from the world at large.
Show me the man who rules his household well: 740
I'll show you someone fit to rule the state.
That good man, my son,
I have every confidence he and he alone
can give commands and take them too. Staunch
in the storm of spears he'll stand his ground,   745
a loyal, unflinching comrade at your side.

But whoever steps out of line, violates the laws
or presumes to hand out orders to his superiors,
he'll win no praise from me. But that man
the city places in authority, his orders   750
must be obeyed, large and small,
right and wrong.
                    Anarchy—
show me a greater crime in all the earth!
She, she destroys cities, rips up houses,
breaks the ranks of spearmen into headlong rout.   755
But the ones who last it out, the great mass of them
owe their lives to discipline. Therefore
we must defend the men who live by law,
never let some woman triumph over us.
Better to fall from power, if fall we must,   760
at the hands of a man—never be rated
inferior to a woman, never.
LEADER: To us,
    unless old age has robbed us of our wits,
    you seem to say what you have to say with sense.
HAEMON: Father, only the gods endow a man with reason,   765
    the finest of all their gifts, a treasure.
    Far be it from me—I haven't the skill,
    and certainly no desire, to tell you when,
    if ever, you make a slip in speech . . . though
    someone else might have a good suggestion.   770

    Of course it's not for you,
    in the normal run of things, to watch
    whatever men say or do, or find to criticize.
    The man in the street, you know, dreads your glance,
    he'd never say anything displeasing to your face.   775
    But it's for me to catch the murmurs in the dark,

the way the city mourns for this young girl.
"No woman," they say, "ever deserved death less,
and such a brutal death for such a glorious action.
She, with her own dear brother lying in his blood — 780
she couldn't bear to leave him dead, unburied,
food for the wild dogs or wheeling vultures.
Death? She deserves a glowing crown of gold!"
So they say, and the rumor spreads in secret,
darkly . . .
　　　　　　　　I rejoice in your success, father — 785
nothing more precious to me in the world.
What medal of honor brighter to his children
than a father's growing glory? Or a child's
to his proud father? Now don't, please,
be quite so single-minded, self-involved, 790
or assume the world is wrong and you are right.
Whoever thinks that he alone possesses intelligence,
the gift of eloquence, he and no one else,
and character too . . . such men, I tell you,
spread them open — you will find them empty.
　　　　　　　　　　　　　　　　No, 795

it's no disgrace for a man, even a wise man,
to learn many things and not to be too rigid.
You've seen trees by a raging winter torrent,
how many sway with the flood and salvage every twig,
but not the stubborn — they're ripped out, roots and all. 800
Bend or break. The same when a man is sailing:
haul your sheets too taut, never give an inch,
you'll capsize, go the rest of the voyage
keel up and the rowing-benches under.

Oh give way. Relax your anger — change! 805
I'm young, I know, but let me offer this:
it would be best by far, I admit,
if a man were born infallible, right by nature.
If not — and things don't often go that way,
it's best to learn from those with good advice. 810

LEADER:　You'd do well, my lord, if he's speaking to the point,
　　to learn from him,

Turning to Haemon.

　　　　　　　　and you, my boy, from him.
　　You both are talking sense.
CREON:　　　　　　　　　　　So,
　　men our age, we're to be lectured, are we? —
　　schooled by a boy his age? 815

HAEMON: Only in what is right. But if I seem young,
    look less to my years and more to what I do.
CREON: Do? Is admiring rebels an achievement?
HAEMON: I'd never suggest that you admire treason.
CREON: Oh? —
    isn't that just the sickness that's attacked her?   820
HAEMON: The whole city of Thebes denies it, to a man.
CREON: And is Thebes about to tell me how to rule?
HAEMON: Now, you see? Who's talking like a child?
CREON: Am I to rule this land for others — or myself?
HAEMON: It's no city at all, owned by one man alone.   825
CREON: What? The city *is* the king's — that's the law!
HAEMON: What a splendid king you'd make of a desert island —
    you and you alone.
CREON:

To the Chorus.

                              This boy, I do believe,
    is fighting on her side, the woman's side.
HAEMON: If you are a woman, yes;   830
    my concern is all for you.
CREON: Why, you degenerate — bandying accusations,
    threatening me with justice, your own father!
HAEMON: I see my father offending justice — wrong.
CREON: Wrong?
    To protect my royal rights?
HAEMON: Protect your rights?   835
    When you trample down the honors of the gods?
CREON: You, you soul of corruption, rotten through —
    woman's accomplice!
HAEMON: That may be,
    but you'll never find me accomplice to a criminal.
CREON: That's what *she* is,   840
    and every word you say is a blatant appeal for her —
HAEMON: And you, and me, and the gods beneath the earth.
CREON: You'll never marry her, not while she's alive.
HAEMON: Then she'll die . . . but her death will kill another.
CREON: What, brazen threats? You go too far!
HAEMON: What threat?   845
    Combating your empty, mindless judgments with a word?
CREON: You'll suffer for your sermons, you and your empty wisdom!
HAEMON: If you weren't my father, I'd say you were insane.
CREON: Don't flatter me with Father — you woman's slave!
HAEMON: You really expect to fling abuse at me   850
    and not receive the same?
CREON: Is that so!

Now, by heaven, I promise you, you'll pay—
taunting, insulting me! Bring her out,
that hateful—she'll die now, here,
in front of his eyes, beside her groom! 855
HAEMON: No, no, she will never die beside me—
don't delude yourself. And you will never
see me, never set eyes on my face again.
Rage your heart out, rage with friends
who can stand the sight of you. 860

Rushing out.

LEADER: Gone, my king, in a burst of anger.
A temper young as his . . . hurt him once,
he may do something violent.
CREON: Let him do—
dream up something desperate, past all human limit!
Good riddance. Rest assured, 865
he'll never save those two young girls from death.
LEADER: Both of them, you really intend to kill them both?
CREON: No, not her, the one whose hands are clean;
you're quite right.
LEADER: But Antigone—
what sort of death do you have in mind for her? 870
CREON: I'll take her down some wild, desolate path
never trod by men, and wall her up alive
in a rocky vault, and set out short rations,
just a gesture of piety
to keep the entire city free of defilement. 875
There let her pray to the one god she worships:
Death—who knows?—may just reprieve her from death.
Or she may learn at last, better late than never,
what a waste of breath it is to worship Death.

Exit to the palace.

CHORUS: Love, never conquered in battle 880
Love the plunderer laying waste the rich!
Love standing the night-watch
                    guarding a girl's soft cheek,
you range the seas, the shepherds' steadings off in the wilds—
not even the deathless gods can flee your onset, 885
nothing human born for a day—
whoever feels your grip is driven mad.
                              Love
you wrench the minds of the righteous into outrage,
swerve them to their ruin—you have ignited this,
this kindred strife, father and son at war 890
                    and Love alone the victor—

warm glance of the bride triumphant, burning with desire!
Throned in power, side-by-side with the mighty laws!
Irresistible Aphrodite,° never conquered—
Love, you mock us for your sport.   895

Antigone is brought from the palace under guard.

But now, even I'd rebel against the king,
I'd break all bounds when I see this—
I fill with tears, can't hold them back,
not any more . . . I see Antigone make her way
to the bridal vault where all are laid to rest.   900
ANTIGONE: Look at me, men of my fatherland,
     setting out on the last road
looking into the last light of day
the last I'll ever see . . .
the god of death who puts us all to bed   905
takes me down to the banks of Acheron° alive—
     denied my part in the wedding-songs,
no wedding-song in the dusk has crowned my marriage—
I go to wed the lord of the dark waters.
CHORUS: Not crowned with glory, crowned with a dirge,   910
     you leave for the deep pit of the dead.
     No withering illness laid you low,
     no strokes of the sword—a law to yourself,
     alone, no mortal like you, ever, you go down
     to the halls of Death alive and breathing.   915
ANTIGONE: But think of Niobe°—well I know her story—
     think what a living death she died,
Tantalus' daughter, stranger queen from the east:
there on the mountain heights, growing stone
binding as ivy, slowly walled her round   920
and the rains will never cease, the legends say
the snows will never leave her . . .
     wasting away, under her brows the tears
showering down her breasting ridge and slopes—
a rocky death like hers puts me to sleep.   925
CHORUS: But she was a god, born of gods,
     and we are only mortals born to die.
     And yet, of course, it's a great thing
     for a dying girl to hear, just hear

---

894 Aphrodite: Goddess of love.   **906 Acheron:** A river in the underworld, to which the dead go.   **916 Niobe:** A queen of Thebes who was punished by the gods for her pride and was turned into stone.

she shares a destiny equal to the gods,   930
during life and later, once she's dead.

ANTIGONE: O you mock me!
Why, in the name of all my fathers' gods
why can't you wait till I am gone —
     must you abuse me to my face?
O my city, all your fine rich sons!   935
And you, you springs of the Dirce,
holy grove of Thebes where the chariots gather,
        you at least, you'll bear me witness, look,
unmourned by friends and forced by such crude laws
I go to my rockbound prison, strange new tomb —   940
     always a stranger, O dear god,
       I have no home on earth and none below,
        not with the living, not with the breathless dead.

CHORUS: You went too far, the last limits of daring —
       smashing against the high throne of Justice!   945
         Your life's in ruins, child — I wonder . . .
       do you pay for your father's terrible ordeal?

ANTIGONE: There — at last you've touched it, the worst pain
     the worst anguish! Raking up the grief for father
       three times over, for all the doom   950
that's struck us down, the brilliant house of Laius.
O mother, your marriage-bed
the coiling horrors, the coupling there —
     you with your own son, my father — doomstruck mother!
Such, such were my parents, and I their wretched child.   955
I go to them now, cursed, unwed, to share their home —
     I am a stranger! O dear brother, doomed
     in your marriage — your marriage murders mine,
       your dying drags me down to death alive!

Enter Creon.

CHORUS: Reverence asks some reverence in return —   960
     but attacks on power never go unchecked,
       not by the man who holds the reins of power.
     Your own blind will, your passion has destroyed you.

ANTIGONE: No one to weep for me, my friends,
     no wedding-song — they take me away   965
     in all my pain . . . the road lies open, waiting.
     Never again, the law forbids me to see
     the sacred eye of day. I am agony!
     No tears for the destiny that's mine,
     no loved one mourns my death.

CREON: Can't you see?   970
If a man could wail his own dirge *before* he dies,
he'd never finish.

To the guards.

                 Take her away, quickly!
Wall her up in the tomb, you have your orders.
Abandon her there, alone, and let her choose —
death or a buried life with a good roof for shelter.   975
As for myself, my hands are clean. This young girl —
dead or alive, she will be stripped of her rights,
her stranger's rights, here in the world above.

ANTIGONE: O tomb, my bridal-bed — my house, my prison
cut in the hollow rock, my everlasting watch!   980
I'll soon be there, soon embrace my own,
the great growing family of our dead
Persephone° has received among her ghosts.
                           I,
the last of them all, the most reviled by far,
go down before my destined time's run out.   985
But still I go, cherishing one good hope:
my arrival may be dear to father,
dear to you, my mother,
dear to you, my loving brother, Eteocles —
When you died I washed you with my hands,   990
I dressed you all, I poured the cups
across your tombs. But now, Polynices,
because I laid your body out as well,
this, this is my reward. Nevertheless
I honored you — the decent will admit it —   995
well and wisely too.
                 Never, I tell you,
if I had been the mother of children
or if my husband died, exposed and rotting —
I'd never have taken this ordeal upon myself,
never defied our people's will. What law,   1000
you ask, do I satisfy with what I say?
A husband dead, there might have been another.
A child by another too, if I had lost the first.
But mother and father both lost in the halls of Death,
no brother could ever spring to light again.   1005

For this law alone I held you first in honor.
For this, Creon, the king, judges me a criminal
guilty of dreadful outrage, my dear brother!
And now he leads me off, a captive in his hands,
with no part in the bridal-song, the bridal-bed,   1010
denied all joy of marriage, raising children —

---

983 Persephone: Queen of the underworld.

deserted so by loved ones, struck by fate,
I descend alive to the caverns of the dead.

What law of the mighty gods have I transgressed?
Why look to the heavens any more, tormented as I am?   1015
Whom to call, what comrades now? Just think,
my reverence only brands me for irreverence!
Very well: if this is the pleasure of the gods,
once I suffer I will know that I was wrong.
But if these men are wrong, let them suffer   1020
nothing worse than they mete out to me —
these masters of injustice!

LEADER: Still the same rough winds, the wild passion
    raging through the girl.

CREON:

To the guards.

                        Take her away.
You're wasting time — you'll pay for it too.   1025

ANTIGONE: Oh god, the voice of death. It's come, it's here.

CREON: True. Not a word of hope — your doom is sealed.

ANTIGONE: Land of Thebes, city of all my fathers —
    O you gods, the first gods of the race!
    They drag me away, now, no more delay.   1030
    Look on me, you noble sons of Thebes —
    the last of a great line of kings,
    I alone, see what I suffer now
    at the hands of what breed of men —
    all for reverence, my reverence for the gods!   1035

She leaves under guard; the Chorus gathers.

CHORUS: Danaë, Danaë° —
    even she endured a fate like yours,
        in all her lovely strength she traded
    the light of day for the bolted brazen vault —
    buried within her tomb, her bridal-chamber,   1040
    wed to the yoke and broken.
        But she was of glorious birth
                   my child, my child
    and treasured the seed of Zeus within her womb,
    the cloudburst streaming gold!   1045
        The power of fate is a wonder,
        dark, terrible wonder —
        neither wealth nor armies

1036 Danaë: Locked in a cell by her father because it was prophesied that her son would kill him, but visited by Zeus in the form of a shower of gold. Their son was Perseus.

      towered walls nor ships
         black hulls lashed by the salt   1050
      can save us from that force.

The yoke tamed him too
         young Lycurgus° flaming in anger
king of Edonia, all for his mad taunts
Dionysus clamped him down, encased   1055
in the chain-mail of rock
      and there his rage
                his terrible flowering rage burst—
sobbing, dying away . . . at last that madman
came to know his god—   1060
         the power he mocked, the power
         he taunted in all his frenzy
         trying to stamp out
         the women strong with the god—
         the torch, the raving sacred cries—   1065
         enraging the Muses° who adore the flute.

And far north where the Black Rocks
         cut the sea in half
and murderous straits
split the coast of Thrace   1070
         a forbidding city stands
where once, hard by the walls
the savage Ares thrilled to watch
a king's new queen, a Fury rearing in rage
         against his two royal sons—   1075
         her bloody hands, her dagger-shuttle
stabbing out their eyes—cursed, blinding wounds—
their eyes blind sockets screaming for revenge!

They wailed in agony, cries echoing cries
         the princes doomed at birth . . .   1080
and their mother doomed to chains,
walled off in a tomb of stone—
         but she traced her own birth back
to a proud Athenian line and the high gods
and off in caverns half the world away,   1085
born of the wild North Wind
         she sprang on her father's gales,
           racing stallions up the leaping cliffs—
child of the heavens. But even on her the Fates

1053 Lycurgus: Punished by Dionysus because he would not worship him.   **1066 Muses:** Goddesses of the arts.

the gray everlasting Fates rode hard 　　　　　　　　　　　1090
　　my child, my child.

Enter Tiresias, the blind prophet, led by a boy.

TIRESIAS:　　　　　　　　Lords of Thebes,
　　I and the boy have come together,
　　hand in hand. Two see with the eyes of one . . .
　　so the blind must go, with a guide to lead the way.
CREON:　What is it, old Tiresias? What news now? 　　　　　1095
TIRESIAS:　I will teach you. And you obey the seer.
CREON:　　　　　　　　　　　　　　　　I will,
　　I've never wavered from your advice before.
TIRESIAS:　And so you kept the city straight on course.
CREON:　I owe you a great deal, I swear to that.
TIRESIAS:　　Then reflect, my son: you are poised, 　　　　　1100
　　once more, on the razor-edge of fate.
CREON:　What is it? I shudder to hear you.
TIRESIAS:　　　　　　　　　　　　You will learn
　　when you listen to the warnings of my craft.
　　As I sat on the ancient seat of augury,°
　　in the sanctuary where every bird I know 　　　　　　　　1105
　　will hover at my hands—suddenly I heard it,
　　a strange voice in the wingbeats, unintelligible,
　　barbaric, a mad scream! Talons flashing, ripping,
　　they were killing each other—that much I knew—
　　the murderous fury whirring in those wings 　　　　　　　1110
　　made that much clear!
　　　　　　　　　　　I was afraid,
　　I turned quickly, tested the burnt-sacrifice,
　　ignited the altar at all points—but no fire,
　　the god in the fire never blazed.
　　Not from those offerings . . . over the embers 　　　　　　1115
　　slid a heavy ooze from the long thighbones,
　　smoking, sputtering out, and the bladder
　　puffed and burst—spraying gall into the air—
　　and the fat wrapping the bones slithered off
　　and left them glistening white. No fire! 　　　　　　　　1120
　　The rites failed that might have blazed the future
　　with a sign. So I learned from the boy here;
　　he is my guide, as I am guide to others.
　　　　　　　　　　　　And it's you—
　　your high resolve that sets this plague on Thebes.
　　The public altars and sacred hearths are fouled, 　　　　　1125

1104 seat of augury: Where Tiresias looked for omens among birds.

one and all, by the birds and dogs with carrion
torn from the corpse, the doomstruck son of Oedipus!
And so the gods are deaf to our prayers, they spurn
the offerings in our hands, the flame of holy flesh.
No birds cry out an omen clear and true —   1130
they're gorged with the murdered victim's blood and fat.
Take these things to heart, my son, I warn you.
All men make mistakes, it is only human.
But once the wrong is done, a man
can turn his back on folly, misfortune too,   1135
if he tries to make amends, however low he's fallen,
and stops his bullnecked ways. Stubbornness
brands you for stupidity — pride is a crime.
No, yield to the dead!
Never stab the fighter when he's down.   1140
Where's the glory, killing the dead twice over?

I mean you well. I give you sound advice.
It's best to learn from a good adviser
when he speaks for your own good:
it's pure gain.

CREON: Old man — all of you! So,   1145
you shoot your arrows at my head like archers at the target —
I even have *him* loosed on me, this fortune-teller.
Oh his ilk has tried to sell me short
and ship me off for years. Well,
drive your bargains, traffic — much as you like —   1150
in the gold of India, silver-gold of Sardis.
You'll never bury that body in the grave,
not even if Zeus's eagles rip the corpse
and wing their rotten pickings off to the throne of god!
Never, not even in fear of such defilement   1155
will I tolerate his burial, that traitor.
Well I know, we can't defile the gods —
no mortal has the power.
                        No,
reverend old Tiresias, all men fall,
it's only human, but the wisest fall obscenely   1160
when they glorify obscene advice with rhetoric —
all for their own gain.

TIRESIAS: Oh god, is there a man alive
who knows, who actually believes . . .

CREON: What now?
What earth-shattering truth are you about to utter?   1165

TIRESIAS: . . . just how much a sense of judgment, wisdom
is the greatest gift we have?

CREON: Just as much, I'd say,
    as a twisted mind is the worst affliction going.
TIRESIAS: You are the one who's sick, Creon, sick to death.
CREON: I am in no mood to trade insults with a seer.   1170
TIRESIAS: You have already, calling my prophecies a lie.
CREON: Why not?
    You and the whole breed of seers are mad for money!
TIRESIAS: And the whole race of tyrants lusts to rake it in.
CREON: This slander of yours —
    are you aware you're speaking to the king?   1175
TIRESIAS: Well aware. Who helped you save the city?
CREON: You —
    you have your skills, old seer, but you lust for injustice!
TIRESIAS: You will drive me to utter the dreadful secret in my heart.
CREON: Spit it out! Just don't speak it out for profit.
TIRESIAS: Profit? No, not a bit of profit, not for you.   1180
CREON: Know full well, you'll never buy off my resolve.
TIRESIAS: Then know this too, learn this by heart!
    The chariot of the sun will not race through
    so many circuits more, before you have surrendered
    one born of your own loins, your own flesh and blood,   1185
    a corpse for corpses given in return, since you have thrust
    to the world below a child sprung for the world above,
    ruthlessly lodged a living soul within the grave —
    then you've robbed the gods below the earth,
    keeping a dead body here in the bright air,   1190
    unburied, unsung, unhallowed by the rites.

    You, you have no business with the dead,
    nor do the gods above — this is violence
    you have forced upon the heavens.
    And so the avengers, the dark destroyers late   1195
    but true to the mark, now lie in wait for you,
    the Furies sent by the gods and the god of death
    to strike you down with the pains that you perfected!

    There. Reflect on that, tell me I've been bribed.
    The day comes soon, no long test of time, not now,   1200
    that wakes the wails for men and women in your halls.
    Great hatred rises against you —
    cities in tumult, all whose mutilated sons
    the dogs have graced with burial, or the wild beasts,
    some wheeling crow that wings the ungodly stench of carrion   1205
    back to each city, each warrior's hearth and home.

    These arrows for your heart! Since you've raked me
    I loose them like an archer in my anger,

arrows deadly true. You'll never escape
their burning, searing force.   1210

Motioning to his escort.

Come, boy, take me home.
So he can vent his rage on younger men,
and learn to keep a gentler tongue in his head
and better sense than what he carries now.

Exit to the side.

LEADER: The old man's gone, my king—   1215
terrible prophecies. Well I know,
since the hair on this old head went gray,
he's never lied to Thebes.
CREON: I know it myself—I'm shaken, torn.
It's a dreadful thing to yield . . . but resist now?   1220
Lay my pride bare to the blows of ruin?
That's dreadful too.
LEADER: But good advice,
Creon, take it now, you must.
CREON: What should I do? Tell me . . . I'll obey.
LEADER: Go! Free the girl from the rocky vault   1225
and raise a mound for the body you exposed.
CREON: That's your advice? You think I should give in?
LEADER: Yes, my king, quickly. Disasters sent by the gods
cut short our follies in a flash.
CREON: Oh it's hard.
giving up the heart's desire . . . but I will do it—   1230
no more fighting a losing battle with necessity.
LEADER: Do it now, go, don't leave it to others.
CREON: Now—I'm on my way! Come, each of you,
take up axes, make for the high ground,
over there, quickly! I and my better judgment   1235
have come round to this—I shackled her,
I'll set her free myself. I am afraid . . .
it's best to keep the established laws
to the very day we die.

Rushing out, followed by his entourage. The Chorus clusters around the altar.

CHORUS: God of a hundred names!
                          Great Dionysus—   1240
          Son and glory of Semele! Pride of Thebes—
Child of Zeus whose thunder rocks the clouds—
Lord of the famous lands of evening—
King of the Mysteries!
                          King of Eleusis, Demeter's plain°

1244 Demeter's plain: The goddess of grain was worshiped at Eleusis, near Athens.

her breasting hills that welcome in the world —   1245
Great Dionysus!
             Bacchus,° living in Thebes
the mother-city of all your frenzied women —
                             Bacchus
          living along the Ismenus'° rippling waters
standing over the field sown with the Dragon's teeth!

You — we have seen you through the flaring smoky fires,   1250
      your torches blazing over the twin peaks
where nymphs of the hallowed cave climb onward
               fired with you, your sacred rage —
we have seen you at Castalia's running spring°
and down from the heights of Nysa° crowned with ivy   1255
the greening shore rioting vines and grapes
        down you come in your storm of wild women
             ecstatic, mystic cries —
                   Dionysus —
down to watch and ward the roads of Thebes!

First of all cities, Thebes you honor first   1260
you and your mother, bride of the lightning —
come, Dionysus! now your people lie
in the iron grip of plague,
come in your racing, healing stride
             down Parnassus'° slopes   1265
or across the moaning straits.
              Lord of the dancing —
dance, dance the constellations breathing fire!
Great master of the voices of the night!
Child of Zeus, God's offspring, come, come forth!
Lord, king, dance with your nymphs, swirling, raving   1270
arm-in-arm in frenzy through the night
      they dance you, Iacchus° —
                Dance, Dionysus
giver of all good things!

Enter a Messenger from the side.

MESSENGER: Neighbors,
friends of the house of Cadmus° and the kings,
there's not a thing in this life of ours   1275

1246 Bacchus: Another name for Dionysus.   **1248 Ismenus:** A river near Thebes where the founders of the city were said to have sprung from a dragon's teeth.   **1254 Castalia's running spring:** The sacred spring of Apollo's oracle at Delphi.   **1255 Nysa:** A mountain where Dionysus was worshiped.   **1265 Parnassus:** A mountain in Greece that was sacred to Dionysus as well as other gods and goddesses.   **1272 Iacchus:** Dionysus.   **1274 Cadmus:** The legendary founder of Thebes.

I'd praise or blame as settled once for all.
Fortune lifts and Fortune fells the lucky
and unlucky every day. No prophet on earth
can tell a man his fate. Take Creon:
there was a man to rouse your envy once,   1280
as I see it. He saved the realm from enemies;
taking power, he alone, the lord of the fatherland,
he set us true on course — flourished like a tree
with the noble line of sons he bred and reared . . .
and now it's lost, all gone.
                    Believe me,   1285
when a man has squandered his true joys,
he's good as dead, I tell you, a living corpse.
Pile up riches in your house, as much as you like —
live like a king with a huge show of pomp,
but if real delight is missing from the lot,   1290
I wouldn't give you a wisp of smoke for it,
not compared with joy.
LEADER: What now?
What new grief do you bring the house of kings?
MESSENGER: Dead, dead — and the living are guilty of their death!
LEADER: Who's the murderer? Who is dead? Tell us.   1295
MESSENGER: Haemon's gone, his blood spilled by the very hand —
LEADER: His father's or his own?
MESSENGER: His own . . .
raging mad with his father for the death —
LEADER: Oh great seer,
you saw it all, you brought your word to birth!
MESSENGER: Those are the facts. Deal with them as you will.   1300

As he turns to go, Eurydice enters from the palace.

LEADER: Look, Eurydice. Poor woman, Creon's wife,
so close at hand. By chance perhaps,
unless she's heard the news about her son.
EURYDICE: My countrymen,
all of you — I caught the sound of your words
as I was leaving to do my part,   1305
to appeal to queen Athena° with my prayers.
I was just loosing the bolts, opening the doors,
when a voice filled with sorrow, family sorrow,
struck my ears, and I fell back, terrified,
into the women's arms — everything went black.   1310
Tell me the news, again, whatever it is . . .
sorrow and I are hardly strangers;
I can bear the worst.

1306 **Athena:** Goddess of wisdom and protector of Greek cities.

MESSENGER: I—dear lady,
  I'll speak as an eye-witness. I was there.
  And I won't pass over one word of the truth.   1315
  Why should I try to soothe you with a story,
  only to prove a liar in a moment?
  Truth is always best.
                So,
  I escorted your lord, I guided him
  to the edge of the plain where the body lay,   1320
  Polynices, torn by the dogs and still unmourned.
  And saying a prayer to Hecate of the Crossroads,
  Pluto° too, to hold their anger and be kind,
  we washed the dead in a bath of holy water
  and plucking some fresh branches, gathering . . .   1325
  what was left of him, we burned them all together
  and raised a high mound of native earth, and then
  we turned and made for that rocky vault of hers,
  the hollow, empty bed of the bride of Death.
  And far off, one of us heard a voice,   1330
  a long wail rising, echoing
  out of that unhallowed wedding-chamber;
  he ran to alert the master and Creon pressed on,
  closer—the strange, inscrutable cry came sharper,
  throbbing around him now, and he let loose   1335
  a cry of his own, enough to wrench the heart,
  "Oh god, am I the prophet now? going down
  the darkest road I've ever gone? My son—
  it's *his* dear voice, he greets me! Go, men,
  closer, quickly! Go through the gap,   1340
  the rocks are dragged back—
  right to the tomb's very mouth—and look,
  see if it's Haemon's voice I think I hear,
  or the gods have robbed me of my senses."

  The king was shattered. We took his orders,   1345
  went and searched, and there in the deepest,
  dark recesses of the tomb we found her . . .
  hanged by the neck in a fine linen noose,
  strangled in her veils—and the boy,
  his arms flung around her waist,   1350
  clinging to her, wailing for his bride,
  dead and down below, for his father's crimes
  and the bed of his marriage blighted by misfortune.
  When Creon saw him, he gave a deep sob,

1322–1323 **Hecate, Pluto:** Gods of the underworld.

he ran in, shouting, crying out to him,   1355
"Oh my child—what have you done? what seized you,
what insanity? what disaster drove you mad?
Come out, my son! I beg you on my knees!"
But the boy gave him a wild burning glance,
spat in his face, not a word in reply,   1360
he drew his sword—his father rushed out,
running as Haemon lunged and missed!—
and then, doomed, desperate with himself,
suddenly leaning his full weight on the blade,
he buried it in his body, halfway to the hilt.   1365
And still in his senses, pouring his arms around her,
he embraced the girl and breathing hard,
released a quick rush of blood,
bright red on her cheek glistening white.
And there he lies, body enfolding body . . .   1370
he has won his bride at last, poor boy,
not here but in the houses of the dead.

Creon shows the world that of all the ills
afflicting men the worst is lack of judgment.

Eurydice turns and reenters the palace.

LEADER: What do you make of that? The lady's gone,   1375
without a word, good or bad.
MESSENGER: I'm alarmed too
but here's my hope—faced with her son's death,
she finds it unbecoming to mourn in public.
Inside, under her roof, she'll set her women
to the task and wail the sorrow of the house.   1380
She's too discreet. She won't do something rash.
LEADER: I'm not so sure. To me, at least,
a long heavy silence promises danger,
just as much as a lot of empty outcries.
MESSENGER: We'll see if she's holding something back,   1385
hiding some passion in her heart.
I'm going in. You may be right—who knows?
Even too much silence has its dangers.

Exit to the palace. Enter Creon from the side, escorted by attendants carrying Haemon's body on a bier.

LEADER: The king himself! Coming toward us,
look, holding the boy's head in his hands.   1390
Clear, damning proof, if it's right to say so—
proof of his own madness, no one else's,
no, his own blind wrongs.
CREON: Ohhh,
so senseless, so insane . . . my crimes,

my stubborn, deadly— 1395
Look at us, the killer, the killed,
father and son, the same blood—the misery!
My plans, my mad fanatic heart,
my son, cut off so young!
Ai, dead, lost to the world, 1400
not through your stupidity, no, my own.

LEADER: Too late,
too late, you see what justice means.

CREON: Oh I've learned
through blood and tears! Then, it was then,
when the god came down and struck me—a great weight
shattering, driving me down that wild savage path, 1405
ruining, trampling down my joy. Oh the agony,
the heartbreaking agonies of our lives.

Enter the Messenger from the palace.

MESSENGER: Master,
what a hoard of grief you have, and you'll have more.
The grief that lies to hand you've brought yourself—

Pointing to Haemon's body.

the rest, in the house, you'll see it all too soon. 1410

CREON: What now? What's worse than this?

MESSENGER: The queen is dead.
The mother of this dead boy . . . mother to the end—
poor thing, her wounds are fresh.

CREON: No, no,
harbor of Death, so choked, so hard to cleanse!—
why me? why are you killing me? 1415
Herald of pain, more words, more grief?
I died once, you kill me again and again!
What's the report, boy . . . some news for me?
My wife dead? O dear god!
Slaughter heaped on slaughter?

The doors open; the body of Eurydice is brought out on her bier.

MESSENGER: See for yourself: 1420
now they bring her body from the palace.

CREON: Oh no,
another, a second loss to break the heart.
What next, what fate still waits for me?
I just held my son in my arms and now,
look, a new corpse rising before my eyes— 1425
wretched, helpless mother—O my son!

MESSENGER: She stabbed herself at the altar,
then her eyes went dark, after she'd raised

a cry for the noble fate of Megareus,° the hero
killed in the first assault, then for Haemon,   1430
then with her dying breath she called down
torments on your head—you killed her sons.
CREON: Oh the dread,
     I shudder with dread! Why not kill me too?—
     run me through with a good sharp sword?
     Oh god, the misery, anguish—   1435
     I, I'm churning with it, going under.
MESSENGER: Yes, and the dead, the woman lying there,
     piles the guilt of all their deaths on you.
CREON: How did she end her life, what bloody stroke?
MESSENGER: She drove home to the heart with her own hand,   1440
     once she learned her son was dead . . . that agony.
CREON: And the guilt is all mine—
          can never be fixed on another man,
          no escape for me. I killed you,
          I, god help me, I admit it all!   1445

To his attendants.

          Take me away, quickly, out of sight.
          I don't even exist—I'm no one. Nothing.
LEADER: Good advice, if there's any good in suffering.
     Quickest is best when troubles block the way.
CREON:

Kneeling in prayer.

          Come, let it come!—that best of fates for me   1450
          that brings the final day, best fate of all.
          Oh quickly, now—
          so I never have to see another sunrise.
LEADER: That will come when it comes;
     we must deal with all that lies before us.   1455
     The future rests with the ones who tend the future.
CREON: That prayer—I poured my heart into that prayer!
LEADER: No more prayers now. For mortal men
     there is no escape from the doom we must endure.
CREON: Take me away, I beg you, out of sight.   1460
          A rash, indiscriminate fool!
          I murdered you, my son, against my will—
          you too, my wife . . .
                              Wailing wreck of a man,
          whom to look to? where to lean for support?

1429 **Megareus:** A son of Creon and Eurydice; he died when Thebes was attacked.

Desperately turning from Haemon to Eurydice on their biers.

CREON: Whatever I touch goes wrong—once more   1465
a crushing fate's come down upon my head.

The Messenger and attendants lead Creon into the palace.

CHORUS: Wisdom is by far the greatest part of joy,
and reverence toward the gods must be safeguarded.
The mighty words of the proud are paid in full
with mighty blows of fate, and at long last   1470
those blows will teach us wisdom.

The old citizens exit to the side.   [c. 441 B.C.E.]

THINKING ABOUT THE TEXT

1. Describe Antigone with at least three adjectives of your own. How much
do you sympathize with her? Do you consider her morally superior to
Creon? Identify specific things that influence your view of her. Do
your feelings about her shift during the course of the play? If so, when
and how?

2. Do you feel any sympathy for Creon? For Ismene? Explain your reasoning. What values seem to be in conflict as Antigone argues with each?

3. Where, if anywhere, do you see the chorus as expressing wisdom? Where,
if anywhere, does the chorus strike you as imperfect people?

4. Here is an issue of genre: Ever since the ancient Greek philosopher Aristotle analyzed tragedy in his *Poetics*, a common definition of this kind of
play is that its central character has a fatal flaw. How well does this definition fit *Antigone*? Must it be altered to accommodate Sophocles' play?
Explain. Here is another issue of genre: In the *Poetics* Aristotle also
argued that a tragedy ends in *katharsis*. After arousing pity and fear in the
audience, it relieves the audience of these feelings. How well does Aristotle's observation apply in the case of *Antigone*?

5. As was customary in Greek tragedy, the violent events in this play occur
offstage and are merely reported. Had they occurred onstage, how might
the audience's reaction have been different? Today, many films and television shows directly confront their audience with violence. Do you prefer this directness to Greek tragedy's way of dealing with violence?
Support your answer by comparing some contemporary presentations of
violence with *Antigone*'s.

BERNARD KNOX

From *The Heroic Temper*

Bernard Knox (b. 1914) is regarded as one of the foremost contemporary scholars of classical literature. The following piece is excerpted from his influential 1964 book The Heroic Temper: Studies in Sophoclean Tragedy. *When he refers to the* polis, *Knox is using the ancient Greek term for a city-state such as Thebes and Athens.*

In both Creon and Antigone the deepest motive for action is individual, particular, inexplicable in any other terms than personal, a passionate, almost irrational impulse. But they have both appealed to greater sanctions, to conflicting institutions and gods. The questions they have raised bulk large in the play, and they must somehow be answered. The answers, such as they are (for this is a play, not a philosophical dialogue), are given to us in the concluding scenes, in what happens to Antigone and Creon.

Creon, to enforce what he considers the good of the *polis*, has defied in action and denied in speech the obligations imposed by membership in the family. Not only has he exposed the corpse of a nephew, condemned a niece to death, and broken the marriage of a son, he has also shown, in many of his speeches, a clear consciousness of what he is doing. His rejection of the claims of the family is deliberate. When disaster comes on him so suddenly, it is precisely in this sphere that the hammer blows strike in swift succession: his own family turns against him in violence and hatred. . . .

But this is not all. Creon cannot even claim, in the end, that what he did was for the best interests of the *polis*. He has turned into a tyrant prepared to impose his own will, right or wrong, on the city he considers his own property; and that will is clearly exposed as contrary to the interests of the *polis*. . . .

The gods too turn away from him. His belated amends made to the gods of death are ignored; Hades has already, through the suicide of Antigone, ensured Creon's punishment. The gods above, whose champion he once claimed to be, repudiate him, as Tiresias comes to tell him. He was wrong, wrong from the start; he does not even have the cold comfort of heroic obstinacy to sustain him. He broke, and tried to make amends, but failed to escape the consequences of his actions. . . .

And Antigone? She was the champion of the family against the *polis*, and though in her last clear vision of her action she realized that she was devoted not to the family as a theoretical principle but simply to her own existing relatives (for so she thinks of them, dead though they are), she can take comfort in the result. She is rightly confident of the gratitude of those beloved dead she goes to join. And even the last living representative of the family, the sister she rejects, shows such love for her that she tries to share her death. The family does not repudiate Antigone, as the *polis*, in the person of Haemon and later of the chorus, repudiates Creon.

5

But she has defied the *polis.* In the particular issue on which she defied it she was right, as the last scenes of the play make clear; the exposure of the corpse of Polynices is *not* in the interest of the *polis.* But, as Sophocles so repeatedly emphasizes in everything Antigone says, her attitude is not that higher, enlightened loyalty to the *polis* which pursues the best policy rather than the immediately expedient; it is an attitude which ignores the interests of the *polis* completely. The fact that she is right about what is best for Thebes is merely accidental; it is all too clear that if the exposure of the corpse of her brother *had* been expedient for the *polis,* she would have buried him just the same. She completely ignores the obligations which membership in the *polis* imposes, and even though Creon, their self-appointed spokesman, is wrong in the demand he makes, those obligations exist and no one in the audience for whom the play was written would have denied their force or sympathized with Antigone's refusal to reckon with them. . . .

But, as always in Sophocles, we are made to feel that the gods recognize the hero's greatness. In Antigone there is something else to recommend her to them, as to us, something not always associated with the heroic temper. Creon's deepest motive for his action was hatred — hatred for the traitor Polynices and for the girl who defied his power. But Antigone's was love. In the last speech where she greets her dead mother, father, and brothers this love is revealed as the source of her heroic strength, the true justification of her action; unlike Creon's hatred, it does not fail her in the testing time but sustains her to the end.   [1964]

MARTHA NUSSBAUM

From *The Fragility of Goodness*

At present, Martha Nussbaum (b. 1947) teaches in the University of Chicago School of Law. Although trained as a philosopher, she often writes about literature, tracing the ways it dramatizes moral conflict. The following passages are excerpted from her 1986 book The Fragility of Goodness, *a study of ethical issues in classical philosophy and literature.*

Creon's strategy of simplification led him to regard others as material for his aggressive exploitation. Antigone's dutiful subservience to the dead leads to an equally strange, though different (and certainly less hideous) result. Her relation to others in the world above is characterized by an odd coldness. "You are alive," she tells her sister, "but my life (*psuche*) is long since dead, to the end of serving the dead." The safely dutiful human life requires, or is, life's annihilation. Creon's attitude towards others is like necrophilia: he aspires to possess the inert and unresisting. Antigone's subservience to duty is, finally, the ambition to be a *nekros,* a corpse beloved of corpses. (Her apparent similarity to martyrs in our own tradition, who expect a fully active life after death, should not conceal from us the strangeness of this goal.) In the world below, there are no risks of failure or wrongdoing.

Neither Creon nor Antigone, then, is a loving or passionate being in anything like the usual sense. Not one of the gods, not one human being escapes the power of *eros*, says the Chorus; but these two oddly inhuman beings do, it appears, escape. Creon sees loved persons as functions of the civic good, replaceable producers of citizens. For Antigone, they are either dead, fellow servants of the dead, or objects of complete indifference. No living being is loved for his or her personal qualities, loved with the sort of love that Haemon feels and Ismene praises. By altering their beliefs about the nature and value of persons, they have, it seems, altered or restructured the human passions themselves. They achieve harmony in this way; but at a cost. The Chorus speaks of *eros* as a force as important and obligating as the ancient *thesmoi* or laws of right, a force against which it is both foolish and, apparently, blameworthy to rebel.

Antigone learns too — like Creon, by being forced to recognize a problem that lies at the heart of her single-minded concern. Creon saw that the city itself is pious and loving; that he could not be its champion without valuing what it values, in all its complexity. Antigone comes to see that the service of the dead requires the city, that her own religious aims cannot be fulfilled without civic institutions. By being her own law, she has not only ignored a part of piety, she has also jeopardized the fulfillment of the very pious duties to which she is so attached. Cut off from friends, from the possibility of having children, she cannot keep herself alive in order to do further service to the dead; nor can she guarantee the pious treatment of her own corpse. In her last speeches she laments not so much the fact of imminent death as, repeatedly, her isolation from the continuity of offspring, from friends and mourners. She emphasizes the fact that she will never marry; she will remain childless. Acheron will be her husband, the tomb her bridal chamber. Unless she can successfully appeal to the citizens whose needs as citizens she had refused to consider, she will die without anyone to mourn her death or to replace her as guardian of her family religion.

We have, then, two narrowly limited practical worlds, two strategies of avoidance and simplification. In one, a single human value has become *the* final end; in the other, a single set of duties has eclipsed all others. But we can now acknowledge that we admire Antigone, nonetheless, in a way that we do not admire Creon. It seems important to look for the basis of this difference.

First, in the world of the play, it seems clear that Antigone's actual choice is   5
preferable to Creon's. The dishonour to civic values involved in giving pious burial to an enemy's corpse is far less radical than the violation of religion involved in Creon's act. Antigone shows a deeper understanding of the community and its values than Creon does when she argues that the obligation to bury the dead is an unwritten law, which cannot be set aside by the decree of a particular ruler. The belief that not all values are utility-relative, that there are certain claims whose neglect will prove deeply destructive of communal attunement and individual character, is a part of Antigone's position left untouched by the play's implicit criticism of her single-mindedness.

Furthermore, Antigone's pursuit of virtue is her own. It involves nobody else and commits her to abusing no other person. Rulership must be rulership *of* something; Antigone's pious actions are executed alone, out of a solitary commitment, she may be strangely remote from the world; but she does no violence to it.

Finally, and perhaps most important, Antigone remains ready to risk and to sacrifice her ends in a way that is not possible for Creon, given the singleness of his conception of value. There is a complexity in Antigone's virtue that permits genuine sacrifice *within* the defense of piety. She dies recanting nothing; but still she is torn by a conflict. . . . This vulnerability in virtue, this ability to acknowledge the world of nature by mourning the constraints that it imposes on virtue, surely contributes to making her the more humanly rational and the richer of the two protagonists: both active and receptive, neither exploiter nor simply victim.   [1986]

CHARLES SEGAL
From *Interpreting Greek Tragedy*

A veteran teacher of classics and comparative literature at Brown University, Charles Segal (b. 1936) has written many books about ancient Greek and Roman works. The following remarks about Creon and Antigone are excerpted from his 1986 book Interpreting Greek Tragedy: Myth, Poetry, Text.

It is . . . among the tragic paradoxes of Antigone's position that she who accepts the absolutes of death has a far fuller sense of the complexities of life. Creon, who lacks a true reverence for the gods, the powers beyond human life, also lacks a deep awareness of the complexities within the human realm. Hence he tends to see the world in terms of harshly opposed categories, right and wrong, reason and folly, youth and age, male and female. . . .

All these categories imply the relation of superior and inferior, stronger and weaker. This highly structured and aggressive view of the world Creon expresses perhaps most strikingly in repeatedly formulating the conflicts between Antigone and himself in terms of the woman trying to conquer the man. . . . He sees in Antigone a challenge to his whole way of living and his basic attitudes toward the world. And of course he is right, for Antigone's full acceptance of her womanly nature, her absolute valuation of the bonds of blood and affection, is a total denial of Creon's obsessively masculine rationality.

Antigone's acceptance of this womanly obligation stands out the more by contrast with Ismene's rejection of it. . . . Ismene feels her womanhood as something negative, as a weakness. Antigone finds in it a source of strength. Ismene capitulates to Creon's view; Antigone resists and finds in her nature a potent heroism that cuts across Creon's dichotomizing of things and has its echoes even after her death in the equally womanly, though less significant, death of Eurydice.

[1986]

MAKING COMPARISONS

1. Both Knox and Nussbaum compare Antigone with Creon. What similarities and differences do they note?

2. Knox celebrates Antigone's capacity to love, whereas Nussbaum finds in her "an odd coldness." Do you agree with one of these scholars more than the other? Why, or why not?

3. Segal contrasts Antigone's "full acceptance of her womanly nature" with Creon's "obsessively masculine rationality." How comfortable are you with Segal's references to gender? Do they strike you as applicable to Sophocles' play? Would you apply Segal's phrases to any people today? If so, whom?

WRITING ABOUT ISSUES

1. Write an essay analyzing a character in Sophocles' play *other* than Antigone or Creon: examples include the chorus (which you can treat as one character), Ismene, Haemon, Tiresias, and Eurydice. Concentrate on explaining the relation between your chosen character and an issue important in the play. (Remember that it's useful to phrase an issue as a question with more than one possible answer.)

2. Imagine that as director of a contemporary production of *Antigone* you make your cast read two of the critical commentaries in this cluster. Write an essay identifying which two you would choose, why you would choose them, how you would contextualize them for your cast, and how you would like the cast to react to them. Keep in mind that you could point out to the cast remarks in your chosen commentaries that you disagree with, as well as remarks you like. If you wish, write your essay to the cast and imagine that they would read it along with the commentaries you have selected.

3. Imagine that a group of producers has invited you to stage a production of *Antigone*, under one condition: that the production be in an area of the world where audiences are apt to find the play's issues relevant. You decide to accept this condition. Write a letter to the producers stating where you will stage the play and why you think audiences there will relate to it. If you wish, also identify how you will stage the play so that those audiences will be even more drawn to it.

4. Choose a real-life case of civil disobedience, past or present, and read at least three articles about it. Write an essay in which you present basic facts of the case, argue for or against the civil disobedience involved, and support your argument. If you wish, compare the case with *Antigone*.

JUDGING SANITY: CULTURAL CONTEXTS FOR CHARLOTTE PERKINS GILMAN'S "THE YELLOW WALLPAPER"

CHARLOTTE PERKINS GILMAN, "The Yellow Wallpaper"

CULTURAL CONTEXTS:
CHARLOTTE PERKINS GILMAN, "Why I Wrote 'The Yellow Wallpaper'"
S. WEIR MITCHELL, From "The Evolution of the Rest Treatment"
JOHN HARVEY KELLOGG, From *The Ladies' Guide in Health and Disease*

When doctors make a medical or psychiatric diagnosis, often they do not simply pinpoint their patient's condition, but also they accept or reject their society's definition of *health.* The social context of diagnoses seems especially worth considering when a particular condition afflicts one gender much more than the other. Today, many more women than men appear to suffer from depression, anorexia, bulimia, and multiple personality disorder. Why? Perhaps traditional female roles encourage these illnesses; perhaps gender bias affects how doctors label and treat them. Charlotte Perkins Gilman raised both these possibilities in her 1892 short story "The Yellow Wallpaper." In her own life, Gilman suffered what we now call postpartum depression after the birth of her daughter. Subsequently Gilman was ordered by her doctor, the well-known S. Weir Mitchell, to undergo a "rest cure" in which she did no work. For Gilman, the cure proved worse than the disease, and through "The Yellow Wallpaper" she suggested that women found to be mentally ill may actually be rebelling against patriarchal constraints. Besides Gilman's story, we include her account of why she wrote it, an excerpt from a lecture by Mitchell about his cure, and some advice about motherhood from John Kellogg, another influential doctor of the time.

BEFORE YOU READ

How is mental illness depicted in particular movies and television shows you have seen? Which representations of mental illness have you appreciated the most? Which have you especially disliked? State your criteria for these judgments.

CHARLOTTE PERKINS GILMAN
The Yellow Wallpaper

Charlotte Perkins Gilman (1860–1935) was a major activist and theorist within America's first wave of feminism. During her lifetime, she was chiefly known for her 1898 book Women and Economics. *In it she argued that women should not be confined to the household and made economically dependent on men. Gilman also advanced such ideas through her many public speaking appearances and her magazine* The Forerunner, *which she edited from 1909 to 1916. Gilman wrote many articles and works of fiction for* The Forerunner, *including a tale called* Herland *(1915) in which she envisioned an all-female utopia. Today, however, Gilman is best known for her short story "The Yellow Wallpaper," which she published first in an 1892 issue of the* New England Magazine. *The story is based on Gilman's struggle with depression right after the birth of her daughter Katharine in 1885. Seeking help for emotional turmoil then, Gilman had gone to the eminent neurologist Silas Weir Mitchell, who prescribed his famous "rest cure." This treatment, which forbade Gilman to work, actually worsened her distress. She improved only after she moved to California, divorced her husband, let him raise Katharine with his new wife, married someone else, and plunged fully into a literary and political career. As Gilman noted in her posthumously published autobiography,* The Living of Charlotte Perkins Gilman *(1935), she never fully recovered from the debilitation that had led her to Dr. Mitchell, but she did manage to be enormously productive after leaving him. Although "The Yellow Wallpaper" is a work of fiction rather than a factual account of her experience with Mitchell, obviously Gilman used the story to criticize his patriarchal approach as well as the efforts of society at large to keep women passive.*

It is very seldom that mere ordinary people like John and myself secure ancestral halls for the summer.

A colonial mansion, a hereditary estate, I would say a haunted house and reach the height of romantic felicity—but that would be asking too much of fate!

Still I will proudly declare that there is something queer about it.

Else, why should it be let so cheaply? And why have stood so long untenanted?

John laughs at me, of course, but one expects that in marriage.   5

John is practical in the extreme. He has no patience with faith, an intense horror of superstition, and he scoffs openly at any talk of things not to be felt and seen and put down in figures.

John is a physician, and *perhaps*—(I would not say it to a living soul, of course, but this is dead paper and a great relief to my mind)—*perhaps* that is one reason I do not get well faster.

You see, he does not believe I am sick!

And what can one do?

If a physician of high standing, and one's own husband, assures friends and   10
relatives that there is really nothing the matter with one but temporary nervous depression—a slight hysterical tendency—what is one to do?

My brother is also a physician, and also of high standing, and he says the same thing.

So I take phosphates or phosphites—whichever it is, and tonics, and journeys, and air, and exercise, and am absolutely forbidden to "work" until I am well again.

Personally, I disagree with their ideas.

Personally, I believe that congenial work, with excitement and change, would do me good.

But what is one to do? 15

I did write for a while in spite of them; but it *does* exhaust me a good deal — having to be so sly about it, or else meet with heavy opposition.

I sometimes fancy that in my condition if I had less opposition and more society and stimulus — but John says the very worst thing I can do is to think about my condition, and I confess it always makes me feel bad.

So I will let it alone and talk about the house.

The most beautiful place! It is quite alone, standing well back from the road, quite three miles from the village. It makes me think of English places that you read about, for there are hedges and walls and gates that lock, and lots of separate little houses for the gardeners and people.

There is a *delicious* garden! I never saw such a garden — large and shady, full 20 of box-bordered paths, and lined with long grape-covered arbors with seats under them.

There were greenhouses, too, but they are all broken now.

There was some legal trouble, I believe, something about the heirs and co-heirs; anyhow, the place has been empty for years.

That spoils my ghostliness, I am afraid, but I don't care — there is something strange about the house — I can feel it.

I even said so to John one moonlight evening, but he said what I felt was a *draught*, and shut the window.

I get unreasonably angry with John sometimes. I'm sure I never used to be so 25 sensitive. I think it is due to this nervous condition.

But John says if I feel so, I shall neglect proper self-control; so I take pains to control myself — before him, at least, and that makes me very tired.

I don't like our room a bit. I wanted one downstairs that opened on the piazza and had roses all over the window, and such pretty old-fashioned chintz hangings! but John would not hear of it.

He said there was only one window and not room for two beds, and no near room for him if he took another.

He is very careful and loving, and hardly lets me stir without special direction.

I have a schedule prescription for each hour in the day; he takes all care from 30 me, and so I feel basely ungrateful not to value it more.

He said we came here solely on my account, that I was to have perfect rest and all the air I could get. "Your exercise depends on your strength, my dear," said he, "and your food somewhat on your appetite; but air you can absorb all the time." So we took the nursery at the top of the house.

It is a big, airy room, the whole floor nearly, with windows that look all ways, and air and sunshine galore. It was nursery first and then playroom and gymnasium, I should judge; for the windows are barred for little children, and there are rings and things in the walls.

The paint and paper look as if a boys' school had used it. It is stripped off — the paper — in great patches all around the head of my bed, about as far as I can reach, and in a great place on the other side of the room low down. I never saw a worse paper in my life.

One of those sprawling flamboyant patterns committing every artistic sin.

It is dull enough to confuse the eye in following, pronounced enough to constantly irritate and provoke study, and when you follow the lame uncertain curves for a little distance they suddenly commit suicide — plunge off at outrageous angles, destroy themselves in unheard of contradictions.

The color is repellant, almost revolting; a smouldering unclean yellow, strangely faded by the slow-turning sunlight.

It is a dull yet lurid orange in some places, a sickly sulphur tint in others.

No wonder the children hated it! I should hate it myself if I had to live in this room long.

There comes John, and I must put this away, — he hates to have me write a word.

We have been here two weeks, and I haven't felt like writing before, since that first day.

I am sitting by the window now, up in this atrocious nursery, and there is nothing to hinder my writing as much as I please, save lack of strength.

John is away all day, and even some nights when his cases are serious.

I am glad my case is not serious!

But these nervous troubles are dreadfully depressing.

John does not know how much I really suffer. He knows there is no *reason* to suffer, and that satisfies him.

Of course it is only nervousness. It does weigh on me so not to do my duty in any way!

I meant to be such a help to John, such a real rest and comfort, and here I am a comparative burden already!

Nobody would believe what an effort it is to do what little I am able, — to dress and entertain, and order things.

It is fortunate Mary is so good with the baby. Such a dear baby!

And yet I *cannot* be with him, it makes me so nervous.

I suppose John never was nervous in his life. He laughs at me so about this wall-paper!

At first he meant to repaper the room, but afterward he said that I was letting it get the better of me, and that nothing was worse for a nervous patient than to give way to such fancies.

He said that after the wall-paper was changed it would be the heavy bedstead, and then the barred windows, and then that gate at the head of the stairs, and so on.

"You know the place is doing you good," he said, "and really, dear, I don't care to renovate the house just for a three months' rental."

"Then do let us go downstairs," I said, "there are such pretty rooms there."

Then he took me in his arms and called me a blessed little goose, and said he would go down cellar, if I wished, and have it whitewashed into the bargain.

But he is right enough about the beds and windows and things.

It is an airy and comfortable room as anyone need wish, and, of course, I would not be so silly as to make him uncomfortable just for a whim.

I'm really getting quite fond of the big room, all but that horrid paper.

Out of one window I can see the garden, those mysterious deep-shaded arbors, the riotous old-fashioned flowers, and bushes and gnarly trees. 60

Out of another I get a lovely view of the bay and a little private wharf belonging to the estate. There is a beautiful shaded lane that runs down there from the house. I always fancy I see people walking in these numerous paths and arbors, but John has cautioned me not to give way to fancy in the least. He says that with my imaginative power and habit of story-making, a nervous weakness like mine is sure to lead to all manner of excited fancies, and that I ought to use my will and good sense to check the tendency. So I try.

I think sometimes that if I were only well enough to write a little it would relieve the press of ideas and rest me.

But I find I get pretty tired when I try.

It is so discouraging not to have any advice and companionship about my work. When I get really well, John says we will ask Cousin Henry and Julia down for a long visit; but he says he would as soon put fireworks in my pillow-case as to let me have those stimulating people about now.

I wish I could get well faster. 65

But I must not think about that. This paper looks to me as if it *knew* what a vicious influence it had!

There is a recurrent spot where the pattern lolls like a broken neck and two bulbous eyes stare at you upside down.

I get positively angry with the impertinence of it and the everlastingness. Up and down and sideways they crawl, and those absurd, unblinking eyes are everywhere. There is one place where two breadths didn't match, and the eyes go all up and down the line, one a little higher than the other.

I never saw so much expression in an inanimate thing before, and we all know how much expression they have! I used to lie awake as a child and get more entertainment and terror out of blank walls and plain furniture than most children could find in a toy-store.

I remember what a kindly wink the knobs of our big, old bureau used to have, and there was one chair that always seemed like a strong friend. 70

I used to feel that if any of the other things looked too fierce I could always hop into that chair and be safe.

The furniture in this room is no worse than inharmonious, however, for we had to bring it all from downstairs. I suppose when this was used as a playroom they had to take the nursery things out, and no wonder! I never saw such ravages as the children have made here.

The wall-paper, as I said before, is torn off in spots, and it sticketh closer than a brother — they must have had perseverance as well as hatred.

Then the floor is scratched and gouged and splintered, the plaster itself is dug out here and there, and this great heavy bed, which is all we found in the room, looks as if it had been through the wars.

But I don't mind it a bit—only the paper.

There comes John's sister. Such a dear girl as she is, and so careful of me! I must not let her find me writing.

She is a perfect and enthusiastic housekeeper, and hopes for no better profession. I verily believe she thinks it is the writing which made me sick!

But I can write when she is out, and see her a long way off from these windows.

There is one that commands the road, a lovely shaded winding road, and one that just looks off over the country. A lovely country, too, full of great elms and velvet meadows.

This wallpaper has a kind of sub-pattern in a different shade, a particularly irritating one, for you can only see it in certain lights, and not clearly then.

But in the places where it isn't faded and where the sun is just so—I can see a strange, provoking, formless sort of figure, that seems to skulk about behind that silly and conspicuous front design.

There's sister on the stairs!

Well, the Fourth of July is over! The people are all gone and I am tired out. John thought it might do me good to see a little company, so we just had mother and Nellie and the children down for a week.

Of course I didn't do a thing. Jennie sees to everything now.

But it tired me all the same.

John says if I don't pick up faster he shall send me to Weir Mitchell° in the fall.

But I don't want to go there at all. I had a friend who was in his hands once, and she says he is just like John and my brother, only more so!

Besides, it is such an undertaking to go so far.

I don't feel as if it was worthwhile to turn my hand over for anything, and I'm getting dreadfully fretful and querulous.

I cry at nothing, and cry most of the time.

Of course I don't when John is here, or anybody else, but when I am alone.

And I am alone a good deal just now. John is kept in town very often by serious cases, and Jennie is good and lets me alone when I want her to.

So I walk a little in the garden or down that lovely lane, sit on the porch under the roses, and lie down up here a good deal.

I'm getting really fond of the room in spite of the wallpaper. Perhaps *because* of the wallpaper.

It dwells in my mind so!

I lie here on this great immovable bed—it is nailed down, I believe—and follow that pattern about by the hour. It is as good as gymnastics, I assure you. I start, we'll say, at the bottom, down in the corner over there where it has not been

75

80

85

90

95

Weir Mitchell: Dr. S. Weir Mitchell (1829–1914) was an eminent Philadelphia neurologist who advocated "rest cures" for nervous disorders. He was the author of *Diseases of the Nervous System, Especially of Women* (1881).

touched, and I determine for the thousandth time that I *will* follow that pointless pattern to some sort of a conclusion.

I know a little of the principle of design, and I know this thing was not arranged on any laws of radiation, or alternation, or repetition, or symmetry, or anything else that I ever heard of.

It is repeated, of course, by the breadths, but not otherwise.

Looked at in one way each breadth stands alone, the bloated curves and flourishes—a kind of "debased Romanesque" with *delirium tremens*—go waddling up and down in isolated columns of fatuity.

But, on the other hand, they connect diagonally, and the sprawling outlines   100
run off in great slanting waves of optic horror, like a lot of wallowing seaweeds in full chase.

The whole thing goes horizontally, too, at least it seems so, and I exhaust myself in trying to distinguish the order of its going in that direction.

They have used a horizontal breadth for a frieze, and that adds wonderfully to the confusion.

There is one end of the room where it is almost intact, and there, when the crosslights fade and the low sun shines directly upon it, I can almost fancy radiation after all,—the interminable grotesques seem to form around a common centre and rush off in headlong plunges of equal distraction.

It makes me tired to follow it. I will take a nap I guess.

I don't know why I should write this.   105
I don't want to.
I don't feel able.
And I know John would think it absurd. But I *must* say what I feel and think in some way—it is such a relief!
But the effort is getting to be greater than the relief.
Half the time now I am awfully lazy, and lie down ever so much.   110
John says I mustn't lose my strength, and has me take cod liver oil and lots of tonics and things, to say nothing of ale and wine and rare meat.

Dear John! He loves me very dearly, and hates to have me sick. I tried to have a real earnest reasonable talk with him the other day, and tell him how I wish he would let me go and make a visit to Cousin Henry and Julia.

But he said I wasn't able to go, nor able to stand it after I got there; and I did not make out a very good case for myself, for I was crying before I had finished.

It is getting to be a great effort for me to think straight. Just this nervous weakness I suppose.

And dear John gathered me up in his arms, and just carried me upstairs and   115
laid me on the bed, and sat by me and read to me till it tired my head.

He said I was his darling and his comfort and all he had, and that I must take care of myself for his sake, and keep well.

He says no one but myself can help me out of it, that I must use my will and self-control and not let any silly fancies run away with me.

There's one comfort, the baby is well and happy, and does not have to occupy this nursery with the horrid wallpaper.

If we had not used it, that blessed child would have! What a fortunate escape! Why, I wouldn't have a child of mine, an impressionable little thing, live in such a room for worlds.

I never thought of it before, but it is lucky that John kept me here after all, I can stand it so much easier than a baby, you see.

Of course I never mention it to them any more—I am too wise, but I keep watch of it all the same.

There are things in the wallpaper that nobody knows but me, or ever will.

Behind that outside pattern the dim shapes get clearer every day.

It is always the same shape, only very numerous.

And it is like a woman stooping down and creeping about behind that pattern. I don't like it a bit. I wonder—I begin to think—I wish John would take me away from here!

It is so hard to talk with John about my case, because he is so wise, and because he loves me so.

But I tried it last night.

It was moonlight. The moon shines in all around just as the sun does.

I hate to see it sometimes, it creeps so slowly, and always comes in by one window or another.

John was asleep and I hated to waken him, so I kept still and watched the moonlight on that undulating wallpaper till I felt creepy.

The faint figure behind seemed to shake the pattern, just as if she wanted to get out.

I got up softly and went to feel and see if the paper *did* move, and when I came back John was awake.

"What is it, little girl?" he said. "Don't go walking about like that—you'll get cold."

I thought it was a good time to talk, so I told him that I really was not gaining here, and that I wished he would take me away.

"Why, darling!" said he, "our lease will be up in three weeks, and I can't see how to leave before.

"The repairs are not done at home, and I cannot possibly leave town just now. Of course if you were in any danger, I could and would, but you really are better, dear, whether you can see it or not. I am a doctor, dear, and I know. You are gaining flesh and color, your appetite is better, I feel really much easier about you."

"I don't weigh a bit more," said I, "nor as much; and my appetite may be better in the evening when you are here but it is worse in the morning when you are away!"

"Bless her little heart!" said he with a big hug, "she shall be as sick as she pleases! But now let's improve the shining hours by going to sleep, and talk about it in the morning!"

"And you won't go away?" I asked gloomily.

"Why, how can I, dear? It is only three weeks more and then we will take a nice little trip of a few days while Jennie is getting the house ready. Really dear you are better!"

120

125

130

135

140

"Better in body perhaps—" I began, and stopped short, for he sat up straight and looked at me with such a stern, reproachful look that I could not say another word.

"My darling," said he, "I beg you, for my sake and for our child's sake, as well as for your own, that you will never for one instant let that idea enter your mind! There is nothing so dangerous, so fascinating, to a temperament like yours. It is a false and foolish fancy. Can you trust me as a physician when I tell you so?"

So of course I said no more on that score, and we went to sleep before long. He thought I was asleep first, but I wasn't, and lay there for hours trying to decide whether that front pattern and the back pattern really did move together or separately.

On a pattern like this, by daylight, there is a lack of sequence, a defiance of law, that is a constant irritant to a normal mind.

The color is hideous enough, and unreliable enough, and infuriating enough, but the pattern is torturing.   145

You think you have mastered it, but just as you get well underway in following, it turns a back-somersault and there you are. It slaps you in the face, knocks you down, and tramples upon you. It is like a bad dream.

The outside pattern is a florid arabesque, reminding one of a fungus. If you can imagine a toadstool in joints, an interminable string of toadstools, budding and sprouting in endless convolutions—why, that is something like it.

That is, sometimes!

There is one marked peculiarity about this paper, a thing nobody seems to notice but myself, and that is that it changes as the light changes.

When the sun shoots in through the east window—I always watch for that   150
first long, straight ray—it changes so quickly that I never can quite believe it.

That is why I watch it always.

By moonlight—the moon shines in all night when there is a moon—I wouldn't know it was the same paper.

At night in any kind of light, in twilight, candlelight, lamplight, and worst of all by moonlight, it becomes bars! The outside pattern I mean, and the woman behind it is as plain as can be.

I didn't realize for a long time what the thing was that showed behind, that dim sub-pattern, but now I am quite sure it is a woman.

By daylight she is subdued, quiet. I fancy it is the pattern that keeps her so   155
still. It is so puzzling. It keeps me quiet by the hour.

I lie down ever so much now. John says it is good for me, and to sleep all I can.

Indeed he started the habit by making me lie down for an hour after each meal.

It is a very bad habit I am convinced, for you see I don't sleep.

And that cultivates deceit, for I don't tell them I'm awake—O, no!

The fact is I am getting a little afraid of John.   160

He seems very queer sometimes, and even Jennie has an inexplicable look.

It strikes me occasionally, just as a scientific hypothesis,—that perhaps it is the paper!

I have watched John when he did not know I was looking, and come into the room suddenly on the most innocent excuses, and I've caught him several times *looking at the paper!* And Jennie too. I caught Jennie with her hand on it once.

She didn't know I was in the room, and when I asked her in a quiet, a very quiet voice, with the most restrained manner possible, what she was doing with the paper—she turned around as if she had been caught stealing, and looked quite angry—asked me why I should frighten her so!

Then she said that the paper stained everything it touched, that she had   165 found yellow smooches on all my clothes and John's, and she wished we would be more careful!

Did not that sound innocent? But I know she was studying that pattern, and I am determined that nobody shall find it out but myself!

Life is very much more exciting now than it used to be. You see I have something more to expect, to look forward to, to watch. I really do eat better, and am more quiet than I was.

John is so pleased to see me improve! He laughed a little the other day, and said I seemed to be flourishing in spite of my wall-paper.

I turned it off with a laugh. I had no intention of telling him it was *because* of the wall-paper—he would make fun of me. He might even want to take me away.

I don't want to leave now until I have found it out. There is a week more, and   170 I think that will be enough.

I'm feeling ever so much better! I don't sleep much at night, for it is so interesting to watch developments; but I sleep a good deal in the daytime.

In the daytime it is tiresome and perplexing.

There are always new shoots on the fungus, and new shades of yellow all over it. I cannot keep count of them, though I have tried conscientiously.

It is the strangest yellow, that wall-paper! It makes me think of all the yellow things I ever saw—not beautiful ones like buttercups, but old foul, bad yellow things.

But there is something else about that paper—the smell! I noticed it the   175 moment we came into the room, but with so much air and sun it was not bad. Now we have had a week of fog and rain, and whether the windows are open or not, the smell is here.

It creeps all over the house.

I find it hovering in the dining-room, skulking in the parlor, hiding in the hall, lying in wait for me on the stairs.

It gets into my hair.

Even when I go to ride, if I turn my head suddenly and surprise it—there is that smell!

Such a peculiar odor, too! I have spent hours in trying to analyze it, to find   180 what it smelled like.

It is not bad—at first, and very gentle, but quite the subtlest, most enduring odor I ever met.

In this damp weather it is awful, I wake up in the night and find it hanging over me.

It used to disturb me at first. I thought seriously of burning the house — to reach the smell.

But now I am used to it. The only thing I can think of that it is like is the *color* of the paper! A yellow smell.

There is a very funny mark on this wall, low down, near the mopboard. A streak that runs round the room. It goes behind every piece of furniture, except the bed, a long, straight, even *smooch*, as if it had been rubbed over and over.

I wonder how it was done and who did it, and what they did it for. Round and round and round — round and round and round — it makes me dizzy!

I really have discovered something at last.

Through watching so much at night, when it changes so, I have finally found out.

The front pattern *does* move — and no wonder! The woman behind shakes it!

Sometimes I think there are a great many women behind, and sometimes only one, and she crawls around fast, and her crawling shakes it all over.

Then in the very bright spots she keeps still, and in the very shady spots she just takes hold of the bars and shakes them hard.

And she is all the time trying to climb through. But nobody could climb through that pattern — it strangles so; I think that is why it has so many heads.

They get through, and then the pattern strangles them off and turns them upside down, and makes their eyes white!

If those heads were covered or taken off it would not be half so bad.

I think that woman gets out in the daytime!

And I'll tell you why — privately — I've seen her!

I can see her out of every one of my windows!

It is the same woman, I know, for she is always creeping, and most women do not creep by daylight.

I see her in that long shaded lane, creeping up and down. I see her in those dark grape arbors, creeping all around the garden.

I see her on that long road under the trees, creeping along, and when a carriage comes she hides under the blackberry vines.

I don't blame her a bit. It must be very humiliating to be caught creeping by daylight!

I always lock the door when I creep by daylight. I can't do it at night, for I know John would suspect something at once.

And John is so queer now, that I don't want to irritate him. I wish he would take another room! Besides, I don't want anybody to get that woman out at night but myself.

I often wonder if I could see her out of all the windows at once.

But, turn as fast as I can, I can only see out of one at one time.

And though I always see her, she *may* be able to creep faster than I can turn!

I have watched her sometimes away off in the open country, creeping as fast as a cloud shadow in a high wind.

If only that top pattern could be gotten off from the under one! I mean to try it, little by little.

I have found out another funny thing, but I shan't tell it this time! It does not do to trust people too much.

There are only two more days to get this paper off, and I believe John is   210
beginning to notice. I don't like the look in his eyes.

And I heard him ask Jennie a lot of professional questions, about me. She had a very good report to give.

She said I slept a good deal in the daytime.

John knows I don't sleep very well at night, for all I'm so quiet!

He asked me all sorts of questions too, and pretended to be very loving and kind.

As if I couldn't see through him!   215

Still, I don't wonder he acts so, sleeping under this paper for three months.

It only interests me, but I feel sure John and Jennie are secretly affected by it.

Hurrah! This is the last day, but it is enough. John to stay in town over night, and won't be out until this evening.

Jennie wanted to sleep with me—the sly thing! But I told her I should undoubtedly rest better for a night all alone.

That was clever, for really I wasn't alone a bit! As soon as it was moonlight   220
and that poor thing began to crawl and shake the pattern, I got up and ran to help her.

I pulled and she shook, I shook and she pulled, and before morning we had peeled off yards of that paper.

A strip about as high as my head and half around the room.

And then when the sun came and that awful pattern began to laugh at me, I declared I would finish it to-day!

We go away to-morrow, and they are moving all my furniture down again to leave things as they were before.

Jennie looked at the wall in amazement, but I told her merrily that I did it   225
out of pure spite at the vicious thing.

She laughed and said she wouldn't mind doing it herself, but I must not get tired.

How she betrayed herself that time!

But I am here, and no person touches this paper but me,—not *alive!*

She tried to get me out of the room—it was too patent! But I said it was so quiet and empty and clean now that I believed I would lie down again and sleep all I could, and not to wake me even for dinner—I would call when I woke.

So now she is gone, and the servants are gone, and the things are gone, and   230
there is nothing left but that great bedstead nailed down, with the canvas mattress we found on it.

We shall sleep downstairs to-night, and take the boat home to-morrow.

I quite enjoy the room, now it is bare again.

How those children did tear about here!

This bedstead is fairly gnawed!

But I must get to work.   235

I have locked the door and thrown the key down into the front path.

I don't want to go out, and I don't want to have anybody come in, till John comes.

I want to astonish him.

I've got a rope up here that even Jennie did not find. If that woman does get out, and tries to get away, I can tie her!

But I forgot I could not reach far without anything to stand on!   240

This bed will *not* move!

I tried to lift and push it until I was lame, and then I got so angry I bit off a little piece at one corner — but it hurt my teeth.

Then I peeled off all the paper I could reach standing on the floor. It sticks horribly and the pattern just enjoys it! All those strangled heads and bulbous eyes and waddling fungus growths just shriek with derision!

I am getting angry enough to do something desperate. To jump out of the window would be admirable exercise, but the bars are too strong even to try.

Besides I wouldn't do it. Of course not. I know well enough that a step like   245
that is improper and might be misconstrued.

I don't like to *look* out of the windows even — there are so many of those creeping women, and they creep so fast.

I wonder if they all come out of that wall-paper as I did?

But I am securely fastened now by my well-hidden rope — you don't get *me* out in the road there!

I suppose I shall have to get back behind the pattern when it comes night, and that is hard!

It is so pleasant to be out in this great room and creep around as I please!   250

I don't want to go outside. I won't, even if Jennie asks me to.

For outside you have to creep on the ground, and everything is green instead of yellow.

But here I can creep smoothly on the floor, and my shoulder just fits in that long smooch around the wall, so I cannot lose my way.

Why, there's John at the door!

It is no use, young man, you can't open it!   255

How he does call and pound!

Now he's crying for an axe.

It would be a shame to break down that beautiful door!

"John dear!" said I in the gentlest voice, "the key is down by the front steps, under a plantain leaf!"

That silenced him for a few moments.   260

Then he said — very quietly indeed, "Open the door, my darling!"

"I can't," said I. "The key is down by the front door under a plantain leaf!"

And then I said it again, several times, very gently and slowly, and said it so often that he had to go and see, and he got it of course, and came in. He stopped short by the door.

"What is the matter?" he cried. "For God's sake, what are you doing!"

I kept on creeping just the same, but I looked at him over my shoulder.   265

"I've got out at last," said I, "in spite of you and Jane. And I've pulled off most of the paper, so you can't put me back!"

Now why should that man have fainted? But he did, and right across my path by the wall, so that I had to creep over him every time!   [1892]

THINKING ABOUT THE TEXT

1. What psychological stages does the narrator go through as the story progresses?

2. How does the wallpaper function as a symbol in this story? What do you conclude about the narrator when she becomes increasingly interested in the woman she finds there?

3. Explain your ultimate view of the narrator, by using specific details of the story and by identifying some of the warrants or assumptions behind your opinion. Do you admire her? Sympathize with her? Recoil from her? What would you say to someone who simply dismisses her as crazy?

4. The story is narrated in the present tense. Would its effect be different if it were narrated in the past? Why, or why not?

5. In real life, Gilman's husband and her doctor were two separate people. In the story, the narrator's husband is her doctor as well. Why do you think Gilman made this change? What is the effect of her combining husband and doctor?

CHARLOTTE PERKINS GILMAN

Why I Wrote "The Yellow Wallpaper"

Gilman published the following piece in the October 1913 issue of her magazine The Forerunner.

Many and many a reader has asked that. When the story first came out, in the *New England Magazine* about 1891, a Boston physician made protest in *The Transcript.* Such a story ought not to be written, he said; it was enough to drive anyone mad to read it.

Another physician, in Kansas I think, wrote to say that it was the best description of incipient insanity he had ever seen, and — begging my pardon — had I been there?

Now the story of the story is this:

For many years I suffered from a severe and continuous nervous breakdown tending to melancholia — and beyond. During about the third year of this trouble I went, in devout faith and some faint stir of hope, to a noted specialist in nervous diseases, the best known in the country. This wise man put me to bed and applied the rest cure, to which a still good physique responded so promptly that, he concluded there was nothing much the matter with me, and sent me home with solemn advice to "live as domestic a life as far as possible," to "have but two hours' intellectual life a day," and "never to touch pen, brush or pencil again as long as I lived." This was in 1887.

I went home and obeyed those directions for some three months, and came   5
so near the border line of utter mental ruin that I could see over.

Then, using the remnants of intelligence that remained, and helped by a wise friend, I cast the noted specialist's advice to the winds and went to work again — work, the normal life of every human being; work, in which is joy and growth and service, without which one is a pauper and a parasite; ultimately recovering some measure of power.

Being naturally moved to rejoicing by this narrow escape, I wrote *The Yellow Wallpaper*, with its embellishments and additions to carry out the ideal (I never had hallucinations or objections to my mural decorations) and sent a copy to the physician who so nearly drove me mad. He never acknowledged it.

The little book is valued by alienists° and as a good specimen of one kind of literature. It has to my knowledge saved one woman from a similar fate — so terrifying her family that they let her out into normal activity and she recovered.

But the best result is this. Many years later I was told that the great specialist had admitted to friends of his that he had altered his treatment of neurasthenia since reading *The Yellow Wallpaper*.

It was not intended to drive people crazy, but to save people from being   10
driven crazy, and it worked.   [1913]

alienists: Nineteenth-century term for psychiatrists.

THINKING ABOUT THE TEXT

1. S. Weir Mitchell was the "noted specialist in nervous diseases" whom Gilman mentions. Yet she does not identify him by name. Why not, do you think? Some historians argue that, contrary to Gilman's claim here, Mitchell continued to believe his "rest cure" valid. Does this issue of fact matter to your judgment of her piece? Why, or why not?

2. Look again at Gilman's last sentence. Do you believe that her story could indeed "save people from being driven crazy"? Why, or why not?

3. Does this piece as a whole affect your interpretation and opinion of Gilman's story? Why, or why not? In general, how much do you think readers of a story should know about its author's life?

S. WEIR MITCHELL
From "The Evolution of the Rest Treatment"

Charlotte Perkins Gilman sought help from Silas Weir Mitchell (1829–1914)
because he was a well-known and highly respected physician who had treated many
women's mental problems. Mitchell developed his "rest cure" while serving as an
army surgeon during the Civil War. Ironically, like Gilman he was also a writer.
Besides producing numerous monographs on medical subjects, he published many
short stories and novels. The following is an excerpt from a lecture that Mitchell
gave to the Philadelphia Neurological Society in 1904, twelve years after "The Yel-
low Wallpaper" appeared. As you will see, Mitchell was still enthusiastic about his
"rest cure," although he had changed it in certain respects since devising it.

I have been asked to come here to-night to speak to you on some subject connected with nervous disease. I had hoped to have had ready a fitting paper for so
notable an occasion, but have been prevented by public engagements and private business so as to make it quite impossible. I have, therefore, been driven to
ask whether it would be agreeable if I should speak in regard to the mode in
which the treatment of disease by rest was evolved. This being favorably received,
I am here this evening to say a few words on that subject.

You all know full well that the art of cure rests upon a number of sciences,
and that what we do in medicine, we cannot always explain, and that our methods are far from having the accuracy involved in the term scientific. Very often,
however, it is found that what comes to us through some accident or popular use
and proves of value, is defensible in the end by scientific explanatory research.
This was the case as regards the treatment I shall briefly consider for you to-night.

The first indication I ever had of the great value of mere rest in disease, was
during the Civil War, when there fell into the hands of Doctors Morehouse,
Keen and myself, a great many cases of what we called acute exhaustion. These
were men, who, being tired by much marching, gave out suddenly at the end of
some unusual exertion, and remained for weeks, perhaps months, in a pitiable
state of what we should call today, Neurasthenia. In these war cases, it came on
with strange abruptness. It was more extreme and also more certainly curable
than are most of the graver male cases which now we are called on to treat.

I have seen nothing exactly like it in civil experience, but the combination of
malaria, excessive exertion, and exposure provided cases such as no one sees
today. Complete rest and plentiful diet usually brought these men up again and
in many instances enabled them to return to the front.

In 1872 I had charge of a man who had locomotor ataxia° with extreme pain   5
in the extremities, and while making some unusual exertion, he broke his right

---

ataxia: An inability to control muscular movements that is symptomatic of some nervous
diseases.

thigh. This confined him to his bed for three months, and the day he got up, he broke his left thigh. This involved another three months of rest. At the end of that time he confessed with satisfaction that his ataxia was better, and that he was, as he remained thereafter, free from pain. I learned from this, and two other cases, that in ataxia the bones are brittle, and I learned also that rest in bed is valuable in a proportion of such cases. You may perceive that my attention was thus twice drawn towards the fact that mere rest had certain therapeutic values.

In 1874 Mrs. G., of B——, Maine, came to see me in the month of January. I have described her case elsewhere, so that it is needless to go into detail here, except to say that she was a lady of ample means, with no special troubles or annoyances, but completely exhausted by having had children in rapid succession and from having undertaken to do charitable and other work to an extent far beyond her strength. When first I saw this tall woman, large, gaunt, weighing under a hundred pounds, her complexion pale and acneous, and heard her story, I was for a time in a state of such therapeutic despair as usually fell upon physicians of that day when called upon to treat such cases. She had been to Spas, to physicians of the utmost eminence, passed through the hands of gynecologists, worn spinal supporters, and taken every tonic known to the books. When I saw her she was unable to walk up stairs. Her exercise was limited to moving feebly up and down her room, a dozen times a day. She slept little and, being very intelligent, felt deeply her inability to read or write. Any such use of the eyes caused headache and nausea. Conversation tired her, and she had by degrees accepted a life of isolation. She was able partially to digest and retain her meals if she lay down in a noiseless and darkened room. Any disturbance or the least excitement, in short, any effort, caused nausea and immediate rejection of her meal. With care she could retain enough food to preserve her life and hardly to do more. Anemia, which we had then no accurate means of measuring, had been met by half a dozen forms of iron, all of which were said to produce headache, and generally to disagree with her. Naturally enough, her case had been pronounced to be hysteria, but calling names may relieve a doctor and comfort him in failure, but does not always assist the patient, and to my mind there was more of a general condition of nervous excitability due to the extreme of weakness than I should have been satisfied to label with the apologetic label hysteria.

I sat beside this woman day after day, hearing her pitiful story, and distressed that a woman, young, once handsome, and with every means of enjoyment in life should be condemned to what she had been told was a state of hopeless invalidism. After my third or fourth visit, with a deep sense that everything had been done for her that able men could with reason suggest, and many things which reason never could have suggested, she said to me that I appeared to have nothing to offer which had not been tried over and over again. I asked her for another day before she gave up the hope which had brought her to me. The night brought counsel. The following morning I said to her, if you are at rest you appear to digest your meals better. "Yes," she said. "I have been told that on that account I ought to lie in bed. It has been tried, but when I remain in bed for a few days, I lose all appetite, have intense constipation, and get up feeling weaker than when I went to bed. Please do not ask me to go to bed." Nevertheless, I did, and a week in bed justified her statements. She threw up her meals undigested, and was manifestly worse for my experiment. Sometimes the emesis° was mere regurgitation, sometimes there was nausea and violent straining, with consequent extreme exhaustion. She declared that unless she had the small exercise of walking up and down her room, she was infallibly worse. I was here between two difficulties. That she needed rest I saw, that she required some form of exercise I also saw. How could I unite the two?

As I sat beside her, with a keen sense of defeat, it suddenly occurred to me that some time before, I had seen a man, known as a layer on of hands, use very rough rubbing for a gentleman who was in a state of general paresis.° Mr. S. had asked me if I objected to this man rubbing him. I said no, and that I should like to see him do so, as he had relieved, to my knowledge, cases of rheumatic stiffness. I was present at two sittings and saw this man rub my patient. He kept him sitting in a chair at the time and was very rough and violent like the quacks now known as osteopaths. I told him he had injured my patient by his extreme roughness, and that if he rubbed him at all he must be more gentle. He took the hint and as a result there was every time a notable but temporary gain. Struck with this, I tried to have rubbing used on spinal cases, but those who tried to do the work were inefficient, and I made no constant use of it. It remained, however, on my mind, and recurred to me as I sat beside this wreck of a useful and once vigorous woman. The thought was fertile. I asked myself why rubbing might not prove competent to do for the muscles and tardy circulation what voluntary exercise does. I said to myself, this may be exercise without exertion, and wondered why I had not long before had this pregnant view of the matter.

Suffice it to say that I brought a young woman to Mrs. G.'s bedside and told her how I thought she ought to be rubbed. The girl was clever, and developed talent in that direction, and afterwards became the first of that great number of people who have since made a livelihood by massage. I watched the rubbing two or three times, giving instructions, in fact developing out of the clumsy massage I had seen, the manual of a therapeutic means, at that time entirely new to me. A few days later I fell upon the idea of giving electric passive exercise and cautiously added this second agency. Meanwhile, as she had always done best when secluded, I insisted on entire rest and shut out friends, relatives, books and letters. I had some faith that I should succeed. In ten days I was sure the woman had found a new tonic, hope, and blossomed like a rose. Her symptoms passed away one by one. I was soon able to add to her diet, to feed her between meals, to give her malt daily, and, after a time, to conceal in it full doses of pyro-phosphates of iron. First, then, I had found two means which enabled me to use rest in bed without causing the injurious effects of unassisted rest; secondly, I had discovered that massage was a tonic of extraordinary value: thirdly, I had learned that with this combination of seclusion, massage and electricity, I could overfeed the patient until I had brought her into a state of entire health. I learned later the

emesis: Vomiting.　　**paresis:** Brain syphilis.

care which had to be exercised in getting these patients out of bed. But this does not concern us now. In two months she gained forty pounds and was a cheerful, blooming woman, fit to do as she pleased. She has remained, save for time's ravage, what I made her.

It may strike you as interesting that for a while I was not fully aware of the   10
enormous value of a therapeutic discovery which employed no new agents, but owed its usefulness to a combination of means more or less well known.

Simple rest as a treatment had been suggested, but not in this class of cases. Massage has a long history. Used, I think, as a luxury by the Orientals for ages, it was employed by Ling in 1813. It never attained perfection in the hands of the Swedes, nor do they to-day understand the proper use of this agent. It was over and over recognized in Germany, but never generally accepted. In France, at a later period, Dreyfus, in 1841, wrote upon it and advised its use, as did Recamier and Lainé in 1868. Two at least of these authors thought it useful as a general agent, but no one seems to have accepted their views, nor was its value as a tonic spoken of in the books on therapeutics or recommended on any text-book as a powerful toning agent. It was used here in the Rest Treatment, and this, I think, gave it vogue and caused the familiar use of this invaluable therapeutic measure.

A word before I close. My first case left me in May, 1874, and shortly afterwards I began to employ the same method in other cases, being careful to choose only those which seemed best suited to it. My first mention in print of the treatment was in 1875, in the Sequin Lectures, Vol. 1., No. 4, "Rest in the Treatment of Disease." In that paper I first described Mrs. G.'s case. My second paper was in 1877, an address before the Medico-Chirurgical faculty of Maryland, and the same year I printed my book on "Rest Treatment." The one mistake in the book was the title. I was, however, so impressed at the time by the extraordinary gain in flesh and blood under this treatment that I made it too prominent in the title of the book. Let me say that for a long time the new treatment was received with the utmost incredulity. When I spoke in my papers of the people who had gained half a pound a day or more, my results were questioned and ridiculed in this city as approaching charlatanism. At a later date in England some physicians were equally wanting in foresight and courtesy. It seems incredible that any man who was a member of the British Medical Association could have said that he would rather see his patients not get well than have them cured by such a method as that. It was several years before it was taken up by Professor Goodell, and it was a longer time in making its way in Europe when by mere accident it came to be first used by Professor William Playfair.

I suffered keenly at that time from this unfair criticism, as any sensitive man must have done, for some who were eminent in the profession said of it and of me things which were most inconsiderate. Over and over in consultation I was rejected with ill-concealed scorn. I made no reply to my critics. I knew that time would justify me: I have added a long since accepted means of helping those whom before my day few helped. This is a sufficient reward for silence, patience and self-faith. I fancy that there are in this room many who have profited for themselves and their patients by the thought which evolved the Rest Treatment as I sat by the beside of my first rest case in 1874. Playfair said of it at the British Association that he had nothing to add to it and nothing to omit, and to this day no one has differed as to his verdict.

How fully the use of massage has been justified by the later scientific studies of Lauder Brunton, myself, and others you all know. It is one of the most scientific of remedial methods.   [1904]

THINKING ABOUT THE TEXT

1. How would you describe Mitchell's tone in this lecture? What self-image does he seem to cultivate? Support your answers by referring to specific words in the text.

2. Why does Mitchell consider Mrs. G——'s case significant? In what ways does she resemble Gilman and the narrator of Gilman's story?

3. Mitchell indicates that his patients have included male as well as female hysterics. Are we therefore justified in concluding that gender did not matter much in his application of the "rest cure"? Why, or why not?

JOHN HARVEY KELLOGG

From *The Ladies' Guide in Health and Disease*

John Harvey Kellogg (1852–1943) was an American physician who wrote much advice about how to discipline one's sexual desires and, in the case of women, how to be a good mother. Perhaps you associate the name "Kellogg" with breakfast cereals. As founder and superintendent of the Battle Creek Sanitarium in Michigan, Dr. Kellogg urged that his patients eat cereals as part of their treatment, and eventually his brother established the cereal company that bears their family name. Dr. Kellogg's keen interest in cereals and health foods is satirized in T. Coraghessan Boyle's 1993 novel The Road to Wellville *and the film based on that book. The following piece is an excerpt from Kellogg's 1882* Ladies' Guide in Health and Disease: Girlhood, Maidenhood, Wifehood, Motherhood. *In this selection, he virtually equates womanhood with motherhood and discusses what a woman must do to produce outstanding children. Kellogg's advice reflects the view that much of his society held about women — or at least about middle- and upper-class white women. His discussion of "puerperal mania" is especially relevant to Gilman's story.*

The special influence of the mother begins with the moment of conception. In fact it is possible that the mental condition at the time of the generative act has much to do with determining the character of the child, though it is generally conceded that at this time the influence of the father is greater than that of the mother. Any number of instances have occurred in which a drunken father has impressed upon his child the condition of his nervous system to such a degree as to render permanent in the child the staggering gait and maudlin manner which in his own case was a transient condition induced by the poisonous influence of alcohol. A child born as the result of a union in which both parents were in a state of beastly intoxication was idiotic.

Another fact might be added to impress the importance that the new being should be supplied from the very beginning of its existence with the very best conditions possible. Indeed, it is desirable to go back still further, and secure a proper preparation for the important function of maternity. The qualities which go to make up individuality of character are the result of the summing up of a long line of influences, too subtle and too varied to admit of full control, but still, to some degree at least, subject to management. The dominance of law is nowhere more evident than in the relation of ante-natal influences to character.

The hap-hazard way in which human beings are generated leaves no room for surprise that the race should deteriorate. No stock-breeder would expect anything but ruin should he allow his animals to propagate with no attention to their physical conditions or previous preparation.

Finding herself in a pregnant condition, the mother should not yield to the depressing influences which often crowd upon her. The anxieties and fears which women sometimes yield themselves to, grow with encouragement, until they become so absorbed as to be capable of producing a profoundly evil impression on the child. The true mother who is prepared for the functions of maternity, will welcome the evidence of pregnancy, and joyfully enter upon the Heaven-given task of molding a human character, of bringing into the world a new being whose life-history may involve the destinies of nations, or change the current of human thought for generations to come.

The pregnant mother should cultivate cheerfulness of mind and calmness of temper, but should avoid excitements of all kinds, such as theatrical performances, public contests of various descriptions, etc. Anger, envy, irritability of temper, and, in fact, all the passions and propensities should be held in check. The fickleness of desire and the constantly varying whims which characterize the pregnant state in some women should not be regarded as uncontrollable, and to be yielded to as the only means of appeasing them. The mother should be gently encouraged to resist such tendencies when they become at all marked, and to assist her in the effort, her husband should endeavor to engage her mind by interesting conversation, reading, and various harmless and pleasant diversions.

If it is desired that the child should possess a special aptitude for any particular art or pursuit, during the period of pregnancy the mother's mind should be constantly directed in this channel. If artistic taste or skill is the trait desired, the mother should be surrounded by works of art of a high order of merit. She should read art, think art, talk, and write about art, and if possible, herself engage in the close practical study of some one or more branches of art, as painting, drawing, etching, or modeling. If ability for authorship is desired, then the mother should devote herself assiduously to literature. It is not claimed that by following these suggestions any mother can make of her children great artists or authors at will;

but it is certain that by this means the greatest possibilities in individual cases can be attained; and it is certain that decided results have been secured by close attention to the principles laid down. It should be understood, however, that not merely a formal and desultory effort on the part of the mother is what is required. The theme selected must completely absorb her mind. It must be the one idea of her waking thoughts and the model on which is formed the dreams of her sleeping hours.

The question of diet during pregnancy as before stated is a vitally important one as regards the interests of the child. A diet into which enters largely such unwholesome articles as mustard, pepper, hot sauces, spices, and other stimulating condiments, engenders a love for stimulants in the disposition of the infant. Tea and coffee, especially if used to excess, undoubtedly tend in the same direction. We firmly believe that we have, in the facts first stated, the key to the constant increase in the consumption of ardent spirits. The children of the present generation inherit from their condiment-consuming, tea-, coffee-, and liquor-drinking, and tobacco-using parents, not simply a readiness for the acquirement of the habits mentioned, but a propensity for the use of stimulants which in persons of weak will-power and those whose circumstances are not the most favorable, becomes irresistible.

The present generation is also suffering in consequence of the impoverished diet of its parents. The modern custom of bolting the flour from the different grains has deprived millions of infants and children of the necessary supply of bone-making material, thus giving rise to a greatly increased frequency of the various diseases which arise from imperfect bony structure, as rickets, caries, premature decay of the teeth, etc. The proper remedy is the disuse of fine-flour bread and all other bolted grain preparations. Graham-flour bread, oatmeal, cracked wheat, and similar preparations, should be relied upon as the leading articles of diet. Supplemented by milk, the whole-grain preparations constitute a complete form of nourishment, and render a large amount of animal food not only unnecessary but really harmful on account of its stimulating character. It is by no means so necessary as is generally supposed that meat, fish, fowl, and flesh in various forms should constitute a large element of the dietary of the pregnant or nursing mother in order to furnish adequate nourishment for the developing child. We have seen the happiest results follow the employment of a strictly vegetarian dietary, and do not hesitate to advise moderation in the use of flesh food, though we do not recommend the entire discontinuance of its use by the pregnant mother who has been accustomed to use it freely.

A nursing mother should at once suspend nursing if she discovers that pregnancy has again occurred. The continuance of nursing under such circumstances is to the disadvantage of three individuals, the mother, the infant at the breast, and the developing child.

Sexual indulgence during pregnancy may be suspended with decided bene- 10
fit to both mother and child. The most ancient medical writers call attention to the fact that by the practice of continence° during gestation, the pains of child-

continence: Chastity, abstinence, or restraint.

birth are greatly mitigated. The injurious influences upon the child of the gratifi-cation of the passions during the period when its character is being formed, is undoubtedly much greater than is usually supposed. We have no doubt that this is a common cause of the transmission of libidinous tendencies to the child; and that the tendency to abortion is induced by sexual indulgence has long been a well established fact. The females of most animals resolutely resist the advances of the males during this period, being guided in harmony with natural law by their natural instincts which have been less perverted in them than in human beings. The practice of continence during pregnancy is also enforced in the harems of the East, which fact leads to the practice of abortion among women of this class who are desirous of remaining the special favorites of the common husband.

The general health of the mother must be kept up in every way. It is espe-cially important that the regularity of the bowels should be maintained. Proper diet and as much physical exercise as can be taken are the best means for accom-plishing this. When constipation is allowed to exist, the infant as well as the mother suffers. The effete products which should be promptly removed from the body, being long retained, are certain to find their way back into the system again, poisoning not only the blood of the mother but that of the developing fœtus. . . .

Puerperal Mania. — This form of mental disease is most apt to show itself about two weeks after delivery. Although, fortunately, of not very frequent occur-rence, it is a most serious disorder when it does occur, and hence we may with pro-priety introduce the following somewhat lengthy, but most graphic description of the disease from the pen of Dr. Ramsbotham, an eminent English physician: —

"In mania there is almost always, at the very commencement, a troubled, agitated, and hurried manner, a restless eye, an unnaturally anxious, suspicious, and unpleasing expression of face; — sometimes it is pallid, at others more flushed than usual; — an unaccustomed irritability of temper, and impatience of control or contradiction; a vacillation of purpose, or loss of memory; sometimes a rapid succession of contradictory orders are issued, or a paroxysm of excessive anger is excited about the merest trifle. Occasionally, one of the first indications will be a sullen obstinacy, or listlessness and stubborn silence. The patient lies on her back, and can by no means be persuaded to reply to the questions of her attendants, or she will repeat them, as an echo, until, all at once, without any apparent cause, she will break out into a torrent of language more or less in-coherent, and her words will follow each other with surprising rapidity. These symptoms will sometimes show themselves rather suddenly, on the patient's awakening from a disturbed and unrefreshing sleep, or they may supervene more slowly when she has been harassed with wakefulness for three or four previous nights in succession, or perhaps ever since her delivery. She will very likely then become impressed with the idea that some evil has befallen her husband, or, what is still more usual, her child; that it is dead or stolen; and if it be brought to her, nothing can persuade her it is her own; she supposes it to belong to some-body else; or she will fancy that her husband is unfaithful to her, or that he and those about her have conspired to poison her. Those persons who are naturally the objects of her deepest and most devout affection, are regarded by her with jealousy, suspicion, and hatred. This is particularly remarkable with regard to her newly born infant; and I have known many instances where attempts have been made to destroy it when it has been incautiously left within her power. Sometimes, though rarely, may be observed a great anxiety regarding the termination of her own case, or a firm conviction that she is speedily about to die. I have observed upon occasions a constant movement of the lips, while the mouth was shut; or the patient is incessantly rubbing the inside of her lips with her fingers, or thrusting them far back into her mouth; and if questions are asked, particularly if she be desired to put out her tongue, she will often compress the lips forcibly together, as if with an obstinate determination of resistance. One peculiarity attending some cases of puerperal mania is the immorality and obscenity of the expressions uttered; they are often such, indeed, as to excite our astonishment that women in a respectable station of society could ever have become acquainted with such language."

The insanity of childbirth differs from that of pregnancy in that in the latter cases the patient is almost always melancholy,° while in the former there is active mania. Derangement of the digestive organs is a constant accompaniment of the disease.

If the patient has no previous or hereditary tendency to insanity, the prospect of a quite speedy recovery is good. The result is seldom immediately fatal, but the patient not infrequently remains in a condition of mental unsoundness for months or even years, and sometimes permanently.

Treatment: When there is reason to suspect a liability to puerperal mania from previous mental disease or from hereditary influence, much can be done to ward off an attack. Special attention must be paid to the digestive organs, which should be regulated by proper food and simple means to aid digestion. The tendency to sleeplessness must be combatted by careful nursing, light massage at night, rubbing of the spine, alternate hot and cold applications to the spine, cooling the head by cloths wrung out of cold water, and the use of the warm bath at bed time. These measures are often successful in securing sleep when all other measures fail.

The patient must be kept very quiet. Visitors, even if near relatives, must not be allowed when the patient is at all nervous or disturbed, and it is best to exclude nearly every one from the sick-room with the exception of the nurse, who should be a competent and experienced person.

When the attack has really begun, the patient must have the most vigilant watchcare, not being left alone for a moment. It is much better to care for the patient at home, when possible to do so efficiently, than to take her to an asylum.

When evidences of returning rationality appear, the greatest care must be exercised to prevent too great excitement. Sometimes a change of air, if the

15

---

melancholy: Mental state characterized by severe depression, somatic problems, and hallucinations or delusions.

patient is sufficiently strong, physically, will at this period prove eminently beneficial. A visit from a dear friend will sometimes afford a needed stimulus to the dormant faculties. Such cases as these of course require intelligent medical supervision. [1882]

THINKING ABOUT THE TEXT

1. What specific responsibilities does Kellogg assign to women? What are some key assumptions he makes about them?

2. Quite possibly Kellogg would have said that the narrator of Gilman's story suffers from puerperal mania. What details of the story would support this diagnosis? What significant details of the narrator's life, if any, would Kellogg be ignoring if he saw her as *merely* a case of puerperal mania?

3. If Kellogg's advice were published today, what parts of it do you think readers would accept? What parts do you think many readers would reject?

WRITING ABOUT ISSUES

1. "The Yellow Wallpaper" ends with the narrator creeping. Write an essay explaining how you think this act should be judged. What should readers take into consideration as they seek to put this act in context?

2. Write an essay discussing "The Yellow Wallpaper" as a response to the kind of thinking expressed in Mitchell's or Kellogg's selection. Refer to specific details of both texts. If you wish, you may refer as well to Gilman's "Why I Wrote 'The Yellow Wallpaper.'"

3. Write an essay about an occasion when you, or someone you know, tried to challenge a medical or psychiatric diagnosis. Above all, analyze how doctor and patient behaved toward each other. (There may have been more than one doctor involved.) If you wish, imagine what Gilman would have said about this experience.

4. As we said in the introduction to this cluster, today many more women than men seek treatment for depression, anorexia, bulimia, and multiple personality disorder. Research one of these conditions and then write an essay in which you try to explain why it seems to afflict mostly women. If you wish, refer to any of the texts in this cluster.

PUNISHMENTS

ROBERT BROWNING, "My Last Duchess"
CAROLYN FORCHÉ, "The Colonel"
SEAMUS HEANEY, "Punishment"
SHERMAN ALEXIE, "Capital Punishment"

Acts of punishment are also acts of judgment. Clearly a punishment reflects the decisions and values of the person ordering it. Similarly, it says something about the ethics of the person willing to carry it out. Even people who merely learn about a punishment wind up judging it. Consciously or unconsciously, they choose to praise it, criticize it, or passively tolerate it. Each of the four poems deals with judgments made by punishers and those who are, in some sense, their audience. Think about what actions you are taking and what principles you are expressing as you judge the people you encounter here.

BEFORE YOU READ

Recall a particular punishment that you considered unjust. What were the circumstances? What experiences, values, and reasoning led you to disapprove of the punishment? Could you have done anything to prevent it or to see that similarly unfair punishments did not recur? If so, what?

ROBERT BROWNING
My Last Duchess

Today, Robert Browning (1812–1889) is regarded as one of the greatest poets of nineteenth-century England, but in his own time he was not nearly as celebrated as his wife, the poet Elizabeth Barrett Browning. He is chiefly known for his achievements with the dramatic monologue, a genre of poetry that emphasizes the speaker's own distinct personality. Often Browning's speakers are his imaginative re-creations of people who once existed in real life. He was especially interested in religious, political, and artistic figures from the Renaissance. The following poem, perhaps Browning's most famous, was written in 1842, and its speaker, Duke of Ferrara, was an actual man.

Ferrara°

That's my last Duchess painted on the wall,
Looking as if she were alive. I call

EPIGRAPH **Ferrara:** In the sixteenth century, the duke of this Italian city arranged to marry a second time after the mysterious death of his very young first wife.

That piece a wonder, now: Frà Pandolf's° hands
Worked busily a day, and there she stands.
Will't please you sit and look at her? I said   5
"Frà Pandolf" by design, for never read
Strangers like you that pictured countenance,
The depth and passion of its earnest glance,
But to myself they turned (since none puts by
The curtain I have drawn for you, but I)   10
And seemed as they would ask me, if they durst,
How such a glance came there; so, not the first
Are you to turn and ask thus. Sir, 'twas not
Her husband's presence only, called that spot
Of joy into the Duchess' cheek: perhaps   15
Frà Pandolf chanced to say "Her mantle laps
Over my lady's wrist too much," or "Paint
Must never hope to reproduce the faint
Half-flush that dies along her throat": such stuff
Was courtesy, she thought, and cause enough   20
For calling up that spot of joy. She had
A heart — how shall I say? — too soon made glad,
Too easily impressed; she liked whate'er
She looked on, and her looks went everywhere.
Sir, 'twas all one! My favor at her breast,   25
The dropping of the daylight in the West,
The bough of cherries some officious fool
Broke in the orchard for her, the white mule
She rode with round the terrace — all and each
Would draw from her alike the approving speech,   30
Or blush, at least. She thanked men, — good! but thanked
Somehow — I know not how — as if she ranked
My gift of a nine-hundred-years-old name
With anybody's gift. Who'd stoop to blame
This sort of trifling? Even had you skill   35
In speech — which I have not — to make your will
Quite clear to such an one, and say, "Just this
Or that in you disgusts me; here you miss,
Or there exceed the mark" — and if she let
Herself be lessoned so, nor plainly set   40
Her wits to yours, forsooth, and made excuse,
— E'en then would be some stooping; and I choose
Never to stoop. Oh sir, she smiled, no doubt,
Whene'er I passed her; but who passed without
Much the same smile? This grew; I gave commands;   45
Then all smiles stopped together. There she stands

3 **Frà Pandolf:** A fictitious artist.

As if alive. Will't please you rise? We'll meet
The company below, then. I repeat,
The Count your master's known munificence
Is ample warrant that no just pretense   50
Of mine for dowry will be disallowed;
Though his fair daughter's self, as I avowed
At starting, is my object. Nay, we'll go
Together down, sir. Notice Neptune, though,
Taming a sea-horse, thought a rarity,   55
Which Claus of Innsbruck° cast in bronze for me!   [1842]

56 Claus of Innsbruck: A fictitious artist.

THINKING ABOUT THE TEXT

1. The duke offers a history of his first marriage. Summarize his story in your own words, including the reasons he gives for his behavior. How would you describe him? Do you admire anything about him? If so, what?

2. Try to reconstruct the rhetorical situation in which the duke is making his remarks. Who might be his audience? What might be his goals? What strategies is he using to accomplish them? Cite details that support your conjectures.

3. When you read the poem aloud, how conscious are you of its rhymes? What is its rhyme scheme? What is the effect of Browning's using just one stanza rather than breaking the poem into several?

4. Going by this example of the genre, what are the advantages of writing a poem as a dramatic monologue? What are the disadvantages?

5. Browning suggests that the setting of this poem is Renaissance Italy. What relevance might his poem have had for readers in mid-nineteenth-century England? What relevance might it have for audiences in the United States today?

CAROLYN FORCHÉ

The Colonel

In her poetry, Carolyn Forché (b. 1950) often addresses contemporary abuses of power. Her first book of poems, Gathering the Tribes *(1976), won the Yale Series of Younger Poets competition. The following poem is from her second,* The Country Between Us *(1981), which won the Lamont Award from the Academy of American Poets. Much of this book is based on Forché's experiences during her stay in El Salvador, which at the time was beset by civil war. Forché's latest book of poetry is* The Angel of History *(1994), and she has also edited a collection entitled* Against

Forgetting: Twentieth-Century Poetry of Witness (1993). *She lives in Rockville, Maryland, and teaches creative writing at George Mason University in Fairfax, Virginia.*

What you have heard is true. I was in his house. His wife carried a tray of coffee and sugar. His daughter filed her nails, his son went out for the night. There were daily papers, pet dogs, a pistol on the cushion beside him. The moon swung bare on its black cord over the house. On the television was a cop show. It was in English. Broken bottles were embedded in the walls around the house to scoop   5 the kneecaps from a man's legs or cut his hands to lace. On the windows there were gratings like those in liquor stores. We had dinner, rack of lamb, good wine, a gold bell was on the table for calling the maid. The maid brought green mangoes, salt, a type of bread. I was asked how I enjoyed the country. There was a brief commercial in Spanish. His wife took everything away. There was some talk   10 then of how difficult it had become to govern. The parrot said hello on the terrace. The colonel told it to shut up, and pushed himself from the table. My friend said to me with his eyes: say nothing. The colonel returned with a sack used to bring groceries home. He spilled many human ears on the table. They were like dried peach halves. There is no other way to say this. He took one of   15 them in his hands, shook it in our faces, dropped it into a water glass. It came alive there. I am tired of fooling around he said. As for the rights of anyone, tell your people they can go fuck themselves. He swept the ears to the floor with his arm and held the last of his wine in the air. Something for your poetry, no? he said. Some of the ears on the floor caught this scrap of his voice. Some of the ears   20 on the floor were pressed to the ground.   [May 1978]

THINKING ABOUT THE TEXT

1. How do you characterize the colonel? List a number of specific adjectives and supporting details. Does your impression of him change as you read, or does it stay pretty much the same? Explain.

2. Forché calls this text a poem, and yet it seems to consist of one long prose paragraph. So, here is an issue of genre: Is it *really* a poem? Support your answer by identifying what you think are characteristics of poetry. What is the effect of Forché's presenting the text as a poem? Note what the colonel says about poetry. How might this text be considered a response to him?

3. Forché uses many short sentences here. What is the effect of this strategy? Even though she quotes the colonel, she does not use quotation marks. What is the effect of this choice?

4. The poem begins, "What you have heard is true." Do you think the situation it describes really occurred? Identify some warrants or assumptions that influence your answer. Where else does the poem refer to hearing? How might it be seen as being about audiences and their responses?

5. Forché wrote "The Colonel" after a stay in El Salvador, and so it is reasonable for her audience to conclude that the poem is set in that country. Yet she does not actually specify the setting. Should she have done so? Why, or why not?

MAKING COMPARISONS

1. Does Browning's duke strike you as the kind of person who would do what Forché's colonel does? Why, or why not?
2. Do the listeners in these two poems both seem passive? Refer to specific details of both texts.
3. "My Last Duchess" is a single stanza; "The Colonel" is a single paragraph. Would you say their forms are basically the same and with similar effects? Or are you more conscious of differences?

SEAMUS HEANEY
Punishment

For his distinguished career as a poet, Seamus Heaney (b. 1939) won the Nobel Prize in Literature in 1995. He was raised as a Catholic in Northern Ireland, where Protestants remained in the majority and frequently conflicted with Catholics. Until the Peace Accord of 1997, the region was controlled by the British government, whereas now it is ruled by a mixed body representing both religions. Several of Heaney's poems deal with Catholic resistance to the longtime British domination of his native land. Heaney moved to Dublin in the Republic of Ireland in the early 1970s, but he has often visited the United States, even holding an appointment as Boylston Professor of Rhetoric at Harvard University. The following poem appears in Heaney's 1975 book North. *It is part of a whole sequence of poems based on P. V. Glob's 1969 book* The Bog People. *Heaney was drawn to Glob's photographs of Iron Age people whose preserved bodies were discovered in bogs of Denmark and other European countries.*

I can feel the tug
of the halter at the nape
of her neck, the wind
on her naked front.

It blows her nipples
to amber beads,
it shakes the frail rigging
of her ribs.

5

◆ ◆ ◆

I can see her drowned
body in the bog,   10
the weighing stone,
the floating rods and boughs.

Under which at first
she was a barked sapling
that is dug up   15
oak-bone, brain-firkin:

her shaved head
like a stubble of black corn,
her blindfold a soiled bandage,
her noose a ring   20

to store
the memories of love.
Little adulteress,
before they punished you

you were flaxen-haired,   25
undernourished, and your
tar-black face was beautiful.
My poor scapegoat,

I almost love you
but would have cast, I know,   30
the stones of silence.°
I am the artful voyeur

of your brain's exposed
and darkened combs,
your muscles' webbing   35
and all your numbered bones:

I who have stood dumb
when your betraying sisters,
cauled in tar,
wept by the railings,°   40

who would connive
in civilized outrage
yet understand the exact
and tribal, intimate revenge.   [1975]

30–31 would have cast . . . of silence: In John 8:7–9, Jesus confronts a mob about to stone an
adulterous woman and makes the famous statement "He that is without sin among you, let him
first cast a stone at her." The crowd retreats, "being convicted by their own conscience."
37–40 I who . . . by the railings: In 1969, the British army became highly visible occupiers of
Northern Ireland. In Heaney's native city of Belfast, the Irish Republican Army retaliated
against Irish Catholic women who dated British soldiers. Punishments included shaving the
women's heads, stripping and tarring them, and handcuffing them to the city's railings.

THINKING ABOUT THE TEXT

1. Summarize your impression of the bog woman. Where does the speaker begin directly addressing her? Why do you suppose Heaney has him refrain from addressing her right away?

2. Who is the main subject of this poem? The bog woman? The "betraying sisters"? The speaker? Some combination of these people?

3. The speaker refers to himself as a "voyeur." Consult a dictionary definition of this word. How might it apply to the speaker? Do you think it is ultimately the best label for him? Explain. Do you feel like a "voyeur" reading this poem? Why, or why not?

4. What are the speaker's thoughts in the last stanza? What connotation do you attach to the word *connive*? (You might want to consult a dictionary definition of it.) What is the speaker's attitude toward "the exact / and tribal, intimate revenge"? Do you see him as tolerating violence?

5. What words in this poem, if any, are unfamiliar to you? What is their effect on you? Each stanza has four lines. Does this pattern create steady rhythm or one more fragmented than harmonious? Try reading it aloud.

MAKING COMPARISONS

1. Do you find the punishments alluded to in Heaney's, Browning's, and Forché's poems equally disturbing? Note specific things that influence your impressions.

2. How does each of these three poems raise the subject of silence? Does each suggest that silence is bad?

3. Which, if any, of the situations referred to in these three poems could happen in the contemporary United States?

SHERMAN ALEXIE
Capital Punishment

Sherman Alexie (b. 1966) is a member of the Spokane/Coeur d'Alene tribe. Born in Spokane, Washington, he currently lives in Seattle and contributes opinion columns to the Seattle Weekly. *Alexie's fiction includes two novels,* Reservation Blues *(1996) and* Indian Killer *(1997). He has also produced a collection of short stories,* The Lone Ranger and Tonto Fistfight in Heaven *(1994), which he adapted for the acclaimed 1998 film* Smoke Signals. *Alexie is a poet, too, with his collections of verse including* The Business of Fancy Dancing *(1992),* Old Shirts & New Skins *(1993),* First Indian on the Moon *(1993), and* Drums Like This *(1996). Having appeared first in a 1996 issue of* Indiana Review, *"Capital Punish-*

ment" was then selected for that year's edition of the volume Best American Poetry. *Alexie was inspired to write the poem by the media's coverage of an actual execution in the state of Washington.*

I prepare the last meal
for the Indian man to be executed

but this killer doesn't want much:
baked potato, salad, tall glass of ice water.

(I am not a witness)   5

It's mostly the dark ones
who are forced to sit in the chair

especially when white people die.
It's true, you can look it up

and this Indian killer pushed   10
his fists all the way down

a white man's throat, just to win a bet
about the size of his heart.

Those Indians are always gambling.
Still, I season this last meal   15

with all I have. I don't have much
but I send it down the line

with the handsome guard
who has fallen in love

with the Indian killer.   20
I don't care who loves whom.

(I am not a witness)

I don't care if I add too much
salt or pepper to the warden's stew.

He can eat what I put in front of him.   25
I just cook for the boss

but I cook just right
for the Indian man to be executed.

The temperature is the thing.
I once heard a story   30

about a black man who was electrocuted
in that chair and lived to tell about it

◆ ◆ ◆

before the court decided to sit him back down
an hour later and kill him all over again.

I have an extra sandwich hidden away   35
in the back of the refrigerator

in case this Indian killer survives
that first slow flip of the switch

and gets hungry while he waits
for the engineers to debate the flaws.   40

(I am not a witness)

I prepare the last meal for free
just like I signed up for the last war.

I learned how to cook
by lasting longer than any of the others.   45

Tonight, I'm just the last one left
after the handsome guard takes the meal away.

I turn off the kitchen lights
and sit alone in the dark

because the whole damn prison dims   50
when the chair is switched on.

You can watch a light bulb flicker
on a night like this

and remember it too clearly
like it was your first kiss   55

or the first hard kick to your groin.
It's all the same

when I am huddled down here
trying not to look at the clock

look at the clock, no, don't   60
look at the clock, when all of it stops

making sense: a salad, a potato
a drink of water all taste like heat.

(I am not a witness)

I want you to know I tasted a little   65
of that last meal before I sent it away.

It's the cook's job, to make sure
and I was sure I ate from the same plate

◆ ◆ ◆

and ate with the same fork and spoon
that the Indian killer used later 70

in his cell. Maybe a little bit of me
lodged in his stomach, wedged between

his front teeth, his incisors, his molars
when he chewed down on the bit

and his body arced like modern art 75
curving organically, smoke rising

from his joints, wispy flames decorating
the crown of his head, the balls of his feet.

(I am not a witness)

I sit here in the dark kitchen 80
when they do it, meaning

when they kill him, kill
and add another definition of the word

to the dictionary. American fills
its dictionary. We write down *kill* and everybody 85

in the audience shouts out exactly how
they spell it, what it means to them

and all of the answers are taken down
by the pollsters and secretaries

who take care of the small details: 90
time of death, pulse rate, press release.

I heard a story once about some reporters
at a hanging who wanted the hood removed

from the condemned's head, so they could look
into his eyes and tell their readers 95

what they saw there. What did they expect?
All of the stories should be simple.

1 death + 1 death = 2 deaths.
But we throw the killers in one grave

and victims in another. We form sides 100
and have two separate feasts.

(I am a witness)

I prepared the last meal
for the Indian man who was executed

◆ ◆ ◆

and have learned this: If any of us   105
stood for days on top of a barren hill

during an electrical storm
then lightning would eventually strike us

and we'd have no idea for which of our sins
we were reduced to headlines and ash.   [1996]   110

THINKING ABOUT THE TEXT

1. Alexie reports that in writing this poem, he aimed "to call for the aboli-
   tion of the death penalty." In reading the poem, do you sense that this is
   his aim? Why, or why not? In what respects might the poem be seen as
   arguing against the death penalty? State how you viewed capital punishment before and after you read it. Did Alexie affect your attitude? If
   so, how?

2. Why do you think Alexie cast the speaker as the condemned man's cook?
   How do you explain the speaker's shift from denying that he is a witness to
   acknowledging that he is one? Identify how he seems to define the term
   witness. What would you say to someone who argues that the speaker is
   unreasonably stretching the meaning of this word, because apparently he
   didn't directly observe the execution?

3. How does race figure in this poem? Should people consider race when
   discussing capital punishment? If so, what about race should they especially ponder? In examining Alexie's poem, should readers bear in mind
   that the author is Native American? Why, or why not?

4. The film *Dead Man Walking* (1995), which deals with arguments about
   capital punishment, shows in chilling detail an execution by injection.
   Yet at the moment the condemned man dies, the film also shows the faces
   of his two victims. By contrast, Alexie doesn't refer to the victims of the
   executed men he writes about. Should he have mentioned them? Identify some of the values reflected in your answer.

5. Summarize and evaluate the lesson delivered by the speaker at the end of
   the poem. What do you think headlines might say about you if you were
   killed in the manner he describes?

MAKING COMPARISONS

1. Forché's first sentence is "What you have heard is true." After noting that
   "It's mostly the dark ones / who are forced to sit in the chair / especially
   when white people die," Alexie's speaker declares "It's true, you can look
   it up." What do these lines imply about each poem's readers?

2. Do you think Alexie would appreciate Heaney's use of the word *tribal*? Why, or why not? Could the word be applied to any of the other poems in this cluster? If so, how?

3. Unlike the other poems in this cluster, Alexie's is in one- and two-line stanzas. Does this difference in pattern lead to a significant difference in effect? Explain.

WRITING ABOUT ISSUES

1. Choose one of the poems in this cluster and write an essay explaining how it can be seen as a poem about witnessing. In your essay, note what definition(s) of "witnessing" seem relevant to the poem, as well as what the poem seems to be saying about ethical issues involved in this act.

2. The eighth amendment to the U.S. Constitution forbids "cruel and unusual punishment." People who argue about capital punishment often find themselves considering whether it is indeed "cruel and unusual." For several years the U.S. Supreme Court considered it so because it was arbitrarily imposed and therefore banned it. Write an essay in which you examine the phrase "cruel and unusual punishment" by choosing a poem from this cluster and discussing whether the phrase applies to anything mentioned in it. In your essay, also discuss whether the phrase applies to the event described in this paragraph from the March 26, 1997, issue of *The Washington Post*:

> Moments after convicted killer Pedro Medina was strapped into Florida's electric chair and 2,000 volts of electricity surged into his body this morning, flames leapt from the inmate's head, filling the death chamber with smoke and horrifying two dozen witnesses.

Does Medina's execution amount to "cruel and unusual punishment"? If you need additional information before firmly deciding, what do you need to know?

3. Today, Amnesty International and PEN International, a writers' organization, regularly bring to the American public's attention cases of what they deem unjust punishment. In fact, Amnesty International has criticized all instances of capital punishment in the United States. Research one of the cases reported by these organizations. Then write an article for your school newspaper in which you (a) present the basic facts of the case; (b) identify values and principles you think your audience should apply to it; (c) point out anything you believe can and should be done about it. If you wish, refer to any of the poems in this cluster.

REVENGE

EDGAR ALLAN POE, "The Cask of Amontillado"
LOUISE ERDRICH, "Fleur"
ANDRE DUBUS, "Killings"

Many people consider revenge abhorrent. They hold that wrongdoers should be forgiven, left to the judgment of God ("Vengeance is mine, saith the Lord"), or dealt with through the supposed fair and rational processes of the judicial system. Yet others believe in getting even. They may tolerate or encourage revenge taken by others, or retaliate themselves against perceived offenders, in effect following the ancient Babylonian principle of "an eye for an eye, a tooth for a tooth." In each of the following stories, a character expresses a judgment of one or more other characters by engaging in an act of revenge. As you read each story here, consider the logic, morality, context, and effects of the vengeance described.

BEFORE YOU READ

Do you believe it is ever justifiable for someone to avenge a crime or wrongdoing by going outside the law? What specific cases do you think about as you address this issue?

EDGAR ALLAN POE
The Cask of Amontillado

The life of Edgar Allan Poe (1809–1849) was relatively brief, its end tragically hastened by his alcohol and drug abuse, but his contributions to literature were unique. As a book reviewer, he produced pieces of literary criticism and theory that are still widely respected. As a poet, he wrote such classics as "The Raven" (1845), "The Bells" (1849), and "Annabel Lee" (1849). Moreover, his short fiction was groundbreaking and continues to be popular, a source for many films and television shows. With works such as "The Murders in the Rue Morgue" (1841), "The Gold Bug" (1843), and "The Purloined Letter" (1944), he pioneered the modern detective story. Others of Poe's tales are masterpieces of horror, including "The Fall of the House of Usher" (1842), "The Pit and the Pendulum" (1842), and the following story, which he wrote in 1846.

The thousand injuries of Fortunato I had borne as I best could; but when he ventured upon insult, I vowed revenge. You, who so well know the nature of my soul, will not suppose, however, that I gave utterance to a threat. *At length* I would be avenged; this was a point definitely settled — but the very definitiveness with which it was resolved precluded the idea of risk. I must not only punish, but punish with impunity. A wrong is unredressed when retribution overtakes its redresser. It is equally unredressed when the avenger fails to make himself felt as such to him who has done the wrong.

It must be understood, that neither by word nor deed had I given Fortunato cause to doubt my good-will. I continued, as was my wont, to smile in his face, and he did not perceive that my smile *now* was at the thought of his immolation.

He had a weak point — this Fortunato — although in other regards he was a man to be respected and even feared. He prided himself on his connoisseurship in wine. Few Italians have the true virtuoso spirit. For the most part their enthusiasm is adopted to suit the time and opportunity — to practise imposture upon the British and Austrian *millionnaires*. In painting and gemmary Fortunato, like his countrymen, was a quack — but in the matter of old wines he was sincere. In this respect I did not differ from him materially: I was skilful in the Italian vintages myself, and bought largely whenever I could.

It was about dusk, one evening during the supreme madness of the carnival season, that I encountered my friend. He accosted me with excessive warmth, for he had been drinking much. The man wore motley. He had on a tight-fitting parti-striped dress, and his head was surmounted by the conical cap and bells. I was so pleased to see him, that I thought I should never have done wringing his hand.

I said to him: "My dear Fortunato, you are luckily met. How remarkably well   5
you are looking to-day! But I have received a pipe° of what passes for Amontillado, and I have my doubts."

"How?" said he. "Amontillado? A pipe? Impossible! And in the middle of the carnival!"

"I have my doubts," I replied; "and I was silly enough to pay the full Amontillado price without consulting you in the matter. You were not to be found, and I was fearful of losing a bargain."

"Amontillado!"

"I have my doubts."

"Amontillado!"   10

"And I must satisfy them."

"Amontillado!"

"As you are engaged, I am on my way to Luchesi. If any one has a critical turn, it is he. He will tell me — "

"Luchesi cannot tell Amontillado from Sherry."

"And yet some fools will have it that his taste is a match for your own."   15

"Come, let us go."

"Whither?"

"To your vaults."

"My friend, no; I will not impose upon your good nature. I perceive you have an engagement. Luchesi — "

"I have no engagement; — come."   20

pipe: A large cask.

"My friend, no. It is not the engagement, but the severe cold with which I perceive you are afflicted. The vaults are insufferably damp. They are encrusted with nitre."

"Let us go, nevertheless. The cold is merely nothing. Amontillado! You have been imposed upon. And as for Luchesi, he cannot distinguish Sherry from Amontillado."

Thus speaking, Fortunato possessed himself of my arm. Putting on a mask of black silk, and drawing a *roquelaire*° closely about my person, I suffered him to hurry me to my palazzo.

There were no attendants at home; they had absconded to make merry in honor of the time. I had told them that I should not return until the morning, and had given them explicit orders not to stir from the house. These orders were sufficient, I well knew, to insure their immediate disappearance, one and all, as soon as my back was turned.

I took from their sconces two flambeaux, and giving one to Fortunato, bowed   25 him through several suites of rooms to the archway that led into the vaults. I passed down a long and winding staircase, requesting him to be cautious as he followed. We came at length to the foot of the descent, and stood together on the damp ground of the catacombs of the Montresors.

The gait of my friend was unsteady, and the bells upon his cap jingled as he strode.

"The pipe?" said he.

"It is farther on," said I; "but observe the white web-work which gleams from these cavern walls."

He turned toward me, and looked into my eyes with two filmy orbs that distilled the rheum of intoxication.

"Nitre?" he asked, at length.   30

"Nitre," I replied. "How long have you had that cough?"

"Ugh! ugh! ugh!—ugh! ugh! ugh!—ugh! ugh! ugh!—ugh! ugh! ugh!—ugh! ugh! ugh!"

My poor friend found it impossible to reply for many minutes.

"It is nothing," he said, at last.

"Come," I said, with decision, "we will go back; your health is precious. You   35 are rich, respected, admired, beloved; you are happy, as once I was. You are a man to be missed. For me it is no matter. We will go back; you will be ill, and I cannot be responsible. Besides, there is Luchesi——"

"Enough," he said; "the cough is a mere nothing; it will not kill me. I shall not die of a cough."

"True—true," I replied; "and, indeed, I had no intention of alarming you unnecessarily; but you should use all proper caution. A draught of this Medoc will defend us from the damps."

Here I knocked off the neck of a bottle which I drew from a long row of its fellows that lay upon the mould.

"Drink," I said, presenting him the wine.

---

roquelaire: A short cloak.

He raised it to his lips with a leer. He paused and nodded to me familiarly, 40
while his bells jingled.

"I drink," he said, "to the buried that repose around us."

"And I to your long life."

He again took my arm, and we proceeded.

"These vaults," he said, "are extensive."

"The Montresors," I replied, "were a great and numerous family." 45

"I forget your arms."

"A huge human foot d'or,° in a field azure; the foot crushes a serpent rampant whose fangs are imbedded in the heel."

"And the motto?"

"*Nemo me impune lacessit.*"°

"Good!" he said. 50

The wine sparkled in his eyes and the bells jingled. My own fancy grew warm with the Medoc. We had passed through walls of piled bones, with casks and puncheons intermingling into the inmost recesses of the catacombs. I paused again, and this time I made bold to seize Fortunato by an arm above the elbow.

"The nitre!" I said; "see, it increases. It hangs like moss upon the vaults. We are below the river's bed. The drops of moisture trickle among the bones. Come, we will go back ere it is too late. Your cough ——"

"It is nothing," he said; "let us go on. But first, another draught of the Medoc."

I broke and reached him a flagon of De Grâve. He emptied it at a breath. His eyes flashed with a fierce light. He laughed and threw the bottle upward with a gesticulation I did not understand.

I looked at him in surprise. He repeated the movement—a grotesque one. 55

"You do not comprehend?" he said.

"Not I," I replied.

"Then you are not of the brotherhood."

"How?"

"You are not of the masons." 60

"Yes, yes," I said; "yes, yes."

"You? Impossible! A mason?"

"A mason," I replied.

"A sign," he said.

"It is this," I answered, producing a trowel from beneath the folds of my 65
roquelaire.

"You jest," he exclaimed, recoiling a few paces. "But let us proceed to the Amontillado."

"Be it so," I said, replacing the tool beneath the cloak, and again offering him my arm. He leaned upon it heavily. We continued our route in search of the Amontillado. We passed through a range of low arches, descended, passed on,

d'or: Of gold.
Nemo me impune lacessit: "No one wounds me with impunity" is the motto on the royal arms of Scotland.

and descending again, arrived at a deep crypt, in which the foulness of the air caused our flambeaux rather to glow than flame.

At the most remote end of the crypt there appeared another less spacious. Its walls had been lined with human remains, piled to the vault overhead, in the fashion of the great catacombs of Paris. Three sides of this interior crypt were still ornamented in this manner. From the fourth the bones had been thrown down, and lay promiscuously upon the earth, forming at one point a mound of some size. Within the wall thus exposed by the displacing of the bones, we perceived a still interior recess, in depth about four feet, in width three, in height six or seven. It seemed to have been constructed for no especial use within itself, but formed merely the interval between two of the colossal supports of the roof of the catacombs, and was backed by one of their circumscribing walls of solid granite.

It was in vain that Fortunato, uplifting his dull torch, endeavored to pry into the depth of the recess. Its termination the feeble light did not enable us to see.

"Proceed," I said; "herein is the Amontillado. As for Luchesi——"   70

"He is an ignoramus," interrupted my friend, as he stepped unsteadily forward, while I followed immediately at his heels. In an instant he had reached the extremity of the niche, and finding his progress arrested by the rock, stood stupidly bewildered. A moment more and I had fettered him to the granite. In its surface were two iron staples, distant from each other about two feet, horizontally. From one of these depended a short chain, from the other a padlock. Throwing the links about his waist, it was but the work of a few seconds to secure it. He was too much astounded to resist. Withdrawing the key I stepped back from the recess.

"Pass your hand," I said, "over the wall; you cannot help feeling the nitre. Indeed it is *very* damp. Once more let me *implore* you to return. No? Then I must positively leave you. But I must first render you all the little attentions in my power."

"The Amontillado!" ejaculated my friend, not yet recovered from his astonishment.

"True," I replied; "the Amontillado."

As I said these words I busied myself among the pile of bones of which I have   75
before spoken. Throwing them aside, I soon uncovered a quantity of building stone and mortar. With these materials and with the aid of my trowel, I began vigorously to wall up the entrance of the niche.

I had scarcely laid the first tier of the masonry when I discovered that the intoxication of Fortunato had in a great measure worn off. The earliest indication I had of this was a low moaning cry from the depth of the recess. It was *not* the cry of a drunken man. There was then a long and obstinate silence. I laid the second tier, and the third, and the fourth; and then I heard the furious vibrations of the chain. The noise lasted for several minutes, during which, that I might hearken to it with the more satisfaction, I ceased my labors and sat down upon the bones. When at last the clanking subsided, I resumed the trowel, and finished without interruption the fifth, the sixth, and the seventh tier. The wall was now nearly upon a level with my breast. I again paused, and holding the flambeaux over the masonwork, threw a few feeble rays upon the figure within.

A succession of loud and shrill screams, bursting suddenly from the throat of the chained form, seemed to thrust me violently back. For a brief moment I hesitated—I trembled. Unsheathing my rapier, I began to grope with it about the recess; but the thought of an instant reassured me. I placed my hand upon the solid fabric of the catacombs, and felt satisfied. I reapproached the wall. I replied to the yells of him who clamored. I reechoed—I aided—I surpassed them in volume and in strength. I did this, and the clamorer grew still.

It was now midnight, and my task was drawing to a close. I had completed the eighth, the ninth, and the tenth tier. I had finished a portion of the last and the eleventh; there remained but a single stone to be fitted and plastered in. I struggled with its weight; I placed it partially in its destined position. But now there came from out the niche a low laugh that erected the hairs upon my head. It was succeeded by a sad voice, which I had difficulty in recognizing as that of the noble Fortunato. The voice said—

"Ha! ha! ha!—he! he!—a very good joke indeed—an excellent jest. We will have many a rich laugh about it at the palazzo—he! he! he!—over our wine—he! he! he!"

"The Amontillado!" I said.   80

"He! he! he!—he! he! he!—yes, the Amontillado. But is it not getting late? Will not they be awaiting us at the palazzo, the Lady Fortunato and the rest? Let us be gone."

"Yes," I said, "let us be gone."

"*For the love of God, Montresor!*"

"Yes," I said, "for the love of God!"

But to these words I hearkened in vain for a reply. I grew impatient. I called   85
aloud:

"Fortunato!"

No answer. I called again:

"Fortunato!"

No answer still, I thrust a torch through the remaining aperture and let it fall within. There came forth in return only a jingling of the bells. My heart grew sick—on account of the dampness of the catacombs. I hastened to make an end of my labor. I forced the last stone into its position; I plastered it up. Against the new masonry I re-erected the old rampart of bones. For the half of a century no mortal has disturbed them. *In pace requiescat!*°   [1846]

In pace requiescat: In peace may he rest (Latin).

THINKING ABOUT THE TEXT

1. Evidently Montresor is recounting the story of his revenge fifty years after it took place. To whom might he be speaking? With what purposes?

2. Montresor does not describe in detail any of the offenses that Fortunato has supposedly committed against him. In considering how to judge Montresor, do you need such information? Why, or why not? State in

your own words the principles of revenge he lays out in the first paragraph.

3. What, if anything, does Poe achieve by having this story take place during a carnival? By repeating the word *amontillado* so much?

4. What does Montresor mean when he echoes Fortunato's words "for the love of God"? What might Fortunato be attempting to communicate with his final "jingling of the bells"?

5. Do you sympathize with Montresor? With Fortunato? Explain. What emotion did you mainly feel as you read the story? Identify specific features of it that led to this emotion.

LOUISE ERDRICH
Fleur

Louise Erdrich (b. 1954) is of German American and Chippewa descent. She was raised in Wahpeton, North Dakota, where both of her parents worked for the Bureau of Indian Affairs. In 1976, she earned a degree in Native American Studies at Dartmouth College; a year later, she received a master's degree in creative writing from the Johns Hopkins University. Although she has published poetry, essays, and a nonfiction book entitled The Blue Jay's Dance: A Birth Year *(1995), Erdrich is chiefly known for her novels about Native American life. Several of these feature a continuing cast of characters, including* Love Medicine *(1984; revised and expanded edition 1993),* The Beet Queen *(1986),* Tracks *(1988),* The Bingo Palace *(1994), and* Tales of Burning Love *(1996). She and her late husband Michael Dorris also collaborated on a novel entitled* The Crown of Columbus *(1991). "Fleur" was first published in a 1986 issue of* Esquire, *and later it became a chapter in* Tracks.

The first time she drowned in the cold and glassy waters of Lake Turcot, Fleur Pillager was only a girl. Two men saw the boat tip, saw her struggle in the waves. They rowed over to the place she went down, and jumped in. When they dragged her over the gunwales, she was cold to the touch and stiff, so they slapped her face, shook her by the heels, worked her arms back and forth, and pounded her back until she coughed up lake water. She shivered all over like a dog, then took a breath. But it wasn't long afterward that those two men disappeared. The first wandered off, and the other, Jean Hat, got himself run over by a cart.

It went to show, my grandma said. It figured to her, all right. By saving Fleur Pillager, those two men had lost themselves.

The next time she fell in the lake, Fleur Pillager was twenty years old and no one touched her. She washed onshore, her skin a dull dead gray, but when George Many Women bent to look closer, he saw her chest move. Then her eyes spun open, sharp black riprock, and she looked at him. "You'll take my place," she hissed. Everybody scattered and left her there, so no one knows how she dragged herself home. Soon after that we noticed Many Women changed, grew afraid, wouldn't leave his house, and would not be forced to go near water. For his caution, he lived until the day that his sons brought him a new tin bathtub. Then the first time he used the tub he slipped, got knocked out, and breathed water while his wife stood in the other room frying breakfast.

Men stayed clear of Fleur Pillager after the second drowning. Even though she was good-looking, nobody dared to court her because it was clear that Misshepeshu, the waterman, the monster, wanted her for himself. He's a devil, that one, love-hungry with desire and maddened for the touch of young girls, the strong and daring especially, the ones like Fleur.

Our mothers warn us that we'll think he's handsome, for he appears with green eyes, copper skin, a mouth tender as a child's. But if you fall into his arms, he sprouts horns, fangs, claws, fins. His feet are joined as one and his skin, brass scales, rings to the touch. You're fascinated, cannot move. He casts a shell necklace at your feet, weeps gleaming chips that harden into mica on your breasts. He holds you under. Then he takes the body of a lion or a fat brown worm. He's made of gold. He's made of beach moss. He's a thing of dry foam, a thing of death by drowning, the death a Chippewa cannot survive. 5

Unless you are Fleur Pillager. We all knew she couldn't swim. After the first time, we thought she'd never go back to Lake Turcot. We thought she'd keep to herself, live quiet, stop killing men off by drowning in the lake. After the first time, we thought she'd keep the good ways. But then, after the second drowning, we knew that we were dealing with something much more serious. She was haywire, out of control. She messed with evil, laughed at the old women's advice, and dressed like a man. She got herself into some half-forgotten medicine, studied ways we shouldn't talk about. Some say she kept the finger of a child in her pocket and a powder of unborn rabbits in a leather thong around her neck. She laid the heart of an owl on her tongue so she could see at night, and went out, hunting, not even in her own body. We know for sure because the next morning, in the snow or dust, we followed the tracks of her bare feet and saw where they changed, where the claws sprang out, the pad broadened and pressed into the dirt. By night we heard her chuffing cough, the bear cough. By day her silence and the wide grin she threw to bring down our guard made us frightened. Some thought that Fleur Pillager should be driven off the reservation, but not a single person who spoke like this had the nerve. And finally, when people were just about to get together and throw her out, she left on her own and didn't come back all summer. That's what this story is about.

During that summer, when she lived a few miles south in Argus, things happened. She almost destroyed that town.

When she got down to Argus in the year of 1920, it was just a small grid of six streets on either side of the railroad depot. There were two elevators, one central, the other a few miles west. Two stores competed for the trade of the three hundred citizens, and three churches quarreled with one another for their souls. There was a frame building for Lutherans, a heavy brick one for Episcopalians, and a long narrow shingled Catholic church. This last had a tall slender steeple, twice as high as any building or tree.

No doubt, across the low, flat wheat, watching from the road as she came near Argus on foot, Fleur saw that steeple rise, a shadow thin as a needle. Maybe in that raw space it drew her the way a lone tree draws lightning. Maybe, in the end, the Catholics are to blame. For if she hadn't seen that sign of pride, that slim prayer, that marker, maybe she would have kept walking.

But Fleur Pillager turned, and the first place she went once she came into town was to the back door of the priest's residence attached to the landmark church. She didn't go there for a handout, although she got that, but to ask for work. She got that too, or the town got her. It's hard to tell which came out worse, her or the men or the town, although the upshot of it all was that Fleur lived.   10

The four men who worked at the butcher's had carved up about a thousand carcasses between them, maybe half of that steers and the other half pigs, sheep, and game animals like deer, elk, and bear. That's not even mentioning the chickens, which were beyond counting. Pete Kozka owned the place, and employed Lily Veddar, Tor Grunewald, and my stepfather, Dutch James, who had brought my mother down from the reservation the year before she disappointed him by dying. Dutch took me out of school to take her place. I kept house half the time and worked the other in the butcher shop, sweeping floors, putting sawdust down, running a hambone across the street to a customer's bean pot or a package of sausage to the corner. I was a good one to have around because until they needed me, I was invisible. I blended into the stained brown walls, a skinny, big-nosed girl with staring eyes. Because I could fade into a corner or squeeze beneath a shelf, I knew everything, what the men said when no one was around, and what they did to Fleur.

Kozka's Meats served farmers for a fifty-mile area, both to slaughter, for it had a stock pen and chute, and to cure the meat by smoking it or spicing it in sausage. The storage locker was a marvel, made of many thicknesses of brick, earth insulation, and Minnesota timber, lined inside with sawdust and vast blocks of ice cut from Lake Turcot, hauled down from home each winter by horse and sledge.

A ramshackle board building, part slaughterhouse, part store, was fixed to the low, thick square of the lockers. That's where Fleur worked. Kozka hired her for her strength. She could lift a haunch or carry a pole of sausages without stumbling, and she soon learned cutting from Pete's wife, a string thin blonde who chain-smoked and handled the razor-sharp knives with nerveless precision, slicing close to her stained fingers. Fleur and Fritzie Kozka worked afternoons, wrapping their cuts in paper, and Fleur hauled the packages to the lockers. The meat was left outside the heavy oak doors that were only opened at 5:00 each afternoon, before the men ate supper.

Sometimes Dutch, Tor, and Lily ate at the lockers, and when they did I stayed too, cleaned floors, restoked the fires in the front smokehouses, while the men sat around the squat cast-iron stove spearing slats of herring onto hardtack bread. They played long games of poker or cribbage on a board made from the planed end of a salt crate. They talked and I listened, although there wasn't much to hear since almost nothing ever happened in Argus. Tor was married, Dutch had lost my mother, and Lily read circulars. They mainly discussed about the auctions to come, equipment, or women.

Every so often, Pete Kozka came out front to make a whist, leaving Fritzie to smoke cigarettes and fry raised doughnuts in the back room. He sat and played a few rounds but kept his thoughts to himself. Fritzie did not tolerate him talking behind her back, and the one book he read was the New Testament. If he said something, it concerned weather or a surplus of sheep stomachs, a ham that smoked green or the markets for corn and wheat. He had a good-luck talisman, the opal-white lens of a cow's eye. Playing cards, he rubbed it between his fingers. That soft sound and the slap of cards was about the only conversation.

Fleur finally gave them a subject.

Her cheeks were wide and flat, her hands large, chapped, muscular. Fleur's shoulders were broad as beams, her hips fishlike, slippery, narrow. An old green dress clung to her waist, worn thin where she sat. Her braids were thick like the tails of animals, and swung against her when she moved, deliberately, slowly in her work, held in and half-tamed, but only half. I could tell, but the others never saw. They never looked into her sly brown eyes or noticed her teeth, strong and curved and very white. Her legs were bare, and since she padded around in bead-work moccasins they never saw that her fifth toes were missing. They never knew she'd drowned. They were blinded, they were stupid, they only saw her in the flesh.

And yet it wasn't just that she was a Chippewa, or even that she was a woman, it wasn't that she was good-looking or even that she was alone that made their brains hum. It was how she played cards.

Women didn't usually play with men, so the evening that Fleur drew a chair up to the men's table without being so much as asked, there was a shock of surprise.

"What's this," said Lily. He was fat, with a snake's cold pale eyes and precious skin, smooth and lily-white, which is how he got his name. Lily had a dog, a stumpy mean little bull of a thing with a belly drum-tight from eating pork rinds. The dog liked to play cards just like Lily, and straddled his barrel thighs through games of stud, rum poker, vingt-un. The dog snapped at Fleur's arm that first night, but cringed back, its snarl frozen, when she took her place.

"I thought," she said, her voice soft and stroking, "you might deal me in."

There was a space between the heavy bin of spiced flour and the wall where I just fit. I hunkered down there, kept my eyes open, saw her black hair swing over the chair, her feet solid on the wood floor. I couldn't see up on the table where the cards slapped down, so after they were deep in their game I raised myself up in the shadows, and crouched on a sill of wood.

I watched Fleur's hands stack and ruffle, divide the cards, spill them to each player in a blur, rake them up and shuffle again. Tor, short and scrappy, shut one eye and squinted the other at Fleur. Dutch screwed his lips around a wet cigar.

"Gotta see a man," he mumbled, getting up to go out back to the privy. The others broke, put their cards down, and Fleur sat alone in the lamplight that glowed in a sheen across the push of her breasts. I watched her closely, then she paid me a beam of notice for the first time. She turned, looked straight at me, and grinned the white wolf grin a Pillager turns on its victims, except that she wasn't after me.

"Pauline there," she said, "how much money you got?"   25

We'd all been paid for the week that day. Eight cents was in my pocket.

"Stake me," she said, holding out her long fingers. I put the coins in her palm and then I melted back to nothing, part of the walls and tables. It was a long time before I understood that the men would not have seen me no matter what I did, how I moved. I wasn't anything like Fleur. My dress hung loose and my back was already curved, an old woman's. Work had roughened me, reading made my eyes sore, caring for my mother before she died had hardened my face. I was not much to look at, so they never saw me.

When the men came back and sat around the table, they had drawn together. They shot each other small glances, stuck their tongues in their cheeks, burst out laughing at odd moments, to rattle Fleur. But she never minded. They played their vingt-un, staying even as Fleur slowly gained. Those pennies I had given her drew nickels and attracted dimes until there was a small pile in front of her.

Then she hooked them with five-card draw, nothing wild. She dealt, discarded, drew, and then she sighed and her cards gave a little shiver. Tor's eye gleamed, and Dutch straightened in his seat.

"I'll pay to see that hand," said Lily Veddar.   30

Fleur showed, and she had nothing there, nothing at all.

Tor's thin smile cracked open, and he threw his hand in too.

"Well, we know one thing," he said, leaning back in his chair, "the squaw can't bluff."

With that I lowered myself into a mound of swept sawdust and slept. I woke up during the night, but none of them had moved yet, so I couldn't either. Still later, the men must have gone out again, or Fritzie come out to break the game, because I was lifted, soothed, cradled in a woman's arms and rocked so quiet that I kept my eyes shut while Fleur rolled me into a closet of grimy ledgers, oiled paper, balls of string, and thick files that fit beneath me like a mattress.

The game went on after work the next evening. I got my eight cents back five   35
times over, and Fleur kept the rest of the dollar she'd won for a stake. This time they didn't play so late, but they played regular, and then kept going at it night after night. They played poker now, or variations, for one week straight, and each time Fleur won exactly one dollar, no more and no less, too consistent for luck.

By this time, Lily and the other men were so lit with suspense that they got Pete to join the game with them. They concentrated, the fat dog sitting tense in Lily Veddar's lap, Tor suspicious, Dutch stroking his huge square brow, Pete steady. It wasn't that Fleur won that hooked them in so, because she lost hands too. It was rather that she never had a freak hand or even anything above a straight. She only took on her low cards, which didn't sit right. By chance, Fleur should have gotten a full or flush by now. The irritating thing was she beat with pairs and never bluffed, because she couldn't, and still she ended up each night with exactly one dollar. Lily couldn't believe, first of all, that a woman could be smart enough to play cards, but even if she was, that she would then be stupid enough to cheat for a dollar a night. By day I watched him turn the problem over, his hard white face dull, small fingers probing at his knuckles, until he finally thought he had Fleur figured out as a bit-time player, caution her game. Raising the stakes would throw her.

More than anything now, he wanted Fleur to come away with something but a dollar. Two bits less or ten more, the sum didn't matter, just so he broke her streak.

Night after night she played, won her dollar, and left to stay in a place that just Fritzie and I knew about. Fleur bathed in the slaughtering tub, then slept in the unused brick smokehouse behind the lockers, a windowless place tarred on the inside with scorched fats. When I brushed against her skin I noticed that she smelled of the walls, rich and woody, slightly burnt. Since that night she put me in the closet I was no longer afraid of her, but followed her close, stayed with her, became her moving shadow that the men never noticed, the shadow that could have saved her.

August, the month that bears fruit, closed around the shop, and Pete and Fritzie left for Minnesota to escape the heat. Night by night, running, Fleur had won thirty dollars, and only Pete's presence had kept Lily at bay. But Pete was gone now, and one payday, with the heat so bad no one could move but Fleur, the men sat and played and waited while she finished work. The cards sweat, limp in their fingers, the table was slick with grease, and even the walls were warm to the touch. The air was motionless. Fleur was in the next room boiling heads.

Her green dress, drenched, wrapped her like a transparent sheet. A skin of 40 lakeweed. Black snarls of veining clung to her arms. Her braids were loose, half-unraveled, tied behind her neck in a thick loop. She stood in steam, turning skulls through a vat with a wooden paddle. When scraps boiled to the surface, she bent with a round tin sieve and scooped them out. She'd filled two dishpans.

"Ain't that enough now?" called Lily. "We're waiting." The stump of a dog trembled in his lap, alive with rage. It never smelled me or noticed me above Fleur's smoky skin. The air was heavy in my corner, and pressed me down. Fleur sat with them.

"Now what do you say?" Lily asked the dog. It barked. That was the signal for the real game to start.

"Let's up the ante," said Lily, who had been stalking this night all month. He had a roll of money in his pocket. Fleur had five bills in her dress. The men had each saved their full pay.

"Ante a dollar then," said Fleur, and pitched hers in. She lost, but they let her scrape along, cent by cent. And then she won some. She played unevenly, as if chance was all she had. She reeled them in. The game went on. The dog was stiff now, poised on Lily's knees, a ball of vicious muscle with its yellow eyes slit in concentration. It gave advice, seemed to sniff the lay of Fleur's cards, twitched and nudged. Fleur was up, then down, saved by a scratch. Tor dealt seven cards, three down. The pot grew, round by round, until it held all the money. Nobody folded. Then it all rode on one last card and they went silent. Fleur picked hers up and blew a long breath. The heat lowered like a bell. Her card shook, but she stayed in.

Lily smiled and took the dog's head tenderly between his palms. 45

"Say, Fatso," he said, crooning the words, "you reckon that girl's bluffing?"

The dog whined and Lily laughed. "Me too," he said, "let's show." He swept his bills and coins into the pot and then they turned their cards over.

Lily looked once, looked again, then he squeezed the dog up like a fist of dough and slammed it on the table.

Fleur threw her arms out and drew the money over, grinning that same wolf grin that she'd used on me, the grin that had them. She jammed the bills in her dress, scooped the coins up in waxed white paper that she tied with string.

"Let's go another round," said Lily, his voice choked with burrs. But Fleur   50
opened her mouth and yawned, then walked out back to gather slops for the one big hog that was waiting in the stock pen to be killed.

The men sat still as rocks, their hands spread on the oiled wood table. Dutch had chewed his cigar to damp shreds, Tor's eye was dull. Lily's gaze was the only one to follow Fleur. I didn't move. I felt them gathering, saw my stepfather's veins, the ones in his forehead that stood out in anger. The dog had rolled off the table and curled in a knot below the counter, where none of the men could touch it.

Lily rose and stepped out back to the closet of ledgers where Pete kept his private stock. He brought back a bottle, uncorked and tipped it between his fingers. The lump in his throat moved, then he passed it on. They drank, quickly felt the whiskey's fire, and planned with their eyes things they couldn't say out loud.

When they left, I followed. I hid out back in the clutter of broken boards and chicken crates beside the stock pen, where they waited. Fleur could not be seen at first, and then the moon broke and showed her, slipping cautiously along the rough board chute with a bucket in her hand. Her hair fell, wild and coarse, to her waist, and her dress was a floating patch in the dark. She made a pig-calling sound, rang the tin pail lightly against the wood, froze suspiciously. But too late. In the sound of the ring Lily moved, fat and nimble, stepped right behind Fleur and put out his creamy hands. At his first touch, she whirled and doused him with the bucket of sour slops. He pushed her against the big fence and the package of coins split, went clinking and jumping, winked against the wood. Fleur rolled over once and vanished in the yard.

The moon fell behind a curtain of ragged clouds, and Lily followed into the dark muck. But he tripped, pitched over the huge flank of the pig, who lay mired to the snout, heavily snoring. I sprang out of the weeds and climbed the side of the pen, stuck like glue. I saw the sow rise to her neat, knobby knees, gain her balance, and sway, curious, as Lily stumbled forward. Fleur had backed into the angle of rough wood just beyond, and when Lily tried to jostle past, the sow tipped up on her hind legs and struck, quick and hard as a snake. She plunged her head into Lily's thick side and snatched a mouthful of his shirt. She lunged again, caught him lower, so that he grunted in pained surprise. He seemed to ponder, breathing deep. Then he launched his huge body in a swimmer's dive.

The sow screamed as his body smacked over hers. She rolled, striking out   55
with her knife-sharp hooves, and Lily gathered himself upon her, took her foot-long face by the ears and scraped her snout and cheeks against the trestles of the pen. He hurled the sow's tight skull against an iron post, but instead of knocking her dead, he merely woke her from her dream.

She reared, shrieked, drew him with her so that they posed standing upright. They bowed jerkily to each other, as if to begin. Then his arms swung and flailed. She sank her black fangs into his shoulder, clasping him, dancing him forward and backward through the pen. Their steps picked up pace, went wild. The two dipped as one, box-stepped, tripped each other. She ran her split foot through his hair. He grabbed her kinked tail. They went down and came up, the same shape and then the same color, until the men couldn't tell one from the other in that light and Fleur was able to launch herself over the gates, swing down, hit gravel.

The men saw, yelled, and chased her at a dead run to the smokehouse. And Lily too, once the sow gave up in disgust and freed him. That is where I should have gone to Fleur, saved her, thrown myself on Dutch. But I went stiff with fear and couldn't unlatch myself from the trestles or move at all. I closed my eyes and put my head in my arms, tried to hide, so there is nothing to describe but what I couldn't block out, Fleur's hoarse breath, so loud it filled me, her cry in the old language, and my name repeated over and over among the words.

The heat was still dense the next morning when I came back to work. Fleur was gone but the men were there, slack-faced, hung over. Lily was paler and softer than ever, as if his flesh had steamed on his bones. They smoked, took pulls off a bottle. It wasn't noon yet. I worked awhile, waiting shop and sharpening steel. But I was sick, I was smothered, I was sweating so hard that my hands slipped on the knives, and I wiped my fingers clean of the greasy touch of the customers' coins. Lily opened his mouth and roared once, not in anger. There was no meaning to the sound. His boxer dog, sprawled limp beside his foot, never lifted its head. Nor did the other men.

They didn't notice when I stepped outside, hoping for a clear breath. And then I forgot them because I knew that we were all balanced, ready to tip, to fly, to be crushed as soon as the weather broke. The sky was so low that I felt the weight of it like a yoke. Clouds hung down, witch teats, a tornado's green-brown cones, and as I watched one flicked out and became a delicate probing thumb. Even as I picked up my heels and ran back inside, the wind blew suddenly, cold, and then came rain.

Inside, the men had disappeared already and the whole place was trembling as if a huge hand was pinched at the rafters, shaking it. I ran straight through, screaming for Dutch or for any of them, and then I stopped at the heavy doors of the lockers, where they had surely taken shelter. I stood there a moment. Everything went still. Then I heard a cry building in the wind, faint at first, a whistle and then a shrill scream that tore through the walls and gathered around me, spoke plain so I understood that I should move, put my arms out, and slam down the great iron bar that fit across the hasp and lock.

Outside, the wind was stronger, like a hand held against me. I struggled forward. The bushes tossed, the awnings flapped off storefronts, the rails of porches rattled. The odd cloud became a fat snout that nosed along the earth and sniffled, jabbed, picked at things, sucked them up, blew them apart, rooted around as if it was following a certain scent, then stopped behind me at the butcher shop and bored down like a drill.

60

I went flying, landed somewhere in a ball. When I opened my eyes and looked, stranger things were happening.

A herd of cattle flew through the air like giant birds, dropping dung, their mouths opened in stunned bellows. A candle, still lighted, blew past, and tables, napkins, garden tools, a whole school of drifting eyeglasses, jackets on hangers, hams, a checkerboard, a lampshade, and at last the sow from behind the lockers, on the run, her hooves a blur, set free, swooping, diving, screaming as everything in Argus fell apart and got turned upside down, smashed, and thoroughly wrecked.

Days passed before the town went looking for the men. They were bachelors, after all, except for Tor, whose wife had suffered a blow to the head that made her forgetful. Everyone was occupied with digging out, in high relief because even though the Catholic steeple had been torn off like a peaked cap and sent across five fields, those huddled in the cellar were unhurt. Walls had fallen, windows were demolished, but the stores were intact and so were the bankers and shop owners who had taken refuge in their safes or beneath their cash registers. It was a fair-minded disaster, no one could be said to have suffered much more than the next, at least not until Fritzie and Pete came home.

Of all the businesses in Argus, Kozka's Meats had suffered worst. The boards of the front building had been split to kindling, piled in a huge pyramid, and the shop equipment was blasted far and wide. Pete paced off the distance the iron bathtub had been flung—a hundred feet. The glass candy case went fifty, and landed without so much as a cracked pane. There were other surprises as well, for the back rooms where Fritzie and Pete lived were undisturbed. Fritzie said the dust still coated her china figures, and upon her kitchen table, in the ashtray, perched the last cigarette she'd put out in haste. She lit it up and finished it, looking through the window. From there, she could see that the old smokehouse Fleur had slept in was crushed to a reddish sand and the stockpens were completely torn apart, the rails stacked helter-skelter. Fritzie asked for Fleur. People shrugged. Then she asked about the others and, suddenly, the town understood that three men were missing.

There was a rally of help, a gathering of shovels and volunteers. We passed boards from hand to hand, stacked them, uncovered what lay beneath the pile of jagged splinters. The lockers, full of the meat that was Pete and Fritzie's investment, slowly came into sight, still intact. When enough room was made for a man to stand on the roof, there were calls, a general urge to hack through and see what lay below. But Fritzie shouted that she wouldn't allow it because the meat would spoil. And so the work continued, board by board, until at last the heavy oak doors of the freezer were revealed and people pressed to the entry. Everyone wanted to be the first, but since it was my stepfather lost, I was let go in when Pete and Fritzie wedged through into the sudden icy air.

Pete scraped a match on his boot, lit the lamp Fritzie held, and then the three of us stood still in its circle. Light glared off the skinned and hanging carcasses, the crates of wrapped sausages, the bright and cloudy blocks of lake ice, pure as winter. The cold bit into us, pleasant at first, then numbing. We must

65

have stood there a couple of minutes before we saw the men, or more rightly, the humps of fur, the iced and shaggy hides they wore, the bearskins they had taken down and wrapped around themselves. We stepped closer and tilted the lantern beneath the flaps of fur into their faces. The dog was there, perched among them, heavy as a doorstop. The three had hunched around a barrel where the game was still laid out, and a dead lantern and an empty bottle, too. But they had thrown down their last hands and hunkered tight, clutching one another, knuckles raw from beating at the door they had also attacked with hooks. Frost stars gleamed off their eyelashes and the stubble of their beards. Their faces were set in concentration, mouths open as if to speak some careful thought, some agreement they'd come to in each other's arms.

Power travels in the bloodlines, handed out before birth. It comes down through the hands, which in the Pillagers were strong and knotted, big, spidery, and rough, with sensitive fingertips good at dealing cards. It comes through the eyes, too, belligerent, darkest brown, the eyes of those in the bear clan, impolite as they gaze directly at a person.

In my dreams, I look straight back at Fleur, at the men. I am no longer the watcher on the dark sill, the skinny girl.

The blood draws us back, as if it runs through a vein of earth. I've come   70
home and, except for talking to my cousins, live a quiet life. Fleur lives quiet too, down on Lake Turcot with her boat. Some say she's married to the waterman, Misshepeshu, or that she's living in shame with white men or windigos, or that she's killed them all. I'm about the only one here who ever goes to visit her. Last winter, I went to help out in her cabin when she bore the child, whose green eyes and skin the color of an old penny made more talk, as no one could decide if the child was mixed blood or what, fathered in a smokehouse, or by a man with brass scales, or by the lake. The girl is bold, smiling in her sleep, as if she knows what people wonder, as if she hears the old men talk, turning the story over. It comes up different every time and has no ending, no beginning. They get the middle wrong too. They only know that they don't know anything.   [1986]

THINKING ABOUT THE TEXT

1. Should this story be called "Pauline" since she is the narrator and commits the climactic act of revenge?

2. Repeatedly Pauline associates Fleur with supernatural forces. What is the effect of these associations on you? If Erdrich had omitted them, would the story's impact have been different? If so, how?

3. In the process of reading the story, did you expect that the men would violently turn on Fleur, or were you surprised when they did? Note specific things that affected your ability to predict what would happen.

4. How do racial differences figure in this story? What role do gender differences play? Are race and gender equally relevant here?

5. Before she closes the door on the men, Pauline evidently feels guilty because she didn't help Fleur fight them. Is Pauline right to feel this way? Why, or why not? Was Pauline justified in taking revenge? Identify some warrants or assumptions behind your answer.

MAKING COMPARISONS

1. In both Poe's story and Erdrich's, the narrator takes revenge by entombing someone. Compare how the stories describe this act. Does one story present it in a more horrifying way?

2. Both Poe's story and Erdrich's end by giving you brief glimpses of the avenger's thoughts some time after the act of revenge. Do these leaps forward have the same effect on you? Identify how each contributes to the overall meaning.

3. At the end of "Fleur," Pauline refers to the old men's talking about the origins of Fleur's child. Her last sentence is "They only know that they don't know anything." Would you apply the same statement to yourself as someone analyzing Erdrich's story? As someone attempting to understand Poe's? Explain your reasoning.

ANDRE DUBUS
Killings

Andre Dubus (1936–1999) served five years in the Marine Corps, attaining the rank of captain before becoming a full-time writer of short stories. Dubus lived in Haverhill, Massachusetts, and much of his fiction is set in the Merrimack Valley north of Boston. This is true of the following story, which appeared in his collection Finding a Girl in America *(1980) and was reprinted in his* Selected Stories *(1988). In 1991, Dubus also published a collection of essays,* Broken Vessels. *In part, the book deals with a 1986 accident that changed his life. Getting out of his car to aid stranded motorists, he was struck by another car; he eventually lost most of one leg and power over the other. Though confined to a wheelchair, Dubus continued to work actively. In 1996, he published his last collection of stories,* Dancing After Hours, *and in 1998, another volume of essays entitled* Meditations from a Moveable Chair.

On the August morning when Matt Fowler buried his youngest son, Frank, who had lived for twenty-one years, eight months, and four days, Matt's older son, Steve, turned to him as the family left the grave and walked between their friends, and said: "I should kill him." He was twenty-eight, his brown hair starting to thin in front where he used to have a cowlick. He bit his lower lip, wiped his eyes, then said it again. Ruth's arm, linked with Matt's, tightened; he looked at her.

Beneath her eyes there was swelling from the three days she had suffered. At the limousine Matt stopped and looked back at the grave, the casket, and the Congregationalist minister who he thought had probably had a difficult job with the eulogy though he hadn't seemed to, and the old funeral director who was saying something to the six young pallbearers. The grave was on a hill and overlooked the Merrimack, which he could not see from where he stood; he looked at the opposite bank, at the apple orchard with its symmetrically planted trees going up a hill.

Next day Steve drove with his wife back to Baltimore where he managed the branch office of a bank, and Cathleen, the middle child, drove with her husband back to Syracuse. They had left the grandchildren with friends. A month after the funeral Matt played poker at Willis Trottier's because Ruth, who knew this was the second time he had been invited, told him to go, he couldn't sit home with her for the rest of her life, she was all right. After the game Willis went outside to tell everyone good night and, when the others had driven away, he walked with Matt to his car. Willis was a short, silver-haired man who had opened a diner after World War II, his trade then mostly very early breakfast, which he cooked, and then lunch for the men who worked at the leather and shoe factories. He now owned a large restaurant.

"He walks the Goddamn streets," Matt said.

"I know. He was in my place last night, at the bar. With a girl."

"I don't see him. I'm in the store all the time. Ruth sees him. She sees him　　5
too much. She was at Sunnyhurst today getting cigarettes and aspirin, and there he was. She can't even go out for cigarettes and aspirin. It's killing her."

"Come back in for a drink."

Matt looked at his watch. Ruth would be asleep. He walked with Willis back into the house, pausing at the steps to look at the starlit sky. It was a cool summer night; he thought vaguely of the Red Sox, did not even know if they were at home tonight; since it happened he had not been able to think about any of the small pleasures he believed he had earned, as he had earned also what was shattered now forever: the quietly harried and quietly pleasurable days of fatherhood. They went inside. Willis's wife, Martha, had gone to bed hours ago, in the rear of the large house which was rigged with burglar and fire alarms. They went downstairs to the game room: the television set suspended from the ceiling, the pool table, the poker table with beer cans, cards, chips, filled ashtrays, and the six chairs where Matt and his friends had sat, the friends picking up the old banter as though he had only been away on vacation; but he could see the affection and courtesy in their eyes. Willis went behind the bar and mixed them each a Scotch and soda; he stayed behind the bar and looked at Matt sitting on the stool.

"How often have you thought about it?" Willis said.

"Every day since he got out. I didn't think about bail. I thought I wouldn't have to worry about him for years. She sees him all the time. It makes her cry."

"He was in my place a long time last night. He'll be back."　　　　　　　　10

"Maybe he won't."

"The band. He likes the band."

"What's he doing now?"

"He's tending bar up to Hampton Beach. For a friend. Ever notice even the worst bastard always has friends? He couldn't get work in town. It's just tourists and kids up to Hampton. Nobody knows him. If they do, they don't care. They drink what he mixes."

"Nobody tells me about him."

"I hate him, Matt. My boys went to school with him. He was the same then. Know what he'll do? Five at the most. Remember that woman about seven years ago? Shot her husband and dropped him off the bridge in the Merrimack with a hundred-pound sack of cement and said all the way through it that nobody helped her. Know where she is now? She's in Lawrence now, a secretary. And whoever helped her, where the hell is he?"

"I've got a .38 I've had for years, I take it to the store now. I tell Ruth it's for the night deposits. I tell her things have changed: we got junkies here now too. Lots of people without jobs. She knows though."

"What does she know?"

"She knows I started carrying it after the first time she saw him in town. She knows it's in case I see him, and there's some kind of a situation—"

He stopped, looked at Willis, and finished his drink. Willis mixed him another.

"What kind of situation?"

"Where he did something to me. Where I could get away with it."

"How does Ruth feel about that?"

"She doesn't know."

"You said she does, she's got it figured out."

He thought of her that afternoon: when she went into Sunnyhurst, Strout was waiting at the counter while the clerk bagged the things he had bought; she turned down an aisle and looked at soup cans until he left.

"Ruth would shoot him herself, if she thought she could hit him."

"You got a permit?"

"No."

"I do. You could get a year for that."

"Maybe I'll get one. Or maybe I won't. Maybe I'll just stop bringing it to the store."

Richard Strout was twenty-six years old, a high school athlete, football scholarship to the University of Massachusetts where he lasted for almost two semesters before quitting in advance of the final grades that would have forced him not to return. People then said: Dickie can do the work; he just doesn't want to. He came home and did construction work for his father but refused his father's offer to learn the business; his two older brothers had learned it, so that Strout and Sons trucks going about town, and signs on construction sites, now slashed wounds into Matt Fowler's life. Then Richard married a young girl and became a bartender, his salary and tips augmented and perhaps sometimes matched by his father, who also posted his bond. So his friends, his enemies (he had those: fist fights or, more often, boys and then young men who had not fought him when they thought they should have), and those who simply knew him by face and

15

20

25

30

name, had a series of images of him which they recalled when they heard of the killing: the high school running back, the young drunk in bars, the oblivious hard-hatted young man eating lunch at a counter, the bartender who could perhaps be called courteous but not more than that: as he tended bar, his dark eyes and dark, wide-jawed face appeared less sullen, near blank.

One night he beat Frank. Frank was living at home and waiting for September, for graduate school in economics, and working as a lifeguard at Salisbury Beach, where he met Mary Ann Strout, in her first month of separation. She spent most days at the beach with her two sons. Before ten o'clock one night Frank came home; he had driven to the hospital first, and he walked into the living room with stitches over his right eye and both lips bright and swollen.

"I'm all right," he said, when Matt and Ruth stood up, and Matt turned off the television, letting Ruth get to him first: the tall, muscled but slender suntanned boy. Frank tried to smile at them but couldn't because of his lips.

"It was her husband, wasn't it?" Ruth said.   35

"Ex," Frank said. "He dropped in."

Matt gently held Frank's jaw and turned his face to the light, looked at the stitches, the blood under the white of the eye, the bruised flesh.

"Press charges," Matt said.

"No."

"What's to stop him from doing it again? Did you hit him at all? Enough so   40
he won't want to next time?"

"I don't think I touched him."

"So what are you going to do?"

"Take karate," Frank said, and tried again to smile.

"That's not the problem," Ruth said.

"You know you like her," Frank said.   45

"I like a lot of people. What about the boys? Did they see it?"

"They were asleep."

"Did you leave her alone with him?"

"He left first. She was yelling at him. I believe she had a skillet in her hand."

"Oh for God's sake," Ruth said.   50

Matt had been dealing with that too: at the dinner table on evenings when Frank wasn't home, was eating with Mary Ann; or, on the other nights—and Frank was with her every night—he talked with Ruth while they watched television, or lay in bed with the windows open and he smelled the night air and imagined, with both pride and muted sorrow, Frank in Mary Ann's arms. Ruth didn't like it because Mary Ann was in the process of divorce, because she had two children, because she was four years older than Frank, and finally—she told this in bed, where she had during all of their marriage told him of her deepest feelings: of love, of passion, of fears about one of the children, of pain Matt had caused her or she had caused him—she was against it because of what she had heard: that the marriage had gone bad early, and for most of it Richard and Mary Ann had both played around.

"That can't be true," Matt said. "Strout wouldn't have stood for it."

"Maybe he loves her."

"He's too hot-tempered. He couldn't have taken that."

But Matt knew Strout had taken it, for he had heard the stories too. He won-　55
dered who had told them to Ruth; and he felt vaguely annoyed and isolated: living with her for thirty-one years and still not knowing what she talked about with
her friends. On these summer nights he did not so much argue with her as try to
comfort her, but finally there was no difference between the two: she had concrete objections, which he tried to overcome. And in his attempt to do this, he
neglected his own objections, which were the same as hers, so that as he spoke to
her he felt as disembodied as he sometimes did in the store when he helped a
man choose a blouse or dress or piece of costume jewelry for his wife.

"The divorce doesn't mean anything," he said. "She was young and maybe
she liked his looks and then after a while she realized she was living with a bastard. I see it as a positive thing."

"She's not divorced yet."

"It's the same thing. Massachusetts has crazy laws, that's all. Her age is no
problem. What's it matter when she was born? And that other business: even if it's
true, which it probably isn't, it's got nothing to do with Frank, and it's in the past.
And the kids are no problem. She's been married six years; she ought to have kids.
Frank likes them. He plays with them. And he's not going to marry her anyway, so
it's not a problem of money."

"Then what's he doing with her?"

"She probably loves him, Ruth. Girls always have. Why can't we just leave it　60
at that?"

"He got home at six o'clock Tuesday morning."

"I didn't know you knew. I've already talked to him about it."

Which he had: since he believed almost nothing he told Ruth, he went to
Frank with what he believed. The night before, he had followed Frank to the car
after dinner.

"You wouldn't make much of a burglar," he said.

"How's that?"　65

Matt was looking up at him; Frank was six feet tall, an inch and a half taller
than Matt, who had been proud when Frank at seventeen outgrew him; he had
only felt uncomfortable when he had to reprimand or caution him. He touched
Frank's bicep, thought of the young taut passionate body, believed he could sense
the desire, and again he felt the pride and sorrow and envy too, not knowing
whether he was envious of Frank or Mary Ann.

"When you came in yesterday morning, I woke up. One of these mornings
your mother will. And I'm the one who'll have to talk to her. She won't interfere
with you. Okay? I know it means—" But he stopped, thinking: I know it means
getting up and leaving that suntanned girl and going sleepy to the car, I know—

"Okay," Frank said, and touched Matt's shoulder and got into the car.

There had been other talks, but the only long one was their first one: a night
driving to Fenway Park, Matt having ordered the tickets so they could talk, and
knowing when Frank said yes, he would go, that he knew the talk was coming
too. It took them forty minutes to get to Boston, and they talked about Mary Ann
until they joined the city traffic along the Charles River, blue in the late sun.

Frank told him all the things that Matt would later pretend to believe when he told them to Ruth.

"It seems like a lot for a young guy to take on," Matt finally said. 70

"Sometimes it is. But she's worth it."

"Are you thinking about getting married?"

"We haven't talked about it. She can't for over a year. I've got school."

"I *do* like her," Matt said.

He did. Some evenings, when the long summer sun was still low in the sky, 75 Frank brought her home; they came into the house smelling of suntan lotion and the sea, and Matt gave them gin and tonics and started the charcoal in the back-yard, and looked at Mary Ann in the lawn chair: long and very light brown hair (Matt thinking that twenty years ago she would have dyed it blonde), and the long brown legs he loved to look at; her face was pretty; she had probably never in her adult life gone unnoticed into a public place. It was in her wide brown eyes that she looked older than Frank; after a few drinks Matt thought what he saw in her eyes was something erotic, testament to the rumors about her; but he knew it wasn't that, or all that: she had, very young, been through a sort of pain that his children, and he and Ruth, had been spared. In the moments of his recognizing that pain, he wanted to tenderly touch her hair, wanted with some gesture to give her solace and hope. And he would glance at Frank, and hope they would love each other, hope Frank would soothe that pain in her heart, take it from her eyes; and her divorce, her age, and her children did not matter at all. On the first two evenings she did not bring her boys, and then Ruth asked her to bring them the next time. In bed that night Ruth said, "She hasn't brought them because she's embarrassed. She shouldn't feel embarrassed."

Richard Strout shot Frank in front of the boys. They were sitting on the living room floor watching television, Frank sitting on the couch, and Mary Ann just returning from the kitchen with a tray of sandwiches. Strout came in the front door and shot Frank twice in the chest and once in the face with a 9 mm auto-matic. Then he looked at the boys and Mary Ann, and went home to wait for the police.

It seemed to Matt that from the time Mary Ann called weeping to tell him until now, a Saturday night in September, sitting in the car with Willis, parked beside Strout's car, waiting for the bar to close, that he had not so much moved through his life as wandered through it, his spirits like a dazed body bumping into furniture and corners. He had always been a fearful father: when his chil-dren were young, at the start of each summer he thought of them drowning in a pond or the sea, and he was relieved when he came home in the evenings and they were there; usually that relief was his only acknowledgment of his fear, which he never spoke of, and which he controlled within his heart. As he had when they were very young and all of them in turn, Cathleen too, were drawn to the high oak in the backyard, and had to climb it. Smiling, he watched them, imagining the fall: and he was poised to catch the small body before it hit the earth. Or his legs were poised; his hands were in his pockets or his arms were folded and, for the child looking down, he appeared relaxed and confident while his heart beat with the two words he wanted to call out but did not: *Don't fall.* In winter he was less afraid: he made sure the ice would hold him before they skated, and he brought or sent them to places where they could sled without ending in the street. So he and his children had survived their childhood, and he only worried about them when he knew they were driving a long distance, and then he lost Frank in a way no father expected to lose his son, and he felt that all the fears he had borne while they were growing up, and all the grief he had been afraid of, had backed up like a huge wave and struck him on the beach and swept him out to sea. Each day he felt the same and when he was able to forget how he felt, when he was able to force himself not to feel that way, the eyes of his clerks and customers defeated him. He wished those eyes were oblivious, even cold; he felt he was withering in their tenderness. And beneath his listless wandering, every day in his soul he shot Richard Strout in the face; while Ruth, going about town on errands, kept seeing him. And at night in bed she would hold Matt and cry, or sometimes she was silent and Matt would touch her tightening arm, her clenched fist.

As his own right fist was now, squeezing the butt of the revolver, the last of the drinkers having left the bar, talking to each other, going to their separate cars which were in the lot in front of the bar, out of Matt's vision. He heard their voices, their cars, and then the ocean again, across the street. The tide was in and sometimes it smacked the sea wall. Through the windshield he looked at the dark red side wall of the bar, and then to his left, past Willis, at Strout's car, and through its windows he could see the now-emptied parking lot, the road, the sea wall. He could smell the sea.

The front door of the bar opened and closed again and Willis looked at Matt then at the corner of the building; when Strout came around it alone Matt got out of the car, giving up the hope he had kept all night (and for the past week) that Strout would come out with friends, and Willis would simply drive away; thinking: *All right then. All right*; and he went around the front of Willis's car, and at Strout's he stopped and aimed over the hood at Strout's blue shirt ten feet away. Willis was aiming too, crouched on Matt's left, his elbow resting on the hood.

"Mr. Fowler," Strout said. He looked at each of them, and at the guns. "Mr.   80
Trottier."

Then Matt, watching the parking lot and the road, walked quickly between the car and the building and stood behind Strout. He took one leather glove from his pocket and put it on his left hand.

"Don't talk. Unlock the front and back and get in."

Strout unlocked the front door, reached in and unlocked the back, then got in, and Matt slid into the back seat, closed the door with his gloved hand, and touched Strout's head once with the muzzle.

"It's cocked. Drive to your house."

When Strout looked over his shoulder to back the car, Matt aimed at his   85
temple and did not look at his eyes.

"Drive slowly," he said. "Don't try to get stopped."

They drove across the empty front lot and onto the road, Willis's headlights shining into the car; then back through town, the sea wall on the left hiding the beach, though far out Matt could see the ocean; he uncocked the revolver; on the right were the places, most with their neon signs off, that did so much business in summer: the lounges and cafés and pizza houses, the street itself empty of traffic, the way he and Willis had known it would be when they decided to take Strout at the bar rather than knock on his door at two o'clock one morning and risk that one insomniac neighbor. Matt had not told Willis he was afraid he could not be alone with Strout for very long, smell his smells, feel the presence of his flesh, hear his voice, and then shoot him. They left the beach town and then were on the high bridge over the channel: to the left the smacking curling white at the breakwater and beyond that the dark sea and the full moon, and down to his right the small fishing boats bobbing at anchor in the cove. When they left the bridge, the sea was blocked by abandoned beach cottages, and Matt's left hand was sweating in the glove. Out here in the dark in the car he believed Ruth knew. Willis had come to his house at eleven and asked if he wanted a nightcap; Matt went to the bedroom for his wallet, put the gloves in one trouser pocket and the .38 in the other and went back to the living room, his hand in his pocket covering the bulge of the cool cylinder pressed against his fingers, the butt against his palm. When Ruth said good night she looked at his face, and he felt she could see in his eyes the gun, and the night he was going to. But he knew he couldn't trust what he saw. Willis's wife had taken her sleeping pill, which gave her eight hours—the reason, Willis had told Matt, he had the alarms installed, for nights when he was late at the restaurant—and when it was all done and Willis got home he would leave ice and a trace of Scotch and soda in two glasses in the game room and tell Martha in the morning that he had left the restaurant early and brought Matt home for a drink.

"He was making it with my wife." Strout's voice was careful, not pleading.

Matt pressed the muzzle against Strout's head, pressed it harder than he wanted to, feeling through the gun Strout's head flinching and moving forward; then he lowered the gun to his lap.

"Don't talk," he said.　　　　　　　　　　　　　　　　　　　　90

Strout did not speak again. They turned west, drove past the Dairy Queen closed until spring, and the two lobster restaurants that faced each other and were crowded all summer and were now also closed, onto the short bridge crossing the tidal stream, and over the engine Matt could hear through his open window the water rushing inland under the bridge; looking to his left he saw its swift moonlit current going back into the marsh which, leaving the bridge, they entered: the salt marsh stretching out on both sides, the grass tall in patches but mostly low and leaning earthward as though windblown, a large dark rock sitting as though it rested on nothing but itself, and shallow pools reflecting the bright moon.

Beyond the marsh they drove through woods, Matt thinking now of the hole he and Willis had dug last Sunday afternoon after telling their wives they were going to Fenway Park. They listened to the game on a transistor radio, but heard none of it as they dug into the soft earth on the knoll they had chosen because elms and maples sheltered it. Already some leaves had fallen. When the hole was deep enough they covered it and the piled earth with dead branches, then cleaned their shoes and pants and went to a restaurant farther up in New Hampshire where they ate sandwiches and drank beer and watched the rest of the game on television. Looking at the back of Strout's head he thought of Frank's grave; he had not been back to it; but he would go before winter, and its second burial of snow.

He thought of Frank sitting on the couch and perhaps talking to the children as they watched television, imagined him feeling young and strong, still warmed from the sun at the beach, and feeling loved, hearing Mary Ann moving about in the kitchen, hearing her walking into the living room; maybe he looked up at her and maybe she said something, looking at him over the tray of sandwiches, smiling at him, saying something the way women do when they offer food as a gift, then the front door opening and this son of a bitch coming in and Frank seeing that he meant the gun in his hand, this son of a bitch and his gun the last person and thing Frank saw on earth.

When they drove into town the streets were nearly empty: a few slow cars, a policeman walking his beat past the darkened fronts of stores. Strout and Matt both glanced at him as they drove by. They were on the main street, and all the stoplights were blinking yellow. Willis and Matt had talked about that too: the lights changed at midnight, so there would be no place Strout had to stop and where he might try to run. Strout turned down the block where he lived and Willis's headlights were no longer with Matt in the back seat. They had planned that too, had decided it was best for just the one car to go to the house, and again Matt had said nothing about his fear of being alone with Strout, especially in his house: a duplex, dark as all the houses on the street were, the street itself lit at the corner of each block. As Strout turned into the driveway Matt thought of the one insomniac neighbor, thought of some man or woman sitting alone in the dark living room, watching the all-night channel from Boston. When Strout stopped the car near the front of the house, Matt said: "Drive it to the back."

He touched Strout's head with the muzzle.   95

"You wouldn't have it cocked, would you? For when I put on the brakes."

Matt cocked it, and said: "It is now."

Strout waited a moment; then he eased the car forward, the engine doing little more than idling, and as they approached the garage he gently braked. Matt opened the door, then took off the glove and put it in his pocket. He stepped out and shut the door with his hip and said: "All right."

Strout looked at the gun, then got out, and Matt followed him across the grass, and as Strout unlocked the door Matt looked quickly at the row of small backyards on either side, and scattered tall trees, some evergreens, others not, and he thought of the red and yellow leaves on the trees over the hole, saw them falling soon, probably in two weeks, dropping slowly, covering. Strout stepped into the kitchen.

"Turn on the light."   100

Strout reached to the wall switch, and in the light Matt looked at his wide back, the dark blue shirt, the white belt, the red plaid pants.

"Where's your suitcase?"

"My suitcase?"

"Where is it?"

"In the bedroom closet." 105

"That's where we're going then. When we get to a door you stop and turn on the light."

They crossed the kitchen, Matt glancing at the sink and stove and refrigerator: no dishes in the sink or even the dish rack beside it, no grease splashings on the stove, the refrigerator door clean and white. He did not want to look at any more but he looked quickly at all he could see: in the living room magazines and newspapers in a wicker basket, clean ashtrays, a record player, the records shelved next to it, then down the hall where, near the bedroom door, hung a color photograph of Mary Ann and the two boys sitting on a lawn — there was no house in the picture — Mary Ann smiling at the camera or Strout or whoever held the camera, smiling as she had on Matt's lawn this summer while he waited for the charcoal and they all talked and he looked at her brown legs and at Frank touching her arm, her shoulder, her hair; he moved down the hall with her smile in his mind, wondering: was that when they were both playing around and she was smiling like that at him and they were happy, even sometimes, making it worth it? He recalled her eyes, the pain in them, and he was conscious of the circles of love he was touching with the hand that held the revolver so tightly now as Strout stopped at the door at the end of the hall.

"There's no wall switch."

"Where's the light?"

"By the bed." 110

"Let's go."

Matt stayed a pace behind, then Strout leaned over and the room was lighted: the bed, a double one, was neatly made; the ashtray on the bedside table clean, the bureau top dustless, and no photographs; probably so the girl — who *was* she? — would not have to see Mary Ann in the bedroom she believed was theirs. But because Matt was a father and a husband, though never an ex-husband, he knew (and did not want to know) that this bedroom had never been theirs alone. Strout turned around; Matt looked at his lips, his wide jaw, and thought of Frank's doomed and fearful eyes looking up from the couch.

"Where's Mr. Trottier?"

"He's waiting. Pack clothes for warm weather."

"What's going on?" 115

"You're jumping bail."

"Mr. Fowler—"

He pointed the cocked revolver at Strout's face. The barrel trembled but not much, not as much as he had expected. Strout went to the closet and got the suitcase from the floor and opened it on the bed. As he went to the bureau, he said: "He was making it with my wife. I'd go pick up my kids and he'd be there. Sometimes he spent the night. My boys told me."

He did not look at Matt as he spoke. He opened the top drawer and Matt stepped closer so he could see Strout's hands: underwear and socks, the socks rolled, the underwear folded and stacked. He took them back to the bed, arranged them neatly in the suitcase, then from the closet he was taking shirts and trousers and a jacket; he laid them on the bed and Matt followed him to the bathroom and watched from the door while he packed those things a person accumulated and that became part of him so that at times in the store Matt felt he was selling more than clothes.

"I wanted to try to get together with her again." He was bent over the suit-   120
case. "I couldn't even talk to her. He was always with her. I'm going to jail for it; if I ever get out I'll be an old man. Isn't that enough?"

"You're not going to jail."

Strout closed the suitcase and faced Matt, looking at the gun. Matt went to his rear, so Strout was between him and the lighted hall; then using his handker-chief he turned off the lamp and said: "Let's go."

They went down the hall, Matt looking again at the photograph, and through the living room and kitchen, Matt turning off the lights and talking, frightened that he was talking, that he was telling this lie he had not planned: "It's the trial. We can't go through that, my wife and me. So you're leaving. We've got you a ticket, and a job. A friend of Mr. Trottier's. Out west. My wife keeps seeing you. We can't have that anymore."

Matt turned out the kitchen light and put the handkerchief in his pocket, and they went down the two brick steps and across the lawn. Strout put the suit-case on the floor of the back seat, then got into the front seat and Matt got in the back and put on his glove and shut the door.

"They'll catch me. They'll check passenger lists."   125

"We didn't use your name."

"They'll figure that out too. You think I wouldn't have done it myself if it was that easy?"

He backed into the street, Matt looking down the gun barrel but not at the profiled face beyond it.

"You were alone," Matt said. "We've got it worked out."

"There's no planes this time of night, Mr. Fowler."   130

"Go back through town. Then north on 125."

They came to the corner and turned, and now Willis's headlights were in the car with Matt.

"Why north, Mr. Fowler?"

"Somebody's going to keep you for a while. They'll take you to the airport." He uncocked the hammer and lowered the revolver to his lap and said wearily: "No more talking."

As they drove back through town, Matt's body sagged, going limp with his   135
spirit and its new and false bond with Strout, the hope his lie had given Strout. He had grown up in this town whose streets had become places of apprehension and pain for Ruth as she drove and walked, doing what she had to do; and for him too, if only in his mind as he worked and chatted six days a week in his store; he wondered now if his lie would have worked, if sending Strout away would have been enough; but then he knew that just thinking of Strout in Montana or what-ever place lay at the end of the lie he had told, thinking of him walking the streets there, loving a girl there (who *was* she?) would be enough to slowly rot the rest

of his days. And Ruth's. Again he was certain that she knew, that she was waiting for him.

They were in New Hampshire now, on the narrow highway, passing the shopping center at the state line, and then houses and small stores and sandwich shops. There were few cars on the road. After ten minutes he raised his trembling hand, touched Strout's neck with the gun, and said: "Turn in up here. At the dirt road."

Strout flicked on the indicator and slowed.

"Mr. Fowler?"

"They're waiting here."

Strout turned very slowly, easing his neck away from the gun. In the moon- 140 light the road was light brown, lighter and yellowed where the headlights shone; weeds and a few trees grew on either side of it, and ahead of them were the woods.

"There's nothing back here, Mr. Fowler."

"It's for your car. You don't think we'd leave it at the airport, do you?"

He watched Strout's large, big-knuckled hands tighten on the wheel, saw Frank's face that night: not the stitches and bruised eye and swollen lips, but his own hand gently touching Frank's jaw, turning his wounds to the light. They rounded a bend in the road and were out of sight of the highway: tall trees all around them now, hiding the moon. When they reached the abandoned gravel pit on the left, the bare flat earth and steep pale embankment behind it, and the black crowns of trees at its top, Matt said: "Stop here."

Strout stopped but did not turn off the engine. Matt pressed the gun hard against his neck, and he straightened in the seat and looked in the rearview mirror, Matt's eyes meeting his in the glass for an instant before looking at the hair at the end of the gun barrel.

"Turn it off." 145

Strout did, then held the wheel with two hands, and looked in the mirror.

"I'll do twenty years, Mr. Fowler; at least. I'll be forty-six years old."

"That's nine years younger than I am," Matt said, and got out and took off the glove and kicked the door shut. He aimed at Strout's ear and pulled back the hammer. Willis's headlights were off and Matt heard him walking on the soft thin layer of dust, the hard earth beneath it. Strout opened the door, sat for a moment in the interior light, then stepped out onto the road. Now his face was pleading. Matt did not look at his eyes, but he could see it in the lips.

"Just get the suitcase. They're right up the road."

Willis was beside him now, to his left. Strout looked at both guns. Then he 150 opened the back door, leaned in, and with a jerk brought the suitcase out. He was turning to face them when Matt said: "Just walk up the road. Just ahead."

Strout turned to walk, the suitcase in his right hand, and Matt and Willis followed; as Strout cleared the front of his car he dropped the suitcase and, ducking, took one step that was the beginning of a sprint to his right. The gun kicked in Matt's hand, and the explosion of the shot surrounded him, isolated him in a nimbus of sound that cut him off from all his time, all his history, isolated him standing absolutely still on the dirt road with the gun in his hand, looking down at Richard Strout squirming on his belly, kicking one leg behind him, pushing himself forward, toward the woods. Then Matt went to him and shot him once in the back of the head.

Driving south to Boston, wearing both gloves now, staying in the middle lane and looking often in the rearview mirror at Willis's headlights, he relived the suitcase dropping, the quick dip and turn of Strout's back, and the kick of the gun, the sound of the shot. When he walked to Strout, he still existed within the first shot, still trembled and breathed with it. The second shot and the burial seemed to be happening to someone else, someone he was watching. He and Willis each held an arm and pulled Strout face-down off the road and into the woods, his bouncing sliding belt white under the trees where it was so dark that when they stopped at the top of the knoll, panting and sweating, Matt could not see where Strout's blue shirt ended and the earth began. They pulled off the branches then dragged Strout to the edge of the hole and went behind him and lifted his legs and pushed him in. They stood still for a moment. The woods were quiet save for their breathing, and Matt remembered hearing the movements of birds and small animals after the first shot. Or maybe he had not heard them. Willis went down to the road. Matt could see him clearly out on the tan dirt, could see the glint of Strout's car and, beyond the road, the gravel pit. Willis came back up the knoll with the suitcase. He dropped it in the hole and took off his gloves and they went down to his car for the spades. They worked quietly. Sometimes they paused to listen to the woods. When they were finished Willis turned on his flashlight and they covered the earth with leaves and branches and then went down to the spot in front of the car, and while Matt held the light Willis crouched and sprinkled dust on the blood, backing up till he reached the grass and leaves, then he used leaves until they had worked up to the grave again. They did not stop. They walked around the grave and through the woods, using the light on the ground, looking up through the trees to where they ended at the lake. Neither of them spoke above the sounds of their heavy and clumsy strides through low brush and over fallen branches. Then they reached it: wide and dark, lapping softly at the bank, pine needles smooth under Matt's feet, moonlight on the lake, a small island near its middle, with black, tall evergreens. He took out the gun and threw for the island: taking two steps back on the pine needles, striding with the throw and going to one knee as he followed through, looking up to see the dark shapeless object arcing downward, splashing.

They left Strout's car in Boston, in front of an apartment building on Commonwealth Avenue. When they got back to town Willis drove slowly over the bridge and Matt threw the keys into the Merrimack. The sky was turning light. Willis let him out a block from his house, and walking home he listened for sounds from the houses he passed. They were quiet. A light was on in his living room. He turned it off and undressed in there, and went softly toward the bedroom; in the hall he smelled the smoke, and he stood in the bedroom doorway and looked at the orange of her cigarette in the dark. The curtains were closed. He went to the closet and put his shoes on the floor and felt for a hanger.

"Did you do it?" she said.

He went down the hall to the bathroom and in the dark he washed his hands   155
and face. Then he went to her, lay on his back, and pulled the sheet up to his
throat.

"Are you all right?" she said.

"I think so."

Now she touched him, lying on her side, her hand on his belly, his thigh.

"Tell me," she said.

He started from the beginning, in the parking lot at the bar; but soon with his   160
eyes closed and Ruth petting him, he spoke of Strout's house: the order, the
woman presence, the picture on the wall.

"The way she was smiling," he said.

"What about it?"

"I don't know. Did you ever see Strout's girl? When you saw him in town?"

"No."

"I wonder who she was."   165

Then he thought: *not was: is. Sleeping now she is his girl.* He opened his eyes,
then closed them again. There was more light beyond the curtains. With Ruth
now he left Strout's house and told again his lie to Strout, gave him again that
hope that Strout must have for a while believed, else he would have to believe
only the gun pointed at him for the last two hours of his life. And with Ruth he
saw again the dropping suitcase, the darting move to the right: and he told of the
first shot, feeling her hand on him but his heart isolated still, beating on the road
still in that explosion like thunder. He told her the rest, but the words had no
images for him, he did not see himself doing what the words said he had done; he
only saw himself on that road.

"We can't tell the other kids," she said. "It'll hurt them, thinking he got away.
But we mustn't."

"No."

She was holding him, wanting him, and he wished he could make love with
her but he could not. He saw Frank and Mary Ann making love in her bed, their
eyes closed, their bodies brown and smelling of the sea; the other girl was faceless,
bodiless, but he felt her sleeping now; and he saw Frank and Strout, their faces
alive; he saw red and yellow leaves falling on the earth, then snow: falling and
freezing and falling; and holding Ruth, his cheek touching her breast, he shuddered with a sob that he kept silent in his heart.   [1979]

THINKING ABOUT THE TEXT

1. Here is an issue of cause and effect: Why, evidently, does Matt kill Richard
   Strout? Consider the possibility that he has more than one reason. Here is
   an issue of evaluation: To what extent should the reader sympathize with
   Matt? Identify some things that readers should especially consider in addressing this question.

2. Identify the argument that Richard Strout makes as he tries to keep Matt
   from killing him. What warrants or assumptions does Strout use? How
   common is his way of thinking?

3. Why does Willis help Matt take revenge? To what extent does Ruth's thinking resemble her husband's?

4. What is Matt's view of Mary Ann, his late son's girlfriend?

5. After beginning with Frank's funeral, the story features several flashbacks. Only gradually does Dubus provide certain seemingly important facts, such as exactly how Matt's son died. ("Richard Strout shot Frank in front of the boys.") What do you think might have been Dubus's purpose(s) in refusing to be more straightforward? In the last several pages, the story is pretty straightforward, moving step by step through the night of Matt's revenge. Why do you suppose Dubus changed his method of storytelling?

MAKING COMPARISONS

1. Montresor and Matt carefully plan their revenge. But Pauline appears to commit revenge spontaneously, not carefully planning it beforehand. Does this difference matter to you as you judge these three acts of revenge? Why, or why not?

2. How guilty does each of these three avengers feel? Compare their degrees of citing specific details from each text to support your impressions.

3. Do Poe, Erdrich, and Dubus seem equally committed to making you feel that the settings they describe really exist? Again, support your answer by referring to specific details from each text.

WRITING ABOUT ISSUES

1. Choose one of the three stories in this cluster and write an essay identifying the extent to which readers ought to feel sorry for the victim or victims of revenge. Argue for your position by citing details of the text.

2. In her book *Bird by Bird: Some Instructions on Writing and Life*, Anne Lamott advises would-be fiction writers that a story must culminate in "a killing or a healing or a domination." She goes on to explain:

> It can be a real killing, a murder, or it can be a killing of the spirit, or of something terrible inside one's soul, or it can be a killing of a deadness within, after which the person becomes alive again. The healing may be about union, reclamation, the rescue of a fragile prize. But whatever happens, we need to feel that it was inevitable, that even though we may be amazed, it feels absolutely right, that of course things would come to this, of course they would shake down in this way.

Choose two of the stories in this cluster and write an essay discussing the extent to which they obey Lamott's advice. Refer to specific words in the passage from her, as well as to specific details of the stories. If you wish, feel free to evaluate Lamott's advice. Do you think fiction writers ought to follow it?

3. Gerald Murphy, a famous socialite of the 1920s, once said that "living well is the best revenge." Murphy did not identify whom it was revenge against. Still, his statement is thought-provoking in its suggestion that revenge is not always recognizable as such. "Living well" may be revenge in disguise. Write an essay showing how a specific action you are familiar with can be seen as an act of revenge, even though many people wouldn't realize this. In your essay, also evaluate the action. Do you approve of this act of revenge? Why, or why not?

4. Write an essay examining a real-life legal case that involved one or more of the acts depicted in these stories: for example, rape, sexual relations between employer and employee, racial discrimination, reactions to perceived insults, acts of revenge. To learn important facts about the case, you may have to do research in the library. In your essay, point out at least one issue raised by the case, identify your position on the issue, and support your position. If you wish, refer to any of the stories in this cluster.

VALUE JUDGMENTS:
A COLLECTION OF WRITINGS BY ALICE WALKER

ALICE WALKER, "Everyday Use"
ALICE WALKER, "Nineteen Fifty-Five"
ALICE WALKER, "In Search of Our Mothers' Gardens"

Alice Walker is a leading contemporary fiction writer, poet, and essayist. She writes on a variety of topics and often addresses the issue of how African American culture should be valued. In the pieces collected here — two stories and an essay — Walker identifies ways in which white Americans as well as African Americans have been tempted to see African American culture as a mere commodity. At the same time, Walker proposes other ways of valuing this culture's artifacts. Moreover, she suggests that many African American artists have yet to be recognized as such. Overall, this cluster encourages you to review your own judgments of artistic value. It encourages you, too, to consider how cultural biases may prevent people from seeing deep worth in other people's achievements.

BEFORE YOU READ

List several people you know, including yourself. Then identify ways in which they might be considered artists. Finally, list some words you associate with the word *art*.

ALICE WALKER
Everyday Use

Alice Walker (b. 1944) is an accomplished writer in many genres. A native of Eatonton, Georgia, she attended Spelman College and Sarah Lawrence College. During the 1960s, she was active in the civil rights movement, an experience reflected in her 1976 novel Meridian. *Also, she has long been involved in the women's movement, among other things being a frequent contributor to* Ms. *magazine. Today, Walker is best known for her 1982 novel* The Color Purple. *Besides winning the Pulitzer Prize and the American Book Award, it was made into a popular film. Walker's other novels include* The Third Life of Grange Copeland *(1970),* The Temple of My Familiar *(1989), and* Possessing the Secret of Joy *(1992), a sequel to* The Color Purple *that criticizes forced clitoridectomies. Walker has continued to examine this practice in a documentary film,* Warrior Marks *(1995), as well as in a nonfiction book with the same title. Her volumes of poetry include* Revolutionary Petunias and Other Poems *(1973) and* Goodnight, Willie Lee, I'll See You in the Morning *(1979). As an essayist, she has produced the collections* In Search of Our Mothers' Gardens: Womanist Prose *(1983),* Living by the Word *(1988),* The Same River Twice *(1995), and* Anything We Love Can Be Saved *(1997). Furthermore, Walker's short stories are collected in* In Love and Trouble: Stories of Black Women *(1973), which includes "Everyday Use," and* You Can't Keep a Good Woman Down *(1981).*

I will wait for her in the yard that Maggie and I made so clean and wavy yesterday afternoon. A yard like this is more comfortable than most people know. It is not just a yard. It is like an extended living room. When the hard clay is swept clean as a floor and the fine sand around the edges lined with tiny, irregular grooves anyone can come and sit and look up into the elm tree and wait for the breezes that never come inside the house.

Maggie will be nervous until after her sister goes: she will stand hopelessly in corners homely and ashamed of the burn scars down her arms and legs, eyeing her sister with a mixture of envy and awe. She thinks her sister has held life always in the palm of one hand, that "no" is a word the world never learned to say to her.

You've no doubt seen those TV shows where the child who has "made it" is confronted, as a surprise, by her own mother and father, tottering in weakly from backstage. (A pleasant surprise, of course: What would they do if parent and child came on the show only to curse out and insult each other?) On TV mother and child embrace and smile into each other's faces. Sometimes the mother and father weep, the child wraps them in her arms and leans across the table to tell how she would not have made it without their help. I have seen these programs.

Sometimes I dream a dream in which Dee and I are suddenly brought together on a TV program of this sort. Out of a dark and soft-seated limousine I am ushered into a bright room filled with many people. There I meet a smiling, gray, sporty man like Johnny Carson who shakes my hand and tells me what a fine girl I have. Then we are on the stage and Dee is embracing me with tears in her eyes. She pins on my dress a large orchid, even though she has told me once that she thinks orchids are tacky flowers.

In real life I am a large, big-boned woman with rough, man-working hands.   5
In the winter I wear flannel nightgowns to bed and overalls during the day. I can kill and clean a hog as mercilessly as a man. My fat keeps me hot in zero weather. I can work outside all day, breaking ice to get water for washing; I can eat pork liver cooked over the open fire minutes after it comes steaming from the hog. One winter I knocked a bull calf straight in the brain between the eyes with a sledge hammer and had the meat hung up to chill before nightfall. But of course all this does not show on television. I am the way my daughter would want me to be: a hundred pounds lighter, my skin like an uncooked barley pancake. My hair glistens in the hot bright lights. Johnny Carson has much to do to keep up with my quick and witty tongue.

But that is a mistake. I know even before I wake up. Who ever knew a Johnson with a quick tongue? Who can even imagine me looking a strange white man in the eye? It seems to me I have talked to them always with one foot raised in flight, with my head turned in whichever way is farthest from them. Dee, though. She would always look anyone in the eye. Hesitation was no part of her nature.

"How do I look, Mama?" Maggie says, showing just enough of her thin body enveloped in pink skirt and red blouse for me to know she's there, almost hidden by the door.

"Come out into the yard," I say.

Have you ever seen a lame animal, perhaps a dog run over by some careless person rich enough to own a car, sidle up to someone who is ignorant enough to be kind to him? That is the way my Maggie walks. She has been like this, chin on chest, eyes on ground, feet in shuffle, ever since the fire that burned the other house to the ground.

Dee is lighter than Maggie, with nicer hair and a fuller figure. She's a   10
woman now, though sometimes I forget. How long ago was it that the other house burned? Ten, twelve years? Sometimes I can still hear the flames and feel Maggie's arms sticking to me, her hair smoking and her dress falling off her in little black papery flakes. Her eyes seemed stretched open, blazed open by the flames reflected in them. And Dee. I see her standing off under the sweet gum tree she used to dig gum out of; a look of concentration on her face as she watched the last dingy gray board of the house fall in toward the red-hot brick chimney. Why don't you do a dance around the ashes? I'd wanted to ask her. She had hated the house that much.

I used to think she hated Maggie, too. But that was before we raised the money, the church and me, to send her to Augusta to school. She used to read to us without pity; forcing words, lies, other folks' habits, whole lives upon us two, sitting trapped and ignorant underneath her voice. She washed us in a river of make-believe, burned us with a lot of knowledge we didn't necessarily need to know. Pressed us to her with the serious way she read, to shove us away at just the moment, like dimwits, we seemed about to understand.

Dee wanted nice things. A yellow organdy dress to wear to her graduation from high school; black pumps to match a green suit she'd made from an old suit somebody gave me. She was determined to stare down any disaster in her efforts. Her eyelids would not flicker for minutes at a time. Often I fought off the temptation to shake her. At sixteen she had a style of her own: and knew what style was.

I never had an education myself. After second grade the school was closed down. Don't ask me why: in 1927 colored asked fewer questions than they do now. Sometimes Maggie reads to me. She stumbles along good-naturedly but can't see well. She knows she is not bright. Like good looks and money, quickness passed her by. She will marry John Thomas (who has mossy teeth in an earnest face) and then I'll be free to sit here and I guess just sing church songs to myself. Although I never was a good singer. Never could carry a tune. I was always better at a man's job. I used to love to milk till I was hooked in the side in '49. Cows are soothing and slow and don't bother you, unless you try to milk them the wrong way.

I have deliberately turned my back on the house. It is three rooms, just like the one that burned, except the roof is tin; they don't make shingle roofs any more. There are no real windows, just some holes cut in the sides, like the portholes in a ship, but not round and not square, with rawhide holding the shutters up on the outside. This house is in a pasture, too, like the other one. No doubt when Dee sees it she will want to tear it down. She wrote me once that no matter where we "choose" to live, she will manage to come see us. But she will never bring her friends. Maggie and I thought about this and Maggie asked me, "Mama, when did Dee ever *have* any friends?"

She had a few. Furtive boys in pink shirts hanging about on washday after school. Nervous girls who never laughed. Impressed with her they worshiped the well-turned phrase, the cute shape, the scalding humor that erupted like bubbles in lye. She read to them. 15

When she was courting Jimmy T she didn't have much time to pay to us, but turned all her faultfinding power on him. He *flew* to marry a cheap gal from a family of ignorant flashy people. She hardly had time to recompose herself.

When she comes I will meet — but there they are!

Maggie attempts to make a dash for the house, in her shuffling way, but I stay her with my hand. "Come back here," I say. And she stops and tries to dig a well in the sand with her toe.

It is hard to see them clearly through the strong sun. But even the first glimpse of leg out of the car tells me it is Dee. Her feet were always neat-looking, as if God himself had shaped them with a certain style. From the other side of the car comes a short, stocky man. Hair is all over his head a foot long and hanging from his chin like a kinky mule tail. I hear Maggie suck in her breath. "Uhnnnh," is what it sounds like. Like when you see the wriggling end of a snake just in front of your foot on the road. "Uhnnnh."

Dee next. A dress down to the ground, in this hot weather. A dress so loud it   20 hurts my eyes. There are yellows and oranges enough to throw back the light of the sun. I feel my whole face warming from the heat waves it throws out. Earrings gold, too, and hanging down to her shoulders. Bracelets dangling and making noises when she moves her arm up to shake the folds of the dress out of her armpits. The dress is loose and flows, and as she walks closer, I like it. I hear Maggie go "Uhnnnh" again. It is her sister's hair. It stands straight up like the wool on a sheep. It is black as night and around the edges are two long pigtails that rope about like small lizards disappearing behind her ears.

"Wa-su-zo-Tean-o!" she says, coming on in that gliding way the dress makes her move. The short stocky fellow with the hair to his navel is all grinning and he follows up with "Asalamalakim, my mother and sister!" He moves to hug Maggie but she falls back, right up against the back of my chair. I feel her trembling there and when I look up I see the perspiration falling off her chin.

"Don't get up," says Dee. Since I am stout it takes something of a push. You can see me trying to move a second or two before I make it. She turns, showing white heels through her sandals, and goes back to the car. Out she peeks next with a Polaroid. She stoops down quickly and lines up picture after picture of me sitting there in front of the house with Maggie cowering behind me. She never takes a shot without making sure the house is included. When a cow comes nibbling around the edge of the yard she snaps it and me and Maggie *and* the house. Then she puts the Polaroid in the back seat of the car, and comes up and kisses me on the forehead.

Meanwhile Asalamalakim is going through the motions with Maggie's hand. Maggie's hand is as limp as a fish, and probably as cold, despite the sweat, and she keeps trying to pull it back. It looks like Asalamalakim wants to shake hands but wants to do it fancy. Or maybe he don't know how people shake hands. Anyhow, he soon gives up on Maggie.

"Well," I say. "Dee."

"No, Mama," she says. "Not 'Dee,' Wangero Leewanika Kemanjo!"   25

"What happened to 'Dee'?" I wanted to know.

"She's dead," Wangero said. "I couldn't bear it any longer being named after the people who oppress me."

"You know as well as me you was named after your aunt Dicie," I said. Dicie is my sister. She named Dee. We called her "Big Dee" after Dee was born.

"But who was *she* named after?" asked Wangero.

"I guess after Grandma Dee," I said.   30

"And who was she named after?" asked Wangero.

"Her mother," I said, and saw Wangero was getting tired. "That's about as far back as I can trace it," I said. Though, in fact, I probably could have carried it back beyond the Civil War through the branches.

"Well," said Asalamalakim, "there you are."

"Uhnnnh," I heard Maggie say.

"There I was not," I said, "before 'Dicie' cropped up in our family, so why   35
should I try to trace it that far back?"

He just stood there grinning, looking down on me like somebody inspecting
a Model A car. Every once in a while he and Wangero sent eye signals over my
head.

"How do you pronounce this name?" I asked.

"You don't have to call me by it if you don't want to," said Wangero.

"Why shouldn't I?" I asked. "If that's what you want us to call you, we'll
call you."

"I know it might sound awkward at first," said Wangero.   40

"I'll get used to it," I said. "Ream it out again."

Well, soon we got the name out of the way. Asalamalakim had a name twice
as long and three times as hard. After I tripped over it two or three times he told
me to just call him Hakim-a-barber. I wanted to ask him was he a barber, but I
didn't really think he was, so I didn't ask.

"You must belong to those beef-cattle peoples down the road," I said. They
said "Asalamalakim" when they met you, too, but they didn't shake hands. Always
too busy: feeding the cattle, fixing the fences, putting up salt-lick shelters, throwing down hay. When the white folks poisoned some of the herd the men stayed
up all night with rifles in their hands. I walked a mile and a half just to see the
sight.

Hakim-a-barber said, "I accept some of their doctrines, but farming and raising cattle is not my style." (They didn't tell me, and I didn't ask, whether Wangero
[Dee] had really gone and married him.)

We sat down to eat and right away he said he didn't eat collards and pork was   45
unclean. Wangero, though, went on through the chitlins and corn bread, the
greens and everything else. She talked a blue streak over the sweet potatoes.
Everything delighted her. Even the fact that we still used the benches her daddy
made for the table when we couldn't afford to buy chairs.

"Oh, Mama!" she cried. Then turned to Hakim-a-barber. "I never knew how
lovely these benches are. You can feel the rump prints," she said, running her
hands underneath her and along the bench. Then she gave a sigh and her hand
closed over Grandma Dee's butter dish. "That's it!" she said. "I knew there was
something I wanted to ask you if I could have." She jumped up from the table
and went over in the corner where the churn stood, the milk in it clabber by now.
She looked at the churn and looked at it.

"This churn top is what I need," she said. "Didn't Uncle Buddy whittle it out
of a tree you all used to have?"

"Yes," I said.

"Uh huh," she said happily. "And I want the dasher, too."

"Uncle Buddy whittle that, too?" asked the barber.   50

Dee (Wangero) looked up at me.

"Aunt Dee's first husband whittled the dash," said Maggie so low you almost
couldn't hear her. "His name was Henry, but they called him Stash."

"Maggie's brain is like all elephant's," Wangero said, laughing. "I can use the churn top as a centerpiece for the alcove table," she said, sliding a plate over the churn, "and I'll think of something artistic to do with the dasher."

When she finished wrapping the dasher the handle stuck out. I took it for a moment in my hands. You didn't even have to look close to see where hands pushing the dasher up and down to make butter had left a kind of sink in the wood. In fact, there were a lot of small sinks; you could see where thumbs and fingers had sunk into the wood. It was beautiful light yellow wood, from a tree that grew in the yard where Big Dee and Stash had lived.

After dinner Dee (Wangero) went to the trunk at the foot of my bed and started rifling through it. Maggie hung back in the kitchen over the dishpan. Out came Wangero with two quilts. They had been pieced by Grandma Dee and then Big Dee and me had hung them on the quilt frames on the front porch and quilted them. One was in the Lone Star pattern. The other was Walk Around the Mountain. In both of them were scraps of dresses Grandma Dee had worn fifty and more years ago. Bits and pieces of Grandpa Jarrell's paisley shirts. And one teeny faded blue piece, about the size of a penny matchbox, that was from Great Grandpa Ezra's uniform that he wore in the Civil War.

"Mama," Wangero said sweet as a bird. "Can I have these old quilts?"

I heard something fall in the kitchen, and a minute later the kitchen door slammed.

"Why don't you take one or two of the others?" I asked. "These old things was just done by me and Big Dee from some tops your grandma pieced before she died."

"No," said Wangero. "I don't want those. They are stitched around the borders by machine."

"That'll make them last better," I said.

"That's not the point," said Wangero. "These are all pieces of dresses Grandma used to wear. She did all this stitching by hand. Imagine!" She held the quilts securely in her arms, stroking them.

"Some of the pieces, like those lavender ones, come from old clothes her mother handed down to her," I said, moving up to touch the quilts. Dee (Wangero) moved back just enough so that I couldn't reach the quilts. They already belonged to her.

"Imagine!" she breathed again, clutching them closely to her bosom.

"The truth is," I said, "I promised to give them quilts to Maggie, for when she marries John Thomas."

She gasped like a bee had stung her.

"Maggie can't appreciate these quilts!" she said. "She'd probably be backward enough to put them to everyday use."

"I reckon she would," I said. "God knows I been saving 'em for long enough with nobody using 'em. I hope she will!" I didn't want to bring up how I had offered Dee (Wangero) a quilt when she went away to college. Then she had told me they were old-fashioned, out of style.

"But they're *priceless!*" she was saying now, furiously; for she has a temper. "Maggie would put them on the bed and in five years they'd be in rags. Less than that!"

"She can always make some more," I said. "Maggie knows how to quilt."

Dee (Wangero) looked at me with hatred. "You just will not understand. The   70
point is these quilts, *these* quilts!"

"Well," I said, stumped. "What would *you* do with them?"

"Hang them," she said. As if that was the only thing you *could* do with quilts.

Maggie by now was standing in the door. I could almost hear the sound her
feet made as they scraped over each other.

"She can have them, Mama," she said, like somebody used to never winning
anything, or having anything reserved for her. "I can 'member Grandma Dee
without the quilts."

I looked at her hard. She had filled her bottom lip with checkerberry snuff   75
and it gave her face a kind of dopey, hangdog look. It was Grandma Dee and Big
Dee who taught her how to quilt herself. She stood there with her scarred hands
hidden in the folds of her skirt. She looked at her sister with something like fear
but she wasn't mad at her. This was Maggie's portion. This was the way she knew
God to work.

When I looked at her like that something hit me in the top of my head and
ran down to the soles of my feet. Just like when I'm in church and the spirit of
God touches me and I get happy and shout. I did something I never had done
before: hugged Maggie to me, then dragged her on into the room, snatched the
quilts out of Miss Wangero's hands and dumped them into Maggie's lap. Maggie
just sat there on my bed with her mouth open.

"Take one or two of the others," I said to Dee.

But she turned without a word and went out to Hakim-a-barber.

"You just don't understand," she said, as Maggie and I came out to the car.

"What don't I understand?" I wanted to know.   80

"Your heritage," she said. And then she turned to Maggie, kissed her, and
said, "You ought to try to make something of yourself, too, Maggie. It's really a
new day for us. But from the way you and Mama still live you'd never know it."

She put on some sunglasses that hid everything above the tip of her nose and
her chin.

Maggie smiled; maybe at the sunglasses. But a real smile, not scared. After
we watched the car dust settle I asked Maggie to bring me a dip of snuff. And
then the two of us sat there just enjoying, until it was time to go in the house and
go to bed.   [1973]

THINKING ABOUT THE TEXT

1. Identify the conflict of values at work in Maggie's and Dee's joint desire
   for the quilts. What values does Mama's ultimate decision reflect?

2. What has influenced Dee's behavior and language? Do you wish she
   would be completely like Mama or Maggie? Why, or why not?

3. What are Mama's physical characteristics? What role do they play in your
   judgment of her?

4. What would you say to someone who argues that Walker stacks the deck too much in Maggie's favor, especially by making her a burn victim?

5. To what extent is this a serious story? How much comedy do you find in it? Refer to specific passages.

ALICE WALKER
Nineteen Fifty-Five

The following short story appears in Walker's second collection of stories, You Can't Keep a Good Woman Down *(1981). Although a work of fiction, it is obviously based on the career of Elvis Presley. Guided by his manager, Colonel Tom Parker, Presley climbed to fame in part by recording his own versions of songs by African American performers such as Big Mama Thornton (the source of Presley's hit "Hound Dog"). Throughout the 1950s and 1960s, several white rock-and-roll stars won success by copying what was then referred to as "race music."*

1955

The car is a brandnew red Thunderbird convertible, and it's passed the house more than once. It slows down real slow now, and stops at the curb. An older gentleman dressed like a Baptist deacon gets out on the side near the house. and a young fellow who looks about sixteen gets out on the driver's side. They are white, and I wonder what in the world they doing in this neighborhood.

Well, I say to J. T., put your shirt on, anyway, and let me clean these glasses offa the table.

We had been watching the ballgame on TV. I wasn't actually watching, I was sort of daydreaming, with my foots up in J. T.'s lap.

I seen 'em coming on up the walk, brisk, like they coming to sell something, and then they rung the bell, and J. T. declined to put on a shirt but instead disappeared into the bedroom where the other television is. I turned down the one in the living room; I figured I'd be rid of these two double quick and J. T. could come back out again.

Are you Gracie Mae Still? asked the old guy, when I opened the door and   5
put my hand on the lock inside the screen.

And I don't need to buy a thing, said I.

What makes you think we're sellin'? he asks, in that hearty Southern way that makes my eyeballs ache.

Well, one way or another and they're inside the house and the first thing the young fellow does is raise the TV a couple of decibels. He's about five feet nine, sort of womanish looking, with real dark white skin and a red pouting mouth. His hair is black and curly and he looks like a Loosianna creole.

◆ ◆ ◆

About one of your songs, says the deacon. He is maybe sixty, with white hair and beard, white silk shirt, black linen suit, black tie and black shoes. His cold gray eyes look like they're sweating.

One of my songs?

Traynor here just *loves* your songs. Don't you, Traynor? He nudges Traynor with his elbow. Traynor blinks, says something I can't catch in a pitch I don't register.

The boy learned to sing and dance livin' round you people out in the country. Practically cut his teeth on you.

Traynor looks up at me and bites his thumbnail.

I laugh.

Well, one way or another they leave with my agreement that they can record one of my songs. The deacon writes me a check for five hundred dollars, the boy grunts his awareness of the transaction, and I am laughing all over myself by the time I rejoin J. T.

Just as I am snuggling down beside him though I hear the front door bell going off again.

Forgit his hat? asks J. T.

I hope not, I say.

The deacon stands there leaning on the door frame and once again I'm thinking of those sweaty-looking eyeballs of his. I wonder if sweat makes your eyeballs pink because his are sure pink. Pink and gray and it strikes me that nobody I'd care to know is behind them.

I forgot one little thing, he says pleasantly. I forgot to tell you Traynor and I would like to buy up all of those records you made of the song. I tell you we sure do love it.

Well, love it or not, I'm not so stupid as to let them do that without making 'em pay. So I says, Well, that's gonna cost you. Because, really, that song never did sell all that good, so I was glad they was going to buy it up. But on the other hand, them two listening to my song by themselves, and nobody else getting to hear me sing it, give me a pause.

Well, one way or another the deacon showed me where I would come out ahead on any deal he had proposed so far. Didn't I give you five hundred dollars? he asked. What white man—and don't even need to mention colored—would give you more? We buy up all your records of that particular song: first, you git royalties. Let me ask you, how much you sell that song for in the first place? Fifty dollars? A hundred, I say. And no royalties from it yet, right? Right. Well, when we buy up all of them records you gonna git royalties. And that's gonna make all them race record shops sit up and take notice of Gracie Mae Still. And they gonna push all them other records of yourn they got. And you no doubt will become one of the big name colored recording artists. And then we can offer you another five hundred dollars for letting us do all this for you. And by God you'll be sittin' pretty! You can go out and buy you the kind of outfit a star should have. Plenty sequins and yards of red satin.

I had done unlocked the screen when I saw I could get some more money out of him. Now I held it wide open while he squeezed through the opening

10

15

20

between me and the door. He whipped out another piece of paper and I signed it.

He sort of trotted out to the car and slid in beside Traynor, whose head was back against the seat. They swung around in a u-turn in front of the house and then they was gone.

J. T. was putting his shirt on when I got back to the bedroom. Yankees beat   25
the Orioles 10–6, he said. I believe I'll drive out to Paschal's pond and go fishing. Wanta go?

While I was putting on my pants J. T. was holding the two checks.

I'm real proud of a woman that can make cash money without leavin' home, he said. And I said *Umph*. Because we met on the road with me singing in first one little low-life jook after another, making ten dollars a night for myself if I was lucky, and sometimes bringin' home nothing but my life. And J. T. just loved them times. The way I was fast and flashy and always on the go from one time to another. He loved the way my singin' made the dirt farmers cry like babies and the womens shout Honey, hush! But that's mens. They loves any style to which you can get 'em accustomed.

1956

My little grandbaby called me one night on the phone: Little Mama, Little Mama, there's a white man on the television singing one of your songs! Turn on channel 5.

Lord, if it wasn't Traynor. Still looking half asleep from the neck up, but kind of awake in a nasty way from the waist down. He wasn't doing too bad with my song either, but it wasn't just the song the people in the audience was screeching and screaming over, it was that nasty little jerk he was doing from the waist down.

Well, Lord have mercy, I said, listening to him. If I'da closed my eyes, it   30
could have been me. He had followed every turning of my voice, side streets, avenues, red lights, train crossing and all. It give me a chill.

Everywhere I went I heard Traynor singing my song, and all the little white girls just eating it up. I never had so many ponytails switched across my line of vision in my life. They was so *proud*. He was a *genius*.

Well, all that year I was trying to lose weight anyway and that and high blood pressure and sugar kept me pretty well occupied. Traynor had made a smash from a song of mine, I still had seven hundred dollars, of the original one thousand dollars in the bank, and I felt if I could just bring my weight down, life would be sweet.

1957

I lost ten pounds in 1956. That's what I give myself for Christmas. And J. T. and me and the children and their friends and grandkids of all description had just finished dinner — over which I had put on nine and a half of my lost ten — when who should appear at the front door but Traynor. Little Mama, Little

Mama! It's that white man who sings ⸺ ⸺ ⸺. The children didn't call it my song anymore. Nobody did. It was funny how that happened. Traynor and the deacon had bought up all my records, true, but on his record he had put "written by Gracie Mae Still." But that was just another name on the label, like "produced by Apex Records."

On the TV he was inclined to dress like the deacon told him. But now he looked presentable.

Merry Christmas, said he.   35

And same to you, Son.

I don't know why I called him Son. Well, one way or another they're all our sons. The only requirement is that they be younger than us. But then again, Traynor seemed to be aging by the minute.

You looks tired, I said. Come on in and have a glass of Christmas cheer.

J. T. ain't never in his life been able to act decent to a white man he wasn't working for, but he poured Traynor a glass of bourbon and water, then he took all the children and grandkids and friends and whatnot out to the den. After while I heard Traynor's voice singing the song, coming from the stereo console. It was just the kind of Christmas present my kids would consider cute.

I looked at Traynor, complicit. But he looked like it was the last thing in the   40
world he wanted to hear. His head was pitched forward over his lap, his hands holding his glass and his elbows on his knees.

I done sung that song seem like a millions times this year, he said. I sung it on the Grand Ole Opry, I sung it on the Ed Sullivan show. I sung it on Mike Douglas, I sung it at the Cotton Bowl, the Orange Bowl. I sung it at Festivals. I sung it at Fairs. I sung it overseas in Rome, Italy, and once in a submarine *underseas.* I've sung it and sung it, and I'm making forty thousand dollars a day offa it, and you know what, I don't have the faintest notion what that song means.

Whatchumean, what do it mean? It mean what it says. All I could think was: These suckers is making forty thousand a *day* offa my song and now they gonna come back and try to swindle me out of the original thousand.

It's just a song, I said. Cagey. When you fool around with a lot of no count mens you sing a bunch of 'em. I shrugged.

Oh, he said. Well. He started brightening up. I just come by to tell you I think you are a great singer.

He didn't blush, saying that. Just said it straight out.   45

And I brought you a little Christmas present too. Now you take this little box and you hold it until I drive off. Then you take it outside under that first streetlight back up the street aways in front of that green house. Then you open the box and see . . . Well, just *see.*

What had come over this boy, I wondered, holding the box. I looked out the window in time to see another white man come up and get in the car with him and then two more cars full of white mens start out behind him. They was all in long black cars that looked like a funeral procession.

Little Mama, Little Mama, what is it? One of my grandkids come running up and started pulling at the box. It was wrapped in gay Christmas paper — the thick, rich kind that it's hard to picture folks making just to throw away.

J. T. and the rest of the crowd followed me out the house, up the street to the streetlight and in front of the green house. Nothing was there but somebody's gold-grilled white Cadillac. Brandnew and most distracting. We got to looking at it so till I almost forgot the little box in my hand. While the others were busy making 'miration I carefully took off the paper and ribbon and folded them up and put them in my pants pocket. What should I see but a pair of genuine solid gold caddy keys.

Dangling the keys in front of everybody's nose, I unlocked the caddy, motioned   50
for J. T. to git in on the other side, and us didn't come back home for two days.

1960

Well, the boy was sure nuff famous by now. He was still a mite shy of twenty but already they was calling him the Emperor of Rock and Roll.

Then what should happen but the draft.

Well, says J. T. There goes all this Emperor of Rock and Roll business.

But even in the army the womens was on him like white on rice. We watched it on the News.

> *Dear Gracie Mae* [he wrote from Germany],
> *How you? Fine I hope as this leaves me doing real well. Before I come in the army I was gaining a lot of weight and gitting jittery from making all them dumb movies. But now I exercise and eat right and get plenty of rest. I'm more awake than I been in ten years.*
> *I wonder if you are writing any more songs?*
>
> > *Sincerely,*
> > *Traynor*

I wrote him back:

> *Dear Son,*
> *We is all fine in the Lord's good grace and hope this finds you the same. J. T. and me be out all times of the day and night in that car you give me — which you know you didn't have to do. Oh, and I do appreciate the mink and the new self-cleaning oven. But if you send anymore stuff to eat from Germany I'm going to have to open up a store in the neighborhood just to get rid of it. Really, we have more than enough of everything. The Lord is good to us and we don't know Want.*
> *Glad to here you is well and gitting your right rest. There ain't nothing like exercising to help that along. J. T. and me work some part of every day that we don't go fishing in the garden.*
> *Well, so long Soldier.*
>
> > *Sincerely,*
> > *Gracie Mae*

He wrote:

> *Dear Gracie Mae,*
> *I hope you and J. T. like that automatic power tiller I had one of the stores back home send you. I went through a mountain of catalogs looking for it — I wanted something that even a woman could use.*

I've been thinking about writing some songs of my own but every time I finish one it don't seem to be about nothing I've actually lived myself. My agent keeps sending me other people's songs but they just sound mooney. I can hardly git through 'em without gagging.

Everybody still loves that song of yours. They ask me all the time what do I think it means, really. I mean, they want to know just what I want to know, Where out of your life did it come from?

Sincerely,
Traynor

1968

I didn't see the boy for seven years. No. Eight. Because just about everybody   55
was dead when I saw him again. Malcolm X, King, the president and his brother, and even J. T. J. T. died of a head cold. It just settled in his head like a block of ice, he said, and nothing we did moved it until one day he just leaned out the bed and died.

His good friend Horace helped me put him away, and then about a year later Horace and me started going together. We was sitting out on the front porch swing one summer night, dusk-dark, and I saw this great procession of lights winding to a stop.

Holy Toledo! said Horace. (He's got a real sexy voice like Ray Charles.) Look *at* it. He meant the long line of flashy cars and the white men in white summer suits jumping out on the drivers' sides and standing at attention. With wings they could pass for angels, with hoods they could be the Klan.

Traynor comes waddling up the walk.

And suddenly I know what it is he could pass for. An Arab like the ones you see in storybooks. Plump and soft and with never a care about weight. Because with so much money, who cares? Traynor is almost dressed like someone from a storybook too. He has on, I swear, about ten necklaces. Two sets of bracelets on his arms, at least one ring on every finger, and some kind of shining buckles on his shoes, so that when he walks you get quite a few twinkling lights.

Gracie Mae, he says, coming up to give me a hug. J. T.   60

I explain that J. T. passed. That this is Horace.

Horace, he says, puzzled but polite, sort of rocking back on his heels, Horace.

That's it for Horace. He goes in the house and don't come back.

Looks like you and me is gained a few, I say.

He laughs. The first time I ever heard him laugh. It don't sound much like a   65
laugh and I can't swear that it's better than no laugh a'tall.

He's gitting fat for sure, but he's still slim compared to me. I'll never see three hundred pounds again and I've just about said (excuse me) fuck it. I got to think-ing about it one day an' I thought: aside from the fact that they say it's unhealthy, my fat ain't never been no trouble. Mens always have loved me. My kids ain't never complained. Plus they's fat. And fat like I is I looks distinguished. You see me coming and know somebody's *there*.

Gracie Mae, he says, I've come with a personal invitation to you to my house tomorrow for dinner. He laughed. What did it sound like? I couldn't place it. See them men out there? he asked me. I'm sick and tired of eating with them. They don't never have nothing to talk about. That's why I eat so much. But if you come to dinner tomorrow we can talk about the old days. You can tell me about that farm I bought you.

I sold it, I said.

You did?

Yeah, I said, I did. Just cause I said I liked to exercise by working in a garden 70 didn't mean I wanted five hundred acres! Anyhow, I'm a city girl now. Raised in the country it's true. Dirt poor — the whole bit — but that's all behind me now.

Oh well, he said, I didn't mean to offend you.

We sat a few minutes listening to the crickets.

Then he said: You wrote that song while you was still on the farm, didn't you, or was it right after you left?

You had somebody spying on me? I asked.

You and Bessie Smith got into a fight over it once, he said. 75

You *is* been spying on me!

But I don't know what the fight was about, he said. Just like I don't know what happened to your second husband. Your first one died in the Texas electric chair. Did you know that? Your third one beat you up, stole your touring costumes and your car and retired with a chorine to Tuskegee. He laughed. He's still there.

I had been mad, but suddenly I calmed down. Traynor was talking very dreamily. It was dark but seems like I could tell his eyes weren't right. It was like some*thing* was sitting there talking to me but not necessarily with a person behind it.

You gave up on marrying and seem happier for it. He laughed again. I married but it never went like it was supposed to. I never could squeeze any of my own life either into it or out of it. It was like singing somebody else's record. I copied the way it was sposed to be *exactly* but I never had a clue what marriage meant.

I bought her a diamond ring big as your fist. I bought her clothes. I built her 80 a mansion. But right away she didn't want the boys to stay there. Said they smoked up the bottom floor. Hell, there were *five* floors.

No need to grieve, I said. No need to. Plenty more where she comes from.

He perked up. That's part of what that song means, ain't it? No need to grieve. Whatever it is, there's plenty more down the line.

I never really believed that way back when I wrote that song, I said. It was all bluffing then. The trick is to live long enough to put your young bluffs to use. Now if I was to sing that song today I'd tear it up. 'Cause I done lived long enough to know it's *true*. Them words could hold me up.

I ain't lived that long, he said.

Look like you on your way, I said. I don't know why, but the boy seemed to 85 need some encouraging. And I don't know, seem like one way or another you talk to rich white folks and you end up reassuring *them*. But what the hell, by now I feel something for the boy. I wouldn't be in his bed all alone in the middle of the night for nothing. Couldn't be nothing worse than being famous the world over for something you don't even understand. That's what I tried to tell Bessie. She wanted that same song. Overheard me practicing it one day, said, with her hands on her hips: Gracie Mae, I'ma sing your song tonight. I *likes* it.

Your lips be too swole to sing, I said. She was mean and she was strong, but I trounced her.

Ain't you famous enough with your own stuff? I said. Leave mine alone. Later on, she thanked me. By then she was Miss Bessie Smith to the World, and I was still Miss Gracie Mae Nobody from Notasulga.

The next day all these limousines arrived to pick me up. Five cars and twelve bodyguards. Horace picked that morning to start painting the kitchen.

Don't paint the kitchen, fool, I said. The only reason that dumb boy of ours is going to show me his mansion is because he intends to present us with a new house.

What you gonna do with it? he asked me, standing there in his shirtsleeves   90
stirring the paint.

Sell it. Give it to the children. Live in it on weekends. It don't matter what I do. He sure don't care.

Horace just stood there shaking his head. Mama you sure looks *good*, he says. Wake me up when you git back.

Fool, I say, and pat my wig in front of the mirror.

The boy's house is something else. First you come to this mountain, and then you commence to drive and drive up this road that's lined with magnolias. Do magnolias grow on mountains? I was wondering. And you come to lakes and you come to ponds and you come to deer and you come up on some sheep. And I figure these two is sposed to represent England and Wales. Or something out of Europe. And you just keeping on coming to stuff. And it's all pretty. Only the man driving my car don't look at nothing but the road. Fool. And then *finally*, after all this time, you begin to go up the driveway. And there's more magnolias — only they're not in such good shape. It's sort of cool up this high and I don't think they're gonna make it. And then I see this building that looks like if it had a name it would be The Tara Hotel. Columns and steps and outdoor chandeliers and rocking chairs. Rocking chairs? Well, and there's the boy on the steps dressed in a dark green satin jacket like you see folks wearing on TV late at night, and he looks sort of like a fat dracula with all that house rising behind him, and standing beside him there's this little white vision of loveliness that he introduces as his wife.

He's nervous when he introduces us and he says to her: This is Gracie Mae   95
Still, I want you to know me. I mean . . . and she gives him a look that would fry meat.

Won't you come in, Gracie Mae, she says, and that's the last I see of her.

He fishes around for something to say or do and decides to escort me to the kitchen. We go through the entry and the parlor and the breakfast room and the dining room and the servants' passage and finally get there. The first thing I notice is that, altogether, there are five stoves. He looks about to introduce me to one.

Wait a minute, I say. Kitchens don't do nothing for me. Let's go sit on the front porch.

Well, we hike back and we sit in the rocking chairs rocking until dinner.

Gracie Mae, he says down the table, taking a piece of fried chicken from the woman standing over him, I gotta little surprise for you. 100

It's a house, ain't it? I ask, spearing a chitlin.

You're getting *spoiled*, he says. And the way he says *spoiled* sounds funny. He slurs it. It sounds like his tongue is too thick for his mouth. Just that quick he's finished the chicken and is now eating chitlins *and* a pork chop. *Me* spoiled, I'm thinking.

I already got a house. Horace is right this minute painting the kitchen. I bought that house. My kids feel comfortable in that house.

But this one I bought you is just like mine. Only a little smaller.

I still don't need no house. And anyway who would clean it? 105

He looks surprised.

Really, I think, some peoples advance *so* slowly.

I hadn't thought of that. But what the hell, I'll get you somebody to live in.

I don't want other folks living 'round me. Makes me nervous.

You *don't?* It *do?* 110

What I want to wake up and see folks I don't even know for?

He just sits there downtable staring at me. Some of that feeling is in the song, ain't it? Not the words, the *feeling*. What I want to wake up and see folks I don't even know for? But I see twenty folks a day I don't even know, including my wife.

This food wouldn't be bad to wake up to though, I said. The boy had found the genius of corn bread.

He looked at me real hard. He laughed. Short. They want what you got but they don't want you. They want what I got only it ain't mine. That's what makes 'em so hungry for me when I sing. They getting the flavor of something but they ain't getting the thing itself. They like a pack of hound dogs trying to gobble up a scent.

You talking 'bout your fans? 115

Right. Right. He says.

Don't worry 'bout your fans, I say. They don't know their asses from a hole in the ground. I doubt there's a honest one in the bunch.

That's the point. Dammit, that's the point! He hits the table with his fist. It's so solid it don't even quiver. You need a honest audience! You can't have folks that's just gonna lie right back to you.

Yeah, I say, it was small compared to yours, but I had one. It would have been worth my life to try to sing 'em somebody else's stuff that I didn't know nothing about.

He must have pressed a buzzer under the table. One of his flunkies zombies up. 120

Git Johnny Carson, he says.

On the phone? asks the zombie.

On the phone, says Traynor, what you think I mean, git him offa the front porch? Move your ass.

So two weeks later we's on the Johnny Carson show.

Traynor is all corseted down nice and looks a little bit fat but mostly good.   125
And all the women that grew up on him and my song squeal and squeal. Traynor says: The lady who wrote my first hit record is here with us tonight, and she's agreed to sing it for all of us, just like she sung it forty-five years ago. Ladies and Gentlemen, the great Gracie Mae Still!

Well, I had tried to lose a couple of pounds my own self, but failing that I had me a very big dress made. So I sort of rolls over next to Traynor, who is dwarfted by me, so that when he puts his arm around back of me to try to hug me it looks funny to the audience and they laugh.

I can see this pisses him off. But I smile out there at 'em. Imagine squealing for twenty years and not knowing why you're squealing? No more sense of endings and beginnings than hogs.

It don't matter, Son, I say. Don't fret none over me.

I commence to sing. And I sound — wonderful. Being able to sing good ain't all about having a good singing voice a'tall. A good singing voice helps. But when you come up in the Hard Shell Baptist church like I did you understand early that the fellow that sings is the singer. Them that waits for programs and arrangements and letters from home is just good voices occupying body space.

So there I am singing my own song, my own way. And I give it all I got and   130
enjoy every minute of it. When I finish Traynor is standing up clapping and clapping and beaming at first me and then the audience like I'm his mama for true. The audience claps politely for about two seconds.

Traynor looks disgusted.

He comes over and tries to hug me again. The audience laughs.

Johnny Carson looks at us like we both weird.

Traynor is mad as hell. He's supposed to sing something called a love ballad. But instead he takes the mike, turns to me and says: Now see if my imitation still holds up. He goes into the same song, *our* song, I think, looking out at his flaky audience. And he sings it just the way he always did. My voice, my tone, my inflection, everything. But he forgets a couple of lines. Even before he's finished the matronly squeals begin.

He sits down next to me looking whipped.   135

It don't matter, Son, I say, patting his hand. You don't even know those people. Try to make the people you know happy.

Is that in the song? he asks.

Maybe. I say.

1977

For a few years I hear from him, then nothing. But trying to lose weight takes all the attention I got to spare. I finally faced up to the fact that my fat is the hurt I don't admit, not even to myself, and that I been trying to bury it from the day I was born. But also when you git real old, to tell the truth, it ain't as pleasant. It gits lumpy and slack. Yuck. So one day I said to Horace. I'ma git this shit offa me.

And he fell in with the program like he always try to do and Lord such a procession of salads and cottage cheese and fruit juice!   140

One night I dreamed Traynor had split up with his fifteenth wife. He said: *You meet 'em for no reason. You date 'em for no reason. You marry 'em for no reason. I do it all but I swear it's just like somebody else doing it. I feel like I can't remember Life.*

The boy's in trouble, I said to Horace.

You've always said that, he said.

I have?

Yeah. You always said he looked asleep. You can't sleep through life if you   145
wants to live it.

You not such a fool after all, I said, pushing myself up with my cane and hobbling over to where he was. Let me sit down on your lap, I said, while this salad I ate takes effect.

In the morning we heard Traynor was dead. Some said fat, some said heart, some said alcohol, some said drugs. One of the children called from Detroit. Them dumb fans of his is on a crying rampage, she said. You just ought to turn on the TV.

But I didn't want to see 'em. They was crying and crying and didn't even know what they was crying for. One day this is going to be a pitiful country, I thought.   [1981]

THINKING ABOUT THE TEXT

1. Although he makes a hit record of Gracie Mae's song, Traynor claims that he can't understand it. What do you make of this repeated confession? What does Gracie Mae understand about the song that Traynor doesn't?

2. Why does Traynor shower Gracie Mae with gifts? Identify things especially important to consider in addressing this issue of cause and effect. What, ultimately, is your evaluation of Traynor? Think of an appropriate epitaph for his tombstone.

3. What is your general impression of Gracie Mae and her life through the years? Give supporting details. Both Gracie Mae and Traynor get fat; for the same reasons, do you think?

4. Gracie Mae resorts to nonstandard English (or what some people call Ebonics). Identify a few examples in the text. What is your reaction to Gracie Mae's language? What would you say to a reader who is put off by her departures from standard English?

5. How do you feel about the appropriation of black performers' songs by white rock and roll stars like Traynor (and Elvis Presley)? Try to think of crossracial borrowings in popular culture today.

MAKING COMPARISONS

1. In "Everyday Use," Mama dreams about being on the Johnny Carson show or a show like it. In "Nineteen Fifty-Five," Gracie Mae actually appears on the Johnny Carson show. Do these scenes have the same function in their respective texts? Compare Mama and Gracie Mae in general. Do they seem to have the same values and perspectives?

2. Compare Traynor and Dee. Do they seem to see African American culture in the same way? Refer to specific details of each story.

3. "Everyday Use" focuses on a single day whereas "Nineteen Fifty-Five" spans many years. Does this difference in time frame amount to a significant difference in effect? Explain.

ALICE WALKER
In Search of Our Mothers' Gardens

Originally, the following was a speech Walker gave at a May 1973 conference on "The Black Woman: Myths and Realities," held at Radcliffe College. Walker later described her audience as "the crème de la crème of educated Black women in America." To a great extent, the conference was a response to the 1965 Moynihan Report, which argued that a major cause of poverty among African Americans was their acceptance of woman-headed families. Walker's speech gained a wider audience when it was subsequently printed in the May 1974 issue of Ms. *It appeared, too, as the title piece of her 1983 essay collection* In Search of Our Mothers' Gardens: Womanist Prose.

> I described her own nature and temperament. Told how they needed a larger life for their expression. . . . I pointed out that in lieu of proper channels, her emotions had overflowed into paths that dissipated them. I talked, beautifully I thought, about an art that would be born, an art that would open the way for women the likes of her. I asked her to hope, and build up an inner life against the coming of that day. . . . I sang, with a strange quiver in my voice, a promise song.
>
> — "Avey," Jean Toomer, *Cane*
> *The poet speaking to a prostitute who falls asleep while he's talking*

When the poet Jean Toomer walked through the South in the early twenties, he discovered a curious thing: black women whose spirituality was so intense, so deep, so *unconscious*, they were themselves unaware of the richness they held. They stumbled blindly through their lives: creatures so abused and mutilated in body, so dimmed and confused by pain, that they considered themselves unworthy even of hope. In the selfless abstractions their bodies became to the men who used them, they became more than "sexual objects," more even than mere women: they became "Saints." Instead of being perceived as whole persons, their bodies became shrines: what was thought to be their minds became temples suitable for worship. These crazy Saints stared out at the world, wildly, like lunatics — or quietly, like suicides; and the "God" that was in their gaze was as mute as a great stone.

Who were these Saints? These crazy, loony, pitiful women?

Some of them, without a doubt, were our mothers and grandmothers.

In the still heat of the post-Reconstruction South, this is how they seemed to Jean Toomer: exquisite butterflies trapped in an evil honey, toiling away their lives in an era, a century, that did not acknowledge them, except as "the *mule* of the world." They dreamed dreams that no one knew — not even themselves, in any coherent fashion — and saw visions no one could understand. They wandered or sat about the countryside crooning lullabies to ghosts, and drawing the mother of Christ in charcoal on courthouse walls.

They forced their minds to desert their bodies and their striving spirits sought   5
to rise, like frail whirlwinds from the hard red clay. And when those frail whirlwinds fell, in scattered particles, upon the ground, no one mourned. Instead, men lit candles to celebrate the emptiness that remained, as people do who enter a beautiful but vacant space to resurrect a God.

Our mothers and grandmothers, some of them: moving to music not yet written. And they waited.

They waited for a day when the unknown thing that was in them would be made known; but guessed, somehow in their darkness, that on the day of their revelation they would be long dead. Therefore to Toomer they walked, and even ran, in slow motion. For they were going nowhere immediate, and the future was not yet within their grasp. And men took our mothers and grandmothers, "but got no pleasure from it." So complex was their passion and their calm.

To Toomer, they lay vacant and fallow as autumn fields, with harvest time never in sight: and he saw them enter loveless marriages, without joy; and become prostitutes, without resistance; and become mothers of children, without fulfillment.

For these grandmothers and mothers of ours were not Saints, but Artists; driven to a numb and bleeding madness by the springs of creativity in them for which there was no release. They were Creators, who lived lives of spiritual waste, because they were so rich in spirituality — which is the basis of Art — that the strain of enduring their unused and unwanted talent drove them insane. Throwing away this spirituality was their pathetic attempt to lighten the soul to a weight their work-worn, sexually abused bodies could bear.

What did it mean for a black woman to be an artist in our grandmothers'   10
time? In our great-grandmothers' day? It is a question with an answer cruel enough to stop the blood.

Did you have a genius of a great-great-grandmother who died under some ignorant and depraved white overseer's lash? Or was she required to bake biscuits for a lazy backwater tramp, when she cried out in her soul to paint watercolors of sunsets, or the rain falling on the green and peaceful pasturelands? Or was her body broken and forced to bear children (who were more often than not sold away from her)—eight, ten, fifteen, twenty children—when her one joy was the thought of modeling heroic figures of rebellion, in stone or clay?

How was the creativity of the black woman kept alive, year after year and century after century, when for most of the years black people have been in America, it was a punishable crime for a black person to read or write? And the freedom to paint, to sculpt, to expand the mind with action did not exist. Consider, if you can bear to imagine it, what might have been the result if singing, too, had been forbidden by law. Listen to the voices of Bessie Smith, Billie Holiday, Nina Simone, Roberta Flack, and Aretha Franklin, among others, and imagine those voices muzzled for life. Then you may begin to comprehend the lives of our "crazy," "Sainted" mothers and grandmothers. The agony of the lives of women who might have been Poets, Novelists, Essayists, and Short-Story Writers (over a period of centuries), who died with their real gifts stifled within them.

And, if this were the end of the story, we would have cause to cry out in my paraphrase of Okot p'Bitek's great poem:

> O, my clanswoman
> Let us all cry together!
> Come,
> Let us mourn the death of our mother,
> The death of a Queen
> The ash that was produced
> By a great fire!
> O, this homestead is utterly dead
> Close the gates
> With *lacari* thorns,
> For our mother
> The creator of the Stool is lost!
> And all the young men
> Have perished in the wilderness!

But this is not the end of the story, for all the young women—our mothers and grandmothers, *ourselves*—have not perished in the wilderness. And if we ask ourselves why, and search for and find the answer, we will know beyond all efforts to erase it from our minds, just exactly who, and of what, we black American women are.

One example, perhaps the most pathetic, most misunderstood one, can provide a backdrop for our mothers' work: Phillis Wheatley, a slave in the 1700s.   15

Virginia Woolf, in her book *A Room of One's Own*, wrote that in order for a woman to write fiction she must have two things, certainly: a room of her own (with key and lock) and enough money to support herself.

What then are we to make of Phillis Wheatley, a slave, who owned not even herself? This sickly, frail black girl who required a servant of her own at times—her health was so precarious—and who, had she been white, would have been easily considered the intellectual superior of all the women and most of the men in the society of her day.

Virginia Woolf wrote further, speaking of course not of our Phillis, that "any woman born with a great gift in the sixteenth century [insert "eighteenth century," insert "black woman," insert "born or made a slave"] would certainly have gone crazed, shot herself, or ended her days in some lonely cottage outside the village, half witch, half wizard [insert "Saint"], feared and mocked at. For it needs little skill and psychology to be sure that a highly gifted girl who had tried to use her gift of poetry would have been so thwarted and hindered by contrary instincts [add "chains, guns, the lash, the ownership of one's body by someone else, submission to an alien religion"], that she must have lost her health and sanity to a certainty."

The key words, as they relate to Phillis, are "contrary instincts." For when we read the poetry of Phillis Wheatley—as when we read the novels of Nella Larsen or the oddly false-sounding autobiography of that freest of all black women writers, Zora Hurston—evidence of "contrary instincts" is everywhere. Her loyalties were completely divided, as was, without question, her mind.

But how could this be otherwise? Captured at seven, a slave of wealthy, doting whites who instilled in her the "savagery" of the Africa they "rescued" her from . . . one wonders if she was even able to remember her homeland as she had known it, or as it really was.   20

Yet, because she did try to use her gift for poetry in a world that made her a slave, she was "so thwarted and hindered by . . . contrary instincts, that she . . . lost her health. . . ." In the last years of her brief life, burdened not only with the need to express her gift but also with a penniless, friendless "freedom" and several small children for whom she was forced to do strenuous work to feed, she lost her health, certainly. Suffering from malnutrition and neglect and who knows what mental agonies, Phillis Wheatley died.

So torn by "contrary instincts" was black, kidnapped, enslaved Phillis that her description of "the Goddess"—as she poetically called the Liberty she did not have—is ironically, cruelly humorous. And, in fact, has held Phillis up to ridicule for more than a century. It is usually read prior to hanging Phillis's memory as that of a fool. She wrote:

> The Goddess comes, she moves divinely fair,
> Olive and laurel binds her *golden* hair.
> Wherever shines this native of the skies,
> Unnumber'd charms and recent graces rise. [My italics]

is obvious that Phillis, the slave, combed the "Goddess's" hair every morning; prior, perhaps, to bringing in the milk, or fixing her mistress's lunch. She took her imagery from the one thing she saw elevated above all others.

With the benefit of hindsight we ask, "How could she?"

But at last, Phillis, we understand. No more snickering when your stiff, struggling, ambivalent lines are forced on us. We know now that you were not an idiot or a traitor; only a sickly little black girl, snatched from your home and country and made a slave; a woman who still struggled to sing the song that was your gift, although in a land of barbarians who praised you for your bewildered tongue. It is   25 not so much what you sang, as that you kept alive, in so many of our ancestors, *the notion of song.*

Black women are called, in the folklore that so aptly identifies one's status in society, "the *mule* of the world," because we have been handed the burdens that everyone else—*everyone* else—refused to carry. We have also been called "Matriarchs," "Superwomen," and "Mean and Evil Bitches." Not to mention "Castraters" and "Sapphire's Mama." When we have pleaded for understanding, our character has been distorted; when we have asked for simple caring, we have been handed empty inspirational appellations, then stuck in the farthest corner. When we have asked for love, we have been given children. In short, even our plainer gifts, our labors of fidelity and love, have been knocked down our throats. To be an artist and a black woman, even today, lowers our status in many respects, rather than raises it: and yet, artists we will be.

Therefore we must fearlessly pull out of ourselves and look at and identify with our lives the living creativity some of our great-grandmothers were not allowed to know. I stress *some* of them because it is well known that the majority of our great-grandmothers knew, even without "knowing" it, the reality of their spirituality, even if they didn't recognize it beyond what happened in the singing at church—and they never had any intention of giving it up.

How they did it—those millions of black women who were not Phillis Wheatley, or Lucy Terry or Frances Harper or Zora Hurston or Nella Larsen or Bessie Smith; or Elizabeth Catlett, or Katherine Dunham, either—brings me to the title of this essay, "In Search of Our Mothers' Gardens," which is a personal account that is yet shared, in its theme and its meaning, by all of us. I found, while thinking about the far-reaching world of the creative black woman, that often the truest answer to a question that really matters can be found very close.

In the late 1920s my mother ran away from home to marry my father. Marriage, if not running away, was expected of seventeen-year-old girls. By the time she was twenty, she had two children and was pregnant with a third. Five children later, I was born. And this is how I came to know my mother: she seemed a large, soft, loving-eyed woman who was rarely impatient in our home. Her quick, violent temper was on view only a few times a year, when she battled with the white landlord who had the misfortune to suggest to her that her children did not need to go to school.

She made all the clothes we wore, even my brothers' overalls. She made all the towels and sheets we used. She spent the summers canning vegetables and fruits. She spent the winter evenings making quilts enough to cover all our beds.

During the "working" day, she labored beside—not behind—my father in the fields. Her day began before sunup, and did not end until late at night. There was never a moment for her to sit down, undisturbed, to unravel her own private thoughts; never a time free from interruption—by work or the noisy inquiries of her many children. And yet, it is to my mother—and all our mothers who were not famous—that I went in search of the secret of what has fed that muzzled and

30

often mutilated, but vibrant, creative spirit that the black woman has inherited, and that pops out in wild and unlikely places to this day.

But when, you will ask, did my overworked mother have time to know or care about feeding the creative spirit?

The answer is so simple that many of us have spent years discovering it. We have constantly looked high, when we should have looked high—and low.

For example: in the Smithsonian Institution in Washington, D.C., there hangs a quilt unlike any other in the world. In fanciful, inspired, and yet simple and identifiable figures, it portrays the story of the Crucifixion. It is considered rare, beyond price. Though it follows no known pattern of quiltmaking, and though it is made of bits and pieces of worthless rags, it is obviously the work of a person of powerful imagination and deep spiritual feeling. Below this quilt I saw a note that says it was made by "an anonymous Black woman in Alabama, a hundred years ago."

If we could locate this "anonymous" black woman from Alabama, she would turn out to be one of our grandmothers—an artist who left her mark in the only materials she could afford, and in the only medium her position in society allowed her to use.   35

As Virginia Woolf wrote further, in *A Room of One's Own*:

> Yet genius of a sort must have existed among women as it must have existed among the working class. [Change this to "slaves" and "the wives and daughters of sharecroppers."] Now and again an Emily Brontë or a Robert Burns [change this to "a Zora Hurston or a Richard Wright"] blazes out and proves its presence. But certainly it never got itself on to paper. When, however, one reads of a witch being ducked, of a woman possessed by devils [or "Sainthood"], of a wise woman selling herbs [or root workers], or even a very remarkable man who had a mother, then I think we are on the track of a lost novelist, a suppressed poet, or some mute and inglorious Jane Austen. . . . Indeed, I would venture to guess that Anon, who wrote so many poems without signing them, was often a woman. . . .

And so our mothers and grandmothers have, more often than not anonymously, handed on the creative spark, the seed of the flower they themselves never hoped to see: or like a sealed letter they could not plainly read.

And so it is, certainly, with my own mother. Unlike "Ma" Rainey's songs, which retained their creator's name even while blasting forth from Bessie Smith's mouth, no song or poem will bear my mother's name. Yet so many of the stories that I write, that we all write, are my mother's stories. Only recently did I fully realize this: that through years of listening to my mother's stories of her life, I have absorbed not only the stories themselves, but something of the manner in which she spoke, something of the urgency that involves the knowledge that her stories—like her life—must be recorded. It is probably for this reason that so much of what I have written is about characters whose counterparts in real life are so much older than I am.

But the telling of these stories, which came from my mother's lips as naturally as breathing, was not the only way my mother showed herself as an artist. For stories, too, were subject to being distracted, to dying without conclusion. Dinners must be started, and cotton must be gathered before the big rains. The artist that was and is my mother showed itself to me only after many years. This is what I finally noticed:

Like Mem, a character in *The Third Life of Grange Copeland,* my mother 40 adorned with flowers whatever shabby house we were forced to live in. And not just your typical straggly country stand of zinnias, either. She planted ambitious gardens—and still does—with over fifty different varieties of plants that bloom profusely from early March until late November. Before she left home for the fields, she watered her flowers, chopped up the grass, and laid out new beds. When she returned from the fields she might divide clumps of bulbs, dig a cold pit, uproot and replant roses, or prune branches from her taller bushes or trees— until night came and it was too dark to see.

Whatever she planted grew as if by magic, and her fame as a grower of flowers spread over three counties. Because of her creativity with her flowers, even my memories of poverty are seen through a screen of blooms—sunflowers, petunias, roses, dahlias, forsythia, spirea, delphiniums, verbena . . . and so on.

And I remember people coming to my mother's yard to be given cuttings from her flowers; I hear again the praise showered on her because whatever rocky soil she landed on, she turned into a garden. A garden so brilliant with colors, so original in its design, so magnificent with life and creativity, that to this day people drive by our house in Georgia—perfect strangers and imperfect strangers—and ask to stand or walk among my mother's art.

I notice that it is only when my mother is working in her flowers that she is radiant, almost to the point of being invisible—except as Creator: hand and eye. She is involved in work her soul must have. Ordering the universe in the image of her personal conception of Beauty.

Her face, as she prepares the Art that is her gift, is a legacy of respect she leaves to me, for all that illuminates and cherishes life. She has handed down respect for the possibilities—and the will to grasp them.

For her, so hindered and intruded upon in so many ways, being an artist has 45 still been a daily part of her life. This ability to hold on, even in very simple ways, is work black women have done for a very long time.

This poem is not enough, but it is something, for the woman who literally covered the holes in our walls with sunflowers:

> They were women then
> My mama's generation
> Husky of voice—Stout of
> Step
> With fists as well as
> Hands
> How they battered down
> Doors
> And ironed
> Starched white

Shirts
How they led
Armies
Headragged Generals
Across mined
Fields
Booby-trapped
Kitchens
To discover books
Desks
A place for us
How they knew what we
Must know
Without knowing a page
Of it
Themselves.

Guided by my heritage of a love of beauty and a respect for strength — in search of my mother's garden, I found my own.

And perhaps in Africa over two hundred years ago, there was just such a mother; perhaps she painted vivid and daring decorations in oranges and yellows and greens on the walls of her hut; perhaps she sang — in a voice like Roberta Flack's — *sweetly* over the compounds of her village; perhaps she wove the most stunning mats or told the most ingenious stories of all the village storytellers. Perhaps she was herself a poet — though only her daughter's name is signed to the poems that we know.

Perhaps Phillis Wheatley's mother was also an artist.

Perhaps in more than Phillis Wheatley's biological life is her mother's signature made clear.   [1974]

50

THINKING ABOUT THE TEXT

1. What are the turning points in this essay? Discuss them as steps in an argument that Walker is making.

2. How does Walker define *art*? What do you think of her definition?

3. To what extent does Walker agree with the views of earlier writers Jean Toomer and Virginia Woolf? In what ways, if any, does she seek to amend their views? What argument does she make on behalf of Phillis Wheatley?

4. Originally, this essay was a speech. Look back at the introduction to it for details of the rhetorical situation in which Walker presented it. In what ways does the text seem designed for this occasion?

5. Walker's original speech ended three paragraphs earlier than the essay version of it does. She added what are now the final three paragraphs when she published the speech in *Ms.* magazine. Evaluate this revision. Does it strike you as a better ending? Why, or why not?

MAKING COMPARISONS

1. Both "Everyday Use" and this essay refer to quiltmaking. Do they find the same significance in it? Refer to specific details of each text.

2. Both "Nineteen Fifty-Five" and this essay refer to song. Again, do they find the same significance in it?

3. Think of Mama in "Everyday Use," Gracie Mae in "Nineteen Fifty-Five," and Walker's mother in this essay. Does their gender affect their lives as much as their race does?

WRITING ABOUT ISSUES

1. Choose one work from this cluster and write an essay identifying what the work leads you to conclude about African American culture. (Keep in mind that you may conclude more than one thing.) Support your conclusions by referring to specific details of the text.

2. In her essay, Walker writes,

> Only recently did I fully realize this: that through years of listening to my mother's stories of her life, I have absorbed not only the stories themselves, but something of the manner in which she spoke, something of the urgency that involves the knowledge that her stories—like her life—must be recorded. It is probably for this reason that so much of what I have written is about characters whose counterparts in real life are so much older than I am.

The passage suggests that you can compare Walker's mother to Mama in "Everyday Use" and Gracie Mae in "Nineteen Fifty-Five." Write an essay showing how what Walker says about her mother in the essay can indeed apply to one of these two fictional characters.

3. Following Walker's lead, write an essay arguing that your mother or someone else close to you is an artist, even though this person doesn't fit conventional notions of the term. Be sure to cite specific artifacts and activities as you argue for this person's artistry.

4. Each work in this cluster reflects historical developments. For instance, as the two short stories indicate, quilts are increasingly considered art objects. Moreover, like Traynor, many performers and artists—including Elvis—have taken material from someone of another race. Also, the Radcliffe conference at which Walker spoke was partly a response to the 1965 Moynihan report (see p. 1438). Choose one of these historical developments and find at least two articles dealing with it. Then, drawing on your research, write an essay connecting the development to Walker's writing. In your essay, refer to the articles you have consulted.

JUDGING WRITING

ROSEMARY CATACALOS, "David Talamántez on the Last Day of Second Grade"
BILLY COLLINS, "Workshop"
PHILIP LARKIN, "Fiction and the Reading Public"

The following poems depict people judging other people's writing, a process you are going through in this course. No doubt you are judging the literature you read, making conscious or unconscious evaluations of it. Your classmates are doing the same, and perhaps you sometimes differ in your judgments. You also are evaluating your own writing *about* literature, finding some aspects of your drafts effective and striving to improve others. Surely your teacher, too, registers judgments about your own work. Perhaps in your course students critique one another's writing. If so, you react to your classmates' work and ponder their judgments of yours. Whatever the case, take this cluster as an occasion for reflecting on the various judgments made about writing during your course. What values, assumptions, and procedures guide these judgments? With what effects?

BEFORE YOU READ

Think of a text about which you changed your mind. You judged it one way when you first read it; you judged it another way when you encountered it again at a later time. What influenced your judgment on both occasions? Why did your judgment change?

ROSEMARY CATACALOS

David Talamántez on the Last Day of Second Grade

Rosemary Catacalos (b. 1944) grew up in San Antonio, Texas. Formerly a reporter and arts columnist, she is now executive director of San Francisco State University's Poetry Center and American Poetry Archives. Her own books of poetry, both published in 1984, are As Long As It Takes *and* Again for the First Time. *The following poem appeared in a 1996 issue of* The Texas Observer *and was subsequently included in the collection* Best American Poetry 1996.

San Antonio, Texas 1988

David Talamántez, whose mother is at work, leaves his mark,
    everywhere in the schoolyard,
tosses pages from a thick sheaf of lined paper high in the air one by
    one, watches them

◆ ◆ ◆

catch on the teachers' car bumpers, drift into the chalky narrow shade   5
    of the water fountain.
One last batch, stapled together, he rolls tight into a makeshift horn
    through which he shouts

David! and *David, yes!* before hurling it away hard and darting across
    Barzos Street against   10
the light, the little sag of head and shoulders when, safe on the other
    side, he kicks a can

in the gutter and wanders toward home. David Talamántez believes
    birds are warm blooded,
the way they are quick in the air and give out long strings of   15
    complicated music, different

all the time, not like cats and dogs. For this he was marked down in
    Science, and for putting
his name in the wrong place, on the right with the date instead on the
    left with Science   20

Questions, and for not skipping a line between his heading and
    answers. The X's for wrong
things are big, much bigger than Talamántez's tiny writing. *Write larger,*
    his teacher says

in red ink across the tops of many pages. *Messy!* she says on others   25
    where he has erased
and started over, erased and started over. Spelling, Language
    Expression, Sentences Using

the Following Words. *Neck. I have a neck name. No!* 20's, 30's. *Think
    again!* He's good   30
in Art, though, makes 70 on Reading Station Artist's Corner, where
    he's traced and colored

an illustration from *Henny Penny.* A goose with red-and-white striped
    shirt, a hen in a turquoise
dress. Points off for the birds, cloud and butterfly he's drawn in   35
    freehand. *Not in the original*

picture! Twenty-five points off for writing nothing in the blank after
    This is my favorite scene
in the book because . . . There's a page called Rules. *Listen! Always*
    working! Stay in your seat!   40

Raise your hand before you speak! No fighting! Be quiet! Rules copied from
    the board, no grade,
only a huge red checkmark. Later there is a test on Rules. *Listen! Alay*
    ercng! Sast in ao snet!

◆ ◆ ◆

Rars aone bfo your spek! No finagn! Be cayt! He gets 70 on Rules, 10 on   45
    Spelling. An old man
stoops to pick up a crumpled drawing of a large family crowded
    around a table, an apartment

with bars on the windows in Alazán Courts, a huge sun in one corner
    saying, *To mush noys!*   50
After correcting the spelling, the grade is 90. *Nice details!* And there's
    another mark, on this paper

and all the others, the one in the doorway of La Rosa Beauty Shop, the
    one that blew under
the pool table at La Tenampa, the ones older kids have wadded up like   55
    big spit balls, the ones run

over by cars. On every single page David Talamántez has crossed out
    the teacher's red numbers
and written in giant letters, blue ink, *Yes! David, yes!*   [1996]

THINKING ABOUT THE TEXT

1. In *Best American Poetry 1996*, Catacalos admits that "David Talamántez is a composite of many Chicano children in many times and places." As you read her poem, do you assume she based it on a real-life individual? Why, or why not? How conscious are you that the boy in this poem is Chicano? Do you think it could just as easily be about someone from a different ethnic background? Explain your reasoning.

2. Sum up and evaluate the teacher's judgments of David's writing and his other work. What are some of her values and assumptions?

3. What are some adjectives of your own for David? Note what he does with the papers he has gotten back. Is he engaging in significant acts of resistance? Explain your view.

4. Here is an issue of policy: What should be done about the kind of situation described in this poem? By whom?

5. Many sentences in this poem run from one line to the next—a technique called *enjambment*. What is the effect?

BILLY COLLINS
Workshop

Born in New York City, Billy Collins (b. 1941) has taught at Lehman College in the Bronx. The following poem was published in a 1995 issue of The Paris Review *and also appeared that year in Collins's book* The Art of Drowning. *His*

other volumes of poetry are The Apple That Astonished *(1988),* Questions about
Angels *(1991), and* Picnic, Lightning *(1998).*

I might as well begin by saying how much I like the title.
It gets me right away because I'm in a workshop now
so immediately the poem has my attention,
like the ancient mariner grabbing me by the sleeve.

And I like the first couple of stanzas,   5
the way they establish this mode of self-pointing
that runs through the whole poem
and tells us that words are food thrown down
on the ground for other words to eat.
I can almost taste the tail of the snake   10
in its own mouth,
if you know what I mean.

But what I'm not sure about is the voice
which sounds in places very casual, very blue jeans,
but other times seems standoffish,   15
professorial in the worst sense of the word
like the poem is blowing pipe smoke in my face.
But maybe that's just what it wants to do.

What I did find engaging were the middle stanzas,
especially the fourth one.   20
I like the image of clouds flying like lozenges
which gives me a very clear picture.
And I really like how this drawbridge operator
just appears out of the blue
with his feet up on the iron railing   25
and his fishing pole jigging — I like jigging —
a hook in the slow industrial canal below.
I love slow industrial canal below. All those *l*'s.

Maybe it's just me,
but the next stanza is where I start to have a problem.   30
I mean how can the evening bump into the stars?
And what's an obbligato of snow?
Also, I roam the decaffeinated streets.
At that point I'm lost. I need help.

The other thing that throws me off,   35
and maybe this is just me,
is the way the scene keeps shifting around.
First, we're in this big aerodrome
and the speaker is inspecting a row of dirigibles,

which makes me think this could be a dream.   40
Then he takes us into his garden,
the part with the dahlias and the coiling hose,
though that's nice, the coiling hose,
but then I'm not sure where we're supposed to be.
The rain and the mint green light,   45
that makes it feel outdoors, but what about this wallpaper?
Or is it a kind of indoor cemetery?
There's something about death going on here.

In fact, I start to wonder if what we have here
is really two poems, or three, or four,   50
or possibly none.

But then there's that last stanza, my favorite.
This is where the poem wins me back,
especially the lines spoken in the voice of the mouse.
I mean we've all seen these images in cartoons before,   55
but I still love the details he uses
when he's describing where he lives.
The perfect little arch of an entrance in the baseboard,
the bed made out of a curled-back sardine can,
the spool of thread for a table.   60
I start thinking about how hard the mouse had to work
night after night collecting all these things
while the people in the house were fast asleep,
and that gives me a very strong feeling,
a very powerful sense of something.   65
But I don't know if anyone else was feeling that.
Maybe that was just me.
Maybe that's just the way I read it.   [1995]

THINKING ABOUT THE TEXT

1. What indications does Collins give that the poem you are reading is the poem being judged?

2. What are the turning points in this poem? Identify places where the speaker's judgment seems to shift.

3. Describe the tone of the speaker. In what settings, if any, have you encountered someone speaking this way? Do you think this kind of talk would help the writer whose work is being judged? Why, or why not?

3. On the basis of this poem, define what a *workshop* is. Would you apply the term to your own class? Why, or why not?

5. Here is an issue of genre: Do you consider the poem a satire or parody? Or would you assign it to some other genre? Explain your reasoning.

MAKING COMPARISONS

1. How might Collins's speaker respond to Catacalos's poem? Write at least a page imagining this response.

2. The teacher in Catacalos's poem puts a lot of emphasis on following rules. Do you get the impression that there are rules in the workshop depicted by Collins? If so, what are they?

3. On the whole, does the workshop in Collins's poem seem better than David Talamántez's classroom? Identify things you believe especially important in addressing this issue of evaluation.

PHILIP LARKIN
Fiction and the Reading Public

Philip Larkin (1922–1985) was a major figure in post–World War II British poetry, producing such influential volumes as The North Ship *(1945),* The Less Deceived *(1955), and* High Windows *(1974). His* Collected Poems *appeared in 1988. But Larkin also published the novels* Jill *(1946) and* A Girl in Winter *(1947). Furthermore, he wrote jazz criticism, which was collected in* All What Jazz: A Record Diary 1961–68 *(1970). Larkin wrote the following poem in 1954 and read it over BBC radio a few months later. The title is the same as that of a 1932 book by Q. D. Leavis that became well known for its highly negative view of mass culture.*

Give me a thrill, says the reader,
Give me a kick;
I don't care how you succeed, or
What subject you pick.
Choose something you know all about   5
That'll sound like real life:
Your childhood, your Dad pegging out,
How you sleep with your wife.

But that's not sufficient, unless
You make me feel good —   10
Whatever you're 'trying to express'
Let it be understood
That 'somehow' God plaits up the threads,
Makes 'all for the best,'
That we may lie quiet in our beds   15
And not be 'depressed.'

For I call the tune in this racket:
I pay your screw,

Write reviews and the bull on the jacket —
So stop looking blue 20
And start serving up your sensations
Before it's too late;
Just please me for two generations —
You'll be 'truly great.' [1954]

THINKING ABOUT THE TEXT

1. Supply a few adjectives for the reader depicted in Larkin's poem. With what tone does this reader address would-be fiction writers? Cite specific words that especially come to mind.

2. To what extent do your tastes in fiction resemble those of the reader depicted in the poem?

3. What would you say to someone who dismisses Larkin's poem, believing that Larkin is merely expressing his bitterness over negative reviews of his work?

4. How does Larkin define "the reading public"? What other definitions of the term are possible? Would you apply this term to any group today? If so, how would you be able to tell that someone is a member of what you consider the present "reading public"?

5. The poem has a simple rhyme scheme. What is its effect? Larkin puts quotation marks around certain words. What is the effect of this technique?

MAKING COMPARISONS

1. What might Larkin's reader say about the two previous poems in this cluster? Support your conjectures with details from all three texts.

2. What words of Larkin's reader, if any, might the teacher in Catacalos's poem and the speaker in Collins's poem use? Again, refer to details of all three texts.

3. The reader in Larkin's poem seems to think that a work of fiction should "sound like real life." Apply this standard to each poem in the cluster. Does each "sound like real life" to you? Why, or why not? Do you believe that a work of fiction or poetry should always meet this standard? Explain.

WRITING ABOUT ISSUES

1. Choose one of the poems in this cluster and write an essay arguing for a certain judgment of the reader depicted in it (consider the teacher in Catacalos's poem as the reader). Be sure to identify specific principles and responsibilities you think the reader you discuss should uphold.

2. Choose two of the poems in this cluster and write an essay judging them. Do you find one better than the other? Be sure to identify the standards you are applying to each. Also, defend those standards, not assuming that your own reader will automatically accept them.

3. Think of a moment in this class or in some other class when people argued about how to judge a certain piece of writing. Perhaps you were directly involved in this argument. At any rate, write an essay analyzing it. Identify the issues involved, the positions expressed, how the argument proceeded, and what you thought of the outcome. If your view of the argument has changed since you witnessed it, explain how. If you wish, refer to one or more of the poems in this cluster.

4. Read at least two published reviews of something you have read, seen, or heard. Then, write an essay analyzing these reviews as arguments. Consider their claims, evidence, warrants, rhetorical strategies, and implied audience. If you wish, evaluate these reviews. You may find it useful to refer to one or more of the poems in the cluster.

JUDGING SOCIETY

WILLIAM BLAKE, "London"
WILLIAM WORDSWORTH, "The World Is Too Much with Us"
MATTHEW ARNOLD, "Dover Beach"
ZBIGNIEW HERBERT, "Report from the Besieged City"

Through literature, many writers judge their society. In many cases, the judgments are negative, part of an effort to make that society change. Ironically, several works that are now required reading in American schools actually engage in social protest; they criticize values and institutions that reigned in the writer's own setting. The poems by Blake, Wordsworth, and Arnold in this cluster have become established classics, what the sociologist Pierre Bourdieu terms "cultural capital." Yet each features a speaker who scorns the predominant ways of his world. Focus on the specific judgments these speakers make; consider why and how they oppose their society. The cluster's last poem is a more recent one by Zbigniew Herbert, a Polish writer who was often at odds with his country's totalitarian regimes. Clearly Herbert's speaker is judging contemporary Poland, but think about how his observations might apply to other "besieged" cities and societies.

BEFORE YOU READ

Get the recent issue of a daily newspaper and look through its first section. What judgments about American society are you inclined to make after reading that section's articles, editorials, and advertisements? Identify particular items that especially influence your view.

WILLIAM BLAKE
London

His contemporaries largely dismissed him as eccentric, even mad, but William Blake (1757–1827) is now regarded as a major figure in British Romanticism. In part, Blake was a painter and engraver, lavishly illustrating his own editions of his poems. Through both his visual and his verbal art, Blake promoted his own self-devised religion that incorporated stories and characters from the Bible. In 1789, he published Songs of Innocence, *and in 1794 he produced a counterpart group of poems,* Songs of Experience, *which included "London."*

I wander through each chartered° street,
Near where the chartered Thames does flow,
And mark in every face I meet
Marks of weakness, marks of woe.

In every cry of every man,   5
In every Infant's cry of fear,
In every voice, in every ban,
The mind-forged manacles I hear.

How the Chimney-sweeper's cry
Every black'ning Church appalls;   10
And the hapless Soldier's sigh
Runs in blood down Palace walls.

But most through midnight streets I hear
How the youthful Harlot's curse
Blasts the new-born Infant's tear,   15
And blights with plagues the Marriage hearse.   [1794]

1 **chartered:** Defined by law.

THINKING ABOUT THE TEXT

1. Where does the poem repeat words? How do these repetitions affect you?
2. What might the speaker have in mind with the phrase "mind-forged manacles"? Is this term applicable to your own society? Why, or why not?
3. Blake might have presented the third and fourth stanzas in reverse order. Why do you suppose he chose to conclude the poem by referring to "the youthful Harlot's curse"?

4. How abstract is this poem? To what extent does it rely on concrete images? Support your answers by referring to particular lines.

5. What would you say to someone who dislikes this poem because it is thoroughly negative, offering no solution to the problems it describes?

WILLIAM WORDSWORTH
The World Is Too Much with Us

Like William Blake, William Wordsworth (1770–1850) is today seen as a major British Romantic poet. Unlike Blake, he was regarded as such in his own lifetime, even being made poet laureate of England. He and his fellow poet Samuel Taylor Coleridge collaborated on Lyrical Ballads *(1798), a collection of verse that became a landmark of Romantic poetry. In his preface to the second edition two years later, Wordsworth famously defined poetry as "emotion recollected in tranquillity," contended that it should draw on "common life," and called for it to incorporate "language really used by men." Although young Wordsworth supported the French Revolution, the established poet increasingly embraced political conservatism. Whatever his ideology of the moment, however, Wordsworth used his writing to engage in social criticism. Probably he wrote the following poem in 1803; in any case, it appeared in his 1807* Poems in Two Volumes.

The world is too much with us; late and soon,
Getting and spending, we lay waste our powers;
Little we see in Nature that is ours;
We have given our hearts away, a sordid boon!
This Sea that bares her bosom to the moon;   5
The winds that will be howling at all hours,
And are up-gathered now like sleeping flowers;
For this, for everything, we are out of tune;
It moves us not. — Great God! I'd rather be
A Pagan suckled in a creed outworn;   10
So might I, standing on this pleasant lea,
Have glimpses that would make me less forlorn;
Have sight of Proteus rising from the sea;
Or hear old Triton blow his wreathèd horn.   [1807]

THINKING ABOUT THE TEXT

1. Wordworth's poem is a sonnet. All sonnets have fourteen lines, but they may differ in their rhyme schemes. What pattern of rhyme does this poem follow? What is its effect?

2. Often the last six lines of a sonnet differ significantly in meaning from the previous section. Is this true of Wordsworth's poem? Why, or why not?

3. What might the speaker have in mind when he claims that "the world is too much with us"? What specific "powers" does he apparently feel we have "wasted"?

4. In the third line, the speaker declares, "Little we see in Nature that is ours." What would you say to someone who argues that this line has become irrelevant, for Nature *has* become "ours" in the sense that our industrial civilization has conquered it? Should we care about nature as much as the poem's speaker does? Why, or why not?

5. What physical senses does the poem refer to? Does it emphasize one of these senses more than others? If so, which one?

MAKING COMPARISONS

1. Notice that Blake's and Wordworth's lives overlapped. Do their poems in this cluster express roughly the same social criticisms? Explain.

2. Whereas Blake's poem is four stanzas long, Wordsworth's poem is one continuous stanza. Does this difference in structure lead to a difference in effect? If so, how? Imagine that Blake's stanzas were run together as one, and that Wordsworth's stanza was divided in two after line 9. How would the effect of each poem change?

3. Whereas Wordsworth criticizes "us," neither that word nor "we" appears in Blake's poem. Does this mean that Blake is less concerned with criticizing the reader than Wordsworth is? Why, or why not?

MATTHEW ARNOLD
Dover Beach

Matthew Arnold (1822–1888) was the son of the headmaster at Rugby, one of England's elite schools, and in adulthood he too served education by working many years as a school inspector. But Arnold also established a considerable reputation as a social critic. In essays such as "The Function of Criticism at the Present Time" (1865) and books such as Culture and Anarchy *(1869), he called for Victorian society to improve its ethics by studying certain literary masterpieces. Arnold expressed similar concerns in his poetry. "Dover Beach," first published in 1867, is probably the best-known example of his verse.*

The sea is calm tonight.
The tide is full, the moon lies fair

Upon the straits; — on the French coast the light
Gleams and is gone; the cliffs of England stand,
Glimmering and vast, out in the tranquil bay.   5
Come to the window, sweet is the night-air!
Only, from the long line of spray
Where the sea meets the moon-blanched land,
Listen! you hear the grating roar
Of pebbles which the waves draw back, and fling,   10
At their return, up the high strand,
Begin, and cease, and then again begin,
With tremulous cadence slow, and bring
The eternal note of sadness in.

Sophocles long ago   15
Heard it on the Aegean, and it brought
Into his mind the turbid ebb and flow
Of human misery;° we
Find also in the sound a thought,
Hearing it by this distant northern sea.   20

The Sea of Faith
Was once, too, at the full, and round earth's shore
Lay like the folds of a bright girdle furled.
But now I only hear
Its melancholy, long, withdrawing roar,   25
Retreating, to the breath
Of the night-wind, down the vast edges drear
And naked shingles° of the world.

Ah, love, let us be true
To one another! for the world, which seems   30
To lie before us like a land of dreams,
So various, so beautiful, so new,
Hath really neither joy, nor love, nor light,
Nor certitude, nor peace, nor help for pain;
And we are here as on a darkling plain   35
Swept with confused alarms of struggle and flight,
Where ignorant armies clash by night.   [1867]

15–18 **Sophocles . . . misery:** In *Antigone* (lines 656–77), Sophocles describes the disasters that beset the house of Oedipus as a "mounting tide."   **28 shingles:** Pebble beaches.

THINKING ABOUT THE TEXT

1. How does the speaker use the image of the sea to make various points?

2. At what moments in the poem does the speaker make clear that he is

addressing a particular person? Identify what you learn about this listener. Do you learn enough? Why, or why not?

3. How does the speaker's vision of the world affect his relationship with his listener?

4. Where does the speaker refer to the present? To the past? To the future? Express the theme of this poem as a statement referring to time.

5. What would you say to a reader who dislikes the speaker because he seems to retreat from society at the end of the poem?

MAKING COMPARISONS

1. Both Wordsworth and Arnold refer to the sea. Are they making much the same point? Explain. By contrast, Blake's poem remains in London. Do you think Blake would therefore see Arnold as dealing with a largely different subject? Why, or why not?

2. Where does Arnold's poem rhyme? It uses an *irregular* rhyme scheme because it never really becomes a consistent, predictable pattern. By contrast, Blake's and Wordsworth's poems feature regular rhyme schemes. Do they therefore have a different effect than Arnold's poem does? Why, or why not?

3. What would you say to someone who criticizes Arnold's speaker as being more self-centered than Blake's and Wordsworth's?

ZBIGNIEW HERBERT
Report from the Besieged City
Translated by John and Bogdana Carpenter

Zbigniew Herbert (1924–1998) was a leading poet of twentieth-century Poland, which was conquered by the Nazis during World War II and later ruled by the Soviets. In many of his poems, Herbert criticizes one or both of these totalitarian regimes, yet often the speaker displays wry, self-mocking humor as well as pain. The poem's translators point out that the speaker alludes to particular episodes in Polish history when he says, "I don't know when the invasion began / two hundred years ago in December in September perhaps yesterday at dawn." In the late 1700s, the countries of Prussia, Russia, and Austria divided Poland up three times. In September 1939, Poland was invaded by the Nazis; in September 1944, the Soviet army arrived. On December 13, 1981, the Polish prodemocracy movement suffered defeat as General Jaruzelski reasserted Communist control. Though Herbert lived to see the increasing democratization of his country in the 1990s, the poem we feature here is from 1982, when Communism still held sway.

Too old to carry arms and fight like the others —

they graciously gave me the inferior role of chronicler
I record — I don't know for whom — the history of the siege

I am supposed to be exact but I don't know when the invasion began
two hundred years ago in December in September perhaps yesterday at dawn   5
everyone here suffers from a loss of the sense of time

all we have left is the place the attachment to the place
we still rule over the ruins of temples specters of gardens and houses
if we lose the ruins nothing will be left

I write as I can in the rhythm of interminable weeks   10
monday: empty storehouses a rat became the unit of currency
tuesday: the mayor murdered by unknown assailants
wednesday: negotiations for a cease-fire the enemy has imprisoned our
               messengers
we don't know where they are held that is the place of torture
thursday: after a stormy meeting a majority of voices rejected   15
the motion of the spice merchants for unconditional surrender
friday: the beginning of the plague saturday: our invincible defender
N.N. committed suicide sunday: no more water we drove back
an attack at the eastern gate called the Gate of the Alliance

all of this is monotonous I know it can't move anyone   20

I avoid any commentary I keep a tight hold on my emotions I write about
               the facts
only they it seems are appreciated in foreign markets
yet with a certain pride I would like to inform the world
that thanks to the war we have raised a new species of children
our children don't like fairy tales they play at killing   25
awake and asleep they dream of soup of bread and bones
just like dogs and cats

in the evening I like to wander near the outposts of the City
along the frontier of our uncertain freedom
I look at the swarms of soldiers below their lights   30
I listen to the noise of drums barbarian shrieks
truly it is inconceivable the City is still defending itself
the siege has lasted a long time the enemies must take turns
nothing unites them except the desire for our extermination
Goths the Tartars Swedes troops of the Emperor regiments of the Transfiguration   35
who can count them
the colors of their banners change like the forest on the horizon
from delicate bird's yellow in spring through green through red to winter's black

and so in the evening released from facts I can think
about distant ancient matters for example our   40

friends beyond the sea I know they sincerely sympathize
they send us flour lard sacks of comfort and good advice
they don't even know their fathers betrayed us
our former allies at the time of the second Apocalypse
their sons are blameless they deserve our gratitude therefore we are grateful   45
they have not experienced a siege as long as eternity
those struck by misfortune are always alone
the defenders of the Dalai Lama the Kurds the Afghan mountaineers

now as I write these words the advocates of conciliation
have won the upper hand over the party of inflexibles   50
a normal hesitation of moods fate still hangs in the balance

cemeteries grow larger the number of defenders is smaller
yet the defense continues it will continue to the end
and if the City falls but a single man escapes
he will carry the City within himself on the roads of exile   55
he will be the City

we look in the face of hunger the face of fire face of death
worst of all — the face of betrayal

and only our dreams have not been humiliated   [1982]

THINKING ABOUT THE TEXT

1. What judgments does the speaker make about the world outside his city? About the city itself? Refer to specific lines.

2. In what ways does the speaker seem concerned about the poem's audience?

3. What is the speaker's relationship to "facts"?

4. In what ways does this poem seem a "report"? In what ways does it seem quite different from a "report," according to your definition of that genre?

5. What might the speaker mean by "he will be the city"?

MAKING COMPARISONS

1. How might the term *besieged* be applied to topics mentioned in Blake's, Wordsworth's, and Arnold's poems? Use Herbert's poem and a dictionary definition of *besieged* to support your answer.

2. Do you think Herbert's poem is more political than Blake's, Wordsworth's, and Arnold's? Explain your reasoning, including how you define *political*.

3. Rank the four poems in this cluster according to their degrees of abstraction, from most abstract to least abstract. Does each poem's degree of abstraction affect your judgment of it? Explain.

WRITING ABOUT ISSUES

1. Choose one of the poems in this cluster and write an essay identifying whatever judgments the speaker makes about his society. In particular, consider whether the speaker makes various judgments or a single one. Refer to specific lines.

2. The poems by Blake, Wordsworth, and Arnold have long been recognized as masterpieces of British literature. Because Herbert's poem was written more recently, whether it will become an established classic is in question. Does it deserve to endure as long as the other three poems have? Write an essay stating and supporting your answer by referring to Herbert's poem and at least one of the others. If you wish, identify what you would say to someone who argues that Herbert's poem is already irrelevant because Poland is now a democracy.

3. Take a line from one of the poems in this cluster and write an essay showing that the line is applicable to a particular trend you have observed in your own community, region, or nation.

4. Choose a newspaper or magazine columnist who regularly criticizes aspects of society. Read at least three of this writer's recent pieces. Then write an essay identifying this writer's basic concerns and rhetorical strategies. If you wish, refer to any of the poems in this cluster.

JUDGING A LIFE

PERCY BYSSHE SHELLEY, "Ozymandias"
STEVIE SMITH, "Not Waving but Drowning"
JAMES WRIGHT, "Lying in a Hammock at William Duffy's Farm
in Pine Island, Minnesota"
SHARON OLDS, "I Go Back to May 1937"

The first poem in this cluster is from the early nineteenth century. The remaining three are more recent; the latest is from the mid-1980s. But all four poems show people judging lives: either their own life, others' lives, or both. Try as we may to avoid making such judgments, we often wind up making them anyway. Plenty of our judgments are automatic and unconscious. Only on certain occasions might we seriously ponder the nature of our own or someone else's existence. But a literature course such as the one you are taking is a wonderful forum for considering lives. While reading various works for the course, you develop opinions about their characters. Maybe literature is most valuable when it conveys the message that summarizing and evaluating a life is difficult, and should be. A literary work may not be worth reading if it endorses snap judgments about people. Consider whether and how these four poems encourage you to complicate the biographies and autobiographies you construct.

BEFORE YOU READ

According to the contemporary writer Reynolds Price, "No one under forty can believe how nearly everything's inherited." In effect, Price is making a claim about the ability of people under forty to judge their lives. What does Price mean? How do you react to his claim?

PERCY BYSSHE SHELLEY

Ozymandias

Before his untimely death by drowning, Percy Bysshe Shelley (1792–1822) composed many poems that are now regarded as masterpieces of British Romanticism. Shelley published the following poem in 1818 after a visit to the British Museum. On exhibit there were artifacts from the tomb of the ancient Egyptian pharaoh Rameses II, called Ozymandias by many of Shelley's contemporaries. These objects included a broken statue of the pharaoh.

I met a traveler from an antique land
Who said: Two vast and trunkless legs of stone
Stand in the desert. . . . Near them, on the sand,
Half sunk, a shattered visage lies, whose frown,
And wrinkled lip, and sneer of cold command,   5
Tell that its sculptor well those passions read
Which yet survive, stamped on these lifeless things,
The hand that mocked them, and the heart that fed:
And on the pedestal these words appear:
"My name is Ozymandias, King of Kings: 10
Look on my works, ye Mighty, and despair!"
Nothing beside remains. Round the decay
Of that colossal wreck, boundless and bare
The lone and level sands stretch far away.   [1818]

THINKING ABOUT THE TEXT

1. "Ozymandias" is a sonnet, a poem consisting of fourteen lines. Often there is a significant division in content between a sonnet's first eight lines and its last six. Is there such a division in Shelley's poem? Explain.

2. How is the poem a comment on the epitaph it quotes from the statue's pedestal? Describe Ozymandias by listing at least three adjectives for him, and identify the specific lines that make you think of them.

3. Although the poem begins by referring to "I," this is not the main speaker of the poem; soon we are presented with the report of the "traveler." Shelley could have had the traveler narrate the whole poem. Why might he have begun with the "I"?

4. Both Shelley and the sculptor are artists. To what extent do they resemble each other? Note that the poem describes the sculptor as someone who "well those passions read." Why does Shelley associate him with the act of reading?

5. According to this poem, what survives? What does not?

STEVIE SMITH
Not Waving but Drowning

Stevie Smith was the pen name of Florence Martin Smith (1902–1971). For much of her adult life, she was anything but a public figure; rather, she spent much time taking care of her aunt in a London suburb. During the 1960s, however, Smith became increasingly known in England for her poetry; she even read from it aloud on numerous radio broadcasts. Her Collected Poems *was published posthumously in 1975. The following poem, Smith's best known, appeared in a 1957 book that was also entitled* Not Waving but Drowning.

Nobody heard him, the dead man,
But still he lay moaning:
I was much further out than you thought
And not waving but drowning.

Poor chap, he always loved larking   5
And now he's dead
It must have been too cold for him his heart gave way,
They said.

Oh, no, no, no, it was too cold always
(Still the dead one lay moaning)   10
I was much too far out all my life
And not waving but drowning.

                                                                      [1957]

THINKING ABOUT THE TEXT

1. In what senses might the dead man have been drowning? In what senses might he have been "too cold" and "much too far out"?

2. How do you think it was possible for "They" to misunderstand the dead man's real situation?

3. Smith might have ended the poem with the first stanza. What do the second and third stanzas contribute?

4. What, if anything, does the dead man hope to achieve through his moaning?

5. Is it unrealistic for Smith to have a dead man speak?

MAKING COMPARISONS

1. Compare the dead man's statements to what Ozymandias says about himself. Does Smith's character seem wiser than Ozymandias? Do you sympathize with him more? Explain.

2. Is it possible that the man in Smith's poem had the same social stature as Ozymandias? Why, or why not?

3. Is there any equivalent in Shelley's poem to the "They" in Smith's? Support your answer by referring to specific lines in both poems.

JAMES WRIGHT

Lying in a Hammock at William Duffy's Farm in Pine Island, Minnesota

James Wright (1927–1980) was born and raised in the industrial town of Martin's Ferry, Ohio. Many of his poems deal with the working-class life he experienced there. Early in his career as a poet, he wrote in conventional forms, but later he became much more experimental. The following poem is from Wright's 1963 book The Branch Will Not Break, *much of which reflects the interest he had then in the crisp, enigmatic style of various classic Chinese poets.*

Over my head, I see the bronze butterfly,
Asleep on the black trunk,
Blowing like a leaf in green shadow.
Down the ravine behind the empty house,
The cowbells follow one another   5
Into the distances of the afternoon.
To my right,
In a field of sunlight between two pines,
The droppings of last year's horses
Blaze up into golden stones.   10
I lean back, as the evening darkens and comes on.
A chicken hawk floats over, looking for home.
I have wasted my life.

[1963]

THINKING ABOUT THE TEXT

1. Does the last line surprise you? Why, or why not? Looking back over the poem, does the last line fit well with the previous ones? Why, or why not?

2. How objective does the speaker seem in each of his observations?

3. Would the poem's meaning and effect be different if the speaker's observations about nature were put in a different order? Explain. What would have been the effect had the speaker begun with the statement that now concludes the poem?

4. The title is quite specific about the poem's setting. Why evidently does Wright point out whose farm it is and exactly where it is located?

5. Despite the specificity of the title, the speaker isn't specific about how he has wasted his life. Why evidently does Wright refuse to provide such detail? What things do you plan to do so that you do not feel that you have wasted your life?

MAKING COMPARISONS

1. Are Shelley's and Smith's poems as much about waste as Wright's poem is? Support your answer by referring to specific lines in all three texts.

2. How does nature play a role in all three poems?

3. Both Shelley's and Smith's poems refer to more than one human being. Wright's poem is different: Aside from the reference to William Duffy in its title, the poem does not refer to any other human beings besides the speaker. Does this difference make for a significant difference in effect? Explain.

SHARON OLDS
I Go Back to May 1937

Sharon Olds (b. 1942) is one of the most widely read contemporary American poets. For the last several years, she has taught poetry writing at New York University. In many of her poems, Olds seems to be discussing her own family relationships, yet increasingly she has resisted critics' efforts to interpret her work as purely autobiographical. Olds won the National Book Critics Circle Award for her 1983 book The Dead and the Living. *She has published four other volumes, the latest of which is* The Wellspring (1997). *The following poem comes from* The Gold Cell (1987).

I see them standing at the formal gates of their colleges,
I see my father strolling out
under the ochre sandstone arch, the

red tiles glinting like bent
plates of blood behind his head, I 5
see my mother with a few light books at her hip
standing at the pillar made of tiny bricks with the
wrought-iron gate still open behind her, its
sword-tips black in the May air,
they are about to graduate, they are about to get married, 10
they are kids, they are dumb, all they know is they are
innocent, they would never hurt anybody.
I want to go up to them and say Stop,
don't do it—she's the wrong woman,
he's the wrong man, you are going to do things 15
you cannot imagine you would ever do,
you are going to do bad things to children,
you are going to suffer in ways you never heard of,
you are going to want to die. I want to go
up to them there in the late May sunlight and say it, 20
her hungry pretty blank face turning to me,
her pitiful beautiful untouched body,
his arrogant handsome blind face turning to me,
his pitiful beautiful untouched body,
but I don't do it. I want to live. I 25
take them up like the male and female
paper dolls and bang them together
at the hips like chips of flint as if to
strike sparks from them, I say
Do what you are going to do, and I will tell about it. [1987] 30

THINKING ABOUT THE TEXT

1. To what extent does this seem a poem about the speaker herself? Are you
   inclined to accept her judgments and predictions? Why, or why not?

2. Does the speaker express significantly different attitudes toward her father
   and mother, or does she seem to regard both parents in much the same
   way? Refer to specific lines.

3. Identify instances of repetition in the poem. What is their effect?

4. Near the end of the poem, the speaker seems to take physical control of
   her parents, as if she is really able to "bang them together." To what extent
   do you sympathize with the speaker at this moment? In the last line, the
   speaker states the following: "Do what you are going to do, and I will tell
   about it." Indeed, the whole poem can be considered a means by which
   the speaker *does* "tell about it." How do you feel about the speaker's desire
   to tell? What would you say to someone who argues that people should
   keep their family's suffering private?

5. In 1988, Olds was interviewed by Terry Gross on the National Public Radio show *Fresh Air*. During the interview, Olds read this particular poem aloud, and Gross proceeded to ask her repeatedly about the poem's relation to Olds's own personal life. Do you think Gross was right to pursue this line of inquiry? In response, Olds insisted that the poem *not* be viewed as autobiographical. Do you think she was being reasonable? Identify some of the warrants or assumptions reflected in your answers to these questions.

MAKING COMPARISONS

1. Does each poem in this cluster deal with past, present, and future? Support your answer by referring to specific lines in each text.

2. How important is setting in each of the four poems?

3. Review all four poems in this cluster. Where do you find a person making a judgment about himself or herself? Where do you find a person judging others? Based on your reading of these poems, compare these two types of judgment. Do you think it important to distinguish them? If so, in what respects?

WRITING ABOUT ISSUES

1. Terry Gross introduced her 1988 interview with Sharon Olds by claiming that every poem by Olds brings together "destruction" and "creation." Write an essay examining the extent to which Gross's claim fits the poem by Olds included here. Or, write an essay in which you focus on another poem in this cluster, examining the extent to which it deals with both "destruction" and "creation."

2. Choose two of the poems in this cluster. Then, write an essay considering the extent to which each indicates that people may make faulty judgments about their own lives or others' lives.

3. Choose a well-known person, living or dead, who you feel has been misjudged by many other people. Then, write an essay in which you state and support your notion of how this person ought to be judged.

4. In recent newspapers and magazines, find some obituaries that present detailed accounts of the deceased person's life. What, basically, do these obituaries suggest are the important aspects of a person's life? Write an essay in which you answer this question by using several examples. If you wish, focus on multiple obituaries about the same person. Also feel free to refer to poems in this cluster.

12

Confronting Mortality

Much literature deals with human hopes and desires. But just as often, literature depicts constraints on them. Among other things, it portrays the human body as vulnerable, aging, destined to die. Perhaps the most interesting and significant works of literature are those that examine how people try to live meaningfully despite their mortality. Whether or not readers believe in an afterlife, literature offers stirring accounts of humans struggling with earthly limits.

Not every writer of literature views mortality as bad. Many suggest that because people know they will die, they are more apt to value their time on earth, whereas they might waste it if they expected it to last forever. For each of the writers in this chapter, death is at least worth serious attention. After all, it is a part of life.

We begin with a cluster of poems (p. 1471) by John Keats, Gerard Manley Hopkins, Robin Becker, and Virginia Hamilton Adair that focus on the passage of time, which leads many of us to contemplate our mortality. Next, a pair of short stories (p. 1480) by Tim O'Brien and Jameson Currier show particular communities of men working to survive in the face of mortal danger. O'Brien's characters are fighting in the Vietnam War; Currier's are threatened by AIDS. The third cluster (p. 1504) features poems about death by Emily Dickinson, who is well known for her many imaginative and thought-provoking death scenes. Because she wrote about death so much, you may think Dickinson was too obsessed with the subject, but each of her poems about it takes a fresh angle.

The death of a stranger can move people to reflect on mortality in the stories comprising the fourth cluster (p. 1510). Katherine Mansfield depicts a girl confronting the body of a dead laborer after a joyous garden party; Gabriel García Márquez details a group of villagers' fascination with an anonymous corpse; and Don DeLillo presents a man similarly fascinated with a killing he sees on videotape. Of course, when people do think about death, a wide variety of positions is available for them to take. In the next cluster (p. 1532), poets John Donne, Dylan Thomas, and Wislawa Szymborska all express scorn toward it. In the pair of essays that follow (p. 1538), George Orwell and Annie Dillard reflect on the cultural differences that can affect how people view the act of killing an animal.

The seventh cluster (p. 1549) features Marsha Norman's play *'night, Mother,* in which a woman seeks to kill herself while her mother tries to prevent her from doing so. Americans are increasingly debating whether suicide is ever appropriate; to help you consider Norman's handling of this issue, we include three commentaries on her play.

Next come two stories (p. 1588) by Elizabeth Bowen and Robert Olen Butler in which a dead person returns to life. Bowen focuses on a living person fearing the reappearance of her dead lover. You can sense the situation of Butler's central character from his story's very title: "Jealous Husband Returns in Form of Parrot." Both stories belong to a whole tradition of tales featuring the return of the dead. You may be familiar with film and television versions of this plot, most of which do little more than titillate audiences. Yet, while Bowen's and Butler's are indeed entertaining, they are also complex, using resurrection to probe human relationships.

In the story that is the focus of our next cluster (p. 1600), Bharati Mukherjee's "The Management of Grief," the heroine Shaila must learn to live with the fact that her husband and sons will never return to her. Along with other members of her Indian-Canadian community, they have perished in an airplane crash over the Irish Sea. We include Muherjee's story because it illustrates the cultural negotiations that often occur with such disasters. As Shaila attempts to come to terms with her loss, she finds herself dealing with native Canadians, Indian immigrants to Canada, her parents in India, and even authorities in Ireland, where she goes in an effort to recover her family's bodies. Although the story is a work of fiction, Mukherjee based it on the real-life crash of an Air India flight in 1985. With her husband Clark Blaise, she has written a book about that actual event, and we include their chapter on the trip to Ireland made by relatives of the victims. Also, we present a 1992 article from the *New York Times* updating the Air India case; specifically, it reports the arrest of a Sikh for bombing the plane. To conclude the cluster, we present a 1996 opinion piece that brings up the cultural context of disaster. In it, author Sam Husseini criticizes airlines suspicious of passengers who belong to particular ethnic groups.

The chapter's final cluster (p. 1628) continues examining real-life brushes with death. In essays, Audre Lorde and June Jordan discuss resolutions they made once they were forced to acknowledge mortality. Lorde discusses how, after finding that she had a tumor, she decided to quit being silent about various things. Recalling the suicide of her mother, Jordan notes that after this terrible event, she grew more determined to become strong herself. Along with the other writers in this chapter, Lorde and Jordan insist on making the reader aware of death, not because they despair but because they believe people can learn much from pondering it.

THE PASSAGE OF TIME

JOHN KEATS, "Ode on a Grecian Urn"
GERARD MANLEY HOPKINS, "Spring and Fall"
ROBIN BECKER, "The Star Show"
VIRGINIA HAMILTON ADAIR, "A Last Marriage"

People often forget about their mortality until some experience reminds them that their life is moving on. The passage of time is one of literature's most frequent concerns. Here we feature poems on this topic by two nineteenth-century British writers, John Keats and Gerard Manley Hopkins, and by two contemporary Americans, Robin Becker and Virginia Hamilton Adair. Keats's poem "Ode on a Grecian Urn" ponders how the urn's images seem frozen in time, but indirectly Keats reminds his reader that, by contrast, flesh-and-blood humans age. To dramatize this process of change, Hopkins and Becker juxtapose youth with later life. Hopkins's speaker is telling a young girl that she will get older, while Becker's speaker looks back at her own childhood. Adair's poem deals with aging, too, although here the speaker is evidently an elderly woman trying to move beyond various losses and make the most of her remaining life. Like many writers, all four of these poets analyze time by referring to seasons. As you read their works, consider what you associate symbolically with summer, fall, winter, and spring.

BEFORE YOU READ

What sorts of occasions typically make people realize that the years are passing? Identify at least two occasions when, unexpectedly, you became quite aware that you are growing older.

JOHN KEATS

Ode on a Grecian Urn

Despite his early death from tuberculosis, John Keats (1795–1821) produced several poems still regarded as masterpieces of British Romanticism. The following poem is from a series of odes that Keats composed in 1819; others include "Ode to a Nightingale" and "Ode on Melancholy." At this period in his life, Keats was experiencing emotional turmoil. Already he was suffering from the disease that would kill him, while he also felt growing passion for a woman named Fanny Brawne. In turning to the genre of the ode, Keats was perpetuating a kind of poem that dates back to ancient Greece, where it adhered to a fixed structure involving three stanzas. By Keats's time, the ode's form had become more flexible. Often it featured more than three stanzas, which could vary in rhythm and length. In subject matter, the modern ode often dealt with topics that Keats addresses here: on the one hand, the speaker's desire for enduring beauty; on the other, the reality of a changing world.

1

Thou still unravished bride of quietness,
   Thou foster-child of silence and slow time,
Sylvan° historian, who canst thus express
   A flowery tale more sweetly than our rhyme:
What leaf-fringed legend haunts about thy shape   5
   Of deities or mortals, or of both,
      In Tempe or the dales of Arcady?°
What men or gods are these? What maidens loath?
   What mad pursuit? What struggle to escape?
      What pipes and timbrels? What wild ecstasy?   10

2

Heard melodies are sweet, but those unheard
   Are sweeter; therefore, ye soft pipes, play on;
Not to the sensual ear, but, more endeared,
   Pipe to the spirit ditties of no tone:
Fair youth, beneath the trees, thou canst not leave   15
   Thy song, nor ever can those trees be bare;
      Bold Lover, never, never canst thou kiss,
Though winning near the goal — yet, do not grieve;
   She cannot fade, though thou hast not thy bliss,
      For ever wilt thou love, and she be fair!   20

3

Ah, happy, happy boughs! that cannot shed
   Your leaves, nor ever bid the Spring adieu;
And, happy melodist, unwearièd,
   For ever piping songs for ever new;
More happy love! more happy, happy love!   25
   For ever warm and still to be enjoyed,
      For ever panting, and for ever young;
All breathing human passion far above,
   That leaves a heart high-sorrowful and cloyed,
      A burning forehead, and a parching tongue.   30

4

Who are these coming to the sacrifice?
   To what green altar, O mysterious priest,

---

3 Sylvan: Rustic; the urn is decorated with a forest scene.   **7 Tempe . . . Arcady:** Beautiful
rural valleys in Greece.

Lead'st thou that heifer lowing at the skies,
　　And all her silken flanks with garlands drest?
What little town by river or sea shore,   35
　　Or mountain-built with peaceful citadel,
　　　　Is emptied of this folk, this pious morn?
And, little town, thy streets for evermore
　　Will silent be; and not a soul to tell
　　　　Why thou art desolate, can e'er return.   40

5

O Attic° shape! Fair attitude! with brede°
Of marble men and maidens overwrought,
With forest branches and the trodden weed;
　　Thou, silent form, dost tease us out of thought
As doth eternity: Cold Pastoral!   45
　　When old age shall this generation waste,
　　　　Thou shalt remain, in midst of other woe
Than ours, a friend to man, to whom thou say'st,
　　Beauty is truth, truth beauty—that is all
　　　　Ye know on earth, and all ye need to know.   [1819]   50

41 Attic: Possessing classic Athenian simplicity;　**brede:** Design.

THINKING ABOUT THE TEXT

1. Visualize the urn based on Keats's lines about it. (You might draw a picture of it and compare your drawing with a classmate's.) How objective does the speaker's description of this object seem?

2. Two of the poem's stanzas are packed with questions. In general, what are these questions about?

3. What image of love does the speaker describe the urn as presenting? To what extent is it an image that you believe should be treasured?

4. What is the effect of the speaker's reference to the deserted town in the fourth stanza? Why do you think the speaker focuses on such an image at this point?

5. Why do you think the speaker calls the urn "cold" in line 45? Critics have long debated how to interpret the poem's last two lines. Do you agree with the speaker's statement that "Beauty is truth, truth beauty" is "all ye need to know"? Explain your reasoning.

GERARD MANLEY HOPKINS
Spring and Fall

Gerard Manley Hopkins (1844–1889) was a Jesuit priest who published few of his poems during his lifetime; they became widely known only after the second collected edition of them appeared in 1930. Hopkins is now especially famous for his development of a technique he called sprung rhythm. As "Spring and Fall" demonstrates, a poem that uses it may include several stressed syllables in each line, and the number of stresses per line may vary. Sprung rhythm allows a poet to emphasize words as he or she sees fit, without following a regular pattern. The following poem was written in 1880.

To a Young Child

Márgarét áre you gríeving
Over Goldengrove unleaving?
Leáves, like the things of man, you
With your fresh thoughts care for, can you?
Áh! ás the heart grows older   5
It will come to such sights colder
By and by, nor spare a sigh
Though worlds of wanwood leafmeal lie;°
And yet you wíll weep and know why.
Now no matter, child, the name: 10
Sórrow's spríngs áre the same.
Nor mouth had, no nor mind, expressed
What heart heard of, ghost° guessed:
It ís the blight man was born for,
it is Margaret you mourn for.   [1880]   15

8 Though worlds of wanwood leafmeal lie: The trees have shed leaves that now lie in piecemeal fashion on the ground. Probably Hopkins is describing these trees as pale, the most common modern meaning of *wan.* He may, however, be seeking to create the opposite impression, for *wan* resembles an Old English word that means "dark." **13 ghost:** Soul.

THINKING ABOUT THE TEXT

1. In what respects does the poem relate to its title, "Spring and Fall"? Refer to specific lines.

2. What do you take to be the reasoning behind the speaker's ultimate claim, "It is Margaret you mourn for"? Why do you suppose the speaker addresses Margaret this way? Could a child actually benefit from hearing such a message? If so, how?

3. Suppose the poem had been about Margaret rather than addressed to Margaret. Might its effect on you have been different? If so, how?

4. As we pointed out in the headnote, Hopkins was a priest. Does the poem seem to have been written by a religious person? What words of the text should someone especially consider in answering this question? How do you define *religious*?

5. Identify places where Hopkins uses alliteration, rhyming, and unusual words. How effective is each of these devices?

MAKING COMPARISONS

1. Hopkins's speaker addresses the child Margaret, while Keats's speaker addresses images on the urn. Do you react to the poems differently because of this difference in audience? Explain.

2. Compare Hopkins's and Keats's references to leaves and spring. Do you think that the two poems express different attitudes toward these things? Why, or why not?

3. To what extent is each of these two poems about mourning?

ROBIN BECKER

The Star Show

Robin Becker (b. 1951) teaches creative writing at Pennsylvania State University. Her books of poetry include Backtalk *(1982),* Giacometti's Dog *(1990), and* All-American Girl, *a 1992 volume in which the following poem appears.*

Though we're flat on our backs
at midnight
under the enormous sky, I know I'm really
in the Fels Planetarium
in Philadelphia, where I've come with the other   5
third-graders for the Star Show.
Tonight the trailing
blazes of white explode
across the darkness like firecrackers
and my companions *ooooh* and point   10
and say *over there*, though the words are too late
to be of use and hang
in the air much longer than light.

What I remember about the Star Show   15
is the commentator's calm voice,

the miracle spreading overhead
as he wooed us in plain English,
as if he didn't need special gear
to show us the sky's mysteries.
He needed only the reclining seats, the artificial   20
ceiling shuddering close with its countless stars,
our willingness to leave the known
earth, our parents, teachers, friends, ourselves
for this uncertain meeting in the dark.

He urged us to let our eyes adjust   25
for the journey, he asked us to relax
as the room began to spin and he whispered
in his knowledgeable voice about Jupiter.
Like my rabbi appearing suddenly in the dome
to discuss Moses, he explained with sorrow   30
that brilliant Galileo
had to retract his scientific
conclusions before the Inquisition.
This made us sad, for we already knew
that Galileo was right,   35
that four stars revolved around Jupiter
as the earth revolved around the sun.

And then, as though someone were shaking out a bedspread,
someone shook the sky and all the stars
shifted, it was winter, night of the lean wolf.   40
His voice grew cold and we buttoned our sweaters
because the temperature was failing, and we wanted
to follow him wherever he was going,
which was December.
                              Across the mountain passes   45
we hunted bear; with the Hopis, we cured buffalo
hides and predicted the hour of sunrise.
Who didn't want to linger on that winter
mesa with the spotted ponies, so close to the stars?

There wasn't time. He was galloping toward   50
summer while I sat weeping for what I'd lost:
a glimpse of the sadness to come, the astronomer's
sure purpose. He guided the constellations
from early spring to June and then the sun
rose higher than we thought possible   55
and the longest day endured; he brought us into
a meadow drenched with light, but it was night,
we knew it, for now we could name every star.
How could he leave us here, now that we had become

his, now that he had asked us   60
to learn his heaven? As the chairs began to tilt
he threw the stars across the sky, flung meteors
carelessly and laughed a grown-up laugh.
He punctured the darkness with white bullets
and the kids began to shout.   65
The seats fell forward and the sun rose
in the auditorium, warming the air.
I sat bereft before the retreating stars.
Row by row we stood and blinked
into that autumn afternoon, as the ordinary jeers   70
and curses filled our mouths.   [1992]

THINKING ABOUT THE TEXT

1. The poem begins with the speaker's present situation. What apparently is going on? Consider whether the first stanza is really necessary. If Becker had omitted it and begun with the second stanza, would the poem's effect have been significantly different? Explain.

2. Where does Becker use the seasons for a framework? Where does she refer to changes in the day? Should she be criticized for using what are, after all, conventional signs of the passing of time? Why, or why not?

3. What psychological changes does the speaker recall going through during the star show? Do you think a child might really have these feelings, or do you suspect they belong more to the adult who is looking back? How important to you is it that the poem be realistic?

4. Describe the commentator as the speaker remembers him. What do you conclude about this figure? What should be made of the fact that the speaker compares him to a rabbi?

5. Trace the poem's references to language. What should readers think when it ends with children's "jeers / and curses"?

MAKING COMPARISONS

1. Compare what Hopkins and Becker imply about a child's state of mind. Do their portraits of childhood seem pretty much the same, or are there important differences?

2. Would you say that Keats's, Hopkins's, and Becker's poems all end with a tone of despair? Why, or why not?

3. Can any words in Becker's description of the commentator be used to describe Keats's speaker or Hopkins's? Explain. Choose two or three particular moments in the star show that Becker describes and imagine that Keats's speaker or Hopkins's speaker was the commentator during these moments. What might the speaker might have said to the children?

VIRGINIA HAMILTON ADAIR
A Last Marriage

Virginia Hamilton Adair (b. 1913) has written poetry for much for her life, and a number of her poems have appeared in magazines over the years. But she was eighty-three years old when she published her first book of poetry, Ants on the Melon *(1996), which includes the following poem. Although she has been blind for several years, Adair continues to write. In this respect, she resembles the seventeenth-century poet John Milton, whose poem on his blindness appears on page 11. Her latest collection of poems is* Belief and Blasphemies *(1998).*

The children gone, grown into other arms,
Man of her heart and bed gone underground,
Powder and chunks of ash in a shamefast urn,
Her mother long since buried in a blue gown,
Friends vanishing downward from the highway crash,   5
Slow hospital dooms, or a bullet in the head,
She came at last alone into her overgrown
Shapeless and forlorn garden. Death was there
Too, but tangible. She hacked and dragged away
Horrors of deadwood, webbed and sagging foliage,   10
Self-strangling roots, vines, suckers, arboreal
Deformities in viperish coils. Sweat, anger, pity
Poured from her. And her flesh was jabbed by thorns,
Hair jerked by twigs, eyes stung by mould and tears.
But day by day in the afterbath she recovered stillness.   15
Day by day the disreputable garden regained
Its green tenderness. They wooed one another. The living
Responses issued from clean beds of earth.
It was a new marriage, reclusive, active, wordless.
Early each morning even in rain she walked   20
The reviving ground where one day she would knock and enter.
She took its green tribute into her arms and rooms.
Through autumn the pruned wood gave her ceremonial
Fires, where she saw lost faces radiant with love.
Beyond the window, birds passed and the leaves with them.   25
Now was a season to sit still with time to know,
Drawing each breath like a fine crystal of snow.   [1996]

THINKING ABOUT THE TEXT

1. Summarize the stages that the woman goes through. In what senses does she experience "a last marriage"?

2. Here is an issue of fact: Should readers assume that the garden is real? Identify the degree to which this issue is important.

3. What is the effect of Adair's referring to the woman merely as "she" rather than naming her or giving her some more specific identity? Do you think gender matters in this poem? If the references had been to a "he," would the effect have been different? Explain your reasoning.

4. The poem ends with a rhyming couplet, and only here does the poem obviously rhyme. What is the effect of this rhyming? Why do you suppose Adair uses rhyme here and not throughout the poem? What should readers conclude from the fact that the poem ends with the word "snow"?

5. Are there any sound similarities besides rhyme among earlier words? If so, what specific patterns do you find?

MAKING COMPARISONS

1. With the exception of Keats's "Ode," all of the poems in this cluster refer to weeping. Does the reason for weeping seem basically the same in each case? Support your answer by noting specific lines.

2. All four poems refer to seasons. Do they seem to make similar associations with them? Again, note specific lines.

3. Compare the garden in Adair's poem to "Goldengrove" in Hopkins's. Is there any equivalent to "Goldengrove" in Keats's poem? In Becker's poem? (Of course, you will need to identify what you think the word *Goldengrove* refers to in the first place.)

WRITING ABOUT ISSUES

1. Choose one of the four poems in this cluster and write an essay identifying its dominant mood or emotion. Support your impression by referring to specific lines. Feel free to mention other moods or emotions at work in the poem as you discuss its main one.

2. Write an essay comparing Hopkins's Margaret to the younger self of Becker's speaker or to Adair's heroine. Focus in particular on their reactions to the passage of time.

3. Write an essay recalling a particular show or ceremony you attended when you were young, one that made you aware that time was passing. Note particular things that gave you this impression and explain how you felt about it. If you wish, distinguish between the self you were then and the self you are now. Feel free to refer to one or more of the poems in this cluster.

4. Write an essay analyzing how the passage of time is represented in a particular artifact of popular culture, such as a film, a television show, a calendar, a greeting card, or a song. (Keep in mind that representation may

take the form of pictures or sounds, not just words.) In your analysis, identify what you assume is the audience for this artifact. You may want to compare the artifact to one or more of the poems in this cluster.

FIGHTING FOR SURVIVAL

TIM O'BRIEN, "The Things They Carried"
JAMESON CURRIER, "What They Carried"

In much literature, characters strive to preserve their own lives or those of others. From Homer's *Iliad* on, one recurring setting for these efforts has been war. Contemporary literature is no exception. For example, even though the war in Vietnam ended more than two decades ago, many poets, playwrights, fiction writers, and essayists continue to chronicle and reflect on the struggles of its participants, in part because they recognize that Americans still argue about whether the war should ever have been fought. Naturally, the Vietnam conflict is particularly a concern for writers who served in it. Here we include a short story by one veteran of it, Tim O'Brien. As indicated by the title, "The Things They Carried," the story depicts the experiences of soldiers in Vietnam by focusing on equipment they used to survive. Though similar in title, Jameson Currier's story reminds readers that the contemporary world has been marked by other kinds of "warfare." Specifically, it details how a group of gay men work together to help a friend of theirs suffering from AIDS. At the start, you might assume that what's principally carried in this story is the AIDS virus. But Currier emphasizes the resources, physical as well as spiritual, with which his characters fight it. As you read both of these stories, compare their depictions of communities—more precisely, male communities—struggling to survive.

BEFORE YOU READ

List the sorts of personalities, emotions, and events that you think might appear in a story about an American military unit in Vietnam. Then, list the sorts that you think might appear in a story about gay men coping with AIDS. Finally, identify differences and similarities between your two lists.

TIM O'BRIEN
The Things They Carried

A native of Minnesota, Tim O'Brien (b. 1946) was drafted after he graduated from Macalester College. Subsequently, he served in the Vietnam War, during which he received a Purple Heart. In one way or another, practically all of his fiction deals

with the war, although he has been repeatedly ambiguous about how and when his
work incorporates his own Vietnam experiences. O'Brien's novels include If I Die in
a Combat Zone *(1973),* Going After Cacciato *(which won the National Book*
Award in 1978), In the Lake of the Woods *(a 1994 book that touches on the mas-*
sacre at My Lai), and Tomcat in Love *(1998). Originally published in* Esquire
magazine, the following story was reprinted in The Best American Short Stories
1987. *It then appeared along with related stories by O'Brien in a 1990 book also*
entitled The Things They Carried.

First Lieutenant Jimmy Cross carried letters from a girl named Martha, a
junior at Mount Sebastian College in New Jersey. They were not love letters, but
Lieutenant Cross was hoping, so he kept them folded in plastic at the bottom of
his rucksack. In the late afternoon, after a day's march, he would dig his foxhole,
wash his hands under a canteen, unwrap the letters, hold them with the tips of his
fingers, and spend the last hour of light pretending. He would imagine romantic
camping trips into the White Mountains in New Hampshire. He would sometimes taste the envelope flaps, knowing her tongue had been there. More than
anything, he wanted Martha to love him as he loved her, but the letters were
mostly chatty, elusive on the matter of love. She was a virgin, he was almost sure.
She was an English major at Mount Sebastian, and she wrote beautifully about
her professors and roommates and midterm exams, about her respect for
Chaucer and her great affection for Virginia Woolf. She often quoted lines of
poetry; she never mentioned the war, except to say, Jimmy, take care of yourself.
The letters weighed ten ounces. They were signed "Love, Martha," but Lieutenant Cross understood that "Love" was only a way of signing and did not mean
what he sometimes pretended it meant. At dusk, he would carefully return the
letters to his rucksack. Slowly, a bit distracted, he would get up and move among
his men, checking the perimeter, then at full dark he would return to his hole
and watch the night and wonder if Martha was a virgin.

The things they carried were largely determined by necessity. Among the
necessities or near necessities were P-38 can openers, pocket knives, heat tabs,
wrist watches, dog tags, mosquito repellant, chewing gum, candy, cigarettes, salt
tablets, packets of Kool-Aid, lighters, matches, sewing kits, Military Payment Cer-
tificates, C rations, and two or three canteens of water. Together, these items
weighed between fifteen and twenty pounds, depending upon a man's habits or
rate of metabolism. Henry Dobbins, who was a big man, carried extra rations; he
was especially fond of canned peaches in heavy syrup over pound cake. Dave
Jensen, who practiced field hygiene, carried a toothbrush, dental floss, and several hotel-size bars of soap he'd stolen on R&R in Sydney, Australia. Ted Lavender, who was scared, carried tranquilizers until he was shot in the head outside
the village of Than Khe in mid-April. By necessity, and because it was SOP,°
they all carried steel helmets that weighed five pounds including the liner and
camouflage cover. They carried the standard fatigue jackets and trousers. Very

SOP: Standard operating procedure.

few carried underwear. On their feet they carried jungle boots — 2.1 pounds — and Dave Jensen carried three pairs of socks and a can of Dr. Scholl's foot powder as a precaution against trench foot. Until he was shot, Ted Lavender carried six or seven ounces of premium dope, which for him was a necessity. Mitchell Sanders, the RTO,° carried condoms. Norman Bowker carried a diary. Rat Kiley carried comic books. Kiowa, a devout Baptist, carried an illustrated New Testament that had been presented to him by his father, who taught Sunday school in Oklahoma City, Oklahoma. As a hedge against bad times, however, Kiowa also carried his grandmother's distrust of the white man, his grandfather's old hunting hatchet. Necessity dictated. Because the land was mined and booby-trapped, it was SOP for each man to carry a steel-centered, nylon-covered flak jacket, which weighed 6.7 pounds, but which on hot days seemed much heavier. Because you could die so quickly, each man carried at least one large compress bandage, usually in the helmet band for easy access. Because the nights were cold, and because the monsoons were wet, each carried a green plastic poncho that could be used as a raincoat or ground sheet or makeshift tent. With its quilted liner, the poncho weighed almost two pounds, but it was worth every ounce. In April, for instance, when Ted Lavender was shot, they used his poncho to wrap him up, then to carry him across the paddy, then to lift him into the chopper that took him away.

They were called legs or grunts.

To carry something was to "hump" it, as when Lieutenant Jimmy Cross humped his love for Martha up the hills and through the swamps. In its intransitive form, "to hump" meant "to walk," or "to march," but it implied burdens far beyond the intransitive.

Almost everyone humped photographs. In his wallet, Lieutenant Cross carried two photographs of Martha. The first was a Kodachrome snapshot signed "Love," though he knew better. She stood against a brick wall. Her eyes were gray and neutral, her lips slightly open as she stared straight-on at the camera. At night, sometimes, Lieutenant Cross wondered who had taken the picture, because he knew she had boyfriends, because he loved her so much, and because he could see the shadow of the picture taker spreading out against the brick wall. The second photograph had been clipped from the 1968 Mount Sebastian yearbook. It was an action shot — women's volleyball — and Martha was bent horizontal to the floor, reaching, the palms of her hands in sharp focus, the tongue taut, the expression frank and competitive. There was no visible sweat. She wore white gym shorts. Her legs, he thought, were almost certainly the legs of a virgin, dry and without hair, the left knee cocked and carrying her entire weight, which was just over one hundred pounds. Lieutenant Cross remembered touching that left knee. A dark theater, he remembered, and the movie was *Bonnie and Clyde,* and Martha wore a tweed skirt, and during the final scene, when he touched her knee, she turned and looked at him in a sad, sober way that made him pull his hand back, but he would always remember the feel of the tweed skirt and the knee beneath it and the sound of the gunfire that killed Bonnie and Clyde, how

5

RTO: Radiotelephone operator.

embarrassing it was, how slow and oppressive. He remembered kissing her good night at the dorm door. Right then, he thought, he should've done something brave. He should've carried her up the stairs to her room and tied her to the bed and touched that left knee all night long. He should've risked it. Whenever he looked at the photographs, he thought of new things he should've done.

What they carried was partly a function of rank, partly of field specialty.

As a first lieutenant and platoon leader, Jimmy Cross carried a compass, maps, code books, binoculars, and a .45-caliber pistol that weighed 2.9 pounds fully loaded. He carried a strobe light and the responsibility for the lives of his men.

As an RTO, Mitchell Sanders carried the PRC-25 radio, a killer, twenty-six pounds with its battery.

As a medic, Rat Kiley carried a canvas satchel filled with morphine and plasma and malaria tablets and surgical tape and comic books and all the things a medic must carry, including M&M's for especially bad wounds, for a total weight of nearly twenty pounds.

As a big man, therefore a machine gunner, Henry Dobbins carried the M-60,   10 which weighed twenty-three pounds unloaded, but which was almost always loaded. In addition, Dobbins carried between ten and fifteen pounds of ammunition draped in belts across his chest and shoulders.

As PFCs or Spec 4s, most of them were common grunts and carried the standard M-16 gas-operated assault rifle. The weapon weighed 7.5 pounds unloaded, 8.2 pounds with its full twenty-round magazine. Depending on numerous factors, such as topography and psychology, the riflemen carried anywhere from twelve to twenty magazines, usually in cloth bandoliers, adding on another 8.4 pounds at minimum, fourteen pounds at maximum. When it was available, they also carried M-16 maintenance gear — rods and steel brushes and swabs and tubes of LSA on — all of which weighed about a pound. Among the grunts, some carried the M-79 grenade launcher, 5.9 pounds unloaded, a reasonably light weapon except for the ammunition, which was heavy. A single round weighed ten ounces. The typical load was twenty-five rounds. But Ted Lavender, who was scared, carried thirty-four rounds when he was shot and killed outside Than Khe, and he went down under an exceptional burden, more than twenty pounds of ammunition, plus the flak jacket and helmet and rations and water and toilet paper and tranquilizers and all the rest, plus the unweighed fear. He was dead weight. There was no twitching or flopping. Kiowa, who saw it happen, said it was like watching a rock fall, or a big sandbag or something — just boom, then down — not like the movies where the dead guy rolls around and does fancy spins and goes ass over teakettle — not like that, Kiowa said, the poor bastard just flat-fuck fell. Boom. Down. Nothing else. It was a bright morning in mid-April. Lieutenant Cross felt the pain. He blamed himself. They stripped off Lavender's canteens and ammo, all the heavy things, and Rat Kiley said the obvious, the guy's dead, and Mitchell Sanders used his radio to report one U.S. KIA° and to

---

KIA: Killed in action.

request a chopper. Then they wrapped Lavender in his poncho. They carried him out to a dry paddy, established security, and sat smoking the dead man's dope until the chopper came. Lieutenant Cross kept to himself. He pictured Martha's smooth young face, thinking he loved her more than anything, more than his men, and now Ted Lavender was dead because he loved her so much and could not stop thinking about her. When the dust-off arrived, they carried Lavender aboard. Afterward they burned Than Khe. They marched until dusk, then dug their holes, and that night Kiowa kept explaining how you had to be there, how fast it was, how the poor guy just dropped like so much concrete. Boom-down, he said. Like cement.

In addition to the three standard weapons—the M-60, M-16, and M-79— they carried whatever presented itself, or whatever seemed appropriate as a means of killing or staying alive. They carried catch-as-catch-can. At various times, in various situations, they carried M-14s and CAR-15s and Swedish Ks and grease guns and captured AK-47s and Chi-Coms and RPGs and Simonov carbines and black-market Uzis and .38-caliber Smith & Wesson handguns and 66 mm LAWs and shotguns and silencers and blackjacks and bayonets and C-4 plastic explosives. Lee Strunk carried a slingshot; a weapon of last resort, he called it. Mitchell Sanders carried brass knuckles. Kiowa carried his grand-father's feathered hatchet. Every third or fourth man carried a Claymore antiper-sonnel mine—3.5 pounds with its firing device. They all carried fragmentation grenades—fourteen ounces each. They all carried at least one M-18 colored smoke grenade—twenty-four ounces. Some carried CS or tear-gas grenades. Some carried white-phosphorus grenades. They carried all they could bear, and then some, including a silent awe for the terrible power of the things they carried.

In the first week of April, before Lavender died, Lieutenant Jimmy Cross received a good-luck charm from Martha. It was a simple pebble, an ounce at most. Smooth to the touch, it was a milky-white color with flecks of orange and violet, oval-shaped, like a miniature egg. In the accompanying letter, Martha wrote that she had found the pebble on the Jersey shoreline, precisely where the land touched water at high tide, where things came together but also separated. It was this separate-but-together quality, she wrote, that had inspired her to pick up the pebble and to carry it in her breast pocket for several days, where it seemed weightless, and then to send it through the mail, by air, as a token of her truest feelings for him. Lieutenant Cross found this romantic. But he wondered what her truest feelings were, exactly, and what she meant by separate-but-together. He wondered how the tides and waves had come into play on that afternoon along the Jersey shoreline when Martha saw the pebble and bent down to rescue it from geology. He imagined bare feet. Martha was a poet, with the poet's sensibilities, and her feet would be brown and bare, the toenails unpainted, the eyes chilly and somber like the ocean in March, and though it was painful, he wondered who had been with her that afternoon. He imagined a pair of shadows moving along the strip of sand where things came together but also separated. It was phantom jealousy, he knew, but he couldn't help himself. He loved her so much. On the march, through the hot days of early April, he carried the pebble in his mouth, turning it with his tongue, tasting sea salts and moisture. His mind wandered. He had difficulty keeping his attention on the war. On occasion he would yell at his men to spread out the column, to keep their eyes open, but then he would slip away into daydreams, just pretending, walking barefoot along the Jersey shore, with Martha, carrying nothing. He would feel himself rising. Sun and waves and gentle winds, all love and lightness.

What they carried varied by mission.

When a mission took them to the mountains, they carried mosquito netting, machetes, canvas tarps, and extra bug juice.   15

If a mission seemed especially hazardous, or if it involved a place they knew to be bad, they carried everything they could. In certain heavily mined AOs,° where the land was dense with Toe Poppers and Bouncing Betties, they took turns humping a twenty-eight-pound mine detector. With its headphones and big sensing plate, the equipment was a stress on the lower back and shoulders, awkward to handle, often useless because of the shrapnel in the earth, but they carried it anyway, partly for safety, partly for the illusion of safety.

On ambush, or other night missions, they carried peculiar little odds and ends. Kiowa always took along his New Testament and a pair of moccasins for silence. Dave Jensen carried night-sight vitamins high in carotin. Lee Strunk carried his slingshot; ammo, he claimed, would never be a problem. Rat Kiley carried brandy and M&M's. Until he was shot, Ted Lavender carried the starlight scope, which weighed 6.3 pounds with its aluminum carrying case. Henry Dobbins carried his girlfriend's pantyhose wrapped around his neck as a comforter. They all carried ghosts. When dark came, they would move out single file across the meadows and paddies to their ambush coordinates, where they would quietly set up the Claymores and lie down and spend the night waiting.

Other missions were more complicated and required special equipment. In mid-April, it was their mission to search out and destroy the elaborate tunnel complexes in the Than Khe area south of Chu Lai. To blow the tunnels, they carried one-pound blocks of pentrite high explosives, four blocks to a man, sixty-eight pounds in all. They carried wiring, detonators, and battery-powered clackers. Dave Jensen carried earplugs. Most often, before blowing the tunnels, they were ordered by higher command to search them, which was considered bad news, but by and large they just shrugged and carried out orders. Because he was a big man, Henry Dobbins was excused from tunnel duty. The others would draw numbers. Before Lavender died there were seventeen men in the platoon, and whoever drew the number seventeen would strip off his gear and crawl in head first with a flashlight and Lieutenant Cross's .45-caliber pistol. The rest of them would fan out as security. They would sit down or kneel, not facing the hole, listening to the ground beneath them, imagining cobwebs and ghosts, whatever was down there — the tunnel walls squeezing in — how the flashlight seemed impossibly heavy in the hand and how it was tunnel vision in the very strictest

AOs: Areas of operations.

sense, compression in all ways, even time, and how you had to wiggle in—ass and elbows—a swallowed-up feeling—and how you found yourself worrying about odd things—will your flashlight go dead? Do rats carry rabies? If you screamed, how far would the sound carry? Would your buddies hear it? Would they have the courage to drag you out? In some respects, though not many, the waiting was worse than the tunnel itself. Imagination was a killer.

On April 16, when Lee Strunk drew the number seventeen, he laughed and muttered something and went down quickly. The morning was hot and very still. Not good, Kiowa said. He looked at the tunnel opening, then out across a dry paddy toward the village of Than Khe. Nothing moved. No clouds or birds or people. As they waited, the men smoked and drank Kool-Aid, not talking much, feeling sympathy for Lee Strunk but also feeling the luck of the draw. You win some, you lose some, said Mitchell Sanders, and sometimes you settle for a rain check. It was a tired line and no one laughed.

Henry Dobbins ate a tropical chocolate bar. Ted Lavender popped a tran- 20 quilizer and went off to pee.

After five minutes, Lieutenant Jimmy Cross moved to the tunnel, leaned down, and examined the darkness. Trouble, he thought—a cave-in maybe. And then suddenly, without willing it, he was thinking about Martha. The stresses and fractures, the quick collapse, the two of them buried alive under all that weight. Dense, crushing love. Kneeling, watching the hole, he tried to concentrate on Lee Strunk and the war, all the dangers, but his love was too much for him, he felt paralyzed, he wanted to sleep inside her lungs and breathe her blood and be smothered. He wanted her to be a virgin and not a virgin, all at once. He wanted to know her. Intimate secrets—why poetry? Why so sad? Why the grayness in her eyes? Why so alone? Not lonely, just alone—riding her bike across campus or sitting off by herself in the cafeteria. Even dancing, she danced alone—and it was the aloneness that filled him with love. He remembered telling her that one evening. How she nodded and looked away. And how, later, when he kissed her, she received the kiss without returning it, her eyes wide open, not afraid, not a virgin's eyes, just flat and uninvolved.

Lieutenant Cross gazed at the tunnel. But he was not there. He was buried with Martha under the white sand at the Jersey shore. They were pressed together, and the pebble in his mouth was her tongue. He was smiling. Vaguely, he was aware of how quiet the day was, the sullen paddies, yet he could not bring himself to worry about matters of security. He was beyond that. He was just a kid at war, in love. He was twenty-two years old. He couldn't help it.

A few moments later Lee Strunk crawled out of the tunnel. He came up grinning, filthy but alive. Lieutenant Cross nodded and closed his eyes while the others clapped Strunk on the back and made jokes about rising from the dead.

Worms, Rat Kiley said. Right out of the grave. Fuckin' zombie.

The men laughed. They all felt great relief. 25

Spook City, said Mitchell Sanders.

Lee Strunk made a funny ghost sound, a kind of moaning, yet very happy, and right then, when Strunk made that high happy moaning sound, when he went *Ahhooooo*, right then Ted Lavender was shot in the head on his way back from peeing. He lay with his mouth open. The teeth were broken. There was a swollen black bruise under his left eye. The cheekbone was gone. Oh shit, Rat Kiley said, the guy's dead. The guy's dead, he kept saying, which seemed profound — the guy's dead. I mean really.

The things they carried were determined to some extent by superstition. Lieutenant Cross carried his good-luck pebble. Dave Jensen carried a rabbit's foot. Norman Bowker, otherwise a very gentle person, carried a thumb that had been presented to him as a gift by Mitchell Sanders. The thumb was dark brown, rubbery to the touch, and weighed four ounces at most. It had been cut from a VC corpse, a boy of fifteen or sixteen. They'd found him at the bottom of an irrigation ditch, badly burned, flies in his mouth and eyes. The boy wore black shorts and sandals. At the time of his death he had been carrying a pouch of rice, a rifle, and three magazines of ammunition.

You want my opinion, Mitchell Sanders said, there's a definite moral here.

He put his hand on the dead boy's wrist. He was quiet for a time, as if counting a pulse, then he patted the stomach, almost affectionately, and used Kiowa's hunting hatchet to remove the thumb.   30

Henry Dobbins asked what the moral was.

Moral?

You know. *Moral.*

Sanders wrapped the thumb in toilet paper and handed it across to Norman Bowker. There was no blood. Smiling, he kicked the boy's head, watched the flies scatter, and said, It's like with that old TV show — Paladin. Have gun, will travel.

Henry Dobbins thought about it.   35

Yeah, well, he finally said. I don't see no moral.

There it *is*, man.

Fuck off.

They carried USO stationery and pencils and pens. They carried Sterno, safety pins, trip flares, signal flares, spools of wire, razor blades, chewing tobacco, liberated joss sticks and statuettes of the smiling Buddha, candles, grease pencils, *The Stars and Stripes*, fingernail clippers, Psy Ops° leaflets, bush hats, bolos, and much more. Twice a week, when the resupply choppers came in, they carried hot chow in green Mermite cans and large canvas bags filled with iced beer and soda pop. They carried plastic water containers, each with a two-gallon capacity. Mitchell Sanders carried a set of starched tiger fatigues for special occasions. Henry Dobbins carried Black Flag insecticide. Dave Jensen carried empty sandbags that could be filled at night for added protection. Lee Strunk carried tanning lotion. Some things they carried in common. Taking turns, they carried the big PRC-77 scrambler radio, which weighed thirty pounds with its battery. They shared the weight of memory. They took up what others could no longer bear. Often, they carried each other, the wounded or weak. They carried infections. They carried chess sets, basketballs, Vietnamese-English dictionaries, insignia of

Psy Ops: Psychological operations.

rank, Bronze Stars and Purple Hearts, plastic cards imprinted with the Code of Conduct. They carried diseases, among them malaria and dysentery. They carried lice and ringworm and leeches and paddy algae and various rots and molds. They carried the land itself—Vietnam, the place, the soil—a powdery orange-red dust that covered their boots and fatigues and faces. They carried the sky. The whole atmosphere, they carried it, the humidity, the monsoons, the stink of fungus and decay, all of it, they carried gravity. They moved like mules. By daylight they took sniper fire, at night they were mortared, but it was not battle, it was just the endless march, village to village, without purpose, nothing won or lost. They marched for the sake of the march. They plodded along slowly, dumbly, leaning forward against the heat, unthinking, all blood and bone, simple grunts, soldiering with their legs, toiling up the hills and down into the paddies and across the rivers and up again and down, just humping, one step and then the next and then another, but no volition, no will, because it was automatic, it was anatomy, and the war was entirely a matter of posture and carriage, the hump was everything, a kind of inertia, a kind of emptiness, a dullness of desire and intellect and conscience and hope and human sensibility. Their principles were in their feet. Their calculations were biological. They had no sense of strategy or mission. They searched the villages without knowing what to look for, not caring, kicking over jars of rice, frisking children and old men, blowing tunnels, sometimes setting fires and sometimes not, then forming up and moving on to the next village, then other villages, where it would always be the same. They carried their own lives. The pressures were enormous. In the heat of early afternoon, they would remove their helmets and flak jackets, walking bare, which was dangerous but which helped ease the strain. They would often discard things along the route of march. Purely for comfort, they would throw away rations, blow their Claymores and grenades, no matter, because by nightfall the resupply choppers would arrive with more of the same, then a day or two later still more, fresh watermelons and crates of ammunition and sunglasses and woolen sweaters—the resources were stunning—sparklers for the Fourth of July, colored eggs for Easter. It was the great American war chest—the fruits of science, the smokestacks, the canneries, the arsenals at Hartford, the Minnesota forests, the machine shops, the vast fields of corn and wheat—they carried like freight trains; they carried it on their backs and shoulders—and for all the ambiguities of Vietnam, all the mysteries and unknowns, there was at least the single abiding certainty that they would never be at a loss for things to carry.

After the chopper took Lavender away, Lieutenant Jimmy Cross led his men   40
into the village of Than Khe. They burned everything. They shot chickens and dogs, they trashed the village well, they called in artillery and watched the wreckage, then they marched for several hours through the hot afternoon, and then at dusk, while Kiowa explained how Lavender died, Lieutenant Cross found himself trembling.

He tried not to cry. With his entrenching tool, which weighed five pounds, he began digging a hole in the earth.

He felt shame. He hated himself. He had loved Martha more than his men, and as a consequence Lavender was now dead, and this was something he would have to carry like a stone in his stomach for the rest of the war.

All he could do was dig. He used his entrenching tool like an ax, slashing, feeling both love and hate, and then later, when it was full dark, he sat at the bottom of his foxhole and wept. It went on for a long while. In part, he was grieving for Ted Lavender, but mostly it was for Martha, and for himself, because she belonged to another world, which was not quite real, and because she was a junior at Mount Sebastian College in New Jersey, a poet and a virgin and uninvolved, and because he realized she did not love him and never would.

Like cement, Kiowa whispered in the dark. I swear to God — boom-down. Not a word.

I've heard this, said Norman Bowker. 45

A pisser, you know? Still zipping himself up. Zapped while zipping.

All right, fine. That's enough.

Yeah, but you had to see it, the guy just —

I *heard*, man. Cement. So why not shut the fuck *up?*

Kiowa shook his head sadly and glanced over at the hole where Lieutenant 50
Jimmy Cross sat watching the night. The air was thick and wet. A warm, dense fog had settled over the paddies and there was the stillness that precedes rain.

After a time Kiowa sighed.

One thing for sure, he said. The Lieutenant's in some deep hurt. I mean that crying jag — the way he was carrying on — it wasn't fake or anything, it was real heavy-duty hurt. The man cares.

Sure, Norman Bowker said.

Say what you want, the man does care.

We all got problems. 55

Not Lavender.

No, I guess not, Bowker said. Do me a favor, though.

Shut up?

That's a smart Indian. Shut up.

Shrugging, Kiowa pulled off his boots. He wanted to say more, just to lighten 60
up his sleep, but instead he opened his New Testament and arranged it beneath his head as a pillow. The fog made things seem hollow and unattached. He tried not to think about Ted Lavender, but then he was thinking how fast it was, no drama, down and dead, and how it was hard to feel anything except surprise. It seemed un-Christian. He wished he could find some great sadness, or even anger, but the emotion wasn't there and he couldn't make it happen. Mostly he felt pleased to be alive. He liked the smell of the New Testament under his cheek, the leather and ink and paper and glue, whatever the chemicals were. He liked hearing the sounds of night. Even his fatigue, it felt fine, the stiff muscles and the prickly awareness of his own body, a floating feeling. He enjoyed not being dead. Lying there, Kiowa admired Lieutenant Jimmy Cross's capacity for grief. He wanted to share the man's pain, he wanted to care as Jimmy Cross

cared. And yet when he closed his eyes, all he could think was Boom-down, and all he could feel was the pleasure of having his boots off and the fog curling in around him and the damp soil and the Bible smells and the plush comfort of night.

After a moment Norman Bowker sat up in the dark.

What the hell, he said. You want to talk, *talk*. Tell it to me.

Forget it.

No, man, go on. One thing I hate, it's a silent Indian.

For the most part they carried themselves with poise, a kind of dignity. Now   65 and then, however, there were times of panic, when they squealed or wanted to squeal but couldn't, when they twitched and made moaning sounds and covered their heads and said Dear Jesus and flopped around on the earth and fired their weapons blindly and cringed and sobbed and begged for the noise to stop and went wild and made stupid promises to themselves and to God and to their mothers and fathers, hoping not to die. In different ways, it happened to all of them. Afterward, when the firing ended, they would blink and peek up. They would touch their bodies, feeling shame, then quickly hiding it. They would force themselves to stand. As if in slow motion, frame by frame, the world would take on the old logic—absolute silence, then the wind, then sunlight, then voices. It was the burden of being alive. Awkwardly, the men would reassemble themselves, first in private, then in groups, becoming soldiers again. They would repair the leaks in their eyes. They would check for casualties, call in dust-offs, light cigarettes, try to smile, clear their throats and spit and begin cleaning their weapons. After a time someone would shake his head and say, No lie, I almost shit my pants, and someone else would laugh, which meant it was bad, yes, but the guy had obviously not shit his pants, it wasn't that bad, and in any case nobody would ever do such a thing and then go ahead and talk about it. They would squint into the dense, oppressive sunlight. For a few moments, perhaps, they would fall silent, lighting a joint and tracking its passage from man to man, inhaling, holding in the humiliation. Scary stuff, one of them might say. But then someone else would grin or flick his eyebrows and say, Roger-dodger, almost cut me a new asshole, *almost*.

There were numerous such poses. Some carried themselves with a sort of wistful resignation, others with pride or stiff soldierly discipline or good humor or macho zeal. They were afraid of dying but they were even more afraid to show it.

They found jokes to tell.

They used a hard vocabulary to contain the terrible softness. *Greased*, they'd say. *Offed, lit up, zapped while zipping*. It wasn't cruelty, just stage presence. They were actors and the war came at them in 3-D. When someone died, it wasn't quite dying, because in a curious way it seemed scripted, and because they had their lines mostly memorized, irony mixed with tragedy, and because they called it by other names, as if to encyst and destroy the reality of death itself. They kicked corpses. They cut off thumbs. They talked grunt lingo. They told stories about Ted Lavender's supply of tranquilizers, how the poor guy didn't feel a thing, how incredibly tranquil he was.

There's a moral here, said Mitchell Sanders.

They were waiting for Lavender's chopper, smoking the dead man's dope.   70

The moral's pretty obvious, Sanders said, and winked. Stay away from drugs. No joke, they'll ruin your day every time.

Cute, said Henry Dobbins.

Mind-blower, get it? Talk about wiggy — nothing left, just blood and brains.

They made themselves laugh.

There it is, they'd say, over and over, as if the repetition itself were an act of   75
poise, a balance between crazy and almost crazy, knowing without going. There it is, which meant be cool, let it ride, because oh yeah, man, you can't change what can't be changed, there it is, there it absolutely and positively and fucking well *is*.

They were tough.

They carried all the emotional baggage of men who might die. Grief, terror, love, longing — these were intangibles, but the intangibles had their own mass and specific gravity, they had tangible weight. They carried shameful memories. They carried the common secret of cowardice barely restrained, the instinct to run or freeze or hide, and in many respects this was the heaviest burden of all, for it could never be put down, it required perfect balance and perfect posture. They carried their reputations. They carried the soldier's greatest fear, which was the fear of blushing. Men killed, and died, because they were embarrassed not to. It was what had brought them to the war in the first place, nothing positive, no dreams of glory or honor, just to avoid the blush of dishonor. They died so as not to die of embarrassment. They crawled into tunnels and walked point and advanced under fire. Each morning, despite the unknowns, they made their legs move. They endured. They kept humping. They did not submit to the obvious alternative, which was simply to close the eyes and fall. So easy, really. Go limp and tumble to the ground and let the muscles unwind and not speak and not budge until your buddies picked you up and lifted you into the chopper that would roar and dip its nose and carry you off to the world. A mere matter of falling, yet no one ever fell. It was not courage, exactly; the object was not valor. Rather, they were too frightened to be cowards.

By and large they carried these things inside, maintaining the masks of composure. They sneered at sick call. They spoke bitterly about guys who had found release by shooting off their own toes or fingers. Pussies, they'd say. Candyasses. It was fierce, mocking talk, with only a trace of envy or awe, but even so, the image played itself out behind their eyes.

They imagined the muzzle against flesh. They imagined the quick, sweet pain, then the evacuation to Japan, then a hospital with warm beds and cute geisha nurses.

They dreamed of freedom birds.   80

At night, on guard, staring into the dark, they were carried away by jumbo jets. They felt the rush of takeoff. *Gone!* they yelled. And then velocity, wings and engines, a smiling stewardess — but it was more than a plane, it was a real bird, a big sleek silver bird with feathers and talons and high screeching. They were flying. The weights fell off, there was nothing to bear. They laughed and held on tight, feeling the cold slap of wind and altitude, soaring, thinking *It's over, I'm gone!* — they were naked, they were light and free — it was all lightness, bright and fast and buoyant, light as light, a helium buzz in the brain, a giddy bubbling in the lungs as they were taken up over the clouds and the war, beyond duty, beyond gravity and mortification and global entanglements — *Sin loi!*° they yelled, *I'm sorry, motherfuckers, but I'm out of it, I'm goofed, I'm on a space cruise, I'm gone!* — and it was a restful, disencumbered sensation, just riding the light waves, sailing that big silver freedom bird over the mountains and oceans, over America, over the farms and great sleeping cities and cemeteries and highways and the golden arches of McDonald's. It was flight, a kind of fleeing, a kind of falling, falling higher and higher, spinning off the edge of the earth and beyond the sun and through the vast, silent vacuum where there were no burdens and where everything weighed exactly nothing. *Gone!* they screamed, *I'm sorry but I'm gone!* And so at night, not quite dreaming, they gave themselves over to lightness, they were carried, they were purely borne.

On the morning after Ted Lavender died, First Lieutenant Jimmy Cross crouched at the bottom of his foxhole and burned Martha's letters. Then he burned the two photographs. There was a steady rain falling, which made it difficult, but he used heat tabs and Sterno to build a small fire, screening it with his body, holding the photographs over the tight blue flame with the tips of his fingers.

He realized it was only a gesture. Stupid, he thought. Sentimental, too, but mostly just stupid.

Lavender was dead. You couldn't burn the blame.

Besides, the letters were in his head. And even now, without photographs, Lieutenant Cross could see Martha playing volleyball in her white gym shorts and yellow T-shirt. He could see her moving in the rain.   85

When the fire died out, Lieutenant Cross pulled his poncho over his shoulders and ate breakfast from a can.

There was no great mystery, he decided.

In those burned letters Martha had never mentioned the war, except to say, Jimmy, take care of yourself. She wasn't involved. She signed the letters "Love," but it wasn't love, and all the fine lines and technicalities did not matter.

The morning came up wet and blurry. Everything seemed part of everything else, the fog and Martha and the deepening rain.

It was a war, after all.   90

Half smiling, Lieutenant Jimmy Cross took out his maps. He shook his head hard, as if to clear it, then bent forward and began planning the day's march. In ten minutes, or maybe twenty, he would rouse the men and they would pack up and head west, where the maps showed the country to be green and inviting. They would do what they had always done. The rain might add some weight, but otherwise it would be one more day layered upon all the other days.

He was realistic about it. There was that new hardness in his stomach.

Sin loi: "Sorry about that!"

No more fantasies, he told himself.

Henceforth, when he thought about Martha, it would be only to think that she belonged elsewhere. He would shut down the daydreams. This was not Mount Sebastian, it was another world, where there were no pretty poems or midterm exams, a place where men died because of carelessness and gross stupidity. Kiowa was right. Boom-down, and you were dead, never partly dead.

Briefly, in the rain, Lieutenant Cross saw Martha's gray eyes gazing back   95
at him.

He understood.

It was very sad, he thought. The things men carried inside. The things men did or felt they had to do.

He almost nodded at her, but didn't.

Instead he went back to his maps. He was now determined to perform his duties firmly and without negligence. It wouldn't help Lavender, he knew that, but from this point on he would comport himself as a soldier. He would dispose of his good-luck pebble. Swallow it, maybe, or use Lee Strunk's slingshot, or just drop it along the trail. On the march he would impose strict field discipline. He would be careful to send out flank security, to prevent straggling or bunching up, to keep his troops moving at the proper pace and at the proper interval. He would insist on clean weapons. He would confiscate the remainder of Lavender's dope. Later in the day, perhaps, he would call the men together and speak to them plainly. He would accept the blame for what had happened to Ted Lavender. He would be a man about it. He would look them in the eyes, keeping his chin level, and he would issue the new SOPs in a calm, impersonal tone of voice, an officer's voice, leaving no room for argument or discussion. Commencing immediately, he'd tell them, they would no longer abandon equipment along the route of march. They would police up their acts. They would get their shit together, and keep it together, and maintain it neatly and in good working order.

He would not tolerate laxity. He would show strength, distancing himself.   100
Among the men there would be grumbling, of course, and maybe worse, because their days would seem longer and their loads heavier, but Lieutenant Cross reminded himself that his obligation was not to be loved but to lead. He would dispense with love; it was not now a factor. And if anyone quarreled or complained, he would simply tighten his lips and arrange his shoulders in the correct command posture. He might give a curt little nod. Or he might not. He might just shrug and say Carry on, then they would saddle up and form into a column and move out toward the villages of Than Khe.   [1986]

THINKING ABOUT THE TEXT

1. Obviously a significant pattern in this story is the repeated references to "the things they carried." How does this pattern affect you? What might O'Brien have hoped to accomplish with it? At what points in the story are there variations on this pattern — changes in the kinds of things that the narrator reports being carried?

2. Describe the structure of this story. Is there a central event? If so, what is it and why do you consider it central?

3. Evaluate Lieutenant Cross's fascination with Martha, including his preoccupation with the issue of whether or not she is a virgin. How sympathetic are you to him? At the end of the story, Cross blames himself for Ted Lavender's death. Is this a fair self-evaluation, or is he too hard on himself? Identify some of the warrants or assumptions behind your answer.

4. Do the other members of the company seem mostly alike, or are there significant differences among them? Explain. What is your evaluation of the company as a whole? List some adjectives for it.

5. Does the war depicted in this story appear significantly different from other wars, such as World War II? If so, in what ways? Is this an antiwar story? Identify characteristics you associate with the genre.

JAMESON CURRIER
What They Carried

A native of Georgia and a graduate of Emory University in Atlanta, Jameson Currier (b. 1955) now lives in Manhattan. Besides writing fiction, he has published essays and written a documentary film, Living Proof: HIV and the Pursuit of Happiness *(1993). In 1998, Currier published his first novel,* Where the Rainbow Ends, *which traces a group of men through the years of the AIDS crisis. The subject is similar to that of the following piece, which appears in a 1993 collection of Currier's stories entitled* Dancing on the Moon: Short Stories about AIDS.

John had carried the flowers since Perry Street, long-stemmed irises wrapped together by a pale-pink tissue. Now he held them across his lap in the taxi; a patch of his khaki pants had turned dark brown from the beads of water which rolled down the stems. Danny thought John would have tired of flowers; once a week he had carried irises to Adam. This afternoon, on their way to Seventh Avenue, John had hesitated in front of the florist, and Danny, recognizing the confused look which had rushed across John's face, had instinctively scooped up the flowers from the white plastic bucket. Shifting the weight of the canvas gym bag he was carrying to his left shoulder, Danny went inside and paid a small Oriental woman, watching her eyes disappear into fine lines as she smiled and wrapped the irises together. Outside again, on the sidewalk, John raised his arms toward Danny, taking the flowers as though offering to hold a child. In the taxi, Danny lifted John's hand and smelled his wrist, wondering why the fragrance of flowers never lasted as long as cologne.

Adam had carried only his briefcase to the emergency room. Inside was his wallet, his address book, a bottle of aspirin, and the reviews of the play he had been publicizing. Adam had tried calling John first, but he was out of the office, so he called Danny, because he was worried and wanted help quickly. When Danny got to the hospital, Adam was already in a private room and had a temperature of 103. Danny took the keys to Adam's apartment and brought back to the hospital Adam's pajamas, bathrobe, slippers, razor, shaving cream, toothbrush, toothpaste, and pillow. By the time Danny returned, Adam was asleep and John was sitting in the chair beside the bed, watching the sun set through the windows that overlooked East 79th Street.

The next day the doctors began their tests. Nurses drew blood and took away urine samples, though nothing was done specifically about the pain in Adam's lower back, which was the reason he had gone to the emergency room in the first place, Adam told Danny. John had to ask the nurses several times about getting some sort of medication to relieve Adam's discomfort, and finally got a doctor to order a prescription for Percodan. While Adam was being examined by yet another doctor, John and Danny sat in the waiting room, and John mentioned it wasn't the pain that had driven Adam to the hospital. He had been working too hard, had been trying to cover for his boss, who was on vacation. The producers were worried because the play wasn't a hit. Stress and exhaustion, John said, were the reasons Adam was here. Danny slumped down in his chair and rested his elbows against his knees, cupping his chin in the palms of his hands. Danny could tell Adam was thinner since last week; the youthful complexion had disappeared from his face, leaving behind an impression of bones and angles. Danny shifted his head till his eyes rested at a point somewhere beyond John. I wish I could believe that was the reason, Danny said. But I know it's not. Don't forget, I've been here before.

The following day John took off work and brought Adam flowers. Adam had not showered or shaved in three days. Lying in bed, he held the flowers across his chest and then asked John to help rearrange the pillows behind his neck. That night, Danny came by after work and brought the fruit salad that Adam had called and said he wanted, because, he added, he could not even stand to smell the hospital food. Danny had stopped at the Korean grocery on Lexington Avenue and bought a container of sliced peaches, melons, and strawberries, as out-of-season as the flowers John had found. John brought a bottle of orange soda Adam had called and asked for. While Adam ate, slowly and uncomfortably, John and Danny sat near the bed and watched *Hollywood Squares* on the wall-mounted television set. Before they left, Adam threw up the food, and John helped Adam change into a clean T-shirt, while Danny wiped the floor and rinsed the soiled pajamas. In the hall outside Adam's room, John mentioned he was surprised Adam was getting worse. Don't people go into the hospital to get better? he asked. Adam had been in the hospital only last month, overnight, for a blood transfusion. Danny said nothing but shifted his feet so he could lean against the wall for support. Danny knew Adam had already passed the point; the virus had become a disease.

Adam told John he didn't want any visitors. Only John and Danny were   5
allowed to come by. I don't want anyone to see me like this, Adam said. They would be upset and hurt. Some would be angry, he explained to Danny. He

would be better in a few days and then would go home. And Adam said no one could bring him anything personal other than clothing and toiletries, not even a book or a radio or a *TV Guide*, anything, he noted, which would suggest he might be in the hospital for a while. After all, he said, I'm not planning on staying here long, and then, lifting his eyes to the ceiling and assessing himself realistically, added, I just don't want it to feel like a long time. In four days, Adam had dropped five pounds. He hated the hospital. He thought the nurses were inept; they couldn't even tell the difference between aspirin and Valium. They won't help me, he said. They can't stop the pain in my back.

And the doctors continued their tests: X rays of his chest, abdomen, and skull. There were bone scans, T scans, CAT scans, spinal taps, and another blood transfusion. By the end of the week, when friends found out Adam had not been at work or at home, the phone beside his hospital bed began ringing, and Danny knew the visitors could not be stopped.

Wes brought a new pair of pajamas after John mentioned Adam had already thrown out three pairs and several hospital gowns. Cheryl, Adam's assistant, brought a bag of Pepperidge Farm Goldfish crackers, which at the moment she spoke with Adam on the phone was what Adam wanted, though they remained unopened in the top drawer of the hospital dresser. Roy brought current copies of *Spy* and *New York* magazines; Elliot brought Archie and Superman comic books. They all tried to smile, joke, catch Adam up on what was happening at work or in the news. They would clear their throats, change the subject, or avert their eyes when necessary, carrying their feelings inside, the way they knew they must, the way they knew Adam wanted. In the evenings, John and Danny would bring whatever food Adam wanted: lemon yogurt, canned peaches, pretzels, or taco chips. Most nights Danny stayed later than visiting hours, in case Adam threw up and needed to be changed.

And the tests continued. Steve brought an advance copy of the book he was editing on the Bloomsbury authors. Elliot brought scissors, which Adam used to clip his nails. Bob brought lip balm, which Adam wanted because he thought the hospital air was so dry. When the new pajamas found their way into the trash, John went to a discount store and bought six irregular large T-shirts, though Adam's favorite was the old gray shirt Danny pulled from his gym bag one night; Adam refused to wear it, instead keeping it rolled up next to his assortment of pillows. The office sent an arrangement of red and white columbines. Millie sent a basket of painted daisies. Roy brought yellow tulips. One night during the second week, Adam asked John to bring the bottle of cologne he kept underneath the towels in the closet of the apartment. If I'm not washing, he said, at least I can smell better than the flowers. When a postcard arrived at the hospital from London, from Harris, Adam spent an hour trying to calculate how long it had taken to arrive by overseas mail, how long he had been in the hospital, and what day Harris had heard he was sick.

Cheryl said to Danny she had never realized the small red bumps on Adam's cheeks were Kaposi's sarcoma; she had thought it was acne that wouldn't go away. After all, she commented softly while Adam was sleeping, he'll bring almost anything back to his desk to eat. Although I do, too, she moaned, but he never had to worry about his weight. Later that week, Adam told John food had lost its taste. It only has a meaning now, he said, and the next day he stopped eating altogether. The nurses began feeding him with a machine suspended on a pole which pumped solutions of fats and minerals and vitamins through plastic tubes connected to a vein in his right arm. Adam seldom moved from the bed now. When he couldn't manage to push the pump to the bathroom, the nurses brought urinals and bedpans but were still sluggish about bringing him medication. John began to have problems coping with Adam's illness. So Danny began to wash Adam at night with warm, wet cloths and brought cups and pans of water from the sink so he could brush his teeth. Adam said he still had the pain in his lower back and the doctors could not find the cause. It's not even a brain tumor, Adam remarked during a commercial between rounds of *Jeopardy.* He turned his head away from the TV set and began to cry. All I want to do is go out and see a movie, he said. At a theatre. With real popcorn and butter. The next day Adam had a biopsy of the lymph glands of his neck. Two days later a doctor brought the news he had Burkitt's lymphoma. Danny made Adam call his mother in New Jersey and tell her he was sick. She's the only family you have, and you have to tell her, Danny said. It's not right to keep it a secret any longer. On Saturday, his mother came to the hospital, stayed two hours, and cried. On Monday, Adam began chemotherapy. Adam told Danny he was honestly going to get better. Because now he was ready to go back home.

Danny was surprised three weeks had passed. Many days he could not find   10
an order or sense of strategy to what had to be done, so he began to make lists: what to carry to the hospital, what he had to buy, whom he had to call, what he had to do when he got home. Danny carried the lists in his gym bag, pressed between the pages of his calendar. Inside, along with a bottle of ibuprofen, Danny carried antihistamine pills, decongestant tablets, and a box of cherry-flavored cough drops, because he never knew if the headaches he got in the late afternoons might actually be the start of the flu or a cold. There was also a comb, two ballpoint pens, a small scratch pad that Danny used to jot down notes, and a combination lock for his gym locker, though Danny had not made it to the gym since Adam first entered the hospital. Some days Danny worried the canvas bag would rip; when he added a book to read on the subway, and an umbrella or gloves because the weather could slip without warning between fall and winter, the weight would almost reach ten pounds.

The day Adam came home, John and Danny carried everything in duffel bags from the hospital to the fourth-floor apartment. Adam had been released and set up on a home-care program. A nurse would visit if needed; every night he would continue the intravenous fluids. Two delivery men from the home-care service carried up the stairs an infusion pump similar to the one that had stood next to the hospital bed, and three large boxes of supplies. Inside were vitamin, lipid, and insulin bottles, and an assortment of needles, syringes, and plastic tubing. Enough supplies for a month, a hospital representative told Danny. Danny cleaned the refrigerator to make room for the plastic bags of nutritional solution which Adam had to have for twelve hours each night. In his gym bag Danny now carried a change of clothing, in case he slept overnight at Adam's apartment; in his calendar he wrote every possible emergency number he might have to use. John made five extra sets of keys to the apartment, one for Danny, one for himself, others for Roy, Wes, and Elliot, so they could come and go as quickly and easily as necessary. Elliot went to the grocery store to get the things Adam wanted to eat: frozen turkey tetrazzini and pizza, potato chips, mocha-nut ice cream, milk, and mint-chocolate-chip cookies. Roy went to the pharmacy to get the medicine the doctor had prescribed: Halcion for sleep, Xanax for anxiety, Nizoral for thrush, Zovirax for the herpes sores in Adam's mouth, and prednisone, Bactrim, allopurinol, and AZT. Adam complained about taking so many pills. His least favorite were the large yellow capsules, which he said were difficult to swallow. His voice sounds so strange now, Danny said to John when they were alone in the kitchen. It sounds as raspy as if he'd spent a lifetime smoking, and he's always coughing to clear away the phlegm.

That night, John and Danny helped Adam hook up the infusion pump, following the instructions a nurse had written for them. Before he left the hospital, Adam had had surgery to implant a catheter in his chest, because his arms had turned into long strands of bruises where the veins had collapsed from being punctured with too many needles. It took John and Danny over two hours to do what the nurse had demonstrated in less than twenty minutes. They injected insulin and liquid vitamins into the clear solution of a plastic bag, connected plastic tubing to the bag and a bottle of lipids, and then suspended them from the poles of the infusion pump. They washed their hands and ran the tubing through the machine, then wiped the end with gauzes soaked in isopropyl and povidone-iodine. John panicked at every step, convinced Adam would be murdered by an air bubble. Danny continued, steadying his hands by placing his arms on Adam's stomach till he had connected the liquid-filled tubing to the tubing that hung from Adam's chest. Adam, too, was anxious and nervous. I don't want to go back, he said, and could not fall asleep. He refused to take the Halcion or Xanax and stayed awake, sweating and worrying and rolling the pump to the bathroom because of his diarrhea.

The first week Adam spent at home, everyone carried the hope he was getting better. Roy picked up Adam's paychecks and did the best he could to sort through what bills could be sent to the insurance company. Cheryl carried more insurance forms to the apartment. John did more grocery shopping; there never seemed to be enough paper towels, tissues, or garbage bags. Bob came by and trimmed Adam's hair. Elliot did the laundry. Wes took afternoons off from work to take Adam to the doctor's office for chemotherapy treatments. Danny arranged a meal service to deliver lunches to Adam in the afternoon. In the evenings, friends brought him dinner. Steve brought Chinese, Millie brought Italian, Bob brought cream of broccoli soup and an omelet from the restaurant where he worked. Adam said there was more food than he would ever eat, even if he did have an appetite.

When Danny arrived in the evenings now, he hung a change of clothing in the bedroom closet. His overnight kit, which contained soap, shampoo, deodorant, shaving cream, and a razor, found a permanent place by the bathroom windowsill. Danny slept on the floor beside Adam's bed; he was afraid of sleeping in the bed with Adam, because he was certain he would become tangled in the plastic tubes. Adam has always been a restless sleeper, John said. Before he became sick, he would toss so violently he would twist the sheet around himself till he cut off his circulation. When Adam could no longer make it to the bathroom in the middle of the night, even with help, Danny bought a bedpan, and John found the large plastic Donald Duck glasses to use as urinals, the ones Adam had brought back from his trip to Disney World.

Adam said afternoons were always the worst. He would be alone in the apartment, watching TV, when the depression would hit. But if anyone called, he refused to answer the phone, afraid of having someone hear the way his voice sounded. There were moments when Danny actually thought Adam vas getting better. At least his spirits seemed to rise. At least he was eating. Every evening Adam would describe for Danny what he had eaten, how many bites he had taken, and if it tasted good or bad. Adam had also started coughing in his sleep, so fitfully Danny thought he wasn't sleeping well; Danny was surprised, then, when he asked Adam one morning how he had slept and Adam answered, I'm sleeping better than ever. 15

Danny learned Adam's thoughts went through a cycle. One day it was, Am I going to die? Another, it would be, Do you think I'm going to die? Danny was never sure how to answer Adam's questions. Once, when Danny decided to be honest and Adam asked, How do I look?, Danny responded by saying, OK. Adam lifted himself out of bed and walked to the mirror that hung on the back of the bedroom door, bracing himself by holding on to the doorknob. Just OK? he questioned, and began brushing his thinning hair. Please, he added, I still have my vanity, and he walked to the window and threw the brush outside.

The second week he was home, Roy and Danny took Adam to see a movie. Danny helped Adam walk down the four flights of stairs, his arms wrapped around Adam's waist so he would not fall because Adam refused to use the cane John had bought. Roy borrowed a car and dropped them off in front of the theatre on 59th Street. Danny found it difficult to concentrate on the movie, even though Adam felt certain it would be nominated for a number of Academy Awards. Roy bought popcorn and sodas, though Adam ate nothing, coughing and squirming in his seat the entire two hours. Afterward, riding in the car back to the apartment, Adam said he wanted to get tickets to see *The Phantom of the Opera* and take a cruise to the Bahamas in the spring. When Roy and Danny were alone in Adam's kitchen, Roy said Adam was setting himself up for disappointments. Danny replied, It's the way Adam has always lived. He needs to look forward to something. Later, in the bedroom, Adam told Danny, Today was the first time I was actually afraid of dying.

Danny was concerned that Adam was telling him things he told no one else. When Roy or John or Wes or Elliot was out of the room, Adam would talk about how he had not had sex since July because of the pain in his back. Adam said he felt safe when Danny slept on the floor, though he knew it was selfish to ask so much of him, but John was too impatient, Roy flustered easily, and they never knew what to do if there was a problem. Once, Adam said to Danny, I'm so afraid you'll be so disgusted you'll walk away. Danny promised him he wouldn't leave, though Danny knew there were moments when he wished Adam would die quickly. Adam himself could be impatient: Danny was too slow bringing the medication or could not pick up the tissues fast enough from the floor. The glass of water was too cloudy or cold, the TV was not loud enough or too loud, or Danny had left his fingerprints on the lens after cleaning Adam's eyeglasses. Adam had now dropped six more pounds; at night, he would stretch out his arms and remark in a rather wry tone, I'm beginning to look worse than a Biafra baby.

On Wednesday, Wes invited friends over to watch *The Wizard of Oz* on TV. Roy decorated the living room with a rainbow of crepe paper. Cheryl made green cookies to eat when Dorothy reached the Emerald City. Danny carried Adam to the couch in the living room a few minutes before the movie was to start. John remarked it was odd it wasn't Sunday. Remember, Bob added, it was always tele-cast on Sunday nights. Elliot said when he was a kid his parents always made sure they stayed late at church that night just to torture him. Adam said the worst pun-ishment his mother ever gave him was not letting him watch it one year. He cried so hard she finally relented, letting him out of his bedroom just as the Wicked Witch disappeared in a puff of smoke on top of the thatched roof. Steve said, Remember when we watched it all in black and white? Or when we had to go to someone's house to watch it in color, John added. Roy said his favorite was still *Peter Pan*. Remember when Mary Martin sang about Never-Never Land?

The next morning Adam said to Danny, We can't go on like this, and   20
laughed weakly. How many men have said that to you in your lifetime? Still trying to shake the sleep from his body, Danny sat on the side of the bed and held Adam's hand. I should go back to the hospital, Adam said. This isn't fair to anyone.

The moment Adam said he felt better was the time he was the most helpless, strapped in a wheelchair whizzing through a hospital corridor. It was almost fun, he told Danny later, all dressed in white, letting people I didn't even know worry about only me for just a few minutes.

The doctors began more tests: EKGs, EEGs, X rays, specimens, and cul-tures. The reason he went back, Adam said, was because he needed stronger chemotherapy, and he wasn't able to function at home alone the day after the dosages. He got angry only once, when a nurse said he wasn't trying hard enough when he refused to take a pill right away. He yelled back at her that she wasn't his mother. In fact, he added, I don't even like you, and besides, I didn't even ask for your opinion. The next day the stitching that held the catheter tubing in place fell apart. The doctor said it was impossible to perform the surgery again to repair it. Adam was too weak; now he weighed a hundred pounds. And an X ray showed a small black spot on his right lung. Another doctor said Adam wouldn't be able to sustain the amount of chemotherapy he would need. By the end of the night, the nurses had set him up on a respiratory system; oxygen rushed through plastic tubing to his nose. The next morning, Danny arranged for twenty-four-hour nurs-ing care so Adam could go home. Adam had decided it was time to die.

It's not like I'm giving up, he said to Danny and John and Roy. It's just that I'm going to die naturally. Without surgery or therapy or treatments which would only prolong my life by a couple of days.

This time, John and Danny carried Adam up the stairs in a wheelchair. Roy went and picked up more prescriptions: Duricef, Compazine, nystatin, propranolol, and dexamethasone. A nurse was always there to give Adam his medication and make sure he would eat. Danny told John he felt somewhat relieved. Now there is someone who knows what to do about the coughing, knows when he needs to drink liquids, knows what time he is supposed to take a pill, knows what to say and how to deal with the pain. Someone is there to help him be comfortable. John answered, It isn't like this is all new to us.

Danny told John, Adam always had a fascination with suicide. Didn't he remember Adam reading *Last Wish* by Betty Rollin? The first time he was in the hospital, Adam had asked if Danny could find someone who could get him Nembutal—his doctor had refused to give him a prescription. Adam mentioned suicide first to Danny because he knew it would upset John. Adam said that he wanted to live, but the quality of his life had deteriorated beyond depression. I've spent the last two months waiting, he said. Waiting for doctors and nurses and medicine and food and visits and friends. Roy cried when Danny told him Adam wanted to die swiftly and painlessly, but Danny knew that Adam would not kill himself, that Adam had carried himself with dignity for so long, he wouldn't want his life to end with disappointments. Roy told Adam he didn't want him to do it, but if that was his decision, then he would do his best to respect it. But no one would help Adam find the medication. Adam complained it had been easy in the book. When Adam asked Danny to just open the window and let him jump, Danny said no, and Adam said he would do it himself. Danny laughed and tried turning it into a joke: How could someone who has not moved from bed in over a week make it to the window and jump from the fire escape? I thought you were going to help me die, Adam replied. I'm sorry I'm disappointing you, Danny answered. Now you know exactly how selfish I am. I'm sorry you're more valuable to me alive than dead.

Five days after coming home from the hospital, Adam died. In the afternoon he began to have respiratory problems. The nurse hooked him up to the oxygen tank which had been placed by his bed. By the time Danny arrived, around 7:00 P.M., Adam was semiconscious, lying on his back, gasping for breath, his arms twitching as if he were asking for help. Danny reached for Adam's hand, thinking he might calm him, but he was shocked that Adam's skin felt as cold and lifeless as vinyl, so Danny rubbed his hands along Adam's arms, hoping it would help the circulation. Thirty minutes later, when the gasping subsided, the nurse rolled Adam over to rest on his side. She turned to Danny and said in a brisk whisper, Have any arrangements been made? Does he want last rites? Danny paced the floor till the breathing stopped.

The only time Danny cried was the day in the hospital when an orderly came into the room and shaved the hair on Adam's chest before the surgery to implant the catheter. John cried after his first visit to the hospital. Roy said he had

25

cried while waiting in line to buy underwear. Cheryl cried when Adam called and said she could have the posters that hung over his desk. Wes said he cried in the steam room at the gym, when he knew no one was looking. Bob and Millie cried while having drinks together at the bar of a Japanese restaurant in the Village after they had tried to get Adam to eat the dinner Millie had brought. Elliot cried during the opening credits when *Auntie Mame* came on TV one night; he and Adam had seen it together on a double bill at the Regency. Steve didn't cry, or so he said, though Danny noticed he had started walking with his fists clenched.

In the hospital a doctor remarked to John that someone might carry this virus in his body for years before it began to deteriorate the immune system. Some people might not be affected at all. Danny turned to the doctor and replied rather sarcastically, Do you think we're all fools? We all know about this disease. Don't you know? Danny added. Haven't you heard? It's the fear every gay man carries today.

The hardest thing, Danny said to John during the ride in the taxi, was carrying the ashes. Danny had picked them up yesterday from the funeral home. They had been placed inside a cardboard box, small and rectangular, and the man at the funeral home had placed the box in a plastic bag. When Danny took the bag, he was surprised it was so heavy for something that small, estimating the weight he held was almost ten pounds. As Danny walked back to the apartment, the weight grew heavier, he couldn't shake the thought of what he carried.

John took the flowers to the kitchen of Wes's apartment, unwrapped them   30
from the tissue, and arranged them in a tall glass vase. He carried them to the dining table and placed them at the center. Around him Roy, Millie, and Elliot took their seats. The extra leaf Wes had added to the table made the room seem smaller; the air was warm and perfumed by the ginger he had used in cooking. Bob dimmed the overhead light, Cheryl lit the candles with the matches she found in her purse, and Steve circled the table, pouring glasses of wine. Danny asked Wes if there was anything he could do to help: Give me something to do, Danny said. Bring these to the table, Wes answered, pointing at two steaming plates of food.

As Danny brought the plates from the kitchen he paused at the window, noticing the way the rain bent the branches of a tree toward the sidewalk. This afternoon Adam's mother had called him. She had found the portrait which had been painted of Adam eight years ago, the summer when Adam was twenty-four. She described the picture, the way the artist had overlapped a sequence of pale-blue and green strokes, like a camera out of focus, yet had remarkably managed to capture the dimples on the left side of his mouth when Adam tried to hold back a smile. Then she apologized for not mentioning at the funeral that, when she saw Adam the day before he died, he had said, I feel so ashamed that it has to end this way. They've made it so much easier for me, and I've only made it harder for them. You know he loved you very much, she said to Danny. He wanted you to have the portrait. I'll send it to you soon, she added, and then said goodbye.

Danny had done everything he knew how to do; why, then, did he feel that wasn't enough? He straightened his shoulders to release the strain from his back and then carried the plates to the table. [1993]

THINKING ABOUT THE TEXT

1. This story has a flashback structure. It begins just before the memorial dinner for Adam, but then recalls the events leading up to his death, ending with the dinner. Would the story's effect have been different if its structure had been strictly chronological? If so, how?

2. List the things carried in this story. What subcategories can they be placed in? Which of these things are especially significant to you? Why?

3. Characterize Danny, Adam, and John. How sympathetic are you to each? What specific details of the story affect your response to each?

4. What are some things you don't learn about the characters in this story? Would the story have been better if Currier had provided more facts about them? If so, what additional information should he have included?

5. Describe the narrator's tone. How emotional is it? Does it seem appropriate? Note that although conversations are reported, there are no quotation marks. Why do you suppose Currier omitted them?

MAKING COMPARISONS

1. Quite possibly, Currier was aware of O'Brien's story when he wrote his. Suppose that he did indeed know it. How might Currier's story be considered a comment on O'Brien's? Which specific features of O'Brien's story might Currier be honoring? Which might he be seen as challenging or ignoring?

2. To what extent does each of these stories undercut stereotypical images of Vietnam veterans and gay men?

3. Do you have the same emotional reaction to each of these stories? Identify what influences your reaction in each case.

WRITING ABOUT ISSUES

1. Write an essay explaining the role of setting in O'Brien's or in Currier's story. If you choose to discuss O'Brien's story, consider how it matters that the setting is the Vietnam War. How does this context shape the characters' thinking and behavior? If you choose to discuss Currier's story, consider at least two key settings featured in it, focusing on how these bring out certain traits in the story's characters.

2. Are the men in O'Brien's story as close to one another as the men in Currier's? Write an essay addressing this issue, referring to specific details of both texts.

3. For the next couple of days, keep a list of the things you carry. Then, write at least three paragraphs in which you identify what your list reveals about you. Next, exchange your list with a classmate's and write at least a paragraph in which you indicate what your classmate's list suggests about him or her. Finally, return the list with your analysis of it, get your list back, together with your classmate's commentary on it, and write at least a paragraph in which you identify what you have learned from this exercise.

4. Find an article that describes a specific American military unit in the Vietnam War or a specific group of men dealing with AIDS. Write an essay comparing O'Brien's story to the military article or Currier's story to the AIDS article. Focus on the two works as pieces of writing. In what ways do they resemble each other? What does the article do that the story doesn't, and vice versa?

IMAGINING THE END: A COLLECTION OF WRITINGS BY EMILY DICKINSON

EMILY DICKINSON, "I like a look of Agony,"
EMILY DICKINSON, "I've seen a Dying Eye"
EMILY DICKINSON, "I heard a Fly buzz — when I died — "
EMILY DICKINSON, "Because I could not stop for Death — "

Through the centuries, works of literature have depicted scenes of death, with all sorts of purposes, styles, and effects. Among the most well-known death scenes in literature are those produced by Emily Dickinson (1830–1886), now regarded as one of the greatest American poets. Although Dickinson spent much of her adult life as a virtual recluse, rarely leaving the Amherst, Massachusetts, home where she was born, her poems constantly reveal a lively, passionate intelligence. Moreover, death was hardly her sole topic; she wrote hundreds of poems on other subjects. Her poems about death are wonderfully creative, even playful in their use of metaphor and detail, and express a range of attitudes toward death, from sadness to curiosity to acceptance. They vary as well in the positions they accord the speaker: the "I" is sometimes the dying person, at other times a witness to someone else's death. The four poems included here illustrate just a few of the diverse approaches that Dickinson took to human mortality. They do have in common the large amount of room they leave for interpretation; see if you and your classmates agree on how to analyze them.

BEFORE YOU READ

Why do you think a poet might be interested in describing scenes of death? Do you assume there is something unhealthy about such a focus? Why, or why not?

EMILY DICKINSON
I like a look of Agony,

Emily Dickinson was an avid reader and a prolific writer, producing almost two thousand poems. Only a few of them were published while she was alive, partly because male editors of her time had difficulty appreciating her sheer originality as a woman writer. Furthermore, posthumous editors of her work have not always reproduced her manuscripts faithfully. Often they have altered the spelling, punctuation, and overall form of her poems in an attempt to make them seem more conventional than they really are. Actually, Dickinson did not even give her poems titles. Following customary practice, we have identified the ones in this cluster by their first lines. The following poem was written around 1861.

I like a look of Agony,
Because I know it's true —
Men do not sham Convulsion,
Nor simulate, a Throe —

The Eyes glaze once — and that is Death — 5
Impossible to feign
The Beads upon the Forehead
By homely Anguish strung. [c. 1861]

THINKING ABOUT THE TEXT

1. What would you say to someone who argues that the speaker is being sadistic in liking "a look of agony," especially when many Americans were dying agonizing deaths in the Civil War? Do you share to any extent the speaker's values?
2. What is the effect of Dickinson's use of capitalization?
3. How does the second stanza of the poem relate to the first?
4. Look up the word *homely* in a dictionary. Is Dickinson using the word in any of the senses you find there? Should she?
5. Note the words *beads* and *strung* at the end of the poem. What object do they normally suggest? How appropriate is this object as a concluding image for the poem?

EMILY DICKINSON
I've seen a Dying Eye

Dickinson wrote this poem around 1862.

I've seen a Dying Eye
Run round and round a Room —
In search of Something — as it seemed —
Then Cloudier become —
And then — obscure with Fog —   5
And then — be soldered down
Without disclosing what it be
'Twere blessed to have seen —   [c. 1862]

THINKING ABOUT THE TEXT

1. To what extent does this poem seem to be about the speaker rather than about the dying person? What adjectives would you use to describe each?

2. What would you say to someone who argues that the word *run* is too active a verb for someone who is dying?

3. Should readers try to guess what the dying person is searching for? Why, or why not? Do you get the impression that he or she was, in fact, "blessed"?

4. Trace the poem's pattern of *m* sounds. What is their effect?

5. What do you conclude from the fact that the word *seen* appears both at the beginning and at the end of the poem?

MAKING COMPARISONS

1. Do you get the impression that this poem depicts the "look of agony" that the speaker in the first poem likes? Refer to specific lines in each text.

2. How vivid is the death scene in this poem compared to that in the first?

3. What words in this poem can be related to the word *glaze* in the first?

EMILY DICKINSON
I heard a Fly buzz — when I died —

Dickinson wrote the following poem, one of her most famous, around 1862.

I heard a Fly buzz — when I died —
The Stillness in the Room

Was like the Stillness in the Air—
Between the Heaves of Storm—

The Eyes around—had wrung them dry— 5
And Breaths were gathering firm
For that last Onset—when the King
Be witnessed—in the Room—

I willed my Keepsakes—Signed away
What portion of me be 10
Assignable—and then it was
There interposed a Fly—

With Blue—uncertain stumbling Buzz—
Between the light—and me—
And then the Windows failed—and then 15
I could not see to see— [c. 1862]

THINKING ABOUT THE TEXT

1. Do you find this poem amusing? Horrifying? Both? Neither? Identify specific lines, as well as any experiences of yours, that influence your response.

2. Many might argue that the poem presents a logical impossibility: No one can recall when he or she died because death extinguishes thought. How would you respond to this charge?

3. Why do you think Dickinson repeats the word *stillness* in the first stanza? Consult a dictionary definition of the word. Why do you think she repeats *see* in the last line?

4. Although Dickinson mentions the fly in the first line, she doesn't return to it until the last line of the third stanza. Why do you think she delays? What might she have been trying to achieve in the intervening lines?

5. Although Dickinson writes "And then the Windows failed," plainly it is the speaker's eyesight that is failing. Why do you think Dickinson states otherwise?

MAKING COMPARISONS

1. In the first two poems, the "I" is a witness to someone else's death. Here, the "I" dies. Do you therefore read this poem with different feelings? Why, or why not?

2. Note the reference to "the King" in the second stanza of this poem. Would someone be justified in concluding that "the King" is what the dying person is searching for in "I've seen a Dying Eye"? Why, or why not? Does the first poem have nothing to do with religion since it does not use expressions like "the King"?

3. The second stanza of this poem refers to "eyes" and "breaths" rather than whole people. Similarly, "I've seen a Dying Eye" refers just to an eye rather than explicitly mentioning a person. Moreover, the second stanza of "I like a look of Agony," focuses purely on the eyes and the forehead. What should readers conclude from Dickinson's emphasis on parts of bodies?

EMILY DICKINSON
Because I could not stop for Death —

This poem, also one of Dickinson's best known, was written about 1863.

Because I could not stop for Death —
He kindly stopped for me —
The Carriage held but just Ourselves —
And Immortality.

We slowly drove — He knew no haste   5
And I had put away
My labor and my leisure too,
For His Civility —

We passed the School, where Children strove
At Recess — in the Ring —   10
We passed the Fields of Gazing Grain —
We passed the Setting Sun —

Or rather — He passed Us —
The Dews drew quivering and chill —
For only Gossamer, my Gown —   15
My Tippet° — only Tulle —

We paused before a House that seemed
A Swelling of the Ground —
The Roof was scarcely visible —
The Cornice — in the Ground —   20

Since then — 'tis Centuries — and yet
Feels shorter than the Day
I first surmised the Horses' Heads
Were toward Eternity —   [c. 1863]

THINKING ABOUT THE TEXT

1. Describe the speaker's tone. What do you think he or she means by "I could not stop for Death"? How, exactly, might "He kindly stopped for me" refer to something different? In what other lines, if any, do you sense the speaker expressing his or her feelings?

2. The first stanza ends by noting that immortality is a passenger in the carriage. Should readers conclude that the speaker is now immortal? Why, or why not?

3. What image of death do you get from this poem? List at least three adjectives of your own.

4. Note the things passed in the third stanza. Why do you think Dickinson chose to include these rather than other things? What is the effect of her making the ultimate destination a house?

5. Do you find this poem comforting? Remember that Dickinson wrote it when she was about thirty-three. If she had identified the speaker as being only that old, would you have reacted to the poem differently?

MAKING COMPARISONS

1. Do the first two lines of this poem seem applicable to the deaths in the other three poems? Explain your reasoning. In general, this poem develops the idea of dying as a journey. Is such a metaphor compatible with the death scenes of the other three poems? Refer to specific lines in them.

2. Is this poem sunnier than the other three? Explain.

3. Rank the four poems in this cluster from the one you like most to the one you like least. Identify the criteria you are using to make your evaluations.

WRITING ABOUT ISSUES

1. Each of the poems in this cluster refers to one or more efforts to see something. Choose one of the poems and write an essay considering what is and isn't accomplished by whatever attempts at vision the poem discusses. Refer to specific lines.

2. Write an essay comparing two of the speakers in this cluster. Focus on identifying the extent to which they resemble each other in their feelings and thoughts. Refer to specific lines in each poem.

3. Choose one of the poems in this cluster and write an essay discussing how you would present the poem to a particular person you know. What about the poem would you emphasize to this person? What about the person's own life would you be thinking of? What kind of response would you hope for? If you wish, your essay can take the form of a letter to the person.

4. Obtain a contemporary sympathy card that features a poem. Then write an essay comparing the card's poem to a poem by Dickinson from this cluster. Focus on just one or two bases of comparison: for example, the poems' attitudes toward death, their language, their potential functions in society, their relative artistic quality. Be sure to quote from each of the two poems you discuss.

CONFRONTING THE DEATH OF A STRANGER

KATHERINE MANSFIELD, "The Garden-Party"
GABRIEL GARCÍA MÁRQUEZ, "The Handsomest Drowned Man
in the World"
DON DELILLO, "Videotape"

When do people really ponder human mortality? For some, it's when some-one close to them dies, or when they themselves are in peril. For others, it's when they witness the deaths of strangers, as is the case in the following three stories. Encountering a workman's body right after her family's party, the well-to-do young heroine of Katherine Mansfield's story finds herself suddenly contemplating the nature of life as well as death. When "the handsomest drowned man in the world" washes up on their island, Gabriel García Márquez's characters are moved to reflect on various limitations of their own. In Don DeLillo's story, which is set in our own electronic era, the narrator repeatedly watches and broods about a child's videotape of a murder. Indeed, nowadays you can witness fatal violence quite eas-ily if you have TV; just turn on the evening news. Precisely because death is a reg-ular feature of television and other media, people may be more apt to consider what it means to them. On the other hand, they may become less sensitive to death and less inclined to consider how to live in the face of it. Try weighing both possibilities as you see how Mansfield's, García Márquez's, and DeLillo's charac-ters treat the demise of someone unknown to them.

BEFORE YOU READ

Describe a death scene that you have read or one that you have seen depicted on television or film. What was your emotional reaction to this scene? What specific aspects of it influenced your reaction most? How realis-tic was the scene? In what ways, if any, could it have been done more realisti-cally? Be sure to identify what you mean by these terms.

KATHERINE MANSFIELD
The Garden-Party

Katherine Mansfield (1888–1923) was one of the leading writers in English during the first decades of the twentieth century. She is chiefly known for her short stories and for her journal, a version of which was published posthumously. Mansfield was born in New Zealand and spent most of her youth there. Eventually, though, she lived in France, Germany, and especially England until her death from tuberculo-sis at the age of thirty-four. The following story appeared in a 1922 collection of her works, also entitled The Garden-Party.

And after all the weather was ideal. They could not have had a more perfect day for a garden-party if they had ordered it. Windless, warm, the sky without a cloud. Only the blue was veiled with a haze of light gold, as it is sometimes in early summer. The gardener had been up since dawn, mowing the lawns and sweeping them, until the grass and the dark flat rosettes where the daisy plants had been seemed to shine. As for the roses, you could not help feeling they understood that roses are the only flowers that impress people at garden-parties; the only flowers that everybody is certain of knowing. Hundreds, yes, literally hundreds, had come out in a single night; the green bushes bowed down as though they had been visited by archangels.

Breakfast was not yet over before the men came to put up the marquee.

"Where do you want the marquee put, mother?"

"My dear child, it's no use asking me. I'm determined to leave everything to you children this year. Forget I am your mother. Treat me as an honoured guest."

But Meg could not possibly go and supervise the men. She had washed her hair before breakfast, and she sat drinking her coffee in a green turban, with a dark wet curl stamped on each cheek. Jose, the butterfly, always came down in a silk petticoat and a kimono jacket.   5

"You'll have to go, Laura; you're the artistic one."

Away Laura flew, still holding her piece of bread-and-butter. It's so delicious to have an excuse for eating out of doors, and besides, she loved having to arrange things; she always felt she could do it so much better than anybody else.

Four men in their shirt-sleeves stood grouped together on the garden path. They carried staves covered with rolls of canvas, and they had big tool-bags slung on their backs. They looked impressive. Laura wished now that she had not got the bread-and-butter, but there was nowhere to put it, and she couldn't possibly throw it away. She blushed and tried to look severe and even a little bit short-sighted as she came up to them.

"Good morning," she said, copying her mother's voice. But that sounded so fearfully affected that she was ashamed, and stammered like a little girl, "Oh — er — have you come — is it about the marquee?"

"That's right, miss," said the tallest of the men, a lanky, freckled fellow, and   10
he shifted his tool-bag, knocked back his straw hat and smiled down at her. "That's about it."

His smile was so easy, so friendly that Laura recovered. What nice eyes he had, small, but such dark blue! And now she looked at the others, they were smiling too. "Cheer up, we won't bite," their smile seemed to say. How very nice workmen were! And what a beautiful morning! She mustn't mention the morning; she must be businesslike. The marquee.

"Well, what about the lily-lawn? Would that do?"

And she pointed to the lily-lawn with the hand that didn't hold the bread-and-butter. They turned, they stared in the direction. A little fat chap thrust out his under-lip, and the tall fellow frowned.

"I don't fancy it," said he. "Not conspicuous enough. You see, with a thing like a marquee," and he turned to Laura in his easy way, "you want to put it somewhere where it'll give you a bang slap in the eye, if you follow me."

Laura's upbringing made her wonder for a moment whether it was quite   15
respectful of a workman to talk to her of bangs slap in the eye. But she did quite
follow him.

"A corner of the tennis-court," she suggested. "But the band's going to be in
one corner."

"H'm, going to have a band, are you?" said another of the workmen. He was
pale. He had a haggard look as his dark eyes scanned the tennis-court. What was
he thinking?

"Only a very small band," said Laura gently. Perhaps he wouldn't mind so
much if the band was quite small. But the tall fellow interrupted.

"Look here, miss, that's the place. Against those trees. Over there. That'll
do fine."

Against the karakas. Then the karaka-trees would be hidden. And they were   20
so lovely, with their broad, gleaming leaves, and their clusters of yellow fruit.
They were like trees you imagined growing on a desert island, proud, solitary, lifting their leaves and fruits to the sun in a kind of silent splendour. Must they be
hidden by a marquee?

They must. Already the men had shouldered their staves and were making
for the place. Only the tall fellow was left. He bent down, pinched a sprig of
lavender, put his thumb and forefinger to his nose and snuffed up the smell.
When Laura saw that gesture she forgot all about the karakas in her wonder at
him caring for things like that — caring for the smell of lavender. How many men
that she knew would have done such a thing? Oh, how extraordinarily nice workmen were, she thought. Why couldn't she have workmen for friends rather than
the silly boys she danced with and who came to Sunday night supper? She would
get on much better with men like these.

It's all the fault, she decided, as the tall fellow drew something on the back of
an envelope, something that was to be looped up or left to hang, of these absurd
class distinctions. Well, for her part, she didn't feel them. Not a bit, not an
atom. . . . And now there came the chock-chock of wooden hammers. Some one
whistled, some one sang out, "Are you right there, matey?" "Matey!" The friendliness of it, the — the — Just to prove how happy she was, just to show the tall fellow how at home she felt, and how she despised stupid conventions, Laura took a
big bite of her bread-and-butter as she stared at the little drawing. She felt just like
a work-girl.

"Laura, Laura, where are you? Telephone, Laura!" a voice cried from the
house.

"Coming!" Away she skimmed, over the lawn, up the path, up the steps,
across the veranda, and into the porch. In the hall her father and Laurie were
brushing their hats ready to go to the office.

"I say, Laura," said Laurie very fast, "you might just give a squiz at my coat   25
before this afternoon. See if it wants pressing."

"I will," said she. Suddenly she couldn't stop herself. She ran at Laurie and
gave him a small, quick squeeze. "Oh, I do love parties, don't you?" gasped Laura.

"Ra-ther," said Laurie's warm, boyish voice, and he squeezed his sister too,
and gave her a gentle push. "Dash off to the telephone, old girl."

The telephone. "Yes, yes; oh yes. Kitty? Good morning, dear. Come to lunch? Do, dear. Delighted of course. It will only be a very scratch meal—just the sandwich crusts and broken meringue-shells and what's left over. Yes, isn't it a perfect morning? Your white? Oh, I certainly should. One moment—hold the line. Mother's calling." And Laura sat back. "What, mother? Can't hear."

Mrs. Sheridan's voice floated down the stairs. "Tell her to wear that sweet hat she had on last Sunday."

"Mother says you're to wear that *sweet* hat you had on last Sunday. Good.   30
One o'clock. Bye-bye."

Laura put back the receiver, flung her arms over her head, took a deep breath, stretched and let them fall. "Huh," she sighed, and the moment after the sigh she sat up quickly. She was still, listening. All the doors in the house seemed to be open. The house was alive with soft, quick steps and running voices. The green baize door that led to the kitchen regions swung open and shut with a muffled thud. And now there came a long, chuckling absurd sound. It was the heavy piano being moved on its stiff castors. But the air! If you stopped to notice, was the air always like this? Little faint winds were playing chase, in at the tops of the windows, out at the doors. And there were two tiny spots of sun, one on the inkpot, one on a silver photograph frame, playing too. Darling little spots. Especially the one on the inkpot lid. It was quite warm. A warm little silver star. She could have kissed it.

The front door bell pealed, and there sounded the rustle of Sadie's print skirt on the stairs. A man's voice murmured; Sadie answered, careless, "I'm sure I don't know. Wait. I'll ask Mrs. Sheridan."

"What is it, Sadie?" Laura came into the hall.

"It's the florist, Miss Laura."

It was, indeed. There, just inside the door, stood a wide, shallow tray full of   35
pots of pink lilies. No other kind. Nothing but lilies—canna lilies, big pink flowers, wide open, radiant, almost frighteningly alive on bright crimson stems.

"O-oh Sadie!" said Laura, and the sound was like a little moan. She crouched down as if to warm herself at that blaze of lilies; she felt they were in her fingers, on her lips, growing in her breast.

"It's some mistake," she said faintly. "Nobody ever ordered so many. Sadie, go and find mother."

But at that moment Mrs. Sheridan joined them.

"It's quite right," she said calmly. "Yes, I ordered them. Aren't they lovely?" She pressed Laura's arm. "I was passing the shop yesterday, and I saw them in the window. And I suddenly thought for once in my life I shall have enough canna lilies. The garden-party will be a good excuse."

"But I thought you said you didn't mean to interfere," said Laura. Sadie had   40
gone. The florist's man was still outside at his van. She put her arm round her mother's neck and gently, very gently, she bit her mother's ear.

"My darling child, you wouldn't like a logical mother, would you? Don't do that. Here's the man."

He carried more lilies still, another whole tray.

"Bank them up, just inside the door, on both sides of the porch, please," said Mrs. Sheridan. "Don't you agree, Laura?"

"Oh, I *do* mother."

In the drawing-room Meg, Jose and good little Hans had at last succeeded in moving the piano.   45

"Now, if we put this chesterfield against the wall and move everything out of the room except the chairs, don't you think?"

"Quite."

"Hans, move these tables into the smoking-room, and bring a sweeper to take these marks off the carpet and — one moment, Hans — " Jose loved giving orders to the servants, and they loved obeying her. She always made them feel they were taking part in some drama. "Tell mother and Miss Laura to come here at once."

"Very good, Miss Jose."

She turned to Meg. "I want to hear what the piano sounds like, just in case   50 I'm asked to sing this afternoon. Let's try over 'This Life is Weary.'"

Pom! Ta-ta-ta *Tee*-ta! The piano burst out so passionately that Jose's face changed. She clasped her hands. She looked mournfully and enigmatically at her mother and Laura as they came in.

> This Life is *Wee*-ary,
> A Tear — a Sigh.
> A Love that *Chan*-ges,
>   This Life is *Wee*-ary,
> A Tear — a Sigh.
> A Love that *Chan*-ges,
> And then . . . *Good*-bye!

But at the word "Good-bye," and although the piano sounded more desperate than ever, her face broke into a brilliant, dreadfully unsympathetic smile.

"Aren't I in good voice, mummy?" she beamed.

> This Life is *Wee*-ary,
> Hope comes to Die.
> A Dream — a *Wa*-kening.

But now Sadie interrupted them. "What is it, Sadie?"

"If you please, m'm, cook says have you got the flags for the sandwiches?"   55

"The flags for the sandwiches, Sadie?" echoed Mrs. Sheridan dreamily. And the children knew by her face that she hadn't got them. "Let me see." And she said to Sadie firmly, "Tell cook I'll let her have them in ten minutes."

Sadie went.

"Now, Laura," said her mother quickly. "Come with me into the smoking-room. I've got the names somewhere on the back of an envelope. You'll have to write them out for me. Meg, go upstairs this minute and take that wet thing off your head. Jose, run and finish dressing this instant. Do you hear me, children, or shall I have to tell your father when he comes home to-night? And — and, Jose, pacify cook if you do go into the kitchen, will you? I'm terrified of her this morning."

The envelope was found at last behind the dining-room clock, though how it had got there Mrs. Sheridan could not imagine.

"One of you children must have stolen it out of my bag, because I remember   60
vividly—cream cheese and lemon-curd. Have you done that?"

"Yes."

"Egg and—" Mrs. Sheridan held the envelope away from her. "It looks like mice. It can't be mice, can it?"

"Olive, pet," said Laura, looking over her shoulder.

"Yes, of course, olive. What a horrible combination it sounds. Egg and olive."

They were finished at last, and Laura took them off to the kitchen. She found   65
Jose there pacifying the cook, who did not look at all terrifying.

"I have never seen such exquisite sandwiches," said Jose's rapturous voice. "How many kinds did you say there were, cook? Fifteen?"

"Fifteen, Miss Jose."

"Well, cook, I congratulate you."

Cook swept up crusts with the long sandwich knife, and smiled broadly.

"Godber's has come," announced Sadie, issuing out of the pantry. She had   70
seen the man pass the window.

That meant the cream puffs had come. Godber's were famous for their cream puffs. Nobody ever thought of making them at home.

"Bring them in and put them on the table, my girl," ordered cook.

Sadie brought them in and went back to the door. Of course Laura and Jose were far too grown-up to really care about such things. All the same, they couldn't help agreeing that the puffs looked very attractive. Very. Cook began arranging them, shaking off the extra icing sugar.

"Don't they carry one back to all one's parties?" said Laura.

"I suppose they do," said practical Jose, who never liked to be carried back.   75
"They look beautifully light and feathery, I must say."

"Have one each, my dears," said cook in her comfortable voice. "Yer ma won't know."

Oh, impossible. Fancy cream puffs so soon after breakfast. The very idea made one shudder. All the same, two minutes later Jose and Laura were licking their fingers with that absorbed inward look that only comes from whipped cream.

"Let's go into the garden, out by the back way," suggested Laura. "I want to see how the men are getting on with the marquee. They're such awfully nice men."

But the back door was blocked by cook, Sadie, Godber's man and Hans.

Something had happened.   80

"Tuk-tuk-tuk," clucked cook like an agitated hen. Sadie had her hand clapped to her cheek as though she had toothache. Hans's face was screwed up in the effort to understand. Only Godber's man seemed to be enjoying himself; it was his story.

"What's the matter? What's happened?"

"There's been a horrible accident," said Cook. "A man killed."

"A man killed! Where? How? When?"

But Godber's man wasn't going to have his story snatched from under his   85
very nose.

"Know those little cottages just below here, miss?" Know them? Of course,
she knew them. "Well, there's a young chap living there, name of Scott, a carter.
His horse shied at a traction-engine, corner of Hawke Street this morning, and he
was thrown out on the back of his head. Killed."

"Dead!" Laura stared at Godber's man.

"Dead when they picked him up," said Godber's man with relish. "They
were taking the body home as I come up here." And he said to the cook, "He's left
a wife and five little ones."

"Jose, come here." Laura caught hold of her sister's sleeve and dragged her
through the kitchen to the other side of the green baize door. There she paused
and leaned against it. "Jose!" she said, horrified, "however are we going to stop
everything?"

"Stop everything, Laura!" cried Jose in astonishment. "What do you mean?"   90

"Stop the garden-party, of course." Why did Jose pretend?

But Jose was still more amazed. "Stop the garden-party? My dear Laura,
don't be so absurd. Of course we can't do anything of the kind. Nobody expects
us to. Don't be so extravagant."

"But we can't possibly have a garden-party with a man dead just outside the
front gate."

That really was extravagant, for the little cottages were in a lane to themselves at the very bottom of a steep rise that led up to the house. A broad road ran
between. True, they were far too near. They were the greatest possible eyesore,
and they had no right to be in that neighbourhood at all. They were little mean
dwellings painted a chocolate brown. In the garden patches there was nothing
but cabbage stalks, sick hens and tomato cans. The very smoke coming out of
their chimneys was poverty-stricken. Little rags and shreds of smoke, so unlike
the great silvery plumes that uncurled from the Sheridans' chimneys. Washer-
women lived in the lane and sweeps and a cobbler, and a man whose house-front
was studded all over with minute bird-cages. Children swarmed. When the
Sheridans were little they were forbidden to set foot there because of the revolting language and of what they might catch. But since they were grown up, Laura
and Laurie on their prowls sometimes walked through. It was disgusting and sordid. They came out with a shudder. But still one must go everywhere; one must
see everything. So through they went.

"And just think of what the band would sound like to that poor woman," said   95
Laura.

"Oh, Laura!" Jose began to be seriously annoyed. "If you're going to stop a
band playing every time some one has an accident, you'll lead a very strenuous
life. I'm every bit as sorry about it as you. I feel just as sympathetic." Her eyes
hardened. She looked at her sister just as she used to when they were little and
fighting together. "You won't bring a drunken workman back to life by being sentimental," she said softly.

"Drunk! Who said he was drunk?" Laura turned furiously on Jose. She said, just as they had used to say on those occasions, "I'm going straight up to tell mother."

"Do, dear," cooed Jose.

"Mother, can I come in your room?" Laura turned the big glass door-knob.

"Of course, child. Why, what's the matter? What's given you such a colour?" And Mrs. Sheridan turned round from her dressing-table. She was trying on a new hat.

"Mother, a man's been killed," began Laura.

"*Not* in the garden?" interrupted her mother.

"No, no!"

"Oh, what a fright you gave me!" Mrs. Sheridan sighed with relief, and took off the big hat and held it on her knees.

"But listen, mother," said Laura. Breathless, half-choking, she told the dreadful story. "Of course, we can't have our party, can we?" she pleaded. "The band and everybody arriving. They'd hear us, mother; they're nearly neighbors!"

To Laura's astonishment her mother behaved just like Jose, it was harder to bear because she seemed amused. She refused to take Laura seriously.

"But, my dear child, use your common sense. It's only by accident we've heard of it. If some one had died there normally—and I can't understand how they keep alive in those poky little holes—we should still be having our party, shouldn't we?"

Laura had to say "yes" to that, but she felt it was all wrong. She sat down on her mother's sofa and pinched the cushion frill.

"Mother, isn't it really terribly heartless of us?" she asked.

"Darling!" Mrs. Sheridan got up and came over to her, carrying the hat. Before Laura could stop her she had popped it on. "My child!" said her mother, "the hat is yours. It's made for you. It's much too young for me. I have never seen you look such a picture. Look at yourself!" And she held up her hand-mirror.

"But, mother," Laura began again. She couldn't look at herself; she turned aside.

This time Mrs. Sheridan lost patience just as Jose had done.

"You are being very absurd, Laura," she said coldly. "People like that don't expect sacrifices from us. And it's not very sympathetic to spoil everybody's enjoyment as you're doing now."

"I don't understand," said Laura, and she walked quickly out of the room into her own bedroom. There, quite by chance, the first thing she saw was this charming girl in the mirror, in her black hat trimmed with gold daisies, and a long black velvet ribbon. Never had she imagined she could look like that. Is mother right? she thought. And now she hoped her mother was right. Am I being extravagant? Perhaps it was extravagant. Just for a moment she had another glimpse of that poor woman and those little children, and the body being carried into the house. But it all seemed blurred, unreal, like a picture in the newspaper. I'll remember it again after the party's over, she decided. And somehow that seemed quite the best plan. . . .

Lunch was over by half-past one. By half-past two they were all ready for the   115
fray. The green-coated band had arrived and was established in a corner of the
tennis-court.

"My dear!" trilled Kitty Maitland, "aren't they too like frogs for words? You
ought to have arranged them round the pond with the conductor in the middle
on a leaf."

Laurie arrived and hailed them on his way to dress. At the sight of him Laura
remembered the accident again. She wanted to tell him. If Laurie agreed
with the others, then it was bound to be all right. And she followed him into
the hall.

"Laurie!"

"Hallo!" He was half-way upstairs, but when he turned round and saw Laura
he suddenly puffed out his cheeks and goggled his eyes at her. "My word, Laura;
You do look stunning," said Laurie. "What an absolutely topping hat!"

Laura said faintly, "Is it?" and smiled up at Laurie, and didn't tell him   120
after all.

Soon after that people began coming in streams. The band struck up; the
hired waiters ran from the house to the marquee. Wherever you looked there
were couples strolling, bending to the flowers, greeting, moving on over the lawn.
They were like bright birds that had alighted in the Sheridans' garden for this one
afternoon, on their way to — where? Ah, what happiness it is to be with people
who all are happy, to press hands, press cheeks, smile into eyes.

"Darling Laura, how well you look!"

"What a becoming hat, child!"

"Laura, you look quite Spanish. I've never seen you look so striking."

And Laura, glowing, answered softly, "Have you had tea? Won't you have an   125
ice? The passion-fruit ices really are rather special." She ran to her father and
begged him. "Daddy darling, can't the band have something to drink?"

And the perfect afternoon slowly ripened, slowly faded, slowly its petals
closed.

"Never a more delightful garden-party . . ." "The greatest success . . ." "Quite
the most . . ."

Laura helped her mother with the good-byes. They stood side by side in the
porch till it was all over.

"All over, all over, thank heaven," said Mrs. Sheridan. "Round up the others,
Laura. Let's go and have some fresh coffee. I'm exhausted. Yes, it's been very successful. But oh, these parties, these parties! Why will you children insist on giving
parties!" And they all of them sat down in the deserted marquee.

"Have a sandwich, daddy dear. I wrote the flag."   130

"Thanks." Mr. Sheridan took a bite and the sandwich was gone. He took
another. "I suppose you didn't hear of a beastly accident that happened to-day?"
he said.

"My dear," said Mrs. Sheridan, holding up her hand, "we did. It nearly
ruined the party. Laura insisted we should put it off."

"Oh, mother!" Laura didn't want to be teased about it.

"It was a horrible affair all the same," said Mr. Sheridan. "The chap was married too. Lived just below in the lane, and leaves a wife and half a dozen kiddies, so they say."

An awkward little silence fell. Mrs. Sheridan fidgeted with her cup. Really, it 135 was very tactless of father. . . .

Suddenly she looked up. There on the table were all those sandwiches, cakes, puffs, all uneaten, all going to be wasted. She had one of her brilliant ideas.

"I know," she said. "Let's make up a basket. Let's send that poor creature some of this perfectly good food. At any rate, it will be the greatest treat for the children. Don't you agree? And she's sure to have neighbours calling in and so on. What a point to have it all ready prepared. Laura!" She jumped up. "Get me the big basket out of the stairs cupboard."

"But, mother, do you really think it's a good idea?" said Laura.

Again, how curious, she seemed to be different from them all. To take scraps from their party. Would the poor woman really like that?

"Of course! What's the matter with you to-day? An hour or two ago you were 140 insisting on us being sympathetic, and now —"

Oh, well! Laura ran for the basket. It was filled, it was heaped by her mother.

"Take it yourself, darling," said she. "Run down just as you are. No, wait, take the arum lilies too. People of that class are so impressed by arum lilies."

"The stems will ruin her lace frock," said practical Jose.

So they would. Just in time. "Only the basket, then. And, Laura!" — her mother followed her out of the marquee — "don't on any account —"

"What, mother?"   145

No, better not put such ideas into the child's head! "Nothing! Run along."

It was just growing dusky as Laura shut their garden gates. A big dog ran by like a shadow. The road gleamed white, and down below in the hollow the little cottages were in deep shade. How quiet it seemed after the afternoon. Here she was going down the hill to somewhere where a man lay dead, and she couldn't realize it. Why couldn't she? She stopped a minute. And it seemed to her that kisses, voices, tinkling spoons, laughter, the smell of crushed grass were somehow inside her. She had no room for anything else. How strange! She looked up at the pale sky, and all she thought was, "Yes, it was the most successful party."

Now the broad road was crossed. The lane began, smoky and dark. Women in shawls and men's tweed caps hurried by. Men hung over the palings; the children played in the doorways. A low hum came from the mean little cottages. In some of them there was a flicker of light, and a shadow, crab-like, moved across the window. Laura bent her head and hurried on. She wished now she had put on a coat. How her frock shone! And the big hat with the velvet streamer — if only it was another hat! Were the people looking at her? They must be. It was a mistake to have come; she knew all along it was a mistake. Should she go back even now?

No, too late. This was the house. It must be. A dark knot of people stood outside. Beside the gate an old, old woman with a crutch sat in a chair, watching.

She had her feet on a newspaper. The voices stopped as Laura drew near. The group parted. It was as though she was expected, as though they had known she was coming here.

Laura was terribly nervous. Tossing the velvet ribbon over her shoulder, she said to a woman standing by, "Is this Mrs. Scott's house?" and the woman, smiling queerly, said, "It is, my lass." 150

Oh, to be away from this! She actually said, "Help me, God," as she walked up the tiny path and knocked. To be away from those staring eyes, or to be covered up in anything, one of those women's shawls even. I'll just leave the basket and go, she decided. I shan't even wait for it to be emptied.

Then the door opened. A little woman in black showed in the gloom.

Laura said, "Are you Mrs. Scott?" But to her horror the woman answered, "Walk in please, miss," and she was shut in the passage.

"No," said Laura, "I don't want to come in. I only want to leave this basket. Mother sent—"

The little woman in the gloomy passage seemed not to have heard her. "Step this way, please, miss," she said in an oily voice, and Laura followed her. 155

She found herself in a wretched little low kitchen, lighted by a smoky lamp. There was a woman sitting before the fire.

"Em," said the little creature who had let her in. "Em! It's a young lady." She turned to Laura. She said meaningly, "I'm 'er sister, Miss. You'll excuse 'er, won't you?"

"Oh, but of course!" said Laura. "Please, please don't disturb her. I—I only want to leave—"

But at that moment the woman at the fire turned round. Her face, puffed up, red, with swollen eyes and swollen lips, looked terrible. She seemed as though she couldn't understand why Laura was there. What did it mean? Why was this stranger standing in the kitchen with a basket? What was it all about? And the poor face puckered up again.

"All right, my dear," said the other. "I'll thenk the young lady." 160

And again she began, "You'll excuse her, miss, I'm sure," and her face, swollen too, tried an oily smile.

Laura only wanted to get out, to get away. She was back in the passage. The door opened. She walked straight through into the bedroom, where the dead man was lying.

"You'd like a look at 'im, wouldn't you?" said Em's sister, and she brushed past Laura over to the bed. "Don't be afraid, my lass,—" and now her voice sounded fond and sly, and fondly she drew down the sheet—"'e looks a picture. There's nothing to show. Come along, my dear."

There lay a young man, fast asleep—sleeping so soundly, so deeply, that he was far, far away from them both. Oh, so remote, so peaceful. He was dreaming. Never wake him up again. His head was sunk in the pillow, his eyes were closed; they were blind under the closed eyelids. He was given up to his dream. What did garden-parties and baskets and lace frocks matter to him? He was far from all those things. He was wonderful, beautiful. While they were laughing and while the band was playing, this marvel had come to the lane. Happy . . . happy. . . . All is well, said that sleeping face. This is just as it should be. I am content.

But all the same you had to cry, and she couldn't go out of the room without saying something to him. Laura gave a loud childish sob.

"Forgive my hat," she said.

And this time she didn't wait for Em's sister. She found her way out of the door, down the path, past all those dark people. At the corner of the lane she met Laurie.

He stepped out of the shadow. "Is that you, Laura?"

"Yes."

"Mother was getting anxious. Was it all right?"

"Yes, quite. Oh, Laurie!" She took his arm, she pressed up against him.

"I say, you're not crying, are you?" asked her brother.

Laura shook her head. She was.

Laurie put his arm round her shoulder. "Don't cry," he said in his warm, loving voice. "Was it awful?"

"No," sobbed Laura. "It was simply marvellous. But, Laurie —" She stopped, she looked at her brother. "Isn't life," she stammered, "isn't life —" But what life was she couldn't explain. No matter. He quite understood.

"*Isn't* it, darling?" said Laurie.   [1922]

THINKING ABOUT THE TEXT

1. Describe in your own words Laura's reaction to the dead man upon encountering him. Does her response seem sound and appropriate, or do you find it shallow? Support your evaluation.

2. Earlier in the story, Laura wonders if her family is being "heartless" in having the party despite the man's death. How fair is it to call the family "heartless"? What warrants or assumptions are reflected in your answer?

3. What distinctions are there between the culture of Laura's family and the culture of the workers? Do these cultures have anything in common? If so, what?

4. Although Mansfield has entitled her story "The Garden-Party" and describes the preparations for that party at length, she barely describes the party itself. Why, do you suppose?

5. To what extent is the story told from Laura's point of view and with her kind of language? Refer to specific passages.

GABRIEL GARCÍA MÁRQUEZ
The Handsomest Drowned Man in the World

A TALE FOR CHILDREN

Translated by Gregory Rabassa

Gabriel García Márquez (b. 1928) has achieved international renown, certified by his 1982 Nobel Prize in Literature. For several years, though, he lived in exile from his native Colombia because he opposed its dictatorship. García Márquez's fiction is often described as "magic realism" because it mixes everyday life and fantastic events. His several novels include the frequently taught One Hundred Years of Solitude *(1967). The following piece is from a 1973 book by García Márquez entitled* Leaf Storm and Other Stories.

The first children who saw the dark and slinky bulge approaching through the sea let themselves think it was an enemy ship. Then they saw it had no flags or masts and they thought it was a whale. But when it washed up on the beach, they removed the clumps of seaweed, the jellyfish tentacles, and the remains of fish and flotsam, and only then did they see that it was a drowned man.

They had been playing with him all afternoon, burying him in the sand and digging him up again, when someone chanced to see them and spread the alarm in the village. The men who carried him to the nearest house noticed that he weighed more than any dead man they had ever known, almost as much as a horse, and they said to each other that maybe he'd been floating too long and the water had got into his bones. When they laid him on the floor they said he'd been taller than all other men because there was barely enough room for him in the house, but they thought that maybe the ability to keep on growing after death was part of the nature of certain drowned men. He had the smell of the sea about him and only his shape gave one to suppose that it was the corpse of a human being, because the skin was covered with a crust of mud and scales.

They did not even have to clean off his face to know that the dead man was a stranger. The village was made up of only twenty-odd wooden houses that had stone courtyards with no flowers and which were spread about on the end of a desertlike cape. There was so little land that mothers always went about with the fear that the wind would carry off their children and the few dead that the years had caused among them had to be thrown off the cliffs. But the sea was calm and bountiful and all the men fit into seven boats. So when they found the drowned man they simply had to look at one another to see that they were all there.

That night they did not go out to work at sea. While the men went to find out if anyone was missing in neighboring villages, the women stayed behind to care for the drowned man. They took the mud off with grass swabs, they removed the underwater stones entangled in his hair, and they scraped the crust off with tools used for scaling fish. As they were doing that they noticed that the vegetation on him came from faraway oceans and deep water and that his clothes were in tatters, as if he had sailed through labyrinths of coral. They noticed too that he bore his death with pride, for he did not have the lonely look of other drowned men who came out of the sea or that haggard, needy look of men who drowned in rivers. But only when they finished cleaning him off did they become aware of the kind of man he was and it left them breathless. Not only was he the tallest, strongest, most virile, and best built man they had ever seen, but even though they were looking at him there was no room for him in their imagination.

They could not find a bed in the village large enough to lay him on nor was there a table solid enough to use for his wake. The tallest men's holiday pants would not fit him, nor the fattest ones' Sunday shirts, nor the shoes of the one with the biggest feet. Fascinated by his huge size and his beauty, the women then decided to make him some pants from a large piece of sail and a shirt from some bridal Brabant linen so that he could continue through his death with dignity. As they sewed, sitting in a circle and gazing at the corpse between stitches, it seemed to them that the wind had never been so steady nor the sea so restless as on that night and they supposed that the change had something to do with the dead man. They thought that if that magnificent man had lived in the village, his house would have had the widest doors, the highest ceiling, and the strongest floor; his bedstead would have been made from a midship frame held together by iron bolts, and his wife would have been the happiest woman. They thought that he would have had so much authority that he could have drawn fish out of the sea simply by calling their names and that he would have put so much work into his land that springs would have burst forth from among the rocks so that he would have been able to plant flowers on the cliffs. They secretly compared him to their own men, thinking that for all their lives theirs were incapable of doing what he could do in one night, and they ended up dismissing them deep in their hearts as the weakest, meanest, and most useless creatures on earth. They were wandering through that maze of fantasy when the oldest woman, who as the oldest had looked upon the drowned man with more compassion than passion, sighed:

"He has the face of someone called Esteban."

It was true. Most of them had only to take another look at him to see that he could not have any other name. The more stubborn among them, who were the youngest, still lived for a few hours with the illusion that when they put his clothes on and he lay among the flowers in patent leather shoes his name might be Lautaro. But it was a vain illusion. There had not been enough canvas, the poorly cut and worse sewn pants were too tight, and the hidden strength of his heart popped the buttons on his shirt. After midnight the whistling of the wind died down and the sea fell into its Wednesday drowsiness. The silence put an end to any last doubts: he was Esteban. The women who had dressed him, who had combed his hair, had cut his nails and shaved him were unable to hold back a shudder of pity when they had to resign themselves to his being dragged along the ground. It was then that they understood how unhappy he must have been with that huge body since it bothered him even after death. They could see him in life, condemned to going through doors sideways, cracking his head on crossbeams, remaining on his feet during visits, not knowing what to do with his soft

5

pink, sealion hands while the lady of the house looked for her most resistant chair and begged him, frightened to death, sit here, Esteban, please, and he, leaning against the wall, smiling, don't bother, ma'am, I'm fine where I am, his heels raw and his back roasted from having done the same thing so many times whenever he paid a visit, don't bother, ma'am, I'm fine where I am, just to avoid the embarrassment of breaking up the chair, and never knowing perhaps that the ones who said don't go, Esteban, at least wait till the coffee's ready, were the ones who later on would whisper the big boob finally left, how nice, the handsome fool has gone. That was what the women were thinking beside the body a little before dawn. Later, when they covered his face with a handkerchief so that the light would not bother him, he looked so forever dead, so defenseless, so much like their men that the first furrows of tears opened in their hearts. It was one of the younger ones who began the weeping. The others, coming to, went from sighs to wails, and the more they sobbed the more they felt like weeping, because the drowned man was becoming all the more Esteban for them, and so they wept so much, for he was the most destitute, most peaceful, and most obliging man on earth, poor Esteban. So when the men returned with the news that the drowned man was not from the neighboring villages either, the women felt an opening of jubilation in the midst of their tears.

"Praise the Lord," they sighed, "he's ours!"

The men thought the fuss was only womanish frivolity. Fatigued because of the difficult nighttime inquiries, all they wanted was to get rid of the bother of the newcomer once and for all before the sun grew strong on that arid, windless day. They improvised a litter with the remains of foremasts and gaffs, tying it together with rigging so that it would bear the weight of the body until they reached the cliffs. They wanted to tie the anchor from a cargo ship to him so that he would sink easily into the deepest waves, where fish are blind and divers die of nostalgia, and bad currents would not bring him back to shore, as had happened with other bodies. But the more they hurried, the more the women thought of ways to waste time. They walked about like startled hens, pecking with the sea charms on their breasts, some interfering on one side to put a scapular of the good wind on the drowned man, some on the other side to put a wrist compass on him, and after a great deal of *get away from there, woman, stay out of the way, look, you almost made me fall on top of the dead man*, the men began to feel mistrust in their livers and started grumbling about why so many main-altar decorations for a stranger, because no matter how many nails and holy-water jars he had on him, the sharks would chew him all the same, but the women kept on piling on their junk relics, running back and forth, stumbling, while they released in sighs what they did not in tears, so that the men finally exploded with *since when has there ever been such a fuss over a drifting corpse, a drowned nobody, a piece of cold Wednesday meat.* One of the women, mortified by so much lack of care, then removed the handkerchief from the dead man's face and the men were left breathless too.

He was Esteban. It was not necessary to repeat it for them to recognize him. If they had been told Sir Walter Raleigh, even they might have been impressed with his gringo accent, the macaw on his shoulder, his cannibal-killing blunder-

10

buss, but there could be only one Esteban in the world and there he was, stretched out like a sperm whale, shoeless, wearing the pants of an undersized child, and with those stony nails that had to be cut with a knife. They had only to take the handkerchief off his face to see that he was ashamed, that it was not his fault that he was so big or so heavy or so handsome, and if he had known that this was going to happen, he would have looked for a more discreet place to drown in; seriously, I even would have tied the anchor off a galleon around my neck and staggered off a cliff like someone who doesn't like things in order not to be upsetting people now with this Wednesday dead body, as you people say, in order not to be bothering anyone with this filthy piece of cold meat that doesn't have anything to do with me. There was so much truth in his manner that even the most mistrustful men, the ones who felt the bitterness of endless nights at sea fearing that their women would tire of dreaming about them and begin to dream of drowned men, even they and others who were harder still shuddered in the marrow of their bones at Esteban's sincerity.

That was how they came to hold the most splendid funeral they could conceive of for an abandoned drowned man. Some women who had gone to get flowers in the neighboring villages returned with other women who could not believe what they had been told, and those women went back for more flowers when they saw the dead man, and they brought more and more until there were so many flowers and so many people that it was hard to walk about. At the final moment it pained them to return him to the waters as an orphan and they chose a father and mother from among the best people, and aunts and uncles and cousins, so that through him all the inhabitants of the village became kinsmen. Some sailors who heard the weeping from a distance went off course, and people heard of one who had himself tied to the mainmast, remembering ancient fables about sirens. While they fought for the privilege of carrying him on their shoulders along the steep escarpment by the cliffs, men and women became aware for the first time of the desolation of their streets, the dryness of their courtyards, the narrowness of their dreams as they faced the splendor and beauty of their drowned man. They let him go without an anchor so that he could come back if he wished and whenever he wished, and they all held their breath for the fraction of centuries the body took to fall into the abyss. They did not need to look at one another to realize that they were no longer all present, that they would never be. But they also knew that everything would be different from then on, that their houses would have wider doors, higher ceilings, and stronger floors so that Esteban's memory could go everywhere without bumping into beams and so that no one in the future would dare whisper the big boob finally died, too bad, the handsome fool has finally died, because they were going to paint their house fronts gay colors to make Esteban's memory eternal and they were going to break their backs digging for springs among the stones and planting flowers on the cliffs so that in future years at dawn the passengers on great liners would awaken, suffocated by the smell of gardens on the high seas, and the captain would have to come down from the bridge in his dress uniform, with his astrolabe, his pole star, and his row of war medals and, pointing to the promontory of roses on the horizon, he would say in fourteen languages, look there, where the wind is so peaceful now that it's gone to sleep beneath the beds, over there, where the sun's so bright that the sunflowers don't know which way to turn, yes, over there, that's Esteban's village.   [1973]

THINKING ABOUT THE TEXT

1. The subtitle of this story is "A Tale for Children." Is García Márquez is being ironic, or does his story indeed fit that genre? How do you think an audience of children might react to it?

2. Identify the villagers' various conceptions of the dead man. What gender differences emerge? What should a reader conclude from the fact that these conceptions change? What would you say to someone who argues that the villagers are being foolish in giving the dead man a name and making so much of him?

3. Do you find humor in this story? If so, in what specific passages?

4. What, if anything, seems realistic about this story? Where, if anywhere, does García Márquez strike you as departing from realism? Elaborate how you are defining *realism*.

5. Identify the various sentence lengths in this story, using specific examples. Note in particular where García Márquez's sentences get quite long. Are these long sentences effective, or should he have broken them into shorter ones? Explain your reasoning.

MAKING COMPARISONS

1. Both Laura and García Márquez's villagers find their respective dead men physically attractive. Is this response sensible in each case? Identify some warrants or assumptions behind your answer.

2. Do you think both Laura and the villagers will be permanently affected by their encounters with these dead men? Support your answer by referring to specific details of both texts.

3. Analyze the role of flowers in Mansfield's and García Márquez's stories. Do flowers have roughly the same function in both?

DON DELILLO
Videotape

Don DeLillo (b. 1936) is a contemporary American writer known mostly for his novels. These include End Zone *(1972),* The Names *(1982),* White Noise *(1985),* Libra *(1988), a fictionalized biography of Lee Harvey Oswald, and* Underworld *(1997). The following story first appeared in the literary journal* Antaeus *in 1994.*

Subsequently, it was included in The Pushcart Prize, XX: Best of the Small Presses 1995–96 *and became part of* Underworld. *Like most of DeLillo's fiction, the story deals with the impact of new media technology on human thought.*

It shows a man driving a car. It is the simplest sort of family video. You see a man at the wheel of a medium Dodge.

It is just a kid aiming her camera through the rear window of the family car at the windshield of the car behind her.

You know about families and their video cameras. You know how kids get involved, how the camera shows them that every subject is potentially charged, a million things they never see with the unaided eye. They investigate the meaning of inert objects and dumb pets and they poke at family privacy. They learn to see things twice.

It is the kid's own privacy that is being protected here. She is twelve years old and her name is being withheld even though she is neither the victim nor the perpetrator of the crime but only the means of recording it.

It shows a man in a sport shirt at the wheel of his car. There is nothing else to   5
see. The car approaches briefly, then falls back.

You know how children with cameras learn to work the exposed moments that define the family cluster. They break every trust, spy out the undefended space, catching mom coming out of the bathroom in her cumbrous robe and turbaned towel, looking bloodless and plucked. It is not a joke. They will shoot you sitting on the pot if they can manage a suitable vantage.

The tape has the jostled sort of noneventness that marks the family product. Of course the man in this case is not a member of the family but a stranger in a car, a random figure, someone who has happened along in the slow lane.

It shows a man in his forties wearing a pale shirt open at the throat, the image washed by reflections and sunglint, with many jostled moments.

It is not just another video homicide. It is a homicide recorded by a child who thought she was doing something simple and maybe halfway clever, shooting some tape of a man in a car.

He sees the girl and waves briefly, wagging a hand without taking it off the   10
wheel—an underplayed reaction that makes you like him.

It is unrelenting footage that rolls on and on. It has an aimless determination, a persistence that lives outside the subject matter. You are looking into the mind of home video. It is innocent, it is aimless, it is determined, it is real.

He is bald up the middle of his head, a nice guy in his forties whose whole life seems open to the hand-held camera.

But there is also an element of suspense. You keep on looking not because you know something is going to happen—of course you do know something is going to happen and you do look for that reason but you might also keep on looking if you came across this footage for the first time without knowing the outcome. There is a crude power operating here. You keep on looking because things combine to hold you fast—a sense of the random, the amateurish, the accidental, the impending. You don't think of the tape as boring or interesting. It is crude, it is blunt, it is relentless. It is the jostled part of your mind, the film that runs through your hotel brain under all the thoughts you know you're thinking.

The world is lurking in the camera, already framed, waiting for the boy or girl who will come along and take up the device, learn the instrument, shooting old granddad at breakfast, all stroked out so his nostrils gape, the cereal spoon baby-gripped in his pale fist.

It shows a man alone in a medium Dodge. It seems to go on forever.   15

There's something about the nature of the tape, the grain of the image, the sputtering black-and-white tones, the starkness — you think this is more real, truer-to-life than anything around you. The things around you have a rehearsed and layered and cosmetic look. The tape is superreal, or maybe underreal is the way you want to put it. It is what lies at the scraped bottom of all the layers you have added. And this is another reason why you keep on looking. The tape has a searing realness.

It shows him giving an abbreviated wave, stiff-palmed, like a signal flag at a siding.

You know how families make up games. This is just another game in which the child invents the rules as she goes along. She likes the idea of videotaping a man in his car. She has probably never done it before and she sees no reason to vary the format or terminate early or pan to another car. This is her game and she is learning it and playing it at the same time. She feels halfway clever and inventive and maybe slightly intrusive as well, a little bit of brazenness that spices any game.

And you keep on looking. You look because this is the nature of the footage, to make a channeled path through time, to give things a shape and a destiny.

Of course if she had panned to another car, the right car at the precise time,   20
she would have caught the gunman as he fired.

The chance quality of the encounter. The victim, the killer, and the child with a camera. Random energies that approach a common point. There's something here that speaks to you directly, saying terrible things about forces beyond your control, lines of intersection that cut through history and logic and every reasonable layer of human expectation.

She wandered into it. The girl got lost and wandered clear-eyed into horror. This is a children's story about straying too far from home. But it isn't the family car that serves as the instrument of the child's curiosity, her inclination to explore. It is the camera that puts her in the tale.

You know about holidays and family celebrations and how somebody shows up with a camcorder and the relatives stand around and barely react because they're numbingly accustomed to the process of being taped and decked and shown on the VCR with the coffee and cake.

He is hit soon after. If you've seen the tape many times you know from the hand wave exactly when he will be hit. It is something, naturally, that you wait for. You say to your wife, if you're at home and she is there, Now here is where he gets it. You say, Janet, hurry up, this is where it happens.

Now here is where he gets it. You see him jolted, sort of wire-shocked — then   25 he seizes up and falls toward the door or maybe leans or slides into the door is the proper way to put it. It is awful and unremarkable at the same time. The car stays in the slow lane. It approaches briefly, then falls back.

You don't usually call your wife over to the TV set. She has her programs, you have yours. But there's a certain urgency here. You want her to see how it looks. The tape has been running forever and now the thing is finally going to happen and you want her to be here when he's shot.

Here it comes all right. He is shot, head-shot, and the camera reacts, the child reacts—there is a jolting movement but she keeps on taping, there is a sympathetic response, a nerve response, her heart is beating faster but she keeps the camera trained on the subject as he slides into the door and even as you see him die you're thinking of the girl. At some level the girl has to be present here, watching what you're watching, unprepared—the girl is seeing this cold and you have to marvel at the fact that she keeps the tape rolling.

It shows something awful and unaccompanied. You want your wife to see it because it is real this time, not fancy movie violence—the realness beneath the layers of cosmetic perception. Hurry up, Janet, here it comes. He dies so fast. There is no accompaniment of any kind. It is very stripped. You want to tell her it is realer than real but then she will ask what that means.

The way the camera reacts to the gunshot—a startle reaction that brings pity and terror into the frame, the girl's own shock, the girl's identification with the victim.

You don't see the blood, which is probably trickling behind his ear and down   30
the back of his neck. The way his head is twisted away from the door, the twist of the head gives you only a partial profile and it's the wrong side, it's not the side where he was hit.

And maybe you're being a little aggressive here, practically forcing your wife to watch. Why? What are you telling her? Are you making a little statement? Like I'm going to ruin your day out of ordinary spite. Or a big statement? Like this is the risk of existing. Either way you're rubbing her face in this tape and you don't know why.

It shows the car drifting toward the guardrail and then there's a jostling sense of two other lanes and part of another car, a split-second blur, and the tape ends here, either because the girl stopped shooting or because some central authority, the police or the district attorney or the TV station, decided there was nothing else you had to see.

This is either the tenth or eleventh homicide committed by the Texas Highway Killer. The number is uncertain because the police believe that one of the shootings may have been a copycat crime.

And there is something about videotape, isn't there, and this particular kind of serial crime? This is a crime designed for random taping and immediate playing. You sit there and wonder if this kind of crime became more possible when the means of taping an event and playing it immediately, without a neutral interval, a balancing space and time, became widely available. Taping-and-playing intensifies and compresses the event. It dangles a need to do it again. You sit there thinking that the serial murderer has found its medium, or vice versa—an act of shadow technology, of compressed time and repeated images, stark and glary and unremarkable.

It shows very little in the end. It is a famous murder because it is on tape and because the murderer has done it many times and because the crime was recorded by a child. So the child is involved, the Video Kid as she is sometimes called because they have to call her something. The tape is famous and so is she. She is famous in the modern manner of people whose names are strategically withheld. They are famous without names or faces, spirits living apart from their bodies, the victims and witnesses, the underage criminals, out there somewhere at the edges of perception. 35

Seeing someone at the moment he dies, dying unexpectedly. This is reason alone to stay fixed to the screen. It is instructional, watching a man shot dead as he drives along on a sunny day. It demonstrates an elemental truth, that every breath you take has two possible endings. And that's another thing. There's a joke locked away here, a note of cruel slapstick that you are willing to appreciate even if it makes you feel a little guilty. Maybe the victim's a chump, a sort of silent-movie dope, classically unlucky. He had it coming, in a sense, for letting himself be caught on camera. Because once the tape starts rolling it can only end one way. This is what the context requires.

You don't want Janet to give you any crap about it's on all the time, they show it a thousand times a day. They show it because it exists, because they have to show it, because this is why they're out there, to provide our entertainment.

The more you watch the tape, the deader and colder and more relentless it becomes. The tape sucks the air right out of your chest but you watch it every time. [1994]

THINKING ABOUT THE TEXT

1. If asked to identify significant features of your own historical context, would you include the ability of people to videotape things? Or do you consider the technology of videotape a relatively insignificant aspect of your times?

2. Describe in your own words the narrator of this story. Does his fascination with the videotape of the murder strike you as legitimate? In general, do you tend to identify with him, or do you consider him quite different from you? What specific features of the story, and of your own experience, come to mind as you evaluate him?

3. Analyze the narrator's repeated references to "you." Who, specifically, might be his audience? How friendly is he toward this "you"? What might be his rhetorical purposes as he addresses this "you"?

4. What do you feel able to say about the child? DeLillo could have had the videotaper be an adult. What, if anything, does DeLillo achieve by making the videotaper so young?

5. What does the narrator apparently mean when he suggests that the murderer "commits the crimes as if they were a form of taped-and-played event"? Compare this story to a videotape. How does it resemble one? Differ from one?

MAKING COMPARISONS

1. Evidently, Mansfield's and García Márquez's stories both take place in a world without videotape. Are the settings of these two stories extremely different from DeLillo's setting as a result? Explain.

2. What would you say to someone who argues that García Márquez's subtitle, "A Tale for Children," applies more to Mansfield's and DeLillo's stories since children actually figure in them?

3. Each of these three stories features a dead man, but none of them tells much about his life. Why do you suppose the author in each case was so uninformative?

WRITING ABOUT ISSUES

1. Choose Mansfield's, García Márquez's, or DeLillo's story and write an essay considering whether any of the characters proves capable of recognizing reality. If you want to argue that no one in the story is capable, spend most of your essay discussing a few specific examples of short-sightedness. In any case, be sure to indicate the particular behavior you have in mind when arguing that a character is or isn't being realistic.

2. Choose two of the stories in this cluster and write an essay discussing each as a portrait of a whole society. Focus above all on the issue of whether one of these portraits is more negative than the other.

3. Probably there are several deceased people whom you admire but who are strangers to all or most of your classmates. Write an essay describing one such person for your classmates, aiming to persuade them that they, too, should admire him or her.

4. Write an essay evaluating how a recent article or television news story reported someone's death. In your essay, be sure to describe precisely how the death was presented and specify the criteria you are using to evaluate that presentation. Feel free to mention any of the stories in this cluster.

DISRESPECTING DEATH

JOHN DONNE, "Death Be Not Proud"
DYLAN THOMAS, "Do Not Go Gentle into That Good Night"
WISLAWA SZYMBORSKA, "On Death, without Exaggeration"

Through their works, writers of literature convey a wide range of attitudes toward death. Some take the opportunity to mourn the demise of a loved one, a friend, or a public figure. Others use the written word to stress that death is inevitable. Many literary works deal with death by expressing both sorrow and resignation. Each of the poems in this cluster expresses still another stance toward death: disrespect. Directly addressing death, John Donne's speaker virtually sneers at it. Addressing someone in danger of dying, Dylan Thomas's speaker portrays death as a force to resist. Finally, Wislawa Szymborska describes death in terms that considerably reduce its significance. As you read all three poems, think about whether disrespect toward death makes sense to you. Perhaps you feel that it is appropriate in certain circumstances but not others. If so, exactly when would you want death scorned? When would you call for acceptance of it, even reverence toward it?

BEFORE YOU READ

If you were to write a poem treating Death as a person and insulting him or her, what specific remarks might you make?

JOHN DONNE

Death Be Not Proud

Long regarded as a major English writer, John Donne (1572–1631) was also trained as a lawyer and clergyman. Around 1594, he converted from Catholicism to Anglicanism; in 1615, he was ordained; and in 1621, he was appointed to the prestigious position of dean of St. Paul's Cathedral in London. Today, his sermons continue to be studied as literature, yet he is more known for his poetry. When he was a young man, he often wrote about love, but later he focused on religious themes. The following poem, one of Donne's "holy sonnets," is from 1611.

Death be not proud, though some have callèd thee
Mighty and dreadful, for thou art not so;
For those whom thou think'st thou dost overthrow
Die not, poor Death, nor yet canst thou kill me.
From rest and sleep, which but thy pictures° be,   *images*   5

Much pleasure; then from thee much more must flow,
And soonest our best men with thee do go,
Rest of their bones, and soul's delivery.°   *deliverance*
Thou art slave to Fate, Chance, kings, and desperate men,
And dost with Poison, War, and Sickness dwell;   10
And poppy or charms can make us sleep as well,
And better than thy stroke; why swell'st° thou then?   *swell with pride*
One short sleep past, we wake eternally
And death shall be no more; Death, thou shalt die.   [1611]

THINKING ABOUT THE TEXT

1. In a sense, Death is the speaker's audience. But presumably Donne expected the living to read his poem. What reaction might he have wanted from this audience?

2. Is the speaker proud? Define what you mean by the term.

3. Evidently the speaker believes in an afterlife. What would you say to people who consider the speaker naive and the poem irrelevant because they don't believe that "we wake eternally"? How significant is this warrant or assumption? Do you share it?

4. Identify the rhyme patterns. How aware of them were you when you first read the poem?

5. Imagine Death writing a sonnet in response to the speaker. Perhaps it would be entitled "Life Be Not Proud." What things might Death say in it?

DYLAN THOMAS
Do Not Go Gentle into That Good Night

Dylan Thomas (1914–1953) was a Welsh poet, short-story writer, and playwright. Among his most enduring works are his radio dramas Under Milk Wood *(1954) and* A Child's Christmas in Wales *(1955). A frequent visitor to the United States, Thomas built a devoted audience in this country through his electrifying public readings. Unfortunately, he was also well known for his alcoholism, which killed him at a relatively young age. He wrote the following poem in 1952, not long before his own death. It takes the form of a villanelle, other examples of which are Theodore Roethke's "The Waking" and Elizabeth Bishop's "One Art" (see Chapter 8, "Teaching and Learning"). A villanelle consists of nineteen lines: five tercets (three-line stanzas) followed by a quatrain (four-line stanza). The first and third lines of the opening tercet are used alternately to conclude each succeeding tercet, and they are joined to form a rhyme at the poem's end.*

Do not go gentle into that good night,
Old age should burn and rave at close of day;
Rage, rage against the dying of the light.

Though wise men at their end know dark is right,
Because their words had forked no lightning they   5
Do not go gentle into that good night.

Good men, the last wave by, crying how bright
Their frail deeds might have danced in a green bay,
Rage, rage against the dying of the light.

Wild men who caught and sang the sun in flight,   10
And learn, too late, they grieved it on its way,
Do not go gentle into that good night.

Grave men, near death, who see with blinding sight
Blind eyes could blaze like meteors and be gay,
Rage, rage against the dying of the light.   15

And you, my father, there on the sad height,
Curse, bless, me now with your fierce tears, I pray.
Do not go gentle into that good night.
Rage, rage against the dying of the light.   [1952]

THINKING ABOUT THE TEXT

1. In what sense could the night possibly be "good," given that people are
   supposed to "rage" at it?

2. Why do you think Thomas has his speaker refer to "the dying of the light"
   instead of simply to "dying"? What other parts of the poem relate to the
   word *light*?

3. The speaker refers to four kinds of "men." Restate in your own words the
   description given of each. Should Thomas's language about them have
   been less abstract? Why, or why not?

4. What is the effect of climaxing the poem with a reference to "you, my
   father"? If the father had been introduced in the first or second stanzas,
   would the effect have been quite different? If so, how?

5. What is the effect of the villanelle form? Judging by Thomas's poem, do
   you think it is worthwhile for a poet to write in this way, despite the technical challenges of the form? Should teachers of poetry writing push their
   students to write a villanelle? Explain your reasoning.

WISLAWA SZYMBORSKA
On Death, without Exaggeration

Translated by Stanislaw Baranczak and Clare Cavanagh

Although she has written several volumes of poetry, Wislawa Szymborska (b. 1923) was little known outside of her native Poland until she won the Nobel Prize for Literature in 1996. Since then, readers in various countries have come to admire the blend of simplicity, wit, and wisdom in her writing. The Polish version of the following poem appeared in Szymborska's 1986 book The People on the Bridge. *Subsequently, Stanislaw Baranczak and Clare Cavanagh included in it in their 1995 English collection of Szymborska's poems,* View with a Grain of Sand. *We present their translation of the text.*

It can't take a joke,
find a star, make a bridge.
It knows nothing about weaving, mining, farming,
building ships, or baking cakes.

In our planning for tomorrow,   5
it has the final word,
which is always beside the point.

It can't even get the things done
that are part of its trade:
dig a grave,   10
make a coffin,
clean up after itself.

Preoccupied with killing,
it does the job awkwardly,
without system or skill.   15
As though each of us were its first kill.

Oh, it has its triumphs,
but look at its countless defeats,
missed blows,
and repeat attempts!   20

Sometimes it isn't strong enough
to swat a fly from the air.
Many are the caterpillars
that have outcrawled it.

All those bulbs, pods,   25
tentacles, fins, tracheae,

nuptial plumage, and winter fur
show that it has fallen behind
with its halfhearted work.

Ill will won't help   30
and even our lending a hand with wars and coups d'état
is so far not enough.

Hearts beat inside eggs.
Babies' skeletons grow.
Seeds, hard at work, sprout their first tiny pair of leaves   35
and sometimes even tall trees fall away.

Whoever claims that it's omnipotent
is himself living proof
that it's not.

There's no life   40
that couldn't be immortal
if only for a moment.

Death
always arrives by that very moment too late.

In vain it tugs at the knob   45
of the invisible door.
As far as you've come
can't be undone.   [1986]

THINKING ABOUT THE TEXT

1. Although the word *death* appears in the title, it doesn't appear in the text
   of the poem until the next-to-last stanza. Up till then, death is repeatedly
   referred to as "it." What is the effect of this pronoun? What might be
   the effect had Szymborska referred to death more explicitly throughout
   the text?

2. Evidently the speaker is trying not to exaggerate death. What sorts of
   remarks about death might the speaker see as an exaggeration of it?
   Define what you mean by *exaggeration*.

3. What images of death does the speaker create? Refer to specific lines.

4. In the eighth stanza, the speaker mentions that human beings are "lending a hand" to death. Do you take the speaker to be criticizing humanity
   at this point? Why, or why not?

5. Does the order of the stanzas matter? Could the speaker's observations
   about death appear in any order and have the same effect? Explain your
   reasoning.

MAKING COMPARISONS

1. Do all three poems in this cluster speak of death "without exaggeration"? Define what you mean by the term.

2. Does Szymborska's poem strike you as lighter, less serious than Donne's and Thomas's? Refer to specific lines in each text.

3. Suppose that you didn't know who wrote these three poems and were told that only one of the authors was female. What specific aspects of these poems, if any, would you consider as you tried to guess the one written by a woman?

WRITING ABOUT ISSUES

1. Choose Donne's, Thomas's, or Szymborska's poem and write an essay analyzing the poem as an argument for a certain position on death. Specify the main claim and the evidence given in support of it. Feel free to evaluate the argument you discuss, although keep in mind that the artistic success of the poem may or may not depend on whether its argument is fully developed.

2. Write an essay comparing two of the poems in this cluster, focusing on the issue of whether they are basically similar or significantly different in the ideas and feelings they express. Refer to specific lines from each text.

3. Write an essay recalling a specific occasion when you had difficulty deciding whether to accept something as inevitable. In your essay, give details of the occasion, the difficulty, and your ultimate reasoning. Indicate as well what your final decision revealed about you. Perhaps you will want to distinguish between the self you were then and the self you are now. If you wish, refer to any of the poems in this cluster.

4. Imagine that you are on the staff of a nursing home. At a staff meeting, the chief administrator asks you and your colleagues to consider framing and hanging Donne's, Thomas's, or Szymborska's poem in the recreation room. Write a letter to the administrator in which you favor one of these poems or reject them all as inappropriate. Be sure to give reasons for your view.

REFLECTING ON KILLING ANIMALS

GEORGE ORWELL, "Shooting an Elephant"
ANNIE DILLARD, "The Deer at Providencia"

When you think about death, probably you think about your own fate or that of other people. But occasions may arise when you have to ponder the death of an animal. At such times, you may experience a moral dilemma, having to decide whether to allow or prevent the animal's demise. Perhaps you have had to consider ending a sick pet's life. Or perhaps you have wondered whether to protest social practices deadly to animals, such as hunting, lab experiments with monkeys, and the slaughter of cattle for human consumption. Of course, your cultural context may greatly influence your attitude toward the killing of animals, as George Orwell and Annie Dillard show in the following essays. Orwell's essay, written in the mid-1930s, is an account of his service as a British colonial policeman in Burma. Specifically, he recalls a day when he shot an elephant merely to preserve his own status in the village he patrolled. In effect, Orwell reminds his readers that the killing of animals can occur within and be influenced by human power struggles. Dillard's essay, which dates from the early 1980s, is about an expedition she made with other Americans to a village in Ecuador. While there, she and the rest of her group came face to face with the mortal suffering of a deer captured by their hosts. Like Orwell's account, Dillard's suggests that cultural differences can significantly affect people's responses when an animal is slain. At the same time, Dillard's essay raises the issue of whether outsiders to a culture should feel free to criticize its treatment of animals. How would you have reacted in these situations?

BEFORE YOU READ

In the contemporary United States, animals are killed in various ways. Make a list of these ways. Which, if any, do you consider tolerable? Which, if any, do you think can and should be prevented?

GEORGE ORWELL
Shooting an Elephant

George Orwell was the pen name of Eric Arthur Blair (1903–1950). Although born in India, he traveled widely. After his schooling in England, he joined the Indian Imperial Police in Burma, where he served from 1922 to 1927. Later, Orwell lived in Paris and London, studied the lives of coal miners in the north of England, and fought on the Republican side in the Spanish Civil War against the fascist forces of General Francisco Franco. Probably Orwell is best known today for two novels he wrote as warnings against totalitarianism, Animal Farm *(1945) and* Nineteen

Eighty-Four *(1949). But he also wrote much journalism and many essays, often exploring through these writings how political ideologies influence human thinking, language, and behavior. The following essay, which tells of an event during his service in Burma, was first published in 1936.*

In Moulmein, in Lower Burma, I was hated by large numbers of people — the only time in my life that I have been important enough for this to happen to me. I was sub-divisional police officer of the town, and in an aimless, petty kind of way anti-European feeling was very bitter. No one had the guts to raise a riot, but if a European woman went through the bazaars alone somebody would probably spit betel juice over her dress. As a police officer I was an obvious target and was baited whenever it seemed safe to do so. When a nimble Burman tripped me up on the football field and the referee (another Burman) looked the other way, the crowd yelled with hideous laughter. This happened more than once. In the end the sneering yellow faces of young men that met me everywhere, the insults hooted after me when I was at a safe distance, got badly on my nerves. The young Buddhist priests were the worst of all. There were several thousands of them in the town and none of them seemed to have anything to do except stand on street corners and jeer at Europeans.

All this was perplexing and upsetting. For at that time I had already made up my mind that imperialism was an evil thing and the sooner I chucked up my job and got out of it the better. Theoretically — and secretly, of course — I was all for the Burmese and all against their oppressors, the British. As for the job I was doing, I hated it more bitterly than I can perhaps make clear. In a job like that you see the dirty work of Empire at close quarters. The wretched prisoners huddling in the stinking cages of the lockups, the grey, cowed faces of the long-term convicts, the scarred buttocks of the men who had been flogged with bamboos — all these oppressed me with an intolerable sense of guilt. But I could get nothing into perspective. I was young and ill-educated and I had had to think out my problems in the utter silence that is imposed on every Englishman in the East. I did not even know that the British Empire is dying, still less did I know that it is a great deal better than the younger empires that are going to supplant it.° All I knew was that I was stuck between my hatred of the empire I served and my rage against the evil-spirited little beasts who tried to make my job impossible. With one part of my mind I thought of the British Raj° as an unbreakable tyranny, as something clamped down, in *saecula saeculorum*,° upon the will of prostrate peoples; with another part I thought that the greatest joy in the world would be to drive a bayonet into a Buddhist priest's guts. Feelings like these are the normal by-products of imperialism; ask any Anglo-Indian official, if you can catch him off duty.

One day something happened which in a roundabout way was enlightening. It was a tiny incident in itself, but it gave me a better glimpse than I had had

younger empires . . . supplant it: In 1936, Hitler and Stalin were in power and World War II was only three years away.   **Raj:** Sovereignty.   *saecula saeculorum:* From time immemorial.

before of the real nature of imperialism — the real motives for which despotic governments act. Early one morning the sub-inspector at a police station the other end of the town rang me up on the phone and said that an elephant was ravaging the bazaar. Would I please come and do something about it? I did not know what I could do, but I wanted to see what was happening and I got on to a pony and started out. I took my rifle, an old .44 Winchester and much too small to kill an elephant, but I thought the noise might be useful *in terrorem.*° Various Burmans stopped me on the way and told me about the elephant's doings. It was not, of course, a wild elephant, but a tame one which had gone "must."° It had been chained up, as tame elephants always are when their attack of "must" is due, but on the previous night it had broken its chain and escaped. Its mahout,° the only person who could manage it when it was in that state, had set out in pursuit, but had taken the wrong direction and was now twelve hours' journey away, and in the morning the elephant had suddenly reappeared in the town. The Burmese population had no weapons and were quite helpless against it. It had already destroyed somebody's bamboo hut, killed a cow, and raided some fruit-stalls and devoured the stock; also it had met the municipal rubbish van and, when the driver jumped out and took to his heels, had turned the van over and inflicted violences upon it.

The Burmese sub-inspector and some Indian constables were waiting for me in the quarter where the elephant had been seen. It was a very poor quarter, a labyrinth of squalid bamboo huts, thatched with palm-leaf, winding all over a steep hillside. I remember that it was a cloudy, stuffy morning at the beginning of the rains. We began questioning people as to where the elephant had gone, and, as usual, failed to get any definite information. That is invariably the case in the East; a story always sounds clear enough at a distance, but the nearer you get to the scene of events the vaguer it becomes. Some of the people said that the elephant had gone in one direction, some said that he had gone in another, some professed not even to have heard of an elephant. I had almost made up my mind that the whole story was a pack of lies, when we heard yells a little distance away. There was a loud, scandalized cry of "Go away, child! Go away this instant!" and an old woman with a switch in her hand came round the corner of a hut, violently shooing away a crowd of naked children. Some more women followed, clicking their tongues and exclaiming; evidently there was something that the children ought not to have seen. I rounded the hut and saw a man's dead body sprawling in the mud. He was an Indian, a black Dravidian coolie, almost naked, and he could not have been dead many minutes. The people said that the elephant had come suddenly upon him round the corner of the hut, caught him with its trunk, put its foot on his back, and ground him into the earth. This was the rainy season and the ground was soft, and his face had scored a trench a foot deep and a couple of yards long. He was lying on his belly with arms crucified and head sharply twisted to one side. His face was coated with mud, the eyes wide open, the teeth bared and grinning with an expression of unendurable agony.

---

in terrorem: In terrorizing him.   **must:** That is, gone into a state of frenzy.   **mahout:** A keeper and driver of an elephant.

(Never tell me, by the way, that the dead look peaceful. Most of the corpses I have seen looked devilish.) The friction of the great beast's foot had stripped the skin from his back as neatly as one skins a rabbit. As soon as I saw the dead man I sent an orderly to a friend's house nearby to borrow an elephant rifle. I had already sent back the pony, not wanting it to go mad with fright and throw me if it smelled the elephant.

The orderly came back in a few minutes with a rifle and five cartridges, and meanwhile some Burmans had arrived and told us that the elephant was in the paddy fields below, only a few hundred yards away. As I started forward practically the whole population of the quarter flocked out of the houses and followed me. They had seen the rifle and were all shouting excitedly that I was going to shoot the elephant. They had not shown much interest in the elephant when he was merely ravaging their homes, but it was different now that he was going to be shot. It was a bit of fun to them, as it would be to an English crowd; besides they wanted the meat. It made me vaguely uneasy. I had no intention of shooting the elephant—I had merely sent for the rifle to defend myself if necessary—and it is always unnerving to have a crowd following you. I marched down the hill, looking and feeling a fool, with the rifle over my shoulder and an ever-growing army of people jostling at my heels. At the bottom, when you got away from the huts, there was a metalled road and beyond that a miry waste of paddy fields a thousand yards across, not yet ploughed but soggy from the first rains and dotted with coarse grass. The elephant was standing eight yards from the road, his left side towards us. He took not the slightest notice of the crowd's approach. He was tearing up bunches of grass, beating them against his knees to clean them and stuffing them into his mouth.

I had halted on the road. As soon as I saw the elephant I knew with perfect certainty that I ought not to shoot him. It is a serious matter to shoot a working elephant—it is comparable to destroying a huge and costly piece of machinery—and obviously one ought not to do it if it can possibly be avoided. And at that distance, peacefully eating, the elephant looked no more dangerous than a cow. I thought then and I think now that his attack of "must" was already passing off; in which case he would merely wander harmlessly about until the mahout came back and caught him. Moreover, I did not in the least want to shoot him. I decided that I would watch him for a little while to make sure that he did not turn savage again, and then go home.

But at that moment I glanced round at the crowd that had followed me. It was an immense crowd, two thousand at the least and growing every minute. It blocked the road for a long distance on either side. I looked at the sea of yellow faces above the garish clothes—faces all happy and excited over this bit of fun, all certain that the elephant was going to be shot. They were watching me as they would watch a conjurer about to perform a trick. They did not like me, but with the magical rifle in my hands I was momentarily worth watching. And suddenly I realized that I should have to shoot the elephant after all. The people expected it of me and I had got to do it; I could feel their two thousand wills pressing me forward, irresistibly. And it was at this moment, as I stood there with the rifle in my hands, that I first grasped the hollowness, the futility of the white man's dominion

5

in the East. Here was I, the white man with his gun, standing in front of the unarmed native crowd—seemingly the leading actor of the piece; but in reality I was only an absurd puppet pushed to and fro by the will of those yellow faces behind. I perceived in this moment that when the white man turns tyrant it is his own freedom that he destroys. He becomes a sort of hollow, posing dummy, the conventionalized figure of a sahib.° For it is the condition of his rule that he shall spend his life in trying to impress the "natives," and so in every crisis he has got to do what the "natives" expect of him. He wears a mask, and his face grows to fit it. I had got to shoot the elephant. I had committed myself to doing it when I sent for the rifle. A sahib has got to act like a sahib; he has got to appear resolute, to know his own mind and do definite things. To come all that way, rifle in hand, with two thousand people marching at my heels, and then to trail feebly away, having done nothing—no, that was impossible. The crowd would laugh at me. And my whole life, every white man's life in the East, was one long struggle not to be laughed at.

But I did not want to shoot the elephant. I watched him beating his bunch of grass against his knees, with the preoccupied grandmotherly air that elephants have. It seemed to me that it would be murder to shoot him. At that age I was not squeamish about killing animals, but I had never shot an elephant and never wanted to. (Somehow it always seems worse to kill a *large* animal.) Besides, there was the beast's owner to be considered. Alive, the elephant was worth at least a hundred pounds; dead, he would only be worth the value of his tusks, five pounds, possibly. But I had got to act quickly. I turned to some experienced-looking Burmans who had been there when we arrived, and asked them how the elephant had been behaving. They all said the same thing: he took no notice of you if you left him alone, but he might charge if you went too close to him.

It was perfectly clear to me what I ought to do. I ought to walk up to within, say, twenty-five yards of the elephant and test his behavior. If he charged I could shoot, if he took no notice of me it would be safe to leave him until the mahout came back. But also I knew that I was going to do no such thing. I was a poor shot with a rifle and the ground was soft mud into which one would sink at every step. If the elephant charged and I missed him, I should have about as much chance as a toad under a steamroller. But even then I was not thinking particularly of my own skin, only of the watchful yellow faces behind. For at that moment, with the crowd watching me, I was not afraid in the ordinary sense, as I would have been if I had been alone. A white man mustn't be frightened in front of "natives"; and so, in general, he isn't frightened. The sole thought in my mind was that if any-thing went wrong those two thousand Burmans would see me pursued, caught, trampled on, and reduced to a grinning corpse like that Indian up the hill. And if that happened it was quite probable that some of them would laugh. That would never do. There was only one alternative. I shoved the cartridges into the maga-zine and lay down on the road to get a better aim.

The crowd grew very still, and a deep, low, happy sigh, as of people who see   10
the theater curtain go up at last, breathed from innumerable throats. They were

---

sahib: Term used among Hindus and Muslims in Colonial India when speaking of an official.

going to have their bit of fun after all. The rifle was a beautiful German thing with cross-hair sights. I did not then know that in shooting an elephant one would shoot to cut an imaginary bar running from ear-hole to ear-hole. I ought, therefore, as the elephant was sideways on, to have aimed straight at his ear-hole; actually I aimed several inches in front of this, thinking the brain would be further forward.

When I pulled the trigger I did not hear the bang or feel the kick — one never does when a shot goes home — but I heard the devilish roar of glee that went up from the crowd. In that instant, in too short a time, one would have thought, even for the bullet to get there, a mysterious, terrible change had come over the elephant. He neither stirred nor fell, but every line on his body had altered. He looked suddenly stricken, shrunken, immensely old, as though the frightful impact of the bullet had paralyzed him without knocking him down. At last, after what seemed a long time — it might have been five seconds, I dare say — he sagged flabbily to his knees. His mouth slobbered. An enormous senility seemed to have settled upon him. One could have imagined him thousands of years old. I fired again into the same spot. At the second shot he did not collapse but climbed with desperate slowness to his feet and stood weakly upright, with legs sagging and head drooping. I fired a third time. That was the shot that did for him. You could see the agony of it jolt his whole body and knock the last remnant of strength from his legs. But in falling he seemed for a moment to rise, for as his hind legs collapsed beneath him he seemed to tower upwards like a huge rock toppling, his trunk reaching skywards like a tree. He trumpeted, for the first and only time. And then down he came, his belly towards me, with a crash that seemed to shake the ground even where I lay.

I got up. The Burmans were already racing past me across the mud. It was obvious that the elephant would never rise again, but he was not dead. He was breathing very rhythmically with long rattling gasps, his great mound of a side painfully rising and falling. His mouth was wide open — I could see far down into the caverns of pale pink throat. I waited a long time for him to die, but his breathing did not weaken. Finally, I fired my two remaining shots into the spot where I thought his heart must be. The thick blood welled out of him like red velvet, but still he did not die. His body did not even jerk when the shots hit him, the tortured breathing continued without a pause. He was dying, very slowly and in great agony, but in some world remote from me where not even a bullet could damage him further. I felt that I had got to put an end to that dreadful noise. It seemed dreadful to see the great beast lying there, powerless to move and yet powerless to die, and not even to be able to finish him. I sent back for my small rifle and poured shot after shot into his heart and down his throat. They seemed to make no impression. The tortured gasps continued as steadily as the ticking of a clock.

In the end I could not stand it any longer and went away. I heard later that it took him half an hour to die. Burmans were bringing dahs° and baskets even before I left, and I was told they had stripped his body almost to the bones by the afternoon.

dahs: Large heavy knives.

Afterwards, of course, there were endless discussions about the shooting of the elephant. The owner was furious, but he was only an Indian and could do nothing. Besides, legally I had done the right thing, for a mad elephant has to be killed, like a mad dog, if its owner fails to control it. Among the Europeans opinion was divided. The older men said I was right, the younger men said it was a damn shame to shoot an elephant for killing a coolie, because an elephant was worth more than any damn Coringhee coolie. And afterwards I was very glad that the coolie had been killed; it put me legally in the right and it gave me a sufficient pretext for shooting the elephant. I often wondered whether any of the others grasped that I had done it solely to avoid looking a fool.   [1936]

THINKING ABOUT THE TEXT

1. Why is the writer focusing on this particular day in his past? What is he using it to illustrate? What other kinds of significance might one find in this episode?

2. On the basis of this essay, how would you describe the younger Orwell's attitude toward the Burmese villagers? Cite specific statements that you find especially helpful in answering this question. Does the older Orwell who is writing the essay seem much different from his younger self? Again, identify specific statements that affect your thinking on this issue.

3. According to the essay, at what points might the shooting of the elephant have been avoided? Why at these points did the younger Orwell nevertheless find himself heading toward the act of killing?

4. Reread the description of the elephant's suffering after he is shot. How does the writer's language encourage you to compare the elephant's physical decline with the eventual decline of the British Empire?

5. "Shooting an Elephant" has appeared in many essay anthologies, especially those intended for composition classes. Why is it anthologized so much, do you think? Should it be? Identify some of your warrants or assumptions in addressing this issue of evaluation.

ANNIE DILLARD
The Deer at Providencia

Annie Dillard (b. 1945) teaches creative writing at Wesleyan University in Middletown, Connecticut. She first came to national attention with her 1975 Pulitzer Prize–winning book Pilgrim at Tinker Creek, *which chronicled her nature walks in Virginia's Roanoke Valley. Since then, she has published several full-length books, including* Holy the Firm *(1978),* Living by Fiction *(1982),* For the Time Being *(1999), an autobiography entitled* An American Childhood *(1987), and a novel called* The Living *(1982). She is also a poet, having produced the collections* Tickets for a Prayer Wheel *(1974) and* Mornings Like This *(1995). But many of her readers are most familiar with Dillard's essays, which often deal with her travels to various places, her explorations of nature, and her spiritual quests. The following piece appears in her 1982 volume of essays* Teaching a Stone to Talk.

There were four of us North Americans in the jungle, in the Ecuadorian jungle on the banks of the Napo River in the Amazon watershed. The other three North Americans were metropolitan men. We stayed in tents in one riverside village, and visited others. At the village called Providencia we saw a sight which moved us, and which shocked the men.

The first thing we saw when we climbed the riverbank to the village of Providencia was the deer. It was roped to a tree on the grass clearing near the thatch shelter where we would eat lunch.

The deer was small, about the size of a whitetail fawn, but apparently full-grown. It had a rope around its neck and three feet caught in the rope. Someone said that the dogs had caught it that morning and the villagers were going to cook and eat it that night.

This clearing lay at the edge of the little thatched-hut village. We could see the villagers going about their business, scattering feed corn for hens about their houses, and wandering down paths to the river to bathe. The village headman was our host; he stood beside us as we watched the deer struggle. Several village boys were interested in the deer; they formed part of the circle we made around it in the clearing. So also did four businessmen from Quito who were attempting to guide us around the jungle. Few of the very different people standing in this circle had a common language. We watched the deer, and no one said much.

The deer lay on its side at the rope's very end, so the rope lacked slack to let it rest its head in the dust. It was "pretty," delicate of bone like all deer, and thin-skinned for the tropics. Its skin looked virtually hairless, in fact, and almost translucent, like a membrane. Its neck was no thicker than my wrist; it was rubbed open on the rope, and gashed. Trying to paw itself free of the rope, the deer had scratched its own neck with its hooves. The raw underside of its neck showed red stripes and some bruises bleeding inside the muscles. Now three of its feet were hooked in the rope under its jaw. It could not stand, of course, on one leg, so it could not move to slacken the rope and ease the pull on its throat and enable it to rest its head.

Repeatedly the deer paused, motionless, its eyes veiled, with only its rib cage in motion, and its breaths the only sound. Then, after I would think, "It has given up; now it will die," it would heave. The rope twanged; the tree leaves clattered; the deer's free foot beat the ground. We stepped back and held our breaths. It thrashed, kicking, but only one leg moved; the other three legs tightened inside the rope's loop. Its hip jerked; its spine shook. Its eyes rolled; its tongue, thick with

5

spittle, pushed in and out. Then it would rest again. We watched this for fifteen minutes.

Once three young native boys charged in, released its trapped legs, and jumped back to the circle of people. But instantly the deer scratched up its neck with its hooves and snared its forelegs in the rope again. It was easy to imagine a third and then a fourth leg soon stuck, like Brer Rabbit and the Tar Baby.

We watched the deer from the circle, and then we drifted on to lunch. Our palm-roofed shelter stood on a grassy promontory from which we could see the deer tied to the tree, pigs and hens walking under village houses, and black-and-white cattle standing in the river. There was even a breeze.

Lunch, which was the second and better lunch we had that day, was hot and fried. There was a big fish called *doncella*, a kind of catfish, dipped whole in corn flour and beaten egg, then deep fried. With our fingers we pulled soft fragments of it from its sides to our plates, and ate; it was delicate fish-flesh, fresh and mild. Someone found the roe, and I ate of that too—it was fat and stronger, like egg yolk, naturally enough, and warm.

There was also a stew of meat in shreds with rice and pale brown gravy. I had asked what kind of deer it was tied to the tree; Pepe had answered in Spanish, "*Gama.*" Now they told us this was *gama* too, stewed. I suspect the word means merely game or venison. At any rate, I heard that the village dogs had cornered another deer just yesterday, and it was this deer which we were now eating in full sight of the whole article. It was good. I was surprised at its tenderness. But it is a fact that high levels of lactic acid, which builds up in muscle tissues during exertion, tenderizes.

After the fish and meat we ate bananas fried in chunks and served on a tray; they were sweet and full of flavor. I felt terrific. My shirt was wet and cool from swimming; I had had a night's sleep, two decent walks, three meals, and a swim—everything tasted good. From time to time each one of us, separately, would look beyond our shaded roof to the sunny spot where the deer was still convulsing in the dust. Our meal completed, we walked around the deer and back to the boats.

That night I learned that while we were watching the deer, the others were watching me.

We four North Americans grew close in the jungle in a way that was not the usual artificial intimacy of travelers. We liked each other. We stayed up all that night talking, murmuring, as though we rocked on hammocks slung above time. The others were from big cities: New York, Washington, Boston. They all said that I had no expression on my face when I was watching the deer—or at any rate, not the expression they expected.

They had looked to see how I, the only woman, and the youngest, was taking the sight of the deer's struggles. I looked detached, apparently, or hard, or calm, or focused, still. I don't know. I was thinking. I remember feeling very old and energetic. I could say like Thoreau that I have traveled widely in Roanoke, Virginia. I have thought a great deal about carnivorousness; I eat meat. These things are not issues; they are mysteries.

Gentlemen of the city, what surprises you? That there is suffering here, or   15
that I know it?

We lay in the tent and talked. "If it had been my wife," one man said with special vigor, amazed, "she wouldn't have cared *what* was going on; she would have dropped *everything* right at that moment and gone in the village from here to there to there, she would not have *stopped* until that animal was out of its suffering one way or another. She couldn't *bear* to see a creature in agony like that."

I nodded.

Now I am home. When I wake I comb my hair before the mirror above my dresser. Every morning for the past two years I have seen in that mirror, beside my sleep-softened face, the blackened face of a burnt man. It is a wire-service photograph clipped from a newspaper and taped to my mirror. The caption reads: "Alan McDonald in Miami hospital bed." All you can see in the photograph is a smudged triangle of face from his eyelids to his lower lip; the rest is bandages. You cannot see the expression in his eyes; the bandages shade them.

The story, headed MAN BURNED FOR SECOND TIME, begins:

"Why does God hate me?" Alan McDonald asked from his hospital bed.
    "When the gunpowder went off, I couldn't believe it," he said. "I just couldn't believe it. I said, 'No, God couldn't do this to me again.'"

He was in a burn ward in Miami, in serious condition. I do not even know if he lived. I wrote him a letter at the time, cringing.

He had been burned before, thirteen years previously, by flaming gasoline.   20
For years he had been having his body restored and his face remade in dozens of operations. He had been a boy, and then a burnt boy. He had already been stunned by what could happen, by how life could veer.

Once I read that people who survive bad burns tend to go crazy; they have a very high suicide rate. Medicine cannot ease their pain; drugs just leak away, soaking the sheets, because there is no skin to hold them in. The people just lie there and weep. Later they kill themselves. They had not known, before they were burned, that the world included such suffering, that life could permit them personally such pain.

This time a bowl of gunpowder had exploded on McDonald.

"I didn't realize what had happened at first," he recounted. "And then I heard that sound from 13 years ago. I was burning. I rolled to put the fire out and I thought, 'Oh God, not again.'
    "If my friend hadn't been there, I would have jumped into a canal with a rock around my neck."

His wife concludes the piece, "Man, it just isn't fair."

I read the whole clipping again every morning. This is the Big Time here, every minute of it. Will someone please explain to Alan McDonald in his dignity, to the deer at Providencia in his dignity, what is going on? And mail me the carbon.

When we walked by the deer at Providencia for the last time, I said to Pepe, with a pitying glance at the deer, *"Pobrecito"* — "poor little thing." But I was trying out Spanish. I knew at the time it was a ridiculous thing to say.   [1982]

THINKING ABOUT THE TEXT

1. Why did the men with whom Dillard was traveling expect her to act differently than she did? How do you think she should have behaved when she saw the villagers tormenting the deer? How do you feel about the satisfaction she derived from the deer-meat stew? Identify some of the warrants or assumptions behind your answers.

2. What do you make of Dillard's obsession with Alan McDonald? Do you believe his case belongs in this essay? Why, or why not?

3. Dillard declares, "These things are not issues; they are mysteries." What distinction does she make between *issues* and *mysteries*? How does she define these terms? Do you agree that the things she reports are better viewed as mysteries than as issues? Explain your reasoning.

4. At the end of the essay, Dillard returns to a moment back in Ecuador; she could have described this moment in the first section of the essay. Why do you think she chooses to conclude with it?

5. What does the word *Providencia* signify? (You may need to consult a classmate or a Spanish-English dictionary.) Why do you suppose Dillard included the word in her title?

MAKING COMPARISONS

1. Does Dillard seem less narrow-minded than Orwell? Identify details of both texts that you think especially important for you to consider as you answer this question.

2. Orwell's essay is pretty much one continuous story, whereas Dillard begins with the story of the deer and then jumps to her ongoing obsession with Alan McDonald. Does Dillard's essay seem less dramatic or intense than Orwell's because it is less continuous? Why, or why not?

3. Obviously gender is relevant to Dillard's essay. Is it as relevant to Orwell's essay? Explain.

WRITING ABOUT ISSUES

1. Choose either Orwell's or Dillard's piece and write an essay explaining how you think the writer should have acted toward the animal discussed.

Take into account the specific circumstances that the writer was in. Also provide reasons for your judgment.

2. Could Dillard's statement "these things are not issues; they are mysteries" be applied to Orwell's essay? Would he consider the statement relevant to his own piece? Write an essay answering these questions. Make clear how Dillard evidently defines *issues* and *mysteries*.

3. Write an essay analyzing your behavior at a time when you had to decide how much to endorse the killing of a certain animal or of a certain group of animals. What thoughts ran through your mind? What specific pressures did you face? How did you believe your conduct would be viewed by others? Indicate any significant differences between your younger self and the kind of person you are now.

4. Research a group that is against hunting, against the killing of animals in lab experiments, or against the killing of animals for human consumption. Find out especially about the rhetorical strategies this group uses to advance its cause. Then write an essay identifying and evaluating some of these methods of persuasion.

ESCAPING LIFE: CRITICAL COMMENTARIES ON MARSHA NORMAN'S *'NIGHT, MOTHER*

MARSHA NORMAN, *'night, Mother*

CRITICAL COMMENTARIES:

LISA J. MCDONNELL, From "Diverse Similitude: Beth Henley and Marsha Norman"

SALLY BROWDER, From "'I Thought You Were Mine': Marsha Norman's *'night, Mother*"

JENNY S. SPENCER, From "Norman's *'night, Mother*: Psycho-drama of Female Identity"

Should people intent on suicide always be stopped from committing it? Is suicide ever justifiable? For the families and loved ones of those who have killed themselves, the act is usually an occasion for pain instead of rejoicing. But increasingly, Americans debate the first two questions. In large part, they do so because of the new prominence given physician-assisted suicide. Even as the Supreme Court considered whether state laws could ban this practice, doctors such as Jack Kevorkian and Timothy Quill publicly confessed to helping physically ill or incapacitated patients kill themselves. Is suicide appropriate if the reasons for it are purely psychological? This question confronts the two characters in Marsha Norman's 1983 play *'night, Mother*. Near the start, Jessie announces to her mother, Thelma, that she will kill herself later that evening, and Thelma does everything she can to change her daughter's mind. As you read the play, consider whether you approve of Jessie's plan or side with Thelma in her efforts to thwart it. To help you weigh their positions, we include three commentaries on their conflict. Lisa McDonnell sees Jessie as using death to achieve selfhood, Sally Browder examines the psychological dynamics of the play's mother-daughter relationship, and Jenny Spencer observes that women's responses to the play differ from men's.

BEFORE YOU READ

What influences your view of suicide? Would you ever approve of someone's committing it? If so, under what circumstances?

MARSHA NORMAN
'night, Mother

Marsha Norman (b. 1947) grew up in Louisville, Kentucky, and has long been associated with the Actors Theatre there. Her plays include Getting Out *(1977),* Traveler in the Dark *(1984), and, most recently,* Trudy Blue *(1995). In 1991, her script for the musical* The Secret Garden *won her a Tony Award. The play* 'night, Mother, *for which Norman won the Pulitzer Prize, premiered at the American Repertory Theatre in Cambridge, Massachusetts, in January 1983. In March of that year, it was produced on Broadway. Both of these productions featured Kathy Bates as Jessie and Anne Pitoniak as Thelma; in the 1986 film version, the roles were played by Sissy Spacek and Anne Bancroft. As a theater piece,* 'night, Mother *has aroused a lot of attention for its treatment of suicide. It is also distinctive in its time span. With plays and movies, hardly ever does the time span represented coincide with the work's actual running time. This play covers about ninety minutes in the lives of its characters and takes the same amount of time to perform. Indeed, in most productions of the play, the time shown by the clocks on the set is the same as the actual time when the play is performed in the evening.*

CHARACTERS

JESSIE CATES, *in her late thirties or early forties, is pale and vaguely unsteady physically. It is only in the last year that Jessie has gained control of her mind and body, and tonight she is determined to hold on to that control. She wears pants and a long black sweater with deep pockets, which contain scraps of paper, and there may be a pencil behind her ear or a pen clipped to one of the pockets of the sweater.*

As a rule, Jessie doesn't feel much like talking. Other people have rarely found her quirky sense of humor amusing. She has a peaceful energy on this night, a sense of purpose, but is clearly aware of the time passing moment by moment. Oddly enough, Jessie has never been as communicative or as enjoyable as she is on this evening, but we must know she has not always been this way. There is a familiarity between these two women that comes from having lived together for a long time. There is a shorthand to the talk and a sense of routine comfort in the way they relate to each other physically. Naturally, there are also routine aggravations.

THELMA CATES, MAMA, *is Jessie's mother, in her late fifties or early sixties. She has begun to feel her age and so takes it easy when she can, or when it serves her purpose to let someone help her. But she speaks quickly and enjoys talking. She believes that things are what she says they are. Her sturdiness is more a mental quality than a physical one, finally. She is chatty and nosy, and this is her house.*

The play takes place in a relatively new house built way out on a country road, with a living room and connecting kitchen, and a center hall that leads off to the bedrooms. A pull cord in the hall ceiling releases a ladder which leads to the attic. One of these bedrooms opens directly onto the hall, and its entry should be visible to everyone in the audience. It should be, in fact, the focal point of the entire set, and the lighting should make it disappear completely at times and draw the entire set into it at others. It is a point of both threat and promise. It is an ordinary door that opens onto absolute nothingness. That door is the point of all the action, and the utmost care should be given to its design and construction.

The living room is cluttered with magazines and needlework catalogues, ashtrays and candy dishes. Examples of Mama's needlework are everywhere — pillows, afghans, and quilts, doilies and rugs, and they are quite nice examples. The house is more comfortable than messy, but there is quite a lot to keep in place here. It is more personal than charming. It is not quaint. Under no circumstances should the set and its dressing make a judgment about the intelligence or taste of Jessie and Mama. It should simply indicate that they are very specific real people who happen to live in a particular part of the country. Heavy accents, which would further distance the audience from Jessie and Mama, are also wrong.

The time is the present, with the action beginning about 8:15. Clocks onstage in the kitchen and on a table in the living room should run throughout the performance and be visible to the audience.

There will be no intermission.

Mama stretches to reach the cupcakes in a cabinet in the kitchen. She can't see them, but she can feel around for them, and she's eager to have one, so she's working pretty hard at it. This may be the most serious exercise Mama ever gets. She finds a cupcake, the coconut-covered, raspberry-and-marshmallow-filled kind known as a snowball, but sees that there's one missing from the package. She calls to Jessie, who is apparently somewhere else in the house.

MAMA (*unwrapping the cupcake*):   Jessie, it's the last snowball, sugar. Put it on the list, O.K.? And we're out of Hershey bars, and where's that peanut brittle? I think maybe Dawson's been in it again. I ought to put a big mirror on the refrigerator door. That'll keep him out of my treats, won't it? You hear me, honey? *(Then more to herself.)* I hate it when the coconut falls off. Why does the coconut fall off?

Jessie enters from her bedroom, carrying a stack of newspapers.

JESSIE: We got any old towels?

MAMA: There you are!

JESSIE *(holding a towel that was on the stack of newspapers)*:   Towels you don't want anymore. *(Picking up Mama's snowball wrapper.)* How about this swimming towel Loretta gave us? Beach towel, that's the name of it. You want it? *(Mama shakes her head no.)*

MAMA: What have you been doing in there?

JESSIE: And a big piece of plastic like a rubber sheet or something. Garbage bags would do if there's enough.

MAMA: Don't go making a big mess, Jessie. It's eight o'clock already.

JESSIE: Maybe an old blanket or towels we got in a soap box sometime?

MAMA: I said don't make a mess. Your hair is black enough, hon.

JESSIE *(continuing to search the kitchen cabinets, finding two or three more towels to add to her stack)*:   It's not for my hair, Mama. What about some old pillows anywhere, or a foam cushion out of a yard chair would be real good.

MAMA: You haven't forgot what night it is, have you? *(Holding up her fingernails.)* They're all chipped, see? I've been waiting all week, Jess. It's Saturday night, sugar.

JESSIE: I know. I got it on the schedule.

MAMA *(crossing to the living room)*:   You want me to wash 'em now or are you making your mess first? *(Looking at the snowball.)* We're out of these. Did I say that already?

JESSIE: There's more coming tomorrow. I ordered you a whole case.

MAMA *(checking the TV Guide)*:   A whole case will go stale, Jessie.

JESSIE: They can go in the freezer till you're ready for them. Where's Daddy's gun?

MAMA: In the attic.

JESSIE: Where in the attic? I looked your whole nap and couldn't find it anywhere.

MAMA: One of his shoeboxes, I think.

JESSIE: Full of shoes. I looked already.

MAMA: Well, you didn't look good enough, then. There's that box from the ones he wore to the hospital. When he died, they told me I could have them back, but I never did like those shoes.

JESSIE *(pulling them out of her pocket)*:   I found the bullets. They were in an old milk can.

MAMA *(as Jessie starts for the hall)*:   Dawson took the shotgun, didn't he? Hand me that basket, hon.

JESSIE *(getting the basket for her)*:   Dawson better not've taken that pistol.

MAMA *(stopping her again)*:   Now my glasses, please. *(Jessie returns to get the glasses.)* I told him to take those rubber boots, too, but he said they were for fishing. I told him to take up fishing.

Jessie reaches for the cleaning spray and cleans Mama's glasses for her.

JESSIE: He's just too lazy to climb up there, Mama. Or maybe he's just being smart. That floor's not very steady.

MAMA *(getting out a piece of knitting)*:   It's not a floor at all, hon, it's a board now and then. Measure this for me. I need six inches.

JESSIE *(as she measures)*:   Dawson could probably use some of those clothes up there. Somebody should have them. You ought to call the Salvation Army before the whole thing falls in on you. Six inches exactly.

MAMA: It's plenty safe! As long as you don't go up there.

JESSIE *(turning to go again)*:   I'm careful.

MAMA: What do you want the gun for, Jess?

JESSIE *(not returning this time. Opening the ladder in the hall.)*:   Protection. *(She steadies the ladder as Mama talks.)*

MAMA: You take the TV way too serious, hon. I've never seen a criminal in my life. This is way too far to come for what's out here to steal. Never seen one.

JESSIE *(taking her first step up)*:   Except for Ricky.

MAMA: Ricky is mixed up. That's not a crime.

JESSIE: Get your hands washed. I'll be right back. And get 'em real dry. You dry your hands till I get back or it's no go, all right?

MAMA: I thought Dawson told you not to go up those stairs.

JESSIE *(going up)*:   He did.

MAMA: I don't like the idea of a gun, Jess.

JESSIE *(calling down from the attic)*:   Which shoebox, do you remember?

MAMA: Black.

JESSIE: The box was black?

MAMA: The shoes were black.

JESSIE: That doesn't help much, Mother.

MAMA: I'm not trying to help, sugar. *(No answer.)* We don't have anything anybody'd want, Jessie. I mean, I don't even want what we got, Jessie.

JESSIE: Neither do I. Wash your hands. *(Mama gets up and crosses to stand under the ladder.)*

MAMA: You come down from there before you have a fit. I can't come up and get you, you know.

JESSIE: I know.

MAMA: We'll just hand it over to them when they come, how's that? Whatever they want, the criminals.

JESSIE: That's a good idea, Mama.

MAMA: Ricky will grow out of this and be a real fine boy, Jess. But I have to tell you, I wouldn't want Ricky to know we had a gun in the house.

JESSIE: Here it is. I found it.

MAMA: It's just something Ricky's going through. Maybe he's in with some bad people. He just needs some time, sugar. He'll get back in school or get a job or one day you'll get a call and he'll say he's sorry for all the trouble he's caused and invite you out for supper someplace dress-up.

JESSIE *(coming back down the steps)*:   Don't worry. It's not for him, it's for me.

MAMA: I didn't think you would shoot your own boy, Jessie. I know you've felt like it, well, we've all felt like shooting somebody, but we don't do it. I just don't think we need . . .

JESSIE *(interrupting)*:   Your hands aren't washed. Do you want a manicure or not?

MAMA: Yes, I do, but . . .

JESSIE *(crossing to the chair)*:   Then wash your hands and don't talk to me any-more about Ricky. Those two rings he took were the last valuable things *I* had, so now he's started in on other people, door to door. I hope they put him away sometime. I'd turn him in myself if I knew where he was.

MAMA: You don't mean that.

JESSIE: Every word. Wash your hands and that's the last time I'm telling you.

Jessie sits down with the gun and starts cleaning it, pushing the cylinder out, check-ing to see that the chambers and barrel are empty, then putting some oil on a small patch of cloth and pushing it through the barrel with the push rod that was in the box. Mama goes to the kitchen and washes her hands, as instructed, trying not to show her concern about the gun.

MAMA: I shoulda got you to bring down that milk can. Agnes Fletcher sold hers to somebody with a flea market for forty dollars apiece.

JESSIE: I'll go back and get it in a minute. There's a wagon wheel up there, too. There's even a churn. I'll get it all if you want.

MAMA *(coming over, now, taking over now)*:   What are you doing?

JESSIE: The barrel has to be clean, Mama. Old powder, dust gets in it . . .

MAMA: What for?

JESSIE: I told you.

MAMA *(reaching for the gun)*:   And I told you, we don't get criminals out here.

JESSIE *(quickly pulling it to her)*:   And I told you . . . *(Then trying to be calm.)* The gun is for me.

MAMA: Well, you can have it if you want. When I die, you'll get it all, anyway.

JESSIE: I'm going to kill myself, Mama.

MAMA *(returning to the sofa)*:   Very funny. Very funny.

JESSIE: I am.

MAMA: You are not! Don't even say such a thing, Jessie.

JESSIE: How would you know if I didn't say it? You want it to be a surprise? You're lying there in your bed or maybe you're just brushing your teeth and you hear this . . . noise down the hall?

MAMA: Kill yourself.

JESSIE: Shoot myself. In a couple of hours.

MAMA: It must be time for your medicine.

JESSIE: Took it already.

MAMA: What's the matter with you?

JESSIE: Not a thing. Feel fine.

MAMA: You feel fine. You're just going to kill yourself.

JESSIE: Waited until I felt good enough, in fact.

MAMA: Don't make jokes, Jessie. I'm too old for jokes.

JESSIE: It's not a joke, Mama.

Mama watches for a moment in silence.

MAMA: That gun's no good, you know. He broke it right before he died. He dropped it in the mud one day.

JESSIE: Seems O.K. *(She spins the chamber, cocks the pistol, and pulls the trigger. The gun is not yet loaded, so all we hear is the click, but it will definitely work. It's also obvious that Jessie knows her way around a gun. Mama cannot speak.)* I had Cecil's all ready in there, just in case I couldn't find this one, but I'd rather use Daddy's.

MAMA: Those bullets are at least fifteen years old.

JESSIE *(pulling out another box)*:   These are from last week.

MAMA: Where did you get those?

JESSIE: Feed store Dawson told me about.

MAMA: Dawson!

JESSIE: I told him I was worried about prowlers. He said he thought it was a good idea. He told me what kind to ask for.

MAMA: If he had any idea . . .

JESSIE: He took it as a compliment. He thought I might be taking an interest in things. He got through telling me all about the bullets and then he said we ought to talk like this more often.

MAMA: And where was I while this was going on?

JESSIE: On the phone with Agnes. About the milk can, I guess. Anyway, I asked Dawson if he thought they'd send me some bullets and he said he'd just call for me, because he knew they'd send them if he told them to. And he was absolutely right. Here they are.

MAMA: How could he do that?

JESSIE: Just trying to help, Mama.

MAMA: And then I told you where the gun was.

JESSIE *(smiling, enjoying this joke)*:   See? Everybody's doing what they can.

MAMA: You told me it was for protection!

JESSIE: It *is!* I'm still doing your nails, though. Want to try that new Chinaberry color?

MAMA: Well, I'm calling Dawson right now. We'll just see what he has to say about this little stunt.

JESSIE: Dawson doesn't have any more to do with this.

MAMA: He's your brother.

JESSIE: And that's all.

MAMA *(stands up, moves toward the phone)*:   Dawson will put a stop to this. Yes he will. He'll take the gun away.

JESSIE: If you call him, I'll just have to do it before he gets here. Soon as you hang up the phone, I'll just walk in the bedroom and lock the door. Dawson will get here just in time to help you clean up. Go ahead, call him. Then call the police. Then call the funeral home. Then call Loretta and see if *she'll* do your nails.

MAMA: You will not! This is crazy talk, Jessie!

Mama goes directly to the telephone and starts to dial, but Jessie is fast, coming up behind her and taking the receiver out of her hand, putting it back down.

JESSIE *(firm and quiet)*:   I said no. This is private. Dawson is not invited.

MAMA: Just me.

JESSIE: I don't want anybody else over here. Just you and me. If Dawson comes over, it'll make me feel stupid for not doing it ten years ago.

MAMA: I think we better call the doctor. Or how about the ambulance. You like that one driver, I know. What's his name, Timmy? Get you somebody to talk to.

JESSIE *(going back to her chair)*:   I'm through talking, Mama. You're it. No more.

MAMA: We're just going to sit around like every other night in the world and then you're going to kill yourself? *(Jessie doesn't answer.)* You'll miss. *(Again there is no response.)* You'll just wind up a vegetable. How would you like that? Shoot your ear off? You know what the doctor said about getting excited. You'll cock the pistol and have a fit.

JESSIE: I think I can kill myself, Mama.

MAMA: You're not going to kill yourself, Jessie. You're not even upset! *(Jessie smiles, or laughs quietly, and Mama tries a different approach.)* People don't really kill themselves, Jessie. No, mam, doesn't make sense, unless you're retarded or deranged, and you're as normal as they come, Jessie, for the most part. We're all *afraid* to die.

JESSIE: I'm not, Mama. I'm cold all the time, anyway.

MAMA: That's ridiculous.

JESSIE: It's exactly what I want. It's dark and quiet.

MAMA: So is the back yard, Jessie! Close your eyes. Stuff cotton in your ears. Take a nap! It's quiet in your room. I'll leave the TV off all night.

JESSIE: So quiet I don't know it's quiet. So nobody can get me.

MAMA: You don't know what dead is like. It might not be quiet at all. What if it's like an alarm clock and you can't wake up so you can't shut it off. Ever.

JESSIE: Dead is everybody and everything I ever knew, gone. Dead is dead quiet.

MAMA: It's a sin. You'll go to hell.

JESSIE: Uh-huh.

MAMA: You will!

JESSIE: Jesus was a suicide, if you ask me.

MAMA: You'll go to hell just for saying that. Jessie!

JESSIE *(with genuine surprise)*:   I didn't know I thought that.

MAMA: Jessie!

Jessie doesn't answer. She puts the now-loaded gun back in the box and crosses to the kitchen. But Mama is afraid she's headed for the bedroom.

MAMA *(in a panic)*:   You can't use my towels! They're my towels. I've had them for a long time. I like my towels.

JESSIE: I asked you if you wanted that swimming towel and you said you didn't.

MAMA: And you can't use your father's gun, either. It's mine now, too. And you can't do it in my house.

JESSIE: Oh, come on.

MAMA: No. You can't do it. I won't let you. The house is in my name.

JESSIE: I have to go in the bedroom and lock the door behind me so they won't
          arrest you for killing me. They'll probably test your hands for gunpowder,
          anyway, but you'll pass.

MAMA: Not in my house!

JESSIE: If I'd known you were going to act like this, I wouldn't have told you.

MAMA: How am I supposed to act? Tell you to go ahead? O.K. by me, sugar?
          Might try it myself. What took you so long?

JESSIE: There's just no point in fighting me over it, that's all. Want some coffee?

MAMA: Your birthday's coming up, Jessie. Don't you want to know what we got
          you?

JESSIE: You got me dusting powder, Loretta got me a new housecoat, pink prob-
          ably, and Dawson got me new slippers, too small, but they go with the robe,
          he'll say. (*Mama cannot speak.*) Right? (*Apparently Jessie is right.*) Be back in
          a minute.

*Jessie takes the gun box, puts it on top of the stack of towels and garbage bags, and
takes them into her bedroom. Mama, alone for a moment, goes to the phone, picks
up the receiver, looks toward the bedroom, starts to dial, and then replaces the
receiver in its cradle as Jessie walks back into the room. Jessie wonders, silently. They
have lived together for so long there is very rarely any reason for one to ask what the
other was about to do.*

MAMA: I started to, but I didn't. I didn't call him.

JESSIE: Good. Thank you.

MAMA (*starting over, a new approach*):   What's this all about, Jessie?

JESSIE: About?

*Jessie now begins the next task she had "on the schedule," which is refilling all the
candy jars, taking the empty papers out of the boxes of chocolates, etc. Mama generally snitches when Jessie does this. Not tonight, though. Nevertheless, Jessie offers.*

MAMA: What did I do?

JESSIE: Nothing. Want a caramel?

MAMA (*ignoring the candy*):   You're mad at me.

JESSIE: Not a bit. I am worried about you, but I'm going to do what I can before
          I go. We're not just going to sit around tonight. I made a list of things.

MAMA: What things?

JESSIE: How the washer works. Things like that.

MAMA: I know how the washer works. You put the clothes in. You put the soap
          in. You turn it on. You wait.

JESSIE: You do something else. You don't just wait.

MAMA: Whatever else you find to do, you're still mainly waiting. The waiting's the
          worst part of it. The waiting's what you pay somebody else to do, if you can.

JESSIE (*nodding*):   O.K. Where do we keep the soap?

MAMA: I could find it.

JESSIE: See?

MAMA: If you're mad about doing the wash, we can get Loretta to do it.

JESSIE: Oh now, that might be worth staying to see.

MAMA: She'd never in her life, would she?

JESSIE: Nope.

MAMA: What's the matter with her?

JESSIE: She thinks she's better than we are. She's not.

MAMA: Maybe if she didn't wear that yellow all the time.

JESSIE: The washer repair number is on a little card taped to the side of the machine.

MAMA: Loretta doesn't ever have to come over here again. Dawson can just leave her at home when he comes. And we don't ever have to see Dawson either if he bothers you. Does he bother you?

JESSIE: Sure he does. Be sure you clean out the lint tray every time you use the dryer. But don't ever put your house shoes in, it'll melt the soles.

MAMA: What does Dawson do, that bothers you?

JESSIE: He just calls me Jess like he knows who he's talking to. He's always wondering what I do all day. I mean, I wonder that myself, but it's my day, so it's mine to wonder about, not his.

MAMA: Family is just accident, Jessie. It's nothing personal, hon. They don't mean to get on your nerves. They don't even mean to be your family, they just are.

JESSIE: They know too much.

MAMA: About what?

JESSIE: They know things about you, and they learned it before you had a chance to say whether you wanted them to know it or not. They were there when it happened and it don't belong to them, it belongs to you, only they got it. Like my mail-order bra got delivered to their house.

MAMA: By accident!

JESSIE: All the same . . . they opened it. They saw the little rosebuds on it. *(Offering her another candy.)* Chewy mint?

MAMA *(shaking her head no)*: What do they know about you? I'll tell them never to talk about it again. Is it Ricky or Cecil or your fits or your hair is falling out or you drink too much coffee or you never go out of the house or what?

JESSIE: I just don't like their talk. The account at the grocery is in Dawson's name when you call. The number's on a whole list of numbers on the back cover of the phone book.

MAMA: Well! Now we're getting somewhere. They're none of them ever setting foot in this house again.

JESSIE: It's not them, Mother. I wouldn't kill myself just to get away from them.

MAMA: You leave the room when they come over, anyway.

JESSIE: I stay as long as I can. Besides, it's you they come to see.

MAMA: That's because I stay in the room when they come.

JESSIE: It's not them.

MAMA: Then what is it?

JESSIE *(checking the list on her note pad)*: The grocery won't deliver on Saturday anymore. And if you want your order the same day, you have to call before ten. And they won't deliver less than fifteen dollars' worth. What I do is tell them what we need and tell them to add on cigarettes until it gets to fifteen dollars.

MAMA: It's Ricky. You're trying to get through to him.

JESSIE: If I thought I could do that, I would stay.

MAMA: Make him sorry he hurt you, then. That's it, isn't it?

JESSIE: He's hurt me, I've hurt him. We're about even.

MAMA: You'll be telling him killing is O.K. with you, you know. Want him to start killing next? Nothing wrong with it. Mom did it.

JESSIE: Only a matter of time, anyway, Mama. When the call comes, you let Dawson handle it.

MAMA: Honey, nothing says those calls are always going to be some new trouble he's into. You could get one that he's got a job, that he's getting married, or how about he's joined the army, wouldn't that be nice?

JESSIE: If you call the Sweet Tooth before you call the grocery, that Susie will take your fudge next door to the grocery and it'll all come out together. Be sure you talk to Susie, though. She won't let them put it in the bottom of a sack like that one time, remember?

MAMA: Ricky could come over, you know. What if he calls us?

JESSIE: It's not Ricky, Mama.

MAMA: Or anybody could call us, Jessie.

JESSIE: Not on Saturday night, Mama.

MAMA: Then what is it? Are you sick? If your gums are swelling again, we can get you to the dentist in the morning.

JESSIE: No. Can you order your medicine or do you want Dawson to? I've got a note to him. I'll add that to it if you want.

MAMA: Your eyes don't look right. I thought so yesterday.

JESSIE: That was just the ragweed. I'm not sick.

MAMA: Epilepsy is sick, Jessie.

JESSIE: It won't kill me. (*A pause.*) If it would, I wouldn't have to.

MAMA: You don't *have* to.

JESSIE: No, I don't. That's what I like about it.

MAMA: Well, I won't let you!

JESSIE: It's not up to you.

MAMA: Jessie!

JESSIE: I want to hang a big sign around my neck, like Daddy's on the barn. GONE FISHING.

MAMA: You don't like it here.

JESSIE (*smiling*):   Exactly.

MAMA: I meant here in my house.

JESSIE: I know you did.

MAMA: You never should have moved back in here with me. If you'd kept your little house or found another place when Cecil left you, you'd have made some new friends at least. Had a life to lead. Had your own things around you. Give Ricky a place to come see you. You never should've come here.

JESSIE: Maybe.

MAMA: But I didn't force you, did I?

JESSIE: If it was a mistake, we made it together. You took me in. I appreciate that.

MAMA: You didn't have any business being by yourself right then, but I can see how you might want a place of your own. A grown woman should . . .

JESSIE: Mama . . . I'm just not having a very good time and I don't have any reason to think it'll get anything but worse. I'm tired. I'm hurt. I'm sad. I feel used.

MAMA: Tired of what?

JESSIE: It all.

MAMA: What does that mean?

JESSIE: I can't say it any better.

MAMA: Well, you'll have to say it better because I'm not letting you alone till you do. What were those other things? Hurt . . . *(Before Jessie can answer.)* You had this all ready to say to me, didn't you? Did you write this down? How long have you been thinking about this?

JESSIE: Off and on, ten years. On all the time, since Christmas.

MAMA: What happened at Christmas?

JESSIE: Nothing.

MAMA: So why Christmas?

JESSIE: That's it. On the nose.

A pause. Mama knows exactly what Jessie means. She was there, too, after all.

JESSIE *(putting the candy sacks away)*:   See where all this is? Red hots up front, sour balls and horehound mixed together in this one sack. New packages of toffee and licorice right in back there.

MAMA: Go back to your list. You're hurt by what?

JESSIE *(Mama knows perfectly well)*:   Mama . . .

MAMA: O.K. Sad about what? There's nothing real sad going on right now. If it was after your divorce or something, that would make sense.

JESSIE *(looking at her list, then opening the drawer)*:   Now, this drawer has everything in it that there's no better place for. Extension cords, batteries for the radio, extra lighters, sandpaper, masking tape, Elmer's glue, thumbtacks, that kind of stuff. The mousetraps are under the sink, but you call Dawson if you've got one and let him do it.

MAMA: Sad about what?

JESSIE: The way things are.

MAMA: Not good enough. What things?

JESSIE: Oh, everything from you and me to Red China.

MAMA: I think we can leave the Chinese out of this.

JESSIE *(crosses back into the living room)*:   There's extra light bulbs in a box in the hall closet. And we've got a couple of packages of fuses in the fuse box. There's candles and matches in the top of the broom closet, but if the lights go out, just call Dawson and sit tight. But don't open the refrigerator door. Things will stay cool in there as long as you keep the door shut.

MAMA: I asked you a question.

JESSIE: I read the paper. I don't like how things are. And they're not any better out there than they are in here.

MAMA: If you're doing this because of the newspapers, I can sure fix that!

JESSIE: There's just more of it on TV.

MAMA *(kicking the television set)*:   Take it out, then!

JESSIE: You wouldn't do that.

MAMA: Watch me.

JESSIE: What would you do all day?

MAMA *(desperately)*:   Sing. *(Jessie laughs.)* I would, too. You want to watch? I'll sing till morning to keep you alive, Jessie, please!

JESSIE: No. *(Then affectionately.)* It's a funny idea, though. What do you sing?

MAMA *(has no idea how to answer this)*:   We've got a good life here!

JESSIE *(going back into the kitchen)*:   I called this morning and canceled the papers, except for Sunday, for your puzzles; you'll still get that one.

MAMA: Let's get another dog, Jessie! You liked a big dog, now, didn't you? That King dog, didn't you?

JESSIE *(washing her hands)*:   I did like that King dog, yes.

MAMA: I'm so dumb. He's the one run under the tractor.

JESSIE: That makes him dumb, not you.

MAMA: For bringing it up.

JESSIE: It's O.K. Handi-Wipes and sponges under the sink.

MAMA: We could get a new dog and keep him in the house. Dogs are cheap!

JESSIE *(getting big pill jars out of the cabinet)*:   No.

MAMA: Something for you to take care of.

JESSIE: I've had you, Mama.

MAMA *(frantically starting to fill pill bottles)*:   You do too much for me. I can fill pill bottles all day, Jessie, and change the shelf paper and wash the floor when I get through. You just watch me. You don't have to do another thing in this house if you don't want to. You don't have to take care of me, Jessie.

JESSIE: I know that. You've just been letting me do it so I'll have something to do, haven't you?

MAMA *(realizing this was a mistake)*:   I don't do it as well as you. I just meant if it tires you out or makes you feel used . . .

JESSIE: Mama, I know you used to ride the bus. Riding the bus and it's hot and bumpy and crowded and too noisy and more than anything in the world you want to get off and the only reason in the world you don't get off is it's still fifty blocks from where you're going? Well, I can get off right now if I want to, because even if I ride fifty more years and get off then, it's the same place when I step down to it. Whenever I feel like it, I can get off. As soon as I've had enough, it's my stop. I've had enough.

MAMA: You're feeling sorry for yourself!

JESSIE: The plumber's helper is under the sink, too.

MAMA: You're not having a good time! Whoever promised you a good time? Do you think I've had a good time?

JESSIE: I think you're pretty happy, yeah. You have things you like to do.

MAMA: Like what?

JESSIE: Like crochet.

MAMA: I'll teach you to crochet.

JESSIE: I can't do any of that nice work, Mama.

MAMA: Good time don't come looking for you, Jessie. You could work some puzzles or put in a garden or go to the store. Let's call a taxi and go to the A&P!

JESSIE: I shopped you up for about two weeks already. You're not going to need toilet paper till Thanksgiving.

MAMA (*interrupting*): You're acting like some little brat, Jessie. You're mad and everybody's boring and you don't have anything to do and you don't like me and you don't like going out and you don't like staying in and you never talk on the phone and you don't watch TV and you're miserable and it's your own sweet fault.

JESSIE: And it's time I did something about it.

MAMA: Not something like killing yourself. Something like . . . buying us all new dishes! I'd like that. Or maybe the doctor would let you get a driver's license now, or I know what let's do right this minute, let's rearrange the furniture.

JESSIE: I'll do that. If you want. I always thought if the TV was somewhere else, you wouldn't get such a glare on it during the day. I'll do whatever you want before I go.

MAMA (*badly frightened by those words*): You could get a job!

JESSIE: I took that telephone sales job and I didn't even make enough money to pay the phone bill, and I tried to work at the gift shop at the hospital and they said I made people real uncomfortable smiling at them the way I did.

MAMA: You could keep books. You kept your dad's books.

JESSIE: But nobody ever checked them.

MAMA: When he died, they checked them.

JESSIE: And that's when they took the books away from me.

MAMA: That's because without him there wasn't any business, Jessie!

JESSIE (*putting the pill bottles away*): You know I couldn't work. I can't do anything. I've never been around people my whole life except when I went to the hospital. I could have a seizure any time. What good would a job do? The kind of job I could get would make me feel worse.

MAMA: Jessie!

JESSIE: It's true!

MAMA: It's what you think is true!

JESSIE (*struck by the clarity of that*): That's right. It's what I think is true.

MAMA (*hysterically*): But I can't do anything about that!

JESSIE (*quietly*): No. You can't. (*Mama slumps, if not physically, at least emotionally.*) And I can't do anything either, about my life, to change it, make it better, make me feel better about it. Like it better, make it work. But I can stop it. Shut it down, turn it off like the radio when there's nothing on I want to listen to. It's all I really have that belongs to me and I'm going to say what happens to it. And it's going to stop. And I'm going to stop it. So. Let's just have a good time.

MAMA: Have a good time.

JESSIE: We can't go on fussing all night. I mean, I could ask you things I always wanted to know and you could make me some hot chocolate. The old way.

MAMA (*in despair*):   It takes cocoa, Jessie.

JESSIE (*gets it out of the cabinet*):   I bought cocoa, Mama. And I'd like to have a caramel apple and do your nails.

MAMA: You didn't eat a bite of supper.

JESSIE: Does that mean I can't have a caramel apple?

MAMA: Of course not. I mean . . . (*Smiling a little.*) Of course you can have a caramel apple.

JESSIE: I thought I could.

MAMA: I make the best caramel apples in the world.

JESSIE: I know you do.

MAMA: Or used to. And you don't get cocoa like mine anywhere anymore.

JESSIE: It takes time, I know, but . . .

MAMA: The salt is the trick.

JESSIE: Trouble and everything.

MAMA (*backing away toward the stove*):   It's no trouble. What trouble? You put it in the pan and stir it up. All right. Fine. Caramel apples. Cocoa. O.K.

Jessie walks to the counter to retrieve her cigarettes as Mama looks for the right pan. There are brief near-smiles, and maybe Mama clears her throat. We have a truce, for the moment. A genuine but nevertheless uneasy one. Jessie, who has been in constant motion since the beginning, now seems content to sit.

Mama starts looking for a pan to make the cocoa, getting out all the pans in the cabinets in the process. It looks like she's making a mess on purpose so Jessie will have to put them all away again. Mama is buying time, or trying to, and entertaining.

JESSIE: You talk to Agnes today?

MAMA: She's calling me from a pay phone this week. God only knows why. She has a perfectly good Trimline at home.

JESSIE (*laughing*):   Well, how is she?

MAMA: How is she every day, Jessie? Nuts.

JESSIE: Is she really crazy or just silly?

MAMA: No, she's really crazy. She was probably using the pay phone because she had another little fire problem at home.

JESSIE: Mother . . .

MAMA: I'm serious! Agnes Fletcher's burned down every house she ever lived in. Eight fires, and she's due for a new one any day now.

JESSIE (*laughing*):   No!

MAMA: Wouldn't surprise me a bit.

JESSIE (*laughing*):   Why didn't you tell me this before? Why isn't she locked up somewhere?

MAMA: 'Cause nobody ever got hurt, I guess. Agnes woke everybody up to watch the fires as soon as she set 'em. One time she set out porch chairs and served lemonade.

JESSIE (*shaking her head*):   Real lemonade?

MAMA: The houses they lived in, you knew they were going to fall down anyway, so why wait for it, is all I could ever make out about it. Agnes likes a feeling of accomplishment.

JESSIE: Good for her.

MAMA *(finding the pan she wants)*:   Why are you asking about Agnes? One cup or two?

JESSIE: One. She's your friend. No marshmallows.

MAMA *(getting the milk, etc.)*:   You have to have marshmallows. That's the old way, Jess. Two or three? Three is better.

JESSIE: Three, then. Her whole house burns up? Her clothes and pillows and everything? I'm not sure I believe this.

MAMA: When she was a girl, Jess, not now. Long time ago. But she's still got it in her, I'm sure of it.

JESSIE: She wouldn't burn her house down now. Where would she go? She can't get Buster to build her a new one, he's dead. How could she burn it up?

MAMA: Be exciting, though, if she did. You never know.

JESSIE: You do too know, Mama. She wouldn't do it.

MAMA *(forced to admit, but reluctant)*:   I guess not.

JESSIE: What else? Why does she wear all those whistles around her neck?

MAMA: Why does she have a house full of birds?

JESSIE: I didn't know she had a house full of birds!

MAMA: Well, she does. And she says they just follow her home. Well, I know for a fact she's still paying on the last parrot she bought. You gotta keep your life filled up, she says. She says a lot of stupid things. *(Jessie laughs, Mama continues, convinced she's getting somewhere.)* It's all that okra she eats. You can't just willy-nilly eat okra two meals a day and expect to get away with it. Made her crazy.

JESSIE: She really eats okra twice a day? Where does she get it in the winter?

MAMA: Well, she eats it a lot. Maybe not two meals, but . . .

JESSIE: More than the average person.

MAMA *(beginning to get irritated)*:   I don't know how much okra the average person eats.

JESSIE: Do you know how much okra Agnes eats?

MAMA: No.

JESSIE: How many birds does she have?

MAMA: Two.

JESSIE: Then what are the whistles for?

MAMA: They're not real whistles. Just little plastic ones on a necklace she won playing Bingo, and I only told you about it because I thought I might get a laugh out of you for once even if it wasn't the truth, Jessie. Things don't have to be true to talk about 'em, you know.

JESSIE: Why won't she come over here?

Mama is suddenly quiet, but the cocoa and milk are in the pan now, so she lights the stove and starts stirring.

MAMA: Well now, what a good idea. We should've had more cocoa. Cocoa is perfect.

JESSIE: Except you don't like milk.

MAMA (*another attempt, but not as energetic*):   I hate milk. Coats your throat as
    bad as okra. Something just downright disgusting about it.

JESSIE: It's because of me, isn't it?

MAMA: No, Jess.

JESSIE: Yes, Mama.

MAMA: O.K. Yes, then, but she's crazy. She's as crazy as they come. She's a
    lunatic.

JESSIE: What is it exactly? Did I say something, sometime? Or did she see me
    have a fit and's afraid I might have another one if she came over, or what?

MAMA: I guess.

JESSIE: You guess what? What's she ever said? She must've given you some
    reason.

MAMA: Your hands are cold.

JESSIE: What difference does that make?

MAMA: "Like a corpse," she says, "and I'm gonna be one soon enough as it is."

JESSIE: That's crazy.

MAMA: That's Agnes. "Jessie's shook the hand of death and I can't take the
    chance it's catching, Thelma, so I ain't comin' over, and you can understand
    or no, but I ain't comin'. I'll come up the driveway, but that's as far as I go."

JESSIE (*laughing, relieved*):   I thought she didn't like me! She's scared of me!
    How about that! Scared of me.

MAMA: I could make her come over here, Jessie. I could call her up right now
    and she could bring the birds and come visit. I didn't know you ever thought
    about her at all. I'll tell her she just has to come and she'll come, all right.
    She owes me one.

JESSIE: No, that's all right. I just wondered about it. When I'm in the hospital,
    does she come over here?

MAMA: Her kitchen is just a tiny thing. When she comes over here, she feels
    like . . . (*Toning it down a little.*) Well, we all like a change of scene, don't we?

JESSIE (*playing along*):   Sure we do. Plus there's no birds diving around.

MAMA: I hate those birds. She says I don't understand them. What's there to
    understand about birds?

JESSIE: Why Agnes likes them, for one thing. Why they stay with her when they
    could be outside with the other birds. What their singing means. How they
    fly. What they think Agnes is.

MAMA: Why do you have to know so much about things, Jessie? There's just not
    that much *to* things that I could ever see.

JESSIE: That you could ever *tell*, you mean. You didn't have to lie to me about
    Agnes.

MAMA: I didn't lie. You never asked before!

JESSIE: You lied about setting fire to all those houses and about how many birds
    she has and how much okra she eats and why she won't come over here. If I
    have to keep dragging the truth out of you, this is going to take all night.

MAMA: That's fine with me. I'm not a bit sleepy.

JESSIE: Mama . . .

MAMA: All right. Ask me whatever you want. Here.

They come to an awkward stop, as the cocoa is ready and Mama pours it into the cups Jessie has set on the table.

JESSIE *(as Mama takes her first sip):*   Did you love Daddy?

MAMA: No.

JESSIE *(pleased that Mama understands the rules better now):*   I didn't think so. Were you really fifteen when you married him?

MAMA: The way he told it? I'm sitting in the mud, he comes along, drags me in the kitchen, "She's been there ever since"?

JESSIE: Yes.

MAMA: No. It was a big fat lie, the whole thing. He just thought it was funnier that way. God, this milk in here.

JESSIE: The cocoa helps.

MAMA *(pleased that they agree on this, at least):*   Not enough, though, does it? You can still taste it, can't you?

JESSIE: Yeah, it's pretty bad. I thought it was my memory that was bad, but it's not. It's the milk, all right.

MAMA: It's a real waste of chocolate. You don't have to finish it.

JESSIE *(putting her cup down):*   Thanks, though.

MAMA: I should've known not to make it. I knew you wouldn't like it. You never did like it.

JESSIE: You didn't ever love him, or he did something and you stopped loving him, or what?

MAMA: He felt sorry for me. He wanted a plain country woman and that's what he married, and then he held it against me the rest of my life like I was supposed to change and surprise him somehow. Like I remember this one day he was standing on the porch and I told him to get a shirt on and he went in and got one and then he said, real peaceful, but to the point, "You're right, Thelma. If God had meant for people to go around without any clothes on, they'd have been born that way."

JESSIE *(sees Mama's hurt):*   He didn't mean anything by that, Mama.

MAMA: He never said a word he didn't have to, Jessie. That was probably all he'd said to me all day, Jessie. So if he said it, there was something to it, but I never did figure that one out. What did that mean?

JESSIE: I don't know. I liked him better than you did, but I didn't know him any better.

MAMA: How could I love him, Jessie. I didn't have a thing he wanted. *(Jessie doesn't answer.)* He got his share, though. You loved him enough for both of us. You followed him around like some . . . Jessie, all the man ever did was farm and sit . . . and try to think of somebody to sell the farm to.

JESSIE: Or make me a boyfriend out of pipe cleaners and sit back and smile like the stick man was about to dance and wasn't I going to get a kick out of that. Or sit up with a sick cow all night and leave me a chain of sleepy stick elephants on my bed in the morning.

MAMA: Or just sit.

JESSIE: I liked him sitting. Big old faded blue man in the chair. Quiet.

MAMA: Agnes gets more talk out of her birds than I got from the two of you. He could've had that GONE FISHING sign around his neck in that chair. I saw him stare off at the water. I saw him look at the weather rolling in. I got where I could practically see the boat myself. But you, you knew what he was thinking about and you're going to tell me.

JESSIE: I don't know, Mama! His life, I guess. His corn. His boots. Us. Things. You know.

MAMA: No, I don't know, Jessie! You had those quiet little conversations after supper every night. What were you whispering about?

JESSIE: We weren't whispering, you were just across the room.

MAMA: What did you talk about?

JESSIE: We talked about why black socks are warmer than blue socks. Is that something to go tell Mother? You were just jealous because I'd rather talk to him than wash the dishes with you.

MAMA: I was jealous because you'd rather talk to him than anything! *(Jessie reaches across the table for the small clock and stars to wind it.)* If I had died instead of him, he wouldn't have taken you in like I did.

JESSIE: I wouldn't have expected him to.

MAMA: Then what would you have done?

JESSIE: Come visit.

MAMA: Oh, I see. He died and left you stuck with me and you're mad about it.

JESSIE *(getting up from the table)*: Not anymore. He didn't mean to. I didn't have to come here. We've been through this.

MAMA: He felt sorry for you, too, Jessie, don't kid yourself about that. He said you were a runt and he said it from the day you were born and he said you didn't have a chance.

JESSIE *(getting the canister of sugar and starting to refill the sugar bowl)*: I know he loved me.

MAMA: What if he did? It didn't change anything.

JESSIE: It didn't have to. I miss him.

MAMA: He never really went fishing, you know. Never once. His tackle box was full of chewing tobacco and all he ever did was drive out to the lake and sit in his car. Dawson told me. And Bennie at the bait shop, he told Dawson. They all laughed about it. And he'd come back from fishing and all he'd have to show for it was . . . a whole pipe-cleaner *family* — chickens, pigs, a dog with a bad leg — it was creepy strange. It made me sick to look at them and I hid his pipe cleaners a couple of times but he always had more somewhere.

JESSIE: I thought it might be better for you after he died. You'd get interested in things. Breathe better. Change somehow.

MAMA: Into what? The Queen? A clerk in a shoe store? Why should I? Because he said to? Because you said to? *(Jessie shakes her head.)* Well I wasn't here for his entertainment and I'm not here for yours either, Jessie. I don't know what I'm here for, but then I don't think about it. *(Realizing what all this means.)* But I bet you wouldn't be killing yourself if he were still alive. That's a fine thing to figure out, isn't it?

JESSIE (*filling the honey jar now*):   That's not true.

MAMA: Oh no? Then what were you asking about him for? Why did you want to
know if I loved him?

JESSIE: I didn't think you did, that's all.

MAMA: Fine then. You were right. Do you feel better now?

JESSIE (*cleaning the honey jar carefully*):   It feels good to be right about it.

MAMA: It didn't matter whether I loved him. It didn't matter to me and it didn't
matter to him. And it didn't mean we didn't get along. It wasn't important.
We didn't talk about it. (*Sweeping the pots off the cabinet.*) Take all these pots
out to the porch!

JESSIE: What for?

MAMA: Just leave me this one pan. (*She jerks the silverware drawer open.*) Get
me one knife, one fork, one big spoon, and the can opener, and put them out
where I can get them. (*Starts throwing knives and forks in one of the pans.*)

JESSIE: Don't do that! I just straightened that drawer!

MAMA (*throwing the pan in the sink*):   And throw out all the plates and cups. I'll
use paper. Loretta can have what she wants and Dawson can sell the rest.

JESSIE (*calmly*):   What are you doing?

MAMA: I'm not going to cook. I never liked it, anyway. I like candy. Wrapped in
plastic or coming in sacks. And tuna. I like tuna. I'll eat tuna, thank you.

JESSIE (*taking the pan out of the sink*):   What if you want to make apple butter?
You can't make apple butter in that little pan. What if you leave carrots on
cooking and burn up that pan?

MAMA: I don't like carrots.

JESSIE: What if the strawberries are good this year and you want to go picking
with Agnes.

MAMA: I'll tell her to bring a pan. You said you would do whatever I wanted! I
don't want a bunch of pans cluttering up my cabinets I can't get down to,
anyway. Throw them out. Every last one.

JESSIE (*gathering up the pots*):   I'm putting them all back in. I'm not taking them
to the porch. If you want them, they'll be here. You'll bend down and get
them, like you got the one for the cocoa. And if somebody else comes over
here to cook, they'll have something to cook in, and that's the end of it!

MAMA: Who's going to come cook here?

JESSIE: Agnes.

MAMA: In my pots. Not on your life.

JESSIE: There's no reason why the two of you couldn't just live here together. Be
cheaper for both of you and somebody to talk to. And if the birds bothered
you, well, one day when Agnes is out getting her hair done, you could take
them all for a walk!

MAMA (*as Jessie straightens the silverware*):   So that's why you're pestering me
about Agnes. You think you can rest easy if you get me a new babysitter?
Well, I don't want to live with Agnes. I barely want to talk with Agnes. She's
just around. We go back, that's all. I'm not letting Agnes near this place. You
don't get off as easy as that, child.

JESSIE: O.K., then. It's just something to think about.

MAMA: I don't like things to think about. I like things to go on.

JESSIE *(closing the silverware drawer)*:   I want to know what Daddy said to you the night he died. You came storming out of his room and said I could wait it out with him if I wanted to, but you were going to watch *Gunsmoke*. What did he say to you?

MAMA: He didn't have *anything* to say to me, Jessie. That's why I left. He didn't say a thing. It was his last chance not to talk to me and he took full advantage of it.

JESSIE *(after a moment)*:   I'm sorry you didn't love him. Sorry for you, I mean. He seemed like a nice man.

MAMA *(as Jessie walks to the refrigerator)*:   Ready for your apple now?

JESSIE: Soon as I'm through here, Mama.

MAMA: You won't like the apple, either. It'll be just like the cocoa. You never liked eating at all, did you? Any of it! What have you been living on all these years, toothpaste?

JESSIE *(as she starts to clean out the refrigerator)*:   Now, you know the milkman comes on Wednesdays and Saturdays, and he leaves the order blank in an egg box, and you give the bills to Dawson once a month.

MAMA: Do they still make that orangeade?

JESSIE: It's not orangeade, it's just orange.

MAMA: I'm going to get some. I thought they stopped making it. You just stopped ordering it.

JESSIE: You should drink milk.

MAMA: Not anymore, I'm not. That hot chocolate was the last. Hooray.

JESSIE *(getting the garbage can from under the sink)*:   I told them to keep delivering a quart a week no matter what you said. I told them you'd run out of Cokes and you'd have to drink it. I told them I knew you wouldn't pour it on the ground . . .

MAMA *(finishing her sentence)*:   And you told them you weren't going to be ordering anymore?

JESSIE: I told them I was taking a little holiday and to look after you.

MAMA: And they didn't think something was funny about that? You who doesn't go to the front steps? You, who only sees the driveway looking down from a stretcher passed out cold?

JESSIE *(enjoying this, but not laughing)*:   They said it was about time, but why didn't I take you with me? And I said I didn't think you'd want to go, and they said, "Yeah, everybody's got their own idea of vacation."

MAMA: I guess you think that's funny.

JESSIE *(pulling jars out of the refrigerator)*:   You know there never was any reason to call the ambulance for me. All they ever did for me in the emergency room was let me wake up. I could've done that here. Now, I'll just call them out and you say yes or no. I know you like pickles. Ketchup?

MAMA: Keep it.

JESSIE: We've had this since last Fourth of July.

MAMA: Keep the ketchup. Keep it all.

JESSIE: Are you going to drink ketchup from the bottle or what? How can you want your food and not want your pots to cook it in? This stuff will all spoil in here, Mother.

MAMA: Nothing I ever did was good enough for you and I want to know why.

JESSIE: That's not true.

MAMA: And I want to know why you've lived here this long feeling the way you do.

JESSIE: You have no earthly idea how I feel.

MAMA: Well, how could I? You're real far back there, Jessie.

JESSIE: Back where?

MAMA: What's it like over there, where you are? Do people always say the right thing or get whatever they want, or what?

JESSIE: What are you talking about?

MAMA: Why do you read the newspaper? Why don't you wear that sweater I made for you? Do you remember how I used to look, or am I just any old woman now? When you have a fit, do you see stars or what? How did you fall off the horse, really? Why did Cecil leave you? Where did you put my old glasses?

JESSIE *(stunned by Mama's intensity)*:   They're in the bottom drawer of your dresser in an old Milk of Magnesia box. Cecil left me because he made me choose between him and smoking.

MAMA: Jessie, I know he wasn't that dumb.

JESSIE: I never understood why he hated it so much when it's so good. Smoking is the only thing I know that's always just what you think it's going to be. Just like it was the last time, right there when you want it and real quiet.

MAMA: Your fits made him sick and you know it.

JESSIE: Say seizures, not fits. Seizures.

MAMA: It's the same thing. A seizure in the hospital is a fit at home.

JESSIE: They didn't bother him at all. Except he did feel responsible for it. It *was* his idea to go horseback riding that day. It was his idea I could do *anything* if I just made up my mind to. I fell off the horse because I didn't know how to hold on. Cecil left for pretty much the same reason.

MAMA: He had a girl, Jessie. I walked right in on them in the toolshed.

JESSIE *(after a moment)*:   O.K. That's fair. *(Lighting another cigarette.)* Was she very pretty?

MAMA: She was Agnes's girl, Carlene. Judge for yourself.

JESSIE *(as she walks to the living room)*:   I guess you and Agnes had a good talk about that, huh?

MAMA: I never thought he was good enough for you. They moved here from Tennessee, you know.

JESSIE: What are you talking about? You liked him better than I did. You flirted him out here to build your porch or I'd never even met him at all. You thought maybe he'd help you out around the place, come in and get some coffee and talk to you. God knows what you thought. All that curly hair.

MAMA: He's the best carpenter I ever saw. That little house of yours will still be standing at the end of the world, Jessie.

JESSIE:　You didn't need a porch, Mama.

MAMA:　All right! I wanted you to have a husband.

JESSIE:　And I couldn't get one on my own, of course.

MAMA:　How were you going to get a husband never opening your mouth to a living soul?

JESSIE:　So I was quiet about it, so what?

MAMA:　So I should have let you just sit here? Sit like your daddy? Sit here?

JESSIE:　Maybe.

MAMA:　Well, I didn't think so.

JESSIE:　Well, what did you know?

MAMA:　I never said I knew much. How was I supposed to learn anything living out here? I didn't know enough to do half the things I did in my life. Things happen. You do what you can about them and you see what happens next. I married you off to the wrong man, I admit that. So I took you in when he left. I'm sorry

JESSIE:　He wasn't the wrong man.

MAMA:　He didn't love you, Jessie, or he wouldn't have left.

JESSIE:　He wasn't the wrong man, Mama. I loved Cecil so much. And I tried to get more exercise and I tried to stay awake. I tried to learn to ride a horse. And I tried to stay outside with him, but he always knew I was trying, so it didn't work.

MAMA:　He was a selfish man. He told me once he hated to see people move into his houses after he built them. He knew they'd mess them up.

JESSIE:　I loved that bridge he built over the creek in back of the house. It didn't have to be anything special, a couple of boards would have been just fine, but he used that yellow pine and rubbed it so smooth . . .

MAMA:　He had responsibilities here. He had a wife and son here and he failed you.

JESSIE:　Or that baby bed he built for Ricky. I told him he didn't have to spend so much time on it, but he said it had to last, and the thing ended up weighing two hundred pounds and I couldn't move it. I said, "How long does a baby bed have to last, anyway?" But maybe he thought if it was strong enough, it might keep Ricky a baby.

MAMA:　Ricky is too much like Cecil.

JESSIE:　He is not. Ricky is as much like me as it's possible for any human to be. We even wear the same size pants. These are his, I think.

MAMA:　That's just the same size. That's not you're the same person.

JESSIE:　I see it on his face. I hear it when he talks. We look out at the world and we see the same thing: Not Fair. And the only difference between us is Ricky's out there trying to get even. And he knows not to trust anybody and he got it straight from me. And he knows not to try to get work, and guess where he got that. He walks around like there's loose boards in the floor, and you know who laid that floor, I did.

MAMA:　Ricky isn't through yet. You don't know how he'll turn out!

JESSIE (*going back to the kitchen*):　Yes I do and so did Cecil. Ricky is the two of us together for all time in too small a space. And we're tearing each other apart, like always, inside that boy, and if you don't see it, then you're just blind.

MAMA: Give him time, Jess.

JESSIE: Oh, he'll have plenty of that. Five years for forgery, ten years for armed assault . . .

MAMA *(furious)*:   Stop that! *(Then pleading.)* Jessie, Cecil might be ready to try it again, honey, that happens sometimes. Go downtown. Find him. Talk to him. He didn't know what he had in you. Maybe he sees things different now, but you're not going to know that till you go see him. Or call him up! Right now! He might be home.

JESSIE: And say what? Nothing's changed, Cecil, I'd just like to look at you, if you don't mind? No. He loved me, Mama. He just didn't know how things fall down around me like they do. I think he did the right thing. He gave himself another chance, that's all. But I did beg him to take me with him. I did tell him I would leave Ricky and you and everything I loved out here if only he would take me with him, but he couldn't and I understood that. *(Pause.)* I wrote that note I showed you. I wrote it. Not Cecil. I said "I'm sorry, Jessie, I can't fix it all for you." I said I'd always love me, not Cecil. But that's how he felt.

MAMA: Then he should've taken you with him!

JESSIE *(picking up the garbage bag she has filled)*:   Mama, you don't pack your garbage when you move.

MAMA: You will not call yourself garbage, Jessie.

JESSIE *(taking the bag to the big garbage can near the back door)*:   Just a way of say-ing it, Mama. Thinking about my list, that's all. *(Opening the can, putting the garbage in, then securing the lid.)* Well, a little more than that. I was trying to say it's all right that Cecil left. It was . . . a relief in a way. I never was what he wanted to see, so it was better when he wasn't looking at me all the time.

MAMA: I'll make your apple now.

JESSIE: No thanks. You get the manicure stuff and I'll be right there.

Jessie ties up the big garbage bag in the can and replaces the small garbage bag under the sink, all the time trying desperately to regain her calm. Mama watches, from a distance, her hand reaching unconsciously for the phone. Then she has a better idea. Or rather she thinks of the only other thing left and is willing to try it. Maybe she is even convinced it will work.

MAMA: Jessie, I think your daddy had little . . .

JESSIE *(interrupting her)*:   Garbage night is Tuesday. Put it out as late as you can. The Davis's dogs get in it if you don't. *(Replacing the garbage bag in the can under the sink.)* And keep ordering the heavy black bags. It doesn't pay to buy the cheap ones. And I've got all the ties here with the hammers and all. Take them out of the box as soon as you open a new one and put them in this drawer. They'll get lost if you don't, and rubber bands or something else won't work.

MAMA: I think your daddy had fits, too. I think he sat in his chair and had little fits. I read this a long time ago in a magazine, how little fits go, just little blackouts where maybe their eyes don't even close and people just call them "thinking spells."

JESSIE *(getting the slipcover out of the laundry basket)*:   I don't think you want this manicure we've been looking forward to. I washed this cover for the sofa, but it'll take both of us to get it back on.

MAMA: I watched his eyes. I know that's what it was. The magazine said some people don't even know they've had one.

JESSIE: Daddy would've known if he'd had fits, Mama.

MAMA: The lady in this story had kept track of hers and she'd had eighty thousand of them in the last eleven years.

JESSIE: Next time you wash this cover, it'll dry better if you put it on wet.

MAMA: Jessie, listen to what I'm telling you. This lady had anywhere between five and five hundred fits a day and they lasted maybe fifteen seconds apiece, so that out of her life, she'd only lost about two weeks altogether, and she had a full-time secretary job and an IQ of 120.

JESSIE *(amused by Mama's approach)*:   You want to talk about fits, is that it?

MAMA: Yes. I do. I want to say . . .

JESSIE *(interrupting)*:   Most of the time I wouldn't even know I'd had one, except I wake up with different clothes on, feeling like I've been run over. Sometimes I feel my head start to turn around or hear myself scream. And sometimes there *is* this dizzy stupid feeling a little before it, but if the TV's on, well, it's easy to miss.

As Jessie and Mama replace the slipcover on the sofa and the afghan on the chair, the physical struggle somehow mirrors the emotional one in the conversation.

MAMA: I can tell when you're about to have one. Your eyes get this big! But, Jessie, you haven't . . .

JESSIE *(taking charge of this)*:   What do they look like? The seizures.

MAMA *(reluctant)*:   Different each time, Jess.

JESSIE: O.K. Pick one, then. A good one. I think I want to know now.

MAMA: There's not much to tell. You just . . . crumple, in a heap, like a puppet and somebody cut the strings all at once, or like the firing squad in some Mexican movie, you just slide down the wall, you know. You don't know what happens? How can you not know what happens?

JESSIE: I'm busy.

MAMA: That's not funny.

JESSIE: I'm not laughing. My head turns around and I fall down and then what?

MAMA: Well, your chest squeezes in and out, and you sound like you're gagging, sucking air in and out like you can't breathe.

JESSIE: Do it for me. Make the sound for me.

MAMA: I will not. It's awful-sounding.

JESSIE: Yeah. It felt like it might be. What's next?

MAMA: Your mouth bites down and I have to get your tongue out of the way fast, so you don't bite yourself.

JESSIE: Or you. I bite you, too, don't I?

MAMA: You got me once real good. I had to get a tetanus! But I know what to watch for now. And then you turn blue and the jerks start up. Like I'm standing there poking you with a cattle prod or you're sticking your finger in a light socket as fast as you can . . .

JESSIE: Foaming like a mad dog the whole time.

MAMA: It's bubbling, Jess, not foam like the washer overflowed, for God's sake; it's bubbling like a baby spitting up. I go get a wet washcloth, that's all. And then the jerks slow down and you wet yourself and it's over. Two minutes tops.

JESSIE: How do I get to the bed?

MAMA: How do you think?

JESSIE: I'm too heavy for you now. How do you do it?

MAMA: I call Dawson. But I get you cleaned up before he gets here and I make him leave before you wake up.

JESSIE: You could just leave me on the floor.

MAMA: I want you to wake up someplace nice, O.K.? *(Then making a real effort.)* But, Jessie, and this is the reason I even brought this up! You haven't had a seizure for a solid year. A whole year, do you realize that?

JESSIE: Yeah, the phenobarb's about right now, I guess.

MAMA: You bet it is. You might never have another one, ever! You might be through with it for all time!

JESSIE: Could be.

MAMA: You are. I know you are!

JESSIE: I sure am feeling good. I really am. The double vision's gone and my gums aren't swelling. No rashes or anything. I'm feeling as good as I ever felt in my life. I'm even feeling like worrying or getting mad and I'm not afraid it will start a fit if I do, I just go ahead.

MAMA: Of course you do! You can even scream at me, if you want to. I can take it. You don't have to act like you're just visiting here, Jessie. This is your house, too.

JESSIE: The best part is, my memory's back.

MAMA: Your memory's always been good. When couldn't you remember things? You're always reminding me what . . .

JESSIE: Because I've made lists for everything. But now I remember what things mean on my lists. I see "dish towels," and I used to wonder whether I was supposed to wash them, buy them, or look for them because I wouldn't remember where I put them after I washed them, but now I know it means wrap them up, they're a present for Loretta's birthday.

MAMA *(finished with the sofa now)*: You used to go looking for your lists, too, I've noticed that. You always know where they are now! *(Then suddenly worried.)* Loretta's birthday isn't coming up, is it?

JESSIE: I made a list of all the birthdays for you. I even put yours on it. *(A small smile.)* So you can call Loretta and remind her.

MAMA: Let's take Loretta to Howard Johnson's and have those fried clams. I *know* you love that clam roll.

JESSIE *(slight pause)*: I won't be here, Mama.

MAMA: What have we just been talking about? You'll be here. You're well, Jessie. You're starting all over. You said it yourself. You're remembering things and . . .

JESSIE: I won't be here. If I'd ever had a year like this, to think straight and all, before now, I'd be gone already.

MAMA *(not pleading, commanding)*:   No, Jessie.

JESSIE *(folding the rest of the laundry)*:   Yes, Mama. Once I started remembering, I could see what it all added up to.

MAMA: The fits are over!

JESSIE: It's not the fits, Mama.

MAMA: Then it's me for giving them to you, but I didn't do it!

JESSIE: It's not the fits! You said it yourself, the medicine takes care of the fits.

MAMA *(interrupting)*:   Your daddy gave you those fits, Jessie. He passed it down to you like your green eyes and your straight hair. It's not my fault!

JESSIE: So what if he had little fits? It's not inherited. I fell off the horse. It was an accident.

MAMA: The horse wasn't the first time, Jessie. You had a fit when you were five years old.

JESSIE: I did not.

MAMA: You did! You were eating a popsicle and down you went. He gave it to you. It's *his* fault, not mine.

JESSIE: Well, you took your time telling me.

MAMA: How do you tell that to a five-year-old?

JESSIE: What did the doctor say?

MAMA: He said kids have them all the time. He said there wasn't anything to do but wait for another one.

JESSIE: But I didn't have another one.

Now there is a real silence.

JESSIE: You mean to tell me I had fits all the time as a kid and you just told me I fell down or something and it wasn't till I had the fit when Cecil was looking that anybody bothered to find out what was the matter with me?

MAMA: It wasn't *all the time*, Jessie. And they changed when you started to school. More like your daddy's. Oh, that was some swell time, sitting here with the two of you turning off and on like light bulbs some nights.

JESSIE: How many fits did I have?

MAMA: You never hurt yourself. I never let you out of my sight. I caught you every time.

JESSIE: But you didn't tell anybody.

MAMA: It was none of their business.

JESSIE: You were ashamed.

MAMA: I didn't want anybody to know. Least of all you.

JESSIE: Least of all me. Oh, right. That was mine to know, Mama, not yours. Did Daddy know?

MAMA: He thought you were . . . you fell down a lot. That's what he thought. You were careless. Or maybe he thought I beat you. I don't know what he thought. He didn't think about it.

JESSIE: Because you didn't tell him!

MAMA: If I told him about you, I'd have to tell him about him!

JESSIE: I don't like this. I don't like this one bit.

MAMA: I didn't think you'd like it. That's why I didn't tell you.

JESSIE: If I'd known I was an epileptic, Mama, I wouldn't have ridden any horses.

MAMA: Make you feel like a freak, is that what I should have done?

JESSIE: Just get the manicure tray and sit down!

MAMA *(throwing it to the floor)*:   I don't want a manicure!

JESSIE: Doesn't look like you do, no.

MAMA: Maybe I did drop you, you don't know.

JESSIE: If you say you didn't, you didn't.

MAMA *(beginning to break down)*:   Maybe I fed you the wrong thing. Maybe you had a fever sometime and I didn't know it soon enough. Maybe it's a punishment.

JESSIE: For what?

MAMA: I don't know. Because of how I felt about your father. Because I didn't want any more children. Because I smoked too much or didn't eat right when I was carrying you. It has to be something I did.

JESSIE: It does not. It's just a sickness, not a curse. Epilepsy doesn't mean anything. It just is.

MAMA: I'm not talking about the fits here, Jessie! I'm talking about this killing yourself. It has to be me that's the matter here. You wouldn't be doing this if it wasn't. I didn't tell you things or I married you off to the wrong man or I took you in and let your life get away from you or all of it put together. I don't know what I did, but I did it, I know. This is all my fault, Jessie, but I don't know what to do about it now!

JESSIE *(exasperated at having to say this again)*:   It doesn't have anything to do with you!

MAMA: Everything you do has to do with me, Jessie. You can't do *anything*, wash your face or cut your finger, without doing it to me. That's right! You might as well kill me as you, Jessie, it's the same thing. This has to do with me, Jessie.

JESSIE: Then what if it does! What if it has everything to do with you! What if you are all I have and you're not enough? What if I could take all the rest of it if only I didn't have you here? What if the only way I can get away from you for good is to kill myself? What if it is? I can *still* do it!

MAMA *(in desperate tears)*:   Don't leave me, Jessie! *(Jessie stands for a moment, then turns for the bedroom.)* No! *(She grabs Jessie's arm.)*

JESSIE *(carefully taking her arm away)*:   I have a box of things I want people to have. I'm just going to go get it for you. You . . . just rest a minute.

Jessie is gone. Mama heads for the telephone, but she can't even pick up the receiver this time and, instead, stoops to clean up the bottles that have spilled out of the manicure tray.

Jessie returns, carrying a box that groceries were delivered in. It probably says Hershey Kisses or Starkist Tuna. Mama is still down on the floor cleaning up, hoping that maybe if she just makes it look nice enough, Jessie will stay.

MAMA: Jessie, how can I live here without you? I need you! You're supposed to tell me to stand up straight and say how nice I look in my pink dress, and drink my milk. You're supposed to go around and lock up so I know we're safe for the night, and when I wake up, you're supposed to be out there making the coffee and watching me get older every day, and you're supposed to help me die when the time comes. I can't do that by myself, Jessie. I'm not like you, Jessie. I hate the quiet and I don't want to die and I don't want you to go, Jessie. How can I . . . *(Has to stop a moment.)* How can I get up every day knowing you had to kill yourself to make it stop hurting and I was here all the time and I never even saw it. And then you gave me this chance to make it better, convince you to stay alive, and I couldn't do it. How can I live with myself after this, Jessie?

JESSIE: I only told you so I could explain it, so you wouldn't blame yourself, so you wouldn't feel bad. There wasn't anything you could say to change my mind. I didn't want you to save me. I just wanted you to know.

MAMA: Stay with me just a little longer. Just a few more years. I don't have that many more to go, Jessie. And as soon as I'm dead, you can do whatever you want. Maybe with me gone, you'll have all the quiet you want, right here in the house. And maybe one day you'll put in some begonias up the walk and get just the right rain for them all summer. And Ricky will be married by then and he'll bring your grandbabies over and you can sneak them a piece of candy when their daddy's not looking and then be real glad when they've gone home and left you to your quiet again.

JESSIE: Don't you see, Mama, everything I do winds up like this. How could I think you would understand? How could I think you would want a manicure? We could hold hands for an hour and then I could go shoot myself? I'm sorry about tonight, Mama, but it's exactly why I'm doing it.

MAMA: If you've got the guts to kill yourself, Jessie, you've got the guts to stay alive.

JESSIE: I know that. So it's really just a matter of where I'd rather be.

MAMA: Look, maybe I can't think of what you should do, but that doesn't mean there isn't something that would help. *You* find it. *You* think of it. You can keep trying. You can get brave and try some more. You don't have to give up!

JESSIE: I'm *not* giving up! This *is* the other thing I'm trying. And I'm sure there are some other things that might work, but *might* work isn't good enough anymore. I need something that *will* work. *This* will work. That's why I picked it.

MAMA: But something might happen. Something that could change everything. Who knows what it might be, but it might be worth waiting for! *(Jessie doesn't respond.)* Try it for two more weeks. We could have more talks like tonight.

JESSIE: No, Mama.

MAMA: I'll pay more attention to you. Tell the truth when you ask me. Let you have your say.

JESSIE: No, Mama! We wouldn't have more talks like tonight, because it's this next part that's made this last part so good, Mama. No, Mama. *This* is how I have my say. This is how I say what I thought about it *all* and I say no. To Dawson and Loretta and the Red Chinese and epilepsy and Ricky and Cecil and you. And me. And hope. I say no! *(Then going to Mama on the sofa.)* Just let me go easy, Mama.

MAMA: How can I let you go?

JESSIE: You can because you have to. It's what you've always done.

MAMA: You are my child!

JESSIE: I am what became of your child. *(Mama cannot answer.)* I found an old baby picture of me. And it was somebody else, not me. It was somebody pink and fat who never heard of sick or lonely, somebody who cried and got fed, and reached up and got held and kicked but didn't hurt anybody, and slept whenever she wanted to, just by closing her eyes. Somebody who mainly just laid there and laughed at the colors waving around over her head and chewed on a polka-dot whale and woke up knowing some new trick nearly every day, and rolled over and drooled on the sheet and felt your hand pulling my quilt back up over me. That's who I started out and this is who is left. *(There is no self-pity here.)* That's what this is about. It's somebody I lost, all right, it's my own self. Who I never was. Or who I tried to be and never got there. Somebody I waited for who never came. And never will. So, see, it doesn't much matter what else happens in the world or in this house, even. I'm what was worth waiting for and I didn't make it. Me . . . who might have made a difference to me . . . I'm not going to show up, so there's no reason to stay, except to keep you company, and that's . . . not reason enough because I'm not . . . very good company. *(Pause.)* Am I.

MAMA *(knowing she must tell the truth):*   No. And neither am I.

JESSIE: I had this strange little thought, well, maybe it's not so strange. Anyway, after Christmas, after I decided to do this, I would wonder, sometimes, what might keep me here, what might be worth staying for, and you know what it was? It was maybe if there was something I really liked, like maybe if I really liked rice pudding or cornflakes for breakfast or something, that might be enough.

MAMA: Rice pudding is good.

JESSIE: Not to me.

MAMA: And you're not afraid?

JESSIE: Afraid of what?

MAMA: I'm afraid of it, for me, I mean. When my time comes. I know it's coming, but . . .

JESSIE: You don't know when. Like in a scary movie.

MAMA: Yeah, sneaking up on me like some killer on the loose, hiding out in the back yard just waiting for me to have my hands full someday and how am I supposed to protect myself anyhow when I don't know what he looks like and I don't know how he sounds coming up behind me like that or if it will hurt or take very long or what I don't get done before it happens.

JESSIE: You've got plenty of time left.

MAMA: I forget what for, right now.

JESSIE: For whatever happens, I don't know. For the rest of your life. For Agnes burning down one more house or Dawson losing his hair or . . .

MAMA *(quickly):*   Jessie, I can't just sit here and say O.K., kill yourself if you want to.

JESSIE: Sure you can. You just did. Say it again.

MAMA *(really startled)*:   Jessie! *(Quiet horror.)* How dare you! *(Furious.)* How dare you! You think you can just leave whenever you want, like you're watching television here? No, you can't, Jessie. You make me feel like a fool for being alive, child, and you are so wrong! I like it here, and I will stay here until they make me go, until they drag me screaming and I mean screeching into my grave, and you're real smart to get away before then because, I mean, honey, you've never heard noise like that in your life. *(Jessie turns away.)* Who am I talking to? You're gone already, aren't you? I'm looking right through you! I can't stop you because you're already gone! I guess you think they'll all have to talk about you now! I guess you think this will really confuse them. Oh yes, ever since Christmas you've been laughing to yourself and thinking, "Boy, are they all in for a surprise." Well, nobody's going to be a bit surprised, sweetheart. This is just like you. Do it the hard way, that's my girl, all right. *(Jessie gets up and goes into the kitchen, but Mama follows her.)* You know who they're going to feel sorry for? Me! How about that! Not you, me! They're going to be *ashamed* of you. Yes. *Ashamed!* If somebody asks Dawson about it, he'll change the subject as fast as he can. He'll talk about how much he has to pay to park his car these days.

JESSIE: Leave me alone.

MAMA: It's the truth!

JESSIE: I should've just left you a note!

MAMA *(screaming)*:   Yes! *(Then suddenly understanding what she has said, nearly paralyzed by the thought of it, she turns slowly to face Jessie, nearly whispering.)* No. No. I . . . might not have thought of all the things you've said.

JESSIE: It's O.K., Mama.

Mama is nearly unconscious from the emotional devastation of these last few moments. She sits down at the kitchen table, hurt and angry and desperately afraid. But she looks almost numb. She is so far beyond what is known as pain that she is virtually unreachable and Jessie knows this, and talks quietly, watching for signs of recovery.

JESSIE *(washes her hands in the sink)*:   I remember you liked that preacher who did Daddy's, so if you want to ask him to do the service, that's O.K. with me.

MAMA *(not an answer, just a word)*:   What.

JESSIE *(putting on hand lotion as she talks)*:   And pick some songs you like or let Agnes pick, she'll know exactly which ones. Oh, and I had your dress cleaned that you wore to Daddy's. You looked real good in that.

MAMA: I don't remember, hon.

JESSIE: And it won't be so bad once your friends start coming to the funeral home. You'll probably see people you haven't seen for years, but I thought about what you should say to get you over that nervous part when they first come in.

MAMA *(simply repeating)*:   Come in.

JESSIE: Take them up to see their flowers, they'd like that. And when they say, "I'm so sorry, Thelma," you just say, "I appreciate your coming, Connie."

And then ask how their garden was this summer or what they're doing for Thanksgiving or how their children . . .

MAMA: I don't think I should ask about their children. I'll talk about what they have on, that's always good. And I'll have some crochet work with me.

JESSIE: And Agnes will be there, so you might not have to talk at all.

MAMA: Maybe if Connie Richards does come, I can get her to tell me where she gets that Irish yarn, she calls it. I know it doesn't come from Ireland. I think it just comes with a green wrapper.

JESSIE: And be sure to invite enough people home afterward so you get enough food to feed them all and have some left for you. But don't let anybody take anything home, especially Loretta.

MAMA: Loretta will get all the food set up, honey. It's only fair to let her have some macaroni or something.

JESSIE: No, Mama. You have to be more selfish from now on. (*Sitting at the table with Mama.*) Now, somebody's bound to ask you why I did it and you just say you don't know. That you loved me and you know I loved you and we just sat around tonight like every other night of our lives, and then I came over and kissed you and said, " 'night, Mother," and you heard me close my bedroom door and the next thing you heard was the shot. And whatever reasons I had, well, you guess I just took them with me.

MAMA (*quietly*):   It was something personal.

JESSIE: Good. That's good, Mama.

MAMA: That's what I'll say, then.

JESSIE: Personal. Yeah.

MAMA: Is that what I tell Dawson and Loretta, too? We sat around, you kissed me, " 'night, Mother"? They'll want to know more, Jessie. They won't believe it.

JESSIE: Well, then, tell them what we did. I filled up the candy jars. I cleaned out the refrigerator. We made some hot chocolate and put the cover back on the sofa. You had no idea. All right? I really think it's better that way. If they know we talked about it, they really won't understand how you let me go.

MAMA: I guess not.

JESSIE: It's private. Tonight is private, yours and mine, and I don't want anybody else to have any of it.

MAMA: O.K., then.

JESSIE (*standing behind Mama now, holding her shoulders*):   Now, when you hear the shot, I don't want you to come in. First of all, you won't be able to get in by yourself, but I don't want you trying. Call Dawson, then call the police, and then call Agnes. And then you'll need something to do till somebody gets here, so wash the hot-chocolate pan. You wash that pan till you hear the doorbell ring and I don't care if it's an hour, you keep washing that pan.

MAMA: I'll make my calls and then I'll just sit. I won't need something to do. What will the police say?

JESSIE: They'll do that gunpowder test, I guess, and ask you what happened, and by that time, the ambulance will be here and they'll come in and get me and you know how that goes. You stay out here with Dawson and Loretta.

You keep Dawson out here. I want the police in the room first, not Dawson, O.K.?

MAMA: What if Dawson and Loretta want me to go home with them?

JESSIE *(returning to the living room)*:   That's up to you.

MAMA: I think I'll stay here. All they've got is Sanka.

JESSIE: Maybe Agnes could come stay with you for a few days.

MAMA *(standing up, looking into the living room)*:   I'd rather be by myself, I think. *(Walking toward the box Jessie brought in earlier.)* You want me to give people those things?

JESSIE *(they sit down on the sofa, Jessie holding the box on her lap)*:   I want Loretta to have my little calculator. Dawson bought it for himself, you know, but then he saw one he liked better and he couldn't bring both of them home with Loretta counting every penny the way she does, so he gave the first one to me. Be funny for her to have it now, don't you think? And all my house slippers are in a sack for her in my closet. Tell her I know they'll fit and I've never worn any of them, and make sure Dawson hears you tell her that. I'm glad he loves Loretta so much, but I wish he knew not everybody has her size feet.

MAMA *(taking the calculator)*:   O.K.

JESSIE *(reaching into the box again)*:   This letter is for Dawson, but it's mostly about you, so read it if you want. There's a list of presents for you for at least twenty more Christmases and birthdays, so if you want anything special you better add it to this list before you give it to him. Or if you want to be surprised, just don't read that page. This Christmas, you're getting mostly stuff for the house, like a new rug in your bathroom and needlework, but next Christmas, you're really going to cost him next Christmas. I think you'll like it a lot and you'd never think of it.

MAMA: And you think he'll go for it?

JESSIE: I think he'll feel like a real jerk if he doesn't. Me telling him to, like this and all. Now, this number's where you call Cecil. I called it last week and he answered, so I know he still lives there.

MAMA: What do you want me to tell him?

JESSIE: Tell him we talked about him and I only had good things to say about him, but mainly tell him to find Ricky and tell him what I did, and tell Ricky you have something for him, out here, from me, and to come get it. *(Pulls a sack out of the box.)*

MAMA *(the sack feels empty)*:   What is it?

JESSIE *(taking it off)*:   My watch. *(Putting it in the sack and taking a ribbon out of the sack to tie around the top of it.)*

MAMA: He'll sell it!

JESSIE: That's the idea. I appreciate him not stealing it already. I'd like to buy him a good meal.

MAMA: He'll buy dope with it!

JESSIE: Well, then, I hope he gets some good dope with it, Mama. And the rest of this is for you. *(Handing Mama the box now. Mama picks up the things and looks at them.)*

MAMA (*surprised and pleased*):   When did you do all this? During my naps, I guess.

JESSIE: I guess. I tried to be quiet about it. (*As Mama is puzzled by the presents.*) Those are just little presents. For whenever you need one. They're not bought presents, just things I thought you might like to look at, pictures or things you think you've lost. Things you didn't know you had, even. You'll see.

MAMA: I'm not sure I want them. They'll make me think of you.

JESSIE: No they won't. They're just things, like a free tube of toothpaste I found hanging on the door one day.

MAMA: Oh. All right, then.

JESSIE: Well, maybe there's one present in there somewhere. It's Granny's ring she gave me and I thought you might like to have it, but I didn't think you'd wear it if I gave it to you right now.

MAMA (*taking the box to a table nearby*):   No. Probably not. (*Turning back to face her.*) I'm ready for my manicure, I guess. Want me to wash my hands again?

JESSIE (*standing up*):   It's time for me to go, Mama.

MAMA (*starting for her*):   No, Jessie, you've got all night!

JESSIE (*as Mama grabs her*):   No, Mama.

MAMA: It's not even ten o'clock.

JESSIE (*very calm*):   Let me go, Mama.

MAMA: I can't. You can't go. You can't do this. You didn't say it would be so soon, Jessie. I'm scared. I love you.

JESSIE (*takes her hands away*):   Let go of me, Mama. I've said everything I had to say.

MAMA (*standing still a minute*):   You said you wanted to do my nails.

JESSIE (*taking a small step backward*):   I can't. It's too late.

MAMA: It's not too late!

JESSIE: I don't want you to wake Dawson and Loretta when you call. I want them to still be up and dressed so they can get right over.

MAMA (*as Jessie backs up, Mama moves in on her, but carefully*):   They wake up fast, Jessie, if they have to. They don't matter here, Jessie. You do. I do. We're not through yet. We've got a lot of things to take care of here. I don't know where my prescriptions are and you didn't tell me what to tell Dr. Davis when he calls or how much you want me to tell Ricky or who I call to rake the leaves or . . .

JESSIE: Don't try and stop me, Mama, you can't do it.

MAMA (*grabbing her again, this time hard*):   I can too! I'll stand in front of this hall and you can't get past me. (*They struggle.*) You'll have to knock me down to get away from me, Jessie. I'm not about to let you . . .

Mama struggles with Jessie at the door and in the struggle Jessie gets away from her and—

JESSIE (*almost a whisper*):   'Night, Mother. (*She vanishes into her bedroom and we hear the door lock just as Mama gets to it.*)

MAMA (*screams*):   Jessie! (*Pounding on the door.*) Jessie, you let me in there. Don't you do this, Jessie. I'm not going to stop screaming until you open this door, Jessie. Jessie! Jessie! What if I don't do any of the things you told me to do! I'll tell Cecil what a miserable man he was to make you feel the way he did and I'll give Ricky's watch to Dawson if I feel like it and the only way you can make sure I do what you want is you come out here and make me, Jessie! *(Pounding again.)* Jessie! Stop this! I didn't know! I was here with you all the time. How could I know you were so alone?

And Mama stops for a moment, breathless and frantic, putting her ear to the door, and when she doesn't hear anything, she stands up straight again and screams once more.

Jessie! Please!

And we hear the shot, and it sounds like an answer, it sounds like No.

Mama collapses against the door, tears streaming down her face, but not screaming anymore. In shock now.

Jessie, Jessie, child . . . Forgive me. *(Pause.)* I thought you were mine.

And she leaves the door and makes her way through the living room, around the furniture, as though she didn't know where it was, not knowing what to do. Finally, she goes to the stove in the kitchen and picks up the hot-chocolate pan and carries it with her to the telephone and holds on to it while she dials the number. She looks down at the pan, holding it tight like her life depended on it. She hears Loretta answer.

MAMA: Loretta, let me talk to Dawson, honey.   [1983]

THINKING ABOUT THE TEXT

1. Here is an issue of cause and effect: Why does Jessie want to kill herself? Does she make her reasons clear or is the audience left to guess them at the end of the play? How important a role does her epilepsy seem to play in her thinking?

2. What are Thelma's main arguments against Jessie's committing suicide? What are Jessie's main arguments in return? Do you side with one character more than the other? Why, or why not?

3. What are the advantages and disadvantages for the playwright in restricting the time span covered by the play to the length of its performance? How surprised were you by the play's ending? In the course of your reading, what elements in the text did you especially consider as you thought about how it might end?

4. Jessie and Thelma refer to several absent characters. Do any of them seem more important than others? If so, which and why? Evaluate Norman's decision to keep all of these characters offstage. Should she have brought any of them on?

5. What would you say to people worried that Norman's play will encourage suicide?

LISA J. MCDONNELL

From "Diverse Similitude: Beth Henley and Marsha Norman"

Lisa J. McDonnell (b. 1949) teaches in the English department at Denison University in Granville, Ohio. The following excerpt is from an article that appeared in a 1985 issue of the journal Southern Quarterly. *As the title suggests, McDonnell compares Norman with another contemporary Southern woman playwright, Beth Henley.*

Disillusioned by life on a number of fronts, Jessie, an overweight, epileptic young woman who has been abandoned by her husband, disappointed by her delinquent son and frustrated by her inability to hold a job, decides to say "no" to hope and to take charge of her own life, thereby reclaiming her dignity as a human being. Although many argue that her death is merely an act of desperation, Jessie's decision to take her own life displays a new confidence in herself; she knows that it is the right decision for her. She goes beyond family expectations to find her own meaning only in the "rest" afforded by death. Her mother's obviously loving feelings are not sufficient reason for Jessie to prolong her miserable life. Unlike Henley's characters, who find hope and some strength for survival in their families, Jessie finds neither, but does manage to find *herself* in the act of dying.

Like Henley, Norman delineates characters and relationships sensitively. The relationship between Jessie and her mother demonstrates Norman's ability, for in *'night, Mother* Norman accomplishes the difficult task of making the audience identify with adversarial characters — Mama, who pleads, "Don't leave me, Jessie," and Jessie, who knows that her peace and dignity as an individual can be achieved only through death. By the end of the play the audience understands that Mama and Jessie's relationship is loving but empty, like the stage set that looks warm and homey until harsh lighting illuminates its sterility and emptiness. Like Arlie,° Jessie removes herself from her family in order to save herself; this movement contrasts with that of Henley's characters, who at their moment of testing draw on the family as a source of strength.   [1985]

Arlie: A character in Norman's 1977 play *Getting Out.*

SALLY BROWDER

From "'I Thought You Were Mine': Marsha Norman's 'night, Mother

Sally Browder is a clinical psychologist. The following excerpt is from an essay that appeared in the 1989 collection Mother Puzzle: Daughters and Mothers in Contemporary American Literature, *edited by Mickey Pearlman.*

At some point, most mothers and daughters recognize that they are pitted in an ageless struggle by their mutual efforts to maintain their relationship in its earliest form or to alter it. Like a complicated primitive dance, they perpetually pull together and move apart. The daughter resists her mother's attempts to control her life, yet at the same time resents the mother for what the mother has not been able to provide for her. The mother, on the other hand, simultaneously pushes her daughter away, in an effort to teach her not to expect nurturance but to give it and yet strives to protect and cling to her daughter, to claim her as an extension or possession. From this struggle emerges the opportunity for daughters to make their own choices, develop a sense of themselves, and participate in relationships as more equal partners.

For daughters, and thus for all women, the struggle is played out continuously in relationships. It is the choice between security and risk, loyalty and self-assertion, submission and power. They must choose to replay intricate patterns of dependency and need or courageously engage in equitable partnerships. Given the unique dynamics of this first important relationship, women are in greatest peril of failing to develop an adequate sense of meaning and autonomy when they confront the temptation to accept a sense of meaning assigned to them by others, assigned to them initially by their mothers.

This is the tragic realization to which Jessie comes too late. Jessie's isolation and exclusive reliance upon her mother as sole companion are insufficient to provide her with a sense of self, to provide her with a sense of power, a sense of meaning in life: "What if you are all I have and you're not enough?" "It's somebody I lost, all right, it's my own self. Who I never was, or who I tried to be and never got there. Somebody I waited for who never came. And never will."

The healthy course, to participate in relationships as an equal partner rather than as a dependent or recipient, requires giving up the security of an unequal relationship. It requires being strong and hopeful about one's own future while tolerating the pain of knowing the limitations and diminishment of the one with whom one may be most identified. It also implies staying around to confront the consequences of honesty, something of which Jessie's choice of suicide relieved her.

Honesty is a casualty of unequal relationships. The lack of honesty in mother-daughter relationships is not always intentional or malicious and usually arises out of a desire to protect. Mothers alter the truth in an effort to shield their daughters from what well may be a harsh reality. In doing so, however, they fail to equip their daughters to deal with reality, whatever it may be. I am reminded of a friend's story of how, as a young girl, she could not tolerate spending even one night away from home. When she called home her mother always insisted that everything was fine in the same tone of voice she always used, even in the presence of disaster. The mother's reassurances became red flags that pitched the young girl into a frenzy of anxiety and fear.

If Thelma is at fault, it is only in believing she could provide everything for this daughter, that she alone could be enough. So pervasive is this expectation, that even Jessie shares it, only realizing the bitter consequences of it on the evening of her death. She says of the decision to return to live with her mother, "If it was a mistake, we made it together."

In the end, whatever this particular mother did would have been wrong, just as whatever any mother does is wrong. As long as she is made to feel ultimately responsible for her daughter's well-being, a mother is thrust into unyielding, conflicting expectations. She encourages her daughter's dependency and identification with her while struggling with her own ambivalence about rearing a child who may serve to remind her of her own limitations. She must enable the daughter to develop a sense of self-sufficiency while being charged by society to engender qualities that may not contribute to a sense of power or well-being. The qualities that we think of as characterizing a good mother are not necessarily qualities that enable young daughters to attain autonomy. Mothers either love their children too much or not enough. And their daughters either love or hate them whatever they do. [1989]

JENNY S. SPENCER

From "Norman's 'night, Mother: Psycho-drama of Female Identity"

Jenny S. Spencer (b. 1951) teaches in the English department of the University of Massachusetts at Amherst. The following excerpt is from an article that appeared in a 1987 issue of the journal Modern Drama.

To say that male viewers can identify with neither the characters of this play nor its central experience would be inaccurate; many obviously have. But I suggest that the play is potentially more terrifying for the female viewer because she *must* identify at one and the same time with both characters on the stage, and moreover, do so in a gender-specific manner. If we assume that the avenues open to male response are similar to the avenues available in "real life," then more than a single possibility exists. Men may react to these characters as "human beings" rather than sexual objects and grant them as much subjective autonomy as men are willing and able to grant women in their own lives. But since the focus of the play is so sharply defined as "private," outside history, and in the normal sphere of women's domination (the home and the family), it presents a relatively unthreatening and possibly uninteresting avenue to the female psyche. Perceiving themselves as relatively detached or capable of objectivity about such matters (women, home and family), men may more easily approach the problems addressed in the play in broadly thematic or symbolic terms: as emblematic of human existential problems involving freedom, determination, and morality; or as a "limited" play about women who are subconsciously denied the kind of individual autonomy that men take for granted. Finally, male response may be affected by the fact that neither woman, as depicted, offers herself as a viable substitute for men's own attachment to women; in other words, men are not bound to the action through structures of desire. In reviews of the play, Stanley

Kauffman and Richard Gilman both describe Norman's characters in a negative manner, Kauffman calling the mother, for example, "a dodo" and "a silly old self-indulgent woman." As a female heroine, Jessie may be too strong and rational to appeal to men's protective instincts and too unemotional, apathetic, sexless, depressed, and unattractive to appeal to male desire. Gilman describes her in three words: "heavyset, slow-moving and morose." Norman goes to great lengths to portray Mama as anything but ideal and Jessie as anything but sexy; but for the female viewer, the characters' sexual identity is simply never in question. Using T. J. Scheff's definition of cathartic effect as "crying, laughing and other emotional processes that occur when an unresolved emotional distress is re-awakened in a properly distanced context," one might suggest that Norman's *'night, Mother* is aesthetically over-distanced for men (producing indifference) and aesthetically under-distanced for women (producing pain). Indeed, the power of the play for women rests not only on the ways in which Norman self-consciously addresses a female audience through subject matter, language, and situation. The text also presents a psycho-dynamically charged situation that symbolically mirrors the female viewer's own — a narrative movement at least partly generated from the desires, fantasies, resentments, and fears originally connected with the very process of gender acquisition.   [1987]

MAKING COMPARISONS

1. Do you agree with McDonnell that Jessie "does manage to find *herself* in the act of dying"? Why, or why not? What would you say to someone who argues that if anything, suicide is a loss of self?

2. Do Browder's comments about mother-daughter relationships make sense to you? Identify some specific things that have influenced your own view of this subject. How does Browder's psychoanalytic approach to Norman's play affect your interpretation of it?

3. Are you surprised by Spencer's claim that men and women tend to react differently to Norman's play? Why, or why not?

WRITING ABOUT ISSUES

1. Write an essay comparing Jessie with Thelma by focusing on what you consider to be the most important statement made by each character. Explain why the statements are noteworthy. In your essay, you may certainly refer to other lines, but concentrate on one for Jessie and one for Thelma.

2. Imagine that the three critics featured in this cluster have all made their comments as part of a conference panel on "Family Relationships in *'night, Mother.*" Now you, as the final panelist, will speak on the same general subject. In your talk, however, you will address this subject by focusing on Jessie's relationship with a man in her family: that is, her

father, her brother, her son, or her ex-husband. Write the talk you would give, referring at some point to at least one statement made by a previous panelist.

3. Write an essay recalling an occasion when you tried to talk a family member or friend out of doing something you considered horribly self-destructive. Identify the specific arguments each of you made and the outcome of the confrontation. If you wish, distinguish between your thinking then and your thinking now. Make comparisons to the conflict between Jessie and Thelma if you feel they are pertinent.

4. Should doctors ever help patients kill themselves? Write an essay arguing your position on physician-assisted suicide. Refer to at least two articles that express different views on the subject.

RETURNING TO LIFE

ELIZABETH BOWEN, "The Demon Lover"
ROBERT OLEN BUTLER, "Jealous Husband Returns in Form of Parrot"

Much of humanity refuses to concede that death is final. Several religions believe in resurrection, reincarnation, or the possibility of communicating with ancestors, and quite a few people argue for the existence of ghosts. Even someone who doubts that the dead truly return may enjoy films, television shows, and works of literature in which they do come back. Through the centuries, such tales have had considerable appeal. In part, their popularity derives from their sensationalism; their audiences love the sheer excitement of seeing a dead person revive. But many examples of the genre are also thought-provoking as they explore relations between the dead and the living. In this category we would include the following two stories. Both are from the twentieth century, although they were written more than fifty years apart. In Elizabeth Bowen's story, written and set during the Nazi bombing of London, a woman fears being reunited with a former fiancé who is supposed to be dead. In Robert Olen Butler's story, written and set in the contemporary United States, a dead man is reincarnated as a parrot and forced to witness his wife's sexual flings. Thus, Bowen focuses on a living person faced with the return of her dead lover, whereas Butler focuses on the dead lover who returns. Consider what difference this difference in perspective makes.

BEFORE YOU READ

Recall an example of this genre that you are familiar with: that is, a film, television show, or literary text in which a dead person returns to life. Does this work have psychological or philosophical substance? Or does it simply try to elicit certain sensations? What was your overall reaction to this work? Identify things that influenced your response to it.

ELIZABETH BOWEN
The Demon Lover

Elizabeth Bowen (1899–1973) was born in Dublin and educated in England. She was the author of many novels, essays, and short stories, including several tales of the supernatural. The following story is Bowen's adaptation of a centuries-old ballad also entitled "The Demon Lover." Bowen wrote her version in 1941 during the period known as the Blitz. Nazi bombers were regularly attacking London, prompting many of its citizens to seek refuge elsewhere in England or in other countries. Bowen's character Mrs. Drover, having fled with her family to the English countryside, is now returning to her London house merely for the day — or so she thinks.

Towards the end of her day in London Mrs. Drover went round to her shut-up house to look for several things she wanted to take away. Some belonged to herself, some to her family, who were by now used to their country life. It was late August; it had been a steamy, showery day: at the moment the trees down the pavement glittered in an escape of humid yellow afternoon sun. Against the next batch of clouds, already piling up ink-dark, broken chimneys and parapets stood out. In her once familiar street, as in any unused channel, an unfamiliar queerness had silted up; a cat wove itself in and out of railings, but no human eye watched Mrs. Drover's return. Shifting some parcels under her arm, she slowly forced round her latchkey in an unwilling lock, then gave the door, which had warped, a push with her knee. Dead air came out to meet her as she went in.

The staircase window having been boarded up, no light came down into the hall. But one door, she could just see, stood ajar, so she went quickly through into the room and unshuttered the big window in there. Now the prosaic woman, looking about her, was more perplexed than she knew by everything that she saw, by traces of her long former habit of life — the yellow smoke-stain up the white marble mantelpiece, the ring left by a vase on the top of the escritoire; the bruise in the wallpaper where, on the door being thrown open widely, the china handle had always hit the wall. The piano, having gone away to be stored, had left what looked like claw-marks on its part of the parquet. Though not much dust had seeped in, each object wore a film of another kind; and, the only ventilation being the chimney, the whole drawing-room smelled of the cold hearth. Mrs. Drover put down her parcels on the escritoire and left the room to proceed upstairs; the things she wanted were in a bedroom chest.

She had been anxious to see how the house was — the part-time caretaker she shared with some neighbours was away this week on his holiday, known to be not yet back. At the best of times he did not look in often, and she was never sure that she trusted him. There were some cracks in the structure, left by the last bombing, on which she was anxious to keep an eye. Not that one could do anything—

A shaft of refracted daylight now lay across the hall. She stopped dead and stared at the hall table—on this lay a letter addressed to her.

She thought first—then the caretaker *must* be back. All the same, who, seeing the house shuttered, would have dropped a letter in at the box? It was not a circular, it was not a bill. And the post office redirected, to the address in the country, everything for her that came through the post. The caretaker (even if he *were* back) did not know she was due in London today—her call here had been planned to be a surprise—so his negligence in the manner of this letter, leaving it to wait in the dusk and the dust, annoyed her. Annoyed, she picked up the letter, which bore no stamp. But it cannot be important, or they would know . . . She took the letter rapidly upstairs with her, without a stop to look at the writing till she reached what had been her bedroom, where she let in light. The room looked over the garden and other gardens: the sun had gone in; as the clouds sharpened and lowered, the trees and rank lawns seemed already to smoke with dark. Her reluctance to look again at the letter came from the fact that she felt intruded upon—and by someone contemptuous of her ways. However, in the tenseness preceding the fall of rain she read it: it was a few lines.

> Dear Kathleen: You will not have forgotten that today is our anniversary, and the day we said. The years have gone by at once slowly and fast. In view of the fact that nothing has changed, I shall rely upon you to keep your promise. I was sorry to see you leave London, but was satisfied that you would be back in time. You may expect me, therefore, at the hour arranged.
> Until then . . .   K.

Mrs. Drover looked for the date: it was today's. She dropped the letter on to the bed-springs, then picked it up to see the writing again—her lips, beneath the remains of lipstick, beginning to go white. She felt so much the change in her own face that she went to the mirror, polished a clear patch in it and looked at once urgently and stealthily in. She was confronted by a woman of forty-four, with eyes starting out under a hat-brim that had been rather carelessly pulled down. She had not put on any more powder since she left the shop where she ate her solitary tea. The pearls her husband had given her on their marriage hung loose round her now rather thinner throat, slipping in the V of the pink wool jumper her sister knitted last autumn as they sat round the fire. Mrs. Drover's most normal expression was one of controlled worry, but of assent. Since the birth of the third of her little boys, attended by a quite serious illness, she had had an intermittent muscular flicker to the left of her mouth, but in spite of this she could always sustain a manner that was at once energetic and calm.

Turning from her own face as precipitately as she had gone to meet it, she went to the chest where the things were, unlocked it, threw up the lid and knelt to search. But as rain began to come crashing down she could not keep from looking over her shoulder at the stripped bed on which the letter lay. Behind the blanket of rain the clock of the church that still stood struck six—with rapidly heightening apprehension she counted each of the slow strokes. "The hour arranged . . . My God," she said, "*what* hour? How should I . . . ? After twenty-five years . . ."

The young girl talking to the soldier in the garden had not ever completely seen his face. It was dark; they were saying goodbye under a tree. Now and then—for it felt, from not seeing him at this intense moment, as though she had never seen him at all—she verified his presence for these few moments longer by putting out a hand, which he each time pressed, without very much kindness, and painfully, on to one of the breast buttons of his uniform. That cut of the button on the palm of her hand was, principally what she was to carry away. This was so near the end of a leave from France that she could only wish him already gone. It was August 1916. Being not kissed, being drawn away from and looked at intimidated Kathleen till she imagined spectral glitters in the place of his eyes. Turning away and looking back up the lawn she saw, through branches of trees, the drawing-room window alight: she caught a breath for the moment when she could go running back there into the safe arms of her mother and sister, and cry: "What shall I do, what shall I do? He has gone."

Hearing her catch her breath, her fiancé said, without feeling: "Cold?"

"You're going away such a long way."

"Not so far as you think."   10

"I don't understand?"

"You don't have to," he said. "You will. You know what we said."

"But that was—suppose you—I mean, suppose."

"I shall be with you," he said, "sooner or later. You won't forget that. You need do nothing but wait."

Only a little more than a minute later she was free to run up the silent lawn.   15
Looking in through the window at her mother and sister, who did not for the moment perceive her, she already felt that unnatural promise drive down between her and the rest of all human kind. No other way of having given herself could have made her feel so apart, lost and foresworn. She could not have plighted a more sinister troth.

Kathleen behaved well when, some months later, her fiancé was reported missing, presumed killed. Her family not only supported her but were able to praise her courage without stint because they could not regret, as a husband for her, the man they knew almost nothing about. They hoped she would, in a year or two, console herself—and had it been only a question of consolation things might have gone much straighter ahead. But her trouble, behind just a little grief, was a complete dislocation from everything. She did not reject other lovers, for these failed to appear: for years she failed to attract men—and with the approach of her 'thirties she became natural enough to share her family's anxiousness on this score. She began to put herself out, to wonder; and at thirty-two she was very greatly relieved to find herself being courted by William Drover. She married him, and the two of them settled down in this quiet, arboreal part of Kensington: in this house the years piled up, her children were born and they all lived till they were driven out by the bombs of the next war. Her movements as Mrs. Drover were circumscribed, and she dismissed any idea that they were still watched.

As things were — dead or living the letter-writer sent her only a threat. Unable, for some minutes, to go on kneeling with her back exposed to the empty room, Mrs. Drover rose from the chest to sit on an upright chair whose back was firmly against the wall. The desuetude of her former bedroom, her married London home's whole air of being a cracked cup from which memory, with its reassuring power, had either evaporated or leaked away, made a crisis — and at just this crisis the letter-writer had, knowledgeably, struck. The hollowness of the house this evening cancelled years on years of voices, habits and steps. Through the shut windows she only heard rain fall on the roofs around. To rally herself, she said she was in a mood — and for two or three seconds shutting her eyes, told herself that she had imagined the letter. But she opened them — there it lay on the bed.

On the supernatural side of the letter's entrance she was not permitting her mind to dwell. Who, in London, knew she meant to call at the house today? Evidently, however, this had been known. The caretaker, *had* he come back, had had no cause to expect her: he would have taken the letter in his pocket, to forward it, at his own time, through the post. There was no other sign that the caretaker had been in — but, if not? Letters dropped in at doors of deserted houses do not fly or walk to tables in halls. They do not sit on the dust of empty tables with the air of certainty that they will be found. There is needed some human hand — but nobody but the caretaker had a key. Under circumstances she did not care to consider, a house can be entered without a key. It was possible that she was not alone now. She might be being waited for, downstairs. Waited for — until when? Until "the hour arranged." At least that was not six o'clock: six has struck.

She rose from the chair and went over and locked the door.

The thing was, to get out. To fly? No, not that: she had to catch her train. As a woman whose utter dependability was the keystone of her family life she was not willing to return to the country, to her husband, her little boys and her sister, without the objects she had come up to fetch. Resuming work at the chest she set about making up a number of parcels in a rapid, fumbling-decisive way. These, with her shopping parcels, would be too much to carry; these meant a taxi — at the thought of the taxi her heart went up and her normal breathing resumed. I will ring up the taxi now; the taxi cannot come too soon: I shall hear the taxi out there running its engine, till I walk calmly down to it through the hall. I'll ring up — But no: the telephone is cut off . . . . She tugged at a knot she had tied wrong.

The idea of flight . . . He was never kind to me, not really. I don't remember him kind at all. Mother said he never considered me. He was set on me, that was what it was — not love. Not love, not meaning a person well. What did he do, to make me promise like that? I can't remember — But she found that she could.

She remembered with such dreadful acuteness that the twenty-five years since then dissolved like smoke and she instinctively looked for the weal left by the button on the palm of her hand. She remembered not only all that he said and did but the complete suspension of *her* existence during that August week. I was not myself — they all told me so at the time. She remembered — but with one white burning blank as where acid has dropped on a photograph: *under no conditions* could she remember his face.

20

So, wherever he may be waiting, I shall not know him. You have no time to run from a face you do not expect.

The thing was to get to the taxi before any clock struck what could be the hour. She would slip down the street and round the side of the square to where the square gave on the main road. She would return in the taxi, safe, to her own door, and bring the solid driver into the house with her to pick up the parcels from room to room. The idea of the taxi driver made her decisive, bold: she unlocked her door, went to the top of the staircase and listened down.

She heard nothing—but while she was hearing nothing the *passé* air of the 25 staircase was disturbed by a draught that travelled up to her face. It emanated from the basement: down there a door or window was being opened by someone who chose this moment to leave the house.

The rain had stopped; the pavements steamily shone as Mrs. Drover let herself out by inches from her own front door into the empty street. The unoccupied houses opposite continued to meet her look with their damaged stare. Making towards the thoroughfare and the taxi, she tried not to keep looking behind. Indeed, the silence was so intense—one of those creeks of London silence exaggerated this summer by the damage of war—that no tread could have gained on hers unheard. Where her street debouched on the square where people went on living, she grew conscious of, and checked, her unnatural pace. Across the open end of the square two buses impassively passed each other: women, a perambulator, cyclists, a man wheeling a barrow signalized, once again, the ordinary flow of life. At the square's most populous corner should be—and was—the short taxi rank. This evening, only one taxi—but this, although it presented its blank rump, appeared already to be alertly waiting for her. Indeed, without looking round the driver started his engine as she panted up from behind and put her hand on the door. As she did so, the clock struck seven. The taxi faced the main road: to make the trip back to her house it would have to turn—she had settled back on the seat and the taxi *had* turned before she, surprised by its knowing movement, recollected that she had not "said where." She leaned forward to scratch at the glass panel that divided the driver's head from her own.

The driver braked to what was almost a stop, turned round, and slid the glass panel back: the jolt of this flung Mrs. Drover forward till her face was almost into the glass. Through the aperture driver and passenger, not six inches between them, remained for an eternity eye to eye. Mrs. Drover's mouth hung open for some seconds before she could issue her first scream. After that she continued to scream freely and to beat with her gloved hands on the glass all round as the taxi, accelerating without mercy, made off with her into the hinterland of deserted streets.   [1941]

THINKING ABOUT THE TEXT

1. What specific features of this story promote suspense?

2. Here is an issue of fact: What do you feel able to say about the demon lover as he was when Mrs. Drover first knew him?

3. Why conceivably is Mrs. Drover having this experience now, after many years of *not* encountering her ex-fiancé? Do you sympathize with her as she goes through this experience? Why, or why not?

4. Why do you think Bowen includes the scene of Mrs. Drover looking at herself in the mirror?

5. At the end of the story, Bowen doesn't really describe the driver. Should she have done so? Why, or why not?

ROBERT OLEN BUTLER

Jealous Husband Returns in Form of Parrot

Robert Olen Butler (b. 1946) is the author of several novels, and he won the Pulitzer Prize for his 1992 volume of short stories A Good Scent from a Strange Mountain. *For several years he has taught creative writing at McNeese State University in Lake Charles, Louisiana. The following story first appeared in a 1995 issue of* The New Yorker *and was then selected for* The Best American Short Stories 1996. *Butler has also included it in his latest collection of short stories,* Tabloid Dreams (1996). *All of the stories in the book were inspired by headlines in tabloid newspapers like* The National Enquirer, The Star, *and* Weekly World News.

I never can quite say as much as I know. I look at other parrots and I wonder if it's the same for them, if somebody is trapped in each of them, paying some kind of price for living their life in a certain way. For instance, "Hello," I say, and I'm sitting on a perch in a pet store in Houston and what I'm really thinking is, Holy shit. It's you. And what's happened is I'm looking at my wife.

"Hello," she says, and she comes over to me, and I can't believe how beautiful she is. Those great brown eyes, almost as dark as the center of mine. And her nose—I don't remember her for her nose, but its beauty is clear to me now. Her nose is a little too long, but it's redeemed by the faint hook to it.

She scratches the back of my neck.

Her touch makes my tail flare. I feel the stretch and rustle of me back there. I bend my head to her and she whispers, "Pretty bird."

For a moment, I think she knows it's me. But she doesn't, of course. I say   5 "Hello" again, and I will eventually pick up "pretty bird." I can tell that as soon as she says it, but for now I can only give her another "Hello." Her fingertips move through my feathers, and she seems to know about birds. She knows that to pet a bird you don't smooth his feathers down, you ruffle them.

But of course she did that in my human life as well. It's all the same for her. Not that I was complaining, even to myself, at that moment in the pet shop when she found me like I presume she was supposed to. She said it again—"Pretty bird"—and this brain that works the way it does now could feel that tiny little voice of mine ready to shape itself around these sounds. But before I could get them out of my beak, there was this guy at my wife's shoulder, and all my feathers went slick-flat to make me small enough not to be seen, and I backed away. The pupils of my eyes pinned and dilated and pinned again.

He circled around her. A guy that looked like a meat-packer, big in the chest and thick with hair, the kind of guy that I always sensed her eyes moving to when I was alive. I had a bare chest, and I'd look for little black hairs on the sheets when I'd come home on a day with the whiff of somebody else in the air. She was still in the same goddamn rut.

A "hello" wouldn't do, and I'd recently learned "good night," but it was the wrong suggestion altogether, so I said nothing and the guy circled her, and he was looking at me with a smug little smile, and I fluffed up all my feathers, made myself about twice as big, so big he'd see he couldn't mess with me. I waited for him to draw close enough for me to take off the tip of his finger.

But she intervened. Those nut-brown eyes were before me, and she said, "I want him."

And that's how I ended up in my own house once again. She bought me a   10
large black wrought-iron cage, very large, convinced by some young guy who clerked in the bird department and who took her aside and made his voice go much too soft when he was doing the selling job. The meat-packer didn't like it. I didn't either. I'd missed a lot of chances to take a bite out of this clerk in my stay at the shop, and I regretted that suddenly.

But I got my giant cage, and I guess I'm happy enough about that. I can pace as much as I want. I can hang upside down. It's full of bird toys. That dangling thing over there with knots and strips of rawhide and a bell at the bottom needs a good thrashing a couple of times a day, and I'm the bird to do it. I look at the very dangle of it, and the thing is rough, the rawhide and the knotted rope, and I get this restlessness back in my tail, a burning, thrashing feeling, and it's like all the times when I was sure there was a man naked with my wife. Then I go to this thing that feels so familiar and I bite and bite, and it's very good.

I could have used the thing the last day I went out of this house as a man. I'd found the address of the new guy at my wife's office. He'd been there a month, in the shipping department, and three times she'd mentioned him. She didn't even have to work with him, and three times I heard about him, just dropped into the conversation. "Oh," she'd say when a car commercial came on the television, "that car there is like the one the new man in shipping owns. Just like it." Hey, I'm not stupid. She said another thing about him and then another, and right after the third one I locked myself in the bathroom, because I couldn't rage about this anymore. I felt like a damn fool whenever I actually said anything about this kind of feeling and she looked at me as though she could start hating me real easy, and so I was working on saying nothing, even if it meant locking myself up. My goal was to hold my tongue about half the time. That would be a good start.

But this guy from shipping. I found out his name and his address, and it was one of her typical Saturday afternoons of vague shopping. So I went to his house, and his car that was just like the commercial was outside. Nobody was around in the neighborhood, and there was this big tree in back of the house going up to a second-floor window that was making funny little sounds. I went up. The shade was drawn but not quite all the way. I was holding on to a limb with my arms and legs wrapped around it like it was her in those times when I could forget the others for a little while. But the crack in the shade was just out of view, and I crawled on till there was no limb left, and I fell on my head. When I think about that now, my wings flap and I feel myself lift up, and it all seems so avoidable. Though I know I'm different now. I'm a bird.

Except I'm not. That's what's confusing. It's like those times when she would tell me she loved me and I actually believed her and maybe it was true and we clung to each other in bed and at times like that I was different. I was the man in her life. I was whole with her. Except even at that moment, as I held her sweetly, there was this other creature inside me who knew a lot more about it and couldn't quite put all the evidence together to speak.

My cage sits in the den. My pool table is gone, and the cage is sitting in that space, and if I come all the way down to one end of my perch I can see through the door and down the back hallway to the master bedroom. When she keeps the bedroom door open, I can see the space at the foot of the bed but not the bed itself. I can sense it to the left, just out of sight. I watch the men go in and I hear the sounds, but I can't quite see. And they drive me crazy. 15

I flap my wings and I squawk and I fluff up and I slick down and I throw seed and I attack that dangly toy as if it were the guy's balls, but it does no good. It never did any good in the other life either, the thrashing around I did by myself. In that other life I'd have given anything to be standing in this den with her doing this thing with some other guy just down the hall, and all I had to do was walk down there and turn the corner and she couldn't deny it anymore.

But now all I can do is try to let it go. I sidestep down to the opposite end of the cage and I look out the big sliding glass doors to the back yard. It's a pretty yard. There are great, placid live oaks with good places to roost. There's a blue sky that plucks at the feathers on my chest. There are clouds. Other birds. Fly away. I could just fly away.

I tried once, and I learned a lesson. She forgot and left the door to my cage open, and I climbed beak and foot, beak and foot, along the bars and curled around to stretch sideways out the door, and the vast scene of peace was there, at the other end of the room. I flew.

And a pain flared through my head, and I fell straight down, and the room whirled around, and the only good thing was that she held me. She put her hands under my wings and lifted me and clutched me to her breast, and I wish there hadn't been bees in my head at the time so I could have enjoyed that, but she put me back in the cage and wept a while. That touched me, her tears. And I looked back to the wall of sky and trees. There was something invisible there between me and that dream of peace. I remembered, eventually, about glass, and I knew I'd been lucky; I knew that for the little, fragile-boned skull I was doing all this thinking in, it meant death.

She wept that day, but by the night she had another man. A guy with a thick Georgia-truck-stop accent and pale white skin and an Adam's apple big as my seed 20 ball. This guy has been around for a few weeks, and he makes a whooping sound down the hallway, just out of my sight. At times like that, I want to fly against the bars of the cage, but I don't. I have to remember how the world has changed.

She's single now, of course. Her husband, the man that I was, is dead to her. She does not understand all that is behind my "Hello." I know many words, for a parrot. I am a yellow-nape Amazon, a handsome bird, I think, green with a splash of yellow at the back of my neck. I talk pretty well, but none of my words are adequate. I can't make her understand.

And what would I say if I could? I was jealous in life. I admit it. I would admit it to her. But it was because of my connection to her. I would explain that. When we held each other, I had no past at all, no present but her body, no future but to lie there and not let her go. I was an egg hatched beneath her crouching body, I entered as a chick into her wet sky of a body, and all that I wished was to sit on her shoulder and fluff my feathers and lay my head against her cheek, with my neck exposed to her hand. And so the glances that I could see in her troubled me deeply: the movement of her eyes in public to other men, the laughs sent across a room, the tracking of her mind behind her blank eyes, pursuing images of others, her distraction even in our bed, the ghosts that were there of men who'd touched her, perhaps even that very day. I was not part of all those other men who were part of her. I didn't want to connect to all that. It was only her that I would fluff for, but these others were there also, and I couldn't put them aside. I sensed them inside her, and so they were inside me. If I had the words, these are the things I would say.

But half an hour ago, there was a moment that thrilled me. A word, a word we all knew in the pet shop, was just the right word after all. This guy with his cowboy belt buckle and rattlesnake boots and his pasty face and his twanging words of love trailed after my wife through the den, past my cage, and I said, "Cracker." He even flipped his head back a little at this in surprise. He'd been called that before to his face, I realized. I said it again, "Cracker." But to him I was a bird, and he let it pass. "Cracker," I said. "Hello, cracker." That was even better. They were out of sight through the hall doorway, and I hustled along the perch and I caught a glimpse of them before they made the turn to the bed and I said, "Hello, cracker," and he shot me one last glance.

It made me hopeful. I eased away from that end of the cage, moved toward the scene of peace beyond the far wall. The sky is chalky blue today, blue like the brow of the blue-front Amazon who was on the perch next to me for about a week at the store. She was very sweet, but I watched her carefully for a day or two when she first came in. And it wasn't long before she nuzzled up to a cockatoo named Willy, and I knew she'd break my heart. But her color now, in the sky, is sweet, really. I left all those feelings behind me when my wife showed up. I am a faithful man, for all my suspicions. Too faithful, maybe. I am ready to give too much, and maybe that's the problem.

The whooping began down the hall, and I focused on a tree out there. A crow flapped down, his mouth open, his throat throbbing, though I could not hear his sound. I was feeling very odd. At least I'd made my point to the guy in the

25

other room. "Pretty bird," I said, referring to myself. She called me "pretty bird," and I believed her and I told myself again, "Pretty bird."

But then something new happened, something very difficult for me. She appeared in the den naked. I have not seen her naked since I fell from the tree and had no wings to fly. She always had a certain tidiness in things. She was naked in the bedroom, clothed in the den. But now she appears from the hallway, and I look at her, and she is still slim and she is beautiful, I think—at least I clearly remember that as her husband I found her beautiful in this state. Now, though, she seems too naked. Plucked. I find that a sad thing. I am sorry for her, and she goes by me and she disappears into the kitchen. I want to pluck some of my own feathers, the feathers from my chest, and give them to her. I love her more in that moment, seeing her terrible nakedness, than I ever have before.

And since I've had success in the last few minutes with words, when she comes back I am moved to speak. "Hello," I say, meaning, You are still connected to me, I still want only you. "Hello," I say again. Please listen to this tiny heart that beats fast at all times for you.

And she does indeed stop, and she comes to me and bends to me. "Pretty bird," I say, and I am saying, You are beautiful, my wife, and your beauty cries out for protection. "Pretty." I want to cover you with my own nakedness. "Bad bird," I say. If there are others in your life, even in your mind, then there is nothing I can do. "Bad." Your nakedness is touched from inside by the others. "Open," I say. How can we be whole together if you are not empty in the place that I am to fill?

She smiles at this, and she opens the door to my cage. "Up," I say, meaning, Is there no place for me in this world where I can be free of this terrible sense of others?

She reaches in now and offers her hand, and I climb onto it and I tremble   30
and she says, "Poor baby."

"Poor baby," I say. You have yearned for wholeness too, and somehow I failed you. I was not enough. "Bad bird," I say. I'm sorry.

And then the cracker comes around the corner. He wears only his rattle-snake boots. I take one look at his miserable, featherless body and shake my head. We keep our sexual parts hidden, we parrots, and this man is a pitiful sight. "Peanut," I say. I presume that my wife simply has not noticed. But that's foolish, of course. This is, in fact, what she wants. Not me. And she scrapes me off her hand onto the open cage door and she turns her naked back to me and embraces this man, and they laugh and stagger in their embrace around the corner.

For a moment, I still think I've been eloquent. What I've said only needs repeating for it to have its transforming effect. "Hello," I say. "Hello. Pretty bird. Pretty. Bad bird. Bad. Open. Up. Poor baby. Bad bird." And I am beginning to hear myself as I really sound to her. "Peanut." I can never say what is in my heart to her. Never.

I stand on my cage door now, and my wings stir. I look at the corner to the hallway, and down at the end the whooping has begun again. I can fly there and think of things to do about all this.

But I do not. I turn instead, and I look at the trees moving just beyond the   35
other end of the room. I look at the sky the color of the brow of a blue-front Amazon. A shadow of birds spanks across the lawn. And I spread my wings. I will fly
now. Even though I know there is something between me and that place where I
can be free of all these feelings, I will fly. I will throw myself there again and
again. Pretty bird. Bad bird. Good night.   [1992]

THINKING ABOUT THE TEXT

1. The narrator begins with the comment "I never can quite say as much as I
   know." What later passages in the story especially relate to this opening
   sentence? What might be concluded from the fact that this is a statement
   a writer might make? (Perhaps you have made it yourself!)

2. Do you find this story humorous? If so, in what respects?

3. Before he died, the narrator was a jealous husband. What should readers
   consider in trying to determine whether his jealousy was reasonable? As a
   parrot, the narrator still seems jealous. Again, what should readers think
   about in evaluating his state of mind? How would you describe his wife?

4. Why do you think Butler positions the narrator outside the bedroom so
   that he can only imagine what is going on inside it? If the parrot had been
   inside the bedroom, how might the story have been different?

5. Is the narrator suicidal at the end of the story? Explain.

MAKING COMPARISONS

1. Do you sympathize with both Mrs. Drover and the parrot? Why, or why
   not? At the end of their respective stories, both of them are imprisoned
   within glass. Does this mean they are similar in other ways?

2. Are you willing to say that both stories are horror stories? What should
   someone especially consider in addressing this issue of genre?

3. Whereas Bowen's story is entirely in past tense, much of Butler's story is in
   present tense. Does this difference make for a significant difference in
   effect?

WRITING ABOUT ISSUES

1. Write an essay arguing for the demon lover or the parrot's wife, using at
   least some details already in the text. If you wish, write as if you were the
   character you are focusing on, taking as your audience another character
   in the same story or the readers of that story. Conclude your essay with a
   paragraph or two in which you identify what you really think of the character whose case you have made.

2. Which does Butler's parrot resemble more, Mrs. Drover or the demon lover? Write an essay answering this question by referring to specific details in each of the two stories.

3. Think of a person whom you haven't seen in years but who continues to haunt you. (This may be someone whom you barely knew in the first place.) Then write an essay analyzing your continuing attachment to this person. The essay can take the form of a letter to him or her. If you wish, refer to either or both of the stories in this cluster.

4. Write an essay comparing Bowen's or Butler's story with an article in a current issue of a tabloid newspaper. Although you can emphasize differences between the two texts, choose an article that resembles the story in at least one respect.

When Disaster Strikes: Cultural Contexts for Bharati Mukherjee's "The Management of Grief"

BHARATI MUKHERJEE, "The Management of Grief"

Cultural Contexts:
CLARK BLAISE AND BHARATI MUKHERJEE, From *The Sorrow and the Terror: The Haunting Legacy of the Air India Tragedy*
NEW YORK TIMES, "India Arrests Sikh in '85 Bombing of Jetliner"
SAM HUSSEINI, "Profile in Unfairness"

The public suddenly grows conscious of death's reality when lots of people perish in some disaster, such as an airplane crash, a train wreck, or the collapse of a building. Attention is especially great when terrorism is a possible cause. Recall, for example, the crash of TWA's New York–Paris Flight 800 in 1996. This disaster aroused considerable interest not only because it took many lives, but also because it seemed a deliberate bombing. Simultaneously, the Flight 800 case turned into a drama of cultural relations. For one thing, the relatives of French passengers became impatient with the American government; they wanted bodies identified more quickly and the crash investigated better. Furthermore, many Americans assumed that any culprits would be from abroad; as with the Oklahoma City bombing, Arabs were the first object of suspicion. Indeed, many disasters result in cultures tangling with one another as people grieve over victims, investigate causes, adopt new safety measures, and attempt to get on with their own lives.

Bharati Mukherjee explores the cultural contexts of disaster in her short story "The Management of Grief," which we present here. Its main characters are a community of Indian immigrants in Canada whose loved ones have suddenly died in an airplane crash. Mukherjee based her story on a real-life incident that occurred on June 23, 1985. Heading from Toronto and Montreal toward New Delhi and Bombay, Air India Flight 182 exploded over the Irish Sea. All 329 people aboard were killed. They included a large number of Canadian citizens who had emigrated from India or who were of Indian descent. After a long investigation, Canadian and Indian authorities found that the explosion resulted from a bomb planted by certain members of India's Sikh religion. Like many, though not all Sikhs, they were agitating for the creation of a separate, independent Sikh state, commonly referred to as Khalistan.

In struggling to "manage" her grief, Mukherjee's narrator Shaila must decide how she will henceforth treat Sikhs. At the same time, she finds herself dealing with authorities in Canada and Ireland, as well as her Indian neighbors. In short, the story's cultural contexts are multiple. To help you think about them, we include a chapter from Mukherjee's 1987 book about the Air India bombing, which she wrote with her husband Clark Blaise. We also include two newspaper articles. The second, from 1996, is an opinion piece on a cultural issue related to the TWA Flight 800 crash. Writer Sam Husseini worries that this disaster will encourage airline officials to harass passengers of Arabic descent, treating them as if they are more prone to terrorism than other groups. The first article, from 1992, is a brief report from the *New York Times* on the capture of one of the Air India bombers. Unfortunately, it took seven years for someone finally to be arrested. Just as unfortunate, many people have forgotten about the bombing by now; in a sense, Air India 182 has slipped off the public's radar screen. As you read about it, think about whether and how you would put it back on.

BEFORE YOU READ

Think about a recent disaster that took many lives and caught your attention. Why were you interested in it? What do you think the other members of this class should note about it?

BHARATI MUKHERJEE
The Management of Grief

A native of Calcutta, Bharati Mukherjee (b. 1942) grew up in India. She attended the universities of Calcutta and Boroda, earning a master's degree in English and Ancient Indian Culture. In 1961, she moved to the United States. There, she attended the University of Iowa's renowned Writers Workshop, where she earned a master of fine arts as well as a doctorate in English. From 1966 to 1980, Mukherjee taught at McGill University in Canada; currently, she is a professor of English at the University of California in Berkeley. Her novels include The Tiger's Daughter *(1971),* Wife *(1972),* Jasmine *(1989), and* The Holder of the World *(1993). In addition, she has published two volumes of short stories,* Darkness *(1985) and* The Middleman and Other Stories *(1988). "The Management of Grief" appears in the*

*latter volume, which won the National Book Critics Circle Award for fiction. The
story was also selected for* The Best American Short Stories 1987. *With her husband Clark Blaise, Mukherjee has written two nonfiction books. In the first,* Days
and Nights in Calcutta (1979), *they each give an account of a trip they made to
India. In the second,* The Sorrow and the Terror: The Haunting Legacy of the Air
India Tragedy (1987), *they examine the real-life disaster on which the following
story is based.*

    A woman I don't know is boiling tea the Indian way in my kitchen. There are
a lot of women I don't know in my kitchen, whispering and moving tactfully.
They open doors, rummage through the pantry, and try not to ask me where
things are kept. They remind me of when my sons were small, on Mother's Day
or when Vikram and I were tired, and they would make big, sloppy omelets. I
would lie in bed pretending I didn't hear them.

    Dr. Sharma, the treasurer of the Indo-Canada Society, pulls me into the hall-
way. He wants to know if I am worried about money. His wife, who has just come
up from the basement with a tray of empty cups and glasses, scolds him. "Don't
bother Mrs. Bhave with mundane details." She looks so monstrously pregnant
her baby must be days overdue. I tell her she shouldn't be carrying heavy things.
"Shaila," she says, smiling, "this is the fifth." Then she grabs a teenager by his
shirttails. He slips his Walkman off his head. He has to be one of her four children; they have the same domed and dented foreheads. "What's the official word
now?" she demands. The boy slips the headphones back on. "They're acting evasive, Ma. They're saying it could be an accident or a terrorist bomb."

    All morning, the boys have been muttering, Sikh bomb, Sikh bomb. The
men, not using the word, bow their heads in agreement. Mrs. Sharma touches
her forehead at such a word. At least they've stopped talking about space debris
and Russian lasers.

    Two radios are going in the dining room. They are tuned to different stations.
Someone must have brought the radios down from my boys' bedrooms. I haven't
gone into their rooms since Kusum came running across the front lawn in her
bathrobe. She looked so funny, I was laughing when I opened the door.

    The big TV in the den is being whizzed through American networks and
cable channels.   5

    "Damn!" some man swears bitterly. "How can these preachers carry on like
nothing's happened?" I want to tell him we're not that important. You look at the
audience, and at the preacher in his blue robe with his beautiful white hair, the
potted palm trees under a blue sky, and you know they care about nothing.

    The phone rings and rings. Dr. Sharma's taken charge. "We're with her," he
keeps saying. "Yes, yes, the doctor has given calming pills. Yes, yes, pills are having necessary effect." I wonder if pills alone explain this calm. Not peace, just a
deadening quiet. I was always controlled, but never repressed. Sound can reach
me, but my body is tensed, ready to scream. I hear their voices all around me. I
hear my boys and Vikram cry, "Mommy, Shaila!" and their screams insulate me,
like headphones.

The woman boiling water tells her story again and again. "I got the news first. My cousin called from Halifax before six A.M., can you imagine? He'd gotten up for prayers and his son was studying for medical exams and heard on a rock channel that something had happened to a plane. They said first it had disappeared from the radar, like a giant eraser just reached out. His father called me, so I said to him, what do you mean, 'something bad'? You mean a hijacking? And he said, *Behn,* there is no confirmation of anything yet, but check with your neighbors because a lot of them must be on that plane. So I called poor Kusum straightaway. I knew Kusum's husband and daughter were booked to go yesterday."

Kusum lives across the street from me. She and Satish had moved in less than a month ago. They said they needed a bigger place. All these people, the Sharmas and friends from the Indo-Canada Society, had been there for the housewarming. Satish and Kusum made tandoori on their big gas grill and even the white neighbors piled their plates high with that luridly red, charred, juicy chicken. Their younger daughter had danced, and even our boys had broken away from the Stanley Cup telecast to put in a reluctant appearance. Everyone took pictures for their albums and for the community newspapers — another of our families had made it big in Toronto — and now I wonder how many of those happy faces are gone. "Why does God give us so much if all along He intends to take it away?" Kusum asks me.

I nod. We sit on carpeted stairs, holding hands like children. "I never once   10 told him that I loved him," I say. I was too much the well-brought-up woman. I was so well brought up I never felt comfortable calling my husband by his first name.

"It's all right," Kusum says. "He knew. My husband knew. They felt it. Modern young girls have to say it because what they feel is fake."

Kusum's daughter Pam runs in with an overnight case. Pam's in her McDonald's uniform. "Mummy! You have to get dressed!" Panic makes her cranky. "A reporter's on his way here."

"Why?"

"You want to talk to him in your bathrobe?" She starts to brush her mother's long hair. She's the daughter who's always in trouble. She dates Canadian boys and hangs out in the mall, shopping for tight sweaters. The younger one, the goody-goody one according to Pam, the one with a voice so sweet that when she sang *bhajans* for Ethiopian relief even a frugal man like my husband wrote out a hundred-dollar check, *she* was on that plane. *She* was going to spend July and August with grandparents because Pam wouldn't go. Pam said she'd rather waitress at McDonald's. "If it's a choice between Bombay and Wonderland, I'm picking Wonderland," she'd said.

"Leave me alone," Kusum yells. "You know what I want to do? If I didn't   15 have to look after you now, I'd hang myself."

Pam's young face goes blotchy with pain. "Thanks," she says, "don't let me stop you."

"Hush," pregnant Mrs. Sharma scolds Pam. "Leave your mother alone. Mr. Sharma will tackle the reporters and fill out the forms. He'll say what has to be said."

Pam stands her ground. "You think I don't know what Mummy's thinking? *Why her?* That's what. That's sick! Mummy wishes my little sister were alive and I were dead."

Kusum's hand in mine is trembly hot. We continue to sit on the stairs.

She calls before she arrives, wondering if there's anything I need. Her name   20
is Judith Templeton and she's an appointee of the provincial government. "Multi-culturalism?" I ask, and she says "partially," but that her mandate is bigger. "I've been told you knew many of the people on the flight," she says. "Perhaps if you'd agree to help us reach the others. . . ?"

She gives me time at least to put on tea water and pick up the mess in the front room. I have a few *samosas* from Kusum's housewarming that I could fry up, but then I think, why prolong this visit?

Judith Templeton is much younger than she sounded. She wears a blue suit with a white blouse and a polka-dot tie. Her blond hair is cut short, her only jewelry is pearl-drop earrings. Her briefcase is new and expensive looking, a gleaming cordovan leather. She sits with it across her lap. When she looks out the front windows onto the street, her contact lenses seem to float in front of her light blue eyes.

"What sort of help do you want from me?" I ask. She has refused the tea, out of politeness, but I insist, along with some slightly stale biscuits.

"I have no experience," she admits. "That is, I have an M.S.W. and I've worked in liaison with accident victims, but I mean I have no experience with a tragedy of this scale —"

"Who could?" I ask.   25

"— and with the complications of culture, language, and customs. Someone mentioned that Mrs. Bhave is a pillar —because you've taken it more calmly."

At this, perhaps, I frown, for she reaches forward, almost to take my hand. "I hope you understand my meaning, Mrs. Bhave. There are hundreds of people in Metro directly affected, like you, and some of them speak no English. There are some widows who've never handled money or gone on a bus, and there are old parents who still haven't eaten or gone outside their bedrooms. Some houses and apartments have been looted. Some wives are still hysterical. Some husbands are in shock and profound depression. We want to help, but our hands are tied in so many ways. We have to distribute money to some people, and there are legal doc-uments—these things can be done. We have interpreters, but we don't always have the human touch, or maybe the right human touch. We don't want to make mistakes, Mrs. Bhave, and that's why we'd like to ask you to help us."

"More mistakes, you mean," I say.

"Police matters are not in my hands," she answers.

"Nothing I can do will make any difference," I say. "We must all grieve in our   30
own way."

"But you are coping very well. All the people said, Mrs. Bhave is the strongest person of all. Perhaps if the others could see you, talk with you, it would help them."

"By the standards of the people you call hysterical, I am behaving very oddly and very badly, Miss Templeton." I want to say to her, *I wish I could scream, starve, walk into Lake Ontario, jump from a bridge.* "They would not see me as a model. I do not see myself as a model."

I am a freak. No one who has ever known me would think of me reacting this way. This terrible calm will not go away.

She asks me if she may call again, after I get back from a long trip that we all must make. "Of course," I say. "Feel free to call, anytime."

Four days later, I find Kusum squatting on a rock overlooking a bay in Ire-   35
land. It isn't a big rock, but it juts sharply out over water. This is as close as we'll ever get to them. June breezes balloon out her sari and unpin her knee-length hair. She has the bewildered look of a sea creature whom the tides have stranded.

It's been one hundred hours since Kusum came stumbling and screaming across my lawn. Waiting around the hospital, we've heard many stories. The police, the diplomats, they tell us things thinking that we're strong, that knowledge is helpful to the grieving, and maybe it is. Some, I know, prefer ignorance, or their own versions. The plane broke into two, they say. Unconsciousness was instantaneous. No one suffered. My boys must have just finished their breakfasts. They loved eating on planes, they loved the smallness of plates, knives, and forks. Last year they saved the airline salt and pepper shakers. Half an hour more and they would have made it to Heathrow.

Kusum says that we can't escape our fate. She says that all those people — our husbands, my boys, her girl with the nightingale voice, all those Hindus, Christians, Sikhs, Muslims, Parsis, and atheists on that plane — were fated to die together off this beautiful bay. She learned this from a swami in Toronto.

I have my Valium.

Six of us "relatives" — two widows and four widowers — chose to spend the day today by the waters instead of sitting in a hospital room and scanning photographs of the dead. That's what they call us now: relatives. I've looked through twenty-seven photos in two days. They're very kind to us, the Irish are very understanding. Sometimes understanding means freeing a tourist bus for this trip to the bay, so we can pretend to spy our loved ones through the glassiness of waves or in sun-speckled cloud shapes.

I could die here, too, and be content.   40

"What is that, out there?" She's standing and flapping her hands, and for a moment I see a head shape bobbing in the waves. She's standing in the water, I on the boulder. The tide is low, and a round, black, head-sized rock has just risen from the waves. She returns, her sari end dripping and ruined, and her face is a twisted remnant of hope, the way mine was a hundred hours ago, still laughing but inwardly knowing that nothing but the ultimate tragedy could bring two women together at six o'clock on a Sunday morning. I watch her face sag into blankness.

"That water felt warm, Shaila," she says at length.

"You can't," I say. "We have to wait for our turn to come."

I haven't eaten in four days, haven't brushed my teeth.

"I know," she says. "I tell myself I have no right to grieve. They are in a better   45
place than we are. My swami says depression is a sign of our selfishness."

Maybe I'm selfish. Selfishly I break away from Kusum and run, sandals slapping against stones, to the water's edge. What if my boys aren't lying pinned under the debris? What if they aren't stuck a mile below that innocent blue chop? What if, given the strong currents. . . .

Now I've ruined my sari, one of my best. Kusum has joined me, knee deep in water that feels to me like a swimming pool. I could settle in the water, and my husband would take my hand and the boys would slap water in my face just to see me scream.

"Do you remember what good swimmers my boys were, Kusum?"

"I saw the medals," she says.

One of the widowers, Dr. Ranganathan from Montreal, walks out to us, carrying his shoes in one hand. He's an electrical engineer. Someone at the hotel   50
mentioned his work is famous around the world, something about the place where physics and electricity come together. He has lost a huge family, something indescribable. "With some good luck," Dr. Ranganathan suggests to me, "a good swimmer could make it safely to some island. It is quite possible that there may be many, many microscopic islets scattered around."

"You're not just saying that?" I tell Dr. Ranganathan about Vinod, my elder son. Last year he took diving as well.

"It's a parent's duty to hope," he says. "It is foolish to rule out possibilities that have not been tested. I myself have not surrendered hope."

Kusum is sobbing once again. "Dear lady," he says, laying his free hand on her arm, and she calms down.

"Vinod is how old?" he asks me. He's very careful, as we all are. *Is,* not was.

"Fourteen. Yesterday he was fourteen. His father and uncle were going to   55
take him down to the Taj and give him a big birthday party. I couldn't go with them because I couldn't get two weeks off from my stupid job in June." I process bills for a travel agent. June is a big travel month.

Dr. Ranganathan whips the pockets of his suit jacket inside out. Squashed roses, in darkening shades of pink, float on the water. He tore the roses off creepers in somebody's garden. He didn't ask anyone if he could pluck the roses, but now there's been an article about it in the local papers. When you see an Indian person, it says, please give them flowers.

"A strong youth of fourteen," he says, "can very likely pull to safety a younger one."

My sons, though four years apart, were very close. Vinod wouldn't let Mithun drown. *Electrical engineering,* I think, foolishly perhaps: this man knows important secrets of the universe, things closed to me. Relief spins me lightheaded. No wonder my boys' photographs haven't turned up in the gallery of photos of the recovered dead. "Such pretty roses," I say.

"My wife loved pink roses. Every Friday I had to bring a bunch home. I used to say, Why? After twenty-odd years of marriage you're still needing proof positive of my love?" He has identified his wife and three of his children. Then others from Montreal, the lucky ones, intact families with no survivors. He chuckles as he wades back to shore. Then he swings around to ask me a question. "Mrs. Bhave, you are wanting to throw in some roses for your loved ones? I have two big ones left."

But I have other things to float: Vinod's pocket calculator; a half-painted   60
model B-52 for my Mithun. They'd want them on their island. And for my husband? For him I let fall into the calm, glassy waters a poem I wrote in the hospital yesterday. Finally he'll know my feelings for him.

"Don't tumble, the rocks are slippery," Dr. Ranganathan cautions. He holds out a hand for me to grab.

Then it's time to get back on the bus, time to rush back to our waiting posts on hospital benches.

Kusum is one of the lucky ones. The lucky ones flew here, identified in multiplicate their loved ones, then will fly to India with the bodies for proper ceremonies. Satish is one of the few males who surfaced. The photos of faces we saw on the walls in an office at Heathrow and here in the hospital are mostly of women. Women have more body fat, a nun said to me matter-of-factly. They float better.

Today I was stopped by a young sailor on the street. He had loaded bodies, he'd gone into the water when — he checks my face for signs of strength — when the sharks were first spotted. I don't blush, and he breaks down. "It's all right," I say. "Thank you." I heard about the sharks from Dr. Ranganathan. In his orderly mind, science brings understanding, it holds no terror. It is the shark's duty. For every deer there is a hunter, for every fish a fisherman.

The Irish are not shy; they rush to me and give me hugs and some are crying.   65
I cannot imagine reactions like that on the streets of Toronto. Just strangers, and I am touched. Some carry flowers with them and give them to any Indian they see.

After lunch, a policeman I have gotten to know quite well catches hold of me. He says he thinks he has a match for Vinod. I explain what a good swimmer Vinod is.

"You want me with you when you look at photos?" Dr. Ranganathan walks ahead of me into the picture gallery. In these matters, he is a scientist, and I am grateful. It is a new perspective. "They have performed miracles," he says. "We are indebted to them."

The first day or two the policemen showed us relatives only one picture at a time; now they're in a hurry, they're eager to lay out the possibles, and even the probables.

The face on the photo is of a boy much like Vinod; the same intelligent eyes, the same thick brows dipping into a V. But this boy's features, even his cheeks, are puffier, wider, mushier.

"No." My gaze is pulled by other pictures. There are five other boys who look   70
like Vinod.

The nun assigned to console me rubs the first picture with a fingertip. "When they've been in the water for a while, love, they look a little heavier." The bones under the skin are broken, they said on the first day — try to adjust your memories. It's important.

"It's not him. I'm his mother. I'd know."

"I know this one!" Dr. Ranganathan cries out, and suddenly from the back of the gallery. "And this one!" I think he senses that I don't want to find my boys. "They are the Kutty brothers. They were also from Montreal." I don't mean to be crying. On the contrary, I am ecstatic. My suitcase in the hotel is packed heavy with dry clothes for my boys.

The policeman starts to cry. "I am so sorry. I am so sorry, ma'am. I really thought we had a match."

With the nun ahead of us and the policeman behind, we, the unlucky ones   75
without our children's bodies, file out of the makeshift gallery.

From Ireland most of us go on to India. Kusum and I take the same direct flight to Bombay, so I can help her clear customs quickly. But we have to argue with a man in uniform. He has large boils on his face. The boils swell and glow with sweat as we argue with him. He wants Kusum to wait in line and he refuses to take authority because his boss is on a tea break. But Kusum won't let her coffins out of sight, and I shan't desert her though I know that my parents, elderly and diabetic, must be waiting in a stuffy car in a scorching lot.

"You bastard!" I scream at the man with the popping boils. Other passengers press closer. "You think we're smuggling contraband in those coffins!"

Once upon a time we were well-brought-up women; we were dutiful wives who kept our heads veiled, our voices shy and sweet.

In India, I become, once again, an only child of rich, ailing parents. Old friends of the family come to pay their respects. Some are Sikh, and inwardly, involuntarily, I cringe. My parents are progressive people; they do not blame communities for a few individuals.

In Canada it is a different story now.   80

"Stay longer," my mother pleads. "Canada is a cold place. Why would you want to be by yourself?" I stay.

Three months pass. Then another.

"Vikram wouldn't have wanted you to give up things!" they protest. They call my husband by the name he was born with. In Toronto he'd changed to Vik so the men he worked with at his office would find his name as easy as Rod or Chris. "You know, the dead aren't cut off from us!"

My grandmother, the spoiled daughter of a rich zamindar,° shaved her head with rusty razor blades when she was widowed at sixteen. My grandfather died of childhood diabetes when he was nineteen, and she saw herself as the harbinger of bad luck. My mother grew up without parents, raised indifferently by an uncle, while her true mother slept in a hut behind the main estate house and took her food with the servants. She grew up a rationalist. My parents abhor mindless mortification.

The zamindar's daughter kept stubborn faith in Vedic rituals; my parents   85
rebelled. I am trapped between two modes of knowledge. At thirty-six, I am too

zamindar: Feudal landlord in British India.

old to start over and too young to give up. Like my husband's spirit, I flutter between worlds.

Courting aphasia, we travel. We travel with our phalanx of servants and poor relatives. To hill stations and to beach resorts. We play contract bridge in dusty gymkhana clubs. We ride stubby ponies up crumbly mountain trails. At tea dances, we let ourselves be twirled twice round the ballroom. We hit the holy spots we hadn't made time for before. In Varanasi, Kalighat, Rishikesh, Hardwar, astrologers and palmists seek me out and for a fee offer me cosmic consolations.

Already the widowers among us are being shown new bride candidates. They cannot resist the call of custom, the authority of their parents and older brothers. They must marry; it is the duty of a man to look after a wife. The new wives will be young widows with children, destitute but of good family. They will make loving wives, but the men will shun them. I've had calls from the men over crackling Indian telephone lines. "Save me," they say, these substantial, educated, successful men of forty. "My parents are arranging a marriage for me." In a month they will have buried one family and returned to Canada with a new bride and partial family.

I am comparatively lucky. No one here thinks of arranging a husband for an unlucky widow.

Then, on the third day of the sixth month into this odyssey, in an abandoned temple in a tiny Himalayan village, as I make my offering of flowers and sweetmeats to the god of a tribe of animists, my husband descends to me. He is squatting next to a scrawny sadhu° in moth-eaten robes. Vikram wears the vanilla suit he wore the last time I hugged him. The sadhu tosses petals on a butter-fed flame, reciting Sanskrit mantras, and sweeps his face of flies. My husband takes my hands in his.

You're beautiful, he starts. Then, *What are you doing here?*   90

Shall I stay? I ask. He only smiles, but already the image is fading. *You must finish alone what we started together.* No seaweed wreathes his mouth. He speaks too fast, just as he used to when we were an envied family in our pink split-level. He is gone.

In the windowless altar room, smoky with joss sticks and clarified butter lamps, a sweaty hand gropes for my blouse. I do not shriek. The sadhu arranges his robe. The lamps hiss and sputter out.

When we come out of the temple, my mother says, "Did you feel something weird in there?"

My mother has no patience with ghosts, prophetic dreams, holy men, and cults.

"No," I lie. "Nothing."   95

But she knows that she's lost me. She knows that in days I shall be leaving.

Kusum's put up her house for sale. She wants to live in an ashram in Hardwar. Moving to Hardwar was her swami's idea. Her swami runs two ashrams, the one in Hardwar and another here in Toronto.

---

sadhu: Ascetic or holy man.

"Don't run away," I tell her.

"I'm not running away," she says. "I'm pursuing inner peace. You think you or that Ranganathan fellow are better off?"

Pam's left for California. She wants to do some modeling, she says. She says   100
when she comes into her share of the insurance money she'll open a yoga-cum-aerobics studio in Hollywood. She sends me postcards so naughty I daren't leave them on the coffee table. Her mother has withdrawn from her and the world.

The rest of us don't lose touch, that's the point. Talk is all we have, says Dr. Ranganathan, who has also resisted his relatives and returned to Montreal and to his job, alone. He says, Whom better to talk with than other relatives? We've been melted down and recast as a new tribe.

He calls me twice a week from Montreal. Every Wednesday night and every Saturday afternoon. He is changing jobs, going to Ottawa. But Ottawa is over a hundred miles away, and he is forced to drive two hundred and twenty miles a day from his home in Montreal. He can't bring himself to sell his house. The house is a temple, he says; the king-sized bed in the master bedroom is a shrine. He sleeps on a folding cot. A devotee.

There are still some hysterical relatives. Judith Templeton's list of those needing help and those who've "accepted" is in nearly perfect balance. Acceptance means you speak of your family in the past tense and you make active plans for moving ahead with your life. There are courses at Seneca and Ryerson we could be taking. Her gleaming leather briefcase is full of college catalogues and lists of cultural societies that need our help. She has done impressive work, I tell her.

"In the textbooks on grief management," she replies — I am her confidante, I realize, one of the few whose grief has not sprung bizarre obsessions — "there are stages to pass through: rejection, depression, acceptance, reconstruction." She has compiled a chart and finds that six months after the tragedy, none of us still rejects reality, but only a handful are reconstructing. "Depressed acceptance" is the plateau we've reached. Remarriage is a major step in reconstruction (though she's a little surprised, even shocked, over *how* quickly some of the men have taken on new families). Selling one's house and changing jobs and cities is healthy.

How to tell Judith Templeton that my family surrounds me, and that like   105
creatures in epics, they've changed shapes? She sees me as calm and accepting but worries that I have no job, no career. My closest friends are worse off than I. I cannot tell her my days, even my nights, are thrilling.

She asks me to help with families she can't reach at all. An elderly couple in Agincourt whose sons were killed just weeks after they had brought their parents over from a village in Punjab. From their names, I know they are Sikh. Judith Templeton and a translator have visited them twice with offers of money for airfare to Ireland, with bank forms, power-of-attorney forms, but they have refused to sign, or to leave their tiny apartment. Their sons' money is frozen in the bank. Their sons' investment apartments have been trashed by tenants, the furnishings sold off. The parents fear that anything they sign or any money they receive will end the company's or the country's obligations to them. They fear they are selling their sons for two airline tickets to a place they've never seen.

The high-rise apartment is a tower of Indians and West Indians, with a sprinkling of Orientals. The nearest bus-stop kiosk is lined with women in saris. Boys practice cricket in the parking lot. Inside the building, even I wince a bit from the ferocity of onion fumes, the distinctive and immediate Indianness of frying ghee, but Judith Templeton maintains a steady flow of information. These poor old people are in imminent danger of losing their place and all their services.

I say to her, "They are Sikh. They will not open up to a Hindu woman." And what I want to add is, as much as I try not to, I stiffen now at the sight of beards and turbans. I remember a time when we all trusted each other in this new country, it was only the new country we worried about.

The two rooms are dark and stuffy. The lights are off, and an oil lamp sputters on the coffee table. The bent old lady has let us in, and her husband is wrapping a white turban over his oiled, hip-length hair. She immediately goes to the kitchen, and I hear the most familiar sound of an Indian home, tap water hitting and filling a teapot.

They have not paid their utility bills, out of fear and inability to write a   110
check. The telephone is gone, electricity and gas and water are soon to follow. They have told Judith their sons will provide. They are good boys, and they have always earned and looked after their parents.

We converse a bit in Hindi. They do not ask about the crash and I wonder if I should bring it up. If they think I am here merely as a translator, then they may feel insulted. There are thousands of Punjabi speakers, Sikhs, in Toronto to do a better job. And so I say to the old lady, "I too have lost my sons, and my husband, in the crash."

Her eyes immediately fill with tears. The man mutters a few words which sound like a blessing. "God provides and God takes away," he says.

I want to say, But only men destroy and give back nothing. "My boys and my husband are not coming back," I say. "We have to understand that."

Now the old woman responds. "But who is to say? Man alone does not decide these things." To this her husband adds his agreement.

Judith asks about the bank papers, the release forms. With a stroke of the   115
pen, they will have a provincial trustee to pay their bills, invest their money, send them a monthly pension.

"Do you know this woman?" I ask them.

The man raises his hand from the table, turns it over, and seems to regard each finger separately before he answers. "This young lady is always coming here, we make tea for her, and she leaves papers for us to sign." His eyes scan a pile of papers in the corner of the room. "Soon we will be out of tea, then will she go away?"

The old lady adds, "I have asked my neighbors and no one else gets *angrezi*° visitors. What have we done?"

---

angrezi: English or Anglo.

"It's her job," I try to explain. "The government is worried. Soon you will have no place to stay, no lights, no gas, no water."

"Government will get its money. Tell her not to worry, we are honorable   120
people."

I try to explain the government wishes to give money, not take. He raises his hand. "Let them take," he says. "We are accustomed to that. That is no problem."

"We are strong people," says the wife. "Tell her that."

"Who needs all this machinery?" demands the husband. "It is unhealthy, the bright lights, the cold air on a hot day, the cold food, the four gas rings. God will provide, not government."

"When our boys return," the mother says.

Her husband sucks his teeth. "Enough talk," he says.   125

Judith breaks in. "Have you convinced them?" The snaps on her cordovan briefcase go off like firecrackers in that quiet apartment. She lays the sheaf of legal papers on the coffee table. "If they can't write their names, an X will do—I've told them that."

Now the old lady has shuffled to the kitchen and soon emerges with a pot of tea and two cups. "I think my bladder will go first on a job like this," Judith says to me, smiling. "If only there was some way of reaching them. Please thank her for the tea. Tell her she's very kind."

I nod in Judith's direction and tell them in Hindi, "She thanks you for the tea. She thinks you are being very hospitable but she doesn't have the slightest idea what it means."

I want to say, Humor her. I want to say, My boys and my husband are with me too, more than ever. I look in the old man's eyes and I can read his stubborn, peasant's message: *I have protected this woman as best I can. She is the only person I have left. Give to me or take from me what you will, but I will not sign for it. I will not pretend that I accept.*

In the car, Judith says, "You see what I'm up against? I'm sure they're lovely   130
people, but their stubbornness and ignorance are driving me crazy. They think signing a paper is signing their sons' death warrants, don't they?"

I am looking out the window. I want to say, *In our culture, it is a parent's duty to hope.*

"Now Shaila, this next woman is a real mess. She cries day and night, and she refuses all medical help. We may have to—"

"Let me out at the subway," I say.

"I beg your pardon?" I can feel those blue eyes staring at me.

It would not be like her to disobey. She merely disapproves, and slows at a   135
corner to let me out. Her voice is plaintive. "Is there anything I said? Anything I did?"

I could answer her suddenly in a dozen ways, but I choose not to. "Shaila? Let's talk about it," I hear, then slam the door.

A wife and mother begins her life in a new country, and that life is cut short. Yet her husband tells her: Complete what we have started. We, who stayed out of politics and came half way around the world to avoid religious and political feuding, have been the first in the New World to die from it. I no longer know what we started, nor how to complete it. I write letters to the editors of local papers and to members of Parliament. Now at least they admit it was a bomb. One MP answers back, with sympathy, but with a challenge. You want to make a difference? Work on a campaign. Work on mine. Politicize the Indian voter.

My husband's old lawyer helps me set up a trust. Vikram was a saver and a careful investor. He had saved the boys' boarding school and college fees. I sell the pink house at four times what we paid for it and take a small apartment downtown. I am looking for a charity to support.

We are deep in the Toronto winter, gray skies, icy pavements. I stay indoors, watching television. I have tried to assess my situation, how best to live my life, to complete what we began so many years ago. Kusum has written me from Hardwar that her life is now serene. She has seen Satish and has heard her daughter sing again. Kusum was on a pilgrimage, passing through a village, when she heard a young girl's voice, singing one of her daughter's favorite *bhajans.* She followed the music through the squalor of a Himalayan village, to a hut where a young girl, an exact replica of her daughter, was fanning coals under the kitchen fire. When she appeared, the girl cried out, "Ma!" and ran away. What did I think of that?

I think I can only envy her.   140

Pam didn't make it to California, but writes me from Vancouver. She works in a department store, giving makeup hints to Indian and Oriental girls. Dr. Ranganathan has given up his commute, given up his house and job, and accepted an academic position in Texas, where no one knows his story and he has vowed not to tell it. He calls me now once a week.

I wait, I listen and I pray, but Vikram has not returned to me. The voices and the shapes and the nights filled with visions ended abruptly several weeks ago.

I take it as a sign.

One rare, beautiful, sunny day last week, returning from a small errand on Yonge Street, I was walking through the park from the subway to my apartment. I live equidistant from the Ontario Houses of Parliament and the University of Toronto. The day was not cold, but something in the bare trees caught my attention. I looked up from the gravel, into the branches and the clear blue sky beyond. I thought I heard the rustling of larger forms, and I waited a moment for voices. Nothing.

"What?" I asked.   145

Then as I stood in the path looking north to Queen's Park and west to the university, I heard the voices of my family one last time. *Your time has come,* they said. *Go, be brave.*

I do not know where this voyage I have begun will end. I do not know which direction I will take. I dropped the package on a park bench and started walking.

[1988]

THINKING ABOUT THE TEXT

1. In what sense does this story involve "culture"? Define the term.

2. In what ways does Shaila develop during the story? Does she go through the stages of grief that Judith Templeton mentions?

3. Consider the title. Can grief be "managed"? Define the term *manage*. What characters in the story, if any, attempt to manage grief? In what ways?

4. Evaluate Judith Templeton's words and actions. Does she deserve any sympathy?

5. Identify the role of gender in the story. If Shaila had been male, what other elements of the story, if any, might have been different?

CLARK BLAISE AND BHARATI MUKHERJEE
From *The Sorrow and the Terror: The Haunting Legacy of the Air India Tragedy*

As we pointed out in the introduction to this cluster, Mukherjee based "The Management of Grief" on the June 23, 1985, crash of Air India Flight 182. Bound for New Delhi and Bombay after leaving Toronto and Montreal, it exploded over the Irish Sea. All 329 people aboard perished. Many of them were, like Shaila, Canadian citizens of Indian descent. The explosion was a bombing, part of an effort by certain members of India's Sikh religion to win from that country a separate, independent state that would be called Khalistan. While not all Sikhs have participated in the campaign for Khalistan, it has raged for several years, and there has been other violence committed during it. For example, in 1984 Sikhs assassinated India's prime minister Indira Gandhi, largely because under her orders the Indian military had stormed a Sikh holy place, the Golden Temple of Amritsar.

Mukherjee and her husband Clark Blaise (b. 1942) wrote about the Air India incident in their 1987 book The Sorrow and the Terror: The Haunting Legacy of the Air India Tragedy. *Like Mukherjee, Blaise is the author of several books, including the novels* Lunar Attractions *(1979) and* Lusts *(1983) as well as the nonfiction work* I Had a Father: A Post-Modern Autobiography *(1993). Currently he teaches in the Writers Workshop at the University of Iowa. Here we present Chapter 6 of their book, which deals with the immediate aftermath of the Air India disaster. Numerous relatives of the passengers journeyed to Cork, Ireland, hoping to identify and repossess the bodies of their loved ones. In this effort, they found themselves dealing with Irish as well as Canadian officials, including the Gardai (Irish police).*

At the Cork Regional Hospital, the relatives were let off at the main entrance in the West Wing. Some local people were in the lobby; patients' visitors, nursing staff, ordinary citizens moved by the tragedy. The counsellors escorted the relatives through the lobby—a short walk—to the stairs leading up to the Nurses' Residence, and upstairs down a corridor lined with glass cases of plaster models of human parts, cases now draped so their contents would not upset the bereaved, to the hall where special Gardai detectives were to talk to them.

The detectives explained the identification process. First, each relative would have to fill out a pink Interpol identification form with the help of the policeman assigned to her or him. Then the Gardai would try to match the physical characteristics listed on the pink form with their own photographs and lists. If the Gardai found a match, the relative would be led away to another room and shown a selection of photographs. If the relative made a positive identification in this photo gallery, the mini-family of mourner, counsellor, and policeman would make the long walk to the East Wing. There the relative would be taken into a room and shown a plastic bag of wet, ripped clothes and jewellery. If the relative recognized the washed-up debris, then and then only, would he or she be led into another, smaller room and shown a coffined body.

The Gardai announced the procedure. The bodies were in their care, and they had to be sure that the right body went to the right relative. Besides, that first day, with the first batch of relatives—it was Wednesday, June 26th—the pathology teams were still working on the retrieved bodies.

The relatives thought they would get to see the bodies of their loved ones right away. They thought they would, at least, see the photographs. They thought they would arrive, claim their dead, and try to make sense out of abominable tragedy. They didn't know what they thought. There were no rules on how to behave well in circumstances like this. Nobody they knew had gone through what they were going through. They knew one thing: they were angry. They didn't want to fill out more forms listing shape of nose, length of playground scars, shade of black hair. They had already done this back home while they'd been kept waiting by the authorities. Agents for the Kenyon Group, the undertakers and the local police, had gone over all that with them. The men had lifted fingerprints from textbooks in neat, suburban homes. Those men had come with Yellow Identification Forms. Pink forms, yellow forms. The relatives wanted to fill out no more forms; they wanted to grieve over bodies.

The counsellors calmed the relatives. The Gardai were patient, sympathetic. 5
They had to be sure, they said. Having the relatives on hand made the filling out of the Pink Identification Forms much easier. The relatives allowed themselves to be comforted. Like them, the Irish were family people, emotional and god-fearing. They filled out the Pink Forms. Separate agencies had their separate forms. The Yellow Forms, not handled by the Irish, were lost, they suspected.

They waited. They told each other how and when they had heard the dreadful news. One man's nephew, a studious immigrant, had been cramming for college exams with the radio on and he'd heard at four in the morning. Nobody had believed the nephew. You fell asleep, they had scolded him.

The counsellors encouraged the relatives to talk. They saw an extraordinary bond forming within that vast, mournful body in the hall of the Nurses' Residence. The bereaved comforted each other. The bereaved accepted solace from other bereaved. More arrived. From India, Canada, the United States, Britain. Here were the nearly three hundred relatives, but they were not screaming; they were demanding nothing. They were private, and noble, in their terrible grief.

The Gardai, the counsellors, and beefed-up staff from consulates and embassies met each flight at Cork Airport. So did TV and print journalists. The Press followed the relatives to the hospital. Do you believe the plane was sabotaged, they asked. Are you satisfied with the hospital's arrangements? How well have Canadian officials handled this tragedy? On camera, one or two men blew up at what they perceived as consular callousness or white-Canadian coldness. "Where are those bastards?" one relative demanded. "Are they sitting tight in cozy chairs?" Back home in Toronto his astounded teenaged son witnessed his father's grief on TV. He had never heard his quiet, hard-working, very correct father use the word "bastard."

The Gardai read through their records. They had 131 bodies. One hundred and ninety-eight bodies were in the plane's wreckage at the bottom of the sea. Most relatives who had come to Cork would have no body to grieve over or to cremate. The Gardai had to be careful. They called in a relative as soon as they felt there was a fair chance of match-up. The relative called in felt "lucky." (Afterwards, John Laurence, the father of the young dancers, said, "Can you imagine how topsy-turvy those days were? We thought we were 'lucky' if the police came in saying that they thought they had a body for viewing!" His two daughters were beautiful. He had photographs of them, eighteen and sixteen, in their splendid dance costumes. Their bodies were not brought back in bodybags to be rephotographed in mutilation.)

In the photo gallery some relatives had trouble recognizing the marked faces   10 and bloated bodies. These were not the faces of the people they had hugged at Pearson International Airport or at Mirabel in Montreal. They had an easier time recognizing the photographs of friends and neighbours. The Gardai was glad of that help. Whole families had been lost on that plane. This was a tight community. The mourners in Cork remembered what departing friends had worn for the vacation trip to India. Those who could identify the pictures went on to the East Wing for the rest of the sad, grim procedure. The others came back to the hall to wait for a change in "luck."

In the hall relatives who had flown in from India had a hard time filling out the forms. Two women, both wives and mothers, both naturalized Canadians, had gone on to India ahead of their families. They did not know what their loved ones had worn on the plane when they had taken off on Saturday. The Indian relatives of Canadian families that had perished without survivors had the hardest time. They had come to identify and mourn brothers or sisters they hadn't seen perhaps in years. The faces had thickened or maybe thinned; many of the women had cut their hair. The infants they had cradled years ago had grown into teenaged math whizzes and dance instructors. Some India-based relatives could not speak English and had a harder time still with the identification.

So the relatives helped each other. Do you remember any birthmarks? Did they write you of any surgery, any illnesses? They felt very close.

Some of the relatives from India had horror stories about the Canadian High Commission in New Delhi. They had tried to get visas to go on to Canada after Cork, so they could at least help look after a devastated brother or sister for a few months. The Canadian High Commission, some said, had not only refused them visas but had behaved badly, had treated them with unnecessary rudeness. They said that the Canadian visa officers had acted suspicious, as though this were not family rallying in time of monumental tragedy, but just one more immigration scam to sneak into Canada.

There was a lot of waiting around in the hall where the Gardai detectives had given their procedural talk. To make the wait a little easier, the Friends of the Hospital, a volunteer group, set themselves up in a corner of another hall. They poured tea, cut cake. Some relatives fell sick during the waiting, and four had to be treated—for assorted ailments such as hysteria, diabetes, bad heart—in the hospital.

The relatives waited and asked each other deep questions about Fate. What 15 if their families had been booked to fly on an airline other than Air India? Would the 329 people on that Air India Flight 182 have all died precisely at the ordained moment on the morning of Sunday, June 23rd? Many had originally reserved tickets on other airlines: British Airways, Kuwait Airways. Some had planned to send their families a week earlier or a week later. Why and how had it happened? The journalists were full of stories of sabotage. The journalists played phrases by them: Sikh terrorists, bag-bombs. (The refinement of phrase from "Sikh" to "Khalistani" would be slow.) Was the destruction of family life, which meant their lives in Canada, the lives they had worked so hard and saved so hard for, caused by the individual wills of *saboteurs*? In those early days, when the pain was real but the loss not yet felt, the Hindu relatives consoled themselves with thoughts of Destiny. When one has fulfilled one's mission on earth, one is recalled by God. Atman, the individual soul, dissolves forever into the Brahman, and the cycle of reincarnation is stopped. This happy fusion is promised to "pure" souls. And their loved ones on that plane had been innocent, pure. They had hurt nobody. The children, in fact, had done good. Many were carrying back money from their piggy-banks to give away to the Indian poor.

Thoughts about Fate consoled the Hindus in Cork. And this fatalism was a temporary boon to government and insurance companies. Angry relatives making emotional remarks about Sikh-Hindu conflicts to the Indian press could set off dreadful communal riots. Delhi had gone through such communal riots the day Mrs. Gandhi was fatally shot. The plane crash, the Indian officials suspected, was an act of Khalistani terrorist revenge—innocent blood for innocent blood—for those very riots. The Canadians and Air India were thankful for the fatalism of these New Canadians, which delayed any ferocious complaints to the Press about Canadian laxity in securing its major airports.

The relatives who were still without bodies tried their best to change their "luck." One man, an engineer, shaved off his mourner's stubble and spruced himself up. "My wife wouldn't go out with me if I didn't shave," he told his nephew who had come from Toronto to look after him in Cork. "I haven't shaved since I heard the news. Who knows, if I shave maybe she'll show up." And his wife's body did. The engineer found the bodies of his wife and son. The son didn't look mangled. His father was told it would be better if he didn't look at the wife's face. He didn't find the body of his teenaged daughter. And he thought to himself that if it is God's will to take a life, then it is also God's will to save life. "Why a miracle can't happen and save her?" he said to his nephew. He remembered what the Gardai had said about ocean currents bearing bodies, very possibly, towards Spain or France. Why not, he thought. Maybe, by a miracle, the daughter was alive. (In India, where he went from Cork, two astrologers assured him that his daughter was still alive. So did a Canadian astrologer when he got back to work. Water was a miraculous medium. He had heard a story of a man drowning in an Indian river, and then returning home alive to his family a year later. There were other stories. He liked especially the one in which a man died in a plane crash in Kashmir, and then two years after the "death," the man walked in the door of his house as though he'd never died in the crash.) He had posters made from his daughter's picture — posters as for a Missing Person — and a year after the crash he went to Málaga, Spain, and put the posters on walls.

The engineer was not the only one who believed that a daughter had survived the terrible fall. One mother brought dry clothes to Cork for her two missing girls. The girls were excellent swimmers. They would swim ashore and need clothes. The daughters were not retrieved by the rescue squads, and for a long time, for months in fact, the mother believed that they had made their way to an island and were waiting to be found.

For some relatives the process of identifying bodies of loved ones they had seen off cheerfully in Toronto just days before was grimly swift and grimly smooth. The young parents of a teenaged dancer rushed into London as early as Monday the 24th, and, dazed, located their daughter's photograph in the Air India office at Heathrow Airport. Their inconsolable grief made gut-wrenching international headline news.

They arrived in Cork, sped through the police identification process, and had the body released to them. Their daughter had loved Toronto. Toronto, not India, had been her home. Toronto was where her soul should rest. The parents wanted to fly back with her casket right away. But the Air India office in Cork had its own cost-effective casket-freighting schedule. The parents were advised to fly home by themselves and wait for the body, which would be freighted into Toronto separately within three days, maybe four. But they would not part with their daughter a second time. They tried Aer-Lingus; they would fly Aer-Lingus if Aer-Lingus could fly the casket and them on the same flight. Aer-Lingus had its own problems; in the middle of this swell of disaster traffic, the local airline was grounded by a strike.

The parents tried the Canadian Embassy as a last resort. Many relatives perceived the Canadian officials as insensitive to their grief and as unhelpful. These

20

officials were correct, but how could they know what was needed. The Canadian Embassy did have an office on the second floor of the hospital, however, and that's where the determined parents went. The Canadian officials served these parents coffee, and confided that they had instructions from External Affairs to get in touch with Ottawa as soon as the family arrived in Cork. The parents sat in that second-floor office while the Canadians called, first Ottawa, then on Ottawa's advice, the Canadian Forces base in West Germany, so that space for the family of living and dead could be freed that evening on a Hercules transport aircraft.

Months later, in Mississauga, the father recalled the soothing words of the Canadian official. "The diplomat said to me, 'The Hercules will be at the airport by 7:30. Get ready. But please don't tell anyone. There are a hundred and fifty other Canadians out there. We can't help anyone else. Let's go. Please get in my car and I'll drive you back to your hotel.' So he took us to the hotel, and he packed up my little suitcase. Then he took us down to the airport, to a small room where nobody could see us, and he waited with us until the Hercules came. Our daughter was lucky. We knew she would have fame, and she did. Her picture was in the papers. She was treated special."

The relatives whose loved ones' descriptions had not yet been matched with photographs of bodies spent many hours by the shores of Bantry Bay. Tony Dawson arranged coach trips. By island standards, Cork to Bantry is a longish way. The mourners left early in the morning and got back to their hotels late in the evening. The ocean calmed them. They felt close to the people they had lost. The water at the bay was still, still enough for good swimmers to stay afloat. They couldn't visualize churning seas or sharks, and the sailors who had plucked or winched or hefted mutilated bodies had been instructed not to talk; at least not about the gory part of their heroic job. The Laurences spent their most peaceful hours at the coast. They remembered their daughters had loved roses. One girl had loved red roses, the other white. They wanted to offer the sea red and white rose petals. There were gardens with rose bushes in Bantry, so they asked the owner of one garden, could they please pluck a rose. And the owner and her neighbours told the Laurences to take not one, not a bunch, but gardensful. In spite of the horror, these were radiant times. Thank God the plane went down off Ireland, the Laurences said. The Irish were sincere people. Anywhere else, in London or Toronto or Delhi, for instance, the same grief would have been unbearable.

But when they came back to Cork, to their hotels, the loss became nightly more real. And there were pictures to see, descriptions to listen to. Just in case. The relatives and the Gardai wanted to be sure, absolutely, positively sure, before they let a relative leave Cork. The Laurences looked through ninety pictures.

One of the relatives, Dr. Bal Gupta, a calm, methodical man not known to be emotional except for one outburst at the invisibility of Canadian officials, had lost his wife in the crash. He came back from Bantry Bay on Saturday evening and found a message from the hospital. The Gardai thought they had a match for Mrs. Gupta. He took the bus back to the hospital at once.

25

He had left his older son in Toronto, and brought with him his younger, a thirteen-year-old who'd suddenly, mysteriously, developed an ulcer. The boy, though sick, had come to Cork to look after his father. Father and son had arrived on Wednesday night. On Thursday Dr. Gupta had filled out forms. Friday had been a nightmare of waiting, but the waiting hadn't been the hospital's fault. He praised John Martin's Group for its generous-spirited management of the mammoth disaster. He praised the counsellor and the policeman who had stayed with him through the long, slow days of ordeal. He praised Kiran and Razia Doshi, the official and the unofficial Indian ambassadors. He had no praise, however, for the staff representing Canada.

"Up through Thursday," he said, "we didn't see the Canadians' faces, nobody's. . . . What happened was on Thursday night all of us were being bused back to our hotels from the hospital. It was very late, and I was probably the last one to come out. I came out and reporters surrounded us. I don't know if they were local TV crews, or CTV or what. They kept asking questions, such as 'Are you satisfied with the arrangements?' I told them that I was disappointed that more bodies could not be identified that day but that I understood why the Gardai had to be slow and meticulous. But when they asked me about the Canadian representatives . . . I don't know, I just burst out. I used some very unparliamentary language right there on tape! That night some Canadian official called me at the hotel, and the next morning, Friday morning, some Canadians came and apologized and said that they were working behind the scenes."

Saturday he and his son had gone on the bus to Bantry Bay. He had prayed on the ride over — he was a licensed Hindu priest back in Toronto — and he had prayed at the shore, tossed flowers in the water and prayed, and prayed again on the ride back to Cork. And in Cork there was the message: come to the hospital.

Dr. Gupta left his sick child in the hotel and rushed to face whatever alien ordeal. This is how he remembers the rest of Saturday night:

"First of all they [the Gardai] sat down and read from the post-mortem report. There were some discrepancies: the height was off by an inch, and the weight was a little different. But those things were all right, I thought, because of water absorption, etc. The description was about right. The clothes they described sounded the same as the *kurta* and *salivar* she'd been wearing. She'd dressed in a long *kurta* dress and tight pyjamas. The design seemed the same. Then the Gardai brought me a bag of effects. They showed me ornaments. I said, 'They don't belong to my wife. She didn't own those.' And they said, 'Well, anyway, we may as well show you the picture.' Then they showed me the picture. I said, 'This isn't my wife. This is my friend's wife. This is Mrs. Sharma.' The Gardai said. 'Well, it hasn't been a waste then. At least a body has been identified.'

"So we — the policeman and counsellor and I — came back up to the hall in the Nurses' Residence in the West Wing. They told us to wait. They said they would call us one by one. There were others waiting. What they had done was put the pictures up in a room, and they were asking people in small batches. Then all of a sudden, I don't know if somebody goofed or what, they opened the door and we went in and we looked at the pictures.

30

"#2 was Mrs. Sharma. #40 was the Sharmas' elder boy. #96 was Mrs. Radha-krishna. And then #97 was my wife's picture. I had no difficulty in identifying. The face was in reasonable shape, except for a cut. We identified two of the Sharma boys. We had some doubts about the third.

"Then I went to the policeman, and I said. 'That's my wife's body.' It was the same policeman. That was very good, you always dealt with the same policeman.

"Around seven or eight in the evening, they came to us and took down our description. Then they led us downstairs [to the East Wing] and showed us a bag of belongings. There were two rings, nothing else. There was no clothing.

"Then they showed us the body. The bodies were very well kept. The Gardai   35 were identifying first through pictures, then they were bringing in the body from the morgue.

"If you requested they would leave you alone with the body in a little room. Otherwise, there were nuns there all the time.

"Then there was a lot of paperwork involved. I made a declaration about my wife's body. Then about the other bodies I'd identified. They made notes. We fin-ished around eleven o'clock. Probably I was the last one to leave the hospital.

"I phoned home that night. I have a brother in Toronto. My brother's opin-ion was that if the body has been found, it should be taken to India for funeral rites. He said that he would call India and let my in-laws know.

"On Sunday the hospital organized a mixed service in the chapel. It was very beautiful. The Laurences read from the Bible, I read from the Gita. There were Muslim prayers. After that we had to do paperwork for the transportation of the body. I spent the whole of Sunday on the paperwork, and still it wasn't com-pleted. The body could only be released by the police authorities. And the police authorities had to make sure that the body could be released. I was told to come back on Monday. I was making all the arrangements for the Sharma family, too. I phoned Sharma's brother in India, but the brother was already on his way to Ire-land. Sunday night I had to take care of my son. He had fever, and I gave him antibiotics. I finished my wife's paperwork by lunchtime on Monday."

There were only two cases of initial misidentification. One husband matched   40 memory with photograph and identified his wife's body, but the dental records on his wife's Yellow Form did not match the dental records from that body's post-mortem. Another body, misidentified and shipped on to London, was recalled in time for correct identification. One man, who had lost his wife and two small chil-dren, found his wife's body fairly quickly, but not those of his children. He remem-bered a year later that towards the end of the identification week when only a few bodies were left and he was hysterical with grief, the nuns had let him into a room so he could view the unclaimed bodies of children. He remembered (or misre-membered) the nuns urging him to take two bodies as his own. He peered into faces, but the faces were alien. In the end, all the bodies retrieved were positively identified. This is unique in the history of air-crash disasters of this magnitude.

But some identifications took a long time. The identifications, for instance, of Ms. Rama Paul's brother's family. The whole Bhat family — mother, father, and two daughters, Bina and Tina—was wiped out. Rama Paul is a nurse at the Princess Margaret Hospital (for cancer patients) in Toronto. Soothing people in pain and in fear of death is her job. She is a remarkable person, remarkable in the Toronto Indo-Canadian community for her energy, her frankness and her ability to live a happy life on her own as a single woman. In this community, women in their forties are invariably wives or widows. Rama Paul devoted herself to her brother's family and to her patients at the Princess Margaret Hospital. She was so devoted, and so capable, that she had packed the Bhat family's suitcases the night before the Air India flight and labelled each one with waterproof markers: BHAT, DOWNSVIEW, ONTARIO. She'd told the family what to wear before they'd driven to the airport: the suit he had graduated in for her brother, bridal red for her sister-in-law, and smart Canadian clothes she herself had bought for her nieces, who slept over more often in her apartment than they did in their own. When tragedy struck—and she had had premonitions strong enough and recurrent enough to urge her family even at the airport not to go— she became an excellent filler of the Pink and Yellow Forms. She knew what each member had worn, what object was in which part of each suitcase. With her nurse's memory for minutiae, she knew about birthmarks and scars. But she did not want to go to Cork as soon as she heard the dreaded, pre-intimated news.

"Air India wanted me to go when it happened," Rama Paul said. "They told me how many bodies had been found. I said to them, 'What guarantee can you give me that of the 329 who died, I'll find even one from my family. No, I don't want to go.' But I told them I wanted them to keep in touch with me. So they used to ring me up. They were very good about that.

"Then one Sunday morning, at about a quarter to five, the phone rang. I thought it was probably my sister in Australia. She sometimes calls. I get up at five on Sundays. It's a work day for me, and there aren't that many buses, so if I miss my bus I have to wait another half-hour. It wasn't my sister on the phone; it was a policeman from Cork. He said that he wanted to ask me some questions. I said, 'Look, I'm going off to work. I have to get ready to catch my bus. I'll be late if I answer your questions.' But he kept on asking questions: what was your niece wearing, and so on. I told him.

"He said, 'Miss Paul, we want you to fly immediately to Cork.'

"I said, 'No way. I'm not flying to Cork. I am going to work.'

"The policeman said, 'You have no choice.'

"I said, 'Look, Monday is my day off. I can fly on Monday.' But he wouldn't agree to that. So I warned him, 'I'm going to work now, and don't call me at work.'

"It was my bus time already, and I hadn't brushed my teeth or had a wash. I just slipped on my uniform and rushed to catch that bus. When I got to the hospital the nursing officer could tell that I was in a panic. In no time there were five calls from Cork, and three from Air India. The girls on the floor were really worried, because the callers identified themselves as police officers and kept asking what kind of passport does Miss Paul hold? I think between 7:30 and 9:30 that morning there must have been ten calls.

45

"Around twelve noon a man from Air India brought me a ticket. And early that evening Chandra's brother and I were off to Cork.

"When we got to Cork, we were treated like VIPs. We were the last relatives   50 to arrive, you see. There were a lot of people there, because they were putting on a big ceremony. A very beautiful ceremony. I think that's why they were rushing to identify bodies."

Rama Paul found three bodies in Cork. She had Kenyons air-freight those coffined bodies to India. At least the souls would finish the trip home.

Of the 132 bodies recovered from the sea, 60 were shipped to India, 13 to Canada, 2 to England, and 1 to the United States. There were 52 bodies cremated in Dublin, 2 bodies buried in Dublin and 2 buried in the serene, green city of Cork. Many had to leave the bodies of their loved ones on the ocean bed. Some day, they promised themselves, they would rent a ship to carry them to the exact spot where the *Emperor Kanishka* had torn through the waves. They would chant the final prayers for their lost families from the ship's deck, and in that way, calm their own bereft, bewildered souls.   [1987]

THINKING ABOUT THE TEXT

1. Compare this chapter to the Ireland section of Mukherjee's story. Does her fictional work seem significantly different in emphasis from her non-fiction one? What specific features of each come most to your mind as you consider this question?

2. Describing the relatives who came to Ireland, Blaise and Mukherjee write that "they were private, and noble, in their terrible grief." Which characters in Mukherjee's short story, if any, fit this description?

3. What do you suppose the two authors want to emphasize with the particular details and anecdotes they report? Where in this chapter, if anywhere, do Blaise and Mukherjee let their personal feelings show? Should they have expressed them more often? Why, or why not?

NEW YORK TIMES
India Arrests Sikh in '85 Bombing of Jetliner

At the time they were in Cork, relatives of the Air India flight's passengers did not know who or what had blown up the plane. In fact, they could not be certain that a bomb had caused the disaster. Even at the time Blaise and Mukherjee wrote their book, no culprits had been precisely identified, although it was clear by then that Sikh terrorists had been involved. Not until seven years after the disaster was someone arrested for it. That arrest was reported in the following article, which appeared in the July 19, 1992, issue of the New York Times *and was supplied to the newspaper by the Reuters wire service.*

Bombay, India, July 18—The authorities have arrested a Sikh separatist in a 1985 bomb explosion aboard an Air India Boeing 747 off the coast of Ireland in which 329 people died, a senior police official said today.

The Bombay Police Commissioner, S. Ramamurthy, said the suspect, Manjit Singh, thirty years old, who used the alias Lal Singh, was seized on Thursday by an anti-terrorist squad that had received a tip that he would be arriving by train in Bombay from the northern state of Punjab.

He said the officers prevented Mr. Singh from biting into a cyanide pill as he was being arrested.

Commissioner Ramamurthy said Mr. Singh has been described as a lieutenant general in the Sikh separatist group that calls itself the Khalistan Liberation Force. He was also wanted on charges of smuggling arms from Pakistan to Punjab state, where Sikh rebels are campaigning for an independent homeland.

An Indian Government inquiry into the Air India blast concluded that it was   5
caused by a bomb that had been hidden in the luggage of a man identified as Mr. Singh.

The official report said Mr. Singh had checked his baggage in Vancouver, British Columbia, for a Canadian Pacific flight to Toronto and on to Bombay on a linking Air India flight. Mr. Singh never boarded the flight in Vancouver and had no confirmed reservation from Toronto, the report said.

The bomb exploded on June 23, 1985, when the airliner was flying at 31,000 feet off the Irish coast. There were no survivors.

Another bomb, in the suitcase of a man registered as L. Singh, exploded the same day as it was being unloaded from a Canadian airliner at the Narita airport in Tokyo. Two people were killed.

That suitcase had also been handled at Vancouver and Toronto. It was being transferred in Tokyo from the Canadian plane to an Air India flight to Bangkok when the bomb went off, the official report on the blast said.

More than 15,000 people have been killed since 1985 in the Sikh campaign   10
for an independent homeland in Punjab state, which the separatists refer to as Khalistan.

Mr. Ramamurthy said Mr. Singh worked on a merchant ship in Canada from 1978 until 1984, the year that Indian Army soldiers invaded the Golden Temple in Amritsar, the holiest Sikh shrine, to root out armed militants.

He said that Mr. Singh joined the militants after the army operation, which was viewed by many Sikhs as a sacrilege.   [1992]

THINKING ABOUT THE TEXT

1. What is the function of each paragraph in this article?

2. The article is quite short. Moreover, the *Times* had not published an article on the Air India disaster since 1986 and has published nothing further on it since reporting the arrest. What would you to say to someone who accuses the newspaper of cultural bias in failing to provide additional information about these foreign events?

3. Imagine that years after "The Management of Grief" ends, Shaila reads this article. What might her thoughts be? Try writing a page or two in her voice.

SAM HUSSEINI

Profile in Unfairness

In "The Management of Grief," Shaila becomes more distrustful of Sikhs because the plane crash appears to have been caused by members of that religion. Similarly, in real life, particular groups have become objects of suspicion when terrorism occurs or seems possible. Immediately following the Oklahoma City bombing, for instance, many Americans assumed that Arabs were responsible. The same suspicion arose when TWA Flight 800 crashed in 1996. If terrorism is to be thwarted, must airlines subject people of certain cultures to special scrutiny? Is such treatment ethical? Sam Husseini, a consultant to the American-Arab Anti-Discrimination Committee, addresses these issues in the following opinion piece. It was published in the November 24, 1996, issue of The Washington Post, *four months after the TWA crash.*

The Gore Commission on Aviation Safety and Security, formed in the wake of the TWA 800 crash, made twenty recommendations—virtually all of which deal with security issues. Most troubling, the commission recommended—and on October 9 Clinton signed into law—a computer passenger "profiling" system to be created by the FAA in conjunction with Northwest Airlines. This pilot program is supposed to serve as a model for other airlines to adopt. If your "profile" fits that of a terrorist, you will undergo more questions and search than other passengers. It's a law that could make institutionalized discrimination more prevalent.

There's an imbalance in the commission's work fueled by fear of terrorism. Most plane crashes are not the result of terrorist attack. The best available evidence on the TWA crash now suggests that mechanical failure, not a bomb, was responsible. The commission's rush to judgment after the events of last July has come at the expense of civil rights in general.

Last August Laura Fadil, a nursing student at Yale University, went to the Newark airport for a flight to visit her relatives in Haifa, Israel, for the first time. As she got to the ticket counter of El Al, the national airline of Israel, security personnel asked her what kind of name "Fadil" was. When she told them it was an Arab name, she was taken to a room and questioned for thirty minutes. She was asked "If you're a student, how could you afford the plane ticket?" and "What's the amount of your scholarship?" Finally, she was told, "You're a security risk." Fadil offered to let the El Al officials hand search her bags, but she was ignored. Instead, she was given a ticket with another airline for the next day. Outraged she came to the American-Arab Anti-Discrimination Committee, where I work, with her story.

"I was raised as an American—we're used to rights," she says. "The experience was so foreign to me—to be treated that way, not because of anything I did. It was extremely humiliating. I don't think I'll ever forget it."

This type of thing isn't supposed to happen any more. "In the past, security   5
officers have sometimes used a crude profile consisting mainly of one factor,
race, to single out minorities for special searches," the *New York Times* recently
editorialized, implying that profiling has been abandoned.

It hasn't been. After the Oklahoma City bombing in April 1995, Abraham
Ahmad was traveling from Oklahoma to Jordan to visit family. He was deemed a
suspect in the bombing because of his ethnicity and travel destination. Law
enforcement authorities detained and questioned him repeatedly over three
days. He was stopped in Chicago and handcuffed and unnecessarily paraded
through the London airport. He was made to answer questions about his religious
practices. He was strip searched. Eventually he got an apology and was allowed to
go on his way

In June, within twenty-four hours after the bombing of the U.S. military residence in Saudi Arabia, Lilia Tawasil and her daughter Zee traveled from the
Philippines to San Francisco. On arrival, U.S. Customs officials asked them
about the veils they were wearing, about their religion, about their prayer rug.
Lilia Tawasil later told me that she and her daughter were asked for numerous
forms of identification, then taken to a room where a security agent frisked her —
a grandmother of three — all because she was a Muslim wearing a veil. The Customs Service later apologized for not explaining why she was searched.

I myself was singled out three times for baggage searches while traveling
from the Mideast to the United States through Europe in the summer of 1993 on
a U.S. carrier.

This is what happens when "profiling" is put in practice. The Customs Service denies that it uses profiling but acknowledges that it does "passenger analysis." Whatever you call it, the practice seems to result in searches based on
stereotypes. As the American Civil Liberties Union recently put it, "at the airport
ticket counter, passengers check only their luggage, not their rights to personal
security, privacy, and equality."

The Gore Commission says it "will establish an advisory board on civil liber-   10
ties questions that arise from the development and use of profiling systems." But
that sounds like these concerns will be at best an afterthought. The FAA recently
stated that none of the criteria of a profiling system they are developing with
Northwest Airlines are based on "race, religion, gender or personal appearance" — but declined to say whether place of birth or travel history would be factors. So, it's possible that anyone who was born in or has visited an Arab country
could be singled out when they're trying to fly from Pittsburgh to Los Angeles.
This would be de facto discrimination.

And while "profiling" is overly broad from a civil rights perspective, it is
overly narrow from a security perspective. Profiling, for example, would probably
not have zeroed in on the white seminarian who recently pled guilty to trying to
board a plane in Tampa with hand grenades. He was caught at a metal detector.

Still, some are all too willing to toss away rights for a false sense of security.
New York Times columnist Thomas Friedman recently complained that it was too

easy for him to get his bags through security: "I was going to TEHERAN, IRAN," Friedman emphasized, as if it belonged on another planet, "and security agents let some yo-yo load my suitcase without a tag or a search. On top of that, I look like [convicted bomber] Ramzi Yousef's twin brother!"

USA Today headlined a recent story "Improving Airport Security: Profiling May Be as Important as Technology." El Al, the airline that developed profiling and refused to seat Laura Fadil, was singled out for praise. Former El Al security official Arik Arad was quoted as saying, "Profiling — asking specific questions to identify travelers who pose the highest security risks — is the most valuable weapon in the war against terrorism." The paper reported that the Israeli carrier's alumni "now teach the airline's methods to other carriers." Is that supposed to be a good thing — to emulate a country that has sacrificed civil liberties in pursuit of illusory security? Since the TWA 800 crash, Arad has been a media darling, appearing on such shows as "This Week with David Brinkley."

In covering the investigation of the cause of the TWA crash, the big media outlets have focused on the apparent precedent of the bombing of Pan Am flight 103 over Lockerbie, Scotland, in 1988. Given the inconclusive results of the TWA 800 inquiry so far, plane crashes related to mechanical failures seem more relevant. For example, a Boeing 747-100 plane — the same kind of plane as TWA 800 — exploded and crashed near Madrid in 1976. The plane had previously been owned by TWA and sold to the Iranian Air Force. The *Seattle Times* reported this summer that investigators compiled evidence that a fuel leak ignited by an electrical spark may have caused the explosion but were never able to say definitively what caused the crash.

Of course, the fact that TWA 800 might have been the result of a mechanical   15
failure doesn't mean that terrorist attacks aren't possible. But in seeking to protect ourselves from terrorism and mechanical failures, we should recall the words of Thurgood Marshall: "History teaches that grave threats to liberty often come in times of urgency, when constitutional rights seem too extravagant to endure."

That seems to have been too often forgotten since the crash of TWA 800. In a recent "NBC Nightly News" segment, reporter Martin Fletcher noted that one of El Al's criteria for a suspicious profile is "young, dark-skinned men." Still, Fletcher reported approvingly, "Any airline can be as safe as El Al, security experts said today. They just need the money and the commitment."

Not to mention the brazenness to single out people because of the color of their skin.   [1996]

THINKING ABOUT THE TEXT

1. At the end of his article, Husseini suggests that "profiling" amounts to "brazenness." What other terms might he use to label the practice he is criticizing? How does he support his argument? Evaluate the case he makes. Does he use anecdotes about specific people as effectively as Blaise and Mukherjee do? What would you say to someone who criticizes him for failing to suggest alternative methods of preventing terrorism?

2. Husseini works for the American-Arab Anti-Discrimination Committee and is presumably of Arab descent. In what ways, if any, does his background matter to you as he criticizes the Israeli airline El Al?

3. In Mukherjee's story, Shaila is more suspicious of Sikhs after the plane crash. Do you suppose Husseini would fault her for being so? Why, or why not? What would you say to someone who argues that the arrest of a Sikh for the real-life Air India disaster indicates that the airline should have profiled Sikhs more in the first place?

WRITING ABOUT ISSUES

1. Write an essay comparing Shaila with another character in Mukherjee's story who has lost a family member in the plane crash. Are the differences between these two characters or their similarities more striking? Refer to specific acts and words of each.

2. Imagine that you are the present-day assistant editor of a newspaper in your hometown. Your boss, the editor, asks your advice: Should the newspaper remind its readers of the 1985 Air India disaster? If so, what are some things about it that are important to emphasize? Write a memo to your boss addressing these questions by referring to at least two of the texts in this cluster.

3. At one point in "The Management of Grief," Shaila claims to "flutter between worlds." Write an essay discussing at least one specific way in which this phrase applies to you. Be sure to identify what you mean by *worlds*.

4. Write an essay explaining how a particular disaster brought a certain cultural issue to the fore and what your position on the issue is. Define what you mean by *culture* and support the position you express. To discuss the disaster in detail, you may need to do research in the library. If you wish, refer in your essay to one or more of the texts in this cluster.

LEARNING FROM PERSONAL ENCOUNTERS WITH MORTALITY

AUDRE LORDE, "The Transformation of Silence into Language and Action"
JUNE JORDAN, "Many Rivers to Cross"

In his 1910 novel *Howards End*, E. M. Forster observed that "death destroys a man" but "the idea of death saves him." Although Forster used the generic male, clearly he aimed to express a universal truth, and his statement does seem to capture one. While death entails physical extinction, recognizing that you will eventually die can motivate you to make your life productive. Here two African American writers discuss how they changed their lives for the better after facing death up close. Audre Lorde reports that the threat of breast cancer made her stop being silent about various matters. Recalling her mother's suicide, June Jordan finds in this terrible event reason to work at developing her own strengths. Although we call Lorde's and Jordan's texts essays, both actually were written as speeches for groups composed mostly of women. Think about how they may have shaped their accounts to inspire their original audiences as well as you, their current reader.

BEFORE YOU READ

If you were to give a speech for an audience of women about silences in your life, what things might you mention? If you were to give a speech for an audience of women about your work experiences, which ones might you emphasize?

AUDRE LORDE

The Transformation of Silence into Language and Action

Audre Lorde (1934–1992) was a poet, essayist, college professor, and political activist. The following text appeared in a 1978 issue of the journal Sinister Wisdom, *in Lorde's 1980 nonfiction book* The Cancer Journals, *and in the 1984 collection* Sister Outsider: Essays and Speeches by Audre Lorde. *But originally it was a speech delivered at the 1977 convention of the Modern Language Association, the leading organization of college faculty who teach literature and language. Lorde spoke as part of a panel on "The Lesbian and Literature," and her audience was primarily female. In her speech, Lorde reported that her breast tumor had turned out to be benign. Subsequently, she did develop breast cancer and died from it.*

I have come to believe over and over again that what is most important to me must be spoken, made verbal and shared, even at the risk of having it bruised or misunderstood. That the speaking profits me, beyond any other effect. I am standing here as a Black lesbian poet, and the meaning of all that waits upon the fact that I am still alive, and might not have been. Less than two months ago I was told by two doctors, one female and one male, that I would have to have breast surgery, and that there was a 60 to 80 percent chance that the tumor was malignant. Between that telling and the actual surgery, there was a three-week period of the agony of an involuntary reorganization of my entire life. The surgery was completed, and the growth was benign.

But within those three weeks, I was forced to look upon myself and my living with a harsh and urgent clarity that has left me still shaken but much stronger. This is a situation faced by many women, by some of you here today. Some of what I experienced during that time has helped elucidate for me much of what I feel concerning the transformation of silence into language and action.

In becoming forcibly and essentially aware of my mortality, and of what I wished and wanted for my life, however short it might be, priorities and omissions became strongly etched in a merciless light, and what I most regretted were my silences. Of what had I *ever* been afraid? To question or to speak as I believed could have meant pain, or death. But we all hurt in so many different ways, all the time, and pain will either change or end. Death, on the other hand, is the final silence. And that might be coming quickly, now, without regard for whether I had ever spoken what needed to be said, or had only betrayed myself into small silences, while I planned someday to speak, or waited for someone else's words. And I began to recognize a source of power within myself that comes from the knowledge that while it is most desirable not to be afraid, learning to put fear into a perspective gave me great strength.

I was going to die, if not sooner then later, whether or not I had ever spoken myself. My silences had not protected me. Your silence will not protect you. But for every real word spoken, for every attempt I had ever made to speak those truths for which I am still seeking, I had made contact with other women while we examined the words to fit a world in which we all believed, bridging our differences. And it was the concern and caring of all those women which gave me strength and enabled me to scrutinize the essentials of my living.

The women who sustained me through that period were Black and white, old and young, lesbian, bisexual, and heterosexual, and we all shared a war against the tyrannies of silence. They all gave me a strength and concern without which I could not have survived intact. Within those weeks of acute fear came the knowledge — within the war we are all waging with the forces of death, subtle and otherwise, conscious or not — I am not only a casualty, I am also a warrior.

5

What are the words you do not yet have? What do you need to say? What are the tyrannies you swallow day by day and attempt to make your own, until you will sicken and die of them, still in silence? Perhaps for some of you here today, I am the face of one of your fears. Because I am woman, because I am Black, because I am lesbian, because I am myself — a Black woman warrior poet doing my work — come to ask you, are you doing yours?

And of course I am afraid, because the transformation of silence into language and action is an act of self-revelation, and that always seems fraught with danger. But my daughter, when I told her of our topic and my difficulty with it, said, "Tell them about how you're never really a whole person if you remain silent, because there's always that one little piece inside you that wants to be spoken out, and if you keep ignoring it, it gets madder and madder and hotter and hotter, and if you don't speak it out one day it will just up and punch you in the mouth from the inside."

In the cause of silence, each of us draws the face of her own fear — fear of contempt, of censure, or some judgment, or recognition, of challenge, of annihilation. But most of all, I think, we fear the visibility without which we cannot truly live. Within this country where racial difference creates a constant, if unspoken, distortion of vision, Black women have on one hand always been highly visible, and so, on the other hand, have been rendered invisible through the depersonalization of racism. Even within the women's movement, we have had to fight, and still do, for that very visibility which also renders us most vulnerable, our Blackness. For to survive in the mouth of this dragon we call America, we have had to learn this first and most vital lesson — that we were never meant to survive. Not as human beings. And neither were most of you here today, Black or not. And that visibility which makes us most vulnerable is that which also is the source of our greatest strength. Because the machine will try to grind you into dust anyway, whether or not we speak. We can sit in our corners mute forever while our sisters and our selves are wasted, while our children are distorted and destroyed, while our earth is poisoned; we can sit in our safe corners mute as bottles, and we will still be no less afraid.

In my house this year we are celebrating the feast of Kwanza, the African-American festival of harvest which begins the day after Christmas and lasts for seven days. There are seven principles of Kwanza, one for each day. The first principle is Umoja, which means unity, the decision to strive for and maintain unity in self and community. The principle for yesterday, the second day, was Kujichagulia — self-determination — the decision to define ourselves, name ourselves, and speak for ourselves, instead of being defined and spoken for by others. Today is the third day of Kwanza, and the principle for today is Ujima — collective work and responsibility — the decision to build and maintain ourselves and our communities together and to recognize and solve our problems together.

Each of us is here now because in one way or another we share a commitment to language and to the power of language, and to the reclaiming of that language which has been made to work against us. In the transformation of silence into language and action, it is vitally necessary for each one of us to establish or examine her function in that transformation and to recognize her role as vital within that transformation. 10

For those of us who write, it is necessary to scrutinize not only the truth of what we speak, but the truth of that language by which we speak it. For others, it is to share and spread also those words that are meaningful to us. But primarily for us all, it is necessary to teach by living and speaking those truths which we believe and know beyond understanding. Because in this way alone we can survive, by taking part in a process of life that is creative and continuing, that is growth.

And it is never without fear — of visibility, of the harsh light of scrutiny and perhaps judgment, of pain, of death. But we have lived through all of those already, in silence, except death. And I remind myself all the time now that if I were to have been born mute, or had maintained an oath of silence my whole life long for safety, I would still have suffered, and I would still die. It is very good for establishing perspective.

And where the words of women are crying to be heard, we must each of us recognize our responsibility to seek those words out, to read them and share them and examine them in their pertinence to our lives. That we not hide behind the mockeries of separations that have been imposed upon us and which so often we accept as our own. For instance, "I can't possibly teach Black women's writing — their experience is so different from mine." Yet how many years have you spent teaching Plato and Shakespeare and Proust? Or another, "She's a white woman and what could she possibly have to say to me!" Or, "She's a lesbian, what would my husband say, or my chairman?" Or again, "This woman writes of her sons and I have no children." And all the other endless ways in which we rob ourselves of ourselves and each other.

We can learn to work and speak when we are afraid in the same way we have learned to work and speak when we are tired. For we have been socialized to respect fear more than our own needs for language and definition, and while we wait in silence for that final luxury of fearlessness, the weight of that silence will choke us.

The fact that we are here and that I speak these words is an attempt to break   15
that silence and bridge some of those differences between us, for it is not difference which immobilizes us, but silence. And there are so many silences to be broken.   [1978]

THINKING ABOUT THE TEXT

1. What does Lorde assume about her audience? What are some things she does to make her listeners feel that they, too, should quit being silent? Refer to specific places in her speech.

2. Does Lorde consider *all* silences bad? Identify specific passages in addressing this question. What things, if any, do you believe people should be less silent about than they currently are? What things, if any, do you believe should be kept silent?

3. "Perhaps for some of you here today," Lorde notes, "I am the face of one of your fears. Because I am woman, because I am Black, because I am lesbian, because I am myself — a Black woman warrior poet doing my work — come to ask you, are you doing yours?" Is Lorde the face of one of your fears? If so, in what ways? In general, do you think your response to her text is influenced by your previous encounters with the kind of person she describes herself as? If so, how?

4. Are you bothered when Lorde refers to the United States as a "dragon"? Why, or why not? What might she mean when she declares that "we were never meant to survive"?

5. Your historical context differs from Lorde's. Among other things, you are reading her 1977 speech knowing that she did eventually die of breast cancer. Does this knowledge affect your response to the speech? If so, how?

JUNE JORDAN
Many Rivers to Cross

Although trained as a city planner, June Jordan (b. 1936) has become much more known as a writer. She has published several collections of poems and essays, in addition to writing plays, biographies, and a regular column for the political magazine The Progressive. *Currently she is a professor of Afro-American studies and women's studies at the University of California at Berkeley. The following text, which appears in Jordan's 1985 book* On Call, *was the keynote address at a 1981 conference on "Women and Work," held at Barnard College in New York City. In the speech, Jordan recalls the suicide of her mother fifteen years earlier.*

When my mother killed herself I was looking for a job. That was fifteen years ago. I had no money and no food. On the pleasure side I was down to my last pack of Pall Malls plus half a bottle of J & B. I needed to find work because I needed to be able fully to support myself and my eight-year-old son, very fast. My plan was to raise enough big bucks so that I could take an okay apartment inside an acceptable public school district, by September. That deadline left me less than three months to turn my fortunes right side up.

It seemed that I had everything to do at once. Somehow, I must move all of our things, mostly books and toys, out of the housing project before the rent fell due, again. I must do this without letting my neighbors know because destitution and divorce added up to personal shame, and failure. Those same neighbors had looked upon my husband and me as an ideal young couple, in many ways: inseparable, doting, ambitious. They had kept me busy and laughing in the hard weeks following my husband's departure for graduate school in Chicago; they had been the ones to remember him warmly through teasing remarks and questions all that long year that I remained alone, waiting for his return while I became the "temporary," sole breadwinner of our peculiar long-distance family by telephone. They had been the ones who kindly stopped the teasing and the queries when the year ended and my husband, the father of my child, did not come back. They never asked me and I never told them what that meant, altogether. I don't think I really knew.

I could see how my husband would proceed more or less naturally from graduate school to a professional occupation of his choice, just as he had shifted rather easily from me, his wife, to another man's wife — another woman. What I could not see was how I should go forward, now, in any natural, coherent way. As a mother without a husband, as a poet without a publisher, a freelance journalist without assignment, a city planner without a contract, it seemed to me that several incontestable and conflicting necessities had suddenly eliminated the whole realm of choice from my life.

My husband and I agreed that he would have the divorce that he wanted, and I would have the child. This ordinary settlement is, as millions of women will testify, as absurd as saying, "I'll give you a call, you handle everything else." At any rate, as my lawyer explained, the law then was the same as the law today; the courts would surely award me a reasonable amount of the father's income as child support, but the courts would also insist that they could not enforce their own decree. In other words, according to the law, what a father owes to his child is not serious compared to what a man owes to the bank for a car, or a vacation. Hence, as they say, it is extremely regrettable but nonetheless true that the courts cannot garnish a father's salary, nor freeze his account, nor seize his property on behalf of his children, in our society. Apparently this is because a child is not a car or a couch or a boat. (I would suppose this is the very best available definition of the difference between an American child and a car.)

Anyway, I wanted to get out of the projects as quickly as possible. But I was   5
going to need help because I couldn't bend down and I couldn't carry anything heavy and I couldn't let my parents know about these problems because I didn't want to fight with them about the reasons behind the problems — which was the same reason I couldn't walk around or sit up straight to read or write without vomiting and acute abdominal pain. My parents would have evaluated that reason as a terrible secret compounded by a terrible crime; once again an unmarried woman, I had, nevertheless, become pregnant. What's more I had tried to interrupt this pregnancy even though this particular effort required not only one but a total of three abortions — each of them illegal and amazingly expensive, as well as, evidently, somewhat poorly executed.

My mother, against my father's furious rejections of me and what he viewed as my failure, offered what she could; she had no money herself but there was space in the old brownstone of my childhood. I would live with them during the summer while I pursued my crash schedule for cash, and she would spend as much time with Christopher, her only and beloved grandchild, as her worsening but partially undiagnosed illness allowed.

After she suffered a stroke, her serenely imposing figure had shrunk into an unevenly balanced, starved shell of chronic disorder. In the last two years, her physical condition had forced her retirement from nursing, and she spent most of her days on a makeshift cot pushed against the wall of the dining room next to the kitchen. She could do very few things for herself, besides snack on crackers, or pour ready-made juice into a cup and then drink it.

In June, 1966, I moved from the projects into my parents' house with the help of a woman named Mrs. Hazel Griffin. Since my teens, she had been my hairdresser. Every day, all day, she stood on her feet, washing and straightening hair in her crowded shop, the Arch of Beauty. Mrs. Griffin had never been married, had never finished high school, and she ran the Arch of Beauty with an imperturbable and contagious sense of success. She had a daughter as old as I who worked alongside her mother, coddling customer fantasy into confidence. Gradually, Mrs. Griffin and I became close; as my own mother became more and more bedridden and demoralized, Mrs. Griffin extended herself — dropping by my parents' house to make dinner for them, or calling me to wish me good luck on a special freelance venture, and so forth. It was Mrs. Griffin who closed her shop for a whole day and drove all the way from Brooklyn to my housing project apartment in Queens. It was Mrs. Griffin who packed me up, so to speak, and carried me and the boxes back to Brooklyn, back to the house of my parents. It was Mrs. Griffin who ignored my father standing hateful at the top of the stone steps of the house and not saying a word of thanks and not once relieving her of a single load she wrestled up the stairs and past him. My father hated Mrs. Griffin because he was proud and because she was a stranger of mercy. My father hated Mrs. Griffin because he was like that sometimes: hateful and crazy.

My father alternated between weeping bouts of self-pity and storm explosions of wrath against the gods apparently determined to ruin him. These were his alternating reactions to my mother's increasing enfeeblement, her stoic depression. I think he was scared; who would take care of him? Would she get well again and make everything all right again?

This is how we organized the brownstone; I fixed a room for my son on the top floor of the house. I slept on the parlor floor in the front room. My father slept on the same floor, in the back. My mother stayed downstairs.   10

About a week after moving in, my mother asked me about the progress of my plans. I told her things were not terrific but that there were two different planning jobs I hoped to secure within a few days. One of them involved a study of new towns in Sweden and the other one involved an analysis of the social consequences of a huge hydro-electric dam under construction in Ghana. My mother stared at me uncomprehendingly and then urged me to look for work in the local post office. We bitterly argued about what she dismissed as my "high-falutin" ideas and, I believe, that was the last substantial conversation between us.

From my first memory of him, my father had always worked at the post office. His favorite was the night shift, which brought him home usually between three and four o'clock in the morning.

It was hot. I finally fell asleep that night, a few nights after the argument between my mother and myself. She seemed to be rallying; that afternoon, she and my son had spent a long time in the backyard, oblivious to the heat and the mosquitoes. They were both tired but peaceful when they noisily re-entered the house, holding hands awkwardly.

But someone was knocking at the door to my room. Why should I wake up? It would be impossible to fall asleep again. It was so hot. The knocking continued. I switched on the light by the bed: 3:30 A.M. It must be my father. Furious, I pulled on a pair of shorts and a t-shirt. "What do you want? What's the matter?" I asked him, through the door. Had he gone berserk? What could he have to talk about at that ridiculous hour?

"OK, all right," I said, rubbing my eyes awake as I stepped to the door and opened it. "What?"   15

To my surprise, my father stood there looking very uncertain.

"It's your mother," he told me, in a burly, formal voice. "I think she's dead, but I'm not sure." He was avoiding my eyes.

"What do you mean," I answered.

"I want you to go downstairs and figure it out."

I could not believe what he was saying to me. "You want me to figure out if my mother is dead or alive?"   20

"I can't tell! I don't know!!" he shouted angrily.

"Jesus Christ," I muttered, angry and beside myself.

I turned and glanced about my room, wondering if I could find anything to carry with me on this mission; what do you use to determine a life or a death? I couldn't see anything obvious that might be useful.

"I'll wait up here," my father said. "You call up and let me know."

I could not believe it; a man married to a woman more than forty years and   25
he can't tell if she's alive or dead and he wakes up his kid and tells her, "You figure it out."

I was at the bottom of the stairs. I halted just outside the dining room where my mother slept. Suppose she really was dead? Suppose my father was not just being crazy and hateful? "Naw," I shook my head and confidently entered the room.

"Momma?!" I called, aloud. At the edge of the cot, my mother was leaning forward, one arm braced to hoist her body up. She was trying to stand up! I rushed over. "Wait. Here, I'll help you!" I said.

And I reached out my hands to give her a lift. The body of my mother was stiff. She was not yet cold, but she was stiff. Maybe I had come downstairs just in time! I tried to loosen her arms, to change her position, to ease her into lying down.

"Momma!" I kept saying. "Momma, listen to me! It's OK! I'm here and everything. Just relax. Relax! Give me a hand, now. I'm trying to help you lie down!"

Her body did not relax. She did not answer me. But she was not cold. Her   30
eyes were not shut.

From upstairs my father was yelling, "Is she dead? Is she dead?"

"No!" I screamed at him. "No! She's not dead!"

At this, my father tore down the stairs and into the room. Then he braked.

"Milly?" he called out, tentative. Then he shouted at me and banged around the walls. "You damn fool. Don't you see now she's gone. Now she's gone!" We began to argue.

"She's alive! Call the doctor!"   35

"No!"

"Yes!"

At last my father left the room to call the doctor.

I straightened up. I felt completely exhausted from trying to gain a response from my mother. There she was, stiff on the edge of her bed, just about to stand up. Her lips were set, determined. She would manage it, but by herself. I could not help. Her eyes fixed on some point below the floor.

"Momma!" I shook her hard as I could to rouse her into focus. Now she fell   40
back on the cot, but frozen and in the wrong position. It hit me that she might be dead. She might be dead.

My father reappeared at the door. He would not come any closer. "Dr. Davis says he will come. And he call the police."

The police? Would they know if my mother was dead or alive? Who would know?

I went to the phone and called my aunt. "Come quick," I said. "My father thinks Momma has died but she's here but she's stiff."

Soon the house was weird and ugly and crowded and I thought I was losing my mind.

Three white policemen stood around telling me my mother was dead. "How 45 do you know?" I asked, and they shrugged and then they repeated themselves. And the doctor never came. But my aunt came and my uncle and they said she was dead.

After a conference with the cops, my aunt disappeared and when she came back she held a bottle in one of her hands. She and the police whispered together some more. Then one of the cops said, "Don't worry about it. We won't say anything." My aunt signalled me to follow her into the hallway where she let me understand that, in fact, my mother had committed suicide.

I could not assimilate this information: suicide.

I broke away from my aunt and ran to the telephone. I called a friend of mine, a woman who talked back loud to me so that I could realize my growing hysteria, and check it. Then I called my cousin Valerie who lived in Harlem; she woke up instantly and urged me to come right away.

I hurried to the top floor and stood my sleeping son on his feet. I wanted to get him out of this house of death more than I ever wanted anything. He could not stand by himself so I carried him down the two flights to the street and laid him on the backseat and then took off.

At Valerie's, my son continued to sleep, so we put him to bed, closed the 50 door, and talked. My cousin made me eat eggs, drink whiskey, and shower. She would take care of Christopher, she said. I should go back and deal with the situation in Brooklyn.

When I arrived, the house was absolutely full of women from the church dressed as though they were going to Sunday communion. It seemed to me they were, every one of them, wearing hats and gloves and drinking coffee and solemnly addressing invitations to a funeral and I could not find my mother anywhere and I could not find an empty spot in the house where I could sit down and smoke a cigarette.

My mother was dead.

Feeling completely out of place, I headed for the front door, ready to leave. My father grabbed my shoulder from behind and forcibly spun me around.

"You see this?" he smiled, waving a large document in the air. "This am insurance paper for you!" He waved it into my face. "Your mother, she left you insurance, see?"

I watched him. 55

"But I gwine burn it in the furnace before I give it you to t'row away on trash!"

"Is that money?" I demanded. "Did my mother leave me money?"

"Eh-heh!" he laughed. "And you don't get it from me. Not today, not tomorrow. Not until I dead and buried!"

My father grabbed for my arm and I swung away from him. He hit me on my head and I hit back. We were fighting.

Suddenly, the ladies from the church bustled about and pushed, horrified, 60 between us. This was a sin, they said, for a father and a child to fight in the house of the dead and the mother not yet in the ground! Such a good woman she was, they said. She was a good woman, a good woman, they all agreed. Out of respect for the memory of this good woman, in deference to my mother who had committed suicide, the ladies shook their hats and insisted we should not fight; I should not fight with my father.

Utterly disgusted and disoriented, I went back to Harlem. By the time I reached my cousin's place I had begun to bleed, heavily. Valerie said I was hemorrhaging so she called up her boyfriend and the two of them hobbled me into Harlem Hospital.

I don't know how long I remained unconscious, but when I opened my eyes I found myself on the women's ward, with an intravenous setup feeding into my arm. After a while, Valerie showed up. Christopher was fine, she told me; my friends were taking turns with him. Whatever I did, I should not admit I'd had an abortion or I'd get her into trouble, and myself in trouble. Just play dumb and rest. I'd have to stay on the ward for several days. My mother's funeral was tomorrow afternoon. What did I want her to tell people to explain why I wouldn't be there? She meant, what lie?

I thought about it and I decided I had nothing to say; if I couldn't tell the truth then the hell with it.

I lay in that bed at Harlem Hospital, thinking and sleeping. I wanted to get well.

I wanted to be strong. I never wanted to be weak again as long as I lived. I   65
thought about my mother and her suicide and I thought about how my father could not tell whether she was dead or alive.

I wanted to get well and what I wanted to do as soon as I was strong again, actually, what I wanted to do was I wanted to live my life so that people would know unmistakably that I am alive, so that when I finally die people will know the difference for sure between my living and my death.

And I thought about the idea of my mother as a good woman and I rejected that, because I don't see why it's a good thing when you give up, or when you cooperate with those who hate you or when you polish and iron and mend and endlessly mollify for the sake of the people who love the way that you kill yourself day by day silently.

And I think all of this is really about women and work. Certainly this is all about me as a woman and my life work. I mean I am not sure my mother's suicide was something extraordinary. Perhaps most women must deal with a similar inheritance, the legacy of a woman whose death you cannot possibly pinpoint because she died so many, many times and because, even before she became your mother, the life of that woman was taken; I say it was taken away.

And really it was to honor my mother that I did fight with my father, that man who could not tell the living from the dead.

And really it is to honor Mrs. Hazel Griffin and my cousin Valerie and all the   70
women I love, including myself, that I am working for the courage to admit the truth that Bertolt Brecht has written; he says, "It takes courage to say that the good were defeated not because they were good, but because they were weak."

I cherish the mercy and the grace of women's work. But I know there is new work that we must undertake as well: that new work will make defeat detestable to us. That new women's work will mean we will not die trying to stand up: we will live that way: standing up.

I came too late to help my mother to her feet.

By way of everlasting thanks to all of the women who have helped me to stay alive I am working never to be late again.　　　　　　　　　　　　[1985]

THINKING ABOUT THE TEXT

1. Although Jordan mentions her mother's suicide in her very first sentence, she doesn't return to it until much later. Instead, she focuses for a long while on her own plight. Does this strike you as appropriate? What, if anything, does she gain by postponing full discussion of her mother's death?

2. In recalling the occasion of her mother's death, Jordan uses a lot of dialogue, quoting herself, her father, and other people. What would you say to someone who argues that Jordan could not possibly have remembered exactly what she and others had said fifteen years before?

3. Near the end of her speech, Jordan refers directly to the conference topic, women, and work. Does she deal with this topic earlier in the speech? If so, in which specific passages?

4. Do you assume that Jordan is fairly describing her father? Why, or why not? To what extent do you agree with Jordan's ultimate evaluation of her mother? What image do you have of Jordan as she was fifteen years before the speech? What is your impression of the June Jordan who is giving the speech?

5. Where does Jordan turn details of her experiences into metaphors? Refer to specific passages.

MAKING COMPARISONS

1. Both Lorde and Jordan refer to work. Do you get the sense that they have pretty much the same vision of it?

2. Jordan uses narrative more than Lorde does. Does this difference matter to you as you evaluate their respective speeches?

3. Identify places where Lorde and Jordan refer to the importance of female support networks. Do you see these references as implying anything about men? If so, what?

WRITING ABOUT ISSUES

1. Choose Lorde's or Jordan's speech and write an essay analyzing it as an argument for a particular idea. Focus on identifying the particular strategies used by the author to make her main point persuasive to her audience.

2. Can Jordan's speech be related to Lorde's remarks about silences? Or is Jordan really dealing with a significantly different subject? Write an essay addressing this issue by referring to specific passages in both texts.

3. Write an essay discussing an experience of your own in light of Lorde's or Jordan's speech. Note that you can disagree with all or part of the speech if you like.

4. Write an essay discussing Lorde's or Jordan's speech in light of a widely known event that has occurred since 1977 (in Lorde's case) or 1981 (in Jordan's case). Choose an event somehow related to the topic of the speech you are considering. Does this event demonstrate the truth of the speech? Does it contradict all or some of what the speaker is claiming? You may have to do research in the library.

APPENDIX

Writing a Research Paper

You may imagine that writing a research paper for your English class is a significantly different, and perhaps more difficult, assignment than others you have had. Because more steps are involved in their writing (for example, additional reading and analysis of sources), research papers tend to be long-range projects. They also tend to be more formal than other kinds of papers because they involve integrating and documenting source material.

These differences, however, are essentially of magnitude and appearance, not of substance. Despite the common misconception (cause of much unnecessary anxiety) that writing a research paper requires a special set of knowledge and skills, it draws principally on the same kind of knowledge and skills needed to write other types of papers. A writer still needs to begin with an arguable **issue** and a **claim**, still needs to marshal **evidence** to defend that claim, and still needs to present that evidence persuasively to convince an audience that the claim has merit. The main difference between research papers and other papers that you will write for this course is that the evidence for a research paper comes from a wider variety of sources.

Writing about literature begins with a **primary research source**—the story, poem, play, or essay on which the paper is focused. In addition to this primary source, however, research papers call on **secondary research sources**—historical, biographical, cultural, and critical documents that writers use to support their claims.

Identifying an Issue and a Tentative Claim

Your first task in writing a research paper is to identify an issue that you genuinely want to think and to learn more about. The more interested you are in your issue, the better your paper will be. You may choose, for example, to write about issues of theme, symbolism, pattern, or genre, or you may prefer to explore contextual issues of social policy, or of the author's biography, culture, or historical period. Any of the types of issues described on pages 19–26 are potentially suitable for research. The type of secondary research materials you use will depend largely on the issue you choose to pursue.

First, read your primary source carefully, taking notes as you do so. If you work with the texts in this book, you will want to read the biographical and contextual information about the author and any questions or commentaries that follow the texts. Then, ask questions of your own to figure out what really interests you about the literature. Do not look for simple issues or questions that can be easily answered with a few factual statements; instead, try to discover a topic that will challenge you to perform serious research and do some hard thinking.

Before you begin looking for secondary research sources for your paper, formulate a tentative claim, much like a scientist who begins research with a hypothesis to be tested and affirmed or refuted. Since this tentative claim is unlikely to find its way into your final paper, do not worry if it seems a little vague or obvious. You will have plenty of opportunities to refine it as your research proceeds. Having a tentative claim in mind—or, better still, on paper—will prevent you from becoming overwhelmed by the multitude of potential secondary sources available to you.

Rebecca Stanley, who wrote the research paper that begins on page 1657, chose to write on Kate Chopin. After reading the three Chopin stories included in this book, she found herself wondering about the racial issues raised by "Désirée's Baby" (p. 776). She was horrified by the racism depicted by Chopin but also fascinated by Chopin's unusual and apparently sensitive treatment of the topic. Still, she knew that she lacked a clear sense of direction for her paper and would have to do more reading and thinking. On her second reading of the story (now that she was no longer concentrating on what would happen next), she began to notice how Chopin's vivid, descriptive language, especially her use of light and dark imagery, seemed to create a mood and comment on the theme of racism. She decided on a tentative claim: that there is a connection between the imagery in "Désirée's Baby" and Chopin's attitude towards race relations in her society. Clearly this claim would need refining, but it gave Rebecca a starting point as she headed to the library to begin her research.

Finding and Using Secondary Sources

Once you have your topic in mind and have sketched a tentative claim, begin looking for secondary research sources. Many different types of sources for literary research are available, and the types you will need will depend largely on the type of claim you choose to defend. If your issue is primarily one of interpretation—about the theme, patterns, or symbolism of the text, for instance—you will most likely need to consult literary criticism to see what has been said in the past about the literature you are discussing. If your issue concerns historical or cultural context, including issues of social policy, you may need to consult newspapers, magazines, and similar sorts of cultural documents. Some topics, like Rebecca's, might require several different types of sources.

Researching your project divides into two main activities. First, you will need to identify several secondary sources and construct a **working bibliography**—that is, a list of the materials you might use. Most researchers find it useful to record this working bibliography on a stack of note cards, with one entry per card containing all the pertinent information to help find the source and later to list it in the paper's bibliography, called the **Works Cited.** (Some researchers who have notebook-style computers prefer to bring them to the library and record their working bibliographies on a computer file instead of a collection of cards.) Once you have compiled a working bibliography, you will be ready to move on to the second stage: tracking down the materials you have identified, reading and evaluating them, and writing notes from (and about) them as a preliminary step to writing your own paper.

As you make note of potentially useful sources, it is important that you include in your working bibliography all of the information—including names, titles, publication information, and page numbers—that will eventually be needed for your Works Cited list. An explanation of the Works Cited format for each type of source (from books and articles to CD-ROMs and Web sites) begins on page 1649. Acquaint yourself with this format before you begin compiling your working bibliography; otherwise, you may forget to record crucial information that you will need when you prepare the final version of your paper.

FINDING SOURCES IN THE LIBRARY

A good place to commence your research is your college or university library's computerized **catalog**. Be aware that scholarly books are often quite specialized, and that you may want to start with one or two fairly general titles to orient you before venturing into more sharply focused scholarship. Because Rebecca was interested in race relations in the South during Chopin's time, she searched the catalog using the very general key words *race relations* and *United States*, which turned up references to a number of books. Among the most interesting titles was Stetson Kennedy's *Jim Crow Guide*, which provided her with a good deal of useful information for her paper.

Perhaps an even better place than the library catalog to begin research for your paper is the **MLA International Bibliography**, published each year by the Modern Language Association. Most college and university libraries carry both the CD-ROM and print versions of this work, which lists scholarly books and articles on a wide range of topics in literary criticism and history. The CD-ROM version is a powerful and flexible tool that allows a researcher to enter a topic or the name of an author or work of literature and then to see on-screen a list of books and articles addressing that topic. These references can be copied by hand, printed out, or downloaded to a floppy disk for your working bibliography.

The print version of the *Bibliography* is also useful, though you must understand its organization to use it efficiently. The bibliographic references are subdivided first by the nationality of the literature, then by its date of publication, then by the author and title of the work. To find information from this source for her paper, Rebecca first located the most recent edition of the *MLA International Bibliography*, then moved to the section devoted to American literature, then to literature of

1800–99, then finally to Kate Chopin and the specific story, "Désirée's Baby." If you find few or no references to your topic in an edition of the bibliography, try the editions for the previous few years. Chances are your topic will show up.

Sources of cultural information other than literary criticism and history can be found by using other excellent options widely available in college and university libraries. These include *infotrac*, a user-friendly electronic index of academic and general-interest periodicals including scholarly journals, magazines, and several prominent newspapers. Many researchers also like to use the *Reader's Guide to Periodical Literature* (available in both print and CD-ROM versions), the *Newspaper Abstracts*, and the many specialized indexes devoted to particular fields of study, from science, to history, to education. Let your topic lead you to the information sources that will be most valuable to you. Your reference librarians will be happy to tell you what is available in your particular library as well as how to use any of these books and databases.

EVALUATING SOURCES

Whatever method you use to locate your research materials, remember that not all sources are created equal. Be sure to allot some time for **evaluating** the materials you find. In general, the best and most reliable sources of information for academic papers are (1) books published by academic and university presses; (2) articles appearing in scholarly and professional journals; and (3) articles in prominent, reputable newspapers, such as the *New York Times* or the *Washington Post*. Many other types of sources — from CD-ROMs to popular magazines — may prove useful to you as well, but if you have any hesitation about the trustworthiness of a source, approach it with healthy skepticism. Also, the more recent your information, the better (unless, of course, you are doing historical research).

In general, basic questions you should ask of your sources include: (1) Is the information recent, and if not, is the validity of the information likely to have changed significantly over time? (2) How credible is the author? Is he or she a recognized expert on the subject? (3) Is the source published by an established, respectable press, or does it appear in a well-respected journal or periodical (the *Los Angeles Times* has more credibility than the *National Enquirer*, for example) or Web site (one supported by a university or library, for instance)? (4) Based on what you've learned about responsible argument, do the arguments in your source seem sound, fair, and thoughtful? Is the evidence convincing? Is the development of the argument logical?

You increase your own credibility with your audience by using the most credible research materials available to you, so do not just settle for whatever comes to hand if you have the opportunity to find a stronger source.

FINDING SOURCES WITH A COMPUTER

These days, reliable information is widely and conveniently available on CD-ROMs, many of which may be found in college and university libraries. These include texts of literary works (often with commentaries on these works), bibliographies and indexes to help you locate more traditional sources of information, and even the texts of historical and cultural documents. (For example, a CD-ROM about Robert Frost includes not only the texts of his poems but also critical commentaries, relevant source materials, biographical and autobiographical passages, and recordings of Frost reading his own poetry.) In addition, standard reference works such as encyclopedias and dictionaries are often available on CD-ROM, where they can be efficiently searched for background information or factual corroboration (names, dates, spelling) for your paper. Keep in mind that you may need to rely on your librarian to tell you about your library's holdings, because many CD-ROMs are not yet indexed in the same way as traditional books and magazines.

A wealth of information is available on the Internet as well, and, as with the information in the library, your goal is to find useful information efficiently, evaluate it carefully, and make effective use of it in your paper. Unfortunately, and unlike a library's sources, the information on the Internet is not indexed and organized to make it easily accessible to researchers. You will need to do a certain amount of "surfing" if you are to find appropriate materials for your project. Probably the most useful place to start your Internet research is with the text-and-graphics portion known as the World Wide Web. A number of **search engines** (programs for finding information) are designed to help you track down documents on the Web, and if you are an old hand on the Internet, you can probably depend on search engines that have served you well in the past. One of the most useful search engines for serious research, called *Yahoo!*, allows you continually to narrow a topic until you arrive at the information desired.

For example, to find information on Kate Chopin, Rebecca launched the Web browser on her computer and went to *Yahoo!* From the menu of categories, she chose the following path, clicking on each entry successively: Arts/Humanities/Literature/Authors/Literary Fiction/Chopin, Kate. *Yahoo!* then provided her with several Web sites she could choose to visit, one of which contained the complete text of Chopin's novel *The Awakening* and several of her short stories. Other sites on the list provided a wealth of biographical and critical information about Chopin and her work as well as contextual information about southern literature, Chopin's contemporaries, and her culture. (Similar information exists on-line for many of the other authors whose works appear in this book.)

Special care is needed to evaluate on-line sources, since anyone can put information on the Net. It will be up to you to determine if you are reading a piece of professional criticism or a middle-school term paper. When using on-line sources for serious research, look especially for work that has been signed by the author and is hosted by a respectable site, such as a university or a library.

Taking Notes: Summarizing, Paraphrasing, Quoting, and Avoiding Plagiarism

Once you have identified a number of sources for your paper and tracked down the books, periodicals, or other materials, it is time to begin reading, analyzing, and taking notes. At this point, it is especially important to keep yourself well organized and to write down *everything* that may be of use to you later. No matter how good your memory, do not count on remembering a few days (or even hours) later which notes or quotations come from which sources. Scrupulously write down page numbers and double-check facts and spellings.

Many researchers find it easier to stay organized if they take notes on large note cards, with each card containing just one key point from one source. The notes you take from sources will fall into one of three basic categories: summaries, paraphrases, and quotations. (A fourth category is notes of your own ideas, prompted by your research. Write these down as well, keeping them separate and clearly labeled, as you would any other notes.)

Student researchers often rely too heavily on **quotations**, copying verbatim large sections from their research sources. Do not make this mistake. Instead, start your note taking with a **summary** of the source in question — just one or two sentences indicating in your own words the author's main point. Such summaries guarantee that you understand the gist of an author's argument and (since they are your own words) can readily be incorporated in your paper. You might think of a summary as a restatement of the author's principal claim, perhaps with a brief indication of the types of supporting evidence he or she marshals. You can also write summaries of supporting points — subsections of an author's argument — if they seem applicable to your paper. A summary should not, however, include quotations, exhaustive detail about subpoints, or a list of all the evidence in a given source. A summary is meant to provide a succinct overview — to demonstrate that you have grasped a point and can convey it to your readers.

Chances are you will want to take more specific notes as well, ones that **paraphrase** the most germane passages in a particular source. Unlike a summary, a paraphrase does not condense an argument or leave out supporting evidence; instead it puts the information into new words. A paraphrase is generally no shorter than the material being paraphrased, but it still has two advantages over a quotation. First, as with a summary, an accurate paraphrase proves that you understand the material you've read. Second, again as with a summary, a paraphrase is easier to integrate into your paper than a quotation, since it is already written in your own words and style. When you include a paraphrase in your notes, indicate on the note the page numbers in the original source.

The rule of thumb about summarizing or paraphrasing is that you must always clearly indicate which ideas are yours and which are those of others. It is **plagiarism** — a serious violation of academic standards — to accept credit for another's ideas, even if you put them in your own words. Ideas in your paper that are not attributed to a source will be assumed to be your own, so to avoid plagiarism it is important to leave no doubt in your reader's mind about when you are summarizing or paraphrasing. Always cite the source.

An exception to the rule is **common knowledge** — factual information that the average reader can be expected to know or is readily available in many easily accessible sources — which need not be referenced. For example, it is common knowledge that Kate Chopin was an American writer. It is also considered common knowledge that her original name was Katherine O'Flaherty, and that she was born in St. Louis in 1851 and died there in 1904, even though most people would have to look that information up in an encyclopedia or biographical dictionary to verify it.

Sometimes, of course, you will want to copy quotations directly from a source. Do so sparingly, copying quotations only when the author's own words are especially succinct and pertinent. When you write down a quotation, enclose it in quotation marks and record the *exact* wording, right down to the punctuation. As with a paraphrase, make note of the original page numbers for the quotation, as you will need to indicate this in your final paper.

Each time you take a note, be it summary, paraphrase, or quotation, take a moment to consider why you wrote it down. Why is this particular note from this source important? Consider writing a brief commentary about the note's importance, maybe just a sentence or a few words, perhaps on the back of the note card (if you are using note cards). When the time comes to draft your paper, such commentaries will help you remember why you bothered to take the note, and may restart your train of thought if it gets stuck.

And do not forget: If something you read in a source sparks an original idea, write it down and label it clearly as your own. Keep these notes with your notes from the primary and secondary sources. Without your own ideas, your paper will be little more than a report, a record of what others have said. Your ideas will provide the framework for an argument that is your own.

Writing the Paper: Integrating Sources

With your research completed (at least for the moment), it is time to get down to drafting the paper. At this point, many students find themselves overwhelmed with information and wonder if they are really in any better shape to begin writing than they were before starting their research. But having read and thought about a number of authors' ideas and arguments, you are almost certainly more prepared to construct an argument of your own. You can, of course, use any method that has worked for you in the past to devise a first draft of your paper. If you are having trouble getting started, though, you might look to Chapters 2 through 6 of this book, which discuss general strategies for exploring, planning, and drafting papers as well as more specific ideas for working with individual literary genres.

Start by revisiting your tentative claim. Refine it to take into account what you have learned during your research. Rebecca Stanley began with the claim that there was a connection between Chopin's imagery and the attitudes she expressed towards race relations in her society. Having done some research, Rebecca was now ready to claim that the patterns of imagery Chopin uses indicate not only the racial heritage of the main characters in the story but also how guilty or innocent they are of racism. While this is still not quite the thesis of Rebecca's final paper, it reflects the major focus of her research.

With your revised-and-refined claim at hand, examine your assembled notes and try to subdivide them into groups of related ideas, each of which can form a single section of your paper, or even a single piece of supporting evidence for your claim. You can then arrange the groups of notes according to a logical developmental pattern—for example, from cause to effect, or from weakest to strongest evidence—which may provide a structure for the body of your essay. As you write, avoid using your own comments as a kind of glue to hold together other people's ideas. Instead, you are constructing an argument of your own, using secondary sources as bricks to build your own structure of claims and evidence.

Anytime you summarize, paraphrase, or quote another author, it should be clear how this author's ideas or words relate to your own argument. Keep in mind that, in your final paper, it is quite unlikely that every note you took deserves a place. Be prepared to discard any notes that do not, in some fashion, support your claim and strengthen your argument. Remember also that direct quotations should be used sparingly for greatest effect; papers that rely too heavily on them make for choppy reading. By contrast, summaries and paraphrases are in your own words and should be a clean and easy fit with your prose style.

Notice how Rebecca uses both summary and paraphrase in her essay (p. 1657). For example, she summarizes two Supreme Court decisions on page 4 of her paper and paraphrases information from *The Jim Crow Guide* on pages 3 and 4. In both cases, her references clearly indicate that the information originated from a particular source. Notice also how smoothly she integrates these summaries and paraphrases into her own discussion of interracial relationships and shows how they connect to the Chopin story and to her claim. The following section on documenting sources (pp. 1649–56) demonstrates the proper format for acknowledging authors whose work you summarize or paraphrase.

When you quote directly from either primary or secondary sources, you will need to follow special conventions of format and style. When quoting up to four lines of prose or three lines of poetry, integrate the quotation directly into your paragraph, enclosing the quoted material in double quotation marks and checking to make sure that the quotation accurately reflects the original. Longer quotations are set off from the text by starting a new line and indenting one inch on the left margin only; these are called **block quotations.** For these, quotation marks are omitted since the indention is enough to indicate that the material is a quotation. Examples of the correct format for both long and short quotations appear in Rebecca's paper.

When a short quotation is from a poem, line breaks in the poem are indicated by slash marks, with single spaces on either side. The example below demonstrates this using a short quotation from William Shakespeare's sonnet, "Let me not to the marriage of true minds." The number in parentheses is a page reference, and the format for these is explained in the next section, "Documenting Sources."

```
Shakespeare tells us that "Love is not love / Which
alters when it alteration finds, / Or bends with the
remover to remove" (716).
```

While it is essential to quote accurately, sometimes you may need to alter a quotation slightly, either by deleting text for brevity, or by adding or changing text to incorporate it grammatically. If you delete words from a quotation, indicate the deletion by inserting an ellipsis (three periods with spaces between them) as demonstrated below with another quotation from the Shakespeare sonnet.

```
Love, Shakespeare tells us, is "not Time's fool . . . But
bears it out even to the edge of doom" (716).
```

If you need to change or add words for clarity or grammatical correctness, indicate the changes with square brackets. If, for instance, you wanted to clarify the meaning of "It" in Shakespeare's line "It is the star to every wandering bark," you could do so like this:

```
Shakespeare claims that "[Love] is the star to every wan-
dering bark" (716).
```

In addition to these format considerations, remember a few general rules of thumb as you deploy primary and secondary sources in your paper. First, without stinting on necessary information, keep quotations as short as possible — your argument will flow more smoothly if you do. Quotations long enough to be blocked should be relatively rare. Second, never assume that a quotation is self-sufficient or its meaning self-evident. Every time you put a quotation in your paper, take the time to introduce it clearly and comment on it, to demonstrate why you chose to include it in the first place. Finally, quote fairly and accurately and stick to a consistent format (such as the MLA style explained below) when giving credit to your sources.

Documenting Sources: MLA Format

Documentation is the means by which you give credit to the authors of all primary and secondary sources cited within a research paper. It serves two principal purposes: (1) it allows your readers to find out more about the origin of the ideas you present; and (2) it protects you from charges of plagiarism. Every academic discipline follows slightly different conventions for documentation, but the method most commonly used for writing about literature is the format devised by the Modern Language Association (MLA). This documentation method encompasses **in-text citations**, which briefly identify within the body of your paper the source of a particular quotation, summary, or paraphrase, and a bibliography, called **Works Cited**, which gives more complete publication information.

While mastering the precise requirements of MLA punctuation and format can be time-consuming and even frustrating, getting it right adds immeasurably to the professionalism of a finished paper. More detailed information, including special circumstances and documentation styles for types of sources not covered here, will be found in the *MLA Handbook for Writers of Research Papers*, Fifth Edition, by Joseph Gibaldi (New York: Modern Language Association, 1999). Of course, if your instructor requests that you follow a different documentation method, you should follow his or her instructions instead.

MLA IN-TEXT CITATION

Each time you include information from any outside source — whether in the form of a summary, a paraphrase, or a quotation — you must provide your reader with a brief reference indicating the author and page number of the original. This reference directs the reader to the Works Cited list, where more complete information is available.

There are two basic methods for in-text citation. The first, and usually preferable, method is to include the author's name in the text of your essay and note the page number in parentheses at the end of the citation. The following paraphrase and quotation from James Joyce's "Araby" (p. 728) show the format to be followed for this method. Note that the page number (without the abbreviation "pg." or additional punctuation) is enclosed within the parentheses, and that the final punctuation for the sentence occurs after the parenthetical reference, effectively making the reference part of the preceding sentence. For a direct quotation, the closing quotation marks come before the page reference, but the final period is still saved until after the reference.

```
Joyce's narrator recounts how he thought of Mangan's sis-
ter constantly, even at the most inappropriate times
(729).
```

```
Joyce's narrator claims that he thought of Mangan's sis-
ter "even in places the most hostile to romance" (729).
```

The method is similar for long quotations (those set off from the main text of your essay). The only difference, as you can see on page 4 of Rebecca's essay, is that the final punctuation comes before the parenthetical page reference.

In those cases where citing the author's name in your text would be awkward or difficult, you may include both the author's last name and the page reference in the parenthetical citation. The example below draws a quotation from Nathaniel Branden's commentary "Immature Love," which appears on page 837. As demonstrated, the last name of the author (or authors) and the page number (or numbers) are the only thing included in such a reference. No additional punctuation or information is needed.

```
According to one psychologist, the relationships of imma-
ture persons "tend to be dependent and manipulative, not
the encounter of two autonomous selves who feel free to
express themselves honestly" (Branden 838).
```

Knowing the last name of the author is enough to allow your reader to find out more about the reference in the Works Cited, and having the page number makes it easy to find the original of the quotation, summary, or paraphrase should your reader choose to. The only time more information is needed is if you cite more than one work by the same author. In this case, you will need to specify from which of the author's works a particular citation comes. Notice that since Rebecca includes more than one of Kate Chopin's works in her Works Cited list, she always makes clear, either in her lead-in to a citation or in the parenthetical reference, which story is the basis of a paraphrase or source of a quotation. Electronic sources, such as CD-ROMs and Internet sources, are generally not divided into numbered pages. If you cite from such a source, the parenthetical reference need only include the author's last name (or, if the work is anonymous, an identifying title).

MLA WORKS CITED

The second feature of the MLA format is the Works Cited list, or bibliography. This list should begin on a new page of your paper and should be double spaced throughout and use hanging indention, which means that all lines except the first are indented one half inch. The list is alphabetized by author's last name (or by the title in the case of anonymous works) and includes every primary and secondary source referred to in your paper. The format for the most common types of entries is given below. If any of the information called for is unavailable for a particular source, simply skip that element and keep the rest of the entry as close as possible to the given format. An anonymous work, for instance, skips the author's name and is alphabetized under the title. In addition to the explanations below, you can see examples of MLA bibliographic format in Rebecca's Works Cited.

Books

Entries in your Works Cited for books should contain as much of the following information as is available to you. Follow the order and format exactly as given, with a period after each numbered element below (between author and title, and so on). Not all of these elements will be needed for most books. Copy the information directly from the title and publication pages of the book, not from a library catalog or other reference, because these sources often leave some information out.

1. The name(s) of the author(s) (or editor, if no author is listed, or organization in the case of a corporate author), last name first.
2. The full title, underlined or in italics. If the book has a subtitle, put a colon between title and subtitle.
3. The name(s) of the editor(s), if the book has both an author and an editor, following the abbreviation "Ed."
4. The name(s) of the translator or compiler, following the abbreviation "Trans.," or "Comp.," as appropriate.
5. The edition, if other than the first.

6. The volume(s) used, if the book is part of a multivolume set.
7. The name of any series to which the book belongs.
8. The city of publication (followed by a colon), name of the publisher (comma), and year.

The examples below cover the most common types of books you will encounter.

A book by a single author or editor.   Simply follow the elements and format as listed above. The first example below is for a book by a single author; note also the abbreviation UP, for "University Press." The second example is a book by a single editor. The third is for a book with both author (Conrad) and an editor (Murfin); note also that it is a second edition and a book in a series, so these facts are listed as well.

Cima, Gay Gibson. <u>Performing Women: Female Char-</u>

   <u>acters, Male Playwrights, and the Modern Stage</u>.

   Ithaca, NY: Cornell UP, 1993.

Tucker, Robert C., ed. <u>The Marx-Engels Reader</u>. New

   York: Norton, 1972.

Conrad, Joseph. <u>Heart of Darkness</u>. Ed. Ross C Murfin.

   2nd ed. Case Studies in Contemporary Criticism.

   Boston: Bedford/St. Martin's, 1996.

A book with multiple authors or editors.   If a book has two or three authors or editors , list all names, but note that only the first name is given last name first and the rest are in normal order. In cases where a book has four or more authors or editors, give only the first name listed on the title page, followed by a comma and the phrase *et al.* (Latin for "and others").

Leeming, David, and Jake Page. <u>God: Myths of the Male</u>

   <u>Divine</u>. New York: Oxford UP, 1996.

Arrow, Kenneth Joseph, et al., eds. <u>Education in a</u>

   <u>Research University</u>. Stanford: Stanford UP, 1996.

A book with a corporate author.   When a book has a group, government agency, or other organization listed as its author, treat that organization in your Works Cited just as you would a single author.

National Conference on Undergraduate Research. <u>Pro-</u>

   <u>ceedings of the National Conference on Under-</u>

   <u>graduate Research</u>. Asheville: U of North Carolina,

   1995.

Short Works from Collections and Anthologies

Many scholarly books are collections of articles on a single topic by several different authors. When you cite an article from such a collection, include the information given below. The format is the same for works of literature that appear in an anthology, such as this one.

1. The name of the author(s) of the article or literary work.
2. The title of the short work, enclosed in quotation marks.
3. Name(s) of the editor(s) of the collection or anthology.
4. All relevant publication information, in the same order and format as it would appear in a book citation.
5. The inclusive page numbers for the shorter work.

A single work from a collection or anthology.   If you are citing only one article or literary work from any given collection or anthology, simply follow the format outlined above and demonstrated in the following examples.

```
Kirk, Russell. "Eliot's Christian Imagination." The

     Placing of T. S. Eliot. Ed. Jewel Spears Brooker.

     Columbia: U of Missouri P, 1991. 136-44.

Silko, Leslie Marmon. "Yellow Woman." Making

     Literature Matter: An Anthology for Readers and

     Writers. Ed. John Schilb and John Clifford.

     Boston: Bedford/St. Martin's, 1999. 720-27.
```

Multiple works from the same collection or anthology.   If you are citing more than one short work from a single collection or anthology, it is often more efficient to set up a **cross-reference**. This means first writing a single general entry that provides full publication information for the collection or anthology as a whole. The entries for the shorter works then contain only the author and title of the shorter work, the names of the editors of the book, and the page numbers of the shorter work. The example below shows an entry for a short story cross-referenced with a general entry for this book; note that the entries remain in alphabetical order in your Works Cited, regardless of whether the general or specialized entry comes first.

```
Faulkner, William. "A Rose for Emily." Schilb and

     Clifford. 849-56.

Schilb, John, and John Clifford, eds. Making Liter-

     ature Matter: An Anthology for Readers and

     Writers. Boston: Bedford/St. Martin's, 1999.
```

Works in Periodicals

The following information should be included, in the given order and format, when you cite articles and other short works from journals, magazines, or newspapers.

1. The name(s) of the author(s) of the short work.
2. The title of the short work, in quotation marks.

3. The title of the periodical, underlined or italicized.
4. All relevant publication information as explained in the examples below.
5. The inclusive page numbers for the shorter work.

A work in a scholarly journal.   Publication information for work from scholarly and professional journals should include the volume number (and also the issue number, if the journal paginates each issue separately), the year of publication in parentheses and followed by a colon, and the page numbers of the shorter work.

```
Charles, Casey. "Gender Trouble in Twelfth Night."
    Theatre Journal 49 (1997): 121-41.
```

An article in a magazine.   Publication information for articles in general-circulation magazines includes the month(s) of publication for a monthly (or bimonthly), and the date (day, month, then year) for a weekly or biweekly, followed by a colon and the page numbers of the article.

```
Cowley, Malcolm. "It Took a Village." Utne Reader
    Nov.-Dec. 1997: 48-49.
Levy, Steven. "On the Net, Anything Goes." Newsweek 7
    July 1997: 28-30.
```

An article in a newspaper.   When citing an article from a newspaper include the date (day, month, year) and the edition if one is listed on the masthead, followed by a colon and the page numbers (including the section number or letter, if applicable).

```
Cobb, Nathan. "How to Dig Up a Family Tree." The
    Boston Globe 9 Mar. 1998: C7.
```

CD-ROMs

CD-ROMs come in two basic types, those published in a single edition — including major reference works like dictionaries and encyclopedias — and those published serially on a regular basis. In a Works Cited list, the first type is treated like a book and the second like a periodical. Details of citation appear in the following examples.

Single-edition CD-ROMs.   An entry for a single-edition CD-ROM is formatted like one for a book, but with the word *CD-ROM* preceding publication information. Most CD-ROMs are divided into smaller subsections, and these should be treated like short works from anthologies.

```
"Realism." The Oxford English Dictionary. 2nd ed.
    CD-ROM. Oxford: Oxford UP, 1992.
```

Serial CD-ROMs.   Treat information published on periodically released CD-ROMs just as you would articles in print periodical, but also include the title of the CD-ROM, underlined or italicized, the word *CD-ROM*, the name of the vendor distributing the CD-ROM, and the date of electronic publication. Many such CD-ROMs contain reprints and abstracts of print works, and in these cases, the publisher and date for the print version should be listed as well, preceding the information for the electronic version.

```
Brodie, James Michael and Barbara K. Curry. Sweet

     Words So Brave: The Story of African American

     Literature. Madison, WI: Knowledge Unlimited,

     1996. ERIC CD-ROM. SilverPlatter. 1997.
```

The Internet

Internet sources fall into several categories — World Wide Web documents and postings to newsgroups, listservs, and so on. Documentation for these sources should include as much of the following information as is available, in the order and format specified.

1. The name of the author(s), last name first (as for a print publication).
2. The title of the section of the work accessed (the subject line for e-mails and postings) in quotation marks.
3. The title of the full document or site, underlined or in italics.
4. Date the material was published or updated.
5. The protocol used for access (World Wide Web, FTP, USENET newsgroup, listserv, and so on).
6. The electronic address or path followed for access, in angle brackets.
7. The date you access a site, or the date specified on an e-mail or posting, in parentheses.

The examples below show entries for a Web site and a newsgroup citation, two of the most common sorts of Internet sources.

```
Brandes, Jay. "Maya Angelou: A Bibliography of

     Literary Criticism." 20 Aug. 1997. <http://

     www.geocities.com/ResearchTriangle/1221/

     Angelou.htm> (10 Feb. 1998).

Broun, Mike. "Jane Austen Video Package Launched."

     1 Mar. 1998. <rec.arts.prose> (11 Mar. 1998).
```

Personal Communication

In some cases you may get information directly from another person, either by conducting an interview or by receiving correspondence. In this case, include in your Works Cited the name of the person who gave you the information, the type of communication you had with that person, and the date of the communication.

```
McCorkle, Patrick. Personal [or Telephone] interview.

     12 Mar. 1998.
```

```
Aburrow, Clare. Letter [or E-mail] to the author. 15
     Apr. 1998.
```

Multiple Works by the Same Author

If you cite more than one work (in any medium) by a single author, the individual works are alphabetized by title. The author's full name is given only for the first citation in the Works Cited, after which it is replaced by three hyphens. The rest of the citation follows whatever format is appropriate for the medium of the source. The two entries below are for a work in an anthology and a book, both by the same author.

```
Faulkner, William. "A Rose for Emily." Making Litera-
     ture Matter: An Anthology for Readers and Writers.
     Ed. John Schilb and John Clifford. Boston:
     Bedford/St. Martin's, 1999. 849-56.
---. The Sound and the Fury. New York: Modern Li-
     brary, 1956.
```

Occasionally, you may have an idea or find a piece of information that seems important to your paper but that you just cannot work in smoothly without interrupting the flow of ideas. Such information can be included in the form of **endnotes**. A small superscript number in your text signals a note, and the notes themselves appear on a separate page at the end of your paper, before the Works Cited. Rebecca Stanley's paper includes an endnote, but for many research papers none will be needed.

Sample Student Research Paper

Of course, not all research follows exactly the pattern we have described; it varies from researcher to researcher and project to project. In working on your own research paper, you may find yourself taking more or less time on certain steps, doing the steps in a slightly different order, or looping back to further refine your claim or do more research. But if you take the time to think your project through, do the research right, and write and revise carefully, you should end up with a paper you can be proud of. Take a look at the paper Rebecca finally wrote, and note the annotations, which point out key features of her text and of the MLA format.

Stanley 1

Rebecca Stanley

Professor Gardner

English 102

15 March ----

      Racial Disharmony and "Désirée's Baby"

    The sensuous quality of Kate Chopin's works, as
well as the Creole and Cajun dialect that flavor
her diction, establish her as one of the nineteenth
century's foremost writers. Both her style and
themes have led to her being considered a precursor
to the "Southern Renaissance" of the 1920s (Evans).
In recent years, critics have especially focused on
the ground-breaking explorations of female autonomy
in her short novel The Awakening and in stories
like "The Story of an Hour." Another trait that
sets Chopin's writing ahead of her contemporaries'
is her advocacy of racial harmony, which is not
characteristic of early southern literature. The
racial issue is explored in "Désirée's Baby," in
which Chopin uses black and white imagery and an
ironic twist at the end to teach her audience a
profound truth about humanity. Rather than make
assumptions based upon appearance, individuals
should look beyond the exterior and notice the common humanity that binds all people together. Many
people in Chopin's audience had never learned this
lesson, and sadly enough, neither have many modern-
day Americans.

    "Désirée's Baby" tells the tragic story of a
young woman's suffering in the face of her society's condemnation of mixed marriages. The reader
is introduced to the main character, Désirée, early
in her life, when she is a vulnerable infant, lacking any familial ties. Désirée has been abandoned
at the Valmondé gates, and a kindhearted Madame
Valmondé takes pity and adopts the child as her

*Separate title page
unnecessary. First page
gives student name,
teacher's name, course,
and due date in upper
left corner. Centered
below is paper's title.
Student's last name
and page number
appear in upper right
corner.*

*Information cited from
World Wide Web
source; no page
number in
parenthetical
reference.*

*Rebecca immediately
introduces issue of race
and makes two related
claims — one about
Chopin's imagery and
one about American
society.*

own. Any doubts lurking in Madame Valmondé's mind
regarding the baby's obscure origin are assuaged as
the child blossoms into a "beautiful and gentle,
affectionate and sincere" young adult--"the idol of
Valmondé" (Chopin 776). This description is
Chopin's first association of Désirée with goodness, suggesting that the baby has been sent to
Madame Valmondé "by a beneficent Providence" (776).
Throughout the story, Chopin continually describes
Désirée as innately good, and she supports this
with imagery of light and undefiled whiteness.

Quotation cited with author's name and page number.

A character foil emerges when Armand Aubigny
enters the scene on horseback. A dark and handsome
knight of sorts, Armand's shadow falls across
Désirée's whiteness as she stands at the gate
of Valmondé. Eighteen years have passed since
Désirée's initial arrival at the gate, and she has
blossomed into an exquisite young woman. Their
encounter ignites a fiery passion in Armand's soul,
which "[sweeps] along like an avalanche, or like a
prairie fire, or like anything that drives headlong
over all obstacles" (776). The young girl's name-
lessness does not concern Armand, for his Aubigny
heritage--one of the oldest and proudest in
Louisiana (776)--will compensate for her lack
thereof. He hastily dismisses all differences,
marrying Désirée as soon as the corbeille arrives
from Paris.

Square brackets indicate alteration to quoted text. With the author's name already known, only the page number appears in parenthetical citation.

Désirée makes the symbolic transition from
undefiled light to darkness when she takes up residence in the Aubigny household, which, like the man
of the house, is immediately characterized by its
dark and somber presence:

> The roof came down steep and black like a cowl,
> reaching out beyond the wide galleries that
> encircled the yellow stuccoed house. Big,

Format for block quotation, indented one inch on left margin only. Ellipses indicate deletion from quota- tion. Note format for page reference.

solemn oaks grew close to it, and their thick-
leaved, far-reaching branches shadowed it like
a pall. Young Aubigny's rule was a strict
one . . . and under it his negroes had forgotten
how to be gay. (776)

Désirée's presence brings sunshine to Armand's previously lonely world, and a new addition to the
Aubigny family further multiplies his joy as the
couple become the proud parents of a baby boy soon
after they are married. Chopin uses light imagery
in the description of Désirée's countenance, which
is "suffused with a glow that [is] happiness itself" (777), when she confides in Madame
Valmondé that Armand has undergone a total character change since the baby's arrival. Désirée
observes that the child's birth has indeed "softened Armand Aubigny's imperious and exacting nature
greatly" (777), marveling at the fact that none of
the blacks have been punished by him since the
baby's arrival. It is obvious that Désirée and
the baby bring an uncharacteristic happiness to
Armand, whose dark, handsome face, "[has] not
often been disfigured by frowns since the day he
fell in love" (777).

As Désirée reclines upon a couch, glowing in
her soft white muslins and laces, she is a vision
of perfect happiness and purity. Unfortunately,
this idyllic existence is short-lived. Something is
wrong with the child, something which will ultimately break many hearts and split the family asunder. Désirée slowly realizes that her child does
not appear to be of entirely white heritage. "Look
at our child," she pleads with Armand. "What does
it mean? tell me" (778). She clutches her husband's
arm in desperation yet he, with his heart of
stone, pushes her hand away in disgust. Finally,

Stanley 4

he replies that the child is not white because the
mother is not white. Eventually, bitter that
Désirée and the child are part black, he coldheart-
edly forces them both to leave.

Although Armand is guilty for harsh treatment
of someone whom he suspects is of mixed heritage,
the racism he demonstrates is common in the place
and time in which he lives. In New Orleans, where
"Désirée's Baby" takes place, personal relationships between the races were clearly forbidden by
society's rules of etiquette, as well as by state
law. Southern society abided by certain unspoken
rules that governed every type of interracial
encounter. Even the shaking of hands between members of different races, under any set of circumstances, was taboo (Kennedy 212). Racist groups,
most notably the Ku Klux Klan, were constantly on
the prowl for those who violated this code of etiquette. For those who dared to exceed the established limits of interracial contact, the social
ramifications were great. Oftentimes, death by
lynching was the punishment for such unacceptable
behavior.

In Armand's society, association with members
of another race was not merely a faux pas--it was a
flagrant violation of the law. Racism was enforced
by the state of Louisiana to the extent that both
races were forbidden to occupy space in the same
apartment building, even with the existence of
walls separating the races and segregated entrances. The only legal exception to this clause
existed where a member of one race was employed as
a servant of the other (Kennedy 74). The legal
system did its best to maintain a stratified class
structure that relegated blacks to the lowest position in society, dehumanizing them in the process.

*Connection
established between
original claims and the
specifics of the story.*

Stanley 5

Since the legal system forbade even such casual
physical contact as handshaking and was known to
punish perpetrators with flogging (Kennedy 212),
interracial sexual relations were clearly taboo.
The language of Louisiana's legislation forbade
"sexual intercourse, cohabitation, concubinage,
and marriage between whites and all 'persons of
color,'" who are "defined by the courts to include
anyone having one-sixteenth or more Negro blood"
(Kennedy 66). However, this racist legislation was
not limited to the state of Louisiana, or even to
the deep South.

Quotation within a quotation: The phrase "persons of color" was in quotation marks in original source, and this is indicated by placing it in single quotation marks within the full quotation.

Legislation that restricted relations between
the races were commonplace in state and federal
laws across the nation. The United States' racial
precedent was set early on when Article I, section
2, of the Constitution specified that each black
was to be counted as three-fifths of a white person
in the determination of the number of each state's
representatives in Congress. However, legalized
racism did not end with the addition of the Fourteenth Amendment to the Constitution, despite its
guarantee of "life, liberty, and property" to every
citizen. Before and after the Fourteenth Amendment
was added, the U.S. Supreme Court repeatedly condoned the dehumanization of blacks in its rulings,
as evidenced in such cases as the Dred Scott decision (1857) and Plessy v. Ferguson (1896). The earlier decision was an outright denial of the black
race's humanity, in which the Court sought to bar
the entire race from the benefits of citizenship
and withhold the rights which are guaranteed to all
through the Constitution (Scott v. Sandford). The
subsequent decision sanctioned the forced segregation of the races (Plessy v. Ferguson). As long
as the involved party rendered lip-service to the

Summaries of constitutional articles and court cases.

Stanley 6

Constitution by stipulating that the facilities
provided were "separate but equal," the U.S. government turned a blind eye to blatant racial injus-
tices (Kennedy 167-69) and relegated blacks to
their inferior position in society.

*Brief summary of
multiple pages in
original source.*

Succumbing to pressure from a social structure
and legal system so permeated with racism, Armand
forces his wife and their child to leave. Countless
happy homes, such as that of the Aubigny family,
have been torn apart by this demon of racism
throughout history. Some individuals in today's
society argue that the problem of race relations,
as well as the controversial issue of racial identity, are merely past conflicts that have been
overcome by a more enlightened people. However,
Louisiana--the very state in which the Aubigny family lived--was the location of a recent racial controversy, proving that the issue of race still
divides American society.

In 1983, an individual named Susie Guillory
Phipps requested that the Louisiana Bureau of Vital
Records change her racial classification from black
to white and attempted to sue the bureau after its
refusal to do so. Since Phipps is a descendent of
an eighteenth-century white planter and a black
slave, her birth certificate automatically classified her as black in accordance with a 1970 state
law that declared anyone with at least one-thirty-
second "Negro" blood to be black (Omi and Winant
13). Although Phipps's attorney argued that most
whites have at least one-twentieth "Negro" ancestry, the Court maintained its support of the
quantification of racial identity, and "in so
doing, affirmed the legality of assigning individuals to specific racial groupings" (13). Even as
late as 1986, Louisiana passed another racially

*Specific evidence
provided to support a
debatable claim.*

Stanley 7

divisive ruling in which a woman with "negligible
African heritage" was legally defined as black
(Cose 78).

These modern court rulings raise the specter of
racism which has haunted the South, and the entire
country to a lesser extent, since the country's
inception. It is the very same system that exists
in Chopin's world, where, according to Michele
Birnbaum:

> The "black," the "mulatto," the "quadroon,"
> and the "Griffe" are subtle indices to social
> status in the white community. Named according
> to the ratio of "Negro blood" in their veins,
> these representative figures function not as
> indictments of an arbitrary colorline, but as
> reminders and reinforcements of cultural tier-
> ing. (308)[1]

The legal system's recent support of classification
based upon percentages of racial heritage only
maintains the rift that has divided the races by
stressing differences and has granted equality a
lesser significance. Countless potential relationships have been thwarted, and even terminated, by
the legal system and the social system's racial
codes. At times, the grounds for interracial
couples' painful separations have been entirely
false.

The agony of rejection undoubtedly breaks
Désirée's heart as she bids farewell to the
husband who has brought her much joy and the happy
home they once shared. The rays from the October
sunset illuminate the golden strands in her tresses
like a halo, and the thin white dress dances in the
breeze like an angel's robe. It is appropriate that
Chopin uses light imagery in her description of
Désirée, for the young woman is truly the only

*Superscript numeral
refers reader to
endnote.*

Stanley 8

sunshine that the miserable Armand has ever known.
Like the sun, the beautiful Désirée is as glorious
in her departure as she is in her arrival. However,
unlike the sun, there is no hope for her return
tomorrow.

A few weeks after Désirée's dramatic farewell,
the miserable Armand presides over a great bonfire
in the backyard of L'Abri. This scene conjures up
vivid images of the devil and is consistent with
the dark imagery that Chopin uses throughout
"Désirée's Baby" to describe Armand. As he sits
high above the spectacle, a half dozen blacks feed
the flames with every reminder of his love affair
and previously joyous existence. After the willow
cradle and the baby's layette as well as Désirée's
silk and velvet robes have been devoured by the
blaze, only the couple's love letters from their
days of espousal remain. Among them lingers a
curious scrap of paper scrawled in his own
mother's handwriting. In the note, she thanks God
for blessing her with the love of her husband. In
conclusion, she declares, "But, above all . . .
night and day, I thank the good God for having so
arranged our lives that our dear Armand will
never know that his mother, who adores him, belongs
to the race that is cursed with the brand of slavery" (779).

One may wish that Armand had only known in time
that it was he--not Désirée--who shared a common
heritage with the slaves! Chopin drops hints about
Armand's black ancestry throughout the story, fore-
shadowing the ending with dark and evil imagery
that mirrors common stereotypes of the black race.
However, the awareness of his own heritage eludes
Armand, who makes the mistake of a lifetime based

Stanley 9

upon societal prejudices. That knowledge would also
save Désirée, and the blacks of L'Abri, from the
misery that Armand has inflicted upon their lives
by treating them as second-class citizens. Readers
may wish he had only realized the "negro blood"
coursing through his veins is no different than the
"white," because the ending would have turned out
so differently. The regrets will undoubtedly haunt
Armand forever.

It is easy for the reader to judge Armand for
rejecting someone he regards as an inferior, yet
countless American citizens and the legal system
are guilty of committing the same crime. American
society has relegated an entire people to second-
class status, while ignoring the fact that the
only difference between the races is skin color.
Most individuals regret America's dark past, if
only due to the selfish realization that a countless number of Mozarts, Einsteins, and Shakespeares
were branded with a stamp of inferiority and
silenced by the legal and social systems. However,
the daily paper reveals that acts of racism are
still being committed, and the lesson of racial
equality has yet to be learned. American society
has done itself an immense disservice by making an
issue of skin color in the past, and it continues
to do so in the present. Until the world is perceived through color-blind eyes, barriers will
divide the races and peace will remain an unattain-
able goal.

Endnote

[1]Birnbaum is referring here to racial classifica-
tions in Chopin's novel The Awakening, but clearly
the same system applies in "Désirée's Baby."

*Endnote provides
information that could
not be easily integrated
into text of paper.*

Stanley 10

Works Cited

Birnbaum, Michele A. "'Alien Hands': Kate Chopin
    and the Colonization of Race." <u>American Litera-
    ture</u> 66 (1994): 301-23.

Chopin, Kate. <u>The Awakening</u>. 1899. Ed. Nancy A.
    Walker. Boston: Bedford/St. Martin's, 1993.

---. "Désirée's Baby." <u>Making Literature Matter: An
    Anthology for Readers and Writers</u>. Ed. John
    Schilb and John Clifford. Boston: Bedford/St.
    Martin's, 1999. 776-79.

---. "The Story of an Hour." <u>Making Literature Mat-
    ter: An Anthology for Readers and Writers</u>. Ed.
    John Schilb and John Clifford. Boston: Bed-
    ford/St. Martin's, 1999. 773-75.

Cose, Ellis. "One Drop of Bloody History." <u>Newsweek</u>
    13 Feb. 1995: 78+.

Evans, Patricia. "Southern Women Writers, An His-
    torical Overview." <u>Literature of the South</u>.
    World Wide Web. <http://falcon.jmu.edu/~ram-
    seyil/southwomen.htm> (8 Mar. 1998).

Kennedy, Stetson. <u>The Jim Crow Guide: The Way It
    Was</u>. N.p.: Lawrence & Wishart, 1959. Boca
    Raton: Florida Atlantic U, 1990.

Omi, Michael, and Harold Winant. "Racial Forma-
    tions." <u>Race, Class, and Gender in the United
    States: An Integrated Study</u>. Ed. Paula Rothen-
    berg. New York: St. Martin's, 1995. 13-22.

Plessy v. Ferguson. 163 US 537. US Supr. Ct. 1896.

Scott v. Sandford. 60 US 393. US Supr. Ct. 1856.

US Const. Amend. XIV, sec. 1.

Citation for an article in a scholarly journal.

Citation for a work in an anthology. Note style for multiple works by the same author.

Citation for an article in a general-circulation periodical. Citation for a World Wide Web source.

Citation for a book.

Citation for a chapter in a book.

Citations for court cases.

Citation for a government document.

Contents by Genre

Short Stories

Poems

Plays

Essays

Critical Commentaries

© 1981 by Carolyn Forché. Originally appeared in Women's International Resource Exchange. Reprinted by permission of HarperCollins Publishers, Inc.

Maurice Friedman. Excerpt from "Bartleby and the Modern Exile" from *Bartleby, the Scrivener: A Symposium*, edited by Howard P. Vincent (*The Melville Annual 1965, Kent Studies in English* 3, pp. 64–81 in the original). Copyright © 1966 by Kent State University Press. Used with permission of the Kent State University Press.

Robert Frost. "Mending Wall," "Stopping by Woods on a Snowy Evening," and "The Road Not Taken" from *The Poetry of Robert Frost*, edited by Edward Connery Lathem. Copyright 1944, 1951, © 1958 by Robert Frost. Copyright © 1967 by Lesley Frost Ballantine. Copyright 1916, 1923, 1930, 1939, © 1969 by Henry Holt and Company, LLC. Reprinted by permission of Henry Holt and Company, LLC.

Howard Gadlin. Excerpt from "Mediating Sexual Harassment" from *Sexual Harassment on Campus: A Guide for Administrators, Faculty and Students*, edited by Bernice R. Sandler and Robert J. Shoop. Copyright © 1997 by Allyn & Bacon. Reprinted by permission of the publisher.

Gabriel García Márquez. "The Handsomest Drowned Man in the World" from *Leaf Storm and Other Stories* by Gabriel García Márquez. Copyright © 1971 by Gabriel García Márquez. Reprinted by permission of HarperCollins Publishers, Inc.

Karen Gershon. "Race" from *Selected Poems* by Karen Gershon. Reprinted by permission of Val Tripp, Executor of the Estate of Karen Gershon.

Nikki Giovanni. "Legacies" from *In My House* by Nikki Giovanni. Copyright © 1974 by Nikki Giovanni. Reprinted by permission of William Morrow & Company.

Louise Glück. "The School Children" from *The House on Marshland* by Louise Glück. Copyright © 1971, 1972, 1973, 1974, 1975 by Louise Glück. Reprinted by permission of the Ecco Press.

Paul Gray. "What Is Love?" from *Time* (February 15, 1993). Copyright © 1993 Time Inc. Reprinted by permission.

Jacob and Wilhelm Grimm. "Cinderella," "Hansel and Gretel," and "Snow White" from *The Complete Fairy Tales of the Brothers Grimm*, translated by Jack Zipes. Translation copyright © 1987 by Jack Zipes. Used by permission of Bantam Books, a division of Random House, Inc.

Forrest Hamer. "Lesson" from *Call and Response* by Forrest Hamer (Alice James Books, 1995). Reprinted by permission of the publisher.

Lorraine Hansberry. "April 23, 1964, Letter to the *New York Times*" from *To Be Young, Gifted and Black: Lorraine Hansberry in Her Own Words*, adapted by Robert Nemiroff. Copyright © 1969 by Robert Nemiroff as Executor of the Estate of Lorraine Hansberry. Reprinted with the permission of Simon & Schuster, Inc. *A Raisin in the Sun*. Copyright © 1958 by Robert Nemiroff, as an unpublished work. Copyright © 1959, 1966, 1984 by Robert Nemiroff. Reprinted by permission of Random House, Inc.

Robert Hayden. "Those Winter Sundays" from *Angle of Ascent: New and Selected Poems* by Robert Hayden. Copyright © 1966 by Robert Hayden. Reprinted by permission of Liveright Publishing Corporation.

Seamus Heaney. "Punishment" from *Opened Ground: Selected Poems 1966–1996* by Seamus Heaney. Copyright © 1998 by Seamus Heaney. Reprinted by permission of Farrar, Straus and Giroux, LLC. From *New Selected Poems 1966–1987* by Seamus Heaney. Reprinted by permission of Faber & Faber Limited.

Essex Hemphill. "Commitments" from *Ceremonies* by Essex Hemphill. Copyright © 1992 by Essex Hemphill. Used by permission of Dutton, a division of Penguin Putnam Inc.

Zbigniew Herbert. "Report from the Besieged City" from *Report from the Besieged City* by Zbigniew Herbert, translated by John Carpenter and Bogdana Carpenter. Copyright © 1985 Zbigniew Herbert. Reprinted by permission of the Ecco Press.

David Hernandez. "Pigeons." Copyright David Hernandez—Street Sounds Media Group, 1998. Reprinted by permission of the author.

Linda Hogan. "Heritage" from *Calling Myself Home* by Linda Hogan. First appeared in *Red Clay* (1991). Reprinted by permission of Greenfield Review Press.

bell hooks. "Inspired Eccentricity." Reprinted by permission of the author.

Pam Houston. "How to Talk to a Hunter" from *Cowboys Are My Weakness* by Pam Houston. Copyright © 1992 by Pam Houston. Reprinted by permission of W. W. Norton & Company, Inc.

permission of Alfred A. Knopf, Inc., and by permission of Writer's House, Inc., on behalf of the Estate of Frank O'Connor.

Dwight Okita. "In Response to Executive Order 9066" from *Crossing with the Light* by Dwight Okita (Tia Chucha Press, 1992). Reprinted by permission of the author.

Sharon Olds. "I Go Back to May 1937" from *The Gold Cell* by Sharon Olds. Copyright © 1987 by Sharon Olds. Reprinted by permission of Alfred A. Knopf, Inc.

Mary Oliver. "Singapore" from *House of Light* by Mary Oliver. Copyright © 1990 by Mary Oliver. Reprinted by permission of Beacon Press, Boston.

Tillie Olsen. "I Stand Here Ironing" from *Tell Me a Riddle* by Tillie Olsen. Copyright © 1956, 1957, 1960, 1961 by Tillie Olsen. Introduction by John Leonard. Used by permission of Delacorte Press/Seymour Lawrence, a division of Random House, Inc.

Robert M. O'Neil. "Protecting Free Speech When the Issue Is Sexual Harassment" from *The Chronicle of Higher Education* (September 13, 1996). Reprinted by permission of the author, Robert O'Neil, Director, Thomas Jefferson Center for the Protection of Free Expression and Professor of Law, University of Virginia.

Daniel Orozco. "Orientation." Originally appeared in *The Seattle Review* (1994). Reprinted by permission of the author.

George Orwell. "Shooting an Elephant" from *Shooting an Elephant and Other Essays* by George Orwell. Copyright 1950 by Sonia Brownell Orwell and renewed 1978 by Sonia Pitt-Rivers. Reprinted by permission of Harcourt, Inc. Copyright © 1936 George Orwell. Reproduced from *The Complete Works of George Orwell* (Secker and Warburg, 1998) by permission of A. M. Heath & Co., Ltd., on behalf of Mark Hamilton as the Literary Executor of the Estate of the Late Sonia Brownell Orwell and Secker and Warburg Ltd.

Linda Pastan. "Ethics" from *Waiting for My Life* by Linda Pastan. Copyright © 1981 by Linda Pastan. Reprinted by permission of W. W. Norton & Company, Inc.

Ann Petry. "Like a Winding Sheet" from *Miss Muriel and Other Stories* by Ann Petry. Copyright © 1945 by Ann Petry. Originally appeared in *The Crisis* (November 1945). Reprinted by permission of Russell & Volkening as agents for the author.

Marge Piercy. "Right to Life" from *The Moon Is Always Female* by Marge Piercy. Copyright © 1980 by Marge Piercy. Reprinted by permission of Alfred A. Knopf, Inc. "To be of use" from *Circles on the Water* by Marge Piercy. Copyright © 1982 by Marge Piercy. Reprinted by permission of Alfred A. Knopf, Inc.

Sylvia Plath. Excerpt from "Daddy" from *Ariel* by Sylvia Plath. Copyright © 1963 by Ted Hughes. Copyright renewed. Reprinted by permission of HarperCollins Publishers, Inc., and Faber & Faber Limited.

Katherine Anne Porter. "He" from *Flowering Judas and Other Stories* by Katherine Anne Porter. Copyright 1930 and renewed 1958 by Katherine Anne Porter. Reprinted Harcourt, Inc.

Minnie Bruce Pratt. "Two Small-Sized Girls" from *Crime Against Nature* by Minnie Bruce Pratt. Copyright © 1990 by Minnie Bruce Pratt. Reprinted by permission of Firebrand Publishing.

Henry Reed. "Naming of Parts" from *Henry Reed: Collected Poems*, edited by John Stallworthy. Copyright © 1991 by the Executor of Henry Reed's Estate. Reprinted by permission of Oxford University Press.

Tomás Rivera. Excerpt from "Richard Rodriguez's *Hunger of Memory* as Humanistic Antithesis" from *Melus*, vol. 2 (1984). Copyright © 1984 by Melus, the Society for the Study of Multi-Ethnic Literature of the United States. Reprinted by permission.

Richard Rodriguez. "Aria" from *Hunger of Memory* by Richard Rodriguez (Boston: David R. Godine, Publisher, 1981). Copyright © 1981 by Richard Rodriguez. Reprinted by permission of Georges Borchardt, Inc., for the author.

Theodore Roethke. "My Papa's Waltz" from *The Collected Poems of Theodore Roethke* by Theodore Roethke. Copyright 1942 by Hearst Magazines, Inc. Used by permission of Doubleday, a division of Random House, Inc. "The Waking" from *The Collected Poems of Theodore Roethke* by Theodore Roethke. Copyright 1953 by Theodore Roethke. Used by permission of Doubleday, a division of Random House, Inc.

Katherine M. Rogers. Excerpt from "Feminism and *A Doll's House*" by Katherine M. Rogers, in

PMLA (January 1989), pp. 28–40. Reprinted by permission of the Modern Language Association of America.

Dylan Thomas. "Do Not Go Gentle into That Good Night" from *Collected Poems* by Dylan Thomas (J. M. Dent, Publishers). Reprinted by permission of David Higham Associates. From *The Poems of Dylan Thomas*. Copyright © 1952 by Dylan Thomas. Reprinted by permission of New Directions Publishing Corp.

Anastasia Toufexis. "The Right Chemistry" from *Time* (February 15, 1993). Copyright © 1993 Time Inc. Reprinted by permission.

Kitty Tsui. "A Chinese Banquet" from *The Words of a Woman Who Breathes Fire* by Kitty Tsui. Reprinted by permission of the author.

University of Maryland at College Park. "Pamphlet on Sexual Harassment." Copyright © 1988 University of Maryland, College Park. Pamphlet content subject to revision as of June 1998. Reprinted by permission.

John Updike. "A & P" from *Pigeon Feathers and Other Stories* by John Updike. Copyright © 1962 by John Updike. Reprinted by permission of Alfred A. Knopf, Inc.

Gore Vidal. "The Desire and the Successful Pursuit of the Whole" from *Palimpsest* by Gore Vidal. Copyright © 1995 by Literary Creations, Inc. Reprinted by permission of Random House, Inc.

Victor Villanueva Jr. Excerpt from "Whose Voice Is It Anyway? Rodriguez' Speech in Retrospect." Originally published in *English Journal* (1987). Reprinted by permission of the National Council of Teachers of English.

David Wagoner. "The Singing Lesson" from *Traveling Light: Collected and New Poems* by David Wagoner. Reprinted by permission of the author.

Alice Walker. "Everyday Use" from *In Love and In Trouble: Stories of Black Women* by Alice Walker. Copyright © 1973 by Alice Walker. Reprinted by permission of Harcourt, Inc. "Nineteen Fifty-Five" from *You Can't Keep a Good Woman Down* by Alice Walker. Copyright © 1981 by Alice Walker. Reprinted by permission of Harcourt, Inc. "In Search of Our Mothers' Gardens" from *In Search of Our Mothers' Gardens: Womanist Prose* by Alice Walker. Copyright © 1974 by Alice Walker. Reprinted by permission of Harcourt, Inc.

Hermann J. Weigand. Excerpt from *The Modern Ibsen: A Reconsideration* by Hermann J. Weigand. Copyright © 1925 by Holt, Rinehart & Winston. Copyright © 1953 by Hermann J. Weigand. Reprinted by permission of Henry Holt and Company, LLC.

Eudora Welty. "A Visit of Charity" from *A Curtain of Green and Other Stories* by Eudora Welty. Copyright © 1941 and renewed 1969 by Eudora Welty. Reprinted by permission of Harcourt, Inc.

E. B. White. "Once More to the Lake" from *One Man's Meat* by E. B. White. Text copyright © 1941 by E. B. White. Reprinted by permission of Tilbury House, Publishers, Gardiner, ME.

Tennessee Williams. *The Glass Menagerie*. Copyright © 1945 by Tennessee Williams and Edwina D. Williams and renewed 1973 by Tennessee Williams. Reprinted by permission of Random House, Inc.

Naomi Wolf. "The Making of a Slut" from *Promiscuities* by Naomi Wolf. Reprinted by permission of Random House, Inc.

Tobias Wolff. "The Rich Brother" from *Back in the World* by Tobias Wolff. Copyright © 1985 by Tobias Wolff. Reprinted by permission of International Creative Management.

James Wright. "Lying in a Hammock at William Duffy's Farm in Pine Island, Minnesota" from *Above the River: The Complete Poems* by James Wright. Copyright © 1990 by Anne Wright, Wesleyan University Press. Reprinted by permission of the University Press of New England.

Yevgeny Yevtushenko. "Babii Yar" from *Collected Poems 1952–1990* by Yevgeny Yevtushenko.

Index of Authors, Titles, First Lines, and Terms

The boldfaced page references indicate where a key term is highlighted in the text.